The Oxford Handbook of Leadership and Organizations

OXFORD LIBRARY OF PSYCHOLOGY

Editor in Chief PETER E. NATHAN

The Oxford Handbook of Leadership and Organizations

Edited by

David V. Day

OXFORD
UNIVERSITY PRESS

OXFORD
UNIVERSITY PRESS

Oxford University Press is a department of the University of Oxford.
It furthers the University's objective of excellence in research, scholarship,
and education by publishing worldwide.

Oxford New York
Auckland Cape Town Dar es Salaam Hong Kong Karachi
Kuala Lumpur Madrid Melbourne Mexico City Nairobi
New Delhi Shanghai Taipei Toronto

With offices in
Argentina Austria Brazil Chile Czech Republic France Greece
Guatemala Hungary Italy Japan Poland Portugal Singapore
South Korea Switzerland Thailand Turkey Ukraine Vietnam

Oxford is a registered trademark of Oxford University Press
in the UK and certain other countries.

Published in the United States of America by
Oxford University Press
198 Madison Avenue, New York, NY 10016

Library of Congress Cataloging-in-Publication Data
The Oxford handbook of leadership and organizations / edited by David V. Day.
pages cm
Includes bibliographical references and index.
ISBN 978-0-19-975561-5
1. Leadership. 2. Organization. I. Day, David V., 1956– editor of compilation.
HD57.7.O966 2014
658.4′092—dc23
2014000017

SHORT CONTENTS

OXFORD LIBRARY OF PSYCHOLOGY

The *Oxford Library of Psychology*, a landmark series of handbooks, is published by Oxford University Press, one of the world's oldest and most highly respected publishers, with a tradition of publishing significant books in psychology. The ambitious goal of the *Oxford Library of Psychology* is nothing less than to span a vibrant, wide-ranging field and, in so doing, to fill a clear market need.

Encompassing a comprehensive set of handbooks, organized hierarchically, the *Library* incorporates volumes at different levels, each designed to meet a distinct need. At one level are a set of handbooks designed broadly to survey the major subfields of psychology; at another are numerous handbooks that cover important current focal research and scholarly areas of psychology in depth and detail. Planned as a reflection of the dynamism of psychology, the *Library* will grow and expand as psychology itself develops, thereby highlighting significant new research that will impact on the field. Adding to its accessibility and ease of use, the *Library* will be published in print and, later on, electronically.

The *Library* surveys psychology's principal subfields with a set of handbooks that capture the current status and future prospects of those major subdisciplines. This initial set includes handbooks of social and personality psychology, clinical psychology, counseling psychology, school psychology, educational psychology, industrial and organizational psychology, cognitive psychology, cognitive neuroscience, methods and measurements, history, neuropsychology, personality assessment, developmental psychology, and more. Each handbook undertakes to review one of psychology's major subdisciplines with breadth, comprehensiveness, and exemplary scholarship. In addition to these broadly conceived volumes, the *Library* also includes a large number of handbooks designed to explore in depth more specialized areas of scholarship and research, such as stress, health and coping, anxiety and related disorders, cognitive development, or child and adolescent assessment. In contrast to the broad coverage of the subfield handbooks, each of these latter volumes focuses on an especially productive, more highly focused line of scholarship and research. Whether at the broadest or most specific level, however, all of the *Library* handbooks offer synthetic coverage that reviews and evaluates the relevant past and present research and anticipates research in the future. Each handbook in the *Library* includes introductory and concluding chapters written by its editor to provide a roadmap to the handbook's table of contents and to offer informed anticipations of significant future developments in that field.

An undertaking of this scope calls for handbook editors and chapter authors who are established scholars in the areas about which they write. Many of the nation's and world's most productive and best-respected psychologists have agreed to edit *Library* handbooks or write authoritative chapters in their areas of expertise.

For whom has the *Oxford Library of Psychology* been written? Because of its breadth, depth, and accessibility, the *Library* serves a diverse audience, including graduate students in psychology and their faculty mentors, scholars, researchers, and practitioners in psychology and related fields. Each will find in the *Library* the information he or she seeks on the subfield or focal area of psychology in which they work or are interested.

Befitting its commitment to accessibility, each handbook includes a comprehensive index, as well as extensive references to help guide research. And because the *Library* was designed from its inception as an online as well as a print resource, its structure and contents will be readily and rationally searchable online. Furthermore, once the *Library* is released online, the handbooks will be regularly and thoroughly updated.

In summary, the *Oxford Library of Psychology* will grow organically to provide a thoroughly informed perspective on the field of psychology, one that reflects both psychology's dynamism and its increasing interdisciplinarity. Once published electronically, the *Library* is also destined to become a uniquely valuable interactive tool, with extended search and browsing capabilities. As you begin to consult this handbook, we sincerely hope you will share our enthusiasm for the more than 500-year tradition of Oxford University Press for excellence, innovation, and quality, as exemplified by the *Oxford Library of Psychology.*

Peter E. Nathan
Editor-in-Chief
Oxford Library of Psychology

ABOUT THE EDITOR

David V. Day

David V. Day is Winthrop Professor and Woodside Chair in Leadership and Management at the University of Western Australia Business School. He is a Fellow of the American Psychological Association and a Fellow of the Association for Psychological Science.

CONTRIBUTORS

Mats Alvesson
Lund University
Lund, Sweden

John Antonakis
Faculty of Business and Economics
University of Lausanne
Lausanne, Switzerland

Richard D. Arvey
Center for Strategic Leadership
National University of Singapore
Singapore

Neal M. Ashkanasy
UQ Business School
The University of Queensland
Brisbane, Australia

Bruce J. Avolio
Management and Organization Department
Michael G. Foster School of Business
University of Washington
Seattle, Washington

Marie-Michèle Beauchesne
Department of Management and International Business
College of Business Administration
Florida International University
Miami, Florida

Talya N. Bauer
Portland State University
School of Business
Portland, Oregon

Samuel Bendahan
Faculty of Business and Economics
University of Lausanne
Lausanne, Switzerland

Jeffrey R. Bentley
State University of New York at Buffalo
Buffalo, New York

Joyce E. Bono
Management Department
Warrington College of Business
University of Florida
Gainesville, Florida

Felix C. Brodbeck
Ludwig-Maximilians-University
Munich, Germany

Michael E. Brown
Sam and Irene Black School of Business
Penn State Erie – The Behrend College
Erie, Pennsylvania

John M. Bryson
Hubert H. Humphrey School of Public Affairs
University of Minnesota
Ann Arbor, Minnesota

Dorothy R. Carter
Georgia Institute of Technology
Atlanta, Georgia

Jean Lau Chin
Derner Institute for Advanced Psychological Studies
Adelphi University
Garden City, New York

Donna Chrobot-Mason
Director of the Center for Organizational Leadership
Center for Organizational Leadership
University of Cincinnati
Cincinnati, Ohio

S. Bartholomew Craig
Department of Psychology
North Carolina State University
Raleigh, North Carolina

Barbara C. Crosby
Hubert H. Humphrey School of Public Affairs
University of Minnesota
Ann Arbor, MI

Leslie A. DeChurch
Department of Psychology
Georgia Institute of Technology
Atlanta, Georgia

D. Scott DeRue
Department of Management & Organizations
University of Michigan
Ann Arbor, Michigan

Jessica E. Dinh
University of Akron
Akron, Ohio

John P. Dugan
Higher Education Program
College of Education
Loyola University Chicago
Chicago, Illinois

Berrin Erdogan
Portland State University
School of Business
Portland, Oregon

Silke A. Eisenbeiss
Department of International Business
Faculty of Business and Economics
Tübingen University
Tübingen, Germany

Colin Fisher
School of Management
Boston University
Boston, Massachusetts

Carter Gibson
The University of Oklahoma
Norman, Oklahoma

Vincent Giorgini
The University of Oklahoma
Norman, Oklahoma

Mark A. Griffin
School of Psychology
The University of Western Australia
Crawley, Australia

Sean T. Hannah
Schools of Business
Wake Forest University
Winston-Salem, North Carolina

James K. Hazy
Department of Management, Marketing, and Decision Sciences
Adelphi University
Garden City, New York

Nathan J. Hiller
Department of Management & International Business
College of Business
Florida International University
Modesto A. Maidique Campus
Miami, Florida

Ernest Hoffman
University of Akron
Akron, Ohio

Emily R. Hoole
Evaluation Center
Center for Creative Leadership
Greensboro, North Carolina

Jia Hu
College of Business
University of Notre Dame
Notre Dame, Indiana

Ronald H. Humphrey
Department of Management
Virginia Commonwealth University
Richmond, Virginia

Herminia Ibarra
INSEAD
Fontainebleau, France

Philippe Jacquart
The Wharton School
University of Pennsylvania
Philadelphia, Pennsylvania

Robert B. Kaiser
Kaiser Leadership Solutions
Greensboro, North Carolina

Karin Klenke
Leadership Development Institute (LDI) International
Richmond, Virginia

Susan R. Komives
Department of Counseling, Higher Education, and Special Education
College of Education
University of Maryland
College Park, Maryland

Rafael Lalive
Faculty of Business and Economics
University of Lausanne
Lausanne, Switzerland

Wendong Li
Department of Psychological Sciences
Kansas State University
Manhattan, Kansas

Robert C. Liden
Department of Managerial Studies
University of Illinois at Chicago
Chicago, Illinois

Songqi Liu
Department of Psychology
The Pennsylvania State University
University Park, Pennsylvania

Robert G. Lord
Durham University Business School
Durham, UK

Jennifer W. Martineau
Vice President, Research, Innovation and Product Development
Center for Creative Leadership
Greensboro, North Carolina

Jensen Mecca
The University of Oklahoma
Norman, Oklahoma

Jeremy D. Meuser
Department of Managerial Studies
University of Illinois at Chicago
Chicago, Illinois

Ketan H. Mhatre
Kravis Leadership Institute
Claremont McKenna College
Claremont, California

Ivana Milosevic
College of Business Administration
University of Nebraska
Lincoln, Nebraska

Michael D. Mumford
Department of Psychology
The University of Oklahoma
Norman, Oklahoma

Christopher G. Myers
Department of Management & Organizations
University of Michigan
Ann Arbor, Michigan

Lisa H. Nishii
School of Industrial and Labor Relations
Cornell University
Ithaca, New York

Richard N. Osborn
Wayne State University
Detroit, Michigan

Alexandra Panaccio
Department of Management
Concordia University
Montreal, Quebec, Canada

Sharon K. Parker
UWA Business School
The University of Western Australia
Crawley, Australia

Ken W. Parry
Bond University
Gold Coast, Australia

Gianpiero Petriglieri
INSEAD
Fontainebleau, France

Ronald E. Riggio
Kravis Leadership Institute
Claremont McKenna College
Claremont, California

Marian N. Ruderman
Group Director, Global Leadership and Diversity
Center for Creative Leadership
Greensboro, North Carolina

Winny Shen
Department of Psychology
University of South Florida
Tampa, Florida

Zhaoli Song
Center for Strategic Leadership
National University of Singapore
Singapore

Raymond T. Sparrowe
Olin Business School
Washington University in St. Louis
St. Louis, Missouri

André Spicer
Cass Business School
London, United Kingdom

Daan Stam
Rotterdam School of Management
Erasmus University Rotterdam
Rotterdam, The Netherlands

Zenobia Talati
School of Psychology
The University of Western Australia
Crawley, Australia

Darren C. Treadway
School of Management
University at Buffalo
Buffalo, New York

Linda K. Treviño
Department of Management and Organization
Smeal College of Business
The Pennsylvania State University
University Park, Pennsylvania

Mary Uhl-Bien
College of Business
University of Nebraska-Lincoln
Lincoln, Nebraska

Daan van Knippenberg
Rotterdam School of Management
Erasmus University Rotterdam
Rotterdam, The Netherlands

Ruth Wageman
Department of Psychology
Harvard University
Cambridge, Massachusetts

David A. Waldman
Department of Management
W. P. Carey School of Business
Arizona State University
Tempe, Arizona

Angela S. Wallace
Department of Organization and Human Resources
State University of New York at Buffalo
Buffalo, New York

Fred O. Walumbwa
Department of Management & International Business
College of Business
Florida International University
Miami, Florida

Mo Wang
Warrington College of Business Administration
Department of Management
University of Florida
Gainesville, Florida

Nan Wang
Center for Strategic Leadership
National University of Singapore
Singapore

Sandy J. Wayne
Department of Managerial Studies
University of Illinois at Chicago
Chicago, Illinois

Lisa M. Williams
College of Business
Niagara University
Niagara University, New York

Sarah Wittman
INSEAD
Fontainebleau, France

Chia-huei Wu
UWA Business School
The University of Western Australia
Crawley, Australia

David J. Yoon
Department of Work and Organizations
Carlson School of Management
University of Minnesota
Minneapolis, Minnesota

Stephen J. Zaccaro
The Mason Institute for Leadership Excellence
George Mason University
Fairfax, Virginia

Le Zhou
Department of Management
University of Florida
Gainesville, Florida

CONTENTS

Part Four • Follower-Centric Theories and Approaches

Part Five • Dyadic and Team-Centric Theories and Approaches

Part Six • Emerging Issues in Organizational Leadership

Part Seven • Emerging Contextual Issues in Leadership

PART 1

History and Background

CHAPTER

1 Introduction: Leadership and Organizations

David V. Day

Abstract

This chapter introduces and briefly summarizes the chapters in *The Oxford Handbook of Leadership and Organizations*. The notion of what it takes to be an effective leader or provide effective leadership has spawned a century or more of research. Yet definitive answers to these straightforward questions have proved elusive. The perspective espoused in this handbook is to encourage more systems-level thinking around leadership that incorporates leaders, followers, dyads, teams, organizations, and contextual concerns. In looking to the future of leadership, ways to interconnect these various perspectives on leadership are encouraged. The handbook is organized into nine parts, addressing history and background to leadership, research issues, leader-centric theories and approaches, follower-centric theories and approaches, dyadic and team-centric theories and approaches, emerging issues in organizational leadership, emerging contextual issues in leadership, special concerns in leadership, and the future of leadership.

Key Words: leadership, followership, leader–member exchange, team leadership, context, leader development

What does it mean to be a good leader or provide effective leadership? These are relatively simple questions that have turned out to have extremely complex answers. More than a century of scholarly research has been devoted to the topics of leaders and leadership, so we should know a few things about leadership from a scholarly research perspective, even though it can safely be assumed that we know much less about leadership than we need to know. For that reason, among others, one purpose for this handbook on leadership and organizations is to compile and summarize the body of scholarly evidence that exists with regard to leadership, as well as to identify areas for future contributions. One of the messages imparted in this handbook is that the leadership field continues to grow, evolve, and change. Some may view this in a negative light, suggesting that leadership is not worthy of scientific scrutiny if the field and the core construct of leadership continue to change over time. Conversely, this makes the field more dynamic and challenging and has no doubt contributed to the longstanding interest in leadership from a scientific and scholarly perspective.

Despite this longevity, there was a time in the 1970s when scholars thought that leadership was pretty much irrelevant to organizational performance. Fortunately, times change. Available evidence suggests that leadership can explain upward of 40 percent of the variance in organizational performance when evaluated using appropriate outcomes and time lags (Day & Lord, 1988). That is a considerable effect, which is one reason why leadership remains a topic of keen interest to academics as well as practitioners.

On the academic side of the equation, several scholarly journals have launched in the latter part of the twentieth century sharing the core focus on publishing research and theory solely devoted to leadership issues. The oldest of these is *The Leadership Quarterly*, which celebrates its twenty-fifth anniversary in 2014. Top-tier journals across various disciplines also publish research and theory on leadership. On the practitioner side of the equation, organizations spend billions of dollars each year on issues related to leadership and its development. This has spawned an entire consulting industry devoted to meeting organizational demands for better leadership. Leadership is not only a major concern in practice, but it continues to be something that interests academics in disciplines as varied as psychology, management, sociology, communications, and evolutionary biology, as well as economics and finance.

Clearly, there is something to leadership that has attracted such sustained interest. But what it is *exactly* about leadership that makes it important remains an elusive ideal. It is widely known in the field that there is no shared, agreed-upon leadership definition (Bass, 2008). Although myriad definitions have been proposed over the years, none fully captures the essence of this important but somewhat mysterious and elusive construct. The difficulty with attempting to provide a concise leadership definition is that it invariably leaves something out or otherwise oversimplifies a complex, dynamic, and evolving process.

This state of affairs with regard to change in the leadership field in terms of research focus and the evolving nature of the construct itself has been a source of irritation and frustration to some who would prefer a set of agreed-upon leadership principles and a universal definition (e.g., Locke, 2003). Although this hard-nosed scientific perspective is commendable in some ways, it is unreasonable to expect complete construct stability given that leadership is dynamic, interpersonal, multifunctional, and multilevel in nature. It is also true that advances in conceptual frameworks and analytical tools have contributed significantly to changes in the way that researchers think about and study leadership.

One example of this pertains to recent advances in multilevel modeling that have helped spur the evolution of leadership theory and research. Leadership can be thought of as inherently multilevel, involving leaders, followers, and situations (i.e., context). Leadership can range from individual to organizational levels of analysis and anything in between—or beyond—as with multiteam systems (see Carter & DeChurch, this volume). In addition, the target of leadership processes can be directed at the level of the organization, the group or team, or individual followers. This raises the possibility of cross-level effects, particularly given that leaders do not treat all followers identically (see Erdogan & Bauer, this volume). Multilevel modeling techniques allow researchers to test the underlying assumptions directly and to model their effects more accurately.

The development and acceptance of meta-analysis as a set of techniques to estimate effects across various studies has also contributed to the evolution of the leadership field. Meta-analysis addresses a key limitation associated with any single study, namely, sampling error. An important question is to what extent the results of any single study are biased because of a small sample size or other artifacts such as less than perfectly reliable measures. Procedures were developed to allow for correcting for various artifacts, such as sampling error between studies, and this helped to provide more accurate population estimates of the effects being studied. A well-known example in the leadership literature involves personality traits and leadership. An early review of the research suggested that there was little consistent effects for leader personality on relevant outcomes (Mann, 1959; Stogdill, 1948); however, subsequent meta-analyses showed that this conclusion was likely an artifact of sampling error and that the effects of leader personality on various outcomes was generalizable (i.e., robust) (Lord, De Vader, & Alliger, 1986).

Another important factor related to these changes in focus concerned increasingly complex challenges requiring leadership. No matter how smart or experienced individual leaders are, they often reach their limits in terms of being able to figure things out and provide effective solutions. As a result, it becomes less and less relevant to study leadership as a person as compared with leadership as a process (Hollander & Julian, 1969).

Nonetheless, the field is still dominated by leader-centric perspectives rather than by leadership process approaches in which the so-called leader plays one role among many in a leadership system. Leader-centric perspectives are not wrong, but they are limited. By focusing only on the person as a leader in studying leadership, one ignores the social and interpersonal context in which leadership takes place. A major change that has occurred in the study of leadership is the move from a sole focus on the leader to a wider view that is more inclusive in terms of considering both leaders and followers or a context in which there is no formally appointed leader and leadership emerges through social interactions.

Given the voluminous nature of the leadership literature, as well as its continuing evolution, the goal of this handbook is not to try to provide a comprehensive treatment of every leadership theory and research stream that has been studied over the evolution of the field. Other tomes have attempted to take on that challenging feat (e.g., Bass, 2008). With that in mind, a primary purpose of this handbook is to bring together those scholars involved in cutting-edge research and theory building on the most vibrant topics in the field.

It is also the case that the title of this handbook addresses leadership *and* organizations. Organizations are an important venue in which leadership plays out—sometimes supportive, other times not. One of the themes in this handbook is in addressing some of the richness found in the context of organizations. Whereas organizations need leadership to run effectively and to fulfill their strategic objectives, they can range from very large to very small, for-profit and nonprofit, business and commercial, or military and educational, among other types. For that reason, it is probably unrealistic to expect leadership to play out identically regardless of organization context. What the present handbook hopes to do is to articulate some of the basic tenets of leadership and how it is researched but also to examine the various organizational contexts in which it is needed. Therefore, the approach adopted in this handbook is both general and more nuanced. It is hoped that readers will appreciate the myriad facets of leadership and how it is enacted and brought about in organizations.

This is an exciting time to be a leadership researcher or student of leadership. The field has matured and evolved in ways that were not anticipated even as recently as 10 or 15 years ago. Some of the questions that early researchers grappled with, such as whether leaders or born or made, have been for the most part resolved (yes, it is both nature *and* nurture; see Arvey et al. in this volume). Advances in research methods and analytical procedures have opened the door to understanding leadership in new ways and to come to new understandings with regard to its importance and relationship to other constructs. Some topics, such as the relationship between individual personality and leadership, that have been studied for many decades continue to attract new research ideas and yield new insights. Other topics, such as behavioral approaches to leadership, have evolved into new forms such as transformational leadership and functional team leadership. And, yet again, there are entirely new fields that have emerged as horizons have broadened and imaginations have deepened; these include complexity approaches to leadership and conceptualizing leadership as a complex adaptive system. For all these reasons, leadership remains not only a viable field of scientific study, but one that is diverse and sophisticated in its topics and approaches. It is hoped that as you read this handbook, this excitement and potential becomes clearly evident.

Plan of This Handbook

This handbook comprises nine different sections reflecting the diversity of topics and perspectives in the field of leadership. In general, the topics range from historical perspectives to research issues, from those perspectives focusing on leaders to those more follower-centric and collective in focus, to emerging issues and special concerns in the field of leadership. Each of these sections is described briefly.

Part I: History and Background

The opening section of the handbook provides historical background on the evolution of leadership theory, as well as on some perspectives on the field from critical management studies, public policy, and the emerging field of sociobiology of leadership. Stephen Zaccaro opens the handbook with a view of leadership from antiquity to modern times in the form of leadership memes. He describes four leader memes that have evolved through human cultural history and are reflected in intergenerational cultural artifacts. These memes depict leaders as *warriors, problem solvers, politicians,* or *teachers*. Each of these memes is grounded in classical and modern sources that define and replicate its core themes about the nature and practice of leadership. They are the stories that novice and apprentice leaders are told in order to explain leadership. It is argued that memes reside at the core of how we practice and study leadership. This provides a novel perspective on the evolution of leadership theory, as well as on its foundation in basic notions of what leadership means from a more layperson or naïve perspective.

Although much of the literature on the topic might be considered pro-leadership, there are emerging critical perspectives on the field that challenge some of the basic assumptions made by researchers. Mats Alvesson and André Spicer offer an alternative set of ideas based on critical theory. They suggest that leadership should be denaturalized and studied reflexively, with research conducted with a noninstrumental intent. They review the growing body of work that has built on these ideas, including topics such as ideology, identity, exclusions and inclusions, and interventions.

Barbara Crosby and John Bryson address the topic of integrative public leadership, which refers to the work of integrating people, resources, and organizations across various boundaries to tackle complex public problems and achieve a common good. This is a more recently developed theoretical approach that draws on research on cross-sector collaboration, corporate social responsibility, and collaborative public management, as well as on practice theory. Their chapter explores the development of integrative leadership theory and discusses key integrative leadership practices through the examination of two case studies involving the creation of a geographic information system for a US region and a global campaign to eradicate polio. Through these cases, the authors consider implications for leadership development and demonstrate the need to learn from unsuccessful as well as successful efforts to lead across sector, cultural, and geographic boundaries.

The final chapter in this section deals with the fascinating topic of the biology of leadership. Richard Arvey, Nan Wang, Zhaoli Song, and Wengdong Li argue that scholars are beginning to recognize important biological elements that may influence who emerges into leadership positions and who is effective in such roles. The authors review a growing literature on the role of biological factors in leadership emergence and effectiveness. In doing this, the authors provide a succinct and useful summary of the various biological factors that have been identified as being associated with various leadership criteria, and they outline directions for future research in these areas.

Part II: Research Issues

Leadership research incorporates various methodological approaches and designs. This section addresses a few of those overarching research issues. John Antonakis, Samuel Bendahan, Philippe Jacquart, and Rafael Lalive address the critical issues of causality and endogeneity in leadership research. They argue that most leadership and management researchers ignore endogeneity threats in their research, thus leading to serious estimation problems that can result in uninterpretable model parameter estimates. They discuss the problem of endogeneity in depth and explain conditions that produce it using examples grounded in the leadership literature. Specifically, they demonstrate how consistent causal estimates can be derived from the randomized experiment in which endogeneity is eliminated by experimental design. Reasons why estimates may become biased (i.e., inconsistent) in nonexperimental designs are reviewed, and useful remedies for examining causal relations with nonexperimental data are provided. This is a critically important area of concern for leadership researchers. If we are to develop a sound, evidence-based approach to leadership, we need to be certain that this evidence is based on rigorous designs that rule out alternative explanations. Endogeneity is one of those alternative explanations that need to be addressed in leadership research.

Karin Klenke addresses a different research perspective in reviewing qualitative approaches to leadership research. Her chapter presents the ontological, epistemological, and axiological assumptions underlying qualitative paradigms and describes some of the major qualitative research methods used in the study of leadership (e.g., interviews, content analysis, case study, grounded theory, narrative analysis, and non–text-based data sources such as photographs, works of art, film, theater, and music). Data collection and analyses are described both collectively and individually for specific qualitative methods such as ethnography and image-based research. Strategies for enhancing the quality and rigor of qualitative leadership research to achieve trustworthiness in a qualitative leadership study are presented. Future directions for qualitative leadership research are reviewed with an eye to increasing the application of qualitative methods and enhancing their legitimacy and potential in advancing the study of leadership.

Mo Wang, Le Zhou, and Songqi Liu next address multilevel issues in leadership research. They point out that leadership is an inherently multilevel phenomenon. For that reason, levels of analysis issues should be considered and addressed in theoretical and empirical studies of leadership. Wang and colleagues discuss levels of analysis issues in the conceptualization and measurement of leadership constructs, as well as levels issues in developing leadership theories, change-related issues in leadership research, and up-to-date statistical methods for testing multilevel leadership theories. They suggest possible ways to further contribute to the understanding of leadership process in organizations through adopting a multilevel focus. Their objective is to facilitate more rigorous leadership studies, help integrate different leadership theories, and inspire new approaches to leadership research. Multilevel methods and analyses have emerged as cutting-edge concerns, especially in leadership research. This chapter provides a very user-friendly approach to understanding core issues with regard to conceptualization and analysis across multiple levels in leadership research.

An Achilles heel of sorts with regard to practical applications of leadership and leadership development concerns the evaluation of such initiatives. Emily Hoole and Jennifer Martineau examine the challenge of evaluating the impact of leadership development. Their chapter explores existing frameworks for evaluating leadership interventions and proposes a more comprehensive framework. They also describe a variety of methods that can be used to effectively evaluate leadership development at multiple levels in alignment with this framework.

Part III: Leader-Centric Theories and Approaches

Traditional approaches to the study of leadership have been primarily leader-centric. That is, the origins of leadership are conceptualized as residing with the leader rather than with some broader set of systems forces. There is a rich history of leader-centric approaches, which continue to be introduced into the literature. Joyce Bono, Winny Shen, and David Yoon address the oldest of these approaches—personality- or trait-based perspectives on leadership. As they note, scholarly and practical interest in the traits and characteristics of effective leaders is longstanding and broad ranging. Their chapter briefly summarizes the empirical literature, with a focus on both traits that have been linked to leadership in the past (i.e., Big Five traits, self-monitoring) and traits that deserve more attention in the future as predictors of leadership success and failure (i.e., traits related to resiliency, proactivity, adaptability, integrity). In an effort to stimulate future research, they advocate for a more complex approach to the study of personality and leadership, including examination of nonlinear associations, trait profiles, and factors that enhance or constrain the personality–leadership association.

Ketan Mhatre and Ronald Riggio review the theoretical frameworks of charismatic and transformational leadership, which have been at the forefront of leadership research and practice for the past several decades. They highlight the developments that have characterized the two areas of study since their conception and attempt to create a foundation for leadership research to progress in the future. Charismatic leadership and transformational leadership are reviewed, in turn, to provide an overview of the different viewpoints that have driven the respective theoretical development of these leadership constructs. In looking to the future, the authors outline several theoretical and research-related questions that will serve to motivate even better understanding of charismatic and transformational leadership.

Daan van Knippenberg and Daan Stam address the related issue of visionary leadership, defined as the communication of a future image of a collective with the intention to persuade others to contribute to its realization. It is widely seen as an effective way of mobilizing and motivating followers. The authors review the state of the science in visionary leadership and come to the conclusion that the effectiveness of visionary leadership is overly optimistic given the current state of the evidence. Their conclusions warn against complacency and satisfaction with the current state of the science with regard to visionary leadership. They close by presenting some specific methodological and conceptual challenges to consider in moving the study of visionary leadership forward.

The next chapter takes more of a "dark side" perspective on leadership through an examination of destructive leadership. Robert Kaiser and S. Bartholomew Craig offer a refined and integrative definition of destructive leadership that establishes the construct as a broad category containing narrower facets at the intersection of leadership and counterproductive work behavior. They review the small but growing evidence basis in destructive leadership in terms of empirical studies that focus on destructive leaders and those that focus on situational factors associated with destructive leadership. The review considers the implications of research on destructive leadership for organizational outcomes, highlights key themes regarding what is known about this phenomenon, identifies gaps in our knowledge, discusses needed future research, and also poses practical recommendations for organizations in detecting, preventing, and, if needed, recovering from destructive leadership.

Herminia Ibarra, Sarah Wittman, Gianpiero Petriglieri, and David Day review the contributions of role identity, social identity, and social construction theories toward comprehending the emergence, effectiveness, and development of leaders. In recent years, leadership scholars have combined two or more of these identity theories to conceptualize and study a range of phenomena including transitions into leadership roles, the challenges faced by women leaders, and the role of identity workspaces in leadership development. They propose areas where further research attention is needed, particularly the process by which non–prototypical leaders emerge, lead effectively, and develop; leader identities in contemporary settings characterized by globally distributed teams and multiple leadership roles; and identity evolution in the context of the life cycle of a leadership career.

Part IV: Follower-Centric Theories and Approaches

This handbook section switches the focus from leaders to followers in exploring various perspectives on how followers contribute meaningfully to effective leadership processes. The first chapter explores state-of-the-art perspectives on leadership perceptions. Jessica Dinh, Robert Lord, and Ernest Hoffman review and integrate recent empirical findings from neuropsychological research and the cognitive sciences to develop an information processing model that explores how symbolic, connectionist, emotional, and embodied architectures dynamically influence leadership perception and information processing. They conceptualize the human mind in terms of four abstract information-processing architectures (symbolic, connectionist, emotional, and embodied systems) that are based on neurobiological adaptive systems. A framework is then presented to explore how these architectures influence the emergence of leadership perceptions and information processing through multiple constraint satisfaction. This framework has the benefit of organizing and identifying new areas for future leadership research.

Bruce Avolio and Fred Walumbwa examine modern discussions regarding what constitutes authentic leadership by primarily focusing on the past decade of work in this area. Their chapter is organized around a series of questions used to frame how authentic leadership and its development are examined. These questions come from both the academic and practice communities and pose: (a) why authentic leadership now; (b) how the academic and practice communities have viewed authentic leadership; (c) the links that have been tested between authentic leadership, followership, and performance outcomes; (d) how authentic leadership relates to ethical outcomes; (e) how the research on authentic leadership can be extended to other domains, such as positive emotions; (f) how authentic leadership became authentic leadership development; (g) whether authentic leaders are born or made; and (h) what we have learned from research on authentic leadership in the past decade. Answers to these questions set the stage for discussing future research needs on the topic of authentic leadership and authentic leadership development.

Turning attention to the topic of servant leadership, Robert Liden Alexandra Panaccio, Jeremy Meuser, Jia Hu, and Sandy Wayne offer a comprehensive theoretical model that captures the development (antecedents) of servant leadership, its consequences (outcomes), and the mediating and moderating processes through which servant leadership behaviors result in key outcomes. They note that psychometrically sound measures of servant leadership are available that demonstrate incremental validity after controlling for the two most widely studied approaches to leadership: leader–member exchange and transformational leadership. Now that servant leadership has established legitimacy in the academic field, additional theory development and testing is needed to guide its further advancement. The model proposed by Liden and colleagues should be very helpful in advancing a science of servant leadership.

Sharon Parker and Chia-huei Wu review the emerging issue of leading for proactivity. In particular, how do leaders' promote proactivity among their staff (i.e., followers) where proactivity is defined as a future-focused, change-oriented, and self-starting ways of behaving? Included in their review is literature on individual innovation, taking charge, voice, proactive socialization, and other such ways of behaving proactively. They propose a model in which multiple pathways by which leaders can influence their staff's motivation and capability to be proactive are identified, as well as the effectiveness of their proactivity. Specifically, team-oriented and person-oriented leadership inputs can have direct effects on motivation and capability via leader actions, as well as through indirect effects on motivation and capability via leader effects on the team climate, work design, or other team-level inputs.

Part V: Dyadic and Team-Centric Theories and Approaches

This section further widens the theoretical lens in terms of examining leadership from more collective perspectives, particularly those dealing with dyads and teams. Berrin Erdogan and Talya Bauer present a comprehensive review of the literature on leader–member exchange (LMX), which is a widely researched, dyadic approach to leadership. They provide a summary of the theoretical underpinnings of LMX, discuss the measurement of LMX quality, provide a detailed review of the antecedents and consequences of LMX, and examine more recent developments aimed at exploring group-level implications of LMX. Future research directions and recommendations for best practices for research methods and dyadic relationship nomenclature are included.

The next chapter takes on the emerging issue of social networks and leadership. Raymond Sparrowe offers a novel approach to integrating leadership theories and social network perspectives by initiating a dialog that is organized in relation to leadership theories. In particular, these theories include exchange, which is the basis of LMX theory; categorization, including implicit leadership theory and other cognitive approaches; and identity processes such as identification, internalization, and the engagement of self-systems. These causal accounts serve as the focal point for initiating dialog with the social network perspective and its emphasis on embeddedness within the structure of relationships. In some cases, opportunities for integration emerge readily; in others, the juxtaposition of leadership theories and the social network perspectives is less easily resolved into a new synthesis. Taken together, this chapter offers a new way to think about social networks in relation to traditional as well as more contemporary approaches to leadership.

In addressing the topic of team leadership, Ruth Wageman and Colin Fisher analyze how specific team leadership challenges and opportunities emerge based on whether the team itself or managers hold legitimate authority for four critical team functions: (a) executing the team task, (b) monitoring and managing work processes, (c) designing the team and its context, and (d) setting overall direction for the team. These four resultant team authority structures (i.e. manager-led, self-managing, self-designing, and self-governing) are used to synthesize relevant research, draw implications for the practice of team leadership, and identify directions for future research.

Expanding the theoretical lens even further to address leadership in multiteam systems, which are composed of two or more teams that share one or more common superordinate goal, Dorothy Carter and Leslie DeChurch argue that, in complex systems involving multiple teams, leadership is often the result of the joint actions of multiple members. That is, leadership is often a shared or collective phenomenon in multiteam systems. They explain how the *form* of leadership (e.g., vertical, shared) can be captured using network analytic techniques across multiple *network foci* (e.g., within teams, between-teams, across the system). This perspective is then extended to describe the application of specific ego-net and network indices to the evaluation of multiteam leadership forms. Example prompts that could be used to elicit leadership *functions* and *goal foci* (e.g., leadership focused on individual, team-level goals, or multiteam system goals) in leadership networks are described, and example research questions that stem from incorporation of network analytic techniques with the study of multiteam leadership are discussed.

Part VI: Emerging Issues in Organizational Leadership

Chapters in this section shift the focus from leadership in organizations to leadership of organizations. In other words, it takes the perspective of different approaches to leading organizations rather than leading individuals, dyads, or teams in organizations. Darren Treadway, Jeffrey Bentley, Lisa Williams, and Angela Wallace seek to dispel notions of politics, and in particular political skill, as necessary evils of leadership and recast them simply as necessary for leadership. By recognizing leadership as a political process revolving around the facilitation of shared meaning, they review the development of the political skill construct and its integration with leadership research, including LMX, relational leadership, political leadership, and the CEO-celebrity effect. They identify areas in which scholarship has been relatively absent and discuss how addressing these areas in future research offer an important step toward developing a more comprehensive theory of politics and leadership.

Linda Treviño and Michael Brown review theory and research in the relatively new are of ethical leadership. They begin with an overview of the construct and its measurement, and then follow the development of a burgeoning literature to date. Thus far, research has mostly focused on the attitudinal and behavioral outcomes of ethical leadership, but researchers have also begun to investigate antecedents, intervening processes, moderators, and multilevel effects of different levels of leadership. Recommendations for future research are offered to extend our understanding of ethical leadership from a broader, systems perspective.

The topic of ethical leadership is related to the emerging field of corporate social responsibility and responsible leadership. David Waldman provides an overview of various societal and academic trends that have led to the need to more precisely consider the concept of responsible leadership. The chapter then presents an overview of alternative definitions of responsible leadership, connections with other leadership topics or models, existing research on responsible leadership, and future theory development and research agendas.

Nathan Hiller and Marie-Michèle Beauchesne review the literature on executive leadership or leadership in the executive context. Their review emphasizes research from the Upper Echelons perspective of strategic management while also considering traditional leadership research approaches and findings. The nature of executive leadership and the role of CEOs, top management teams, and boards of directors in producing organizational-level strategic, cultural, and performance outcomes are each considered. They also suggest seven methodological and conceptual possibilities for future research that appear to hold significant promise for advancing our understanding of the nature, mechanisms, and effects of executive leadership.

Part VII: Emerging Contextual Issues in Leadership

Contextual approaches to leadership have emerged as some of the most active areas of leadership research in the last decade (Day & Antonakis, 2012). Rather than one particular theory, contextual approaches represent a class of different theories relating to various contexts in which leadership is needed. Richard Osborn, Mary Uhl-Bien, and Ivana Milosevic explore the role context has played in leadership research over the past 100 years and offer a historical description of diverse perspectives and understandings of this interplay. Three approaches to studying the context of leadership are reviewed: (a) leadership as "nested" in hierarchy, (b) leadership as "pervasive" in social processes, and (c) leadership as a "hybrid" approach that is a combination of (a) and (b). The development of each approach is reviewed and alternative avenues for future research are suggested to achieve richer theoretical depiction and inspire continuous progress toward a more complete understanding of leadership and leadership effectiveness.

Sean Hannah and Ken Parry point out that in extreme (i.e., dangerous and unpredictable) contexts, the contextualization of leadership is pronounced and should be understood by researchers and incorporated into conceptualizations and models of leadership. They discuss the study and practice of leadership in extreme events and the nesting of those events in extreme contexts, and they describe the various unique and significant causations, constraints, contingencies, and other influences extreme contexts place on those in leadership positions, their followers, and the overall leadership processes. A deeper understanding of the relationships and interactions between leadership and contextual factors are needed, particularly if research is to inform ways to prepare leaders to operate effectively in extreme contexts.

Mark Griffin and Zenobia Talati address the important contextual concern of safety leadership or leadership in safety-critical environments, which pose a number of complex challenges for leaders. At the interpersonal level, leaders must devote their time to monitoring safety behaviors, providing feedback, setting goals and providing rewards to improve the behaviors of their followers. At the organizational level, leaders must work to create a positive safety culture in which employees feel a sense of trust in management and empowerment. In addition to managing human error, leaders need to maintain the integrity of machines and technology used in the work environment. Their review of the literature demonstrates the positive impact of these leader behaviors on safety performance at different organizational levels. They also review how leaders can balance the safety goals that are intrinsic to high reliability with goals to support and produce a proactive workforce that goes beyond compliance and actively participates in the safety process.

The role of leadership in global and cross-cultural contexts is addressed by Felix Brodbeck and Silke Eisenbeiss. The progress achieved in the field is critically reviewed along fundamental research questions, such as: which definitions of leadership are appropriate for cross-cultural study, which approaches to culture are suitable for studying leadership, which focus on leadership to take (leadership differences or communalities across cultures), the magnitude of cultural effects on leadership, the moderating role of culture on the relationship between leadership and other relevant variables, and the methodological issues that have been and still need to be resolved in cross-cultural leadership research. Targeting the future, seven recommendations are offered that specify fundamental conceptual, theoretical, methodological, and practical issues in which significant progress can be made with regard to global and cross-cultural leadership.

Donna Chrobot-Mason, Marian Ruderman, and Lisa Nishii address the challenges and opportunities associated with understanding leadership in a diverse organizational context. Although there is a significant need to understand the implications of increasing demographic diversity for leadership, surprisingly little research has been conducted on the topic. The review is organized into three sections: (a) how leaders lead themselves, (b) how they lead others, and (c) how they lead the organization. Issues related to social identity, the qualities that leaders are likely to need when managing employees who are from diverse backgrounds, and what it takes to develop quality relationships, cultivate an inclusive climate, span boundaries, and frame diversity initiatives. Research related to the role leaders play in setting their organization's diversity strategy, implementing diversity practices, managing conflict, responding to diversity crises, and measuring progress are also discussed.

James Hazy and Mary Uhl-Bien review the study of complexity theory and how it has become an important lens through which to view and understand the causes and potencies of individual action and interaction in organizations, as well as their meaning for leadership research and practice. This review of key complexity ideas and their theoretical implications for leadership describes emerging theories in the field, highlights the growing empirical support for these approaches, and sets an agenda for future research. Just as complexity has become an overarching theoretical paradigm in the natural sciences, it is providing the basis for a paradigm shift in the social sciences, particularly in leadership and organizational studies. Complex systems leadership theory describes the process whereby the rules governing local interactions are changed in response to and in anticipation of changing circumstances. In shifting the focus from the individual to the organizing process itself, the complexity leadership perspective has important implications for both research and practice.

Jean Lau Chin addresses the gendered context of leadership in which differences and similarities between men and women are identified in the research on women and leadership. The contexts of leadership that are relevant to this topic include follower perceptions and expectations, as well as the nature of the leadership–member relationships, which are important influences in how women lead. Underrepresentation and the existence of gender bias frame the context of leadership for women. It is noted that current theories of leadership typically omit any discussion of gender, feminist values, or principles of diversity. Chin argues that organizational cultures remain male dominated and do not strive toward gender-equitable work environments, although ethics-based leadership, diversity leadership, collaborative leadership, and transformational leadership styles, which favor the leadership of women, are considered to be important dimensions of leadership today. Whereas the behavior of men and women leaders is similar in many ways, leadership for women remains a different experience. Future directions must consider the importance of leadership contexts and leader identity including work–family interface, affirmative paradigms, lived experience, and multiple dimensions of self-identity

Part VIII: Special Concerns in Leadership

The eighth section addresses various special topics or concerns in leadership such as creativity, emotions, and training and development. Michael Mumford, Carter Gibson, Vincent Giorgini, and Jensen Mecca note that the success of many organizations depends on creativity (i.e., the production of original problem solutions) and innovation (i.e., the translation of these solutions into viable new products or processes). The traditional perspectives hold that leaders have little influence on the work of creative people. More recent research, however, indicates that leadership may be critical to the success of creative efforts in organizations. The review focuses on three key functions that leaders of creative efforts must execute: (a) directing the work, (b) leading people doing the work, and (c) managing relationships with the organization. Key issues arising in the execution of each of these functions are examined.

Neal Ashkanasy and Ronald Humphreys argue that leadership and emotion are intimately connected at five levels of organizing. At Level 1, leaders generate and manage affective events for their followers that result in emotional states, which in turn lead to positive or negative attitudes and behaviors. At Level 2, leaders exhibit individual differences in their ability to perceive and manage emotions, both in themselves and in their followers, usually referred to as emotional intelligence. At Level 3, which concerns interpersonal relationships, leadership effectiveness is associated with the idea of leading with emotional labor, in which a leader's ability to manage followers is determined in part by the leader's ability to model the right type and amount of emotion in the right circumstance. At Level 4, group leadership is discussed, whereby processes of emotional contagion are important. At Level 5, emotions and leadership are viewed as organization-wide processes in which culture becomes a "fossilization" of patterns of behavior. As such, leaders have a responsibility to engender a positive emotional work environment, resulting in effective outcomes for the organization as a whole.

Susan Komives and John Dugan address the important topic of student leadership development. They advance a lifespan approach to the process of leadership development through the exploration of educational contexts experienced by adolescents and college students as powerful venues for building leadership capacity. Considerations from developmental psychology are positioned as critical influences on the processes of leadership development. The chapter synthesizes existing theories, research, and practical applications designed specifically for youth and college student populations.

Scott DeRue and Christopher Myers develop a conceptual framework called PREPARE that helps organize and synthesize key insights from the literature on leadership development. In this framework, attention is directed to the strategic purpose and desired results of leadership development in organizations. They emphasize how organizations can deliberately and systematically leverage a range of developmental experiences for enhancing the leadership capabilities of individuals, relationships, and collectives. They also highlight how individuals and organizations vary in their approach to and support for leadership development and how these differences explain variation in leadership development processes and outcomes. As an organizing mechanism for the existing literature, the PREPARE framework advances our understanding of what individuals and organizations can do to develop leadership talent and highlights important questions for future research.

Part IX: Future of Leadership

In the sole chapter in the final section, I review the progress made in advancing a complex, systems perspective on leadership that incorporates leaders, followers, dyads, teams, organizations, and contextual concerns. In looking to the future of leadership, ways to interconnect these various perspectives on leadership are encouraged. It is hoped that this handbook provides readers with fresh and innovative ways to think about leadership and how its scientific foundation can be strengthened, as well as how ideas into action (i.e., practice) can be facilitated.

Acknowledgments

I gratefully acknowledge the Australian Research Council (DP #1093209) for support that, in part, assisted in the composition of this chapter and in editing this handbook.

References

Bass, B. M. (2008). *The Bass handbook of leadership: Theory, research, and managerial applications* (4th ed.). New York: Free Press.

Day, D. V., & Antonakis, J. (2012). Leadership: Past, present, and future. In D. V. Day & J. Antonakis (Eds.), *The nature of leadership* (2nd ed., pp. 3–25). Los Angeles: Sage.

Day, D. V., & Lord, R. G. (1988). Executive leadership and organizational performance: Suggestions for a new theory and methodology. *Journal of Management, 14*, 453–464.

Hollander, E. P., & Julian, J. W. (1969). Contemporary trends in the analysis of leadership processes. *Psychological Bulletin, 71*, 387–397.

Locke, E. A. (2003). Foundations for a theory of leadership. In S. E. Murphy & R. E. Riggio (Eds.), *The future of leadership development* (pp. 29–46). Mahwah, NJ: Erlbaum.

Lord, R. G., De Vader, C. L., & Alliger, G. M. (1986). A meta-analysis of the relation between personality traits and leadership perceptions: An application of validity generalization procedures. *Journal of Applied Psychology, 71*, 402–409.

Mann, R. D. (1959). A review of the relationships between personality and performance in small groups. *Psychological Bulletin, 56*, 241–270.

Stogdill, R. M. (1948). Personal factors associated with leadership: A survey of the literature. *Journal of Psychology, 25*, 35–71.

CHAPTER 2

Leadership Memes: From Ancient History and Literature to Twenty-First Century Theory and Research

Stephen J. Zaccaro

Abstract

Leadership has fascinated people since antiquity. This fascination has given rise to countless intergenerational transmissions and replications of leadership stories, legends, fables, and lessons. These transmissions have coalesced into at least the four leader memes described here: *leader-warrior, leader–problem solver, leader-politician,* and *leader-teacher*. In this chapter, each meme is presented along with a brief summary of historical and cultural replicated exemplars that provide memetic content. The influences of memes are seen in modern theories and models of leadership. Thus, this chapter indicates the scientific frameworks of leadership that reflect the core ideas of each leader meme. Finally, memes can influence the weight people place on particular traits and attributes in their leader prototypes. Likewise, their orientation to and interpretation of leadership experiences are in turn influenced by memetic-infused leader self-identities. These dynamics determine a person's selection of leader development activities. This chapter concludes with a discussion of these relationships.

Key Words: leader memes, leader prototypes, leader self-identities, leader development

Concepts of leadership have been part of the human vocabulary since antiquity. Van Vugt, Hogan, and Kaiser (2008) grounded leadership emergence back in earliest human history on the functional requirements of collective action. They opined that human ancestral groups displaying particular types of organization were more likely to be successful in accomplishing daily tasks, noting that "collective foraging and hunting, food sharing, division of labor, group defenses, and communal parenting provided a buffer against external threats" (p. 183). Such collective action would require decisions about direction and organization of collective effort, and those primitive groups that could make such decisions more effectively were more likely to thrive. Decision making about initiative and direction is the province of leadership (Van Vugt, et al., 2008; Zaccaro, Heinen, & Shuffler, 2009). Moreover, Van Vugt et al. noted that the likely constancy of conflict in human ancestral groups heightened the need for "central command" (p. 184) in such contexts; accordingly, the utility of individuals who could act as either peacekeepers or conquerors fostered the evolutionary functionality of leadership dynamics. They surmised that groups that evolved effective leadership dynamics were likely to survive and thrive over those that did not foster such processes: "In this way, psychological mechanisms supporting leadership and followership could eventually spread through a population" (p. 184).

The centrality of leadership to ancestral group survival and success suggests that individuals who provided leadership at various critical moments in the group's history were likely to be the subjects and themes of repeated intra- and intergenerational storytelling within the group. Bass (2008) described the ubiquity of leadership in both human mythology and history. He noted that "myths and legends about great leaders were important in the development of civilized societies" (p. 4), and described how leader stories occupied the core of ancient literary references and classics from Babylonian, Greek, Latin, Hindu, Asian, Christian, and most other cultures. These stories were told and retold in many forms such that they transcended the boundaries of any particular group or culture, and infused their themes across many generations and societies. Members of each generation and society absorb, imitate, revise, and pass on the ideas and actions derived from these themes. This evolution of leadership themes reflects what Richard Dawkins (1976) referred to more generally as "memes," or replicators that serve as cultural analogues of biological genes.

The vast array of anecdotes, myths, and stories of leadership from antiquity to the present do not reflect a single monolithic theme that is uniformly reflected in every telling. Human literature is replete with great variety in the nature of leadership memetic genotypes (see Blackmore, 1999, for an explication of meme genotypes and phenotypes). In this chapter, I will describe four such leader memes that have evolved through human cultural history and that are reflected in many intergenerational cultural artifacts. These memes depict leaders as *warriors, problem solvers, politicians*, or *teachers*. Each of these memes is grounded in a rich set of classical and modern sources that define and replicate its core themes about the nature and practice of leadership. They are the stories that novice and apprentice leaders are told in order to explain leadership.

The Role of Leader Memes in the Science of Leadership

Leader memes play several important roles in scientific leadership theories and models. First, theories and models of leadership can reflect at their core one or more of these memes. For example, the leader-warrior meme emphasizes the leader as overcoming competitors and establishing dominance in a particular space. This notion is reflected in several models of strategic management (Barney, 1991; Jaques, 1976; 1989; Porter, 1979, 1980, 2008; Miles & Snow, 1978) as well as (obviously) in frameworks of military leadership (Hannah, Uhl-Bien, Avolio, & Cavarretto, 2009; Wong, Bliese, & McGurk, 2003). Leader-politician reflects the theme that leaders gain power and influence by acquiring leadership authority, or the acquiescence to lead, from a critical threshold of followers (cf. Hollander, 1964; Hollander & Julian, 1970). This idea has prompted theories of how follower perceptions and prototypes of leaders affect leadership dynamics (Dinh & Lord, 2012; Eden & Leviatan, 1975; Lord, Foti, & Phillips, 1982; Rush, Thomas, & Lord, 1977). This influence of leader memes on modern leadership models and theories exist as well for the memes of leader–problem solver (e.g., Jacobs & Jaques, 1987; Mumford, Zaccaro, Harding, Jaocbs, & Fleishman, 2000), and leader-teacher (e.g., Bass, 1985; Greenleaf, 1970/2008; Hackman & Wageman, 2005; Kozlowski, Gully, McHugh, Salas, & Cannon-Bowers, 1996; Kozlowski, Watola, Jensen, Kim, & Botero, 2009).

Leader memes and their content are also implicated in the traits, personal qualities, and attributes that individuals ascribe as ideal for effective leaders. The identification of the traits that distinguish leaders from nonleaders and good leaders from bad leaders is perhaps the oldest theme in leadership scholarship. Indeed, many literary classics that have contributed to current leader memes emphasize this theme (e.g., Plato's *Republic*, Machiavelli's *The Prince*). The stories that serve as the foundation of each leader meme highlight different attributes of focal leaders. For example, the leader-warrior meme may emphasize courage, honor, integrity, and strategic cunning as key leader attributes for success; the leader–problem solver meme primes such attributes as cognitive capacity, divergent thinking, and wisdom. Leader-politician memes would place a premium on communication skills, social acumen, and political savvy, while leader-teacher memes emphasize attributes such as empathy, integrity, humility, and a service orientation.

Lord and his colleagues have shown how beliefs about leader attributes become organized in cognitive structures, or prototypes, that in turn become influential in follower perceptions of leaders and leadership behaviors (Dinh & Lord, 2012; Lord, 1985; Lord, Brown, Harvey, & Hall, 2001; Lord, Foti, & DeVader, 1984; Lord & Maher, 1993; Phillips & Lord, 1982). Following Rosch (1975, 1978), Lord et al. (1984) described these cognitive structures as having three levels. The superordinate level consists of those core attributes that differentiate leaders from nonleaders. All leaders are expected to share those attributes, and these qualities would be absent in the descriptions of nonleaders. At the basic level, separate categories of leaders would be denoted with sets of attributes and characteristics that differentiate different types of leaders (e.g., political, military, religious). Finally the subordinate level reflects characteristics that further differentiate leaders within a particular type (e.g., progressive versus conservative political leaders).

Lord et al. (2001; see also Dinh & Lord, 2012) extended this perspective by suggesting that leader prototypes can reflect connectionist networks containing attributes as nodes, with linkages among the attributes forming an overall leader attribute pattern. Contextual parameters activate these networks in alternative ways, such that different cultural, leader, follower, and task characteristics foster greater (or less) weight on certain attributes and linkages among attributes. For example, Lord, et al. (2001) proposed that contrasting attribute networks could be activated by male versus female leaders and followers; prototypes activated by males would emphasize dominance and masculinity, while female-activated prototypes would weight flexibility more heavily and dominance and masculinity less so. Support for this proposition was offered by Johnson, Murphy, Zewdie, & Reichard (2008) who found that certain attributes (strength, masculinity, tyranny) were primed by male leaders, while sensitivity as an attribute was more primed by female leaders. Both types of leaders primed the attributes of dedication, charisma, attractiveness, and intelligence.

In a similar manner, leader memes are likely to imbue the core values, beliefs, self-identities, and goal orientations of leaders and followers that in turn contribute to the differential activation of leader prototypes. The memes described in this chapter are reflected in the earliest and most frequent leadership stories that individuals attend to and resonate with, placing them at the core of emerging leader self-identities and values. Accordingly, different leader memes can activate different patterns among connected leader attributes. For example, Dinh and Lord (2012) suggest,

> In a *competitive* environment, for instance, leadership prototypes may center more on individual characteristics that emphasize "dominance" and "aggression." However, in contexts that center on *cooperation,* a different type of leadership prototype may become active—e.g., one that views traits such as being "sensitive" and "generous" as being important leadership characteristics. (p. 655)

While not necessarily reflecting different environments or contexts, leader memes can give rise to similar differential emphases. Thus, the leader-warrior meme is more likely to lead to the perception of leader contexts as competitive and therefore emphasize the importance of leader dominance and aggression. Alternatively, the leader-teacher meme may lead to perceptions of leader contexts as entailing cooperation and empowerment, and would therefore trigger sensitivity and generosity as critical leader attributes.

To be clear, leader memes are not the same as leader prototypes or implicit leadership theories. The latter are cognitive representations of leadership that emerge from early and frequent experiences with leaders. Memes are rooted in the true stories, myths and fables about leaders and leadership that are replicated across persons. Thus, they reside fundamentally in cultures, and are passed from generation to generation through repeated storytelling. Recipients of these memes may then use them when interpreting their personal experiences of leaders and forming subsequent leader prototypes. Memes are somewhat analogous to, although not the same as, Jungian archetypes or the kinds of myths described by Joseph Campbell (e.g., Campbell & Moyers, 1988). Jung described archetypes as psychic elements that form the basis of ancient myths, reside in a collective unconscious, and are present in all of us (Jung, trans. 2010). Memes evolve and derive from the stories, events, and myths that reflect these archetypes. They are not present in a collective unconscious nor do they exist in the same ways in all individuals who receive them. The kinds of myths described by Campbell and Moyers (1988) serve as forms of memetic transmission. However, memes are derived (and replicated) not only through myths, but also from oft-cited historical events and treatises of behavioral prescriptions (e.g., Machiavelli's *The Prince*; Benjamin Franklin's *Poor Richard's Almanack*).

If memes influence perceptions of which leader attribute patterns are primary drivers of leader emergence and effectiveness, they can influence those aspects of leadership that are in turn affected by such perceptions, including leader and follower behaviors, leadership development, and processes of selecting leaders in organizations. Thus, leader memes may serve as important drivers in multiple theories and models of leadership emergence, effectiveness, and development. Later in this chapter I will explore these linkages between concepts of leadership memes and leadership theories, but for now the critical point is that leadership memes infuse not only our culture but also our scholarship about leadership.

In the next sections of this chapter I will describe the notion of memes and their application to leadership. A full discourse on the nature of memes is beyond this chapter, and I refer interested readers to the references that are offered in the text. However, I will offer a brief description on the mechanisms of memes and memetic influence as they may apply to leadership. I will follow this section with some elaboration on how leadership memes influence leadership phenomena.

The heart of this chapter describes each of the specified leadership memes. For each meme, I will (1) provide a definition of its substance; (2) briefly trace its ancestral lineage, (3) point to conceptual models of leadership that appear to most reflect that meme; and (4) delineate leader traits and attributes that are primed by that meme. Through this explication, I hope to sharpen understanding of the cultural evolution of core leadership concepts in our scientific models and theories.

The Nature and Transmission of Leadership Memes

Memes: Basic Principles

The term *meme* was first coined by Dawkins (1976/2006), who defined it as "a unit of cultural transmission, or a unit of *imitation*" (p. 192, italics in original). Blackmore (1999, p. 4) defined a meme as "as idea, an instruction, a behaviour, a piece of information" and "instructions for carrying out behaviour, stored in brains (or other objects) and passed on by imitation" (p. 17). Dawkins (1976/2006) stated,

> Examples of memes are tunes, ideas, catch-phrases, clothes fashions, ways of making pots or of building arches. Just as genes propagate themselves in the gene pool by leaping from body to body via sperms or eggs, so memes propagate themselves in the meme pool by leaping from brain to brain via a process which, in the broad sense, can be called imitation. If a scientist hears, or reads about, a good idea, he passes it on to his colleagues and scientists. He mentions it in his articles and his lectures. If the idea catches on, it can be said to propagate itself, spreading from brain to brain. (p. 192)

A meme, then, is defined not so much by its initiation, but rather by its imitation and replication. An idea becomes a meme when people begin to imitate its expression. It gains in power as this imitation is replicated across groups, populations, cultures, and generations (Blackmore, 1999; Dennett, 1991). Imitation and replication occurs through many modes—verbal histories and stories perhaps at first, followed by texts and written words, and, in the modern era, web-based links and other forms of electronic media. For example, Dawkins (1999, p. xiv) uses the Internet or web search engines to assess the widespread usage (and therefore power) of a meme (in his example, the concept "meme"). Wikipedia represents perhaps a most interesting example of meme transmission, as the entries in this electronic encyclopedia are prepared by volunteers. The entry for "Wikipedia" in *Wikipedia* notes, "A topic [to be included] should... meet Wikipedia's standards of 'notability,' which usually means that it must have received significant coverage in reliable secondary sources such as mainstream media or major academic journals that are independent of the subject of the topic" ("Wikipedia," n.d.). The choice to add a topic into *Wikipedia*, then, depends upon it rising to a level of an oft-imitated or replicated meme.

According to Dawkins (1976/2006; see also Blackmore, 1999), the process of imitation and replication is an evolutionary one, in which some memes have greater ability or tendency to be replicated than others. Blackmore (1999) defined three characteristics of memes as replicators: *variation, retention*, and *selection*. When transmitted across persons, memes change in some elements—the original idea, description, or story mutates, is embellished, with some particulars rearranged or even dropped. Multiple imperfect copies of the original meme create variation in the population. However, Blackmore's notion of retention means that "something of the original meme must be retained for us to call it imitation or copying or learning by example" (p. 14). Thus, the core nature, idea, lesson, or principle of the meme gets transmitted, even though its more peripheral details can be lost or changed across multiple transmissions.

Regarding memetic selection, Blackmore (1999, p. 14) noted that "some memes grab the attention, are faithfully remembered and passed on to other people, while others fail to get copied at all." The key question then is this: What gives a meme greater (or less) "replicator power" (Blackmore, 1999, p. 5)? Blackmore argues that such power resides both in the cognitive characteristics of humans (e.g., attention, memory, information processing capacity) and in elements of the memes themselves. The attention and memory capacity of meme receivers is likely to influence their degree of retention and subsequent transmission. Moreover, features of the memes can determine the degree to which they attract attention and facilitate encoding; memes that are novel, rich in detail, useful, and expressed by authoritative sources are more likely to be replicated (Heylighen, 1997, 2001).

Heath, Bell, and Sternberg (2001) argued that the memes survive and succeed because of both their information value and their evocation of shared and widespread emotional reactions among recipients. The researchers noted that memes can evoke both positive and negative emotions, and they specified two social functions of such emotions. First, emotion-laden memes address recipients' "emotional consumption" needs (Heath, et al., 2001, p. 1030). According to Heath et al., people enjoy experiencing emotions, particularly positive ones, and will choose to attend and pass on items that elicit such emotions. They argued that memes are often replicated "based on their ability to evoke consistent emotions across people" (p. 1030). Their second argument was that the emotional aspects of memes can create "social bonding" among recipients; they note that "people may choose to pass along rumors and legends that create emotion not because they enjoy consuming the emotion directly, but because the shared emotion enhances their social interactions" (p. 1030). Thus, for both reasons, more emotion-laden memes have an increased likelihood of being imitated and replicated in a culture. In support of this argument, Heath, et al. found in a study of the transmission of urban legends that those memes with an ability to elicit stronger emotions were more likely to be replicated

Application to Leader-Memes

This short summary of the nature of memes suggests several key elements in the cultural transmission and assimilation of leader memes. First, many core leadership principles and ideas have a very long history of imitation and replication. As an example, consider the expression "know thyself," a phrase that prescribes greater self-awareness and, when used in leadership contexts, refers to a necessary component of effective leader development (Day, 2000; McCauley, Van Velsor, & Ruderman, 2010). *Wikipedia*'s entry for this phrase (itself attesting to strong power as a meme) delineates its long history in human discourse and literature ("Know thyself," n.d.). The earliest rendition of this idea is an inscription on the temple of Luxor in ancient Egypt, which dates back to about 1400 B.C. (Hill, 2010). The inscription was also on the temple of Apollo at Delphi, dating to about the 6th century B.C. This *Wikipedia* entry for "know thyself" does not mention Sun Tzu's *Art of War* (trans. 2011), but in that text, which also dates to about the 6th century B.C., Sun Tzu summarized strategic prescriptions for military leadership by noting "hence the saying: If you know the enemy and know yourself, you need not fear the result of a hundred battles (p.10). " His use of the phrase "hence the saying" suggests that "know thyself" was already a replicated meme and was being applied at least to military leadership. *Wikipedia*'s entry for this phrase also noted its widespread use in Plato's descriptions of Socrates' teaching, dating toward the end of the 5th century B.C.

The strong replicator power of this meme is also evidenced in the summary by *Wikipedia* of its literary use in 1651 by Thomas Hobbes, 1734 by Alexander Pope, 1750 by Benjamin Franklin, 1831 by Ralph Waldo Emerson, 1832 by Samuel T. Coleridge, and 1999 in the movie *The Matrix* ("Know thyself," n.d.). As of this writing, a Google search of the phrase "know thyself" elicited close to 3 million results. Indeed, its relevance for modern leadership theory and research is evidenced by three recent research articles on strategic leadership and leadership development that used the phrase "know thyself" as part of their titles (Grotas, 2004; Riantoputra, 2010; Turesky & Gallagher, 2011). Thus, the replicator power of this particular meme has endured for approximately 3,500 years and has come to illustrate a core principle of leadership and leader development. It provides one example of an ancient meme that has survived to influence present leadership philosophy, theory, and research.

Leadership memes have been—and continue to be—replicated through all forms of verbal and written modes of communication. These transmitted memes have taken mostly three major forms: fictionalized legends and myths, biographical stories, and prescriptive treatises. Bass (2008) described leadership principles found in early Egyptian literature in 2300 B.C. He also noted such principles found in the Greek mythology texts by Homer, the *Iliad* and the *Odyssey*, which date back to around 700 B.C. Another mythological source of leadership memes, Virgil's *Aeneid* describes the story of Aeneas establishing the settlements that give rise to Rome and the Roman Empire. Such leadership myths are not limited to ancient sources. Celebrations of George Washington's birthday every year give rise to repeated renditions of the fable that he chopped down a cherry tree and, when asked, could not tell a lie. The core of this myth, of course, was the personal integrity of our first president.

Biographical accounts, although they are sometimes open to questions of full validity and accuracy, provide another source of replicated leadership memes. Several accounts of ancient Grecian leaders, including Alexander the Great, were provided in early biographies by Arrian (trans. 1958), Herodotus (trans. 2002), and Plutarch (trans. 1960). Early Roman leaders were the source of biographies by Suetonius (trans. 1957), Livi (trans. 1960), and Plutarch (trans. 1965). Another source, *Plutarch's Lives* (Plutarch, trans. 2001), represents an interesting comparison of early Roman and Greek leaders that illustrates how similar these leaders were in several core leadership traits (Zaccaro, LaPort, & José, 2013). The Bible also provides a rich compendium of biography-derived leadership ideas and memes (Woolfe, 2002). Indeed, David, Solomon, and Jesus provided roots for three of the four leader memes described in this chapter.

Biographical accounts of more modern leaders remain a popular form of meme transmission in contemporary literature and other forms of discourse. A scan of the *New York Times* Best Sellers list for the last three months of 2012 and the first month of 2013 produced mention of no fewer than 12 biographies, autobiographies, and memoirs about leaders in political, business, military and sports contexts.[1] Abraham Lincoln was not only the source of one of these books (Goodwin, 2005), but of an acclaimed movie in 2012, as well. The re-emergence of the book on the best sellers list was perhaps prompted by the success of the movie; indeed, its title, *Team of Rivals,* reflects the leadership meme of "keeping your enemies close."

Leadership memes have also derived from leadership prescriptions offered by successful leaders. One of the earliest of such literature is Sun Tzu's *Art of War* (trans. 2011). Others include Plato's *Republic* (trans. 1993), Machiavelli's The *Prince* (trans. 2003), and von Clausewitz's *On War* (1832/1976). Books offering leadership prescriptions are ubiquitous in modern literature as well; a search on Amazon.com on the word *leadership* produced more than 85,000 titles. Many of these sources build on prior leadership memes or initiate some of their own.

The drivers of strong memetic selection proposed by Blackmore (1999), Heath et al. (2001), and Heylighen (1997, 2001) are well-evidenced in the most persistent leadership memes. Leadership stories that provided the sources for memes passed intra- and intergenerationally were likely to reflect major and critical events in a culture's history. Because of their historical centrality, these stories, beginning as oral traditions, were likely to be rich in details that were replicated faithfully across transmissions. The most vivid leadership successes (or failures, when the goal is to impart leadership lessons) were likely to be the basis of these stories. For example, George Washington lost many battles in the American Revolution, yet one of his most iconic painted images shows him leading his troops across the Delaware in a stealth attack on the Hessians. Depictions such as this one, together with such sources as Sun Tzu's *Art of War* (trans. 2011) and the story of David and Goliath in the Bible provide part of the foundation for the leader-warrior meme.

Because leadership is crucial to collective success (Burke et al., 2006; Morgeson, DeRue, & Karam, 2010; Zaccaro et al., 2009), memetic leadership content provides important sources of information on how to engage effectively as a leader. The stories become vehicles for imparting leadership lessons to leader-apprentices. Moreover, the vividness of leadership stories and their rooting in major events in a culture's history are likely to foster high emotional consumption (Heath et al., 2001). Stories of leadership successes in a culture or community evoke pride among its inhabitant tellers and listeners. The positive emotions evoked by most leadership stories, their informative content, and their facilitative effects on community cohesion provide strong replicator power to corresponding leader memes. Accordingly, they continue to endure powerfully across multiple cultures.

Dawkins (1999) raises an interesting question: What size unit denotes a meme (p. xiv)? While the answer is yet unknown, or at least undefined, leader memes are probably more accurately described as integrated clusters of memes, or "memeplexes" (Speel, 1995, cited in Blackmore, 1999, p. 19). Multiple memetic ideas likely cohere around a core meaning of leadership and its practice. Until more clarity exists around the notion of memeplexes, their size, and their character, for the purposes of this chapter, I will use the word *meme* to refer to these core meanings, rather than to any particular memetic idea.

Four Leadership Memes

Earlier I described four leadership memes that have exhibited strong replicator power in human discourse: *leader-warrior; leader–problem solver; leader-politician*; and *leader-teacher*. In this section, I will elaborate on each of these memes. Note that I have not labeled these memes leader *as* warrior or leader *as* problem solver; these are not analogies, metaphors, or symbols of leadership. Instead they reflect core values and beliefs about the nature of leadership and the relationship between leaders and followers. They are ideas about leadership that are transmitted in relatively stable form from person to person, across and within generations, through multiple cultural modes.

For each meme, I will offer (1) a definition and description of its content; (2) a brief summary of its historical roots and cultural evolution; (3) illustrations of how the meme has influenced or appeared in modern leadership theory and research; and (4) a listing of primed personal attributes. Table 2.1 presents a summary of each of these elements for each meme. The content of a leader meme will reflect core leadership values and prescribe certain functional leadership activities. Functional leadership perspectives suggest that the fundamental role of

Table 2.1. A Summary of Leader Memes, Their Historical and Cultural Roots, and Their Influences on Leadership Science

Leader Meme	Leadership Frame	Sample of Historical and Cultural Memetic Replications	Influenced Leadership Theories and Models	Primed Leader Attributes
Leader-warrior	• Leadership as overcoming enemies and competitors • Motivating and leading followers into battle	• Sun Tzu, *The Art of War* • Biblical story of David & Goliath • Early Greek and Roman war heroes (e.g., Alexander the Great; Julius Caesar) • von Clausewitz's *On War* • Modern war heroes (Washington, Napoleon, Churchill)	• Strategic management theories • Stratified systems theory • Resource-based theory	• Courage • Risk-taking • Honor • Integrity • Strategic cunning
Leader–problem solver	• Leadership as generating wise solutions	• Lao Tzu, *Tao Te Ching* • Biblical story of King Solomon • Plato's *Republic* • Benjamin Franklin	• Initiating structure • Models of leader problem-solving processes • Models of leader wisdom	• Complex problem-solving skills • Wisdom • Divergent thinking skills
Leader-politician	• Leadership as accruing the loyalty and leader role endorsement of followers	• Cicero • Machiavelli, *The Prince* • Leaders who were great communicators (e.g., Martin Luther King; Abraham Lincoln, Winston Churchill) • Leaders who enacted far-reaching political bargains (e.g., Thomas Jefferson, Abraham Lincoln, Franklin Roosevelt, Lyndon Johnson)	• Hollander's leader legitimacy model • Leader categorization theory; models of follower information processing • Charismatic leadership models	• Communication skills • Interpersonal skills • Social acumen • Political savvy • Negotiation skills
Leader-teacher	• Leadership as teaching, coaching, and empowering followers	• Lao Tzu, *Tao Te Ching* • Jesus	• Servant leadership • Transformational leadership • Leader-member exchange theory • Models of team leadership	• Empathy • Integrity • Authenticity • Humility • Service orientation • Coaching and pedagogical skills

leaders is to provide for the satisfaction of collective needs (McGrath, 1962; Hackman & Walton, 1986). Because each meme defines collective success in relatively different terms, each implies a different set of team and follower needs that require address by leaders. Accordingly, different leadership activities will be primed by different leader-memes as more or less instrumental for collective success.

Different leader memes will also highlight different leader attributes. Earlier in this chapter, I summarized work by Lord and his colleagues describing how leaders and followers retain elaborated cognitive structures linking multiple personal attributes together in a leader prototype. These prototypes become instrumental in how followers perceive leaders and leadership acts (Dinh & Lord, 2012; Lord et al., 2001; Lord & Maher, 1993). Dinh and Lord (2012) argued that contextual parameters can place greater (or less) weight on the influence of certain attributes and certain attribute linkages on leadership perceptions. Because leadership memes prime certain perspectives and qualities of leadership behavior, they too can increase or decrease weights assigned to particular traits, or combination of traits in leader prototypes. Accordingly, in the descriptions below of each leadership meme, I include personal qualities that are suggested by each meme as critical leader attributes.

Leader-Warrior Meme

DEFINITION

The leader-warrior meme describes leaders as conquerors of enemies, and defenders of followers against enemies. Functional leadership activities reflected by this meme include understanding the enemy; developing tactical, operational, and strategic plans to overcome enemies; and motivating and leading followers into a battle. Leadership success is thus defined relative to the status of enemies, opponents, or competitors. Memetic elements of the leader-warrior include stories of heroism by leaders in competition, and leadership strategies developed to overcome enemies. They contain informational and motivational leadership prescriptions offered as critical to competitive success (e.g., "Know thy enemy"[2]; "Keep friends close, and enemies closer"[3]; "Winning isn't everything, it's the only thing"[4]).

HISTORICAL AND CULTURAL EVOLUTION

The earliest leadership stories most likely reflected the leader-warrior meme. Sun Tzu's *Art of War* (trans. 2011) summarizes a number of leadership prescriptions that contribute to the content of this meme. According to Sun Tzu, successful leadership is to be grounded in effective strategic thinking that takes into account not only the strengths and weaknesses of one's own followers, but those of the enemy as well. Both leader self-awareness and understanding of the enemy are also defined as a critical for success ("If you know the enemy and know yourself, you need not fear the result of a hundred battles" p. 10). The relationship of the leader to follower is an instrumental one in which the former motivates the latter to persist in battle to the point of death; leaders are to act toward followers in such a way as to foster high referent power (French & Raven, 1959).

This definition of leadership, which entails conquering enemies and motivating followers into battle, has been replicated in multiple leader fables, stories, prescriptive texts, and biographies across many generations and cultures. Near contemporaneous biographies of Alexander the Great (Arrian, trans. 1958) and Julius Caesar (Suetoniuus, trans. 1957) highlighted their military achievements for Greece and Rome, respectively. The Biblical account of David defeating Goliath (1 Samuel 17) is a prime example of the leader-warrior meme, one that has been replicated many times in art.[5] Von Clausewitz's *On War* (1832/1976) represents the 19th-century follow-up to Sun Tzu's text. Accounts of the military achievements of George Washington, Napoleon, and Winston Churchill have also furthered this meme. A constant theme in most replications of this meme, perhaps exemplified best by the David and Goliath story, is how a military leader (e.g., George Washington, Winston Churchill) defeats an apparently stronger and more powerful foe. This particular quality imbues the leader-warrior meme with an emotional tone that enhances its replicator power (Heath et al., 2001).

INFLUENCE IN LEADERSHIP THEORY AND RESEARCH

The core elements of the leader-warrior meme emphasize leadership in competitive contexts directed toward overcoming opponents and enemies. Within this meme, leadership also entails inspiring subordinates to follow leaders into competitions with high risks for personal losses. These elements appear obviously in models and research on military leadership (Wong et al., 2003); they are also prominent, however, in conceptions of strategic business leadership (Jaques, 1976, 1989). Stratified systems theory represents one leadership model that was rooted originally in strategic management (Jaques, 1976) but applied extensively to military leadership (Hunt, 1991; Jacobs & Jaques, 1990; Wong et al., 2003).

This theory articulates three fundamental levels of organizational leadership—*direct, organizational,* and *systems.* As leaders move up through levels, the time span of their work extends further into the future, and the scope and scale of their work responsibilities expand considerably (Hunt, 1991; Jacobs & Jaques, 1987; Jacques, 1989; Zaccaro, 2001). Wong et al. (2003) argued that because this model "parallels the military's stratification of warfare," (p. 662) it was particularly applicable to military leadership:

> The three levels of war are the strategic, operational, and tactical levels.... At the strategic level, national policy is at stake and national resources are used to accomplish strategic military objectives derived from National Command Authority guidance. At the operational level, major operations and campaigns are fought. This level links the tactical employment of forces to strategic objectives. Finally, it is at the tactical level that battles and engagements are fought. The tactical level, like the direct leadership level, is the realm of close combat. The extended multilevel leadership model corresponds well to the military's delineation of levels in warfare, doctrine, leader development, and command. (p. 662)

The leadership tasks and activities specified at each level correspond to those necessary to overcome enemies and inspire subordinates in battle. According to Wong et al. (2003; see also Hunt, 1990), systems-level leadership entails the development of long-term strategy to position the organization to overcome present and future enemies; organizational leadership involves managing large-scale organizational units to reflect strategic initiatives developed at the systems level; direct military leadership includes the execution of orders from operational levels and the development and training of soldiers to be combat-ready. Across the levels, leadership is ideally integrated to maximize the system's readiness to confront and defeat enemies. Research on stratified systems theory has extended the framework from military to business contexts (Zaccaro, 2001).

Recent research on leadership in extreme conditions also reflects the leader-warrior meme. This research examines how leaders help their followers, units, and organization "to overcome great challenges or peril" (Hannah, Uhl-Bein, Avolio, & Cavarretto, 2009, p. 897). Hannah, Uhl-Bein, et al. (2009) defined several types of extreme organizational contexts, reflecting situations in which leaders are required to confront and resolve circumstances, either by themselves or with others; a subset of these contexts entailed confrontations with enemies. They offered a taxonomy of dimensions characterizing extreme contexts, some of which prescribe leadership requirements echoing those offered by Sun Tzu. For example, they defined extreme contexts in terms of time and temporal ordering, and argued that preparatory and post-event leadership activities were as important to success as action-oriented leadership during the event. The researchers noted that "leadership is critical in preparation for an extreme event to provide foresight, planning, training, and other preparedness events (p. 902). Compare this to Sun Tzu (trans. 2011): "Now the general who wins a battle makes many calculations in his temple ere the battle is fought. The general who loses a battle makes but few calculations beforehand" (p. 5); and "He who exercises no forethought but makes light of his opponents is sure to be captured by them" (p. 29).

Hannah, Uhl-Bein, et al. (2009) also defined the psychosocial distance between the leader and follower as a critical aspect of leadership in extreme contexts; they pointed to a "duality" (p. 907) of leadership-follower distance whereby leaders need to maintain a distance from followers in order to enforce command, yet be close enough to engender strong loyalty and devotion. This duality of orientation to followers reflects elements of the leader-warrior, again harkening back to Sun Tzu (trans. 2011):

> If soldiers are punished before they have grown attached to you, they will not prove submissive; and unless submissive, then will be practically useless. If, when the soldiers have become attached to you, punishments are not enforced, they will still be useless.... Therefore, soldiers must be treated in the first instance with humanity, but kept under control by means of iron discipline. (p. 29)

> Regard your soldiers as your children, and they will follow you into the deepest valleys; look upon them as your own beloved sons, and they will stand by you even unto death. (p. 32)

Principles reflected in the leader-warrior meme also pervade theories and models of strategic management and leadership in business. Indeed a recent posting on the business-oriented *Forbes* website noted that "the most common scorecard that most businesses use is financially beating their competition," although this article also touted the value of "keeping your enemies closer" as a way of achieving mutual goals ("Keep your enemies closer," 2012). Such sentiments appear in several frameworks of strategic management, which argue that the key role of leaders is to determine and establish the means of competitive advantage, defined as "an ability to generate above normal returns relative to competitors" (Ployhart, 2012, p. 62). Resource-based theory (RBT) states that competitive advantage accrues to those organizations that manage resources (e.g., financial resources, material resources, human capital, social capital) in ways that increase the probability of above-normal returns (Barney, 1991; Ployhart, 2012; Sirmon, Hitt, & Ireland, 2007). Sirmon et al. (2007) argued that the enhancement of a company's competitive advantage depends on decisions strategic leaders make about specific ways to structure, bundle, and leverage organization resourses under conditions of high environmental uncertainty. Several empirical studies have linked managerial decision-making to strategic competitive advantage, that is, to higher performance of a firm relative to its competitors (Adner & Helffat, 2003; Hitt, Bierman, Shimizu, & Kochhar, 2001; Morrow, Sirmon, Hitt, & Holcomb, 2007; Ndofor, Sirmon, & He, 2011; Sirmon, Gove, & Hitt, 2008; Sirmon & Hitt, 2009).

The leader-warrior meme is also reflected in the competitive strategy framework offered by Miles and Snow (1978; 1984). They articulated four types of strategic orientations. *Defenders* are those firms that adopt a strategy of improving the sustainability of current product lines and the efficiency of product operations. Thus, they shore up their ability to withstand market confrontations with competitors. *Prospectors* seek to capitalize on multiple product lines and create new products that catch competitors off guard. Miles and Snow (1984, p. 37) noted, "[Prospector] organizations often are the creators of change and uncertainty to which competitors must respond." Firms that adopt an *analyzer* strategic orientation focus on a defensive strategy of maximizing efficiency in stable markets, but they adopt a more proactive strategy of product innovation under different market conditions, depending upon actions of competitors. In the latter case, analyzer "managers watch their competitors closely for new ideas, and then they rapidly adopt those that appear to be the most promising" (Miles & Snow, 1984, p. 38). Companies that adopt the fourth strategic orientation, *reactor*, tend not to offer consistent responses to environmental dynamics and typically fail to prosper (i.e., they are defeated by competitors).

Much research in the area of strategic management and leadership has focused on the characteristics of top management teams as they adopt and implement one of these strategic orientations relative to competitors. For example, Hambrick (1981) found that managerial power was associated with the degree to which managers were in areas of the firm primed by defender versus prospector strategies, and when they engaged in scanning and coping activities related to those domains. Hambrick (1994) proposed that the degree of behavioral integration in top management teams was associated in part with their adoption of different strategies. Lord and Maher (1993) argued that these four strategic orientations are examples of what "can be thought of as the 'implicit theories' of top executives" (p. 226). They also argued that managers differing on their implicit theories of strategy will vary with regard to how they process strategic information. Finkelstein, Hambrick, and Cannella (2009) summarized prior research in a model that linked top management executives' values, cognitive styles, cognitive representations, and prior experiences to their adoption of particular strategic choices and their strategic performance relative to competitors. In sum, many studies in strategic management have focused on leadership actions in juxtaposition to those of competitors, including defining the executive attributes and processes that drive such actions.

PRIMED LEADER ATTRIBUTES

I have noted that while there is likely a set of core attributes that are prototypic of all types of leaders, different leadership memes can emphasize certain leader traits and attributes as being more critical than others for leadership success. Using the notions of attribute connectionist networks offered by Lord and his colleagues (Dinh & Lord, 2012; Lord et al., 2001), each leader meme may increase (or decrease) the weight of some attributes as well as strengthen (or weaken) the linkages among others. Many replicated stories that are the sources of the leader-warrior meme highlight such attributes as courage/risk-taking, honor/integrity, and strategic cunning. For example, Sun Tzu (trans. 2011) cited courage and honor as one of the attributes of a commander in the *Art of War*, as did von Clausewitz in his treatise *On War* (1832/1976). In the Biblical story of David and Goliath, David proclaims, "Let no man's heart fail because of him; thy servant will go and fight with this Philistine" (1 Samuel 17:32, King James Version). As king he instructs his son and successor Solomon to "be strong and of good courage, and do it: fear not, nor be dismayed" (1 Chronicles 28:20). Biographical accounts of Alexander the Great (Arrian, trans., 1958; Curtius, trans., 2004); Augustus, the first emperor of Rome (Suetonius, trans., 1957), Hannibal (Livy, trans., 1965; Gabriel, 2011), George Washington (Brookhiser, 2008), Robert E. Lee (Crocker, 2000), and Winston Churchill (Manchester & Reid, 2012) feature prominently the traits of courage and daring in each of the described leaders. A document summarizing famous leadership quotes prepared by the Army—itself a means of memetic transmission—offered twelve specific quotes on courage and six on honor/integrity as key attributes of military leadership (U.S. Department of the Army, 1985). The latest Army manual of leadership (U.S. Department of the Army, 2012) also has specific sections on courage (pp. 3–4) and integrity (p. 6) as central leader attributes.

Sun Tzu (trans. 2011) also touted the importance of skills in outthinking or outwitting your opponents. Such strategic cunning reflects contingent thinking about enemy actions and corresponding responses. For example, in a summary of interviews with senior U.S. Army officers about leading in combat, one officer said that a key process for preparation was to "think about how you expect the enemy will come, and importantly, what you are going to do about it" (Command and General Staff College, 2000, p. 11).

The leader attributes primed by the leader-warrior meme have been supported in empirical research on determinants of leader emergence and effectiveness. Zaccaro, et al. (2013) summarized twenty-five major reviews of leader traits and attributes that appeared between 1924 and 1911. Courage was mentioned in 4 such reviews and integrity was mentioned in 9 of these reviews.

Leader–Problem Solver Meme

DEFINITION

The Leader–problem solver meme depicts leaders as wise individuals who develop solutions to complex societal or community problems. Leadership processes that are related to this meme include developing problem awareness and making sense of complex issues, generating complex problem solutions, and planning and solution implementation. While such cognitive processes can be found reflected in the replicated stories behind each of the leader memes, this meme emphasizes the wisdom and sagacity of individuals when leading societies. Leader effectiveness is defined by the quality and success of generated problem solutions. Thematic elements of the leader–problem solver meme include stories of wise decision-making by leaders, the generation of novel or innovative solutions, and the development of complex strategic frames.

HISTORICAL AND CULTURAL EVOLUTION

One of the earliest works reflecting the leader–problem solver meme was Lao Tzu's *Tao Te Ching* (trans. 2012). This was a prescriptive treatise written in the 5th century B.C. to offer advice on how to wisely lead a society (Heider, 1985). While elements of this work also reflected the leader-teacher meme (see below), many themes pertained to the leader's need to be reflective and thoughtful in the enactment of leadership. Heider (1985) offered a modern version of the *Tao Te Ching*, with corresponding leadership prescriptions. For example, according to Heider's interpretation, leaders were to "allow regular time for silent reflection" (p. 23); and to "be still. Follow your inner wisdom" (p. 45). The leader's "job is to facilitate process and clarify conflicts. This ability depends less on formal education than on common sense and traditional wisdom" (p. 39). Confucius in the 6th century B.C. also spoke to wisdom as a prerequisite for leadership. Durant (2002, p. 12) interpreted a Confucian prescription as follows: "The greatest fortune of a people would be to keep ignorant persons from public office, and secure their wisest men to rule them."

The Biblical story of King Solomon reflects another historio-cultural contribution to the leader–problem solver meme. When offered by God any leadership quality he wanted, Solomon requested wisdom (1 Kings 3:9–12). The classic story of Solomon solving the problem of the mothers claiming the same child (1 Kings 3:16–27) has been memetically replicated in many ways through generations as a lesson in leadership. The Book of Proverbs in the Bible included Solomon's prescriptions on leadership and wisdom (Williams, 2010).

Another classical contribution to this meme is Plato's *Republic* (trans. 1993). In this treatise, Plato argued that society is best governed by "philosopher-kings," noting that "unless communities have philosophers as kings . . . or the people who are currently called kings and rulers practice philosophy...there can be no end to political troubles . . . or even to human troubles in general (p. 193). According to Plato, philosophers seek wisdom, using reasoning skills to uncover knowledge and truth. Thus, leadership is to be grounded in the use of higher-order thinking skills and processes that seek wise and truthful solutions to societal ills. While Plato's prescriptions have often been dismissed as antidemocratic and not workable in today's society (see, for example, Popper, 1966), Williamson (2008) distilled three core ideas from *The Republic* that still resonate in modern leadership ideas, theories, and research. These were (1) "the best educated people, who are able to distinguish knowledge and truth from mere opinion and belief, should have the principal leadership positions and principal positions of responsibility"; (2) "leaders should have a broader moral horizon than followers; leaders are to look beyond immediate desires and concerns and see a larger picture, and to take action on behalf of a broader, public good"; and (3) "the character of leaders makes a large difference in whether they are able to rule effectively on behalf of the community" (p. 402).

Another exemplar of the leader–problem solver meme that has been cited by modern leadership scholars is Benjamin Franklin (Mumford & Van Doorn, 2001). His work as an inventor and scientist indicated a strong orientation toward practical problem-solving. His actions as one of the preparers of the Declaration of Independence, as the first postmaster general, as ambassador to France during the American Revolution, and as a delegate at the Philadelphia Convention, which drafted the U.S. Constitution, speaks to his application of this problem-solving approach to political leadership. Regarding Franklin's personal philosophy, Isaacson (2003) noted that "what he found more satisfactory—more than metaphysics or poetry or exalted romantic sentiments—was looking at things in a pragmatic and practical way" (pp. 93–94). Indeed, Franklin's famous *Poor Richard's Almanack* is a widely replicated memetic source of wisdom and practical advice. Mumford and Van Doorn (2001) described ten cases of leadership displayed by Franklin and showed how they illustrated several elements of pragmatic leadership (see also Mumford, 2002). The elements they identified in Franklin's leadership approach pertained to aspects of social problem-solving, including problem analysis; generation and evaluation of functional solutions; analysis of downstream and long-term consequences; consideration of and planning for obstacles to solution implementation; and using elites and other social connections to foster solution implementation. Thus, the memetic exemplar of Benjamin Franklin complements the wise leadership models of Lao Tzu, Solomon, and Plato with practical problem-solving leadership.

INFLUENCE IN LEADERSHIP THEORY AND RESEARCH

The leader–problem solver meme emphasizes the generation and implementation of wise solutions. An integral part of these leadership activities reflects the leader's role in providing instruction and structure to the work of followers; accordingly its influence can be perceived in one half of the classic Ohio State two-factor model of leadership behavior—*initiating structure* (Fleishman, 1953; Hemphill & Coons, 1957). Behaviors linked to this factor included "tries out...new ideas," and "offers new approaches to problems" (Fleishman, 1953, p. 3). The leadership style of structuring solutions to task problems is prominent in many leadership theories and models, including Fiedler's (1964) contingency model, Blake and Mouton's (1964) managerial grid, House's (1971) path goal theory, and Hersey and Blanchard's (1984) situational leadership theory, among others. In most of these models and theories, problem-solving and task structuring are listed as key leadership behavioral styles. Yukl's (1994) integrative taxonomy of managerial behavior lists thirteen other dimensions in addition to "planning and organizing" and "problem-solving" (p. 68). Thus, problem-solving is not the defining element of leadership except under certain conditions or circumstances (e.g., Hersey & Blanchard, 1977; House, 1971).

Alternatively, several other models of leadership activity and leader attributes have centrally emphasized wisdom and complex problem-solving as core aspects of effective leadership. For example, Fleishman et al. (1991) argued,

> Leadership behavior represents a form of *organizationally-based problem solving*, implemented in a social context, where an attempt is made to bring about goal attainment by influencing the actions of other subsystems. Leadership behavior is viewed as a complex, opportunistic, social problem solving syndrome involving many cognitive capacities... in the generation, selection, and implementation of influence attempts. (pp. 258–259, italics in the original text)

Mumford, et al. (2000) elaborated on this approach to leadership as social problem-solving by delineating critical leadership processes such as problem definition, information acquisition, meaning-making, solution generation, identification of solution restrictions, and formulating plans. They also defined several leader attributes, such as divergent thinking skills, social judgment skills, wisdom, and knowledge, as central leader attributes for effectiveness. As noted earlier, Mumford and Van Doorn (2001; see also Mumford, 2002) applied this conceptual approach in a case analysis of Benjamin Franklin's leadership, thereby directly linking a memetic leadership exemplar with the testing of a modern leadership framework.

Other scholars have also placed wisdom at the center of their leadership frameworks. Kilburg (2006) offered a model of executive wisdom that emphasized intuitive and rational perception, decision-making, and action. He noted,

> For leaders, being able to discover or create the right thing to do is never enough; they also need to do the right thing in the right way and against the right time frame. It is the unique combination of thinking, deciding, and acting wisely through time on behalf of groups of humans, and sometimes on behalf of every human, that separates Executive Wisdom from normal human wisdom. (p. 47)

This framework emphasizes the same problem-solving processes articulated by Mumford et al. (2000): problem analysis, solution analysis and choice, and solution implementation. Kilburg (2006) also illustrated nicely the memetic replication of a leadership meme, as he grounded his conceptual framework in the contributions of Confucius, Socrates, Plato, and others, as well as in a range of historical developments and events that illustrated wise leadership (e.g., the Magna Carta, the Columbus voyages, and the Marshall Plan).

Sternberg (2007, 2013) too offered a leadership model that roots effectiveness in the leader's display of wisdom, creativity, and problem-solving prowess. His framework "views leadership as a matter of how one formulates, makes, and acts on decisions" (Sternberg, 2007, p. 34). He delineated several types of skill-based processes used by leaders to derive complex, wise, and creative solutions. For example, leaders define problems in different and creative ways; they "do not define a problem, the way everyone else does, simply because everyone else defines the problem that way" (Sternberg, 2007, p. 36). They also engage in analysis to determine "whether their solution is the best one possible" (Sternberg, 2007, p. 36). They engage in selective encoding, selective comparison, and selective combination, which entail (1) "distinguishing irrelevant from relevant information in one's field of experience"; (2) "novel relating of new information to old information"; and (3) "taking selectively encoded information and combining it in a novel but productive way" (pp. 36–37). Sternberg asserts that "leaders need wisdom" (p. 38), and defines wisdom in terms using complex problem-solving skills and capacities "for a common good" (p. 38). Thus, his model, like those of Mumford et al. (2000) and Kilburg (2006), reflects the theme, dating back to Confucius, Lao Tzu, Solomon, and Plato, of leaders employing wisdom and other higher-order cognitive processes for the gain of society.

PRIMED LEADER ATTRIBUTES

The leader–problem solver meme places cognitive capacities and skills, particularly wisdom, prominently in a constellation or prototype of critical leader traits. King Solomon defined "wisdom" as the prime leader quality (1 Kings 3:9–12). Plato argued that higher-order reasoning should be the key characteristic of kings. Lao Tzu's prescriptions were focused on how leaders can act wisely in their rule. The central theme, which is memetically replicated as these accounts are transmitted across generations, is that good leaders are those who possess higher-order cognitive capacities.

Intelligence has been the trait perhaps most linked with leadership (Mann, 1959; Lord, DeVader, & Alliger, 1986; Zaccaro et al., 2013). Zaccaro et al. (2013), in their summary of 25 leadership reviews published between 1924 and 2011, found that intelligence was mentioned in more reviews—23—than any other leader trait. Thus, cognitive ability has often been associated with leadership emergence and effectiveness in research studies of these outcomes. However, the leader–problem solving meme specifically emphasizes cognitive capacities other than (or rather in addition to) intelligence. Sternberg emphasizes the integration of both wisdom and creativity with academic and practical intelligence as a central leadership trait pattern. Mumford et al. (2000) included divergent thinking skills, complex problem solving skills, and higher order social judgment skills (comparable to wisdom) as companion attributes to intelligence in predicting leadership effectiveness. Connelly et al. (2000) reported that creativity and problem-solving skills explained unique variance in leader achievement beyond verbal reasoning, an index of intelligence. Intelligence is a quality that is prominent in the leader prototypes emphasized in several of the leader memes described in this chapter. The difference between the ideas and historio-cultural sources that reflect the leader–problem solver meme and those of the other memes is that in the leader-problem solver meme additional higher-order conceptual capacities, in addition to intelligence, are also defined as central to the practice of leadership.

Leader-Politician Meme

DEFINITION

The leader-politician meme defines leadership as the process of winning the hearts and minds of followers—and the power to influence them. The criterion for effective leadership becomes the support and loyalty of followers. Functional leadership activities reflected in this meme include understanding social and follower dynamics, engaging in inspirational communications, shaping and fulfilling follower expectations of leadership, and enacting self-presentation strategies that enhance follower endorsement and attachment. Memetic exemplars include leaders who are great communicators as well as leadership stories of wide-ranging political bargains and victories. Leader prescriptions in these exemplars speak to strategies about how to gain and keep the loyalty of followers.

The term *politician* to describe this meme is on one hand a bit constraining, because many memetic exemplars were not necessarily involved in political office. However, leaders reflecting this meme are known both as (1) great communicators capable of appealing to masses of followers and (2) influential deal-makers able to achieve bargains and agreements with potential adversaries and turn them into allies: two oft-cited attributes of great politicians. Thus, both charismatic leaders and master negotiators fit under this theme. While the thematic core of the leader-warrior meme is on defeating and overcoming enemies, and of the leader–problem solver on generating wise and grand solutions, the core of the leader-politician is on gaining the strong and emotional endorsement and loyalty of followers, and on co-opting potential adversaries.

HISTORICAL AND CULTURAL EVOLUTION

Cicero offers an early memetic exemplar of the leader-politician meme. Described by Everitt (2001) as Rome's greatest politician, Cicero was known for his oratorical skills and political acumen. Indeed, he worked to develop his public speaking skills to increase his ability to move followers (Everitt, 2001; Plutarch, trans. 2001). The early Roman biographer, Plutarch (trans. 2001), noted that early in his life Cicero "was defective in his delivery" (p. 411) and sought counsel from actors and playwrights, successfully improving his skills: "Such afterwards was Cicero's delivery that it did not a little contribute to render his eloquence persuasive" (p. 411). Later in his life, Cicero wrote instructional treatises describing the qualities of great orators, and teaching others on how to be similarly great. Cicero, then, provides an early memetic exemplar of linking leadership with communication skills. Everitt (2001) wrote that "the cadences of [Cicero's] oratory can be heard in the speeches of Thomas Jefferson and William Pitt (not to mention Abraham Lincoln and, only a half a century ago, Winston Churchill)" (p. viii).

Cicero's political skills were grounded in the belief that successful influence required a deep understanding of one's potential followers. Plutarch noted (trans. 2001, p. 412),

> On beginning to apply himself more resolutely to public business, [Cicero] remarked it as an unreasonable and absurd thing that... the statesman, whose instruments for carrying out public measures are men, should be negligent and careless of the knowledge of persons. And so, he not only acquainted himself with the names, but also knew the particular place where everyone of the more eminent citizens dwelt, what lands he possessed, the friends he made use of, and those that were of his neighbourhoods, and when he travelled on any road in Italy, he could readily name and show the estates and seats of his friends and acquaintance.

The necessity of social acumen and understanding of followers was instrumental in Cicero's run for the office of consul, the highest office in the Rome at that time (64 B.C.). His brother and campaign manager, Quintus, summarized for him in a letter (Cicero, trans. 2012) the political tactics he would need to garner enough support to win the election. He emphasized the importance of powerful communication and the need to cultivate loyal followers and the right kinds of relationships from key groups in Roman society. Thus, early in the evolution of this particular meme, the acquisition of a leadership position is tied directly to fostering perceptions of greatness and effectiveness among potential followers, and such activities were in turn grounded in having an acute awareness of the needs, motives, and agendas of these followers.

Machiavelli's *The Prince* (trans. 2003) represents another classic memetic exemplar for the leader-politician meme. While this work has typically been defined in terms of the manipulative and inauthentic leader, Machiavelli's core point was the necessity of leaders to secure the endorsement of the governed (albeit by any means necessary) to be effective. Two of the most famous ideas to derive from *The Prince*, themselves replicated memes, are (1) "it is better to be feared than loved," and (2) "the end justifies the means." Regarding the first, Machiavelli argued that the preference of the prince was to be both feared and loved but that this combination was difficult to achieve in a populace; he believed the endorsement of the governed was more reliably stable under fear than love (Harrison, 2011). Regarding the second notion, Rebhorn in an introduction to his translation of *The Prince* (trans. 2003) argued that the critical point was not on the use of ruthless means to engender a desired end, but rather that followers pay more attention to outcomes rather than processes in judging the effectiveness of a leader, and therefore in making an endorsement decision; Rebhorn notes (p. xxiii), "what [Machiavelli] is really saying is that people will judge a prince's means to be good as long as he succeeds and the outcome is beneficial to them." The notion that outcomes matter greatly in perceptions of leader effectiveness has resonated in modern leadership research (e.g., Meindl, Ehrlick, & Dukerich, 1985).

The subthemes in the leader-politician meme—leaders as displaying great political acumen and being great communicators—have been reinforced by other memetic exemplars. In American history, Presidents Thomas Jefferson, Andrew Jackson, Abraham Lincoln, Franklin Roosevelt, and Lyndon Johnson have all been cited by bibliographers for their extraordinary political skills (Caro, 2003; Goodwin, 2005; Meacham, 2008, 2012; Smith, 2007). Each of these exemplars is especially known and often cited for his skill in garnering the endorsement and support of followers, as well as his adeptness in negotiating with opponents to turn them into allies. Replicated memetic exemplars of the leader as a great communicator include Lincoln, Franklin Roosevelt, Winston Churchill, and Martin Luther King. The fealty of their followers was based as much on these leaders' oratory skills as their political acumen.

INFLUENCE IN LEADERSHIP THEORY AND RESEARCH

The notion that leader legitimacy and power rests on follower perceptions and endorsement has a rich history in leadership theory and research. Hollander's work on leader legitimacy (1958; 1961; 1964; Hollander & Julian, 1970) emphasized the transactional nature of the relationship between the leader and the led. He noted (1961, p. 30, emphasis added) that "leaders [derive] status from followers who may accord or withdraw it, in an essentially free interchange within a group context. *Group consent is therefore a central feature in the leader-follower [relationship].*" Hollander (1958) argued that leaders acquired the status to lead groups in different directions only after "accumulation of positively disposed impressions residing in the perceptions of relevant others" (p. 120). Hollander and Julian (1970, p. 117) specified more clearly the transactional nature of the leader-follower relationship:

> Put in transactional terms, the leader who fulfills expectations and helps to achieve group goals provides a rewarding resource for others which is exchanged for status, esteem, and greater influence. Thus, he gives something and gets something. And what he gets contributes to his legitimacy insofar as he is "validated" in his role by followers. It is the leader's sense of this legitimacy which then serves as the base on which he may operate to exert influence.

The leader's role legitimacy and validation are grounded in the perceptions and impressions of followers who accord him or her status. The leader is not viewed as passive in this relationship; Hollander (1958) suggested that leaders possess a heightened sensitivity to relevant group norms and attitudes, and can act more readily in accordance with these group standards. This sensitivity reflects the nature of political acumen residing at the heart of the leader-politician meme.

Hollander's work emphasized the social perceptions of followers as a critical factor in leadership dynamics. Lord and his colleagues expanded this focus by examining (1) the followers' cognitive activities in the granting of leader role legitimacy, and (2) the cognitive representations that were used in these activities (Dinh & Lord, 2012; Lord & Maher, 1993; Shondrick, Dinh, & Lord, 2010). According to Lord and colleagues, followers develop cognitive models that serve as templates for the evaluation and categorization of individuals as leaders. When making such evaluations, followers compare the observed behaviors and inferred attributes of individuals to their cognitive representations of prototypical leaders. Perceived legitimacy, therefore, is based on how closely a target's behaviors and attributes match those encoded in the followers' leader schema. Dinh and Lord (2012) described the complexity of these leadership prototypes, noting that they can vary by a number of contextual parameters. They also note that leaders' individual differences influence the display of leadership behavior, and that leaders can vary behavioral displays in accordance with contextual cues. Leader qualities such as social and political acumen can determine the success of such situational responsiveness (Ahearn,

Ferris, Hochwarter, Douglas, & Ammeter, 2004; Ferris et al., 2005; Zaccaro, Foti, & Kenny, 1991; Zaccaro, Gilbert, Thor, & Mumford, 1991). Indeed, Zaccaro, Foti, et al., (1991) found that leaders higher in situational responsiveness skills were more likely to emerge as leaders across situations varying in role requirements. Ferentinos (1996) extended this work by finding that successfully emergent leaders indeed varied their behaviors to match situational requirements more so than individuals who were not endorsed as leaders. Taken together, this body of work by Hollander and Lord, respectively, reflects two key themes of the leader-politician meme: that leader influence depends on the endorsement of followers, and that effective leaders can alter their behavioral responses to followers in ways necessary to secure such endorsement.

Charismatic leadership theories echo these themes of the leader-politician meme, but also emphasize the high-level communication skills noted by Cicero. Weber (1947) argued that charisma, rather than being an innate quality of an individual, derived instead from perceptions of followers. According to Trice and Beyer (1986), these perceptions were driven by (1) the existence of crisis, for which (2) a charismatic leader offered a solution that (3) attracted followers, and (4) whose perceptions of extraordinary leadership were maintained by continued successful outcomes. House (1977) provided a theory of charismatic leadership that specified a set of leadership behaviors that fostered perceptions of charisma. These behaviors included the communication of a powerful vision in an expressive and engaging style that resonated with followers (See also Conger, 1991; Holladay & Coombs, 1993, 1994). A number of empirical studies have supported the role of leader communication content and style as driving perceptions of leader charisma (Awamleh & Gardner, 1999; Holladay & Coombs, 1993, 1994; Howell & Frost, 1989; Shamir, Arthur, & House, 1994). These studies and the theoretical models they support provide a scientific analogue to the stories replicated as part of the leader-politician meme.

Charismatic leadership models also emphasize another theme in the leader-politician meme, the notion that leaders carefully manage the impressions they convey to followers. Gardner and Avolio (1998) defined this impression management as "the packaging of information in order to lead target audiences to desired conclusions" (p. 33). Such packaging is intended to provide followers with messages and images that foster their commitment and loyalty (Conger, 1989). Gardner and Avolio define four elements of leader impression management—*framing, scripting, staging,* and *performing.* Framing refers to the meaning-making aspects of leader communication. Scripting reflects how leaders shape the delivery of meaning for followers, including the use of metaphors, nonverbal and emotional expressions, and role definitions. Staging entails "the development and manipulation of symbols, including the physical appearances, settings, props, and other types of artifactual displays" in ways that magnify the impact of the impression being made to followers (Gardner & Avolio, 1998, p. 43). Finally, performing refers to the actual delivery of scripted and staged communication. Gardner and Avolio identified "exemplification" as the most typical performance strategy of charismatic leaders, in which these leaders

> portray themselves as exceptionally trustworthy and morally responsible individuals. They may also stress their similarity to followers with regard to their background and experiences in order to establish themselves as trusted representatives of their followers' interest. (p. 44)

Gardner and Avolio's "dramaturgical perspective" of the leader-follower relationship, as well as empirical research on the style of leader rhetoric, track closely with both Cicero's and Machiavelli's contributions to the leader-politician meme, particularly their advice regarding leader communications:

> Words must not only be well chosen, but properly disposed, and the speaker must have a thorough knowledge of all the affections which nature has implanted in the soul of man, because it demands the whole energy and power of speaking to awaken and to sooth the passions of an audience.... Why need I to mention *action* itself, which must be regulated by the motion of the body, the gesture, the look, joined to the justness of accent and command of voice? (Cicero, trans. 1822/2011, chapter V, italics in the original)

> A prince must therefore take great care that nothing slips from his lips which is not full of the five qualities mentioned above [mercy, loyalty, humaneness, forthrightness, and religiousness], and when one sees or hears him, he should seem to be all mercy, all loyalty, all sincerity, all humanity, all religion.... Everyone sees what you appear to be, few feel what you are. *(Machiavelli, trans. 2003, pp. 76–77)*

PRIMED LEADER ATTRIBUTES

Leaders are portrayed in the leader-politician meme has having (1) strong dominance and motivation to lead, (2) heightened communication and interpersonal skills, and (3) high levels of social and political acumen. Office seekers who undergo the process of trying to gain the leadership endorsements of followers are presumed to have high motivation for the position, although they use their interpersonal skills and social/political acumen to portray this need for power as a desire to provide service. Accordingly, these attributes are likely to be represented prominently in those leader prototypes that reflect this meme. Prior research has also supported their relevance for leader effectiveness. Zaccaro et al. (2013) reported that interpersonal and communication skills as well as different aspects of social acumen have appeared in 17 of 25 reviews of critical leader attributes. Dominance, drive, ambition, need for power, and motivation to lead have been cited in 18 such reviews.

Leader-Teacher Meme

DEFINITION

The leader-teacher meme articulates a perspective of leadership as reflecting *service* to followers, with the goal of helping them grow their individual and collective capacity for action. Thus, leadership is construed as the empowerment and elevation of followers. Accordingly, leader effectiveness is defined more in terms of follower growth and achievements than those of the leader. Leader activities reflected in this meme include teaching and coaching followers, encouraging them to higher levels of achievement, and providing them with developmental activities. More recently, this idea has been expanded to include leaders helping and teaching followers how to enact effective leadership and become leaders themselves (Kozlowski et al., 2009; Zaccaro et al., 2009).

HISTORICAL AND CULTURAL EVOLUTION

Lao Tzu's *Tao Te Ching* (trans. 2012) replicates the leader–problem solver meme, depicting wisdom as a key element of leadership. However, this work also emphasizes the importance of wise leaders not elevating themselves above followers, serving instead as guides for group action. The work of the group as a whole, rather than the leader, is the central focus. Note the difference from other memes, where leaders provide the main force in collective action. While followers are more instrumental in the leader-politician meme, they serve exclusively to provide endorsement and action to the leader's influence and direction. Lao Tzu's treatise places greater emphasis on the group's capacities and actions, with the leader serving more in the background as a facilitator and teacher. Heider (1985) translated and adapted the *Tao Te Ching* into more direct leadership prescriptions that reflect these principles:

> Enlightened leadership is service, not selfishness. (p. 13)
>
> The group members need the leader for guidance and facilitation. The leader needs people to work with, people to serve. (p. 53)
>
> The wise leader is of service: receptive, yielding, following. The group member's vibration dominates and leads, while the leader follows. But soon it is the member's consciousness which is transformed, the member's vibration which is resolved. The relationship is reciprocal. It is the job of the leader to be aware of the group member's process; it is the need of the group member to be received and paid attention to. Both get what they need, if the leader has the wisdom to serve and follow, to be open and below. (p. 121)

This meme of leader as teacher and servant is also exemplified by the account of Jesus in the New Testament. Described as "the best known servant-leader" (Woolfe, 2002, p. 83), Jesus preached "whoever desires to be great among you, let him be your servant" (Matthew 20:26, NKJV). His action at the Last Supper of washing the feet of his disciples was meant to emphatically convey this theme.

In his book *The Servant as Leader,* Greenleaf (1970/2008) recounts a story from Hermann Hesse's 1932 novel, *Journey to the East,* that replicates the meme of leadership as service in the form of teaching and offering guidance. In the story, a servant, Leo, guides a group of men on a difficult journey, taking care of their needs and maintaining their motivation for the journey. However, during the journey, Leo disappears and the group collapses, ending the journey. Years later, a member of the party finds Leo, who takes him home, where he discovers that Leo is actually head of an Order, in which, as described by Greenleaf, he was "its guiding spirit, a great and noble *leader*" (p. 7, emphasis in the original). Greenleaf credited his reading of this story as the source of his work on servant leadership, arguing the central moral of the story of Leo was that "*the great leader is seen as servant first,* and that simple fact is the key to his greatness" (p. 7, emphasis in the original). This represents perhaps the most direct link between a memetic replication of a leadership story and the development of a modern leadership model.

INFLUENCE IN LEADERSHIP THEORY AND RESEARCH

The notion of leaders as individuals who nurture and foster the growth of followers has become a staple of several current leadership theories and models. Perhaps the framework that is most prototypical of the leader-teacher meme is servant leadership, which dates to the original coining of the term by Greenleaf (1970/2008), although construct clarity has been elusive despite more than 10 years of empirical research (van Dierendonk, 2011). The servant leader is one who places followers' interest first, ahead of his or her own; Greenleaf (1997/2008) noted that for such leaders, "the best test... is: do those served grow as persons; do they, *while being served*, become healthier, wiser, freer, more autonomous, more likely themselves to become servants?" (p. 14) emphasis in the original. Greenleaf suggests, then, that the goal is not only personal growth, but growth in a follower's specific capacity to be a leader. Van Dierendonk (2011) reviewed and synthesized the empirical research on servant leadership, defining six characteristics of such leadership: (1) a focus on "empowering and developing people" (p. 1232); (2) displaying humility, defined as willing to "benefit from the expertise of others" and placing the "interests of others first" (p. 1233); (3) displaying authenticity and integrity; (4) displaying interpersonal acceptance, perspective taking, and empathy; (5) providing direction that is tailored for follower abilities, needs, and requirements for growth; and (6) displaying stewardship, or "the willingness to take responsibility for the larger institution and to go for service instead of control and self-interest" (p. 1234). Research has linked servant leadership to such outcomes as follower work attitudes (Hebert, 2003; Jaramillo, Grisaffe, Chonko, & Roberts, 2009a), follower task performance (Jaramillo, Grisaffe, Chonko, & Roberts, 2009b), follower citizenship behavior (Ehrhart, 2004), team effectiveness (Hu & Liden, 2011; Irving & Longbotham, 2007), and firm performance, defined as return on assets (Peterson, Galvin, & Lange, 2012).

The notion of leaders empowering followers is a key element of two other major leadership models—transformational leadership theory and leader-member exchange (LMX) theory. Bass, (1985, 1996) defined transformational leadership as emphasizing leaders as models, inspirations, and mentor/coaches for followers. One component of transformational leaderhsip, "individualized consideration," particularly reflects the leader-teacher meme. Bass (1996) noted that "transformational leaders pay special attention to each individual's needs for achievement and growth by acting as coach or mentor. Followers and colleagues are developed to successively higher levels of potential" (p. 6). Unlike servant leadership, the primary emphasis of transformational leadership remains organizational growth and performance (Stone, Russell, & Patterson, 2004), but follower empowerment and growth is defined as a critical driver of organizational progress.

LMX theory defines two types of relationships leaders may have with followers (Dansereau, Graen, & Haga, 1975). One emphasizes a distant connection to the leader in which most exchanges between leader and follower are highly structured and transactional. The other emphasizes the leader providing greater autonomy and self-direction to followers, along with more individualized attention. As with transformational leadership theory, this model also emphasizes organizational progress (Graen & Uhl-Bien, 1995), but follower growth is defined as a product of a high-quality relationship with leaders. Thus, both theories reflect central elements of the leader-teacher meme, although not as strongly as does servant leadership theory.

The leadership models discussed under this meme emphasize leaders helping individual followers or followers in an aggregate. Other models have focused on leaders acting as coaches and teachers for follower teams (Hackman & Wageman, 2005), where the role of the leader is to foster effective team synergy (Zaccaro, et al., 2009). Thus, leaders are defined in a sense as servants of teams. Functional leadership models describe leaders as responsible for providing teams with whatever they need to help them accomplish their goals (Hackman & Walton, 1986; McGrath, 1962; Morgeson et al., 2010). Within this perspective, some researchers have suggested that leaders serve teams by fostering the emergence of shared leadership capacity within the team (Kozlowski et al., 2009; Zaccaro et al., 2009). Day, Gronn, and Salas (2004) argued for "leadership [that] emerges or is drawn from teams as a function of working on and accomplishing shared work" (p. 859). Thus, team leadership capacity derives from team members engaging and learning from the resolution of team problems. Zaccaro et al. (2009) described an analogous concept, shared leadership expertise, and posited team leader actions as instrumental in the emergence of such expertise. These actions include developing individual member expertise, and coaching the team to engage in such leadership actions as setting team direction, planning, role assignment, and information processing. Hackman and Wageman (2005) offered a model of such team coaching, emphasizing the leader's role in providing motivational, consultative, and educational coaching to the team. Kozlowski and his colleagues (Koslowski, Gully, McHugh, Salas, & Cannon-Bowers, 1996; Kozlowski, Gully, Salas, & Cannon-Bowers, 1996; Koslowski et al., 2009) also provided a framework of how leaders guide teams through several developmental phases; the final phase is one in which team members are engaging effectively in a variety of team self-management, shared leadership, and adaptation functions. All of these models of team leadership emphasize the idea from the leader-teacher meme of not only fostering growth in followers, but helping them to collectively become leaders as well.

PRIMED LEADER ATTRIBUTES

The leader-teacher meme portrays leaders as having such attributes as empathy, integrity/authenticity, humility, and a service orientation (van Dierendonck, 2011). Skills in developing, coaching, and teaching others are prominent as well. Empathy relates to an ability to understand and connect psychologically with others (Bass, 2008). Such an attribute is highly related to social acumen (Zaccaro, Gilbert, et al., 1991), an attribute that is also primed by the leader-politician meme. However, the pairing of social acumen skills with humility, integrity/authenticity, and a service orientation differentiates its use here from its use in the leader-politician meme. A service orientation represents a core value in the leader-teacher constellation of attributes. Army leadership manuals describe selfless service as a primary leader quality: Officers are instructed to "put the welfare of the Nation, the Army, and subordinates before your own" (U.S. Department of the Army, 2006, p. 4–6). Van Dierendonck (2011) offers a similar concept, "stewardship," in his model of servant leadership. He define stewardship as "the willingness to take responsibility for the larger institution and go for service instead of control and self-interest" (p. 1234). Several proposed conceptual models and empirical studies support the primacy of these attributes for leadership (Dennis & Bocarnea, 2005; Peterson et al., 2012; Russell & Stone, 2002; van Dierendonck, 2011; van Dierendonck & Nuijten, 2011; Washington, Sutton, & Feild, 2006).

Summary

Leadership is a prime example of a meme that has been transmitted, imitated, and replicated across cultures and generations. However, leader memes are not monolithic in terms of their core ideas and themes about the practice of leadership. I have suggested four memes that have emerged with strong replicator power across history and cultures. Each meme rests on a different set of historical exemplars and prescriptions about leaders. While many attributes are common across all four portrayals of leaders, each meme offers different core attributes that would reside centrally in constellations of attributes that guide perceptions of leadership. These memes, then, provide powerful representations of how people may think about leadership. These memes are not symbols, analogies, or metaphors about leadership. Instead, they define core value–based beliefs about what leadership means, and what combination of attributes should be possessed by individuals who would serve as leaders. As such, they become the wellspring of early leader development and the formation of leader self-identity. When asking individuals to describe who they are as leaders, or what kind of leaders they should be, they will likely describe themselves predominantly in terms of one of these memes. Because leader memes reflect very different perspectives of what leadership entails, individuals cannot likely hold two or more such memes simultaneously in their core identities as leaders. In the last section of this chapter, I will elaborate on the importance of leader memes in leader and leadership development.

The Role of Leader Memes in Leader Self-Identity and Leadership Development

Figure 2.1 portrays a model of how leader memes can influence both the emergence of leader self-identity and an orientation to particular leader development experiences. Such experiences in the form of early exposure to leadership models play a role in the emergence of a leader self-identity, which in turn influences the type of growth experiences leaders will select later in their development (Day & Harrison, 2007; Hannah, Woolfolk, & Lord, 2009). Replicated elements of leader memes provide the seeds for early development, and they are reinforced, or even substantially revised (Lord & Hall, 2005), by later developmental experiences.

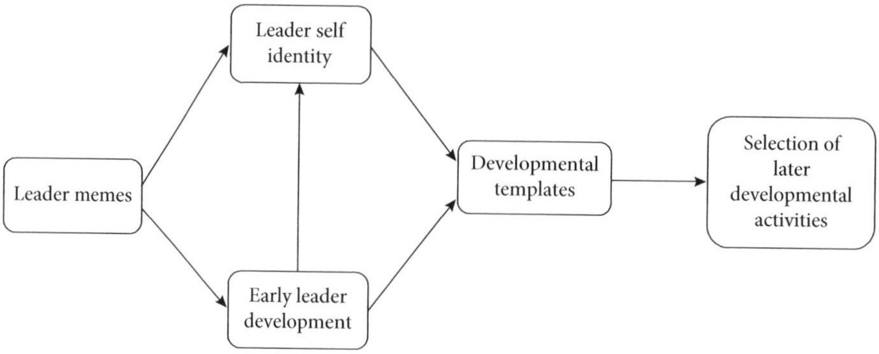

Figure 2.1. A Model of the Influences of Leader Memes on Leader Self-Identity and Leader Development.

Leader Memes and Leader Self-Identity

Several researchers have offered leader self-identity or self-concept as a key construct in leader development and performance (Day & Harrison, 2007; Hannah, Woolfolk, et al., 2009; Lord & Hall, 2005). According to Day and Harrison (2007), "Identity is the culmination of an individual's values, experiences, and self-perceptions" (p. 365). People carry multiple subidentities within their self-concept, but only one at a time is primed or activated in particular contexts (Day & Harrison, 2007; Hannah, Woolfolk, et al., 2009; Lord & Brown, 2004; Markus & Wurf, 1987). Individuals' conception of themselves as leaders reflects a leader subidentity or leader self-concept (Day & Harrison, 2007). According to Hannah et al. (2009), leader self-concepts can be characterized in terms of both their content and their structures. Content refers to beliefs, values, and self-knowledge that individuals have about the nature of leadership and, in particular, the attributes they associate with their effective conduct of leadership (Hannah, Woolfolk, et al., 2009; Lord & Hall, 2005). For example, Hannah, Woolfolk, et al. (2009) illustrate a leader self-concept containing attributes such as "motivating," "visionary," "empowering," "trustworthy," and "ethical" (p. 272).

According to Hannah, Woolfolk et al. (2009), the structure of a leader self-concept reflects how leader content is organized in a representation that links attributes, beliefs, and actions. Some attributes in such representations are more strongly related to one another than others; moreover, different situational features and parameters will activate different attributes and linkages among attributes (Dinh & Lord, 2012; Hannah, Woolfolk, et al., 2009; Shoda, Tiernan, & Mischel, 2002). Leader self-concepts can differ in terms of their degree of complexity, with more complex self-structures reflecting higher degrees of leader role/attribute differentiation and integration (Hannah, Woolfolk, et al., 2009; Lord, Hannah, & Jennings, 2011). However, leader self-structures also have a core set of interconnected attributes that reside more centrally in such structures and contribute to self-concept clarity (Hannah, Woolfolk, et al., 2009); these core attributes are connected to sets of more peripheral leader attributes that in turn have greater susceptibility to fluctuating influence across different leadership contexts (Dinh & Lord, 2012). Core or central attributes in a leader self-structure produce a relative degree of stability in beliefs and values activated across such contexts (Dinh & Lord, 2012; Rosch & Mervis, 1975; Shoda et al., 2002).

Leader memes reflect values and beliefs about how one should engage in leadership; accordingly, they are likely to provide the material for the core of newly forming or emerging leader self-identities. As I have noted earlier, leader memes activate and emphasize different sets of leader qualities and attributes. Leader self-identities can be distinguished by these different attribute sets. Thus, for example, a leader self-identity that encodes themes from a leader-warrior meme would emphasize competitiveness and dominance as part of an identity core, and feature core attributes such as courage, risk-taking, and strategic cunning. Alternatively, a leader self-identity based on a leader-teacher meme would encode such leadership themes as empowerment and a focus on follower growth, and feature attributes such as humility and a service orientation. Leader–problem solver and leader-politician memes would also produce core identity elements and attributes that correspond to the themes and ideas replicated in their respective cultural phenotypes or exemplars.

Leader Memes and Leader Development

The replicated and imitated stories, fables, and anecdotes that derive leader memes are often the first leadership ideas communicated to neophyte leaders. For example, children growing up within a Judeo-Christian tradition hear and read stories from the Bible that feature David and Goliath, the wise decisions of Solomon, and the teachings of Jesus, each reflecting one of the aforementioned memes. Indeed, some children's readings are fictionalized derivations from these Bible stories. For example, a children's book by Gat and Prital (2012) recounts the fable of *Wise King Solomon and the Honey Bee* (from an 1882 poem by John Godfrey Saxe): King Solomon spares the life a bee that stung him; the bee later helps him resolve a confounding problem. This story replicates the leader–problem solver meme.

A children's story from another culture, the Navajo creation legend recounted by Joseph Campbell (Oakes, King, & Campbell, 1943/1991), reflects the leader-warrior meme: it tells of two young heroes who journey on a quest and return home to defeat their enemies. Children receive other such leadership parables and fables about imaginary and real leaders. For example, Bennett's (1995) collection of widely replicated children's memetic stories of virtue contains several leadership-related fables, including the tale of George Washington and the cherry tree. Boulais (2000; 2002) completed an analysis based on Kouzes and Posner's (1995) leadership themes of children's literature (Caldecott Medal winners or Honor books). She found that about 70 percent of her sample "did contain metaphors and images representing one of the five leadership practices defined by Kouzes and Posner (1995)" (Boulais, 2002, p. 56). Many of the books reviewed reflected themes related to the leader–problem solver and leader-teacher memes.

Leader memes are also transmitted in the stories and fables told by parents and other influential models to children. These transmissions can be quite powerful, because they evoke the level of emotional tone that strengthens memetic replication (Heath et al., 2001). Both the content of the story and the identity of the storyteller (parents, models) contribute to emotion activation. Adler (2011) tells of how the experience of her mother and father confronting the evils of World War II, which they recounted repeatedly to her as a child, shaped her own views of leadership. She noted that "each of us has a personal story embedded in a cultural and family history that has shaped us as individuals and has given us our unique and highly personal combination of values, inspiration, and courage—our humanity—that we draw on in our day-to-day and larger leadership efforts" (p. 169).

Adler's account of her family history exemplifies how memetic transmissions come to influence later leader self-identities. As future leaders hear leadership stories, certain themes hold more resonance than others, based on their (1) constant retelling in ways that become deeply encoded in memory (Blackmore, 1999), and (2) informational content and emotional connection to both the storyteller and story-receiver (Heath et al., 2001). These themes coalesce around a leader self-identity or concept.

As leader self-concepts emerge, with identifiable leader memetic themes at their core, they begin to influence choices of early leader developmental experiences (Day & Harrison, 2007; Hannah, Woolfolk et al., 2009). Mumford, Stokes, and their colleagues argue that early life experiences cohere into developmental trajectories that reflect relatively stable choices about different activities and experiences consonant with one's developmental preferences (Mumford & Owens, 1987; Mumford, Stokes, & Owens, 1990; Stokes, Mumford, & Owens, 1989). Mumford, Snell, and Reiter-Palmon (1994; see also Mumford, Ulhman, & Kilcullen, 1992) suggested that individuals who are presented with a significant array of possible developmental activities use a heuristic template to evaluate and select among possible alternatives. Situational features are used to evaluate fit with elements in the template. Mumford et al. (1992, p. 113) noted that this template was "an idealized image about. . . what life should be like," and it "[emerged] from an integration of needs, values, beliefs about oneself, and beliefs about the world in relation to available role models" (p. 113).

Extending this concept to leadership development, decision-making templates derived from early leadership experiences become instrumental in helping leaders select among possible developmental activities. Those activities that best match elements featured in one's developmental template are more likely to be evaluated positively and selected (see Mumford et al., 1992). Leader memes are likely to be closely entwined with these elements. Thus, for example, individuals who have a leader self-concept reflecting a leader-warrior meme are likely to accrue competitive leadership experiences that reinforce their self-concept, and will form a developmental template that favors choices of similar experiences. The other memes would similarly give rise to templates favoring experiences congruent with their particular perspectives of leadership. In this way, leader memes, through their influences on leader self-identity and leader choices of developmental experiences, become powerful purveyors of leader maturation.

Research Questions

Figure 2.1 provides some fodder for research questions based on the role of leader memes in leader and leadership development. Leader self-identity is presented as a key mechanism for this influence. However, little is known or has been validated about (1) how such identity emerges from early leadership experiences, and (2) how memes are implicated in both early experiences and the growth of leader self-identity. Leader self-identity is not wholly idiosyncratic—it derives from not only one's personal experiences, but also from those reflected and replicated within one's social context. How such memetic influences translate into different types of leader self-identities becomes an important question, particularly given the crucial role of such identities in leader development (Lord & Hall, 2005).

Developmental templates reflect another key secondary mediator of memetic influences on leader development. Insufficient attention has been paid to the idea that leaders select their developmental activities, and to the factors that influence these choices. Mumford et al.'s (1994) notion of developmental templates is an important mechanism for framing and explaining such choices. Mumford et al. noted that these templates form fairly early in one's life, certainly before one begins to obtain formal adult leadership roles. What individual and contextual factors influence the formation of such templates? I have speculated that different leader memes give rise to different primed early developmental experiences and the content of early leader self-identity. An important research question, then, is how leader memetic transmissions become encoded eventually in the developmental templates and choices of nascent leaders.

Conclusion

Leadership has fascinated people since antiquity. This fascination has given rise to countless intergenerational transmissions of leadership stories, legends, fables, and lessons. These transmissions have coalesced into at least four leader memes that are described in this chapter. People's ideas about leadership, and their leader self-identities (or follower self-identities) are rooted in these memes. Their orientation to and interpretation of leadership experiences are in turn influenced by memetic-infused leader identities. Leader memes are also reflected in the fundamentals of most leadership scientific models and theories. Thus, leader memes reside at the core of how we practice and study leadership. Leadership is deeply embedded in historical/cultural events and dynamics. Leader memes are the links between cultural history and leadership practice. They can also serve as another important conceptual mechanism for understanding more deeply how people evolve a leader self-identity and how that identity matures through self-selected leadership experiences.

Notes

1. Winston Churchill, Terry Francona, Benjamin Franklin, Thomas Jefferson, Steve Jobs, Joseph P. Kennedy, Tony La Russa, Abraham Lincoln, Stanley A. McChrystal, Arnold Schwarzenegger, Sonia Sotomayor, and an account of more than 20 military generals from World War II to the present.
2. Sun Tzu, *The Art of War*
3. Michael Corleone, *Godfather Part II*
4. Henry "Red" Saunders; Vince Lombardi
5. Versions of this story have been depicted in art as early as 629–630 A.D. (Byzantine plate in the Metropolitan Museum of Art), and by some of the greatest artists in history, including Donatello, Michelangelo, Raphael, Titian, Caravaggio, Rembrandt, Bernini, and Turner.

References

Adler, N. J. (2011). I am my mother's daughter: Early developmental influences on leadership. In S. E. Murphy & R. J. Reichard (Eds.), *Early development and leadership: Building the next generation of leaders* (pp. 159–178). New York, NY: Routledge.

Adner, R., & Helfat, C. E. (2003). Corporate effects and dynamic managerial capabilities. *Strategic Management Journal, 24*, 1011–1025.

Ahearn, K. K., Ferris, G. R., Hochwarter, W. A., Douglas, C., & Ammeter, A. P. (2004). Leader political skill and team performance. *Journal of Management, 30*, 309–327.

Arrian (trans. 1958). *The campaigns of Alexander* (A. de Sélincourt, Trans.). London, UK: Penguin Books.

Awamleh, R., & Gardner, W. L. (1999). Perceptions of leader charisma and effectiveness: The effects of vision, content, delivery, and organizational performance. *Leadership Quarterly, 10*, 345–373.

Barney, J. B. (1991). Firm resources and sustained competitive advantage. *Journal of Management, 17*, 99–120.

Bass, B. M. (1985). *Leadership and performance beyond expectations*. New York, NY: Free Press.

Bass, B. M. (1996). *A new paradigm of leadership: An inquiry into transformational leadership*. Alexandria, VA: U.S. Army Research Institute for the Behavioral and Social Sciences.

Bass, B. M. (2008). *The Bass handbook of leadership: Theory, research, and managerial applications* (4th ed.). New York, NY: Free Press.

Bennett, W. J. (1995). *The children's book of virtues*. New York, NY: Simon & Schuster.

Blackmore, S. (1999). *The meme machine*. Oxford, UK: Oxford University Press.

Blake, R. R., & Mouton, J. S. (1964). *The managerial grid*. Houston, TX: Gulf Publishing.

Boulais, N. A. (2000). *A content analysis of children's literature using Kouzes and Posner leadership themes in Caldecott Medal winners and selected Honor books.* (Doctoral dissertation, University of Mississippi) Dissertation Abstracts International, 62-01A, 31.

Boulais, N. A. (2002). Leadership in children's literature: Qualitative analysis from a study based on the Kouzes and Posner leadership framework. *The Journal of Leadership Studies, 8,* 54–63.

Brookhiser, R. (2008). *George Washington on leadership.* New York, NY: Basic Books.

Burke, S., Stagl, K. C., Klein, C., Goodwin, G. F., Salas, E., & Halpin, S. M. (2006). What type of leadership behaviors are functional in teams? A meta-analysis. *Leadership Quarterly, 17,* 288–307.

Campbell, J., & Moyers, B. (1988). *The power of myth.* New York, NY: Anchor Books, Random House.

Caro, R. A. (2003). *Master of the Senate: The years of Lyndon Johnson.* New York, NY: Vintage Books.

Cicero, M. T. (2011). *On oratory* (W. Guthrie, Trans.). E-book: Evergreen Books.

Cicero, Q. T. (2012). *How to win an election: An ancient guide for modern politicians* (P. Freeman, Trans.). Princeton, NJ: Princeton University Press.

Command and General Staff College (2000). *66 stories of battle command.* Fort Leavenworth, KS: U.S. Army Command and General Staff College Press.

Conger, J. A. (1989). *The charismatic leader. Behind the mystique of exceptional leadership.* San Francisco, CA: Jossey-Bass.

Conger, J. A. (1991). Inspiring others: The language of leadership. *Academy of Management Executive, 5,* 31–45.

Connelly, M. S., Gilbert, J. A., Zaccaro, S. J., Threlfall, K. V., Marks, M. A., & Mumford, M. D. (2000). Cognitive and temperament predictors of organizational leadership. *Leadership Quarterly, 11,* 65–86.

Crocker, H. W., III (2000). *Robert E. Lee on leadership: Executive lessons in character, courage, and vision.* New York, NY: Three Rivers Press.

Curtius, Q. (2004). *The history of Alexander* (J. Yardley, Trans.). London: Penguin Books.

Dansereau, F., Graen, G., & Haga, W. J. (1975). A vertical dyad linkage approach to leadership within formal organizations: A longitudinal investigation of the role making process. *Organizational Behavior and Human Performance, 13,* 46–78.

Dawkins, R. (1976). *The selfish gene.* Oxford, UK: Oxford University Press.

Dawkins, R. (1999). Foreword. In S. Blackmore, *The meme machine* (pp. iv–xvi). Oxford, UK: Oxford University Press.

Day, D. V. (2000). Leadership development: A review in context. *Leadership Quarterly, 11,* 581–613.

Day, D. V., Gronn, P., & Salas, E. (2004). Leadership capacity in teams. *Leadership Quarterly, 15,* 857–880.

Day, D. V., & Harrison, M. M. (2007). A multilevel, identity-based approach to leadership development. *Human Resource Management Review, 17,* 360–373.

Dennis, R. S., & Bocarnea, M. (2005). Development of the servant leadership assessment instrument. *Leadership and Organization Development Journal, 26,* 600–615.

Dennett, D. (1991). *Consciousness explained.* New York, NY: Penguin Books.

Dinh, J. & Lord, R. G. (2012). Implications of dispositional and process views of traits for individual difference research in leadership. *Leadership Quarterly, 23,* 651–669.

Durant, W. (2002). *The greatest minds and ideas of all time* (compiled and edited by J. Little). New York, NY: Simon & Shuster.

Eden, D., & Leviatan, U. (1975). Implicit leadership theory as a determinant of the factor structure underlying supervisory behavior scales. *Journal of Applied Psychology, 60,* 736–741.

Ehrhart, M. G. (2004). Leadership and procedural justice climate as antecedents of unit-level organizational citizenship behavior. *Personnel Psychology, 57,* 61–94.

Everitt, A. (2001). *Cicero: The life and times of Rome's greatest politician.* New York, NY: Random House.

Ferentinos, C. H. (1996). Linking social intelligence and leadership: An investigation of leaders' situational responsiveness under conditions of changing group tasks and membership. *Dissertation Abstracts International: Section B: The Sciences & Engineering, 57(4-B),* 2920.

Ferris, G. R., Treadway, D. C., Kolodinsky, R. W., Hochwarter, W. A., Kacmar, C. J., Douglas, C., & Frink, D. D. (2005). Development and validation of the political skill inventory. *Journal of Management, 31,* 126–152.

Fiedler, F. E. (1964). A contingency model of leadership effectiveness. In L. Berkowitz (Ed.), *Advances in experimental social psychology* (Vol. 1, pp. 149–190). New York, NY: Academic Press.

Finkelstein, S., Hambrick, D. C., & Cannella, A. A., Jr. (2009). *Strategic leadership: Theory and Research on executives, top management teams, and boards.* Oxford, UK: Oxford University Press.

Fleishman, E. A. (1953). The description of supervisory behavior. *Personnel Psychology, 37,* 1–6.

Fleishman, E. A., Mumford, M. D., Zaccaro, S. J., Levin, K. Y., Korotkin, A. L., & Hein, M. B. (1991). Taxonomic efforts in the description of leader behavior: A synthesis and functional interpretation. *Leadership Quarterly, 2,* 245–287.

French, J. R. P., & Raven, B. H. (1959). The bases of social power. In D. Cartwright (Ed.), *Studies of social power* (pp. 150–167). Ann Arbor, MI: Institute for Social Research.

Gabriel, R. A. (2011). *Hannibal: The military biography of Rome's greatest enemy.* Dulles, VA: Potomac Books, Inc.

Gardner, W. L., & Avolio, B. J. (1998). The charismatic relationship: A dramaturgical perspective. *Academy of Management Review, 23,* 32–58.

Gat, I., & Prital, M. (2012). *Wise King Solomon and the honey bee.* E-book: CreateSpace Independent Publishing Platform.

Goodwin, D. K. (2005). *Team of rivals: The political genius of Abraham Lincoln.* New York, NY: Simon & Schuster.

Graen, G. B., & Uhl-Bien, M. (1995). Relationship-based approach to leadership: Development of leader-member exchange (LMX) theory of leadership over 25 years: Applying a multi-level multi-domain approach. *Leadership Quarterly, 6,* 219–247.

Greenleaf, R. K. (1970/2008). *The servant as leader.* Westfield, IN: Greenleaf Center for Servant Leadership.

Grotas, J. M. (2004). To know thyself: The roles of accuracy of self-assessment, personality, and cognitive intelligence in assessment center performance. Rutgers University: Unpublished dissertation.

Hackman J. R., & Wageman, R. (2005). A theory of team coaching. *Academy of Management Review, 30,* 269–287.

Hackman, J. R., & Walton, R. E. (1986). Leading groups in organizations. In P. S. Goodman & Associates (Eds.), *Designing effective work groups* (pp. 72–119). San Francisco, CA: Jossey-Bass.

Hambrick, D. C. (1981). Environment, strategy, and power within top management teams. *Administrative Science Quarterly, 26*, 253–276.

Hambrick, D. C. (1994). Top management groups: A conceptual integration and reconsideration of the "team" label. *Research in organizational behavior, 16*, 171–213.

Hannah, S. T., Uhl-Bien, M., Avolio, B. J., & Cavarretta, F. L. (2009). A framework for examining leadership in extreme contexts. *The Leadership Quarterly*, 20, 89–919.

Hannah, S. T., Woolfolk, R. L., & Lord, R. G. (2009). Leader self-structure: A framework for positive leadership. *Journal of Organizational Behavior, 30*, 269–290.

Harrison, R. P. (2011). What can you learn from Machiavelli? *Yale Insights*. Retrieved from (http://qn.som.yale.edu/content/what-can-you-learn-machiavelli)

Heath, C., Bell, C., & Sternberg, E. (2001). Emotional selection in memes: The case of urban legends. *Journal of Personality and Social Psychology, 81*, 1028–1041.

Hebert, S. C. (2003). *The relationship of perceived servant leadership and job satisfaction from the follower's perspective*. Doctoral dissertation, Cappella University, UMI No. 3112981.

Heider, J. (1985). *The Tao of leadership: Lao Tzu's Tao Te Ching adapted for a new age*. Atlanta, GA: Humanics New Age.

Hemphill, J. K., & Coons, A. E. (1957). Development of the leader behavior description questionnaire. In R. M. Stogdill and A. E. Coons (Eds.), *Leader behavior: Its description and measurement* (pp. 6–38). Columbus, OH: Bureau of Business Research, Ohio State University.

Herodotus (2002). *The histories* (J. Marincola, Trans.). London, UK: Penguin Books.

Hersey, P., & Blanchard, K. H. (1984). *Management of organizational behavior* (4th ed.). Englewood Cliffs, NJ: Prentice-Hall.

Heylighen F. (1997). Objective, subjective and intersubjective selectors of knowledge. *Evolution and Cognition, 3*, 63–67.

Heylighen, F. (2001). Memetic selection criteria. Retrieved from http://pespmc1.vub.ac.be/MEMSELC.html

Hill, J. (2010). Luxor temple. Retrieved from http://www.ancientegyptonline.co.uk/luxortemple.html

Hitt M. A., Bierman, L., Shimizu, K., Kochhar, R. (2001). Direct and moderating effects of human capital on strategy and performance in professional service firms: a resource-based perspective. *Academy of Management Journal, 44*, 13–28.

Holladay. S. J., & Coombs, W. T. (1993). Communicating visions: An exploration of the role of delivery in the creation of leader charisma. *Management Communication Quarterly, 6*, 405–427.

Holladay, S. J., & Coombs, W. T. (1994). Speaking of visions and visions being spoken: An exploration of the effects of content and delivery on perceptions of leader charisma. *Management Communication Quarterly, 8*, 165–189.

Hollander, E. P. (1958). Conformity, status, and idiosyncrasy credit. *Psychological Review, 65*, 117–127.

Hollander, E. P. (1961). Emergent leadership and social influence. In L. Petrullo & B. M. Bass (Eds.), *Leadership and interpersonal behavior* (pp. 30–47). New York, NY: Holt, Rinehart, and Winston, Inc.

Hollander, E. P. (1964). *Leaders, groups, and influence*. New York, NY: Oxford University Press.

Hollander, E. P., & Julian, J. W. (1970). Studies in leader legitimacy, influence, and motivation. *Advances in experimental social psychology, 5*, 33–69.

House, R. J. (1971). A path goal theory of leader effectiveness. *Administrative Science Quarterly, 16*, 321–339.

House, R. J. (1977). A 1976 theory of charismatic leadership. In J. G. Hunt & L. Larson (Eds.), *Leadership: The cutting edge*. Carbondale, IL: Southern Illinois University Press.

Howell, J. M., & Frost, P. J. (1989). A laboratory study of charismatic leadership. *Organizational Behavior and Human Decision Process, 43*, 243–269.

Hu, J., & Liden, R. C. (2011). Antecedents of team potency and team effectiveness: An examination of goal and process clarity and servant leadership. *Journal of Applied Psychology, 96*, 851–862.

Hunt, J. G. (1991). *Leadership: A new synthesis*. Newbury Park, CA: Sage.

Irving, J. A., & Longbotham, G. J. (2007). Team effectiveness and six essential servant leadership themes: A regression model based on the items in the Organizational Leadership Assessment. *International Journal of Leadership Studies, 2*, 98–113.

Isaacson, W. (2003). *Benjamin Franklin: An American life*. New York: Simon & Schuster.

Jacobs, T. O., & Jaques, E. (1987). Leadership in complex systems. In J. Zeidner (Ed.), *Human productivity enhancement*. New York, NY: Praeger.

Jacobs, T. O., & Jaques, E. (1990). Military executive leadership. In K. E. Clark, & M. B. Clark (Eds.), *Measures of leadership* (pp. 281–296). West Orange, NJ: Leadership Library of America.

Jaques, E. (1976). *A general theory of bureaucracy*. Exeter, NH: Heinemann.

Jaques, E. (1989). *Requisite organization*. Arlington, VA: Cason Hall.

Jaramillo, F., Grisaffe, D. B., Chonko, L. B., & Roberts, J. A. (2009a). Examining the impact of servant leadership on salesperson's turnover intention. *Journal of Personal Selling and Sales Management, 29*, 351–365.

Jaramillo, F., Grisaffe, D. B., Chonko, L. B., & Roberts, J. A. (2009b). Examining the impact of servant leadership on sales force performance. *Journal of Personal Selling and Sales Management, 29*, 257–275.

Johnson, S. K., Murphy, S. E., Zewdie, S., & Reichard, R. J. (2008). The strong, sensitive type: Effects of gender stereotypes and leader prototypes on the evaluation of male and female leaders. *Organizational Behavior and Human Decision Processes, 106*, 39–60.

Jung, C. (2010). *Four archetypes* (R. F. C. Hull, Trans.). Princeton, NJ: Princeton University Press.

Keeping your enemies closer. (2012). *Forbes*. Retrieved from http://www.forbes.com/sites/aileron/2012/12/27/keeping-your-enemies-closer

Kilburg, R. R. (2006). *Executive wisdom: Coaching and the emergence of virtuous leaders*. Washington, DC: American Psychological Association.

Know thyself (n.d.). In *Wikipedia*. Retrieved from http://en.wikipedia.org/wiki/Know_thyself

Kouzes, J. M., & Posner, B. Z. (1995). *The leadership challenge: How to keep getting extraordinary things done in organizations* (2nd ed.). San Francisco, CA: Jossey-Bass.

Kozlowski, S. W. J., Gully, S. M., McHugh, P. P., Salas, E., & Cannon-Bowers, J. A. (1996). A dynamic theory of leadership and team effectiveness: Developmental and task contingent leader roles. *Research in Personnel and Human Resources Management, 14*, 253–305.

Kozlowski, S. W. J., Gully, S. M., Salas, E., & Cannon-Bowers, J. A. (1996). Team leadership and development: Theory, principles, and guidelines for training leaders and teams. In M. M. Beyerlein, D. Johnson, & S. T. Beyerlein (Eds.), *Interdisciplinary studies of work teams* (Vol. 3: Team Leadership). Greenwich, CT: JAI Press.

Kozlowski, S. W. J., Watola, D. J., Jensen, J. M., Kim, B. H., & Botero, I. C. (2009). Developing adaptive teams: A theory of dynamic team leadership. In E. Salas, G. F. Goodwin, & C. S. Burke (Eds.), *Team effectiveness in complex organizations* (pp. 113–155). New York, NY: Routledge.

Lao Tzu. (2012). *Tao Te Ching* (D. Waller, Trans.). Bedford, TX: D. Waller.

Livy, T. (trans. 1965). *The war with Hannibal* (A. de Sélincourt, Trans.). London: Penguin Books.

Lord, R. G. (1985). An information processing approach to social perceptions, leadership perceptions and behavioral measurement on organizational settings. In B. M. Staw & L. Cummings (Eds.), *Research in organizational behavior* (pp. 87–128). Greenwich, CT: JAI Press.

Lord, R. G., & Brown, D. J. (2004). *Leadership processes and follower self-identity.* Mahwah, NJ: Lawrence Erlbaum Associates.

Lord, R. G., Brown, D. J., Harvey, J. L., & Hall, R. J. (2001). Contextual constraints on prototype generation and their multilevel consequences for leadership perceptions. *The Leadership Quarterly, 12*, 311–338.

Lord, R. G., De Vader, C. L., & Alliger, G. M. (1986). A meta-analysis of the relation between personality traits and leadership perceptions: An application of validity generalization procedures. *Journal of Applied Psychology, 71*, 402–410.

Lord, R. G., Foti, R. J., & De Vader, C. L. (1984). A test of leadership categorization theory: Internal structure, information processing, and leadership perceptions. *Organizational Behavior and Human Performance, 34*, 343–378.

Lord, R. G., Foti, R. J., & Phillips, J. S. (1982). A theory of leadership categorization theory: Internal structure, information processing, and leadership perceptions. *Organizational Behavior and Human Performance, 34*, 343–378.

Lord, R. G., & Hall, R. J. (2005). Identity, deep structure and the development of leadership skills. *The Leadership Quarterly, 16*, 591–615.

Lord, R. G., Hannah, S. T., & Jennings, P. L. (2011). A framework for understanding leadership and individual requisite complexity. *Organizational Psychology Review, 1*, 104–127.

Lord, R. G., & Maher, K. J. (1993). *Leadership and information processing: Linking perceptions and performance.* New York, NY: Routledge.

Machiavelli, N. (2003). *The prince and other writings* (W. A. Rebhorn, Trans.). New York, NY: Barnes & Noble Classics.

Manchester, W., & Reid, P. (2012). *The last lion: Winston Spencer Churchill: Defender of the Realm.* New York, NY: Little, Brown, and Company.

Mann, R. D. (1959). A review of the relationship between personality and performance in small groups. *Psychological Bulletin, 56*, 241–270.

Markus, H. R., & Wurf, E. (1987). The dynamic self-concept: A social psychological perspective. *Annual Review of Psychology, 38*, 299–337.

McCauley, C. D., Van Velsor, E., & Ruderman, M. N. (2010). Introduction: Our view of leadership development. In E. Van Velsor, C. D. McCauley, & M. N. Ruderman, (Eds.), *The Center for Creative Leadership handbook of leadership development* (3rd ed.) (pp. 1–26). San Francisco, CA: Jossey-Bass.

McGrath, J. E. (1962). *Leadership behavior: Some requirements for leadership training.* Washington, DC: U.S. Civil Service Commission, Office of Career Development.

Meacham, J. (2008). *American lion: Andrew Jackson in the White House.* New York, NY: Random House.

Meacham, J. (2012). *Thomas Jefferson: The art of power.* New York, NY: Random House.

Meindl, J. R., Ehrlich, S. B., & Dukerich, J. M. (1985). The romance of leadership. *Administrative Science Quarterly, 30*, 78–102.

Miles R. E., & Snow C. C. (1978). *Organizational strategy, structure, and process.* McGraw-Hill: New York.

Miles R. E., & Snow C. C. (1984). Designing strategic human resources systems. *Organizational Dynamics, 13*(1), 36–52.

Morgeson, F. P., DeRue, D. S., & Karam, E. P. (2010). Leadership in teams: A functional approach to understanding leadership structures and processes. *Journal of Management, 36*, 5–39.

Morrow, J. L., Sirmon, D. G., Hitt, M. A., & Holcomb, T. R. (2007). Creating value in the face of declining performance: firm strategies and organizational recovery. *Strategic Management Journal, 28*, 271–283.

Mumford, M. D. (2002). Social innovation: Ten cases from Benjamin Franklin. *Creativity Research Journal, 14*, 253–266.

Mumford, M. D., Zaccaro, S. J., Harding, F. D., Jacobs, T. O., & Fleishman, E. A. (2000). Leadership skills for a changing world: Solving complex social problems. *Leadership Quarterly, 11*, 11–35.

Mumford, M. D., & Owens, W. A. (1987). Methodology review: Principles, procedures, and findings in the application of background data measures. *Applied Psychological Measurement, 11*, 1–31.

Mumford, M. D., Snell, A. F., & Reiter-Palmon, R. (1994). Personality and background data: Life history and self concepts in an ecological system. In G. S. Stokes, M. D. Mumford, & W. A. Owens (Eds.), *Handbook of background data research: Theories, measures, and applications* (pp. 583–625). Palo Alto, CA: Consulting Psychologists Press.

Mumford, M. D., Stokes, G. S., & Owens, W. A. (1990). *Patterns of life adaptation: The ecology of human individuality.* Hillsdale, NJ: Lawrence Erlbaum Associates, Inc.

Mumford, M. D., Uhlman, C. E., & Kilcullen, R. N. (1992). The structure of life history: Implications for the construct validity of background data scales. *Human Performance, 5*, 109–137.

Mumford, M. D., & Van Doorn, J. R. (2001). The leadership of pragmatism: Reconsidering Franklin in the age of charisma. *The Leadership Quarterly, 12*, 279–309.

Ndofor, H. A., Sirmon D. G., He X. (2011). Firm resources, competitive actions, and performance: Investigating a mediated model with evidence from the in-vitro diagnostics industry. *Strategic Management Journal, 32*, 640–657.

Oakes, M., King, J., & Campbell, J. (1943/1991). *Where the two came to their father.* Princeton, NJ: Princeton University Press.

Peterson, S. J., Galvin, B. M., & Lange, D. (2012). CEO servant leadership: Exploring executive characteristics and firm performance. *Personnel Psychology, 65*, 565–596.

Phillips, J. S., & Lord, R. G. (1982). Schematic information processing and perceptions of leadership in problem-solving groups. *Journal of Applied Psychology, 67*, 486–492.

Plato. (1993). *The republic* (R. Waterfield, Trans.). New York: Oxford University Press.

Ployhart, R. E. (2012). The psychology of competitive advantage: An adjacent possibility. *Industrial and Organizational Psychology, 5*, 62–81.

Plutarch. (1960). *Nine Greek lives* (I. Scorr-Kilvert, Trans.). London, UK: Penguin Books.
Plutarch. (1965). *Nine Roman lives* (I. Scorr-Kilvert, Trans.). London, UK: Penguin Books.
Plutarch (2001). *Plutarch's lives* (Vol. 2). New York, NY: The Modern Library.
Popper, K. R. (1966). *The Open Society and Its Enemies. Volume I. The Spell of Plato.* London, UK: Routledge & Kegan Paul.
Porter, M. E. (1979). How competitive forces shape society. *Harvard Business Review, 57,* 137–145.
Porter, M. E. 1980. *Competitive strategy.* New York, NY: The Free Press.
Porter, M. E. (1979). The five competitive forces that shape strategy. *Harvard Business Review, 86,* 78–93.
Rebhorn, W. A. (2003). Introduction. In N. Machiavelli, *The prince and other writings* (W. A. Rebhorn, Trans.). New York, NY: Barnes & Noble Classics.
Riantoputra, C. D. (2010). Know thyself: Examining factors that influence the activation of organizational identity concepts in top managers' mind. *Group & Organization Management, 35,* 8–38.
Rosch, E. (1975). Cognitive representations of semantic categories. *Journal of Experimental Psychology: General, 104,* 192–233.
Rosch, E. (1978). *Principles of categorization.* In E. Rosch & B. B. Lloyd (Eds.), *Cognition and categorization.* Hillsdale, NJ: Erlbaum.
Rosch, E., & Mervis, C. B. (1975). Family resemblances: Studies in the internal structure of categories. *Cognitive Psychology, 7,* 573–605.
Rush, M. C., Thomas, J. C., & Lord, R. G. (1977). Implicit leadership theory: A potential threat to the internal validity of leader behavior questionnaires. *Organizational Behavior and Human Performance, 81,* 756–765.
Russell, R. F., & Stone, A. G. (2002). A review of servant leadership attributes: Developing a practical model. *Leadership and Organization Development Journal, 23,* 145–157.
Shamir, B., Arthur, M. B., & House, R. J. (1994). The rhetoric of charismatic leadership: A theoretical extension, a case study, and implications for research. *Leadership Quarterly, 5,* 25–42.
Shoda, Y., Tiernan, S. L., & Mischel, W. (2002). Personality as a dynamical system: Emergence of stability and distinctiveness from intra- and interpersonal interactions. *Personality and Social Psychology Review, 4,* 316–325.
Shondrick, S. J., Dinh, J. E., & Lord, R. G. (2010). Developments in implicit leadership theory and cognitive science: Applications to improving measurement and understanding alternatives to hierarchical leadership. *The Leadership Quarterly, 21,* 959–978.
Sirmon, D. G., Gove, S., & Hitt, M. A. (2008). Resource management in dyadic competitive rivalry: the effects of resource bundling and deployment. *Academy of Management Journal, 51,* 918–935.
Sirmon, D. G., & Hitt, M. A. (2009). Contingencies within dynamic managerial capabilities: interdependent effects of resource investment and deployment on firm performance. *Strategic Management Journal, 30,* 1375–1394.
Sirmon, D. G., Hitt, M. A., & Ireland, R. D. (2007). Managing firm resources in dynamic environments to create value: Looking inside the black box. *Academy of Management Review, 32,* 273–292.
Smith, J. E. (2007). *FDR.* New York, NY: Random House.
Speel, H. C., (1995) Memetics: On a conceptual framework for cultural evolution. Paper presented at the symposium "Einstein meets Magrittte." Free University of Brussels, June.
Sternberg, R. J. (2007). The systems model of leadership: WICS. *American Psychologist, 62,* 34–42.
Sternberg, R. J. (2013). The WICS model of leadership. In M. G. Rumsey (Ed.), *The Oxford handbook of leadership* (pp. 47–62). New York, NY: Oxford University Press.
Stokes, G. S., Mumford, M. D., & Owens, W. A. (1989). Life history prototypes in the study of human individuality. *Journal of Personality, 57,* 509–545.
Stone, A. G., Russell, R. F., & Patterson, K. (2004). Transformational versus servant leadership: A difference in leader focus. *Leadership and Organization Development Journal, 25,* 349–361.
Suetonius, G. (1957). *The twelve Caesars* (R. Graves, Trans.). London, UK: Penguin Books.
Sun Tzu (2011). The art of war (L. Giles, Trans.). Retrieved from http://www.seedboxpress.com.
Trice, H. M., & Beyer, J. M. (1986). Charisma and its routinization in two social movement organizations. In B. M. Staw & L. L. Cummings (Eds.), *Research in organizational behavior* (pp. 113–164). Greenwich, CT: JAI Press.
Turesky, E. F., & Gallagher, D. (2011). Know thyself: Coaching for leadership using Kolb's experiential learning theory. *The Coaching Psychologist, 7,* 5–14.
U.S. Department of the Army (1985). *Leadership statements and quotes* (Pam. 600–64). Washington, DC: U.S. Government Printing Office.
U.S. Department of the Army (2006). *Army leadership* (FM 6-22). Washington, DC: U.S. Government Printing Office.
U.S. Department of the Army (2012). *Army leadership* (ADP 6-22). Washington, DC: U.S. Government Printing Office.
Van Dierendonck, D. (2011). Servant leadership: A review and synthesis. *Journal of Management, 37,* 1228–1261.
Van Dierendonck, D., & Nuijten, I. (2011). The servant leadership survey: Development and validation of a multidimensional measure. *Journal of Business and Psychology, 26,* 249–267.
Van Vugt, M., Hogan, R., & Kaiser, R. B. (2008). Leadership, followership, and evolution. *American Psychologist, 63,* 182–196.
von Clausewitz, C. (1832/1976). *On war* (M. Howard & P. Paret, Trans.). Princeton, NJ: Princeton University Press.
Washington, R. R., Sutton, C. D., & Feild, H. S. (2006). Individual differences in servant leadership: The roles of values and personality. *Leadership and Organization Development Journal, 27,* 700–716.
Weber, M. (1947). *The theory of social and economic organization* (T. Parsons, Trans.). New York, NY: Free Press.
Wikipedia (n.d.). In *Wikipedia.* Retrieved from http://en.wikipedia.org/wiki/Wikipedia
Williams, P. (2010). *The leadership wisdom of Solomon.* Cincinnati, OH: Standard Publishing.
Williamson T. (2008). The good society and the good soul: Plato's Republic on leadership. *The Leadership Quarterly, 19,* 397–408.
Wong, L., Bliese, P., & McGurk, D. (2003). Military leadership: A context specific review. *The Leadership Quarterly, 14,* 657–692.
Woolfe, L. (2002). *Leadership secrets from the Bible.* New York, NY: MJF Books.
Yukl, G. (1994). *Leadership in organizations* (3rd ed.). Englewood Cliffs, NJ: Prentice-Hall.

Zaccaro, S. J. (2001). *The nature of executive leadership: A conceptual and empirical analysis of success.* Washington, DC: APA Books.

Zaccaro, S. J., Foti, R. J., & Kenny, D. A. (1991). Self-monitoring and trait-based variance in leadership: An investigation of leader flexibility across multiple group situations. *Journal of Applied Psychology, 76*, 308–315.

Zaccaro, S. J., Gilbert, J., Thor, K., & Mumford, M. (1991). Leadership and social intelligence: Linking social perceptiveness and behavioral flexibility to leader effectiveness. *Leadership Quarterly, 2*, 317–342.

Zaccaro, S. J., Heinen, B., & Shuffler, M (2009). Team leadership and team effectiveness. In E. Salas., J. Goodwin, & C. S. Burke (Eds.), *Team effectiveness in complex organizations: Cross disciplinary perspective and approaches* (pp. 83–111). San Francisco, CA: Jossey-Bass.

Zaccaro, S. J., LaPort, K., & Jose, I. (2013). Attributes of successful leaders: A performance requirements approach. In M. Rumsey (Ed.), *The Oxford handbook of leadership* (pp. 11–36). Oxford, UK: Oxford University Press.

CHAPTER

3 Critical Perspectives on Leadership

Mats Alvesson *and* André Spicer

Abstract

This chapter reviews the emerging body of literature on critical theories of leadership. It begins by putting critical approaches to leadership in the context of broader debates about leadership. It notes that most existing work builds on either functional or interpretive assumptions. After noting some of the shortcomings with these directions, this chapter offers an alternative set of ideas based on critical theory. These suggest that leadership should be denaturalized and studied reflexively, and that this research should be done with a noninstrumental intent. The chapter then reviews the growing body of work that has built on these ideas. This work addresses issues including ideology, identity, exclusions and inclusions, and interventions. The chapter concludes by outlining a range of areas for future research.

Key Words: critical leadership studies, ideology, identity, performativity

Calls for more leadership are everywhere. Businesses large and small, the government, public administration, and the nonprofit sector are abuzz with demands for increased leadership. We are told that almost any problem—including the global financial crisis, failing schools, the spread of HIV/AIDS, and global warming—is solvable through more or better leadership. Millions of dollars and thousands of hours are invested in developing better leaders. Indeed, leadership seems to have become a kind of universal solution for any issue, irrespective of context. We assume that, no matter what the problem, leadership is the solution. A whole industry is devoted to manufacturing leaders and creating demand for "leadership." Those believed to be good leaders are paid enormous amounts of money. Of course, there are cases where even the greatest proponents of leadership recognize that leaders clearly have not offered magical solutions. Proponents excuse such cases as being examples of lack of leadership or perhaps the wrong form of leadership; these cases are labeled as examples of inauthentic, toxic, or laissez-faire leadership, or simply a form of stuffy management. This kind of reasoning leads to a widespread and stubborn assumption that leadership is always needed and always good. (The reasoning here is often tautological—leadership is typically defined in broad and functional terms, thus, it is by definition highly significant and always good.)

The astonishing spread of this idea suggests that leadership may have overtaken management as one of the dominant social myths of our time (Gemmill & Oakley, 1992). In many instances, embracing the idea of leadership does not involve any significant change to practice, but merely indicates an interest in relabeling managerial work as "leadership" to make it sound more fashionable and impressive. The term *leadership* is seductive, has a strong rhetorical appeal, and is therefore heavily overused. In today's business world, it is important to appear impressive and remarkable and to produce positive images (Alvesson, 2013). One must persuade others and oneself of the importance and superiority of one's job, activities, and achievements. In such a context, leadership—and preferably impressive forms of it, like transformational or, more recently, post-transformational leadership—becomes attractive. Instead of supervision, management, administration, or bureaucracy, we find leadership. Instead of initiating structure or personnel orientation, we find transformational, visionary, strategic, authentic leadership. Instead of peer influence and teamwork, we find shared leadership. Instead of motivating or organizing yourself, we find self-leadership. Instead of lobbying or influencing people higher up in an organization, we get upward leadership. Leadership, it seems, is a word that can be and often is used to describe nearly any kind of activity. It gives us a way of talking about what is often mundane and pedestrian work as if it was particularly impressive and grandiose (Alvesson, 2013; Alvesson & Sveningsson, 2003a).

Talk and text about leadership is appealing and widely shared, but, on closer inspection, it is not particularly convincing. Like many popular management fashions, much of the discussion about leadership is based on shaky foundations. It is often superficial, appeals to wishful thinking, uses popular symbols as a persuasive resource, resorts to vague and confused thinking, and is ultimately founded on bandwagon effects and (pseudo)intellectual opportunism. Academic studies of leadership are not exempt from these problems. The field has rapidly become a hothouse for all manner of peculiar (quasi) scholastic ventures that assume that leadership is an altogether desirable and necessary activity. This is, of course, not meant to deny the pluralism and variety of academic studies of leadership. Instead, we want to point out that the vast majority of studies of leadership do not subject the issue of leadership to much serious scrutiny. Rather, many leadership researchers concentrate on getting the numbers right, without worrying too much about whether undergraduate students, people participating in management education, or those responding to online requests offer much valuable knowledge when they fill in research questionnaires. If our ideas about leadership are so questionable, then perhaps some careful reflection and critical thinking is needed.

In this chapter, we review a small but growing field of research that seeks to provide a more critical understanding of leadership (e.g., Alvesson & Spicer, 2011, 2012; Collinson, 2011; Ford, Harding, & Learmouth, 2008; Gemmill & Oakley, 1992; Knights & Willmott, 1992; Zoller & Fairhurst, 2007). Although critical leadership studies is made up of different concerns, some common themes include (a) asking whether leadership is always desirable; (b) considering the possibility that, in many cases, leadership may be more about creating domination, excess control, and self-enhancing images rather than effective organization and direction of tasks; (c) unpacking the blind faith in the curative powers of leadership; and (d) being skeptical about whether leadership is actually needed (or happening) in many situations.

In this chapter, we seek to provide an overview of critical studies of leadership. We start by clarifying what we mean by leadership. We then look at how leadership has been studied through functionalist and interpretive frameworks and outline some of the central problems with these approaches. We then put forward critical leadership studies as a way of addressing many of these shortcomings. We outline common assumptions underpinning many critical studies of leadership. Then, we examine different foci of critical leadership studies including identities, images, ideology, incapacitation, and intervention. We conclude the chapter by drawing out some paucities and areas for future research in the field.

Defining Leadership

The meaning of leadership has always been a great source of ambiguity and confusion. To avoid such confusion, many studies simply refrain from defining it. Researchers agree that it is some kind of influencing process, but this does not really say anything. There are all sorts of ways to influence people that are perhaps not best defined as leadership. Many studies start by identifying some of the basic ingredients of leadership, such as the presence of a leader and one or more followers and interaction among the follower(s) and leader (e.g., Antonakis, Cianciolo, & Sternberg, 2004; Fiedler 1996). Whether the distinction between leader and follower is necessarily a good way to capture social relations at work is seldom considered. In these studies, the world is divided up into two kinds of people (leaders and followers), and seldom is any effort made to reflect or empirically check whether this makes much sense. Some researchers try to sharpen up the definition by adding what may be influenced: behavior, commitment, thinking, goal attainment, and so on (Yukl 1989). Others have tried to shift the focus from leaders and followers to the underlying processes of leadership, such as developing direction, creating alignment, and building commitment (Drath et al., 2008). However, these attempts to broaden what is meant by leadership can mean that almost any kind of organizing or coordinating activity is counted as leadership. Such definitions (or the absence of definitions) lead to uses of the leadership label that are vague or all-embracing, thus making it possible to address leadership as everything or nothing. As a result, leadership becomes an empty signifier—a word that can be stuffed with almost any content one wishes. This vagueness has also caused many commentators to bemoan the lack of clear ideas or definitions (e.g., Barker, 1997) and has led some to conclude that leadership is an essentially contestable concept (Grint, 2000). This suggests that the difficulties in nailing down a definition of leadership are somehow part of the essence of leadership. Yet such essential ambiguity does not seem to prevent researchers from studying leadership in all sorts of ways. Rather, it seems to actually spur them on. Vagueness and ambiguity actually become resources for people addressing a wide set of different phenomena that appear to do something important and relevant under the label "leadership."

One way researchers have sought to tackle the endemically vague concept of leadership has been by introducing a distinction between management and leadership (Nichols, 1987; Zaleznik, 1977). Researchers typically point out that managers rely on their formal position for authority and work with bureaucratic processes such as planning, budgeting, organizing, and controlling. In contrast, leaders rely on their personal abilities; work at creating vision, agendas, and coalition building; and mainly use noncoercive means to affect people's feelings and thinking (e.g., Kotter, 1985; Zaleznik, 1977). The focus of leadership thus becomes influence through "altering moods, evoking images and expectations, and in establishing specific desires and objectives...The net result of this influence is to change the way people think about what is desirable, possible and necessary" (Zaleznik, 1977: 71). This split between symbol-manipulating leaders and administrative managers seems appealing. It makes leadership sound like a glamorous, challenging, almost mystical pursuit. In contrast, management appears as a humdrum set of administrative tasks. Given such an alluring image, people easily identify with leadership and feel themselves to be "leaders, not managers," although lying behind this desire to present and see themselves as leaders is often much confusion (Alvesson & Sveningsson, 2003b, c; Carroll & Levy, 2008).

This rigid distinction between leaders and managers is questionable. Leadership often involves a significant component of management. Most people who claim to be leaders or who are believed to be leaders in organizations occupy a formal position (such as manager, committee chair, union representative, or the like). Formal positions often tap into our deeply held belief that people can legitimately exercise influence over us when they are in official positions of authority: A statement may have different effects when said by the CEO or by her assistant. Similarly, management is often shot through with leadership. People usually gain access to these formal positions on the basis of perceived "informal" leadership capabilities. Those promoted to management positions are expected to have some of the qualities usually associated with leadership and to "look" like a leader. In practice, managers can seldom rely purely on bureaucracy or output control but need to create commitment for—or at least acceptance of—plans, rules, goals, and instructions and thus use an element of leadership. We are not trying to say that all management is leadership or that leadership is purely management. Rather, leadership seldom appears in any pure form and is frequently intertwined with management (Bolden et al., 2011). Despite the fact that leadership and management are difficult to separate in reality, we think it is important to draw some kind of analytical distinctions. To see leadership as "everything" is meaningless. We believe that a lot of what is called leadership is so labeled without any good reasons—apart from rhetorical appeal. As Spoelstra and ten Bos (2011) note, laissez-faire and transformational leadership have little to do with leadership but can be much better described and understood in other ways.

For us, leadership involves a strong ingredient of *meaning management* (Ladkin, 2010; Sandberg & Targama, 2007; Smircich & Morgan, 1982; Zaleznik, 1977), in which the shaping of the ideas, values, perceptions, and feelings is central. The idea of leadership as the management of meaning, as we see it, is neutral with regards to the change/stability dimension. Management can be central to change, and leadership can be very much about maintaining, revising, or strengthening ideas, beliefs, morale, values, and understandings. It is important to recognize that leadership, despite being about meanings, can also involve coercive elements (seen as legitimately enacted). Behind the "purely" convincing and appealing is typically a system of norms encouraging respect and compliance with authority figures (like managers) and a contingent feeling that the leader (or others in the environment) also can create problems for those not receptive to meaning management. People disinclined to see themselves as followers, who insist on thinking autonomously and critically, may disrupt organizational order and be targeted for more or less subtle discipline. The power element in leadership is typically neglected or trivialized in most studies of leadership. This seriously reduces its value because power issues are crucial in organizations (Clegg, 1989; Pfeffer, 1981) and are a key aspect of leader–follower relations (Collinson, 2005).

Studying Leadership

The ongoing struggles to define leadership have contributed to the many different perspectives outlined in this handbook. At first glance, such a variety of different approaches may seem confusing or as little more than varied attempts to carve up the field. For instance, some researchers have identified five broad approaches to studying leadership, focusing on leader traits, leader behavioral style, contingency approaches, transformational leadership, and postheroic leadership (House & Aditya, 1997; Parry & Bryman, 2006). Conversely, we think one particular useful way of understanding the study of leadership is to identify some of the deeper underlying paradigmatic assumptions on which the literature is based. These are the shared and often implicit ontological, epistemological, and political assumptions that underpin research (Alvesson & Sandberg, 2011) and that the broader field of organization and management studies has long recognized as the underlying paradigmatic assumptions underpinning research in their field (e.g., Burrell & Morgan, 1979).

The great majority of studies of leadership are firmly grounded in functionalist assumptions. Researchers working in this tradition assume that leadership is an objective phenomenon that is amenable to scientific inquiry and is primarily grounded in shared interests of system functioning and survival (Burrell & Morgan, 1979). Functionalist studies approach leadership as a fairly stable object that exists in the world and can be tracked down with the help of correct analytical tools. Studies in this tradition have sought to identify those traits that are correlated with leadership, such as physical and psychological characteristics (for a review, see House & Aditya, 1997). They have also investigated leadership behaviors, such as task-centric and people-centric styles (House & Aditya, 1997). A third broad focus has been on those situations in which leadership takes place (e.g., Fiedler, 1967). A fourth focus has considered a leader's ability to formulate visions and transform followers (Bass, 1985; Bennis & Nanus, 1985; Hartnell & Walumbwa, 2011; Sashkin, 2004). Finally, researchers have begun to move their focus away from the role of the leader and to that of the follower (Bligh, 2011; Hollander, 1992; Meindl, 1995). Although each of these approaches tends to focus on different explanatory variables, they all share similar underlying assumptions. Ontologically, they assume that leadership is something existing independently out there in the world, located within a web of causal relationships. Epistemologically, they assume leadership can be known in a value-free way, through what is claimed to be the rigorous application of the scientific method. Politically, they aim to increase the efficiency and effectiveness of current modes of leadership.

The dominance of functionalist assumptions about leadership was rarely questioned, even though strong doubts about the level of progress being made under this paradigm were expressed in the 1970s and '80s (Andriessen & Drenth, 1984; Yukl, 1989). More recently, however, a number of important shortcomings in functionalist studies of leadership have become apparent. First, functionalist studies typically ignore the issue of *meaning*. In particular, they do not capture divergent meanings that are attributed to leadership by different actors. Respondents are typically asked to answer questionnaires without much consideration of the degree that constrained response alternatives limit how people in leadership relations actually experience their situations (Alvesson, 1996). Second, functionalist studies frequently ignore processes of *interaction* involved in leadership. Few studies consider what the leader brings to an interaction, what she does, how followers attribute meaning to these action, and how followers' perceptions shape the actions of a leader (Alvesson & Sveningsson, 2012). Third, functionalist studies are often *acontextual*. Leadership is studied in splendid isolation. By this we mean that these studies do not consider various "extraneous" factors like national specificity, hierarchical level, industry, historical period, and economic conditions (to name just a few issues). Nor do they account for local organizational conditions that may profoundly shape what is understood as leadership and how leader–follower relations are framed (Fairhurst, 2009; Liden & Antonakis, 2009). Fourth, many functionalist studies are plagued by a *common source bias* (Avolio et al., 1991). By this we mean that studies of leadership often rely on only one source. Subordinates might be asked to describe their manager (leader), or managers may be asked to describe their own leadership. But research shows that when several sources are used, different subjects do not agree (Cogliser, Schriesheim, Scandura, & Gardner, 2009). Although there is increased awareness of this problem, most published research still relies on a single source. Fifth, studies of leadership are often framed and designed in such a way that results comes close to being mere tautologies. This happens when research is designed to link positively formulated indicators of leadership with good outcomes. This is, for example, salient in much transformational leadership research. This result may reflect all sorts of researcher-based bias, such as a positive (or a negative) view of managers informing all responses or a desire to avoid cognitive dissonance (Alvesson, 1996). Finally, functionalist studies are often imprisoned by a *pro-leadership ideology*. By this we mean that many studies are founded on the assumption that leadership is associated with positive outcomes (Alvesson, 2011c). Any attempts to stray from these assumptions are often marginalized (Bryman, 2011).

These criticisms of functionalist approaches have led some researchers to explore alternative assumptions that emphasize the meaning-laden aspects of leadership (e.g., Alvesson, 1996). This has involved a shift toward interpretive assumptions that see leadership as socially constructed through actors "recognizing" a set of activities as leadership (Fairhurst & Grant, 2010). This calls for qualitative methodological approaches such as ethnography, in-depth case studies, and various forms of linguistic analysis that sensitize us to multiple understandings of leadership (for reviews, see Bryman, 2004; Fairhurst, 2007). Interpretive approaches to leadership have come in a range of formats. Some have looked at symbolic leadership and how leaders try to influence frames, cognitions, and meanings. This occurs when "leadership is realized in the process whereby one or more individuals succeed in attempting to frame and define the reality of others" (Smircich & Morgan, 1982: 258; see also Fairhurst, 2007; Ladkin, 2010; Sandberg & Targama, 2007). Another strand of literature has investigated the processes of social constructions (e.g., Fairhurst, 2009; Fairhurst & Grant, 2010; Uhl-Bien, 2006). For some, this has involved considering how leadership "continuously emerges" from the ongoing interactions between superiors and subordinates (Wood, 2005). Others have looked at leadership as a language game, considering how and when the term is used (Kelly, 2008; Pondy, 1978). Still others have investigated the clashing constructions and languages that are used to interpret and understand acts of leadership (Alvesson & Sveningsson, 2003b). Although these studies exhibit some important differences, they all share a common set of assumptions. Ontologically, leadership is thought to be constructed through ongoing processes of intersubjective understanding. Epistemologically, leadership is seen as a process that can only be accessed through examining these value-laden understandings and interpretations that actors use to understand leadership. Many interpretive studies seek to surface different understandings of leadership in the hope of supporting increasingly shared meaning.

Interpretive assumptions have opened up new vistas by highlighting how leadership is constructed, as well as the ambiguities and uncertainties associated with it. However, interpretive approaches have some important shortcomings, partly shared by functionalist approaches. First, an interpretive approach can be fairly uncritical, even naïve. By this we mean those interpretive approaches that do not question discourses of leadership as presented by interviewees. Interpretivists often assume that there is a clear and coherent set of meanings informing people and their actions, thus indicating that a coherent worldview and understanding guide what they do. This ignores the possibility that presentations of leadership in interviews and talk in organizations may be more than just a wish to express experience and meaning in a straightforward way. These researchers may underestimate the cultural and social forces operating unconsciously on people (Alvesson, 2011a). The second shortcoming of interpretive approaches is that the strict focus on issues of meaning can divert our attention from systematic structural and ideological issues. That is, just looking at the local meaning that actors attribute to notions of leadership diverts our attention from the possibility that very different people—from CEOs to deacons to supermarket supervisors—may want to identify themselves as "leaders" and as eager to "do leadership." The third shortcoming of interpretive studies is that they can miss issues of power and domination. By looking at processes such as shared or distributed leadership, many interpretive researchers can miss the various forms of inequality that seem essential to leadership. This is because power differentials often mean that one person is in a stronger position to impose his or her definition of what good leadership is, particularly if there is strong institutional and ideological support for this definition that normalizes leader–follower distinctions and relations. The final shortcoming of many interpretive studies of leadership is that they find it difficult to account for some of the nondiscursive aspects of leadership; they cannot adequately capture the various forms of economic, human, cultural, and social capital that place one person in a more conducive position to engage in leadership whereas another is unable to do so (Spillane, Hallet, & Diamond, 2003).

These shortcomings are in some ways similar to those of functionalism and reflect a narrow view of the subject matter, a strong belief in the capacity of informants to report data about behavior and meaning, a shortage of critical thinking in methodological terms, and an underestimation of the complexities of force that shape leadership practices.

Critical Leadership Studies

To address the shortcomings of both functionalist and interpretive studies, a limited number of researchers have developed critical approaches to leadership (e.g., Alvesson & Spicer, 2012; Alvesson & Sveningsson, 2003b; 2012; Calás & Smircich, 1991; Collinson 2005, 2011; Ford, 2010; Ford et al., 2008; Fryer, 2012; Gemmill & Oakley, 1992; Grint, 2005; Harding, Lee, Ford, & Learmouth, 2011; Knights & Willmott, 1992; Western, 2008). These researchers often draw on insights and methodological protocols associated with interpretive approaches, such as in-depth qualitative methods and a focus on processes of social construction (Fairhurst & Grant, 2010). Critical scholars do not simply seek to understand how leadership is given meaning in different situations (as interpretivists do). Rather, they seek to go further by examining the patterns of power and domination associated with leadership and relating these patterns to broader ideological and institutional conditions. Critical theories have sought inspiration from a set of assumptions associated with critical management studies (e.g., Alvesson, Bridgman, & Willmott, 2009; Alvesson & Willmott, 2012; Fournier & Grey, 2000). Critical leadership studies have also built on feminism by emphasizing gendered notions of leadership that support and legitimize male domination (Alvesson & Billing, 2009; Calás & Smircich, 1991).

Critical studies adopt a set of assumptions quite different from those found in functionalist or interpretive studies. The guiding principle here is the critical exploration of institutions, ideologies, practices, and identities in order to encourage *emancipation* from forms of domination and socially unjustified forms of constraint. The latter can be partly self-produced, occurring when we talk ourselves into situations of followership. It can also occur when we refrain from taking active responsibility for ourselves and our organizations in ways not initiated and sanctioned by "leaders." Critical researchers seek to *denaturalize* leadership by showing it to be the outcome of an ongoing process of social construction and negotiation. They try to study it *reflexively* by reflecting on how the researcher and her assumptions and methods are implicated in producing the phenomena of leadership. Finally, they aim to treat it *nonperformatively* (noninstrumentally) by breaking away from attempts to optimize leadership.

These four broad commitments are only loosely adhered to in critical studies of leadership (but for a fairly strict application see Ford & Harding, 2007). However, all research in this tradition questions whether leadership is something overwhelmingly positive and necessary that can be treated as an objective entity (a thing). This research seeks to uncover the "darker side" of leadership, typically by breaking with much of the positive rhetoric surrounding leadership and emphasizing how leadership can be a dominating discourse in contemporary organizations. That is, leadership can be seen as a form of talk or text that organizational members increasingly use to express and understand their work lives. This discourse is far from an innocent way of describing organizational reality. Rather, it can have constructive effects insofar as it shapes how people experience, negotiate, and reconstruct organizations in specific ways. It is orchestrated by dominant ideology and produces and reinforces certain asymmetrical relations. By doing so, it favors those who are labeled as "leaders" doing "leadership." It also marginalizes others in terms of status, significance, and agency. Leadership can then become the dominant way in which people understand, experience, and negotiate organizational reality. This is, of course, not the only possibility. Leadership discourse may be questioned, rejected, strategically used, or even ignored by organizational actors. The central focus of critical studies of leadership is on which dominant discourses of leadership are established; how these might be reinforced, negotiated, rejected, or embraced by their targets; and what implications this might have for organizational members.

To address these core issues, some researchers have looked at particular forms of leadership. For instance, Tourish and Pennington (2002) sought to uncover the less seemly side of "transformational leadership" by drawing parallels with cult behavior. Tourish and Vatcha (2006) pointed out how notions of charismatic leadership have led to the suppression of dissent and the creation of conditions supporting various forms of unethical behavior—a situation that eventually led to the implosion of Enron. Robinson and Kerr (2009) explored how one British organization became attached to charismatic leadership, with subsequent negative consequences such as a preponderance of symbolic violence within the organization. Others have gone further, arguing that leadership per se is highly problematic. These "antileadership" researchers approach "the very idea of leadership as an anathema" (Gronn, 2002: 427), and many of the "antileadership" scholars that Gronn (2002) mentions question the usefulness of leadership as a scientific construct (e.g., Kerr & Jermier, 1978; Pfeffer, 1977). Others of a more explicitly critical bent have pointed out the negative effects that our attachment to leadership can have, including depersonalization and domination (e.g., Marcuse, 2008), the propagation of conformity and blind commitment (Kets de Vries, 1980), and individual relinquishment of autonomy (Gemmill & Oakley, 1992). These darker themes are picked up by Calás and Smircich (1991), who note that the idea of leadership often presents a very heroic and masculine image that is usually very seductive to both leader and led. A follow-up study shows how important aspects of seduction were marginalized in typical analyses of charismatic leadership (Calás, 1993).

In seeking to subject leadership to critical inquiry, researchers have explored a range of diverse but somewhat overlapping themes. In what follows, we will explore four themes of critical leadership studies in a more detail. These are issues of ideology, identity, inclusion (and exclusion), and intervention.

Ideology

One predominant way that people have looked at leadership is as an ideology. This strand of work looks at how discourses of leadership shape ideas and values in a way that reinforces dominant social relationships. The focus of this research is not on how leaders in organizations propagate a dominant ideology (or corporate culture); rather, it examines how leadership itself can become an ideology that is widely believed by leaders and followers alike. Indeed, many studies of leadership appear to be accepted, even celebrated, not because of their scientific rigor (which is often remarkably weak if one goes beneath the number crunching to consider the limitations of one-source studies, the taken-for-grantedness of leaders and followers, and tautological statements about "good" leadership leading to "good" results), but because of their ideological appeal (Alvesson, 2011c). This strand of research investigates what ideals and values are embodied in talk and texts about leadership, how this works, and how this reproduces dominant social relations.

Studies of leadership as a form of ideology have identified the range of different forms it has taken in recent years. Tourish and Pinnington (2002) explored transformational leadership as a form of ideology having many of the features of cults. This led them to conclude that ideas of transformational leadership can create the same kind of unthinking attachment to leaders and lack of careful criticism that characterize strongly ideological cults. Another aspect of ideology-based research concerns theory as such, viewing much leadership theory as largely positive, celebratory, and legitimizing of truth claims that present leaders and leadership in a way that reinforces elitism, privilege, and subordination. Alvesson (2011c), for example, argues that ideas of transformational leadership are better considered a form of ideology rather than a focus of scientific research because this view often arbitrarily lumps positively defined elements together in a way that presents a positive image rather than an accurate description of leadership dynamics. "New" forms of leadership that purport to be democratic are not immune. Notions such as authentic leadership and servant leadership, which emphasize the moral basis of leadership, can be seen to have a highly ideological tenor.

The idea of authentic leadership relies on ideas about the perfection of self-esteem, self-knowledge, and self-determination. Ideas of servant leadership also rely on highly appealing images of the leader as someone who puts "followers first, organizations second, their own needs last" (Sandjaya, Sarros, & Santora., 2008: 403). Such ideas create highly appealing images of leadership as a kind of saintly, moral, peak-performance state (Alvesson, 2011b). The leader is represented as an extremely good person who is able to inspire his or her followers simply through his or her own goodness. But this attractive image may clash with the realities of most organizations, particularly in businesses exposed to hard competition (Jackall, 1988). People trying to be authentic and engage in service leadership can also create a lot of confusion and difficulties in organizations that call for flexible behavior and tactful interaction with superiors, subordinates, customers, and others.

Some critical studies have looked at how leadership ideas legitimize the exercise of power. Mainstream studies of leadership either avoid or reduce this issue by claiming that only bad leaders are interested in power in itself, whereas good leaders use power only for the benefit of the organizations they are leading (e.g., McClelland & Burnham, 1976). This can be interpreted as managerialist ideology invoked to cleanse leadership of any negative association with power (Alvesson, 1987).

Studies of leadership as ideology have identified a range of ways in which ideology works. Some claim that leadership works as a kind of "myth" that hides, obfuscates, or represses the (difficult) truth of a situation. In this sense, positive talk about leadership is a way of disguising more brutal relations of power and domination or uncomfortable realities of responsibility. For instance, Gemmill and Oakley (1992) argue that leadership is a dominant social myth that helps to reify the necessity of hierarchy and authority in organizations. It also creates a sense of alienation and helplessness in followers by making them feel fairly deskilled in organizing and leading their own work. As well as creating a "mythical" representation of social reality, ideology also paints a positive and appealing picture that legitimates certain interests and specific social orders (Alvesson, 1987). Part of this involves presenting leadership in an unfalteringly positive light. Leadership is framed seductively. It is typically represented as being positive, involving good qualities (such as vision, inspiration, and so forth), and associated with desirable outcomes. This happens as "leadership scholars generally produce all sorts of beautiful images of leadership" (Spoelstra & ten Bos, 2011: 182).

Another aspect of ideology-based research is that leadership studies on the whole represent leadership as being altogether necessary for the smooth and efficient functioning of organizations. Many accounts reinforce the widespread belief that leadership is required if organizations are to operate in an orderly and organized fashion. This is well illustrated in O'Reilly and Reed's (2010, 2011) work on the rise of "leaderism" in the U.K. public sector. They argue that this new discourse has appeared alongside notions of professionalism and managerialism as a way of justifying elite social relations and the structuring of power relationships in the public sector. For them "leaderism" is a language that presents a particular form of agency, which is to be privileged and seen as necessary in the reform of the public sector. In this sense, the notion of leadership provides justification for existing or, in some cases, new forms of status. Privilege and power are reinforced because people who claim to "do leadership" often receive support for their elite positions. This finding chimes with other research on the spread of notions of leadership (particularly distributed or democratic ideas of leadership) in the U.K. school system (Currie, Lockett, & Suhomlinova, 2009). O'Reilly and Reed (2010, 2011) find that new practices of leadership were frequently adopted not because they were particularly effective, but because they were deeply institutionalized and came to be seen as the "correct" way of leading a school.

An ideology like leadership can have many effects. It can provide *legitimation* for a social order by portraying reality in a positive light, creating hope, and offering ideals worth striving for (Alvesson, 1987). Leadership works in this way by creating a positive aura around what are often mundane bureaucratic hierarchies or repressive authority relationships. It also provides middle managers with attractive ideals to strive for in their often difficult and frequently unrewarding work. Leadership ideology can also provide strong *justification* for existing specific power relations. It does this by providing a whole language and set of values that explain the necessity for (surplus) repression and inequalities. For instance, discourses of "leaderism" support the necessity of leadership as a driver of modernization in public service (O'Reilly & Reed, 2011). Finally, ideologies of leadership work to *reify* leadership by turning it from a contingent social demand into something that is altogether necessary and required by organizations. This can have the effect of alienating employees from their own sense of agency. Through these three processes, notions of leadership typically serve to reinforce and reproduce dominant relations of power in an organization (Knights & Willmott, 1992) or, in some cases, introduce new forms of power relations into an organization (O'Reilly & Reed, 2011).

In sum, ideology-based research highlights how notions of leadership are loaded with particular values and ideals. In this sense, the ideology of leadership "structures observations so thoroughly that researchers come to actually believe that they are observing harmonious systems" (Fleming &

Mandarini 2009: 331). The result is that all good things are identified with leadership, whereas negative aspects are marginalized and demonized as "toxic" leadership or as not being leadership at all. "True leadership" is seen to be unfalteringly "good." Unlike much of the research found in conventional studies, critical work on leadership seeks to call this ideology into question and identify some of the more negative consequences of this talk and text.

Identity

A second related strand of critical leadership studies investigates the question of identity. This work examines how discourses of leadership shape people's sense of self in the workplace (and sometimes beyond the workplace). Some have pointed out how discourses of leadership tend to construct particular kinds of viable subject positions (such as follower and leader). These subject positions are often strongly asymmetrical relations, where it is taken as self-evident that some are supposed to be led by their betters. But discourses also provide people with the appropriate "identity material" for elevating what are usually seen as rather mundane and boring tasks into more exciting and inspiring activities.

One of the more well-trodden issues in critical studies of leadership is how leadership discourse can shape what is accepted as an appropriate sense of self. One aspect of this research involves looking at how leaders seek to shape the identities and sense of self of followers. Such studies look at the various processes through which leaders seek to create and manipulate the subject positions of their followers, as well as how followers respond to and in some cases resist these subject positions (Collinson, 2006). Other research has focused primarily on the identities of leaders. This involves tracing out how managers within organizations come to see themselves not as professionals, managers, or administrators (or any other potential formal role available to them within the organization) but as "leaders." Knights and Willmott (1992) examined how notions of leadership were mobilized during a meeting in a U.K. insurance company. They show how social reality was reconstructed during a meeting to reinforce dominant identities (such as the CEO as the leader who has the prerogative to do things "his way" and as his subordinates as followers). Later work has examined how notions of leadership have played an important part in reconstructing professional roles. Ford and colleagues (2008) explored how discourses of leadership have reconstructed health care professionals' understandings of their identities. For instance, they trace out how the rise of discourses of leadership (often propagated through training courses explicitly aimed at instilling leadership skills) have played an important role in changing how health care professionals think about and represent themselves. They illustrate how these health care professionals have struggled to adopt this identity and how they have made it performative in their own professional lives. For instance, they show how hospital CEOs have mobilized heroic notions associated with leadership in attempts to justify their own position and role. The central point they make is that these discourses of leadership construct the very identities that they are supposed to describe. But Ford et al. are also aware that discourses of leadership and the subject position they provide are not particularly totalizing. Rather, these discourses involve a kind of gap or absence, in which individuals' constant strivings to represent themselves as leaders are open to congenital failures. Although people continue to strive to see themselves and be seen by others as leaders, they often fall short of this identity. For instance, in a study of a health care setting, Parker (2000) noted that physicians tend to see hospital managers as "administrators" and hardly as "leaders" (as they liked to fashion themselves). Ford and Harding (2011) also point out how recent forms of leadership discourse (such as "authentic leadership") push issues of personal identity to the fore and make concerns with being true to oneself important. In more recent work, Ford (2010) explored how managers pulled together a range of different discourses in an attempt to bring together different identities. This work reminds us that when professionals and managers are required to negotiate discourses of leadership, they are also required to negotiate their own sense of self.

Another related stream of literature on leadership has explored how the discourses of leadership are used in various identity projects by managers and professionals. Here, the focus is on how managers try to "consume" or incorporate leadership ideas as part of their own individual strivings (rather than as part of a collective response, as occurs when a profession is required to reinvent itself and all members need to adapt). This research examines how discourses of leadership offer appealing *identity material* for managers (Alvesson & Sveningsson, 2003b; Sveningsson & Larsson, 2006). By taking on discourses of leadership, the mundane, instrumental, and operative sides of managerial work can be forgotten in favor of far more impressive and ego- and status-boosting activities. In this sense, the identity of being a leader can help to reduce frustration. Managers caught in bureaucratic administrative and technical work find that the creation of deliverables and the maintenance of corporate machinery take up most of their time (Holmberg & Tyrstrup, 2010). By drawing on discourses of leadership, they are able to frame their work and fantasize about themselves in an appealing way. By representing leadership as embracing an "open-door policy," for example, an ordinary thing like engaging in small talk with subordinates takes on a special, almost magical luster—at least for the manager (Alvesson & Sveningsson, 2003a). In this sense, leadership can then fuel (and conceal) a form of escapism that allows managers to imagine their work in rather grandiose terms and avoid a too painful consciousness of many of the more boring, mundane, or even trying aspects of leadership. In this sense, discourses of leadership do not simply act as a mechanism of domination through "making up" new subject positions, they also can act as a mechanism of escape. This is something that can have equally troubling consequences. One of these is the neglect of many of the bureaucratic processes that ensure equity and due process in organizational life. Another troubling outcome is the painful clashes that may occur between the grandiose fantasies of leadership and the humdrum realities of managerial work (Sveningsson & Alvesson, 2003).

To summarize, a vital way that discourses of identity work is through the construction of identities and subject positions while replacing other potential occupational identities, such as being a professional or a manager. But such discourses also work as a form of escapism used by middle managers to flee from the disturbing realities of managerial work. In this sense, leader identities can both provide a form of domination and also a fantasy. This can help to secure the middle manager's sense of self, but, at the same time, it can also undermine many important practices typically associated with managerial work and organizational administration. Clashes between idealized versions of being a leader and the realities of everyday managerial and administrative work may also lead to disappointment and suffering.

Inclusion and Exclusion

A third central strand in critical studies of leadership is the issue of how discourses of leadership tend to include some people and exclude others in a way that produces differentiation and marginalization. The naturalization of the great leader–follower divide means that nonleaders are marginalized and reduced to followers. In this sense, discourses of leadership create idealized images of leadership that clearly favor some people, who are upgraded in terms of status, influence, and rewards. At the same time, others find that demotion to "followership" status results in influence, rewards, and status being removed from their grasp. Of course, differentiation and making people more or less central in influencing processes can be useful. People do vary in abilities, skills, and experiences. But there is the tendency for many leadership scholars to exaggerate this variation and produce a world full of leaders and followers.

Other differentiations are also problematic, especially those associated with the unrecognized propagation of leadership ideals favoring certain categories of people, such as white middle-class males. The central stream of work on this topic has largely investigated how leadership discourses are gendered. However, more recent work has explored the ethnic marking (Ospina and Foldy, 2009) and implicit heterosexism (Harding, Lee, Ford, & Learmonth, 2011) of leadership discourses.

There is a long history of studies of women in leadership (for review, see Alvesson & Billing, 2009). Much of this work tends to focus on comparisons of the leadership of women and men. However, an equally strong strand points out how women have been systematically excluded from managerial positions and how stereotypical claims of "women's ways of leading" have often been devalued. Many liberal approaches see this as a problem that can be rectified by ensuring that more women are involved in leadership roles through removing obstacles (e.g., Eagly & Carli, 2007). In contrast, more critical assessment of leadership tends to focus on the various inclusions and exclusions that are implicit within the discourse of leadership. The gendered nature of dominant ideas of leadership is emphasized. An exemplar here is Calás and Smircich's (1991) analysis of the seductive nature of leadership discourse. They point out that, typically, leadership is set up in opposition to seduction. However, through a deconstructive reading of some core academic texts on the subject, Calás and Smircich (1991) note how seduction is deeply bound up with notions of leadership. Importantly, they point out that the discourse of leadership "seduces only those who are of the same kind—masculine or masculine-identified—and promotes, as leadership knowledge only a homosocial system of organization, i.e. based on the values of masculinity, including masculine definitions of femininity" (p. 571). The central point then is that leadership discourse is a masculine discourse that celebrates masculine norms such as competition, aggression, and individualism. To be a leader then becomes an act of attempting to comply with these norms. Pullen and Rhodes (2008) have noted how many accounts of narcissism and leadership are largely characterized by masculine assumptions of aggression, self-centeredness, and domination. A number of field studies have sought to demonstrate how difficult these stances are for many women. For instance, in a study of a U.K. public sector organization, Ford (2006) found that the propagation of discourses of leadership reinforced a masculine "androcentric" norm around what it meant to be a leader. This created a series of difficult contradictions that women managers were required to negotiate. This study reminds us that the masculine norms implicit within much leadership research exclude women and feminine values not simply from academic discussions of leadership, but also from more practical "performance" leadership discourses (see also Ford, 2010). Fletcher (1994) has pointed out that many of the assumptions associated with postheroic leadership are loaded with particular gendered assumptions. There has been some critique of feminist work for assuming a rigid, unitary, almost "essentialistic" masculine norm (Billing 2011), and the idea of masculinity and the idea of the male as norm are not unproblematic. Researchers often impose their own view of what is culturally masculine and create a conflict between these views and those of women, possibly underestimating both the pluralism of leadership discourses and the diversity of females (and males).

Along with the substantial literature looking at the gendered nature of much leadership discourse, a growing body of work also highlights how notions of leadership frequently imply other kinds of exclusions and marginalizations. One recent stream of work highlights how discourses of leadership are caught within a "heterosexist matrix" (Bowring, 2004) and emphasize a set of heteronormative assumptions (e.g., Harding et al., 2011). This work points out how leadership often works through seduction and often evokes strong homoerotic desires toward the leader. However, they note that these homoerotic desires are typically oppressed and marginalized because they fall afoul of the dominant heteronormative assumptions associated with leadership. This suggests that leadership is often based on the exclusion and marginalization of homosexual desires and identities at the very same time that actually evokes these identities. In this sense, leadership can be seen as having a strong heterosexist emphasis. Others researchers have noted how ethnicity and race often play an important role in excluding people from engaging with discourses of leadership (for review, see Ospina & Foldy, 2009). For instance, in a study of leadership education, Rusch (2004) points out that issues of ethnicity are typically excluded from the curriculum—the result being that these issues are often also avoided or skirted around during training programs. More recent work points out that racialized discourses around leadership do not simply form a limitation or a suppressed issue; rather, they can be used as a resource by "non-Anglo" leaders (e.g., Ospina & Su, 2009).

To briefly summarize, one important implication of leadership discourse is that it tends to marginalize (or at least make it difficult for) many people who do not fit white, male, heterosexist norms to occupy positions of leadership or managerial positions from which it is easy to exercise leadership because of a series of culturally marked assumptions (masculine, heteronormative, and Anglo-Saxon) that are implicit within much leadership discourse. Of particular importance are the heroic models of leadership, such as charismatic and transformational leadership. This can make it difficult, and sometimes impossible, for people from the "wrong" groups to occupy and make use of the subject position of "leader." However, it can be possible to rearticulate or rework leadership discourse in a way that creates space and the potential for alternatives.

Intervention

The final strand of work in critical leadership studies examines how critical thinking can intervene in leadership thinking and practices. Such interventions often aim to combine critical and normative-pragmatic considerations. Instead of assuming that discourses of leadership are largely about domination and should be resisted and minimized, these studies explore how various actors can seek to unseat and transform notions of leadership in more democratic and critically grounded ways.

One important aspect of intervention into discourses of leadership involves active processes of follower influencing. Collinson (2005) points out that leadership is not simply a discourse that establishes relations of power and domination but that leadership action is often the target of efforts to reduce asymmetries. Thus, notions of leadership are frequently questioned, rejected, or sometimes ignored by employees. In this sense, leadership is often a far less powerful and influential discourse than it is made out to be. For instance, targets of leadership discourse may seek to avoid it, resist it, or opt for alternative available identities, such as that of being a "professional." A person defining herself as such is not primarily inclined to be a follower. In other cases, efforts to "do leadership" may prove awkward or unconvincing. In addition, bureaucracy or a focus on delivering results may significantly constrain the space for leadership. Leadership discourses may also become a resource that actors seek to turn to their own purposes. For instance, Zoller and Fairhurst (2007) point out that leadership may be used by various groups as an important part of resistance processes. By making this argument, they highlight how leadership can actually be turned away from the dynamics of domination and used for more emancipatory purposes. Here, leadership continues to be represented as something negative to be avoided or minimized (even though some form of leadership may also exist in resistance projects).

Other researchers have taken the position that "critical theorists must go beyond identifying 'bad leadership practice' and aim to create and support successful ethical frameworks for leadership" (Western, 2008: 21; see also Fryer, 2012). To do this, they have suggested engagement with the concept in a way that draws out the potential of leadership ideas and practices, avoids or minimizes domination, and intervenes productively in social relations (Alvesson & Spicer, 2012). Broadly put, this entails recognizing the limits of leadership at the same time that we consider the emancipatory potential lurking within possible uses of leadership ideas. It also calls for a consideration of the significance of exercising legitimate forms of authority to accomplish organizational goals. This is a difficult balance to strike and certainly does not allow for universal solutions. Rather, it requires detailed and situationally specific engagement with leadership in action. This calls for moving between an affirmative and a pragmatic position (which largely accepts present conditions and constraints) and a distanced and critical position (which emphasizes independent thinking and aims for less constraining social relations—being more "antileadership"). To do this, Alvesson and Spicer (2012) offer the concept of *critical performativity*. This stance aims to capture the importance of critical work that seeks to engage with existing dominant discourses of leadership in a way that allows a creative and critical reconstruction of these discourses. It combines intellectual stimulation through radical questioning with an ambition to use discourse in an impactful way, both in terms of emancipatory effect and practical organizational work. This is achieved through adopting an affirmative stance to the target of critique, engaging an ethic of care with regards to the views of those whom we research, following a more pragmatic approach, attempting to engage emancipatory potential within a discourse, and developing a more normative orientation based on reflection and critique (Spicer, Alvesson, & Kärreman, 2009: 545–554).

To summarize, this strand of critical leadership studies emphasizes how leadership discourses can be engaged with to produce a more positive outcome than the standard version, which sees leaders as exerting one-directional influence on followers. It encourages researchers to view leadership as a target of resistance that might be actively reworked by nonleaders and leaders alike. It outlines how leadership is sometimes central to collective resistance efforts and notes that discourses of leadership may be the target for critical performative reworking and rearticulation. Ultimately, this strand of work seeks to also remind critical researchers that leadership is not simply a form of domination. Rather, it can create new and potentially more emancipatory forms of leading and following.

Conclusion

Critical leadership studies is a relatively new subfield within the broader area of leadership studies. As we have argued here, critical studies of leadership try to avoid much of the fairly empty celebration of leadership. As a field, it rejects functionalist attempts to use scientific methods to treat leadership as purportedly objective phenomena that can be measured effectively using self-report questionnaires. Critical studies also move beyond interpretive approaches that seek to uncover the various meanings that actors give to notions of leadership and how leadership processes are negotiated in practice. Instead, critical studies examine leadership as a dominant discourse that can create problematic relations of power and domination. Critical studies show how leadership thinking often favors elitism and the marginalization of most people. Critics question the significance of leadership, particularly when it is presented as vital for organizational performance, as well as the ethical behavior of followers and their well-being at work. Critiques include the examination of how leadership discourse creates dominant values and ideas. Critical studies have also examined how leadership discourse works through the construct and propagation of the "leader" as a dominant or attractive identity that replaces or substitutes other occupational identities, such as professional or manager. Leadership ideas do not simply aim to seduce people into becoming devoted followers; they also have the potential for seducing managers into identifying with fashionable leadership templates. A third focus of critical studies has been on how this process of identity construction has frequently marginalized many people who do not neatly fit within the purview of leadership discourse, and critical studies have demonstrated how leadership discourse includes a number of biases that effectively marginalize people from this discourse. The final issue that critical studies of leadership has examined is how discourses of leadership may be resisted or used in a more progressive and less leader-centric way. This research tries to encourage researchers to consider how discourses of leadership can open up space for reconfiguring how we think about and enact discourses of leadership.

This small but growing body of literature provides some novel insights that are often ignored in more conventional analyses of leadership. For instance, critical researchers have pointed out that leadership theory and most studies accomplished under its influence might not actually be an accurate description of reality, but rather work to enforce a dominant social myth or discourse (e.g., Gemmill & Oakley, 1992). In this sense, many leadership studies contain an important normative bias that leadership is something inherently good, desirable, and necessary, thus covering up the ambiguity, messiness, and imperfections of organizations and people's aims and acts. This set of widely shared normative assumptions is beneficial for researchers who associate themselves with the topic of leadership. It provides an attractive collective label that opens up job opportunities, publication possibilities, and other material rewards. It is also a discourse that many managers and other practitioners find particularly attractive because it provides them with an identity boost (Sveningsson & Alvesson, 2003): It allows them to claim that "I am a leader, not just a manager." A large management education industry—business schools, institutes, publishers and consultants—benefits from leadership being seen as central to good organizational performance. Furthermore, critical studies remind us that discourses of leadership are often consumed more as a kind of fantasy text. It allows many managers to imagine a sense of hero worship and indulge their own grandiosity (Alvesson, 2013). But discourses of leadership can have broader societal implications. In particular, they can serve as an ideological resource that social elites and their advocates draw on to justify their own interests and reinforce inequality between leaders and nonleaders. Perhaps one of the most glaring examples of this shows how discourses of leadership have frequently been used to justify the continued centralization of power in many organizations, increasing the steep pay differentials between those at the top and the bottom of the organization, thus reducing to "followers" those who actually help to lay the groundwork for the success of the leaders. But we have also tried to highlight that discourses of leadership are often characterized by ambiguity and confusion. Thus, notions of leadership are potentially open to alternative interpretations and frames of understanding. It means that they need not be used simply as a tool for justifying extreme income differentials or as a source of managerial fantasy. Discourses of leadership can also provide a resource for emancipatory practices, such as resistance and critical performative interventions.

Future Research

Critical studies of leadership have certainly provided some novel and interesting findings. However, much still remains to be explored. To close this chapter, we would like to build on the research that we have already reviewed and highlight some issues that might be developed in future studies of the topic.

Ideological Impacts of Leadership

First, studies of the ideological impacts of leadership might be further examined. For instance, we know little about the history of leadership ideology. It would be of interest to explore in more depth how the ideas and values contained within discourses of leadership have shifted over time. For instance, future research might trace the rise of leadership discourse following World War II, the rise of transformational leadership during the 1980s, and the more recent rise of neo-humanist visions of leadership, such as authentic, servant, or shared leadership. We also do not know how the ideological impact of different forms of leadership discourse differ across industries, nations, and levels within an organization. For instance, future research might explore differences in leadership ideology between different countries in Europe or between developing and developed countries. It would also be interesting to see if the "leaderism" identified by O'Reilly and Reed (2010, 2011) is as prevalent in other countries as it is in the U.K. It would also be interesting to look at different organizations and occupations. Has leadership also started to imprint groups traditionally reluctant to follow this trend (e.g., professions)? Leadership rhetoric seems to be increasingly common across sectors, but determining how many take it seriously is another question.

Impact of Leadership Discourse on Identity

A second strand of future research would explore in more depth how leadership discourse has impacted and shaped identities. This research could extend existing findings to trace out how the rise of "leader" identities has played out in different sectors. Much of the existing work is in the public sector. Existing work might examine how "leader" identities have worked in the private as well as the nonprofit sector. Furthermore, research might also explore what happens when managers adopt "leader"-based identities when these are not accepted by their "followers." There is also much more work to be done on how leader identities are propagated through a wider "economy of leadership," which includes leadership education providers, consultants, academics, and a whole range of leadership consumers.

Exclusions and Inclusions of Leadership Discourse

A third strand of future work for critical studies might explore the various exclusions and inclusions implicit within leadership discourse. We have noted that many researchers have already looked at exclusions associated with gender, ethnicity, and sexuality. However, many more dimensions of diversity have not been explored in relation to leadership discourse. Four key dimensions we would like to highlight here are age, disability, religion, and class. We think exploring the implicit biases associated with each of these dimensions in leadership discourse may yield some interesting insights. For instance, it would be interesting to trace whether idealized images of leaders have become progressively younger in recent years and how this may have the effect of excluding older people from leadership positions (and possibly prematurely including young people into these positions). We also think it is important to look at moments when predicted patterns of exclusion and domination do not work. For instance, this appears to happen when various marginalized groups have sought to develop indigenous models of leadership to replace hegemonic "white" leadership models.

Leadership Work

A fourth stream of research would investigate the work involved in doing leadership. We also note a shortage of in-depth studies of leadership practices and relations. This is a limitation that critical research shares with mainstream studies, which are, in most cases, satisfied with questionnaire-based research and interviews conducted with managers about their leadership. Critical studies need to move forward in exploring what happens outside of texts promoting leadership. They need to look at the dirty and depressing everyday work of leadership, preferably using ethnographic methods. This entails asking how leaders seek to do leadership, when is it that doing leadership works, and what happens when these attempts to do leadership fail. Such a close-range analysis would focus on leadership work—that is, the purposeful activities involved in attempts to influence and coordinate people. But it would also look at leadership identity work—that is, the difficult work involved in attempts to maintain the identity of being a leader. A study of these issues would reveal the actual labors involved in the day-to-day activities of doing leadership. In addition, it might consider the labor process of leadership work—those attempts made to control the work done by leaders in an organization. Leadership ideas often assume that the manager-leader is the agent and source of leadership—usually in interaction with followers; however, most people expected to do leadership are located below the top of an organization and are hardly free to lead as they want. Research on this issue would delineate how leaders are themselves the targets of attempts to control and direct their work.

The Leadership Industries

A fifth stream of work that critical studies of leadership might develop is an examination of the leadership industries. This would entail the whole economy involved in the production, distribution, and consumption of leadership discourse. This work would investigate the vast industry of consultants, institutes, centers, and business schools that make their living through the promotion of ideas about leadership. Research in this tradition would involve mapping this leadership economy, tracing out its history, and considering which kinds of discourses about leadership are circulated. The point would be to consider the institutional and economic bases of leadership discourse and the differences these aspects make. It would also try to find out how leadership industries provide a space for identity work by middle managers, how they create particular inclusions and exclusions in who might be considered a leader, and how they further propagate the broader ideology of leadership. One might even go further by considering how leadership industries set out not simply to convince, but also to entertain. This would alert our attention to the seductive, pleasurable, and fantastic aspects of leadership ideas. Indeed, one might consider leadership theory as a kind of more organizationally acceptable alternative to Hollywood films for the bored middle manager. We might also begin thinking about leadership training as an extension of the tourism industry—an opportunity for executives to get away from the office and enjoy all sorts of fun activities (e.g., horseback riding, climbing, meditation, spending time in nice conference environments) on the company coin.

Transforming Leadership Discourse

The final strand of future work we would like to highlight here those are attempts made to intervene into discourses of leadership based on critical thinking. A potentially fertile issue here would be to explore how various forms of leadership are resisted and to encourage "productive" forms of resistance. Are the kinds of resistance to notions of leadership similar to those that other researchers have found in response to managerialism? Or do struggles against leadership take on a different tenor? An important issue here is how leadership involves a "voluntary" acceptance of the ideas of the leader. This makes the situation different from management, in which coercion and behavioral-material effects typically are more salient. Also, under what alternatives, if any, do groups seek to resist leadership? Another interesting issue would be to explore how various forms of collective resistance are led, organized, or simply erupt. For instance, studies may ask questions about what kinds of coordination appear in explicitly or implicitly antileadership movements in organizations. Finally, it is important for critical leadership studies to begin to develop a range of tactics for intervening in and limiting the reach of "leaderism." An important part of this work might involve articulating and reinforcing alternatives to leadership, such as the mobilization of peers for support, direction, and feedback.

References

Alvesson, M. (1987). *Organization Theory and Technocratic Consciousness*. Berlin: de Gruyter.

Alvesson, M. (1996). Leadership studies: From procedure and abstraction to reflexivity and situation. *Leadership Quarterly, 7*(4), 455–485.

Alvesson, M. (2011a). *Interpreting Interviews*. London: Sage

Alvesson, M. (2011b). Leaders as saints: Leadership through moral peak performance. In M. Alvesson & A. Spicer (Eds.), *Metaphors We Lead By: Understanding Leadership in the Real World* (pp. 51–75). London: Routledge.

Alvesson, M. (2011c). *The leadership researcher goes to Hollywood – and the Vatican*. Working Paper, Lund University.

Alvesson, M. (2013). *The Triumph of Emptiness*. Oxford: Oxford University Press.

Alvesson, M., & Billing, Y. (2009). *Understanding Gender and Organization*. London: Sage

Alvesson, M., Bridgman, T., & Willmott, H. (Eds.). (2009). *Oxford Handbook of Critical Management Studies*. Oxford: Oxford University Press.

Alvesson, M., & Sandberg, J. (2011). Generating research questions through problematization. *Academy of Management Review, 36*(2), 247–271.

Alvesson, M., & Spicer, A. (Eds.). (2011). *Metaphors We Lead By: Understanding Leadership in the Real World*. London: Routledge.

Alvesson, M., & Spicer, A. (2012). Critical leadership studies. *Human Relations, 65*(3), 367–390.

Alvesson, M., & Sveningsson, S. (2003a). Managers doing leadership. The extraordinarization of the mundane. *Human Relations, 56*(12), 1435–1459.

Alvesson, M., & Sveningsson, S. (2003b). The good visions, the bad micro-management and the ugly ambiguity: Contradictions of (non-)leadership in a knowledge-intensive company. *Organization Studies, 24*(6), 961–988.

Alvesson, M., & Sveningsson, S. (2003c). The great disappearance act: Difficulties in doing leadership. *Leadership Quarterly, 14*(3), 359–381.

Alvesson, M., & Sveningsson, S. (2012). Un- and repacking leadership: Context, relations, constructions and politics. In M. Uhl-Bien & S. Ospina (Eds.), *Advancing Relational Leadership Theory: A Conversation among Perspectives* (pp. 203–226). Greenwich: Information Age Publishing.

Alvesson, M., & Willmott, H. (2012). *Making Sense of Management: A Critical Introduction*. 2nd ed. London: Sage.

Andriessen, E., & Drenth, P. (1984). Leadership: Theories and models. In P. Drenth, H. Thierry, P. J. Williams, & C. J. de Wolff (Eds.), *Handbook of Work and Organizational Psychology* (Vol. 1, pp. 481–520). Chichester: Wiley.

Antonakis, J., Cianciolo, A. T., & Sternberg, R. J. (2004). Introduction. In J. Antonakis, A. T. Cianciolo, & R. J. Sternberg (Eds.), *The Nature of Leadership* (pp. 3–15). Thousand Oaks, CA: Sage.

Barker, R. (1997). How can we train leaders if we don't know what leadership is? *Human Relations, 50*(4), 343–362.

Bass, B. (1985). *Leadership and Performance Beyond Expectations*. New York: Free Press.

Bennis, W. G., & Nanus, B. (1985). *Leaders: Strategies for Taking Charge*. New York: Harper & Row.

Billing, Y. D. (2011). Are women in management victims of the phantom of the male norm?, *Gender, Work and Organization, 18*(3), 298–317.

Bligh, M. (2011). Followership and follower-centric approaches. In A. Bryman et al. (Eds.), *The SAGE Handbook of Leadership* (pp. 425–436). London: Sage.

Bolden, R., Gosling, J., Hawkins, B., & Taylor, S. (2011). *Exploring Leadership: Individual, Organizational, and Societal Perspectives.* Oxford: Oxford University Press.

Bowring, M. A. (2004). Resistance is *not* futile: Liberating Captain Janeway from the masculine-feminine dualism of leadership. *Gender, Work and Organization, 11*(4), 381–405.

Bryman, A. (2004). Qualitative research in leadership: A critical but appreciative review. *Leadership Quarterly, 15*(6), 729–769.

Bryman, A. (2011). Research methods in the study of leadership. In Bryman, A. et al. (Eds.), *The SAGE Handbook of Leadership* (pp. 15–28). London: Sage.

Burrell, G., & Morgan, G. (1979). *Sociological Paradigms and Organizational Analysis.* London: Heinemann.

Calás, M. (1993). Deconstructing charismatic leadership: Re-reading Weber from the darker side. *Leadership Quarterly, 4*(3–4), 305–328.

Calás, M., & Smirchich, L. (1991). Voicing seduction to silence leadership. *Organization Studies, 12*(4), 567–601.

Carroll, B., & Levy, L. (2008). Defaulting to management: Leadership defined by what it is not. *Organization, 15*(1), 75–96.

Clegg, S. R. (1989). *Frameworks of Power.* London: Sage.

Cogliser, C., Schriesheim, C., Scandura, T., & Gardner, W. (2009). Balance in leader and follower perceptions of leader-member exchange: Relationships with performance and work attitudes. *Leadership Quarterly, 20,* 452–465.

Collinson, D. (2005). Dialectics of leadership. *Human Relations, 58,* 1419–1442.

Collinson, D. (2006). Rethinking followership: A post-structural analysis of follower identities. *Leadership Quarterly, 17,* 179–189.

Collinson, D. (2011). Critical leadership studies. In A. Bryman et al. (Eds.), The SAGE *Handbook of Leadership* (pp. 181–194). London: Sage

Currie, G., Lockett, A., & Suhomlinova, O. (2009). The institutionalization of distributed leadership: A "Catch-22" in English public services. *Human Relations, 62*(11), 1735–1761.

Drath, W., McCauley, C., Palus, C., Van Velsor, E., O'Connor, P., & McGuire, J. (2008). Direction, alignment, commitment: Toward a more integrative ontology of leadership. *Leadership Quarterly, 19,* 635–653.

Eagly, A., & Carli, L. (2007, September). Women and the labyrinth of leadership. *Harvard Business Review, 75,* 62–71.

Fairhurst, G. (2007). *Discursive Leadership.* Thousand Oaks, CA: Sage.

Fairhurst, G. (2009). Considering context in discursive leadership research. *Human Relations, 62,* 1607–1633.

Fairhurst, G., & Grant, D. (2010). The social construction of leadership: A sailing guide. *Management Communication Quarterly, 24*(2), 171–210.

Fiedler, F. E. (1967). *A Theory of Leadership Effectiveness.* New York: McGraw-Hill.

Fiedler, F. (1996). Research on leadership selection and training: One view of the future. *Administrative Science Quarterly, 41,* 241–250.

Fleming, P., & Mandarini, M. (2009). Towards a workers' society? New perspective on work and emancipation. In M. Alvesson, H. Willmott, & T. Bridgman (Eds.), *Oxford Handbook of Critical Management Studies* (pp. 328–344). New York: Oxford University Press.

Fletcher, J. (1994). Castrating the female advantage. Feminist standpoint research and management science. *Journal of Management Inquiry, 3,* 74–82.

Ford, J. (2006). Discourses of leadership: Gender, identity and contradiction in a UK public sector organization. *Leadership, 2,* 77–79.

Ford, J. (2010). Studying leadership critically: A psychosocial lens on leadership identities. *Leadership, 6,* 1–19.

Ford, J., & Harding, N. (2007). Move over management: We are all leaders now. *Management Learning, 38,* 475–494.

Ford, J., & Harding, N. (2011). The impossibility of the "true self" of authentic leadership: A critique through object relations theory. *Leadership, 7*(4), 463–479.

Ford, J., Harding, N., & Learmonth, M. (2008). *Leadership as Identity: Constructions and Deconstructions.* London: Palgrave.

Fournier, V., & Grey, C. (2000). At the critical moment: Conditions and prospects for critical management studies. *Human Relations, 53,* 7–32.

Fryer, M. (2012). Facilitative leadership: "Drawing Habermas" model of ideal speech to propose a critically sensitive way to lead. *Organization, 19,* 25–43.

Gemmill, G., & Oakley, J. (1992). Leadership: An alienating social myth. *Human Relations, 45,* 113–129.

Grint, K. (2000). *The Art of Leadership.* Oxford: Oxford University Press.

Grint, K. (2005) *Leadership: Limits and Possibilities.* London: Palgrave.

Gronn, P. (2002). Distributed leadership as a unit of analysis. *Leadership Quarterly 13,* 423–451.

Harding, N. Lee, H. Ford, J., & Learmonth, M. (2011). Leadership and charisma: A desire that cannot speak its name. *Human Relations, 64,* 927–949.

Hartnell, C., & Walumbwa, F. (2011). Transformational leadership and organizational culture. In. N. Ashkanasy, C. P. M. Wilderorn, & M. F. Peterson (Eds.), *The Handbook of Organizational Culture and Climate* (2nd ed., pp. 225–248) Thousand Oaks, CA: Sage.

Hollander, E. P. (1992). Leadership, followership, self and other. *Leadership Quarterly, 3,* 43–54.

Holmberg, I., & Tyrstrup, M. (2010). Well then—what now? An everyday approach to managerial leadership. *Leadership, 6,* 353–372.

House, R., & Aditya, R. (1997). The social scientific study of leadership: Quo vadis? *Journal of Management, 23,* 409–473.

Jackall, R. (1988). *Moral Mazes. The World of Corporate Manager.* New York: Oxford University Press.

Kelly, S. (2008). Leadership: A categorical mistake? *Human Relations, 61,* 763–782.

Kerr, S., & Jermier, J. M. (1978). Substitutes for leadership: Their meaning and measurement, *Organization Behaviour and Human Performance, 22,* 375–403.

Kets de Vries, M. (1980). *Organizational Paradoxes.* London: Tavistock.

Knights, D., & H. Willmott. (1992). Conceptualizing leadership processes: A study of senior managers in a financial services company. *Journal of Management Studies, 29,* 761–782.

Kotter, J. (1985). *Power and Influence: Beyond Formal Authority.* New York: Free Press.

Ladkin, D. (2010). *Rethinking Leadership: A New Look at Old Leadership Questions.* Cheltenham: Edward Elgar.

Liden, R., & Antonakis, J. (2009). Considering context in psychological leadership research. *Human Relations, 62,* 1587–1606.

Marcuse, H. (2008). *A Study on Authority*. London: Verso.
McClelland, D., & Burnham, D. (1976, March–April). Power is the great motivator. *Harvard Business Review. 54,* 100–110.
Meindl, J. (1995). The romance of leadership as a follower-centric theory: A social constructionist approach. *Leadership Quarterly, 6*, 329–341.
Nichols, J. (1987). Leadership in organisations: Meta, macro and micro. *European Management Journal, 6*, 16–25.
O'Reilly, D. & Reed, M. (2010) Leaderism: An evolution of managerialism in UK public service reform. *Public Administration, 88*, 960–978.
O'Reilly, D., & Reed, M. (2011). The grit in the oyster: Professionalism, managerialism and leaderism as discourses of UK public services modernization. *Organization Studies, 32,* 1079–1101.
Ospina, S., & Foldy, E. (2009). A critical review of race and ethnicity in the leadership literature: Surfacing context, power and the collective dimensions of leadership. *Leadership Quarterly, 26*, 876–896.
Ospina, S., & Su, C. (2009). Weaving color lines: Race, ethnicity, and the work of leadership in social change organizations. *Leadership, 5*, 131–170.
Parker, M. (2000). *Organizational Culture: Unity and Division at Work*. London: Sage.
Parry, K., & A. Bryman (2006). Leadership in organizations. In S. Clegg, C. Hardy, & W. Nord (Eds.), *The SAGE handbook of organization studies.* 2nd ed., pp. 447–468. London: Sage.
Pfeffer, J. (1977). The ambiguity of leadership. *Academy of Management Review, 2*, 104–112.
Pfeffer, J. (1981). *Power in Organizations*. Boston: Pitman.
Pondy, L. R. (1978). Leadership is a language game. In M. W. McCall & M. M. Lombardo (Eds.), *Leadership: Where else can we go?* (pp. 87–99). Durham, NC: Duke University Press.
Pullen, A., & Rhodes, C. (2008). "It's all about me!": Gendered narcissism and leaders' identity work. *Leadership, 4*, 5–25.
Robinson, S. K., & Kerr, R. (2009). The symbolic violence of leadership: A critical hermeneutic study of leadership and succession in a British organization in the post-Soviet context. *Human Relations, 62*, 875–903.
Rusch, E. A. (2004). Gender and race in leadership preparation: A constrained discourse. *Education Administration Quarterly, 40*, 16–48.
Sandberg, J., & Targama, A. (2007). *Managing Understanding in Organizations*. London: Sage.
Sandjaya, S. Sarros, J. C., & Santora, J. C. (2008). Defining and measuring servant leadership behaviour in organization. *Journal of Management Studies, 45*, 402–424.
Sashkin, M. (2004). Transformational leadership approaches: A review and synthesis. In Antonakis, J. et al. (Eds.), *The Nature of Leadership* (pp. 171–196). Thousand Oaks, CA: Sage.
Smircich, L., & Morgan, G. (1982). Leadership: The management of meaning. *Journal of Applied Behavioural Science, 18*, 257–273.
Spicer, A., Alvesson, M., & Kärreman, D. (2009). Critical performativity: The unfinished business of critical management studies. *Human Relations, 62*, 537–560.
Spillane, J. P., Hallet, T., & Diamond, J. B. (2003). Forms of capital and the construction of leadership: Instructional leadership in urban elementary schools. *Sociology of Education, 76*, 1–17.
Spoelstra, S. & ten Bos, R. (2011). Leadership. In R. ten Bos & M. Painter-Moreland (Eds.), *Business Ethics and Contemporary Philosophy*. Cambridge: Cambridge University Press.
Sveningsson, S., & Alvesson, M. (2003). Managing managerial identities: Organizational fragmentation, discourse and identity struggle. *Human Relations, 56*, 1163–1193.
Sveningsson, S., & Larsson, M. (2006). Fantasies of leadership: Identity work. *Leadership, 2*, 203–224.
Tourish, D., & Pinnington, A. (2002). Transformational leadership, corporate cultism and the spirituality paradigm. An unholy trinity in the workplace? *Human Relations, 55*, 147–152.
Tourish, D., & Vatcha, N. (2006). Charismatic leadership and corporate cultism at Enron: The elimination of dissent, the promotion of conformity and organizational collapse. *Leadership, 1*, 455–480.
Uhl-Bien, M. (2006). Relational leadership theory: Exploring the social processes of leadership and organizing. *The Leadership Quarterly, 17*, 654–676.
Western, S. (2008). *Leadership: A Critical Text.* Thousand Oaks, CA: Sage.
Wood, M. (2005). The fallacy of misplaced leadership. *Journal of Management Studies, 42*, 1101–1121.
Yukl, G. (1989). Managerial leadership: A review of theory and research. *Journal of Management, 15*, 251–289.
Zaleznik, A. (1977, May–June). Managers and leaders: Are they different? *Harvard Business Review, 55,* 67–68.
Zoller, H. M., & Fairhurst, G. T. (2007). Resistance leadership: The overlooked potential in critical organization and leadership studies. *Human Relations, 60*, 1331–1360.

CHAPTER 4

Public Integrative Leadership

Barbara C. Crosby *and* John M. Bryson

Abstract

Integrative public leadership refers to the work of integrating people, resources, and organizations across various boundaries to tackle complex public problems and achieve the common good. The theory of public integrative leadership has been developed relatively recently and draws from research on cross-sector collaboration, corporate social responsibility, and collaborative public management, as well as from practice theory. This chapter explores the development of integrative leadership theory and discusses key integrative leadership practices. Two cases-the creation of a geographic information system (GIS) for a U.S. region and a global campaign to eradicate polio-illustrate the practices. The chapter also considers implications for leadership development and emphasizes the need to learn from unsuccessful as well as successful efforts to lead across sector, cultural, and geographic boundaries.

Key Words: public integrative leadership, collaborative leadership, cross-boundary leadership, interorganizational leadership, common good, leadership practice, practice theory

Leaders seeking to sustain their organizations in today's interconnected, interdependent world must pay attention to the well-being of surrounding communities and societies, as well as to their own organizations' well-being (Gerencser, Van Lee, Napolitano, & Kelly, 2008; Senge, Smith, Schley, & Laur, 2008). They have to collaborate with other organizations and groups to tackle problems like unemployment, climate change, and disease, and respond to societal opportunities presented by new technologies or demographic changes.

To be effective in these collaborative endeavors, leaders need to be adept in the practices of public integrative leadership—that is, leading across various types of boundaries to integrate people, resources, and organizations into semipermanent arrangements to achieve the common good (Crosby & Bryson, 2010). The boundaries may be between sectors (e.g., business, government, nonprofits), between geographic areas (e.g., neighborhoods or countries), or between cultures (e.g., religious or ethnic groups).

This chapter discusses the theory of public integrative leadership and uses two cases to illustrate integrative leadership practices. One of the cases—the creation of a geographic information system (GIS) for a U.S. region—was initiated by leaders in government. The other case—a global campaign to eradicate polio—was initiated by leaders in a transnational nonprofit organization. The main portion of the chapter describes the practices of public integrative leadership; this is followed by a discussion of its implications for leadership development and by a concluding section that discusses future research directions.

Development of Public Integrative Leadership Theory

The foundations for a theory of public integrative leadership have been laid in recent years by scholars recognizing the increased demand for (and practice of) interorganizational, collaborative leadership and management. Some focused mainly on government and nonprofit organizations facing the need to collaborate with each other and with businesses (see, for example, Bingham & O'Leary, 2008; Morse, Buss & Kinghorn, 2007; O'Leary & Bingham, 2009; Osborne, 2010). Others focused mainly on businesses and the demand that they be socially responsible (Crane, McWilliams, Matten, & Moon, 2008; Scherer & Palazzo, 2007; Waddock, 2007). Others, including the authors of this chapter, have focused on cross-sector collaborations initiated by any sector (see, for example, Bryson, Crosby, & Stone, 2006; Ernst & Chrobot-Mason, 2011).

Much of this research draws on practitioners' experiences with crafting effective and ineffective cross-sector collaborations and responds to practitioners' desire for better understanding of how to lead across organizational, sectoral, geographical, and cultural boundaries. Indeed, it was a corporate leader, Marilyn Carlson Nelson (then CEO of Carlson Companies, a prominent global tourism company), who called specifically for a new brand of leadership that would be integrative and work across sectoral boundaries to tackle social challenges (Nelson, 2008). She has been a strong supporter of the development of the Center for Integrative Leadership at the University of Minnesota, which has organized conferences, community consultations, and research projects aimed at understanding and promoting integrative leadership.

In 2010, *The Leadership Quarterly* published a special issue on integrative public leadership. Articles focused on, for example, the integrative practices of county emergency managers, the Seattle mayor's office, social movement leaders, federal agency leaders, and the organizers of the GIS system described in this chapter. One article also explored how leadership development programs can increase integrative leadership. More specifically, the article by Morse (2010) deepened understanding of how integrative leadership is enacted through people, processes, and structures. Page (2010) measured the use of three key leadership tactics—framing the agenda, convening stakeholders, and structuring deliberation—in civic engagement initiatives in Seattle and found that extensive use of these tactics is likely to increase political will, civic capacity, and policy performance—key desirable results of collaborative public problem solving. Silvia and McGuire (2010) found that when county emergency managers led across organizational boundaries, they engaged in more people-oriented behavior than they did when leading within their own agency. Redekop (2010) and Ospina and Foldy (2010) examined the ways integrative leaders in social change organizations bring together diverse constituencies within their organizations, build interorganizational coalitions, and fundamentally challenge the dominant ways of understanding particular public problems. Fernandez, Cho, and Perry (2010) analyzed the relationship between integrated leadership (defined as a combination of task-, relations-, change-, diversity-, and integrity-oriented leadership styles) and federal program performance. They found that integrated leadership has a positive and sizeable effect on the performance of federal subagencies. Bono, Shen, and Snyder (2010) found that businesspeople and other community residents who participated in North American community leadership programs engaged in their communities in new ways following the programs.

In that same issue, the authors of this chapter also presented a framework for public integrative leadership consisting of five elements: initial conditions, processes and practices, structure and governance, contingencies and constraints, and outcomes and accountabilities (Crosby & Bryson, 2010). The article developed several propositions about what contributes to successful integrative leadership (see Table 4.1). A condensed version of this framework will be used to describe key practices of integrative leadership in the next section. (Contingencies and constraints will be incorporated into the other elements.)

Focusing on leadership practices fits with the "practice turn" in the social sciences (Corley & Gioia, 2011; Reckwitz, 2002; Schatzki, Knorr-Cetina, & Savigny 2001). It also fits with the "pragmatic turn" in philosophy, in which actors' practical wisdom is accorded new respect (Egginton & Sandbothe 2004; Innes & Booher, 2010; Menand, 2001). Although practice recently has become a prominent research focus in the social sciences, its intellectual roots are deep (Corley & Gioia, 2011; Johnson, Langley, Melin, & Whittington, 2007; Latour, 2005; Nicolini, Gherardi, & Yanow, 2003; Sennett, 2008). "Practice theory" is the term typically used to indicate important commonalities across a range of theoretical approaches to the study of practice. Schatzki (1996) and Reckwitz (2002) are the most frequently cited authors, with Reckwitz identifying Bourdieu, Foucault, Giddens, Butler, Garfinkel, Charles Taylor, and Schatzki as significant contributors.

Table 4.1. Propositions About the Relationship of Integrative Leadership and Cross-sector Collaborations

Proposition 1: Like all interorganizational relationships, cross-sector collaborations are more likely to form in turbulent environments. Leaders will have more success at launching these collaborations when they take advantage of opportunities opened up by driving forces (including helping create or favorably altering them) while remaining attuned to constraining forces.
Proposition 2: Leaders are most likely to try cross-sector collaboration if they believe that separate efforts by several sectors to address a public problem have failed and the actual failures cannot be fixed by a separate sector alone.
Proposition 3: Cross-sector collaborations are more likely to succeed when one or more linking mechanisms, such as powerful sponsors and champions, general agreement on the problem, or existing networks are in place at the time of their initial formation.
Proposition 4: Cross-sector collaborations are more likely to succeed when sponsors, champions, and other leaders pay careful attention to the wise design and use of forums, arenas, and courts, including the creation of helpful boundary groups, experiences, and objects.
Proposition 5: The form and content of a collaboration's initial agreements, as well as the processes leaders use to formulate them, will affect the outcomes of the collaboration's work.
Proposition 6: Leaders are more likely to guide cross-sector collaborations to success if they help participants combine deliberate and emergent planning, with deliberate planning probably being emphasized more in mandated collaborations and emergent planning probably being emphasized more in nonmandated collaborations.
Proposition 7: Leaders of cross-sector collaborations are more likely to succeed if they ensure planning processes include stakeholder analyses, emphasize responsiveness to key stakeholders, use the process to build trust and the capacity to manage conflict, and build on the general competencies and distinctive competencies of the collaborators.
Proposition 8: Because conflict is common in partnerships, cross-sector collaborations are more likely to succeed if leaders use resources and tactics to help equalize power and manage conflict effectively.
Proposition 9: Cross-sector collaborations are more likely to succeed if they have committed sponsors and effective champions at many levels who provide formal and informal leadership.
Proposition 10: Cross-sector collaborations are more likely to succeed if leaders make sure that trust-building activities (including nurturing cross-sector understanding) are continuous.
Proposition 11: Leaders of cross-sector collaborations are more likely to succeed if they establish with both internal and external stakeholders the legitimacy of collaboration as a form of organizing, as a separate entity and as a source of trusted interaction among members.
Proposition 12: Collaborative structure—and therefore leadership effectiveness—is influenced by environmental factors, such as system stability and the collaboration's strategic purpose. Astute leaders will ensure that the structure of the collaboration is flexible and adaptive enough to deal with system shifts and accomplish strategic purposes.
Proposition 13: Collaborative structure—and therefore the effectiveness of particular leaders—is also likely to change over time due to ambiguity of membership and complexity in local environments. Astute leaders will recognize these dynamics and plan for incorporation of new members and for leader succession.
Proposition 14: Leadership is crucial in matching governing mechanisms to context appropriately; subsequently, governing mechanisms, at both formal and informal levels, are likely to influence collaboration effectiveness and, consequently, the effectiveness of network leadership.
Proposition 15: The process leaders follow to develop collaboration structures and governance mechanisms is likely to influence the effectiveness of the structures and mechanisms.
Proposition 16: Collaboration leaders are likely to have more leeway in designing structures and governance mechanisms in bottom-up collaborations, but those structures and mechanisms are likely to emerge more slowly than in top-down collaborations.

(continued)

Table 4.1. Continued

Proposition 17: Leaders in cross-sector collaborations should tailor investment in negotiation among stakeholders to the level of the collaboration. Collaborations involving system-level planning activities are likely to involve the most negotiation, followed by collaborations focused on administrative-level partnerships, followed by service delivery partnerships.
Proposition 18: Cross-sector collaborations are more likely to succeed if leaders build in resources and tactics for dealing with power imbalances and shocks.
Proposition 19: Competing institutional logics are likely within cross-sector collaborations and may significantly influence the extent to which collaboration leaders can agree on essential elements of process and structure, as well as outcomes. Astute leaders will reframe disputes in ways that can appeal across sectors.
Proposition 20: Cross-sector collaborations are most likely to create public value if leaders design them (or help them emerge) in such a way that they build on individuals' and organizations' self-interests, along with each sector's characteristic strengths, while finding ways to minimize, overcome, or compensate for each sector's characteristic weaknesses.
Proposition 21: Cross-sector collaborations are most likely to create public value if leaders explicitly seek the production of positive first-, second-, and third-order effects.
Proposition 22: Cross-sector collaborations are more likely to be successful if leaders insist that there be an accountability system that tracks inputs, processes, and outcomes; use a variety of methods for gathering, interpreting, and using data; and use a results management system built on strong relationships with key political and professional constituencies.
Proposition 23: Cross-sector collaborations are most likely to create public value if leaders demonstrate resilience and engage in regular reassessments.
Proposition 24: The normal expectation ought to be that success will be very difficult to achieve in cross-sector collaborations, regardless of leadership effectiveness.

Schatzki and Reckwitz provide the outlines of a coherent approach to studying practices. As summarized by Shove, Watson, Hand, and Ingram (2007: 12–14), the premises of that approach are as follows. *First*, according to Reckwitz (2002: 249), a practice may be defined as "a routinized type of behavior which consists of several elements, interconnected to one another: forms of bodily activities, forms of mental activities, 'things' and their use, [and] a background knowledge in the form of understanding, know-how, states of emotion and motivational knowledge." The definition clearly entails a caution to practitioners and researchers not to overly reify "things" like leadership. Leadership in practice, although it may be represented or described simply, is thus a very complex *process*—as "reflective practitioners" (Schön, 1987) all know.

Second, practice is a fundamental component of social existence, since both individuality and social order result from practices (Schatzki, 1996). Leadership as practice involves ideas, behaviors, and collective actions determined by both individual human agency and by structural and institutional forces. Strategic choices are made by individuals and groups embedded in social structures that are reproduced and shaped by individual and group actions. Practice theory, in Shove et al.'s (2007: 12) words, "emphasizes tacit and unconscious forms of knowledge and experience through which shared ways of understanding and being in the world are established, through which purposes emerge as desirable, and norms [are seen] as legitimate." There is, thus, typically more going on than meets the eye.

Third, viewing a practice as simply what people do is simplistic. Schatzki (1996) helps clarify how much more is involved than "just doing" by distinguishing between practice as a coordinated entity and practice as a performance. As an *entity*, practice has a relatively enduring existence across both actual and potential performances, although its existence depends on its recurrent enactment by practitioners. When people have discussions about leadership or cross-sector collaboration *in the abstract*, they are talking about it as an *entity*. In contrast, *practice-as-performance* refers to the action through which a practice-as-entity is maintained, reproduced, and possibly changed. This distinction leads to the assertion that practices cannot be reduced simply to what people do. Instead, as Shove et al. (2007: 13) note, "doings are performances, shaped by and constitutive of the complex relations—of materials, knowledges, norms, meanings and so on—which comprise the practice-as-entity."[1]

Fourth, practice theory expands the central foci of dominant social theories—minds, conversations, texts, and/or specific behaviors and interactions—as Reckwitz (2002: 259) notes, by "simultaneously [shifting] bodily movements, things, practical knowledge and routine to the center of the vocabulary." Practice theories thus "contend with and seek to account for the integration and reproduction of the diverse elements of social existence" (Shove et al., 2007: 13). Viewing leadership in cross-sector collaborations as practice(s) thus requires that it be seen as quite richly constituted when done well and not as easily reduced to the scaled variables of variance studies (e.g., Bryson, Crosby, & Bryson, 2009; Crosby & Bryson, 2012; Forester, 1999; Jarzabkowski, 2005).

A final point comes from Wenger (1998: 4–9), who emphasizes the importance of "communities of practice." Practices are sustained or changed in communities (which themselves may be sustained or changed). More to the point, leadership in cross-sector collaborations occurs in communities of practice that vary in permanence. Indeed, temporary cross-boundary communities, such as collaboration coordinating committees, task forces, or teams, are often intentionally created to shake up people's thinking, acting, and learning. The knowledge brought to bear or produced (learned) should relate to understanding and/or achieving the purposes of an enterprise or its parts. Knowing and learning, however partial, are a matter of actively engaging in the pursuits of such enterprises and working to make the engagement meaningful. Learning is, thus, an ongoing issue of sustaining the interconnected communities of practice that comprise any organization or network and through which the enterprise knows what it knows and, as a result, becomes effective and valuable.

The notions of boundary experiences, boundary objects, and boundary groups may be particularly helpful in shaping and reshaping communities of practice (Carlile, 2002, 2004; Feldman, Khademian, Ingram, & Schneider, 2006; Kellogg, Orlikowski, & Yates, 2006). Boundary experiences provide opportunities for diverse stakeholders to get to know each other, see an issue from each other's perspective, and co-produce solutions. Boundary objects are "physical objects that enable people to understand other perspectives" (Feldman et al., 2006; 95) and, thus, are important in helping people create shared meaning (Carlile, 2002, 2004; Star & Griesemer, 1989). They help translate the language of diverse groups to each other (Akkerman & Bakker (2011). Examples of boundary objects include mission statements, stakeholder diagrams, action-oriented strategy maps (Bryson, Ackermann, Eden, & Finn, 2004), reports, websites, and GIS maps. Boundary experiences and the production of boundary objects can lay the groundwork for formal boundary groups such as steering committees, working groups, task forces, or advisory teams.

Of necessity, issues of personal and collective identity are salient in communities of practice, which means changes in practices and organizations also necessarily prompt at least marginal changes in personal and collective identity (Fiol, 2001) or organizational culture more broadly (Schein, 2010). From a practice perspective, leadership becomes a fluid, relational enterprise, embedded in and shaping communities of practice. In sum, integrative leadership is best understood as a set of interrelated practices and not as an entity abstracted far from practice.

Two Cases of Public Integrative Leadership

The two cases highlighted here are similar in their involvement of diverse stakeholders from multiple sectors, in the need to lead across geographic boundaries, in the importance of technological innovation, and in leaders' engagement in extensive collaborative deliberation about shared purpose and how to achieve it. They also are dissimilar in several important ways. Leaders in the MetroGIS case had to cope with difficult political barriers among local governments and between local governments and the regional government. The main cultural differences they encountered were likely between technical experts, on the one hand, and management- and/or process-oriented people, on the other. In the case of PolioPlus, leaders had to deal with boundaries among nations, the differing agendas of major international organizations, and multiple national and ethnic cultures. The campaign was based in a century-old service organization, Rotary International, comprised of thousands of clubs worldwide.

The Metro GIS Case

The Metro GIS case is an example of a bottom-up collaboration. MetroGIS is the regional GIS in the Twin Cities area of Minnesota (http://www.metrogis.

org). MetroGIS was initiated in 1995 and has grown into an award-winning regional system serving the seven-county Minneapolis-St. Paul metropolitan area. MetroGIS is coordinated and staffed by the Metropolitan Council (MC), the regional government, but is perhaps most usefully viewed as a voluntary collaboration—and what interviewees call a "virtual organization"—involving more than 300 local and regional governments, partners in the state and federal governments, and academic institutions, nonprofit organizations, and businesses. MetroGIS provides a regional forum to promote and facilitate widespread sharing and use of geospatial data, very little of which is owned by the MC. The organization is a clear example of "collaborative planning" by multiple units of government, nonprofits, and businesses (Healey, 2006) and of "inclusive management" (Feldman & Khademian 2000, 2007), with high levels of inclusion, democratic and consensus-based decision-making processes, and varying levels of participation depending on the situation.

The conversations leading to development of MetroGIS grew out of the intersection of need and opportunity. Local government leaders and planners in the Minneapolis-St. Paul region were frustrated by what they believed were faulty population, employment, and land use data and projections issued by the MC. Local governments had to rely on these data to compile their land use plans for incorporation into the council's regional plans. The availability of new geographic information technology, however, provided the opportunity to adopt an effective method to gather information at the parcel level in each local jurisdiction and then compile it at the regional level. An MC manager convinced the MC deputy administrator that the organization should explore the creation of a regional GIS and that someone should be hired to handle the exploration. As a result, the MC hired an experienced planner for one of the area's suburbs to become the council's GIS liaison, and he went to work convening stakeholder conversations.

A Strategic Planning Forum held at the end of 1995 and including representatives of government, nonprofit, and business interests resulted in a statement of intent to proceed, identification of strategic issues, and an initial structure for a collaborative regional GIS. Subsequently, stakeholders agreed on a mission statement, goals, guiding principles, strategic projects, and a formal structure. For the next 12 years, the MetroGIS network implemented its strategic projects, resulting in national and international recognition. Among its outstanding creations was the DataFinder Café, a state-of-the-art, Internet-enabled, geographic data distribution system.

In 2007, stakeholders came together in a second major strategic planning workshop, revised their mission, and agreed to focus on eight major activity areas for the next three to five years, including building advocacy and awareness of the benefits of collaborative solutions. More details on this case may be found in Bryson, Crosby, and Bryson (2009) and at www.metrogis.org.

POLIO PLUS

PolioPlus is basically a bottom-up collaboration as well, although its formation was strongly influenced by top decision makers in Rotary International (Rotary), a nongovernmental organization with about 1.2 million members in 33,000 clubs worldwide. The roots of PolioPlus go back decades, to the time when Rotary presidents began fostering partnerships between clubs in the so-called developing and developed countries, resulting in a number of joint service projects and exchanges. By the late 1970s, the Rotary Board of Directors became even more ambitious and instituted a Health, Hunger, and Humanity (3H) Program aimed at using Rotary's massive volunteer resources to tackle major problems affecting poorer nations. One of the program's early initiatives was a response to a Rotary member and physician who urged the organization to help immunize children around the world against communicable diseases. In 1979, Rotary's 3H Committee approved a pilot project aimed at eradicating polio in the Philippines through an intensive immunization campaign. At the time, the country had one of the highest rates of polio cases in the world. Rotarians carried out the project in cooperation with the Philippine Ministry of Health, the United Nations Children's Fund (UNICEF), and the World Health Organization (WHO), and achieved 90 percent immunization of children under five. Building on this success, Rotary launched similar projects in several other countries.

In the early 1980s, a Rotarian who was chief of the infectious diseases branch of the National Institutes of Health in the United States proposed that Rotary set its sights even higher by adopting the goal of wiping out polio worldwide by 2005. The Rotary Board approved the idea for a 20-year campaign ending in 2005, which would be the organization's 100th anniversary. The board also pledged to raise $120 million to support the campaign and established an international committee to oversee it.

During the first year of the campaign, organizers focused on educating Rotary members about the project, training campaign leaders, and developing fundraising logistics. With UNICEF, WHO, and others, they worked carefully with political decision makers in countries where polio was endemic. In 1988, WHO announced the Global Polio Eradication Initiative, aimed at eradicating polio by the turn of the new century. The initiative partners were Rotary, WHO, the U.S. Centers for Disease Control and Prevention, and UNICEF. Rotary agreed to provide the polio vaccine, assist with political support, and mobilize communities.

One of the most successful and visible components of the PolioPlus campaign is national immunization days, in which massive numbers of volunteers assist health professionals in administering vaccines, then follow-up by going door-to-door to make sure all families have a chance to have their children immunized. On just one of these days in India, 650,000 immunization booths were set up, 1.3 million volunteers participated, and 150 million children were immunized.

In 1985, 350,000 cases of polio were reported. By end of 2009, as a result of the global eradication campaign, fewer than 1,600 had been reported for the year. By that point, 2.5 billion children worldwide had been immunized and 20 million volunteers had been involved. More than $8 billion had been committed to the project by Rotary, foundations, UN organizations, businesses, governments, and individuals. The disease remained endemic in only four countries: Nigeria, India, Pakistan, and Afghanistan. The milestone of Rotary's 100th anniversary had passed, and supporters of PolioPlus could not claim complete success, but they could claim amazing results, and the organization committed itself anew to continuing the campaign and adapting to the unique challenges posed by conditions in the four remaining countries. More details on this case can be found in Mooty (2010) and on the Rotary International website (http://www.rotary.org/en/SERVICEANDFELLOWSHIP/POLIO/Pages/ridefault.aspx).

Practices of Public Integrative Leadership

A variety of leadership practices appears to be associated with effective cross-sector collaboration in these two cases and numerous others (see Crosby & Bryson, 2012; Ernst & Chrobot-Mason, 2011; Senge et al., 2008). We group these practices according to major elements of cross-sector collaboration identified in our previous work: initial conditions, structure and process, and outcomes and accountabilities (Bryson, Crosby & Stone, 2006; Crosby & Bryson, 2010, 2012).

Initial Conditions

Diagnosing context is the leadership practice focus associated with initial conditions. Three general types of practices are part of diagnosing context: shaping and taking advantage of windows of opportunity, developing strategic cross-boundary relationships, and deploying personal assets on behalf of a policy change (Crosby & Bryson, 2012). Each of these is discussed here, and specific practices are identified.

PRACTICE: SHAPING AND TAKING ADVANTAGE OF WINDOWS OF OPPORTUNITIES

Shaping windows of opportunity (Kingdon, 2003) appears to be a crucial leadership practice. As part of this practice, leaders and their constituents attend to political, social, economic, technological, and ecological conditions, shifts, and trends, identifying how the shifts and trends—such as the growing sophistication of GIS technologies, the availability of an oral polio vaccine, or a change in top leaders—open up a window of opportunity. The practice also involves the construction of meaning, or "sensegiving" (Weick, Sutcliffe, & Obstfeld, 2005), around whether a condition is alterable, what kind of problem it is, its urgency, and whether the time is right for innovative action. Successful efforts at meaning making and sensegiving appear in both of the cases.

In the MetroGIS case, specialists built understanding via reports and conferences about the potential of GIS to support policy makers and improve the quality of their planning and decision making. In the PolioPlus case, Rotary presidents began recasting Rotary as a truly international organization as far back as the 1960s, when they fostered transnational partnerships between clubs. In the 1970s, Rotary members with public health expertise worked to convince the organization's decision makers that polio actually could be eradicated in Latin America, Africa, Asia, and the Middle East through the combined efforts of clubs around the world.

To facilitate detecting and opening windows of opportunity, organizations and individuals practice *scanning*: They peruse journals, read web postings and newspapers, participate in forums, attend conferences, or respond to requests for proposals (RFPs), job offers, or organizational routines that provide chances to advance their desired policy change. For example, the suburban planner responded to an offer to become GIS liaison for the MC; other GIS enthusiasts responded to his invitation to begin thinking about a regional GIS system. The physician who initially championed Rotary's involvement with immunization brought his recommendation for immunizing children against polio to Rotary's International Board of Directors, and it fit precisely with the objectives of Rotary's new 3H Program. The first 3H grant was for the pilot immunization program in the Philippines. The Rotarian who proposed the 2005 goal of wiping out polio recognized the symbolic significance of Rotary's 100th anniversary as an opportunity for launching an ambitious 20-year antipolio campaign.

PRACTICE: BUILDING STRATEGIC CROSS-BOUNDARY RELATIONSHIPS

Cross-sector collaboration doesn't just happen. It occurs in part through the medium of relationships that cross boundaries of many sorts, both intra- and interorganizationally (Ernst & Chrobot-Mason, 2011; Ospina & Foldy, 2010; Senge et al., 2008).

In the MetroGIS case, the GIS liaison moved from a planning position in local government to a job in regional government; he negotiated a direct reporting relationship with the MC deputy administrator, and he found University of Minnesota partners to contribute needed expertise. By its nature, MC, in effect, mandates a relationship between local planners and officials and regional planners and officials (although the relationship has experienced plenty of friction).

In PolioPlus, the pairing of Rotary clubs in developed countries with clubs in developing countries was an exercise in strategic relationship building. To undertake the pilot project in the Philippines, Rotarians developed cooperative relationships with the country's Ministry of Health and UN agencies.

Stakeholder analysis methods (Bryson, 2004) can help integrative leaders understand which important cross-boundary relationships exist and which must be built to make progress on a public problem. Stakeholder interviewing (Senge et al., 2008) is a useful way of gauging stakeholders' experiences and perspectives. Using these methods, leaders and their constituents identify key individuals, groups, and organizations with a stake in the problem, characterize the connections that exist among the stakeholders, and lay the groundwork for inclusive, creative processes and structures.

PRACTICE: DEPLOYING PERSONAL AND ORGANIZATIONAL ASSETS ON BEHALF OF A POLICY CHANGE

Open windows of opportunity and initial supportive relationships are not enough to nurture collaboration. Individuals and organizations involved must draw on a variety of resources, including formal authority, in order to take the actions necessary to create, govern, and manage cross-sector collaboration (Crosby & Bryson, 2005). People we call *sponsors* are a particularly important kind of leader in cross-sector collaboration because they provide the formal authority, much of the legitimacy, and other resources (such as staff and money) necessary to support effective collaboration. For example, in the MetroGIS case, the MC deputy administrator used his authority and resources to persuade the MC to authorize hiring new staff to explore the potential for a regional GIS system. In PolioPlus, Rotary presidents used their position to introduce transformative initiatives like club pairing and the 3H Program to legitimize the proposal for the PolioPlus campaign.

Champions are also an important resource (Crosby & Bryson, 2005; Taylor, Cocklin, Brown, & Wilson-Evered, 2011). Sponsors are typically not involved in the day-to-day work of a collaboration; *champions* are. They make use of informal authority, passion, and process expertise to initiate change. In the MetroGIS case, a middle manager and the GIS liaison used their knowledge of the friction between local and regional planners and of problems with the council's data-gathering system to pressure MC policy makers to authorize change. In PolioPlus, Rotary members drew on their professional expertise and sense of Rotary's potential for mobilizing volunteers to champion the idea of massive immunization campaigns. The campaign structure also facilitated the emergence of numerous champions throughout Rotary.

Structure and Process

Structure and process constantly interact in collaborative settings. Structure provides a basic architecture within which processes and social mechanisms build commitment among people and institutions to enable collective decision making. Rules about collective decision making provide a bridge between structure and process (Stone, Crosby & Bryson, 2010). The practices associated with structure and process are design and use of forums, design and use of governance structures and decision-making processes, influencing and authorizing decision makers, enforcing and reinforcing formal and informal rules and norms in courts, and maintaining structural flexibility. The practices draw on, build, and activate stakeholder relationships, power, and interests, and develop shared understandings (including common language), commitments, and new policies and practices. They both reproduce and alter existing institutional arrangements (Crosby & Bryson, 2005; Sydow, Lerch, Huxham, & Hibbert, 2011).

PRACTICE: DESIGN AND USE OF FORUMS

The work of collaborative forums can be thought of as a boundary-spanning experience involving boundary-spanning groups producing boundary objects. The result is typically social learning, which could include development of shared understanding (along with particularized understanding on the part of individual stakeholders) and development of a shared identity alongside preexisting identities (Akkerman & Bakker, 2011). The design and use of forums (such as task forces, public meetings, committee meetings, informal gatherings, and interactive websites) include reasonably inclusive convening that fosters systems thinking and builds coalitions for action. In both the MetroGIS and PolioPlus cases, diverse stakeholders were brought together to engage in social learning and problem solving. Initial forums may be small gatherings of people who are concerned about a public problem or challenge, but leaders seeking to build effective collaborations will eventually have to convene representatives of all relevant parts of the system (Senge et al., 2008).

A related practice is fostering dialog and deliberation within forums. In simplest terms, dialog refers to an exchange of ideas and perspectives between two or more people. Senge et al. (2008) argue that productive dialog is more likely when participants are able to suspend assumptions, balance inquiry and advocacy, and tap group members' values. Barzelay and Thompson (2010) say that deliberative argumentation consists of engaging with others in careful observation; rich (rather than thin or superficial) description; normative reasoning about what constitutes a good outcome; consideration of various strategies for accomplishing outcomes; and evaluation that reflects different attitudes, beliefs, and values. Fletcher and Kaüfer (2003) and Scharmer (2009) offer especially helpful guidelines for engaging in generative dialog.

To foster systems thinking, leaders can engage in the iceberg exercise described by Senge et al. (2008). Participants begin by talking about observable events (the tip of the iceberg) connected to the problem or challenge that concerns them. They then move below the surface to observe underlying patterns and trends, then even deeper to identify forces that cause the patterns, and finally, at the deepest level, explore mental models that allow the problem to persist Leaders can also offer an overview of the policy change process (Crosby & Bryson, 2005), so that participants see the process as a whole, develop appropriate strategies for different phases of the process, and establish timelines for change.

A desired outcome in cross-sector collaboration would be creation of shared meaning and commitment to pursue a plan of action. Dialog and deliberation in forums are also useful for purposes of designing new decision-making structures, especially those that govern the collaboration. Forums should be intentionally designed to foster personal relationships that can be "strategically leveraged" (Ernst & Chrobot-Mason, 2011; Mandell & Keast, 2011) on behalf of the collaborative work. This often means postponing in-depth focus on the challenge prompting the dialog and, instead, focusing on personal interests and experiences.

In designing and using forums, sponsors and champions are called on to be visionary leaders—that is, leaders who help participants create and communicate shared meaning (Crosby & Bryson, 2005). They help participants envision a desired future—such as a world free of polio or a region with a world-class GIS—and a path for reaching it. They help connect the vision to key participant values—such as Rotary's tradition of humanitarian service or pride in the Minneapolis-St. Paul region's reputation for public innovation. They help constituents develop new ways of seeing or framing the challenges that concern them. Champions, in particular, will be called on to exercise the arts of "foruming": inviting, facilitating, developing agendas and other boundary objects, managing conflict, balancing power, and tracking agreements.

The use of deliberative forums is prominent in both the MetroGIS and PolioPlus cases. For example, in 1995, the GIS liaison convened two major forums of 75-plus stakeholders each to explore pursuit of a regional GIS system and whether the MC should lead the initiative. Participants included local and county government representatives, GIS experts, and academic advocates. Subsequently, he organized a Strategic Planning Forum, in which 22 invited representatives of government, nonprofit, and business organizations produced strategy maps that would guide development of the MetroGIS system. Another strategic planning workshop 12 years later included approximately 40 stakeholders who focused on sustaining the success of the regional network and pursuing new directions. These forums and follow-up processes resulted in a living vision for a regional GIS system and helped participants reframe geographic data gathered by local governments, utilities, and consultants: They reframed the data from a possession to be hoarded to a pooled resource generating mutual benefits.

Rotary International is a committee-oriented organization. The proposal for the PolioPlus campaign was initially considered and endorsed by a committee. Once the International Board of Directors approved it, the Rotary president appointed the Polio 2005 Committee that developed a plan for the campaign. During the first year, Rotary leaders held meetings with other international organizations, especially WHO and UNICEF, to win their support, and activated thousands of volunteers to communicate the campaign's vision in club meetings around the world. Rotary leaders helped their own organization and their many partners reframe polio in developing nations from a condition that could only be contained to a disease that could be wiped out with the right combination of professional, volunteer, and political effort along with adequate vaccines.

PRACTICE: DESIGN AND USE OF GOVERNANCE STRUCTURES (OR ARENAS) AND DECISION-MAKING PROCESSES

In the two cases, leaders devoted attention to designing and using arenas that set policies for the collaboration and that were suited to the collaboration's needs and characteristics. At times, forums and arenas overlapped. What is noteworthy is that, almost always, dialog and deliberation (the work of forums) preceded actual decision making in arenas.

For example, the forums convened by the GIS liaison gave participants a chance to learn about the potential of a regional GIS and consider how it might be implemented. The forums resulted in strong support for the idea of a regional GIS system and agreement that the council should take the lead in creating it. Through dialog and deliberation, participants agreed on elements of a mission and goals for the system, identified strategic issues to be addressed over the next four months, established a Coordinating Committee, and proposed a set of "guiding principles" for the system. Subsequent dialog and deliberation in the committee, advisory groups, and the MC helped establish the full-fledged MetroGIS governance structure with decision-making authority.

In the PolioPlus campaign, the deliberations of the Polio 2005 Committee and the Rotary International Board resulted in top-level commitment to the campaign, an ambitious fundraising goal, and initial strategies. To oversee the campaign, the board established a new decision-making arena, the International PolioPlus Committee. It would be supported by an extensive structure for carrying out the campaign: an executive director, 11 international coordinators, 84 national coordinators, 44 national or regional committees, and 3,300 area coordinators. Also part of the structure was the Rotary International Foundation, governed by a board of trustees, which was key to campaign fundraising.

PRACTICE: INFLUENCING AND AUTHORIZING DECISION MAKERS

This practice focuses on continual awareness of nodes of power and authority affecting a collaborative effort. It includes lobbying, bargaining, and negotiating. In addition, an important part of this practice is building and sustaining substantial coalitions of decision makers to exert pressure on others and mobilize financial and human resources.

From the outset, the GIS liaison made sure he had a guaranteed direct line to the MC's deputy administrator, who ensured that council members kept MetroGIS on their agenda and gave due consideration to its funding and policy requests. By establishing a Policy Board mainly consisting of Twin Cities-area elected officials, the builders of MetroGIS incorporated key political decision makers into the system. These people could be expected to lobby their government units to participate in MetroGIS. By building a record of money-saving achievements, the architects of MetroGIS maintained support from the MC. A strong coalition—consisting of data users, local officials, and GIS advocates—grew out of the inclusive forums convened by the GIS liaison. It was sustained by several structures: the Coordinating Committee, the Policy Board, and the Technical Advisory Team. As databases and their functionality grew, they directly benefited many members of the coalition and, ultimately, the residents of the participating counties.

The advocates of Rotary's polio eradication campaign worked hard to build support for the campaign from top to bottom. Even the name PolioPlus was a sort of boundary object that communicated a compromise between members who wanted a laser focus on polio and those who argued Rotary should focus more broadly on immunization against childhood disease. The "Plus" referred to Rotary's development of political and grassroots support, campaign management expertise, and fundraising not only to combat polio but to bolster national governments' and international organizations' broader immunization efforts.

PolioPlus leaders also had to overcome considerable turf issues and some skepticism to persuade organizations like WHO and UNICEF to become campaign partners. Rotary leaders won them over by adopting strategies through which Rotary's work would complement, rather than supplant, the work of these organizations. For example, Rotary pledged to provide polio vaccine, help develop political support, and spread awareness of the benefits of immunization. An effective strategy for building political support was having national health departments take responsibility for the campaign in their countries. At the local level, the national immunization days were effective modes for influencing community- and household-level decision makers.

PolioPlus leaders realized that Rotarians could not raise all the money needed for eradicating polio. They worked with their UN partners and the UN Foundation to secure funding from governments, corporations, and foundations; a $25 million pledge from the Gates Foundation was one very significant result.

A key mechanism for building and sustaining a supportive coalition is achieving a series of accomplishments that add up to an eventual "big win" (Crosby & Bryson, 2005). Senge et al. (2008) emphasize the value of pilot projects and prototypes. MetroGIS leaders could highlight the creation of datasets and various computer applications, as well as the DataFinder Café. Rotary's leaders used the pilot project in the Philippines both to build the organization's capacity and demonstrate it could carry out a successful immunization campaign. As the PolioPlus campaign proceeded, it touted success in eliminating the disease first in one region and then another.

PRACTICE: ENFORCING AND REINFORCING FORMAL AND INFORMAL RULES AND NORMS IN COURTS

Rules—and perhaps especially norms—are crucial mechanisms for ensuring effective communication, coordination, and collaboration. Even in top-down collaborations, power is dispersed, so the rules and norms collaborators choose to observe via their practices of engagement strongly influence the effectiveness of collaboration. Enforcing and reinforcing rules and norms is the work of formal and informal courts. In both the MetroGIS and PolioPlus cases, formal courts were in the background, ready to enforce laws, but other kinds of courts were also at work. These included hierarchical superiors able to resolve or manage conflict between subordinates. Perhaps most importantly, they also included the court of public opinion.

In the MetroGIS case, the key principle of mutual data sharing among system participants was enforced mainly by peer pressure. The MC and counties had sanctioning power over the system via their funding authority and, at one point, the council even conducted an audit to assess whether the system met the basic criteria of cost-effectiveness. The GIS liaison and other participants mitigated government's sanctioning power by obtaining nongovernmental grants to carry out some projects. The awards they obtained from prestigious national and international groups also were positive sanctions or assurances of MetroGIS's legitimacy.

Rotary's antipolio campaigners had to be sure they were observing national laws and not running afoul of rules established by international bodies like WHO, and they had to be attuned to cultural norms. At times, they reached out to religious leaders and health professionals to overcome myths about immunization.

PRACTICE: MAINTAINING STRUCTURAL FLEXIBILITY

In the course of a major collaborative initiative, partners experience multiple shocks and shifts in the environment. If they are to sustain the collaboration, they must use flexible structures and processes to respond to and even shape these changes. The foci of practices associated with maintaining structural flexibility are working within both hierarchies and networks and forming and maintaining boundary groups. One such practice is navigating hierarchical and network structures.

The MetroGIS system is a network of individuals and organizations tied together in different ways and working with a sophisticated set of databases. Key decisions are made by the system's Policy Board, Coordinating Committee, and Technical Advisory Team. At the same time, champions of the system have to comply with the decision-making processes of hierarchical government organizations at the regional and county level. The Policy Board has been a key link between the network and hierarchical structures. (The Policy Board, Coordinating Committee, and Technical Advisory Team enjoy a certain legitimacy within the network and the hierarchies since they emerged from the inclusive initial strategic planning process.)

MetroGIS also is affected by changes in the MC's membership and in the composition of the governing bodies that contribute to it. Several years after its creation, MetroGIS came under fire from an MC member, who questioned the wisdom of continuing investment in it. The council undertook a system evaluation that not only highlighted the system's achievements but showed that every dollar invested in the system produced six dollars in benefits. This example indicates the importance of producing results along the way that can be used to justify the collaboration's work in the face of shocks and shifts. Even so, MetroGIS remains vulnerable because it has never been able to secure a cost-sharing agreement from participating governments and remains reliant on grants and funding from the MC.

Rotary International is itself a blend of hierarchical and network structure. Local clubs have considerable autonomy, but organizational policy and grand strategy are determined by the Rotary International Board and carried out by a president and secretariat; district-level structures govern regional groups of clubs. The structure of the organization and of the PolioPlus campaign offers paths for mutual influence between top decision makers and club members.

Rotary leaders established numerous formal partnerships with large, bureaucratic UN agencies and governments. Meanwhile, the worldwide network of Rotarians used their connections, credibility, and zeal to influence their government officials, fellow professionals, and donors.

A practice related to maintaining structural flexibility involves managing the blend of diversity and unity within boundary groups. Although leaders of cross-boundary collaborations seek to build shared vision and commitment through boundary experiences, they benefit from recognizing that some degree of diversity is both desirable and unavoidable. Most participants in the collaboration will still have ties of loyalty and responsibility to their own organizations, sectors, cultures, and communities, and, indeed, their different ties, perspectives, and knowledge bases are prime resources in the collaboration's ongoing work. Collaboration leaders also should recognize the need for affirming some boundaries between groups, since they are likely to resist efforts to submerge their identity or dilute their power. The most effective collaborations create a supra-identity that all collaboration participants can claim; they also accept that participants have other identities and loyalties (Ernst & Chrobot-Mason, 2011).

By establishing the Policy Board and Technical Advisory Team, MetroGIS architects provided opportunities for diverse stakeholders to share an interest in advancing MetroGIS along with their service as officials, senior managers, or technical experts. Randall Johnson was an important link between the two groups.

In the PolioPlus case, division of labor was an important mechanism for managing diverse competencies within the shared mission of polio eradication. In organizing National Immunization Days, a partner like the U.S. Centers for Disease Control and Prevention could provide trained epidemiologists and virologists to understand and monitor the spread of polio cases, while Rotary leaders could take responsibility for supplying volunteers, funding, and political support.

Outcomes and Accountabilities

Leaders seeking to develop effective cross-sector collaborations must have means of assessing outcomes and feeding assessment data back to people carrying out the collaboration's activities so they can make adequate midcourse corrections. These assessments can hold particular people or organizations accountable through the practices associated with design and use of courts.

PRACTICE: ASSESSING OUTCOMES AND MANAGING RESULTS

In both cases, an important leadership practice was assessing outcomes and figuring out what to do about results. In MetroGIS, the GIS liaison and his staff, along with other partners, continually collect information from system users to ensure the system is meeting their needs and to invent new applications. They have always been mindful to demonstrate the effectiveness of MetroGIS, although the audit forced them to do an explicit cost-benefit analysis of inputs compared to outcomes.

In the PolioPlus campaign, the criterion for declaring a country polio-free is very precise—a reliable surveillance program must find no cases of polio for three consecutive years. In the initial stage of the campaign, organizers learned the only true way to eradicate polio was to develop a reporting network that would report every single incidence of the disease. The campaign developed a results management system that promoted routine immunization and national immunization days and used surveillance data to target regions with residual cases of polio.

Implications for Leadership Development

Formal and informal leadership development programs or experiences should focus on developing the personal and group assets, skills, and habits that promote the practices highlighted in the previous section. Day, Harrison, and Halpin (2009) suggest that effective leadership development experiences integrate understandings of human development, identity, and expertise. They, like other scholars (Crosby & Bryson, 2005; Hooijberg, Hunt, & Dodge, 1997), recognize that to be effective in today's interdependent, complex organizational and social worlds, leaders require cognitive, social, and behavioral complexity. (Behavioral complexity is the ability to draw on cognitive and social skills appropriately in a particular situation.) These requirements seem even more important for people engaged in public integrative leadership. Developing such complexity requires self-understanding, as well as understanding of self in relation to others (Avolio & Luthans, 2006; Day et al., 2009). It requires the ability to engage in critical and integrative thinking (Martin, 2002) and make reflective judgments. Important social skills include the ability to gauge and regulate one's and others' emotions and to promote shared identity and a sense of high-performing possible selves among followers (Day et al., 2009; Pittinsky, 2009).

Key elements of programs aimed at developing effective integrative public leaders include self-awareness and moral reflection, and skill development and practice.

Self-Awareness and Moral Reflection

Participants should have the opportunity to identify and evaluate personal passions or commitments (Crosby & Bryson, 2005), a practice that resonates with the understanding of moral development emphasized by Day, Harrison, and Halpin (2009), Stephen Brookfield's narrative of commitment, and Marshall Ganz's (2008) public narrative. Participants should identify other personal assets and liabilities that help or hinder boundary-crossing work. For example, they might be prompted to ask themselves: Which professional expertise—such as the GIS liaison's planning experience or some Rotarians' medical experience—do I have that allows me to move across geography, sector, or culture with legitimacy? What formal or informal experiences—such as international travel or multisector employment/volunteer experiences—do I have that allow me to understand other cultures or sectors? What networks do I have that I can rely on for support? Do I have a generally optimistic view of the possibility of joining with others to tackle complex public challenges? What lessons can I learn from previous experiences leading across boundaries? What intentions do I have for engaging in cross-boundary experiences or acquiring other assets needed for my leadership work?

Skill Development and Practice

Participants should have opportunities through role plays, simulations, or action learning projects (see Raelin, 2006) to practice skills involved in diagnosing context, creating inclusive and flexible processes and structures, and assessing outcomes and managing results. Instructors should explain or demonstrate conceptual frameworks, tools, and techniques for employing these skills. They engage in reflection on what worked and what didn't in these learning experiences. Program instructors should build in assessment and feedback at various points of the learning process and highlight the importance of learning from feedback and reflection (Day et al., 2009; Van Velsor & McCauley, 2004).

Conclusion

A number of conclusions emerge from this examination of public integrative leadership. First, active and engaged sponsors and champions are crucial for the creation and effective operation of cross-boundary collaborations. Second, focusing on leadership practices directs attention to what groups of people actually and regularly do in particular settings and across settings. What people actually do is a blend of intentionality and design, affective response and strategic behavior, engagement in task accomplishment and socioemotional maintenance, identity creation and identity change, and so on. What people—and especially sponsors and champions—do is often quite complex and multifunctional; that very complexity and multifunctionality merits attention. A practice focus draws attention to the multiple and complex behaviors of leaders as they draw on and build (or perhaps diminish) human, intellectual, social, and political capital in pursuit of collaboration purposes.

Third, leadership in cross-sector collaborations involves managing often complex arrangements of hierarchy and lateral relationships. This calls for a kind of ambidexterity —again, especially on the part of sponsors and champions—that requires cognitive, behavioral, social, and political skill sets that are both demanding and probably unusual. Again, a practice focus draws attention to this.

Research on public integrative leadership and related topics such as collaborative public management continues to advance. Cases of successful and unsuccessful public integrative leadership continue to be documented; they focus mainly on successful endeavors. In the interest of balanced learning, researchers should increase their attention to failures. Published research in this area tends to be conducted by U.S. and European scholars. Ideally, scholars from elsewhere will become more involved and perhaps partner with their U.S. and European counterparts; scholars themselves are likely to benefit from working together across boundaries. Attention to China, India, Brazil, and the Middle East seems especially warranted due to these regions' impact on global affairs. More empirical studies might be done to test the propositions about public integrative leadership drawn from case studies (see Crosby & Bryson, 2010). The role of 21st-century computer and web-based technology in facilitating integrative leadership also merits considerable further research (see Brown & Adler, 2008; and Bryson, Crosby, Stone, & Saunoi-Sandgren, 2011; Shirky, 2008).

Future Directions

Some specific questions for future research would be:

- What are suitable measures for testing the propositions generated by Bryson, Crosby, and Stone (2006)?
- How do sponsors and champions of integrative work influence each other, and how can they work together most effectively?
- What distinguishes failed cases of public integrative leadership from successful ones?
- What are the distinguishing characteristics of public integrative leadership in China (India, Brazil, the Middle East)?
- How do social media facilitate and hinder public integrative leadership?

Note

1. In the management literature, Feldman and Pentland (2008: 302–303) have developed this idea in relation to a particular kind of practice: routines. They refer to the *ostensive* aspects of a routine-as-entity as the abstract patterns formed out of many performances. They refer to the *performative* aspects as what we observe: "real actions, by real people, in specific times and places." Of course, the ostensive and performative aspects are linked: The ostensive parts "are the embodied understandings of the routine that we act out in specific instances... [T]hey guide performances, and are used to account for and refer to performances." The performative parts "create, maintain, and modify the ostensive aspects of the routine." In other words, actual performances can change what we think of as the "routine in principle" (ibid.; see also Feldman & Pentland, 2003, 2005).

References

Akkerman, S. F., & Bakker, A. (2011). Boundary crossing and boundary objects. *Review of Educational Research, 81*(2), 132–169.

Avolio, B. J., & Luthans, F. (2006). *The High Impact Leader: Moments Matter in Accelerating Authentic Leadership Development.* New York: McGraw Hill.

Barzelay, M., & Thompson, F. (2010). Back to the future: Making public administration a design science. *Public Administration Review, 70*(Supplement 1), S295–S297.

Bingham, L. B., & O'Leary, R. (2008). *Big Ideas in Collaborative Public Management.* Armonk, NY: M.E. Sharpe, Inc.

Bono, J. E., Shen, W., & Snyder, M. (2010). Fostering integrative community leadership. *Leadership Quarterly, 21*(2), 324–335.

Brown, J. S., & Adler, R. P. (2008). Minds on fire: Open education, the long tail, and learning 2.0. *EDUCAUSE Review,* January/February, 17–32.

Bryson, J. M. (2004). What to do when stakeholders matter: Stakeholder identification and analysis techniques. *Public Management Review, 6*(1), 21–53.

Bryson, J. M., Ackermann, F., Eden, C., & Finn, C. (2004). *Visible Thinking: Unlocking Causal Mapping for Practical Business Results.* New York: Wiley.

Bryson, J. M., Crosby, B. C., & Bryson, J. K. (2009). Understanding strategic planning and the formulation and implementation of strategic plans as a way of knowing: The contributions of actor-network theory. *International Public Management Journal, 12*(2), 172–207.

Bryson, J. M., Crosby, B. C., & Stone, M. M. (2006). The design and implementation of cross-sector collaborations: Propositions from the literature. *Public Administration Review, 66*(s1), 44–55.

Bryson, J. M., Crosby, B. C., Stone, M. M., & Saunoi-Sandgren, E. (June 2-4, 2011). *Dynamics of cross-sector collaboration: Minnesota's Urban Partnership Agreement from start to finish.* Syracuse, New York: Paper presented at the National Public Management Research Conference, Maxwell School of Citizenship and Public Affairs, Syracuse University.

Carlile, P. R. (2002). A pragmatic view of knowledge and boundaries: Boundary objects in new product development. *Organization Science, 13*(4), 442–455.

Carlile, P. R. (2004). Transferring, translating, and transforming: An integrative framework for managing knowledge across boundaries. *Organization Science, 15*(5), 555–568.

Corley, K. G., & Gioia, D. A. (2011). Building theory about theory building: What constitutes a theoretical contribution? *Academy of Management Review, 36*(1), 12–32.

Crane, A., McWilliams, A., Matten, D., & Moon, J. (Eds.). (2008). *Oxford Handbook of Corporate Social Responsibility.* Oxford: Oxford University Press.

Crosby, B. C., & Bryson, J. M. (2005). *Leadership for the Common Good: Tackling Public Problems in a Shared-Power World*. San Francisco, CA: Jossey-Bass.

Crosby, B. C., & Bryson, J. M. (2010). Integrative leadership and the creation and maintenance of cross-sector collaborations *Leadership Quarterly, 21*(2), 211–230.

Crosby, B. C., & Bryson, J. M. (2012). Integrative leadership and policy change: A hybrid relational view In S. Ospina, & M. Uhl-Bien (Eds.), *Advancing Relational Leadership Theory: A Conversation Among Perspectives*. Charlotte, NC: Information Age Publishing.

Day, D. V., Harrison, M. M., & Halpin, S. M. (2009). *An Integrative Approach to Leader Development: Connecting Adult Development, Identity, and Expertise*. New York: Routledge.

Egginton, M., & Sandbothe, M. (2004). *The Pragmatic Turn in Philosophy*. Albany, NY: SUNY Press.

Ernst, C., & Chrobot-Mason, D. (2011). *Boundary Spanning Leadership*. New York: McGraw Hill.

Feldman, M. S., & Khademian, A. M. (2000). Managing for inclusion: Balancing control and participation. *International Journal of Public Management, 3*(2), 149–168.

Feldman, M. S., & Khademian, A. M. (2007). The role of the public manager in inclusion: Creating communities of participation. *Governance, 20*(2), 305–324.

Feldman, M. S., Khademian, A. M., Ingram, H., & Schneider, A. S. (2006). Ways of knowing and inclusive management practices. *Public Administration Review, 66*, 89–99.

Feldman, M. S., & Pentland, B. T. (2003). Reconceptualizing organizational routines as a source of flexibility and change. *Administrative Science Quarterly, 48*, 94–118.

Feldman, M., & Pentland, B. (2005). Organizational routines and the macro-actor. In B. Czarniawska & T. Hernes (Eds.), *Actor-Network Theory and Organizing* (pp. 91–111). Malmo, Sweden: Elanders Berling.

Feldman, M. S., & Pentland, B. T. (2008). Routine dynamics. In D. Barry & H. Hansen (Eds.), *The SAGE Handbook of New Approaches in Management and Organization* (pp. 302–315). London: SAGE Publications Ltd.

Fernandez, S., Cho, Y. J., & Perry, J. L. (2010). Exploring the link between integrated leadership and public sector performance. *Leadership Quarterly, 21*(2), 308–323.

Fiol, C. M. (2001). Revisiting an identity-based view of sustainable competitive advantage. *Journal of Management, 27*, 691–699.

Fletcher, J. K., & Kaüfer, K. (2003). Shared leadership: Paradox and possibility. In C. L. Pearce & J. A. Conger (Eds.), *Shared Leadership: Reframing the Hows and Whys of Leadership*. Thousand Oaks, CA: Sage.

Forester, J. (1999). *The Deliberative Practitioner*. Cambridge, MA: MIT Press.

Ganz, M. (2008). What Is Public Narrative? Retrieved July 12, 2011, from http://grassrootsfund.org/docs/WhatIsPublicNarrative08

Gerencser, M., Van Lee, R., Napolitano, F., & Kelly, C. (2008). *Megacommunities: How Leaders of Government, Business and Non-Profits Can Tackle Today's Global Challenges Together*. New York: Palgrave Macmillan.

Healey, P. (2006). *Collaborative Planning: Shaping Places in Fragmented Societies*. 2nd ed. London: Palgrave Macmillan.

Hooijberg, R., Hunt, J. G., & Dodge, G. E. (1997). Leadership complexity and development of the leaderplex model. *Journal of Management, 23*(3), 37–408.

Innes, J. E., & Booher, D. E. (2010). *Planning with Complexity: An Introduction to Collaborative Rationality for Public Policy*. New York: Routledge.

Jarzabkowski, P. (2005). *Strategy as Practice: An Activity-Based Approach*. London: SAGE Publications.

Johnson, G., Langley, A., Melin, L., & Whittington, R. (2007). *Strategy as Practice: Research Directions and Resources*. New York: Cambridge University Press.

Kellogg, K. C., Orlikowski, W. J., & Yates, J. (2006). Life in the trading zone: Structuring coordination across boundaries in postbureaucratic organizations. *Organization Science, 17*(1), 22–44.

Kingdon, J. W. (2003). *Agendas, Alternatives, and Public Policies*. 2nd ed. New York: Harper Collins.

Latour, B. (2005). *Reassembling the Social*. New York: Oxford University Press.

Mandell, M. P., & Keast, R. (June 2011). *Strategic Leveraging: A Revised Framework of Managing Strategically in Collaborative Networks*. Newark, NJ: 7th Trans-Atlantic Dialogue Conference.

Martin, R. (2002). Integrative thinking: A model takes shape. *Rotman Management*, Fall, 8–11.

Menand, L. (2001). *The Metaphysical Club: A Story of Ideas in America*. New York: Farrar, Strauss, and Giroux.

Moosty, P. R. (2010). *Rotary International Polio Eradication: A Case Study in Integrative Leadership*. Minneapolis: Center for Integrative Leadership, University of Minnesota.

Morse, R. (2010). Integrative public leadership: Catalyzing collaboration to create public value. *Leadership Quarterly, 21*(2), 231–245.

Morse, R. S., Buss, T. F., & Kinghorn, C. M. (Eds.). (2007). *Transforming Public Leadership for the 21st Century*. Armonk, NY: M. E. Sharpe.

Nelson, M. C. (2008). *How We Lead Matters: Reflections on a Life of Leadership*. New York: McGrawHill.

Nicolini, D., Gherardi, S., & Yanow, D. (2003). *Knowing in Organizations: A Practice-Based Approach*. Armonk, NY: M. E. Sharpe.

O'Leary, R., & Bingham, L. B. (Eds.) (2009). *The Collaborative Public Manager*. Washington, DC: Georgetown University Press.

Osborne, S. P. (2010). *The New Public Governance?* New York: Routledge.

Ospina, S., & Foldy, E. (2010). Building bridges from the margins: The work of leadership in social change organizations. *Leadership Quarterly*, 292–307.

Page, S. (2010). Integrative leadership for collaborative governance: Civic engagement in Seattle. *Leadership Quarterly, 21*(2), 246–263.

Pittinsky, T. L. (Ed.). (2009). *Crossing the Divide: Intergroup Leadership in a World of Difference*. Boston: Harvard Business Press.

Raelin, J. A. (2006). Does action learning promote collaborative leadership? *Academy of Management Learning & Education, 5*(2), 152–168.

Reckwitz, A. (2002). The status of the "material" in theories of culture: From "social structure" to "artifacts." *Journal for the Theory of Social Behaviour, 32*(2), 195–217.

Redekop, B. W. (2010). Physicians to a dying planet: Helen Caldicott, Randall Forsberg, and the anti-nuclear weapons movement of the early 1980s. *Leadership Quarterly, 21*(2), 278–291.

Scharmer, C. O. (2009). *Theory U: Leading from the Future as It Emerges*. San Francisco: Berrett-Koehler.

Schatzki, T. (1996). *Social Practices: A Wittgensteinian Approach to Human Activity*. Cambridge: Cambridge University Press.

Schatzki, T. R., Knorr-Cetina, K., & Savigny, E. (2001). *The Practice Turn in Contemporary Theory*. London, New York: Routledge.
Schein, E. H. (2010). *Organizational Culture and Leadership*. San Francisco: Jossey-Bass.
Scherer, A. G., & Palazzo, G. (2007). Toward a political conception of corporate responsibility: Business and society seen from a Habermasian perspective. *Academy of Management Review, 32*(4), 1096–1120.
Schön, D. (1987). *Educating the Reflective Practitioner*. San Francisco: Jossey-Bass.
Senge, P. M., Smith, B., Schley, S., & Laur, J. (2008). *The Necessary Revolution: How Individuals and Organizations Are Working Together to Create a Sustainable World*. New York: Doubleday.
Sennett, R. (2008). *The Craftsman*. New Haven, CT: Yale University Press.
Shirky, C. (2008). *Here Comes Everybody: The Power of Organizing Without Organizations*. New York: Penguin.
Shove, E., Watson, M., Hand, M., & Ingram, J. (2007). *The Design of Everyday Life*. New York: Berg.
Silvia, C., & McGuire, M. (2010). Leading public sector networks: An empirical examination of integrative leadership behaviors. *Leadership Quarterly, 21*(2), 264–277.
Star, S. L., & Griesemer, J. R. (1989). Institutional ecology, "translations" and boundary objects: Amateurs and professionals in Berkeley's museum of vertebrate zoology, 1907–39. *Social Studies of Science, 19*(3), 387–420.
Stone, M. M., Crosby, B. C., & Bryson, J. M. (2010). Governing public-nonprofit collaborations: Understanding their complexity and the implications for research. *Voluntary Sector Review, 1*(3), 309–334.
Sydow, J., Lerch, F., Huxham, C., & Hibbert, P. (2011). A silent cry for leadership: organizing for leading (in) clusters. *Leadership Quarterly, 22*(2), 328–343.
Taylor, A., Cocklin, C., Brown, R., & Wilson-Evered, E. (2011). An investigation of champion-driven leadership processes. *Leadership Quarterly, 22*(2), 412–433.
Van Velsor, E., & McCauley, C. D. (2004). Our view of leadership development. In C. D. McCauley, & E. Van Velsor (Eds.), *Center for Creative Leadership Handbook for Leadership Development*. 2nd ed. (pp. 1–22). San Francisco: Jossey-Bass.
Waddock, S. (2007). Leadership integrity in a fractured knowledge world. *Academy of Management Learning & Education, 6*(4), 543–557.
Weick, K. E., Sutcliffe, K. M., & Obstfeld, D. (2005). Organizing and the process of sensemaking. *Organization Science, 16*(4), 409–421.
Wenger, E. (1998). *Communities of Practice: Learning, Meaning, and Identity*. Cambridge: Cambridge University Press.

CHAPTER

5 The Biology of Leadership

Richard D. Arvey, Nan Wang, Zhaoli Song, *and* Wendong Li

Abstract

Scholars are beginning to recognize important biological elements that may influence those who move into leadership positions and who are effective in such roles (Arvey, Rotundo, Johnson, Zhang, & McGue, 2006; Balthazard, Waldman, Thatcher, & Hannah, 2012). Although consistent with the general "trait" model of individual differences as influencing leadership emergence and effectiveness, other biologically based influences also may play a similar role in determining those who move into and are effective in such leadership capacities. A growing literature on the role of biological factors has not yet been abstracted and summarized. It is the aim of this chapter to provide a succinct and useful summary of the various biological factors that have been identified as being associated with various leadership criteria and to provide directions for future research in these areas.

Key Words: leadership, biology, evolution, gene, environment, hormones, cognitive neuroscience

This chapter reviews literatures associated with a number of biological factors and research themes dealing with the topic of leadership. We cover research domains including evolutionary psychology; behavioral genetics; physical factors; hormonal, neurological, and brain functioning; and comparative studies with animals. This list represents a relatively large scope and although we wish to be comprehensive, our review is somewhat selectively narrowed due to the relatively small number of studies dealing with leadership issues across these domains. These areas of research often go unlinked, suggesting that such efforts are marching down their own, separate paths. As such, we attempt to find relevant connections and points of conversion. In addition, we deal with leadership that is defined rather loosely, as the term is typically used differently across the studies we review. Van Vugt, Hogan, and Kaiser (2008) considered leadership as both a resource for groups and an attribute of individuals, one whose primary significance concerns group performance. At a basic level, we use the term "leadership" as signifying one person exerting influence on followers to achieve certain kind of goals, but we also embrace the view that leadership is sometimes viewed as role-inherent. That is, people in formal management roles, in which they are supervising the work of others, are also considered "leaders" by nature of the power and authority invested in these "leadership positions." This notion is consistent with the view expressed by Bass (1990: 19), who says that people in such role positions "lead as a consequence of their status—the power of the position they occupy." This construal of leadership is also consistent with various empirical studies that define leadership from a role occupancy perspective. For example, Day, Sin, and Chen (2004) used the team captain position of professional (National Hockey League) teams as indicative of leadership role occupancy and studied the impact of role occupancy on later individual performance. The authors also pointed out that being appointed as an NHL team captain conferred special leadership privileges on those role occupants.

Why Examine Biological Processes in Leadership?

There is evidence that the recognition and incorporation of biological constructs and variables in theorizing and research in organizational behavior is mounting. Research is being published in top-tier journals about the role of genetics, hormones, physiological variables, evolutionary processes, and the like on organizational behavior (e.g., Arvey, Bouchard, Segal, & Abraham, 1989; Judge & Cable, 2004; Zyphur, Narayanan, Koh, & Koh, 2009). Thus, variables such as job satisfaction, vocational choices, decision making, and the like, which are somewhat under the influence of biological factors, are making their way into our literatures. This is not happening without resistance. Colarelli and Arvey (in preparation) make the observation that traditional scholars in the field of organizational behavior continue the tradition that organizational behavior can be "managed," working under mechanistic models of rationality, conscious, deliberation, and volition. The notion that biological elements could be involved somewhat violates this basic cognitive model of behavior. Moreover, most scholars maintained the belief that much of the variation in human behavior was due to environmental factors, such as developmental experiences and interventions, as well as to culture—what Cosmides and Tooby (1992) call the *standard social science model.* This model was developed out of the behaviorism model popularized by Watson in the 1920s (Watson, 1913, 1928).

Although it is now recognized that biological factors are indeed involved in organizational behavior, there is also a growing literature focusing on biological influences on the discipline of leadership. Such biological features may represent both barriers and enhancements in terms of one's likelihood of emerging as a leader and of being effective as a leader. Thus, our review summarizes these various biological features. It is important to recognize at the outset that we are not arguing that leadership is entirely due to biological factors. Indeed, the evidence presented will show that such factors are associated but, with a few exceptions, not highly coupled with leadership emergence and effectiveness.

Before we delve into a review of previous research, we discuss a question many people may ask: How can a biological perspective contribute to leadership research in general?

Leadership research has long recognized that a person's traits (e.g., general mental ability, personality, values, and physical features) play a critical role in leadership emergence and leadership effectiveness. Incorporating a biological perspective can enhance our understanding of the nature of the leader, the environment to which a leader is attracted and/or selected in (e.g., leadership experience), and how the leader and the environment interdependently shape leadership effectiveness.

First, a biological perspective of leadership can contribute to leadership research by promoting our understanding of the very nature of the person, beyond simply looking at leader traits. State-of-the-art technological developments in biology, neuroscience, and genetics allow us to tap into a leader's brain function, neurotransmitter activities, and genetic architecture. These new technologies have been widely used in such social sciences as economics, sociology, political science, and social and personality psychology. Leadership research can surely benefit from capitalizing on these developments.

Second, a biological perspective can also shed light on a deeper understanding of a leader's environment. For instance, research on leader development investigates how challenge experiences promote a leader's development of his capabilities. However, these challenge experiences are not entirely environmental: Leaders are likely to self-select or be selected into environments corresponding to their biological architecture. Incorporating a biological perspective could help tease apart biological influences on environmental factors and provide a deeper understanding of the relationship between putative environmental factors and leader development. Third, a biological perspective provides us ample opportunities to examine the interplay between the person and the environment in general. The notion that human behaviors are shaped by both the person and the environment has long been accepted in the organizational behavior area, yet extant research has predominantly used personality traits as a manifestation of the person. However, personality traits are also prone to environmental influence. A biological perspective, especially a molecular genetics approach focusing on the effect of specific genes, can carry forward the stream of research focusing on the interplay between person and environment. In the next sections, we review a range of biological approaches.

Evolutionary Approaches

It is a universal given that leadership positions exist and that these positions are filled by someone. Such leadership roles are required for the direction of and planning for "followers," for the swift execution of tasks, for the provision of resources, and more. Van Vugt, Hogan, and Kaiser (2008) and King, Johnson, and Van Vugt (2009) present evolutionary perspectives on leadership. These authors essentially reflect on two major issues: the origins of leadership (how did the need for leadership arise?) and the characteristics of individuals who move into these leadership roles. Both studies suggest that leadership arose in the context of both followers and leaders needing to adapt and compromise in order to maximize their gains for survival. For example, King et al. (2009) noted that cooperation and collaborations within animal or early human groups are of crucial importance for the efficiency and survival of the whole group, but that order is seldom acquired without a leader. Thus, King et al. (2009) suggest that the key to the emergence of leadership and followership was (and is) the need to coordinate and that the need for such coordination began quite early in the history of humans, who faced severe challenges from a primitive and dangerous world, and who needed to acquire basic resources (e.g., food, shelter, etc.). Game theory analyses are cited as supporting the need for coordination between leaders and followers. Because the need for leadership promoted the survival of our forbearers, it became part of our evolved psychology. Thus, there is almost universal societal recognition of the need for leaders and the acceptance of individuals who move into these roles.

Both King et al. (2009) and Van Vugt et al. (2008) outline the stages in human history for which different types of leadership existed to meet the conditions encountered in the environment. Van Vugt et al. (2008) describe four different stages (i.e., pre-human leadership (stage 1), band and tribal leadership (stage 2), chefs, kings and warlords (stage 3), state and business leadership (stage 4)) under which the kind of leadership involved differed substantially. King et al. (2009) suggest five major transitions in the evolution of human leadership: (1) leadership emerged in prehuman species as a mechanism to solve simple group coordination problems, in which any individual initiated an action and others followed; (2) leadership was co-opted to foster collective action in situations involving significant conflicts of interest, in which dominant or socially important individuals evolved as leaders; (3) dominance was attenuated to pave the way for democratic and prestige-based leadership to facilitate group coordination; (4) the increase in human group size created the need to select leaders based on powerful social and cognitive mechanisms; and (5) the increase in social complexity produced the need for more powerful and formal leaders to manage complex relationships. Another factor, of course, is the increased complexity of the technical environment surrounding humans in business settings; this created the need for cognitively smart and socially adept leaders. Of note is that particular environments in our history were salient with regard to the need for adaptation among our ancestors. This is an important ingredient in the co-evolution of situations and leadership.

King et al. (2009) and Van Vugt et al. (2008) also articulate the kinds of leader characteristics that are implicated in their evolutionary analyses. The typical suspects of personality traits (e.g. extraversion, dominance), social skills (e.g., perceiving the needs of followers), physical factors (i.e., height, weight, health), and motivation are suggested.

In summary, these two articles provide provocative perspectives on how leadership roles and the characteristics of leaders (and followers) evolved in the context of different situations. They pave the way for the rest of our chapter by providing a nice starting point and in laying a foundation for other literatures.

Animal Studies of Leadership

Much of the literature on human evolutionary processes refers to associated research on animals. The argument is that animal behavior was and is shaped by evolutionary processes, and similar processes were most probably operative for humans as well. The Discovery Channel and other media are replete with examples of the competition between males for mates, the role of dominance in the animal kingdom, and the like (although these accounts often describe competition for mates, rather than leadership).

The scientific literature also contains similar and fascinating material regarding leadership in animals. A variety of studies examine the phenomenon of leadership existence and of individuals exhibiting leadership among the species studied, as well as the factors that seem to be correlated with leadership. For example, a relatively early study by Allee, Allee, Ritchey, and Castles (1947) showed that there was some (but not complete) consistency in the leadership of a flock of white ducks, as indicated by which ducks generally were in front of others in going out the door of a duck house and going to food. Rabb, Woolpy, and Ginsburg (1967) observed the social organization of a group of wolves in an outdoor enclosure over several breeding seasons. They found the more dominant animals restricted the courtship activities of inferior wolves of their own sex.

Among some studies, personality factors, knowledge, and information, as well as environmental conditions appear to influence the likelihood of certain animals taking on leadership roles. For example, Kurvers et al. (2009) studied barnacle geese and showed that a leadership score (i.e., marking when the goose arrived at a food patch when matched against other geese) was significantly correlated with a variable called "novel object," which represented whether the goose would be relatively fast or slow in moving toward an object of unknown status. Other studies found that information could be crucial. Using minnows, Reebs (2000, 2001) showed that a small minority of informed individual fish would lead others to food at the right place and time of day and that such behavior was a function of body size and experience. Similar results were found by Leblond and Reebs (2006). Other animals such as elephants (Foley, Pettorelli, & Foley, 2008), ravens (Wright, Stone, & Brown, 2003), and hawks (Maransky & Bildstein, 2001) have been similarly identified as leaders as a function of being better informed and able to lead followers to resources. More generally, King et al. (2009: R912) observed that, across species, "individuals are more likely to emerge as leaders if they have a particular morphological, physiological, or behavioral trait increasing their propensity to act first in coordination problems." They remark that motivation, temperament, dominance, and knowledge are factors that increase the likelihood of individuals emerging as leaders among animal groups. Moreover, Hofmann, Benson, and Fernald (1999) studied the consistency of social status (measured by whether a fish was under threatening or nonthreatening conditions) among African cichlid fish as a function of changes in the environment, and their data indicated that changes in social status were a function of several underlying environmental conditions.

These and other articles generally provide evidence about leadership in the animal kingdom. Several themes fall out: (1) there is certainly evidence for leader–follower relationships; (2) particular individuals take on leadership roles; (3) some correlates exist between leadership and certain characteristics (i.e., body size, dominance, experience, etc.), although there is some evidence that the individuals that take on such roles are not always consistent across time and/or tasks; and (4) there appears to be some evidence that environmental factors influence which and when individuals take up leadership roles (e.g., environmental turbulence, particular task involved). These are also familiar themes in the literature pertaining to leadership among humans.

Genetic Factors

There are strong opinions regarding the degree to which leadership has a genetic basis compared to various environmental and developmental factors. For example, Sorcher and Brant (2002: 81) hold that "our experience has led us to believe that much of leadership talent is hardwired in people before they reach their early or mid-twenties." Conversely, Kellaway (2002) reports the efforts of a major bank to develop all of its employees (95,000 of them) into leaders, reflecting the belief that leadership is predominately influenced by developmental factors.

Methods to Examine the Genetic Influence

There is, however, growing evidence that genetic factors are associated with leadership. What was once an intractable problem of separating the impact of environments from genetic factors on particular variables of interest has now been solved via behavioral genetics methodologies using twin samples. The observation that talent or "leadership" runs in the family is frequently made, and there are certain well-known examples of this, particularly in political contexts (e.g., the Bush or Kennedy families). However, families have both common genetic endowments and common environments. The use of twin samples allows researchers to estimate the separate influences of both genetics and environments on observed or latent variables. Several methodologies are involved. The first method is to calculate the similarity of monozygotic (MZ) twins reared apart. Because this type of twins has 100 percent of their genes in common, but were raised in (presumably) different environments, a measure of similarity (i.e., the intraclass correlation coefficient) gives a direct estimate of the proportion of variance accounted for by genetics (or the heritability). Arvey, Bouchard, Segal, and Abrahams (1989) used this methodology to estimate the heritability of job satisfaction, showing that about 30 percent of the variance in overall job satisfaction can be accounted for by genetic factors.

Because obtaining samples of MZ (identical) twins reared apart is difficult, and such twin pairs are rare, an alternate methodology uses mono- and dizygotic (DZ, or fraternal) twins as samples. Because MZ twins hold 100 percent of their genes in common, whereas DZ twins hold on average only 50 percent of their genes in common, greater similarity among the MZ twins on the variable of interest compared to the DZ twins indicates that genetic factors are operative. The assumption here is that the twin pairs were raised in common environments (e.g., same father and mother, housing, income levels, etc.). This methodology basically allows for variation in the genetic makeup of the two types of twin pairs, but with a common shared environment (at least when growing up); conversely, in reared-apart twin studies, the variation is in the environment, with the genetic factors held constant. Examples of the use of this methodology are studies by Arvey, McCall, Bouchard, Taubman, and Cavanaugh (1994) on work values, and by McCall, Cavanaugh, Arvey and Taubman (1997) on job switching (see Ilies, Arvey, and Bouchard [2006] for a review of this research).

The assumption that MZ and DZ twins (within each pair) share a common environment (the equal environment assumption or EEA) is frequently challenged, and it is worthwhile commenting on this issue. There is some research testing the hypothesis that environmental similarity would affect twin similarity for the construct or behavior of interest. The issue is not necessarily that MZ twins experience more similar environments than do DZ twins, but whether such similarity is related to what is being studied. This assumption has been tested with personality. Borkenau, Riemann, Angleitner, and Spinath (2002) showed that MZ twins reported more similar experiences than did DZ twins but that treatment similarity was unrelated to personality resemblance. More relevant to the research on leadership reviewed here, using the male sample of MZ and DZ twins described by Arvey, Rotundo, Johnson, Zhang, and McGue (2006), Zhang (unpublished data analysis) found that although the MZ twins were indeed more similar when describing their parental environment than were DZ twins, this stronger resemblance was unrelated to any resemblance with regard to the leadership variable used in this study (leadership role occupancy). These data are consistent with the statement by Plomin et al. (2008: 79) that the "equal environments assumption has been tested in several ways and appears reasonable for most traits."

More sophisticated modeling procedures (structural equation modeling) now allow researchers to separate the factors that account for variance in a variable into three independent factors: *genetic factors* (A), the proportion of variance due to one's genetic background; *shared environmental factors* (C), the proportion of variance due to common influences from one's family and/or common experiences for both twins; and *nonshared environmental factors* (E), essentially, all possible exogenous events and developmental personal experiences that could influence the variable of interest. Behavioral genetics research has firmly established that almost every human attribute has some genetic influence (McGue & Bouchard Jr., 1998; Plomin, DeFries, McClearn, & McGuffin, 2008).

Several recent articles examine the influence of genetic factors on leadership. Before reviewing this literature, it is worthwhile understanding why there may be such a relationship. One helpful model is given in Figure 5.1, showing the potential pathways by which genes could exert an impact on leadership. This figure indicates that genetic factors may have both a direct effect on leadership, as well as operate indirectly through a variety of biological and psychological pathways. The question becomes: What empirical evidence is there for the role of genetics in relationship to leadership?

Evidence of Genetic Influences on Leadership

Several studies bear directly on this issue. An earlier study by Johnson, Vernon, McCarthy, Molson, Harris, and Jang (1998) used MZ and DZ twins to estimate the heritability of two leadership style measures—transformational and transactional leadership. Their results showed that, respectively, 48 and 59 percent of the variance of the transactional and transformational leadership measures were accounted for by genetic factors. A later study using these same subjects was reported by Johnson, Vernon, Harris, and Jang (2004) showing that a number of personality variables were likewise under considerable genetic influence and that the same genetic factors were involved in their influence on the leadership measures—a finding of genetic correlation. Another study examined the heritability of a particular personality variable—leadership potential—drawn from the California Psychological Inventory (CPI) comparing twins reared apart and twins reared together (Bouchard, McGue, Hur, & Horn, 1998). The data indicated that a substantial portion of the variance on this variable was heritable—about 49 percent.

Arvey, Rotundo, Johnson, Zhang, and McGue (2006) used 238 MZ male twins and 188 DZ male twins to examine the heritability of leadership role occupancy—that is, whether these individuals had

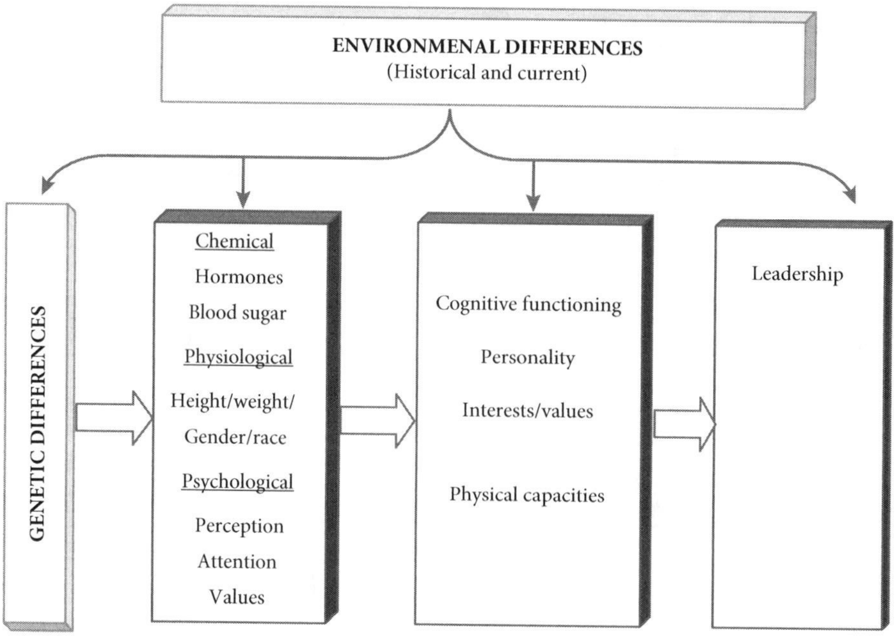

Figure 5.1. Pathways from Genes to Leadership.

moved up into leadership positions and the relative nature of these positions (i.e., whether they were in presidential, vice-presidential, director, supervisory roles). This variable is consistent with the definition of leadership having an "emergent" quality, in contrast to "leadership effectiveness" (see Judge, Bono, Ilies, & Gerhardt [2002] for an operational definition of these two broad types of leadership). The data indicated that the estimated genetic component on this leadership variable was 31 percent, whereas the remaining variance (69 percent) was accounted for by the nonshared environment. Interestingly, no influence was observed for the shared environmental factor, which is a consistent finding in the behavioral genetics domain—shared environment seems to play little or no role relative to genetic and nonshared environmental factors. Also measured were a number of personality variables (i.e., social potency, achievement) hypothesized to mediate the path between the genetic and leadership variables. Although both these personality factors were likewise shown to be under considerable genetic influence (54 percent and 43 percent of variance respectively), no mediation effects were detected due to low statistical power.

A similar study was conducted by Arvey, Zhang, Avolio, and Krueger (2007), this time using female twin samples. In this study, 178 DZ and 214 MZ female twins were investigated with regard to the heritability of leadership role occupancy. Findings were consistent with the previously cited male sample—a heritability of 32 percent was found. This study also examined more specifically what kinds of nonshared environmental factors were associated with the movement of these subjects into positions of leadership. Two broad general developmental factors were identified. One involved formal work experiences (e.g., training and development experiences, prior successes in leadership, unexpected opportunities), whereas the other factor was a more general family experience factor involving parents, siblings, and religious experiences. Although both these factors were correlated with the leadership role occupancy variable, when the genetic factor was parceled out, the work factor was significantly related to leadership role occupancy. Thus, this study suggests that, although people might attribute their success in becoming leaders to their families, their actual success might actually work through their common genetic backgrounds and developmental activities in work settings.

Using meta-analysis–derived correlations between the "big five" personality dimensions of emotional stability, extraversion, openness, agreeableness, and conscientiousness, and adding the dimension of intelligence, Ilies, Gerhardt, and Le (2004) estimated the genetic contribution to leadership emergence as mediated through these other variables. Their analyses indicated that approximately 17 percent of the variance of the latent construct of leadership emergence could be accounted for by genetics, as mediated through these personality and IQ variables. However, as noted earlier in other studies, the generally consistent value is about 30 percent, so other variables may also mediate the genetic–leadership linkage and/or there is a direct effect that is operative.

What is quite clear based on these studies is that a fairly powerful genetic component is associated with leadership emergence. However, equally clear is that environmental factors also play the major role in influence. Again, we do not argue a deterministic point of view on the part of "nature."[1]

Gene and Environmental Interplays

The finding that leadership has a fairly sizable genetic component is not particularly exciting at this stage of frontier research programs. As is evident from the literature abstracts cited earlier, recent research is looking at various, more complex models that incorporate both genetic and environmental factors.

The notion that there may be genetic and environmental *interactions* that are important to look at in studying leadership was suggested by Ilies, Arvey, and Bouchard (2006) and more recently by Zhang, Ilies, and Arvey (2009). Zhang et al. (2009: 118) state: "Apart from the main effects of genetics, the environmental and the developmental efforts stemming from the environment could have an active influence on the extent to which one capitalizes on his or her genetic endowments for leadership." Zhang et al. (2009) conducted one such study examining whether early family conflict (an environmental experience) would interact with genetic factors in influencing whether individuals moved into positions of leadership. They developed two possible scenarios: One possibility was that early conflict would act to allow greater genetic influence in leadership capacity; the other scenario was that a more benign (or enriched) early environment would permit greater genetic influence on later leadership emergence. Based on the same male twin sample used by Arvey et al. (2006), their data showed that, in terms of moving into leadership positions, genetic influences were weaker for twins reared in the more enriched family environments, but stronger for twins who had relatively poorer social environments. These data are consistent with those suggesting that challenge, adversity, and negative situations are the environmental developmental components that allow individuals to learn from these circumstances and become better equipped to move into leadership positions (e.g., Bennis, 1994; Coutu, 2002). A perplexing issue in examining such interaction is *which* specific component of the environment one should examine. There are an infinite number of specific environmental factors (e.g., work, family, school) that individuals experience in early and later life. What is needed is a better taxonomic system to further categorize such exogenous factors and to use theoretical frameworks to choose which to use in exploring such environmental–genetic interactions.

It is also useful to explore *gene–environmental correlations* in conducting further research on genetics and leadership. This posits the possibility that there may be a genetically based tendency for individuals either to seek out or avoid certain environments. At a broader level, Johnson (2007: 424) states that "the environment is not a unitary set of circumstances, and individuals' efforts to seek or create environments compatible with their genetic endowments are fundamental to the process of evolution." For example, it might be that individuals who are genetically predisposed to moving into leadership roles would seek out more challenging and complex work environments, whereas others who are not so predisposed might avoid such environments. Two studies looking at other workplace phenomenon demonstrate such a correlation. First, Arvey et al. (1989) showed that identical twins reared apart were working in similarly complex jobs—the heritability for job complexity was 0.44. Similarly, Hershberger, Lichtenstein, and Knox (1994) found descriptions of organizational climate, a variable thought to be almost entirely a function of environmental factors, was heritable. The upshot of this is that researchers must consider what kinds of environments individuals who become leaders are most attracted to. In addition, is it possible to engineer such environmental components early in development, so as to capitalize on these genetic tendencies for later movement into and effectiveness in leadership roles?

New Approaches to Study the Relationship Between Genetics and Leadership

Other types of designs incorporating longitudinal approaches could also have great value in studying genetic forces at play during developmental periods, and these kinds of designs have been used in other contexts. Although currently published findings on specific genes and their possible association with leadership variables are scarce, ongoing research does shed light on other variables often related to leadership. For example, the serotonin transporter gene 5-HTTLPR has been shown to be related to the stress resilience of individuals (e.g., Munafò, Brown, & Hariri, 2008). These findings lend support to promising future application of molecular genetics in leadership research. As a matter of fact, some initiatives demonstrating the value of molecular genetics in the organizational behavior paradigm are already under way. Song, Li, and Arvey, in their series of studies about molecular genetics and job satisfaction, have found some interesting results. One of their studies found statistically significant (although relatively weak) associations with job satisfaction between dopamine receptor gene DRD4 and serotonin transporter gene 5-HTTLPR, and that participants' level of pay mediated the relationship between DRD4 and job satisfaction (Song, Li & Arvey, 2011). A second study found the moderating effect of the DRD4 gene on the relationship between job complexity and job satisfaction. The relationship is stronger among people who have a larger number of the DRD4 7R gene. Also in this study, they found that job complexity partially mediated the relationship between the DRD4 gene and job satisfaction (Li, Song, & Arvey, unpublished). Meanwhile, another group of researchers has begun to investigate the genetic basis of leadership by combining twin studies with genetic association methodologies (De Neve, Mikhaylov, Dawes, Fowler, & Christakis, 2013).Thus, we expect more research examining specific genes and how they correlate—as well as interact—with other variables in influencing leadership.

Anthropomorphic Factors

If we borrow from evolutionary psychology and the comparative animal literature, we would suspect that a number of physical factors might be correlated with leadership. A number of studies have indicated positive relationships between various physical factors and leadership emergence and effectiveness. Bass and Bass (2008) provide a good review of many of these studies. The variables examined include height, weight, physique, health, athletic prowess, energy, and energy level.

With regard to height, accumulating evidence from general research suggests being taller has a number of positive outcomes for individuals. Bass et al. (2008) report a correlation of about 0.30 between height and leadership. A more recent meta-analysis by Judge and Cable (2004) showed that height was moderately correlated with leadership emergence (0.24) and leader performance (0.18), in addition to being significantly correlated with income and other psychological variables (e.g., self-esteem). Thus, although one cannot discount the potential impact of greater nutritional environments, the evidence clearly indicates a correlation between individual height and leadership.

When examining weight, some theorize that the relationships between this variable and a variety of success variables may differ by gender (see Judge & Cable, 2011). It is believed that, for males, those who weight more (up to the point of obesity) may be more successful than those who weigh less. For females, it seems that excessive weight is disadvantageous, but excessive thinness is disadvantageous as well.

Judge and Cable (2011) analyzed data from two large databases and generally confirmed the complex relationship of the impact of weight on income: Weight is generally positively related to income up to a particular weight level for men, and that weight is negatively related to income for women. However, we acknowledge here that the relationship between weight and income is probably much more complex than Judge and Cable's study claimed. Another study (Han, Norton, & Stearns, 2009) analyzed the same dataset (National Longitudinal Survey of Youth 1979) used by Judge and Cable (2011) but reached different conclusions. That study found a stronger negative relationship between body mass index (BMI) and wages in occupations requiring more interpersonal skills. For those beyond their mid-twenties, the negative relationship between BMI and wage is even stronger. Furthermore, they found that being overweight and obese tended to be associated with less income for all race–gender subgroups except black women and black men. Assuming leadership emergence is related to income, these results would probably generalize to the leadership domain.

Superior physique can also be an advantageous characteristic for leaders. Bass and Bass (2008) presented early studies showing small but reliable evidence for a relationship between physique and leadership variables. Most likely, such physical characteristics may facilitate leader role acquisition via the projection of a favorable image, although physique per se may not be specifically related to being a better leader. Studies show that people have stereotypes regarding particular body shapes (or "somatotypes"). For males, physical traits and strength are key factors in the evaluation of their masculinity and, subsequently, their fitness for leadership. For example, Gacsaly and Borges (1979) found that a well-muscled, sportsman-like body shape (a *mesomorph* body type in their study) was associated with more socially desirable personality traits, whereas a body build with more fat and less muscle (an *endomorph* body type) was associated with individuals who lack social skills as well as leadership capability.

According to a group of studies summarized in Bass and Bass (2008 [refer to p. 32]), leaders generally appear to be superior in health to nonleaders Early scholars (i.e., Stogdill, 1948) proposed that situational factors may be involved in the explanatory effectiveness of physical characteristics with regard to leadership. In situations where physical requirements are high, a relationship will be manifested. For example, in their study of male cadets at the U.S. Military Academy, Rice, Yoder, Adams, Priest, and Prince (1984) found significant positive relationship between physical fitness and leadership ability evaluations. Similarly, Atwater, Dionne, Avolio, Camobreco, and Lau (1999) tracked the leadership development of 236 males in a military college from matriculation to graduation and found that physical fitness measured early in the first year of college predicted leadership effectiveness in the fourth year.

Several studies present evidence that in boys' gangs and groups, athletic ability and physical prowess are related to leadership status (Bass & Bass, 2008). One later study by Atwater and Yammarinol (1993), studying midshipmen at the U.S. Naval Academy, found that athletic participation was an effective predictor of followers' ratings of transformational leadership.

A higher level of energy is also considered an important characteristic of leaders, who usually deal with heavy workloads (e.g., extensive travel, long hours.) and complex relationships. Five earlier studies summarized in Bass and Bass (2008) showed that those who emerge as leaders were generally characterized by high energy levels.

Another physical feature of interest to researchers studying leadership is physical appearance. In general, human beings show a preference for better looking faces. As early as infancy, such preferences are readily observable (e.g., Langlois et al., 1987). Physical attractiveness not only offers advantages in romantic relationships, but facilitates the acquisition of social status. Eleven studies reviewed in Bass and Bass (2008) found leaders to be better looking, although it should be noted that observed relationships between appearance and leadership are not unconditional. For example, students emphasize appearance more when choosing leaders for social activities compared to choosing leaders for intellectual and religious activities (Dunkerley, 1940). Furthermore, such a relationship may be more salient for boys than for girls in leadership contexts (Tryon, 1939). Moreover, facial appearance often serves to provide intuitive shortcuts for inferring individual competence in leader elections (e.g., Antonakis & Dalgas, 2009; Todorov, Mandisodza, Goren, & Hall, 2005). When asking a group of Swiss children to pick a leader from a pair of photos, Antonakis and Dalgas (2009) surprisingly found that children make predictions quite consistent with assumedly more rational and experienced adults. This may suggest that, as electors, we are subject to so-called *facial effects* more by nature than by nurture.

Appearance may also function differently under different conditions. Mazur et al. (1984) found that facial dominance of West Point cadets had a substantially positive relationship with cadet rank while at West Point but a weaker positive relationship with rank in military service 30 years later. Livingston and Pearce (2009) also showed that, despite its stereotyped correlation with immaturity and lack of competence, having a "baby face" nonetheless benefits black CEOs, as a "baby face is disarming" and makes them seem more trustworthy. Another interesting study showed that people prefer leaders to have more masculine faces when imagining their nation is under threat of war, whereas they are more accepting of feminine faces when imaging the nation in peace-keeping roles (Brian, Homan, Grabo, & Van Vugt, 2012; Spisak, Homan, Grabo, & Van Vugt, 2012). Despite the specific conditions in which the criteria of a preferable appearance may differ, the research evidence generally supports a relationship between appearance and leadership.

Endocrinology and Leadership

The endocrine system is made up of glands, each of which secretes a type of hormone into the bloodstream to regulate the body. Hormones are chemical mediators released from endocrine tissue that allow communication among cells and regulate many functions of an organism, including mood, growth and development, tissue function, and metabolism. Hormones generally act more slowly in controlling biological processes compared to their activity in the nervous system (Brown, 1994), but the endocrine system usually interacts closely with the nervous system. The study of such interactions is called *neuroendocrinology*. Neurotransmitters are mainly responsible for transmitting neural information.

Several types of important hormones and neurotransmitters are considered to demonstrate reliable influences on a variety of social behaviors and have been widely studied. Here, we focus on studies concerning testosterone, serotonin, and oxytocin as they pertain to leadership. Some of the studies bear directly on the issue of leadership; others may not concentrate on this specific topic but offer meaningful findings contributing to the growing literature in this area of leadership research. Our choice of these three particular hormones was guided simply by the number of previous studies showing relationships between them and other social behaviors associated with leadership (e.g., dominance).

Testosterone

As Anderson et al. (2007) noticed, testosterone (T) has received the most attention among potential hormones or neurotransmitters that may be antecedents of dominance (a particularly reliable correlate of leadership). Testosterone is the androgen (male sex hormone) that relates to the development and maintenance of masculine features, and it is found in both males and females (Brown, 1994). It has been associated with dominance, status seeking, aggressive behaviors, and sexuality in a wide range of studies, although inconsistent findings exist. Males generally have seven times as much serum T as do females (Mazur & Booth, 1998), and three times as much in saliva (Granger, Shirtcliff, Booth, Kivligham, & Schwartz, 2004). Nonetheless, it has been shown that T has a similar impact on psychological and behavioral outcomes in both sexes when controlling for gender (Josephs, Newman, Sellers, & Metha, 2006). It has also been shown that T levels have a rather high heritability (0.40) (Meilke, Stringham, Bishop, & West, 1987), indicating that there may be a persistent and stable difference among individuals regarding their observed T levels. Compelling evidence has documented an association between testosterone and dominance using both animal and human subjects. The association between T and dominance is observed in primates with a more developed social structure, such as rhesus macaques (Rose, Holaday, & Bernstein, 1971), squirrel monkeys (Coe, Smith, Mendoza, & Levine, 1983), mountain gorillas (Robbins & Czekala, 1997), bonobos (Marshall & Hohmann, 2005), and chimpanzees (Anestis, 2006; Muehlenbein, Watts, & Whitten, 2004).

Similar influences of T on dominance and status seeking in humans have been shown in a large collection of studies (Archer, 2006; Mazur & Booth, 1998). Testosterone also has been shown to effect motivation to gain power and social dominance (Gray, Jackson, & McKinlay, 1991; Sellers, Mehl, & Josephs, 2007) or make one alert to status threats (Josephs, Newman, Brown, & Beer, 2003; Schultheiss & Brunstein, 2001). Boys recognized by peers as leaders have higher basal T levels (Rowe, Maughan, Worthman, Costello, & Angold, 2004). Within the context of organizational settings, T was found to be related to higher status positions in occupations (Cristiansen & Knussman, 1987; Purifoy & Koopmans, 1979).

Another piece of evidence about the relationship between T and leadership comes from studies on the ratio of second-to-fourth–digit length (2D:4D), which is considered a marker for the concentration of prenatal testosterone relative to estrogen. One study found that those with lower 2D:4D ratio (an indication of higher prenatal T concentrations relative to estrogen) had stronger preference for an enterprise career orientation, which is characterized by management, organizing, trade, and leadership (Weis, Firker, & Hennig, 2007). Another study also reported that a lower 2D:4D ratio was related to higher perceived dominance and masculinity for males (Neave, Laing, Fink, & Manning, 2003). A recent study by Zyphur, Narayanan, Koh, and Koh (2009) revealed that, rather than being a direct predictor, T level may play a more implicit and subtle role at the basic psychological level. Their results showed that whether members end up with a higher status in a group is not necessarily related to their T levels, but that a greater mismatch between T levels and status can lead to lower collective efficacy for the group.

Notwithstanding the large volume of studies on T, several issues are still in contention. These include:

1. *Is there is a direct causal relationship between T and dominance?* Some evidence suggests reversed or reciprocal relationships. For example, Rose, Berstein, and Gordon (1975) found that not only did T levels predict dominance, but that changes in dominance or social status also affected T levels.
2. *Are dominance and aggression affected similarly?* Mazur and Booth (1998) favored the hypotheses that T level has a more direct relationship with dominance than aggression. This may be a more reasonable hypothesis for humans, for whom being dominant is much more complex than simply being strong and aggressive, as in many animal species.

3. *What are the conditions under which T and dominating behavior is aroused?* Interesting studies have suggested that T level may increase under perceived social hierarchy instability (Josephs, Newman, Brown, & Beer, 2003; Josephs et al., 2006) or when facing challenges, as was predicted by the challenge hypothesis (see Mazur & Booth, 1998).

4. *Do other hormones in combination with T affect dominance?* Mehta and Josephs (2010) recently found that T was positively related to dominance, but only in individuals with low cortisol. Such studies are informative because studies of single biological factors usually have difficulty in consistently explaining or predicting phenomena.

Serotonin

The neurotransmitter serotonin also has been related to aggression and establishment of social status. Serotonin shows important functions in regulating emotions, eating behaviors, biological rhythms, behavioral arousal, and motor activity (e.g., Challet, Pévet, & Malan, 1997); pathologically, it is involved in a range of emotional disorders including anxiety, stress, depression, and schizophrenia (Dinan, 1996a, b; Graeff, 1997; Graeff, Guimarães, De Andrade, & Deakin, 1996). Anderson and Summers (2007) discuss the serotonergic system and its possible relevance to leadership, proposing that any relationship exists mainly through the serotonergic regulation of mood and aggression. They presented studies showing that both serotonin and T actively influence aggression through anterior hypothalamus, by acting on vasopressinergic cells. Human studies are very rare in this area. Madsen (1985) proposed that whole blood serotonin (WBS) was related to power seekers and type-A personality behavior patterns, but his methods were criticized as suffering from conceptual imprecision and improper operationalization (Vatz & Weinberg, 1991). Although much progress has been made in studying the functions of serotonin, questions about a serotonin–leadership relationship remain largely unanswered, especially for human beings.

Oxytocin

Dominance and aggression may facilitate leadership emergence in some situations. Nonetheless, trust and the feelings of attachment also play important roles in the development and maintenance of relationships among social animals, including human. And relationships between leaders and followers are no exception. Trust and attachment are key concepts in important leadership areas such as transformational and charismatic leadership (e.g., Dirks & Ferrin, 2002; Kirkpatrick & Locke, 1996; Popper, Mayseless, & Castelnovo, 2000). Transformational leaders usually show keen interest in followers with emotional investment. They value trust and have positive models of both themselves and others in an attachment relationship.

There are apparent individual differences in the tendency to become a transformational leader, and it is of great interest to review which biological factors may influence key components of transformational leadership, such as trust, empathy, personal consideration, and attachment. Kosfeld et al. (2005) showed that oxytocin may be part of the biological basis of trust among humans, considering its important role in social attachment and affiliation in nonhuman animals. They found that intranasal administration of oxytocin causes a substantial increase in trust. Particularly, oxytocin has no effect on a general increase in the readiness to bear risks, but specifically affects the willingness to bear social risks through interpersonal interactions. Oxytocin is also related to trustworthiness between humans (Zak, Kurzban, & Matzner, 2005), and higher oxytocin levels are associated with trustworthy behavior or others' intention to trust. In addition, oxytocin was also related to empathy and attachment, or affiliative behaviors (e.g., Hurlemann et al., 2010; Insel & Young, 2001). Thus, we may tentatively infer that leaders with higher levels of oxytocin may be more likely to consider building and maintaining trust an easy and comfortable task, and that the empathy abilities associated with oxytocin also enable the leader to stand in the shoes of subordinates. In turn, subordinates aware of the leader's benign intentions would be more willing to put their trust in him or her, according to Zak et al. (2005). In addition, oxytocin is also involved in stress reduction. For example, oxytocin can mediate the effects of social supports in reducing psychological stress in humans (Heinrichs, Baumgartner, Kirschbaum, & Ehlert, 2003).

Unfortunately, despite the exciting fact that social behaviors associated with oxytocin have important implications in leadership research, we are not aware of any study investigating the possible association of oxytocin and leadership styles. Thus, we can only propose that some interesting relationships may exist, but more theoretical and empirical efforts are needed to verify them.

Cognitive Neuroscience and Leadership

The *Annals of the New York Academy of Sciences* devoted an entire issue (no. 1118) in November 2007 to discuss social cognitive neuroscience in organizational studies, thus implicating the value of this emerging area of interest in organizational paradigms. In their recent review, Senior, Lee, and Butler (2010) offer further illustrations about the organizational cognitive neuroscience (OCN) perspective, the research benefits of using OCN, and the techniques that organizational cognitive neuroscientists may use. In discussing the application of neuroscience to leadership research, they mention that, although certain leadership traits are heritable, recent finding in mice showed that through training and learning processes parts of the brain may engage in functional reorganization (Yin et al., 2009). Thus, cognitive neuroscience may help to resolve the debates on how much of leadership is influenced by nature and how much by nurture. Moreover, by integrating cognitive neuroscientific knowledge about other interesting variables, such as creativity and empathy, we may come to know more about what constitutes leadership (Senior, Lee, & Butler, 2010).

Conversely, as Senior et al. have noted, few organizational researchers have applied cognitive neuroscience within their research models. Consequently, possible connections between leadership research and neuroscience are rather implicit. In addition, direct linkages are also less likely to be found due to the complexity of the leadership phenomenon. Thus, a better strategy is to decompose leadership variables and explore the neural basis for the key elements. We first talk about decision making. This important topic is of mutual interest in both leadership and neuroscience studies, and there are also relatively more studies available in the area of cognitive neuroscience. Then, we introduce some recent studies that explore the neuroscientific explanations of leadership.

Before discussing those specific topics, it is worth mentioning that Senior et al. (2010) provided concise and comprehensive instructions about the techniques that organizational cognitive neuroscientists can utilize. The relatively common techniques are electro- and magnetoencephalography (EEG and MEG) and functional magnetic resonance imaging (fMRI). In their review, Senior et al., using an illustration, show how each technique is placed in its unique area according to limitations of spatial resolution (the size of the minimum area of brain activity measurable) and temporal resolution (the time it takes to record a measurement). EEG and MEG are superior in their depiction of temporal resolution; fMRI has relatively poor temporal resolution but very high spatial resolution, which makes it a popular technique. Other available techniques, such as electrodermal activity (EDA) and transcranial magnetic stimulation (TMS), are also discussed in their review. Refer to Senior et al. (2010) for more information.

Decision Making

Decision making is a major task of particular importance in situations of risk and uncertainty. Leaders are often challenged to make risky choices and decide how various choices might benefit or harm their organizations. Real-life observation show abundant evidence that leaders vary in their tendency and style of risk taking and decision making. As to the neural basis of decision making, neuroeconomic researchers are blazing the trail with remarkable findings. People generally tend to avoid risky options involving a potential loss until the gain is at least twice as much as the loss, a phenomenon known as "loss aversion." In risky choice studies, a consistent finding is that increased activity in insular cortex (a part of the cerebral cortex that regulates perception, motor control, self-awareness, cognitive functioning, and interpersonal experience) accompanies higher risk outcomes (Platt & Huettel, 2008), and people who score higher on neuroticism and harm avoidance also have the greatest magnitude of insular activation. When insular activity is higher before a decision is made, one may make an inferior choice to ensure safety even when the risky choice was actually a superior choice and in situations where such behaviors are maladaptive (Kuhnen & Knutson, 2005).

For leaders as well, when facing challenges and uncertainty, it might not always be effective to adhere to the safest strategy. Making decisions not only involves identifying risk, but also evaluating reward probabilities. It is usually difficult for leaders to obtain the complete information necessary, and they must learn how to make a choice under conditions of ambiguity both by analysis and trial and error over time (Platt & Huettel, 2008). The medial prefrontal cortex[2] has been proposed to be associated with subjects' learning about uncertainty by trial and error (Elliott & Dolan, 1998; Schubotz & von Cramon, 2002). Platt and Huettel (2008) also mentioned other brain regions that may be associated with selection of behaviors under uncertainty. For example, insular, lateral prefrontal, and parietal cortices show increased activation under high uncertainty when a probabilistic classification task is based on the relative accumulation of information between two choices. These regions also overlap with the neural control systems involved in behavioral control and executive processing. Fellows (2004) proposed that frontal lobe plays an important role in decision making, according to evidence from lesion studies[3], such that a less functional frontal lobe leads to impaired decisions. Another study indicates that genetic variation in the serotonin transporter gene (5-HTTLPR) may mediate bias in decision making, in that the genetic variation is associated with altered amygdala[4] reactivity and lack of prefrontal regulatory control, which in turn is related to people's susceptibility to context and risk while making decisions (Roiser et al., 2009).

These studies are rather selective, given the large volume of neuroeconomic studies in decision making, yet they are helpful in giving organizational researchers a sense of the current findings on decision making, as well as possible ways to conduct such studies. Understanding how the brain functions in decision-making processes is valuable in estimating and predicting how leaders make their decisions. Moreover, neuroscientific findings about decision-making efficiency in leaders may offer tests of leadership development efforts. If some learning processes do involve neural reorganization, such research would provide a valuable guide for more elegant development program designs.

Emerging Efforts in Leadership Neuroscience

A group of researchers from Arizona State University has tried to understand the distinguishable features of effective leaders' brain functions by using quantitative electroencephalographs (qEEG). In their recent review, Waldman, Balthazard, and Peterson (2011) reported their study by conducting qEEG assessments for 50 senior leaders from a variety of industries and they found that right frontal brain coherence[5] predicted leaders' behavioral charisma, as perceived by followers. This process was likely to be mediated by *socialized visionary communication*, which is an important feature of charismatic or transformational leadership. The activities of the right frontal brain, according to these researchers, is linked to emotional control of balance, foresight or "big picture" thinking, and insight. The authors believe that enhanced right frontal coherence may help individuals to be more flexible and insightful when balancing multiple concerns in the formation of a more socialized vision and to effectively deal with possible emotional strains and uncertainties.

Although neuroscientists may not reach agreement about the functions of the right frontal portion of the brain, and charismatic leadership can involve more complex cooperation of different parts of the brain, their findings are still informative and encouraging. Accumulated research efforts, especially those with reasonable theoretical guidance and supportive evidence, are necessary before any final conclusion can be reached.

Effective leaders interacting with individuals, groups, and organizations in dynamic environments are assumed to possess certain level of cognitive and affective complexity. Thus, in another research project, researchers (Hannah, Balthazard, Waldman, Jennings, & Thatcher, 2013) were interested in what constitutes complex adaptive leadership. They used qEEG to detect the brain activity of military leaders differing in psychometric assessments of self-complexity, and some preliminary results seem to suggest that observable differences in certain areas of the brain are related with high or low self-complexity. Moreover, these researchers are attempting to determine the usefulness of neurofeedback, which depends on an operant conditional procedure by which individuals can modify their neurophysiological activities, in the development of leadership ability. Although this brain training technique for leaders sounds like science fiction, it is a brave move forward. Interested readers are referred to Waldman, Balthazard and Peterson's (2011) review about inspirational leadership and neuroscience, which offers a detailed summary of their current research effort.

Other Neurological Findings Related to Leadership

In addition to discussions on leadership skills and their neurological basis, some interesting findings in neurologic studies about status-seeking motivation are worth mentioning. For example, a recent study using fMRI found that ventromedial prefrontal cortex (VLPFC) showed increased signals to higher status cues, relative to neutral and low status cues (Marsh, Blair, Jones, Soliman, & Blair, 2008). Zink, Tong, Chen, Bassett, Stein, and Meyer-Lindenberg (2008) found that viewing a superior individual was related to activity in dorsolateral prefrontal cortex. They stated that in unstable hierarchical settings additional regions (such as amygdala) relating to emotional processing, social cognition (medial prefrontal cortex), and behavioral readiness are recruited. Awareness of being at a lower status can cause stress. In vertebrates, stress hormones mediate such influence and eventually have physical consequences on immune and brain systems, including neurogenesis[6] (Robinson, Grozinger, & Whitfield, 2005). These studies help explain status-seeking motivations as being driven by neurological regulation.

Conclusion

This chapter has wound its way through a wide variety of topics and literatures. Although diverse, several important conclusions can be made:

1. There is abundant evidence that biological factors are clearly associated with a number of different leadership variables.
2. These associations are probably based on different kinds of direct and indirect mediating processes (e.g., through cognitive processes, personality, etc.).
3. Even though the evidence for the relationships between biological factors and leadership is strong and compelling, the environment is clearly more strongly associated.
4. There are good arguments based on evolutionary explanations as to why various biological factors demonstrate such associations.
5. The interplay between environmental and biological factors is complex, but will most likely provide a more comprehensive and accurate account of leadership.

Given the plethora of previous research on biological features reviewed and the broad concept of leadership, it seems difficult to give specific directions for future research. Thus, we offer only five general directions that we believe would be fruitful future research adopting a biological perspective, while we acknowledge there may be other promising avenues. We hope our suggestions stimulate more interest in the relationship between biology and leadership (and organizational behavior in general).

1. Future research should continue to examine associations between biological features (e.g., specific genes, hormones, and brain functions) and leadership. We view these types of association studies as a first step toward incorporating a biological view of leadership that shows the "main effect" of biological features.
2. Researchers should examine the pathways/mechanisms through which biological factors influence leadership. For instance, do specific genes shape leadership emergence by modulating protein formation, hormone activities, brain functions, and personality traits?
3. Researchers should investigate how biological features and environmental factors jointly (i.e., through interactions) influence leadership and the interactive effect of biological factors.
4. Researchers should conduct longitudinal studies to unpack more nuanced relationships among biological factors, the environment, and leadership. For instance, how do environmental influences modulate the expression of specific genes, signal feedback to the endocrine system, and adjust brain functioning over time? How do biological features and environmental forces interdependently influence leader development in the long run? How do genetic architecture and culture co-evolve in the emergence of a social hierarchy?
5. From a practical perspective, it would be helpful to generate evidence to support the notion that biological factors can be targets of intervention to promote leadership effectiveness. We believe endeavors in all of these directions can push forward our knowledge about leadership.
6. Finally, it is interesting to consider if similar factors are involved in "followership." That is, are the biological factors associated with who becomes a leader also involved in determining who is a follower?

It is time to get on with the pursuit of research that focuses on biological processes and how they influence leadership, a new paradigmatic approach that needs to be explored much more fully.

Acknowledgments

We thank Dr. John Antonakis for his helpful comments on an earlier version of this chapter.

Notes

1. Even highly heritable factors can be modified by environmental intervention. For example, eyeglasses and surgery can "correct" for poor vision, which is highly heritable.
2. Medial prefrontal cortex is a part of the brain cortex that is located in the frontal lobe.
3. A classical method to understand the functions and dysfunctions of the human nervous system by studying patients with deficits that follow specific brain damage.
4. The amygdala is an almond-shaped group of nuclei located deep within the medial temporal lobes of the brain. It has been found to perform a primary role in the processing and memory of emotional reactions.

5. According to the authors, coherence here refers to the strength of connectedness between various regions of the brain.
6. The concept of neurogenesis refers to the process by which neurons are generated.

References

Allee, W. C., Allee, M. N., Ritchey, F., & Castles, E. W. (1947). Leadership in a flock of white Pekin ducks. *Ecology, 28*(3), 310–315.

Anderson, W. D., & Summers, C. H. (2007). Neuroendocrine mechanisms, stress coping strategies, and social dominance: Comparative lessons about leadership potential. *Annals of the American Academy of Political and Social Science, 614*, 102–130.

Anestis, S. F. (2006). Testosterone in juvenile and adolescent male chimpanzees (Pan troglodytes): Effects of dominance rank, aggression, and behavioral style. *American Journal of Physical Anthropology, 130*(4), 536–545.

Antonakis, J., & Dalgas, O. (2009). Predicting elections: Child's play! *Science, 323*(5918), 1183.

Archer, J. (2006). Testosterone and human aggression: An evaluation of the challenge hypothesis. *Neuroscience and Biobehavioral Reviews, 30*, 319–345.

Arvey, R., Bouchard, T., Segal, N., & Abraham, L. (1989). Job satisfaction: Environmental and genetic components. *Journal of Applied Psychology, 74*(2), 187–192.

Arvey, R., McCall, B., Bouchard, T., Taubman, P., & Cavanaugh, M. A. (1994). Genetic influences on job satisfaction and work values. *Personality and Individual Differences, 17*(1), 21–33.

Arvey, R., Rotundo, M., Johnson, W., Zhang, Z., & McGue, M. (2006). The determinants of leadership role occupancy: Genetic and personality factors. *Leadership Quarterly, 17*, 1–20.

Arvey, R., Zhang, Z., Avolio, B. J., & Krueger, R. F. (2007). Developmental and genetic determinants of leadership role occupancy among women. *Journal of Applied Psychology, 92*(3), 693–706.

Atwater, L. E., Dionne, S. D., Avolio, B., Camobreco, J. F., & Lau, A. W. (1999). A longitudinal study of the leadership development process: Individual differences predicting leader effectiveness. *Human Relations, 52*(12), 1543–1562.

Atwater, L. E., & Yammarinol, F. J. (1993). Personal attributes as predictors of superiors' and subordinates' perceptions of military academy leadership. *Human Relations, 46*(5), 645–668.

Balthazard, P. A., Waldman, D. A., Thatcher, R. W., & Hannah, S. T. (2012). Differentiating transformational and non-transformational leaders on the basis of neurological imaging. *Leadership Quarterly, 23*(2), 244–258.

Bass, B. M. (1990). *Handbook of leadership*. New York: The Free Press.

Bass, B. M., & Bass, R. (2008). *The Bass Handbook of Leadership: Theory, Research, and Managerial Applications*. New York: The Free Press.

Bennis, W. G. (1994). An Invented Life: Reflections on Leadership and Change. Reading, MA: Addison-Wesley.

Borkenau, P., Riemann, R., Angleitner, A., & Spinath, F. M. (2002). Similarity of childhood experiences and personality resemblance in monozygotic and dizygotic twins: a test of the equal environments assumption. *Personality and Individual differences, 33*(2), 261–269.

Bouchard, T. J., McGue, M., Hur, Y.-M., & Horn, J. M. (1998). A genetic and environmental analysis of the California Psychological Inventory using adult twins reared apart and together. *European Journal of Personality, 12*, 307–320.

Brian, R., Homan, A., Grabo, A., & Van Vugt, M. (2012). Facing the situation: Testing a biosocial contingency model of leadership in intergroup relations using masculine and feminine faces. *Leadership Quarterly, 23*(2), 273–280.

Brown, R. (Ed.). (1994). *An Introduction to Neuroendocrinology*. Cambridge: Cambridge University Press.

Challet, E., Pévet, P., & Malan, A. (1997). Lesion of the serotonergic terminals in the suprachiasmatic nuclei limits the phase advance of body temperature rhythm in food-restricted rats fed during daytime. *Journal of Biological Rhythms, 12*(3), 235–244.

Coe, C. L., Smith, E. R., Mendoza, S. P., & Levine, S. (Eds.). (1983). *Varying Influence of Social Status on Hormone Levels in Male Squirrel Monkeys*. New York: Spectrum Publications.

Colarelli, S., & Arvey, R. D. (Eds.). (In Preparation). *The Biological Foundations of Organizational Behavior*. Chicago: University of Chicago Press.

Cosmides, L., & Tooby, J. (1992). Cognitive adaptations for social exchange. In J. Barkow, L. Cosmides, & J. Tooby (Eds.), *The adapted mind: Evolutionary psychology and the generation of culture* (pp. 163–228). New York: Oxford University Press.

Coutu, D. L. (2002). How resilience works. *Harvard Business Review, 80*(5), 46–50.

Cristiansen, K., & Knussman, R. (1987). Androgen levels and components of aggressive behavior in men. *Hormones and Behavior, 21*, 170–180.

Day, D. V., Sin, H. P., & Chen, T. T. (2004). Assessing the burdens of leadership: Effects of formal leadership roles on individual performance over time. *Personnel Psychology, 57*(3), 573–605.

De Neve, J. E., Mikhavlov S., Dawes, C. T., Christaki, N. A., & Fowler, J. H. (2013). Born to lead? A twin design and genetic association study of leadership role occupancy. *Leadersh Quarterly, 24*(1), 45–60.

Dinan, T. (1996a). Serotonin and the regulation of hypothalamic-pituitary-adrenal axis function. *Life Sciences, 58*(20), 1683–1694.

Dinan, T. (1996b). Serotonin: Current understanding and the way forward. *International Clinical Psychopharmacology, 11*, 19–22.

Dirks, K. T., & Ferrin, D. L. (2002). Trust in leadership: Meta-analytic findings and implications for research and practice. *Journal of Applied Psychology, 87*(4), 611–628.

Dunkerley, M. D. (1940). *A statistical study of leadership among college women,*. 4(6). Catholic: University of America Press.

Elliott, R., & Dolan, R. J. (1998). Activation of different anterior cingulate foci in association with hypothesis testing and response selection. *Neuroimage, 8*, 17–29.

Fellows, L. K. (2004). The cognitive neuroscience of human decision making: A review and conceptual framework. *Behavioral and Cognitive Neuroscience Reviews, 3*(3), 159–172.

Foley, C., Pettorelli, N., & Foley, L. (2008). Severe drought and calf survival in elephants. *Biology Letters, 4*(5), 541–544.

Gacsaly, S. A., & Borges, C. A. (1979). The male physique and behavioral expectancies. *Journal of Psychology: Interdisciplinary and Applied, 101*, 97–102.

Graeff, F. (1997). Serotonergic systems. *Psychiatric Clinics of North America, 20*(4), 723–739.

Graeff, F., Guimarães, F., De Andrade, T., & Deakin, J. (1996). Role of 5-HT in stress, anxiety, and depression. *Pharmacology Biochemistry and Behavior, 54*(1), 129–141.

Granger, D. A., Shirtcliff, E. A., Booth, A., Kivligham, K. T., & Schwartz, E. B. (2004). The "trouble" with salivary testosterone *Psychoneuroendocrinology, 29*, 1229–1240.

Gray, A., Jackson, D. N., & McKinlay, J. B. (1991). The relation between dominance, anger, and hormones in normally aging men: Results from the Massachusetts male aging study. *Psychosomatic Medicine, 53*, 375–385.

Han, E., Norton, E. C., & Stearns, S. C. (2009). Weight and wages: Fat versus lean paychecks. *Health Economics, 18*(5), 535–548.

Hannah, S. T., Balthazard, P. A., Waldman, D. A., Jennings, P. L., & Thatcher, R. W. (2013). The psychological and neurological bases of leader self-complexity and effects on adaptive decision-making. *Journal of Applied Psychology, 98*(3), 393–411.

Heinrichs, M., Baumgartner, T., Kirschbaum, C., & Ehlert, U. (2003). Social support and oxytocin interact to suppress cortisol and subjective responses to psychosocial stress. *Biological Psychiatry, 54*, 1389–1398.

Hershberger, S. L., Lichtenstein, P., & Knox, S. S. (1994). Genetic and environmental influences on perceptions of organizational climate. *Journal of Applied Psychology, 79*(1), 24–33.

Hofmann, H. A., Benson, M. E., & Fernald, R. D. (1999). Social status regulates growth rate: Consequences for life-history strategies. *Proceedings of the National Academy of Sciences of the United States of America, 96*(24), 14171–14176.

Hurlemann, R., Patin, A., Onur, O., Cohen, M., Baumgartner, T., Metzler, S., et al. (2010). Oxytocin enhances amygdala-dependent, socially reinforced learning and emotional empathy in humans. *Journal of Neuroscience, 30*(14), 4999–5007.

Ilies, R., Arvey, R. D., & Bouchard, T. J. (2006). Darwinism, behavioral genetics, and organizational behavior: A review and agenda for future research. *Journal of Organizational Behavior, 27*(2), 121–141.

Ilies, R., Gerhardt, M. W., & Le, H. (2004). Individual differences in leadership emergence: Integrating meta analytic findings and behavioral genetics estimates. *International Journal of Selection and Assessment, 12*(3), 207–219.

Insel, T. R., & Young, L. J. (2001). The neurobiology of attachment. *Nature Review Neuroscience, 2*(2), 129–136.

Johnson, W. (2007). Genetic and environmental influences on behavior: capturing all the interplay. *Psychological review, 114*(2), 423–440.

Johnson, A. M., Vernon, P. A., McCarthy, J. M., Molson, M., Harris, J. A., & Jang, K. L. (1998). Nature vs nurture: Are leaders born or made. A behavior genetic investigation of leadership style. *Twin Research, 1*(4), 216–223.

Johnson, A. M., Vernon, P. A., Harris, J. A., & Jang, K. L. (2004). A behavior genetic investigation of the relationship between leadership and personality. *Twin Research, 7*(1), 27–32.

Josephs, R., Newman, M., Brown, R., & Beer, J. (2003). Status, testosterone, and human intellectual performance: Stereotype threat as status concern. *Psychological Science, 14*(2), 158–163.

Josephs, R., Newman, M., Sellers, J., & Metha, P. (2006). The mismatch effect: When testosterone and status are at odds. *Journal of Personality and Social Psychology, 90*, 999–1013.

Judge, T., Bono, J. E., Ilies, R., & Gerhardt, M. W. (2002). Personality and leadership: A qualitative and quantitative review. *Journal of Applied Psychology, 87*(4), 765–779.

Judge, T. A., & Cable, D. M. (2004). The effect of physical height on workplace success and income: Preliminary test of a theoretical model. *Journal of Applied Psychology, 89*(3), 428–440.

Judge, T. A., & Cable, D. M. (2011). When it comes to pay, do the thin win? The effect of weight on pay for men and women. *Journal of Applied Psychology, 96*(1), 95–112.

Kellaway, L. (2002, September 2). Leaders of the bank unite. *Financial Times*, 10.

King, A. J., Johnson, D.D., & Van Vugt, M. (2009). The origins and evolution of leadership. *Current biology, 19*(19), R911–R916.

Kirkpatrick, S. A., & Locke, E. A. (1996). Direct and indirect effects of three core charismatic leadership components on performance and attitudes. *Journal of Applied Psychology, 81*(1), 36–51.

Kosfeld, M., Heinrichs, M., Zak, P. J., Fischbacher, U., & Fehr, E. (2005). Oxytocin increases trust in humans. *Nature, 435*(7042), 673–676.

Kuhnen, C., & Knutson, B. (2005). The neural basis of financial risk taking. *Neuron, 47*(5), 763–770.

Kurvers, R. H. J. M., Eijkelenkamp, B., van Oers, K., van Lith, B., van Wieren, S. E., Ydenberg, R. C., et al. (2009). Personality differences explain leadership in barnacle geese. *Animal Behaviour, 78*(2), 447–453.

Langlois, J. H., Roggman, L. A., Casey, R. J., Ritter, J. M., Rieser-Danner, L. A., & Jenkins, V. Y. (1987). Infant preferences for attractive faces: Rudiments of a stereotype? *Developmental Psychology, 23*(3), 363–369.

Leblond, C., & Reebs, S. G. (2006). Individual leadership and boldness in shoals of golden shiners (*Notemigonus crysoleucas*). *Behaviour, 143*(10), 1263–1280.

Li, W. D., Song, Z. L. & Arvey, R. (unpublished). DRD4, job complexity and job satisfaction: A moderated mediation model.

Livingston, R. W., & Pearce, N. A. (2009). The teddy-bear effect. *Psychological Science, 20*(10), 1229–1236.

Madsen, D. (1985). A biochemical property relating to power seeking in humans. *The American Political Science Review, 79*(2), 448–457.

Maransky, B. P., & Bildstein, K. L. (2001). Follow your elders: Age-related differences in the migration behavior of broad-winged hawks at Hawk Mountain Sanctuary, Pennsylvania. *The Wilson Bulletin, 113*(3), 350–353.

Marsh, A. A., Blair, K. S., Jones, M. M., Soliman, N., & Blair, R. J. R. (2008). Dominance and submission: The ventrolateral prefrontal cortex and responses to status cues. *Journal of Cognitive Neuroscience, 21*(4), 713–724.

Marshall, A., & Hohmann, G. (2005). Urinary testosterone levels of wild male bonobos (*Pan paniscus*) in the Lomako Forest, Democratic Republic of Congo. *American Journal of Primatology, 65*, 87–92.

Mazur, A., & Booth, A. (1998). Testosterone and dominance in men. *Behavioral and Brain Sciences, 21*, 353–397.

Mazur, A., Mazur, J., & Keating, C. (1984). Military rank attainment of a West Point class: Effects of cadets' physical features. *The American Journal of Sociology, 90*(1), 125–150.

McCall, B., Cavanaugh, M. A., Arvey, R., & Taubman, P. (1997). Genetic influences on job and occupational switching. *Journal of Vocational Behavior, 50*(1), 60–77.

McGue, M., & Bouchard Jr., T. J. (1998). Genetic and environmental influences on human behavioral differences. *Annual Review of Neuroscience, 21*(1), 1–24.

Mehta, P. H., & Josephs, R. A. (2010). Testosterone and cortisol jointly regulate dominance: Evidence for a dual-hormone hypothesis. *Hormones and Behavior, 58*, 898–906.

Meilke, A. W., Stringham, J. D., Bishop, D. T., & West, D. W. (1987). Quantitating genetic and nongenetic factors influencing androgen production and clearance rates in men. *Journal of Clinical Endocrinology and Metabolism 67*(1), 104–119.

Muehlenbein, M., Watts, D. P., & Whitten, P. L. (2004). Dominance rank and fecal testosterone levels in adult male chimpanzees (*Pan troglodytes schweinfurthii*) at Ngogo, Kibale National Park, Uganda. *American Journal of Primatology, 64*, 71–82.

Munafò, M., Brown, S., & Hariri, A. (2008). Serotonin transporter (5-HTTLPR) genotype and amygdala activation: A meta-analysis. *Biological Psychiatry, 63*(9), 852–857.

Neave, N., Laing, S., Fink, B., & Manning, J. T. (2003). Second to fourth digit ratio, testosterone and perceived male dominance. *Proceedings of the Royal Society of London. Series B: Biological Sciences, 270*(1529), 2167–2172.

Platt, M. L., & Huettel, S. A. (2008). Risky business: The neuroeconomics of decision making under uncertainty. *Nature Neuroscience, 11*(4), 398–403.

Plomin, R., DeFries, J., McClearn, G., & McGuffin, P. (2008). *Behavioral Genetics* (Vol. 5). New York: Worth.

Popper, M., Mayseless, O., & Castelnovo, O. (2000). Transformational leadership and attachment. *Leadership Quarterly, 11*(2), 267–289.

Purifoy, E. E., & Koopmans, L. H. (1979). Androstenedione, testosterone, and free testosterone concentration in women in various occupations. *Social Biology, 26*, 179–188.

Rabb, G. B., Woolpy, J. H., & Ginsburg, B. E. (1967). Social relationships in a group of captive wolves. *American Zoologist, 7*(2), 305–311.

Reebs, S. G. (2000). Can a minority of informed leaders determine the foraging movements of a fish shoal? *Animal Behaviour, 59*(2), 403–409.

Reebs, S. G. (2001). Influence of body size on leadership in shoals of golden shiners, *Notemigonus crysoleucas. Behaviour, 138*(7), 797–809.

Rice, R. W., Yoder, J. D., Adams, J., Priest, R. F., & Prince, H. T. (1984). Leadership ratings for male and female military cadets. *Sex Roles, 10*(11), 885–901.

Robbins, M. M., & Czekala, N. M. (1997). A preliminary investigation of urinary testosterone and cortisol levels in wild male mountain gorillas. *American Journal of Primatology, 43*, 51–64.

Robinson, G. E., Grozinger, C. M., & Whitfield, C. W. (2005). Sociogenomics: Social life in molecular terms. *Nature Review Genetics, 6*(4), 257–270.

Roiser, J. P., de Martino, B., Tan, G. C. Y., Kumaran, D., Seymour, B., Wood, N. W., et al. (2009). A genetically mediated bias in decision making driven by failure of amygdala control. *Journal of Neuroscience, 29*(18), 5985–5991.

Rose, R., Berstein, I., & Gordon, T. (1975). Consequences of social conflict on plasma testosterone levels in rhesus monkeys. *Psychosomatic Medicine, 37*(1), 50–61.

Rose, R. M., Holaday, J. W., & Bernstein, I. S. (1971). Plasma testosterone, dominance rank and aggressive behaviour in male rhesus monkeys. *Nature, 231*, 366–368.

Rowe, R., Maughan, B., Worthman, C. M., Costello, E. J., & Angold, A. (2004). Testosterone, antisocial behavior, and social dominance in boys: Pubertal development and biosocial interaction. *Biological Psychiatry, 55*, 546–552.

Schubotz, R. I., & von Cramon, D. Y. (2002). A blueprint for target motion: fMRI reveals perceived sequential complexity to modulate premotor cortex. *Neuroimage, 16*, 920–935.

Schultheiss, O. C., & Brunstein, J. C. (2001). Assessment of implicit motives with a research version of the TAT: Picture profiles, gender differences, and relations to other personality measures. *Journal of Personality Assessment, 77*, 71–86.

Sellers, J. G., Mehl, M. R., & Josephs, R. A. (2007). Hormones and personality: Testosterone as a marker of individual differences. *Journal of Research in Personality, 41*(1), 126–138.

Senior, C., Lee, N., & Butler, M. (2010). Organizational cognitive neuroscience. *Organization Science*, 1–12.

Song, Z., Li, W., & Arvey, R. D. (2011). Associations between dopamine and serotonin genes and job satisfaction: Preliminary evidence from the Add Health Study. *Journal of Applied Psychology, 96*(6), 1223–1233.

Sorcher, M., & Brant, J. (2002). Are you picking the right leaders? *Harvard Business Review, 80*(2), 78–87.

Spisak, B. R., Homan, A. C., Grabo, A., & Van Vugt, M. (2012). Facing the situation: Testing a biosocial contingency model of leadership in intergroup relations using masculine and feminine faces. *Leadership Quarterly, 23*(2), 273–280.

Stogdill, R. M. (1948). Personal factors associated with leadership: A survey of the literature. *Journal of Psychology, 25*(1), 35–71.

Todorov, A., Mandisodza, A. N., Goren, A., & Hall, C. C. (2005). Inferences of competence from faces predict election outcomes. *Science, 308*(5728), 1623.

Tryon, C. M. (1939). Evaluations of adolescent personality by adolescents. *Monographs of the Society for Research in Child Development, 4*(4), i–83.

Van Vugt, M., Hogan, R., & Kaiser, R. B. (2008). Leadership, followership, and evolution: Some lessons from the past. *American Psychologist, 63*(3), 182–196.

Vatz, R. E., & Weinberg, L. S. (1991). Biochemistry and power-seeking. *Politics and the Life Sciences, 10*(1), 69–75.

Waldman, D. A., Balthazard, P. A., & Peterson, S. J. (2011). Leadership and Neuroscience: Can We Revolutionize the Way That Inspirational Leaders Are Identified and Developed?. *The Academy of Management Perspectives, 25*(1), 60–74.

Watson, J. (1913). Psychology as the behaviorist views it. *Psychological Review, 20*, 158–177.

Watson, J. (1928). *The Ways of Behaviorism.* New York: Harper & Brothers

Weis, S. E., Firker, A., & Hennig, J. (2007). Associations between the second to fourth digit ratio and career interests. *Personality and Individual Differences, 43*(3), 485–493.

Wright, J., Stone, R. E., & Brown, N. (2003). Communal roosts as structured information centres in the raven, *Corvus corax. Journal of Animal Ecology, 72*(6), 1003–1014.

Yin, H., Mulcare, S., Hilário, M., Clouse, E., Holloway, T., Davis, M., et al. (2009). Dynamic reorganization of striatal circuits during the acquisition and consolidation of a skill. *Nature Neuroscience, 12*(3), 333–341.

Zak, P. J., Kurzban, R., & Matzner, W. T. (2005). Oxytocin is associated with human trustworthiness. *Hormones and Behavior, 48*(5), 522–527.

Zhang, Z., Ilies, R., & Arvey, R. D. (2009). Beyond genetic explanations for leadership: The moderating role of the social

environment. *Organizational Behavior and Human Decision Processes, 110*(2), 118–128.
Zink, C. F., Tong, Y., Chen, Q., Bassett, D. S., Stein, J. L., & Meyer-Lindenberg, A. (2008). Know your place: Neural processing of social hierarchy in humans. *Neuron, 58*(2), 273–283.
Zyphur, M. J., Narayanan, J., Koh, G., & Koh, D. (2009). Testosterone-status mismatch lowers collective efficacy in groups: Evidence from a slope-as-predictor multilevel structural equation model. *Organizational Behavior and Human Decision Processes, 110*(2), 70–79.

PART 2

Research Issues

CHAPTER

6 Causality and Endogeneity: Problems and Solutions

John Antonakis, Samuel Bendahan, Philippe Jacquart, *and* Rafael Lalive

Abstract

Unfortunately, most researchers in leadership studies (and management in general) ignore one key design and estimation problem rendering parameter estimates uninterpretable: *endogeneity*. This chapter discusses the problem of endogeneity in depth and explains conditions that engender it. It shows how consistent causal estimates can be derived from the randomized experiment, in which endogeneity is eliminated by experimental design. It then reviews the reasons why estimates may become biased (i.e., inconsistent) in nonexperimental designs and presents a number of useful remedies for examining causal relations with nonexperimental data. This chapter is written in intuitive terms using nontechnical language to make it accessible to a large audience, irrespective of discipline.

Key Words: causality, common-method bias, endogeneity, instrumental variables, quasi-experimentation, randomized experiments

> "Man is impelled to invent theories to account for what happens in the world. Unfortunately, he is not quite intelligent enough, in most cases, to find correct explanations. So that when he acts on his theories, he behaves very often like a lunatic."
>
> —Aldous Huxley *(Texts and Pretexts, 1932, p. 270)*

Theory is the ultimate aim of science (Kerlinger & Lee, 2000). Contrary to the lay individuals described in Aldous Huxley's opening quote, scientists put their theories to the empirical test in order to determine whether or not the theories are plausible. As stated by Murphy (1997, p. 4), "the methods chosen should be appropriate to the research question and the inferences drawn should be consistent with what was actually attempted in [the] study." Given the importance of theory testing for understanding and predicting how the world works, the choice of research design and analysis method is of the utmost importance, particularly because research findings influence policy and practice.

As explained in detail in this chapter, the randomized experiment is the gold standard to identify and test causal relationships. However, be it for practical or ethical considerations, it may not always be possible to conduct randomized experiments (see Cook, Shadish, & Wong, 2008; Rubin, 2008). Although most researchers undoubtedly know that the randomized experiment is the method of choice to infer causality, many of them ignore two key issues:

1. Experimental design is not the only method available to make valid causal inferences; that is, there are other designs available to make valid causal claims, which do not require manipulation of the exogenous variables on the part of the researcher.
2. Nonexperimental designs that do not address problems of endogeneity are pretty much useless for understanding phenomena; that is, finding a relationship between an endogenous regressor x—that has not been purged from endogeneity somehow—and y does not help theory one bit!

The way in which we state these two points, particularly the second, is admittedly rather harsh and blunt; however, going through the chapter will make readers realize that this bluntness is actually an understatement. To help research advance in leadership (and other social sciences) more researchers must join the effort to stomp out endogeneity; this problem is far bigger than we dared to imagine.

We recently conducted a review of leadership studies showing that the conditions and designs that allow to uncover causal relationship with nonexperimental data are not well understood by the majority of leadership researchers (Antonakis, Bendahan, Jacquart, & Lalive, 2010). This problem is not isolated to the field of leadership. In fact, aside from the field of economics, which starting addressing this problem a couple of decades ago, many social sciences disciplines face a similar situation (Bascle, 2008; Duncan, Magnusson, & Ludwig, 2004; Foster & McLanahan, 1996; Gennetian, Magnuson, & Morris, 2008; Halaby, 2004; Larcker & Rusticus, 2010; Shaver, 1998).

For example, a recent review has found that fewer than 10 percent of the papers published in the top strategy journal (i.e., *Strategic Management Journal*) properly analyzed the nonexperimental data they presented (Hamilton & Nickerson, 2003). In our review, where we examined a random sample of 110 leadership papers published in top scientific journals, we found that researchers failed to correct between 66 and 90 percent of design and estimation conditions that threaten estimate validity (refer to Table 6.1 for a summary of the threats). We also found that 109 of the articles had at least one threat to validity and that 100 articles had three or more validity threats (discussed in more detail later). This sad state of affairs has to be changed because policy

Table 6.1. Threats to Validity

Validity Threat	Explanation
1. Omitted variables:	(a) Omitting a regressor, that is, failing to include important control variables when testing the predictive validity of dispositional or behavioral variables (e.g., testing predictive validity of "emotional intelligence" without including IQ or personality; not controlling for competing leadership styles) (b) Omitting fixed effects (c) Using random-effects without justification (d) In all other cases, independent variables not exogenous (if it is not clear what the controls should be)
2. Omitted selection:	(a) Comparing a treatment group to other nonequivalent groups (i.e., where the treatment group is not the same as the other groups) (b) Comparing entities that are grouped nominally where selection to group is endogenous (e.g., comparing men and women leaders on leadership effectiveness where the selection process to leadership is not equivalent) (c) Sample (participants or survey responses) suffers from self-selection or is nonrepresentative
3. Simultaneity:	(a) Reverse causality (i.e., an independent variable is potential caused by the dependent variable)
4. Measurement error:	(a) Including imperfectly measured variables as independent variables and not modeling measurement error
5. Common-methods variance:	(a) Independent and dependent variables are gathered from the same rating source.
6. Inconsistent inference:	(a) Using normal standard errors without examining for heteroscedasticity (b) Not using cluster-robust standard errors in panel data
7. Model misspecification:	(a) Not correlating disturbances of potentially endogenous regressors in mediation models (and not testing for endogeneity using a Hausman test or augmented regression) (b) Using a full information estimator (e.g., maximum likelihood, three-stage least squares) without comparing estimates to a limited information estimator (e.g., two stage-least squares)

Note: Reprinted from Antonakis, J., Bendahan, S., Jacquart, P., & Lalive, R. (2010). On making causal claims: A review and recommendations, *The Leadership Quarterly, 21*(6), 1086–1120, with permission from Elsevier.

implications that stem from research that is incorrectly undertaken will be wrong.

When we refer to causal analysis of nonexperimental data, we are referring to designs that will produce coefficients that capture the magnitude of the true (causal) relationship rather than just an association or a correlation (which could be spurious). True estimates are called *consistent*. To say that an estimate is consistent suggests that it will converge to the true population parameter as sample size goes to infinity (i.e., asymptotically).

The main threat to consistency is *endogeneity*; much of what is discussed in this chapter focuses on explaining what it is and how to deal with it. If an estimate is inconsistent, it is purely and simply uninterpretable. A coefficient may appear to adequately reflect the hypothesized relationship—for example, it is the right direction and the effect is highly significant—but in the presence of endogeneity it will be inconsistent and will not reflect the true population parameter. Reporting it is pretty much useless to help understand a phenomenon because the observed correlation may be far off from the true relation; that is, the true relation could be *higher, lower, zero*, or of a *different sign* from the observed association (correlation). This is why understanding the nature of causal designs is crucial.

Our goal in this chapter is to present some of the methods available to researchers for testing theory correctly. It begins by discussing what theories are and why causality is important to theory testing; a simple example of endogeneity is presented with simulated data and the problem is extended to leadership research to show that models with endogenous regressors are simply not very useful (these data will prove to be very useful as a teaching aid for those teaching methods courses). Next, the randomized experiment is presented as a failsafe way to make causal claims; an understanding of what, precisely, random assignment does is essential for understanding how endogeneity is engendered, and why it renders estimates biased. Some methods are then presented that can be used to analyze nonexperimental data causally. The chapter closes with a discussion of future directions in leadership research.

What Is Causality?

A theory consists in a set of interrelated constructs and data connecting these constructs with the empirical world—within certain boundaries and under certain constraints (Antonakis et al., 2004); a theory is constructed so as to answers a number of questions: *What* elements are being studied and *how* do they relate? *Why* and *when* (*where* and to *whom*) does the theory apply? To be acceptable, a theory should be devoid of contradictions and be consistent with the empirical world—that is, it should have internal and external consistency; moreover, a theory should be testable, have both generality and parsimony (for in-depth treatment see Bacharach, 1989; Dubin, 1976; Kerlinger & Lee, 2000). More importantly, a theory should present a causally valid explanation of a phenomenon.

What causality is and how it should be tested has important implications for understanding natural phenomena (and the theories that explain them); it also has important implications regarding how scientific research should be conducted. Causality is a fascinating topic that has been examined in depth by many philosophers and scientists (cf. Mulaik, 2009; Pearl, 2009). In this chapter, we steer clear from philosophical considerations and adopt a pragmatic and broadly accepted view on causality. Here, the focus is on understanding how one can assess and quantify a causal effect. Classically, x is said to have an effect on y if the following three conditions are met (Holland, 1986; Kenny, 1979):

1. y follows x temporally.
2. y changes as x changes (and this relationship is statistically significant).
3. No other causes should eliminate the relation between x and y.

The first two conditions are quite straightforward; regarding the first condition, caution is warranted in the case where x and y simultaneously affect each other; also, that y follows x in no mean suggests that x caused y (i.e., it is possible that an omitted lagged cause of x also predicts y). This latter point will become clear in the first simulation we present. Also, we should note that from the second condition it follows that the constructs being studied should be operationalized (measured) and statistically analyzed. Although necessary, it is clear that these two first conditions are not sufficient to establish causality. They are, however, sufficient for one to fall prey to the *post hoc, ergo propter hoc* fallacy, which consists in wrongly interpreting causality by inferring that x is the cause of y precisely because it occurred before y (Kerlinger & Lee, 2000). The third condition has more to do with design and analysis issues than it has with theoretical arguments, though theory is important too (see also James, Mulaik, & Brett, 1982; Mulaik & James, 1995). It is also the more troublesome condition and the one with which much of this chapter is concerned.

This third condition can be restated by simply saying that changes in x produce changes in y holding all other things equal. This is clearly the case if x varies randomly and independently from the system of variables under study; if x depended on some unmodeled causes that also drive other variables in the model then x would be said to be *endogenous*—hence the problem of *endogeneity*. As alluded to in the introduction, the consequences of endogeneity are dire. If the necessary precautions are not taken to purge the endogenous variable of endogeneity then estimated coefficients are devoid of any meaning and cannot be interpreted.

Endogeneity: Two Inconvenient Demonstrations

We start with a very simple demonstration, presented by John Antonakis in the podcast *Endogeneity: An Inconvenient Truth* (available on YouTube), and previously discussed by Antonakis (in Fairhurst & Antonakis, 2012): A philosopher is sent out on a field to observe a naturally occurring phenomenon and is required to piece together a theoretical account of what she saw. She observes 50 trials of the phenomenon, which consists of a disk streaking across the sky that almost always shatters soon after a loud "crack" is heard; the disk never shatters when the crack is not heard. She carefully gathers the data, including number of trials, whether the crack was present or not (and how loud it was in decibels), and whether the disc disintegrated or not. Refer to Table 6.2A for a summary of the data regarding the relation between the presence of the "crack" and the disc.

The *observed* (and it is important to highlight the word *observed*), correlation between the two variables, noise (heard or not) and disk (shattering or not), is very strong and statistically significant: ϕ = .92, $\chi^2(1)$ = 42.32, p < .001 (see Table 6.2B). The data spoke clearly: Thus, the philosopher concludes that the soundwaves from this loud crack—which emanate from some yet-to-be-established source—caused the disks to shatter into smithereens. She writes an extensive theory around this explanation; for the sake of argument several policy implications follow, which have a military focus (i.e., building jamming defenses against the "noise," which would potentially be a very dangerous weapon against her city state).

The research efforts of the philosopher are nothing more than futile, as are the policy implications; unbeknown to the philosopher is the true causal model behind the data. The noise is caused by a hidden shooter who fires a rifle shot at the disk. The noise and the disk shattering are both caused by the rifle that is being fired by the shooter. Thus, the sound is in no way related to the disk shattering; they both share a common cause. What relation is observed is coincidental—spurious. Reporting it and building policies around it pointless.

Table 6.2. What Caused the Disk to Shatter

A: Summary data with omitted cause

	Disc not shattered	Disc shattered	Total
Noise not heard	19	0	19
Noise heard	2	29	31
Total	21	29	50

B: Correlation matrix and descriptive statistics

Variable	Mean	Std. Dev.	1	2	3
1. Rifle (fired = 1; else = 0)	.62	.49			
2. Disk shattered	.58	.50	.92		
3. Noise (db)	75.48	6.22	.99	.90	
4. Noise (heard =1; else = 0)	.62	.49	1.00	.92	.99

Note: Data from "Endogeneity: An Inconvenient Truth" (simulated data).
The data can be downloaded at: http://www.hec.unil.ch/jantonakis/disk.xls.

Knowing the true causal structure behind these data allows us to estimate whether there is a correlation between the noise and the disk; we use the decibels as the variable of interest (because hearing the crack and whether the rifle fires are perfectly collinear). We thus estimate the following multivariate least-squares regression:

$$Disk = \beta_0 + \beta_1 Rifle + e \quad (1)$$

$$Noise = \gamma_0 + \gamma_1 Rifle + u \quad (2)$$

where Disk = whether the disk shatters (= 1) or not (= 0); Noise = noise measured in decibels; Rifle = whether the rifle was fired (= 1) or not (= 0). Note, Eq. (1) is estimated using a linear probability model (ordinary least squares [OLS]), which is perfectly fine to use, particularly in this case where rifle = 0, which is always associated with noise = 0 (Caudill, 1988). Given that standard errors might not be consistent for Eq. (1), we bootstrap the standard errors (using 1000 replications; we could also have used a robust variance estimator). We also bootstrap the standard error for the test of the significance of the residual correlation (Breusch & Pagan, 1980) between Disk and Noise to determine whether they are still related once the phenomenon is correctly modeled.

The estimated parameters are: $\beta_1 = .93$, SE = .04, $z = 22.47$, $p < .001$, and $\gamma_1 = 121.74$, SE = 1.81, $z = 67.34$, $p < .001$. However, the test for the significance of the residual correlation is not significant: $\chi^2(1) = 2.94$, SE = 2.34, $p > .10$. Thus, once the correct causal structure of the data is accounted for, it is clear that the noise is unrelated to the disk shattering. Thus, these variables have been "*d*-separated" or directionally separated (Hayduk et al., 2003; Pearl, 2009). The noise was endogenous; thus regressing anything on the noise is pretty much a useless endeavor unless the true model is being estimated (or some corrective procedures are undertaken). Granted, we admit that there may be some very limited use to studying correlations in the initial phases of understanding a phenomenon. However, after studying the phenomenon for some time, we sincerely hope that researchers will go beyond merely studying associations; we do not see this being the case in leadership research (or organizational behavior, management, and applied psychology research in general).

A direct analog in leadership research to the "crack" in the preceding example is any endogenous variable that does not vary randomly or independently of the specified model variables or omitted variables (i.e., it has a theoretical cause or several causes that correlate with the modeled variables). Consider Leader–Member Exchange (LMX), that is, quality of leader–member relations. LMX has been linked to several outcomes (*y*). However, LMX does not vary randomly in organizations. It depends on some factors that may stem from the leader, the follower, and the organization, which may correlate with a supposed outcome of LMX. If these factors are omitted from the model and if they predict *y* too, the effects of LMX on *y* cannot be correctly estimated. LMX (i.e., the "crack") depends on something (i.e., the "rifle shot"); if this "something" is not modeled when using LMX as regressor then what correlations are reported are really not very useful in advancing leadership research.

To understand this problem better, and how LMX (or any another other endogenous variable that is studied in leadership) relates to the "crack" assume the causal structure as described in Eqs. (3) and (4), which we have simulated. This account of what drives the two endogenous variables is theoretically plausible; it is, however, a simple model and not necessarily an adequate model that will suffice for the demonstration (note, all the coefficients in the model are "1"; the intercepts are –250 and 150 respectively):

$$\begin{aligned} LMX = \beta_0 &+ \beta_1 L\_Extra \\ &+ \beta_2 L\_Incent \\ &+ \beta_3 L\_IQ + \beta_4 F\_IQ \\ &+ \beta_5 F\_Consc \\ &- \beta_6 F\_Neuro + 3 * e \end{aligned} \quad (3)$$

$$\begin{aligned} Turnover = \gamma_0 &- \gamma_1 L\_Incent \\ &- \gamma_2 L\_IQ - \gamma_3 C\_Policies \\ &+ \gamma_4 F\_Neuro + 3 * u \end{aligned} \quad (4)$$

Where LMX = quality of leader-member relations; L_Extra = leader extraversion; L_Incent = leader use of incentives; L_IQ = leader IQ; F_IQ = follower IQ; F_Consc = Follower conscientiousness; F_Neuro = Follower neuroticism; Turnover = Follower turnover intentions; and C_Policies = company policies (including pay, working conditions, etc.); *e* and *u* are random independent variables that are normally distributed. Also, suppose that the modeled independent variables are random variables (i.e., exogenous with respect to the two endogenous ones LMX and Turnover), and are measured without error, and that model is a correct causal account of what drives LMX and follower turnover. The summary data are listed in Table 6.3 (we generated these data using Stata and random seed 1234; note, because a covariance matrix can be generated from the summary data, those who are interested can replicate this analysis using a Structural Equation Modeling program). Interesting to note is that the observed correlation between LMX and Turnover is high and significant, $r(1000) = -.50$, $p < .001$.

We then estimated a multivariate regression model (saturated), where we predicted LMX and Turnover from the independent variables (see Table 6.4A). What is interesting to observe in this case is whether the residual correlation between LMX and Turnover is significantly different from zero: It is not, whether we estimate the model using OLS or maximum likelihood ($r = .02$, $p > .10$). Thus, whatever observed correlation is found between LMX and turnover is a false account of the relation between LMX and turnover (refer to the similarity of this conclusion with that which is presented later in discussing the two-stage least squares estimator).

Now, we estimate the following naïve model (Table 6.4B):

$$Turnover = \delta_0 + \delta_1 LMX + \delta_2 C\_Policies + \psi \quad (5)$$

From the above specification, LMX appears to affect turnover intentions on the part of subordinates, $\delta_1 = -.46$, $p < .001$. However, because theoretically, LMX is endogenous, this coefficient is devoid of any meaning. This point—and again, we are using LMX as an example and leadership research is replete with such potentially endogenous regressors (e.g., authentic leadership)—has not garnered much interest from leadership scholars and is not well understood. For instance, House and Aditya (1997) noted that "While it is almost tautological to say that good or effective leadership consists in part of good relationships between leaders and followers, there are several questions about such relationships to which answers are not intuitively obvious. . . . A specification of the attributes of high-quality LMX—trust, respect, openness, latitude of discretion—is as close as the theory comes to describing or prescribing specific leader behaviors. The theory implies that any leader behavior that has a positive effect on LMX quality will be effective. However, precisely what these behaviors are is not explicitly stated, as the appropriate leader behavior is dependent on anticipated subordinate response" (pp. 431–432).

Meta-analyses have established correlates of LMX, both antecedents and consequences (Dulebohn, Bommer, Liden, Brouer, & Ferris, 2011; Gerstner & Day, 1997); interestingly, Gerstner and Day (1997, p. 829) had noted: "we avoid discussing [the relationships found] in terms of causal inferences regarding the direction of these relationships. For purposes of the present analyses, we treat them all as correlates." Fifteen years later, Dulebohn et al. (2011) noted: "In addition, many of the studies included in our analysis were based on a cross-sectional correlation design, which prevents the establishment of causal

Table 6.3. Summary Data Showing Regarding LMX-Turnover Relation (simulated data)

	Mean	SD	1	2	3	4	5	6	7	8
1. Leader extraversion	50.04	2.93								
2. Leader use of incentives	9.86	2.99	−.03							
3. Leader IQ	110.07	2.90	.05	.03						
4. Follower IQ	105.00	2.94	.02	−.02	.03					
5. Follower conscientiousness	39.91	2.89	.01	.01	−.05	.01				
6. Follower neuroticism	35.04	3.08	.00	−.02	−.02	−.01	.02			
7. Company policies	19.98	3.12	.00	−.05	−.01	−.07	.00	.01		
8. LMX	29.78	7.88	.37	.40	.40	.39	.34	−.40	−.08	
9. Turnover	45.01	6.70	−.02	−.43	−.45	.02	.03	.48	−.45	−.50

$N = 1{,}000$.

Table 6.4. Regressions Regarding LMX and Turnover (simulated data)

	Coef.	SE	*t*	*p*
A: Multivariate regression estimates				
Dependent variable: LMX				
Leader extraversion	.94	.03	29.05	.00
Leader use of incentives	1.05	.03	33.21	.00
Leader IQ	.99	.03	3.45	.00
Follower IQ	.99	.03	3.81	.00
Follower conscientiousness	.97	.03	29.62	.00
Follower neuroticism	–1.00	.03	–32.71	.00
Company policies	–.05	.03	–1.78	.08
Constant	–243.36	5.43	–44.82	.00
$F(8,991) = 857.15$, $p < .001$, $r^2 = .86$				
Dependent variable: Turnover				
Leader extraversion	–.04	.03	–1.17	.24
Leader use of incentives	–.98	.03	–31.85	.00
Leader IQ	–.98	.03	–31.03	.00
Follower IQ	–.02	.03	–.66	.51
Follower conscientiousness	.01	.03	.22	.83
Follower neuroticism	1.02	.03	34.31	.00
Company policies	–1.02	.03	–34.89	.00
Constant	151.04	5.26	28.71	.00
$F(8,991) = 626.61$, $p < .001$, $r^2 = .82$				
B: Naïve regression estimates				
Dependent variable: Turnover				
Leader–member exchange	–.46	.02	–23.75	.00
Company policies	–1.04	.05	–21.41	.00
Constant	79.52	1.18	67.49	.00
$F(2,997) = 474.74$, $p < .001$, $r^2 = .49$				

Note: the residual correlation for the model in A, between LMX and turnover, is zero.

direction." Yet, Dulebohn et al. conducted tests of mediation to establish whether LMX mediates the effects of certain regressors on outcomes. These tests, however, reported biased coefficients because as we become clear later mediation must be undertaken using the 2SLS estimator (in the case of an endogenous mediator). Also, the problem with "causal direction" does not have to do with finding a coefficient of, say –.30, while not knowing whether this effect captures how x influences y or how y influences

x; that is not the point. If the regressor is endogenous, this coefficient capturing the true effect of x on y or of y on x could be higher, lower, zero or of a different sign!

As it has become clear in the introduction, establishing the true (causal) relationship between two (or more) variables is not a simple matter. We show how one can establish the true relation even when the regressor is endogenous. We first discuss the workings of the experimental design and how it eliminates endogeneity (i.e., by manipulating the regressors); then we show methods can be used to recover causal estimates even if the regressor has not been manipulated.

Counterfactuals and the Randomized Experiment

The Counterfactual Argument

The counterfactual argument is at the heart of the experimental design and serves as a main foundation of causal analysis. Let us consider a simple experiment in which individuals, in a treatment or control group (captured by the dichotomous variable x), are measured on an observed variable y. Assuming that x preceded y temporally, and that x and y are significantly correlated beyond chance, how could we establish that x has a *causal* effect on y? In other words, how can we rule out alternate explanations as to why x could affect y? To do so, we need to consider either one of the two possible counterfactual conditionals—only in this way can causality be determined (Morgan & Winship, 2007; Rubin, 1974; Winship & Morgan, 1999).

If we consider the situation from the standpoint of the individuals in the treatment group, the counterfactual conditional would ask, "What would we have observed on y for the individuals in the treatment group had they not received the treatment?" Alternatively, if we first consider individuals in the control group, the counterfactual conditional would ask, "What would we have observed on y for the individuals in the control group had they received the treatment?" Comparing two given states of the world (i.e., what currently is vs. the counterfactual condition) allows us to establish causality. This is precisely what is done in the randomized experiment, which is achieved by randomizing participants to treatment, which is a failsafe way to eliminate endogeneity.

Kerlinger and Lee (2000) refer to the laboratory experiments as one of the greatest inventions in history because of its ability to identify and test causal relationships in uncontaminated conditions. The randomized experiment establishes causality through the counterfactual argument. By randomly allocating participants to treatment and control groups, the experimental design ensures that both groups of individuals are similar on all (observable and unobservable) characteristics. Thus, each group serves as the counterfactual conditional for the other and consequently, the causal effect of the experimental treatment can be observed as the difference between the treatment and control groups on the dependent variable.

Let us focus on how statistical analysis of experimental data produces causal *estimates*, which brings to light the problem of endogeneity and why experimental data can support causal claims. We here examine the OLS estimator—the estimator commonly used in regression (or ANOVA models)—which derives estimates by reducing the sum of squared residuals (hence its name) between observed and predicted values. We use a simple model in which two groups (i.e., an experimental and a control group) are measured on a dependent variable y. We use a dummy variable x, which is 1 if an individual receives the treatment and to 0 otherwise, to model the experimental effect. For this example, we also assume that participants are pre-measured on z, indicating participant sex (female = 1, else 0), which is a predictor of y. The inclusion of the covariate z serves to increase statistical power and should consequently make it easier for the researcher to identify the effect of x on y (Keppel & Wickens, 2004; Maxwell, Cole, Arvey, & Salas, 1991). In addition, the covariate may correct for small differences remaining between the control and treatment groups despite randomization (Shadish, Cook, & Campbell, 2002); including covariates (as in an ANCOVA) design is thus a very good idea, particularly if the sample will not be very large. We thus estimate:

$$y_i = \beta_0 + \beta_1 x_i + \beta_2 z_i + e_i \qquad (6)$$

Important to note is that the error (or disturbance) term e captures all unobserved sources of variance in y along with any other sources of error (such as measurement error for example). To avoid any confusion, note that the error or disturbance term is not the same as the residual term. The error term refers to all unobserved and unmodeled sources of variance in y, whereas the residual term is the difference between the predicted and observed values of y (and the OLS estimator is concerned with minimizing the sum of the squares of these differences).

By design, the residual term is orthogonal to the independent variables, which is not necessarily the case with the error term.

There is a key assumption made by the OLS estimator that is central to understanding how and when causal analysis is possible with nonexperimental data. The OLS estimator assumes that the error term e is uncorrelated with any of the independent variables. If we consider only x, the manipulated variable in our example, OLS assumes that e is uncorrelated to x, which is the same to say that e and x are orthogonal, or that x is *exogenous*. This brings us back to the problem of endogeneity, which refers precisely to the situation were x and e correlate. In the randomized experiment, x and e are uncorrelated by design, because of two conditions: (1) the researcher has total control over x and (2) participants are randomly assigned to conditions. Because factors that explain y beyond the treatment, e, are unrelated with x (or other covariates) estimates are consistent. If these two conditions are not met, it will be very likely that x and e will correlate.

Suppose an organization wants to assess the effectiveness of a leadership training it offers to its employees. To do so, participants are randomly assigned either to the leadership training or to a control condition (who receive no training), and are measured on leader prototypicality at the outcome of the training. We are keeping the problem simple with two groups; however, we may have alternative treatments and can also cross designs as in the typical 2 × 2 ANOVA. Of course, at the outset of the experiment some participants will possess characteristics that make them more prototypical of leaders (e.g., being more charismatic). But because of random assignment, the proportion of participants high (or low) on these characteristics will be roughly the same in both groups. Therefore, any difference we observe between groups on leader prototypicality at the end of the experiment can be attributed only to the experimental manipulation.

Following on the same example, let us imagine now that rather than randomly assigning participants to treatment and control conditions, the organization compares managers from one division (Division 1) who were chosen to complete the training, to a group of managers from another division (Division 2) who do not attend training. What if participants who were chosen to do the leadership training program differ from those participants who did not attend the training on some characteristics? For example, Division 1 might spend a lot of time in carefully choosing whom they promote to positions of leadership (i.e., they use 360-degree ratings to take the best leaders); however, suppose that Division 2 does not have these mechanisms (and instead only the division boss is the person who appoints leaders based on production figures). If the characteristics on which Division 1 and 2 participants are selected predict leader prototypicality, then the effect of the treatment is confounded. In other words, the treatment will correlate with the error term. Why? Because some of the characteristics (e.g., leadership styles) are higher in the treatment group (Division 1 leaders) and these factors correlate with y too; thus, because these factors were not randomly assigned and they are omitted from the model, their effects are pooled into the error term, which will correlate with x and induce endogeneity.

Such conditions violate the orthogonality assumption (of e with x) of the OLS estimate and also of the maximum likelihood estimator. As a consequence, the estimator, in an attempt to satisfy this assumption, will "adjust" the estimate of the problematic (i.e., endogenous) variable. The estimate of the endogenous variable will become inconsistent, meaning that it will not converge to the true population parameters as sample size increases. The estimate is therefore useless; furthermore, the endogenous variable will also render inconsistent all other variables in the model with which it correlates even if these are not endogenous (refer to Figure 6.1 for a graphic representation).

Whereas the randomized experiment is the fail-safe design to test theoretical propositions, it may not always be possible for researchers to implement a randomized experiment—be it for practical or ethical reasons. Also, randomized experiments typically concern small and quite specific populations, thus limiting their external validity. Consequently, researchers must often rely on nonexperimental data to test their theories. In nonexperimental settings, scientists neither have direct *control* over independent variables, nor do they have the possibility to use random assignment—the two elements that allow one to make causal claims with the experimental method. Thus, the important question to ask is: How can causal claims be made on the basis of nonexperimental data? To answer this question, we must understand the causes of inconsistent estimates.

The Pitfalls of Nonexperimental Research

Endogeneity can stem from a plethora of situations wherein a regressor x correlates with the

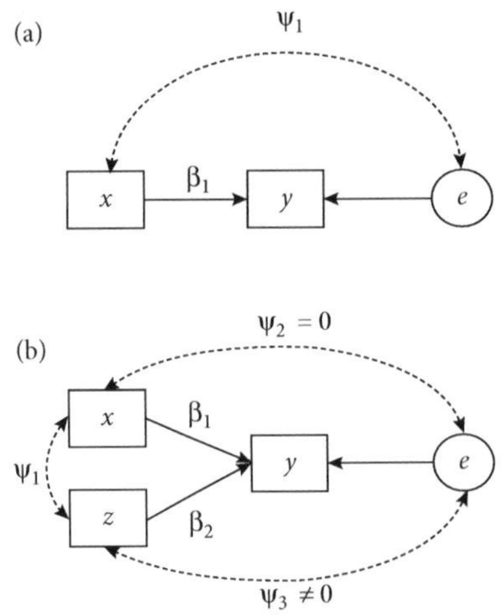

Panel	Condition	β_1	β_2	Explanation
A	$\psi_1 = 0$	Consistent		x does not correlate with e thus β_1 is consistent.
A	$\psi_1 \neq 0$	Inconsistent		x correlates with e and thus β_1 is inconsistent.
B	$\psi_1 = 0$	Consistent	Inconsistent	z correlates with e and thus β_2 is inconsistent. β_1 is consistent because x is uncorrelated both with z and with e.
B	$\psi_1 \neq 0$	Inconsistent	Inconsistent	z correlates with e thus β_2 is inconsistent. Although x is uncorrelated with e, β_1 it inconsistent because it is affected by the bias in z through x's correlation with z.

Figure 6.1. Endogeneity and the Consistency of Estimates.

model's error term e (thus violating one of the underlying assumptions of OLS of maximum likelihood). Below we present conditions that potentially cause endogeneity and threaten estimate validity. We also cover an additional area researchers should be wary of when testing theoretical models, which are concerned not with the consistency of estimates, but with the consistency of inferences (i.e., the validity of the standard errors). We also discuss proper model specification in the context of simultaneous equations models. Following Antonakis et al. (2010), we use some basic algebra to show how endogeneity is engendered, particularly for the case of an omitted regressor and common-method variance (which are discussed in more detail). The advantage of using algebra is that we show very specifically how x correlates with the error term. We cover the rest of the threats briefly; readers can refer to Antonakis et al. (2010) for further details.

Omitting a Regressor

Consider the following model in which each individual i is measured on a dependent variable y, and on two independent variables x and z:

$$y_i = \beta_0 + \beta_1 x_i + \beta_2 z_i + e_i \qquad (7)$$

The assumption of the estimator is that x and z are exogenous; in other words, they are not predicted by the workings of this specific model. Thus, neither x nor z should correlate with any of the unobserved sources of variances in y (i.e., they do not correlate with e). Now, suppose a researcher is interested in understanding whether x, one's ability to wait before obtaining a desired outcome (i.e., delayed gratification), predicts leader effectiveness (y). Because delayed gratification correlates in part to cognitive ability z, and because cognitive ability predicts leader effectiveness, the researcher must control for z. If the researcher fails to do so, the estimate of x will be biased because x will correlate with e. This can be easily seen in the following equations. This is the misspecified model omitting z:

$$y_i = \varphi_0 + \varphi_1 x_i + v_i \quad (8)$$

If z and x correlate (irrespective of the direction), then we can note that:

$$z_i = \gamma_1 x_i + u_i \quad (9)$$

The endogeneity is evident when substituting Eq. (9) into Eq. (7):

$$y_i = \beta_0 + \beta_1 x_i + \beta_2(\gamma_1 x_i + u_i) + e_i, \quad (10)$$

Multiplying out gives (notice, the error term v_i, which is the error term of Eq. (8):

$$y_i = \beta_0 + \beta_1 x_i + (\beta_2 \gamma_1 x_i + \beta_2 u_i + e_i) \quad (11)$$

$$v_i$$

Or, rearranging as a function of x gives

$$y_i = \beta_0 + (\beta_1 + \beta_2 \gamma_1) x_i + (\beta_2 u_i + e_i) \quad (12)$$

In the presence of endogeneity, one does not estimate β_1 of Eq. (7), but φ_1 in Eq. (8); these two estimates will not be equal except under two conditions: If (a) $\beta_2 = 0$ or if (b) $\gamma_1 = 0$. In these cases, then v_i reduces to e_i and there is no omitted variable when excluding z from the model. Also, whether φ_1 is increases or decreases when excluding z will depend on the signs and magnitudes of β_2 and γ_1.

Given the consequences of omitting a variable, when in doubt about whether a given variable should be included or not in a model, it is always best to stay on the safe side by including this additional variable (Cameron & Trivedi, 2005); this is not the advice that management methodologists usually provide (e.g., Spector & Brannick, 2011). Indeed, the cost of including additional variables is higher standard errors (i.e., reduced efficiency); if the sample is large enough to detect significant effects then this is a small cost to pay. If there is a choice to be made, we will always prefer consistency to efficiency. What is the value of inconsistent estimates having precise standard errors?

How does a researcher determine whether there are omitted variables? There is only one rather limited test to examine whether polynomial terms are omitted from the model. This is called Ramsey's (1969) regression-error-specification (RESET); however, this test *cannot* determine whether there are other types of omitted variables. Thus, the most important guide is "theory, theory, and more theory" (Antonakis & Dietz, 2011, p. 218); there are no direct tests to determine whether there is an omitted variable, which could be a main effect or an interaction effect too in a particular model (apart from comparing random-effects to fixed-effects estimators, as discussed later). One way to suggest that there are omitted variables is to compare the target model to a model that is known to be consistent (e.g., from an instrumental-variable model, discussed later). The parameter(s) of interest is tested using a Hausman (1978) test. This is a very versatile test that can be used to compare estimators. Basically, the test shows that if an estimate (from the efficient but not consistent model) is different from that of the consistent model, this difference must come from the fact that the variable correlates with the disturbance in the efficient model.

In its simplest form, the Hausman test may be computed for one parameter, where δ is the element of β being tested (Wooldrige, 2002); the efficient estimate is compared to the consistent estimate using a t test that follows an asymptotic standard normal distribution. Note too that the Hausman test for one parameter is also useful in situations where the test for an overall model is not defined and the researcher is concerned about whether a specific variable may be endogenous (note that Hausman tests can be conducted using other ways, e.g., Wald tests in the context of "seemingly unrelated" regression models). The formula for the one-parameter test is:

$$z = \frac{(\hat{\delta}_{CONSISTENT} - \hat{\delta}_{EFFICIENT})}{\sqrt{SE(\hat{\delta}_{CONSISTENT})^2 - SE(\hat{\delta}_{EFFICIENT})^2}}$$

We discussed the basic case of omitted variable bias in depth using two examples (i.e., the "inconvenient demonstrations") and with simple algebra. We now briefly discuss other types of endogeneity bias. For in-depth discussion and detailed explanation regarding these forms of endogeneity refer to Antonakis et al. (2010).

Measurement Error (Errors-in-Variables)

Measurement error is a common problem in leadership research, yet it remains largely unaddressed (with the exception of researchers using structural equation models that correct for measurement error as discussed in the following section of this chapter; however, these researchers make another critical error by ignoring the overidentification test). There are many examples of how estimates can be severely compromised by measurement error (for demonstrations see Fiori & Antonakis, 2011; Schulte, Ree, & Carretta, 2004; von Wittich & Antonakis, 2011).

Many constructs of interest in social sciences cannot be perfectly observed; consequently measurement of these constructs includes some degree of measurement error. For example, imagine that we want to measure the intelligence of leaders. Intelligence in a "pure" theoretical form, which we will call x^*, cannot be directly observed. Rather, what we observe is x which consists of the x^*, the pure construct, and an error term u reflecting measurement error (see Cameron & Trivedi, 2005; Maddala, 1977). So, if our goal is to understand the relationship between follower motivation (y) and leader intelligence x^*, we would consider the following model:

$$y_i = \beta_0 + \beta_1 x_i^* + e_i \qquad (13)$$

We cannot directly observe x^*, but what we observe is a proxy of x^*, x as follows:

$$x_i = x_i^* + u_i \; or \; x_i^* = x_i - u_i \qquad (14)$$

So, substituting Eq. (14) in Eq. (13) gives:

$$y_i = \beta_0 + \beta_1 (x_i - u_i) + e_i \qquad (15)$$

which is equivalent to the following model:

$$y_i = \beta_0 + \beta_1 x_i + (e_i - \beta_1 u_i) \qquad (16)$$

As it is clear from Eq. (16), the rearranged error term correlates with x and therefore the estimates of the effect of x will be inconsistent. Thus, we see that if we do not explicitly model u, we create endogeneity by omitting a source of variance in y. This omission results in an attenuated estimate of the effect of x. As with the omitted variable bias, measurement error in x will affect all variables correlated with the problematic variable (Bollen, 1989; Kennedy, 2003).

Measurement error can easily be modeled by constraining the variance of disturbance of x to (1−reliability$_x$) * Variance$_x$ (Bollen, 1989). Estimates of the reliability of a measure can be obtained by, for example, using the test–retest reliability or Cronbach's alpha (which is a lower-bound correction). Alternatively, if reliability is not known, estimates can be derived theoretically to constrain the disturbance (Hayduk, 1996; Onyskiw & Hayduk, 2001).

In terms of technical implementation, measurement error can be modeled in a regression using, for example, the least-squares eivreg (errors-in-variables) command in Stata; one could also use maximum likelihood estimation in a structural equation modeling program. When measurement error concerns a measure with a single indicator, the eivreg routine should be chosen over structural equation modeling solutions because it is much less restrictive in terms of assumptions and sample size (e.g., see Bollen, 1996; Draper & Smith, 1998; Kmenta, 1986). Structural equation modeling is the method of choice for treating measurement error in latent constructs with multiple indicators. In practice—and assuming item indicators are valid measures of the construct—if one uses a parcel (i.e., average of indicators) and models this as one indicator of a latent variable, structural estimates will be similar to those obtained from a full specification (e.g., Bandalos & Finney, 2001; Hall, Snell, & Singer Foust, 1999; Liang, Lawrence, Bennett, & Whitelaw, 1990). The instrumental variable method we discuss later also provides a solution to measurement error bias.

Common Source, Common Method Variance

Another cause for inconsistent estimates is common method variance (cf. Podsakoff, Mackenzie, & Podsakoff, 2010); this problem is related to measurement error. Common method variance refers to the situation where the relationship between x and y is dependent on a third variable q. At best, researchers acknowledge that common method variance can bias estimates, but with the erroneous assumption that estimates can be biased only upwards. At worse, some researchers suggest that this bias is exaggerated (e.g., Spector, 2006); unfortunately, it is not possible to know how exaggerated the bias is unless the correct procedures are used (e.g., instrumental-variable regression).

A prevalent example of common method variance is one in which subordinates are asked to provide ratings on independent and dependent measures on their leaders (there are 50 leaders in this sample)—for example, ratings of leader prototypicality (x) and ratings of leader ethical behavior (y). In this situation, subordinates will seek to maintain cognitive consistency between both ratings (Podsakoff, MacKenzie, Lee, & Podsakoff, 2003; Podsakoff & Organ, 1986), which may be driven by a third variable(s) q (e.g., affect for the leader, knowledge of the effectiveness of the leader, and other biases). Assume we collected measures on leader$_j$ from follower$_i$, in a model in which we control for leader fixed-effects too using $k - 1$ leader dummy variables (i.e., 49 dummy variables; refer to the later section on fixed-effects):

$$y^*_{ij} = \beta_0 + \beta_1 x^*_{ij} + \sum_{k=2}^{50} + e_{ij} \tag{17}$$

As with measurement error, we do not directly observe y^* or x^*; rather we observe y and x, which can be modeled as a function of q and y^*:

$$y_{ij} = y^*_{ij} + \gamma_y q_{ij} \tag{18}$$

$$x_{ij} = x^*_{ij} + \gamma_x q_{ij} \tag{19}$$

The two later equations can be rearranged as follows:

$$y^*_{ij} = y_{ij} - \gamma_y q_{ij} \tag{20}$$

$$x^*_{ij} = x_{ij} - \gamma_x q_{ij} \tag{21}$$

We can substitute y^* and x^* in Eq. (17), which gives:

$$(y_{ij} - \gamma_y q_{ij}) = \beta_0 + \beta_1 (x_{ij} - \gamma_x q_{ij}) + \sum_{k=2}^{50} \beta_k D_{jk} + e_{ij} \tag{22}$$

This equation can be rearranged to obtain:

$$y_{ij} = \beta_0 + \beta_1 x_{ij} + \sum_{k=2}^{50} \beta_k D_{jk} + (e_{ij} - \beta_1 \gamma_x q_{ij} + \gamma_y q_{ij}) \tag{23}$$

We now see that the expanded and rearranged error term correlates with x. Once again, this results in an inconsistent estimate of the effect of x (and of all covariates correlating with x). The resulting bias may cause *inflated* or *attenuated* estimates (and cannot be eliminated with fixed-effects estimation; see next section).

A common (but incorrect) solution to the common source bias is that common source bias can be eliminated by including an unmeasured latent method factor in the model (Podsakoff et al., 2003). In order to work, this solution would require the researcher to know how the variables are affected by the unmeasured cause—which is not possible (cf. Antonakis et al., 2010; Richardson, Simmering, & Sturman, 2009). Furthermore, simulations shown that this solution cannot recover correct model estimates (cf. Antonakis et al., 2010; Richardson et al., 2009).

Several solutions to the common source bias have been proposed (cf. Antonakis et al., 2010; Podsakoff et al., 2010; Richardson et al., 2009). The most intuitive solution is to gather data on q; however, this solution is not practical because the researchers must know of all sources of q. Researchers could gather independent and dependent measures from difference sources (i.e., "objective" or hard measures of leader performance such as profits). The independent variables must of course be exogenous; otherwise there will still be endogeneity in the model. Another solution is to use a split-sample design (e.g., Koh, Steers, & Terborg, 1995) in which one half of the sample is used for ratings on the dependent measure and the other half is used for the independent measures; this solution is not ideal because with the split-sample design only half of the data is used and therefore the estimates of standard errors will be less precise (i.e., efficiency is reduced) and estimates will be less precise too given that fewer raters are used (Mount & Scullen, 2001; Scullen, Mount, & Goff, 2000). We later discuss another solution (i.e., instrumental variables models).

Omitting Fixed Effects

Researchers often have data on entities that are repeatedly measured over time (i.e., a longitudinal panel); data might also be hierarchically nested (i.e., a hierarchical or pseudo-panel) where entities under higher-level units are measured, as for example, companies nested under countries, leaders nested under companies, team members nested under leaders (cf. Liden & Antonakis, 2009). In either case, what we have are observations (Level 1) nested either in time or in a higher level entity of sorts (Level 2). Thus, with panel data, it is possible that Level 2 "fixed-effects" drive a part of the variance in the dependent variable and also correlate with other regressors. For example, when we observe leaders nested in organizations, leaders within organizations would share certain characteristics (e.g., as result of firm recruiting policies for example), which may affect the modeled variables. Thus, firm-level factors may predict performance outcomes; however, they may also correlate with leader-level characteristics (which were used by some firms to select leaders). Under the proviso that these Level 2 fixed-effects have an effect on the dependant variable and correlate with leader level (Level 1) characteristics, they will be pooled in the error term along with all other unmodeled sources of variance if they are not explicitly modeled; in this way, estimates of model become inconsistent (Cameron & Trivedi, 2005; Wooldridge, 2002).

How can this situation be avoided? The easy solution is to explicitly model these fixed-effects by using $k - 1$ company dummy variables (which capture all unobserved difference in firms). The difficult solution, which leads to what we call here the "*HLM problem*," is to attempt to include all relevant Level 2 predictors (i.e., company level regressors such as firm size, etc.) and estimate the model using a random-effects estimator (e.g., HLM). The problem here is what if all sources of Level 2 variance are not included? If an important Level 2 variable is omitted, then endogeneity is engendered. This endogeneity can be tested for using a Hausman test (1978); that is, the random-effects estimates (efficient) are compared to the fixed-effects estimates (consistent). If there is a significant difference, it means that the efficient estimator is not consistent and must be rejected. If there is not a significant difference, the efficient estimator is not rejected.

Unfortunately, this point *is still not understood* by those who estimate HLM-type models (Antonakis et al., 2010; Halaby, 2004); omitting fixed-effects is a major problem that must be taken seriously by researchers estimating HLM models. The only way to ensure that Level 2 fixed-effects are included is to model the Level 2 dummy variables. However, doing so precludes modeling Level 2 variables (because they will be perfectly collinear with the dummies). Researchers using HLM models can have their cake and eat it too, however. That is, it is possible to include both Level 2 fixed-effects and Level 2 variables by using the Mundlak (1978) procedure; refer to Antonakis et al. (2010) for intuitive explanations.

Omitting Selection

Without random assignment, treatment is endogenous unless selection is explicitly modeled. Consider the equation below:

$$y_i = \beta_0 + \beta_1 x_i + \beta_2 z_i + e_i \qquad (24)$$

Say that x is equal to 1 if the individual receives the treatment (i.e., a leadership-training program), or is equal to 0 if the individual is in the control condition. The dependent variable y is how prototypical of a leader the individual is and z is a dummy variable indicating participant sex (female = 1). Assume now that individuals have been self selected to the conditions. Because of this selection, both groups will differ on a number of characteristics on the outset (recall that they would have been roughly equivalent had x been randomly assigned). This specification is problematic because differences between both groups may correlate with the dependent variable causing x to correlate with e. Assume that the selection x^* can be modeled in the following probit (or logit) equation (Cong & Drukker, 2001):

$$x_i^* = \gamma_0 + \sum_{k=1}^{q} \gamma_k d_{kj} + u_i \qquad (25)$$

where we have k regressors and a disturbance term u. Individuals are selected (i.e., $x = 1$) if $x^* > 0$. The problem of omitted selection arises because u will correlate with e (called $\rho_{e,u}$) and as a result of which x will correlate with e.

For example, it is possible that individuals with high levels of extraversion are more likely to self-select to the leadership training, and it is also possible that because of their extraversion these individuals are perceived as more leaderlike than their counterparts. Therefore, we are here again in a situation where an unmodeled source of variance (pooled in e) correlates with x, thus creating endogeneity and yielding inconsistent parameters (Kennedy, 2003). The only way causality can be assessed with nonrandom assignment of participants to conditions is by explicitly modeling the selection process so as to create a clean counterfactual (Cong & Drukker, 2001; Maddala, 1983).

Researchers must be cautious not only of the selection process to treatment and control conditions, but also of the selection of their samples. Indeed, nonrepresentative, or censored, samples will result in inconsistent estimates. For example, studying the effect of cognitive abilities on leader effectiveness will produce misleading results in that there is little variance on cognitive abilities in the study sampled (e.g., because participants are all highly intelligent). In this latter example, the researcher will find attenuated estimates of the effect of cognitive abilities on leader effectiveness. In the case in which participants are nonrandomly selected (either self-selected or selected on another basis), the researcher should ensure that participants are representative of the general population on relevant factors. If this is not the case, estimates could be misleading. Take, for example, the situation in which leader performance ratings are obtained from followers who have been selected by the leader to provide these ratings. We can expect that the leader will select followers who are most likely to give positive feedback. If this is the case, again, selection must be explicitly modeled.

A final example of the problem of omitted selection is samples in which a certain range of data is missing on the dependant variable (i.e., the dependent variable is censored). It is possible to deal with such problems by using censored regression models (Tobin, 1958) or truncated regression models or sorts (Long & Freese, 2006).

Simultaneity

The problem of simultaneity, although quite simple to understand, can be quite troublesome for researchers. Simultaneity happens when two variables *simultaneously* affect each other (hence the name). Note that this is different from what researchers sometimes name "backward causality," which is when the estimated effect of x on y is proposed to be caused by y affecting x.

A good example of simultaneous causality is the relation between levels of crime and number of police officers discussed by Steven Levitt (see Levitt, 1997, 2002). The standard expectation is that that hiring more police officers will reduce crime. Thus, we would expect the estimate of the relationship between the number of police officers and crime to be negative. However, crime can also affect the number of police officers. Indeed, a response to rising crime levels might be to increase the police force. Because of this simultaneous relation, the number of police officers will be endogenous. Such a type of simultaneity can be evident in leadership research too (e.g., a leader style of leading could depend on follower performance). Refer to Antonakis et al. (2010) for further discussion.

Consistency of Inference

Up to now, we have discussed consistency only with regard to the consistency of estimates. However, consistency of standard errors (i.e., the consistency of inference) is also important but overlooked. Work on this topic stems from the work of Huber (1967) and White (1980).

Consistent standard errors can be derived from OLS estimation under the assumption that regression residuals are identically and independently distributed (or, simply, i.i.d.). This assumption regarding residuals is twofold. First, residuals are assumed to be homoskedastic (i.e., identically distributed); in other words, they are assumed to have been drawn from the same population and have a uniform variance. Second, residuals are assumed to be neither clustered (nested under a higher level entity) nor serially correlated (i.e., they are assumed to be independently distributed).

It is noteworthy that non-i.i.d. residuals affect only the consistency of the standard errors and not the consistency of estimates. This problem is nevertheless a serious threat to validity because in the presence of heteroskedasticity, standard errors will be biased and p-values will be either under- or overstated. Thus, conclusions about the significance of parameter estimates will be wrong. The assumption of i.i.d. residuals, or lack thereof, can be tested using a number of tests readily available in programs akin to Stata.

If the homoskedasticity assumption is violated, variance has to be estimated using a variance estimator based on the works of Huber and White. Hence these standard errors are called Huber–White standard errors, sandwiched standard errors, or robust standard errors (i.e., robust to heteroskedasticity). Alternatively, consistent standard errors can also be estimated using bootstrapping.

Standard errors could also become inconsistent because of clustered data, which directly violates the assumption that residuals are independently distributed. If this is case, standard errors must be cluster corrected using a specific variance estimator. Interestingly, this problem is often overlooked, and was so until recently even in economics (see Bertrand, Duflo, & Mullainathan, 2004). Note that data may involve multiple (independent or hierarchical) dimensions of clustering that must be taken into account by researchers (Cameron, Gelbach, & Miller, 2011).

Quasi-Experimental and Structural Equation Methods

This section presents methods available to researchers to test theoretical models (i.e., causal relationships) in nonexperimental settings. We begin with and devote a greater part of this section to two-stage least squares estimation. We then briefly discuss other methods too; for further details refer to Antonakis et al. (2010).

Two-Stage Least Squares Estimation

The two-stage least squares (2SLS), or instrumental-variable estimation, allows for *consistent* estimation of simultaneous equations with endogenous predictors. We have made reference to this method several times throughout this chapter as a means to treat endogeneity; 2SLS is one of the most potent and versatile tools available in this regard. This reason undoubtedly explains why this method is the workhorse of econometrics. Unfortunately, this method is scarcely used in other social sciences (see Cameron & Trivedi, 2005; Foster & McLanahan, 1996; Gennetian et al., 2008). We hope that in the future researchers will reap the benefits of this method: It truly is a cure to endogeneity resulting from omitted variables, measurement error, simultaneity, and common method bias (Cameron & Trivedi, 2005; Greene, 2008; Kennedy, 2003)! This estimator seems almost too good to be true, but 2SLS really is a clean and elegant way to purge models of endogeneity.

How does the 2SLS estimator correct for endogeneity? Recall that inconsistent estimates result from a regressor (x) correlating with the model's error term (e). If x and e did not correlate, we would obtain consistent estimates. This is precisely what the 2SLS estimation does: It removes the portion of variance in x that correlates with e. To do so, the 2SLS estimator relies on instrumental variables, which are exogenous regressors of the problematic (endogenous) variable. By definition, the instruments are uncorrelated with e, and therefore they can be used in a first estimation stage to obtain predicted values of the endogenous variable that will be uncorrelated with e (for ideas about where to find instrumental variables refer to Antonakis et al., 2010). These predicted values can then be used in a second stage to predict the dependent variable. In essence, the instrumental variables purge the endogenous variable from variance that overlaps with the error term. In this way consistent estimates of the endogenous variable are obtained. However, consistency here comes at the cost efficiency, which is reduced given that less of the available information is used.

Note, endogeneity can also arise in an experiment in which the causal effect of one dependent variable on another is estimated (i.e., the effect of $y1$ on $y2$). If the 2SLS estimator is not used, what is estimated will be biased. Thus, the 2SLS estimator is also useful to test mediation models (in the context of experiments or otherwise) to identify the causal effect of one endogenous regressor on another (stemming from the instrument/s). However, to estimate such models correctly one cannot use the simple mediation approaches that are popular in management and applied psychology research, that is, $x \rightarrow y1 \rightarrow y2$ (no matter how much estimates or standard errors are bootstrapped using the method of Preacher & Hayes, 2004). The problem is not necessarily with the standard errors of the indirect effect of x on $y2$; the problem has to do with the estimates and acknowledging that the mediator is endogenous (which is done by correlating the cross-equation disturbances of the endogenous variables: this is the 2SLS estimator). Refer to Figure 6.2 for a graphic depiction of this estimator. Failing to model the causal system correctly gives the same incorrect estimate that OLS gives.

To derive consistent estimates, the researcher needs to identify instruments to predict the endogenous variable x. There should be at least as many instruments as there are endogenous variables (this constitutes the order condition), although it would be desirable to have more instruments than endogenous variables to test overidentifying restrictions, as discussed later. Instruments should be significant and strong predictors of x, and predict y only through its effect on x; of course, instruments must also be uncorrelated with the model's error term—recall instruments must be exogenous. Having strong instruments (and non-redundant elements in the variance-covariance matrix) constitutes the rank condition. Only if both the order and rank conditions are satisfied can parameters be identified (Wooldridge, 2002). Note too that the instruments *may* correlate with y (in Antonakis et al., 2010 we had stated *must*; to be clear, the "must" is relevant in the case that x is truly a predictor of y—if not the instruments need not correlate with y to be valid instruments).

The more instruments are included in a model, the more information will be used to obtain the predicted values of x (i.e., $\hat{x}$). It is consequently desirable to include all available exogenous variables as instruments. Also, all predictors must be used as instruments (even if they only are theorized to predict y) in case they correlate with first-stage instruments; this can also avoid certain pitfalls that would otherwise result in inconsistent estimates (see Baltagi, 2002, for more information).

As explained earlier, consistency is ensured through the 2SLS estimation procedure, because only the "clean" (i.e., uncorrelated with the model error term) portion of variance in x is used to predict y. This clean portion is obtained by predicting x from the exogenous regressor, which is uncorrelated with the model error term (see Kennedy, 2003). Furthermore, consistency can be ensured only when cross-equation error terms are correlated

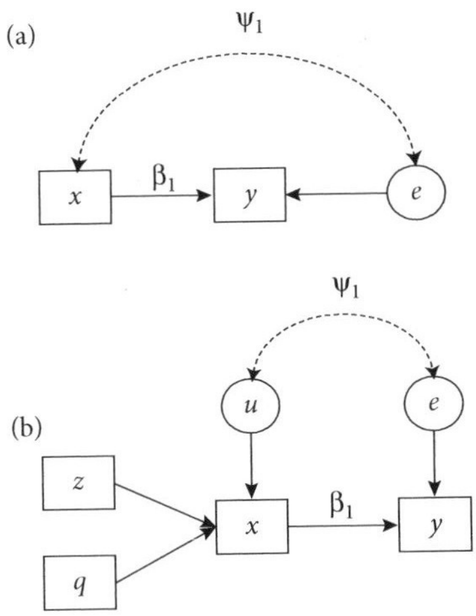

Panel	Condition	Estimator	β_1	Explanation
A	$\psi_1 \neq 0$	OLS	Inconsistent	x correlates with e thus β_1 is inconsistent.
B	$\psi_1 \neq 0$	Instrumental Variable (e.g., 2SLS)	Consistent	ψ_1 is estimated. β_1 is consistent because the instruments z and q are truly exogenous. In this case, β_1 (Panel A) $\neq \beta_1$ (Panel B)
B	$\psi_1 \neq 0$	OLS	Inconsistent	ψ_1 is constrained to zero; therefore β_1 is inconsistent. In this case, β_1 (Panel A) = β_1(Panel B)

Figure 6.2. Endogeneity and the Consistency of Estimates in Simultaneous Equation (Mediatory) Models.

(see Figure 6.2). Not estimating this correlation is akin to assuming that *x* is exogenous and will produce the same estimates as OLS (Maddala, 1977)—which will of course be inconsistent (unless *x* is exogenous). A Hausman test can be conducted to compare the (consistent) 2SLS estimates with the (efficient) OLS estimates obtained without instrumenting. A significant difference indicates that the estimates obtained through OLS are inconsistent and that *x* should be instrumented.

Estimation by 2SLS is imprecise if instruments only weakly predict the endogenous regressor *x*. Moreover, inference with weak instruments can be seriously biased (Bound, Jaeger, & Baker, 1995). Though the good news is that weak instruments can easily be detected; instruments are weak if the *F*-test for joint significance of instruments falls below a rule of thumb threshold of 10. Stock and Yogo (2002) present exact threshold values and extensions for multivariate models (see also Stock & Watson, 2007; Stock, Wright, & Yogo, 2002).

For increased efficiency, researchers can use a three-stage least square (3SLS) estimator (e.g., Zellner & Theil, 1962) or a maximum likelihood estimator (Baltagi, 2002; Bollen, 1996; Bollen, Kirby, Curran, Paxton, & Chen, 2007). These estimators produce more precise standard errors because they are full information estimators. However, before retaining full information estimates, the researcher must make sure these are consistent. A Hausman test can be used to compare the estimates from the efficient (e.g., 3SLS) and the consistent (i.e., 2SLS) estimators. A significant difference indicates that the consistent estimator must be retained.

The 2SLS estimator (i.e., a least-squares instrumental-variance estimator) can also be used in the context of structural equations models too. The same logic applies as previously (though the estimator is now a maximum likelihood instrumental-variable estimator). For more details refer to Antonakis et al. (2010).

Two-Stage Least Squares in Practice: An Example

Turning back to the LMX example (from the data generated by Eqs. [3] and [4], as presented in Table 6.3), to determine whether there is a causal effect of LMX on turnover, we should estimate a model where LMX is first purged from endogeneity bias by using the instruments to predict it (first-stage model); then in the second stage, the predicted value of LMX is used as a regressor of turnover. That is, in the general form we estimate:

$$\begin{aligned} LMX = \lambda_0 + \lambda_1 L\_Extra \\ +\lambda_2 F\_IQ \\ +\lambda_3 F\_Consc \\ +controls + \varpi \end{aligned} \quad (26)$$

$$Turnover = \mu_0 - \mu_1 LMX + controls + \xi \quad (27)$$

Refer to Table 6.5 for model estimates. In Model 1 we estimated the system of equations using OLS, where the cross-equation disturbances are not correlated; using maximum likelihood, where the correlation between the disturbances is constrained to be zero would give the same result (i.e., refer to Figure 6.2).

The estimate of LMX no turnover is –.43, $p < .001$. Given the causal structure of the model that generated the data, this estimate is wrong. Thus, an important lesson to retain here is that simple estimating system of equations where the potentially problematic regressor (LMX) is modeled as an outcome of antecedents will not produce the correct estimates in predicting *y* if (1) the problematic regressor is endogenous and (2) the 2SLS estimator is not used (i.e., the cross-equation disturbances are constrained to be zero, which is what the OLS estimator does). If, and only if, LMX is not endogenous would OLS estimates be consistent.

Model 2 is like Model 1 except that the 2SLS estimator is used; LMX is predicted in the first-stage equation by Leader Extraversion, Follower IQ, and Follower Conscientiousness and turnover is regressed on the predicted value of LMX. Here it is clear that LMX does not predict turnover. Models 3 and 4 provide similar estimates. Interesting to note is that even including omitted predictors of turnover does not significantly change the estimates of the relation between LMX to turnover. Of course, in this case, the data were simulated such that there was no relation between LMX and turnover (which is evident too from the fact that the instruments overlap very little with turnover too). For other examples in which the sign of the endogenous regressor is flipped when instrumented see Antonakis et al. (2010).

A Note on Overidentification

When estimating simultaneous equation models, like that in the previous examples, and also with more complex path models or Structural Equation Models, it is important that the overidentifying restrictions hold. That is, are the constraints that are made valid? If the answer is "no" the model parameters are suspect and cannot be trusted (because it suggests that the exogenous variables correlate with the disturbance/s of the endogenous variable/s). This point is very important to understand, and we show in the text that follows why researchers must pay attention to the overidentification statistic (and not dismiss it as is often the case).

Important to note is that if the model is correctly specified this statistic will not be significant, no matter how large the sample size (Bollen, 1990; Hayduk, Cummings, Boadu, Pazderka-Robinson, & Boulianne, 2007; McIntosh, 2007). If researchers do not trust the chi-square test then they should not trust tests of parameter estimates either (as we show later, the chi-square test uses the same statistical theory that researchers use to estimate parameters and their significance levels).

In the case of the previous 2SLS examples, we will use Model 2 in Table 6.5 to demonstrate how the overidentification statistic is derived. Notice that there are three instruments that predict LMX (Leader Extraversion, Follower IQ, and Follower conscientiousness); however, they are excluded from the turnover equation wherein only LMX is the predictor. By being excluded from the second-stage equation, the constraints that are made are that the relationships of the instruments with omitted sources of variance *y* are zero.

In this system of equations we have five variables. Thus, the variance–covariance matrix has $v(v + 1)/2$ bits of information (variance–covariance matrix) or $5(5 + 1)/2 = 15$ elements. We estimated the following parameters:

Regression coefficients	4
Correlations (between exogenous variables):	3
Correlations (between disturbances):	1
Variances (of endogenous variables):	2
Variances (of exogenous variables):	3
Total:	13

Table 6.5. Predicting Turnover from LMX Using OLS and 2SLS Regression (simulated data)

	Model (1)	Model (1)	Model (2)	Model (2)	Model (3)	Model (3)	Model (4)	Model (4)
Variables	Turnover	LMX	Turnover	LMX	Turnover	LMX	Turnover	LMX
LMX	−.43**		.02		−.00		−.02	
	(18.35)		(.42)		(0.03)		(0.94)	
Leader extraversion		.95**		.95**		.99**		.94**
		(14.32)		(14.35)		(22.17)		(29.17)
Follower IQ		1.01**		1.01**		1.02**		.99**
		(15.22)		(15.25)		(23.03)		(30.93)
Follower conscientiousness		.91**		.91**		.92**		.97**
		(13.42)		(13.45)		(20.22)		(29.74)
Leader use of incentives					−.95**	1.09**	−.96**	1.05**
					(14.74)	(24.81)	(26.82)	(33.35)
Follower neuroticism					1.03**	−1.02**	1.00**	−1.00**
					(16.51)	(24.08)	(28.83)	(32.84)
Leader IQ							−.97**	.99**
							(26.38)	(30.58)
Company policies							−1.02**	−.05
							(35.01)	(1.79)
Constant	57.72**	−160.19**	44.46**	−160.19**	18.41**	−138.82**	146.64**	−243.36**
	(80.56)	(19.82)	(33.85)	(19.86)	(6.98)	(24.58)	(38.35)	(45.00)
R^2	.25	.39	.25	.39	.41	.73	.82	.86

n = 1,000; t-statistics in parentheses;
** $p < 0.01$,
*$p < 0.05$. Model 1 is estimated with OLS. Models 2, 3 and 4 are estimated with 2SLS. Note for the Turnover equation in Model 2 the r^2 was negative (this is not necessarily a problem in simultaneous equation models, see: http://www.stata.com/support/faqs/stat/2sls.html): We calculated it by correlating (and squaring) the predicted and observed value of turnover; this correlation is the actually same as that in Model 1. The coefficients of LMX in Models 2, 3, and 4 are not significantly different from each other; the coefficient of LMX in Model 1 is significantly different from those in Models 2, 3, and 4. The Sargan chi-square test for Models 2, 3, and 4 is nonsignificant.

The overidentification test has 15 – 13 = 2 degrees of freedom (DF). For simple mediation models the DF are the number of instruments less mediators (i.e., endogenous variables). The overidentification statistic of interest is the Sargan chi-square statistic, which is also often called the Hansen–Sargan statistic or the J-Test (Hansen, 1982; Sargan, 1958). This test is an analog to the chi-square test of fit commonly used in structural equation modeling programs, though it is calculated in a different way. What this test examines is whether the residuals of the turnover equation correlate with the instruments. If they do, it suggests that the model is misspecified (because there is systematic variance in the residuals that can be predicted by the instruments). Thus, parameters estimates are biased and cannot be trusted.

Using Stata's overidentification routine shows that the test is insignificant, $\chi^2(2) = 1.47$, $p = .48$. To do this test manually one would first generated model predicted values of turnover ($\hat{t}$) from the second-stage equation. That is, $\hat{t}$ = 44.46 + .02*

LMX (note, we have rounded the values of the intercept and slope, which originally were 44.4598 and .0184804 respectively). The residuals are simply calculated, for each observation, as turnover $-\hat{t}$ (i.e., the residual is the observed value of turnover minus the predicted value of turnover for each observation). Next, the residuals are regressed on the three instruments (Leader Extraversion, Follower IQ, and Follower conscientiousness); the Sargan statistic is simply N^*R^2 (where N is the sample size and R^2 is the r-square from this regression model). This statistic is distributed as a chi-square statistic with DF as described previously. The r^2 is .0014733, which when multiplied by the N size (1000), gives 1.4732984. At 2 DF, the p-value of this statistic is .47871531, which is precisely what the Stata program gave. Estimating the model with the structural equation modeling program (SEM) MPlus gives a chi-square value of 1.473 and a p-value of .4788 (note, how this statistic is calculated in the context of a SEM model is different and requires matrix algebra, see Jöreskog, 1967). Also, with more complicated models the test is an omnibus test of model fit; this test may differ when using a full- information (e.g., 3SLS, limited-information maximum likelihood, or maximum likelihood) versus a limited-information estimator. Also, misspecifications in full-information estimators may spread bias in the model, which is why it is always good to check estimates against a limited-information estimator (Baltagi, 2002; Bollen, 1996; Bollen et al., 2007).

Now, suppose we estimated the following wrong model:

$$LMX = \kappa_0 + \kappa_1 L\_IQ + \kappa_2 L\_Incent + \kappa_3 L\_Extra + \kappa_4 F\_IQ + \Xi \quad (28)$$

$$Turnover = \omega_0 - \omega_1 LMX + \omega_2 L\_Extra + \omega_3 F\_IQ + \Upsilon \quad (29)$$

We know that this model is wrong, because Leader Incentives are a direct cause of Turnover (as well as of LMX). Thus, Leader Incentives should also be used as regressor in Eq. (29). Estimating this model shows that the data do not fit the model, $\chi^2(1) = 3.89$, $p < .05$. Also, the coefficient of LMX is now –.94, $p < .001$. Given the significant chi-square test, this coefficient cannot be interpreted. Researchers in management, organizational behavior, applied psychology, MIS (and probably other disciplines) but certainly not in economics, oftentimes ignore this chi-square test of fit test and use what they called approximate indexes fit (e.g., Comparative Fit Index [CFI] and the Root Mean Squared Error of Approximation [RMSEA], among others); in the case of the above misspecified model the approximate indexes show great fit: CFI = 1.00, RMSEA = .05 (which shows that they forgive really bad models). Such researchers argue that the chi-square test is too powerful and that even minute discrepancies in the model will cause the model to be rejected by the chi-square test; thus, the chi-square test should be ignored in favor of approximate fit (i.e., the thinking here is that if the model is approximately good then it is still interpretable). However, using that line of thinking would suggest that if the sample size is too large for the chi-square test, it is also too large for the tests of the model parameters; thus, tests of model parameters should be summarily dismissed as well. This attitude is ludicrous, defeatist, and wrong. If this chi-square test cannot be trusted then we cannot trust any other statistic either that uses the same statistical theory.

Other Methods for Inferring Causality

Other methods can be used to obtain consistent estimates in nonexperimental settings (Cook et al., 2008; Meyer, 1995; Shadish & Cook, 1999, 2009; Shadish et al., 2002). We briefly introduce four methods in the following subsection. For further details on these, refer to Antonakis et al. (2010).

PROPENSITY SCORE ANALYSIS

Propensity score analysis (PSA) can be used to recover causal estimates in situations where treatment has been nonrandomly assigned. Had treatment been randomly assigned (into one of two conditions), the probability of receiving treatment would be 50 percent. By determining the probability that an individual would have received treatment based on observable factors, a counterfactual can be recreated by comparing individuals from the treatment and control groups who have the same propensity (i.e., probability) of being assigned to the treatment condition (D'Agostino, 1998).

To use PSA, the researcher must be able to know which variables determine the probability that an individual would have received treatment. Furthermore, unmodeled sources of variance in determining selection should be uncorrelated with unmodeled sources of variance in the main model (Cameron & Trivedi, 2005). If this latter assumption is not met, a treatment effects model (Maddala, 1983) should be used.

Selection Models (Heckman Models)

Heckman-type two-step selection model (Heckman, 1979) or *treatment effects model* (see Cong & Drukker, 2001; Maddala, 1983) are two-stage models that allow one to recover causal estimates in presence of nonrandom assignment to treatment. In these models, in the first stage the probability being selected in the treatment group is predicted from exogenous instruments. In the second stage, the main model is estimated addition a control variable capturing the difference between treatment and control group resulting from unmodeled sources of variance in the selection process. Thus, the correlation between the error term and selection is removed and consistent estimates can be obtained.

Regression Discontinuity Models

These are used when selection to treatment is nonrandom but is based a known threshold or cutoff value. The idea behind the RDD is to explicitly model selection procedure. By doing so, the RDD very closely emulates the randomized experiment (Cook et al., 2008). As with the randomized experiment, the error term is uncorrelated with the selection variable, which results from explicitly modeling the selection process. In this way, there are no unmodeled sources of variance in the selection variable that could otherwise correlate with the model's error term.

The RDD is easy to implement and is an excellent design to test for policy effects. Another advantage of the RDD is that it allows the researcher to oftentimes give treatment to those individuals who need it the most (e.g., in terms of training needs). Lee and Lemieux (2009) provide a comprehensive review of the RDD.

Difference-in-Differences Models

Differences-in-differences models compare two similar groups before and after treatment is administered. The underlying idea is that by comparing two similar groups over time, it is possible to remove confounding factors affecting both groups, and thus recover causal estimates. Under a number of assumptions—the more important being that difference between groups remain stable over time and that the onset of the treatment is exogenous—causal estimates of the treatment effect can be correctly recovered (see Angrist & Krueger, 1999; Angrist & Pischke, 2008; Meyer, 1995). In psychology, the differences-in-differences design is known as an untreated control group design with pre- and post-test (Shadish et al., 2002).

Conclusions

Lewin (1945, p. 129) once noted "nothing is as practical as a good theory." The point of all our research efforts is to develop theoretical models that explain natural phenomena. Doing so means undertaking different sorts of studies and ideally to do more fieldwork that emulates "natural experiments" (Meyer, 1995); the latter can be particularly useful for making strong and relevant causal claims *if* certain design and estimation conditions are respected. We trust that we have made it clear that that researchers in leadership and other applied areas must pay more attention to the problems of endogeneity and correct model estimation. Researchers have mostly been ignorant of these problems (Antonakis et al., 2010) and graduate training in statistics has not been sufficient to ensure the needed methodological standards (Aiken, West, & Millsap, 2008). It is vital to understand endogeneity and how to deal with it; facing this "inconvenient truth" will be difficult because many researchers have to break with past practices that produced specious estimates. Theories may have to be revamped and new ways of clean causal thinking and testing have to become the order of the day.

As the world economy hits crisis after crisis, and as research budgets get squeezed, it becomes all the more vital to ensure that research monies are well invested in approaches that can help make a real difference to practice. Relevance must go hand in hand with rigor (Vermeulen, 2005); for that to occur, models must be build around rigorous methods that can be applied to practical problems.

Future Directions

Insofar as future directions in causal analysis are concerned, we hope that advances on par with those that allowed causal research to be done in the field will continue to be made (Heckman, 1979; Rubin, 1974; Thistlethwaite & Campbell, 1960). With respect to leadership research, our expectations are that researchers begin to use these tools (which are standard in other sciences, e.g., medical or economics) and teach them to their students. In our recent review (Antonakis et al., 2010) we showed that these methods are foreign to leadership scholars; we also identified 10 best practices for ensuring valid causal claims, as noted in Table 6.6, which we hope leadership scholars will begin to adopt.

Table 6.6. The 10 Commandments of Causal Analysis

1. Avoid omitted variable bias by including appropriate control variables; if these are difficult to identify, use fixed-effects estimation or instrument the endogenous variables.
2. Prior to using HLM models, ensure that the estimator is consistent with respect to the fixed-effects estimator; test for differences between the estimators using a Hausman test.
3. Show that modeled independent variables are exogenous; if there is doubt, instrument them with truly exogenous variables.
4. Do not compare groups unless assignment to group was randomized or the selection procedure to group has been appropriately modeled.
5. Test overidentifying restrictions in simultaneous equations with a chi-square test of fit; if failed, do not interpret parameter estimates.
6. Use errors-in-variables regression, SEM, or instruments (in 2SLS models) to correct estimates for measurement bias.
7. Avoid common-methods bias; use instrumental-variable models to correct for it if unavoidable.
8. Use robust variance estimators as the default (unless residuals are i.i.d). Use cluster-robust variance estimators with nested data.
9. Use the 2SLS estimator in mediation models (and correlate disturbances of endogenous regressors); examine endogeneity with a Hausman test.
10. Use full-information estimators (i.e., maximum likelihood) if estimates are equivalent to limited information (2SLS) estimators. Never use PLS (which cannot test for overidentifying restrictions).

Note: Adapted from Antonakis, J., Bendahan, S., Jacquart, P., & Lalive, R. (2010). On making causal claims: A review and recommendations. *The Leadership Quarterly, 21*(6), 1086–1120, with permission from Elsevier.

Only when nonexperimental models are correctly tested we will be in a position to better evaluate current theories of leadership and better answer questions like:

1. Do potentially endogenous regressors (e.g., LMX, authentic leadership, etc.) matter for organizational outcomes?
2. To what extent do multilevel leadership models estimated using HLM-type models (random effects/coefficients) still explain increment outcomes when controlling for omitted fixed effects?
3. Do leader individual differences (e.g., cognitive style, emotional intelligence, self-monitoring, etc.) matter in predicting leader behaviors or outcomes beyond established personality (e.g., the big five) and cognitive ability models?
4. How would multifactorial models look like (e.g., the Multifactor Leadership Questionnaire) when stronger modeling procedures are undertaken (e.g., using MIMIC models; see Bollen, 1989; Muthén, 1989) while paying attention to real tests of overidentification?

At this time, we do not have enough well-designed studies to answer these questions, as well as many other questions that are implied from the validity threats we have identified in Table 6.1. We hope that leadership scholars will rise to the challenge and test their causal models correctly.

References

Aiken, L. S., West, S. G., & Millsap, R. E. (2008). Doctoral training in statistics, measurement, and methodology in psychology—Replication and extension of Aiken, West, Sechrest, and Reno's (1990) survey of PhD programs in North America. *American Psychologist, 63*(1), 32–50.

Angrist, J. D., & Krueger, A. B. (1999). Empirical strategies in labor economics. In O. C. Ashenfelter & D. Card (Eds.), *Handbook of labor economics* (Vol. 3,Part 1, pp. 1277–1366). Amsterdam, The Netherlands: Elsevier.

Angrist, J. D., & Pischke, J.-S. (2008). *Mostly harmless econometrics: An empiricist's companion.* Princeton, NJ: Princeton University Press.

Antonakis, J., Bendahan, S., Jacquart, P., & Lalive, R. (2010). On making causal claims: A review and recommendations. *The Leadership Quarterly, 21*(6), 1086–1120.

Antonakis, J., & Dietz, J. (2011). More on testing for validity instead of looking for it. *Personality and Individual Differences, 50*(3), 418–421.

Antonakis, J., Schriesheim, C. A., Donovan, J. A., Gopalakrishna-Pillai, K., Pellegrini, E., & Rossomme, J. L. (2004). Methods for studying leadership. In J. Antonakis, A. T. Cianciolo, & R. J. Sternberg (Eds.), *The nature of leadership* (pp. 48–70). Thousand Oaks, CA: SAGE.

Bacharach, S. B. (1989). Organizational theories: Some criteria for evaluation. *Academy of Management Review, 14*(4), 496–515.

Baltagi, B. H. (2002). *Econometrics*. New York, NY: Springer Science+Business Media.

Bandalos, D. L., & Finney, S. J. (2001). Item parceling issues in structural equation modeling. In G. A. Marcoulides & R. E. Schmacker (Eds.), *New developments and techniques in structural equation modeling* (pp. 269–296). Mahwah, NJ: Academic Press.

Bascle, G. (2008). Controlling for endogeneity with instrumental variables in strategic management research. *Strategic Organization, 6*(3), 285–327.

Bertrand, M., Duflo, E., & Mullainathan, S. (2004). How much should we trust differences-in-differences estimates? *Quarterly Journal of Economics, 119*(1), 249–275.

Bollen, K. A. (1989). *Structural equations with latent variables*. New York, NY: John Wiley & Sons.

Bollen, K. A. (1990). Overall fit in covariance structure models—2 types of sample-size effects. *Psychological Bulletin, 107*(2), 256–259.

Bollen, K. A. (1996). An alternative two stage least squares (2SLS) estimator for latent variable equations. *Psychometrika, 61*, 109–121.

Bollen, K. A., Kirby, J. B., Curran, P. J., Paxton, P. M., & Chen, F. N. (2007). Latent variable models under misspecification—two-stage least squares (2SLS) and maximum likelihood (ML) estimators. *Sociological Methods & Research, 36*(1), 48–86.

Bound, J., Jaeger, D. A., & Baker, R. M. (1995). Problems with instrumental variables estimation when the correlation between the instruments and the endogeneous explanatory variable is weak. *Journal of the American Statistical Association, 90*(430), 443–450.

Breusch, T. S., & Pagan, A. R. (1980). The Lagrange multiplier test and its applications to model specification in econometrics. *Review of Economic Studies, 47*, 239–253.

Cameron, A. C., Gelbach, J. B., & Miller, D. L. (2011). Robust Inference with multiway clustering. *Journal of Business & Economic Statistics, 29*(2), 238–249.

Cameron, A. C., & Trivedi, P. K. (2005). *Microeconometrics: Methods and applications*. New York, NY: Cambridge University Press.

Caudill, S. B. (1988). An advantage of the linear probability model over probit or logit. *Oxford Bulletin of Economics and Statistics, 50*(4), 425–427.

Cong, R., & Drukker, D. M. (2001). Treatment effects model. *Stata Technical Bulletin, 10*(55), 25–33.

Cook, T. D., Shadish, W. R., & Wong, V. C. (2008). Three conditions under which experiments and observational studies produce comparable causal estimates: New findings from within-study comparisons. *Journal of Policy Analysis and Management, 27*(4), 724–750.

D'Agostino, R. B. (1998). Propensity score methods for bias reduction in the comparison of a treatment to a non-randomized control group. *Statistics in Medicine, 17*(19), 2265–2281.

Draper, N. R., & Smith, H. (1998). *Applied regression analysis* (3rd ed.). New York, NY: John Wiley & Sons.

Dubin, R. (1976). Theory building in applied areas. In M. D. Dunnette (Ed.), *Handbook of industrial and organizational psychology* (pp. 17–40). Chicago, IL: Rand McNally.

Dulebohn, J. H., Bommer, W. H., Liden, R. C., Brouer, R. L., & Ferris, G. R. (2011). A meta-analysis of antecedents and consequences of leader-member exchange: Integrating the past with an eye toward the future. *Journal of Management.*

Duncan, G. J., Magnusson, K. A., & Ludwig, J. (2004). The endogeneity problem in developmental studies. *Research in Human Development, 1*(1&2), 59–80.

Fairhurst, G. T., & Antonakis, J. (2012). A research agenda for relational leadership. In M. Uhl-Bien & S. Ospina (Eds.), *Advancing relational leadership theory: A conversation among perspectives* (pp. 433–459). Greenwich, CT: Information Age Publishing.

Fiori, M., & Antonakis, J. (2011). The ability model of emotional intelligence: Searching for valid measures. *Personality and Individual Differences, 50*(3), 329–334.

Foster, E. M., & McLanahan, S. (1996). An illustration of the use of instrumental variables: Do neighborhood conditions affect a young person's change of finishing high school? *Psychological Methods, 1*(3), 249–260.

Gennetian, L. A., Magnuson, K., & Morris, P. A. (2008). From statistical associations to causation: What developmentalists can learn from instrumental variables techniques coupled with experimental data. *Developmental Psychology, 44*(2), 381–394.

Gerstner, C. R., & Day, D. V. (1997). Meta-analytic review of leader-member exchange theory: Correlates and construct issues. *Journal of Applied Psychology, 82*(6), 827–844.

Greene, W. H. (2008). *Econometric analysis* (6th ed.). Upper Saddle River, NJ: Prentice–Hall.

Halaby, C. N. (2004). Panel models in sociological research: Theory into practice. *Annual Review of Sociology, 30*, 507–544.

Hall, R. J., Snell, A. F., & Singer Foust, M. (1999). Item parceling strategies in SEM: Investigating the subtle effects of unmodeled secondary constructs. *Organizational Research Methods, 2*(3), 233–256.

Hamilton, B. H., & Nickerson, J. A. (2003). Correcting for endogeneity in strategic management research. *Strategic Organization, 1*(1), 51–78.

Hansen, L. P. (1982). Large sample properties of generalized method of moments estimators. *Econometrica, 50*, 1029–1054.

Hausman, J. A. (1978). Specification tests in econometrics. *Econometrica, 46*(6), 1251–1271.

Hayduk, L. A. (1996). *LISREL issues, debates, and strategies*. Baltimore, MD: Johns Hopkins University Press.

Hayduk, L. A., Cummings, G., Boadu, K., Pazderka-Robinson, H., & Boulianne, S. (2007). Testing! testing! one, two, three: Testing the theory in structural equation models! *Personality and Individual Differences, 42*(5), 841–850.

Hayduk, L. A., Cummings, G., Stratkotter, R., Nimmo, M., Grygoryev, K., Dosman, D., et al. (2003). Pearl's D-separation: One more step into causal thinking. *Structural Equation Modeling, 10*(2), 289–311.

Heckman, J. J. (1979). Sample selection bias as a specification error. *Econometrica, 47*(1), 153–161.

Holland, P. W. (1986). Statistics and causal inference. *Journal of the American Statistical Association, 81*(396), 945–960.

House, R. J., & Aditya, R. N. (1997). The social scientific study of leadership: Quo vadis? *Journal of Management, 23*(3), 409–473.

Huber, P. J. (1967). The behavior of maximum likelihood estimates under nonstandard conditions. *Fifth Berkeley Symposium on Mathematical Statistics and Probability, 1*, 221–233.

James, L. R., Mulaik, S. A., & Brett, J. M. (1982). *Causal analysis: Assumptions, models, and data*. Beverly Hills, CA: SAGE.

Jöreskog, K. G. (1967). Some contributions to maximum likelihood factor analysis. *Psychometrika, 32*(4): 443–482.
Kennedy, P. (2003). *A guide to econometrics* (5th ed.). Cambridge, MA: MIT Press.
Kenny, D. A. (1979). *Correlation and causality*. New York, NY: Wiley-Interscience.
Keppel, G., & Wickens, T. D. (2004). *Design and analysis: A researcher's handbook*. Upper Saddle River, NJ: Pearson.
Kerlinger, F., & Lee, H. B. (2000). *Foundations of behavioral research* (4th ed.). Forth Worth, TX: Harcourt.
Kmenta, J. (1986). *Elements of econometrics* (2nd ed.). New York: Macmillan.
Koh, W. L., Steers, R. M., & Terborg, J. R. (1995). The effects of transformational leadership on teacher attitudes and student performance in Singapore. *Journal of Organizational Behavior, 16*(4), 319–333.
Larcker, D. F., & Rusticus, T. O. (2010). On the use of instrumental variables in accounting research. *Journal of Accounting and Economics, 49*(3), 186–205.
Lee, D., & Lemieux, T. (2009). Regression discontinuity designs in economics. *National Bureau of Economic Research*, Working Paper 14723.
Levitt, S. D. (1997). Using electoral cycles in police hiring to estimate the effects of police on crime. *American Economic Review, 87*(3), 270–290.
Levitt, S. D. (2002). Using electoral cycles in police hiring to estimate the effects of police on crime: Reply. *American Economic Review, 92*(4), 1244–1250.
Lewin, K. (1945). The research center for group dynamics at Massachusetts Institute of Technology. *Sociometry, 8*(2), 126–136.
Liang, J., Lawrence, R. H., Bennett, J. M., & Whitelaw, N. A. (1990). Appropriateness of composites in structural equation models. *Journal of Gerontology: Social Sciences, 45*(2), 52–59.
Liden, R. C., & Antonakis, J. (2009). Considering context in psychological leadership research. *Human Relations, 62*(11), 1587–1605.
Long, J. S., & Freese, J. (2006). *Regression models for categorical dependent variables using Stata* (2nd ed.). College Station, TX: StataCorp LP.
Maddala, G. S. (1977). *Econometrics*. New York, NY: McGraw-Hill.
Maddala, G. S. (1983). *Limited-dependent and qualitative variables in econometrics*. Cambridge, UK: Cambridge University Press.
Maxwell, S. E., Cole, D. A., Arvey, R. D., & Salas, E. (1991). A comparison of methods for increasing power in randomized between-subjects designs. *Psychological Bulletin, 110*(2), 328–337.
McIntosh, C. N. (2007). Rethinking fit assessment in structural equation modelling: A commentary and elaboration on Barrett (2007). *Personality and Individual Differences, 42*(5), 859–867.
Meyer, B. D. (1995). Natural and quasi-experiments in economics. *Journal of Business & Economics Statistics, 13*(2), 151–161.
Morgan, S. L., & Winship, C. (2007). *Counterfactuals and causal inference: Methods and principles for social research*. New York, NY: Cambridge University Press.
Mount, M. K., & Scullen, S. E. (2001). Multisource feedback ratings: What do they really measure? In M. London (Ed.), *How people evaluate others in organizations* (pp. 155–176). Mahwah, NJ: Lawrence Erlbaum.
Mulaik, S. A. (2009). *Linear causal modeling with structural equations*. Boca Raton, FL: CRC Press.
Mulaik, S. A., & James, L. R. (1995). Objectivity and reasoning in science and structural equation modeling. In R. H. Hoyle (Ed.), *Structural equation modeling: Concepts, issues, and applications* (pp. 118–137). Thousand Oaks, CA: SAGE.
Mundlak, Y. (1978). Pooling of time-series and cross-section data. *Econometrica, 46*(1), 69–85.
Murphy, K. R. (1997). Editorial. *Journal of Applied Psychology, 82*(1), 3–5.
Muthén, B. O. (1989). Latent variable modeling in heterogenous populations. *Psychometrika, 54*(4), 557–585.
Onyskiw, J. E., & Hayduk, L. A. (2001). Processes underlying childern's adjustment in families characterized by physical aggression. *Family Relations, 50*, 376–385.
Pearl, J. (2009). *Causality: Models, reasoning, and inference* (2nd ed.). Cambridge, UK: Cambridge University Press.
Preacher, K. J. & Hayes, A. F. (2004). SPSS and SAS procedures for estimating indirect effects in simple mediation models. *Behavior Research Methods, Instruments, & Computers, 36*(4): 717–731.
Podsakoff, P. M., MacKenzie, S. B., Lee, J.-Y., & Podsakoff, N. P. (2003). Common method biases in behavioral research: A critical review of the literature and recommended remedies. *Journal of Applied Psychology, 89*(5), 879–903.
Podsakoff, P. M., Mackenzie, S. B., & Podsakoff, N. P. (2010). Sources of method bias in social Science Research and Recommendations on How to Control It. *Annual Review of Psychology*.
Podsakoff, P. M., & Organ, D. W. (1986). Self-reports in organizational research: Problems and prospects. *Journal of Management, 12*(4), 531–544.
Ramsey, J. B. (1969). Tests for specification errors in classical linear least-squares regression analysis. *Journal of the Royal Statistical Society B, 31*, 350–371.
Richardson, H. A., Simmering, M. J., & Sturman, M. C. (2009). A tale of three perspectives: Examining post hoc statistical techniques for detection and correction of common method variance. *Organizational Research Methods, 12*(4), 762–800.
Rubin, D. B. (1974). Estimating causal effects of treatments in randomized and nonrandomized studies. *Journal of Educational Psychology, 66*(5), 688–701.
Rubin, D. B. (2008). For objective causal inference, design trumps analysis. *Annals of Applied Statistics, 2*(3), 808–840.
Sargan, J. D. (1958). The estimation of economic relationships using instrumental variables. *Econometrica, 26*, 393–415.
Schulte, M. J., Ree, M. J., & Carretta, T. R. (2004). Emotional Intelligence: Not much more than g and personality. *Personality and Individual Differences, 37*(5), 1059–1068.
Scullen, S. E., Mount, M. K., & Goff, M. (2000). Understanding the latent structure of job performance ratings. *Journal of Applied Psychology, 85*(6), 956–970.
Shadish, W. R., & Cook, T. D. (1999). Comment-design rules: More steps toward a complete theory of quasi-experimentation. *Statistical Science, 14*(3), 294–300.
Shadish, W. R., & Cook, T. D. (2009). The renaissance of field experimentation in evaluating interventions. *Annual Review of Psychology, 60*, 607–629.
Shadish, W. R., Cook, T. D., & Campbell, D. T. (2002). *Experimental and quasi-experimental designs for generalized causal inference*. Boston, MA: Houghton Mifflin.
Shaver, J. M. (1998). Accounting for endogeneity when assessing strategy performance: Does entry mode choice affect FDI survival? *Management Science, 44*(4), 571–585.

Spector, P. E. (2006). Method variance in organizational research—Truth or urban legend? *Organizational Research Methods, 9*(2), 221–232.

Spector, P. E., & Brannick, M. T. (2011). Methodological urban legends: The misuse of statistical control variables. *Organizational Research Methods, 14*(2), 287–305.

Stock, J. H., & Watson, M. W. (2007). *Introduction to econometrics* (2nd ed.). Boston, MA: Pearson Addison Wesley.

Stock, J. H., Wright, J. H., & Yogo, M. (2002). A survey of weak instruments and weak identification in generalized method of moments. *Journal of Business & Economic Statistics, 20*(4), 518–529.

Stock, J. H., & Yogo, M. (2002). Testing for weak instruments in linear IV regression. *NBER Technical Working Papers 0284.*

Thistlethwaite, D. L., & Campbell, D. T. (1960). Regression-discontinuity analysis: An alternative to the ex post facto experiment. *Journal of Educational Psychology, 51*(6), 309–317.

Tobin, J. (1958). Estimation of relationships for limited dependent variables. *Econometrica, 26*, 24–36.

Vermeulen, F. (2005). On rigor and relevance: Fostering dialectic progress in management research. *Academy of Management Journal, 48*(6), 978–982.

von Wittich, D., & Antonakis, J. (2011). The KAI cognitive style inventory: Was it personality all along? *Personality and Individual Differences, 50*(7), 1044–1049.

White, H. (1980). A heteroskedasticity-consistent covariance matrix estimator and a direct test for heteroskedasticity. *Econometrica, 48*, 817–830.

Winship, C., & Morgan, S. L. (1999). The estimation of causal effects from observational data. *Annual Review of Sociology, 25*, 659–706.

Wooldridge, J. M. (2002). *Econometric analysis of cross section and panel data.* Cambridge, MA: MIT Press.

Zellner, A., & Theil, H. (1962). 3-Stage least-squares—simultaneous estimation of simultaneous-equations. *Econometrica, 30*(1), 54–78.

CHAPTER

7

Sculpting the Contours of the Qualitative Landscape of Leadership Research

Karin Klenke

Abstract
This chapter presents the ontological, epistemological, methodological, and axiological assumptions underlying qualitative paradigms and describes some of the major qualitative research methods used in the study of leadership including interviews, content analysis, case study and grounded theory, narrative analysis, and a brief introduction into non-text-based data sources such as photographs, works of art, film, theater, and music. Data collection techniques and data analyses are described both collectively as well as individually for specific qualitative methods such as ethnography and image-based research. Strategies for enhancing quality standards that enhance the quality and rigor of qualitative leadership research to achieve trustworthiness and credibility are presented. The chapter concludes with an overview of future directions for qualitative leadership research that will increase the utilization of qualitative methods, enhance their legitimacy, and potential as critical contributors to advance the study of leadership.

Key Words: Qualitative paradigms, methodology, qualitative research methods; data collection techniques, data analyses, quality standards

Introduction

Qualitative research has come into its own over the last few decades and is recognized as making significant contributions to leadership research, theory, and practice (Conger, 1998). The evolution of applications of qualitative methods in the study of leadership reveals several noteworthy trends. First, it involves a shift from a marginalized position to a position of greater legitimacy and credibility. For example, Lowe and Gardner (2000), in a content analysis of articles published in the first decade of *The Leadership Quarterly* (1990-1999), the premier outlet for scholarly leadership research, reported that 39 percent of the articles were based on qualitative data; for most volumes of the journal, the ratio of quantitative to qualitative studies was at least 2 to 1 (p. 475). Second, the growth of qualitative research was also spurred by a variety of other factors including the growing dissatisfaction with the hegemony of survey research in the study of leadership using self-report measures (e.g., Bryman, 2004), the lack of attention to context (e.g., Klenke, 2008; Osborn, Jauch & Hunt, 2002; Porter & McLaughlin, 2006), the leader-centric nature of many leadership theories, the tendency of leadership researchers to succumb to fads, fashions, or leadership zeitgeist (Hunt & Dodge, 2000), and the emergence of a new genre of leadership theories that require theory development more than theory testing as well as external factors resulting from changes in the macro environment in which leaders operate.

Although the hegemony of the quantitative paradigm in leadership remains undisputed, the qualitative paradigm, after decades of paradigm wars, is slowly gaining recognition and legitimacy as qualitative leadership research has come into its own right over the last few decades. As a result, leading academic journals that traditionally favored quantitative articles have opened the doors for submissions of qualitative studies or commissioned special issues dealing with theoretical and methodological issues in qualitative leadership research along with the publication of empirical qualitative articles. For example, Gebhardt (2004) in an editorial in the *Academy of Management Journal* (AMJ) issued a statement describing the journal's commitment to and vision of a qualitative agenda to advance management research. This commitment was reflected in the appointment of two associate editors assigned exclusively to managing qualitative manuscripts through the review process (Bansal & Corley, 2011). The authors pointed out that strong norms pertaining to the quality of qualitative research have emerged that are evidenced in the 11 percent publication rate of qualitative articles that appeared in AMJ between 2001 and 2011. At the same time, the authors called for greater diversity in the qualitative articles appearing in AMJ (p. 233).

The Changing Terrain of Organizations

Over the past decades, organizations and individuals have witnessed significant social, cultural, political, and economic changes that have had a profound effect on leadership research and theory. The changes include,

- The growing recognition of the importance of context in leadership theory and research; it is now widely acknowledged that leadership is context-dependent and context- sensitive (Klenke, 2011; Osborn, Jauch, & Hunt, 2002).
- The emergence of post-bureaucratic organizational structures such as boundaryless, networked, and virtual organizations (e.g., Arthur & Rousseau, 1996; Shamir, 1999).
- The replacement of single, omnipotent CEO by top management teams (TMT) as a coalition of the firm's most powerful executives (e.g., Finkelstein, 1992; Finkelstein & Hambrick 1990; Hambrick, 2007).
- The transition from a command-and-control leadership style to a range of different styles including transformational (e.g., Bass, 1985; Bass & Bass, 2008), charismatic (Conger & Kanungo, 1998), visionary (Sashkin, 1999; Sashkin & Sashkin, 2003), servant (e.g., Greenleaf, 1970; Spears, & Lawrence, 1997; Greenleaf, Spears, & Covey, 2002), and relational leadership (Uhl-Bien, 2006).
- The shift from leader-centric theories to the inclusion of followers in leader-follower equation (e.g., Kellerman, 2008; Shamir & Pilai, 2006).
- The increasing importance of shared, dispersed leadership (e.g., Day, Gronn, & Salas, 2006; Pearce & Conger, 2003; Zacarro, Rittman, & Marks, 2001).
- Increased emphasis on multiple levels of analysis (individual, group/team, organizational) (e.g., Yammarino, Dionne, Chun, & Dansereau, 2005).

These changes have led to the development of a wide range of emergent leadership theories with different foci, which are depicted in Table 7.1.

Table 7.1. Emergent Theories of Leadership

Spiritual leadership (Fry, 2003, 2005)	**Quiet leadership (Badaracco, 2002)**
Post-heroic leadership (Fletcher, 2004)	Ethical leadership (Bass & Steidlmeier; Brown & Trevino, 2006; Ciulla, 2004)
Servant leadership (Greenleaf, 1997; Spears, 2004)	Chaos and complexity theory (Marion & Uhl-Bien, 2001; Uhl-Bien, Marion, & McKelvey, 2007; Schneider & Sommers, 2006)
Authentic leadership (Avolio & Gardner,2005; Klenke, 2005)	Self-sacrificial leadership (DeCremer & van Knippendorf, 2005)
Aesthetic leadership (Ladkin, 2008; Strati, 1992, 1996)	Paradoxical leadership (Kark, Shamir, & Chen, 2003)
Relational Leadership (Uhl-Bien, 2006)	Terror management theory (Cohen et al.; 2004; Hoyt, Simon & Reid, 2009)
Team leadership (Day, Gronn, & Salas, 2006; Zacarro, Rittman, & Marks, 2001)	

Note: The studies in the table are arranged according to the qualitative research methods used; alphabetical or chronological arrangement would make little sense.

New-genre leadership theories which include - authentic, spiritual, ethical, relational, team, servant and chaos and complexity theory, to name a few - opened new vistas for qualitative research because in the early stages of development of emergent theories, theory building takes precedence over theory testing thus calling for qualitative designs. Qualitative methods such as case study and grounded theory are examples of research techniques intended for the primary purpose of inductively building theory (e.g., Eisenhardt, 1989; Kan & Parry, 2005; Yin, 1994, 2003). Sonpar and Golden-Biddle (2008) argued that content analysis is also well suited to refine and elaborate adolescent theories (Scott, 1987), that is, theories that have not been adequately developed or tested. By theory elaboration, the authors refer to refinement through specification of concepts, relationships, and their explanatory limits (Sonpar & Golden-Biddle, 2008, p. 795). In the development of new-genre theories, researchers are taking a more holistic approach by transcending the focus on leader-centric models to casting a wider net that includes not only the leader, but the followers, contexts, levels of analysis, and their dynamic interaction. They are also particularly sensitive to the importance of context, acknowledging that information taken out of context can mean something different from what was originally intended (Gummerson, 2006).

One of the hallmarks of qualitative research is sensitivity to and dependence on the context in which leaders, followers, and other stakeholders operate. According to Miles and Huberman (1994), qualitative research "provides thick descriptions that are vivid, nested in real context and have a ring of truth" (p. 11). Thick descriptions are the opposite of thin descriptions which consist of generalized findings, factual statement, observations or coded data (Cunliffe, 2010).

The potential of qualitative research is often elucidated by placing it in opposition to quantitative research. For example, Strauss and Corbin (1990) defined qualitative research as "any kind of research that produces findings not arrived at by means of statistical procedures or other means of quantification" (p. 17). Whereas quantitative researchers seek causal determination, prediction, and generalization of findings, qualitative researchers, pursue thick descriptions of the lived experience of their research participants; they seek illumination and understanding of complex phenomena in context-specific settings. The widespread disenchantment with much of the leadership research is due to a combination of factors including the pervasive use of static surveys, which make up the bulk of quantitative leadership research; the presence of measurement artifacts; the cross-sectional nature of many leadership studies; a body of empirical data bedeviled with conflicting findings; and the pervasive emphasis on rationality and objectivity that drives the quantitative paradigm.

The purpose of this chapter is to present a holistic approach to qualitative research in the study of leadership. Figure 7.1 provides a road map for the organization of this chapter, which takes the reader on a journey. Beginning with the critical but often overlooked discussions of the philosophical assumptions undergirding qualitative research to include ontology, epistemology and methodology, a review of qualitative research methods used in the study of leadership and a critical assessment of rigor and quality of quality standards applied to qualitative research.

Qualitative Paradigms

Unlike positivism and its closely related cousin, post-positivism, qualitative research draws on a number of different paradigms, which include interpretivism, constructionism, symbolic interactionism, pragmatism and realism. Qualitative paradigms provide new means of investigating previous unexplored questions, thus enabling leadership researchers to conduct studies that lead to new forms of knowledge about leadership and organizations (Sandberg, 2005). Although there are differences across these qualitative paradigms, many of them share fundamental philosophical assumptions concerning ontology, epistemology, and methodology. For example, most qualitative paradigms stress to differing degrees the importance of the role of meaning, language, and symbols in human and social interactions and claim that knowledge is constructed in and out of interactions between human beings and their world, that is developed and transmitted within an essentially social context (Golafshani, 2003).

Philosophical Foundations of Qualitative Research

Ontology addresses the paradigmatic question, "What is the nature of reality?" Qualitative researchers believe reality is subjective and therefore they embrace multiple realities, which reside in the mental models of the researcher and the researched. Qualitative researchers endorse a relativistic ontology that is always intersubjective and multiple, that

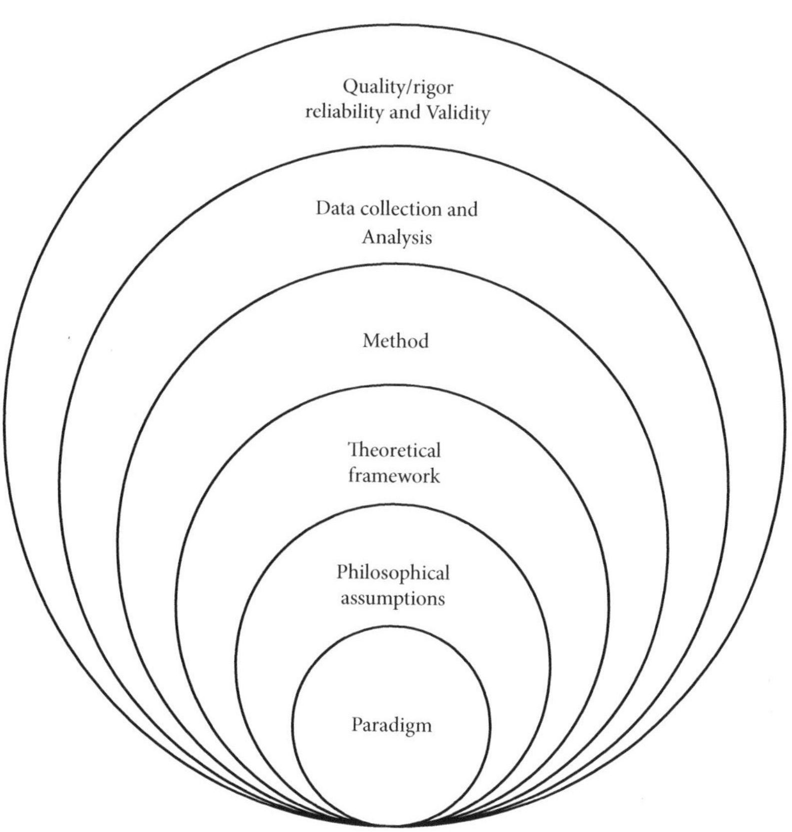

Figure 7.1. Conceptual Model of Qualitative Research (Courtesy of Jennifer Lovelette).

is socially constructed and shaped by the context in which the researcher and the researched live. Qualitative researchers argue that our perceptions of reality are always colored by "our specific historical, cultural, ideological, gender-based, and linguistic understanding of reality" (Sandberg, 2005, p. 45). Unlike quantitative researchers who assume that language is a mirror of reality, qualitative researchers claim that language is not a representational system that can be used to describe reality (Sandberg, 2005).

Epistemology refers to the position a researcher takes pertaining to his or her theory of knowledge creation. Across the different qualitative paradigms, researchers assume that knowledge is co-created through interactions between the researcher and the researched. Whereas in quantitative research the investigator assumes the dominant role in the generation of new knowledge, in qualitative research the relative contributions to knowledge creation of the researcher and the informants is more egalitarian. In fact, in most qualitative studies, it is the voices of the participants that carry the greatest weight in knowledge creation. Moreover, researchers from different traditions within the qualitative paradigm such as critical theory or symbolic interactionism claim that objective knowledge is unattainable. Conceptions of knowledge are grounded in theories, beliefs, values, and different epistemological views that have an influence on the methods of inquiry used. Taken together, a researcher's ontological and epistemological perspectives and beliefs determine what counts as knowledge (King & Horrocks, 2010).

Methodology, sometimes also referred to as theoretical framework, addresses the role of theory that underlie qualitative research methods and the extent to which theory informs the use and choice of research methods (Merriam & Associates, 2002). Methodology, as part of paradigm, sets the boundaries for the development of theoretical or methodological frameworks. According to Anfara and Mertz (2006), a theoretical framework has "the ability to: (1) focus a study; (2) reveal and conceal meaning and understanding; (3) situate the research in a scholarly conversation and provide a vernacular, and (4) reveal its strength and weaknesses" (p. 192). As a result, discussions of the role of theory vary greatly; some researchers give it little or no consideration, others clearly link theory to methodology. For example, according to Denzin and Lincoln (2003), "the researcher approaches the world with set of ideas, a framework (theory, ontology) that specifies a set of questions (epistemology) that he or she then examines in specific ways (methodology)" (p. 30). For this type of researcher, the theoretical framework guides and illuminates a qualitative study through all phases of the research process; in the formulation of research questions; in the design and method choice and in the data collection, analysis and interpretation. Methodologies, as explanatory systems of theory and practice, represent the glue that undergirds the various facets of a qualitative study and are highly contingent on epistemological positions, researcher interests, rapport, and confidentiality, among a host of other concerns.

Richards and Morse (2007) introduced the concept of *methodological congruence* to refer to the necessity that qualitative research requires consistent ways of thinking about all elements of a study. Methodological congruence results from a well-constructed theoretical framework and results in "fit" – fit between the research problem and the question; fit among the method, data collection and data interpretation. Finally, the distinction between methodology and method is important. Like Morrow (2005), I see methodology in a philosophical sense as a broader explanatory system of theory and practice within which certain methods, or forms of inquiry, are nested. According to Morrow (1994), the term *method* refers to specific research techniques such as interviewing or case study whereas *methodology* implies an overall strategy for constructing specific types of knowledge and is justified by a set of metatheoretical assumptions (p. 36).

I have added *axiology* to the paradigmatic triad of ontology, epistemology and methodology. Axiology refers to the values a qualitative researcher brings to his or her study that must be made transparent, because they potentially represent a source of bias. The values embraced by a qualitative researcher may include integrity, honesty, reflexivity, subjectivity and transparency and they reflect both early socialization and academic training. Figure 7.2 depicts the expanded paradigm triangle.

In sum, qualitative paradigms, compared to positivism, operate under different philosophical assumptions and require new ways of thinking about the research process and the role of the researcher and the researched to avoid the lingering influence of positivistic concepts such as reliability and validity which

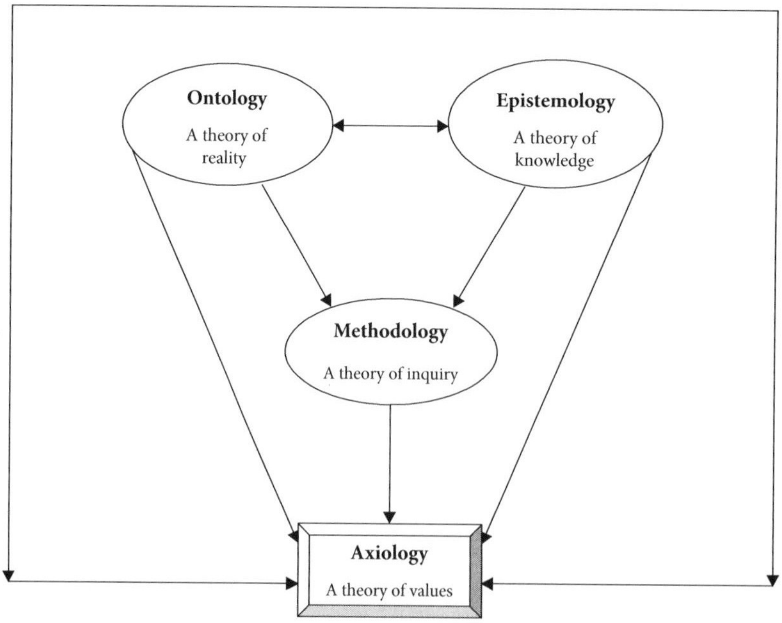

Figure 7.2. Expanded Paradigm Triangle.

Taken from Klenke, K. (2008), Qualitative Research in the Study of Leadership, Emerald Group Publishing Ltd, UK, reprinted with permission of the Emerald Group Ltd.

according to Strauss and Corbin (1990), require redefinition in order to fit the realities of qualitative research (p. 250). Qualitative researchers who feel compelled to conduct their studies in a way that is true to the ideological framework underlying a specific qualitative research method are bound by the assumptions of the paradigm used to frame their research.

Research Methods Used in Qualitative Leadership Research

The majority of qualitative research designs employ interviews, case studies and content analysis. However, a much wider repertoire of research methods exists, including grounded theory, ethnography, phenomenology and narrative analysis, many of which are underutilized in the study of leadership. Moreover, the traditional repertoire of research methods that require the analyses of bodies of text is now augmented by non-text-based or image-based data sources derived from photography, video, and various works of art and music. My selection of the research methods for this section was based on considerations such as providing the reader with an appreciation of the richness of qualitative methods and calling attention to missed opportunities in terms of research designs that have yet to find their way into leadership research such as image-based leadership studies that promise to generate new insights into leadership dynamics and processes. At the same time, the selection of the methods presented here, like other choices, reflect my own biases and current understanding of the field. For example, compared the more frequently used and better understood interview and content analysis methods, I offer a more detailed description of underutilized methods such as grounded theory, narrative analysis and visual methods compared to the more frequently used and better understood interview and content analysis methods because I believe that these methods deserve more attention from leadership scholars.

Interviews in Leadership Research

Interviews are pervasive in our society which is sometimes described as an "interview culture" because of the pervasiveness of interviews in our daily lives. We constantly encounter interviews of one type or another: job interviews, life history interviews, celebrity interviews, forensic interviews, admissions interviews, and therapeutic interviews. According to Gubrium and Holstein (2002), the interview is not only a tool that enables us to inquire about our social world; the interview; the interview is actually a significant part of the society we live in.

Hence it comes as no surprise that interviews have always been a staple in the repertoire of a qualitative researcher, especially since they cut across a variety of different research methods. For example, ethnographers, phenomenologists, narrative analysts and case study researchers use qualitative interviewing as their primary data collection method. Many of them consider the interview as a conversation with empathetic understanding (Alvesson, 2003) that places the interviewer and interviewee on equal footing. Structured, semi-structured, and unstructured interviews are the most commonly used basic types which have been augmented by such variations such as increased use of focus groups, e-interviews, and photo interviews also known as inter-*views*. Conger (1998) is critical of the overreliance on interviewing as a principal method in qualitative research. According to the author, "By relying solely on interviews as a research strategy, qualitative researchers in the leadership field fall into a similar trap as questionnaire survey researchers - dependence on a single method... It is imperative that we increasingly utilize observation and other qualitative strategies in conjunction with interviews to ensure not only between-method triangulation of data but also multiple perspectives on the phenomena being studied" (1998, p. 111).

At the heart of qualitative interviewing is the in-depth interview that often takes an unstructured format or a semi-structured format consisting of open-ended questions followed by prepared or unplanned probes and follow-up. The development of the interview protocol may be guided by the theoretical framework the interviewer has established. For example, Wengraf (2006) developed an interview protocol known as the pyramid model that starts with a central research question (CRQ), followed by a series of theory-derived question (TQs) that are couched in conceptual terms and finally by general interview questions (IQs) that may be derived from the context and experiences of the research participants and the researcher. Regardless of the specific interview methods used, effective interviewers demonstrate theoretical and contextual sensitivity, are empathetic listeners, and manage their own emotions well, and respond appropriately to the emotions of interviewees.

The outcome of an unstructured or semi-structured interview is a thick description of the leadership phenomenon under investigation, which manages to capture the participants voice. The term *thick description,* which originated as a research tool for ethnographers (Geertz, 1973), became one of the most important concepts in the lexicon of qualitative researchers. As noted earlier, thick description captures the thoughts and feelings of the research participants as well as the often complex interrelationships among them and gives the reader a sense of verisimilitude, which they can use to cognitively and emotionally place themselves within the research context (Ponterotto, 2006).

Upon completion the responses of the interview protocol are transcribed by the researcher or a professional transcriptionist. Since much detail can be lost or subtly altered when an oral account is transcribed into text, researchers have called into question the commonly held notion that a transcript is a truthful representation of some objective reality (e.g., Kvale, 1996). As Green, Franquiz, and Dixon (1997) pointed out, "a transcript is a text that re-presents an event; it is not the event itself. Following this logic, what is represented is data constructed by the researcher (or transcriptionist) for a particular purpose, not just talk written down" (p. 172). As Bernard and Ryan (2010) pointed out, the sheer work of transcribing is overwhelming. For example, a researcher with 40 hours of recorded interviews who plans on working eight hours a day, every day for 30 days to convert the interview data to text files may spend several months on the task.

Transcripts are influenced by the researcher's interpretive and theoretical lenses, which that shape the analysis and interpretation of the text. To overcome biases that may be inherent in such lenses, some qualitative researchers engage the services of a professional transcriptionist. However, hiring individuals for transcription work does not guarantee accuracy and objectivity either because transcriptionists may become emotionally involved in the work connecting to the characters they construct based on the recordings (Tilley, 2003). The author argued that researchers can ensure that decisions related to transcription are included in the research design and related to the purposes of the research as well as plans for data analysis. In addition, making the complexity of transcription work visible can strengthen claims of trustworthiness (p. 771).

Treviño, Brown and Pincus's (2003) examination of senior executives' and ethics officers' perceptions ethical leadership in their organizations is typical of a qualitative study using semi-structured interviews conducted via telephone as well as face-to-face. The findings from the manifest content analysis revealed several dimensions, including ethical awareness, personal morality, and setting ethical standards and accountability. The authors concluded that in order to be perceived as an ethical leader, executives must engage in behaviors that are socially salient and stand out as ethical exemplars again an ethically neutral ground (p. 34).

Content Analysis in Leadership Research

Krippendorff (2004) defined content analysis as a "research technique for making replicable and valid inferences from text" (p. 18). The author furthermore noted that this qualitative research method consists of a well-developed set of protocols and procedures to make sense of multiple sources of data including texts, visual data, works of art, and interview transcripts. Content analyses of text and non-text- based data can take on a variety of forms: some methods of content analysis are highly quantitative; they rely on computer-assisted analyses, especially in the early stages of word crunching, and on the development of code families that are intended to reduce the data from word frequency counts to fewer content categories and themes. The quantitative content analyses produce a variety of statistics including t-tests, correlations, and log-linear models (e.g., Krippendorff, 2004; Neuendorf, 2002). Among the computer programs used in content analysis are Atlas.ti, NVivo and winMAX. One statistic often used in content analyses is the computation of an index of intercoder agreement which works like a reliability coefficient. Among the available coefficients to measure intercoder reliability are Scott's π, Cohen's ķ, and Krippendorff's α, the latter being the most versatile and, according to the author, the most general measure of agreement between two or more coders. Bligh, Kohles and Meindl's (2004) content analysis of the rhetorical content of George Wt Bush's speeches before and after 9/11 illustrates a highly quantitative content analysis with statistics such as means, standard deviations, intercorrelations between content categories and analysis of covariance.

At the other end of the spectrum, the content analysts who pursues a qualitative strategy often follow the coding sequence developed by Glaser and Strauss (1967) and further refined by Strauss and Corbin (1990) in the context of grounded theory. This sequence begins with open coding, which captures the data in the form of word frequencies and word families followed by axial coding which according to Strauss and Corbin (1990) is "more focused and geared toward discovering and relating categories in terms of the paradigm model" (p. 114). The final stage, selective coding, operates at the highest level of abstraction and is aimed at the integration of codes, categories, and themes developed in the previous phases, resulting in a few core categories or supercodes which reflect the central phenomenon of the study. Themes and core categories emerge both from the data and researchers' theoretical understanding of the leadership phenomena they are studying.

Boyatzis (1998) further expanded approaches to qualitative coding by introducing a multi-step procedure known as thematic content analysis which makes a distinction between manifest codes - codes that are observable at the surface of the data - and latent codes which underlie the phenomenon under investigation. According to Morse and Field (1995) thematic analysis involves the search for and identification of common threads that extend throughout an entire data set. As the authors note, threads are usually quite abstract and difficult to identify. Bartlett (2004), in a study of ethical decision making among managers of large private sector companies in the U.K., conducted a thematic content analysis of interview data and found that personal values, organizational characteristics such as organizational culture and affect in managerial ethical decision making were the major themes that were abstracted from a large number of lower level codes.

Data reduction in content analysis, similar to factor analysis in quantitative research, may be performed at the level of words, sentences, paragraphs, or the entire text (Weber, 1990), and it results in a set of codes that are compiled in a codebook. A typical codebook contains three types of codes: (1) structural codes, which describe characteristics of the environment in which the data are collected, attributes of the respondents and characteristics of the researcher; (2) theme codes, which show where the themes identified by the content analyst actually occur in a text; and (3) memos, which are field notes about the coding process; they are the researcher's reflective journal of the research process (Strauss & Corbin, 1990).

Although computerized coding greatly facilitates the task of the researcher, in the final analysis, especially at the higher levels of abstracting that involve the development of themes and patterns, it is the human analyst who has to extract meaning from the data and interpret them. Despite the fact that qualitative software programs can be useful in organizing and coding data, they are no substitute for the researcher's interpretation of the data. Like other researchers, Martin (2008) combined computerized and thematic analysis in a content analysis of Mary Parker Follett's major books, collections of papers, and speeches, which amounted to 1450 pages of text. Given the size of the corpus of text analyzed in this research, word crunching, autocoding, and line-by-line coding functions in Atlas.ti (followed by hand coding using Boyatzis' thematic coding procedure, it would have almost been impossible to complete this research in a reasonable time period.

Case Study Research and Grounded Theory in Leadership Research

In addition to interviews and content analysis, case study research is also well represented in qualitative leadership research. However, despite its popularity as a method, Yin (2009) believes that case studies have "long been (and continue to be) stereotyped as a weak sibling among social science research methods" (p. xiii), largely because of arguments over the ability to generalize from case studies, Flyvberg (2005) concurs, stressing that social science is about generalizing and one cannot generalize from a single case or other small sample sizes However, many have argued that case study owes its legitimacy and power to the exemplary knowledge, especially theoretical insights, generated by case studies, rather than their generalizability (e.g., Eisenhardt, 1989, 2009; Thomas, 2010). Thus a single case can be a powerful tool, because cases are often instrumental in generating new research questions, concepts and emergent theories. Immersion in rich case data serves as an inspiration for new ideas and, perhaps most importantly, "Research involving case data can usually get much closer to theoretical constructs and provide a much more persuasive argument about causal forces than broad empirical research can" (Siggelow, 2007, pp. 22-23). A substantial body of empirical research using case study has demonstrated that this qualitative method can provide us with a better understanding of the explanatory power of competing theories (e.g., Langley, 1999; Lee, 1989).

Stake (1995, 2005) developed a typology of case studies. He categorized as "intrinsic cases" those cases in which the researcher is convinced of the inherent value of the case and wants to learn something more about the underlying problem underlying. By contrast, he categorized as "instrumental cases" those cases in which the researcher is driven by a need for general understanding beyond the particularities of the case. Yin (2009) added that multiple cases provide a stronger base for theory building and are chosen for theoretical reasons such as replication, extension of theory, and elimination of alternative explanations. According to Pauwels and Mattyson (2004), four pillars define multiple case study research: theoretical sampling, triangulation, pattern matching logic, and analytic generalization; the latter two concepts are discussed in the section on data analyses.

I have grouped case study and grounded theory together because both methods have certain commonalities: building theory inductively from the data (Eisenhardt, 1989; Yin, 2009); they both employ theoretical sampling, and emphasize analytical generalization over statistical generalization Both methods also use interviews as primary sources of data that may be augmented by archival records or participant observation. In contrast to deductive theory testing associated with the positivistic paradigm and quantitative social science research methods, inductive theory building is the primary purpose 'in both the case study method and grounded theory'. Grounded theory was developed by Glaser and Strauss (1967) as a reaction against the extreme positivism that permeated most social science research at a time when the prevalent assumption was that only quantitative or deductive studies could provide systematic scientific research, with linear regression and structural functionalism going strong (e.g., Alvesson & Scølberg, 2002; Suddaby, 2006). Grounded theory is a qualitative tradition built on the constant comparison method in which concepts are categorized and iteratively compared to help the researcher understand their interrelationships through a continual interplay between data collection and analysis to produce theory pertaining to a phenomenon (Strauss & Corbin, 1990). In grounded theory,. theory is said "to lay grounded in the data from the field and to emerge by constantly comparing, fractioning, coding, and analyzing observational and interview data until saturation is reached" (Fendt & Sachs, 2008, p. 431). The literature review usually follows after data analyses have produced theory as opposed to preceding it. As Gephard (2004) pointed out, the purpose of grounded theory is to make knowledge claims not about objective reality but how the researcher and the researched interpret reality, that is, to analyze and conceptualize the "actual production of meanings and concepts used by actors in real settings" (p. 457).

There are a number of different ways of conducting a grounded theory leadership study. The orthodox procedure calls for the application of the method developed by Glaser and Strauss (1967). Modifications have called for a more intentional move toward constructivism (e.g., Chamaz, 2006) or for more "regrounding" (e.g., Bryant, 2003). Chamaz (2006), for example, added an interpretive twist to the analytic interpretations of grounded theory which focuses on the creation of a contextualized emergent understanding rather than the creation of testable theoretical structures (O'Connor, Netting, & Thomas, 2008, p. 30). As pointed out by Locke (2001), few researchers apply grounded theory in its pure or orthodox form. Nevertheless, all approaches to grounded theory stress the importance of the constant comparison method of data collection and analysis and theoretical sampling in which data collection decisions driven by the researcher's intent "to develop plausible propositions of the relationships among concepts and clusters of concepts that can be traced back to the data" (Fendt & Sachs, 2008, p. 448).

Grounded theorists work reflectively through the coding sequence from open to axial and selective coding. They are acting very much like investigative reporters, asking questions of what, when, where, why, how, and with what result or consequence (Strauss & Corbin, 1998). Using the constant comparison method, the researcher is constantly gathering more data, analyzing them, comparing the analyses to past analyses and then collecting and analyzing more data to clarify the emerging relationships among variables (Parry, 1998). Context (e.g., the organization, actors, researcher- method fit, culture, and temporality) is of critical importance in grounded theory research and is "expected to convey a conceptual understanding of the issues that make up the naturalistic world, that is, permit theoretical generalization" (Fendt & Sachs, 2008, p. 431).

Data are grouped according to patterns, categories, and themes that emerge from the data analysis, and they examined to capture the essence of the meaning or experiences drawn from varied situations and contexts (Bowen, 2006). At successive stages, categories and themes move from low levels of abstraction to become major, overarching themes rooted in the concrete evidence located in the data (Bowen, 2006). Once the data are assigned to coded categories and subcategories and relationships among the categories have been established, they are broken down into units and reconstructed into categories with greater and greater degrees of abstraction (O'Connor, Netting, & Thomas, 2008, p. 41). This process continues until a small number of categories captures the entire data set.

The iterative process of data collection and data analysis is discontinued when the point of saturation is reached, which occurs when no new information can be extracted from the data, or the existing conceptual categories become redundant. Thus saturation pertains to the question of what constitutes sufficient data, especially because the volume of data in a grounded theory study quickly becomes overwhelming. According to Glaser and Strauss (1967), saturation is determined by "a combination of the empirical limits of the data, the integration and density of the theory, and the analyst's theoretical sensitivity" (p. 62). However, as Suddaby (2006) pointed out, " Because grounded theory research uses iteration and sets no discrete boundary between data collection and analysis, saturation it not always obvious, even to experienced researches" (p. 693). Once the point of saturation is reached, the grounded theorist usually conducts the review of the extant literature the data collection and analysis have been completed.

One of the controversial issues in grounded theory concerns the degree to which existing theory shapes the design of a grounded theory study since the purpose of this qualitative method is to build theory. Grounded theory always involves trade-offs between a lot of prior theorizing to identify themes versus starting fresh with no or little attention to existing theory. At the one end of this continuum, Strauss and Corbin (1990) recommend that researchers should have no preconceived ideas about expected findings. Yet grounded theory researchers do not approach their study as a tabula rasa excluding all pre-analytic knowledge; existing theory enters into several elements of the research, particularly the design of the interview protocol. Researchers are expected to demonstrate theoretical sensitivity, open mindedness, introspection and reflexivity based on their reading of the literature. Therefore, it is necessary for the grounded theory analyst to have some understanding of the theories that may influence their study. For example, leadership is often defined as an influence process or related to change. In both of these two areas a considerable amount of theory exists which may shape the researcher's methodological framework. However, as recommended by Glaser (1978), the grounded theory analyst should avoid, for example, asking explicit questions about influence processes or change dynamics derived from existing theories. Chamaz (2006) captures this conundrum by concluding that prior theorizing can inhibit the emergence of new ideas while assiduous theory avoidance runs the risk of not connecting the data to the research questions.

Two empirical studies capture the essence of case study and grounded theory research. Simpson (2007) analyzed the case of an organizational simulation, a developmental activity in an MBA program, in which some unexpected and unusual leadership and organizational dynamics emerged. More specifically, the author treated the simulation as a novel, creative organization defined by a self-organizing process of communication mimicking the challenges of organizing under conditions of chaos and complexity. Moreover, the research participants viewed leadership as a collective activity, which was engaged in the group as members shared decision making responsibilities leaving participants without a clear leadership structure.

Grounded theory using the procedures established by Strauss and Corbin (1998) was the research method of choice for Wilson-Stronks, Mutha, and Swedish (2010) to examine hospital CEOs' motivation to embrace cultural competence. Following interviews with 59 CEOs, the transcriptions were analyzed using NVivo. Among the themes that emerged using the constant comparison method were alignments with the organization's mission or strategic plans, meeting patient needs. Among the less frequently mentioned motivators were perception of benefits associated with embracing cultural competence, compliance with laws and regulation and efforts to seek external funding to support cultural competence activities.

Ethnography in Leadership Research

Van Maanen (1988) has stated that "ethnography is a written representation of culture" (p. 1). It is through the interpretation of local culture, seen through the cultural lenses of ethnography that this research method makes its greatest contribution. Culture is defined differently by ethnographers from various disciplinary backgrounds; however, as Agar (1996) stated,

> One of the things ethnographers must deal with is culture shock. Culture shock comes from the sudden immersion in the lifeways of a group different from yourself. Suddenly you do not know the rules anymore. You do not know how to interpret the stream of motions and noises that surround you. You have no idea what is expected of you. Many of the assumptions that form the bedrock of your existence are mercilessly ripped out from under you. The more you cling to them, the less you will understand about the people with whom you work (p. 100).

Almost 25 years later, the same author (Van Maanen, 2010), in a reflective essay on changes in ethnography over the past 20 years, noted that with the rise of market globalization, which led to widespread social interconnectivity and multiculturalism, the standard model of an ethnographic study as a single-site, year- in-the- field, one-tribe-one-scribe enterprise is being challenged as a new generation of ethnographers searches for new modes of inquiry and innovations in tale telling that reflect contemporary social, historical, cultural, and political contingencies. The changes we have witnessed around the world over the last two decades not only make conventional fieldwork difficult but, in some cases, obsolete, because they challenge our ways of thinking about culture. Eisenhart, (2001) asks, "What views of culture can guide the ethnography of postmodernity, the ethnography of groups and sites of permeable boundaries, multiple influences, dispersed group networks and improvised responses" (p. 20)? Van Maanen (2010) concluded that today a good deal more topical variety, methodological imagination, and stylistic diversity are used in ethnographic studies compared to 1998 when his *Tales of the Field* book was published.

Fieldwork is one the most characteristic elements of ethnographic research, particularly fieldwork of the immersive sort, which, according to Van Maanen (2010), is by and large definitional of the trade in ethnography. Cultural immersion, the second hallmark of an ethnographic study, means that the researcher lives and works in the community chosen for the study for six month to a year, 'going native' by learning the language, ritual, symbols, and beliefs of the community or social group. According to Emerson (1987), "long-term and intimate involvement in the routine, everyday worlds of others is a methodological sine qua non" (p. 71).

Moreover, ethnographers need to be sensitive to how their "ethnographic accounts are subject to the disciplinary authorial voice of the ethnographer and how they judge the cultures they are studying through their own ethnocentric norms, practices, and cultural lenses" (Cunliffe, 2010, p. 228). Like their grounded theory colleagues, ethnographers leave the field when they believe that enough data have been gathered to describe the culture or problem, that is, when the point of saturation has been reached. However, although much has been written about the various meanings of culture, there have been relatively few discussions of how ethnographic research methods should or could vary accordingly (Eisenhart, 2001, p. 16).

In an illustrative ethnographic study, Iszatt-White (2009) studied educational leaders in the UK to examine practices leaders use to make themselves and their followers feel valued and to what extent valuing practices involve the exercise of emotional labor. Examples of valuing practices included receiving constructive feedback, praise, recognition or opportunities for personal development. The results of the fieldwork, which consisted of interviews with staff members of educational leaders were presented in the form of direct participant quotes, which provided examples of valuing practices in specific context and leaders' accounts of valuing practices as emotional labor.

Narratives in Leadership Research

Narratives have played a central role in understanding the social construction of organizational phenomena (Czarniawska, 2004). Narratives encompass a wide genre of writing - stories, self-narratives, life histories, biographies and autobiographies. According to Polkinghorne (1995), "A storied narrative is the linguistic form that preserves the complexity of human action with its interrelationship of temporal sequence, human motivation, chance happenings, and changing interpersonal and environmental contexts" (p. 7). According to Pentland (1999), people do not simply tell their stories - they enact them.

In order to qualify as narrative, stories must include three criteria: temporality or the chronology of events; causality; and evaluation. In a seminal paper, Labov and Waletzky (1967) stated that narrative provides "a method of recapitulating past experiences by matching a verbal sequence of clauses to the sequence of events that actually occurred" (p. 12). This statement captures the first two central features: temporality and causality. Aristotle in his *Poetics* provided the simplest definition of temporality when he described a story as a narrative with a beginning, a middle, and an end assuming that time has a unilateral direction moving from past, to present to future. Intimately linked with the temporal qualities of narrative is the notion of plot. The plot within a narrative relates events to each other by linking a prior happening to a subsequent event (Polkinghorme, 1995). For example, Denning (2004) suggests that a story is a narrative that links a series of events in some kind of causal sequence. Although storytelling is subject to cultural variation (Burger & Miller, 1999), people from all walks of life can and do make sense of their experience by linking events through plot lines, thereby constructing narratives (Polkinghorne, 1988).

The second defining feature of narrative is causality. Baumeister and Neuman's (1994) work suggests that narratives depend on causal structures to give them coherence and to provide the foundations for events that are not simply temporally ordered but linked together like cogs and wheels of a machine. The third characteristic of narrative is evaluation identified by Labov and Waletzkey (1967) as an expression of the narrator's attitude toward, or feelings about, the content of the narrative. According to the author, a narrative without an evaluation lacks significance simply because it has no point.

The academic literature distinguishes narrative from story. Boje and colleagues (Boje, 2001, Boje, Rosile, & Gardner, 2004) argue that a narrative is distinguished from a story in that it has a plot. Asimov (1996) argued that a tale is something to be told (from the Anglo-Saxon) and a narrative is something that is narrated (from the Latin). One specific type of narrative is the life story defined as a narrated process that reconstructs rather than resurrects the past. Life narratives or life stories have been described as an economic summary of life's experiences. According to McAdams (2001), this narrative summation is used as an explanatory structure that allows people to maintain a sense of personal identity. As Ligon, Hunter and Mumford (2008) noted, although events, especially those of an unusual or unpredicted nature, are important for understanding the life stories of leaders, the content or thematic underpinnings of the events are equally important. The authors cited the work of McAdams (2001) and his collaborators (McAdams, Hoffman, Mansfield, & Ray, 1996) whose research showed that the content of life narratives is especially relevant for identifying individual differences in personal goals and motives, coping strategies, values and beliefs. The authors concluded that such content differences should be helpful in distinguishing leadership styles as well (p. 345). Shamir and Eilam (2005) added that in constructing their life stories leaders explain and justify their present self which includes their leadership motivations and experiences and the meanings they attach to them.

Narratives offer a view of leadership from the ground up by building theories and developing ideas that are based on human experience (Boudens, 2005). Narratives of leaders take multiple forms, from life stories to fairy tales; they tell stories of heroes and villains, supermen and superwomen. Sternberg (2008) proposed that leaders who engage in storytelling succeed to the extent that they: (1a) have a story that fits their followers' need; (2b) communicate that story in a compelling way; (3c) implement the story in a way that suggests it is succeeding; and (4d) persuade followers that in the end the story accomplished what it set out to accomplish. Conversely, leaders' stories fail if they do not fit followers' needs, fail to communicate the intended message, do not get implemented and lack coherence or allow a story of successful leadership to be replaced by a story of personal failings.

Storytelling can be a powerful leadership tool, especially when there is a need for cultural change within the organization. There is ample evidence that storytelling in organizations helps in training and development, in reinforcing organizational socialization and identity, and in promoting change (Parkin, 2004). Conveying meaning through life narratives may foster identification with followers, providing a basis for common understanding which permits more intuitive social interaction between followers and leaders (Keller, 2003). Denning (2004) suggested that leaders keep the following goals in mind when building their stories: to spark action (transformation), to communicate who you are (to build empathy and trust), to transmit values, to foster collaboration, to tame rumors, to share knowledge, and to lead people into the future. However, the demands made on leaders in contemporary organizations operating in complex, uncertain, and unpredictable environments require the development of new narratives, as old narratives espousing predictability and control based on assumptions and beliefs which are no longer tenable (Woodward & Funk, 2010) lose their explanatory power.

The life narrative approach is exemplified by a study conducted by Ligon, Hunter, and Mumford (2008) which traced the development of outstanding leaders. The researchers examined 120 biographies of historically notable 20th century leaders which were content analyzed using the life story approach. The researchers categorized the historical leaders as ideological (i.e., Susan B. Anthony and Theodore Roosevelt), charismatic (i.e., John F. Kennedy and Eva Peron) and pragmatic (i.e., Martha Stewart and Sam Walton) to determine differences in development experiences among these three types of leaders. After identifying a number of different events in the life experiences of the leaders such as turning points or concrete events that necessitated them to revise their goals and direction, the results of both quantitative and qualitative analyses highlighted the importance of events experienced early in the leader's life. The authors found significant differences in pathways to outstanding leadership between ideological, charismatic, and pragmatic leaders in this historical sample of eminent leaders in a wide range of contexts including politics, social movements, and business.

Image-Based Methods in Leadership Research

One of the new frontiers in qualitative research involves the use of images as sources of data including photographs, films, videos or works of art which have been more widely applied in other disciplines such as education, sociology, health care and anthropology. The basic premise in image-based research is that images are data. As Jackson and Guthey (2006) noted, we live in an era in which visual images have become paramount, taking center stage in politics news, corporations, and the media (see also Frosh, 2003; Schroeder, 2002; Thompson, 2000). The authors set out to make a case for the importance of visual images in the construction of leadership drawing on the work of Meindl (e.g., Bligh, Kohles, & Meindl, 2004; Chen & Meindl, 1991; Meindl, Ehrlich, Dukerich, 1985) who studied leadership imagery in a wide range of contexts. Images of fallen leaders such as Jeffrey Skillings of Enron being led out of court in handcuffs or pictures of Martha Stewart before and after her downfall, are much more powerful than verbal accounts of these events, because they juxtapose previous celebratory images of the same individuals at the height of their success with negative photographs or TV coverage of theit fall from grace. Newsweek reporter Sloan (2004) observed that the media finally got the photo op that so many people wanted for so long: Ken Lay doing the perp walk, almost three years after Enron's collapse touched off the current corporate scandal fest. According to Jackson and Guthey (2006), "Visual images of CEOs and top executives deserve close scrutiny because they serve as an important window into how business, celebrity, firm reputation, and corporate legitimacy are constructed and deconstructed in the media" (p. 169). Yet, the visual dimension of leadership has only received limited research attention.

What might this new frontier have to offer to leadership research? How should work in this new frontier be assessed? What additional training do qualitative researchers need to become effective image-based researchers? Although the use of visual methods is limited in leadership studies, there is nevertheless a slow increase in the use of arts-based methods as part of a broader cross-fertilization between business and the arts (Taylor & Ladkin, 2009). Adler (2006) argued that business has turned to the arts because of five trends: (1) increasing global connectedness; (2) increasing domination of market forces; (3) an increasingly complex and chaotic environment; (4) decreased cost of experimentation, and (5) yearning for significance. Gayá Wicks and Rippin (2010) propose that arts-based inquiry allows participants to reflect on the inherent tensions and ambiguities of leadership in a world characterized by inherent complexity, tensions, and contradictions. Stanczak (2007) noted that the historical use of images in social research has recently changed from an emphasis of visual images that functioned as illustrations to a phase where "Visual or image-based research is reemerging with significant untapped potential and vigor across a broader scope of disciplines" (p. 3). He added, "Images are not merely appendages to the research but rather inseparable components to learning about our social worlds" (p. 3).

Among the visual research methods leadership researchers have at their disposal are inter-*views* also known as photo-elicitation in which the researcher and the respondent produce photos and then collaboratively discuss images or photographs to generate data. Anthropologists Bateson and Mead (1942) took more than 25,000 photographs over a two-year field experience, from which they selected 759 for their book *Balinese Character*. These photographs were sorted into Balinese cultural categories such as spatial orientation and levels, rites of passage, and integration and disintegration of the body. According to Strati (2000), a prominent theorist of organizational aesthetics, photographs arouse aesthetic experiences which attest to the power of photography. Other sources of data derived from visual methods include cartoons, quilts, works of art, film, corporate logos, websites and multimedia sources, which blend image, video and audio. According to Warren (2008), the widespread availability of images through the Internet and social media sites have facilitated their use as sources of data for qualitative researchers. In a world dominated by multimedia, it is not surprising that visual representations are increasingly recognized as valid data (Richards, 2006).

Early examples of the use of images come from Dougherty and Kinda (1990) who applied content analysis to photographs in the annual reports of five major corporations. Vince and Broussine (1996) used drawings of managers in six public service organizations as the catalyst to enable them to bring out the often paradoxical emotions and work with them as part of the change management process. Meyer (1991) explored the use of visual data in organizational research and argued that drawings are capable of communicating information about multi-dimensional organizational attributes with clarity and precision and that research respondents often possess complex cognitive maps of their organizations that they cannot verbalize. Siles (2004) questioned why academics are so reluctant to embrace the pictorial form as a means of understanding their world, especially given the power images convey, in an era when the United States is becoming an increasingly visual society where knowledge is constructed through images (Rose, 2003).

Theater and music are two art forms that have been examined as relevant to leadership. Vail (1991) referred to leadership as a performing art while Mangham and Overington (1983) noted that both theater and leadership have strong performance components and that there is a tradition of comparing organizations to theater and leaders to actors. Life as drama and the world as a stage are idioms familiar to most of us. According to Mangham (1978), the life-as-drama analogy holds that the social world is capable of being "conceptualized in terms of the stage, that social reality is realized theatrically, that life is theatre, and that action is inherently dramatic" (p. 20). Gardner and Avolio (1998) were the first to advance the relevance of dramaturgical approach to leadership by examining the roles that the environment, actor (leader), and audience (followers) play in defining a situation and in jointly constructing a charismatic leadership. The authors defined the dramaturgical process as framing, scripting, staging, and performing, they and adopted the approach first proposed by Goffman (1959) and applied to charismatic leadership. Leaders have often been compared to actors with the most obvious parallel stemming from the principle of performing, which both engage in. According to Mangham (2001), the theater is a place for challenge, reflection, and instructions, functions in which leaders are also involved.

Biehl-Missal (2010) explored leadership as an art by having leaders investigate theatrical themes where the audience is confronted with contentious and problematic heroes. Dysfunctional leaders have populated the stage for millennia from Sophocles to Shakespeare. Lehman (2006), in discussing Sophocles "Antigone" as an indecisive heroine unable to manage her destiny, showed that the style of performing can be used to support the deconstruction of self-confident leadership. The author concluded that "The lessons from theatre consist of a more nuanced understanding of leadership that is based on a felt and emotional experience because an appreciation of theatre includes the bodily experience of a performance situation and is accompanied by a constant questioning of realities and of the nature and necessity of role-playing and appearance" (p. 290).

Music is very much unexploited as a medium for the study of leadership. Daykin (2004) explored the expressive potential of music and noted that in itself and by itself, music has neither a textual or visual basis, which may explain why it is so infrequently used in art-based research. The author cites the collaborative work of British jazz composer/saxophonist John Surman and American drummer Jack DeJohnette, in which woodwinds and brass represent different "voices" in an underlying text concerning troubled world politics and serve as a reminder of the principles of the United Nations 1946 Universal Declaration of Human Rights.

The Aesthetics of Leadership

Theoretically, the use of image-based research methods is often linked to organizational aesthetics (e.g., Carr & Hancock, 2003; Guillet de Monthoux, 2004; Strati, 1996, 1999, 2000). Visual representations of leadership have been enhanced by the aesthetic turn in organization studies. Numerous theorists (e.g., Strati, 1996, 1999; Taylor, 2002; Taylor & Hansen, 2005) have called attention to the need of engaging all of our senses, including the visual, in the construction of knowledge. Like other facets of organizational life, leadership too has been associated with arts and aesthetics (e.g. Adler, 2006). Grint (2001) makes a persuasive case that rather than being considered a science, leadership should be viewed as an art.

Like art, leadership has the power to inspire, transform, heal, and connect us to something larger than ourselves (Klein & Diket, 1999). Art, as Aristotle noted, is a way of knowing. It is *poiesis,* knowing by making, as contrasted with *theoria,* knowing by observing, and *praxis,* knowing by taking action. Like artists, leaders can create "spaces that may be psychological illusionary, theatrical, metaphysical, physical as in the case of sculpture or architecture, or virtual as in cyber-generated spaces" (Klein & Diket, 1999, p. 25). According to Watrin (1999) art is at times like qualitative research in that it "seizes the fullness of the lived experience by describing, interpreting, creating, reconstituting, and revealing meaning" (p. 93). Guillett de Monthoux, Gustafson and Sjotrend (2007) concluded that aesthetic leadership is "The ability to organize muddled realities, to move easily between spaces (fields of flow) by providing an inviting yet defined container for the emergence of creative thought and action" (p. 263).

However, as Eisner (1997) pointed out, new forms of data representation have their perils as well as their promises. Among the reasons visual methods are rarely used in leadership research are subjectivity in interpretation, extreme variations in artistic ability, technical publishing difficulties and an academic orthodoxy that still regards images as subjective, inferior or even an eccentric form of data compared to words and numbers (Siles, 2004). For example, because respondents vary in visual aptitude, image-based techniques carry a risk of overgeneralizing the responses of artistic informants. Meyer (1991) added that that image-based researcher face an insidious risk: visual data can be enormously compelling, even when their validity is low. In addition, visual methods require expertise above and beyond competency in qualitative methods, such as the ability to appraise non-text-based research that does not fit conventional paradigms, including aesthetic sensitivity and technical expertise, for example, in the choice of medium and equipment (digital versus analog, black and white versus color, etc.)

Moreover, leadership researchers who pursue visual approaches may be marginalized because they do not conform to mainstream theories. Historically, the arts have often challenged dominant political, religious and aesthetic conventions while serving as a lightning rod for social change (Slattery, 2003, p. 1951). As Hooks (1990) stated, "There can never be one critical paradigm for the evaluation of artistic work...a realistic aesthetic acknowledges that we are constantly changing positions, locations that our needs and concerns vary, that these diverse directions must correspond with our shifts in critical thinking" (p. 111). Likewise, Pink (2001) argued that images cannot and should not fit into existing methodologies while Stanczak (2007) emphasized that "Images and videos add an additional layer of data from which the critical reader may triangulate between statistics, theoretical or conceptual triangulation, and the subjectively interpreted lived experience of the participants" (p. 12).

Two New Zealand scholars, a leadership researcher and an art historian, teamed up to examine how commissioned leadership portraits serve not only as commemorative images of leaders but, more important illustrate and reinforce the power of the institutions that commissioned the paintings (Griffey & Jackson, 2008). The authors mounted an exhibition entitled "The Power of Portraiture" which featured 40 portraits that were commissioned by local government agencies, businesses, and private individuals and featured major public figures in New Zealand. In the article, the authors singled out seven paintings of New Zealand's formal leaders that included the country's first sovereign Queen Victoria, a Maori chief, Sir Edmund Hillary in whom "the media and portrait painters found an icon of visual leadership built on physical strength, mental determination, and public humility" (p. 147) and New Zealand's first female prime minister, Jenny Shipley. The authors used techniques from art history to analyze the portraits and showed that "commissioned portraits in New Zealand promote leadership not as a born right to rule but a privilege achieved by hard work, determination and the desire to be a productive member of society, even when the subject has inherited their leadership role" (p. 142). The leaders in the portraits showed virtues such as humility and excellence; they exuded an air of quiet heroism indicating that that formal power and authority were not hallmarks of their leadership. The authors concluded that although commissioned portraits are merely inanimate surrogates of leaders, they can exert an enduring influence beyond the time and space they inhabited and attest to the power of the institutions. Finally, Griffey and Jackson suggested that leadership may not only be treated as an art but the other way around, asking to consider art as leadership (p. 155)

Table 7.2 presents illustrative examples of qualitative leadership studies that utilized the research methods discussed here. The diversity of topics, nationality of authors and reporting quality are all noteworthy here. My primary motivation in the search for current articles illustrating the qualitative methods discussed here was to identify recent research not reviewed in Klenke (2008). An interesting by-product of my search was the discovery of the diversity of the types of journals in which these studies are published.

Data Collection and Analyses

Interviews, observations, and gathering records of secondary data, such as organizational documents and inspection physical artifacts, are the primary data collection methods in qualitative research. Interviews rank as the foremost data collection method in several qualitative designs, including phenomenology, ethnography, and narrative analysis. Other specific methods of data collection

Table 7.2. Empirical Leadership Studies Illustrating the Qualitative Research Methods Discussed in this Chapter

Author/Date	Title	Data Collection/Sources	Analysis	Journal
Interviews				
Campbell, 2003	Leadership and academic culture in the senate presidency	Semi-structured telephone interviews with 42 UK faculty senate presidents	Thematic coding	*American Behavioral Scientist*
Lineham & Scullion, 2002	Repatriation of European female corporate executives: An empirical study	Interviews with 50 European senior managers	Thematic coding	*Int. J. of Human Resource Management*
Pina de Cuna, Campos e Cuna & Rego, 2009	Exploring the role of leaders-subordinate interactions in the construction of organizational positivity	Semi-structured interviews with 89 Portuguese participants	Critical incidents, constant comparison, coding and conceptualization	*Leadership*
Treniño, Brown & Pincus, 2003	A qualitative investigation of perceived executive ethical leadership: Perceptions from inside and outside the executive suite	Semi-structured interviews with 20 senior executives and 20 US ethics officers	Manifest and latent coding (Boyatzis)	*Human Relations*
Content Analysis				
Ahmend, 2005	Desired competencies and job duties of non-profit CEOs in relation to the current challenges: Through the lens of CEOs job advertisements	Collecting 242 US job advertisements for CEO positions	Content analysis	*Journal of Management*
Bartlett, 2004	A comparative study of ethical decision making amongst managers in large private sector U.K. companies	Qualitative research interviews with 40 UK managers, critical incidents	NUD*IST assisted content analysis; code book development	*Book chapter*
Calogero, & Mullen, 2008	About face: Facial prominence of George W. Bush in cartoons as a function of war	Identifying 253 images of George W. Bush showing facial prominence as a function of involvement in wars in political cartoons	Quantitative content analysis using descriptive and statistic and ANOVA	*The Leadership Quarterly*
Case Studies				
McCabe, D., 2002	'Waiting for dead men's shoes': Toward a cultural understanding of management innovation. 'Waiting for dead men's shoes': Toward cultural understanding of management innovation	Interviews with 50 staff, 10 supervisors, 4 assistant managers, 2 department managers, and IT and personnel managers in US	Not reported; data were presented in form of participant quotation to questions followed by author's comments	*Human Relations*

(continued)

Table 7.2. Continued

Author/Date	Title	Data Collection/Sources	Analysis	Journal
Simpson, 2007	Organizing in the mist: A case study of leadership and complexity	Organizational simulation used in group interviews with 20 UK MBA students	Development of themes, analytical method not reported	*Leadership and Organization Development Journal*
Grounded Theory				
Parry, 1999	Enhancing adaptability: Leadership strategies to accommodate change in local government settings	43 unstructured interviews with employees from three US organizations	Theoretical coding based on Glaser & Strauss (1967), categorization, linking categories, higher order explanatory categories	*Journal of Organizational Change Management*
Wilson-Stroks & Terrance, 2010	From the perspective of CEOs: What motivates hospitals to embrace cultural competence?	Secondary data derived from an earlier study that used semi-structured interviews with 59 US hospital CEOs	Thematic NVIVO assisted coding, constant comparison method to develop categories	*Journal of Health Care Management*
Ethnography				
Iszatt-White, 2009	Leadership as emotional labour: The effortful accomplishment of valuing practices.	Field notes, participant observation, shadowing, interviews with a small number of educational leaders in the U.K.	Coding for themes from fieldwork abstracts	*Leadership*
Narrative				
Bosch, 2008	Telling stories, creating (and saving) her life. An autobiography of Ayaan Hirsi Ali.	Ghost written autobiography of Somalian refugee who immigrated to the Netherlands	Description of plots in the context of the extant literature	*Women's International Business Journal*
Carroll & Levy, 2008	Defaulting to management: leadership define by what it is not	Semi-structured interviews with 53 managers enrolled in leadership development programs in Australia	Interpretation of quotes	*Organization*
Americ, Craig & Tourish, 2007	The transformational leaders as *pedagogue, physician, architect, commander, and saint:* Five root metaphors in Jack Welch's letters to stockholders of General Electric	Collecting letters written by Jack Welch to stockholders; 52,894 word corpus of text	Metaphor analysis, classification of letter content in terms of metaphors; emergence of five dominant metaphors	*Human Relations*

Table 7.2. Continued

Author/Date	Title	Data Collection/Sources	Analysis	Journal
Visual Methods				
Griffey & Jackson, 2010	The portrait as leader: Commissioned portraits and the power of tradition	Seven commissioned portraits selected from a New Zealand art exhibition depicting leaders in different contexts	Techniques (unspecified) from art history	*Leadership*
Islam, 2009	Animating leadership: Crisis and renewal of governance in 4 mythic narrative	Four animated films dealing with leadership emergence and the relationship between leaders and society	Lacanian psychoanalysis used in cinema studies; structural analysis underlying central themes	*The Leadership Quarterly*
Guethy & Jackson, 2005	CEO portraits and the authenticity paradox	7 executive portraits painted by Danish photographer	Description of portraits through analysis of the artist as CEO photographer	*Journal of Management Studies*

techniques include direct observation, participant observation, and analysis of archival records such as memoranda, newspaper articles, or annual reports. Most qualitative studies use theoretical or purposive sampling, which means that "cases are selected that are particularly useful for illumination and extending the relationships and logic among constructs" (Eisenhardt & Graebner, 2007, p. 27); the cases represent unusually revelatory or extreme exemplars as well as opportunities for unusual research access (Yin, 2009). Graebner and Eisenhardt (2004) introduced "polar types " (similar to Yin's extreme exemplars) as an important concept in theoretical sampling, in which the researcher samples extremes such as very high- and very low-performing leaders in order to observe contrasting patterns in the data. This sampling, according to Eisenhardt and Graebner, "Leads to very clear recognition of the central constructs, relationships, and logic of the focal phenomenon" (p. 27). Purposive sampling is aimed at theory construction and not the representativeness of a population. Qualitative researchers are expected to gather rich descriptive data and ground conclusions and understandings in the data mined, not in prior theories (Bruce, 2007).

Bernard and Ryan (2010) defined qualitative data as reductions of our experiences. That is, when qualitative researchers reduce informants' thoughts, behaviors, emotions, artifacts, and environments to words, pictures, or sounds, they produce qualitative data. Although data analytic procedures have been well documented (e.g., Bernard & Ryan, 2010; Richards, 2006; Richard & Morse, 2007), it is important to note that there is no single method for analyzing qualitative data; instead data are created in a particular form according to the method used. However, qualitative researchers generally use inductive data analyses as their predominant approach, resulting in reports that are "Descriptive, incorporating expressive language and the presence of voice in the text" (Eisner, 1991, p. 36). Qualitative researchers pay attention to the idiosyncratic as well as pervasive and seek the unique of each case (Patton, 2002).

Some qualitative methods share analytical strategies, such as content analysis, which is used in a number of methods based on qualitative interviewing such as case study, ethnography, and grounded theory. Content analysis procedures are described in the section on content analysis as a research method earlier in this chapter. Although the process of data analysis may appear as a linear coding sequence, in actuality, it is more of a circular process during which data collection and analysis occur in an iterative fashion. Codes are developed to identify themes, which refer to entities more encompassing than topics or categories. These themes represent the first step of abstracting and always require categorization

(Richards & Morse, 2007). With categorization the researcher puts a first foot on the ladder of abstraction (Carney, 1990) and then moves up the ladder to conceptualizations, which utilize more abstract concepts and mental images.

Many qualitative methods produce thick descriptions, which are attained through interactions with the research participants: recordings of field notes, meetings, and from the analyses of unstructured or semi-structured interviews. Analyses in many qualitative methods involve reading and re-reading interview transcripts, reviewing other data sources and gradually piecing together each of the main protagonist's narrative of events (Brown, Stacy, & Nandhakuma, 2008).

For many qualitative methods, including qualitative interviewing, ethnography and narrative analysis, there are no standardized procedures detailing how textual data should be analyzed. However, a common feature in these methods is the transformation of oral accounts provided by the researcher, participants and their interactions with the researcher into a body of text through transcription. The difficulty of producing a text from speech, which manages to preserve the meaning embedded in the communications between the researcher and participants, is widely recognized. As Wengraf (2006) recommended, rather than treating transcription as occurring prior to the analysis, it is more appropriate to understand it as part of the analytic process. Since it is all but impossible to produce a transcription that captures all of the meaning of the communications between the researcher and the researched, any transcription of speech must be understood as a compromise (Elliott, 2006)

Other qualitative research methods employ data analytical techniques unique to a given method. For example, in a case study, pattern-matching is a major mode of analysis, which involves comparing an empirical pattern found in the data with a predicted one (Yin, 2009). Yin recommends that in order to produce an analysis of the highest quality, authors should, (1) show that the analysis relied on all the relevant evidence; (2) include all major rival interpretations in the analysis; (3) address the most significant aspect of the case study; and (4) use their own prior expert knowledge to further the analyses. All that pattern matching requires is "a theoretical pattern of expected outcomes, an observed pattern of effects, and an attempt to match the two" (Troachim, 1989, p. 360). Stake (1995) recommended categorical aggregation as another means of analysis in case study research: researchers assemble a collection of incidents from the data from which they expect relevant issues to emerge. Silverman (2001) emphasized the use of "deviant-case-analysis" (p. 239), also known as negative case sampling, as an approach where discrepant instances help to sharpen the conceptual clarity of categories and cases.

Likewise, grounded theory research relies on the constant comparison method for data collection and analyses. Here, too, analytical procedures have been well documented (e.g., Glaser & Strauss, 1967; Glaser & Strauss, 1990; Strauss & Corbin; Strauss & Corbin, 1998; Chamaz, 2006). Qualitative data analysis procedures for grounded theory have been widely documented: what is less transparent, however, are the details of how data collection and data analysis interact in a practical sense (Bruce, 2007). Bruce suggested the use of diagrams to explicitly illustrate the practical interaction between data collection and analysis.

Ethnographers obtain their data by immersing themselves in a social group or culture. They often use participant observation as an adjunct to unstructured or semi-structured interviews and focus on language, rituals, cultural artifacts, stories, symbols, and their interrelationships. Since ethnographies are all about the culture of a social group, ethnographers "go native"- that is, they spend a long time in the field to assimilate themselves into the culture they are studying. Whereas for a quantitative researchers going native may be seen as a liability because it represents a potential source of bias and loss of objectivity, for qualitative researchers it is a research strategy that allows them to capture the voices of the participants in an authentic way.

Fieldwork and observations comprise the core of an ethnographic study. According to Goodall (2000), a number of activities are necessary to become an ethnographer: (1) learning how to do fieldwork; (2) learning how to write; (3) figuring out who you are as a person/fieldworker/writer; and (4) knowing how, when, and where these all connect (p. 7). Many ethnographic studies involve triangulation of data collection methods, such as participant observation, semi-structured or autobiographical interviews, life histories of members of the local community and the collection of folktales. Among the equipment used in data collection are digital voice recorders, personal digital assistants (PDA), GPS technology, cameras, digital camcorders and digital video (Fetterman, 2010). In the final analysis, ethnographers must integrate the analyses of the various data sources, field notes, and digital recordings to draw an overall picture of the group or culture. They must couch the ethnographic report in a language that the audience understands. Conveying the findings in the most appropriate medium is a critical, but often overlooked, last step in ethnographic reporting.

Analyses of visual representation of leadership are evolving and often lack methodological detail and precision. Rose (2003) reviewed several methods, three of which are briefly mentioned here: compositional interpretation, content analysis, and semiology. Compositional interpretation focuses on the image itself. What does the image show in terms of color, spatial organization, geometrical perspective, light, and expressive content, which Taylor (1957) defined as the "Combined effect of subject matter and visual form" (p. 43). As Taylor pointed out, separate consideration of expressive content is necessary because breaking an image into its component parts – spatial organization, color, light – does not necessarily capture the look of an image. According to Rose (2003), the major shortcoming of compositional interpretation is its lack of concern with the social practices of visual imagery.

Content analysis of visual images follows the rules and procedures established for content analysis of text – it basically involves counting what you see. Sampling here involves locating images that are appropriate to the research questions followed by the establishment of strategies for coding the images. Once each image has a number of codes attached to, it the researcher proceeds with frequency counts and generates categories. Lutz and Collins (1993) stressed the importance of the analyst's dependence on a theorized connection between the image and the broader cultural context in which meaning is made. The authors use the term *theorized* because making this connection entails drawing on a theoretical and empirical understanding of the images under consideration.

Unlike compositional description, which is simply descriptive, or content analysis, which relies on quantitative analyses, semiology (sometimes also called semiotics) offers a repertoire of tools for taking an image apart and tracing how it works in relation to a broader system of meaning (Williamson, 1978). Semiology often takes the form of detailed case studies of relatively few images. It makes a crucial distinction between the two parts of a sign: the signified and the signifier. The signified is a concept or an object such as a leaderless group or the statue of a leader. The signifier is a sound or image that is attached to the signified; in this case, the words *toxic leadership*. This distinction, according to Rose (2003), enables semiology to focus on the transfers of signifieds between signs. Examples of signs in humans include age, gender, body, and hair, which have symbolic meanings. For example, women's hair is often used to signify seductive beauty as seen in many commercials of hair enhancing products. In finding meaning in images, semiology focuses on the construction of social differences through signs and the ideologies underlying these differences.

Quality Standards and Rigor in Qualitative Research

Qualitative research designs have become so diverse that applications of standards of quality and rigor are become an increasing challenge (Patton, 2002; Shek, Tnag, & Han, 2005). Although reliability, validity, and generalizability are traditional standards that define the quality of research conducted under the auspices of positivism, they continue to influence the way in which methodological rigor in qualitative research is defined and evaluated. These criteria are tools of a positivistic epistemology, and they continue to spill over into qualitative research. However, as many researchers have noted (e.g., Guba, 1981; Strauss & Corbin, 1990; Easterby, Golden-Biddle, & Locke, 2008), the criteria by which objectivistic, positivistic, quantitative research is evaluated are not necessarily appropriate for judging the quality of qualitative research.

As Eisner (1997) observed, "When everybody is quantifying the world, it looks like there are no other options. When everyone requires random selection of a sample from a population as a condition for generalization, it looks as though that idea is made in heaven. When almost everyone conceptualizes validity in terms of its four canonical conditions, the meaning of validity becomes a kind of catechism that novices memorize" (p. 265). Demonstrating that qualitative data analysis is reliable and valid and that the study was conducted in a rigorous manner is especially important given a common criticism that qualitative results are often presented in an anecdotal manner. Likewise, overcoming perceptions of qualitative research as not being reliable and rigorous, developing more rigorous quality standards remains an important priority with regard to procuring funding for qualitative research.

What constitutes quality in qualitative research is a thorny question for many qualitative methodologists. While there is broad agreement among quantitative researchers on how to evaluate the quality of a quantitative study, there is less relatively less agreement on what constitutes a rigorous qualitative study. At the Congress of Qualitative Inquiry (2005), Burbules offered the following epistemological virtues as a basis for assessing the quality of a qualitative study: (1) make your position, stakes, and value presuppositions explicit; (2) subject yourself to internal and external criticism; (3) take the chance of being mistaken; (4) make findings public; and (5) share data, not just conclusions, with the audience. However, although qualitative researchers, like their quantitative counterparts, desire to produce research that is well written, methodologically appropriate, and makes a theoretical contribution, there is still no boilerplate for how to achieve these aims for qualitative researchers (Pratt, 2009).

As a result, qualitative researchers have created their own quality standards to include credibility, which corresponds to reliability in quantitative research; transferability, which requires that rich descriptions of qualitative data collection and analysis methods allow for potential application in other contexts (the qualitative analog of external validity or generalizability); and dependability, or the need to articulate an audit trail made transparent for the reader. Demands for demonstrations of new quality standards resonate with the qualitative research community and were described by Demerath (2006) as "The elucidative response for reducing marginalization of qualitative research referring to the need for achieving greater transparency in research design, development of inferences and theory, and quality criteria" (p. 98).

Some scholars (e.g., Lincoln & Guba, 1985) refer to the concepts of trustworthiness or authenticity in qualitative research and compare these to the concepts of reliability and validity in the quantitative research process. The authors proposed that "There exist substitute criteria (called credibility, transferability, dependability, and confirmability) together with corresponding empirical procedures that adequately (if not absolutely) affirm the trustworthiness of naturalistic approaches" (p.43). The four terms presented by Lincoln and Guba, credibility, transferability, dependability, and confirmability, are the qualitative equivalents of the quantitative criteria of internal validity, external validity, reliability, and objectivity. The authors affirm that "The basic issue in relation to trustworthiness is simple: how can an inquirer persuade his or her audiences (including self) that the findings of an inquiry are worth paying attention to, worth taking account of" (p. 290). According to Bansal & Corley, (2011, p. 236) methodological rigor in qualitative research is conveyed through the authenticity and candor of the text by "Describing the who, what how, and when in such a way that the reader sees clearly how the researcher moved from the raw data to the theoretical insights." According to Sandberg (2005), the principal question of validity concerns how qualitative researchers justify that their interpretations are truthful to the lived experience of the research participants within the theoretical and methodological perspectives taken (p. 58), while Bamberg (2007) claims that determinants of validity should to be considered in the light of qualitative methodologies. Hence, the criteria for assessing the trustworthiness of qualitative findings are not so much a matter of whether the outcome is statistically significant but whether it is meaningful. As Bruner (1996) noted, the purpose is to achieve understanding rather than explanation, and in the process, we construct meaning.

Validity in image-based research is an even more complex issue since data representation and trustworthiness of data analysis are central to all qualitative methods, including image-based research (Prosser, 1998). Simco and Warin (1997) argue that the concept of validity is particularly problematic when applied to image-based research and presents a "Strategy for ensuring trustworthiness based on five key criteria: completeness, adequacy of interpretation, transparency, self-reflection and the aggregation of conflicting interpretation" (p. 661). Bamberg (2007) proposed that in qualitative, arts-based research, notions of form provide a more appropriate way of determining the merit and value of research than traditional notions of validity, because they imply the creation of expressive frames that are visually, audibly and/or imaginatively perceivable. The author goes on to say that form requires immersion, sympathy, openness, and awareness on part of both the researcher and the researched.

To enhance the validity of visual analyses, most researcher (e.g., Prosser, 1998; Van Leeuwen & Jewitt (2001) recommend that researchers not to rely solely on visual data but triangulate visual techniques with interviews, narratives, or life stories. As Pels, Hetherington and Vandenberge (2002) remind us " [images] need symbolic framings, storylines and human spokespersons in order to acquire social lives" (p. 11). In the final analysis, as Wilson and Chaddha (2009) suggested in the context of ethnographic research, the extent to which [ethnographic] research "Can withstand critical and prolonged scrutiny in the context of validation will be based in large measure on the researcher's creative insights in the discovery and integration of empirical findings and theoretical ideas" (p. 560).

Future Directions

Attention to the following issues will further enhance the legitimacy and increased utilization of qualitative research methods in the study of leadership:

1. Greater utilization of less frequently used qualitative research methods such as phenomenology, narrative analyses, or historiometry.
2. Use of nontextual data which include photographs, cartoon, works of art, dance and other performing arts. Many scholars (e.g. Hervey, 2000; Taylor & Hanson, 2005) call for more research that employs image-based and other non-text based methods such as drama or music to explore aesthetic issues in organizational life including leadership. This type of research requires the collaborative efforts of leadership scholars and art historians, which was illustrated by Griffey and Jackson (2010) in their analysis of commissioned portraits of formal leaders against the background of multiculturalism that defines New Zealand politically and socially.
3. Better training in the design of qualitative research – currently there is a lack of training in qualitative research methods, especially for doctoral students, regarding qualitative research in leadership studies. Few graduate programs offer qualitative research methods courses. As Van Maanen (2010) noted, "Most of us have little training or aptitude for analyzing metaphors, deciphering tropes, recognizing voice, or examining rhetorical ploys. Literary practices are terra incognita" (p. 241).
4. More focused efforts by authors to make paradigm assumptions explicit and by editors to insist that authors make the philosophical assumptions underlying their studies more transparent. Alise and Teddlie (2010) pointed out that in contrast to authors of theoretical papers who often explicitly discuss their paradigmatic orientation, qualitative researchers reporting the results of empirical studies seldom do so. The authors noted that only a handful of researchers identified their paradigmatic grounding, and those who did typically employed an orientation other than postpositivism or constructivism, such as critical theory, contexualism or pragmatism (p. 122).
5. Greater transparency in the description of data analyses including graphic representations of qualitative data. For example, in the analyses of case studies, pattern matching is often mentioned as the primary analytic technique, yet researchers seldom proceed to specify the set of variables, the observed outcomes, and the actual matching operations performed (Biketine, 2008). Eisenhardt and Graebner (2007) stress that when presenting empirical evidence in qualitative studies, " Is critical to invest in developing well-crafted tables, appendices, and visual aids to demonstrate the theory's underlying empirical support and the anticipated richness of the case data, and tie those tables clearly to the text (p. 29). Just as discussions of the paradigmatic assumptions underlying a particular research method are often absent in published qualitative leadership studies, so are discourses concerning unique features of certain methods such as the criticality of transcription in interview studies, researchers' ethical responsibilities or the role of reflexivity. Anafara, Brown, and Mangione (2002) also made a cogent argument for making the qualitative research process more public by providing readers with detailed explanations of how research questions are related to data sources, how themes or categories are developed, and how triangulation is accomplished (p. 30). According to Suddaby (2006), devotion to transparency and rigor will be hallmarks of future qualitative leadership studies.
6. Better description in the development of inferences and theory, that is, the reasoning through which a qualitative research moves from data to coding to inferences and ultimately interpretations and emergent theory. Anafara, Brown and Mangione's (2002) code map, and Harry, Sturges and Klingner's (2005) data analysis map provide models of visual flow of how, in an empirical study, researchers progress from open codes, through categories and themes, and ultimately to theory. Often qualitative researchers stop short of extending theoretically their findings and fail to generate compelling theoretical formulations or illuminate clearly some extant theory (Snow, 2004, p. 133).
7. Development of more salient criteria by which to judge qualitative research. For example, a qualitative study may be judged by how well it employs flexibility in design. This would demonstrate that the researcher has followed the emergent twists and turns of the data, rather than adhering rigidly to the original formulation

of the problem (Blee, 2004). Accuracy of the data or breadth of analysis may be examples of alternative quality criteria. In fact, according to Blee, the criterion of breadth may be the closest that qualitative methodologists are willing to come to developing a correlate of statistical power. Stenbacka (2001) adds carefulness to her set of quality standards referring to the care taken in the design and execution of a qualitative study.

8. Increased use of multiparadigmatic research to promote the interplay between the positivistic and different interpretive paradigms, that is, within and between method triangulation. In the post-paradigm war era, Romani, Primecz and Topçu (2011) defined paradigm interplay as a "Respectful interaction between analyses performed in different paradigms and compared this interaction to a conversation" (p. 433). They go on to say that by "Respecting paradigmatic integrity, the interaction builds upon the tension created by the simultaneous consideration of how the analyses are connected and what differentiates them" (p. 433). The authors offer an example of a multiparadigmatic study in the area of crosscultural management and metaphorically presented it as a conversation between a positivist and an interpretive researcher. Moreover, they outlined a three-step process for conducting bi-paradigm research: (1) perform separate analyses for each paradigm; (2) contrast the two analyses in light of each other; and (3) place the analysis in interaction. According to Romani et al. (2011), the interplay is successful if it can respect both types of analyses and generates new contributions (p. 450). While multiparadigm research and the mastery of several methodologies along with the need to adopt distinct languages in the separate analyses associated with it is extremely challenging, this approach holds considerable promise for the study of leadership because potentially it offers the possibility of reconciling contradictory findings obtained in single paradigm research.

Conclusions

Qualitative leadership research is entering an exciting phase that has the potential of significantly advancing our current theoretical and empirical knowledge. This phase is driven by the confluence of several factors, including new theoretical, methodological, analytical, and technological developments. Undoubtedly quantitative research has been and will continue to be instrumental in advancing our knowledge and understanding of leadership; however, not every cobbler thinks leather is the only thing. Qualitative approaches do not merely offer different ways of doing research, but different ways of thinking about leadership phenomena. Concepts and constructs are operationalized to collect data from which theoretical propositions can be deduced. However, since these theoretical propositions may be provisional but explain phenomena that can be verified and generalized, qualitative research presupposes that knowledge and insights emanate as much from intuition and reflexivity. Moreover, interpretive research methods are based on the premise that participants bring implicit and tacit understanding to a leadership problem and that their interactions with the researcher converge with existing knowledge systems to yield new insights.

Qualitative research continues to be important in leadership scholarship because it addresses research questions and issues that quantitative methods are poorly equipped to answer. Much of leadership defies rationality and objectivity, poses the types of research questions that ask "why" rather than "how many," and is shaped by the context in which leaders and followers interact. Qualitative research is context -sensitive and context- dependent and therefore encourages the introduction of a wide range of contextual variables. It produces thick, detailed descriptions of leadership phenomena, exposes instead of imposes meaning based in interactions between the researcher and the researched and utilizes a flexible theoretical framework that may be subject to change as the study progresses.

Qualitative research methods, such as phenomenology, historiometry, and narrative analysis, beg to be applied to leadership problems. One of the new frontiers, image- based leadership research that employs documentaries, videos, film, TV, or other works of art, is still very underexploited despite the fact that we live in a visual, image-rich society surrounded by a diverse array of media capable of producing high-quality images, whether conventional or digital. Aesthetically informed leadership is a new, promising frontier in leadership research that has only begun to be explored. New research methods and analytical techniques that are draws from visual research methods as a new frontier in leadership research offer opportunities to create new relationships among theories, contexts, research participants, and researchers. Finally, there is a need for continued search for broader quality criteria and strategies beyond those employed by quantitative researchers such as form, reflexivity, and transparency of the research process. Researchers need to continue to demonstrate the rigor of their work, which remains a central issue in qualitative leadership studies. Implementation of the proposed directions for advancing the state-of-the-art of qualitative methods will lead to greater methodological rigor and analytical defensibility of the qualitative paradigm.

Note: I wish to thank Professor David Day for his assistance in the early stages of the development of this article.

References

Adler, N. (2006). The arts & leadership: Now that we can do anything, what will we do? *Academy of Management Learning & Education, 5*(4), 486–499.

Ahmend, S. (2005). Desired competencies and job duties of non-profit CEOs in relation to the current challenges: Through the lens of CEOs job advertisements. *Journal of Management Development, 24*(10), 913–928.

Alise, M., & Teddlie, C. (2010). A continuation of the paradigm wars? Prevalence rates of methodological approaches across social/behavioral sciences. *Journal of Mixed Methods Research, 4*(2), 103–1226.

Alvesson, M. (2003). Beyond neopositivists, romantics, and localists: A reflexive approach to interviews in organizational research. *Academy of Management Review, 28*, 13–33.

Alvesson, M., & Scølberg, K. (2002). *Reflexive Methodology: New Vistas for Qualitative Research.* London: Sage.

Americ, J., Craig, R., & Tourish, D. (2007). The transformational leaders as *pedagogue, physician, architect, commander, and saint*: Five root metaphors in Jack Welch's letters to stockholders of General Electric. *Human Relations, 60*(2), 1839–1872.

Anafara, V., Brown, K., & Mangione, T. (2002). Qualitative analysis on stage: Making the research process more public. *Educational Researcher, 31*(7), 28–38.

Anfara, V., & Martz, N. (2006). *Theoretical Frameworks in Qualitative Research.* Thousand Oaks, CA: Sage.

Arthur, M., & Rousseau, D. (1996). Conclusion: A lexicon for a new organizational era. In M. Arthur & D. Rousseau (Eds.), *The Boundaryless Career: A New Employment Principle for a New Organizational Era* (pp. 370–382). New York: Oxford University Press.

Asimov, I. (1996). *Gold.* London: HarperCollins.

Avolio, B., & Gardner, W. (2005). Authentic leadership development: Getting to the root of positive forms of leadership. *The Leadership Quarterly, 16*(3), 315–338.

Badaracco, J. (2003). *Leading Quietly: An Unorthodox Way of Doing the Right Thing.* Boston, MA: Harvard Business School Press.

Bamberg, A. (2007). Form: An alternative to validity in qualitative, arts-based research. Retrieved July 21, 2010 from http://www.aare.edu.au/00pap/bam00016.htm.

Bansal, P., & Corey, K. (2011). The coming of age of qualitative research: Embracing the diversity of qualitative methods. *Academy of Management Journal, 54*(2), 233–237.

Bartlett, D. (2004). A comparative study of ethical decision making amongst managers in large private sector U.K. companies. In L. Pava (Ed.), *Spiritual Intelligence at Work: Meaning, Morals Metaphors, and Morals* (pp. 213–237). New York: Elsevier.

Bass, B. (1985). *Leadership: Performance beyond expectations.* New York: Harper & Row.

Bass, B., & Bass, R. (2008). *The Bass Handbook of Leadership: Theory, Research, and Managerial Applications.* New York: Free Press.

Bateson, G., & Mead, M. (1942). *Balinese Character: A Photographic Analysis.* New York: New York Academy of Sciences.

Baumeister, R., & Neuman, S. (1994). How stories make sense of personal experiences: motives that shape autobiographical narratives. *Personality and Social Psychology Bulletin, 20*, 676–690.

Bernard, R., & Ryan, G. (2010). *Analyzing Qualitative Data.* Thousand Oaks, CA: Sage.

Biehl-Missal, M. (2010). Hero takes a fall: A lesson learned from theatre for leadership. *Leadership, 6*(3), 279–294.

Biketine, A. (2008). Prospective case study design. *Organizational Research Methods, 11*(1), 160–180.

Blee, K. (2004). Evaluating qualitative research. Paper presented at the National Science Foundation Workshop on Scientific Foundations of Qualitative Research, Arlington, VA.

Bligh, M., Kohles, J., & Meindl, J. (2004). Charisma under crisis: Presidential leadership, rhetoric, and media responses before and after the September 11 terrorist attacks. *The Leadership Quarterly, 15*(2), 211–239.

Boje, D. (2001). *Narrative Methods in Organizational and Communication Research.* London: Sage.

Boje, D., Rosile, G., & Gardner, C. (2004, August). Antenarratives, narratives, and anaemic stories. Paper presented at the Academy of Management Meeting, New Orleans, LA.

Boudens, C. (2005). The story of work: A narrative analysis of workplace emotion. *Organization Studies, 26*(4), 1285–1306.

Bowen, G. (2006). Grounded theory and sensitizing concepts. *International Journal of Qualitative Methods, 5*(3), Article 2. Retrieved July 10 from http://www.ualbeta.ca/~ijqm/backissues/5_3/pdf/bowen/pdf.

Boyatzis, R. (1998). *Transforming Qualitative Information: Thematic Analysis and Code Development.* Thousand Oaks, CA: Sage.

Brown, A., Stacey, P., & Nandhakumar, J. (2008). Making sense of sensemaking narratives. *Human Relations, 61*(8), 1035–1064.

Bruce, C. (2007). Questions arising about emergence, data collection and its interaction with analysis in a grounded theory study. *International Journal of Qualitative Methods, 6*(1), Article 4. Retrieved July 10, 2011 from http://ww.ualberta.ca/~ijqm/backissues/6_1/bruce.htm.

Bruner, J. (1990). *Acts of Meaning.* Cambridge, MA: Harvard University Press.

Bryant, A. (2003). A constructivist response to Glaser. *Forum: Qualitative Social Research, 4*(1), 25–42.

Bryman, A. (2004). Qualitative research on leadership: A critical but appreciative review. *The Leadership Quarterly, 15*, 729–769.

Burbules, N. (2005). Beyond method: The role of epistemological virtues in social inquiries. Paper presented at the Congress of Qualitative Inquiry, Urbana-Champaign, IL.

Burger, L., & Miller, p. (1999). Early talk about the past revisited: Affect in working-class and Middle-class children's co-narrations. *Journal of Child Language, 26*, 133–162.

Calogero, R., & Mullen, B. (2008). About face: Facial prominence of George W. Bush in cartoons as a function of war. *The Leadership Quarterly, 19*, 107–116.

Campbell, D. (2003). Leadership and academic culture in the senate presidency. *The American Behavioral Scientists, 46*(7), 946–959.

Carney, T. (1990). *Collaborative Inquiry Methodology.* Windsor, ON: University of Windsor: Division of Instructional Development.

Carr, A., & Hancock, P. (2003). *Arts and Aesthetics at Work.* New York: Palgrave Macmillan.

Carroll, B., & Levy, L. (2008). Defaulting to management: leadership define by what it is not. *Organization, 15*(1), 75–96.

Chamaz, K. (2006). *Constructing Grounded Theory: A Practical Guide Through Qualitative Analysis.* London: Sage.

Chen, C., & Meindl, J. (1991). The construction of leadership images in the popular press: The Case of Donald Burr and People Express. *Administrative Science Quarterly, 36*(4), 521–551.

Cohen, F., Solomon, S., Maxfield, M., Pyszcynki, R., & Greenberg, T (2004). Fatal attraction: Effects of mortality salience on evaluations of charismatic, task-oriented, and relationship-oriented leaders. *Psychological Science, 15*(2), 486–651.

Conger, J. A. (1998). Qualitative research as the cornerstone methodology for understanding leadership. *The Leadership Quarterly, 9*(1), 107–121.

Conger, J., & Kanungo, R. (1998). *Charismatic Leadership in Organizations.* Thousand Oaks, CA: Sage.

Cunliffe, A. (2010). Retelling tales from the field: In search of organizational ethnography 20 years. *Organizational Research Methods, 13*(3), 224–239.

Czarniawska, B. (2004). *Narratives in Social Science Research.* Thousand Oaks, CA: Sage.

Day, D., Gronn, P., & Salas, E. (2006). Leadership in team-based organizations: On the threshold of a new era. *The Leadership Quarterly, 17*(3), 211–216.

Daykin, N. (2004). The role of music in art-based qualitative research. *International Journal of Qualitative Research, 3*(2). Article 3. Retrieved July 21, 2011, from http://www.ualberta.ca/~iiqm/backssues/3_2/pdf/daykin.pdf.

DeCremer, D., & van Knippenberg, D. (2004). Leader self-sacrifice and leadership effectiveness: The moderating role of self-confidence. *Organizational Behavior and Human Decision Processes, 95*(2), 140–155.

Demerath, P. (2006). The science of context: Modes of response for qualitative researchers in Education. *International Journal of Qualitative Studies in Education, 19*(1), 97–113.

Denning, S. (2004). Telling tales. *Harvard Business Review, 82*(5), 122–129.

Denzin, N. & Lincoln, Y. (2003). *The Landscape of Qualitative Research* (2nd ed.). Thousand Oaks, CA: Sage.

Dougherty, D., & Kunda, G. (1990). Photograph analysis; A method to capture organizational belief systems. In P. Gagliardi (Ed.). *Symbols and Artifacts: Views from the Corporate Landscape* (pp. 185–206). Piscataway, NJ: Aldine Transaction.

Easterby-Smith, M., Golden-Biddle, K., & Locke, K. (2008). Working with pluralism: Determining quality in qualitative research. *Organizational Research Methods, 11*(3), 419–429.

Eisenhardt, K. (1989). Building theories from case study research. *Academy of Management Review, 14*(4), 532–550.

Eisenhardt, K. (2009). Generalization from qualitative inquiry. In K. Ercikan & W. Roth (Eds.), *Generalizing from Educational Research* (pp. 51–66). London: Routledge.

Eisenhardt, L., & Graebner, M. (2007). Theory building from cases: Challenges and opportunities. *Academy of Management Journal, 50*(1), 25–32.

Eisenhart, M. (2001). Educational ethnography past, present, and future: Ideas to think with. *Educational Researcher, 30*(8), 16–27.

Eisner, E (1991). *The Enlightened Eye: Qualitative Inquiry and the Enhancement of Educational Practice.* New York, NY: Macmillan Publishing Company.

Eisner, E. (1997). The new frontier in qualitative methodology. *Qualitative Inquiry, 3*(3), 259–271.

Elliott, J. (2006). *Using Narrative in Social Research.* Thousand Oaks, CA: Sage.

Emerson, R. (1987). Four ways to improve the craft of fieldwork. *Journal of Contemporary Ethnography, 16*(1), 69–89.

Fendt, J., & Sachs, W. (2008). Grounded theory method in management researcher: Users' perspectives. *Organizational Research Methods, 11*(3), 430–455.

Fetterman, D. (2010). *Ethnography* (3rd ed). Los Angeles, CA: Sage.

Finkelstein, S. (1992). Power in top management teams. *Academy of Management Journal, 35*, 505–538.

Finkelstein, S. & Hambrick, D. (1990). Top management team tenure and organizational outcomes: The moderating role of managerial discretion. *Administrative Science Quarterly, 35*, 484–503.

Fletcher, J. (2004). The paradox of postheroic leadership: An essay on gender, power, and transformational change. *The Leadership Quarterly, 15*(5), 647–661.

Frosh, P. (2003). Image factory: Consumer culture, photography, and the visual content industry. Oxford, UK: Berg.

Flyvberg, B. (2006). Five misunderstanding about case study research. *Qualitative Inquiry, 12*, 219–245.

Fry, L. (2003). Toward a theory of spiritual leadership. *The Leadership Quarterly, 14*(6), 693–727.

Fry, L. (2005). Toward a theory of ethical and spiritual well-being and corporate social responsibility through spiritual leadership. In R. Giacalone, C. Jurkiewisz, & C. Dunn (Eds.). *Positive psychology in Business Ethics and Corporate Social Responsibility* (pp. 47–83). Greenwich, CT: Information Age Publishing.

Gardner, W. & Avolio, B. (1998). The charismatic relationship: A dramaturgical perspective. *Academy of Management Review, 23*, 32–58.

Gayá Wicks, P., & Rippin, A. (2010). Art as an experience: An inquiry into art and leadership using dolls and doll making. *Leadership, 6*(3), 259–278.

Gebhart, R. (2004). Qualitative research and the Academy of Management Journal. *Academy of Management Journal, 47*(4), 414–431.

Geertz, C. (1973). *The Interpretation of Cultures.* New York: Basic Books.

Glaser, B. (1978). *Theoretical Sensitivity.* Mill Valley, CA: The Sociology Press.

Glaser, B. & Strauss, A. (1967). *The Discovery of Grounded Theory: Strategies for Qualitative Research.* New York: De Gruyter.

Goffman, E. (1959). *The Presentation of Self in Everyday Life.* Garden City, NY: Doubleday Anchor.

Golafshani, N. (2003). Understanding reliability and validity in qualitative research. *The Qualitative Report, 8*(4), 597–607.

Goodall, H. (2000). *Writing the New Ethnography.* Lanham, MD: Altamira Press.

Graebner, M., & Eisenhardt, K. (2004). The seller's side of the story: Acquisition as courtship and governance as syndicate in entrepreneurial firms. *Administrative Science Quarterly, 49*, 366–403.

Green, J. Franquiz, M., & Dixon, C. (1997). The myth of the objective transcript: Transcribing as a situated act. *TESOL Quarterly, 31*, 172–176.

Greenleaf, R., Spears. L., & Covey, S. (2002). *Servant Leadership: A Journey into Legitimate Power and Greatness.* Minneapolist, MN: Paulist Press.

Greenleaf, R. K. (1970). The servant as leader. In L. C. Spears (Ed.), *Servant Leadership: A Journey into the Nature of Legitimate Power and Greatness* (pp. 21–61). New York: Paulist Press.

Griffey, E., & Jackson, B. (2010). The portrait as leader: Commissioned portraits and the power of tradition. *Leadership, 6*(2), 133–157.

Grint, K. (2001). *The Arts of Leadership.* Oxford: Oxford University Press.

Guba, E. (1981). Criteria for assessing the trustworthiness of naturalistic inquiries. *ECT, 19*, 75–109.

Guba, E., & Lincoln, Y. (1994). Competing paradigms in qualitative research. In N. Denzin & Y. Lincoln (Eds.), *Handbook of Qualitative Research* (pp. 75–109). Thousand Oaks, CA: Sage.

Gubrium, J., & Holstein, J. (2002). From the individual interview to the interview society. In J. Gubrium & J. Holstein (Eds.), *Handbook of Interview Research: Context and Methods* (pp. 3–32). Thousand Oaks, CA: Sage.

Guillett de Monthoux, P. (2004). *The Art Firm: Aesthetic Management and Metaphysical Marketing.* Palo Alto: CA: Stanford University Press.

Guillett de Monthoux, P., Gustafson, C., & Sjostrend, S. (Eds.) (2007). *Aesthetic Leadership: Managing Fields of Flow in Art and Business.* New York: Palgrave Macmillan.

Gummesson, E. (2006). Qualitative research in management: addressing complexity, context, and persona. *Management Decision, 44*(2), 167–179.

Hambrick, D. (2007). Upper echelon theory: An update. *Academy of Management Review, 32*(2), 334–343.

Harry, B., Sturges, K., & Klingner, J. (2005). Mapping the process: An exemplar of process and Challenge in grounded theory analysis. *Educational Researcher, 34*(2), 3–13.

Hervey, L. (2000). *Artistic Inquiry in Dance/Movement Therapy.* Springfield, IL: Charles C. Thomas Publisher.

Hooks, B. (1990). *Yearning: Race, Gender, and Cultural Politics.* Boston, MA: South End.

Hoyt, C., Simon, S., & Reid, L. (2009). Choosing the best (wo) man for the job: The effects of mortality, sex, and gender stereotypes on leader evaluations. *The Leadership Quarterly, 20*, 233–246.

Hunt, J., & Dodge, G. (2000). Leadership déjà vu all over again. *The Leadership Quarterly, 11*(4), 435–458.

Islam, G. (2009). Animating leadership: Crisis and renewal of governance in 4 mythic narratives. *The Leadership Quarterly, 20*, 828–836.

Iszatt-White, M. (2009). Leadership as emotional labour: The effortful accomplishment of valuing practices. *Leadership, 5*(4), 447–467.

Jackson, B., & Guthey, E. (2006). Putting the visual into the social construction of leadership. In B. Shamir & R. Pillai (Eds), *Follower-centered perspectives on leadership: A tribute to James R. Meindl* (pp. 167–168). Charlotte, NC: Information Age Publishing.

Kan, M.M., & Parry, K.W. (2004). Identifying paradox: A grounded theory of leadership in overcoming resistance to change. *The Leadership Quarterly, 15*, 467–491.

Kark, R., Shamir, B., & Chen G. (2003). The two faces of transformational leadership: Empowerment and dependency. *Journal of Applied Psychology, 88*(2), 246–255.

Keller, J. (2003). Parental images as a guide to leadership sensemaking: An attachment perspective on implicit leadership theories. *Leadership Quarterly, 14*, 141–160.

Kellerman, B. (2008). *Followership: How followers are creating and changing leaders.* Boston, MA: Harvard Business Press.

King, N., & Horrocks, C. (2010). *Interviews in Qualitative Research.* London: Sage.

Klein, S., & Diket, R.(1999). Creating artful leadership. *International Journal of Leadership in Education, 2*(1), 23–30.

Klenke, K. (2005). The internal theater of the authentic leader: Integrating cognitive, affective and spiritual facets of authentic leadership. In W. Gardner, B. Avolio, & F. Walumba (Eds.). *Authenic Leadership: Origins, Effects, and Developments* (pp. 155–182). New York: Elsevier.

Klenke, K. (2007). Authentic leadership: A self, leader, and spiritual identity perspectives. *Journal of International Leadership Studies, 3*(1), 68–97.

Klenke, K. (2008). *Qualitative Research in the Study of Leadership.* Bingley, UK: Emerald Group Publishing Limited.

Krippendorff, K. (2004). *Content Analysis: An Introduction to Its Methodology.* London: Sage.

Kvale, S. (1996). *Interviews: An Introduction to Qualitative Research Interviewing.* Thousand Oaks, CA: Sage.

Ladkin, D. (2008). Leading Beautifully: How mastery, congruence and purpose create the aesthetic of embodied leadership practice, *The Leadership Quarterly, Volume, 19*(1), 31–41.

Langley, A. (1999). Strategies for theorizing from process data. *Academy of Management Review, 38*(2), 48–352.

Labov, W., & Waletzkey, J. (1967). Narrative analysis. In J. Helm (Ed.), *Essays on Verbal and Visual Arts.* Seattle, WA: American Ethnological Society.

Lee, A. (1989). A scientific methodology for MIS case studies. *MIS Quarterly, 13*(1), 33–50.

Lehman, H. (2006). Postdramatic theatre. London: Routledge.

Ligon, G., Hunter, S., & Mumford, M. (2008). Development of outstanding leadership: A life narrative approach. *The Leadership Quarterly, 19*, 312–334.

Lincoln, Y., & Guba, E. (1985). *Naturalistic Inquiry.* Newbury Park, CA: Sage.

Lineham, M., & Scullion, H. (2004). Repatriation of European female corporate executives: an empirical study. *International Journal of Human Resource Management, 13*(2), 254–267.

Locke, K. (2001). *Grounded Theory in Management Research.* London: Sage.

Lowe, K., & Gardner, W. (2000). Ten years of the leadership quarterly: Contributions and Challenges for the future. *The Leadership Quarterly, 11*(4), 495–514.

Lutz, C., & Collins, J. (1993). *Reading National Geographics.* Chicago, IL: Chicago University Press.

Mangham, I. (1978). *Interactions and Interventions in Organization.* Chichester: Wiley.

Mangham, I., & Overington, M. (1983). Dramatism and the theatrical metaphor. In G. Morgan (Ed.), *Beyond method* (pp. 219–233). Thousand Oaks, CA: Sage.

Marion, R. & Uhl-Bien, M. (2001). Leadership in complex organizations. *The Leadership Quarterly, 12*(4), 241–270.

Martin, S. (2008). Content analysis of the writings of Mary Parker Follett. In K. Klenke. *Qualitative Research in the Study of Leadership* (pp. 289–316). Bingley, UK: Emerald Group Publishing Limited.

McAdams, D. (2001). The psychology of life stories. *Review of General Psychology, 5*, 100–123.

McAdams, D., Hoffman, B., Mansfield, E., & Ray, R. (1996). Themes of agency and communion in significant autobiographical scenes. *Journal of Personality, 64*, 339–378.

McCabe, D. (2002). 'Waiting for dead men's shoes': Toward cultural understanding of management innovation. *Human Relations, 35*(3), 505–536.

Meindl, J., Ehrlich, S., & Dukerich, J. (1985). The romance of leadership. *Administrative Science Quarterly, 30*(1), 78–102.

Merriam, S., & Associates (2002). *Qualitative Research in Practice*. San Francisco, CA: Jossey-Bass.

Meyer, A. (1991). Visual data in organizational research. *Organization Science, 2*(2), 218–236.

Miles, M., & Huberman, A. (1994). *Qualitative Data Analysis.* Thousand Oaks, CA: Sage.

Morse, J., & Field, P. (1994). *Qualitative Research for Health Professionals.* Thousand Oaks, CA: Sage.

Morrow, S. (2005). Quality and trustworthiness in qualitative research in counseling psychology. *Journal of Counseling Psychology, 52*, 250–260.

Neuendorf, K. (2002). *Content Analysis Guidebook.* Thousand Oaks, CA: Sage.

O'Connor, M., Netting, F., & Thomas, M. (2008). Grounded theory: Managing the challenge of those facing institutional review board oversight. *Qualitative Inquiry, 14*(1), 28–45.

Osborn, R., Hunt, J., & Jauch, L. (2002). Toward a contextual theory of leadership. *The Leadership Quarterly, 13*, 797–837.

Parkin, M. (2004). *Tales for Change: Using Storytelling to Develop People and Organizations.* London: Kogan Page.

Parry, K. (1998). Grounded theory and social process: A new direction for leadership research. *Leadership Quarterly, 9*(1), 85–105.

Patton, M. (2000). *Qualitative Evaluation and Research Methods* (3rd ed). Newbury Park, CA: Sage.

Patton, M. (2002). Two decades of development in qualitative inquiry. *Qualitative Social Work, 1*, 2261–2283.

Pauwels, P. & Mattyson, P. (2004). The architecture of multiple case studies in international business. In R. Marshan-Piekkari & C. Welch (Eds.), *Handbook for Qualitative Research Methods for International Business* (pp. 124–143). Cheltenham, UK: Edward Elgar.

Pearce, C., & Conger, J. (2002). *Shared Leadership: Reframing the Hows and Whys of Leadership.* Thousand Oaks, CA: Sage.

Pels, D., Hetherington, K., Vanderberge, F. (2002). The status of the object: performances, mediations and techniques. *Theory, Culture, and Society, 19*(5/6), 1–21.

Pentland, B. (1999). Building process theory with narrative; from description to explanation. *Academy of Management Review, 24*(4), 711–724.

Pina de Cuna, M., Campos e Cuna, R., & Rego, A. (2009). Exploring the role of leaders-subordinate interactions in the construction of organizational positivity. *Leadership, 5*(1), 81–101.

Pink, S. (2001). *Doing Visual Ethnography: Images, Media, and Representation in Research.* Thousand Oaks, CA: Sage.

Polkinghorne, D. (1995). Narrative configuration in qualitative analysis. In J. Hatch & R. Wisniewski (Eds.), *Life History and Narrative* (pp. 5–24). Washington, DC: Palmer.

Polkinghorne, D. (1988). *Narrative Knowing and Human Science.* Albany, NY: State University of New York.

Ponterotto, J. (2006). A brief note on the origin, evolution, and meaning of the qualitative research concept of transcription. Retrieved July 8, 2011, from http://www.nova.edu/ssss/QR/QR11-3/ponterotto.pdf.

Porter, L., & McLaughlin, G. (2006). Leadership and the organizational context: Like the weather. *The Leadership Quarterly, 17*(6), 559–576.

Pratt, M. (2009). For the lack of a boilerplate: Tips on writing up (and reviewing) qualitative research. *Academy of Management Journal, 52*, 856–862.

Prosser, J. (1998). The status of image-based research. In J. Prosser (Ed.), *Image-Based Research: A Sourcebook for Qualitative Researchers* (pp. 97–112). Bristol, PA: Falmer Press.

Richards, L. (2005). *Handling Qualitative Data: A Practical Guide.* Thousand Oaks, CA: Sage.

Richards, L., & Morse, J. (2007). *User's Guide to Qualitative Methods.* Thousand Oaks, CA: Sage.

Romani, L., Primecz, H., & Topçu, K. (2011). Paradigm interplay for theory development: A methodological example with the Kulturstandard method. *Organizational Research Methods, 14*(3), 432–455.

Rose, G. (2003). *Visual Methodologies: An Introduction to the Interpretation of Visual Materials.* Thousand Oaks, CA: Sage.

Sandberg, J. (2005). How do we justify knowledge produced within interpretive approaches? *Organizational Research Methods, 8*(1), 41–68.

Sashkin, M. (1996). *Becoming a Visionary Leader.* New York: Blackwell.

Sashkin, M., & Sashkin, M. (2003). *Leadership That Matters. Critical Factors in People's Lives and Organizations' Success.* San Francisco, CA: Berrett-Koehler.

Schneider, M., & Somers, M. (2006). Organizations in complex adaptive systems: Implications of complexity theory for leadership research. *The Leadership Quarterly, 17*(4), 351–365.

Schroeder, J. (2002). *Visual Consumption.* London: Routledge.

Scott, W. (1987). The adolescence of institutional theory. *Administrative Science Quarterly, 32*, 493–511.

Shamir, B. (1999). Leadership in boundaryless organizations: Disposable or indispensible? *European Journal of Work and Organizational Psychology, 8*(1), 49–71.

Shamir, B., & Eilam, G. (2005). "What's your story?" A life-stories approach to authentic leadership development. *The Leadership Quarterly, 16*(3), 395–417

Shek, D., Tang, V., & Han, X. (2005). Evaluation of evaluation studies using qualitative research methods in social work literature (1900–2003): Evidence that constitutes a wake-up call. *Research on Social Work Practice, 15*(3), 180–194.

Siggelow, N. (2007). Persuasion with case studies. *Academy of Management Journal, 50*(2), 20–24.

Siles, D. (2004). Pictoral representation. In G. Symon & C. Cassell (Eds.), *Essential Guide to Qualitative Methods in Organizational Research* (pp. 127–139). London: Sage.

Silverman, D. (2001). *Interpreting Qualitative Data: Methods of Analyzing Talk, Text, and Interaction* (2nd. ed). London: Sage.

Simco, N. & Warin, J. (1997). Validity in image-based research: An elaborated illustration of the issues. *British Educational Journal, 23*(5), 661–672.

Simpson, P. (2007). Organizing in the mist: a case study of leadership and complexity. *Leadership and Organization Development Journal, 28*(5), 465–482.

Slattery, P. (2003). Troubling the contours of arts-based educational research. *Qualitative Inquiry, 9*(3), 192–197.

Sloan, A. (2004, July 19). Lay's a victim? Not a chance. If Enron's indicted former CEO was Clueless as he claims to be, he should return all the money he made for running the

company. Retrieved July 10, 2011from http://www.highbeam.com/doc/1G1-119232675.html.
Snow, D. (2004). Thoughts on alternative pathways to theoretical development: Theory generation and extension. Paper presented at the National Science Foundation Workshop on Scientific Foundations of Qualitative Research, Arlington, VA.
Sonpar, K., & Goldon-Biddle, K. (2008). Using content analysis to elaborate adolescent theories of organization. *Organizational Research Methods, 11*(4), 795–814.
Spears, L. & M. Lawrence (2006). *Insights on Leadership: Stewardship, Spirit and Servant Leadership.* New York: Wiley.
Stake, B. (1995). *The Art of Case Research.* Thousand Oaks, CA: Sage.
Stake, B. (2005). Qualitative case studies. In N. Denzin & Y. Lincoln (Eds.), *The Sage Handbook of Qualitative Research* (3rd. ed.) (pp. 443–466). Thousand Oaks, CA: Sage.
Stanczak, G. (2007). *Visual Research Methods: Images, Society, and Representation.* Los Angeles, CA: Sage.
Stenbaka, C. (2001). Qualitative research requires quality concepts of its own. *Management Decision, 39*(7), 551–555.
Sternberg, R. (2008). The WICS approach to leadership: Stories of leadership and the structures and processes that support them. *The Leadership Quarterly, 19,* 360–371.
Strati, A. (1996). Organizations viewed through the lenses of aesthetics. *Organization, 3*(2), 209–218.
Strati, A. (1999). *Organization and Aesthetics.* London: Sage.
Strati, A. (2000). Putting people in the picture: Art and aesthetics in understanding organizational life. *Organization Studies, 21,* 53–69.
Strauss, A., & Corbin, J. (1990). *Basics of Qualitative Research: Grounded Theory Procedures and Techniques.* Newbury Park, CA: Sage.
Strauss, A., & Corbin, J. (1998). *Basics of Qualitative Research: Techniques and Procedures for Developing Grounded Theory* (2nd ed.). Thousand Oaks, CA: Sage.
Suddaby, R. (2006). From the editors: What grounded theory is not. *Academy of Management Journal, 49*(4), 633–642.
Taylor, J. (1957). *Learning to Look: A Handbook for the Visual Arts.* Chicago, IL: Chicago University Press.
Taylor, S. (2002). Overcoming aesthetic muteness: researching organizational members' aesthetic experiences. *Human Relations, 57*(7), 821–840.
Taylor, S., & Hansen, H. (2005). Finding form: Looking at the field of organizational aesthetics. *Journal of Management Studies, 42*(6), 1211–1230.
Taylor, S., & Ladkin, D. (2009). Understanding arts-based methods in managerial development. *Academy of Management Learning & Education, 8*(1), 55–69.
Thomas, G. (2010). Doing case study: Abduction not induction, phronesis not theory. *Qualitative Inquiry, 16*(7), 575–583.
Thompson, J. (2000). *Political Scandal: Power and Visibility in the Media Age.* London: Polity Press.
Tilley, S. (2003). "Challenging" research practices: Turning a critical lens on the work of transcription. *Qualitative Inquiry, 9*(5), 750–773.
Treniño, L., Brown, M., & Pincus, L. (2003). A qualitative investigation of perceived executive ethical leadership: Perceptions from inside and outside the executive suite. *Human Relations, 56*(1), 5–27.
Troachim, W. (1989). Outcome pattern matching and program theory. *Evaluation and Program Planning, 12,* 355–366.
Uhl-Bien, M. (2006). Relational leadership theory: Exploring the social processes of leadership and organizing. *The Leadership Quarterly, 17*(6), 654–676.
Uhl-Bien, M., Marion, R., & McKelvey, B. (2007). Complexity theory and leadership: Shifting leadership from the industrial age to the knowledge era. *The Leadership Quarterly, 18,* 298–318.
Vail, P. (1991). *Leadership as Performing Art: New Ideas for a World of Chaotic Change.* San Francisco, CA: Jossey-Bass.
Van Leeuen, T., & Jewitt, C. (2001). *Handbook of Visual Analysis.* Thousand Oaks, CA: Sage.
Van Maanen, J. (1979). Fact and fiction in organizational ethnography. *Administrative Science Quarterly, 24*(4), 539–550.
Van Maanen, J. (1988). *Tales of the Field: On Writing Ethnography.* Chicago, IL: University of Chicago Press.
Van Maanen, J. (2010). A song for my supper: More tales of the field. *Organizational Research Methods, 13*(2), 240–255.
Vince, R., & Broussine, M. (1996). Paradox, defense and attachment: Accessing and working with emotions and relations underlying organizational change. *Organization Studies. 17*(1), 1–21.
Warren, S. (2008). Empirical challenges in organizational aesthetics research: Towards a sensual methodology. *Organization Studies, 29*(4), 559–580.
Watrin, R. (1999). Art as research. *Canadian Review of Art Education, 26*(2), 92–100.
Weber, R. (1990). *Basic Content Analysis.* London: Sage.
Wengraf, T. (2006). *Qualitative Research Interviewing.* Thousand Oaks, CA: Sage.
Williamson, J. (1978). *Decoding Advertisements: Ideology and Meaning in Advertising.* London: Marion Boyars.
Wilson, W., & Chaddha, A. (2009). The role of theory in ethnographic research. *Ethnography, 10*(4), 249–264.
Wilson-Stroks, A., & Terrance, O. (2010). From the perspective of CEOs: What motivates hospitals to embrace cultural competence? *Journal of Health Care Management, 55*(5), 339–352.
Yammarino, F., Dionne, S., Chun, & Danserau, F. (2005). Leadership and levels of analysis: A state- of-science review *The Leadership Quarterly, 16*(6), 879–919.
Yin, R. (2009). *Case Study Research: Design and Methods.* Beverly Hills, CA: Sage.
Yin, R. (2003). *Case Study Research.* Beverly Hills, CA: Sage.
Zacarro, S., Rittman, A., & Marks, M. (2001). Team leadership. *The Leadership Quarterly, 12*(4), 451–483.

CHAPTER

8

Multilevel Issues in Leadership Research

Mo Wang, Le Zhou, *and* Songqi Liu

Abstract

Leadership is a multilevel phenomenon. Accordingly, levels-of-analysis issues should be considered and addressed in theoretical and empirical studies of leadership. This chapter discusses levels-of-analysis issues in the conceptualization and measurement of leadership constructs, levels-of-analysis issues in developing leadership theories, change-related issues in leadership research, and up-to-date statistical methods for testing multilevel leadership theories. In this chapter's discussions, levels-of-analysis issues are illustrated by reviewing leadership literature and suggesting possible ways to further contribute to the understanding of leadership process in organizations. The authors hope this chapter can facilitate more rigorous leadership studies, help integrate different leadership theories, and inspire new approaches to leadership research.

Key Words: Leadership, levels-of-analysis issues, multilevel, leadership constructs, leadership theories, longitudinal

Multilevel Issues in Leadership Research

In leadership research it is important to consider levels-of-analysis issues for both theoretical and empirical reasons. First, in different theories, leadership constructs may manifest at different levels. It is necessary to articulate and justify which level the focal leadership construct originates from and manifests in the given theory. Here, constructs refer to abstractions used in theories to describe and explain phenomena of interest. Like other formal organizational theories, leadership theories use constructs as their building blocks in explaining leadership-related phenomena. The level of a construct is "the level at which it is hypothesized to be manifest in a given theoretical model—the known or predicted level of the phenomenon in question" (Kozlowski & Klein, 2000, p. 27). Depending on its scope, a leadership theory can focus on constructs at the same level, or it can involve constructs that reside at multiple levels. For example, in leadership theories focusing on leaders (e.g., transformational leadership, Bass & Riggio, 2006; ethical leadership, Brown, Treviño, & Harrison, 2005), the focal constructs are at individual level. In leadership theories taking a relational approach (e.g., leader-member exchange [LMX] theory; Graen & Uhl-Bien, 1995), the focal construct is at dyadic level. In theories on team leadership, such as shared or distributed leadership (Gronn, 2002; Pearce & Sims, 2002), the focal constructs originate from the individual level and operate at the collective level (i.e., team level). Moreover, in theories describing leadership processes at multiple levels of analysis, the single label "leadership" can mean different constructs at different levels of analysis (e.g., Chen & Bliese, 2002; Chen & Kanfer, 2006). Therefore, without explaining the level of the leadership construct, it is difficult to accurately test the theory and to compare and combine theories from multiple theoretical perspectives.

Second, in a given theory, a leadership construct and its antecedents and outcomes might manifest at different levels of analysis. For example, researchers might be interested in the relationship between behaviors of formal team leaders and individual team members' job performance (e.g., Chen, Kirkman, Kanfer, Allen, & Rosen, 2007). In this case, the focal leadership construct is at the team level, because behaviors of formal team leaders target the team as a whole (Morgeson, DeRue, & Karam, 2010), whereas the outcome of interest (i.e., individual performance) is at the individual level. In addition, the antecedents of focal leadership construct might also span across multiple levels. For example, Mumford, Antes, Caughron, and Friedrich (2008) investigated predictors at environmental, organizational, group, and individual levels for leader emergence. Leadership researchers might also be interested in whether the relationship between leaders' characteristics and subordinates' perceptions varies depending on the broader context, such as societal culture and norms (e.g., Lord, Brown, Harvey, & Hall, 2001). In this case, the contextual variables typically operate at a higher level than leadership constructs. In essence, in leadership theories that include constructs at different levels, levels issues should be explicitly addressed to explain how phenomena at different levels are connected (Kozlowski & Klein, 2000).

Moreover, levels-of-analysis issues are relevant for studying leadership phenomena that are dynamic (i.e., change- or time-related phenomena). Models about longitudinal change patterns are multilevel in nature because the repeated observations from different time points are nested within individuals. In other words, in longitudinal models there are at least two levels of analysis involved: the between-unit level and the within-unit level (Chan, 2002; Mehta & Neale, 2005; Mehta & West, 2000; Raudenbush, 2001). Examples of dynamic leadership phenomena include leader development (Day, Harrison, & Halpin, 2009), leader-follower dyadic relationship development (Graen & Uhl-Bien, 1995), and ongoing activation and reconstruction of leaders' and followers' identities over time (DeRue & Ashford, 2010; Lord & Brown, 2004). Considering levels-of-analysis issues in this research context can help articulate *what* is changing, *why* change happens, *the time intervals* needed to observe change, and *how* change is related to other variables.

Furthermore, levels-of-analysis issues should be addressed with special attention in theories and research regarding leadership-related collective processes. For example, leadership in work groups or teams without an appointed leader, such as self-management teams or voluntary groups, can be distributed among team members. It is argued that this distributed or shared form of leadership is a type of group process in which leadership originates from interactions among individuals and manifests as collective actions or capacities (Day, Gronn, & Salas, 2004; Gronn, 2002; Pearce & Sims, 2002; Yukl, 1998). To understand the structure and function of this shared or distributed type of leadership, levels-of-analysis issues should be clearly addressed, as the inter-individual interactions and resulted collective actions obviously operate across both individual and group levels.

Finally, it is important to consider levels of constructs and relationships in the empirical examination of leadership-related research questions. Organizations are multilevel systems (Kozlowski & Klein, 2000). Individuals are nested in work groups and teams, which are nested in organizations, industries, and societies. Data collected in leadership studies are seldom completely independent observations free of any higher level grouping factors (Bliese & Hanges, 2004). From a statistical standpoint, ignoring this nested structure of the data can result in inflated Type I or Type II error rate in hypothesis testing (Bliese & Hanges, 2004; Bryk & Raudenbush, 2002; Kenny & Judd, 1986). Specifically, when only relationships between lower-level variables (e.g., the relationship between subordinate's interaction frequency with leader and subordinate's job satisfaction) are examined, ignoring the fact that lower-level units (i.e., subordinates) are nested within higher level units can result in inflated Type II error rates. This is because when nonindependence is ignored, the estimation of lower-level residual variance is inflated, thus the standard error of the lower-level relationship estimate is upwardly biased. When a leadership construct at a higher level is hypothesized to influence a lower-level outcome (e.g., the effect of leader charisma on subordinate's work motivation), ignoring nonindependence can result in a downwardly biased estimate of standard error, thus resulting in increased Type I error rates.

For all the reasons discussed above, levels-of-analysis issues have been explicitly discussed in leadership theories and incorporated into research design in recent empirical studies (Yammarino, & Dansereau, 2008; Yammarino, Dionne, Chun, & Dansereau, 2005). However, it is still quite common for studies to ignore these issues in leadership research (Lord & Dinh, 2012). In addition, the misalignment in levels between theory, construct, measurement, design, and analyses is still frequently seen in leadership studies. As such, in the following sections of this chapter, we discuss levels-of-analysis issues in the conceptualization and measurement of leadership constructs, leadership theory building, and statistical analysis for leadership studies. We also devote one section to discussing dynamic issues in leadership research. In this way, this chapter aims to provide an up-to-date qualitative review of the levels-of-analysis issues in leadership research building on prior work on this topic (Dansereau, Yammarino, & Markham, 1995; Hunt & Dodge, 2000; Markham, 2010; Yammarino & Dansereau, 2008; Yammarino et al., 2005) and to point out potential ways to extend and integrate leadership theories.

Level-Related Issues in Conceptualization and Measurement of Leadership Constructs

Regardless of whether the researcher is interested in building a multilevel theory of leadership, levels issues in conceptualization and measurement of leadership constructs cannot be overlooked. This is because in order to build a clear and generalizable theory, theorists need to articulate the origins of the focal constructs and use conceptualization of the constructs as the basis for measurement methods. Without a clear specification of level and origin of constructs, misalignment of theory and measurement may occur, which then challenges construct validity and generalizability of the findings (Kozlowski & Klein, 2000; Yammarino et al., 2005). Specifically, according to Kozlowski and Klein, in order to explicate the level of a construct, theorists must develop a targeted theory (mini theory) to explain the formation and manifestation of the construct (also see Morgeson and Hofmann, 1999, on structure and function of collective constructs). Based on this mini theory, an appropriate measurement strategy can be decided. In the remainder of this section, we discuss possible ways for different types of leadership research to develop a mini theory on the level of leadership construct and to align measurement of the construct to its conceptualization.

Leadership as an Individual-Level Construct

Researchers are often interested in identifying what traits, behaviors, or behavior styles distinguish leaders from non-leaders. For example, trait theories study leader personality and traits (e.g., Judge, Bono, Ilies, & Gerhardt, 2002; Judge, LePine, & Rich, 2006), and behavioral theories study leader behaviors or behavioral styles, such as initiating structure and consideration behaviors (Stogdill & Coons, 1957) and transformational leadership behaviors (Bass & Riggio, 2006). Studies based on these theories typically conceptualize leadership as an individual-level construct that originates from leaders' personal developmental history, training, experience, or other individualized influences. For example, to study CEO personality and its strategic influence, a CEO's core self-evaluation can be defined as a leadership trait that reflects an individual's overall self-concept and influences individual's behaviors (Resick, Whitman, Weingarden, & Hiller, 2009). To provide a detailed account on how a leader's core self-evaluation forms as a stable individual difference, evolutionary theories can be drawn to explain why, how, when, and where it originates and manifests its effect on individual-level outcomes (e.g., Judge, Piccolo, & Kosalka, 2009).

Given the individual-level conceptualization, leader traits or behaviors can be measured via leader self-report (e.g., NEO Personality Inventory; Costa & McCrae, 1992; Transformational Leadership Behavior Inventory; Podsakoff, MacKenzie, Moorman, & Fetter, 1990). Researchers can also collect information about focal leader traits or behaviors from other sources, such as trained assessors (e.g., Resick et al., 2009) or subordinates (e.g., Brown et al., 2005; Hu & Liden, 2011; Judge & Bono, 2000). Using information from other sources to measure individual-level leadership constructs should be supported by evidence showing that the leader traits or behaviors studied are observable to the sources. When ratings are collected from multiple sources (e.g., multiple subordinates), they can be aggregated across rating sources to reduce measurement error that may be caused by potential rating biases in self- or other-reports of personal traits and behaviors (Atwater, Wang, Smither, & Fleenor, 2009; Watson, Hubbard, & Wiese, 2000).

Leadership as a Dyadic-Level Construct

Researchers taking a relational approach to leadership are interested in the relations, ties, and links between leaders and followers (e.g., vertical dyad linkage approach to leadership, Dansereau, Graen, & Haga, 1975; LMX theory, Graen & Uhl-Bien, 1995). Leader-follower relationship can be conceptualized as a dyadic-level construct that originates from the relationship development process in leader-follower dyad and manifests its effect on social exchange between the dyad. To explicate the origin of a leader-follower relationship as a dyadic-level construct, researchers can draw on social exchange theory to explain why, how, where, and when supervisors develop different exchange relationships with different followers (Cropanzano & Mitchell, 2005).

When the relationship between leader and follower is conceptualized as a dyadic-level construct, it can be measured in at least three ways: leader's perspective, subordinate's perspective, and third-party observation. A majority of prior research on leader-follower relationship has measured the dyadic relationship solely from the subordinate's perspective despite consistent evidence from prior research that there is only low to medium agreement between the leader's and the subordinate's perceptions about their relationship (Gerstner & Day, 1997; Sin, Nahrgang, & Morgeson, 2009). Prior research also suggests that agreement, or disagreement, between a leader's and his/her subordinate's perceptions of their relationship itself is a variable of theoretical importance. Thus, studies taking a relational approach to leadership can also conceptualize the agreement of relationship perceptions as a dyadic-level construct.

Leadership as a Unit-Level Construct

Unit-level constructs describe properties of collectives composed of more than one individual. There are three basic types of unit-level constructs: global, shared, and configural (Kozlowski & Klein, 2000). Shared and configural constructs are formed by demographics, emotions, cognitions, or behaviors, and interactions of individual unit members, whereas global constructs do not originate from lower level but from the unit level itself. In addition, for shared constructs, the meanings of the constructs are similar at the unit and individual levels, whereas for configural constructs, their meanings are different from their individual-level components. We demonstrate below how leadership constructs may manifest as global, shared, or configural properties of the units and the different theoretical meanings they carry.

Global construct. Global constructs describe unit properties that cannot be broken down into individual-level parts. This is because global constructs do not have individual level counterparts. Global constructs usually originate from the units' structure or function in a larger system, such as units' size or geographic location. Thus, when conceptualizing leadership as a global property of a unit, it is necessary to explicitly identify where leadership originates and why within-unit variation does not exist or is not of interest. By conceptualizing leadership as a global construct, the research focus shifts from individual followers to units themselves.

Specifically, studies that examine the effect of a leader on a team as a whole essentially theorize the relationship between a global construct and some global, shared, or configural properties of the unit (Chen & Kanfer, 2006). For example, in studies that examine the relationship between leader traits and unit financial performance, the relationship between two global constructs is the focus of research (e.g., Baum & Locke, 2004). In addition, in studies that examine the relationship between leader behaviors and unit climate, the relationship between a global construct and a shared construct is the focus of research (e.g., Zohar & Luria, 2005). Moreover, in studies that examine leader behaviors and density of advice network in work units (e.g., Zhang & Peterson, 2011), the relationship between a global construct and a configural property of the unit is the focus of research.

In addition, studies that examine the average influence of a leader on all individual unit members also view leader traits or behaviors as a global construct (Chen & Kanfer, 2006). For example, in studies that examine the main effect of leader behaviors on individual subordinates' outcomes, it is usually implicitly assumed that leaders influence all subordinates through the same mechanism thus changing the unit average of subordinates' individual outcomes (Preacher, Zyphur, & Zhang, 2010). This implicit assumption is also often held in studies that examine the cross-level moderating effects of leader behaviors on relationships between lower-level variables (e.g., subordinate's perceived leader-follower relationship and individual empowerment; Chen et al., 2007).

When leadership is conceptualized as a global construct, it is appropriate to measure it from leader self-report or objective ratings (e.g., Baum & Locke, 2004). When measured from subordinates' reports (e.g., Zhang & Peterson, 2011), within-unit (i.e., within-leader) variations may exist in the ratings. This variation is typically considered as error due to measurement procedure rather than a characteristic of the theoretical construct, because global construct does not conceptualize within-unit variation (Kozlowski & Klein, 2000).

Shared construct. Shared constructs describe units' properties that are shared by all members of the unit. They originate from unit members' individual demographics, emotions, cognitions, behaviors, and interactions among unit members, and emerge as a collective property characterizing the unit as a whole. Shared constructs retain the same content, meaning, and function as their individual-level elements. Thus, when conceptualizing leadership as shared constructs, a critical task is to explain why and how consensus emerges from unit members' individual properties and interactions among unit members. For example, leader charisma can be conceptualized as unit members' common view of the leader that emerges from social interactions among unit members, and between leader and the whole unit (Balkundi, Kilduff, & Harrison, 2011; Klein & House, 1995). Further, leader effectiveness can be conceptualized as a shared construct influenced by unit members' collective cognitive schema and leaders' actual behaviors (e.g., Hall & Lord, 1995).

Referent shift composition model is most appropriate for measuring shared leadership constructs (Chan, 1998b). Specifically, subordinates within the units are asked how they perceive their leader or team leadership. If there is consensus among unit members' ratings, an average score of their ratings can be used to indicate leaders' or units' standing on the construct (e.g., Balkundi et al., 2011). It should be noted that assessing the consensus among unit members' ratings is a requisite before aggregating them to form a single score, because systematic variation among unit members' ratings imply potential problems in conceptualizing the shared construct (Kozlowski & Klein, 2000). Interested readers can refer to other sources for guidance on technique aspects of consensus tests (Bliese, 2000; James, Demaree, & Wolf, 1984; Lebreton & Senter, 2008).

Configural construct. Configural constructs describe pattern, configuration, distribution, or variability of unit members in certain properties (Kozlowski & Klein, 2000). Configural constructs originate from individual level and emerge at unit level. Different from shared constructs, configural constructs have different content and meaning than their individual-level components because the configuration process is nonlinear and complex. For example, demographical diversity within a team is a configural construct that describes distribution of all unit members' demographical characteristics, while the individual-level component describes an individual's standing on a demographic variable. Therefore, when conceptualizing a configural construct, researchers should explicate what is the process through which individual-level properties configure into a unit-level property and why the process yields a qualitatively different unit-level construct.

In leadership research, to study charisma as a social construal phenomenon, homogeneity of perceived leader charisma may be conceptualized as variation in subordinates' perception of leader's charisma (e.g., Klein & House, 1995). Moreover, in studies on differentiated leadership in groups, variation in leader-follower relationships within the same unit (e.g., Boies & Howell, 2006; Henderson, Wayne, Shore, Bommer, & Tetrick, 2008) or disparity of leader treatment of subordinates (Wu, Tsui, & Kinicki, 2010) can be conceptualized as configural constructs. Finally, shared leadership in teams can also be conceptualized as a configural construct when it is studied as the pattern of interpersonal influence among team members (e.g., Carson, Tesluk, & Marrone, 2007).

To be consistent with conceptualizing leadership as a unit-level configural construct, researchers need to collect information at the individual level and summarize the pattern or configuration according to their theory on the configuration process. For example, researchers may define LMX differentiation as the variation of LMX within a unit (e.g., Boies & Howell, 2006). Accordingly, information about each dyad's LMX needs to be measured, and variance or standard deviation of LMX in the unit is the indicator of LMX differentiation of the unit. To measure configural constructs, sources of information do not have to be unit members. For example, gender diversity in top management teams can be measured by using information from company records. In addition, depending on the theory, instead of standard deviation or variation, other indices may indicate the configural construct more accurately, such as coefficient of variation, Blau's index, or the Gini coefficient (Harrison & Klein, 2007; Wu et al., 2010).

Leadership as a Process

More recently, a growing number of studies have examined leadership as a process. In these studies, researchers are interested in how leaders or leadership emerge through multiple episodes of social interactions (e.g., DeRue & Ashford, 2010), develop over time (e.g., Day & Sin, 2011), or operate as a dynamic system (e.g., Klein, Ziegert, Knight, & Xiao, 2006). As the diversity of this body of literature shows, leadership can be conceptualized as processes at multiple levels and happening at different paces. Despite the complexity of the phenomenon, some general rules of conceptualizing and measuring process constructs apply. Specifically, when conceptualizing a phenomenon (e.g., leadership) as a process in a multilevel system (e.g., organization), researchers need to specify the lower-level change process or mechanism, identify critical parameters and their relationships, and specify higher-level analogues of the critical parameters (Chan, 1998b; Kozlowski & Klein, 2000).

To apply this set of general rules to leadership research, the first step to conceptualize leadership as a process is to specify the change process at the lower level. Lower level could be the event level when the researchers are examining leader development trajectories, or it could be the individual level when researchers are examining team leadership emergence. Researchers need to explicate which lower-level mechanism drives the change and the specific form of interrelationships among variables (e.g., leader identity is related to leader effectiveness over time; Day & Sin, 2011). Based on this explication, leadership can be conceptualized as a change parameter of a system at the higher level or a homologous process at both higher and lower levels. For example, leadership in self-management teams can be conceptualized as a homologous process. At the individual level, leadership is fulfilled through members regulating their own behaviors toward individual performance goal; while at the team level, leadership is fulfilled through members collectively regulating their behaviors toward team goal (Manz & Sims, 1980; Tesluk & Mathieu, 1999).

Level-Related Issues in Leadership Theory Building

In this section, we review and discuss how level-related issues (e.g., Klein, Dansereau, & Hall, 1994; Kozlowski & Klein, 2000; Rousseau, 1985) have been addressed in leadership theory building. There are a formidable number of leadership theories in the social science literature. To analyze each leadership theory in the literature is beyond the scope of this chapter. However, aiming to provide a comprehensive review, we include major leadership theories that were covered in prior reviews on levels-of-analysis issues in leadership research (Markham, 2010; Yammarino et al., 2005) and some leadership theories that are gaining more attention recently. We group these theories into several categories according to their research focus or theoretical approach (Graen & Uhl-Bien, 1995; Hernandez, Eberly, Avolio, & Johnson, 2011), including leader-focused theories, contingency theories, follower-focused theories, relational approach, and team-focused theories. For each category of leadership theories, the following level-related issues are reviewed: (1) the focal construct or process examined and its level of analysis, (2) assumptions of the relationship between wholes and parts, i.e., whether individuals within units are viewed as homogenous, independent, or heterogeneous, and (3) which multilevel models described in Kozlowski and Klein's (2000) typology, including individual-level models, unit-level models, cross-level models, and homologous multilevel models, have been examined and can be examined in future research.

Leader-focused Leadership Theories

Leadership theories focusing on analyzing leader individual differences have a long history with its origin in the great man theory on changes in human history and society (Carlyle, 1907; Cowley, 1928). A basic assumption of leader-focused theories is that there are certain traits, behaviors, or behavioral styles that can be used to differentiate leaders from non-leaders or place all leaders on a continuum of a trait or behavior. Among theories taking this approach, trait theories and behavioral theories from studies conducted by Ohio State University and University of Michigan (Stogdill & Coons, 1957) are considered as classical paradigms of leadership research (House & Aditya, 1997). Several neoclassic leadership theories that appeared in the 1970s also took a leader-focused approach, including charismatic leadership (Conger & Kanungo, 1987; House, 1977), transformational leadership (Bass & Riggio, 2006), and servant leadership (Greenleaf, 1977). More recently, there emerged some newer theories focusing on leader traits, behaviors, or behavioral styles, including authentic leadership (Avolio, Gardner, Walumbwa, Luthans, & May, 2004), ethical leadership (Brown et al., 2005), influence tactics (Yukl & Falbe, 1990), leaderplex theory (Hooijberg, Hunt, & Dodge, 1997), and abusive supervision (Tepper, 2000).

In leadership theories taking a leader-focused perspective, leader traits (e.g., Big Five personality) and behaviors (e.g., task-oriented supervisory behaviors) are the focal constructs of interest. Thus, these types of theories are often developed at the individual level. Research that focuses on leader individual differences (i.e., variance at the individual level) and their relationships with other individual-level constructs often assumes that individuals and individual-level processes are independent of higher-level units (e.g., work groups, companies, or industries) or lower-level units (e.g., subordinates' individual differences, daily fluctuation within leaders). This independence assumption is most typically held in research using classical traits or behavioral paradigm of leadership (Yammarino et al., 2005).

Although the initial focus and basic assumption of leader-focused theories are rooted in individual differences, a recent development in leader-focused theories is to take variables or processes at the collective or within-individual level into consideration (e.g., Ohio State Model, Schriesheim, Cogliser, & Neider, 1995; charismatic leadership, Howell & Shamir, 2005). When extending leader-focused theories using multilevel lenses, researchers have held homogeneity or heterogeneity assumptions regarding individuals within units. When implicitly or explicitly assuming homogeneity, theorists argue that subordinates are similar to each other with respect to the focal leadership process studied (Klein et al., 1994). When implicitly or explicitly assuming heterogeneity, leadership theorists study within-leader and between-leader differences simultaneously. In other words, leader-level variance is no longer the only theoretical focus in the study.

Studies applying leader-focused theories can specify models including constructs at the same or different levels of analysis to explicate the leadership process. First, studies can specify a model only including relationships between individual-level constructs to examine the individual-level antecedents and outcomes of leader traits and behaviors, such as a model including the relationship between impression management strategies used by leaders and charismatic leadership (e.g., Sosik, Avolio, & Jung, 2002) and a model including the relationship between leader's initiating structure and consideration behaviors and leader's job performance rating (e.g., Judge, Piccolo, & Ilies, 2004). Second, studies based on leader-focused theories can also specify unit-level models that only include global, shared, or configural constructs to explicate unit-level leadership processes. For example, relationship between two global constructs can be specified to examine the relationship between leader traits and behaviors and unit financial performance (Barling, Weber, & Kelloway, 1996; Baum & Locke, 2004; Tosi, Misangyi, Fanelli, Waldman, & Yammarino, 2004). In addition, a relationship between a global and a shared construct can be specified to examine the relationship between leader traits and behaviors with unit potency (e.g., Hu & Liden, 2011), unit climate (e.g., Zohar & Luria, 2005), and group deviance (e.g., Detert, Treviño, Burris, & Andiappan, 2007). Moreover, relationship between a global and a configural construct can be specified to examine the relationship between leader behaviors and properties of networks in the unit (Zhang & Peterson, 2011). Finally, cross-level models that include constructs at two different levels of analysis can be specified to examine the direct effect of leader traits and behaviors on subordinates' outcomes (e.g., direct effect of transformational leadership on subordinate's job satisfaction; Bono & Judge, 2003) or their moderating effect on relationships between lower-level variables (e.g., moderating effect of transformational leadership on the relationship between subordinate's emotional regulation and job satisfaction; Bono, Foldes, Vinson, & Muros, 2007).

Contingency Theories of Leadership

The basic proposition of contingency theories of leadership is that leadership effectiveness is determined by the interaction between leader attributes and the situation (Vroom & Jago, 2007). Fiedler's (1967) contingency model of leadership is the most influential leadership theory taking a contingency approach. Other theories taking a contingency approach include Vroom and colleagues' theory of participation in decision-making (Vroom & Jago, 1988; Vroom & Yetton, 1973), path-goal theory of leadership (House, 1971), situational leadership (Hersey & Blanchard, 1977), substitutes for leadership (Kerr & Jermier, 1978; Manz & Sims, 1980), and multiple linkage model (Yukl, 1998). In contingency models, the leader attribute examined can be leader traits (e.g., motivational orientation) or leader behaviors (e.g., telling, delegating, and task behaviors); the situational factor examined can be characters of leaders (e.g., personal control), followers (e.g., maturity, motivation), or groups (e.g., group climate). Therefore, in a specific contingency model, depending on the personal, situational, and outcome variables included, the study may examine within-group variation, between-group variation, or variations at both levels (Ayman, Chemers, & Fiedler, 1995).

Studies that apply contingency theories can specify individual-level, unit-level, or cross-level models to explicate leadership processes. Individual-level examinations often focus on the interaction effect between leader characters and leader situation on leader outcomes, such as leader well-being or performance (e.g., Chemers & Ayman, 1985; Vroom & Jago, 1988). Unit-level models can be specified to examine the interaction effect of leader characters and group climate on unit performance or average job satisfaction of unit members (e.g., Ayman et al., 1995; Csoka & Fiedler, 1972). Moreover, cross-level models can be specified to examine the facilitating effect of leader characters on the relationship between individual subordinate's characters and outcomes (e.g., Fernandez & Vecchio, 1997; House, 1971; Podsakoff, MacKenzie, & Bommer, 1996). In summary, contingency theories provide a meta-proposition that leadership is a process through which leader traits or behaviors complement or facilitate subordinate abilities and environment to increase subordinate's satisfaction and performance, as well as the unit performance (Yammarino et al., 2005). This proposition itself describes a multilevel relationship and can be directly tested. Moreover, other leadership theories can be further extended by integrating a contingency perspective.

Follower-focused Leadership Theories

Drawing on cognitive theories, follower-focused leadership theories examine the content of followers' leadership-related knowledge and how followers process leadership-related information. Theories focusing on followers include implicit leadership theory (Lord & Maher, 1993), cognitive theory of leadership perception (Lord & Brown, 2004), and romance of leadership theory (Meindl, Ehrlich, & Dukerich, 1985). In these theories, the focal construct and process of interest are often at the individual level of analysis. Research that only examines individual-level factors often assumes that the individual-level process specified is independent from higher-level units. However, both within- and between-unit levels of analysis have been examined in recent research that examines the within-person dynamics in leadership perception (e.g., DeRue & Ashford, 2010) and contextual influence on followers' implicit leadership beliefs (e.g., GLOBE, House, Hanges, Javidan, Dorfman, & Gupta, 2004).

Studies taking a follower-focused approach can specify models including constructs at the same or different levels of analysis. Specifically, individual-level models can be specified to examine the relationship between followers' individual differences and their implicit beliefs of leadership (e.g., Hall & Lord, 1995; Keller, 1999). In addition, unit-level models can be specified to examine how cognitive schema of a group influences shared perception of group leader. Moreover, cross-level models can be specified to examine the cross-level effect of context (e.g., societal culture) on individuals' and groups' perception of leadership (e.g., House et al., 2004).

Relational Approach to Leadership

In theories taking a relational approach, leader-follower dyad is the smallest unit examined. Thus, theory is often developed at dyadic level of analysis. For example, vertical dyadic linkage approach to leadership (Dansereau et al., 1975) examines how leader-follower dyads form different types of relationships and exchange resources based on the type of their relationship. Similarly, LMX theory (Graen & Uhl-Bien, 1995) examines the relationship between leader's expectations about a particular subordinate and the quality of their dyadic relationship developed. Accordingly, in studies taking a relational approach, dyadic-level models are often specified to explicate the antecedents and outcomes of dyadic relationship (e.g., Wayne, Shore, & Liden, 1997). Moreover, cross-level models can also be specified to examine the effect of leader-level characteristics on dyadic-level variables. For example, Venkataramani, Green, and Schleicher (2010) specified a cross-level model on the effect of leader's centrality in advice network on leader-follower's dyadic relationship quality.

A recent trend in leadership research taking a relational approach is to examine heterogeneity of leader-follower dyads within the same work group. In these studies, unit-level models and cross-level models are specified. For example, unit-level models including a configural and a shared construct can be specified to examine how LMX differentiation is related to team potency (Boies & Howell, 2006). Moreover, cross-level models can be specified to examine organization-level antecedents or individual-level outcomes of LMX differentiation (e.g., Henderson, Liden, Glibkowski, & Chaudhry, 2009).

Team-Focused Leadership Theories

Team-focused leadership theories include theories on a team of leaders (e.g., board of directors or top management team, TMT) and theories on leadership in a team setting. In research on top organizational leaders, traits and behaviors of CEO and other organizational leaders are studied by applying traditional leadership theories (e.g., trait theory; Baum & Locke, 2004) or by examining leadership structure in boards of directors (e.g., Dalton, Daily, Ellstrand, & Johnson, 1998) and composition of senior executives (e.g., Hambrick, Cho, & Chen,

1996). The focus in team leadership research can be viewed as on a continuum with a single person responsible for leading a team at one end and the leadership being distributed to everyone in the team at the other end (Gronn, 2002; Morgeson et al., 2010). Studies that focus on examining formally designated leaders either extend traditional leadership theories to team context (e.g., transformational leadership, Lim & Ployhart, 2004; LMX theory, Zhou, Wang, Chen, & Shi, 2012) or develop new theories to explicate leader behaviors (e.g., empowering leadership; Chen & Kanfer, 2006; Chen et al., 2007; Kirkman & Rosen, 1999). At the other end of the continuum, shared, collective, and distributive leadership theories are developed to explain how leadership manifests as a team process or a collective property (Carson et al., 2007; Hiller, Day, & Vance, 2006; Pearce & Sims, 2002). In addition, there are integrated theoretical frameworks explicating the relations between different types of team leadership (e.g., Morgeson et al., 2010; Zaccaro, Rittman, & Marks, 2001).

Despite different focuses in these team leadership theories, one thing in common is that the level of analysis is at the unit level. Focal constructs in team-focused leadership theories can be global, shared, or configural unit-level constructs, or processes that operate at the unit level. Consistent with its focus on the team, team leadership studies examine within- and between-unit variation simultaneously. Depending on the specific phenomenon examined, within-unit components are assumed to be homogenous or heterogeneous. Specifically, in theories on formal team leaders, followers within the team can be assumed to have similar cognitions, emotions, and behaviors. Based on this homogenous assumption, average influence of formal team leaders (e.g., empowering leadership) on all team members can be examined (Chen & Kanfer, 2006). In contrast, in theories on shared or distributed team leadership, heterogeneity among team members' roles or perceptions is assumed. Based on this heterogeneous assumption, a pattern or distribution of team members' influence on each other and its effect on the team as a whole can be studied (e.g., Carson et al., 2007).

Team-focused leadership research often specifies unit-level models or cross-level models to explicate the leadership process. For example, in research that examines the relationship between the composition of board of directors or TMT members and firm performance, a unit-level model including a configural and a global construct is specified (e.g., Dalton et al., 1998; Hambrick et al., 1996). In addition, in studies on the influence of formal team leader behaviors on team motivational states, a unit-level model including a global and a shared construct is specified (e.g., Kirkman & Rosen, 1999). Moreover, cross-level main effect models can be specified to examine the main effect of team leader behaviors on individual team members (e.g., Chen, Sharma, Edinger, Shapiro, & Farh, 2011). Finally cross-level moderating effect models can be specified to examine the boundary effect of team leader behaviors on individual-level processes (e.g., Mathieu, Ahearne, & Taylor, 2007).

Dynamic Issues in Leadership Research

Time- or change-related issues have to be addressed in any organizational theory that explains a relationship between two variables (Mitchell & James, 2001; Ployhart & Vandenberg, 2010). This is because in order to explicate causality, a good theory needs to specify why an independent variable happens before the dependent variable and how changes or differences in an independent variable are associated with changes or differences in the dependent variable over time. Leadership theory is not an exception. Special attention should be paid to change- or time-related issues when researchers are interested in developing a longitudinal theory on leadership, such as theory on growth trajectory of leader abilities and skills (e.g., Day et al., 2009), fluctuations in followers' emotions, motivations, and cognitions (e.g., Bono et al., 2007), changes in team leadership capacity (e.g., Day et al., 2004), and emergence of leader or leadership (e.g., DeRue & Ashford, 2010).

Issues in Developing Change-Related Theories

What is the form of change? Research on changes can start with describing the form of change of one variable over time (Chan, 1998a; Wang & Bodner, 2007). To provide a clear description, a series of questions should be answered. Is the change continuous or discrete over time? When does change start, and when/whether does change end? If change is discrete, when does the status shift happen? Is the change linear or nonlinear? What is the rate or pace of change at a given time point? Answering these questions helps accurately describe the form of change and clarify the level of change-related construct. Misspecification of the form of change may result in problems in the conceptualization of relationships between variables, and misalignment between theory and research design (Ployhart & Vandenberg, 2010).

What is the level of change? In time- or change-related research, another issue to explicate is to determine the levels of variables examined. For example, in studies that examine development of leader effectiveness over time, leader effectiveness at a given time point is at the within-unit (i.e., within-leader) level, while growth parameters, including initial status and growth rate of leader effectiveness, are at the unit (i.e., leader) level. In a more complicated model that examines the effect of a time-varying predictor (e.g., experience) and leader individual differences on development of leader effectiveness, experience and leader effectiveness at a given time point are at the within-leader level of analysis while growth parameters of both experience and leader effectiveness, and leader individual differences are at the leader level of analysis. Moreover, in studies that examine whether different groups of leaders have qualitatively different growth trajectories of leader effectiveness (Day & Sin, 2011), leader effectiveness is at the within-leader level of analysis, leader individual differences are at leader level of analysis, and characteristics of the groups are at a higher group level of analysis

Why does change happen in variable(s)? After describing the form of change in one or more variables and the levels of analysis of all variables included, theorists should go further to explain why change in variables(s) happens. In theories on change, it would hardly be convincing to merely argue that change in a variable is *caused by* time itself. Instead, theories should specify what caused change in the focal variable *over* time (Ployhart & Vandenberg, 2010). Thus, it is always necessary to introduce another variable to explain why and how change in the focal variable happens. There are several different ways in which one variable can cause change in anther variable over time (Mitchell & James, 2001). First, change in one variable could be triggered by another static, that is, time-invariant, variable (e.g., the influence of gender on career progress of leaders). Second, change in one variable could be caused by change in another variable over time (e.g., effect of leader experience on leadership effectiveness over time). Third, change in one variable could cause status shift of another variable (e.g., leader effectiveness over time and promotion to top management team). Finally, two variables can influence each other cyclically (e.g., recursive influence between leadership identity and followership identity). In a given theory, mechanisms driving change in one of the above forms, or a mix, should be specified.

Changes in Development of Leaders

Clarifying change-related issues are necessary in research on leader development. Day et al.'s (2009) integrative model of leader develop provides an example on how to clarify forms of leader development, levels of change, and mechanisms underlying change. Specifically, Day et al. (2009) describe the form of change in leader development as a continuous process across a life span. Different leaders start at a varying initial status due to different personal history before assuming the leadership position. It is also argued that the rate of growth is not always positive. Instead, it could be negative or reduce to zero over time. A nonlinear growth pattern is expected due to changing growth rate. In addition, they argue that leader development can be examined at multiple levels of analysis, including changes in leader competence (expertise and effectiveness) and skills at within-leader level, between-leader differences in growth parameters, and qualitatively different growth patterns at the group level (e.g., Day & Sin, 2011). Moreover, Day et al. (2009) specify several underlying mechanisms of leader development at different levels of analysis by drawing on previous studies (DeRue & Wellman, 2009; Dragoni, Tesluk, & Oh, 2009; Foti & Hauenstein, 2007). In particular, they argue that the initial status of leader competence and skills can be influenced by leaders' biological characteristics, personality, previous experience, leadership efficacy, self-identity, goal orientation, and ability to learn. These time-invariant factors can also influence growth rate, thereby shaping the form of growth trajectory. During the development process, growth rate is constantly influenced by self-regulation processes (e.g., feedback, goal orientation), ongoing reconstruction of knowledge structures and mental models (e.g., self-identity) and other adult developmental processes (e.g., selection, optimization, and compensation). By addressing change-related issues, these researchers provide a clear and testable theory on leader development.

Changes in Followers' Cognitions, Affect, and Behaviors

Change-related issues are also relevant for research on dynamics in followers' cognition, affect, and behaviors. For example, it is suggested that followers' affective states can demonstrate a fluctuating form of change over time (Bono et al., 2007).

Therefore, studies on followers' affect need to specify how often the valence (positive vs. negative) and intensity of followers' affects change. Further, studies on dynamics in followers should also clarify levels of analysis of the changes. Studies may examine within-follower changes across events (e.g., different reactions to different affective events) and/or between-follower differences in change parameters (e.g., average magnitude and direction of affective state, strengths of associations between affective event and affective reaction). Finally, studies on dynamics in followers should explain the mechanisms underlying changes (e.g., Bono et al., 2007; Epitropaki & Martin, 2004; Keller, 1999; Lord & Brown, 2004). It is possible that time-varying factors, such as external events or interactions with leaders and coworkers, may influence change of followers' motivational states. It is also possible that between-follower differences in change parameters are influenced by dispositional factors, such as positive and negative affectivity, personality, and higher-order self-identity.

Changes in Development of Leader-Follower Relationship

Studies on development of the leader-follower dyadic relationship also need to address change-related issues. First, it is necessary to describe the form of change in development of the leader-follower relationship over time. It is possible that a plateau period appears and continues after a stable relationship is formed. Thus, a complete description of the development of the leader-follower relationship should specify when the plateau is reached and how long it is going to last until a potential decline or transformation happens. Second, studies should clarify the levels of analysis of variables in the relationship development process examined. Studies may examine changes within a leader-follower dyad, differences in change processes between different leader-follower dyads, and/or changes of a set of dyads (i.e., a network) over time. In addition, it is important for studies to explicate the mechanisms driving development of leader-follower relationships over time. For example, it is suggested that similarity and fit between leader and follower, leader's expectation of follower, follower's implicit theory of leadership, and mutual liking can all facilitate the formation of a relationship (Chen & Klimoski, 2003; Epitropaki & Martin, 2005; Liden, Wayne, & Stilwell, 1993; Wayne et al., 1997; Zhang, Wang, & Shi, 2012). In addition, some time-varying factors at within-dyad level may influence the speed of relationship development and its stability, such as member performance over time (Bauer & Green, 1996). Moreover, contextual factors such as organizations' HR practices and strategies may influence how networks among multiple leaders and followers develop over time (Collins & Clark, 2003).

Changes in Team Leadership Capacity

Finally, change-related issues should be considered in research on development of team leadership. Different forms of change have been described in prior studies on team leadership (e.g., Day et al., 2004; Klein et al., 2006; Morgeson, 2005; Morgeson & DeRue, 2006), including changes in formal team leaders' interventions on ongoing team events, changes of team leadership capacity, and changes in delegation of leadership roles in action teams. Studies on development of team leadership can examine change at different levels of analysis. For example, research can examine how team leadership capacity coevolves with individual team members' self-management capacity. Moreover, research on development of team leadership should explicate mechanisms underlying changes in team leadership. It is possible that change in team leadership capacity is influenced by time-varying factors such as characteristics of team tasks, accumulation of collective knowledge due to ongoing team learning, and flow of personnel of the team. Some static factors can also trigger and influence changes in team leadership, such as organizational human resource practices.

Statistical Methods for Testing Multilevel Leadership Theories

Like other organizational researchers, leadership researchers are often interested in the main effects of predictors on outcome variables or the moderation or mediation effects of variables at the same or different levels. When the predictor and outcome variables are both at the highest level of analysis, the main effect of one variable on the other can be tested using ordinary least squares (OLS) regression. When the predictor and the outcome variables are at the same level but are both nested within a higher level unit, or when the outcome variable is at a lower-level of analysis than the predictor variable, multilevel modeling (MLM) should be used to test the main effect. MLM should also be used for analyzing complex multilevel models that include cross-level moderation and/or multilevel mediation effects. As we pointed out at the beginning of this chapter, data collected for leadership studies are seldom free from non-independence problems. Therefore, MLM is typically the appropriate method for analyzing nested data to test leadership theories.

Several MLM techniques developed from different statistical perspectives are available, including repeated measure analysis of variance (ANOVA), hierarchical linear modeling, or random coefficient modeling (RCM, e.g., Bryk & Raudenbush, 2002; Snijders & Bosker, 1999), structural equation modeling (SEM), and time series analysis. In this section, we first introduce the basic ideas of two popular MLM approaches, RCM and SEM, and how they can be used to analyze main effects of predictors on one outcome variable, the moderating relationship in a three-variable system, and longitudinal data. We then introduce a more integrated framework, multilevel structural equation modeling (MSEM), which is more suitable for analyzing multilevel mediation models and complex models involving both mediation and moderation relationships (Preacher et al., 2010).

It is important to note that examining the measurement properties of multilevel constructs should be the first step in the empirical analysis before testing the relationships between constructs. Interested readers can refer to other sources for explanations of statistical procedures used in data aggregation and measurement quality assessment (e.g., Bliese, 2000; James et al., 1984; LeBreton & Senter, 2008). Here we mainly focus on introducing analytical methods for estimating multilevel models and testing relationships among variables.

Random Coefficient Modeling

Random coefficient modeling specifies a multilevel model in two steps (please refer to Bliese, 2002; Bryk & Raudenbush, 2002; Hofmann & Gavin, 1998, for detailed mathematical expressions). First, a lower-level regression equation is specified in which there is one lower-level outcome variable as a function of one or multiple lower-level predictor variables and a within-unit level residual. Using the intercepts and slopes from the lower-level regression equations as the outcome variables at the unit-level, multiple unit-level regression equations can be specified to include unit-level predictors and unit-level residuals. As such, unit-level residuals capture the random variation of the within-unit intercept and slopes across units that cannot be predicted by unit-level variables. Parameters in the within- and between-unit levels are estimated simultaneously in RCM, which can be conveniently done in several software packages including HLM, PROC MIXED in SAS, lme in R, Mplus, and MLwiN.

Analyzing main effects using RCM. In random coefficient models without moderators, the main effect of a lower-level predictor on the outcome variable (which is always at the lower-level in RCM) is described by two parameters in the higher-level equation with slope as outcome: the intercept of the higher-level equation describes its fixed effect pooled across all units, and the unit-level residual variance describes the variation of its effect across units. When the predictor is at the higher level, its main effect on the outcome variable, often referred to as cross-level main effect, is described by the slope in the higher-level equation with intercept as the outcome. To test the significance of a main effect in RCM, its fixed effect is usually tested by *t*-test, and its variation is tested by Chi-square tests (Bryk & Raudenbush, 2002).

Analyzing moderation effects using RCM. In random coefficient models, the moderating effect of a higher-level variable on the relationship between two lower-lever variables is described by the slope in the higher-level equation with slope as the outcome. When the moderating variable is also at the lower-level of analysis, an interaction term can be formed by multiplying the group-mean-centered lower-level predictors. This interaction term can be treated as a lower-level predictor on the outcome variable. In the higher-level equation with the random slope of this interaction term as the outcome, the intercept captures the average within-unit interaction effect (Enders & Tofighi, 2007). Similar to testing other fixed effects, the moderating effect can be tested by *t*-tests in RCM.

Analyzing longitudinal data using RCM. Repeated measures nested within individuals form a special case of multilevel data. Literature within the RCM framework has demonstrated how longitudinal data can be analyzed in a RCM framework (e.g., Bryk & Raudenbush, 2002). Within organization studies, Bliese and Ployhart (2002) provides an illustration of how to analyze longitudinal data to model growth curves by using RCM. The basic idea of their procedure is to treat time as a lower-level predictor in the random coefficient model. Thus, parameters of the growth curve can be described by the fixed effect of time (i.e., the growth rate) and the fixed effect of the lower-level intercept (i.e., the initial status). The effect of individual differences on the growth parameters can be modeled by including them as predictors in higher-level regression equations with growth parameters as outcomes.

Structural Equation Modeling Approach

Multilevel data can also be analyzed in conventional SEM framework. Research has shown that under some conditions, the multilevel models specified in RCM and SEM are mathematically equivalent (Curran, 2003; Mehta & Neale, 2005; Mehta & West, 2000; Rovine & Molenaar, 2000). Differences between RCM and SEM approaches mainly lie in methods for estimating random parameters, how missing data are handled, and specific features associated with each analytic framework. For example, multilevel modeling in SEM can provide model fit indices to help evaluate and compare different models, and it is not restricted to models with a single outcome; while RCM can be more flexible with modeling data that have more than two levels (see Bliese & Ployhart, 2002; Mehta & Neale, 2005, for discussions on choosing the analytical strategy). When the researchers are interested in estimating main effects or simple moderation effects as discussed above, RCM can sometimes be a better option because of its intuitive two-stage model specification procedure. However, as part of a generalized structural equation modeling framework (Muthén, 2001), SEM approach to multilevel modeling is especially suitable for modeling data from longitudinal design with complex data structure.

Model growth curves. Latent growth modeling (LGM) within SEM framework describes a growth curve by specifying the within-individual repeated observations as indicators of growth parameters (e.g., linear growth factor, quadratic growth factor, and intercept factor). The means of the growth parameters describe the average growth pattern in the population. The variances and covariances of the growth parameters describe the variation of the growth curves between individuals (e.g., variation of the initial status or the linear growth rate across people) and their interdependence (e.g., the higher the initial status, the slower the growth rate). As a special case of mean structure and covariances analysis in SEM framework, LGM can be estimated by maximum-likelihood estimation methods, which can be conducted in conventional SEM software, such as LISREL and Mplus.

Longitudinal data analysis in SEM frameworks can also accommodate models with categorical outcomes, different types of covariates (e.g., continuous or categorical, observed or latent) of growth factors, and population heterogeneity (Muthén, 2001). Interested readers can refer to other works introducing longitudinal data analysis in SEM framework for technical details (Bollen & Curran, 2005; Duncan, Duncan, & Strycker, 2006; Langeheine & van de Pol, 2002; Muthén, 2004). Examples of applications of longitudinal data analysis in organizational research are also available (e.g., Chan, 2002; Wang & Bodner, 2007; Wang & Chan, 2011; Wang, & Hanges, 2011).

Multilevel Structural Equation Modeling

Leadership researchers are often interested in testing mediation hypotheses about the intermediate mechanisms linking two variables. In Krull and MacKinnon's (2001) taxonomy, three variables in a multilevel model can form a 2-2-1 (i.e., the predictor and mediator are at the higher level, and the outcome is at the lower level), 2-1-1 (i.e., the predictor is at the higher level, and the mediator and the outcome are at the lower level), or 1-1-1 (i.e., the predictor, the mediator, and the outcome are all at the lower level) mediation relationship. An example for a 2-2-1 mediation model would be empowering team leadership relates to team empowerment, which in turn influences individual outcomes (e.g., Chen et al., 2007). An example of a 2-1-1 mediation model would be the mediation relationship between transformational leadership, subordinates' motivational states, and subordinates' job satisfaction and job performance (e.g., Bono & Judge, 2003). An example of a 1-1-1 mediation model would be the mediation relationship between subordinates' perceived leader-follower relationship quality, subordinates' perceived empowerment, and subordinates' job satisfaction (e.g., Liden, Wayne, & Sparrowe, 2000). Moreover, leadership researchers can be interested in whether one or multiple mediation links are dependent on another higher-level variable, which forms a moderated multilevel mediation relationship (e.g., Chen et al., 2007; Zhou et al., 2012).

Analyzing complex methods as illustrated in these examples using an RCM approach have two major limitations. First, estimating models with multiple outcomes (e.g., mediation models) in RCM requires additional data rearrangement (see Bauer et al., 2006, for an example of rearranging data for analyzing a 1-1-1 model in RCM), because RCM is not designed for multivariate modeling. Second, RCM cannot handle models with outcome variables at the higher level of analysis (e.g., subordinate's mood moderates the relationship between leader's behavior and subordinate's rating of leader). Analyzing these complex models in SEM also has some limitations, mainly due to its limited ability to accommodate multiple random slopes, missing data, and unbalanced unit sizes (e.g., Bauer, 2003; Curran, 2003; Mehta & Neale, 2005).

To address the limitations of RCM and SEM approach, recent methodological research on MLM has advocated the framework of MSEM; Asparouhov & Muthén, 2008; Preacher et al., 2010). In MSEM, the variance of a variable at the lower level can be partitioned into within- and between-unit latent components, which are orthogonal to each other (Asparouhov & Muthén, 2006). Thus, a variable's between-unit variance component is also orthogonal to any other variable's within-unit variance component. Therefore, the relationships between the between (or within) unit components can be considered as pure between (or within) unit effects. It should be noted that the between-unit component is a *latent* factor which is different from the observed means of the lower-level scores. Lüdtke, Marsh, Robitzsch, Trautwein, Asparouhov, and Muthén's (2008) simulation study has demonstrated that the mean of lower-level scores can be a biased measure of the higher-level unit's standing on the latent factor.

Partitioning the variances of variables and the covariances among variables into two orthogonal latent components offers MSEM several advantages over traditional RCM and SEM approaches. First, in MSEM, the within- and between-unit effects are estimated separately to provide a more accurate test of the hypothesized relationship at either within or between-unit level of analysis. In conventional RCM, if not particularly specified, an estimate of the relationship between two lower-level variables is a conflated estimate of their within-unit relationship and between-unit relationships (see Enders & Tofighi, 2007, for mathematical and pictorial illustrations). This can be problematic, especially when the two relationships are of different directions. A researcher may detect a close to zero effect when in reality the effect is positive at one level and negative at the other level.

Moreover, compared to RCM or SEM, MSEM is more flexible with outcomes in the model estimated. MSEM can accommodate multiple outcomes, hence alleviating problems associated with a piecemeal approach in testing multilevel mediation models (Bauer, Preacher, & Gil, 2006; Edwards & Lambert, 2007). In addition, MSEM can accommodate models with outcome variables at a higher level. Traditional MLM assumes that the outcome variable is only at the lowest level of analysis (Krull & MacKinnon, 2001). Some methods have been proposed to extend traditional MLM to include higher-level outcome variables, such as Griffin's (1997) two-step analysis and Pituch, Stapleton, and Kang's (2006) procedure. However, MSEM outperforms these two-stage analyses in terms of efficiency and accuracy of estimation and ease in manipulation of data (Preacher et al., 2010).

Finally, within the generalized structural equation modeling framework, missing data on outcome variables can be modeled by the full-information maximum-likelihood (FIML) method assuming that data are missing at random (i.e., missing depends on observed data, MAR; Little & Rubin, 2002). It is suggested that in estimation of longitudinal models, FIML performs better than other available missing data solutions, such as pairwise deletion, listwise deletion, and stochastic regression imputation (Newman, 2003). Modeling missing data with different assumptions about the underlying nature of the missing data (e.g., MAR or missing completely at random), is available in software Mplus (Muthén & Muthén, 2007).

Therefore, based on recent advances in methodological research, we recommend using the MSEM framework to analyze complex multilevel models. Preacher et al. (2010) provided detailed nontechnical guidelines and examples on how to conduct different types of MSEM in software Mplus. Other references on technical details of MSEM are also available (e.g., Asparouhov & Muthén, 2006, 2008).

Estimating Indirect Effect and Its Standard Error

The distribution of indirect effect in single or multiple level models seldom follows normal distribution (MacKinnon, Lockwood, & Williams, 2004). Thus, to estimate the indirect effect and to construct the sampling distribution of the statistic more accurately, several methods not relying on normality assumptions have been developed (Bauer et al., 2006; MacKinnon et al., 2004). Most of these methods developed are resampling techniques. The first category of methods uses resampling of parameter estimates, sometimes called Monte Carlo simulation, which has been used to construct confidence intervals of multilevel indirect effects (e.g., Preacher et al., 2010). Specifically, estimates of each mediation path and its standard error are obtained from estimating the hypothesized model using the original data. Then in each round of resampling, an estimate of each link can be sampled from its sampling distribution. Multiplying the two estimates from respective sampling distribution forms a new estimate of the indirect effect. Repeating this procedure a certain number of times can generate a simulated sampling distribution of the indirect effect. Parametric resampling procedures can be conducted in software R, SAS, or Matlab (R codes are available at http://www.quantpsy.org).

In addition to resampling parameters, it is also possible to test indirect effects by resampling residual variance. In a procedure developed by Pituch et al. (2006), the original data is first estimated using multilevel modeling. In each simulation round, residuals are sampled from the distribution based on the estimates from the original data. A new data set is constructed using information from the sample sizes of the units, the original value of the predictors, the fixed effects of the predictors, and the resampled residuals. The hypothesized model is estimated using each set of simulated data, thus generating a new indirect effect estimate. After repeating the resampling-estimating procedure a certain number of times, a sampling distribution of the indirect effect is constructed and the confidence interval at a certain confidence level can be obtained.

Conclusions

We would like to end this chapter by discussing some overarching levels-of-analysis issues in leadership research and highlighting some future research directions. First, although repeatedly discussed in levels literature (e.g., Klein et al., 1994; Rousseau, 1985; Yammarino & Dansereau, 2011; Yammarino et al., 2005), it is worthwhile to emphasize again the alignment of level of theory, level of construct, measurement of constructs, and statistical analysis. If the theory is about individual-level relationship and independence of the individual-level constructs from higher-level units is assumed, data should be collected from independent observations of individuals. Given that organizations are multilevel systems by nature, it may be difficult to ensure independence in design (Bliese & Hanges, 2004). Thus, it is necessary for researchers to explicitly articulate how they address the alignment issue even when the theory is at the individual level of analysis. If the theory is about unit-level or cross-level relationship(s), measurement should reflect the conceptualization of unit-level constructs and aggregation tests may be necessary.

In addition, alignment is important for refining and integrating theories. A construct is the connection between observations and theories (Shadish, Cook, & Campbell, 2001). When there is a misalignment between measurement and a construct, it is impossible to tell whether the phenomenon observed is the phenomenon explicated in the theory. Alignment between theory and research can also help avoid fallacies in conclusions drawn from research. Two types of fallacies may mislead leadership theory development: ecological fallacy occurs when researchers generalize findings from a higher level of analysis to a lower-level relationship, and individualistic fallacy occurs when individual-level relationships are aggregated to infer higher-level relationships (Alker, 1969; Robinson, 1950). By paying attention to levels-of-analysis issues in theory, measurement, and analysis, researchers should be more aware of the generalizability of their findings. In this way, alignment can further facilitate refining and integrating leadership theories.

Another issue potentially hindering improvement of the quality of leadership research is that some studies only describe relationships between leader traits and behaviors with an outcome instead of explaining why the outcome results from the leadership processes (Lord & Dinh, 2012). As we discussed above, to explain mechanisms underlying leadership processes, change- and time-related issues should be explicitly addressed, regardless of whether theorists are interested in developing a longitudinal model (Mitchell & James, 2001). Thus, future research should take dynamic issues into consideration in developing leadership theories.

Finally, person-centered analysis is an important yet underused approach in leadership research. A variable- or dimension-centered approach describes and explains the associations between variables, while a person-centered approach answers questions about groupings of individuals according to qualitatively different patterns among variables (Wang & Hanges, 2011). Conventional ways of theorizing in leadership research follow a variable-centered approach. Nevertheless, some research questions may be answered more clearly by taking a person-centered approach (e.g., Foti & Hauenstein, 2007; Mumford, Zaccaro, Johnson, Diana, Gilbert, & Threlfall, 2000) or a combination of both person- and variable-centered analyses (e.g., Day & Sin, 2011; Foti, Bray, Thompson, & Allgood, 2012). Moreover, inconsistencies in predictions from different theories may be reconciled by considering potential heterogeneity in the population studied. Theory development should not be constrained by availability of research methods (Bamberger, 2008). On the other hand, with the rapid developments of research methodology, it is important that leadership theories move beyond describing a static linear relationship between two variables and advance to providing theoretical guidance for more complicated empirical research. Taking a person-centered view may help reach this aim.

FUTURE RESEARCH DIRECTIONS

There also exist several areas in leadership research that can potentially be advanced by better incorporating levels theory and analyses. First, with the advancement of MSEM analysis framework, research on homologous processes in leadership may be advanced by delineating the processes more clearly and testing the relationships more accurately. Like other social scientists, leadership researchers are also interested in to what extent relationships at one level of analysis can generalize to another level (i.e., homology; Kozlowski & Klein, 2000). For example, whether the relationship between leadership and subordinates' individual motivational state can generalize to group level (Chen & Kanfer, 2006), or whether the relationship between leadership and collective performance can generalize across different organizational levels (Zaccaro & Klimoski, 2001). Recent methodological development (Chen, Bliese, & Mathieu, 2005; Preacher et al., 2010) provides tools to address research questions like these. In addition to helping us refine and test extant theories, homologous analysis framework may also facilitate integrating leadership literature from both micro and macro perspectives.

Second, there is a growing interest in using social network measures to operationalize leadership constructs (e.g., Carson et al., 2007; Venkataramani et al., 2010). Leadership research can borrow more from social network literature by studying the larger network among leaders, subordinates, and other people in and outside the organization. For example, future research can examine how ties between leaders and subordinates across multiple organizational levels influence organizational performance and individual career outcomes (e.g., Burt, 2004). Future research can also examine how leaders' ties with people outside the organization (e.g., clients, competitors, classmates at schools, family, and friends) influence leadership development. Another interesting and important issue to study is how leaders develop their ties, or relationships, with multiple people in the organization (e.g., subordinates; Sparrowe & Liden, 1997) and succeed or fail to become the center of the network (Balkundi et al., 2011).

Third, research on leader-subordinate congruence or leader-team congruence can be advanced by taking a levels perspective. Research taking a person-environment fit perspective or leader-subordinate relational perspective is often curious about how the similarity, distance, or fit between leader and subordinate influence dyadic or individual outcomes (e.g., Tsui & O'Reilly, 1989). Earlier studies usually only examine a single leader-subordinate dyad in one unit despite the fact that multiple subordinates may report to the same leader (e.g., Lam, Hui, & Law, 1999). With development of cross-level polynomial regression procedures (Jansen & Kristof-Brown, 2005), recent studies have examined how congruence between leader and multiple subordinates in the same work group influences dyadic and individual outcomes (Zhang et al., 2012). Future research can also examine how fit between leader and organizational context or congruence between external team leader and attitudes of the team influence team-level outcomes.

References

Alker, H. R., Jr. (1969). A typology of ecological fallacies. In M. Dogan & S. Rokkan (Eds.), *Quantitative ecological analyses in the social sciences* (pp. 69–86). Cambridge, MA: MIT Press.

Asparouhov, T., & Muthén, B. (2006). Constructing covariances in multilevel regression (Mplus Web Notes No. 11). Retrieved from http://www.statmodel.com

Asparouhov, T., & Muthén, B. (2008). Multilevel mixture models. In G. R. Hancock & K. M. Samuelsen (Eds.), *Advances in latent variable mixture models* (pp. 27–51). Charlotte, NC: Information Age Publishing, Inc.

Atwater, L., Wang, M., Smither, J. W., & Fleenor, J. W. (2009) Are cultural characteristics associated with the relationship between self and others' ratings of leadership? *Journal of Applied Psychology, 94,* 876–886.

Ayman, R., Chemers, M. M., & Fiedler, F. (1995). The contingency model of leadership effectiveness: Its levels of analysis. *The Leadership Quarterly, 6,* 147–167.

Avolio, B. J., Gardner, W. L., Walumbwa, F. O., Luthans, F., & May, D. R. (2004). Unlocking the mask: A look at the process by which authentic leaders impact follower attitudes and behaviors. *The Leadership Quarterly, 15,* 801–823.

Balkundi, P., Kilduff, M., & Harrison, D. A. (2011). Centrality and charisma: Comparing how leader networks and attributions affect team performance. *Journal of Applied Psychology, 96,* 1209–1222.

Bamberger, P. (2008). Beyond contextualization: Using context theories to narrow the micro-macro gap in management research. *Academy of Management Journal, 51,* 839–846.

Barling, J., Weber, T., & Kelloway, E. K. (1996). Effects of transformational leadership training on attitudinal and financial outcomes: A field experiment. *Journal of Applied Psychology, 81,* 827–832.

Bass, B. M., & Riggio, R. E. (2006). *Transformational leadership* (2nd ed.). Mahwah, NJ: Lawrence Erlbaum.

Bauer, D. J. (2003). Estimating multilevel linear models as structural equation models. *Journal of Educational and Behavioral Statistics, 28,* 135–167.

Bauer, D. J., Preacher, K. J., & Gil, K. M. (2006). Conceptualizing and testing random indirect effects and moderated mediation in multilevel models: New procedures and recommendations. *Psychological Methods, 11*, 142–163.
Bauer, T. N., & Green, S. G. (1996). Development of leader-member exchange: A longitudinal test. *Academy of Management Journal, 39*, 1538–1567.
Baum, J. R., & Locke, E. A. (2004). The relationship of entrepreneurial traits, skill, and motivation to subsequent venture growth. *Journal of Applied Psychology, 89*, 587–598.
Bliese, P. D. (2000). Within-group agreement, non-independence, and reliability: Implications for data aggregation and analyses. In K. J. Klein and S.W.J. Kozlowski (Eds.), *Multilevel theory, research, and methods in organizations: Foundations, extensions, and new directions* (pp. 349–381). San Francisco: Jossey-Bass.
Bliese, P. D. (2002). Multilevel random coefficient modeling in organizational research: Examples using SAS and S-PLUS. In F. Drasgow & N. Schmitt (Eds.), *Measuring and analyzing behavior in organizations: Advances in measurement and data analysis* (pp. 401–445). San Francisco: Jossey-Bass.
Bliese, P. D., & Hanges, P. J. (2004). Being both too liberal and too conservative: The perils of treating grouped data as though they were independent. *Organizational Research Methods, 7*, 400–417.
Bliese, P. D., & Ployhart, R. E. (2002). Growth modeling using random coefficient models: Model building, testing, and illustrations. *Organizational Research Methods, 5*, 362–387.
Boies, K., & Howell, J. M. (2006). Leader-member exchange in teams: An examination of the interaction between relationship differentiation and mean LMX in explaining team-level outcomes. *The Leadership Quarterly, 17*, 246–257.
Bollen, K. A., & Curran, P. J. (2005). *Latent curve models: A structural equation perspective*. New York: John Wiley & Sons.
Bono, J. E., & Judge, T. A. (2003). Self-concordance at work: Toward understanding the motivational effects of transformational leaders. *Academy of Management Journal, 46*, 554–571.
Bono, J. E., Foldes, H. J., Vinson, G., & Muros, J. P. (2007). Workplace emotions: The role of supervision and leadership. *Journal of Applied Psychology, 92*, 1357–1367.
Brown, M.E., Treviño, L. K., & Harrison, D. A. (2005). Ethical leadership: A social learning perspective for construct development and testing. *Organizational Behavior and Human Decision Processes, 97*, 117–134.
Bryk, A. S., & Raudenbush, S. W. (2002). *Hierarchical linear models* (2nd ed.). Thousand Oaks, CA: Sage.
Burt, R. S. (2004). Structural holes and good ideas. *American Journal of Sociology, 110*, 349–399.
Carlyle, T. (1907). *On heroes, hero-worship, and the heroic in history*. Boston: Houghton Mifflin.
Carson, J. B., Tesluk, P. E., & Marrone, J. A. (2007). Shared leadership in teams: An investigation of antecedent conditions and performance. *Academy of Management Journal, 50*, 1217–1234.
Chan, D. (1998a). The conceptualization and analysis of change over time: An integrative approach incorporating longitudinal mean and covariance structures analysis (LMACS) and multiple indicator latent growth modeling (MLGM). *Organization Research Methods, 1*, 421–483.
Chan, D. (1998b). Functional relations among constructs in the same content domain at different levels of analysis: A typology of composition models. *Journal of Applied Psychology, 83*, 234–246.
Chan, D. (2002). Longitudinal modeling. In S. G. Rogelberg (Ed), *Handbook of research methods in industrial/organizational psychology* (pp. 412–430). Malden, MA: Blackwell Publishers, Inc.
Chemers, M. M., & Ayman, R. (1985). Leadership orientation as a moderator of the relationship between job performance and job satisfaction of Mexican managers. *Personality and Social Psychology Bulletin, 11*, 359–367.
Chen, G., & Bliese, P. D. (2002). The role of different levels of leadership in predicting self- and collective efficacy: Evidence for discontinuity. *Journal of Applied Psychology, 877*, 549–556.
Chen, G., Bliese, P. D., & Mathieu, J. E. (2005). Conceptual framework and statistical procedures for delineating and testing multilevel theories of homology. *Organizational Research Methods, 8*, 375–409.
Chen, G., & Kanfer, R. (2006). Toward a systems theory of motivated behavior in work teams. *Research in Organizational Behavior, 27*, 223–267.
Chen, G., Kirkman, B. L., Kanfer, R., Allen, D., & Rosen, B. (2007). A multilevel study of leadership, empowerment, and performance in teams. *Journal of Applied Psychology, 92*, 331–346.
Chen, G., & Klimoski, R. J. (2003). The impact of expectations on newcomer performance in teams as mediated by work characteristics, social exchanges, and empowerment. *Academy of Management Journal, 46*, 591–607.
Chen, G., Sharma, P. N., Edinger, S., Shapiro, D. L., & Farh, J. L. (2011). Motivating and de-motivating forces in teams: Cross-level influences of empowering leadership and relationship conflict. *Journal of Applied Psychology, 96*, 541–557.
Collins, C. J., & Clark, K. D. (2003). Strategic human resource practices, top management team social networks, and firm performance: The role of human resource practices in creating organizational competitive advantage. *Academy of Management Journal, 46*, 740–751.
Conger, J. A., & Kanungo, R. N. (1987). Toward a behavioral theory of charismatic leadership in organizational setting. *Academy of Management Review, 12*, 637–647.
Costa, P. T., Jr., & McCrae, R. R. (1992). *Revised CEO personality inventory (NEO-PI-R) and NEO five-factor (NEO-FFI) inventory professional manual.* Odessa, FL: Psychological Assessment Resources.
Cowley, W. H. (1928). Three distinctions in the study of leaders. *Journal of Abnormal and Social Psychology, 23*, 144–157.
Cropanzano, R., & Mitchell, M. S. (2005). Social exchange theory: An interdisciplinary review. *Journal of Management, 31*, 874–900.
Csoka, L. S., & Fiedler, F. E. (1972). The effect of military leadership training: A test of the contingency model. *Organizational Behavior and Human Performance, 8*, 395–407.
Curran, P. J. (2003). Have multilevel models been structural equation models all along? *Multivariate Behavioral Research, 38*, 529–569.
Dalton, D. R., Daily, C. M., Ellstrand, A. E., & Johnson, J. L. (1998). Meta-analytic reviews of board composition, leadership structure, and financial performance. *Strategic Management Journal, 19*, 269–290.
Dansereau, F., Graen, G., & Haga, W. J. (1975). A vertical dyad linkage approach to leadership within formal organizations: A longitudinal investigation of the role making process. *Organizational Behavior and Human Performance, 13*, 46–78.

Dansereau, F., Yammarino, F. J., & Markham, S. E. (1995). Leadership: The multi-level approaches. *The Leadership Quarterly, 6,* 97–109.

Day, D. V., Gronn, P., & Salas, E. (2004). Leadership capacity in teams. *The Leadership Quarterly, 15,* 857–880.

Day, D. V., Harrison, M. M., & Halpin, S. M. (2009). *An integrative approach to leader development: Connecting adult development, identity, and expertise.* New York: Routledge.

Day, D. V., & Sin, H. (2011). Longitudinal tests of an integrative model of leader development: Charting and understanding developmental trajectories. *The Leadership Quarterly, 22,* 545–560.

DeRue, D. C., & Ashford, S. J. (2010). Who will lead and who will follow? A social process of leadership identity construction in organizations. *Academy of Management Review, 35,* 627–647.

DeRue, D. S., & Wellman, N. (2009). Developing leaders via experience: The role of developmental challenge, learning orientation, and feedback availability. *Journal of Applied Psychology, 94,* 859–875.

Detert, J. R., Treviño, L. K., Burris, E. R., & Andiappan, M. (2007). Managerial modes of influence and counterproductivity in organizations: A longitudinal business-unit-level investigation. *Journal of Applied Psychology, 92,* 993–1005.

Dragoni, L., Tesluk, P. E., & Oh, I. (2009). Understanding managerial development: Integrating developmental assignments, learning orientation, and access to developmental opportunities in predicting managerial competencies. *Academy of Managerial Journal, 52,* 731–743.

Duncan, T. E., Duncan, S. C., & Strycker, L. A. (2006). *An introduction to latent variable growth curve modeling: Concepts, issues, and applications* (2nd ed.). Mahwah, NJ: Lawrence Erlbaum.

Edwards, J. R., & Lambert, L. S. (2007). Methods for integrating moderation and mediation: A general analytical framework using moderated path analysis. *Psychological Methods, 12,* 1–22.

Enders, C. K., & Tofighi, D. (2007). Centering predictor variables in cross-sectional multilevel models: A new look at an old issue. *Psychological Methods, 12,* 121–138.

Epitropaki, O., & Martin, R. (2004). Implicit leadership theories in applied settings: Factor structure, generalizability, and stability over time. *Journal of Applied Psychology, 89,* 293–310.

Epitropaki, O., & Martin, R. (2005). From ideal to real: A longitudinal study of the role of implicit leadership theories on leader-member exchanges and employee outcomes. *Journal of Applied Psychology, 90,* 659–676.

Fernandez, C. F., & Vecchio, R. P. (1997). Situational leadership theory revisited: A test of an across-jobs perspective. *The Leadership Quarterly, 8,* 67–84.

Fiedler, F. E. (1967). *A theory of leadership effectiveness.* New York: McGraw Hill.

Foti, R. J., Bray, B. C., Thompson, N. J., & Allgood, S. F. (2012). Know thy self, know thy leader: Contributions of a pattern-oriented approach to examining leader perceptions. *Leadership Quarterly, 23,* 702–717.

Foti, R. J., & Hauenstein, N.M.A. (2007). Pattern and variable approaches in leadership emergence and effectiveness. *Journal of Applied Psychology, 92,* 347–355.

Gerstner, C. R., & Day, D. V. (1997). Meta-analytic review of leader-member exchange theory: Correlates and construct issues. *Journal of Applied Psychology, 82,* 827–844.

Graen, C. B., & Uhl-Bien, M. (1995) Relationship-based approach to leadership development of leader-member exchange (LMX) theory of leadership over 25 years: Applying a multi-level multi-domain perspective. *The Leadership Quarterly, 6,* 219–247.

Greenleaf, R. K. (1977). *Servant leadership: A journey into the nature of legitimate power and greatness.* Mahwah, NJ: Paulist Press.

Griffin, M. A. (1997). Interaction between individuals and situations: Using HLM procedures to estimate reciprocal relationships. *Journal of Management, 23,* 759–773.

Gronn, P. (2002). Distributed leadership as a unit of analysis. *The Leadership Quarterly, 13,* 423–451.

Hall, R. J., & Lord, R. G. (1995). Multi-level information-processing explanations of followers' leadership perceptions. *The Leadership Quarterly, 6,* 265–287.

Hambrick, D. C., Cho, T. S., & Chen, M. (1996). The influence of top management team heterogeneity on firms' competitive moves. *Administrative Science Quarterly, 41,* 659–684.

Harrison, D. A., & Klein, K. J. (2007). What's the difference? Diversity constructs as separation, variety, or disparity in organizations. *Academy of Management Review, 32,* 1199–1228.

Henderson, D. J., Liden, R. C., Glibkowski, B. C., & Chaudhry, A. (2009). LMX differentiation: A multilevel review and examination of its antecedents and outcomes. *The Leadership Quarterly, 20,* 517–534.

Henderson, D. J., Wayne, S. J., Shore, L. M., Bommer, W. H., & Tetrick, L. E. (2008). Leader-member exchange, differentiation, and psychological contract fulfillment: A multilevel examination. *Journal of Applied Psychology, 93,* 1208–1219.

Hernandez, M., Eberly, M. B., Avolio, B. J., & Johnson, M. D. (2011). The loci and mechanisms of leadership: Exploring a more comprehensive view of leadership theory. *The Leadership Quarterly, 22,* 1165–1185.

Hersey, P., & Blanchard, K. (1977). *Management of organization behavior: Utilizing human resources* (3rd ed.). Englewood Cliffs, NJ: Prentice Hall.

Hiller, N. J., Day, D. V., & Vance, R. J. (2006). Collective enactment of leadership roles and team effectiveness: A field study. *The Leadership Quarterly, 17,* 387–397.

Hofmann, D. A., & Gavin, M. B. (1998). Centering decisions in hierarchical linear models: Implications for research in organizations. *Journal of Management, 24,* 623–641.

Hooijberg, R., Hunt, J. G., & Dodge, G. E. (1997). Leadership complexity and development of the leaderplex model. *Journal of Management, 23,* 375–408.

House, R. J. (1971). A path-goal theory of leadership effectiveness. *Administrative Science Quarterly, 16,* 321–339.

House, R. J. (1977). A 1976 theory of charismatic leadership. In J. G. Hunt & L. L. Larson (Eds.), *Leadership: The cutting edge* (pp. 189–207). Carbondale: Southern Illinois University Press

House, R. J., & Aditya, R. N. (1997). The social scientific study of leadership: Quo vadis? *Journal of Management, 23,* 409–473.

House, R. J., Hanges, P. W., Javidan, M., Dorfman, P., & Gupta, V. (2004). *Culture, leadership, and organizations: The GLOBE study of 62 societies.* Thousand Oaks, CA: Sage.

Howell, J. M., & Shamir, B. (2005). The role of followers in the charismatic leadership process: Relationship and their consequences. *Academy of Management Review, 30,* 96–112.

Hu, J., & Liden, R. C. (2011). Antecedents of team potency and team effectiveness: An examination of goal and process clarity and servant leadership. *Journal of Applied Psychology, 96,* 4, 851–862.

Hunt, J. G., & Dodge, G. E. (2000). Leadership déjà vu all over again. *The Leadership Quarterly, 11*, 435–458.
James, L. R., Demaree, R. G., & Wolf, G. (1984). Estimating within-group interrater reliability with and without response bias. *Journal of Applied Psychology, 69*, 85–98.
Jansen, K. J., & Kristof-Brown, A. L. (2005). Marching to the best of a different drummer: Examining the impact of pacing congruence. *Organizational Behavior and Human Decision Processes, 97*, 93–105.
Judge, T. A., & Bono, J. E. (2000). Five-factor model of personality and transformational leadership. *Journal of Applied Psychology, 85*, 751–765.
Judge, T. A., Bono, J. E., Ilies, R., & Gerhardt, M. W. (2002). Personality and leadership: A qualitative and quantitative review. *Journal of Applied Psychology, 87*, 765–780.
Judge, T. A., LePine, J. A., & Rich, B. L. (2006). Loving yourself abundantly: Relationship of the narcissistic personality to self- and other perceptions of workplace deviance, leadership, and task and contextual performance. *Journal of Applied Psychology, 91*, 762–776.
Judge, T. A., Piccolo, R. F., & Ilies, R. (2004). The forgotten ones? The validity of consideration and initiating structure in leadership research. *Journal of Applied Psychology, 89*, 36–51.
Judge, T. A., Piccolo, R. F., & Kosalka, T. (2009). The bright and dark sides of leader traits: A review and theoretical extension of the leader trait paradigm. *The Leadership Quarterly, 20*, 855–875.
Keller, T. (1999). Images of the familiar: Individual differences and implicit leadership theories. *The Leadership Quarterly, 10*, 589–607.
Kenny, D. A., & Judd, C. M. (1986). Consequences of violating the independence assumption in analysis of variance. *Psychological Bulletin, 99*, 422–431.
Kerr, S., & Jermier, J. (1978). Substitutes for leadership: Their meaning and measurement. *Organizational Behavior & Human Performance, 22*, 375–403.
Kirkman, B. L., & Rosen, B. (1999). Beyond self-management: Antecedents and consequences of team empowerment. *Academy of Management Journal, 42*(1), 58–74.
Klein, K. J., Dansereau, F., & Hall, R. J. (1994). Levels issues in theory development, data collection, and analysis. *Academy of Management Review, 19*, 195–229.
Klein, K. J., & House, R. J. (1995). On fire: Charismatic leadership and levels of analysis. *The Leadership Quarterly, 6*, 183–198.
Klein, K. J., Ziegert, J. C., Knight, A. P., & Xiao, Y. (2006). Dynamic delegation: Shared, hierarchical, and deindividualized leadership in extreme action teams. *Administrative Science Quarterly, 51*, 590–621.
Kozlowski, S. W. J., & Klein, K. J. (2000). A multilevel approach to theory and research in organizations: Contextual, temporal, and emergent processes. In K. J. Klein & S. W. J. Kozlowski (Eds.), *Multilevel theory, research, and methods in organizations: Foundations, extensions, and new directions* (pp. 3–90). San Francisco: Jossey-Bass.
Krull, J. L., & MacKinnon, D. P. (2001). Multilevel modeling of individual and group level mediated effects. *Multivariate Behavioral Research, 36*, 249–277.
Lam, S. S. K., Hui, C., & Law, K. S. (1999). Organizational citizenship behavior: Comparing perspectives of supervisors and subordinates across four international samples. *Journal of Applied Psychology, 84*, 594–601.
Langeheine, R., & van de Pol, F. (2002). Latent Markov chains. In J. A. Hagenaars & A. L. McCutcheon (Eds.), *Applied latent class analysis* (pp. 304–341). New York: Cambridge University Press.
LeBreton, J. M., & Senter, J. L. (2008). Answers to 20 questions about interrater reliability and interrater agreement. *Organizational Research Methods, 11*, 815–852.
Liden, R. C., Wayne, S. J., & Stilwell, D. (1993). A longitudinal study on the early development of leader-member exchanges. *Journal of Applied Psychology, 78*, 662–674.
Liden, R. C., Wayne, S. J., & Sparrowe, R. T. (2000). An examination of the mediating role of psychological empowerment on the relations between the job, interpersonal relationships, and work outcomes. *Journal of Applied Psychology, 85*, 407–416.
Lim, B., & Ployhart, R. E. (2004). Transformational leadership: Relations to the five-factor model and team performance in typical and maximum contexts. *Journal of Applied Psychology, 89*, 610–621.
Little, R. J., & Rubin, D. B. (2002). *Statistical analysis with missing data* (2nd ed.). New York: John Wiley & Sons.
Lord, R. G., & Brown, D. J. (2004). *Leadership processes and follower self-identity.* Mahwah, NJ: Lawrence Erlbaum.
Lord, R. G., Brown, D. J., Harvey, J. L., & Hall, R. J. (2001). Contextual constraints on prototype generation and their multilevel consequences for leadership perceptions. *The Leadership Quarterly, 12*, 311–338.
Lord, R. G., & Dinh, J. E. (2012). Aggregation processes and levels of analysis as organizational structures for leadership theory. In D. V. Day & J. Antonakis (Eds.), *The nature of leadership* (2nd ed., pp. 29–65). Los Angeles: Sage.
Lord, R. G., & Maher, K. J. (1993). *Leadership and information processing: Linking perceptions and performance.* Boston: Rutledge.
Lüdtke, O., Marsh, H. W., Robitzsch, A., Trautwein, U., Asparouhov, T., and Muthén, B. (2008). The multilevel latent covariate model: A new, more reliable approach to group-level effects in contextual studies. *Psychological Methods, 13*, 203–229.
MacKinnon, D. P., Lockwood, C. M., & Williams, J. (2004). Confidence limits for the indirect effect: Distribution of the product and resampling methods. *Multivariate Behavioral Research, 39*, 99–128.
Manz, C. C., & Sims, H. P., Jr. (1980). Self-management as a substitute for leadership: A social learning theory perspective. *Academy of Management Review, 5*, 361–367.
Markham, S. E. (2010). Leadership, levels of analysis, and déjà vu: Modest proposals for taxonomy and cladistics coupled with replication and visualization. *The Leadership Quarterly, 21*, 1121–1143.
Mathieu, J., Ahearne, M., & Taylor, S. R. (2007). A longitudinal cross-level model of leader and salesperson influences on sales force technology use and performance. *Journal of Applied Psychology, 92*, 528–537.
Mehta, P. D., & Neale, M. C. (2005). People are variables too: Multilevel structural equation modeling. *Psychological Methods, 10*, 259–284.
Mehta, P. D., & West, S. G. (2000). Putting the individual back into individual growth curves. *Psychological Methods, 5*, 23–43.
Meindl, J. R., Ehrlich, S. B., & Dukerich, J. M. (1985). The romance of leadership. *Administrative Science Quarterly, 30*, 78–102.
Mitchell, T. R., & James, L. R. (2001). Building better theory: Time and the specification of when things happen. *Academy of Management Review, 26*, 530–547.

Morgeson, F. P. (2005). The external leadership of self-managing teams: Intervening in the context of novel and disruptive events. *Journal of Applied Psychology, 90*, 497–508.

Morgeson, F. P., & DeRue, D. S. (2006). Event criticality, urgency, and duration: Understanding how events disrupt teams and influence team leader intervention. *The Leadership Quarterly, 17*, 271–287.

Morgeson, F. P., DeRue, D. S., & Karam, E. P. (2010). Leadership in teams: A functional approach to understanding leadership structures and processes. *Journal of Management, 36*, 5–39.

Morgeson, F. P., & Hofmann, D. A. (1999). The structure and function of collective constructs: Implications for multilevel research and theory development. *Academy of Management Review, 24*, 249–265.

Mumford, M. D., Antes, A. L., Caughron, J. J., & Friedrich, T. L. (2008). Charismatic, ideological, and pragmatic leadership: Multi-level influences on emergence and performance. *The Leadership Quarterly, 19*, 144–160.

Mumford, M. D., Zaccaro, S. J., Johnson, J. F., Diana, M., Gilbert, J. A., & Threlfall, K. V. (2000). Patterns of leader characteristics: Implications for performance and development. *The Leadership Quarterly, 11*, 115–133.

Muthén, B. (2001). Second-generation structural equation modeling with a combination of categorical and continuous latent variables: New opportunities for latent class-latent growth modeling. In L. Collins & A. Sayer (Eds.), *New methods for the analysis of change* (pp. 291–322). Washington, DC: American Psychological Association.

Muthén, B. (2004). Latent variable analysis: Growth mixture modeling and related techniques for longitudinal data. In D. Kaplan (Ed.), *Handbook of quantitative methodology for the social sciences* (pp. 345–368). Thousand Oaks, CA: Sage.

Muthén, L. K., and Muthén, B. O. (2007). *Mplus User's Guide. Fifth Edition*. Los Angeles: Muthén & Muthén.

Newman, D. A. (2003). Longitudinal modeling with randomly and systematically missing data: A simulation of ad hoc, maximum likelihood, and multiple imputation techniques. *Organizational Research Methods, 6*, 328–362.

Pearce, C. L., & Sims, H. P., Jr. (2002). Vertical versus shared leadership as predictors of the effectiveness of change management teams: An examination of aversive, directive, transactional, transformational, and empowering leader behaviors. *Group Dynamics: Theory, Research, and Practice, 6*, 172–197.

Pituch, K. A., Stapleton, L. M., & Kang, J. Y. (2006). A comparison of single sample and bootstrap methods to assess mediation in cluster randomized trials. *Multivariate Behavioral Research, 41*, 367–400.

Ployhart, R. E., & Vandenberg, R. J. (2010). Longitudinal research: The theory, design, and analysis of change. *Journal of Management, 36*, 94–120.

Podsakoff, P. M., MacKenzie, S. B., & Bommer, W. H. (1996). Meta-analysis of the relationships between Kerr and Jermier's substitutes for leadership and employee job attitudes, role perceptions, and performance. *Journal of Applied Psychology, 81*, 380–399.

Podsakoff, P. M., MacKenzie, S. B., Moorman, R. H., & Fetter, R. (1990). Transformational leader behaviors and their effects on followers' trust in leader, satisfaction, and organizational citizenship behaviors. *The Leadership Quarterly, 1*, 107–142.

Preacher, K. J., Zyphur, M. J., & Zhang, Z. (2010). A general multilevel SEM framework for assessing multilevel mediation. *Psychological Methods, 15*, 209–233.

Raudenbush, S. W. (2001). Comparing personal trajectories and drawing causal inferences from longitudinal data. *Annual Review of Psychology, 52*, 501–525.

Resick, C. J., Whitman, D. S., Weingarden, S. M., & Hiller, N. J. (2009). The bright-side and dark-side of CEO personality: Examining core self-evaluations, narcissism, transformational leadership, and strategic influence. *Journal of Applied Psychology, 94*, 1365–1381.

Robinson, W. S. (1950). Ecological correlations and the behavior of individuals. *American Sociological Review, 15*, 351–357.

Rousseau, D. M. (1985). Issues of level in organizational research: Multi-level and cross-level perspectives. *Research in Organizational Behavior, 7*, 1–37.

Rovine, M. J., & Molenaar, P. C. (2000). A structural modeling approach to a multilevel random coefficients model. *Multivariate Behavioral Research, 35*, 51–88.

Schriesheim, C. A., Cogliser, C. C., & Neider, L. L. (1995). Is it "trustworthy"? A multiple-levels-of-analysis reexamination of an Ohio state leadership study, with implications for future research. *The Leadership Quarterly, 6*, 111–145.

Shadish, W. R., Cook, T. D., & Campbell, D. T. (2001). *Experimental and quasi-experimental designs for generalized causal inference* (pp. 64–102). Boston: Houghton Mifflin Company.

Sin, H., Nahrgang, J. D., & Morgeson, F. P. (2009). Understanding why they don't see eye to eye: An examination of leader-member exchange (LMX) agreement. *Journal of Applied Psychology, 94*, 1048–1057.

Snijders, T.A.B., & Bosker, R. J. (1999). *Multilevel analysis: An introduction to basic and advanced multilevel modeling*. London: Sage.

Sosik, J. J., Avolio B. J., & Jung, D. I. (2002). Beneath the mask: Examining the relationship of self-presentation attributes and impression management to charismatic leadership. *The Leadership Quarterly, 13*, 217–242.

Sparrowe, R. T., & Liden, R. C. (1997). Process and structure in leader-member exchange. *Academy of Management Review, 22*, 522–552.

Stogdill, R. M., & Coons, A. E. (1957). *Leader behavior: Its dispersion and measurement*. Columbus: Ohio State University Press for Bureau of Business Research.

Tepper, B. J. (2000). Consequences of abusive supervision. *Academy of Management Journal, 43*, 178–190.

Tesluk, P. E., & Mathieu, J. E. (1999). Overcoming roadblocks to effectiveness: Incorporating management of performance barriers into models of work group effectiveness. *Journal of Applied Psychology, 84*, 200–217.

Tosi, H. L., Misangyi, V. F., Fanelli, A., Waldman, D. A., & Yammarino, F. J. (2004). CEO charisma, compensation, and firm performance. *The Leadership Quarterly, 15*, 405–420.

Tsui, A. S., & O'Reilly, C. A., III. (1989). Beyond simple demographic effects: The importance of relationship demography in supervisor-subordinate dyads. *Academy of Management Journal, 32*, 402–423.

Venkataramani, V., Green, S. G., & Schleicher, D. J. (2010). Well-connected leaders: The impact of leaders' social network ties on LMX and members' work attitudes. *Journal of Applied Psychology, 95*, 1071–1084.

Vroom, V. H., & Jago, A. G. (1988). *The new leadership: Managing participation in organizations*. Englewood Cliffs, NJ: Prentice Hall.

Vroom, V. H., & Jago, A. G. (2007). The role of the situation in leadership. *American Psychologist, 62*, 17–24.

Vroom, V. H., & Yetton, P. W. (1973). *Leadership and decision making*. Pittsburgh, PA: University of Pittsburgh Press.

Wang, M., & Bodner, T. E. (2007). Growth mixture modeling: Identifying and predicting unobserved subpopulations with longitudinal data. *Organizational Research Methods, 10*, 635–656.

Wang, M., & Chan, D. (2011). Mixture latent Markov modeling: Identifying and predicting unobserved heterogeneity in longitudinal qualitative status change. *Organizational Research Methods, 14*, 411–431.

Wang, M., & Hanges, P. J. (2011). Latent class procedures: Applications to organizational research. *Organizational Research Methods, 14*, 24–31.

Watson, D., Hubbard, B., & Wiese, D. (2000). Self-other agreement in personality and affectivity: The role of acquaintanceship, trait visibility, and assumed similarity. *Journal of Personality and Social Psychology, 78*, 546–558.

Wayne, S. J., Shore, L. M., & Linden, R. C. (1997). Perceived organizational support and leader-member exchange: A social exchange perspective. *Academy of Management Journal, 40*, 82–111.

Wu, J. B., Tsui, A. S., & Kinicki, A. J. (2010). Consequences of differentiated leadership in groups. *Academy of Management Journal, 53*, 90–106.

Yammarino, F. J., & Dansereau, F. (2008). Multi-level nature of and multi-level approaches to leadership. *The Leadership Quarterly, 19*, 135–141.

Yammarino, F. J., & Dansereau, F. (2011). Multi-level issues in evolutionary theory, organization science, and leadership. *The Leadership Quarterly, 22*, 1042–1057.

Yammarino, F. J., Dionne, S. D., Chun, J. U., & Dansereau, F. (2005). Leadership and levels of analysis: A state-of-the-science review. *The Leadership Quarterly, 16*, 879–919.

Yukl, G. A. (1998). *Leadership in organizations*. Englewood Cliffs, NJ: Prentice Hall.

Yukl, G. A., & Falbe, C. M. (1990). Influence tactics in upward, downward, and lateral influence attempts. *Journal of Applied Psychology, 75*, 132–140.

Zaccaro, S. J., & Klimoski, R. J. (2001). *The nature of organizational leadership*. New York: John Wiley & Sons.

Zaccaro, S. J., Rittman, A. L., & Marks, M. A. (2001). Team leadership. *The Leadership Quarterly, 12*, 451–483.

Zhang, Z., & Peterson, S. J. (2011). Advice networks in teams: The role of transformational leadership and members' core self-evaluations. *Journal of Applied Psychology, 96*, 1004–1017.

Zhang, Z., Wang, M., & Shi, J. (2012). Leader-follower congruence in proactive personality and work outcomes: The mediating role of LMX. *Academy of Management Journal, 55*, 111–130.

Zhou, L., Wang, M., Chen, G., & Shi, J. (2012). Supervisors' upward exchange relationships and subordinates' outcomes: Testing the multilevel mediation role of empowerment. *Journal of Applied Psychology, 97*, 668–680.

Zohar, D., & Luria, G. (2005). A multilevel model of safety climate: Cross-level relationships between organizational and group-level climates. *Journal of Applied Psychology, 90*, 616–628.

CHAPTER 9

Evaluation Methods

Emily R. Hoole *and* Jennifer W. Martineau

Abstract

The challenge of evaluating the impact of leadership development is significant, and practitioners and researchers alike attempt to address this challenge through the use of multiple approaches and methods. This chapter explores existing frameworks for evaluating leadership development and proposes a more comprehensive framework. It will then describe a variety of methods that can be used to effectively evaluate leadership development at multiple levels in alignment with this framework.

Key Words: Evaluation, leadership development, multiple methods, individual, group, team, organizational, societal, impact

Introduction

While there are disagreements in the field about what leadership is and how to best develop it, one idea that most practitioners and researchers agree on is that we need to better understand how to develop leadership and how to understand the impact of leadership development. We approach this challenge using a variety of models, frameworks, and methodologies—some of which are inappropriately used given the intent of the development initiative and/or the anticipated outcomes.

One of the major fallacies, however, is that we can effectively measure change and demonstrate impact from leadership development solely through using pre- and post-measures of change. Evaluation is not just about pre-post measurement, however. It tells a story that includes the context in which leadership development is taking place, the values and beliefs inherent in leaders and the people and entities surrounding them, as well as the changes that are occurring (and why). In addition to telling the story, evaluation must also help to create the story. Evaluation is not only used to indicate success, failure, or growth—it is used to actually enable the leadership development efforts to be most effective. In other words, it must be integrated with leadership development from the needs assessment and design phases. Used effectively, evaluation can both map *and* track the story.

In this chapter, we will explore the similarities and differences between research and evaluation. We will present existing frameworks for evaluating leadership development, and propose a more comprehensive framework. We will then describe a variety of methods that can be used to effectively evaluate leadership development at multiple levels aligned with this framework.

Evaluation of leadership development faces a challenge in that it does not often stand up to the methodological rigor required for publication in top-tier research journals. Some of this can be addressed by the use of more rigorous methods and designs, yet the problem will persist because there is resistance in organizations to using nontreatment designs such as control groups. The proportion of evaluation studies accepted for publication are unlikely to grow significantly unless organizations are more interested in using research designs in evaluation. Thus, our intent with this chapter is to use a more comprehensive framework for evaluating leadership development and illustrate the methods that can be used at various levels in this framework so that we can extend both the quality and quantity of leadership development evaluation used in practice so that our field, as a whole, can continue to improve its effectiveness.

First, we will review some current areas of confusion with regard to evaluation of leadership and organizational development. These areas of confusion are opportunities for advancement in the field if clarity can be attained. Later in the chapter we will provide our own thinking regarding how to address a troubling issue in the field: the lack of clear linkage and measurement between the different levels of the targets and levels of impact.

Target of the Intervention versus Outcomes Desired

A significant challenge for the evaluation of the impact of leadership and organizational interventions is the implicit assumption made about the link from individual to organizational outcomes. According to Collins and Holton (2004), "Organizations believe improving knowledge and skills of individual employees automatically enhances the organizations' effectiveness" (p. 218). While this may be the case, the lack of clear models identifying the direct and indirect ways improved leadership skills and behaviors at the individual level translates into group or organizational-level outcomes hampers our ability to definitively answer this question. The challenge is further compounded when leadership development programs are implemented with nebulous outcomes that make the linkage to other levels of outcomes tenuous at best (Craig & Hannum, 2007).

So the first element in addressing this challenge is in understanding the difference that exists between the target of the intervention (most often the individual) and the type and level of impact desired. A scan of the field in 2002 (Kellogg) found organizational effects frequently mentioned as desired outcomes, regardless of whether the program was truly designed to achieve such a goal. The scan provided a caution to programs that lay claim to organizational impact based on feedback from individual participants, arguing that organizational-level claims require corroborating data from other sources, as well as a longitudinal perspective.

The second element to address is the difficulty of evaluating impact when the target of the intervention and the outcomes are at different levels. Many models assume a clear and direct causal chain in training that simply does not exist. As Brinkerhoff & Mooney (2010) write, "Training alone does not produce results" (p. 129). Since so few formal evaluations of interventions are conducted or published, the many moderating and mediating factors are not well known, measured, or tested. Brinkerhoff's Success Case Method provides a viable means of examining the transfer issues that occur at the individual level and impact behavior change and application, but the list of possible moderators and mediators grows as impact is desired at higher levels. A bright spot is in the field of education, which has developed a model of principal leadership that takes into account the many variables by which principals influence student performance in the classroom. This model has determined the indirect effect of leadership, which accounts for a quarter of the total schools effects (explaining 10–20 percent of the variance in student achievement) (Leithwood, Louis, Anderson, & Walstrom, 2004).

DeChurch, Hiller, Murase, Doty, and Salas (2010) argue strenuously for more research on the ways in which leadership impacts team and unit-level outcomes, and the way specific leadership theories and constructs affect bottom-up emergent constructs at multiple levels. This clearly indicates that neither research nor evaluation has clear models or mechanisms by which leaders at the individual or collective level impact performance of other levels through these emergent or indirect means.

In areas where leadership is considered critical and investments in development are high, the "lack of an evaluation model that adequately measures the effect of the interventions on the performance of the organization" is a serious detriment for all researchers, evaluators, and practitioners (Collins & Holtin, 2004, pp. 218–219). A serious question to consider is whether the inability to find impact at the group, organization, or community level is a failure of measurement or of the intervention. Day (2000) argues against the common practice of implementing interventions without linkage to current organizational initiatives and strategic focus and which lack accountability and evaluation. If interventions fail because they have no connection to the reality within an organization (Sirianni & Frey, 2001), or are not planned properly to have impact at the organizational level (Mabey 2002; Mabey & Thomson, 2000), evaluation then has a key role to play in clarifying these areas of confusion.

Evaluation and Research

If evaluation has a role in helping organizations and the field understand the linkages between interventions and outcomes, what then is the difference between evaluation and research? In this section we attempt to articulate as Mathison (2008) put it, "what is distinct about evaluation?" Much of the ongoing discussion is fueled by the rise of evaluation as a field and profession, as well as the desire to articulate unique features and requirements for practice in the field.

A clear starting point in distinguishing between evaluation and research is the purpose. Leaders in the field point to three main functions of evaluation: accountability, judgment of merit and worth, and decision making. Mark, Henry, and Julnes (2000) approach the issue through the lens of accountability for social programs and articulate the purpose of evaluation to review the merit of programs and value to society. Evaluation also serves the purpose of improving an organization and its services, ensuring that a program complies with mandates, and to build knowledge and expertise for future programs. Implicit in Mark, Henry and Jules's viewpoint on evaluation purpose is the perspective of Michael Scriven (1967) who strongly contends that placing a value on data—determining merit and worth—is the quintessential role of the evaluator. The third area of focus has been on use of evaluation data for decision making. Beyond making a determination of merit or worth and establishing accountability, this aspect is focused in making use of evaluation data and results for program or organizational changes (Alkin & Christie, 2004).

Narrowing our discussion to the field of training and development, which deals most specifically with leadership and organizations, evaluation is considered an important component of the instructional design process but also serves the same purposes as listed above. Organizations investing in training and development at the individual, team, and group level desire a level of accountability for funds invested and an understanding of the merit and worth of such efforts. The need for making data-based decisions regarding changes, improvements, and continuation of interventions are also strong drivers for evaluation in this space. Evaluators continue to call for new models for evaluation of training and development and more and better evaluation given the pressure on HRD to show value to the organization (Holton, 1996; Martineau & Patterson, 2010).

A number of evaluation theorists have also argued the competencies necessary to be a skilled evaluator differ from those needed for social science research. For Scriven (Coffman, 2003–2004) these include the ability to search for side effects; deal with controversial values and issues; and most important, the ability to synthesize evaluative and factual conclusions. Stevahn, King, Ghere, and Minnema (2005) embarked on an ambitious project to establish the essential competencies for program evaluators. What emerges from their work is that what differentiates an evaluator from a researcher is the ability to engage in situational analysis. For both Scriven and Stevah et al., interpersonal competencies, as they relate to working with stakeholders, are much more important in an evaluation context than in a research context.

Some additional areas of distinction between research and evaluation are audience, theory, and questions. Russ-Eft and Preskill (2009) list audience as one of their key differentiators between evaluation and research, recognizing the different reasons that drive evaluation and research ultimately lead to different questions, needs, and communication (p. 8). Audiences for evaluation may be small (the staff of a single program) or very broad (legislators and policy makers). Within an organizational context, the audience may range from the facilitator of a program to the company's board of directors, depending upon the purpose of evaluation. But the primary focus is on identifying, balancing, and meeting the needs of the stakeholders. Researchers may have a less-defined audience, often attempting to influence the field or policy and practice, with much greater freedom in research questions, designs, and reporting (Mathison, 2008).

In evaluation the theory is most often that of the program, which may have a basis in social science research but is unique to a specific context. For example, the intervention may be based upon a specific approach (leader development–individual vs. leadership development–collective, Day, 2000), but the program theory and desired outcomes will potentially be unique for all programs. A program theory provides the same boundaries and playing field that LMX theory, for example, does for research studies in the leadership space. Research studies are based upon social science theories and focus on extension of theory, testing of theory, or development of new theories not tied to a specific program or context. Therefore, evaluation can be said to be field dependent rather than theory dependent (Levin-Rozalis, 2003).

Evaluation and research also differ in the types of questions that are asked. Asking whether a program met the needs of participants and/or the organization is a value judgment and evaluative in nature—not research. Research may ask, "How does content from a program translate into behavior changes which can be transferred to a work context?" This question will be of interest to evaluators as they work to design and improve programs, but the question is not evaluative in nature. When making determinations of merit or worth, evaluation questions need to go beyond what traditional research methods can tell us. "These are questions about feasibility, practicability, needs, costs, intended and unintended outcomes, ethics, and justifiability" (Mathison, 2008, p. 186). For example, evaluators may ask for whom was the impact the greatest and why, and if the investment in the development intervention was worth the cost.

The differences in purpose and questions have resulted in the development of a variety of frameworks and approaches to guide evaluators in effective practice. Frameworks ensure that studies generate findings of sufficient rigor and validity to make judgments. Because evaluation is judged not only by its accuracy, but also by its propriety, utility, and feasibility (Yarbrough, Shulha, Hopson, & Caruthers, 2011), evaluation frameworks and approaches provide a broad range of perspectives on effective evaluation in general, and detailed guidance regarding specific types of evaluation or program areas. We provide an overview and critique of frameworks and approaches specific to the evaluation of leadership development in the next section of the chapter.

Despite the differences above, evaluation and social science research also share many similarities. In general practice, the methods used in evaluation and applied social science research are identical, and issues of rigor, reliability, and validity apply equally to both. Both fields have standards that guide ethical practice and establish acceptable work in the field with crossover between the two, such as the Standards for Educational and Psychological Testing. While the similarities outnumber the differences, keeping the differences in perspective is essential in practice so that the appropriate outcomes are achieved.

Best Practices in Evaluation of Leadership Development

The need to generate results of sufficient accuracy, reliability, and validity in the leadership and organizational field has fueled the development of best practices for the evaluation of development interventions. These best practices can be directly tied to standards in the field requiring that evaluation data support valid interpretations based on sound designs and analysis (Yarbrough, Shulha, Hopson, & Caruthers, 2011). While striving for a high level of rigor to generate confidence in results (Wells, 2008), evaluation must also balance respect for people and the welfare of society as a whole in determining what constitutes credible evidence (Rollis, 2009). Current standard practice in evaluation of training and development uses self-report data of quality, effectiveness, and impact compromises the utility of such evaluation data (Lockheed, 2009). What is needed are evaluations using the following best practices balanced with contextual understanding of "what works" in certain situations or populations so that multicultural validity or the "accuracy and trustworthiness of understandings, actions and consequences across multiple, intersecting dimensions of cultural diversity" (Kirkhart, 2010) can be achieved.

MULTISOURCE

The first best practice for which we advocate is the use of multiple sources of data. Studies have clearly indicated that perceptual data regarding behavior is best measured from multiple perspectives. Taylor, Russ-Eft, and Taylor (2009) suggest studies should use supervisor and direct report ratings because these are distinct sources of information when compared with self-report ratings. We and many others (Baldwin & Ford, 1988; Burke & Hutchins, 2007; Hoole & Martineau, 2010) have also argued for multisource data for effective measurement of leadership development outcomes.

MULTIMETHOD

Another best practice for increasing the rigor of evaluation is the use of multiple methods. Multiple methods to evaluate the effectiveness of leadership are recommended to increase validity (Leskiw & Singh, 2007). Multiple methods also create a fuller picture of program impact (Kellogg, 2002), allow for triangulation of results (Black & Earnest, 2009), and are necessary for assessing impact at various levels (Hannum, 2004).

LONGITUDINAL

Because individual and organizational interventions are meant to have both immediate and long-lasting impact at various levels, longitudinal research designs are most appropriate for measuring and documenting the change associated with these interventions. Longitudinal research is defined as having at least three waves of data collection of a substantive construct (Ployhart & Vandenberg, 2010). Multiple, accurate measurement of changes over time is essential for understanding what works, for whom, and under what conditions. Rigorous evaluation should focus on measuring the developmental trajectories of individuals (Day & Sin, 2011), and the sustainability of such changes at multiple levels (Gentry & Martineau, 2010).

MEASUREMENT

This brings us to the area of measurement. Data collection methods used in evaluation, from instruments to interviews to observations, need to yield reliable and valid data. If "validity is the heart of good evaluation" (Kirkhart, 2010), then effective measurement is the foundation. Best practice would encourage researchers and evaluators alike to investigate the psychometric properties of assessments and surveys used, and to utilize other recognized methods to investigate the reliability and validity of any qualitative data gathered.

ISOLATION

The most difficult practice to achieve in evaluation is the implementation of methods to isolate the impact of the development. Use of control or comparison group, delayed treatment, trend analysis, and regression discontinuity designs are relatively rare in practice (Lockheed, 2009). Yet increased use of isolation techniques, such as experimental or quasi-experimental designs, not only builds a stronger evidence base for individual or organizational interventions, it is also a means to start addressing the challenge of linking targets of interventions to multiple levels of impact.

In conclusion, applying these best practices to the conduct of evaluation of leadership development is critical to effective evaluation. With these aspects clarified, we now turn to the frameworks used in evaluation of leadership development.

Frameworks for Designing Evaluation

In this section, we provide an overview of frameworks used for designing evaluation. This is important because deciding which methods to use for the evaluation will depend on the overall intent and purpose of the evaluation. Selecting or designing methods without first identifying the guiding framework will result in an evaluation plan that is a hodge-podge of data collection techniques that may or may not produce the data needed to answer the key evaluation questions identified.

A point of clarity for the reader: The Center for Creative Leadership (CCL) defines leadership from the perspective of three outcomes: *Direction* (widespread agreement in a collective on overall goals, aims, and mission); *Alignment* (the organization and coordination of knowledge and work in a collective); and *Commitment* (the willingness of members of a collective to subsume their own interests and benefits within those of the collective). *Leadership* is the production of direction, alignment, and commitment. *Leadership development* is the expansion of a collective's capacity to produce direction, alignment, and commitment (Drath et al., 2008). When we write about the development (and subsequently the evaluation) of leadership, we are intentional about the multiple levels at which leadership is developed and demonstrated. Therefore, some of the frameworks we highlight below do not provide adequate methodologies or processes, or even mindset, to enable the full evaluation of leadership development as defined by CCL.

Current Leadership Development Evaluation Frameworks

In research and evaluation fields, professionals test and work within the structure of models or frameworks. The American Heritage Dictionary (2000, 2009.) defines models as *schematic descriptions or representations of something, especially a system or phenomenon that accounts for its properties and is used to study its characteristics* and frameworks as *a set of assumptions, concepts, values, and practices that constitute a way of viewing reality.* The reality of leadership development evaluation is that a program or intervention may never occur in exactly the same way twice because creating a controlled environment where the participants are selected for certain characteristics, exposed to the exact same treatment, and closely observed for their behaviors is rare. Rather, evaluation of leadership development takes place in a broader context of change and transformation, and the truth is that using the same objectives and design with two different groups may result in significantly different "treatment" based entirely on the combination of individuals involved and the context in which they are leading.

Therefore, the use of frameworks for designing evaluation is appropriate because we are not testing a specific model (which has its own methods associated) but we are attempting to understand the process and outcomes related to the development of leadership capability in distinct individuals, groups, organizations, and other entities. This section will overview some of the more frequently used frameworks in the evaluation of leadership development.

KIRKPATRICK'S FOUR-LEVEL EVALUATION MODEL

One of the most widely used frameworks was created by Donald Kirkpatrick (1959 a, b; 1960 a, b) when he observed that most of the outcomes of training and development could be described as reactions, learning, behaviors, and results. Kirkpatrick categorized these types of outcomes as Level 1 (Reactions), Level 2 (Learning), Level 3 (Behaviors), and Level 4 (Results). Level 1 (Reactions) captures outcomes related to how people think and feel about the training. Although Level 1 of this framework has been historically misused as a measure of general reactions to the program, it is more broadly defined as both general reactions as well as how relevant the training is to the participants' work.

Level 2 (Learning) is most rigorously used as a cognitive measure of whether participants have built knowledge about specific models, policies, and frameworks included in the training. For example, participants of leadership development may be expected to learn their organization's stated values so that they can role model those values for their employees. Level 2 outcomes are focused on whether participants have learned and remembered those values.

Level 3 (Behaviors) outcomes include whether the participants' behaviors and individual performance have improved since the training. Appropriate use of Level 3 measurement will take place in the context of the work—after the participant has returned to the workplace and is performing their work as leaders. It focuses on whether they are using the new skills on the job. In the case of values, Level 3 would examine whether participants are demonstrating their organization's values in their day-to-day performance, and how effective they are at doing so.

Finally, Level 4 (Results) outcome measurement is focused on whether the organization is achieving the results intended from the training. If part of the intent of a training program was to improve the use of an organization's values in the workplace, and if Level 3 measures are indicating that leaders are more effectively demonstrating those values, Level 4 measures would attempt to assess the impact of improved individual performance on organizational indicators such as retention rate of employees or customer satisfaction.

Although Kirkpatrick intended his model to be a set of categories of possible outcomes (i.e., a framework), researchers and evaluators have misinterpreted it as a model. As a result, they have designed studies testing the predictive nature of each of the levels toward the next level, as if the levels form a hierarchy or a linear set of outcomes. In other words, the interpretation is that positive reactions will produce positive learning, that positive learning produces positive behaviors, and that positive behaviors produce positive results at the organizational level. However, research studies have demonstrated that it is actually possible for positive results to be produced in the absence of measurable behavior change. For example, Martineau (1995) found that job performance following training was influenced by both individual and situational characteristics such as achievement motivation and the presence of a continuous learning culture, more strongly than by use of the behavior itself during the training program.

How prevalent is Kirkpatrick's model? A review by Hilbert, Preskill, and Russ-Eft (1997) shows that 44 of 57 journal articles focused on training evaluation included Kirkpatrick's model. Only 13 articles used a model other than Kirkpatrick's.

SWANSON & SLEEZER TRAINING EFFECTIVENESS EVALUATION SYSTEM

The Training Effectiveness Evaluation System (TEE) (Swanson & Sleezer, 1987) is built off of the Kirkpatrick model. The special focus of this model is on three evaluation processes: creating a training effectiveness evaluation plan, developing tools for measuring training effectiveness, and compiling an evaluation report. Like Kirkpatrick's model, it also focuses on four levels of outcomes. More specifically, however, the TEE system requires a minimum of four tools to be used in evaluating training: two satisfaction measures, one learning measure, and one performance measure. This model works by calculating scores from each tool before creating the evaluation report, and requires the comparison of scores on a specific performance goal both before and after training.

PHILLIPS' RETURN ON INVESTMENT MODEL

After two decades of use of Kirkpatrick's four-level framework, Phillips extended the use of these levels by refining Level 4 and adding Level 5 (Phillips, 1983). Beginning in the early 1970s,

Phillips created a more standardized and rigorous methodology for the measurement of each of the five levels and used cost/benefit analysis formulas to identify the financial return gained from training programs. Today, the ROI (return on investment) methodology is widely used in training and development evaluations in general (Phillips & Phillips, 2008). Although its utilization in the leadership development field is more limited, our field is gradually expanding the use of this framework in our evaluation studies. Indeed, Phillips and Schmidt (2004) applied this methodology to leadership development by creating a focused "scorecard" approach to evaluating leadership development using the ROI methodology.

The ROI methodology uses a series of steps that are crucial to obtaining as accurate as possible a measure of the return on investment for a given program. Some of these steps are the isolation of program effects, conversion of data to financial figures, documentation of intangible benefits (data that cannot be converted to financials), identification of program costs, and finally the calculation of return on investment. The ultimate outcome is represented as a percentage (e.g., 10 percent ROI, 355 percent ROI), and enables comparison of program value across different types of programs such as leadership development versus customer service training.

RETURN ON DEVELOPMENT INVESTMENT

Like Phillips's ROI methodology, the Return on Development Investment (RODI; Avolio, Avey, & Quisenberry, 2010) methodology is intended to predict the financial return of organizations' investments in leadership development. The RODI is based on Cascio and Boudreau's (2008) methodology, which allows for investigation of leadership development impact that occurs over multiple points in time, rather than in a prescribed period of time.

The RODI methodology uses a combination of computations including fully loaded costs and estimates of impact. Using effect sizes, confidence intervals, estimated leader salary levels, program costs, and other data from their meta-analysis (Avolio, Hannah, Reichard, Chan, & Walumbwa, 2009), Avolio and his colleagues estimated the financial return from a range of leadership development interventions.

Where Phillips's ROI methodology can be used either to predict the anticipated return on investment of a program being planned and to determine the return of a program by examining the actual data coming from that program, the RODI methodology is intended primarily as a predictive tool that organizations can use to estimate the anticipated return from their investment on leadership development before investing in a given program or initiative.

EVALULEAD

The EvaluLead framework (Grove, Kibel, & Haas, 2005) was created as a way of moving to a more open-systems approach to evaluation of leadership development programs. Sponsored by the Population Leadership Program of the Public Health Institute, the framework emerged through the collaborative work of the Leadership Evaluation Advisory Group and was field tested by a variety of programs with the support of the W. K. Kellogg Foundation and the United States Agency for International Development (USAID). The purpose behind EvaluLead was to provide the framing and methodology to capture a wider variety of outcomes that can emerge from leadership development, especially when the ultimate goal of a program is in the changes that occur to a community or population served by the individuals who participate in leadership development.

The EvaluLead framework is intended to identify the outcomes of leadership development programs at multiple levels and in the context in which the program is taking place. Context is central to this framework—it assumes that the context within which a program is taking place will influence both the program and the outcomes themselves, as well as be influenced by the program and the outcomes. The model provides evidence of the outcomes that are used to justify leadership development programs such as creating improved health outcomes in communities or greater leadership capacity in organizations. It identifies outcomes at the individual, organizational, and societal/community levels as well as outcomes considered "evidential" or more tangible (such as improved job-related skills/performance, increased organizational outputs, or environmental improvements) and those that are "evocative" or less tangible (such as new personal insights, shift in organizational values, or shift in community norms).

LOGIC MODELING/THEORIES OF CHANGE

Logic models (Bickman, 1987) have been used in program planning and evaluation since the 1980s. These models included the inputs, processes, outputs, and outcomes of a given program. Theory of

Change models have come into use more recently, in the mid 1990s. Weiss (1995) described theories of change as frameworks created by both designers and key stakeholders to map the assumptions of why various program elements would create specific outcomes.

The terminology of "logic models" and "theory of change models" are often used interchangeably but can take different forms. A valuable tool for understanding the similarities and differences can be found in the W. K. Kellogg Foundation's *Logic Model Development Guide* (2003). This guide delineates the key components, including the theory of change that influenced the design of an evaluation, the activities that comprise the program being evaluated, and the outcomes anticipated from the program. Gutiérrez and Tasse (2007) define a theory of change as including (1) the underlying assumptions about how and why the program will achieve its anticipated results, (2) the identification of anticipated outcomes over time, and (3) the connections between strategies and outcomes.

SUCCESS CASE METHOD

The Success Case Method (SCM; Brinkerhoff, 2003) was created as a way of using the traditional practice of storytelling to evaluate the business outcomes of training. Like the EvaluLead framework, SCM acknowledges that development is complex and is affected by many factors beyond the program and the participants only. It begins by collecting data through surveys from a broad representation of people involved in a leadership development initiative and looking through these data for cases where success has resulted. By using a structured process, SCM creates a comprehensive picture of the impact of a program through four essential questions:

1. What is really happening?
2. What results, if any, is the program helping to produce?
3. What is the value of the results?
4. How could the initiative be improved?

The SCM involves surveys and interviews. Both are customized in the context of the initiative being evaluated and the organization sponsoring the initiative. The work to design the evaluation is done in collaboration with the initiative's key stakeholders, and data from the initial surveys are analyzed with the stakeholders to determine the best subset of promising success cases for the interviews. Through a two-phase interview process, successful cases are vetted and selected for inclusion in the full study. The result is a story of impact that illustrates not only *what* impact occurred at both individual and organizational levels, but *why* it occurred. The latter enables the organization to refine the initiative in ways that create even greater opportunities for success.

Proposed Leadership Development Evaluation Framework: SOGI

The richness of existing frameworks, models, and approaches for evaluating leadership development provides evaluators and others with a variety of ways of thinking about how to document and measure what is occurring with a leadership development program or initiative. Yet for us, none of these is quite comprehensive enough to provide an overarching framework that addresses multiple purposes for leadership development, outcomes ranging from individual to societal levels, and recommended methods that align with the myriad of purposes and outcomes possible.

We begin by rethinking the source of leadership—moving from only thinking of leadership capability as located within individuals, to also thinking of it within a much larger domain—as people creating shared direction, alignment, and commitment (DAC) in all sorts of interesting and potentially generative ways. In our own research and practice over the last 20 years, this has been a liberating idea, allowing our constituencies and ourselves to see and enact new possibilities for developing more collaborative, connected, adaptive, and vital—interdependent—forms of leadership.

Thus, we are recommending a higher-order way of thinking about evaluating leadership development. This framework, which we call SOGI (pronounced *so' ji*), represents the full spectrum of human social engagement, simplified as four levels: society, organizational, group, and individual. The *societal* level includes relationships among organizations and their value webs, entire fields and industries, regional and demographic cultures, and global society (Ospina & Foldy, 2010; Quinn & Van Velsor, 2010). The *organizational* level includes multipart organizations and communities. The *group* level includes smaller subcollectives such as divisions, functions, teams, small businesses, work groups, and task forces. The *individual* level includes the personal and interpersonal domain, including the qualities of individual leaders, followers, and members.

In our experience evaluating leadership development initiatives, we have seen firsthand the benefit of "designing with the end in mind"—that is, including evaluation thinking from the initial needs assessment phases so that the ultimate leadership development program or initiative is designed in a way that is most likely to result in the desired outcomes at multiple levels. Too often, stakeholders have a preconceived notion of using traditional (i.e., classroom-based, individually focused) leadership development with the intent of creating organizational level outcomes. By designing leadership development through the lens of evaluation, an initiative intended to create behavior change in a certain population of leaders will be more effective at doing so, and an initiative intended to result in organizational culture transformation will be designed much differently than one intended to help a single team be more effective in their work together.

The SOGI framework aligns with the contemporary view by scholars that calls for awareness of the multiple social levels at which leadership functions (Hannum, Martineau, & Reinelt, 2007; Wilber, 2000; Yammarino & Dansereau, 2008). A common trap is to define one level solely in terms of another level, for example, by viewing the organizational level as simply the sum of individual leaders, or only as the activity of the senior leader group. However, when leadership development is designed with the end in mind, it is more likely that the resulting design will include approaches and interventions that produce the intended level of outcome because they are, indeed, interventions targeted at the right level to produce those outcomes.

Another important feature of the SOGI concept is that we understand the levels to be intertwined and overlapping. SOGI enables the integration of these levels rather than separating them into four distinct categories. SOGI represents the entire spectrum of social activity from the I to the S. One level shades into the next, and all levels can be identified as vital in any scenario that requires direction, alignment, and commitment. SOGI helps us embrace the entire domain of leadership and its impact, including, yet going beyond, the individual leader.

SOGI is framed in Figure 9.1. In the next section, we will describe methods that can be used to evaluate leadership development at each level. As we do so, the reader will understand that methods can be used for multiple levels and purposes, but that there are categories of methods that are best for evaluating certain types of outcomes.

Evaluation Methods

Individual Methods

We begin with the evaluation methods appropriate for measuring the individual level of outcomes.

SURVEYS

Surveys are one of the most frequently used methods for evaluating leadership development. In their meta-analyses, Ely, Boyce, Nelson, Zaccaro, Hernez-Broome, & Whyman (2010) and DeMeuse et al. (2009) found that most studies they examined used surveys as either the main evaluation method or one of a small number of methods used.

Developing surveys that yield reliable, valid data can be time consuming to develop, but they can be relatively inexpensive to administer. They allow for responses from a large sample of people and can collect easily analyzed quantitative data. They allow for anonymity or confidentiality of responses, are useful when respondents are geographically dispersed, allow respondents to respond on their own time, and require that all respondents answer the same set of questions. On the minus side, they don't allow for changes to or clarification of questions. Intuition can be misleading when developing a survey. Even seemingly simple choices, such as what response options to use, can have an unintended impact on results. If you plan to develop your own survey and do not have training in survey development, it is wise to seek advice from measurement or psychometric publications or from measurement professionals.

Surveys are used in a variety of ways depending on the level and type of outcome being measured. In this section we will illustrate various types of surveys and the reason for using each.

Participant Expectation Surveys

One purpose of surveys is to gather information about *participant expectations* before an initiative. This is a useful way to help participants understand the initiative in which they are participating. Information from an expectations survey provides initiative designers and trainers information about whether or not participant expectations differ from initiative objectives and they can also compare objectives with what participants perceive as benefits (if the survey asks about perceived benefits or relevance). The use of expectation surveys can increase the potential for the initiative to accomplish its intended outcomes by enabling designers, sponsors, and facilitators to shape participants' expectations as well as customize the design in response to their expectations.

	Outcomes that Occur *Within* each Level INSIDE	Outcomes Created by Development at Each Level OUT	Evaluation Methods for Measuring Impact at each Level
Societal (capabilities)	• Collaboration • DAC • Culture • Values • Execution • Growth mentality • Responsiveness • Dialogue • Shared responsibility • Social capital	• Participation/engagement • Policies • Environmental improvement • Health, etc. • Alleviation of poverty/ economic growth • Diversity • Quality of life • Peace	• Community-wide surveys (social capital) • Some SNA • Photovoice • Q-sort • Secondary data analysis • Document analysis • Interviews • Focus groups • Storytelling • Observation
Organizational (capabilities)	• Culture • Values • Innovation • DAC • Adaptability • Sustainability • Leadership pipeline • Learning • Collaboration	• Networks/partnerships • Business/org outcomes • Leadership strategy • Diversity	• SNA, ONA • Measures of culture transformation • Business-level surveys • Secondary data • Document analysis • Storytelling • Visual methods-photovoice • Appreciative inquiry • Q-sort • Specific measures for outcomes • Ethnography/observation
Group (capabilities)	• DAC • Learning • CCL team capabilities • Dialogue • Collaboration • Values • Execution • Boundary spanning	• Increased resources • Credibility/recognition • Effectiveness/efficiency • Networks/partnerships • Problem solving	• SNA • Observation • Simulations/performance assessment • Surveys of team constructs • Focus groups • Appreciative inquiry • Q-sort • Visual methods • Secondary data analysis
Individual (competencies)	• KSA • Behavior (incl boundary spanning) • Identity/perspective	• Career/work • Personal • Visibility • Confidence	• Survey • Interviews • Observation • Visual methods • Document analysis • Performance assessment

Figure 9.1. SOGI Framework.

Learning Surveys

Another purpose of surveys is to measure the extent to which participants have learned new content during the leadership development initiative. The *learning survey* is valuable when participants are expected to retain factual information (such as their organization's leadership or competency models or its business policies or practices) or learn specific steps for implementing leadership responsibilities (such as giving feedback and coaching others).

There are generally two ways to assess the attainment of factual information: (1) to administer the learning survey twice (once before the initiative and once immediately afterward, and (2) administer a survey after an initiative. The first approach has two advantages over the latter. The pretest, a survey before the initiative, provides a means of assessing the needs of participants: this can guide you in focusing the measures you will use in the evaluation. This approach also allows you to create a logical tie to what has been learned with the initiative. However, it should be considered that a prepost survey design for measuring learning (or behavior change, for that matter) will allow conclusions only about the amount of measurable learning that has occurred—not about the underlying learning process that has been experienced by the individual.

Change Surveys

Many programs use surveys to measure change, yet they use different formats to do so. *Change surveys* are useful in assessing whether change has occurred as a result of a development initiative. They are typically used to measure changes in attitudes or behaviors specific to the initiative in question. A well-developed change survey should be based on what is already known about the impact of the initiative and/or the objectives of the initiative. Evaluators should test survey questions for clarity and reliability in a pilot test. They should also ensure that the response scale used in the change survey facilitates the measurement of change. Change surveys are most effective when the focus of the evaluation is on behavioral changes as measured by quantitative data. Administering a change survey at different points in time has different purposes. For example, using a survey before an initiative allows the evaluator to identify behavioral shifts after an initiative so that the changes can be noted and measured. When administered several months after the initiative has ended, a change survey can be used to measure the associated behavioral change resulting from the initiative.

Daily or End-of-Program Surveys

Surveys are also used at the end of each day of a program. These *daily evaluations* have two key purposes. First, they give participants an opportunity to reflect on their daily experiences, which reinforces what they've learned (especially when questions are written in a way that requires such reflection). Second, they provide program staff with information that enables them to make any immediate necessary adjustments to the initiative, thereby enhancing its effectiveness. This method is somewhat limited in that it does not offer participants much time to reflect on their experiences and may not provide a comprehensive picture of the experience.

Many programs make use of *end-of-program evaluations*. Participants complete end-of-initiative evaluation forms at the conclusion of each component of the leadership development initiative. These forms can be designed to capture the extent to which a specific component met its target objectives, how participants intend to apply what they've learned in the workplace, and how well facilitators, facilities, and logistics met a specified standard. They should be used to gather evidence regarding how participants intend to use lessons learned, to collect impressions of how relevant and valuable the initiative is to potential participants, and to capture suggestions for changing the initiative. Capturing this information while it is fresh on the minds of participants is helpful, but this method doesn't measure the actual implementation of the intended changes—only the intent to apply what has been learned.

Pre- and Post-Surveys

One of the most popular methods for measuring change is to use the same assessment survey before and after the leadership development initiative takes place—*pre- and post-initiative assessments*. This is popular because many leadership development programs use a survey prior to the program to gather baseline data. Rather than create a new method to use after the program has ended, some organizations may find it cost effective to readminister the same survey after the program has ended. This technique works best in situations where what you want to measure is very specific and concrete—in other words, it is easily observable.

360-Degree Surveys

There are several ways in which 360-degree surveys are used to measure change. First, some programs use *Pre-post Assessments* (360-degree assessments) as the survey both before and after the program. Using the same instrument allows organizations another snapshot at a particular point in time from a particular group of people and enables comparisons across broad themes and patterns. Although this process seems to make sense, it does have some problems. For example, if different raters are used (which is often the case), there may be changes in scores simply because different raters are providing information. Also, participants revisiting the same 360-degree instrument will need access to a coach or trainer who is can help them interpret the meaning of the differences shown in the pre and post ratings. Scores on scales, and particularly on questions, can fluctuate even though a person's "true" score remains the same. Comparing scores (question by question or scale by scale) to measure change over time or to measure the impact of an initiative or other leadership development experience may provide misleading information. CCL's experience with 360-degree retests has demonstrated the difficulty in accurately measuring behavioral change using this method (Martineau, 1997). There are many factors other than the development initiative itself that could cause a change (positive or negative) in pre- and post-initiative assessments. Response-shift bias is one example; another is a change in the organization (restructuring, layoffs, or new compensation systems, to name a few).

An alternative survey process developed to counteract some of the challenges found in pre-post assessments such as response-shift bias is the use of retrospective pretest and posttest surveys (Howard & Dailey, 1979). This format requires two ratings at the *same time after* participants have completed the initiative. One rating is given to describe an individual participant before the intervention, while the second rating assesses the person's skills and behaviors at the time the survey is completed. The participants, their bosses, and other stakeholders can be involved in the rating process. It is beneficial to include ratings from multiple perspectives. Some evaluators doubt the merits of this method, perceiving it to create a "demand characteristic" that would automatically result in increased ratings of effectiveness from the "before" to the "now" ratings. However, CCL's research and other research in the field argue for its validity (Pratt, McGuigan, & Katzev, 2000; Rohs, 1999; Rohs & Langone, 1997). Ratings of change are highly correlated with objective measures of change such as performance appraisals.

Finally, d*egree-of-change surveys* are another method that is used with measuring individual change resulting from leadership development. A single rating is provided that evaluates the extent of change observed using a response scale, such as a five-point scale ranging from "no change" to "great change." Research has shown this to be an effective method; there seems to be more agreement across rater groups (peers, direct reports, and bosses, for example) as to the amount of change when all groups are rating change directly, as compared with evaluations that measure change using pre- and posttest ratings (Peterson, 1993).

INTERVIEWS

In addition to surveys, interviews are frequently used for evaluating the impact of leadership development at the individual level (Ely et al., 2010). Interviews are an excellent method to collect qualitative data to determine how a participant's knowledge, skills, attitudes, and behaviors have evolved as a result of an initiative, as well as to assess perception of the initiative from a stakeholder's perspective (Hannum and Martineau, 2008). Interviews can be conducted face to face, or through virtual means such as VOIP, videoconference, or telephone. Interviews are particularly effective when the evaluation requires examples and details related to the question at hand, rather than only quantitative data. However, one significant downside of interviews is that they are expensive to conduct given the intense time required on the part of evaluators, and can be complex to schedule. If resources don't allow for one-on-one interviews yet individual level information is required, interview questions can be adapted to open-ended questionnaires that participants can complete at their convenience. To get the most value from interviews, we suggest using them for more than one purpose (e.g., prior to an initiative, conducting needs assessment to understand both organizational and individual needs; after an initiative, to further interpret earlier survey results and determine additional growth that has occurred since the initiative).

OBSERVATION

Observation is a method that produces both qualitative and quantitative data by observing a set of activities, the people involved in those activities, and the environment in which the activities are taking place. Evaluators who use observation for data collection produce field notes as well as ratings, rankings, or frequencies related to the activities being observed. In CCL's evaluation work, our most frequent uses of observation are of program activities themselves (e.g., small group dialogues and role plays, simulations, large group debriefs of critical experiences) as well as team interactions to document team dynamics both before and after an intensive leadership development event has occurred. Observation can also be used to determine levels of interaction, engagement, skill development, and satisfaction with the initiative.

Because observation can be conducted in the work setting where behaviors and mindsets learned are being put to action in real-world situations, the validity of the measures is relatively strong compared to self-report methods such as survey and interview. Trained observers are also able to see nuances that others involved in or close to the initiative may miss. Finally, the observation process can illuminate issues that participants may be unwilling or uncomfortable to talk about in interviews.

On the other hand, observation requires well-trained observers in order to be fully effective, which can increase the costs of evaluation. When multiple observers are engaged, analysis and synthesis can be more challenging unless time is allocated to ensuring that observers are interpreting what they see in the same way. Another downside to evaluation is that participants may feel uncomfortable being observed and may not interact normally, resulting in data that are not completely reflective of true behavior or mindset and disruptions to participants' effectiveness in the workplace. Finally, observations can be an expensive method to employ, especially if large samples are required.

VISUAL METHODS

A more recent type of method being used for evaluative purposes is the use of visual artifacts to gather data from participants. Carefully selected for use in an evaluation (or created by participants themselves as part of the initiative), visual images have significant power to cross boundaries in terms of perspectives, culture, and language. Researchers at CCL have created a set of compelling images (e.g., photos and drawings), which are used to create opportunities for mediated dialogue for both developmental and evaluative purposes. The evocative nature of the images can prompt deeper reflection on the experience and illustrate the impact of the program to stakeholders more effectively than reports and presentations. Images can also serve as a powerful mechanism for communicating findings that can "speak to" different stakeholder groups in a way that may convey the evaluation results more meaningfully and accurately than many other methods (Hoole & Hannum, 2008).

Visual methods are used for a variety of purposes, including surfacing opportunities for dialogue and shared meaning making through inquiry (Palus & Drath, 2001), qualitative research and anthropological methods (Brace-Govan, 2007; Schwartz, 1989; Weade & Ernst, 2001), and using metaphors to move groups beyond facts and details to deeper interpretations of meaning based on what is seen (Weade & Ernst, 2001). Images can be used in interviews, focus groups, and large group settings effectively. In addition to creating the space for a reflective dialogue for evaluative purposes, we have also used visual methods for creating a storyboard that allows individuals and groups to create a visual image of their developmental journey over time, collages to illustrate patterns and connections, and in needs assessment to help individuals and groups to understand both current and desired future states leadership competence and capabilities.

DOCUMENT ANALYSIS

There are many forms of documents that can provide valuable information for evaluative purposes. Russ-Eft and Preskill (2009) address several of these, including the positions achieved by individuals during their career growth and performance appraisals by superiors. Documents can be collected by organizations (e.g., absenteeism, communication issues, grievances, performance appraisals), communities (e.g., events captured in news articles), and individuals (e.g., e-mail exchanges, journals) (Hannum & Martineau, 2008). We have used document analysis to track individual progress on their action plans based on leadership development initiatives by tracking changes over time in the goals set and actions achieved toward those goals.

A best practice is to have participants create documents as part of their program intervention (e.g., action plans, journals) that are used for both developmental purposes and evaluative purposes. The efforts participants put into creating these documents for their own developmental purposes is valuable above and beyond the value created for evaluative purposes—this double use of time and resources is highly advised to facilitate the most unobtrusive data collection form documents. On the other hand, it is also possible that participants will not use as much candor if they know that their documents and reflections will be viewed by others, so the data collected from these methods are at risk of not accurately reflecting the change or development intended.

PERFORMANCE ASSESSMENT

Noting the difficulties in measuring leader behavior (e.g., differences in perception of what is important by leaders and their raters, complexities of gathering data that consistently represent behavior or knowledge/skill), Mumford, Friedrich, Caughron, and Antes (2009) proposed an alternative model for leader assessment and discussed the empirical evidence to support the model. The authors focused on assessing individual differences in leader cognition (a.k.a. knowledge) as an indicator of performance. For example, they hypothesize that leaders could be presented with a change event as well as a series of cases that help them understand the change event. They could then be asked questions about the relevance of the various cases for explaining the change event. Their responses provide insights to their thought process, knowledge, and potential performance choices. The authors recommend that leader development programs make better use of methods to assess leader cognition as a means of determining whether a program's objectives have been met and as a predictive measure of objective leader performance (Mumford et al., 2009).

Group Methods

When evaluating leadership development that is targeted at group-level outcomes, a set of methods that is both unique from and somewhat overlapping with individual methods is used. These are described below.

SOCIAL NETWORK ANALYSIS

Social Network Analysis (SNA) refers to a body of quantitative methodologies based upon graph theory, combinatrics, and matrix mathematics applied to the study of social, communal, communication, and transactional relations (Cross, Borgatti, & Parker, 2001). It is based on the broader practice of network analysis and provides the tools to structurally and objectively quantify the characteristics of a network at the individual, the group, and the network levels. SNA can empirically identify the roles and advantages of individuals within the network, and provide graphical images of the network's structure.

Various forms of social network analysis have been developed over the past decade for use in understanding the nature of collective relationships (Borgatti & Foster, 2003). Hoppe and Reinelt (2010) demonstrate the use of social network analysis in the evaluation of leadership development initiatives. SNA can be used to identify whether and how leadership development initiatives are improving the strength and number of connections between peers, peer groups, organizations, and networks within a field. They can be used to determine whether connections are uni- or bidirectional, whether specific individuals are at the center of a network or on its periphery, and where clusters within a network reside.

According to Hoppe and Reinelt (2010), networks can be evaluated for their connectivity, their overall health, and the outcomes of the network. Networks can be examined from a variety of perspectives such as the level of trust among network members, the frequency of communication, the relative value of network members to one's overall effectiveness, and how decisions are made within the network. From a leadership development evaluation perspective, social network analysis can be used to determine whether the outcomes of an initiative have been achieved, as well as how the network and/or changes in the network may have had an influence on the implementation and outcomes of the initiative.

The use of SNA can strengthen the design and potential impact of a leadership development initiative as well. For example, by understanding the informal network in an organization, the design can be created to leverage key connectors as participants, project sponsors, or coaches.

In terms of challenges, social network analysis is not always perceived as useful as an evaluation tool. Too often, SNA is used to get a picture of current collaboration efforts but isn't then put into action to determine how to best improve the efforts. Rather, a social network map can be used to inappropriately penalize those who are not central to the network, or congratulate those who are. To be used effectively, SNA users need to understand how the results can help to improve their collaboration efforts as a developmental rather than solely an evaluative tool.

SNA can also be costly, depending on the complexity and number of questions involved as well as the number of people asked to complete the survey. The costs can be both direct and indirect in the form of the amount of time required by participants to thoroughly respond to all of the questions.

Finally, SNA can present confidentiality issues. SNA is most useful if individual and group names are provided as part of the maps resulting from analysis. However, participants need to be aware that their names and other identifiers will be shared before they provide the data so that they respond will full knowledge.

OBSERVATION

In addition to being useful in individual evaluation, observation can be used to understand how a team works together in either their own setting or a simulated exercise. All of the benefits and challenges of using observation for individual level evaluation are found when using the method for team observation. In addition, observing a team in their own context may illuminate behavior and interaction styles for which the team is not even aware and would not be able to raise or discuss during a focus group or dialogue.

For example, we have used observation of team interactions when an executive team has been working on their organizational strategy or a significant organizational decision. When developing leadership capability among a team, it is critical that the team be able to practice new ways of collaborating together. The best case is when the evaluator can observe a team in one of its regularly scheduled meetings or working sessions and be able to see them work to influence, discuss, debate, decide, and take action together. Interacting in the naturally complex environments of team work—with the knowledge that they are developing greater leadership capability as a team—often provides the context for teams and team members to take the work seriously to achieve real outcomes *and* to take more risks than they may outside of the context of development.

Because observation can be conducted in the work setting where behaviors and mindsets learned are being put to action in real-world situations, the validity of the measures is relatively strong compared to self-report methods such as survey and interview. Trained observers are also able to see nuances that others involved in or close to the initiative may miss. Finally, the observation process can illuminate issues that participants may be unwilling or uncomfortable to talk about in interviews.

On the other hand, observation requires well-trained observers to be fully effective, which can increase the costs of evaluation. When multiple observers are engaged, analysis and synthesis can be more challenging unless time is allocated to ensuring that observers are interpreting what they see in the same way. Another downside to observation is that participants may feel uncomfortable being observed and may not interact normally, resulting in data that are not completely reflective of true behavior or mindset and disruptions to participants' effectiveness in the workplace. Finally, observations can be an expensive method to employ, especially if large samples are required.

SIMULATIONS AND PERFORMANCE ASSESSMENT

When a development initiative includes a real-world simulation where team members are assigned roles and a task that is real (for example, running an organization through a merger versus building toy trains that will run on a track), there is the opportunity for an evaluation to include an assessment of the group or team's performance in a real yet nonwork environment. Through both observation (above) and performance assessment tools, an evaluation design can utilize the developmental value of a simulation and the relatively controlled environment of the training context to create an assessment that measures what a team is expected to accomplish during the simulation. The assessment (usually a survey) can be completed by team members, trainers, professional coaches working with the initiative, and evaluators. The results can simultaneously provide developmental feedback for a team in terms of how well they were able to employ newly learned capabilities together to be successful in the simulation and provides data for the evaluation about the team's performance.

SURVEY OF TEAM CONSTRUCTS

Surveys are certainly a frequently used method in evaluation, and many times a survey targeting individual constructs will be used to aggregate to the group or team level. The problem is that the data are merely an aggregation of individual-level outcomes rather than a measure of change that is happening at the team level. To appropriately measure team outcomes, a survey should be designed and implemented in a way that accurately reflects team-level constructs.

Morgeson, Lindoerfer, and Loring (2010) present a model of team leadership development that addresses the components of team actions, feelings, and learning, as well as team needs (e.g., charter, goals), and the context in which teams function (the team itself, organization, and environment). To assess the level of team leadership capability for a given team, the authors recommend an assessment process that could take the form of a survey (as well as other methods) and asks five key questions that align with the model:

1. How did the team do? (Team effectiveness)
2. What were the top two or three challenges the team faced? (Team challenges)
3. What were the top two or three needs the team had? (Team needs)
4. What leadership was displayed by the team? (Leadership displayed)
5. How effective was the team's leadership? (Leadership effectiveness)

A survey of team leadership capability development would be given to team members individually or as a team as well as stakeholders from outside the team, such as superiors, other teams, and recipients of the team's work.

Gentry and Martineau (2010) describe the use of a survey designed to assess change in team leadership capability over time. A five-phase development process was designed for teams of leaders from 21 schools within a single school district. Each phase was designed to address the same nine areas of capability (e.g., Leading with Purpose), while for each phase the way in which the teams were expected to develop and perform varied: the first phase focused on individual development; the second on team development; the third on the role the team as a collective was having an impact at the school level; and the fourth and fifth phases focused on the impact of the team within the school district (4) and surrounding community (5). A team survey was developed for each year according to the expected outcomes, and completed by team members as well as stakeholders outside of the team. A random coefficients model indicated that teams demonstrated growth over time according to increases in ratings on the team survey.

FOCUS GROUPS

Focus groups are generally used to gather qualitative perspectives from a team or group that has shared a leadership development experience. Focus groups are frequently used in evaluation, and there are numerous resources available to help evaluators in designing and facilitating focus groups (Greenbaum, 1998; Morgan, 1993; Morgan & Krueger, 1997). A focus group is essentially a group interview, where the evaluator will pose questions to the group and allow team members to respond. As with team surveys, the questions should be focused on the leadership capability and experiences of the team as a whole, rather than at the individual level. When properly structured, a team-level focus group should elicit more "we" than "me" responses—in other words, team members' responses should reflect what the team did, challenges of the team, etc., rather than of individual team members.

As is true with interviews, focus groups can be conducted either face to face or virtually through various technologies. Unlike surveys, however, focus groups require that the team members be able to hear and respond to each other's responses interactively, so it must enable synchronous participation. To be effective, focus groups must be conducted in a way that provides a "safe environment" for team members to openly share their perspectives, which means that the evaluator is responsible for designing and asking questions that are not threatening and facilitating the discussion in a way that enables a productive exchange of thoughts and ideas.

A benefit of focus groups for use in evaluation is that they are flexible in the role they can play. Evaluations include focus groups before leadership development begins (to understand needs and better define potential outcomes), during the development process (as a way of making formative improvements to the process), and after a development process has ended (to understand whether and how outcomes were achieved as well as help the group focus on their future work together). These uses of focus groups can actually enable the creation of more impact by focusing the needs, challenges, and strengths of teams related to leadership development.

Although focus groups can be less time consuming to conduct than individual interviews, the evaluator must have strong facilitation skills to keep the team focused on the questions being asked rather than drifting off into other areas of discussion. Focus groups can be challenging to schedule due to the need to coordinate the schedules of multiple people.

DIALOGUE

While focus groups are structured and the evaluator facilitates the direction of the interactions through a series of questions, group dialogue enables a deeper conversation to take place among team members. In fact, the role of the evaluator in team dialogue is primarily to set up the conversation and then move into the background in an observer role. This allows the evaluator to unobtrusively observe the discussion and interaction of the team. This method does require a specific set of steps or guidelines in which team members must listen to each other's perspectives objectively and in an inquiry-based mindset rather than waiting for the next opportunity to jump in and respond (McGuire & Palus, 2003). Some of the guidelines of the dialogue method are that everyone has a voice and an equal place in the conversation, team members should find a balance between advocacy (i.e., statements of belief) and inquiry (i.e., questions of clarification), the team should use the opportunity to explore multiple perspectives and possibilities, and a debrief of the process itself should take place at the end of the dialogue (Hannum et al., 2008). There are a variety of techniques that can be used to create the desired environment, such as having team members sit in a circle without tables or other obstructions between them and using visual methods to "put something in the middle" and enable more exploratory conversation (Palus & Drath, 2001).

Just as is true with focus groups, a challenge of the dialogue method is that the team must be gathered simultaneously (and in fact, in the same room) for effective dialogue to occur, thus schedules become an issue. However, the benefits of dialogue over focus group is that team members have the opportunity to explore each other's' perspectives and insights in a deeper way than when the evaluator is structuring the interaction through questions, which can help them grow as a team through building more effective skills for communicating.

APPRECIATIVE INQUIRY

Appreciative inquiry (AI) is an approach to understanding what is good and working in individuals, groups, organizations, and communities. Based on the discovery that focusing on the positive actually leads to more positive outcomes, the AI methodology has been widely used for both studying and creating change (Cooperrider, Whitney, & Stavros, 2003). As an evaluative method, AI is participatory, collaborative, and allows for the expression of many different perspectives (Coghlan, Preskill, & Catsambas, 2003) in developing a picture of what is working with a particular leadership development initiative or program. Because AI has a strong intent of learning, it can remove the fear of "being judged" from evaluation and enable participants to focus instead on what they have accomplished. Preskill and Catsambas (2006) also illustrate the positive influence on the power and effectiveness of an evaluation when groups are brought together rather than divided through a focus on the problems that exist.

AI can be used in evaluation to identify the growth of groups through leadership development by asking questions such as "describe a time when this group or team successfully accomplished a challenge together," and "how did the program help the team to accomplish their challenge?" By asking questions of the group members together as a group, both the reflections about the accomplishment and lessons learned become visible and spoken, and therefore become part of the ongoing shared learning by the group that can be accessed the next time a similar challenge arises.

AI is criticized as focusing only on the positive outcomes of interventions and not looking for the problems that can be solved. Evaluators who use the AI method in its true form counter that problems do get addressed through shifting the conversation and lessons learned to a focus on possibilities based on past experience rather than a focus on problems, issues, and challenges (Preskill & Catsambas, 2006).

Q-SORT

The Q-methodology was developed in the 1930s as a method for allowing individuals to share their perspectives on a given question by ranking or prioritizing a set of stimuli without being overly structured by the researcher (Dziopa & Ahern, 2011). The process of sorting the stimuli as part of this methodology is known as Q-sort. Often the Q-sort process is used to document the opinions or perspectives of individuals and then, through analytical steps, the data are examined for patterns in responses across individuals.

Militello and Benham (2010) used the Q-sort methodology to evaluate the development of collective leadership among a group, rather than looking at the data from the individual level. To reframe their evaluation at the right level of focus, the authors defined collective leadership as a "dynamic process that engages a diverse and intergenerational group of people who learn together to honor their place, and share and generate power to address common challenges in an effort to build broad-based knowledge and action that leads to constructive, community-based systems change" (Benham, Militello, & Halladay, 2005). They asked participants to sort a set of statements that were outcome oriented and descriptive of the participants' training, development, and work together. Participants sorted the statements from most to least representative of their work in the program. Using a combination of the factor-analyzed Q-sort data and data from several other methods, the evaluation team identified deeper meaning from the sorted data within each collective group, as well as themes across the six groups participating in the program.

This case illustrates the value of using the Q-sort methodology as part of a longitudinal, multisource evaluation of a program focused on building capability at the group and community levels. The authors also caution against several limitations of the Q-methodology for evaluation purposes. Two in particular are raised here. First, they recommend against using Q-methodology alone—using it as the sole source of data would not have enabled the same level of richness in interpretation and understanding of the program's impact. Second, they caution that by capturing statements to be sorted, participants are indeed somewhat limited (versus open-ended response style questions) in the perspectives they provide to evaluators.

VISUAL METHODS

We find the use of visual methods particularly useful in groups and teams. Regardless of whether the presenting challenge from an organization for leadership development is greater innovation, improved global capability, or better ability to respond to the complex changes an organization experiences, one of the essential elements of leadership development is often enabling the team to communicate with greater authenticity and ability to understand and respect alternate perspectives (Schwartz, 1989). Visual methods often take the pressure off of relying on one's expertise ("I am the expert engineer of the group so therefore when we have a group conversation I need to reflect best practices from an engineering perspective") to relying on communicating beliefs, values, concerns, insights, and so on in a way that can create a deeper exploration of the issue at hand (Palus & Drath, 2001).

SECONDARY DATA

When evaluating the development of groups, a relatively unobtrusive method is the use of secondary data. As is true of using secondary data for individual-level evaluation, the ideal situation is when the data are collected as a normal part of either the development process or the work of the team itself.

For example, when CCL includes strategic projects during a development initiative for a team of leaders from an organization, part of the project deliverables include both the documentation of what was accomplished by the team as well as what they learned from a developmental perspective (Hannum & Martineau, 2008). The specific type of data used will vary depending on the objectives of the leadership development initiative. As part of a development initiative intended to create stronger collaboration among leaders in multiple functions in a financial services organization, a project may require that members of the group study and then make recommendations to their executive team regarding potential improvements in the organization's annual incentive plan that appropriately considers the contribution to annual net revenues of both line and staff functions. The team would capture (at a minimum) the summary of its research, its recommendations, and the lessons the team learned about collaboration during the course of the project. The report or presentation in which these insights were captured would be analyzed by the evaluator for themes related to the expected outcomes of the team's work.

Organizational Methods

Within the field, methods for evaluating change at the individual level, while not perfect, are fairly well developed and understood. Linking and measuring changes from the individual level to the organizational level becomes much more challenging methodologically. Issues of reliability and validity of data and inferences, for both quantitative *and* qualitative methods become ever more complex at higher levels. The ability to generalize findings from surveys and samplings of individuals is always a concern, given the complexity of organizational life. This section introduces some well-known and possibly less well-known methods to examine changes and impact at the organizational level of the SOGI framework.

ORGANIZATIONAL SURVEYS

Employee surveys are commonly used for data collection by researchers and evaluators to understand organizations, assess performance, benchmark, and measure change (Kraut, 1996). When evaluating a development intervention a number of different types of surveys may be used: either standardized instruments to measure constructs of interest, or custom surveys designed to specifically measure the impact of the intervention.

To evaluate the impact of leadership or organizational interventions at the organizational level, pre- and post-test measures of the constructs of interest can be given and changes measured over time. Careful consideration of the level of intervention (individual leader development vs. organizational leadership development) needs to be given in deciding whether organizational-level constructs are likely to change as a result. When the organizational leadership culture is the target for change, individual level development of leaders may not be sufficient to change overall cultural values, norms, practices, and procedures.

When focusing on changes in organizational culture, a wide variety of standardized instruments exist. These instruments can be categorized into having either a typological approach or a dimensional approach (Scott, Mannion, Davies, & Marshall, 2003). Typological culture surveys categorize culture by type. An example is the Competing Values Framework (Cameron and Freeman 1991; Gerowitz 1998; Gerowitz, Lemieux-Charles, Heginbothan, &

Johnson 1996), which categorizes culture into four types: clan, adhocracy, hierarchy, and market types. CCL's Leadership Culture Survey falls into this assessment type and categorizes organizational leadership cultures as Dependent, Independent, or Interdependent (McCauley et al 2008). As with the Competing Values Framework, more than one type of organizational leadership culture can exist within an organization at the same or multiple levels.

Dimensional approaches to assessing organizational culture include the Organizational Culture Survey, which measures six dimensions: teamwork and conflict, climate and morale, information flow, involvement, supervision, and meetings (Glaser, Zamanou, & Hacker, 1987). Separate from culture surveys, there is also the option of using a climate survey. These surveys measure organizational practices and procedures at the individual level, and data are then aggregated (West, 2008). Often climate is specified for certain areas, such as service climate, safety climate, or ethical climate. The fields of IO Psychology, Organizational Behavior, Management, and other social sciences contain a wide variety of additional constructs and measures that could be considered as evaluation measures if there is alignment with the goals of the initiative. These include employee engagement (Harter, Schmidt, Killham, & Agrawal, 2009), organizational trust (Butler, 1991, Cummings & Bromiley, 1996), organizational citizenship behavior (Becker & Randall, 1994), and innovation culture and climate (Amabile, Conti, Coon, Lasenby, & Herron, 1996).

An alternative to established measures, one which may provide greater sensitivity to measuring change, would be the development of a customized survey. While allowing for greater targeting of questions to the intent of the intervention, creating custom surveys require a rigorous development and testing process to ensure the validity of the results (Russ-Eft & Preskill, 2009). Based on stakeholder need and data usage, custom organizational surveys can range from rapid and low cost, to time consuming and expensive depending upon scope, size, and rigor needed.

The psychometric issues related to survey data at the organizational level deal primarily with issues of aggregation. Determining the level of measurement, whether individual (How engaged are you....) or group level (How well do senior leaders in the organization....) is the first step. The answer to this question then drives the type of aggregation. If measurement is at the individual level, then the individual responses are aggregated to get an organizational level variable. If measurement is at the group level, examining the level of intragroup agreement is important using various indicators such as R_{wg} and Interclass Correlations. For a full discussion of the issues related to multilevel measurement and analysis, see Yammarino, Dionne, Chun, and Dansereau (2005).

ORGANIZATIONAL/SOCIAL NETWORK ANALYSIS

Social network analysis (SNA) holds much promise for the field for needs assessment/discovery, as an intervention at the individual, group, organizational or societal levels, and as a way to examine changes over time. At the individual level, use of SNA to map a leader's personal network can increase effectiveness (e.g., Balkundi, Kilduff, & Harrison, 2011; Cross & Thomas, 2008; Mehra, Kilduff, & Brass, 2001). At the team level, SNA can assist senior leadership teams to restructure committees and processes to speed decision making and increase execution of strategy and operational initiatives (Cross, Ehrlich, Dawson, & Helferich, 2008; Susskind, Odom-Reed, & Viccari, 2011). At the organizational level, especially for change efforts, organizational network analysis can identify critical individuals in the network who can either facilitate change, or serve as a roadblock to change (Cross, Yan, & Louis, 2000; Johnson-Cramer, Parise, Cross, 2007). By using SNA in these types of ways, the potential impact of the leadership development initiative can be strengthened.

For evaluation at the organizational level, examining network changes over time can be useful when increased collaboration and trust are the goals. By measuring the meaning in the links, such as level of trust and collaboration, the value of the network structure emerges and can be tracked over time. New linkages between groups formerly unconnected or the development of new network relationships with key stakeholders external to the organization can substantiate successful development efforts and can ultimately serve to build a base of knowledge regarding the relationship between network changes and other desired organizational outcomes, such as innovation, integrated supply chains, or entry into new markets.

Yet for all the promise of SNA, its use for evaluation, and to measure changes over time, remains problematic. From an evaluative perspective, there is no clear understanding or consensus to understand the value in changing network metrics. As Hoppe and Reinelt (2010) point out, "Established standards for evaluating networks do not currently exist" (p. 47). This is clearly an area in need of additional research to understand changing network metrics, individual and organizational perceptions and use of social network maps, and the relationship between network changes and other organizational outcomes.

SECONDARY DATA

Using secondary data to measure progress and determine impact at the organizational level provides the benefits of leveraging current data collection activities and is less intrusive when compared to other methods such as interview, focus group, and observation (Russ-Eft & Preskill, 2009). Businesses track a wide variety of metrics and Key Performance Indicators (KPIs) across different domains such as

- HR/Talent (retention, employee grievances, absenteeism, promotions, performance ratings);
- Profit and Loss (sales, top line revenue, expenses, bottom line revenue);
- Marketing (customer satisfaction, brand awareness, and image); and
- Operations (productivity, returns, rework, safety, task completion).

Tracking these metrics over time can provide evidence of changes or trends over time.

For use as an evaluation measure, there needs to be clear linkage between the design of the program and the business metric. Ideally this linkage is clear and direct, but if the linkage is indirect, a clear logic or theory of change is needed to articulate how the intervention is expected to impact the metric, as well as identification of other variables that may also positively or negatively impact the trend. For individuals participating in a leadership development intervention, those involved need to see a clear linkage between the development process and the outcome—so they are able to apply new knowledge, skills, and capabilities to achieve the business outcome.

With secondary data and business metrics, there are multiple options for analysis, including trend-line analysis, forecasting, time series analysis, and multilevel/hierarchical modeling. With these models, taking into account the multiple variables that may impact the metric over time or for a specific period of time is a serious challenge. The ability of these methods to truly isolate the impact of the intervention is low (Phillips & Aaron, 2008).

DOCUMENT ANALYSIS

Document analysis, as separate from a method of gathering secondary data, can also be utilized in studying an organization's communications internally and externally to examine changes over time. Document analysis might be a useful approach to examine culture change, cross-group communication, organizational climate, and changes in external relationship management. The documents may represent the official communications of the organization to employees, customers, shareholders, partners, and the field; or the documents may represent the more informal daily communication between groups, divisions, and functions.

Qualitative approaches and methods like content analysis, discourse analysis, semiotics, grounded theory, and linguistic approaches are all options, as well as newer social media analytics examining both the content and network structure of the data. Discourse analysis may range from a focus on the meaning of the texts and interactions in an organization to the use of language in social contexts (Alvesson & Karreman, 2000). These approaches provide a rich means of understanding how the social context changes due to interventions, how the social context can change the intervention, and ultimately how the interaction between the existing social structures and the introduction of new structures creates a new social reality.

PHOTOVOICE

While most use of Photovoice has been at the societal level (see following section), the method may hold promise at the organizational level to investigate changes in such phenomena as culture, climate, and engagement. Photovoice is a participatory method engaging individuals in diagnosing and understanding their current experience in a context, along with documenting changes using photographs and critical dialogue. Participants in the process are trained in the method and given cameras and then asked to take pictures representing their current reality. A critical group dialogue process is used to select the photos that best represent and communicate the current situation. Within an organization, participants can be selected to take photos signifying the cultural values of the organization. After a culture change intervention, the process can be used by participants again to document perceived and visible changes to the symbols and behavior representing the organizational culture.

APPRECIATIVE INQUIRY

As described earlier, Appreciative Inquiry is a participatory approach incorporating a wide range of different perspectives into a multidimensional representation of what is working well, or what is positive within a group, organization, or community (Coghlan, Preskill, & Catsambas, 2003). At the organizational level, AI can help an organization identify and build on the positive values and norms (culture), behaviors and practices (climate), and business processes currently existing and envisioning what could be. This could happen within a certain division, with a level of leaders, leadership as a whole, or the entire organization.

From an evaluation perspective, an AI process would uncover the ways in which building on strengths has benefited the organization and the means by which the organization increased its capacity. A large-scale AI project and evaluation would gather sufficient input to build a strong evidence base to substantiate the changes and impacts uncovered through the process, as well as facilitate organizational learning. AI utilizes storytelling methods to generate the aspirational vision, foster organizational learning, create positive reinforcement, communicate changes, and track progress (Finegold, Holland, & Lingham, 2002).

To effectively use AI for evaluation at the organizational level, all the conditions for success necessary for AI to succeed as a change intervention must be in place. This includes process integrity, human change integrity, perseverance, and narrative-rich communication (Cooperrider & Whitney, 1999). Ultimately, the process must include those in the organization targeted by the intervention, and the people involved must be open to and willing to change with the persistence to persevere through a nonlinear change process.

STORYTELLING—MOST SIGNIFICANT CHANGE

The Most Significant Change method (Davies, 1996) was developed as an approach to evaluating a complex development program in rural Bangladesh. The participatory program required a different type of evaluation to fully understand and document its impact. Rather than traditional quantitative methods and hypothesized outcomes, stories are collected that answer the question "During the last month, in your opinion, what was the most significant change that took place in _____?" The specific target of the question, such as a particular program, an organization, or a community, provides the context for the response. The stories collected are then analyzed through several phases, where each successive phase narrows down the stories to those that illustrate the most significant change that has occurred. The iterative process also results in the rationale for why each story was selected at the highest level of review, resulting in a report that includes both the stories and the rationale for including them. The report is organized by domain so that key stakeholders can easily understand what type of change is being described by each. The process provides ongoing information for program improvement, as well as building a database of significant stories to document the impact of the program in the various domains.

Q-SORT

By allowing evaluators to compare individual Q-sorts to the group Q-sort, as well as compare group Q-sorts across the organization, this method offers insight into subjective perceptions in a quantifiable way. When the development of collective practices, values, culture, and beliefs are the goal, using a Q-sort method allows for comparison across individuals regarding areas of consensus or disagreement and the creation of a group aggregate (model sort)—and correlation of each individual's sort to the group's model sort (Militello & Benham, 2010). By highlighting these areas of convergence or divergence, a rich dialogue can occur regarding these perceptions. When using Q-sort across groups, functions or divisions in an organization, individual and group perceptions can be examined pre- and post-intervention, merger, or reorganization. Along with additional methods such as interviews and focus groups, a deeper understanding can be achieved regarding the organizational reality experienced by employees.

The opportunity afforded by Q-sort to quantify subjective perceptions creates possibilities of using such data in multilevel models for research as well. Data are aggregated in such a way that the level of collective agreement is reflected in the results, leading to interesting questions regarding the relationship between strength of agreement and group or organizational results. How strong is the relationship between a collective sense of direction, alignment, and commitment within the organization to organizational results such as revenue, sales, and productivity or efficiency measures?

The drawbacks of the method remain the same at the various levels. Q-sort is a complicated and time-consuming method that artificially constrains the process to a specific set of statements. These statements, the Q-sample, need to reflect the domain(s) of interest but not be so many as to overwhelm participant's cognitive ability to distinguish between the statements and sort them in a comparative manner. Quite often the most illuminating information comes from interviewing participants during the Q-sort process, requiring a significant investment of time by participant and evaluator.

OBSERVATION/ETHNOGRAPHY

Observation can play a variety of roles in evaluating interventions at the organizational level. Observational methods can involve organizational members as internal actors or outside observers, can include short-term observation to validate mastery of new behaviors, or can be a long-term field study in which the outside observer/evaluator becomes a part of the daily life of the organization. Observation has the potential to provide objective, quantifiable data regarding new collaborative behaviors and practices through the use of checklists and observation forms, which might require a short time frame. Longer immersions or full ethnographic studies can provide baseline data, real-time feedback for improvement, represent the multiple perspectives present in organizations, identify opportunities for additional research, and provide greater context than survey data (McGarvey & Volkman, 2006).

There are several limitations in using observation. If the observers are organizational members, proper training is essential to ensure valid and reliable data are collected (Russ-Eft & Preskill, 2009). When external evaluators are used, especially over a long period of time, the costs can be quite high. Trust is essential between the observed and observer, or the behaviors and environment the observer experiences will be false and yield invalid inferences (McGarvey & Volkman, 2006). If trust exists, however, ethnography can be very powerful for the organization in understanding itself, the progress of interventions, areas of improvement, and the results of development efforts.

Societal Methods

Especially at the level of society, evaluation methods need to focus on process and progress to help guide the intervention over a longer period of time. With interventions targeted at complex systems like communities and nations, evaluation is critical at providing ongoing feedback to guide changes in the intervention and generate learning for those involved. Issues of measurement become even greater at the societal level. Who represents society for an intervention—A neighborhood, and entire community, a region, a country, a continent, the world? Howard and Reinelt (2007) articulate the challenge well, "Community change is difficult to evaluate precisely because the effects of movement building are often invisible over a long period of time, with many battles seemingly lost before any are won."

COMMUNITY-WIDE SURVEYS

When well-established measures exist for society or community outcomes targeted for impact, pre- and post-administration, or trend analysis over time, can provide some insight into changes. Often initiatives may target the development of social capital, empowerment, developmental assets, cohesion, capacity or volunteering at a metalevel. Measures exist for a number of these areas: social capital (Saguaro Seminar, 2006; Social Capital Questions Bank, 2002; World Bank), developmental assets (Oman, Vesely, & McLeroy, 2002), cohesion, empowerment, and volunteering (The Citizenship Survey, UK, 2008), values (World Values Survey, 2005), and others that organizations and governments have developed and administer over time.

Surveys in communities and societies are conducted in various ways, through the mail with paper and pencil, telephone, face to face, and door to door. Most of these constructs are measured at the individual level and then aggregated to the group level. Issues of sampling would be critical in generalizing to the larger society. Along with generalization challenges, the sensitivity of these measures to interventions may not be well understood, so potential shifts may not be evident for some period of time. Therefore it is recommended that additional methods be incorporated to capture the changes from a longer-term process.

SOCIAL NETWORK ANALYSIS

As a method, social network analysis (SNA) can be applied at the individual, group, organizational, or community/societal level. Evaluation uses at the societal level have focused on the development and changes to networks within communities, coalitions, fields, and communities of practice. Along with capturing a "picture" of a network, SNA surveys can also gather data regarding many factors associated with a relationship, such as information exchange, trust, relationship quality, and evidence of collaboration (Luque et al., 2010).

Our own use of SNA at the community level in public health allowed us to look at both the individual network of participants and changes over time, and also to examine the organization to organization relationships and how they were impacted by the leadership development intervention. In many instances, social networks can be used as an intervention and as an evaluation method (Cross, Laseter, Parker, & Velasquez, 2006). When seeking to impact change within an organization, community or society as a whole, understanding the current relationships and identifying people who serve as hubs, bridgers, and pulse takers/energizers in the system, then building new and different connections can facilitate the change process (Stephenson, 2007). Follow-up SNA can then document the changes to the network and be linked to the desired outcomes for the intervention.

PHOTOVOICE

Photovoice is a popular participatory method at the community level and has been used extensive with groups who have less power within a certain society including youth (Wilson et al., 2007), women (Duffy, 2011), and mentally ill residents (Thompson et al., 2008). As a method it has been used for needs assessment, community and economic development, health promotion, and empowerment. The images and discussions provide a powerful way to document changes as a result of societal level leadership development. The images and discussion uncover visible and hidden aspects of the community context and dynamics that can communicate powerfully to a broad range of stakeholder groups.

For an effective Photovoice project, well-trained individuals organize the process, gathering the key participant group and providing framing questions, such as "What activities best show collective leadership in action to improve XXX in your community?" Participants are then given cameras (still and/or video) and asked to capture images they feel reflect the framing questions. The cameras are then returned to the team, who develop and compile the images. Work is then done at the individual level to select the images that best represent the person's personal point of view. A larger group session is then conducted using dialogue to generate deeper inquiry into the meaning and to generate a group perspective and understanding of the image's meaning. This meaning-making process is powerful for the group, facilitates public learning, and generates effective communication messages about impact at the societal level.

In a resource poor context, or when using the method with individuals who have little experience with technology (e.g., developing contexts, rural contexts), skilled practitioners and close management of the design and process is necessary for success (Krone & Dlamini et al, 2010). The process can also be very time consuming and costly. Though the process generates valuable stories and meanings, it does not provide data that can be causally linked to interventions, nor used in comprehensive models examining development and societal change.

Q-SORT

As outlined earlier in the chapter, Q-sort is a process in which individuals sort a number of statements (Q-sample) into a specified forced distribution of how descriptive a statement is of the area of interest. A the community level the descriptor could be, "Our community has experienced visible shifts in the public's willingness to engage in community improvement efforts," or "Our Fellowship efforts have led to policy changes to improve teaching and learning in our academic institutions." The distribution of the statements is then analyzed at the individual and group level using principal components analysis to provide z-scores for each statement in a factor. This allows a correlation to be computed between the individual and the model sort (Militello & Benham, 2010).

Q-sort has been used as a method of comparing changes across communities for a place-based collective leadership development intervention (Militello & Benham, 2010). The ability to measure the subjective level of agreement within a group, and then compare across groups holds promise as a quantitative method to build our understanding of impact at the societal level. And the ability to build and test models of interventions at the societal level is sorely needed within the field. Comparing across groups could occur at the community level, as in the evaluation of the Kellogg Leadership for Community Change, or across specific groups within a community, state, or country. Since changes at the societal level are unlikely to be consistent across subgroups, understanding the differences in timing and process of an intervention and the resulting changes is critical.

SECONDARY DATA/SOCIAL INDICATORS

Social indicators are used quite broadly at the community, state, national and international levels to track a variety of "objective" indicators of economic and social well-being and subjective measures of social well-being to look at changes and trends over time (Diener & Suh, 1997). While use of indicators is not without both measurement issues and political issues, they provide a way to look at macro indicators of valued outcomes and how they may change and be impact over time by interventions targeted at the societal level.

A variety of organizations have developed or compiled indicators or indexes, such as the World Bank, the UNDP, OECD, U.S. Government, and the European Union. The UN Development Program (UNDP) has a Human Development Index (HDI) that provides global data at the country level. The European Values Study allows for comparison across European countries and trends over time on basic human values, attitudes. and preferences. Quite often consortiums, governments, universities. or research organizations provide data at the community level. Ferriss (2001) argues that the use of social indicators to track changes over time should become a key empirical approach to evaluation at the societal level.

DOCUMENT ANALYSIS

There are several perspectives to take in approaching the use of document analysis at the societal level. The field of policy analysis examines the policy development and impact at various levels of governments—local, regional and national. Policy analysis frameworks focused on process, content, and performance can track efforts of collective leadership focused on social change efforts (O'Conner & Netting, 2008). On the technical end of the spectrum, leveraging social media data from blogs, Twitter feeds, and sites such as Facebook can be accomplished using text mining and sentiment analysis. These methods can be used to measure group and societal communication, interaction and emotional states and have been tested as a leading indicator for consumer confidence and presidential job approval polls in the USA (O'Conner, Balasubramanyan, Routledge, & Smith, 2010), predict presidential election results in Germany, (Tumasjan, Sprenger, Sandner, & Welpe, 2011), and to measure conflict dynamics in the Middle East (Zeitzoff, 2011).

INTERVIEWS/FOCUS GROUPS

Examining process and impact from multiple perspectives through interviews and focus groups can provide a holistic view of community and society-level interventions. Involving staff, participants, beneficiaries (if any) and the broader community can serve as a method of further refining indicators, testing emerging findings, and opportunity for additional data collection (e.g., surveys), and networking opportunities for participants (Howard & Reinelt, 2007). Use of key stakeholder interviews and broad-based community member interviews can efficiently gather information to provide a wide variety of perspectives. A challenge with this approach is that it is hard to conduct enough interviews and focus groups to truly generalize data because this approach is unlikely to capture all possible perspectives within a societal group.

STORYTELLING

Storytelling methods such as Most Significant Change (MSC) and newer methods such as crowd-sourcing narrative capture can make sense of highly contextualized experiences and uncover important themes, findings and unexpected results. MSC was developed for use within communities, and the participatory nature and learning focus provide significant benefits to long-term interventions when combined with more quantitative methods such as social indicators or exclusively when use of indicators is not feasible. Narrative capture as an approach provides a participant/beneficiary view and measures level of consensus through stories collected and analyzed by the community itself. Sense making of micronarratives at a large scale have provided great value in the social investment community (Boss, 2011). It is likely this value could be transferred to community leadership development interventions as well. This process combines the basics of human storytelling and technology to catalog and visualize the meaning participant's identify in the story.

OBSERVATION/ETHNOGRAPHY

Ethnography can be thought of as an approach, as opposed to a method, since it can combine multiple qualitative methods such as observation, interviews inventories, and photographs, for example. The areas of focus in ethnography to evaluate community-level interventions are understanding the meaning, context, and process of the intervention, working collaboratively with the community but engaging in reflexivity to understand bias in an effort to provide multiple voicing to the community (Jarrett, 2000). The Annie E. Casey Foundation's March 1997 Research and Evaluation Conference report on Evaluating Comprehensive Community Change believes that, "Through interviews with community members, ethnographic researchers create a detailed description of the way of life in a culture or society, including people's beliefs, attitudes and understandings. The goal is to produce conceptual or theoretical data about social life that are tied to empirical data" (p. 17). Use of ethnography can be especially important for ethnically diverse communities to capture varying perceptions among groups. Various issues and challenge exist when engaging in an ethnographic approach. Sample selection can introduce bias, and inability to gain trusted access to the community can compromise the validity of the data and results; data quality can vary greatly, again threatening validity, and as with any method, but more so for an approach that includes longer engagement at the community level, ethical issues abound.

Of all the levels outlined in this chapter, the development and application of appropriate methods to evaluate the impact of leadership interventions meant affect large-scale populations such as communities or whole societies is most needed. Intervention at this level hold the most promise for creating large-scale positive change, but the field's inability to understand and leverage complex community interventions limits the value such efforts are able to achieve.

Future Directions

There are four major areas we would highlight as holding potential in moving the field forward. These areas focus on model building, use of new and more sophisticated methods, development of standards and benchmarks, and use of evaluation as a part of the intervention process. These areas impact practice, use, and theory.

Model Building and Testing

As we articulate earlier in the chapter, the lack of fully developed and tested models of how leadership development at different levels leads to and results in different outcomes, along with important mediating and moderating factors, is a significant shortcoming. More rigorous application of models would also increase the validity and generalizability of evaluation results, building a stronger knowledge base of what works for the field. We would propose the SOGI framework as one such was to approach developing appropriate models to test multilevel development. Another aspect to be investigated within this area is questions of dosage. How much of a certain activity or intervention is necessary to achieve the desired outcomes. Having well-constructed models would make investigating this question easier to accomplish. A final area of model building of great interest to the training field is learning transfer. A better understanding of the individual, contextual, and intervention variables and interactions among them would lead to better designed and executed interventions. Future work on the model development discussed here has great potential to impact both the evaluation of development interventions, as well as the conceptualization and use of development interventions within organizations, communities, and societies.

Use of Technology to Collect, Share, and Make Sense of Information

As much of the world begins to benefit from the increased availability and use of technology, new approaches in data collection, sharing, and analysis have the potential to transform the way evaluation occurs, allowing for greater participation and engagement of participants in the evaluation process and interpretation of findings. Social media methods of cocreation of evaluation content and even analysis raise the idea of empowerment and participatory evaluation to a whole new level. Crowdsourcing methods can engage participants and others throughout the entire evaluation process—from data collection, analysis, and reporting—a constant member check to ensure accuracy and credibility of the results. With the proliferation of smartphones throughout the developed and developing world, accessing individuals electronically for data collection becomes much simpler, allowing for greater data collection and potentially more valid results. In the moment, data collection methods such as sociometers (Pentland, 2010) make collecting and reporting objective data regarding interactions and collaborations possible in unobtrusive ways. Sociometers can measure personal interactions, conversations, physical location, and activity to better understand individual and collective behavior.

Technology developments in software and methods allow evaluators to use more sophisticated analysis techniques such as social network analysis/organizational network analysis. We have highlighted this approach several times in the chapter and believe it holds great promise at the individual and collective level for understanding relationships, interactions, and the development of collective leadership. Advances in data visualization, of which network analysis is one, mean relevant findings and patterns can be uncovered and shared more effectively. Interactive data sets with multiple visualization possibilities can engage broader communities in sense making—academics, practitioners, and participants alike.

Metrics: Standards and Benchmarks

As evaluation in the learning and development field continues to mature, there is a greater movement toward the development of agreed-upon standards in the field, such as the Talent Development Reporting Principles (Barnett & Vance, 2012). These principals aim to serve the same purpose as the Generally Accepted Accounting Principles (GAAP) do in accounting to guide organizations in the collection and reporting of data related to learning and development activities and functions (Vance, 2011). Work to date includes the development of eight general principles, development of standard definitions and measures, three foundational statements, and recommendation of three executive reports. This effort continues to build upon previous work to establish benchmarks for efficiency, effectiveness, learning outcomes, and impact. Internal and external benchmarking of data across types of programs, participants, industries, regions, etc., also helps to build the knowledge base of the field in understand the results achieved for whom and how. This approach can also start to address the dosage question looking at program, participants, and outcomes.

Clearer articulation and closer linkage of interventions with organizational metrics at the talent level and with business results would advance the felt need by organizations to understand the value and ROI of investments in development at various levels. CCL's model of Talent Sustainability (Smith & Campbell, 2007) identifies eight critical areas for organizations to focus on for successful talent efforts:

1. Executive commitment and engagement
2. Critical talent identification, development, and succession
3. Learning and development
4. Competency model development and deployment
5. Knowledge management
6. Performance management
7. Rewards and recognition
8. Sourcing and recruiting

Identifying and linking organizational systems and processes, development interventions, and change efforts to metrics in these areas can provide a comprehensive picture of impact in the talent area. Some possible metrics include (Lamoureux, Campbell, & Smith, 2009):

- Percent of key roles likely to become vacant in the next one–three years with successor identified
- Percent of successors with development plans in place
- Strength of pipeline—Percent of leadership roles with ready-now successors
- Retention rate of high-potential talent
- Success rate of succession plans

This move toward standardization could prove foundational for the field.

Evaluation as an Intervention

As development interventions target multiple levels within organizations or communities, complexity increases, and the possible role of evaluation as an ongoing organizational learning process and key part of the actual intervention becomes greater. Using an approach such as Developmental Evaluation (DE), as opposed to more typical formative and summative approaches provides various benefits (Patton, 2011):

- The process supports innovation and adaptation during implementation.
- It is ideal for evolving situations where fidelity to a program design is not the issue and a logic model is of limited use.
- DE uses a systems change focus
- DE enables cocreation with stakeholders to guide the development of the most relevant and useful measures for each stage of the intervention.
- DE is utilization focused and focused on in the moment development of measures and data collection to help determine possible future directions
- DE is learning oriented and fosters an evaluative mindset, rather than being summative in nature

Use of approaches such as Developmental Evaluation can lead to greater integration of evaluation from the beginning, allowing the evaluation process to both shape the story as well as tell the story.

Along with the four future directions outlined above, we would continue to call for more publishing of evaluations to showcase current best practice in the field and encourage increased rigor in design, execution, and analysis. To achieve this goal, more active solicitation and acceptance of evaluation-oriented papers by journal editors will be required. Editors can create special issues dedicated to evaluation of developmental interventions and search out the best examples to showcase. On the other side, organizations and groups need to be more willing to share their program experience and the results, be they positive, neutral, or negative.

Only through continued sharing of ideas, theories, and work can the field advance and play a key role in advancing leadership at multiple levels and in multiple places.

Conclusion

Our firm belief is that evaluation plays a critical role in leadership development as a mechanism for creating sustainable learning. As we stated in the introduction, evaluation can be effectively used to set and understand the context for leadership development, influence the design and implementation of an initiative, measure changes that occur and identify the causes of the changes, and influence changes to be made at multiple levels.

To be most effective, evaluation must measure and address change at multiple levels, using multiple methods, and be implemented longitudinally. It must also be an integral part of the needs assessment and design of the initiative.

Because leadership development has powerful potential for impact at multiple levels, we offer a framework for evaluating it that addresses change at four levels: individual, group, organizational, and societal. This framework, abbreviated as SOGI, forms a useful way of both designing and evaluating leadership development. Evaluation methods can be appropriate and relevant for use at multiple levels of SOGI, but their design and use must be adapted to measure change at each specific level.

Finally, we encourage greater sharing of evaluation studies and findings in refereed journals through effective management of what may seem to be polarities—rigor and reality. There is no doubt that evaluation studies cannot be as tightly controlled as laboratory studies, but the value from their contribution is significant. Evaluators, organizations, and academia must continue to stretch the field of evaluation through publishing both the design and results of evaluation studies.

References

Alkin, M. C., & Christie, C. A. (2004). An evaluation theory tree. In M. C. Alkin (Ed.), *Evaluation roots: Tracing theorists' views and influences.* Thousand Oaks, CA: Sage.

Alvesson, M., & Karreman, D. (2000). Varieties of discourse: On the study of organizations through discourse analysis. *Human Relations, 53*(9), 1125–1149.

Amabile, T. M., Conti, R., Coon, H., Lasenby, J., & Herron, M. (1996). Assessing the work environment for creativity. *The Academy of Management Journal, 39*(5), 1154–1184.

The American Heritage® Dictionary of the English Language, Fourth Edition copyright ©2000 by Houghton Mifflin Company. Updated in 2009. Published by Houghton Mifflin Company. All rights reserved.

Avolio, B. J., Avey, J. B., & Quisenberry, D. (2010). Estimating return on leadership development investment. *The Leadership Quarterly, 21*(4), 633–644.

Avolio, B. J., Hannah, S., Reichard, R., Chan, A., & Walumbwa, F. (2009). 100 years of leadership intervention research. *Leadership Quarterly, 20,* 764–784.

Baldwin, T. T., & Ford, J. K. (1988), Transfer of training: A review and directions for future research. *Personnel Psychology, 41,* 63–105.

Balkundi, P., Kilduff, M., & Harrison, D. A. (2011). Centrality and charisma: Comparing how leader networks and attributions affect team performance. *Journal of Applied Psychology, 96,* 1209–1222.

Barnett, K, & Vance, D. (2012). TRDp whitepaper. Accessed on May 11, 2012, from http://www.tdrprinciples.org/pdfs/whitepaper-full-version.pdf

Becker, T. E., & Randall, D. M. (1994). Validation of a measure of organizational citizenship behavior against an objective behavioral criterion. *Educational and Psychological Measurement, 54*(1), 160–167.

Benham, M., Militello, M., & Halladay, P. (2005). *Kellogg leadership for community change: Focus on teaching and learning.* Final evaluation. Battle Creek, MI: The W.K.K. Foundation.

Bickman, L. (1987). The functions of program theory. *New Directions in Program Evaluation: Using Program Theory in Evaluation, 1987*(33), 5–18.

Borgatti, S. P., & Foster, P. C. (2003). The network paradigm in organizational research: A review and typology. *Journal of Management, 29*(6), 991–1013.

Boss, S. (2011, Summer). Amplifying local voices: GlobalGiving's storytelling project turns anecdotes into useful data. *Stanford Social Innovation Review, 9*(3), 67–68.

Brace-Govan, J. (2007). Participant photography in visual ethnography. *International Journal of Market Research, 49*(6), 735–750.

Brinkerhoff, R. O. (2003). *The success case method.* San Francisco: Berrett-Koehler.

Brinkerhoff, R. O., & Mooney, T. P. (2010). The success case method. In P. P. Phillip (Ed.), Handbook of *Measuring and Evaluating Training* (pp. 125–134). Alexandria, VA: ASTD.

Burke, L. A., & Hutchins, H. M. (2007). Training transfer: An integrative literature review. *Human Resource Development Review, 6*(3), 263–296.

Butler, J. K. (1991). Toward understanding and measuring conditions of trust: Evolution of a conditions of trust inventory. *Journal of Management, 17*(3), 643–663.

Cameron, K., & Freeman, S. (1991). Culture, congruence, strength and type: Relationship to effectiveness. *Research in Organizational Change and Development, 5,* 23–58.

Cascio, W. F., & Boudreau, J. W. (2008). *Investing in people: Financial impact of human resource initiatives.* Saddle River, New Jersey: FT Press.

The Citizenship Survey (2008) Accessed on August 28, 2011, from http://www.communities.gov.uk/documents/statistics/pdf/1133115.pdf

Coffman, J. (2003–2004). Michael Scriven on the differences between evaluation and social sciences research. *The Evaluation Exchange 9*(4). Retrieved August 31, 2012, from http://www.hfrp.org/evaluation/the-evaluation-exchange/issue-archive

Coghlan, A. T., Preskill, H., & Catsambas, T. T. (2003). An overview of appreciative inquiry in evaluation. In Preskill, H. & Coghlan, A. T. (Eds.), *Using appreciative inquiry in evaluation* (pp. 5–22). San Francisco: Jossey-Bass.

Collins, D. B., Holton, E. F. (2004). The effectiveness of managerial leadership development programs: A meta-analysis of studies from 1982 to 2001. *Human Resource Development Quarterly, 15*, 217–248.

Cooperrider, D. L., & Whitney, D. (1999). Collaborating for change: Appreciative inquiry. Accessed from web.me.com/davidnsaunders/dns/papers/AppreciativeInquiry.doc on August 30, 2011.

Cooperrider, D. L., Whitney, D., & Stavros, J. M. (2003). *Appreciative inquiry handbook.* Bedford Heights, OH: Lakeshore Publishers.

Craig, S. B., & Hannum, K. M. (2007). Experimental and quasi-experimental evaluations. In K. M. Hannum, J. W. Martineau, & C. Reinelt (Eds.), *The handbook of leadership development evaluation* (pp. 19–47). San Francisco: Jossey-Bass.

Cross, R., Borgatti, S. P., & Parker, A. 2001. Beyond Answers: Dimensions of the Advice Network. *Social Networks, 23*(3): 215–235.

Cross, R., Ehrlich, K., Dawson, R., & Helferich, J. (2008) Managing collaboration: Improving team effectiveness through a network perspective. *California Management Review, 50*, 74–99.

Cross, R., Laseter, T., Parker, A., & Velasquez, G. (2006). Using social network analysis to improve communities of practice. *California Management Review, 49*(1), 32–60.

Cross, R., & Thomas, R. (2008). How top talent uses networks and where rising stars get trapped. *Organizational Dynamics, 37*, 165–180.

Cross, R., Yan, A., & Louis, M. (2000). Boundary activity in "Boundaryless" organizations: A case study of a transformation to a team-based structure. *Human Relations, 53*(6), 841–868.

Cummings, L. L., & Bromiley, P. (1996). The organizational trust inventory (OTI): Development and validation. In T. K. Tyler (Ed.), *Trust in organizations: Frontiers of theory and research* (pp. 302–330). Thousand Oaks, CA: Sage Publications.

Davies, R. J. (1996). An evolutionary approach to facilitating organisational learning: An experiment by the Christian Commission for Development in Bangladesh. Swansea, UK: Centre for Development Studies [online]: http://www.swan.ac.uk/cds/rd/ccdb.htm. This paper has also been published, with some variations, in Mosse, D., Farrington, J., & Rew, A. (1998). *Development as process: Concepts and methods for working with complexity.* London: Routledge/ODI (pp 68–83); and in Impact assessment and project Appraisal, 16. No. 3, September 1998, 243–250.

Day, D. (2000). Leadership development: A review in context. *Leadership Quarterly, 15*, 857–880.

Day, D., & Sin, H-P. (2011). Longitudinal tests of an integrative model of leader development: Charting and understanding developmental trajectories. *The Leadership Quarterly, 22*, 545–560.

DeChurch, L. A., Hiller, N. J., Murase, T., Doty, D., & Salas, E. (2010). Leadership across levels: Levels of leaders and their levels of impact. *The Leadership Quarterly, 21*, 1069–1085.

De Meuse, K. P., Dai, G., & Lee, R. J. (2009). Evaluating the effectiveness of executive coaching: Beyond ROI? *Coaching: An International Journal of Theory, Research and Practice, 2*(2), 117–134.

Diener, E., & Suh, E. (1997). Measuring quality of life: Economic, social, and subjective indicators. *Social Indicators Research, 40*, 189–216.

Drath, W. H., McCauley, C. D., Palus, C. J., Van Velsor, E., O'Connor, P.M.G., & McGuire, J. B. (2008). Direction, alignment, commitment: Toward a more integrative ontology of leadership. *Leadership Quarterly, 19*, 635–653.

Duffy, L. (2011). Step-by-Step we are stronger: Women's empowerment through photovoice. *Journal of Community Health Nursing, 28*(2), 105–116.

Dziopa, F., & Ahern, K. (2011). A Systematic literature review of the applications of Q-technique and its methodology. *Methodology, 7*(2), 39–55.

Ely, K., Boyce, L. A., Nelson, J. K., Zaccaro, S. J., Hernez-Broome, G., & Whyman, W. (2010). Evaluating leadership coaching: A review and integrated framework. *The Leadership Quarterly*, (21), 585–599.

Ferriss, A. L. (2001). The uses of social indicators. *Social Indicators, 66*(3), 601–617.

Finegold, M. A., Holland, B. M., & Lingham, T. (2002). Appreciative inquiry and public dialogue: An approach to community change. *Public Organization Review: A Global Journal, 2*, 235–252.

Gentry, W. A., & Martineau, J. W. (2010). Hierarchical linear modeling as an example for measuring change over time in a leadership development evaluation context. *The Leadership Quarterly, 21*, 654–656.

Gerowitz, M., Lemieux-Charles, L., Heginbothan, C., & Johnson, B. (1996). Top management culture and performance in Canadian, UK and US hospitals. *Health Services Management Research, 6*(3), 69–78.

Gerowitz, M. B. (1998). Do TQM interventions change management culture? *Quality Management in Health Care, 6*(3), 1–11.

Glaser, S., Zamanou, S., & Hacker, K. (1987). Measuring and interpreting organizational culture. *Management Communication Quarterly, 1*(2), 173–198.

Greenbaum, T. L. (1998). *The handbook for focus group research.* London: Sage.

Grove, J., Kibel, B., & Haas, T. (2005). *EvaluLEAD: A guide for shaping and evaluating leadership development programs.* Chicago: W. K. Kellogg Foundation and Public Health Institute.

Gutierrez, M., & Tasse, T. (2007). Leading with theory: Using a theory of change approach for leadership development evaluations. In K. M. Hannum, J. W. Martineau, & C. Reinelt (Eds.), *The handbook of leadership development evaluation* (pp. 48–70). San Francisco: Jossey-Bass.

Hannum, K. M., & Martineau, J. W. (2008). *Evaluating the impact of leadership development.* San Francisco: Jossey-Bass.

Hannum, K. M., Martineau, J. W., & Reinelt, C. (2007). *The handbook of leadership development evaluation.* San Francisco: Jossey-Bass.

Harter, J. K., Schmidt, F. L., Killham, E. A., & Agrawal, S. (2009, August). *Q12 meta-analysis: The relationship between engagement at work and organizational outcomes.* Omaha, NE: Gallup Press.

Hilbert, J., Preskill, H., & Russ-Eft, D. (1997). Evaluating training. In L. J. Bassi & D. Russ-Eft (Eds.), *What works: Assessment, development, and measurement* (pp. 109–150). Alexandria, VA: ASTD.

Holton, E. F. III (1996). The flawed four-level evaluation model. *Human Resource Development Quarterly, 7*(1), 5–21.

Hoole, E., & Hannum, K. (2008, September). *Picture this: Using images to gather and communicate evaluation data.* Paper presented at the Australasian Evaluation Society annual meeting, Perth, Australia.

Hoole, E., & Martineau, J. W. (2010). Evaluating leadership development. In P. P. Phillips (Ed.), *ASTD handbook of measuring and evaluating training* (pp. 321–336). Alexandria, VA: ASTD.

Hoppe, B., & Reinelt, C. (2010). Social network analysis and the evaluation of leadership networks. *The Leadership Quarterly, 21*, 600–619.

Howard, G. S., & Dailey, P. R. (1979). Response-shift bias: A source of contamination of self-report measures. *Journal of Applied Psychology, 64*, 144–150.

Howard, K. A., & Reinelt, C. (2007). Evaluating leadership development for social change. In Hannum, K. M., Martineau, J. W., & Reinelt, C. (Eds.), *The handbook of leadership development evaluation* (pp. 343–376). San Francisco: Jossey-Bass.

Jarrett, R. L. (2000). Voices from below: The use of ethnographic research for informing public policy. In J. M. Mercier, S. Garasky, & M C. Shelley II (Eds.), *Redefining family policy: Implications for the 21st century* (pp. 67–84). Iowa City, IA: Iowa State University Press.

Johnson-Cramer, M., Parise, S., & Cross, R. (2007). Managing change through networks and values: How a relational view of culture can facilitate large scale change. *California Management Review, 49*(3), 85–109.

Kirkhart, K. E. (2010). Eyes on the prize: Multicultural validity and evaluation theory. *American Journal of Evaluation, 31*, 400–413.

Kirkpatrick, D. L. (1959a). Techniques for evaluating training programs. *Journal of American Society of Training Directors, 13*(11), 3–9.

Kirkpatrick, D. L. (1959b). Techniques for evaluating training programs—Part 2: Learning. *Journal of the American Society of Training Directors, 13*(11), 21–26.

Kirkpatrick, D. L. (1960a). Techniques for evaluating training programs—Part 3: Behavior. *Journal of the American Society of Training Directors, 14*(1), 13–18.

Kirkpatrick, D. L. (1960b). Techniques for evaluating training programs—Part 4: Results. *Journal of the American Society of Training Directors, 14*(1), 28–32.

Kraut, A. I. (1996). Organizational surveys: *Tools for assessment and change*. San Francisco: Jossey-Bass.

Krone, A., & Dlamini, N. (2010, June 28–30). PhotoVoice as a tool for planning and measuring impact of community-based economic development initiatives. *Montpellier*, France: ISDA.

Lamoureux, K., Campbell, M., & Smith, R. (2009). *High impact succession management*. Bersin & Associates and Center for Creative Leadership Industry Report.

Leithwood, K., Louis, K. S., Anderson, S., & Wahlstrom, K. (2004). *How leadership influences student learning*. Center for Applied Research and Educational Improvement, Ontario Institute for Studies in Education. Accessed on July, 14, 2013 from http://www.wallacefoundation.org/knowledge-center/school-leadership/key-research/Pages/How-Leadership-Influences-Student-Learning.aspx.

Leskiw, S. L., & Singh, P. (2007). Leadership development: Learning from best practices. *Leadership and Organization Development Journal, 28*(5), 444–464.

Levin-Rozalis, M. (2003). Evaluation and research: Differences and similarities. *The Canadian Journal of Program Evaluation, 18*(2), 1–31.

Lockheed, M. E. (2009). Evaluating development learning: The world bank experience. *Evaluation, 15*(1), 113–126.

Luque, J., Tyson, D. M., Lee, J., Gwede, C., Vadaparampil, S., Noel-Thomas, S., & Meade, C. (2010). Using social network analysis to evaluate community capacity building of a regional community cancer network. *Journal of Community Psychology, 38*(5), 656–668.

Mabey, C. (2002, Dec.). Mapping management development practice. *Journal of Management Studies, 39*(8), 1139–1160.

Mabey, C., & Thomson, A. (2000). The determinants of management development. *British Journal of Management, 11*, Special Issue, S3–SI6.

Mark, M. M., Henry, G. T., & Julnes, G. (2000). *Evaluation: An integrated framework for understanding, guiding, and improving policies and programs*. San Francisco: Jossey-Bass.

Martineau, J. W. (1995). *A contextual examination of the effectiveness of a supervisory skills training program*. Doctoral dissertation, The Pennsylvania State University at University Park, Pennsylvania.

Martineau, J. W. (1997). Using 360-degree surveys to assess change. In W. W. Tornow & M. London (Eds.), *Maximizing the value of 360-degree feedback* (pp. 217–248). San Francisco: Jossey-Bass.

Martineau, J. W., & Patterson, T. E. (2010). Evaluating leader development. In C. D. McCauley, M. N. Ruderman, & E. Van Velsor (Eds.), *The Center for Creative Leadership handbook of leadership development* (3rd ed., pp. 251–281). San Francisco: Jossey-Bass.

Mathison, S. (2008). What is the difference between evaluation and research, and why do we care? In N. L. Smith & P. R. Brandon (Eds.), *Fundamental issues in evaluation* (pp. 183–196). New York: Guilford Press.

McCauley, C. D., Palus, C. J., Drath W., Hughes, R. L., McGuire, J., O'Connor, P. M. G., & Van Velsor, E. (2008). Interdependent leadership in organizations: Evidence from six case studies. CCL Research Report no. 190. Greensboro, NC: Center for Creative Leadership.

McCauley, C., Smith, R., & Campbell, M. (2007). *Talent sustainability: Orchestrators, accelerators, and influencers*. Paper presented in ASTD 2008, International Conference & Exposition, Washington, DC, USA.

McGarvey, C., & Volkman, T. (2006). Getting inside the story: Ethnographic approaches to evaluation. Accessed on August 18, 2011, from http://www.grantcraft.org/index.cfm?fuseaction=Page.ViewPage&pageId=1539

McGuire, J. B., & Palus, C. J. (2003). Conversation piece: Using dialogue as a tool for better leadership. *Leadership in Action, 23*(1), 8–11.

Mehra, A., Kilduff, M., & Brass, D. J. (2001). The social networks of high and low self-monitors: Implications for workplace performance, *46*, 121–146.

Militello, M., & Benham, M. K. P. (2010). "Sorting Out" collective leadership: How Q-methodology can be used to evaluate leadership development. *The Leadership Quarterly, 21*(4), 620–632.

Morgan, D. L. (1993). *Success focus groups: Advancing the state of the art*. Thousand Oaks, CA: Sage.

Morgan, D. L., & Krueger, R. A. (1997). *Focus group kit, volumes 1–6*. Thousand Oaks, CA: Sage.

Morgeson, F. P., Lindoerfer, D., & Loring, D. J. (2010). Developing team leadership capability. In C. D. McCauley, M. N. Ruderman, & E. Van Velsor (Eds.), *The Center for Creative Leadership handbook of leadership development* (3rd ed., pp. 251–281). San Francisco: Jossey-Bass.

Mumford, M. D., Friedrich, T. L., Caughron, J. J., & Antes, A. (2009). Leadership development and assessment: Describing and rethinking the state of the art. In K. Ericsson (Ed.), *Development of professional expertise: Toward measurement of expert performance and design of optimal learning environments* (pp. 84–107). New York: Cambridge University Press.

O'Conner, B., Balasubramanyan, R., Routledge, B. R., & Smith, N. A. (2010.) *From tweets to polls: Linking text sentiment to public opinion time series*. Fourth International AAAI Conference on Weblogs and Social Media.

O'Conner, M. K., & Netting, F. E. (2008). Teaching policy analysis as research: Consideration and extension of options. *Journal of Social Work Education, 44*(3), 159–172.

Oman, R. F., Vesely, S. K., & McLeroy, K. R. (2002). Reliability and validity of the Youth Asset Survey (YAS). *Journal of Adolescent Health, 31*(3):247–255.
Ospina, S., & Foldy, E. (2010). Building bridges from the margins: The work of leadership in social change organizations. *The Leadership Quarterly, 21*(2), 292–307.
Palus, J. C., & Drath, W. H. (2001). Putting something in the middle: An approach to dialogue. *REFLECTIONS: The SoL Journal, 3*(2), 28–39.
Patton, M. Q. (2011). *Developmental evaluation.* New York: The Guilford Press.
Pentland, A. (2010). To signal is human. *American Scientist, 98,* 204–211.
Phillips, J. J. (1983). *Handbook of training and evaluation methods.* (1st ed.). Houston, TX: Gulf Publishing.
Phillipps, J. J., & Aaron, B. C. (2008). *Isolation of results: Defining the impact of the program.* San Francisco: Pfeiffer.
Phillips, J. J., & Schmidt, L. (2004). *The leadership scorecard.* Burlington, MA: Elsevier.
Phillips, P. P., & Phillips, J. J. (2008). *ROI fundamentals: Why and when to measure return on investment.* San Francisco: Wiley.
Ployhart, R. E., & Vandenberg, R. J. (2010). Longitudinal research: The theory, design, and analysis of change. *Journal of Management, 36*(1), 94–120.
Pratt, C., McGuigan, W., & Katzev, A. (2000). Measuring program outcomes: Using retrospective pretest methodology. *American Journal of Evaluation, 21*(3), 341–349.
Preskill, H., & Catsambas, T. T. (2006). *Reframing evaluation through appreciative inquiry.* Thousand Oaks, CA: Sage.
Quinn, L., & Van Velsor, E. (2010). Developing globally responsible leadership. In C. D. McCauley, E. Van Velsor, & M. N. Ruderman (Eds.), *The Center for Creative Leadership handbook of leadership development* (3rd ed.) (pp. 345–374). San Francisco: Jossey-Bass.
Rohs, F. R. (1999). Response shift bias: A problem in evaluating leadership development with self-report pretest-posttest measures. *Journal of Agricultural Education, 40*(4), 28–37.
Rohs, R. R., & Langone, C. A. (1997). Increased accuracy in measuring leadership impacts. *Journal of Leadership Studies, 4*(1), 150–158.
Rozalis, M. L. (2003). Evaluation and research: Differences and similarities. *The Canadian Journal of Program Evaluation, 18*(2), 1–31.
Russ-Eft, D., & Preskill, H. (2009). *Evaluation in organizations: A systematic approach to enhancing learning, performance, and change.* New York: Basic Books.
Saguaro Seminar (2009). SK 2006 community survey. Accessed on August 28, 2011, from http://www.hks.harvard.edu/saguaro/measurement/2006sccs.htm
Schwartz, D. (1989). Visual ethnography: Using photography in qualitative research. *Qualitative Sociology, 12*(2), 119–154.
Scott, T., Mannion, R., Davies, H., & Marshall, M. (2003). The quantitative measurement of organizational culture in health care: A review of the available instruments. *Health Services Research, 38*(3), 923–945.
Scriven, M. (1967). The methodology of evaluation. In R. Tyler, R. Gagne, & M. Scriven (Eds.), *Perspectives of curriculum evaluation* (pp. 39–83). Chicago: Rand McNally.
Sirianni, P. M., & Frey, B. A. (2001). Changing a culture: Evaluation of a leadership development program at Mellon Financial Services. *International Journal of Training and Development, 5,* 290–301.
Social Capital Question Bank (2002). Accessed on August 28, 2001, from http://www.ons.gov.uk/ons/guide-method/user-guidance/social-capital-guide/the-question-bank/index.html
Stephenson, K. (2007). The community network solution, *strategy+business* Issue 49, Winter 2007. Accessed on March 8, 2012, from: http://www.strategy-business.com/article/07403?pg=all
Stevahn, L., King, J. A., Ghere, G., & Minneman, J. (2005). Establishing essential competencies for evaluators. *American Journal of Evaluation, 26,* 43–59.
Susskind, A. M., Odom-Reed, P. R., & Viccari, A. E. (2011). Team leaders and team members in interorganizational networks: An examination of structural holes and performance. *Communication Research, 38,* 613–633.
Swanson, R. A., & Sleezer, C. M. (1987). Training effectiveness evaluation. *Journal of European Industrial Training, 11*(4), 7–16.
Taylor, P. J., Russ-Eft, D. F., & Taylor, H. (2009). Transfer of management training from alternative perspectives. *Journal of Applied Psychology, 94*(1), 104–121.
Thompson, N. C., Hunter, E. E., Murray, L., Ninci, L., Rolfs, E. M., & Pallikkathayil, L. (2008). The experience of living with chronic mental illness: A photovoice study. *Perspectives in Psychiatric Care, 44*(1), 14–24.
Tumasjan, A., Sprenger, T. O., Sandner, P. G., & Welpe, I. M. (2011). Election forecasts with Twitter—how 140 characters reflect the political landscape. *Social Science Computer Review, 29*(4), 402–418.
Vance, D. (2011). Talent development reporting: An evolving standard for L&D. Chief learning Officer. Accessed on May 11, 2012, from http://clomedia.com/articles/view/5190/
Weade R., & Ernst, G. (2001). Pictures of life in classrooms, and the search for metaphors to frame them. *Theory Into Practice, 29*(2), 133–140.
Wells, J. B. (2008, October). How rigorous should your training evaluation be? *Corrections Today,* 116–118.
West, M. (2008). Organizational climate. In S. R. Clegg & J. R. Bailey (Eds.), *International encyclopedia of organization studies* (vol. 3, pp. 1028–1030). Thousand Oaks, CA: Sage.
W. K. Kellogg Foundation. (2002). *Evaluating outcomes and impacts: A scan of 55 leadership development programs.* Battle Creek, MI: Authors.
W. K. Kellogg Foundation (2003). *Logic Model Development Guide.* Battle Creek, MI: W. K. Kellogg Foundation.
The World Bank has a number of resources on measuring social capital at the country level (http://web.worldbank.org/WBSITE/EXTERNAL/TOPICS/EXTSOCIALDEVELOPMENT/EXTTSOCIALCAPITAL/0,,contentMDK:20193049~menuPK:418220~pagePK:148956~piPK:216618~theSitePK:401015,00.html)
World Values Survey 2005 Official Data File v.20090901, 2009. World Values Survey Association (www.worldvaluessurvey.org)
Yammarino, F. J., & Dansereau, F. (2008). Multi-level nature of and multi-level approaches to leadership. *The Leadership Quarterly, 19*(2), 135–141.
Yammarino, F. J., Dionne, S. D., Chun, J. U., & Dansereau, F. (2005). Leadership and levels of analysis: A state-of-the-science review. *The Leadership Quarterly, 16,* 879–919.
Yarbrough, D. B., Shulha, L. M., Hopson, R. K., & Caruthers, F. A. (2011). *The program evaluation standards: A guide for evaluators and evaluation users* (3rd ed.). Thousand Oaks, CA: Sage.
Zeitzoff, T. (2011). Using social media to measure conflict dynamics. An application to the 2008–2009 Gaza conflict. *Journal of Conflict Resolution, 55*(6), 938–969.

PART 3

Leader-Centric Theories and Approaches

CHAPTER

10 Personality and Leadership: Looking Back, Looking Ahead

Joyce E. Bono, Winny Shen, *and* David J. Yoon

Abstract

Scholarly and practical interest in the traits and characteristics of effective leaders is long-standing and broad ranging. This chapter briefly summarizes the empirical literature with a focus on both traits that have been linked to leadership in the past (i.e., Big Five traits, self-monitoring), and traits that deserve more attention in the future as predictors of leadership success and failure (i.e., traits related to resiliency, proactivity, adaptability, integrity). In an effort to stimulate future research, the authors advocate for a more complex approach to the study of personality and leadership, including examination of nonlinear associations, trait profiles, and factors that enhance or constrain the personality–leadership association.

Key Words: destructive leadership, leadership effectiveness, personality, trait configurations

Introduction

Scholarly and practical interest in the traits and characteristics of effective leaders is longstanding and broad ranging. Terman's study of gifted children in the early 1900s (Terman & Oden, 1947) was motivated in part by a belief that intelligence (or more specifically, genius) was a characteristic of leaders. In *Outliers*, a recent popular book on exceptional performance, Gladwell (2008) attempts to debunk the myth that individuals who are top performers in their field are fundamentally different from others. His central argument is that opportunity, practice, and hard work are better predictors of success (in leadership, piano, hockey, or any other domain) than are stable characteristics of individuals. But a careful analysis of his writing begs this question: What characteristics might be the source of the magical 10,000 hours of practice that leads one to be an expert (or leader)? Why do some people practice 10,000 hours and others do not? The notion that personality traits are not the basis of leadership is also taken up in writings by Bill George, Harvard professor of management practice and former Medtronic CEO. George, along with Sims, McLean, and Mayer (2007), argues that it is not personality that makes a leader; it is how a person deals with crucible events in life: "Leadership emerges from your life story" (p. 130). This approach also begs the question of what leads one individual to react to major life events with resilience and fortitude while another reacts with depression and anger. The assumption of personality psychologists is that such differences (in willingness to devote long hours to practice or in resilience to difficult events) may be rooted in stable individual differences, including personality.

The existing literature on personality and leadership is large: 63 million hits on Google, 691 thousand hits in Google scholar, thousands of journal pages on the topic, hundreds of empirical studies, and multiple meta-analyses linking personality to some type of leadership criteria (e.g., Bono & Judge, 2004; Judge, Bono, Ilies, & Gerhardt, 2002; Lord, De Vader, & Alliger, 1986). Yet, some decry how little we know about the characteristics of effective leaders (see Judge, Piccolo, & Kosalka, 2009, for a comprehensive review of this position). Our inability to reach strong and clear conclusions about the traits of effective leaders is not surprising given how broad, dynamic, relational, and contextually driven the leadership process is; how many ways that leadership and leadership effectiveness can be measured; and how many broad and narrow personality traits exist in the literature. When leadership is defined at its most fundamental level as guiding, influencing, and directing others, it is clear that certain personality traits (e.g., extraversion, especially the tendency toward dominance and positive emotionality) might be associated with leadership success. Yet, the process of guiding and influencing others can be achieved by many means, and not all of them would be well matched with extraversion. Sometimes inspiration derives from a leader with a clear vision; sometimes it comes from the quiet confidence a leader puts in employees; sometimes it is the result of active participation by employees in setting an organizational direction; and sometimes it is the effect of a leader who stands up for what is "right" for an organization or its people in the long run. Moreover, guiding and influencing others is only one small part of effective leadership. Thus, identifying the "traits of leaders" is a challenging proposition and one not likely to result in a wholly satisfying conclusion, especially those looking to select effective leaders based on their personality traits (Morgeson et al., 2007).

Nonetheless, our position in this chapter is that those who study leadership, those who select and train leaders, and those who teach leadership would be remiss not to consider personality. Research focused on the personality traits of effective leaders helps us better understand the behaviors that are necessary for leadership success both within specific situations and across a broad variety of situations, even when those traits are not explicitly used for selection. Given the complexity of leadership and the contexts in which it occurs, we do not apologize for reporting some small effect sizes linking personality to leadership, considering that these effects are found across people, companies, markets, cultures, goals, and in spite of vast differences in regulatory constraints, organizational politics and policies, and employee knowledge, skills, motivation, and abilities. Rather, given the vast array of personality traits that could be (and have been) studied, the many ways of defining and measuring leadership, and the broad variety of situations in which it occurs, we find it impressive that some consistent links between personality and leadership have been found. But, we also acknowledge that the field as a whole has taken a rather narrow view of the link between personality and leadership; we believe that increased understanding will result from the adoption of a more holistic and complex approach to the study of this association.

In this chapter, we begin with a brief summary of what is known about the personality traits associated with leadership success, drawing on existing qualitative and quantitative reviews. After summarizing existing knowledge, we turn our focus to areas where we believe more research attention is needed in the future. A fundamental assumption underlying our discussion of personality and leadership—whether it concerns organizations, teams, individuals, or even the self—is that leadership in the future is becoming more complex and dynamic than it is today. Influencing others will always be at the core of the leadership process, but more attention is needed on broad leader capabilities, such as initiative, resilience, adaptability, and integrity, as such capabilities may loom larger as predictors of leadership success in the future. After summarizing the current state of the personality–leadership literature, we seek to stimulate future research by discussing (1) traits that may be relevant for leadership in the future, but that have been understudied (Judge et al., 2009), including traits of destructive leaders (e.g., Wang, Sinclair, & Deese., 2010); (2) nonlinear and configural approaches to the measurement of traits (e.g., Benson & Campbell, 2007); and (3) the role of context (e.g., follower traits, gender, level in the organizational hierarchy) in the association between personality and leadership.

A Few Things We Know about Personality and Leadership

There are a number of excellent reviews and book chapters on the topic of personality and leadership (Bono & Judge, 2004; Judge et al., 2002; Lord et al., 1986, among others). We especially point out a recent, comprehensive, article on the topic that provides a broad and theoretically grounded framework for understanding links between personality and leadership (Judge et al., 2009) and a recent special Issue of *Leadership Quarterly* that focuses on leadership traits (Zaccaro, 2012). With much written on the topic, we do not provide a comprehensive review of the literature in this chapter. Rather, we focus this introductory section on some important highlights of the existing literature, with a specific focus on questions and issues that have been the subject of considerable research or debate.

Born versus Made

Individuals who share common genes are significantly more alike in their tendency to emerge as leaders than those who do not. Using meta-analytic correlations among and between traits and leadership, along with the estimated heritability of each, Ilies, Gerhardt, and Le (2004) estimated that 17 percent of the heritable variance in leadership emergence can be explained by intelligence and the Big Five personality traits. Although their study made an important contribution to the literature, it was limited in that estimates were based on extrapolations from data in existing meta-analyses, rather than on direct examination of twin data. Taking a different approach, Arvey, Zhang, Avolio, and Krueger (2007) studied genetic and developmental influence on leadership emergence (i.e., role occupancy) using a large sample of female fraternal and identical twins. They found that genetics influenced both leadership emergence and two developmental factors that predicted leadership influence (i.e., family experience and work experience). The percent variance explained by genetics for each factor was family experience (8.7 percent), work experience (6.9 percent), and leadership (16.3 percent). This study focused only on women and only on the genetic basis of leadership emergence and did not deal specifically with the role that personality plays in that process. Research by Arvey, Rotundo, Johnson, Zhang, and McGue (2006) used a similar sample of male twins and examined genetic influences on both personality and leadership role occupancy; they found genetic influences on both but tests of mediation were not conclusive with respect to the question of whether the genetic influences on leadership operate through personality (i.e., a partial mediation model was not a better fit for the data than a no mediation model, where genetics and personality both had direct effects on leadership). Taking a slightly different approach (but also using fraternal and identical twins), Johnson, Vernon, Harris, and Jang (2004) report statistically significant and positive genetic correlations between transformational leadership and the personality factors of conscientiousness, extraversion, and openness to experience. Considering this line of research as a whole, there is considerable evidence in support of genetic influences on leadership emergence and transformational leadership behavior and weaker, but suggestive, evidence that these genetic effects operate via personality.

Traits of Leaders

Across time, a wide variety of personality traits have been associated with various leadership criteria, including perceptions of leadership, leadership effectiveness, leadership behaviors, emergence into leadership positions, and effective team performance. There have been several attempts to summarize the results of those studies both qualitatively (e.g., Hogan Curphy, & Hogan, 1994; Kirkpatrick & Locke, 1991; Stogdill, 1948) and quantitatively via meta-analysis (Lord et al., 1986). The list of traits important enough to be considered in these reviews is long, including masculinity, dominance, extraversion, adjustment, conservatism, leadership motivation, honesty and integrity, self-confidence, intelligence, knowledge of business, sociability, ambition or achievement, diplomacy, cooperative, emotional control, mood, and surgency, among others. Subsequent to these reviews, the emergence and popularity of the Big Five personality traits as a broad taxonomy into which narrower traits could be organized was as useful in leadership as it has been in other domains (e.g., job performance).

Big Five Traits

Using the Big Five framework, it is easier to identify key leadership traits. All the Big Five traits have been linked to leadership in some way (Bono & Judge, 2004; Judge et al., 2002) and are listed here in their order of importance as correlates of leadership, broadly construed.

EXTRAVERSION

If there is a single leadership trait, this would be it; nearly half of the adjectives listed in earlier reviews can be mapped onto various dimensions of extraversion. Extraverts are sociable, dominant, and energetic, and they experience and express positive emotions. They seek out leadership positions, exude confidence, and can articulate a compelling vision for the future, leading them to be perceived to be leader-like (Hogan et al., 1994). In addition to emerging as leaders, extraverts are also more likely (than leaders low on this trait) to be successful in leadership positions (Judge et al., 2002). Judge et al. (2002) also directly examined facets of extraversion and found significant associations between both sociability and dominance and leadership. Extraversion has also been identified as a consistent correlate of transformational leadership behaviors (Bono & Judge, 2004). When considered in concert with the other Big Five traits, extraversion has the largest association with leader emergence (tied with conscientiousness) and effectiveness (tied with openness to experience), though its status as the most important leadership predictor is not confirmed in government or military settings (Judge et al., 2002).

CONSCIENTIOUSNESS

This trait is associated primarily with achievement motivation; the tendency to be well-organized and dependable; and to have decisions guided by rules, laws, and principles. As leaders, individuals who score high on this trait have integrity (see also the subsequent section on this topic), have a clear plan for the future and know how to set goals to achieve those plans, and persist in carrying them out. Terms associated with conscientiousness also show up in past reviews (e.g., honesty and integrity, achievement) though to a much smaller degree than do terms associated with extraversion. In meta-analyses, conscientiousness has been positively and significantly associated with leadership emergence, but there is considerably more variability in its association with effectiveness (i.e., the 80 percent credibility interval includes zero; Judge et al., 2002). When the Big Five traits were considered together, conscientiousness was significantly associated with leadership emergence, but not effectiveness. This may be related to the finding by Judge and colleagues that showed that conscientiousness was not significantly associated with leadership in business settings, though it was in government and military settings and among student samples. When leadership criteria (emergence and effectiveness) were combined in the Judge et al., (2002) meta-analysis, both facets of conscientiousness they studied (achievement and dependability) were positively associated with leadership. Bono and Judge (2004) also found considerable variability (a nonsignificant meta-analytic association) in the association between conscientiousness and transformational leadership behaviors. Considered as a whole, existing research suggests that conscientious individuals tend to emerge as leaders but may be effective only in some situations, or that the association between conscientiousness and leadership effectiveness maybe nonlinear (see subsequent section on nonlinear associations).

OPENNESS TO EXPERIENCE

Although openness to experiences has been the trait of least interest to organizational scholars over time (especially those who study job performance), there is evidence that this trait may be important to leadership. In terms of facet structure, openness is least understood, but its association with general mental ability is highest among the Big Five (McCrae, 1987). Individuals high on this trait are curious, creative, and imaginative; openness has been linked to divergent thinking as well. It may be that openness predicts leadership, at least in part, because individual high on this trait are better at the analytic and problem-solving elements of leadership, or because they cope better with change (Judge, Thoresen, Pucik, & Welbourne, 1999). In the Judge et al. (2002) meta-analysis, openness was positively associated with both leader emergence and leader effectiveness, but this association disappeared in government and military settings. Considered together with the other Big Five traits, openness remained a significant predictor of both leadership emergence and effectiveness (Judge et al., 2002), but it was not significantly associated with the overall transformational leadership composite (i.e., the 80 percent credibility interval included zero; Bono & Judge, 2004).

NEUROTICISM

Given that anxiety, negative emotions, and emotional instability are the hallmarks of neuroticism, and that confidence is one of the commonly used words in describing leaders, it is not surprising that neuroticism is negatively associated with leadership effectiveness, though it has not been significantly associated with emergence (i.e., the 80 percent confidence interval for emergence includes zero; Judge et al., 2002). When the Big Five traits are regressed on leadership emergence and effectiveness, no significant associations between neuroticism and leadership emerge, but this trait is significantly (negatively) associated with transformational leadership behaviors (Bono & Judge, 2004).

AGREEABLENESS

When considering the relational aspects of leadership, it is plausible to expect that agreeableness, which includes the propensity to be altruistic, cooperative, kind, and conflict avoidant, might be helpful. But the aspects of leadership that require hard decisions and especially those that require choices between what is good for individuals and what is good for the group or organization might be particularly challenging for individuals high on agreeableness (Judge et al., 2009). In the Judge et al., (2002) meta-analysis, agreeableness was associated neither with leadership emergence nor with effectiveness. Moreover, when the Big Five traits were considered together, a significant, negative, association between agreeableness and leadership emergence was found, but the association between agreeableness and leadership effectiveness was not significant (Judge et al., 2002). Agreeableness was not linked to transformational leadership (Judge et al., 2004).

SELF-MONITORING

The Big Five trait taxonomy is useful because it allows researchers to organize results of studies linking many specific traits into a single framework. But the trait of self-monitoring, which has also been linked to leadership, does not neatly fall into the Big Five taxonomy.

Being alert to the surrounding environment and patterning one's behavior accordingly are marks of a good leader (Kenny & Zaccaro, 1983; Stogdill, 1948; Zaccaro, Gilbert, Thor, & Mumford, 1991). Thus, it is not surprising that self-monitoring—a trait related to monitoring and controlling one's behavior according to external cues (Snyder, 1974)—has been studied in connection with leadership. Self-monitoring consists of three characteristics: (1) sensitivity to social cues, (2) consideration for social appropriateness, and (3) ability to alter one's behavior based on external cues (Snyder, 1974). Self-monitoring was positively associated with leader emergence and leadership perceptions (Day, Schleicher, Unckless, & Hiller, 2002; Ellis, 1988; Foti & Hauenstein, 2007; Garland & Beard, 1979; Zaccaro, Foti, & Kenny, 1993) and leadership effectiveness (Foti & Hauenstein, 2007). This may be in part because individuals with high scores on self-monitoring are more sensitive to emotional cues from followers and are thus able to respond to them more appropriately. It may also be because individuals who score high on this trait are skilled at presenting information that is tailored to the needs of a particular audience.

Effect Sizes

Although the literature clearly links personality traits to leadership outcomes, one question that needs to be answered is whether these associations are large enough to have any practical value (Morgeson et al., 2007). Using Cohen's (1992) criteria for effects sizes, we conclude that for the most part, the association between individual personality traits and leadership are small to medium in magnitude, but the real question is whether they are large enough to be important. For the traits reviewed earlier, most correlations between individual traits and a single leadership criterion range from the high teens to the low. 30s. Perhaps more important than the individual trait–leadership correlations however, is the amount of variance that can be explained by the traits as a group. In the Judge et al. (2002) meta-analysis, the multiple correlations for the Big Five traits was .53 for leadership emergence, .39 for leadership effectiveness, and .48 for the combined leadership criteria. Thus, traits explain between 15 percent and 28 percent of the differences between people in their attainment of leadership position (emergence) and in their success in such positions (effectiveness). Moreover, the Big Five explain 9 percent of the variance in transformational leadership behaviors and 12 percent of the variance in charisma (Bono & Judge, 2004). We are not aware of any summary studies that consider the Big Five and self-monitoring together, but given the associations between self-monitoring and the Big Five, it would be reasonable to expect a small increment in the R^2 if self-monitoring was also considered in a multiple regression. The question of what is enough variance to matter is not an easy one, but our review strongly suggests that across raters and situations, the Big Five traits are important predictors of who will emerge and be effective as a leader.

Summary

Twin research suggests genetic bases for leadership emergence, and provides preliminary evidence that these effects are due to heritable personality traits. Based on quantitative and qualitative reviews, the individual traits that seem to matter most for leadership emergence and effectiveness are extraversion, openness to experience, conscientiousness, and self-monitoring. Considered together, these traits explain approximately 15–25 percent of the variance in leadership effectiveness and emergence.

Leadership Traits That Deserve More Attention

A key advantage of using the Big Five framework to describe the traits of leaders is that it allows researchers to organize the literature, revealing personality–leadership associations that might otherwise be obscured. However, this approach comes with a downside, in that it focuses on broad multidimensional traits and may mask the importance of narrower traits that are not well represented in the broad Big Five dimensions or traits that lie at the intersection of the five broad traits (i.e., compound traits). With this is mind, we focus next on traits that address four broad leadership capabilities expected to become increasingly important for leadership in the future: resiliency, adaptability, integrity, and initiative. In addition, we examine traits that may be associated with destructive leadership or leadership derailment (i.e., dark side traits).

Resiliency, Adaptability, Integrity, and Initiative

CORE SELF-EVALUATIONS

Core self-evaluations (CSE) is a trait cluster introduced by Judge, Locke, and Durham (1997). It represents an individual's fundamental evaluation of his or her self-worth, capabilities, and competence (Judge et al., 1997) and manifests in four self-evaluative traits: self-esteem, generalized self-efficacy, neuroticism, and internal locus of control. CSE has been most often studied in the context of job satisfaction (Judge & Bono, 2001) and life satisfaction (Judge, Bono, Erez, & Locke, 2005). It has also been positively associated with goal-setting, motivation, and the pursuit of goals for intrinsic and value-based reasons (Erez & Judge, 2001; Judge et al., 2005), as well as with resilience in the face of stress (Chang, Ferris, Johnson, Rosen, & Tan, 2012; Erez & Judge, 2001; Harris, Harvey, & Kacmar, 2009; Kammeyer-Mueller, Judge, & Scott, 2009), and negatively with burnout (Best, Stapleton, & Downey, 2005). In a meta-analysis, Chang and colleagues (2012) shows that individuals high in CSE are more focused on the positive aspects of their surroundings and view their workplace to be more attractive than those low in CSE, set more challenging goals and are more committed to fulfilling them, perform tasks better and display organizational citizenship behaviors more frequently, and are less prone to display counterproductive work behaviors than those with low in CSE.

Although there has been little research linking CSE with leadership, there are reasons to suspect that this trait might play a role in the leadership process. First, individuals high in CSE evaluate themselves and their capabilities positively, which is a fundamental requirement for leadership; one of the most common leadership descriptors found in the literature is confidence. Second, one of the key challenges of the leadership role is to adapt successfully to challenges provided by the context, including employees, organizational climate, and the broader market conditions; CSE is associated with resilience and the ability to adapt to change (Judge et al., 1999). Recent research also shows that high-CSE leaders were more likely to steer a firm toward entrepreneurial orientation when the firm is in an unstable, fluctuating market environment (Simsek, Heavey, & Veiga, 2010). Considering this trait and its correlates, CSE may be a trait worthy of more attention by leadership scholars. The confidence, optimism, and resiliency that characterize this trait should serve leaders when they face problems and need to show followers a path forward. Positive self-regard in the form of self-esteem and internal locus of control have been linked to leadership (Judge et al., 2002), and they may provide psychological security for the followers (Eden, 1992; House & Howell, 1992; Shamir, House, & Arthur, 1993). Wang and colleagues (2010) also include CSE as part of a "resilience cluster" of traits—traits that they identify as important for the prevention of destructive leader behavior, largely via improved self-regulatory capacity.

HARDINESS

Hardy individuals believe that they control the events they experience (control dimension), have the ability to feel deeply committed to the activities of their lives and finding meaning in such activities (commitment dimension), and construe change as a challenge for further learning and growth (challenge dimension; Kobasa, 1979). Researchers have extensively studied the relationship between hardiness and stress. In her study of executives, Kobasa (1979) found that executives that were hardy—strong commitment to self, vigor toward the environment, strong sense of meaningfulness, internal locus of control—were less physically ill when faced with high-stress events than those who were less hardy. Hardiness positively affected health in other studies involving managers (Kobasa, Maddi, & Khan, 1982) because it affected the managers' use of social resources in coping with stress (Kobasa & Puccetti, 1983). More specifically, the commitment and control dimensions directly affect health, but also do so by buffering the impact of stressful life events (Hull, Van Treuren, & Virnelli, 1987). Hardy individuals are confident and employ a number of proactive measures such as active coping and utilizing social support to overcome their distress (Florian, Mikulincer, & Taubman, 1995). A leader's hardiness also predicts performance beyond general mental ability and Big Five traits (Bartone, Eid, Johnsen, Laberg, & Snook, 2009). Leaders who have high levels of hardiness are resistant to stressful events and better utilize social resources when faced with challenges, making this an important trait for both resilience and adaptability. The extent to which this trait overlaps with CSE needs further examination in the literature.

PROACTIVE PERSONALITY

Bateman and Crant (1993) define proactive personality as the "relatively stable tendency to effect environmental change" (p. 103). Proactive personality has also been associated with charismatic leadership (Crant & Bateman, 2000), explaining additional variance beyond the Big Five traits. Leader's proactive personality has been linked to proactive cognitive and motivational states as well. For instance, Parker, Williams, and Turner (2006) found that proactive personality was a positive predictor of the tendency to adapt—specifically, role breadth self-efficacy and flexible role orientation—and this in turn, positively predicted the initiation of problem-solving procedures. Parker and her colleagues (Parker, Bindl, & Strauss, 2010) argued that proactive personality, core self-evaluations, openness, and conscientiousness (among others) are important traits for proactive motivation, which leads to proactive goal generation (e.g., envisioning a future from a different angle and planning accordingly) and proactive goal striving (e.g., persevering throughout the difficulties that come up when fulfilling their vision). Proactive goal generation and goal striving are important to adaptive leadership, especially when leaders face new situations where their previous training or experience cannot directly inform them of solutions.

INTEGRITY

At the heart of integrity is coherence—a state in which one's beliefs are consistent with one another as well as a state in which one's beliefs are consistent with one's actions (McFall, 1987). Integrity, when considered in an organizational setting, emphasizes consistency between belief and action. According to Becker (1998: 158), integrity is the quality that describes "the extent to which a person acts on rational principles and values" and is not synonymous to honesty and conscientiousness. An individual can lack integrity on the basis of (1) having desires that are inconsistent with moral values or rational convictions or (2) not being able to practice moral values in the face of resistance (Becker, 1998). Hence, the discussion of integrity from a personality standpoint requires a view that encompasses a *combination* of traits that not only steers a leader toward having moral principles but also serves as tools for acting on those principles; Ones and Viswesvaran (2001) construe integrity as a combination of Big Five traits (conscientiousness, neuroticism, agreeableness). Wang et al. (2010) construed integrity as a cluster of traits and linked the integrity cluster with lower capability to deal with stressors via self-regulation, poorer attitude toward others, prescribing to a lenient view toward mistreatment of others, and being more receptive to destructive norms. Thus, the integrity cluster of traits may be both associated with effective leadership (e.g., Becker, 1998) and lack of the integrity cluster of traits may also be a predictor of destructive leadership. For this reason the integrity cluster is especially important for leadership.

Destructive Leadership and Leadership Derailment

In addition to traits that predict leadership success, there has been more recent attention to another set of traits, those that predict destructive leadership (Wang, et al., 2010) and leadership derailment (Hogan & Hogan, 2001). Our focus here is on a different set of outcomes (destructive leadership and leadership derailment) and a different set of traits, though Judge et al. (2009) make the point that some traits associated with leadership effectiveness may also have a dark side (and dark side traits may have bright sides as well), an issue that is addressed directly in the section on nonlinear associations. In their dual-process model, Wang et al. (2010) suggest that destructive leadership may be due to either failed self-regulation or intentional behavior, or both. They suggest that traits associated with destructive leadership tend to fall into three clusters: resiliency, integrity, and dark side traits. In their examination of the bright and dark side of leadership personality, Judge et al. (2009) also include some dark traits that represent more than high or low levels of bright traits. In this section we briefly review these dark traits.

HOGAN DEVELOPMENT SURVEY

Prior to the 1970s, dark side personality traits were viewed mostly as extreme neuroticism, exhibited as depression and anxiety (Hogan & Hogan, 2001). However, the understanding of dark side personality in the managerial literature deepened over the past 20 years with the increasing juxtaposition between the Big Five personality traits and personality disorders. Hogan and Hogan (1997) developed a measure (Hogan Development Survey [HDS]) that taps into the traits between the range of the Big Five and the *Diagnostic and Statistical Manual of Mental Disorders*, Fourth Editon (DSM-IV) that captures factors associated with managerial derailment. They mapped dysfunctional personality traits onto the dimensions from Horney's (1950) model of flawed interpersonal characteristics: (1) moving away from people (i.e., individuals who distance themselves from others to deal with their insecurity; Excitable, Cautious, Reserved, Skeptical, Leisurely); (2) moving against people (i.e., individuals who use manipulation and intimidation to deal with their insecurities; Mischievous, Bold, Colorful, Imaginative) and (3) moving toward people (i.e., individuals who conform to others to deal with their insecurities; Diligent and Dutiful). An important issue, relative to leadership, is that individuals with these traits may also have good social skills, leading their dark side traits to be invisible in traditional selection settings, yet they are particularly insidious for leaders because the behaviors associated with these characteristics erode trust (Hogan & Kaiser, 2005). Another reason these traits present problems for leadership is that some of them are positively associated with effective leadership behaviors, such as charisma. For example, Khoo and Burch (2008) showed that the Colorful dimension (i.e., histrionic personality) was a positive predictor of transformational leadership. Moreover, research by Benson and Campbell (2007) suggests nonlinear associations between these traits and both task and interpersonal leadership, such that at lower levels there is little association between the traits and leadership, but as dark side trait levels increase, a negative association emerges. This same curvilinear association emerged in another sample of managers from a variety of industries, and predicted four types of leadership: results-, business-, people-, and self-leadership.

NARCISSISM

Understanding narcissism as a trait requires examining its origin as a clinical disorder (American Psychiatric Association, 1994). The clinical symptoms of narcissism denote a pattern of grandiosity, need for admiration, and a strong sense of entitlement. It is a sign of insecurity that manifests in overcompensation, which is actually a defense mechanism against such a negative view of self (Jordan, Spencer, Zanna, Hoshino-Browne, & Correll, 2003; Zeigler-Hill, 2006). However, personality researchers view milder manifestation of such narcissism to be a personality type rather than a disorder (O'Boyle, Forsyth, Banks, & McDaniel, in press; Rhodewalt & Peterson, 2009); these views consider narcissism to be relatively prevalent in organizations in distorting others' perceptions and behaviors (Brown, 1997). Leaders with high levels of trait narcissism are likely to feel important; exaggerate personal achievements; demand praise despite unwarranted levels of achievements; delve into fantasies of success, power, and beauty, and feel as though they can be understood only by superior individuals, like themselves. From the trait perspective, narcissism has often been associated with an extreme case of self-esteem, extraversion, or even hostility (Judge, LePine, & Rich, 2006), but research suggests that narcissism is not isomorphic to very high sense of self-esteem though the two are positively related (r =. 35; Brown & Zeigler-Hill, 2004).

The most devastating aspect of narcissism in leaders is that that they become easily agitated, angered, and jealous of others who receive attention and respect that they believe they themselves should receive (see American Psychiatric Association, 1994). Judge and colleagues (2006) found that narcissistic leaders have a distorted perspective of themselves as good leaders. For instance, narcissistic leaders rate themselves as effective leaders, but their followers did not agree with such an assessment (Judge et al., 2006). Furthermore, narcissistic leaders consider themselves to be good organizational citizens and hard workers even when they are not. Narcissism is positively related to leader emergence, perhaps in part because narcissistic individuals can be charismatic (e.g., Sankowsky, 1995), but once in a leadership position, narcissistic leaders are not effective (Judge et al., 2006; Rosenthal & Pittinsky, 2006) and do not display transformational behaviors (Khoo & Burch, 2008).

MACHIAVELLIANISM

The idea of Machiavellianism as a trait was first introduced by Christie and Geis (1970) and reflects the leadership traits and beliefs advocated by the 16th century Italian politician Niccolo Machiavelli in *The Prince*. According to Machiavelli, effective leaders are those who are opportunistic, do not consider emotions in relationships, dismiss assumptions on human nature, and are independent from the confines of conventional morality. Leaders who have high levels of Machiavellianism are manipulative and use deception toward their followers to achieve their goals (Judge et al., 2009; McHoskey, 1999). Their goals are neither to benefit the organization nor to uphold societal values (Becker & O'Hair, 2007).

Empirical studies on Machiavellianism show that individuals with these traits often emerge as leaders and are effective at influencing others. Studies show that Machiavellians have a higher motivation to lead and end up in positions of formal authority (Mael,

Waldman, & Mulqueen, 2001), as these positions make it easier for them to achieve their personal goals. Unlike narcissistic leaders, Machiavellian leaders are aware of their followers' psychological tendencies and strategically influence them accordingly (Judge et al., 2009). In their experimental study, Drory and Gluskinos (1980) found that Machiavellian leaders were indeed more responsive to situational demands and tailored their influential tactics to the situation. Machiavellian leaders gave more directives but were not involved in easing tensions within the group when the situation was more favorable (e.g., when the group had the technical capability for the task), similar to the tendencies of narcissistic leaders. In contrast, when the situation of the group was more unfavorable (e.g., when the group did not have the technical capability for the task), Machiavellian leaders were less directive and more frequently asked for assistance. Deluga (2001) found that presidential Machiavellianism was a positive predictor of charismatic leadership, creativity, and rated performance.

HUBRIS

Hubris is an exaggerated sense of pride or arrogance (Kroll, Toombs, & Wright, 2000). Similar to narcissistic leaders, hubristic leaders overinflate their self-evaluations of their talent and ability than is warranted (Judge et al., 2009). The major difference between narcissism and hubris is how the trait is activated. Although all personality traits have both genetic and situational components, narcissism is considered a self-regulatory defense mechanism in service of a positive self-image (Morf & Rhodewait, 2001). In contrast, the trait of hubris arises largely in response to particular situations, but is considered trait-like because it is a stable response of some individuals to such situations. Leader hubris has four interrelated sources: (1) a series of successes that a leader experienced, (2) the leader's uncritical acceptance of accolades from these successes, (3) the leader's exemption from the organizational rules (often because of the organization's beliefs that the leader's success warrants such a benefit of the doubt), and these circumstantial factors are exacerbated by (4) the leader's narcissism (Kroll et al., 2000).

Hubristic leaders often emerge as leaders because these individuals can maintain high self-esteem in difficult times (Zuckerman & O'Loughlin, 2006). Thus, when an organization faces difficult times, these leaders emerge as a voice of hope and power in dealing with such crises, and become a source of inspiration to their followers. But they are not capable of sustaining success as they often make decisions based on their beliefs of themselves rather than on the negative and critical evaluations of the situation that their peers and followers provide (Hayward & Hambrick, 1997; Smalley & Stake, 1996). This erroneous decision making from a leader's hubris happens in a three-step process (Kroll et al., 2000), whereby confidence turns into arrogance, which then leads a leader to believe that future successes can be obtained using the same means as past successes were, and finally causes the leader to stick to a formula for success without considering new information.

SOCIAL DOMINANCE ORIENTATION

Social dominance orientation (SDO) is a personality variable that involves the desire to be superior to others, especially those who are different from the self (Pratto, Sidanius, Stallworth, & Malle, 1994). Those with high SDO have a preference toward hierarchical versus equal relationships (e.g., superior–inferior paradigms). Social dominance (the desire to be superior to others) is different than the dominance facet of extraversion (Judge et al., 2002, 2009); it is also distinct from interpersonal dominance and authoritarianism (Pratto et al., 1994). Empirical studies suggest that SDO may be important for leadership. Leaders with high SDO are less likely to exhibit characteristics of successful leaders, as the trait is associated negatively with empathy, altruism, communality, and tolerance (Pratto et al., 1994). In a managerial role-playing experimental study, Son Hing, Bobocel, Zanna, and McBride (2007) found that individuals with high SDO are likely to emerge as leaders, but are also likely to make unethical decisions when facing a trade-off between profits and ethics.

Unlike research on the Big Five, there has been little integration and examination of underlying taxonomies of the dark side traits. Nonetheless, existing research strongly suggests that these traits do not fall neatly into either psychopathology nor into existing taxonomies of normal personality, though they may represent space between the two. From the perspective of understanding leadership, it appears that one set of traits best predicts leader emergence, effectiveness, and behaviors, whereas another set of traits best predicts leadership derailment and destructive leadership, but further integration of these paradigms may advance our understanding of leadership and personality.

Examining Complex Associations between Personality and Leadership

Zaccaro and colleagues note that research examining the relationship between personality traits and leadership (whether defined as behaviors, emergence, effectiveness, or outcomes) tends to focus on additive, univariate, and linear relationships (Zaccaro, 2007; Zaccaro, Gulick, & Khare, 2008). Evidence of this approach can be found in our review section, which draws heavily on bivariate correlations and the independent or unique predictive validity of each trait, sometimes while holding the effects of the other traits constant (e.g., Bono & Judge, 2004; Judge & Bono, 2000; Judge et al., 2002). This approach constrains the relationship between personality and leadership to be linear and does not consider potential effects of the interplay between the traits (i.e., configuration or pattern of personality traits). Given the complexity of influencing and directing collective or group effort toward organizational goals (Uhl-Bien, Marion, & McKelvey, 2007), we propose that important advances in our understanding of the trait basis of leadership behavior and effectiveness might be made by examining nonlinear and configural relationships between personality traits and leadership criteria.

Nonlinear Relationships

In the vast majority of psychological research, monotonically linear associations have been assumed (e.g., greater extraversion is linearly associated with greater likelihood of leadership emergence). Grant and Schwartz (2011) argue instead that many relationships between psychological traits (or individual differences generally) and outcomes may be nonlinear, in the form of an inverted-U shape, wherein too much or too little of a trait leads to less desirable outcomes than moderate trait levels. They draw on Aristotle's philosophical teachings that promote moderation as the pathway to happiness and success. For example, they argue that a moderate level of pleasing others is the virtuous behavior of friendliness, whereas an excessive need to please others is viewed as obsequiousness and a deficiency in pleasing others is perceived as surliness. Reviewing a broad spectrum of research, Grant and Schwartz illustrate how many seemingly positive traits and behaviors are nonlinearly related to outcomes following the inverted-U shape, including: practice and performance (e.g., Berman, Down, & Hill, 2002), optimism and well-being (e.g., Milam, Richardson, Marks, Kemper, & McCutchan, 2004), empathy and prosocial behavior (e.g., Eisenberg et al., 1994), and choice and performance (e.g., Iyengar & Lepper, 2000). They argue that many such "virtues" are nonlinearly related to criteria because of conflicts between virtues. In the preceding example, pleasing others can be considered a virtue because of self-transcendence and the value typically placed on maintaining social ties, while similarly, pleasing and being true to oneself can be considered a virtue owing to self-actualization of one's own needs and desires. Thus, moderation on a given trait is often the most successful way to balance competing, desirable virtues.

In the leadership domain, Judge and colleagues (2009) have similarly argued that there are bright sides to dark side traits and dark sides to bright sides traits, which supports nonlinear associations between personality traits and leadership outcomes. In discussing the Big Five personality traits, they argue that excessive levels of conscientiousness could manifest in rigidity, inflexibility, and extreme caution, leading to poor innovation and micromanagement of others; excessive extraversion could result in aggressive behaviors and self-aggrandizement leading to poor decision making and failure to share credit; excessive agreeableness could result in becoming a pushover, leading to conflict avoidance; excessive emotional stability (extremely low neuroticism) could manifest as a lack of emotional expressions, leading to perceptions of low charisma and credibility; and excessive openness could lead to flights of fancy and pursuit of the latest fads to the detriment of organizational performance and stability. Supporting the idea of nonlinear associations between Big Five traits and leadership is recently emerging research in the domain of personality and job performance, where inverted U-shaped associations between conscientiousness and job performance have been found (LaHuis, Martin, & Avis, 2005; Le et al., 2011; Whetzel, McDaniel, Yost, & Kim, 2010).

Another trait that may have a nonlinear association with leadership is core self-evaluations (Judge et al., 2009). Specifically, Judge and colleagues argue that hyper-CSE, characterized by extremely positive views of the self, may resemble narcissism or hubris, resulting in overconfidence and poor decision making due to the inability to assess one's own ideas objectively and critically. We argue that integrity may also have nonlinear relationships with leadership outcomes. Given that integrity is a compound trait associated with conscientiousness, agreeableness, and emotional stability, individuals who score very high on integrity may adhere to rules within social structures rigidly and be unable to evaluate the unique circumstances surrounding the situation when exceptions should be considered. Thus, moderate levels of integrity may be most beneficial for leadership, with both extreme high and low levels being dysfunctional. With regard to the bright sides of dark side traits, Judge and colleagues argue that narcissism and hubris both reflect positive self-regard and confidence and at moderate levels will likely be positively viewed by others as being leader-like. Most of these arguments also suggest nonlinear associations in the shape of an inverted-U, with moderate levels of each trait resulting in the most successful leadership.

To our knowledge, two studies have empirically examined nonlinear relationships between personality traits and leadership criteria. In the first study, Ames and Flynn (2007) found that leader assertiveness was nonlinearly related to ratings of leader performance in the shape of an inverted-U, with effective leaders being characterized by moderate levels of assertiveness. It was found that low levels of assertiveness were associated with more positive relational (i.e., interpersonal) outcomes while high levels of assertiveness were associated with more positive instrumental (i.e., performance) outcomes. Thus, the most effective leaders had to be assertive in moderation in order to balance both relational and instrumental goals. This finding is in line with Grant and Schwartz's (2011) suggestion that virtues may often come into conflict with each other, resulting in moderation being the most successful course of action. In the second study, Benson and Campbell (2007) found that dark side personality traits (i.e., a derailing composite based on the ego-centered, intimidating, manipulating, micro-managing, and passive aggressive scales of the Global Personality Inventory [Schmitt, Kihm, & Robie, 2000] and the moving against composite from the HDS; Hogan & Hogan 1997) were nonlinearly related to leadership performance ratings (i.e., assessment center ratings of leadership skills and competencies and multisource ratings of leader performance) in the form of an inverted-U shape. Thus, leaders with modest (or average) levels of self-confidence, vision, and entitlement were rated as the best performers compared to those leaders who either did not possess these traits or possessed high (or extreme) levels of these traits.

Given the nascent state of research and theory on nonlinear relationships between personality and leadership, there is a lack of specificity in the current literature regarding what aspects (or facets) of traits might exhibit nonlinear associations with leadership. For example, if conscientiousness is found to be curvilinearly related to leadership effectiveness in the form of an inverted-U, it could be that it was due to the leader being wrapped up in minor details (i.e., facet of order), inflexibly adhering to rules and norms (i.e., facet of traditionalism), or being so highly achievement-motivated that he or she was single-mindedly focused on achieving their goal without considering the goals of his or her subordinates (i.e., facet of achievement orientation), or the combined effects of all three of these dimensions. Indeed, it is plausible that for some traits, some facets have nonlinear associations with leadership, whereas the association for other facets or the global trait (i.e., common variance among the facets) may be linear.

Although many traits may be dysfunctional for leadership at extreme high or low levels, we are not suggesting nonlinear associations between all traits and leadership effectiveness. For example, we expect the relationship between resilience and proactivity and various leadership criteria to be monotonically linear in form. Both resilience and proactivity are associated with effective self-regulation. Resilience centers on how individuals regulate their reactions (both behavioral and emotional) to adverse and unexpected circumstances while proactive personality centers on how individuals approach and regulate their progress toward goals. Existing research suggests that self-control, another trait related to self-regulation, may be a trait that is linearly related to positive outcomes (Finkenauer, Engels, & Baumeister, 2005; Tangney, Baumeister, & Boone, 2004). In arguing that there is no such thing as too much self-control, Tangney et al. (2004) contends that clinical disorders reflecting over-control (i.e., obsessive–compulsive disorder, anorexia) also reflect poor self-control (i.e., inability to regulate their desire to control the situation) and that effective regulation may always be beneficial.

Trait Configurations and Profiles

Whereas the previously reviewed research has sought to examine nonlinearity in the relationships between personality traits and leadership, another more complex approach would be to focus on the interactions, configurations, or patterns among a set of personality traits in predicting leadership criteria. Given the adaptive nature of personality functioning, researchers have argued that personality traits do not develop in isolation; instead, they form coherently into an overall system, Gestalt, and that—owing to environmental and adaptive pressures—there are a limited number of systems or meaningful "subgroups" or "sub-types" (Allport, 1937; Bergman & Magnusson, 1997). These theorists argue that our tradition of looking at relationships between variables using correlational methods can be supplemented and complemented by a person-oriented approach where the focus is on the person and how organized systems develop within individuals (Bergman & Trost, 2006).

Within the leadership literature, Foti and colleagues (Foti & Hauenstein, 2007; O'Shea, Foti, Hauenstein, & Bycio, 2009; Smith & Foti, 1998) have spearheaded the application of pattern-oriented methodologies. Using a sample of student cadets, Foti and Haunstein (2007) used cluster analysis to identify three subgroups. They found that individuals in the subgroup characterized by high scores on cognitive ability, dominance, self-efficacy, and self-monitoring outperformed individuals in the mixed pattern (some of these traits were high and some were low) and low pattern (scores on all traits were low) subgroups in both leadership emergence and effectiveness. In addition, subgroup membership predicted incrementally over the combined linear effects of the traits for two of the leadership criteria they examined, promotion and peer ratings of leadership emergence. Similarly, in an experimental study using student teams, Smith and Foti (1998) found that members of the subgroup characterized by high scores on intelligence, dominance, and general self-efficacy, were more likely to emerge as leaders compared to mixed pattern and low pattern subgroups. In other words, there was a statistically significant three-way interaction between the three traits in predicting leadership emergence in this study.

In another configural study, McClelland and Boyatzis (1982) found that a conceptually derived pattern of leadership motives derived from Thematic Apperception Test responses, characterized by moderate to high need for power, low need for affiliation, and high activity inhibition, predicted the promotions of entry-level managers over a period of 16 years. Individuals with this pattern of leadership motives were compared to individuals without this pattern, with no attempt to identify whether there were other meaningful subgroups; thus, it is possible that individuals with other motive patterns may also have been promoted. Mumford et al. (2000) also took a profile approach, using cluster analysis to identify profiles of personality and cognitive ability that predicted leadership success in Army officers. They identified seven types that were similarly represented among the junior officers (10–20 percent of the sample fell into each type), but the relative frequency of these types differed among senior officers, suggesting that promotion was linked to two specific subtypes: motivated communicators and thoughtful innovators (40 percent and 26 percent of senior officers, respectively). In addition, motivated communicators and thoughtful innovators self-reported higher numbers of career achievements, received higher scores for critical incidents of best performance behaviors, and were rated most highly by experts for their solutions to complex military problems.

Taking yet another approach to personality configurations, Dilchert (2007) utilized a criterion-related profile methodology developed by Davison and Davenport (2002) to identify personality profiles associated with interest in leadership and managerial roles. This approach explicitly examines whether a trait profile explains significant incremental variance over mean trait levels (i.e., elevation across the predictor scores). Dilchert found that a personality profile characterized by elevated scores on extraversion and lowered scores on agreeableness (relative to a person's mean) was consistently related to interest in leadership roles across industries.

Traits in Context

Given the relatively modest links between personality traits and leadership criteria reported in the literature, another question worthy of examination is whether we gain a different picture of the relationship between personality and leadership when we take context into consideration. Is the link between personality and leadership stronger for certain groups? Are there certain situations that activate trait expressions and thus elicit stronger links between leadership and personality? We explore three contextual variables: follower personality, leader gender, and level in the organizational hierarchy.

Partner (Follower) Personality

Despite the inherently dyadic nature of leadership, we rarely examine the personality traits of followers, or the personality fit between leader and follower traits as predictors of leadership outcomes. There is an entire literature on dyadic relationships (e.g.., Back et al., 2011; Cuperman & Ickes, 2009; Jackson, Dimmock, Gucciardi, & Grove, 2010; Kenny & La Voie, 1984) and within that literature there are studies examining the role of personality fit between leaders and followers. Perhaps because the primary outcome of interest in such studies is the relationship itself, the leader–member exchange (LMX) literature tends not to be well cited in the personality–leadership literature. Nonetheless, we find value in considering the role that follower traits play in in the link between leader traits and outcomes. This is especially true when considered from the standpoint of the trait-activation theory (Tett & Burnett, 2003; Tett & Guterman, 2000), which suggests that situations, including social factors such as the traits of others, affect trait manifestation.

Follower traits and leader–follower personality fit may be especially important when considering the impact of leader's dark side traits. Padilla, Hogan, and Kaiser (2007) propose a "toxic triangle" where the situation—the follower and a conducive environment—in combination with leader traits work in concert to elicit destructive leadership. More specifically, when leaders high on dark side traits are paired with sycophantic followers, leader behaviors associated with dark side traits are augmented. For example, narcissistic leaders feed off of such sycophants' flattery, as flattery provides license for the narcissistic leader to continue on with destructive behavior (Padilla et al., 2007; Sheng, 2001). In addition, Son Hing et al. (2007) found that a leader who has a high level of social dominance orientation tends to make more unethical decisions when a follower has a high level of agreeableness, presumably because agreeable individuals strive for harmonious relationships and avoid conflict (Graziano, Jensen-Campbell, & Hair, 1996).

Destructive leadership behaviors may also be more evident with followers low on CSE, because they are less sure of themselves and are more prone to be taken advantage of by leaders with dark side personality traits (Luthans, Peterson, & Ibrayevna, 1998). Followers with low self-esteem, low self-efficacy, or an external locus of control are particularly susceptible as they are easily enticed and enamored by the façade of confidence that leaders with high levels of dark side personality traits project.

Gender

Although there has been longstanding interest in studying gender differences in leadership, the vast majority of research has focused on mean (or average) differences between men and women in leadership emergence (Eagly & Karau, 1991), evaluations (Eagly, Makhijani, & Klonsky, 1992), effectiveness (Eagly, Karau, & Makhijani, 1995), and style (Eagly & Johnson, 1990). Relatively little research has examined whether gender *moderates* the relationship between personality and leadership, even though several theories suggest that may be the case.

Role congruity theory (Eagly & Karau, 2002) argues that our expectations regarding female leaders are based on their dual roles in society as a woman and a leader, roles that seem to require incompatible behaviors (i.e., communion versus agency). These expectations lead to stereotypes that are not only descriptive (i.e., how people *would* behave) but also prescriptive (i.e., how people *should* behave), resulting in punishments against those who violate stereotypes. Thus, women might be both (1) perceived as less worthy of leadership positions because their female role is inconsistent with leadership stereotypes and (2) evaluated less favorably when practicing the same behaviors as male leaders, because they violate their female role stereotypes. If women alter their behavior to fit leadership role requirements, the result would be diminished associations between personality and behaviors, leading to smaller correlations between personality and leadership criteria for women, as compared to men.

Shifting standards theory (Biernat, 2003) also provides reason to expect differential personality–leadership associations for men and women. Studies with objective indices of leadership effectiveness are rare; observer ratings of effectiveness are far more common. Such subjective evaluations inherently involve reference to some standard, typically the behavior of others (i.e., this manager is effective, compared to other managers). Shifting standards theory posits the use of different standards of evaluation for men and women leaders. Male and female manager demonstrating equivalent behaviors and outcomes might be rated differently because they are compared to different reference groups. For example, a woman might be rated poorly because she is not as good at developing employees as other women (developing others fits a female stereotype of communality) or she might be rated highly because she is exceptional at developing people compared to the average male leader (developing others does not fit with a male stereotype of agency). Shifting standards theory makes no prediction that men will be rated more highly then women (or vice versa). Instead, the prediction is that different standards will be used in their evaluations. The effect of shifting standards is to introduce error into the measurement of leadership effectiveness, error that reduces the personality–leadership association, potentially doing so differently for men and women.

In yet another approach to this topic, Lord and colleagues (e.g., Lord, Foti, & De Vader, 1984) argue that people hold certain assumptions (implicit leadership theories [ILT]) about the traits necessary to be successful in a leadership role; these assumptions lead to cognitive schemas through which leaders' actions and behaviors are interpreted (Offermann, Kennedy, & Wirtz, 1994). Research on ILTs shows that they differ for men and women leaders, such that women leaders were expected to conform to both sensitivity and masculinity prototypes to be effective, while men only had to conform to the masculinity prototype (Johnson, Murphy, Zewdie, & Reichard, 2008). Consistent with this idea, Scott and Brown (2006) demonstrated that people have more difficulty encoding leadership behaviors that are nonprototypical for each gender, suggesting that trait-linked behaviors associated with gender (such as nurturing others, or being decisive) might be differentially noticed and recalled for male and female leaders.

Considered as a whole, these lines of theory converge in suggesting differential associations between personality and leadership for men and women. Although empirical tests of this notion are rare, Duehr (2007) examined the association between personality and leadership for men and women leaders and found evidence of systematic predictive bias against women managers. In each case of differential prediction, women's positive leadership behaviors (i.e., transformational leadership) were underpredicted by the personality trait (i.e., extraversion, neuroticism, and agreeableness). This study suggests that a common regression line predicting the leadership effectiveness of men and women may not be appropriate and that personality–leadership relationships are not invariant across gender.

Organizational Level

There are two central reasons that the association between personality and leadership might differ by organizational level: (1) differences in the nature of leadership performance (i.e., leadership role requirements) and (2) differences in situational strength. In the organizational literature, scholars recognize that leaders at different levels of the organization face different issues. In Stratified Social Systems Theory, Jaques (1978) asserts that the organizational hierarchy can be meaningfully separated into five levels: (1) front-line supervisors, (2) departmental managers, (3) general manager, (4) leader of a small organization, and (5) leader or senior officer of a large organization. At the lowest level, supervisors are responsible primarily for ensuring that job tasks are carried out, while at the highest level, senior leaders of a large corporation are responsible for strategic choices in managing the business environment and building alliances and external relationships.

Research has shown that different leadership skills (e.g., cognitive, interpersonal, business, and strategic skills) are required for success at different organizational levels, with greater business and strategic skills requirements at higher organizational levels relative to cognitive and interpersonal skill requirements (Mumford, Campion, & Morgeson, 2007). Dai, Tang, and DeMeuse (2011) also demonstrated that the skills needed for leadership success are different across organizational levels. Different traits have also been linked to leadership success at various organizational levels; positions higher in the organizational hierarchy require more agentic or masculine traits (Hunt, Boal, & Sorenson, 1990; Lord & Maher, 1993). Because we expect that the development of leadership skills is based—at least in part—on stable personality traits, we expect different associations between leadership effectiveness and personality for entry level and senior managers.

Another reason to expect differential personality–leadership associations across organizational levels (and across organizations) is due to differences in the strength of situational constraints. In some situations, strong behavioral norms constrain behavior, resulting in weaker relationships between personality traits and behaviors or outcomes (Meyer, Dalal, & Hermida, 2010). For example, leaders at the lower levels of the organizational hierarchy (i.e., entry level supervisors) may operate in strong situations, whereby their actions are circumscribed by their role in the organization and by organizational policies, leaving them with little flexibility in terms of their actions. In contrast, leaders at the top of the organizational hierarchy (i.e., CEOs, executives) may have considerably weaker situations, allowing them a wider range of behavior. In such a case, the personality–leadership association would be stronger for executives than for entry-level managers. Differences across industries and sectors may also vary in the extent to which they constrain behavior, which may explain why Judge et al. (2002) found somewhat different personality–leadership associations in business and in government/military organizations.

Conclusion

The study of personality and leadership is dead; long live the study of personality and leadership! Much is known about the personality traits of leaders. Emergence of the Big Five traits as an organizational tool for the study of personality has moved the field forward in an important way, allowing us to clearly and cleanly summarize what is known about the correlation between personality traits and leadership perceptions, emergence, effectiveness, and behavior. Moreover, recent research on the heritability of both personality and leadership suggests that stable individual differences in personality, which appear to have a genetic basis, are associated with the propensity to seek out and attain positions of leadership. But, much is yet to be learned about the traits that predict leadership in an increasingly fast-paced and complex world, both the personality traits that are associated with success and those associated with destructive leadership and derailment. Our review suggests that a new set of traits, many of which are not cleanly captured within the Big Five framework, may be important additions to our understanding and prediction of leadership in the future. We also believe that nonlinear and more holistic approaches to the study of leadership personality may be fruitful avenues to explore, as the use of univariate and additive methods (i.e., correlation, regression) may have inadvertently constrained knowledge of the personality–leadership relationship.

Future Research

Although the literature on personality and leadership has made great strides, there are many critical questions that remain unanswered. In the following section, we lay out the five key questions we view as critical in moving the literature forward, which are summarized in Figure 10.1.

Question 1: What Is the Optimal Trait Profile for Effective Leadership?

There has been little theory or empirical research focusing on the *set of traits* (and what level of those traits) that best predict who will be effective in leading others in the pursuit and attainment of organizational goals, who will be resilient in the face of challenges and obstacles, who can cope with change and help others to do so, who can lead with integrity, and who can avoid the types of destructive behaviors that lead to derailment. With dual goals of simplicity (parsimony) and complexity (trait profiles or configurations), we see three possible starting points to identifying an optimal leader trait profile: (1) investigate configurations of broad trait clusters that are associated with resiliency, initiative, adaptability, and integrity; (2) remain within the Big Five framework, but examine Big Five

Trait Configurations	- Big Five Trait Profiles - Resiliency, Adaptability, Proactivity Clusters - Bright and Dark Side Traits - Individual Differences Profiles (Personality, Ability, Interest)
Leadership Criteria	- Attainment of Group Objectives - Destructive Leadership and Derailment - Objective Assessment of Behaviors Across Situations - Consistency vs. Adaptability
Methodology	- Dyadic Analysis - Configural or Pattern-Oriented Approaches - Experience Sampling Methodology - Multi-Level Moderated Mediation - Growth Mixture Modeling
Moderators	- Gender - Organizational Level - Personality of Interaction Partner or Group - Trait Activation Potential of Context
Abuse of Power	- Situational Facilitators - Trickle-Down Effects (Role Modeling of Negative Behaviors)

Figure 10.1. What's Next for the Study of Personality and Leadership?

profiles rather than focusing on individual traits; or (3) combine personality with other individual differences.

Throughout our review, we identified a number of potential trait clusters that have been written about, some with implications for leadership. For example, the model of Parker et al. (2010) identifies a set of traits (e.g., proactive personality, core self-evaluations) that may be the basis of proactive motivation, a motivational style that is particularly relevant for the initiative aspects of leadership. Similarly Wang et al. (2010) describe a resiliency cluster of traits (i.e., psychological capital, core self-evaluations, hardiness) that describe individual characteristics that aid in withstanding stressful events.

Big Five personality would also be a good place for researchers to *begin* their nonlinear and configural investigations. First, Big Five personality traits have been consistently found to be related to leadership criteria (e.g., Bono & Judge, 2004; Judge et al., 2002). Second, the five traits are only modestly correlated with each other, leading to the possibility of differentiation in personality profiles across individuals. Third, given that the Five Factor Model has emerged as generalizable across cultures (e.g., McCrae & Costa, 1997), these traits can be considered fundamental building blocks of personality, making it more likely that configural examinations will find coherent "systems" or organizations of traits. Fourth, the Big Five traits have been integrated into a hierarchical taxonomy of personality, allowing researchers to move coherently from the Big Five traits downward to increased levels of specificity (e.g., facets) and upward to examine compounds traits or meta-traits.

Another approach would be to broaden our scope to include other individual differences variables (i.e., abilities, interests, motivation) as researchers in other domains have already done. As an avenue of pursuit and theoretical framework, we highlight Ackerman's intelligence-as-Process, Personality, Interests, and intelligence-as-Knowledge (PPIK) theory, which integrates the previously disparate domains of cognitive ability, personality, and interests into meta-trait complexes that better capture the interrelationships between these areas (Ackerman & Heggestad, 1997). These meta-trait complexes have been linked to differences in domain knowledge (e.g., Ackerman, 2003), and may hold promise in predicting leadership behaviors since a leader's responsibilities include complex decision making (Mumford, Zaccaro, Harding, Jacobs, & Fleishman, 2000).

Given the strong conceptual arguments for nonlinear and configural relationships between personality and leadership criteria, there is an extreme dearth of empirical research examining this question. Existing studies, though promising and suggestive, are few and unsystematic, leaving considerable room for advancement in this area.

Question 2: What Leadership Criteria Should We Assess and How?

Within the leadership domain, researchers have traditionally studied two leadership criteria: leader emergence (i.e., being perceived as leader-like by others or personal desire to seek out and attain positions of power and status) and leader effectiveness (i.e., successfully directing the group to goal accomplishment). Kaiser, Hogan, and Craig (2008) reviewed the literature and found that leadership effectiveness has typically been operationalized in three ways: (1) evaluations of leader effectiveness, (2) assessment of leader behaviors, or (3) group performance, but the vast majority of research relies on the first two, typically using supervisor or follower ratings. Hogan and colleagues (1994) have argued that group performance—whether the group being led achieves its goals—is the most appropriate operationalization. We urge future research to examine links between personality traits (and configurations) with all three measures of leader effectiveness because it is not clear that the personality traits or profiles that predict supervisor ratings of effectiveness will be the same as those predicting group performance.

In addition to clarity in theory and measurement of leader effectiveness, there is also a need to broaden the leadership criterion domain. Recently, leadership scholars have called for increased research on the nature of ineffective or destructive leadership behaviors and leadership derailment (Hackman & Wageman, 2007; Hogan & Hogan, 2001; Hunter, Bedell-Avers, & Mumford, 2007; Wang et al., 2010). At this point in time, neither the nature of the associations between effective and ineffective leadership, nor the association between various ineffective leadership constructs (e.g., managerial derailment, Leslie & Van Velsor, 1996; abusive supervision, Tepper, 2000; leader bullying, Ferris, Zinko, Brouer, Buckley, & Harvey, 2007) has been well established. Thus, another unanswered question is whether a common set of personality traits predicts both effective and ineffective leadership.

In addition to clarifying leadership criteria, leadership researchers have long struggled with how to best assess leadership behaviors. Almost complete reliance on subordinate ratings of leader behaviors is problematic given that these raters have ongoing relationships with the leader and view the leader's behaviors through a nonobjective lens. They may rely on cognitive or affective heuristics (e.g., implicit leadership theories) in reporting on leader behaviors rather than basing their responses on actual behavioral incidents and observations. For example, previous research has established that rater affect toward the leader (i.e., liking) strongly influences reports of leader behavior (Brown & Keeping, 2005). Although this potential bias in behavioral ratings is not necessarily problematic when predicting follower reactions to a leader, it does cause a problem for finding associations between leaders' personalities and their behaviors. We strongly urge the utilization of innovative approaches in future research; two possible avenues occur to us. The first is to use neutral (i.e., third-party) observers to assess leadership behaviors, either trained researchers from outside the organization or organizational insiders who do not have relationships with the focal leader. Although potentially costly and time-consuming, this approach would likely yield more objective behavioral measures and could be compared to the ratings of individuals with established relationships with the leader (i.e., subordinates, peers, and supervisors), as a way of establishing the validity of their observations. The second avenue would be to utilize short-term assessments of leadership behaviors longitudinally, perhaps using momentary ecological assessments (i.e., experience-sampling; Beal & Weiss, 2003; see also Dinh & Lord, 2012). Behavioral observations should be more accurate when they are restricted to a defined timeframe and when they are recorded soon after the behavior occurs (i.e., end of the workday). Another strength of this approach is that idiosyncratic, momentary, and contextual influences on leadership behaviors could be removed if behavior reports were aggregated across days. Such an approach would also aid our understanding of the extent to which behavioral flexibility or behavioral consistency best predict leadership success; variability in leader behavior across employees may be an important criterion.

Question 3: What New Methodologies Should We Be Using?

Careful consideration of methodology will be necessary to move forward as we have suggested. For example, our review of the literature reveals many modestly sized samples in leadership studies, sample sizes that are incompatible with the stringent data requirements needed to test for departures from linearity (cf. Coward & Sackett, 1990). Multiple operationalizations of both personality (e.g., self and observer reports) and leadership criteria (e.g., ratings of effectiveness along with objective measures of group output) are also needed.

Future research should also capitalize on advanced statistical techniques that allow examination of within-leader variability in behavior or person-oriented approaches to personality. As we develop increasingly sophisticated methodologies for analyzing trait configurations (e.g., Bergman & Magnusson, 1997; Davison & Davenport, 2002), for examining patterns of success over time (Wang & Bodner, 2007), and for considering complex associations at multiple levels of analysis (Preacher, Zyphur, Zhang, 2010), our ability to understand better the traits associated with effective leadership and leadership derailment is enhanced. For example, many configural investigations use "internal" subgrouping methods (e.g., cluster analysis) to generate profiles, so the creation of profiles is not linked to an external criterion. Moreover, once a limited number of subgroups (or types) are identified, group membership was found to have limited predictive or incremental value (see Foti & Hauenstein, 2007 for an exception). Given recent advances in statistical methodology, future research might benefit from using criterion-related configural methods (e.g., Davison & Davenport, 2002). We also urge for an increased use of cross-validation techniques because the extent to which findings of studies using nonlinear and configural approaches are stable, generalizable, and replicable is at present unclear.

In addition to thinking about innovative methods of analysis, measurement practices for personality also deserve attention. Colbert and colleagues (Colbert, Judge, Choi, & Wang, 2012) recently found that the link between traits and leadership was stronger when observer reports were used for both leader traits and leadership outcomes. This is consistent with recent work in personality psychology suggesting that other reports of personality can be both accurate and valid predictors of behavior (Connelly & Ones, 2010).

Question 4: What Are Some Important Moderators?

In the present chapter, we highlight three potential moderators for future research: leader gender, organizational level of the leader, and the personality of the dyadic partner. Although we believe that there are strong conceptual bases for these three moderators, we encourage researchers to incorporate the examination of moderators with some of the other ideas we have put forward in this chapter. For example, there may not only be differential associations between extraversion and transformational leadership for men and women (e.g., Duehr, 2007), but the personality profiles (or configurations) of effective men and women leaders may differ as well. We also see the opportunity for extension of our ideas. Whereas we focused on the role of follower personality in dyadic leader–follower relationships, this could be extended to examine the effects of fit between leader personality and team personality (e.g., mean personality level and dispersion or variability) in predicting group performance.

We also encourage theoretically driven investigations examining the situational or contextual factors that activate trait-relevant behaviors. Trait activation theory (Tett & Guterman, 2000) posits that trait-specific situational cues activate or elicit the expression of trait-relevant behavior. This perspective argues against a one-size fits all approach in terms of which aspect of the situation will moderate the relationship between personality and leadership behaviors, as the effects of context will vary based on the personality trait (or personality profile) of interest. Future research should seek to identify aspects of the environment that are trait-relevant (i.e., other persons, features of the job, features of the organization, etc.) for the expression of leadership behaviors across a wide range of previously identified leadership-relevant traits (e.g., extraversion, resilience, integrity, dark-side traits).

Another related area that deserves more attention in the future is the role of personality and ideal leader prototypes in assessments of and reactions to leaders. There is existing evidence that the prototypes individuals hold about effective leadership influence how they attend to and recall leader behaviors and that ideal leader prototypes can be predicted based on personality (e.g., Bono, Hooper, & Yoon, 2012; Keller, 1999). Recent research (Foti, Bray, Thompson, & Algood, 2012) shows that for some individuals there is a similarity between self and ideal leader profiles whereas for others self and ideal leader profiles are different. Given that ideal leader profiles affect reactions to leaders, this research suggests the link between traits and effectiveness may vary depending on the extent to which leader behavior matches follower self and ideal leader profiles. This line of research also suggests that it is important to consider leadership as a dynamic process negotiated between leaders and followers (see also DeRue & Ashford, 2010).

Question 5: What Leads Some to Abuse Power?

An area that has received little attention in the literature is personality traits and leaders' abuse of power. To some extent, abuse of power is included in the destructive leadership paradigm, and thus the trait clusters associated with destructive leadership (Wang, et al., 2010) would be linked to abuse of power as well. But the association between dark side traits and abuse of power is likely to be enhanced under certain conditions. An organization that has an authoritarian culture wherein the top leaders are abusive and such behavior is tolerated tend to have a trickle-down effect down the organizational hierarchy, such that destructive behaviors are accepted and justified by those who are at the receiving end of such abuse as performance-enhancing gestures rather than as abuse (Liu, Liao, & Loi, 2012). Because dark side traits such as a leader's narcissism and Machiavellianism are strong predictors of the leader's abusive supervision (Kiazad, Restubog, Zagenczyk, Kiewitz, & Tang, 2010; Tepper, 2007) and workplace deviance (Judge et al., 2006), we suspect that when combined with an authoritarian culture, the leader behaviors stemming from their dark side traits would trickle down throughout the organization, perpetuating the abuse of power. Muddling the issue of dark side traits and the abuse of power are findings that point toward the bright sides of dark side traits. Existing research on dark side traits suggest that they are also associated with effective leadership (e.g., histrionic personality was positively associated with transformational leadership [Khoo & Burch, 2008] and hubris was associated with innovation and new venture formation [Hayward, Shepherd, & Griffin, 2006]). It strikes us that understanding who will abuse power and when can be better understood by a combination of approaches, including use of pattern and configural approaches to personality that may include specific combinations of bright and dark side traits, and examining moderators such as organizational and follower characteristics. Moreover, full understanding of abuse of power requires analysis over time.

These five questions fail to tap the myriad ways that researchers might advance our understanding of the association between personality and leadership, but we believe they provide a strong jumping off point for future research.

References

Ackerman, P. L. (2003). Aptitude and trait complexes. *Educational Psychologist, 38*, 85–93.

Ackerman, P. L., & Heggestad, E. D. (1997). Intelligence, personality, and interest: Evidence for overlapping traits. *Psychological Bulletin, 121*, 219–245.

Allport, G. W. (1937). *Personality: A psychological interpretation.* New York, NY: Holt.

American Psychiatric Association (1994). *Diagnostic and statistical manual of mental disorders*, fourth edition: *DSM-IV.* Washington, DC: American Psychiatric Association.

Ames, D. R., & Flynn, F. J. (2007). What breaks a leader: The curvilinear relationship between assertiveness and leadership. *Journal of Personality and Social Psychology, 92*, 307–324.

Arvey, R. D., Rotundo, M., Johnson, W., Zhang, Z., & McGue, M. (2006). The determinants of leadership role occupancy: Genetic and personality factors. *Leadership Quarterly, 17*, 1–20.

Arvey, R. D., Zhang, Z., Avolio, B. J., & Krueger, R. F. (2007). Developmental and genetic determinants of leadership role occupancy among women. *Journal of Applied Psychology, 92*, 693–706.

Back, M. D., Baumert, A., Denissen, J. J. A., Hartung, F-M., Penke, L., Schmukle, S. C., . . . Wrzus, C. (2011). PERSOC: A unified framework for understanding the dynamic interplay of personality and social relationships. *European Journal of Personality, 25*, 90–107.

Bartone, P. T., Eid, J., Johnsen, B. H., Laberg, J. C., & Snook, S. A. (2009). Big five personality factors, hardiness, and social judgment as predictors of leader performance. *Leadership & Organization Development, 30*, 498–521.

Bateman, T. S., & Crant, J. M. (1993). The proactive component of organizational behavior: A measure and correlates. *Journal of Organizational Behavior, 14*, 103–118.

Beal, D. J., **&** Weiss, H. M. (2003). Methods of ecological momentary assessment in organizational research. *Organizational Research Methods, 6*, 440–464.

Becker, T. E. (1998). Integrity in organizations: Beyond honesty and conscientiousness. *Academy of Management Review, 23*, 154–161.

Becker, J. A. H., & O'Hair, H. D. (2007). Machiavellians' motives in organizational citizenship behavior. *Journal of Applied Communication Research, 35*, 246–267.

Benson, M. J., & Campbell, J. P. (2007). To be, or not to be, linear: An expanded representation of personality and its relationship to leadership performance. *International Journal of Selection and Assessment, 15*, 232–249.

Bergman, L. R., & Magnusson, D. (1997). A person-oriented approach in research on developmental psychopathology. *Development and Psychopathology, 9*, 291–319.

Bergman, L. R., & Trost, K. (2006). The person-oriented versus the variable-oriented approach: Are they complementary, opposites, or exploring different worlds? *Merrill-Palmer Quarterly, 52*, 601–632.

Berman, S. L., Down, J., & Hill, C. W. L. (2002). Tacit knowledge as a source of competitive advantage in the National Basketball Association. *Academy of Management Journal, 45*, 13–31.

Best, R. G., Stapleton, L. M., & Downey, R. G. (2005). Core self-evaluations and job burnout: The test of alternative models. *Journal of Occupational Health Psychology, 10*, 441–451.

Biernat, M. (2003). Toward a broader view of social stereotyping. *American Psychologist, 58*, 1019–1027.

Bono, J. E., Hooper, A. C., & Yoon, D. (2012). Impact of rater personality on transformational and transactional leadership ratings. *Leadership Quarterly, 23*, 132–145.

Bono, J. E., & Judge, T. A. (2004). Personality and transformational and transactional leadership: A meta-analysis. *Journal of Applied Psychology, 89*, 901–910.

Brown, A. D. (1997). Narcissism, identity, and legitimacy. *Academy of Management Review, 22*, 643–686.

Brown, D. J., & Keeping, L. M. (2005). Measuring transformational leadership with the MLQ: The role of affect. *The Leadership Quarterly, 16*, 245–272.

Brown, R. P., & Zeigler-Hill, V. (2004). Narcissism and the non-equivalence of self-esteem measures: A matter of dominance? *Journal of Research in Personality, 38*, 585–592.

Chang, C-H, Ferris, D. L., Johnson, R. E., Rosen, C. C., & Tan, J. A. (2012). Core self-evaluations: A review and evaluation of the literature. *Journal of Management, 38*, 81–128.

Christie, R., & Geis, F. L. (1970). *Studies in Machiavellianism.* New York, NY: Academic Press

Cohen, J. (1992). A power primer. *Psychological Bulletin, 12*, 155–159.

Colbert, A. E., Judge, T. A., Choi, D., & Wang, G. (2012). Assessing the trait theory of leadership using self and observer ratings of personality: The mediating role of contributions to group success. *Leadership Quarterly, 23*, 670–685.

Connelly, B. S., & Ones, D. S. (2010). Another perspective on personality: Meta-analytic integration of observers' accuracy and predictive validity. *Psychological Bulletin, 136*, 1092–1122.

Coward, W. M., & Sackett, P. R. (1990). Linearity of ability-performance relationships: A reconfirmation. *Journal of Applied Psychology, 75*, 297–300.

Crant, J. M., & Bateman, T. S. (2000). Charismatic leadership viewed from above: The impact of proactive personality. *Journal of Organizational Behavior, 21*, 63–75.

Cuperman, R., & Ickes, W. (2009). Big Five predictors of behavior and perceptions in initial dyadic interactions: Personality similarity helps extraverts and introverts, but hurts "disagreeables." *Journal of Personality and Social Psychology, 97*, 667–684.

Dai, G., Tang, K. Y., & DeMeuse, K. P. (2011). Leadership competencies across organizational levels: A test of the pipeline model. *Journal of Management Development, 30*, 366–380.

Davison, M. L., & Davenport, E. C., Jr. (2002). Identifying criterion-related patterns of predictor scores using multiple regression. *Psychological Methods, 7*, 468–484.

Day, D. V., Schleicher, D. J., Unckless, A. L., & Hiller, N. J. (2002). Self-monitoring personality at work: A meta-analytic investigation of construct validity. *Journal of Applied Psychology, 87*, 390–401.

Deluga, R. J. (2001). American presidential Machiavellianism: Implications for charismatic leadership and rated performance. *Leadership Quarterly, 12*, 339–363.

DeRue, D. S., & Ashford, S. J. (2010). Who will lead and who will follow? A social process of leadership identity construction in organizations. *Academy of Management Review, 35*, 627–647.

Dilchert, S. (2007). Peaks and valleys: Predicting interests in leadership and managerial positions from personality profiles. *International Journal of Selection and Assessment, 15*, 317–334.

Dinh, J. E., & Lord, R. G. (2012). Implications of dispositional and process views of traits for individual difference research in leadership. *Leadership Quarterly, 23*, 651–669.

Drory, A., & Gluskinos, U. M. (1980). Machiavellianism and leadership. *Journal of Applied Personality, 65*, 81–86.

Duehr, E. E. (2007). Personality, gender, and transformational leadership: Investigating differential prediction for male

and female leaders. *Dissertation Abstracts International, 67* (9-B), 5453.
Eagly, A. H., & Johnson, B. T. (1990). Gender and leadership style: A meta-analysis. *Psychological Bulletin, 108*, 233–256.
Eagly, A. H., & Karau, S. J. (1991). Gender and the emergence of leaders: A meta-analysis. *Journal of Personality and Social Psychology, 60*, 685–710.
Eagly, A. H., & Karau, S. J. (2002). Role congruity theory of prejudice toward female leaders. *Psychological Review, 109*, 573–598.
Eagly, A. H., Karau, S. J., & Makhijani, M. G. (1995). Gender and the effectiveness of leaders: A meta-analysis. *Psychological Bulletin, 117*, 125–145.
Eagly, A. H., Makhijani, M. G., & Klonsky, B. G. (1992). Gender and the evaluations of leaders: A meta-analysis. *Psychological Bulletin, 111*, 3–22.
Eden, D. (1992). Leadership and expectations: Pygmalion effects and other self-fulfilling prophecies in organizations. *Leadership Quarterly, 3*, 271–305.
Eisenberg, N., Fabes, R. A., Murphy, B., Karbon, M., Maszk, P., Smith, M.,...Suh K. (1994). The relations of emotionality and regulation to dispositional and situational empathy-related responding. *Journal of Personality and Social Psychology, 66*, 776–797.
Ellis, R. J. (1988). Self-monitoring and leadership emergence in groups. *Personality and Social Psychology Bulletin, 14*, 681–693.
Erez, A., & Judge, T. A. (2001). Relationship of core self-evaluations to goal setting, motivation, and performance. *Journal of Applied Psychology, 86*, 1270–1279.
Ferris, G. R., Zinko, R., Brouer, R. L., Buckley, M. R., & Harvey, M. G. (2007). Strategic bullying as a supplementary, balanced perspective on destructive leadership. *Leadership Quarterly, 18*, 195–206.
Finkenauer, C., Engels, R. C. M. E., & Baumeister, R. F. (2005). Parenting behaviour and adolescent behavioural and emotional problems: The role of self-control. *International Journal of Behavioral Development, 29*, 58–69.
Florian, V., Mikulincer, M., & Taubman, O. (1995). Does hardiness contribute to mental health during a stressful real-life situation? The roles of appraisal and coping. *Journal of Personality and Social Psychology, 68*, 687–695.
Foti, R. J., Bray, B. C., Thompson, N. J., & Allgood, S. F. (2012). Know thy self, know thy leader: Contributions of a pattern-oriented approach to examining leader perceptions. *Leadership Quarterly, 23*, 702–717.
Foti, R. J., & Hauenstein, N. M. A. (2007). Pattern and variable approaches in leadership emergence and effectiveness. *Journal of Applied Psychology, 92*, 347–355.
Garland, H., & Beard, J. F. (1979). Relationship between self-monitoring and leader emergence across two task situations. *Journal of Applied Psychology, 64*, 72–76.
George, B., Sims, P., McLean, A. N., & Mayer, D. (2007, February). Discovering your authentic leadership. *Harvard Business Review*, 129–138.
Gladwell, M. (2008). *Outliers: The story of success.* New York, NY: Little, Brown and Company.
Grant, A. M., & Schwartz, B. (2011). Too much of a good thing: The challenge and opportunity of the inverted U. *Perspectives on Psychological Science, 6*, 61–76.
Graziano, W. G., Jensen-Campbell, L. A., & Hair, E. C. (1996). Perceiving interpersonal conflict and reacting to it: The case for agreeableness. *Journal of Personality and Social Psychology, 70*, 820–835.
Hackman, J. R., & Wageman, R. (2007). Asking the right questions about leadership: Discussion and conclusions. *American Psychologist, 62*, 43–47.
Harris, K. J., Harvey, P., & Kacmar, K. M. (2009). Do social stressors impact everyone equally? An examination of the moderating impact of core self-evaluations. *Journal of Business Psychology, 24*, 153–164.
Hayward, M. L. A., & Hambrick, D. C. (1997). Explaining the premiums paid for large acquisitions: Evidence of CEO hubris. *Administrative Science Quarterly, 42*, 103–127.
Hayward, M. L. A., Shepherd, D. A., & Griffin, D. (2006). A hubris theory of entrepreneurship. *Management Science, 52*, 160–172.
Hogan, R., Curphy, G. J., & Hogan, J. (1994). What we know about leadership: Effectiveness and personality. *American Psychologist*, 49, 493–504.
Hogan, R., & Hogan, J. (1997). *Hogan Development Survey manual.* Tulsa, OK: Hogan Assessment Systems.
Hogan, R., & Hogan, J. (2001). Assessing leadership: A view from the dark side. *International Journal of Selection and Assessment, 9*, 40–51.
Hogan, R., & Kaiser, R. B. (2005). What we know about leadership. *Review of General Psychology, 9*, 169–180.
Horney, K. (1950). *Neurosis and human growth.* New York, NY: W. W. Norton.
House, R. J., & Howell, J. M. (1992). Personality and charismatic leadership. *Leadership Quarterly, 3*, 81–108.
Hull, J. G., Van Treuren, R. R., & Virnelli, S. (1987). Hardiness and health: A critique and alternative approach. *Journal of Personality and Social Psychology, 53*, 518–530.
Hunt, J. G., Boal, K. B., & Sorenson, R. L. (1990). Top management leadership: Inside the black box. *Leadership Quarterly, 1*, 41–65.
Hunter, S. T., Bedell-Avers, K. E., & Mumford, M. D. (2007). The typical leadership study: Assumptions, implications, and potential remedies. *Leadership Quarterly, 18*, 435–446.
Ilies, Gerhardt, Le (2004). Individual differences in leadership emergence: Integrating meta-analytic findings and behavioral genetics estimates. *International Journal of Selection and Assessment, 12*, 207–219.
Iyengar, S. S., & Lepper, M. (2000). When choice is demotivating: Can one desire too much of a good thing? *Journal of Personality and Social Psychology, 79*, 995–1006.
Jackson, B., Dimmock, J. A., Gucciardi, D. F., & Grove, J. R. (2010). Relationship commitment in athletic dyads: Actor and partner effects for Big Five self- and other-ratings. *Journal of Research in Personality, 44*, 641–648.
Jaques, E. (1978). *General theory of bureaucracy.* Exter, NH: Heinemann Books.
Johnson, S. J., Murphy, S. E, Zewdie, S., & Reichard, R. J. (2008). The strong, sensitive type: Effects of gender stereotypes and leadership prototypes on the evaluation of male and female leaders. *Organizational Behavior and Human Decision Processes, 1*, 39–60.
Johnson, A. M., Vernon, P. A., Harris, J. A., & Jang, K. L. (2004). A behavior genetic investigation of the relationship between leadership and personality. *Twin Research, 7*, 27–32.
Jordan, C. H., Spencer, S. J., Zanna, M. P., Hoshino-Browne, E., & Correll, J. (2003). Secure and defensive high self-esteem. *Journal of Personality and Social Psychology, 85*, 969–978.
Judge, T. A., & Bono, J. E. (2000). Five-factor model of personality and transformational leadership. *Journal of Applied Psychology, 85*, 751–765.

Judge, T. A., & Bono, J. E. (2001). Relationship of core self-evaluations traits—self-esteem, generalized self-efficacy, locus of control, and emotional stability—with job satisfaction and job performance: A meta-analysis. *Journal of Applied Psychology, 86*, 80–92.

Judge, T. A., Bono, J. E., Erez, A., & Locke, E. A. (2005). Core self-evaluations and job and life satisfaction: The role of self-concordance and goal attainment. *Journal of Applied Psychology, 90*, 257–268.

Judge, T. A., Bono, J. E., Ilies, R., & Gerhardt, M. W. (2002). Personality and leadership: A qualitative and quantitative review. *Journal of Applied Psychology, 87*, 765–780.

Judge, T. A., LePine, J. A., & Rich, B. L. (2006). Loving yourself abundantly: Relationship of the narcissistic personality to self-and other perceptions of workplace deviance, leadership, and task and contextual performance. *Journal of Applied Psychology, 91*, 762–776.

Judge, T. A., Locke, E. A., & Durham, C. C. (1997). The dispositional causes of job satisfaction: A core evaluations approach. *Research in Organizational Behavior, 19*, 151–188.

Judge, T. A., Piccolo, R. F., & Kosalka, T. (2009). The bright and dark sides of leader traits: A review and theoretical extension of the leader trait paradigm. *Leadership Quarterly, 20*, 855–875.

Judge, T. A., Thoresen, C. J., Pucik, V., & Welbourne, T. M. (1999). Managerial coping with organizational change: A dispositional perspective. *Journal of Applied Psychology, 84*, 107–122.

Kaiser, R. B., Hogan, R., & Craig, S. B. (2008). Leadership and the fate of organizations. *American Psychologist, 63*, 96–110.

Kammeyer-Mueller, J. D., Judge, T. A., & Scott, B. A. (2009). The role of core self-evaluations in the coping process. *Journal of Applied Psychology, 94*, 177–195.

Keller, T. (1999). Images of the familiar: Individual differences and implicit leadership theories, *Leadership Quarterly, 10*, 589–607.

Kenny, D. A., & La Voie, L. (1984). The social relations model. *Advances in Experimental Social Psychology, 18*, 141–182.

Kenny, D. A., & Zaccaro, S. J. (1983). An estimate of variance due to traits in leadership. *Journal of Applied Psychology, 68*, 678–685.

Khoo, H. S., & Burch, G. S. J. (2008). The "dark side" of leadership personality and transformational leadership: An exploratory study. *Personality and Individual Differences, 44*, 86–97.

Kiazad, K., Restubog, S. L. D., Zagenczyk, T. J., Kiewitz, C., & Tang, R. L. (2010). In pursuit of power: The role of authoritarian leadership in the relationship between supervisors' Machiavellianism and subordinates' perceptions of abusive supervisory behavior. *Journal of Research in Personality, 44*, 512–519.

Kirkpatrick, S. A., & Locke, E. A. (1991). Leadership: Do traits matter? *Academy of Management Executive, 5*, 48–60.

Kobasa, S. C., Maddi, S. R., & Kahn, S. (1982). Hardiness and health: A prospective study. *Journal of Personality and Social Psychology, 42*, 168–177.

Kobasa, S. C., & Puccetti, M. C. (1983). Personality and social resources in stress resistance. *Journal of Personality and Social Psychology, 45*, 839–850.

Kroll, M. J., Toombs, L. A., & Wright, P. (2000). Napoleon's tragic march home from Moscow: Lessons in hubris. *Academy of Management Executive, 14*, 117–128.

LaHuis, D. M., Martin, N. R., & Avis, J. M. (2005). Investigating nonlinear conscientiousness- job performance relations for clerical workers. *Human Performance, 18*, 199–212.

Le, H., Oh, I., Robbins, S. B., Ilies, R., Holland, E., & Westrick, P. (2011). Too much of a good thing: Curvilinear relationships between personality traits and job performance. *Journal of Applied Psychology, 96*, 113–133.

Leslie, J. B., & Van Velsor, E. (1996). *A look at derailment today: North America and Europe*. Greensboro, NC: Center for Creative Leadership.

Liu, D., Liao, H., & Loi, R. (2012). The dark side of leadership: A three level investigation of the cascading effect of abusive supervision on employee creativity. *Academy of Management Journal*, 55, 1187–1212.

Lord, R. G., De Vader, C. L., & Alliger, G. M. (1986). A meta-analysis of the relation between personality traits and leadership perceptions: An application of validity generalization procedures. *Journal of Applied Psychology, 71*, 402–410.

Lord, R. G., Foti, R. J., & De Vader, C. L. (1984). A test of leadership categorization theory: Internal structure, information processing, and leadership perceptions. *Organizational Behavior and Human Performance. 34*, 343–378.

Lord, R. G., & Maher, K. J. (1993). *Executive leadership and information processing: Linking perceptions and organizational performance*. New York, NY: Routledge.

Luthans, F., Peterson, S. J., & Ibrayeva, E. (1998). The potential for the "dark side" of leadership in post-communist countries. *Journal of World Business, 33*, 185–201.

Mael, F. A., Waldman, D. A., & Mulqueen, C. (2001). From scientific careers to organizational leadership: Predictors of the desire to enter management on the part of technical personnel. *Journal of Vocational Behavior, 59*, 132–148.

McClelland, D. C., & Boyatzis, R. E. (1982). Leadership motive pattern and long term success in management. *Journal of Applied Psychology, 67*, 737–743.

McCrae, R. R. (1987). Creativity, divergent thinking, and openness to experience. *Journal of Personality and Social Psychology*, 52, 1258–1265.

McCrae, R. R., & Costa, P. T., Jr. (1997). Personality structure as a human universal. *American Psychologist, 58*, 509–516.

McFall, L. (1987). Integrity. *Ethics, 98*, 5–20.

McHoskey, J. W. (1999). Machiavellianism, intrinsic versus extrinsic goals, and social interest: A self-determination theory analysis. *Motivation and Emotion, 23*, 267–283.

Meyer, R. D., Dalal, R. S., & Hermida, R. (2010). A review and synthesis of situational strength in the organizational sciences. *Journal of Management, 36*, 121–140.

Milam, J. E., Richardson, J. L., Marks, G., Kemper, C. A., & McCutchan, A. J. (2004). The roles of dispositional optimism and pessimism in HIV disease. *Psychology and Health, 19*, 167–181.

Morf, C. C., & Rhodewait, F. (2001). Unraveling the paradoxes of narcissism: A dynamic self-regulatory processing model. *Psychological Inquiry, 12*, 177–196.

Morgeson, F. P., Campion, M. A., Dipboye, R. L., Hollenbeck, J. R., Murphy, K., & Schmitt, N. (2007). Are we getting fooled again? Coming to terms with limitations in the use of personality tests for personnel selection. *Personnel Psychology, 60*, 1029–1049.

Mumford, T. V., Campion, M. A., & Morgeson, F. P. (2007). The leadership skills strataplex: Leadership skill requirements across organizational levels. *Leadership Quarterly, 18*, 154–166.

Mumford, M. D., Zaccaro, S. J., Harding, F. D., Jacobs, T. O., & Fleishman, E. A. (2000). Leadership skills for a changing world solving complex social problems. *The Leadership Quarterly, 11*, 11–35.

Mumford, M. D., Zaccaro, S. J., Johnson, J. F., Diana, M., Gilbert, J. A., & Threlfall, K. V. (2000). Patterns of leader

characteristics: Implications for performance and development. *Leadership Quarterly, 11*, 115–133.
O'Boyle, E. H., Jr., Forsyth, D. R., Banks, G. C., & McDaniel, M. A. (2012). A meta-analysis of the Dark Triad and work behavior: A social exchange perspective. *Journal of Applied Psychology*, 97, 557–579.
Offermann, L. R., Kennedy, J. K., Jr,. & Wirtz, P. W. (1994). Implicit leadership theories: Content, structure, and generalizability.*Leadership Quarterly, 5*, 43–58.
Ones, D. S., & Viswesvaran, C. (2001). Personality at work: Criterion-focused occupational personality scales used in personnel selection. In B. W. Roberts & R. Hogan (Eds.), *Personality psychology in the workplace* (pp. 63–92). Washington, DC: APA Books.
O'Shea, P. G., Foti, R. J., Hauenstein, N. M. A., & Bycio, P. (2009). Are the best leaders both transformational and transactional? A pattern-oriented analysis. *Leadership, 5*, 237–259.
Padilla, A., Hogan, R., & Kaiser, R. B. (2007). The toxic triangle: Destructive leaders, susceptible followers, and conducive environments. *Leadership Quarterly, 18*, 176–194.
Parker, S. K., Bindl, U. K., & Strauss, K. (2010). Making things happen: A model of proactive motivation. *Journal of Management, 36*, 827–856.
Parker, S. K., Williams, H. M., & Turner, N. (2006). Modeling the antecedents of proactive behavior at work. *Journal of Applied Psychology, 91*, 636–652.
Pratto, F., Sidanius, J., Stallworth, L. M., & Malle, B. F. (1994). Social dominance orientation: A personality variable predicting social and political attitudes. *Journal of Personality and Social Psychology, 67*, 741–763.
Preacher, K. J., Zyphur, M. J., & Zhang, Z. (2010). A general multilevel SEM framework for assessing multilevel mediation. *Psychological Methods, 15*, 209–233.
Rhodewalt, F., & Peterson, P. (2009). Narcissism. In M. R. Leary & R. H. Hoyle (Eds.), *Handbook of individual differences in social behavior* (pp .547–560). New York, NY: Guilford Press.
Rosenthal, S. A., & Pittinsky, T. L. (2006). Narcissistic leadership. *Leadership Quarterly, 17*, 617–633.
Sankowsky, D. (1995). The charismatic leader as narcissist: Understanding the abuse of power. *Organizational Dynamics, 23*, 57–71.
Schmitt, M. J., Kihm, J. A., & Robie, C. (2000). Development of a global measure of personality. *Personnel Psychology, 53*, 153–193.
Scott, K. A., & Brown, D. J. (2006). Female first, leader second? Gender bias in the encoding of leadership behavior. *Organizational Behavior and Human Decision Processes, 101*, 230–242.
Shamir, B., House, R. J., & Arthur, M. B. (1993). The motivational effects of charismatic leadership: A self-concept based theory. *Organization Science, 4*, 577–594.
Sheng, M. M. (2001). Mao Zedong's narcissistic personality disorder and China's road to disaster. In O. Feldman & L. O. Valenty (Eds.), *Profiling political leaders* (pp. 111–127). Westport, CT: Praeger.
Simsek, Z., Heavey, C., & Veiga, J. F. (2010). The impact of CEO core self-evaluation on the firm's entrepreneurial orientation. *Strategic Management Journal, 31*, 110–119.
Smalley, R., & Stake, J. E. (1996). Evaluating sources of ego-threatening feedback: Self-esteem and narcissism effects. *Journal of Research in Personality, 30*, 483–495.
Smith, J. A., & Foti, R. J. (1998). A pattern approach to the study of leader emergence. *Leadership Quarterly, 9*, 147–160.
Snyder, M. (1974). The self-monitoring of expressive behavior. *Journal of Personality and Social Psychology, 30*, 526–537.
Son Hing, L. S., Bobocel, D. R., Zanna, M. P., & McBride, M. V. (2007). Authoritarian dynamics and unethical decision making: High social dominance orientation leaders and high right-wing authoritarianism followers. *Journal of Personality and Social Psychology, 92*, 67–81.
Stogdill, R. M. (1948). Personal factors associated with leadership: A survey of the literature. *Journal of Personality, 25*, 35–71.
Tangney, J. P., Baumeister, R. F., & Boone, A. L. (2004). High self-control predicts good adjustment, less pathology, better grades, and interpersonal success. *Journal of Personality, 72*, 271–322.
Tepper, B. J. (2000). Consequences of abusive supervision. *Academy of Management Journal, 42*, 100–108.
Tepper, B. J. (2007). Abusive supervision in work organizations: Review, synthesis, and research agenda. *Journal of Management, 33*, 261–289.
Terman, L. M. & Oden, M. H. (1947). The gifted child grows up: Twenty-five years' follow-up of a superior group. In L. M. Terman (Ed.), *Genetic studies of genius* (Vol. 4, 1–10). Stanford, CA: Stanford University Press.
Tett, R. P., & Burnett, D. D. (2003). A personality trait-based interactionist model of job performance. *Journal of Applied Psychology, 88*, 500–517.
Tett, R. P., & Guterman, H. A. (2000). Situation trait relevance, trait expression, and cross-situational consistency: Testing a principle of trait activation. *Journal of Research in Personality, 34*, 397–423.
Uhl-Bien, M., Marion, R., & McKelvey, B. (2007). Complexity leadership theory: Shifting leadership from the industrial age to the knowledge era. *The Leadership Quarterly, 18*, 298–318.
Wang, M., & Bodner, T. E. (2007). Growth mixture modeling: Identifying and predicting unobserved populations with longitudinal data. *Organizational Research Methods, 10*, 635–656.
Wang, M., Sinclair, R. R., & Deese, M. N. (2010). Understanding the causes of destructive leadership: A dual process model. In T. Hansbrough & B. Schyns (Eds.), *When leadership goes wrong: Destructive leadership, mistakes and ethical failures* (pp. 73–97). Charlotte, NC: Information Age Publishing.
Whetzel, D. L., McDaniel, M. A., Yost, A. P., & Kim, N. (2010). Linearity of personality-performance relationships: A large-scale examination. *International Journal of Selection and Assessment, 18*, 310–320.
Zaccaro, S. J. (2007). Trait-based perspectives of leadership. *American Psychologist, 62*, 6–16.
Zaccaro, S. J. (2012). Individual differences and leadership: Contributions to a third tipping point. *Leadership Quarterly, 23*, 718–728.
Zaccaro, S. J., Foti, R. J., & Kenny, D. A. (1993). Self-monitoring and trait-based variance in leadership: An investigation of leader flexibility across multiple group situations. *Journal of Applied Psychology, 76*, 308–315.
Zaccaro, S. J., Gilbert, J. A., Thor, K. K., & Mumford, M. D. (1991). Leadership and social intelligence: Linking social perceptiveness and behavioral flexibility to leader effectiveness. *Leadership Quarterly, 2*, 317–342.
Zaccaro, S. J., Gulick, L. M. V., & Khare, V. P. (2008). Personality and leadership. In J. Ciculla (Ed.), *Leadership at the crossroads*, Vol. 1 (pp. 13–29). Westport, CT: Praeger.
Zeigler-Hill, V. (2006). Discrepancies between implicit and explicit self-esteem: Implications for narcissism and self-esteem instability. *Journal of Personality, 74*, 119–143.
Zuckerman, M., & O'Loughlin, R. E. (2006). Self-enhancement by social comparison: A prospective analysis. *Personality and Social Psychology Bulletin, 32*, 751–760.

CHAPTER

11 Charismatic and Transformational Leadership: Past, Present, and Future

Ketan H. Mhatre *and* Ronald E. Riggio

Abstract

The theoretical frameworks of charismatic and transformational leadership have been at the forefront of leadership research and practice for the last several decades. This review highlights the developments that have characterized the two areas of study since their conception and attempts to create a solid foundation for leadership research to progress in the future. This review opens with an examination of charismatic leadership and provides an overview of the different viewpoints that have driven its theoretical development. Next the chapter reviews existing literature on charismatic leadership by offering a brief summary of empirical research that has been done to date and follows that with a discussion of some criticisms and limitations of charismatic leadership. A similar review and critique is then conducted on the construct of transformational leadership. Finally, it closes with avenues for future research to proceed along, with an outline of several theoretical and research questions.

Key Words: Charisma, charismatic leadership, transformational leadership

Introduction

Ever since the systematic study of leadership commenced in the early 1900s, research on leadership has evolved in a rather dramatic manner. In a sense, its evolution has mirrored our ability as a species to comprehend the intricacies and complexities associated with objective reality. As we get better at understanding the objective reality that surrounds us, so does our understanding of what constitutes effective leadership and the multitude of psychosocial processes that accompany it. Such increments in our understanding of effective leadership have paved the way for the creation of newer, better, and more comprehensive conceptualizations and theories of leadership that have provided us with an enhanced understanding of the constitution and enactment of leadership across political, social, organizational, and other domains.

One such conceptualization of leadership that has arguably been at the vanguard of leadership research over the last several decades views leadership from an emotional, symbolic, and influence perspective. According to this conceptualization, leaders use emotional appeals, symbolic gestures, and a combination of several different influence mechanisms to lead their followers to "perform beyond expectations" (Bass, 1985). This perspective on leadership—which in several ways is markedly different from most of its predecessors—has received widespread research support across several different domains, contexts, and cultures. This perspective is the family of charismatic and transformational leadership models and theories. Together, charismatic and (especially) transformational leadership have been the most-studied theories of leadership in the past 20 years (Gardner, Lowe, Moss, Mahoney, & Cogliser, 2010; Lowe & Gardner, 2000). Although charismatic leadership has been discussed for nearly a century, and theories of transformational leadership for more than three decades, there is still much that research can do to further our understanding of these complex models of effective leadership.

For decades, early research on leadership focused on leader traits (e.g., intelligence, dominance, achievement, self-confidence, drive, motivation, etc.) or other attributes of leaders (e.g., competencies) that contributed to their success (Lord, DeVader, & Alliger, 1986; Mann, 1959; Stogdill, 1948, 1974). This "trait-based" paradigm of studying leadership was followed by the behavioral approach, which involved an examination of the actual behaviors of effective leaders (Katz, Maccoby, Gurin, & Floor, 1951; Stogdill & Coons, 1957). Throughout the 1960s and 1970s, contingency or interactional models of leadership effectiveness dominated. These theories saw leadership as an interaction of leaders' behavior, followers, and situational elements (Fiedler, 1996). Although these theories were popular as research models (e.g., Fiedler, 1964, 1967; Vroom & Jago, 1988; Vroom & Yetoon, 1973) and with practitioners (Fiedler & Chemers, 1974; Hersey & Blanchard, 1969, 1977), there was dissatisfaction in some circles, and a sense of stagnation. For example, Miner (1975) suggested that leadership research was not particularly "successful in building a viable theory of organization" and that "current theories of leadership tend to exist in an organizational vacuum" (p. 295). He argued for a better paradigm to govern leadership thinking and research than what had existed in the past.

In spite of the continuing advances in the field of leadership theory and research, there were several questions that remained unanswered. For instance, why do some leaders succeed at getting their followers to go above and beyond their call of duty while others fail to accomplish similar outcomes? Why do followers of some leaders value the collective vision and mission more than they do their own individual materialistic goals and aspirations? Why do some leaders succeed in persuading followers to perform self-sacrificial behaviors for the collective benefit while others don't? What specific steps do such leaders take to elicit such self-sacrificial behaviors from their followers? Why are some leaders more effective at generating emotional arousal in their followers than others?

Existing theories, such as the interactional models, did not seem to address these processes. So, leadership researchers turned to the long-dormant concept of leader charisma (Weber, 1947), and extended it with the development of more modern versions of charismatic leadership and with transformational theories of leadership.

The advent of charismatic and transformational theories of leadership introduced a new way of thinking about leadership. Leaders were not merely seen as "repertoires" of traits (as suggested by the Universalist paradigm). Neither were they viewed as enactors of a series of specific behaviors (like the Behavioral paradigm seemed to suggest). Leadership scholars started viewing leaders as change agents who—through the use of a combination of several different influence mechanisms—"transform" followers into highly inspired, energized, and motivated teams. Research from these theoretical perspectives began to seek answers to some of the elusive questions that in many ways inhibited the advancement of the field. This new line of inquiry and exploration thus provided a much-needed impetus to the field of leadership research and helped rejuvenate the research process that seemed to have stalled. As a result, charismatic theory, and transformational leadership theory, in particular, have been the dominant paradigm in leadership research for the past 25 years.

The current review is aimed at outlining the evolutionary trajectory of charismatic and transformational leadership. We begin this chapter by providing a comprehensive overview of the different approaches that fall under the respective categories of Charismatic and Transformational Leadership. We follow this with a brief summary of important empirical research that has helped advance the two theoretical frameworks. Next, we cite the limitations of the theories, along with some criticisms that have been voiced by the community of leadership researchers and scholars. In doing so, our goal is to aid the facilitation of a more robust transformation of these fields of study and pave the way for continued development. And finally, we offer guidelines and directions for future research on charismatic and transformational leadership to progress further.

Charismatic Leadership

Conception of Charisma

Although some of the earliest vestiges of charisma can be traced back to the writings of Aristotle (circa 4th century BC), the modern-day conception of charisma has been largely attributed to the works of Max Weber. Weber (1947) borrowed from the literal Greek meaning of the word *charisma*—which means "divine gift"—and described a breed of leaders who seem to possess certain "gifts" that allow them to lead in novel and inspiring ways that are markedly different from other traditional forms of leadership (e.g., leadership on the basis of formal authority). According to Weber, followers of charismatic leaders perceive their leaders to be gifted and to possess unique abilities that allow them to perform feats that are beyond the capacity of average individuals. Moreover, the key to success for charismatic leaders lies solely in the extent to which they are perceived to be gifted by their followers. If followers fail to recognize their leaders as having charisma, then the charismatic influence mechanism breaks down, and leaders can no longer exert their influence over followers. A quote from Weber (1968) summarizes this leadership predicament quite appropriately.

> The holder of charisma seizes the task that is adequate for him and demands obedience and a following by virtue of his mission. His success determines whether he finds them. His charismatic claim breaks down if his mission is not recognized by those to whom he feels he has been sent. If they recognize him, he is their master—so long as he knows how to maintain recognition through 'proving' himself. But he does not derive his 'right' from their will, in the manner of an election. Rather, the reverse holds: it is the duty of those to whom he addresses his mission to recognize him as their charismatically qualified leader. (p. 20)

In addition to describing the attributional nature of charisma, Weber suggested that charismatic leaders tend to arise during times of economic, social, political, and/or other forms of unrest. He argued that it is during such crisis situations that charismatic leaders get the opportunity to utilize their "divine gifts" and are able to lead effectively and successfully. These "divine gifts" often take the form of an emotional appeal to inspire and rouse followers, a radical vision to instill hope for the future, or bold steps that a leader may take to attenuate the negative effects of a crisis at hand. Once followers get a small taste of success, they tend to become more inclined to believe in the leader's powers to perform extraordinary feats resulting in a further consolidation of the leader's influence over followers.

Weber conceptualized charisma mostly as a perception of being divinely gifted and possessing certain extraordinary capacities. This reflects the premise of the trait-based Universalist theories of leadership, which maintain that leaders are born with a certain collection of traits that make them effective/successful in their respective roles. Weber also attempted to outline (albeit not in as detailed a manner as done by some later researchers) the behavioral repertoire of charismatics that leads to follower obedience and compliance. Lastly, Weber's conception of charismatic leadership can be seen as a special case of the contingency-based theories of leadership in the sense that Weber suggested the prevalence of a crisis, or some form of a social turmoil as a precondition for charismatic leadership to emerge. Thus, it may be of interest to note that even though subsequent conceptualizations of charismatic leadership have borrowed from the groundwork that Weber laid out, Weber's own conception of charisma and charismatic leadership seems consistent with the reigning leadership paradigms of the century—thus highlighting the cumulative nature of the evolution of leadership research.

Modern Development of Charismatic Leadership Theory

Decades after Weber, House (1977) was the first to present a comprehensive theoretical framework to describe the nature of charismatic leadership, explain the psychological processes through which charismatics end up influencing their followers, and outline subsequent follower outcomes that accrue as a result. His contribution to leadership research was especially significant because it brought the concept of charisma and the process of charismatic leadership from a relatively abstract to a more concrete plane—a plane where actual leader behaviors could be observed and examined, propositions could be formulated and empirically tested, and meaningful inferences that informed leadership research and practice could be derived. If Weber was the founding father of the modern-day "charisma movement," House could arguably be described as one of the chief architects who laid the plans for a scientific and systematic study of charismatic leadership.

According to House (1977), the key to successful relationships between charismatic leaders and their followers is the ability of leaders to inspire and emotionally arouse their followers. Successful charismatics are able to energize their followers by championing an appealing and potentially radical vision for the future. Followers of charismatic leaders often end up developing strong emotional bonds with their leaders, which serve as a foundation for their willingness to be compliant and committed to their leaders' agendas. The perception of leader charisma leads to a belief that charismatic leaders are blessed with extraordinary strengths that are likely to lead to a realization of the radical vision articulated by leaders. Moreover, given that charismatic leadership is more likely to emerge in times of acute crises and/or contexts characterized by distress, the presence of a leader with extraordinary abilities serves as a source of reassurance and hope, which further strengthens the influence that charismatic leaders tend to exert on their followers.

House's (1977) theory of charismatic leadership was further developed by Shamir and colleagues (Shamir, House, & Arthur, 1993) to include a more elaborate articulation of the behaviors of charismatic leaders, the mediating processes through which charismatic leaders motivate and influence followers, and the outcomes that follow as a result of leaders' influence. According to this self-concept-based theory of charismatic leadership, "charismatic leaders achieve transformational effects through implicating the self-concept of followers" (p. 584). They "increase the intrinsic value of efforts and goals by linking them to valued aspects of the follower's self-concept, thus harnessing the motivational forces of self-expression, self-consistency, self-esteem, and self-worth" (p. 584). Through the use of positive evaluations and by communicating higher performance expectations to their followers, charismatic leaders express confidence in their followers' abilities to meet those higher performance expectations and end up elevating the self-efficacy and collective efficacy of their followers. Additionally, their messages to their followers often consist of references to values, morals, and ideals, and this creates a sense of a higher purpose that followers associate with their own roles and actions.

Shamir and colleagues also outlined other mediating processes that contribute to charismatic leaders' influence over their followers. Charismatic leaders use social identification, personal identification, and value internalization as sources of influence over followers. Followers of charismatic leaders define themselves in terms of the social category in which they are embedded (e.g., their group or their organization). They take pride in being a part of that social category and perceive their membership in that category to be an important part of their social identity. This high level of social identification often leads to followers going out of their way with regard to their duties, roles, and functions, and performing at levels that are often above and beyond those of average expectations.

Followers of charismatic leaders often identify personally with their leaders. Due to the perception that charismatic leaders possess "extraordinary" qualities, followers oftentimes make an attempt to be like the leader whom they admire and emulate the leader psychologically as well as behaviorally. Psychologically, they may subscribe to the same value systems, morals, and ideals that their leader is known to embody; and behaviorally, followers may end up enacting the same leadership behaviors that they observe their leader performing. Like social identification, personal identification also moves followers to go above and beyond their call of duty.

Finally, Shamir and colleagues described internalization as one more mechanism that is responsible for the influence that charismatic leaders exert on their followers. Internalization "refers to the incorporation of values within the self as guiding principles" (p. 586). When charismatic leaders use ideological explanations to communicate their vision to followers, they portray their vision as noble, heroic, and having high moral standards. When followers internalize the values, ideals, and goals inherent in their leaders' vision, those values, ideals, and goals become part of the followers themselves. They "come to view their work role as inseparably linked to their self-concept and self-worth" and "carry out the role because it is a part of their essential nature and destiny" (Yukl, 2006, p. 253).

In addition to describing leader behaviors and mediating influence processes associated with charismatic leadership, Shamir and colleagues also outlined the organizational conditions under which charismatic leadership is more likely to emerge and be effective. According to the self-concept theory of charismatic leadership, charismatic leaders are most effective when their espoused vision is congruent with the values, ideals, and identities of their followers. Such congruence allows charismatic leaders to generate higher levels of social and personal identification as well as value internalization. Charismatic leaders do not have to work extra to convince or persuade their followers to adopt new value systems, and they are able to use their charisma to elicit follower outcomes such as commitment to the leader, commitment to the leadership mission and vision, self-sacrificial behaviors, and performance beyond expectations.

Charismatic Leadership—An Attributional Perspective

Building on the theoretical groundwork established by Weber, House, Shamir, and others, Conger and Kanungo (1987, 1998) proposed an alternative theory that highlighted the attributional nature of charismatic leadership. According to this conception, the phenomenon of leader charisma was described as a function of the attributional processes that followers utilize to ascribe charismatic qualities to their leaders. Although there are several similarities between the conception and function of charisma between this new attributional perspective and the previous self-concept-based perspective, there were significant deviations as well, which makes this theory a significant step forward in the evolution of theories of charismatic leadership.

According to Conger and Kanungo (1987, 1998), the source of leader charisma lies in the attributions that followers make about their leaders. In essence, it reflects the adage, "charisma lies in the eye of the beholder." The attribution of charismatic qualities to a leader depends on how the leader behaves, the perceptions of the leader's competence and ability to handle problems and difficult situations, and the characteristics of the context/situation that the leader-followers are embedded in. The right mix of the three ingredients leads to followers attributing charismatic qualities to the leader, which marks the beginning of the influence process of charismatic leaders.

Conger and Kanungo (1987, 1998) outlined several traits and behaviors of leaders that cause followers to make charismatic attributions. Foremost among them is the portrayal of confidence by the leader. Leaders are seen as more charismatic when they exhibit a sense of self-efficacy in their beliefs and actions. When followers see their leaders taking decisive steps toward the attainment of collective goals, and acting confidently to overcome persistent problems/hurdles, they are more likely to believe that their leaders have the "divine gift," and tend to make attributions of charisma.

Followers also tend to attribute charisma to leaders who espouse radical and ideological visions that are distinct from the status quo. The fortitude and courage that is displayed in communicating a vision that serves to challenge the status quo leads to perceptions of leader boldness and decisiveness, both seductive attributes in their own right. When followers realize and understand the positive outcomes associated with the radical vision, they are compelled to make charismatic attributions; for without the leader's foresight, the path to success would not have been possible. One caveat, however, is that if the espoused vision is perceived to be too radical or too much of a deviation from what seems possible, the leader runs the risk of being perceived as incompetent or outlandish.

Another quality that adds to the charismatic image of leaders is the ability to use emotional appeals in a strategic manner to stir and inspire followers. Through the use of symbols, slogans, and other similar means, successful charismatic leaders inject a jolt of inspiration into the thoughts and lives of their followers. They offer their followers a new purpose and meaning, and inspire them to strive hard to attain their radical vision by denouncing the status quo in favor of a better collective future. Such influx of inspiration often leads to attributions of charisma. Additionally, by acting in unconventional ways to achieve their vision and collective goals, charismatic leaders communicate a willingness to deviate from the norm for the sake of the collective good. For instance, a leader who is seen making self-sacrifices and taking personal risks for the benefit of the collective is often revered and enjoys the kind of influence and respect that is seldom afforded to noncharismatic leaders. Moreover, by conveying a sense of selflessness and making personal sacrifices for the sake of the collective, a charismatic leader manages to earn followers' trust—a very critical and influential variable in the leader-follower relationship. Followers who trust their leaders are more likely to make self-sacrifices themselves, and go above and beyond the call of duty for the attainment of the leader's vision, mission, and goals. Such behavior invites attributions of charisma and further strengthens the charismatic appeal of leaders.

The attributional theory of charismatic leadership also offered a description of the mediating influence processes through which charismatic leaders have an impact on their followers. While social identification and internalization seem to be the two key influence processes associated with the self-concept theory of charismatic leadership proposed by House and colleagues, the attribution theory of charismatic leaders views the process from a slightly different lens, in that it suggests personal identification with the leader as one of the key influence processes in the leader-follower relationship. According to Conger (1989), because followers perceive their leaders to possess extraordinary qualities, they tend to idolize them and are likely to imitate them. To be like the leader becomes a supplementary goal, and followers yearn for approval from their admired leaders. Praise and recognition from leaders have a significant impact on followers, and they seem willing to walk the extra mile in order to earn the coveted attention from their idols. Moreover, this desire to please the leader tends to act as a driving force that motivates followers to continue on the path that has been laid out in front of them.

In addition to personal identification, Conger (1989) also described internalization as one of the mediating influence processes associated with charismatic leadership. As mentioned earlier, if a vision is perceived to be too radical or unrealistic, then leaders run the risk of being labeled incompetent or outlandish. Thus, for successful leader influence to materialize, followers' internalization of the goals, values, ideals, and vision espoused by the leader becomes an imperative. Followers who internalize leaders' beliefs, values, and agenda are more likely to invest their psychological, physical, social, and other resources into the attainment of the leader's vision. Successful charismatics—through the use of their unusual gifts—are able to persuade, convince, and/or cajole their followers into buying into the collective agenda.

From a contextual perspective, the attribution theory of charismatic leadership is distinct from the self-concept theory of charismatic leadership in the sense that the prevalence of a crisis is not deemed to be a necessary precondition for the emergence of charismatic leadership. Whereas House and colleagues considered crises to be a relatively necessary condition for charismatic leadership to emerge, Conger and Kanungo (1998) proposed that charismatic leadership can emerge even in the absence of a crisis. They suggested that leaders often are motivated to create a discord with the status quo and use that as a foundation to further their visionary ideas for a better future. Reframing the situation as a crisis (when in fact it might not qualify as one) and presenting unconventional ways to overcome it was not considered to be beyond the behavioral repertoire of charismatic leaders according to the attributional theory of charismatic leadership.

Competing Conceptions of Charisma

In addition to the two theoretical frameworks proposed by Shamir and colleagues (1993) and Conger and Kanungo (1998), the period between 1976 and 2000 saw several alternative perspectives and conceptualizations of charisma and charismatic leadership. A majority of those perspectives were instituted with the objective of filling the gaps in the explanatory and predictive potential of existing frameworks. Their addition to the domain of research on charismatic leadership served two main purposes. First, by perpetuating theorizing and research efforts in the field, they made the domain of charismatic leadership popular among emerging leadership researchers and scholars as well as practitioners, thus facilitating a more thorough examination of leadership, in general, and charismatic leadership, in particular. Second, it fueled research designed to empirically test these theoretical frameworks, and explore this new paradigm further.

Kets de Vries (1988) and Lindholm (1988) utilized a Freudian lens and looked at charisma from a psychoanalytic perspective. They sought to explain the reasons behind followers' personal identification with their leaders and the subsequent effect that it has on followers. According to this perspective, followers can derive a sense of empowerment and positive energy by merging their identity with that of the charismatic leader whom they admire and cherish. Through the process of transference (i.e., unconscious redirection of feelings from one person to another), followers often seek to compensate for fractured self-identities, inchoate value systems and morals, and unfulfilled needs/desires by identifying with a charismatic leader who is seen as a walking example of what they seem to want or lack. They derive a sense of vicarious fulfillment of their needs and desires by associating with their leader, and the leader often becomes a source of continual motivation and inspiration. This view of how followers come to identify and "worship" charismatic leaders sheds light on the influence processes associated with cult leadership and leaders with compromised moral standards who nevertheless are able to command strong support and devotion from their followers.

Around this same time, Riggio and colleagues (Friedman, Riggio, & Casella, 1988; Riggio, 1987) argued that the charismatic qualities that cause a leader to be labeled "charismatic" were highly developed interpersonal and social skills, particularly skills in emotional and nonverbal communication (e.g., "emotional expressiveness"; Riggio, 1998). Emphasis was placed on the emotional contagion processes between charismatic leaders and followers, a topic of research that has continued up to the present time (Bono & Ilies, 2006; Johnson, 2009).

In an attempt to explain why certain followers make attributions of charisma toward leaders with whom they have never had close contact or personal interactions, Meindl (1990) proposed an alternate conceptualization of the process by which attributions of charisma emerge and are perpetuated among followers. Dubbing the process as "social contagion," Meindl (1990) suggested that followers often look for means or reasons to act on their desires to fight for a just or righteous cause that would allow them the opportunity to make self-sacrifices for the greater good. Such desires are often in a state of repression due to inhibiting social norms and/or conflicting social identities. However, when a leader (especially in the context of a crisis) challenges existing social norms and behaves in unconventional ways, he or she sparks a chain reaction or a "social contagion" that provides followers with an outlet to vent their repressed desires and emotions and allows them to pursue a just and righteous cause. Followers try to imitate the unconventional behavior displayed by their leader and indulge in activities that support and further their newly realized purpose. To understand, justify, and rationalize this change, followers often tend to attribute charisma to their leader, and such attributions often become exaggerated as they channel across multitudes of followers.

To distinguish between a charismatic relationship in which leaders are in close contact with their followers and one in which leaders are physically distant from their followers, Shamir (1995) and Yagil (1998) conducted exploratory studies to determine how followers make attributions of charisma when they are in close contact with their leaders and when they are distant from them. Shamir (1995) found that attributions of charisma for distant leaders stem from the achievements that the leader is known for; and attributions of charisma for close leaders originate on the basis of leader identification, the leader's interpersonal skills, and the leader's ability to motivate and inspire followers. These were interesting results and helped to uncover an interesting dynamic associated with how charisma works across different situations and contexts. However, subsequent studies did not fully support these results, which left the door open for future studies to address the topics of charisma and leader distance.

Several organizational researchers and leadership scholars (e.g., Bass & Steidlmeier, 1999; Conger, 1989; Conger & Kanungo, 1998; Hogan, Raskin, & Fazzini, 1990; House & Howell, 1992; Mumford, Gessner, Connelly, O'Connor, & Clifton, 1993) suggested the existence of a negative aspect to the influence of charisma and charismatic leadership. Referring to it as "the dark side of charisma," it was proposed that because followers are in awe of their "gifted" leaders, they might be less likely to speak up against the ideas and the propositions of their leader, and refrain from offering criticism regarding certain actions or practices. The "awe" might result in a perception that their leader is infallible and can potentially create a context that is divorced from objective reality. Given that charismatic leaders often challenge the status quo and partake in risky decisions, a less-than-optimal strategy to see their radical vision to fruition may result in serious failures and/or catastrophic and irrecoverable losses; and this does not augur well for any leadership situation. Moreover, such failures can potentially result in forces of opposition that may work toward removing the charismatic leader from his/her leadership position.

House and Howell (1992) offered a distinction between two different kinds of charismatic leaders, viz., personalized charismatic leaders and socialized charismatic leaders. Personalized charismatic leaders were described as self-aggrandizing, non-egalitarian, and exploitative leaders whose primary goal is to act in the interest of their own selves. Socialized charismatic leaders, on the other hand, were described as collectively oriented, egalitarian, and nonexploitative and whose primary goal is to act in the interest of others. Furthermore, personality traits such as need for power, authoritarianism, Machiavellianism, locus of control, etc., were the moderating factors that contributed to the distinction between personalized and socialized charismatic leaders.

Charismatic leadership, thus, is not without its own set of pitfalls, and efforts to further understand this "dark side of charisma" should continue if we are to acquire a better understanding of the overall process of leadership, both "positive" and productive, and "negative" and (potentially) destructive.

Charismatic Leadership—Brief Summary of Empirical Research

The different theoretical frameworks and conceptualizations of charismatic leadership have received varying degrees of empirical support over the years—some more so than others. Leadership researchers and organizational scholars have conducted numerous laboratory and field studies to test the propositions associated with the multiple conceptions of charisma and those of charismatic leadership. In the following section, we organize empirical research in this field into four main categories: (1) empirical research validating the relationships between charismatic leadership and common follower/organizational outcomes, (2) empirical research exploring and validating the factors that aid or impede perceptions/attributions of leader charisma, (3) empirical research validating and/or supporting the mediating mechanisms associated with the influence of charismatic leaders, and (4) research outlining other factors that exert an impact on perceptions/attributions of leader charisma. Additionally, it needs to be noted that the following section is more a summary of empirical research on charismatic leadership than a comprehensive overview, and space limitations prohibit us from listing all the studies that have contributed toward the validation and establishment of research on charismatic leadership.

Charismatic leadership and follower/organizational outcomes. Howell and Frost (1989) found that charismatic leadership was associated with high task performance, task adjustment, and adjustment to leader and group. Additionally, group productivity norms (i.e., high and low group productivity norms) did not have an impact on the relationship between charismatic leadership and the above-mentioned outcomes. Kirkpatrick and Locke (1996) examined the effects of visioning, highly expressive communication style, and providing advice to followers and found that visioning was associated with followers' perceptions of their task as more interesting, challenging, and important. Additionally, leader visioning led followers to set higher performance goals, display higher trust in the leader, and perceive the leader to be more charismatic, inspirational, and intellectually stimulating. In an attempt to explore the effects of charismatic leadership on negative organizational outcomes such as workplace aggression, Hepworth and Towler (2004) explored the relationship of charismatic leadership and workplace aggression and found that the effect of charismatic leadership on workplace aggression was small but significant. In a similar effort, Brown and Treviño (2006) investigated the relationship between socialized charismatic leadership and deviance in work groups and found that work groups managed by socialized charismatic leaders (i.e., charismatic leaders who motivate followers to achieve collective organizational goals without regard to their personal needs or agendas) exhibited less workplace deviance.

Cicero and Pierro (2007) found that charismatic leadership was positively related to work effort, job involvement, job satisfaction, performance, and negatively related to turnover intention. Erez, Misangyi, Johnson, LePine, and Halverson (2008) reported leader charisma to be positively related to followers' positive affect and negatively related to followers' negative affect. De Hoogh and Den Hartog (2009) found that charisma was associated with lower burnout, and that relationship was especially salient for individuals who were low in internal locus of control. Michaelis and Stegmaier (2009) found that charismatic leadership was positively related to innovation implementation behavior. Rowold and Laukamp (2009) found that charismatic leadership was negatively related to follower absenteeism and was positively related to follower training and development activity. Additionally, charismatic leadership was reported to be positively associated with profit, thus confirming the hypothesis that charismatic leadership might be related to objective and organizationally relevant indicators. Such (and other) research efforts helped corroborate the theoretical propositions of several charismatic leadership models and paved the way for a better understanding of the impact that charismatic leadership has on follower and organizational outcomes.

Research identifying/validating precursors of charismatic perceptions/attributions. In addition to examining the relationship between charismatic leadership and several individual/group level outcomes, several researchers explored the factors that are responsible for followers perceiving leaders as charismatic and attributing charisma to them. In one of the first attempts at understanding the effects of leaders' vision content, delivery, and organizational performance on perceptions of leader charisma and effectiveness, Awamleh and Gardner (1999) conducted an experiment and found that strength of delivery played a key role in determining whether a leader was perceived as charismatic and effective. Choi and Mai-Dalton (1999) conducted two studies to explore the impact of self-sacrificial behaviors on attributions of leader charisma and found that followers tend to attribute charisma to leaders who exhibit self-sacrificial behaviors. Additionally, they found that followers of self-sacrificial leaders intend to reciprocate such leader behaviors, and these effects are stronger when leaders are perceived to be competent. House, Spangler, and Woycke (1991) conducted a comparative study on charismatic leadership of U.S. presidents and found that presidents with a socialized power orientation (i.e., concern with others' welfare instead of their own) exhibited more behaviors that were characteristic of charismatic leadership. Additionally, such presidents were more likely to be perceived as charismatic, and their performance was rated higher than those of noncharismatic presidents. Halverson, Murphy, and Riggio (2004) examined the effects of evaluation stress and situational crisis on ratings of charismatic leadership and found that perceptions of leader charisma were more likely when the context was characterized by stress.

In an attempt to explore whether individuals could be taught how to be more charismatic, Antonakis, Fenley, and Liechti (2011) tested the efficacy of a theoretically designed intervention aimed at making "individuals appear more charismatic to independent observers." Using a field and lab study, the researchers manipulated individuals' charisma ad measured its impact on observer perceptions of charisma. They found that charisma training led to an increase in perceptions of charisma, leader prototypicality, and leader emergence (i.e., trained individuals were perceived as more prototypical leaders and more leader like). These are only but a few studies that have identified the precursors or antecedents of charismatic attributions/perceptions, and research on charismatic leadership continues to grow.

Research on mediating processes associated with charismatic leadership. Several researchers have contributed to the body of research on charismatic leadership by identifying the mediating processes through which charismatic leadership influences follower/organizational outcomes. Erez et al. (2008) reported that the relationships between leader charisma and followers' positive and negative affect were mediated by leaders' positive affect, positive expression, and aroused behavior. Cicero and Pierro (2007) found that the relationships between charismatic leadership and work effort, job involvement, job satisfaction, performance, and turnover intention were mediated by follower work-group identification. Michaelis and Stegmaier (2009) found that the relationship between charismatic leadership and innovation implementation behavior was mediated by followers' affective commitment to change.

Other factors impacting perceptions of charisma. Groves (2005) examined the role of gender in attributions of charisma and found that female leaders were perceived to be higher on social and emotional skills as well as on followers' ratings of charismatic leadership. Den Hartog, House, Hanges, Ruiz-Quintanilla, and Dorfman (1999) explored leader attributes reflecting charismatic (and transformational) leadership across 62 cultures around the world and found that leader attributes such as motive arouser, foresight, encouraging, communicative, trustworthy, dynamic, positive, confidence builder, and motivational were universally endorsed. This seems to suggest that although the vast majority of theoretical frameworks and conceptualizations of charismatic leadership are products of Western cultures, their relevance, pertinence, and applicability tends to cross-cultural barriers and might not be limited to Western cultures. In a related study, Van De Vliert (2006) conducted secondary analysis of managerial survey data from 61 countries and found that charismatic organizational leadership is endorsed more in countries with higher income and more demanding climates.

Thus, it is evident that the theoretical framework of charismatic leadership has received ample empirical support from numerous research efforts and as the number of studies to test the various propositions and mechanisms associated with charismatic leadership continues to grow, so does our understanding of the antecedents, mediators, and outcomes associated with this branch of leadership.

Criticism and Limitations of Charismatic Leadership Theory

The accumulation of theoretical and empirical research on charismatic leadership was met with several criticisms by numerous leadership scholars. Turner (1993) argued that the secular view of charisma that was introduced by Weber (1947) was unable to explain how leaders impact followers' expectations and internalization of attitude and behavioral changes. Beyer (1999) and House (1999) argued that a majority of the emphasis of charismatic leadership is skewed toward an examination of the influence of charismatic leaders on individual followers and fails to account for the influence that charismatic leaders may have on groups, teams, and organizations.

Yukl (1999) cited concerns regarding the ambiguity associated with the multiple conceptions and definitions of charisma. According to him, the differences between the leading construct definitions of charisma (viz., Conger & Kanungo's (1988, 1998) attributional view of charisma and House (1977) and Shamir et al.'s (1993) behavioral and follower influence-oriented view of charisma) created a "need for more clarity and consistency in how the term charismatic is defined and used" (p. 294).

Yukl (1999) also cited concerns with the ambiguity associated with the underlying influence processes in charismatic leadership. While the attributional theory of charismatic leadership (Conger & Kanungo, 1987, 1998) described personal identification and internalization as the primary influence processes of charismatic leaders, the self-concept theory of leadership (House, 1977; Shamir et al., 1993) identified internalization and collective identification as the key influence processes. This is a cause for concern because the identification of dominant influence processes in leader-follower relationships is critical for understanding and predicting leadership effectiveness (Howell, 1988; Shamir, 1991).

Some other concerns with charismatic leadership cited by Yukl (1999) were differences in behavioral repertoires associated with different theories of charismatic leadership, confusion regarding necessary conditions for attributions of charisma to surface (e.g., essential characteristics of followers in a charismatic leader-follower relationship, contextual variables such as the presence/absence of uncertainty or crises, etc.), and ambiguity regarding the reasons for the loss of charisma.

Charismatic leadership is not without its own set of limitations. The use of impression management, information restriction, unconventional behavior, and personal risk taking by charismatic leaders leads to the perception that such leaders are extraordinarily competent (Yukl, 2006). In the process, they might pay less attention to follower empowerment, appropriate delegation of authority, development of follower skills and self-efficacy, and the development of a strong empowering culture (Yukl, 2006). This implies that followers of charismatic leaders are more likely to be dependent on the "extraordinariness" of the charismatic leader and in the event that the leader is absent, followers might be unable to meet the challenges associated with their work task/roles. Thus, charismatic leadership seems to foster an unhealthy dependence on leaders that may lead to undesirable consequences in the long run.

Another limitation of charismatic leadership is that its emergence seems to depend on the existence of certain favorable contextual variables (Bass, 1985; Shamir & Howell, 1999). Although it may not be a necessary condition for charismatic leadership to emerge, the presence of some form of uncertainty or crisis creates a fertile ground for the emergence of charismatic leadership. This implies that the applications of charismatic leadership in everyday life may be of a restrictive nature.

While research on charismatic leadership reemerged in the late 1970s and 1980s to reenergize research on leadership, it was the theory of transformational leadership that led to explosive growth in leadership research. Transformational leadership theory, which incorporated aspects of charisma, but went beyond charisma, captured the attention of students of leadership, and the development of instruments to measure transformational leadership, facilitated scholars' research.

Transformational Leadership

It was in part the criticisms of and limitations to charismatic leadership theories that spurred the development of conceptualizations of transformational leadership. In some ways, transformational leadership theory, as developed by Bass and colleagues (Bass, 1985, 1998; Bass & Avolio, 1994), includes the notion of charisma, but goes well beyond in terms of its scope. As a result, transformational leadership has been the most-studied theory of leadership over the past two decades (Bass & Riggio, 2006; Gardner, Lowe, Moss, Mahoney, & Cogliser, 2010).

The origin of transformational leadership theory can be traced to the book, *Leadership*, by political scientist and presidential historian James MacGregor Burns. Burns (1978) laid down the foundation for transformational leadership by describing leadership from a transactional and a transformational perspective, the latter of which he labeled "transforming leadership." According to Burns (1978), transactional leadership is based on the principle of exchange.

> Such leadership occurs when one person takes the initiative in making contact with others for the purpose of exchange of valued things. The exchange could be economic or political or psychological in nature: a swap of goods or of one good for money; a trading of votes between candidate and citizen or between legislators; hospitality to another person in exchange for willingness to listen to one's troubles. (p. 19)

Transactional leadership does not go beyond the exchange. There is nothing holding the leader and follower together except for the mutual benefits each receives.

Transforming leadership on the other hand is based on the principle of raising the consciousness of followers to a higher moral plane and encouraging them to aspire to high ethical standards. The following paragraph taken from Burns's (1978) *Leadership* summarizes the concept of transforming leadership quite effectively.

> Such leadership occurs when one or more persons engage with others in such a way that leaders and followers raise one another to higher levels of motivation and morality. Their purposes, which might have started out as separate but related, as in the case of transactional leadership, become fused... But transforming leadership ultimately becomes moral in that it raises the level of human conduct and ethical aspiration of both leader and led, and thus it has a transforming effect on both." (p. 20)

By describing leadership along a continuum ranging from "transactional" to "transforming," Burns laid down the foundation for what would be later conceptualized as the Transactional-Transformational model of leadership.

The term "transformational leadership" was first introduced by Downton (1973) to describe a model of transactional, charismatic, and inspirational leadership. Bass (1985) proposed a different model of transformational leadership in which he further extended the theoretical frameworks earlier proposed by Burns (1978) and the charismatic leadership theory of House (1977). Central to Bass's model was the concept that different leadership styles and behaviors exist along a continuum. On the one end of the continuum was transformational leadership that consisted of four different factors. Following that was transactional leadership that consisted of two discrete factors, and it was followed by a single factor denoting the absence of leadership, or what Bass labeled "laissez-faire" leadership. Taken together, this continuum became known as the Full Range of Leadership model (Avolio & Bass, 2002).

The four factors that composed transformational leadership were termed *idealized influence, inspirational motivation, intellectual stimulation,* and *individualized consideration.* These components of transformational leadership are briefly described in Table 11.1.

The four transformational leadership factors, along with the three forms of transactional leadership (labeled Contingent Reward, Active Management-by-Exception, and Passive Management-by-Exception), and Laissez-Faire leadership are all measured by the Multifactor Leadership Questionnaire (MLQ). Perhaps more than any other single element, the MLQ spurred the increase in research on transformational leadership in the 1990s and beyond (see Antonakis, 2012).

Interestingly, there seems to be a significant amount of overlap between the influence processes associated with charismatic leadership and those associated with transformational leadership. Given that transformational leadership had charisma as an integral part of its factor structure, personal and social identification with the leader were common to both theoretical frameworks. Moreover, given that transformational leaders take active efforts to link tasks to followers' value systems and beliefs, followers are likely to perceive their tasks as a part of their own and thus experience the process of internalization.

Other Models of Transformational Leadership

Bennis and Nanus (1985) presented a model of transforming leadership that outlined four common strategies used by leaders in transforming organizations. They described transforming leaders as (1) having a clear vision of the future state of their organization, (2) social architects capable of

Table 11.1. The Four Components of Transformational Leadership (Bass, 1998; Bass & Riggio, 2006)

Idealized Influence (II)—is the leader's ability to serve as a positive role model for followers. Transformational leaders convey an ideological vision to their followers and give followers a higher sense of purpose—persuading followers to let go of self-interests for the benefit of collective goals. By setting high moral standards and establishing ethical codes of conduct, such leaders garner respect and trust from followers.
Idealized influence was initially considered a single factor, yet it was later divided into idealized influence-attributed—charisma attributed to leaders from followers—and idealized influence-behavioral, which refers to observable leader behaviors that constitute a leader's charismatic appeal.
Inspirational Motivation (IM)—is the ability of transformational leaders to inspire and motivate followers. Leaders communicate high-performance expectations and convey a sense of confidence that followers can meet those expectations.
Taken together, idealized influence and inspirational motivation best represent the notion of a leader's *charisma* (Bass & Riggio, 2006).
Intellectual Stimulation (IS)—is the ability to spur innovative and creative thinking through challenging followers to solve problems and think "outside the box." Because transformational leaders encourage followers to approach problems in novel and perhaps unconventional ways, leaders convey to followers that they are trusted and empowered.
Individualized Consideration (IC)—is the leader's ability to provide for the needs, and be responsive to, each individual follower. The leader provides support, guidance, and mentorship with the result of improving followers' performance, potential, and leadership capacity.

mobilizing followers to accept a new group identity or philosophy for their organizations, (3) creators of trust within their organizations, and (4) leaders capable of using creative deployment of self through positive self-regard.

Kouzes and Posner (1987, 2002) interviewed several middle and senior managers and used content analysis to come up with their model of leadership. According to this model, there are five fundamental practices that allow leaders to accomplish extraordinary things. These practices are (1) modeling the way, (2) inspiring a shared vision, (3) challenging the process, (4) enabling others to act, and (5) encouraging the heart. There is a great deal of similarity between these factors and the components of transformational leadership in Bass's model (Bass & Riggio, 2006).

Podsakoff, MacKenzie, Moorman, and Fetter (1990) presented another model of transformational leadership that was conceptually similar to the one presented by Bass (1985). It contained six transformational leadership factors that were (1) articulating a vision, (2) providing an appropriate model, (3) fostering the acceptance of group goals, (4) high-performance expectations, (5) providing individualized support, and (6) individualized consideration.

Kouzes and Posner (1988) produced the *Leadership Practices Inventory*, which is widely used in their work in developing leaders, but rarely used as a research tool. Podsakoff et al. (1990) also produced a measure of transformational leadership that has been used in research, but research using the MLQ predominates in the literature.

Transformational Leadership—Summary of Empirical Research

The theory of transformational leadership arguably has been the most researched of all leadership theories. Since its conception circa 1980, many researchers have devoted a great deal of effort toward testing and validating the various aspects of this popular theoretical framework. Given that there is quite a bit of overlap between charismatic leadership and transformational leadership (e.g., idealized influence or charisma is an integral element of transformational leadership), much empirical research aimed at testing the propositions of charismatic leadership inadvertently ends up testing some theoretical propositions associated with transformational leadership, and vice versa. While a comprehensive overview of all the research associated with transformational leadership is beyond the scope of this chapter, the following sections outline some of the research findings associated with this theory of leadership.

Transformational leadership and follower/organizational outcomes. There has been a great deal of research devoted to exploring the relationships between transformational leadership (usually using the MLQ) and follower, team, and organizational outcomes, that several meta-analyses have been conducted. The results suggest that transformational leadership has had a major impact on key variables such as individual and team performance, satisfaction with the leader, and positive workplace attitudes and behaviors.

Meta-analytic results show that all of the components of transformational leadership (e.g., idealized influence, inspirational motivation, etc.) and total score on the transformational leadership components of the MLQ are associated with higher ratings of unit performance (mean *r*s in the .4–.6 range) and objective measures of positive unit performance (mean *r*s .2–.3). Interestingly, transactional leadership, as represented by the contingent reward scale of the MLQ, has an estimated r of .45 with rated performance, but only .07 with objective performance. More recently, Wang, Oh, and Colbert (2011) found that transformational leadership was positively related to individual, team, and organizational level performance. The authors also reported that transformational leadership had an augmentation effect over transactional leadership in predicting individual-level contextual performance and team-level performance. These results suggest, in line with the title of Bass's 1985 book that transformational leadership does indeed lead to "performance beyond expectations." (Dumdum, Lowe, & Avolio, 2002; Lowe, Kroek, & Sivasubramaniam, 1996).

The effects of transformational leadership on follower attitudes are even stronger, (although this is partly due to common method bias as followers rate their leaders on the MLQ and also complete the attitude measures). Followers of transformational leaders tend to be more satisfied and show stronger organizational commitment than followers of non-transformational leaders (DeGroot, Kiker, & Cross, 2000; Dumdum et al., 2002). There is also a negative relationship between transformational leadership and turnover intentions (e.g., Martin & Epitropaki, 2001).

In addition to the effects of transformational leadership on employee attitudes and job performance, followers of transformational leaders engage in more organizational citizenship behaviors (i.e., employee behaviors that go beyond the required duties of followers' jobs; Cho & Dansereau, 2010; Podsakoff, Mackenzie, & Bommer, 1996; Purvanova, Bono, & Dzieweczynski, 2006). Transformational leadership also seems to have positive effects on followers' well-being and resistance to stress and burnout. For example, Seltzer, Numerof, and Bass (1989) show that followers of transformational leaders report lower levels of stress and burnout.

An important element of transformational leadership theory is the concept that transformational leaders develop followers' leadership capacity. In other words, followers of transformational leaders should themselves be more effective when put in a leadership role than followers of non-transformational leaders. As a result, there is an expectation that transformational leaders should have a positive developmental impact on followers. Dvir, Eden, Avolio, and Shamir (2002) used a longitudinal randomized field experiment to test the impact of transformational leadership on follower development and performance. They found that leaders receiving transformational leadership training had a more positive impact on direct followers' leader development, as defined by a group of measures including internalized moral values, an orientation toward the collective, and a sense of self-efficacy, than did leaders in the comparison group (which received eclectic leadership training). Moreover, these followers, once in leadership positions, led higher performing groups than did leaders receiving eclectic leadership training. Sosik and colleagues (Sosik & Godshalk, 2000; Sosik, Godshalk, & Yammarino, 2004) have suggested that transformational leaders develop followers through effective mentoring processes, including providing career guidance, enhancing self-esteem/efficacy, and providing networking opportunities.

Understanding the transformational leadership process. Much of the process by which transformational leaders affect followers and individual, group, and organizational outcomes has been touched on in our discussion of charismatic leadership given that charisma is a component of transformational leadership. For example, Shamir, et al. (1993) noted how charismatic leaders enhance the self-concept and esteem of followers, and this leads them to greater commitment and performance. It has also been suggested that transformational leaders enhance a collective sense of self-efficacy that facilitates group performance (Hoyt, Murphy, Halverson, & Watson, 2003; Sosik, Avolio, Kahai, & Jung, 1998).

In addition to developing a sense of self-efficacy in followers, transformational leaders also tend to empower followers; and consistent with the intellectual stimulation component, transformational leaders delegate important tasks to challenge followers. This allows followers to "stretch" and grow in their positions, and develop their own leadership potential (Bass & Riggio, 2006).

Another aspect of the dynamics of transformational leadership is that followers tend to identify with the leader and develop a sense of trust in him or her. Pillai, Schriesheim, and Williams (1999) suggest that it is trust in the leader and perceptions of leader fairness that are partially responsible for the positive impact transformational leaders have on followers. Deluga (1995) and Podsakoff et al. (1990) found that trust in the leader mediated the relationship between transformational leadership and follower engagement in organizational citizenship behaviors.

As far as an explanation for the finding that transformational leadership is negatively associated with follower stress and burnout goes, it has been suggested that transformational leaders are able to cognitively reframe potentially stressful situations as challenges (Bass & Riggio, 2006). Through enhancing followers' collective sense of efficacy and motivating them to rise to the challenge, followers are buffered against the negative aspects of difficult and taxing situations.

Additional research on transformational leadership. As noted, there has been a huge number of studies and scholarly papers on transformational and charismatic leadership. For example, Wang et al., (2011) found 113 separate studies that looked at the relationship between transformational leadership and follower performance. Antonakis (2012) found 200 papers published on charismatic and transformational leadership in 2009 alone. Therefore, it would be impossible to review all of the categories and subcategories of research and the multitude of variables that have been explored. What follows is a sampling of additional research topics that have been studied.

One area of research has explored the antecedents to transformational leadership, with the greatest emphasis on the relationship between personality and transformational leadership. Bono and Judge (2004) conducted a meta-analysis to determine the nature of the relationship between personality variables and ratings of transformational and transactional leader behaviors and found that the personality variables of extraversion and neuroticism showed a positive and negative association, respectively, particularly with the charisma-related dimensions of transformational leadership (i.e., idealized influence and inspirational motivation). Self-confidence/self-esteem, dominance, openness to experience, and resiliency/hardiness have also been associated with transformational leadership (Bass & Riggio, 2006).

Another important concern is whether transformational leadership theory is U.S.- or Western-centric, or whether it applies to other countries and cultures. Bass (1997) suggests that transformational leadership is more or less universal in its applicability across cultures, and the GLOBE studies suggest that charisma (although it may take different forms in different nations and cultures) is universally valued (House et al., 2004).

Another well-researched topic concerns gender differences in transformational leadership. In their meta-analysis, Eagly, Johannesen-Schmidt, and van Engen (2003) explored gender differences across transformational, transactional, and laissez-faire leadership styles and found that female leaders were more transformational, engaged in more contingent reward behaviors, and were less likely to manifest aspects of transactional leadership (viz. active and passive management-by-exception) and laissez-faire leadership than male leaders.

Criticisms and Limitations of Transformational Leadership Theory

Similar to charismatic leadership, transformational leadership too has its own set of problems and pitfalls, and numerous researchers have voiced their concerns and criticisms about this theoretical framework (Antonakis, 2012; Antonakis & House, 2002; Yukl, 1999). For example, the original concept of transformational/transactional leadership, emanating from Burns (1978), suggests that transformational leadership is, in many, or perhaps all, ways, superior to transactional leadership. Yet, evidence suggests that transactional leadership, at least as represented by the Contingent Reward subscale of the MLQ, does a good job of predicting positive group and follower outcomes (Bass & Riggio, 2006). Perhaps a better conceptualization has been suggested (Bass, Avolio, Jung, & Berson, 2003; Bass & Riggio, 2006) that transformational leadership augments the positive effects of transactional leadership.

Another criticism of transformational (as well as of charismatic) leadership is that it tends to be leader-centric and only marginally accounts for the role of followers in the leadership process. House (1999) suggested that charismatic/transformational models place too much emphasis on the effects that leaders have on followers while simultaneously neglecting leaders' effects on group and organizational performance. This criticism has been addressed—to a certain extent—since House (1999) first voiced his concern, however, much needs to be done to fully understand the macrolevel impact that transformational leadership has on group and organizational level outcomes.

Yukl (2006) suggested that "most theories of transformational and charismatic leadership lack sufficient specification of underlying influence processes" (p. 272). For example, the self-concept theory of charismatic leadership seems to lack a detailed description of how the different types of leader influence processes interact and the extent to which they are compatible with each other. Another concern voiced by Yukl (2006) is that most of the theories emphasize leadership from a dyadic perspective and neglect to appropriately explain how leaders build high performing teams. In order to overcome this potential problem, Yukl (2006) suggested that "the theories could be strengthened by a better explanation of how leaders enhance mutual trust and cooperation, empowerment, collective identification, collective efficacy, and collective learning" (p. 273).

Yet another concern expressed by Yukl (2006) is that the theories of charismatic and transformational leadership are unable to appropriately explain the external roles that leaders have to play (e.g., monitoring the environment for opportunities and threats, boundary spanning activities, acting as spokespersons for their organizations, seeking political support, building networks, negotiating, etc.). Such roles are of significant importance for organizational success, and the theories of charismatic and transformational leadership do not offer details regarding leaders' roles and responsibilities in this arena.

Brown and Lord (1999) argued that transformational leadership as a field of leadership research tends to exhibit an overdependence on survey and field studies. According to them, more experimental research needs to be done in order to be able to fully understand the underlying mediating processes associated with how transformational leaders influence their followers—and, in turn, their organizations.

Transformational (as well as charismatic) leadership theories have been accused of overemphasizing universal leader attributes that are relevant across all contexts and situation. This "one size fits all" approach to leadership seems to forgo the significance and impact of contextual variables that might play a role in critical leader-follower processes. Accordingly researchers have called for more attention to situational variables in order to determine the extent to which charismatic and transformational leadership will be effective across different situations (Beyer, 1999; Bryman, 1992). Even though research on the effect of situational factors is emerging (e.g., Antonakis & Atwater, 2002), much more work still needs to be done to accurately decipher the true nature and impact of charismatic and transformational leadership.

Another line of criticism has been leveled at the means for measuring transformational leadership. Criticisms of the MLQ have led to the development of alternative measures (e.g., Alimo-Metcalfe & Alban-Metcalfe, 2001; Podsakoff, et al., 1990), and the factor structure of the MLQ has been criticized. For example, some researchers (e.g. Den Hartog, Van Muijen, & Koopman, 1997; Tejeda, Scandura, & Pillai, 2001; Tracey & Hinkin, 1998) have reported a significant overlap between the four components of transformational leadership, and an inability to replicate the factor structure of the Full Range of Leadership model. However, Antonakis and colleagues (Antonakis, 2012; Antonakis et al., 2003), have suggested that the factor structure of transformational leadership, as measured by the MLQ, does indeed support the four factors outlined above. However, a legitimate criticism is the overreliance on rated, questionnaire measures for assessing transformational leadership, an issue we will discuss in the next section that will deal with future directions needed to increase our understanding of charismatic and transformational leadership.

Directions for Future Theory and Research on Charismatic and Transformational Leadership

Future Theoretical Direction: Charismatic leadership theory still suffers from a lack of consensus regarding the definition of "charisma." This is also a problem for the charisma elements of transformational leadership theory.

Because of its magical and mystical overtones, any attempt to define charisma is met with skepticism (as in "I don't know exactly how to define it, but I know it when I see it, and your definition isn't it."). It may very well be that during the 1990s and early 2000s, research on transformational leadership flourished, while research on leader charisma floundered, simply because of transformational leadership's four well-defined components, and accepted measurement tool (i.e., the MLQ). Yet, the lack of an agreed-upon definition of charisma is still a problem. Researchers have been trying to determine both the elements that seem to contribute to charismatic behavior (e.g., emotional expressiveness, the type and quality of rhetoric, use of metaphor, etc.), and there has been research that has tried to capture aspects of the charisma process (e.g., emotional contagion between leaders and followers, perceptions of leader charisma, etc.). This search for a better understanding of charisma may reinvigorate theorizing and research on charismatic leadership (and on the role of charisma in transformational leadership).

Future Theoretical Direction: Neither charismatic nor transformational leadership theories have dealt adequately with "dark side" leaders.

There is an underlying assumption that charismatic and transformational leadership represent ideals of effective leadership, yet there are many examples of charismatic leaders who were/are horrible dictators, despots, and heads of dangerous and deadly cults. Transformational leadership theory has also been concerned with "pseudo-transformational" leaders (Bass & Steidlmeier, 1999). Indeed, it is this issue that has driven research on authentic leadership (e.g., Avolio & Gardner, 2005; Gardner, Avolio, Walumbwa, 2005) in an effort to focus only on the positive or "authentic" forms of leadership. It is clear that future theory and research on both charismatic and transformational leadership need to clearly define and distinguish the "light" and "dark" forms.

Future Research Direction: The need for additional measures of charismatic and transformational leadership.

In addition to the need for clearer definitions within these leadership theories, there is a need for additional attention given to the measurement of charismatic and transformational leadership. Aside from the authors' own work, few researchers have adopted the Conger and Kanungo (1988, 1998) measure of charismatic leadership. More typically, researchers interested in charismatic leadership have used the charisma subscales from the MLQ, or they use the terms "charismatic" and "transformational" interchangeably. However, the MLQ is not without its critics (e.g., Tejeda, Scandura, & Pillai, 2001; Yukl, 1999), although the instrument has received strong support (e.g., Antonakis. Avolio,

& Sivasubramaniam, 2003) and usage. Still there are limitations to the MLQ. It has been suggested, however, that other methods and approaches for assessing transformational leadership should be developed. Specifically, Bass and Riggio (2006) suggest the need for a diary-based measurement of transformational leadership behaviors, as well as observational coding.

Future Research Direction: Greater emphasis on the multilevel phenomenon of charismatic and transformational leadership, which involves leaders, followers, and situational elements.

Both charismatic and transformational leadership are very leader-centric theories, focusing primarily on the leader's role in influencing followers. In reality, leadership is a multilevel phenomenon, with leaders and followers collaboratively creating leadership in groups and organizations. Moreover, the role of the situation is theoretically implicated in both charismatic (e.g., crisis situations) and transformational (e.g., stagnant groups and organizations needing change strategies) leadership. Leadership research in general has been moving toward multilevel analyses of leadership (Yammarino & Dansereau, 2008), and research on charismatic and transformational leadership needs to move in this direction.

Future Research Direction: There is a need for evidence that transformational leaders actually "transform" followers (as well as organizations).

A critical and defining element of transformational leadership is the idea of leader "transformation" of followers—the idea that transformational leaders encourage and catalyze the development of leadership potential/capacity in those they lead (see also Antonakis, 2012). However, there has been virtually no evidence, in terms of solid longitudinal investigations, that have demonstrated that transformational leadership actually leads to increases in follower leadership capacity. This research needs to be done. Indeed, leadership research in general suffers from a lack of longitudinal studies of both leader development and leadership processes over time (Day, 2011; Riggio & Mumford, 2011).

Future Research Direction: A clearer articulation of the successful influence tactics that enhance the effectiveness of Charismatic and Transformational leadership.

Research on influence tactics has come a long way since they were introduced into leadership/organizational contexts by Kipnis, Schmidt, and Wilkinson (1980) and Jones and Pittman (1982). Multiple efforts have been directed at identifying the effectiveness of specific influence tactics across a plethora of agents, targets, and situations (see Higgins, Judge, & Ferris (2003) for a meta-analytic review of influence tactics' impact on work related outcomes). Although most current models of Charismatic and Transformational leadership outline several influence processes that mediate the impact of Charismatic and Transformational leadership, efforts to associate specific influence tactics with models of Charismatic and Transformational leadership have been relatively scant (Charbonneau, 2004; Clarke & Ward, 2006; Howell & Higgins, 1990). More research needs to be done to identify and validate the specific influence tactics that charismatic and transformational leaders use to effect leadership outcomes. Furthermore, exploring the impact of several different combinations of influence tactics across different situations, cultures, as well as followers of varying demographics can yield a better understanding of the how the current models work and can potentially pave the way for more refined theories.

Future Research Direction: More comprehensive descriptive as well as normative models of Charismatic and Transformational leadership need to be developed for leading in multi- and cross-cultural environments.

Although research on Charismatic and Transformational leadership is transcending the typical Western contexts (Den Hartog et al., 1999; Leong & Fischer, 2011; Lian, Brown, Tanzer, Che, 2011; Van De Vliert, 2006), more work needs to go into the development of theoretically and empirically validated models of Charismatic and Transformational leadership that are best suited for specific cultures around the world. Most cross-cultural research on Charismatic and Transformational leadership seems to be aimed at empirically testing the efficacy of current models across different cultures. Although this has significantly added to our understanding of the different processes and outcomes associated with these theories, a necessary next step is to adapt and refine current models so that they are more culturally specific and accurate. Such efforts at theory revision should focus more on introducing necessary increments/decrements to current models to suit particular cultures—rather than a revolutionary upheaval of established theory. Adopting this route will have tremendous implications for not only the theoretical advancement of the field, but also have implications for the practice of charismatic and transformational leadership across the globe.

Conclusion

Charismatic and transformational leadership are popular theories with research scholars and with the general public. Both involve the elusive, but fascinating, construct of charisma—that special "gift" discussed by Weber more than a century ago. Yet, there is still some disagreement over the definition and proper assessment of charisma. These theories are also appealing because they represent superior, and perhaps even ideal, forms of leadership. In the case of transformational leadership, there is substantial evidence that transformational leaders do indeed lead better than their non-transformational counterparts. Moreover, because of the availability of reasonably well-validated measurement instruments, particularly the MLQ, research efforts to further understand the intermediary processes and outcomes associated with transformational leadership have flourished, and will likely continue into the foreseeable future. Several challenges to such efforts, however, loom on the horizon. Given the porous nature of organizational, cultural, political, and social boundaries, coupled with the ever-evolving role played by rapid technological innovation, the form and function of charismatic, as well as transformational leadership, as we understand them today might change. Followers today have the means to witness and minutely scrutinize each and every action of leaders. Social media platforms such as Facebook, Twitter, YouTube, etc., have made contemporary leaders more visible. Due to such widespread visibility, a relatively minor mistake or a faux pas on the part of leaders has the potential to cause their downfall. This calls for greater transparency between leaders and followers—a component of a relatively new model of leadership, viz. Authentic leadership (but also hinted at in discussions of "authentic" transformational leadership (Bass & Riggio, 2006). We speculate that with passing time and changing contexts, newer prerequisites, antecedents, and moderators will be introduced to the present conceptualizations of charismatic and transformational leadership thus prolonging their applicability and deferring their *potentially impending* obsolescence. Whether models of charismatic and transformational leadership become obsolete or not will be a question that will be answered in due course of time, however, following Thomas Kuhn's (1962) suggestion, their place in the history and progression of the field of leadership will remain irreplaceable as we stand in the face of new frontiers of leadership science and thought.

References

Antonakis, J. (2012). Transformational and charismatic leadership. In D. V. Day & J. Antonakis (Eds.), *The nature of leadership* (2nd ed., pp. 256–288). Thousand Oaks, CA: Sage.

Antonakis, J., & Atwater, L. (2002). Leader distance: A review and a proposed theory. *Leadership Quarterly, 13*(6), 673–704.

Antonakis, J., Avolio, B. J., & Sivasubramaniam, N. (2003). Context and leadership: An examination of the nine-factor full-range leadership theory using the Multifactor Leadership Questionnaire. *The Leadership Quarterly, 14*(3), 261–295.

Avolio, B. J., & Bass, B. M. (Eds.). (2002). *Developing potential across a full range of leadership: Cases on transactional and transformational leadership*. Mahwah, NJ: Lawrence Erlbaum Associates.

Avolio, B. J., & Gardner, W. L. (2005). Authentic leadership development: Getting to the root of positive forms of leadership. *Leadership Quarterly, 16*, 315–338.

Awamleh, R., & Gardner, W. L. (1999). Perceptions of leader charisma and effectiveness: The effects of vision content, delivery, and organizational performance. *Leadership Quarterly, 10*(3), 345.

Bass, B. M. (1985). *Leadership and performance beyond expectations*. New York: Free Press.

Bass, B. M. (1997). Does the transactional/transformational leadership paradigm transcend organizational and national boundaries? *American psychologist, 52*, 130–139.

Bass, B. M. (1998). *Transformational leadership: Industrial, military, and educational impact*. Mahwah, NJ: Lawrence Erlbaum Associates.

Bass, B. M., & Avolio, B. J. (1994). *Improving organizational effectiveness through transformational leadership*. Thousand Oaks, CA: Sage.

Bass, B. M., Avolio, B. J., Jung, D. I., & Berson, Y. (2003). Predicting unit performance by assessing transformational and transactional leadership. *Journal of Applied Psychology, 88*, 207–218.

Bass, B. M., & Riggio, R. E. (2006). *Transformational Leadership* (2nd ed.). Mahwah, NJ: Lawrence Erlbaum Associates.

Bass, B. M., & Steidlmeier, P. (1999). Ethics, character, and authentic transformational leadership. *Leadership Quarterly, 10*, 181–217.

Bennis, W. G., & Nanus, B. (1985). *Leaders: The strategies for taking charge*. New York: Harper & Row.

Beyer, J. M. (1999). Taming and promoting charisma to change organizations. *Leadership Quarterly, 10*, 307–330.

Bono, J. E., & Ilies, R. (2006). Charisma, positive emotions, and mood contagion. *The Leadership Quarterly, 17*, 317–334.

Bono, J. E., & Judge, T. A. (2004). Personality and transformational and transactional leadership: A meta-analysis. *Journal of Applied Psychology, 89*, 901–910.

Brown, D. S., & Lord, R. G. (1999). The utility of experimental research in the study of transformational/charismatic leadership. *Leadership Quarterly, 10*, 531–539.

Brown, M. E., & Treviño, L. K. (2006). Socialized charismatic leadership, values congruence, and deviance in work groups. *Journal of Applied Psychology, 91*(4), 954–962.

Bryman, A. (1992). *Charisma and leadership in organizations*. London: Sage.

Burns, J. M. (1978). *Leadership*. New York: Harper & Row.

Charbonneau, D. (2004). Influence tactics and perceptions of transformational leadership. *Leadership & Organization Development Journal, 25*(7), 565–576.

Cho, J., & Dansereau, F. (2010). Are transformational leaders fair? A multi-level study of transformational leadership, justice perceptions, and organizational citizenship behaviors. *Leadership Quarterly, 21*(3), 409–421.

Choi, Y., & Mai-Dalton, R. R. (1999). The model of followers' responses to self-sacrificial leadership: An empirical test. *Leadership Quarterly, 10*(3), 397–421.

Cicero, L., & Pierro, A. (2007). Charismatic leadership and organizational outcomes: The mediating role of employees' work-group identification. *International Journal of Psychology, 42*(5), 297–306.

Clarke, S., & Ward, K. (2006). The role of leader influence tactics and safety climate in engaging employees' safety participation. *Risk Analysis: An International Journal, 26*(5), 1175–1185.

Conger, J. A. (1989). *The charismatic leader: Behind the mystique of exceptional leadership*. San Francisco: Jossey-Bass.

Conger, J. A., & Kanungo, R. (1987). Toward a behavioral theory of charismatic leadership in organizational settings. *Academy of Management Review, 12*, 637–647.

Conger, J. A., & Kanungo, R. (1998). *Charismatic leadership in organizations*. Thousand Oaks, CA: Sage.

Day, D. V. (2011). Integrative perspectives on longitudinal investigations of leader development: From childhood through adulthood. *The Leadership Quarterly, 22*, 561–571.

DeGroot, T., Kiker, D. S., & Cross, T. C. (2000). A meta-analysis to review organizational outcomes related to charismatic leadership. *Canadian Journal of Administrative Sciences, 17*, 356–371.

Den Hartog, D. N., House, R. J., Hanges, P. J., Ruiz-Quintanilla, S. A., & Dorfman, P. W. (1999). Culture specific and cross-culturally generalizable implicit theories: Are attributes of charismatic/transformational leadership universally endorsed? *Leadership Quarterly, 10*(2), 219.

De Hoogh, A.H.B., & Den Hartog, D. N. (2009). Neuroticism and locus of control as moderators of the relationships of charismatic and autocratic leadership with burnout. *Journal of Applied Psychology, 94*(4), 1058–1067.

Deluga, R. J. (1995). The relationship between trust in the supervisor and subordinate organizational citizenship behavior. *Military Psychology, 3*, 25–39.

Downton, J. V. (1973). *Rebel leadership: Commitment and charisma in the revolutionary process*. New York: Free Press.

Dumdum, U. R., Lowe, K. B. & Avolio, B. J. (2002). A meta-analysis of transformational and transactional leadership correlates of effectiveness and satisfaction: An update and extension. In B. J. Avolio & F. J. Yammarino (Eds.), *Transformational and charismatic leadership: The road ahead* (pp. 35–66). Oxford: JAI/Elsevier.

Dvir, T., Eden, D., Avolio, B. J., & Shamir, B. (2002). Impact of transformational leadership on follower development and performance: A field experiment. *Academy of Management Journal, 45*, 735–744.

Eagly, A. H., Johannesen-Schmidt, M. C., & van Engen, M. L. (2003). Transformational, transactional, and laissez-faire leadership styles: A meta-analysis comparing men and women. *Psychological Bulletin, 129*, 569–591.

Erez, A., Misangyi, V. F., Johnson, D. E., LePine, M. A., & Halverson, K. C. (2008). Stirring the hearts of followers: Charismatic leadership as the transferal of affect. *Journal of Applied Psychology, 93*(3), 602–616.

Fiedler, F. E. (1964). A contingency model of leadership effectiveness. In L. Berkowitz (Ed.), *Advances in experimental social psychology* (vol. 1, pp. 149–190). New York: Academic Press.

Fiedler, F. E. (1967). *A theory of leadership effectiveness*. New York: McGraw-Hill.

Fiedler, F. E., & Chemers, M. M. (1974). *Leadership and effective management*. Glenview, IL: Scott, Foresman.

Friedman, H. S., Riggio, R. E., & Casella, D. (1988). Nonverbal skill, personal charisma, and initial attraction. *Personality and Social Psychology Bulletin, 14*, 203–211.

Gardner, W. L., Avolio, B. J., & Walumbwa, F. O. (2005). Authentic leadership development: Emergent trends and future directions. In W. L. Gardner, B. J. Avolio, & F. O. Walumbwa (Eds.), *Authentic leadership theory and practice: Origins, effects, and development* (pp. 387–406). Oxford: Elsevier Science.

Gardner, W. L., Lowe, K. B., Moss, T. W., Mahoney, K. T., & Cogliser, C. C. (2010). Scholarly leadership of the study of leadership: A review of the Leadership Quarterly's second decade, 2000–2009. *The Leadership Quarterly, 21*(6), 922–958.

Groves, K. S. (2005). Gender differences in social and emotional skills and charismatic leadership. *Journal of Leadership and Organizational Studies, 11*(3), 30–46.

Halverson, S. K., Murphy, S. E., & Riggio, R. E. (2004). Charismatic leadership in crisis situations: A laboratory investigation of stress and crisis. *Small Group Research, 35*(5), 495–514.

Hepworth, W., & Towler, A. (2004). The effects of individual differences and charismatic leadership on workplace aggression. *Journal of Occupational Health Psychology, 9*(2), 176–185.

Hersey, P., & Blanchard, K. H. (1969). *Management of organizational behavior: Utilizing human resources*. Englewood Cliffs, NJ: Prentice Hall.

Hersey, P., & Blanchard, K. H. (1969). *Management of organizational behavior: Utilizing human resources* (3rd ed.). Englewood Cliffs, NJ: Prentice Hall.

Hersey, P., & Blanchard, K. H. (1969). *Management of organizational behavior: Utilizing human resources* (5th ed.). Englewood Cliffs, NJ: Prentice Hall.

Higgins, C. A., Judge, T. A., & Ferris, G. R. (2003). Influence tactics and work outcomes: a meta-analysis. *Journal of Occupational Behavior, 24*, 89–106.

Hogan, R. J., Raskin, R., & Fazzini, D. (1990). The dark side of charisma. In K. E. Clark & M. B. Clark (Eds.), *Measures of leadership* (pp. 343–354). West Orange, NJ: Leadership Library of America.

House, R. J. (1977). A 1976 theory of charismatic leadership. In J. G. Hunt & L. L. Larson (Eds.), *Leadership: The cutting edge* (pp. 189–207). Carbondale: Southern Illinois University Press.

House, R. J. (1999). Weber and the neo-charismatic paradigm: A response to Beyer. *Leadership Quarterly, 10*, 563–574.

House, R. J., & Howell, J. M. (1992). Personality and charismatic leadership. *Leadership Quarterly, 3*(2), 81–108.

House, R. J., Spangler, W. D., & Woycke, J. (1991). Personality and charisma in U.S. presidency: A psychological theory of leader effectiveness. *Administrative Science Quarterly, 36*(3), 364–396.

Howell, J. M. (1988). Two faces of charisma: Socialized and personalized leadership in organizations. In J. A. Conger & R. N. Kanungo (Eds.), *Charismatic leadership: The elusive factor in organizational effectiveness* (pp. 213–236). San Francisco: Jossey-Bass.

Howell, J. M., & Frost, P. J. (1989). A laboratory stud of charismatic leadership. *Organizational Behavior and Human Decision Processes, 43*(2), pp. 243–269.

Howell, J. M., & Higgins, C. A. (1990). Leadership behaviors, influence tactics, and career experiences of champions of technological innovation. *The Leadership Quarterly, 1*(4), 249–264.

Hoyt, C. L., Murphy, S. E., Halverson, S. K., & Watson, C. B. (2003). Group leadership: Efficacy and effectiveness. *Group Dynamics: Theory, Research, and Practice, 7*, 259–274.

Johnson, S. K. (2009). Do you feel what I feel? Mood contagion and leadership outcomes. *The Leadership Quarterly, 20*(5), 814–827.

Jones, E. E., & Pittman, T. S. (1982). Toward a general theory of strategic self presentation. In J. Suls (Ed.), *Psychological perspectives on the self* (pp. 231–262). Hillsdale, NJ: Lawrence Erlbaum Associates.

Katz, D., Maccoby, N., Gurin, G., & Floor, L. G. (1951). *Productivity, supervision and morale among railroad workers.* Ann Arbor, MI: Institute for Social Research, University of Michigan.

Kets de Vries, M.F.R. (1988). Prisoners of leadership. *Human Relations, 41*(3), 261–280.

Kipnis, D., Schmidt, S.M., & Wilkinson, I. (1980). Intraorganizational influence tactics: Exploration in getting one's way. *Journal of Applied Psychology, 65*(4), 440–452.

Kirkpatrick, S. A., & Locke, E. A. (1996). Direct and indirect effects of three core charismatic leadership components on performance and attitudes. *Journal of Applied Psychology, 81*(1), 36–51.

Kouzes, J. M., & Posner, B. Z. (1987). *The leadership challenge: How to get extraordinary things done in organizations.* San Francisco: Jossey-Bass.

Kouzes, J. M., & Posner, B. Z. (2002). *The leadership challenge* (3rd ed.). San Francisco: Jossey-Bass.

Kuhn, T. S. (1962). *The structure of scientific revolutions.* Chicago: University of Chicago Press.

Leong, L., & Fischer, R. (2011). Is transformational leadership universal? A meta-analytical investigation of multifactor leadership questionnaire means across cultures. *Journal of Leadership & Organizational Studies, 18*(2), 164–174.

Lian, H., Brown, D., Tanzer, N., & Che, H. (2011). Distal charismatic leadership and follower effects: An examination of Conger and Kanungo's conceptualization of charisma in China. *Leadership, 7*(3), 251–273.

Lindholm, C. (1988). Lovers and leaders: comparative models of romance and charisma. *Social Science Information, 27*(1), 3–45.

Lord, R. G., DeVader, C. L., & Alliger, G. M. (1986). A meta-analysis of the relation between personality traits and leadership perceptions: An application of validity generalization procedures. *Journal of Applied Psychology, 71*, 402–410.

Lowe, K. B., & Gardner, W. L. (2000). Ten years of *The Leadership Quarterly*: Contributions and challenges for the future. *The Leadership Quarterly, 11*, 459–514.

Lowe, K. B., Kroeck, K. G., & Sivasubramaniam, N. (1996). Effectiveness correlates of transformational and transactional leadership: A meta-analytic review of the MLQ literature. *The Leadership Quarterly, 7*(3), 385–425.

Mann, R. D. (1959). A review of the relationship between personality and performance in small groups. *Psychological Bulletin, 56*, 241–270.

Martin, R., & Epitropaki, O. (2001). Role of organizational identification on implicit leadership theories (ILTs), transformational leadership and work attitudes. *Group Processes and Intergroup Relations, 4*, 247–262.

Meindl, J. R. (1990). On leadership: An alternative to the conventional wisdom. In B. M. Staw & L. L. Cummings (Eds.), *Research in organizational behavior* (vol. 12, pp. 159–203). Greenwich, CT: JAI Press.

Michaelis, B., Stegmaier, R., & Sonntag, K. (2009). Affective commitment to change and innovation implementation of behavior: The role of charismatic leadership and employees' trust in top management. *Journal of Change Management, 9*(4), 399–417.

Miner, J. B. (1975). The uncertain future of the leadership concept. An overview. In J. G. Hunt & L. L. Larson (Eds.), *Leadership frontiers* (pp. 197–208). Kent, OH: Kent State University Press.

Mumford, M. D., Gessner, T. L., Connelly, M. S., O'Connor, J. A., & Clifton, T. C. (1993). Leadership and destructive acts: Individual and situational influences. *Leadership Quarterly, 4*, 115–147.

Pillai, R., Schriesheim, C. A., & Williams, S. E. (1999). Fairness perceptions and trust as mediators for transformational and transactional leadership: A two-sample study. *Journal of Management, 25*, 897–933.

Podsakoff, P. M., MacKenzie, S. B., & Bommer, W. H. (1996). Transformational leader behaviors and substitutes for leadership as determinants of employee satisfaction, commitment, trust, and organizational, citizenship behaviors. *Journal of Management, 22*, 259–298.

Podsakoff, P. M., MacKenzie, S. B., Moorman, R. H., & Fetter, R. (1990). Transformational leader behaviors and their effects on follower's trust in leader, satisfaction, and organizational citizenship behaviors. *Leadership Quarterly, 1*, 107–142.

Purvanova, R. K., Bono, J. E., & Dzieweczynski, J. (2006). Transformational leadership, job characteristics, and organizational citizenship performance. *Human Performance, 19*(1), 1–22.

Riggio, R. E. (1987). *The charisma quotient.* New York: Dodd-Mead.

Riggio, R. E. (1998). Charisma. In H. S. Friedman (Ed.), *Encyclopedia of mental health.* (pp. 387–396). San Diego, CA: Academic Press.

Riggio, R. E., & Mumford, M. D. (2011). Introduction to the special issue: Longitudinal studies of leadership development. *The Leadership Quarterly, 22*, 453–456.

Rowold, J., & Laukamp, L. (2009). Charismatic leadership and objective performance. *Applied Psychology: An International Review, 58*(4), 602–621.

Seltzer, J., Numerof, R. E., & Bass, B. M. (1989). Transformational leadership: Is it a source of more or less burnout or stress? *Journal of Health and Human Resources Administration, 12*, 174–185.

Shamir, B. (1991). The charismatic relationship: Alternative explanations and predictions. *Leadership Quarterly, 2*, 81–104.

Shamir, B. (1995). Social distance and charisma: Theoretical notes and an exploratory study. *Leadership Quarterly, 6*, 19–47.

Shamir, B., House, R. J., & Arthur, M. B. (1993). The motivational effects of charismatic leadership: A self-concept based theory. *Organizational Science, 4*, 1–17.

Shamir, B., & Howell, J. M. (1999). Organizational and contextual influences on the emergence and effectiveness of charismatic leadership. *Leadership Quarterly, 10*, 257–283.

Sosik, J. J., Avolio, B. J., Kahai, S. S., & Jung, D. I. (1998). Computer-supported work group potency and effectiveness: The role of transformational leadership, anonymity, and task interdependence. *Computers in Human Behavior, 14*, 491–511.

Sosik, J. J., & Godshalk, V. M. (2000). Leadership styles, mentoring functions received and job-related stress: A conceptual model and preliminary study. *Journal of Organizational Behavior, 21*, 365–390.

Sosik, J. J., Godshalk, V. M., & Yammarino, F. J. (2004). Transformational leadership, learning goal orientation, and expectations for career success in mentor-protégé relationships: A multiple levels of analysis perspective. *The Leadership Quarterly, 15*, 241–261.

Stogdill, R. M. (1948). Personal factors associated with leadership: A survey of the literature. *Journal of Psychology, 25*, 35–71.

Stogdill, R. M. (1974). *Handbook of leadership: A survey of theory and research* New York: Free Press.

Stogdill, R. M., & Coons, A. E. (Eds.). (1957). *Leader behavior: Its description and measurement.* Columbus: Ohio State University, Bureau of Business Research.

Tejeda, M. J., Scandura, T. A., & Pillai, R. (2001). The MLQ revisited: Psychometric properties and recommendations. *The Leadership Quarterly, 12*, 31–52.

Tracey, J. B., & Hinkin, T. R. (1998). Transformational leadership or effective managerial practices? *Group & Organization Management, 23*(3), 220–236.

Turner, S. (1993). Charisma and obedience: A risk cognition approach. *Leadership Quarterly, 4*(3–4), 235–256.

Van De Vliert, E. (2006). Climatic ecology of charismatic leadership ideals. *European Journal of Work and Organizational Psychology, 15*(4), 385–403.

Vroom, V. H., & Jago, A. G. (1988). *The new leadership: Managing participation in organizations.* Englewood Cliffs, NJ: Prentice Hall.

Vroom, V. H., & Yetton, P. W. (1973). *Leadership and decision-making.* Pittsburgh, PA: University of Pittsburgh Press.

Wang, G., Oh, I., & Colbert, A. E. (2011). Transformational leadership and performance across criteria and levels: A meta-analytic review of 25 years of research. *Group & Organization Management, 36*(2), 223–270.

Weber, M. (1947). *The theory of social and economic organization* (T. Parsons, Trans.). New York: Free Press.

Weber, M. (1968). *Max Weber on charisma and institutional building* (S. N. Eisenstadt, Ed.). Chicago: The University of Chicago Press.

Yagil, D. (1998). Charismatic leadership and organizational hierarchy: Attribution of charisma to close and distant leaders. *Leadership Quarterly, 9*, 161–176.

Yammarino, F. J., & Dansereau, F. (2008). Multi-level nature and multi-level approaches to leadership. *The Leadership Quarterly, 19*(2), 135–141.

Yukl, G. (1999). An evaluation of conceptual weaknesses in transformational and charismatic leadership potential. *Leadership Quarterly, 10*, 285–305.

Yukl, G. (2006). *Leadership in Organizations.* NJ: Prentice-Hall.

CHAPTER

12 Visionary Leadership

Daan van Knippenberg *and* Daan Stam

Abstract

Visionary leadership, the communication of a future image of a collective with the intention to persuade others to contribute to its realization, is widely seen as a particularly effective way of mobilizing and motivating followers. In this chapter, we take stock of the state of the science in visionary leadership and conclude that conclusions regarding the effectiveness of visionary leadership are overly optimistic at least in the sense that the existing evidence base leaves much to be desired. The conclusions we highlight from a review of the evidence warn against complacency and satisfaction with the current state of the science. We identify methodological and conceptual issues to take into consideration in moving the study of visionary leadership forward.

Key Words: charisma, charismatic leadership, inspirational leadership, leadership, leadership effectiveness, transformational leadership, vision, visionary leadership

Oh, the vision thing.

—*George H. W. Bush*

Those who consider what makes leaders successful in mobilizing and motivating followers seem to converge on one thing at least: vision. The communication of an inspiring vision is seen to lie at the core of the exceptional leadership that mobilizes the masses, unites countries, and spurs organizations toward exceptional performance. These notions are most evident in theories of charismatic and transformational leadership where the communication of an inspiring vision probably more than anything else is seen to distinguish charismatic-transformational leadership from other forms of leadership (Bass, 1985; Bryman, 1992; Burns, 1978; Conger & Kanungo, 1987; Shamir, House, & Arthur, 1993). For leaders to be really effective in mobilizing and motivating followers to pursue collective objectives, visionary leadership presumably is the thing. But what *is* this thing called visionary leadership?—and what do we know about it from sound academic research? These are the questions this chapter aims to answer.

To clarify one issue upfront, we note that we understand visionary leadership to be more narrowly defined than charismatic and transformational leadership. The communication of a vision may be a core element of charismatic and transformational leadership, and the communication of an inspiring vision may lead to the perception that the leader is charismatic, but charismatic-transformational leadership is also understood to include elements that are conceptually distinct from the communication of a vision (e.g., self-sacrifice, individualized consideration; Bass, 1985; Conger & Kanungo, 1987; Shamir et al., 1993). In contrast to these broader perspectives on leadership, we understand visionary leadership as exclusively concerning the communication of a vision, an image of the future of a collective (e.g., team, organization, nation), and the evidence we review also concerns leader communication of visions specifically and not the broader body of evidence in charismatic-transformational leadership that collapses assessment of leader vision communication into broader measures of charismatic-transformational leadership (cf. Bass & Riggio, 2006).

From the perspective that ultimately any theory is only as strong as the evidence supporting it (Ferris, Hochwarter, & Buckley, 2012), we place a strong emphasis on empirical, hypothesis-testing research in our review of the state of the science in visionary leadership.[1] For research in visionary leadership this is no minor point, because the study of visionary leadership in particular is riddled by writings invoking "the vision thing" without much clarity as to the evidence base from which conclusions are drawn. Should we take all these writings at face value, we would be led to believe that it is proven beyond a shadow of a doubt that visionary leadership is particularly effective, and moreover that we know what it is that makes visionary leadership effective. As our chapter shows, this is an overly optimistic impression.

What the current chapter shows, in contrast, is that our knowledge of visionary leadership is actually surprisingly fragmented. There is little if any programmatic research on visionary leadership, and there is so much diversity in empirical research, focusing on different independent as well as different dependent variables, that findings are very hard to integrate. Inevitably then, we find ourselves at least as much concluding what we do not know than what we do know. Moreover, research in visionary leadership is associated with a couple of serious methodological concerns and our chapter emphasizes as much the implications for future research in terms of methods as it does in terms of conceptual developments. In a sense then, this chapter is at least as much a call to arms to leadership research as it is an integration of research evidence. Despite its critical tone, however, this chapter is not intended to call the effectiveness of visionary leadership into doubt. Indeed, we would contend there is scope for solid theory and research to capture the effectiveness of visionary leadership. Rather, the current chapter aims to inspire the more systematic and scientific study of visionary leadership.

To set the stage for our review, we first briefly outline the broader issue of leadership effectiveness in leadership research. This allows us to better position the study of visionary leadership and the field's excitement with it as a presumably particularly effective form of leadership. In assessing the empirical evidence, leadership is a field where it pays off to also first consider some of the methodological problems associated with the field's research, and this might be particularly true for visionary leadership. Before we turn to a review of empirical studies in visionary leadership in terms of how they speak to theory, we therefore first consider some of these methodological issues that provide important caveats in assessing this evidence.

Vision and Leadership Effectiveness

Leadership is a fundamental element of human groups (Hogg & van Knippenberg, 2003), and for better or worse one with great potential impact on the functioning, performance, and well-being of groups and their members. It is therefore not surprising that leadership has been on the agenda of behavioral research for more than 100 years—a "classic" field of study as behavioral research goes. The key question in leadership research is what makes leaders effective in mobilizing and motivating followers—what makes individuals in leadership positions successful in influencing others to pursue collective objectives (Bass, 2008; van Knippenberg, 2012; Yukl, 2002).

At the core of this question lies an interest in social influence—an interest in leadership's influence on the thoughts and actions of others. More specifically, the issue of leadership effectiveness as described in the previous paragraph narrows the social influence of interest down in at least two ways worth mentioning to understand the emphasis on visionary leadership in research in leadership effectiveness. First, leadership effectiveness concerns influence that motivates pursuit of *collective* rather than individual ends. This influence would thus typically take place in the context of a social grouping (e.g., work group, team, organization, nation; van Knippenberg & Hogg, 2003), and leadership effectiveness in part resides in the leader's ability to move followers beyond self-interest and to embrace the collective interest (Burns, 1978; Shamir et al., 1993; van Knippenberg, van Knippenberg, De Cremer, & Hogg, 2004). Second, leadership effectiveness concerns influence regarding ends for which leaders have substantial discretion in their communication. Often, these will be ends that are in fact defined by the leader, but such leadership arguably could also include the way leaders frame and make sense of more widely shared organizational visions. Merely passing on orders from above (e.g., handing down a corporate communiqué) would not typically be understood as leadership (or alternatively as bad, ineffective leadership). This means that the ability of leaders to define, frame, and communicate collective ends is part of effective leadership. Considering these issues, it is not surprising that visionary leadership looms large in discussions of leadership effectiveness.

We define a vision as what is conceived and communicated by the leader in terms of an image of a future for a collective. Visionary leadership is defined as *the verbal communication of an image of a future for a collective with the intention to persuade others to contribute to the realization of that future.* All definitions of vision share the notion that visions are images of the future (going back to the roots of research in charismatic leadership in the work of Weber, 1947). Scholars advancing these definitions would most likely agree that these concern a future for a collective rather than a single individual. Several of these scholars would define visions a bit more specifically, however, as not only an image of the future but as also containing one or more elements that are presumed to render visions effective in motivating followers. To some visions by definition are *idealized* futures (e.g., Conger, 1999; Strange & Mumford, 2002; Yukl, 2002), images capturing shared values and identity (e.g., Boal & Bryson, 1988; Kirkpatrick & Locke, 1996; Shamir et al., 1993; Tichy & Devanna, 1986), or images shared by followers (Conger & Kanungo, 1998). Our perspective on this is that these are better seen as elements that can make a vision more or less effective than as elements that determine whether an image of the future warrants the label vision.

In considering what makes leadership effective, visionary leadership is important in that it concerns the definition of ends for a collective (i.e., the vision to pursue) and the attempt to persuade followers to contribute to the achievement of these ends as a collective interest. Indeed, no other element of leadership identified in the literature probably speaks so directly to these aspects of leadership effectiveness as visionary leadership. This is not to say that the communication of collective objectives is seen as the sole domain of visionary leadership; both goal-setting, which can be understood as an aspect of leadership (Locke & Latham, 1990), and the notion of task-oriented leadership (or initiating structure; e.g., Judge, Piccolo, & Ilies, 2004) include the communication of collective objectives. Goal-setting theory is particularly articulate in this respect, and indeed visions could be argued to be goals.

In goal-setting theory, however, effective goals are seen quite differently than visions. Goal-setting is proposed to be most effective when it concerns goals with a clearly defined end state in the not too distant future for which both the reaching of the end state and progress toward the end state can be unambiguously assessed (Locke & Latham, 1990). Effective goal-setting would typically concern in-role performance with quantifiable targets to be reached over a period of time that individuals can oversee with reasonable ease (e.g., a 10 percent sales increase over the next quarter). Visions, in contrast, are typically understood to be defined more in qualitative than in quantitative terms and to concern imagery that elicits sensory sensations such as a mental picture or a sound (Emrich, Brower, Feldman, & Garland, 2001). Moreover, as compared with the goals highlighted in goal-setting theory (and for task-oriented leadership), visions are understood to be more distal in time, or even ongoing (e.g., visions capturing enduring qualities of an organization's products or services), with greater challenges in monitoring progress and self-regulating behavior toward their achievement than goals. The importance of these distinctions should lie in the notion that visionary leadership thus should lend itself better than goal-setting to successfully motivating more uncertain and open-ended endeavors such as innovation, collective change, and extraordinarily high performance—outcomes for which leadership is sought in particular (e.g., Bass, 1985; van Knippenberg, van Knippenberg, & Bobbio, 2008). In short, it is not unreasonable to see visions as goals, but they should be understood as specific types of goals that are distinct from the goals emphasized in goal-setting theory.

It may also be noted that in many writings visionary leadership and vision tend to be used almost interchangeably. This is not unreasonable from the perspective that the communication of a vision implies its conception. Even so, in studying visionary leadership it is instructive to make a distinction between the influence of the content of the vision per se (i.e., some characteristics of the vision may render visionary leadership more effective) and the influence of the way in which the vision is communicated (i.e., some ways of communicating a vision may be more effective than others; e.g., Awamleh & Gardner, 1999; Holladay & Coombs, 1993; Tichy & Devanna, 1986). Different elements of visionary leadership can thus be studied in isolation as well as in interaction. This not only holds for the distinction between vision and vision communication, but also for different elements of vision content or vision communication. Thus, visionary leadership should be seen as a multidimensional construct.

The present chapter emphasizes leader agency as an essential element in visionary leadership. To clarify and illustrate this point, consider a study by Paul, Costley, Howell, Dorfman, and Trafimow (2001). Paul et al. experimentally compared the effectiveness of visionary communication originating from a leader with the same communication ostensibly being routinely put together by a service team. Whereas the former would be seen as visionary leadership, the latter would (typically) not. The finding of Paul et al. that the vision was more effective when originating from a leader than when it was routinized speaks to the importance of leader agency in visionary leadership, and thus is valuable in developing our understanding of visionary leadership. Once we move to the study of visions without leader agency but either as shared understanding within a team (Pearce & Ensley, 2004) or perceived as a depersonalized project vision (Lynn & Akgün, 2001) or organizational vision (Oswald, Mossholder, & Harris, 1997; Testa, 1999), however, evidence becomes more indirectly relevant to visionary leadership and receives no priority in the present review.

Methodological Issues in Visionary Leadership Research

For an accurate assessment of the state of the science in visionary leadership an appreciation of some of the methodological problems in visionary leadership research is important. Because several of these problems are shared by many studies, it is more instructive to consider these upfront than to discuss these problems in a piecemeal fashion inspired by individual studies. In this section we identify the methodological issues we see as posing the greatest challenges to the advancement of our understanding of visionary leadership. The problems we identify in this section should both be seen as important caveats in assessing the empirical evidence base and as important considerations for future research in visionary leadership.

Theorizing about Visions but Studying Goal-setting?

As discussed in the previous section, conceptually visions can be distinguished from goals more generally and especially from goals as understood in goal-setting theory in that visions are more qualitative and imagery-based, and concern longer time horizons than goal-setting. A pervasive problem in survey research in visionary leadership is that this understanding of visions as different from more concrete and shorter-term goals is not reflected in operationalizations of visionary leadership.

Questionnaire measures of visionary leadership arguably as easily could be measuring goal-setting as visionary leadership. Many measures explicitly refer to goals (e.g., Lynn & Akgün, 2001) or are phrased in ways that would make it possible to respond positively on the basis of visionary leadership as well as goal-setting (e.g., "has a clear understanding of where we are going" [Podsakoff, Mackenzie, Moorman, & Fetter, 1990; Rafferty & Griffin, 2004]; "provides inspiring strategic and organizational goals" [Conger & Kanungo, 1994]). These may be descriptions that apply to visionary leadership, but they are not unique to visionary leadership. They may capture goal-setting too. As it is, it is not clear to what extent current findings from survey research relying on such "goal" measures speak to visionary leadership, goal-setting, or a combination of both. This forms an important caveat in drawing conclusions from survey research in visionary leadership.

For evidence from survey measures to uniquely speak to visionary leadership, it would be important to develop measures that more explicitly and unambiguously uniquely capture visionary leadership. This would mean developing measurement that describes the visionary leadership in ways that would not also apply to goals as understood in goal-setting, for instance by explicitly capturing notions of imagery and extended time horizons (unfortunately, we could currently not quote a measure that is free of the ambiguity identified here and uniquely captures vision communication). This could also entail including a separate measure of goal-setting as control in research on visionary leadership. Inclusion of such a goal-setting measure would also allow for theoretically interesting comparisons of goal-setting and visionary leadership influences that would help develop our understanding of visionary leadership.

Apples and Oranges: Reliance on Confounded Comparisons

We noted earlier in our discussion that there are no well-developed multidimensional conceptualizations of visionary leadership. Even so, it stands to reason that the effectiveness of visionary leadership is determined by both aspects of the vision and aspects of the way in which the vision is communicated.

This understanding is at least implicitly shared in the field, judging by the variety of aspects of visionary leadership that have been studied (as per our review presented in the next main section). When multiple aspects are at stake, it is important that they are studied in a systematic way to avoid confounded comparisons (i.e., comparing leader communications that differ on multiple aspects). More common practice in research in visionary leadership seems to be, however, to rely on comparisons that reflect multiple differences at once, confounding the influence of one aspect of visionary leadership with the influence of others. The end result is that we cannot reach conclusions about the aspects of visionary leadership that are the "active ingredients" in the observed effects of visionary leadership or about the extent to which these concern additive or interactive influences. Comparing apples and oranges in this way slows down development of the field much more than many researchers seem to realize.

The issue is most easily illustrated for experimental research with its comparisons between distinct experimental conditions even when the problem is not limited to experimental research. A widely cited experimental study by Kirkpatrick and Locke (1996), for instance, was designed to compare the effectiveness of visionary leadership and nonvisionary leader communication through speeches delivered by a confederate. The visionary condition differed in multiple aspects from the nonvisionary condition, however, such as the topic of speech, appeal to interfirm competition, and appeal to self-efficacy. It may indeed be the case that these are all elements that would differentiate more effective from less effective leader communication (or visionary from nonvisionary communication). The problem is that by varying multiple differences simultaneously rather than independently in a full factorial design, Kirkpartrick and Locke made it impossible to determine to what extent each difference contributed to effects on the dependent variables (i.e., either as a main effect or in interaction with other elements). The problem is not unique to the Kirkpatrick and Locke study, and in effect such studies can inform us only to a modest extent about the effects of visionary leadership. Comparisons sometimes also confound leadership with context. Hunt, Boal, and Dodge (1999), for example, compared (among others) visionary leadership in times of crisis with another form of leadership that was only studied in a non-crisis situation, confounding crisis and leadership.

This confounding of multiple aspects of leadership in the study of visionary leadership is not limited to experimental research. Ruvio et al. (2010), for instance, drew a comparison of visionary leadership in a profit and a nonprofit sector. Sectors differed, however, in the strategies organizations were likely to follow. This was not captured by the vision measure, but may be assumed to be reflected in the content of the visions. Their observation that visionary leadership was differentially related to venture performance and growth for profit and nonprofit organizations might thus reflect differences in the content of the visions between sectors, differences between the importance of visionary leadership between sectors, or both (and controlling for the reported strategies does not address this issue).

Again, this example is not to single out a particular study for criticism. Rather, it is to illustrate a common problem in survey research in visionary leadership. Survey measures of visionary leadership are "content-free" (e.g., Conger & Kanungo, 1994; Podsakoff et al., 1990; Rafferty & Griffin, 2004). They aim to capture the extent to which the leader has or communicates a vision, but not the content of that vision. As a result, differential relationships for visionary leadership and outcomes may reflect differences in the content of visions as well as differences in the importance of visionary leadership. Without more specific measures, there is no way of knowing.

Such confounded comparisons are problematic from the perspective of sound academic research, because they render conclusions ambiguous at best. The obvious solution here is to pursue greater methodological rigor in research designs to yield more unconfounded comparisons—in field research as well as in lab research. As a showcase example of how visionary communication can be studied systematically and without confounds, let us point to a study by Naidoo and Lord (2008). Naidoo and Lord were interested in the role of speech imagery, and ran an experiment in which they took great care to limit differences between leader speech conditions to imagery only. To illustrate, here is what they did:

> For the other speech, each imagery-based word or phrase was carefully replaced with a concept-based equivalent, yielding a low-imagery speech with essentially the same meaning as the original. For example, one excerpt reads "Small wonder that confidence languishes, for it thrives only on honest..." in the high imagery condition, and

"Small wonder that confidence decreases, for it increases only on honesty..." in the low imagery (concept-based words) version. (Naidoo & Lord, 2008: 286)

Naidoo and Lord thus produced two speeches that were exactly the same except for the extent to which imagery-based rhetoric was used. As a result, any difference between conditions could unambiguously be attributed to image-based rhetoric. Clearly, for field research relying on naturally occurring visions, such clean comparisons are unlikely to be realized. In recognition of this problem, however, field research may search for opportunities in which leader communications would be maximally comparable (e.g., situations in which different top management team members each communicate the same organizational vision) or strive for coding of vision content and delivery to render variables that would otherwise be potential confounds as much as possible part of the actual data analysis.

Confounding Visionary Leadership with Its Effects

Another problem found in survey research on visionary leadership is that measurement confounds visionary leadership with the outcomes it is supposed to predict. Common measures of visionary leadership include items soliciting a rating of perceived effectiveness: "inspires others with his/her plans for the future," "is able to get others committed to his/her dream" (Podsakoff et al., 1990); "inspirational, able to motivate by articulating effectively the importance of what organizational members are doing" (Conger & Kanungo, 1994). The problem with such measurement becomes evident when these measures are used to predict leadership effectiveness, especially when indicators of effectiveness are derived from subjective ratings provided by followers (the most common measures of leadership effectiveness in leadership research; Kaiser, Hogan, & Craig, 2008; van Knippenberg, 2012). Follower ratings of visionary leadership in terms of its effectiveness in inspiring and instilling commitment more or less inevitably correlate highly with subjective ratings such as leadership evaluations and work attitudes. It seems a legitimate question what exactly can be concluded on the basis of positive relationships between such ratings. They seem to prove very little.

Some may argue that it is perfectly legitimate to study what leads to the attribution that a leader is visionary. Indeed, it is perfectly legitimate to study attributions of visionary qualities. We disagree, however, with the practice to confound a behavioral understanding of visionary leadership (i.e., what the leader does) with an attributional perspective on visionary leadership (i.e., what the leader is perceived to effectuate). By and large conceptual analyses of visionary leadership emphasize the behavioral perspective, and from this perspective it is bad practice to confound the measurement of visionary leadership with follower attributions of leadership effects. What this means, then, is that we should interpret findings relying on hybrid measures of visionary leadership (i.e., combining ratings of leader behavior and of the perceived effects of leadership) with extreme caution—a level of caution that can probably not be overstated. Clearly, for future research this means that there is substantial value-added in the development of visionary leadership measures that avoid confounding leader behavior with its perceived effects.

Subjective Ratings of Visions and Outcomes

Most research in leadership relies on subjective ratings provided by the same source (i.e., followers) to assess leadership as well as the indicators of leadership effectiveness (e.g., leadership evaluations, work attitudes). Research in visionary leadership is no exception and in assessing the state of the science in visionary leadership it is important to consider the methodological problems associated with this practice.

A first concern here is with the subjective assessment of visionary leadership. This is a particular concern for leadership research, because (implicit) beliefs about leadership may strongly color leadership perceptions (Eden & Leviatan, 1975; Lord, 1977; Lord & Maher, 1991; Meindl, Ehrlich, & Dukerich, 1985). Positive evaluations of visionary leadership may reflect these preconceptions as much as "objective" visionary leadership, for instance in response to the observation that the team or organization is doing well. There thus is a legitimate concern with what subjective leadership ratings reflect, especially when they have stronger evaluative connotations (as ratings of visionary leadership clearly do).

A second concern is with the practice to relate subjective ratings of leadership to dependent variables that also are subjective ratings provided by the same source. Many visionary leadership studies rely on attitudinal-evaluative ratings by subordinates as indicators of leadership effectiveness (i.e., rather than the more objective behavioral indicators that would be preferable; Kaiser et al., 2008). Combined with subordinate ratings of leadership, this means that common method variance is an issue: the fact that both leadership and its outcomes are rated by the same source in and of itself can be the cause of the observed relationships, or at least inflate the magnitude of relationship (Podsakoff, MacKenzie, Lee, & Podsakoff, 2003).

As alternative to follower ratings, some studies rely on leader self-ratings of their vision (e.g., Larwood, Falbe, Kriger, & Miesing, 1995; Ruvio, Rosenblatt, & Hertz-Lazarowitz, 2010). This introduces two additional concerns. The first is that self-ratings in particular are colored by a desire to present a favorable rating of visionary leadership (cf. Judge, LePine, & Rich, 2006). The second concern is the possibility that at least the existing self-rating measures overemphasize the vision itself over the communication of the vision (i.e., items solicited evaluations of the vision, not of the communication of the vision). That is, they do not tell us how or to what extent the vision is communicated.

Evidence regarding visionary leadership thus is stronger if it originates from more objective operationalizations, such as content coding of written vision statements (e.g., Baum, Locke, & Kirkpatrick, 1998) or experimental manipulations of visionary communication (e.g., Naidoo & Lord, 2008). It is also stronger when it concern more objective outcome indicators rather than attitudinal-evaluative ratings. An obvious call to research in visionary leadership thus is to prioritize such evidence over more subjective ratings, as it is critical to the development of our understanding of visionary leadership that we can exclude alternative interpretations in terms of methodological shortcomings.

Studying the Relationship between Visionary Leadership and Charismatic-Transformational Leadership Including Visionary Leadership

In visionary leadership research there is a strong focus on showing that the communication of a vision predicts charismatic-transformational leadership or that charismatic-transformational leadership predicts the communication of a vision. All major theories of charismatic and transformational leadership see visionary leadership as an integral part of charismatic-transformational leadership (i.e., more narrowly defined than, but completely overlapping with charismatic-transformational leadership). From the perspective of validation, it thus makes sense to show that visionary leadership is perceived as charismatic-transformational, or that leaders perceived to be charismatic-transformational are also perceived to engage in visionary leadership. Setting aside the issue that the study of the relationship between visionary leadership and charismatic-transformational leadership does not add anything beyond validation because the relationship is there by definition, there is actually a problem with this particular research focus: in much of the available research the relationship is there also "by design."

The measures used to assess charismatic-transformational leadership probably without exception include items referring to the communication of a vision (e.g., Bass & Avolio, 1995; Conger & Kanungo, 1994; Podsakoff et al., 1990; Rafferty & Griffin, 2004). The conclusion then is that communicating a vision leads to the perception that one communicates a vision (Awamleh & Gardner, 1999; Johnson & Dipboye, 2008) or, when charismatic/transformational leadership is the predictor variable, that a measure including the perception that one communicates an inspiring vision predicts visionary leadership (Sosik & Dinger, 2007). That is, research inducing the communication of a vision shows that this results in the perception that a vision is communicated (i.e., as part of a measure of charismatic-transformational leadership) and research measuring the communication of a vision (i.e., as part of a measure of charismatic-transformational leadership) shows that this predicts a measure of vision communication. In experimental terminology, this is a manipulation check, not a proper dependent variable.

What is required to make such validations meaningful at the operational level, is an operationalization of charismatic-transformational leadership that does not include the perception that the leader communicates a vision. At the same time, such a measure would beg the conceptual question what the measure represents when vision communication is explicitly excluded from charismatic-transformational leadership. For such research to be meaningful then, it would seem to make more sense to focus on a construct that is not overlapping conceptually with visionary leadership. For instance, the perception that the leader is inspiring could be meaningfully studied as a function of visionary leadership, where different elements of vision content and vision delivery could be measured or manipulated to predict the perception of inspirational qualities.

Visionary Leadership as Part of Broader Conceptualizations/Operationalizations of Charismatic-Transformational Leadership

In assessing the empirical evidence it is also important to realize that most evidence regarding visionary leadership is "hidden" in measures of charismatic-transformational leadership. The communication of an inspiring vision is such an integral part of conceptualizations of charismatic and transformational leadership (e.g., Bass, 1985; Conger & Kanungo, 1987) that all major operationalizations of charismatic-transformational leadership in questionnaire measures include items or subscales referring to leader vision (Bass & Avolio, 1995; Conger & Kanungo, 1994; Podsakoff et al., 1990; Rafferty & Griffin, 2004). Yet, the measurement of visionary leadership in most studies is lost in larger measures, either because the measurement of vision is part of a broader subscale to begin with (Bass & Avolio, 1995) or because subscales are collapsed into broader measures of charismatic and transformational leadership (which is the more common practice in research in charismatic-transformational leadership; cf. Khatri, Ng, & Lee, 2001).

A similar problem is encountered in some experimental operationalizations of charismatic-transformational leadership that include but are not limited to the communication of a vision, rendering it impossible to isolate the effects of visionary leadership (e.g., Towler, 2003). Thus, an important conclusion in assessing the field of visionary leadership research is that much of the work—in fact most of the work—that also includes measurement or manipulations relating to vision confounds visionary leadership with other elements of leadership.

Accordingly, in terms of our intention to set a research agenda for research in visionary leadership, an important issue is to study visionary leadership in its own right and not confounded with other elements of leadership (even when these can be included in the study, they should be conceptually and empirically distinct). Likewise, our chapter concerns only studies that focus on visionary leadership specifically and does not include studies that include reference to visions as part of broader measures.

Caveats and Lessons Learned

To recap, then, the consideration of methodological concerns in research in visionary leadership points to a couple of caveats in assessing the available evidence as well as issues to take into account in designing future studies in visionary leadership. Interestingly, much of these caveats and design considerations concern confounds—confounding of visionary leadership with other elements (goal-setting, perceiver attributions of effects, other aspects of charismatic-transformational leadership), and drawing comparisons concerning multiple differences simultaneously. Note that these concerns in part are concerns with existing measures of visionary leadership—new measurement development is in order. Addressing these concerns in lab and field studies that are carefully designed to eliminate these confounds or reduce these to the minimum is of great importance to the further development of visionary leadership research. In addition, such studies would ideally avoid the problems associated with subjective ratings (not including expert ratings) as much as possible. With these caveats in mind, we now turn to an evaluation of the available evidence.

What Does the Evidence Say?

Although clearly a consideration of methodological issues is part of the assessment of the state of the science in visionary leadership, now that we have considered these issues we can move on to considering what the evidence says in terms of conceptual propositions. To do so, we first consider evidence pertaining to the effects of visionary leadership per se. We then move on to the consideration of moderators of the relationship between visionary leadership and outcomes, and we conclude with an assessment of potential precursors to visionary leadership.

Main Effects of Visionary Leadership

ATTRIBUTIONS OF CHARISMA AND OTHER LEADERSHIP EVALUATIONS

As outlined in the previous section, theories of charismatic-transformational leadership dictate that visionary leadership should predict attributions of charisma, and it does. We already described the visionary versus nonvisionary leader communication in Kirkpatrick and Locke (1996). This manipulation was found to predict ratings of charismatic-transformational leadership as predicted. In addition, Kirkpatrick and Locke (1996) found that visionary leadership resulted in greater trust in the leader.

Holladay and Coombs (1994) experimentally manipulated the content of a (confederate) leaders' speech to make it visionary versus nonvisionary—unfortunately also with many differences between conditions—as well as the charismatic versus noncharismatic delivery of the vision (understood as a combination of eye contact, facial expressions, gestures, and body movement). They found that these two manipulations interacted to produce the highest charisma ratings on a measure including the perception that the leader communicates a vision for a charismatic vision with charismatic delivery (i.e., given that these are both aspects of visionary leadership, we consider the interaction as part of the "main effects" of visionary leadership). Johnson and Dipboye (2008) found very similar main effects on charisma for very similar vision and delivery manipulations. Also using a very similar design, Awamleh and Gardner (1999) manipulated leader speech/vision content (confounding inspirational themes, symbolic elements, and rhetoric devices), vision delivery (cf. Holladay & Coombs, 1993), and company performance (good and improving vs. bad and declining). They observed main effects of these three factors on ratings of charisma (including the perception of vision) and leadership effectiveness.

Hunt et al. (1999) compared visionary leadership (operationalized through a confederate in a way closely resembling the Holladay & Coombs, 1993, and Awamleh & Gardner, 1999, studies) with other forms of leadership (exchange-based leadership and low-expressiveness leadership) differing in multiple ways from the visionary leadership condition and found that visionary leadership resulted in higher charisma ratings. Hunt et al. (1999) also found that visionary leadership was more effective than exchange-based leadership or low-expressiveness leadership in eliciting ratings of leader inspirational qualities and ratings of leader self-confidence (which arguably both can be seen as elements of charisma) as well as positive evaluations of the leader.

Revisiting a methodological concern we identified earlier we may note that what all these studies have in common is that they compare visionary and nonvisionary communication in comparisons involving multiple differences simultaneously and using measures of charisma including the perception of vision. Whereas all these studies thus to a certain extent validate the proposition that visionary leadership results in attributions of charisma, their conclusions come with important caveats regarding confounded manipulations and the use of overlapping operationalizations of independent and dependent variables.

Other studies looked not so much at the communication of a vision as compared with nonvisionary communication as they looked at an element of leader communication that may play an important role in successfully communicating a vision—leader rhetoric. Emrich et al. (2001) focused on the influence of imaged-based rhetoric (i.e., the extent to which a word of phrase easily elicits a sensory experience). This "arousing" effect of image-based rhetoric was expected to result in attributions of charisma. Coding of US presidential speeches for image-based rhetoric showed that imagery predicted expert ratings of presidential charisma and greatness. Naidoo and Lord (2008) build on these findings in a carefully constructed experiment in which they manipulated imagery in an otherwise identical speech as described in the previous. This unconfounded comparison confirmed earlier findings by Emrich et al. (2001). Moreover, this study showed that the relationship between imagery and leadership perceptions was partially mediated by positive affect, speaking to the positive arousing potential of imagery. Related work also focused on US presidential rhetoric as predictor of perceptions of presidential charisma. Mio, Riggio, Levin, and Reese (2005) coded presidential speeches for the use of metaphors, expecting that the use of metaphors as a rhetoric device would similarly predict expert ratings of charisma. This was found to be the case.

These studies of leader rhetoric are important to our understanding of visionary leadership in their isolation of elements of leader communication that may add to the effectiveness of visionary leadership. On a more critical note, however, we may observe that charisma and other leadership evaluations are not the most important outcomes when it comes to assessing the effectiveness of visionary leadership (cf. Kaiser et al., 2008). Future research prioritizing the relationship between such rhetoric and more behavioral outcomes would be particularly worthwhile from that perspective.

OTHER PERCEPTUAL-EVALUATIVE OUTCOMES

Research has also yielded some evidence regarding the relationship between visionary leadership and perceptual-evaluative ratings other than leadership evaluations. Paul et al. (2001) experimentally studied the effects of an appeal to values (seen as an element that makes visions more inspiring) and an appeal to the individual needs of followers on collective self-conception. Collective self-conception is a potential precursor to contributions to collective interests (Ashforth & Mael, 1989), and thus potentially important in terms of visionary leadership's ability to motivate the pursuit of collective interests (cf. Shamir et al., 1993). They found that these two elements combined yielded greater salience of self-conception in collective terms than either factor alone, provided the message originated from a leader and not from a service team (a finding referred to earlier as illustrating the importance of leader agency). It is not clear, however, whether the influence of these elements of leader communication is interactive or additive, because there was no condition without either appeal.

Somewhat related through its focus on affective organizational commitment is a study by Dvir, Kass, and Shamir (2004)—commitment too arguably would be associated with a willingness to contribute to organizational interests. These authors found that commitment was predicted by survey measures of vision formulation, appeal to social values in vision, and perceived appropriateness of the vision, but not by ratings of instrumental values in the vision (the latter was not expected either, as inspiring visions would be expected to concern social values more than instrumental values), suggesting that visionary leadership may build affective commitment. This conclusion is corroborated by the findings of Khatri et al. (2001), who also found a positive relationship between survey measures of visionary leadership and commitment (as well as with motivation and self-ratings of unit performance). Findings from both studies come with the caveat that they concern single-source percept-percept relationships that may be inflated by common method variance.

Showing that the issue of the visionary leadership-commitment relationship is not that clear-cut, however, Rafferty and Griffin (2004) found no relationship between survey measures of vision and affective commitment. They did find a negative relationship between vision and continuance commitment (commitment out of necessity)—a relationship that Dvir et al. (2004) also tested but did not find. Moreover, vision was negatively related to role-breadth self-efficacy, a finding that does not sit well with the suggestion that visionary leadership would build self and collective efficacy (cf. Shamir et al., 1993). Arguably, however, there is a difference between what visionary leadership would *ideally* do (cf. Shamir et al., 1993) and what it may do in practice. It is possible that at least for some visions or under some circumstances visionary leadership is perceived as overly directive or restrictive.

PERFORMANCE-RELATED OUTCOMES

Methodological concerns with subjective ratings as indicators of leadership effectiveness set aside, visionary leadership is ultimately understood as being about motivating follower action—contributions to the pursuit and realization of the vision. This is consistent with a more general concern in research in leadership effectiveness with behavioral outcomes, not attitudinal-evaluative judgments, as the "bottom line" indicator of leadership effectiveness (Kaiser et al., 2008). Ultimately, then, in evaluating the effectiveness of visionary leadership, behavioral evidence takes precedence over subjective ratings. Some studies in a sense come halfway in speaking to this issue in that they focus on behavioral outcomes but rely on self-ratings to assess these. We already noted the findings of Kathri et al. (2001) regarding self-rated unit effectiveness in the previous.

There is evidence that visionary leadership may affect objective performance outcomes. Baum et al. (1998) content-coded vision statements for visionary qualities resulting in one overall score reflecting the extent to which the statement had qualities associated with inspiring visions, and in addition coded vision statements for growth imagery. They also gathered ratings of the extent to which the vision was communicated. All three variables predicted venture growth, which is a relevant performance outcome in their entrepreneurial sample, and for the growth imagery variable at least also an outcome directly reflective of vision pursuit. Vision communication was found to only partly mediate the relationships for visionary quality and growth imagery, suggesting that their relationship with venture growth does not work exclusively through vision communication but also presumably through such actions as leader strategic decisions (cf. Finkelstein, Hambrick, & Canella, 2009).

Kirkpatrick, Wofford, and Baum (2002), using the same database as Baum et al. (1998), show that coding for motive imagery—distinguishing power, affiliation, and achievement motives, it was the power motive that predicted venture growth. The same motive coding for another dataset focusing on ratings of unit and leader effectiveness yielded only a relationship for need for affiliation and unit effectiveness and no relationships for leader effectiveness, thus yielding inconsistent results that fail to support a consistent role for motive imagery.

Fanelli, Misangyi, and Tosi (2009) looked at the relationship between CEO vision, content-coded for reference to the past, present, and future (cf. Shamir et al., 1993) based on text analysis, as a predictor of securities analysts' recommendations. They found that the extent to which visions were rated as charismatic predicted favorability of recommendation as well as the uniformity of recommendations across analysts, but interestingly also greater errors in analysts' forecasting of future firm performance.

Wood, Owens, and Durham (2005) studied US presidential speeches and focused on expressions of optimism in particular—thus singling out an element of rhetoric rather than visionary leadership as a whole. Complementing findings for rhetoric and charisma, they found that the expression of optimism predicted economic growth.

In sum, there is main effect evidence that (elements of) visionary leadership may predict leadership evaluations and other attitudinal-evaluative responses as well as more objective (performance) indicators of leadership effectiveness.

Moderators of the Impact of Visionary Leadership

In view of the overwhelming evidence that leadership models benefit from the consideration of contingencies of the effects of leadership (e.g., van Knippenberg, 2012), however, potential moderators of the effectiveness of visionary leadership are worthy of close consideration. Only a modest number of studies have investigated moderators of the effects of visionary leadership.

Johnson and Dipboye (2008) build on earlier work by Holladay and Coombs (1993) and Awamleh and Gardner (1999) by focusing on a very similar operationalization of the content and delivery manipulations from these studies, but extended the design with the inclusion of variations in the task performed. They argued that more complex, open-ended tasks would be more conducive to the effectiveness of charismatic leadership, and therefore predicted that the interaction of visionary communication and charismatic delivery would emerge primarily on the most open-ended task in their design—a creative thinking task. The predicted three-way interaction on performance was obtained, supporting the conclusion that some task contexts are more conducive to positive performance effects of visionary leadership than others.

In an experimental study, Shipley and Michela (2006) focused on the contributions individuals were willing to make to a cause advocated by the leader, but these were hypothetical contributions—in a sense thus taking the issue halfway to behavioral outcomes. Using unconfounded manipulations, they showed that leader communication to mobilize support for a collective cause was more effective as a function of the interaction of two factors. The first factor was whether or not the values underlying the cause were made explicit in the communication (cf. Shamir et al., 1993, 1994)—the communication was otherwise identical across conditions. The second factor was whether or not audience groups reflected on the values underlying the cause after exposure to the leader's communication. The findings for the role of an appeal to values can be seen to complement the findings from the Paul et al. (2001) and Dvir et al. (2004) studies discussed earlier, in that these studies all underscore the effectiveness of an appeal to (social) values in visionary communication. The Shipley and Michela study adds to this by showing that this influence is greater if people take the time to carefully "digest" the leader's message and reflect on these values.

Taking a different perspective, Platow, van Knippenberg, Haslam, van Knippenberg, and Spears (2006) focused on leader rhetoric, experimentally manipulating whether a leader suggested that subscribing to the leader's appeal would serve the follower's self-interest or the collective interest (otherwise, leader communications were identical). Consistent with analyses of charismatic leadership, an appeal to collective interest should lead to stronger attributions of charisma (cf. Shamir et al., 1993). The concern of Platow et al. was not with this main effect, however, but with the prediction based on the social identity theory of leadership (Hogg & van Knippenberg, 2003; van Knippenberg & Hogg, 2003) that a leader who was seen to be group prototypical—an embodiment of the shared group identity—would be seen as relatively charismatic regardless of the nature of the leader's appeal, whereas leaders that were seen as more marginal to the group's identity would need to appeal to the collective interest to invite attributions of charisma. This prediction was supported.

Griffin, Parker, and Mason (2010) focused on self-rated proactivity and adaptability—behavioral outcomes that can be expected to be important to visionary leadership's ability to engender change and innovation (even when they should not be equated with them, and with the caveat that self-ratings of behavior should not be equated with objective measures of behavior). They predicted and found that visionary leadership is more strongly related to follower adaptivity for followers higher in openness to work role change, and to proactivity for followers higher in role breath self-efficacy. In combination, this suggests that visions may be more effective in stimulating change- and innovation-oriented behaviors for those employees more open to such activities to begin with.

The notion that follower characteristics may be an important moderator of visionary leadership's effectiveness is also found in a series of studies on follower regulatory focus. Regulatory focus theory (Higgins, 1996, 1997) distinguishes two fundamental and independent mechanisms in behavioral self-regulation to which individuals can be inclined to a greater or lesser extent: promotion focus, an orientation on realizing positive outcomes, and prevention focus, an orientation on preventing negative outcomes. Interestingly, promotion focus may motivate the same behavior but for different reasons (e.g., effort to achieve success or effort to prevent failure), but it also colors attention to and processing of information and thus may moderate responses to social stimuli—such as leadership. Brockner and Higgins (2001; also see Kark & van Dijk, 2007) argued that transformational leadership has a focus on achieving positive outcomes and would thus fit more with promotion focus than with prevention focus.

Stam, van Knippenberg, and Wisse (2010a) extended this analysis to focus specifically on visionary leadership and the role of follower regulatory focus. They argued that the communication of a vision of an idealized future would appeal more to individuals with a (stronger) promotion focus. This was predicted to be especially the case when the vision rhetoric invited them to reflect on what the vision meant for them personally, because this would invite them to form a "possible self" (Markus & Nurius, 1986) based on the vision—an idealized image of who they could become by pursuing the vision. Possible selves have motivating power—they drive behaviors that serve the realization of the possible self (Markus & Nurius, 1986). Accordingly, Stam et al. predicted that the formation of a vision-based possible self would result in the behavioral pursuit of the vision. In two experiments in which they manipulated leader rhetoric for otherwise identical visions, they found support for this prediction both for a situational induction of regulatory focus (i.e., a state) and for a dispositional measure of regulatory focus (i.e., a trait).

In further development of this analysis, Stam, van Knippenberg, and Wisse (2010b) took on the field's preoccupation with visions as idealized images, arguing that visionary leadership may also revolve around negative images of the future (cf. Bruch, Shamir, & Eilam-Shamir, 2007)—Nobel Prize winner Al Gore's *An Inconvenient Truth* would be a recent and highly visible example. Stam et al. argued that the more typically considered idealized vision could be qualified as a promotion-focused appeal that would appeal to more promotion-focused individuals (cf. Stam et al., 2010a). In contrast, visions revolving around dark images of the future could be seen as prevention-focused appeals (i.e., the point is to prevent the dark future from becoming reality) that would appeal more to a prevention-focused audience. In short, they predicted that the effectiveness of visionary leadership would be a function of the interaction between the promotion-focused or prevention-focused nature of the vision and the regulatory focus of the follower. This is exactly what they found across two experiments that established behavioral effects across a state and a trait operationalization of regulatory focus.

Whitford and Moss (2009) also focused on the moderating role of follower regulatory focus on similar grounds as Stam et al. (2010a) in their study of idealized visions and leader rhetoric, but added a complication in comparing virtual and face-to-face teams. They predicted that the fit of visionary leadership with promotion focus, as evidenced in the relationship between visionary leadership and work attitudes, should be evident more in virtual teams than in face-to-face teams. In contrast, a misfit with prevention focus would be more pronounced in face-to-face teams. No statistical decomposition of the three-way interactions is reported but what they seem to find is that for followers with high promotion focus, visionary leadership had a positive relationship with job satisfaction regardless of team setting, whereas for individuals with low promotion focus this relationship obtained only in face-to-face teams. Visionary leadership seemed to be essentially unrelated to work engagement, except for the *positive* relationship (i.e., contrary to predictions) that obtains for followers with a stronger prevention focus in face-to-face teams. What to make of this is not clear, but we are tempted to conclude that this is another instance where it would be important to have information about vision *content* to aid interpretation (cf. Stam et al., 2010b).

The evidence for the moderating role of follower characteristics also points to a multilevel issue (cf. Klein & Kozlowski, 2000) that so far does not seem to have been considered in research in visionary leadership. Different followers may respond differently to the same vision from the same leader, and sometimes the more appropriate analysis may be one of followers "nested" within leader. This would seem to be no minor point as visionary leadership in particular seems to hold the connotation of "speaking to the masses," which could be understood as a one-size-fits-all approach to leadership. The evidence for the moderating role of follower characteristics that has started to accumulate in recent years would suggest that collectively shared effects of visionary leadership are far from a given, and that this is an issue worthy of consideration in its own right.

Determinants of Visionary Leadership

If a particular form of leadership is effective, an obvious question is what leads individuals to engage in such leadership—what are the determinants of the leader behavior in question? Some researchers have raised this question for leader visions. Berson et al. (2001) coded visions for four inspirational elements (optimism, specificity, values, and challenges) argued to represent the visions' "inspirational strength" (cf. Shamir et al., 1993, 1994). They focused on how transformational leadership (measured with items referring to visioning) predicted this inspirational strength, and it did for two out of four dimensions (optimism and specificity). In view of the fact that the relationship between the transformational leadership measure and inspirational vision amounts to validation, one might be tempted to conclude that the fact that the relationship was obtained for only two out of four indicators reflects poorly on measurement validity. Organizational size was negatively related to vision strength and moderated the relationship between passive leadership and vision strength, which was negative but only in small organizations.

Using the Berson et al. (2001) coding scheme for vision strength, Sosik and Dinger (2007) also focused on the relationship between rated charismatic-transformational leadership and vision strength, but only using the charisma subdimension from the transformational leadership scale (i.e., which includes the items referring to visioning). Providing validating evidence for the questionnaire and coded vision measures, results showed that charisma ratings predicted inspirational content of the vision. Charisma was also found to be more predictive of inspirational content with lower need for approval, higher self-monitoring, and higher need for power of the leader, suggesting that the "content-free" charisma rating contains variability in content that can be captured (indirectly) only by focusing also on leader personality (we see this as a case in point in our plea for the development of measures of visionary leadership that do capture content). In addition, Sosik and Dinger found that contingent reward (a non-transformational form of leadership based in social exchange) predicted instrumental content in the visions, and more strongly so with higher need for approval, lower self-monitoring, and higher need for power of the leader.

A line of research by Mumford and colleagues speaks to the "developmentability" of visionary skills. Strange and Mumford (2005) experimentally show that the interaction of high-quality background information and reflection on own relevant experience and goals for the organization result in higher quality visions as rated from written vision statements. In a similar vein, Shipman, Byrne, and Mumford (2010) show that the extent to which individuals invested in forecasting related to the intended vision outcome positively predicted vision quality as rated from written vision statement. In combination, these studies suggest that vision quality improves through deliberate investment in background information, reflection, and elaboration. To a certain extent this may not be a particularly surprising conclusion, as most if not all intellective work would seem to improve with intellective investment. Even so, the conclusion here is therefore no less important: visionary leadership is to a certain degree under the volitional control of leaders and can thus also presumably be trained and developed.

This conclusion is corroborated by a recent study by Antonakis, Fenley, and Liechti (2012). These authors trained MBA students in the skills required for charismatic delivery of speech through targeted feedback on student speeches. By also recording post-intervention speeches, coding these for use of the charismatic delivery techniques, and gathering ratings of student charisma, they were able to show that these delivery skills could indeed be developed (cf. Towler, 2003).

A bottom line problem with this research in the determinants of visionary leadership, or vision quality, is that research on the effectiveness of visionary leadership is insufficiently clear on what makes for an effective vision—and what are the contingencies of the answer to this question. To a certain extent then, research in the determinants of visionary leadership is studying something for which the effectiveness needs yet to be determined. This should not discourage the study of the determinants of visioning, even when it may prioritize the study of the effectiveness of visionary leadership. What it does suggest, however, is that research in the determinants of visionary leadership is much more valuable when it also includes indicators of the effectiveness of visionary leadership—when it treats visionary leadership as a mediating variable rather than as a bottom line outcome.

A Summary of the Evidence

Figure 12.1 provides a summary of the evidence regarding elements of visionary leadership, moderator variables, and outcomes of visionary leadership reviewed in this section. The display in Figure 12.1 is not intended to represent a conceptual model but rather to give a summary overview of the research findings reviewed (and it comes with all the caveats we identified in our discussion of methodological concerns). On the independent variable side, the elements of visionary leadership studied are somewhat of a mixed bag with several elements from the Shamir et al. (1993, 1994) analysis, more specific rhetorical aspects, and some miscellaneous others. Moderator variables can roughly be categorized into variables concerning the source of the vision, the task context in which the vision is communicated, and characteristics of the followers. On the outcome variable side, a distinction can be made between follower leadership evaluations, follower psychological states, and behavioral/performance outcomes, where the latter can be subdivided in concerning the individual level or the collective (team, organization, nation) level.

As a summary of the state of the science in quantitative research on visionary leadership, this overview of independent, dependent, and moderator variables is useful to identify some overarching issues. A first issue to emerge from this overview is that there is only modest structure to the current body of empirical research. There is no clear conceptual framework to tie the different elements of visionary leadership studied together or to tie these in with the different moderator variables studied. What also stands out here is the relative inattention to mediating processes. Yet, the outcome variables studied can be divided in those concerning leadership evaluations, those concerning follower psychological states, and those concerning behavioral outcomes. Follower psychological states would be obvious mediating processes in translating visionary leadership into follower action (cf. Naidoo & Lord, 2008; Stam et al., 2010a), and a straightforward conclusion for future research would be to consider the psychological states identified as potential mediating influences in relationships with the behavioral outcomes identified. Indeed, leadership research as well as organizational behavior research more generally provides solid ground to link these psychological states to behavioral outcomes (e.g., van Knippenberg et al., 2004).

Another issue to emerge from this overview is that of levels of analysis. Clearly, visionary leadership and leader characteristics reside at the leader level, as would the task context presumably typically do. Follower characteristics as moderator reside at the

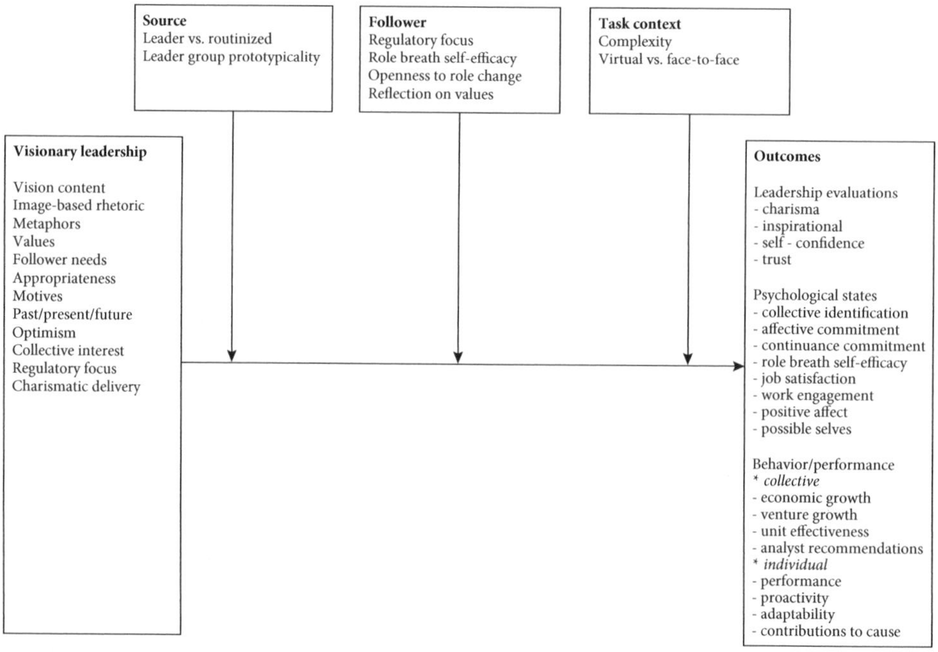

Figure 12.1. A Summary of Research Findings.

level of the individual follower, and suggest potential multilevel models in which the same visionary leadership has different effects for different followers. Developing such models would be important to understand when and how visionary leadership may *collectively* motivate followers (i.e., rather than speak to some but perhaps not others). In a related vein, most of the outcome variables studied (leadership evaluations, psychological states, a number of the behavioral outcomes) are individual-level variables, but a number of the behavioral outcomes also concern collective-level variables. This too suggests a number of multilevel issues to consider, for instance, whether outcomes of different levels of analysis involve different mediating and moderating processes, or how individual-level processes combine to produce collective-level outcomes.

Where Do We Go from Here?

Reading the literature on visionary leadership (and indeed on charismatic-transformational leadership) one could easily get the impression that it is proven beyond a shadow of a doubt that visionary leadership is highly effective, and moreover that we know reasonably well what it is that makes visions effective. The great confidence with which many claims regarding the effectiveness of visionary leadership are posited seems to be based by and large on measures of transformational, charismatic, or visionary leadership that include, but more often than not are not limited to, "content-free" reference to visioning. Our analysis suggests that this confidence is unjustified, and that we in fact know far less about visionary leadership and its effectiveness than the field likes to believe. Measures that confound visioning with other elements of leadership cannot be taken as evidence regarding the effectiveness of visionary leadership. The available evidence regarding content-free measures that specifically target visionary leadership suggests that their content-free nature seriously compromises the interpretation of findings and the ability to reach unambiguous conclusions. Moreover, whereas studies that do speak to vision content are scarce, many of these rely on confounded comparisons to reach conclusions about the effectiveness of visionary leadership. If we limit our conclusions to studies that speak to the content of visions (or leader rhetoric) without confounded comparisons, very few studies remain.

The good news is that the studies that allow us to reach relatively unambiguous conclusions about visionary leadership do support the conclusion that visionary leadership can be effective—but also that its effects are contingent on leader, follower, and situational characteristics, and—of no minor importance—that the nature of the vision itself plays a role such that no one particular "type" of vision is uniformly more effective. The importance of these conclusions should not be underestimated, because the going flavor in the charismatic-transformational leadership literature seems to posit visionary leadership effectiveness as a strong main effect, and moreover conceptualizes inspiring visions as one particular type of vision (i.e., a "charismatic" vision). It seems safe to conclude that the available evidence suggests that this conclusion is not supported.

What then is needed to paint a fuller, richer picture of the contingencies of visionary leadership effectiveness? Our analysis points to a number of issues to consider. Rather than produce a laundry list of issues big and small in repeating all of the observations made in the previous, we highlight three issues here that we believe benefit most from explicit articulation at this point.

Broaden the Conceptual Perspective

First, it would seem advisable to move beyond charismatic-transformational leadership in conceptualizing and operationalizing visions and visionary leadership. The evidence speaking to prevention-focused visions (Stam et al., 2010b) is a case in point here, but no doubt the issue is not limited to the regulatory orientation of the vision. Effective visionary leadership may include elements identified in charismatic-transformational leadership theory, but need not be limited to this, nor would "charismatic style" necessarily be the only relevant variable in vision delivery. Note that this is not to deny that the elements of visionary leadership identified in charismatic-transformational leadership research can contribute to leadership effectiveness, but rather to point out that they may not always do so and moreover that elements not identified in this perspective can add to visionary leadership effectiveness too. Integrating insights from a variety of literatures—leadership and non-leadership alike—will be essential to move beyond the inherent limitations of the currently dominant charismatic-transformational paradigm.

Measurement Development

A second issue is the development of better survey measurement for visionary leadership. Unless the current content-free measurement of visionary leadership is replaced by measures tapping into the content of visions (e.g., in terms of regulatory orientation, appeals to values, etc.), research will continue to produce ambiguous and seemingly inconsistent findings. This would be important not only in terms of speaking to vision content per se, but also in more unambiguously differentiating visionary leadership from leader goal-setting (or alternatively treating this as a variable of interest in visionary leadership). Moreover, it would be an important step toward aligning survey measures of visionary leadership and measures based on content-coding of vision statements. The latter currently do speak to vision content, even if in a variety of ways and sometimes collapsing content into one vision variable (e.g., Baum et al., 1998), and there currently is a disconnect between this content-coding and content-free survey measures that stands in the way of drawing firm conclusions from findings obtained across methodologies. The exact same logic holds for the connection between findings from survey research and experimental research. Experimental research can and does identify specific vision content. Once survey measures do to, findings can be better understood across methodologies and stronger theory can be build.

Mediation Models

The third issue is the consideration of mediating processes. With few exceptions, research in visionary leadership does not assess mediating processes. This is unfortunate for a number of reasons. Theory development benefits from assessing rather than assuming mediating processes. Especially when predictions are not supported it is highly informative to know whether the expected influence on the mediator did or did not materialize as well as whether the mediator predicted the outcome, because this informs researchers where to seek conceptual improvement. A more careful consideration of mediating processes also helps identify moderating influences (e.g., Stam et al., 2010a, identified regulatory focus as a moderator through the consideration of possible selves as a mediator)—or put differently, the consideration of moderating influences can help develop our understanding of mediating processes. In addition, a consideration of mediators helps integrate findings across studies, where it is informative to know whether different factors affect the same or different mediating processes. The issue of mediation is no minor point, as several mediating processes are implied by different studies. For instance, research in leader rhetoric points to the arousing potential of visions (e.g., Naidoo & Lord, 2008), Stam et al. (2010a) point to the role of ideal (possible) selves in the effectiveness of idealized future images, and research conceptualizing visionary leadership following Shamir et al. (1993, 1994) points to the role of self- and collective efficacy (cf. Kirkpatrick & Locke, 1996). This is not to say that all of these processes would always play a role nor that these processes offer alternative interpretations, but rather that different aspects of visionary leadership could speak to different mediating processes—and thus, for instance, be more effective in different circumstances.

In Conclusion

As critical as our assessment of the state of the science in visionary leadership research may be, the good news as we see it is that many of the building blocks to move ahead are in fact already in place. We have theory to move beyond the dominant charismatic-transformational paradigm even when it needs further development, we have theory to develop content measures of visionary leadership for survey research even when it needs further development, and we have theory to develop our understanding of mediation even when it needs further development. We also have the methodological savvy to walk away from confounded operationalizations of visionary leadership and to address the other issues we identified in our analysis. In short, the field is in good shape to address the challenges we identified here. The only precondition is that we recognize and accept these challenges.

Recognizing and addressing these challenges is important, because we otherwise run the risk of fooling ourselves into believing that we know more about visionary leadership than in fact we do. Research in visionary leadership has great potential to yield actionable knowledge: insights about visionary leadership most likely are of great importance to leader training and development efforts. Such efforts should be evidence based, however, and not based on conceptual models that have not received proper testing. Meeting the research challenges we identify here should thus also provide a firm basis for the translation of these insights to leadership practice.

To in a sense "come full circle" and return to some of our opening observations, there is also great academic importance in meeting these research challenges. Visionary leadership, probably more than any other element of leadership, is associated with leadership that accomplishes great things. Visionary leadership potentially has tremendously importance as a motivator of change and innovation and may indeed more than anything else lie at the core of effective leadership. The critical reading of the visionary leadership literature we present in the current chapter is not to deny this potential—it is only to point out that the evidence base from which to conclude that visionary leadership has the effects that are attributed to it by and large does not allow for these attributions. Rather, the current review should be seen as a call to arms to address these research challenges for an aspect of leadership that is particularly worthy of such research efforts.

Note

1. Research in visionary leadership has its share of qualitative case studies. Though we embrace the potential of this qualitative work to develop new theory, we take the not unusual position that only quantitative research can test theory. Only quantitative research can thus qualify as evidence in assessing the merits of theoretical notions, even when the theory tested may have a solid basis in qualitative research.

References

Antonakis, J., Fenley, M., & Liechti, S. (2011). Can charisma be taught? Test of two interventions. *Academy of Management Learning & Education, 10,* 374–396.

Ashforth, B. E., & Mael, F. (1989). Social identity theory and the organization. *Academy of Management Review, 14,* 20–39.

Awamleh, R., & Gardner, W. L. (1999). Perceptions of leader charisma and effectiveness: The effects of vision content, delivery, and organizational performance. *The Leadership Quarterly, 10,* 345–373.

Bass, B. M. (1985). *Leadership and performance beyond expectations.* New York, NY: Free Press.

Bass, B. M. (2008). *The Bass handbook of leadership* (4th ed.). New York: Simon & Schuster.

Bass, B. M., & Avolio, B. J. (1995). *Manual for the multifactor leadership questionnaire: Rater form (5X short).* Palo Alto, CA: Mind Garden.

Bass, B. M., & Riggio, R. E. (2006). *Transformational leadership.* Mahwah, NJ: Lawrence Erlbaum.

Baum, J. R., Locke, E. A., & Kirkpatrick, S. A. (1998). A longitudinal study of the relation of vision and vision communication to venture growth in entrepreneurial firms. *Journal of Applied Psychology, 83,* 43–54.

Berson, Y., Shamir, B., Avolio, B. J., & Popper, M. (2001). The relationship between vision strength, leadership style, and context. *The Leadership Quarterly, 12,* 53–73.

Boal, K. B., & Bryson, J. M. (1988). Charismatic leadership: A phenomenological and structural approach. In J. G. Hunt, B. R. Baliga, H. P. Dachler, & C. A. Schriesheim (Eds.), *Emerging leadership vistas* (pp. 11–28). Lexington, MA: Lexington Books.

Brockner, J., & Higgins, E. T. (2001). Regulatory focus theory: Implications for the study of emotions at work. *Organizational Behavior and Human Decision Processes, 86,* 35–66.

Bruch, H., Shamir, B., & Eilam-Shamir, G. (2007). Managing meanings in times of crisis and recovery: CEO prevention-oriented leadership. In R. Hooijberg, J. Hunt, J. Antonakis, K. Boal, & N. Lane (Eds.), *Being there even when you are not: Leading through strategy, structures, and systems* (pp. 131–158). Oxford, England: JAI Press.

Bryman, A. (1992). *Charisma and leadership in organizations.* London: SAGE.

Burns, J. M. (1978). *Leadership.* New York, NY: Harper & Row.

Conger, J. A. (1999). Charismatic and transformational leadership in organizations: An insider's perspective on these developing streams of research. *The Leadership Quarterly, 10,* 145–179.

Conger, J. A., & Kanungo, R. N. (1987). Towards a behavioral theory of charismatic leadership in organizational settings. *Academy of Management Review, 12,* 637–647.

Conger, J. A., & Kanungo, R. N. (1994). Charismatic leadership in organizations: Perceived behavioral attributes and their measurement. *Journal of Organizational Behavior, 15,* 439–452.

Conger, J., & Kanungo, R. (1998). *Charismatic leadership in organizations.* Thousand Oaks, CA: SAGE.

Dvir, T., Kass, N., & Shamir, B. (2004). The emotional bond: Vision and organizational commitment among high-tech employees. *Journal of Organizational Change Management, 17,* 126–143.

Eden, D., & Leviatan, V. (1975). Implicit leadership theory as a determinant of the factor structure underlying supervisory behavior. *Journal of Applied Psychology, 60,* 736–741.

Emrich, C. G., Brower, H. H., Feldman, J. M., & Garland, H. (2001). Images in words: Presidential rhetoric, charisma, and greatness. *Administrative Science Quarterly, 46,* 527–557.

Fanelli, A., Misangyi, V. F., & Tosi, H. L. (2009). In charisma we trust: The effects of CEO charismatic visions on securities analysts. *Organization Science, 20,* 1011–1033.

Ferris, G. R., Hochwarter, W. A., & Buckley, M. R. (2012). Theory in the organizational sciences: How will we know it when we see it? *Organizational Psychology Review, 2,* 94–106.

Finkelstein, S., Hambrick, D. C., & Canella, A. A. (2009). *Strategic leadership.* New York, NY: Oxford University Press.

Griffin, M. A., Parker, S. K., & Mason, C. M. (2010). Leader vision and the development of adaptive and proactive performance: A longitudinal study. *Journal of Applied Psychology, 95,* 174–182.

Higgins, E. T. (1987). Self-discrepancy: A theory relating self and affect. *Psychological Review, 94,* 319–340.

Higgins, E. T. (1996). The "self digest": Self knowledge serving self-regulatory functions. *Journal of Personality and Social Psychology, 71,* 1062–1083.

Higgins, E. T. (1997). Beyond pleasure and pain. *American Psychologist, 52,* 1280–1300

Hogg, M. A., & van Knippenberg, D. (2003). Social identity and leadership processes in groups. *Advances in Experimental Social Psychology, 35,* 1–52.

Holladay, S. J., & Coombs, W. T. (1993). Communicating visions. *Management Communication Quarterly, 6,* 405–427.

Holladay, S. J., & Coombs, W. T. (1994). Speaking of visions and visions being spoken. *Management Communication Quarterly, 8,* 1 165–189.

Hunt, J. G., Boal, K. B., & Dodge, G. E. (1999). The effects of visionary and crisis-responsive charisma on followers: An experimental examination of two kinds of charismatic leadership. *The Leadership Quarterly, 10,* 423–448.

Johnson, S. K., & Dipboye, R. L. (2008). Effects of charismatic content and delivery on follower task performance. *Group & Organization Management, 33,* 77–106.

Judge, T. A., LePine, J. A., & Rich, B. L. (2006). Loving yourself abundantly: Relationship of the narcissistic personality to self- and other perceptions of workplace deviance, leadership, and task and contextual performance. *Journal of Applied Psychology, 91*, 762–776.

Judge, T. A., Piccolo, R. F., & Ilies, R. (2004). The forgotten ones? A re-examination of consideration, initiating structure, and leadership effectiveness. *Journal of Applied Psychology, 89*, 36–51.

Kaiser, R. B., Hogan, R., & Craig, S. B. (2008). Leadership and the fate of organizations. *American Psychologist, 63*, 96–110.

Kark, R., & Van Dijk, D. (2007). Motivation to lead, motivation to follow: The role of the self-regulatory focus in leadership processes. *Academy of Management Review, 32*, 500–528.

Khatri, N., Alvin Ng, H., & Lee, T. (2001). The distinction between charisma and vision: An empirical study. *Asia Pacific Journal of Management, 18*, 373–393.

Kirkpatrick, S. A., & Locke, E. A. (1996). Direct and indirect effects of three core charismatic leadership components on performance and attitudes. *Journal of Applied Psychology, 81*, 36–51.

Kirkpatrick, S. A., Wofford, J. C., & Baum, J. R. (2002). Measuring motive imagery contained in the vision statement. *The Leadership Quarterly, 13*, 139–150.

Klein, K. J., & Kozlowski, S. W. J. (2000). *Multilevel theory, research, and methods in organizations: Foundations, extensions, and new directions*. San Francisco, CA: Jossey-Bass.

Larwood, L., Falbe, C. M., Kriger, M. P., & Miesing, P. (1995). Structure and meaning of organizational vision. *Academy of Management Journal, 38*, 740–769.

Locke, E. A., & Latham, G. P. (1990). *A theory of goal setting and task performance*. Englewood Cliffs, NJ: Prentice-Hall.

Lord, R. G. (1977). Functional leadership behavior: Measurement and relation to social power and leadership perceptions. *Administrative Science Quarterly, 22*, 114–133.

Lord, R. G., & Maher, K. J. (1991). *Leadership and information processing: Linking perceptions and performance*. Boston, MA: Unwin Hyman.

Lynn, G. S., & Akgün, A. E. (2001). Project visioning: Its components and impact on new product success. *Journal of Product Innovation Management, 18*, 374–387.

Markus, H. R., & Nurius, P. (1986). Possible selves. *American Psychologist, 41*, 954–969.

Meindl, J. R., Ehrlich, S. B., & Dukerich, J. M. (1985). The romance of leadership. *Administrative Science Quarterly, 30*, 78–102.

Mio, J., Riggio, R., Levin, S., & Reese, R. (2005). Presidential leadership and charisma: The effects of metaphor. *The Leadership Quarterly, 16*, 287–294.

Naidoo, L. J., & Lord, R. G. (2008). Speech imagery and perceptions of charisma: The mediating role of positive affect. *The Leadership Quarterly, 19*, 283–296.

Oswald, S. L., Mossholder, K. W., & Harris, S. G. (1997). Relations between strategic involvement and managers' perceptions of environment and competitive strengths. *Group & Organization Management, 22*, 343–365.

Paul, J., Costley, D. L., Howell, J. P., Dorfman, P. W., & Trafimow, D. (2001). The effects of charismatic leadership on followers' self-concept accessibility. *Journal of Applied Social Psychology, 31*, 1821–1842.

Pearce, C. L., & Ensley, M. D. (2004). A reciprocal and longitudinal investigation of the innovation process: The central role of shared vision in product and process innovation teams (PPITs). *Journal of Organizational Behavior, 25*, 259–278.

Platow, M. J., van Knippenberg, D., Haslam, S. A., van Knippenberg, B., & Spears, R. (2006). A special gift we bestow on you for being representative of us: Considering leader charisma from a self-categorization perspective. *British Journal of Social Psychology, 45*, 303–320.

Podsakoff, P. M., MacKenzie, S. B., Lee, J., & Podsakoff, N. P. (2003). Common method biases in behavioral research: A critical review of the literature and recommended remedies. *Journal of Applied Psychology, 88*, 879–903.

Podsakoff, P. M., Mackenzie, S. B., Moorman, R. H., & Fetter, R. (1990). Transformational leader behaviors and their effects on followers' trust in leader, satisfaction, and organizational citizenship behaviors. *The Leadership Quarterly, 1*, 107–142.

Rafferty, A. E., & Griffin, M. A. (2004). Dimensions of transformational leadership: Conceptual and empirical extensions. *The Leadership Quarterly, 15*, 329–354.

Ruvio, A., Rosenblatt, Z., & Hertz-Lazarowitz, R. (2010). Entrepreneurial leadership vision in nonprofit vs. for-profit organizations. *The Leadership Quarterly, 21*, 144–158.

Shamir, B., Arthur, M. B., & House, R. J. (1994). The rhetoric of charismatic leadership: A theoretical extension, a case study, and implications for research. *The Leadership Quarterly, 5*, 25–42.

Shamir, B., House, R., & Arthur, M. B. (1993). The motivational effects of charismatic leadership: A self-concept based theory. *Organization Science, 4*, 577–594.

Shipley, R., & Michela, J. L. (2006). Can vision motivate planning action? *Planning, Practice & Research, 21*, 223–244.

Shipman, A. S., Byrne, C. L., & Mumford, M. D. (2010). Leader vision formation and forecasting: The effects of forecasting extent, resources, and timeframe. *The Leadership Quarterly, 21*, 439–456.

Sosik, J. J., & Dinger, S. L. (2007). Relationships between leadership style and vision content: The moderating role of need for social approval, self-monitoring, and need for social power. *The Leadership Quarterly, 18*, 134–153.

Stam, D., van Knippenberg, D., & Wisse, B. (2010a). Focusing on followers: The role of regulatory focus and possible selves in explaining the effectiveness of vision statements. *The Leadership Quarterly, 21*, 457–468.

Stam, D., van Knippenberg, D., & Wisse, B. (2010b). The role of regulatory fit in visionary leadership. *Journal of Organizational Behavior, 31*, 499–518.

Strange, J. M., & Mumford, M. D. (2002). The origins of vision: Charismatic versus ideological leadership. *The Leadership Quarterly, 13*, 343–377.

Strange, J. M., & Mumford, M. D. (2005). The origins of vision: Effects of reflection, models, and analysis. *The Leadership Quarterly, 16*, 121–148.

Testa, M. R. (1999). Satisfaction with organizational vision, job satisfaction and service efforts: An empirical investigation. *Leadership & Organization Development Journal, 20*, 154–161.

Tichy, N., & Devanna, M. (1986). *The transformational leader.* Toronto, ON, Canada: John Wiley & Sons.

Towler, A. J. (2003). Effects of charismatic influence training on attitudes, behavior, and performance. *Personnel Psychology, 56*, 363–381.

van Knippenberg, D. (2012). Leadership: A person-in-situation perspective. In K. Deaux & M. Snyder (Eds.), *The Oxford*

handbook of personality and social psychology (pp. 673–700). New York, NY: Oxford University Press.
van Knippenberg, D., & Hogg, M. A. (2003). A social identity model of leadership effectiveness in organizations. *Research in Organizational Behavior, 25*, 243–295.
van Knippenberg, D., van Knippenberg, B., & Bobbio, A. (2008). Leaders as agents of continuity: Self-continuity and resistance to collective change. In F. Sani (Ed.), *Self-continuity: Individual and collective perspectives* (pp. 175–186). New York, NY: Psychology Press.
van Knippenberg, D., van Knippenberg, B., De Cremer, D., & Hogg, M. A. (2004). Leadership, self, and identity: A review and research agenda. *Leadership Quarterly, 15*, 825–856.
Weber, M. (1947). *The theory of social and economic organization.* New York: Oxford University Press.
Whitford, T., & Moss, S. A. (2009). Transformational leadership in distributed work groups: The moderating role of follower regulatory focus and goal orientation. *Communication Research, 36*, 810–837.
Wood, B., Owens, C., & Durham, B. (2005). Presidential rhetoric and the economy. *The Journal of Politics, 6*, 627–645.
Yukl, G. (2002). *Leadership in organizations* (5th ed.). New York: Prentice Hall.

CHAPTER

13 Destructive Leadership in and of Organizations

Robert B. Kaiser *and* S. Bartholomew Craig

Abstract

This chapter provides a refined and integrative definition of destructive leadership that establishes the construct as a broad category containing narrower facets at the intersection of leadership and counterproductive work behavior. The authors then review the nascent, but growing, research literature on destructive leadership in terms of studies that focus on destructive leaders and those that focus on situational factors associated with destructive leadership. Their review considers the implications of research on destructive leadership for organizational outcomes, highlights key themes regarding what is known about this phenomenon, identifies gaps in our knowledge, and discusses needed future research. Practical recommendations for organizations are also provided, including suggestions for preventing, detecting, and recovering from destructive leadership.

Key Words: Destructive leadership, toxic leadership, abusive supervision, counterproductive work behavior, dark side

Introduction

Consider the term "leadership" for a moment. Chances are, especially if you are an American, the images and thoughts conjured up were positive: a world leader offering a vision of hope, a coach guiding a team to victory, a grassroots organizer bringing together a small group of citizens around a common interest. The scholarly study of leadership is shot through with this positivity bias, nearly conceiving the concept as favorable by definition. One eminent theorist went so far as to claim that Adolph Hitler was not a leader despite his astonishing ability to mobilize people and resources to conduct horrifying atrocities on a grand scale (Burns, 2003). Even if implicit, there seems to be an ideology of goodness that pervades leadership theory and research.

The same positivity bias also pervades leadership practice, perhaps even more so than it does theory and research. Rare indeed is the leadership training program that warns those in positions of power about temptations to exploit their post for personal gain at the expense of the greater good. Similarly, methods used for assessing the performance of managers are increasingly based on competency models defined in terms of desirable dimensions of behavior. Imagine the reaction if one proposed using *incompetency* models to assess corporate executives.

Nonetheless, we are reminded that such a rosy view of the topic of leadership is incomplete by a shocking string of events over the last decade, starting with scandals like those at Enron, WorldComm, and Tyco, running through the near collapse of the global economy in 2008, and including the 2009 British Parliament Ministry wrongdoings as well as the cover-up of decades of predatory sexual abuse by members of the clergy made public in recent years. One could also point to the ideological divide and partisan politics displayed by the U.S. federal government in August of 2011 as another example of leadership gone wrong, given how sharply it undermined market confidence and nearly caused a financial default by the world's largest economy.

In our view, leadership is a social process of influence and guidance, neither inherently good nor inherently bad, but which can be put to better or worse uses. Additionally, it may be the case that the harm that some leaders do outweighs the good that other leaders may do. As two extreme examples, the fraud and malfeasance of Chairman Kenneth Lay, CEO Jeffrey Skilling, and CFO Andrew Fastow that resulted in the Enron implosion effectively destroyed over USD$60 billion in market capitalization. Even more ghastly, over 130 million citizens were murdered by their own governments in the 20th century (Rummel, 1994). Beyond these examples, research across a sweeping range of topics in psychology supports the contention that "bad is stronger than good" by showing that negative information, experiences, and people have a stronger effect than positive ones (Baumeister, Bratslavsky, Finkenauer, & Vohs, 2001). Why should this principle not generalize to leadership? Consider the following.

From 1996 to 2002, the former French Finance Minister Jean-Marie Messier was the CEO of the Parisian company, Compagnie Generale des Eaux (CGE). Messier was regarded as confident, charismatic, and completely self-absorbed. His autobiography was titled *J6M.com*; the six M's stood for "(Jean)-Marie Messier, moi-même, maître du monde," which translates into English as "Jean-Marie Messier, me myself, master of the world" (Messier, 2000). In the 1990s, CGE was a highly profitable global leader in water, electrical, and waste utilities, and analysts believed its long-term outlook favored steady growth. Nonetheless, Messier was not satisfied to simply run a "boring" utilities company and, with no background in the entertainment industry, he conducted a series of overpriced and ill-advised acquisitions to transform CGE into Vivendi Universal, a film and music conglomerate that resulted in financial disaster and Messier's forced resignation. Although he left with a severance package of €20.5 million in 2002, Vivendi reported corporate losses of €23.3 billion (Johnson & Orange, 2003).

While working with Dean Witter as a McKinsey consultant in the 1970s, Philip J. Purcell became popular with senior management at the retail brokerage firm. So enamored were they that they hired him to become CEO. According to the *New York Times* (Nocera, 2005), as a CEO, Purcell was "...ruthless, autocratic, and remote. He had no tolerance for dissent or even argument. He pushed away strong executives and surrounded himself with yes men and women. He demanded loyalty to himself over the organization. He played power games...," and had little contact with employees, preferring to hole up in his office to contemplate deals. Despite widespread criticism on the grounds of a poor culture fit, Purcell steamrolled a merger with the merchant banking firm, Morgan Stanley. And it was here that his abrasive interpersonal style was writ large. The *Times* article reported that "He belittled the investment bankers [at Morgan Stanley]. Executives learned that it was pointless to argue with Mr. Purcell about anything—all it did was make him mad and he didn't even pretend to be listening." Many Morgan Stanley executives left in a mass exodus, and Purcell gave their old jobs to friends and loyalists. Angry and offended, former executives petitioned the board, creating such a stir that the board fired the controversial CEO. Although Purcell claimed the merger with Morgan Stanley was a success and that his ouster was little more than a personal vendetta, the result of his last year in office was a 20-percent decline in quarterly earnings and the loss of some of the most talented investment bankers in the industry.

The stories of Messier and Purcell may be dramatic in the scope and scale of their destructiveness, but they are not that different in form and function from daily episodes of destructive leadership that take place deep in the bowels of organizations far from the public eye. Both cases illustrate undesirable outcomes that were caused primarily, not by the absence of some desirable features of leadership, but by the *presence* of undesirable features. Moreover, these two examples also illustrate the two primary channels through which destructive leaders have their effects: in the case of Messier, through disastrous decisions; and in the case of Purcell, through abusive interpersonal behavior.

In this chapter we will consider the defining characteristics of destructive leadership, along with some more narrowly defined concepts that constitute facets of this broad construct, and what distinguishes these from other phenomena in the leadership domain. We will also review the current state of research in this nascent but rapidly developing area of inquiry. Our review considers both behaviors and individual differences that distinguish destructive leaders, as well as situational factors associated with the operation of destructive leadership. Finally, we will offer some practical recommendations for minimizing the effects of destructive leadership in organizations and identify gaps in our current knowledge that suggest some potentially fruitful avenues for future researchers to pursue.

Definitional Issues

Early research in this area was slow to define exactly what constitutes destructive leadership. In discussions of the dark side of charisma, for instance, Howell and Avolio (1992, p. 44) warned about "blind fanaticism in the service of megalomaniacs and dangerous values"; Sankowsky (1995, p. 57) described how narcissists "abuse power"; Conger (1990, p. 44) referred to "problematic or even disastrous outcomes"; while O'Connor, Mumford, Clifton, Gessner, and Connelly (1995, p. 529) discussed "destructive acts" and noted that some charismatic leaders "may be more interested in personal outcomes" (p. 529). But until only recently, scholars did not explicitly define destructive leadership, per se. Rather, it was treated as a "know it when you see it" phenomenon.

What Is Destructive Leadership?

It seemed that that the adjective "destructive" was simply used to modify the noun "leadership" until a 2007 special issue of *The Leadership Quarterly* (Tierney & Tepper, 2007) was devoted to the topic. Two articles in that special issue developed independent definitions for the term "destructive leadership" (Einarsen, Aasland, & Skogstad, 2007; Padilla, Hogan, & Kaiser, 2007). Building on this important conceptual work, in a recent chapter we proposed the following definition of destructive leadership as an integration and extension of the definitions provided by these two views. Specifically, we defined destructive leadership as *behavior by a leader, supervisor, or manager that knowingly violates, or inappropriately risks violating, the legitimate interest of the organization, its members, or other legitimate stakeholders by undermining or sabotaging their goals, tasks, resources, motivation, well-being, or effectiveness* (Craig & Kaiser, 2013).

This definition establishes destructive leadership as a type of counterproductive work behavior (CWB) specific to incumbents in leadership roles, and is consistent with accepted definitions of CWB in its emphasis on harm to the legitimate interests of the organization and on the intentionality of the actor (e.g., Robinson & Bennett, 1995; Sackett & DeVore, 2002; Spector & Fox, 2002). Unique to this notion of CWB committed by leaders is the inclusion of "other legitimate stakeholders" as potential victims of destructive leadership, which takes into account how the special responsibilities of leaders in setting direction and managing the interface with external constituents makes their on-the-job behavior relevant, not only for members of their own organizations, but also for stakeholders outside their own organizations, such as the larger society. For example, a plant manager who increased her factory's profitability by dumping toxic waste into a nearby river rather than transporting it away for proper disposal would be considered a destructive leader under this definition, even though her own organization actually benefited from her externally destructive behavior (at least in the short term, and potentially in the long term if the practice was not discovered and sanctioned).

Another key aspect of this definition is its requirement of intentionality for leaders' destructive behavior. Intentionality, either to produce harm or to disregard the risk of producing harm, distinguishes this "dark side" approach to the study of leadership from the "bright side" approaches that have been the traditional focus of most leadership theory and research. For example, the various behavioral approaches derived from the Ohio State (e.g., Fleishman, 1953) and University of Michigan (e.g., Katz, Maccoby, & Morse, 1950) studies, Path-Goal Theory (House, 1996), Leader-Member Exchange (LMX) Theory (Dansereau, Graen, & Haga, 1975), Charismatic Leadership Theory (Conger & Kanungo, 1987; House, 1977), Transformational Leadership Theory (Bass, 1985; Burns, 1978), and most trait-based approaches (Judge, Bono, Ilies, & Gerhardt, 2002; Zaccaro, 2007) all identify aspects of leadership that enhance effectiveness through their *presence*, with ineffectiveness arising correspondingly from the *absence* of one or more of these features.

In contrast, destructive leadership specifically implies actively counterproductive behaviors rather than simply the absence of productive or effective ones and, further, that those behaviors be executed willfully and knowingly. In the case examples above, both Messier's unbridled lust for fame and self-glory and Purcell's dictatorial acts to suppress dissenting opinions were active behavior patterns that produced dire consequences. This feature of our definition distinguishes destructive leadership from simple incompetence, which is arguably already addressed by the traditional bright side approach (i.e., via the consideration of low levels of desirable behavior). Neither of those two executives' negative impacts on their organization was caused by lack of ability, but rather were the results of their willfully making decisions and engaging in behaviors designed to serve their personal goals without proper regard for the interests of their organizations.

We also exclude from our definition *self-destructive* leadership, where the negative consequences of intentionally harmful or negligent leadership are primarily experienced by the destructive leader him- or herself. Our emphasis in destructive leadership is on negative collective outcomes, whereas self-destructive leadership is focused on negative personal outcomes. For instance, a large body of research on the topic of career derailment considers factors associated with managers who get fired, demoted, or otherwise stall in their careers (McCall & Lombardo, 1983). This research has identified such factors as a lack of strategic thinking, inability to motivate others and build a team, troubled relationships, and a lack of self-awareness as commonly associated with failing in a managerial career (Hogan, Hogan, & Kaiser, 2010). We regard this topic as distinct, although in some regards related, to destructive leadership because of its focus on negative career outcomes for the leader. However, there is often overlap between behaviors that bring harm to organizations and those which harm leaders themselves; for instance, not only did Messier and Purcell destroy economic value and make employees miserable, they also lost their jobs. Thus, the difference between self-destructive leadership and the more general concept of destructive leadership is a matter of perspective and point of emphasis. Since leadership is a collective phenomenon, we focus on collective harm in our conception of destructive leadership, leaving self-destructiveness to other established areas of inquiry such as career derailment.

Lastly, because of its breadth, our definition of destructive leadership establishes the construct as a meso-level category representing the inclusion of leadership in the domain of counterproductive work behavior (see Figure 13.1). As such, it allows for a variety of related, but narrower, concepts to be subsumed as specific forms of destructive leadership. For example, the concepts of "abusive supervision" (Tepper, 2000, 2007), "petty tyranny" (Ashforth, 1994), "bad leadership" (Kellerman, 2004), "brutal bosses" (Hornstein, 1996), and "toxic leadership" (Lipman-Blumen, 2005; Schmidt, 2008) can all be classified under the general umbrella of destructive leadership, but still retain unique elements within their own definitions.

The Selfish Nature of Destructive Leadership

A defining feature of destructive leadership worth emphasizing is how it involves a selfish motivational orientation on the part of the destructive leader (Liden, 2010). Early discussions routinely acknowledged how the destructive leader's interpersonal behavior and/or decision making focused on his or her personal objectives and goals, as opposed to serving the needs of constituents and the larger social organization (Conger, 1990; O'Connor et al., 1995; Sankowsky, 1995). Self-interest is a powerful human motive, perhaps the most powerful one, and is a chief reason for exploitative, manipulative, unethical, and negligent leader behavior.

Scholars have long recognized that the power conferred by a leadership role can be used for personal benefit or the benefit of the larger social system. It was this observation that prompted McClelland (1970, 1975) to distinguish between personal needs

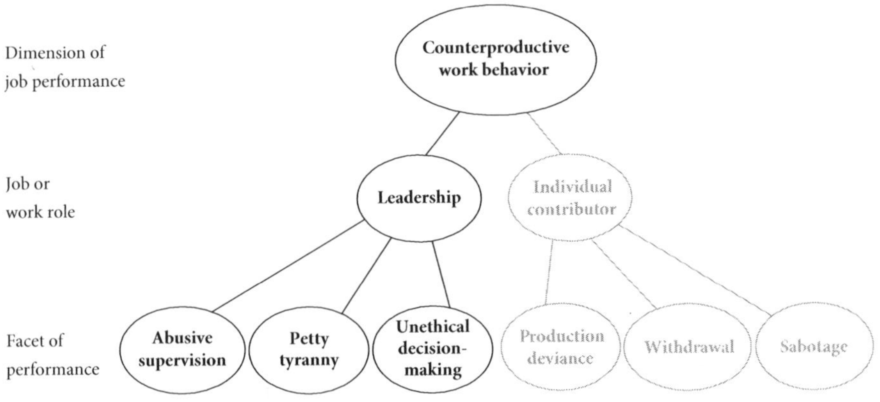

Figure 13.1. Conceptualizing Destructive Leadership as a Form of Counterproductive Work Behavior.

Note. Specific facets are illustrative examples and not intended to be exhaustive. Facets of counterproductive work behavior for individual contributor roles are presented as an example to distinguish facets of destructive leadership.

for power versus socialized needs for power. Leaders with personalized needs for power desire power *over* people, and use authority "...in an impetuously aggressive manner for self-aggrandizing purposes, to the detriment of their subordinates and organizations" (House & Aditya, 1997, p. 414). They lack self-control, a sense of responsibility, guilt or conscience, and impulse inhibition. In contrast, leaders with socialized needs for power desire power *through* people and use their authority to motivate, coordinate, and guide a group to the successful accomplishment of collective goals. This distinction has been used to distinguish desirable and prosocial forms of charismatic leadership from undesirable and selfish forms of charismatic leadership, where leaders use their charm and influence skills to satisfy personal needs (Hogan, Raskin, & Fazzini, 1990; House & Howell, 1992; Howell & Avolio, 1992).

An evolutionary analysis of leadership gives greater depth and insight to this critical distinction. There are two competing explanations for the emergence of the leadership role that is universally present among all known human societies: social dominance theory and social coordination theory (Kaiser, 2010; Van Vugt et al., 2008). Social dominance theory views human leadership as an extension of the alpha-male control structure seen in other primates, where "might makes right" and the strongest individual member of a group can use the threat of force to get others to comply. Social coordination theory, on the other hand, views human leadership as an elaboration on the mechanisms that allow species such as fish, birds, and many social insects to synchronize efforts in elaborate patterns of movement among many individuals. Critical to this line of thinking is the concept of multilevel selection, the idea that natural selection occurs at multiple levels of analysis, such as individuals versus groups. A principle of multilevel selection is that adaptations that are advantageous at one level tend to undermine adaptations at other levels (Wilson & Wilson, 2007). Thus, social dominance may confer benefits to the dominant alpha, but at the expense of the group. Similarly, social coordination may require self-sacrifice by the leader but nonetheless benefit the group.

We believe that destructive leadership typically takes the form of social dominance, whereas desirable leadership reflects effective social coordination. Further, we believe that the underlying motivations in destructive leadership are often selfish, whereas motivation is prosocial in effective leadership. There is, however, a temporal element to evaluating the eventual impact of both forms of leadership. Like most forms of self-defeating behavior (Baumeister & Scher, 1988), selfish leader behavior may deliver short-term benefits to the egocentric leader but typically results in long-term costs that exceed the initial benefit. As a recent example, the Egyptian dictator Hosni Mubarak was able to hold on to power and enrich his family during 30 years of autocratic rule. However, soon after the Arab Spring uprising of 2011, he was arrested and brought to trial on charges of corruption and complicity in the killing of protesters. Images of the aged and ailing Mubarak being dragged into court in a caged hospital bed captured for the relieved Egyptian citizenry a fitting picture of his eventual fate.

Shades of Gray

Sharp distinctions may help to elucidate conceptual differences, but they can also convey a false sense of absolutism. Although we talk about destructive leadership as having a negative impact on the legitimate interests of the organization and about desirable leadership as prosocial in nature, there are shades of gray. For instance, destructive leaders are not invariably bad; even the most destructive leaders may also bring some good to their constituents (Padilla et al., 2007). It has been argued and empirically shown that most leaders display some combination of constructive and destructive behaviors (Einarsen, Skogstad, & Aasland, 2010). Additionally, we do not necessarily believe that effective leadership is exclusively self-sacrificial and prosocial; more likely, the net effects of effective leadership benefit the larger social system as well as the individual leader, even if it requires self-sacrifice from time to time. Again, it is a question of emphasis and the more a leader's intentional effects harm the organization and its stakeholders, the more we can say that destructive leadership has occurred.

Destructive Leadership and Organizational Outcomes

Functional theories of leadership emphasize how leadership is a resource for group performance. For instance, McGrath's (1962) application of the functionalist view defines leadership responsibilities in terms of providing whatever a group needs to accomplish its goals. Evolutionary analyses of the origin and ultimate reason for the emergence of leadership as a social role emphasize its centrality to the survival of early human bands and tribes (Van Vugt, Hogan, & Kaiser, 2008). In other words, since leadership exists for the benefit of group performance, leadership should be evaluated in terms of team or organizational performance (Hogan, Curphy, & Hogan, 1994; Hogan & Kaiser, 2005; Kaiser, Hogan, & Craig, 2008). It follows that destructive leadership should be examined in terms of its impact on organizational outcomes and processes related to those outcomes. Although numerous taxonomies of leader behavior have been proposed (cf. Borman & Brush, 1993; Fleishman et al., 1991; Pearce, et al., 2003; Yukl, 2005), some of which are quite extensive, we believe that leaders' effects on group-level outcomes can be conceived as operating through two primary channels: decision making and interpersonal influence (cf. Kaiser & Hogan, 2007; Kaiser et al., 2008; Kaiser & Overfield, 2010). Destructive leadership, like desirable leadership, can be analyzed in terms of its impact on group outcomes through these two channels.

Leader decision making. Leadership positions typically afford the occupants of those positions some latitude of authority within which they decide what will happen (Finkelstein & Hambrick, 1990). Within the latitude afforded by their roles, leaders make myriad decisions that affect group-level performance, including decisions about what goals the group (or organization) will adopt (strategy), which group members will occupy which roles (staffing), how work will be distributed among roles (structure), and the processes by which work will be accomplished (systems; cf. Hambrick & Abrahamson, 1995). Key decisions affect organizational performance by guiding and constraining organization members' choices and behavior. This is not to say that leaders are the only members of organizations who make decisions, or that leaders do not incorporate input from non-leaders into their decision making. Our point is that making decisions—especially decisions about group direction—is integral to the role of "leader" in a more centrally fundamental way than it is to non-leadership roles.

Interpersonal influence. In addition to making decisions, leaders also influence others, both inside and outside the organization, to behave in ways that move the group toward its goals (or, in the case of destructive leadership, away from them). Any leader social behavior that exerts a causal influence on the behavior of others would fall into this category. Interpersonal influence activity includes most of the leadership phenomena that have been studied by organizational psychology since the early 20th century, such as power, influence, inspiration, and social exchange. Leaders' effects on organizational performance through this channel are mediated through follower variables such as attitudes, effort, and teamwork (Hogan & Kaiser, 2005). As with decision making, we do not mean to imply that leaders are the only individuals in organizations who exert interpersonal influence; indeed, the truth is quite to the contrary. But we do argue that influencing and motivating others is more centrally and formally a part of the "leader" role than it is for nonleader roles.

It is worth pointing out that the distinction we make between the decision-making and interpersonal influence channels is similar to distinctions made by other authors who have considered the means by which leaders influence performance. For instance, Dubin (1979) distinguished leadership *in* an organization (interpersonal influence) from leadership *of* an organization (structural influence). Zaccaro and Horn (2003) contrasted *direct influence* of the interpersonal variety with impersonal, *indirect influences* that guide and constrain followers through direction, goals, plans, and policies. We prefer to refer to these two channels as decision making and interpersonal influence because these labels seem more descriptive of the activities in which leaders engage.

The twin activities of decision making and influencing are so intertwined in many cases that it is often difficult to draw a clear line between making a decision and influencing others to execute it, to know where one activity stops and the other starts. But for the present purposes it is usually not necessary to draw such lines within a single task sequence. Rather, we offer this twin-channel structure simply as a framework for examining the implications of specific destructive leadership behaviors for organizational outcomes. For example, destructive decision making, such as the tendency for narcissistic executives to make bold acquisitions that make headlines but do not make business sense (cf., Hayward & Hambrick, 1997; Malmendier & Tate, 2005)—like Messier did to transform CGE into Vivendi—may be a qualitatively different phenomenon from destructive influence, such as when abusive supervisors motivate through intimidation and ridicule (Tepper, 2007)—as Purcell did with Morgan Stanley executives. We will invoke this framework as we next review research on destructive leadership.

Research on Destructive Leadership

Research on destructive leadership has been fragmented, with different researchers often applying different terms to the same phenomena or different definitions to the same terms. The various streams of research, however, can be categorized according to whether they focus on characteristics of the leader or on characteristics of the situation within which the leader operates. We use the person-situation distinction to organize our review of the blossoming research literature on destructive leadership.

Person Factors in Destructive Leadership

Most previous research on destructive leadership falls into the category of person factors; specifically, factors associated with the individual considered to be a destructive leader. Person factors include both traditional personality traits and also stable behavior patterns and preferred patterns of decision making. A key distinction here is the method of measurement, with personality traits typically having been assessed using data collected from leaders themselves, and behavior patterns usually being assessed via observations by coworkers or other subject matter experts.

Abusive supervision. Abusive supervision is arguably the most well developed and extensively researched type of destructive leadership. Tepper (2000) defined abusive supervision as the "sustained display of hostile verbal and nonverbal behaviors, excluding physical contact" by supervisors toward subordinates (p. 178). On Tepper's definition, the experience of hostility and abuse from the supervisor depends on the subjective perception of the subordinate; the same supervisory behavior might be perceived as abusive by one subordinate but not by another in the same work group. The exclusion of leader behaviors involving physical contact from Tepper's definition differentiates this construct from supervisor aggression (Grandey & Kern, 2004), which is otherwise similar. Tepper's concept of abusive supervision also overlaps with Ashforth's (1994) description of "petty tyranny," although the latter was not specific to leadership settings and could apply to any situation where one individual holds power or influence over others. Another distinguishing characteristic of the abusive supervision construct is the emphasis on hostility, which differentiates abusive supervision from petty tyranny and from the otherwise similar notion of supervisor undermining (Duffy, Ganster, & Pagon, 2002).

In terms of the two primary channels through which leaders affect group-level outcomes, the abusive supervision construct seems more directly relevant to the interpersonal influence path than to the decision-making path. That is, we would expect abusive supervisory behaviors to affect organization-level outcomes primarily though effects on subordinates tasked with doing the organization's work, such as reduced motivation and productivity and higher costs from turnover and health care.

A considerable amount of research has adopted Tepper's framework (including his scale items, sometimes with minor modifications) to investigate antecedents, consequences, and moderators of abusive supervision (see Tepper, 2007, for an extensive review of research on abusive supervision and several related constructs). We review research considering contextual antecedents to and moderators of abusive supervision later in this chapter, in the section on situational factors, and focus here on research concerning consequences of abusive supervision.

A variety of undesirable consequences have been linked to abusive supervision. It has been found to be negatively related to subordinates' job satisfaction (Tepper, 2000) and organizational commitment (Duffy et al., 2002) and positively related to subordinates' intentions to quit (Tepper, 2000), to their resistance to following supervisors' instructions (Tepper, Duffy, & Shaw, 2001), and to their display of counterproductive behavior toward the supervisor (Inness, Barling, & Turner, 2005; Mitchell & Ambrose, 2007), as well as toward the organization and their coworkers (Mitchell & Ambrose, 2007). Victims of abusive supervision have been found to respond less favorably to their coworkers' organizational citizenship behaviors (Tepper, Duffy, Hoobler, & Ensley, 2004), perhaps because they are more likely to interpret the coworkers' behaviors as attempts to curry favor with the abusive supervisor (Tepper, 2007). Victims of supervisory abuse have also been found to engage in lower levels of organizational citizenship behaviors themselves (Aryee et al., 2007; Zellars, Tepper, & Duffy, 2002) and to receive lower performance appraisal ratings (Harris, Kacmar, & Zivnuska, 2007). Subordinates of abusive supervisors show higher levels of anxiety, depression, burnout, and work-family conflict, along with lower levels of life satisfaction (Tepper, 2000), as well as reduced self-efficacy, more frequent health complaints (Duffy et al., 2002), and higher levels of problem drinking behavior (Bamberger & Bacharach, 2006). Extrapolating from what is known about the outcomes of abusive supervision, Tepper, Duffy, Henle, and Lambert (2006) estimated its total cost at USD$23.8 billion per year in the United States alone.

Although not an explicit focus of research on abusive supervision as Tepper (2000) defined it, it is also possible that abuse of subordinates may correlate with making destructive decisions. For example, it may turn out that the same leaders who engage in abusive supervisory practices also tend to make decisions that take their groups in destructive directions. But we are not aware of any research that has directly addressed this question. Future researchers could investigate whether abusive supervisors also tend to make destructive decisions for their organizations or whether their destructiveness is limited to the interpersonal path.

Unethical leadership. Interest in issues of ethics and integrity has grown in recent years, largely in response to a wave of high-profile moral lapses among business executives and government officials (e.g., Brown & Treviño, 2006a; Ciulla, 2004). It is interesting that it took the field so long to focus on such issues, especially since research on implicit leadership theories shows that the single-most important diagnostic category people use for deciding whether or not someone is worth following is "honesty"; "fair" and "believable" also are high on the list (Lord, Foti, & De Vader, 1984). Curiously, most of the recent theory and research on leader ethics and integrity is focused on the positive side, and tends to assume that unethical leadership is defined by a lack of ethical leadership (Kaiser & Hogan, 2010).

Consistent with our conceptual and definitional position on destructive leadership, research suggests that the presence of unethical leader behavior may not be isomorphic with the absence of ethical leader behavior. Rather, unethical leadership may be better conceptualized as actively devious, manipulative, and dishonest behavior (Craig & Gustafson, 1998). Further, it is the presence of the undesirable components that account for the empirical links between unethical leadership and destructive outcomes. For instance, Kaiser and Hogan (2010) showed that measures that focus on observed behaviors at the ethical end of the integrity continuum identify only a negligible proportion of managers with potential integrity issues and are minimally related to indices of leader effectiveness. On the other hand, measures that focus on the unethical end of the continuum identify a much larger proportion of managers as being at risk for behaving unethically and are highly related to less favorable employee attitudes and lower ratings of the leader's perceived effectiveness.

Although not as common as studies that operationalize ethical leadership in terms of desirable behaviors, a number of studies have analyzed destructive leadership by examining leaders who have a dubious reputation among individuals who have had the opportunity to observe the leader over time. In one of the first efforts to create a psychometrically sound measure of destructive leadership, Craig and Gustafson (1998; see also Craig, 1995) developed the Perceived Leader Integrity Scale (PLIS) to assess observers' impressions of leaders' likelihood of engaging in destructive behavior (i.e., a "dubious reputation"). Despite the word "integrity" in the title, the PLIS is focused on unethical behavior and assesses almost exclusively destructive behaviors. Based on findings that coworkers form overall impressions of leaders' integrity that are primarily a function of discrete and negative behaviors, Craig and Gustafson identified the specific leader behaviors that predicted observers' impressions of unethical leadership and developed items to measure those behaviors, along with the overall impression of the leader as a person of lower or higher integrity. The behavioral items concern both character flaws (e.g., "is vindictive") and misconduct (e.g., "would steal from the organization"), and expectations about whether a manager would mistreat the person providing the ratings (e.g., "would lie to me," "would allow me to be blamed for his/her mistakes"). The specific behaviors assessed by the PLIS have been found to account for more than 80 percent of the variance in observers' overall impressions of leader destructiveness (Baker & Craig, 2006).

Research using the PLIS has found unethical leadership to correlate positively with followers' desire to quit (Craig & Gustafson, 1998), and negatively with follower job satisfaction and perceptions of leader effectiveness (Kaiser & Hogan, 2010), organizational effectiveness (Parry & Proctor-Thomson, 2002), and leader-member exchange quality (Mahsud, Yukl, & Prussia, 2010). Lin, Che, and Leung (2009) found that subordinates with unethical leaders were less accepting of unfavorable outcomes than those with more ethical leaders. The PLIS has also been translated into Spanish (Arredondo, 2004) and Mandarin Chinese (Ho, Shih, & Craig, 2011) to facilitate future research on destructive leadership across cultures.

The construct of unethical leadership has implications for both the decision-making and interpersonal influence links between leader behavior and organizational outcomes. As discussed above, research has shown how unethical leaders have undesirable direct interpersonal effects on followers, such as reduced motivation and increased deviance and turnover, which could cascade to the organizational level as lower group performance and productivity.

Additionally, because the unethical leadership construct includes components such as dishonesty, neglecting commitments and obligations, and breaking rules, scores on a measure such as the PLIS (Craig & Gustafson, 1998) would also be expected to predict self-serving and counterproductive biases in decision making. For example, unethical leaders might be more likely to choose a course of action for their organization that violates a law or regulation, such as failing to comply with an environmental protection requirement. That decision could then produce an organizational outcome in the form of money lost to fines and customer backlash due to a damaged corporate reputation. Similarly, the fraudulent accounting practices endorsed at Enron by CEO Jeffrey Skilling and CFO Andrew Fastow were clear examples of unethical decision making that led to what was, at the time, the largest bankruptcy in U.S. history.

Dark side of charisma. Interest in charismatic leadership surged in the late 1970s and 1980s (Conger & Kunungo, 1987; House, 1977). Alongside this research came the closely related concept of transformational leadership (Bass, 1985; Burns, 1978). Hundreds of studies have addressed these emotion-based modes of interpersonal influence and generally found them to be effective leadership styles in a wide variety of settings. Meta-analyses show transformational leadership to correlate with a host of follower motivation and group performance criteria (Judge & Piccolo, 2004; Lowe, Kroeck, & Sivasubramaniam, 1996). Charisma, however, is more controversial. On one hand are findings such as those showing that charismatic U.S. presidents were more effective leaders than noncharismatic presidents (House, Spangler, & Woycke, 1991). On the other hand are studies showing no relationship between charisma and leadership effectiveness. One review noted that studies of CEO charisma have not found a direct relationship with organizational performance, but have found a direct relationship with CEO compensation (Kaiser et al., 2008). Charisma seems to benefit leaders more than their constituents and organizations.

Early on, authors raised questions about a possible dark side of charisma (Conger, 1990; Hogan et al., 1990; Howell & Avolio, 1992), and a stream of inquiry arose to consider the relations among charisma, transformational leadership, and destructive outcomes. Hogan et al. (1990) coined the phrase, "dark side of charisma," in explaining how selfish and manipulative leaders seem charming and have good social skills that they use to conceal their ulterior motives. Conger (1990) speculated that the unusual degree of influence that charismatic leaders have over their followers could exert a corrupting influence, creating temptations for the leader to replace organizational goals with personal goals and to circumvent normal organizational checks and balances. Bass and Steidlmeier (1999) responded to concerns about leaders using their charisma for personal and counterproductive purposes by arguing that leaders who gave in to such temptations should be considered pseudo-transformational leaders at best, and offered a definition of authentic transformational leadership that included morality as a requirement. Similarly, as mentioned earlier, House and Howell (1992) and O'Connor et al. (1995) distinguished between socialized charismatics, who are primarily motivated by a desire to serve a greater good, and personalized charismatics, who are primarily motivated by self-interest.

Despite a great deal of theoretical interest, little systematic empirical research has isolated the destructive effects of charismatic or transformational leadership. In the transformational literature, research shows that ratings of transformational leadership are highly associated with lower scores on measures of unethical leadership (Parry & Proctor-Thomson, 2002) as well as highly and positively related with scores on an objective test of moral development (Turner et al., 2002). Further, meta-analyses show that transformational leadership correlates reliably with a range of desirable leadership outcomes across a variety of settings (Judge & Piccolo, 2004; Lowe et al., 1996). Consistent with our conceptual position distinguishing bright and dark side factors in leadership, there is little empirical evidence for a link between transformational leadership and destructive leadership.

In contrast, charisma has been linked to destructive leadership, but this effect depends on the motives of the leader. For example, Brown and Treviño (2006b) found leaders' socialized charisma to be negatively related to followers' deviant behavior. On the other hand, personalized charisma has been empirically linked to inflicting harm on the larger social system (O'Connor et al., 1995). This research also shows that, compared to socialized charismatics, the destructive personalized type of charismatic leader is distinguished by having an excessive need for power, a narcissistic sense of entitlement and grandiosity, seeing other people as objects, and espousing negative life themes that convey images of abuse, hatred, and violence. Thus, there is empirical evidence for a link between charisma and destructive leadership; although not all charismatic leaders are destructive, many destructive leaders are charismatic. Padilla et al. (2007), for instance, note that history is replete with examples of larger-than-life charismatic figures who used their charm and influence to seduce others to carry out their bidding and manipulate governance systems to minimize checks and balances, thereby consolidating power and control that they used to purse a selfish agenda (e.g., Hitler, Stalin, Castro).

Research on the dark side of charisma has obvious implications for leaders' destructive effects on organizational outcomes via the interpersonal path. First, personalized charismatics tend to neglect the needs and rights of other people. They see others as objects and have no compunctions against manipulating them for self-serving instrumental purposes. Second, the enhanced personal influence of a destructive charismatic leader would likely affect followers in ways that would create organizational level outcomes, such as by shifting their loyalty from the organization to the charismatic leader, distracting from the pursuit of legitimate organizational interests if not actively undermining those interests in the service of the leader's personal interests.

Due to little systematic research on the topic, it is less clear whether personalized charismatic leaders would necessarily engage in more destructive decision making, but the possibility seems likely. First, due to their greater social influence and ability to secure power and control, personalized charismatics may enjoy more discretion and latitude to make independent decisions (Hambrick & Abrahamson, 1995). Second, self-interest and other egocentric biases are more likely to influence those decisions if they are subject to less scrutiny and governance (Kaiser & Hogan, 2007). For instance, observers have noted that it was chiefly Messier's spellbinding influence over the board of directors of Compagnie Generale des Eaux that allowed him to coax approval for several acquisitions that made little business sense (Johnson & Orange, 2003). Despite being experienced financiers and savvy business people, the board was so mesmerized by Messier that they attributed to him a quasi-magical power to turn dross into gold. In retrospect, it was obvious that Messier pursued these acquisitions primarily to build his own personal empire and position himself as a mogul in the glamorous world of entertainment. But, dazzled by charisma, the board was blind to Messier's motives and neglected its governance role as a check and balance to his leadership.

Narcissism. Narcissism refers to a dysfunctional personality syndrome involving arrogance, grandiosity, self-absorption, and a sense of entitlement (Rosenthal & Pittinsky, 2006). Common expressions of narcissism include feelings of superiority and entitlement to special privileges, exploitation and manipulation of other people, and a constant need for attention and admiration (Bogart, Benotsch, & Pavlovic, 2004). On the positive side, narcissists can be charming and inspirational. It is the obsessive focus on the self that links the narcissistic personality with personalized charisma (House & Howell, 1992; Sankowsky, 1995).

Leadership theorists with backgrounds in clinical psychology have maintained that narcissism is a common attribute of powerful leaders (Kets de Vries & Miller, 1985; Maccoby, 2007). Moreover, narcissism is often seen as a double-edged sword. On the one hand, a certain degree of narcissism is seen as useful and perhaps even necessary for leaders, providing the self-confidence, vision, and inspiration needed to motivate people to take on ambitious collective projects. But on the other hand, the grandiose belief systems of narcissistic leaders defy reality testing, and can lead them to pursue big plans that are ultimately unrealistic and cannot be successfully implemented. Further, their excessive needs for power and admiration and obsessive self-focus often preclude empathetic concern for others, particularly their followers.

Despite great popular interest and a good deal of theoretical work, there has been relatively little empirical research on narcissism and leadership. Most of this work has been based on case studies and clinical evaluations of high-profile CEOs (e.g., Kets de Vries et al., 1985; Maccoby, 2007). Recent empirical work has relied on two primary means of measurement for narcissism: the Narcissistic Personality Inventory (Raskin & Hall, 1979), a self-report questionnaire; and content analysis of public records to quantify objective indicators of narcissism. For instance, investigators in one study developed a reliable unobtrusive measure of CEO narcissism defined in terms of four components (Chatterjee & Hambrick, 2007): how often the CEO's photograph appeared in the company's annual report, how frequently the CEO was mentioned in company press releases, how often the CEO used the term "I" in public statements, and the ratio of the CEO's salary to the salary of the next highest paid person in the organization.

Research on narcissistic leaders is relevant to both the interpersonal influence and decision-making paths linking leaders to organizational performance. More narcissistic leaders would be expected to have a greater tendency to make big, bold, and risky decisions that garner public attention. Further, these decisions often have negative consequences for the organization. Leader narcissism is associated with frequent changes in strategy that lurch the organization from one vision to another without sufficient opportunity to make progress, making headlines with high-profile acquisitions that often involve paying more than market value and actually losing value for the acquiring firm, and increased variability in performance with a few major wins to punctuate many big losses (Chatterjee & Hambrich, 2007; Hayward & Hambrick, 1997; Malmendier & Tate, 2005). At least part of the problem underlying these costly decisions is that, in the pursuit of self-glory, narcissistic leaders make rash decisions without sufficient objective information, discount or ignore negative feedback, and surround themselves with loyal supporters who will not disagree with them.

In terms of interpersonal influence, the confidence projected by narcissistic leaders can, over time, come to be seen as arrogance. Further, narcissistic leaders tend to devalue and belittle employees as well as to ignore them altogether, have difficulty forming mutually satisfying work relationships, and make large and unreasonable demands on their staff, all of which can impair employee motivation and harm their well-being (Hogan & Fico, 2011). Narcissistic leaders also neglect the development of their staff and have difficulties grooming a successor and executing a plan for orderly succession, often leaving a leadership vacuum when they retire or depart (Sankowsky, 1995).

Although empirical work on narcissism in leadership is growing, researchers continue to disagree about the nature and definition of narcissistic leadership and how it should be assessed. Some see it as its own distinct style of leadership whereas others see it as overlapping with other established leadership constructs such as personalized charisma (House & Howell, 1992). Rosenthal and Pittinsky (2006) reviewed this literature and noted this problem, along with the complicating factor that narcissism can be associated with both desirable features of leadership (e.g., confidence, vision) as well as undesirable features (e.g., grandiosity, entitlement, manipulation, selfishness). They further proposed distinguishing between narcissistic *leadership* and narcissistic *leaders*. They viewed narcissistic *leadership* as a style that reflects elements of the narcissism personality syndrome but could also be influenced by situation factors and narcissistic *leaders* as individuals who have elevated levels of this personality trait. Whether this distinction will help advance research remains to be seen; after all, narcissism is as narcissism does.

The dark side of personality. Narcissism is the personality trait historically most often associated with destructive leadership, but recent research suggests it may only be the tip of the iceberg. The development and widespread acceptance of the Five-Factor Model (FFM) of personality as a taxonomy for classifying traits and predicting job performance has led to an explosion of research on the role of personality in the workplace. Recent research has begun to explore the personality domain beyond the FFM to consider also dysfunctional personality traits like narcissism and several others, a view that has been referred to as "the dark side" of personality (Hogan & Hogan, 2001; Judge, Piccolo, & Kosalka, 2009). There is evidence that "dark side" traits are distinct from the "bright side" traits captured by the FFM, and contribute unique variance in the prediction of work behavior (Moscoso & Salgado, 2004; Schmit, Kilm, & Robie, 2000; Wu & LeBreton, 2011). Moreover, a consensus is forming that dark side traits may be more important than bright side traits for understanding counterproductive leader behavior and managerial failure (J. Hogan et al., 2010; Judge et al., 2009; Wu & LeBreton, 2011).

As a new area of inquiry, the field has yet to settle on an accepted taxonomy of dark side personality traits, and empirical research has yet to coalesce around a large body of reliable findings, such as that which characterizes the literature on the Five-Factor Model. Different theorists have proposed different conceptual models, with varying degrees of overlap. For instance, Wu and LeBreton (2011) focus on "the Dark Triad" of Narcissism, Machiavellianism, and Psychopathy. As one of the first efforts to provide conceptual guidance, Hogan and Hogan (2001) proposed an 11-dimension taxonomy of dysfunctional traits that disrupt work relationships and corrupt judgment. This taxonomy was originally guided by the Axis-II personality disorders as defined in the *Diagnostic and Statistical Manual of Mental Disorders IV* (American Psychiatric Association [DSM-IV-TR], 2000). However, the emerging view is that "dark side" personality traits are not clinical personality disorders because they do not impair significant life functioning in the manner or degree required for a clinical diagnosis

(Wu & LeBreton, 2011). Rather, dark side traits are viewed as part of normal personality that operates within healthy individuals, although they do interfere with relationships and judgment and therefore compromise leadership performance (J. Hogan et al., 2010; Hogan & Kaiser, 2005).

Theorizing on the nature of dark side traits characterize them in terms of *schemas*, cognitive structures derived from experience that help people interpret their social environment and decide how to respond (Kihlstrom & Klein, 1994; Young, Klosko, & Weishaar, 2003). Schemas function automatically and outside conscious awareness; they serve as mental filters and heuristics that cause us to interpret information in ways that fit with our expectations (Baldwin, 1992). According to R. Hogan and J. Hogan, the dysfunctional dispositions that constitute the dark side of personality reflect the effects of maladaptive schemas designed to enhance one's interests, either by protecting the individual from the repeat of a past injury or by justifying a self-serving course of action (J. Hogan et al., 2010; Hogan & Hogan, 2001). The schemas that underwrite various dark side traits have in common a neglect to consider the rights and needs of other people.

As of this writing, there are three published inventories of dysfunctional personality designed to assess counterproductive variations in normal personality and are nonclinical (Hogan & Hogan, 2009; Moscosco & Salgado, 2004; Schmit, Kilm, & Robie, 2000). There is a large degree of conceptual overlap across these three inventories. The relations among them, organized in terms of the 11 Axis-II personality disorders used in their original conceptualization (Hogan & Hogan, 2001), are summarized in Table 13.1.

Although research has established relationships between leaders' dark side traits and a range of undesirable organizational outcomes, some research has also shown relationships with desirable outcomes (e.g., Harms, Spain, & Hannah, 2011). The resolution to this apparent paradox may depend on time. According to Hogan and Hogan (2001), dark side traits coexist with well-developed social skills that can conceal their selfish and counterproductive nature, and can even make them appear as desirable qualities at first. For instance, Messier's grandiose sense of self and delusional belief system appeared as confidence early in his tenure at CGE; over time, it came to be viewed as narcissistic arrogance. The Dean Witter management team was initially impressed with Purcell's no-nonsense ability to analyze deals and not allow emotions and other people's feelings to complicate his analysis; in the end this same reserved trait was better understood in terms of the cold, aloof, and insensitive qualities that alienated his staff. Dark side traits have a seductive quality, and we encourage longitudinal research designs to better disentangle their dynamic temporal relationships with measures of perceived leader behavior and undesirable organizational processes and outcomes.

Negligent, or laissez-faire leadership. Passive forms of leadership traditionally have been thought of as the absence of leadership, or non-leadership, which fails to result in positive outcomes, but not necessarily as resulting in negative outcomes. Viewed this way, negligent or laissez-faire leadership may not satisfy our definition for destructive leadership. However, it could also be argued that passive forms of leadership represent negligence on the part of leaders who knowingly abdicate their authority and intentionally avoid their responsibilities in influencing employees and making organizational decisions (Craig & Kaiser, 2013). Cases involving such knowing and willful negligence to perform role requirements or to prevent harm to the organizations' legitimate interests *would* meet our definitional requirements for destructive leadership. Moreover, other recent theorists have also taken the position that laissez-faire leadership is not just the absence of desirable leadership but is a form of negligent and destructive leadership, perhaps even the most common form of destructive leadership (Aasland, Skogstad, Notelaers, Nielsen, & Einarsen, 2010).

There is empirical support for this reasoning. For example, studies using the Multifactor Leadership Questionnaire have found laissez-faire behaviors to be empirically distinct from transformational and transactional leader behavior, and not simply the polar opposite of these active forms of desirable leadership (Antonakis, Avolio, & Sivasubramaniam, 2003). Further, the absence of this passive form of destructive leadership is associated with better leadership outcomes. Meta-analytic research has reported strong and consistent negative relationships between laissez-faire leadership behavior and leader effectiveness, subordinate job satisfaction, and subordinate satisfaction with their leader (Judge & Piccolo, 2004). Laissez-faire leader behavior is also associated with subordinate role ambiguity and role conflict and a variety of workplace stressors (Skogstad, Einarsen, Torsheim, Aasland, & Hetland, 2007).

Table 13.1. An Integrative Summary of Dark Side Personality Traits and Measurement Scales

		Measurement Scales		
Axis-II Dimension	**Analogous dark side tendencies among normal adults**	**Hogan & Hogan (2001)**	**Moscosco & Salgado (2004)**	**Schmit, Kilm, & Robie (2000)**
Borderline	Moody; intense but short-lived enthusiasm for people, projects, and things; hard to please.	Excitable	Ambivalent	
Avoidant	Reluctant to take risks for fear of being rejected or negatively evaluated.	Cautious	Shy	
Paranoid	Cynical, distrustful, and doubtful of others' true intentions.	Skeptical	Suspicious	Intimidating[1]
Schizoid	Aloof, and uncommunicative; lacking awareness and care for others' feelings.	Reserved	Lone	Intimidating[1]
Passive-Aggressive	Casual; ignoring people's requests and becoming irritated or excusive if they persist.	Leisurely	Pessimistic	Passive-Aggressive
Narcissism	Extraordinarily self-confident; grandiosity and entitlement; overestimation of capabilities.	Arrogant	Egocentric	Ego-Centered
Antisocial	Enjoy taking risks and testing limits; manipulative, deceitful, cunning, and exploitive.	Mischievous	Risky	Manipulation
Histrionic	Expressive, animated, and dramatic; wanting to be noticed and the center of attention.	Colorful	Cheerful	
Schizotypal	Acting and thinking in creative but sometimes odd or unusual ways.	Imaginative	Eccentric	
Obsessive-Compulsive	Meticulous, precise, and perfectionistic; inflexible about rules and procedures.	Diligent	Reliable	Micro-Managing
Dependent	Eager to please; dependent on the support and approval of others; reluctant to disagree with others, especially authority figures.	Dutiful	Submitted	

Note: Analogous dark side tendencies based on Hogan and Hogan (2001) and Hogan and Kaiser (2005). Scales presented in the same row are measures of the same dark side trait.

[1] The Intimidating scale from Schmit, Kilm, & Robie (2000) blends elements of the Skeptical and Reserved dimensions from Hogan & Hogan (2001).

Follow-up studies have clarified the nature of the link between laissez-faire leadership and negative effects on employees. For example, role conflict, role ambiguity, and conflict with coworkers explain the effects of laissez-faire leadership on bullying from coworkers. Workplace stressors—especially bullying—have been found to mediate the link between laissez-faire leadership and subordinates' levels of distress (Skogstad et al., 2007). Negligent leaders allow conflict among employees to fester to the point where harmful levels of stress and discord undermine organizational performance.

Separate lines of research extend these findings and demonstrate the sweeping destructive effects of passivity and negligence. Hinkin and Schriesheim (2008) reported a series of four studies showing that when leaders do not provide rewards for high performance or enforce accountability for poor performance, subordinates are less satisfied and don't perform as well. Subordinates also had more negative perceptions of passive leaders. Research in the area of employee safety shows how laissez-faire leadership amounts to "sins of omission" in terms of negligence and disregard for employee well-being. Kelloway, Mullen, and Francis (2006) found that passive leaders shirk their leadership responsibilities and are unlikely to be involved in promoting safety behaviors at work. Their results indicated that safety-specific passive leadership behaviors were negatively related to safety-related outcomes, even after controlling for the positive effects of safety-specific transformational leadership behavior.

This research shows how laissez-faire leadership negatively affects organizational outcomes via the interpersonal influence path. For example, the failure of laissez-faire leaders to give clear direction and to deal with conflict among followers is likely to result in reduced follower productivity, work group cohesion, and group performance. Although not explicitly addressed by extant research, it seems likely that a laissez-faire leadership style would also include a tendency to avoid making timely decisions, especially when decisions are important, high risk, and visible to stakeholders like senior managers or boards of directors. Such hesitation or abdication of decision-making responsibilities could produce undesirable organizational consequences in the form of missed opportunities as well as unaddressed problems.

Situational Factors Related to Destructive Leadership

Our review of the literature indicates that there is more research on destructive leadership that concerns person factors than concerns situational factors. Nonetheless, destructive leadership cannot be fully understood without considering the situations within which leaders exhibit destructive behaviors (Einarsen et al., 2010). Padilla et al. (2007) proposed that destructive leadership involves an interplay between toxic leaders, susceptible followers, and conducive environments—a configuration they called a "toxic triangle." They then offered retrospective examinations of historical incidents of destructive leadership to support their propositions. Einarsen et al. (2010) made the interesting point that it is important to understand situational factors that inhibit or allow destructive leadership in order to establish early detection systems and preventative measures through means such as organizational design, organizational culture, and training and development programs.

In general, research on situational variables focuses on two general classes of mechanisms: those that allow destructive individuals to exert their destructive influence and those that encourage otherwise productive individuals to behave counterproductively. These two contrasting perspectives can be distinguished as the bad apple approach versus the bad barrel approach, respectively (cf. Kish-Gephart, Harrison, & Treviño, 2010). For instance, the *Toxic Triangle* model (Padilla et al., 2007) focused on destructive leaders as "bad apples" and the conducive environments in which they could exert their destructive influence. Later, Mulvey and Padilla (2010) reconsidered situational factors from a "bad barrel" perspective to more fully elaborate a framework for describing situations likely to elicit destructive leadership. A central assumption in this later work was that environmental factors can overwhelm otherwise "good" leaders and followers to produce destructive outcomes. Next, we review the literature on situational variables associated with destructive leadership in terms of these contrasting perspectives.

The bad apple perspective. A key factor associated with whether or not destructive individuals are able to exert influence concerns their degree of *discretion* (Kaiser & Hogan, 2007). Discretion is a multifaceted variable that reflects the degree to which leaders can turn their intentions into reality—what Hambrick and Finkelstein (1987) called "latitude of action." When discretion is low, leader judgment and behavior are constrained. When discretion is high, leaders are relatively free to do as they wish. A key factor that determines the degree of discretion for any individual leader is the organizational level at which he or she is employed. The higher up the leader, the greater the degrees of freedom in choice and action with executives having the greatest degree of discretion, and therefore also the greatest opportunity to cause harm and destruction (Kaiser & Hogan, 2007).

Other factors that influence the degree to which leaders are constrained include agents or institutions, either within or outside the organization, that function as checks on leaders' managerial discretion. Mulvey and Padilla (2010) identified several factors that might function as checks, including news media, external experts or pundits, government agencies, and boards of directors or governors. They hypothesized that levels of destructive leadership would increase as the availability of such checks on leader power decreased.

Organizations operating in more complex environments, such as those in fast-cycle industries with rapid innovation, are hypothesized to display more specialization and differentiation in their structures than those operating in less-complex environments. This additional complexity in structure is expected to allow for higher levels of destructive leadership due to there being less transparency and greater difficulty in regulating individuals' behavior (Fleming & Zyglidopoulos, 2008). As one example, the complexity created by the proliferation of credit default swaps, collateralized debt obligations, securitized mortgages, and other exotic financial instruments in the first decade of the 21st century is thought to have overwhelmed the ability of internal auditors to assess risk and external regulatory agencies to monitor the financial industry in the lead-up to the recent meltdown in the global markets (Kaufman, 2007; Tett, 2009).

Instability and rapid change may also permit leaders to more easily centralize power and control, thereby increasing their degree of discretion. Leaders are often granted more authority during uncertain times because instability demands quick action and unilateral decision making (Janis & Mann, 1977). However, once decision making becomes centralized, it is difficult to take back (Kipnis, 1972). The structural stability of the governance system (Cell, 1974)—the degree to which rules are explicit and consistently applied—is also important. Destructive leaders have more latitude for control when the governance structure is less stable.

The perception of threat by organization members also facilitates destructive leadership because people are more willing to accept authoritarian leadership when they feel threatened. Research on terror management theory illustrates how threat increases followers' support and identification with charismatic leaders, particularly those who are not participative. One study found that people who were made aware of their mortality showed an increased preference for charismatic leaders and a decreased preference for participative leaders (Cohen, Solomon, Maxfield, Pyszczynski, & Greenberg, 2004). Another study found that emphasizing the mortal dangers of terrorism increased subjects' support for U.S. President George W. Bush and his counterterrorism policies shortly after the 9/11 attacks (Landau et al., 2004). Three points about the role of threat are important. First, objective threats are not necessary; it is followers' perceptions of threat that have the motivating effects. Second, destructive leaders often perpetuate the perception of threat in order to draw support and strengthen their power. Third, the perception of threat on the part of leaders can also be associated with destructive leadership. For instance, personalized charismatics are more likely to inflict harm and use coercive methods in conditions in which uncertainty and fear produce anxiety around issues of power, control, and security (O'Connor et al., 1995).

Finally, certain cultural values may make it easier for destructive individuals to wield power. Hofstede (1991) identified several values on which societies differ, and three have been postulated to facilitate destructive leaders: uncertainty avoidance, collectivism, and power distance (Luthans, Peterson, & Ibrayeva, 1998). Uncertainty avoidance, the preference for order and predictability, is expected to be negatively related to destructive leadership because of the higher levels of structure, regulation, and transparency in cultures with high uncertainty avoidance. Individuals in more collectivistic cultures are less inclined to question or challenge authority, making destructive leadership more likely. Finally, cultures higher on power distance are more accepting of centralized power, which provides destructive leaders more discretion.

The bad barrel perspective. On the other hand is research that considers the kinds of environmental factors that influence otherwise good leaders to behave destructively. The classic study often cited in support of this position is the famous 1971 Stanford Prison experiment, in which typical undergraduate students were screened for normality and mental health and then randomly assigned to play the role of guard or prisoner over the course of a two-week simulation (Zimbardo, 1973). The experimenters had to stop the exercise on the sixth day because many "guards" began to dominate the "prisoners" with increasingly coercive and hostile tactics, humiliating and dehumanizing treatment, and abuse. The researchers concluded that the situation overrode the good character of those guards and made them behave in a cruel manner. Rather than some dispositional qualities or personality traits, they proposed that the alchemy of ambiguity, authority, and an "us versus them" social structure with one group defined as morally inferior made healthy, normal, average young adults behave like evil sadists.

Support for the influence of situational variables eliciting destructive influence behavior has been claimed in several studies of abusive supervision. Abusive supervisory behavior has been related to supervisors' own experiences of procedural injustice and their resultant depression (Tepper et al., 2006) as well as to supervisors' perceptions of psychological contract breach (Hoobler & Brass, 2006) and interpersonal mistreatment (Aryee, Chen, Sun, & Debrah, 2007) on the part of their organizations. The pattern of results found was consistent with the idea of abusive supervision as displaced aggression; after suffering perceived wrongs at the hands of their organizations, supervisors redirected their hostility toward subordinates who were relatively safer targets (Tepper, 2007). Tepper et al. (2006) found that subordinates higher in negative affectivity were more likely to report being the victims of abusive supervision, creating some question as to whether they are actually the targets of greater supervisory abuse or are merely more likely to report it (Aquino, Grover, Bradfield, & Allen, 1999). Moreover, it is also important to note that this research does not preclude the possibility of "bad apples"; it is possible that these situational factors stimulated a latent propensity toward abusive behavior rather than directly caused "good" managers to act abusively.

Research on decision making also points to the power of contextual factors to encourage managers to make unethical choices. From a recent meta-analysis of research on ethical decision making in organizations, Kish-Gephart, Harrison, and Treviño (2010) concluded that features of both the organizational environment and of the decisions themselves can influence unethical decision making. When decisions involved cases where the probability, magnitude, and immediacy of harm were greater, unethical decision making was more likely. This tendency was exacerbated in organizations where the prevailing culture emphasized self-promotion over concern for others such as coworkers, customers, or the community. Additionally, organizational cultures in which the range of acceptable behavior and the consequences of unacceptable behavior were not clearly communicated to organization members, such as by unambiguous statements or leaders' role modeling, produced higher rates of unethical decision making.

Applying Ashforth and Anand's (2003) model describing the routinization of corruption to these findings, it is easy to see how a small number of situationally induced unethical decisions by only a few leaders—or even one—might initiate a chain reaction resulting in widespread destructive behavior by multiple leaders in the same organization. Specifically, Ashforth and Anand proposed that an initial corrupt act can become institutionalized by being embedded in organizational structures or processes, leading to the development of self-serving ideologies that justify the embedded corruption. Eventually, even new entrants into the organization begin to be socialized into the corrupt ideologies, allowing for the effects of the original destructive leader to extend far beyond his or her own reach or tenure. The infamous Enron case seems to represent a particularly clear example of this process, where the initial success of a few "creative" new products and methods for manipulating markets, subverting standard accounting oversight controls, and providing immediate and sizable compensation bonuses ultimately resulted in a culture that spawned destructive acts by numerous leaders and non-leaders at an alarming rate (McLean & Elkind, 2005).

A series of social psychological experiments conducted by Galinsky and colleagues provides compelling evidence that situational factors can induce people in leadership positions to behave destructively. This body of research shows that status and power have a distorting effect on one's outlook, making it harder to see matters from another person's point of view and easier to rationalize and justify self-serving actions and decisions. For instance, with simple primes such as asking people to recall situations in which they had power over others versus those in which others had power over them, or arbitrarily assigning individuals to high- or low-status positions in a brief role play, these researchers found that subjects in the high-power conditions were more likely to lie, believe that they were entitled to cheat on taxes whereas other people are not, and that their own morally deviant behavior was more acceptable than a hypothetical other doing the same behavior (Lammers, Stapel, & Galinsky, 2010). Another experiment showed how power literally increases the tendency to view the world from one's own perspective. Subjects were told to write the letter "E" with a marker on their foreheads. Those in the high-power condition were three times more likely to write the letter so it appeared normal from their perspective, but backwards from an observer's perspective (Galinsky, Magee, Inesi, & Gruenfeld, 2006). Not surprisingly, subsequent studies showed how subjects in a high-power condition were more likely to objectify other people and see them as an instrumental tool to be used for one's self-interested purposes (Gruenfeld, Inesi, Magee, & Galinksi, 2008).

The research by Galinsky and colleagues is startling. Although each study used a somewhat different manipulation to create high- and low-power conditions, they each represent relatively simple and temporary inductions of mental states or brief differences in social status in low-stakes situations. Moreover, subjects were randomly assigned to conditions. However, when generalizing the findings to leadership in organizations, the experience of power for, say, executives is amplified significantly.

Status-seeking individuals who desire power self-select into these positions. Moreover, the greater pay, prestige, and control of resources in an executive career represent a relatively permanent change in social status and power. This increase in status is reinforced by the acquisition of material objects and a privileged lifestyle, deference by subordinates in the organizational hierarchy, and respect from one's community. As Kenneth Lay famously remarked at the sentencing trial at the end of the Enron scandal, "It's the type of lifestyle that's difficult to turn off like a spigot" (Flood, 2006). If college students can be easily manipulated by a brief experience of power to feel entitled to special privileges, see themselves as above the law, and ignore other people's rights and objectify them, how strong might be the effects of the kind of power provided to individuals at the highest levels of organizational status?

Field research has produced results consistent with the idea that these effects are pervasive and operate in the real world of organizations, although it is important to note that this research does not include the kinds of design controls needed to infer causality. It is also important to note that this research does not indicate that all executives are bad people. Nonetheless, the pattern of naturally occurring trends distinguishing executives from lower-level managers suggests that, as a population, many senior managers in organizations do resemble to some degree the subjects who experienced the corrupting influence of power in Galinsky's experiments. For example, De Meuse, Dai, and Wu (2011) compared competency ratings between 431 middle managers and 241 executives from a variety of corporations. The executives were rated higher on competencies having to do with business strategy and financial acumen, but were rated *lower* on competencies concerning relationships and people skills. In particular, the executives were rated lower on the competency, *Integrity and Trust.* In a study of critical incidents of destructive leadership behavior reported by subordinates, Rasch, Shen, Davies, and Bono (2008) found that out of the nine categories of bad behavior they identified, the one that had the most toxic impact on staff morale was "Failure to consider human needs." More to the point, the frequency of this behavior increased with organizational level; the more senior the manager, the more likely the neglect of the needs and rights of other people.

Future Research Directions

Our review of existing research on destructive leadership revealed that, although some is known about this phenomenon, our empirically based knowledge is both incomplete and fragmented. Below, we highlight several areas where further research or conceptual development would be particularly valuable for advancing the state of our knowledge in this area.

Mapping the Nomological Net for Destructive Leadership

As noted above, researchers and theorists have addressed many different facets of destructive leadership (e.g., abusive supervision, petty tyranny, unethical leadership, etc.), but we are aware of no single study that has simultaneously examined multiple facets in an effort to determine their relations with each other. Although we believe that definitions proposed here by us and others have adequately positioned destructive leadership relative to other forms of leadership and counterproductive work behavior, we still need further empirical work to position the elements *within* the destructive leadership domain relative to each other. Such work would go far toward standardizing terminology and eventually producing an integrated framework that could reduce redundancy and highlight unaddressed areas.

Multidimensional Measurement

Related to the point above, this area of inquiry would benefit from the availability of a more comprehensive measurement tool that encompasses most or all of the identified facets of destructive leadership. By virtue of including any facet of destructive leadership in which a researcher might be interested, more researchers would be encouraged to use the same measure, thus facilitating future meta-analyses and integrative frameworks.

Person X Situation Interactions

As we have seen here, research has tended to focus on person factors or situational factors, with interactions among these rarely being examined. In other domains of inquiry into human behavior, it has been well established that person factors and situational factors interact to determine behavior, so it seems reasonable to suspect that similar conclusions would be reached with regard to destructive leadership, were the appropriate research to be conducted. A useful early step along these lines might be to develop a taxonomy of situations, based on factors identified as relevant to destructive leadership, which would provide a consistent metric for classifying situations across studies and facilitate an integrated approach to research on interactions with person factors.

Longitudinal Research

As noted earlier, there is reason to believe that destructive behavior develops over time, but little or no research has examined the process by which this occurs. Although admittedly unwieldy and potentially expensive, longitudinal designs could shed light on how environmental and personal factors influence destructive leadership behaviors, both before and after their initial conduct. For example, does the frequency of destructive behavior tend to increase, decrease, or stay constant over time? Do different individuals exhibit different trajectories of destructive behavior, depending on the combinations of person and situation factors present?

Group-Level Outcomes

Very little research has specifically addressed the consequences of destructive leadership at the group or organization level, especially as related to objective performance criteria. Research relating destructive leader behaviors to distal, objective outcomes would help to map the channels through which destructive effects propagate, and may eventually suggest means by which those effects could be interrupted, even after they are set in motion.

Evaluation of Interventions

More business schools have begun including ethics training in their curricula in recent years, and ethics training is becoming more common in organizations as well. Additionally, the prevalence of corporate values statements and ethics officers in organizations appears to be on the rise. Research evaluating the effectiveness of these various interventions could provide valuable information about what works and what does not, so as to facilitate the development of progressively more effective interventions.

Minimizing the Effects of Destructive Leadership

Stakeholders in organizations are understandably concerned with the practical question of how to minimize the effects due to destructive leadership, whether by reducing the likelihood of destructive leadership occurring in the first place, minimizing the time that elapses before destructive behaviors are detected and addressed, or by methods of "damage control" that can be applied after the fact. Unfortunately, evidence from direct evaluations of specific strategies is virtually nonexistent. But some recommendations can be extrapolated from other relevant research and from theory.

Prevention

Selection. Perhaps the most straightforward way for an organization to avoid having to cope with a destructive leader is to avoid placing destructive individuals into leadership roles in the first place, though this is almost certainly more easily said than done. Part of the challenge is that the qualities that make one appealing as a candidate for a leadership position may not necessarily make for constructive leadership. As Napoleon Bonaparte is said to have observed, to get power one needs to display absolute pettiness but to exercise power one needs character. A recent paper reporting three experiments comparing what qualities people say they prefer in a leader to the qualities of the individuals they selected for leadership roles lends credence to Napoleon's observation: most subjects chose leaders who were dominant (rather than generous) and who valued their own power over the well-being of the group (Halevy, Chou, Cohen, & Livingston, in press).

One underutilized technique for identifying the potential for destructive leadership among candidates in a leadership selection process is the assessment of dark side personality factors. Historically, personality assessments have not been commonly used in executive selection (Sessa, Kaiser, Taylor, & Campbell, 1998), and when they are used, they usually involve tests focused on the "bright side," neglecting the "dark side" factors discussed above and described in Table 13.1. However, dark side assessments are designed to identify counterproductive personality traits that may appear desirable at first, making them well-suited for candidate screening and evaluation (Hogan & Hogan, 2001; Hogan & Kaiser, 2005).

Beyond formal testing and assessment, it is also advisable to evaluate relevant samples of behavior among leadership candidates. In considering the facets of destructive leadership that were discussed above, two related themes emerge that might serve as red flags signaling the potential for destructive behavior: selfish entitlement and inadequate self-regulation.

Selfish entitlement refers to a consistent history of putting one's own self-interest before those of other legitimate stakeholders. In individual contributor roles, a sense of selfish entitlement might manifest as an unwillingness to share credit for success with others or even instances of attempting to take credit where it is undeserved. Selfishly entitled individuals might exhibit an inappropriate sense of personal ownership of organizational resources or other property that does not belong to them, and they may show a blatant disregard for rules, policies, or even the law. The entitled individual's credo is "rules are for everyone else." For example, Gustafson and Ritzer (1995) found that aberrant self-promoters received significantly more parking tickets than their less destructive counterparts.

Inadequate self-regulation refers to a consistent pattern of failing to maintain composure or keep emotions in check. Coworkers might have noticed that an individual reacts violently to criticism or other frustrations, that he frequently says things without thinking and that he ends up apologizing for later (or should have apologized for), or demonstrates unusual tendencies to hold grudges against others. A consistent tendency to write off or declare as an enemy forever anyone who frustrates the individual in some trivial way could be a sign of inadequate self-regulation, by suggesting that the individual is unable to make rational judgments about the severity of the perceived insult or the value of maintaining relationships, or unable to direct his attention away from the source of his frustration.

Organizational decision makers may be able to detect these warning signs before hiring or promoting potentially destructive individuals. References from previous employers and coworkers, and criminal background checks may be useful for uncovering information about external hires. In promotion and succession settings, confidential conversations with current coworkers and, if available, 360-degree ratings from personnel files may be useful. The recommendation to consult such sources during the selection process is certainly nothing new, but if avoiding destructive leadership is a concern, the key is to actively seek out—and not ignore—warning signs related to selfish entitlement and inadequate self-regulation.

Deterrence. As the discussion of situation factors above indicated, destructive behavior often results from an interaction of person characteristics and features of the situation. Some individuals may be inclined to behave destructively regardless of the situation, but others with the potential for counterproductive behavior may never actualize it if the situation can be maintained as nonconducive. Extrapolating from the themes discussed earlier, key aspects of the organizational environment that should be attended to include transparency, accountability, and climate. Organizations that are characterized by these features may not only deter destructive behavior from incumbents, but they may also appear less attractive to external bad actors who are considering joining the organization.

Transparency refers to established norms for open communication. In a high-transparency organization, information is shared freely, and group members generally know what their coworkers are doing—there are few, if any, secrets. Destructive behavior often begins with clandestine acts, such as bad-mouthing coworkers behind their backs or seeking special privileges that not everyone has. For example, Babiak (1995) found that corporate psychopaths depended on being able to disseminate conflicting misinformation to different coworkers and not be discovered because the coworkers never got together to compare notes. If there is a norm for transparency and a lack of secrets, it may be more difficult for a potentially destructive individual to get started with such a behavior pattern, because she knows that her actions will become known.

Related to transparency, *accountability* refers to the presence of limits on individual discretion. As discussed earlier, the risk of destructive leadership is likely to increase when individual power is less constrained. Accountability could include boards of directors acting as checks on CEOs' power, supervisors applying consequences to individual contributors for misdeeds, or HR departments actively investigating complaints and grievances.

Finally, a well-established norm or *climate* for ethical behavior within the organization, in combination with transparency and accountability, may deter destructive behaviors by clearly communicating what standards of behavior are expected from organization members. It can be tempting to avoid explicit talk of ethics in organizations because it is assumed that "everyone knows what is expected here." But salient signals, such as posted ethics mission statements, comments in corporate communications, and inclusion of ethics as a dimension in performance assessments can serve to reinforce the perception of an organization as one that does not tolerate unethical behavior. That perception, in turn, may help deter incumbents' unethical behavior or discourage potentially destructive individuals from seeking to enter the organization.

Detection

Transparency and accountability. As discussed above, transparency and accountability may serve to deter destructive leadership behavior from occurring in the first place. But these same two situational features are also organizations' first line of defense for detecting destructive leaders after they have a foothold. Destructive leaders do their damage over time, so the sooner a destructive behavior pattern is recognized and terminated, the less damage the organization will incur. A key challenge to detection is that, as leaders are promoted into roles of larger and larger responsibility, the number of individuals in the organization with the formal power to check their behavior naturally decreases. This requires organizational watchdogs at the top of the hierarchy, such as boards of directors, to be particularly vigilant regarding the behavior of top leadership. A clear risk factor for destructive leadership is the population of the board (or other governing body) by members who have personal relationships with top executives or who have business relationships with them that lie outside the focal organization. To minimize potential damage from destructive leaders, organizations should maintain clarity regarding exactly whom each leader is accountable to, and systematically analyze potential threats to that system of accountabilities. Top leaders are likely to resist being held strictly accountable in this way, but a firmly established ethical climate can help reduce such resistance.

Whistle-blowing. Even with accountability watchdogs in place, transparency is still required to ensure they receive the information necessary to act. In addition to the usual systems of organizational results reporting, a climate and infrastructure that supports whistle-blowing can also be valuable. Systems that allow organization members to provide anonymous tips, such as telephone hotlines or dedicated e-mail systems, can make it more likely that destructive behavior will come to the attention of watchdogs quickly. Further, a climate that values whistle-blowing, rather than stigmatizing it, and written policies offering protections to informants can increase the likelihood that whistle-blowing infrastructures will be utilized when needed.

Mitigation

By the time a pattern of destructive behavior by a leader has been detected, it is likely that the organization has already sustained some degree of damage, some of which may be readily quantifiable and some not. Because of the many forms that destructive leadership may take, the different types of stakeholders potentially affected, and because some types of damage may take months or years to fully surface, specific recommendations for mitigating damage to the organization and other stakeholders are difficult to offer. However, we offer a general process framework that may serve as a useful guide to organizations grappling with the aftermath of this phenomenon. Broadly, we recommend that organizations seeking to mitigate damages caused by a destructive leader should systematically form an investigation team, assess the damage across multiple domains, develop an action plan, and execute that plan.

Forming a team. The key idea behind forming an investigation team is that dealing with the aftermath of a destructive leader is unlikely to fall within anyone's normal job description, so doing this well means creating a new entity dedicated to this purpose. Further, the damage and corresponding steps needed are likely to span multiple domains of expertise, such that no single individual is likely to be able to execute the entire project. The specific position held by the destructive leader and the exact nature of the misdeeds will determine what expertise is needed on the team. But functions likely needing to be represented include accounting, public relations/marketing, regulatory compliance, human resources, and legal counsel. The last two are particularly important; representation of both legal counsel and human resources is likely to be needed on the team regardless of the specifics of the situation. This is because, even if no external stakeholders are involved, these two constituencies will be needed to advise on how to deal with the destructive leader him- or herself. Options could include termination, civil lawsuits, or criminal charges, all of which are relevant to the legal and human resources functions.

Damage and threat assessment. Once the team is assembled, it should construct a plan for investigating the incidents suspected to have occurred, which should include assignment of team members to roles, specification of deliverables, and timelines. Broadly, the objectives of the investigation should be to (1) ascertain what events occurred, (2) determine what harm has already occurred, and (3) identify threats of future harm that may yet occur or be discovered. An important element of this process will be to document the various domains in which harm has occurred or is likely to occur. For example, the organization may have suffered immediate financial losses, damage to physical resources such as equipment or property, damage to its reputation, harm to specific organization members; and be exposed to civil, regulatory, or even criminal liability. For each domain affected, the team should document what occurred and what the likely costs are, including trajectories for those costs over time.

Action plan. After assessing the situation, the expertise of the team members should be leveraged to develop a list of recommendations to be presented to the organization's leadership. The specific actions recommended will depend on the nature of the harm done in each domain. As with the damage assessment plan, the damage control action plan should include assignment of individuals to roles, specific deliverables, and timelines for accomplishing tasks. Additionally, the plan should identify one or more individuals who will have accountability for ensuring the plan is executed. After an appropriate period of time since the plan's implementation, it may be desirable to revisit the original damage assessments—particularly for those damages that were expected to occur over time—to determine whether any revisions are called for. After the forecast time frames for damages have elapsed, it may be useful to compile an overall assessment of the total costs incurred due to the destructive leader. Aside from the obvious accounting utility, such an assessment can serve as a useful reinforcer of the importance—and relative cost effectiveness—of preventing destructive leadership rather than attempting to mitigate its effects after the fact.

Conclusion

In this chapter we have refined an integrative definition of destructive leadership that establishes it as a form of counterproductive work behavior and as a high-level category encompassing multiple narrower facets. We have reviewed extant research on specific types of destructive leadership, considered what is known about each in terms of consequences for organization-level outcomes, highlighted gaps in our current knowledge, and provided suggestions for future avenues of research. We have also offered practical recommendations for dealing with destructive leadership in organizations. Leadership positions will continue to afford power to their occupants, and humans can be expected to continue to be motivated by self-interest, so the threat of destructive leadership will always be with us. But we are hopeful that a commitment to continuing the advance of our knowledge of this phenomenon can help to identify, design, and apply methods that reduce the frequency and severity of the damage caused by destructive leadership.

References

Aasland, M. S., Skogstad, A., Notelaers, G., Nielsen, M. B., & Einarsen, S. (2010). The prevalence of destructive leadership behavior. *British Journal of Management, 21,* 438–452.

Antonakis, J., Avolio, B. J., & Sivasubramaniam, N. (2003). Context and leadership: An examination of the nine-factor full-range leadership theory using the Multifactor Leadership Questionnaire. *The Leadership Quarterly, 14,* 261–295.

Aquino, K., Grover, S. L., Bradfield, M., & Allen, D. G. (1999). The effects of negative affectivity, hierarchical status, and self-determination on workplace victimization. *Academy of Management Journal, 42,* 260–272.

Arredondo, F. (2004). *La integridad del líder de empresa y su relación con el liderazgo.* Unpublished doctoral dissertation, Tecnológico de Monterrey.

Aryee, S., Chen, Z. X., Sun, L., & Debrah, Y. A. (2007). Antecedents and outcomes of abusive supervision: Test of a trickle-down model. *Journal of Applied Psychology, 92,* 191–201.

Ashforth, B. (1994). Petty tyranny in organizations. *Human Relations, 47,* 755–778.

Ashforth, B. E., & Anand, V. (2003). The normalization of corruption in organizations. *Research in Organizational Behavior, 25,* 1–52.

Baker, R., & Craig, S.B. (2006). When actions speak louder than words: The relative importance of leader behaviors in predicting global impressions of integrity. In M. Hargis (chair), *Leadership, It's All Relative: Applying Relative Importance Statistics to Leadership.* Symposium presented at the annual conference of the Academy of Management in Atlanta, Georgia.

Babiak, P. (1995). When psychopaths go to work: A case study of an industrial psychopath. *Applied Psychology: An International Review, 44,* 171–188.

Baldwin, M. W. (1992). Relational schemas and the processing of social information. *Psychological Bulletin, 112,* 461–484.

Bamberger, P. A., & Bacharach, S. B. (2006). Abusive supervision and subordinate problem drinking: Taking resistance, stress, and subordinate personality into account. *Human Relations, 59,* 1–30.

Bass, B. M. (1985). *Leadership and performance beyond expectations.* New York: Free Press.

Bass, B. M., & Steidlmeier, P. (1999). Ethics, character, and authentic transformational leadership behavior. *The Leadership Quarterly, 10,* 181–217.

Baumeister, R., Bratslavsky, E., Finkenauer, C., & Vohs, K. (2001). Bad is stronger than good. *Review of General Psychology, 5,* 323–370.

Baumeister, R. F., & Scher, S. J. (1988). Self-defeating behavior patterns among normal individuals. *Psychological Bulletin, 104,* 3–22.

Bogart, L. M., Benotsch, E. G., & Pavlovic, J. D. (2004). Feeling superior but not threatened: The relation of narcissism to social comparison. *Basic and Applied Social Psychology, 26,* 35–44.

Borman, W. C., & Brush, D. H. (1993). More progress toward a taxonomy of managerial performance requirements. *Human Performance, 6,* 1–21.

Brown, M. E., & Treviño, L. K. (2006a). Ethical leadership: A review and future directions. *Leadership Quarterly, 17,* 595–616.

Brown, M. E., & Treviño, L. K. (2006b). Socialized charismatic leadership, values congruence, and deviance in work groups. *Journal of Applied Psychology, 91,* 954–962.

Burns, J. M. (1978). *Leadership.* New York: Harper & Row.

Burns, J. (2003). *Transformational leadership.* New York: Atlantic Monthly Press.

Cell, C. (1974). Charismatic heads of state: The social context. *Behavior Science Research, 9*, 255–305.
Chatterjee, A., & Hambrick, D. (2007). It's all about me: Narcissistic chief executive officers and their effects on company strategy and performance. *Administrative Science Quarterly, 52*, 351–386.
Ciulla, J. (2004). Ethics and leadership effectiveness. In J. Antonakis, A. T. Cianciolo, & R. J. Sternberg (Eds), *The nature of leadership* (pp. 302–327). Thousand Oaks, CA: Sage.
Cohen, F., Solomon, S., Maxfield, M., Pyszczynski, T., & Greenberg, J. (2004). Fatal attraction: The effects of mortality salience on evaluations of charismatic, task-oriented, and relationship-oriented leaders. *Psychological Science, 15*, 846–851.
Conger, J. (1990). The dark side of leadership. *Organizational Dynamics, 19*, 44–55.
Conger, J. A., & Kanungo, R. (1987). Toward a behavioral theory of charismatic leadership in organizational settings. *Academy of Management Review, 12*, 637–647.
Craig, S. B. (1995). Perceptions of leader integrity: A psychological climate dimension with implications for subordinate job satisfaction. Unpublished master's thesis, Virginia Polytechnic Institute and State University.
Craig, S. B., & Gustafson, S. B. (1998). Perceived leader integrity scale: An instrument for assessing employee perceptions of leader integrity. *The Leadership Quarterly, 9*, 127–145.
Craig, S. B., & Kaiser, R. B. (2013). Destructive leadership. In M. Rumsey (Ed.), *Oxford handbook of leadership* (pp. 439–454). New York: Oxford University Press.
Dansereau, F., Graen, G. B., & Haga, W. (1975). A vertical dyad linkage approach to leadership in formal organizations. *Organizational Behavior and Human Performance, 13*, 46–78.
De Meuse, K. P., Dai, G., & Wu, J. (2011). Leadership skills across organizational levels: A closer examination. *The Psychologist-Manager Journal, 14*, 120–139.
Dubin, R. (1979). Metaphors of leadership. In J. G. Hunt & L. L. Larson (Eds.), *Crosscurrents in leadership* (pp. 225–238). Carbondale: Southern Illinois University Press.
Duffy, M. K., Ganster, D., & Pagon, M. (2002). Social undermining in the workplace. *Academy of Management Journal, 45*, 331–351.
Einarsen, S., Aasland, M. S., & Skogstad, A. (2007). Destructive leadership behaviour: A definition and conceptual model. *The Leadership Quarterly, 18*, 207–216.
Einarsen, S., Skogstad, A., & Aasland, M. S. (2010). The nature, prevalence, and outcomes of destructive leadership: A behavioral and conglomerate approach. In B. Schyns and T. Hansbrough (Eds.), *When leadership goes wrong: Destructive leadership, mistakes, and ethical failure* (pp. 145–171). Charlotte, NC: Information Age.
Finkelstein, S., & Hambrick, D. C. (1990). Top-management-team tenure and organizational outcomes: The moderating role of managerial discretion. *Administrative Science Quarterly, 35*, 484–503.
Fleishman, E. A. (1953). The description of supervisory behavior. *Personnel Psychology, 37*, 1–6.
Fleishman, E. A., Mumford, M. D., Zaccaro, S. J., Levin, K. Y., Korotkin, A. L., & Hein, M. B. (1991). Taxonomic efforts in the description of leader behavior: A synthesis and functional interpretation. *The Leadership Quarterly, 2*, 245–287.
Fleming, P., & Zyglidopoulos, S. C. (2008). The escalation of deception in organizations. *Journal of Business Ethics, 81*, 837–850.
Flood, M. (2006). Lay defends lavish lifestyle, cash withdrawals. Retrieved on August 17, 2011 from http://www.chron.com/business/enron/article/Lay-defends-lavish-lifestyle-cash-withdrawals-1897799.php
Galinsky, A. D., Magee, J. C., Inesi, M. E., & Gruenfeld, D. H. (2006). Power and perspective not taken. *Psychological Science, 17*, 1068–1074.
Grandey, A. A., & Kern, J. (2004). Biting the hand that serves them: When does customer aggression predict employee exhaustion? Unpublished manuscript, Penn State University, University Park.
Gruenfeld, D. H., Inesi, M. E., Magee, J. C., & Galinksi, A. D. (2008). Power and the objectification of social targets. *Journal of Personality and Social Psychology, 95*, 111–127.
Gustafson, S. B., & Ritzer, D. R. (1995). The dark side of normal: A psychopathy-linked pattern called aberrant self-promotion. *European Journal of Personality, 9*, 147–183.
Halevy, N., Chou, E. Y., Cohen, T. R., & Livingston, R. W. (2012). Status conferral in intergroup social dilemmas: Behavioral antecedents and consequences of prestige and dominance. *Journal of Personality and Social Psychology, 102*, 351–366.
Hambrick, D., & Abrahamson, C. (1995). Assessing the amount of managerial discretion in different industries: A multi-method approach. *Academy of Management Journal, 38*, 1427–1441.
Hambrick, D. C., & Finkelstein, S. (1987). Managerial discretion: A bridge between polar views of organizations. *Research in Organizational Behavior, 9*, 369–406.
Harms, P. D., Spain, S. M., & Hannah, S. (2011). Leader development and the dark side of personality. *Leadership Quarterly, 22*, 495–509.
Harris, K. J., Kacmar, K. M., & Zivnuska, S. (2007). An investigation of abusive supervision as a predictor of performance and the meaning of work as a moderator of the relationship. *The Leadership Quarterly, 18*, 252–263.
Hayward, M., & Hambrick, D. C. (1997). Explaining the premiums paid for large acquisitions: Evidence of CEO hubris. *Administrative Science Quarterly, 42*, 103–127.
Hinkin, T. R., & Schriesheim, C. A. (2008). An examination of nonleadership: From laissez- faire leadership to leader reward omission and punishment omission. *Journal of Applied Psychology, 93*, 1234–1248.
Ho, C., Shih, S., & Craig, S. B. (2011). *A Chinese version of the Perceived Integrity Leadership Scale.* Unpublished manuscript.
Hofstede, G. (1991) *Cultures and organizations: Software of the mind.* New York: McGraw-Hill.
Hogan, J., Hogan, R., & Kaiser, R. B. (2010). Management derailment: Personality assessment and mitigation. In S. Zedeck (Ed.), *American Psychological Association handbook of industrial and organizational psychology* (vol. 3, pp. 555–575). Washington, DC: American Psychological Association.
Hogan, R., Curphy, G. J., & Hogan, J. (1994). What we know about leadership: Effectiveness and personality. *American Psychologist, 49*, 493–504.
Hogan, R., & Fico, J. (2011). Leadership. In W. K. Campbell & J. D. Miller (Eds.), *The handbook of narcissism and narcissistic personality disorder: Theoretical approaches, empirical findings, and treatments* (pp. 393–402). New York: Wiley.
Hogan, R., & Hogan, J. (2001). Assessing leadership: A view from the dark side. *International Journal of Selection and Assessment, 9*, 40–51.

Hogan, R., & Hogan, J. (2009). *Hogan Development Survey manual* (2nd ed.). Tulsa, OK: Hogan Assessment Systems.

Hogan, R., & Kaiser, R. (2005). What we know about leadership. *Review of General Psychology, 9*, 169–180.

Hogan, R., Raskin, R., & Fazzini, D. (1990). The dark side of charisma. In K. Clark & M. Clark (Eds.), *Measures of leadership* (pp. 343–354). West Orange, NJ: Leadership Library of America.

Hoobler, J., & Brass, D. (2006). Abusive supervision and family undermining as displaced aggression. *Journal of Applied Psychology, 91*, 1125–1133.

Hornstein, H. A. (1996). *Brutal bosses and their prey.* New York: Riverhead Books.

House, R. J. (1977). A 1976 theory of charismatic leadership. In J. G. Hunt & L. L. Larson (Eds.), *Leadership: The cutting edge* (pp. 189–207). Carbondale: Southern Illinois University Press.

House, R. J. (1996). Path-goal theory of leadership: Lessons, legacy, and a reformulated theory. *The Leadership Quarterly, 7*, 323–352.

House, R., & Aditya, R. (1997). The social scientific study of leadership: Quo Vadis? *Journal of Management, 23*, 409–473.

House, R. J., & Howell, J. M. (1992). Personality and charismatic leadership. *The Leadership Quarterly, 3*, 81–108.

House, R. J., Spangler, W. D., & Woycke, J. (1991). Personality and charisma in the U.S. presidency: A psychological theory of leader effectiveness. *Administrative Science Quarterly, 36*, 364–396.

Howell, J. M., & Avolio, B. J. (1992). The ethics of charismatic leadership: Submission or liberation? *Academy of Management Executive, 6*, 43–54.

Inness, M., Barling, J., & Turner, N. (2005). Understanding supervisor-targeted aggression: A within-person, between-jobs design. *Journal of Applied Psychology, 90*, 731–739.

Janis, I., & Mann, L. (1977). *Decision making: A psychological analysis of conflict, choice, and commitment.* New York: Free University Press.

Johnson, J., & Orange, M. (2003). *The man who tried to buy the world: Jean-Marie Messier and Vivendi Universal.* New York: Portfolio.

Judge, T. A., Bono, J. E., Ilies, R., & Gerhardt, M. W. (2002). Personality and leadership: A qualitative and quantitative review. *Journal of Applied Psychology, 87*, 765–780.

Judge, T. A., & Piccolo, R. F. (2004). Transformational and transactional leadership: A meta-analytic test of their relative validity. *Journal of Applied Psychology, 89*, 755–768.

Judge, T. A., Piccolo, R. F., & Kosalka, T. (2009). The bright and dark sides of leader traits: A review and theoretical extension of the leader trait paradigm. *Leadership Quarterly, 20*, 855–875.

Kaiser, R. B. (2010, April). *Right or responsibility? The costs of real leadership.* Presented at the 25th Annual Conference of the Society for Industrial and Organizational Psychology, Atlanta, GA.

Kaiser, R. B., & Hogan, R. (2007). The dark side of discretion. In R. Hooijberg, J. Hunt, J. Antonakis, & K. Boal (Eds.), *Being there even when you are not: Leading through strategy, systems and structures* (pp. 177–197). London: Elsevier Science.

Kaiser, R. B., & Hogan, R. (2010). How to (and how not to) assess the integrity of managers. *Consulting Psychology Journal: Practice and Research, 62*, 216–234.

Kaiser, R. B., Hogan, R. T., & Craig, S. B. (2008). Leadership and the fate of organizations. *American Psychologist, 63*, 96–110.

Kaiser, R. B., & Overfield, D. V. (2010). The leadership value chain. *The Psychologist-Manager Journal, 13*, 164–183.

Katz, D., Maccoby, N., & Morse, N. (1950). *Productivity, supervision, and morale in an office situation.* Ann Arbor, MI: Institute for Social Research.

Kaufman, H. (2007). The dangers of the liquidity boom. *Financial Times.* Retrieved from http://www.ft.com/intl/cms/s/0/d256d17c-3ea8-11dc-bfcf-0000779fd2ac.html#axzz1MpN9v4gr

Kellerman, B. (2004). *Bad leadership: What it is, how it happens, why it matters.* Boston: Harvard Business School Press.

Kelloway, E. K., Mullen, J., & Francis, L. (2006) Divergent effects of transformational and passive leadership on employee safety. *Journal of Occupational Health Psychology, 11*, 76–86.

Kets de Vries, M.F.R., & Miller, D. (1985). Narcissism and leadership: An object relations perspective. *Human Relations, 38*, 583–601.

Kihlstrom, J. F., & Klein, S. B. (1994). The self as a knowledge structure. In R. S. Wyer Jr. & T. K. Strull (Eds.), *Handbook of social cognition* (pp. 153–208). Hillsdale, NJ: Lawrence Erlbaum Associates.

Kipnis, D. (1972). Does power corrupt? *Journal of Personality and Social Psychology, 24*, 33–41.

Kish-Gephart, J. J., Harrison, D. A., & Treviño, L. K. (2010). Bad apples, bad cases, and bad barrels: Meta-analytic evidence about sources of unethical decisions at work. *Journal of Applied Psychology, 95*, 1–31.

Lammers, J., Stapel, D. A., & Galinsky, A. D. (2010). Power increases hypocrisy: Moralizing in reasoning, immorality in behavior. *Psychological Science, 21*, 737–744.

Landau, M. J., Solomon, S., Arndt, J., Greenberg, J., Pyszczynski, T., Miller, C., . . . Cook, A. (2004). Deliver us from evil: The effects of mortality salience and reminders of 9/11 on support for President George W. Bush. *Personality and Social Psychology Bulletin, 30*, 1136–1150.

Liden, R. C. (2010). Preface. In B. Schyns and Hansbrough (Eds.), *When leadership goes wrong* (pp. ix–xii). Charlotte, NC: Information Age Publishing.

Lin, X., Che, H., & Leung, K. (2009). The role of leader morality in the interaction effect of procedural justice and outcome favorability. *Journal of Applied Social Psychology, 39*, 1536–1561.

Lipman-Blumen, J. (2005). *The allure of toxic leaders: Why we follow destructive bosses and corrupt politicians—and how we can survive them.* Oxford: Oxford University Press.

Lord, R., Foti, R. J., & De Vader, C. L. (1984). A test of leadership categorization theory. *Organizational Behavior and Human Performance, 34*, 343–378.

Lowe, K. B., Kroeck, K. G., & Sivasubramaniam, N. (1996). Effectiveness correlates of transformational and transactional leadership: A meta-analytic review of the MLQ literature. *The Leadership Quarterly, 7*, 385–425.

Luthans, F., Peterson, S. J., & Ibrayeva, E. (1998). The potential for the "dark side" of leadership in post-communist countries. *Journal of World Business, 33*, 185–201.

Maccoby, M. (2007). *Narcissistic leaders: Who succeeds and who fails.* Boston: Harvard Business School Press.

Mahsud, R., Yukl, G., & Prussia, G. (2010). Leader empathy, ethical leadership, and relations-oriented behaviors as

antecedents of leader-member exchange quality. *Journal of Managerial Psychology, 25*, 561–577.
Malmendier, U., & Tate, G. (2005). CEO overconfidence and corporate investment. *Journal of Finance, 60*, 2661–2700.
McCall, M. W. Jr., & Lombardo, M. M. (1983). *Off the track: Why and how successful executives get derailed.* Technical Report No. 21. Greensboro, NC: Center for Creative Leadership.
McClelland, D. C. (1970). The two faces of power. *Journal of International Affairs, 24*, 29–47.
McClelland, D. C. (1975). *Power: The inner experience.* New York: Irvington.
McGrath, J. E. (1962). *Leadership behavior: Some requirements for leadership training.* Washington, DC: U.S. Civil Service Commission.
McLean, B., & Elkind, P. (2005). *The smartest guys in the room.* New York: Penguin.
Messier, J. (2000). *J6M.COM: Faut-il avoir peur de la nouvelle économie?* Paris: Hachette.
Mitchell, M. S., & Ambrose, M. L. (2007). Abusive supervision and workplace deviance and the moderating effects of negative reciprocity beliefs. *Journal of Applied Psychology, 92*, 1159–1168.
Moscoso, S., & Salgado, J. F. (2004). "Dark side" personality styles as predictors of task, contextual, and job performance. *International Journal of Selection and Assessment, 12*, 356–362.
Mulvey, P. W., & Padilla, A. (2010) The environment of destructive leadership. In B. Schyns, & T. Hansbrough (Eds.), *When leadership goes wrong: Destructive leadership, mistakes, and ethical failures* (pp. 49–71). Greenwich, CT: Information Age Publishing.
Nocera, J. (2005, June 18). In business, tough guys finish last. New York Times. Retrieved August 17, 2011, from http://www.nytimes.com/2005/06/18/business/18nocera.html?pagewanted=1
O'Connor, J., Mumford, M., Clifton, T., Gessner, T., & Connelly, M. (1995). Charismatic leaders and destructiveness: An historiometric study. *The Leadership Quarterly, 6*, 529–555.
Padilla, A., Hogan, R., & Kaiser, R. B. (2007). The toxic triangle: Destructive leaders, vulnerable followers, and conducive environments. *The Leadership Quarterly, 18*, 176–194.
Parry, K. W., & Proctor-Thomson, S. B. (2002). Perceived integrity of transformational leaders in organizational settings. *Journal of Business Ethics, 35*, 75–96.
Pearce, C. L., Sims, H. P., Cox, J. F., Ball, G., Schnell, E., Smith, K. A., & Trevino, L. (2003). Transactors, transformers and beyond: A multi-method development of a theoretical typology of leadership. *Journal of Management Development, 22*, 273–307.
Rasch, R., Shen, W., Davies, S. E., & Bono, J. (2008, April). *The development of a taxonomy of ineffective leadership behaviors.* Paper presented at the 23rd Annual Conference of the Society for Industrial and Organizational Psychology, San Francisco, CA.
Raskin, R. N., & Hall, C. S. (1979). A narcissistic personality inventory. *Psychological Reports, 45*, 590.
Robinson, S. L., & Bennett, R. J. (1995). A typology of deviant workplace behaviors: A multidimensional scaling study. *Academy of Management Journal, 38*, 555–572.
Rosenthal, S. A., & Pittinsky, T. L. (2006). Narcissistic leadership. *Leadership Quarterly, 17*, 617–633.
Rummel, R. J. (1994). *Death by government.* New Brunswick, NJ: Transaction Publishers.
Sackett, P. R., & DeVore, C. J. (2002). Counterproductive behaviors at work. In N. Anderson et al. (Eds.), *Handbook of industrial, work, & organizational psychology, Volume 1: Personnel Psychology.* Thousand Oaks, CA: Sage.
Sankowsky, D. (1995). The charismatic leader as a narcissist: Understanding the abuse of power. *Organizational Dynamics, 23*, 57–71.
Schmidt, A. A. (2008). *Development and validation of the toxic leadership scale.* Unpublished master's thesis, University of Maryland at College Park.
Schmit, M. J., Kilm, J. A., & Robie, C. A. (2000). Development of a global measure of personality. *Personnel Psychology, 53*, 153–193.
Sessa, V. I., Kaiser, R. B., Taylor, J. K., & Campbell, R. J. (1998). *Executive selection: A research report on what works and what doesn't.* Greensboro, NC: Center for Creative Leadership.
Skogstad, A., Einarsen, S., Torsheim, T., Aasland, M. S., & Hetland, H. (2007). The destructiveness of laissez-faire leadership behavior. *Journal of Occupational Health Psychology, 12*, 80–92.
Spector, P. E., & Fox, S. (2002). An emotion-centered model of voluntary work behavior: Some parallels between counterproductive work behavior and organizational citizenship behavior. *Human Resource Management Review, 12*, 269–292.
Tepper, B. J. (2000). Consequences of abusive supervision. *Academy of Management Journal, 43*, 178–190.
Tepper, B. J. (2007). Abusive supervision in work organizations: Review, synthesis, and research agenda. *Journal of Management, 33*, 261–289.
Tepper, B. J., Duffy, M. K., Henle, C. A., & Lambert, L. S. (2006). Procedural injustice, victim precipitation, and abusive supervision. *Personnel Psychology, 59*, 101–123.
Tepper, B. J., Duffy, M. K., Hoobler, J. M., & Ensley, M. D. (2004). Moderators of the relationship between coworkers' organizational citizenship behavior and fellow employees' attitudes. *Journal of Applied Psychology, 89*, 455–465.
Tepper, B. J., Duffy, M. K., & Shaw, J. D. (2001). Personality moderators of the relationships between abusive supervision and subordinates' resistance. *Journal of Applied Psychology, 86*, 974–983.
Tett, G. (2009). *Fool's gold.* New York: Simon and Schuster.
Tierney, P., & Tepper, B. J. (Eds.). (2007). *The Leadership Quarterly, 18*, 171–292. [special issue: Destructive Leadership]
Turner, N., Barling, J., Epitropaki, O., Butcher, V., & Milner, C. (2002). Transformational leadership and moral reasoning. *Journal of Applied Psychology, 87*, 304–311.
Van Vugt, M., Hogan, R., & Kaiser, R. B. (2008). Leadership, followership, and evolution: Some lessons from the past. *American Psychologist, 63*, 182–196.
Wilson. D. S., & Wilson, E. O. (2007). Rethinking the theoretical foundation of sociobiology. *Quarterly Review of Biology, 82*, 327–348.
Wu, J. & LeBreton, J. M. (2011). Reconsidering the dispositional basis of counterproductive work behavior: The role of aberrant personality. *Personnel Psychology, 64*, 593–626.
Young, J. E., Klosko, J. S., & Weishaar, M. E. (2003). *Schema therapy.* New York: Guilford.

Yukl, G. A. (2005). *Leadership in organizations* (6th ed.). Englewood Cliffs, NJ: Prentice Hall.

Zaccaro, S. J. (2007). Trait- based perspectives of leadership. *American Psychologist, 62*, 6–16.

Zaccaro, S. J., & Horn, Z. N. J. (2003). Leadership theory and practice: Fostering an effective symbiosis. *Leadership Quarterly, 14*, 769–806.

Zellars, K. L., Tepper, B. J., & Duffy, M. K. (2002). Abusive supervision and subordinates' organizational citizenship behavior. *Journal of Applied Psychology, 86*, 1068–1076.

Zimbardo, P. G. (1973). On the ethics of intervention in human psychological research: With special reference to the Stanford prison experiment. *Cognition, 2*, 243–256.

CHAPTER

14 Leadership and Identity: An Examination of Three Theories and New Research Directions

Herminia Ibarra, Sarah Wittman, Gianpiero Petriglieri, *and* David V. Day

Abstract

Identity has emerged as a potent force in understanding leadership. This chapter reviews the contributions of role identity, social identity, and social construction theories toward comprehending the emergence, effectiveness, and development of leaders. In recent years leadership scholars have combined two or more of these identity theories to conceptualize and study a range of phenomena including transitions into leadership roles, the challenges faced by women leaders, and the role of identity workspaces in leadership development. Based on the authors' review they propose areas where further research attention is needed, in particular the process by which non-prototypical leaders emerge, lead effectively, and develop; leader identities in contemporary settings characterized by globally distributed teams and multiple leadership roles; and identity evolution in the context of the life cycle of a leadership career.

Key Words: gender, identity, identity workspaces, leader identity, leader identity development, social identity

While the self as an organizing construct in the behavioral and social sciences has a long history going back to the foundational work of William James (Leary & Tangney, 2003), the notion of identity has received little attention among leadership scholars until relatively recently. As workplaces become more globalized, mobile and diverse—rendering identities more malleable and their maintenance problematic—scholars have increasingly focused on the dynamics that give leaders their standing beyond the formal position they occupy. The common definition of leadership as a social process of mutual and reciprocal influence in the service of accomplishing a collective goal (Bass, 2008; Yukl, 2010) inherently implies basic identity processes such as categorization, identification, and identity change. Accordingly, a new perspective has been emerging that more explicitly links leadership and such identity processes (e.g., Carroll & Levy, 2010; Day & Harrison, 2007; Hogg, 2001; Ibarra, Snook, & Guillen, 2010; Lord & Brown, 2004; Lord & Hall, 2005; Petriglieri G., 2011; van Knippenberg & Hogg, 2003; van Knippenberg B., van Knippenberg D., Cremer, & Hogg, 2004), pointing attention to the role that leaders' identities play in their emergence, effectiveness, and development. As leadership (and followership) is increasingly conceptualized not as a static superior–subordinate exchange but as a complex and adaptive interaction process (DeRue, 2011), ideas about identity increasingly provide the foundation for theorizing and empirical research.

Our objective in this chapter is to consolidate and extend this burgeoning line of thinking, by comparing perspectives from different theories of identity, identifying gaps in our current understanding of the relationship between identity and leadership processes, and pointing to new and promising research directions. The chapter is organized into three sections. We first provide an overview of three strains of identity theorizing that are relevant to the study of leadership—role-based, social identity, and social constructionist theories—comparing and contrasting their potency for enhancing our understanding of leadership phenomena. Next, we focus on three areas of recent empirical and theoretical attention that combine ideas drawn from several theoretical traditions: transitions into, and identification with, formal and informal leadership roles; the emergence and effectiveness of leaders from "non-prototypical" groups, in particular women in male-dominated contexts; and the role of "identity workspaces" in facilitating the identity work that underpins leaders' development. We conclude with a look to the future, charting specific areas where further attention by researchers is needed.

Identity Theories: Roles, Social Identities, and Identity Construction Processes

Identity refers to the various meanings attached to oneself by self and others (Gecas, 1982). These meanings or self-conceptions are based on the social roles and group memberships a person holds (social identities) as well as the personal and character traits they display, and others attribute to them, based on their conduct (personal identities) (Ashforth, 2001; Gecas, 1982). Both personal and social identities aid us in answering the questions "who am I?" and "who do other people know me to be?" Identities are claimed and granted in social interaction (Cooley, 1902; Goffman, 1959; DeRue & Ashford, 2010) and evolve over time with varied experiences and meaningful feedback that allow people to gain insight about their central and enduring preferences, talents, and values (Lord & Hall, 2005; Schein, 1978). Although people have many, frequently mutating identities, some are more central to a person's overall self-definition, and are more deeply embedded in his or her social life, while others are relevant only in specific contexts and situations (Ashforth & Johnson, 2001; Ebaugh, 1988; Stryker & Serpe, 1982).

Adding further complexity to this idea, Brewer and Gardner (1996) argued that identities or self-concepts range along a continuum of inclusiveness. An individual identity emphasizes the uniqueness of an individual and how he or she is different from others. A relational identity defines the self in terms of relationships with others, and a collective identity defines the self in terms of membership in and endorsement by groups or organizations. Whereas people understand themselves and others through all three kinds of identity, any single identity may incorporate meanings drawn from personal idiosyncrasies, interpersonal relations, and collective demands. Further, specific contexts trigger differentially the salience of different levels: the construction of a person's various identities implies a continuous interaction between the self and the environment—the individual may propose different selves as a result of sequential attention being paid to certain contextual cues or patterns, but it is ultimately the environment that will determine which particular selves are active (Yost & Strube, 1992).

Identities also have enduring, trans-situational components. Relevant for our purposes is the idea that a professional identity such as "leader" can combine individual, relational, and collective identities, as the relatively stable and enduring constellation of attributes, beliefs, values, motives, and experiences in terms of which people define themselves in a professional role (Schein, 1978). From this perspective, a leader identity is not simply the counterpart to a formally held leadership position but rather evolves as a person internalizes and tailors a leader identity and is recognized by others as 'leader' (DeRue & Ashford, 2010). For example, a person may hold a social role as a group head, a personal identity as someone who takes initiative and is good at getting things done through people, and social relationships that reinforce this self-conception; over time he or she may increasingly seek out roles and assignments in which there are more opportunities to lead, and these experiences will also shape his or her evolution as a leader.

Three distinct but related streams of theorizing are relevant to understanding leadership phenomena: identity theory, which focuses on the roles that individuals adopt in their personal and professional lives; social identity theory, which focuses on social categories and processes of categorization; and theories about how the self is constructed in social interaction that have focused on identity work. By examining the self though the lens of role-based identity, social identity theory, and social construction we hope to advance a more general understanding of identity processes in leadership. As reviewed in the text that follows, leaders' development, emergence and effectiveness involves the internalization of a leader identity, the integration of this identity within an individual's broader self-concept and life narrative, and its enactment, refinement, and validation in social interactions.

Identity Theory: Leadership as a Social Role

According to structural interactionists, identity theory provides a view of individuals through the roles they take on or have ascribed to them (Gecas, 1982). For example, a person may define him- or herself, or be defined, as a friend, parent, spouse, co-worker, boss, and so forth. From this perspective, *leader* would be one possible role that, once internalized, would form a part of a person's identity. Roles are the different "hats" a person wears: demarcated positions in a social structure, with different roles potentially overlapping (one's roles as spouse and parent, for example, may be active simultaneously in some situations), conflicting, or being ascribed to completely different and bounded areas of a person's life. Each is associated with socially defined expectations as to what behaviors a particular role requires (Gecas, 1982), and the degree to which a role is internalized (or committed to) will determine how influential that role is to a person's behavior (i.e., "role-person merger;" Turner, 1978).

The perspective of leader identities as social roles permits the exploration of the socialization processes and motivational factors that spur people to assume or grow into leadership roles, or, alternatively, distance themselves from them (Lord & Hall, 2005; DeRue & Ashford, 2010). People learn new roles by identifying with role models, experimenting with provisional identities, and evaluating experiments against internal standards and external feedback (Ibarra, 1999). Although most leadership scholars distinguish between leadership as a formal position and leadership as an informal role, most existing empirical and conceptual work concerns formal leadership roles (see DeRue [2011] for a recent review) and transitions into them (Hill, 1992; Ibarra, 1999), processes in which shifts in identity are clearly linked to changes in the position the individual occupies in the social structure, and concomitant changes in the expectations of, and exchanges with, those with whom the person interacts in performing the new role.

Proponents of viewing leader development through the lens of role-based identity argue that acquiring leadership skills, much as other forms of expertise, is done through deliberate practice (i.e., Day & Harrison, 2007; Day, Harrison, & Halpin, 2009; Lord & Hall, 2005). Lord and Hall (2005), for example, posit a model of development in which increasingly sophisticated systems guide manager's behavior, knowledge and perceptions; these systems develop along with emerging personal identities in which leadership roles and skills become more central to a person's sense of self.

Whereas putting forth a clear and compelling argument that, over time, leadership skills and knowledge become inextricably integrated with the development of a self-concept as a leader, research and theorizing on leadership development has yet to specify the processes and moderating conditions that account for this identity transition and change. For example, once a person assumes a formal leader role, it may or may not become a part of his or her identity, depending on his or her level of commitment to the role. What happens when a person occupies a leadership role without having a leader identity, and what impact would this have on his or her effectiveness as a leader? Alternatively, how does internalizing the role identity affect a person's hierarchy of possible salient leader sub-roles? And what about other identities a person holds, which may impinge on the internalization or enactment of the leader role-identity? Whereas some extant identities may more easily be revised or discarded to better fit the requirement of the leader identity one aspires to, other identities—such as those based on personal history or deeply ingrained habits—may prove harder to dislodge, hence generating potentially dysfunctional intrapsychic and interpersonal conflicts (Petriglieri G. & Stein, 2012). Recent research on how individuals cope with multiple, conflicting, and/or ambiguous identities (Ashforth et al. 2000; Bartel & Dutton, 2001; Elsbach, 1999; Pratt & Foreman, 2000a; Sveningsson & Alvesson, 2003) and adapt role identities to fit better their sense of self and vice versa (Ibarra, 1999; Kreiner et al., 2006; Pratt, Rockmann, & Kaufmann, 2006; Van Maanen, 1997) can be applied to leadership studies in order to delineate ways in which individuals clarify, tailor, and/or manage conflicts between their leadership and other role or social identities.

Social Identity Theory: Leadership and Social Categorization

A rich vein of contemporary scholarship examines the emergence and effectiveness of leaders through the lens of social identity theory (for a review, see van Knippenberg and Hogg [2003]), and suggests that "the secret of successful leadership lies in the capacity of the leader to induce followers to perceive him or her as the embodiment of a positive social identity that they have in common and that distinguishes them from others" (Ellemers et al., 2004: 469).

Whereas identity theory is concerned with the various roles people play in organizations and society (Hogg, 2003; Stets & Burke, 2000), social identity theory focuses on the social categories and group-level processes. People both define themselves and enable others to define them based on the groups to which they belong (Hogg, 2003; Tajfel & Turner, 2010). When a social identity is activated, people see themselves as part of a larger group; this process entails depersonalization, which causes the individual to classify people, including him- or herself, not as individuals but as in- versus out-group members (Brewer, 2003).

Van Knippenberg and Hogg (2003) suggested that this depersonalization process promotes the emergence of prototypical leaders, who embody the values and identity of the group, producing a range of outcomes including shared norms/normative behavior, collective behavior, high levels of cohesion and positive attitudes among the in-group, mutual influence, cooperation, altruism, empathy and emotional contagion, stereotyping and ethnocentrism (Hogg, 2003). As group identities are activated, individuals come to see as ideal whatever the prototype of the group is, motivating them to strive for the relevant group characteristics and thus creating a more cohesive and likeminded collective.

The principal contribution of social identity theory to leadership research is Hogg (2001) and van Knippenberg & Hogg's (2003) notion of prototypicality, in which people who embody prototypical characteristics of the group are more likely to emerge and be effective as leaders. Ellemers et al. (2004) developed the argument further, demonstrating that prototypical leadership results in higher levels of motivation in groups, and Hirst et al. (2009) showed that leader prototypicality is related to creative effort and, as a result, creative performance. Ruderman and Ernst (2004) proposed that leadership effectiveness arises in part due to self-knowledge of social identity, the groups a person belongs to and those that are ascribed by others to him or her. Taking a longitudinal approach, Hogg and Terry (2000) argued that leaders have an inherent self-interest in constructing the group's identity in such a way so that they remain prototypical.

Building on the work of Hogg and colleagues, Haslam, Reicher, and Platow (2011) argued that there are four social identity bases for effective leadership. The first basis, "being one of us" is the prototypicality argument: the more representative someone is of the group the more influential or leader-like he or she will be in the group. The second basis entails "doing it for us," or advancing the collective interests of the group and showing that a leader's actions are not simply self-serving, but rather are for the benefit of the group. This notion is founded on research indicating that leaders are most effective when they pursue purposes that are aligned with their personal values and oriented toward advancing the collective good (Fu et al., 2010; Lord & Hall, 2005: 594; Quinn, 2004). The third basis is "crafting a sense of us," or shaping and communicating a collective identity. Fourth, leaders engage in "making us matter," by embedding identity more deeply, casting the group's identity and purpose as valuable in a broader context beyond the group. Leaders who advance such purposes experience themselves and are experienced by others as authentic (Fu et al., 2010). When leaders are connected and connect others to larger purposes, they inspire trust, increase others' sense of urgency, and help them find greater meaning in their work (Jung & Avolio, 2000; Podolny et al., 2005; Quinn & Spreitzer, 2006).

Two unresolved issues arising out of this stream of research concern leadership in complex intergroup or multiple identity settings, and the emergence and effectiveness of non-prototypical leaders as organizations become more diverse. First, with regard to what leaders lead best in groups with various sub-identities or when intergroup collaboration is required, van Knippenberg et al. (2004) have suggested that effective leaders create overarching "superordinate identities" and Hogg et al. (2012) have proposed the notion of "intergroup relational identity" in which leaders recognize different identities as legitimate and distinguishable parts of a whole. Research is needed, however, to discern conditions under which these forms of leadership are effective, as current theorizing leaves open questions about leadership of multiple-identity groups (i.e., religion and health, as discussed by Pratt & Foreman, 2000a) or groups for which the boundaries are not entirely clear.

Second, while all social identity theories hinge on the notion of prototypicality, scholars disagree on its definition and proxies. One of the earliest references is Rosch's (1978) definition of a prototype as a set of characteristics that describe the essence of a group. Hogg (2001) defined the prototypical leader as one who is perceived to embody the group's identity. But, on what bases are people perceived to be prototypical? While van Knippenberg and his collaborators argue that the values the group cherishes will be the *fons et origo* for prototypical leader emergence, what of visible signals such as personal history, gender, or race that people use as proxies for less easily observable traits? Integration and equal rights, for example, defined the U.S. Civil Rights

Movement, and one can hardly imagine a Jesse Jackson or Martin Luther King, Jr. emerging who had never experienced segregation or the African American struggle.

Pratt (2001) suggested that visible signals could denote group characteristics, depending on their ease of accessibility. A group that values strength, for example, depending on the socio-cultural understanding of the definition of "strength," may see brawn, brains, or courage as the proper embodiment of that value; this may, in turn, lead to the emergence of leaders of certain genders, levels of education or personal history. Thus, whereas values may be the underlying foundation for judgments about prototypicality, in reality prototypicality will likely be expressed and understood through proxies that serve as shorthand in defining the group itself.

A focus on prototypicality and ways in which leaders embody their groups necessarily raise questions about the pathologies of overidentification. Dukerich et al. (1998) highlighted the negative consequences of overidentification for the individual, such as diminished willingness to question organizational practices and take responsibility to change them, and/or increased vulnerability to identity threat. Overidentification is riskier for individuals in "highly visible, high status, and intrinsically motivating roles, which offer highly seductive identities for their incumbents" (Ashforth et al., 2008: 338). In other words, just as overidentification "may be a substitute for something that is missing in one's life" (Dukerich et al., 1998: 254), it may also generate pressure to protect the status quo on which one's leader identity is grounded, and to distance oneself from or even attack those who may question or simply differ from it (Petriglieri G. & Stein, 2012).

Social Constructionism: Leadership as Identity Work

If identities are claimed and granted in social interaction, they are partially defined by how a person's social entourage views him or her (Baumeister, 1998; Bartel & Dutton, 2001; Goffman, 1959). Recent scholarship on identity work, defined as people's engagement in forming, repairing, maintaining, strengthening, or revising their identities (Snow & Anderson, 1987; Svenigsson & Alvesson, 2003), has been used as a foundation for understanding the social processes involved in becoming a leader. As conceptualized by DeRue and Ashford (2010), internalizing a leader identity entails a set of relational and social processes through which one comes to see oneself, and is seen by others, as a leader. A person takes actions aimed at asserting leadership, others affirm or disaffirm those actions, encouraging or discouraging further assertions, and so on. Through this back and forth, the would-be leader accumulates experiences that inform his or her sense of self as a leader, as well as feedback about his or her fit for enacting the leader role. Based on the preceding review of role identity and social identity theories, identity work for leaders can be defined as the process through which individuals acquire, internalize, and validate a leader identity and refine, revise, and enact their other identities so as to minimize conflict with the leader identity and maximize group prototypicality.

The recursive and mutually reinforcing nature of the leader identity-construction process can produce positive or negative spirals (DeRue & Ashford, 2010; DeRue, Ashford, & Cotton, 2009). On the positive side, receiving validation for one's self-view as a leader bolsters self-confidence, which increases one's motivation to lead (Chan & Drasgow, 2001; Kark & van Dijk, 2007) and to seek new opportunities to practice leadership (Day & Harrison, 2007; Day, Harrison, & Halpin, 2009). As one's opportunities and capacity for exercising leadership grow, so too does the likelihood of receiving collective endorsement from the organization more broadly, such as assignments to formal leadership roles (DeRue & Ashford, 2010). Recognition and affirmation strengthen one's self-identity as a leader, which in turn fuels the search for new opportunities and growth. Internalizing a leader identity helps to sustain the level of interest and fortitude needed to develop and practice complex leadership skills (Lord & Hall, 2005) and to take the risks of experimenting with unfamiliar aspects of the emerging identity (Ibarra, 1999). In this positive spiral, the leader identity moves from being a peripheral, provisional aspect of the self, indicative of one's leadership potential, to being a more central and enduring one, grounded in actual achievement (Lord & Hall, 2005). On the negative side, failing to receive validation for one's leadership attempts diminishes self-confidence as well as the motivation to seek developmental opportunities, experiment, and take on new leadership roles (Day et al., 2009), thus weakening one's self-identity as a leader (DeRue & Ashford, 2010).

Building on McAdams's (1999) definition of identity as "the internalized and evolving story that results from a person's selective appropriation of past, present and future" (486), scholars have also argued that a central task of identity work is crafting, experimenting with, and revising identity narratives, or stories about the self (Ashforth et al., 2008; Ibarra & Barbulescu, 2010; Snow & Anderson, 1987). This is both an introspective and a social process, whereby the narrative that endures is the one that one feels to best account for his or her experience and aspirations, accrues the most social validation from interaction partners, and fits the narrative repertoire available within one's culture (Ibarra & Barbulescu, 2010; Shamir & Eilam, 2005). In this respect, leaders' identity work entails selecting a suitable narrative of the self as a leader, as much as accepting to be cast within a narrative that followers hold dear (Gardner & Laskin, 1995).

This conceptual approach to leader–follower interactions highlights the importance of identity construction in developing leadership and social capital through interactions between leaders and followers rather than a sole focus on developing the leader and his or her human capital (Day, 2000). This view resonates with theorizing on authentic leadership development (Avolio, this volume; Shamir & Eilam, 2005) as well as psychodynamic perspectives on identity and leadership (Petriglieri G. & Petriglieri J. L., 2010; Petriglieri G., 2011).

A view of leadership as acquired and sustained (or lost) through constant social interactions shifts power away from the leader and transfers it to the relationship between leader and followers, and the latter's identification with the former. Whereas this may accurately reflect the fate of leaders in the flat, informal, and fast-changing organizations of this day and age, it also puts them in the position of having to deal with the insecurity, anxiety, and potential for loss that experiencing a valuable identity as unstable entails (Alvesson & Wilmott, 2002). Although there is mention of struggle in the literature on identity work, much of the focus is on the crafting of identities, rather than on the identity undoing (Nicholson & Carroll, 2013), emotional distress, and existential puzzlement (Petriglieri G., Wood & Petriglieri J. L., 2011) that are part and parcel of the experience of developing and practicing leaders. Identity work research has recognized that valued identities are sources of pride and self-esteem, and identity voids are often filled with anxiety and hope. Scholarship in this field, however, has focused on the dynamics of shifting self-conceptions and enactments more than on the emotional undercurrents of acquiring, sustaining, or losing a leader identity. And although some of these emotions may be dealt with consciously, some of them are likely to be dealt with through less conscious defensive processes (Petriglieri & Stein, 2012). Given the role of implicit affect in influencing decisions and behavior (for a review, see Barsade, Ramarajan, & Westen, 2009), this is a fruitful area for future investigation.

A view of identity as constantly negotiated throughout the life span also challenges traditional scholarship in adult development (Day, Harrison, & Halpin, 2009). In his seminal work, Erikson (1959/1980) posited that resolution of identity questions in late adolescence was necessary to be able to focus on the adult endeavors of forming lasting intimate bonds, serving others, and building a legacy (Erikson, 1959/1980). Developmental psychologists have since moved away from an age-related view of identity formation and suggested that the development of identity at different levels of complexity continues throughout the life span (Kegan, 1982). Nevertheless, the question of whether a preoccupation with their own identity vis à vis their social context may distract leaders from other fundamental pursuits remains a pertinent one.

Table 14.1 summarizes three existing strands of identity theory and research reviewed in the preceding text as they pertain to leader emergence, effectiveness, and development.

Personal Identity as Linchpin cross Identity Theories

Although some proponents of social identity theory see major differences with role-based identity (e.g., Hogg, Terry, & White, 1995), others see substantial similarities and overlap between the two approaches to identity (Stets & Burke, 2000). The basis of the claims of similarity and overlap lie in the practicality of trying to disentangle group identities from role identities, which cannot be easily separated from personal identities constructed over time with experience and social interaction. Stets (1995) argued that personal identities and role identities are related through a common system of meaning. The gist of the argument is that an individual cannot be guided by role or group identities and have his or her personal identities unaffected by them. For example, a leader role identity may be linked to a personal identity such as self-perception of self-efficacy and mastery, that is, being a competent person. Thus, when acting to influence someone or otherwise exercise leadership, behaviors are often enacted in the service of role, group, and personal identities.

If leaders are most authentic (Avolio, this volume) and effective when they internalize, not just

Table 14.1. Leadership Implications of Identity Theories

	Identity theory	Social identity theory	Social construction
Leader emergence	Individuals take on role or have it ascribed to them (Gecas, 1982).	Prototypical group members gain influence by embodying the characteristics that define the group's essence (Hogg, 2001; van Knippenberg et al., 2000).	Individuals claim or are granted the leader role in a given social interaction (DeRue & Ashford, 2010).
Leader development	Development may occur through experimentation, personalization, and internalization (commitment) of the leader role (Ibarra, 1999; Turner, 1978) and through practice (Day & Harrison, 2007; Day, Harrison, & Halpin, 2009; Lord & Hall, 2005).	Members may adapt behavior to group prototypes in order to gain power; leaders may guide group's identity to maintain prototypicality and preserve power (Hogg & Terry, 2000).	Positive spirals of being repeatedly granted leader claims (DeRue & Ashford, 2010; DeRue, Ashford & Cotton, 2009) result in increased confidence, motivation (Chan & Drasgow, 2001; Kark & van Dijk, 2007) and seeking of leadership opportunities (Day & Harrison, 2007; Day, Harrison, & Halpin, 2009).
Leader effectiveness	Through adaptation and growth into the role, understanding and living up to expectations associated with the role schema (Gecas, 1982) and followers' specific needs (Lord & Hall, 2005).	Leader prototypicality engenders member trust (e.g., van Knippenberg & van Knippenberg, 2005), allows for wider range of acceptable action (e.g., van Knippenberg & Hogg, 2003), and can protect perceptions of leader effectiveness even in the case of failure (Giessner & van Knippenberg, 2008).	With practice and exposure to different situational requirements, leaders are better able to judge what is needed by different followers and adapt their leadership style to them (Lord & Hall, 2005).

enact, the identities that followers hold dear, leader development is likely to result in a "deep identification," with a dissolution of the boundary between one's role requirements and personal identity—so that the person experiences an overlap "between self-at-work and one's broader self-concept" (Rousseau, 1998: 218). This implies that although there are different pathways to the development of valued identities at work (Dutton, Morgan Roberts, & Bednar, 2010), in the case of aspiring leaders the development of personal identities will be tightly interwoven with the development of leader identities and vice versa. Anecdotal evidence for this view can be found in the popularity of leadership development programs that focus on leaders' personal foundations and aspirations (Petriglieri G. et al., 2011).

For these reasons, Stets and Burke (2000) have argued that an analysis of the group, the role, and the person might foster a deeper understanding of motivational processes such as self-esteem, self-efficacy, and authenticity. As they noted: "It is possible that people largely feel *good* about themselves when they associate with particular groups, typically feel *confident* about themselves when enacting particular roles, and generally feel they are "real" or *authentic* when their person identities are verified" (p. 234, italics in original). They argued that working to merge these identity approaches will result in stronger social psychology theory that can address macro-, meso-, and micro-level social processes. As noted earlier in this chapter, little work to date has been conducted to achieve this end but it remains a potentially important area of further theory development and research in linking identity and leadership.

New Research and Theorizing on Leadership and Identity

The idea of identity as multiple, relatively fluid, and highly contextual is especially pertinent for the study of leadership today, when individuals increasingly aspire to mobile careers that unfold across organizational boundaries (Arthur, 2008; Sennett, 2006). In the subsections that follow, we first extend current theorizing about leadership development as identity transitions, call attention to the impact of gender on the processes of claiming and granting a leader identity, and highlight the role of identity workspaces in leadership development.

Transitions into Leadership Roles

Conceptualizing leaders as both occupying social roles and continuously engaging in processes of claiming and being granted or denied leader identities is helpful in understanding career development dynamics, notably how people transition into formal leadership roles, and the relationship between leader development and adult development (Day et al., 2009). Lord and Hall (2005) proposed that the knowledge and information processing capabilities required as leaders develop differ qualitatively as the leader progresses from novice to intermediate to expert, at each expertise stage. In particular, identity, meta-cognitive processes, and emotional regulation are proposed as factors that are pivotal in developing the deeper cognitive structures associated with leadership capability. Furthermore, the self-regulation needed to acquire leadership expertise depends at least partly on the currently active identity held by an individual. It is thought that as leaders develop, there is a systematic shift in identity from relatively independent to more inclusive (i.e., collective) forms.

At the heart of the Lord and Hall (2005) model is the notion that as people develop leadership skills they also shift their identity focus. This is a relatively simple but important point. Novice leaders emphasize individual identities in terms of differentiating themselves from followers and other leaders. Novices focus on acquiring basic leadership skills and being seen as a leader by others. As these basic skills are mastered, the focus changes from self to others in which building numerous, differentiated relationships with followers is seen as the key to effective leadership. This is supported by a shift from an individual to a relational identity. As collective group membership becomes more important to developing leaders, there is corresponding development of a more principled and contextually based capacity to promote and enact alternative identities. This type of shift to a deeper structure is indicative of expert level knowledge and expert performance.

Building on this theoretical perspective, Day and Harrison (2007) investigated changes in self-identity (individual, relational, and collective) across developing leaders' career stages. They proposed that identity level changes from an individual focus at lower organizational levels to a more collective identity focus at higher levels. In order for these identity shifts to occur it is necessary for individuals to engage in *letting go to develop* across career stages, especially in areas of technical expertise that are tied to identity. In a similar vein, others have taken a role-based perspective on leader identity in arguing that leader development unfolds as an identity transition in which people disengage from central, behaviorally anchored identities while exploring alternative possible selves (Ibarra, Snook, & Guillen Ramo, 2010). When making major role transitions, individuals co-mingle new and old identities while trying on and refining provisional selves (Ibarra, 1999). The notion of letting go to develop is evident in this approach as well if old selves (e.g., technical experts) are discarded in favor of new possible selves (e.g., leader of others) that occur through role transitions and career progression.

Women's Leader Identity Development

Conceptualizing leaders as simultaneously occupying social roles, belonging to social categories, and continuously engaging in processes of claiming and granting social identities sheds light on the leadership development challenges faced by members of underrepresented, and therefore, non-prototypical group members, notably women in business leadership. Building on these foundational theories Ely, Ibarra, and Kolb (2011) recently argued that subtle, institutionalized forms of gender bias—stemming from workplace structures, cultures, and patterns of interaction that inadvertently favor men—shape, and often interfere with, the identity work of women leaders.

Gender researchers argue that the social interactions in which people claim and grant leader identities, and the status accorded to social categories such as gender do not occur *ex nihilo* but are shaped by culturally available ideologies about what it means to be a leader. In most cultures, the meaning is masculine, making the prototypical leader a quintessentially masculine man: decisive, assertive, and independent (Bailyn, 2006; Calás & Smircich, 1991; Dennis & Kunkel, 2004; Epitropaki & Martin, 2004; Powell, Butterfield, & Parent, 2002; Willemsen, 2002). By contrast, women are thought to be communal—friendly, unselfish, care-taking—and thus lacking in the qualities required for success in leadership roles (Heilman, Block, Martell, & Simon, 1989; Schein, 2001; Fletcher, 2004).

The mismatch between personal qualities attributed to women and qualities thought necessary for leadership places women leaders in a double bind and subjects them to a double standard. Women in positions of authority are thought too aggressive or not aggressive enough, and what appears assertive, self-confident, or entrepreneurial in a man often looks abrasive, arrogant, or self-promoting in a woman (for a review, see Heilman & Parks-Stamm, 2007). In experiment after experiment, women who achieve in distinctly male arenas are seen as competent but are less well liked than equally successful men (Heilman, Wallen, Fuchs, & Tamkins, 2004: 416). Merely being a successful woman in a male domain can be regarded as a violation of gender norms warranting sanctions (e.g., Heilman & Okimoto, 2007). By the same token, when women performing traditionally male roles are seen as conforming to feminine stereotypes, they tend to be liked but not respected (Rudman & Glick, 2001): they are judged too soft, emotional, and unassertive to make tough decisions and to come across as sufficiently authoritative (Eagly & Carli, 2007). In short, women face trade-offs between competence and likability in leadership roles.

These cultural norms are reinforced and amplified by women's underrepresentation in formal, top leadership roles in business and society. For example, women currently constitute only 2.2 percent of *Fortune* 500 CEOs (Catalyst, 2011a) and about 15 percent of these companies' board seats and corporate officer positions (Catalyst, 2011b). How work is valued informally may similarly favor men, making their bids for leadership seem more valid. Research suggests that visible, heroic work, such as setting strategic direction (Ibarra & Obodaru, 2009) or taking charge of a turnaround (Ruderman & Ohlott, 2002), more often the purview of men, is recognized and rewarded, whereas equally vital, behind-the-scenes work (e.g., building a team, avoiding crises), more characteristic of women, tends to be overlooked (Fletcher, 1994).

If a central developmental task for an aspiring leader is to integrate the leader identity into the core self, then this task is fraught at the outset for a woman, who must establish credibility in a culture that is deeply conflicted about her authority (Ely & Rhode, 2010). Workplace conditions, including the lack of role models for women (Ely, 1994; Ibarra, 1999), gendered career paths and gendered work (Baron & Bielby, 1985; Bielby & Baron, 1986), and women's lack of access to networks and sponsors (Ely, Ibarra, & Kolb, 2011) exacerbate the problem, posing challenges for women at every stage of their career development. The result is a vicious cycle: people see men as a better fit for leadership roles partly because the paths to such roles were designed with men mind; the belief that men are a better fit propels more men into leadership roles, which in turn reinforces the perception that men are a better fit, leaving gendered practices intact. Thus, a challenge for women is to construct leader identities in spite of the subtle barriers organizations erect to women's leadership advancement.

Identity Workspaces and Leadership Development

While acknowledging that the development of leaders' identities involves both intrapsychic and social processes, theorizing and research on leaders' development, emergence and effectiveness has mostly focused on *how* leaders' identity work unfolds, as opposed to *where*. Once we conceptualize the exercise and development of leadership as social accomplishments, however, examining the social settings in which they take place becomes of utmost importance. These settings are neither just background for leaders' growth and deeds, nor simply targets of their influencing efforts. They are constitutive and reflective of leaders themselves. That is, they provide—or fail to—the raw material from which leaders' identities are crafted, and the social validation on which the consolidation and ongoing enactment of those identities rests.

Not all social settings are equally favorable for the development of leaders' identities. Identity workspaces, defined as social settings that are conducive to the development and maintenance of leaders' identities, are institutions or groups that provide a holding environment (Winnicott, 1975) for identity work, that is, a social context that reduces disturbing affect, facilitates sense making, and eases the transition to a new identity and/or the consolidation of an existing one (Petriglieri G. & Petriglieri J. L., 2010).

The notion of identity workspaces rests on two common assumptions in identity scholarship. The first is that, by definition, individuals cannot craft or validate identities on their own (Kreiner et al., 2006; Snow & Anderson, 1987); the second is that identity work is often sparked by, and always involves, experiences of uncertainty, destabilization, fragmentation, and anxiety (Alvesson & Wilmott, 2002). Identity work, therefore, can be facilitated by a holding environment that supports the individual in the cognitive, emotional, and social process of elaborating, experimenting with, and consolidating the meanings associated with the self (Petriglieri G. & Petriglieri J. L., 2010).

Three elements enable a social setting to potentially become an identity workspace for its members—viable social defenses, a sentient community, and meaningful rites of passage. Social defenses are collective arrangements, shared beliefs, interpretive schemes, accepted routines, that allow the individual to understand, and act in, the world in a way that minimizes his or her experience of uncertainty and anxiety, be it related to the work or to broader existential concerns (Jaques, 1955; Menzies, 1960; Halton, 1994; Long, 2006). Sentient communities are social groups that provide clarification, advice, support, feedback, validation and, most important, a felt experience of belonging (Miller & Rice, 1967). Rites of passage are ceremonial events that manage major role transitions within a social system (Trice & Morand, 1989). Such rites have multiple functions, including the transmission of practical and cultural knowledge to role incumbents and the collective affirmation of a valued social narratives and mores (Campbell, 1972; Van Gennep, 1960).

Identity workspaces can be located within an established organization. For example, a corporate management training scheme involving job rotations, mentoring, and in-house educational opportunities and transition ceremonies, may serve as an identity workspace that accelerates individuals' acquisition and affirmation of an identity as an organizational member, or as a manager of that specific organization. They can also be located at the periphery of established organizations. For example, a medical residency program may be designed to facilitate the acquisition of a "pediatrician" or "radiologist" identity that, although requiring ongoing maintenance, is legitimate and relatively transferable across different hospitals.

Petriglieri G. & Petriglieri J. L. (2010) argued that the more individuals aspire to mobile careers that unfold across organizational boundaries (Arthur, 2008; Sennett, 2006), the less likely they are to entrust work organizations—the traditional context for leader development—as identity workspaces. The reasons are twofold. The expectation that organizational membership may last but for a limited time makes one less likely to want to alter one's personal identity too much to fit organizational requirements. The second is that such careers require the development of a work identity that may generate and facilitate access to opportunities elsewhere. As a result individuals are likely to seek identity workspaces that facilitate the development of personal and professional identities that can be transferred across organizations, for example, those provided by professional schools and leadership courses.

To function as an identity workspace, a social setting needs to help its members address two fundamental identity questions: "Who am I as a leader?" and "What does leading mean to us?" (Petriglieri G., 2011). Whereas some identity workspaces are be designed to indoctrinate individuals to adopt prescribed answers, the most valuable ones are those in which identity questions are openly addressed rather than pushed aside. This occurs through two processes: personalization and contextualization.

Personalization is a process through which individuals examine their experience and revisit their life story as part and parcel of learning to lead (Petriglieri G. et al., 2011). This allows them to examine the influence of their personal identities, and of the groups and social systems they are embedded in, on the ways they think, feel, act, and are perceived as leaders. Through the process of personalization, individuals integrate their personal identities with their identity as leaders, which allows them to give themselves more fully to their leadership roles. *Contextualization* is a process through which individuals acquire and reflect on the language, skills and cultural scripts that are expected of those who aspire to lead in a specific social context. This involves not only practicing a language, a set of skills, and requisite behaviors. It also involves taking ownership, individually and with one's peers, of the existence of language, skills, and requisite behavior; its maintenance, and if necessary, change.

Despite an organization or group's best efforts to provide access to viable social defenses, valuable sentient communities, and vital rites of passage not all members will entrust it as an identity workspace (Petriglieri G. & Petriglieri J. L., 2010), as evident in the recurrent empirical finding that even organizations explicitly designed to be identity-transforming succeed only with a portion of their members (Greil & Rudi, 1984; Pratt, 2000). The notion of identity workspaces calls us to examine the cultural assumptions upon which the meanings associated with being a "leader" rest—and to whom those meanings are more likely to be attributed. This mindfulness marks the difference between identity workspaces used only for cultural replication versus those that enable cultural reflection and change. A conceptualization of identity workspaces for leadership development, therefore, would suggest that interventions revisit the meanings traditionally associated with leadership.

Future Research Directions

Calls for tackling the inherent multiplicity and dynamism of identity processes have multiplied (e.g., Albert, Ashforth, and Dutton, 2000), as have attempts to shift the focus of leadership research and theorizing from a concern with the personal characteristics of leaders and followers to a dynamic and fluid leading-following process that is contextually embedded. Yet the potential of combining these two areas of inquiry remains largely underexploited. When viewed through the perspective of identity, the study of leadership broadens into an exploration of a process that is experimental (Ibarra, 1999), interactive and iterative (DeRue & Ashford, 2010), and context dependent (Yost & Strube, 1992). Our discussion in this chapter points to several avenues for furthering our understanding of identity processes as they relate to leadership.

Diversity and Non-Prototypical Leadership

If roles are socially constructed (Gecas, 1982), social context matters to leader identity development and effectiveness. Leaders developing in different situational and cultural contexts will necessarily relate in distinct ways to their subordinates—a leader whose tenure has been altogether peaceful will have a different understanding of the leader identity than one whose experience has been rife with fragmentation and group in-fighting. Although a leader in a hierarchical culture may develop the capacity to guide subordinates in a paternalistic manner, he or she will probably not have developed the understanding of leader as a collaborative member of a team that leaders from more egalitarian cultures would espouse. This is all the more likely if the leader's primary identity workspaces have all been consistent with that culture, rather than exposing him or her to diverse contexts and their differing leadership mores.

Whereas certainly leadership across cultures has been explored (e.g., House et al., 2004), an examination of a cross-cultural process of leader identity development, grounded in context-specific role interpretation and experimentation, may add explanatory depth to the process of becoming a leader in transnational contexts. If the leader identity developed in one sociocultural context manifests itself in a different way from those of leaders developed in others, what is required to show oneself a leader and be accepted as such across contexts? Cultural and contextual processes of leader identity development have implications for multinational organizations that require leadership across national boundaries.

Similarly, if prototypical leaders are more likely to emerge and be effective (van Knippenberg, 2011; van Knippenberg & Hogg, 2003), our theories need to account for the emergence and effectiveness of leaders who are not prototypical of their groups by virtue of their gender, race, age, or national culture. That ascribed characteristics are not the only factor at play in leader selection is highlighted by examples of such leaders as Condoleezza Rice, who after growing up in the segregated US South became the youngest, first woman, and first minority member to be appointed as Stanford University's Provost, and later became the first female African American United States Secretary of State. How do non-prototypical group members develop a leader identity and gain respect as effective in environments in which social identity theorists would suggest that they are unlikely to be viewed as leaders from the start? Future research is needed to clarify the ways in which the identity work of leadership development is complicated by cultural differences and intractable biases in the workplace and society.

New Settings for Leadership: Global, Virtual, and Multiple Identities

As organizations become more international and globally connected through technology, leaders are required to work across borders and cyberspace. Distributed groups and multiple team memberships have become commonplace in organizations, fundamentally changing the nature of the social units being led to accomplish common goals (e.g., O'Leary & Mortensen, 2010; O'Leary, Mortensen, & Woolley, 2011; Mortensen & Hinds, 2001). From product development to scientific discovery, a range of work today is conducted via distributed leadership of multiple actors using social media across organizational and national boundaries. Although the emergence, development, and effectiveness of leaders for virtual and broadly distributed teams is likely to differ from that of small face-to-face groups, the bulk of the research on which identity theories are based concerns the latter. Research questions here include: What kinds of leaders emerge in virtual teams? What kinds of leaders are effective in virtual contexts? Are leader identities developed in a dispersed, virtual community more or less portable than those developed in face-to-face social groups?

In today's careers and organizations, people may also play multiple, sometimes competing, leadership roles. For example, surveys estimate that 65 to 95 percent of knowledge workers across a wide range of industries and occupations are members of more than one project team at a time, while in some companies it is common for people to be members of five, ten, or twelve or more teams at a time (O'Leary, Mortensen, & Woolley, 2011). As a leader identity becomes more central to an individual's self-concept, it moves up an identity salience hierarchy (Gecas, 1982; Stryker, 1980). The more central the identity, the more a person will seek out opportunities to enact it (Shamir, 1991), and successful enactments will lead people to seek out further roles that allow expression of the underlying identity. Once a leader identity is internalized and developed, new opportunities to take on a leader role will be seen as compatible with the "leader" part of the individual's self-concept; these will not violate the individual's need for self-consistency (Gecas, 1982). Thus, there will be affinity between the already established leader identity and extra-role leadership opportunities (see Pratt, 1998 and Ashforth et al., 2008 for relation of affinity to the taking on of organizational roles). A multiplicity of leader roles, then, can be viewed as manifestations of a unifying leader identity.

Although identity synergy (Pratt & Foreman, 2000b) may result from having a common identity base across roles, high levels of intra-identity permeability can produce identity spillover (Kreiner et al., 2006) and role blurring (Ashforth & Kreiner, 2000). Questions for further exploration include how holding multiple leadership roles affects a person's ability to transition into the roles for which he or she is not leader—is it a more difficult balance when one is a pluri-leader than when one holds one or very few leadership positions? To what degree is it possible to integrate various leader roles, on what does this integration depend, and what are the results of such integration? On the other hand, when and how is it possible or beneficial to build boundaries (Ashforth & Kreiner, 2000) between these integrated leadership role identities? Finally, what are the implications of exiting a formal leadership role (Ebaugh, 1988) on the person's other leader roles? Table 14.2 outlines findings from the three identity theories reviewed in this chapter that may be used to develop hypotheses about identity and leadership in virtual and multiple roles.

The Lifecycle of Leader Identities

Identities are taken on, adapted, made more or less salient, or sloughed off depending on their relevance in how a person defines him- or herself. This can be viewed as a sort of identity life-cycle that may or may not end in death—identities are born through exposure, develop to different degrees through experience (Yost & Strube, 1992), become more or less salient through use and necessity, and are abandoned when or if they become incompatible with a person's understanding of him- or herself in light of the demands of his or her context (cf. Bouchikhi & Kimberly, 2003, for a discussion of organizational identity obsolescence). Leader as an identity is no different; however, it is important to differentiate between a leader identity that is tied

Table 14.2. Leadership and Identity in the Current Organizational Landscape

	Identity theory	Social identity theory	Social constructionist
Multiple leadership roles	The more a leader role is internalized, the more likely a person will be to seek opportunities to enact this role (Day & Harrison, 2007). This may lead to leader role transference across boundaries.	The leader would be prototypical of each group's characteristics, likely resulting in leadership across similar types of groups.	Positive spirals would result in confidence in enacting leader role in different social contexts. Experience and practice in one context would enable adaptation to follower needs in another.
Leading across boundaries and in diverse groups	The leader can be effective as long as the groups have non-conflicting leader role expectations.	Either build an overarching superordinate identity (van Knippenberg et al., 2004) or a coalition of different identity groups (Hogg et al., 2012).	Inexperienced leaders would focus on their leader identity, restricting the range of leader action to their understanding of the leader role; experienced leaders would have the capacity to adapt their leadership style to different followers' needs (Lord & Hall, 2005).

exclusively to a position or role and a leader identity that permeates and is used as a lens through which to best interpret the obligations of leader roles in various aspects of a person's life, as described earlier. In the former case, the losing of a position may result in an identity loss for the identity embedded in a role (cf. Ebaugh [1988] on "becoming an ex"); whereas in the latter, the role is simply one expression of the underlying identity. Because an acutely developed leader identity can have manifestations across a range of roles, the process of abandoning a meta-leader identity will be a more complex process than leaving an identity that is tied to a discrete and well-demarcated role. In a world where attaining and keeping leadership status is seen as overwhelmingly positive, and losing it is seen as failure, there is no body of literature that we know of that explicitly focuses on the process of *un*becoming a leader. In the case of exit for a leader identity based on multiple leadership roles, it is unclear what viable alternative identities would be available.

Conclusions

In this chapter we have discussed what leader identity emergence, development, and effectiveness entail from three theoretical perspectives. First, in the case of identity theory, leader is a *role* whose adoption and enactment is defined by societal expectations. From this perspective, "practice makes perfect": the leader role is internalized and a leader gains competence through increased exposure to different role situations and time-in-role. Questions not fully satisfied by our current knowledge of leader identity based in identity theory include change and transitions to and from leader roles; internalization of the leader role and to what degree this affects leader effectiveness; and how an established leader identity affects other—including other leader—roles. Second, social identity theory sees leader identity in terms of representing a *category*. Those who lead are they who best embody what it means to be a member of their social group. It is due to this representativeness or prototypicality that they are entrusted with opportunities to pursue leadership, and the practice of leadership in turn serves to influence the group's identity. A leader's status as a prototypical group member who knows the group (because he or she *is* the group) vests him or her with the expertise necessary to lead appropriately. The questions, however, that social identity theory has not yet satisfied are definitions and proxies used to establish prototypicality, and leadership in complex groups, such as those with multiple identities. Finally, social constructionism proposes leader identity as a *process*—of identity acquisition, internalization, and validation—involving continuous interplay between a leader and his or her current and prospective followers. Although leaders' development is indeed important according to this perspective, followers play an equally important role because of their interaction and identification with the leader. Thus, followers here are both enablers (or inhibitors) of leader development and arbiters of effectiveness. We propose that understanding leader identity from these three theoretical perspectives permits evaluation of the strengths and limitations of the approaches, and an integration of these can serve to impel further investigation.

Combining the different perspectives, we have explored transitions into leadership and identity work; the granting or denial of leadership based on sociocultural understandings of who is considered appropriate and prototypical leader material; and the social settings where leaders can emerge and develop. Transitioning into and between positions of leadership requires changes in identity and self-understanding, and openness to "letting go to develop"—exploration of what identity personalization entails for both the leader and his or her followers. This space of leader-follower interaction and exploration is bounded by sociocultural expectations, and leadership positions are not necessarily open to every aspirant. In the case of women leaders, in particular, many times what is seen to be prototypical of "leader" is seen as incongruent with what is prototypical of "woman." Thus, women face the challenge of both gaining leadership and being effective in arenas where traditionally few women have tread. We propose that identity workspaces provide a setting to craft and experiment with leader identities, allowing people a safe environment to internalize and maintain what it means for them to be leaders. These workspaces can be located within an organization, but when subtle barriers to leadership positions exist in many organizations and this in a world of rapid job change and mobile careers, aspiring leaders seek validation and development of identities outside of the traditional milieu.

The field of leader identity is ripe for further research. In leader emergence, there is much room to expand our current knowledge of how non-prototypical leaders emerge, develop, and are effective, even when theory proposes lack of support by prospective followers. The burgeoning area of cross-cultural research in management offers the opportunity to develop theory on leadership capacity transfer across cultural and national boundaries. From technological developments questions arise on new leader capabilities in virtual and distributed teams. Teamwork in diverse and numerous environments creates meta-leaders who must understand and deploy their leader identity (or identities) across contexts—we have yet to understand this process. While our chapter has provided an overview of existing theory and ideas for future discussion and investigation, we encourage and look forward to new and exciting voices and directions in research on leadership and leaders' identities.

References

Albert, S., Ashforth, B. E., & Dutton, J. E. (2000). Organizational identity and identification: Charting new waters and building new bridges. *Academy of Management Review, 25*(1), 13–17.

Alvesson, M., & Willmott, H. (2002). Identity regulation as organizational control: Producing the appropriate individual. *Journal of Management Studies, 39*, 619–644.

Arthur, M. B. (2008). Examining contemporary careers: A call for interdisciplinary inquiry. *Human Relations, 61*(2), 163–186.

Ashforth, B. E. (2001). *Role transitions in organizational life: An identity-based perspective.* Mahwah, NJ: Lawrence Erlbaum.

Ashforth, B. E., Harrison, S. H., & Corley, K. G. (2008). Identification in organizations: An examination of four fundamental questions. *Journal of Management, 34*(3), 325–374.

Ashforth, B. E., & Johnson, S. A. (2001). Which hat to wear? The relative salience of multiple identities in organizational contexts. In M. A. Hogg & D. J. Terry (Eds.), *Social identity processes in organizational contexts* (pp. 31–48). Philadelphia, PA: Psychology Press.

Ashforth, B. E., Kreiner, G. E., & Fugate, M. (2000). All in a day's work: Boundaries and micro role transitions. *Academy of Management Review, 25*(3), 472–491.

Bailyn, L. (2006). *Breaking the mold: Redesigning work for productive and satisfying lives.* Ithaca, NY: Cornell University Press.

Baron, J. N., & Bielby, W. T. (1985). Organizational barriers to gender equality: Sex segregation of jobs and opportunities. In A. S. Rossi (Ed.), *Gender and the life course* (pp. 233–251). Chicago, IL: Aldine.

Barsade, S. G., Ramarajan, L., & Westen, D. (2009). Implicit affect in organizations. *Research in Organizational Behavior, 29*, 125–162.

Bartel, C. A., & Dutton, J. E. (2001). Ambiguous organizational memberships: Constructing organizational identities in interactions with others. In M. A. Hogg & D. J. Terry (Eds.), *Social identity processes in organizational contexts* (pp. 115–130). Philadelphia, PA: Psychology Press.

Bass, B. M. (2008). *The Bass handbook of leadership: Theory, research, and managerial applications* (4th ed.). New York, NY: Free Press.

Baumeister, R. F. (1998). The self. In G. L. Gardner (Ed.), *The handbook of social psychology*, Vol. 1 (4th ed., pp. 680–726). New York, NY: McGraw-Hill.

Bielby, W. T., & Baron, J. N. (1986). Men and women at work: Sex segregation and statistical discrimination. *American Journal of Sociology, 91*, 759–799.

Bouchikhi, H., & Kimberly, J.R. (2003). Escaping the identity trap. *MIT Sloan Management Review, 44*(3), 20–26.

Brewer, M. B. (2003). Optimal distinctiveness, social identity and the self. In M. R. Leary & J. P. Tangney (Eds.), *Handbook of self and identity* (pp. 480–491). New York, NY: Guilford Press.

Brewer, M. B., & Gardner, W. (1996). Who is this "we"? Levels of collective identity and self-representations. *Journal of Personality and Social Psychology, 71*(1), 83–93.

Campbell, J. (1972). The importance of rites. In *Myths to live by* (pp. 44–60). London, UK: Penguin.

Carroll, B., & Levy, L. (2010). Leadership development as identity construction. *Management Communication Quarterly, 24*, 211–231.

Catalyst. (2011a). *U.S. women in business.* New York, NY: Author. Retrieved April 30, 2011 from http://www.catalyst.org/publication/132/us-women-in-business.

Catalyst. (2011b). *Women in U.S. management.* New York, NY: Author. Retrieved April 30, 2011, from http://www.catalyst.org/publication/206/women-in-us-management.

Chan, K. Y., & Drasgow, F. (2001). Toward a theory of individual differences and leadership: Understanding the motivation to lead. *Journal of Applied Psychology, 86*(3), 481–498.

Cooley, C. H. (1902). *Human nature and the social order.* New York, NY: Scribner's.

Day, D. V., & Harrison, M. M. (2007). A multilevel, identity-based approach to leadership development. *Human Resource Management Review, 17*(4), 360–373.

Day, D. V., Harrison, M. M., & Halpin, S. M. (2009). *An integrative approach to leader development: Connecting adult development, identity, and expertise.* New York, NY: Routledge.

Dennis, M. R., & Kunkel, A. D. (2004). Perceptions of men, women, and CEOs: The effects of gender identity. *Social Behavior and Personality: An International Journal, 32*(2), 155–172.

DeRue, D. S. (2011). Adaptive leadership theory: Leading and following as a complex adaptive process. *Research in Organizational Behavior, 31*, 125–150.

DeRue, D. S., & Ashford, S. J. (2010). Who will lead and who will follow? A social process of leadership identity construction in organizations. *Academy of Management Review, 35*(4), 627–647.

DeRue, D. S., Ashford, S. J., & Cotton, N. C. (2009). Assuming the mantle: Unpacking the process by which individual internalize a leader identity. In L. M. Roberts & J. E. Dutton (Eds.), *Exploring positive identities and organizations: Building a theoretical and research foundation* (pp. 213–232). New York, NY: Taylor & Francis.

Dukerich, J. M., Kramer, R., & McLean Parks, J. (1998). The dark side of organizational identification. In D. A. Whetten & P. C. Godfrey (Eds.), *Identity in organizations: Building theory through conversations* (pp. 245–256). Thousand Oaks, CA: SAGE.

Dutton, J. E., Morgan Roberts, L., & Bednar, J. (2010). Pathways for positive identity construction at work: Four types of positive identity and the building of social resources. *Academy of Management Review, 35*, 265–293.

Eagly, A. H., & Carli, L. C. (2007). *Through the labyrinth: The truth about how women become leaders.* Boston, MA: Harvard Business School Press.

Ebaugh, H. R. F. (1988). *Becoming an ex.* Chicago, IL: University of Chicago Press.

Ellemers, N., de Gilder, D., & Haslam, S. A. (2004). Motivating individuals and groups at work: A social identity

perspective on leadership and group performance. *Academy of Management Review, 29*(3), 459–478.
Elsbach, K. D. (1999). An expanded model of organizational identification. *Research in Organizational Behavior, 21*, 163–200.
Ely, R. J. (1994). The effects of organizational demographics and social identity on relationships among professional women. *Administrative Science Quarterly, 39*(2), 203–238.
Ely, R. J., Ibarra, H., & Kolb, D. M. (2011). Taking gender into account: Theory and design for women's leadership development programs. *Academy of Management Learning & Education, 10*(3), 474–493.
Ely, R. J., & Rhode, D. L. (2010). Women and leadership: Defining the challenges. In N. Nohria & R. Khurana (Eds.), *Handbook of leadership theory and practice* (pp. 377–410). Boston, MA: Harvard Business School Press.
Epitropaki, O., & Martin, R. (2004). Implicit leadership theories in applied settings: Factor structure, generalizability, and stability over time. *Journal of Applied Psychology, 89*(2), 293–310.
Erikson, E. H. (1980). *Identity and the life cycle.* New York, NY: W. W. Norton & Company. (Original work published 1959).
Fletcher, J. K. (1994). Castrating the female advantage. *Journal of Management Inquiry, 3*(1), 74–82.
Fletcher, J. K. (2004). The paradox of post heroic leadership: An essay on gender, power and transformational change. *Leadership Quarterly, 15*(5), 647–661.
Fu, P. P., Tsui, A. S., Liu, J., & Li, L. (2010). Pursuit of whose happiness? Executive leaders' transformational behaviors and personal values. *Administrative Science Quarterly, 55*, 222–254.
Gardner, H., & Laskin, E. (1995). *Leading minds: An anatomy of leadership.* New York, NY: Basic Books.
Gecas, V. (1982). The self concept. *Annual Review of Sociology, 8*, 1–33.
Giessner, S. R., & van Knippenberg, D. (2008). "Licence to fail": Goal definition, leader group prototypicality, and perceptions of leadership effectiveness after leader failure. *Organizational Behavior and Human Decision Processes, 105*, 14–35.
Goffman, E. (1959). *The presentation of self in everyday life.* Garden City, NY: Doubleday.
Greil, A. L., & Rudy, D. R. (1984). Social cocoons: Encapsulation and identity transformation organizations, *Sociological Inquiry, 54*, 260–278.
Halton, W. (1994). Some unconscious aspects of organizational life: Contributions from psychoanalysis. In A. Obholzer & V. Z. Roberts (Eds.), *The unconscious at work: Individual and organizational stress in the human services* (pp. 11–18). London, UK: Routledge.
Haslam, S. A., Reicher, S. D., & Platow, M. J. (2011). *The new psychology of leadership: Identity, influence, and power.* New York, NY: Psychology Press.
Heilman, M. E., Block, C. J., Martell, R. F., & Simon, M. (1989). Has anything changed? Current characterizations of men, women and managers. *Journal of Applied Psychology, 74*(6), 935–942.
Heilman, M. E., & Okimoto, T. G. (2007). Why are women penalized for success at male tasks? The implied communality deficit. *Journal of Applied Psychology, 92*(1), 81–92.
Heilman, M. E., & Parks-Stamm, E. J. (2007). Gender stereotypes in the workplace: Obstacles to women's career progress. In S. J. Correll (Ed.), *Social psychology of gender: Advances in group processes* (pp. 47–77). Greenwich, CT: JAI Press.
Heilman, M. E., Wallen, A. S., Fuchs, D., & Tamkins, M. M. (2004). Penalties for success: Reactions to women who succeed at male gender-typed tasks. *Journal of Applied Psychology, 89*(3), 416–427.
Hill, L. A. (1992). *Becoming a manager: Mastery of a new identity.* Boston, MA: Harvard Business School Press.
Hirst, G., van Dick, R., & van Knippenberg, D. (2009). A social identity perspective on leadership and employee creativity. *Journal of Organizational Behavior, 30*(7), 963–982.
Hogg, M. A. (2001). A social identity theory of leadership. *Personality and Social Psychology Review, 5*(3), 184–200.
Hogg, M. A. (2003). Social identity. In M. R. Leary & J. P. Tangney (Eds.), *Handbook of self and identity* (pp. 480–491). New York, NY: Guilford Press.
Hogg, M. A., & Terry, D. J. (2000). The dynamic, diverse, and variable faces of organizational identity. *Academy of Management Review, 25*(1), 150–152.
Hogg, M. A., Terry, D. J., & White, K. M. (1995). A tale of two theories: A critical comparison of identity theory with social identity theory. *Social Psychology Quarterly, 58*(4), 255–269.
Hogg, M. A., van Knippenberg, & D., Rast, III, D. E. (2012). Intergroup leadership in organizations: Leading across group and organizational boundaries. *Academy of Management Review, 37*(2), 232–255.
House, R. J., Hanges, P. J., Javidan, M., Dorfman, P. W., & Gupta, V. (Eds.). (2004). *Culture, leadership and organizations: The GLOBE study of 62 societies.* Thousand Oaks, CA: SAGE.
Ibarra, H. (1999). Provisional selves: Experimenting with image and identity in professional adaptation. *Administrative Science Quarterly, 44*(4), 764–791.
Ibarra, H., & Barbulescu, R. (2010). Identity as narrative: Prevalence, effectiveness, and consequences of narrative identity work in macro role work transitions. *Academy of Management Review, 35*(1), 135–154.
Ibarra, H., & Obodaru, O. (2009). Women and the vision thing. *Harvard Business Review, 87*(1), 62–70.
Ibarra, H., Snook, S., & Guillen Ramo, L. (2010). Identity-based leader development. In N. Nohria & R. Khurana (Eds.), *Handbook of leadership theory and practice* (pp. 657–678). Boston, MA: Harvard Business School Press.
Jaques, E. (1955). Social systems as a defence against persecutory and depressive anxiety. In M. Klein, P. Heimann, & R. Money-Kyrle (Eds.), *New directions in psycho-analysis* (pp. 478–498). London, UK: Tavistock.
Jung, D. I., & Avolio, B. J. (2000). Opening the black box: An experimental investigation of the mediating effects of trust and value congruence on transformational and transactional leadership. *Journal of Organizational Behavior, 21*(8), 949–964.
Kark, R., & van Dijk, D. (2007). Motivation to lead, motivation to follow: The role of the self-regulatory focus in leadership processes. *Academy of Management Review, 32*(2), 500–528.
Kegan, R. (1982). *The evolving self: Problem and process in human development.* Cambridge, MA: Harvard University Press.
Kreiner, G. E., Hollensbe, E. C., & Sheep, M. L. (2006). On the edge of identity: Boundary dynamics at the interface of individual and organizational identities. *Human Relations, 59*(10), 1315–1341.
Leary, M. R., & Tangney, J. P. (2003). The self as an organizing construct in the behavioral and social sciences. In M. R. Leary, & J. P. Tangney (Eds.), *Handbook of self and identity* (pp. 3–14). New York, NY: Guilford Press.

Long, S. (2006). Organisational defenses against anxiety: What has happened since the 1955 Jaques paper? *International Journal of Applied Psychoanalytic Studies, 3*(4), 279–295.

Lord, R. G., & Brown, D. J. (2004). *Leadership processes and follower self-identity.* Mahwah, NJ: Lawrence Erlbaum.

Lord, R. G., & Hall, R. J. (2005). Identity, deep structure and the development of leadership skill. *The Leadership Quarterly, 16*(4), 591–615.

McAdams, D. P. (1999). Personal narratives and the life story. In L. Pervin & O. John (Eds.), *Handbook of personality: Theory and research* (2nd ed., pp. 478–500). New York, NY: Guilford Press.

Menzies, I. E. P. (1960). A case-study in the functioning of social systems as a defence against anxiety: A report on a study of the nursing service of a general hospital. *Human Relations, 13,* 95–121.

Miller, E. J., & Rice, A. K. (1967). *Systems of organization: Tasks and sentient groups and their boundary control.* London, UK: Tavistock Publications.

Mortensen, M., & Hinds, P. J. (2001). Conflict and shared identity in geographically distributed teams. *International Journal of Conflict Management, 12*(3), 212–238.

Nicholson, H. & Carroll, B. (2013). Identity undoing and power relations in leadership development. *Human Relations, 66*(9), 1225–1248.

O'Leary, M., & Mortensen, M. (2010). Go (con)figure: The role of competing subgroups in geographically dispersed teams. *Organization Science, 21*(1), 115–131.

O'Leary, M., Mortensen, M., & Woolley, A. W. (2011). Multiple team membership: A theoretical model of its effects on productivity and learning for individuals and teams. *Academy of Management Review, 36*(3), 461–478.

Petriglieri, G. (2011). Identity workspaces for leadership development. In S. Snook, N. Nohria & R. Khurana (Eds.) *The handbook for teaching leadership* (pp. 295–312). London, UK: SAGE.

Petriglieri, G., & Petriglieri, J. L. (2010). Identity workspaces: The case of business schools. *Academy of Management Learning & Education, 9,* 44–60.

Petriglieri, G., & Stein, M. (2012). The unwanted self: Projective identification in leaders' identity work. *Organization Studies, 33,* 1217–1236.

Petriglieri, G., Wood, J. D., & Petriglieri J. L. (2011). Up close and personal: Building foundations for leaders' development through the personalization of management learning. *Academy of Management Learning and Education, 10,* 430–450.

Petriglieri, J. L. (2011). Under threat: Responses to and the consequences of threats to individuals' identities. *Academy of Management Review, 36*(4), 641–662.

Podolny, J. M., Khurana, R., & Hill-Popper, M. (2005). Revisiting the meaning of leadership. *Research in Organizational Behavior, 26,* 1–36.

Powell, G. N., Butterfield, D. A., & Parent, D. (2002). Gender and managerial stereotypes: Have the times changed? *Journal of Management, 28*(2), 177–193.

Pratt, M. G. (1998). To be or not to be? Central questions in organizational identification. In D. A. Whetten & P. C. Godfrey (Eds.), *Identity in organizations: Building theory through conversations* (pp. 171–207). Thousand Oaks, CA: SAGE.

Pratt, M. G. (2000). The good, the bad, and the ambivalent: Management identification among Amway distributors. *Administrative Science Quarterly, 45*(3), 456–495.

Pratt, M. G. (2001). Social identity dynamics in modern organizations: An organizational psychology/organizational behaviour perspective. In. M. A. Hogg & D. J. Terry (Eds.), *Social identity processes in organizational contexts* (pp. 13–30). Philadelphia, PA: Psychological Press.

Pratt, M. G., & Foreman, P. O. (2000a). Classifying managerial responses to multiple identity organizations. *Academy of Management Review, 25*(1), 18–42.

Pratt, M. G., & Foreman, P. O. (2000b). Identity dialogues: The beauty of and barriers to organizational theories of identity. *Academy of Management Review, 25*(1), 141–143.

Pratt, M. G., Rockmann, K. W., & Kaufmann, J. B. (2006). Constructing professional identity: The role of work and identity learning cycles in the customization of identity among medical residents. *Academy of Management Journal, 49*(2), 235–262.

Quinn, R. E. (2004). Building the bridge as you walk on it. *Leader to Leader,* (34), 21–26.

Quinn, R. E., & Spreitzer, G. M. (2006). Entering the fundamental state of leadership: A framework for the positive transformation of self and others. In R. Burke & C. Cooper (Eds.), *Inspiring leaders* (pp. 67–83). Oxford, England: Routledge.

Rosch, E. (1978). Principles of categorization. In E. Rosch & B. B. Lloyd (Eds.), *Cognition and categorization* (pp. 28–48). Hillsdale, NJ: Lawrence Erlbaum.

Rousseau, D. M. (1998). Why workers still identify with organizations. *Journal of Organizational Behavior, 19*(3), 217–233.

Ruderman, M. N., & Ernst, C. (2004). Finding yourself: How social identity affects leadership. *Leadership in Action, 24*(3), 3–7.

Ruderman, M. N, & Ohlott, P. J. (2002). *Standing at the crossroads: Next steps for high-achieving women.* San Francisco, CA: John Wiley & Sons.

Rudman, L., & Glick, P. (2001). Prescriptive gender stereotypes and backlash toward agentic women. *Journal of Social Issues, 57*(4), 743–762.

Schein, E.H. (1978). *Career dynamics: Matching individual and organizational needs.* Reading, MA: Addison Wesley.

Schein, V. E. (2001). A global look at the psychological barriers to women's progress in management. *Journal of Social Issues, 57*(4), 675–688.

Sennett, R. (2006). *The culture of the new capitalism.* London, UK: Yale University Press.

Shamir, B. (1991). Meaning, self and motivation in organizations. *Organization Studies, 12*(3), 405–424.

Shamir, B., & Eilam, G. (2005). "What's your story?" A life-stories approach to authentic leadership development. *Leadership Quarterly, 16,* 395–417.

Snow, D. A., & Anderson, L. (1987). Identity work among the homeless: The verbal construction and avowal of personal identities. *The American Journal of Sociology, 92*(6), 1336–1371.

Stets, J. E. (1995). Role identities and person identities: Gender identity, mastery identity, and controlling one's partner. *Sociological Perspectives, 38*(2), 129–150.

Stets, J. E., & Burke, P. J. (2000). Identity theory and social identity theory. *Social Psychology Quarterly, 63*(3), 224–237.

Stryker, S. (1980). *Symbolic interactionism: A social structural version.* Menlo Park, CA: Benjamin Cummings.

Stryker, S., & Serpe, R. T. (1982). Commitment, identity salience, and role behavior: Theory and research example. In W. Ickes & E. S. Knowles (Eds.), *Personality, roles, and social behavior* (pp. 199–218). New York, NY: Springer-Verlag.

Sveningsson, S., & Alvesson, M. (2003). Managing managerial identities: Organizational fragmentation, discourse and identity struggle. *Human Relations, 56*, 1163–1193.

Tajfel, H., & Turner, J. C. (1986). The social identity theory of intergroup behaviour. In S. Worchel & W. G. Austin (Eds.), *Psychology of intergroup relations* (pp. 7–24). Chicago, IL: Nelson-Hall.

Tajfel, H., & Turner, J. C. (2010). An integrative theory of intergroup conflict. In T. Postmes & N. R. Branscombe (Eds.), *Rediscovering social identity* (pp. 173–190). New York, NY: Psychology Press.

Trice, H. M., & Morand, D. A. (1989). Rites of passage in work careers. In M. B. Arthur, D. T. Hall & B. S. Lawrence (Eds.), *Handbook of career theory* (pp. 397–416). Cambridge, UK: Cambridge University Press.

Turner, R. H. (1978). The role and the person. *American Journal of Sociology, 84*(1), 1–23.

Van Gennep, A. (1960). *The rites of passage* (M. B. Vizedom & G. L. Cafee, Trans.). Chicago, IL: University of Chicago Press. (Original work published 1908).

van Knippenberg, D. (2011). Embodying who we are: Leader group prototypicality and leadership effectiveness. *Leadership Quarterly, 22*(6), 1078–1091.

van Knippenberg, D., & Hogg, M. A. (2003). A social identity model of leadership effectiveness in organizations. *Research in Organizational Behavior, 25*, 243–295.

van Knippenberg, B., & van Knippenberg, D. (2005). Leader self-sacrifice and leader effectiveness: The moderating role of leader prototypicality. *The Journal of Applied Psychology, 90*, 25–37.

van Knippenberg, B., van Knippenberg, D., De Cremer, D., & Hogg, M. A. (2004). Leadership, self, and identity: A review and research agenda. *Leadership Quarterly, 15*(6), 825–856.

van Knippenberg, D., van Knippenberg, B., & van Dijk, E. (2000). Who takes the lead in risky decision making? Effects of group members' individual riskiness and prototypicality. *Organizational Behavior and Human Decision Processes, 83*, 213–234.

Van Mannen, J. (1997). *Identity work: Notes on the personal identity of police officers* (MIT Working Paper). Cambridge, MA: Massachusetts Institute of Technology.

Willemsen, T. M. (2002). Gender typing of the successful manager: A stereotype reconsidered. *Sex Roles, 46*(11–12), 385–391.

Winnicott, D.W. (1975). Transitional objects and transitional phenomena. In D. W. Winnicott, (Ed.), *Through pediatrics to psychoanalysis* (pp. 229–242). London, UK: Karnac. (Original work published 1958).

Yost, J. H., & Strube, M. J. (1992). The construction of the self: An evolutionary view. *Current Psychology, 11*(2), 110–121.

Yukl, G. (2010). *Leadership in organizations* (7th ed.). Upper Saddle River, NJ: Prentice-Hall.

PART 4

Follower-Centric Theories and Approaches

CHAPTER

15 Leadership Perception and Information Processing: Influences of Symbolic, Connectionist, Emotional, and Embodied Architectures

Jessica E. Dinh, Robert G. Lord, *and* Ernest Hoffman

Abstract

This chapter reviews and integrates recent empirical findings from neuropsychological research and the cognitive sciences to develop an information processing model that explores how symbolic, connectionist, emotional, and embodied architectures dynamically influence leadership perception and information processing. The authors begin by conceptualizing the human mind in terms of four abstract information processing architectures (symbolic, connectionist, emotional, and embodied systems) that are based on neurobiological adaptive systems. They then present a framework to explore how these architectures influence the emergence of leadership perceptions and information processing through multiple constraint satisfaction. This framework has the benefit of organizing and identifying new areas for future leadership research.

Key Words: symbolic architectures, connectionist architectures, emotional architectures, embodied architectures, dynamic adaptive systems, information processing, leadership perception, multiple constraint satisfaction

Leadership Perception and Information Processing: Influences of Symbolic, Connectionist, Emotional, and Embodied Architectures

Leaders in the 21st century experience unique challenges as they operate within complex, dynamic organizational systems (Uhl-Bien & Marion, 2009) that are internally diverse and geographically expansive (Osland, 2010). For instance, leaders must make sense of changing social contexts, evolving organizational processes, and disruptive events that vary in duration, magnitude, and severity (e.g., Balogun & Johnson, 2004; Morgeson, 2005). In addition, leaders must make accurate assessments of others, including their values, motives, and talents. It is no surprise then, a leader's ability to discern and process these subtle environmental cues has profound consequences on individual and organizational outcomes.

In this chapter, we explain that efforts to understand emergent leadership phenomena, including how leaders perceive and interpret their changing social environments, require that we closely explore the dynamics among four types of cognitive architectures (symbolic, connectionist, emotional, embodied), which provide qualitatively different frames for information processing. In brief, *cognitive architectures* refer to fixed (or slowly varying) structures that provide an abstract framework for understanding processes related to cognition, learning, and performance (Newell, 1990; Newell, Rosenbloom, & Laird, 1989). Although early work on cognitive architectures focused on the abstract processing capabilities of *symbolic* and *connectionist* architectures (Newell et al., 1989; Rumelhart, Hinton, & McClelland, 1986), recent thinking in social and neurocognitive sciences supports the need to consider the effects of emotional and embodied systems on a person's information processing capabilities (Blanchette & Richards, 2010; Lord & Shondrick, 2011; Pfeifer & Bongard, 2006). As Iacoboni (2007) argues, the need to broaden our perspective and develop a more holistic understanding of informational processing systems arises because meaning is not just conveyed by abstract internal representations of the outside world. Rather, it is also constructed through the experiences and effects of a body that is *physically embedded in the world.*

Our perspective highlights three issues that are relevant to understanding leadership processes. First, recent advances in neuroimaging show that the brain is a highly complex structure composed of dense, interconnected layers of neurons (Bassett & Gazzaniga, 2011) that function together as a *dynamic adaptive system*. We maintain that conceptualizing the brain as a flexible, dynamic structure produces many constructs and models for integrating processes over time, such as how leaders adjust to varying constraints within changing environments (Dinh & Lord, 2012). Second, although neurological research clearly indicates that the brain is composed of multiple systems that evolved over time and bear on different processing tasks (Stone, 2007), the brain's complexity limits the value of understanding leadership perception and information processing from a purely neurological perspective. However, by using the concept of dynamic adaptive systems to ground our theory, we explain how intelligent systems can be modeled by representing neurological systems in terms of four cognitive architectures as shown in Figure 15.1. Third, we use this framework to show the relevance of lower order (embodied and emotional) systems in explaining emergent leadership outcomes by reviewing and integrating important domains within the social-cognitive literature. Finally, we discuss the implications of our perspective for leadership theory and practice. We make note that throughout this chapter, we present terminology that may be unfamiliar to some readers. To ease interpretation, however, these terms are listed and defined in Table 15.1.

A Micro-Level Perspective for Understanding Event and Person Perceptions

Research on leadership and information processing often focuses on person or global level features (Lord & Dinh, 2012). However, efforts to understand fully the dynamics of leadership perception require that we examine perceptual processes that evolve over a few milliseconds rather than those that occur over minutes, hours, or days. At this level, information is processed "in situation" as the brain incorporates feedback from the physical body, as well as the environmental cues and the historical context of a given event.

We assert that there are two advantages of creating a framework that focuses explicitly on micro-level features. First, perceptions and reactions to events can be conceptualized as dynamic, emergent stimulus-driven processes rather than as an outcome of static, top-down processes. Second,

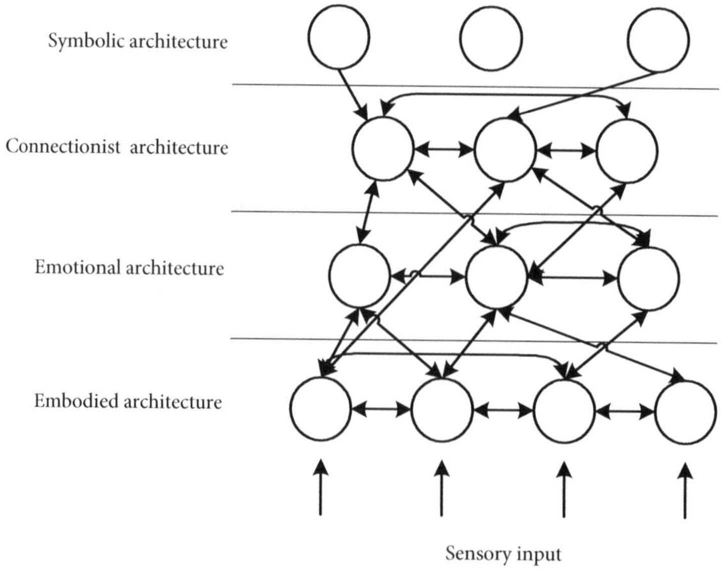

Figure 15.1. Integrative Processing Framework for Symbolic, Connectionist, Emotional, and Embodied Architectures.

Table 15.1. Glossary

Term	Definition
Attractor	Point of stability or convergence in a dynamic system
Brain modularity	Specialized subcomponents of the brain that perform unique functions and can adapt or evolve to external demands
Brain scale	System-wide processing of the brain
Events	Temporally contained units of activity that are distinguishable to the perceiver
Cognitive architecture	Abstract information processing structures with distinct basic operations, control mechanisms, and memory systems that influence cognition, learning, and performance
Complex system	A system whose overall behavior can be characterized as more than the sum of its parts
Connectionist architecture	Network-based processing structure that quickly and automatically transmits activation or inhibition to connected units to create meaningful patterns. Learning occurs as the weights connecting units are changed.
Embodied architecture	Processes sensory information received from the body's morphology and organic material. Sensitive to the body's physiological reactions and the surrounding environment.
Emotional architecture	Processing structure for evolutionary based emotions occurring in lower cortical regions of the brain. Emotional stimuli are processed quickly and automatically with distinct facial systems for the detection of emotions.
Parallel processing	Information is processed simultaneously across different cortical systems or brain areas.
Phase space	Multidimensional surfaces or landscapes that represent the trajectory of a dynamic system
Prototype	Collection of typical features that define a category
Symbols	Abstract representations of an idea or physical entity
Symbolic architecture	Rule-based processing structure that uses conscious and attentional resources to process information serially. Information is represented abstractly in symbol structures and is processed in higher order cortical networks.

it illuminates how sensory information is integrated across diverse cognitive systems to form more encompassing cognitions. The connections in Figure 15.1 address this issue. For example, faster processing systems (i.e., embodied and emotional) appear near the bottom of the figure and are believed to "take the lead" in processing incoming sensory information (Lord & Harvey, 2002). However, higher order systems may also constrain the sensitivity and functioning of lower order systems through these connections. Consequently, each cognitive system may influence the local processing of information in other cognitive systems (Abbott & Regehr, 2004; Bassett & Gazzanigna, 2011), which affects how sensory and cognitive information interact to emerge in a holistic manner. Given the bidirectional influence of information processing systems (Freeman & Ambady, 2011), it is likely insufficient to examine such dynamics at a person level, and moving down to a micro-level allows for a more fine-grained perspective of how diverse systems are integrated together.

It is helpful to describe some properties of *dynamic adaptive systems* before focusing on the integrative framework shown in Figure 15.1. Using a micro-level perspective, we then use this framework to understand leadership processes.

Dynamic Adaptive Systems and Information Processing

DYNAMIC SYSTEMS

The human brain is a complex structure that consists of differentiated networks and subsystems for processing unique sensory and abstract information (Bassett & Gazzanigna, 2011). Importantly, the neuronal connections within a subsystem are typically stronger than those linking together different subsystems (Kirschner & Gerhart, 1998). As such, there is partial independence between different subsystems. From an evolutionary standpoint, partial independence, or brain modularity, is advantageous as it enables subsystems to adapt to dynamic environmental changes without being restricted by other subsystems (Basset & Gazzanigna, 2011). Thus, adaption can be a local, rather than a global brain-scale event, and change can occur simultaneously in multiple locations as different modules process information in parallel.

It is important to note that despite brain modularity, brain subsystems are also highly interconnected, and there are soft or flexible constraints among these subsystems that enable one to influence the activation (or inhibition) of another (Thagard & Nerb, 2002). Through such mutual influences, various brain systems can self-organize as they create coherent responses to events or form social perceptions (Carver & Scheier, 2002). Often, these organized responses function as an *attractor*, which represent a point of stability in various brain modalities that attracts a system's movements toward a predictable end state (Bectel & Abrahamsen, 2002; Ikegaya et al., 2004). For example, a leadership prototype (an image of our ideal leader) is frequently described in terms of a perceptual attractor (Lord & Maher, 1991).

Attractors are important as they can create momentary frames that guide information processing. Although similar, we note that attractors differ from cognitive architectures in that architectures are *enduring* (vs. momentary) frames that guide information processing. Abstractly, attractors can be represented as deep wells in a phase space that tracks the output of a dynamic system over time. As shown in Figure 15.2, a *phase space* is a multidimensional surface or landscape that helps one visualize the behavioral trajectory of a system. Using this analogy, attractors define the nature of dynamic systems by capturing and changing the trajectory of variable entities, such as ideas and perceptions, that enter its basin; moving them toward points of stability as defined by the attractor. These systems operate much like a watershed directs the flow of water toward lakes or rivers in its domain. Similarly, Eiser (1994) maintains that attractors can be thought of as being carved out by learning processes that organize thoughts and actions in a consistent or schematic way, or they can be created "on-the-fly" as a means to make sense of novel situations. Changes in social perceptions, such as in leadership, reflect shifts from one attractor to another (Foti, Knee, & Backert, 2008; Hanges, Lord, Godfrey, & Raver, 2002).

Leaders can also influence the development of attractors. As shown in Figure 15.2, leaders can create behavioral attractors that "pull" or normalize team members' behaviors to create a safety climate when leaders are consistent in prioritizing safety goals (Dragoni, 2005). However, when leaders are inconsistent in prioritizing safety goals, team members may weakly adhere to such safety regulations (as represented by a shallow attractor). In this example, the consistency of a leader's behavior is a key factor in the development of homogenous organizational norms. When leaders are inconsistent, however, their actions may weaken the strength of an attractor and cause team members to gravitate toward different behavioral norms, which introduces heterogeneity in organizational safety values.

The preceding paragraphs suggest that attractors can create consistency or variability in one's behaviors and perceptions of others. We have also offered a parsimonious view of how different types

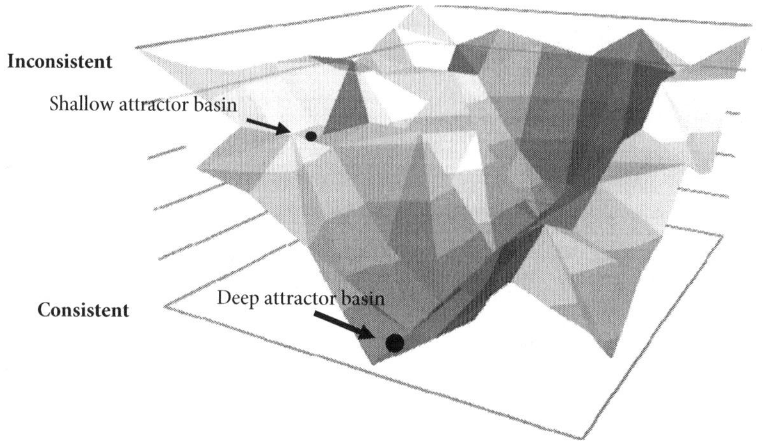

Figure 15.2. Phase Space and Leadership Attractors.

of attractors (e.g., perceptual, behavioral) can independently influence leadership perception and information processing. However, it is more accurate to suggest that although attractors are situated in local brain modalities and subsystems, their effects can extend to other cortical regions to affect how cognition and perception emerge on a more global brain scale. The dynamics of multiple attractors is well illustrated in neurological studies on the origins and prevention of epileptic seizures (e.g., Kalitzin, Velis, & Lopes da Silva, 2010), which demonstrates that systems of attractors maintain cerebral "steady states" or stable patterns of neural activity. Seizures occur, however, when attractor networks deform during mental shifts or transitions and cause some neural signals to surpass a critical threshold. Thus, the processing dynamics among multiple attractors creates coherency and continuity in information processing especially during periods when individuals transition between mental states.

Generally, systems of attractors affect the generation (or maintenance) of thoughts, ideas, and actions on a moment-to-moment basis. This implies that networks of attractors may span diverse perceptual and cognitive systems (e.g., emotional, embodied, symbolic), which together, introduce dynamic constraints that color one's perceptual experiences and motivational processes. To demonstrate, O'Reilly, Braver, and Cohen (1999) show that affective states can modulate or bias the processes that maintain goal structures in the prefrontal cortex, and goal structures, in turn, shape conscious thoughts and memory processes. Thus, at least three qualitatively different attractors (affect, goals, and consciousness) are linked by dynamic, cross-modular, feedback systems. O'Reilly et al. also show that positive affective states occur when one anticipates that actions will be successful. Hence, leadership activities that increase follower expectations, such as Eden's Pygmalion effect (1992), may have far-reaching effects that stabilize motivational and cognitive systems. Supportive leaders also may help stabilize processing systems in others as they move individuals from one attractor state (e.g., negative affect) to another (e.g., positive affect) (George & Zhou, 2007).

COGNITIVE ARCHITECTURES AND INFORMATION PROCESSING

Over the last 50 years, cognitive scientists have developed several types of operating models to represent information processing systems which they refer to as *cognitive architectures*. In this section, we discuss information processing in terms of four cognitive architectures, which are briefly summarized in Table 15.2. We then illustrate the relation of architectures to dynamic systems. Architectures are one step removed from the physical systems that implement cognitive operations, but much can be learned by thinking about how brain structures can implement a specific architecture (e.g., Newell, 1990). Because architectures provide an abstract system for theorizing about cognitive operations, these systems can provide a basis for learning about artificial intelligence, as well as human information processing.

There are three notable characteristics of an architecture that structures how it influences information processing. First, architectures have systems that are dedicated to performing specific operations (also referred to as *basic operations*) that the system can perform quickly and efficiently. For example, emotional architectures have highly efficient systems located in the temporal lobes that specialize in detecting and processing facial emotions (i.e., fusiform face area; Nestor, Plaut, & Behrmann, 2011). In humans, basic operations involve primitive processing structures that had evolved millions of years ago and are shared with other species (Stone, 2007). Second, architectures have *control mechanisms* that specify the sequence of cognitive operations needed to provide coherence, order, and purpose to information processing. Often, control mechanisms rely on an integration of multiple parameters (e.g., current goals, sensory inputs, recent thoughts, and active identities) through spreading activation to automatically trigger appropriate operations. Control mechanisms thereby provide a mechanism for integrating information across different architectures. Third, architectures contain *memory systems* that allow for the storage and retrieval of information. For example, symbolic architectures have long-term and short-term memory stores that differ in the capacity and the speed with which each can access and retrieve memory (Jonides et al., 2008).

In addition to these structural characteristics, architectures must address the need for purposeful interaction with a relevant environment (e.g., task, social, or organizational), as well as conform at some level to the parameters of human interactions. For instance, Allport (1989) notes that memory and selective attention mechanisms must make information required for action available precisely when it is

Table 15.2. Parameters for Symbolic, Connectionist, Emotional, and Embodied Architectures

	Cognitive architecture			
	Symbolic	Connectionist	Emotional	Embodied
Time frame	500 milliseconds–10 seconds	200–500 milliseconds	≥10 milliseconds	≥5 milliseconds
Supporting technology	Serial processing system that retrieves, transforms in rule-based manner, and restores symbol structures	Parallel processing network that transmits activation and inhibition among units to create meaningful patterns while satisfying constraints	Coherent neuroanatomical and neurochemical circuits that connect to expressive and motivational systems. Connections to cognitive systems are optional.	Sensorimotor pressure sensors in the body's joints, epidermis, and musculature
Memory system	Separate units	Activation (inhibition) pattern	Neurochemical	Motor memory
Sequencing mechanism	Executive unit, serial processing	Parallel summing of activation, emergent	Stimulus and evolution based; fixed mechanism	Stimulus and evolution based; fixed mechanism
Storage/learning	Development of new symbol structures in long-term and short-term memory systems	Modification of connection weights	Modification of genetic information and cognition	Muscle memory, elasticity in skin, sensori-motor habituation
Retrieval	Access unit	Recreate pattern	Neural and physical activation	Sensorimotor activation
Supporting processing regions	Prefrontal and frontal cortices	Distributed neural networks	Amygdala, insula, precunis, limbic system	Muscles, sensori-motor receptors, pressure receptors

needed, a principle he calls *selection-for-action*. This principle applies when responding to social, as well as task relevant information within an environment. Selection-for-action often operates automatically outside of consciousness, and may reflect cumulative learning such as experience. For example, implicit voice theories, which guide the decision to speak or remain silent, use information based on a supervisor's abusive or supportive leadership style to automatically to guide social interactions (Detert & Edmondson, 2011).

As shown in Table 15.2, processing time is an important factor that differs among architectures. Symbolic operations, which involve conscious states of awareness, operate slowly and often require several seconds to be completed. In contrast, connectionist architectures can assimilate large quantities of information in less than a fraction of a second. Among the fastest, emotional and embodied architectures require only a few milliseconds to perform operations such as detecting an angry face in a crowd (Öhman, 2002), or adjusting the body's movements based on feedback from its morphology (Pfeifer & Bongard, 2006). Although all four architectures operate simultaneously, each architecture fulfills different functions based on its unique processing style. For example, emotional architectures can provide a protective defense mechanism by quickly alerting individuals to potential dangers or opportunities in their environment due to its fast processing speed (Le Doux, 1996). Connectionist and embodied architectures, in contrast, enable the mind and body to adjust flexibly to contextual demands by using more automatic forms of informational processing (Lord, Brown, Harvey, & Hall, 2001; Pfeifer & Bongard, 2006). Traditionally, different cognitive architectures have been modeled as independent systems. By applying properties of dynamic adaptive systems (Bassett & Gazzanigna, 2011), however, we can conceptualize architectures as interacting systems that spontaneously create emergent structures that constrain or facilitate leadership perceptions and information processing.

In the following section, we begin by discussing symbolic architectures, which has received the most attention in traditional cognitive research. As we proceed downwards in Figure 15.1, we also differentiate between symbolic, connectionist, emotional, and embodied architectures. In doing so, we draw on dynamic systems and multiple constraints theory (Holyoak & Thagard, 1989; 1995; Rumelhart et al., 1986), and explain how these theories can be applied to better understand emergent leadership phenomena.

A Systems Approach to Understanding Leadership Processes

Symbolic Architectures

Symbolic types of informational processing has received much attention in cognitive research, and it has served as the default model for how knowledge is mentally represented (Norman, 1993). According to symbolic perspectives, knowledge and concepts are represented abstractly as symbols that are disconnected from the body and external events (Lord & Shondrick, 2011; Schooler et al., 2011). *Symbols* are representations that stand for something else, such as *words* in a language. Symbols can also be combined to create higher order symbol structures, just as words are combined into sentences. Other examples of symbol structures include goals, thoughts, beliefs, and case-based knowledge (Mumford, Blair, & Marcy, 2007), such as scripts or schemas (Lord & Shondrick, 2011). Importantly, all of these symbol structures can be maintained independently of perceptual input (Schooler et al., 2011).

Symbolic architectures are characterized by several important characteristics. First, they process information serially and slowly based on rules (e.g., if-then statements), much like a modern computer. Generally, information is processed intentionally and consciously within symbolic architectures (Smith & DeCoster, 2000), which makes this architecture particularly good for explaining leadership processes that involve highly abstract forms of thinking such as logical reasoning (Lord & Shondrick, 2011) or processes such as vision communication (Stam, van Knippenberg, & Wisse, 2010). Second, the processing capacity of symbolic architectures are constrained by its limited attentional capacity (Fiske & Taylor, 2008). Symbolic architectures are therefore affected by situational constraints, such as the effects of stress or distractions that divert one's attention from processing a focal object or task. For example, multitasking (e.g., driving and talking on a cell phone) has been shown to adversely affect an individual's sensitivity to environmental cues (e.g., noticing pedestrians, road hazards) by taxing one's attentional resources (Strayer, Drews, & Crouch, 2006). Similar effects can limit a leader's ability to acquire new skills and knowledge. In fact, although leaders generally benefit from developmental challenges and experiences that encourage them to reflect on their behavioral strategies (Day, 2012; Day, Harrison, & Halpin, 2009), challenges can interfere with learning when they overtax their cognitive and attentional resources (DeRue & Wellman, 2009).

In the past decade, neurocognitive research has shown that a significant proportion of human thought processes occur independently of sensory input and external events (about 50 percent; Killingsworth & Gilbert, 2010). According to Schooler et al. (2011), periods of *stimulus-independent thought*, such as mind wandering or symbolic thinking, have important adaptive functions. For instance, by momentarily decoupling conscious thought processes from sensory input, individuals are able to reflect on different goals, as well as formulate future plans. Stimulus-independent thought also encourages creativity and learning by allowing individuals to consciously switch between tasks, incubate ideas, or renew needed cognitive resources for later dedicated processing (Schooler et al., 2011).

SYMBOLIC ARCHITECTURES AND INFORMATION PROCESSING

Symbol structures, such as goals, plans, or identities can influence how individuals process sensory information (Engle, Fries, & Singer, 2001). This top-down effect occurs as symbolic structures highlight aspects in the environment that are particularly self-relevant while competing information becomes automatically suppressed (Lord, Diefendorf, Schmidt, & Hall, 2010). For example, neurological research shows that goal-directed cognition, which is processed in the prefrontal and parietal cortical regions (Koechlin, Basso, Pietrini, Panzer, & Grafman, 1991), influences information processing by modulating the temporal activation patterns of large neuronal assemblies that respond to stimulus-evoked activity (Dehaene & Naccache, 2001; Engle et al., 2001). Therefore, as incoming sensory information is received, anticipatory activity and expectations can create "bias signals" in sensorimotor loops that increase the coherence and processing speed of relevant information across diverse neuronal networks (Engel et al., 2001). By influencing the temporal synchronization of large neuronal assemblies, selective attention and top-down processing influences not only how sensory information binds together, it also facilitates the access and conscious processing of stored memories (Engel et al., 2001).

An important function of symbolic architectures and top-down processes is that they increase the efficiency with which sensory information can be extracted and interpreted from complex visual scenes or experienced events (Corbetta & Schulman, 2002; Engle et al., 2001). When applied to leadership, this idea suggests that leaders with greater cognitive complexity (e.g., knowledge and experience) may be better at managing complex organizational events based on their ability to anticipate or recognize relevant patterns in the environment, and their ability to communicate these observations to others (Hannah, Lord, & Pearce, 2011; Lord & Hall, 2005). For instance, complexity in extant knowledge provides leaders with a larger and a much more diverse repertoire of procedural operations and strategies that can be matched to specific situations (Hooijberg, Hunt, & Dodge, 1997). Complexity also enables needed structures to emerge spontaneously that afford leaders greater flexibility and the ability to adapt to changing work settings (Lord, Hannah, & Jennings, 2011). As Morgeson (2005) showed, the value of leadership activities for autonomous work teams may depend on whether they are appropriately matched to situational factors (e.g., novel events, distress among team members, strenuous production period). For example, he found that leadership activities related to sensemaking or team preparation was positively related to performance, but only when events were novel. This example illustrates that cognitively complex leaders may have a greater sense of when to appropriately (vs. inappropriately) intervene in team processes.

However, selective attention and top-down processes that are controlled by symbolic architectures may also interfere with a leader's ability to accurately interpret organizational events and communicate to others. This effect is similar to experiencing functional fixedness (Adamson, 1952), in which prior expectations and goals limit one's ability to recognize alternative solutions to problems or attend to different aspects of one's visual field. Selective attention and top-down processes are exemplified in organizational research showing that those with performance-goal orientations frequently attend to environmental cues that validate their personal belief that feedback has little developmental value. In contrast, those with a mastery-goal orientation selectively attend to situational cues that promote learning (VandeWalle, 2003). The influence of top-down processes is also evident in Pygmalion effects (Eden, 1992), in which a leader's expectation of their subordinates' performance level causes subordinates to focus on performance cues that are consistent with their higher self-expectations, resulting in greater motivation, effort, and performance.

CONTROLLED AND AUTOMATIC PROCESSES IN SYMBOLIC ARCHITECTURES

Symbolic architectures have generally been thought of as involving conscious, controlled forms of processing. However, research also shows that under certain conditions, knowledge and concepts may be processed automatically. It has been shown for instance, that with extensive practice, rule-based processes can become much less dependent on attentional working memory resources (Shiffrin & Schneider, 1977). Initially, the process of learning a new skill may be highly dependent on working memory as individuals must deliberately monitor and revise their action sequences. With experience, however, working memory processes become much less critical as these skills become more automatized (Kanfer & Ackerman, 1989). Interestingly, once actions become automatized, conscious thoughts may actually interfere with the execution of automatic behavioral routines.

There are significant implications associated with the fact that symbolic architectures operate using both controlled and automatic forms of processing. From a dynamic systems perspective, this fact suggests that consciousness involves multiple cognitive systems. This is because consciousness is thought to emerge from interactive processes among diverse cortical regions in response to incoming sensory stimuli (Baars, 2005; Dehaene & Naccache, 2001). Indeed, there is evidence to suggest that once a stimulus' activation pattern surpasses a critical threshold, these patterns can gain access to long-distance neural networks that integrates the information with other cortical areas (Dehaene & Naccache, 2001). Hence, there is a shift from local to more global forms of neural processing as symbolic forms of thinking are engaged, and it is here that individuals become consciously aware of the *outcome* of perceptual processes. However, knowledge of how these interpretations are derived remains largely unknown to perceivers.

The processing dynamics among multiple cognitive architectures are shown in Figure 15.1, which reveal how symbolic modes of thinking can be influenced by more automatic processes. To illustrate, *trust* is fundamental to leadership processes, and humans have evolutionary-based predispositions to follow individuals whom they trust (Van Gugt, 2012). Trust may be based on careful evaluations about the context, or it may involve recalling past experiences with a particular individual (Mayer, Davis, & Schoorman, 1995). This controlled type of conscious processing is likely to be slow and effortful based on our portrayal of symbolic architectures.

It is often the case, however, that trust can be developed through the use of faster processing architectures. In fact, employees may develop affective-based trust from experiencing subtle bodily or affective cues (e.g., touch, approach behavior, Duchene smiles; Levav & Argo, 2010), or it may be based on the interpersonal relationship that employees have with their leader or manager (McAllister, 1995; Yang, Mossholder, & Peng, 2009). Affective-based trust (or mistrust) may in turn, color one's rational assessment of a target individual (e.g., Ballenger & Rockmann, 2010). In short, the aforementioned research not only suggests that symbol structures, such as trust, may be derived from other cognitive architectures, it also demonstrates that symbolic architectures are integrated with other architectures operating below the level of conscious awareness. These more automatic architectures are discussed in the following sections.

Connectionist Architectures

Although symbolic architectures can account for a variety of perceptual phenomena that involve conscious, deliberative processing, this perspective does not fully address how ideas, thoughts, and behavior may emerge in a dynamic manner (Lord et al., 2011; Vallacher, Read, & Nowak, 2002). One weakness of symbolic architectures is that they conceptualize knowledge and memory as being stored at a fixed location, much like files in a filing drawer. As such, the ability to interpret and perceive an object or entity depends on the accessibility and correct retrieval of knowledge from memory. In addition, symbolic architectures are highly dependent on attentional resources, and they process information in a serial manner (Lord & Shondrick, 2011). Yet, research has shown that people can process perceptual stimuli automatically and unconsciously (Bargh, 1989; Greenwald & Banaji, 1995).

To represent the complexity of the human brain, connectionist networks had been lauded by cognitive researchers for their ability to model how the mind can simultaneously integrate multiple sources of information. In their most rudimentary form, connectionist networks represent systems as being composed of simple units (i.e., nodes) and connections that feed activation to other neurons in input–output, feed-forward systems. However, such systems can select different responses when (a) different input patterns are experienced, or (b) when networks have "hidden layers" that allow different nodes to interact (Churchland & Sejnowski, 1990). In this section, we focus on *recurrent connectionist networks*, which have richer structures of interconnected nodes that allow feedback loops to maintain activation independently of stimulus input (Smith, 1996), as well as allow systems to "dynamically interact to adapt to their environments" (Bechtel & Abrahamsen, 1996: 22).

A critical feature of recurrent connectionist networks is that each unit or node is associated with an activation value that affects how information is processed holistically in the network. For instance, nodes can be excitatory (i.e., a positive activation value) or inhibitory (i.e., a negative activation value), which influences the activation patterns of nearby nodes much like systems of neurons in the brain. Compared to simple feed-forward networks, recurrent connectionist networks can pass information *bidirectionally* from node to node (Freeman & Ambady, 2011). Therefore, as information is received by a node (e.g., an excitatory node), a signal is relayed to other interconnected nodes that are distributed across the network. As this occurs, a feedback signal that may be either excitatory or inhibitory, is returned to the original sending node. Consequently, feedback mechanisms allow nodes to learn and adapt by changing the connection strength among nodes. At a more global level, these bidirectional processes can culminate to affect how patterns of activation are actively (re)generated across the network with each successive activation cycle (Bechtel & Abrahamsen, 1996). Importantly, such processes allow interactive networks to spontaneously create attractors (Eiser, 1994; Hopfield, 1982), which serve as momentary guides for information processing.

Recurrent connectionist networks are well suited to explain how perceptions can vary as different activation patterns spread across the same units at various points in time (Hanges, Lord, & Dickson, 2000). Such variation is much more difficult to represent or explain in traditional symbolic models of cognition because they posit that information is represented in higher order knowledge structures as symbols (e.g., schemas, traits, prototypes) that are static, are accessed serially, and require the support of conscious attentional resources (Bechtel & Abrahamsen, 1996). In contrast, recurrent connectionist networks can incorporate contextual constraints, as well as the interaction between top-down structures (e.g., expectations, motivation) and bottom-up input (e.g., sensory information) as they "settle in" to create solutions, such as leadership perceptions (Foti et al., 2008; Hanges, et al., 2000; Lord et al., 2001).

Spreading activation within connectionist networks can also explain how perceptual information is constructed or "filled in," as shown when individuals falsely recall past memories and experiences by inserting in plausible details (e.g., eyewitness testimonies; Loftus & Palmer, 1974). Memory construction is also evident when individuals infer leadership characteristics based on their *implicit leadership theories* (Shondrick, Dinh, & Lord, 2011), which occur when unobserved prototypical leadership behaviors are falsely remembered because they are consistent with leadership prototypes (Phillips, 1984). Spreading activation from behaviors that were actually observed provides one viable explanation of such effects. Because memory in a connectionist network involves both the reactivation and the filling-in of information through a pattern completion process, it is said to have a *content addressable memory.* This property avoids the need to have a pointer or index (e.g., a category label) to find information as is required in a symbolic system. Thus, "memory" for leadership activities and leadership impressions can be activated by leadership content such as the traits, qualities, and behaviors that are associated with leadership.

ATTRACTORS AND MULTIPLE CONSTRAINT SATISFACTION

In connectionist networks, the final activation of a node is determined by the satisfaction of multiple constraints, which are determined by the connections and activation patterns of nearby nodes (Freeman & Ambady, 2011). Therefore, as each node in the network constrains (or facilitates) the activation of other nodes, an activation pattern is generated that represents the best fitting solution that accounts for the incoming sensory information and the constraints that had been created by the structure of the existing network. A good analogy of multiple constraint satisfaction can be obtained from how people form decisions in complex, ambiguous situations. For instance, when individuals are presented with pieces of information, such as evidence in a jury trial, decision makers must weigh how the evidence and rival arguments fit together to create a coherent story. As Holyoak and Simon (1999) show (see also Holyoak & Thagard, 1997), the development of a coherent story follows a constraint satisfaction model in that an individual's understanding of the jury case is shaped by the constraints given by each piece of information. Therefore, a juror's final decision is the best fitting solution that accounts for all of the received information (and constraints given by the information), much like how an overall activation pattern satisfies the constraints given by nodes across a connectionist network.

When the properties of connectionist networks are applied to explain leadership perceptions, this architecture suggests that the perceptions and memories of a leader are actively (re)constructed in ways that conform to current attractors (Lord et al., 2001), instead of being drawn from static memory "bins" as symbolic categorization theories would suggest (Srull & Wyer, 1989). Consequently, an individual's prototypical image of a leader may vary across contexts and events, which allows for the emergence of very different leaders in different situations (Brown, Diekman, & Schneider, 2011; Hanges et al., 2000; Sy et al., 2010). This concept applies especially to modern organizations, which have become globalized and include diverse cultures (Osland, 2010). According to Hanges et al. (2000), culture provides a knowledge system that allows people to make sense of encountered events and people. Importantly, because cultural beliefs impose multiple constraints on specific traits associated with leadership (e.g., a leader's language, height, ethnicity, age, gender), it constrains the prototype that is used to evaluate potential leaders. At the same time, connectionist architectures can evaluate the fit of potential leaders, such that an individual who fits the active pattern of constraints is likely seen as a leader than someone with a less congruent profile. Thus, leadership perceptions seem to reflect the effects of patterns in addition to the effects of specific leadership characteristics (Foti & Hauenstein, 2007; Smith & Foti, 1998). These findings also illustrate that leadership perception is a dynamic process (Lord et al., 2001), where a person's features (e.g., gender) can shape the prototype that is used to form leadership perceptions (Foti et al., 2008), just as the prototype being used can shape the qualities of potential leaders that are noticed and remembered.

Other leadership outcomes can be understood as the product of multiple constraint satisfaction in organizational systems. For instance, the development of creative ideas and leadership visions often require mutual collaboration among multiple individuals who each have different backgrounds and perspectives. Although heterogeneous team compositions may facilitate a team's innovative capacities by allowing leaders and team members to draw on a diverse pool of skills and resources (Hannah et al., 2011), constraints may emerge as interpersonal differences make it more difficult for members to cooperate with others (Cannella, Park, & Lee, 2008; Page, 2007). Thus, innovation in teams represents the satisfaction of multiple constraints that are created by each team member within a leader's immediate social network. The same types of processes can be used to understand shared or distributive leadership, and how different individuals may emerge as leaders at different points in time as the constraints created by a particular situation brings out the best (or worst) in certain individuals (Carson, Tesluk, & Marrone, 2007). However, leadership is embedded within a larger social context (Day et al., 2009; Lord & Brown, 2004), and larger macro-level constraints, such as organizational and national policies, also apply as leaders and team members learn to adapt their ideas and visions in ways that are consistent with their organization's structure and values.

CONTROLLED AND AUTOMATIC PROCESSES IN CONNECTIONIST ARCHITECTURES

Our knowledge of the external world is acquired primarily through the output of perceptual processes and the mental models they engender (Johnson-Laird, 1989). Although generally operating outside of awareness, mental structures and incoming information typically interact. Through such interactions, select streams of information can become conscious when there is sufficient amplification from bottom-up and top-down attentional resources (Baars, 2005; Dehaene & Naccache, 2001). For instance, when perceptual stimuli resonate within long-term memory structures (Grossberg, 1999), or when they are discrepant from one's expectations, bottom-up stimuli can "capture" one's focus of attention. Such occurrences are easily demonstrated in visual *pop out effects,* or the *cocktail party effect,* where hearing one's own name causes them to turn their attention toward the source of the sound.

Conceptualizing connectionist architectures as a highly interconnected constraint satisfying network helps clarify how perceptual processes can be subconsciously influenced by many different cognitive architectures. To demonstrate, Dijksterhuis and Nordgren (2006) argue that subconscious information processing incorporates more information and can be more accurate under certain circumstances compared to when information is consciously integrated. Supporting this argument, they demonstrated that decision making for various events (e.g., buying a home) was more accurate when individuals made their decisions *automatically* based on "gut feelings," compared to when they deliberated their choices. Thus, automatic processes that occur within connectionist architectures may be enhanced by cross-system effects from lower and higher order systems.

The connections that link connectionist architectures to other architectures also provides a means by which leaders can implicitly or subconsciously influence their followers' perceptions and behaviors. For example, Lord and Brown (2004) maintain that leaders can symbolically prime alternative follower goals and identities by emphasizing different pronouns (We vs. I), and thereby modify follower behavior. Also illustrating such effects, research has demonstrated that human beings have a natural tendency to mimic or embody the behaviors of others, which may result in emotional contagion (i.e., nonconscious transferal of emotional experiences; Chartrand & Bargh, 1999; Niedenthal, Barsalou, Winkielman, Krauth-Gruber, & Rie, 2005). Research also shows that these embodied processes can promote social cohesion. By subtlety copying a target's behavior (e.g., touching one's chin, rubbing one's hands), for example, a leader can subconsciously induce an interdependent self-construal (a collective orientation) within the target that promotes the engagement of prosocial behaviors (Ashton-James, van Baaren, Chartrand, Decety, & Karremans, 2007). Prosocial behavior, in turn, benefit organizations by increasing its performance (e.g., customer satisfaction, lower turnover and absenteeism; Podsakoff, Whiting, Podsakoff, & Blume, 2009), and social capital (Bolino, Bloodgood, & Turnley, 2002).

Hence, the mind's ability to simultaneously integrate multiple streams of sensory information through connectionist architectures is socially adaptive as it helps manage the task of interpreting complex social and organizational environments. At a broader level, connectionist systems are intricately connected with other architectures, which enables leaders and followers to reciprocally influence one another symbolically through words or symbolism, and implicitly through their emotions, gestures, and embodiment. We suggest that this perspective differs from a large part of the leadership literature, which has focused largely on how explicit, symbolic forms of communication and decision making affect leadership phenomena.

Emotional Architectures

Emotional architectures have unique computational capacities that set them apart from symbolic and connectionist architectures. For instance, information processing occurs within a matter of milliseconds, which allows individuals to quickly detect external threats. Hence, there is a unique survival function associated with emotional architectures (Cosmides & Tooby, 2000). Neurologically, emotional architectures are also distinct from symbolic and connectionist architectures in that informational processing occurs in the lower, more primitive regions of the brain (amygdala and limbic systems), rather in areas that are known for higher order cognitive processing (prefrontal cortex and medial temporal lobe; LaBar & Cabeza, 2006; LeDoux & Phelps, 2008). Within our framework, emotional architectures primarily process the emotional and the affective content of perceptual stimuli, and structurally, there is evidence to suggest that basic human emotions (e.g., happy, sad, fear) are associated with specific neurotransmitter systems in the brain (Cahill & McGaugh, 1998; LeDoux, 2007). In this way, experiencing a specific kind of emotion can be understood in terms of an attractor that emerges after constraints from an individual's external and internal environment are satisfied to trigger these neurotransmitter systems (Thayer & Lane, 2000).

Emotions can be conceptualized as a class of affective phenomena that originate from an individual's conscious or subconscious assessment of stimuli (Fredrickson, 2001). Emotions are also more closely tied to specific events, and are more transient than moods, which describe feelings that are pervasive and objectless. Universally, people experience several basic emotions that include fear, anger, disgust, sadness, and happiness, which are innate rather than learned (Ekman & Friesen, 1971). In addition, emotions are distinctively conveyed by specific facial expressions and nonverbal vocalizations that also appear to be universally represented (Ekman & Davidson, 1994; Sauter, Eisner, Ekman, & Scott, 2010). In short, emotional systems operate as an architecture in two respects. First, there are dedicated physiological systems for processing emotions, which allows processing to be fast and independent of other cognitive operations; second, there are distinct muscular systems for expressing emotions, which enable the communication of emotional experiences.

These features facilitate several adaptive social functions. Foremost, the ability to experience and convey emotions is valuable not only for survival purposes, but also for effective social functioning. This is not surprising as humans are social animals and have survived through group activities. Emotions allow groups to rapidly experience the same motivational structures and respond to the same emotional cues—approaching pleasant or joyful stimuli—while avoiding angry individuals or disgusting stimuli. The ability to engage in coordinated social action increases the efficiency with which groups can address situational or social issues. Thus, leadership processes that make use of these efficient, emotionally guided reactions may be particularly powerful in achieving leadership outcomes. For example, charismatic and transformational leadership have strong affective components, where conveying positive affect (both verbally and nonverbally) is an important criterion that determines charismatic leadership perceptions (Bono & Ilies, 2006; Erez, Misangyi, Johnson, LePine, & Halverson, 2008; Naidoo & Lord, 2008). However, the importance of affect may extend further than influencing leadership emergence. As Brown and Keeping (2005) show, the overall performance evaluation of a transformational leader may be encoded in affective as well as behavioral terms.

EMOTIONAL ARCHITECTURES AND INFORMATION PROCESSING

Research on emotional systems in the past two decades has advanced our understanding of how emotional stimuli are processed. To date, research suggests that after sensory information is initially received by the retina, information is processed in one of two distinct pathways or "roads" that differ in the amount of perceptual detail available, and the processing speed that is used to analyze emotional stimuli (LeDoux, 1996). According to LeDoux's (1996) model of fear activation, sensory information may be processed through a "low road" where information is transferred directly from subcortical structures (the thalamus and superior colliculus) to the amygdala. This pathway allows information to be processed quickly, and it is useful for the detection of threats (LeDoux, 1996; LeDoux & Phelps, 2008). For instance, an involuntary jump backwards after seeing a coiled black "snake" in the grass exemplifies the rapid processing of visual stimuli through direct thalamo–amygdala connections. However, because this pathway bypasses the cortex (LeDoux, 1996), information is processed coarsely without great perceptual detail.

However, when sensory information is processed using a "high road," information is first relayed from the lateral geniculate nuclei of the thalamus to the cortex, where it is then projected to the amygdala (LeDoux, 1996). In this path, stimuli are processed at a much slower rate as neural signals must travel greater cortical distances; as a result, the perceptual representation of stimuli becomes more detailed, and individuals are also more likely to become consciously aware of processing that occurs in this path. For example, a "high road" interpretation of the aforementioned situation may involve individuals becoming consciously aware that they had (mistakenly) overreacted to a nonlethal garden hose. Applied to leadership, sensemaking that uses the high road may depend on a leader's verbal communication, whereas sensemaking that uses the low road may be more dependent on a leader's emotions or nonverbal behavior.

The distinction between a low and high road of information processing also parallels the distinction between primary and secondary appraisals. *Primary appraisal* involves the automatic assessment of self-relevance and the potential harm that is associated with a person or event. It is this assessment that creates an initial positive or negative valence appraisal, similar to a low road type of processing. For example, the initial framing of an event as being either a threat or an opportunity (Dutton & Jackson, 1987) may produce emotional responses through a primary appraisal process. In contrast, *secondary appraisal* involves a more thoughtful assessment of causality for actions as well as an evaluation of one's available resources to cope with an event (Frijda, 1986; Lazarus, 1991). Consequently, secondary appraisals are slower and deliberate as they draw forth resources and integrate information from diverse areas of the brain. It is possible, however, that subconscious processes can influence secondary appraisals. For example, Medvedeff (2008) showed in an experimental study that when experimenters coupled negative feedback with positive emotional expressions, secondary appraisal resulted in problem-focused coping, whereas pairing negative feedback with negative emotional expressions produced emotion-based coping responses. The practical relevance of this research becomes apparent by recognizing that leaders fulfill an important sensemaking function (Weick, 1995) that draws on primary and secondary appraisal processes.

Often, sensemaking can become dependent on emotional architectures, and specifically on primary appraisal processes. For instance, in many types of industries and professions (e.g., armed forces, law enforcement), the exposure to threatening situations is an anticipated element of an individual's job. However, an individual's response to these sudden and fearful situations may emerge automatically without conscious thought. As Artwohl's (2002) survey on active law enforcement officers shows, this was the case for approximately 74 percent of officers who were involved in shootings. Although such automatic reactions may be adaptive in threatening situations, mistakes are often costly as reports of civilian casualties and cases of mistaken identities demonstrate (for an example, see Correll, Park, Judd, & Wittenbrink, 2002). For this reason, professionals within these fields train extensively for scenarios that involve threat, which helps make appropriate responses more automatic. It also helps individuals acquire symbolic rules of engagement that allow them to better manage more automatic emotional responses. Consistent with our framework, this shows that multiple architectures are involved in the processing of perceptions, decisions, and behaviors.

Because the ability to cope can depend on how an individual manages his or her social resources, leaders must be adept at forming secondary appraisals by recognizing and managing emotions in oneself and others. However, this ability may depend on a leader's level of *emotional complexity* (having a profound sense of emotional knowledge). In a recent study, Tavares and colleagues (2010) showed that compared to less emotionally complex individuals, those with high emotional complexity were more likely to activate brain areas known to process semantic concepts and emotional perspective taking (i.e., left temporal poles) when reacting to emotional stimuli. The activation of these higher order semantic areas also attenuated activity in the hypothalamus, which is known to process emotional stimuli in a more vicarious or reflexive manner. When applied to leadership, this finding suggests that emotionally complex leaders would be better adept at tuning into emotional and social information. Illustrating such effects, Kellet, Humphrey, and Sleeth (2006) found that the capacity to empathize with others and express emotions predicted leadership perceptions among followers. Emotionally complex leaders may also be more skilled at influencing how followers self-regulate and respond to affective events that involve both positive and negative emotions (George, 2011). As a number of authors have argued (e.g., Caruso, Mayer, & Salovey, 2002; Rubin, Munz, & Bommer, 2005), it is only when leaders are able to perceive accurately how followers *feel* that they can understand their needs; express empathy, authenticity, excitement, and enthusiasm; and develop a deeper sense of trust with followers. Indeed, Rubin et al. (2005) showed that the ability to recognize emotions accurately in others is an important individual difference that underlies one's perception as a transformational leader.

CONTROLLED AND AUTOMATIC PROCESSES IN EMOTIONAL ARCHITECTURES

The literature reviewed in the preceding text suggests that information processing within emotional architectures may be effortful or automatic, and that there are identifiable neural pathways which process affect (LeDoux, 1996). As shown in Figure 15.1, however, emotional architectures are also highly integrated with other cognitive architectures. Supporting this statement, research has shown that the amygdala is intricately connected to cortical regions that process higher and lower order cognitions, which allows this structure to modulate activity in other cognitive systems (LeDoux, 2007). For example, the amygdala can capture conscious attention when implicit expectations guided by connectionist level schemas are not met (Lieberman, Gaunt, Gilbert, & Trope, 2002). Using Figure 15.1, cross-system interactions are shown as emotions manage the shift from connectionist to symbolic processing that reflects the onset of conscious attention. On a more abstract level, we can represent emotional architectures as being intricately interwoven with architectures that involve symbolic, connectionist, or embodied processing (Damasio, 1994). Thus, many of the more interesting effects of emotions involve cross-system interactions among various architectures, which can also coincide with the transition from automatic to more controlled forms of information processing.

Cross-system interactions between emotional and nonaffective architectures have important consequences on individual outcomes. One outcome is that individuals may become consciously aware of their emotions (Damasio, 2003) as patterns of neural impulses temporally and spatially summate at a micro-level (Baars, 2005; Dehaene & Naccache, 2001). Another is that emotions can shape the nature of more symbolic or abstract forms of thinking. Fredrickson's (2001) broaden-and-build theory suggests, for instance, that by broadening action-repertoires to include exploration and risk-taking, positive emotions can promote learning and skill development in connectionist systems. Positive emotions can also facilitate the development of symbolic processes such as trust (Harkner & Keltner, 2001) or creative thinking (George, 2011; George & Zhou, 2007). Thus, the fact that transformational and charismatic leadership can manage change is perhaps not too surprising given that the positive emotions that these leaders convey can promote broader, more flexible ways of thinking, as well as encourage the development of new skills.

Dynamic processes between emotional and nonaffective architectures can also culminate to influence organizational outcomes. As Bolino et al. (2002) argued, organizations that can foster unity among employees have an unparalleled advantage as they are more effective at disseminating information and resources across the organization. Consequently, organizational policies and managerial practices that make positive emotional experiences particularly salient can influence the development of creativity, trust, and interpersonal relationships at a more symbolic and connectionist level (George, 2011; George & Zhou, 2007; Harker & Keltner, 2001). Therefore, leaders who can convey positive affect or create positive organizational climates can have profound, but often unrecognized effects on group and organizational functioning (Cameron, Dutton, & Quinn, 2003; Isen, 2001).

Although our focus was on how emotional architectures can facilitate connectionist and symbolic thinking, we note that less positive emotions (e.g., anger, fear) also have important consequences on information processing. At a symbolic level, research has shown that negative affect can reduce creativity and the accuracy of social judgments by narrowing one's attention to local details (Ambady & Gray, 2002). In addition, by heightening the production of stress hormones (i.e., glucocorticoid), negative affect can interfere with connectionist systems in the processing of sensory information and the encoding of memory (Fuchs

& Flügge, 1998; McGaugh & Roozendaal, 2002). However, under certain conditions, negative affect can facilitate problem solving. George and Zhou (2007; see also George, 2011) convincingly demonstrated that by encouraging individuals to meticulously examine problems, negative affect can be a precursor of innovative solutions, but this occurred only when positive affect and supervisory support were also experienced. Specifically, when supervisors were perceived as being trustworthy and just, employees experienced personal safety that encouraged exploration and risk-taking. There are many ways in which supervisors can build employee trust. As we will discuss, leaders and supervisors can symbolically develop trust by enacting procedural or distributive forms of justice (Johnson & Lord, 2010; Yang et al., 2009), but it is also possible that leaders develop trust through physical embodiment, such as through a slight touch on the back (Levav & Argo, 2010).

In short, emotional architectures have important consequences on information processing. Yet, the biological interconnections of the amygdala and limbic system with lower and higher order brain areas suggest that emotional architectures also interact with other cognitive architectures to influence the emergence of leadership perceptions and behaviors. In the following section, we address embodied architectures as a final, but often overlooked system that is involved in leadership processes.

Embodied Architectures

Over the last century, *functionalism* had been the dominant approach in understanding the relationship between the mind and the body. According to functionalists, the mind represents the "external" world by manipulating abstract "internal" mental symbols separately and independently from the functioning body (Fodor, 1987; Pylyshyn, 1984). Although this theoretical interpretation of cognition was instrumental in the design of the computer (Hodges, 1983), the practice of separating the mind from the body has been reevaluated by modern cognitive science (Iacoboni, 2007; Thompson & Varela, 2001). Instead, embodied approaches to information processing argues that there exists *continuity* between mind and body, where cognition is fundamentally rooted in the actions of the physical self (Pfeifer & Bongrad, 2006). From this perspective, the body has an influential role on rational thought, and as Dewey famously stated, "to see the organism *in* nature, the nervous system in the organism, the brain in the nervous system, the cortex in the brain is the answer to the problem which haunt philosophy" (1988: 198).

Embodied architectures have an influential role on the way we think. As individuals interact with their environment, their experience of the physical world is shaped by their physical morphology (e.g., body shape and limb configurations, placement of sensors) and the physical constraints of the body (e.g., the positioning of the eye sockets in the skull; Pfeifer & Bongrad, 2006). At a neuronal level, the coupling of a human being's morphology and the structural capabilities of the human body create *action patterns* as individuals interact with the environment that then become encoded subconsciously by kinetic sensors in the skin, joints, and limbs.

Action patterns have a prominent role in providing meaning by defining the contours of the physical world as individuals move in and out of their physical environments (Johnson & Rohrer, 2007). For example, the downward pull of gravity on our spinal column and the resistance experienced in our pivotal hip joints and knees allows us to experience verticality and horizontal dimensions as we stand (or sit), or move forward (or backwards) across space. In the same way, pressure sensors on one's feet and skin can inform the body of the terrain, which allows the musculoskeletal system to adjust its movements accordingly. As these examples demonstrate, the forces that act on the physical body have characteristic patterns and qualities that constrain our actions (Johnson & Rohrer, 2007), which we encode and embody through interactive experience. In this process, attractors can form as behavioral responses emerge from the interaction between the body and environment and "settle in" into recognizable physical movements, such as a particular gait. Importantly, these body–environmental analyses are computed using the physiology and the morphology of the body, rather than the brain (Pfeifer & Bongard, 2006).

Embodied architectures offer several notable evolutionary advantages. Foremost, the processing capabilities enabled by the body's musculoskeletal (mechanical) and sensory systems allows for emergent, self-stabilizing behaviors with minimal conscious processing. As an example, one can compare an artificial intelligent robot against a human being running across an uneven terrain. Whereas the robot would require a significant amount of computational processing to sense and detect every detail in the terrain (e.g., angle, curve) to adjust its mechanical arms effectively, the elasticity and spring in a human being's leg muscles could accommodate locally for uneven surface changes. Thus, embodiment reduces the computational demands needed from higher cognitive systems (Pfeifer & Bongard, 2006).

In addition, organic systems can learn and store response sequences to similar action patterns by strengthening or modifying its materials (e.g., musculature strength, joint flexibility), which further increase its efficiency. In humans, the *fist reflex* (clenching of the hands) is a common hand reflex that activates during high stress situations. This reflex is acquired naturally at birth, but it can be reinforced through job training that uses fist defensive tactics or intensive sports (e.g., boxing; Messina & Czarnecki, 2002). Although evolutionarily adaptive in response to threats, the "fist reflex" has also been attributed as a leading cause of involuntary weapon discharge in law enforcement as individuals reflexively clench on the trigger (Messina, 1994). Interestingly, this has led to the removal and replacement of fisted strikes with open hand techniques in law enforcement training programs (Messina & Czarnecki, 2002).

As physical entities, embodied architectures play an important role in guiding how human beings interact and respond to their surrounding environments. Naturally, these principles apply to larger collectives including teams and how leaders perceive and operate within dynamic organizational settings. As leaders move through an organization's space, embodiment enables the body to adjust to spatial and physical changes on a moment-to-moment basis. This capability reduces the information processing demands on higher cognitive systems, which allows leaders to reallocate resources to learn or process more central work tasks. Findings by DeRue and Wellman (2009) offer an example of when embodiment may be helpful in leader developmental training. They show that a leader's ability to learn declines as the difficulty level of a task continually increases. However, increased automaticity and coordination between the body and the environment (e.g., reflexive movement patterns in the musculature of the body's arms, hands, legs, and head) may signal when leaders are ready to handle more complex challenges as they are better equipped to automatically process lower-level operations.

Although the examples above illustrate how embodied architectures can influence leaders' performance and how they understand the contours of their environment, leaders are embedded within a larger social context (Day et al., 2009; Lord & Brown, 2004). As such, leaders must be able to process how others (e.g., their morphology, physical presence, postures, and emotional expressions) might influence organizational outcomes through embodiment. As we will show, embodied architectures can also influence how leaders and followers perceive others and their surrounding environments. However, these processes also involve the interaction among multiple cognitive architectures that operate above and below the level of conscious awareness.

EMBODIED ARCHITECTURES AND INFORMATIONAL PROCESSING

Heretofore, we focused on aspects of embodiment that are locally represented in the musculoskeletal and sensorimotor systems of the body. However, it is likely that these activation patterns are also represented cortically in distinct topological neural maps (for touch, pressure, kinetics; Buccino et al., 2001; Rizzolatti, Fogassi, & Gallese, 2002), which provides a seamless connection that grounds the mind with the body. An important concept is that sensorimotor experiences are not typically represented in a single topological neural map; rather multiple neural maps and areas of the cortex are connected in representing these experiences. For instance, when a physical object or entity is experienced, populations of neurons (known as feature detectors) become active in the brain's modality-specific systems. Importantly, these neurons capture relevant modality-specific features, such as sound, sight, and touch. When stepping onto a frozen surface, for example, sensorimotor neurons in one's joints and muscles (and corresponding cells in the somatorsensory cortex) may encode torque as one's feet slides forward. Simultaneously, neurons in other primary processing areas, such those involved with sight or sound, may encode the white hue of the ice or the crackling sound made by the frozen surface. Neurologically, these activation patterns become linked by *conjunction neurons* (Damasio, 1989; Martin, 2001) to create "image schemas" (Johnson, 1987), which are cross-modal representations of an embodied experience.

Conjunction neurons are notable in several respects. Rather than accessing modality specific memories independently, conjunction neurons provide a neurological mechanism that allows information processing to occur in parallel across multiple sensory modalities and cognitive systems. As such, sensory experiences from one modality can trigger activation patterns in another cortical region through spreading activation. This process may result in *offline embodiment* (Niedenthal et al., 2005), where perceptual experiences that were previously encoded by a sensory modality are recreated, although they may not be physically present. For example, a particular smell (e.g., an odor) can reactivate an embodied sensation of disgust (Schnall, Haidt, Clore, & Jordan, 2008a). Likewise, clenching one's fists or maintaining an upright posture can increase one's perception of power (Huang, Galinskey, Gruenfeld, & Guillory, 2011; Schubert, 2004). For social perceptions, visualizing previous experiences using these offline embodied processes can increase accuracy in recall and the role of affect in leadership processes (Naidoo, Kohari, Lord, & Dubois, 2010). Finally, different forms of touch can elicit a wide range of emotional experiences (e.g., angry, happy, sad, love; Thompson & Hampton, 2010). As these studies show, embodied architectures have significant effects on one's perpetual experiences including how one perceives and remembers others or events. Moreover, these perceptions may reflect dynamic processes that spread across several cognitive architectures (e.g., emotional, symbolic, embodied, connectionist) that settle on an attractor that locates the body in a social and physical environment.

The idea that continuity exists between the mind and body (Dewey, 1988; Thompson & Varela, 2001) explains how leaders can influence followers through their actions and words. According to Johnson and Rohrer (2007), abstract thoughts and human language are imbued with embodied concepts that are acquired from interacting with our physical environments. This linkage may explain why words or concepts such as "important" and "power" carry a metaphorical meaning that originates in the logic of our bodily experiences (Isanski & West, 2010). For instance, *importance* is a metaphor that is grounded in our bodily experience of weight. Thus, experiencing *weight* (e.g., holding a heavy object) can make our perception of people and situations appear more important (Ackerman, Nocera, & Bargh, 2010). Similarly, *power* is represented in the bodily experience of obtaining a higher vantage point or vertical distance. Thus, those who appear to be tall or upright, are perceived to have more power than lesser individuals (Giessner & Schubert, 2007). Other bodily expressions, such as maintaining an expansive posture (Huang et al., 2011), also help to convey the perception of dominance and power.

The effects of embodied architectures in leadership perceptions also apply to how leaders (and followers) construe events. In fact, our conceptualization of time, specifically the *future* or *past*, can be influenced by our physical location in space (*at the front* or *in the back*). As Boroditsky and Ramscar (2002) show, the temporal proximity of an event, as being closer in the future or in the past, changes depending on whether one currently stands at the front or at the end of a line. These types of embodied processes are critical to understanding how leaders and followers form perceptions and understand events (see Lord & Shondrick, 2011 for a review), and they are a fundamental aspect of leadership sensemaking processes (O'Malley, Ritchie, Gregory, Lord, & Young, 2009).

We suggest that leaders, by way of using sensory-rich metaphors (e.g., *heavy, cold*) can elicit embodied representations that influence how followers perceive others and their organizational surroundings. Research has shown that the use of metaphorical concepts that convey *forward movement* (e.g., being ahead of our time) can evoke the perception of *safety*, whereas those that convey *coldness* (e.g., a cold shoulder) or *weight* (e.g., a heavy topic) can evoke perceptions of *isolation* that causes individuals to experience social distance or to slow down (see Isanski & West, 2010). Indeed, the use of visual imagery is an important factor that underlies the perception of a charismatic leader (Naidoo & Lord, 2008), and these embodied sensory cues may be important for granting leaders influence over their followers' actions.

The continuity between the mind and body also explains how a leader's actions and gestures can impact symbolic and emotional architectures in the self and others. Research in this domain has been advanced by the discovery of the mirror neuron circuit, which are neural circuits that are activated by performing an action, and by watching others perform the same action (Rizzolatti et al., 2002). These circuits are crucial in conveying one's embeddedness in a social environment (Iacoboni, 2007), and mechanically they also underlie the tendency of people and animals to mimic the gestures and motions of an interacting partner (Chartrand & Bargh, 1999). As leaders and followers interact, mirror neuron circuits have powerful effects on social cognition and the transfer of emotions. Studies show that a simple act of nodding along with dyadic partner (e.g., a leader) increases the likelihood that one will agree with the partner's arguments (e.g., Tom, Ramli, Zapanta, Demir, & Lopez, 2006), and mirroring another's actions can foster the experience of empathy for another (Pfeifer, Iacoboni, Mazziotta, & Dapretto, 2008).

Facial expressions are also closely mimicked as people interact. One outcome of copying another's facial expressions (e.g., smiles, frowns) is that emotional experiences can be transferred between different people, which is referred to as *emotional contagion*. In this way, leaders can influence followers' positive or negative affect by expressing facial expressions that correspond with these emotions (Erez et al., 2008). Indeed, there is evidence to suggest that charismatic or transformational leaders are particularly effective at creating emotional contagion, perhaps because they are particularly effective at expressing positive emotions (Naidoo & Lord, 2008), which in turn, can exacerbate mimicry (Kuhbandner, Pekrun, & Maier, 2010). However, emotional contagion can also occur horizontally in an organization as followers mimic another person's facial expressions (Brown, 2012). The contagion of positive or negative emotions can in turn, positively or adversely influence follower's perception of their leader or social others (Brown & Geis, 1984).

CONTROLLED AND AUTOMATIC PROCESSES IN EMBODIED ARCHITECTURES

In this section, we have shown the role embodied architectures have on perceptual processes, which operate automatically and primarily below the level of conscious awareness. However, embodied architectures and the cognitive systems used to analyze actions and sensorimotor experiences are also highly interconnected with other architectures and systems that are involved with emotions and abstract thought. For example, skin conductance changes precede the conscious awareness of affect (Damasio, 2003), and the ability to form the corresponding facial expression is integral to understanding the meaning of emotion related words or expressions (Neal & Chartrand, 2011; Neidenthal, Winkeilman, Mondilon, &Vermeulen, 2009). Similarly, moving forward or backward can help form the basis for social categorization related to inclusive or exclusive group membership (Paladino & Castelli, 2008). As previously noted, a slight touch on the back by another can help develop a sense of trust (Levav & Argo, 2010).

As shown in Figure 15.1, the interconnectivity among these cognitive architectures enables consciousness of embodied processes, particularly those related to emotions. In fact, research in cybernetic robotics demonstrates that awareness of physiological processes can occur when the actions and movements of another (e.g., the stochastic movements of a human-like robot) are discrepant with one's own sensorimotor experiences (Saygin, Chaminade, Ishiguro, Driver, & Frith, 2011). In this way, cross-system interactions from symbolic and connectionist architectures (e.g., expectations, scripts) amplify discrepancies in embodied processing systems, which also activate emotional structures as individuals experience a sense of detachment and unfamiliarity with the perceptual target (Saygin et al., 2011). We suggest that similar processes allow one to judge the authenticity of a leader's statements. For example, research shows that perceivers are adept at detecting subtle facial, vocal, and body expressions that may signal deceit or mal-intent (Ekman, O'Sullivan, Friesen, & Scherer, 1991; Frank & Ekman, 1997). Although these processes may at operate subconsciously, the effects of nonverbal behavior may become salient and influential in the conscious evaluation of another's sincerity (Ekman et al., 1991; Frank & Ekman, 1997).

Theoretical and Practical Implications for Leadership

In this chapter, we used theoretical and practical issues related to leadership to illustrate how attention to four cognitive architectures can uniquely inform leadership processes. The value of our framework, however, lies in understanding how various architectures interact to influence emergent leadership phenomena. In many instances, we described these interactions as we covered the literature for each of the four architectures. These interactions are summarized in Table 15.3, in which we list the architecture typically investigated on the left under the "interaction" column. These interactions indicate that many fundamental aspects of social cognitions and leadership phenomena cannot be adequately represented by a single architecture. This is because leadership involves real people who are embodied and embedded in specific contexts, and who experience emotions as they respond to familiar patterns and think abstractly about leadership.

As this table highlights, thinking about how architectures interact is a new way to conceptualize and model the potential effects of leaders on followers (and followers on leaders). We offer this summary table as a template for thinking about areas for theoretical development, which we illustrate in the final three sections of this chapter. As this table shows, there are many examples of cross-system interactions that have no analog in leadership research, and they suggest new areas for leadership research and practice.

Table 15.3. Interactions of Symbolic, Connectionist, Emotional, and Embodied Architectures: Social Cognitive and Leadership Research

Interaction	Social cognitive research	Leadership research
C x S	Memories "filled in" with false but plausible details (Levidow & Duensing, 1992; Loftus, 1979) Automatic decision making (Dijksterhuis & Nordgren, 2006)	Characteristics inferred from implicit leadership theories (Shondrick et al., 2011) Priming of goals or identity (Lord & Brown, 2004)
Em x S	Positive emotions encourage innovation or creativity (Fredrickson, 2001; Harkner & Keltner, 2001)	Positive/negative emotions and creative processing (George, 2011; George & Zhou, 2007)
Eb x S	Mimicry of head movements influences likeability or persuasion (Tom et al., 1991) Weight influences perceived importance (Ackerman, Nocera, & Bargh, 2010) Clenching fists influences perception of power (Schubert, 2004)	Experience visualization and recall accuracy (Naidoo et al., 2010) Upright posture, height increases perception of power (Giessner & Schubert, 2007; Huang et al., 2011)
Em x C or S	Negative emotions interferes with information processing (McGaugh & Roozendaal, 2002)	Conveying positive affect affects perceptions of charismatic leadership and performance (Bono & Ilies, 2006; Brown & Geis, 1984; Naidoo & Lord, 2008)
Eb x C or S	Somatic markers used to guide decisions (Damasio, 1994) Embodied approach or avoidance affects ingroup–outgroup categorization (Paladio & Castelli, 2008) Nonverbal nuances of deceit (Ekman et al., 1991; Frank & Ekman, 1997)	No known analogue
Eb x Em	Touch elicits range of emotional experiences (Hernstein et al., 2006; Thompson & Hampton, 2010) Experience of trust through touch (Levav & Argo, 2010)	Facial mimicry of leader influences positive affect (Erez et al., 2008)
Em x C x S	Affective modulation of goal structures (O'Reilly, Braver, & Cohen, 1999)	No known analogue
Eb x Em x S	Unpleasant smell elicits disgust and influences moral perceptions (Schnall et al., 2008) Mimicry elicits empathy and influences moral awareness (Immordino-Yang, 2011)	Emotional contagion from mimicking facial expressions influences perceived charisma (Erez et al., 2008)

Note. S = symbolic; C = connectionist; Em = emotional; Eb = Embodied.

An Integrated Approach to Understanding Leadership Processes

In addition to the advantages of using an integrated approach, there are two additional implications that can be inferred from our framework. First, cross-system effects are often subtle and occur outside of consciousness awareness. However, they can have profound consequences on the trajectory of dynamic systems. For example, gestures signifying approach or avoidance tendencies operate in embodied architectures, whereas positive and negative affect operate in emotional architectures. However, leaders can, and often do use both gestures and emotional expressions in their communications as a means of catalyzing the emergence of regulatory focus in connectionist or symbolic architectures. We suspect that to be effective, leaders need a coherent approach that utilizes all four architectures to catalyze social systems, much like a chemist who adds precise mixtures of different compounds to create complex chemical solutions.

The second implication of using this integrative approach is that it encourages viewing leaders as individuals who can guide the functioning of dynamic systems, rather than as individuals who can directly control organizational processes. As noted by complexity theorists (Marion & Uhl-Bien, 2001), leaders can catalyze, but they cannot control systems that continually evolve. In this chapter, we argued that the organization and functioning of the brain can be compared to a complex dynamic system; therefore, the principles suggested by complexity theorists also apply for understanding a leader's influence on the emergence of human thought and behavior. To illustrate this idea, consider the demands on a leader as a sensegiver when organizations encounter a novel event. In this situation, leaders can attempt to convey meaning exclusively through symbolic statements. However, our theory suggests that leaders might also influence the emergence of meaning in others through nonsymbolic information processing systems such as connectionist, emotional, and embodied architectures. For example, followers may pay more attention to how a leader reacts in an embodied and emotional sense than to what he or she *says* about an event. Although indirect, these embodied and emotional systems may have a greater influence on sensemaking as they better represent the reality of the physical environment within which followers are embedded. Leaders who are unaware of such embodied/emotional processes are not likely to be effective sensegivers. In short, our description of four interrelated architectures suggests that there are multiple ways in which one system can affect processes in another. Thus, it creates a broader framework for considering how leaders can influence the emergence of phenomena in social systems.

Leadership and Modeling Holistic System Functioning

One difficulty that leaders face in influencing organizations is that it is hard to predict the consequences of one's actions as their effects and trajectories are at best, non-linear (Cilliers, 1998). However, the availability of free software and computer modeling programs (e.g., PDPtool software, McClelland, 2011; Vensim, see Vancouver, Putka, & Scherbaum, 2005) may provide researchers with the tools to simulate how specific leadership processes can influence the dynamics of complex systems. This approach has been used by Freeman and Ambady (2011) to explore the dynamics of social perceptions by using a dynamic systems approach similar to that depicted in Figure 15.1. For example, they were able to explore how multiple constraint satisfaction among hierarchically arranged perceptual levels (e.g., sensory cues, categories, and stereotypes) underlies the dynamics of social perception and how person construal can shift as different contextual cues are entered into the system. We suggest that the same methods can be used to understand leadership phenomena, including how organizational dynamics are affected by parameters within each of the four cognitive architectures.

Although this might appear to be just an example of computational modeling approaches applied to leadership, we suggest that an advantage of adopting a holistic view of information processing is that it encourages thinking in terms of modeling specific architectures, their interconnections, and how these systems relate to leadership outcomes. For example, complex systems create effects that evolve over time, and each of the architectures that we have described have clear time parameters (see Table 15.2) that could be used as modeling constraints. We suggest that these models could be developed to address issues that include understanding which architecture would be critical for catalyzing emergent systems; how this process may vary across different situations or tasks; or how the consistency or variability across levels might influence the effects of leadership. Because the cognitive architectures that we have described are grounded in neurological brain systems, findings from these models can open new doors for using brain imaging methodologies. Work in this domain can complement the growing body of neuropsychological research that explores how different brain systems may interact to influence outcomes that are relevant to leadership (e.g., morality, emotional sensitivity toward others; Immordino-Yang, 2011; Tavares et al., 2011).

This approach could also provide an agenda for leadership research programs that initially focus on modeling individuals, but could then be extended to model larger collectives, such as teams or groups. Hazy (2007) provides an extensive discussion of computational modeling of leadership processes. Researchers interested in individual level leadership processes might model variables such as perceptions, motivation, learning, development, and decision making. However, these variables could be extended to model analogous outcomes at a group level. For example, leadership and requisite complexity could be modeled at an individual (Lord et al., 2011) or at a group level (Hannah et al., 2011). One might also consider the effects of leadership on group dynamics and how individual inputs are combined to produce group level outcomes (see Lord & Dinh, 2012 for an extensive discussion of this issue).

However, one limitation of computational approaches is that they are not grounded in specific bodies or specific contexts (Pfeifer & Bongrad, 2006). Thus, output from any modeling approach needs to be compared to the emotions, thoughts, and behaviors of real subjects in real situations, and such comparisons should be made at a fine-grained level. Thus, we envision research programs in leadership that alternate between using simulations, experiments, and survey methodologies, much like Freeman and Ambady (2011), who built on their prior experimental research to develop their simulations.

Grounding Systems in Real Events

Using an integrative information processing framework requires that we examine leadership processes within a time frame that is much shorter than what is typically considered in the majority of leadership research. The value of using a chronometric approach to examine how dynamic team and organizational processes unfold has been voiced by a number of authors (e.g., Harrison, Mohammed, McGrath, Florey, & Vanderstoep, 2003; Morgeson, 2005). Adding to this discussion, we suggest that adopting an event level perspective—that is, understanding phenomena occurring within a bounded period of time—and applying event-level methodologies, will provide much needed insight into dynamic informational processing systems as they apply to leadership.

Dinh and Lord (2012) maintain that an event-level focus can capture the transitory cues and patterns of social and environmental information that interact to produce emergent outcomes, such as leadership perception or performance. This potential is especially important because emotional and embodied experiences are transitory, and are not captured by conventional measures that ask participants to retrospectively report their experienced emotions or physical sensations after lengthy periods of time (see Shondrick et al., 2010 for greater discussion of this issue). Although event level research methodologies for emotions have been developed recently (e.g., using experience sampling techniques), efforts to develop comparable event level techniques for capturing embodied processes remains an area in need of development.

Another advantage of event level perspectives is that it helps ground leadership processes within a specific context. Scholars have long noted that leadership is a social process and that leaders are embedded within a larger social environment (Day et al., 2009; Lord & Brown, 2004; Porter & McLaughlin, 2006). As such, understanding the contexts of leadership, including the constraints stemming from constructs such as climate, structures, and goals, can provide insight into the dynamics of specific leadership events and how they might influence information processing within each of the four cognitive architectures. Thus, efforts to understand leadership at an event level is especially important because causal dynamics likely reflect the joint effects of event characteristics, contextual features, and the dynamics among information processing architectures, which can vary at different points in time.

Conclusion

The dynamics of leadership perception and information processing can be understood from multiple perspectives and across a number of disciplines. In this chapter, we showed that pairing findings from various domains in leadership research with recent developments in neurophysiology and the cognitive sciences can yield new insight that provides a springboard for new theory and advances in leadership research. We argued that a dynamic systems approach that examines how information is processed across four neurologically grounded cognitive architectures provides a comprehensive understanding of emergent leadership phenomena. We assert that without this richer approach to conceptualizing leadership and information processing, fundamental aspects of leadership phenomena cannot be adequately represented. We also maintain that an event level perspective that emphasizes the uniqueness of context and research that incorporates dynamic systems modeling can advance understanding of emergent leadership phenomena.

Discussion Questions for Future Research

1. What methodologies can be developed to capture how embodied and emotional processing systems influence leadership perceptions and information processing? What level of analysis would be most informative in understanding these phenomena?
2. Can an integrative information processing model similar to the one presented in this chapter be applied to understanding the emergence of leadership perception and information processing within larger collectives, such as work teams and organizations?

3. How can the use of computational modeling programs help researchers understand nonlinear dynamics among different information processing systems to predict future leadership outcomes? What are some limitations or difficulties that need to be addressed in this kind of research?

4. Is the magnitude of each of the four information processing architectures stable or variable in influencing leadership perceptions and information processing? What kinds of events and situations might be relevant in determining a specific system's influence?

5. What are the applied implications of applying this framework to leadership perceptions? Does it offer new insights on access to leadership positions and garnering social influence by women and minorities?

References

Abbott, L. F., & Regehr, W. G. (2004). Synaptic computation. *Nature, 431*, 796–803.

Ackerman, J. M., Nocera, C. C., & Bargh, J. A. (2010). Incidental haptic sensations influence social judgment and decision making. *Science, 328*, 1712–1715.

Adamson, R. E. (1952). Functional fixedness as related to problem solving: A repetition of three experiments. *Journal of Experimental Psychology, 44*, 288–291.

Allport, A. (1989). Visual attention. In M. I. Posner (Ed.), *Foundations of cognitive science* (pp. 631–682). Cambridge, MA: MIT Press

Ambady, N., & Gray, H. M. (2002). On being sad and mistaken: Mood effects on the accuracy of thin-slice judgments. *Journal of Personality and Social Psychology, 83*, 947–961.

Artwohl, A. (2002). Perceptual and memory distortion during officer-involved shootings. *FBI Law Enforcement Bulletin, 71*, 18–24.

Ashton-James, C., van Baaren, R. B., Chartrand, T. L., Decety, J., & Karremans, J. (2007). Mimicry and me: The impact of mimicry on self-construal. *Social Cognition, 25*, 518–535.

Baars, B. J. (2005). Global workspace theory of consciousness: Toward cognitive neuroscience of human experience? *Progressing Brain Research, 150*, 45–54.

Ballenger, G. A., & Rockmann, K. W. (2010). Chutes versus ladders: Anchoring events and a punctuated-equilibrium perspective on social exchange relationships. *Academy of Management Review, 35*, 373–391.

Balogun, J., & Johnson, G. (2004). Organizational restructuring and middle manager sensemaking. *Academy of Management Journal, 47*, 523–549.

Bargh, J. A. (1989). Conditional automaticity: Varieties of automatic influence in social perception and cognition. In J. S. Uleman & J. A. Bargh (Eds.), *Unintended thought* (pp. 3–51). New York, NY: Guilford Press.

Bassett, D. S., & Gazzaniga, M. S. (2011). Understanding complexity in the human brain. *Trends in Cognitive Sciences, 15*, 200–210.

Bechtel, W., & Abrahamsen, A. (1996). *Connectionism and the mind: Parallel processing, dynamics, and evolution in networks* (2nd ed.). Oxford, England: Blackwell.

Blanchette, I., & Richards, A. (2010). The influence of affect on higher level cognition: A review of interpretation, judgment, decision making, and reasoning. *Cognition and Emotion, 24*, 561–595.

Bolino, M. C., Turnley, W. H., & Bloodgood, J. M. (2002). Citizenship behavior and the creation of social capital in organizations. *Academy of Management Review, 27*, 505–522.

Bono, J. E., & Ilies, R. (2006). Charisma, positive emotions, and mood contagion. *The Leadership Quarterly, 17*, 317–334.

Boroditsky, L., & Ramscar, M. (2002). The roles of body and mind in abstract thought. *Psychological Science, 13*, 185–189.

Brown, D. J. (2012). In the minds of followers: Follower-centric approaches to leadership. In D. V. Day & J. Antonakis (Eds.), *The nature of leadership*, 2nd ed. (pp. 331–363). Thousand Oaks, CA: SAGE.

Brown, E. R., Diekman, A. B., & Schneider, M. C. (2011). A change will do us good: Threats diminish typical preferences for male leaders. *Personality and Social Psychology Bulletin, 37*, 930–941.

Brown, V., & Geis, F. L. (1984). Turning leads into gold: Evaluations of men and women leaders and the alchemy of social consensus. *Journal of Personality and Social Psychology, 46*, 881–824.

Brown, D. J., & Keeping, L. M. (2005). Elaborating the construct of transformational leadership: The role of affect. *The Leadership Quarterly, 16*, 245–273.

Buccino, F., Binkofski, Fink, G. F., Fadiga, L., Fogassi, L., Gallese, V., . . . Freund, H. J. (2001). Action observation activates premotor and parietal areas in a somatotopic manner: An fMRI study. *European Journal of Neuroscience, 13*, 400–404.

Cahill, L., & McGaugh, J. L. (1998). Mechanisms of emotional arousal and lasting declarative memory. *Trends in Neuroscience, 21*, 294–299.

Cameron, K. S., Dutton, J. E., & Quinn, R. E. (2003). *Positive organizational scholarship*. San Francisco, CA: Berrett-Koehler.

Cannella, A. A., Park. J. H., & Lee, H. U. (2008). Top management team functional background diversity and firm performance: Examining the roles of team member collocation and environmental uncertainty. *Academy of Management Journal, 51*, 768–784.

Carson, J. B., Tesluk, P. E., & Marrone, J. A. (2007). Shared leadership in teams: An investigation of antecedent conditions and performance. *Academy of Management Journal, 50*, 1217–1234.

Caruso, D. R., Mayer, J. D., & Salovey, P. (2002). Emotional intelligence and emotional leadership: Multiple intelligences and leadership. In R. E. Riggio, S. D. Murphey, & J. Francis (Ed.), *Multiple Intelligences and leadership, LEA's organizational and management series* (pp. 55–74). Mahwah, NJ: Lawrence Erlbaum.

Carver, C. S., & Scheier, M. F. (2002). Control processes and self-organization as complementary principles underlying behavior. *Personality and Social Psychology Review, 6*, 304–315.

Chartrand, T. L., & Bargh, J. A. (1999). The chameleon effect: The perception-behavior link and social interaction. *Journal of Personality and Social Psychology, 76*, 893–910.

Churchland, P. S., & Sejnowski, T. J. (1990). Neural representation and neural computation. *Philosophical Perspectives, 4*, 343–382.

Cilliers, P. (1998). *Complexity and postmodernism: Understanding complex systems*. London: Routledge.

Corbetta, M., & Shulman, G. L. (2002). Control of goal-directed and stimulus-driven attention in the brain. *Nature Reviews Neuroscience, 3,* 201–215.

Correll, J., Park, B., Judd, C. M., & Wittenbrink, B. (2002). The police officer's dilemma: Using ethnicity to disambiguate potentially threatening individuals. *Journal of Personality and Social Psychology, 83,* 1314–1329.

Cosmides, L., & Tooby, J. (2000). Evolutionary psychology and the emotions. In M. Lewis & J. M Haviland-Jones (Eds.), *Handbook of emotions,* 2nd ed. New York, NY: Guilford Press.

Damasio, A. R. (1989). Time-locked multiregional retroactivation: A systems-level proposal for the neural substrates of recall and recognition. *Cognition, 33,* 25–62.

Damasio, A. R. (1994). *Descartes' error: Emotion, reason, and the human brain.* New York, NY: Grosset/Putnam.

Damasio A. R. (2003). *Looking for Spinoza: Joy, sorrow, and the feeling brain.* New York, NY: Harcourt.

Day, D. V. (2012). The nature of leadership development. In D. V. Day & J. Antonakis (Eds.), *The nature of leadership, second edition* (pp. 108–140). Thousand Oaks, CA: SAGE.

Day, D. V., Harrison, M. M., & Haplin, S. M. (2009). *An integrative theory of leadership development: Connecting adult development, identity, and expertise.* New York, NY: Psychology Press.

Dehaene, S., & Naccache, L. (2001). Towards a cognitive neuroscience of consciousness: Basic evidence and a workspace framework. *Cognition, 79,* 1–37.

DeRue, D. S., & Wellman, N. (2009). Developing leaders via experience: The role of developmental challenge, learning orientation, and feedback availability. *Journal of Applied Psychology, 94,* 859–875.

Detert, J. R., & Edmondson, A. C. (2011). Implicit voice theories: Taken-for-granted rules of self-censorship at work. *Academy of Management Journal, 54,* 461–488.

Dewey, J. (1988). *The later works of John Dewey, 1925–1953.* Vol. I: *1925. Experience and Nature.* Carbondale, IL: Southern Illinois University Press.

Dijksterhuis, A., & Nordgren, L. F. (2006). A theory of unconscious thought. *Perspectives on Psychological Science, 1,* 95–109.

Dinh, J. E., & Lord, R. G. (2012). Implications of dispositional and process views of traits for individual difference research in leadership. *The Leadership Quarterly, 23,* 651–669.

Dragoni, L. (2005). Understanding the emergence of state goal orientation in organizational work groups: The role of leadership and multilevel climate perceptions. *Journal of Applied Psychology, 90,* 1081–1095.

Dutton, J. E., & Jackson, S. E. (1987). Categorizing strategic issues: Links to organizational actions. *Academy of Management Review, 12,* 76–90.

Eden, D. (1992). Leadership and expectations: Pygmanion effects and other self-fulling prophecies in organizations. *The Leadership Quarterly, 3,* 271–305.

Eiser, J. R. (1994). *Attitudes, chaos and the connectionist Mind.* Oxford, England: Blackwell.

Ekman, P., & Davidson, R. (1994). *The nature of emotion: Fundamental questions.* New York, NY: Oxford University Press.

Ekman, P., & Friesen, W. V. (1971). Constants across cultures in face and emotion. *Journal of Personality and Social Psychology, 17,* 124–129.

Ekman, P., O'Sullivan, M., Friesen, W. V., & Scherer, K. R. (1991). Invited article: Face, voice, and body in detecting deceit. *Journal of Nonverbal Behavior, 15,* 125–135.

Engle, A. K., Frieds, P., & Singer, W. (2001). Dynamic predictions: Oscillations and synchrony in top-down processing. *Nature, 2,* 704–716.

Erez, A., Misangyi, V. F., Johnson, D. E., LePine, M. A., & Halverson, K. C. (2008). Stirring the hearts of followers: Charismatic leadership as the transferal of affect. *Journal of Applied Psychology, 93,* 602–615.

Fiske, S., & Taylor, S. (2008). *Social cognition, from brains to culture.* New York, NY: McGraw-Hill.

Fodor, J. A. (1987). Modules, frames, frigeons, sleeping dogs and the music of the spheres. In Z. Pylyshyn (Ed.), *The robot's dilemma: The frame problem in artificial intelligence* (pp. 111–118). Norwood, NJ: Ablex.

Foti, R. J., & Hauenstein, N. M. A. (2007). Pattern and variable approaches in leadership emergence and effectiveness. *Journal of Applied Psychology, 92,* 347–355.

Foti, R. J., Knee, R. E., & Backert, R. S. G. (2008). Multi-level implications of framing leadership perceptions as a dynamic process. *The Leadership Quarterly, 19,* 178–194.

Frank, M. G., & Ekman, P. (1997). The ability to detect deceit generalizes across different types of high-stake lies. *Journal of Personality and Social Psychology, 72,* 1429–1439.

Fredrickson, B. L. (2001). The role of positive emotions in positive psychology: The broaden-and-build theory of positive emotions. *American Psychologist, 56,* 218–226.

Freeman, J. B., & Ambady, N. (2011). A dynamic interactive theory of person construal. *Psychological Review, 118,* 247–279.

Frijda, N. H. (1986). *The emotions.* Cambridge, England: Cambridge University Press.

Fuchs, E., & Flügge, G. (1998). Stress, glucocorticoids and structural plasticity of the hippocampus. *Neuroscience and Biobehavioral Reviews, 23,* 295–300.

George, J. M. (2011). Dual tuning: A minimum condition for understanding affect in organizations. *Organizational Psychology Review, 1,* 147–164.

George, J. M., & Zhou, J. (2007). Dual tuning in a supportive context: Joint contributions of positive mood, negative mood, and supervisory behaviors to employee creativity. *Academy of Management Journal, 50,* 605–622.

Giessner, S. R., & Schubert, T. W. (2007). High in the hierarchy: How vertical location and judgments of leaders' power are interrelated. *Organizational Behavior and Human Decision Processes, 104,* 30–44.

Greenwald, A. G., & Banaji, M. R. (1995). Implicit social cognition: Attitudes, self-esteem, and stereotype. *Psychological Review, 102,* 4–27.

Grossberg, S. (1999). The link between brain learning, attention, and consciousness. *Consciousness and Cognition, 8,* 1–44

Hanges, P., Lord, R. G., & Dickson, M. (2000). An information-processing perspective on leadership and culture: A case for connectionist architecture. *Applied Psychology, 49,* 133–161.

Hanges, P. J., Lord, R. G., Godfrey, E. G., & Raver, J. L. (2002). Modeling nonlinear relationships: Neural networks and catastrophe analysis. In S. Rogelberg (Ed.), *Handbook of research methods in industrial and organizational psychology* (pp. 431–455). Malden, MA: Blackwell.

Hannah, S. T., Lord, R. G., & Pearce, C. L. (2011). Leadership and collective requisite complexity. *Organizational Psychology Review, 1,* 215–238.

Harker, L., & Keltner, D. (2001). Expressions of positive emotion in women's college yearbook pictures and their relationship

to personality and life outcomes across adulthood. *Journal of Personality and Social Psychology, 80*, 112–124.
Harrison, D. A., MoHammed, S., McGrath, J. E., Florey, A. T., & Vanderstoep, S. W. (2003). Time matters in team performance: Effects of member familiarity, entrainment, and task discontinuity on speed and quality. *Personnel Psychology, 56*, 633–669.
Hazy, J. K. (2007). Computer models of leadership: Foundation for a new discipline or meaningless diversions? *The Leadership Quarterly, 18*, 391–410.
Hodges, A. (1983). *Alan Turing: The enigma*. London, England: Simon & Schuster.
Holyoak, K. J., & Simon, D. (1999). Bidirectional reasoning in decision making by constraint satisfaction. *Journal of Experimental Psychology: General, 128*, 3–31.
Holyoak, K. J., & Thagard, P. (1989). Analogical mapping by constraint satisfaction. *Cognitive Science, 13*, 295–355.
Holyoak, K. J., & Thagard, P. (1995). *Mental leaps: Analogy in creative thought*. Cambridge, MA: MIT Press.
Holyoak, K. J., & Thagard, P. (1997). The analogical mind. *American Psychologist, 52*, 35–44.
Hooijberg, R., Hunt, J. G., & Dodge, G. E. (1997). Leadership complexity and development of the leaderplex model. *Journal of Management, 23*, 375–408.
Hopfield, J. J. (1982). Neural networks and physical systems with emergent collective computational abilities. *Proceedings of the National Academy of Sciences of the United States of America, 79*, 2554–2558.
Huang, L., Galinskey, A. D., Gruenfeld, D. H., & Guillory, L. E. (2011). Powerful postures versus powerful roles: Which is the proximate correlate of thought and behavior? *Psychological Science, 22*, 95–102.
Iacoboni, M. (2007). The quiet revolution of existential neuroscience. In E. Harmon-Jones & P. Winkielman (Eds.), *Social neuroscience: Integrating biological and psychological explanations of social behavior* (pp. 439–453). New York, NY: The Guilford Press.
Ikegaya, Y., Aaron, G., Cossart, R., Aronov, D., Lampi, I., Ferster, D., & Yuste, R. (2004). Synfire chains and cortical songs: Temporal modules of cortical activity. *Science, 304*, 559–564.
Immordino-Yang, M. H. (2011). Me, my "self" and you: Neuropsychological relations between social emotion, self-awareness, and morality. *Emotional Review, 3*, 313–315.
Isanski, B., & West, C. (2010). The body of knowledge: Understanding embodied cognition. *Association for Psychological Science, 23*, 14–18.
Isen, A. M. (2001). An influence of positive affect on decision making in complex situations: Theories and practical implications. *Journal of Consumer Psychology, 1*, 75–85.
Johnson, M. (1987). *The Body in the mind: The bodily basis of meaning, imagination and reason*. Chicago, IL: University of Chicago Press.
Johnson, M., & Rohrer, T. (2007). We are live creatures: Embodiment, American Pragmatism, and the cognitive organism. *Body, Language, and Mind, 1*, 17–54.
Johnson, R. E., & Lord, R. G. (2010). Implicit effects of justice on self-identity. *Journal of Applied Psychology, 95*, 681–695.
Johnson-Laird, P. N. (1989). *The computer and the mind: An introduction to cognitive science*. Cambridge, MA: Harvard University Press.
Jonides, J., Lewis, R. L., Nee, D. E., Lustig, C. A., Berman, M. G., & Moore, K. S. (2008). The mind and brain of short-term memory. *Annual Review of Psychology, 59*, 193–224.
Kalitzin, S. N., Velis, D. N., & Lopes da Silva, F. H. (2010). Stimulation-based anticipation and control of state transition. *Epilepsy & Behavior, 17*, 310–323.
Kanfer, R., & Ackerman, P. L. (1989). Motivation and cognitive abilities: An integrative/aptitude-treatment interaction approach to skill acquisition. *Journal of Applied Psychology, 74*, 657–690.
Kellet, J. B., Humphrey, R. H., & Sleeth, R. G. (2006). Empathy and the emergence of task and relations leaders. *The Leadership Quarterly, 17*, 146–162.
Killingsworth, M. A., & Gilbert, D. T. (2010). A wandering mind is an unhappy mind. *Science, 330*, 932.
Kirschner, M., & Gerhart, J. (1998). Evolvability. *Proceedings of the National Academy of Sciences of the United States of America, 95*, 8420–8427.
Koechlin, E., Basso, G., Pietrini, P., Panzer, S., & Grafman, J. (1991). The role of the anterior prefrontal cortex in human cognition. *Nature, 399*, 148–151.
Kuhbandner, C., Pekrun, R., & Maier, M. A. (2010). The role of positive and negative affect in "mirroring" of the other persons' actions. *Cognition and Emotion, 24*, 1182–1190.
LaBar, K. S., & Cabeza, R. (2006). Cognitive neuroscience of emotional memory. *Nature, 7*, 54–64.
Lazarus, R. S. (1991). *Emotion and adaptation*. New York, NY: Oxford University Press.
LeDoux, J. E. (1996). *The emotional brain*. New York, NY: Simon & Schuster.
LeDoux, J. E. (2007). The amygdale. *Current Biology, 17*, R868–R874.
LeDoux, J. E., & Phelps, E. A. (2008). Emotional networks in the brain. In M. Lewis, J. M. Haviland-Jones, & L. F. Barrett (Eds.), *Handbook of emotions* (pp. 159–179). New York, NY: The Guilford Press.
Levav, J., & Argo, J. J. (2010). Physical contact and financial risk taking. *Psychological Science, 1*, 1–7.
Lieberman, M. D., Gaunt, R., Gilbert, D. T., & Trope, Y. (2002). Reflexion and reflection: A social cognitive neuroscience approach to attributional inference. In M. P. Zanna (Ed.), *Advances in experimental social psychology* (Vol. 34, pp. 199–249). New York: Academic Press.
Loftus, E. F., & Palmer, J. C. (1974). Reconstruction of automobile destruction: An example of the interaction between language and memory. *Journal of Verbal Learning and Verbal Behavior, 13*, 585–589.
Lord, R. G., & Brown, D. J. (2004). *Leadership processes and follower self-identity*. Mahwah, NJ: Lawrence Erlbaum.
Lord, R. G., Brown, D. J., Harvey, & Hall, R. J. (2001). Contextual constraints on prototype generation and their multilevel consequences for leadership perceptions. *The Leadership Quarterly, 12*, 311–338.
Lord, R. G., Diefendorff, J. M., Schmidt, A. M., & Hall, R. J. (2010). Self-regulation at work. *Annual Review of Psychology, 61*, 543–568.
Lord, R. G., & Dinh, J. E. (2012). Aggregation processes and levels of analysis as organizing structures for leadership theory. In. D. V. Day & J. Antonakis (Eds.), *The nature of leadership*, 2nd ed. (p. 29–65). Thousand Oaks, CA: SAGE.
Lord, R. G., & Hall, R. J. (2005). Identity, deep structure and the development of leadership skills. *The Leadership Quarterly, 16*, 591–615.
Lord, R. G., Hannah, S. T., & Jennings, P. L. (2011). A framework for understanding leadership and individual requisite complexity. *Organizational Psychology Review, 1*, 1–29.

Lord, R. G., & Harvey, J. L. (2002). An information processing framework for emotional regulation. In R. G. Lord, R. J. Klimoski, & R. Kanfer (Eds.), *Emotions in the workplace: Understanding the structure and role of emotions in organizational behavior* (pp. 115–146). San Fransisco, CA: Jossey-Bass.

Lord, R. G., & Maher, K. J. (1991). *Leadership and information processing.* London, England: Routledge.

Lord, R. G., & Shondrick, S. J. (2011). Leadership and knowledge: Symbolic, connectionist, and embodied perspectives. *The Leadership Quarterly, 22,* 207–222.

Marion, R., & Uhl-Bien, M. (2001). Leadership in complex organizations. *Leadership Quarterly, 12,* 389–418.

Martin, A. (2001). Functional neuroimaging of semantic memory. In R. Cabeza & A. Kingstone (Eds.), *Handbook of functional neuroimaging of cognition* (pp. 153–186). Cambridge, MA: MIT Press.

Mayer, R. C., Davis, J. H., & Schoorman, F. D. (1995). An integrative model of organizational trust. *Academy of Management Review, 20,* 709–734.

McAllister, D. J. (1995). Affect- and cognition-based trust as foundations for interpersonal cooperation in organizations. *Academy of Management Journal, 38,* 24–59.

McClelland, J. L. (2011). Explorations in parallel distributed processing: A handbook of models, programs, and exercises. 2nd ed. draft of March 21, 2011. Retrieved from http://www.stanford.edu/group/pdplab/pdphandbook/

McGaugh, J. L., & Roozendaal, B. (2002). Role of adrenal stress hormones in forming lasting memories in the brain. *Current Opinion in Neurobiology, 12,* 205–210.

Medvedeff, M. (2008). Leader affective displays during a negative work event: Influences on subordinate appraisals, affect, and coping strategies. (Unpublished doctoral dissertation). University of Akron, Ohio.

Messina, P. (1994). Involuntary discharge experiment. *International Defensive Tactics Journal, 1,* 2–3.

Messina, P., & Czarnecki, F. (2002). Martial arts for cops: The dark side. *The Police Marksman, 26,* 16–17.

Morgeson, F. P. (2005). The external leadership of self-management teams: Intervening in the context of novel and disruptive events. *Journal of Applied Psychology, 90,* 497–508.

Mumford, M. D., Blair, C., & Marcy, R. T. (2007). Alternative knowledge structures in creative thought: Schema, associations, and cases. In J. Kaufman & J. Baer (Eds.), *The relationship between creativity, knowledge, and reason.* Cambridge, England: Cambridge University Press.

Naidoo, L. J., Kohari, N. E., Lord, R. G., & DuBois, D. A. (2010). "Seeing" is retrieving: Recovering emotional content in leadership ratings through visualization. *The Leadership Quarterly, 21,* 886–900.

Naidoo, L. J., & Lord, R. G. (2008). Speech imagery and perceptions of charisma: The mediating role of positive affect. *The Leadership Quarterly, 19,* 283–296.

Neal, D. T., & Chartrand, T. L. (2011). Embodied emotion perception: Amplifying and dampening facial feedback modulates emotion perception accuracy. *Social Psychological and Personality Science, 1,* 1–6.

Nestor, A., Plaut, D. C., & Behrmann, M. (2011). Unraveling the distributed neural code of facial identity through spatiotemporal pattern analysis. *Proceedings of the National Academy of Sciences of the United States of America, 108,* 9998–10,003.

Newell, A. (1990). *Unified theories of cognition.* Cambridge, MA: Harvard University Press.

Newell, A., Rosenbloom, P. S., & Lard, J. E. (1989). Symbolic architectures for cognition. In M. D. Posner (Ed.), *Foundations of cognitive science* (pp. 93–113). Cambridge, MA: Bradford Books/MIT Press.

Niedenthal, P. M., Barsalou, L. W., Winkielman, P., Krauth-Gruber, S., & Rie, F. (2005). Embodiment in attitudes, social perception, and emotion. *Personality and Social Psychology Review, 9,* 184–211.

Niedenthal, P. M., Winkielman, P., Mondillon, L., & Vermeulen, N. (2009). Embodiment of emotion concepts. *Journal of Personality and Social Psychology, 96,* 1120–1136.

Norman, D. A. (1993). *Things that make us smart: Defending human attributes in the age of the machine.* Reading, MA: Addison-Wesley.

Öhman, A. (2002). Automaticity and the amygdala: Nonconscious responses to emotional faces. *Psychological Science, 11,* 62–66.

O'Malley, A. L., Ritchie, S. A., Lord, R. G., Gregory, J. B., & Young, C. M. (2009). Incorporating embodied cognitions into sensemaking theory: A theoretical examination of embodied processes in a leadership context. *Current Trends in Management, 14,* 158–178.

O'Reilly, R. C., Braver, T. S., & Cohen, J. D. (1999). A biologically-based computational model of working memory. In A. Miyake, P. Shah (Ed.), *Models of working memory: Mechanisms of active maintenance and executive control* (pp. 375–411). New York, NY: Cambridge University Press.

Osland, J. (2010). An overview of the global leadership literature. In M. Mendenhall, J. Osland, A. Bird, G. Oddou, & M. Maznevski (Eds.), *Global leadership: Research, practice, and development* (pp. 23–40). New York, NY: Routledge.

Page, S. E. (2007). *The difference: How the power of diversity creates better groups, firms, schools, and societies.* Princeton, NJ: Princeton University Press.

Paladino, M-P., & Castelli, L. (2008). On the immediate consequences of intergroup categorization: Activation of approach and avoidance motor behavior toward ingroup and outgroup members. *Personality and Social Psychology Bulletin, 34,* 755–768.

Pfeifer, R., & Bongard, J. (2006). *How the body shapes the way we think.* London, England: The MIT Press.

Phillips, J. S. (1984). The accuracy of leadership ratings: A cognitive categorization perspective. *Organizational Behavior and Human Performance, 33,* 125–138.

Podsakoff, N. P., Whiting, S. W., Podsakoff, P. M., & Blume, B. D. (2009). Individual and organizational-level consequences of organizational citizenship behavior: A meta-analysis. *Journal of Applied Psychology, 94,* 122–141.

Porter, L. W., & McLaughlin, G. B. (2006). Leadership and the organizational context: Like the weather? *The Leadership Quarterly, 17,* 559–576.

Pylyshyn, Z. W. (1984). *Computation and cognition: Toward a foundation for cognitive science.* Cambridge, MA: MIT Press, a Bradford Book.

Rizzolatti, G., Fogassi, L., & Gallese, V. (2002). Motor and cognitive functions of the ventral premotor cortex. *Current Opinion in Neurobiology, 12,* 149–154.

Rubin, R. S., Munz, D. C., & Bommer, W. H. (2005). Leading from within: The effects of emotion recognition and personality on transformational leadership behavior. *Academy of Management Journal, 48,* 845–858.

Rumelhart, D. E., Hinton, G. E., & McClelland, J. L. (1986). *A general framework for parallel distributed processing.* Cambridge, MA: MIT Press.

Sauter, D. A., Eisner, F., Ekman, P., & Scott, S. (2010). Cross-cultural recognition of basic emotions through nonverbal emotional vocalization. *PNSA, 6*, 2408–2412.

Saygin, A. P., Chaminade, T., Ishiguro, H., Driver, J., & Frith, C. (2011). The thing that should not be: Predictive coding and the uncanny valley in perceiving human and humanoid robot actions. *Scan, 6*, 1–10.

Schnall, S., Haidt, J., Clore, G. L., & Jordan, A. H. (2008). Disgust as embodied moral judgment. *Personality and Social Psychology Bulletin, 34*, 1096–1109.

Schooler, J. W., Smallwood, J., Christoff, K., Handy, T. C., Reichie, E. D., & Sayette, M. A. (2011). Meta-awareness, perceptual decoupling and the wandering mind. *Trends in Cognitive Sciences, 15*, 39–326.

Schubert, T. W. (2004). The power in your hand: Gender differences in bodily feedback from making a fist. *Personality and Social Psychology Bulletin, 30*, 757–769.

Srull, T. K., & Wyer, R. S. (1989). Person memory and judgment. *Psychological Review, 96*, 53–83.

Shiffrin, R. M., & Schneider, W. (1977). Controlled and automatic human information processing: Perceptual learning, automatic attending and a general theory. *Psychological Review, 84*, 127–190.

Shondrick, S. J., Dinh, J. E., & Lord, R. G. (2010). Developments in implicit leadership theory and cognitive science: Applications to improving measurement and understanding alternatives to hierarchical leadership. *The Leadership Quarterly, 21*, 959–078.

Smith, E. R. (1996). What do connectionism and social psychology offer each other? *Journal of Personality and Social Psychology, 70*, 893–912.

Smith, E. R., & DeCoster, J. (2000). Dual-process models in social and cognitive psychology: Conceptual integration and links to underlying memory systems. *Personality and Social Psychology Review, 4*, 108–131.

Smith, J. A., & Foti, R. J. (1998). A pattern approach to the study of leader emergence. *The Leadership Quarterly, 9*, 147–160.

Stam, D., van Knippenberg, D., & Wisse, B. (2010). Focusing on followers: The role of regulatory focus and possible selves in visionary leadership. *The Leadership Quarterly, 21*, 457–468.

Stone, V. E. (2007). An evolutionary perspective on domain specificity in social intelligence. In E. Harmon-Jones & P. Winkielman (Eds.), *Social neuroscience: Integrating biological and psychological explanations of social behavior* (pp. 316–349). New York, NY: The Guilford Press.

Strayer, D. L., Drews, F. A., & Crouch, D. J. (2006). A comparison of the cell phone driver and the drunk driver. *Human Factors, 48*, 381–391.

Sy, T., Shore, L. M., Strauss, J., Shore, T. H., Tram, S., Whiteley, P., & Ikeda-Muromachi, K. (2010). Leadership perceptions as a function of race-occupation fit: The case of Asian Americans. *Journal of Applied Psychology, 95*, 902–919.

Tavares, P., Barnard, P. J., & Lawrence, A. D. (2010). Emotional complexity and the neural representation of emotion in motion. *Scan, 6*, 98–108.

Thagard, P., & Nerb, J. (2002). Emotional gestalts: Appraisal, change, and the dynamics of affect. *Personality and Social Psychological Review, 6*, 274–282.

Thayer, J., F., & Lane, R. D. (2000). A model of neurovisceral integration in emotion regulation and dysregulation. *Journal of Affective Disorders, 61*, 201–216.

Thompson, E. H., & Hampton, J. A. (2010). The effect of relationship status on communicating emotions through touch. *Cognitions and Emotion, 1*, 1–12.

Thompson, E., & Varela, F. J. (2001). Radical embodiment: Neural dynamics and consciousness. *Trends in Cognitive Sciences, 5*, 418–426.

Tom, G., Ramil, E., Zapanta, I., Demir, K., & Lopez, S. (2006). The role of overt head movement and attention in persuasion. *The Journal of Psychology, 140*, 247–253.

Uhl-bien, M., & Marion, R. (2009). Complexity leadership in bureaucratic forms of organizing: A meso model. *The Leadership Quarterly, 20*, 631–650.

Vallacher, R. R., Read, S. J., & Nowak, A. (2002). Dynamic perspective in personality and social psychology. *Personality and Social Psychology Review, 6*, 264–273.

Vancouver, J. B., Putka, D. J., & Scherbaum, C. A. (2005). Testing a computational model of the goal-level effect: An example of a neglected methodology. *Organizational Research Methods, 8*, 100–129.

VandeWalle, D. (2003). A goal orientation model of feedback-seeking behavior. *Human Resource Management Review, 13*, 581–604.

Van Vugt, M. (2012). The nature in leadership: Evolutionary, biological, and social neuroscience perspectives. In D. V. Day & J. Antonakis (Eds.), *The nature of leadership*, 2nd ed. (pp. 141–178). Thousand Oaks, CA: SAGE.

Weick, K. E. (1995). *Sensemaking in organizations*. London: SAGE.

Yang, J., Mossholder, K. W., & Peng, T. K. (2009). Supervisory procedural justice effects: The mediating roles of cognitive and affective trust. *The Leadership Quarterly, 20*, 143–154.

CHAPTER

16 Authentic Leadership Theory, Research and Practice: Steps Taken and Steps that Remain

Bruce J. Avolio *and* Fred O. Walumbwa

Abstract

In this chapter, we provide an updated review and integration of the advances in theory and research associated with authentic leadership. Our primary purpose was to provide the reader with a representative sampling of the emerging literature in this new area of leadership inquiry, and therefore we do not necessarily include every published or unpublished paper on the topic. Nevertheless, we believe the reader will get a sufficient understanding of the progress that has been made in this area of leadership research since the foundational theoretical models were published back in 2004 and 2005. We also have addressed some of the practical implications of this work, in a world that each day seems to require more and more authentic leaders and leadership at every organizational level, including those serving in follower roles.

Key Words: Authentic leadership, authentic leadership theory, higher-order construct, authentic development

We might ask a reasonable question regarding whether we need yet another theory of leadership, in this case one focusing on explaining what constitutes authentic leadership. Although authors have been debating what constitutes authenticity and, more recently, authentic leadership for at least two millennia, there has actually been very little done to understand what systematically differentiates a leader or leadership from being seen as "authentic" versus "inauthentic." In this article, we set out to examine the "modern" discussions regarding what constitutes authentic leadership by primarily focusing on the last decade of work in this area. Although we will cover some of the earlier research and discussions that addressed the issue of authentic leadership, the best resource for such earlier work is Gardner, Cogliser, Davis, and Dickens (2011).

Our article will be organized around a series of questions that we use to frame how authentic leadership and its development will be examined. The questions that we have provided below come from both the academic and practice communities. For example, we start with this question: *why has so much interest been placed in examining authentic leadership over the last decade in both the practice and research literature?*

Why Authentic Leadership Now?

As is true of most prior work on leadership, there is frequently a need for what might be a different kind of leadership to address particular challenges facing organizations or societies that emerge, from time to time. Such challenges once evident and clearly articulated are typically addressed by someone who provides a "new" framework for examining and understanding the "type of leadership" needed to deal with the challenge. However, most of these "new" frameworks for explaining leadership and addressing those challenges typically have deep roots in prior literature. For example, in the early 1980s, discussions in the leadership literature that were largely centered in the United States examined the type of leadership that was needed to transform organizations to address the growing threats from an emerging global economy, and, in particular, Japan.

Authors such as Bass (1985), Tichy and Devanna (1986), and Bennis and Nanus (1985) responded to the global challenges facing organizations and societies by calling for a new kind of leadership, one that could transform individuals, groups, and organizations and therefore went beyond the traditional transactional models of leadership. However, like most "new" theories, the work on transformational leadership was deeply rooted in earlier work by House (1976), Burns (1978), and Weber (1924/1947). Each of these prior authors had already introduced and examined various component constructs that eventually became part of transformational leadership theory, but it was not until the early 1980s, and in terms of empirical research well into the 1990s, that the full range theory of transformational and transactional leadership proposed by Avolio and Bass (1991) was firmly established in the literature (Bass & Bass, 2008).

Similar evolutionary patterns have been evident with most theories of leadership. For example, back in the mid-1990s, Avolio and his colleagues published a paper on shared leadership, which corresponded with similar research being pursued by Craig Pearce and Hank Sims on the same topic (Pearce & Sims, 2002). However, the focus on shared leadership didn't take hold in the literature until the last several years. We believe there were several reasons for this acceptance lag in the leadership literature. First, there wasn't a compelling need that captured the interests of researchers or practitioners. Certainly, many organizations at that time were moving towards team-based structures, which was highlighting the need for more collaborative leadership; however very few would be described as sharing in leadership.

Second, there were some doubts raised by researchers as to whether one could escalate leadership constructs such as transformational, from an individual to a team or shared level. Specifically, did shared leadership represent a new and unique construct in terms of its *content* and *process*? Today, this debate has largely been resolved with authors agreeing that constructs such as transformational or transactional leadership can be escalated across levels of analysis, without any loss in meaning. For instance, using the team as referent, we can observe and evaluate transactional or transformational leadership styles as characterizing the overall teams' aggregate behavior, each individual's behavior aggregated to the team level, the consensus ratings of the team's aggregate leadership, and so forth (Avolio, 2011).

Third, there has been a great deal of debate regarding the most appropriate ways to measure shared leadership. Many researchers asked whether it should be measured by using social network analysis, consensus ratings, each member rating everyone else in the team, each member rating the team as referent, or by using some other method, such as narratives that can be used to describe the way team members influence each other. Although the answer to these respective questions has not yet been fully resolved, we believe that in the end, we can use all of these means to assess shared leadership.

Returning to trying to understand why there has been an emerging interest in authentic leadership over the last decade, we suspect it has been due, in part, to a growing concern regarding the falling levels of trust in leaders throughout the world. We see in polls produced by the Kennedy School at Harvard University that the U.S. index of leadership has shown declines in terms of the level of trust that Americans have in their leaders. Specifically, in a 2007 national study by Harvard University on the confidence Americans have in their leaders, 77 per cent of participants agreed or strongly agreed that there was a crisis of confidence regarding leaders in America (Rosenthal, Pittinsky, Purvin, & Montoya, 2007). Business and government leaders were rated as being in the lower third of all occupations, with respondents indicating they had moderate or not much trust at all in these leaders.

Ghoshal (2005) specifically criticized business schools for the leader products they were producing stating, "by propagating amoral theories business schools have actively freed their students from any sense of moral responsibility" (p. 76). The growing concerns about the state of American business leadership, led a group of Harvard MBA students and faculty to establish an oath, to essentially commit to being ethical stewards of their organizations after graduation. If there wasn't a felt need, would there have been a need to create such an oath?

It seems that hardly a day goes by where there is not a government, business, religious, or sports leader, who is not in the news charged with doing something "inauthentic" or, worse yet, unethical or illegal. How many business leaders do we need to see on the front page of the *New York Times* or

Financial Times in handcuffs, before we begin to conclude that too many leaders in big business are simply not authentic? How many billions of dollars does the Catholic Church need to pay for protecting their priests or for compensating victims of child abuse before we consider at least some religious leaders not authentic? How many politicians have to stand in front of cameras along with their wives apologizing to their constituents and their spouses for poor moral conduct, before we begin to question the authenticity of our public leaders? Many would say, not many more, if at all. Others would say the leaders who have always been inauthentic or immoral are just getting caught more often due to higher levels of transparency and oversight of our leaders.

We do know that the growing awareness of unethical conduct regarding today's leaders has promoted writings by popular leadership authors such as former Medtronic CEO Bill George (George, 2003; George & Sims, 2007), who has called for more genuine or authentic leadership. Paralleling these popular concerns, Luthans and Avolio (2003, p. 244) expressed "a need for a theory-driven model identifying the specific construct variables and relationships that can guide authentic leader development and suggest researchable propositions." Luthans and Avolio's work was motivated in part by how many of the American public thought their leaders were authentic (Avolio & Luthans, 2006). Specifically, based on a 2004 U.S. poll of working adults, only one-third of the American public indicated their leaders were authentic frequently if not always. This poll also revealed that only 22 per cent of the respondents felt their leaders were willing to admit their mistakes or were willing to sacrifice for the good of the organization. At the time the U.S. poll on authenticity was being created and deployed, it was reported that there was a 25 per cent growth in ethics officers in U.S. corporations from 2003–2004 based on findings from the Ethics Officer Association. In combination, these findings motivated Avolio and Luthans to explore not only what constituted authentic leaders, but whether it could be developed (Avolio & Luthans, 2006).

Given the call for more authenticity in leaders, how has and how should we define authenticity to determine what it is we need more of in our leaders? Sartre (1966) defined authenticity of individuals as the absence of self-deception, or being true to who you are as an individual. Brumbaugh (1971) characterized authenticity as representing the ability to make individual choices, take responsibility for one's errors, and recognize your drawbacks, while working toward the fulfillment of your potential. Kernis (2003) described authenticity as the "unobstructed operation of one's true, or core, self in one's daily enterprise" (p. 1). And Harter (2002) described authenticity, as owning one's personal experiences, including one's thoughts, emotions, needs, desires, or beliefs.

Luthans and Avolio primarily used Harter's definition of what constituted the authentic self, to suggest that being self-aware and acting in accord with one's true self by being transparent with what one genuinely thinks and believes (Luthans & Avolio, 2003), could represent in large part what constitutes authentic leadership. Luthans and Avolio (2003) defined authentic leadership as "a process that draws from both positive psychological capacities and a highly developed organizational context, which results in both greater self-awareness and self-regulated positive behaviors on the part of leaders and associates, fostering positive self-development" (p. 243).

The authentic qualities described above are the attributes typically associated with leaders that have been characteristically described as authentic, such as the famed investor Warren Buffett, who runs Berkshire Hathaway, or the highly successful Indian entrepreneur Narayana Murthy, who is the founding chairman of Infosys. Indeed, we see in the behavior and brand of both of these iconic leaders the challenge to be authentic with your constituents. With Buffett, his name has become synonymous with the idea of examining your choices against whether you would want your family members to read about what you did on the front page of the *New York Times*.

With Mr. Murthy, we can identify numerous examples based on his decisions throughout his career to protect the authenticity of his organization. For instance, at the start-up of Infosys, he and his six cofounders refused to take or give bribes to get things done in India—which was standard business practice in India—everyone did it (Barney, 2010)! It took over a year to get their initial phones hooked up at Infosys because Murthy and his cofounders refused to bribe the individuals who did the hook-ups. Repeatedly, the leadership of this highly successful organization that essentially launched the outsourcing movement in IT, refused to behave in any way that would detract from their authentic brand, separating them out among global giants in the technology industry.

Perhaps as noted by Avolio and Luthans (2006), because leadership is under much closer scrutiny today as systems and processes become more transparent, we are more motivated to search for the authentic leader. Websites such as glassdoor.com or wiki-leaks are forcing organizational leaders to address the reality of being more exposed in terms of not only their decisions, but literally every single communication they have had through electronic correspondence. The practice community has certainly responded to this need by offering a growing number of training programs on ethical and authentic leadership. We believe these efforts are likely premature, in that we have not fully validated the model that captures what constitutes authentic leadership. Without validation work, we submit that the authentic leader training programs, like many leadership development efforts in the past, will end up on the junk heap of popular leadership programs.

How Then Has the Academic and Practice Community Viewed Authentic Leadership?

Looking back to earlier discussions linking authenticity to leadership, Gardner et al. (2011) identified that the first "modern" attempt in the academic literature to define and operationalize the constructs of leader authenticity was made by Henderson and Hoy (1983). Henderson and Hoy conceptualized leader authenticity as encompassing three components: (1) acceptance of personal and organizational responsibility for actions, outcomes, and mistakes; (2) the nonmanipulation of others; and (3) the salience of the self over role requirements, which we interpret to mean core values having precedent over demands in the leadership context: for example, a willingness to take a stand for doing the right thing.

Although the components proposed by Henderson and Hoy overlap with the constructs discussed by Kernis and Goldman (2005), as well as more recent theoretical work on authentic leadership cited above, they do not include all of the components now being used in measures of authentic leadership (see Walumbwa, Avolio, Gardner, Wernsing, & Peterson, 2008). Nevertheless, the emphasis that Henderson and Hoy placed on the salience of self is clearly linked to the historically based conception of authenticity, as it "refers to the tendency to behave in a genuine manner relatively unconstrained by traditional role requirements... such a person is viewed as being real and authentic" (Henderson & Hoy, 1983, p. 66).

The emerging literature on authentic leadership emphasizes the importance of positive role modeling represented by honesty, integrity, and high ethical standards and how each relates to the development of authentic leader-follower relationships (Avolio & Walumbwa, 2006; Gardner, Avolio, Luthans, May, & Walumbwa, 2005a; Gardner, Avolio, & Walumbwa, 2005b; Walumbwa et al., 2008). Authentic leaders have been depicted as being open and transparent in their relationships with followers, displaying high levels of congruence between their words and deeds. Followers of authentic leaders are able to count on them to display their true selves, to be predictable, and to follow through on promises.

Recent work on authentic leadership theory (Avolio & Gardner, 2005), has been linked to prior discussions of what constituted an individual's level of authenticity and has included four component constructs: (1) awareness, (2) unbiased processing, (3) authentic behavior exhibited, and (4) the relational orientation of the individual (Kernis, 2003; Kernis & Goldman, 2006). This earlier conceptualization of authenticity provided the basis for recently emerging theories of authentic leadership, as well as providing some guidance as to how authentic leadership has been measured over the last five years in the leadership literature (Gardner et al., 2005a; Ilies, Morgeson, & Nahrgang, 2005; Spitzmuller & Ilies, 2010).

From the practice side, George (2003) and George and Sims (2007) discussed five dimensions associated with authentic leadership including (1) pursuing purpose with passion. (2) exhibiting solid values, (3) leading with empathy or heart, (4) establishing enduring relationships, and (5) demonstrating self-discipline. Although the terms used here were meant to make authentic leadership concepts more accessible to a broader audience, several of these dimensions map well to the components of authenticity identified by Kernis and Goldman (2006). For example, establishing enduring relationships is consistent with what Kernis and Goldman described as a leader who has a relational orientation.

Luthans and Avolio (2003) introduced authentic leadership into the management/leadership research literature by examining what constitutes the core components of authentic leadership, followed by extensions of their work to authentic leadership development, which parallels some of the arguments made by Day (2000) examining leadership development in context over time. Avolio and Luthan's work connected the emerging research in positive psychology, positive organizational behavior, positive organizational scholarship, and transformational leadership. This stream of research largely grew out of a concern that was raised as far back as 1988 (e.g., Avolio & Gibbons, 1988) concerning whether charismatic transformational leaders were *also* authentic.

The question of whether transformational leadership could be genuine or not, led Bass and Steidlmeier's (1999) to label leaders considered to be genuinely transformational leaders as "authentic" and those who were not were labeled "pseudo-transformational" leaders. These latter leaders looked like and behaved like transformational leaders, but they were missing the ethical and moral foundation associated with authentic leaders, and therefore could not be considered transformational. Why? Burns (1978) specifically defined transforming leadership as morally uplifting, and therefore absent a moral foundation, such leaders should not be considered transformational.

Avolio and Gardner (2005) took a very clear stand on this issue describing authentic leadership as being inherently moral, which led Walumbwa and colleagues (2008) to suggest that internalized moral perspective was a core component of authentic leadership. Subsequently, much of the emerging leadership literature over the last six years has included a discussion of moral perspectives when examining authentic leadership, which may also have blurred the boundaries between the ongoing research on ethical leadership by Trevino and her colleagues (Brown, Trevino, & Harrison, 2005) and the emerging work on authentic leadership (Ladkin & Taylor, 2010). The convergence of these literatures has raised a growing concern regarding how authentic leaders and leadership differ from other positive forms of leadership, such as transformational or ethical leadership.

Luthans and Avolio's (2003) conceptualization of authentic leadership also included a focus on what constituted the leader's characteristics and style, as well as how such leadership was developed. Luthans and Avolio set out to extend the work that had been done on transformational and other similar and positive forms of leadership to get at what was referred to by Avolio, Gardner, Walumbwa, Luthans, and May (2004) as a "root" construct underlying all positive forms of leadership. These authors suggested that at the base of all positive forms of leadership was a level of genuineness they labeled authentic leadership. Luthans and Avolio went on to assert that authentic leaders "can incorporate transformational, charismatic, servant, spiritual or other forms of leadership" (p. 329).

Avolio and colleagues (e.g., Avolio & Gardner, 2005; Gardner et al., 2005a) offered a comprehensive view of authentic leadership by examining what constitutes authentic leadership and its impact on performance. Their framework involved an examination of 9 major facets including (1) Positive psychological capital—efficacy, hope, optimism, and resiliency; (2) Positive moral perspective; (3) Leader self-awareness; (4) Leader self-regulation; (5) Leadership processes/behaviors; (6) Follower self-awareness/regulation; (7) Follower development; (8) Organizational Context; and (9) Veritable and sustainable performance beyond expectations.

At the time that Avolio and colleagues were developing the broader framework above that was eventually published in a special issue of the *Leadership Quarterly* back in 2005, Ilies, Morgeson, and Nahrgang (2005) were also developing a model of authentic leadership based on the framework put forth by Kernis noted above. A conference that was held at the University of Nebraska in 2004 to launch discussions on what constituted authentic leadership included a solicitation for papers to be published in a special issue on authentic leadership. Near the start of the conference, both sets of authors discovered they had independently built nearly identical theories for what constituted authentic leadership. Subsequently, these frameworks became the basis for measuring what Walumbwa and colleagues established as representing authentic leadership.

Examining Authentic Leadership as a Higher-Order Construct

Before discussing the work on examining authentic leadership as a higher-order construct, it is worth noting that there are a number of issues and concerns that have been raised by other authors on what generally constitutes a higher-order construct. These issues include how such constructs are conceptualized and analyzed. For example, one concern that has been raised in the literature relates to whether the higher-order construct is best modeled as a formative (aggregate) versus a reflective (superordinate) construct (Edwards, 2011; Johnsen, Rosen, Chang & Djurdjevic & Taing 2012). Formative constructs are defined as being created by their indicators, where well-being might be "created" by one's socioeconomic status, emotional stability, and friendship network. Conversely, a reflective construct is caused by its indicators, such that the perceived ease of use of a particular technology is a function of how clear the directions for use are, how easy it is to learn to use, and how one is enabled to control the technology. Thus, reflective measures are caused by the latent construct versus formative measures, which cause the latent construct (Bollen & Lennox, 1991).

Johnson, Rosen, and Djurjevic (2011) raise some additional concerns regarding the development and testing of higher-order constructs. Specifically, they suggest that some of the shared variance one might associate with the component constructs comprising a higher-order construct may be due to measurement error such as common method variance. Johnson et al. (2011) also suggest there should be a very clear theoretical rationale for including specific lower-order constructs into a higher-order aggregate construct, as well as empirical evidence that shows how the higher-order construct predicts relevant criterion measures above and beyond the component constructs. The three general criteria that Johnson and his colleagues recommend include (1) specifying the theoretical framework and criteria for construct inclusion, (2) specifying the empirical criteria for inclusion, and (3) testing the component indicators against the conceptual and empirical criteria specified above.

Johnson et al. (2011) examined one of the more prominent higher-order constructs in the personality literature, which has been referred to as the core self-evaluation construct (see Judge, Erez, Bono, & Thoresen, 2003), showing that some of the shared variance associated with the components of this construct may indeed be due error or common method variance. Based on their findings, Johnson et al. (2011, p. 247) concluded, "whether or not to combine stand alone indicators into a higher-order construct is a complicated issue, one requiring much theoretical consideration and empirical evidence."

To direct future research on examining higher-order constructs going forward, Johnson et al. (2011) recommended some specific steps should be taken when advocating such higher-order constructs, which included the following: (1) Theory should drive the inclusion of indicators or component constructs; (2) One must distinguish if the construct is an aggregate or superordinate construct; (3) Provide empirical evidence to judge the final indicators included that will represent the higher-order construct; (4) An obligation to collect data to test the modeling and inclusion of indicators; (5) Ruling out common method variance as a cause of shared variance and other unmeasured causal variables; (6) Demonstrating the incremental importance of the higher-order construct using dominance or usefulness analysis; and (7) Finally, testing alternative modeling of indicators. With respect to the development of authentic leadership and the continuing research on this construct, most of these specific steps have already been followed.

Authentic leadership as higher-order construct. The higher-order authentic leadership construct examined by Walumbwa and his colleagues is comprised of four unique constructs or components, which include self-awareness, transparency, balanced processing, and moral perspective. As noted above, developing a multidimensional higher-order construct involves providing evidence for the validity of both the higher-order construct and its component dimensions, as well as the inclusion of constructs being guided by clear theoretical guidelines for identifying the appropriate indicators of the higher-order construct (see Johnson et al., 2011; Johnson et al., 2012).

Considering the criteria noted above by Johnson et al. (2011), the higher-order authentic leadership construct was developed based on an extensive review of all relevant literature and through the independent development of two theoretical frameworks that were created to explain what constitutes authentic leadership as a guiding framework for the inaugural conference on authentic leadership and its development. Using both deductive and inductive strategies to determine what constituted the higher-order construct of authentic leadership, Walumbwa and colleagues (2008) initially identified five constructs comprising the authentic leadership construct: self-awareness, relational transparency, balanced information processing, internalized regulation, and positive moral perspective. This initial list of component constructs was then examined by an independent group of leadership scholars and graduate students, who were asked to further define these construct domains and to generate items for each of the five component constructs. After going through the item generation process, the research group concluded that the best representation of authentic leadership was to use four dimensions, with the internalized regulation and positive moral perspective dimensions combined into one dimension. Beyond the lack of conceptual clarity noted by this research group for these two constructs, the behavioral descriptions generated in a series of pilot studies of what described authentic leaders failed to differentiate between them, as both involved exhibiting behavior that was consistent with one's internal values and standards.

Again, as part of the inaugural conference, a second and independent group of researchers were also working on developing a theoretical framework to define and conceptualize what constituted authentic leadership in part being guided by the work on authenticity by Kernis (2003) with a greater emphasis on linking authentic leadership to well-being. Nevertheless, Ilies et al. (2005) specified the same four components prior to the onset of the foundational conference noted above, providing independent verification for these component constructs.

The next step by Walumbwa and colleagues involved specifying the nature of the higher-order multidimensional authentic leadership construct. As noted in previous literature a multidimensional construct can be measured reflectively or formatively (Bollen & Lennox, 1991; Edwards & Bagozzi, 2000). A reflective or superordinate (Johnson et al., 2011) construct is posited as the common cause of items or indicators such that items or indicators are reflective manifestations of underlying construct (Edwards, 2011). Specifically, the causal action flows from the latent construct to the items or indicators such that any change in the construct creates changes in the items or indicators (Bollen & Lennox, 1991). In a reflective model, if items or indicators are manifestations of a higher-order construct, dropping an indicator should not alter the meaning of the construct because the indicators all reflect the same underlying construct (Johnson et al., 2012).

A formative or aggregate (Johnson et al., 2012) construct is considered to be composed of independent, albeit correlated, variables. The causal action flows from the items or indicators to the composite construct such that any change in the items or indicators will produce meaningful change in the higher-order construct; items or indicators are not interchangeable and, thus, are formative (Bollen & Lennox, 1991; Johnson et al., 2012; Peterson, Straub & Rai, 2007).

Although these two models are conceptually, substantively, and psychometrically different (Bollen & Lennox, 1991), researchers should be aware of an alternative of using a combination of reflective and formative specifications (e.g., first-order reflective, second-order formative) to operationalize complex, higher-order construct (Diamantopoulos & Siguaw, 2006; Jarvis, MacKenzie, & Podsakoff, 2003). In terms of authentic leadership, we view the higher-order construct as being created by the four component constructs, and therefore is formative at the second-order level. Each of the four component constructs can be viewed as reflective constructs whereby the items for each dimension reflect or represent the unobserved latent construct.

In the early validation work on measuring authentic leadership, Walumbwa and colleagues pursued the strategy of identifying items that would reflect each of the component constructs, not the overall higher-order construct. They also suggested that alternative measures of these constructs may be developed in the future to reflect these constructs, but these four component constructs were essential to operationalizing authentic leadership. Consequently, future research may use fewer items to reflect each component construct, but in combination (the four components), they would still represent authentic leadership. For example, in a recent study involving a multidimensional measure of empowerment leadership (e.g., Arnold, Arad, Rhoades, & Drasgow, 2000), Srivastava, Bartol, and Locke (2006) adopted three items for each of the five factors as listed in Arnold et al. (2000). A similar validation strategy was used by Walumbwa, Luthans, Avey, and Oke (2011c) when they measured psychological capital (PCQ; e.g., Luthans, Avolio, Avey, & Norman, 2007). Walumbwa et al. (2011c) used two items from the validated PCQ to measure each of the four resource components of psychological capital of hope, efficacy, optimism, and resilience. In both cases, although the authors used fewer items to capture each dimension, the choice of items did not significantly affect the dimensions relationships or the fit with the overall higher-order construct.

However, as noted above, the higher-order authentic leadership construct should be considered a formative or aggregate construct because it comprises four interrelated components that each contributes uniquely to leaders' overall levels of perceived authenticity. This is in line with Walumbwa and colleagues' original position that the four components (i.e., self-awareness, transparency, balanced processing, and moral perspectives) jointly determine the conceptual and empirical meaning of authentic leadership. Thus the component dimensions are conceptualized as reflective, while the higher-order construct is modeled as formative, which up to this point has not been as clearly articulated or tested in prior literature on authentic leadership.

Another defining feature of formative constructs is that the nomological network for the indicators may differ. In other words, indicators are not required to have the same antecedents and consequences (Jarvis et al., 2003; Petter et al., 2007). Walumbwa and colleagues suggest that the four components of authentic leadership do not need to have equal contribution, and that it is possible that certain authentic leadership components may be more or less important to predicting the outcomes of leadership across different contexts, but that does not in any way mean that some of the components are not relevant (Walumbwa et al., 2008).

To summarize, based on a series of prior confirmatory factor analyses, Walumbwa and colleagues provided consistent support for a higher-order, multidimensional model of authentic leadership that encompasses the four subdimensions noted above. Evidence for a four-component model of authentic leadership has also been provided by other authors in a broad range of samples (e.g., military to industrial) and contexts (e.g., across cultures, industry, and leadership levels) (see Avolio, 2011). The results noted above have recently been confirmed by Moriano, Molero, and Mangin (2011) using a sample of more than 600 Spanish employees and by Caza, Bagozzi, Woolley, Levy, and Caza (2010) using a random, nationally representative sample of working adults in New Zealand. What remains for future research is to test the models now using the formative and reflective framing combination that we have discussed above.

In their initial validation study of the Authentic Leadership Questionnaire or ALQ, Walumbwa et al. (2008) also demonstrated that their assessment of authentic leadership accounted for variance beyond more traditional measures of transformational (Multifactor Leadership Questionnaire, MLQ, Form 5x; Bass & Avolio, 2004 and ethical leadership (Brown et al., 2005), in predicting performance. This initial validation work provided evidence for the discriminant validity of the authentic leadership higher-order construct. In terms of performance outcomes in this initial set of studies, authentic leadership also positively related to follower satisfaction with one's supervisor, job satisfaction, organizational citizenship behavior, organizational commitment, and job performance.

More recently, Spitzmuller and Ilies (2010) examined the relationship between a leader's relational authenticity and follower assessments of that leader's transformational leadership. Spitzmuller and Ilies hypothesized that a strong relational orientation exhibited by an authentic leader would foster open and trusting leader-follower relationships, follower identification with the leader, and attributions of leader integrity, yielding elevated perceptions of individualized consideration, idealized influence, and inspirational motivation—three core components of transformational leadership. Implied in the relational aspects of authentic leadership is the assumption that authenticity has behavioral components that can be reliably perceived by others. This reliability of transmission is enhanced when one considers the developmental nature by which authenticity is achieved. Consequently, authenticity involves being true to one's self with the leader knowing this to be true, as well as his or her followers through the transmission of authentic leadership behaviors. For instance, while a skilled actor may be able to manage perceptions of authenticity in the short run, as followers assess the cross-situational consistency of the actor's words and deeds over time, the correspondence between perceived and actual authenticity should be enhanced (Schlenker, 2003).

Both practitioner and scholarly authors have emphasized the importance of authentic followership (Gardner et al., 2005a; George, 2003; Shamir & Eilam, 2005), as being central to understanding the authentic leadership process. Indeed from the very outset, the model of authentic leadership emphasized both the leader and follower in explaining what constituted authentic leadership. For example, in early formulations of the theory of authentic leadership it was posited that positive ethical climate would facilitate the development of both authentic leaders and followers, thereby fostering what Gardner and colleagues (2005a) proposed as being authentic leader x follower relationships. Gardner and colleagues (2005a) focused on describing the "follower" component as part of a more dynamic authentic leadership framework, which provided for a multilevel view of authentic leadership, which also incorporated leader and follower development. Authentic followership was described as being an integral component and outcome of the process of authentic leadership development.

Gardner and colleagues (2005) described the process through which authentic leaders use positive role modeling to develop authentic followers, who like the leaders themselves, possess higher levels of self-awareness and self-regulatory behaviors that mirror the values and beliefs of their authentic leaders. These authors suggested that personal history and trigger events act as antecedents of both authentic leadership and authentic followership and the authentic relationship, which was predicted to positively influence outcomes such as higher levels of follower trust, engagement, workplace well-being, and sustainable and veritable performance. Again, within their multilevel framework, Gardner and colleagues (2005) also highlighted the role played by an ethical and strengths-based organizational climate in fostering the development of authentic leaders and authentic followers.

To a large degree, although not necessarily specifically noted in the academic literature on authentic leadership, the locus of what constituted authentic leadership was evolving past more traditional models of leadership. What we mean here and describe in more detail below is that the leader and follower were now emerging as the loci of leadership in authentic leadership theory, as opposed to focusing just on the leader as the locus or source of leadership. This more complex view of the loci of leadership in our view does a better job from the outset of viewing the complex leadership dynamic we witness every day in organizations.

What Are the Locus and Mechanisms of Authentic Leadership?

Authenticity has been defined as "owning one's personal experiences, be they thoughts, emotions, needs, wants, preferences, or beliefs, processes represented by most authors as an individual who is coming to know 'him or herself'" (Harter, 2002). As with any leadership model, one might then ask, where does such authentic leadership come from, and how is such leadership transmitted to others? Hernandez, Eberly, Avolio, and Johnson (2011) define the *locus* of leadership, as the source from which leadership arises, while the *mechanism* of leadership was defined as the means through which leadership is transmitted or enacted within context.

Hernandez and colleagues used Weick's (1979) "double interact" concept to examine how complex interactions between the loci and mechanisms of leadership can provide for a more comprehensive view of what constitutes leadership in general and more specifically authentic leadership. When considering the locus of leadership, one must determine whether the leader is the source initiator of leadership, or if other loci give rise to leadership. As we noted above, Gardner and colleagues (2005a) take the position that the loci of leadership includes an authentic relationship between the leader and the follower. Thus, we would argue that the loci lie in the relationship with the leader and follower, and not necessarily in one versus the other. This is not to say, that the locus can't reside in the individual, but that to fully understand authentic leadership, we will have to examine the authentic leader x follower dynamic.

A main premise of authentic leadership theory is that authenticity, which is represented in one's ability to remain true to one's values and ideals, should be highly valued by followers and indeed emulated in that followers would come to identify with and trust authentic leaders to a greater extent (Avolio et al., 2004; Avolio & Walumbwa, 2006; Gardner et al., 2005a; George & Sims, 2007). Early writings on authentic leadership (Gardner et al., 2005; Luthans & Avolio, 2003) emphasized the role of authentic leaders in bolstering their followers' authenticity through the mechanism of positive role modeling. Along these lines, Gardner et al. (2005) proposed that authentic leaders and followers interacted and reinforced the formation and development of authenticity in each other, subsequently establishing more authentic relationships where authenticity within and between leaders and followers was reinforced. Similarly, George and Sims (2007) suggested that as they develop as authentic leaders, they are more concerned about serving others than they are about their own success or recognition. And they are constantly looking for ways to grow personally. This early work described followers as an active component in the leadership dynamic or process, unlike earlier models of leadership such as charismatic, visionary, or even transformational that at least initially tended to treat followers as a passive component of the leadership process (Bass, 1985; Shamir, House, & Arthur, 1993; Yukl, 2010).

How might the follower then emulate the leader's authenticity? It has been suggested that to the extent to which the leaders' authentic behaviors become prototypical behaviors in a group or organization, that followers would come to identify with those prototypical behaviors, thereby replicating their leader's authenticity by mirroring the leader's behaviors (Chan, Hannah, & Gardner, 2005; Hogg, 2001). As originally proposed by Gardner and colleagues (2005a), to the degree that authentic leadership is seen as desirable by followers, such leadership should result in followers behaving more authentically themselves, thus reinforcing the authenticity in themselves as well as in their interactions with their leader. With this conceptualization of leadership, one can see the locus of leadership is no longer centrally fixed just within the leader.

Building on the leader-and-follower dynamic described above, it has also been suggested that we can escalate the locus of authentic leadership to the group level. Specifically, Yammarino, Dionne, Schriesheim, and Dansereau (2008) proposed that authentic leadership could be viewed as shared authentic leadership in teams (Kozlowski & Ilgen, 2006), where team members, including the leader, view authentic leadership behaviors being distributed (not necessarily equally) throughout the entire team. Authentic leadership would then be expected to represent the way team members interact with each other, with such shared leadership becoming part of the shared knowledge structure within the team, and therefore driving how the team members behave (Yammarino et al., 2008).

Hmieleski, Cole, and Baron (2012) using affective events theory (AET) to understand the relationship between new venture top management teams' (TMTs) shared authentic leadership and the performance of their firms found a positive indirect effect of shared authentic leadership behavior on firm performance, an effect that operated through TMTs' positive affective tone. Walumbwa et al. (2011c) examined how authentic leadership affects group-level processes, exploring the mediating role of "collective" or group-level psychological capital and trust on the relationship between authentic leadership and work group outcomes. Walumbwa and colleagues (2011c) reported that collective psychological capital and trust mediated the relationship between ratings of authentic leadership and group citizenship behavior and group performance, while considering the effects of transformational leadership. Replicating the findings reported by Walumbwa and colleagues (2008), Walumbwa and colleagues (2011c) offered evidence that provided support for the predictive validity of authentic leadership over and above transformational leadership.

Notwithstanding these foundational arguments to escalate authentic leadership to the group level, like other leadership research (see Gardner et al., 2011), most prior studies that have focused on authentic leadership have primarily examined authentic leadership at an individual level of analysis. However, there are two important exceptions to this norm. In one study, Hannah, Walumbwa, and Fry (2011b) set out to examine how the team leader's level of authenticity predicted the average levels of authenticity exhibited in their teams. Their findings showed that the modeling of authentic leadership proposed by Gardner and colleagues (2005) with respect to the leader-and-follower relationship, also emerged at the team level as proposed by Yammarino et al. (2008). Hannah and colleagues (2011b) were able to show what appeared to be some transference of authentic leadership behaviors to a broader set of team members. For instance, their findings suggest that teams composed of self-aware team members who have established normative behaviors that are more transparent, balanced, and ethical are more likely to interact in ways that enhance their team's aggregate level of authentic leadership. Those teams that reported both higher mean levels of authentic leadership, as well as greater consistency (or lower variance) in authentic leadership behaviors across all team members were also higher performing teams. Hannah and colleagues (2011b) concluded that authenticity strength (high agreement) within teams was positively related to higher levels of team performance. In another study, Walumbwa, Hartnell, Aryee, and Christensen (2011b) tested a model that examined creativity in work groups by focusing on authentic leadership, communication climate, and knowledge sharing. Their findings revealed that authentic leadership was positively related to work group creativity, with this relationship mediated by communication climate and knowledge sharing controlling for transformational leadership and group size. Importantly, they also found that authentic leadership accounted for an additional 14 per cent of variance in the group's creativity beyond transformational leadership, providing further evidence of incremental validity of authentic leadership.

As we can see from the research reviewed above, what constitutes the loci of authentic leadership, relatively early in the emergence of research in this area, includes individual, dyadic as well as group levels of analysis. Starting with this more dynamic set of loci avoids the common criticism leveled against prior leadership research that has been more traditionally focused on the leader as locus of leadership, sacrificing work on other loci such as the follower or team. Hernandez and colleagues (2011) define mechanisms of leadership as the means by which leadership is enacted. Specifically, "the leader behaves authentically," and the followers can also behave authentically, with each being a mechanism for transmitting authentic leadership. According to Weick (1979), individual behaviors within organizations do not occur in isolation, but rather through interlocking events called "interacts." Using the double interact framework, the leader initiates an authentic behavior that influences followers authentic behaviors, and these in turn could then influence the leader's authentic leadership behavior in subsequent events. Morgeson and Hofmann (1999, p. 252) describe the double interact as "the basic building block upon which all larger collective structures are composed."

Osborn, Hunt, and Jauch (2002, p. 805) captured the interaction denoted above by stating that "leadership is not something one does by itself. Its dimensions emerge from actions and interactions," which supports the position proposed by Gardner et al. (2005), about the leader x follower authentic leadership. Gardner, Fischer, and Hunt (2009) advanced a model of leader authenticity in which they examined how the emotional labor exhibited by the leader played a role in transmitting authentic leadership. Specifically, they discussed how the level of emotional labor exhibited by leaders would affect follower perceptions of authenticity. Gardner and colleagues (2011) argued that the degree of surface acting, deep acting, and genuine emotions transmitted by the leader would predict followers' perceptions of a leader's authenticity. The leader's level of perceived authenticity would also be related to the trust that followers experience working with the leader.

In a similar vein, Ladkin and Taylor (2010) argued that followers' perceptions of leader authenticity are dependent upon the manner in which the leader's "true self" is transmitted. The way authentic leadership is transmitted according to Ladkin and Taylor depends on three key aspects: (1) self-exposure, (2) relating to others, and (3) leaders' choices. However, other authors have criticized the foundational theory of authentic leadership suggesting that "it is not clear from authentic leadership theory how deeply self-referent aspects of a leader's self (authenticity) and the leader's underlying moral values (integrity) become apparent to followers" (Fields, 2007, p. 196). Pittinsky and Tyson (2005) suggested that the follower was critical to assessing how authentic leadership was perceived stating that "on a practical level, followers' perceptions of the authenticity of a leader are as important to consider as are the actual thoughts and actions of the leader" (p. 254).

In sum, the loci and mechanism view of leadership provides a useful framework for understanding what constitutes authentic leadership and followership and how each may affect the other in interactions across time and levels of analysis. We now move to exploring some of the other links that have been uncovered between authentic leaders, followers, and performance in the emerging empirical literature on this topic.

What Are Links That Have Been Tested Between Authentic Leadership, Followership, and Performance Outcomes?

One would be hard pressed to pick up an article in any top research outlet, and not see the authors focusing on the ubiquitous "black box" of leadership. The black box metaphor represents the "things" that happen between when the leader does something, and the follower reacts, at least in terms of more traditional models of leadership. Filling the black box involves focusing on mediators, sometimes one or more than one, as well as including the context as a moderator of the hypothesized relationships.

The focus on what was in the black box was evident at the 2004 summit on authentic leadership held at the University of Nebraska and critiques of this work that appeared in the special issue of the *Leadership Quarterly* by Cooper, Scandura, and Schriesheim (2005). As one would naturally expect, the need was raised to examine how authentic leadership was not only different from other positive forms of leadership, but also how it affected mediating links between leadership and performance differently as compared to other positive leadership constructs. Specifically, calls were made to examine how authentic leadership related to followers' engagement, trust, levels of identification, independence, positivity, and ownership in the work they did in organizations.

Gardner and his colleagues (2011) conducted a review of the authentic leadership research literature reporting that there have been 91 scholarly publications on authentic leadership at the time when their review of the leadership literature was completed. This emerging line of research has primarily focused on examining what constitutes authentic leadership and its impact on followers and performance. Gardner and his colleagues note that nearly two-thirds of the articles focusing on authentic leadership during this period of time have been theoretical papers, so a lot more work remains on the empirical front.

Representative of the empirical work on examining the mediating links for authentic leadership is Clapp-Smith and colleagues' (2009) investigation on the relationships between authentic leadership, trust in management, psychological capital (efficacy, hope, optimism, and resiliency) and work group performance. Their results revealed that trust in management partially mediated the relationship between ratings of an individual leaders' authentic leadership and group performance. Similarly, Walumbwa, Wang, Wang, Schaubroeck, and Avolio (2010) focused on examining the direct and indirect effects of authentic leadership on followers' work engagement and organizational citizenship behaviors (OCBs). Using a sample of managers and their direct reports, they showed that authentic leadership was related to elevated levels of follower work engagement and OCB, and that these relationships were mediated by feelings of empowerment and identification with the supervisor, as posited by the foundational authentic leadership models (Gardner et al., 2005a; Ilies et al., 2005; Shamir & Eilam, 2005).

A number of authors have also focused on examining the links between authentic leadership and OCB because prior theoretical work suggests that authentic leaders, through their ethical role modeling, transparency, and balanced decision making, create the conditions that promote positive extra-role behaviors with followers (Avolio & Luthans, 2006; Van Dyne & LePine, 1998). Prior research has also focused on examining employee work engagement because engagement has been related to a variety of important organizational outcomes, including employee productivity and retention, customer satisfaction, turnover, and overall profitability (Harter, Schmidt, & Hayes, 2002).

The work by Walumbwa and colleagues suggests that leaders who are perceived to be more authentic promote employee-helping behavior by making them more aware of the importance of helping one another, as well as modeling the importance of transparently sharing information to optimize individual and unit performance (Walumbwa et al., 2010; Walumbwa et al., 2011c). Paralleling the research on authentic leadership, Mayer, Kuenzi, Greenbaum, Bardes, and Salvador (2009) demonstrated a significant and positive relationship between ethical leadership, a component of authentic leadership, and ratings of OCBs. Similarly, prior research has shown that employees experiencing more honest and trusting relationships with their supervisor also tend to display higher levels of OCB (Mayer & Gavin 2005). One would therefore expect authentic leaders to promote more prosocial organizational behaviors among their followers as shown by Kernis and Goldman (2005), who reported higher levels of self-reported authenticity to be related to higher student engagement scores.

Authentic leaders also transparently share information and utilize followers' inputs in making their decisions, thus it would be expected that their followers would be more likely to experience self-determination in their work as they take greater responsibility for their actions. Spreitzer (2006) reported that followers who were in more inclusive unit climates where leaders readily shared information, both of which characterize authentic leadership, reported higher levels of psychological empowerment. Previous research has shown that higher levels of self-reported authenticity were significantly related to higher levels of student self-determination (Kernis & Goldman, 2005).

Authentic leaders strengthen followers' positive states through their own positive states and heightened self-awareness (Luthans & Avolio, 2003) by transmitting these positive states through their actions and behaviors. Prior research has provided evidence linking a leader's level of psychological capital including hope, optimism, self-efficacy, and resilience, and followers' positive attitudes (Larson & Luthans, 2006), as well as with their performance (Luthans, Avolio, Walumbwa, & Li, 2005; Luthans et al., 2007). For instance, Jensen and Luthans (2006) reported that entrepreneurial leaders who had higher self-ratings on these core positive states were also rated higher on their authentic leadership.

The above evidence provides very preliminary support for the positive relationship between leader authenticity and positive psychological states, as proposed by Luthans and Avolio (2003), as well as Avolio and Luthans (2006). It can be argued that followers who identify with their authentic leader, are in turn, also more likely to be aware of the positive strengths and capacities of their leader, which should promote higher levels of efficacy, hope, optimism, and resilience in themselves. Support for this position comes from research on emotional contagion effects, which has shown that positivity can spread between leaders and followers (Johnson, 2008), or can be linked through the mechanism of role modeling (Kark, Shamir, & Chen, 2003). Specifically, followers would be expected to be more capable of identifying with a transparent and self-aware leader, and that the process of personal identification should strengthen the follower's self-concept, promoting their positive psychological states (Avolio et al., 2004).

Trust has been defined in the literature as representing a willingness on the part of one individual to be vulnerable based on expected behaviors and motives of another (Schoorman, Mayer, & Davis, 2007). To the extent that authentic leaders are more transparent, we would expect their followers to become more aware of the leader's true character, values, beliefs, and motives, resulting in followers seeing a greater level of alignment between the leader's values and their own, thus enhancing their levels of trust (Tomlinson & Mayer, 2009). Jones and George (1998) argued that when leaders and followers share congruent values, they are more likely to develop unconditional levels of trust in each other, which would be very difficult to undermine.

Gardner and colleagues (2005a) suggest that followers who personally identify with their leader would be more likely to adopt the leader's styles and attributes that are associated with authenticity. Authentic leaders are said to be aware of and to remain true to their values and beliefs, transparently communicating those beliefs, and soliciting multiple points of view before making a decision or devising a course of action. We suggest that this should result in facilitating stronger personal follower identification as the follower emulates the leader's authenticity. Furthermore, followers of authentic leaders may trust that it is safe to be vulnerable with a leader when that leader also demonstrates high levels of moral integrity, openness, and consistency (Lapidot, Kark, & Shamir, 2007). This suggests identification with one's leader may mediate the relationship between authentic leadership and trust in one's leader. Adopting these attributes and styles may also be reinforcing to the extent that being described by others as "authentic" has positive effects on one's self-concept. For example, Kernis (2003) suggests that as we come to know and accept ourselves in terms of what we are capable and not capable of doing, then we also would be expected to exhibit higher and more consistent levels of self-esteem. Authentic leaders, by definition, know and accept themselves and thus present a model of certainty, stability, and consistency associated with their self-concept and therefore should be more self-assured and demonstrate higher levels of self-esteem.

Sluss and Ashforth (2008) suggested that interpersonal levels of identification could be based in role-related relationships, such as the ones that exist between supervisors and their direct reports. Sluss and Ashforth (2008) suggested that through the process of identifying with a role relationship such as leader and follower, each individual would be more likely to internalize the performance standards and norms that define that relationship. Walumbwa and colleagues (2010) reasoned that relational identification offers one way to understand how individuals define themselves with respect to the type of leaders they are more (less) willing to follow and indeed become over time.

Ilies and colleagues (2005) also suggested that more authentic leaders' relational orientation would encourage their followers to personally identify with both the leader and their organization. For example, because authentic leaders are seen as promoting transparency in terms of how they express their stands on important issues, values, and beliefs, their followers in turn would be more likely to identify with them (Avolio & Gardner, 2005; Ilies et al., 2005). Moreover, to the extent that authentic leaders set a personal example of high moral standards and balance in making critical decisions, they would be expected to promote a stronger sense of identification among followers that would elevate followers' own self-awareness about what are the moral and ethical standards that the follower should promote and support.

Walumbwa and colleagues (2010) built on Sluss and Ashforth's operational definition of relational identification suggesting that authentic leaders by exhibiting respect for each follower, would be more likely to create openness or transparency, as well as accountability in their relationships with them (Gardner et al., 2005; Ilies et al., 2005; Luthans & Avolio, 2003). Walumbwa and colleagues (2010) then predicted that authentic leader behaviors would be associated with a higher level of relational identification. Moreover, based on the available research, Walumbwa and colleagues (2010) also predicted a positive relationship between authentic leadership and empowerment. Their results showed that empowerment was an important motivational mechanism through which authentic leaders can affect follower work-related outcomes. Their findings also indicated that a follower's interpersonal identification with his or her supervisor might also be a critical intervening variable linking leader and follower work outcomes.

Overall, the pattern of results reported by Walumbwa and colleagues (2010) suggest that the more leaders are seen as authentic, the more employees are likely to identify with them, feel psychologically empowered, engaged in their roles, and demonstrate more citizenship-rated behaviors. Other studies also show that authentic leadership is positively related to health care quality, employee engagement, job satisfaction, and voice behavior among registered nurses. For instance, Giallonardo, Wong, and Iwasiw (2010) reported that authentic leadership was not only positively related to nurses' job satisfaction, but that this relationship was partially mediated by the nurses' work engagement. In another related study, Wong, Laschnger, and Cummings (2010) found that authentic leadership was positively related to employee voice behavior and perceived unit care quality by enhancing nurses' trust in their managers and work engagement.

We also are beginning to learn that authentic leadership positively relates to intervening constructs such as trust in ways that may differ from other positive forms of leadership. For instance, Walumbwa and colleagues (2008) suggested that transformational leaders may impact a follower's level of personal identification through their inspiration or compelling vision, while authentic leaders route to enhancing a follower's level of relational identification with the leader might occur through the leader being more transparent about his or her values, or just in terms of making hard decisions in a fair and balanced way and modeling high moral conduct.

Bass and Riggio (2006) suggested that transformational leaders could enhance their followers' trust by paying greater attention to understanding their individual needs, strength, and weaknesses, and then providing appropriate growth opportunities to stretch their followers' development and performance. In addition, transformational leaders may enhance follower trust, by demonstrating their willingness to self-sacrifice for the good of their organization (Shamir et al., 2003) and/or by promoting others to challenge their ideas through the use of intellectual stimulation. Indeed, leaders who are clear on setting expectations and following through on commitments and goals from a transactional sense could also enhance followers trust in their leader to deliver on promises.

Authentic leaders may also engender follower trust through the consistency between their words and actions based on having a keen sense of their own level of self-awareness and the ability to adjust the way they interact and address follower concerns to make adjustments in their relationships to arrive at the most balanced decisions. Followers of authentic leaders also may assign greater trust to their leaders because of the leaders promoting greater transparency and positivity in their interactions with their followers, thus followers feeling that nothing will be hidden minimizing risk and likely enhancing feelings of psychological safety (Luthans et al., 2007; Macik-Frey, Quick, & Cooper, 2009).

In sum, over the last seven years, there have been numerous studies examining the proposed links between authentic leadership and various interim and ultimate outcome measures. These studies have examined a range of mediating and outcome variables including personal identification with the leader, social identification with the organization, work and life satisfaction, trust, positive emotions, engagement, well-being, burnout, turnover, absenteeism, and work effectiveness. For example, ratings of authentic leadership were positively related to identification with one's supervisor (Walumbwa et al., 2010); communication climate, and knowledge sharing (Walumbwa et al., 2011b); trust in leadership (Clapp-Smith et al., 2009; Wong & Cummings, 2009); follower job satisfaction (Jensen & Luthans, 2006); organizational commitment (Jensen & Luthans, 2006); follower citizenship behavior; voice and work engagement (Giallonardo et al., 2010; Walumbwa et al., 2011c; Wong et al., 2010); follower job performance (Wong & Cummings, 2009); and psychological well-being (Toor & Ofori, 2009) as well as group creativity (Walumbwa et al., 2011b), team productivity (Hannah et al., 2011b), and firm performance (Hmieleski et al., 2011). What we can take away from the accumulated research is that most of the original predictions in the foundational models of authentic leadership have largely been supported. We now extend our examination of authentic leadership to address how it relates to outcomes that would be more aligned with leaders and followers doing the right thing, or ethical outcomes.

How Does Authentic Leadership Relate to Ethical Outcomes?

Authentic leadership has been hypothesized as being positively related to follower ethical behaviors and outcomes (Avolio et al., 2004; Gardner et al., 2005a). Brown and Mitchell (2010) suggested that since authentic leadership has a "strong emphasis on the ethical dimension of leaders, future research linking authentic leadership to important ethics-related outcomes is promising." Yet, there has still been relatively little research that has examined linkages between authentic leadership and ethical outcomes.

Related research examining the links between leadership and ethical outcomes has shown that leaders who are seen as more ethical by their followers have followers who are more likely to be committed to their organization and have a greater propensity to report issues and problems (Avey, Palanski, & Walumbwa, 2010; Brown et al, 2005; Neubert, Carlson, Kacmar, Roberts, & Chonko, 2009). Lester et al. (2009) proposed that leaders who are seen as moral exemplars by their followers can be effective role models for developing higher levels of courage in their followers to take a stand on addressing ethical issues. Authentic leaders are expected to transmit behaviors that would be consistent with the leader's moral and ethical values/beliefs and subsequent actions, promoting confidence in the leader to do "the right thing." Based on social learning theory (Bandura, 1977), leaders who transmit authentic behaviors would signal to their followers that they should stand up and act in line with their moral values. This process occurs as the authentic leader models or transmits the expected set of behaviors, and through the social learning process, followers then develop ideas for taking courageous action (Hannah, Avolio, & Walumbwa, 2011a).

Leaders seen as authentic by their followers also demonstrate a well-developed moral perspective and tend to work to create ethical organizational cultures that align with their moral perspective (Hannah et al., 2005). Ethical cultures not only communicate the appropriate normative expectations to guide follower behavior, they also make desired values evident in the organization (Treviño & Youngblood, 1990; Verschoor, 2003). When core values and beliefs are activated, the behavior that is encouraged in individuals would be expected to be in line with those core values and beliefs (Verplanken & Holland, 2002). Consequently, authentic leaders would be expected to highlight the values and beliefs in the workplace that employees should strive to achieve (Gardner et al., 2005), while also modeling those values and beliefs to reinforce that in others.

Hannah and colleagues (2011a) argue that authentic leaders will create a climate where followers' believe that they can openly share their beliefs and align them with their behaviors, with the expectation that their behaviors will be reinforced by their leader and others in the environment. Ilies and colleagues argued this is partly because authentic leaders set the conditions for *relational authenticity* where both leader and followers feel at ease to disclose and act in accordance with their thoughts and ideals. In combination, this should foster higher levels of moral courage to stand up and exhibit ethical behavior. Authentic leaders do this in part by being balanced and fair with their decision making, allowing their decisions to be challenged (Avolio & Gardner, 2005).

We suggest that when faced with ethical dilemmas, followers operating in a more open, transparent climate that has a clear set of ethical values that are well articulated will be more compelled to stand up and act in line with their beliefs even if there is pressure to act otherwise. Consequently, authentic leaders are expected to activate higher levels of moral agency or efficacy in their followers, which in turn should promote engagement in ethical behaviors, while at the same time, limiting moral disengagement that may otherwise occur when individuals seek to justify their omission of ethical, or commission of unethical acts (Bandura, 1999; Hannah, et al., 2005; Lester, et al., 2009).

In sum, there is a clear rationale and some preliminary evidence to support the proposed links between authentic leadership and behaving more ethically in organizations. Clearly, a lot of work remains to determine under what conditions authentic leadership may be more or less likely to foster ethical outcomes. For example, would the reward system where one is recognized for self-interest impact the link between authentic leadership and ethical outcomes? Moreover, how will authentic leadership impact ethical outcomes for followers when the leader and follower are working in more extreme environments and organizations? Do decisions that represent life and death outcomes moderate the impact of authentic leadership on ethical outcomes? Finally, how does authentic leadership generalize across cultures? Do the core attributes representing authentic leadership and their links to ethical outcomes vary as a consequence of leaders and followers operating in different cultural settings?

How Can We Extend the Work on Authentic Leadership to Other Domains Such as Positive Emotions?

As noted at the outset of this article, one of the things that differentiated authentic leadership theory was the focus taken by Luthans and Avolio (2003) to integrate the work on authentic leadership with positive psychology and positive organizational behavior. Part of the logic for taking this focus was expressed by Avolio and Luthans (2006) whereby they suggested that authentic leaders would not only have a more positive view of themselves, but also would transfer those levels of positivity to their followers. It was expected that leaders who really knew themselves (highly self-aware) and were comfortable being transparent with others, would more likely be positive about themselves, their own leadership and their roles in working with others.

Gardner et al. (2011) review of the authentic leadership literature indicated that authors have now begun to examine how authentic leadership theory relates to work on emotions including considering linkages with affective events theory (Weiss & Cropanzano, 1996). Taking this focus supports arguments presented by Luthans and Avolio (2003) whereby they discussed potential conceptual links between authentic leadership and positive constructs such as positive self-regulation, optimism, hope, resiliency and efficacy, as noted. To date, Gardner et al. (2011) indicated that only five articles have focused on linking affective constructs/

process theories to the leader and/or follower's positive emotions (see Gardner et al., 2009).

In addition to the foundational work on authentic leadership, subsequent authors have suggested that authentic leaders can raise the emotions of followers by creating positive, supportive, fair, and transparent climates that help to facilitate followers achieving higher levels of authenticity themselves (Dasborough & Ashkanasy, 2005). In one of the first studies to examine the link between authentic leadership and follower positivity and performance, Peterson, Walumbwa, Avolio, and Fredrickson (2007) examined how the authentic leadership of police officers predicted the positive emotions of their direct reports over time. The preliminary results indicated that leaders in the police organization rated by followers as more authentic had followers who were rated as more effective performers by their supervisors. More important, these authors reported that authentic leadership predicted follower job performance partially through the leader's ability to influence their followers' level of positive emotions over time. Followers who worked for an authentic leader reported experiencing more positive emotions and fewer negative emotions than those who worked for a less authentic leader, which translated into more effective police performance. Results of their study also indicated that the positive relationship between authentic leadership and followers' job performance was partially mediated by followers' positive emotions. Importantly, the authors did not find any evidence to support the mediating effect of negative emotions on performance, although they did report ratings of authentic leadership were negatively related to followers' negative emotions. This suggests that followers of more authentic leaders were more likely to experience less negative emotions over a several months period of time.

How Did Authentic Leadership Become Authentic Leadership Development?

We know that about one-quarter of the $50 billion that organizations spend on organizational learning and development is specifically focused on leadership development (O'Leonard, 2010). Yet, in 2011, we still know very little regarding the best ways to accelerate genuine or authentic leadership development. In recent critiques of the leadership literature, perhaps one of the most interesting conclusions that has been drawn is that leadership development among all major topics in the field of leadership has been the least explored (Avolio, 2007; Avolio, Walumbwa, & Weber, 2009c; Day, 2000; Day, Harrison & Halpin, 2009). More importantly, research examining what promotes genuine leadership development is very sparse in the leadership literature, as are theories of leadership development (Avolio & Luthans, 2006; Day et al., 2009).

However, there have been some attempts made to examine what constitutes effective leadership development with growing interest over the last decade in this topic. For example, Burke and Day (1986) completed the first meta-analysis on research that focused on leadership development reporting that there was a moderately positive effect in 12 out of 17 studies included in their quantitative review (Burke & Day, 1986). Collins and Holton (2004) built on the foundational meta-analysis reported by Burke and Day with their quantitative review of the literature that included 83 intervention studies that focused on managerial training published between 1982 and 2001. Collins and Holton replicated the earlier results reported by Burke and Day (1986), demonstrating that managerial training had a positive impact on various performance outcomes that ranged from being a moderate to strong effect. Finally, Avolio, Reichard, Hannah, Walumbwa, and Chan (2009a) conducted a comprehensive meta-analysis of all types of leadership interventions, including experimental, quasi-experimental, training and development looking back over the last 100 years of leadership research. Paralleling the results above, Avolio et al. (2009a) reported that there were moderately positive effects for leadership development with development programs based on Pygmalion theory and transformational leadership demonstrating some of the strongest effects.

What is interesting about the leadership development literature is that most prior research efforts have not examined the impact of leadership training on whether the leaders actually changed or not in terms of style, ways of thinking about leadership, and impact on others (see Day, 2000). Over three decades ago, this prompted Stogdill (1974) to criticize research on leadership development because there were very few studies that had examined whether the interventions had actually changed leaders, and more important whether the changes had any impact on organizational performance outcomes. Over two decades later, Yukl (2006) similarly criticized leadership research again pointing out that most prior research had not shown if the improvement in performance outcomes was causally due to a theory-driven leadership development process.

These criticisms notwithstanding, there have actually been a growing number of rigorous attempts in both lab and field experiments that have shown positive and significant effects that were attributable to leader development interventions (e.g., Barling, Loughlin, & Kelloway, 2002). For example, Dvir, Eden, Avolio, and Shamir (2002) demonstrated using the gold standard for field research, a longitudinal, randomized field experiment, that transformational leadership was enhanced by training, as well as the leader's performance. More importantly, the experimental training had a more positive impact on followers' development and performance compared to a comparison group, who received an alternative form of transformational leadership training. This alternate form was less behaviorally based, which was the primary focus of the experimental intervention—to change the leadership of these participants to exhibit more transformational leadership behaviors. In fact, the program that had the greater impact was considered to be more genuine or authentic, in that it focused on how to best lead in real incidents applying transformational and transactional leadership behaviors.

In combination, the prior meta-analytic research, as well as growing number of field research projects focusing on leadership development offers consistent and positive evidence regarding the effects of leadership training on improvements in leader behavior and performance (Arthur, Bennett, Edens, & Bell, 2003; Avolio et al., 2009a). In fact, Avolio and colleagues (2009a) reported that even short leadership interventions that lasted a day or less were shown to have a positive impact on leader development.

Back in 2003 when the 100 year meta-analysis was begun, discussions regarding the state of research and practice on leadership development prompted Avolio and his colleagues at the University of Nebraska to set a standard that much of the work that would come from the new leadership institute being initiated there, would focus on determining what constituted "genuine" or authentic leadership development. This initiative was prompted in part by comments by Ralph Stogdill regarding the lack of theory and research on leadership development. At that time and currently, one could say that the practice community was so far out ahead of the research community, that there was little if any connection between the two domains. This conclusion lead to an obvious question: *what did practitioners know about developing authentic leadership that the scholarly community did not know?* Moreover, *what did the scholars need to know in order to provide a foundation for the considerable investment that was being made in authentic leadership development?* What became obvious over time was that the practice community was "practicing" the development of leadership, and whether it had an impact on changing leaders, was largely ignored in terms of any systematic attempt to determine the effects of leadership development. Billions were being invested in leadership development, but no one knew the return-on-investment (ROI).

Since Avolio and his colleagues also set out to examine the "root construct" of all positive forms of leadership, which they labeled as authentic, it seemed appropriate at the time to connect the focus on examining authentic leadership with authentic leadership development. Specifically, they set out to examine what actually developed leadership in leaders and more important what developed them to become more authentic leaders. What was evident back in the early part of the current century was that there were more discussions and speculation about what constituted authentic leadership development than there were empirical findings (Avolio, 2005; Day et al., 2009).

There were essentially two initiatives launched back in 2003 to examine what constituted "authentic" leadership development, which were captured in the title of a book published by Avolio (2005), *Leadership development in balance: Made/Born*. What Avolio (2005) intended to initiate in this book was an examination of the balance between determining the innate qualities of an individual that promoted his emergence as a leader or what he called the "denominator" in the made over born fraction. Conversely, the numerator represented the life experiences that constituted the "made" component of leadership development. Avolio (2005) suggested that there would be some leader attributes that were more heritable that would contribute to promoting leadership emergence, such as the energy level that an individual inherits from one's parents (Bass, 1990; Zaccaro, Kemp, & Bader, 2004). Yet, Avolio (2005) also suggested that life experiences including formal training, mentoring, coaching, challenges, education, and other such interventions would impact the "numerator" in the *made* over *born* fraction. The simple idea proposed by Avolio (2005) was we could take the heritable qualities represented in "the denominator" and optimize them through various experiences as represented in "the numerator."

Extending the metaphor of the fraction described above, there are some that are endowed with many more qualities that promote leadership emergence, who will never emerge as leaders. We might say these individuals can have become a smaller fraction than their genetic potential would have predicted. This insight prompted a renewed focus on life events and how they shaped and triggered a leader's emergence and development (Luthans & Avolio, 2003).

In line with the focus on the "made" aspects of leadership, Bennis and Thomas (2002) concluded after interviewing 50 well-known young and older leaders, that in every instance, leadership had emerged after a defining or "crucible" experience in life—signaling the numerator's impact on leader emergence and development. Extending this work, one could ask, what are the heritable traits *and* life experiences that develop an authentic versus inauthentic leader? Is it possible to start out with heritable traits that would lean one more toward being inauthentic and then due to some life altering experiences, having the individual end up as being more authentic? Conversely, are some of our worst examples of leaders who ruined companies and even societies, if given the right crucible events, could have become authentic leaders?

The questions above guided the early foundational work on authentic leadership and its development. Indeed, Shamir and Eilam (2005) proposed the use of life stories at the inaugural conference on authentic leadership for examining how authentic leadership development occurred. Shamir and Eilam argued that by examining a leader's life story, one could derive a number of insights into the meanings that the leader attached to prior life events and how those events promoted subsequent development. Shamir and Eilam further proposed that life stories provide followers with significant sources of information to base their judgments about the authenticity of their leaders and to use in terms of their own development.

Currently, we are seeing much more attention to understanding the individual leader, whether in the work appearing in the practice community by authors such as Gardner and Schermerhorn (2004); George and Sims (2007); and Walumbwa, Christensen, and Hailey, (2011a); or in terms of research studies. For example, Orvis and Langkamer-Ratwani (2010) indicated we are seeing much more attention to leadership development that focuses on self-development. At the same time, we are also seeing much more of a focus on bringing development into the workspace, where authors such as Avolio (2005, 2011) argue that authentic leadership development more than likely occurs. Given the rapid shifts with mobile technology and the ability to push information to leaders as well as pull what they request in terms of support, it certainly appears that more genuine leadership development will be embedded at work versus accomplished at off-site training locations, which will serve other useful purposes (Boyce, Zaccaro, & Wisecarver, 2010; Walumbwa et al., 2011a).

In the next section, we will address the question that appears to remain at the top of the list in terms of figuring out where leaders come from. The question essentially focuses on what is the "ultimate" source code for leadership?

So Is Authentic Leadership Born or Made?

This question pervades almost every discussion one has regarding leadership. The question is so pervasive that one might consider it to be part of the evolution of humankind. Indeed, if we examine the field of leadership from an evolutionary perspective, we still find today and for most societies no more than three generations back, that those countries were run by kings or queens. In those situations, in order to become a leader, one had to be born into the role, which didn't necessarily mean that the individual was an effective leader, nor transformational or authentic. All it meant was that one of the fundamental prerequisites for leadership was to be born into the right family. Consequently, as the world has changed in terms of who emerges as leaders, certainly providing more opportunities for individuals to be "made" into leaders, one wonders how much of our evolutionary implicit model of leadership still relates back to kings and queens being "the leader."

Avolio and his colleagues chose as a starting point for research on authentic leadership development to examine how much of it was born or heritable and how much of it was made. This jumping-off point led to a series of studies examining identical versus fraternal twins and their emergence as leaders. Twin databases were chosen for research because with twins one can account for heritability, in that identical twins have 100 per cent the same genes while fraternal have about 50 per cent. Knowing these two figures allows one to effectively control for heritability, while examining what researchers in this area call the "shared" and "unshared" environments in which these twins had developed. A shared environment might typically mean growing up in the same household. With regards to an unshared environment, this might result where one twin has a great mentor in high school, while the other twin does not have a mentor.

The accumulated research on the heritability of leadership has consistently shown that approximately 30 per cent of the variation in leadership style (self-rated) and emergence can be accounted for by heritability. The remaining variation is attributed to nonshared environmental influences such as individuals being exposed to different role models and early opportunities for leadership development (Arvey, Rotundo, Johnson, Zhang, & McGue, 2006; Arvey, Zhang, Avolio, & Krueger, 2007; Ilies, Gerhardt, & Le, 2004). It is also important to recognize that even unshared environments may be similar to the degree the two environments provide similar experiences for each twin member.

The initial findings reported above support Plomin and Daniels (1987, p. 1) conclusion regarding heritability whereby, "behavioral-genetic research seldom finds evidence that more than half of the variance in complex behavioral traits is due to genetic differences among individuals... most behavioral variability among individuals is environmental in origin." Moreover, this also supports Mumford, Stokes, and Owens's (1990) earlier conclusion that with respect to leadership development, heredity and environmental influences appear to work hand in hand.

Looking to explore the numerator further, Avolio, Rotundo, and Walumbwa (2009b) examined the impact of different types of childhood events/experiences comparing identical and fraternal twins. These authors focused on the level of rule-breaking behavior associated with individuals during their adolescence, and the type of parenting style they received, in determining how each predicted the ascendance of the respective twin pairs into adult leadership roles, while controlling for personality and genetic predispositions. Based on earlier parenting research, Avolio et al. (2009b) proposed that parents who promoted more prosocial behavior using authoritative parenting with their children, would facilitate their development as leaders (see Caprara, Barbaranelli, Pastorelli, Bandura, & Cimbardo, 2000). They based their prediction on the idea that with authoritative parenting, adolescents would be provided with specific guidance on how to avoid future rule breaking that could be harmful to their success in life or in this instance in leadership roles. Authoritative parenting was considered a fair and disciplined way of developing adolescents to overcome and learn from past mistakes, thus preparing them to take on future life leadership challenges.

Avolio and colleagues (2009b) also referred to earlier writings by Avolio (2005), who suggested that one of the first significant trainers that leaders experience in life were their parents or significant others. Avolio and Gibbons (1988) reported that leaders who were evaluated as more transformational described their parents through in-depth life history interviews as being extremely challenging and directive—authoritative, but nevertheless also supportive when the child failed at the challenge. They consistently reported, that when they failed, their parents were described as helping them sort of "pick up the pieces" and getting them refocused to try again.

Other prior research has also shown that authoritative parenting style has been predictive of ascendance into leadership roles (Bass, 1990; Yukl, 2006). For instance, children who reported having parents who exhibited more authoritative parenting exhibited later in life higher levels of achievement orientation, self-confidence, internal locus of control, levels of moral reasoning, industriousness, independence, self-efficacy, and generativity (Baumrind, 1991; Darling & Steinberg, 1993; Lawford, Pratt, Hunsberger, & Pancer, 2005; Parker & Gladstone, 1996; Pratt, Skoe, & Arnold, 2004; Rest, 1979).

Avolio and colleagues (2009b) reported evidence to support a direct link between the effects of rule-breaking behavior and parenting style with regards to the ascendance of twins into leadership roles later on in life. In line with findings reported by Avolio and Gibbons (1988), when adolescents challenge the status quo and authority early in life, coupled with authoritative parenting, they appear to learn from those experiences why the choices they made were not appropriate. They also learn how they might have achieved their goals using strategies that could have avoided breaking rules. Avolio and colleagues (2009b) also reported that approximately 30 per cent of the variance associated with ascending into leadership roles could be accounted for by heritability, and the rest was "made."

Accordingly, the locus of authentic leadership development is not just the individual's personality, self-awareness, and self-regulation; it encompasses the interactions between loci, such as with followers and context. For example, with respect to the context, McCauley (2001) suggests designing leadership interventions to examine how "natural" learning experiences in the work context trigger development in leaders. Along these lines, Dragoni, Tesluck, Russell, and Oh (2009) examined the extent to which job assignments that were associated with observable and meaningful leadership development predicted effective leader performance, concluding that managers who were in jobs that had a higher focus on developmental assignments achieved higher levels of leadership competencies.

What Have We Learned from Research on Authentic Leadership in the Past Decade?

Based on the accumulated research, we have seen that authentic leadership can be reliably measured, and is comprised of four component factors representing a higher-order construct (Walumbwa et al., 2008), however construct validation work still remains in examining the higher-order construct as being formative, while the component constructs are modeled as reflective. Nevertheless, the foundational measure of authentic leadership has been shown to have discriminant validity in several different field studies across multiple cultures and samples when compared to measures of transformational and ethical leadership.

In terms of future research, Avolio and his colleagues have also indicated that other factors may remain uncovered, which may also explain what constitutes authentic leadership. For example, constructs such as humility may be important to fully describing what constitutes authentic leadership, and remains an area for future research to explore. In addition, the authors of the Authentic Leadership Questionnaire (see www.mindgarden.com) have indicated that using survey methods is one way of examining authentic leadership, while clearly there are other potential methods that can be used as well. For example, they suggest that one way to assess authentic leadership in the field is to triangulate data collected via survey, observation as well as archival data. Along these lines, one could assess the incidence of authentic leadership, by asking individuals who work with the leader to respond to questions sent via text messaging. Specifically, using an experience-sampling methodology, researchers could push a question to individuals who work with the leader to describe a specific behavior they have observed that characterized the leader's interaction with them that day. Using this methodology over a several-month period of time would help confirm the results collected via survey.

In addition to these experience-sampling approaches, researchers could also examine archival data, such as reports written by the leaders, e-mail communications, speeches, and so forth to determine through content analysis evidence for authentic leadership. At more senior levels, it is also possible to evaluate how top management team members relate to investors, in calls that are made quarterly that could be analyzed for authentic leadership content.

Beyond field research described above, there has been relatively little work examining how authentic leadership could be manipulated in experimental settings. For example, Mhatre (2009) conducted a true field experimental study using a sample of 221 working adults randomly assigned to four separate conditions. The goal of this study was to examine the impact of perceived leader authenticity and ability on shifts in attitude that participants displayed in each of the four conditions in this field experiment. Written scenarios were used to depict a fictitious leader who was represented as being high (low) in terms of the authentic leadership behavior and high (low) in terms of their ability. These conditions were set up to examine how they affected the rational persuasion/arguments used by the leader to get followers to change their views on the back dating of stock options. Essentially, the focus of the experiment was to determine how the authenticity of the leader and his expressed capability, would interact to change followers' views about the organization, which based on the pilot testing of the back dating scenarios were expected to be more negative.

Mhatre's (2009) results indicated that leaders who were seen as more authentic and capable had a more positive impact on attitude change in targets. There was a significant interaction between the perceptions of leader authenticity and leader ability that in combination predicted higher levels of trust in the leader. Trust in the leader also mediated the relationship between perceptions of leader authenticity and leader ability and also whether participants were willing to become an advocate for and to invest resources in the leader's organization. This type of experimental research provides very useful insights into not only testing the causal effects of authentic leadership, but also how we might go about developing it in leaders using the types of scripts and vignettes employed in this and previous experimental research.

In terms of directions for future research, there are a number of important areas that still remain to be examined including additional predicted moderators such as the nature of the organization and work; national culture; tenure of the follower with the leader; individual differences such as age, gender, personality and values; organizational structure; organizational climate; and type of performance outcome. Some interesting mediators requiring further research include the goal orientation of followers, openness to new experiences, perspective-taking capacity/moral reasoning, cognitive complexity, self-concept clarity, and motivation to lead and learn. Future research should also determine how the authentic leadership exhibited by the leader can impact the follower in terms of his or her perceived authenticity. We would expect that for leaders who role model authenticity, that followers would in turn exhibit more positive aspects of authentic leadership based on the relational focus of the foundational model of authentic leadership.

Prior research has also supported the augmentation effects of authentic leadership over transformational and ethical leadership, thus clearly demonstrating its discriminant validity. However, it still remains unclear whether authentic leadership enhances positive emotions in one's followers, or fosters performance thereby enhancing one's positive emotions, or through some interaction effect. Like most prior leadership research, there is a need for using longitudinal research designs to address each of these questions, as well as the experimental frameworks depicted above. Additionally, the components may also be moderated in different ways by the context in which leaders and followers are embedded, or based on the followers' attributes. For example, in an organization where transparency is limited, how would the authentic leaders focus on being transparent end up being perceived by others including their direct and indirect followers? This question relates to earlier comments by Pittinsky and Tyson (2005) about the importance of including follower perceptions in how leader *transmissions* of authentic leadership behavior are perceived, while also examining the context in which the leader's leadership is observed.

Although the initial validation studies on the ALQ did include samples outside of Western cultures, still a great deal of the theorizing and research on authentic leadership has been conducted within Western cultures (Gardner et al., 2011). One might then ask the question, how does authentic leadership emerge in different cultures, and in industries around the world? Generalizing the current findings regarding authentic leadership to other cultural contexts, would further generalize the conceptual and empirical contribution of authentic leadership to the broader field of leadership studies.

Other areas requiring further exploration include focusing on the impact of gender, ethnicity, and race on perceptions of authentic leadership. Given that the proportion of women assuming leadership positions is on the rise around the world, it makes sense to examine if there are systematic differences in the way authenticity is enacted and perceived (authentic behaviors) across men and women leaders (followers), as well as for race and ethnicity. It would also make sense to look at the normative gender characteristics of an industry or occupation, for example, highly male dominated careers, to determine how gender x industry effects impact what constitutes people's implicit theory of authentic leadership, and how that in turn affects their ratings of authentic leadership.

Avolio and Luthans (2006) suggested examining how the effects of authentic leadership cascade across different levels in terms of its effects on cognitive, emotional, and performance outcomes, examining the direct and indirect followers or surrogates of authentic leaders. This research will need to examine the extent to which there are cascading effects across time, levels of analysis, and levels of organizations. For example, does authentic leadership cascade in different ways versus other forms of leadership based on the hypothesized leader and follower authentic relationship in the foundational models? Extending this relationship, how does authentic leadership become part of an organization's culture, where we then witness higher levels of transparency and authenticity in the culture at the broader collective level? Moreover, we might ask, what is the "half-life" of an authentic leader in an organization, community or society? For instance, Medtronic after Bill George served as its CEO has had several recent incidents that could be used to question the authenticity of its culture without necessarily linking any of these incidents to Bill George himself.

For example, Dr. Gossman who was a cardiologist at the Lahey Clinic near Boston observed what he argues are violations of ethical guidelines concerning the clinic's financial relationship with Medtronic. Dr. Gossman claims that Medtronic was willing to give them early access to a new product called the CoreValve if, in return, the hospital made the purchasing of this product over others a priority. Dr. Gossman also claimed that a Dr. Thomas Piemonte in the clinic had a significant financial interest in Medtronic, while also serving on the speaker's bureau for Medtronic. Dr. Piemonte's wife is both a Medtronic employee and a stockholder.

In another case, Medtronic has been under scrutiny by the FDA regarding a product they call Infuse, which is a major product for Medtronic bringing in nearly $750 million. The issue being investigated by the Department of Justice and U.S. Senate regards clinical testing of the product done by investigators and reported in 13 studies primarily paid for by Medtronic that concluded little if any negative side effects for the product. In contrast, in an independently funded research project the authors reported that there were significant threats to using this product, including life-threatening events.

In fairness to Medtronic, Bill George, and the current leadership, the events described above are claims that will need to be worked through the various bodies reviewing evidence. We simply raise these examples to suggest that even an organization that has been considered synonymous with authentic leadership, may not sustain that type of leadership over time, depending on the subsequent leadership that is in place. Unfortunately, it is not just the act of unethical behavior, but the presumption that can negatively impact an organization's credibility and culture.

How Does All of this Work Impact the Practice of Leadership?

There are numerous practical implications of the ongoing work on authentic leadership and authentic leadership development. For example, what are the methods and mechanisms for developing authentic leadership when working with adolescents versus mature adults? Do the trigger and crucible events that foster authentic leadership differ earlier in life versus later on in one's careers? For now, we know that early life events impact the way leaders view their leadership, but would those same events or experiences have the same impact later in life? The focus on adolescents versus more experienced adult leaders might suggest that how one goes about genuinely developing authentic leadership could likely differ for someone with relatively little organizational experience versus someone who is at their mid-career point. If crucible events are so consequential to developing leadership, then how can we take greater advantage of those events prior to and following their occurrence? Are there strategies that we can use to develop greater mindfulness to such events, and how they can be translated into development?

Taking a less dramatic focus, Avolio and Luthans (2006) suggested that life "trigger events" that may seem less consequential than crucibles, may be equally relevant to accelerating the development of authentic leadership (also see Bennis & Thomas, 2002; Bennis, 2011). For instance, based on numerous interviews with leaders around the globe, Avolio and Luthans found that leaders oftentimes could recall a "trigger event" that didn't seem consequential at the time, but throughout their career the leader realized how it became foundational in their personal theory of leadership and its development. Avolio and Luthans cite one example of an aspiring leader who was told by a mentor, to always remember that, "every conversation matters." This trigger event led to a 10-year focus on making sure that everyone in her organization was always heard by her, which she felt boosted her transparency, self-awareness, as well as how fairly and ethically she was perceived.

One of the most exciting areas to now explore is to determine how via training and education, we can enhance the root construct of other positive forms of leadership. So often, leadership development is focused on enhancing particular styles of leadership, without necessarily building the base upon which trust and credibility are established. We suggest that by developing one's level of authentic leadership, all other positive forms of leadership impact would be enhanced.

Challenges withstanding notwithstanding, we are confident that authentic leadership can be reliably and validly measured using surveys, and/or other observation techniques, which suggests that feedback can be provided to those leaders who aspire to be more authentic. We suggest that training interventions that are based on well-validated models and methods, some of which could be designed based on what we have learned from experimental research, will provide a more authentic basis for developing authentic leaders.

We also have come to the realization that developing authentic leaders may also mean developing authentic followers. Specifically, how followers perceive and reinforce authenticity in their leaders could be a key component to how authentic leadership is in fact developed over time. One can imagine a training effort to develop what constitutes authentic followership such that leaders know what it means to be both an authentic leader and follower, since in most organizations they have to serve in both respective roles usually within the same teams and time periods. Moreover, evidence supporting the escalation of the effects of authentic leadership to the group level, suggests that developing team authentic leadership is something future intervention work needs to consider. By developing authentic leadership at the team level, we would also envision that the team can reinforce the learning of authentic leadership and followership at these respective individual levels, which ultimately then impacts the type of organizational climate and culture observed.

Conclusion

In sum, there has been an extraordinary amount of progress made into understanding what constitutes authentic leadership and its development. It is also true that we could spend yet another millennium obsessing over what constitutes the "true self" or what it means to be "self-aware." And some reading this article may say we have circumvented these debates by focusing in on what we have called the "modern" discussions of authenticity and authentic leadership. We don't disagree with this interpretation, but rather simply say, we were transparent about our intentions from the start, and believe the progress that has been made thus far in this area of leadership research and practice provides ample justification for getting beyond the traditional problematic and philosophical issues, to what we consider to be the more enduring and practical aspects of authentic leadership and its development. In the end, the world simply can't wait any longer for more authentic leaders and leadership.

References

Arnold, J. A., Arad, S., Rhoades, J. A., & Drasgow, F. (2000). The empowering leadership questionnaire: The construction and validation of a new scale for measuring leader behaviors. *Journal of Organizational Behavior*, 21, 249–269.

Arvey, R. D., Rotundo, M., Johnson, W., Zhang, Z., & McGue, M. (2006). The determinants of leadership role occupancy: Genetic and personality factors. *The Leadership Quarterly, 17*, 1–20.

Arvey, R. D., Zhang, Z., Avolio, B. J., & Krueger, R. (2007). Understanding the developmental and genetic determinants of leadership among females. *Journal of Applied Psychology, 92*, 693–706.

Arthur, W., Bennett, W., Edens, P. S., & Bell, S. T. (2003). Effectiveness of training in organizations: A meta-analysis of design and evaluation features. *Journal of Applied Psychology, 88*, 234–245.

Avey, J. B., Palanski, M., & Walumbwa, F. O. (2010). When leadership goes unnoticed: The moderating role of follower self-esteem on the relationship between ethical leadership and follower behaviors. *Journal of Business Ethics, 98*(4), 573–582.

Avolio, B. J. (2005). *Leadership development in balance: Made/Born*. NJ: Lawrence Erlbaum & Associates.

Avolio, B. J. (2007). Promoting more integrative strategies for leadership theory building. *American Psychologist, 62*, 25–33.

Avolio, B. J. (2011). *Full range leadership development*. Thousand Oaks, CA: Sage.

Avolio, B. J., & Bass, B. M. (1991). *Full range leadership development: Technical manual*. Binghamton, NY: SUNY.

Avolio, B. J., & Gardner, W. L. (2005). Authentic leadership development: Getting to the root of positive forms of leadership. *Leadership Quarterly, 16*, 315–338.

Avolio, B. J., Gardner, W. L., Walumbwa, F. O., Luthans, F., & May, D. R. (2004). Unlocking the mask: A look at the process by which authentic leaders' impact follower attitudes and behaviors. *Leadership Quarterly, 15*, 801–823.

Avolio, B. J., & Gibbons, T. G. (1988). Developing transformational leaders: A life span approach. In J. A. Conger, & R. N. Kanungo (Eds.), *Charismatic Leadership: The elusive factor in organizational effectiveness* (pp. 276–308). San Francisco, CA: Jossey-Bass Publishers.

Avolio, B. J., & Luthans, F. (2006). *High impact leader: Moments matter in authentic leadership development*. New York, NY: McGraw-Hill.

Avolio, B. J., Reichard, R. J., Hannah, S. T., Walumbwa, F. O., & Chan, A. (2009a). A meta-analytic review of leadership impact research: Experimental and quasi-experimental studies. *Leadership Quarterly, 20*, 764–784.

Avolio, B. J., Rotundo, M., & Walumbwa, F. O. (2009b). Early life experiences as determinants of leadership role occupancy: The importance of parental influence and rule breaking behavior. *Leadership Quarterly, 20*, 329–342.

Avolio, B. J., & Walumbwa, F. O. (2006). Authentic leadership: Moving HR leaders to a higher level. In J. J. Martocchio (Ed.), *Research in personnel and human resources management* (vol. 25, pp. 273–304). Amsterdam: Elsevier.

Avolio, B. J., Walumbwa, F. O., & Weber, T. (2009c). Leadership: Current theories, research and future directions. *Annual Review of Psychology, 60*, 421–449.

Bandura, A. (1977). Self-efficacy: Toward a unifying theory of behavioral change. *Psychological Review, 84*, 191–215.

Bandura, A. (1999). Moral disengagement in the perpetuation of inhumanities. *Personality and Social Psychology Review*, 33, 193–209.

Barling, J., Loughlin, C., & Kelloway, E. K. (2002). Development and test of a model linking safety-specific transformational leadership and occupational safety. *Journal of Applied Psychology, 87*, 488–496.

Barney, M. (2010). *Leadership @ Infosys*. India: Portfolio Penguin

Bass, B. M. (1985). *Leadership and performance beyond expectations*. New York, NY: Free Press.

Bass, B. M. (1990). *The Bass Stogdill handbook of leadership*. New York, NY: Free Press.

Bass, B. M., & Avolio, B. J. (2004). *Multifactor leadership questionnaire: Manual leader form, rater, and scoring key for MLQ* (form 5x-short). Redwood City, CA: Mind Garden.

Bass, B. M., & Bass, R. (2008). *The Bass handbook of leadership; Theory, research and applications*. New York, NY: The Free Press.

Bass, B. M., & Riggio, R. E. (2006). *Transformational leadership* (2nd ed.). Mahwah, NJ: Lawrence Erlbaum & Associates.

Bass, B. M., & Steidlmeier, P. (1999). Ethics, character, and authentic transformational leadership. *Leadership Quarterly, 10*, 181–218.

Baumrind, D. (1991). The influence of parenting style on adolescent competence and substance use. *Journal of Early Adolescence, 11*, 56–95.

Bennis, W. G. (2011). The crucibles of authentic leadership. In D. V. Day & J. Antonakis (Eds.), *The nature of leadership* (2nd ed., pp. 543–556). Thousand Oaks, CA: Sage.

Bennis, W. G., & Nanus, B. (1985). *Leaders: The strategies for taking charge*. New York, NY: Harper & Row.

Bennis, W. G., & Thomas, R. J. (2002). *Geeks and geezers: How era, values and defining moments shape leaders*. Boston, MA: Harvard Business School.

Bollen, K., & Lennox, R. (1991). Conventional wisdom on measurement: A structural equation perspective. *Psychological Bulletin, 110*(2), 305–314.

Boyce, L. A., Zaccaro, S. J., & Wisecarver, M. Z. (2010). Propensity for self-development of leadership attributes: Understanding, predicting, and supporting performance of leader self-development. *Leadership Quarterly, 21*, 159–178.

Brumbaugh, R. B. (1971). Authenticity and theories of administrative behavior. *Administrative Science Quarterly, 16*, 108–112.

Brown, M. E., & Mitchell, M. S. (2010). Ethical and unethical leadership: Exploring new avenues for future research. *Business Ethics Quarterly, 20*, 583–616.

Brown, M. E., Trevino, L. K., & Harrison, D. A. (2005). Ethical leadership: A social learning theory perspective for construct development. *Organizational Behavior and Human Decision Process, 97*, 117–134.

Burke, M. J., & Day, R. R. (1986). A cumulative study of the effectiveness of managerial training. *Journal of Applied Psychology, 71*, 232–245

Burns, J. M. (1978). *Leadership*. New York, NY: Harper & Row.

Caprara, G. V., Barbaranelli, C., Pastorelli, C., Bandura, A., & Cimbrado, P. G. (2000). Social foundations of children's academia achievement. *Psychological Science, 11*, 306–310.

Caza, A., Bagozzi, R. P., Woolley, L., Levy, L., & Caza, B. B. (2010). Psychological capital and authentic leadership: Measurement structure, gender comparison, and cultural extension. *Asia Pacific Journal of Business Administration, 2*(1), 53–70.

Chan, A., Hannah, S. T., & Gardner, W. (2005). Veritable authentic leadership: Emergence, functioning, and impacts. In W. B. Gardner, B. J. Avolio, & F. O. Walumbwa (Eds.), *Authentic leadership theory and practice: Origins, effects, and development* (pp. 3–42). Oxford, UK: Elsevier.

Clapp-Smith, R., Vogelgesang, G. R., & Avey, J. B. (2009). Authentic leadership and positive psychological capital: The mediating role of trust at the group level of analysis. *Journal of Leadership and Organizational Studies, 15*, 227–240.

Collins, D. B., & Holton, E. F. (2004). The effectiveness of managerial leadership development programs: A meta-analysis of studies from 1982 to 2001. *Human Resource Development Quarterly, 15*, 217–248.

Cooper, C., Scandura, T. A., & Schriesheim, C. A. (2005). Looking forward but learning from our past: Potential challenges to developing authentic leaders. *Leadership Quarterly, 16*, 475–493.

Diamantopoulos, A., & Siguaw, J. A. (2006). Formative versus reflective indicators in organizational measure development: A comparison and empirical illustration. *British Journal of Management, 17*, 263–282.

Darling, N., & Steinberg, L. (1993). Parenting style as context: An integrative model. *Psychological Bulletin, 113*, 487–496.

Dasborough, M. T., & Ashkanasy, N. M. (2005). Follower emotional reactions to authentic and inauthentic leadership influence. In W. L. Gardner, B. J. Avolio, & F. O. Walumbwa (Eds.), *Authentic leadership theory and practice: Origins, effects and development.* (pp. 281–300). Oxford, UK: Elsevier Science.

Day, D. V. (2000). Leadership development: A review in context. *Leadership Quarterly, 11*, 581–613.

Day, D. V., Harrison, M. M., & Halpin, S. M. (2009). *Integrative approach to leader development: Connecting adult development, identity, and expertise*. New York, NY: Taylor & Francis Group, LLC.

Dragoni, L, Tesluk, P. E., & Russell, E. A. (2009). Understanding managerial development: Integrating developmental assignments, learning orientation, and access to developmental opportunities in predicting managerial outcomes. *Academy of Management Journal, 52*, 731–743.

Dvir, T., Eden, D., Avolio, B. J., & Shamir, B. (2002). Impact of transformational leadership training on follower development and performance: A field experiment. *Academy of Management Journal, 45*, 735–744.

Edwards, J. R. (2011). The fallacy of fomrative measurement. *Organizational Research Methods, 14*(2), 370–388. doi: 10.1177/1094428110378369

Edwards, J. R., & Bagozzi, R. P. (2000). On the nature and direction of relationships between constructs and measures. *Psychological Methods, 5*, 155–174.

Fields, D. L. (2007). Determinants of follower perceptions of a leader's authenticity and integrity. *European Management Journal, 25*, 195–206.

Gardner, W. L., Avolio, B. J., Luthans, F., May, D. R., & Walumbwa, F. O. (2005a). "Can you see the real me?" A self-based model of authentic leader and follower development. *Leadership Quarterly, 16*, 343–372.

Gardner, W. L., Avolio, B. J., & Walumbwa, F. O. (2005b). *Authentic leadership theory and practice: Origins, effects and development.* Amsterdam: Elsevier JAI Press.

Gardner, W. L., Cogliser, C. C., Davis, K. M., & Dickens, M. (2011). Authentic leadership: A review of the literature and research agenda. *Leadership Quarterly, 22*, 1120–1145.

Gardner, W. L., Fischer, D., & Hunt, J. G. (2009). Emotional labor and leadership: A threat to authenticity? *Leadership Quarterly, 20*, 466–482.

Gardner, W. L., & Schermerhorn, J. R. (2004). Unleashing individual potential: Performance gains through positive organizational behavior and authentic leadership. *Organizational Dynamics, 33*, 270–281.

George, W. (2003). *Authentic leadership: Rediscovering the secrets to creating lasting value.* San Francisco, CA: Jossey-Bass.

George, W., & Sims, P. (2007). *True north: Discover your authentic leadership.* San Francisco, CA: Jossey-Bass.

Ghoshal, S. (2005). Bad management theories are destroying good management practices. *Academy of Management Learning and Education, 4*, 75–91.

Giallonardo, L. M., Wong, C. A., & Iwasiw, C. L. (2010). Authentic leadership of preceptors: Predictor of new graduate nurses' work engagement and job satisfaction. *Journal of Nursing Management, 18*, 993–1003.

Hannah, S. T., Avolio, B. J., & Walumbwa, F. O. (2011a). Relationships between authentic leadership, moral courage, ethical and pro-social behaviors. *Business Ethics Quarterly, 21*, 555–578.

Hannah, S. T., Lester, P. B., & Vogelgesang, G. R. (2005). Moral leadership: Explicating the moral component of authentic leadership. In W. B. Gardner, B. J. Avolio, & F. O. Walumbwa (Eds.), *Authentic leadership theory and practice: Origins, effects, and development. Monographs in leadership and management* (pp. 43–82): Oxford, UK: Elsevier/JAI Press.

Hannah, S. T., Walumbwa, F. O., & Fry, J. (2011b). Leadership in action teams: Team leader and members' authenticity, authenticity strength, and performance outcomes. *Personnel Psychology*, 64, 771–801.

Harter, J. K., Schmidt, F. L., & Hayes, T. L. (2002). Business-unit-level relationship between employee satisfaction, employee engagement, and business outcomes: A meta-analysis. *Journal of Applied Psychology, 87*, 268–279.

Harter, S. (2002). Authenticity. In C. S. Snyder & S. J. Lopez (Eds.), *Handbook of positive psychology* (pp. 382–394). Oxford: Oxford University Press.

Henderson, J. E., & Hoy, W. K. (1983). Leader authenticity: The development and test of an operational measure. *Educational and Psychological Research, 3*, 63–75.

Hernandez, M., Eberly, M. B., Avolio, B. J., & Johnson, M. D. (2011). The loci and mechanisms of leadership: Exploring a more comprehensive view of leadership theory. *Leadership Quarterly, 22*, 1165–1185.

Hmieleski, K. M., Cole, M. S., & Baron, R. A. (2012). Shared authentic leadership and new venture performance. *Journal of Management, 38*, 1476–1499.

Hogg, M. A. (2001). A social identity theory of leadership. *Personality and Social Psychology Review, 5*, 184–200.

House, R. J. (1977). A 1976 theory of charismatic leadership. In J. G. Hunt & L. L. Larson (Eds.), *Leadership: The cutting edge* (pp. 189–207). Carbondale: Southern Illinois University Press.

Ilies, R., Morgeson, F. P., & Nahrgang, J. D. (2005). Authentic leadership and eudaemonic well-being: Understanding leader-follower outcomes. *Leadership Quarterly, 16*, 373–394.

Ilies, R., Gerhardt, M. W., & Le, H. (2004). Individual differences in leadership emergence: Integrating meta-analytic findings and behavioral genetics estimates. *International Journal of Selection and Assessment, 12*, 207–219.

Jarvis, C. B., MacKenzie, S. B., & Podsakoff, P. M. (2003). A critical review of construct indicators and measurement model misspecification in marketing and consumer research. *Journal of Consumer Research, 30*, 199–218.

Jensen, S. M., & Luthans, F. (2006). Entrepreneurs as authentic leaders: Impact on employees' attitudes. *Leadership & Organization Development Journal, 27*(8), 646–666.

Jones, G. R., & George, J. M. (1998). The experience and evolution of trust: Implications for cooperation and teamwork. *Academy of Management Review, 23*, 531–546.

Johnson, R. E., Rosen, C. C., Chang, C.-H., Djurdjevic, E., & Taing, M. U. (2012). Recommendations for improving the construct clarity of higher-order multidimensional constructs. *Human Resource Management Review, 22*, 62–72.

Johnson, R. E., Rosen, C. C., & Djurdjevic, E. (2011). Assessing the impact of common method variance on higher order multidimensional constructs. *Journal of Applied Psychology*, 96, 744–761.

Johnson, S. K. (2008). I second that emotion: effects of emotional contagion and affect at work on leader and follower outcomes. *Leadership Quarterly, 19*, 1–19.

Judge, T. A., Erez, A., Bono, J. E., & Thoresen, C. J. (2003). The Core Self- Evaluations Scale: Development of a measure. *Personnel Psychology, 56*, 303–331.

Kark, R., Shamir, B., & Chen, G. (2003). The two faces of transformational leadership: Empowerment and dependency. *Journal of Applied Psychology, 88*, 246–255.

Kernis, M. H. (2003). Toward a conceptualization of optimal self-esteem. *Psychological Inquiry, 14*, 1–26.

Kernis, M. H., & Goldman, B. M. (2005). From thought and experience to behavior and interpersonal relationships: A multicomponent conceptualization of authenticity. In A. Tesser, J. V. Wood & D. Stapel (Eds.), *On building, defending and regulating the self: A psychological perspective* (pp. 31–52). New York, NY: Psychology Press.

Kozlowski, S. W. J., & Ilgen, D. R. (2006). Enhancing the effectiveness of work groups and teams (Monograph). *Psychological Science in the Public Interest, 7*, 77–124.

Ladkin, D., & Taylor, S. S. (2010). Enacting the "true self": Towards a theory of embodied authentic leadership. *Leadership Quarterly, 21*, 64–74.

Lapidot, Y., Kark, R., & Shamir, B. (2007). The impact of situational vulnerability on the development and erosion of followers' trust in their leader. *Leadership Quarterly, 18*, 16–34.

Larson, M., & Luthans, F. (2006). Potential added value of psychological capital in predicting work attitudes. *Journal of Leadership and Organizational Studies, 13*, 75–92.

Lawford, H., Pratt, M. W., Hunsberger, B., & Pancer, S. M. (2005). Adolescent generativity: A longitudinal study of two possible contexts for learning concern for future generations. *Journal of Research on Adolescence, 15*, 261–273.

Lester, P. B., Vogelgesang, G., Hannah, S. T., & Kimmey, T. (2009). Developing courage in followers: Theoretical and applied perspectives. In C. Pury & S. Lopez (Eds.), *The psychology of courage: Modern research on an ancient virtue* (pp. 210–245). Washington, DC: American Psychological Association.

Luthans, F., & Avolio, B. J. (2003). Authentic leadership development. In K. S. Cameron, J. E. Dutton, & R. E. Quinn (Eds.), *Positive organizational scholarship* (pp. 241–258). San Francisco, CA: Berrett-Koehler.

Luthans, F., Avolio, B. J., Avey, J. B., & Norman, S. M. (2007). Positive psychological capital: Measurement and relationship with performance and satisfaction. *Personnel Psychology*, 60, 541–572.

Luthans, F., Avolio, B.J., Walumbwa, F.O., & Li, W. (2005). The psychological capital of Chinese workers: Exploring the relationship with performance. *Management and Organization Review, 1*, 249–271.

Macik-Frey, M. Quick, J. C., & Cooper, C. L. (2009). Authentic leadership as a pathway to positive health. *Journal of Organizational Behavior, 30*, 453–458.

Mayer, R. C., & Gavin, M. B. (2005). Trust in management and performance: Who minds the shop while the employees watch the boss? *Academy of Management Journal, 48*, 874–888.

Mayer, D. M., Kuenzi, M., Greenbaum, R., Bardes, M., & Salvador, R. (2009). How low does ethical leadership flow? Test of a trickle-down model. *Organizational Behavior and Human Decision Processes, 108*, 1–13.

McCauley, C. D. (2001). Leader training and development. In J. S. Zaccaro & R. J. Klimoski (Eds.), *The nature of organizational leadership: Understanding the imperatives confronting today's leaders* (pp. 347–383). San Francisco, CA: Jossey-Bass.

Mhatre, K. (2009). *Rational persuasion and attitude change: The impact of perceived leader authenticity and perceived leader ability on follower outcomes.* Doctoral Dissertation, University of Nebraska, Lincoln.

Morgeson, F. P., & Hofmann, D. A. (1999). The structure and function of collective constructs: Implications for multilevel research and theory development. *Academy of Management Review, 24*, 249–265.

Moriano, J. A., Molero, F., & Mangin, J. P. L. (2011). Authentic leadership. Concept and validation of the ALQ in Spain. *Psicothema, 23*(2), 336–341.

Mumford, M., Stokes, G. S., & Owens, W. A. (1990). Patterns of life history: The ecology of human development. Mahwah, NJ: Lawrence Erlbaum & Associates.

Neubert, M. J., Carlson, D. S., Kacmar, K. M., Roberts, J. A., & Chonko, L. B. (2009). The virtuous influence of ethical leadership behavior: Evidence from the field. *Journal of Business Ethics, 90*, 157–170.

O'Leonard, K. (2010). *The corporate learning factbook 2009: Benchmarks, trends and analysis of the U.S. training market.* Oakland, CA: Bersin & Associates.

Orvis, K. A., & Langkamer-Ratwani, K. (2010). Leader self-development: A contemporary context for leader development evaluation. *Leadership Quarterly, 21*, 657–674.

Parker, G., & Gladstone, G. L. (1996). Parental characteristics as influences on adjustment in adulthood. In G. R. Pierce, B. R. Sarason, & I. G. Sarason (Eds.), *Handbook of social support and the family* (pp. 193–218). New York, NY: Plenum Press.

Pearce, C. L., & Sims, H. P. (2002). Vertical versus shared leadership as predictors of the effectiveness of change management teams: An examination of aversive, directive, transactional, transformational, and empowering leader behaviors. *Group Dynamics: Theory, Research, & Practice, 6*, 172–197.

Peterson, S. J., Walumbwa, F. O., Avolio, B. J., & Fredrickson, B. (2007). *Examining how authentic leadership and psychological capital predict human flourishing and performance with police officers.* Paper presented at the Annual Academy of Management Meetings. Philadelphia, PA.

Petter, S., Straub, D. W., & Rai, A. (2007). Specifying formative constructs in IS research. *MIS Quarterly, 31*(4), 623–656.

Pittinsky, T. L., & Tyson, C. J. (2005). Leader authenticity markers: Findings from a study of perceptions of African–American political leaders. In W. L. Gardner, B. J. Avolio, & F. O. Walumbwa (Eds.), *Authentic leadership theory and practice: Origins, effects and development* (pp. 253–280). London: Elsevier.

Plomin, R., & Daniels, D. (1987). Why are children in the same family so different from each other? *Behavioral and Brain Sciences, 10*, 1–16.

Pratt, M. W., Skoe, E. E., & Arnold, M. L. (2004). Care reasoning development and family socialization patterns in later adolescence: A longitudinal analysis. *International Journal of Behavioral Development, 28*, 139–147.

Rest, J. (1979). *Development in judging moral issues.* Minneapolis: University of Minnesota Press.

Rosenthal, S. A., Pittinsky, T. L., Purvin, D. M., & Montoya, R. M. (2007). *National Leadership Index 2007: A National Study of Confidence in Leadership.* Center for Public Leadership, John F. Kennedy School of Government, Harvard University, Cambridge, Massachusetts.

Sartre, J. P. (1966). *The age of reason.* New York, NY: A. A. Knopf.

Schlenker, B. R. (2003). Self-presentation. In M. R. Leary and J. P. Tangney (Eds.), Handbook of self and identity (pp. 492–518). New York: Guilford.

Schoorman, F. D., Mayer, R. C., & Davis, J. H. (2007). An integrative model of organizational trust: Past, present and future. *Academy of Management Review, 32*, 344–354.

Shamir, B., & Eilam, G. (2005). "What's your story?" A life-stories approach to authentic leadership development. *Leadership Quarterly, 16*, 395–417.

Shamir, B., House, R. J., & Arthur, M. B. (1993). The motivational effects of charismatic leadership: A self-concept based theory. *Organization Science, 4*, 577–593.

Sluss, D. M., & Ashforth, B. E. (2008). How relational and organizational identification converge: Processes and conditions. *Organizational Science, 19*, 807–823.

Spitzmuller, M., & Ilies, R. (2010). Do they [all] see my true self? Leader's relational authenticity and followers' assessments of transformational leadership. *European Journal of Work and Organizational Psychology, 19*, 304–332.

Spreitzer, G. M. (2006). Leading to grow and growing to lead: Leadership development lessons from positive organizational studies. *Organizational Dynamics, 35*, 305.

Stogdill, R. (1974). *Handbook of leadership* (1st ed.). New York, NY: Free Press.

Srivastava, A., Bartol, K. M., & Locke, E. A. (2006). Empowering leadership in management teams: Effects on knowledge sharing, efficacy, and performance. *Academy of Management Journal, 49*, 1239–1251.

Tichy, N. N., & Devanna, M. A. (1986). *The transformational leader.* New York, NY: Wiley.

Tomlinson, E. C., & Mayer, R. C. (2009). The role of causal attribution dimensions in trust repair. *Academy of Management Review, 34*, 85–104.

Toor, S.-u.-R., Ofori, G., & Arain, F. M. (2007). Authentic leadership style and its implications in project management. *Business Review, 2(1)*, 31–55.

Treviño, L. K., & Youngblood, S. A. (1990). Bad apples in bad barrels: A causal analysis of ethical decision making behavior. *Journal of Applied Psychology, 75*, 447–476.

Van Dyne, L., & LePine, J. A. (1998). Helping and voice extra-role behavior: Evidence of construct and predictive validity. *Academy of Management Journal, 41*, 108–119.

Verplanken, B., & Holland, R. W. (2002). Motivated decision making: Effects of activation and self-centrality of values on choices and behavior. *Journal of Personality and Social Psychology, 82*, 434–447.

Verschoor, C. C. (2003). Eight ethical traits of healthy organization. *Strategic Finance, 85*, 20–33.

Walumbwa, F. O., Avolio, B. J., Gardner, W. L., Wernsing, T. S., & Peterson, S. J. (2008). Authentic leadership: Development and validation of a theory-based measure. *Journal of Management, 34*, 89–126.

Walumbwa, F. O., Christensen, A. L., & Hailey, F. (2011a). Authentic leadership and the knowledge economy: Sustaining motivation and trust among knowledge workers. *Organizational Dynamics, 40*,110–118.

Walumbwa, F. O., Hartnell, A. L., Aryee, S., & Christensen, C. A. (2011b). *Fostering creativity in work groups: Authentic leadership, communication climate, and knowledge sharing.* Paper presented at the Academy of Management Annual Meetings. San Antonio, TX.

Walumbwa, F. O., Luthans, F., Avey, J., & Oke, A. (2011c). Authentically leading groups: The mediating role of positivity and trust. *Journal of Organizational Behavior, 32*, 43–24.

Walumbwa, F. O., Wang, P., Wang, H., Schaubroeck, J., & Avolio, B. J. (2010). Psychological processes linking authentic leadership and follower behavior. *Leadership Quarterly, 21*, 901–914.

Weber, M. (1947). *The theory of social and economic organizations.* Translated by T. Parsons. New York, NY: The Free Press.

Weick, K. E. (1979). *The social psychology of organizing* (2nd ed.). New York, NY: McGraw-Hill.

Weiss, H. M., & Cropanzano, R. (1996). Affective Events Theory: A theoretical discussion of the structure, causes, and consequences of affective experiences at work. In B. M. Staw and L. L. Cummings (Eds.), *Research in Organizational Behavior,* Vol. 18 (pp. 1–74). Greenwich, CT: JAI Press.

Wong, C. A., & Cummings, G. G. (2009). The influence of authentic leadership behaviors on trust and work outcomes of health care staff. *Journal of Leadership Studies, 3*, 6–23.

Wong, C. A., Laschnger, H. K. S., & Cummings, G. G. (2010). Authentic leadership and nurses' voice behavior and perceptions of care quality. *Journal of Nursing Management, 18*, 889–900.

Yammarino, F. J., Dionne, S. D., Schriesheim, C. A., & Dansereau, F. (2008). Authentic leadership and positive organizational behavior: A meso, multi-level perspective. *Leadership Quarterly, 19*, 693–707.

Yukl, G. (2006). *Leadership in Organizations* (6th ed.). New York, NY: Prentice Hall.

Yukl, G. (2010). *Leadership in Organizations* (7th ed.). New York, NY: Prentice Hall.

Zaccaro, S. J., Kemp, C., & Bader, P. (2004). Leader traits and attributes. In J. Antonakis, A. T. Cianciolo, & R. J. Sternberg (Eds.), *The nature of leadership* (pp. 101–124). Thousand Oaks, CA: Sage.

CHAPTER

17 Servant Leadership: Antecedents, Processes, and Outcomes

Robert C. Liden, Alexandra Panaccio, Jeremy D. Meuser, Jia Hu, *and* Sandy J. Wayne

Abstract

Servant leadership was first introduced in 1970, but was slow to attract the attention of academic researchers until recently. Today, research on servant leadership is being conducted at an accelerated pace. Psychometrically sound measures are available, and servant leadership has passed the test of showing incremental validity after controlling for the two most widely studied approaches to leadership, leader-member exchange, and transformational leadership. Now that servant leadership has established legitimacy in the academic field, theory development is needed to guide its further advancement. The purpose of the current chapter is to offer a comprehensive theoretical model that captures the development (antecedents) of servant leadership, its consequences (outcomes), and the mediating and moderating processes through which servant leadership behaviors result in key outcomes.

Key Words: Servant leadership, leader awareness, core self-evaluation, empowerment, trust, organizational citizenship behaviors, emotional intelligence, leader prototypes, community citizenship, identity

Our goal in this chapter is to provide an overview of servant leadership and recommend future directions. In doing so, we hope to stimulate interest in servant leadership so as to entice researchers to devote increased attention to this intriguing form of leadership. We attempt to accomplish this by developing theory on the antecedents and outcomes of servant leadership, as well as articulating the underlying processes through which this form of leadership operates. We illustrate our theory with a model depicted in Figure 17.1. In our theory, we identify individual characteristics of leaders and followers that are conducive to servant leadership, as well as the mediating mechanisms through which servant leader behaviors lead to attitudinal and behavioral outcomes. Finally, we suggest several elements in the context thought to moderate proposed relationships between servant leadership and outcomes. Prior to the introduction of our theoretical model, we present a brief overview of servant leadership research.

Although aspects of servant leadership appeared in writings of Confucianism and in the Bible, modern servant leadership was introduced in a now-classic article by Robert K. Greenleaf (1970). Greenleaf worked for American Telephone & Telegraph (AT&T) from 1926 to 1964, rising from a job as a laborer on a line construction crew to head of management research. Greenleaf also introduced many creative training programs during his tenure at AT&T. Following retirement, Greenleaf taught university classes, served as a consultant, and inspired the formation of the Center for Creative Leadership in North Carolina. But he is best known for forming the Center for Applied Ethics, which after several name changes continues to exist as the Greenleaf Center for Servant Leadership (Frick, 2004). Greenleaf asserted that being a truly effective leader requires a focus on

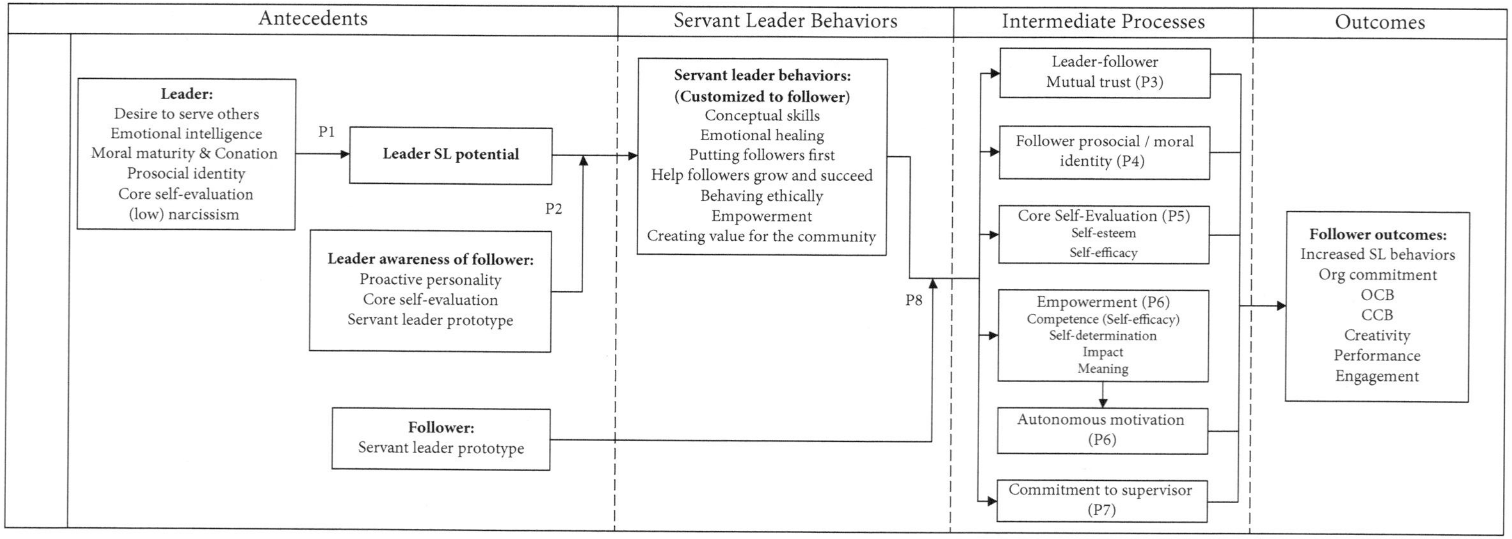

Figure 17.1. Model of Servant Leadership: Ancedents, Processes, and Outcomes.

Note: SL=Servant leadership; Org commitment= Organizational commitment; OCB= Organizational citizenship behavior; CCB= Community citizenship behavior.

serving others, particularly one's followers. Due in part to the positive response to Greenleaf's (1970) essay, Greenleaf formed a center devoted to the promotion of servant leadership, which later bore his name. Over the years, the Greenleaf Center has successfully introduced servant leadership to many practitioners. However, with the exception of an article by Jill Graham in the inaugural issue of *Leadership Quarterly* back in 1991, servant leadership attracted little interest in the academic community until the 2000s. In the last few years, there has been a noted increase in scientific research on servant leadership that has been published in top academic journals (Ehrhart, 2004; Hu & Liden, 2011; Hunter et al., 2013; Liden, Wayne, Liao, & Meuser, in press; Liden, Wayne, Zhao, & Henderson, 2008; Neubert, Kacmar, Carlson, Chonko, & Roberts, 2008; Peterson, Galvin, & Lange, 2012; Schaubroeck, Lam, & Peng, 2011; Van Dierendonck, 2011; Walumbwa, Hartnell, & Oke, 2010).

In order for rigorous empirical research on servant leadership to proceed, it was recognized that a servant leadership measure developed using sound psychometric practices was essential. Van Dierendonck (2011) argued that of the attempts to measure servant leadership, only scales by Liden and colleagues (2008) and by Van Dierendonck and Nuijten (2011) meet adequate psychometric standards. The Liden et al. scale (2008), used in research by Hu and Liden (2011), Schaubroeck and colleagues (2011), and by Peterson and colleagues (2012), captures seven dimensions of servant leadership: putting subordinates first, helping subordinates grow and succeed, empowering, emotional healing, creating value for the community, behaving ethically, and conceptual skills. Consistent with the work of Greenleaf, a servant leader serves others by prioritizing the needs of followers above the leader's needs. This includes assisting subordinates in recognizing their full potential, which is done partially through empowerment. Paralleling Greenleaf's emphasis on servant leaders being genuine only if they behave as a servant leader in all realms of life, another dimension of servant leadership identified by Liden and colleagues (2008) is helping to create value for the community in which the organization is embedded, both by directly contributing service to the community as well as encouraging followers to do the same. Finally, Liden and colleagues found support for the dimension of promoting ethical behavior by acting with honesty and integrity.

Although support was found for multiple dimensions of servant leadership through factor analyses and differential relations between dimensions and outcomes (Liden et al., 2008), the seven dimensions have been shown to map onto a higher order or global "servant leadership" factor (see Hu & Liden, 2011, for analyses). Indeed, as with many multidimensional constructs in organizational behavior, most researchers (Ehrhart, 2004; Hu & Liden, 2011; Neubert et al., 2008; Schaubroeck et al., 2011; Walumbwa et al., 2010) have employed global servant leadership, rather than investigating the dimensions separately. But even when a global factor is used exclusively in research, multidimensional scales more clearly reveal the full domain of the construct under study, as each dimension represents a different component of the content contained in the realm of the construct. Due to space constraints and for greater clarity, the relationships proposed in this chapter refer only to global servant leadership and not the separate dimensions. We do, however, encourage researchers to further explore the dimensions of servant leadership presented by Liden and his colleagues (2008).

While there is a dedicated ethical leadership model (for a review, see Brown and Treviño, 2006) defined as "the demonstration of normatively appropriate conduct through personal actions and interpersonal relationships, and the promotion of such conduct to followers through two-way communication, reinforcement, and decision-making" (Brown, Treviño, & Harrison, 2005, p. 120), servant leadership is a different, more holistic leadership approach. Essentially, ethical leaders make ethics a salient feature of the workplace by modeling and communicating fair ethical values, and providing for a reward and punishment schema in line with those values. In contrast to the ethical leadership model, which is a single dimensional construct with three main foci (ethical role clarification, which includes transparency; concern for morality and fairness; and power sharing, or voice; De Hoogh & Den Hartog, 2008), servant leadership includes ethical behavior as a component that represents only one of seven servant leadership dimensions. So, for the servant leader, ethical behavior is only one mode of service. [See Van Dierendonck, 2011, for a review of the differences between servant leadership and other leadership models.]

To date, many scholars have contributed to our understanding of the impact of the servant leader in the workplace, but research on servant leadership is still in its infancy, as evidenced by a servant leadership literature review by Van Dierendonck (2011) that uncovered a modest 14 refereed journal articles. To avoid redundancy, for our review we have selected the key articles among those 14, as well as select articles published subsequent to Van Dierendonck's (2011) review.

Ehrhart (2004) is one of the first published authors of an empirical article on servant leadership. Ehrhart developed his own scale from seven dimensions of servant leadership based upon his review of the literature and used this scale in a cross-sectional study involving a grocery store chain. While scale development was not the focus of this paper, it is important to note that a three-factor confirmatory factor analysis (CFA) with servant leadership, leader-member exchange (LMX; Dansereau, Graen, & Haga, 1975; Liden & Maslyn, 1998), and transformational leadership (Bass, 1985) showed adequate fit, which provides evidence that servant leadership is empirically distinct from these other two leadership styles. Support was found for a relationship between servant leadership and organizational citizenship behavior (OCB). The relationship was partially mediated by procedural justice climate. This suggests that servant leadership promotes a fair workplace environment, and this fair environment along with servant leadership, promotes discretionary helping behaviors that benefit the organization.

Liden and colleagues (2008), in the process of developing their servant leadership scale, showed a positive relationship between servant leadership and the outcome variables of in-role performance, organizational commitment, and community citizenship behaviors even after controlling for both LMX and transformational leadership in an organizational field sample. Like Ehrhart (2004), these scholars contributed evidence that servant leadership is distinct from LMX and transformational leadership (Bass, 1985).

Neubert and colleagues (2008) investigated the impact of initiating structure and servant leadership in the same model. These authors used the 14-item Ehrhart (2004) servant leadership measure and collected same source data, with three weeks separating collection of IV/mediator and DVs. Neubert and colleagues conducted a CFA that revealed separate factors for servant leadership and initiating structure. Their results suggest that promotion (vs. prevention) focus mediates the relationship between servant leadership and helping and creative behaviors, suggesting that servant leadership can shift followers' focus from prevention to promotion. Essentially, followers of servant leaders, relative to followers of supervisors high in initiating structure, are more likely to focus on nurturance rather than dwelling on security needs. Their analyses for servant leadership also controlled for initiating structure, adding to a growing body of evidence that servant leadership is not redundant with previously researched leadership models.

Walumbwa and colleagues (2010) extended Ehrhart's (2004) findings. The focus of their study was to show group and individual-level intermediary processes that explain how servant leadership increases OCB. These authors used Ehrhart's (2004) 14-item scale in a longitudinal study involving multisource data from seven multinational corporations operating in Kenya, Africa. Findings supported partial mediation between servant leadership and OCB for procedural justice climate and service climate at the group level, and self-efficacy and commitment to supervisor at the individual level. Procedural justice and service climate were proposed to moderate the impact of the individual-level variables on OCB, but support was only found for the impact of procedural justice climate and service climate on the relationship between commitment to the supervisor and OCB. LMX and transformational leadership were not controlled for in this study. Nevertheless, this study provides important support for the theoretical expectations of servant leadership. Specifically, servant leaders are expected to "grow" their followers into more capable members of the organization who eventually become servant leaders themselves. Finding servant leadership to be associated with increased self-efficacy, OCB, and climates of justice and service provide empirical support for this theoretical expectation.

Hu and Liden (2011), using Liden and colleagues' (2008) 28-item scale, investigated the impact of servant leadership on the team-level variables of team potency and team OCB in a sample of five banks in China. In this study, support was found for a moderated-mediation model, showing that servant leadership has direct positive effects on team effectiveness as well as effects that are partially mediated by team potency. Team potency also mediated the impact of goal clarity and process clarity on team effectiveness. Interestingly, both mediated relationships were strongly impacted by servant leadership, such that servant leadership increased the importance of goal and process clarity for team potency. In fact, in the absence of a servant leader, results showed that potency was higher in teams with *lower* goal clarity. Evidently, if the leader did not provide the support associated with servant leadership, it was better *not* to have a clear idea of the goal. Having a clear picture of the goal, but not getting the leader support needed to accomplish the goal, was evidently frustrating for team members. However, with a servant leader, the relationship between goal clarity and team potency was strong and positive. Therefore, this study provides evidence that servant leadership provides important benefits to teams, including enhanced team potency and team effectiveness.

Schaubroeck and colleagues (2011) conducted a cross-sectional study sampling United States and Hong Kong branches of the same bank using the Liden et al. (2008) 28-item scale. This study is similar to Neubert and colleagues (2008) in that the impact of two different leadership models was investigated in the same study. Here, servant leadership and transformational leadership were shown to relate to increased team performance, but through differing mechanisms. Servant leadership appears to operate through affect-based trust and increased team psychological safety, whereas transformational leadership seems to manifest itself via cognitive-based trust and increased team potency. But clearly the key finding of the study was that servant leadership explained an additional 10 percent of the variance in team performance when controlling for variance explained by transformational leadership.

Peterson and colleagues (2012) examined antecedents and outcomes of CEO servant leadership in a sample of 126 technology organizations in the United States, using a shortened 16-item version of the Liden et al. (2008) scale. Data were collected over four time periods. This study's results showed a negative relationship between CEO narcissism and servant leadership, and a positive relationship between CEO founder status (vs. non-founder) and servant leadership. Further, CEO organizational identification partially mediated these two relationships. More interesting, a positive relationship was found between CEO servant leadership and firm performance measured as return on assets, even after controlling for transformational leadership. This study provides evidence that top management servant leadership enhances organizational-level performance. This study also contributed to the growing body of evidence that supports the differentiation between servant leadership and transformational leadership.

Van Dierendonck (2011) provided a six-point comprehensive review of servant leadership research. First, he provided a brief overview and background of the construct. Second, he assessed the key components of servant leadership. Third, he addressed the empirical and theoretical differences between servant leadership and other leadership models, specifically transformational leadership, authentic leadership, ethical leadership, empowering leadership, spiritual leadership, self-sacrificing leadership, and Level 5 leadership. Level 5 leadership, identified by Collins (2001) as the best form of leadership in terms of organizational effectiveness, stresses the importance of leaders to be guided by humility. Fourth, Van Dierendonck reviewed current methods for measuring servant leadership. Fifth, he reviewed antecedents and consequences of servant leadership based upon the extant empirical evidence. Sixth, and finally, he offered suggestions for future research. In order to avoid redundancy, we refer the reader to Van Dierendoncks' review of the past literature, extant servant leader measures, and differences between servant leadership and other leadership models. Our goal then, is to address new issues and to provide a theoretical model accompanied by propositions that are designed to guide future research.

Challenges of Servant Leadership

Before proceeding with the presentation of our model, we must acknowledge that some scholars have identified potential challenges to the servant leadership approach. First, it is likely that not all followers or organizations will openly receive servant leadership as an appropriate or valid leadership style. Further, servant leaders must balance the concerns and preferences of multiple stakeholders (organization, supervisor, followers, community, and personal life and family), which can be both logistically and emotionally taxing. These issues elucidate potential challenges for implementing servant leadership.

Follower leadership preferences may be an important issue that impacts the way in which servant leaders' actions are perceived (Meuser, Liden, Wayne, & Henderson, 2011). Quite simply, not all people may desire the benevolent behaviors of a servant leader. A mismatch between follower comfort with or desire for servant leadership and actual leadership style may cause deleterious effects in the workplace (e.g., reduced follower performance or OCB) when servant leadership is applied, and in extreme cases may even result in followers not perceiving their immediate superiors to be leaders.

Research into the scarcity paradigm (e.g., Greenhaus & Beutell, 1985) provides a basis for understanding the complexities and challenges of the role and resource conflicts a servant leader may experience. All stakeholders place a claim on the servant leader's finite time, energy, and financial resources, and there may simply not be enough to go around. Emotional labor costs (see Ashforth & Humphrey, 1993; Beal, Trougakos, Weiss, & Green, 2006; Morris & Feldman, 1996) are likely to be high for servant leaders. The more traditional way to lead via directing and controlling is much less demanding than engaging in servant leadership, which requires listening, empathy, mentoring, guidance, and emotional support. This approach to leadership may be emotionally taxing due to the emotional regulation that is required when attempting to serve others. In addition to the cost of emotional regulation, making oneself so readily available to followers as a source of help and support, also raises the possibility of role conflicts in attempting to serve all relevant "others" first. The problem becomes exacerbated by demands placed on the servant leader by other role set members, such as the immediate superior. Servant leadership is defined as putting others' needs first. Doing so is essential for becoming a genuine servant leader. However, if servant leaders put the needs of all members first, they themselves may risk stress and eventual burnout. Further, the servant leader may be susceptible to manipulation by more savvy followers, who might exploit the servant leader for personal gain, thus placing an inordinate emotional and logistical burden on the leader (Whetstone, 2002).

Indeed, due to role and resource conflict, servant leaders may struggle to defend their leadership style in some organizations. Anderson (2009), for example, criticized the servant leader model as detrimental to organizational goals. To him, servant leadership represents an agency problem, where concern with followers reduces the concern and energy applied to organizational goals. When the immediate superior of a servant leader holds a view similar to Anderson or the organizational culture is unsupportive, the servant leader encounters additional obstacles that can increase the emotional labor associated with being a servant leader.

Role conflict may not only occur with respect to attempting to satisfy the competing demands of followers and others at work. Indeed, servant leaders, who by definition should be servants in *all* realms of life, may also experience conflict between demands of followers, family members, and members of the community. Conflicts may not only occur within the work context, such as between satisfying the needs of multiple followers and/or the immediate superior, but also across contexts, such as wanting to serve a follower at the same time that a family member needs help. In attempting to satisfy all relevant others, the servant leader likely engages in high levels of emotional labor. Tremendous stress can result from situations in which the servant leader is faced with multiple simultaneous demands to put others first. Sometimes the role conflict is such that the servant leader must decide who to help, and who cannot be helped at the moment. For example, a leader's daughter needs help on a school project, but followers need the leader to stay at work late to provide guidance on an important report. Using a role conflict framework, research integrating work, family, and community is needed to fully understand the potential competing demands of servant leadership.

Antecedents of Servant Leadership

While the servant leadership literature has devoted considerable attention to the study of what constitutes a servant leader and the outcomes of servant leadership, scarce attention has been paid to the development of servant leadership, or the antecedents of servant leadership behaviors. Drawing from servant leadership's theoretical underpinnings, we identified six leader characteristics that arm leaders with the potential to engage in servant leadership behaviors. However, because servant leadership does not occur in a vacuum, context likely influences the degree to which these leader characteristics result in manifestations of servant leadership. In line with recent calls to account for individual differences in the study of servant leadership (e.g., Walumbwa et al., 2010), we propose that follower characteristics alert leaders to the receptiveness of each follower to servant leadership, and the leader's awareness of follower desire for servant leadership moderates the relationships between leader characteristics and servant leader behaviors.

Leader Characteristics

Six leader characteristics are proposed as antecedents of servant leadership potential: the desire to serve others, emotional intelligence, moral maturity and conation, prosocial identity, core self-evaluation, and (low) narcissism.

Desire to serve others. Readiness and motivation to lead have been portrayed as key prerequisites for effective leadership (Hannah & Avolio, 2010). Servant leaders, however, are thought to be driven by an additional force, which is the desire to serve (Ng, Koh, & Goh, 2008). This desire is viewed as the prime motivation for engaging in servant leadership behaviors. In essence, servant leaders make a conscious choice to lead as a means of serving others (Greenleaf, 1977). Greenleaf's description of the servant leader as one who "wants to serve, to serve first" (1977, p. 13) and one who is genuinely concerned with serving followers, clearly places the notion of service at the core of servant leadership. This emphasis on serving others epitomizes the selfless or altruistic motives of servant leaders, and contributes to setting servant leadership apart from other leadership theories, which make serving the organization the main focus.

In line with Greenleaf's seminal work, the desire to serve has been embedded in one form or another in several conceptualizations of servant leadership (e.g., Barbuto & Wheeler, 2006; Graham, 1991; Russell & Stone, 2002; Sendjaya, Sarros, & Santora, 2008; Van Dierendonck, 2011). Following our view of servant leadership as a set of behaviors, rather than a combination of personal characteristics, we argue that desire to serve others is best seen as an antecedent of these behaviors, because desires and needs foster motivation, which in turn drives behavior (Kanfer, 1990). Specifically, we propose that servant leaders' desire to serve fosters a motivation to serve, which predisposes one toward servant leadership behaviors. In our view, the desire to serve others includes, but goes beyond, the propensity to be concerned for others, or other orientation (Meglino & Korsgaard, 2004), because it corresponds to an intrinsic motivation to engage in serving behaviors rather than a mere predisposition to be concerned for the well-being of others. Further, a desire to serve also motivates leaders to know their followers in order to better serve each individual's needs.

Emotional intelligence. Emotional intelligence, "the ability to understand and manage moods and emotions in the self and others" (George, 2000, p. 1027), represents an integration of emotion with cognition (Wolff, Pescosolido, & Druskat, 2002). Recent theoretical work proposes a cascading model of emotional intelligence, which views emotion perception (the ability to identify emotions in oneself and in others), emotion understanding (knowledge of the origins and consequences of emotions), and emotion regulation (influencing how one experiences and expresses emotions) as elements of a sequential process (Joseph & Newman, 2010). This model further proposes that conscientiousness, cognitive ability, and emotional stability, respectively, contribute to these dimensions of emotional intelligence, and that the latter partially mediate their impact on job performance. These antecedents of emotional intelligence also present links with servant leadership. For instance, a leader with a high level of cognitive ability is more likely to possess a high level of conceptual skills. Similarly, because conscientious individuals are methodical, dependable, organized and tend to perform at high levels (Dudley, Orvis, Lebiecki, & Cortina, 2006), conscientious leaders are likely to demonstrate a high level of conceptual skills and the propensity to provide valuable assistance in helping followers grow and succeed. Lastly, because emotionally stable leaders tend to experience less negative affect and are generally happier, more satisfied people (Steel, Schmidt, & Shultz, 2008), they may be in a better position to provide emotional healing. Empathy, "the ability to comprehend another's feelings and to re-experience them oneself," is also seen as a central characteristic of emotional intelligence (Salovey & Mayer, 1990, p. 194) and highly relevant to servant leadership.

We contend that individuals who possess a high degree of emotional intelligence are more likely to manifest servant leader behaviors. Indeed, serving others requires knowledge and awareness of how followers need to be helped. Specifically, most servant leader behaviors require empathy, an awareness and understanding of others' emotions, and/or the ability to manage emotions (emotion regulation). For example, in order to effectively provide emotional healing, the leader must correctly identify a need for such healing. Because of their awareness (perception and understanding) and empathy, individuals high on emotional intelligence may possess the sensitivity to recognize each individual's unique needs and consequently be more apt to soothe others than would a less emotionally intelligent leader (Goleman, 1995; Humphrey, 2002).

We also contend that in order to engage in servant leadership behaviors, leaders need an awareness and ability to manage their own emotions (i.e., perception and understanding of one's own emotions). For example, in times of crisis, putting followers' needs first and providing emotional healing may require the leader to acknowledge and overcome his or her own negative emotions. This may be easier for emotionally intelligent individuals, because they understand their emotions better, and are more likely to regulate them appropriately (Antonakis, Ashkanasy, & Dashborough, 2009). The servant leader behavior, "empowering followers" (Liden et al., 2008), includes acceptance of the risk associated with follower mistakes that may result from the increased influence and control granted to them by the servant leader. Whereas non-servant leaders may be reluctant to assume such risks, servant leaders accept the risks as a necessary part of the process through which followers reach their full potential. Dealing with the disappointment that is natural when followers make mistakes may be easier for emotionally intelligent leaders, who by definition are more adept at managing feelings of frustration (emotion regulation). Finally, empathy, a key element of emotional intelligence, is a driver for altruistic behavior (Batson, 1990) that should predispose individuals to adopt behaviors that are, by nature, selfless.

We contend that emotional intelligence is a necessary—but not sufficient—prerequisite for servant leader behaviors. This view is consistent with prior theoretical work on servant leadership, which views empathy and awareness as important attributes of servant leaders (e.g., Barbuto & Wheeler, 2006; Spears, 1998), and empirical work on emotional intelligence, which suggests that emotionally intelligent leaders tend to engage in altruistic behaviors (Carmeli, 2003), including behaviors associated with serving followers.

Moral maturity and moral conation. From its inception, servant leadership has explicitly included an ethical or moral dimension (e.g., Graham, 1991; Greenleaf, 1970; Liden et al., 2008; Sendjaya et al., 2008; Van Dierendonck & Nuijten, 2011), which acts to distinguish servant leadership from other leadership theories. For example, neither LMX, transformational, transactional, charismatic, behavioral, contingent nor situational leadership theories include a "moral safeguard" (Walumbwa et al., 2010).

The relationship between morality and the ethical behaviors of a servant leader can be understood in light of the theoretical contribution of Hannah, Avolio, and May (2011). Hannah and his colleagues (2011) offer a taxonomy for moral processes with two categories of individual differences that are relevant for moral thought and action: moral maturation and moral conation.

Moral maturity reflects a high capacity for moral judgment resulting from the adoption of personal moral codes and the ability to think in an independent way (Kohlberg, 1984; Rest et al., 1999). Moral maturation is comprised of three components: moral complexity (the ability to recognize, organize, and categorize moral phenomena), metacognitive ability (the ability to consider and refine those mental categorizations), and moral identity (the centrality of "moral" to the focal person's self-view). We propose that moral complexity and metacognitive ability are antecedents to the ethical behaviors contained within servant leadership, as one cannot behave in a consistently moral fashion if one has not developed the ability to recognize and categorize moral situations.

An identity is a self-definition that guides behavior (Erikson, 1964; Reynolds & Ceranic, 2007). Moral identity, "a specific kind of identity that revolves around the moral aspects of one's self" (Reynolds & Ceranic, 2007, p. 1611) is an important determinant of moral behavior. Moral identity goes beyond mere thoughts about moral phenomena, capturing the extent to which "being a moral person" is central to an individual's self-concept, thus compelling him or her to think, judge, *and* act in a moral manner (Aquino & Reed, 2002; Hannah et al., 2011). Recent empirical work by Mayer, Aquino, Greenbaum, and Kuenzi (2012) supports a connection between leader moral identity and moral behaviors that are consistent with that self-definition.

Leaders who possess moral maturity likely behave in a way that is consistent with their personal moral or ethical norms (i.e., their moral identity), as behaving otherwise would create cognitive dissonance. Consistent with this view, leaders' cognitive moral development has been found to be significantly and positively related to ethical decision making (Ashkanasy, Windsor, & Treviño, 2006), perceived leader integrity, and to servant leader behaviors (Washington, Sutton, & Feild, 2006). Leader moral maturity may also foster other types of servant leader behaviors, as individuals who have achieved high cognitive moral development are less likely to behave in a self-serving manner (Schminke, Ambrose, & Neubaum, 2005). In line with a recent review of the servant leadership literature (Van Dierendonck, 2011), we view leader moral maturity as an antecedent to servant leadership behaviors.

However, moral maturity, the understanding of right vs. wrong, alone is not sufficient to secure moral action. *Moral conation* (Hannah et al., 2011) is the capacity to believe one is morally responsible and act in a moral way, even in the presence of obstacles to moral action. Moral conation is comprised of three components: moral ownership (extent to which one feels responsible for moral action, either on behalf of oneself or a larger group), moral efficacy (belief that one can act in a moral way in a given situation), and moral courage (tenacity to engage in moral behaviors and overcome obstacles to moral action). We propose that the attainment of moral conation is also an antecedent to the ethical behaviors contained within servant leadership. Servant leaders, therefore, are expected to have a high degree of moral ownership, moral efficacy, and moral courage, and as such, feel responsible for moral action, believe they can act morally, and do so in the face of obstacles.

Prosocial identity. Identity theory and empirical research suggest that individuals hold multiple identities, which influence behavior as a function of their salience (Grant, Molinsky, Margolis, Kamin, & Schiano, 2009; Stryker & Burke, 2000). Similar to moral identity, a strong prosocial identity, "the dimension of the self-concept focused on helping and benefiting others" (Grant et al., 2009, p. 321), may predispose individuals to adopt servant leadership behaviors. This can be expected, because helping and being of service to others—followers and the broader community—are at the very core of servant leadership theory (Liden et al., 2008; Van Dierendonck, 2011). As servant leader behaviors are by nature prosocial, a strong prosocial identity should predispose individuals to manifest them.

Core self-evaluation. Core self-evaluation (CSE; Erez & Judge, 2001; Judge, Erez, & Bono, 1998; Judge, Erez, Bono, & Thoresen, 2003) is a combination of four lower-level personality traits. Specifically, CSE is comprised of self-esteem, self-efficacy, locus of control, and neuroticism and can be summarized in terms of one's fundamental view of one's self as a competent, worthy, and effective person. We contend that individuals with higher CSE are more likely to manifest servant leadership behaviors. Indeed, it has been suggested that those with positive self-concepts would be more likely to adopt altruistic behaviors, as they are less preoccupied with themselves (Rushton, 1980). More specifically, leaders with high self-esteem are less likely to seek approval and self-gratification through leadership roles, and their belief in their self-worth may shield them against the risks of failure associated with servant leadership behaviors, such as empowering and developing followers. Individuals with high self-efficacy, because they believe in their own abilities, are more likely to go beyond traditional leadership and engage in the more challenging servant leadership behaviors of empowering followers and helping them grow, or creating value for the community. Having an internal locus of control should also predispose leaders to engaging in servant leadership behaviors as these behaviors require a belief in one's ability to actively influence one's environment, including followers and the broader community. Lastly, as low neuroticism leads one to focus on the positive side of things, leaders low on neuroticism are more likely to see, and thus want to develop, followers' strengths. Conversely, leaders high on neuroticism are less likely to "involve themselves in their subordinates' efforts" (Bass, 1985, p. 173).

Narcissism. Narcissism can be broadly defined as a "grandiose sense of self-importance" (Judge, LePine, & Rich, 2006, p. 762). Narcissists require excessive admiration, have a sense of entitlement, are interpersonally exploitive and lack empathy. Insensitive to others' needs, narcissists tend to focus on their goals at the expense of others' goals (Judge et al., 2006; Morf & Rhodewalt, 2001). Clearly, this self-serving tendency contrasts with servant leadership's prioritization of others' needs and goals. Specifically, an individual with such a pervasive self-focus is unlikely to put subordinates first, help them grow and succeed, and empower them, as these behaviors are based on a prioritization of subordinates' (rather than one's own) needs. We thus contend that individuals with higher narcissism are less likely to engage in servant leadership behaviors. In line with our view, Peterson and colleagues (2012) recently found a negative relationship between narcissism and servant leadership behaviors among CEOs.

Proposition 1: Leader desire to serve others, emotional intelligence, moral maturity and moral conation, prosocial identity, and core self-evaluation are positively, and narcissism negatively, related to servant leadership potential.

Follower Characteristics

Although leadership does not exist without followers, most attention in leadership theory and research is on leaders. Perhaps this is due to the fact that the trait theories dominated thinking on leadership since early Greek philosophers. Indeed, leaders alter their behaviors based on the characteristics and behaviors of followers (Herold, 1977; Lowin & Craig, 1968). Servant leaders act on their knowledge of their followers' needs, desires, and potential, by adjusting their leader behaviors accordingly. For example, one follower may require more individual guidance and mentoring than a proactive follower who mainly seeks empowerment.

Although relationships are important to many leadership approaches (Ferris et al., 2009), they are central to servant leadership. The servant leader forms unique relationships with each follower, and these relationships enable the servant leader to focus followers' motivation and behavior, modifying the application of the servant leader dimensions to each particular case. The servant leader can thereby draw out the best from each follower by providing tailored attention to each follower's needs. We consider three follower characteristics that may influence leader engagement in servant leadership: proactive personality, CSE, and servant leader prototype. We contend that servant leaders' perceptions of follower characteristics drive the specific way in which servant leader behaviors are employed for each follower.

Proactive personality. Proactive people "select, create, and influence work situations that increase the likelihood of career success" (Seibert, Kraimer, & Crant, 2001, p. 847), and these individuals engage in proactive behaviors, or personal initiative directed toward improving a current situation. A meta-analysis on proactive personality (Fuller & Marler, 2009) found positive population correlation coefficients for the proactive behaviors of voice ($\rho = .26$), taking change ($\rho = .28$), networking ($\rho = .31$), and career initiative ($\rho = .35$). Servant leaders, given their focus on service versus authority and power, are particularly well situated to allow those followers with proactive personalities to shine. Consistent with Greenleaf's arguments (1970), rather than attempting to stifle alternative points of view, servant leaders welcome followers to express different points of view. In essence, the servant leader is comfortable with those who show initiative and enact voice, and this is manifested by empowering and helping subordinates grow and succeed. Conversely, servant leaders recognize that followers low on proactive personality need a more active "hands on" leader, and the servant leader, given his or her relational orientation with followers, discerns when to apply assistance in order to maximize follower potential (Liden et al., 2008).

Core self-evaluation. Social cognitive theory (SCT; Bandura, 1991) suggests that people higher on CSE will be more willing and motivated to engage in productive workplace behaviors to the extent that they perceive their actions will result in positive outcomes (either tangible or intangible, e.g., higher self-evaluation after accomplishing a desired goal). The self-regulation and motivation that results in performance will depend on the cognitive regulation that occurs within a person. Self-esteem and self-efficacy are fundamental components in the social cognitive theory of motivation (SCT; Bandura, 1991; Wood & Bandura, 1989). SCT views a person as an influencer of the environment as well as influenced by the environment (Bandura, 1999). Those with higher self-esteem and self-efficacy view themselves as capable of exercising influence and control over their environment. Internal locus of control, therefore, joins with self-esteem and self-efficacy as important predictors of one's belief that he or she can affect the environment. Under the SCT view, the possession of relevant knowledge, skills, and abilities is necessary but not sufficient for performance. Individuals must believe that they can effectively influence their environment in order to be motivated to do so. As such, the type of servant leadership applied to a follower depends on the follower's CSE. We propose that followers high in CSE react more favorably to empowerment opportunities and more readily benefit from the servant leader's attempts to help a subordinate grow and succeed. Conversely, followers low in CSE benefit from more emotional healing in order to address the negative psychological well-being that can accompany low self-esteem and self-efficacy. Thus, we argue that follower CSE positively influences the leader's engagement in servant leader behaviors.

Servant leader prototype. Category theory (Rosch, 1978) describes a process by which people develop and use mental shortcuts, grouping similar things together, at least for some purposes. Lord and colleagues have leveraged Rosch's work, applying it to the domain of leadership. Leadership category theory (Lord, Foti, & Devader, 1984) suggests that all followers have their own mental representation of "leader," which is built and refined over time (Lord, Brown, Harvey, & Hall, 2001). Leadership prototypes are an individual difference (Gerstner & Day, 1994), and as such, a priori agreement on leadership preferences should not be assumed, even for servant leadership.

A servant leader is a benevolent, supportive, and caring leader. One may expect that all followers would desire a servant leader, and that more servant leadership yields more positive outcomes. However, theory and research support a contrary perspective (Meuser et al., 2011). There is variability in the extent to which followers form implicit perceptions or prototypes of an ideal leader that is consistent with servant leadership theory. Specifically, there is variance in the degree to which followers desire a leader who engages in servant leadership behaviors. Because servant leaders are empathic and sensitive to the needs of followers, we contend that in forming relationships with followers, servant leaders become aware of follower leadership preferences (Graham, 1991).

The literature is silent with respect to leader awareness of follower preferences. Servant leadership theory emphasizes that in order to be in a position to help followers, leaders must be attentive to the unique qualities and aspirations of each follower. In fact, a hallmark of servant leadership is that servant leaders take the time to learn about the backgrounds, interests, and preferences of each follower, which is crucial if the leader is to place the needs of followers first in serving followers (Greenleaf, 1970). Extending beyond the individualized consideration of transformational leadership theory, servant leaders empathize with followers and not only attempt to provide task assignments and rewards based on individual needs as described by transformational leadership theory, but also providing emotional support and guidance. Thus, we contend that relative to non-servant leaders, servant leaders are especially attuned to the unique aspirations and preferences of each follower and individually customize the application of servant leader behaviors based upon these perceptions. We further argue that the more accurately leaders perceive followers' servant leadership prototypes, the stronger the positive relationships between servant leader potential and servant leader behaviors.

Proposition 2: Servant leader awareness of follower characteristics (proactive personality, core self-evaluation, and servant leader prototype) moderates the relationship between servant leader potential and servant leader behaviors.

Intermediate Processes and Outcomes

We propose that servant leader behaviors influence follower outcomes via the following individual-level processes: leader-follower mutual trust, follower prosocial/moral identity, follower CSE (specifically self-esteem and self-efficacy), empowerment, autonomous motivation, and commitment to the supervisor. We argue that these processes in turn lead to favorable follower-level outcomes, such as creativity/innovation, servant leadership behaviors, organizational commitment, organizational citizenship behaviors (OCBs), community citizenship behaviors, in-role performance, and engagement. These processes and outcomes are discussed in the following subsections.

Leader-follower mutual trust. Although trust has been discussed with respect to LMX and transformational leadership, it is critical for servant leadership. The notion of trust has been present in the servant leadership literature since its inception with Robert Greenleaf's seminal essay (1970), either as an attribute of servant leaders, or as a state elicited by them (e.g., Farling, Stone, & Winston, 1999; Russell & Stone, 2002). Servant leadership and trust are positively related (Joseph & Winston, 2005), which is salient given that trust in the leader has been found to influence follower outcomes, such as job performance, job satisfaction, and organizational commitment (Dirks & Ferrin, 2002). Theory and empirical evidence point to trust as a key mediating mechanism through which servant leader behaviors influence follower outcomes.

Trust is "a psychological state comprising the intention to accept vulnerability based upon positive expectations of the intentions or behavior of another" (Rousseau, Sitkin, Burt, & Camerer, 1998, p. 395). Conceptual work suggests that perceived ability, benevolence, and integrity are important predictors of trust (Hosmer, 1995; Mayer, Davis, & Schoorman, 1995). Ability refers to the skills that enable an individual to have influence within a specific domain (Mayer et al., 1995). This overlaps with servant leaders' conceptual skills, which involves possessing the knowledge of the organization and tasks to support and assist others (Liden et al., 2008). The second antecedent of trust, benevolence, refers to the extent an individual believes the other party is concerned for his or her welfare (Mayer et al., 1995). Servant leaders' helping subordinates grow and succeed, putting subordinates first, and emotional healing behaviors are likely seen as providing evidence of benevolence. Lastly, integrity is the extent to which individuals believe that the other party adheres to principles that they find acceptable (Mayer et al., 1995). As servant leaders behave ethically and interact openly, fairly, and honestly with others (Liden et al., 2008), they are likely perceived to have integrity. The conceptual proximity between predictors of trust and servant leadership behaviors suggests that the latter contribute to the development of leader-follower trust.

Moreover, empirical evidence suggests that concern for employees, a defining characteristic of servant leadership, and open communication, which servant leaders are thought to favor (Humphreys, 2005; Liden et al., 2008) are related to trust in the leader (Korsgaard, Brodt, & Whitener, 2002). In addition to inspiring trust, servant leaders likely convey to followers a sense of their own trustworthiness by showing concern, empathy, dependability, and full acceptance of them (Greenleaf, 1977) and by sharing information freely (Humphreys, 2005). Indeed, theoretical (Brower, Schoorman, &

Tan, 2000; Sparrowe & Liden, 1997) and empirical research clearly suggests that via social exchange mechanisms, when one party of a dyad trusts the other individual, the dyadic partner tends to feel the same sense of trust (Sparrowe & Liden, 2005). Given that servant leaders tend to form high LMX relationships with followers (Liden et al., 2008), it follows that the trust that characterizes servant leader-follower relationships is mutual.

We contend that mutual trust, in turn, leads to favorable outcomes, such as enhanced creativity/innovation. Innovation-related behaviors involve proactive idea implementation and proactive problem solving (Parker, Williams, & Turner, 2006). Proactive idea implementation involves promulgating new and creative ideas, as well as self-implementation and the support of others who also may implement the new and creative ideas within the workplace (Axtell et al., 2000). Innovative behaviors encourage new ideas and processes, and involve stepping "outside the box" in order to improve group or organizational processes and procedures. Because of the inherent risk associated with innovative behaviors due to the fact that these behaviors, by definition, challenge the status quo (Neubert et al., 2008), employees are more likely to manifest such behaviors only if they feel safe (Hülsheger, Anderson, & Salgado, 2009). Research suggests that employees are more likely to engage in innovative behaviors in a climate of supervisory benevolence, security, and trust (Mumford & Gustafson, 1988; Oldham & Cummings, 1996), such as that likely created by servant leaders. Indeed, the leader is thought to be particularly impactful in the emergence of innovative behaviors (Amabile, Schatzel, Moneta, & Karmer, 2004; Scott & Bruce, 1994). Because of the mutual trust that we argue characterizes the servant leader-follower relationship, servant leadership should thus contribute to enhanced employee creativity and innovation.

Proposition 3. Leader-follower mutual trust mediates relationships between servant leader behaviors and follower outcomes.

Follower prosocial/moral identity. Scholars have emphasized the importance of modeling as an important element of servant leadership (Russell & Stone, 2002). For instance, Graham (1991) viewed the emulation of leaders' service orientation as the distinctive follower response to this leadership. Servant leaders may thus influence follower outcomes through role modeling, a phenomenon that can be understood using social learning theory (Bandura, 1986). According to this theory, individuals learn by observing the behavior of role models chosen based on their attractiveness and credibility. While leaders naturally tend to be seen as role models (Neubert et al., 2008), those who enact servant leadership behaviors are particularly likely to become role models, because these behaviors enhance their attractiveness and credibility in the eyes of followers. Specifically, their concern for others and strong ethics may enhance attractiveness, and the trust that they inspire in others as well as their expertise (conceptual skills) likely translate into greater credibility (Brown & Treviño, 2006; Farling et al., 1999; Walumbwa et al., 2010).

In terms of outcomes, an important tenet of servant leadership theory is that servant-led followers will themselves tend to become servant leaders (Greenleaf, 1970; Liden et al., 2008), which implies that they engage in prosocial behaviors, as servant leader behaviors are, by nature, prosocial. We argue that this may occur through the development of followers' prosocial/moral identity. The service mentality and orientation of the servant leader imply that the servant leader is interested in the holistic growth of his or her followers. As followers grow and their prosocial/moral identity becomes more salient, they become more capable of behaving as servant leaders. Social identity theory (Tajfel, 1972; Tajfel & Turner, 1979) and social categorization theory (Turner, 1985; Turner et al., 1987) explain why followers act on this capability. The leader leads the in-group to which the follower desires to belong. This desire may be motivated by a predilection to increase self-esteem (Turner, 1982; J. C. Turner, Brown, & Tajfel, 1979) or to decrease uncertainty (Hogg, 2000; Hogg & Abrams, 1993; Hogg & Mullin, 1999). Through a process of self-categorization and depersonalization, followers come to see themselves as prototypical group members, that is, those who behave according to the social norms of the group: in our case, norms established by the servant leader. As such, the prototypical in-group members behave as the servant leader does. The follower can be sure that servant leader behaviors are the "right" behaviors to model within the group, which provides a strong incentive for adopting such behaviors.

Organizational and community citizenship behaviors are also likely associated with servant leadership behaviors through follower prosocial/moral identity. Citizenship behaviors are prosocial activities that may be directed toward a variety of recipients. OCBs are behaviors that contribute to organizational effectiveness, but are not explicitly required of employees nor formally rewarded (Organ, 1997). These behaviors can be directed toward the organization (OCB-O) or an individual within the organization (OCB-I; Williams & Anderson, 1991). The same prosocial concern may be extended outside of the organization via community citizenship behaviors, which are prosocial actions directed at benefiting recipients outside of the organization (Liden et al., 2008). A unique feature of servant leadership as compared to other leadership approaches is that concern is *not* restricted to purely organizational goals, but follower and community goals as well (Graham, 1991). Concern for stakeholders beyond the organization manifests itself for the servant leader in the creating value for the community dimension. As such, the servant leader is concerned with prosocial actions toward a multitude of stakeholders. Previous research has supported a connection between servant leadership and follower OCBs (e.g., Ehrhart, 2004; Hu & Liden, 2011; Walumbwa et al., 2010) as well as community citizenship behaviors (Liden et al., 2008). We contend that this relationship occurs due to servant leaders' activation of a prosocial identity within followers. In sum, we propose that servant leaders elicit followers' prosocial/moral identity through role modeling and repeated exposure to servant leader behaviors, and the increased salience of this identity results in followers engaging in prosocial behaviors, such as servant leadership behaviors, and organizational and community citizenship behaviors in order to maintain consistency with their own identity.

Proposition 4. Follower prosocial/moral identity mediates relationships between servant leader behaviors and follower outcomes (in particular, follower servant leader behaviors, organizational citizenship behaviors, and community citizenship behaviors).

Core self-evaluation. CSE is positioned in our model as an initial follower characteristic, but also as a mediator of relationships between servant leader behaviors and individual outcomes. Of the four components of CSE, we contend that servant leadership behaviors are most likely to positively influence self-esteem and self-efficacy. The remaining two components of CSE, locus of control and neuroticism, are relatively more stable personality traits and thus not likely to be influenced to the same degree as self-esteem and self-efficacy.

Self-esteem is a self-evaluation reflecting one's perceived value as an individual (Pierce & Gardner, 2004). It has been shown to exert a positive influence on employee outcomes, such as job satisfaction, performance, and well-being (e.g., Judge & Bono, 2001). While theoretical and empirical work suggests that leaders have the ability to enhance their followers' self-esteem (e.g., Kark, Shamir, & Chen, 2003; Shamir, House, & Arthur, 1993), we propose that servant leaders are particularly likely to do so for two reasons. First, servant leader behaviors, such as putting subordinates first, providing emotional healing, and helping them grow and succeed convey to followers the message that they are worthy and valuable individuals. This likely contributes to self-esteem, as messages sent by "significant others in one's social environment," such as mentors and role models, are important determinants of self-esteem (Pierce & Gardner, 2004, p. 593). Leaders generally represent a highly salient significant other in followers' work environments, and servant leaders are likely to become mentors (as mentoring is one way to help subordinates succeed) and, as argued above, role models. In addition to messages sent by significant others, another important determinant of self-esteem is successful experiences for which individuals take credit (Pierce & Gardner, 2004). As a result of servant leaders' empowering behaviors, followers may have such successful experiences when their own decisions lead to positive outcomes (Conger & Kanungo, 1988). Servant leaders may thus contribute to enhancing their followers' self-esteem via empowering behaviors.

With regard to outcomes, follower self-esteem may be another mechanism, in addition to follower prosocial/moral identity, through which servant leaders motivate followers to engage in servant leadership behaviors themselves. Indeed, research suggests that those who identify with a group and adhere to group norms often operate from a prevention focus (Higgins, 1997, 1998), where they are restricted by the norms of the group. This is not conducive to the development of servant leader characteristics, especially within those who do not yet exhibit these characteristics, because in such a state, one is motivated to avoid loss and minimize cost and thus less likely to manifest new behaviors. However, the cultivation of a supportive environment and the bolstering of follower self-esteem helps shift employees from a prevention focus to a promotion focus (Higgins, 1997, 1998), and employees with a promotion focus are inclined to try new behaviors in order to maximize gains and benefits over the long term (Wang & Lee, 2006). Through the direction of a servant leader, we contend that the majority of new behaviors benefit others and are not focused on self-promotion. As servant leaders create positive work climates and engage in behavior that increase follower self-esteem (Liden et al., 2008), we propose servant leaders have the ability to develop followers into servant leaders themselves through increasing their self-esteem.

Although other forms of leadership, such as transformational leadership, have been shown to be positively related to follower self-efficacy (Den Hartog & Belschak, 2012), we contend that servant leaders are especially well-positioned to enhance follower self-efficacy (Walumbwa et al., 2010). Self-efficacy reflects one's belief in his/her capacity to skillfully perform an activity (Bandura, 1986). Servant leaders provide opportunities for followers to have successful experiences through increased responsibility associated with empowering behaviors, and feedback to further enhance self-efficacy (Gist & Mitchell, 1992). Furthermore, in helping followers grow and succeed, servant leaders may assist them in improving and developing new skills, and using their knowledge of the work and the organization (conceptual skills). This helps followers to successfully solve problems at work, which likely results in more successful experiences (Walumbwa et al., 2010). Servant leaders' emotional healing behaviors may also contribute to increasing self-efficacy via positive affective states, as their followers may experience less psychological strain at work. Finally, servant leaders may enhance follower self-efficacy by putting subordinates first and empowering followers, giving them increased confidence in their ability to perform well.

Proposition 5: Follower core self-evaluation (specifically self-esteem and self-efficacy) mediates relationships between servant leader behaviors and follower outcomes (in particular, follower servant leader behaviors).

Empowerment. Empowerment has long held a prominent place in the servant leadership literature, with many conceptualizations including empowerment (or empowering) as a dimension of servant leadership (Russell & Stone, 2002). Empowerment is conceptualized as a psychological state resulting from an enabling process that comprises four dimensions: self-determination, impact, meaning, and competence (Conger & Kanungo, 1988; Spreitzer, 1995; Thomas & Velthouse, 1990). We contend that empowerment is a mediating process through which servant leader behaviors impact follower outcomes. As can be seen from our model in Figure 17.1, we propose that empowerment impacts these outcomes in part via autonomous motivation. In the following paragraphs, we present our rationale for expecting followers of servant leaders to experience empowerment; relationships involving autonomous motivation are discussed in the next subsection.

Self-determination, the first dimension of empowerment, represents the perception of having choice in initiating and regulating actions; it corresponds to the notion of autonomy (Spreitzer, 1995). The empowering dimension in Liden and colleagues' (2008) servant leadership conceptualization is closely related to this facet of empowerment, as it focuses on giving followers latitude in decision making. Empowering behaviors are also likely to give followers a sense of impact, empowerment's second dimension, which reflects the degree to which employees feel they can influence outcomes at work (Spreitzer, 1995). Indeed, giving followers decision-making power increases their perception of making a difference at work. Meaning, the third dimension, refers to the perceived value of work goals, or the degree to which employees care about their tasks (Spreitzer, 1995; Thomas & Velthouse, 1990). Because servant leaders are committed to creating value for the community and society as a whole, follower work goals should be aligned with this mission, making it likely that followers perceive work goals as being meaningful.

Competence, empowerment's fourth dimension, is synonymous with the concept of self-efficacy (Bandura, 1986; Thomas & Velthouse, 1990), which has also been identified as a key dimension of CSE (Judge & Bono, 2001). Followers of servant leaders may develop a heightened sense of competence due to the perception of having their leader's trust and of being worthy of his or her attention and support, which also likely results in positive affective states (Chen & Bliese, 2002; Conger & Kanungo, 1988). Empowerment, as comprised of the four dimensions described above, is proposed to lead to autonomous motivation as captured in self-determination theory (Deci & Ryan, 1985).

Autonomous motivation. Self-determination theory (Deci & Ryan, 1985, 2000) distinguishes autonomous motivation, an internalized form of behavioral regulation based on volition and choice, from controlled motivation, which results from external pressures. We propose autonomous motivation as another mechanism through which servant leadership leads to positive follower outcomes. Autonomous motivation is thought to stem from the satisfaction of three basic, universal needs: autonomy, competence, and relatedness (Deci & Ryan, 2000). Empowerment, through its self-determination (autonomy) and competence dimensions, fulfills needs for autonomy and competence. As servant leaders are expected to empower followers, it follows that servant leaders should foster autonomous motivation through feelings of empowerment. In addition, by providing emotional healing and putting subordinates first, servant leaders may contribute to fulfilling followers' need for relatedness, which is a need to feel connected to others, loved and cared for (Deci & Ryan, 2000). The idea that servant leaders cultivate followers' autonomous motivation by fulfilling their basic needs is consistent with servant leadership's emphasis on serving others. Indeed, a core characteristic of servant leaders is that they place their followers' needs above their own and strive to fulfill them (Graham, 1991; Liden et al., 2008), as evidenced by positive relationships found between servant leadership and the three basic needs (Mayer, Bardes, & Piccolo, 2008).

Self-determination theory purports autonomous motivation to be most beneficial in terms of employee outcomes, and empirical evidence supports this contention, as autonomous motivation has been linked to in-role performance, prosocial behaviors, job satisfaction, organizational commitment, and employee well-being, among other outcomes (Gagné & Deci, 2005). We propose that autonomous motivation mediates relationships between servant leader behaviors and in-role performance and engagement. Indeed, research has shown servant leadership to have a positive relationship with individual job performance (Liden et al., 2008). This relationship likely occurs in part because the servant leader enhances followers' sense of competence/self-efficacy. In turn, this heightened sense of competence likely promotes autonomous motivation (Deci & Ryan, 1985), which leads to increased in-role performances (Gagné & Deci, 2005).

Engagement is defined as the complete investment of one's entire self in a role (Rich, LePine, & Crawford, 2010). This concept has close conceptual ties with autonomous motivation, as engagement is defined as a motivational concept (Christian, Garza, & Slaughter, 2011), and the underlying mechanisms leading to the development of autonomous motivation have been proposed as drivers of engagement (Meyer & Gagné, 2008). Furthermore, empirical evidence suggests that autonomous motivation leads to employee engagement (e.g., Van Beek, Hu, Schaufeli, Taris, & Schreurs, 2012). We thus propose that servant leadership behaviors contribute to employee engagement via empowerment and autonomous motivation.

Proposition 6: Via autonomous motivation, psychological empowerment mediates relationships between servant leader behaviors and follower outcomes.

Commitment to the supervisor. Commitment to the supervisor is proposed as the last mediating variable between servant leader behaviors and follower outcomes. Theory and empirical evidence suggest commitment to the supervisor can take various forms (e.g., Clugston, Howell, & Dorfman, 2000; Meyer & Herscovitch, 2001). Affective commitment to the supervisor, an employee's emotional attachment to his or her leader (Meyer & Herscovitch, 2001), is thought to develop following social exchange and reciprocity mechanisms (Blau, 1964; Gouldner, 1960) as a result of positive work experiences perceived to be offered by the supervisor (Meyer, Irving, & Allen, 1998). Specifically, support and fair treatment received from the supervisor have been shown to influence this commitment mindset (Liao & Rupp, 2005; Stinglhamber & Vandenberghe, 2003). Similar processes are thought to lead to the development of normative commitment to the supervisor, which is based on a sense of loyalty and duty toward the leader (Clugston et al., 2000; Meyer & Herscovitch, 2001). As servant leaders are likely to provide support (via emotional healing and helping subordinates grow and succeed), fairness (through ethical behaviors), and, generally, to offer followers a positive work experience in the broad sense of the word (by putting subordinates' needs first, for example), followers are likely to become affectively and normatively committed to them in return.

With regard to outcomes, research suggests commitment to the supervisor enhances organizational commitment, the psychological force that binds employees to their employing organization (e.g., Hunt & Morgan, 1994; Panaccio & Vandenberghe, 2011). This may be due to the fact that the supervisor is seen as a key representative of the organization (Levinson, 1965), and when one experiences favorable treatment from the supervisor, one develops a positive view of the organization and experiences a need to reciprocate this favorable treatment. One form of reciprocation is to increase one's organizational commitment (Tsui, Pearce, Porter, & Tripoli, 1997). Commitment to the supervisor has also been shown to contribute to in-role performance and OCBs (e.g., Becker, Billings, Eveleth, & Gilbert, 1996; Becker & Kernan, 2003). This is likely due to the fact that these behaviors also represent ways to reciprocate for the favorable treatment received from the organization via its representative, the supervisor. We thus propose that commitment to the supervisor mediates relationships between servant leader behaviors and follower outcomes, such as organizational commitment, in-role performance, and OCBs. In line with our view, commitment to the supervisor has been shown to partially mediate the relationship between servant leadership and OCBs (Walumbwa et al., 2010).

Proposition 7: Commitment to the supervisor mediates relationships between servant leader behaviors and follower outcomes (in particular, organizational commitment, in-role performance, and OCBs).

Impact of Servant Leadership Prototype

We contend that follower servant leadership prototypes, previously presented as a moderator of associations between servant leadership potential and actual servant leader behaviors, also moderate relationships between servant leader behaviors and the intermediate processes. Our proposition is based on the linkage between followers' leadership prototypes and their self-identities. Social identity theory (Tajfel, 1972) suggests that one's surroundings impact one's self-image through a process of self-identification. Social identity has been defined as "the individual's knowledge that he belongs to certain social groups together with some emotional and value significance to him of this group membership" (Tajfel, 1972, p. 292). Essentially, one defines in- and out-groups based upon salient group characteristics, sees oneself as a member of the in-group, defines oneself (at least in part) by that group's characteristics, and becomes concerned with group goals, making them his or her own (Hogg, 2001; Sedikides & Brewer, 2001; Turner et al., 1987).

Congruence with follower mental representation of the ideal leader (i.e., the follower's leadership prototype) yields higher follower ratings of leader effectiveness (e.g., Hogg & Terry, 2000; Nye & Forsyth, 1991), and charisma (Platow, Van Knippenberg, Haslam, Van Knippenberg, & Spears, 2006), and impacts follower perceptions of leader legitimacy, power, and discretion (Maurer & Lord, 1991). Such a leader is seen as one to follow, a leader of the social "in-group" to which it is advantageous and attractive to belong. Belonging increases follower self-esteem (Tajfel & Turner, 1986; Turner, 1982; Wagner, Lampen, & Syllwasschy, 1986) and reduces uncertainty (Hogg, 2000). That is, congruency between actual and expected leadership behaviors activates (makes salient) the subordinate's identity as a follower of the leader. We submit that these general effects of leadership prototypes on follower identity hold for servant leader prototypes. It follows that followers will see themselves as part of the in-group to the extent that their servant leadership prototype is congruent with the behaviors of the servant leader. Forehand, Deshpandé, and Reed (2002) found empirical support for their hypothesis that exposure to identity primes is positively related to identity salience, and in this case, servant leader prototype congruency is that identity prime.

We contend that a servant leader primes a particular identity within followers. The behaviors of the servant leader are fundamentally prosocial, and serve as an environmental factor that primes a prosocial identity (Aquino & Reed, 2002; Forehand et al., 2002; Grant, Dutton, & Rosso, 2008). Activation of a prosocial identity within a follower in turn motivates the follower to perform actions consistent with that identity, that is, prosocial actions that benefit the collective "we" of the group. Specifically, this motivates other orientation and further cements commitment to the supervisor, as a moral referent (Aquino & Reed, 2002) that at least in part informs the focal employee's prosocial identity.

Empirically, Grant et al. (2008) demonstrated that providing tangible and emotional support to employees strengthens their prosocial identity and organizational commitment. Similar results have been found with charismatic leaders, who are able to connect individual contributions to a larger group identity (Conger, Kanungo, & Menon, 2000; Shamir et al., 1993). Even though leaders may be able to influence the leadership prototypes that followers develop, because leaders vary in the extent to which they engage in servant leadership, there similarly are differences in the extent to which followers form leadership prototypes that are consistent with servant leadership. As a result, we contend that the congruence between follower servant leadership prototypes and servant leader behaviors moderates the relationships between servant leadership behaviors and intermediate processes, consistent with the initial findings of Meuser and colleagues (2011). Note that the "moderation arrow" in Figure 17.1 from follower servant leader prototype to the relationship between servant leader behaviors and intermediate processes does not refer to traditional cross-product moderation analysis, but rather response surface methodology

(Edwards, 2007), which is better suited to analyzing hypotheses dealing with congruence or fit (e.g., person-environment fit, follower-leader fit, etc.)

Proposition 8: Congruence between follower servant leader prototype and the behaviors of his or her servant leader moderates the relationship between servant leader behaviors and intermediate processes.

Propositions 3 through 8 focus on the intermediate processes between servant leadership behaviors and outcomes that involve a single level of analysis. Although beyond the scope of our chapter, many team and cross-level propositions could also be developed using the model in Figure 17.1 as a general framework. For example, the trust that is engendered through servant leadership at the individual level may enhance team identification, as it has been shown that followers tend to trust coworkers who are trusted by the leader (Lau & Liden, 2008). When team members trust one another, they should identify more with the team.

Future Directions

Although servant leadership pre-dates key leadership approaches studied today, such as LMX and transformational leadership, far fewer empirical studies have been conducted on this theory of leadership. Our proposed model suggests many avenues for enhancing knowledge of servant leadership and, in turn, providing insights on the practical value of this approach for organizations. While each proposition merits attention by scholars, in this section we prioritize the numerous opportunities for advancing research on servant leadership. Specifically, we offer five recommendations for future research that we believe have potential for establishing servant leadership as a dominant theory of leadership among researchers and practitioners. While we recognize that initial empirical studies provide support for the distinctiveness of servant leadership compared to other leadership approaches, our future research recommendations would provide even further evidence of the value of servant leadership to the leadership literature.

Determine Key Antecedents of Servant Leadership. What's More Important: Nature or Nurture?

There is a definite need for research on antecedents of servant leadership. Our model identifies specific characteristics of the leader such as desire to serve others, emotional intelligence, moral maturity and conation, and prosocial identity. In terms of priorities, future research should examine a broad set of predictors including those that might be personality based (nature) as well as those that may be more malleable (nurture). In order for servant leadership to gain prominence, it is important to understand how to increase these behaviors or create servant leaders, especially through management development programs. For example, some studies suggest that emotional intelligence can be enhanced through training. However, at this point we do not know the relative importance of various predictors of servant leadership and the extent to which they are malleable through training. We believe this should be a high priority of scholars interested in servant leadership.

Explore the Process by Which Servant Leadership Proliferates within an Organization

Research is also needed on the contention that servant leaders groom some of their followers to be servant leaders. No other leadership approach stresses the notion of propagating the leader's behaviors through followers as does servant leadership. This defining feature of servant leadership which separates it from other leadership approaches, is in need of empirical research. At a microlevel, what is the process through which leaders identify followers with the potential to be developed into servant leaders? And once identified, how are followers transformed into servant leaders? We have suggested that modeling may be critical, but direct forms of mentoring followers to adopt servant leader behaviors may also be in evidence.

As more and more followers are transformed into servant leaders within an organization, a serving culture emerges in the organization (Greenleaf, 1977; Liden et al., in press). Essentially, the process involves moving from the presence of isolated servant leaders in an organization to a culture that promotes serving others. Exploring the processes, however, represents a formidable challenge, as an adequate sample of teams or organizations to produce adequate variance in culture is necessary for exploring this idea. Yet, the value of exploring servant leadership at the macro level is significant.

Investigate the Process by Which Servant Leadership Impacts Follower and Team Outcomes and How This Process Compares to Other Approaches to Leadership

Our model identifies a number of intermediate processes by which servant leader behaviors may impact follower outcomes. We argue that one way by which servant leadership impacts follower outcomes is through follower moral identity. With the exception of the ethical leadership model, behaving ethically is not emphasized in other leadership frameworks to the extent that it is in servant leadership theory. Thus, in order to demonstrate the uniqueness of servant leadership, examining whether servant leaders enhance followers' moral identity should be a priority. Furthermore, given the importance of moral identity to ethical behavior, demonstrating that a workplace leader could enhance the salience of others' moral identity through servant leader behaviors, and in turn influence ethical behavior, would be noteworthy.

In addition to the growing attention on the influence of servant leadership on follower outcomes, a small group of research highlights the value of servant leadership in work teams and focuses on processes between servant leadership and team effectiveness. For example, following the lead of Walumbwa and his colleagues' (2010) individual-level research revealing the mediating effect of service climate on relationships between servant leadership behaviors and individual OCBs, we recommend that scholars place a priority on examining service climate as a mediator between servant leadership and team outcomes. Especially in the service industry, we expect that servant leadership will have a significant impact on team outcomes through service climate. An ideal setting for such a study may be branches of banks or a restaurant chain where there are few layers of management such that leaders interact frequently with followers, who directly serve customers. In these settings, we expect that service climate may be an important mediator. In addition to service climate, other potential mediators of the relationship between servant leadership and team outcomes include team potency, cohesiveness, communal sharing, and procedural justice climate.

Examine the Outcomes of Servant Leadership beyond Follower Performance and OCB

Because scientifically designed empirical research published in top academic outlets on servant leadership in organizations is recent, with the first study appearing in 2004 by Ehrhart, the set of outcomes considered has been limited. Most of the studies have linked servant leadership to individual performance and OCB. Few studies have investigated outcomes of servant leadership that may be unique to this particular theory of leadership. In addressing this gap, we suggest that scholars focus their attention on the individual outcome of community citizenship behavior, which has been addressed in only one study (Liden et al., 2008) to our knowledge. One of the distinguishing characteristics of servant leadership is the emphasis on caring about the needs of others, including those in the community. No other theory of leadership focuses attention on this behavior, despite the growing interest among researchers and practitioners in corporate social responsibility (CSR), which includes improving the larger community. If future research finds the relation between servant leadership and follower community citizenship behavior reported by Liden and colleagues generalizes across situations, this would further discern servant leadership from prevailing theories of leadership. It would also offer insights on how leadership may be instrumental in enabling organizations to achieve their CSR goals.

Another priority for research on servant leadership outcomes is to continue investigating team-level performance to better understand the boundary conditions associated with the relationships between servant leadership and team performance demonstrated by Hu and Liden (2011) and Schaubroeck and his colleagues (2011) and the relationship between servant leadership and team-level OCBs shown in Ehrhart's (2004) study. An underlying assumption is that servant leaders attempt to meet the needs and provide support to all followers, not just a subset. This is in contrast to LMX, which argues that due to a lack of time and resources the leader develops a high-quality exchange with some followers, but not all. Because servant leaders attempt to meet the needs of each member, the question is whether servant leadership enhances interpersonal relations among team members, engendering synergistic effects, such that team performance exceeds the cumulative performance of the individual members. Conducting research that examines additional contextual and moderating variables not examined by Ehrhart (2004), Hu and Liden (2011), and Schaubroeck (2011) would lay the groundwork for establishing servant leadership as a driver of effective team dynamics.

Identify Boundary Conditions for Servant Leadership, Including Cross-Cultural Comparisons

As would be expected in an emerging area of study, servant leadership needs to be examined at multiple levels of analysis and include a wider range of job types, organizations, and cultures.

Ehrhart studied grocery store workers in the United States and focused on the team level. Liden and colleagues (2008) examined production, distribution, and marketing employees of a small building products organization located in the United States. Walumbwa and colleagues (2010) investigated clerical, administrative, professional, and managerial employees representing seven multinational organizations located in Kenya, Africa. Schaubroeck et al.'s study (2011) was conducted in both the United States and Hong Kong within the same banking organization. Hu and Liden's (2011) study was based on data collected in banks located in the People's Republic of China. The latter two studies were conducted only at the team level. Neuberg and colleagues (2010) employed an online research services company to collect their data, and thus the country(ies) from where the data originated do not appear to be known. Peterson et al. (2012) studied CEOs in technology companies in the Western United States. These studies suggest that servant leadership may be impactful in a broad range of jobs and in different cultures. However, we encourage scholars to explore cultural factors within the context of servant leadership. Specifically, servant leadership studies that are able to investigate national culture as a moderator between leader characteristics and engagement in servant leadership would make great strides in determining boundary conditions for this form of leader behavior. Although culture may need to be assigned based on country tendencies, the preferred approach is to directly measure cultural values so that both within- and between-group variance can be assessed, and so that tests involving culture as a moderating variable are more accurate.

Conclusion

Although over 40 years have passed since the publication of Greenleaf's (1970) seminal essay, empirical research beginning with Ehrhart (2004) has shown great promise for servant leadership. Results have demonstrated that servant leadership influences important work outcomes, such as OCBs and performance, at both the individual and team levels, even when controlling LMX and/or transformational leadership. With recent accusations that economic downturns are often caused by greed and excessive self-interest, servant leadership holds promise for the future of organizations and society. We hope that our model and accompanying propositions will stimulate continued interest and further research on servant leadership.

References

Amabile, T. M., Schatzel, E. A., Moneta, G. B., & Kramer, S. J. (2004). Leader behaviors and the work environment for creativity: Perceived leader support. *Leadership Quarterly, 15*, 5–32.

Anderson, J. A. (2009). When a servant leader comes knocking. *Leadership & Organization Development Journal, 30*, 4–15.

Antonakis, J., Ashkanasy, N. M., & Dasborough, M. T. (2009). Does leadership need emotional intelligence? *Leadership Quarterly, 20*, 247–261.

Aquino, K., & Reed, A. II. (2002). The self-importance of moral identity. *Journal of Personality and Social Psychology, 83*, 1423–1440.

Ashforth, B. E., & Humphrey, R. H. (1993). Emotional labor in service roles: The influence of identity. *The Academy of Management Review, 18*, 88–115.

Ashkanasy, N. M., Windsor, C. A., & Treviño, L. K. (2006). Bad apples in bad barrels revisited: Cognitive moral development, just world beliefs, rewards, and ethical decision-making. *Business Ethics Quarterly, 16*, 449–473.

Axtell, C. M., Holman, D. J., Unsworth, K. L., Wall, T. D., Waterson, P. E., & Harrington, E. (2000). Shopfloor innovation: Facilitating the suggestion and implementation of ideas. *Journal of Occupational and Organizational Psychology, 73*, 265–285.

Bandura, A. (1986). *Social foundations of thought and action: A social cognitive theory*. Englewood Cliffs, NJ: Prentice Hall.

Bandura, A. (1991). Social cognitive theory of self-regulation. *Organizational Behavior and Human Decision Processes, 50*, 248–287.

Bandura, A. (1999). Social cognitive theory of personality. In D. Cervone & Y. Shoda (Eds.), *The coherence of personality: Social-cognitive bases of consistency, variability, and organization* (pp. 185–241). New York: Guilford.

Barbuto, J. E., & Wheeler, D. W. (2006). Scale development and construct clarification of servant leadership. *Group and Organization Management, 31*, 300–326.

Bass, B. M. (1985). *Leadership and performance beyond expectations*. New York: Free Press.

Batson, C. D. (1990). How social an animal? The human capacity for caring. *American Psychologist, 45*, 336–346.

Beal, D. J., Trougakos, J. P., Weiss, H. M., & Green, S. G. (2006). Episodic processes in emotional labor: Perceptions of affective delivery and regulation strategies. *Journal of Applied Psychology, 91*, 1053–1065.

Becker, T. E., Billings, R. S., Eveleth, E. M., & Gilbert, N. L. (1996). Foci and bases of employee commitment: Implications for job performance. *Academy of Management Journal, 39*, 464–482.

Becker, T. E., & Kernan, M. (2003). Matching commitment to supervisors and organizations to in-role and extra-role performance. *Human Performance, 16*, 327–348.

Blau, P. M. (1964). *Exchange and power in social life*. New York: Wiley.

Brower, H. H., Schoorman, F. D., & Tan, H. H. (2000). A model of relational leadership: The integration of trust and leader–member exchange. *The Leadership Quarterly, 11*(2), 227–250.

Brown, M. E., & Treviño, L. K. (2006). Ethical leadership: A review and future directions. *Leadership Quarterly, 17*, 595–616.

Brown, M. E., Treviño, L. K., & Harrison, D. A. (2005). Ethical leadership: A social learning perspective for construct

development and testing. *Organizational Behavior and Human Decision Processes, 97*, 117–134.
Carmeli, A. (2003). The relationship between emotional intelligence and work attitudes, behavior and outcomes. *Journal of Managerial Psychology, 18*, 788–813.
Chen, G., & Bliese, P. D. (2002). The role of different levels of leadership in predicting self- and collective efficacy: Evidence for discontinuity. *Journal of Applied Psychology, 87*, 549–556.
Christian, M. S., Garza, A. S., & Slaughter, J. E. (2011). Work engagement: A quantitative review and test of its relations with task and contextual performance. *Personnel Psychology, 64*, 89–136.
Clugston, M., Howell, J. P., & Dorfman, P. W. (2000). Does cultural socialization predict multiple bases and foci of commitment? *Journal of Management, 26*, 5–30.
Collins, J. (2001). *Good to great: Why some companies make the leap and others don't.* New York: Harper-Collins.
Conger, J. A., & Kanungo, R. N. (1988). The empowerment process: Integrating theory and practice. *Academy of Management Review, 13*, 471–482.
Conger, J. A., Kanungo, R. N., & Menon, S. T. (2000). Charismatic leadership and follower effects. *Journal of Organizational Behavior, 21*, 747–767.
Dansereau, F., Graen, G., & Haga, W. (1975). A vertical dyad approach to leadership within formal organizations. *Organizational Behavior and Human Performance, 13*, 46–78.
Deci, E. L., & Ryan, R. M. (1985). *Intrinsic motivation and self-determination in human behavior.* New York: Plenum.
Deci, E. L., & Ryan, R. M. (2000). The "what" and the "why" of goal pursuits: Human needs and the self-determination of behavior. *Psychological Inquiry, 11*, 227–268.
De Hoogh, A.H.B., & Den Hartog, D. N. (2008). Ethical and despotic leadership, relationships with leader's social responsibility, top management team effectiveness and subordinates' optimism: A multi-method study. *Leadership Quarterly, 19*, 297–311.
Den Hartog, D. N., & Belschak, F. D. (2012). When does transformational leadership enhance employee proactive behavior? The role of autonomy and role breadth self-efficacy. *Journal of Applied Psychology, 97*, 194–202.
Dirks, K. T., & Ferrin, D. L. (2002). Trust in leadership: Meta-analytic findings and implications for research and practice. *Journal of Applied Psychology, 87*, 611–628.
Dudley, N. M., Orvis, K. A., Lebiecki, J. E., & Cortina, J. M. (2006). A meta-analytic investigation of conscientiousness in the prediction of job performance: Examining the intercorrelations and the incremental validity of narrow traits. *Journal of Applied Psychology, 91*, 40–57.
Edwards, J. R. (2007). Polynomial regression and response surface methodology. In C. Ostroff & T. A. Judge (Eds.), *Perspectives on organizational fit* (pp. 361–372). San Francisco: Jossey-Bass.
Ehrhart, M. G. (2004). Leadership and procedural justice climate as antecedents of unit-level organizational citizenship behavior. *Personnel Psychology, 57*, 61–94.
Erez, A., & Judge, T. A. (2001). Relationship of core self-evaluations to goal setting, motivation, and performance. *Journal of Applied Psychology, 86*, 1270–1279.
Erikson, E. H. (1964). *Insight and responsibility.* New York: Norton.
Farling, M. L., Stone, A. G., & Winston, B. E. (1999). Servant leadership: Setting the stage for empirical research. *Journal of Leadership Studies, 6*, 49–72.
Ferris, G. R., Liden, R. C., Munyon, T. P., Summers, J. K., Basik, K. J., & Buckley, M. R. (2009). Relationships at work: Toward a multidimensional conceptualization of dyadic work relationships. *Journal of Management, 35*, 1379–1403.
Forehand, M. K., Deshpandé, R., & Reed II, A. (2002). Identity salience and the influence of differential activation of the social self-schema on advertising response. *Journal of Applied Psychology, 87*, 1086–1099.
Frick, D. M. (2004). *Robert K. Greenleaf: A life of servant leadership.* San Francisco: Berrett-Koehler.
Fuller, B. & Marler, L.E. (2009). Change driven by nature: A meta-analytic review of the proactive personality literature. *Journal of Vocational Behavior, 75*, 329–345.
Gagné, M., & Deci, E. L. (2005). Self-determination theory and work motivation. *Journal of Organizational Behavior, 26*, 331–362.
George, J. M. (2000). Emotions and leadership: The role of emotional intelligence. *Human Relations, 53*, 1027–1055.
Gerstner, C. R., & Day, D. V. (1994). Cross-cultural comparison of leadership prototypes. *Leadership Quarterly, 5*, 121–134.
Gist, M. E., & Mitchell, T. R. (1992). Self-efficacy: A theoretical analysis of its determinants and malleability. *Academy of Management Review, 17*, 183–211.
Goleman, D. (1995). *Emotional intelligence.* New York: Bantam Books.
Gouldner, A. W. (1960). The norm of reciprocity: A preliminary statement. *American Sociological Review, 25*, 161–178.
Graham, J. W. (1991). Servant-leader in organizations: Inspirational and moral. *Leadership Quarterly, 2*, 105–119.
Grant, A. M., Dutton, J. E., & Rosso, B. D. (2008). Giving commitment: Employee support programs and the prosocial sensemaking process. *Academy of Management Journal, 51*(5), 898–918.
Grant, A. M., Molinsky, A., Margolis, J., Kamin, M., & Schiano, W. (2009). The performer's reactions to procedural injustice: When prosocial identity reduces prosocial behavior. *Journal of Applied Social Psychology, 39*, 319–349.
Greenhaus, J. H., & Beutell, N. J. (1985). Sources of conflict between work and family roles. *Academy of Management Review, 10*, 76–88.
Greenleaf, R. K. (1970). *The servant as leader.* Newton Centre, MA: The Robert K. Greenleaf Center.
Greenleaf, R. K. (1977). *Servant leadership: A journey into the nature of legitimate power and greatness.* New York: Paulist Press.
Hannah, S. T., & Avolio, B. J. (2010). Ready or not: How do we accelerate the developmental readiness of leaders? *Journal of Organizational Behavior, 31*, 1181–1187.
Hannah, S. T., Avolio, B. J., & May, D. R. (2011). Moral maturation and moral conation: A capacity approach to explaining moral thought and action. *Academy of Management Review, 36*, 663–685.
Herold, D. M. (1977). Two-way influence processes in leader-follower dyads. *Academy of Management Journal, 20*(2), 224–237.
Higgins, E. T. (1997). Beyond pleasure and pain. *American Psychologist, 52*, 1280–1300.
Higgins, E. T. (1998). Promotion and prevention: Regulatory focus as a motivational principle. In M. P. Zanna (Ed.), *Advances in experimental social psychology* (vol. *30*, pp. 1–46). New York: Academic Press.
Hogg, M. A. (2000). Subjective uncertainty reduction through self-categorization: A motivational theory of social identity processes. *European Review of Social Psychology, 11*, 223–255.

Hogg, M. A. (2001). A social identity theory of leadership. *Personality and Social Psychology Review, 5*, 184–200.
Hogg, M. A., & Abrams, D. (1993). Towards a single-process uncertainty-reduction model of social motivation in groups. In M. A. Hogg & D. Abrams (Eds.), *Group motivation: Social psychological perspectives* (pp. 173–190). London: Harvester-Wheatsheaf.
Hogg, M. A., & Mullin, B. A. (1999). Joining groups to reduce uncertainty: Subjective uncertainty reduction and group identification. In D. Abrams & M. A. Hogg (Eds.), *Social identity and social cognition* (pp. 249–279). Oxford: Blackwell.
Hogg, M. A., & Terry, D. J. (2000). Social identity and self-categorization process in organizational contexts. *Academy of Management Journal, 25*, 121–140.
Hosmer, L. T. (1995). Trust: The connecting link between organizational theory and philosophical ethics. *Academy of Management Review, 20*, 379–403.
Hu, J., & Liden, R. C. (2011). Antecedents of team potency and team effectiveness: An examination of goal and process clarity and servant leadership. *Journal of Applied Psychology, 96*, 851–862.
Hülsheger, U. R., Anderson, N., & Salgado, J. F. (2009). Team-level predictors of innovation at work: A comprehensive meta-analysis spanning three decades of research. *Journal of Applied Psychology, 94*, 1128–1145.
Humphrey, R. H. (2002). The many faces of emotional leadership. *Leadership Quarterly, 13*, 493–504.
Humphreys, J. H. (2005). Contextual implications for transformational and servant leadership: A historical investigation. *Management Decision, 43*, 1410–1431.
Hunt, S. D., & Morgan, R. M. (1994). Organizational commitment: One of many commitments or key mediating construct? *Academy of Management Journal, 37*, 1568–1587.
Hunter, E. M., Mitchell, J., Neubert, M. J., Perry, S. J., Witt, L. A., Penney, L. M., & Weinberger, E. (2013). Servant leaders inspire servant followers: Antecedents and outcomes for employees and the organization. *Leadership Quarterly, 24*, 316–331.
Joseph, D. L., & Newman, D. A. (2010). Emotional intelligence: An integrative meta-analysis and cascading model. *Journal of Applied Psychology, 95*, 54–78.
Joseph, E. E., & Winston, B. E. (2005). A correlation of servant leadership, leader trust, and organizational trust. *Leadership & Organization Development Journal, 26*, 6–22.
Judge, T. A., & Bono, J. E. (2001). Relationships of core self-evaluations traits—self-esteem, generalized self-efficacy, locus of control, and emotional stability—with job satisfaction and job performance: A meta-analysis. *Journal of Applied Psychology, 86*, 80–92.
Judge, T. A., Erez, A., Bono, J. E., & Thoresen, C. J. (2003). The core self-evaluations scale: Development of a measure. *Personnel Psychology, 56*, 303–331.
Judge, T. A., Erez, A., & Bono, J. E. (1998). The power of being positive: The relation between positive self-concept and job performance. *Human Performance, 11*, 167–187.
Judge, T. A., LePine, J. A., & Rich, B. A. (2006). Loving yourself abundantly: Relationship of the narcissistic personality to self- and other perceptions of workplace deviance, leadership, and task and contextual performance. *Journal of Applied Psychology, 91*, 762–776.
Kanfer, R. (1990). Motivation theory and industrial and organizational psychology. In M. D. Dunnette & L. M. Hough (Eds.), *Handbook of industrial and organizational psychology* (2nd ed., vol. *1*, pp. 75–171). Palo Alto, CA: Consulting Psychologists Press.
Kark, R., Shamir, B., & Chen, G. (2003). The two faces of transformational leadership: Empowerment and dependency. *Journal of Applied Psychology, 88*, 246–255.
Kohlberg, L. (1984). *The psychology of moral development: The nature and validity of moral stages*. San Francisco: Harper & Row.
Korsgaard, M. A., Brodt, S. E., & Whitener, E. M. (2002). Trust in the fact of conflict: The role of managerial trustworthy behavior and organizational context. *Journal of Applied Psychology, 87*, 312–319.
Lau, D. C., & Liden, R. C. (2008). Antecedents of coworker trust: Leaders' blessings. *Journal of Applied Psychology, 93*, 1130–1138.
Levinson, H. (1965). Reciprocation: The relationship between man and organization. *Administrative Science Quarterly, 9*, 370–390.
Liao, H., & Rupp, D. E. (2005). The impact of justice climate and justice orientation on work outcomes: A cross-level multifoci framework. *Journal of Applied Psychology, 90*, 242–256.
Liden, R. C., & Maslyn, J. M. (1998). Multidimensionality of leader-member exchange: An empirical assessment through scale development. *Journal of Management, 24*, 43–72.
Liden, R. C., Wayne, S. J., Liao, C., & Meuser, J. D. (in press). Servant leadership and serving culture: Influence on individual and unit performance. *Academy of Management Journal.*
Liden, R. C., Wayne, S. J., Zhao, H., & Henderson, D. (2008). Servant leadership: Development of a multidimensional measure and multilevel assessment. *Leadership Quarterly, 19*, 161–177.
Lord, R. G., Brown, D. J., Harvey, J. L., & Hall, R. J. (2001). Contextual constraints on prototype generation and their multilevel consequences for leadership perceptions. *Leadership Quarterly, 12*, 311–338.
Lord, R. G., Foti, R. J., & de Vader, C. D. (1984). A test of leadership categorization theory: Internal structure, information processing, and leadership perception. *Organizational Behavior and Human Decision Processes, 34*, 343–378.
Lowin, A., & Craig, J. R. (1968). The influence of level of performance on managerial style: An experimental object-lesson in the ambiguity of correlational data. *Organizational Behavior & Human Performance, 3*, 440–458.
Maurer, T. J., & Lord, R. G. (1991). An exploration of cognitive demands in group interaction as a moderator of information processing variables in perceptions of leadership. *Journal of Applied Social Psychology, 21*, 821–839.
Mayer, D. M., Aquino, K., Greenbaum, R. L., & Kuenzi, M. (2012). Who displays ethical leadership, and why does it matter? An examination of antecedents and consequences of ethical leadership. *Academy of Management Review, 37*, 151–171.
Mayer, D. M., Bardes, M., & Piccolo, R. F. (2008). Do servant-leaders help satisfy follower needs? An organizational justice perspective. *European Journal of Work and Organizational Psychology, 17*, 180–197.
Mayer, R. C., Davis, J. H., & Schoorman, F. D. (1995). An integrative model of organizational trust. *Academy of Management Review, 20*, 709–734.
Meglino, B. M., & Korsgaard, M. A. (2004). Considering rational self-interest as a disposition: Organizational implications of other orientation. *Journal of Applied Psychology, 89*, 946–959.
Meuser, J. D., Liden, R. C., Wayne, S. J., & Henderson, D. J. (2011, August). *Is servant leadership always a good thing? The moderating influence of servant leadership prototype?*

Paper presented at the annual meeting of the Academy of Management, San Antonio, Texas.
Meyer, J. P., & Gagné, M. (2008). Employee engagement from a self-determination theory perspective. *Industrial and Organizational Psychology, 1*, 60–62.
Meyer, J. P., & Herscovitch, L. (2001). Commitment in the workplace: Toward a general model. *Human Resource Management Review, 11*, 299–326.
Meyer, J. P., Irving, P. G., & Allen, N. J. (1998). Examination of the combined effects of work values and early work experiences on organizational commitment. *Journal of Organizational Behavior, 19*, 29–52.
Morf, C. C., & Rhodewalt, F. (2001). Unraveling the paradoxes of narcissism: A dynamic self-regulatory processing model. *Psychological Inquiry, 12*, 177–196.
Morris, J. A., & Feldman, D. C. (1996). The dimensions, antecedents, and consequences of emotional labor. *Academy of Management Review, 21*(4), 986–1010.
Mumford, M. D., & Gustafson, S. B. (1988). Creativity syndrome: Integration, application, and innovation. *Psychological Bulletin, 103*, 27–43.
Neubert, M. J., Kacmar, K. M., Carlson, D. S., Chonko, L. B., & Roberts, J. A. (2008). Regulatory focus as a mediator of the influence of initiating structure and servant leadership on employee behavior. *Journal of Applied Psychology, 93*, 1220–1233.
Ng, K.-Y., Koh, C. S.-K., & Goh, H.-C. 2008. The heart of the servant leader. Leader's motivation-to-serve and its impact on LMX and subordinates' extra-role behavior. In G. B. Graen & J. A. Graen (Eds.), *Knowledge driven corporation-complex creative destruction* (pp. 125–144). Charlotte, NC: Information Age.
Nye, J. L., & Forsyth, D. R. (1991). The effects of prototype-based biases on leadership appraisals: a test of leadership categorization theory. *Small Group Research, 22*, 360–379.
Oldham, G. R., & Cummings, A. (1996). Employee creativity: Personal and contextual factors at work. *Academy of Management Journal, 39*, 607–634.
Organ, D. W. (1997). Organizational citizenship behavior: It's construct clean-up time. *Human Performance, 10*, 85–97.
Panaccio, A., & Vandenberghe, C. (2011). The relationships of role clarity and organization-based self-esteem to commitment to supervisors and organizations and turnover intentions. *Journal of Applied Social Psychology, 41*, 1455–1485.
Parker, S. K., Williams, H. M., & Turner, N. (2006). Modeling the antecedents of proactive behavior at work. *Journal of Applied Psychology, 91*, 636–652.
Peterson, S., Galvin, B. M., & Lange, D. (2012). CEO servant leadership: Exploring executive characteristics and firm performance. *Personnel Psychology, 65*, 565–596.
Pierce, J. L., & Gardner, D. G. (2004). Self-esteem within the work and organizational context: A review of the organization-based self-esteem literature. *Journal of Management, 30*, 591–622.
Platow, M. J., Van Knippenberg, D., Haslam, S. A., Van Knippenberg, B., & Spears, R. (2006). A special gift we bestow on you for being representative of us: Considering leader charisma from a self-categorization perspective. *British Journal of Social Psychology, 45*, 303–320.
Rest, J., Narvaez, D., Bebeau, M. J., & Thoma, S. J. (1999). *Postconventional moral thinking: A neo-Kohlbergian approach.* Mahwah, NJ: Lawrence Erlbaum Associates.
Reynolds, S. J., & Ceranic, T. L. (2007). The effects of moral judgment and moral identity on moral behavior: An empirical examination of the moral individual. *Journal of Applied Psychology, 92*, 1610–1624.
Rich, B. L., Lepine, J. A., & Crawford, E. R. (2010). Job engagement: Antecedents and effects on job performance. *Academy of Management Journal, 53*, 617–635.
Rosch, E. (1978). Principles of categorization. In E. Rosch & B. B. Lloyd (Eds.), *Cognition and categorization* (pp. 27–84). Hillsdale, NJ: Lawrence Erlbaum Associates.
Rousseau, D. M., Sitkin, S. B., Burt, R. S., & Camerer, C. (1998). Not so different after all: A cross-discipline view of trust. *Academy of Management Review, 23*, 393–404.
Rushton, J. (1980). *Altruism, socialization, and society.* Englewood Cliffs, NJ: Prentice-Hall.
Russell, R. F., & Stone, G. A. (2002). A review of servant leadership attributes: developing a practical model. *Leadership and Organization Development Journal, 23*, 145–57.
Salovey, P., & Mayer, J. D. (1990). Emotional intelligence. *Imagination, Cognition, and Personality, 9*, 185–211.
Schaubroeck, J., Lam, S.S.K., & Peng, A. C. (2011). Cognition-based and affect-based trust as mediators of leader behavior influences on team performance. *Journal of Applied Psychology, 96*, 863–871.
Schminke, M., Ambrose, M. L., & Neubaum, D. O. (2005). The effect of leader moral development on ethical climate and employee attitudes. *Organizational Behavior and Human Decision Processes, 97*, 135–151.
Scott, S. G., & Bruce, R. A. (1994). Determinants of innovative behavior: A path model of individual innovation in the workplace. *Academy of Management Journal, 37*, 580–607.
Sendjaya, S., Sarros, J. C., & Santora, J. C. (2008). Defining and measuring servant leadership behaviour in organizations. *Journal of Management Studies, 45*, 402–424.
Sedikides, C., & Brewer, M. B. (2001). *The social self: The quest for identity and the motivational primacy of the individual self.* New York: Psychology Press.
Seibert, S. E., Kraimer, M. L., & Crant, J. M. (2001). What do proactive people do? A longitudinal model linking proactive personality and career success. *Personnel Psychology, 54*, 845–874.
Shamir, B., House, R. J., & Arthur, M. (1993). The motivational effects of charismatic leadership: A self-concept based theory. *Organization Science, 4*, 566–594.
Sparrowe, R. T., & Liden, R. C. (1997). Process and structure in leader-member exchange. *Academy of Management Review, 22*, 522–552.
Sparrowe, R. T., & Liden, R. C. (2005). Two routes to influence: Integrating leader-member exchange and social network perspectives. *Administrative Science Quarterly, 50*, 505–535.
Spears, L. C. (1998). Tracing the growing impact of servant leadership. In L. C. Spears (Ed.), *Insights on leadership: Service, stewardship, spirit, and servant-leadership* (pp. 1–12). New York: John Wiley and Sons.
Spreitzer, G. M. (1995). Psychological empowerment in the workplace: Dimensions, measurement, and validation. *Academy of Management Journal, 38*, 1442–1465.
Steel, P., Schmidt, J., & Shultz, J. (2008). Refining the relationship between personality and subjective well-being. *Psychological Bulletin, 134*, 138–161.
Stinglhamber, F., & Vandenberghe, C. (2003). Organizations and supervisors as sources of support and targets of commitment: A longitudinal study. *Journal of Organizational Behavior, 24*, 251–270.

Stryker, S., & Burke, P. J. (2000). The past, present, and future of identity theory. *Social Psychology Quarterly, 63*, 284–297.

Tajfel, H. (1972). Social categorization. English manuscript of "La categorization sociale." In S. Moscovici (Ed.), *Introduction a la Psychologie Sociale* (vol. *1*, pp. 272–302). Paris: Larousse.

Tajfel, H., & Turner, J. C. (1979). An integrative theory of intergroup conflict. In W. G. Austin & S. Worchel (Eds.), *The social psychology of intergroup relations* (pp. 33–47). Monterey, CA: Brooks/Cole.

Tajfel, H., & Turner, J. (1986). The social identity theory of intergroup behavior. In S. Worchel & W. Austin (Eds.), *Psychology of intergroup relations* (pp. 7–24). Chicago: Nelson-Hall.

Thomas, K. W., & Velthouse, B. A. (1990). Cognitive elements of empowerment: An "interpretive" model of intrinsic task motivation. *Academy of Management Review, 15*, 666–681.

Tsui, A. S., Pearce, J. L., Porter, L. W., & Tripoli, A. M. (1997). Alternative approaches to the employee–organization relationship: Does investment in employees pay off? *Academy of Management Journal, 40*, 1089–1121.

Turner, J. C. (1982). Towards a cognitive redefinition of the social group. In H. Tajfel (Ed.), *Social identity and intergroup relations* (pp. 15–40). Cambridge: Cambridge University Press.

Turner, J. C. (1985). Social categorization and the self-concept: A social cognitive theory of group behavior. In E. J. Lawler (Ed.), *Advances in group processes: Theory and research* (vol. *2*, pp. 77–122). Greenwich, CT: JAI.

Turner, J. C., Brown, R. J., & Tajfel, H. (1979). Social comparison and group interest in ingroup favouritism. *European Journal of Social Psychology, 9*(2), 187–204.

Turner, J. C., Hogg, M. A., Oakes, P. J., Reicher, S. D., & Wetherell, M. S. (1987). *Rediscovering the social group: A self-categorization theory*. Oxford: Blackwell.

Van Beek, I., Hu, Q., Schaufeli, W. B., Taris, T. W., & Schreurs, B. H. J. (2012). For fun, love, or money: What drives workaholic, engaged, and burned-out employees at work? *Applied Psychology: An International Review, 61*, 30–55.

Van Dierendonck, D. (2011). Servant leadership: A review and synthesis. *Journal of Management, 37*, 1228–1261.

Van Dierendonck, D., & Nuijten, I. (2011). The Servant-Leadership Survey: Development and validation of a multidimensional measure. *Journal of Business and Psychology, 26*, 249–267.

Wagner, U., Lampen, L., & Syllwasschy, J. (1986). In-group inferiority, social identity and out-group devaluation in a modified minimal group study. *British Journal of Social Psychology, 25*, 15–23.

Walumbwa, F. O., Hartnell, C. A., & Oke, A. (2010). Servant leadership, procedural justice climate, service climate, employee attitudes, and organizational citizenship behavior: A cross level investigation. *Journal of Applied Psychology, 95*, 517–529.

Wang, J., & Lee, A. Y. (2006). The role of regulatory focus in preference construction. *Journal of Marketing Research, 43*, 28–38.

Washington, R. R., Sutton, C. D., & Feild, H. S. (2006). Individual differences in servant leadership: The role of value and personality. *Leadership and Organization Development Journal, 27*, 700–716.

Whetstone, J. T. (2002). Personalism and moral leadership—the servant leader with a transforming vision. *Business Ethics: A European Review, 11*, 385–392.

Williams, L. J., & Anderson, S. E. (1991). Job satisfaction and organizational commitment as predictors of organizational citizenship and in-role behaviors. *Journal of Management, 17*, 601–617.

Wolff, S. B., Percosolido, A. T., & Druskat, V. U. (2002). Emotional intelligence as the basis of leadership emergence in self-managing teams. *Leadership Quarterly, 13*, 505–522.

Wood, R., & Bandura, A. (1989). Social cognitive theory of organizational management. *Academy of Management Review, 14*, 361–384.

CHAPTER

18 Leading for Proactivity: How Leaders Cultivate Staff Who Make Things Happen

Sharon K. Parker *and* Chia-huei Wu

Abstract

How do leaders promote proactivity among their staff? This chapter focuses on how leaders cultivate individual-level proactivity, with proactivity being defined as a future-focused, change-oriented, and self-starting way of behaving. Behaviors from many domains can be carried out more or less proactively, so we include in our review literature on individual innovation, taking charge, voice, proactive socialization, and other such ways of behaving proactively. After describing existing research on how leadership relates to proactivity, the authors propose a model in which we identify multiple pathways by which leaders can influence their staff's motivation and capability to be proactive, as well as the effectiveness of their proactivity. They propose that both team-oriented and person-oriented leadership inputs can have direct effects on motivation and capability via leader actions, as well as indirect effects on motivation and capability via leader effects on the team climate, work design, or other team-level inputs. The authors then identify several ways that this model can be expanded, as well as directions for future research.

Key Words: capability, individual innovation, individual-oriented inputs, motivation, job performance, proactivity, taking charge, voice, team-oriented inputs

Introduction

Being proactive is about making things happen. It involves anticipating events and taking charge to bring about a different future, such as by speaking out with ideas, self-initiating improved work methods, and actively seeking feedback (Parker, Bindl, & Strauss, 2010). A great deal of research shows the value of behaving proactively for outcomes such as career success (e.g., Seibert, Kraimer, & Crant, 2001), job performance (e.g., Thomas, Whitman, & Viswesvaran, 2010), organizational innovation (e.g., Gumusluoglu & Ilsev, 2009), and entrepreneurship (e.g., Unger, Keith, Hilling, Gielnik, & Frese, 2009).

However, proactivity can be a challenging way of behaving within organizations. Behaving proactively is often psychologically risky for individuals: its emphasis on change means others do not always welcome proactivity, and its emphasis on self-initiation increases individual vulnerability to blame if proactive efforts are not successful. At the same time, there are many forces in organizations that act to stifle proactivity. The notion of passive obedience to authority (Milgram, 1974), well embedded in most individuals' psyche by adulthood, is reinforced by hierarchical organizational structures that place leaders in authority over others. Similarly, an array of leader biases can serve to stifle voice and proactivity, such as a confirmation bias, in which leaders attend only to information that supports their own thinking (Ashford, Sutcliffe, & Christianson, 2009). These scholars concluded: "for a variety of reasons, leaders discourage, resist, and ignore voice" (p. 195). Proactivity is also focused on the long term, yet many aspects in organizations reinforce short-term and reactive approaches to problems. For example, Repenning and Sterman (2002) demonstrated how, because managers often believe getting people to work harder is the key to improvement, they tend to introduce changes to technology that tightly monitor and control worker activities, which in turn generates short-term and inflexible thinking among those in the system. Altogether, several forces operate to create and reinforce employee passivity in organizations.

In light of these forces, we suggest that leaders in organizations who want to cultivate staff proactivity will need to take deliberate, intentional steps both to motivate individuals' willingness to behave proactively as well as to enhance their capability for this way of behaving. In this chapter, we propose a model of leading for proactivity in which we identify multiple pathways by which leaders can influence their staff's motivation and capability to be proactive. This model contributes to existing research by suggesting a set of precise and testable pathways by which leaders can shape proactivity. A further important contribution of this model is that we distinguish team-oriented leader inputs that have cross-level effects on individuals' motivation and proactivity from person-oriented inputs that have individual-level effects on motivation and proactivity. We also distinguish direct effects and indirect effects of leadership on proactivity, showing how leaders can shape proactivity not only by their particular actions, but also by the work designs, climate, and practices they put in place.

First we describe how we conceptualize proactivity in this chapter. We then describe existing research regarding how leadership relates to proactive behaviors. We then put forward our model of leading for proactivity. We conclude by identifying various ways to extend this model, such as considering leading for the proactivity of higher-level entities (e.g., teams and organizations) and other directions for research, such as the value of identifying individual attributes that are likely to be associated with leading for proactivity.

Understanding Proactivity

Proactivity has been conceptualized from different perspectives, including an individual difference, a behavioral, and a goal process perspective. From the individual difference perspective, Bateman and Crant (1993: 105) proposed the concept of proactive personality to describe a person "who is relative unconstrained by situational forces and who effects environmental change." Proactive personality is distinct from the big five personality dimensions and related personality variables (Bateman & Crant, 1993), and predicts various proactive behaviors, such as network building (Lambert, Eby, & Reeves, 2006; Thompson, 2005); proactive socialization (Kammeyer-Mueller & Wanberg, 2003); career initiative (Seibert et al., 2001); and change-oriented behaviors such as taking charge, individual innovation, problem prevention, and voice (Parker & Collins, 2010). Nevertheless, although a personality-based approach explains why some individual are more proactive than others, considering proactivity as a trait does not help us to understand the role that environmental factors—such as leadership—have in shaping proactive action.

A more useful perspective from this stance is to consider proactive *behavior*. Studies have focused on a range of proactive behaviors, such as proactive socialization (e.g., Thompson, 2005), career initiative (e.g., Seibert et al., 2001), individual innovation (e.g., Scott & Bruce, 1994), taking charge (e.g., Morrison & Phelps, 1999), and proactive feedback seeking (e.g., Ashford, Blatt, & VandeWalle, 2003). In recent times, scholars have sought to understand what these diverse proactive behaviors have in common. Conceptually, it has been recognized that, even though in different domains, these behaviors all involve self-initiated and future-focused efforts to change the situation and/or oneself (Grant & Ashford, 2008; Parker, Williams, & Turner, 2006). Empirically, in an effort to synthesize this literature, Parker and Collins (2010) identified three higher order factors that have in common behaviors that are proactive but that vary in the goals of this proactivity. The higher order categories include proactive goals: to achieve a better fit between the individual and their environment ("proactive person–environment fit" behavior, such as feedback inquiry, job-role negotiation, career initiative); to improve the internal organizational environment ("proactive work behavior," such as taking charge, voice, individual innovation, and problem prevention), and to achieve a better fit between the organization or unit and its wider environment ("proactive strategic behavior," such as strategic scanning and issue selling).

From this behavioral perspective, it is important to be clear why proactivity is distinct from related ways of behaving. An early confusion concerned whether proactive behavior is just a type of citizenship. However, scholars have argued that citizenship behaviors such as helping can be executed in a passive, reactive way, or they can be executed in a more proactive, anticipatory way (Grant & Ashford,

2008; Parker et al., 2010). Consistent with this idea, a recent meta-analysis showed more proactive forms of citizenship involving bringing about positive modifications at work were distinct from less proactive forms of citizenship involving maintaining the social context at work (Chiaburu, Oh, Berry, Li, & Gardner, 2011). Behaving proactively is also distinct from creativity, when the latter is defined as "the production of novel and useful ideas" (Amabile, Conti, Coon, Lazenby, & Herron, 1996). Proactivity involves actively trying to bring about a future change, and this might or might not be a "new" idea. A similar distinction applies to proactivity and individual-level innovation. Conceptually, individual-level innovation is broader than individual-level proactivity because innovation includes idea generation whereas proactivity does not, as well as narrower than proactivity because innovation applies to novel ideas only[1].

A further and more recent conceptual development, beyond considering proactivity as a way of behaving, has been to recognize that proactivity is not a single action but involves a broader goal process (Bindl, Parker, Totterdell, & Hagger-Johnson, 2012; Frese & Fay, 2001; Grant & Ashford, 2008; Parker et al., 2010). Based on the two-stage motivation theory (Chen & Kanfer, 2006), Parker et al. (2010) suggested that when an individual tries to bring about a different future, he or she engages in conscious goal-directed processes, including both goal generation and goal striving. Goal generation involves envisioning, setting, and planning to bring about a proactive goal, whereas goal striving involves the concrete steps to achieve this goal, including persisting in the face of obstacles, as well as reflecting on these actions and their consequences. In support of a process view of proactivity, Bindl et al. (2012) showed evidence for the distinctiveness of two elements of both proactive goal generation (envisioning and planning) and proactive goal striving (enacting and reflecting), and showed these elements have distinct antecedents.

In sum, proactivity has been conceptualized as a personality trait, as a way of behaving that is applicable across many domains, and as a goal process. In this chapter, we draw particularly on the latter two perspectives because our interest is in how proactivity can be enhanced through leadership.

Leadership and Proactivity: Existing Studies

Because proactive behavior aims to bring about change, which can feel psychologically risky to the initiator, leaders' appreciation, encouragement, and support of new ideas and changes have been consistently found to be associated with more proactive behavior of their subordinates. Supportive and empowering behaviors such as encouraging free expression of ideas in a nonevaluative atmosphere, encouraging employee participation, keeping employees informed, and rewarding good performance predict various forms of proactive behavior, such as the number of rewarded suggestions of an employee (Frese, Teng, & Wijnen, 1999), innovation behavior (Janssen, 2005; Pieterse, Van Knippenberg, Schippers, & Stam, 2010), personal initiative (Ohly, Sonnentag, & Pluntke, 2006), and proactive service performance (Rank, Carsten, Unger, & Spector, 2007). Studies have also shown that transformational leadership—which includes establishing a clear vision, providing individualized support, stimulating thinking, and demonstrating integrity—is positively associated with employees' innovation (Jansen, Vera, & Crossan, 2009; Rank, Nelson, Allen, & Xu, 2009), organizationally oriented proactivity (e.g., suggesting ideas for solutions for company problems), and interpersonally oriented proactivity (e.g., helping to orient new colleagues) (Belschak & Den Hartog, 2010).

In a related vein, factors such as trust in leaders and leaders' emotional intelligence can lead to more voice behavior or creativity (Gao, Janssen, & Shi, 2011; Rego, Sousa, Pina e Cunha, Correia, & Saur-Amaral, 2007), although sometimes these relationships have been shown to be contingent. For example, Premeaux and Bedeian (2003) reported that trust in a supervisor can enhance speaking up, in particular among employees who tend to focus on their own inner attitudes, emotions, and dispositions (low self-monitoring).

Coincident with evidence for the effects of positive leader behaviors, negative leader behaviors appear to inhibit proactivity. For example, abusive leadership was associated with lower ratings of prosocial voice behaviors, in part because it reduced perceptions of interactional justice (Rafferty & Restubog, 2011). In a similar study, abusive supervision predicted lowered voice through increased psychological detachment (Burris, Detert, & Chiaburu, 2008). Rank et al. (2009) showed that active management by exception (involving close monitoring of subordinates to detect errors) was associated with lower levels of innovation behavior, especially for low self-monitoring individuals (who the authors suggested are more likely to reject the controlling influences of negative leaders).

The quality of the exchange relationship between leader and employee can also affect proactive behavior. For example, higher leader–member exchange (LMX) has been positively related to individual innovation and creativity (Janssen & Van Yperen, 2004; Scott & Bruce, 1994; Tierney, Farmer, & Graen, 1999; Van Dyne, Jehn, & Cummings, 2002), voice (Botero & Van Dyne, 2009; Burris et al., 2008; Van Dyne, Kamdar, & Joireman, 2008), and change-oriented organizational citizenship behaviors (Bettencourt, 2004). Tierney et al. (1999) further indicated that the impact of LMX relationships on individual creativity is stronger among people who are "cognitive adaptors" rather than "cognitive innovators" because adaptors tend to be compliant and easily influenced by the quality of LMX toward creativity. Van Dyne et al. (2002) also indicated that better LMX relationships buffer the negative impact of work or home strain on creative performance at work. This is because employees in better LMX relationships are more likely to obtain substantial resources (e.g., higher autonomy, more time), individualized consideration, and guidance from their leaders and thus minimize distracting aspects of work and home strain due to this supportive basis and can devote more time and effort to think beyond the job requirement.

Finally, some studies have found null or inconsistent findings of leader behavior on proactive outcomes. For example, Axtell et al. (2000) reported a null relationship between team leader support and individual innovation; and Parker et al. (2006) reported that, once autonomy was controlled, there was no positive effect of supervisory support on wire makers' proactivity.

The preceding review shows that leadership matters—at least some of the time—for individual proactivity. In general, positive leader behaviors such as support and empowerment appear to predict proactivity whereas negative leader behaviors such as aggression suppress proactivity. However, this body of work does not provide a coherent framework for guiding further research, in part because little attention has been given to the pathways linking leadership and proactivity. Without a more precise understanding of why leadership relates to proactivity, it is difficult to integrate the literature and to make sense of potential contingency factors. Moreover, insufficient attention has been given to what sort of leadership is most important for proactivity, relative to other behaviors. We therefore propose an integrating framework to guide future research on leadership and proactive work behavior[2], which we elaborate next.

Proposed Model of Leading for Proactivity

The model has as its ultimate outcome individual job performance, or observable actions individuals take that are relevant to the goals of the organization (Campbell, McHenry, & Wise, 1990). We propose that proactive goal regulation, involving the generation of a proactive goal and striving to achieve that goal, will lead to higher individual job performance. This is consistent with prior research showing that proactivity predicts job performance (Crant, 1995; Grant, Parker, & Collins, 2009; Morrison, 1993; Thompson, 2005; Van Dyne & Le Pine, 1998) (Figure 18.1).

Next, the model indicates that proactive goal regulation is shaped by three motivational states: can do, reason to, and energized to. This part of the model derives from the integrative model of Parker et al. (2010) summarizing how motivation can shape proactivity. Regarding the can do pathway, drawing on theoretical perspectives such as self-regulation theory, scholars have argued that various proactive acts such as taking charge likely involve a deliberate decision process in which the individual assesses the likely outcomes of his or her efforts (Dutton & Ashford, 1993; Morrison & Phelps, 1999; Parker et al., 2006). In essence, individuals ask themselves can do questions such as "Can I do this?"; "Is it feasible?"; and "How high are the costs?" Individuals with high self-efficacy, or a belief in their own capabilities for proactive action, are more likely to weigh potential costs of proactivity more positively, believe they can cope with setbacks, and perceive a higher likelihood of success relative to individuals with low self-efficacy. Empirically, there is strong evidence for the role of self-efficacy in predicting several types of proactivity (e.g., Axtell et al., 2000; Bledow & Frese, 2009; Brown, Cober, Kane, & Shalhoop, 2006; Frese, Garst, & Fay, 2007; Gruman, Saks, & Zweig, 2006; Kanfer, Wanberg, & Kantrowitz, 2001; Ohly & Fritz, 2007; Raub & Liao, 2012; Saks & Ashforth, 1999; Speier & Frese, 1997). Likewise, evidence suggests that beliefs about whether one can exert control or have an impact also influence proactivity. For example, Ashford and her colleagues (1998) showed that women are more likely to voice gender equity issues when they perceive a higher chance of gaining attention for their issue. Beliefs about potential costs or image risks are also important. For example, Tidwell and Sias (2005) found that the perceived social cost in information seeking in organizations has a negative impact on overt information-seeking behavior among newcomers.

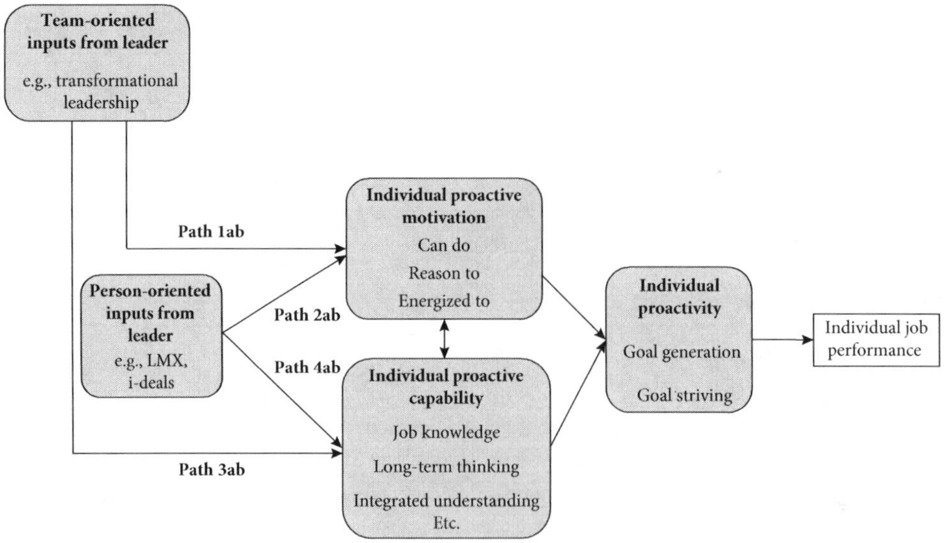

Figure 18.1. Summarizes our Proposed Framework. In this Section, we Describe the Overall Model Moving from Right to Left, Prior to Delving More Deeply into the Leadership Pathways.

The second motivation pathway is summarized as a "reason to" path. As described by (Eccles & Wigfield, 2002: 112): "[E]ven if people are certain they can do a task, they may have no compelling reason to do it." Parker et al. (2010) argued for the importance of internalized or autonomous, rather than controlled, forms of motivation for prompting proactivity. Internalized forms of motivation can be derived from meeting fundamental needs, such as indicated by studies showing that a desire for control prompts proactive socialization (Ashford & Black, 1996). Internalized forms of motivation can also be derived from one's commitment toward career, teams, and organizations. Studies have shown, for example, that affective commitment predicts proactive behavior (Belschak & Den Hartog, 2010; Burris et al., 2008; Chiaburu, Marinova, & Lim, 2007; Den Hartog & Belschak, 2007; M. A. Griffin, Neal, & Parker, 2007; Rank et al., 2007; Strauss, Griffin, & Rafferty, 2009). Internalized forms of motivation can also result from the internalization of external goals or values, or an identified regulation process. As example of this is having a broader role perception in which individuals define their role in a flexible way (Parker, Wall, & Jackson, 1997) or a sense of felt responsibility to bring about changes (Morrison & Phelps, 1999). These types of identified regulation have been shown to predict an array of forms of proactivity, such as personal initiative (Bledow & Frese, 2009), taking charge (Morrison & Phelps, 1999), voice (Fuller, Marler, & Hester, 2006; Grant & Mayer, 2009; Parker & Collins, 2010; Tangirala & Ramanujam, 2008), change-oriented behavior (Choi, 2007), proactive problem solving (Dorenbosch, Engen, & Verhagen, 2005; Parker et al., 2006), and feedback seeking (Ashford & Cummings, 1985).

The third motivation pathway is an affective one, which Parker et al. (2010) summarized as "energized to" motivation. Positive affect is likely to influence the selection of proactive goals because it expands thinking and results in more flexible cognitive processes (Fredrickson, 1998, 2001; Isen, 1999), and will likely promote proactive goal striving because affect invokes feelings of energy (Shraga & Shirom, 2009) and can facilitate self-efficacy and persistence (Tsai, Chen, & Liu, 2007). Several studies have shown that positive affect links to proactive behavior, such as proactive socialization (Ashforth, Sluss, & Saks, 2007), personal initiative (Den Hartog & Belschak, 2007), and taking charge (Fritz & Sonnentag, 2009). Bindl et al. (2012) presented evidence for the more specific role of activated positive affect (feelings of enthusiasm, inspiration, etc.) for multiple elements of proactive goal regulation, and showed the incremental role of activated positive affect in predicting proactivity beyond self-efficacy and commitment.

Next, the model proposes that proactive goal regulation can be shaped by individual capabilities, or individual knowledge, skills, and abilities (KSAs). This pathway reflects evidence, albeit less well-developed than that for motivation, regarding the role of capabilities such as depth and breadth of knowledge and long-term thinking for proactivity. For example, Frese and Fay (2001) argued that deep job knowledge and cognitive ability are resources that allow the individual to handle the job challenges more effectively, thereby promoting the development of mastery, self-efficacy, and stronger aspirations for control, which in turn lead to personal initiative. Studies support the role of KSAs in boosting proactivity. In their eastern German longitudinal study, cognitive ability predict personal initiative (Fay & Frese, 2001), and in a further study (Frese & Hilligloh, 1994 cited in Frese & Fay, 2001), job qualifications (a summary measure of job knowledge and skill) predicted personal initiative. Other studies have reported links (albeit of relatively modest size) between educational background and proactive outcomes, such as proactive job search (Kanfer et al., 2001) and voicing suggestions (LePine & Van Dyne, 1998). In a study that compared innovation champions against non-champions, Howell and Boies (2004) showed that contextual knowledge predicted individuals' packaging ideas for promotion. Other cognitive variables have also been shown to be important. Because proactive behavior involves bringing about future change, individuals need to engage in future-focused thinking, such as envisioning opportunities in the future, identifying potential problems, and paying attention to and processing information in the environment. Consistent with this reasoning, Parker and Collins (2010) identified that individuals with a future-oriented time perspective are more likely to report higher levels of some types of proactivity.

The model thus proposes two key determinants of proactive goal regulation—motivation and capability—which is consistent with models that identify motivation and knowledge/skill as the two primary determinants of job performance (Tesluk & Jacobs, 1998). The model also recognizes that these sets of determinants can influence each other, as depicted by the double-headed arrow between them. For example, showing how motivation influences capabilities, individuals with high proactive motivation will put more cognitive effort into thinking, which will develop their thinking styles and cognitive complexity in the long term. Likewise, showing how capabilities influence motivation, individuals who have strong interpersonal skills will likely experience stronger self-efficacy for introducing change, and therefore experience stronger can do proactive motivation.

Next the model proposes that leadership can shape proactive goal regulation through motivation and capability. Whereas the elements of the model discussed earlier have been articulated elsewhere (Parker et al., 2010), little systematic attention has been given to the various ways that leadership might influence motivation and capability. As we elaborate shortly, we propose that leadership influences motivation and capability through team-oriented inputs (Paths 1ab, 3ab) as well as person-oriented inputs (paths 2ab, 4ab), a distinction identified by Chen and Kanfer (2006) in their multilevel model of individual and team motivation. These effects can be both direct (paths 1a, 2a, 3a, 4a) or indirect (paths 1b, 2b, 3b, 4b). We discuss these pathways next, focusing first on the links between leadership and motivation, and next on the links between leadership and capability.

Leading for Proactive Motivation

We distinguish between team-oriented and person-oriented leadership inputs as influences on proactive motivation. Chen and Kanfer (2006: 226) made this distinction to recognize "the dynamic, mutual influences of the individual and the team context on individual and team motivation and motivation outcomes." This differentiation between types of inputs helps to understand how a leader can shape employees' proactive motivation via a team-oriented, cross-level process as well as via an individual-oriented process. Team-oriented stimuli affect the team as a whole, or all team members, and so represent a contextual effect on individual motivation, whereas person-oriented stimuli affect a specific team member, rather than all team members, and so represent an individual effect on motivation. In understanding how leaders can shape employees' work motivation, Chen and Kanfer (2006: 253) argued that leader behaviors such as transformational leadership should be considered as team-oriented inputs because "transformational leadership theory suggests that effective leaders motivate their group of followers by transforming the values and priorities of followers and motivating them to perform beyond their expectations." In contrast, leader behavior in a LMX relationship between a leader and a specific subordinate should be considered as person-oriented inputs because a leader can develop different LMX relationships with different subordinates (Graen & Uhl-Bien, 1995), and thus behaviors in each relationship will differ across subordinates. Both team-oriented and person-oriented leadership inputs can have direct effects because what a leader says or does can directly affect employee motivation (path 1a, path 2a), as well as indirectly affect on motivation because leaders can shape climate, work design, and other practices, which in turn affect employee motivation (path 1b, path 2b).

Direct Effects of Team-oriented Leadership on Motivation

Theoretically, there are many ways that leaders can directly influence individual's "can do" motivation. Self-efficacy beliefs are constructed from four sources: mastery experiences, vicarious experiences, social persuasion, and physical and emotional states (Bandura, 1999). Accordingly, leaders can enhance employees' self-efficacy by providing opportunities to master tasks, being a role model for engaging in proactive behavior, verbally expressing confidence in employees that they can engage in proactive behavior, and generating positive feelings while reducing negative feelings such as anxiety. It is also important that individuals experience a sense that their proactive actions will be worthwhile, that they can impact the situation. For example, leaders can shape the perceived instrumentality of voice through how they react when an individual speaks out (Detert & Trevino, 2010). Ashford et al. (2009) proposed various ways that leaders can convey to employees that their voice can make a difference, including actively attending to the information they raise, incorporating employees' ideas into their actions or decisions, providing credible explanations as to why ideas were not used, and repeatedly communicating a strong rationale for the importance of voice.

In one of the few studies that have considered leader behavior operationalized as a team-level input, and that has also considered proactivity-oriented outcomes, Chen, Sharma, Edinger, Shapiro, and Farh (2011) showed that team-level empowering leadership positively related to individuals' psychological empowerment, which in turn predicted individual innovative behavior. Psychological empowerment encompasses the concept of can do motivation because it includes as dimensions perceived competence (similar to self-efficacy) and perceived impact at work (similar to perceptions of controllability). It also includes self-determination and meaning, which relates to the idea of having an internalized reason to be proactive (see next). In another study, Chen, Farh, Campbell-Bush, Wu, and Wu (2013) showed that team-level transformational leadership positively related to individuals' role breadth self-efficacy, which in turn predicted innovative behavior at the individual level.

Related studies considering leadership at the individual rather than the team level also demonstrate similar roles of leadership. Although these studies have operationalized leadership at the individual level, rather than considering leadership as a team-oriented influence, we report them in this section because, theoretically, we believe the effect to be a cross-level one. Thus, transformational leadership has been found to be positively related to creative self-efficacy and creativity (Gong, Huang, & Farh, 2009), psychological empowerment, and creativity (Gumusluoglu & Ilsev, 2009; X. Zhang & Bartol, 2010), as well as to role breadth self-efficacy and more proactive behavior (Strauss et al., 2009).

Regarding a "reason to" pathway, leadership can affect individual's intrinsic motivation for proactive behavior, or their desire to engage in proactivity for its own sake because it is interesting, enjoyable, or challenging (Deci & Ryan, 2000). In the current literature, most studies examining this intrinsic motivation pathway consider leadership only at the individual level. One exception is Chen et al. (2013), who reported that team-level transformational leadership positively related to individuals' intrinsic motivation, which in turn predicted individual innovative behavior. Similarly, empowering leadership assessed at the individual level has been found to be positively associated with intrinsic motivation and thus more creative performance, including idea implementation (X. Zhang & Bartol, 2010).

Leadership can also potentially enhance individuals' feelings of commitment and responsibility (Detert & Burris, 2007). Studies suggest these types of outcomes shape proactivity. For example, several studies have indicated that leaders can enhance employees' affective commitment, which in turn enhances proactive behavior because higher affective commitment can lead an individual to devote more effort to pursue changes at work. Specifically, Michaelis, Stegmaier, and Sonntag (2009) reported that charismatic leadership and trust in top management can lead to higher affective commitment to change and thus more innovation implementation behavior of employees. Strauss et al. (2009) indicated that team leader transformational leadership can lead to higher team commitment and thus more team-oriented proactive behavior, whereas organizational leader transformational leadership can lead to higher organizational commitment and thus more organizationally oriented proactive behavior.

Whether commitment is the best indicator of an individual's "reason to" motivation needs further investigation. For example, Parker et al. (2006) reported that, with other reason-to indicators in the model (e.g., flexible role orientation), commitment did not predict proactivity. These scholars argued that individuals can be committed to an organization or work unit, but this could manifest itself with passive behaviors such as loyalty rather than proactivity. Chen et al. (2011) also found that empowerment leadership at the team level related to employees' affective commitment, but affective commitment only led to teamwork behavior and not innovative behavior. Graham and Van Dyne (2006) reported a similar finding. These authors suggested that strong attachment might motivate some employees to try to bring about improvement whereas others might like the organization because they like how it is, thereby emphasizing sustaining the status quo (see also Ashford & Barton, 2007).

Leadership can also build other forms of internal motivation, such as identified motivation, in which individuals internalize external requirements and incorporate them into their values or identity. Role expectations from leaders can provide a reason for an employee to be proactive because they shape employees' self-expectation and subsequent motivation and behavior through a self-fulfilling (Pygmalion) effect. For example, Scott and Bruce (1994) found role expectations for being innovative from leaders predicted individual innovation behavior. As a further example, Krause (2004) showed that influence-based leadership, such as using expert knowledge and information, granting of autonomy, and openness in decision-making, predicted employees' perceived need for change, which was associated with greater self-reported implementation of innovation.

In a similar vein, self-concept-based leadership theory (van Knippenberg, van Knippenberg, De Cremer, & Hogg, 2004) suggested that leaders can shape one's relational self via personal identification, or identification with one particular other person, and can shape one's collective self via social identification, or identification with a social group. Accordingly, leaders who are characterized as encouraging change, such as those high in transformational leadership, might enhance employees' proactive behavior via an identification process. Supporting this view, transformational leadership assessed at the individual level has been found to lead to more voice via personal identification and social identification (Liu, Zhu, & Yang, 2010). Authentic leadership (i.e., high in balanced information processing, authentic behavior, relational transparency, and self-awareness) assessed at the individual level can also lead to more employees' voice behavior via a personal identification process because authentic leaders are more likely to form a positive relationship with subordinates and thus generate more trust in leaders and higher work engagement (Wong, Laschinger, & Cummings, 2010).

Although a "reason to" mediating process was not measured, Griffin, Parker, and Mason (2010) showed that leader vision predicted an increase in proactivity over time for individuals high in self-efficacy. The authors argued that when leaders present a compelling vision of the future, they highlight the discrepancy between now and the future, which creates an impetus for change, or a reason to be proactive. Those with high self-efficacy respond to the discrepancy by increasing their proactivity.

Promoting the self-relevance of an issue can also increase employees' motivation to engage in thinking, which in turn will increase proactive goal regulation. Research on attitudes and persuasion indicates that individuals are more likely to devote more cognitive effort to scrutinizing presented arguments in judgment tasks when they perceive the issue at hand is relevant to themselves (Petty, Wheeler, & Tormala, 2003). In this regard, supervisors can try to increase self-relevance of issues at work to promote employees' proactive behavior for those issues. As discussed earlier, presenting a vision to employees can generate a sense of self-relevance for making the vision come true (Griffin et al., 2010), thereby prompting individuals to put in greater cognitive effort to achieving their proactive goals.

Finally, leaders can energize employees to engage in proactive behavior by activating positive feelings at work. Madjar, Oldham, and Pratt (2002) reported that support from supervisors related to employees' positive mood, which then predicted higher individual creative performance rated by supervisors. Through mood contagion effect, leaders' feelings and expression of positive emotion can also influence followers' feelings and the affective tone of teams (Bono & Ilies, 2006; Sy, Côté, & Saavedra, 2005). Thus, it is likely that when leaders are in a positive mood, their subordinates will also be in a positive mood, which can prompt greater proactive behavior.

In sum, through positive leader behaviors such as providing a vision or behaving in an empowering way, leaders can boost individual-level proactivity by boosting staff' confidence in themselves and their belief they can make a difference (can do motivation), by building staff's internalized motivation behave proactively such as through self-identification processes (reason to motivation), and by cultivating experiences of positive affect and feelings of energy (energized to motivation). We have theorized these effects as team-level leadership inputs, although thus far almost all studies (with the exception of some studies by Chen and colleagues) have operationalized them as individual-level inputs.

Indirect Effects of Team-oriented Leadership on Proactive Motivation

As well as the direct effects described in the preceding text, team-oriented leadership can indirectly affect staff motivation via its effect on other team-oriented inputs such as climate, work design, and other practices.

Information obtained from interactions with leaders will shape employees' understanding and perception of the work climate. Leaders are representatives of management practices within an organization and, as such, serve as interpretive filters of events and processes that occur in the work unit (Kozlowski & Doherty, 1989). Therefore leadership might have its effect on individual proactive motivation through climate. In a study of this pathway, Chen et al. (2013) showed that team-level support for innovation mediated the effect of transformational leadership on individual-level role breadth self-efficacy. In other words, although causal direction still needs testing, the findings suggest that transformational leadership boosts can do motivation because these leaders cultivate a climate that staff experience as supporting innovation. Such a finding makes sense. Indeed, it is possible that several of the direct effects of leadership reported in the previous section are mediated through team climate variables, such as a climate of psychological safety.

Leadership can also influence the extent to which there is a psychologically safe climate in which team members feel confident they can engage in potentially risky proactive behavior. In support of this process, a combined measure of transformational leadership and managerial openness had its effect on voice via psychological safety (Detert & Burris, 2007). Leaders' attributes or behaviors that are relevant to building a good relationship with employees, such as trust (Madjar & Ortiz-Walters, 2009), individual consideration (VandeWalle, Ganesan, Challagalla, & Brown, 2000), and availability (Carmeli, Reiter-Palmon, & Ziv, 2010), all potentially increase psychological safety (or decrease perceived costs of proactivity). Leaders' ethical behavior and promotion of justice can also promote employees' sense of safety because employees know that they will be treated fairly when they propose challenging ideas. Supporting this, Walumbwa and Schaubroeck (2009) reported that ethical leadership was associated with follower's perception of psychological safety, and in turn, their level of voice.

Several other studies have shown how leader behavior shapes climate, although not necessarily shown a link to individual-level motivation or behavior. For example, Gonzalez-Roma, Peiro, and Tordera (2002) reported that leaders use of informing behaviors, such as communicating role expectation, predicted the strength of innovation climate perceptions, and Gil, Rico, Alcover, and Barrasa (2005) reported that change-oriented leadership predicted a positive team climate. Other studies similarly show how leadership relates to team climates likely to support proactivity (e.g., Chen, 2007; Eisenbeiss, van Knippenberg, & Boerner, 2008; D. Jung, Wu, & Chow, 2008; Sarros, Cooper, & Santora, 2008).

Leadership might also have an indirect influence on proactive motivation through work design. There is strong evidence and theory to suggest that work design shapes employees' proactive motivation. In the sphere of proactivity, most attention has been given to job autonomy because job autonomy can develop expertise (Leach, Wall, & Jackson, 2003) and facilitate learning (Daniels, Boocock, Glover, Hartley, & Holland, 2009), provide mastery experiences at work that can help to enhance employees' self-efficacy at work (Parker, 1998), and boost positive affect (e.g., Parker & Wall, 1998). Job autonomy also denotes a weak situation (Meyer, Dalal, & Hermida, 2010) that allows employees to take actions that challenge the status quo. Leaders can influence the team-level work design of employees by changing the objective characteristics of jobs for team members such as by giving the team more decision-making responsibility. Indeed, suggesting a degree of conceptual confusion between leadership and work design, some leadership styles are characterized in terms of work design. For example, empowering leadership is typically defined in terms of delegating employees' greater decision-making authority. Leaders can also influence how individuals perceive their job characteristics—regardless of their actual job characteristics—because individuals rely on cues from their social contexts to make assessments about work environments

(Salancik & Pfeffer, 1977). Supporting this perspective, Griffin (1981) reported that leader behaviors changed employees' perceptions of their work after three months even without tangible changes to actual jobs. In another study, Piccolo and Colquitt (2006) reported that transformational leaders can shape employees' perceptions of core job characteristics, which in turn affects their level of citizenship behavior.

Finally, although often constrained as a result of broader organization-wide policies, leaders can sometimes shape processes and systems such as performance appraisals or reward systems that in turn affect proactivity. Leaders' justice in appraisal practices is likely to be especially important. Proactive behavior is typically not tied to formal rewards and penalty systems in organizational systems because it is self-initiated and not part of an explicit job description (Van Dyne & Le Pine, 1998). As such, leaders' justice in carrying out appraisals potentially signals to employees whether or not they will be treated fairly when pursuing risky proactive behaviors. Supervisors' procedural justice has been found to be positively related to employees' taking charge behavior, although only when taking charge was also regarded as a part of one's job role (McAllister, Kamdar, Morrison, & Turban, 2007). Leaders can also influence selection and hiring, which in turn shapes proactivity. Ashford et al. (2009) reported studies suggesting that Lincoln selected presidential rivals and actively sought their views, whereas Bush selected individuals with similar perspectives and backgrounds, potentially stifling speaking out and other such proactive behaviors.

In sum, leaders have the possibility to influence proactivity not only through what they directly say and do, but also through the climate, work design, and practices/systems that they can establish or shape. Of course, we recognize each of these elements is influenced by other forces that are often beyond the control of individual leaders, such as organizational-level structures and policies and technological constraints (Parker, Wall, & Cordery, 2001).

Direct Effects of Person-oriented Leadership on Motivation

Beyond team-level leadership, leaders can influence individual-level states and processes via *person-oriented stimuli* (also referred to by Chen & Kanfer, 2006, as discretionary stimuli). Person-oriented leadership is directed to specific team members rather than the team as a whole. Leader-member exchange, as well as the provision of individual feedback or the establishing of "i-deals" (idiosyncratic deals), are examples of person-oriented stimuli provided by leaders (other person-oriented stimuli relevant to proactivity include, for example, individual attributes such as proactive personality[3]). As with team-level leadership, we recognize that person-oriented inputs from leaders can operate directly (e.g., a leader behaves in a particular way, which shapes the motivation of the employee, path 2a) or indirectly (the leader might give high performers more job discretion, and this greater job autonomy motivates more proactivity, path 2b). We discuss the direct pathways here.

Leader–member exchange refers to the quality of the relationship developed between leaders and their followers (Graen & Uhl-Bien, 1991). Much research has investigated how high-quality relationships develop, as well as the positive outcomes of high-quality exchange for leaders, followers, work units, and organizations, including innovation outcomes.

We expect that a high-quality LMX will enhance can do, reason to, and energized to motivation for proactivity. Several studies have shown that LMX predicts innovation (Basu & Green, 1997; Scott & Bruce, 1994; Tierney et al., 1999), with these findings being explained in terms of those with quality relationships being given greater resources, decision-latitude, and autonomy, as well as the associated trust in the relationship being a resource that mitigates against image risks and threats, thereby enhancing can do motivation by reducing perceived costs of proactivity. When supervisors trust and respect an employee they are also more likely to evaluate the ideas of this individual more favorably (Zhou & Woodman, 2003), which again is likely to promote can do motivation. A good quality relationship between leaders and employees potentially enhances an individual's sense of psychological safety that they have room to deviate their work behavior from norms (Graen & Uhl-Bien, 1995). For example, Liao, Liu, and Loi (2010) showed that a higher LMX relationship is associated with employee creativity via self-efficacy, although only when LMX differentiation is low because it is then that employees are more likely to perceive injustice in the flow of resources.

Consistent with a reason to process, Yuan and Woodman (2010) reported that higher quality LMX relationships predicted individual innovation via increasing individual's belief that innovation will enhance job performance, and via expected image gains. LMX did not relate to expected image risks. In the same vein, Burris et al. (2008) reported that employees with poor quality LMX relationships are less likely to engage in voice because they experience detachment, and are essentially withdrawing from the organization. Interestingly, commitment did not predict voice in this study, consistent with our earlier argument that commitment may not be enough to promote voice, whereas detachment is enough to stifle voice.

Leadership studies that highlight the need for different leader behaviors for different individuals can be seen as similar to LMX studies, and are best classified as person-oriented leadership stimuli. Thus, Wang and Casimir (2007) reported that whether leaders encourage subordinates to be creative depends on leaders' trust in the reliability and loyalty of their subordinates. The authors concluded that encouraging staff creativity might expose leaders to risks, so leaders are perhaps willing to do only this if they trust their staff, consistent with a person-oriented approach.

Indirect Effects of Person-oriented Leadership on Proactive Motivation

In the same way that team-oriented leadership can indirectly influence proactivity, we propose that LMX can operate more indirectly. One possible indirect process is through i-deals, which are personalized employment conditions that individuals have negotiated. Hornung, Rousseau, and Glaser (2008) have described how supervisors make i-deals regarding employee development, flexibility, and work load reduction. By definition, these deals are with individuals rather than with the whole team. Evidence suggests that i-deals have various positive motivational and performance consequences, such as organizational commitment (Ng & Feldman, 2010), work performance and job involvement (Hornung, Rousseau, & Glaser, 2009), and citizenship behavior (Anand, Vidyarthi, Liden, & Rousseau, 2010). Therefore it is reasonable to expect that leaders might promote employee proactivity through i-deals, although there are currently no studies supporting this possibility. For example, offering a developmental i-deal in which an individual can participate in more on-the-job development opportunities (Hornung et al., 2008) is likely to boost an individual's self-efficacy, as well as generate a desire to reciprocate to the supervisor.

Scott and Bruce (1994) showed that a higher quality LMX not only directly predicted innovation behavior, but also predicted a perception that there is support from the organization for innovation and employees' perception of resources supply. Thus in this case, LMX indirectly affected individual innovation through individual-climate perceptions.

Leading for Proactive Capability Development

Earlier we argued that there are many paths by which leaders' can shape their team members' proactive motivation, which in turn leads them to set and strive for proactive goals. However, as discussed earlier in this chapter, individual proactivity is also potentially shaped by team members' knowledge, skills, and abilities, or their capability. In this section, we suggest that leaders can influence the proactivity of their team members through fostering the development of knowledge, skills, and abilities that are important for proactivity.[4] We discuss the direct effects of leadership (both team-oriented, path 3a, and person-oriented, path 4a) on individual-level capabilities, as well as the indirect effects of both types of leadership (path 3b, 4b) on individual-level capabilities. In our discussion, although we recognize them as theoretically distinct processes, we discuss team-oriented and person-oriented leadership effects together as the existing research is insufficiently well developed to consider this nuance.

Leadership and Its Direct Effects on Individual Capability

Can leadership influence individuals' knowledge and cognitive capabilities? This is a question that has had surprisingly little attention. Clearly, leaders can influence the acquisition of staff knowledge through supporting staff training and development, both in terms of formal learning and development opportunities and through on-the-job assignments and projects. However, there are other potential paths. Lord, Hannah, and Jennings (2011) argued that leaders can enhance or inhibit the development of "requisite complexity" in their staff. Requisite complexity encompasses cognitive complexity, self-complexity, affective complexity, and social complexity, and refers to "the ability of an individual to perceive and react to the internal and external organizational environment from multiple and sufficiently complexity perspectives to that the complexity of individual understanding achieves congruence with the complexity of the situation" (p. 109). Lord et al. argued two key ways that leaders enhance requisite complexity: through promoting goal structures that facilitate learning (e.g., a learning goal orientation), and by using feedback processes that encourage creativity and invention. These possibilities are supported by DeRue and Wellman (2009), who showed that engaging in greater developmental challenges on-the-job predicted learning and skill development, but only for individuals with a learning orientation and who receive feedback from the context. Similarly, Smircich and Morgan (1982: 258) suggested that leaders can influence employees by "mobilizing meaning, articulating and defining what has previously remained implicit or unsaid, by inventing images and meanings that provide a focus for new attention, and by consolidating, confronting, or changing prevailing wisdom."

As a further example, Dutton and colleagues (2001) identified three types of knowledge that facilitate effective issue selling to top management: relational knowledge (e.g., understanding who will be affected by the issue), normative knowledge (e.g., understanding legitimate decision making approaches in the context), and strategic knowledge (e.g. understanding the organization's goal). These scholars argue that individuals who possess this knowledge and understanding are more likely to engage in particular issue selling "moves" (such as the way to present issues, the way to connect an issue to other issues or goals), which in turn enhance the likelihood that issue selling will be successful. These categories of knowledge are potentially important for other types of proactivity, such as taking charge and individual innovation. For example, if individuals have a good understanding as to who will be effective by their proactivity, they can then take steps to incorporate the perspectives of these individuals, enhancing the likelihood that the change will be successful. Leaders can enhance their staff's relational, normative, and strategic knowledge directly, through their communication, as well as indirectly through work design.

Individuals' thinking and cognition is also expanded by positive mood. In the broaden and build model, Fredrickson (2001) argued that positive affect expands thought–action repertoires, and that over the longer term, this builds enduring personal resources such as psychological resilience. As mentioned previously, positive affect can widen an individual's perspective and increase perceived possibilities to bring about constructive changes. Because of this cognitive expansion, positive affect can also lead an individual to see more alternatives to achieve a proactive goal when he or she encounters obstacles, enhancing psychological resilience and persistency in leading proactive changes (Frese & Fay, 2001). Therefore by creating a positive climate, in which team members experience positive feelings, leaders can potentially build the capacity of their workforce for proactivity. Studies have indicated approaches that leaders can induce subordinates' positive feelings at work such as presenting transformational leadership behaviors (Bono, Foldes, Vinson, & Muros, 2007), supporting subordinates (Cole, Bruch, & Vogel, 2006), and expressing positive emotion (Bono & Ilies, 2006).

We discussed earlier in the chapter how leaders can motivate greater deliberative thinking and cognitive effort by enhancing situational relevance. Leaders can potentially influence long-term thinking through processes such as vision, reinforcing long-term perspectives in decision making, and long-term goal setting.

Leaders can also actively prompt employees to generate proactive ideas by influencing employees' perception of situations. For example, in the problem-solving context, Reiter-Palmon and Illies (2004) suggested that leaders can promote cognitive processes for creative problem solving by: (1) setting a problem-solving goal to find a construction for an ill-defined problem that usually has multiple, even competing goals, (2) providing more time, (3) creating a team with higher diversity to maximize opportunities to expose to different ideas, (4) ensuring accessibility of information, and (5) motivating the integration of new concepts. In addition, by challenging employees' existing concepts and way of thinking (i.e., intellectual stimulation), supervisors also directly shape employees' thinking to see different side of issues and thus more proactivity. Intellectual stimulation is one dimension of transformational leadership. As noted earlier, there is good evidence that transformational leadership is associated with proactivity, and it is possible (although currently untested) that one explanation for the association is that transformational leaders cultivate and develop the thinking skills required for proactivity. For example, Redmond et al. (1993) found that leaders can enhance employees' creative ideas by helping an individual to find more alternative solutions and to formulate better plans for problem solving.

Leaders can also shape how the team coordinates and communicates, which in turn potentially facilitates employees proactivity because it enhances team members' knowledge. For example, Anderson (1966) reported that leaders' initiation of structure (i.e., establishing well-defined channels of communication, patterns of organization, and other means of getting the job done) was positively related to student group creativity. This finding was explained in terms of the leadership style facilitating a flow of information that builds individuals' knowledge-based and opportunity-recognition skill. In another study, leaders trained to pose a problem, avoid suggesting solutions, and share information and make it part of the statement of the problem are more likely to lead their teams to generate innovative and effective solutions during a team discussion than untrained leaders (Maier & McRay, 1972). This is because the trained leader behavior encourages an idea-generation process by delaying an idea-evaluation process.

Leadership and Indirect Effects on Individual Capability

Leaders can also support capability development through work design. Studies have shown a link between enhanced autonomy and cognitive development (Kohn & Schooler, 1978); the acquisition of new task knowledge (Leach et al., 2003; Wall, Jackson, & Davids, 1992); and the acquisition of broader knowledge about the organization, or "integrated understanding" (Parker & Axtell, 2001). Theoretically, for example, job autonomy promotes a deeper understanding of the task (Frese & Zapf, 1994). Similar learning and development mechanisms have been proposed for group work design. For example, it has been suggested that autonomous work group members learn from each other (Pearce & Ravlin, 1987) and, because they assume more responsibility for external coordination with others in other organizations, they also gain more understanding of the broader work process (Batt, 1999).

Summary

Although considerable prior research has shown that leadership relates to proactivity, the lack of an integrating model makes it difficult to understand when and why leadership makes a difference to subordinates' proactivity. In the preceding text we have suggested a testable set of pathways by which leadership can shape individuals' proactive motivation and capability, and thereby prompt individuals to set and strive for proactive goals. An important contribution of this model is to explicitly distinguish team-oriented leadership that affects all team members from more person-oriented forms that focus on individual relationships. Most prior research linking leadership and proactivity has tended to assume leadership is a person-oriented input, whereas theoretically it is often more accurately considered as a team-oriented input. We particularly urge more studies like that of Chen et al. (2013), which is one of the few studies to consider leadership as a team-level input that has cross-level influences on individual-level motivation and proactive behavior. It is also the case that most prior research has focused on how leadership affects employee motivation, with significantly less attention given to how leaders might build employees' capability for proactivity. A further contribution of the model is that it highlights not only the direct ways in which leaders' shape employee proactivity, but also how leaders can shape work climates, job design, performance appraisals, and other such team-level inputs, thereby indirectly influencing proactivity. Practically, our model suggests there are multiple vehicles through which leaders can seek to overcome some of the natural forces toward passivity in organizations that we identified earlier.

Extensions to the Model and Other Future Research Directions

We recognize several ways that the proposed model can be developed further, including considering team-level effects, reciprocal processes, moderating pathways, and distinguishing goal generation and goal striving. We also recommend the need for research that more explicitly compares proactive behaviors relative to other behaviors; considers multiple types of leader behavior simultaneously; attends to the role of more senior leaders on individual-level proactivity; and identifies leader attributes associated with leading for proactivity and how these can be developed. We elaborate these directions next.

Extensions to the Leading for Proactivity Model

Our focus in this chapter has been on individual-level mediating processes. However, beyond the aforementioned paths, an alternative way that leadership could affect individuals' proactive motivation is through team-level proactive motivation. That is, leaders can affect team-level motivation states that, via bottom-down processes, then influence individual proactive motivation. As an example, leaders might build team identification, the degree that individuals define themselves as members of a group, which then trickles down to enhance an individual's reason to engage in team-oriented proactivity. For example, Liu and Phillips (2010) reported that, because they enhance a collective vision, transformational leaders can help to build a strong team identity. A strong team identity is likely to motivate individuals to exert effort into finding solutions to enhance team effectiveness (Hirst, van Dick, & van Knippenberg, 2009), as well as to be willing to share knowledge with team members (Y. Liu & Phillips, 2010), which potentially builds team-member capability. No studies on proactivity have examined this type of process, although Zhou, Wang, Chen, and Shi, (2012) and Chen, Lam, and Zhong (2007) reported that team-level empowerment had a cross-level effect in predicating individual-level empowerment. Because an individual's sense of empowerment has been found to be positively related to proactive behavior as we reviewed previously, their findings therefore suggest that team-level motivation covered by the concept of empowerment (i.e., competence, impact, and self-determination and meaning) can enhance individual-level motivation and thus proactive behavior.

In addition, for proactive action to make a difference to organizations, individual proactive efforts need to be coordinated effectively. It is therefore ultimately important to move beyond considering individual-level proactivity to consider how leaders can promote proactivity at higher levels of analysis, such as team proactivity or organizational proactivity. A small number of such studies exist. For example, Williams, Parker, and Turner (2010) showed that team-level transformational leadership predicted team proactive performance (for similar studies in the innovation domain, see Burpitt & Bigoness, 1997; Krause, Gebert, & Kearney, 2007), although in a contrasting study, Wilson-Evered, Hartel, and Neale (2001) did not identify a significant relationship between transformational leadership and team innovation. Some of these higher-level studies have examined potential team-level of organizational-level mechanisms underpinning leadership styles/leaders' behavior and proactive performance, such as the mediating roles of climate for innovation (Eisenbeiss et al., 2008), favorable team norms (Williams et al., 2010), team identification and cooperation (Paulsen, Maldonado, Callan, & Ayoko, 2009), and knowledge sharing and collective efficacy (A. Y. Zhang, Tsui, & Wang, 2011). Focusing on the organizational level, Garcia-Morales, Llorens-Montes, and Verdu-Jover (2008) reported that transformational leadership at the organization level helps to build knowledge slack, absorptive capacity, and other outcomes that are positive for innovation; and Jung, Chow, and Wu (2003) reported that having a transformational CEO/president is positively associated with an organizational climate that supports creativity and tolerates differences, which in turn predicts higher levels of organizational innovation. However, almost none of these studies have considered cross-level or individual-level processes that might underpin these pathways, such as the possibility that team leadership promotes the development of team-level proactive motivation, which in turn shapes individual-level proactive motivation, or the possibility that team leadership motivates individual proactivity while at the same time resulting in effective coordination and integration (i.e., bottom-up processes from individual proactivity to team-level proactivity). We recommend that these team-level extensions to the model be considered.

Our model also focused on causal effects flowing in one direction: from leadership to proactivity. It is also important to recognize possible reciprocal processes and positive spirals between the variables in the model. So far, we have focused on proactive performance as the ultimate outcome, and have assumed that leadership effects flow through to motivation which flows through to better performance. Nevertheless, higher performance could also trigger a change in leadership inputs (Clegg & Spencer, 2007) and thereby shape motivation and goal-regulation processes. The possibility that subordinates can obtain more resources, such as job autonomy or tolerance for deviation, from supervisors, when they have higher job performance has been discussed in LMX theory (Graen & Uhl-Bien, 1991, 1995). Ultimately one might see positive spirals in which positive outcomes reinforce further change and development, as well as, of course, negative spirals where, for example, abusive leadership causes individuals to fear being proactive, stifling their performance, and incurring yet further abusive supervision. The model would benefit from a deeper consideration of these reciprocal processes.

Thus far, the model has focused on nonmoderated paths. For example, the model assumes a positive link from proactive goal regulation to job performance. However, not all proactivity is of equal value, and proactivity can be more or less effective from the perspective of different stakeholders. For example, studies have demonstrated that proactivity that lacks situational judgment (Chan, 2006) and is guided by non-prosocial values or high negative work affect (Grant et al., 2009) does not contribute to supervisory assessments of job performance. Other scholars have speculated about the importance for effective proactivity of goal alignment (Campbell, 2000), as well as systems thinking and interpersonal skills (Parker et al., 2010). All of these variables potentially mitigate whether proactive goal regulation translates into job performance, or into actions that contribute to organizational goals.

Moreover, it is possible that leaders can shape these moderating processes. In other words, leaders might influence not just the occurrence of proactivity, but also its effectiveness. For example, proactive goal regulation is more likely to result in job performance when individuals direct their proactivity toward organizational ends such as efficiency rather than purely individuals' ends like career development. Leaders can potentially enhance the effectiveness of individuals' proactivity by increasing their personal-organizational fit, such as by communicating management practices and filtering information within an organization (Kozlowski & Doherty, 1989), and through actively providing feedback about whether ideas fit with organizational goals (Reiter-Palmon & Illies, 2004). Likewise, having flexible approaches to thinking is also likely to shape the extent to which an individual's proactivity predicts job performance. For example, a manager contemplating a proactive change who adopts systems thinking principles (Checkland, 1985) will recognize that a change in one element of a system will have implications for other elements, and therefore will be more likely to recognize and seek to consider wider interests, thereby bring about more effective change. We would expect that leaders, through role modeling, encouragement, and appropriate questioning, could potentially facilitate higher levels of systems thinking (Lord et al., 2011), although such studies have yet to be conducted. We suggest this as a promising area of inquiry.

Finally, we identified proactive goal generation and proactive goal striving as two important elements of proactive goal regulation in our model, but we did not consider how leadership might influence these elements in different ways. For example, it might be that leaders need to provide inspiration to promote the setting of proactive goals, yet create a positive climate in which mistakes are tolerated in order to support striving to achieve the goal. Future developments of the model could include more detailed consideration of how leadership, motivation, and capability influence goal generation distinctly from goal striving.

Comparisons of Proactive Behavior versus Other Behaviors

One problem with the literature we have considered so far is that researchers infrequently consider proactive outcomes alongside less proactive outcomes, making it difficult to discern what leader behaviors are uniquely or differentially important for proactivity. Yet the nature of proactivity suggests that some types of leadership might be more important for this behavior relative to others. First, proactivity is explicitly future focused and change oriented, which highlights the potential importance of leader behaviors that support this emphasis. Griffin et al. (2010) showed that leader vision predicted an increase in proactivity over time for individuals with high scores in role breadth self-efficacy, as well as an increase in "adaptivity" for individuals high in openness, but that vision was not important for predicting a growth in proficiency (core task performance). The authors explained their finding thus: "By providing a discrepant view of the future, a strong vision disturbs the equilibrium and motivates behaviors necessary for achieving a different end-state. Achieving a different end-state requires individuals to adjust well to changes initiated by others (adaptivity) and individuals to initiate changes themselves (proactivity). In contrast, vision is less important for motivating an increase in proficiency, which is likely because proficiency is neither oriented towards change nor achieving a different future" (p. 180). The suggestion therefore is that leadership that emphasizes a focus on the future is potentially more important for proactivity than non-proactive behavior.

Second, proactivity has been identified as psychologically risky, which means that leader behaviors that act to mitigate the risk are likely to be particularly important. As an illustration, Rank et al. (2009) found that active management by exception (a focus on close monitoring of mistakes) was not related to task performance, but it was negatively associated with innovation. It might be that leaders' negative behaviors are "more negative" in their effects when it comes to proactivity relative to task performance because the latter is expected and prescribed behavior, rather than more risky self-initiated behavior.

Third, although empowering leadership (and associated leader actions that encourage employee decision-making and discretion) has been shown to predict several types of performance, we expect it might be especially important for proactive behavior because empowerment builds ownership and internalization of the desire to be proactive. For example, Chen et al. (2011) showed that whereas psychological empowerment predicted innovative behavior, it did not predict team work behaviors such as helping.

Ultimately, more research is required that systematically compares the effects of leadership on different types of performance.

Comparisons of Different Types of Leader Behaviors

Another issue in the literature is that studies often include only one type of leadership, reducing insights into which type of leadership is relatively more important. Examining different leadership constructs at the same time can provide theoretical and practical implications. For example, in one study, higher quality LMX relationship predicted individual innovation, and was more important than transformational leadership (Basu & Green, 1997). Indeed, transformational leadership was negatively related when exchange quality was in the equation, leading the authors to suggest that transformational leaders might have negative features, such as squashing the desire for innovation because of a high need for approval. This finding suggests that transformational leadership has a dark side, and this negative aspect is shown when its association with other leadership constructs is controlled. Moreover, their finding raises the possibility that individual-level leadership input (i.e., LMX) is more important than the team-level leadership input (i.e., transformational leadership) in leading individual innovation. However, this speculation should be tested further because in Basu and Green's study, transformational leadership was not operationalized as a team-level input.

In a further study that also highlights the value of examining transformational leadership along with other leader behaviors, Detert and Burris (2007) found that the combination of transformational leadership and managerial openness predicted employee voice, but that openness was more consistently predictive of voice than transformational leadership. The effect of openness on voice was mediated by employee perceptions of psychological safety, and had its strongest effect for the best-performing employees. They suggesting that some transformational leaders can be both empowering and confining, and that a very vocal transformational leader might be seen as overly dominant. Altogether, these authors concluded that openness conveys a stronger signal for employees to engage in voice.

Examining different leadership constructs at the same time also can help to understand the relationship among these constructs in shaping one's proactive behavior. For example, Bettencourt (2004) reported that both leaders' transformational leadership behaviors and contingent reward leadership behaviors can build a positive LMX relationship, and thus enhance an individual's change-oriented citizenship behavior. In this case, team-level leadership input (i.e., transformational and contingent reward leadership) influenced individual-level leadership input (i.e., LMX), which was more proximal to proactive behavior. In our proposed model, we did not discuss the relationship between team-level leadership inputs and individual-level leadership inputs, but according to Bettencourt's (2004) finding, it is possible that when a leader adopts a specific leadership style to lead a team, the adopted particular leadership style may also determine the inputs that a subordinate can receive from the leader.

Skip-level Leadership and the Role of More Senior Leaders on Individual-level Proactivity

Most research focuses on the immediate manager when examining leadership. Yet it might be important for employees to perceive support not only from their immediate supervisors, but also from more powerful individuals in the organization at higher hierarchical levels, in order to risk the engagement in proactive behaviors. In this vein, top managements' appreciative attitude toward proactive behaviors seems to be helpful: Axtell et al. (2000) found that management support facilitated the implementation of ideas over and above the positive influence of supervisor support. Further, Morrison and Phelps (1999) found that top managements' openness to change was positively related with employees' willingness to engage in taking charge behaviors. Similarly, Dutton and colleagues (1997), in a qualitative research approach based on grounded theory, explored that top management's willingness to listen to employees as well as a supportive organizational culture were positively related to employees' perception that it was favorable to engage in issue-selling behaviors. Premeaux and Bedeian (2003) also reported that top management openness can enhance speaking up among some employees.

In a qualitative study involving interviews of employees, Detert and Trevino (2010) identified ways in which "skip-level leaders" (leaders two to five levels above themselves) influenced employees' propensity to engage in voice. They showed that the cross-level nature of workflows means that employees often work closely with their most distal managers, and indeed it is often only skip-level leaders who have the authority to authorize resources or solve problems. Through their indirect effects on structures and practices, and also more directly through the stories they tell and through their behavior (e.g., humiliating an individual on the spot), skip-level leaders can powerful influence employees' can do motivation. These authors highlight how employees are particularly strongly inclined to "rely on general authority scripts" (p. 48) when dealing with skip-level leaders, and therefore suggest it will be especially difficult for these leaders to create perceptions that it is safe to speak up.

Leader Attributes Associated with Leading for Proactivity and How These Might Be Developed

A further important future direction concerns identifying which personality and contextual attributes are likely to facilitate leaders "leading for proactivity." For example, extroversion appears to reduce the likelihood of being an effective leader for proactivity (Grant, Gino, & Hofmann, 2011). In line with dominance complementarity theory (Kiesler, 1983), Grant et al. (2011) found that passive (proactive) teams achieved higher performance when leaders acted high (low) in extraversion. This is because complementarity of dominance avoids confusion and chaos that would occur when both parties in an interaction try to master the situation. Thus, if leaders are themselves dominant, as implied in extroversion, this might reduce their likelihood of leading for proactivity.

From this perspective, it is better for leaders to play a passive but supporting role to encourage, enable, and allow their subordinate to act on their initiative. This point of view is in line with the caregiving perspective in understanding the leadership process (Popper & Mayseless, 2003), and in particular, attachment theory (Bowlby, 1969/1982), in explaining how a caregiver can help a child to engage in exploration behavior in novel situations. In brief, attachment theory suggests that if a caregiver is available to provide appropriate support when it is needed, a child will form a secure attached relationship with the caregiver and will use the caregiver as a secure base to explore new and unfamiliar environments. This positive attachment–exploration association has been supported in child studies (see Grossmann, Grossmann, Heinz, & Zimmermann, 2008), and also adult studies (e.g., Elliot & Reis, 2003; Green & Campbell, 2000; Mikulincer, 1997). In general, these findings suggest that attachment security is a key antecedent of exploration behavior. Because proactive behavior can be regarded as a form of exploration behavior in adulthood (Wu & Parker, 2012), we would suggest that when leaders act as warm, wise, and attentive caregivers to provide attachment security, they are more likely to cultivate their subordinate to be proactive in exploring new possibilities and leading change. This perspective identifies the importance of leaders with attributes that are more likely to form secure attached relationships with subordinates, such as having a secure attachment style, or being attentive to others problems (i.e., perspective taking) or being compassionate and willing to help (Mikulincer & Shaver, 2007).

Ashford et al. (2009) summarized several cognitive and motivational biases that reduce leaders' propensity to listen to others and encourage voice. For example, leaders have a confirmation bias (Evans, 1989), which leads them to believe that employees don't have valuable opinions, and leaders tend to have an action bias (resulting from that fact that leaders often get to their position based on advocating and action, rather than listening). It is important to investigate further what individual difference variables, or contextual variables, might reduce or mitigate such biases. As noted by Ashford et al. (2009: 188) "the factors that influence how receptive a leader is to voice are largely unexplored." We suggest that a potentially important attribute is humility, or the willingness to see one's self accurately (e.g., being aware of one's strengths and weaknesses) and to put oneself in perspective (e.g., a recognition of the "small role that one plays in a vast universe" (Morris, Brotheridge, & Urbanski, 2005: 1331). Humility can be thought of as "that crest of human excellence between arrogance and lowliness" (p. 1331). We expect that leaders who have humility will be more likely to engage in behaviors such as empowerment, listening, and perspective taking, all of which potentially support employee proactivity. Edmondson (2003), for example, reported that nurses (who are lower status members of the team) are more likely to speak out in operating rooms if surgeons acknowledge their own limits.

There are several further directions that deserve more attention beyond those articulated in the preceding text. A nonexhaustive list includes identifying the training/developmental experiences most likely to enhance leaders' propensity to lead for proactivity; contextual influences on leaders' propensity to lead for proactivity; the identification of when leading for proactivity is most important; the possible role of distributed leadership models in leading for proactivity (see Hunter, Thoroughgood, Myer, & Ligon, 2011, who argued, for example, that having a leader with domain-relevant expertise at the same time as having a leader with people-management expertise might be a powerful way to stimulate innovation); the need to examine leaders' "lived experience" in regard to promoting proactivity (see Ashford et al., 2009: 196); and cultural differences in leading for proactivity. A further direction is to consider not leading "for" proactivity, but leading "with" proactivity. Thus far, although some behaviors frequently engaged in by leaders (such as issue selling) have been investigated, there are likely additional behaviors that have had little systematic attention. Ashford et al. (2009) proposed the need to further leaders' "lateral voice" (voice to their peers, such as within the top management team), their "downward voice" (constructively challenging those below), and their voice to external stakeholders. We also suggest that many core aspects of management and leadership can be carried out more or less proactively, such as "scanning" one's staff to proactively identify if they are experiencing problems.

Conclusion

Many forces act to inhibit employees' speaking out, taking charge to bring about change, introducing new ideas, and other such forms of proactive work behavior. Example forces include the hierarchical nature of organizations, the uncertainty and risk involved in being proactive, individuals' general propensity to obey authority, and an array of cognitive and motivational biases that lead those in power to disregard the views of those less powerful. We have suggested in this chapter that leaders play a potentially key role in offsetting these forces. We have argued that, through what they say and do, as well as through the practices, climate, and work designs they create, leaders can reduce some of the risks of being proactive and can increase employees' belief they can make a difference (can do motivation). They can also foster employees' internalized commitment (reason to motivation) and enhance their positive affect (energized to motivation). We have also argued that leaders can assist employees in developing the broader knowledge and particular thinking styles required for proactivity, such as by activating learning orientations that in turn stimulate employee knowledge acquisition. However, leaders must be willing to invest concerted effort into encouraging proactivity because the forces against it are pervasive. If leaders just give lip service to cultivating a supportive climate, or preach but not actually practice behaviors like empowerment, then these changes in motivation or capability are unlikely to occur. We hope this chapter provides a helpful framework for gaining enhanced insights into how to lead for proactivity.

Notes

1. Although creativity and individual innovation are conceptually distinct from proactivity, confusion can arise because operationally, measures of these aspects can be very similar to some forms of proactive behavior. For example, individual-level innovation and taking charge have been shown to be highly correlated (Parker & Collins, 2010). Even measures of creativity often include items that assess idea implementation. In the current chapter, therefore, we include studies that focus on individual innovation and/or creativity *if* they use measures that assess idea implementation. We exclude creativity or innovation studies that focus solely on idea generation or the production of novel ideas.
2. We recognize that leadership can influence proactive person–environment fit behavior and proactive strategic behavior (Parker & Collins, 2010), but for simplicity, we focus our model on predicting proactive work behavior.
3. Note that recent developments in LMX theory and research propose and investigate "leadership making," which is when managers are encouraged and trained to offer high-quality relationship building to all of their subordinates (Graen & Uhl-Bien, 1991). If such an approach were to be adopted and directed toward all members of a work unit, we believe this approach is a type of team-oriented leadership, and in fact might look similar to transformational leadership.
4. Leaders can also shape team members' knowledge, skills, and abilities at the team level through, for example, selecting particular team members and not others. These team-level processes are not the focus here.

References

Amabile, T. M., Conti, R., Coon, H., Lazenby, J., & Herron, M. (1996). Assessing the work environment for creativity. *Academy of Management Journal, 39*, 1154–1184.

Anand, S., Vidyarthi, P. R., Liden, R. C., & Rousseau, D. M. (2010). Good citizens in poor-quality relationships: Idiosyncratic deals as a substitute for relationship quality. *Academy of Management Journal, 53*, 970–988.

Anderson, L. R. (1966). Leader behavior, member attitudes, and task performance of intercultural discussion groups. *The Journal of Social Psychology, 69*(2), 305–319.

Ashford, S. J., & Barton, M. A. (2007). Identity-based issue selling. In C. A. Bartel, S. Blader & A. Wrzesniewski (Eds.), *Identity and the modern organization* (pp. 223–244). Mahwah, NJ: Lawrence Erlbaum.

Ashford, S. J., & Black, J. S. (1996). Proactivity during organizational entry: The role of desire for control. *Journal of Applied Psychology, 81*(2), 199–214.

Ashford, S. J., Blatt, R., & VandeWalle, D. (2003). Reflections on the looking glass: A review of research on feedback-seeking behavior in organizations. *Journal of Management, 29*(6), 773–799.

Ashford, S. J., & Cummings, L. L. (1985). Proactive feedback seeking: The instrumental use of the information environment. *Journal of Occupational Psychology, 58*, 67–79.

Ashford, S. J., Rothbard, N. P., Piderit, S. K., & Dutton, J. E. (1998). Out on a limb: The role of context and impression management in selling gender-equity issues. *Administrative Science Quarterly, 43*(1), 23–57.

Ashford, S. J., Sutcliffe, K. M., & Christianson, M. K. (2009). Leadership, voice, and silence. In J. Greenberg & M. S. Edwards (Eds.), *Voice and silence in organizations* (pp. 175–201). Bingley, England: Emerald Publishing Group.

Ashforth, B. E., Sluss, D. M., & Saks, A. M. (2007). Socialization tactics, proactive behavior, and newcomer learning: Integrating socialization models. *Journal of Vocational Behavior, 70*, 447–462.

Axtell, C. M., Holman, D. J., Unsworth, K. L., Wall, T. D., Waterson, P. E., & Harrington, E. (2000). Shopfloor innovation: Facilitating the suggestion and implementation of ideas. *Journal of Occupational and Organizational Psychology, 73*, 265–285.

Bandura, A. (1999). A social cognitive theory of personality. In L. Pervin & O. John (Eds.), *Handbook of personality* (2nd ed., pp. 154–196). New York, NY: Guilford Press.

Basu, R., & Green, S. G. (1997). Leader-member exchange and transformational leadership: An empirical examination of innovative behaviors in leader-member dyads. *Journal of Applied Social Psychology, 27*(6), 477–499.

Bateman, T. S., & Crant, J. M. (1993). The proactive component of organizational behavior: A measure and correlates. *Journal of Organizational Behavior, 14*(2), 103–118.

Batt, R. (1999). Work organization, technology, and performance in customer service and sales. *Industrial and Labor Relations Review, 52*, 539–564.

Belschak, F. D., & Den Hartog, D. N. (2010). Pro-self, pro-social, and pro-organizational foci of proactive behavior: Differential antecedents and consequences. *Journal of Occupational and Organizational Psychology, 83*, 475–498.

Bettencourt, L. A. (2004). Change-oriented organizational citizenship behaviors: The direct and moderating influence of goal orientation. *Journal of Retailing, 80*, 165–180.

Bindl, U. K., Parker, S. K., Totterdell, P., & Hagger-Johnson, G. (2012). Fuel of the self-starter: How mood relates to proactive goal regulation. *Journal of Applied Psychology, 97*, 134–150.

Bledow, R., & Frese, M. (2009). A situational judgment test of personal initiative and its relationship to performance. *Personnel Psychology, 62*, 229–258.

Bono, J. E., Foldes, H. J., Vinson, G., & Muros, J. P. (2007). Workplace emotions: The role of supervision and leadership. *Journal of Applied Psychology, 92*, 1357–1367.

Bono, J. E., & Ilies, R. (2006). Charisma, positive emotions and mood contagion *Leadership Quarterly, 17*(4), 317–334.

Botero, I. C., & Van Dyne, L. (2009). Employee voice behavior: Interactive effects of LMX and power distance in the United States and Colombia. *Management Communication Quarterly, 23*(1), 84–104.

Bowlby, J. (1969/1982). *Attachment and loss*, Vol. 1: *Attachment*. London, England: Pimlico.

Brown, D. J., Cober, R. T., Kane, K., Levy, P. E., & Shalhoop, J. (2006). Proactive personality and the successful job search: A field investigation with college graduates. *Journal of Applied Psychology, 91*(3), 717–726.

Burpitt, W. J., & Bigoness, W. J. (1997). Leadership and innovation among teams: The impact of empowerment. *Small Group Research, 28*(3), 414–423.

Burris, E. R., Detert, J. R., & Chiaburu, D. S. (2008). Quitting before leaving: The mediating effects of psychological attachment and detachment on voice. *Journal of Applied Psychology, 93*, 912–922.

Campbell, D. J. (2000). The proactive employee: Managing workplace initiative. *Academy of Management Executive, 14*(3), 52–66.

Campbell, J. P., McHenry, J. J., & Wise, L. L. (1990). Modeling job performance in a population of jobs. *Personnel Psychology, 43*, 313–333.

Carmeli, A., Reiter-Palmon, R., & Ziv, E. (2010). Inclusive leadership and employee involvement in creative tasks in the workplace: The mediating role of psychological safety. *Creativity Research Journal, 22*(3), 250–260.

Chan, D. (2006). Interactive effects of situational judgment effectiveness and proactive personality on work perceptions and work outcomes. *Journal of Applied Psychology, 91*(2), 475–481.

Checkland, P. (1985). From optimizing to learning: A development of systems thinking for the 1990s. *Journal of Operational Research Society, 9*, 757–767.

Chen, G., Farh, J. L., Campbell-Bush, E. M., Wu, Z., & Wu, X. (2013). Teams as innovative systems: Multilevel motivational antecedents of innovation in R&D teams. *Journal of Applied Psychology*.

Chen, G., & Kanfer, R. (2006). Toward a systems theory of motivated behavior in work teams. *Research in Organizational Behavior, 27*, 223–267.

Chen, G., Sharma, P. N., Edinger, S. K., Shapiro, D. L., & Farh, J.-L. (2011). Motivating and demotivating forces in teams: Cross-level influences of empowering leadership and relationship conflict. *Journal of Applied Psychology, 96*, 541–557.

Chen, M.-H. (2007). Entrepreneurial leadership and new ventures: Creativity in entrepreneurial teams. *Creativity and Innovation Management, 16*(3), 239–249.

Chen, Z., Lam, W., & Zhong, J. A. (2007). Leader-member exchange and member performance: A new look at individual-level negative feedback-seeking behavior and team-level empowerment climate. *Journal of Applied Psychology, 92*(1), 202–212.

Chiaburu, D. S., Marinova, S. V., & Lim, A. S. (2007). Helping and proactive extra-role behaviors: The influence of motives, goal orientation, and social context. *Personality and Individual Differences, 43*, 2282–2293.

Chiaburu, D. S., Oh, I.-S., Berry, C. M., Li, N., & Gardner, R. G. (2011). The five-factor model of personality traits and organizational citizenship behaviors: A meta-analysis. *Journal of Applied Psychology, 96*, 1140–1166.

Choi, J. N. (2007). Change-oriented organizational citizenship behavior: Effects of work environment characteristics and intervening psychological processes. *Journal of Organizational Behavior, 28*(4), 467–484.

Clegg, C., & Spencer, C. (2007). A circular and dynamic model of the process of job design. *Journal of Occupational and Organizational Psychology, 80*, 321–339.

Cole, M. S., Bruch, H., & Vogel, B. (2006). Emotion as mediators of the relations between perceived supervisor support and psychological hardiness on employee cynicism. *Journal of Organizational Behavior, 27*, 463–484.

Crant, J. M. (1995). The proactive personality scale and objective job performance among real estate agents. *Journal of Applied Psychology, 80*(4), 532–537.

Daniels, K., Boocock, G., Glover, J., Hartley, R., & Holland, J. (2009). An experience sampling study of learning, affect,

and the demands control support model. *Journal of Applied Psychology, 94*(4), 1003–1017.
Deci, E. L., & Ryan, R. M. (2000). The what and why of goal pursuits: Human needs and the self-determination of behavior. *Psychological Inquiry, 11*, 227–268.
Den Hartog, D. N., & Belschak, F. D. (2007). Personal initiative, commitment and affect at work. *Journal of Occupational and Organizational Psychology, 80*, 601–622.
DeRue, D. S., & Wellman, N. (2009). Developing leaders via experience: the role of developmental challenge, learning orientation, and feedback availability. *Journal of Applied Psychology, 94*, 859–875.
Detert, J. R., & Burris, E. R. (2007). Leadership behavior and employee voice: Is the door really open? *Academy of Management Journal, 50*(4), 869–884.
Detert, J. R., & Trevino, L. K. (2010). Speaking up to higher-ups: How supervisors and skip-level leaders influence employee voice. *Organization Science, 21*(1), 249–270.
Dorenbosch, L., Engen, M. L. v., & Verhagen, M. (2005). On-the-job Innovation: The impact of job design and human resource management through production ownership. *Creativity and Innovation Management, 14*, 129–141.
Dutton, J. E., & Ashford, S. J. (1993). Selling issues to top management. *Academy of Management Review, 18*(3), 397–428.
Dutton, J. E., Ashford, S. J., O'Neill, R. M., Hayes, E., & Wierba, E. E. (1997). Reading the wind: How middle managers assess the context for selling issues to top managers. *Strategic Management Journal, 18*(5), 407–425.
Dutton, J. E., Ashford, S. J., O'Neill, R. M., & Lawrence, K. A. (2001). Moves that matter: Issue selling and organizational change. *Academy of Management Journal, 44*(4), 716–736.
Eccles, J. S., & Wigfield, A. (2002). Motivational beliefs, values, and goals. *Annual Review of Psychology, 53*(1), 109–132.
Edmondson, A. C. (2003). Speaking up in the operating room: How team leaders promote learning in interdisciplinary action teams. *Journal of Management Studies, 40*(6), 1419–1452.
Eisenbeiss, S. A., van Knippenberg, D., & Boerner, S. (2008). Transformational leadership and team innovation: Integrating team climate principles. *Journal of Applied Psychology, 93*(6), 1438–1446.
Elliot, A. J., & Reis, H. T. (2003). Attachment and exploration in adulthood. *Journal of Personality and Social Psychology, 85*, 317–331.
Evans, J. (1989). *Bias in human reasoning: Causes and consequences.* Hillsdale, NJ: Lawrence Erlbaum.
Fay, D., & Frese, M. (2001). The concept of personal initiative: An overview of validity studies *Human Performance, 14*(1), 97–124.
Fredrickson, B. L. (1998). What good are positive emotions? *Review of General Psychology, 2*(3), 300–319.
Fredrickson, B. L. (2001). The role of positive emotions in positive psychology: The broaden-and-build theory of positive emotions. *American Psychologist, 56*(3), 218–226.
Frese, M., & Fay, D. (2001). Personal initiative (PI): An active performance concept for work in the 21st century. In B. M. Staw & R. M. Sutton (Eds.), *Research in organizational behavior* (Vol. 23, pp. 133–187). Amsterdam, the Netherlands: Elsevier Science.
Frese, M., Garst, H., & Fay, D. (2007). Making things happen: Reciprocal relationships between work characteristics and personal initiative in a four-wave longitudinal structural equation model. *Journal of Applied Psychology, 92*(4), 1084–1102.
Frese, M., Teng, E., & Wijnen, C. J. D. (1999). Helping to improve suggestion systems: Predictors of making suggestions in companies. *Journal of Organizational Behavior, 20*(7), 1139–1155.
Frese, M., & Zapf, D. (1994). Action as the core of work psychology: A German approach. In H. C. Triandis, M. D. Dunnette, & L. M. Hough (Eds.), *Handbook of industrial and organizational psychology*, 2nd ed. (Vol. 4, pp. 271–340). Palo Alto, CA: Consulting Psychologists Press.
Fritz, C., & Sonnentag, S. (2009). Antecedents of day-level proactive behavior: A look at job stressors and positive affect during the workday. *Journal of Management, 35*, 94–111.
Fuller, J. B., Marler, L. E., & Hester, K. (2006). Promoting felt responsibility for constructive change and proactive behavior: Exploring aspects of an elaborated model of work design. *Journal of Organizational Behavior, 27*, 1089–1120.
Gao, L., Janssen, O., & Shi, K. (2011). Leader trust and employee voice: The moderating role of empowering leader behaviors *Leadership Quarterly, 22*, 787–798
Garcia-Morales, V. J., Llorens-Montes, F. J., & Verdu-Jover, A. J. (2008). The effects of transformational leadership on organizational performance through knowledge and innovation. *British Journal of Management, 19*(4), 299–319.
Gil, F., Rico, R., Alcover, C. M., & Barrasa, A. (2005). Change-oriented leadership, satisfaction and performance in work groups: Effects of team climate and group potency. *Journal of Managerial Psychology, 20*(3–4), 312–328.
Gong, Y., Huang, J.-C., & Farh, J.-L. (2009). Employee learning orientation, transformational leadership, and employee creativity: The mediating role of employee creative self-efficacy. *Academy of Management Journal, 52*(4), 765–778.
Gonzalez-Roma, V., Peiro, J. M., & Tordera, N. (2002). An examination of the antecedents and moderator influences of climate strength. *Journal of Applied Psychology, 87*(3), 465–473.
Graen, G. B., & Uhl-Bien, M. (1991). The transformation of professionals into self-managing and partially self-designing contributions: Toward a theory of leadership-making. *Journal of Management Systems, 3*, 25–39.
Graen, G. B., & Uhl-Bien, M. (1995). Relationship-based approach to leadership: Development of leader-member exchange (LMX) theory of leadership over 25 years: Applying a multi-level multi-domain perspective. *Leadership Quarterly, 6*(2), 219–247.
Graham, J. W., & Dyne, L. V. (2006). Gathering information and exercising influence: Two forms of civic virtue organizational citizenship behavior. *Employee Responsibilities and Rights Journal, 18*, 89–109.
Grant, A. M., & Ashford, S. J. (2008). The dynamics of proactivity at work. *Research in Organizational Behavior, 28*, 3–34.
Grant, A. M., Gino, F., & Hofmann, D. A. (2011). Reversing the extraverted leadership advantage: The role of employee proactivity. *Academy of Management Journal, 54*(3), 528–550.
Grant, A. M., & Mayer, D. M. (2009). Good soldiers and good actors: Prosocial and impression management motives as interactive predictors of affiliative citizenship behaviors. *Journal of Applied Psychology, 94*(4), 900–912.
Grant, A. M., Parker, S. K., & Collins, C. G. (2009). Getting credit for proactive behavior: Supervisor reactions depend on what you value and how you feel. *Personnel Psychology,* (62), 31–55.

Green, J. D., & Campbell, W. K. (2000). Attachment and exploration in adults: Chronic and contextual accessibility. *Personality and Social Psychology Bulletin 26*, 452–461.

Griffin, M. A., Neal, A., & Parker, S. K. (2007). A new model of work role performance: Positive behavior in uncertain and interdependent contexts. *Academy of Management Journal, 50*(2), 327–347.

Griffin, M. A., Parker, S. K., & Mason, C. M. (2010). Leader vision and the development of adaptive and proactive performance: A longitudinal study. *Journal of Applied Psychology, 95*, 174–182.

Griffin, R. W. (1981). Supervisory behaviour as a source of perceived task scope. *Journal of Occupational Psychology, 54*, 175–182.

Grossmann, E., Grossmann, K., Heinz, K., & Zimmermann, P. (2008). A wider view of attachment and exploration: The influence of mothers and fathers on the development of psychological security from infancy to young adulthood. In J. Cassidy & P. R. Shaver (Eds.), *Handbook of attachment: Theory, research, and clinical applications*, 2nd ed. (pp. 857–879). New York, NY: Guilford Press.

Gruman, J. A., Saks, A. M., & Zweig, D. I. (2006). Organizational socialization tactics and newcomer proactive behaviors: An integrative study. *Journal of Vocational Behavior, 69*, 90–104.

Gumusluoglu, L., & Ilsev, A. (2009). Transformational leadership, creativity, and organizational innovation. *Journal of Business Research, 62*(4), 461–473.

Hirst, G., van Dick, R., & van Knippenberg, D. (2009). A social identity perspective on leadership and employee creativity. *Journal of Organizational Behavior, 30*(7), 963–982.

Hornung, S., Rousseau, D. M., & Glaser, J. (2008). Creating flexible work arrangements through idiosyncratic deals. *Journal of Applied Psychology, 93*(3), 655–664.

Hornung, S., Rousseau, D. M., & Glaser, J. (2009). Why supervisors make idiosyncratic deals: Antecedents and outcomes of i- deals from a managerial perspective. *Journal of Managerial Psychology, 24*, 738–764.

Howell, J. M., & Boies, K. (2004). Champions of technological innovation: The influence of contextual knowledge, role orientation, idea generation, and idea promotion on champion emergence. *The Leadership Quarterly, 15*(1), 123–143.

Hunter, S. T., Thoroughgood, C. N., Myer, A. T., & Ligon, G. S. (2011). Paradoxes of leading innovative endeavors: Summary, solutions, and future directions. *Psychology of Aesthetics, Creativity and the Arts, 5*, 54–66.

Isen, A. M. (1999). On the relationship between affect and creative problem solving. In S. Russ (Ed.), *Affect, creative experience, and psychological adjustment* (pp. 3–17). Philadelphia, PA: Taylor & Francis.

Jansen, J. J., Vera, D., & Crossan, M. (2009). Strategic leadership for exploration and exploitation: The moderating role of environmental dynamism. *The Leadership Quarterly, 20*(1), 5–18.

Janssen, O. (2005). The joint impact of perceived influence and supervisor supportiveness on employee innovative behaviour. *Journal of Occupational and Organizational Psychology, 78*(4), 573–579.

Janssen, O., & Van Yperen, N. W. (2004). Employees' goal orientations, the quality of leader-member exchange, and the outcomes of job performance and job satisfaction. *Academy of Management Journal, 47*(3), 368–384.

Jung, D., Wu, A., & Chow, C. W. (2008). Towards understanding the direct and indirect effects of CEOs' transformational leadership on firm innovation. *The Leadership Quarterly, 19*(5), 582–594.

Jung, D. I., Chow, C., & Wu, A. (2003). The role of transformational leadership in enhancing organizational innovation: Hypotheses and some preliminary findings. *The Leadership Quarterly, 14*(4–5), 525–544.

Kammeyer-Mueller, J. D., & Wanberg, C. R. (2003). Unwrapping the organizational entry process: Disentangling multiple antecedents and their pathways to adjustment. *Journal of Applied Psychology, 88*(5), 779–794.

Kanfer, R., Wanberg, C. R., & Kantrowitz, T. M. (2001). Job search and employment: A personality-motivational analysis and meta-analytic review. *Journal of Applied Psychology, 86*(5), 837–855.

Kiesler, D. J. (1983). The 1982 Interpersonal Circle: A taxonomy for complementarity in human transactions. *Psychological Review, 90*, 185–214.

Kohn, M. L., & Schooler, C. (1978). The reciprocal effects of the substantive complexity of work and intellectual flexibility: A longitudinal assessment. *American Journal of Sociology, 84*, 24–52.

Kozlowski, S. W. J., & Doherty, M. L. (1989). Integration of climate and leadership: Examination of a neglected issue. *Journal of Applied Psychology, 74*(4), 546–553.

Krause, D. E. (2004). Influence-based leadership as a determinant of the inclination to innovate and of innovation-related behaviors: An empirical investigation. *The Leadership Quarterly, 15*(1), 79–102.

Krause, D. E., Gebert, D., & Kearney, E. (2007). Implementing process innovations: the benefits of combining delegative-participative with consultative-advisory leadership. *Journal of Leadership & Organizational Studies, 14*, 16–25.

Lambert, T. A., Eby, L. T., & Reeves, M. P. (2006). Predictors of networking intensity and network quality among white-collar job seekers. *Journal of Career Development, 32*, 351–365.

Leach, D. J., Wall, T. D., & Jackson, P. R. (2003). The effect of empowerment on job knowledge: An empirical test involving operators of complex technology. *Journal of Occupational and Organizational Psychology, 76*, 27–52.

LePine, J. A., & Van Dyne, L. (1998). Predicting voice behavior in work groups. *Journal of Applied Psychology, 83*(6), 853–868.

Liao, H., Liu, D., & Loi, R. (2010). Looking at both sides of the social exchange coin: A social cognitive perspective on the joint effects of relationship quality and differentiation on creativity. *Academy of Management Journal, 53*(5), 1090–1109.

Liu, W., Zhu, R., & Yang, Y. (2010). I warn you because I like you: Voice behavior, employee identifications, and transformational leadership. *The Leadership Quarterly, 21*(1), 189–202.

Liu, Y., & Phillips, J. S. (2010). Examining the antecedents of knowledge sharing in facilitating team innovativeness from a multilevel perspective. *International Journal of Information Management, 31*(1), 44–52.

Lord, R. G., Hannah, S. T., & Jennings, P. L. (2011). A framework for understanding leadership and individual requisite complexity. *Organizational Psychology Review, 1*, 104–127.

Madjar, N., Oldham, G. R., & Pratt, M. G. (2002). There's no place like home? The contributions of work and non-work creativity to support employee's creative performance. *Academy of Management Journal, 45*, 757–767.

Madjar, N., & Ortiz-Walters, R. (2009). Trust in supervisors and trust in customers: Their independent, relative, and joint effects on employee performance and creativity. *Human Performance, 22*(2), 128–142.

Maier, N. R. F., & McRay, E. P. (1972). Increasing innovation in change situations through leadership skills. *Psychological Reports, 31*(2), 343–354.

McAllister, D. J., Kamdar, D., Morrison, E. W., & Turban, D. B. (2007). Disentangling role perceptions: How perceived role breadth, discretion, instrumentality, and efficacy relate to helping and taking charge. *Journal of Applied Psychology, 92*, 1200–1211.

Meyer, R. D., Dalal, R. S., & Hermida, R. (2010). A review and synthesis of situational strength in the organizational sciences. *Journal of Management 36*, 121–140.

Michaelis, B., Stegmaier, R., & Sonntag, K. (2009). Affective commitment to change and innovation implementation behavior: The role of charismatic leadership and employees' trust in top management. *Journal of Change Management, 9*(4), 399–417.

Mikulincer, M. (1997). Adult attachment style and information processing: Individual differences in curiosity and cognitive closure. *Journal of Personality and Social Psychology, 72*, 1217–1230.

Mikulincer, M., & Shaver, P. R. (2007). *Attachment in adulthood: Structure, dynamics, and change.* New York, NY: Guilford Press.

Milgram, S. (1974). *Obedience to authority.* New York, NY: Harper & Row.

Morris, J. A., Brotheridge, C. M., & Urbanski, J. C. (2005). Bringing humility to leadership: Antecedents and consequences of leader humility. *Human Relations, 58*, 1323–1350.

Morrison, E. W. (1993). Newcomer information seeking: Exploring types, modes, sources, and outcomes. *Academy of Management Journal, 36*(3), 557–589.

Morrison, E. W., & Phelps, C. C. (1999). Taking charge at work: Extrarole efforts to initiate workplace change. *Academy of Management Journal, 42*(4), 403–419.

Ng, T. W. H., & Feldman, D. C. (2010). Idiosyncratic deals and organizational commitment. *Journal of Vocational Behavior, 76*, 419–427.

Ohly, S., & Fritz, C. (2007). Challenging the status quo: What motivates proactive behavior? *Journal of Occupational and Organizational Psychology, 80*, 623–629.

Ohly, S., Sonnentag, S., & Pluntke, F. (2006). Routinization, work characteristics and their relationships with creative and proactive behaviors. *Journal of Organizational Behavior, 27*(3), 257–279.

Parker, S. K. (1998). Enhancing role breadth self-efficacy: The roles of job enrichment and other organizational interventions. *Journal of Applied Psychology, 83*(6), 835–852.

Parker, S. K., & Axtell, C. M. (2001). Seeing another view point: Antecedents and outcomes of employee perspective-taking. *Academy of ManagementJournal, 44*, 1085–1100.

Parker, S. K., Bindl, U. K., & Strauss, K. (2010). Making things happen: A model of proactive motivation. *Journal of Management, 36*, 827–856.

Parker, S. K., & Collins, C. G. (2010). Taking stock: Integrating and differentiating multiple proactive behaviors. *Journal of Management, 36*, 633–662.

Parker, S. K., & Wall, T. D. (1998). *Job and work design: Organizing work to promote well- being and effectiveness.* Thousand Oaks, CA: SAGE.

Parker, S. K., Wall, T. D., & Cordery, J. (2001). Future work design research and practice: Towards an elaborated model of work design. *Journal of Occupational and Organizational Psychology, 74*, 413–440.

Parker, S. K., Wall, T. D., & Jackson, P. R. (1997). "That's not my job": Developing flexible employee work orientations. *Academy of Management Journal, 40* (4), 899–929.

Parker, S. K., Williams, H. M., & Turner, N. (2006). Modeling the antecedents of proactive behavior at work. *Journal of Applied Psychology, 91*(3), 636–652.

Paulsen, N., Maldonado, D., Callan, V. J., & Ayoko, O. (2009). Charismatic leadership, change and innovation in an R&D organization. *Journal of Organizational Change Management, 22*(5), 511–523.

Pearce, J. A., III, & Ravlin, E. C. (1987). The design and activation of self-regulating work groups. *Human Relations, 40*, 751–782.

Petty, R. E., Wheeler, C. S., & Tormala, Z. L. (2003). Persuasion and attitude change. In T. Millon & M. J. Lerner (Eds.), *Handbook of psychology* (Vol. 5, pp. 353–382). New York, NY: John Wiley & Sons.

Piccolo, R. F., & Colquitt, J. A. (2006). Transformational leadership and job behaviors: The mediating role of core job characteristics. *Academy of Management Journal 49*, 327–340

Pieterse, A. N., Van Knippenberg, D., Schippers, M., & Stam, D. (2010). Transformational and transactional leadership and innovative behavior: The moderating role of psychological empowerment. *Journal of Organizational Behavior, 31*(4), 609–623.

Popper, M., & Mayseless, O. (2003). Back to basics: applying a parenting perspective to transformational leadership. *Leadership Quarterly, 14*, 41–65.

Premeaux, S. F., & Bedeian, A. G. (2003). Breaking the silence: The moderating effects of self-monitoring in predicting speaking up in the workplace. *Journal of Management Studies, 40*(6), 1537–1562.

Rafferty, A. E., & Restubog, S. L. D. (2011). The influence of abusive supervisors on followers' organizational citizenship behaviours: The hidden costs of abusive supervision. *British Journal of Management, 22*(2), 270–285.

Rank, J., Carsten, J. M., Unger, J. M., & Spector, P. E. (2007). Proactive customer service performance: Relationships with individual, task, and leadership variables. *Human Performance, 20*(4), 363–390.

Rank, J., Nelson, N. E., Allen, T. D., & Xu, X. (2009). Leadership predictors of innovation and task performance: Subordinates' self-esteem and self-presentation as moderators. *Journal of Occupational and Organizational Psychology, 82*, 465–489.

Raub, S., & Liao, H. (2012). Doing the right thing without being told: Joint effects of initiative climate and general self-efficacy on employee proactive customer service performance. *Journal of Applied Psychology,97* (3), 651–667.

Redmond, M. R., Mumford, M. D., & Teach, R. (1993). Putting creativity to work: Effects of leader behavior on subordinate creativity. *Organizational Behavior and Human Decision Processes, 55*(1), 120–151.

Rego, A., Sousa, F., Pina e Cunha, M., Correia, A., & Saur-Amaral, I. (2007). Leader self-reported emotional intelligence and

perceived employee creativity: An exploratory study. *Creativity and Innovation Management, 16*(3), 250–264.
Reiter-Palmon, R., & Illies, J. J. (2004). Leadership and creativity: Understanding leadership from a creative problem-solving perspective. *The Leadership Quarterly, 15*(1), 55–77.
Repenning, N. P., & Sterman, J. D. (2002). Capability traps and self-confirming attribution errors in the dynamics of process improvement. *Administrative Science Quarterly, 47*, 265–295.
Saks, A. M., & Ashforth, B. E. (1999). Effects of individual differences and job search behaviors on the employment status of recent university graduates. *Journal of Vocational Behavior, 54*, 335–349.
Salancik, G. R., & Pfeffer, J. (1977). An examination of need-satisfaction models of job attitudes. *Administrative Science Quarterly, 22*, 427–456.
Sarros, J. C., Cooper, B. K., & Santora, J. C. (2008). Building a climate for innovation through transformational leadership and organizational culture. *Journal of Leadership & Organizational Studies, 15*(2), 145–158.
Scott, S. G., & Bruce, R. A. (1994). Determinants of innovative behavior: A path model of individual innovation in the workplace. *Academy of Management Journal, 37*(3), 580–607.
Seibert, S. E., Kraimer, M. L., & Crant, J. M. (2001). What do proactive people do? A longitudinal model linking proactive personality and career success. *Personnel Psychology, 54*(2), 845–874.
Shraga, O., & Shirom, A. (2009). The construct validity of vigor and its antecedents: A qualitative study. *Human Relations, 62*, 271–291.
Smircich, L., & Morgan, G. (1982). Leadership: The management of meaning. *Journal of Applied Behavioral Science, 18*.
Speier, C., & Frese, M. (1997). Generalized self-efficacy as a mediator and moderator between control and complexity at work and personal initiative: A longitudinal study in East Germany. *Human Performance, 10*(2), 171–192.
Strauss, K., Griffin, M. A., & Rafferty, A. E. (2009). Proactivity directed toward the team and organization: The role of leadership, commitment, and role-breadth self-efficacy. *British Journal of Management, 20*, 279–291.
Sy, T., Côté, S., & Saavedra, R. (2005). The contagious leader: impact of the leader's mood on the mood of group members, group affective tone, and group processes. *Journal of Applied Psychology, 90*, 295–305.
Tangirala, S., & Ramanujam, R. (2008). Exploring nonlinearity in employee voice: The effects of personal control and organizational identification. *Academy of Management Journal, 51*, 1189–1203.
Tesluk, P. E., & Jacobs, R. R. (1998). Toward an integrated model of work experience. *Personnel Psychology, 51*, 321–355.
Thomas, J. P., Whitman, D. S., & Viswesvaran, C. (2010). Employee proactivity in organizations: A comparative meta-analysis of emergent proactive constructs. *Journal of Occupational and Organizational Psychology, 83*, 275–300.
Thompson, J. A. (2005). Proactive personality and job performance: A social capital perspective. *Journal of Applied Psychology, 90*(5), 1011–1017.
Tidwell, M., & Sias, P. (2005). Personality and information seeking: Understanding how traits influence information-seeking behaviors. *Journal of Business Communication, 42*, 51–77.
Tierney, P., Farmer, S. M., & Graen, G. B. (1999). An examination of leadership and employee creativity: The relevance of traits and relationships. *Personnel Psychology, 52*(3), 591–620.
Tsai, W.-C., Chen, C.-C., & Liu, H.-L. (2007). Test of a model linking employee positive moods and task performance. *Journal of Applied Psychology, 92*, 1570–1583.
Unger, J. M., Keith, N., Hilling, C., Gielnik, M. M., & Frese, M. (2009). Deliberate practice among South African small business owners: Relationships with education, cognitive ability, knowledge, and success *Journal of Occupational and Organizational Psychology, 82*, 21–44.
Van Dyne, L., Jehn, K. A., & Cummings, A. (2002). Differential effects of strain on two forms of work performance: Individual employee sales and creativity. *Journal of Organizational Behavior, 23*(1), 57–74.
Van Dyne, L., Kamdar, D., & Joireman, J. (2008). In-role perceptions buffer the negative impact of low LMX on helping and enhance the positive impact of high LMX on voice. *Journal of Applied Psychology, 93*(6), 1195–1207.
Van Dyne, L., & Le Pine, J. A. (1998). Helping and voice extra-role behaviors: Evidence of construct and predictive validity. *Academy of Management Journal, 41*(1), 108–119.
van Knippenberg, D., van Knippenberg, B., De Cremer, D., & Hogg, M. A. (2004). Leadership, self, and identity: A review and research agenda. *Leadership Quarterly, 15*, 825–856.
VandeWalle, D., Ganesan, S., Challagalla, G. N., & Brown, S. P. (2000). An integrated model of feedback-seeking behavior: Disposition, context, and cognition. *Journal of Applied Psychology, 85*(6), 996–1003.
Wall, T. D., Jackson, P. R., & Davids, K. (1992). Operator work design and robotics system performance: A serendipitous field study. *Journal of Applied Psychology, 77*, 353–362.
Walumbwa, F. O., & Schaubroeck, J. (2009). Leader personality traits and employee voice behavior: Mediating roles of ethical leadership and work group psychological safety. *Journal of Applied Psychology, 94*(5), 1275–1286.
Wang, K. Y., & Casimir, G. (2007). How attitudes of leaders may enhance organizational creativity: Evidence from a Chinese study. *Creativity and Innovation Management, 16*(3), 229–238.
Williams, H. M., Parker, S. K., & Turner, N. (2010). Proactively performing teams: The role of work design, transformational leadership, and team composition. *Journal of Occupational and Organizational Psychology, 83*, 301–324.
Wilson-Evered, E., Härtel, C. E. J., & Neale, M. (2001). A longitudinal study of work group innovation: The importance of transformational leadership and morale. *Advances in Health Care Management, 2*, 315–340.
Wong, C. A., Laschinger, H. K., & Cummings, G. G. (2010). Authentic leadership and nurses' voice behaviour and perceptions of care quality. *Journal of Nursing Management, 18*(8), 889–900.
Wu, C.-H., & Parker, S. K. (2012). The role of attachment styles in shaping proactive behavior: An intra-individual analysis. *Journal of Occupational and Organizational Psychology, 85*, 523–530
Yuan, F., & Woodman, R. W. (2010). Innovative behavior in the workplace: The role of performance and image outcome expectations. *Academy of Management Journal, 53*, 323–342.
Zhang, A. Y., Tsui, A. S., & Wang, D. X. (2011). Leadership behaviors and group creativity in Chinese organizations: The role of group processes. *The Leadership Quarterly, 22*(5), 851–862.

Zhang, X., & Bartol, K. M. (2010). Linking empowering leadership and employee creativity: The influence of psychological empowerment, intrinsic motivation, and creative process engagement. *Academy of Management Journal*, *53*, 107–128.
Zhou, J., & Woodman, R. W. (2003). Managers' recognition of employees' creative ideas. In V. S. Larisa (Ed.), *The international handbook on innovation.* Hillsdale, NJ: Lawrence Erlbaum.
Zhou, L., Wang, M., Chen, G., & Shi, J. (2012). Effects of supervisors' upward exchange relationships on subordinates: Testing the multilevel mediation role of empowerment. *Journal of Applied Psychology*, *97* (3), 668–680.

PART 5

Dyadic and Team-Centric Theories and Approaches

CHAPTER

19 Leader-Member Exchange (LMX) Theory: The Relational Approach to Leadership

Berrin Erdogan *and* Talya N. Bauer

Abstract

Leader-Member Exchange (LMX) is the foremost dyadic approach to leadership. This paper presents a comprehensive review of the LMX literature. It includes a summation of the theoretical underpinnings of LMX, a discussion of the measurement of LMX quality, a detailed review of the antecedents and consequences of LMX, and more recent developments aimed at exploring group-level implications of LMX. Future research directions and recommendations for best practices for research methods and dyadic relationship nomenclature are included.

Key Words: Leader-member exchange, relational leadership, LMX differentiation, social exchange, dyadic leadership

Leader-member exchange (LMX) theory is the foremost dyadic theory in the leadership literature (Erdogan & Liden, 2002; Liden, Sparrowe, & Wayne, 1997). Whereas contemporary leadership theories such as transformational, servant, or authentic leadership theories are focused on the effects of leader behaviors on employee attitudes, motivation, and team outcomes, LMX theory views the dyadic relationship quality between leaders and members as the key to understanding leader effects on members, teams, and organizations. According to the LMX approach, leaders are closer, friendlier, more inclusive, and more communicative with some members who report to them. In other words, leaders form high-quality, trust, affect, and respect-based relationships with a subset of their team, while with other members they tend to have a lower-quality exchange that is limited to the employee and the leader's job description.

Since its early beginnings as Vertical Dyad Linkage (VDL) theory (Dansereau, Graen, & Haga, 1975), LMX theory has been the subject of hundreds of studies (Dulebohn et al., 2012; Gerstner & Day, 1997). As can be seen in Figure 19.1, as of December 2011, the PsycInfo database, a major online collection of abstracts in behavioral sciences, contained over 700 references to articles with leader-member exchange as a key word in their abstract. In addition, the research pace in this area is currently accelerating, as we found 353 articles (or nearly 50 per cent of the total number of articles in the database) were published between 2006–2010. Given the overwhelming amount of interest in this theory in the past four decades, we feel that taking stock of the literature to examine its roots, what is currently known, what research gaps may exist, and what areas are in need of the most urgent research attention is needed in order to further stimulate future research and open up new research streams. In established fields such as LMX, the large number of studies in the literature may make it difficult to see what remains to be done or areas where little progress has been made. Moreover, the rapid growth of this literature makes it difficult for new scholars to appreciate the main contributions in the field. In this review, it is our intention to summarize the

Date	1971-1975	1976-1980	1981-1990	1986-1990	1991-1995	1996-2000	2001-2005	2006-2010	2011
Frequency	1	1	8	17	44	111	126	353	74

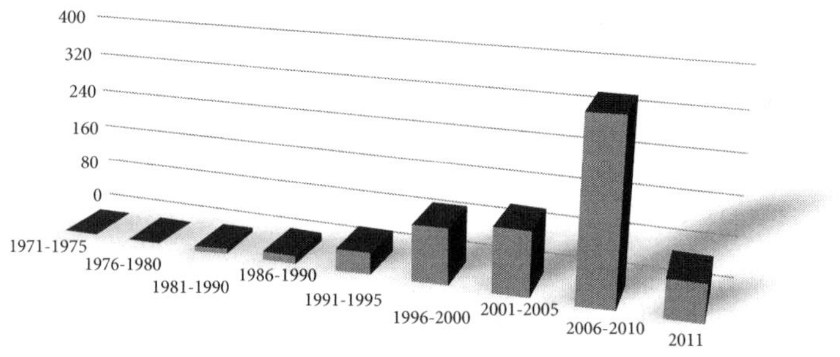

Figure 19.1. Frequency Count of Articles Containing LMX in the Title and/or Abstract in Five-year Increments from 1971 to 2010 Plus 2011.

major developments in the LMX literature so that scholars interested in this field will find it easier to get up to speed quickly and efficiently.

In this article, we start with a summary of the theoretical underpinnings of the theory. We first present an overview of the literature examining antecedents and consequences of LMX quality. Next, we summarize the recent efforts to examine the effects of LMX at the team level. Finally, we postulate on the next steps for future researchers as we see them.

Theoretical Underpinnings of LMX Theory

One of the key premises of LMX theory is that leaders have differentiated relationships with their employees. Although it is theoretically possible that leaders may be equally trusting and affectionate with all their members, the reality is that their followers bring differing levels of competence, motivation, and willingness to spend effort toward their work as well as toward building a relationship. Moreover, developing high-quality relationships is costly to the leader due to the amount of time and energy that needs to be invested in the relationship development. The end result is that leaders tend to differentiate more often than not (Liden & Graen, 1980).

Differentiation is not necessarily an intentional phenomenon. Instead, it is theorized to occur naturally as a result of a "role making" process (Dienesch & Liden, 1986; Graen & Scandura, 1987). Graen and Uhl-Bien (1995) define LMX development as a process where the dyad members move from being *strangers* (lower-quality relationships) to *acquaintances* (moderate-quality relationships) to *maturity* (higher-quality relationships). The role-making process relies on mutual testing during early tenure. When the leader and member first start working together, they start on neutral ground. The leader tests the member by delegating additional responsibilities and by making an offer for a higher-quality relationship. How the member responds to this offer determines whether the leader starts trusting the member. In fact, LMX development may be regarded as a trust-building process where each party is likely to pay attention to cues suggesting how much ability, benevolence, and integrity the other person possesses, and research supports these attributes as the major tenets of role making (Bauer & Green, 1996). As a result, relatively early in the tenure of the new employee-manager dyad, some relationships emerge that are of higher quality than others.

In addition to mutual testing inherent in the role theory, social exchange theory (Blau, 1964) constitutes a solid theoretical basis for both LMX development and how LMX quality affects member and leader actions. According to social exchange theory, relationships are initiated by one party doing a favor for another, and the other party reciprocating. In fact, when a person does a favor for his/her exchange partner, the norm of reciprocity (Gouldner, 1960) dictates that the other party will be motivated to reciprocate within a reasonable time period. As each party does favors for the other they build trust, which results in moving from an "economic exchange" to a "social exchange" relationship. In other words, once the relationship becomes mature and of higher quality, parties to the relationship stop keeping count, and they are motivated to go above and beyond their formal job description to protect and help the other. Therefore, social exchange theory is often used as an explanation for why leaders provide high-quality LMX members with challenging tasks and resources, and why members are motivated to perform and engage in voluntary behaviors at levels exceeding minimum expectations.

Whereas members reciprocate to the attention, support, and resources received from the leader, they may not necessarily reciprocate in kind. Wilson, Sin, and Conlon (2010) developed a model of resource exchange between leaders and members, and contended that members reciprocate with comparable resources such as providing the leader with information in exchange for money and other tangible resources, providing affiliation in return for status, and the like. The element of reciprocity is regarded as a key element in LMX theory, but high-quality exchanges rely on generalized as opposed to immediate reciprocity (Sparrowe & Liden, 1997). In other words, in high-quality exchanges, members and leaders are motivated to benefit each other, but they do not necessarily keep count.

Measurement of LMX Quality

Although early LMX studies showed much variation in which survey items were used to assess exchange quality, the last three decades have seen convergence on two instruments that are used to capture LMX. The LMX-7 (Graen & Uhl-Bien, 1995; Scandura & Graen, 1984) is probably the most frequently used measure of LMX quality. LMX-MDM (Liden & Maslyn, 1998), presented in Table 19.1, is a 12-item instrument based on the idea that LMX is a multidimensional construct (Dienesch & Liden, 1986), consisting of affect, respect, loyalty, and a desire to contribute to the goals of others. Both measures seem to have adequate psychometric properties (Gerstner & Day, 1997). Studying LMX-MDM in more depth, Scherbaum, Finlinson, Barden, and Tamanini (2006) used item response theory and showed that LMX-MDM does a good job of distinguishing between people who have high- and low-quality relations with the leader. Even though LMX-MDM is multidimensional, the majority of research studies have employed this instrument as a measure of overall LMX quality, and studies reporting relationships with individual dimensions did not reveal dimensions that had greater predictive validity. Whichever measure is used, it seems important to use the entire measure instead of selecting subsets of items. This is because Keller and Dansereau (2001) showed that adding or dropping items affected the psychometric properties of LMX measures.

Figure 19.2 depicts a variety of related dyadic and network relationships and summarizes them.

Table 19.1. Original Items and Subscales from the LMX-MDM Scale

Originally published in Liden, R. C., & Maslyn, J. M. (1998). Multidimensionality of leader-member exchange: An empirical assessment through scale development. *Journal of Management, 24,* 43–72. Reprinted by permission of Sage Publications.
Affect
1. I like my supervisor very much as a person.
2. My supervisor is the kind of person one would like to have as a friend.
3. My supervisor is a lot of fun to work with.
Loyalty
4. My supervisor defends my work actions to a superior, even without complete knowledge of the issue in question.
5. My supervisor would come to my defense if I were "attacked" by others.
6. My supervisor would defend me to others in the organization if I made an honest mistake.
Contribution Subscale
7. I do work for my supervisor that goes beyond what is specified in my job description.
8. I am willing to apply extra efforts, beyond those normally required, to meet my supervisor's work goals.
9. I do not mind working my hardest for my supervisor.
Professional Respect
10. I am impressed with my supervisor's knowledge of his/her job.
11. I respect my supervisor's knowledge of and competence on the job.
12. I admire my supervisor's professional skills.

LMX is a dyadic phenomenon, and can potentially be measured from the employee or from the manager's perspective (see Liden et al., 1993; and Greguras & Ford, 2006, for measures of LMX from the supervisor's perspective, or SLMX). However, a review of the literature indicated that 83 per cent of the time, LMX was measured from the employee's perspective (Hiller, DeChurch, Murase, & Doty, 2011). Moreover, leader and member perceptions of LMX tend to display low levels of convergence. For example, a recent meta-analysis based on 63

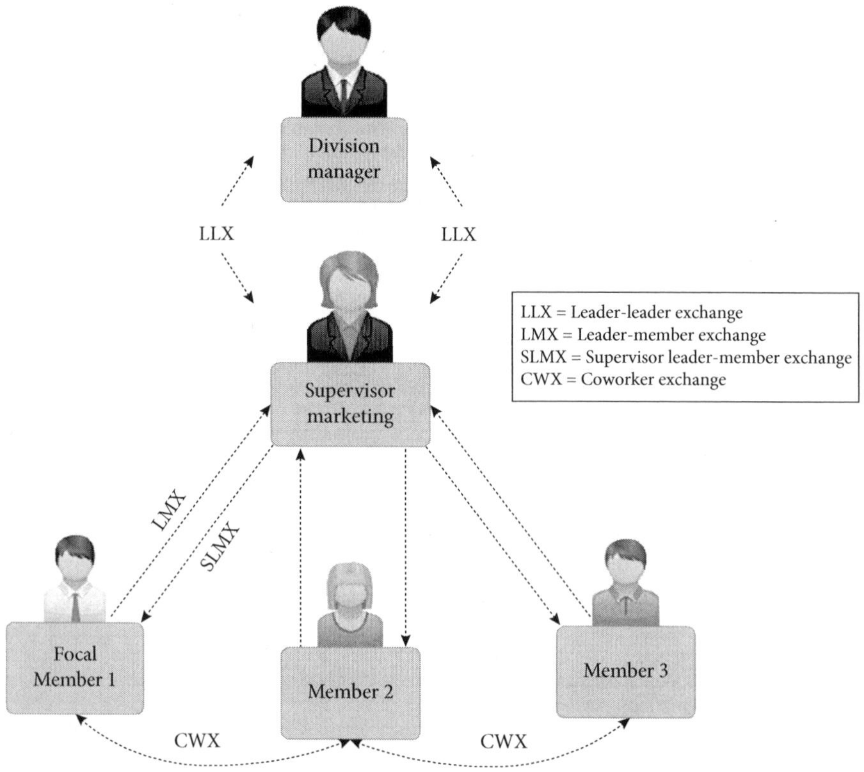

Figure 19.2. Relationships at Work: Summarizing the Nomenclature for Peer, Upward, and Downward Dyadic Relationships.

studies revealed a true score correlation of .37. (Sin, Nahrgang, & Morgeson, 2009). One reason for the lack of convergence could be impression management concerns on the part of leaders, as stating that they do not have a good quality relationship with an employee may reflect poorly upon them. Moreover, it seems that leaders and members pay attention to different aspects of the exchange relationship when reporting relationship quality: managers are more likely to use task-oriented aspects such as member competence or contributions, whereas employees are more likely to use social dimensions such as leadership attention (Zhou & Schriesheim, 2010). Finally, researchers have shown that convergence depended on a number of factors including dyad tenure (Nahrgang, Morgeson, & Ilies, 2009), intensity of communication within the dyad, and sampling methodology (Sin et al., 2009).

Reasons why leader and member assessments of LMX do not converge is an interesting research question. It seems natural that leaders and members may have different perceptions of their shared as well as observed relationships, which is partly dependent on their dyad partner, and partly their own relationship history, relational style, expectations from the other, and implicit leadership/followership theories. As a result, investigating antecedents and consequences of convergence in leader-member views is an interesting future research direction. Therefore, instead of getting discouraged by the lack of convergence between perspectives, treating convergence as an outcome of interest may increase our understanding of LMX quality.

Antecedents of LMX Quality

Why do some relationships never mature into high-quality, partnership relationships? Identifying antecedents of relationship quality has long been a key research question in this literature. To date, examinations of LMX antecedents have lagged behind studies examining consequences of LMX quality. Furthermore, with a few notable exceptions (Bauer & Green, 1996; Dansereau et al., 1975; Liden, Wayne, & Stilwell, 1993; Murphy & Ensher, 1999; Nahrgang, Morgeson, & Ilies, 2009), examinations of LMX antecedents in samples of newly formed dyads have been relatively rare. Instead, researchers have tended to study dyads that have been working together for an extensive period of time. Therefore, whereas a large number of studies have explored the relationship between LMX quality and its theoretical antecedents, in some cases it is unclear whether a particular variable is actually an antecedent or a consequence of LMX quality given the established nature of the relationship. This issue is unlikely to be resolved unless more researchers adopt longitudinal designs and trace the development of newly forming dyads from an acquaintance to a partnership relationship.

Member Demographics and Personality

In our review of over 400 studies, we did not see a consistent relationship between member demographic variables and LMX quality. For example, age showed correlations ranging between -.08 (Schyns, Kroon, & Moors, 2008) to .19 (Pelled & Xin, 2000), and the highest reported correlation with gender was .05 (Pelled & Xin, 2000). The only exception to a demographic that related to LMX quality was dyad tenure. Even though there are studies showing a nonsignificant relation to dyad tenure, there are others with a correlation as high as .22 (Wayne, Shore, Bommer, & Tetrick, 2002). However, it is unclear whether dyad tenure is a causal antecedent. Given that members are more likely to leave groups where they do not get along with their leader, higher dyad tenure may be a natural consequence of high LMX quality, rather than causing it.

There is some evidence that members with certain personalities may be at an advantage in LMX development. Lapierre and Hackett's (2007) meta-analysis (based on just eight correlations) revealed a modest correlation of .13 with conscientiousness, and Dulebohn et al. (2012) found an average correlation of .17 based on nine studies. In other words, how organized and responsible an employee is by itself may not make or break the relationship. However, goal orientation, another personality trait with potential influence over member performance, has been related to LMX (Janssen & van Yperen, 2004) such that, those with mastery goal orientation, or employees who were driven to become proficient at work had higher LMX, whereas those with high-performance goal orientation, or those employees driven to look successful had lower LMX. Furthermore, Li, Liang, and Crant (2010) showed that employees with a proactive personality, or those with a drive to take action and change their environment for the better without being given explicit directions, had higher levels of LMX quality. Internal locus of control is another trait with positive links to LMX quality (Kinicki & Vecchio, 1994; Martin, Thomas, Charles, Epitropaki, & McNamara, 2005), with an average correlation of .22 (Dulebohn et al., 2012). Finally, Murphy and Ensher's (1999) longitudinal study of new interns showed self-efficacy as a predictor of LMX. These findings are consistent with a trust-building explanation proposed by Bauer and Green (1996) in explaining LMX development. Employees with personality traits that may serve as an advantage at work are more likely to develop high-quality relations.

Furthermore, LMX development is not solely task based, as shown by studies looking at personality traits that smooth and facilitate empathy or positive interactions with others. For example, positive affectivity, agreeableness, and extraversion have been shown to have correlations of .28, .16, and .13 with LMX quality respectively (Dulebohn et al., 2012). Recent work also showed a positive link with emotional intelligence (Jordan & Troth, 2011; Sears & Holmvall, 2010).

Member Behaviors and Competence

Another explanation of LMX development concerns the degree to which the member actually displays behaviors that indicate that one is trustworthy and has the potential to be effective. Bauer and Green (1996) found support for the argument that early performance has implications for LMX quality at later periods. Basu and Green (1995), utilizing a cross-sectional design, regarded performance and citizenship as antecedents of LMX. Their study showed that citizenship, but not performance, predicted LMX quality. Lapierre and Hackett's (2007) meta-analytic model found support for a model in which citizenship behaviors predicted LMX. Gerstner and Day's (1997) meta-analysis shows a correlation of .26 between member competence and LMX.

Members appear to play an important role in LMX development not only by signaling that they will be trustworthy and competent, but also by signaling that they are interested in building a high-quality relationship with the leader. Maslyn and Uhl-Bien (2001) showed that leader perceptions that the member is spending effort toward building a relationship is a significant predictor of LMX quality assessed from the leader's perspective. Furthermore, Wayne and Ferris (1990) showed that ingratiation was an effective behavior with regard to relationship development. The effects of ingratiation seem to be more pronounced for employees with visible disabilities who are in a position to be dissimilar from their leaders (Colella & Varma, 2001). Finally, Lam, Huang, and Snape (2007) showed that feedback seeking from one's manager was another effective LMX development technique, to the degree that leaders attributed member feedback seeking to performance improvement and not to impression management motives.

Leader Behaviors and Characteristics

Several studies explored what leaders can do to enhance the relationship quality with followers. Considering LMX development as trust building, several researchers showed that leader delegation is related to higher LMX quality (Bauer & Green, 1996; Yukl, O'Donnell, & Taber, 2009). Viewing delegation as a way in which leaders test their members, delegation may be a causal antecedent of LMX quality, even though some of these studies are cross-sectional. Leaders may also build effective relations by being ethical (Mahsud, Yukl, & Prussia, 2010; Tumasjan, Strobel, & Welpe, 2011; Walumbwa et al., 2011), showing empathy toward members (Mahsud et al., 2010), spending effort toward LMX development (Maslyn & Uhl-Bien, 2001), behaving in ways that will increase perceived fairness of their interactions with members (Erdogan, Liden, & Kraimer, 2006; Masterson, Lewis, Goldman, & Taylor, 2000), and avoid violating psychological contracts (Restubog, Bordia, & Bordia, 2011). Finally, leaders may also enable higher quality LMX development by displaying leader behaviors that communicate a vision and create excitement around the vision, such as transformational leadership behaviors (Wang, Law, Hackett, Wang, & Chen, 2005).

One of the challenges of relating leader behaviors to LMX quality is that high-quality LMX members are likely to engage in positive halo error when assessing behaviors or characteristics of their leaders. As a result, correlations between LMX, leader fairness, positive leader behaviors, and transformational leadership tended to be very high. When the source of measurement is the same, it is likely that assessments of leader behaviors are affected by the relationship quality. High correlations between LMX and leader behaviors reported by employees may not necessarily reflect bias, given that members with higher LMX likely experience different leader behaviors. Still, depending on the leader behavior in question, incorporating observer ratings of leader behaviors that do not rely on dyad members to assess each other may reveal a more accurate picture of what leaders actually do in order to develop high-quality LMXs.

Finally, it seems that leaders who are in a position to benefit their members may be at an advantage in LMX development, as evidenced by a study in which leader centrality in organizational advice networks predicted member assessment of LMX quality (Goodwin, Bowler, & Whittington, 2009). Members may have more to gain when they develop a high-quality exchange with powerful leaders, which may mean that members spend more energy building a relationship with leaders who have greater social capital.

Dyadic Similarity

In addition to leader and member characteristics and behaviors, a large number of studies have investigated the effects of similarity-attraction phenomenon (Byrne, 1971) for LMX development. A relationship is unlikely to be developed solely based on strategic reasons such as how much potential the other party has to further one's goals. Instead, mutual liking (i.e., positive affect) is more likely to develop if each party sees areas of similarity in the other. In fact, Liden, Wayne, and Stilwell's (1993) longitudinal investigation showed that perceived similarity was a stronger predictor of subsequent LMX quality compared with member competence or performance. In other words, while simple demographics such as sex or age do not seem to relate to LMX quality, similarity, particularly perceived similarity, seems influential in the LMX development process.

Among the many different dimensions of actual (as opposed to perceived) demographic similarity, some have shown no relation to LMX quality. For example, age similarity or education similarity showed no relation to LMX quality (Basu & Green, 1995; Green, Anderson, & Shivers, 1996), while there are some studies showing effects for gender similarity (Green et al., 1996; Pelled & Xin, 2000). Similarly, no consistent pattern of relations emerged for race similarity, with correlations of LMX with race similarity ranging from -.19 (Suazo, Turnley, & Mai-Dalton) to .19 (Pelled & Xin, 2000) with most of the studies showing nonsignificant correlations. It seems that either demographic similarity effects do not exist, or researchers have not been able to uncover these relationships as of yet. One possibility is that the effects may be asymmetric. To date, studies of demographic similarity tended to examine the effects of similarity in a nondirectional manner, hypothesizing that dissimilarity (regardless of the direction of dissimilarity) would have negative effects. However, given the status difference between leaders and members, it may be more acceptable for members to work with a leader who is older, more experienced, and more educated than them. When reporting to someone who is younger and less educated, social comparison processes may interfere with relationship development, and the member may start questioning whether he/she made sufficient progress given one's education level and age. Similarly, supervising someone with greater experience and education may be more challenging for supervisors due to greater threats to one's legitimate authority. As a result, it may be worthwhile to examine these relationships further, and consider the direction of similarity in future investigations.

There is some evidence that personality similarity may make a difference in exchange development. For example, Bernerth, Armenakis, Feild, Giles, and Walker (2008) showed that similarity in four dimensions of big five personality traits (except extraversion similarity) predicted LMX quality. However, this study did not control for the main effects of personality on LMX, and therefore it is not clear whether personality or personality similarity makes a difference. Sears and Holmwall (2010) did not find support for core self-evaluation or conscientiousness similarity, but showed that similarity in emotional intelligence had positive effects on LMX. Attitude similarity (Basu & Green, 1995; Phillips & Bedeian, 1994) and positive affectivity similarity (Bauer & Green, 1996) are among other positive correlates of LMX quality.

Finally, an interesting look at the idea of fit between supervisors and employees comes from the implicit leadership theory (ILT) literature. Engle and Lord (1997) held that supervisors have implicit performance theories, or ideas about what the ideal employee looks and behaves like. Similarly, followers have implicit leadership theories, or ideas about their ideal leader. They showed that similarity between leader implicit performance theories and followers' self schemas about performance predicted LMX quality. In other words, if leaders and members can agree on how the ideal member behaves, a higher relationship quality is more likely. Building on the idea of ILTs, Epitropaki and Martin (2005) showed that the congruence between the ILT's employees hold and the actual behaviors the leader displays was related to LMX quality, aside from how similar the leader is to oneself, the similarity of the leader to the leadership prototypes in the employee's mind was key to understanding relationship development.

The Context

One final category of antecedents relates to the work group and organizational characteristics. Are higher LMXs more likely to be developed in some cultures, sectors, or groups of a certain size? Some studies have shown that size matters: there is a negative correlation between group size and LMX (Green et al., 1996; Green, Blank, & Liden, 1983). Work group climate is also positively correlated with LMX (Aryee & Chen, 2006; Cogliser & Schriesheim, 2000), but again, these correlations are based on employee self-reports, and may be affected by the tendency of high-quality LMX members to view their environment in a more positive light. Finally, Erdogan et al. (2006) have shown that leader behaviors resulting in higher LMX seem to depend on organizational culture. In their study of teachers working in 30 schools in Turkey, LMX depended more strongly on interpersonal justice in organizational cultures that were people oriented, whereas fairness of reward distribution was a stronger correlate of LMX quality in aggressive cultures.

Future Research Directions

There are only a handful of studies examining LMX development on newly formed dyads and over time. Moreover, most studies of LMX quality and its antecedents are potentially biased by common source and common method bias. High correlations may be observed due to respondents' desire to achieve consistency between their cognitions and attitudes or between their implicit theories about leadership and their LMX quality, or simply as a function of their affectivity and mood (Podsakoff, MacKenzie, Lee, & Podsakoff, 2003). Therefore, future research examining leader behaviors and contextual characteristics from the perspective of observers who are not part of the focal dyad would increase confidence in earlier findings, and provide more useful tools to members and leaders interested in developing a better relationship with their leaders.

Furthermore, our review of the literature did not reveal any studies examining critical junctures in the leader-member exchange development. In fact, the small number of longitudinal studies (e.g., Liden et al., 1993; Nahrgang et al., 2009) showed that, once formed, the trajectory of LMX quality tends to be stable. In the case of Liden et al. (1993), stable LMX quality was formed as early as within the first two weeks. However, what we do not know is what may damage the relationship over time, and whether relationships may recover from damage and trust violations (Tierney, Bauer, & Rogers, 2002). Dyads exist in an evolving landscape with leaders leaving and new members joining the work group Thus, it is unclear how shifts in the group membership, or broader organizational changes may impact LMX development, resulting in change. We feel that there is a need for research on these critically important topics.

Consequences of Leader-Member Exchange

The majority of the studies on leader-member exchanges have, to date, had the objective of uncovering the implications of LMX quality for member attitudes and behaviors. In many of these studies, LMX quality and the outcome of interest have been measured simultaneously using the same survey instrument, suggesting the possibility that common method and common source bias may have influenced at least some of the relationships observed. Still, results point out to LMX quality being an influential aspect of employee attitudes and behaviors. Moreover, the effects of LMX quality do not seem dependent on culture, as several studies explored and found support for the effects of LMX quality in a number of collectivistic and power distant, as well as individualistic and egalitarian cultures (e.g., Chen, Tsui, & Zhong, 2008; Pellegrini & Scandura, 2006; Pillai, Scandura, & Williams, 1999).

Day-to-Day Implications of LMX quality

Mutual influence. Employees who have a favorable relationship quality with their managers experience a dramatically different work atmosphere on a daily basis. Research has shown that members with higher LMX quality communicate with their managers more frequently (Kacmar, Witt, Zivnuska, & Gully, 2003; Sin, Nahrgang, & Morgeson, 2009). At the same time, the content of their communication with the leader seems to be different from those with low-quality exchanges. Specifically, conversations of leaders and high-quality LMX members seem to reflect lower levels of power distance and higher levels of mutual influence compared to interactions of leaders with lower LMX members. In an ethnographic study in which conversations between managers and their high-, low-, and medium-quality exchange members were taped, Fairhurst and Chandler (1989) observed that leaders were more likely to use mutual influence and persuasion with their high-quality LMX members. In these conversations, members and leaders challenged and disagreed with each other, whereas with medium- and low-quality LMX members, leaders were more likely to use direct authority. In fact, due to the inherent lack of trust, leaders may find that their attempts to influence their employees through inspirational appeals and making promises actually end up backfiring in low-quality LMX relationships (Sparrowe, Soetjipto, & Kraimer, 2006). Similarly, Fairhurst, Rogers, and Sarr (1987) utilized social interaction analysis and recorded conversations of 45 dyads. The analyses of these recordings showed that leader dominance in conversations was higher within the conversations of low-quality LMX dyads. In a study of over 350 dyads in five organizations, Krone (1991) showed that high-quality LMX members were more likely to report using persuasion, and less likely to use manipulation in their communications with the leader. In return, leaders are more likely to delegate authority and responsibility and ask for the opinions of their high-quality LMX followers (Yukl & Fu, 1999).

Given the comfort level with their leaders, it is no surprise that the LMX quality of high-performing members has been shown to predict their decision influence (Scandura, Graen, & Novak, 1986). Several studies have shown higher psychological empowerment levels for higher LMX members (Chen, Kirkman, Kanfer, Allen, & Rosen, 2007; Chen, Lam, & Zhong, 2007; Liden, Wayne, & Sparrowe, 2000). Psychological empowerment encompasses a sense of being autonomous in relation to one's own work as well as impactful with regard to the happenings in other areas of the workplace. The finding that LMX quality is positively related to perceived empowerment suggests that high-quality LMX members see themselves as powerful and independent agents in the workplace.

Access to resources and information. In addition to the relative power balance and mutual influence in high-quality LMX dyads, it seems that high-quality LMX members are in a position to access greater material and informational resources in their organizations. Perhaps one of the greatest advantages high-quality LMX members benefit from is their greater access to the leader's attention (Dansereau, Graen, & Haga, 1975). Leader attention is often a scarce resource and may resolve many problems employees encounter on a day-to-day basis. In terms of tangible resources high-quality LMX members receive, Klein and Kim (1998) have shown that high-quality LMX members were less likely to complain about lack of information, training, supplies, and time. Scott and Bruce (1994) found that LMX quality was positively related to the degree to which members were satisfied with the amount of organizational resources. Finally, high-quality LMX members have access to informational resources in their organizations and are more likely to be "in the know" about the organization. For example, members closer to the leader are more likely to be informed about upcoming organizational changes (van Dam, Oreg, & Schyns, 2008; Yrle, Hartman, & Galle, 2002). Having access to resources and information is likely to set high-quality LMX members up for success and help them achieve their objectives, as well as emerge as influential members in their work group (Sparrowe & Liden, 2005).

Conflict management. Conflict in any relationship is inevitable. However, LMX quality seems to be related to how dyad members approach conflict as well as the frequency of conflict. To begin with, those members with higher LMX quality are less likely to experience conflict with their leaders (Paglis & Green, 2002). There are several reasons for this observation. First, Heneman, Greenberger, and Anonyuo (1989) argued that leaders would interpret behaviors of members with higher LMX quality in such a way that they would receive more credit for their high performance and would be given the benefit of the doubt for their low performance. Supporting this argument, these researchers have shown that LMX was positively related to leader tendency to make internal attributions for high performance. Similarly, Bowler, Halbesleben, and Paul (2010), in a conceptual article, make a similar prediction that positive behaviors of high-quality LMX members are more likely to be attributed to prosocial motives by their managers. High-quality LMX members may also resist influence attempts of their leaders by negotiating, and they do not suffer the negative consequences low-quality LMX members encounter (Tepper et al., 2006). Cumulatively, these findings suggest that leaders are more inclined to see things the way employees see them.

Second, just as leaders seem to be more forgiving and empathetic toward their employees, employees are more forgiving toward their managers if they are in a high-quality LMX relationship. For example, Shapiro, Boss, Salas, Tangirala, and von Glinow (2011) have shown that employees were less likely to be punitive toward a leader who violates their trust in high-quality LMX dyads. Rosen, Harris, and Kacmar (2011) as well as Johnson, Truxillo, Erdogan, Bauer, and Hammer (2009) showed that perceptions of unfairness negatively affected work performance of only lower-quality LMX members. In other words, even when the leader misbehaves, they have greater "idiosyncrasy credit" with their employees, buffering minor and daily transgressions, as well as occasional major ones.

In addition to their lower tendency to engage in conflict, high-quality LMX members also seem to use different tactics in their management of actual conflict. LMX quality is a correlate of conflict management styles as well as actual occurrence of conflict. High-quality LMX members are more likely to use cooperative strategies such as collaboration and compromise, and less likely to resort to avoidance and dominating (Green, 2008).

Learning and growth opportunities. Finally, members with high-quality LMX are in a position to grow, learn, and be effective at work due to selective assignments and growth opportunities they have access to, as well as the amount of coaching and mentoring they receive from their managers. High-quality LMX relationships are characterized by greater levels of trust. As a result, high-quality LMX members are more likely to be chosen for desirable, challenging assignments (Law, Wong, Wang, & Wang, 2000). In return, these members report greater motivation for training (Scaduto, Lindsay, & Chiaburu, 2008), and greater engagement in learning activities (Bezuijen, van Dam, van den Berg, & Thierry, 2010). Thus, high-quality LMX members report greater levels of satisfaction with the amount of growth opportunities (Seers & Graen, 1984).

High-quality LMX members have access to growth opportunities and challenging tasks, and they have greater motivation to improve. Furthermore, they receive more help along the way to improve their skills and effectiveness. Their psychological closeness and comfort with the leader affords them the key advantage of seeking feedback without being afraid of negative repercussions such as disclosing weaknesses and admitting failure. Studies have shown that high-quality LMX members report greater amounts of feedback seeking (Kudisch, Fortunato, & Smith, 2006; Peng, Ngo, Shi, & Wong, 2009), direct feedback seeking (Lee, Park, Lee, & Lee, 2007), and negative feedback seeking (Chen et al., 2007). High-quality LMX members also reported higher expectations regarding future feedback they would receive from their managers (Lee, 1999), and reported greater amounts of feedback received from their managers (Harris, Harris, & Eplion, 2007). Of course, simply because managers provide feedback does not mean that employees would be willing to accept and act on that feedback. However, studies have shown that high-quality LMX members reported lower feedback avoidance behavior (Moss, Sanchez, Brumbaugh, & Borkowski, 2009), and had more positive reactions to the performance feedback and performance evaluations received from their managers (Dobbins, Cardy, & Platz-Vieno, 1990; Elicker, Levy, & Hall, 2006; Snyder, Williams, & Cashman, 1984).

One final piece of the growth and learning opportunities available to high-quality LMX members comes in the form of greater access to mentoring provided by managers. McManus and Russell (1997) argued that developing a high-quality relationship with one's leader would increase opportunities for the leader to serve as a mentor. These authors predicted that, because LMX quality develops relatively early in the relationship life cycle, mentoring would be one of the outcomes of LMX quality, as opposed to preceding LMX. Moreover, these authors predicted that high-quality LMX would increase the desirability of the member as a potential protégé to powerful others in the organization, due to the vetting process implicit in a high-quality exchange. Supporting this argument, several studies found correlations ranging from moderate to high between LMX and mentoring (Chen, Tsui, & Zhong, 2008; Kraimer, Seibert, Wayne, Liden, & Bravo, 2011; Thibodeaux & Lowe, 1996). In sum, greater learning and growth opportunities seem to be a key benefit for high LMX members.

Job Attitudes

Given how LMX quality has implications for the way in which employees experience the workplace, the amount of resources and information they have access to, the nature of their interactions with their supervisor, and the degree to which they can feel challenge and growth at work, it is no surprise that scholars have identified positive relations between LMX quality and job attitudes. Job satisfaction and organizational commitment are the most frequently studied of these work attitudes. Gerstner and Day's (1997) meta-analysis of the literature suggested an average correlation of .46 between LMX and job satisfaction, and .35 for organizational commitment.

High-quality LMX members view the organization through a different lens compared to their lower LMX counterparts. For example, even when reporting their feelings toward the same organization, high-quality LMX members were more likely to characterize the organization as having a more positive work climate (Ansari, Hung, & Aafaqi, 2007; Dunegan, Tierney, & Duchon, 1992; Kozlowski & Doherty, 1989; Mueller & Lee, 2002; Tierney, 1999), lower levels of organizational politics (Atinc, Darrat, Fuller, & Parker, 2010), and higher support for employee development (Kraimer, Seibert, Wayne, Liden, & Bravo, 2011). Moreover, members with higher LMX quality were less likely to report a psychological contract violation (Dulac, Coyle-Shapiro, Henderson, & Wayne, 2008; Henderson, Wayne, Shore, Bommer, & Tetrick, 2008; Suazo et al., 2008), and express higher levels of trust in the organization (Dulac et al., 2008).

LMX quality seems to be associated with more positive attitudes toward the organization and more positive evaluations of the organization. Taking this argument one step further, researchers have shown that one's assessment of LMX quality is a key aspect of how employees view their exchange quality with the organization. The quality of the exchange relationship between the employee and the organization is captured by the construct of Perceived Organizational Support (POS; Eisenberger, Huntington, Hutchison, & Sowa, 1986). Researchers have identified a strong link between LMX quality and POS (Andrews & Kacmar, 2001), with evidence utilizing panel data also suggesting that the direction of the relationship is likely to be from LMX to POS and not the other direction (Eisenberger, Stinglhamber, Vandenberghe, Sucharski, & Rhoades, 2002). Given that the leader is the person that employees look up to for interpretation and implementation of organizational policies and procedures, how employees feel about the organization's treatment of employees seems to be largely shaped by the nature of the relationship employees have with their managers. The correlation between LMX and POS seems to get stronger for leaders who are more powerful in the organization because of their level in the hierarchy (Self, Holt, & Schaninger, 2005), or because of their exchange quality with their own supervisors one level up (Tangirala, Green, & Ramanujam, 2007).

Are all employees affected by the nature of their relationship quality to the same degree? Scholars investigating moderators of LMX to job attitude relationship identified key contingencies that make LMX quality more or less relevant for individuals. It seems that individuals who lack the skills to navigate organizational politics are more dependent on their LMX quality in their assessments of work attitudes (Harris, Harris, & Brouer, 2009). Moreover, employees who are not in a position to interact with their colleagues and with their manager frequently because they perform a greater proportion of their work on a virtual basis are more strongly influenced by LMX quality in their assessments of job satisfaction and organizational commitment (Golden & Veiga, 2008). These results are consistent with the argument that frequent interactions and employee personality may act as substitutes for LMX.

With respect to job characteristics, it seems that employees who have greater levels of autonomy or challenge at work may need a higher-quality LMX relationship. To support this point, Ozer (2008) showed that LMX quality was more positively related to job satisfaction when task autonomy was high. In an earlier study treating LMX quality as the moderator, Schriesheim, Neider, and Scandura (1998) showed that for high-quality LMX members, there was a more positive relationship between leader delegation and job satisfaction. It is plausible that leaders may delegate more meaningful tasks and provide more support to higher-quality LMX members, resulting in greater levels of success with delegated tasks and intrinsic satisfaction. In short, the strength of the relationship between LMX and work attitudes seems to depend on employee personality, working conditions, and the nature of the tasks. Finally, Eisenberger et al. (2010) showed that employees differ in the extent to which they identify the supervisor with the organization, and supervisor's organizational embodiment determines the degree to which LMX quality is related to organizational commitment. In other words, in some contexts members distinguish their relationship with their manager from their relationship with the organization, which also results in some divergence between LMX and job attitudes targeting the organization.

Workplace Behaviors

As discussed earlier, LMX theory is built on the rationale that leaders and members in a high-quality exchange have a social, rather than an economical exchange relationship. A social exchange relies on the norm of reciprocity (Blau, 1964). In return for the goods, services, support, and help obtained from the leader, employees feel motivated to reciprocate to their leader by behaving in ways that will benefit the leader. Whereas each party in the dyad behaves in ways that will benefit the other, they build trust and respect toward one another. In other words, member behavior is expected to be a function of the exchange quality between leaders and members, and members in high-quality relationships are expected to behave in ways that go above and beyond their formal job descriptions (Graen, Novak, & Sommerkamp, 1982). In sum, the nature of the exchange quality between leaders and members is a key influence factor with regard to the type of behaviors employees feel accountable for performing (Erdogan, Sparrowe, Liden, & Dunegan, 2004).

Job Performance. Job performance is one of the key criteria for leadership effectiveness and is one of the outcomes most frequently studied in LMX research. There are several reasons why LMX quality should relate to job performance. First, based on social exchange theory (Blau, 1964), high-quality LMX members are likely to have greater levels of motivation and desire to benefit the leader and the organization. Second, based on the role-making perspective (Graen & Scandura, 1987), high-quality LMX members may tailor their roles in ways that will allow them to shine in their positions. In fact, LMX quality is positively correlated with both intrinsic motivation and job characteristics (e.g., Piccolo & Colquitt, 2006), supporting these two assertions. Finally, given greater access of high-quality LMX members to leader help and support, those engaged in a high-quality relationship with their leader are likely to be more successful in their tasks, resulting in performance advantages for high-quality LMX members.

Even though several reasons exist for expecting high-quality LMX members to outperform their colleagues, studies examining the relation between LMX and objective performance do not point to a strong link. Gerstner and Day's (1997) meta-analysis reported a correlation of only .10. In individual studies, the magnitude of correlations ranged between .07 (Duarte, Goodson, & Klich, 1994) to .31 (Chen, Lam, & Zhong, 2007), and in some studies the relation was negative (Ma & Qu, 2010). Of course, these correlations do not necessarily imply that LMX quality does not relate to job performance, given that there may not be meaningful objective indicators for the performance of every job, making objective indicators deficient in capturing an employee's true performance. Moreover, members with high LMX quality may be assigned to tasks that will result in lower levels of objective performance as a type of developmental "stretch" assignment. For example, these members may be assigned to more demanding clients or more temperamental machinery, resulting in their call completion times and magnitude of errors to be higher but still benefiting team performance in the aggregate.

In addition to objective criteria, LMX quality has been studied with respect to leader ratings of job performance, with an average correlation of .28 when LMX was assessed from the employee perspective and .41 when assessed from the manager's perspective (Gerstner & Day, 1997). A review of the literature indicates that the strength of the relationship varies from study to study. Liden, Wayne, and Sparrowe (2000) noted a correlation of .12 in a study of employees of a service organization, while Varma, Srinivas, and Stroh (2005) observed correlations as high as .79 in their sample of an electronics company.

Interestingly, the literature to date has not examined what particular mechanisms tie LMX quality to job performance, which seems like an important omission. Moreover, supervisor ratings of job performance are not without their problems. While objective criteria may be deficient indicators of actual performance, supervisor ratings are likely to be contaminated, because they are likely to capture a leader's overall affect toward employees and an inclination to see the employee in a positive light. In fact, Duarte et al. (1994) showed that leaders have a tendency to rate high-quality LMX members highly, irrespective of their objective performance, whereas performance ratings of lower-quality LMX members are more likely to reflect their objective performance. In other words, it is often unclear whether job performance ratings simply reflect an assessment of LMX from the supervisor's perspective. In some studies, LMX measured from the supervisor perspective and supervisor ratings of performance showed correlations exceeding .60 (Schriesheim, Castro, & Yammarino, 2000; Schriesheim, Neider, & Scandura, 1998; Stark & Poppler, 2009; Townsend, Phillips, & Elkins, 2000; Varma et al., 2005), providing support for this speculation.

Studies examining the moderators of LMX to performance link have identified a number of relevant variables. Dunegan, Duchon, and Uhl-Bien (1992) showed that LMX to performance link was stronger when the task at hand was either very simple, or very complex. This is likely because demanding tasks necessitate a leader's support and help for successful achievement, while very simple tasks that are not intrinsically motivating may still be performed well when employees feel an obligation to their leader to perform well. Supporting this argument, studies have shown that LMX is more positively related to job performance when members have high levels of autonomy (Ozer, 2008), but also when members have low levels of empowerment (Harris, Wheeler, & Kacmar, 2009), when jobs are performed mostly virtually (Golden & Veiga, 2008), and when jobs are at the low level (Fernandez & Vecchio, 1997). Furthermore, employee personality also determines the degree to which employees may access the resources inherent in a high-quality LMX relationship through alternative means, and whether employees may take advantage of greater expectations and demands involved in being close to the leader. Bauer, Erdogan, Liden, and Wayne (2006) showed that LMX to performance link was stronger for introverted executives than extraverted ones whereas Ozer (2008) showed that the link was more positive for employees with an internal locus of control.

Organizational citizenship behaviors (OCBs). In addition to performing their core jobs well, LMX researchers contended that high-quality LMX members tend to exceed their role definition by performing in ways that benefit the organization but are not required of their jobs. In fact, high-quality LMX members tend to define their jobs more broadly compared to their lower LMX counterparts (Hsiung & Tsai, 2009; Van Dyne, Kamdar, & Joireman, 2008) and feel accountable for performing a larger number of tasks that lower-quality LMX members see as outside their job purview. In a meta-analysis based on 50 samples, Ilies, Nahrgang, and Morgeson (2007) found the average correlation between LMX and OCBs to be .33 for OCBs targeting the supervisor and coworkers, and .27 for OCBs targeting the organization.

The nature of the citizenship behaviors employees perform in reaction to their relationship with their manager depends on the organizational context, and different contexts may make different types of behaviors salient for members. What seems to matter is that LMX results in behaviors that managers value and care about. For example, in a sample of restaurant supervisors and their respective managers, LMX predicted expressing ideas with the intention to make improvements (Burris, Detert, & Chiaburu, 2008). Among field sales personnel, LMX has been shown to be related to adaptive selling and customer-oriented selling techniques (Paparoidamis & Guenzi, 2009). In the context of two organizations that recently experienced organizational change, high-quality LMX members were the ones who displayed lowest amounts of resistance to change (Furst & Cable, 2008). In a sample of US army personnel, LMX was related to safety citizenship behaviors (Hofmann, Morgeson, & Gerras, 2003). Finally, in a manufacturing sample, LMX quality was positively related to safety communication, which in turn was negatively related to accidents (Hofmann & Morgeson, 1999). In a study conducted of Mexican white-collar employees working in Mexico, Tierney, Bauer, and Potter (2002) found that organizational commitment partially mediated LMX and extra role behavior. While the nature of OCBs may be context dependent, it seems that high-quality LMX members are in a position to make positive contributions to their teams as a result of their prosocial actions.

Even though LMX quality predicts OCBs, there are conditions that may mitigate the negative effects of lower-quality LMX on citizenship. For example, Anand, Vidyarthi, Liden, and Rousseau (2010) showed that the degree to which the leader and member strike up idiosyncratic deals (or "i-deals") substituted for the effects of LMX on OCBs. This study suggests that the sense of obligation to the leader and the organization that stems from high-quality LMX may be replicated by unique organizational conditions that allow the leader to extend more favorable working conditions to the member.

Creativity. A final category of LMX outcomes critical for contemporary organizations is employee creativity in the workplace, or the degree to which the employee comes up with novel and useful solutions to challenging problems. High-quality LMX members are likely to have greater levels of psychological security that is necessary to challenge the status quo and come up with unique and different solutions to problems. Supporting this expectation, several studies have shown that LMX is positively related to supervisor ratings of innovative and creative behaviors (Basu & Green, 1997; Scott & Bruce, 1994, 1998; Tierney, Farmer, & Graen, 1999) as well as the amount of bonuses obtained for creative behaviors (Liao, Liu, & Loi, 2010), and self-rated creative behaviors (Atwater & Carmeli, 2009). Moreover, LMX quality seems to serve as an equalizer between those who have an innate ability to be creative and those who do not, as evidenced by Tierney et al.'s (1999) work in which it was shown that creativity levels of employees varied by employee cognitive style only for lower-quality LMX members.

Few studies examined why LMX quality would relate to creative performance. Liao et al. (2010) have shown that the effects of LMX quality on creative performance were mediated by employee self-efficacy. Scott and Bruce (1994) showed that perceived support for innovation and resource supply were the mediators. Atwater and Carmeli (2009) argued that an effective relationship with one's manager creates a sense of autonomy, belonging, and competence, and they showed that feelings of energy mediated the LMX to creative performance link. Finally, Dunegan et al. (1992) showed that LMX quality related to the degree to which employees perceive the organizational climate as innovative, which again may result in higher levels of innovativeness.

Organizational deviance. Finally, in addition to its implications for positive organizational behaviors, LMX quality has been negatively related to more destructive work behaviors such as retaliation (Townsend, Phillips, & Elkins, 2000) and deviance (El Akremi, Vandenberghe, & Camerman, 2010). Given their privileged status in the work group, it follows that high-quality LMX members have less motivation to engage in negative behaviors and have more at stake as a result of behaving in counterproductive ways.

Future research opportunities. LMX quality has been associated with a large number of employee behaviors that are beneficial to the organization and to the supervisor. At the same time, our feeling is that there is need for better integration across these findings. One future direction is to examine the mechanisms linking LMX to employee behaviors, unlocking the black box linking the two. Researchers have offered a large number of potential explanations to explain why LMX is related to employee behaviors, invoking mechanisms such as felt obligation, intrinsic motivation, greater levels of access to resources and information, greater self-efficacy, and greater energy among others. Directly measuring the proposed mediators and exploring whether different mechanisms operate for different outcomes would be useful in order to better understand why higher LMX results in better-behaved employees.

Second, any time supervisor rated behaviors are treated as an outcome of LMX, there is the possibility that the measures are capturing supervisor's perceptions of the exchange quality in addition to the actual behaviors of the employee. Therefore, supplementing measures of citizenship, performance, or creativity by utilizing the perspective of others who are not a member of the dyad would result in more information about the actual effects of LMX quality. Furthermore, given that supervisor ratings of different employee behaviors will likely be subject to halo error, studying different kinds of employee behaviors simultaneously would allow us to more firmly establish consequences of LMX quality. Only focusing on one behavior at a time may result in the omission of the key behaviors leaders are basing their ratings on, potentially resulting in spurious correlations.

Career Success

One of the early findings of LMX researchers that was supported and validated by subsequent studies relates to the implications of LMX quality for the success of the individual in an organization. Graen, Wakabayashi, and colleagues (Graen, Dharwadkar, Grewal, & Wakabayashi, 2006; Wakabayashi & Graen, 1984; Wakabayashi et al., 1980) published a series of articles reporting their findings from a longitudinal study, following the careers of 85 male college graduates starting in a Japanese department store for 23 years. These studies have shown that LMX within the first year had significant implications for newcomer career success, because of a model they termed as the "hidden investment model." High-quality LMX members received more support and more opportunities for development early on, which resulted in a lasting impact for their career trajectories. These studies have shown that assessed potential of the employee early on and LMX quality within the first few years interacted with each other to determine the speed of promotion, promotability assessments, and bonuses received within 7 and 13 years (Wakabayashi & Graen, 1984; Wakabayashi et al., 1988), and speed of upward progress over 23 years (Graen et al., 2006). Moreover, Wakabayashi, Graen, and Uhl-Bien (1990) found in a larger sample from five Japanese organizations that employees with higher LMX reported greater company investment in them. Leaders of high-quality LMX supervisors tend to report greater desire to promote their employees (Law, Wong, Wang, & Wang, 2000).

Along with their accelerated advancement up the organizational hierarchy, there is also some evidence that the paycheck the high-quality LMX members take home may be larger than that of their colleagues. LMX has been positively related to percent salary increase (Golden & Veiga, 2008), salary of the employee 13 years after they start their jobs (Wakabayashi & Graen, 1989; Wakabayashi, Graen, Graen, & Graen, 1988), salary progression within an 18-month period (Wayne, Liden, Kraimer, & Graf, 1999), as well as merit and base pay (Chen, Tsui, & Zhong, 2008). Benson and Pattie (2009) also showed that LMX is related to expected salary growth.

Finally, in addition to objective indicators of career advancement, LMX quality has been related to intrinsic career success, or more subjective assessments of the employee with respect to one's career, including indicators such as career satisfaction (Wayne et al., 1999), pay satisfaction (Seers, 1989; Stepina, Perrewe, Hassell, Harris, & Mayfield, 1991), and satisfaction with pay raises (DeConinck, 2009).

What explains the link between LMX quality and career success? Even though researchers have not yet investigated the mechanisms linking LMX quality to career advancement, there are many potential reasons for this link. Graen (1990) reported, based on a descriptive study of 50 managers, that 47 per cent of high-quality LMX managers, and only 12 per cent of lower-quality LMX managers reported providing advice to their employees about their careers. In fact, LMX quality and the amount of career mentoring employees receive seems to be correlated (Kraimer et al., 2011). Scandura and Schriesheim (1994) showed that employees do not distinguish between LMX quality and supervisor career mentoring, seeing the two as practically the same. While it is possible for employees to receive advice about the politics of an organization and the route to success from others in the organization, not all employees are equally politically savvy. Therefore, LMX quality seems to be even more critical for the career success of employees with low levels of political skills. Breland, Treadway, Duke, and Adams (2007) demonstrated that political skills moderated the relationship between LMX and intrinsic career success. Furthermore, it has been proposed that LMX quality would result in greater sponsorship of the employee by the leader (Sparrowe & Liden, 1997). If the leader introduces the member to his/her network and makes member activities and accomplishments visible to upper management, the employee will be poised to advance quickly. Sparrowe and Liden (2005) found support for this argument, with the further qualifier that leaders who were sponsored by their own supervisors and who were centralized in the organization's network were in a better position to sponsor members they had a high-quality relationship with.

Future research opportunities. In sum, the LMX literature has established that LMX quality has distinct advantages for career advancement. What seems to be missing from this line of inquiry at the moment is an investigation of the mechanisms resulting in greater advancement for members with high-quality LMX, as well as a greater understanding of the conditions under which LMX quality is necessary for career advancement. Whereas studies have shown that LMX relates to career advancement beyond a person's potential, it is unclear if it makes a difference beyond the performance of the employee. In other words, are the effects on career success due to greater opportunities to develop the employee job performance, or due to greater visibility and political sponsoring of the employee? This point deserves future investigation.

Employee Withdrawal

In light of the reported advantages of being in an effective, trust-based relationship with one's leader, it is expected that members with higher LMX quality display greater desire to remain in their organization, and stay within the organization longer. One immediate reason for this is that LMX quality is related to greater job embeddedness (Harris, Wheeler, & Kacmar, 2011; Sekiguchi, Burton, & Sablynski, 2008; Wheeler, Harris, & Harvey, 2010): They have a bond with their manager resulting in an environment that supports the employee autonomy, growth, and effectiveness and which is not easily replicable in a different organization. Even when they experience problems on a day-to-day basis, high-quality LMX members will have greater belief that these problems will be resolved, and give the organization more chances before they make the decision to depart. Sturges, Conway, and Liefooghe (2010) also showed that high-quality LMX members are less likely to manage their careers using external strategies. This could be because they tend to believe that they can reach career goals within their current organization (Benson & Pattie, 2009).

Several studies have linked LMX quality to turnover intentions in the expected direction, with an average sample weighted correlation of -.28 in Gerstner and Day's (1997) meta-analysis. The same study revealed a nonsignificant relationship with turnover, but at the time of the meta-analysis, there were only a handful of studies linking LMX quality to actual turnover. Dulebohn et al.'s (2012) recent meta-analysis based on nine studies revealed an average observed correlation of –.15.

In recent years, we have seen a larger number of studies, this time also looking at moderators of the relationship and using more sophisticated analyses, such as the use of survival analysis and treating number of days stayed at the outcome of interest instead of examining turnover as a dichotomous variable. For example, Bauer et al. (2006) showed that LMX was negatively related to turnover for introverted employees, supporting the argument that the benefits provided by high LMX quality may be more critical and important for members who lack the skills or inclination to proactively obtain them within the organization. Others have investigated and found support for a curvilinear relationship (Morrow, Suzuki, Crum, Ruben, & Pautsch, 2005). Members in a high-quality LMX relationship may be more marketable and may find it easier to find alternative jobs while members in a lower-quality LMX relationship have more reasons to leave, resulting in higher turnover for both high- and low-quality LMX members.

A recent study by Ballinger, Lehman, and Schoorman (2010) is a key advancement in the study of LMX to turnover relationship because of their investigation of the role played by leader turnover. To date, LMX studies tended to measure LMX quality early on, and then obtain turnover data from organizational records one year after the study to examine the degree to which LMX and actual turnover are related. However, a neglected possibility in this research design is the possibility that the leader may have left within this time period, removing the incentive of the member to stay. Ballinger et al. (2010) showed that LMX was negatively related to actual turnover to the degree to which the leader remained in the organization. Moreover, lower-quality LMX members in this study had more positive reactions to their leader's leaving and reported greater expectations of a positive relationship with their new leader, which predicted their turnover intentions following the departure of their leader. We feel that the recognition of the role played by leader departures and their differential effects on high- and lower-quality LMX members is a key development for LMX literature.

Studies investigating the link between LMX, turnover intentions, and actual turnover were more careful to study the mediators of these relationships, shedding some light to the underlying processes. A broad range of mediator variables have been investigated, including job embeddedness (Harris, Wheeler, & Kacmar, 2011), organizational commitment (DeConinck, 2009, 2011), and job performance (DeConinck, 2011).

Future research directions. Despite recent advances, the number of studies examining the implications of LMX quality for employee withdrawal, and particularly actual turnover has been lagging. We feel that this area of investigation would benefit from identifying conditions under which

LMX and turnover are related, including a continued investigation of how turnover of one's leader, or changing leaders within the same organization may have implications for LMX-turnover studies. Furthermore, the possibility of a curvilinear link between LMX and turnover is intriguing and seems deserving of further investigation. Under what conditions are members in a high-quality relationship more, rather than less, likely to leave the organization? In a high-quality exchange, leaders are likely to take a greater interest in member career success and well-being, and it is plausible that under conditions in which internal advancement does not seem feasible nor desirable to the leader or the employee, leaders may encourage, or even enable, members to leave. This possibility has not yet been investigated and may benefit LMX literature.

Stress and Well-Being

Interestingly, even though sufficient theoretical reason exists to expect a relationship between LMX quality and experienced stress, there are only a small number of studies looking at the connection between the two, and these studies tended to rely on cross-sectional methodology and employee self-reports. In other words, we are not currently aware of studies capturing stress using biometric measures to examine whether LMX quality may have consequences for employee health and well-being.

High-quality LMX members are less likely to experience role stress in the form of role ambiguity, role conflict (Gerstner & Day, 1997), or role overload (Rosse & Kraut, 1983; Tordera, González-Romá, & Peiró, 2008). As a result, LMX has been negatively related to overall stress reported by employees (Tanner, Dunn, & Chonko, 1993) and burnout (Huang, Chan, Lam, & Nan, 2010; Thomas & Lankau, 2009). Moreover, studies have shown that LMX tends to alleviate the negative effects of stressful work conditions on employee attitudes and behaviors, such as low levels of person-organization fit (Erdogan, Kraimer, & Liden, 2004), home strain, and work strain (Van Dyne, Jehn, & Cummings, 2002).

Only a handful of studies explored the relationship between LMX quality and work-life conflict. Major and Morganson (2011) theorized that high-quality LMX members may negotiate roles with their leaders in a way that will minimize work-family interference. Moreover, these authors predicted that leaders would provide more family-friendly options to members with whom they have a high-quality exchange, or encourage their members to take advantage of family-friendly policies, resulting in work-life balance. Supporting positive effects of LMX quality for work-life balance, Culbertson, Huffman, and Alden-Anderson (2010) showed that LMX quality resulted in lower levels of hindrance stress, which resulted in lower levels of work-family conflict.

Despite some evidence that LMX quality results in more family-friendly conditions, we feel that there is room for more research investigating the implications of LMX quality for the family domain. It is clear based on the accumulated research on LMX quality that LMX has positive implications for work life. However, it is less clear whether being highly engaged in the work domain will have uniformly positive implications for the family domain. For example, Bernas and Major (2000) showed on a sample of employed women that while LMX quality had a negative indirect effect on work-family interference mediated by job stress, it also had a positive main effect. In other words, while there may be fewer deterrents in one's work life due to high-quality LMX, it is plausible that hours spent at work, one's commitment to work and the supervisor may come at the expense of well-being in the family domain, which is a possibility that deserves more attention. There is some evidence that the LMX-stress link is curvilinear (Harris & Kacmar, 2006; Hochwarter, 2005), suggesting that members in a high-quality LMX are not necessarily immune to stress.

Finally, we were able to identify only one study that examined LMX quality along with an indicator of an individual's overall well-being (as opposed to job-related well-being), which is a study where LMX and life satisfaction was significantly correlated at .22 (Kacmar, Carlson, & Brymer, 1999). A high-quality LMX affords individuals more opportunities to achieve quality of work life, as well as contribute to an individual's feelings about one's self worth, which are key elements of a person's life satisfaction (Erdogan, Bauer, Truxillo, & Mansfield, 2012).

Future research directions. It seems that there is still room for research exploring the effects of LMX quality for stress and well-being of employees. First, we currently know little about the LMX to stress relationship beyond studies based on employee self-reports. Utilizing biomarkers of stress to explore whether LMX quality may affect how a person physiologically experiences stress would make a stronger case for the importance of LMX for employee well-being. Second, the implications of LMX quality for nonwork domains of an employee's life are still unclear. We expect that work orientation and workaholism of a person's manager, degree to which the manager values work-life balance, and personality of the manager (particularly whether the manager has Type A personality) are all factors that would contribute to whether LMX quality results in more or less work-family interference. Finally, we still have a long way to go in investigating the net effects of LMX quality for individual mental well-being. Leaders help shape the work domain, and they may make a person feel a sense of belonging and meaning at work, resulting in greater levels of well-being. If such a link exists, and if a cost to employee physical and mental health exists for lower-quality LMX members, understanding this link would help make a case for more systematic management of manager-employee relationships.

LMX at the Team Level: LMX Mean and Differentiation

As stated up front, LMX theory is based on the idea of differentiation. Early on, researchers have discovered that 90 per cent of the time leaders develop differentiated exchanges with their members (Liden & Graen, 1980). It is only recently that differentiation itself became a construct of interest in the LMX literature. The focus of LMX differentiation studies is an examination of the effects of LMX differentiation (or within group variation in LMX quality) and LMX mean on individual and group outcomes. Does the degree of differentiation make a difference for the individual, above and beyond the focal individual's own LMX quality? Does differentiation have implications for group processes and outcomes or for individual attitudes and behaviors?

Examination of these research questions has been gaining speed in the recent years, even though much remains to be done. Given that LMX development is a function of role differentiation, it is natural that LMX relations are differentiated. A small number of studies examined leader and group characteristics that may add to the degree of differentiation. For example, Ma and Qu (2010) showed that leader values have a role to play in LMX differentiation, whereas Vecchio and Brazil (2007) showed that unit heterogeneity and LMX differentiation were positively correlated. We still do not know whether leader personality traits and the broader organizational culture may play a role.

There are a larger number of studies that have examined the outcomes of differentiation, but it is unclear whether differentiation is a positive or negative influence over outcomes. On the positive side, Boies and Howell (2006) showed that coupled with high LMX mean, differentiation was associated with higher team potency and lower team conflict. Liden, Erdogan, Wayne, and Sparrowe (2006) showed that when task interdependence was high, LMX differentiation was positively related to task performance. Stewart and Johnson (2009) showed that in teams with high gender diversity, LMX differentiation was positively related to team performance. On the negative side, Liao, Liu, and Loi (2010) showed that LMX quality was more positively related to self-efficacy and creativity in teams with low LMX differentiation. LMX differentiation was negatively related to job satisfaction and well-being due to its positive relation with team conflict (Hooper & Martin, 2008). LMX differentiation negatively related to group-level job satisfaction and commitment (Schyns, 2006), and positively predicted inflation in performance ratings (Ma & Qu, 2010). Finally, in teams with low differentiation and high LMX mean, or when leaders were more inclusive in their LMX development, the detrimental effects of team diversity on team level turnover were alleviated.

These results suggest that LMX differentiation does not seem to have unequivocally positive or negative effects on team or individual processes. Instead, a more situational approach may increase our understanding of the differentiation phenomenon. For example, Van Knippenberg and Hogg (2003) postulate that if employees identify with the group, having a leader who has differentiated relations with the team members may potentially be more divisive. This is because differentiation would go against the team spirit that exists within the team. In other words, whether differentiation is a negative or a positive influence likely depends on peer-to-peer relationships that exist within the team. Second, one of the likely effects of differentiation will be greater salience of fairness within the team. Sias and Jablin (1995) showed that differentiated treatment within the team results in greater discussion of fairness concerns within the team for the purposes of emotional expression as well as sense making. Erdogan and Bauer (2010) showed that LMX differentiation was a negative influence on job attitudes, relationships among coworkers, and withdrawal behavior only to the degree to which justice climate did not exist.

LMX differentiation at the group level is an interesting and exciting future research direction for

Table 19.2. Best Practices When Studying LMX Differentiation

✓ Confirm that there are at least three members before considering them a "group."
✓ Confirm that all employees in the group report to the same manager.
✓ Confirm that all employees in the group report to only one manager.
✓ Ensure that you have either (a) sampled the entire group, or (b) employed true randomly sampling to select participants (i.e., snowball sampling is not random sampling and poses special threats to validity to studies of LMX differentiation due to potential sampling bias).
✓ Ensure that 60+% of all direct reports for one manager are included in the final sample.
✓ Control for average LMX before including dispersion statistics (e.g., r_{wg}, SD, or within-group variance).

LMX theory. Henderson, Liden, Glibkowski, and Chaudhry (2009) present a model of antecedents and consequences of LMX differentiation that will likely be a great starting point for future scholars in this area. In addition, we feel that a few measurement issues are noteworthy to mention (see Table 19.2 for a summary). First, most scholars examining LMX differentiation measure LMX at the individual level, and then aggregate individual scores to the group level using metrics such as standard deviation, variance, or r_{wg}. This method assumes that the exchange qualities of the sample of employees drawn from an intact team represent the actual variation that exists within the team. However, if only a small percentage of employees are sampled, or if there is response bias, the conclusions drawn from these studies may have limited generalizability or validity. For example, if five people who are close friends are sampled from a large work group, any effects observed for LMX differentiation may be inflated, because heterogeneity of LMX in a group of close friends will likely be more divisive and disturbing compared to the effects of heterogeneity over the remainder of the group. By the same token, if members with low LMX quality do not respond to the study, the captured LMX differentiation will not represent the real differentiation that exists within the team, which could result in underestimating the effects of differentiation. As a result, one way of dealing with the problem is to make an effort to reach all members of an intact work group and ensuring a large response rate, or conducting a true random sampling of members when this is not feasible. Past researchers customarily used a 60 per cent cutoff for an acceptable response rate (e.g., Liden et al., 2006; Ma & Qu, 2010).

Another alternative method of studying LMX differentiation is an examination of perceived LMX differentiation, rather than using statistical methods of calculating LMX differentiation. Hooper and Martin (2008) have developed a measure of perceived differentiation that has been used for this purpose. The advantage of this method is that it does not require sampling all members of a team, given that employees are reporting on their perceptions of a group-level phenomenon. At the same time, it is likely that actual differentiation that exists within a team and perceived differentiation may not have perfect overlap. Perceived differentiation will likely be affected by a person's own LMX quality, LMX quality of one's close colleagues, as well as expectations about how much differentiation is acceptable. While its convergence with actual differentiation may be limited, it may be a more salient driver of member attitudes and behaviors and therefore is an important construct to study further.

One final caution to future scholars of LMX differentiation relates to the necessity to measure overall LMX quality within the team using LMX mean or LMX median. LMX mean and differentiation tend to be strongly and negatively correlated (e.g., Kinicki & Vecchio, 1994; McClane, 1991; Nishii & Mayer, 2009). Therefore, in order to ascertain whether it is the variation or level of LMX within the team that makes the difference, it seems important to include LMX mean and differentiation simultaneously into models.

LMX in the Context of Peer and Supervisor LMXs

The concept of LMX differentiation explores group-level as well as cross-level effects of LMX theory. A related but distinct direction in the literature is an examination of how peer and supervisor LMXs affect focal members. The idea that members will pay attention to the exchange qualities their peers develop with the leader is not a new one. Duchon, Green, and Taber (1986) showed that individuals accurately perceive the nature of the relationships their peers have with the leader. In other words, LMX relationships are visible to others outside of the immediate dyad. Moreover, the relationship quality peers have with the leader likely matters to the individual, because employees are likely to base their expectations of future treatment on their perceptions of peer LMXs. For example, Erdogan (2002) proposed that employees will expect peer LMXs to relate to peer performance ratings, which would mean that peer LMXs have implications for expectations of future organizational fairness. Furthermore, the exchanges peers have with the leader have the potential to affect one's relations with the peer in question, or coworker exchanges (CWX). Supporting this view, Sherony and Green (2002) showed that when two peers had LMXs of similar quality, their CWX quality tended to be higher as well.

One way in which recent research started examining the effects of peer LMXs on the focal individual is through the concepts of Relative LMX (Henderson, Wayne, Shore, Bommer, & Tetrick, 2008) and LMX social comparisons (Vidyarthi, Liden, Anand, Erdogan, & Ghosh, 2010). These constructs essentially tap into the same phenomenon of how one's LMX quality compares to the LMXs of one's team members. Relative LMX uses the statistical method of subtracting LMX mean from individual LMX to arrive at one's standing, while LMX social comparisons utilize a newly developed survey instrument to capture the perception that one's LMX is of higher or lower-quality compared to one's peers. These studies have shown that controlling for one's LMX quality, having *higher* LMX seems to matter for work behaviors such as performance and citizenship. These findings are interesting and challenge the assumption that the benefits of LMX quality may be maximized if leaders have high-quality LMXs with all members. Instead, it seems that being the one *closer* to the leader has advantages that go beyond simply having a close relationship with the leader.

In other words, a high-quality exchange may become more or less advantageous to the member depending on whether the other members in the group also have high-quality exchanges or whether they have lower-quality exchanges. Having higher-quality LMXs compared to one's peers seems to have advantages for the member, as Relative LMX likely results in greater feelings of security, greater access to organizational information and resources, and greater organizational well-being due to one's proximity to the leader. At the same time, there may be conditions under which being similar to one's peers as opposed to having higher quality LMXs may be more advantageous, such as the condition where work group identification is high. We believe that exploring the conditions under which being similar to one's peers versus being closer to the leader will result in better outcomes for the focal individual is a noteworthy research direction.

In addition to paying attention to the LMXs of their peers, LMX researchers explored the implications of the LMX quality their manager has with their own manager one level up. This concept has been recently labeled as Leader-Leader Exchange (LLX, Tangirala, Green, & Ramanujam, 2007), even though the idea is based on earlier LMX studies exploring the "Pelz Effect" (Graen, Cashman, Ginsburg, & Schiemann, 1977). The Pelz Effect is named after Pelz (1952)'s work where he found that when supervisors have upward influence, their employees are more satisfied with the supervision they receive. Later on, Jablin (1980) termed the moderating effects of leader upward influence on leader behaviors the Pelz Effect. When leaders have a high-quality exchange with their own leaders, they are better positioned to benefit the high-quality LMX members reporting to them, because they can provide more valuable resources, scarcer information, or better visibility to higher levels in the organization.

Prior research has shown a number of effects for LLX. For example, Lee (1998) found that employee perceptions of LLX determines the communication style employees use to approach their leaders. Tangirala et al. (2007) showed that LLX strengthens the relationship between LMX and outcomes. Venkataramani, Green, and Schleicher (2010) showed that LLX results in greater perceived status for the leader, resulting in more favorable job attitudes. Finally, supporting the idea that a leader's relations with those who are higher up have the potential to affect lower-level employees one level below, Erdogan and Enders (2007) found that the leader's exchange quality with the overall organization strengthened the positive effects of LMX on employee satisfaction and performance.

It seems that viewing LMX as a relationship embedded within the context of other relationships opens up a number of intriguing research avenues. Does LLX benefit the select few employees who have high-quality LMX, or does it have broader consequences for the group? How are members affected from their standing in the LMX distribution, and under what conditions different types of distributions may be favored? Taking these ideas a step further, it is easy to postulate a relationship between LMX distribution within the group and social network structure. One's LMX standing may be a reason why some members may be chosen by peers interested in seeking advice, while others are shunned by their peers. The implications of the pattern of LMXs that exist within a work group are interesting and important to investigate.

The Future of LMX Theory

We feel that much is known about the motivating potential of leader-employee exchanges. The breadth and depth of theory and research on the subject are informative about the consequences of a high-quality LMX, and to a lesser extent, about the process of LMX development. Still, we feel that there is much more work to be done by future scholars. We will briefly present an overview of the gaps in the literature as we see them to help provide direction for future researchers interested in LMX phenomena.

Does LMX fit the realities of current organizations? We believe that relationships established with leaders matter more than ever. But which leader? In today's organizations, it is common for employees to report to several leaders for different aspects of their jobs. We were able to identify only two studies that looked at an employee's relations with multiple leaders: Benson and Pattie (2009) explored the differential effects of an expatriate's home and host country managers, and Self, Holt, and Schaninger (2005) explored employee's LMX with immediate supervisor as well as managers one level up, and again found that LMXs with different managers had effects on different outcomes. Instead of making the assumption that one's immediate manager is the most important relation to have, exploring how LMXs with different leaders affect each other, supplement or substitute for each other, may be more in line with the organizational realities professional employees face.

How does LMX relate to one's relationships with coworkers? To date, there are hundreds of investigations examining how LMX is related to one's job attitudes and work behaviors. However, how does LMX affect exchanges with coworkers? Coworker exchanges may covary with LMX similarity (Sherony & Green, 2002). Coworkers may be envious of members with high LMX quality, affecting the relationships among coworkers (Bowler et al., 2010). High-quality LMX members may be regarded as the "teacher's pet" or a liaison to the leader (Sias & Jablin, 1995). Despite the multitude of studies exploring LMX and its outcomes, we do not have systematic investigations of how LMX affects relationships and interactions among coworkers.

Is there a dark side to LMX? To date, studies tended to adopt the belief that high LMX quality is advantageous for members, while low-quality LMX has detrimental consequences. Are there any conditions when high LMX quality may be a curse? The only study we were able to identify as revealing a dark side of LMX was that of Ballinger et al. (2010), which showed that members with high LMX quality were more likely to leave if their leaders left the organization. We feel that there may be more here that deserves investigating. For example, is it possible that high LMX members of workaholic leaders burn out faster and experience greater work-life conflict? Are there conditions under which high-quality LMX members are burdened by too much information about the organization that they are not ready to handle or find it hard to carry the emotional burden of being the one the leader relies on in the most challenging circumstances? We feel that considering the possibility that high-quality LMX relationships may have downsides for the member and the organization is noteworthy to consider.

What are the benefits of LMX to leaders? This is an important research question that has not received any direct research attention (Wilson et al., 2010). To date, the benefits that were examined tended to be in the realm of positive organizational behaviors on the part of employees. However, there may be direct personal benefits to the leaders in question that comes as a result of having high-quality exchanges with one's subordinates, including lower work stress, greater well-being, and greater effectiveness as perceived by one's higher ups. Exploring what leaders get out of high-quality exchanges seems important to determine.

Conclusion

We set out to provide a review article that would serve as a comprehensive primer for those new to the LMX literature, as well as a detailed summary and ideas for future research for research veterans in the area. As we noted earlier, the growth in work done on LMX has been explosive. This is no wonder given that LMX is related to key outcomes such as job satisfaction, turnover, and performance. Further understanding LMX's antecedents is the key to unlocking the full potential of LMX at the dyadic, group, and organizational levels.

References

Anand, S., Vidyarthi, P. R., Liden, R. C., & Rousseau, D. M. (2010). Good citizens in poor-quality relationships: Idiosyncratic deals as a substitute for relationship quality. *Academy of Management Journal, 53*, 970–988.

Andrews, M. C., & Kacmar, K. M. (2001). Discriminating among organizational politics, justice, and support. *Journal of Organizational Behavior, 22*, 347–366.

Ansari, M. A., Hung, D. K. M., & Aafaqi, R. (2007). Leader-member exchange and attitudinal outcomes: Role of procedural justice climate. *Leadership and Organization Development Journal, 28*, 690–709.

Aryee, S., & Chen, Z. X. (2006). Leader-member exchange in a Chinese context: Antecedents, the mediating role of psychological empowerment and outcomes. *Journal of Business Research, 59*, 793–801.

Atinc, G., Darrat, M., Fuller, B., & Parker, B. W. (2010). Perceptions of organizational politics: A meta-analysis of theoretical antecedents. *Journal of Managerial Issues, 22*, 494–513.

Atwater L., & Carmeli, A. (2009). Leader-member exchange, feelings of energy, and involvement in creative work. *Leadership Quarterly, 20*, 264–275.

Ballinger, G. A., Lehman, D. W., & Schoorman, F. D. (2010). Leader-member exchange and turnover before and after succession events. *Organizational Behavior and Human Decision Processes, 113*, 25–36.

Basu, R., & Green, S. G. (1995). Subordinate performance, leader-subordinate compatibility, and exchange quality in leader-member dyads: A field study. *Journal of Applied Social Psychology, 25*, 77–92.

Basu, R., & Green, S. G. (1997). Leader-member exchange and transformational leadership: An empirical examination of innovative behaviors in leader-member dyads. *Journal of Applied Social Psychology*, 27, 477–499.

Bauer T. N., Erdogan, B., Liden, R. C., & Wayne, S. J. (2006). A longitudinal study of the moderating role of extraversion: Leader-member exchange, performance, and turnover during new executive development. *Journal of Applied Psychology, 91*, 298–310.

Bauer, T. N., & Green, S. G. (1996). Development of leader-member exchange: A longitudinal test. *Academy of Management Journal*, 39, 1538–1567.

Benson, G. S., & Pattie, M. (2009). The comparative roles of home and host supervisors in the expatriate experience. *Human Resource Management, 48*, 49–68.

Bernas, K. H., & Major, D. A. (2000). Contributors to stress resistance: Test a model of women's work-family conflict. *Psychology of Women Quarterly, 24*, 170–178.

Bernerth, J., Armenakis, A., Feild, H., Giles, W., & Walker, H. (2008). The influence of personality differences between subordinates-supervisors on perceptions of LMX: An empirical investigation. *Group & Organization Management, 33*, 216–240.

Bezuijen, X. M., van Dam, K., van den Berg, P. T., & Thierry, H. (2010). How leaders stimulate employee learning: A leader-member exchange approach. *Journal of Occupational and Organizational Psychology, 83*, 673–693.

Blau, P. M. (1964). *Exchange and power in social life.* NY: John Wiley & Sons.

Boies, K., & Howell, J. M. (2006). Leader-member exchange in teams: An examination of the interaction between relationship differentiation and mean LMX in explaining team-level outcomes. *Leadership Quarterly, 17*, 246–257.

Bowler, W. M., Halbesleben, J. R. B., & Paul, J. R. B. (2010). If you're close with the leader, you must be a brownnose: The role of leader-member relationships in follower, leader, and coworker attributions of organizational citizenship behavior motives. *Human Resource Management Review, 20*, 309–316.

Breland, J. W., Treadway, D. C., Duke, A. B., & Adams, G. L. (2007). The interactive effect of leader-member exchange and political skill on subjective career success. *Journal of Leadership & Organizational Studies, 13*, 1–14.

Burris, E. R., Detert, J. R., & Chiaburu, D. S. (2008). Quitting before leaving: The mediating effects of psychological attachment and detachment on voice. *Journal of Applied Psychology, 93*, 912–922.

Byrne, D. (1971). *The attraction paradigm.* NY: Academic Press.

Chen, G., Kirkman, B. L., Kanfer, R., Allen, D., & Rosen, B. (2007). A multilevel study of leadership, empowerment, and performance in teams. *Journal of Applied Psychology, 92*, 331–346.

Chen, Z., Lam, W., & Zhong, J. A. (2007). Leader-member exchange and member performance: A new look at individual-level negative feedback-seeking behavior and team-level empowerment climate. *Journal of Applied Psychology, 92*, 202–212.

Chen, Z. X., Tsui, A. S., & Zhong, L. (2008). Reactions to psychological contract breach: A dual perspective. *Journal of Organizational Behavior, 29*, 527–548.

Cogliser, C. C., & Schriesheim, C. A. (2000). Exploring work unit context and leader-member exchange: A multi-level perspective. *Journal of Organizational Behavior, 21*, 487–511.

Colella, A., & Varma, A. (2001). The impact of subordinate disability on leader-member exchange relationships. *Academy of Management Journal, 44*, 304–315.

Culbertson, S. S., Huffman, A. H., & Alden-Anderson, R. (2010). Leader-member exchange and work-family interactions: The mediating role of self-reported challenge-and hindrance-related stress. *Journal of Psychology, 144*, 15–36.

Dansereau, F., Graen, G., & Haga, W. J. (1975). A vertical dyad linkage approach to leadership within formal organizations: A longitudinal investigation of the role making process. *Organizational Behavior and Human Performance, 13*, 46–78.

DeConinck, J. B. (2009). The effect of leader-member exchange on turnover among retail buyers. *Journal of Business Research, 62*, 1081–1086.

DeConinck, J. B. (2011). The effects of leader-member exchange and organizational identification on performance and turnover among salespeople. *Journal of Personal Selling & Sales Management, 1*, 21–34.

Dienesch, R. M., & Liden, R. C. (1986). Leader-member exchange model of leadership: A critique and further development. *Academy of Management Journal, 11*, 618–634.

Dobbins, G. H., Cardy, R. L., & Platz-Vieno, S. J. (1990). A contingency approach to appraisal satisfaction: An initial investigation of the joint effects of organizational variables and appraisal characteristics. *Journal of Management, 16*, 619–632.

Duarte, N. T., Goodson, J. R., & Klich, N. R. (1994). Effects of dyadic quality and duration on performance appraisal. *Academy of Management Journal, 37*, 499–521.

Duchon, D., Green, S. G., & Taber, T. D. (1986). Vertical dyad linkage: A longitudinal assessment of antecedents, measures, and consequences. *Journal of Applied Psychology, 71*, 56–60.

Dulac, T., Coyle-Shapiro, J.A.M., Henderson, D. J., & Wayne, S. J. (2008). Not all responses to breach are the same: The interconnection of social exchange and psychological contract processes in organization. *Academy of Management Journal, 51*, 1079–1098.

Dulebohn, J. H., Bommer, W. H., Liden, R. C., Brouer, R. L., & Ferris, G. R. (2012). A meta-analysis of antecedents and consequences of leader-member exchange: Integrating the past with an eye toward the future. *Journal of Management, 38*, 1715–1759.

Dunegan, K. J., Duchon, D., & Uhl-Bien, M. (1992). Examining the link between leader member exchange and subordinate performance: The role of task analyzability and variety as moderators. *Journal of Management, 18*, 59–76.

Dunegan, K. J., Tierney, P., & Duchon, D. (1992). Perceptions of an innovative climate: Examining the role of divisional affiliation, work group interaction, and leader/subordinate exchange. *IEEE Transactions on Engineering Management, 39*, 227–236.

Eisenberger, R., Huntington, R., Hutchison, S., & Sowa, D. (1986). Perceived organizational support. *Journal of Applied Psychology, 71*, 500–507.

Eisenberger, R., Karagonlar, G., Stinglhamber, F., Neves, P., Becker, T. E., Gonzalez-Morales, M. G., & Steiger-Mueller, M. (2010). Leader-member exchange and affective organizational commitment: The contribution of supervisor's organizational embodiment. *Journal of Applied Psychology, 95*, 1085–1103.

Eisenberger, R., Stinglhamber, F., Vandenberghe, C., Sucharski, I. L., & Rhoades, L. (2002). Perceived supervisor support: Contributions to perceived organizational support and employee retention. *Journal of Applied Psychology, 87*, 565–573.

El Akremi, A., Vandenberghe, C., & Camerman, J. (2010). The role of justice and social exchange relationships in workplace deviance: Test of a mediated model. *Human Relations, 63*, 1687–1717.

Elicker, J. D., Levy, P. E., & Hall, R. J. (2006). The role of leader-member exchange in the performance appraisal process. *Journal of Management, 32*, 531–551.

Engle, E. M., & Lord, R. G. (1997). Implicit theories, self-schemas, and leader-member exchange. *Academy of Management Journal, 40*, 988–1010.

Epitropaki, O., & Martin, R. (2005). From ideal to real: A longitudinal study of the role of implicit leadership theories on leader-member exchanges and employee outcomes. *Journal of Applied Psychology, 90*, 659–676.

Erdogan, B. (2002). Antecedents and consequences of justice perceptions in performance appraisals. *Human Resource Management Review, 12*, 555–578.

Erdogan, B., & Bauer, T. N. (2010). Differentiated leader-member exchanges (LMX): The buffering role of justice climate. *Journal of Applied Psychology, 95*, 1104–1120.

Erdogan, B., Bauer, T. N., Truxillo, D. M., & Mansfield, L. (2012). Whistle while you work: A review of the life satisfaction literature. *Journal of Management, 38*, 1038–1083.

Erdogan, B., & Enders, J. (2007). Support from the top: Supervisors' perceived organizational support as a moderator of leader-member exchange to satisfaction and performance relationships. *Journal of Applied Psychology, 92*, 321–330.

Erdogan, B., Kraimer, M. L., & Liden, R. C. (2004). Work value congruence and intrinsic career success: The compensatory roles of leader-member exchange and perceived organizational support. *Personnel Psychology, 57*, 305–332

Erdogan, B., & Liden, R. C. (2002). Social exchanges in the workplace: A review of recent developments and future research directions in leader-member exchange theory. In L. L. Neider & C. A. Schriesheim (Eds.), *Leadership* (pp. 65–114). Greenwich, CT: Information Age Press.

Erdogan, B., Liden, R. C., & Kraimer, M. L. (2006). Justice and leader-member exçhange: The moderating role of organizational culture. *Academy of Management Journal, 49*, 395–406.

Erdogan, B., Sparrowe, R. T., Liden, R. C., & Dunegan, K. J. (2004). Implications of organizational exchanges for accountability theory. *Human Resource Management Review, 14*, 19–45.

Fairhurst, G. T., & Chandler, T. A. (1989). Social structure in leader-member interaction. *Communication Monographs, 56*, 215–239.

Fairhurst, G. T., Rogers, L. E., & Sarr, R. A. (1987). Manager-subordinate control patterns and judgments about the relationship. In M. McLaughlin (Ed.), *Communication Yearbook* (pp. 395–415). Thousand Oaks, CA: Sage Publications.

Fernandez, C. F., & Vecchio, R. P. (1997). Situational leadership theory revisited: A test of an across-jobs perspective. *Leadership Quarterly, 8*, 67–84.

Furst, S. A., & Cable, D. M. (2008). Employee resistance to organizational change: Managerial influence tactics and leader-member exchange. *Journal of Applied Psychology, 93*, 453–462.

Gerstner, C. R., & Day, D. V. (1997). Meta-analytic review of leader–member exchange theory: Correlates and construct issues. *Journal of Applied Psychology, 82*, 827–844.

Golden, T. D., & Veiga, J. F. (2008). The impact of superior-subordinate relationships on the commitment, job satisfaction, and performance of virtual workers. *Leadership Quarterly, 19*, 77–88.

Goodwin, V. L., Bowler, M., & Whittington, J. L. (2009). A social network perspective on LMX relationships: Accounting for the instrumental value of leader and follower networks. *Journal of Management, 35*, 954–980.

Gouldner, A. W. (1960). The norm of reciprocity: A preliminary statement. *American Sociological Review, 25*, 161–178.

Graen, G. B. (1990). Designing productive leadership systems to improve both work motivation and organizational effectiveness. In U. Kleinbeck, H-H. Quast, H. Thierry, & H. Häcker (Eds.), *Work motivation* (pp. 133–156). Hillsdale, NJ: Lawrence Erlbaum Associates.

Graen, G., Cashman, J. F., Ginsburg, S., & Schiemann, W. (1977). Effects of linking-pin quality on the quality of working life of lower participants. *Administrative Science Quarterly, 22*, 491–504.

Graen, G., Dharwadkar, R., Grewal, R., & Wakabayashi, M. (2006). Japanese career progress: An empirical examination. *Journal of International Business Studies, 37*, 148–161.

Graen, G., Novak, M. A., & Sommerkamp, P. (1982). The effects of leader-member exchange and job design on productivity and satisfaction: Testing a dual attachment model. *Organizational Behavior and Human Performance, 30*, 109–131.

Graen, G., & Scandura, T. (1987). Toward a psychology of dyadic organizing. In B. Staw & L. L. Cummings (Eds.), *Research in Organizational Behavior, 9,* (pp. 175–208). Greenwich, CT: JAI Press.

Graen, G., & Uhl-Bien, M. (1995). Relation-based approach to leadership: Development of leader-member exchange (LMX) theory of leadership over 25 years: Applying a multi-level multi-domain perspective. *Leadership Quarterly, 6*, 219–247.

Green, C. (2008). Leader member exchange and the use of moderating conflict management styles: Impact on relationship quality. *International Journal of Conflict Management, 19*, 92–111.

Green, S. G., Anderson, S. E., & Shivers, S. L. (1996). Demographic and organizational influences on leader-member exchange and related work attitudes. *Organizational Behavior and Human Decision Processes, 66*, 203–214.

Green, S. G., Blank, W., & Liden, R. C. (1983). Market and organizational influences on bank employees' work attitudes and behaviors. *Journal of Applied Psychology, 68*, 298–306.

Greguras, G. J., & Ford, J. M. (2006). An examination of the multidimensionality of supervisor and subordinate perceptions of leader-member exchange. *Journal of Occupational and Organizational Psychology, 79*, 433–465.

Harris, K. J., Harris, R. B., & Brouer, R. L. (2009). LMX and subordinate political skill: Direct and interactive effects on turnover intentions and job satisfaction. *Journal of Applied Social Psychology, 39*, 2373–2395.

Harris, K. J., Harris, R. B., & Eplion, D. M. (2007). Personality, leader-member exchanges, and work outcomes. *Journal of Behavioral and Applied Management, 8*, 92–107.

Harris, K. J., & Kacmar, K. M. (2006). Too much of a good thing: The curvilinear effect of leader-member exchange on stress. *Journal of Social Psychology, 146*, 65–84.

Harris, K. J., Wheeler, A. R., & Kacmar, K. M. (2009). Leader-member exchange and empowerment: Direct and interactive effects on job satisfaction, turnover intentions, and performance. *Leadership Quarterly, 20*, 371–382.

Harris, K. J., Wheeler, A. R., & Kacmar, K. M. (2011). The mediating role of organizational job embeddedness in the LMX-outcomes relationships. *Leadership Quarterly, 22*, 271–281.

Henderson, D. J., Liden, R. C., Glibkowski, B. C., & Chaudhry, A. (2009). LMX differentiation: A multilevel review and examination of its antecedents and outcomes. *Leadership Quarterly, 20*, 517–534.

Henderson, D. J., Wayne, S. J., Shore, L. M., Bommer, W. H., & Tetrick, L. E. (2008). Leader-member exchange: Differentiation, and psychological contract fulfillment: A multilevel examination. *Journal of Applied Psychology, 93*, 1208–1219.

Heneman, R. L., Greenberger, D. B., & Anonyuo, C. (1989). Attributions and exchanges: The effects of interpersonal factors on the diagnosis of employee performance. *Academy of Management Journal, 32*, 466–476.

Hiller, N. J., DeChurch, L. A., Murase, T., & Doty, D. (2011). Searching for outcomes of leadership: A 25-year review. *Journal of Management, 37*, 1137–1177.

Hochwarter, W. (2005). LMX and job tension: Linear and non-linear effects and affectivity. *Journal of Business and Psychology, 19*, 505–520.

Hofmann, D. A., & Morgeson, F. P. (1999). Safety-related behavior as a social exchange: The role of perceived organizational support and leader-member exchange. *Journal of Applied Psychology, 84*, 286–296.

Hofmann, D. A., Morgeson, F. P., & Gerras, S. J. (2003). Climate as a moderator of the relationship between leader-member exchange and content specific citizenship: Safety climate as an exemplar. *Journal of Applied Psychology, 88*, 170–178.

Hooper, D. T., & Martin, R. (2008). Beyond personal leader-member exchange (LMX) quality: The effects of perceived LMX variability on employee reactions. *Leadership Quarterly, 19*, 20–30.

Hsiung, H.-H., & Tsai, W.-C. (2009). Job definition discrepancy between supervisors and subordinates: The antecedent role of LMX and outcomes. *Journal of Occupational and Organizational Psychology, 82*, 89–112.

Huang, X., Chan, S., Lam, W., & Nan, X. S. (2010). The joint effect of leader-member exchange and emotional intelligence on burnout and work performance in call centers. *International Journal of Human Resource Management, 21*, 1124–1144.

Ilies, R., Nahrgang, J. D., & Morgeson, F. P. (2007). Leader-member exchange and citizenship behaviors: A meta-analysis. *Journal of Applied Psychology, 92*, 269–277.

Jablin, F. M. (1980). Superior's upward influence, satisfaction, and openness in superior-subordinate communication: A reexamination of the "Pelz effect." *Human Communication Research, 6*, 210–220.

Janssen, O., & van Yperen, N. W. (2004). Employees' goal orientations, the quality of leader-member exchange, and the outcomes of job performance and job satisfaction. *Academy of Management Journal, 47*, 368–384.

Johnson, J., Truxillo, D. M., Erdogan, B., Bauer, T. N., & Hammer, L. (2009). Perceptions of overall fairness: Are effects on job performance moderated by leader-member exchange? *Human Performance, 22*, 432–449.

Jordan, P. J., & Troth, A. (2011). Emotional intelligence and leader member exchange: The relationship with employee turnover intentions and job satisfaction. *Leadership & Organization Development Journal, 32*, 260–280.

Kacmar, K. M., Carlson, D. S., & Brymer, R. A. (1999). Antecedents and consequences of organizational commitment: A comparison of two scales. *Educational and Psychological Measurement, 59*, 976–994.

Kacmar, K. M., Witt, L. A., Zivnuska, S., & Gully, S. M. (2003). The interactive effect of leader-member exchange and communication frequency on performance ratings. *Journal of Applied Psychology, 88*, 764–772.

Keller, T., & Dansereau, F. (2001). The effect of adding items to scales: An illustrative case of LMX. *Organizational Research Methods, 4*, 131–143.

Kinicki, A. J., & Vecchio, R. P. (1994). Influences on the quality of supervisor-subordinate relations: The role of time-pressure, organizational commitment, and locus of control. *Journal of Organizational Behavior, 15*, 75–82.

Klein, H. J., & Kim, J. S. (1998). A field study of the influence of situational constraints, leader-member exchange, and goal commitment on performance. *Academy of Management Journal, 41*, 88–95.

Kozlowski, S.W.J., & Doherty, M. L. (1989). Integration of climate and leadership: Examination of a neglected issue. *Journal of Applied Psychology, 74*, 546–553.

Kraimer, M. L., Seibert, S. E., Wayne, S. J., Liden, R. C., & Bravo, J. (2011). Antecedents and outcomes of organizational support for development: The critical role of career opportunities. *Journal of Applied Psychology, 96*, 485–500.

Krone, K. J. (1991). Effects of leader-member exchange on subordinates' upward influence attempts. *Communication Research Reports, 8*, 9–18.

Kudisch, J. D., Fortunato, V. J., & Smith, A.F.R. (2006). Contextual and individual difference factors predicting individuals' desire to provide upward feedback. *Group & Organization Management, 31*, 503–529.

Lam, W., Huang. X., & Snape, E. (2007). Feedback-seeking behavior and leader-member exchange: Do supervisor-attributed motives matter? *Academy of Management Journal, 50*, 348–363.

Lapierre, L. M., & Hackett, R. D. (2007). Trait conscientiousness, leader-member exchange, job satisfaction and organizational citizenship behaviour: A test of an integrative model. *Journal of Occupational and Organizational Psychology, 80*, 539–554.

Law, L. S., Wong, C.-S., Wang, D., & Wang, L. (2000). Effect of supervisor-subordinate guanxi on supervisory decisions in China: An empirical investigation. *International Journal of Human Resource Management, 11*, 751–765.

Lee, H. E., Park, H. S., Lee, T. S., & Lee, D. W. (2007). Relationships between LMX and subordinates' feedback-seeking behaviors. *Social Behavior and Personality, 35*, 659–674.

Lee, J. (1998). Maintenance communication in superior-subordinate relationships: An exploratory investigation of group social context and the "Pelz effect." *Southern Communication Journal, 63*, 144–157.

Lee, J. (1999). Leader-member exchange, gender, and members' communication expectations with leaders. *Communication Quarterly, 47*, 415–429.

Li, N., Liang, J., & Crant, J. M. (2010). The role of proactive personality in job satisfaction and organizational citizenship behavior: A relational perspective. *Journal of Applied Psychology, 95*, 395–404.

Liao, H., Liu, D., & Loi, R. (2010). Looking at both sides of the social exchange coin: A social cognitive perspective on the joint effects of relationship quality and differentiation on creativity. *Academy of Management Journal, 53*, 1090–1109.

Liden, R. C., Erdogan, B., Wayne, S. J., & Sparrowe, R. T. (2006). Leader-member exchange, differentiation, and task interdependence: Implications for individual and group performance. *Journal of Organizational Behavior, 27*, 723–746.

Liden, R. C., & Graen, G. (1980). Generalizability of the vertical dyad linkage model of leadership. *Academy of Management Journal, 23*, 451–465.

Liden, R. C., & Maslyn, J. M. (1998). Multidimensionality of leader-member exchange: An empirical assessment through scale development. *Journal of Management, 24*, 43–72.

Liden, R. C., Sparrowe, R. T., & Wayne, S. J. (1997). Leader-member exchange theory: The past and potential for the future. *Research in Personnel and Human Resources Management, 15*, 47–119.

Liden, R. C., Wayne, S. J., & Sparrowe, R. T (2000). An examination of the mediating role of psychological empowerment on the relations between the job, interpersonal relationships, and work outcomes. *Journal of Applied Psychology, 85*, 407–416.

Liden, R. C., Wayne, S. J., & Stilwell, D. (1993). A longitudinal study on the early development of leader-member exchanges. *Journal of Applied Psychology, 78*, 662–674.

Ma, L., & Qu, Q. (2010). Differentiation in leader-member exchange: A hierarchical linear modeling approach. *Leadership Quarterly, 21*, 733–744.

Mahsud, R., Yukl, G., & Prussia, G. (2010). Leader empathy, ethical leadership, and relations-oriented behaviors as antecedents of leader-member exchange quality. *Journal of Managerial Psychology, 25*, 561–577.

Major, D. A., & Morganson, V. J. (2011). Coping with work-family conflict: A leader-member exchange perspective. *Journal of Occupational Health Psychology, 16*, 126–138.

Martin, R., Thomas, G., Charles, K., Epitropaki, O., & McNamara, R. (2005). The role of leader-member exchanges in mediating the relationship between locus of control and work reactions. *Journal of Occupational and Organizational Psychology, 78*, 141–147.

Maslyn, J. M., & Uhl-Bien, M. (2001). Leader-member exchange and its dimensions: Effects of self-effort and other's effort on relationship quality. *Journal of Applied Psychology, 86*, 697–708.

Masterson, S. S., Lewis, K., Goldman, B. M., & Taylor, M. S. (2000). Integrating justice and social exchange: The differing effects of fair procedures and treatment on work relationships. *Academy of Management Journal, 43*, 738–748.

McClane, W. E. (1991). The interaction of leader and member characteristics in the leader-member exchange (LMX) model of leadership. *Small Group Research, 22*, 283–300.

McManus, S. E., & Russell, J.E.A. (1997). New directions for mentoring research: An examination of related constructs. *Journal of Vocational Behavior, 51*, 145–161.

Morrow, P. C., Suzuki, Y., Crum, M. R., Ruben, R., & Pautsch, G. (2005). The role of leader-member exchange in high turnover work environments. *Journal of Managerial Psychology, 20*, 681–694.

Moss, S. E., Sanchez, J. I., Brumbaugh, A. M., & Borkowski, N. (2009). The mediating role of feedback avoidance behavior in the LMX performance relationship. *Group & Organization Management, 34*, 645–664.

Mueller, B. H., & Lee, J. (2002). Leader-member exchange and organizational communication satisfaction in multiple contexts. *Journal of Business Communication, 39*, 220–244.

Murphy, S. E., & Ensher, E. A. (1999). The effects of leader and subordinate characteristics in the development of leader-member exchange quality. *Journal of Applied Social Psychology, 29*, 1371–1394.

Nahrgang, J. D., Morgeson, F. P., & Ilies, R. (2009). The development of leader-member exchanges: Exploring how personality and performance influence leader and member relationships over time. *Organizational Behavior and Human Decision Processes, 108*, 256–266.

Nishii, L. H., & Mayer, D. M. (2009). Do inclusive leaders help to reduce turnover in diverse groups? The moderating role of leader-member exchange in the diversity to turnover relationship. *Journal of Applied Psychology, 94*, 1412–1426.

Ozer, M. (2008). Personal and task-related moderators of leader-member exchange among software developers. *Journal of Applied Psychology, 93*, 1174–1182.

Paglis, L. L., & Green, S. G. (2002). Both sides now: Supervisors and subordinate perspectives on relationship quality. *Journal of Applied Social Psychology, 32*, 250–276.

Paparoidamis, N. G., & Guenzi, P. (2009). An empirical investigation into the impact of relationship selling and LMX on salespeople's behaviours and sales effectiveness. *European Journal of Marketing, 43*, 1053–1075.

Pelled, L. H., & Xin, K. R. (2000). Relational demography and relationship quality in two cultures. *Organization Studies, 21*, 1077–1094.

Pellegrini, E. K., & Scandura, T. A. (2006). Leader-member exchange (LMX), paternalism and delegation in the Turkish

business culture: An empirical investigation. *Journal of International Business Studies, 37*, 264–279.
Pelz, D. C. (1952). Influence: A key to effective leadership in the first-line supervisor. *Personnel, 29*, 209–217.
Peng, K. Z., Ngo, H.-Y., Shi, J., & Wong, C.-S. (2009). Gender differences in the work commitment of Chinese workers: An investigation of two alternative explanations. *Journal of World Business, 44*, 323–335.
Phillips, A. S., & Bedeian, A. G. (1994). Leader-follower exchange quality: The role of personal and interpersonal attributes. *Academy of Management Journal, 37*, 990–1001.
Piccolo, R. F., & Colquitt, J. A. (2006). Transformational leadership and job behaviors: The mediating role of core job characteristics. *Academy of Management Journal, 49*, 327–340.
Pillai, R., Scandura, T. A., & Williams, E. A. (1999). Leadership and organizational justice: Similarities and differences across cultures. *Journal of International Business Studies, 30*, 763–779.
Podsakoff, P. M., MacKenzie, S. M., Lee, J., & Podsakoff, N. P. (2003). Common method variance in behavioral research: A critical review of the literature and recommended remedies. *Journal of Applied Psychology,* 88, 879–903.
Restubog, S.L.D., Bordia, P., & Bordia S. (2011). Investigating the role of psychological contract breach on career success: Convergent evidence from two longitudinal studies. *Journal of Vocational Behavior, 79*, 428–437.
Rosen, C. C., Harris, K. J., & Kacmar, K. M. (2011). LMX, context perceptions, and performance: An uncertainty management perspective. *Journal of Management, 37*, 819–838.
Rosse, J. G., & Kraut, A. I. (1983). Reconsidering the vertical dyad linkage model of leadership. *Journal of Occupational Psychology, 56*, 63–71.
Scaduto, A., Lindsay, D., & Chiaburu, D. S. (2008). Leader influences on training effectiveness: Motivation and outcome expectation processes. *International Journal of Training and Development, 12*, 158–170.
Scandura, T. A., & Graen, G. B. (1984). Moderating effects of initial leader-member exchange status on the effects of a leadership intervention. *Journal of Applied Psychology, 69*, 428–436.
Scandura, T. A., Graen, G. B., & Novak, M. A. (1986). When managers decide not to decide autocratically: An investigation of leader-member exchange and decision influence. *Journal of Applied Psychology, 71*, 579–584.
Scandura, T. A., & Schriesheim, C. A. (1994). Leader-member exchange and supervisor career mentoring as complementary constructs in leadership research. *Academy of Management Journal, 37*, 1588–1602.
Scherbaum, C. A., Finlinson, S., Barden, K., & Tamanini, K. (2006). Applications of item response theory to measurement issues in leadership research. *Leadership Quarterly, 17*, 366–386.
Schriesheim, C. A., Castro, S. L., & Yammarino, F. J. (2000). Investigating contingencies: An examination of the impact of span of supervision and upward controllingness on leader-member exchange using traditional and multivariate within-and between-entities analysis. *Journal of Applied Psychology, 85*, 659–677.
Schriesheim, C. A., Neider, L. L., & Scandura, T. A. (1998). Delegation and leader-member exchange: Main effects, moderators, and measurement issues. *Academy of Management Journal, 41*, 298–318.
Schyns, B. (2006). Are group consensus in LMX and share work values related to organizational outcomes? *Small Group Research, 37*, 20–35.
Schyns, B., Kroon, B., & Moors, G. (2008). Follower characteristics and the perception of leader-member exchange. *Journal of Managerial Psychology, 23*, 772–788.
Scott, S. G., & Bruce, R. A. (1994). Determinants of innovative behavior: A path model of individual innovation in the workplace. *Academy of Management Journal, 37*, 580–607.
Scott, S. G., & Bruce, R. A. (1998). Following the leader in R&D: The joint effect of subordinate problem-solving style and leader-member relations on innovative behavior. *IEEE Transactions on Engineering Management, 45*, 3–10.
Sears, G. J., & Holmvall, C. M. (2010). The joint influence of supervisor and subordinate emotional intelligence on leader-member exchange. *Journal of Business and Psychology, 25*, 593–605.
Seers, A. (1989). Team-member exchange quality: A new construct for role-making research. *Organizational Behavior and Human Decision Processes, 43*, 118–135.
Seers, A., & Graen, G. B. (1984). The dual attachment concept: A longitudinal investigation of the combination of task characteristics and leader-member exchange. *Organizational Behavior and Human Performance, 33*, 283–306.
Sekiguchi, T., Burton, J. P., & Sablynski, C. J. (2008). The role of job embeddedness on employee performance: The interactive effects with leader-member exchange and organization-based self-esteem. *Personnel Psychology, 61*, 761–792.
Self, D. R., Holt, D. T., & Schaninger, W. S. (2005). Work-group organizational support: A test of distinct dimensions. *Journal of Occupational and Organizational Psychology, 78*, 133–140.
Shapiro, D. L., Boss, A. D. Salas, S., Tangirala, S., & von Glinow, M. A. (2011). When are transgressing leaders punitively judged? An empirical test. *Journal of Applied Psychology, 96*, 412–422.
Sherony, K. M., & Green, S. G. (2002). Coworker exchange: Relationships between coworkers, leader-member exchange, and work attitudes. *Journal of Applied Psychology, 87*, 542–548.
Sias, P. M., & Jablin, F. M. (1995). Differential superior-subordinate relations, perceptions of fairness, and coworker communication. *Human Communication Research, 22*, 5–38.
Sin, H. P., Nahrgang, J. D., & Morgeson, F. P. (2009). Understanding why they don't see eye-to-eye: An examination of leader-member exchange (LMX) agreement. *Journal of Applied Psychology, 94*, 1048–1057.
Snyder, R. A., Williams, R. R., & Cashman, J. F. (1984). Age, tenure, and work perceptions as predictors of reactions to performance feedback. *Journal of Psychology, 116*, 11–21.
Sparrowe, R. T., & Liden R. C. (1997). Process and structure in leader-member exchange. *Academy of Management Review, 22*, 522–552.
Sparrowe, R. T., & Liden, R. C. (2005). Two routes to influence: Integrating leader-member exchange and network perspectives. *Administrative Science Quarterly, 50*, 505–535.
Sparrowe, R. T., Soetjipto, B. W., & Kraimer, M. L. (2006). Do leaders' influence tactics relate to members' helping behavior? It depends on the quality of the relationship. *Academy of Management Journal, 49*, 1194–1208.
Stark, E., & Poppler, P. (2009). Leadership, performance evaluations, and all the usual suspects. *Personnel Review, 38*, 320–338.

Stepina, L. P., Perrewe, P. L., Hassell, B. L., Harris, J. R., & Mayfield, C. R. (1991). A comparative test of the independent effects of interpersonal, task, and reward domains on personal and organizational outcomes. *Journal of Social Behavior and Personality, 6*, 93–104.

Stewart, M. M., & Johnson, O. E. (2009). Leader–member exchanges as a moderator of the relationship between work group diversity and team performance. *Group & Organization Management, 34*, 507–535.

Sturges, J., Conway, N., & Liefooghe, A. (2010). Organizational support, individual attributes, and the practice of career self-management behavior. *Group & Organization Management, 35*, 108–141.

Suazo, M. M., Turnley, W. H., & Mai-Dalton, R. R. (2008). Characteristics of the supervisor-subordinate relationship as predictors of psychological contract breach. *Journal of Managerial Issues, 20*, 295–312.

Tangirala, S., Green, S. G., & Ramanujam, R. (2007). In the shadow of the boss's boss: Effects of supervisors' upward exchange relationships on employees. *Journal of Applied Psychology, 92*, 309–320.

Tanner, J. F., Dunn, M. G., & Chonko, L. B. (1993). Vertical exchange and salesperson stress. *Journal of Personal Selling and Sales Management, 13*, 27–36.

Tepper, B. J., Uhl-Bien, M., Kohut, G. F., Rogelberg, S. G., Lockhart, D. E., & Ensley, M. D. (2006). Subordinates' resistance and managers' evaluations of subordinates' performance. *Journal of Management, 32*, 185–209.

Thibodeaux, H. F., & Lowe, R. H. (1996). Convergence of leader-member exchange and mentoring: An investigation of social influence patterns. *Journal of Social Behavior and Personality, 11*, 97–114.

Thomas, C. H., & Lankau, M. J. (2009). Preventing burnout: The effects of LMX and mentoring on socialization, role stress, and burnout. *Human Resource Management, 48*, 417–432.

Tierney, P. (1999). Work relations as a precursor to a psychological climate for change: The role of work group supervisors and peers. *Journal of Organizational Change Management, 12*, 120–133.

Tierney, P., Bauer, T. N., & Potter, R. E. (2002). Extra-role behavior among Mexican employees: The impact of LMX, group acceptance, and job attitudes. *International Journal of Selection and Assessment, 10*, 292–303.

Tierney, P., Bauer, T. N., & Rogers, R. (2002). *Destructive leadership and LMX*. In P. Tierney and T. N. Bauer (Symposium Co-Chairs) with T. Scandura (Discussant), Showcase Symposium on Destructive Leader Behaviors. Academy of Management Annual Meeting, Denver, CO.

Tierney, P., Farmer, S M., & Green, G. N. (1999). An examination of leadership and employee creativity: The relevance of traits and relationships. *Personnel Psychology, 52*, 591–620.

Trodera, N., González-Romá, V., & Peiró, J. M. (2008). The moderator effect of psychological climate on the relationship between leader—member exchange (LMX) quality and role overload. *European Journal of Work and Organizational Psychology, 17*, 55–72.

Townsend, J., Phillips, J. S., & Elkins, T. J. (2000). Employee retaliation: The neglected consequence of poor leader-member exchange relations. *Journal of Occupational Health Psychology, 5*, 457–463.

Tumasjan, A., Strobel, M., & Welpe, I. (2011). Ethical leadership evaluations after moral transgression: Social distance makes the difference. *Journal of Business Ethics, 99*, 609–622.

van Dam, K., Oreg, S., & Schyns, B. (2008). Daily work contexts and resistance to organizational change: The role of leader-member exchange, development climate, and change process characteristics. *Applied Psychology: An International Review, 57*, 313–334.

Van Dyne, L., Jehn, K. A., & Cummings, A. (2002). Differential effects of strain on two forms of work performance: Individual employee sales and creativity. *Journal of Organizational Behavior, 23*, 57–74.

Van Dyne, L., Kamdar, D., & Joireman, J. (2008). In-role perceptions buffer the negative impact of low LMX on helping and enhance the positive impact of high LMX on voice. *Journal of Applied Psychology, 93*, 1195–1207.

Van Knippenberg, D., & Hogg, M. A. (2003). A social identity model of leadership effectiveness in organizations. *Research in Organizational Behavior, 25*, 243–295.

Varma, A., Srinivas, E. S., & Stroh, L. K. (2005). A comparative study of the impact of leader-member exchange in US and Indian samples. *Cross Cultural Management: An International Journal, 12*, 84–95.

Vecchio, R. P., & Brazil, D. M. (2007). Leadership and sex-similarity: A comparison in a military setting. *Personnel Psychology, 60*, 303–335.

Venkataramani, V., Green S. G., & Schleicher, D. J. (2010). Well-connected leaders: The impact of leaders' social network ties on LMX and members' work attitudes. *Journal of Applied Psychology, 95*, 1071–1084.

Vidyarthi, P. R., Liden, R. C., Anand, S., Erdogan, B., & Ghosh, S. (2010). Where do I stand? Examining the effects of leader-member exchange social comparison on employee work behaviors. *Journal of Applied Psychology, 95*, 849–861.

Wakabayashi, M., & Graen, G. B. (1984). The Japanese career progress study: A 7-year follow-up. *Journal of Applied Psychology, 69*, 603–614.

Wakabayashi, M., & Graen, G. (1989). Human resource development of Japanese managers: Leadership and career investment. *Research in Personnel and Human Resources Management, 1*, 235–256.

Wakabayashi, M., Graen, G., Graen, M., & Graen, M. (1988). Japanese management progress: Mobility into middle management. *Journal of Applied Psychology, 73*, 217–227.

Wakabayashi, M., Graen, G., & Uhl-Bien, M. (1990). The generalizability of the hidden investment hypothesis in leading Japanese corporations. *Human Relations, 43*, 1099–1116.

Wakabayashi, M., Minami, T., Hashimoto, M., Sano, K., Graen, G., & Novak, M. (1980). Managerial career development: Japanese style. *International Journal of Intercultural Relations, 4*, 391–420.

Walumbwa, F. O., Mayer, D. M., Wang, P., Wang, H., Workman, K., & Christensen, A. L. (2011). Linking ethical leadership to employee performance: The roles of leader-member exchange, self-efficacy, and organizational identification. *Organizational Behavior and Human Decision Processes, 115*, 204–213.

Wang, H., Law, K. S., Hackett, R. D., Wang, D., & Chen, Z. X. (2005). Leader-member exchange as a mediator of the relationship between transformational leadership and followers' performance and organizational citizenship behavior. *Academy of Management Journal, 48*, 420–432.

Wayne, S. J., & Ferris, G. R. (1990). Influence tactics, affect, and exchange quality in supervisor-subordinate interactions: A laboratory experiment and field study. *Journal of Applied Psychology, 75*, 487–499.

Wayne, S. J., Liden, R. C., Kraimer, M. L., & Graf, I. K. (1999). The role of human capital, motivation and supervisor sponsorship in predicting career success. *Journal of Organizational Behavior, 20*, 577–595.

Wayne, S. J., Shore, L. M., Bommer, W. H., & Tetrick, L. E. (2002). The role of fair treatment and rewards in perceptions of organizational support and leader-member exchange. *Journal of Applied Psychology, 87*, 590–598.

Wheeler, A. R., Harris, K. J., & Harvey, P. (2010). Moderating and mediating the HRM effectiveness—intent to turnover relationship: The roles of supervisors and job embeddedness. *Journal of Managerial Issues, 2*, 182–196.

Wilson, K. S., Sin, H. P., & Conlon, D. E. (2010). What about the leader in leader-member exchange? The impact of resource exchanges and substitutability on the leader. *Academy of Management Review, 35*, 358–372.

Yrle, A. C., Hartman, S., & Galle, W. P. (2002). An investigation of relationships between communication style and leader-member exchange. *Journal of Communication Management, 6*, 257–268.

Yukl, G., & Fu, P. P. (1999). Determinants of delegation and consultation by managers. *Journal of Organizational Behavior, 20*, 219–232.

Yukl, G., O'Donnell, M., & Taber, T. (2009). Influence of leader behaviors on the leader-member exchange relationship. *Journal of Managerial Psychology, 24*, 289–299.

Zhou, X., & Schriesheim, C. A. (2010). Quantitative and qualitative examination of propositions concerning supervisor-subordinate convergence in descriptions of leader-member exchange (LMX) quality. *Leadership Quarterly, 21*, 826–843.

CHAPTER

20 Leadership and Social Networks: Initiating a Different Dialog

Raymond T. Sparrowe

Abstract

This chapter offers a novel approach to integrating leadership theories and social network perspectives. Unlike previous efforts that are organized around social network concepts, the author initiates a dialog that is organized in relation to leadership theories. He begins by identifying several of the primary explanatory accounts whereby leadership is held to affect the discretionary attitudes and behaviors of organizational members. These explanatory accounts include exchange, the basis of Leader–Member Exchange (LMX) theory; categorization, including Implicit Leadership Theory (ILT) and other cognitive approaches; and identity processes, such as identification, internalization, and the engagement of self-systems. These causal accounts then serve as the focal point for initiating dialog with the social network perspective and its emphasis on embeddedness within the structure of relationships. In some cases, opportunities for integration emerge readily; in others, the juxtaposition of leadership theories and the social network perspectives is less easily resolved in a new synthesis.

Key Words: embeddedness, identification, implicit leadership theories, internalization, leader–member exchange theory, self-concept, social networks

Introduction

This chapter joins an emerging stream of research that engages contemporary leadership theories from the social network perspective. It is both retrospective and prospective. It aims to indicate in a meaningful way where researchers have come so far, calling attention to the novel insights the social network perspective has brought to our understanding of the nature of leadership. The chapter also looks forward, identifying opportunities for further dialog with the social network perspective that hold the potential of illuminating in greater detail the nuances of organizational leadership.

In addition to being retrospective and prospective, this chapter is constructive and, at times, critical. In characterizing the distinctive nature of the social network perspective it stresses its emphasis on the structure of social relationships. Although there are important exceptions (Kilduff, Crossland, Tsai, & Krackhardt, 2008; Kilduff & Krackhardt, 1994), the attributes of individuals have played a subordinate role within social network theory and research.[1] Contrast this structural view with leadership theories that attribute outcomes to individual differences, whether those differences are based on personality (Antonakis, Day, & Schyns, 2012; Judge, Piccolo, & Kosalka, 2009) or behavior (DeRue, Nahrgang, Wellman, & Humphrey, 2011; Lambert, Tepper, Carr, Holt, & Barelka, 2012), and a sense of the potential for opposing views readily emerges. Similarly, within the social network perspective there is a clear sense that network structure constrains the opportunities for individual agency, whereas, in some leadership theories, the actions of leaders are described in ways that make them appear to be almost completely unfettered. Where there are such potentially opposing views, they deserve to be brought out and their limits tested through critical reflection and constructive elaboration.

This is not the first effort in framing a dialog between leadership theories and the social network perspective. Brass (2001) introduced social network concepts under the general framework of "social capital" and related those concepts to a number of leadership perspectives. A similar approach is found in Brass and Krackhardt (1999), where the emphasis is on how leaders in "network organizations" benefit from particular strategies based on strong or weak relationships. A third example is that of Balkundi and Kilduff (2006), who develop a model of leadership effectiveness in which the antecedents are dimensions of leaders' individual and organizational networks.

Why yet another discussion of leadership and social networks, and what differentiates this chapter from previous treatments of the topic? The organization of topics in the aforementioned examples is drawn from social network concepts; each concept is described and implications for leadership are drawn. Here, in contrast, the integration is organized around several of the primary leadership perspectives and the underlying question being posed is whether, and in what ways, the network perspective offers novel insight. This difference in organization means that those instances in which the social network perspective and leadership theories stand in uneasy opposition will be more evident.

The potential value of this approach can be seen by means of an initial example. Following Yukl (2010), leadership can be conceptualized in terms of influence. From the leadership perspective, then, it follows that leaders exert influence over members by virtue of their traits, behavior, character, and charisma, etc. The network perspective also is interested in the antecedents of influence, but its focus is on how one's structural position within a network (i.e., centrality) lends influence through access to resources and control over their flow (Brass, 1984). Based on this common interest in interpersonal influence, questions about the effectiveness leaders' social networks can then be posed and strategies for using networks to enhance influence can be elaborated (e.g., Brass, 2001; Brass & Krackhardt, 1999). This approach has led to important insights regarding the opportunities and constraints leaders face in influencing others within organizations; however, the relationships of network position and leadership to influence thus remain additive because each relies on an independent causal mechanism. The objective of this chapter is to engage a dialog between leadership theories and the social network perspective in terms of their underlying explanatory mechanisms.

A Typology of Explanatory Accounts

Given the large number of leadership theories that have engaged the efforts of scholars in recent years, a simplifying typology is necessary to make a dialog with the social network perspective tractable. There are several ways one might imagine carving up this complex domain, but for the purposes of this chapter it is useful to entertain the possibility that these theories draw from a much smaller number of explanatory accounts of the impact of leadership on member outcomes, and the similarities and differences in those accounts describe boundaries that allow for categorization. Further, by focusing on these underlying leadership mechanisms, the potential for dialog with the social network perspective is enhanced because any effort at integration can be built "from the inside out."

Before turning to the specific mechanisms, it is worthwhile to pause briefly at the question of what defines the domain of leadership and what are its most important outcomes. Yukl's (2010) definition is a helpful point of departure: "Leadership is the process of influencing others to understand and agree about what needs to be done and how to do it, and the process of facilitating individual and collective efforts to accomplish shared objectives" (p. 8). Implied in this description of leadership are several relevant points. To the extent that leaders influence, members defer. Similarly, if leadership is a process of facilitation, then members contribute effort toward those shared objectives. The source of this deference and investment of effort lies at the foundation of leadership because it explains how and why leadership "works" to accomplish shared objectives. Further, these objectives encompass a variety of discretionary outcomes addressed in leadership research such as commitment to the organization, in-role and extra-role performance, cooperation with members of the team, and intentions to stay.

In developing taxonomies of leadership theories, a number of scholars (Avolio, Walumbwa, & Weber, 2009; House & Aditya, 1997; Yukl, 2010) discuss the mechanisms through which members defer to leaders in ways that are evidenced by discretionary attitudes and behaviors. DeRue et al. (2011) develop and test a model in which the relationships between leadership traits and outcomes are mediated by two broad categories of variables: leader behaviors, such as initiating structure and consideration, and member cognitions, such as categorizations and identification. Hernandez, Eberly, Avolio, and Johnson (2011) map leadership theories into a two-dimensional matrix with the locus of leadership (leader, follower, dyad, etc.) on the *x*-axis and four basic "mechanisms"—affect, cognitions, behaviors, and traits—on the *y*-axis. So, there is no shortage of explanatory accounts for the effects of leadership on member outcomes! Further, as Hernandez and her colleagues (2011) point out, any single theory can rely on multiple mechanisms in understanding leadership effectiveness.

Fortunately, a small number of such explanatory mechanisms appear with relative frequency across multiple leadership theories and, as the examples mentioned earlier indicate, they lend themselves readily to being organized under larger categories. This chapter identifies and focuses on three fundamental classes of explanatory mechanisms: those based in exchange theory; those drawing from implicit leadership theories (ILTs) and matching, which I call categorization explanations; and those based on identity theories. A number of more specific causal logics are then arrayed under each.

Exchange-based explanations represent leaders and members as parties to exchanges for valued resources, be those resources economic or social (Blau, 1964). Simple—indeed, simplistic—explanations that see member compliance to leader requests as a function of rewards (incentives) fall within this category. But so also do more nuanced explanations that are based on social exchange, such as the leader–member exchange (LMX) perspective, which has seen several efforts at integration with social network theories (Goodwin, Bowler, & Whittington, 2009; Sparrowe & Liden, 2005; Venkataramani, Green, & Schleicher, 2010).

Explanatory mechanisms based on categorization describe how members hold implicit leadership theories (ILTs) that serve as prototypes of ideal leaders against which the behavior of their leaders is compared in a matching process (Eden & Leviatan, 1975; Offermann, Kennedy, & Wirtz, 1994). Leaders, in turn, hold implicit followership theories (IFTs) that they match to the behavior of members (Sy, 2010). Because much of this work seeks to explain how members come to categorize their leaders—say, as effective or ineffective—through the matching process, I refer to this explanatory mechanism as categorization. How members' categorizations of their leaders are related to discretionary attitudes and behaviors often takes an indirect path through other leadership constructs such as LMX (Engle & Lord, 1997; Epitropaki & Martin, 2005).[2]

Within the domain of categorization-based accounts, leadership scholars have developed in considerable detail the proposition that ILTs are connectionist networks or knowledge structures (Foti, Knee, & Backert, 2008; Hanges, Lord, & Dickson, 2000; Lord & Shondrick, 2011). This proposition is interesting in its own right given work from the social network perspective on "cognitive networks" (Kilduff et al., 2008; Krackhardt, 1987; Krackhardt & Kilduff, 1990). Although different in important respects, their apparent similarities prompt critical reflection.

The third category of explanatory mechanisms attributes the effects of leadership to process related to identity. Within this category, I further distinguish between explanatory accounts based on (a) member' identification and internalization and (b) the engagement of self systems. Identification and internalization are common explanations for the effects of charismatic and transformational leadership (Kark, Shamir, & Chen, 2003; Walumbwa, Avolio, & Zhu, 2008), authentic leadership (Avolio, Gardner, Walumbwa, Luthans, & May, 2004; Walumbwa, Wang, Wang, Schaubroeck, & Avolio, 2010), and ethical leadership (Walumbwa et al., 2011). Although internalization implies the involvement of members' self-concepts (Lord & Brown, 2004), I distinguish the engagement of self-systems from internalization because the underlying conceptualizations of the self differ in subtle ways.

Relating Leadership Explanations to Social Network Theories

Exchange-Based Mechanisms

The fundamental idea of exchange-based mechanisms in explaining member outcomes is that leadership is an exchange process with resources of value to either the leader or member. Economic incentives represent a simple case; that is., members perform in accord with the requirements of their jobs to receive financial (and other) rewards. The more interesting cases for dialog with social network theory are those that explain discretionary attitudes and behaviors in relation not solely to economic exchange, but to social exchange (Blau, 1964) as well.

Such an account is one of the primary explanations for members' discretionary attitudes and behaviors in Leader–Member Exchange (LMX)[3] perspective on leadership (Liden, Sparrowe, & Wayne, 1997). It holds that members engage in discretionary attitudes and behaviors in exchange for resources, both social and material, with their leaders. Because social exchange is dyadic, and because dyads are embedded in larger sets of relationships, LMX theory presents itself as an especially attractive candidate for integration with social network perspectives. The dyadic relationships between leaders and members are ties, the dyads within groups constitute networks, and the chain of vertical reporting relationships constitutes a yet larger network—all of which potentially convey valued resources. Further, early formulations of LMX theory specifically reached beyond the leader–member dyad, treating the formal organizational hierarchy (the "understructure" [Cashman, Dansereau, Graen, & Haga, 1976; Dansereau, Graen, & Haga, 1975]) as a network of "linking pin" relations that benefitted those whose vertical ties were of high quality and constraining those whose vertical ties were not.

EXCHANGE-BASED MECHANISMS AND SOCIAL NETWORKS AT THE DYADIC LEVEL

These parallels have led to several studies integrating leadership and social networks within the LMX perspective. Building on earlier theoretical work (1997), a study by Sparrowe and Liden (2005) treats LMX and social networks as complementary perspectives, demonstrating how member influence is a function of LMX, member centrality, their leaders' "sponsorship," and the leader's own centrality. The central ideas in their model involve the moderating roles of sponsorship (the extent to which members share the trust contacts of their leaders) and leader centrality. Sponsorship enhances the relationships of both LMX and member centrality with influence; these positive relationships, however, depend on the leader's own centrality in the advice network. Sponsorship by leaders low in centrality defeats the benefits of members' own social capital: in such cases, influence falls as advice centrality rises.

Goodwin et al. (2009) examine how the network positions of leaders and members within and beyond the workgroup are related to the quality of their LMX. They approach this question in the context of two established antecedents of LMX quality: interaction frequency and leader–member similarity. They specify and test a model in which leader and member network centrality moderate the relationships between interaction frequency and similarity and LMX quality. Interestingly, their results speak to the importance of advice network centrality beyond the work group for members: "When the leader perceives that the follower has a power base outside the workgroup, which allows the follower access to diverse information and to exert influence throughout the organization, the leader's evaluation of the relationship quality is enhanced" (p. 974).

Venkataramani et al. (2010) also examine the network antecedents in and beyond the work group of LMX quality. They argue that leaders' networks, by virtue of the potential they hold for accessing resources, function as signals of status for members. Such status signals "enhance [leaders'] attractiveness as exchange partners for these subordinates in forming high-quality LMX" (p. 1072). Further, this perceived status indirectly affects members' discretionary attitudes through LMX quality.

Much of the research from the LMX perspective focuses on one participant in the dyad, the member, and thus overlooks how exchanges benefit leaders. Drawing from Foa and Foa (1974), Wilson, Sin, and Conlon (2010) develop a theoretical model specifying how the exchange of particular resources, such as information, status, and affiliation (interpersonal support and loyalty), are related to leaders' outcomes. A key feature of their model is that the "currency" of exchanges differs; what leaders offer members are not identical to what members offer leaders. Rather, they are substitutes. So, for example, leaders exchange information from the top of the organization with members' knowledge of what is going on with peers. Just as the resources leaders can exchange with members depend on the structure of leaders' networks (e.g., Sparrowe & Liden, 2005; Venkataramani et al., 2010), so also might the resources leaders' gain depend on the structure of their members' networks. Thus, for example, leaders whose members who are not central in information or gossip networks may be at a disadvantage in acting strategically to benefit their groups.

EXCHANGE-BASED MECHANISMS AND SOCIAL NETWORKS AT THE GROUP LEVEL

The three studies summarized above exemplify how the initial formulation of LMX theory, in which resources cascade through formal organization lines of authority, create an opportunity for theoretical integration with the social network perspective and its emphasis on resources flowing through the structure of informal networks (Sparrowe & Liden, 1997). In this work, however, the focus is on the leader–member dyad as the pivotal unit of theory and analysis. Within the LMX perspective, a growing stream of research investigates the antecedents and outcomes of differentiation, where differentiation is treated as a group-level phenomenon reflecting the extent to which leader-member relations vary in relationship quality. (Figure 20.1a depicts a group with a leader and six members; the quality of each dyadic relationship is reflected in the width of the tie [line]).

Questions addressed in this line of research include how differentiation affects members' discretionary attitudes and behaviors, such as job performance (Liden, Erdogan, Wayne, & Sparrowe, 2006), creativity (Liao, Liu, & Loi, 2010), psychological contract fulfillment (Henderson, Wayne, Shore, Bommer, & Tetrick, 2008), and turnover (Nishii & Mayer, 2009); and whether these relationships depend on perceptions of fairness (Erdogan & Bauer, 2010). At the group level, relatively little research has examined empirically relationships between differentiation and outcomes such as team performance (exceptions include Liden et al., 2006 and Schyns, 2006); however, it is a question of ongoing theoretical interest (Henderson, Liden, Glibkowski, & Chaudhry, 2009).

From the network perspective, a stream of work that models only the variability in ties between the leader and his or her subordinates risks seeing only part of the informal social structure of the group. An entire set of potentially relevant ties—those linking group members to one another—is overlooked. Figure 20.1b depicts one possible configuration of the informal social structure within the group. One member (6), with whom the leader has a low-quality relationship, enjoys good relationships with the others in the leader's "out-group" (members 4 and 5) as well as with several of the members of the leader's "in-group" (members 2 and 3). This pattern can be interpreted to suggest that member 6 can readily withhold support, stall, or even sabotage the leader's initiatives. An entirely different interpretation would follow were the leader's in- and out-groups reversed so that members 4, 5, and 6 were the in-group and members 1, 2, and 3 were the out-group. In this scenario, the centrality (and presumed influence) of member 6 might be put to use supporting the leader's initiatives. So, although it is true that variability in LMX quality reflects the importance of the leader in defining the informal status hierarchy within groups, there are other factors at play as well in determining who enjoys influence and prestige—and social network analysis is ideal for pinpointing such factors.

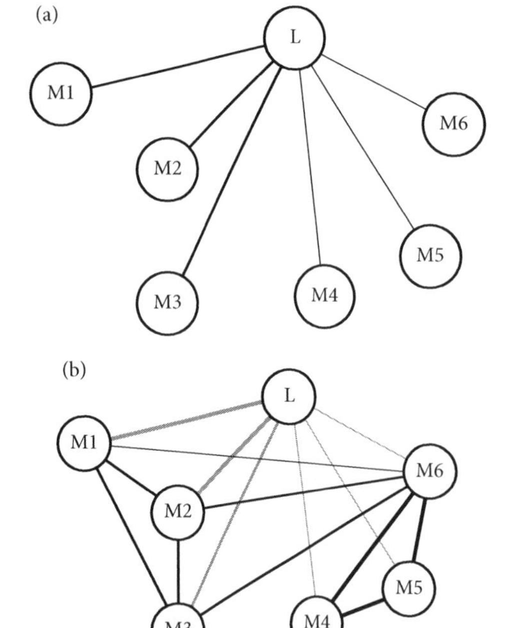

Figure 20.1. Group Structure as Represented in LMX Differentiation Research. **(a)** A Leader, (L) with Six Members (M), with Varying LMX Quality Represented by Tie (line) Width. **(b)** Informal Network Structure Among Members Within the Same Group. Six Members, with the Strength of Relationships Among them Represented by Tie (line) Width.

From the social network perspective, LMX differentiation research is even more vulnerable to the criticism that, in focusing only on the dyadic ties with the leader, performance-relevant information about the overall informal social structure within the team is overlooked. An interest in the overall informal structure within the group is precisely what motivates the work of Mehra, Dixon, Brass, and Robertson (2006), who argue that group performance depends on the formal leader's centrality within his or her team. Further, Mehra et al. demonstrate empirically that leaders' network position beyond the immediate group of members is related to group performance. These two studies suggest that LMX differentiation is not simply a within-group phenomenon; differentiated leader-member relations are embedded in larger networks whose structure is relevant for outcomes.

It is only fair to point out how the network approach is incomplete as well. Although Mehra et al. (2006) do model the informal network within the team, they don't offer theory that integrates differentation with the overall informal structure within the group. So, research from the LMX differentiation side comes tantalizingly close to fully modeling informal group structure, while research from the social network perspective hasn't yet teased out the distinctive contribution of differentiation in the quality of the formal leader's relationships with group members. The as-yet-unsolved puzzle is whether and under what conditions LMX differentiation versus informal social structure matter for group performance. This puzzle is mentioned again at the end of this chapter with regard to directions for future research. Is, for example, the impact of LMX differentiation on group performance dependent on the leader's position in the group's network of advice, trust, or friendship relations? Further, given the evidence that leaders' network centrality moderates the relationships among LMX, sponsorship, and individual performance (Sparrowe & Liden, 2005), how might the leader's position in networks beyond the team interact with LMX differentiation in predicting team performance?

Categorization-based Explanations

The categorization account, most evident in implicit leadership theory, holds that members have mental representations—prototypes—of what an ideal leader should be (Eden & Leviatan, 1975); when leaders behave in ways that are consistent with these ideals, they are perceived—categorized—as effective by their followers (Offermann et al., 1994). Much of the work in this stream of research focuses on the nature of ILTs; evaluating, for example, the extent to which prototypes are context sensitive (Lord, Brown, Harvey, & Hall, 2001), vary as a function of individual differences (Keller, 1999), or vary across cultures (Den Hartog, House, Hanges, Ruiz-Quintanilla, & Dorfman, 1999). Recent work draws from cognitive psychology to describe the nature of activation of prototypes in leaders and members, orienting expectations and shaping behavior (Lord & Shondrick, 2011; Shondrick, Dinh, & Lord, 2010). These elaborations of implicit leadership theory offer a nuanced understanding of how mental representations shape leadership categorization, yet remain largely within the general explanatory framework whereby leadership is inferred when prototypes are activated (Shondrick et al., 2010).

Although research within the ILT framework has focused largely on the categorization of effective leadership by members rather than on members' discretionary attitudes and behaviors, several studies examine relationships between prototypes and the kinds of discretionary attitudes and behaviors often studied from other leadership perspectives (and of interest here). One study focuses on relationship quality, offering empirical evidence that members' prototypes are related to LMX (Engle & Lord, 1997), and through LMX to organizational commitment and job satisfaction (Epitropaki & Martin, 2005). Similarly, leaders' implicit theories about followers have been related to relationship quality and followers' job satisfaction (Sy, 2010).

It bears notice, however, that in explaining discretionary attitudes and behaviors the explanatory logic of prototype matching borrows from exchange-based explanations for leadership. In Engle and Lord (1997) a match between leader and member in implicit performance theories enhances interpersonal liking and increases LMX. Similarly, in Epitropaki and Martin (2005), the logic holds that the extent to which followers' perceptions of their leaders match their ideal prototypes enhances relationship quality by aligning perceptions and expectations. Finally, in Sy (2010), leaders evaluate members' match with their implicit follower prototypes, and the more positive the evaluation, the greater the trust and the better the relationship quality. Because leaders treat members in ways consistent with their evaluations, the more positive the evaluation, the better the treatment will be, and thus members' job satisfaction should increase. So, in these examples, a match between prototypes and observed behavior enhances relationship quality, yet it is relationship quality—social exchange, liking, and trust—that drives members' discretionary attitudes and behaviors. Prototype matching (categorization) thus is located "upstream" in the explanatory flow linking leadership to outcomes. It might therefore appear leadership theories based on implicit prototypes are poor candidates for integration with network theory—except insofar as they set the stage for exchange-based explanations. Further reflection is needed, however, before reaching this conclusion.

ILTS AND SOCIAL NETWORKS

Although the growing emphasis on cognitive psychology locates the domain of implicit leadership theory "between the ears" of members (so to speak), there remains an opportunity for dialog with social network theories. Interestingly enough, this opportunity lies in how cognitive psychology, in particular connectionist and embodied models of cognition, provides an account of the activation of prototypes that is both nuanced and contextually sensitive. Recall that the contribution initially offered by implicit leadership theory was dependent on followers' prototypes of ideal leaders being exogenous. That is, members were understood to bring mental representations of ideal leadership into a situation in which they were compared against a leader's behavior (Foti & Lord, 1987; Lord, Foti, & de Vader, 1984; Lord & Maher, 1993; Offermann et al., 1994). The novel insight consisted in demonstrating that members' evaluations of their leaders' behaviors, as well as the categorizations of their leaders' effectiveness that follow, are contingent on the degree to which those behaviors matched their prototypes. Inherent in this insight is the assumption that prototypes demonstrate both stability through time and generalizability across settings.

There are solid warrants for this assumption. The content of an individual's prototypes is enduring, in part because it was shaped by early childhood attachment models that endure into adulthood (Keller, 2003). Studies from the GLOBE research program demonstrate that dimensions of charismatic and transformational leadership generalize across cultures (Den Hartog et al., 1999; House, Javidan, Hanges, & Dorfman, 2002). Further, there are aspects of leadership prototypes, such as gender, that have roots in evolutionary processes and so would be considered universals (Spisak, Homan, Grabo, & Van, 2011). Finally, as noted previously, Epitropaki and Martin (2004) find empirical support for a multidimensional implicit leadership theory that generalizes relatively well across employee groups and demonstrates stability through time.

If ILTs, once developed, are constant in time and place, then the best one might hope from dialog with the social network perspective is a discussion of how the content of mental representations of the ideal leader are derived from exemplars in the social networks of individuals. In and of itself, however, this idea is hardly remarkable: where else would individuals find exemplars apart from their social worlds? A more compelling dialog begins when it is evident that ILTs are not fixed in time and place but, instead, are context-sensitive, and if their dynamic adaptation takes place in a relational context that can be illuminated by network concepts and frameworks in ways that implicit leadership theory cannot otherwise discern.

The approach to ILTs that is informed by connectionist and embodied perspectives on cognition (Lord & Shondrick, 2011; Lord et al., 2001; Shondrick & Lord, 2010; Shondrick et al., 2010) offers a challenge to the stability and generalizability of prototypes. By categorizing the prototype matching process as a form of symbolic knowledge, space is created to develop the implications for leadership categorization of two other forms, and embodied/embedded knowledge. Context triggers transitions among these three forms of knowledge:

> [E]ach of these representations of knowledge may vary in their utility at different moments during the leadership process. This is because the leadership process involves information processing in real-time while leaders and followers interact with each other and dynamically adapt to changing environments, goals, and ideas, which may lead to shifts in the accessibility of specific representations of knowledge. (Lord & Shondrick, 2011, p. 217)

On this view, ILTs are less "unitary constructs" whose content is immutable than they are multi-faceted, dynamic ensembles of meaning that are arrayed from the basic and general (discriminating between who is a leader and who is not) to the specific (discriminating between an ideal business leader and an ideal political leader) (Shondrick et al., 2010, p. 962). Of the three, symbolic knowledge structures are the most stable and enduring; connectionist structures are malleable as different elements in the network are called forth in the situation, and embodied/embedded knowledge structures are yet more dynamic as they are inextricably bound to perception, physiology, and context. Because symbolic, connectionist and embodied/embedded forms of knowledge are substantively different, exploring options for dialog best proceeds through reflection on each in turn.

ILTS AS SYMBOLIC KNOWLEDGE STRUCTURES AND SOCIAL NETWORKS

When construed as symbolic knowledge structures, ILTs are assumed to be relatively stable across time and place (Lord & Shondrick, 2011). When symbolic knowledge ILTs do change it is because situational or contextual factors have made different elements in the underlying connectionist network more salient and others less salient. Further, because connectionist network representations are, in part, shaped by embodiment and embeddedness, which particular elements become salient in a given ILT may be highly context dependent. So, changes come slowly to symbolic network structures; their dynamism occurs in connectionist and embodied/embedded knowledge structures. So, dialog with social network theory best begins where context matters and matters substantively: connectionist and embodied/embedded knowledge structures.

ILTS AS CONNECTIONIST KNOWLEDGE STRUCTURES AND SOCIAL NETWORKS

The connectionist model describes knowledge structures in terms of networks that organize information in patterns (Hanges et al., 2000; Lord & Emrich, 2000; Smith & Foti, 1998). Lord et al.

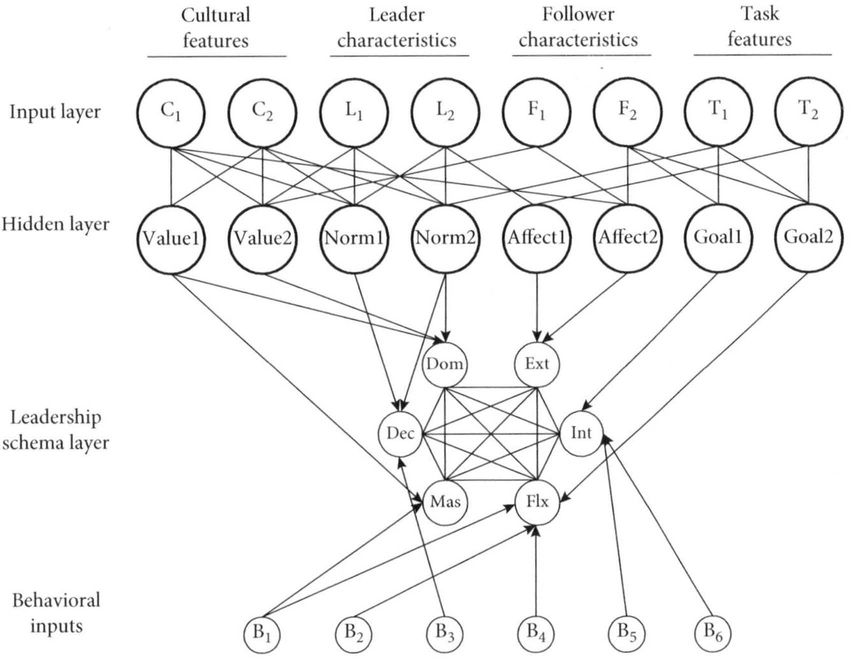

Figure 20.2. The Graph-theoretic Representation of Connectionist Leadership Prototypes. (From Lord, Brown, Harvey, & Hall, 2001, p. 321.)

(2001, pp. 321–324) present increasingly specific schematic illustrations of such networks that underly the formation and activation of implicit leadership prototypes. Figure 20.2 reproduces the most complete of the illustrations of Lord et al. (2001). It is graph-theoretic in the same way as social network representations, in that it features nodes and ties, and the particular configuration of the elements (nodes) defines the implicit leadership theory that is activated: "The differential activation of ILTs in various contexts is produced by dynamic, connectionist network-based processes that create new, contextually tuned ILTs each time they are used" (Lord & Emrich, 2000, p. 562).

This graph-theoretic-like formulation of the dynamics of ILTs signals an interesting opportunity for dialog with network theory and methods. Clearly, cognitive networks are in a different domain than social networks. But network research is not limited to relations among social actors. Carley and her colleagues (Carley, 1997; Carley & Palmquist, 1992) have developed techniques for analyzing and representing mental models graphically—"cognitive mapping"—that is based on individuals' written texts, spoken words, or other meaning-laden expressions. This approach is capable of comparing an individual's cognitive maps across multiple contexts as well as integrating multiple individual cognitive maps (as to create a "team mental model"). So, this technique makes it feasible to test several of the key assumptions of the connectionist theory of ILTs.

One such assumption holds that specific features are activated within an individual's ILT because they are cued contextually; changing the context along the relevant dimensions should result in a commensurate reformulation of the same individual's ILT. That assumption is difficult to test empirically without a means for mapping leadership-related concepts and relations dynamically under conditions of changes in context. Unlike responses to scales, in which measurement invariance across multiple individual responses or multiple respondents is a criterion of validity, cognitive mapping can represent dynamic changes in concepts and the relations among them. Experiments could be designed to manipulate a series of contextual factors in a leadership scenario and, after each manipulation, subjects' would respond by speaking or writing about the scenario in relation to leadership.

ILTS AS EMBODIED/EMBEDDED KNOWLEDGE STRUCTURES AND THE SOCIAL NETWORK PERSPECTIVE

The literature on "situated cognition" traverses the domains cognitive psychology (Clark & Chalmers, 2010), perception (Noë, 2004), neuroscience

(Damasio, 1994), and philosophy of mind (Gallagher, 2005; Wheeler, 2005), and involves a number of different claims about the relationship between cognition and the world (Wilson, 2002). In bringing the embodied/embedded knowledge perspective into leadership theory, Lord and his colleagues (Shondrick & Lord, 2010) are interested in how both the mind and the body are involved in cognition: "not only are the perceiver's abstract mental structures involved in the perceptual processes but knowledge is also literally embodied in that it is dependent on the perceptual structures, the anticipated motor responses to these structures, and affective reactions in the perceiver" (p. 22). This ensemble of ideas draws Lord and Shondrick into a discussion of how leadership perceptions, attributions of causality, leadership behaviors, and decision making are shaped by sensorimotor processes ("embodied") and situated within specific contexts ("embedded"). Lord and Shondrick (2011, p. 211) thus describe "leadership by example" in relation to the processes of mimicry that are made possible by mirror neurons.

These implications that Lord and Shondrick (2011) draw from embedded/embodied knowledge structures focus primarily on individual cognitive processes or on dynamic adjustments in the relationship between leaders and members. However, the idea that cognition is embedded in the immediate external world, and its contents are partially constituted by that context, has a counterpart in network theory. Within social network theory, the concept of embeddedness carries an economic meaning (Borgatti & Foster, 2003; Kilduff & Brass, 2010). In network theory, "[a]ctors are embedded in a network to the extent that they show a preference for transacting with network members or to the extent that social ties are forged, renewed, and extended through the community" (Kilduff & Brass, 2010, p. 319). Behind these surface differences, the two conceptualizations share a strong claim that context matters—not just incidentally, but substantively. In the situated cognition perspective, it might be said that cognition is "forged, renewed, and extended" through the embodiment of perception in action and the embeddedness in opportunities and constraints for action (Gallagher, 2005; Wheeler, 2005).

How might this correspondence between embeddedness in social networks and embedded cognition inform broader questions in leadership theory and research? One obvious candidate is that of shared or distributed leadership (Pearce & Conger, 2003). Carson, Tesluk, and Marrone (2007) measure shared leadership in teams using the network property of density, and demonstrate that density is positively related to external ratings of team performance. A more extensive conceptual and methodological treatment of how the social network perspective can inform research on distributed leadership is found in Contractor, DeChurch, Carson, Carter, and Keegan (2012), who differentiate forms of collective leadership in relation to three dimensions: the concentration of leadership among members, the multiplexity of roles (navigator, engineer, social integrator, and liaison) assumed by members, and the rotation or dynamics of movement of members through roles.

What is intriguing about the Contractor et al. (2012) model is how it offers a topology for the pattern or form of distributed leadership. Similar topologies of shared leadership—also informed by social network concepts—are those of Seibert, Sparrowe, and Liden (2003) and Mehra et al. (2006); all of these examples offer important advantages over focusing only on network density or centralization. Network density is a coarse measure of shared leadership because, being based on calculating within-group means, it fails to differentiate between groups in which leadership is equally shared among members and those in which it is high in some members and low in others. Even network centralization, a measure that reflects the leadership is concentrated in a small proportion of members, lacks the fidelity of these topological approaches, especially the richness of the dynamic and multidimensional model proposed by Contractor et al. (2012).

Despite impressive strengths, these approaches are about distributed leadership and not about embodied or embedded cognition—not, that is, in ways that build from the ideas of Lord and his colleagues (Lord & Shondrick, 2011; Shondrick et al., 2010); nor were they intended to be. A theoretical model of distributed leadership developed by Friedrich, Vessey, Schuelke, Ruark, and Mumford (2009) draws somewhat closer because it focuses on how collective leadership is a function of the ways teams identify and make use of distributed knowledge and expertise; how that knowledge is shared depends in part on the structure of the networks of the leader and members of the team. Note, however, that in the Friedrich et al. model, knowledge is the " 'currency of collective leadership" (p. 940) and leadership qua influence is replaced by mutual coordination. And, although this model holds that there are both leaders and members, "the behavioral roles that often fall under the leadership umbrella may be taken up by multiple individuals." Leadership thus "depend[s] upon the selective and dynamic emergence of individuals whose skills and expertise are most appropriate to a given situation" (p. 933). So, when distributed, leadership takes on a different "currency" (knowledge) and is not a property of a person but instead emerges in the dynamic processes of a team.

CONNECTIONIST AND COGNITIVE NETWORKS

Before moving forward to consider identity-based explanatory leadership accounts, it is worthwhile to explore the relationship between connectionist networks and "cognitive networks" (Krackhardt, 1987) in social network research. This exploration is prompted by an explicit reference to social network concepts by Lord and Emrich (2000). Pointing to work by Hooijberg and his colleagues (1997), Lord and Emrich suggest that the richness of leaders' cognitive representations of their social contexts are manifest in their actual social networks: "Using [social network] analysis, one could measure the number of ties that a leader has with others, the range and closeness of these ties, a leader's access to others, and the asymmetry between a leader's in-coming and out-going interactions. The higher a given leader's scores on these indicators, the greater his or her social complexity" (p. 567). Social complexity, according to Hooijberg et al. (1997), is a measure of a "leader's capacity to differentiate the personal and relational aspects of a social situation and integrate them in a manner that results in increased understanding or changed action-intention valences" (p. 382).

Recent work by Balkundi and Kilduff (2006) seeks to capitalize on this correspondence between "cognitive networks" in the work of Lord and Emrich (2000) and "cognitive networks" as understood in social network research (e.g., Kilduff & Krackhardt, 1994; Krackhardt, 1987, 1990). In social network theory, a cognitive network is an individual's perception (mental representation) of others and his or her beliefs regarding the relations among them. The important implication here is that an individual's belief may or may not accurately reflect an "objective" relation between any two contacts; they "... are conceptually distinct; correlations become a theoretical and empirical question..." (Krackhardt, 1987, p. 114). It is precisely this implication that serves as a bridge between cognitive models of leadership and cognitive social networks in Balkundi and Kilduff's integrative model of leadership effectiveness. Indeed, in the Balkundi and Kilduff (2006) model, all else follows from the accuracy with which a leader perceives her or his network:

> [A]ccuracy is likely to improve the extent to which a leader occupies a strategic position in three social network structures relevant to organizational behavior: the ego network, comprising the individuals immediately connected to the leader; the complete organizational network, comprising not just direct connections but also the leaders' indirect connections to everyone in the organization; and the interorganizational network of relationships important to the leader's work outside the focal organization. (p. 427)

Accuracy, in turn, is dependent on cognitive schemas that facilitate "the match between leaders' perceptions of networks and actual networks" (p. 427). So, in a nutshell, accurate perception of networks facilitates leadership effectiveness because it enables leaders to exert influence locally, within the organization as a whole, and outside of the organization's boundaries.

This idea that leadership effectiveness depends on relationships up close, through the organization, and beyond organizational boundaries is persuasive; it is also the case that social network analysis offers a rich and nuanced approach to understanding the opportunities and constraints for action that leaders face. However, as indicated in the Introduction to this chapter, the internal logic of the Balkundi and Kilduff (2006) model lies within the domain of social network concepts and relationships. The "cognitive turn" taken in recent leadership research serves as an occasion for Balkundi and Kilduff to develop their social network model of leadership effectiveness, but the internal logic of their model owes very little to the kinds of careful distinctions between symbolic, connectionist, and embodied knowledge made by Lord and Shondrick (2011). Further, the importance of accuracy in the mental representations of social networks emerges from the domain of cognitive social network research (e.g., Krackhardt, 1990), rather than from the domain of leadership research. This is not a criticism but an observation intended to move the dialog between leadership theories and the network perspective forward. What, then, might these two perspectives, so similar in surface terminology, suggest going forward?

One direction for additional dialog on this front involves clarifying the nature of leaders' mental representations of their social networks within the larger framework of symbolic, connectionist, and embedded/embodied knowledge structures. The emphasis Balkundi and Kilduff (2006) place on accuracy implies that cognitive social networks are symbolic knowledge structures; subject, however, to bias and distortion. Noting how difficult it is to recall all of one's friends—not to mention the all of the relations among them—Balkundi and Kilduff explain that people rely on schemas and heuristics such as balance (two friends are likely to be friends of each other) and small world (grouping people in clusters on similar dimensions) to make sense of complex social relations. And it is precisely these schemas and heuristics that introduce discrepancies between one's cognitive network and the actual relations among friends and other contacts.

One might argue that errors in the perception and representation of complex network relations reflect nothing more than a shortcoming in human rationality, on the same order as other instances of cognitive bias. I prefer a different account: the fact that heuristic and/or schematic thinking regularly introduces bias and error into the mental representations of social networks suggests that social cognition, in its natural, everyday manifestation, operates not at the level of symbolic knowledge, but should instead be understood as situated cognition—that is, at its most primitive level, as a case of embedded/embodied knowledge. In support of this approach, Levine and Kurzban (2006) explain that seeing the social world in clusters ("small world") and presuming that one's friends are friends of each other ("balance" bias) have long evolutionary histories whose roots lie in solving problems of whom to select as a partner or ally to maximize tertiary benefits. Further, these mechanisms need not operate at the explicit or conscious level; rather, "selection pressures on human cognition" over time are sufficient to explain their prevalence (Levine & Kurzban, 2006, p. 175) in social perception.

It is the case, of course, that the cognitive networks elicited from leaders using the network analytic techniques described by Balkundi and Kilduff (2006) and analyzed in the ways suggested by Lord and Emrich (2000) to measure social complexity are symbolic knowledge structures. But if social relations originate in embodied and embedded knowledge, and then are tentatively represented in connectionist knowledge, the question of accuracy takes on a wholly different significance for understanding leadership effectiveness. Why leaders, or any persons, are inaccurate in their social perceptions becomes a substantive question (Casciaro, 1998; Casciaro, Carley, & Krackhardt, 1999).

The second direction for furthering the dialog between cognitive networks and cognitive perspectives on leadership recalls a theme discussed earlier, namely, the interplay between explanations based on attributes of individuals versus the structure of the relations in which they are embedded. In Balkundi and Kilduff (2006), cognitive networks serve instrumental goals. Leaders whose cognitive networks accurately reflect the structure of actual relations are better able to "...uncover political conflicts, spot communication problems between culturally divided groups, avoid reliance on problematic individuals for the transmission of important resources, achieve strategic objectives through the appointment of key people to influential positions, and manage relations within and across departments" (p. 426). It is characteristic of the leadership field to formulate theories in relation to individual differences (Antonakis et al., 2012), and the "Leaderplex" model (Hooijberg et al., 1997) to which Lord and Emrich (2000) appeal is no exception: networks serve indicators of an individual difference ("social complexity") that, like cognitive complexity, is expected to be related to leadership effectiveness. The difference between these two ways of relating networks to leadership is subtle but important because it brings into relief how leadership theories focus on attributes of leaders whereas network perspectives focus on leaders embedded in relations among individuals.

A closer reading suggests that each is a relatively incomplete explanation of the phenomenon, but taken together they can be seen as complementary. Balkundi and Kilduff's (2006) emphasis on accuracy in cognitive networks as a condition for effectiveness doesn't explain how leaders then are able to reap the benefits of networks, i.e., to "...uncover political conflicts...spot communication problems...avoid reliance on problematic individuals...achieve strategic objectives through the appointment of key people...and manage relations within and across departments" (p. 426). Identifying opportunities and constraints for strategic action depends on having accurate cognitive networks but, in and of itself, accuracy cannot realize opportunities or work around constraints. Further, accuracy may enable leaders to represent mentally who is connected to whom, but identifying "strategic positions" within those networks and how to make one's way into them takes more than perceptual acuity. Might those capabilities, taken together, sum up to social complexity?

With respect to the Lord and Emrich side, in reducing networks to an individual difference like "social complexity" (p. 576), the opportunities and constraints on action faced by leaders in their social networks lose much of their explanatory force. When located in the knowledge structures of leaders, the implication that social complexity originates with leaders rather than their actual social networks readily follows. On reaching that conclusion, the social complexity of leaders becomes endogenous rather than reflecting their positions in the actual social networks of their organizations—a view wholly atomistic rather than embedded. So, a leader needs networks in which to enact his or her "social competence." A genuine integration between these two points of view would treat leaders as firmly embedded in the social networks of their organizations, facing real constraints and seizing genuine opportunities, and yet would specify what individual difference makes some individuals in leadership roles more effective than others.

Identification, Internalization, and Engagement of Self-Systems

Three closely related explanations for the effects of leadership on members' discretionary outcomes are based on identity: identification, internalization, and engagement of self-systems. These explanations characterize not only charismatic and transformational leadership, but also ethical, servant, authentic, and similar leadership theories. Disentangling these three explanations is complicated because their meanings overlap and are not applied consistently in explaining the effects of leadership on member outcomes (Yukl, 1999).[4] Nevertheless, it is possible to tease apart three distinct ideas even though they are often joined in the literature.

Identification is often based in shared values, as shown in the following example drawn from Ilies, Morgeson, and Nahrgang (2005): "Authentic leaders' high levels of self-awareness, in combination with their authentic behavioral and relational orientation, can influence followers' feelings of identification with the leader and the organization, especially when a high degree of value-congruence exists among leaders and their followers" (p. 383). Further, members identify not only with their leaders but also with their groups or their organization. Drawing from the work of Kark and Shamir (2002; 2003), Avolio et al. (2004) propose that authentic leadership engages both personal and social identification "We suggest that authentic leaders are able to enhance the engagement, motivation, commitment, satisfaction, and involvement required from followers to constantly improve their work and performance outcomes through the creation of personal identification with the follower and social identification with the organization" (p. 804).

Internalization differs from identification in that members' self-concepts and sense of self-worth are implicated in ways that go beyond the recognition of shared values even though the two processes often are joined in explaining the effects of leadership. Drawing on a definition of identification proposed by Pratt (1998), Kark et al. (2003) describe the impact of transformational leadership as "(a) evoking followers' self-concept in the recognition that they share similar values with the leader and (b) giving rise to followers' desire to change their self-concept so that their values and beliefs become more similar to those of the leader" (p. 247).

Articulating how members' internalization involves both their leaders and their organizations requires a conceptualization of the self-concept that reflects multiple levels of identification. Brewer and Gardner's (1996) definition of the self as personal, relational, and collective in which the self concept provides the necessary framework (Howell & Shamir, 2005; Kark & Shamir, 2002; Lord, Brown, & Freiberg, 1999); Howell and Shamir (2005) summarize this approach:

> Drawing on Brewer and Gardner's work and its extension to the domain of leadership by Lord et al. (Lord et al., 1999), Kark and Shamir (2002) propose that there are two types of charismatic relationships: one in which the relational self is activated and the primary mechanism of influence is followers' personal identification with the charismatic leader, and one in which the collective self is activated and the primary mechanism of influence is followers' social identification with the group or the organization. Personal identification is characterized by the attribution of desirable qualities to the leader, a definition of self in terms of the relationship with the leader, and a desire to become like the leader. Social identification is characterized by self definition in terms of group membership and a perception of group successes and failures as personal successes and failures. (Ashforth & Mael, 1989, p. 100)

Because identification and internalization are so closely joined in the literature I treat them together as a single explanatory mechanism when exploring opportunities for dialog with social network theory.

ENGAGEMENT OF SELF-SYSTEMS

There are several alternative approaches to identity that do not draw from Brewer and Gardner's (1996) tripartite division of the self-concept and that offer interesting implications for a dialog between leadership theories and the social network perspective. These approaches are based on different conceptualizations of the self, including provisional selves (Ibarra, 1999; Ibarra, Kilduff, & Wenpin, 2005; Stam, van Knippenberg, & Wisse, 2010) and the narrative self (Shamir & Eilam, 2005; Sparrowe, 2005). These approaches are collected under the general heading of engagement of self-systems.

SOCIAL NETWORKS AND IDENTIFICATION/ INTERNALIZATION

Integrating leadership with social network theory explicitly through the explanatory mechanisms of identification and internalization is relatively uncharted territory, perhaps because they frequently are conceived as psychological processes occurring in a dyadic context. That is, through a relevant form of leadership, a member identifies with and internalizes the values of her or his leader (Kark et al., 2003, p. 247). But it is also important to offer an explanatory account for how the effects of these forms of leadership reach beyond the immediacy of dyads (Galvin, Balkundi, & Waldman, 2010). A growing number of studies employ social network theories and methods to examine the ways in which leaders come to be seen as charismatic or transformational (Balkundi, Kilduff, & Harrison, 2011; Bono & Anderson, 2005; Galvin et al., 2010; Pastor, Meindl, & Mayo, 2002).

An early example is that of Pastor et al. (2002), who trace attributions of charisma through the structure of informal networks. In their "network effects" model, "the opinions and beliefs of individual followers regarding their leader are viewed as conditioned by the social systems in which they are embedded" (p. 411). More recently, Galvin, Balkundi, and Waldman (2010) describe how individuals in a leader's network serve as "surrogates" who promote and defend the leader and model followership, resulting in the spread of "perceptions of charisma among distant subordinates" (p. 479). A third example is that of Bono and Anderson (2005), who find that transformational leaders, as well as their followers, enjoy central positions in informal advice and influence networks. Their explanatory logic gives causal priority to transformational leadership; that is, centrality follows from the transformational behaviors of leaders:

> Charismatic leaders communicate high standards of ethical and moral conduct using rhetoric that appeals to values, ideals, and emotions (Bass, 1998). Because transformational leaders promote values and ideas that are broadly appealing and communicate their ideas with optimism and enthusiasm, employees are drawn to them and are likely to seek and trust their advice. (p. 1307)[5]

In these three examples the point of origin is the leader; attributions of charisma or transformational behavior cascade through the structure of informal social networks. One can imagine, however, an alternative direction: network centrality precedes members' categorizations of charisma to their leaders and the discretionary attitudes and behaviors of members (or teams) are mediated by such categorizations. In light of the assumptions of decades of research on charismatic and transformational leadership, this direction goes against the flow. Nevertheless, these accounts are evaluated empirically in a series of two studies by Balkundi et al. (2011). In both studies, categorizations of charisma mediate the relationship between network centrality and outcomes (team performance), whereas centrality does not mediate the relationships between charismatic leadership and performance. Especially important is their Study 2, in which centrality and charisma were measured at two points in time and performance at a third: "leaders who were central at T1 were later seen as charismatic at T2... however... leader charisma at T1 did not significantly predict leader centrality at T2" (p. 1215).

Balkundi and his colleagues (2011) interpret this pattern of results to suggest that "a leadership-relevant aspect of personality—charisma—may derive from occupation of a structural position in the network, compatible with a social personality approach to leadership emergence" (p. 1217). Perhaps sensing that attributing a trait to the social context is a radical statement, Balkundi et al. qualify their view by saying that although the potential to exert charismatic leadership might well be an individual difference, the formation of categorizations of charisma by others is a social process. Charisma, they point out, is "an individual trait that requires considerable social construction in the minds of others" (p. 217).

In attributing a leadership-relevant individual difference to the social context, Balkundi et al.

(2011) reprise one of the guiding themes of this chapter: in the dialog between leadership theories and the social network perspective, how might the relationship between explanations based on individual attributes and those based on social structure be formulated? My intent here is not to rekindle the flames of the person–situation debate (Kenrick & Funder, 1988; Mischel, 1968); rather, it is to sharpen the differences between leadership theories and the social network perspective so that dialog is substantive.

An important first step would be to gain greater clarity on the mechanisms through which charismatic or transformational leadership flow through social networks, gather in followers or teams, and there foster discretionary attitudes and behaviors. Do they involve social influence conditioned on "network effects" (Pastor et al., 2002); the attractiveness of the leader's appeals to values, ideals, and emotions (Bono & Anderson, 2005); the witness of surrogates (Galvin et al., 2010); or the sharing of advice (Balkundi et al., 2011)? Or, are there actually experiences of personal and social identification and internalization that flow at greater and greater social distances from the leader? If identification and internalization are occurring, then charismatic relationships (Howell & Shamir, 2005) are emergent through the network. If not; if attributions of charisma are simply the result of the social influence of surrogates, then those attributions should be seen as based in reputation rather than being the effects of leadership.

Social identification and internalization with the group, the second element in identity-based explanations of leadership (Hogg, 2001; van Knippenberg, van Knippenberg, De Cremer, & Hogg, 2004), reprises considerations of ILTs, prototypes, and categorization processes. In the shift from the dyadic (personal) to group (social) levels of analysis, explanations of which prototypes matter take on more complexity. In its simplest formulation, social identification occurs when a member subsumes his or her self concept to a prototype (cognitive representation) of the exemplary members or ideal types (Hogg & Terry, 2000) of the group. This process, called self-categorization, is the process responsible for producing "positive in-group attitudes and cohesion, cooperation and altruism, emotional contagion and empathy, collective behavior, shared norms, and mutual influence" (p. 123).

The process of defining the group prototype shapes an informal influence hierarchy as the members who most exemplify the group's valued characteristics enjoy influence and those who do not find themselves in the position of deferring. Self-categorization and depersonalization, then, are the processes by which members emerge as informal leaders in their groups (Hogg, 2001; Hogg & Terry, 2000).

What complicates matters is the presence of a formally designated leader in the group. Members bring into the group their implicit theories and schemas of ideal leadership; however, "[a]s group membership becomes more salient, and members identify more strongly with the group, prototypicality becomes an increasingly influential basis for leadership perceptions" (Hogg, 2001, p. 189; Hogg, Hains, & Mason, 1998; van Knippenberg, 2011). Thus, these processes of self-categorization and depersonalization have the potential of overshadowing individually-held implicit leadership theories. Further, depending on the salience of group identity, they determine the extent to which a formal leader is seen as effective and enjoys the deference of the group. It is thus possible to imagine a group having multiple leaders: there may be an emergent leader who ranks as high or higher in prototypicality than the formally designated leader (Hogg et al., 1998).

THE SOCIAL IDENTITY MODEL OF LEADERSHIP AND THE NETWORK PERSPECTIVE

The social identity model relies on psychological processes of identification (self-categorization) and internalization (depersonalization) to explain emergent leadership. However, the hierarchies of influence and deference that result from these psychological processes are informal social structures and are potentially amenable to network approaches. Network techniques and measures have been employed to assess which members are seen as influential (Bunderson, 2003), how centralization is related to group outcomes (Grund, 2012; Shaw, 1964; Sparrowe, Liden, Wayne, & Kraimer, 2001), and the extent to which shared leadership affects performance (Carson et al., 2007; Mehra et al., 2006). This convergence signals an opportunity for dialog similar to what was proposed in relation to LMX differentiation. That groups evidence distinctive internal network patterns or structures (Mehra et al., 2006; Seibert et al., 2003), and that the position of formally designated leaders within these networks is relevant for how their effectiveness is perceived as well as for the performance of their groups. The guiding hypothesis then becomes whether prototypicality, through the processes of self-categorization and depersonalization, is the organizing principle for informal networks.

The network perspective offers an alternative hypothesis, one based homophily. In this view, much as would be predicted by status characteristics theory (Berger, Fisek, Norman, & Zelditch, 1977), members' affiliations within the group would align with similarity in ascribed characteristics such as gender or race. One study (Hogg et al., 2006) speaks to this question, offering empirical evidence that an ascribed characteristic (gender) matters for perceptions of leadership effectiveness when in relationship with prototype salience and the nature of the perceivers' gender stereotypes, but not as a "main effect," thereby supporting the social identity explanation. Further research is warranted, especially insofar as homophily shapes the composition of groups through the structures of opportunity for interaction in societies (McPherson, Popielarz, & Drobnic, 1992; McPherson, Smith-Lovin, & Cook, 2001). Exogeneously formed groups, such as students recruited for a laboratory experiment, as well as groups studied within organizations, rarely reflect the compositional constraints on voluntary affiliation naturally occurring in the population (Ruef, Aldrich, & Carter, 2003).

ENGAGEMENT OF SELF-SYSTEMS AND THE SOCIAL NETWORK PERSPECTIVE

Drawing from Markus and Nurius's (Markus & Nurius, 1986) concept of "possible selves," Ibarra (1999) advances the view that individuals navigate transitions in their careers by experimenting with provisional identities. Like "possible selves," albeit much more "provisional, even makeshift until they have been rehearsed and refined," they involve "observing role models, experimenting with provisional selves, and evaluating the results according to internal standards and external feedback" (p. 782) and, through iteration, "are practices and eventually incorporated into a more enduring repertory" (p. 783).

Subsequently, Ibarra et al. (2005) bring together provisional selves and social networks in a dynamic model of identify formation. In this approach, the selection and imitation of models for identity experiments are given by social networks: "the number and diversity of models, the emotional closeness of relationships, and the extent to which models share with the individual salient social and personal characteristics are likely to affect what possible selves people try and test." (2005, p. 363). Conversely, "visible and salient aspects of identity also affect individuals' social networks," as when ascribed characteristics like gender or race lead to "heightened preferences for same-race or gender ties as a basis for shared identity" (p. 364).

This conceptualization of identity as being composed of possible or provisional selves has been brought into the leadership domain in work by Stam et al. (2010) and by Sparrowe (2005). Stam et al. (2010) build their ideas on the foundation of Markus and Nurius (1986), and are especially interested in how the communication of vision by leaders generates in members "ideal selves," that comprise "future images of the self that represent what or whom an individual aspires to become [and] may be relevant in explaining vision effectiveness, because visions by definition concern ideal, possible futures." As members adapt ideal selves that are oriented to the fulfillment of the leader's vision, they are motivated to "make the ideal self (and thus the vision) reality" (p. 457). Sparrowe (2005), drawing from the work of the philosopher Ricoeur (1992), treats provisional selves as "alternative plot lines" in the creation of the narrative self; a process that "involves experimentation with provisional story lines, counterfactual pasts, and hypothetical futures" (p. 431). Like Ibarra et al. (2005), he argues that leaders and members derive these "plot lines" from their social networks; and, in logic similar to Stam et al. (2010), he suggests that leaders shape the identities of members by offering novel, vision-related "plots" through which alternative selves can be glimpsed.

It is useful to compare these approaches based on provisional selves (Stam et al., 2010) and the self as a narrative project (Sparrowe, 2005) with those based on the tripartite self of Brewer and Gardner (1996), such as Kark et al. (2003) and Lord et al. (1999). Although the underlying conceptualizations of the self differ in subtle ways, each describes how the self is constituted in and by relations with others. Further, they are compatible and can be integrated, as Lord and Brown (2004, p. 45) demonstrate in their discussion of how the personal, relational, and collective levels of the self engage the process of developing and evaluating provisional selves.

Conclusions

In contrast to earlier discussions relating social networks and leadership that are organized around social network concepts and theories (Balkundi & Kilduff, 2006; Brass, 2001; Brass & Krackhardt, 1999), this chapter frames the dialog in terms of several of the central explanatory mechanisms whereby leadership is understood to influence the discretionary attitudes and behaviors of members. Where a leadership theory shares an explanatory account with social networks, integration is relatively straightforward—as in the case of the LMX perspective and its original emphasis on how valued resources flow through the "organizational understructure" composed of networks (Cashman et al., 1976).

In other cases, though, finding genuine common ground is not altogether simple or straightforward, as even the use of similar concepts—such as "cognitive networks" (Balkundi & Kilduff, 2006) and "connectionist networks" (Lord & Shondrick, 2011)—belies substantive differences. Even just elaborating these differences, however, can open up opportunities for dialog. The beginnings of dialog between leadership and social networks offered here are not intended to declare one the winner over the other. Rather, it is—where feasible—to frame the issues in such a way as to make it evident how one is the thesis and the other the antithesis.

Perhaps none of these differences are as sharp as whether outcomes should be explained in terms of the attributes of individuals (leadership) or the structure of the relations among them (social networks), as this reprises the long standing debate of person versus situation. Nevertheless, there are possibilities, hints of synthesis, that can be glimpsed along the way by looking in the direction of situated cognition (Robbins & Aydede, 2009).

Future Directions

Alternative Explanatory Mechanisms

In sketching out the foundations for dialog between leadership and social networks, I limited the domain to explanatory accounts based on exchange, categorization, identification and internalization, and the engagement of self-systems. There are other explanatory mechanisms, such as social learning theory (Bandura, 1977, 1986) and empowerment (Conger & Kanungo, 1988; Thomas & Velthouse, 1990), that also offer interesting opportunities for dialog with the social network perspective. Social learning theory (Brown, Treviño, & Harrison, 2005) and self-efficacy (Walumbwa et al., 2011) explain the effects of leadership through the role played by modeling; social network analysis might be used to elaborate how modeling occurs not only dyadically but also in a larger social context. Empowerment has been modeled as a psychological state of leaders (Spreitzer, De Janesz & Quinn, 1999) and members (Chen, Kirkman, Kanfer, Allen, & Rosen, 2007), as well as being a form of leadership in its own right (Srivastava, Bartol, & Locke, 2006). Whether empowered leaders or members enjoy greater actual influence, and whether empowering leadership grants greater actual influence, are questions social network analysis is especially well suited to address. Future dialog might pursue these opportunities.

Exchange-based Accounts

In the discussion of exchange-based accounts, I identified an as-yet-unsolved puzzle: whether and under what conditions LMX differentiation versus informal social structure matter for group performance. The social network perspective is especially well equipped to illuminate group-level problems such as this one because of its emphasis on the structure of relationships internal to the group. Specific research questions that might be addressed include the following: Is the impact of LMX differentiation on group performance dependent on the leader's position in the group's network of advice, trust, or friendship relations? Given the evidence that leaders' network centrality moderates the relationships among LMX, sponsorship, and individual performance (Sparrowe & Liden, 2005), how might the leader's position in networks beyond the team interact with LMX differentiation in predicting team performance?

Categorization-based Accounts

The discussion of categorization-based accounts concluded with the observation that treating leaders' social networks as an indicator of an individual difference—"social complexity" in the work of Lord and Emrich (2000, p. 576) and Hooijberg et al. (1997)—risks removing leaders from the very networks in which they face opportunities and constraints on action. At the same time, however, the emphasis on accuracy in cognitive networks—as represented by the network approach to leadership of Balkundi and Kilduff (2006)—leaves important questions unanswered about how accuracy in network perceptions leads to strategic action, or why some individuals are more accurate than others. How might an integrated approach treat leaders as firmly embedded in the social networks of their organizations, facing real constraints and seizing genuine opportunities, and yet specify what individual difference makes some individuals in leadership roles more effective than others?

One strategy would focus on individual difference variables that are related both to leadership and skill in navigating networks. Self-monitoring is one such candidate; existing research links this trait to network brokerage (Oh & Kilduff, 2008) as well as to leadership (Day et al., 2002). Is the relationship between self-monitoring and leadership effectiveness mediated by leaders' network positions? Other possible candidates include political skill (Ferris et al., 2007) as well as measures of social competence, such as perspective taking (Russell & Kuhnert, 1992). Also of importance, however, is to investigate whether ascribed traits of leaders, such as empathy (Sadri, Weber, & Gentry, 2011), precede network position or follow from it—much as was the case with charisma and centrality in Balkundi, Kilduff and Harrison (2011).

Identity-based Accounts

So much of the theory and research on identification and internalization invokes dimensions the self; rarely, however, is the implied nature of the self made explicit. Indeed, there could be substantially greater consensus around the nature of the self.[6] No single conceptualization—certainly none discussed here—has achieved prominence (Gallagher, 2011). My focus on provisional selves (Ibarra et al., 2005) and the narrative self (Ricoeur, 1992) is motivated by how both conceptualizations take seriously how identity is constituted in the social context, thereby creating opportunities for dialog with social network theories. As Boyer, Robbins, and Jack (2005) characterize the situation, cognitive science is not concerned with "the self itself but rather the cognitive processes which allow us to construct and maintain representations of ourselves" (p. 647). The more mentally representing the self relies on the very same mechanisms that facilitate social perception, such as empathy and theory of mind, the less the "self" is separable or distinct from the social world out of which it is constituted (p. 647).[7]

Although debates about the nature of the self take place in fields far from leadership or networks, the questions raised in such discussions become important for framing the processes of identification, internalization, and engagement of self-systems. As the "self" comes to be seen as an ensemble of systems, precisely how leaders construct themselves in relation to "whom and what [they] identify with" (Boyer et al., 2005, p. 657) and the world in which they are situated becomes problematic for conceptualizations of leaders as unitary individuals of consistent character and intentionality. Questions that research might address include: To what extent are mental representations of the self of leaders and members reflective of the characteristics of central individuals in their networks? Are the self-concepts of leaders and followers shaped by the dynamics of the relationships in their shared social networks, such that changes in network cohesion are reflected similarity of self-representations? Are identification and internalization manifest in the plots by which members "narrate" themselves in relation to potentialities for action vis-à-vis their leaders?

A Theory of Situated Leadership

It is difficult to imagine a theory of leadership that is embodied, extended, and embedded that is not at the same time a network theory of leadership. The precise form such a theory might take is work for another day, but it would certainly be a theory in which leadership is distributed or emergent in the situational context rather than being identified solely with a single individual or network node. Although not read as an essay in leadership, Hutchins's "How a Cockpit Remembers Its Speeds" (Hutchins, 1995) is certainly an evocative example of such embeddedness. Or, perhaps such a theory would explain how leadership ebbs and flows from one node through a coordinated network, much as described by Klein, Ziegert, Knight, and Xiao (2006) in their analysis of trauma teams. There is much to be done to give shape and substance to situated "network" theory of leadership, but the growing emphasis in theory and research from psychology, philosophy of mind, and neuroscience on situated cognition (e.g., Robbins & Aydede, 2009) suggest that the effort will prove worthwhile.

Notes

1. Recent work by Burt (2012) indicates that there are personality-related differences in the networks of individuals, but those differences are largely irrelevant for reaping the benefits of network structure.
2. Explanations of the nature and effects of leadership based on categorization lie at the origin of what has been called the "cognitive revolution in leadership research" (Lord & Emrich, 2000). Its importance leads Hernandez et al. (2011) to treat cognition as distinct from affect, traits, and behaviors as explanatory mechanisms for the effects of leadership. Although I recognize the distinction, I don't accept the implication that other mechanisms—exchange, for example in this chapter, or affect, behavior or traits in the Hernandez et al. typology—operate independently of cognition.
3. Role theory has also served as a primary explanatory framework for LMX theory (Graen & Scandura, 1987).
4. Kelman's (1958) distinctions among compliance, identification, and internalization would seem to be an obvious foundation for understanding why members defer to the influence of their leaders. However, his framework only occasionally has informed identification-based explanations for

leadership (Shamir, House, & Arthur, 1993; Shamir, Zakay, Brainin, & Popper, 2000). And, as Yukl (1999, p. 294) has pointed out, these applications have not always been consistent with Kelman's original conceptualization.

5. Although Bono and Anderson explain the effects of transformational leadership in relation to behaviors (charisma, individualized consideration, and intellectual stimulation), it is plausible to suggest that the underlying psychological mechanisms involve the identification of members with leaders, in which members see their leaders as sources of expert advice and as influential persons with whom they wish to associate.
6. See Gallagher (2011) for a compendium of perspectives on the self from a variety of disciplines.
7. To claim that representing the self relies largely on the same systems as social cognition is not to deny the "ecological sense of bodily ownership and agency associated with active behavior" (Boyer et al., 2005; p. 648). Following Gallagher's distinction, the latter is the minimal self whereas the former, the narrative self, "supports the self image that associates our identity with various episodes" (p. 648).

References

Antonakis, J., Day, D. V., & Schyns, B. (2012). Leadership and individual differences: At the cusp of a renaissance. *The Leadership Quarterly, 23*, 643–650.

Ashforth, B. E., & Mael, F. (1989). Social identity theory and the organization. *Academy of Management Review, 14*, 20–39.

Avolio, B. J., Gardner, W. L., Walumbwa, F. O., Luthans, F., & May, D. R. (2004). Unlocking the mask: A look at the process by which authentic leaders impact follower attitudes and behaviors. *The Leadership Quarterly, 15*, 801–823.

Avolio, B. J., Walumbwa, F. O., & Weber, T. J. (2009). Leadership: Current theories, research, and future directions. *Annual Review of Psychology, 60*, 421–449.

Balkundi, P., & Kilduff, M. (2006). The ties that lead: A social network approach to leadership. *The Leadership Quarterly, 17*(4), 419–439.

Balkundi, P., Kilduff, M., & Harrison, D. A. (2011). Centrality and charisma: Comparing how leader networks and attributions affect team performance. *Journal of Applied Psychology, 96*, 1209–1222.

Bandura, A. (1977). *Social learning theory*. Upper Saddle River, NJ: Prentice Hall.

Bandura, A. (1986). *Social foundations of thought and action: A social cognitive theory*. Upper Saddle River: Pearson.

Bass, B. M. (1998). *Transformational leadership: Industrial, military, and educational impact*. Manwah, NJ: Lawrence Erlbaum.

Berger, J., Fisek, M. H., Norman, R. Z., & Zelditch, J. M. (1977). *Status characteristics and social interaction: An expectation states approach*. New York, NY: Elsevier.

Blau, P. M. (1964). *Exchange and power in social life*. New York, NY: John Wiley & Sons.

Bono, J. E., & Anderson, M. H. (2005). The advice and influence networks of transformational leaders. *Journal of Applied Psychology, 90*, 1306–1314.

Borgatti, S. P., & Foster, P. C. (2003). The network paradigm in organizational research: A review and typology. *Journal of Management, 29*, 991.

Boyer, P., Robbins, P., & Jack, A. I. (2005). Varieties of self–systems worth having. *Consciousness and Cognition, 14*, 647–660.

Brass, D. J. (1984). Being in the right place: A structural analysis of individual influence in an organization. *Administrative Science Quarterly, 29*, 518–539.

Brass, D. J. (2001). Social capital and organizational leadership. In S. J. Zaccaro & R. J. Klimoski (Eds.), *The nature of organizational leadership: Understanding the performance imperatives confronting today's leaders* (pp. 132–152). San Francisco, CA: Jossey-Bass.

Brass, D. J., & Krackhardt, D. (1999). The social capital of twenty-first-century leaders. In J. G. J. Hunt, G. E. Dodge, & L. Wong (Eds.), *Out-of-the-box leadership: Transforming the twenty-first-century army and other top-performing organizations* (pp. 179–194). Manwah, NJ: Elsevier Science/JAI Press.

Brewer, M. B., & Gardner, W. (1996). Who is this "we?" Levels of collective identity and self representations. *Journal of Personality and Social Psychology, 71*, 83–93.

Brown, M. E., Treviño, L. K., & Harrison, D. A. (2005). Ethical leadership: A social learning perspective for construct development and testing. *Organizational Behavior and Human Decision Processes, 97*, 117–134.

Bunderson, J. S. (2003). Recognizing and utilizing expertise in work groups: A status characteristics perspective. *Administrative Science Quarterly, 48*, 557–591.

Burt, R. S. (2012). Network-related personality and the agency question: Multi-role evidence from a virtual world. *American Journal of Sociology, 118*, 543–591.

Carley, K., & Palmquist, M. E. (1992). Extracting, representing, and analyzing mental models. *Social Forces, 70*, 601–636.

Carley, K. M. (1997). Extracting team mental models through textual analysis. *Journal of Organizational Behavior, 18*, 533–558.

Carson, J. B., Tesluk, P. E., & Marrone, J. A. (2007). Shared leadership in teams: An investigation of antecedent conditions and performance. *Academy of Management Journal, 50*, 1217–1234.

Casciaro, T. (1998). Seeing things clearly: Social structure, personality, and accuracy in social network perception. *Social Networks, 20*, 331–351.

Casciaro, T., Carley, K. M., & Krackhardt, D. (1999). Positive affectivity and accuracy in social network perception. *Motivation and Emotion, 23*, 285–306.

Cashman, J., Dansereau, F., Graen, G., & Haga, W. J. (1976). Organizational understructure and leadership: A longitudinal investigation of the managerial role-making process. *Organizational Behavior and Human Performance, 15*, 278–296.

Chen, G., Kirkman, B. L., Kanfer, R., Allen, D., & Rosen, B. (2007). A multilevel study of leadership, empowerment, and performance in teams. *Journal of Applied Psychology, 92*, 331–346.

Clark, A., & Chalmers, D. J. (2010). The extended mind. In R. Menary (Ed.), *The extended mind* (pp. 27–42). Cambridge, MA: MIT Press.

Conger, J. A., & Kanungo, R. N. (1988). The empowerment process: Integrating theory and practice. *Academy of Management Review, 13*, 471–482.

Contractor, N. S., DeChurch, L. A., Carson, J., Carter, D. R., & Keegan, B. (2012). The topology of collective leadership. *The Leadership Quarterly, 23*, 994–1011.

Damasio, A. R. (1994). *Descartes' error: Emotion, reason and the human brain*. New York, NY: Quill.

Dansereau, F., Graen, G., & Haga, W. J. (1975). A vertical dyad linkage approach to leadership within formal

organizations: A longitudinal investigation of the role making process. *Organizational Behavior and Human Performance, 13*, 46–78.
Day, D. V., Schleicher, D. J., Unckless, A. L., & Hiller, N. J. (2002). Self-monitoring personality at work: A meta-analytic investigation of construct validity. *Journal of Applied Psychology, 87*, 390–401.
Den Hartog, D. N., House, R. J., Hanges, P. J., Ruiz-Quintanilla, S. A., & Dorfman, P. W. (1999). Culture specific and cross-culturally generalizable implicit leadership theories: Are attributes of charismatic/transformational leadership universally endorsed? *The Leadership Quarterly, 10*, 219–256.
DeRue, D. S., Nahrgang, J. D., Wellman, N., & Humphrey, S. E. (2011). Trait and behavioral theories of leadership: An integration and meta-analytic test of their relative validity. *Personnel Psychology, 64*, 7–52.
Eden, D., & Leviatan, U. (1975). Implicit leadership theory as a determinant of the factor structure underlying supervisory behavior scales. *Journal of Applied Psychology, 60*, 736–741.
Engle, E. M., & Lord, R. G. (1997). Implicit theories, self-schemas, and leader-member exchange. *Academy of Management Journal, 40*, 988–1010.
Epitropaki, O., & Martin, R. (2004). Implicit leadership theories in applied settings: Factor structure, generalizability, and stability over time. *Journal of Applied Psychology, 89*, 293–310.
Epitropaki, O., & Martin, R. (2005). From ideal to real: A longitudinal study of the role of implicit leadership theories on leader-member exchanges and employee outcomes. *Journal of Applied Psychology, 90*, 659–676.
Erdogan, B., & Bauer, T. N. (2010). Differentiated leader—member exchanges: The buffering role of justice climate. *Journal of Applied Psychology, 95*, 1104–1120.
Ferris, G. R., Treadway, D. C., Perrewe, P. L., Brouer, R. L., Douglas, C., & Lux, S. (2007). Political skill in organizations. *Journal of Management, 33*, 290–320.
Foa, U. G., & Foa, E. B. (1974). *Societal structures of the mind.* Springfield, IL: Charles C Thomas.
Foti, R. J., Knee, R. E., Jr., & Backert, R. S. G. (2008). Multi-level implications of framing leadership perceptions as a dynamic process. *The Leadership Quarterly, 19*, 178–194.
Foti, R. J., & Lord, R. G. (1987). Prototypes and scripts: The effects of alternative methods of processing information on rating accuracy. *Organizational Behavior and Human Decision Processes, 39*, 318–340.
Friedrich, T. L., Vessey, W. B., Schuelke, M. J., Ruark, G. A., & Mumford, M. D. (2009). A framework for understanding collective leadership: The selective utilization of leader and team expertise within networks. *The Leadership Quarterly, 20*, 933–958.
Gallagher, S. (2005). *How the body shapes the mind.* Oxford, UK: Clarendon Press.
Gallagher, S. (Ed.). (2011). *The Oxford handbook of the self.* Oxford, UK: Oxford University Press.
Galvin, B. M., Balkundi, P., & Waldman, D. A. (2010). Spreading the word: The role of surrogates in charismatic leadership processes. *Academy of Management Review, 35*, 477–494.
Goodwin, V. L., Bowler, W. M., & Whittington, J. L. (2009). A social network perspective on LMX relationships: Accounting for the instrumental value of leader and follower networks. *Journal of Management, 35*, 954–980.
Graen, G. B., & Scandura, T. A. (1987). Toward a psychology of dyadic organizing. *Research in Organizational Behavior, 9*, 175–208.
Grund, T. U. (2012). Network structure and team performance: The case of English Premier League soccer teams. *Social Networks, 34*, 682–690.
Hanges, P. J., Lord, R. G., & Dickson, M. W. (2000). An information-processing perspective on leadership and culture: A case for connectionist architecture. *Applied Psychology: An International Review, 49*, 133–161.
Henderson, D. J., Liden, R. C., Glibkowski, B. C., & Chaudhry, A. (2009). LMX differentiation: A multilevel review and examination of its antecedents and outcomes. *The Leadership Quarterly, 20*, 517–534.
Henderson, D. J., Wayne, S. J., Shore, L. M., Bommer, W. H., & Tetrick, L. E. (2008). Leader-member exchange, differentiation, and psychological contract fulfillment: A multilevel examination. *Journal of Applied Psychology, 93*, 1208–1219.
Hernandez, M., Eberly, M. B., Avolio, B. J., & Johnson, M. D. (2011). The loci and mechanisms of leadership: Exploring a more comprehensive view of leadership theory. *The Leadership Quarterly, 22*, 1165–1185.
Hogg, M. A. (2001). A social identity theory of leadership. *Personality and Social Psychology Review, 5*, 184–200.
Hogg, M. A., Fielding, K. S., Johnson, D., Masser, B., Russell, E., & Svensson, A. (2006). Demographic category membership and leadership in small groups: A social identity analysis. *The Leadership Quarterly, 17*, 335–350.
Hogg, M. A., Hains, S. C., & Mason, I. (1998). Identification and leadership in small groups: Salience, frame of reference, and leader stereotypicality effects on leader evaluations. *Journal of Personality and Social Psychology, 75*, 1248–1263.
Hogg, M. A., & Terry, D. J. (2000). Social identity and self-categorization processes in organizational contexts. *Academy of Management Review, 25*, 121–140.
Hooijberg, R., Hunt, J. G., & Dodge, G. E. (1997). Leadership complexity and development of the Leaderplex model. *Journal of Management, 23*, 375–408.
House, R., Javidan, M., Hanges, P., & Dorfman, P. (2002). Understanding cultures and implicit leadership theories across the globe: An introduction to Project Globe. *Journal of World Business, 37*, 3–10.
House, R. J., & Aditya, R. N. (1997). The social scientific study of leadership: Quo vadis? *Journal of Management, 23*, 409–473.
Howell, J. M., & Shamir, B. (2005). The role of followers in the charismatic leadership process: Relationships and their consequences. *Academy of Management Review, 30*, 96–112.
Hutchins, E. (1995). How a cockpit remembers its speeds. *Cognitive Science, 19*, 265–288.
Ibarra, H. (1999). Provisional selves: Experimenting with image and identity in professional adaptation. *Administrative Science Quarterly, 44*, 764–791.
Ibarra, H., Kilduff, M., & Wenpin, T. (2005). Zooming in and out: Connecting individuals and collectivities at the frontiers of organizational network research. *Organization Science, 16*, 359–371.
Ilies, R., Morgeson, F. P., & Nahrgang, J. D. (2005). Authentic leadership and eudaemonic well-being: Understanding leader-follower outcomes. *The Leadership Quarterly, 16*, 373–394.
Judge, T. A., Piccolo, R. F., & Kosalka, T. (2009). The bright and dark sides of leader traits: A review and theoretical extension of the leader trait paradigm. *The Leadership Quarterly, 20*, 855–875.
Kark, R., & Shamir, B. (2002). The dual effect of transformational leadership: Priming relational and collective selves and

further effects on followers. In B. J. Avolio & F. J. Yammarino (Eds.), *Transformational and charismatic leadership*: The Road Ahead (Vol. 2, pp. 67–91) Stamford, CT: JAI Press.
Kark, R., Shamir, B., & Chen, G. (2003). The two faces of transformational leadership: Empowerment and dependency. *Journal of Applied Psychology, 88*, 246–255.
Keller, T. (1999). Images of the familiar: Individual differences and implicit leadership theories. *The Leadership Quarterly, 10*, 589–607.
Keller, T. (2003). Parental images as a guide to leadership sensemaking: An attachment perspective on implicit leadership theories. *The Leadership Quarterly, 14*, 141–160.
Kelman, H. C. (1958). Compliance, identification, and internalization: Three processes of attitude change. *Journal of Conflict Resolution, 2*, 51–60.
Kenrick, D. T., & Funder, D. C. (1988). Profiting from controversy: Lessons from the person-situation debate. *American Psychologist, 43*, 23–34.
Kilduff, M., & Brass, D. J. (2010). Organizational social network research: Core ideas and key debates. *Academy of Management Annals, 4*, 317–357.
Kilduff, M., Crossland, C., Tsai, W., & Krackhardt, D. (2008). Organizational network perceptions versus reality: A small world after all? *Organizational Behavior and Human Decision Processes, 107*, 15–28.
Kilduff, M., & Krackhardt, D. (1994). Bringing the individual back in: A structural analysis of the internal market for reputation in organizations. *Academy of Management Journal, 37*, 87–108.
Klein, K., J., Ziegert, J., C., Knight, A., P., & Xiao, Y. (2006). Dynamic delegation: Hierarchical, shared and deindividualized leadership in extreme action teams. *Administrative Science Quarterly, 51*, 590–621.
Krackhardt, D. (1987). Cognitive social structures. *Social Networks, 9*, 109–134.
Krackhardt, D. (1990). Assessing the political landscape: Structure, cognition, and power in organizations. *Administrative Science Quarterly, 35*, 342–369.
Krackhardt, D., & Kilduff, M. (1990). Friendship patterns and culture: The control of organizational diversity. *American Anthropologist, 92*, 142–154.
Lambert, L. S., Tepper, B. J., Carr, J. C., Holt, D. T., & Barelka, A. J. (2012). Forgotten but not gone: An examination of fit between leader consideration and initiating structure needed and received. *Journal of Applied Psychology, 97*, 913–930.
Levine, S. S., & Kurzban, R. (2006). Explaining clustering in social networks: Towards an evolutionary theory of cascading benefits. *Managerial & Decision Economics, 27*, 173–187.
Liao, H., Liu, D., & Loi, R. (2010). Looking at both sides of the social exchange coin: A social cognitive perspective on the joint effects of relationship quality and differentiation on creativity. *Academy of Management Journal, 53*, 1090–1109.
Liden, R. C., Erdogan, B., Wayne, S. J., & Sparrowe, R. T. (2006). Leader-member exchange, differentiation, and task interdependence: Implications for individual and group performance. *Journal of Organizational Behavior, 27*, 723–746.
Liden, R. C., Sparrowe, R. T., & Wayne, S. J. (1997). Leader-member exchange theory: The past and potential for the future. In G. R. Ferris (Ed.), *Research in Personnel and Human Resources Management* (Vol. 15, pp. 47–119). Greenwich, CT: Elsevier Science/JAI Press.
Lord, R. G., & Brown, D. J. (2004). *Leadership processes and follower self-identity.* Manwah, NJ: Lawrence Erlbaum.
Lord, R. G., Brown, D. J., & Freiberg, S. J. (1999). Understanding the dynamics of leadership: The role of follower self-concepts in the leader/follower relationship. *Organizational Behavior and Human Decision Processes, 78*, 167–203.
Lord, R. G., Brown, D. J., Harvey, J. L., & Hall, R. J. (2001). Contextual constraints on prototype generation and their multilevel consequences for leadership perceptions. *The Leadership Quarterly, 12*, 311–338.
Lord, R. G., & Emrich, C. G. (2000). Thinking outside the box by looking inside the box: Extending the cognitive revolution in leadership research. *The Leadership Quarterly, 11*, 551–579.
Lord, R. G., Foti, R. J., & de Vader, Christy L. (1984). A test of leadership categorization theory: Internal structure, information processing, and leadership perceptions. *Organizational Behavior & Human Performance, 34*, 343–378.
Lord, R. G., & Maher, K. J. (1993). *Leadership and information processing: Linking perceptions and performance.* New York, NY: Routledge.
Lord, R. G., & Shondrick, S. J. (2011). Leadership and knowledge: Symbolic, connectionist, and embodied perspectives. *Leadership Quarterly, 22*, 207–222.
Markus, H., & Nurius, P. (1986). Possible selves. *American Psychologist, 41*, 954–969.
McPherson, J. M., Popielarz, P. A., & Drobnic, S. (1992). Social networks and organizational dynamics. *American Sociological Review, 57*, 153–170.
McPherson, M., Smith-Lovin, L., & Cook, J. M. (2001). Birds of a feather: Homophily in social networks. *Annual Review of Sociology, 27*, 415–444.
Mehra, A., Dixon, A. L., Brass, D. J., & Robertson, B. (2006). The social network ties of group leaders: Implications for group performance and leader reputation. *Organization Science, 17*, 64–79.
Mehra, A., Smith, B. R., Dixon, A. L., & Robertson, B. (2006). Distributed leadership in teams: The network of leadership perceptions and team performance. *Leadership Quarterly, 17*, 232–245.
Mischel, W. (1968). *Personality and assessment.* Hoboken, NJ: John Wiley & Sons.
Nishii, L. H., & Mayer, D. M. (2009). Do inclusive leaders help to reduce turnover in diverse groups? The moderating role of leader-member exchange in the diversity to turnover relationship. *Journal of Applied Psychology, 94*, 1412–1426.
Noë, A. (2004). *Action in perception.* Cambridge, MA: MIT Press.
Offermann, L. R., Kennedy, J. K., & Wirtz, P. W. (1994). Implicit leadership theories: Content, structure, and generalizability. *The Leadership Quarterly, 5*, 43–58.
Oh, H. & Kilduff, M. (2008). The ripple effect of personality on social structure: Self-monitoring origins of network brokerage. *Journal of Applied Psychology, 93*, 1155–1164.
Pastor, J.-C., Meindl, J. R., & Mayo, M. C. (2002). A network effects model of charisma attributions. *Academy of Management Journal, 45*, 410–420.
Pearce, C. L., & Conger, J. A. (Eds.). (2003). *Shared leadership: Reframing the hows and whys of leadership.* Thousand Oaks, CA: SAGE.
Pratt, M. G. (1998). To be or not to be: Central questions in organizational identification. In D. A. Whetten & P. C. Godfrey (Eds.), *Identity in organizations: Building theory through conversations* (pp. 171–207). Thousand Oaks, CA: SAGE.
Ricoeur, P. (1992). *Oneself as another.* Chicago, IL: University of Chicago Press.

Robbins, P., & Aydede, M. (Eds.). (2009). *The Cambridge handbook of situated cognition.* New York, NY: Cambridge University Press.

Ruef, M., Aldrich, H. E., & Carter, N. M. (2003). The structure of founding teams: Homophily, strong ties, and isolation among U.S. entrepreneurs. *American Sociological Review, 68,* 195–222.

Russell, C. J., & Kuhnert, K. W. (1992). Integrating skill acquisition and perspective taking capacity in the development of leaders. *The Leadership Quarterly, 3,* 335–353.

Sadri, G., Weber, T. J., & Gentry, W. A. (2011). Empathic emotion and leadership performance: An empirical analysis across 38 countries. *The Leadership Quarterly, 22,* 818–830.

Schyns, B. (2006). Are group consensus in leader-member exchange (LMX) and shared work values related to organizational outcomes? Small Group Research, 37, 20–35.

Seibert, S. E., Sparrowe, R. T., & Liden, R. C. (2003). A group exchange structure approach to leadership in groups. In C. Pierce & J. Conger (Eds.), *Shared leadership: Reframing the "hows" and "whys" of leadership* (pp. 173–192). Newbury Park, CA: SAGE.

Shamir, B., & Eilam, G. (2005). "What's your story?" A life-stories approach to authentic leadership development. *The Leadership Quarterly, 16,* 395–417.

Shamir, B., House, R. J., & Arthur, M. B. (1993). The motivational effects of charismatic leadership: A self-concept based theory. *Organization Science, 4,* 577–594.

Shamir, B., Zakay, E., Brainin, E., & Popper, M. (2000). Leadership and social identification in military units: Direct and indirect relationships. *Journal of Applied Social Psychology, 30,* 612–640.

Shaw, M. E. (1964). Communication networks. *Advances in Experimental Social Psychology, 1,* 111–147.

Shondrick, S. J., Dinh, J. E., & Lord, R. G. (2010). Developments in implicit leadership theory and cognitive science: Applications to improving measurement and understanding alternatives to hierarchical leadership. *The Leadership Quarterly, 21,* 959–978.

Shondrick, S. J., & Lord, R. G. (2010). Implicit leadership and followership theories: Dynamic structures for leadership perceptions, memory, and leader-follower processes. In G. P. Hodgkinson & J. K. Ford (Eds.), *International review of industrial and organizational psychology* (pp. 1–33). Hoboken, NJ: Wiley-Blackwell.

Smith, J. A., & Foti, R. J. (1998). A pattern approach to the study of leader emergence. *The Leadership Quarterly, 9,* 147–160.

Sparrowe, R. T. (2005). Authentic leadership and the narrative self. *The Leadership Quarterly, 16,* 419–439.

Sparrowe, R. T., & Liden, R. C. (1997). Process and structure in leader-member exchange. *Academy of Management Review, 22,* 522–552.

Sparrowe, R. T., & Liden, R. C. (2005). Two routes to influence: Integrating leader-member exchange and social network perspectives. *Administrative Science Quarterly, 50,* 505–535.

Sparrowe, R. T., Liden, R. C., Wayne, S. J., & Kraimer, M. L. (2001). Social networks and the performance of individuals and groups. *Academy of Management Journal, 44,* 316–325.

Spisak, B. R., Homan, A. C., Grabo, A., & Van Vugt, M. (2011). Facing the situation: Testing a biosocial contingency model of leadership in intergroup relations using masculine and feminine faces. *The Leadership Quarterly, 23,* 273–280.

Spreitzer, G. M., De Janesz, S. C., & Quinn, R. E. (1999). Empowered to lead: The role of psychological empowerment in leadership. *Journal of Organizational Behavior, 20,* 511–526.

Srivastava, A., Bartol, K. M., & Locke, E. A. (2006). Empowering leadership in management teams: Effects on knowledge sharing, efficacy, and performance. *Academy of Management Journal, 49,* 1239–1251.

Stam, D., van Knippenberg, D., & Wisse, B. (2010). Focusing on followers: The role of regulatory focus and possible selves in visionary leadership. *The Leadership Quarterly, 21,* 457–468.

Sy, T. (2010). What do you think of followers? Examining the content, structure, and consequences of implicit followership theories. *Organizational Behavior and Human Decision Processes, 113,* 73–84.

Thomas, K. W., & Velthouse, B. A. (1990). Cognitive elements of empowerment: An interpretative model of intrinsic task motivation. *Academy of Management Review, 15,* 666–681.

van Knippenberg, D. (2011). Embodying who we are: Leader group prototypicality and leadership effectiveness. *The Leadership Quarterly, 22,* 1078–1091.

van Knippenberg, D., van Knippenberg, B., De Cremer, D., & Hogg, M. A. (2004). Leadership, self, and identity: A review and research agenda. *The Leadership Quarterly,* 15, 825–856.

Venkataramani, V., Green, S. G., & Schleicher, D. J. (2010). Well-connected leaders: The impact of leaders' social network ties on LMX and members' work attitudes. *Journal of Applied Psychology, 95,* 1071–1084.

Walumbwa, F. O., Avolio, B. J., & Zhu, W. (2008). How transformational leadership weaves its influence on individual job performance: The role of identification and efficacy beliefs. *Personnel Psychology, 61,* 793–825.

Walumbwa, F. O., Mayer, D. M., Wang, P., Wang, H., Workman, K., & Christensen, A. L. (2011). Linking ethical leadership to employee performance: The roles of leader-member exchange, self-efficacy, and organizational identification. *Organizational Behavior and Human Decision Processes, 115,* 204–213.

Walumbwa, F. O., Wang, P., Wang, H., Schaubroeck, J., & Avolio, B. J. (2010). Psychological processes linking authentic leadership to follower behaviors. *The Leadership Quarterly, 21,* 901–914.

Wheeler, M. (2005). *Reconstructing the cognitive world: The next step.* Cambridge, MA: Bradford/MIT Press.

Wilson, K. S., Sin, H-P., & Conlon, D. E. (2010). What about the leader in leader-member exchange? The impact of resource exchanges and substituability on the leader. *Academy of Management Review, 35,* 358–372.

Wilson, M. (2002). Six views of embodied cognition. *Psychonomic Bulletin & Review, 9,* 625–636.

Yukl, G. (1999). An evaluation of conceptual weaknesses in transformational and charismatic leadership theories. *The Leadership Quarterly, 10,* 285–305.

Yukl, G. A. (2010). *Leadership in organizations* (7th ed.). Upper Saddle River, NJ: Prentice Hall.

CHAPTER

21 Who's in Charge Here? The Team Leadership Implications of Authority Structure

Ruth Wageman *and* Colin Fisher

Abstract

Although team leadership can be enacted in many ways, a team's formal authority structure shapes how key leadership functions are fulfilled and by whom. This chapter analyzes how specific team leadership challenges and opportunities emerge, whether the team itself or managers hold legitimate authority for four critical team functions (Hackman, 2002): (1) executing the team task, (2) monitoring and managing work processes, (3) designing the team and its context, and (4) setting overall direction for the team. It then uses the four resultant team authority structures (manager-led, self-managing, self-designing, self-governing) to synthesize relevant research, draw implications for the practice of team leadership, and identify directions for future research. This chapter is intended to give practitioners and scholars a way to explore the characteristics of a particular situation that suggest a particular authority structure and the ways in which members and formal leaders may effectively operate within that structure.

Key Words: team leadership, authority, leadership functions, self-managing teams, self-governing teams, self-designing teams, manager-led teams

While teams accomplish much of the work in modern organizations (Hills, 2001 Kozlowski & Bell, 2003; Lawler, Mohrman, & Ledford, 1995), the meaning of team leadership remains elusive. Two factors contribute to this ambiguity. First, team leadership encompasses a wide variety of activities—it can mean everything from deciding to form a team in the first place, to composing the team, to exhorting members to exert more effort (Burke, Stagl, Klein, Goodwin, Salas, & Halpin, 2006; Fleishman, Mumford, Zaccaro, Levin, Korotkin, & Hein, 1991; Hackman & Walton, 1986; Morgeson, DeRue, & Karam, 2010; Zaccaro, Rittman, & Marks, 2001). Second, team leadership can be enacted by multiple people; indeed, it would be a tall order for any one individual to provide all the leadership necessary for a well-functioning team. Because team leadership involves a wide variety of behaviors enacted by multiple people, many scholars and practitioners have embraced a functional view of team leadership (Ginnett, 1993; Morgeson et al., 2010; Wageman & Hackman, 2010). In the functional view, team leadership is defined as "to do, or get done, whatever is not being adequately handled for group needs" (McGrath, 1962, p. 5).

Therefore, one critical implication of the functional view is that asking if someone is "team leader" is less helpful than asking who fulfills critical team leadership functions. Leadership functions *can* be fulfilled by a designated leader with formal authority, but also by team members themselves, or by external coaches with no formal authority over the team. The functional perspective therefore takes as given that team leadership is almost invariably shared leadership (Pearce & Conger, 2003). In other words, anyone can exercise team leadership, and a wide range of activities aimed at creating the conditions for team effectiveness count as acts of leadership. In the functional view, therefore, such team design choices as determining team membership, articulating team purposes clearly, designing team tasks, and establishing its reward structure all count as acts of team leadership, because they are necessary for a group to accomplish its purposes. Indeed, significant research evidence exists to support the view that such design choices are among the most important acts of team leadership, because they account for so much of the variance in team effectiveness (Hackman & O'Connor, 2004; Wageman, 2001).

Nonetheless, there are differences in who fulfills critical team leadership functions in different contexts, and these differences are strongly driven by the authority structure within which teams operate (Pearce & Conger, 2003). While front-line team managers typically have the authority to clarify team objectives and to offer hands-on coaching (Zaccaro et al., 2001), for example, they often lack the authority within their organizations to establish the teams' purposes and structures, or to alter contextual conditions to support a team's work (Manz, 1992). Those organization-wide elements may lie within the authority of much more senior managers, and may be designed for reasons having little to do with the impact on front-line teams. Leadership functions, in such contexts, are shared among different groups of managers. While in theory anyone can exercise leadership for a team, in fact the authority structure in a given context places expectations and constraints on who may legitimately fulfill key leadership functions. Therefore, the location of the *authority* to alter a team's design features and to manage its work processes is a key determinant both of who fulfills critical team leadership functions, the degree to which those are shared, and whether and how well they are fulfilled (Mannix & Sauer, 2006).

Hackman (2002) proposed four key team functions for which teams themselves or external managers of the teams may have authority. These are (1) executing the team task, (2) monitoring and managing work processes, (3) designing the team (e.g., choosing members) and its context (e.g., its information system), and (4) setting overall direction for the team.

Teams can be classified into distinct types depending on whether it is the team itself or managers who hold legitimate authority for these critical team functions. As shown in Figure 21.1, teams that have authority only for the completion of their own tasks are classified as *manager-led* (because all authority to exercise leadership belongs to managers); those that can monitor and manage their own work processes are *self-managing;* teams that also have authority to compose the team and shape their own context are termed *self-designing;* those that have authority over all four functions, including the authority to determine their own purposes, are classified as *self-governing.*

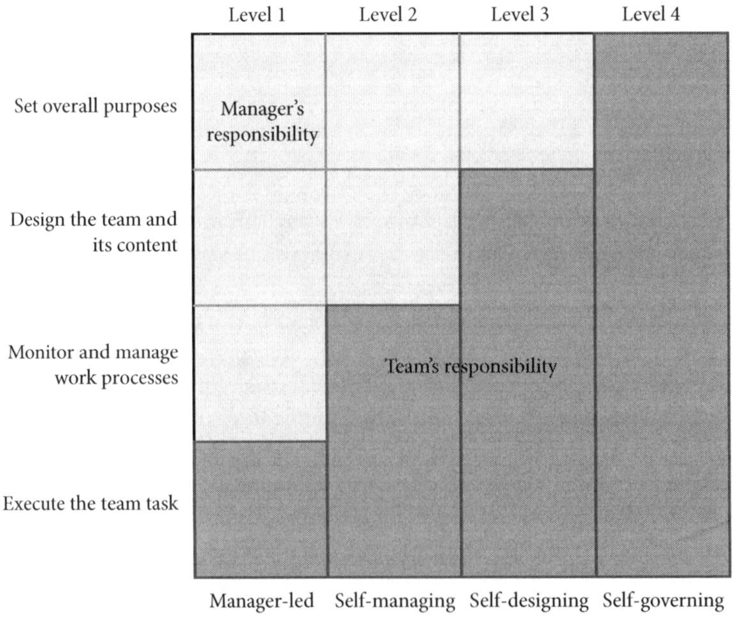

Figure 21.1. Levels of Team Authority.

From J. Richard Hackman (2002). Leading teams: Setting the stage for great performances. Harvard Business School Press.

In this chapter, we use this classification to explore how each type of team authority structure presents different team leadership challenges and opportunities. We summarize and synthesize research relevant to each of these authority structures, draw implications for the practice of team leadership, and identify areas where relatively little is known, offering directions for the future of research. Given several excellent reviews of group processes and functioning in recent years (i.e., Ilgen, Hollenbeck, Johnson, & Jundt, 2005; Larson, 2011; Morgeson et al., 2010; Straus, Parker, & Bruce, 2011; Zaccaro et al., 2001), we do not review research that focuses primarily on the relationships between specific internal group processes and emergent states (e.g., conflict as a driver of information sharing within a team); instead we place our focus on research on the influence of team leadership functions on key team processes and outcomes.

Leadership of Manager-Led Teams

Many scholars and practitioners think of team leadership in terms of an individual team leader vested with formal authority (Day, Gronn, & Salas, 2004; Hackman, 2002). While it is true that many teams have designated individual leaders, not all teams with a formal team leader should be considered "manager-led." Instead, we define manager-led teams as teams in which members "have authority only for actually executing the task... in such teams, managers manage, workers work, and the two functions are kept as separate as possible" (Hackman, 2002). Manager-led teams are ubiquitous in contexts such as orchestras, surgical teams, airline cockpit crews, assembly line manufacturing, and sports teams. For instance, in cardiac surgery teams, leadership is generally "hierarchical, demanding, and direct" (Edmondson, Bohmer, & Pisano, 2001, p. 704); many surgeons lead the teams by controlling even who speaks during surgery. As one perfusionist said,

> Once when we were having trouble with the venous return, and I mentioned it, the surgeon said, "Jack, is that you?" I said yes. He said, "Are you pumping [being the first rather than second, or assisting,] this case?" I said, "No I'm assisting." "Well in the future, if you are not pumping the case, I don't want to hear from you." You see it's a very structured communication. (Edmondson, Bohmer, & Pisano, 2003, p. 704)

This kind of tight control of the group process is common in surgery and the medical profession more generally (Nembhard & Edmonson, 2006). In fact, many surgeons view the team as a mere support system for them as individuals. As one cardiac surgeon said, "Once I get the team set up, I never look up [from the operating field]... it's they who have to make sure that everything is flowing" (Edmondson, Bohmer, & Pisano, 2001, p. 128).

Professional symphony orchestra conductors also tend to tightly control and supervise the process of their work groups (Allmendinger, Hackman, & Lehman, 1996). Like surgeons, conductors often experience the work of their team as a mere vehicle for their individual work. Composer/conductor Eberhard Weber described his experience, saying, "I like to create the music I hear in my interior. As a conductor, you have the ability to squeeze the sounds and interpretation you asked for from 50 to 80 people" (Weber, n.d.). Former Boston Symphony Orchestra music director Charles Munch echoed this view, saying, "The conductor must breathe life into the score. It is you and you alone who must expose it to the understanding, reveal the hidden jewel to the sun at the most flattering angles" (Munch, 1955).

As the examples above show, manager-led teams exist in contexts in which individual team leaders are expected to exert a great deal of control. While a manager-led structure provides unique opportunities for teams to accomplish certain types of work, this structure also produces some well-evidenced challenges. In the following section, we review these opportunities and challenges. Based on this analysis, we suggest imperatives for leaders of manager-led teams and directions for future research.

Opportunities for Manager-Led Teams

As one might imagine, opportunities for manager-led teams generally require a highly competent leader. An incompetent leader with control over team design and work processes can easily undermine a team (Wageman, 2001). In contrast, a superb team leader can help develop and improve even the most competent of performing units. Assuming the leader is qualified, we propose two primary opportunities in implementing and maintaining a manager-led authority structure in teams: (1) the opportunity to bridge an expertise gap between the leader and other team members; and (2) the opportunity to quickly observe and adjust when it is difficult for team members to perceive the whole of the task.

BRIDGING AN EXPERTISE GAP

A common reason to implement and maintain a manager-led structure is that a given leader is significantly more expert than other team members.

When a team leader knows a great deal more about a task or decision than does the team, the leader must provide some direction to the team about how to perform the task or what decision to make. For instance, when novice players participate in team sports, the players may know very little about strategies, roles, or even the rules of the game. It is thus incumbent on the head coach to tightly manage the processes and performance strategies until players understand the rules, tasks, and tactics. In the domain of management, Vroom and colleagues have well-developed research that shows that leaders who have more information than their followers are more effective when they use an autocratic style, in which they dictate both the processes and outcomes of decisions (Vroom & Yetton, 1973; Vroom & Jago, 1988).

Further, it is well-documented that teams predictably and repeatedly fail to facilitate their own decision-making processes; without direction, most groups fail to pool sufficient decision-relevant information before making a decision. However, a leader who knows how to direct such decision-making processes can mitigate these problems by structuring the team interactions. For instance, Larson and colleagues (1998) found that having a formal leader improved information processing and decision-making when those leaders asked questions and highlighted unique information. Additionally, Peterson (1997) found that leaders who use a directive style to advocate for an inclusive decision process (rather than for a particular alternative) tend to promote more information sharing and better group decisions. Similarly, Eisenhardt's (1989) study of strategic decisions in the microcomputing industry found that those CEOs who put an emphasis on processing more information, who considered more alternatives simultaneously, and who imposed processes for sharing information quickly tended to make better quality decisions. In sum, when leaders used their authority to impose processes that stimulate information processing (rather than to advocate for a particular outcome), better and faster decisions tended to result.

OBSERVING THE WHOLE TEAM AND TASK

Beyond the ability to structure and direct processes that groups often find difficult, team leaders may be better positioned than members to observe the complex dynamics of large, fast-moving teams. For instance, in American football, coaches craft and control the strategy and plays, which dictate the precise movements of players on the field (Katz & Koenig, 2001; Keidel, 1987). When playing, no one player can monitor all players simultaneously; in fact, players can seldom see more than one or two others at a time. Similarly, orchestral conductors are positioned such that they can hear all the orchestra members simultaneously, while those sitting in the orchestra often hear only those sitting near them as they are playing. When team members cannot monitor their own processes as they perform the work, giving a single leader the authority to monitor and manage the process may be desirable.

Challenges for Manager-Led Teams

Because manager-led teams require a single individual to fulfill a host of functions, such teams are extremely demanding for individual team leaders (Day, Sin, & Chen, 2004), creating critical leadership challenges. Indeed, much of the literature on manager-led teams has focused on their disadvantages relative to self-managing teams. We view the three most critical leadership challenges for manager-led teams as (1) preventing motivation losses, (2) minimizing evaluative pressure, and (3) avoiding conformity pressure.

PREVENTING MOTIVATION LOSSES

The most common problem specified is that team members tend to be less motivated and satisfied than those on self-managed teams (i.e. Cohen & Ledford, 1994; Goodman, Devadas, & Hughson, 1988), often leading to less productivity (Beekun, 1989; Guzzo, Jette, & Katzell, 1985; Kirkman & Rosen, 1999). Research on work motivation has shown that when workers lack autonomy over their own work processes they feel less responsibility for work outcomes, and they are less motivated to work on their tasks (Gagné & Deci, 2005; Grant & Parker, 2009; Hackman & Oldham, 1980). Thus, leaders of manager-led teams must often take potent steps to counteract this motivational decrement.

MINIMIZING EVALUATIVE PRESSURE

Another structural disadvantage of a manager-led team is that team leaders keep sole authority to monitor and evaluate the team's work processes. Because team leaders need to observe the team at work to fulfill this function, team members often experience such surveillance as evaluative. Increased evaluative surveillance tends to increase psychological arousal in ways that inhibit learning, experimentation, and performance on novel tasks (see Zajonc, 1965) and may also decrease intrinsic motivation (Deci, Koestner, & Ryan, 1999) and creativity

(Amabile, 1983, 1996; Amabile & Fisher, 2009). Further, using talented people in surveillance roles is often an inefficient use of human resources (Pfeffer, 1997); and an underuse of team member knowledge and skills (Allmendinger, Hackman, & Lehman, 1996).

AVOIDING CONFORMITY PRESSURES

Last, while having a leader who can direct decision-making can sometimes be beneficial, it also introduces strong conformity pressures that lead to suboptimal information processing and decision-making. Because it is often difficult to identify which group members hold decision-relevant knowledge (Gardner, Gina, & Staats, 2012; Stasser & Stewart, 1992), formal team leaders often hold influence disproportionate to their expertise, as members often inappropriately use their status as a proxy for task-relevant expertise (Bunderson, 2003; Gardner, Gina, & Staats, 2012). Further, when team leaders are also responsible for monitoring and evaluating member performance, members feel obliged to agree with the leader, which can lead to dysfunctional conformity pressures (Janis, 1982; Leana, 1985).

Imperatives for Leaders of Manager-Led Teams

While we can speculate on the advantages of manager-led teams, these advantages have seldom been documented by research. Instead, most extant research documents the advantages of self-management. Therefore, the imperative for those who hold authority over manager-led teams is to minimize the negative effects of such authority in three ways.

USE MANAGER-LED STRUCTURES SPARINGLY

The most important choice for leaders of manager-led teams is to decide the degree to which they will maintain a manager-led structure as opposed to promoting greater self-management among their members. Although manager-led teams prevail in a few industries, they are seldom the structure of choice in modern, knowledge-intensive organizations. Even in unique contexts, such as orchestras or operating rooms, leaders of manager-led teams would be well-served to consider promoting self-management in at least part of the work.

PROMOTE PSYCHOLOGICAL SAFETY

Leaders of manager-led teams must balance their function to monitor and evaluate team members with the need for those members to learn from mistakes, ask questions, and exercise their own creativity. One of the most fruitful areas of research along these lines has been research into how leaders create a climate of psychological safety (Edmondson, 1999, 2003a). Psychological safety is "a shared belief held by members of a team that the team is safe for interpersonal risk taking" (Edmondson, 1999, p. 350). When team members fear that others will criticize or ridicule their ideas, they are often hesitant to admit mistakes or make suggestions. Thus, psychological safety has been an important determinant of learning behavior in a variety of settings, including manufacturing (Edmondson, 1999), cardiac surgery teams (Edmondson, Bohmer, & Pisano, 2001), and neonatal care units (Nembhard & Edmondson, 2006). Leaders of teams of all types can promote psychological safety by being accessible to members, explicitly asking for input, and modeling their own fallibility by admitting mistakes as an opportunity for learning (Edmondson, Bohmer, & Pisano, 2003; Nembhard & Edmondson, 2006).

AVOID EXCESS ATTENTION TO MANAGING TASK PROCESSES IN REAL TIME

Next, leaders must make sure that they use their legitimate authority when necessary. Because leaders of manager-led teams have more responsibility than individuals in teams with different authority structures, it is easy to become overwhelmed and to ignore crucial aspects of team leadership (Wageman & Hackman, 2010). Top management teams are among the most guilty, with CEOs frequently failing to provide adequate direction or boundaries for the team (Wageman, Nunes, Burruss, & Hackman, 2008). Even the title of "team leader" has been found to make leaders more directive and intervene more frequently (Fisher, 2010) and to induce more interaction with team members (Cohen and Zhou, 1991), which increases the need for the leader to spend time and attention on managing group process.

Further, leaders of manager-led teams must look to the structure and organizational context of the team to solve problems, rather than simply relying on their authority over task and process. Manager-led teams are most prevalant in industries with well-defined task and role structures, as shown in the orchestral, medical, and sports examples earlier in this chapter. Most significantly, leaders in these industries tend to have little control over the task itself. As will be seen in the remainder of this chapter, task design is a critical lever for team effectiveness: in sports, task design cannot account for variations in performance because the basic rules of the game are predetermined; in health care and the military, many tasks have standard operating procedures that are difficult to change and inflexible roles that support these procedures. Such domains can be hotbeds of manager-led teams because there is little debate about what the task is or which role qualifies one to be a team leader. However, because such practices have become so standardized, the lowest hanging fruits for leaders may be in the structure and context— including the manager-led authority structure itself.

Directions for Future Research on Manager-Led Teams

Given that manager-led teams have both challenges and opportunities, the obvious question for future research is when best to use them. In other words, under what conditions do the theoretical advantages of manager-led teams outweigh the advantages of increased self-management? As we noted, manager-led teams seem to be most common when the task and role structure of teams is well-defined. Given the dearth of research supporting the use of manager-led teams, is that authority structure truly the optimal strategy in domains such as surgery, orchestras, or sports? Further, it seems likely that institutional forces play a critical role in sustaining leader-led teams (Hackman & Wageman, 2005b). Future research about manager-led teams should also address how and why manager-led teams have been sustained in the contexts we listed and whether these mechanisms are functional for team performance.

As we noted, manager-led teams also give a great deal of responsibility to the team leader. Most significantly, if a team leader is solely responsible for monitoring and managing the team's process, he or she must have some skill in diagnosing group processes as they unfold and intervening at opportune moments. While existing research has sketched what team leaders should do to improve group processes, there have been few investigations into when to act (or when to wait) and how skilled leaders make such assessments. Thus, a crucial area for future research is the diagnostic and interpretive process of team leaders and their relationship to the timing of process interventions (Fisher, 2010; Wageman, Fisher, & Hackman, 2009).

Finally, it is clear that many sophisticated team leaders pave the way for their teams to become more self-managing, just as many self-managing teams may voluntarily appoint a team leader that eventually consolidates his or her authority. Thus, two crucial yet unanswered questions are these: how do manager-led teams become self-managing and how do self-managing teams become manager-led? Indeed, examining the conditions under which manager-led teams increase their level of self-management may be the most crucial area of research for this authority structure.

Leadership of Self-Managing Teams

Self-managing teams are teams in which members have the authority not only to execute the work, but also to monitor their own performance quality and manage their own processes. In other words, they can make choices, in the absence of managerial instructions, about the main procedures, timing, and sequencing of their own work, as well as their coordination with other groups and individuals. Managing the quality of the work and making decisions about intra-team processes, therefore, are leadership functions that are fulfilled by the team members themselves.

Self-managing teams typically have a formally designated leader who retains authority to provide feedback or rewards to the team and to alter or determine team composition, and who holds responsibility for articulating group purposes (Druskat & Pescosolido, 2002; Gersick & Hackman, 1990; Langfred, 2000; Wageman, 2001). Those purposes may originate well above the teams' immediate leaders, as might other important team design features, such as how reward systems are designed and workloads allocated. For example, in customer service settings in which self-managed teams share accountability for an identified set of customers, a front-line supervisor provides hands-on coaching and feedback, but team memberships are assigned by higher-level managers, and reward systems are designed at the corporate level. Therefore, the array of individuals fulfilling leadership functions for such teams tends to be broad. Nevertheless, in self-managing teams, unlike in manager-led teams, team members themselves have considerable autonomy to determine their own work processes and therefore have a substantial leadership role themselves.

Examples of some common self-managing teams include multidisciplinary health care teams, often led by a nurse manager, and composed of nurses, physicians, perhaps physical and occupational therapists, and other health care workers. Such teams do not choose their own members or determine how rewards are distributed, but they have great latitude in how the work is executed for the care of their patients. Team members share responsibility for the well-being of patients and for coordinating their activities with each other (Edmondson, 1999; Nembhard & Edmondson, 2006; West, Borrill, Dawson, Brodbeck, Shapiro, & Haward, 2003). Other kinds of self-managing teams include production teams, in which quality assurance, production line pace, team member task assignments, and some fabrication processes are determined and executed by the workers themselves, although the teams typically have a supervisor responsible for worker schedules (and therefore team composition), ongoing coaching, and establishing production goals (Druskat & Wheeler, 2003; Kirkman & Rosen, 1999; Manz & Sims, 1987). Finally, many knowledge-work teams such as product and software development teams also belong to the category of self-managing teams. Though members hold full authority to decide how to deploy their collective resources in creating a new product, they typically report to a team leader who has additional authority and responsibilities (such as forming, launching, and coaching the team). Self-managing teams may well comprise the largest category of teams in modern workplaces—as well as being the type of team most frequently studied. Many teams that are typically thought of as self-managing but that also have authority over aspects of their own design or context are in fact what we call self-designing teams, a form of team we will address in the next section of this chapter. Here we address the key opportunities and challenges of self-managing teams, and the critical leadership capacities necessary to support their effectiveness.

Opportunities for Self-Managed Teams

Self-managed teams became common in U.S. organizations during the 1980s because of growing beliefs that they offered certain performance advantages that manager-led teams did not, stemming from two trends. First, the competitive losses of American companies to those from Japan led to the explosion of total quality management, a program that relies heavily on front-line workers devising, monitoring, and managing improvements in the work processes to enhance quality, and "empowered" work teams that make decisions to address the needs of customers in real time. At the same time, manufacturing firms in Europe and Asia had begun altering traditional assembly line designs, creating teams of individuals who shared collective responsibility for the process and quality of building whole subassemblies of various product, such as automobiles (Adler, 1995; Fleishman et al., 1991; Hackman & Walton, 1986; Morgeson, DeRue, & Karam, 2010; Sexton, 1994). These management trends had as their basic underpinnings the assumption that the people actually doing the work are best able to figure out better ways to do it. Moreover, scholars of the time observed that managing the quality of one's own work and interactions with the end users of that work has a powerful motivating effect (thereby enhancing employee engagement and productivity), and that the kinds of structured improvement processes involved in the quality movement produced not only a better process in the short-term but a more capable workforce in the long term (Beekun, 1989; Fleishman et al., 1991; Hackman & Walton, 1986; Morgeson, DeRue, & Karam, 2010; Pearce & Ravlin, 1987). Self-managing teams have tasks that drive positive internal work motivation to a greater degree than do manager-led teams: (1) they have more autonomy over their work processes; (2) they frequently have greater direct interaction with the users of their work; and (3) they often build whole products or share accountability for whole customer territories, rather than perform small and routinized pieces of a larger task (Cohen & Spreitzer, 1994; Cummings, 1981; Hackman & Oldham, 1980). As a consequence, leader intervention to enhance effort is relatively unneeded, with the work itself operating as a "substitute for leadership" (Kerr & Jermier, 1978; Hackman & Wageman, 2005b). The implementation of self-managing teams also involves a major investment in training, thus building the knowledge and skill of team members beyond what they had under manager-led authority structures (Kolodny & Kiggundu, 1980; Wall, Kemp, Jackson, & Clegg, 1986). All these benefits bode well for their effectiveness in comparison to manager-led teams.

Significant amounts of research have examined the performance impact of implementing self-managing teams in settings that were previously manager-led. While some studies showed performance advantages on key indicators of performance, such as customer satisfaction and quality of workmanship (Beekun, 1989; Guzzo, Jette, & Katzell, 1985), attempts to create team self-management just as often result in poor team performance, individualistic behavior, and avoidance of decision-making (Cohen & Ledford, 1994; Fleishman et al., 1991; Hackman &

Walton, 1986; Morgeson, DeRue, & Karam, 2010; Langfred, 2007). As a consequence, much of the subsequent research undertook to identify the antecedents of self-managing team effectiveness. Among the key leadership functions identified as major drivers of self-managing team effectiveness are (1) changes to the existing structures and systems of the firm that elicit, promote, and reward increased interdependence among workers and independent decision making by teams; and (2) changing the behavior of the external leader of the team, most particularly the hands-on coaching of teams' decision processes.

ALTERING STRUCTURES AND SYSTEMS TO PROMOTE INTERDEPENDENCE

Research has demonstrated that team self-management is facilitated by a supportive organizational climate for teamwork (e.g., Hempel, Zhang, & Han, 2012); team-based human resources systems, such as training, development, and information (e.g., Subramony, 2009; Wageman, 2001); and teams composed of members who welcome working interdependently and embrace the added responsibility for decision-making (Cohen & Spreitzer, 1994; Kirkman & Rosen, 1999). Moreover, team self-management also results in improved performance to the extent that the reward system recognizes and rewards excellent team performance over individual performance (Cohen, Spreitzer, & Ledford, 1996; Fleishman et al., 1991; Hackman & Walton, 1986; Morgeson, DeRue, & Karam, 2010; Rosenbaum et al., 1980; Shea & Guzzo, 1987; Wageman, 1995, 2001). Finally, self-managing teams benefit from an organizational education system that provides cross-training in multiple skills, or technical consultation for any aspects of the work that members are not themselves competent to handle (Klaus & Glaser, 1970; Liang, Moreland, & Argote, 1995; Fleishman et al., 1991; Hackman & Walton, 1986; Morgeson, DeRue, & Karam, 2010; Salas, Cannon-Bowers, & Blickensderfer, 1993). In modern workplaces such as professional service firms, where work is typically completed by self-managing teams that have no history of manager-led practice, these same contextual supports also have positive effects (Stewart, 2006). In sum, critical leadership functions for developing self-managing teams are predominantly about making significant investments in creating an organizational context that elicits, reinforces, and supports interdependence among peers and collective decision-making about work processes.

COACHING

Both scholars and practitioners who write about self-managing teams' effectiveness focus a great deal of attention on what leaders do in their day-to-day interactions with team members—that is, they focus on hands-on coaching (e.g. Bass, 1957; Berkowitz, 1953; Druskat & Wheeler, 2003; Fiedler, 1958; Jackson, 1953; Likert, 1958; Lippitt, 1940; Manz, 1986; Manz & Sims, 1987; Schlesinger, Jackson, & Butman, 1960). Coaching refers to direct interaction with the team intended to shape team processes to produce good performance. Pervading the literature on team coaching is the view that leader coaching behaviors can directly affect team members' engagement with their task, their ability to work through interpersonal problems that may be impeding progress, and the degree to which members accept collective responsibility for performance outcomes. Manz and Sims (1987) showed that the external leadership of self-managing teams, especially coaching (such as eliciting self-observation, self-evaluation, and self-reinforcement by members), were a significant differentiator of effective and ineffective self-managing team processes. Similarly, reinforcement by external leaders has been shown to enhance team psychological empowerment (e.g., Cohen & Spreitzer, 1994; Kirkman & Rosen, 1999).

At the same time, Cohen, Ledford, and Spreitzer (1996) found that "encouraging behavior" (providing feedback intended to enhance team motivation) from supervisors was negatively associated with team performance as assessed both by managers and by customers, and Beekun (1989) found that self-managing teams that had no coaches significantly outperformed those that did. Morgeson (2005) showed that active interventions by leaders had a negative impact on team's perceptions of the leader, though when events were sufficiently routine, the impact of those interventions on performance was positive. In sum, existing research evidence suggests that leaders' coaching in some circumstances fosters team self-management, the quality of members' interpersonal relationships, and member satisfaction with the team and its work. Yet in others it had either negative or neutral effects.

Challenges for Self-Managing Teams

The main challenges identified in the research literature on self-managing teams are (1) resistance to change, both among team members and among managers in the transition from manager-led to self-managing teams; (2) a concomitant tendency of so-called self-managing teams to devolve into manager-led teams; and (3) an excessive focus by both leaders and team members on teams' own internal processes.

OVERCOMING RESISTANCE TO SHARED DECISION-MAKING

There are significant challenges to leaders in getting front-line teams to accept managerial responsibilities for the processes and quality of their work, especially in instances in which rewards for improved productivity are not shared with the teams themselves (Barker, 1993; Kirkman & Rosen, 1999; Stewart & Manz, 1995). Moreover, research has shown that organizations face significant challenges in changing the behaviors of those holding supervisory roles to one of coaching rather than supervision. A critical question raised by the conflicting findings of research on the effectiveness of self-managed teams was the degree to which these teams were self-managing in name only.

The difficulties of fostering genuine self-management have been well-documented. These difficulties include the inability of managers to release control of work processes to teams (Golembiewski, 1995; Hut & Molleman, 1998), as well as resistance from team members to taking on self-management (Balkema & Molleman, 1999; Wellins, Byham & Wilson, 1991).

Most research on self-managing teams has focused on introducing such teams into formerly manager-led and individualistic front-line environments such as production lines, sales, and customer service. Members of these newly formed teams held a history of working independently of their peers. Moreover, in such highly structured workplaces, work processes had been dictated by supervisors or by the technology of the assembly line itself. In this environment, introducing self-managing teams both increases teams' authority and accountability for the quality of work processes and increases interdependence with peers, creating a host of leadership challenges. The environments in which these changes take place frequently are unionized as well, and therefore have the history of considerable suspicion between management and workers and a transactional relationship between the firm and the worker typified by control-type environments (Hackman & Walton, 1986; Walton, 2003; Walton & Hackman, 1986).

There is evidence that when teams are given greater accountability for decisions they may view this greater authority as an attempt by the organization to ask them to produce more and take on added responsibility without experiencing the tangible benefits of those changes themselves (Marks & DeMeuse, 2003; Silver, Randolph, & Siebert, 2006). Moreover, workers with strong preferences to work autonomously may continue to pursue their own approaches to the work, resisting the obligations of joint decision-making with their teammates (Wageman, 1995). Organizational culture characteristics such as power distance (Kirkman & Shapiro, 2001), which refers to a collective desire for large differences in the authority of leaders and followers to be maintained (Hofstede, 1984), can exacerbate the desire to avoid taking on authority that was previously the domain of managers.

Parallel to these challenges based in the perceptions, values, and motives of workers are similar sources of psychological resistance from leaders. For example, Manz and Sims (1987) showed that front-line managers can experience the change of authority toward more team self-management as a direct threat to their value and power in the organization, and they frequently lack the skills to offer coaching and consultation rather than issuing orders and setting goals (Manz, 1992). Organizational and national culture can influence leader resistance to sharing authority as well. While the high collectivist values of China, for example, make working in teams relatively natural, the dominant leadership style, which invests all authority in leaders, undermines the development of team behavioral self-management (Bell, 2007; Cheng, Chou, Wu, Huang, & Farh, 2004). Thus, the theoretical improvement in worker autonomy intended by a change to self-management can be undermined by the actual behaviors of leaders and teams. For those who would exercise leadership to realize the benefits of team self-management, then, one critical leadership function is to create conditions to prepare team leaders for coaching roles by building their sense of efficacy and providing direct experience of a new way of working with teams (Golembiewski, 1995; Hut & Molleman, 1998; Manz, 1986).

PREVENTING SELF-MANAGED TEAMS FROM BECOMING DE FACTO MANAGER-LED TEAMS

One common consequence, then, of the less-than-natural transition from manager-led to self-managing teams is for team leaders to recapture control over work processes, making the teams "self-managing" in name only. Research has suggested that the behaviors of teams and leaders are a dynamic, exerting mutual influence over one another. For example, senior leadership teams frequently are initially designed by chief executives to be self-managing—that is, the chief executive intends to hold authority for deciding the purpose and composition of the team, but asks members to take on shared accountability for key decisions affecting the organization. Yet senior teams are frequently ineffective (Edmondson, Roberto, & Watkins, 2003; Hambrick, 1994; Wageman et al., 2008). While some writers suggest that their ineffectiveness is a direct result of the leader's unwillingness to share power and create a genuine consensus decision process (Katzenbach, 1997), it may also be the case that leaders *take back* authority when the team is poor at making decisions together, having become embroiled instead in turf battles and conflicts (Wageman, et al., 2008). A challenge for leaders of self-managing teams, then, may be to exercise self-control at moments when the team is struggling to operate effectively, and avoiding taking over their work. While this pattern has been observed and has sparked commentary, there has yet to be a systematic study of the potentially dynamic relations between team and leader behavior with respect to team authority.

PROMOTING ADEQUATE EXTERNAL FOCUS

The necessity to learn how to make team decisions effectively and to monitor and manage the quality of their teammates' work and work processes can capture much of the attention of self-managing team members. Moreover, significant evidence has accumulated that interpersonal and task-based conflict (De Dreu & Weingart, 2003; Jehn & Bendersky, 2003; Langfred, 2007), shifts in trust levels, and struggles to manage behavioral interdependence (Langfred, 2004; Porter & Lilly, 1996), can captivate the attention of members—and all at the expense of attention to key external relationships and events, such as customer needs and relations with other teams.

Evidence for the importance of external activities to self-managing team performance has been mounting. Ancona and her colleagues have most fully developed this area of research by mapping the range of activities that groups use to engage with their environments, clients, and other external individuals and groups (cf. Gladstein, 1984; Ancona & Caldwell, 1987; 1992; Ancona, 1990). She showed that teams were significantly less effective when they remained relatively isolated from their environments, focused instead on internal activities, or merely observed the outside environment without actively engaging outsiders (Ancona, 1990). Similarly, Gersick (1988) showed that project teams that had an external focus at the calendar midpoints of their projects were significantly more likely to complete their tasks effectively.

The main advantages of self-managing teams—enhanced commitment to the work, better performance strategies, and excellent use of team member capabilities—all have been shown to be significantly better when the team actively engages in some form of task-relevant attentiveness to its external environment. At the same time, while the virtues of external focus have been well documented by Ancona and her colleagues (cf. Gladstein, 1984; Ancona & Caldwell, 1987; Ancona, 1990), the leadership functions that promote adequate external focus have not. There is significant variation in self-managing teams' attentiveness to their environments and in their tendency to focus their energies on internal versus external processes. Relatively little is known about the influences on teams' external activities, or the leadership actions by members and authorities that enable self-managed teams to address this balance effectively.

Imperatives for Leaders of Self-Managing Teams

What has research shown to be the kinds of leader activities that are most critical to enabling self-managing team effectiveness? Two particular patterns emerge with respect to the activities of external leaders and their impact on self-managing teams: (1) the relative influence of designing a team well versus coaching it well and (2) the importance of timing.

DESIGN BEFORE COACHING

Leadership functions divide into two basic conceptual categories: (1) establishing (or influencing) the design features of teams; and (2) providing hands-on coaching and consultation. In a longitudinal field study of customer service teams, Wageman (2001) directly measured the impact of these two main functions of leaders of self-managing teams. The primary influences on effective self-management were the design choices of front-line leaders and *their* leaders, including (1) the design of the task in terms of its interdependence (accomplished in this case by the front-line manager); (2) the clarity of team-level purposes; and (3) rewards for group performance (determined by the manager one level up). Only when these basic design conditions were well-established did front-line leaders' hands-on coaching make a positive difference in the overall effectiveness of self-managing teams. Moreover, the magnitude of the effect of poor coaching (including leaders taking back authority by identifying the teams' problems for them and asserting their own solutions) was also determined by quality of team design. That is, well-designed teams were more robust—less undermined by poor coaching—than those whose basic design features were shaky.

In this view, leaders have the opportunity to coach a team to higher levels of self-management and superior performance only when the team is relatively well-designed. If design conditions are stacked in favor of good performance, the team coach can help the team exploit its favorable circumstances (Hackman, 2011). If the team is poorly designed, on the other hand, attempts to foster team effectiveness through hands-on coaching may be futile or even backfire. In such cases, the flawed design may create dysfunctional processes so strong and preoccupying that coaching interventions risk merely adding to the disarray (Woodman & Sherwood, 1980).

PAY ATTENTION TO TIMING

The efficacy of leaders' interventions may depend not just on their focus but also on the time in the group's life cycle when a team leader chooses to provide them (Wageman, Fisher, & Hackman, 2009; Hackman & Wageman, 2005a). In recent years there has been an outpouring of research findings on temporal aspects of group behavior, much of which bears directly on team leader decision-making about the timing of interventions (see, for example, Ancona & Chong, 1999; Fisher, 2010; Gersick & Hackman, 1990; Langfred, 2000; Orlikowski & Yates, 2002). Gersick's (1988) findings are particularly relevant. In a field study of the life histories of a number of self-managing project teams whose performance periods ranged from several days to several months, she found that each of the groups she tracked developed a distinctive approach toward its task as soon as it commenced work, and stayed with that approach until precisely halfway between its first meeting and its project deadline. At the midpoint of their lives, almost all teams underwent a major transition. In a concentrated burst of changes, they dropped old patterns of behavior, re-engaged with outside supervisors, and adopted new perspectives on their work. Following the midpoint transition, groups entered a final phase of focus on executing their tasks to the point of completion.

The findings of Gersick (1988) and others raise the possibility that the readiness of self-managing teams for external leaders' interventions changes systematically across their life cycles. Specifically, there are three times in a team's life when members may be especially open to interventions that address each of the three key performance processes. At the beginning, when a team is just starting its work, it is especially open to interventions that focus on the effort members will apply to their work. At the midpoint, when the team has completed about half its work (or half the allotted time has elapsed), it is especially open to interventions that help members reflect on their task performance strategy. And at the end, when the work is finished, the team is ready to entertain interventions aimed at helping members draw on their experiences to build the team's complement of knowledge and skill (Hackman & Wageman, 2005a).

Directions for Future Research on Self-Managing Teams

The findings of the scholarly research on self-managing teams raise several intriguing questions and promising avenues for future investigation. These include (1) the dynamic relationship between team and leader behavior in fulfilling key leadership functions; and (2) the challenges of developing leadership capacity to support self-managing team effectiveness. These are described briefly, in turn, below.

DYNAMIC RELATIONS OF TEAM AND LEADER BEHAVIOR

Recall that among the challenges of self-managing teams is the difficulty of implementing them de novo—and the subsequent risk that external leaders undermine team authority by taking back their decision rights over task processes. There exists the possibility that leaders take over the management of the tasks of poorly functioning teams because members themselves are not fulfilling those functions effectively. Feeling accountable for teams' performance, leaders may respond to low team self-management and poor performance by monitoring team performance more closely, by increasing their own interventions in the work of their teams, and by providing fewer cues and rewards for team self-management. This hypothesis is consistent with other research on how follower behavior can shape leader style (e.g., Farris & Lim, 1969; Lowin & Craig, 1968), and it merits additional investigation in the context of self-managing teams.

DEVELOPING THE CAPABILITIES OF SELF-MANAGING TEAMS' EXTERNAL LEADERS

While a great deal is known about the conditions that influence self-managing team effectiveness, the kinds of coaching that do and do not help self-managing teams, and the ways in which predictable times in the life of a group can be used to shape effectiveness, these findings raise important questions relevant to improving the effectiveness of such teams: how and under what conditions are external leaders best able to learn these practices? There are significant conceptual, behavioral, and emotional challenges to learning to lead self-managing teams. For example, understanding what the basic design features are that such teams need, recognizing the degree to which they are in place, and formulating a strategy for getting them in place are significant conceptual challenges (Wageman & Hackman, 2010). At the same time, refraining from intervening in team process, choosing an effective time to do so, and intervening in ways that encourage self-management can be significant emotional and behavioral challenges (Manz & Sims, 1987). Almost no research has yet focused on the personal characteristics, leadership development interventions, or organizational conditions that enhance these team leadership capacities, and we suggest this may be a fruitful avenue for additional investigation into the leadership of self-managing teams.

Leadership of Self-Designing Teams

Self-designing teams are self-managing teams in which members also can determine key features of the team and/or their own organizational context, but not their overall purposes. Most often, self-designing teams can alter their own membership, how rewards are distributed, and what information or technical consultation is offered to the team. Because self-designing teams can influence both their structure and their processes, they control many of the key conditions that foster team effectiveness (Hackman, 2002). While the term *self-designing teams* is rare in the research literature (Bennett & Kidwell, 2001), many teams that are referred to in particular studies as "self-managing" also have authority over some aspect of their own design and thus would be called "self-designing teams" in our terminology.

For instance, many front-line teams have some authority over their own membership and rewards, in addition to managing and monitoring their own work processes. Barker (1993) described how teams at a telecommunications manufacturing facility could interview, hire and fire their own members, as well as dock members' pay for violating team norms. Other examples of self-designing teams include academic research teams (Bennett & Kidwell, 2001) and task forces charged with leveraging new market opportunities (Gersick, 1990) or identifying the causes of organizational performance problems and proposing solutions (Gabarro & Clawson, 1984). Self-designing teams may also be more common in flat or entrepreneurial organizations where who holds authority over team design is often ambiguous.

While self-managing teams are often deliberately implemented to boost motivation and productivity, self-designing teams may come about less intentionally. When organizations implement self-managing teams, they often do so to minimize traditional hierarchical leadership (Manz, 1992) and leave as many decisions as possible to the teams. However, because in complex matrix organizations and multi-national firms authority and resources are jointly held by multiple managers (Cummings & Haas, 2012; Janz, 1999; O'Leary, Mortenson, & Woolley, 2011), teams often have accountabilities they share with other teams and members with diverse goals. Thus, self-managed teams in these organizations may spend much of their time figuring out how to construe the task or negotiating team design features, gradually taking authority over those design features themselves. In taking a functional view of team leadership, we view all of these activities as an exercise of leadership, regardless of whether they are done by a nominal team leader, other team members, or those external to the team.

Opportunities for Self-Designing Teams

The opportunities afforded to self-designing teams are simple: their authority over team, task, or organizational context gives them a range of ways to adjust their design as task demands shift over time. Because team members are likely to be the most familiar with the task demands, client needs, and optimal work processes, they theoretically are better positioned to understand the team's design needs – especially in novel or uncertain tasks with which external leaders have had little experience. Thus, self-designing teams have the opportunity to (1) adjust their membership to meet task demands; (2) structure rewards to maximize motivation and distributive justice; (3) requisition the information they need in real time; and (4) increase their members' leadership capacity (Manz, 1992; Wageman et al., 2008).

REFINING TEAM MEMBERSHIP

One specific opportunity for self-designing teams is to recognize the need for additional knowledge or skills, and to add new team members to address it. Because knowledge-intensive tasks are frequently nonroutine or uncertain (e.g., Cross, Erlich, Dawson, & Helferich, 2008; Rulke & Galaskiewicz, 2000), teams may encounter problems that were unanticipated at team launch. Thus, teams with the authority to add people with relevant needed expertise are best positioned to succeed. For instance, in their study of teams in a design firm, Fisher, Amabile, and Pillemer (2010) found that many senior designers and engineers worked on teams only on an as-needed basis: "project mentors" kept some of their time flexible so that teams could "buy" their hours if their expertise was required. Similarly, Ancona, Bresman, and Caldwell (2009) described how a Microsoft software engineering team self-designed, adding and shedding members as the team moved from brainstorming to design. They further proposed that such self-designed membership flexibility is a key characteristic of innovative, externally focused teams.

REMOVING MEMBERS

Self-designing teams can also use authority over membership to attract more productive individuals or to rid themselves of habitual social loafers (Barker, 1993; Delong, Mody, & Ager, 2003). For instance, teams in C&S Grocer's distribution warehouse had authority over their membership, such that they could dismiss underperforming members, and all members were free to join other teams. This arrangement led to an intense internal marketplace for labor. Because the teams were paid based on productivity, extremely productive individuals could earn more by joining better-performing teams. Top management at C&S Grocers saw these self-designing teams as the key to the organization's growing profits and market share (Delong, Mody, & Ager, 2003). Further, self-designing teams who can dismiss their own members also have considerable authority to punish those who do not conform to team norms (Barker, 1993), which can increase their control over member motivation and behavior.

DISTRIBUTING REWARDS AND PUNISHMENTS

Beyond using team membership as a mechanism for rewarding and punishing members, self-designing teams may also have some control over performance evaluation or pay distribution. Like the ability to hire and fire members, giving a team control over its own reward system will give it greater control over the effort members exert (Barker, 1993). However, giving teams the authority to decide how to evaluate each other and distribute rewards accordingly presents many difficulties, which are detailed in the next section. If self-designing teams are to benefit from authority over their rewards, they would be well-served to agree on a collective reward. Although rewarding individuals with recognition, promotions, and money is common in organizations, rewarding the team as a collective is often more effective at engendering and sustaining collective effort (Druskat & Kayes, 2000; Lawler, 2000; Spreitzer, Noble, Mishra, & Cooke, 1999). However, such teams must be cautious to avoid "hybrid" rewards that simultaneously reward group and individual performance. In her study of self-managing service technicians at Xerox, Wageman (2001) found that the pure individual and pure team reward systems led to better performance than did hybrid reward systems.

OBTAINING KEY INFORMATION

One of the most overlooked design features that self-designing teams may have control over is their access to task-relevant information. In order to develop and maintain a task-appropriate work strategy, teams often need up-to-date, trustworthy information about their work environment, including what is happening with customers, supply chains, or other parts of the organization. However, in modern, knowledge-intensive organizations, information is one of the most valuable resources and can be hoarded by the powerful; front-line, self-managing teams may find it difficult to get task-relevant information when management feels such information is too "competitively sensitive" (Hackman, 2002). Thus, a self-designing team with the authority to requisition whatever information it needs, whenever it needs it, will be much better able to make well-considered decisions about its strategy and deliverables.

BUILDING MEMBERS' LEADERSHIP CAPACITY

Last, self-designing teams have a significant opportunity to build members' capacity for leadership by giving them experience managing membership, rewards, and information systems—tasks often reserved for upper management. In settings such as senior leadership teams, such teams may be a vehicle for leaders of particular areas to think strategically about the whole enterprise, rather than about their particular domain (Wageman & Hackman,

2010; Wageman et al., 2008). Even at lower levels of organizational bureaucracy, individuals who are asked to think strategically about team structure and environment will be encouraged to learn about the organization and to hone their strategic thinking skills (Manz, 1992; Ancona & Caldwell, 1992), thus building the leadership capacity of the organization.

Challenges for Self-Designing Teams

The main challenges for self-designing teams also stem from the broad scope of their authority: their varied responsibilities can lead to the underuse or misuse of team design. Here, we summarize three of these challenges: (1) managing competing demands for attention; (2) having difficult conversations in a team of equals; and (3) limiting the overuse of authority.

MANAGING COMPETING DEMANDS FOR ATTENTION

Self-design inherently invites teams to consider both design and process changes when seeking to improve their teamwork. Many aspects of design – such as bringing in new members or requisitioning information – require a working knowledge of a team's external environment (e.g., the skills of others in the organization; where relevant information might be located; see Ancona, Bresman, & Caldwell, 2009). Thus, a self-designing team will need to keep its attention focused in more directions than a self-managing one would. Because attention is a scarce resource in knowledge-intensive organizations (March & Simon, 1958; Hansen & Haas, 2001), teams responsible for their own design may have difficulty both completing their task and attending to their own design, especially when improving the design is time-consuming. Such multitasking can be especially problematic when team members have many other accountabilities besides the team (Cummings & Haas, 2012; O'Leary et al., 2011) or when it requires the team to increase monitoring of its external environment (Waller, 1997).

HAVING DIFFICULT CONVERSATIONS IN A TEAM OF EQUALS

Even when a self-designing team is attentive to its own structure, it may still be "under-designed" (Ancona & Nadler, 1989) because exercising its authority would be interpersonally difficult. Specifically, research has found that many teams have difficulty managing their own membership or evaluating their teammates because they perceive the costs to them as individuals as greater than the benefits to the team (Peiperl, 1999). For instance, many teams will willingly add new members to address shifting task demands, but do not simultaneously shed members whose expertise is no longer needed (Hackman, 2002; Wageman & Hackman, 2010). Many boards of directors and top management teams suffer from this problem (Wageman, et al., 2008), leading to the team becoming too large to make decisions or have effective discussions (Levine & Moreland, 1998; Hackman & Vidmar, 1970). When teams become too large, members often become frustrated and begin to complete the work individually or in smaller groups, neutering the original team purpose (Hackman & Wageman, 2009).

Similarly, when a team can distribute rewards to its own members, team members must honestly evaluate each other to distribute them equitably. However, members often distort their evaluations of their peers when those evaluations are used to distribute rewards to individuals (Peiperl, 1999). Often, teams evenly distribute rewards, regardless of merit, rather than have the difficult conversation about whether one member worked slightly harder than another (Hackman, 2002). While the authority to distribute rewards may give teams a mechanism to punish social loafers and reward extraordinary contributors, it may also beget difficult conversations that members wish to avoid. Thus, the intended benefits of peer evaluation and reward distribution are rarely realized (Peiperl, 1999).

LIMITING OVERUSE OF AUTHORITY

Another challenge of self-designing teams is that they have more potential to misuse their authority (Cohen & Bailey, 1997; Wageman & Mannix, 1998). A number of scholars have wondered whether increasing a team's autonomy is a way to tighten surveillance and control over individual effort (Barker, 1993; Gryzb, 1984; Sinclair, 1992). For instance, in his ethnography of manufacturing teams with control of team membership and rewards, Barker (1993) found that, over time, some self-designing teams set rules more draconian than any organization would (e.g., "If you're more than 5 minutes late, you're docked a day's pay"; Barker, 1993, p. 428). Because self-designing teams are often more self-contained and independent, the danger of coercive norms developing is perhaps higher than in self-managing or manager-led teams.

Self-designing teams also face a danger of focusing excessively on information search when they have both the authority to requisition information and little oversight into whether they achieve their task. When teams have unclear goals or deadlines (Eisenhardt, 1989) or assume a defensive orientation (Woolley, 2011), they may request and process information as a substitute for working on the task (Hackman, 2011). Because information takes time to process and there is a seemingly endless supply of it, the authority to requisition information can be a dangerous lure. Further, even when such teams receive relevant information, it may not be in a form convenient for them to process (Hackman, 2002), adding to the time required to complete the task. Because self-designing teams are likely to requisition information that they do not routinely access, it is more likely to be in a form preferred by others. Thus, self-designing teams should ask for only the information they need and work quickly to make streams of necessary real-time information available and digestible (Eisenhardt, 1989).

Imperatives for Leaders of Self-Designing Teams

Overall, self-designing teams have many opportunities to match their design to idiosyncratic task demands and member preferences. However, each aspect of team and task design may present costly problems, which teams must learn to minimize. Formal leaders can play an important role in developing those capacities within teams.

SUPPORT GOOD QUALITY MEMBERSHIP CHOICES

First, leaders of self-designing teams can provide coaching and consultation to help those teams manage well the changeover of membership. Leaders can help self-designing teams to identify potential new members with task-relevant expertise, while creating norms that allow current members to leave the team without hard feelings or political repercussions.

PROMOTE EXCELLENT SELF-DIAGNOSIS

Leaders of self-designing teams can support their effectiveness by helping their team create structured processes to conduct effective peer review and to distribute rewards in ways that create both perceived fairness and performance-contingency. Such reviews have been shown to be most effective when they are tied to collective (rather than individual) rewards and are strongly supported by the organization (Peiperl, 1999). However, for self-designing teams to best realize the learning and motivational benefits of peer evaluation and reward distribution, leaders should encourage a discussion of the most meaningful dimensions of performance to be evaluated.

KEEP THE PURPOSE CLEAR

Last, but most important, leaders of self-designing teams can play a critical role in clearly articulating the team's purpose – and reiterating it frequently. Self-designing teams have many tools at their disposal and risk diffusing member attention or drowning in information. Articulating a clear, challenging, and compelling direction to orient, energize, and motivate such teams is thus one of the most important tasks of leaders of self-designing teams.

Directions for Future Research

While the conclusions above about self-designing teams can be gleaned indirectly from the research literature, this body of work is quite underdeveloped. Thus, the next steps in research on self-designing teams are likely to be descriptive, addressing questions such as how prevalent self-designing teams are in organizations, what tasks they are used for, and what design features they most commonly control. From this descriptive platform, further research on the conditions under which self-managing teams can be given authority over specific design features can be conducted.

EXPLORING GOOD USES OF SELF-DESIGNING TEAMS

For what tasks or purposes might self-designing teams be most effective? When is it most useful for a team to have authority over its own membership and when is it counterproductive? Self-designing teams are seldom intended to control all of their own design features. However, it is possible that high-functioning self-managing teams would benefit from increased control of their reward structures, membership, and resources. The question, though, is when self-managing teams should be given control over certain design features. Much more research is needed to understand the types of tasks that such teams do well and the conditions under which they thrive. Because it can be very challenging and demanding to have all of the design features under team control, those designing the authority system must be judicious in deciding which design features a team controls and think through why giving the team this authority will help with the task.

Leadership of Self-Governing Teams

Self-governing teams are teams that convene for their own self-defined purposes or who have the authority to define purposes both for themselves and for others. Self-governing teams have authority over their own design, including the membership of the team and the context within which it operates. Examples of self-governing teams include entrepreneurial startup teams in which the team is formed by a partnership of peers who share leadership of the entity that they jointly create. Other kinds of common self-governing teams include worker cooperatives and kibbutzim, small family-owned businesses, partnerships in professional service firms, some performing arts groups, some (but not all) boards of directors, and even revolutionary groups, such as teams that might lead a mutiny in an organization or start a social movement in public life.

Note that many of these above-named teams can and do have less than self-governing authority structures. For example, some entrepreneurial startups can be self-managing or even manager-led teams, depending on the degree of shared authority over team purposes and the team's design. In some cases, an initial inventor convenes a team of members of her or his own choice, and retains authority for devising team purposes, thereby making the leadership team of the enterprise into a self-managing team rather than a self-governing one. Similarly, while there are string quartets and chamber orchestras who share authority over determining their musical repertoire (team purposes), collaborate in selecting new members (team design), and devising their own rehearsal practices (work processes), there are musical ensembles in which all these choices are under the authority of a conductor, making such teams manager-led. Finally, in contexts in which the chair of a board of directors also is the chief executive, the other board members have far less authority than the leader, making them more typically self-managing or manager-led entities. Nonetheless, there are many examples of self-governing teams, and, as will be seen, this may be the fastest-growing—and least researched—authority structure for teams.

Opportunities of Self-Governing Teams

Teams that hold collective authority over their purposes, as well as their composition, context, and processes, have significant potential for promoting high levels of collaborative accomplishment. Much of the work on such teams has focused on two key virtues: (1) the fit between members' values and team purposes and the impact that fit has on commitment and viability; and (2) the teams' flexibility and capacity to provide leadership to solve complex multistakeholder problems.

ENHANCING VALUES-PURPOSE FIT

Self-governing teams are especially well-poised, compared with other kinds of teams, to create high levels of values-based commitment to the team and to its purposes, precisely because the team itself has full authority to compose and launch a team expressly for activities of great value to its members. There is some evidence that a modern trend in younger generations toward seeking greater work-values fit is spawning an interest in creating new entities and work opportunities, many of which begin as self-governing teams (Bornstein, 1998, 2004; Boschee, 1995; Smola & Sutton, 2002). The increasing individualism of personal career choices around the globe means that countless more people are crafting unique career paths for themselves, oriented by a determination to find personal meaning and autonomy in what they do. As a consequence, they are not seeking employment in traditional firms. At the same time, digitalization and globalization are creating ready access via technology to many more people, greatly increasing the chances of an individual finding a handful of others that share his or her aims. Indeed, one Internet-based organization that supports the self-formation of teams has seen the launch of more than 45,000 self-governing teams in the last few years (About Meetup, n.d.). Nevertheless, it is difficult to find research in organizational behavior, organizational psychology, or social psychology about self-governing teams. Most of the work appears in sociology and political science, where the phenomena of egalitarian and democratic societies, social movements, and citizen voice are of great interest.

Research evidence in support of the commitment advantages of self-governing teams emphasizes the unusual longevity and low turnover of some examples, combined with a long waiting list of candidates who wish to join and high selectivity of induction processes. The research on worker cooperatives, for example, emphasizes the sizeable differences between such organizations and traditional businesses in worker commitment, and behavioral evidence for such commitment, such as low turnover and absenteeism (Oliver, 1984; Rhodes & Steers, 1981). Similarly, the Orpheus Chamber Orchestra and the London Symphony Orchestra are member-led performing ensembles of long duration, in which individual commitment and satisfaction are notably elevated above that of similar manager-led ensembles (Judy, 1999; Hackman, 2002; Stearns, 2002).

In each of these instances, deeply shared values—both around the purposes of the organization and around its determination to maintain democratic practices—serve to elevate a lasting commitment to keeping the entity thriving. Research on these groups emphasizes that self-governing entities offer extensive participation in making critical decisions that affect members' own lives and work (Bart, 1995; Pierce, Rubenfeld, & Morgan, 1991; Whyte, 1991) and membership that is based on deeply shared values (Banai, Niremberg, & Menachem, 2000; Campbell, Keen, Norman, & Oakshott, 1977; Whyte, 1991).

PROVIDING LEADERSHIP FOR COMPLEX SOCIETAL PROBLEMS

Much has been written in sociology about self-governing teams, though not under that term: typically, such groups are part of civic organizations, are leading social movements, or are termed volunteer groups. This research stream emphasizes the prevalence and value of such groups in public life. Self-governing teams have significant benefits, for example, when complex problems require the resources and capabilities of multiple, independent entities, a kind of problem that is increasing in prevalence in the world (Sayles & Chandler, 2009). In the public sector and in civic life, for instance, we are beginning to see an increase in climate-related crises, such as flooded cities, droughts, severe wildfires, oil spills, and epidemics, which are creating the necessity for cross-entity and cross-sector collaborations with people working together from municipalities, NGOs, and the private sector, all with critical leadership roles in the process. These multistakeholder collaborations require active coordination, and they benefit from shared authority held by members appointed from relevant stakeholder groups. These individuals form complex leadership teams, with shared authority to govern the action (Mendonca, Beroggi, & Wallace, 2001; Sayles & Chandler, 2009; Leonard & Howitt, 2010).

Similarly, self-governing teams are taking on problems in civic life for which there is no single institutional accountability, such as promoting conservation and "green" activity among citizens or protecting shared public lands. Civic associations are entities that have volunteer members, are governed by elected leaders, and pursue public voice as a core organizational outcome (Skocpol & Fiorina, 1999). Many teams operate within large civic associations, but nevertheless hold authority to decide the unique focus of their teams. The volunteer leaders in civic associations fulfill essential functions by mobilizing others both to devise and to implement collective strategies. Leadership tasks include motivating people to work together, dealing strategically with a range of external threats and opportunities, and adapting to the novel and challenging circumstances that accompany the work of advocacy (Campbell, 2005; Day, 2000; Morris & Staggenborg, 2004).

These governance groups have the ability to develop context-specific strategies to solve unique local problems. For example, in a longitudinal study of leadership teams in a U.S. civic association whose purpose is to mobilize volunteers to protect the natural environment, Ganz and Wageman (2008) found that teams that were better able to articulate and define genuinely shared purposes among diverse and independent members were better able to mobilize others to accomplish collective aims. Relatedly, Ostrom's (1990; Ostrom, Gardner, & Walker, 1994) ground-breaking research identifying the conditions under which communities avoid the tragedy of the commons shows repeatedly the necessity of community self-governing leadership teams for sustainable agreements. Self-convened, community-authorized, and representative leadership teams are a key design principle for using and preserving publicly held goods such as forests, fisheries, and grazing land (Ostrom, 1990).

Challenges for Self-Governing Teams

While the great strengths and potential of self-governing teams are compelling, it is also the case that such teams struggle with significant challenges to their effectiveness. In particular, there are three relative weaknesses of such teams compared to those in which certain individuals hold some authority over purposes and processes: (1) articulating purposes is not a natural team task; (2) emphasis on consensus elicits the worst dysfunctions of group decision-making; and (3) as a consequence of struggles for clarity and consensus, these teams risk devolving into hierarchies or disbanding.

ARTICULATING PURPOSE COLLABORATIVELY

Clear, shared purpose, which is an essential condition for team effectiveness, is not a strength of this authority structure. Self-governing teams can struggle to arrive at a sharp enough direction statement to guide collective action. Further, defining and clarifying the purpose drawing on multiple perspectives is often a particularly difficult challenge for very diverse groups like the multistakeholder leadership teams described above. Articulating purpose is not a function that is well-executed by groups, but is rather done more effectively by individuals with considerable conceptualization ability and dexterity with language (Hackman, 2002, pp. 224-225). In the study of activist teams described earlier (Wageman & Hackman, 2010), clarity of team purpose was significantly lower for the self-governing environmental activist teams than for any other kinds of front-line task-performing teams or for senior leadership teams, all of which typically have purposes established by an individual.

Self-governing teams often have lofty but abstract aspirations and values. This lack of clarity about where the team is headed can spawn an inability of such teams to reach any agreement on key decisions or to make well-coordinated strategic choices when team members are not together. Hackman (2002) describes, for example, a small cooperative newspaper, in which members of the cooperative were personally committed to the values of democracy and wanted to enact those values by involving all members in setting aspirations. In spite of considerable time and energy invested in the debate, they were never able to reach agreement on a sharp collective purpose concrete enough to guide behavior. Because decisions about purpose always involve choosing what *not* to do (as well as what to do), articulating a direction together requires members to forgo goals that some deem personally valuable (Hackman, 2002). The expression "a camel is a horse designed by a committee" is about this very issue: the tendency of peer groups to sand down the sharpest edges of individuals' visions in the interest of including all their personal goals.

In her classic article "The Tyranny of Structurelessness," Freeman (1973) underscores how a norm of organic growth and egalitarianism in self-governing entities may work to counteract the efforts of any individual to create necessary structures that might support collective action. And when the ensuing chaos and disorientation prevent groups from accomplishing their purposes, there can be a sharp inclination for the pendulum to swing in the opposite direction, establishing rigid structures and a return to hierarchy as a means of creating clarity.

PROMOTING A DECISION-MAKING REPERTOIRE BEYOND CONSENSUS

Self-governing teams are much more likely than other kinds of teams to hold ideologies that insist on democratic processes. They are much more insistent on seeking consensus than groups in which some authority is held by an individual (who might, for example, use his or her authority to decide when it is time to acknowledge the impossibility of consensus and call for a majority vote). As a consequence, they are especially vulnerable to the dysfunctions of consensus decision-making processes that are well-documented in teams. Much of the research on groups in the last 50 years has, in one way or another, underscored the problems that arise when groups of peers are asked to make decisions together. Evidence from juries, real or mock, who are obligated by law to reach consensus (Bray, 1978; MacCoun, 1989; Penrod & Hastie, 1980; Sommers, 2006), and scores of different kinds of problem-solving groups formed in the laboratory (Hollingshead, 1996; Stasser & Titus, 1985; Van de Ven & DelBecq, 1974) all illustrate an array of ways in which the social processes in groups of peers systematically lead them away from the norm of rational decision-making.

Consensus processes can result in phenomena such as group polarization—that is, the tendency for consensus groups to make either riskier or more conservative decisions than is warranted (Isenberg, 1986; Mackie, 1986). They also induce attending excessively to information that all members have at the expense of relevant information held uniquely by certain team members (Stasser & Titus, 1985). They can result in dominance by individuals with higher-status demographic characteristics instead of recognizing the most knowledgeable members (Hollingshead, 1996), and are also vulnerable to some forms of groupthink (Leana, 1985), which refers to an excessive focus on agreement and smoothness of process at the expense of critical evaluation of alternatives.

It is important to note that some studies show that these negative patterns are exacerbated by the presence of a strong leader relative to true self-governing teams (Hollingshead, 1996; Janis, 1971; Mullen, Anthony, Salas, and Driskell, 1994). The critical relevance of these processes to self-governing teams is not that they are especially dysfunctional for such teams, but rather that special challenges to overcoming them exist in such authority structures. While each of these dysfunctions of consensus decision-making *can* be overcome by the introduction of structured processes designed to combat them (Van de Ven & DelBecq, 1974), creating and using a structured decision-making process is not a natural act in peer groups. The presence of an individual authority—absent in self-governing groups—can increase the chances that a team will use a well-structured process. As they grow, many self-governing entities such as kibbutzim, worker cooperatives, and performance ensembles develop electoral processes to create leadership groups that are small enough to make decisions dexterously in comparison to large groups, but they still involve consensus processes within those groups (Hahnel, 2005; Mansbridge, 1980).

How might self-governing groups go about creating for themselves the kinds of structured decision-making processes that help diminish the dysfunctions of natural group processes without resorting to nondemocratic processes or removing the interaction among members altogether (as is frequently done in such structured processes as the nominal group technique; Van de Ven & DelBecq, 1974)? One possibility is for individual members to exercise leadership by taking responsibility for proposing such a process. But in the Wageman and Ganz (2010) study cited earlier, the self-governing teams of environmental activists held widely shared norms of equality, which militated against members claiming the authority to intervene in team processes. It may be something of an art to act as a peer and still engage the group in enacting effectively structured team processes, neither usurping authority one does not have nor abdicating responsibility for creating the conditions for effective teamwork. It remains an important and under-researched question: how can self-governing teams make collective decisions without losing their self-governing character?

PREVENTING DEVOLUTION INTO HIERARCHY

Some scholars have argued that the very egalitarian nature of self-governing groups is something of an unnatural act for humans. Evolutionary psychology suggests that one product of human biological heritage is the inevitability of hierarchies whenever groups form. The logic is that individuals that win a competition for dominance in groups, though they also pay costs for it, have a better chance to pass their genes on to the next generation. The formation of hierarchies in social species is seen in creatures from insects to primates, and is considerably more common than equality of status among conspecifics (Cowlishaw & Dunbar, 1991; Ellis, 1995). Self-governing teams have all the authority they possibly could need to chart their own course and to shape their own structure and context. But authority dynamics *within* a team can compromise members' ability to take concerted collective action. We already have addressed the difficulty of articulating purpose collectively. Observers of social experiments like communes and cooperative business organizations underscore the slow pace of decision-making in large groups, and the crisis-management literature emphasizes a powerful tendency for groups to short-cut collective processes under stress and rely on individual authority (Boehm & Ross, 1989; Burke & Greenstein, 1989; Howitt & Leonard, 2006; Lagadec, 1990; Meyers, 1987; Smart & Stanbury, 1978). Self-governing groups frequently struggle to maintain egalitarian practices that allow the group to fulfill critical leadership functions in a concerted manner. Relatively little research has addressed the conditions under which groups are able to maintain their egalitarian authority structure *and* make rapid and well-coordinated shifts in action when the environment demands responsiveness. Is a true sharing of power a stable arrangement, or are certain kinds of asymmetries necessary for groups' long-term existence? One fruitful avenue for future research, then, is to study the kinds of collective processes—and the kinds of leadership actions that might develop them—that enable members of self-governing groups to sustain their unique democratic character.

IMPERATIVES FOR SHARED LEADERSHIP

The challenges of leadership of self-governing teams are primarily about members developing certain habits and capacities, sharing responsibility for noticing what critical team leadership functions are not yet being fulfilled and taking responsibility to fulfill them. There are two particular aspects of self-governing team functioning that are worth explicit attention by team members, precisely because the automatic processes that emerge in teams of peers around these matters are likely to be ineffective. These are (1) paying explicit attention to what is done by the team as compared with what is attended to by individuals working independently of one another; and (2) creating structured decision processes that support effective shared information processing and democratic decision-making.

IDENTIFY WHAT INDIVIDUALS ARE GOOD FOR . . . AND WHAT TEAMS ARE GOOD FOR

In a field study of student project teams, Wageman & Gordon (2005) showed that teams operate on autopilot when it comes to determining what is done as a whole group and what is done by individuals working independently of one another. This automaticity, driven by shared values in the group, frequently resulted in poor task-process fit, in which whole groups, for example, sat around reading materials together in silence, or groups disaggregated writing tasks that required coherence and a single voice. Egalitarian groups in particular were especially likely to miss opportunities to assign to individuals work that is best done independently. The challenge, then, for the leadership of self-governing teams and their tendency toward shared responsibilities, is to identify that handful of team functions that are better served by individuals while keeping for the group those functions—like creative idea generation and generating commitment to strategic choices—that belong to the group. The irony is that all the individuals in a self-convened group must have—or acquire—an understanding of those kinds of choices in order for the group to evolve excellent self-leadership practices. Some writers in political sociology note that some of the institutions that best help individuals acquire these skills in public life—civic and religious volunteer organizations—are declining, rather than increasing, in prevalence (Putnam, 1994). It remains an important question how the essential skills of self-governance can be developed and transmitted in ways that enable self-governing teams to be maximally effective in addressing their core purposes.

CREATE NORMS OF SHARED ACCOUNTABILITY FOR DEVISING AND SELF-ASSESSING STRUCTURED PROCESSES

Well-designed teams develop norms of attentiveness to changes in environmental demands, and they craft and execute task performance strategies that are fully appropriate to their task and situation, rather than fall mindlessly into the execution of habitual routines (Gersick & Hackman, 1990 Wageman, 1995, 2001). Such norms are likely to emerge naturally when the tasks undertaken by the team are meaningful and when team purposes are clear (Wageman, 2001). But self-governing teams need additional attention to norms about behavior to help them deal constructively with the authority dynamics and challenges of democratic processes that make collective decision-making difficult. For self-managing teams, the usefulness of coaching the team process has been well-established. But in such teams the responsibility to introduce and coach effective processes is squarely placed on a clear team leader. For self-governing teams, widely shared norms of equality can militate against members claiming the authority to intervene in team processes. Member coaching of team processes is by no means impossible, but requires explicit conversation, initiated by members themselves, to get it in place. The establishment of shared responsibility for intervening in team processes may be a critical norm to establish at the launch of a self-governing team, increasing the chances that the kinds of interventions typically the domain of a single leader may be taken up by multiple members in turn.

Directions for Future Research

The recent explosion in the number of self-governing teams is only beginning to attract the attention of teams researchers. There is much descriptive work to be done on the phenomenon, as well as the development of normative theories of effectiveness. First, it would be intriguing to explore the question of the kinds of purposes for which self-governing groups typically convene. Given the complete authority to form teams for any purpose, what are the arenas in which we see people deciding that more typical organizational arrangements are underserving some need, or offering little opportunity to engage with others for a given purpose?

There are many research frontiers available for studying self-governing teams. We have identified a number of normative questions that are relatively underexplored for such teams: Under what conditions do self-governing teams make excellent collaborative decisions in line with their own self-defined purposes? Under what conditions do such teams revert to hierarchies instead of maintaining collective self-governance, and avoid the perverse consequences of that reversion? Do self-governing teams that develop norms of shared responsibility for intervening in team process at launch outperform and outlast those that don't? Under what conditions are members able to sustain collective self-governance and create alignment across multiple such teams? What are the critical challenges to self-formed and self-determining teams in developing their own capacity to learn?

If teams researchers are to address these modern phenomena in team formation and leadership, we will need new ways of thinking about different antecedents to their internal processes (e.g., there are no external leaders whose actions or styles we can study; there is no organizational evaluation, reward, or training system to assess). And we will need new ways of thinking about team processes, such as team self-formation and launch processes, interteam governance processes, and multilevel (individual and team) learning processes, to name a few. Finally, we will need to evolve new or less common ways of studying teams—identifying them when they are born online, finding them outside organizational boundaries, observing them in real time—to begin getting a handle on what the future holds for such teams.

Conclusion

The teams research literature, when seen through the lens of the authority structure within which teams operate, offers a clearly differentiated set of opportunities and challenges for those who would exercise leadership of teams. As we have seen, authority structure influences the exercise of leadership in teams in two important ways: (1) constraining who can lead; and (2) creating particular virtues and weaknesses in the team that open the door for leadership activity to have important impacts on team effectiveness.

First, authority structure constrains who is likely to be able to have an impact on team effectiveness, because it specifies the groups and individuals who have legitimate authority to fulfill certain leadership functions. For example, in manager-led teams, the ability of team members to exercise leadership over some of the most important influences on team effectiveness—such as team membership and the process by which the work gets done—is severely constrained. By contrast, in self-governing teams, members have all the authority they need to influence any aspect of team functioning.

But each of these levels of constraint places specific requirements on those who would exercise leadership. In the first instance, the manager of the team has a particular leadership burden that arises directly from the fact that only he or she can decide work processes, and that is to take steps to manage the motivation losses for the team that are inherent in low-autonomy work. For the self-governing team, a consequence of that shared leadership responsibility is that members have upon them a requirement to exercise leadership around managing the authority dynamics and challenges of democratic processes. In other words, the authority structure itself results in the need to exercise leadership for particular purposes.

We can summarize for each authority structure both the key leadership requirements and the functions that are likely to be in especially good shape, without much intervention, as a result of how authority is partitioned. To do so, it is useful to draw upon three key team processes that together influence the performance effectiveness of teams. Hackman and Wageman (2005a) posited that team effectiveness is a joint function of three performance processes: (1) the level of *effort* group members collectively expend carrying out task work; (2) the appropriateness to the task of the *performance strategies* the group uses in its work; and (3) the amount of *knowledge and skill* members bring to bear on the task. In other words, to the degree that the conditions under which a team works elicit and reinforce high levels of collective energy and attention to the work, enable and support superb strategizing, and result in high levels of knowledge and skill being developed and deployed to do the work, the team members are almost certainly going to perform their work well. The authority structures we have explored in this chapter have some direct effects on these team processes and, as a consequence, direct the leadership needs of the team to particular functions—for example, enhancing motivation or managing knowledge and skill levels—while others will be well fulfilled without direct intervention either by a formal leader or by members themselves.

For manager-led teams, the leadership requirements are considerable and constant: acting in ways that can sustain effort, given the low autonomy of such teams, providing the strategic direction for the group, and compensating for and building the capabilities of low-skill members. For self-managing teams, the leadership requirements to manage these processes shifts to members themselves, and the formal team leader can support them through coaching. The increase in work autonomy makes the burden of motivating the group less onerous, but the demand to attend to creating interdependent structures that promote team decision-making, providing hands-on coaching, and promoting a focus on external constituencies grows.

For self-designing teams, the leadership functions demanded of the team members expand to include attentiveness to managing knowledge and skill—understanding the necessary capabilities and resources to do their work well, and developing their own members, because they hold the authority and therefore the responsibility to compose the team and structure its work. At the same time they also tend to have much more impact on their own motivation, because they collectively share responsibility for how rewards, punishments, and other extrinsic consequences are allocated to members. Formal leaders can be especially helpful to such teams in taking off their plates the responsibility to manage all external relations and obtain and synthesize information that the team can use. Perhaps most critically, formal leaders can help keep collective purposes clear while the team members themselves attend to a complex array of leadership functions to support their own work.

Finally, self-governing teams that define their purposes well have little reason to need to exercise leadership deliberately to enhance effort levels—the combination of work autonomy, shared rewards, and purpose-values fit is a recipe for high motivation. They do, however, have the added burden of fulfilling certain key leadership functions collectively—like defining shared purposes and being explicit about their decision rules—at which teams do not often excel. And so appointing particular individuals to take on certain leadership functions for the team at certain times—that is, designing the internal authority structure—becomes part of their required leadership functions as well.

In this chapter we provide guidance about the trade-offs inherent in each team authority structure and outline the key demands for leadership that are created by those structures. We hope this chapter gives practitioners and scholars a way to identify both the tradeoffs in a particular situation to choose an authority structure, and the ways in which members and formal leaders may effectively operate within that structure.

There remain three significant research questions identified by this approach that have yet to be addressed. We end by summarizing them here. (1) What are the conditions under which particular authority structures are most effective for conducting collaborative work? We know very little about that question from empirical research. What little research has been done to directly address it shows that self-managing teams generally produce superior outcomes on all three criteria of effectiveness compared to manager-led teams, at least when the conditions have been created for formerly manager-led teams to operate in a genuinely self-managing fashion. It remains an open question and one worthy of additional research about when each of the types of teams we have addressed here is most effective—*and for what outcomes of interest*. That is, while the demands of functioning in a self-designing team may be especially enabling of individual team members' leadership capacities, such authority structures may be less able to promote decision-making speed. This observation suggests a further research question: (2) Under what conditions are particular authority structures for teams chosen or enacted? How common are each of the types, and in what organizational or societal circumstances? For example, while we suspect that self-designing teams are increasing in prevalence in workplaces, and that the increase almost certainly reflects a perceived need for teams to have more authority over their own membership and context than they have had in the past, we know very little about what the underlying challenges are that such teams address. Finally, (3) what is the *process* by which team authority structures are determined? Our review of the existing literature suggests that authority dynamics in teams are, indeed, dynamic—that is, in many circumstances they represent a complex negotiation and structuration process over time (Poole & McFee, 2005), with formal leaders' explicit choices, team members' interactions, and other systemic features all interacting to shape the emergent authority structure under which teams operate.

We hope the framework and analysis provided in this chapter offer a starting point for such explorations and a structure for identifying the conditions under which different team authority structures emerge over time and are especially effective for different purposes.

References

About Meetup. (n.d.) Meetup.com. Retrieved from http://www.meetup.com/about

Adler, P. S. (1995). Interdepartmental interdependence and coordination: The case of the design/manufacturing interface. *Organization Science*, 6, 147–167.

Allmendinger, J., Hackman, J. R., & Lehman, E. V. (1996). Life and work in symphony orchestras. *The Musical Quarterly*, 80, 194–219.

Amabile, T. M. (1983). The social psychology of creativity: A componential conceptualization. *Journal of Personality and Social Psychology*, 45, 357–376.

Amabile, T. M. (1996). *Creativity in context.* Boulder, CO.: Westview Press.

Amabile, T.M., & Fisher, C.M. (2009). Stimulate creativity by fueling passion. In E. Locke (Ed.), *Handbook of principles of organizational behavior* (2nd ed.) (pp. 481–497). West Sussex, UK: John Wiley & Sons.

Ancona, D. G. (1990). Outward bound: Strategies for team survival in an organization. *Academy of Management Journal*, 33, 334–365.

Ancona, D. G., Bresman, H., & Caldwell, D. (2009). Six steps to leading high-performing X-teams. *Organizational Dynamics*, 38, 217–224.

Ancona, D. G., & Caldwell, D. F. (1987). Management issues in new product teams in high technology companies. *Advances in Industrial and Labor Relations*, 4, 199–221.

Ancona, D. G., & Caldwell, D. (1988). Beyond task and maintenance: Defining external functions in groups. *Group & Organization Management, 13*(4), 468–494.

Ancona, D. G., & Caldwell, D. F. (1992). Bridging the boundary: External activity and performance in organizational teams. *Administrative Science Quarterly*, 37, 634–665.

Ancona, D. G., & Chong, C. (1999). Cycles and synchrony: The temporal role of context in team behavior. *Research on Managing in Groups and Teams*, 2, 33–48.
Ancona, D. G., & Nadler, D. (1989). Teamwork at the top: Creating high performing executive teams. *Sloan Management Review*, 19, 41–53.
Balkema, A., & Molleman, E. (1999). Barriers to the development of self-organizing teams. *Journal of Managerial Psychology*, 14, 134–150.
Banai, M., Nirenberg, J., & Menachem, M. (2000). Leadership in self-managing organizations: Orpheus and a date plantation. *Journal of Leadership & Organizational Studies*, *7*(3), 3–17.
Barker, J. R. (1993). Tightening the iron cage: Concertive control in self-managing teams. *Administrative Science Quarterly*, 38, 408–437.
Bart, J. (1995). Acceptance criteria for using individual-based models to make management decisions. *Ecological Applications*, 5, 411–420.
Bass, B. M. (1957). Undiscriminated operant acquiescence. *Educational and Psychological Measurement*, 17, 83–85.
Beekun, R. I. (1989). Assessing the effectiveness of sociotechnical interventions: Antidote or fad? *Human Relations*, 42, 877–897.
Bell, S. T. (2007). Deep-level composition variables as predictors of team performance: A meta-analysis. *Journal of Applied Psychology*, 92, 595.
Bennett, N., & Kidwell, R. E. (2001). The provision of effort in self-designing work groups. *Small Group Research*, 32, 727–744.
Berkowitz, L. (1953). Sharing leadership in small, decision-making groups. *The Journal of Abnormal and Social Psychology*, *48*(2), 231–238.
Boehm, B. W., & Ross, R. (1989). Theory-W software project management principles and examples. *Software Engineering, IEEE Transactions*, 15, 902–916.
Bornstein, D. (1998). Changing the world on a shoestring. *Atlantic Monthly*, 281(1), 34–39.
Bornstein, D. (2004). *How to change the world: Social entrepreneurs and the power of new ideas.* Oxford, UK: Oxford University Press.
Boschee, J. (1995). Social entrepreneurship. *Across the Board*, 32(3), 20–25.
Bray, R. M. (1978). Authoritarianism and decisions of mock juries: Evidence of jury bias and group polarization. *Journal of Personal Social Psychology*, 36, 1424–1430.
Bunderson, J. S. (2003). Recognizing and utilizing expertise in work groups: A status characteristics perspective. *Administrative Science Quarterly*, 48, 557–591.
Burke, J. P., & Greenstein, F. I. (1989). *How presidents test reality: Decisions on Vietnam, 1954 and 1965*. New York, NY: Russell Sage Foundation.
Burke, C. S., Stagl, K. C., Klein, C., Goodwin, G. F., Salas, E., & Halpin, S. M. (2006). What type of leadership behaviors are functional in teams? A meta-analysis. *The Leadership Quarterly*, 17, 288–307.
Campbell, D. P. (2005). Globalization: The basic principles of leadership are universal and timeless. *Advances in global leadership, 4*, 143–158.
Campbell, A., Keen, C., Norman, G., & Oakshott, R. (1977). *Worker-owners: The Mondragon achievement*. London, UK: Anglo-German Foundation for the Study of Industrial Society.
Cheng, B. S., Chou, L. F., Wu, T. Y., Huang, M. P., & Farh, J. L. (2004). Paternalistic leadership and subordinate responses: Establishing a leadership model in Chinese organizations. *Asian Journal of Social Psychology*, 7(1), 89–117.
Cohen, B. P., & Zhou, X. (1991). Status processes in enduring work groups. *American Sociological Review*, 56, 179–188.
Cohen, S., & Spreitzer, G. (1994). *Employee involvement: The impact of self-managing work teams on productivity customer satisfaction and employee quality of work life*. Paper presented at Academy of Management, Dallas, TX.
Cohen, S. G., & Bailey, D. E. (1997). What makes teams work: Group effectiveness research from the shop floor to the executive suite. *Journal of Management*, 23, 239–290.
Cohen, S. G., Ledford, G. E., & Spreitzer, G. M. (1996). A predictive model of self-managing work team effectiveness. *Human Relations*, 49, 643–676.
Cohen, S. G., & Ledford, G. E. (1994). The effectiveness of self-managing teams: A quasi-experiment. *Human Relations*, 47(1), 13.
Cowlishaw, G., & Dunbar, R. I. M. (1991). Dominance rank and mating success in male primates. *Animal Behaviour*, 41, 1045–1056.
Cross, R., Ehrlich, K., Dawson, R., & Helferich, J. (2008). Managing collaboration at the point of execution: Improving team effectiveness with a network perspective. *California Management Review*, 50, 74–98.
Cummings, T. G. (1981). Designing effective work groups. *Handbook of Organizational Design*, 2, 250–271.
Cummings, J., & Haas, M. (2012). So many teams, so little time: Time allocation matters in geographically dispersed teams. *Journal of Organizational Behavior.*
Day, D. V. (2000). Leadership development: A review in context. *The Leadership Quarterly*, 11, 581–613.
Day, D. V., Gronn, P., & Salas, E. (2004). Leadership capacity in teams. *The Leadership Quarterly*, 15, 857–880.
Day, D. V., Sin, H. P., & Chen, T. T. (2004). Assessing the burdens of leadership: Effects of formal leadership roles on individual performance over time. *Personnel Psychology*, 57, 573–605.
Deci, E. L., Koestner, R.,& Ryan, R.M. (1999). A meta-analytic review of experiments examining the effects of extrinsic rewards on intrinsic motivation. *Psychological Bulletin*, *125*(6), 627–668.
De Dreu, C. K. W., & Weingart, L. R. (2003). Task versus relationship conflict, team performance, and team member satisfaction: A meta-analysis. *Journal of Applied Psychology*, 88, 741–749.
Delong, T.,. Mody, T., & Ager, D. (2003). *C&S Wholesale Grocers: Self-managed teams.* Cambridge, MA: Harvard Business School Case 404–025.
Druskat, V.U., & Pescosolido, A. (2002). The content of effective teamwork mental models in self-managing teams: Ownership, learning and heedful interrelating. *Human Relations*, *55*, 283–318.
Druskat, V. U., & Kayes, D. C. (2000). Learning versus performance in short-term project teams. *Small Group Research*, 31(3), 328–353.
Druskat, V. U., & Wolff, S. B. (1999). Developmental peer appraisals in self-managing work groups. *Journal of Applied Psychology*, 84(1), 58–74.
Druskat, V. U., & Wheeler, J. V. (2003). Managing from the boundary: The effective leadership of self-managing work teams. *Academy of Management Journal*, 46, 435–457.

Edmondson, A. (1999). Psychological safety and learning behavior in work teams. *Administrative Science Quarterly*, 44, 350–383.
Edmondson, A., Bohmer, R., & Pisano, G. (2001). Speeding up team learning. *Harvard Business Review*, 79(9), 125–134.
Edmondson, A. C. (2003a). *Managing the risk of learning: Psychological safety in work teams.* Division of Research, Harvard Business School.
Edmondson, A. C. (2003b). Speaking up in the operating room: How team leaders promote learning in interdisciplinary action teams. *Journal of Management Studies*, 40, 1419–1452.
Edmondson, A. C., Roberto, M. A., & Watkins, M. D. (2003). A dynamic model of top management team effectiveness: Managing unstructured task streams. *The Leadership Quarterly*, 14, 297–325.
Edmondson, A. C., & I. Nembhard. (2009) Product development and learning in project teams: the challenges are the benefits. *Journal of Product Innovation Management* (*26*)2, 123–138.
Eisenhardt, K. M. (1989). Building theories from case study research. *Academy of Management Review*, 14, 532–550.
Ellis, L. (1995). Dominance and reproductive success among nonhuman animals: A cross-species comparison. *Ethology and Sociobiology*, 16, 257–333.
Farris, G. F., & Lim, F. G. (1969). Effects of performance on leadership, cohesiveness, influence, satisfaction, and subsequent performance. *Journal of Applied Psychology*, 53, 490–497.
Fiedler, F. E. (1958). *Leader attitudes and group effectiveness.* Urbana, IL: University of Illinois Press.
Fisher, C. M. (2010). Better lagged than never: The lagged effects of process interventions on group decisions. In L. A. Toombs (Ed.), *Best Paper Proceedings of the Seventieth Annual Meeting of the Academy of Management (CD)*, ISSN 1543–8643.
Fisher, C. M., & Amabile, T. (2009). Creativity, improvisation and organizations. In T. Rickards, M.A. Runco, & S. Moger (eds.) *The Routledge companion of creativity.* Routledge: New York, 13–24.
Fisher, C. M., Amabile, T. M., & Pillemer, J. (2010, August). Helping in creative teams. In R. Livne-Tarandach & S. Harrison (Chairs), *Fantastical food, inspirational buildings, implausible products, and whimsical shirts: Creativity as process, creativity as social accomplishment.* Symposium presented at the meeting of the Academy of Management, Montreal, Quebec.
Fleishman, E. A., Mumford, M. D., Zaccaro, S. J., Levin, K. Y., Korotkin, A. L., & Hein, M. B. (1991). Taxonomic efforts in the description of leader behavior: A synthesis and functional interpretation. *The Leadership Quarterly*, 2, 245–287.
Freeman, J. (1973). The tyranny of structurelessness. *Berkeley Journal of Sociology*, 17, 151–165.
Gabarro, J. J., & Clawson, J. G. (1984). *Meeting of the overhead reduction task force: Harvard Business School,* case 478–013. Cambridge, MA: Harvard Business Publishing.
Gagné, M., & Deci, E. L. (2005). Self-determination theory and work motivation. *Journal of Organizational Behavior*, 26, 331–362.
Ganz, M., & Wageman, R. (2008). *Leadership development in a civic organization: Multi-level influences on Effectiveness,* Working Paper, Harvard Kennedy School of Government.
Gardner, H.K., Gina, F., & Staats, B.R. (2012). Dynamically integrating knowledge in teams:Transforming resources into performance. *Academy of Management Journal*, 55(4), 998–1022.
Gersick, C. J. G. (1988). Time and transition in work teams: Toward a new model of group development. *Academy of Management Journal*, 31(1), 9–41.
Gersick, C. J., & Davis-Sacks, M. L. (1990). Summary: task forces. *Groups that work and those that don't*, 146–153.
Gersick, C. J. G., & Hackman, J. R. (1990). Habitual routines in task-performing groups. *Organizational Behavior and Human Decision Processes*, 47(1), 65–97.
Ginnett, R. C. (1993). Crews as groups: Their formation and their leadership. In E. Weiner, B. Kanki, & R. Helmreich (Eds.), *Cockpit Resource Management,* (pp. 71–98). San Diego, CA: Academic Press.
Gladstein, D. L. (1984). Groups in context: A model of task group effectiveness. *Administrative Science Quarterly*, 29, 499–517.
Golembiewski, R. T. (1995). *Managing diversity in organizations.* Tuscaloosa, AL: The University of Alabama Press.
Goodman, P. S., Devadas, R., & Hughson, T. L. G. (1988). Groups and productivity: Analyzing the effectiveness of self-managing teams. In J. P. Campbell & R. JC & Associates (Eds), Productivity in Organisations (pp. 295–327).
Grant, A. M., & Parker, S. K. (2009.) Redesigning work design theories: The rise of relational and proactive perspectives. *Academy of Management Annals*, 3, 317–375.
Gryzb, G. (1984). Tailored work groups: Managerial recollectivization and class conflict in the workplace. *Research in Social Movements, Conflict, and Change*, 6, 143–166.
Guzzo, R. A., Jette, R. D., & Katzell, R. A. (1985). The effects of psychologically based intervention programs on worker productivity: A meta-analysis. *Personnel Psychology*, 38, 275–291.
Haas, M. R., & Hansen, M. T. (2007). Different knowledge, different benefits: Toward a productivity perspective on knowledge sharing in organizations. *Strategic Management Journal*, *28*(11), 1133–1153.
Hackman, J. R. (2002). *Leading teams: Setting the stage for great performances.* Boston, MA: Harvard Business Press.
Hackman, J. R. (2011). *Collaborative intelligence: Using teams to solve hard problems.* San Francisco, CA: Berrett-Koehler.
Hackman, J. R., & O'Connor, M. (2004). *What makes for a great analytic team? Individual vs. team approaches to intelligence analysis.* Washington, DC: Intelligence Science Board, Office of the Director of Central Intelligence.
Hackman, J. R., & Oldham, G. R. (1980). *Work redesign.* Reading, MA: Addison-Wesley.
Hackman, J. R., & Vidmar, N. (1970). Effects of size and task type on group performance and member reactions. *Sociometry*, 33, 37–54.
Hackman, J. R., & Wageman, R. (2005a). A theory of team coaching. *The Academy of Management Review*, 30, 269–287.
Hackman, J. R., & Wageman, R. (2005b). When and how team leaders matter. *Research in Organizational Behavior*, 26, 37–74.
Hackman, J.R., & Wageman, R. (2009). Foster team effectiveness by fulfilling key leadership functions. In E. Locke (Ed.), *Handbook of principles of organizational behavior.* New York: Wiley-Blackwell.
Hackman, J. R., & Wageman. R. (2007). Asking the right questions about leadership. *American Psychologist*, *62*, 43–47.
Hackman, J. R., & Walton, R. E. (1986). Leading groups in organizations. In P. S. Goodman (Ed.), *Designing effective work groups* (pp. 72–119). San Francisco, CA: Jossey-Bass.

Hambrick, D. C. (1994). Top management groups: A conceptual integration and reconsideration of the "team" label. *Research in Organizational Behavior*, 16, 171–213.

Hahnel, R. (2005). *Economic justice and democracy: From competition to cooperation.* New York, NY: Routledge.

Hansen, M. T., & Haas, M. R. (2001). Competing for attention in knowledge markets: Electronic document dissemination in a management consulting company. *Administrative Science Quarterly*, 46, 1–28.

Hastie, R., Penrod, S., & Pennington, N. (2002). *Inside the jury.* Clark, NJ: The Lawbook Exchange, Ltd.

Hempel, P. S., Zhang, Z. X., & Han, Y. E. (2012). Team empowerment and the organizational context: Decentralization and the contrasting effects of formalization. *Journal of Management, 38*, 475–501.

Hills, H. (2001). *Team-based learning.* Aldershot, Hamsphire, England: Gower Publishing Company.

Hofstede, G. H. (1984). *Culture's consequences: International differences in work-related values.* Beverly Hills, CA: Sage Publications, Inc.

Hollingshead, A. B. (1996). The rank order effect in group decision making. *Organizational Behavior and Human Decision Processes*, 68, 181–193.

Howitt, A. M., & Leonard, B. L. (2006). Katrina as prelude: Preparing for and responding to Katrina-class disturbances in the United States—testimony to U.S. Senate committee, March 8, 2006. *Journal of Homeland Security and Emergency Management*, 3(2), article 5.

Hut, J., & Molleman, E. (1998). Empowerment and team development. *Team Performance Management*, 4(2), 53–66.

Ilgen, D. R., Hollenbeck, J. R., Johnson, M., & Jundt, D. (2005). Teams in organizations: From input-process-output models to IMOI models. *Annual Review of Psychology*, 56, 517–543.

Isenberg, D. J. (1986). Group polarization: A critical review and meta-analysis. *Journal of Personality and Social Psychology*, 50, 1141–1151.

Jackson, J. M. (1953). The effect of changing the leadership of small work groups. *Human Relations*, 6, 25–44.

Janis, I. L. (1971). *Stress and frustration: Personality variable in social behavior.* New York, NY: Harcourt Brace Jovanovich.

Janis, I. L. (1982). *Groupthink.* Boston, NY: Houghton Mifflin.

Janz, B. D. (1999). Self-directed teams in IS: Correlates for improved systems development work outcomes. *Information & Management*, 35(3), 171–192.

Jehn, K. A., & Bendersky, C. (2003). Intragroup conflict in organizations: A contingency perspective on the conflict-outcome relationship. *Research in Organizational Behavior*, 25, 187–242.

Judy, P. (1999). Organizational effectiveness: The role of the Board of Directors. *Harmony*, 9, 47–57.

Katz, N., & Koenig, G. (2001). Sports teams as a model for workplace teams: Lessons and liabilities. *The Academy of Management Executive*, 15, 56–69.

Katzenbach, J. R. (1997). The myth of the top management team. *Harvard Business Review*, 75, 82–92.

Keidell, R. W. (1987). Team sports models as a generic organizational framework. *Human Relations*, 40, 591–612.

Kerr, S., & Jermier, J. M. (1978). Substitutes for leadership: Their meaning and measurement. *Organizational Behavior and Human Performance*, 22, 375–403.

Kirkman, B. L., & Rosen, B. (1999). Beyond self-management: Antecedents and consequences of team empowerment. *Academy of Management Journal*, 42, 58–74.

Kirkman, B. L., & Shapiro, D. L. (2001). The impact of cultural values on job satisfaction and organizational commitment in self-managing work teams: The mediating role of employee resistance. *Academy of Management Journal*, 44, 557–569.

Klaus, D. J., & Glaser, R. (1970). Reinforcement determinants of team proficiency. *Organizational Behavior and Human Performance*, 5, 33–67.

Kolodny, H. F., & Kiggundu, M. N. (1980). Towards the development of a sociotechnical systems model in woodlands mechanical harvesting. *Human Relations*, 33, 623–645.

Kozlowski, S. W. J., & Bell, B. S. (2003). Work groups and teams in organizations. *Handbook of Psychology.* Wiley Online, 333–375.

Lagadec, P. (1990). *States of emergency: Technological failures and social destabilization.* London, UK: Butterworth-Heinemann.

Langfred, C. W. (2000). The paradox of self-management: Individual and group autonomy in work groups. *Journal of Organizational Behavior*, 21, 563–585.

Langfred, C. W. (2004). Too much of a good thing? Negative effects of high trust and individual autonomy in self-managing teams. *The Academy of Management Journal*, 47, 385–399.

Langfred, C. W. (2007). The downside of self-management: A longitudinal study of the effects of conflict on trust, autonomy, and task interdependence in self-managing teams. *The Academy of Management Journal*, 50, 885–900.

Larson, J. R. (2011). *In search of synergy in small group performance.* London, UK: Psychology Press.

Larson, J. R., Foster-Fishman, P. G., & Franz, T. M. (1998). Leadership style and the discussion of shared and unshared information in decision-making groups. *Personality and Social Psychology Bulletin*, 24, 482–495.

Lawler, E. E. (2000). *Rewarding excellence.* San Francisco, CA: Jossey-Bass.

Lawler, E. E., Mohrman, S. A., & Ledford, G. E. (1995). *Creating high performance organizations: Practices and results of employee involvement and total quality management in Fortune 1000 companies.* San Francisco, CA: Jossey-Bass.

Leana, C. R. (1985). A partial test of Janis' groupthink model: Effects of group cohesiveness and leader behavior on defective decision making. *Journal of Management*, 11(1), 5–18.

Leonard, H. B., & Howitt, A. M. (2010). Organising response to extreme emergencies: the Victorian Bushfires of 2009. *Australian Journal of Public Administration, 69*(4), 372–386.

Levine, J. M., & Moreland, R. L. (1998). Small groups. *The Handbook of Social Psychology*, 2, 415–469.

Liang, D. W., Moreland, R., & Argote, L. (1995). Group versus individual training and group performance: The mediating role of transactive memory. *Personality and Social Psychology Bulletin*, 21, 384–393.

Likert, R. (1958). Effective supervision: An adaptive and relative process 1. *Personnel Psychology*, 11, 317–332.

Lippitt, R. (1940). An experimental study of the effect of democratic and authoritarian group atmospheres. *University of Iowa Studies: Child Welfare*, 16, 43–195.

Lowin, A., & Craig, J. R. (1968). The influence of level of performance on managerial style: An experimental object-lesson in the ambiguity of correlational data. *Organizational Behavior and Human Performance*, 3, 440–458.

MacCoun, R. J. (1989). Experimental research on jury decision-making. *Science*, 244, 1046–1050.

Mackie, D. M. (1986). Social identification effects in group polarization. *Journal of Personality and Social Psychology, 50*, 720–728.

Mannix, E. A., & Sauer, S. J. (2006). Status and power in organizational group research: Acknowledging the pervasiveness of hierarchy. In E. Lawler and S. Thye (Eds.), *Advances in Group Processes: Social Psychology of the Workplace*, 23, 149–182.

Mansbridge, J. (1980). *Beyond adversary democracy*. New York: Basic Books.

Manz, C. C. (1986). Self-leadership: Toward an expanded theory of self-influence processes in organizations. *Academy of Management Review*, 11, 585–600.

Manz, C. C. (1992). Self-leading work teams: Beyond self-management myths. *Human Relations*, 45, 1119–1140.

Manz, C. C., & Sims, H. P. (1987). Leading workers to lead themselves: The external leadership of self-managing work teams. *Administrative Science Quarterly*, 32, 106–129.

Manz, C. C., & Stewart, G. L. (1997). Attaining flexible stability by integrating total quality management and socio-technical systems theory. *Organization Science*, *8*(1), 59–70.

March, J. G., & Simon, H. A. (1958). *Organizations*. New York, NY: Wiley.

Marks, M.A., Mathieu, J.E. & Zaccaro, S.J. (2001). A temporally based framework and taxonomy of team processes. *Academy of Management Review*, *26*: 355–376.

Marks, M. L., & De Meuse, K. P. (2003). The realities of resizing. In M. L. Marks and K. P. Meuse, *Resizing the Organization: Managing Layoffs, Divestitures, and Closings* (J-B SIOP Professional Practice Series, pp. 1–38). USA: Pfeiffer.

McGrath, J. E. (1962). *Leadership behavior: Some requirements for leadership training*. Washington, DC: U.S. Civil Service Commission, Office of Career Development.

Mendonca, D., Beroggi, G. E. G., & Wallace, W. A. (2001). Decision support for improvisation during emergency response operations. *International Journal of Emergency Management*, 1(1), 30–38.

Morgeson, F. P. (2005). The external leadership of self-managing teams: Intervening in the context of novel and disruptive events. *Journal of Applied Psychology*, 90(3), 497–508.

Morgeson, F. P., DeRue, D. S., & Karam, E. P. (2010). Leadership in teams: A functional approach to understanding leadership structures and processes. *Journal of Management*, 36(1), 5–39.

Morris, A. D., & Staggenborg, S. (2004). Leadership in social movements. In D. A. Snow, S. A. Soule, & H. Kriesi (Eds.), *The Blackwell Companion to Social Movements* (pp. 171–196). Malden, MA: Blackwell.

Mullen, B., Anthony, T., Salas, E., & Driskell, J. E. (1994). Group cohesiveness and quality of decision making. *Small Group Research*, 25(2), 189–204.

Munch, C. (1955). *I am a conductor* (L. Burkat, Trans.). London, UK: Oxford University Press: Greenwood Pub Group.

Nembhard, I. M., & Edmondson, A. C. (2006). Making it safe: The effects of leader inclusiveness and professional status on psychological safety and improvement efforts in health care teams. *Journal of Organizational Behavior*, 27(7), 941–966.

Oliver, N. (1984). An examination of organizational commitment in six workers' cooperatives in Scotland. *Human Relations*, 37(1), 29–45.

O'Leary, M. B., Mortensen, M., & Woolley, A. W. (2011). Multiple team membership: A theoretical model of its effects on productivity and learning for individuals and teams. *The Academy of Management Review*, 36(3), 461–478.

Orlikowski, W. J., & Yates, J. A. (2002). It's about time: Temporal structuring in organizations. *Organization Science*, 13(6), 684–700.

Ostrom, E. (1990). *Governing the commons: The evolution of institutions for collective action*. Cambridge, UK: Cambridge University Press.

Ostrom, E., Gardner, R., & Walker, J. (1994). *Rules, games, and common-pool resources*. Ann Arbor, MI: University of Michigan Press.

Pearce, C. L., & Conger, J. A. (2003). *Shared leadership: Refining the hows and whys of leadership*. Thousand Oaks, CA: Sage.

Pearce, J. A., & Ravlin, E. C. (1987). The design and activation of self-regulating work groups. *Human Relations*, 40(11), 751–782.

Peiperl, M. A. (1999). Conditions for the success of peer evaluation. *The International Journal of Human Resource Management*, 10(3), 429–458.

Penrod, S., & Hastie, R. (1980). A computer simulation of jury decision making. *Psychological Review*, *87*(2), 133.

Peterson, R. S. (1997). A directive leadership style in group decision making can be both virtue and vice: Evidence from elite and experimental groups. *Journal of Personality and Social Psychology*, 72(5), 1107–1121.

Pfeffer, J. (1997). *New directions for organization theory: Problems and prospects*. New York, NY: Oxford University Press.

Pierce, J. L., Rubenfeld, S. A., & Morgan, S. (1991). Employee ownership: A conceptual model of process and effects. *Academy of Management Review*, 16, 121–144.

Poole, M. S., & McFee, R. (2005). Structuration theory. In D. Mumby & S. May (Eds.), *Engaging organizational communication: Theory and research* (pp. 171–196). Newbury Park, CA: Sage.

Porter, T.W., & Lilly, B.S. (1996) "The effects of conflict, trust, and task commitment onproject team performance", *International Journal of Conflict Management*, *7*, 361–376

Putnam, R. D. (1994). *Making democracy work: Civic traditions in modern Italy*. Princeton, NJ: Princeton University Press.

Putnam, R. (1996). The strange disappearance of civic America. *Policy, Autumn*, 3–15.

Rhodes, S. R., & Steers, R. M. (1981). Conventional vs. worker-owned organizations. *Human Relations*, 34(12), 1013–1035.

Robinson, P. B., & Sexton, E. A. (1994). The effect of education and experience on self-employment success. *Journal of Business Venturing*, *9*(2), 141–156.

Rosenbaum, M., Moore, D., Cotton, J., Cook, M., Hieser, R., Shovar, M., & Gray, M. (1980). Group productivity and process: Pure and mixed reward structures and task interdependence. *Journal of Personality and Social Psychology*, 39, 626–642.

Rulke, D. L., & Galaskiewicz, J. (2000). Distribution of knowledge, group network structure, and group performance. *Management Science*, 46, 612–625.

Salas, E., Cannon-Bowers, J. A., & Blickensderfer, E. L. (1993). Team performance and training research: Emerging principles. *Journal of the Washington Academy of Sciences*, 83(2), 81–106.

Sayles, L. R., & Chandler, M. K. (2009). *Managing large systems: Organizations for the future*. New York, NY: Harper & Row.

Schlesinger, L., Jackson, J., & Butman, J. (1960). Leader-member interaction in management committees. *The Journal of Abnormal and Social Psychology*, 61(3), 360–364.

Sexton, C. (1994). Self-managed work teams: TQM technology at the employee level. *Journal of Organizational Change Management*, 7(2), 45–52.

Shea, G. P., & Guzzo, R. A. (1987). Group effectiveness: What really matters. *Sloan Management Review*, 28(3), 25–31.

Silver, S., Randolph, W. A., & Seibert, S. (2006). Implementing and sustaining empowerment. *Journal of Management Inquiry*, 15(1), 47.

Sinclair, A. (1992). The tyranny of a team ideology. *Organization Studies*, 13(4), 611–626.

Skocpol, T., & Fiorina, M. P. (1999). Making sense of the civic engagement debate. In T. Skocpol and M. P. Forinia (Eds.), *Civic Engagement in American Democracy* (pp. 1–26). Washington, DC: The Brookings Institution: Russell Sage Foundation.

Smart, C. F., & Stanbury, W. T. (1978). *Studies on crisis management.* Toronto, Canada: Institute for Research on Public Policy; distributed by Butterworth & Co.

Smola, K., & Sutton, C. D. (2002). Generational differences: Revisiting generational workvalues for the new millennium. *Journal of organizational behavior, 23*(4), 363–382.

Sommers, S. R. (2006). On racial diversity and group decision making: Identifying multiple effects of racial composition on jury deliberations. *Journal of Personality and Social Psychology*, 90(4), 597–612.

Spreitzer, G., Noble, D., Mishra, A., & Cooke, W. (1999). Predicting process improvement team performance in an automotive firm: Explicating the roles of trust and empowerment. *Research on Managing Groups and Teams*, 2, 71–92.

Stasser, G., & Titus, W. (1985). Pooling of unshared information in group decision making: Biased information sampling during discussion. *Journal of personality and social psychology, 48*(6), 1467.

Stasser, G., & Stewart, D. (1992). Discovery of hidden profiles by decision-making groups: Solving a problem versus making a judgment. *Journal of Personality and Social Psychology*, 63(3), 426–434.

Stasser, G., & Titus, W. (1985). Pooling of unshared information in group decision making: Biased information sampling during discussion. *Journal of Personality and Social Psychology, 48*(6), 1467.

Stearns, R. (2002). *Improving the effectiveness of small groups within the symphony organization.* Deerfield, IL: Symphony Orchestra Institute.

Stewart, G. L. (2006). A meta-analytic review of relationships between team design features and team performance. *Journal of Management*, 32(1), 29–55.

Stewart, G. L., & Manz, C. C. (1995). Leadership for self-managing work teams: A typology and integrative model. *Human Relations*, 48, 747–770.

Straus, S. G., Parker, A. M., & Bruce, J. B. (2011). The group matters: A review of processes and outcomes in intelligence analysis. *Group Dynamics: Theory, Research, and Practice*, 15(2), 128–146.

Subramony, M. (2009). A meta-analytic investigation of the relationship between HRM bundles and firm performance. *Human Resource Management*, 48, 745–768.

Van de Ven, A. H., & DelBecq, A. L. (1974). The effectiveness of nominal, Delphi, and interacting group processes. *Academy of Management Journal*, 17, 605–621.

Vroom, V. H., & Jago, A. G. (1988). *The new leadership: Managing participation in organizations.* Englewood Cliffs, NJ: Prentice-Hall, Inc.

Vroom, V. H., & Yetton, P. W. (1973). *Leadership and decision-making.* Pittsburgh, PA: University of Pittsburgh Press.

Wageman, R. (1995). Interdependence and group effectiveness. *Administrative Science Quarterly*, 40, 145–180.

Wageman, R. (2001). How leaders foster self-managing team effectiveness: Design choices versus hands-on coaching. *Organization Science*, 12, 559–577.

Wageman, R., Fisher, C. M., & Hackman, J. R. (2009). Leading teams when the time is right: Finding the best moments to act. *Organization Dynamics*, 38, 192–203.

Wageman, R., & Ganz., M. (2010). Leadership development in volunteer organizations. Working paper.

Wageman, R., & Gordon, F. M. (2005). As the twig is bent: How group values shape emergent task interdependence in groups. *Organization Science*, 16, 687–700.

Wageman, R., & Hackman, J. R. (2010). What makes teams of leaders leadable? In N. Nohria & R. Knurana (Eds.), *Handbook of leadership theory and practice* (pp. 475–506). Boston, MA: Harvard Business School Press.

Wageman, R., & Mannix, E. A. (1998). Uses and misuses of power in task-performing teams. In R. Kramer and M. Neale (Eds.) *Power and influence in organizations.*, pp 365–383. Thousand Oaks, CA: Sage Publications.

Wageman, R., Nunes, D., Burruss, J., & Hackman, J. (2008). *Senior leadership teams: What it takes to make them great.* Boston, MA: Harvard Business School Press.

Wall, T. D., Kemp, N. J., Jackson, P. R., & Clegg, C. W. (1986). Outcomes of autonomous workgroups: A long-term field experiment. *Academy of Management Journal*, 29, 280–304.

Waller, M. J. (1997). Keeping the pins in the air: How work groups juggle multiple tasks. *Advances in Interdisciplinary Studies of Work Teams*, 4, 217–247.

Walton, R. E., & Hackman, J. R. (1986). Groups under contrasting management strategies. In P. S. Goodman (Ed.), *Designing effective work groups* (pp. 168–201). San Francisco, CA: Jossey-Bass.

Walton, R. (2003). From control to commitment in the workplace. In M.J. Handel (Ed.), *The sociology of organizations: Classic, contemporary, and critical readings.* Thousand Oaks, CA: Sage, 114–123.

Weber, E. (n.d.). BrainyQuote.com <http://BrainyQuote.com>. Retrieved October 23, 2013, from BrainyQuote.com

Wellins, R., Byham, W., & Wilson, J. (1991). *Empowered teams: Creating self-managing working groups and the improvement of quality, productivity and participation.* San Francisco, CA: Jossey-Bass.

West, M. A., Borrill, C. S., Dawson, J. F., Brodbeck, F., Shapiro, D. A. & Haward, R. (2003). Leadership clarity and team innovation in health care. *The Leadership Quarterly*, 14, 393–410.

Wey Smola, K., & Sutton, C. D. (2002). Generational differences: Revisiting generational work values for the new millennium. *Journal of Organizational Behavior, 23*(4), 363–382.

Whyte, W. F. E. (1991). *Participatory action research.* Thousand Oaks, CA: Sage Publications, Inc.

Woodman, R. W., & Sherwood, J. J. (1980). The role of team development in organizational effectiveness: A critical review. *Psychological Bulletin*, 88(1), 166–186.

Woolley, A. W. (2011). Playing offence vs. defense: The effects of strategic orientation on team process in competitive environments. *Organization Science*, 22, 1384–1398.

Zaccaro, S. J., Rittman, A. L., & Marks, M. A. (2001). Team leadership. *The Leadership Quarterly*, 12, 451–483.

Zajonc, R. B. (1965). Social facilitation. *Science*, 149, 269–274.

CHAPTER

22 Leadership in Multiteam Systems: A Network Perspective

Dorothy R. Carter *and* Leslie A. DeChurch*

Abstract

Multiteam systems (MTSs) are complex collective entities comprising two or more teams that share one or more common superordinate goal. In these systems, leadership is often the result of the joint actions of multiple members. In other words, MTS leadership is often a shared or collective phenomenon. The current chapter explains how the *form* of MTS leadership (e.g., vertical, shared) can be captured using network analytic techniques across multiple MTS *network foci* (e.g., within teams, between-teams, across the system). It extends this perspective to describe the application of specific ego-net and network indices to the evaluation of MTS leadership forms. Finally, it provides example prompts that could be used to elicit leadership *functions* and *goal foci* (e.g., leadership focused toward individual, team-level goals, or MTS-level goals) in MTS leadership networks, and it provides example research questions that stem from incorporation of network analytic techniques with the study of MTS leadership.

Key Words: collective leadership, multiteam systems, social network analysis

Leadership in Multiteam Systems: A Network Perspective

The scientific study of leadership has long recognized that the behavior of leaders can have extraordinary effects on collectives including teams, units, and organizations (Kaiser, Hogan, & Craig, 2008). Although much of the empirical research on leadership focuses on predicting outcomes that reside at the individual level of analysis (DeChurch, Hiller, Murase, Doty, & Salas, 2010), many of the situations in which leaders are potentially most pivotal require complex collective interactions (DeChurch et al., 2011; Zaccaro, Rittman, & Marks, 2001). Hurricane disaster response, vaccine development, and provincial reconstruction are examples of goals that require collective effort, and thus require leaders who impact the orchestration of effort within the collective (Weick, 1993).

Three painful events in modern American history exemplify the inadequacies of current approaches to organizational leadership and mandate the need for a new era of leadership research: September 11, 2001, August 29, 2005, and April 20, 2010. Pre-9/11, intelligence-gathering teams working within the CIA and FBI failed to share the unique and critical information needed to understand fully the planned attacks. Post Katrina, emergency response teams failed to coordinate joint actions critical to saving lives and property. And post *Deepwater Horizon*, science teams working inside and outside of BP struggled to rapidly integrate ideas needed to produce a fast and innovative engineering solution to the gushing oil pouring into the Gulf of Mexico.

These events share three commonalities: (1) teams are the basic unit of effort (i.e., individuals are interdependent); (2) teams share a common fate with one

* Authors contributed equally to this publication and are listed alphabetically. This research was made possible by support from the National Science Foundation, OCI-1056217.

another (i.e., teams are interdependent); and (3) the social forces that sustain and gel the team as a social unit may well simultaneously inhibit collaboration across team boundaries (e.g., Tajfel, 1982; Tajfel & Turner, 1985). The nature of the common-fate goals differed substantially across the three events: unique information sharing (9/11), effort synchronization (Katrina), and knowledge innovation (*Deepwater Horizon*). However, across all three of these catastrophic varietals, naturally occurring social dynamics prevented effective organization. A core scientific problem in need of solution is to understand how leadership can serve as an extraordinary force counteracting natural dysfunctional intergroup dynamics. We need to understand how leadership can orchestrate and sustain the effective networked organizational structures that are needed to tackle complex, high-impact societal problems. The urgent problems of today require complex virtually linked collectives that do not resemble singular cohesive task-performing teams. The current chapter considers the problem of leadership in these complex collectives, hereafter viewed through the lens of multiteam systems. The premise of this chapter is that major advancements in understanding the leadership of complex collectives will follow from a greater integration of network analytic concepts.

The chapter flows as follows. First, current theory and research on leadership in multiteam systems are reviewed. Second, a brief overview of the network perspective and the particular insights regarding leadership that have stemmed from this research are presented. Third, the chapter lays out a new framework for integrating MTS leadership and network analytic techniques, which we believe is critical for future knowledge advancement in this area.

Theory and Research on Multiteam Leadership

Practical Importance of Multiteam Systems

The past decade has witnessed an increase in attention to a new organizational form: the multiteam system (i.e., MTS; Mathieu, Marks, & Zaccaro, 2001). While Mathieu et al. were observing large military exercises with their lenses set on the "team setting" a notable pattern caught their attention. They observed conflict, breaks in cohesion, and communication problems. However, these problems were not located *within* the teams. Rather problems emerged *between* the component teams in the system. The challenges were interpersonal and coordinative, but they were not team problems (Mathieu et al., 2001).

Defining MTS

Broadly defined, MTSs are "tightly coupled constellations of teams" that contribute unique knowledge, skills, expertise, and functions in pursuit of the accomplishment of goals too large to be performed by a single team (DeChurch & Marks, 2006, p. 311). The increased reliance on MTSs has been fueled by globalization, digitization, and empowerment.

Ultimately the rise of MTSs has been an outgrowth of the move for organizations to become flatter and to organize work into teams. Teams allow organizations to draw quickly on the skills and expertise of multiple individuals to solve complex problems (Gully, 2000; Kozlowski & Bell, 2003). Because many important organizational tasks span the expertise of multiple teams, and are too large in scope to be tasked to a single team, teams often link up with other teams. Through carefully orchestrated coordination and collaboration, these complex collectives of teams can address large-scale organizational issues. Moreover, MTSs emerge often as one type of complex collective entity that allows for adaptive responses to environmental challenges (Davison, Hollenbeck, Barnes, Sleesman, & Ilgen, 2012; Zaccaro, Marks, & DeChurch, 2012).

We draw attention to the core characteristics of MTSs stemming from their initial formal definition as:

> Two or more teams that interface directly and interdependently in response to environmental contingencies toward the accomplishment of collective goals. MTS boundaries are defined by virtue of the fact that all teams within the system, while pursuing different proximal goals, share at least one common distal goal; and in doing so exhibit input, process, and outcome interdependence with at least one other team in the system. (Mathieu et al., 2001, p. 289)

Accordingly, MTSs are larger than teams, but can be smaller than the organization(s) that they are embedded within (Mathieu, et al., 2001). In fact, MTSs often traverse organizations such that individuals embedded within the same MTS may hail from multiple organizations.

In recent years, MTS research has challenged organizational scholars to consider the inadvertent consequences of building strong teams in organizations. Although creating a system of strong teams maximizes goal attainment *within* each team individually, if the ultimate system-level goal requires synchronization across teams, then building better teams may not necessarily benefit these valued outcomes (Lanaj, Hollenbeck, Ilgen, Barnes, & Harmon,

2013). DeChurch and Zaccaro (2010) argue that social scientists attempting to solve the problem of how systems deal with time-sensitive multifaceted problems could benefit by focusing more attention on the macro-level dynamics that are central to the resolution of such issues. They contend that organizational scientists may have their "microscopes set at the wrong magnification" (DeChurch & Zaccaro, 2010, p. 329). Although there exists much research to date about the basic building blocks of successful systems (i.e., teams; Kozlowski & Ilgen, 2006) and about the strategic behaviors of leaders in the "upper echelons" of organizations (e.g., CEOs; Finkelstein & Hambrick, 1996), research is still needed regarding the unique requirements of *MTS* effectiveness.

For example, research is warranted that identifies the ways in which team processes and emergent states found to impact component team effectiveness (e.g., Kozlowski & Ilgen, 2006; Mayer, Davis, & Schoorman, 1995; McAllister, 1995) may emerge and impact effectiveness at the system level. The increased use of technology and virtual communication tools that allow geographically distributed teams to work together presents MTS researchers with new problems to solve with regard to methods of promoting and maintaining system-level effectiveness. New methodologies for systematic data collection in MTSs in the field need to be developed to address these new developments (DeVries, Walter, Van der Vegt, Essents, & Vogelaar, 2011).

Finally, more research is needed that identifies the aspects of leadership that enable MTS effectiveness. Leadership of MTSs is a unique challenge owing to the complexity inherent within these systems. MTS leadership must operate to direct the actions of component team members, while simultaneously facilitating the synchronization of distinct teams in the system (Marks, DeChurch, Mathieu, Panzer, & Alonso, 2005).

MTS Leadership Functions

Past work on leadership in MTSs took a functional view, directly extending functional team leadership to the MTS context. Functional leadership theory has been presented as especially appropriate for conceptualizing the role of a team leader. This theory addresses the leader's broad relationship to the team (Hackman & Walton, 1986; Lord, 1977) in that the core duty of the leader is "to do, or get done, whatever is not being adequately handled for group needs" (McGrath, 1962, p. 5). Functional leadership theory is consistent with the systems view of organizations (Katz & Kahn, 1978) as well as the input–process–output (I–P–O) team effectiveness model (McGrath, 1984), or the more recent input mediator output input (IMOI) model (Ilgen, Hollenbeck, Johnson, & Jundt, 2005), in that leadership *inputs* shape interaction processes, emergent states, and other types of mediators, which in turn shape system-level outcomes.

Kozlowski and colleagues further established functional leadership theory in the team context by suggesting that a team leader's role is to deliver inputs aligned with the teams' needs (Kozlowski, Gully, McHugh, Salas, & Cannon-Bowers, 1996). Team leaders are thought to develop effective teamwork throughout team development and team performance management cycles (Bell & Kozlowski, 2002). Moreover, the functional perspective views leadership as a *role* that facilitates team needs over time. The key role of a team leader is one of *problem solver*; involving behaviors that allow leaders to identify problems in the team, generate solutions, and implement those solutions within social domains (Fleishman et al., 1991).

Fleishman et al. (1991) organized the leader activities that are thought to impact effective problem identification, solution generation, and solution implementation into four superordinate dimensions of behavior: (1) information search and structuring; (2) information use in problem solving; (3) managing personnel resources; and (4) managing material resources. Information search and structuring involve a leader's systematic search for information within and outside of the team. Information use in problem solving refers to the leader's synthesis of acquired information and generation of solutions to identified problems. Thus, one major function of the team leader is to generate plans and communicate these plans to team members (Zaccaro et al., 2001). The final two superordinate dimensions—managing personnel resources and managing material resources, refer to activities that involve the implementation of plans and solutions. In particular, managing personnel resources in a team context involves motivating, coordinating, monitoring, and developing team members (Zaccaro et al., 2001). In sum, functional leadership theory would suggest there are three general types of leader activities that directly involve *interactions* between team leaders and other team members. Team leaders generate and communicate plans to team members, and monitor team members as they carry out plans (i.e., *direction-setting activities*). Team leaders also coordinate the collective actions of multiple individuals toward team-level goals (i.e., *coordination activities*) and motivate and develop individual team members (i.e., *motivational activities*).

The view of team leaders through the functional leadership lens has, in recent years, been extended to the MTS context. A MTS leader typically is responsible for interpreting and defining MTS task requirements (Mathieu et al., 2001). MTS leadership, consistent with the functional leadership viewpoint, is conceptualized as including discretion and choice in the solutions applied to a given problem. For example, when requirements shift, as is the case in dynamically changing environments, and entrained team/MTS responses are no longer appropriate; MTS leaders must define or redefine new directions (e.g., vision, task requirements) for the system (Mathieu et al., 2001).

MTS Leadership Focus

Similar to the leadership of teams, key MTS leadership activities include setting directions for MTS members, coordinating collective endeavors, and ensuring motivation throughout the system. However, MTS effectiveness depends on accomplishment of proximal individual and team-level goals, and, in addition, on how well the MTS as a whole collectively coordinates and accomplishes distal goals shared by multiple teams in the system (Mathieu et al., 2001). This view of MTSs as defined by their multilevel goal hierarchy suggests that MTS leadership activities should be focused toward multiple goal levels (e.g., team, system). In other words, the direction setting, motivation, and coordination activities leaders engage in (e.g., DeChurch & Marks, 2006; Zaccaro et al., 2001) should be focused toward goals throughout the system—individual-level, team-level, and system-level goals.

Previous MTS leadership conceptualizations (DeChurch & Marks, 2006; Marks et al., 2005; Mathieu et al., 2001) have emphasized the importance of examining the influence of MTS leadership at multiple levels. Effective MTS leadership ensures that component team efforts throughout the system are aligned appropriately. Specifically, Marks et al. (2005) argued that effective MTS leadership must balance the management of component team actions while, at the same time, leadership must maintain cross-team interdependencies. DeChurch and Marks (2006) found that training manipulations focused on leader strategizing and coordinating between teams, enhanced functional MTS leadership behaviors, and interteam coordination and, in turn, enhanced MTS-level performance.

The concept of MTS leadership focused toward multiple levels was advanced further in a recent historiometric study that examined and classified critical incidents of leadership in emergency response MTSs (e.g., systems of disaster relief teams; DeChurch et al., 2011). Consistent with prior theorizing, these researchers were able to categorize many of the critical incidents as relating to leadership functions (e.g., strategizing and coordination) focused toward goal accomplishment within teams and throughout the system. However, many of the critical incidents referenced leader functions that occurred across the boundaries of the MTS with entities in the greater environment that do not share common goals with MTS component teams (DeChurch et al., 2011).

First, these findings reiterate the *multilevel* nature of MTS leadership focus. Second, they emphasize the inherent *embeddedness* of the MTS as a whole within the greater environment and the importance of the *relationships* that exist within teams, among the component teams, and with external individuals or groups outside of a MTS's boundaries. Furthermore, they highlight the importance of *boundary spanning* activities for MTS leadership. Team and MTS leaders are responsible for boundary activities, such as linking component teams within the MTS to one another or linking the MTS to its broader environment. As such, MTS leaders serve as the "liaison" (Zaccaro & Marks, 1998) between the component teams in the MTS and between the MTS and the outside environment by learning of developments and events occurring within and outside the MTS and then, by interpreting and defining these events.

In sum, MTS leadership functions to facilitate MTS effectiveness by providing direction and motivation for individuals, teams, and the system as a whole. Furthermore, MTS leadership serves to coordinate the collective actions of individuals within teams, component teams within the system, and the system with the external environment. As such, leadership functions are focused toward goal accomplishment across multiple levels of the MTS goal hierarchy.

MTS Leadership Forms

A third aspect of leadership in multiteam systems that moves toward a structural conceptualization is MTS leadership is *form*. Researchers have been careful to acknowledge that the leadership role is not always the sole responsibility of a "formal" leader. Rather, within teams, important leadership functions can be shared among multiple team members (e.g., Day, Gronn, & Salas, 2004; Hackman & Walton, 1986; McGrath, 1962; Morgeson, DeRue, & Karam, 2009). This shared or collective view of leadership is often contrasted with traditional "top-down" vertical perspectives (e.g., Pearce & Conger, 2003).

Vertical leadership refers to a hierarchical structure in which one or a few individuals are held accountable for the functioning of the group (Friedrich, Vessey, Schuelke, Ruark, & Mumford, 2009). In this form of leadership, an appointed leader "serves as the primary source of influence, wisdom, and guidance for team members" (Houghton, Neck, & Manz, 2003, p. 125). On the other hand, the shared or collective perspective views leadership as emerging throughout a group through the collective efforts of many individuals. Rather than viewing leadership as centered on formal leaders and their followers, the shared perspective contends leadership is the result of the joint actions of multiple individuals and it emerges through these interactions (Pearce & Conger, 2003).

In their theoretical conceptualization of possible MTS leadership forms, Zaccaro and DeChurch (2012) highlighted the notion that multiple members can enact MTS leadership functions, simultaneously, or over time. Specifically, these authors offered an initial description of possible leadership forms that may occur within MTSs (Zaccaro & DeChurch, 2012). These forms ranged from highly vertical to highly shared.

Zaccaro and DeChurch (2012) delineated two forms of vertical MTS leadership: fully centralized vertical leadership and multilevel vertical leadership. In *fully centralized vertical leadership* forms, all MTS members are subordinated to a single MTS leader. This formal leader is held accountable to stakeholders for all aspects of system functioning and performance. On the other hand, in many systems, subordinate leaders are also held accountable for key leadership responsibilities. In these *multilevel vertical leadership* forms, lower level leaders are subordinated to higher level leaders (Jaques, 1990, 1996).

Zaccaro and DeChurch (2012) described three general forms of *shared* MTS leadership: rotated, distributed, and simultaneously shared. *Rotated leadership* forms are those in which different members assume the leadership role across time (Carson, Tesluk, & Marrone, 2007; Erez, LePine, & Elmms, 2002). At any point in time, the leadership structure is primarily hierarchical, but the MTS member who is the "leader" changes (e.g., to fit task demands). Leadership in these rotated forms is be considered analogous to a "baton" that is be passed from person to person (Klein, Ziegert, Knight, & Xiao, 2006). Erez and colleagues (2002) argued that rotated leadership allows all team members to feel responsibility for the team's success. They also reported that such leadership increased the degree to which members offer suggestions for change in the team, and the overall level of cooperation within the team. However, rotated leadership may reduce continuity over time, and this form may not always be matched to team or task needs.

Distributed leadership refers to situations in which members of a collective take on different leadership functions at the same time. For example, groups might have a leader that manages internal dynamics (i.e., internal leaders), another that manages external relationships (i.e., external leaders), and another that focuses on strategies for collective actions (i.e., executive coordinators; Zaccaro, Heinen, & Shuffler, 2009). The key advantage of this form of leadership is that it maximizes goal accomplishment by placing those individuals most suited for a given task in a position that allows optimal control over the task.

Finally, the most extreme form of shared leadership—*simultaneous shared leadership*—refers to those instances when all members of the collective are mutually engaged in leadership activities throughout all phases of a performance cycle (Mehra, Smith, Dixon, & Robertson, 2006). In such instances, "every person is a leader and a follower" in the same performance cycle (Mehra, et al., 2006, p. 235).

A NEED FOR NEW MEASUREMENT TECHNIQUES FOR MTS LEADERSHIP FORMS

The traditional approach to the study of leadership focused on the traits (e.g., Judge, Bono, Ilies, & Gerhardt, 2002; Stogdill, 1948), behaviors (Kerr, Schriesheim, Murphy, & Stogdill, 1974; Judge, Piccolo, & Illies, 2004), and/or relationships of formal leaders and followers (e.g., Bass, 1985; Burns, 1978; Dansereau, Graen, & Haga, 1975). This prior work has generated a considerable body of knowledge and many important insights into the nature of leadership. However, the commonly employed technique of investigating the traits, behaviors, and relationships of *one* (or a few) formal leader(s) does not provide a clear picture of the way in which leadership can be distributed among many individuals within a team or across a system. Specifically, these prior methods do not capture the various leadership *forms* that can emerge in MTSs.

Because of the characteristics that often describe MTSs (e.g., large size, functional diversity, geographic distribution, distributed power) MTS leadership is quite often the role of multiple individuals (Zaccaro & DeChurch, 2012). As such, researchers should employ methods of analysis that fully capture the way that leadership is distributed in the study of MTS leadership. We argue that social network analysis (SNA) techniques (Wasserman & Faust, 1994) hold particular promise for the evaluation of leadership distribution (Bavelas, 1950; Carson et al., 2007; Mehra et al., 2006). In the reminder of this chapter, we advance a framework to study MTS leadership from a network perspective.

Network Leadership Theory

Social Networks

Organizational systems can be viewed as social networks. A social network is a set of nodes or actors (i.e., people) joined together through a variety of relationships (i.e., ties; Tichy, Tushman, & Fombrun, 1979). These relationships affect and are affected by system-level outcomes. Typically studied relationships in network research include communication, affect, workflow, advice, and friendship (Brass & Krackhardt, 1999). For example, actors in a network could be asked to respond to prompts such as "Whom do you communicate with?" or "Who do you consider an important source of advice?" Existing ties between actors are typically captured using one of two key survey formats—full network methods (i.e., sociometric measures) or snowball methods (Hanneman & Riddle, 2005). Full network methods require that each actor in the network respond about each other actor. In other words, this method takes a census of ties in a population of actors. Snowball methods, on the other hand, begin by targeting an initial focal group of actors. These focal actors are asked to generate a list of some or all of their ties (e.g., all of the people they communicate with on a regular basis). These new actors are then identified and surveyed. Researchers continue this process until no new actors are identified. To survey the relationships within a MTS, the more appropriate of these two methods is to use the full network or *sociometric* approach to measurement. Because the MTS boundary is likely to be defined, researchers should be able to identify and survey each actor within the system without using the snowball method.

Leadership in Social Networks

In their theory of network leadership, Balkundi and Kilduff (2006) draw from social network theory (e.g., Kilduff & Tsai, 2003), the acknowledgment that cognition is important to leadership effectiveness (e.g., the cognitive revolution; Lord & Emrich, 2001) and research extending the LMX perspective (e.g., Graen & Uhl-Bien, 1995; Liden, Sparrowe, & Wayne, 1997) to assert that leadership is the *social capital* that collects around certain individuals and groups of individuals in a social structure (Balkundi & Kilduff, 2006). Leadership in networks begins with the cognitions of the actors (e.g., leaders) themselves, and then these cognitions lead to dynamic interactions between the organizational and interorganizational (external) networks. In other words, leadership enables and is enabled by network structure.

Balkundi and Kilduff (2006) illustrate how four key network principles—(1) relations between actors, (2) embeddedness, (3) social capital, and (4) structural patterning—are fundamental to the study of leadership in networks. The success of leadership is thought to derive from the relational patterns or ties between actors within and outside of the system. Moreover, network analysis allows researchers to assess the patterns of ties that exist between individuals and how such patterns impact leadership.

RELATIONS BETWEEN ACTORS

Just as leadership is a relational concept, a key emphasis in social network theory is on the *relations between actors.* The specific content of the relations between actors in the network has implications for leadership. The occupancy of a central position (i.e., centrality; Wasserman & Faust, 1994) in a network of positive relationships (e.g., communication, friendship) can lead to beneficial outcomes for a leader. For example, centrality in an organization's advice or friendship network (i.e., those networks reflecting who people turn to for advice/friendship) has been shown to lead to leadership-relevant outcomes including influence, access to information, and positive performance ratings (Baldwin, Bedell, & Johnson, 1997; Brass, 1984). On the other hand, centrality in a network of negative relationships such as adversarial networks (i.e., those networks reflecting who others in the network find it difficult to interact with) is related to negative outcomes such as feelings of discomfort and dissatisfaction within the organization (Baldwin et al., 1997; Sparrowe, Liden, Wayne, & Kraimer, 2001).

EMBEDDED RELATIONSHIPS

Another key focus of network theory is the realization that relationships within a system are not random. Rather, they are inherently *embedded* within the system as a whole. People are embedded in their own networks of existing interpersonal relationships. They tend to enter more frequently into exchange relationships with those who are already closer to them (e.g., family, friends, or close acquaintances) as opposed to individuals whom they have less direct contact with (Balkundi & Kilduff, 2006).

In their examination of the relationship between network structure and team effectiveness, Balkundi and Harrison (2006) emphasized the importance of considering both a team's internal environment as well the greater environment that they are embedded within. These researchers found the density (i.e., the ratio of observed relationships divided by possible relationships in the network; Wasserman & Faust, 1994) of advice and friendship ties within teams as well as the centrality of team leaders within internal team advice and friendship networks is positively predictive of team performance. Furthermore, the centrality of the *team* within the greater environment (i.e., the intergroup network) is positively associated with team performance (Balkundi & Harrison, 2006).

SOCIAL CAPITAL

Network theory emphasizes the idea that network connections represent *social capital* with inherent *value* (e.g., social support, monetary value, access to resources; Balkundi & Kilduff, 2006; Burt, 1997). For example, a friendship link to a prominent organizational member relates to an increase in an individual's performance reputation (Kilduff & Krackhardt, 1994). Close relationships with influential individuals, in or outside of the system, who have access to resources necessary to system functioning, might be beneficial to leader effectiveness (e.g., Brass, 1984; Galbraith, 1973). However, relationships take time and effort to develop and maintain. Certain relationships are more valuable to leadership effectiveness than others. Relationships that are draining and/or time consuming, but do not offer needed resources (e.g., social support, advice, etc.) may be detrimental.

Social capital relates to important organizational activities, such as exchanges and collaborations between units (Adler & Kwon, 2002). Thus, Bilhuber Galli and Müller-Stewens (2012) argue that leadership development should combine traditional individual-level "human capital" approaches with systematic development of optimal levels (dependent on context) of social capital. Specifically, they suggest that complementing the development of individual-level competencies with experiences leading to social capital development can lead to greater impact at the organizational level (Bilhuber Galli & Müller-Stewens, 2012).

Not only is social capital vital to individual effectiveness, but it is also relevant for group performance. At the team level, Oh, Chung, and Labianca (2004) found that optimal *configurations* of members' relations (i.e., social capital) within and outside of the team can maximize group-level effectiveness. For instance, access to heterogeneous knowledge through relationships with external individuals who possess different functional expertise may yield information necessary to effective team innovation (Hansen, 1999; Rodan & Galunic, 2004).

STRUCTURAL PATTERNING

A final key principle of social network research is the emphasis on structural patterning (Balkundi & Kilduff, 2006). Structural patterning refers to the patterns of connections (or lack thereof) that exist within a system. In combination with the other key network principles, structural patterning has significant implications for leadership. Balkundi and Kilduff (2006) argue that one cannot conceptualize leadership in a network without examining the specific social-structural position occupied by the person or persons enacting leadership.

Leadership as a Network

The notion that the structural patterning of relationships is central to the study of leadership can be further extended to the study of shared or collective leadership by conceptualizing the system as a network of *leadership relationships*. Whereas the patterning of ties such as communication, friendship, or advice may impact the degree to which leaders can function effectively in a system, the patterning of leadership ties can yield important information about the way in which leadership is *distributed* in the system. Rather than viewing leadership as impacted by a network of relationships (e.g., friendship ties) the leadership phenomena, itself, can be considered a network. Rather than asking organizational members: "Whom do you communicate with?" researchers can elicit leadership networks by asking: "Whom do you rely on for leadership?" Evaluation of leadership networks elicited in this manner can enable identification of leadership forms in teams and multiteam systems.

The study of leadership networks dates back over 50 years (Bavelas, 1950; Stogdill, 1948; Shaw, 1964). For example, Bavelas (1950) found that manipulating team members' ability to pass information to one another influenced members' perceptions of how leadership was distributed in the team. In recent years, empirical studies examining shared leadership in teams have begun to adopt the leadership network approach (e.g., Carson et al., 2007; Mehra et al., 2006). Whereas aggregating team members' perceptions regarding the degree of shared leadership within the team does not provide precise information about how or where collective leadership emerges and functions, evaluating leadership as a network of ties provides a viable alternative to this practice.

Carson and colleagues (2007) conceptualized shared leadership in teams as the density of the team's leadership network. In a leadership network, density is defined as the number of observed leadership ties divided by the number of leadership ties that could exist. For example, in a five-person team, if every person views and is viewed by every other person as enacting leadership, there are 20 possible leadership connections in the team. If only one person is viewed as the leader, then there are 4 out of 20 leadership ties. Thus, pure vertical leadership (i.e., one hierarchical leader) would have a density score of 0.20. The absence of leadership in the team would correspond to a density of 0. The purest case of collective leadership, in which all five members are seen and see all other teammates as leading the team, would correspond to a density of 1.0. Carson et al. (2007) found that shared leadership, defined as the density of leadership ties, was predictive of consultant team performance as rated by external clients.

Mehra and colleagues (2006) also compared vertical to shared leadership by examining leadership network structures. However, rather than calculating density scores, this study categorized team leadership structures visually into one of four categories: leader centered, distributed, distributed-coordinated, and distributed-fragmented. The structures these authors termed "leader-centered" refer to a strict vertical form of leadership with only one leader, whereas the structures referred to as "distributed" were those where leadership was shared by all members of the team. The distributed-coordinated structure referred to a leadership form in which leadership was distributed among more than one team member (but not all members) and those "leaders" relied on one another for leadership. The distributed-fragmented structure was a leadership form in which leadership was distributed among more than one team member but those leaders did *not* rely on one another for leadership. Interestingly, Mehra et al. (2006) did not find support for the notion that distributed leadership in teams is superior in terms of generating more effective performance as compared to vertical structures. However, the comparison among the three types of distributed leadership structures (i.e., all members sharing, a few connected leaders, a few disconnected leaders) revealed that the most effective structure of these three is one in which leadership is distributed among a few members who are connected to one another through leadership ties. Moreover, this study revealed that coupling in the leadership network (i.e., sharing in leadership) might be more relevant to team performance at certain network locations than others.

MTS Leadership as Leadership Networks

For leadership of MTSs, viewing the leadership network as a strict continuum ranging from highly vertical (low density) to highly shared (high density) may miss important information concerning the multilevel nature of MTS leadership. There are numerous leadership structures possible within a MTS context. In fact, leadership could be highly shared or highly vertical within component teams, but demonstrate a different structure across the system as a whole. For example, members of each component teams may share in leadership functions within their respective teams, while one group of individuals in the system serves as the "leadership team" enacting a more vertical leadership structure across the system as a whole (Zaccaro & DeChurch, 2012). In alignment with the findings of Mehra et al. (2006), MTS leadership forms that display some combination of shared and vertical leadership may be more effective for aligning the efforts of multiple teams as compared to simultaneously shared leadership. SNA allows researchers to identify and differentiate among relationships that exist within subgroups in a network and across the network as a whole. Therefore, SNA is a particularly appropriate method of illustrating the leadership structures that exist within MTS component teams and across the entire MTS.

In the remainder of this section, we first explain how indices that describe the position a MTS member occupies within the leadership structure (i.e., ego-net indices) and those that describe the relationships of two or more actors in the network (i.e., network indices) can be calculated within teams and across the MTS. These indices can provide a comprehensive method of illustrating MTS leadership forms across multiple locations in the network (i.e., network foci). Next, we describe how sociometric prompts can be worded to elicit leadership networks that describe specific leadership functions (e.g., direction setting, coordination, motivation) and goal foci (e.g., individual-level goals, component team goals, MTS-level goals). Such sociometric prompts could allow for better integration of psychosocial leadership research with network analytic techniques. Finally we provide exemplar research questions that stem from the leadership network approach to MTS leadership.

Network Indices for MTS Leadership Forms and Network Foci

Social network indices allow researchers to evaluate network structure at multiple levels of analysis. First, there are a variety of indices that capture the nature of an *individual's* relationship with the network (i.e., ego-net indices). These individual-level indices evaluate the structure of an individual's ego-net (his or her personal network; Wasserman & Faust, 1994). Using ego-net indices, researchers can assess the role that specific individuals play in the MTS leadership structure. Second, there are many indices that assess the structure of relations that exist among *multiple* actors. Indices that evaluate relationships between dyads, triads, and groups can provide a thorough description of the network structure of leadership. Each of these indices can be calculated within teams and across the system as a whole to provide a full description of the structure of MTS leadership across network foci. Table 22.1 lists example network indices that evaluate an individual actor's relationship with the network (i.e., ego-net indices), and those that

Table 22.1. Exemplars of Ego-Net and Network Indices and Insights for Leadership Ego-net Relationships

Centrality	Degree: Number of ties connected to a node Betweenness: Connecting two unconnected nodes Closeness: Proximity of a node to another node Eigenvector: Measure of the importance of a node in a network	Centrality in informal communication networks related to promotion (Brass, 1984).
		Centrality within advice and friendship networks leads to influence, access to information, positive performance ratings, pay raises (Baldwin et al., 1997; Brass, 1984). The degree to which teams are central in the interteam network within which they are embedded is positively related to team performance (Balkundi & Harrison, 2006).
		Followers attribute charisma to those leaders who are socially active in terms of giving and receiving advice (i.e., those who are central in influence/advice networks; Balkundi, Kilduff, & Harrison, 2011).
Brokerage	Degree to which an actor in the network bridges structural holes (i.e., gaps in interpersonal relationships; Burt, 1995)	People with more bridging ties tend to hear about a wider range of information and opportunities earlier than their peers (and those with more open networks have greater ability to convey complex ideas to diverse audiences) (Burt, 1992; Grannovetter, 1973). Ties to those with other functional expertise yield unique/heterogeneous knowledge (Hansen, 1999; Rodan & Galunic, 2004). Optimal configurations of group social capital maximize group effectiveness (Oh, Chung, & Labianca, 2004).
Actor Attributes	Attributes related to position in social network	Demographic characteristics, values, and personality influence acquisition of central positions within advice, friendship, and adversarial networks. High education and low neuroticism leads to high advice and friendship centrality (Klein et al., 2004).
		Attribute similarity (homophily) facilitates dyadic friendship ties, network centrality, and social position (Gibbons & Olk, 2003).

(continued)

Table 22.1. Continued

Dyadic Relationships		
Reciprocity	The propensity for directional ties to be mutual (Wasserman & Faust, 1994)	Reciprocity in trust (important to transactions) is more likely to develop between dyads who are strongly tied (Granovetter, 1985).
Triadic Relationships		
Transitivity	Property in which two nodes that are both connected to the same node have a heightened probability of being connected (Girvan & Newman, 2002)	Group performance is highest when there is network closure within groups and brokerage beyond or between groups (Burt, 2004).
Group Relationships—Within teams, Across MTS		
Cliques	Cluster of actors connected to one another through cohesive bonds	Cohesive teams or cliques may experience less difficulty in communication and coordination (Balkundi et al., 2007).
		Cohesion might promote consistent norms, trust, cooperation, and knowledge sharing (Coleman, 1988; Granovetter, 1985).
		Closed or highly cohesive cliques may experience highly validating interactions and a deficiency in new information (Mizruchi & Stearns, 2001).
Diameter	"The largest geodesic distance in the (connected) network...The diameter of a network tells us how "big" it is, how many steps are necessary to get from one side of it to another" (Hanneman & Riddle, 2005, pp. 7.14)	Groups with longer path links in communication networks (i.e., fewer opportunities for direct communication with all members) have better long-term problem solving ability (Lazer & Friedman, 2007), suggesting MTS leadership may need to limit direct communication among all members when the MTS is engaged in creativity-based tasks.
Centralization	Degree to which links in a network are dispersed around one or a few nodes	Certain kinds of decentralized leadership structures are associated with better team performance than others (Mehra et al., 2006).
Density	Degree to which actors in network are connected to one another	Shared leadership in teams (defined as leadership network density) positively predicts consultant team performance (Carson et al., 2007).

Note. Definitions are from Hanneman & Riddle (2005) unless otherwise indicated.

evaluate the relationship structures of dyads, triads, and groups. In addition, Table 22.1 lists example insights from past research applicable to the study of leadership.

EGO-NET INDICES

As mentioned previously, each actor in a network has a unique ego-net. An actor's ego-net refers to the structure of his or her relationships with other members of the network. One prominent ego-net index is *centrality*. Centrality, broadly construed, describes the extent to which an actor is at a positional advantage in the network (Wasserman & Faust, 1994). Centrality is a structural indicator that can be calculated based on any type of relational tie. There are several indices of centrality that can be calculated for a given actor (e.g., degree, betweenness, eignevector; Hanneman & Riddle, 2005). However, the simplest conceptualization of centrality is degree centrality (i.e., the number of ties connected to an actor). An actor's degree centrality can be calculated based on the number of ties that are connected to the actor (i.e., undirected ties). Or, more specific degree centrality scores can be calculated based on the number of incoming ties (i.e., other members of the network nominated the individual) or outgoing ties (i.e., the focal actor nominated other members of the network). In terms of leadership networks, a high incoming degree centrality implies that a large proportion of other actors in the network identified the focal actor as a leader. In MTSs, members' incoming degree centrality scores can be calculated within component teams to indicate the degree to which a member is considered a leader within his or her team. Centrality scores can also be calculated across the system as a whole to identify individuals who have emerged as central MTS leaders. Thus, centrality scores within teams and across the MTS represent one way to examine the nature of MTS leadership across multiple network foci.

Another ego-net index with implications for MTS leadership networks is *brokerage*. Brokerage is calculated by considering the number of pairs of other actors the focal actor is connected to who are *not* connected to one another. Brokerage implies the degree to which an actor in the network bridges *structural holes* (i.e., gaps in interpersonal relationships; Burt, 1992). According to structural hole theory, actors that bridge structural holes between disconnected groups of others are at an advantage in terms of access to diverse ideas and control of information flow. As such, the position of broker between two unconnected groups implies power (Burt, 2005). Brokerage in communication networks has been shown to lead to positive outcomes for the brokering individual. For example, those actors who bridge more structural holes tend to hear about a wider variety of opportunities as compared to their peers and, in turn, are more likely to receive early promotions, have greater career mobility, and be adept at changing environments (Burt, 1992; Grannovetter, 1973). However, the brokerage position in the leadership network of a complex system is less clear. For example, in a MTS leadership structure, one central MTS leader who serves as the "leadership broker" might connect two disconnected component teams by setting directions for both teams. In alignment with structural hole theory, this may be a powerful position for this individual to occupy, as he or she may direct the activities of two or more component teams. However, this implies a vertical leadership form between teams, which might not be appropriate within some MTS contexts.

NETWORK INDICES

Examination of structural formations at the network-level allows researchers to identify patterns of relations that are of importance to system-level effectiveness (e.g., leadership emergence, communication breakdowns, opportunities for collaboration). There are several key network indices that are important to consider when conceptualizing leadership as a network. The following network indices capture the structure of relationships within dyads, triads, and groups. Note that each of these indices can be calculated for multiple network foci within MTS leadership networks. For example, each index could capture the patterns of relationships that occur within teams—by considering the team as its own "network," or could capture the patterning of relationships across the entire MTS.

Dyadic Relationships

Dyads constitute the smallest possible social structure (Hanneman & Riddle, 2005), and dyadic relationships (i.e., the configurations of ties between two system members) represent a basic unit of network analysis (Wasserman & Faust, 1994). *Reciprocity* is a dyadic measure that assesses the extent to which relationships between actors are mutual. Lack of reciprocation in relationships can have negative consequences. For example, low reciprocation in support relationships with colleagues and supervisors is associated with negative affect (Buunk, Doosje, Jans, & Hopstaken, 1993). Reciprocity in a dyadic leadership relationship indicates that Person A relies on Person B for leadership and Person B relies on Person A for leadership. MTS leadership networks may demonstrate reciprocity at multiple network foci. For example, within component teams, leadership ties may be unidirectional (i.e., not reciprocated), but the leadership ties that link teams together may be highly reciprocated (i.e., between-team reciprocation in leadership).

Triadic Relationships

Triads have a much wider range of possible relational structures than do dyads (Hanneman & Riddle, 2005). Thus, examination of triads allows researchers to answer many more interesting questions about small group interactions. For undirected data (i.e., ignoring the direction of ties and considering whether or not there is a tie present), three nodes can demonstrate four possible triadic relations: (1) no ties, (2) one tie, (3) two ties, or (4) three ties. For directed data (i.e., accounting for the direction of ties), there are, in fact, a total of 16 possible triadic relations. Examination of the complex directional relationships in triads can allow for initial identification of hierarchical structures, equality in relations, or the presence/absence of exclusive groups and isolated individuals (Hanneman & Riddle, 2005).

Triads have a tendency toward equilibrium in relationships. In particular, the property of *transitivity* implies that two nodes that are both connected to the same node have a heightened probability of being connected to one another (Girvan & Newman, 2002). The theoretical basis for this idea can be traced to balance theory (Heider, 1958), which argued that if two individuals were friends, they were likely to have the same evaluations of a given object. Network theorists extended this position by arguing that this object could be a third person in a network (e.g., Harary, Norman, & Cartwright, 1965; Holland & Leinhardt, 1979). Closure (i.e., all actors are connected to one another) within triads is thought to allow for more consistency in affect and behavior between members. These norms could, in turn, lead to positive outcomes such as satisfaction and performance (Krackhardt & Porter, 1985). As with reciprocity, the degree to which triads demonstrate transitivity in leadership may differ depending on the network foci of interest (i.e., network location) such that leadership ties *within* a certain team may demonstrate more or less transitivity as compared to the MTS as a whole.

Figure 22.1 displays a simplified diagram of a nine-person MTS network. The MTS in Figure 22.1 is composed of three teams, each with three team members. The boxes represent the three different teams, and the circles represent the nine members of the teams. The arrows in the diagram represent directional leadership ties that were identified by each person in the network. For example, if one MTS member has an arrow pointing to another, it implies that the first MTS member relies on the second for leadership. The diagram highlights network properties of centrality, reciprocity, and transitivity. First, in Team 1, MTS member 3 is highly central within his or her component team. Both of other members of Team 1 have directional ties to MTS member 3 but are unconnected to one another. Similarly, MTS member 3 is highly central in the MTS because he or she has more incoming leadership ties than any other MTS member. Second, the property of reciprocity in leadership ties within teams is demonstrated between MTS members 4 and 5 such that member 4 nominated member 5 as a leader, and member 5 nominated member 4 as a leader. The property of reciprocity is also demonstrated between teams because MTS members 3 and 4 (members of two different component teams) rely on one another for leadership. Finally, the property of transitivity is demonstrated within Team 3 such that that all three team members in this team rely on one another for leadership.

Group Relationships

Cliques. A clique is a highly cohesive subset of actors in a network in which the actors are more closely tied to one another as compared to other network members (Hanneman & Riddle, 2005; Knoke & Kuklinski, 1982). Network analysis allows researchers to identify the degree to which highly cohesive

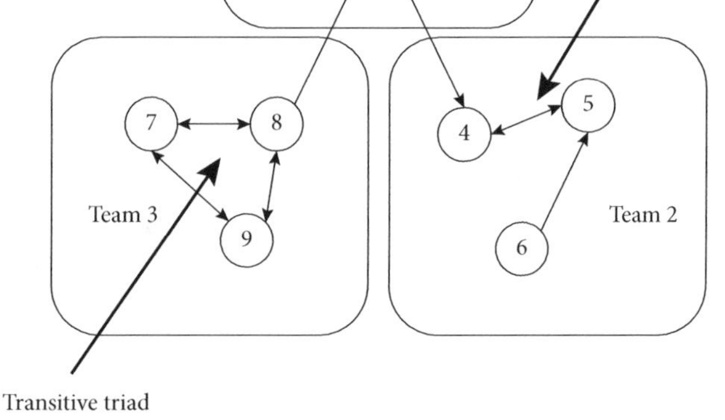

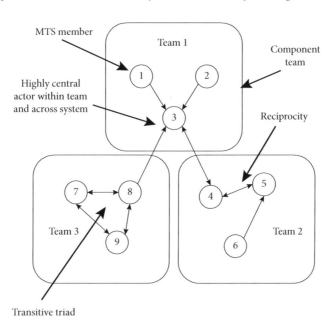

Figure 22.1. Nine-person MTS with Three Component Teams Demonstrating Network Concepts of Centrality, Reciprocity, and Transitivity.

cliques exist in the network. The presence of highly cohesive cliques in a network may be a double-edged sword. Highly cohesive bonds within a team are likely to promote consistent norms, trust, cooperation, and sharing of information (Coleman, 1988; Granovetter, 1985). Because of this consistency, highly cohesive teams or cliques may experience far less difficulty in communication and coordination within their teams (Balkundi, Kilduff, Barsness, & Michael, 2007). However, overly cohesive cliques may experience validating interactions with no dissenting or questioning opinions, and may not have enough exposure to outside information (e.g., Mizruchi & Stearns, 2001). In a MTS leadership network, cliques could be identified that represent component teams or subsets of component teams with highly shared leadership structures. Or across the MTS, cohesive "leadership cliques" with members from multiple teams who are linked together through mutual leadership ties could be identified.

Diameter. The measure of a network's *diameter* indicates the largest "geodistic" distance in the network. Geodistic distance is the number of relations in the shortest possible path from one actor to another in a given network (Hanneman & Riddle, 2005). In terms of leadership, a large diameter indicates the presence of many intermediaries between two members who directly influence one another. Large diameters may negatively impact group performance because of the delay in communication and coordination that is likely to occur when one member needs to work with another. However, systems with large diameters—those whose members are not closely and densely connected—may be better able to generate more unique solutions to challenging problems because the members may not be as susceptible to the "groupthink" phenomenon. In a MTS leadership network, a large diameter across the system might indicate that leadership efforts are not coordinated. For example, Figure 22.2a and b displays two identical nine-person MTSs, each comprising three teams of three members. For clarity, all leadership ties are reciprocated in both of these MTSs. The only difference between the two MTSs shown is the *size* of the networks. Whereas Figure 22.2a shows MTS with a large leadership network diameter, Figure 22.2b shows a MTS with a smaller network diameter. In Figure 22.2a, for the two individuals who are farthest away from one another to influence each other, this influence must traverse eight leadership ties—or in network terms it takes eight steps for these people to reach one another. In Figure 22.2b, the two of individuals farthest away from one another in MTS 2 are separated by only four leadership network steps.

Density. Density of ties indicates the degree to which actors in a network or subset of a network are connected to one another. As described in previous sections, density is calculated by dividing the number of observed ties by the number of possible ties in a network. In past work on shared leadership, the density of leadership ties in a team has been conceptualized

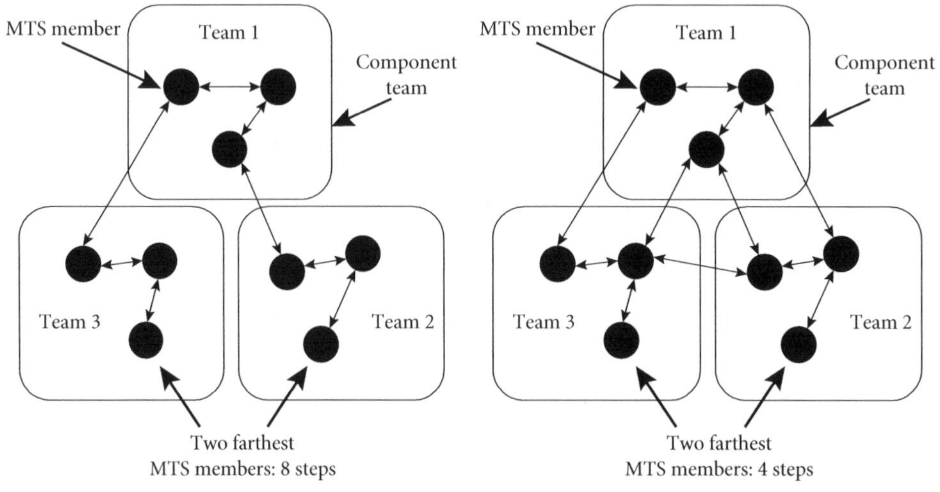

(a) Larger diameter

(b) Smaller diameter

Figure 22.2. Two Identical Nine-person MTSs, Each with Three Component Teams, Representing Larger **(a)** and Smaller **(b)** Leadership Network Diameters.

as a proxy for the amount of shared team leadership (Carson et al., 2007). In a MTS leadership network, shared leadership can be assessed at multiple network foci. For example, researchers could identify the degree to which leadership is shared *within* teams or *across* the MTS as a whole by calculating the density of ties within teams or the density of ties across the system. Furthermore, the degree to which leadership is shared *between teams* could be evaluated by dividing the number of observed leadership ties that traverse multiple teams by the total possible leadership ties that could traverse multiple teams. Finally, researchers can identify the degree to which leadership is shared among specific members of the MTS (e.g., formal leaders) by calculating the density among these members. Figure 22.3 provides examples of these four conceptualizations of MTS leadership network density. Figure 22.3a depicts high density within component teams but zero density between. Figure 22.3b depicts a MTS with zero density within teams but higher density between teams. Figure 22.3c displays the degree of shared leadership among specific MTS members. Figure 22.3d depicts MTSs with high density across the entire MTS.

Centralization. Finally, a measure of *centralization* indicates the degree to which ties in a network are dispersed around one or a few nodes (Hanneman & Riddle, 2005). In a leadership network, centralization could be considered a measure of vertical leadership. As with the previous network indices, centralization could be calculated within teams or across the entire system to assess vertical leadership forms across multiple network foci. For example, component teams could each display high levels of centralization—with leadership power in the hands of one or a few individuals. However, these central team leaders may or may not share in leadership. Figure 22.4 demonstrates the importance of considering centralization across these multiple network foci levels. Figure 22.4a depicts centralized leadership structures within teams, but shared structures among central team leaders. Figure 22.4b shows

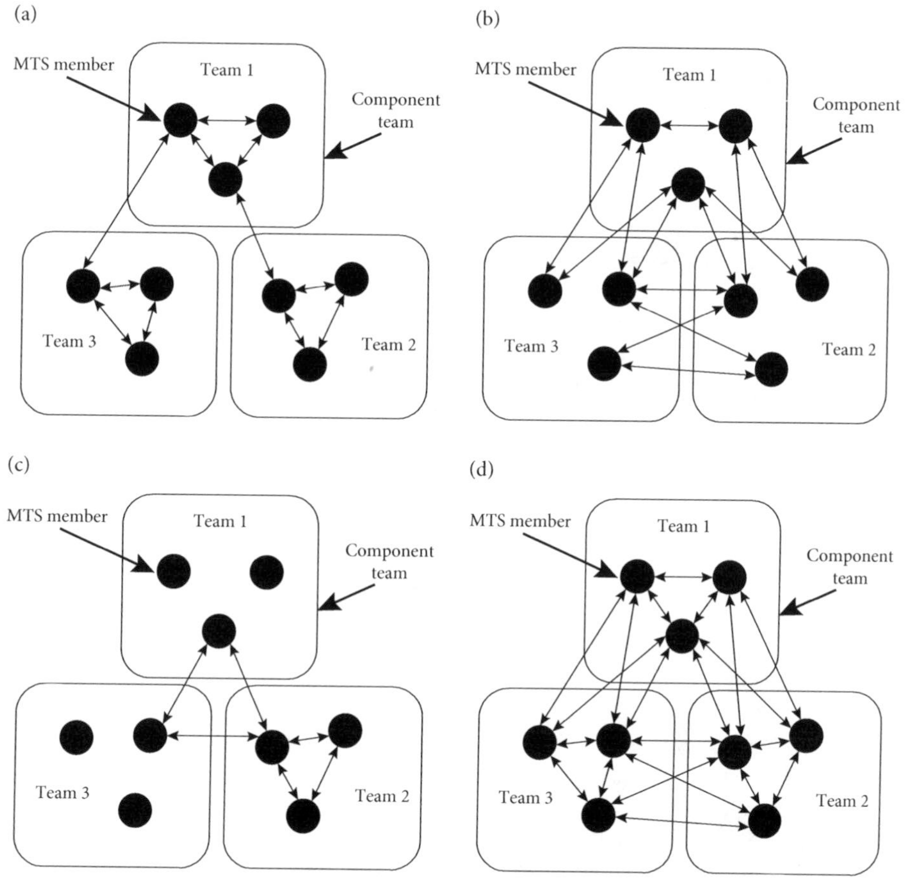

Figure 22.3. Four Nine-person, Three-team MTSs Demonstrating Leadership Density Across Multiple Network Foci. Leadership Density **(a)** Within Teams, **(b)** Between Teams, **(c)** Among Specific MTS Members, and **(d)** Across the MTS.

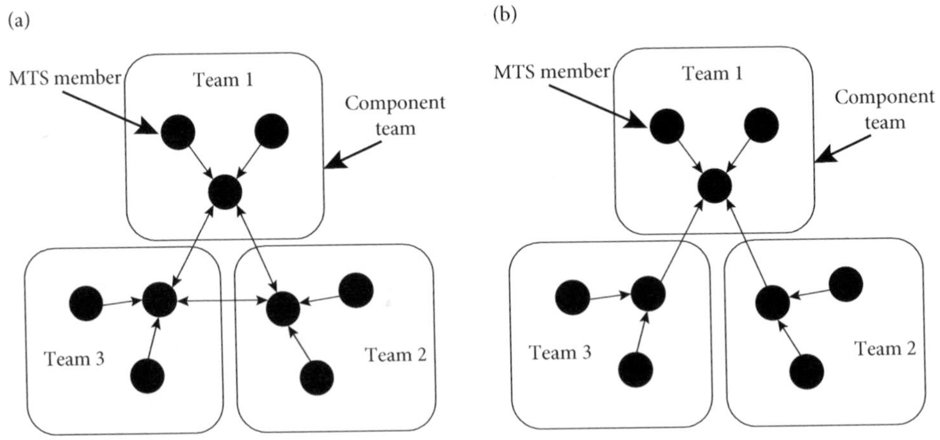

Figure 22.4. Centralized Leadership Network Structures Within Teams and **(a)** Shared (Decentralized) Structures Among Central Team Leaders or **(b)** Centralized Structure Among Central Team Leaders.

a multitier vertical leadership structure such that leadership is centralized within each component team, and each component team leader is subordinated to a higher-level MTS leader.

Sociometric Prompts to Incorporate Leadership Forms, Functions, and Foci

As described in the previous section, leadership structural forms may differ depending on the portion of the MTS leadership network that is examined (i.e., *network foci*; within teams, between teams, across the entire MTS). However, leadership structures may also differ based on the content of the leadership relationships. Sociometric prompts (i.e., network measures) that elicit different aspects of leadership may yield highly different patterns of relations. Initial work examining leadership networks (e.g., Mehra et al., 2006; Stogdill, 1948) used prompts that asked respondents to nominate individuals whom they perceived to be a leader. These initial studies did not clarify what was meant by the term "leader." This technique allows researchers to capture respondents' innate perceptions of leadership. However, years of leadership theory development and research have provided much guidance regarding the specific behaviors and interactions that are involved in successful leadership of groups (e.g., Ohio State studies; Halpin & Winer, 1957, transformational leadership theories; Bass, 1985; Burn, 1978; functional leadership; Fleishman et al., 1991; Zaccaro et al., 2001; Leader–Member Exchange [LMX] theories; Deluga, 1998; Liden et al., 1997). Thus, we propose that incorporating prior work on leadership activities with the network perspective could yield a more comprehensive picture of the leadership structures that emerge within complex systems. Specifically, sociometric prompts could more thoroughly integrate psychosocial work on leadership with the network perspective by eliciting networks that refer directly to leadership activities rather than members' own innate theories of leadership.

In the MTS context, leadership networks can be elicited that identify the leadership *functions* MTS members engage in and to what level of the MTS goal hierarchy these functional leadership activities are *focused* (i.e., goal foci). As mentioned previously, in the description of past theory on MTS leadership, three key MTS leadership activities that involve interactions between "leaders" and "followers" include (1) direction setting (i.e., planning, organizing, problem solving; DeChurch & Marks, 2006; DeChurch et al., 2011; Hiller, Day, & Vance, 2006); (2) coordination (e.g., DeChurch & Marks, 2006; DeChurch et al., 2011); and (3) motivation (e.g., Zaccaro et al., 2001). The inherent interactive nature of these three leadership activities makes them particularly suited for evaluation using network analysis techniques, which identify the presence or absence of relationships between actors.

Furthermore, leadership activities impact individuals, teams, and systems at multiple levels of the system's goal hierarchy. Individuals nested within MTSs work simultaneously toward their own personal goals, the collective goals of their component teams, and the superordinate collective goals of the system as a whole. At times these different goals may be in conflict (Mathieu et al., 2001). MTS leadership exists to create emergence in the higher level patterning of the behavior of lower level units (Marks et al., 2005). Individual-level leadership focuses and motivates individuals to achieve their personal goals. Team-level leadership routinizes the thoughts, feelings, and interactions among individuals toward the goal of the team. MTS-level leadership routinizes the thoughts feelings and interactions of teams with those of other teams and aligns the MTS with the external embedding environment. Examining the degree to which individuals are directed, motivated, and/or coordinated in regards to their personal-, team-, and/or MTS-level goals can improve the knowledge base regarding how leadership can best align goals across multiple levels. Thus, we suggest the use of sociometric prompts that generate MTS leadership structures containing information about both the *function* and the *goal focus* of MTS leadership.

Table 22.2 displays this two-dimensional view of MTS leadership supported by prior research. The functional dimension captures the particular leadership activities that are enacted within the system. The goal-focus dimension captures the level of goals these behaviors impact. Table 22.2 includes illustrative prompts to elicit person-to-person leadership networks containing information regarding leadership functions and goal foci. For example, to assess direction setting for individual-level goals, MTS members could be prompted: "Who provides you with direction in working toward your individual goals?" To assess direction setting for team-level goals, the members could be asked: "Who provides you with direction in working toward your team's goals?" Lastly, to assess direction setting for MTS-level goals, members could be asked: "Who provides you with direction in working toward MTS goals?"

Responses to these prompts can be binary (i.e., 0 or 1) or valued (e.g., Likert-type scale). The prompts in Table 22.2 are worded to elicit binary ties, creating an adjacency matrix filled with 1's for individuals who are exhibiting a particular function/leadership relation, and 0's for individuals not exhibiting a particular function/level of leadership. These leadership network prompts could easily be adapted to use valued ties. For example, the direction setting team network prompt could read: "To what extent does each person provide you with direction in working toward the team goals?" Responses might be on a 5- or 7-point Likert-type scale ranging from "Not at all" to "To a great extent." Although valued ties capture greater gradation in the underlying construct of leadership enactment, many network analytic methods using ties as a dependent variable will require ties to be represented as binary data (e.g., ERGM, Siena).

Once leadership networks are elicited, leadership structural *forms* can be represented using the ego-net and network indices discussed in the preceding section. Finally, these structural forms can be examined at multiple *network foci* throughout the leadership structure (within teams, between teams, across the MTS). Combining these four dimensions of MTS leadership—forms, functions, network foci, and goal foci—can provide a comprehensive view of the way that MTS leadership emerges and impacts system-level effectiveness.

Table 22.2. Leadership Sociometric Prompts to Elicit Forms and Foci

			Focus		
			Individual goals	**Team goals**	**MTS goals**
Function	*Direction Setting*	(i.e., Planning, organizing, problem solving; DeChurch & Marks, 2006; DeChurch et al., 2011; Hiller et al., 2006)	"Who provides you with direction in working toward your individual goals?"	"Who provides you with direction in working toward your team's goals?"	"Who provides you with direction in working toward your MTS's goals?"
	Motivation	(e.g., Zaccaro et al., 2001)	"Who energizes you to work toward your individual goals?"	"Who energizes you to work toward your team's goals?"	"Who energizes you to work toward your MTS's overall goals?"
	Coordination of Collective Actions	(i.e., Task; DeChurch & Marks, 2006; DeChurch et al., 2011)	—	"Who helps you coordinate with members of your team?"	"Who helps you coordinate with members of your MTS?"

Summary, Conclusions, and Future Research Directions

We have discussed four key concepts regarding MTS leadership networks. First, using network analysis indices, leadership *forms* (i.e., structures) that emerge within MTSs can be identified. Second, these indices can be used to capture leadership structure at multiple *network foci* within a MTS leadership network (e.g., within teams, throughout the system). Third, sociometric prompts can be used to identify the leadership *functions* (e.g., direction setting, coordination, motivation) MTS members enact. Finally, these sociometric prompts can be modified to identify the *focus* of leadership activities. Namely, the goals (i.e., individual-level, team-level, MTS-level) can be identified that are most affected by MTS leadership activities.

For each of the ego-net and network indices discussed, we offer exemplar research questions that drive future investigation into this new genre of MTS leadership by incorporating network structure (i.e., forms) with leadership function, network foci, and goal foci. Incorporating a network perspective into MTS leadership research allows us to ask new questions regarding leadership capacity. Table 22.3 presents a mapping of network concepts to future MTS leadership research questions. This list is a far from exhaustive. We offer it as an illustration of the type of questions about leadership in MTSs that this network approach enables us to answer.

Ego-Net Structure Questions

The first category of questions centers on the positioning of particular individuals within the network. In the context of a MTS, these individuals may be formal leaders of teams, or emergent leaders defined by their influence. Two broad types of questions related to individuals' positional features are: (1) What gives rise to these network positions? and (2) What are the consequences that stem from occupation of these positions? Research on personality, values, and skills relevant to leadership can ground predictions that detail how individual differences enable certain MTS members to occupy positions in the functional leadership networks within teams and across systems. Thus, our example question is: What individual differences

Table 22.3. Example Research Questions for MTS Leadership Networks

Relationship Structure	Network Construct(s)	Example MTS Leadership Research Question(s)
Ego-Net Structure	Centrality Brokerage	RQ1: What individual differences predict occupancy of different positions in a leadership network (i.e., across functions, goal foci, and network foci)?
Dyadic Structures	Reciprocity	RQ2: Does the extent to which leadership network ties (i.e., across functions, goal foci, and network foci) are mutual predict MTS effectiveness?
Triadic Structures	Transitivity	RQ3: To what extent does triadic closure in leadership networks (i.e., a high percentage of closed triads across functions, goal foci, and network foci) predict MTS effectiveness?
Group Structures	Cliques	RQ4: To what extent does the emergence of cohesive cliques in leadership networks (i.e., across functions, goal foci, and network foci) augment or detract from MTS effectiveness?
	Diameter	RQ5: To what extent does the overall size of leadership networks (i.e., across functions, goal foci, and network foci) enable MTS effectiveness?
	Centralization Density	RQ6: To what extent does centralization and/or density of leadership networks (i.e., across functions, goal foci, and network foci) enable MTS effectiveness? RQ7: To what extent does the relative density and/or centralization of leadership networks at one network foci (e.g., within teams) compared to another (e.g., across the entire system) enable MTS effectiveness? RQ8: To what extent does the optimal configuration of within team and across MTS centralization and/or density differ based on the stage of development and/or task cycle of the MTS?

predict occupancy of different positions in a leadership network (i.e., across functions, goal foci, and network foci)?

Dyadic Relationship Structure Questions

A second set of questions examines the predictors and consequences of dyadic relationships. In the case of leadership networks, reciprocity in a dyad refers to the degree to which leadership influence is mutual between two individuals. Thus, our second example question is: Does the extent to which leadership network ties (i.e., across functions, goal foci, and network foci) are mutual predict MTS effectiveness?

Triadic Relationship Structure Questions

The third set of questions concern the triadic structures in leadership networks. Triads have been found to be influential stabilizing forces in networks. However, the extent to which teams and MTSs benefit from closure in their leadership networks is an open question. For example, if person A is energized to work on behalf of the team by person B, and person B is energized by person C, what is the likelihood that person C will also be energized by person A, and does this balance in the leadership motivational function underlie effectiveness? Thus, our example question related to triads is: To what extent does triadic closure in leadership networks (i.e., a high percentage of closed triads across functions, goal foci, and network foci) predict MTS effectiveness?

Group Relationship Structure Questions

A final set of questions concerns the effects of group-level leadership structures. In MTSs, there are a variety of questions about the leadership cliques that emerge. For example: To what extent does the emergence of cohesive cliques in leadership networks (i.e., across functions, goal foci, and network foci) augment or detract from MTS effectiveness? With diameter (i.e., the size of MTS leadership networks), to what extent does the overall size of leadership networks (i.e., across functions, goal foci, and network foci) enable MTS effectiveness? For centralization (i.e., leadership in the hands of a few) and for density (i.e., degree of sharing in leadership) we wonder: To what extent does centralization and/or density of leadership networks (i.e., across functions, goal foci, and network foci) enable MTS effectiveness?

Interesting multilevel questions arise when evaluating leadership structure at multiple network foci. For example, within MTSs, centralization can have influence, not only within and across teams, but also in their relative combination. There are likely to be combinative effects when leadership is centralized at one level but decentralized at another. One set of predictions would suggest that alignment in structure at multiple levels would allow members to achieve cognitive congruence, and would benefit the MTS by creating a common set of expectations regarding the structural patterning of leadership. For example, if leadership is centralized within teams, and centralized across the MTS, members expect and normalize hierarchical influence. An alternative set of predictions might suggest that differences in structures across levels are beneficial. For example, perhaps patterns reflecting decentralization within teams and centralization across MTSs are effective. The decentralization within teams would afford the benefits of motivation and empowerment stemming from flat leadership structures, whereas the centralization present in the larger system affords needed efficiency in combining the efforts of a large number of individuals. Thus, an exemplar question in this area is: To what extent does the relative density and/or centralization of leadership networks at one network foci (e.g., within teams) compared to another network foci (e.g., across the entire system) enable MTS effectiveness?

Lastly, we call attention to questions about the impact of structure over time. Perhaps a particular leadership structure is needed in one task cycle (i.e., transition versus action phases; Marks, Mathieu, & Zaccaro, 2001) or particular stage of team development (e.g., team formation versus role compilation; Kozlowski et al., 1996) but a restructuring of leadership is needed in another task cycle or stage. Therefore, we advance the question: To what extent does the optimal configuration of within team and across MTS centralization and/or density differ based on the stage of development and/or task cycle of the MTS?

We opened this chapter by drawing attention to the dire consequences that arise when leadership fails to unite constituent teams within MTSs. This chapter builds on two research traditions—one on multiteam leadership and one on social networks—to suggest a new way to conceptualize and test relationships about the configurations of enactment of leadership within complex systems. We hope that these ideas stimulate additional thinking in this area, and ultimately, that empirical research testing of these ideas will follow.

References

Adler, P. S., & Kwon, S. W. (2002). Social capital: Prospects for a new concept. *Academy of Management Review, 27*, 17–40.

Baldwin, T. T., Bedell, M. D., & Johnson, J. L. (1997). The social fabric of a team-based M.B.A. program: Network effects on student satisfaction and performance. *Academy of Management Journal, 40*, 1369–1397.

Balkundi, P. & Harrison, D. A. (2006). Ties, leaders, and time in teams: Strong inferences about network structure's effects on team viability and performance. *Academy of Management Journal, 49*, 49–68.

Balkundi, P., & Kilduff, M. (2006). The ties that lead: A social network approach to leadership. *The Leadership Quarterly, 17*, 419–439.

Balkundi, P., Kilduff, M., Barsness, Z. I., & Michael, J. H. (2007). Demographic antecedents and performance consequences of structural holes in work teams. *Journal of Organizational Behavior, 28*, 241–260.

Balkundi, P., Kilduff, M., & Harrison, D. A. (2011). Centrality and charisma: Comparing how leader networks and attributions affect team performance. *Journal of Applied Psychology, 96*, 1209–1222.

Bass, B. M. (1985). *Leadership and performance beyond expectations*. New York, NY: Free Press.

Bavelas, A. (1950). Communication patterns in task-oriented groups. *The Journal of the Accoustical Society of America, 22*, 725–730.

Bell, B. S., & Kozlowski, S. W. J. (2002). A typology of virtual teams: Implications for effective leadership. *Group and Organization Management, 27*, 14–49.

Bilhuber Galli, E., & Müller-Stewens, G. (2012). How to build social capital with leadership development: Lessons from an explorative case study of a multibusiness firm. *The Leadership Quarterly, 23*, 176–201.

Brass, D. J. (1984). Being in the right place: A structural analysis of individual influence in an organization. *Administrative Science Quarterly, 29*, 518–539.

Brass, D. J., & Krackhardt, D. (1999). The social capital of twenty-first-century leaders. In J. G. Hunt & R. L. Phillips (Eds.), *Out-of-the-box leadership challenges for the 21st century army*, 179–194. Amsterdam, the Netherlands: Elsevier B.V.

Burns, J. M. (1978). *Leadership*. New York, NY: Harper & Row.

Burt, R. S. (1992). *Structural holes: The social structure of competition*. Cambridge, MA: Harvard University Press.

Burt, R. S. (1997). The contingent value of social capital. *Administrative Science Quarterly, 42*, 339–365.

Burt, R. S. (2005). *Brokerage and closure: An introduction to social capital*. New York, NY: Oxford University Press.

Buunk, B. P., Doosje, B. J., Jans, L. G. J. M., & Hopstaken, L. E. M. (1993). Perceived reciprocity, social support, and stress at work: The role of exchange and communal orientation. *Journal of Personality and Social Psychology, 65*, 801–811.

Carson, J. B., Tesluk, P. E., & Marrone, J. A. (2007). Shared leadership in teams: An investigation of antecedent conditions and performance. *Academy of Management Journal, 50*, 1217–1234.

Coleman, J. S. (1988). Social capital in the creation of human capital. *The American Journal of Sociology, 94*, S95–S120.

Dansereau, F. Jr., Graen, G., & Haga, W. J. (1975). A vertical dyad linkage approach to leadership within formal organizations: A longitudinal investigation of the role making process. *Organizational Behavior and Human Performance, 13*, 46–78.

Davison, R. B., Hollenbeck, J. R., Barnes, C. M., Sleesman, D. J., Ilgen, D. R. (2012). Coordinated action in multiteam systems. *Journal of Applied Psychology, 97*, 808–824.

Day, D. V., Gronn, P., & Salas, E. (2004). Leadership in team-based organizations: On the threshold of a new era. *Leadership Quarterly, 17*, 211–216.

DeChurch, L.A., Burke, C.S., Shuffler, M., Lyons, R., Doty, D., & Salas, E. (2011). A historiometric analysis of leadership in mission critical multiteam environments. *Leadership Quarterly, 22*, 152–169.

DeChurch, L. A., Hiller, N. J., Murase, T., Doty, D., & Salas, E. (2010). Leadership across levels: Levels of leaders and their levels of impact. *Leadership Quarterly, 21*, 1069–1085.

DeChurch, L. A., & Marks, M. A. (2006). Leadership in multiteam systems. *Journal of Applied Psychology, 2*, 311–329.

DeChurch, L. A., & Zaccaro, S. J. (2010). Perspectives: Teams won't solve this problem. *Human Factors: The Journal of Human Factors and Ergonomics Society, 52*, 329–334.

Deluga, R. J. (1998). Leader-member exchange quality and effectiveness ratings: The role of subordinate-supervisor conscientiousness similarity. *Group and Organization Management, 23*, 189–216.

DeVries, T. A., Walter, F., Van der Vegt, G. S., Essens, P. J. M. D., & Vogelaar, A. L. W. (2011). Boundary spanning within multiteam systems: The roles of functional experience and identification. Paper presented at the Annual Academy of Management Conference, San Antonio, TX.

Erez, A., LePine, J. A., & Elms, H. (2002). Effects of rotated leadership and peer evaluation on the functioning and effectiveness of self-managed teams: A quasi-experiment. *Personnel Psychology, 55*, 929–948.

Finkelstein, S., & Hambrick, D. (1996). *Strategic leadership: Top executives and their effects on organizations*. Minneapolis/St. Paul, MN: West.

Fleishman, E. A., Mumford, M. D., Zaccaro, S. J., Levin, K. Y., Korotkin, A. L., & Hein, M. B. (1991). Taxonomic efforts in the description of leader behavior: A synthesis and functional interpretation. *The Leadership Quarterly, 2*, 245–287.

Friedrich, T. L., Vessey, W. B., Schuelke, M. J., Ruark, G. A., & Mumford, M. D. (2009). A framework for understanding collective leadership: The selective utilization of leader and team expertise within networks. *The Leadership Quarterly, 20*, 933–958.

Galbraith, J. R. (1973). *Designing complex organizations*. Boston, MA: Addison-Wesley Longman.

Gibbons, D., & Olk, P. M. (2003). Individual and structural origins of friendship and social position among professionals. *Journal of Personality and Social Psychology, 84*, 340–351.

Girvan, M., & Newman, M. E. J. (2002). Community structure in social and biological networks. *Proceedings of the National Academy of Sciences of the United States of America, 99*, 7821–7826.

Graen, G. B., & Uhl-Bien, M. (1995). Relationship-based approach to leadership: Development of leaders-member exchange (LMX) theory over 25 years: Applying a multi-level multi-domain perspective. *Leadership Quarterly, 6*, 219–247.

Grannovetter, M. S. (1973). The strength of weak ties. *American Journal of Sociology, 78*, 1360–1380.

Granovetter, M. S. (1985). Economic action and social structure. The problem of embeddedness. *American Journal of Sociology, 91*, 481–510.

Gully, S. M. (2000). Work teams research: Recent findings and future trends. In M. M. Beyerlein (Ed.), *Work teams: Past, present and future* (pp. 25–44). Dordrecht, the Netherlands: Kluwer Academic.

Hackman, J. R., & Walton, R. E. (1986). Leading groups in organizations. In P. S. Goodman (Ed.), *Designing effective work groups*. San Francisco, CA: Jossey-Bass.

Halpin, A.W. and Winer, B.J. (1957). A factorial study of the leader behavior descriptions. In R. M. Stogdill & A. E. Coons (Eds.), *Leader behavior: Its description and measurement*. Columbus, OH: Bureau of Business Research, Ohio State University.

Hanneman, R. A., & Riddle, M. (2005). *Introduction to social network methods*. Riverside, CA: University of California, Riverside. Available at http://faculty.ucr.edu/~hanneman/

Hansen, M. T. (1999). The search-transfer problem: The role of weak ties in sharing knowledge across organization subunits. *Administrative Science Quarterly, 44*, 82–111.

Harary, F., Norman, R., & Cartwright, D. (1965). *Structural models: Introduction to theory of directed graphs*. New York, NY: John Wiley & Sons.

Heider, F. (1958). *The psychology of interpersonal relations*. New York, NY: John Wiley & Sons.

Hiller, N. J., Day, D. V., & Vance R. J. (2006). Collective enactment of leadership roles and team effectiveness: A field study. *The Leadership Quarterly, 17*, 387–397.

Holland, P. W., & Leinhardt, S. (1979) *Perspectives on social network research*. New York, NY: Academic Press.

Houghton, J. D., Neck, C. P., & Manz, C. C. (2003). Self-leadership and superleadership. In C. E. Pearce & J. A. Conger (Eds.), *Shared leadership: Reframing the hows and whys of leadership* (pp. 123–140). Thousand Oaks, CA: SAGE.

Ilgen, D. R., Hollenbeck, J. R., Johnson, M., & Jundt, D. (2005). Teams in organizations: From I-P-O Models to IMOI Models. *Annual Review of Psychology, 56*, 517–543.

Jaques, E. (1990, January–February). In praise of hierarchy. *Harvard Business Review*, 127–133.

Jaques, E. (1996). *Requisite organization: A total system for effective managerial organization and managerial leadership for the 21st century*. Arlington, VA: Cason Hall.

Judge, T. A., Bono, J. E., Ilies, R., & Gerhardt, M. W. (2002). Personality and leadership: A qualitative and quantitative review. *Journal of Applied Psychology, 87*, 765–780.

Judge, T. A., Piccolo, R. F., & Ilies, R. (2004). Transformational and transactional leadership: A meta-analytic test of their relative validity. *Journal of Applied Psychology, 89*, 755–768.

Kaiser, R. B., Hogan, R., & Craig, S. B. (2008) Leadership and the fate of organizations. *American Psychologist, 63*, 96–110.

Katz, D., & Kahn, R. L. (1978). *The social psychology of organizations* (2nd ed.). New York, NY: John Wiley & Sons.

Kerr, S., Schriesheim, C. A., Murphy, C. J., & Stogdill, R. M. (1974). Toward a contingency theory of leadership based upon the consideration and initiating structure literature. *Organizational Behavior and Human Performance, 12*, 62–82.

Kilduff, M., & Krackhardt, D. (1994). Bringing the individual back in: A structural analysis of the internal market for reputation in organizations. *Academy of Management Journal, 37*, 87–108.

Kilduff, M., & Tsai, W. (2003). *Social networks and organizations*. London, UK: SAGE.

Klein, K., Lim, B. C., Saltz, J. L., & Mayer, D. M. (2004). How do they get there? An examination of the antecedents of centrality in team networks. *Academy of Management Journal, 47*, 952–963.

Klein, K. J., Ziegert, J. C., Knight, A. P., & Xiao, Y. (2006). Dynamic delegation: Shared, hierarchically, and deindividualized leadership in extreme action teams. *Administrative Science Quarterly, 51*, 590–621.

Knoke, D., & Kuklinski, J. H. (1982) *Network analysis*. Newbury Park, CA: SAGE.

Kozlowski, S. W. J., & Bell, B. S. (2003). Work groups and teams in organizations. In W. C. Borman, D. R. Ilgen, & R. J. Klimoski (Eds.), *Handbook of psychology: Industrial and organizational psychology* (Vol. 12, pp. 333–375). London, UK: John Wiley & Sons.

Kozlowski, S. W. J., Gully, S. M., McHugh, P. P., Salas, E., & Cannon-Bowers, J. A. (1996). A dynamic theory of leadership and team effectiveness: Developmental and task contingent leader roles. *Research in Personnel and Human Resources Management, 14*, 253–306.

Kozlowski, S. W. J., & Ilgen, D. R. (2006). Enhancing the effectiveness of work groups and teams (monograph). *Psychological Science in the Public Interest, 7*, 77–124.

Krackhardt, D., & Porter, L. W. (1985). The snowball effect: Turnover embedded in communication networks. *Journal of Applied Psychology, 71*, 50–55.

Lanaj, K., Hollenbeck, J. R., Ilgen, D. R., Barnes, C. M., & Harmon, S. J. (2013). The double-edged sword of decentralized planning in multi-team systems. *Academy of Management Journal, 56*, 735–757.

Lazer, D., & Friedman, A. (2007). The network structure of exploration and exploitation. *Administrative Science Quarterly, 52*, 667–694.

Liden, R. C., Sparrowe, R. T., & Wayne, S. J. (1997). Leader–member exchange theory: The past and potential for the future. *Research in Personnel and Human Resources Management, 15*, 47–119.

Lord, R. G. (1977). Functional leadership behavior: Measurement and relation to social power and leadership perceptions. *Administrative Science Quarterly, 22*, 114–133.

Lord, R. G., & Emrich, C. G. (2001). Thinking outside the box by looking inside the box: Extending the cognitive revolution in leadership research. *Leadership Quarterly, 11*, 551–579.

Marks, M. A., DeChurch, L. A., Mathieu, J. E., Panzer, F. J., & Alonso, A. (2005). Teamwork in multiteam systems. *Journal of Applied Psychology, 90*, 964–971.

Marks, M. A., Mathieu, J. E., & Zaccaro, S. J. (2001). *Academy of Management Review, 26*, 356–376.

Mathieu, J. E., Marks, M. A., & Zaccaro, S. J. (2001). Multiteam systems. In N. Anderson, D. S. Ones, H. K. Sinangil, & C. Viswesvaran (Eds.), *Handbook of industrial, work, and organizational psychology* (Vol. 2, pp. 289–313). London: Sage Publications.

Mayer, R. C. Davis, J. H., & Schoorman, F. D. (1995). An integration model of organizational trust. *Academy of Management Review, 20*, 709–734.

McAllister, D. J. (1995). Affect—and cognition-based trust as foundations for interpersonal cooperation in organizations. *The Academy of Management Journal, 38*, 24–59.

McGrath, J. E. (1962). *Leadership behavior: Some requirements for leadership training* [Mimeographed]. Washington, DC: U.S. Civil Service Commission.

McGrath, J. E. (1984). *Groups: Interaction and performance*. Englewood Cliffs, NJ: Prentice-Hall.

Mehra, A., Smith, B. R., Dixon, A. L., & Robertson, D. (2006). Distributed leadership in teams: The network of leadership perceptions and team performance. *The Leadership Quarterly, 17*, 232–245.

Mizruchi, M. S., & Stearns, L. B. (2001). Getting deals done: The use of social networks in bank decision making. *American Sociological Review, 5*, 647–671.

Morgeson, F. P., DeRue, D. S., & Karam, E. P. (2009) Leadership in teams: A functional approach to understanding leadership structures and processes. *Journal of Management 36*, 5–39.

Oh, H., Chung, M. H., & Labianca, G. (2004). Group social capital and group effectiveness: The role of informal socializing ties. *Academy of Management Journal, 47*, 860–875.

Pearce, C. L., & Conger, J. A. (Eds.) (2003). *Shared leadership: Reframing the hows and whys of leadership.* Thousand Oaks, CA: SAGE.

Rodan, S., & Galunic, C. (2004). More than network structure: How knowledge heterogeneity influences managerial performance and innovativeness. *Strategic Management Journal, 25*, 541–562.

Shaw, M. E. (1964). Communication networks. In L. Nerkowitz (Ed.), *Advances in experimental social psychology* (Vol. 1, pp. 111–147). New York, NY: Academic Press.

Sparrowe, R., Liden, R. C., Wayne, S. J., & Kraimer, M. L. (2001). Social networks and the performance of individuals and groups. *Academy of Management Journal, 44*, 316–325.

Stogdill, R. M. (1948). Personal factors associated with leadership: A survey of the literature. *The Journal of Psychology: Interdisciplinary and Applied, 25*, 35–71.

Tajfel H. (1982). Instrumentality, identity, and social comparisons. In H. Tajfel (Ed.), *Social identity and intergroup relations* (pp. 483–507). Cambridge, UK: Cambridge University Press.

Tajfel, H., & Turner, J. C. (1985). The social identify theory of intergroup behavior. In S. Worchel & W. G. Austin (Eds.), *Psychology of intergroup relations* (2nd ed., pp. 7–24). Chicago, IL: Nelson-Hall.

Tichy, N. M., Tushman, M. L., & Fombrun, C. (1979). Social network analysis for organizations. *Academy of Management Review, 4*, 507–519.

Wasserman, S., & Faust, K. (1994). *Social network analysis: Methods and applications.* New York, NY: Cambridge University Press.

Weick, K. E. (1993). The collapse of sensemaking in organizations: The Mann Gulch disaster. *Administrative Science Quarterly, 38*, 628–652.

Zaccaro, S. J., & DeChurch, L. A. (2012). Leadership forms and functions in multiteam systems. In S. J. Zaccaro, M. A. Marks, & L. A. DeChurch (Eds.), *Multiteam systems: An organizational form for dynamic and complex environments* (pp. 253–288). New York: Routledge.

Zaccaro, S. J., Heinen, B., & Shuffler, M. (2009). Team leadership and team effectiveness. In E. Salas, G. E. Goodwin, & C. S. Burke (Eds.), *Team effectiveness in complex organizations: Cross-disciplinary perspectives and approaches* (pp. 83–111). New York, NY: Routledge.

Zaccaro, S. J., & Marks, M. A. (1998). The role of leaders in high-performance teams. In E. Sundstrom (Ed.), *Supporting work team effectiveness: Best management practices for fostering high performance* (pp. 95–125). San Francisco, CA: Jossey-Bass.

Zaccaro, S. J., Marks, M. A., & DeChurch, L. A. (2012). *Multiteam systems: An organizational form for dynamic and complex environments.* Management & Organization Series. New York, NY: Routledge.

Zaccaro, S. J., Rittman, A. L., & Marks, M. A. (2001). Team leadership. *Leadership Quarterly, 12*, 451–483.

PART 6

Emerging Issues in Organizational Leadership

CHAPTER

23 The Skill to Lead: The Role of Political Skill in Leadership Dynamics

Darren C. Treadway, Jeffrey R. Bentley, Lisa M. Williams, *and* Angela S. Wallace

Abstract

While perhaps viewed as the dark side of leadership, few academics or practitioners would not acknowledge that effective leaders are skilled politicians. The current chapter seeks to dispel notions of politics in general, and political skill in specific, as necessary evils of leadership and cast them simply as necessary for leadership. By recognizing leadership as a political process revolving around the facilitation of shared meaning, we review the development of the political skill construct and its integration with leadership research, including leader-member exchange (LMX), relational leadership, political leadership, and the CEO-celebrity effect. The authors then identify areas in which scholarship has been relatively absent and discuss how addressing these areas in future research offer an important step toward developing a more comprehensive theory of politics and leadership.

Key Words: Leadership, political skill, organizational politics, relational leadership, leader-member exchange

Introduction

General Stanley McChrystal was, from all accounts, an American hero: a man uniquely qualified by experience, expertise, and education to lead the allied fight in Afghanistan. Routinely commended for his intellectual brilliance, tenacity, and courage, McChrystal appeared to be the perfect leader for America's difficult war in Afghanistan. Thus, it is either shocking, tragic, or both (depending on your end of the looking glass) that his time as leader of the Afghanistan war was effectively ended by an article in *Rolling Stone* magazine. Looking back with the benefit of time, Michael Hastings's (2010) article is not particularly scathing or malicious. It details a general who believes strongly in a position, whose actions as a commander were valiant and extraordinary, but whose inability to successfully navigate the complexities of policy selling to his superiors, subordinates, and the public at large and to effectively understand the political context within which he operated were an inadequate complement to his brilliance and bravado. It is not surprising then that his resignation as the commander in Afghanistan was characterized as not a failure of strategy or competence, but of political skill (Jaffe, 2010) and that his replacement, General David H. Petraeus, is widely praised not just for his strategic acumen on the battlefield, but also in the halls of Congress, the Pentagon and the White House (e.g., Cockburn, 2007; Rubin & Filkins, 2010).

The story of General McChrystal (ret) and his fall from grace is far from unique. History is littered with the epitaphs of leaders who, despite their knowledge, accomplishments, and reputation, could not overcome the institutional and political pitfalls that every leader encounters. The idea of leaders needing to recognize both the opportunities and dangers of political activity, as well as act as an effective political operator, are widely recognized within the popular press. However, the academic pursuit of understanding organizational politics in general, and leader political skill in specific, has been too often stunted by the general notion of those in academe that politics is solely associated with the "dark side" of organizational activity. We see this view as naïve and misinformed. Indeed, we challenge the reader to consider any leader of social or political change in the history of the world who was not an adept organizational politician. In our view, political activity is the dominant mode of organizational functioning and the ability to effectively operate within the political arena as the most critical skill a leader can possess.

Scholarly advancements in the area of political skill can be attributed to an ongoing stream of research by Ferris, Treadway, and their colleagues. Among these authors' contributions were their precise definition of the construct and their extensive development of a measure of the political skill, the Political Skill Inventory (Ferris et al., 2005). Ferris and his colleagues defined political skill as "the ability to effectively understand others at work, and to use such knowledge to influence others to act in ways that enhance one's personal and/or organizational objectives" (Ferris et al., 2005, p. 127). This definition provides the basis from which researchers could move beyond the anecdotal suggestions of early scholars and armchair theories of practitioners and begin to develop a broad base of knowledge regarding the political abilities of leaders and followers alike.

The current chapter seeks to provide the reader with a broad understanding of political skill and its importance in leadership. It will offer a brief description of the political perspective of leadership to provide the background for our understanding of the phenomenon. Next, we discuss the nature of political skill to offer insights into the abilities that make politically leaders essential to an organization's success. We then move on to outline the state of our knowledge by discussing both the conceptual models and empirical evidence that define our current thinking on political skill and leadership. Finally, we offer several avenues for future research into this area and discuss some initial studies that provide glimpses into the utility of these approaches.

The Political Nature of Leadership

For centuries, leadership was thought to exist in the realm of the gods or god-like humans (Bavelas, 1960). This mystical guise seemed to veil scholarly work until relatively recent times when researchers began to explore such illusions of leadership (Meindl, Ehrlich, & Dukerich, 1985) and reveal its inner workings and complexity. Bennis (1959, p. 259) states "...the concept of leadership eludes us or turns up in another form to taunt us again with its slipperiness and complexity...still the concept is not sufficiently defined." Thus, leadership may be viewed as a kaleidoscope of sorts. Many pieces create the entire pattern, and if you close one eye or the other you will have a slightly different focus. Divergent from most approaches to leadership, we recognize this complexity and view leadership as a political process in which leaders and followers engage in social influence behavior to develop shared meaning, drive change, and improve effectiveness. Thus, we adopt Yukl's (1998) definition of leadership:

> leadership is viewed broadly as the process wherein an individual member of a group or organization influences the interpretation of events, the choice of objectives and strategies, the organization of work activities, the motivation of people to achieve objectives, the maintenance of cooperative relationships, the development of skills and confidence by members, and the enlistment of support and cooperation from people outside the group or organization. (p. 5)

A political view of leadership is developed through two basic assumptions. First, at the center of effective leadership is the need to develop shared meaning within the organization and among followers. Second, leadership is assumed to be a political process in which shared meaning evolves as a product of both leader and follower influence behaviors crafted to advance their understandings of personal and organizational interests. As a result of divergent interests and viewpoints among leaders and between leaders and their followers, leadership is a political process in which ideas, coalitions, and personal agendas compete for resources and validation. While an extensive discussion of these assumptions is beyond the scope of this chapter, we briefly outline each of these processes in the section below to better contextualize the nature of political skill and leadership.

Leadership as the Development of Shared Meaning

The perspective of leadership as the development of shared meaning was alluded to when scholars commented that organization members understand their environments through expectations that are created through the interaction between the organization and its members (Stogdill, 1950), and shared outlooks that are related to social reality (Hollander & Julian, 1969). Bavelas (1960) emphasized the idea that this occurs in uncertain environments where organizations, as social inventions, can innovate to survive. Smircich and Morgan (1982) built on these foundations to provide an elaborated and explicit treatise on the topic. They stated that leadership is social action focused on defining and framing reality, creating meaning that can be used for organization, and shaping contexts that lead to collective direction and understanding. From this perspective, organizations are the collection of meanings that arise from these various social processes, and influence and rewards are among the primary tools used to shape any given organizational contexts (Smircich & Morgan, 1982).

Current work on leadership and the management of meaning presents arguments for leadership as sensemaking (Weick, 1995) and sensegiving (Gioia & Chittipeddi, 1991; Maitlis, 2005). Sensemaking is based on individual and social information or events that provide data about the organization and its relation to the environment that can be used for future action. Yet as Weick states, "sense may be in the eye of the beholder, but beholders vote and the majority rules" (Weick, 1995, pp. 5–6). So in organizational settings, sensemaking occurs within individuals, and the strength of its salience is dependent on its collective acceptance. In this approach to leadership, leaders receive ambiguous cues from the environment and must create for themselves a clear understanding of a pathway toward their objectives. Once they have gathered social information and experience in their environment, leaders can use their new view to inspire confidence in followers and guide them along a sensible course that can further adapt to new cues (Weick, 1995).

Sensegiving is defined as a leader's attempt to signal his or her understanding of social-organizational cues and energize followers toward actions congruent with his or her vision; sensegiving is considered an essential component of leadership (Gioia & Chittipeddi, 1991). Based on a case study, Maitlis (2005) investigated the process of sensegiving and determined that leaders tend to use either a high or low sensegiving approach, each of which has unique characteristics. For example, in high sensegiving situations, leaders use a controlled process and meet face to face with others individually through formal authority and channels such as formal meetings or committees. In low sensegiving contexts, there is less structure and control, with information flowing continuously through multiple channels. Using these processes, sensegiving occurs through downward and upward influence (Maitlis, 2005).

The framework of managed meaning implies distinct and unique processes and criteria for those who emerge and are effective as leaders. Specifically, leaders are sensegivers who interpret and give meaning to the world in ways that provide a vision of what the future might be (Weick, 1995), along with a template for specific actions (Smircich & Morgan, 1982). Smircich and Morgan (1982, p. 259) offer four components of the successful leader candidate. First, as a process, leadership as the management of shared meaning is based on social interactions. Second, leadership provides a definition of reality that is accessible to followers. Third, it creates a dependence relationship where followers allow the leader to make these interpretations. Last, leadership is institutionalized through roles and authority relationships.

The criteria for leaders who manage meaning revolve around acting as a conduit between the environment and followers. Specifically, leaders, from environmental uncertainty or chaos (Burke, 1966; Weick, 1995), are able to create meaning and organized action through their words and deeds (Smircich & Morgan, 1982). This notion is seen by researchers who are developing complexity leadership theory in assertion that meaning is created in the spaces that occur between individuals (peer- or leader-follower relations) who develop a shared worldview, rather than through a defined leader role (Lichtenstein et al., 2006). Leaders who cannot do this find themselves with followers who are tense and engage in disruptive behaviors (Burke, 1966). Thus, the development of shared meaning is paramount to leader effectiveness and occurs through the use of influence behavior.

Leadership as a Political Process

The existence of politics, defined as "the exercise or use of power, with power being defined as a potential force" (Pfeffer, 1992, p. 14) in organizational life, requires that effective leaders possess the political savvy necessary to successfully navigate the political landscape (Pfeffer, 1992, 2010). The possession of political savvy to exercise power (i.e,. the political process) differs from the social influence process. The social influence process is a method by which leaders use their power to effectuate a change in the attitudes and behaviors of others. However, the adjusted attitudes and behaviors may not manifest themselves desirably. It is through the political process that leaders are able to use their power to exact changes in attitudes and behaviors that are desired. Thus the political process entails the effective use of power through the use of politics. Mintzberg (1985) provided an early treatise on organizational politics and recognized both dysfunctional and functional aspects. He characterized organizations as political arenas that were primarily characterized by conflict and politics. He further argued that organizational politics are the illegitimate alternative to organizationally ordained power structures and are the result of weak structures or conflict generated through sanctioned structures. Different forms of political games, such as alliance building and expertise, are used to structure and regulate power in ways that create organization (Mintzberg, 1985, p. 134), and these political games coexist, conflict with, or act as substitutes for legitimate power.

In contrast to Mintzberg's view, Pfeffer (1992) did not consider organizational politics to be illegitimate, but rather considered them an effective and necessary means by which to manage the success of organizations and careers. In general, Pfeffer asserted that organizations contain multiple interests, sometimes aligned and sometimes not, that need to be well understood if they are to be well managed. But it is not enough to understand: individuals must also possess power, understand its use by others, and know how to employ it themselves in order to effectively manage these varied interests. As Pfeffer states, "[g]etting things done requires power" (p. 343). In his view, politics are the antidote to the status quo, and the way in which innovation and great success occurs through the alignment of multiple interests or behaviors toward a specific objective.

Following this line of reasoning, Yukl (1998) discussed the idea that the amount of power one has should be related to the amount of power required to reach an objective, and how well power is used by that individual. Those who are less skillful in the exercise of power, or are trying to implement major change, will need more of it to get things done (Yukl, 1998, p. 193). Furthermore, Yukl made distinctions between position and personal power. Position power—such as legitimate, reward, and coercion (French & Raven, 1959)—is less likely to be diminished because it is organizationally supported. On the other hand, he suggested that personal power (i.e., referent and expert power) would lose its effectiveness if the individual's objectives do not promote the well-being of the collective. Mechanisms to check the inappropriate use of power include policies and rules, as well as reciprocal influence (Yukl, 1998, p. 195).

Kotter (1985) adopted a different focus on organizational politics. He spoke of the need for leaders to manage interdependent relationships often characterized by diversity because of their potential to promote dysfunctional conflict. He asserts that effective leaders manage these relationships so that conflict results in desirable outcomes such as firm competitiveness, adaptability, responsiveness, and "more exciting" organizational life (Kotter, 1985, p. 36). Ineffective management of conflict results in infighting, parochial politics, and power struggles that reduce efficiency, increase costs, decrease innovation, alienate people, and "frustrate everyone etc" (p. 36).

Kotter's point is that the productive leadership of organizations and the relationships within and between them require the ability to understand and effectively use a complex social environment in goal-oriented ways. Based on this assumption, he asserted that managing networks and individuals to serve not one stakeholder but rather all stakeholders in the organization is critical. This requires cognitive and interpersonal skills that include the ability to (1) recognize individual differences that include, for example, values and perceptions; (2) assess the interdependencies between and among others; (3) understand the implications of these interdependencies; and (4) use this information to influence and manage these differences and interdependencies. The following section reviews a recent and important development to this end: the conceptualization and related research on political skill.

Political Skill

With the acceptance of organizations as political arenas comes the realization that some people are more effective at navigating this environment than others (Mintzberg, 1983; Pfeffer, 1981a). Some appear self-interested and abrasive, while others appear genuine, generous, and powerful. Cognizant of this fact, both Pfeffer (1981a) and Mintzberg (1983, 1985) independently proposed political skill constructs that described individuals' effectiveness in the social realms of organizations. Politically skilled individuals were those who were able to most effectively gather and use power to obtain desired ends through others. In its simplest form, political skill was social skill in the work domain and represented the interpersonal style with which one influenced others (Jones, 1990).

Yet after Pfeffer's (1981a) and Mintzberg's (1983, 1985) initial thoughts on political skill, no further conceptual or empirical work was conducted on the topic until nearly the turn of the century. At that time, Ferris and colleagues (Ferris et al., 1999, 2005, 2007) built on the work of Pfeffer and Mintzberg by refining the political skill construct to emphasize informal power and social influence effectiveness in general (Ferris, Treadway, Brouer, & Munyon, 2012). Their work launched a rapidly growing body of research that highlights the utility of political skill in explaining aspects of organizational behavior ranging from stress (e.g., Hochwarter et al., 2007; Perrewé et al., 2004, 2005) to job performance (e.g., Blickle et al., 2008; Harris, Kacmar, Zivnuska, & Shaw, 2007; Semadar, Robins, & Ferris, 2006; Treadway, Ferris, Duke, Adams, & Thatcher, 2007) to team effectiveness (Ahearn, Ferris, Hochwarter, Douglas, & Ammeter, 2004). In the paragraphs below we provide an extensive review of the literature, to date, on political skill to provide grounding for our discussion of political skill and leadership.

Conceptual Development of Political Skill

Working within a coalitional perspective (Cyert & March, 1963; March, 1962; Simon, 1959), Pfeffer viewed an organization not as a single cooperative decision-making entity, but as a conglomerate of groups and individuals with both divergent and convergent objectives. Political skill, in his view, described an organizational member's ability to effectively acquire, maintain, and use resources in order to navigate those multifaceted interests and ultimately be perceived as powerful (Ferris, Treadway, Brouer, & Munyon, 2012).

Similarly, Mintzberg (1983) recognized that politically skilled individuals excel at obtaining and using some base of informal power (e.g., referent, expert, reward; French & Raven, 1959) in order to influence other people's thoughts and behaviors. Mintzberg's conceptualization emphasized personal characteristics such as interpersonal sensitivity and savvy, as well as the abilities to successfully negotiate, persuade, bargain, and build alliances (Mintzberg, 1983). His definition of political skill included two important concepts: (1) social intelligence in terms of social situational understanding and behavioral adaptability, and (2) effectiveness in engaging in influence behaviors. Although not specifically recognized, Mintzberg's conceptualization is general and diverse enough to infer the presence of multiple distinct facets or dimensions of political skill, and it is this potential that drove the next phase of political skill research guided by Ferris and colleagues.

Taking into account previous work (Jones, 1990; Mintzberg, 1983; Pfeffer, 1981a), Ferris and colleagues described the politically skilled as characterized by social awareness, confidence, sincerity, charm, and effective communication skills (Ferris et al., 1999; Perrewé, Ferris, Frink, & Anthony, 2000). Their social perceptiveness and behavioral flexibility was believed to allow the politically skilled to perceive and meet the needs of changing situational circumstances in order to elicit desired attributions (e.g., genuineness, confidence, trustworthy) and responses (e.g., compliance, trust) from others (Ferris, Kolodinsky, Hochwarter, & Frink, 2001; Ferris, Perrewé, & Douglas, 2002).

Nomological Network with Social Effectiveness Constructs

Like most social effectiveness constructs, political skill involves social perceptiveness or understanding of social phenomena, and behavioral flexibility in acting on that social knowledge (Ferris, Adams, Kolodinsky, Hochwarter, & Ammeter, 2002). Perceptiveness and flexibility are underlying themes throughout the various definitions of social intelligence, which include the ability to develop goals and engage in goal-directed activity, self-efficacy, skill in bringing about valued social rewards, and cognitive or emotional empathy skills (Marlowe, 1986).

To differentiate political skill from other social effectiveness constructs under the umbrella of social effectiveness, political skill was positioned as "specific to interactions aimed at achieving success in organizations" (Ferris, Perrewé, Anthony, & Gilmore, 2000, p. 31). Ferris and colleagues postulated that political skill was based in practical intelligence (Sternberg, 1997) wherein goal-relevant tacit or experiential social knowledge was the key to personal success at work (Perrewé et al., 2000). They further argued that while they were distinct, political skill shared conceptual overlap with other social effectiveness constructs such as emotional intelligence and self-monitoring.

Emotional intelligence is conceptualized as either a mix of traits and dispositions (e.g., self-esteem, self-management, social awareness, etc.; Ashkanasy & Daus, 2005; Mayer, Salovey, & Caruso, 2008), or a distinct type of intelligence or ability that develops in people over time and through experiences (Mayer & Salovey, 1997; Roberts, Zeidner, & Matthews, 2001; Van Rooy & Viswesvaran, 2004). Both perspectives describe individuals' abilities to know their own emotions, manage those emotions, recognize emotions in others, and influence others' emotions. And meta-analytic evidence links the ability-intelligence model to job performance above and beyond the effects of personality (Joseph & Newman, 2010). Internally, the perception and management of one's own emotions may aide the politically skilled in handling stress and maintaining their composure when interacting with others. Externally, understanding and influencing others' emotions is critical for obtaining the power and resources necessary to facilitate goal advancement, especially individuals with jobs that involve social interaction. Thus, similar to emotionally intelligent leaders, politically skilled leaders are capable of understanding and influencing a large portion of emotion-related social dynamics. Yet beyond emotions, their perceptual acuity and behavioral tendencies also focus on remaining aspects of the social environment and may reside in the domain of their personality.

Among the personality characteristics that may be related to political skill, self-monitoring has, to the casual observer, the most obvious conceptual overlap. Possessing a dispositional tendency to pay close attention to social cues given by others in various situations and adapt their behavior to meet social expectations in order to elicit desired positive reactions from others (Snyder, 1974), high self-monitors have been referred to as social chameleons (Kilduff & Day, 1994). They typically regulate their behavioral self-presentation to meet external constraints or cues (Caldwell & O'Reilly, 1982; Snyder, 1979) rather than adhere to internal affective states and attitudes. Given their almost compulsive propensity to meet others' needs, it is not surprising that self-monitors also likely possess some degree of political skill.

Theoretically, however, the relational and goal achievement capabilities of the politically skilled are broader and more diverse than of those who are solely self-monitors. For instance, self-monitoring is at times compulsive or nonconscious (Cheng & Chartrand, 2003), and has been consistently linked to lower commitment to any one given organization or person (Day, Schleicher, Unckless, & Hiller, 2002; Kilduff & Day, 1994). Politically skilled individuals, in contrast, may use or suspend their self-monitoring tendencies to the extent that it meets their goals. That is, a politically skilled individual may have very high organizational commitment if it serves the purpose of meeting their goals (e.g., maintaining tenure at an organization, working into the dominant coalition, etc.). Thus while political skill is related to self-monitoring, the latter is a deeper more dispositional effect while the former is intertwined in part with conscious-level self-control (i.e., emotional intelligence) and also shaped over time with experience (e.g., practical intelligence, tacit knowledge).

In recognition of the above conceptual overlap and others, political skill researchers sought to demonstrate political skill as empirically distinct from other social effectiveness constructs. In their seminal piece on the measurement of political skill, Ferris and his colleagues (2005) provided evidence that the Political Skill Inventory was related yet empirically distinct from self-monitoring ($r = .39, .33$), political savvy ($r = .47$), and emotional intelligence ($r = .53$). Subsequent research has also confirmed that political skill is correlated, but not redundant with emotional intelligence ($r = .54$, Kisamore, Jawahar, Ligouri, Tagonie, & Stone, 2010; $r = .71$, Semadar et al., 2006; $r = .57$, Vigoda-Gadot & Meisler, 2010) and self-monitoring ($r = .28$, Kisamore et al., 2010; $r = .27$, Semadar et al., 2006). More impressively, Semadar, Robins, and Ferris (2006) demonstrated that when competitively tested with emotional intelligence, self-monitoring, and leadership efficacy, political skill was the most dominant predictor of leadership performance.

Characteristics of the Politically Skilled

Political skill was defined by Ferris and colleagues as "the ability to effectively understand others at work, and to use such knowledge to influence others to act in ways that enhance one's personal and/or organizational objectives" (Ferris et al., 2005, p. 127). Reflecting on this definition, the Political Skill Inventory was developed to measure four aspects of political skill: social astuteness, interpersonal influence, networking ability, and apparent sincerity.

Social astuteness is the extent to which an individual accurately discerns others' motives and understands the forces and dynamics of social situations. Astuteness can best be described as a combination of social perceptiveness, awareness of emotions in others, and understanding of learned social norms and processes. In close complement, the next second dimension of political skill, interpersonal influence, represents the extent to which an individual's interpersonal style draws on his or her social knowledge to act confident, friendly, competent, and therefore induce and influence compliance from others. This conceptually draws on the idea of behavioral flexibility, goal-oriented behavior, and adaptability, and implies that fundamentally influential aspects of an individual's interpersonal style (i.e., warmth, charm, confidence, etc.) are used effectively by politically skilled individuals based on their knowledge of the target or context.

While the first two components are reminiscent of the social perceptiveness and behavioral flexibility dimensions of social intelligence (Ferris, Adams, Kolodinsky, Hochwarter, & Ammeter, 2002; Sternberg, 1997), the latter two are unique to political skill. Networking ability embodies the success with which individuals build relationships with others who have access to resources and information, develop alliances and coalitions, and position themselves in their networks such that they can most effectively use social capital assets. Last, the fourth dimension, apparent sincerity, deals with the extent to which the politically skilled appear genuine, honest, trustworthy, and forthright when influencing others. Appearing genuine can have a dramatic impact on others' acceptance of one's communication and behavior. The four dimensions do not necessarily imply that a politically skilled person is hiding something or engaging in subversion, but merely that he or she is effectively meeting his or her goals through social means. Indeed, it can, for instance, take a great degree of skill to accurately portray oneself or authentically communicate one's message to diverse audiences with divergent interests.

The Political Skill Inventory was developed as a multidimensional measure of political skill. However, subsequent research has not tested the dimensions independently but has used an aggregation of the 18 items. Despite concerns regarding the aggregation of multidimensional constructs, both empirical research and conceptual underpinnings suggest that political skill may be most appropriately measured in this fashion. Ferris and his colleagues (2008) found that the Political Skill Inventory possessed both a four-factor structure and a single higher-order factor; and they concluded that either usage was statistically appropriate. Conceptually, the four dimensions of political skill are not meant to be assessed independently, but are reinforcing skills that may only yield effectiveness when the full range of characteristics is expressed.

By clarifying the nature of political skill, its place in the nomological network of social effectiveness constructs becomes clearer. While political skill shares conceptual space with other social effectiveness constructs, it maintains a fundamental focus on the workplace and work processes, and thus only draws partially from each. To emphasize the importance of the workplace, political skill is defined by work-oriented dimensions such as networking ability and apparent sincerity, in addition to larger more applicable social effectiveness dimensions (i.e., social astuteness, interpersonal influence). Ultimately, political skill is also a learnable and experiential quantity that combines affective and cognitive traits and skills in a comprehensive pattern manifesting in a large variety of behaviors.

Antecedents of Political Skill

Ferris and colleagues (2007, 2008) theorized that several personality characteristics serve as dispositional antecedents to an individual's development of political skill. They suggested that these antecedents could be grouped into four themes. The first of these themes was perceptiveness, which "reflects the ability of individuals to monitor and regulate their own behavior" (Ferris et al., 2007, p. 296), and is believed to be related most strongly to self-monitoring and conscientiousness because of the role both play in focusing externally and understanding social expectations and rules. Perceptiveness was then theoretically related to enhanced social astuteness, interpersonal influence, and networking ability. Empirically these assumptions were supported in that conscientiousness and self-monitoring have been found to strongly correlate with astuteness, influence, and networking in multiple samples (Ferris et al., 2005, 2008).

The next major antecedent theme outlined was control, which describes politically skilled individuals' senses of self-confidence and beliefs in their abilities to control social interactions (Ferris et al., 1999; Perrewé et al., 2004). Control was theorized to consist of high internal locus of control, or beliefs that control over outcomes in one's life are self-determined (Perrewé & Spector, 2002; Spector, 1982), and generalized self-efficacy beliefs that a person can successfully engage in a certain behavior and achieve desired outcomes (Bandura, 1997). Interestingly, while these were conceptually (Ferris et al., 2007) related to interpersonal influence and networking ability, only self-efficacy was empirically predictive of influence (Ferris et al., 2008). However, self-efficacy was also predictive of astuteness and apparent sincerity, which may imply that some degree of overall confidence is necessary for the politically skilled to function in proximal interpersonal interactions (Perrewé et al., 2004).

Moving past control, the politically skilled are also believed to have a base in affability, which is a tendency to be outgoing and socially engaging, and to generate a positive social presence. Extraversion and positive affectivity, both of which involve experiencing positive emotions such as enthusiasm and energetically interacting with their environments (McCrae & John, 1992; Perrewé & Spector, 2002), were conceptualized to predict all three behavior-based dimensions (i.e., interpersonal influence, networking ability, apparent sincerity) since they involve direct interactions with other individuals (Ferris et al., 2007, 2008). Only extraversion predicted influence and sincerity (Ferris et al., 2008) and political skill in general (Liu et al., 2007). This is not too surprising since positive affectivity and extraversion tend to correlate (Perrewé & Spector, 2002), and extraversion is a slightly more diverse construct (e.g., includes components of willpower; Digman, 1990) that would be expected to more strongly relate to political skill, which is also a broad social construct. Last, in continued support of affability, other studies (Ferris et al., 2005; Perrewé et al., 2004) have found trait anxiety and negative affectivity negatively related to political skill.

The fourth theme of political skill is active influence, and it has received the most mixed results and support of the five. Active influence describes politically skilled individuals' tendencies to remain focused on, and engaged in, goal-oriented activities (Ferris et al., 2008). It has been theorized (Ferris et al., 2007, 2008) to be based in action-state orientation (Perrewé & Spector, 2002), proactive personality (Crant, 1995), dominance (Jackson, 1974), and instrumentality/masculinity (Bozionelos, 2001), and to predict interpersonal influence and networking ability. Empirical results, however, only validate a general link between proactive personality and political skill (Liu et al., 2007). While active influence is definitely evident in the actions of the politically skilled, its dispositional sources remain unspecified.

While the first four characteristic themes of political skill are dispositional in nature, a final theme, developmental experiences, is growth related and changeable over time. Mentoring and role modeling are two of the most common means of learning skills within organizations today (Ferris et al., 2007). They provide individuals with the feedback and guidance necessary to accurately assess and improve upon their social awareness and behavioral effectiveness. Empirically, mentoring seems to have the strongest effect on networking ability and apparent sincerity (Ferris et al., 2008). The effects of experience and mentoring on the development of political skill are still mostly unknown and a ripe area for future research in this diverse and multifaceted construct.

Political Skill and Leadership

House and Aditya (1997) explicitly called for the development of a political theory of leadership that married the power and influence aspects of organizing. They suggested that much research has been conducted on constructs (e.g., individual differences, power, influence, political forces, motivation, the effective use of behavioral tactics, and legitimizing political behavior) that recognized the importance of developing this perspective as well as informed it. Recently, some scholars have moved toward this call for a more inclusive political theory by offering initial models articulating how leader and follower political skill impact the interpretation of the leadership context and the execution of leadership behaviors.

Political Theory of Leadership

One of the first major contributions to the integration of political skill and leadership was a conceptual model by Ammeter, Douglas, Gardner, Hochwarter, and Ferris (2002) developed before political skill was validated as an empirical construct. Ammeter et al. (2002) referred to political skill as form of "interpersonal style" and posited that it would enhance the effectiveness with which a leader could convincingly perform political behavior (e.g., symbolic influence, ingratiation, persuasion, impression management, etc.). Like Pfeffer (1981b), Ammeter and colleagues believed that successful management revolved around the effective manipulation of shared meaning by engaging in political behaviors (e.g., rationality, assertiveness, inspirational appeals, ingratiation, consultation, etc.) that reduced ambiguity in work stimuli and guided followers' behaviors and perception of future incidents.

Ammeter and colleagues' model of political leadership highlights both the moderating and mediating effects of political skill on leader and follower outcomes. In particular, leaders' interpersonal style, accurate mental map of the power relations between individuals, interest in engaging in political behavior, and social capital all enhance the likelihood that they will select the appropriate combination of political behaviors to proactively engage in at the appropriate organizational level (e.g., individual, dyadic, network, etc.). This reflects the importance of the social astuteness, networking ability, and interpersonal influence qualities of the politically skilled.

Within the Ammeter et al. model, contextually appropriate political behaviors lead to positive outcomes for the leader (e.g., performance, promotions, power) and follower (e.g., satisfaction, performance) if these behaviors are executed in a convincing and genuine manner. Effective tactic usage is thus enhanced by political skill, more specifically astuteness, influence, and apparent sincerity. Vision promotion (Gardner & Avolio, 1998); exemplification and self-promotion (Jones & Pittman, 1982); and rational persuasion, inspirational appeals, and consultation (Yukl, Kim, & Falbe, 1996; Yukl & Tracey, 1992), are political behaviors that Ammeter and colleagues believe to be especially influential in enhancing leadership effectiveness. Thus, politically skilled leaders are not only astute enough to know which tactics to engage in and when, but they are also able to engage in those tactics in a manner promoting perceptions of authenticity and concern.

Finally, Ammeter and colleagues recognized that successful application of political behavior reinforces the use of those behaviors and over time impacts organizational culture, leaders' positions in the firm (Mintzberg, 1983) and their networks (Brass, 1984, 2001), and leaders' accountability for certain actions. By subtly shaping their organizational functioning and their own images, the successful application of political behavior in turn enhances politically skilled leaders' abilities to enact those behaviors, enhances their understanding of social dynamics, and heightens their propensity for using such behaviors in the future. Ammeter and colleagues laid the groundwork for further development of political skill by recognizing that it acts both as a driver and a facilitator in emergent and ongoing leadership success.

Political Skill and LMX Development

In a comprehensive attempt to explore the link between political skill and leadership, Treadway, Breland, Williams, Wang, and Yang (2008) outlined the means by which leader political skill may enhance the strength of the leader-member relationship at all points in its development via contextual, relational, and partner level effects. First, during the perception phase, politically skilled leaders will be better able to assess the social relationships that make up their political landscapes and thus understand their current and potential relations with their subordinates. Preliminary evidence supports this position in that self-monitors have been found to accurately assess their own (Oh & Kilduff, 2008) and others' social relations and status (Flynn, Reagans, Amanatullah, & Ames, 2006). Since self-monitoring is an antecedent to political skill, politically skilled leaders may excel at identifying the social capital in their own and subordinates' networks, and carefully choosing optimal interaction partners.

During the enactment phase of the exchange relationship, leaders' assessments of their network positions will lead them to engage in political behavior motivated by identity presentation concerns (Kivetz & Tyler, 2007; Tyler & Feldman, 2005). This drive to generate a positive impression and induce positive evaluations from others can be resolved by enhancing the favorability of their image in their followers' eyes (Wayne & Liden, 1995). These political influence behaviors may then lead to enhanced subordinate liking and leader-member exchange quality (Wayne & Ferris, 1990), yet will be more effective to the extent that the behaviors are supported by the organization's climate (Christiansen, Villanova, & Mikulary, 1997) and the leader is politically skilled (Ferris et al., 2007; Harris et al., 2007; Treadway, Ferris et al., 2007). The enactment phase will likely be quickly followed by the interpretation phase where followers determine the extent to which they will reciprocate their leader's affect and interpersonal gestures. Politically skilled followers will be able to accurately discern the sincerity, depth (Dienesch & Liden, 1986), and motives of their leaders' political behaviors, and thus continue or abandon the relationship.

The final phase of the leader-member exchange relationship, the reciprocation phase, is the phase where the leader's behavior combine with their followers' behavior to actually affect follower functioning. Leaders provide their followers with high-quality relationships that may offer loyalty, trust, affect, participation in decision making, autonomy, respect, advantageous treatment, or some combination of those benefits (Dienesch & Liden, 1986; Graen & Uhl-Bien, 1995), which, if perceived as genuine, will enhance followers' perceptions of the quality of their relationship with their leaders. Perceptions of a high-quality relationship will ultimately incur on the part of the subordinate a desire to reciprocate in ways viewed favorably by the leader (Cialdini, 2001; Gouldner, 1960); this drive will lead to enhanced performance (Gerstner & Day, 1997), as well as enhanced political behaviors if the followers is motivated and capable (Treadway et al., 2008).

Politically skilled followers may ultimately enhance their image in the eyes of their superiors, despite their usage of political influence tactics

(Treadway, Ferris et al., 2007). If leaders perceive their followers as prosocial employees (Bolino, 1999; Grant & Mayer, 2009) who contribute to the leaders' well-being, those leaders may then reciprocate in turn by continuing to offer benefits and even potentially granting the follow access to favorable social network benefits (Sparrowe & Liden, 1997; Treadway et al., 2008). In many ways, political skill maximizes the effectiveness of the leader-member exchange for both parties involved. A key insight of Treadway and colleagues' political view of leader-member relations is that there exists a balance of forces between the political skill of the leader and that of the follower: political skill enhances the effectiveness of either in interacting with the other and can lead to greater returns. The balance of power then may shift depending on how much stronger the political skill of the leader or follower is than the other.

Political Skill and Relational Leadership

The traditional leader-member exchange theories follow an entity approach wherein the focus is on the leader or the follower rather than the relationship itself. Uhl-Bien (2006) suggested that distinct from this entity approach was relational leadership which was concerned with the processes through which leader-member relations were constructed. Treadway, Breland, Williams, Williams, and Yang (2007) took a different approach by integrating the entity perspective with a relational one. They describe the impact of the relationship events and relational selves of leaders and followers on one another in terms of social influence, politics, and power, rather than the effects on material and attitudinal outcomes.

With their high level of self-confidence and accepting presence, politically skilled leaders may be more likely to use communication strategies surrounding dominance or equivalence, rather than submission. These methods are generally perceived as more assertive and socially competent when performed by individuals in leadership roles (Burgoon & Dunbar, 2000; Falbe & Yukl, 1992; Kipnis, Schmidt, & Wilkinson, 1980), and typically include the use of influence tactics like rationality, assertiveness, inspirational appeals, or bargaining. Beyond selecting a tactic, politically skilled individuals will also be highly effective in performing those relevant influence tactics in order to elicit desired feelings and thoughts in the minds of followers. These cognitions will not only affect how followers view their leader, but how the followers view themselves (Treadway, Breland, Williams, Williams, & Yang, 2007).

Part of an individual's self-concept, his relational self, is based in his relationships and interactions with meaningful others, and develops through reinforcement of roles and exchange of relational characteristics (Andersen & Chen, 2002; Brewer & Gardner, 1996). Treadway, Breland, and colleagues (2007) asserted that politically skilled leaders will be better able than less politically skilled leaders to elicit feelings of self-concept threat in followers when using hard tactics (e.g., intimidation, assertiveness), and self-concept enhancement when using soft tactics (e.g., ingratiation, inspirational appeals) or rationality. By communicating with followers in believable ways and confidently constructing followers' understanding of any given relational exchange, politically skilled leaders will be able to project personal characteristics on followers and define their role subtly rather than explicitly.

Political Skill and CEO Celebrity

Leader effectiveness operates, at least partially, through the cultivation and leveraging of the leader's reputation (Zinko, Ferris, Blass, & Laird, 2007). From this perspective, Treadway, Adams, Ranft, and Ferris (2009) outlined the role of a CEO's political skill in leveraging his celebrity to create competitive advantage for the company and the CEO by effectively translating that celebrity into reputational capital. In their conceptualization, political skill acts as the initial catalyzing agent that solidifies the situational celebrity status of leaders into an enduring strategic reputational quality, and enhances the likelihood of securing personal and organizational success. In line with a social constructionist perspective, politically skilled leaders have a clearer understanding of the reasons for their celebrity (e.g., social context, parties involved, powerful audience members, etc.) and will then more appropriately select the political behaviors that will elicit attributions of credibility and authenticity from followers (Treadway et al., 2009). Political skill, then, may not only exert immediate effects on a leader's performance, but long-term effects on widespread audiences as well.

Empirical Studies of Political Skill and Leadership

The conceptual models presented above offer eclectic perspectives on the role of political skill in leadership processes. Beyond this theoretical development, a series of empirical investigations have begun to provide much-needed clarification of the mechanisms through which political skill operates within the leadership context. These studies can be broadly classified as addressing political skill as a driver of leader effectiveness, a facilitator of leadership processes, and an aspect of leader-member exchange.

Political Skill as an Antecedent to Leadership Outcomes

A large part of a leader's job consists of directly affecting subordinates and the social work environment; political skill has been found to have direct effects on both leader and subordinate outcomes. Political skill leads to enhanced managerial performance, especially the social astuteness dimension (Ferris et al., 2005), and contributes more to performance than does leadership self-efficacy, emotional intelligence, or self-monitoring as a group (Semadar et al., 2006). The adaptability and social capital of politically skilled leaders also enhances the performance of their teams, beyond the effects of preexisting team empowerment and leader experience (Ahearn, et al. 2004). Much of the success of political skill in predicting leader and team performance beyond other constructs likely has to do with the goal- and achievement-oriented mindset of the politically skilled, tied with their ability to successfully fulfill those motives (Semadar et al., 2006; Treadway, Hochwarter, Kacmar, & Ferris, 2005). By tapping into a person's ability as well as his will to influence others, political skill provides a more comprehensive view of social influence effectiveness than most dispositional or leadership constructs alone.

Subordinates typically prefer to have powerful and skilled leaders; political skill is one means by which leaders can send the appropriate signals to others that will help them optimize their reputations (Ferris, Blass, Douglas, Kolodinsky, & Treadway, 2003) and exhibit a wide range of behaviors that would be deemed effective by subordinates (Hooijberg, 1996; Zaccaro, Gilbert, Thor, & Mumford, 1991). While all aspects are likely important, empirical evidence suggests that the higher a team believes to be the networking ability of their leaders, the more effective they rate those leaders, even after considering the effects of demographics and general social skill (Douglas & Ammeter, 2004). This may be in large part because networking is one of the most visible leader actions, and perception of networking seems to vary within the group between members more so than does interpersonal influence, which is more ubiquitous among all specifically managers (i.e., contains across-team variation).

Beyond image benefits in the eyes of followers, developing resource-sharing relationships, and coordinating with others is also essential for leaders to develop their social capital. By building alliances, partnerships, coalitions, and obtaining superior network positions (e.g., central, access to diverse information), leaders are able to provide opportunities and resources to their followers, and thus enhance their and their teams' effectiveness (Ahearn et al., 2004; Brass, 2001; House, 1995). The networking ability of politically skilled individuals may help them obtain central positions with many different means to access information, thereby reducing their dependency on others, as well as control over information that flows between unconnected social groups within the organization. Popularity and bridging is then leveraged to enhance the success of a leader's team or personal efforts (Balkundi & Harrison, 2006; Friedkin & Slater, 1994; Mehra, Kilduff, & Brass, 2001) and heighten others' perceptions of that person as a leader (Mullen & Salas, 1991).

Social capital, in general, is the sum of resources embedded in and available for activation through an individual's network of relationships (Nahapiet & Ghoshal, 1998). Cognitive resources, such as shared representations or unique information; and relational resources, such as trust or incurred obligations, may be leveraged to facilitate the effectiveness of individuals, yet are contingent on the structural dimensions (e.g., density, connectivity, centrality) of individuals' networks (Balkundi & Kilduff, 2006; Nahapiet & Ghoshal, 1998). Structurally, an individual's social network will tend toward one of two formations: (1) closure (Coleman, 1988), which is characterized by strong ties that are redundant among the same people and offer benefits such as cohesion or internal efficiency; and (2) diversity (Burt, 1992), wherein individuals maintain ties between resource-rich segments of their network that provide unique non-redundant information. Since closure and diversity can both bring unique benefits to leaders through their social network, the best leaders typically maintain a balance of the two (Balkundi & Kilduff, 2006).

Tight-knit cohesive networks help leaders generate and maintain relational benefits like trust (Coleman, 1988; Granovetter, 1973) or the capacity to communicate rich information with ease (Hansen, 1999; Levin & Cross, 2004) through shared jargon and understanding, and even foster strong team performance once strong their social bonds have matured (Soda, Usai, & Zaheer, 2004). Diverse networks, however, offer the benefit of unique information (Granovetter, 1973) unobtainable by subordinates themselves, as well as opportunities to control the flow of resources in a larger social network (e.g., the organization as a whole) and enhanced team performance (Balkundi & Harrison, 2006; Mehra et al., 2001; Soda et al., 2004). Leaders benefit from diversity in their network to the extent that they bridge structural holes between powerful cliques (e.g., the dominant coalition, high-performing teams in other departments, etc.), which exist when contacts from those cliques are not connected to one another in any way that could bypass the leader (Burt, 1992). Leaders who optimize the viability and effectiveness of their subordinates by balancing closure with diversity, will be among the most effective when they ultimately embed themselves and their subordinates in strategically important (e.g., visible, powerful) networks in their organization (Balkundi & Harrison, 2006; Brass, 1984; Uzzi, 1996).

Networking, in combination with the aforementioned astuteness effect (Ferris et al., 2005), may in large part lead to leadership success because of the direct effects they have on subordinate's views of the organizations as well. As primary representatives of their organization as a whole, the actions and perceived motives of leaders have a large impact on how subordinates perceive the processes of, and events within, their organization (Eisenberger, Huntington, Huntington, & Sowa, 1986; Rhoades & Eisenberger, 2002). Politically skilled leaders may then enhance subordinate loyalty by appearing to act in ways that are wholly supportive of the subordinate's well-being, and leveraging their social skill and capital to treat subordinates fairly and grant them more resources on the job (Ferris et al., 2005, 2007; Treadway, et al., 2004).

The importance of managers as representatives of the organization was demonstrated empirically, where leader political skill directly enhanced perceptions of organizational support, which in turn enhanced trust, reduced opinions of cynicism toward the organization, and enhanced job satisfaction (Treadway et al., 2004). Reduced cynicism and enhanced satisfaction both then led to greater organizational commitment among subordinates. Thus, empirical evidence demonstrates that political skill in total allows leaders not only to coordinate resources and heighten the effectiveness of their teams, but also grants them the ability to influence subordinates' sentiments and social cognitions in ways that support the leader and, through them, the organization for which the leader stands.

Political Skill as a Facilitating Ability

The politically skilled are successful because they are able to perceive social information and engage in social influence behaviors in a "manner that inspires trust, confidence, and genuineness, and effectively influences and controls the responses of others" (Ammeter et al., 2002, p. 764). Tapping into the dimensional space that would eventually define political skill, Ammeter and colleagues asserted that political skill allowed socially astute managers to leverage personal and network resources in interpersonal influence interactions in ways that appeared sincere and covered all ulterior motives (Douglas, Ferris, & Perrewé, 2005). Given the many dimensions and aspects that make up political skill, it is not surprising that political skill facilitates the leadership process in multiple ways.

First, as mentioned above, political skill acts as an enabler of political behavior (Ammeter et al., 2002; Ferris et al., 2002; Ferris, Fedor, & King, 1994). Indeed, past research has found that politically skilled individuals are able to ingratiate without appearing ingratiatory (Treadway, Ferris et al., 2007), and receive higher performance ratings when using impression management tactics than those who are not politically skilled (Harris et al., 2007). Moreover, their perceptiveness and welcoming presence lets them excel at communication both with individual subordinates and with the workgroups as a whole (Yammarino & Mumford, 2012). There exists strong support that political skill moderates many relationships between a leader's political influence behaviors and outcomes or perceptions.

Second, social skill and leader style in general have been found to enable the effects of more stable personal qualities such as general mental ability and personality (Ammeter et al., 2002; Hogan & Shelton, 1998). Among workers high in social skill, which was measured by Witt and Ferris (2003) in a way very similar to political skill, conscientiousness more strongly predicted job performance than among those low in social skill (Witt & Ferris, 2003). Similar effects have been found for agreeableness (Blickle et al., 2008) and extraversion (Blickle, Wendel, & Ferris, 2010). Further, social skill has been found to more strongly predict job performance and salary when accompanied by high general mental ability (Ferris, Witt, & Hochwarter,

2001). Thus, social or political skill allows leaders to more successfully integrate with peers and followers, and more appropriately and effectively express their intellectual and personal strengths.

Finally, in addition to impression management and enabling personal characteristics, political skill has been found to help people deal with workplace stressors. The politically skilled derive a sense of self-confidence and personal security from the awareness that they have their ability to deal with threats, a strong network upon which to draw resources, and past success in stressful social situations (Ferris et al., 2005, 2007; Perrewé et al., 2000, 2004). Politically skilled individuals experience lower anxiety, fewer somatic complaints, and less reductions in feelings of personal accomplishment when faced with role stressors (Jawahar, Stone, & Kisamore, 2007; Perrewé et al., 2004, 2005), and also suffer fewer depressive symptoms when in political environments (Brouer, Ferris, Hochwarter, Laird, & Gilmore, 2006). Leaders and managers face challenging social situations every day, and the ability to remain calm and confident under social stress is critical not only for enhancing their functioning, but also to model positive qualities to followers.

Political Skill and the Leader-Follower Relationship

Emerging work accentuates the importance of political skill for enhancing feelings and thoughts via the LMX relationship, as well as the role of followers' political skill in that development. LMX describes the quality of the relationship between a leader and a follower, which has been most popularly conceptualized in terms of trust, respect, and obligation (Graen & Uhl-Bien, 1995), as well as affect, loyalty, and perceived contribution to the relationship (Dienesch & Liden, 1986). LMX has received copious amounts of research and been meta-analytically linked to subordinate job performance, satisfaction with supervisor, job satisfaction overall, organizational commitment, reduced turnover intentions, and reduced role stressors (Gerstner & Day, 1997), as well as subordinate organizational citizenship behavior (Ilies, Nahrgang, & Morgeson, 2007).

Whereas Treadway and his colleagues (2008) have offered a model of political skill and LMX in which the importance of both leader and follower political skill is highlighted, current research on LMX and political skill has focused on the role of follower political skill. For example, political skill has been found to help followers cope with racial dissimilarity in their leader-member exchange relationships (Brouer, Duke, Treadway, & Ferris, 2009), and lead followers to perceive higher levels of subjective career success despite low quality relationships (Breland, Treadway, Duke, & Adams, 2007). When combined with other empirical work on leader political skill, these results lend evidence to the idea that political skill is an important aspect of both the leader and followers' experience of leadership.

Conclusions

The extant research on political skill and leadership is growing rapidly with an influx of models and disconnected studies. Admittedly, the research on political skill to date has consistently positioned the construct in a positive light. That is, political skill has been seen to aid individuals in achieving greater performance and reputation, being a more effective leader, and as a resource to overcome stressful situations. However, in order to fully develop our understanding of political skill in the workplace, researchers must more specifically define the personal and environmental characteristics in which employees utilize their political skill to detrimental effect. Moving forward, we view the answers to several broad questions as offering supplemental and unifying treatments toward developing an overarching theory of political leadership in organizations. Specifically, we wonder what role motivation or political will plays in the activation and implementation of political skill? What impact does political skill have on the selection and execution of counterproductive work behavior? Finally, we question the use of political skill as a selection and development mechanism.

What Role Does Political Will Play in the Activation and Implementation of Political Skill?

Despite an inability to point to any great leader without acknowledging that he or she possessed a superior level of political skill, many academics and practitioners do not like the term "political" and view the construct as being inherently concerned with self-interest and gamesmanship. Even we, as researchers, have had to couch the term "political skill" in the broader idea of social skill in our initial research discussions with companies. Perhaps in light of these challenges, researchers have uniformly positioned political skill as a personal characteristic with only positive qualities for employees and organizations such as higher performance, better relationships, or decreased job stress. Whereas these studies have provided unquestionable depth to our understanding of political skill in the workplace, they have been guilty of accepting the notion that politics is considered inherently negative, and therefore to demonstrate the neutrality of political skill we must show the abundance of positive organizational outcomes that it affects. We suggest that if the functional vs. dysfunctional nature of political skill is to truly be assessed, researchers must engage in research that identifies the combination of motivations and contexts that encourage individuals to engage their political skill in both negative and positive ways.

Inherent in this call is the need to understand the motivation of political actors in organizations. Mintzberg (1983) discussed this idea as "political will," and the popular press routinely references political will in discussions of governmental initiatives, but, until recently no comprehensive treatment of political will in organizations existed and across disciplines the definition of political will was shifting and incomplete. Treadway (2012) noted these concerns and offered both a definition and multidimensional conceptualization of the construct that, when coupled with Mintzberg's notion of the interaction of political will and political skill, may serve as a basis for envisioning how political skill may accentuate both cooperative and detrimental behaviors in organizations.

Treadway (2012) expanded on Mintzberg's notion of political will when he integrated views from sociology and political science to establish a comprehensive definition of political will. He suggested that political represented the "the motivation to engage in strategic, goal-directed behavior that advances the personal agenda and objectives of the actor that inherently involves the risk of relational or reputational capital" (p. 535). His conceptualization suggested that political will was comprised of two sets of competing drives that while resident in each individual, were activated to relative degrees and in specific contexts. Their activation would ultimately predict the likelihood and type of political behavior. In his model, the two competing drives identified were a concern for self versus a concern for others and a focus on a relational or instrumental outcome.

Does Political Skill Impact the Selection and Execution of Counterproductive Work Behavior?

Using Treadway's (2012) conceptualization, it becomes obvious that political skill, when activated by selfish motivations can yield behaviors that are potentially detrimental to the organization and other coworkers. This view maps onto the standard definition provided by Kacmar and Baron (1999) that describes political behavior as being motivated by self-interest and may or may not be injurious to the organization or others. However, in agreement with Treadway (2012), we argue that while individuals may have a general tendency to more or less self-interested, across situations they may engage their resources to aid others, to maintain relationships, or simply achieve individual or personal objectives. Thus, we begin to see how acting politically is the keystone for achieving not only a leader's goals, but in leading social changes that benefit the common good. As such we point to two research streams that are early in their development that address the use of political skill for the personal gain and for public good.

The first research stream looks at not just selfish employees, but abusive employees. Using Crick and Dodge's (1994) social information processing framework of childhood abuse, Treadway et al. (2013) argued that politically skilled individuals will engage their political skill and aggressive reputation to promote their own work performance. Similar ideas regarding political skill and abuse come from the work of Kisamore and her colleagues (Kisamore et al., 2010). In their work they found that when highly politically skilled employees were confronted with conflict, they were more likely to engage in abusive behavior. While Kisamore et al.'s study is intriguing, they did not offer theory regarding why the politically skilled would retaliate rather than engage in other more constructive reactions. It could be argued that an unmeasured variable such as political will or ego threat was at the core of explaining these reactions rather than political skill. Thus, it is evident that a fully developed understanding of the nature of political skill and leadership requires not just a consideration of political skill, but a much more concerted effort to understand the motivations that encourage politically skilled leaders to use their abilities in counterproductive ways. In doing so, researchers can begin to explain the leadership dynamics inherent in areas such as unethical behavior and abusive supervision.

Political Skill as a Selection and Developmental Area?

A highly unique and intriguing research endeavor is the ongoing analysis of the political skill of politicians in the United Kingdom. Silvester and Dykes

(2005) acknowledged the importance of developing the political skills of candidates and sought to determine what the manifestation of those skills were. While not directly addressing political skill, their work highlights the mechanisms through which candidates achieve successful outcomes. They found that a candidate's critical thinking skills and public speaking competency were related to their election performance. Obviously these results have important implications for political skill researchers. To the degree that success as a political leader is dependent on these critical thinking skills, then researchers must begin to assess how politically skilled individuals process social information. Implicitly, researchers have suggested that politically skilled individuals are better capable of accurately assessing their environment, yet this may be because they process more information, appropriate information, or that their mental maps are efficient. Similarly, we know very little about the selection or delivery of influence behavior or strategy as it relates to the politically skilled.

The fruition of these research projects naturally lends itself to programmatic research that assesses and develops political skill. Indeed, a consistent theme within the political skill research is the idea that political skill can, on the margins, be developed (e.g., Ferris, Davidson, & Perrewé, 2005; Ferris et al., 2002; Harvey & Novicevic, 2004). Despite these arguments, research has not yet substantiated these claims. However, the work of Silvester on selecting political candidates and the work of Ferris et al. (2008) suggests that political skill may be an appropriate aspect of selection decisions due to its relation with in-role job performance. If that is the case, then developing the political skill of leaders has a great deal of utility for organizations. Despite an abundance of emotional intelligence training in organizations today there is disturbingly little, if any, political skill training available for current or future leaders. This is more problematic given political skill's demonstrated impact on leader performance.

Thus, we suggest that work by Silvester and Dykes (2005) on the selection of political leaders be expanded to encompass the role of socialization and training on leader's political proficiency. Ferris, Perrewé, and Davidson (2005) suggested that political skill could be developed through self-awareness and role play exercises, but we suggest that additional research is needed to identify the most appropriate techniques for improving the political skill of leaders. This research stream should not focus simply on improving aggregate scores of political skill through training, but must direct itself toward uncovering the mechanisms through which politically skilled leaders operate. Once these critical pathways are identified can we begin to craft training and mentoring programs that will lead to both the development and more effective utilization of leader political skill.

Summary

Despite the increasing awareness that political considerations, such as political skill and will, are critical in the leadership process, we still echo House and Aditya's (1997) call for a broader theory of political leadership. Certainly the ongoing work of Ferris, Treadway, and their colleagues is creating a mosaic of studies that are providing important insights into the phenomenon. Yet despite conceptual models and numerous empirical investigations, no dominant perspective of political skill and leadership has emerged. Perhaps it will simply take time for one of these viewpoints to take hold in the literature. Or perhaps the complexities inherent in the political organization are too voluminous to be succinctly explained by one theory, and as such scholars will be forced to continue cobbling together theories and anecdotes to explain the phenomenon. While we recognize this as a possibility, we feel that larger theory of political leadership is on the horizon, and efforts to such end are most critical to understanding political skill and leadership.

References

Ahearn, K. K., Ferris, G. R., Hochwarter, W. A., Douglas, C., & Ammeter, A. P. (2004). Leader political skill and team performance. *Journal of Management, 30*, 309–327.

Ammeter, A., Douglas, C., Gardner, W., Hochwarter, W., & Ferris, G. (2002). Toward a political theory of leadership. *The Leadership Quarterly, 13*, 751–796.

Andersen, S., & Chen, S. (2002). The relational self: An interpersonal social-cognitive theory. *Psychological Review, 4*, 619–645.

Ashkanasy, N. M., & Daus, C. S. (2005). Rumors of the death of emotional intelligence in organizational behavior are vastly exaggerated. *Journal of Organizational Behavior, 26*, 441–452.

Balkundi, P., & Harrison, D. A. (2006). Ties, leaders, and time in teams: Strong inference about network structure's effects on team viability and performance. *Academy of Management Journal, 49*, 49–68.

Balkundi, P., & Kilduff, M. (2006). The ties that lead: A social network approach to leadership. *Leadership Quarterly, 17*, 419–439.

Bandura, A. (1997). *Self-efficacy: The exercise of control.* New York: Freeman.

Bavelas, A. (1960). Leadership: Man and function. *Administrative Science Quarterly, 4*, 491–498.

Bennis, W. G. (1959). Leadership theory and administrative behavior: The problem of authority. *Administrative Science Quarterly, 4*, 259–301.

Blickle, G., Meurs, J. A., Zettler, I., Solga, J., Noethen, D., Kramer, J., & Ferris, G. R. (2008). Personality, political skill, and job performance. *Journal of Vocational Behavior, 72*, 377–387.

Blickle, G., Wendel, S., & Ferris, G. R. (2010). Political skill as a moderator of personality-job performance relationships in socioanalytic theory: Test of the getting ahead motive in automobile sales. *Journal of Vocational Behavior, 76*, 326–335.

Bolino, M. (1999). Citizenship and impression management: Good soldiers or good actors? *Academy of Management Review, 24*, 82–98.

Bozionelos, N. (2001). The relationship of instrumental and expressive traits with computer anxiety. *Personality and Individual Differences, 31*, 955–974.

Brass, D. J. (1984). Being in the right place: A structural analysis of individual influence in an organization. *Administrative Science Quarterly, 29*, 518–539.

Brass, D. J. (2001). Social capital and organizational leadership. In S. J. Zaccaro & R. J. Klimoski (Eds.), *The nature of organizational leadership: Understanding the performance imperatives confronting today's leaders* (pp. 132–152). San Francisco: Jossey-Bass.

Breland, J. W., Treadway, D. C., Duke, A. B., & Adams, G. L. (2007). The interactive effect of leader-member exchange and political skill on subjective career success. *Journal of Leadership and Organizational Studies, 13*, 1–14.

Brewer, M. B., & Gardner, W. (1996). Who is this "We"? Levels of collective identity and self representations. *Journal of Personality and Social Psychology, 71*, 83–93.

Brouer, R. L., Duke, A., Treadway, D. C., & Ferris, G. R. (2009). Moderating effect of political skill on the demographic dissimilarity—leader-member exchange quality relationship. *Leadership Quarterly, 20*, 61–69.

Brouer, R. L., Ferris, G. R., Hochwarter, W. A., Laird, M. D., & Gilmore, D. C. (2006). The strain-related reactions to perceptions of organizational politics as a workplace stressor: Political skill as a neutralizer. In E. Vigoda-Gadot & A. Drory (Eds.), *Handbook of organizational politics* (pp. 187–206). Northampton, MA: Edward Elgar Publishing, Inc.

Burgoon, J. K., & Dunbar, N. E. (2000). An integrationist perspective on dominance-submission: Interpersonal dominance as a dynamic, situationally contingent social skill. *Communication Monographs, 67*, 96–121.

Burke, P. (1966). Authority relations and disruptive behavior in small discussion groups. *Sociometry, 29*, 237–250.

Burt, R. (1992). *Structural holes: The social structure of competition*. Cambridge, MA: Harvard University Press.

Caldwell, D. F., & O'Reilly, C. A. (1982). Boundary spanning and individual performance: The impact of self-monitoring. *Journal of Applied Psychology, 67*, 124–127.

Cheng, C. M., & Chartrand, T. L. (2003). Self-monitoring without awareness: Using mimicry as a nonconscious affiliation strategy. *Journal of Personality and Social Psychology, 85*, 1170–1179.

Christiansen, N., Villanova, P., & Mikulay, S. (1997). Political influence compatibility: Fitting the person to climate. *Journal of Organizational Behavior, 18*, 709–730.

Cialdini, R. B. (2001). *Influence: Science and practice* (5th ed.). Boston: Pearson.

Cockburn, P. (2007, September 10). Two big skeletons in Petraeus' closet. *CounterPunch*. Retrieved from http://www.counterpunch.org.

Coleman, J. S. (1988). Social capital in the creation of human capital. *American Journal of Sociology, 94*, S95–S120.

Crant, J. M. (1995). The proactive personality scale and objective job performance among real estate agents. *Journal of Applied Psychology, 80*, 532–537.

Crick, N. R. & Dodge, K. A. (1994). A review and reformulation of social information-processing mechanisms in children's social adjustment. *Psychological Bulletin, 115*, 74–101.

Cyert, R. M., & March, J. G. (1963). *A behavioral theory of the firm*. Englewood Cliffs, NJ: Prentice Hall.

Day, D. V., Schleicher, D. J., Unckless, A. L., & Hiller, N. J. (2002). Self-monitoring personality at work: A meta-analytic investigation of construct validity. *Journal of Applied Psychology, 87*, 390–401.

Digman, J. M. (1990). Personality Structure: Emergence of the five-factor model. *Annual Review of Psychology, 41*, 417–440.

Dienesch, R. M., & Liden, R. C. (1986). Leader-member exchange model of leadership: A critique and further development. *Academy of Management Review, 11*, 618–634.

Douglas, C., & Ammeter, A. P. (2004). An examination of leader political skill and its effects on ratings of leader effectiveness. *Leadership Quarterly, 15*, 537–550.

Douglas, C., Ferris, G. R., & Perrewé, P. L. (2005). Leader political skill and authentic leadership. In W. L. Gardner, B. J. Avolio, & F. O. Walumbwa (Eds.), *Authentic leadership theory and practice: Origins, effects, and development* (Vol. 3, pp. 139–154 of the *Monographs in Leadership Management* series, J. G. Hunt, senior editor). Oxford, UK: Elsevier Science.

Eisenberger, R., Huntington, R., Huntington, S., & Sowa, D. (1986). Perceived organizational support. *Journal of Applied Psychology, 71*, 500–507.

Falbe, C. M., & Yukl, G. (1992). Consequences for managers of using single influence tactics and combinations of tactics. *Academy of Management Journal, 35*, 638–653.

Ferris, G. R., Adams, G., Kolodinsky, R. W., Hochwarter, W. A., & Ammeter, A. P. (2002). Perceptions of organizational politics: Theory and research directions. In F. J. Yammarino & F. Dansereau (Eds.), *Research in multi-level issues, Volume 1: The many faces of multi-level issues* (pp. 179–254). Oxford, UK: JAI Press/Elsevier Science.

Ferris, G. R., Anthony, W. P., Kolodinsky, R. W., Gilmore, D. C., & Harvey, M. G. (2002). Development of political skill. In C. Wankel & D. DeFillippi (Eds.), *Rethinking management education for the 21st century* (pp. 3–25). Charlotte, NC: Information Age Publishing.

Ferris, G. R., Berkson, H. M., Kaplan, D. M., Gilmore, D. C., Buckley, M. R., Hochwarter, W. A., & Witt, L. A. (1999). *Development and initial validation of the political skill inventory*. Paper presented at the Academy of Management, 59th Annual National Meeting, Chicago.

Ferris, G. R., Blass, R., Douglas, C., Kolodinsky, R. W., & Treadway, D. C. (2003). Personal reputation in organizations. In J. Greenberg (Ed.), *Organizational behavior: The state of the science* (2nd ed., pp. 211–246). Mahwah, NJ: Lawrence Erlbaum.

Ferris, G. R., Blickle, G., Schneider, P. B., Kramer, J., Zettler, I., Solga, J., Noethen, D., & Meurs, J. A. (2008). Political skill construct and criterion-related validation: A two-study investigation. *Journal of Managerial Psychology, 23*, 744–771.

Ferris, G. R., Davidson, S. L., & Perrewé, P. L. (2005). *Political skill at work: Impact on work effectiveness*. Mountain View, CA: Davies-Black Publishing.

Ferris, G. R., Fedor, D. B., & King, T. R. (1994). A political conceptualization of managerial behavior. *Human Resource Management Review, 4*, 1–34.

Ferris, G. R., Kolodinsky, R. W., Hochwarter, W. A., & Frink, D. D. (2001). *Conceptualization, measurement, and validation of the political skill construct.* Paper presented at the Academy of Management, 61st Annual National Meeting, Washington, DC.

Ferris, G. R., Perrewé, P. L., Anthony, W. P., & Gilmore, D. C. (2000). Political skill at work. *Organizational Dynamics, 28,* 25–37.

Ferris, G. R., Perrewé, P. L., & Douglas, C. (2002). Social effectiveness in organizations: Construct validity and research directions. *Journal of Leadership and Organizational Studies, 9,* 49–63.

Ferris, G. R., Treadway, D. C., Brouer, R. L., & Munyon, T. P. (2012). Political skill in the organizational sciences. In G. R. Ferris & D. C. Treadway (Eds.), *Politics in organizations: Theory and research considerations* (pp. 487–529). New York: Routledge/Taylor and Francis.

Ferris, G. R., Treadway, D. C., Kolodinsky, R. W., Hochwarter, W. A., Kacmar, C. J., Douglas, C., & Frink, D. D. (2005). Development and validation of the political skill inventory. *Journal of Management, 31,* 126–152.

Ferris, G. R., Treadway, D. C., Perrewé, P. L, Brouer, R., Douglas, C., & Lux, S. (2007). Political skill in organizations. *Journal of Management, 33,* 290–320.

Ferris, G. R., Witt, L. A., & Hochwarter, W. A. (2001). Interaction of social skill and general mental ability on job performance and salary. *Journal of Applied Psychology, 86,* 1075–1082.

Flynn, F. J., Reagans, R. E., Amanatullah, E. T., & Ames, D. R. (2006). Helping one's way to the top: Self-monitors achieve status by helping others and knowing who helps whom. *Journal of Personality and Social Psychology, 91,* 1123–1137.

French, J. R. P. & Raven, B. H. (1959). The bases of social power. In D. Cartwright (Ed.), *Studies in social power.* Ann Arbor: University of Michigan Press.

Friedkin, N. E., & Slater, M. R. (1994). School leadership and performance: A social network approach. *Sociology of Education, 67,* 139–157.

Gardner, W. L., & Avolio, B. J. (1998). The charismatic relationship: A dramaturgical perspective. *Academy of Management Review, 23,* 32–58.

Gerstner, C. R., & Day, D. V. (1997). Meta-analytic review of leader-member exchange theory: Correlates and construct issues. *Journal of Applied Psychology, 82,* 827–844.

Gioia, D. A., & Chittipeddi, K. (1991). Sensemaking and sensegiving in strategic change initiation. *Strategic Management Journal, 12,* 433–448.

Gouldner, A. (1960). The norm of reciprocity: A preliminary statement. *American Sociological Review, 25,* 161–178.

Graen, G. B., & Uhl-Bien, M. (1995). Relationship-based approach to leadership: Development of leader-member exchange (LMX) theory of leadership over 25 years: Applying a multi-level multi-domain perspective. *Leadership Quarterly, 6,* 219–247.

Granovetter, M. S. (1973). The strength of weak ties. *American Journal of Sociology, 78,* 1360–1380.

Grant, A. M., & Mayer, D. M. (2009). Good soldiers and good actors: Prosocial and impression management motives as interactive predictors of affiliative citizenship behaviors. *Journal of Applied Psychology, 94,* 900–912.

Hansen, M. T. (1999). The search-transfer problem: The role of weak ties in sharing knowledge across organizational subunits. *Administrative Science Quarterly, 44,* 82–111.

Harris, K. J., Kacmar, K. M., Zivnuska, S., & Shaw, J. D. (2007). The impact of political skill on impression management effectiveness. *Journal of Applied Psychology, 92,* 278–285.

Harvey, M., & Novicevic, M. M. (2004). The development of political skill and political capital by global leaders through global assignments. *International Journal of Human Resource Management, 15,* 1173–1188.

Hastings, M. (2010, June 22). The runaway general. *Rolling Stone.* Retrieved from http://www.rollingstone.com.

Hochwarter, W. A., Ferris, G. R., Gavin, M. B., Perrewé, P. L., Hall, A. T., & Frink, D. D. (2007). Political skill as neutralizer of felt accountability-job tension effects on job performance ratings: A longitudinal investigation. *Organizational Behavior and Human Decision Processes, 102,* 226–239.

Hogan, R., & Shelton, D. (1998). A socioanalytic perspective on job performance. *Human Performance, 11,* 129–144.

Hollander, E. P., & Julian, J. W. (1969). Contemporary trends in the analysis of leadership processes. *Psychological Bulletin, 71,* 387–397.

Hooijberg, R. (1996). A multidimensional approach toward leadership: An extension of the concept of behavioral complexity. *Human Relations, 49,* 917–946.

House, R. J. (1995). Leadership in the twenty-first century. In A. Howard (Ed.), *The changing nature of work* (pp. 411–450). San Francisco: Jossey–Bass.

House, R. J., & Aditya, R. N. (1997). The social scientific study of leadership: quo vadis? *Journal of Management, 23,* 409–473.

Ilies, R., Nahrgang, J. D., & Morgeson, F. P. (2007). Leader-member exchange and citizenship behaviors: A meta-analysis. *Journal of Applied Psychology, 92,* 269–277.

Jackson, D. N. (1974). *Manual for the personality research form.* Goshen, NY: Research Psychology Press.

Jaffe, G. (2010, June 24). McChrystal's lack of political skills led to downfall. *The Washington Post.* Retrieved from http://www.washingtonpost.com

Jawahar, I. M., Stone, T. H., & Kisamore, J. L. (2007). Role conflict and burnout: The direct and moderating effects of political skill and perceived organizational support on burnout dimensions. *International Journal of Stress Management, 14,* 142–159.

Jones, E. E. (1990). *Interpersonal perception.* New York: W. H. Freeman.

Jones, E. E., & Pittman, T. S. (1982). Toward a general theory of strategic self presentation. In J. Suls (Ed.), *Psychological perspectives on the self* (pp. 231–262). Hillsdale, NJ: Lawrence Erlbaum.

Joseph, D. L., & Newman, D. A. (2010). Emotional intelligence: An integrative meta-analysis and cascading model. *Journal of Applied Psychology, 95,* 54–78.

Kacmar, K. M., & Baron, R. A. (1999). Organizational politics: The state of the field, links to related processes, and an agenda for future research. In G. R. Ferris (Ed.), *Research in personnel and human resources management* (Vol. 17, pp. 1–39). Stamford, CT: JAI Press.

Kilduff, M., & Day, D. V. (1994). Do chameleons get ahead? The effects of self-monitoring on managerial careers. *Academy of Management Journal, 37,* 1047–1060.

Kipnis, D., Schmidt, S. & Wilkinson, I. (1980). Intraorganizational influence tactics: Exploration of getting one's way. *Journal of Applied Psychology, 65,* 440–452.

Kisamore, J. L., Jawahar, I. M., Liguori, E. W., Mharapara, T. L., & Stone, T. H. (2010). Conflict and abusive workplace

behaviors: The moderating effects of social competencies. *Career Development International, 15*, 583–600.
Kivetz, Y. & Tyler, T. (2007). Tomorrow I'll be me: The effect of time perspective on the activation of idealistic versus pragmatic selves. *Organizational Behavior and Human Decision Processes, 102*, 193–211.
Kotter, J. P. (1985). *Power and influence: Beyond formal authority*. New York: The Free Press.
Levin, D. Z., & Cross, R. (2004). The strength of weak ties you can trust: The mediating role of trust in effective knowledge transfer. *Management Science, 50*, 1477–1490.
Lichtenstein, B., Uhl-Bien, M., Marion, R., Seers, A., Orton, J. D., & Schreiber, C. (2006). Complexity leadership theory: An interactive perspective on leading in complex adaptive systems. *Emergence: Complexity and Organization, 8*, 2–12.
Liu, Y., Ferris, G. R., Zinko, R., Perrewé, P. L., Weitz, B., & Xu, J. (2007). Dispositional antecedents and outcomes of political skill in organizations: A four-study investigation with convergence. *Journal of Vocational Behavior, 71*, 146–165.
Maitlis, S. (2005). The social processes of organizational sensemaking. *Academy of Management Journal, 48*, 21–49.
March, J. G. (1962). The business firm as a political coalition. *Journal of Politics, 24*, 662–678.
Marlowe, H. A. (1986). Social intelligence: Evidence for multidimensionality and construct independence. *Journal of Educational Psychology, 78*, 52–58.
Mayer, J., & Salovey, P. (1997). What is emotional intelligence? In P. Salovey & D. Sluyter (Eds.), *Emotional development and emotional intelligence: Implication for educators* (pp. 3–31). New York: Basic Books.
Mayer, J., Salovey, P., & Caruso, D. (2008). Emotional intelligence: New ability or eclectic traits? *American Psychologist, 63*, 503–517.
McCrae, R. R. & John, O. P. (1992). An introduction to the five-factor model and its applications. *Journal of Personality, 60*, 176–215.
Mehra, A., Kilduff, M., & Brass, D. J. (2001). The social networks of high and low self-monitors: Implications for workplace performance. *Administrative Science Quarterly, 46*, 121–146.
Meindl, J. R., Ehrlich, S. B., & Dukerich, J. M. (1985). The romance of leadership. *Administrative Science Quarterly, 30*, 78–102.
Mintzberg, H. (1983). *Power in and around organizations*. Englewood Cliffs, NJ: Prentice-Hall.
Mintzberg, H. (1985). The organization as political arena. *Journal of Management Studies, 22*, 133–154.
Mullen, B., & Salas, C. J. (1991). Effects of communication network structure: Components of positional centrality. *Social Networks, 13*, 169–185.
Nahapiet, J., & Ghoshal, S. (1998). Social capital, intellectual capital, and the organizational advantage. *Academy of Management Review, 23*, 242–266.
Oh, H., & Kilduff, M. (2008). The ripple effect of personality on social structure: Self-monitoring origins of network brokerage. *Journal of Applied Psychology, 93*, 1155–1164.
Perrewé, P. L., Ferris, G. R., Frink, D. D., & Anthony, W. P. (2000). Political skill: An antidote for workplace stressors. *Academy of Management Executive, 14*, 115–123.
Perrewé, P. L., & Spector, P. E. (2002). Personality research in the organizational sciences. In Ferris, G. R. (Ed.), *Research in personnel and human resources management* (Vol. 21, pp. 1–64). Oxford, UK: JAI Press, Elsevier Science, Inc.
Perrewé, P. L., Zellars, K. L., Ferris, G. R., Rossi, A. M., Kacmar, C. J., & Ralston, D. A. (2004). Neutralizing job stressors: Political skill as an antidote to the dysfunctional consequences of role conflict. *Academy of Management Journal, 47*, 141–152.
Perrewé, P. L., Zellars, K. L., Rossi, A. M., Ferris, G. R., Kacmar, C. J., Liu, Y., Zinko, R., & Hochwarter, W. A. (2005). Political skill: An antidote in the role overload-strain relationship. *Journal of Occupational Health Psychology, 10*, 239–250.
Pfeffer, J. (1981a). *Power in organizations*. Boston: Pitman.
Pfeffer, J. (1981b). Management as symbolic action: The creation and maintenance of organizational paradigms. In L. L. Cummings & B. M. Staw (Eds.), *Research in organizational behavior* (Vol. 3, pp. 1–52). Greenwich, CT: JAI Press.
Pfeffer, J. (1992). *Managing with power: Politics and influence in organizations*. Boston: Harvard Business School Press.
Pfeffer, J. (2010). Power play. *Harvard Business Review, 88*, 84–92.
Rhoades, L., & Eisenberger, R. (2002). Perceived organization support: A review of the literature. *Journal of Applied Psychology, 87*, 698–714.
Roberts, R. D., Zeidner, M., & Matthews, G. (2001). Does emotional intelligence meet traditional standards for an intelligence? Some new data and conclusions. *Emotion, 1*, 196–231.
Rubin, A. J., & Filkins, D. (2010, June 23). Petraeus is now taking control of a "tougher fight." *The New York Times*. Retrieved from http://www.nytimes.com.
Semadar, A., Robins, G., & Ferris, G. R. (2006). Comparing the validity of multiple social effectiveness constructs in the prediction of managerial job performance. *Journal of Organizational Behaviour, 27*, 443–461.
Silvester, J., & Dykes, C. (2005). Selecting political candidates: A longitudinal study of assessment centre performance and political success in the 2005 UK General Election. *Journal of Occupational and Organizational Psychology, 80*, 11–25.
Simon, H. A. (1959). Theories of decision-making in economics and behavioral science. *American Economic Review, 49*, 253–283.
Smircich, L., & Morgan, G. (1982). Leadership: The management of meaning. *Journal of Applied Behavioral Science, 18*, 257–273.
Snyder, M. (1974). Self-monitoring of expressive behavior. *Journal of Personality and Social Psychology, 30*, 526–537.
Snyder, M. (1979). Self-monitoring processes. In L. Berkowitz (Ed.), *Advances in experimental social psychology* (Vol. 12, pp. 85–128). New York: Academic Press.
Soda, G., Usai, A., & Zaheer, A. (2004). Network memory: The influence of past and current networks on performance. *Academy of Management Journal, 47*, 893–906.
Sparrowe, R., & Liden, R. (1997). Process and structure in leader-member exchange. *Academy of Management Review, 22*, 522–552.
Spector, P. E. (1982). Behavior in organizations as a function of employee's locus of control. *Psychological Bulletin, 91*, 482–497.
Sternberg, R. J. (1997). Managerial intelligence: Why IQ isn't enough. *Journal of Management, 23*, 475–493.
Stogdill, R. M. (1950). Leadership, membership, and organization. *Psychological Bulletin, 47*, 1–14.
Treadway, D. C. (2012). Political will in organizations. In G. R. Ferris & D. C. Treadway (Eds.), *Political in organizations: Theory and*

research considerations (pp. 531–556). New York: Routledge/Taylor and Francis.

Treadway, D. C., Adams, G. L., Ranft, A. L., & Ferris, G. R. (2009). A meso-level conceptualization of CEO celebrity effectiveness. *Leadership Quarterly, 20*, 554–570.

Treadway, D. C., Breland, J. W., Williams, L. A., Wang, L., & Yang, J. (2008). The role of politics in the development of LMX relationships: A multi-level approach. In G. B. Graen & J. A. Graen (Eds.), *Knowledge-driven corporation: Complex creative destruction* (pp. 145–180). Charlotte, NC: Information Age Publishing.

Treadway, D. C., Breland, J. W., Williams, L. A., Williams, L. V., & Yang, J. (2007). Political skill, relational control, and the self in relational leadership processes. In M. Uhl-Bien (Ed.), *Leadership frontiers series*. Charlotte, NC: Information Age Publishing.

Treadway, D. C., Ferris, G. R., Duke, A. B., Adams, G. L., & Thatcher, J. B. (2007). The moderating role of subordinate political skill on supervisors' impressions of subordinate ingratiation and ratings of subordinate interpersonal facilitation. *Journal of Applied Psychology, 92*, 848–855.

Treadway, D. C., Hochwarter, W. A., Ferris, G. R., Kacmar, C. J., Douglas, C., Ammeter, A. P., & Buckley, M. R. (2004). Leader political skill and employee reactions. *Leadership Quarterly, 15*, 493–515.

Treadway, D. C., Hochwarter, W. A., Kacmar, C. J., & Ferris, G. R. (2005). Political will, political skill, and political behavior. *Journal of Organizational Behavior, 26*, 229–245.

Treadway, D. C., Shaughnessy, B. A., Breland, J. W., Yang, J., Reeves, M., & Roberts, M. (2013). Political skill and the job performance of bullies. *Journal of Managerial Psychology, 28*, 273–289.

Tyler, J., & Feldman, R. (2005). Deflecting threat to one's image: Dissembling personal information as a self-presentation strategy. *Basic and Applied Social Psychology, 27*, 371–378.

Uhl-Bien, M. (2006). Relational leadership theory: Exploring the social processes of leadership and organizing. *Leadership Quarterly, 17*, 654–676.

Uzzi, B. (1996). The sources and consequences of embeddedness for the economic performance of organizations: The network effect. *American Sociological Review, 61*, 674–698.

Van Rooy, D. L., & Viswesvaran, C. (2004). Emotional intelligence: A meta-analytic investigation of predictive validity and nomological net. *Journal of Vocational Behavior, 65*, 71–95.

Vigoda-Gadot, E., & Meisler, G. (2010). Emotions in management and the management of emotions: The impact of emotional intelligence and organizational politics on public sector employees. *Public Administration Review, 70*, 72–86.

Wayne, S., & Ferris, G. (1990). Influence tactics, affect, and exchange quality in supervisor-subordinate interactions. A laboratory experiment and field study. *Journal of Applied Psychology, 75*, 487–499.

Wayne, S., & Liden, R. (1995). A longitudinal study on the effects of impression management on performance ratings. *Academy of Management Journal, 38*, 232–260.

Weick, K. E. (1995). *Sensemaking in organizations.* Thousand Oaks, CA: Sage Publications, Inc.

Witt, L. A., & Ferris, G. R. (2003). Social skill as moderator of the conscientiousness–performance relationship: Convergent evidence across four studies. *Journal of Applied Psychology, 88*, 809–820.

Yammarino, F. J., & Mumford, M. D. (2012). Leadership and organizational politics: A multi-level review and framework for pragmatic deals. In G. R. Ferris & D. C. Treadway, *Politics in organizations: Theory and research considerations* (pp. 323–354). New York: Routledge/Taylor and Francis.

Yukl, G. (1998). *Leadership in organizations* (4th ed.). Englewood Cliffs, NJ: Prentice-Hall.

Yukl, G., Kim, H., & Falbe, C. M. (1996). Antecedents of influence outcomes. *Journal of Applied Psychology, 81*, 309–317.

Yukl, G., & Tracey, J. B. (1992). Consequences of influence tactics used with subordinates, peers, and the boss. *Journal of Applied Psychology, 77*, 525–535.

Zaccaro, S. J., Gilbert, J. A., Thor, K. K., & Mumford, M. D. (1991). Leadership and social intelligence: Linking social perceptiveness and behavioral flexibility to leader effectiveness. *Leadership Quarterly, 2*, 317–342.

Zinko, R., Ferris, G. R., Blass, F. R., & Laird, M. D. (2007). Toward a theory of reputation in organizations. In J. J. Martocchio (Ed.), *Research in personnel and human resources management* (Vol. 26, pp. 163–204). Bingley, UK: JAI Press.

CHAPTER

24 Ethical Leadership

Linda K. Treviño *and* Michael E. Brown

Abstract

This chapter reviews the ethical leadership research. It begins with the introduction of the construct and measure and then follows the development of a burgeoning literature to date. Thus far, research has mostly focused on the attitudinal and behavioral outcomes of ethical leadership, but researchers have also begun to investigate antecedents, intervening processes, moderators, and multilevel effects of different levels of leadership. Recommendations for future research are offered.

Key Words: ethical leadership, unethical leadership, hypocritical leadership, ethically neutral leadership, moral person, moral manager, ethics, integrity

Introduction

The ethical dimension of leadership is increasingly being highlighted as essential to the well-being of our organizations and our society. Certainly, when all kinds of organizations find themselves under scrutiny for improper or illegal conduct (from businesses to governments to sports teams to education and religious organizations), fingers quickly point to the ethical failure of leadership, heads often roll, and new leadership is brought in to right the ethically rocky ship. Sometimes it's too late as it was in the case of Arthur Andersen, the long-renowned auditing firm that was associated with the accounting scandals at Enron and was dissolved as a result.

A more recent example is Rupert Murdoch and other leaders of his wide-ranging News Corp media empire. Inquiring minds wanted to know whether top leaders were aware of illegal practices at their tabloid newspaper, including hacking into people's telephones, and whether such practices were widespread and condoned (or simply ignored) in the broader organization. The "News of the World" tabloid at the center of the hacking scandal was shuttered, a number of top leaders resigned, and a British parliamentary investigation labeled Murdoch "unfit to lead" his media empire (euronews.com 5/1/2012). Similarly, investigations into the causes of the US financial crisis were frequently directed at senior leaders who were hauled before congressional committees and questioned at length. Clearly, people perceive that leadership matters when it comes to organizational ethics and, when something goes terribly wrong, we tend to believe that "the buck stops" at the top.

On a more positive note, senior leadership has long been thought to set the ethical "tone at the top" of organizations (Clinard, 1983), providing a moral (not just a technical) foundation for a firm (Barnard, 1938) and creating positive values that undergird and strengthen an organization's culture (Schein, 1985). We can cite legendary CEOs such as James Burke who was at the helm at Johnson & Johnson at the time of the Tylenol cyanide poisoning in Chicago in the 1980s. His decision to recall all Tylenol (despite government and other recommendations not to do so) won him and the company accolades for sticking to the firm's long-standing credo and caring more for customers than for the short-term bottom line. Given the company's recent manufacturing problems and product safety tribulations in the same McNeil Laboratories Division, some may wish that James Burke were back at the helm. More recently, one can think of Bill George who led medical device manufacturer Medtronic for years. George has written about the challenges of being a values-driven CEO (George, 2003) in today's business environment with its intense focus on quarterly profits, and he has taught business ethics at the Harvard Business School. Of course, vaunted ethical leaders are not limited to the United States. Ratan Tata, leader of the Tata conglomerate in India, is widely renowned (especially in India) for his ethical leadership, his care for employees and the communities they live in, and the generally responsible way he conducts business (Singh, 2008).

The importance of ethical leadership is certainly not limited to senior-level leaders. At supervisory leadership levels, traits such as honesty, integrity, fairness, and credibility have long been associated with perceptions of effective leadership (Bass, 1990; Kouzes & Posner, 1993; Posner & Schmidt, 1992). In addition, an ethical dimension has been considered to be an important aspect of specific types of exceptional leadership such as transformational leadership (Bass & Steidlmeier, 1999; Burns, 1978) and authentic leadership (Avolio & Gardner, 2005; Walumbwa, Avolio, Gardner, Wernsing, & Peterson, 2008). But until relatively recently, the ethical dimension of leadership was not treated separately or given unique attention from social scientists. Because ethical behavior in organizations is so important, it seems essential that we consider this dimension of leadership as a separate phenomenon. Brown and Treviño (2006) discussed how ethical leadership is both similar to and different from a variety of other types of positive leadership already in the literature. All of these positive leaders are characterized by integrity and are altruistically motivated and concerned for people. As we will see below, what is most different about ethical leaders is that they are proactively involved in influencing the ethical behavior of their followers, often in quite "transactional" ways.

Before moving on, we should note that the topic of ethical leadership has received, and continues to receive, significant attention in the normative literature from philosophers who write about what leaders "should" do if they are to lead followers in an ethical direction (e.g., Ciulla, 2004; Gini, 1997). We value the extraordinary contributions of these scholars, but consistent with our expertise, we will limit this entry to the treatment of ethical leadership in the social scientific literature. At the same time, we acknowledge that our interest in ethical leadership makes a strong normative assumption that ethical leadership is a good that should be pursued and valued in organizations.

Ethical Leadership as a Social Scientific Construct

In the late 1990s, Treviño and colleagues became interested in developing a greater understanding of the ethical dimension of leadership. The field of organizational ethics had been growing for some time, along with the recognition that understanding the drivers of ethical and unethical conduct requires systematic attention from social scientists. Simultaneously, more and more organizations, especially in business and government, but also in civil society, were setting up formal ethics programs and appointing ethics officers to manage them. Much of this activity in the United States was precipitated by the 1991 Sentencing Guidelines for Organizations that offered management a "carrot" for explicitly managing employees to avoid legal violations. The US Sentencing Commission (the author of the guidelines) offered seven guidelines for an effective legal compliance program that included leadership by a senior executive, development of clear rules and policies, communication of those policies to employees, systems for reporting and investigating violations, and discipline for rule violators, among others.

An organization being investigated or charged with illegal conduct would be treated less harshly if it could demonstrate that it had made a good faith effort to avoid such problems by managing its employees in a particular way. Many organizations appointed ethics or compliance officers who were tasked with managing this entire process. They developed codes of ethics, trained employees, established telephone hotlines to seek advice or report problems, and developed systems to investigate claims of misconduct. Along the way, many of these ethics officers became convinced that leadership at all levels was essential to their effectiveness. For example, they could not do their jobs well if, after an ethics training program, an employee returned to meet with a manager who scoffed at the time spent away from tasks more closely related to the bottom line.

Ethics officers were especially concerned that executive leaders in many companies did not understand the importance of their role as the *C*hief *E*thics *O*fficer who needed to regularly convey the importance of ethical conduct to all employees. A small group of ethics officers at top companies who were a part of the Ethics Resource Center Fellows Program at the time put leadership at the top of their agenda as an issue that they thought required additional research. In response to their call for attention to the issue, a research program began. The first effort involved a qualitative study of executive ethical leadership (Treviño, Hartman, & Brown, 2000; Treviño, Brown, & Hartman, 2003). The researchers interviewed 20 ethics officers and 20 senior executives at a wide range of large companies. The goal was to understand how the interviewees defined ethical leadership (and an alternative the researchers referred to as ethically neutral leadership). In the first part of the interview, interviewees were asked to think of an executive ethical leader from their experience and (without identifying that person) to answer a series of questions about that individual's personal qualities, behaviors, and motivations. The good news was that all interviewees quickly thought of someone, suggesting that ethical leadership was common enough to quickly bring someone to mind. Preliminary analysis of the interviews produced a number of important insights about executive ethical leadership (Treviño, Hartman, & Brown, 2000) that included

1. Executive ethical leadership is a reputational phenomenon. Employees who are distant from senior executives have little to go on when evaluating their ethical leadership because they do not interact directly with them. Therefore, executives must make ethics a clear and explicit part of their leadership agenda in order to be perceived as ethical leaders by followers.
2. Executive ethical leadership is not just about perceptions of the person and his or her character and behavior (what the authors called the "moral person"). Instead, the authors identified what they called a "moral manager" aspect to ethical leadership. Ethical leaders were those who were seen as explicitly and visibly role modeling ethical action, communicating to followers about ethical standards and holding employees accountable to those standards through the performance management system. It was obviously also important to be seen as having ethical traits such as integrity, trustworthiness, and honesty, and to engage in behaviors that demonstrated openness, concern for people, and personal morality. Finally, in the decision-making realm, ethical leaders were seen as being fair, values based, as following ethical decision rules, and being concerned for societal welfare beyond the short-term bottom line. Perhaps the primary insight was that it wasn't enough for the leader to be seen as an ethical "person." She or he had to be perceived to be a moral manager as well, a leader who communicates about ethics, sets expectations for others, and holds them accountable.

In their first practitioner-oriented paper resulting from this study (Treviño, Hartman, & Brown, 2000), the authors combined the moral manager aspect of ethical leadership with the moral person aspect to create a 2x2 matrix. They proposed that only those leaders who were perceived to be BOTH strong moral persons and strong moral managers would be characterized as ethical leaders. Those who were weak on both could be characterized as unethical leaders. Despite the fact that the interviewers never asked about unethical leadership, Al Dunlap, then of Sunbeam infamy, was the interviewees' favorite example of an unethical leader because of his mistreatment of employees, and his apparent willingness to do anything to achieve bottom line results.

Leaders who were good communicators about ethics and what was expected of others (strong moral managers) who didn't live up to ethical expectations themselves (weak moral people) were labeled hypocritical leaders because their actions didn't match their words. They didn't "walk the ethical talk." The authors labeled the final category ethically neutral (or silent) leaders. These were leaders who may be quite successful in business. They may also be ethical persons, but they aren't moral managers. They don't make ethics a part of their leadership agenda. They don't communicate about ethics or about setting standards, and therefore followers simply don't know where they stand.

A more systematic analysis of the interview data produced an academic paper (Treviño, Brown, & Hartman, 2003) that reemphasized that ethical leadership clearly has a "transactional" component, what the authors had earlier referred to as the "moral manager" aspect of ethical leadership. In addition, the authors noted that executive ethical leaders were rarely described as charismatic. This insight began to differentiate ethical leadership from other forms of positive leadership (i.e., charismatic or transformational leadership). The authors also learned more about what they termed "ethically neutral leaders" by looking more closely at the second part of the interview and by contrasting interview results from ethics officers with those from senior executives.

In the second part of the interview, once interviewees had answered all questions related to the ethical leader, they were asked to think of someone who would not qualify as an ethical leader, but who would also not be on an "unethical" leader list. Rather, they were asked to think of someone who may be a successful business person but who was somewhere in the middle in relation to their perceptions of the person's ethical leadership. All of the ethics officers were able to quickly think of someone while about half of the senior executives were able to do so. For those who responded to questions about this category, ethically neutral leaders were characterized as having a narrow view of the organization (as compared to a broad long-term view toward multiple stakeholders for ethical leaders), as less ethically aware, as self-centered rather than caring about others, and as more focused on personal gain and the short-term bottom line. For those who resisted responding to questions about this category of leader, they seemed to be focused on ethical leadership as a function of decision making (rather than traits or actions). They thought that leaders make ethical or unethical decisions and therefore must fit into either the extreme ethical or unethical leadership category. No other category made sense to them. But, these senior executives seemed to be blind to the fact that most organization members are rarely aware of the decision processes that senior executives engage in, and often they don't know about many of the executives' decisions at all. The ethics officers, by contrast, understood that senior executives and their decisions are quite distant from most employees in large organizations. They realized that executives who wanted to convey an ethics message needed to be socially salient, to stand out from a busy background full of messages about bottom line performance. Only behaviors that are salient enough to stand out against this background are noticed and taken into account by lower-level employees. So, visible action and decision making, perhaps unexpected or even courageous, will get followers' attention, as will rewards and punishments that are highly salient to organization members.

The next step was to build upon what had been learned in the qualitative investigation and integrate it with other literature related to ethics and leadership. The objective was to further define and develop the ethical leadership construct, and to develop a survey instrument that could be used to advance ethical leadership research in field studies. Brown, Treviño, and Harrison (2005) embarked on just such an investigation that resulted in a clear definition of the construct and a parsimonious scale that has now been used in many studies. It was important to provide a clear constitutive definition of the construct. Based upon their previous work, and additional interviews the authors conducted to ensure that ethical leadership could be similarly characterized at the supervisory level, the authors defined ethical leadership as "the demonstration of normatively appropriate conduct through personal actions and interpersonal relationships, and the promotion of such conduct to followers through two-way communication, reinforcement, and decision making" (Brown et al., 2005, p. 120). They relied primarily on social learning theory (Bandura, 1986) to explain what ethical leadership is and how ethical leaders could be expected to influence followers. Essential to social learning theory is the concept of modeling. People observe and attend to the behavior of models and learn from them. But, to be effective models, individuals must be attractive, legitimate, and credible. Leaders are likely models because of their status in the organization and their power to influence outcomes of importance to followers. For example, organization members pay close attention to behavior that is rewarded and punished. Leaders are also likely to gain legitimacy by acting in a manner that is considered to be normatively appropriate. So, followers should emulate ethical leaders because these leaders are attractive, legitimate models who behave in ways that are perceived to be normatively appropriate and that let followers know what is expected and what will be rewarded and disciplined.

The authors developed and validated a 10-item ethical leadership scale (the ELS). Across seven studies, they demonstrated that ethical leadership was associated in expected ways with a number of other variables in its nomological network such as leader consideration, interactional fairness, affective trust, leader honesty, and the idealized influence dimension of transformational leadership. They also demonstrated that ethical leadership was associated with outcomes such as satisfaction with the leader, perceptions of leader effectiveness, job dedication, and willingness to report problems to management. It was negatively related to perceptions of abusive supervision. Finally, the research demonstrated that the ethical leadership measure significantly influenced predicted outcomes (perceived supervisor effectiveness, satisfaction with the supervisor, extra effort and willingness to report problems) beyond the idealized influence dimension, its closest competitor from the transformational leadership literature.

The scale items (with responses on a 1 = strongly disagree to 5 = disagree scale) are listed below and are available for researchers to use:

The leader

1. Conducts his/her personal life in an ethical manner
2. Defines success not just by results but also the way that they are obtained
3. Listens to what employees have to say
4. Disciplines employees who violate ethical standards
5. Makes fair and balanced decisions
6. Can be trusted
7. Discusses business ethics or values with employees
8. Sets an example of how to do things the right way in terms of ethics
9. Has the best interests of employees in mind
10. When making decisions, asks "what is the right thing to do?"

Clarity about the construct and the availability of this parsimonious, valid, and reliable scale has helped to unleash a burgeoning of interest in ethical leadership among researchers and practitioners, and a lengthening list of studies has been conducted since the 2005 publication. These include studies on the antecedents and outcomes of ethical leadership, along with work on mediating processes and moderating influences. We begin by reviewing the research on antecedents.

Antecedents of Ethical Leadership

Given the importance of ethical leadership, understanding the factors that are associated with its development has enormous theoretical and practical significance. "How does leader personality affect ethical leadership?," and "What aspects of a leader's context promote or discourage ethical leadership?" are two examples of the kinds of questions related to antecedents that researchers might ask. In a review paper, Brown and Treviño (2006) proposed a number of potential antecedents of ethical leadership that include both individual differences such as personality traits as well as situational factors. However, compared to research on the outcomes of ethical leadership (reviewed below), there have been relatively few empirical studies of the antecedents of ethical leadership to date.

One of the first to test the relationship between personality traits and ethical leadership was Walumbwa and Schaubroeck (2009). These authors argued that personality traits are important antecedents because "ethical leadership is by definition constant and therefore requires a stable dispositional foundation in the leader" (p. 1277). They tested three personality traits that Brown & Treviño (2006) had proposed should be related to ethical leadership—agreeableness, conscientiousness, and neuroticism. According to Walumbwa and Schaubroeck, agreeableness is associated with greater concern for and more positive helping behaviors toward others. Agreeable individuals are interpersonally sensitive, trusting, and cooperative in their relationships (Costa & McCrae, 1992). They are also well liked by those who interact with them. These relational tendencies are essential aspects of ethical leadership and are consistent with a social learning theoretic approach to this construct (Brown & Trevino, 2006) in that they would promote the attractiveness of the ethical leader as a role model to others.

Conscientiousness should be positively related to ethical leadership because highly conscientious leaders feel a strong moral obligation, are honest, and are reliable and dutiful. These characteristics have obvious overlap with the qualities and behaviors of ethical leaders. Conscientious individuals are responsible and dependable, which gives them credibility as models according to social learning theory. Conscientiousness manifests itself in ethical leaders through their setting and enforcing of standards for others and living up to those standards themselves (Brown & Trevino, 2006).

Neuroticism should be negatively related to ethical leadership because high neuroticism is associated with individuals who experience strong negative emotions such as anger, anxiety, fear, and depression. Leaders who experience such strong negative emotions are unattractive from a social learning perspective, making them less likely to be seen as ethical leaders by those around them (Brown & Trevino, 2006).

Walumbwa and Schaubroeck (2009) found support for the first two traits, agreeableness and conscientiousness, but not neuroticism. Subsequent research by Kalshoven, Den Hartog, and De Hoogh (2011a) tested the relationships between these traits and ethical leadership and yielded a different pattern of results. Consistent with previous research, these authors found evidence of a relationship between conscientiousness and ethical leadership. However, unlike Walumbwa and Schaubroeck, these researchers' results supported a negative relationship between neuroticism and ethical leadership and failed to support a hypothesized relationship between agreeableness and ethical leadership.

These conflicting findings indicate that much more research is needed to untangle the relationship between personality traits and ethical leadership. Researchers may need to extend beyond the five-factor model of personality (Tupes & Christal, 1961) to consider how other individual differences such as locus of control (Rotter, 1954) and self-monitoring (Snyder, 1974) are related to ethical leadership (see Brown & Treviño, 2006).

Moving to a type of individual difference explicitly related to the moral realm, researchers have begun to explore how moral identity is related to ethical leadership. Mayer and colleagues (2012) studied the relationship between moral identity, a self-conception organized around a set of moral traits (Aquino & Reed, 2002), and ethical leadership. Aquino and Reed (2002) argued that moral identity can vary. For some individuals, moral identity is more central to their overall self-conception compared to others, making it more readily available for regulating moral conduct. Individuals who have a strong moral identity should be motivated to engage in ethical behavior—to do otherwise would produce self-condemnation (Aquino et al., 2009; Aquino & Reed, 2002).

Moral identity has two dimensions: *symbolization*, which is externally directed (e.g., moral traits are displayed through moral behavior); and *internalization*, which is internally directed (e.g., moral traits are a self-regulatory mechanism rooted in one's self concept). Mayer and colleagues (2012) hypothesized that symbolization encourages leaders to engage in outward displays of moral behaviors related to ethical leadership. They also argued that internalization challenges leaders to behave morally themselves and to ensure that others are engaging in morally appropriate behavior also. Both hypotheses were supported.

Other researchers (Jordan, Brown, Treviño, & Finklelstein, 2013) have considered how cognitive moral development (CMD; Kohlberg, 1969) is related to ethical leadership. Kohlberg studied the process of how people think about moral issues and decide what is morally correct. His research indicated that an individual's moral reasoning moves through three levels—*preconventional* (reasoning based on egocentric criteria), *conventional* (others-focused reasoning that looks to others for guidance), and *postconventional* (more autonomous principled reasoning based upon theories of justice and rights). Research shows that higher levels of CMD are positively related to various types of ethical behavior (Kish-Gephart, Treviño, & Harrison, 2010).

Jordan and colleagues (2013) hypothesized that leader CMD would be positively related to followers' perceptions of ethical leadership. They argued that leaders who reason at higher levels of moral reasoning would demonstrate greater concern for others and commitment to principles such as justice, which are important elements of ethical leadership. They also hypothesized a more complicated relationship between leader-follower CMD and ethical leadership. More specifically, they argued that perceptions of ethical leadership would be highest when leader moral reasoning was more advanced than the moral reasoning of their followers. According to the researchers (Jordan et al., 2013) ethical leaders are more salient and attractive as role models if they operate a step ahead in terms of their ethical reasoning. These authors found support for both of the hypotheses but also suggested that future research on the relationship between CMD and ethical leadership was necessary.

Theoretical work by Hannah and colleagues (Hannah, Avolio, & May, 2011) seems relevant here. These researchers propose that more than moral judgment is required for moral action. They develop research propositions arguing that moral maturation capacities (moral complexity, meta-cognitive ability, and moral identity) drive cognition while moral conation capacities (moral ownership, moral efficacy, and moral courage) drive motivation. But they argue that all of these are necessary for ethical decision making and behavior to occur. If this is so, researchers may want to study these as antecedents of ethical leadership.

Even less is known about how social and other contextual factors might impact ethical leadership. In one of the few studies to look beyond individual differences, Brown & Treviño (in press) studied the relationship between leader role models and ethical leadership. Building on previous work that identified the importance of ethical role modeling in the workplace (Weaver, Treviño, & Agle, 2005), the researchers examined the relationship between three different types of role models (childhood, career mentors, top managers) and ethical leadership. They found that having had a childhood model was positively associated with follower-rated ethical leadership but that this effect was weaker for older leaders. The researchers also found a positive relationship between career role models and ethical leadership, and that this association was stronger for older leaders. They found no link between top management models and ethical leadership. Overall, the results were generally consistent with social learning theory and suggest that future research ought to expand the search for antecedents of ethical leadership beyond leader characteristics.

Outcomes of Ethical Leadership

In reviewing studies on the outcomes of ethical leadership, the list of dependent variables is long, given the short time the construct has been available for study. Researchers have studied relationships between ethical leadership and attitudes such as job satisfaction, commitment, culture and climate perceptions, perceptions of psychological safety, and organizational attractiveness. They have studied positive behavioral outcomes such as organizational citizenship, voice, unit ethical behavior, job performance, and the leader's promotion potential. They have also studied ethical leadership's effect on reducing negative behavioral outcomes such as deviance, bullying, conflict, counterproductive behavior, and unethical behavior.

We begin by reviewing the research on ethical leadership and attitudes, perceptions, and intentions. In their construct development process, Brown and colleagues (Brown et al., 2005) found a significant relationship between ethical leadership and job satisfaction, perceptions of supervisor effectiveness, extra effort, and willingness to report problems to management, and they explained these relationship theoretically within a social learning framework. They noted that employees should be more satisfied with leaders who are high on ethical leadership characteristics, and they should perceive these leaders to be more effective. Employees seek out and learn from nurturing and benevolent individuals who are more likely to be attractive models. Employees are also willing to exert extra effort for leaders who treat them well and fairly. And, they should be more willing to report problems to a leader who can be trusted to take action and to protect the employee who reported.

Ruiz and colleagues (Ruiz, Ruiz, & Martinez, 2011) found that ethical leadership at both the top-manager level and the supervisory level was associated with employee job satisfaction, affective commitment, and reduced turnover intentions. Subsequent research (Hansen, Alge, Brown, Jackson, & Dunford, in press) has teased out the relationship between ethical leadership at top manager and supervisory levels and different types of employee commitment (commitment to the organization and commitment to the supervisor). They found that within-foci effects (e.g., the relationship between organizational ethical leadership and commitment to the organization) are stronger than cross-foci effects (e.g., the relationship between supervisory ethical leadership and commitment to the organization). Neubert and colleagues (2009) also found associations between ethical leadership and both job satisfaction and affective commitment. They found that these relationships were mediated by ethical climate and were strengthened when perceptions of interactional justice were high. Beyond social learning theory, they drew upon attachment theory and virtue theory to argue that ethical leaders meet followers' needs for safety and security by being considerate, trustworthy, and virtuous. Further, Kim and Brymer (2011), as part of a larger study in the hospitality industry, found a relationship between executive ethical leadership and middle manager job satisfaction and organizational commitment.

Finally, Tanner and colleagues (Tanner, Brugger, van Schie, and Lebherz, 2010) developed a 35-item measure of ethical leadership. They found that this measure of ethical leadership was also positively related to attitudes such as job satisfaction, affective commitment, and work engagement and mostly indirectly related to other outcomes such as less emotional exhaustion and absenteeism. The above studies provide substantial support for the notion that ethical leadership is associated with positive attitudinal outcomes in employees at multiple organizational levels who are more satisfied with their jobs and who feel more committed to their organizations under strong ethical leadership.

Ethical leadership has also been associated with follower behavior, including increases in positive behavior (e.g., citizenship, voice, job performance) and decreases in negative behavior such as deviance or unethical dealings. For example, Kacmar and colleagues (Kacmar, Bachrach, Harris, & Zivnuska, 2011) were interested in the relationship between ethical leadership and citizenship behavior, using social exchange theory to explain the relationship. The authors proposed that ethical leadership characteristics and behaviors such as treating people fairly, setting expectations, and following through on those would create a sense of indebtedness that would increase OCBs in employees. They supported this proposition, finding a main effect for ethical leadership on two types of OCBs. But, they also used social role theory to propose and support moderating effects for gender and perceptions of organizational politics.

Avey, Palanski, and Walumbwa (2010) similarly found a relationship between ethical leadership and increased organizational citizenship behaviors. But they also included reduced deviant behavior as a dependent variable. In addition, they proposed, based upon the behavioral plasticity hypothesis, that these relationships would be stronger for individuals lower on self-esteem because cues from the context are more salient for these individuals. Their hypotheses were supported. Thus, both of these studies took into account the effect of follower characteristics in explaining the relationship between ethical leadership and outcomes.

In their 2009 study of personality traits and ethical leadership, Walumbwa and Schaubroeck (2009) also investigated ethical leadership's effect on voice behavior, via perceptions of the psychological safety of speaking up. This voice behavior variable is broader than the reporting of problems to management that had been studied by Brown and colleagues (2005). Here, voice refers to a more routine type of behavior that involves willingness to speak up with ideas and to make recommendations on issues that affect work life in the group. It can be thought of as a kind of citizenship behavior in that it is helpful to the group. The results supported the authors' hypothesis. The effects of personality traits (agreeableness and conscientiousness) on voice were fully mediated through ethical leadership and through psychological safety. Ethical leaders help to promote employee voice in part by creating a more psychologically safe environment for speaking up about all kinds of issues. But, ethical leaders also have a more direct effect on voice (even when the idealized influence dimension of transformational leadership is in the predictive model).

Piccolo and colleagues (Piccolo, Greenbaum, Den Hartog, and Folger, 2010) found that ethical leadership was positively associated with both organizational citizenship behavior as well as job performance via job characteristics and effort. The authors theorized that ethical leaders increase two types of job characteristics. They increase autonomy by listening and providing employees a say in their own work. They also increase task significance by giving moral meaning to the work at hand. These relationships were supported. The influence of task significance on citizenship and task performance was mediated by extra effort. The resulting model demonstrated that ethical leadership influences the outcomes through these job characteristics. These authors went beyond social learning theory to consider other theoretical mechanisms that are likely to help explain the influence of ethical leadership on employee outcomes.

Walumbwa and colleagues (Walumbwa, Mayer, Wang, Wang, Workman, & Christensen, 2011) also studied the relationship between ethical leadership and the job performance of the leaders' direct reports. They found a positive relationship. Importantly, they also proposed and found support for multiple mediators of this relationship, which was fully mediated by leader-member exchange, the subordinates' self-efficacy, and organizational identification. The authors explained the self-efficacy mediation via social learning theory, leader-member exchange mediation using social exchange theory, and the organizational identification mediation using social identity theory of leadership. Social learning theory and social exchange theory have been used in prior studies. But, the link between identification and ethical leadership had been suggested (Brown & Mitchell, 2010) but not tested in previous research. An identity approach represents a somewhat new way of thinking about why ethical leaders might influence subordinates' job performance—by increasing their identification with the organization. Previous studies have demonstrated that ethical leadership is associated with attachment to the organization in the forms of organizational commitment and reduced intention to leave. This study makes the link to general job performance.

Rather than focusing on subordinate performance, Rubin and associates (Rubin, Dierdorff, & Brown, 2010) investigated the association between ethical leadership and *leader* promotability. They found that ethical leadership was associated with superiors' ratings of the leader's promotability to senior leadership (but was unrelated to "near term" promotability, meaning promotability in the next year). The relationship with promotability to senior management was stronger in organizations with a stronger ethical culture and in high pressure to perform contexts, again suggesting the importance of taking into account organizational context. The findings caution us to consider that being an ethical leader is not enough to be considered promotable in the short term. Other job performance factors may be more important. In fact, the authors speculated about the existence of an "ethical ceiling" whereby leaders are rewarded in the shorter term for achieving bottom line results rather than for ethical leadership. Finally, the results for promotability to senior leadership held only when job performance was held constant.

At the executive level, De Hoogh and Den Hartog (2008) found that CEOs' ethical leadership was associated with the CEO's sense of social responsibility (based upon interviews with the CEOs). In addition, ethical leadership was related to perceptions of effectiveness of the top management team, and optimism among direct reports about the organization's future and their role in that future.

Finally, Strobel and colleagues (Strobel, Tumasjan, & Welpe, 2010) proposed that ethical leadership at the middle management level would be associated with perceptions of organizational attractiveness. In two scenario studies with undergraduate students, these researchers found that ethical leadership was positively associated with perceptions of organizational attractiveness and with intentions to pursue employment with firms led by ethical leaders.

In addition to studying the effects of ethical leadership on positive outcomes such as OCBs and job performance, researchers have been investigating its association with reducing negative outcomes such as deviance, counterproductive work behavior, and unethical behavior. Mayer and colleagues (Mayer, Kuenzi, Greenbaum, Bardes, & Salvador, 2009) incorporated two levels of ethical leadership in their study: executive and supervisory-level ethical leadership. They proposed that ethical leadership would flow from the executive level to influence supervisory level leaders and ultimately work group outcomes (both citizenship behaviors and deviance in the group). They relied on social learning theory and social exchange theory to explain these relationships. This study found a direct relationship between both levels of leadership and increased organizational citizenship behaviors and reduced deviance. Importantly, they also found that the effects of executive ethical leadership were mediated by supervisory-level ethical leadership, suggesting that ethical leadership effects "trickle down" from one level to the next. Taking into account multiple levels of leadership simultaneously is an important advance in the study of ethical leadership and its effects on important organizational outcomes.

In two studies (cited above for its study of moral identity as an antecedent of ethical leadership), Mayer and colleagues (Mayer, Aquino, Greenbaum, & Kuenzi, 2012) also investigated work unit-level consequences of ethical leadership on unethical behavior (behavior that is considered to be morally unacceptable by community standards) and relationship conflict. The authors relied on social learning theory to theorize both relationships, and found support for them. Ethical leadership was associated with reduced unethical behavior and reduced work group conflict even when controlling for alternative leadership measures such as interpersonal justice, informational justice, and idealized influence. These findings add to the growing support for the uniqueness of the ethical leadership construct in its ability to predict ethics-related employee outcomes. To our knowledge, this was the first time relationship conflict was studied as an outcome and suggests that ethical leaders have further-reaching effects than first anticipated. Observing good or virtuous behavior may spread to related behaviors such as the desire to achieve cooperation rather than conflict.

One study predicted, but did not find support for a relationship between ethical leadership and counterproductive work behavior (Detert, Treviño, Burris, & Andiappan, 2007). These researchers measured ethical leadership of restaurant general managers and proposed that it would be related to counterproductive work behavior, as measured by an objective food loss outcome. Abusive supervision and managerial oversight were significant predictors of food loss, but ethical leadership was not. The authors speculated that ethical leadership may be less influential (than decent treatment and close supervision) for these low-level, low-paid restaurant employees who face relatively straightforward ethical issues such as whether to waste food, take it, or give it away. This suggests that organizational context may matter and should be taken into account in future research.

Stouten and colleagues (Stouten, Baillien, Van den Broeck, Camps, De Witte, & Euwema, 2010) focused on the relationship between ethical leadership and bullying behavior. They argued that ethical leaders should be negatively associated with being bullied and that ethical leaders would have this effect by altering the work environment (workload and working conditions). Ethical leaders care about their employees and would thus be more likely to create a positive work environment. The authors found that ethical leadership was negatively associated with employees' reports of having been bullied. Ethical leadership was also negatively related to employee perceptions of poor working conditions and quantitative workload, and these variables were found to mediate the relationship between ethical leadership and having been bullied.

In a comprehensive multilevel study, Schaubroeck and colleagues (Schaubroeck et al., 2012) examined ethical leadership and ethical culture across three levels of Army units in Iraq. The researchers found limited support for direct trickle down of ethical leadership from one level to another. They found more support for ethical leaders at various levels influencing the ethical culture (Schein, 1985, 2010; Treviño, 1986, 1990) of their units as well as evidence of ethical leaders influencing ethical culture in lower-level units. They then found that ethical culture at the unit level, in turn, influences ethical cognitions (moral efficacy, intentions to report misconduct) and unethical behavior (e.g., transgressions against noncombatants). Finally, they found a moderating effect, whereby higher-level ethical leadership enhances the influence of subordinate leaders' ethical leadership on unit ethical culture.

This review suggests that we have learned a great deal about ethical leadership, its antecedents, outcomes, and processes in the short time since the construct was introduced to the management literature. Some evidence exists related to antecedents (from personality to moral identity to cognitive moral development), but we do not yet have enough consistent evidence to make clear statements about what we know, leaving the antecedents arena much in need of future research. We know more about the influence of ethical leadership on a range of outcomes that include attitudes (increased job satisfaction, affective commitment, and work engagement and reduced turnover intentions), and behaviors. Ethical leadership is associated with increases in positive behaviors such as voice and citizenship, and it has even been associated with increases in job performance. It has also been associated with decreases in negative behaviors such as deviance. Conceptual and empirical work has also been done on a variety of mediators and moderators. The evidence supports the social learning theory approach to understanding ethical leadership offered by Brown and colleagues but has also gone beyond this conceptualization to consider social exchange and other processes. Although knowledge has advanced considerably, much remains to be learned about the outcomes of ethical leadership and the processes involved.

Future Directions

As the above review makes clear, the empirical study of ethical leadership is flourishing, but the need for additional research remains strong. We will not attempt to be exhaustive here as others have addressed the future research issue in some detail and quite recently (Brown & Mitchell, 2010; Brown & Treviño, 2006). But, we do wish to raise some issues that are particularly important to the future of ethical leadership research.

Antecedents

Important questions about the antecedents of ethical leadership remain unanswered. Where does ethical leadership come from? Are ethical leaders "born or made?" Much of the initial work on antecedents has focused on attributes of the leader such as personality, moral identity, and cognitive moral development. More research is clearly needed on such attributes. But, researchers might also want to broaden the research agenda beyond dispositional factors to include situational factors. For example, how does the ethical climate or culture of an organization affect the development of ethical leadership over time? Preliminary research suggests that ethical culture can enhance an ethical leader's long-term promotion potential (Rubin et al., 2010). Therefore, it seems likely that a strong ethical culture would foster ethical leadership within organizations and enhance its relationships to important outcomes. But, today's employees do not expect to remain with a single organization long term. How might this more macro feature of the work environment influence the development of ethical leadership? Will leaders carry these styles from one organization to another, or is the local context a more important influence?

Another feature of the ethical context relates to an organization's ethics/compliance program orientation (Weaver, Treviño, & Cochran, 1999). Most large organizations have such programs today, but they vary a great deal in their orientation and how employees perceive them. Some are perceived by employees to emphasize a kind of "check the box" compliance with an emphasis on forced compliance with externally imposed rules and regulations while others are perceived to emphasize aspirations and values. Might an organization's program orientation influence ethical leadership? It seems likely that values-oriented programs would foster ethical leadership more than would compliance-oriented programs, given the latter's emphasis on simply obeying the law rather than going beyond it.

How does the more immediate social environment affect ethical leadership? Previous research has shown that individual antisocial behavior is related to coworker antisocial behavior (Robinson & O'Leary-Kelly, 1998). But we know little about whether a peer leadership environment can influence ethical leadership development? Might having peers who are ethical leaders influence an individual's ethical leadership such that a leader models himself or herself after a peer who is clearly an ethical leader? What might such a relationship depend upon?

Some research suggests that ethical leadership trickles down from the top of an organization as supervisors learn from their superiors (Mayer et al., 2009). However, a strong trickle-down effect was not found in other research (Schaubroeck et al., 2012). Clearly, more multilevel studies are needed to fully understand these relationships across multiple levels of leadership. We also recommend that researchers investigate peer and leader influence processes simultaneously so as to assess their relative impact on ethical leadership.

Finally, does experience with ethical leaders in one's career influence development of ethical leadership? Social learning provides the basis for understanding how ethical leaders influence followers. But, it may also help us to understand how ethical leaders learn to be ethical leaders (if they do). Previous research on ethical role models (Brown & Treviño, in press; Weaver, Treviño, & Agle, 2005) suggests that ethical mentors might play a role in developing ethical leadership within the workplace, but additional research is needed to better understand these relationships.

Outcomes

Although we have learned a great deal about the influence of ethical leaders on a variety of outcomes, ethical leadership should affect important follower attitudes, behaviors, and decision-making processes beyond those already studied. For example, although we know that moral identity is an antecedent of ethical leadership, future research might explore whether and how ethical leadership impacts *follower* moral identity (Aquino & Reed, 2002) as well as whether follower moral identity interacts with ethical leadership to influence important ethical outcomes.

One outcome of executive ethical leadership is the organizational ethical context. Previous research has linked ethical leadership to ethical climate (Neubert et al., 2009) and unit ethical culture (Schaubroeck et al., 2012). However, little research has actually examined the relationship between executive ethical leadership and organizational ethical climate or culture. It is assumed that for better (and sometimes for worse), executives set the ethical tone at the top of their organizations. Therefore, future research should focus on executive-level ethical leaders. Researchers should also consider potential moderating influences of the ethical leadership-ethical climate relationship. For example, do other aspects of climate neutralize the impact of ethical leadership on ethical climate? Perhaps an ethical leader's impact on ethical climate is minimized in organizations that have strong instrumental climates.

Also, one would hope that ethical leaders would influence followers' decision making. Certainly, many well-established steps in the ethical decision making process such as moral awareness, moral reasoning, and moral motivation can be studied to better understand how ethical leadership might enhance follower ethical decision making. In addition, new research on moral attentiveness (Reynolds, 2008) and automatic ethical decision making (Reynolds et al., 2010) might provide fruitful new areas for testing how ethical leadership influences less deliberative aspects of ethical decision-making processes.

Measurement of Ethical Leadership

An important issue concerns measurement of the ethical leadership construct. Prior to publication of the ELS, a systematically and rigorously developed ethical leadership instrument was unavailable to researchers. But, research on ethical leadership has exploded since the publication of the ethical leadership scale (Brown et al., 2005). The benefits of the ELS are that it is parsimonious, it was developed in a series of seven studies that provide solid evidence of construct validity, and it has an emerging track record of being used successfully in research that has been published in top research journals.

But, since the development of the ELS, other researchers have begun to develop alternative measures such as the Ethical Leadership at Work Questionnaire (ELW) developed by Kalshoven and colleagues (Kalshoven, Den Hartog, & De Hoogh, 2011b). Like the ELS, the ELW is based on the assumption that ethical leadership represents multiple types of behaviors. The ELW is multidimensional, with 38 items measuring 7 dimensions of ethical leadership. Compared to the ELS, the ELW contains some unique content such as a dimension that reflects a leader's concern for sustainability. The other six dimensions overlap substantially with the ELS (integrity, role clarification, power sharing, fairness, and people orientation). For example, as reported in Study 1 from Kalshoven et al. (2011b), the uncorrected correlations between the ELS and the ELW's dimensions for integrity (Pearson's r = .74), people orientation (.79), ethical guidance (.75), and power sharing (.74) indicate substantial overlap. Additional research will be needed on the construct validity, including discriminant validity, of this new measure.

A final measurement issue concerns executive ethical leadership and social responsibility. A careful examination of the ELS's content reveals that the ELS is focused on internal ethics management within an organization, and not explicitly on issues relating to the ethical and socially responsible treatment of external stakeholders. Socially responsible leadership has recently drawn the deserved attention of leadership scholars (Waldman & Siegel, 2008). Measures such as the ELW, which begin to capture external aspects of leadership such as concern for sustainability represent a start in terms of measurement. However, internal ethics management (ethical leadership) and ethical treatment of external stakeholders (socially responsible leadership) likely represent overlapping but separate constructs and, therefore, require separate measures.

Unethical Leadership?

An important question for future research concerns the relationship between ethical leadership and unethical leadership. We know that being low on ethical leadership has negative outcomes, but it does not make someone an "unethical" leader. Brown and colleagues (2005) did not set out to develop a measure of unethical leadership. So, exactly what characteristics make one an unethical leader, and how should unethical leadership be defined and measured? One construct that seems related to this question is abusive supervision. It has been defined as "subordinates' perception of the extent to which their supervisors engage in the sustained display of hostile verbal and nonverbal behaviors, excluding physical contact" (Tepper, 2000, p. 178). When interviewees talked about Al Dunlap as an unethical leader, they referred to his abusive treatment of employees. So, abusive employee treatment would seem to be a contributor to perceptions of unethical leadership. Abusive supervision has also been associated with employee deviance (e.g., Tepper, 2007) and therefore seems ripe for further study of its effects on ethical and unethical behavior.

In addition, Craig and Gustafson (1998) introduced what they labeled the "leader integrity scale," but a close look at the scale's items suggests that it actually measures employee perceptions of the leader's *lack* of integrity. Perhaps this scale or some variation of it can also be used in future development of an unethical leadership scale.

A related construct that has been recently introduced to the literature is a leader's bottom line mentality (Greenbaum, Mawritz, & Eissa, 2012). Greenbaum and colleagues define bottom line mentality as a narrow frame of mind that focuses almost exclusively on bottom line financial outcomes to the exclusion of other priorities. This seems opposed to the long-term orientation taken by ethical leaders. The researchers found that bottom line mentality was related to social undermining behavior. We hypothesize that having such a bottom line mentality would be negatively related to ethical leadership. But, is such a mentality associated with "unethical leadership?" Once a measure of unethical leadership is developed and validated, researchers can begin to ask questions about the relationship between these constructs, the relative influence of them on outcomes, the antecedents of unethical leadership, and other questions.

Cross-Cultural Research

Researchers should also address the issue of ethical leadership in cross-cultural settings. First, measures of ethical leadership may need to be developed to reflect cultural differences. Some researchers have used a measure developed by the Project GLOBE leadership study to investigate ethical leadership (Resick et al., 2006). Although these data are valuable as researchers begin to attempt to understand ethical leadership across cultures, future cross-cultural research on ethical leadership will require evidence of measurement invariance and equivalence of existing ethical leadership instruments. Perhaps the construct of ethical leadership is not culturally universal. Might cultural differences affect how ethical leadership is conceptualized in different cultures? If so, specific measures of ethical leadership should be developed that reflect these cultural differences. Even if the ethical leadership construct is universal, it is likely that national culture might impact what is considered "normatively appropriate" within a particular society. Also, we speculate that culture might affect the relationship between ethical leadership and its antecedents and outcomes. For example, would the relationship between ethical leadership and employees' willingness to report problems (Brown et al., 2005) hold in cultures that are high on power distance? National culture represents many potential avenues for future research for ethical leadership researchers.

Ethics Education

Another future direction for ethical leadership research involves questions about education for ethical leadership. In the aftermath of so many scandals, business schools have been criticized for not properly preparing their graduates to handle ethical challenges. The Association to Advance Collegiate Schools of Business (AACSB) Ethics Education task force (AACSB, 2004) called for a strong emphasis on teaching ethical leadership in the business curriculum. But we actually know almost nothing about how to do that, leading to important questions that ethical leadership scholars should incorporate into their research agendas.

Can ethical leadership be developed among undergraduate and graduate students, and if so, how? What teaching methods are most effective? For example, is the case study method, which is so popular in graduate business programs, effective in developing ethical leadership behavior? If so, do students best learn about ethical leadership from positive examples of ethical leadership, which is consistent with the literature on ethical role modeling (Weaver et al., 2005)? Or is learning more effective when students are taught what "not to do" from case studies about anti-role models who practiced unethical leadership. Along these lines, can exposing students to guest speakers impact the development of ethical leadership? Do negative models such as Andrew Fastow, who recently spoke to MBA students after serving time in a federal prison for his wrongdoing at Enron (Di Meglio, 2012) make students "scared straight"? Will it make them more inclined to be ethical leaders? Is some combination of negative and positive role models the best answer? Perhaps ethical behavior is best learned from personal experience. Therefore, service and other types of experiential learning might represent an effective teaching method. But, does such experience transfer to the development of ethical leadership? Researchers can (and should) play an important role in advancing our understanding of whether ethical leadership can be taught as well as how best to approach it. They need to begin by developing a conceptual framework for guiding this work. Research in this area will be important because it has implications not only for university pedagogy but also for practice as effective teaching methods are likely transferrable to corporate training and leadership development initiatives.

Finally, in keeping with the AACB's emphasis on assurance of learning, what is the best way to measure learning outcomes related to ethical leadership in student (or executive) populations? In other words, can faculty who teach ethical leadership demonstrate that their students are becoming better ethical leaders; and, if so, how?

Temporal Issues

Finally, longitudinal research would help us to understand how long it takes to develop a reputation for ethical leadership and how resistant it is to change. For example, using an idiosyncrasy credit argument (Hollander, 1958), is a leader with a reputation for ethical leadership somewhat immune from charges of unethical behavior and damage to the reputation? Or, is such a leader more at risk because being on an ethical leadership pedestal makes one more susceptible to reputation harm especially given today's media environment? Recent events at the Pennsylvania State University (home to the authors) seem relevant here. Coach late Joe Paterno earned a well-deserved reputation for ethical leadership during his more than 40 years as head football coach at the university. In addition to winning football games, he focused on ensuring that his players received a solid university education, and his stated goal was to develop them into young men who would contribute to society. His program was never cited for an NCAA violation and was held up as an exemplar of "success with honor," the program's tagline. The Paterno family also became major university benefactors to the library, liberal arts education, and campus spiritual centers. However, when a former assistant coach, Jerry Sandusky, was accused of having a lengthy history of child sexual abuse in November 2011, Coach Paterno's ethical leadership was open to question. The public learned that in 2001, a graduate assistant had reported to Paterno an incident between Sandusky and a young boy that he (the graduate assistant) observed in the locker room after hours. Paterno told his superior (the athletic director) what he had been told and then relied on the athletic director and other administrators to investigate and act. In hindsight, Paterno made clear that he thought he should have done more, and he called the situation the greatest sorrow of his life. Nevertheless, Paterno was pilloried by some in the media and the public. Within a week of the revelation, he was terminated as head coach because the university's Board of Trustees determined that he had failed in his moral responsibility as a leader. Subsequently, many former students, alumni, players, friends, and acquaintances came to Paterno's defense, arguing that the trustees terminated Paterno without an investigation or due process, that others were to blame for not adequately following through on the report, or that a single failure to do more should not stain a stellar reputation for ethical leadership that had been built and sustained over so many decades. But, the question for researchers remains. Can a legacy of ethical leadership be maintained despite such a stain? What does it take to sustain a reputation for ethical leadership over the long term?

Conclusion

We have reviewed the history of the ethical leadership construct and the developing research on ethical leadership in organizations. In a very short time, we have seen significant advances in understanding the antecedents and consequences of ethical leadership as well as the intervening processes. We have learned that ethical leadership increases positive attitudinal and behavioral outcomes and reduces negative ones. Yet, leadership is a complex, multilevel construct that operates over time, and a full understanding of ethical leadership will require additional investigation. We fully expect much more research to come, and we have offered some of our own ideas for future directions. We hope that this future work will help to advance ethical leadership in organizations and society.

References

AACSB International—The Association to Advance Collegiate Schools of Business. (2004). *Ethics education in business schools: Report of the ethics education task force to AACSB International's board of directors*. St. Louis, MO: AACSB International.

Aquino, K., Freeman, D., Reed, A. II., Lim, V. K. G., & Felps, W. (2009). Testing a social-cognitive model of moral behavior: The interactive influence of situations and moral identity centrality. *Journal of Personality and Social Psychology, 97*, 123–141.

Aquino, K. F., & Reed, A., II. (2002). The self-importance of moral identity. *Journal of Personality and Social Psychology, 83*, 1423–1440.

Avey, J. B., Palanski, M. E., & Walumbwa, F. O. 2010. When leadership goes unnoticed: The moderating role of follower self-esteem on the relationship between ethical leadership and follower behavior. *Journal of Business Ethics, 98*, 573–582.

Avolio, B. J., & Gardner, W. L. (2005). Authentic leadership development: Getting to the root of positive forms of leadership. *Leadership Quarterly, 16*, 315–338.

Bandura, A. (1986). *Social foundations of thought and action*. Englewood Cliffs, NJ: Prentice-Hall.

Barnard, C. I. (1938). *The functions of the executive*. Cambridge, MA: Harvard University Press.

Bass, B. M. (1990). *Bass & Stogdill's handbook of leadership*. New York: The Free Press.

Bass, B. M., & Steidlmeier, P. (1999). Ethics, character, and authentic transformational leadership behavior. *The Leadership Quarterly, 10*, 181–217.

Brown, M. E. & Mitchell, M. S. (2010). Ethical and unethical leadership: Exploring new avenues for future research. *Business Ethics Quarterly, 20*, 583–616.

Brown, M. E., Treviño, L. K., & Harrision, D. A. (2005). Ethical leadership: A social learning perspective for construct development and testing. *Organizational Behavior and Human Decision Processes, 97*, 117–134.

Brown, M. E., & Treviño, L. K. (2006). Ethical leadership: A review and future directions. *The Leadership Quarterly, 17*, 595–616.

Brown, M. E. & Treviño, L. K. (in press). Do Role Models Matter? An Investigation of Role Modeling as an Antecedent of Perceived Ethical Leadership. *Journal of Business Ethics*. DOI: 10.1007/s10551-013-1769-0

Burns, J. M. (1978). *Leadership*. NY: Harper & Row.

Ciulla, J. (2004). *Ethics, the heart of leadership*. 2nd edition. Westport, CT: Quorum Books.

Clinard, M. B. (1983). *Corporate ethics and crime: The role of middle management*. Beverly Hills, CA: Sage Publications.

Costa, P. T., Jr., & McCrae, R. R. (1992). *Revised NEO Personality Inventory (NEO-PI-R) and NEO Five-Factor Inventory (NEO-FFI) professional manual*. Odessa, FL: PAR.

Craig, S. B. & Gustafson, S. B. (1998). Perceived leader integrity scale: An instrument for assessing employee perceptions of leader integrity. *Leadership Quarterly, 9*, 127–145.

De Hoogh, A. H. B., & Den Hartog, D. N. 2008. Ethical and despotic leadership, relationships with leader's social responsibility, top management team effectiveness, and subordinates' optimism: A multi-method study. *Leadership Quarterly, 19*, 297–311.

Detert, J. R., Treviño, L. K., Burris, E. R., & Andiappan, M. (2007). Managerial modes of influence and counterproductivity in organizations: A longitudinal business unit level investigation. *Journal of Applied Psychology, 92*, 993–1005.

Di Meglio, F. (2012). Enron's Andrew Fastow: The Mistakes I Made. *Bloomberg Businessweek*. Retrieved from: http://www.businessweek.com/articles/2012-03-22/enrons-andrew-fastow-the-mistakes-i-made on April 23, 2012.

George, B. (2003). *Authentic leadership: Rediscovering the secrets to creating lasting value*. San Francisco: Jossey-Bass.

Gini, A. (1997). Moral leadership: An overview. *Journal of Business Ethics, 16*(3), 323–330.

Greenbaum, R. L. Mawritz, M. B., & Eissa, G. (2012). Bottom-line mentality as an antecedent of social undermining and the moderating roles of core self-evaluations and conscientiousness. *Journal of Applied Psychology, 92*(2), 343–359.

Hansen, S. D., Alge, B. J., Brown, M. E., Jackson, C. J., & Dunford, B. B. (in press). Ethical Leadership: Assessing the Value of a Multifoci Social Exchange Perspective. *Journal of Business Ethics*. DOI: **10.1007/s10551-012-1408-1**

Hannah, S. T., Avolio, B. J., and May, D. R. (2011). Moral maturation and moral conation: A capacity approach to explaining moral thought and action. *Academy of Management Review, 36*, 663–685.

Hollander, E. P. (1958). Conformity, status and idiosyncrasy credit. *Psychological Review, 65*, 117–127.

Jordan, J., Brown, M. E., Treviño, L. K., & Finkelstein, S. (2013). Someone to look up to: Executive-follower ethical reasoning and perceptions of ethical leadership. *Journal of Management, 39*(3), 660–683.

Kacmar, K. M., Bachrach, D. G., & Harris, K. J., Zivnuska, S. (2011). Fostering good citizenship through ethical leadership: Exploring the moderating role of gender and organizational politics. *Journal of Applied Psychology, 96*, 633–642.

Kalshoven, K., Den Hartog, D. N., & De Hoogh, A. H. B. (2011a). Ethical leader behavior and big five factors of personality. *Journal of Business Ethics, 100*, 349–366.

Kalshoven, K., Den Hartog, D. N., & De Hoogh, A. H. B. (2011b). Ethical leadership at work questionnaire (ELW): Development and validation of a multidimensional measure. *Leadership Quarterly, 22*, 51–69.

Kim, W. G,. & Brymer, R. A. (2011). The effects of ethical leadership on manager job satisfaction, commitment, behavioral outcomes, and firm performance. *International Journal of Hospitality Management, 30*, 1020–1026.

Kish-Gephart, J. J., Harrison, D. A., & Treviño, L. K. (2010). Bad apples, bad cases, and bad barrels: Meta-analytic evidence about sources of unethical decisions at work. *Journal of Applied Psychology, 95*, 1–31.

Kohlberg, L. (1969). State and sequence: The cognitive-development approach to socialization. In D. Goslin (Ed.), *Handbook of socialization theory and research* (pp. 347–480). Chicago: Rand–McNally.

Kouzes, J. M., & Posner, B. Z. (1993). *Credibility: How leaders gain and lose it, why people demand it*. San Francisco: Jossey-Bass.

Mayer, D. M., Aquino, K., Greenbaum, R. S., & Kuenzi, M. (2012). Who displays ethical leadership and why does it matter? An examination of antecedents and consequences of ethical leadership. *Academy of Management Journal, 55*(1), 151–171.

Mayer, D. M., Kuenzi, M., Greebaum, R., Bardes, M., & Salvador, R. (2009). How low does ethical leadership flow? Test of a trickle down model. *Organizational Behavior and Human Decision Processes, 108*, 1–13.

Neubert, M. J., Carlson, D. S., Kacmar, K. M., Roberts, J. A., & Chonko, L. B. (2009). The virtuous influence of ethical leadership behavior: Evidence from the field. *Journal of Business Ethics, 90*, 157–170.

Piccolo, R. F., Greenbaum, R., Den Hartog, D. H., & Folger, R. (2010). The relationship between ethical leadership and core job characteristics. *Journal of Organizational Behavior, 31*, 259–278.

Posner, B. Z., & Schmidt, W. H. (1992). Values and the American manager: An update updated. *California Management Review, 34*, 80–94.

Resick, C., Hanges, P., Dickson, M., & Mitchelson, J. (2006). A cross-cultural examination of the endorsement of ethical leadership RID A-8347-2009. *Journal of Business Ethics, 63*(4), 345–359.

Reynolds, S. J. (2008). Moral attentiveness: Who pays attention to the moral aspects of life? *Journal of Applied Psychology, 93*(5), 1027–1041.

Reynolds, S. J., Leavitt, K., & DeCelles, K. A. (2010). Automatic ethics: The effects of implicit assumptions and contextual cues on moral behavior. *Journal of Applied Psychology, 95*(4), 752–760.

Robinson, S. L., & O'Leary-Kelly, A. M. (1998). Monkey see, monkey do: The influence of work groups on the antisocial behavior of employees. *Academy of Management Journal, 41*(6), 658–672.

Rubin, R. S., Dierdorff, E. C., & Brown, M. E. (2010). Do ethical leaders get ahead? Exploring ethical leadership and promotability. *Business Ethics Quarterly, 20*, 215–236.

Ruiz, P., Ruiz, C., & Martinez, R. (2011). Improving the "leader-follower" relationship: Top manager or supervisor? The ethical leadership trickle-down effect on follower job response. *Journal of Business Ethics, 99*, 587–608.

Schaubroeck, J., Hannah, S., Avolio, B., Kozlowski, S., Lord, R., Treviño, L. K., Dimotakis, N, & Peng, C. (2012). Embedding ethical leadership within and across organizational levels. *Academy of Management Journal, 55*(5), 1053–1078.

Schein, E. H. (1985). *Organizational culture and leadership* (1st ed.). San Francisco: Jossey-Bass.

Schein, E. H. (2010). *Organizational culture and leadership* (4th ed.). Hoboken, NJ: Jossey-Bass.

Singh, J. (2008). Tightrope walk at Tata Steel. *South Asian Journal of Management, 15*(1): 118–136.

Snyder, M. (1974). The self-monitoring of expressive behavior. *Journal of Personality and Social Psychology, 30*, 526–537.

Strobel, M., Tumasjan, A., & Welpe, I. (2010). Do business ethics pay off? The influence of ethical leadership on organizational attractiveness. *Journal of Psychology, 218*, 213–224.

Stouten, J., Baillien, E., Van, d. B., Camps, J., De Witte, H., & Euwema, M. (2010). Discouraging bullying: The role of ethical leadership and its effects on the work environment. *Journal of Business Ethics, 95*, 17–27.

Tanner, C., Bruegger, A., van Schie, S., & Lebherz, C. (2010). Actions speak louder than words: The benefits of ethical behaviors of leaders. *Zeitschrift Fur Psychologie-Journal of Psychology, 218*, 225–233.

Tepper, B. J. (2000). Consequences of abusive supervision. *Academy of Management Journal, 43*, 178–190.

Tepper, B. J. (2007). Abusive supervision in work organizations: Review, synthesis, and research agenda. *Journal of Management, 19*, 230–255.

Treviño, L. K. (1986). Ethical decision making in organizations: A person-situation interactionist model. *Academy of Management Review, 11*, 601–617.

Treviño, L. K. (1990). A cultural perspective on changing and developing organizational ethics. *Research in Organizational Change and Development, 4*, 195–230.

Treviño, L. K., Brown, M., & Hartman, L. P. (2003). A qualitative investigation of perceived executive ethical leadership: Perceptions from inside and outside the executive suite. *Human Relations, 56*, 5–37.

Treviño, L. K., Hartman, L. P., & Brown, M. (2000). Moral person and moral manager: How executives develop a reputation for ethical leadership. *California Management Review, 42*, 128–142.

Tupes, E. C., & Christal, R. E. (1961). *Recurrent personality factors based on trait ratings*. (Tech. Rep. ASD-TR-61–97). Lackland Air Force Base, TX: Air Force.

Waldman, D. A., & Siegel, D. (2008). Defining the socially responsible leader. *The Leadership Quarterly, 19*, 117–131.

Walumbwa, F. O., Avolio, B. J., Gardner, W. L., Wernsing, T. S., & Peterson, S. J. (2008). Authentic leadership: Development and validation of a theory-based measure. *Journal of Management, 34*, 89–126.

Walumbwa, F. O., Mayer, D. M., Wang, P., Wang, H., Workman, K., & Christensen, A. L. (2011). Linking ethical leadership to employee performance: The roles of leader-member exchange, self-efficacy, and organizational identification. *Organizational Behavior and Human Decision Processes, 115*, 204–213.

Walumbwa, F. O., & Schaubroeck, J. (2009). Leader personality traits and employee voice behavior: Mediating roles of ethical leadership and work group psychological safety. *Journal of Applied Psychology, 94*, 1275–1286.

Weaver, G. R., Treviño, L. K., & Agle, B. (2005). Somebody I look up to: Ethical role modeling in organizations. *Organizational Dynamics, 34*, 313–330.

Weaver, G. R., Treviño, L. K., & Cochran, P. L. (1999). Corporate ethics programs as control systems: Influences of executive commitment and environmental factors. *Academy of Management Journal, 42*, 41–57.

CHAPTER

25 Bridging the Domains of Leadership and Corporate Social Responsibility

David A. Waldman

Abstract

The concept of responsible leadership has commanded increased attention in recent years. Indeed, as evidenced in corporate scandals and polling information, irresponsibility on the part of people in leadership positions is an area of growing concern to the greater public and policy makers. In addition, responsibility is an issue that is being increasingly addressed by leadership scholars in terms of linking organizational leadership to social issues and corporate social responsibility (CSR). The chapter begins with a consideration of various societal and academic trends that have led to the need to more precisely consider the concept of responsible leadership. The chapter then presents an overview of alternative definitions of responsible leadership, connections with other leadership topics or models, existing research on responsible leadership, and future theory development and research agendas.

Key Words: Leadership, responsible leadership, corporate social responsibility, social issues

Introduction

Since the 1970s, there has been a continuing, theoretical, and empirical literature on corporate social responsibility (CSR). In line with prior work (e.g., McWilliams & Siegel, 2001, Waldman, Siegel, & Javidan, 2006), I define CSR as actions on the part of the firm that appear to advance or promote some socially based good, beyond the immediate financial interests of the firm and its shareholders, and beyond that which is required by law. A number of different targets of such actions are possible. For example, a firm may include socially responsible attributes in their products or services that might be of benefit to both consumers and the environment (e.g., the use of organic ingredients). As another example, firms may engage in actions toward employees that would be construed as socially responsible, such as avoidance of layoffs, promotion of women and minorities, and so forth. Other stakeholders, including suppliers, community groups, and government may also derive satisfaction from a firm's CSR actions.

From this definition, it is clear that CSR brings together a number of different interests or constituent groups that might be relevant to managers and their decisions. Accordingly, it is not surprising that stakeholder theory has been the predominant theoretical basis of CSR research (Donaldson & Preston, 1995; Freeman, 1984; Garriga & Melé, 2004). A key premise of stakeholder theory is that "each group of stakeholders merits consideration for its own sake and not merely because of its ability to further the interests of some other group, such as the shareowners" (Garriga & Melé, 2004, p. 60). In other words, organizations and their management should balance the needs and concerns of a variety of stakeholder entities. However, the precise meaning of "balance" continues to be a point of contention for those who espouse more normative versus instrumental views of both CSR and stakeholders (Donaldson & Preston, 1995; Margolis & Walsh,

2003). I will return to this contention later when the concept of responsible leadership is formally defined.

It is also evident that CSR could be relevant to multiple levels of analyses. That is, CSR pertains to individuals, groups, organizations, and societies. But with that said, the CSR literature has been largely macro in its orientation with much attention devoted to phenomena at organizational, industry, and even societal levels. For example, a large focus of study has been the possible relationship between CSR strategies or practices and firm performance (e.g., Hillman & Keim, 2001; Margolis & Walsh, 2001; Orlitzky, Schmidt, & Rynes, 2003). Much less attention has been directed to the behavior or characteristics of individuals who might be associated with CSR-related decisions or actions, such as leaders.

Accordingly, the overall purpose of this chapter is to consider responsible leadership. With that said, I fully realize that the topic of leadership represents an already crowded, conceptual space. Conceptualizations and prescriptions for effective leadership abound, and they include such things as transformational, ethical/moral, servant, and authentic depictions of leadership. In this chapter, I will make the argument that while related to each of these depictions, the concept of responsible leadership can add an important, as well as truly unique, perspective to considerations of effective leadership. Specifically, the goals of this chapter are fivefold. First, I will describe why the timing is right to bridge leadership and CSR. In so doing, both societal events and recent research and theoretical developments will be overviewed. Second, I will address complex, and even controversial, definitional issues regarding the amalgamation of leadership and CSR, which is referred to as responsible leadership in this chapter. Third, existing leadership topics or perspectives will be addressed in relation to responsible leadership. Fourth, research to date relevant to responsible leadership will be reviewed. Fifth, I will attempt to establish future theoretical and research agendas to move the concept of responsible leadership forward.

Has the Time Come to Understand the Nexus of Leadership and Responsibility?

There are two trends that would suggest that the answer to this question is yes: (1) public opinions pertaining to capitalistic systems and their leaders/stewards, and (2) evolving theoretical and empirical perspectives pertaining to the study of leadership processes. I overview each of these trends below and consider their implications for understanding the linkage between leadership and responsibility.

Public Opinion of Capitalism and Its Leaders

People in leadership positions in the business world operate in the context of a capitalistic system. A key premise of capitalism is that owner/shareholder wealth maximization has a positive influence on the greater social welfare, or the greater good of society. Simply stated, when individual businesses profit, the wealth that is generated allows for societal issues to be addressed through such means as additional tax revenue. However, Jones and Felps (2013) have recently questioned this premise, and as described in more detail below, popular opinion would suggest that capitalism itself is under attack, and a lack of responsible decisions or actions on the part of leaders may be largely the reason. Decades ago, Novak (1982) pointed toward the growing suspicion of the term "capitalism" in the lexicon of Western civilization. He noted that the concept of capitalism was rapidly becoming unpopular because it seemed devoid of spiritual meaning and even potentially disruptive of any sense of community in a society. Furthermore, the term was increasingly associated with selfishness and greed, exploitation, inequality, and even corruption—an image that if anything, has accelerated in more recent times. However, Novak (1982) also noted an upside in that capitalism could also enhance a society through its inherent promulgation of hard work and discipline, self-restraint, and even generosity and integrity. On balance, Novak viewed capitalism as an economic/social system that is at least potentially far superior to socialism, but at the same time, the self-interest encouraged by capitalism had to be balanced with appropriate values.

In more recent times, it is not an exaggeration that capitalism has come under increased scrutiny and attack by the media and society at large, with resulting backlash from government. Recent corporate scandals, especially in the financial industry, have only served to add fuel to the fire with regard to the image of capitalism, as well as perceived failures of people in leadership positions. Over the past decade, names like Lay, Skilling, Ebbers, and Madoff have become etched into the American psyche and have helped to create an image of irresponsibility, whether accurate or not, which is widely attributed to the leaders of corporations and capitalistic endeavors.

In turn, the scandals that are associated with them have fueled legislative backlash, such as the Sarbanes-Oxley Act of Congress, which is designed to ensure the proper enactment and reporting of financial activities on the part of firms (Geiger & Taylor, 2003). This piece of legislation requires significant expenditures by firms to ensure compliance, but such expenditures do little to actually support real productivity or innovation. Indeed, one estimate suggested that even for companies with revenues less than $1 billion, the average annual cost of compliance is approximately $3.4 million (Solomon, 2005). As such, Sarbanes-Oxley could be viewed as an example of an unfortunate drain on organizational performance and financial returns that is necessitated by a capitalistic system in which leaders of firms need policing in terms of responsible behavior. In short, the image of corporate leadership has been tarnished, with employees and the public as a whole largely perceiving them in a suspicious, at best, manner including attributions of distrust and greed—that is, they are no longer trusted to act responsibly as leaders.

In recent times, some interesting polls have emerged that are reflective of the trends mentioned above. One poll taken in the United States by *Rasmussen Reports* (2009) indicated that the term "capitalism" was increasingly being viewed with skepticism or distrust in that only 53 percent of the American public favored the concept, while 20 percent favored socialism, and 27 percent were not sure. Perhaps even more astounding, the percentages favoring capitalism versus socialism were nearly equivalent for young adults under the age of thirty. On the other hand, 70 percent of the public were still favorable toward the notion of a free-market economic system. Evidently for some individuals, the term capitalism connotes potentially insidious actions or motives, and it does not equate to free markets.

Another poll taken by *Harris Interactive* (2009) in the United States and five European countries (i.e., France, Germany, Great Britain, Spain, and Italy) may help provide a better understanding of the above numbers. In that poll, 76 percent of Americans and between 65 and 81 percent of adults in the European countries believe that the recent behavior of business leaders in general has been unethical or irresponsible (e.g., too much executive pay that is not linked to the performance of their firms, not enough concern on the part of executives for the job security of their employees, and so forth). Analyses of these polls numbers would suggest that when businesses and their leaders become unpopular, it affects how the media handles business events and stories, as well as the extent to which governments adopt tough antibusiness policies (e.g., through regulations and taxation) (*Harris Interactive*, 2009). Thus, as suggested above with regard to the Sarbanes-Oxley Act of the U.S. Congress, the unpopularity of business and its leaders might give government officials incentives to pursue more socialist policies in society as a whole.

These conclusions based on the polls presented above should be tempered with the notion that when it comes to perceptions of leaders and the responsibility that they show, bigger may not be better. An earlier poll (*Harris Interactive*, 2007) conducted just in the United States showed that 47 percent of respondents were highly confident in the leaders of small business companies, while only 5 percent said that they had "hardly any" confidence in these leaders.

So in total, what can the above information reveal, and how is it relevant to an understanding of responsible leadership? As suggested by Waldman (2011), the implication may actually be quite straightforward. Specifically, it may be that increasingly, people are associating capitalism directly with the leaders of major corporations, and what they perceive is not favorable. At least in terms of the image portrayed by media reporting, and subsequently digested in the psyche of the public, hypocrisy and personal greed seem to be the predominant modus operandi on the part of corporate leaders. In other words, the public does not perceive a widespread adherence to a larger sense of responsibility on the part of business leaders. Since these leaders represent the face or stewards of capitalism, perhaps there should be no wonder that the public is losing faith in corporations—and even the concept of capitalism itself. But in line with the arguments of Novak (1982), it may be that capitalism per se is not the problem. Instead, certain practices associated with leadership, and specifically irresponsible leadership, may be largely to blame.

With that said, there does seem to be a realization among many business leaders that they face increasingly skeptical publics, volatile environments, and a variety of stakeholders with their own sets of needs and backgrounds. Firms such as Southwest Airlines and Starbucks have leveraged leadership practices at multiple organizational levels to present a better image to the public and to help realize sustained effectiveness. But the point for now is that there is a nexus between effective leadership practices and responsibility in the eyes of the public. Accordingly, it would behoove leadership scholars to pay more systematic attention to this connection. Fortunately, there are both theoretical and empirical developments in recent years that can move such scholarship forward. I will overview these developments next.

Recent Developments Relevant to the Study of Responsible Leadership

There are several developments in recent times that are relevant to the study of responsible leadership. For example, in the study of leadership as a whole, there is increasing recognition of the relevance of ethics and morality (e.g., Bass & Steidlmeier, 1999; Brown & Trevino, 2006a; Brown, Trevino, & Harrison, 2005). But while there is some overlap between ethical and responsible leadership, they are not the same thing. Further, as will be discussed in more detail below, the conceptualization and study of ethical leadership is somewhat problematic, and the concept of responsible leadership may provide a better way forward for theorists and researchers.

Perhaps even more important, as is evident in earlier discussion, a full consideration of responsible leadership will necessarily mean going beyond the dyadic and small-group levels, which have been the predominant, targeted levels of leadership study (Yukl, 2010). In other words, the study of responsible leadership will inherently involve formulations that cross levels of analyses and even organizational boundaries. As an example, how might elements of CSR that are depicted in a CEO's vision affect the identity and commitment of individuals at lower organizational levels? Should the assessment of a CEO's leadership behavior or qualities take into account actions toward, or even perceptions of, external stakeholders? Is responsible leadership in an organization all about the actions of a single individual (e.g., the CEO), or does it inherently involve a more distributed set of individuals? In short, these questions suggest a broadened perspective of leadership processes.

Fortunately, several key perspectives or research trends have emerged in recent years that are relevant to the study of responsible leadership phenomena. First, given the more macro emphasis to date with regard to CSR research efforts, it would seem worthwhile to borrow ideas from the field of strategic management. To that end, the upper echelons perspective has evolved over the past few decades. It would suggest that characteristics of managers or executives affect their strategic choices that, in turn, can affect firm outcomes such as performance (Finkelstein, Hambrick, & Cannella, 2009). As noted by McWilliams and Siegel (2001), strategic choices can pertain specifically to CSR, for example, an initiative for a firm to "go green" in terms of environmental policies and actions.

Regarding the original conceptualization of the upper echelons perspective, Hambrick and Mason (1984) suggested that leaders' behavioral or psychological qualities, such as charisma, were not viable in relation to research endeavors. In essence, their thinking was that such qualities either could not be validly assessed, or executives would not be willing to devote the time to filling out the sorts of surveys that are associated with behavioral phenomena like leadership. It is not surprising that the majority of research based on the upper echelons perspective has primarily involved demographic or background characteristics, such as age, tenure, functional background, and so forth (Finkelstein & Hambrick, 1996). However, more recently, upper echelons theory and research has focused on behavioral characteristics, including leadership qualities, and their effects across organizational levels (Flynn & Staw, 2004; Galvin, Balkundi, & Waldman, 2010; Ling, Simsek, Lubatkin, & Veiga, 2008; Waldman, Ramirez, House, & Puranam, 2001). Indeed, as described in more detail later, some of that research has dealt specifically with managerial characteristics relevant to CSR-related decisions and outcomes.

Second, the vast majority of leadership theory and research has focused on individual *leaders* who occupy formal hierarchical roles. A broader perspective would suggest the consideration of effective *leadership* as a process of positive influence occurring within organizations in which formal leaders are only a part (Day, 2000). A perspective of this nature is indicative of emerging research and theory on shared leadership (e.g., Pearce & Conger, 2003), complexity leadership (Uhl-Bien, Marion, & McKelvery, 2007), and leadership capacity (Day, Gronn, & Salas, 2006). Indeed, Pearce and Conger (2003) defined shared leadership in terms of a dynamic process of mutual influence among peers or individuals at differing hierarchical levels in an organization. The potential need for leadership to be shared more broadly is driven by several forces. For example, the senior-most leaders of organizations do not possess sufficient, relevant information, or even the time, to make all of the decisions in a fast-changing and complex world. People lower in the hierarchy may be more highly informed on a variety of issues, and therefore, in a better position to provide leadership. Nowhere may this be more evident than the realm of CSR. For example, people at lower levels may be more in tune to the needs and desires of stakeholder groups, such as employees and customers. Thus, the overall achievement of responsible leadership in organizations may hinge on a perspective that centers on shared or distributed leadership.

Third, we are also starting to see more theory and research dealing with the effects of leader behavior across organizational boundaries and networks. Bono & Anderson (2005) examined the influence networks of transformational leaders, including such network characteristics as centrality. Ferris and colleagues (Ferris et al., 2005, 2007) examined political skills and savvy of leaders including their ability to form effective, network-based relationships within and between their own organizational units. Given the theoretical grounding of CSR in stakeholder theory, it is necessary for viable conceptualizations of responsible leadership to take into account firm stakeholders broadly considered—not just immediate or even distant followers who are within organizational boundaries.

In sum, theoretical perspectives and research precedence are now squarely established that lay the groundwork for scholarly work on responsible leadership. But with that said, there are some complex and even controversial issues surrounding the definition of responsible leadership. I now explore those issues and their implications for theory and research.

Defining Responsible Leadership

Before attempting definitions of responsible leadership, it is informative to consider the broader concept of responsibility. The dictionary defines responsibility in terms of legal, moral, *or* mental accountability. Indeed, some people might view responsibility as largely a legal matter. Based on such thinking, if the law is followed, one is acting responsibly. Others may see responsibility in more than just legal terms. Specifically, they would argue that there are moral considerations, and as such, a deeper set of values come into play in the pursuit of responsibility. Furthermore, the mental accountability aspect involves a felt obligation to act responsibly. Moreover, accountability can be directed toward individual people, or to animate (e.g., animals) or more inanimate objects or systems (e.g., an organization, an institution, the physical environment, and so forth). In other words, responsibility has multiple bases and can be directed toward multiple objects (Winter, 1991). As shown below, there is potentially a broad or even controversial platform upon which responsibility can be perceived and acted upon by individuals in leadership roles.

At its broadest level, responsible leadership represents a sort of fusion between CSR and the concept of leadership. As such, it is different from most leadership concepts that have been popular in recent years that typically have their basis in the realms of psychology and organizational behavior.[1] But given that different viewpoints exist with regard to the precise meaning of CSR and its effective implementation, it should not be surprising to learn that there are differing viewpoints about the meaning of responsible leadership. Here I present two distinct conceptualizations that have emerged that I label as follows: (1) stakeholder, and (2) economic/instrumental.

The Stakeholder Leader

Perspectives of CSR that have largely taken hold in the literature include what Garriga & Melé (2004) would term either integrative or ethical theories. The former suggests the idea that business should integrate social demands with business decision making, since business depends on society for its continuity and growth. Indeed, the point of much of the polling information that was presented earlier is reflective of integrative thinking. Ethical theories stress that the relationship between business and society is embedded within a normative, ethical framework that suggests that firms should accept social responsibilities as an obligation. In other words, firms should accept the needs and desires of stakeholder groups as legitimate and equal to that of owners/shareholders. It should thus not be surprising that a definition of responsible leadership that seems to be largely taking hold in the literature is in line with both integrative and ethical theories of CSR (Garriga & Melé, 2004). I refer to it as a stakeholder approach to responsible leadership, and it characterizes effective leadership in terms of efforts to take into account and balance or integrate the needs of stakeholders, in addition to shareholders, who may have legitimate interests in a firm's activities (Maak & Pless, 2006; Margolis & Walsh, 2001, 2003). With the stakeholder approach, leaders realize that a broad set of stakeholders have a legitimate claim on the policies and actions of the firm, and thus, there is an obligation to serve their interests.

The above definition of stakeholder-based, responsible leadership is apparent in the work of Waldman and colleagues (e.g., Pless, Maak,

& Waldman, 2012; Waldman & Galvin, 2008; Waldman & Siegel, 2008), as well as Maak and Pless (2006). Moreover, it mirrors ideas about responsible leadership that have been put forth by a number of prominent business leaders, such as Anita Roddick of the Body Shop, Herb Kelleher of Southwest Airlines, and John Mackey of Whole Foods (e.g., see *Reason*, 2005). For example, Waldman and Galvin (2008) discussed Mackey's emphasis on balancing the needs of multiple stakeholders (e.g., employees, customers, and the local community) and the natural environment.

The Economic/Instrumental Leader

The stakeholder approach may seem quite logical, and one might even be tempted to conclude that there is no other viable conceptualization of responsible leadership. However, in an exchange of letters (Waldman & Siegel, 2008), as well as in additional work (Siegel, 2009), Siegel has emphasized a viewpoint of responsible leadership based upon a strategic perspective of CSR (Husted & de Jesus Salazar, 2006; McWilliams & Siegel, 2001). As summarized by Garriga and Melé (2004), this more economic/instrumental perspective would suggest that the firm is simply a wealth creation device. Accordingly, actions on the part of the firm and its leader(s) that might help to generate some sort of social good should only be pursued if those actions can be clearly linked to wealth creation (Pless et al., 2012).

On that basis, Siegel (2009) challenged the notion that leaders should balance the needs of various stakeholder groups in their actions and decision making. Instead, he emphasized the more economic/instrumentally based notion that the priority (or responsibility) of leaders should be to maximize productivity and profits, while controlling costs. Accordingly, leaders who are truly acting responsibly will only invest in CSR efforts if those efforts can be shown to be cost effective and provide a clear financial return on investment. It follows that according to this definition of responsible leadership, the only real stakeholder whose needs or desires the leader should serve is the owner or shareholder. Thus, unlike normative stakeholder theory (Donaldson & Preston, 1995), or integrative and ethical theories of CSR (Garriga & Melé, 2004), those groups other than owners/shareholders would not be viewed as having legitimate interests in the activities of firms.

At its core, Siegel's definition is actually not very different from ideas put forth originally by Milton Friedman that the only social responsibility of a firm is to make profits for its shareholders (Friedman, 1970). To Friedman, managerial actions oriented toward anything other than profit maximization would actually run counter to leader responsibility. However, Siegel (2009) acknowledged that times had changed since the earlier pronouncements of Friedman in that there are increased pressures, as well as potential rewards, for firms to engage in CSR. Thus, Siegel argued that leaders could take carefully reasoned and calculative actions that would benefit broader stakeholder groups—that is, as long as those actions could be justified in terms of return on investment. The problem that he identified is that if not carefully controlled, leaders might make decisions that would benefit their own personal predilections or causes, potentially leading to "corporate misadventures" (Margolis & Walsh, 2003, p. 271). Alternatively stated, if not carefully controlled and monitored, CSR actions on the part of managers might not lead to benefits for firm owners/shareholders, and quite the opposite, could be very costly.

The economic/instrumental definition of responsible leadership would seem to make at least some sense. Agency theory suggests the need to carefully monitor and control the actions of executives (Jensen & Meckling, 1976; Walsh & Seward, 1990). In real life, this is accomplished largely through board of director approval of strategic decisions, the formation of contracts, and even disciplinary actions against executives if necessary. According to the agency perspective, if such monitoring and control are not exercised, opportunistic behavior that would not be of benefit to the firm's owners or shareholders becomes more likely. Many years ago, Adam Smith suggested that in agent-managed firms, "negligence and profusion, therefore, must always prevail [because hired managers are stewards of] other people's money" (1937, p. 122). In line with Siegel's (2009) concerns, the profusion in modern times to which Smith originally referred could pertain to particular CSR-related projects or interests of hired managers.

Conversely, stewardship theorists would argue that while managers and executives may pursue their own best interests or predilections (e.g., pet projects pertaining to CSR), most can be trusted to act consistently in the best interests of their firms (Davis, Schoorman, & Donaldson, 1997). This trust includes actions or expenditures that might, on the surface, appear to be more in the interests of stakeholders other than shareholders. In reality, if strong controls are placed on executives and their discretion, they might lose their identity with the firm, and thus, their intrinsic motivation and commitment (Ashforth & Mael, 1996). Accordingly, stewardship theorists, as well as other skeptics of agency theory (e.g., Ghoshal, 2005), would suggest that rather than restrain and control executives, they should be given maximum freedom to pursue CSR by using resources to help address the concerns of multiple stakeholder entities.

An example might help to illustrate the differences between stakeholder and economic approaches to responsible leadership. In recent years, a number of firms have allowed employees to use paid work hours to engage in community-based projects. For example, Timberland, Inc. has a record of allowing employees 40 paid hours of leave annually to pursue volunteer activities, which can involve either projects that the company supports, or those of the employees' own choosing (Reingold, 2005). From the stakeholder perspective to which the firm appears to be adhering, such policies are warranted since the firm is based in communities, and thus has an obligation to give back in terms employee time. Moreover, employees may find such activities to be intrinsically rewarding, thus fostering their identification and commitment to Timberland, which could ultimately have positive effects on their performance. On the other hand, an economic/instrumental approach to responsible leadership might be more circumspect in allowing such policies. Before pursuing policies similar to those of Timberland, leaders adhering to the economic/instrumental approach might want to see tangible, cost/benefit evidence that the lost productive time would not damage employee and firm performance. Conversely, they would want to see evidence of returns on initiatives of this type, such as good will or "favors" granted toward the firm.

The Moral Basis of Responsible Leadership Conceptualizations

Waldman (2011) noted that the stakeholder and economic/strategic approaches to responsible leadership differ in terms of their moral bases. As already described, the stakeholder portrayal of responsible leadership emphasizes the serving or balancing of the needs of a broad set of stakeholders (see Maak & Pless, 2006; Pless et al., 2012; Waldman & Galvin, 2008). As such, it tends to emphasize a broad moral imperative directed toward anyone or any entity that is affected by, or can affect, the firm. Maak and Pless (2006, p. 105) stated that "having a good character and being a moral person are at the core of being a responsible leader." Agle, Mitchell, and Sonnenfeld (1999) operationalized executive attitudes toward CSR in terms of firms' ethical treatment of a broad set of stakeholder entities. These examples follow from ethical approaches to CSR (Garriga & Melé, 2004), and they are predominant in the existing CSR literature, as well as the growing literature on responsible leadership.

However, in a different take, Milton Friedman was famous for his own assertions regarding executives and social responsibility. In his later years, he added a moral element, as is evident in the following quote, "There is but one 'social responsibility' for corporate executives... they must make as much money as possible for their shareholders. This is a moral imperative. Executives who choose social and environmental goals over profits—who try to act morally—are in fact immoral" (Bakan, 1994, p. 34). In other words, Friedman believed that to not have a single-minded pursuit of profits would inevitably lead executives to do things that would be immoral in relation to the needs of the firm and its only legitimate stakeholders—owners/shareholders. Disciples of Friedman such as Siegel (2009) would probably concur.

In line with the thinking of Agle et al. (1999), Jones, Felps, and Bigley (2007) characterized the morality and ethics of firms in terms of the extent to which their organizational cultures are largely other-regarding, rather than emphasizing a more narrow, self-regard. An other-regarding culture would value and take into account the needs of a broad set of stakeholder entities. Jones et al. (2007) would refer to the type of context that Friedman (see Bakan, 1994) exhorted as a corporate egoist or instrumentalist, organizational culture. As such, Jones et al. (2007) would not characterize such a context as depicting a broad *moral* imperative, since it is limited in terms of other-regard to concerns for owners/shareholders. In contrast, what I have labeled as a stakeholder approach to responsible leadership is more indicative of a moralist or altruist culture, as portrayed by Jones et al. (2007). But as already stressed above, the pure economic/instrumentalist approach to responsible leadership (e.g., Siegel, 2009) might argue that other-regarding could actually become immoral if it is spread too thin among a broad set of stakeholders, when in reality the only presumably legitimate stakeholder is the owner/shareholder.

The goal here is not to argue for the validity or moral legitimacy of the stakeholder, versus a more economic/instrumental approach, to defining responsible leadership. Rather, my goal is to simply point out that both definitions exist, have at least some moral basis, and are viable given the nascent stage of theory and empirical work pertaining to responsible leadership. Indeed, I foresee a danger in researchers forming a bias toward one particular definition prior to substantiation through research. The objective task of researchers is to provide evidence for these or other conceptualizations of responsible leadership that might arise in the future. Only then can we move toward a bona fide, normative theory of responsible leadership. In a later section, I will describe a research agenda that could lead toward such theory development. For now, it is important to put responsible leadership in the context of other approaches toward understanding effective leadership.

Responsibility in the Context of Existing Leadership Theory

The notion of responsibility is evident at least to some degree in a number of existing leadership theories. Accordingly, it is important to consider the overlap, while also pointing out what is missing in those theories with regard to a comprehensive consideration of responsible leadership. In this section, I will briefly consider the following approaches, each of which has been conceived to varying degrees in terms of responsibility: (1) leader-member exchange, (2) authentic leadership, (3) transformational leadership, (4) ethical/moral leadership, and (5) servant leadership. But before proceeding, it is important to point out that the responsibility component for these perspectives has heretofore been largely considered in terms of leader relations with internal organizational members. With that in mind, below I will offer potential theoretical extensions that could more fully reflect responsible leadership through a consideration of leader relations with individuals and entities external to the organization.

Leader-Member Exchange (LMX)

LMX is concerned with the one-on-one social exchange between a formal leader and a follower. According to LMX theory, a formal leader develops relationships of differing quality with different members of work groups during the ongoing process of role negotiation and role taking (on the part of the follower); delegation of tasks; and the follower not meeting, meeting, or exceeding expectations (Bauer & Green, 1996; Dienesch & Liden, 1986; Gerstner & Day, 1997). A low-quality LMX relationship is characterized by lower performance and a lack of responsibility showed by the follower, matched by close supervisory monitoring and lower-level or instrumental exchanges on the part of the leader. In contrast, a high-quality relationship features mutual trust, loyalty, and responsibility (Liden & Maslyn, 1998). In short, followers with high-quality LMX display more responsibility toward the leader and their work, and, in return, the leader shows a high degree of responsibility toward high LMX followers. Such responsibility is displayed through the granting of privileges, access to special resources such as information, and more opportunities for taking on higher-level tasks (Graen & Uhl-Bien, 1995; Liden, Sparrowe, & Wayne, 1997).

As should be apparent, at its current stage of theoretical development, the relevance of LMX to responsible leadership is rather limited. That is, as depicted above, responsible leadership is a concept largely applied to more strategic levels and across organizational boundaries, while LMX has generally been applied to dyadic relationships within formal work groups. But with that said, there may be opportunities for theoretical extensions. Specifically, through the partnership building concept (Graen & Uhl-Bien, 1995), it may be possible to extend LMX concepts to relations with key members of external stakeholders, such as leaders of consumer groups, environmentalists, communities, and so forth. Indeed, the concept of political skill or savvy could come into play as a means of analyzing the quality of such relationships (Ferris et al., 2005, 2007). Issues could be addressed such as the manner in which organizational leaders develop strong relationships with key external stakeholders and how these relationships may pertain to leader and organizational effectiveness.

Authentic Leadership

Avolio, Walumbwa, and Weber (2009) noted multiple definitions and components associated with authentic leadership in the literature. However, two dimensions appear to be consistent in definitions of authentic leadership and relevant to the conceptualizations of responsible leadership presented earlier. First, internal moral perspective involves being guided by one's internalized moral standards that, in turn, are used to consistently self-regulate one's behavior (Bass & Steidlmeier, 1999; Walumbwa, Avolio, Gardner, Wernsing, & Peterson, 2008). It is interesting how this dimension could apply to either a stakeholder or economic/

instrumental interpretations of responsible leadership. Regarding the former, Waldman and Galvin (2008) and Pless et al. (2012) might argue that the stakeholder leader shows his or her internalized moral standards by consistently attempting to serve the needs of all stakeholders who are affected by, or could affect, the operations of the firm. But at the same time, consistent with an economic/instrumental interpretation, Siegel (2009) might argue that an authentic leader with an internal moral perspective will recognize the moral imperative of consistently and exclusively targeting the needs of owners/shareholders. Again, the issue of morality can become somewhat relative or controversial.

Second, relational transparency involves presenting one's true self through openly sharing information and feelings that are appropriate for particular contexts (Walumbwa et al., 2008). In other words, and in plain terms, such transparency involves being up front and genuine. Relational transparency would seem to be quite consistent with prior characterizations of the stakeholder version of responsible leadership. Indeed, example leaders (e.g., John Mackey of Whole Foods) mentioned by Waldman and Galvin (2008) would appear to be up front and genuine in their beliefs and feelings pertaining to stakeholders.

On the other hand, it is not so clear that relational transparency is consistent with an economic/instrumental interpretation of responsible leadership, which would recognize that intangible benefits may occur for firms through the image/reputation building that accompanies CSR (McWilliams & Siegel, 2001; Siegel, 2009). Bakan (2004, p. 32) cynically noted that "pious social responsibility themes now vie with sex for top billing in corporate advertising, whether on television or in the pages of glossy magazines and newspapers." However, proponents of the economic/instrumental perspective would encourage leaders to take advantage of all of the positive image/reputation building that CSR might yield.

Again, a good example is Milton Friedman. Friedman was always leery of any actions taken toward CSR by firms and their leaders—instrumental or non-instrumental in nature. But shortly before his death in 2006, he did acknowledge that there is nothing wrong for leaders to use CSR as a means to maximize shareholders' wealth, as long as CSR is not an ends in itself. While not mentioning advertising per se, he noted that the instrumental use of CSR is like "putting a good-looking girl in front of an automobile to sell an automobile... that's not in order to promote pulchritude... that's in order to sell cars" (see Bakan, 2004, p. 34). In further describing CSR actions, he has said that "If our institutions and the attitudes of the public make it in their [corporate executives] self-interest to cloak their actions in this way, I cannot summon much indignation to denounce them" (*Reason*, 2005). In short, Friedman seemed to have suggested that a lack of leader authenticity, specifically in terms of relational transparency, might actually be a good thing.

Although research is sparse, some recent research would suggest that Friedman might be wrong. Beckman, Colwell, and Cunningham (2009) showed that leader authenticity might be relevant to the effective implementation of CSR. Their work coincides somewhat with that of Carmeli, Gilat, and Waldman (2007) who found that when a firm's reputation is based largely on CSR-related actions, employees tend to form stronger identification with the firm. Despite such initial findings, more research is necessary to understand the effects of leader authenticity with regard to CSR decisions and actions. For example, how do leaders demonstrate authenticity, or lack thereof, in terms of their CSR initiatives? Is authenticity best assessed by surveying multiple stakeholder groups, not just employees? Research addressing these and related questions could provide useful insights relevant to both authentic and responsible leadership.

Transformational Leadership

Following the work of House and Aditya (1997), Avolio et al. (2009) characterized "new-genre" theories of leadership as depicting leader characteristics and processes that could account for extraordinary effects on individuals, groups, and organizations. Among these theories, the transformational leadership paradigm has been predominant in the literature over the past 25 years and has been the focus of numerous studies (Judge & Piccolo, 2004; Lowe, Kroeck, & Sivasubramaniam, 1996). This model has been applied at multiple levels of organizations, and it emphasizes how exceptionally effective leaders relate to followers in a manner that inspires them to higher levels of commitment, identity, and performance. Transformational leaders do so through the articulation of strongly held beliefs and values and visionary communication (Bass & Bass, 2009). As described by various authors (e.g., Brown & Trevino, 2006b; Waldman & Javidan, 2009), vision associated with transformational leadership is oftentimes socialized in nature, thereby directed toward the greater good of the organization (rather than the individual leader) and society as a whole. As such, the vision of transformational leaders is likely to emphasize the role of the firm within the context of the greater community or society, the serving of customers, and so forth—all of which are in line with the stakeholder perspective or responsible leadership. In addition, transformational leaders are likely to show additional behaviors in line with responsible leadership, such as the individualized consideration of the developmental needs of followers (Bass & Bass, 2009). Further, they encourage innovative thinking and problem solving through intellectual stimulation that, as described further below, may be instrumental to the realization of CSR.

Transformational leadership has been contrasted with transactional leadership, which is characterized more in terms of maintaining the status quo and tangible exchanges (e.g., money, resources, and so forth) between leaders and followers (Lowe et al., 1996). Accordingly, it may be interesting to compare transactional leadership with the economic/instrumental approach to responsible leadership. While transactional leadership has traditionally emphasized exchanges between leaders and followers, the economic/instrumental conceptualization of responsible leadership is more strategic in nature, stressing how CSR initiatives or strategies should only be pursued if there are clear returns on investment. Thus, both are built on the phenomenon of exchanges.

In sum, because of its apparent applicability to higher levels of leadership, as well as its consideration of socialized visions and pursuits, the transformational/transactional leadership paradigm is perhaps most applicable of the leadership models reviewed thus far to the concept of responsible leadership. However, there are important differences. For example, as mentioned earlier, to fully understand responsible leadership, researchers will need to cross organizational boundaries. Yet, most transformational leadership research has dealt exclusively with internal follower evaluations of leadership and internal effects (e.g., firm performance). One exception is the theoretical work of Fanelli and Misangyi (2006), which considered the potential effects of CEO charisma, a key component of transformational leadership, on external stakeholders of a firm. It would be interesting to see research along these lines, perhaps asking representatives of key stakeholder groups, other than internal followers, about the transformational qualities of firm leaders.

Ethical/Moral Leadership

Among the perspectives presented here, perhaps ethical/moral leadership is most intuitively connected to responsible leadership. Indeed, ethical/moral leadership has received increased attention in recent times (Brown & Trevino, 2006; Brown et al., 2005), perhaps for some of the same, societal-driven reasons that I considered earlier. It is based on values and principles, as are considerations of responsible leadership. Yet, as suggested earlier, the ethics or morals surrounding responsible leadership are not commonly agreed upon. At the same time, I would suggest that any confusion or controversy pertaining to the concept of responsible leadership may actually be less than that associated with ethical/moral leadership.

I would argue that, as compared to the emerging paradigm surrounding ethical/moral leadership, a focus on leader responsibility can potentially be applied in more beneficial ways. First, Brown and Trevino (2006) discussed how the conceptualization and measurement of ethical/moral leadership to date have tended to be focused upon dyadic and group levels of analyses. In other words, ethical/moral leadership has stressed supervisory-level leadership behavior directed toward immediate subordinates. They acknowledged that although the issue of ethics or morality is clearly relevant to strategic-level leaders (e.g., Thomas, Schermerhorn, & Dienhart, 2004), its conceptualization at such levels of leadership is not so clear. In contrast, the concept of responsible leadership has emerged largely out of the CSR literature and stakeholder perspective. As such, responsible leadership may be uniquely situated to address the ethical/moral concerns of executive leaders, which include both internal and external constituencies. In short, at least at strategic levels, the concept of responsible leadership may help to elevate the discussion of leadership ethics or morality.

Second, an advantage of responsible leadership is that it might help researchers and practitioners alike avoid some of the ambiguity pertaining to ethical/moral leadership. To be sure, as already discussed, there are multiple interpretations of the morality surrounding responsible leadership. But the existing controversy is at least focused in terms of considerations of relevant stakeholder groups to whom leaders may be obligated. However, the emerging paradigm of ethical/moral leadership has defined that concept in local terms as it pertains to leader actions relevant to the norms and values of particular contexts or collectives of individuals (Brown & Trevino, 2006; Brown et al., 2005). Following such thinking, it is conceivable for things such as alcohol consumption (even in the course of doing business), occasional swearing, or certain sexual behavior/orientations (e.g., homosexuality) to be considered as unethical or immoral in one context, but not in another context. As an example of the controversy that can surround a contextual viewpoint, consider the following example. If relatively mild forms of sexual harassment are in line with the norms of a particular context (e.g., sexual jokes or innuendo in staff meetings), should such behavior be considered to be within the bounds of what might be termed ethical/moral? Such inconsistencies and questions, at best, lead to ambiguity with regard to the meaning of ethical/moral leadership.

Jones et al. (2007) attempted to deal with the above dilemma and inconsistencies. Specifically, they discussed how local communities or collectives could develop their own standards or "moral free space" (p. 140) as long as universal standards or "hypernorms" are not violated. To date, this sort of resolution has apparently not been fully considered by the ethical/moral leadership paradigm—either conceptually or through measurement processes (e.g., see Brown et al., 2005). Jones et al. (2007) converged on the notion of concern for self versus others as an overarching principle of how ethics could be applied to an understanding of stakeholder cultures, and I would argue, an understanding of responsible leadership as well. In a similar vein, Gini (2004) largely equated ethical and responsible leadership through the common denominator of showing a strong concern for others. In sum, although ethics and morality are inextricably bound to considerations of responsible leadership, emerging definitions of this construct may at least provide a more straightforward way to deal with the pertinent ethical/moral issues facing leaders.

Servant Leadership

Finally, the concept of servant leadership stresses the idea of how leaders should be responsive to, and serve the needs of, followers, rather than their own self-interests (Barbuto & Wheeler, 2006; Greenleaf, 1977). Thus, servant leadership could be considered as a concept stressing a high degree of responsibility shown by leaders toward followers. It differs from LMX in that there is no consideration of a two-way relationship or differing qualities of relationships. Rather, it is the obligation of leaders to serve the needs of *all* followers. As shown by Liden, Wayne, Zhao, and Henderson (2008), servant leadership is also at least somewhat unique vis-à-vis transformational leadership, although there is some overlapping, conceptual content (e.g., idealized influence and individualized consideration). Moreover, conceptualizations and measures of servant leadership consistently include moral/ethical content (e.g., Ehrhart, 2004; Graham, 1991; Liden et al., 2008).

Heretofore, much of the thinking in the servant leadership literature has been internal to the organization. That is, leaders serve the needs of followers within organizational boundaries. However, it is not a great intellectual leap to potentially apply the servant leadership concept to stakeholder entities outside of an organization's boundaries. Along such lines, it is interesting to note that the philosophy behind servant leadership is very much in line with ethical theories of CSR, which would suggest that firms (and their leaders) should accept responsibilities to serve the needs of stakeholder groups as an ethical obligation (Garriga & Melé, 2004).

Graham (1991) specifically considered how servant leadership could extend beyond organizational boundaries, including service to multiple stakeholder groups, communities, and even society as a whole. Indeed, more recent thinking has emphasized the potential role of servant leadership in relation to stakeholders beyond employees (Ehrhart, 2004; Liden et al., 2008). But with that said, like other leadership research, recent research involving servant leadership has focused on internal outcomes relevant to followers, such as effects on follower organizational commitment, organizational citizenship, and in-role job performance (Ehrhart, 2004; Liden et al., 2008; Walumbwa, Hartnell, & Oke, 2010). Perhaps future research could apply the servant leadership concept and measures (e.g., Barbuto & Wheeler, 2006; Ehrhart, 2004; Liden et al., 2008) to leader actions directed toward external stakeholders that go beyond community-oriented service.

Responsible Leadership Research to Date

Given the connections that have been made here between responsible leadership and existing leadership theories, it might be tempting to view research in this area with a broad brush. In other words, responsible leadership research could potentially be viewed as encompassing any research that deals with the effects of leadership on any stakeholder group, including employees of a firm. If that was the case, then the domain of responsible leadership research would be so broad as to be rendered meaningless.

With that acknowledged, I will now explicitly consider two types of research that are directly relevant to responsible leadership as defined in this chapter. First, I examine existing research that has looked at leadership phenomena in relation to CSR outcomes. Second, given the connection of responsible leadership with stakeholder theory, I will consider research that has examined leader characteristics in relation to behavior or values toward multiple stakeholder groups.

Leadership and CSR Outcomes

To date, there has been at least some research examining the effects of leadership on CSR outcomes. Waldman et al. (2006) used CEO transformational leadership to predict subsequent measures of corporate social performance, as is frequently measured through Kinder, Lydenberg, and Domini (KLD) data. KLD is a firm that provides data for investors who wish to ensure that their investment portfolios include firms with strong CSR policies, while excluding companies that may violate their social principles. This information is based on KLD analysts' interpretations of various sources of data, including surveys, financial statements, articles on companies in the popular press and academic journals, and government reports. Waldman et al. (2006) found that CEO intellectual stimulation and, to a lesser degree, charisma were predictive of what they termed strategically oriented CSR, but not for more socially oriented CSR. They reasoned that intellectually stimulating leaders focus their CSR efforts on areas that are most germane to strategic concerns of the firm, such as product quality and environmental performance. In contrast, CSR issues that have more of a social basis (i.e., community relations and diversity) were not significantly related to either CEO intellectual stimulation or charisma. Perhaps attention to these latter issues could be due to managerial phenomena other than transformational leadership qualities, such as the desire to maintain a positive firm image.

While providing a good start, the Waldman et al. (2006) research does not address a number of questions that might be relevant to understanding the relationship between leadership behavioral qualities and firm-level, CSR outcomes. For example, what mediating variables may intercede in this relationship? Can leadership on the part of a single individual (e.g., a CEO) best account for firm-level CSR, or are shared/distributed leadership processes more relevant? These and other questions represent viable topics for future responsible leadership research.

At a more micro level, Liden et al. (2008) found that an aspect of servant leadership, creating value for the community, was related to the extent to which followers show community citizenship behavior. This aspect involves the extent to which the leader emphasizes the importance of giving back to the community through helping people, as well as whether s/he encourages others to do so as well. It should be noted that the findings of Liden et al. (2008) are somewhat limited in scope and could be due to artifact. That is, both servant leader behavior and follower community citizenship behavior were evaluated by followers, and both measures had similarly worded items. Nevertheless, their work does suggest new avenues for responsible leadership research that will be considered below.

Responsible leadership is largely about the interface between leaders and the stakeholders of a firm, and some interesting research has examined the manner in which leaders view and react toward these stakeholders. Agle et al. (1999) found that the perceptions of CEOs of stakeholders' power, legitimacy, and urgency were related to precisely which stakeholders CEOs actually pay attention. However, despite their predictions, these researchers failed to establish a link between perceived stakeholder salience and firm financial or social performance.

Agle et al. (1999) also established some theoretical and empirical connections between CEO values and perceptions of stakeholders. Sully de Luque, Washburn, Waldman, and House (2008) built on their work by examining the specific economic or stakeholder criteria that leaders use when engaging in critical, strategic decision making. They referred to such criteria in terms of decision-making values. On the one hand, leaders may put emphasis on economically based values, thereby emphasizing profits, cost control, and so forth. On the other hand, leaders may emphasize a range of stakeholders in their strategic decisions, such as customers, employees, environmental concerns, and the greater community in which the firm is located. Sully de Luque et al. found that leaders (i.e., firm CEOs) who value a range of stakeholders in their strategic decision making are associated with more inspiring leadership, as well as more highly effective firms. In contrast, leaders who emphasize economic values are associated with autocratic leadership and no subsequent relationships with firm effectiveness. In short, this study provides at least some initial, normative support for a stakeholder-based definition or responsible leadership, as opposed to a more economic/instrumental definition.

Future Theory Development and Research Agenda

As should be evident from the above review, research on responsible leadership is at a nascent

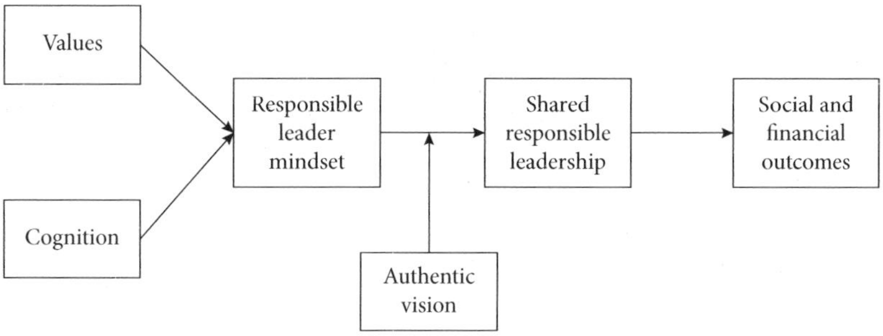

Figure 25.1. A Model of Responsible Leadership and its Effects.

stage of development. I see a number of reasons for the slow evolution of research along these lines. For example, responsible leadership is inherently tied to strategic concerns, and an examination of leadership phenomena at strategic levels has not been the norm in leadership research. In addition, research on responsible leadership will necessarily lead scholars to conceive of leadership processes and effects beyond organizational boundaries—territory into which few researchers have explored.

With that said, I see a clear need for theory development pertaining to responsible leadership as a process. My hope is that the current chapter sets the groundwork for such theory, at least in terms of providing a consideration of definitional issues. But beyond basic definitions, in Figure 25.1, I also offer what may be the beginning of a theoretical framework upon which responsible leadership might be based. There are several features of the model to note. First, in line with the work of Sully de Luque et al. (2008), it begins with the idea that values and cognition form the foundation of an understanding of responsible leadership. As an example of cognitive elements, Sonenshein (2007) considered how different identities, perspectives, and social anchors (i.e., group[s] to which an individual has a strong identification) could determine how individuals cognitively construct issues like responsibility. For example, someone with a strong identity or social anchor as a Milton Friedman(ish) economist would likely construct responsibility issues along the lines of an economic/instrumental perspective. That is, s/he would view owners/shareholders as the only legitimate stakeholders of the firm. Conversely, an individual with a strong identity or social anchor in the more traditional business and society realm would be likely to construct responsibility issues along the lines of a stakeholder approach. That is, s/he would view stakeholders as having a legitimate claim on the firm and its actions, and hence, leaders should balance their concerns in their decision making.

Second, values, beliefs, and cognitive structures combine to form what has been termed "mindsets." As suggested by Levy, Beechler, Taylor, and Boyacigiller (2007), mindsets are likely to guide one's attention and interpretation of information, and thus, may be very relevant to the realization and outcomes of different forms of responsible leadership. For example, in line with the alternative definitions provided here, responsible leader mindsets could vary from being more economic/instrumental in nature, to being more concerned with balancing the perceived, legitimate needs of a broad set of stakeholders.

Third, Figure 25.1 portrays how a responsible leader mindset can potentially result in shared responsible leadership. In other words, there is a recognition that a key formal leader (e.g., CEO) may need to form the impetus for the firm's orientation toward CSR (Waldman et al., 2006). However, for CSR initiatives and a particular form of stakeholder culture to take hold (e.g., Jones et al., 2007), there needs to be shared vision (Pearce & Ensley, 2004) or strategic consensus (Mathieu, Maynard, Rapp, & Gilson, 2008), which reflects a shared understanding of strategic priorities among managers at various organizational levels. Furthermore, Figure 25.1 would suggest that the relationship between leader mindset and shared responsible leadership is moderated by the extent to which the formal leader's vision is authentic in nature (Bass & Steidlmeier, 1999). For example, it may seem politically correct for a leader to present a vision in stakeholder terms (e.g., giving deference to the needs of consumers, the local community, the environment, and so forth). However, on a daily basis, it could become apparent that the leader leans more toward an economic/instrumental, rather than stakeholder, mindset. If that were to be the case, the leader is not likely to be seen as up front and genuine in his vision, with little resulting shared vision/leadership throughout the organization to pursue and effectively implement CSR initiatives.

Finally, the model in Figure 25.1 would suggest that shared aspects of responsible leadership (e.g., shared vision, strategic consensus, and servant leadership) will result in positive outcomes for the firm in terms of both social and financial performance. Obviously, the theory summarized here should be considered both initial and somewhat cursory in scope. But at the same time, it is suggestive of the somewhat complex nature of responsible leadership. I now turn our attention to the type of research agenda that could result from such theory development.

Toward a Research Agenda for Responsible Leadership

Coinciding with the development of conceptualizations of leadership, researchers have concomitantly developed survey measures with followers commonly used as raters. Indeed, leadership research has a long been associated with survey-based, measurement instruments and data based on perceptions of the followers of leaders. For example, the Multifactor Leadership Questionnaire has received much prominence as a tool to assess transformational leadership (Bass & Avolio, 1997). As another example, Graen and Uhl-Bien's (1995) developed the LMX-7 scale. Moreover, Brown et al. (2005) developed a measure of ethical/moral leadership, and Liden et al. (2008) presented a new measure of servant leadership.

But what should be evident in Figure 25.1 is that responsible leadership is a multifaceted process, and its assessment is likely to encompass some combination of leader mindsets, leader behaviors, and shared leadership phenomena. In addition, it may be appropriate to get the input of multiple stakeholder groups. For example, items pertaining to the leader and his/her actions could be posed to a range of stakeholders, including community members, suppliers, customers, representatives of environmental groups, and so forth. In sum, the assessment of responsible leadership is likely to break somewhat from the norm of leadership measurement that has developed over the years.

Beyond measurement and data collection procedures, consideration should also be given to how research strategies could move us closer to a normative theory of responsible leadership. It should be evident that the model posed in Figure 25.1 is descriptive in nature, and as such, represents an appropriate theoretical approach, given the current state of knowledge concerning responsible leadership. It is also in line with the thinking put forth by Margolis and Walsh (2003) in terms of a pragmatic, as opposed to partisan, CSR research agenda. In the context of responsible leadership per se, I propose that research efforts in the near future should be quite descriptive without deference to any particular conceptualization as being either "right" or "wrong."

Important questions could be addressed in such a research agenda. For example, do alternative forms of responsible leadership lead to more or less corporate social or financial performance at the firm level? What exactly are the roles of leader authenticity or shared leadership processes in the realization of these performance outcomes? Furthermore, as noted earlier, some economists would suggest that the economic/instrumental approach to responsible leadership aggregates across firms to produce more favorable societal-level outcomes (Friedman, 1970; Jensen, 2001). However, Jones and Felps (2013) provided evidence and arguments that would make such linkages equivocal at best. The fallout also mentioned earlier with regard to public opinion of large corporations and its leaders may be at least partially due to a predominant economic/instrumental stance on their part toward CSR. In sum, by pursuing descriptive research of this nature at the present time, we may eventually move closer to a research-based, normative theory of responsible leadership.

I should also note that journals are likely to increasingly see the need for research linking leadership to CSR and its outcomes. For example, *Personnel Psychology* recently published a special issue on the connection between HR/OB and CSR (Morgeson, Aguinis, Waldman, & Siegel, 2013). The time may be especially ripe for the research agenda that I have posed here.

Concluding Thoughts

As should be apparent from the above discussion, the topics of CSR, in general, and responsible leadership, more specifically, are inherently value laden and ideological in nature. Accordingly, individuals including scholars are likely to have strong feelings pertaining to these topics. It is somewhat reasonable to assume that many, if not most, researchers who are interested in responsible leadership might inherently lean toward the stakeholder perspective. Using the language of Sonenshein (2007), their social anchors might include networks and affiliations that recognize the claims of stakeholders. These anchors, in turn, could potentially bias the conceptualizations and methods used by researchers. In others words, problems can potentially arise when underlying values and ideologies of a scholar start to affect, or even bias, one's writings and research efforts. Thus, I suggest that researchers who develop theory and investigate responsible leadership should, at a minimum, be aware of their own ideological values, and understand how those values could potentially bias their efforts or advice provided to practitioners.

Responsible leadership should be placed clearly within the realm of leadership theory. It may be tempting to characterize organizations as a whole in terms of displaying (or not displaying) responsible leadership. However, leadership is a process that involves individuals serving as either lone leaders or in a more shared/distributed capacity. In terms of the latter, Day, Gronn, and Salas (2004) proposed that the overall leadership capacity of an entity is a form of social capital that involves the sharedness, distributedness, and connectivity of its members. In line with the work of Day et al. (2004), with regard to responsible leadership, I would propose that leadership capacity could encompass individuals beyond organizational boundaries, such as representatives of stakeholder groups.

But the point here is that for the purposes of understanding responsible leadership, it is necessary to focus on formal leaders in the hierarchy and/or individuals more distributed. Somewhat counter to this notion, it is important to recognize that term "leadership" has been used in an all-encompassing manner when depicting an organizational entity. In other words, it may be tempting to apply it to an organization as a whole, rather than individuals or processes shared by individuals (e.g., distributed or shared leadership). For example, an organization as a whole could be characterized as exhibiting "responsible leadership" because aspects of its policies, practices, or CSR outcomes appear to be in line with a particular way of thinking about responsibility. Perhaps leadership as defined here is indeed present in such an organization. Nevertheless, for the sake of placing the concept of responsible leadership squarely within the realm of leadership theory and research, it should not be confused with organizational-level phenomena (e.g., HR policies) that do not pertain directly to individual leaders. Thus, responsible leadership should not be considered as being the same as responsible organizations. Leaders, not firms, make decisions or take actions pertaining to responsibility or CSR.

In conclusion, it is clear that for both practical and scholarly reasons, responsible leadership is a topic whose time has come. But with that said, for leadership scholars, it may require some "out-of-the-box" thinking. As suggested in this chapter, the topic of responsible leadership presents challenges for theorists and researchers alike. These challenges include expanding the scope of thinking of what leadership is all about and the levels at which it exists, what constitutes its morality or immorality, and how it should be approached in terms of research methods. In this chapter, I have attempted to outline the nature of some of these challenges and suggest ways to move forward. By addressing these challenges, not only will the field of leadership become enriched, but we may also witness increased viability of our academic pursuits in the eyes of practitioners and the greater society at large.

Note

1. Note that one exception is the topic of strategic leadership, which has bridged together concepts from various leadership theories (e.g., transformational leadership) with strategic management concerns or perspectives. For example, see the work of Finkelstein et al. (2009).

References

Agle, B. R., Mitchell, R. K., & Sonnenfeld, J. A. (1999). Who matters to CEOs? An investigation of stakeholder attributes and salience, corporate performance, and CEO values. *Academy of Management Journal, 42*, 507–525.

Ashforth, B. E., & Mael, F. A. (1996). Organizational identity and strategy as a context for the individual. In J. A. C. Baum & J. E. Dutton (Eds.), *Advances in strategic management* (vol. 13, pp. 19–64). Greenwich, CT: JAI Press.

Avolio, B. J., Walumbwa, F. O., & Weber, T. J. (2009). Leadership: Current theories, research, and future directions. *Annual Review of Psychology, 60*, 421–449.

Bakan, J. (2004). *The corporation: The pathological pursuit of profit and power.* New York: Free Press.

Barbuto, J. E., & Wheeler, D. W. (2006). Scale development and construct clarification of servant leadership. *Group and Organization Management, 31*, 300–326.

Bass, B., & Avolio, B. 1997. *Multifactor leadership questionnaire manual.* Palo Alto, CA: Mindgarden.

Bass, B. M., & Bass, R. (2009). *Bass handbook of leadership: Theory, research, and managerial applications* (4th ed). New York: Free Press.

Bass, B. M., & Steidlmeier, P. (1999). Ethics, character, and authentic transformational leadership behavior. *The Leadership Quarterly, 10*, 181–217.

Bauer, T. N., & Green, S. G. (1996). Development of leader-member exchange: A longitudinal test. *Academy of Management Journal, 39*, 1538–1567.

Beckman, T., Colwell, A., & Cunningham, P. H. (2009). The emergence of corporate social responsibility in Chile: The importance of authenticity and social networks. *Journal of Business Ethics, 86*(S2), 191–206.

Brown, M. E., & Trevino, L. K. (2006a). Ethical leadership: A review and future directions. *The Leadership Quarterly, 17*, 595–616.

Brown, M. E., & Trevino, L. K. (2006b). Socialized charismatic leadership, values congruence, and deviance in work groups. *Journal of Applied Psychology, 91*, 954–962.

Brown, M. E., Trevino, L. K., & Harrison, D. A. (2005). Ethical leadership: A social learning perspective for construct development and testing. *Organizational Behavior and Human Decision Processes, 97*, 117–134.
Carmeli, A., Gilat, A., & Waldman, D. A. (2007). The role of perceived organizational performance in organizational identification, adjustment and job performance. *Journal of Management Studies, 44*, 972–992.
Davis, J. H., Schoorman, F. D., & Donaldson, L. (1997). Toward a stewardship theory of management. *Academy of Management Review, 22*, 20–47.
Day, D. V. (2000). Leadership development: A review in context. *The Leadership Quarterly, 11*, 581–613.
Day, D. V., Gronn, P., & Salas, E. (2004). Leadership capacity in teams. *The Leadership Quarterly, 15*, 857–880.
Day, D. V., Gronn, P., & Salas, E. (2006). Leadership in team-based organizations: On the threshold of a new era. *The Leadership Quarterly, 17*, 211–216.
Dienesch, R. M., & Liden, R. C. (1986). Leader-member exchange model of leadership: A critique and further development. *Academy of Management Review, 11*, 618–634.
Donaldson, T., & Preston, L. (1995). The stakeholder theory of the corporation: Concepts, evidence, and implications. *Academy of Management Review, 20*, 65–91.
Ehrhart, M. G. (2004). Leadership and procedural justice climate as antecedents of unit-level organizational citizenship behavior. *Personnel Psychology, 57*, 61–94.
Fanelli, A., & Misangyi, V. F. (2006). Bringing out charisma: CEO charisma and external stakeholders. *Academy of Management Review, 31*, 1049–1061.
Ferris, G. R., Treadway, D. C., Kolodinsky, R. W., Hochwarter, W. A., Kacmar, C. J., Douglas, C., & Frink, D. D. (2005). Development and validation of the political skill inventory. *Journal of Management, 31*, 126–152.
Ferris, G. R., Treadway, D. C., Perrewe, P. L., Brouer, R. L., Douglas, C., & Lux, S. (2007). Political skill in organizations. *Journal of Management, 33*, 290–320.
Finkelstein, S., & Hambrick, D. C. (1996). *Strategic leadership: Top executives and their effects*. St. Paul, MN: West Publishing.
Finkelstein S., Hambrick D., & Cannella B. (2009). *Strategic leadership: Top executives and their effects on organizations* (2nd ed). St. Paul, MN: West Publishing.
Flynn, F. J., & Staw, B. M. (2004). Lend me your wallets: The effect of charismatic leadership on external support for an organization. *Strategic Management Journal, 25*, 309–330.
Freeman, R. E. (1984). *Strategic management: A stakeholder approach*. Boston: Pitman.
Friedman, M. (1970). The social responsibility of business to increase its profits. *New York Times*, September 13, 122–126.
Galvin, B., Balkundi, P., & Waldman, D. A. (2010). Spreading the word: The role of surrogates in charismatic leadership processes. *Academy of Management Review, 35*, 477–494.
Garriga, E., & Melé, D. (2004). Corporate social responsibility theories: Mapping the territory. *Journal of Business Ethics, 53*, 51–71.
Geiger, M. A., & Taylor, P. L., III (2003). CEO and CFO certifications of financial information. *Accounting Horizons, 17*, 357–368.
Gerstner, C. R., & Day, D. V. (1997). Meta-analytic review of leader-member exchange theory: Correlates and construct issues. *Journal of Applied Psychology, 82*, 827–844.
Ghoshal, S. (2005). Bad management theories are destroying good management practices. *Academy of Management Learning and Education, 4*, 75–91.
Gini, A. (2004). Moral leadership and business ethics. In J. B. Ciulla (Ed.), *Ethics, the heart of leadership* (pp. 25–43). Westport, CT: Praeger.
Graen, G. B., & Uhl-Bien, M. (1995). Development of leader-member exchange (LMX) theory of leadership over 25 years: Applying a multi-level multi-domain perspective. *The Leadership Quarterly, 6*, 219–247.
Graham, J. W. (1991). Servant leadership in organizations: Inspirational and moral. *The Leadership Quarterly, 2*, 105–119.
Greenleaf, R. K. (1977). *Servant leadership: A journey into the nature of legitimate power and greatness*. Mahwah, NJ: Paulist Press.
Hambrick, D. C. & Mason, P. A. (1984). Upper echelons: The organization as a reflection of its top managers. *Academy of Management Review, 9*, 193–206.
Harris Interactive. (2007). http://www.harrisinteractive.com/vault/Harris-Interactive-Poll-Research-Conf-in-Institutions-2007-02.pdf
Harris Interactive. (2009). http://www.harrisinteractive.com/vault/Harris-Interactive-Poll-Research-FT-2009-Business-leaders-4.pdf
Hillman, A. J., & Keim, G. D. (2001). Shareholder value, stakeholder management, and social issues: What's the bottom line? *Strategic Management Journal, 22*, 125–139.
House, R. J., & Aditya, R. (1997). The social scientific study of leadership: Quo vadis? *Journal of Management, 23*, 409–474.
Husted, B. W., & de Jesus Salazar, J. (2006). Taking Friedman seriously: Maximizing profits and social performance. *Journal of Management Studies, 43*, 75–91.
Jensen, M. C. (2001). Value maximization, stakeholder theory, and the corporate objective function. *European Financial Management, 7*, 297–317.
Jensen, M. C., & Meckling, M. (1976). Theory of the firm: Managerial behavior, agency costs and ownership structure. *Journal of Financial Economics, 3*, 305–360.
Jones, T. M., & Felps, W. (2013). Shareholder wealth maximization and social welfare: A utilitarian critique. *Business Ethics Quarterly, 23*, 207-238.
Jones, T. M., Felps, W., & Bigley, G. A. (2007). Ethical theory and stakeholder-related decisions: The role of stakeholder culture. *Academy of Management Review, 32*, 137–155.
Judge, T. A., & Piccolo, R. F. (2004). Transformational and transactional leadership: A meta-analytic test of their relative validity. *Journal of Applied Psychology, 89*, 755–768.
Levy, O., Beechler, S., Taylor, S., & Boyacigiller, N. A. (2007). What we talk about when we talk about "global mindset": Managerial cognition in multinational corporations. *Journal of International Business Studies, 38*, 231–258.
Liden, R. C., & Maslyn, J. M. (1998). Multi-dimensionality of leader-member exchange: An empirical assessment through scale development. *Journal Management, 24*, 43–72.
Liden, R. C., Sparrowe, R. T., & Wayne, S. J. (1997). Leader-member exchange theory. The past and potential for the future. *Research in Personnel and Human Resources Management, 15*, 47–119.
Liden, R. C., Wayne, S. J., Zhao, H., & Henderson, D. (2008). Servant leadership: Development of a multidimensional measure and multi-level assessment. *The Leadership Quarterly, 19*, 161–177.

Ling, Y., Simsek, Z., Lubatkin, M., & Veiga, J. (2008). The impact of transformational CEOs on the performance of small- to medium-sized firms: Does organizational context matter?" *Journal of Applied Psychology, 93*, 923–934.

Lowe, K. B, Kroeck, K. G., & Sivasubramaniam, N. (1996). Effectiveness correlates of transformational and transactional leadership: A meta-analytic review of the MLQ literature. *The Leadership Quarterly, 7*, 385–425.

Maak, T., & Pless, N. M. (2006). Responsible leadership in a stakeholder society—A relational Perspective. *Journal of Business Ethics, 66*, 99–115.

Margolis, J. D., & Walsh, J. P. (2001). *People and profits? The search for a link between a company's social and financial performance*. Mahwah, NJ: Lawrence Erlbaum.

Margolis, J. D., Walsh, J. P. (2003). Misery loves companies: Rethinking social initiatives by business. *Administrative Science Quarterly, 48*, 268–305.

Mathieu, J., Maynard, M. T., Rapp, T., & Gilson, L. (2008). Team effectiveness 1997–2007: A review of recent advancements and a glimpse into the future. *Journal of Management, 34*, 410–476.

McWilliams, A., & Siegel, D. (2001). Corporate social responsibility: A theory of the firm perspective. *Academy of Management Review, 26*, 117–227.

Morgeson, F. P., Aguinis, H., Waldman, D. A., & Siegel, D. S. (2013). Extending corporate social responsibility research to the human resource management and organizational behavior domains: A look to the future. *Personnel Psychology, 66*, 805–824.

Novak, M. (1982). *The spirit of democratic capitalism*. New York: Simon & Schuster.

Orlitzky M., Schmidt F. L. & Rynes, S. (2003). Corporate social and financial performance: A meta-analysis. *Organization Studies, 24*, 403–411.

Pearce, C. L., & Conger, J. A. (2003). All those years ago: The historical underpinnings of shared leadership. In C. L. Pearce and J. A. Conger (Eds.), *Shared leadership: Reframing the hows and whys of leadership* (pp. 1–18). Thousand Oaks, CA: Sage.

Pearce, C. L., & Ensley, M. D. (2004). A reciprocal and longitudinal investigation of the innovation process: The central role of shared vision in product and process innovation teams (PPITs). *Journal of Organizational Behavior, 25*, 259–278.

Pless, N. M., Maak, T., & Waldman, D. A. (2012). Different approaches toward doing the right thing: Mapping the responsibility orientations of leaders. *Academy of Management Perspectives, 26*(4), 51-65.

Rasmussen Reports. (2009). Just 53 per cent say capitalism better than socialism. April: http://www.rasmussenreports.com/public_content/politics/general_politics/just_53_say_capitalism_better_than_socialism

Reason. (2005). Rethinking the social responsibility of business: A *Reason* debate featuring Milton Friedman, Whole Foods' John Mackey, and Cypress Semiconductor's T. J. Rodgers. October: http://www.reason.com/news/show/32239.html

Reingold, J. (2005). Walking the walk. *Fast Company*, November, 81–85.

Siegel, D. S. (2009). Green management matters only if it yields more green: An economic/strategic perspective. *Academy of Management Perspectives, 23*(3), 5–16.

Smith, A. (1937). *An inquiry into the nature and causes of the wealth of nations*. New York: Modern Library.

Solomon, D. (2005). Corporate governance (a special report): At what price? Critics say the cost of complying with Sarbanes-Oxley is a lot higher than it should be. *Wall Street Journal*, Oct. 17, R3.

Sonenshein, S. (2007). The role of construction, intuition, and justification in responding to ethical issues at work: The sensemaking-intuition model. *Academy of Management Review, 32*, 1022–1040.

Sully de Luque, M., Washburn, N. T., Waldman, D. A. & House, R. J. (2008). Unrequited profit: How stakeholder and economic values relate to subordinates' perceptions of leadership and firm performance. *Administrative Science Quarterly, 53*, 626–654.

Thomas, T., Schermerhorn, J. R., Jr. & Dienhart, J. W. (2004). Strategic leadership of ethical behavior in business. *Academy of Management Executive, 18*(2), 56–66.

Uhl-Bien, M., Marion, R., & McKelvery, B. (2007). Complexity leadership theory: Shifting leadership form the industrial age to the knowledge era. *The Leadership Quarterly, 18*, 298–318.

Waldman, D. A. (2011). Moving forward with the concept of responsible leadership: Three caveats to guide theory and research. *Journal of Business Ethics, 98*, 75–83.

Waldman, D. A., & Galvin, B. (2008). Alternative perspectives of responsible leadership. *Organizational Dynamics, 37*(4), 327–341.

Waldman, D. A., & Javidan, M. (2009). Alternative forms of leadership in the integration of mergers and acquisitions. *The Leadership Quarterly, 20*, 130–142.

Waldman D. A., Ramirez, G. G., House, R. J., & Puranam, P. (2001). Does leadership matter?: CEO leadership attributes under conditions of perceived environmental uncertainty. *Academy of Management Journal, 44*, 134–143.

Waldman, D. A., & Siegel, D. (2008). Defining the socially responsible leader. *The Leadership Quarterly, 19*, 117–131.

Waldman, D. A., Siegel, D., & Javidan, M. (2006). Components of transformational leadership and corporate social responsibility. *Journal of Management Studies, 43*, 1703–1725.

Walsh, J. P., & Seward, J. K. (1990). On the efficiency of internal and external corporate control mechanisms. *Academy of Management Review, 15*, 133–152.

Walumbwa, F. O, Avolio, B. J., Gardner, W. L., Wernsing, T. S., & Peterson, S. J. (2008). Authentic leadership: Development and validation of a theory-based measure. *Journal of Management, 34*, 89–126.

Walumbwa, F. O., Hartnell, C. A., & Oke, A. (2010). Servant leadership, procedural justice climate, service climate, employee attitudes, and organizational citizenship behavior: A cross-level investigation. *Journal of Applied Psychology, 95*, 517–529.

Winter, D. G. (1991). A motivational model of leadership: Predicting long-term management success from TAT measures of power motivation and responsibility. *The Leadership Quarterly, 2*, 67–80.

Yukl, G. (2010). *Leadership in organizations* (7th ed.). Upper Saddle River, NJ: Prentice-Hall.

CHAPTER

26 Executive Leadership: CEOs, Top Management Teams, and Organizational-Level Outcomes

Nathan J. Hiller *and* Marie-Michèle Beauchesne

Abstract

This chapter provides an overview of the topic of leadership in the executive context, emphasizing research from the upper echelons perspective of strategic management while also considering traditional leadership research approaches and findings. The nature of executive leadership and the role of CEOs, top management teams, and boards of directors in producing organizational-level strategic, culture, and performance outcomes are each considered. The authors suggest seven methodological and conceptual possibilities for future research that appear to hold significant promise for advancing our understanding of the nature, mechanisms, and effects of executive leadership.

Key Words: Strategic leadership, upper echelons, top management team, CEO, organizational performance, discretion, personality, core self-evaluation (CSE), narcissism

Much ado is made of senior organizational leaders—they are both lionized and vilified for their personal actions, strategic pursuits, and for the success (or failure) of the organizations they lead (Kaiser, Hogan, & Craig, 2008). Is this attention from the media, researchers, shareholders, and organizational observers really much ado about nothing? How is leadership enacted by senior strategic leaders, both successfully and unsuccessfully? How do the idiosyncrasies of top executives manifest in the strategic directions and performance of organizations? This chapter first reviews the growing body of work on the topic of senior executive leadership, seeking to address the questions posed above. Specifically, this chapter explores five themes: the ways that senior executive leadership is unique (and not unique) from other manifestations of leadership, the scope (and limits) of executive impact, predictors of executive behavior, and the various ways that executive individual differences impact strategic action and organizational outcomes. Consideration of future research possibilities and needs are examined in a section at the end of the chapter.

We assert that a rich path forward for systematically understanding executive leadership is possible and present seven methodological and conceptual recommendations for future research, including (1) measurement of executive characteristics from the perspective of familiar others; (2) better use and sophisticated validation of proxy measures; (3) attention to the relevance of affect, emotions, and emotional regulation; (4) more complex theorizing and analysis of interactions and nonlinear effects; (5) reframing of top management team research to include both team emergent states and team processes; (6) differentiating the unique positions and roles of top management team (TMT) members and inner circles; and (7) empirical attention to the possibility of executive leadership development. These foci necessitate more systematic bridging of strategic management with core leadership approaches and require drawing from (among other fields and approaches) psychology, networks, and team process literatures.

A relatively greater amount of space in this chapter is spent discussing the nature, outcomes, and contingencies of the CEO role as compared with other top management team members (e.g., COO, CFO, CTO), the top management team as an entity, or boards of directors. This is not to diminish the importance of these other actors and structures in the leadership process, and indeed, we argue that a more nuanced examination of the top management team, in particular, is a critical avenue for future strategic leadership research.

It is important at the outset to acknowledge that by writing a chapter on executive *leadership*, we could perhaps be viewed as falling prey to the fallacy that leadership and formal organizational position are synonymous. We make no such general claims, but in the case of senior executives, their potential impact is so great that we believe they are a population worthy of study under the rubric of leadership, regardless of whether a particular individual exhibits behaviors traditionally associated with effective leadership. What is particularly important to us is the question of whether (and how) they are effective, and how their idiosyncrasies lead to strategic actions, wins, and missteps. We do not hold them with high (or low) esteem simply because of their formal leadership position.

Roles, Tasks, and Functions of Executive Leadership

What does executive leadership entail? The roles, tasks, and functions associated with leadership at the executive level have been noted and described by a number of researchers over the past 75 years using a variety of approaches. These various research approaches have resulted in the characterization of executive leadership in somewhat different ways, yet although different tasks, roles, and functions are emphasized and noted by different researchers, a general picture of the nature of executive leadership emerges when this body of work is considered in totality. As a result, it is best to think of each of these roles, tasks and functions described as being complementary and contributing to the total picture of the nature of executive leadership.

The first explication of the functions of executive leadership in modern organizations comes from Chester Barnard (1938). His description of executive leadership was multifaceted, but at its core emphasized two major roles: (1) motivating employees to collective effort through a common purpose, and (2) coordinating and maintaining organizational systems. Both of these primary roles and the subordinate roles and tasks emphasize leadership of a closed system that operates largely independently of the external environment.

The inwardly focused emphasis of Barnard contrasts with later depictions of the nature of executive leadership, which include consideration of the executive role vis-à-vis the external environment. Katz and Kahn (1978) noted the importance of interfacing with the external environment (e.g., shareholders, policy makers, competitors, potential partners, environmental groups, and unions) as a critical executive function. Jacobs and Jaques (1987) similarly noted the importance of the external environment and emphasized the CEO role of ensuring adaptation of the institution with the broader environment, also known as boundary spanning. Boundary-spanning activities are not just reactive, however, but include both adaptation to the external environment (e.g., adapting to technological changes) and active management and change of the external environment (e.g., making acquisition decisions or lobbying for regulation changes).

Perhaps the most well-known examination of managerial roles was undertaken by Mintzberg (1973), who interviewed CEOs and concluded that there are 10 principal roles, which can be clustered into three categories: interpersonal, informational, and decision related. These roles (figurehead, liaison, leader, monitor, disseminator, spokesman, entrepreneur, disturbance handler, resource allocator, and negotiator) are all considered critical for effective senior leadership, and when taken together with the descriptions of Barnard, Katz and Kahn, and Jacobs and Jaques, paint a picture of the multifaceted nature of executive leadership.

Describing the roles, tasks, and functions of executive leadership, however, does not tell us how executive leadership is or is not different from leadership at other organizational levels. Many of these executive leadership functions and roles described above are not solely the exclusive domain of the senior-most leaders in an organization. Other nonexecutive individuals, both formally appointed leaders and informal leaders, may at times enact many of these roles to varying degrees. Yet for senior executives who function at the top of an organization's hierarchy, the requirements and scope of leadership differ in some important ways from lower organizational levels.

(How) Is Executive Leadership Different?

The preponderance of evidence is that, although leaders at various levels may enact roles and functions associated with senior executives, there appear to be systematic differences in the nature of leadership at the executive level when compared with leadership at other levels. Based largely on the work of Zaccaro (2001), Katz and Kahn (1978), and Porter and Nohria's (2010) research on 135 CEOs from the New CEO Workshop at Harvard, we suggest that the tasks and requirements of senior executive leadership are unique in five primary and important ways.

First, senior executive leaders have a primary responsibility for setting the organization's overall strategy. Should the organization enter a new market? How should the firm raise funds for a new initiative or building? These are questions that must be asked and addressed as part of the senior executive role. A critical component to this is not only the task of organizational-level strategy making itself, but the time horizon of the strategies. At lower organizational levels, planning and goal setting are done with more proximal time frames. Executive leadership, on the other hand, requires a significant amount of attention to longer-term goals (measured in years) and actions that are tied to the long-term strategies. The emphasis on strategy making and long-term time horizons, however, does not mean that executive leadership is all about long-term planning and strategies—CEOs must think also in the short term, and balance proactivity with reactivity to events as they unfold (Porter & Nohria, 2010).

Second, executive leaders participate in significantly more boundary spanning with the external environment and engage with a diverse set of stakeholders outside the organization including shareholders, analysts, board members, industry groups, regulators, politicians, and other constituencies that expect to have direct contact with the CEO. At lower organizational levels, boundary spanning is more (or exclusively) internally focused. For example, boundary spanning by middle-level organizational leaders primarily involves management of the interface between their units or divisions and other units of the organization (Zaccaro, 2001). The boundary spanning required of senior executives can be quite difficult, and senior executives need to possess significant complexity in their cognitions and behaviors in order to deal with the multiple and competing demands of various parts of the organizational system (including external stakeholders) and subsystems (Denison, Hooijberg, & Quinn, 1995; Hodgkinson & Clarke, 2007; Jaques, Clement, Rigby, & Jacobs, 1986; Zaccaro, 2001).

Third, while leaders at other organizational levels work within organizational systems and structures, senior executive leaders *create* those organizational systems and structures (Katz & Kahn, 1978). In essence, executive leaders need to spend significant time in "elaborating the shell" (Hackman & Wageman, 2005)—setting the conditions in motion and launching the organizational system as well as possible so that it can be viable (see Day, Gronn, & Salas, 2006), and making adjustments to ensure alignment with strategy when necessary. Creating systems and structures includes the broad-based design of such features as reporting structures and systems, the ways performance is evaluated and rewarded, the location of work, and how different parts of the organization interface with each other. Leaders at other organizational levels may have the ability and responsibility to design and tweak parts of the system, but the extent and scope are typically limited.

Fourth, the influence of executive leadership has a critical indirect component to it when compared with leadership at lower levels. For example, senior executives are typically involved in hiring leaders at the next organizational level, who in turn are responsible for operational leader hiring. The goals, ideals, and principles that an executive leader considers critical for all employees can't be closely monitored by the executive, but needs to be disseminated to the next level down. This creates an onus on senior executives to be clear about the overall strategic direction and vision of the organization, and to clearly articulate expectations in the hopes that the vision and principles are successfully disseminated and reinforced down and throughout the organization.

Fifth, and finally, executive leadership has much more of a symbolic component to it. Instituting and using symbols both through presence, actions, words, and artifacts is critical in order to convey meaning and help employees and other stakeholders understand principles and ideas about the organization's values (Porter & Nohria, 2010). Beyond commonly noted symbols such as office layout or company folklore that can be carefully (or haphazardly) propagated by senior executive actions, the symbolic component of senior executive leadership can also be more subtle. Simply deciding whether (or not) to attend a meeting, event, or gathering is taken as having implications for what the executive (and thus the company) value. And what he or she chooses to wear can also matter.

In *Who Says Elephants Can't Dance* (Gerstner, 2002, p.33), Lou Gerstner recounts that when he had his first meeting as the new CEO of IBM with the top 50 people in the company, he showed up wearing a blue shirt. At IBM, this was quite a departure from the "uniform" of a white shirt and dark blue suit, which symbolized the traditional conservative culture of the company. At his next meeting with the corporate management board, he again donned a blue shirt, and noted that his top staff were now wearing blue (and other colored) shirts. Not only were people watching (and emulating), but his actions were sending symbolic signals beyond the attire itself about what was important at the "new IBM."

Private actions such as personal donations to political and controversial causes may also be parsed and given meaning about the entire organization's values and intentions. Both Jeff Bezos, CEO of Amazon; and Dan Cathy, CEO of the U.S.-based fast-food restaurant Chick-fil-A made headlines with their private donations to organizations that were lobbying for, and against, same-sex marriage, and risked alienating strongly opinionated customers on the "opposing" side who perceived the CEO's private actions as being indicative of the corporation's values.

Taken together, these five factors significantly differentiate senior executive leadership from leadership at other levels of the organization.

Do Executive Leaders Actually Matter?

The decisions and actions of senior executives can lead an organization to failure. And the adept leadership of a senior executive team can place an organization in a position to be wildly successful. Entering a new market, navigating a crisis, and dealing with environmental shifts are critical tasks that executives can handle well, or poorly. So it appears as a given that senior executives matter to organizations. There is widespread acceptance by most lay people and leadership scholars that the leadership actions of senior executives have real consequences (Carpenter, 2011); however this view is not universal.

A view foreign to many leadership scholars, although held by some organizational theorists, is that leaders in organizations are greatly constrained—by the pre-existing configuration of their resources, cultures, and by strategic and operational inertia that is embedded in the organizational system (e.g., Carroll & Hannan, 2000; Hannan & Freeman, 1989; Powell & DiMaggio, 1991). In these views of organizations, the inertia of organizations and pressure to mimic other organizations in an industry leaves little room for leadership actions to really matter. Indeed, this is not just a scholarly argument—firms (and leaders who set strategy) *do* copy each other, are subject to inertial pressures, and senior executive leaders often admit that they do not have the freedom to do whatever they want. As a result, the possibility for a given senior leader to have a unique and significant effect on organizational-level outcomes may not always be unlimited, and in some cases may be quite limited.

Two studies are often cited as evidence that senior executives are not particularly important to organizational performance (Zaccaro, 2001). The first study, by Lieberson and O'Connor (1972), examined executive succession over a 20-year period. Using a variance decomposition analysis, they estimated that a change in leadership (which is the method they used to estimate the inferred impact of leadership) was associated with changes in sales, earnings, and profit margins of between 6 per cent and 32 per cent, three years after succession, which is taken to be evidence of a small effect of leadership. The second study examined changes in city expenditures attributable to mayoral changes in 30 U.S. cities over an 18-year period (Salancik & Pfeffer, 1977). Their findings suggest mayoral changes explained between 6 per cent and 10 per cent of the variance in city income and expenditures, which again is interpreted as being indicative of a small effect of leadership.

A more recent and comprehensive variance decomposition study was recently undertaken by Wasserman, Nohria, and Anand (2010), who examined the impact of leadership changes in 531 firms across 42 diverse industries. This study examined two different organizational-level financial performance variables: return on assets and Tobins Q (a ratio of the firm's market value divided by its book value). Return on assets represents how efficiently the organization uses its assets (i.e., an internal indicator of performance), whereas Tobins Q is an indicator of the market's perception of the future prospects of a firm's profitability or use of assets. The overall CEO effect was similar using both metrics (13 per cent and 15 per cent).

As others have pointed out (Day & Lord, 1988; Finkelstein, Hambrick, & Cannella, 2009), the heavily biasing methodological choices made by most of this leadership succession research (e.g., not controlling for size of the city budget in the Salancik and Pfeffer study) has led to a significant underestimation of leadership effects. In the first two studies (Lieberson & O'Connor and Salancik & Pfeffer) mentioned above, the leadership effects have been reestimated using a slightly different methodology at between 20 per cent and 45 per cent (Day & Lord, 1988)—much higher than the original estimates.

Perhaps an even bigger point with regard to these studies, however, has to do with the interpretation of even the smallest estimated effects. Rather than concluding that 10 per cent is a small effect indicative of little evidence for the importance of leadership, this result is more appropriately interpreted as being indicative of a substantial effect (Day & Lord, 1988; Zaccaro, 2001). In organizational research, attributing a 10 per cent change to a single variable is almost never seen as being indicative of that variable's marginality. And finally, examination of organizational performance outcomes are certainly important (as these studies have done), but executive leadership also has significant effects on important organizational strategies and structure variables (Hambrick, 2007).

So do senior executive leaders matter? Yes. Are they the only important factor in determining organizational outcomes? Certainly not. Industry, momentum, patents, macroeconomic conditions, and a host of other factors are important determinants of organizational-level outcomes, and a leader's latitude of possible action can be significantly constrained (discussed more later in the chapter).

With the question of "if" senior executives matter being answered in the affirmative (and with noting of constraints), the questions that scholars are now concerned with have squarely shifted (Carpenter, 2011) to understanding the various *ways* that senior organizational leaders affect not only organizational-level outcomes (such as ROA or other measures of success), but also the mechanisms and predictors of strategic decisions and organizational action.

What can go wrong? Are certain strategies and behaviors more or less effective in certain industries or environments? How can we predict the strategic actions of a given executive if we know something about his experience, personality, or values? These are the broad types of questions that are of interest to scholars of senior executive leadership, and are described in the following sections—but before exploring the existing research on predictors, we provide a brief overview of the three broad types of organizational-level outcomes that have been examined: strategy, culture, and performance.

Organizational Outcomes Associated with Senior Executive Leadership

Just as the nature of executive leadership tasks, roles, and functions is different in some important ways from leadership at lower organizational levels, so is the nature of the criterion variables that are possible (and relevant) at the executive level (DeChurch, Hiller, Murase, & Doty, 2010). The primary difference is that senior executives have the potential to impact the organization's overall strategy and, ultimately, performance.

Positional leadership at the lowest managerial level (e.g., a foreman) may be related to individual-level outcomes (such as satisfaction), and team-level outcomes. Middle-level leaders who are responsible for managing other managers (i.e., those responsible for a unit or division) may impact individuals, teams, and their unit or division (Palanski & Yammarino, 2009). Executive leadership is the only level of leadership at which one individual (i.e., the CEO) or a small group of individuals (i.e., the top management team) can have such a direct impact on firm-level strategies and outcomes. This does not diminish the fact that leaders at all levels are key contributors to organizational success—indeed collective efforts at lower levels can be important to organizational-level outcomes (Yukl, 2008), but the decision power of the CEO and its top management team members allow for a clear and direct relationship between their idiosyncrasies, decisions, and behaviors with firm-level outcomes (Kaiser et al., 2008).

Senior executives undoubtedly influence individuals and teams as well, but because these mechanisms of leadership on individuals and nonexecutive teams are, to a great extent, similar to more general leadership mechanisms of influence and impact (and are covered well by other chapters in this book), we focus here on the unique organizational-level effects that senior executive leadership can have. Research in the field of executive leadership has examined a wide variety of organizational-level outcomes, the vast majority of which can be classified within three broad categories: (1) strategy, (2) culture, and (3) performance.

Strategy

Firm strategy (both the enactment of and decisions about) is the most frequently used category of outcome variable in strategic leadership research. Senior executives (and in particular the CEO) are the primary actors responsible for setting a firm's direction and, within notable boundaries, have significant ability to develop and enact strategy. A firm's strategy is sometimes the result of copying peers or moving along an inertial path, but often the development and enactment of strategy is an idiosyncratic cognitive process that flows from the way senior executives understand and interpret their organization and the environment (Miller, Burke, & Glick, 1998). Firm strategy represents a more proximal outcome variable than firm performance (which can be influenced by many factors), thus suggesting that the effect sizes should be greater when predicting firm strategies with leader and leadership characteristics than when predicting firm performance (Finkelstein et al., 2009)—although this generally held assumption has never been comprehensively examined.

Prior work has examined multiple specific firm-level strategies such as innovation (Miller, Kets De Vries, & Toulouse, 1982; Papadakis & Bourantas, 1998), acquisitions (Chatterjee & Hambrick, 2007), geographic and product diversification decisions (Wiersema & Bantel, 1992), firm risk taking (Li & Tang, 2010), and entry mode choices (Herrmann & Datta, 2002). Scholars have explored the influence of executive leadership on organizational structure, which is both a strategy in its own right (e.g., strategic organizational restructuring) and a means to support other strategic actions. Structurally related outcomes include variables such as centralization and formalization (e.g. Miller et al., 1982; Miller & Droge, 1986; Miller & Toulouse, 1986a; 1986b).

In the literature on executive succession, strategic outcomes have most often been examined in terms of strategic change (Hutzschenreuter, Kleindienst, & Greger, 2012), including: shifts in core business (Wiersema, 1995), diversification (Bigley & Wiersema, 2002; Boeker, 1997a, 1997b; Kraatz & Moore, 2002; Sakano & Lewin, 1999) and divestiture of businesses (Barron, Chulkov, & Waddell, 2011; Denis & Denis, 1995; Shimizu & Hitt, 2005; Weisbach, 1995).

In studies using publicly traded (and typically larger) organizations, researchers have generally relied on measures of strategic behavior collected indirectly from databases, such as inferring strategic internationalization from a measure of foreign sales divided by total sales or the number of countries in which the firm operates (e.g., Carpenter, Sanders, & Gregersen, 2001). Direct-measure surveys of executives are more commonly used in sampling small- and medium-sized organizations.

Culture

Organizational culture, defined as the basic assumptions shared by organizational members (Schein, 2010) is often thought to be linked to senior organizational leaders, and particularly founding CEOs (Davis, 1984; Morgan, 1997). There is limited empirical evidence examining this set of outcome variables, but what research there is tends to suggest that CEO leadership behaviors, values, and personality generally influence organizational culture (see Tsui, Zhang, Wang, Xin, & Wu, 2006, for a nuanced qualitative study within the Chinese context). For example, Berson, Oreg, and Dvir (2008) examined how CEOs' values predict the type of culture in place within organizations (e.g., bureaucratic, supportive, and innovation oriented), and Giberson and colleagues (2009) examined the link between CEO personality and the cultural values of employees. Culture has generally been measured using reports from top management or employee perceptions, and, due to the fact that culture is a multifaceted construct, it is perhaps not surprising that culture has been assessed along a variety of dimensions and frameworks.

Performance

Together, strategy, structure, and culture are seen as some of the mediating mechanisms through which CEOs are likely to impact the ultimate category of organizational outcomes—firm performance, although CEO characteristics are sometimes also linked directly with organizational performance (e.g., Chatterjee & Hambrick, 2007). A wide variety of objective firm performance indicators have been examined in the executive leadership literature, including various accounting measures of performance (e.g., return on assets, return on investment, return on equity), market-based measures of performance (e.g., sales growth, market-to-book ratios, stock price), and firm survival. Notably, recent work has taken a broader view of firm performance by expanding the criterion domain to include indicators such as corporate social performance (e.g., Manner, 2010).

Generally, these performance measures are examined using independently verifiable data that is part of the financial and stock-price record of publicly traded companies, but when examining private firms (for which objective measures of performance are difficult to obtain) self-report measures of performance have also been used (e.g., Di Zhang & Bruning, 2011; Ling, Simsek, Lubatkin, & Veiga, 2008; Ling, Zhao, & Baron, 2007). Perceptual measures of performance usually ask the CEO or the TMT members to rate their organizations in comparison with their major competitors on different performance measures such as total sales, profitability, and growth (see Gupta and Govindarajan, 1986, for an example).

In sum, a key differentiator in the study of executive leadership is the level of the outcome variables predominantly used to assess leadership effects. It is hard to imagine examining organizational-level outcomes resulting from a particular team foreman, yet it is much easier to conceptualize (and find evidence for) organizational strategies and organizational performance resulting from senior executive leadership characteristics and behaviors. This difference in the level of manifestation and analysis of outcome variables makes the study of executive leadership unique from the examination of leadership at other hierarchical levels and unique from informal (nonpositional) leadership.

Predicting Organizational-Level Outcomes

One of the primary ways that research on senior executive leadership has sought to understand the effects that leaders can have is through examining stable individual difference variables. Researchers have studied personality characteristics, background and prior experiences, values, and a host of related visible and underlying characteristics of both individuals and top management teams. The logic is that, rather than being a function of a perfectly rational and omniscient calculus, the decisions and actions that executives take are—to a significant degree—a function of their idiosyncrasies, behavioral styles and tendencies, and backgrounds. Although there is still much to be understood, the last 30 years of research findings have shown significant evidence that organizational strategies and outcomes can be better comprehended by understanding the nature of the senior executives who perceive, interpret, decide, and act on behalf of their organizations (Hambrick, 2007; Kaiser et al., 2008).

An instance of how an executive's individuality can affect strategic actions of an organization is evident in the case of Google in mainland China. After four years of operating in China, Google ceased operations there in 2010, which many observers chided as foolish given the size and growth of the Chinese market (Vascellaro, 2010). So why did they decide to pull out of China at a time of rapid growth? The answer lies largely in knowing something about one of Google's cofounders—Sergey Brin. Brin, who spent his early years in the Soviet Union, saw his family experience significant religious discrimination and harassment in the totalitarian regime of his homeland. Decades later, as a key decision maker at Google, his dislike for governments and regimes that he saw as invasive and totalitarian reemerged. After becoming suspicious that the Chinese government was attempting to spy on dissidents by breaking into their Google e-mail accounts, and also seeing the apparent theft of Google's intellectual property in China, he argued that the cost of doing business in China was morally and ethically too high. The purported actions in China reminded Brin of the repression and censorship that his family fled, and led him to note that "in some aspects of their policy, particularly with respect to censorship, with respect to surveillance of dissidents, I see the same earmarks of totalitarianism, and I find that personally quite troubling" (Vascellaro, 2010, para. 3). In the end, these events weighed heavily on Brin and became the deciding factor in leading Brin to convince his cofounder Larry Page, as well as Eric Schmidt (the CEO at the time) to pull business operations out of mainland China.

Despite all of the business reasons to continue operating in China, the previous experiences and values of Sergey Brin ultimately led the company to take a major strategic action that was not otherwise going to take place. More than merely the occasional anecdote, the systematic study of strategic leaders and their characteristics has proven to be a valuable lens for understanding strategic actions and outcomes in organizations. We turn first to demographic predictors, followed by a discussion of research on the impact of executive personality and values.

Demographic Variables

Age. Increasing age has been linked with a general preference for greater stability and increasing levels of cognitive inflexibility in the general population—which not surprisingly has notable implications for executives who are involved in strategic decision making and organizational actions (Child, 1974; Hart & Mellons, 1970; Herrmann & Datta, 2006; Taylor, 1975). As one of the most studied demographic variables in the field of strategic management, increasing executive age has been shown to be related to lower levels of strategic change (Wiersema & Bantel, 1992), choice of less risky/resource intensive modes of entry into a new market (i.e., joint ventures as opposed to greenfields) (Herrmann & Datta, 2006), pursuit of safer strategies (Karami, Analoui, & Kakabadse, 2006) including lower R&D spending (Barker & Mueller, 2002), commitment to the status quo (McClelland, Liang, & Barker III, 2010), and lower corporate growth (Child, 1974; Hart and Mellons, 1970).

While there is some agreement on the influence of top executives' age (and collective TMT age) on strategic decisions, recent research has most frequently used top executive age as a control variable as opposed to a substantive variable of interest.

Tenure. Tenure is the single most studied demographic variable at the top management level. Hambrick and Mason (1984) suggested top executives with longer tenure are more likely to take the organization "as is", and thus less likely to adopt new ways of doing things. Similar to the rationale and findings with executive age, longer organizational tenure has been linked to less corporate strategic change and greater commitment to the status quo (Boeker, 1997b; Finkelstein & Hambrick, 1990; Hambrick, Geletkanycz, & Fredrickson, 1993; Wiersema & Bantel, 1992), more conservative attitude toward change (Musteen, Barker, & Baeten, 2006), and less innovation adoption (Kimberly & Evanisko, 1981).

Tenure and age are not identical variables. What they are taken to represent are in some cases similar, but tenure is often considered to be representative of a variety of additional variables that are not associated with age. In other words, although both age and tenure have been found to be negatively associated to similar outcome variables such as innovation adoption and strategic change, the mechanisms that explain these relationships are fundamentally different. For example, the logic by which tenure is negatively related to strategic changes and innovations is that new externally appointed executives (with new perspectives) are likely to have fewer obligations to internal constituencies, making them more successful in introducing changes and innovations (Kimberly & Evanisko, 1981).

Tenure has also been used as a proxy for power. Finkelstein and Hambrick (2006) suggested that CEOs with longer tenure have more power since some bases of power require time before taking effect. For example, over time CEOs might be able to select board members that will be sympathetic to them, thus increasing their power.

As is apparent with the case of tenure, one of the difficulties with demographic variables is that the same variable may be taken to be representative of several different constructs from study to study. Tenure may be correlated with both power and commitment to the status quo (for example), but care needs to be taken in inferring that these demographic variables are actual representations of the underlying constructs of power or commitment to the status quo. In the case of tenure, perhaps part of the answer lies in three different operationalizations of tenure that have been used: tenure in position (i.e., tenure as a CEO), organizational tenure, and industry tenure. These three operationalizations of tenure likely provide slightly different information about executives. For example, tenure in position might be more appropriately representative of CEO power, organizational tenure might be better to assess CEOs' commitment to strategic status quo, and industry tenure may be used as more of a general past experience measure. In a recent paper, Weng and Lin (in press) start to shed some additional light on the conceptualization and measurement of tenure in predicting strategic change by suggesting that prior CEO experience should be measured not only through one of the typical measures (e.g., tenure in the position), but also prior board experience and prior experience as the heir apparent as an indicator of "newness". Clearly, care needs to be taken in making appropriate inferences from demographic variables.

Background: Experience and education. The work-related and academic backgrounds and qualitative previous experiences of executives are another class of individual difference variables that have been shown to have relevance in the strategic leadership context. Work-related experience has been operationalized as functional diversity (i.e., breadth of exposure to different functional areas such as marketing, accounting, general administration, HR, etc.), general functional background, throughput versus output background (i.e., production, process R&D, and accounting are considered "throughput" backgrounds and marketing and sales, merchandising, product R&D, and entrepreneurship are defined as "output" backgrounds), entrepreneurial experience, executive management experience, and international experience.

As opposed to other demographic variables that are used to predict strategic decisions and other proximal strategy variables, past experience has been regularly related to firm-level performance outcomes. For example, CEO international experience (Slater & Dixon-Fowler, 2009) and breadth of functional experience (Manner, 2010) were found to be positively associated with corporate social performance, whereas TMT functional diversity (Buyl, Boone, Hendriks, & Matthyssens, 2011), CEO executive-level management experience (Stone & Tudor, 2005), and CEO international experience (Roth, 1995) were found to be related to firm performance (operationalized as ROS, ROA, and income growth respectively). These studies also emphasized potential moderators likely to explain prior conflicting results in the literature. For example, Buyl and colleagues (2011) found that TMT functional diversity will have a greater impact on firm performance when the CEO's expertise and background characteristics facilitate the exchange and integration of the diverse views within the TMT.

The other subcategory of what we refer to as background is education. After tenure and age, education is the single most studied individual difference at the top executive level. Education has generally been operationalized in two different ways: level of education and field of study. Both the level and type of formal education of top executives provide some measure of their competencies and individual knowledge (Hambrick & Mason, 1984; Hitt & Tyler, 1991).

Some scholars have suggested that level of education reflects an individual's cognitive capacity and skills (Wieserma & Bantel, 1992). For example, top executives with higher levels of formal education have more tools to envision creative solutions when confronted with complex situations (Karami, Analoui, & Kakabadse, 2006). Level of education has been associated with different firm-level outcomes such as change in corporate strategy (Wieserma & Bantel, 1992) and openness to innovation (Kimberly & Evanisko, 1981).

Field of education has also received some attention under the logic that the type of content studied has the power to alter values and behavioral beliefs (Frank, Gilovich, & Regan, 1993), although it is also likely to be an indicator of preexisting beliefs, values, and preferences (Holland, 1959). As an example of this type of research, Manner (2010) found that organizations led by CEOs with degrees in humanities had stronger corporate social performances than those led by CEOs with degrees in economics.

Gender. The vast majority of senior executives in large organizations (the primary focus of strategic leadership research in the past), have historically been male (Ragins, 1998). And even as of early 2014, only 23 women were CEOs of the 500 largest publicly traded companies in the U.S. Perhaps partly because of the lower propensity of female senior executives (and particularly CEOs), gender is rarely used as a substantive variable of interest, and little is known about the impact of gender on strategic decision making and outcomes, although it is typically used as a control variable in more recent research (e.g., Ciavarella, Buchholtz, Riordan, Gatewood, & Stokes, 2004; Wallace, Little, Hill, & Ridge, 2010; Wang, Tsui, & Xin, 2011). In one of the few empirical studies that has tested the main effect of gender, Musteen and colleagues (2006) found that female CEOs were more open to change. Their rationale was that, in making their way up in an organization, a female executive is conditioned differently. By the time she reaches the C-suite, she has had to prove herself so many times in so many different ways that she has become accustomed to demonstrating considerable entrepreneurial initiative and finding innovative solutions to work problems—which leads her to be more open to strategic change than a male counterpart.

Executive Personality and Values

A more clearly psychological approach to understanding executive leadership comes in utilizing stable dispositional characteristics as predictors of executive strategic action and firm outcomes. In contrast with a general indifference about the substantive use of demographic variables by many current executive leadership scholars, research examining the impact of executive personality, values, and beliefs has been of significant interest since the birth of strategic leadership research and is gaining momentum—these variables generally allow for a deeper and richer conceptual explanation of executive decisions and actions.

Locus of control. The study of executive personality's influence on organizational outcomes was first systematically investigated by Danny Miller and colleagues, who examined the effects of internal locus of control—the extent to which one believes that life is within one's control rather than due to chance or fate (Rotter, 1966)—on both strategy and organizational performance. Whereas various other personality variables are often more distally or complexly related to firm-level performance indicators, there appears to be fairly consistent support for a linkage between locus of control and firm performance. CEOs who have a higher internal locus of control lead companies to better performance than CEOs with a more external locus of control (Miller & Toulouse, 1986a; 1986b; Sidek & Zainol, 2011; Van de Ven, Hudson, & Schroeder, 1984). More recently, executive locus of control has been examined in entrepreneurial settings, and has been positively related to both business performance and venture growth (Lee & Tsang, 2001; Sidek & Zainol, 2011).

The growth and performance effects of locus of control may result from a number of mechanisms. First, it may be that executives work harder and are more effective in implementing whatever strategy they choose (Boone, De Brabander, & Witteloostuijn, 1996). Second internals, who are more agentic in their outlook and who possess significant self-control and persistence, may pursue more innovative strategies and seek out new opportunities (Miller et al., 1982; Ng, Sorensen, & Eby, 2006). For example, Halikias and Panayotopoulou (2003), using a sample of small-to-medium enterprises from Greece, found a positive relationship between CEO internal orientation and a firm's export involvement. Third, although not empirically examined in the upper echelons literature, there is evidence that leaders possessing an internal locus of control are more likely to be perceived as being transformational (Howell & Avolio, 1993), which could result in increased effort by others and enhanced leadership legitimacy.

In sum, executives who more strongly believe in self-control of life's outcomes (i.e., internal locus) seem to manifest this belief in the organizations they run—they embrace (rather than avoid) challenges, adapt through innovative firm strategies, take advantage of opportunities, even those that require significant effort and foresight. Their choices and style, in turn, are positively related to the performance of the organizations they lead.

Views of self: Hubris, narcissism, and core self-evaluation. Research interest in CEOs' views of self-worth and potency is traceable most directly not to psychologists or strategists, but to economist Richard Roll's (1986) "hubris hypothesis" of corporate takeovers, in which he argues that overpaying for a target company is the result of hubris (i.e., exaggerated self-confidence) on the part of the bidding CEO. From this initial conceptual work, empirical research on views of self in the executive arena has considered three related but distinct variables: hubris, narcissism, and core self-evaluations (Chatterjee & Hambrick, 2007; Hayward & Hambrick, 1997; Hiller & Hambrick, 2005; Li & Tang, 2010; Resick et al., 2009; Simsek, Heavey, & Veiga, 2010; Zhang, Peterson, & Reina, 2013).

Hubris. Drawing directly from Roll's postulations about overpaying during corporate takeovers, Hayward and Hambrick (1997) examined a number of proxy measures for hubris to predict overpayment in corporate takeovers. The rationale is that CEOs who possess exaggerated self-confidence in their abilities are not likely to be concerned with quibbling over purchase price. Why worry about what you pay when you, as CEO, believe that the company will be worth many times more when you and your superior skills get ahold of it? Or as famed investor Warren Buffett noted: "If investors instead bankroll princesses who wish to pay double for the right to kiss the toad, those kisses had better pack some real dynamite. We've observed many kisses but very few miracles. Nevertheless, many managerial princesses remain serenely confident about the future potency of their kisses" (Buffett & Cunningham, 2001, pp. 12–13). Indeed, it appears that CEOs inflicted with hubris are veritable royalty in their own minds, and whatever they pay for a company when they acquire it is seen to be a worthy investment because of the value they can add to the acquired company.

Using observable variables as approximations of CEO hubris (such as recent media praise for the CEO that is believed to "puff" him or her up, and the CEO's pay relative to the next highest paid executive), Hayward and Hambrick (1997) were able to substantially predict overpayment in corporate acquisitions—in line with Warren Buffett's observation. The effect size from their findings translates such that, for example, in a billion-dollar acquisition, a CEO would be expected to overpay for the target company by $48 million for every media article previously written about him or her. Celebrity appears to have real consequences.

In a recent study of firm risk taking, Li and Tang (2010) hypothesized that hubris would lead CEOs to overestimate the likelihood of success associated with their strategic initiatives and thus take greater strategic risks. Using the deviation between the CEOs' subjective evaluation of firm performance and an objective accounting performance measure as an indicator of hubris in a sample of 2,790 Chinese CEOs and firms, they found evidence that CEO hubris was positively associated to firm risk taking.

Although the idea of hubris (exaggerated self-confidence) has merit, the concept is less rigorous than two well-validated psychological constructs that can be used to conceptualize executive self-worth: narcissism and core self-evaluations (Hiller & Hambrick, 2005). Both of these constructs enjoy a more research-validated psychological tradition (including definition and measurement) than hubris, and as such, have garnered the bulk of research attention on this general topic in the past decade. Yet it should be noted that at the same time that narcissism and core self-evaluations are both constructs related to "self-worth," or what we might colloquially term "ego"—the two constructs are distinct, and evidence is beginning to suggest that these individual differences are often differentially predictive of outcomes.

Narcissism. Narcissism in the context of senior leadership is a topic that has garnered significant media attention, conceptual thinking, and increasing empirical work in the last decade. Although on the surface it may be difficult to distinguish narcissists from those with a very high and stable sense of self-esteem and worth (CSE), and narcissists may be plagued by exaggerated self-confidence (hubris), narcissism is both conceptually and empirically distinct. As both an enduring personality trait that can also be affected by life circumstances, narcissism is characterized by a number of markers, including a grandiose sense of self-importance, entitlement, a continuous need for validation and admiration, lack of empathy, and envy.

A critical distinguishing feature of narcissism is that although individuals high on this trait exhibit behaviors consistent with an extremely high sense of self-worth and often engage in grandiose displays, true narcissists—and narcissistic leaders—actually have a fragile sense of self-worth and feelings of inferiority that need continual validation. Thus, they are hypersensitive to criticism and prone to envy and other threats to their fragile sense of self (see Rosenthal & Pittinsky, 2006, for a summary and also description of some of the debates about the construct in the general context of leadership). Although narcissists are often painted as being wholly negative in the context of leadership and their effect on organizations, it is also important to recognize that a simple "good or bad" distinction when it comes to narcissism actually requires a bit more nuance.

In the context of senior executive leadership, CEO narcissism has been related to glory-seeking behaviors: sometimes these initiatives appear to be successful, and at other times they are not successful. For example, narcissistic CEOs were found to make more large-scale strategic changes and have resulting larger fluctuations in firm performance than their counterparts who were lower in narcissism (Chatterjee & Hambrick, 2007), but there was no overall main effect of narcissism on firm performance. So, it appears that their glory-seeking behaviors sometimes led to glory (in the form of return on assets), and sometimes lead to underperformance. Understanding the specific conditions under which narcissism may be positive and/or negative for firm performance is an avenue that could benefit from further study, although a new paper (discussed below) sheds some light on this topic.

In a follow-up paper with two separate studies, the same two authors took a trait-by-situation approach and argued that the effects of narcissism may be pronounced or muted depending on the situation (Chatterjee & Hambrick, 2011). They argued that, because of their desire for validation from others, narcissistic CEOs who get validation in the form of media praise and awards (which, as noted above, has previously been used as an indicator of hubris in Hayward & Hambrick, 1997) will be emboldened to make even riskier and large-scale growth and investment decisions than narcissistic CEOs who didn't receive this type of praise.

ARE NARCISSISTIC CEOS LESS TRANSFORMATIONAL?

Two studies have examined the connection between narcissism and transformational leadership: one providing evidence for a negative relationship and the other finding no effect. In a sample of 80 CEOs in New Zealand who were evaluated with a self-report direct measure, narcissism was negatively related to transformational leadership (Khoo & Burch, 2008), but in a study of Major League Baseball presidents over a 100-year period (Resick et al., 2009), an archival historiometric measure of narcissism was unrelated to transformational leadership.

Conceptually, narcissistic senior executives, who are focused on themselves and their own goals and who may get envious of others are likely to have difficulty engaging in a developmental and bidirectional social process characteristic of transformational leadership (Rosenthal & Pittinsky, 2006). Yet on the other hand, their grandiosity may allow them to hold and paint a vision of future organizational wins that others can buy into, and their desire for validation from others can make them compellingly charming and charismatic. So, in total it appears that the verdict is still out on whether and how narcissism is related to transformational leadership, but the self-focus of narcissism is likely to be negatively related to another form of leadership: servant leadership.

Consistent with the idea that narcissists are focused largely on themselves and maintaining their superior status, Peterson, Galvin, and Lange (2012) examined narcissism and servant leadership. Their study of 126 technology CEOs found that narcissists are less likely to have a self-identity tied to the organization, and that this lower level of organizational identification is a partial mediating mechanism in explaining lower levels of servant leadership.

Core self-evaluation. The third self-focused variable that has been examined in strategic leadership research is the variable of core self-evaluation (CSE) - the global and stable evaluation one makes about one's own self-worth and capabilities (Chang, Ferris, Johnson, Rosen, & Tan, 2012; Judge, Locke, Durham, & Kluger, 1998). High CSE individuals view themselves positively and as capable and active agents in the world. They possess a high degree of confidence, but in contrast with hubris, it is not necessarily exaggerated confidence. CSE, by definition, sits conceptually at the intersection of four well-studied psychological traits: self-esteem, generalized self-efficacy, locus of control, and emotional stability (i.e., the inverse of the neuroticism component of the Big Five personality dimension). Thus, at the intersection of these traits, high CSE individuals see themselves as valuable, worthy, agentic, and they are relatively free from anxiety. Although most CEOs are likely to have a healthy dose of CSE (Hiller & Hambrick, 2005), variability has been shown (just as with other traits in the executive arena) to predict a variety of strategic and organizational outcomes.

Using the most commonly validated self-report measure of core self-evaluation (Judge, Erez, Bono, & Thoresen, 2003), Simsek and colleagues (2010) found that CSE levels of a sample of 129 CEOs were related to the firm's entrepreneurial orientation—with higher CSE CEOs perceiving less threat and more opportunities—and thus creating an environment where the top management team took more entrepreneurial risks. The results are suggestive of a trickle-down effect of the leader (CEO) on the top management team's strategic orientation, and also perhaps a selection effect (that high CSE CEOs may select entrepreneurial team members). Consistent with a premise of upper echelons theory (Hambrick & Mason, 1984)—that CEO individual differences are more pronounced in dynamic environments—results were pronounced in environments characterized by greater levels of change.

Contrary to the reported null findings on the relationship between narcissism and transformational leadership (mentioned above), Resick and colleagues (2009) predicted and found evidence for a positive relationship between CSE and transformational leadership.

Narcissism interacting with CSE. In a recent study examining the effects of both narcissism and CSE on firm performance, Zheng and colleagues (Zheng, Peterson, & Reina, 2012) considered the interactive effects of these two personality variables using self-report data from 155 CEOs in the computer software and hardware industries. They found evidence for a moderated curvilinear relationship between narcissism and firm performance (ROA measured one year later). When CEOs had a high level of CSE, there was a positive curvilinear relationship between narcissism and firm performance. However, when CEOs were low on CSE, there was a negative curvilinear relationship between narcissism and firm performance, suggesting that narcissism, in moderation, can have positive effects on firm performance (perhaps when it is of the "constructive" form as indicated by a concomitant high level of CSE). One of the key implications of this study is that researchers may be well served to take note of the explanatory power that comes from a more nuanced, interactionist examination of narcissism—rather than simply searching for main effects. Additionally, this study serves as another indicator that narcissism and CSE are two separate constructs that have unique implications for the strategic leadership literature.

The Big Five. In the last three decades, evidence for the robustness of five broad and distinct personality traits across cultures and measures, as well as evidence that they are predictive of a variety of outcomes in both work and nonwork settings, has led to widespread acceptance and use of the Five Factor Model among personality and organizational researchers (Judge & Bono, 2000). The five traits (known often as the Big Five) are seen to do a fairly good job in representing the broad dimensions on which people most centrally differ: openness to experience, conscientiousness, extraversion, agreeableness, and neuroticism (Costa & McCrae, 1992). This does not mean that the investigation of other traits is irrelevant or that these five are sufficient in evaluating personality, but these five traits are an important conceptual mechanism for understanding individuals, and by extension, executive personality.

In the top executive arena, research examining one or more of these traits has only taken place relatively recently, although it is gaining significant momentum (and is likely to continue). Research into the Big Five traits has considered a direct link between traits and firm performance, but has generally conceptualized and examined the traits as leading to mediating action mechanisms (such as top management team flexibility or strategic actions), which in turn lead to performance.

Peterson and colleagues' (2003) often-cited paper was the first empirical study of executive characteristics and strategy to investigate the five traits—examining the relationship between CEO characteristics and top management team dynamics using archival sources to gauge both CEO personality and TMT dynamics, and ultimately firm performance. The authors found empirical support for their general claim that CEO personality impacts TMT dynamics, which in turn are predictive of firm performance. They found, for example, that CEO agreeableness was positively related to TMT cohesion and decentralization of power, and that these and other indicators of TMT processes and dynamics were in turn related to organizational performance (operationalized as income growth). Despite significant questions about the robustness of their findings due to their small sample of only 17 firms (Hollenbeck, DeRue, & Mannor, 2006), the study was a frontrunner in suggesting and investigating a process mechanism (i.e., TMT dynamics) through which CEO personality is related to organizational performance.

In a similar vein to the Peterson et al. paper, Nadkarni and Herrmann (2010) examined the link between self-reported Big Five traits and firm performance using a sample of 195 CEOs, finding that CEO personality impacts firm performance via the "mechanism" of strategic flexibility. Emotional stability, extraversion, and openness were each positively related to firm strategic flexibility. CEO conscientiousness, on the other hand, was negatively related to strategic flexibility, and CEO agreeableness had an inverted-U relationship with strategic flexibility. This study is one of the rare pieces of research that hypothesized (and found support) for a nonlinear relationship between top executive personality and firm-level outcomes—a possibility that holds great promise for future research.

In another paper examining the Big Five, Giberson and colleagues (2009) found evidence that CEO agreeableness and emotional stability are positively related to the extent to which their organizations are characterized by Clan culture values (i.e., cultures that focus on flexibility and internal maintenance).

Last, in the entrepreneurship literature, Ciavarella and colleagues (2004) studied the Big Five in the context of venture survival. They hypothesized and found support for a positive relationship between an entrepreneur's conscientiousness and long-term venture survival, and somewhat surprisingly (and contradictory to the initial hypothesis), they found a negative relationship between an entrepreneur's openness to experience (i.e., a preference for trying new things) and venture survival.

Considering that the Five Factor Model is one of the most robust and widely accepted operationalizations of personality (Judge & Bono, 2000), it is surprising that there have not been more studies of these traits in the executive leadership arena. One potential explanation is that scholars of senior leadership and strategy have yet to suggest or develop proxy measures of the five traits. In comparison to the study of narcissism or hubris for which scholars have suggested proxy measures, Big Five research in the executive context has not developed such indirect measures, although evidence from other fields of study suggests that they could be developed (e.g., Back et al., 2010; Gosling, Ko, Mannarelli, & Morris, 2002).

Need for achievement. Need for achievement, an individual's need to be successful and reach a high level of performance (McClelland, 1961) has also been shown to be relevant in trait studies of senior executive leadership. The first few studies on the topic came from Miller and colleagues in the 1980s. They found that executives with a high need for achievement prefer to have control over their environment, thus favoring formalized and centralized structures (Miller & Droge, 1986), broad aggressive marketing-oriented strategies (Miller & Toulouse, 1986a; 1986b), and proactive decision making (Miller & Toulouse, 1986a; 1986b). Papadakis and Bourantas (1998) found that CEOs' need for achievement is positively associated with technological innovation. Relating need for achievement with organizational performance, Lee and Tsang (2001) found that entrepreneurs' need for achievement had a positive impact on venture growth.

Risk propensity. Top executives' risk propensity has received considerable attention in the executive leadership literature over the past two decades. Researchers have used multiple terminologies for ideas that fall under the same general idea: tolerance for risk (Wally & Baum, 1994), risk orientation (Hitt & Tyler, 1991), and risk attitude (Papadakis & Bourantas, 1998), to capture top executives' attitudes toward risk. Individuals with a higher tolerance and/or propensity toward risk prefer speedy decisions (Wally & Baum, 1994), are assertive and responsive in decision making (March & Shapira, 1982), prefer decentralized decision making (Papadakis., 2006), and this may lead to higher technological innovation (Papadakis & Bourantas, 1998) and performance (Sidek & Zainol, 2011). In a novel study, Cain & McKeon (2012) used U.S. federal pilot license records as an indicator of risk propensity and found that CEOs who held a private pilot's license led companies with higher amounts of leverage and produced greater stock market return volatility because of their presumed willingness to seek and accept risk and take big chances.

Executive values/integrity/authenticity. Values represent another class of relevant individual characteristics by which to differentiate among executives. Rokeach (1973) defined values as "enduring beliefs that a specific mode of conduct of existence is personally and socially preferable to alternative modes of conduct or end-states of existence." Values are generally believed to be relatively enduring and appear to be linked to strategic decisions and actions. Values can affect both initial perceptions of situations and subsequent strategic decisions. In other words, not only do executives differ in how they perceive and interpret situations based on their values, but they ultimately also discard (or lean toward) certain choices on the basis of values (Hambrick & Mason, 1984).

Despite the apparent implications for strategic action, individual differences in the form of values have rarely been examined. Berson, Oreg, and Dvir (2008) examined the relationship between CEO values and organizational cultures and found that CEOs with self-directing values had more innovative organizational cultures, security values were associated with bureaucratic cultures, and benevolence values were related to supportive cultures. In another paper, Ling, Zhao, and Baron (2007) examined the influence of founders-CEOs' values (novelty and collectivism) on new venture performance. Using a self-report measure of novelty and collectivism at the individual level developed by Simsek et al. (2005), the authors found that CEOs' values for collectivism had a stronger beneficial impact in larger and older firms, whereas CEOs' values for novelty had a stronger beneficial impact in younger firms. Giberson and colleagues (2009), on the other hand, found limited support for a linkage between CEO personal values and organizational culture. In fact, out of the 10 personal values they measured, only CEO status value (i.e., the need to be recognized and desired by others) was related to organizational culture.

In a recent study of the connection between values, perceptions of leadership, and performance (Sully de Luque, Washburn, Waldman, & House, 2008), CEOs who emphasized economic values (i.e., who see their role as maximizing shareholder value) were perceived as autocratic leaders by their followers, whereas CEOs who emphasized stakeholder values (i.e., see their roles as taking into consideration the needs of multiple constituencies) were perceived as being visionary. In turn, visionary leadership was positively related to employees' extra effort and a perceptual measure of comparative firm performance, suggesting that maximizing firm performance (and perhaps even economic or shareholder value) may result somewhat paradoxically from a de-emphasis on economic value creation. In other words, this study suggests that for employees to be engaged and committed to the organization (and its performance)—a more holistic leadership narrative about the firm's values and stakeholders may be critical.

Conceptually related to the idea of values is the notion of virtues. In an investigation of behavioral manifestations of virtues in a sample of 191 executives, Sosik, Gentry, and Chun (2012) found that integrity, bravery, and perspective taking each accounted for individual performance beyond a host of control variables. The extent to which virtues (or the related concept of authentic leadership) of the CEO and/or TMT are related to firm-level outcomes are unknown, but a cascading effect of CEO virtues and authenticity (Palanski & Yammarino, 2009) might certainly be related to a host of team processes, strategies, and firm-outcome variables.

Another interesting possibility with regard to values lies not in individual differences in values, but in country-level differences. A group of executives in a given country are likely to vary between each other in terms of their values, but we would also expect, on balance, general values differences between executives in different countries (England, 1975). Buda and Elsayed-Elkhouly (1998) found evidence for this—US executives were more motivated by social recognition, whereas Egyptian executives displayed more interest in keeping a comfortable life. Although this stream of research on nationally based differences in executives' values and the link to strategic actions has not been empirically evaluated, there are clearly implications for predicting broad, national patterns of executive and firm behavior based on values that executives from those cultures possess.

Cognition

Beyond differences in executive personality and values discussed above, the cognitions of executives are also important to consider. In the executive domain, cognition research has focused on understanding how the cognitive structures and processes of senior leaders affect strategy formulation, strategic choice, and even organizational performance

(Narayanan, Zane & Kemmerer, 2011; Porac & Thomas, 2002). Although cognitions are sometimes presumed from demographic variables such as experience, gender, or age, these demographic variables are poor approximations of cognition (Barr, Stimpert, & Huff, 1992; Markoczy, 1997). Direct assessment of cognitive structures and processes is quite difficult, and is one reason why executive cognitions are less often the focus for researchers interested in executive leadership as compared with other forms of explanation of executive effects; but cognition research is possible, and has progressed.

For instance, Kaplan (2008) examined the cognitive construct of attention by examining annual letters to shareholders as a way to gauge the kinds of things that a given executive was paying attention to. He found that CEO attention to technological innovation impacts the subsequent level of investment in new technologies, and further, that it interacts with the capabilities of the organization to predict strategy adoption. Researchers have also studied the linkages between CEO cognitive complexity (i.e., the understanding of the structure of the environment of the firm and its dynamics) and firm performance. Hackner (1991), for example, found that the relationship between CEO cognitive complexity and firm performance followed an inverted U-shaped curve. In a subsequent study by Calori, Johnson and Sarnin (1994), the relationship between CEO cognitive complexity and firm performance was found to be moderated by the environmental complexity, such that in high complexity environments, high degrees of cognitive complexity led to more effective behaviors. Nadkarni, Perez, & Morganstein (2006) used the cognitive constructs of executive complexity and reactivity to explain why one UK-based firm's internationalization efforts were successful, whereas another was unsuccessful.

Discretion: When Do Executives Matter More or Less?

Thus far in this chapter, we have considered some of the general evidence about whether executive leadership appears to matter to organizational outcomes and how it appears to matter. Yet there is an important caveat about executive effects that is critical to understanding the potential impact of senior executive leadership. This caveat is that the potential impact depends on the situation; there are situations and conditions in which senior executive leadership has a muted (or conversely, a pronounced) impact on strategy and organizational outcomes. This idea—that a given executive may have differing latitudes of action (and impact) from another executive is referred to as *executive discretion* (Hambrick & Finkelstein, 1987).

When an executive is greatly constrained (i.e., has a relatively low amount of discretion)—the potential for their leadership actions to affect the organization is relatively less than when they are unconstrained. Having a degree of discretion, however, does not necessarily mean that an executive will always act in a way that is any different from an executive who has less discretion, but rather it implies the potential to do so—and it is this potential that sometimes manifests in actual actions and performance.

A CEO who is also the chair of the board and the largest shareholder of a company is likely to be able to consider and act in whatever strategic direction she wants. And further, we would expect that her preferences and idiosyncrasies will thus be more likely to be reflected in her strategic actions, as compared to a CEO who has relatively less power (i.e., a CEO who is not the chair of the board and who has few shares). In other words, the ability of executive personality and values to predict strategic action and organizational performance is moderated by the degree to which the CEO can manifest those individual differences in action.

What determines executive discretion? There are three general categories of factors that influence an executive's potential to act in divergent or novel ways: characteristics of the environment, characteristics of the organization, and characteristics of the individual executive.

Environmental determinants of discretion. Characteristics of the environment that an organization operates in can have a significant impact on the level of discretion afforded to executive leaders. These characteristics include macro factors such as country-level institutions and industry characteristics such as industry-level regulations and the amount of change or dynamism in an industry.

In the context of national-level environmental discretion, Crossland and Hambrick (2007) found that CEO effects on organizational outcomes in Japan were the smallest, whereas Germany and US firms showed larger CEO effects (with the United States showing the greatest variance attributable to the CEO). They conjecture that differences in national values (such as collectivism and uncertainty avoidance), ownership structure (how tightly the firm is owned and who those institutional owners are), and board governance arrangements are the drivers of these national-level differences.

Industry is another factor impacting executive latitude of action and potential impact. Higher discretion is afforded to firms operating in less-regulated and higher-growth industries structure (e.g., Finkelstein & Hambrick, 1990; Hambrick & Abrahamson, 1995)—for which there is a wide range of options to meet the firm objectives—as well as to executives in firms operating in more turbulent industries (Haleblian & Finkelstein, 1993).

Two recent papers continue to show the importance of industry-level factors in setting the boundaries for potential leadership impact. First, Wasserman and colleagues (2010) found that industry effects were critical to differences in performance outcome variance attributable to the CEO. They found, for example, that the CEO effect in the communications equipment industry (where CEO action is much less constrained) was 10 times greater than in the meat products industry, where CEOs are significantly constrained by a variety of factors, most notably tight regulations. Second, Simsek and colleagues (2010) examined the importance of industry dynamism (the degree of change in an industry) as an indicator of discretion. Consistent with their argument that greater dynamism leads to greater discretion, they found that in dynamic industries, individual characteristics of the CEO (specifically, CSE) were more predictive of firm-level outcomes than in stable environments.

Organizational determinants of discretion. Organizations may also display characteristics that limit or enhance executive discretion. The two most common organizational-level determinants of discretion discussed in the literature are firm size and firm age. Large mature firms are known for their stronger cultures and significant inertial forces (Hannan & Freeman, 1977), and thus executives have a greater impact on organizational outcomes in smaller and younger firms that have fewer inertial and historical cultural forces. For example, Miller, Kets de Vries, and Toulouse (1982) found that CEO locus of control was strongly related to firm strategy and structure in small firms, but not in large ones.

Individual determinants of discretion. At the individual level, the discretion of a given executive is largely a function of their power within the organization (Bigley & Wiersema, 2002; Finkelstein, 1992). For example, when a CEO is also the chair of the board, it increases his discretion (Bigley & Wiersema, 2002), and CEOs who are founders of the organization have higher levels of discretion in comparison to CEOs who are not (e.g., Adams, Almeida, & Ferreira, 2005). Although it has not been investigated, we might also expect that transformational behaviors and executive charisma would lead to increased discretion.

In sum, managerial discretion is an important concept in refining our understanding of the linkages between executive leadership and firm-level outcomes, and it may also help reconcile variations in prior findings about executive effects (Hutzschenreuter et al., 2012).

Top Management Teams

While significant research (and media) attention is often paid to the CEO (Mooney & Amason, 2011), the CEO does not decide and act in isolation. Other senior executives, usually known as the top management team, can be involved in a variety of ways. Specific individuals or the team collectively may be consulted when framing and making actual decisions, or their influence can sometimes be more indirect. TMT members are also often critical for the implementation of strategy, which may again take the form of a top-down process or a more collective shared process. From a core leadership perspective, an explicit examination of the role and influence of the top management team (not just the CEO) helps to shift the focus away from conceptualizing executive leadership as being primarily about an individual leader to a more realistic recognition that leadership can, at the same time, be distributed and/or may be the property of the entire team (Denis, Langley, & Sergi, 2012).

Team Composition/Demography

A significant amount of research on top management teams has focused on explaining organizational strategy and performance outcomes using team composition variables—typically examining demographic characteristics such as age, tenure, gender, and functional background of team members, or characteristics of the team itself such as team size. This composition/demographic approach has fairly consistently shown that the composition of the top management team is predictive of strategic actions and organizational outcomes and has been aided by the relative ease in collecting demographic characteristics of TMT members from existing and reliable databases (e.g., ExecuComp).

One of the most cited papers using a team composition approach (Wiersema & Bantel, 1992) found that TMTs characterized by lower average age, shorter organizational tenure, higher education heterogeneity, and higher education level tend to pursue more changes in corporate strategies. Carpenter (2002) predicted return on assets with TMT educational, tenure and functional heterogeneity, and TMT demographics have been used to explain other strategy/outcome variables such as commitment to innovation (Daellenbach, McCarthy, & Schoenecker, 1999), expansive global strategies (Sanders & Carpenter, 1998), new venture performance (Amason, Shrader, & Thompson, 2006), and ability to successfully complete an initial public offering (Beckman, Burton, & O'Reilly, 2007).

As with demographic and other surface-level variables in CEO-focused research, demographic or observable composition variables alone have some limitations in terms of being able to explain the underlying processes and mechanisms of action (Hambrick, 2007), and often the actual underlying mechanisms through which demographic variables have their effect are simply inferred. For example, greater diversity in the type of education of top management team members is taken to be representative of a higher degree of cognitive processing capacity from which the team can draw (Carpenter & Fredrickson, 2001) and team size is inferred to be an indicator of a team's ability to process complex information (Sanders & Carpenter, 1998). In some cases the veracity of the mechanisms inferred from the compositional characteristics may be acceptable, but in other cases there should be cause for question. Team size, for example, is not particularly representative of the information processing capacity of a team (Mesmer-Magnus & DeChurch, 2009).

At the same time that there are some significant hurdles and limits with the composition/demographic approach, it is certainly not devoid of examination of mechanisms and processes. In an attempt to mitigate concerns about the ambiguous link between composition and outcomes, some research has explicitly examined process or team properties such as cohesion variables as a mediator (e.g., Smith et al., 1994; Peterson et al., 2003). And further, even when composition is considered without explicitly examining possible intervening mechanisms and states, there is value in examining organizational demography of the top management team in future research (Beckman & Burton, 2011). One possibility, for example, would be to de-emphasize a focus on psychological mechanisms and examine the existence of roles and structures in TMTs over time, both within and between organizations—answering perhaps a different set of questions that cannot be considered using the psychological approach to examining these teams.

Team States and Processes

In research on nonexecutive teams, a significant amount of the "action" in predicting team outcomes comes from the dynamics and interactions of team members, as well as the emergent characteristics of the team. This emphasis on processes and team properties is not particularly concerned with who the team members are, but is rather focused on carefully describing the "state" of the team and how they interact. In the top executive team arena, this topic has rarely been investigated and has rarely borrowed from advances being made by teams researchers.

One of the ways that TMT research has begun to make some headway in understanding team states and processes is through the broad construct of behavioral integration, which is a construct that simultaneously encompasses a host of component team states and processes (Simsek, Veiga, Lubatkin, & Dino, 2005). The construct of behavioral integration is composed of three main indicators: the level of collaborative behavior in the team, the quantity and quality of information exchanged, and the emphasis on joint decision making (Hambrick, 1994) by the team. In other words, behaviorally integrated teams collaborate and work well together, regularly share lots of nonredundant information, and are collectively involved in the decision-making process. And behavioral integration does appear to be important in predicting outcomes. For example, using a sample of 96 service firms, Carmeli (2008) found that TMT behavioral integration of top management teams was positively related to perceptions of both human resource performance and economic performance. Behaviorally integrated TMTs have also been found to positively contribute to their organization's capacity to pursue new strategic initiatives (Lubatkin, Simsek, Ling, & Veiga, 2006) and are more able to implement transformations such as product innovations (Hambrick, 1998). It appears that behavioral integration may be an important construct both in its own right, and it also may be conceptualized as a key moderator of the relationship between TMT characteristics and organizational outcomes (Hambrick, 2005; Ling, Simsek, Lubatkin, & Veiga, 2008).

Similar to the findings demonstrating that the broad construct of behavioral integration is beneficial, much (but not all) of the more fine-grained research on team process has resulted in findings that are perhaps similarly intuitive. Teams characterized by a high degree of each of cohesiveness, communication, and flexibility are generally taken to be more effective and produce better organizational outcomes. For example, Peterson and colleagues (2003) found that top management team flexibility and cohesiveness were positively related to firm income growth; Iaquinto and Fredrickson (1998) found that TMT agreement was positively related to firm performance (operationalized as ROA); and Ensley, Pearson, and Amason (2002) found that TMT cohesiveness was positively related to new venture growth. Despite these findings, we assert that these "positive" team processes may not always be positive and may be dependent on characteristics of the environment and tasks that need to be done. In top management teams where the nature of the work is such that individual team members do not need to closely work together to get their work done (i.e., a low degree of interdependence), a higher degree of cohesiveness and communication may actually be detrimental to performance (Barrick, Bradley, Kristof-Brown, & Colbert, 2007). Additional research would be beneficial in helping to untangle likely nuanced relationships between team states and team processes with outcomes (discussed later in this chapter).

Core Leadership Concepts and Constructs at the Executive Level

Up to this point in the chapter, we have focused largely on research that comes out of the strategic management tradition, and more specifically, the upper echelons perspective of strategic management. But senior executive leadership can also be examined from a core leadership perspective. Certainly, the nature of leadership at the executive level is qualitatively unique from leadership and leadership phenomena at other organizational levels (Day & Lord, 1988), but some of the processes and mechanisms of action *may* (and are likely to) be similar across organizational levels. As such, an investigation of core leadership constructs (such as authentic, transformational, and shared leadership) in the context of executive leadership is informative. This cannot be the only path forward for executive leadership, but certainly a clearer understanding of the applicability and nonapplicability of core leadership constructs to the executive arena will help us develop a clearer picture of the nature and parameters of executive leadership. And at the same time, it may also shed light on and help to advance core leadership constructs.

A significant amount of core leadership research has emerged from organizational behavior and micro-oriented perspectives (Waldman, Siegel, & Javidan, 2006). Most core leadership research focuses on lower-level leaders influencing individual and group-level outcomes, with very little attention to the role of executive leadership in explaining higher-level organizational outcomes (DeChurch, et al., 2010; Yukl, 2008). Several recent empirical papers have examined the nature and dynamics of executive leadership using core leadership constructs (most notably, transformational leadership) as they relate to organizational strategy and outcomes, but these types of studies are quite rare. Although we cannot presume isomorphism of constructs and linkages at the executive level, some of the constructs and linkages may be similar.

Executive Transformational Leadership

Of the empirical examinations of transformational leadership, several studies have examined an overarching transformational leadership factor and in other cases, researchers have separated out two of the components of transformational leadership: charisma and intellectual stimulation. There appears to be building evidence that executive transformational leadership (and the facets) is predictive of organizational-level outcomes. For example, using an overarching transformational leadership factor, Resick and colleagues (2009) examined 75 newly appointed Major League Baseball team presidents and found that transformational leadership of a newly appointed team president was positively related to changes in team winning percentage and fan attendance in the following three years as compared with team presidents who were lower in transformational leadership. Transformational leadership (as a general factor) has also been linked to increased TMT effectiveness (Flood et al., 2000), and visionary leadership has been linked to effort and organizational performance (Sully de Luque et al., 2008).

Charisma. Charisma has been the most frequently examined component of transformational leadership. In general, most studies have found a positive effect of CEO charisma on organizational performance, but these effects may exist primarily (or be more pronounced) under conditions of uncertainty when followers are thought to be more prone to the influence of charisma (Weber, 1947). Both Waldman and colleagues (Waldman, Ramirez, House, & Puranam, 2001) and Tosi and colleagues (Tosi, Misangyi, Fanelli, Waldman, & Yammario, 2004) found that CEO charisma predicted organizational-level outcomes in uncertain conditions, although Bacha (2010) found that CEO charisma predicted organizational performance regardless of the uncertainty in the environment.

One of the biggest difficulties in determining charisma (which exists only as a perceptual measure) is the complexity associated with disentangling the direction of causality between the perception of charisma and performance. The evidence appears equivocal, thus we need to be careful in asserting that the charisma-performance relationship is necessarily unidirectional. On the one hand, Waldman, Javidan, and Varella (2004) found that CEO charisma predicted profit margin and return on equity, and that these effects were not the result of charisma perceptions being a function of prior performance. Agle and colleagues (Agle, Nagarajan, Sonnenfeld, & Srinavasan, 2006), however, provide a more pessimistic overall assessment by finding that CEO charisma was not predictive of a variety of performance measures (stock return, ROA, ROS, ROE, and a perceptual measure of performance), and that TMT perceptions of CEO charisma, rather, were a function of previous organizational performance.

Intellectual stimulation. Another component of transformational leadership, intellectual stimulation, has received significantly less attention, although it is likely to be critical to the leadership process (Locke, 2003). Using a sample of 56 CEOs, Waldman, Siegel, and Javidan (2006) found that CEO intellectual stimulation (as evaluated by senior managers) was related to independent evaluations of corporate social responsibility. Their suggestion was that intellectual stimulation involves encouraging others to question assumptions and authority, to think complexly and innovatively about problems and their solutions, and to consider the broader environmental context. In turn, this emphasis on thinking about systems, stakeholders, and problems would help strategic actors in the organization to first consider social responsibility issues, and then find solutions that balance social responsibility and financial performance. Less intellectually stimulating leaders, on the other hand, would fail to promote sophisticated thinking required to either consider or develop effective and complex solutions to social responsibility issues that the organization faces. It should be noted that they also examined the effect of charisma, but found no effect for charisma on social responsibility performance.

In total, it appears that there is likely two-way causality operating between performance and charisma—and that transformational leadership (particularly charisma and intellectual stimulation) may result in better performance on some metrics. Conceptually linking each of the components of transformational leadership to an appropriate outcome measure is important, and future research that moves beyond the overarching transformational component is likely to be more useful in helping to get a better idea of specific leadership behaviors that influence various outcomes and in various contexts.

Other core leadership constructs. We know significantly less about the influence of other leadership concepts and constructs at the executive level, but a few recent studies have demonstrated their potential relevance. Wang, Tsui, and Xin (2011), for example, studied the organizational performance impact of task versus relationship behaviors at the CEO level using a sample of 125 Chinese firms, and Peterson, Galvin, and Lange (2012) found that servant leadership was positively predictive of return on assets. Utilizing the concepts of both shared leadership and authentic leadership—defined as an ongoing, mutual influence process among top management team members that promotes a positive climate consistent with members' values and beliefs—shared authentic leadership was found to be positively related to firm performance in new venture top management teams (Hmieleski, Cole, & Baron, 2012). Given the breadth of leadership ideas and concepts that have proven to be relevant in nonexecutive domains, these studies are the first that help to paint a more complete picture of executive leadership.

Boards of Directors

Beyond CEOs and top management teams, boards of directors are another group that is part of the landscape of executive leadership. A review of the vast and varied literature on boards of directors and the effects they can have is beyond the scope of this brief section, but here we describe some of the key features and functions of boards and some of the general findings and approaches from research in this area.

Public companies and many other for-profit, not-for-profit, and educational institutions are overseen by a board of directors, which is an entity that is separate from the top management team, but involved in some critical organizational functions. Also referred to as a board of trustees or board of governors in some instances (to name a few possibilities), boards have varying degrees of responsibility in functions including: hiring and firing the CEO; monitoring the environment for opportunities and threats; setting strategic direction; providing advice and counsel to the CEO; approving major initiatives such as acquisitions and divestitures; and ensuring that stakeholders are being fairly represented, including attempts to align CEO and stakeholder interests through the setting of executive pay (Arthaud-Day, Certo, Dalton, & Dalton, 2006; Daily, Dalton, & Cannella, 2003; Hillman, Withers, & Collins, 2009; Zald, 1969).

Just as CEO and TMT individual difference variables have been shown to predict firm-level outcome variables, the compositional make-up of boards are predictive of the strategy and performance of an organization (Johnson, Schnatterly, & Hill, 2013). For example, the gender composition, proportion of outside versus inside members, age, and national origins of board members lead to differences in corporate social performance (Post, Rahman, & Rubow, 2011).

One of the key distinctions between boards and the top management team is that boards do not actively participate in the implementation of strategies and day-to-day operations of the firm (Fama & Jensen, 1983). Their role is primarily limited to monitoring and influence, although they sometimes play a more active role during crisis. Boards also tend to be fairly large (i.e., average of 13 directors, whereas TMTs average 6 members) and include members with potentially differing interests (e.g., insider directors versus outsider directors) (Forbes & Milliken, 1999). They function only periodically, and are mostly confronted with complex tasks. The output of their work is mostly cognitive, since they do not concretely participate to the implementation of their recommendations.

With the board playing a primary role as overseer of the organization, the CEO, then, must ultimately answer to the board of directors, or at least in theory. But in reality the situation is not so simple. At the same time the CEO is required to be held accountable to the board, he also sits on the board—oftentimes alongside several other full-time executives of the organization, and can wield significant influence on the board in framing and guiding information presented, discussions, and decisions. A CEO's influence is particularly enhanced when she also holds the position as chair of the board—a situation which can raise significant questions about the true independence of the board. In 2004 in the United States, 74.3 per cent companies in the Fortune 500 had a CEO who was also chair of the board, and as of May 2012, this percentage was lower but still a majority at 57.2 per cent (Lamb, 2012, para. 5).

In addition to internal players on the board such as the CEO and other the top management team members, boards also usually have members who are not full-time employees of the organization. At a broad level, scholars have differentiated between inside directors (i.e., the top managers of the firm), independent directors (i.e., representatives of other organizations that do very limited or no business with the firm), affiliated directors (i.e., representatives of other organizations that conduct business with the firm), and family directors (i.e., members of the founding family or relatives of top managers).

The nature of the interplay between the CEO, other senior executives, and the board is evolving and needs to be continually understood in the context of a rapidly changing legislative environment (e.g., Sarbanes-Oxley Act of 2002 in the United States, the Companies Act of 2006 in the UK) and general governance environment (Beck & Wiersema, 2011). The changes affect the nature, responsibility, and liability of the board—such that boards, are generally required to be more active and are held more responsible than in the past. Thus, research on boards of directors and their influence on organizations are increasingly important.

Future Directions

Research on senior executive leadership has increased exponentially over the last several decades, and we are starting to better understand the nature, mechanisms, and effects of this unique form of leadership. Yet the phenomena we are trying to understand is highly complex and multifaceted, and as such, acknowledgment of advances need to be tempered with acknowledgment that there is significant work still to be done. We suggest seven possibilities for future research that we believe hold significant promise for advancing the understanding of executive leadership. These seven possibilities include issues and recommendations spanning methodological and conceptual domains.

Future Possibility 1: Understand Executive Characteristics through the Eyes of Others

Scholars interested in understanding the effect of executive individual differences on strategy and performance variables have typically used self-report and proxy measures of psychological characteristics (see Peterson et al., 2003, and Resick et al., 2009, for rare exceptions), and have long lamented that there is significant difficulty in obtaining data from senior executives (Cycyota & Harrison, 2006; Finkelstein,

Hambrick, & Cannella, 2009). Researchers should consider measuring a focal executive's psychological characteristics through ratings provided by familiar others who know the individual. There are at least two potential advantages to obtaining information about an executive from a knowledgeable other.

First, reports by knowledgeable others can be a valuable alternative source of data when direct access to the executive is not possible. Second, and more important, collecting information from knowledgeable others may usefully advance our understanding of senior executive leadership beyond what is possible using only self-report and proxy measures because of the unique information that others can provide. In self-reports of personality, which have long been considered the gold standard in assessing psychological characteristics, it is well known that individuals may intentionally and/or unintentionally distort their responses because of both self-impression motives and/or an inability to properly describe themselves (Paulhus, 1991). Other-reports are less prone to some of these sources of distortion. Solid evidence for the potential benefits of other-reports of personality comes from a large-scale meta-analysis of the predictive validity of other-rated Big Five traits in nonexecutive work settings. Oh, Wang, and Mount (2011) found that other-rated Big Five traits were more predictive of overall job performance than self-reported Big Five traits. Further, they found that other-rated Big Five traits were incrementally predictive beyond the effects of self-reported traits, suggesting that unique and valuable information is being assessed beyond that resulting from self-reported personality. If this were to similarly be true in the executive arena (and there is no reason to believe it would not be), reports of executive personality provided by others may in fact be better in predicting outcomes than self-reports.

Future Possibility 2: Increased Emphasis on Validated (and Creative) Proxy Measures

To circumvent the problem of access to personality data for senior executives, researchers have often relied on "proxy" or indirect observable evidence that can be collected through archival means including company reports of various kinds and purchased databases with information about executives and companies. The standing of an executive on an underlying personality trait is then inferred from this indirect and often biographical evidence. The validity of the construct in measuring what we presume it is measuring, however, is not always well understood.

Is narcissism appropriately measured by the prominence of the CEO's photograph in the company's annual report, or their use of first-person singular pronouns (Chatterjee & Hambrick, 2007)? Is having a pilot's license a reflection of risk propensity/sensation seeking (Cain & McKeon, 2012)? Certainly there appears to be good reasons to believe that the underlying traits of narcissism and sensation seeking would be correlated with these proxy measures, and attempts to provide some evidence for the validity of the construct are occasionally made (see Chatterjee & Hambrick, 2007, for example). Yet, in many cases there is very little evidence presented as to the validity of the inferences about the underlying construct. Perhaps a pilot's license also reflects a love of travel (and perhaps then *openness to experience*) or *need for control* (the pilot does the flying so that someone else isn't in control)—indeed it could be reflective of all three of these underlying constructs to some extent. In order to make appropriate inferences, then, caution needs to be taken in presuming that a particular indicator is truly reflective of the variable of interest and not also reflective of a variety of other potential variables. Simply having predictive validity (a relationship between a proxy measure and an outcome) is not indicative that a measure is actually measuring what we are inferring it to measure. Thus, to the extent that proxy measures in executive leadership research do not provide construct validity evidence, they should be met with caution.

Providing validity evidence will require additional work by researchers, and may include avenues such as demonstrating that an unobtrusive and/or proxy measure is highly correlated to the proposed personality construct in a similar and accessible sample. For example, as a starting point, a researcher interested in validating a proxy measure of narcissism might use an accessible sample of practicing senior managers and measure both their use of first-person pronouns and their scores on a well-known pencil-and-paper measure of narcissism. To the extent that the proxy measure is correlated with the more established pencil-and-paper measure, researchers can be more confident about what the proxy measure is actually measuring. It would also be helpful to show that the proxy measure is not related (or more weakly related) to similar psychological constructs.

If researchers were to take the idea of construct validity seriously, we believe significant strides could be made in studying executive leadership. Once the construct validity evidence for a proxy measure has been established in multiple studies, the measure could be more confidently used in future research. This validation work is not likely to be easy, and it is possible that our inferred underlying constructs are not as well represented by our proxy measures as we currently believe. However, the potential difficulty and messiness that may result from more validation of proxy measures does not mean it should not be undertaken, as it is critical to the veracity of our assertions about the role (or not) of psychological characteristics in executive leadership.

Future Possibility 3: Understanding the Influence of Emotions and Emotional Capabilities

Affect and emotions—including the understanding and regulation of emotions, the interpretation of emotions and affect in others, and using emotions for influence—are important in the nonexecutive context, and may be particularly relevant in the executive domain (Hodgkinson & Healey, 2011).

One of the ways that affect, emotions, and emotion regulation may be critical in the executive context is in decision making (Andrade & Ariely, 2009; Delgado-Garcia & de la Fuente-Sabate, 2010), which is a major task of executive leadership. Senior executives need to react to events, new ideas, and possible strategic paths, and make decisions among alternatives—and oftentimes they have an automatic, gut reaction to those ideas. When those reactions are based on emotional triggers, false beliefs and assumptions, or are clouded or enhanced by an emotional state, they can significantly impact cognitive processes and decision making (Daniels, 1999). Meta-cognitive capabilities, including the proper understanding (self-awareness) and regulation of these emotional and affective states are thus a valuable skill and capacity (e.g., Nelson, 1996; Ochsner, Bunge, Gross, & Gabrieli, 2002), and we should not presume that all executives have similar tendencies and capacities. Understanding an executive's ability/tendency may thus help us predict their decision making in both specific domains and in a global sense. From a prescriptive standpoint, emotional awareness and regulation may be a skill that could be enhanced—such that an executive may be able to learn to better identify a potentially problematic emotional state and actively regulate it in order to maximize decision-making effectiveness (Barrett, 2007).

In addition to understanding decision making and strategic actions, examination of affective states and emotions may also be critical in understanding dynamics of the CEO/TMT interface and executive influence on organizational culture, as group dynamics are influenced by emotion displays (Chi, Chung, & Tsai, 2011), and emotional abilities are likely to be important in a leader's ability to influence others (Coté & Hideg, 2011) and set the tone for the organization. Certainly, the conditions that make the broad topic of emotions relevant in nonexecutive work contexts (Elfenbein, 2007; Grandey, 2008) apply, perhaps even more, in the executive context—thus we see this as an exciting and valuable avenue for future research. Researchers may have to get creative in collecting data as some of the methods used in this stream of research in nonexecutive settings (such as diary studies) are not likely to be practical. Advances in collection of physical reactions from sociometric badge data (worn by an executive) could be one possibility for future research (Olguín et al., 2009), as could emotional coding of executive reactions by trained experts who can recognize subtle emotional cues that an executive may give in public situations.

Future Possibility 4: Increased Sophistication in Theorizing—Interactions and Nonlinear Effects

Explicitly conceptualizing and examining more sophisticated models with interaction and curvilinear effects will expand understanding of executive leadership. Most of the executive leadership literature that is focused on predicting strategic actions and organizational outcomes has explored the substantive impact of single individual characteristics alone or in interaction with situational characteristics. Not only have we left a number of potentially interesting individual differences totally unstudied (such as performance/learning orientation; DeRue & Wellman, 2009) but we could significantly benefit from more sophistication in theorizing and modeling (Blettner, Chaddad, & Bettis, 2012). Outcomes of interest are likely to be predicted by a combination of factors at various stages, and curvilinear relationships may be present, although they are rarely conceptualized or tested.

Two recent examples point the way in terms of more sophisticated multivariate theorizing, which we hope will become more commonplace. First, Nadkarni and Herrmann (2010) examined all five of the Big Five traits simultaneously in a structural equation model and found significant paths from each of the traits to strategic flexibility, and additionally hypothesized and found evidence for an inverted-U relationship between agreeableness and strategic flexibility. The second exemplar is from Zhang and colleagues (Zhang, Peterson, & Reina, 2013), who found interactive effects of narcissism with both CSE and organizational identification of the CEO.

As an unstudied possibility, perhaps there's an inverted U in the relationship between conscientiousness and performance. A certain dose of conscientiousness will benefit firm performance since the CEO needs to be diligent in assessing potential threats and opportunities the firm is facing. However, at high levels, CEO conscientiousness may cause the CEO to become too bogged down in details (one of the markers of conscientiousness) and fail to prioritize properly. These effects may be more pronounced in large and rapidly changing organizations, and they may be less pronounced (or take a different shape) when the CEO has a chief operating officer. Many other possibilities for theorizing complex models not only exist, but are necessary for enhancing our understanding of the realities of executive leadership phenomena.

Future Possibility 5: Reframe the Study of Top Management Teams—Team Emergent States, Leadership Capacity, Processes, Behaviors, and Conditions

The meaning-making, decision, and action processes of executive leadership are often affected by (and involve) the properties, processes, and interactions of the top management team, and research has only begun to scratch the surface in understanding these dynamics (Carpenter, 2011; Hambrick, 2007). We assert that gains in understanding leadership within top management teams are most likely to come by reframing top management team processes and differentiating team processes from team emergent states.

In their seminal paper on team process, Marks, Mathieu, and Zaccaro (2001) differentiate between team processes and team emergent states. They define team processes as the "interdependent team activities that orchestrate taskwork in employees' pursuit of goals" (p. 358), and they describe behaviors and actions such as: monitoring the progress toward goals, strategy formulation, goal specification, team monitoring and back-up behavior, conflict management, affect management, confidence building, and sense making. On the other hand, emergent states characterize the team's perceptions of the current state of the team or the team's attitudes, cognitions, motivations, capacities, and values and are a product of a team's experiences and previous processes. In this way, team cohesion and team potency are *not* process variables but emergent states because they do not describe the nature of member interactions but rather perceptions of the state of the team. Similarly, the collective capacity for leadership within the team may also be an emergent state (Day, Gronn, & Salas, 2004).

Some of the research being done in the domain of nonexecutive teams is likely to be informative to our understanding of top management teams (see DeChurch & Mesmer-Magnus, 2010; Mathieu, Maynard, Rapp, & Gilson, 2008), although the nature of the tasks, the composition of the team, and other differences will need to be carefully considered (Finkelstein, Hambrick, & Cannella, 2009). We realize that this avenue of research is quite behaviorally specific in orientation, and data collection is not likely to be easy, but a systematic conceptualization of top management teamwork that differentiates cognitive and behavioral emergent states and team processes is likely to lead to more specific understanding of some of the critical dynamics of top management teams. This behavioral and specific focus also allows for conceptualization of leadership of and by the team as a series of behaviors, or functions including composing the team, structuring and planning, establishing expectations and goals, sense making, monitoring, solving problems, and providing resources (Morgeson, DeRue, & Karam, 2010). These (and other) functions can be performed by the CEO or by other individuals, or even collectively by the team (Hiller, Day, & Vance, 2006).

If we begin to understand the behaviors and actions (i.e., team processes) and shared emergent states that are critical drivers of top management team functioning,—we will be in a better position to suggest interventions to the structure, resources, composition, and behaviors of the team. And similarly, we may avoid focusing on non-causal remnants that are not the key drivers of TMT success. For example, consider the emergent state of team cohesion. If we focus centrally and blindly on cohesion, we are in danger of implying that cohesion is the actual mechanism of importance, and thus may try to improve team cohesion itself in order to enhance executive team performance. However, helping teams with specific behaviors and processes may be a better locus for intervention (and investigation) than trying to simply promote cohesion. Cohesion is likely to be a remnant, and not the actual cause of team performance. Careful and sophisticated examination of team processes, although difficult, would certainly be a useful avenue for understanding the context of executive team leadership. In order to do so, researchers would need to borrow heavily from the increasingly sophisticated research on teams and multi-team systems emanating from research traditions outside of the management domain. At the same time that we are suggesting the need for an informed fine-grained perspective in understanding teams, we are not suggesting abandonment of work in the meta-construct of behavioral integration (communication, collaborative behavior, and joint decision making). We view the broad construct of behavioral integration as continuing to add value in helping to understand that the overall state and process of an executive team is critical in a variety of ways to the strategic functioning of an organization. Research on behavioral integration may give us clues about where to look (and not look) deeper in order to understand top management teams. Where behavioral integration is less valuable is in diagnosis of critical states, and specific behaviors and actions.

Future Possibility 6: Differentiating TMT Members and Inner Circles

In executive leadership research focused on the top management team, the team has been treated as an undifferentiated collection of equals. In reality, there is certainly disproportionate influence of an "inner circle" or core within the top management team (Mooney & Amason, 2011). If we are to seriously explore the possibility that top management teams matter and hope to understand their processes, it is critical that we identify and test multiple possibilities about where the locus of leadership is best operationalized.

The first research issue in this domain is *who* should be considered to be a member of the top management team (Jones & Cannella, 2011). Researchers have used many different operationalizations of who is on the team, such as: the top two tiers of the organization's management, all the officers above the level of vice president, or the five highest paid executives (Carpenter & Fredrickson, 2001; Carpenter et al., 2001; Wiersema & Bantel, 1992). Finkelstein and Hambrick (2005) suggested in survey research that scholars should first ask CEOs who is in their TMT, and then send out questionnaires to those executives.

For certain strategic decisions or actions, with certain types of CEOs, in certain firms, and in certain industries, it seems that the most-appropriate locus of analysis may differ. What are the conditions under which the CEO may be the best locus of analysis? Does the team matter less in the presence of a narcissistic and powerful CEO who is unlikely to listen to others and is endowed with discretion to choose how she desires? The inner circle in a given firm may be a starting point, but it may also depend on the nature of the strategic action or outcome of interest. The chief human resource officer may have no impact on an organization's propensity to engage in acquisitions, but might be a critical actor when studying organizational culture.

Determining differential relationships and influence within the top management team may be partly related to the role (e.g., the chief operating officer is likely to be closer to and more influential with the CEO than other team members), but also might be a function of homophily and previous experience of an individual in working with a given CEO. If we conceptualized the dyadic relationships between the CEO and team members as part of a leader-member exchange process (Graen & Uhl-Bien, 1995), there may be implications for understanding who has disproportionate influence and also who is likely to be an outlier.

Disproportionate influence and inner circles may be manifest in networks (Contractor, Wasserman, & Faust, 2006), and sociometric badges and e-mail communication patterns are two possible sources of data. Mapping this data with perceptions of relationship quality, strategic decisions, and organizational outcomes could be particularly informative. Examining the patterns of in- and out-flow of executives in organizations (and inner circles) could also be informative (Beckman & Burton, 2011). These possibilities, however, will require sociological and network perspectives and theories as opposed to the more psychological perspective that has dominated much of the thinking about executive leadership.

Conceptualizing the top management team as a monolithic structure with equal participants is likely to hinder advances in understanding top management teams, and subsequently, will likely limit our understanding of their influence on strategy, culture, and performance outcomes. Recognizing channels of disproportionate influence and differentiated relationships are likely to help us understand the foci of leadership most appropriate for a given phenomenon, be it the CEO, the top management team, or inner circle of disproportionate influence.

Future Possibility 7: Focus on Executive Skills, Abilities, and Development

We know relatively little (from an empirical standpoint) about the development of executive leadership, both before an individual reaches an executive role and after they are in the role (Zaccaro, 2001). What, if any, are the skills and abilities of executive leadership that can be developed? How can these skills and abilities be developed? Is it through life or work experiences, enhancement of self-awareness, training sessions and seminars, or other means?

In order to start to understand development, it is requisite that careful attention is given to research findings about factors related to executive success, both globally and in different industries, governance conditions, countries, and when considering different criteria of success (to name a few of the possible contingencies discussed in this chapter). From an understanding of what is required of successful executive leadership, we may then start to think about development and observe how it occurs, as well as seek to intervene. Executives have effects on other executives, teams, and the entire organization, and certain characteristics, skills, and abilities that are effective for one level and with one criteria may not be effective for the other (Hiller, DeChurch, Murase, & Doty, 2011)—so we may discover some skills and behaviors that apply across all levels, but there is also likely to be significant nuance in what is both recommended and possible at executive levels in comparison to nonexecutive leadership development.

Our understanding of dispositional traits and their effects could be of some value in development if executives can become more self-aware of their tendencies to incorrectly act a certain way or make certain decisions, and then design workaround solutions. Skills and abilities, on the other hand, may be better candidates for development to the extent that they are more likely to be trainable or developable. For example, getting buy-in from others, thinking more systemically, and emotional regulation are better candidates for development than any type of intervention involving a personality trait. There is often a fine line between the conceptualization of a disposition and a skill, but a focus on skills and abilities inherently allows for more possibilities for development than dispositions and traits, which are largely immutable.

Only recently have scholars begun to systematically investigate the process and trajectories of leadership development of managers (e.g., Day & Sin, 2011, Dragoni, Tesluk, Russell, & Oh, 2009) and have demonstrated that gains in competencies and effectiveness are not simply a result of tenure, but that individuals differ in their growth trajectories. Part of an individual's growth trajectory may be open to systematic intervention, and some differences in growth may be due to more stable interindividual differences. To the extent that some individuals by nature are simply likely to keep developing as leaders, this may then shift the emphasis away from emphasizing leadership development interventions by others, and shift the focus toward selection of executives who are inherently focused on development.

In sum, an understanding of the possibilities, limits and trajectories of executive leadership development is sorely needed. If general leadership development is an unspoiled section of land waiting to be better mapped, then executive leadership development is a piece of that land that surveyors have not yet seen.

Conclusion

Significant progress has been made in understanding the nature of executive leadership despite the difficulty in gaining direct access to primary data from senior executives. Our review here attempts to summarize and synthesize large swaths of this research (with a particular emphasis on recent research) and to suggest a number of paths forward for future investigation, but by no means should this review and our recommendations be considered exhaustive in breadth or depth.

In many respects, the understanding of executive-level leadership has come a long way since Day and Lord's (1988) admonition that researchers explicitly consider executive leadership as an important domain in its own right and thus in need of unique theoretical and empirical attention—yet there is considerable room and need for more research and more researchers to contribute to the discussion. In addition to the possibility for understanding organizational strategy, culture, and outcomes, increased theorizing and research attention on executive leadership has significant potential to also inform general leadership theories and approaches, our understanding of boundary conditions of leadership (such as discretion and situational moderators), and mechanisms of leadership impact.

References

Adams, R. B., Almeida, H., & Ferreira, D. (2005). Powerful CEOs and their impact on corporate performance. *Review of Financial Studies, 18*, 1403–1432.

Agle, B. R., Nagarajan, N. J., Sonnenfeld, J. A., & Srinivasan, D. (2006). Does CEO charisma matter? An empirical analysis of the relationships among organizational performance, environmental uncertainty, and top management team

perceptions of CEO charisma. *Academy of Management Journal, 49*, 161–174.
Amason, A. C., Shrader, R. C., & Thompson, G. H. (2006). Newness and novelty: Relating top management team composition to new venture performance. *Journal of Business Venturing, 21*, 125–148.
Andrade, E., & Ariely, D. (2009). The enduring impact of transient emotions on decision making. *Organizational Behavior and Human Decision Processes, 109*, 1–8.
Arthaud-Day, M. L., Certo, S. T., Dalton, C. M., & Dalton, D. R. (2006). A changing of the guard: Executive and director turnover following corporate financial restatements. *Academy of Management Journal, 49*, 1119–1136.
Bacha, E. (2010). The relationships among organizational performance, environmental uncertainty, and employees' perceptions of CEO charisma. *Journal of Management Development, 29*, 28–37.
Back, M. D., Stopfer, J. M., Vazire, S., Gaddis, S., Schmukle, S. C., Egloff, B., & Gosling, S. D. (2010). Facebook profiles reflect actual personality not self-idealization. *Psychological Science, 21*, 372–374.
Barker, V., & Mueller, G. (2002). CEO characteristics and firm R&D spending. *Management Science, 48*, 782–801.
Barnard, C. I. (1938). *The functions of the executive*. Cambridge, MA: Harvard University Press.
Barr, P. S., Stimpert, J. L., & Huff, A. S. (1992). Cognitive change, strategic action, and organizational renewal. *Strategic Management Journal, 13*, 15–36.
Barrett, L. F. (2007). Being emotional during decision making—Good or bad? An empirical investigation. *Academy of Management Journal, 50*, 923–940.
Barrick, M. R., Bradley, B. H., Kristof-Brown, A. L., & Colbert, A. E. (2007). The moderating role of top management team interdependence: Implications for real teams and working groups. *Academy of Management Journal, 50*, 544–557.
Barron, J. M., Chulkov, D. V., & Waddell, G. R. (2011). Top management team turnover, CEO succession, and strategic change. *Journal of Business Research, 64*, 904–910.
Beck, J. B., & Wiersema, M. F. (2011). CEO dismissal: The role of the broader governance context. In M. A. Carpenter (Ed.), *The handbook of research on top management teams* (pp. 396–414). New York, NY: Edward Elgar Publishing.
Beckman, C. M., & Burton, M. D. (2011). Bringing organizational demography back in: Time, change and structure in top management team research. In M. A. Carpenter (Ed.), *The handbook of research on top management teams* (pp. 49–70). New York, NY: Edward Elgar Publishing.
Beckman, C. M., Burton, M. D., & O'Reilly, C. (2007). Early teams: The impact of team demography on VC financing and going public. *Journal of Business Venturing, 22*, 147–173.
Berson, Y., Oreg, S., & Dvir, T. (2008). CEO values, organizational culture and firm outcomes. *Journal of Organizational Behavior, 29*, 615–633.
Bigley, G. A., & Wiersema, M. F. (2002). New CEOs and corporate strategic refocusing: How experience as heir apparent influences the use of power. *Administrative Science Quarterly, 47*, 707–727.
Blettner, D. P., Chaddad, F. R., & Bettis, R. A. (2012). The CEO performance effect: Statistical issues and a complex fit perspective. *Strategic Management Journal, 33*, 986–999.
Boeker, W. (1997a). Executive migration and strategic change: The effect of top manager movement on product-market entry. *Administrative Science Quarterly, 42*, 213–236.
Boeker, W. (1997b). Strategic change: The influence of managerial characteristics and organizational growth. *Academy of Management Journal, 40*, 152–170.
Boone, C., De Brabander, B., & Witteloostuijn, A. (1996). CEO locus of control and small firm performance: An integrative framework and empirical test. *Journal of Management Studies, 33*, 667–699.
Buda, R., & Elsayed-Elkhouly, S. M. (1998). Cultural differences between Arabs and Americans—Individualism collectivism revisited. *Journal of Cross-Cultural Psychology, 29*, 487–492.
Buffett, W. E., & Cunningham, L. A. (2001). *The essays of Warren Buffett: Lessons for corporate America* (1st ed.). The Cunningham Group.
Buyl, T., Boone, C., Hendriks, W., & Matthyssens, P. (2011). Top management team functional diversity and firm performance: The moderating role of CEO characteristics. *Journal of Management Studies, 48*, 151–177.
Cain, M. D., & Mckeon, S. B. (2012). Cleared for takeoff? CEO personal risk-taking and corporate policies. Working Paper, University of Notre Dame.
Calori, R., Johnson, G., & Sarnin, P. (1994). CEOs' cognitive maps and the scope of the organization. *Strategic Management Journal, 15*, 437–457.
Carmeli, A. (2008). Top management team behavioral integration and the performance of service organizations. *Group & Organization Management, 33*, 712–735.
Carpenter, M. A. (2002). The implications of strategy and social context for the relationship between top management team heterogeneity and firm performance. *Strategic Management Journal, 23*, 275–284.
Carpenter, M. A. (2011). *Handbook of top management team research*. New York, NY: Edward Elgar Publishing.
Carpenter, M. A., & Fredrickson, J. W. (2001). Top management teams, global strategic posture, and the moderating role of uncertainty. *Academy of Management Journal, 44*, 533–546.
Carpenter, M. A., Sanders, W. G., & Gregersen, H. B. (2001). Bundling human capital with organizational context: The impact of international assignment experience on multination firm performance and CEO pay. *Academy of Management Journal, 44*, 493–512.
Carroll, G. R., & Hannan, M. T. (2000). *The demography of corporations and industries*. Princeton, NJ: Princeton University Press.
Chang, C. H., Ferris, D. L., Johnson, R. E., Rosen, C. C., & Tan, J. A. (2012). Core self-evaluations: A review and evaluation of the literature. *Journal of Management, 38*, 81–128.
Chatterjee, A., & Hambrick, D. C. (2007). It is all about me: Narcissistic chief executive officers and their effects on company strategy and performance. *Administrative Science Quarterly, 52*, 351–386.
Chatterjee, A., & Hambrick, D. C. (2011). Executive personality, capability cues, and risk taking: How narcissistic CEOs react to their successes and stumbles. *Administrative Science Quarterly, 56*, 202–237.
Chi, N. W., Chung, Y. Y., & Tsai, W. C. (2011). How do happy leaders enhance team success? The mediating roles of transformational leadership, group affective tone, and team processes. *Journal of Applied Social Psychology, 41*, 1421–1454.
Child, J. (1974). Managerial and organizational factors associated with company performance. *Journal of Management Studies, 11*, 13–27.

Ciavarella, M. A., Buchholtz, A. K., Riordan, C. M., Gatewood, R. D., & Stokes, G. S. (2004). The Big Five and venture survival: Is there a linkage? *Journal of Business Venturing, 19*, 465–483.

Contractor, N. S., Wasserman, S., & Faust, K. (2006). Testing multitheoretical, multilevel hypotheses about organizational networks: An analytic framework and empirical example. *Academy of Management Review, 31*, 681–703.

Costa, P. T., Jr., & McCrae, R. R. (1992). *Revised NEO personality inventory (NEO-PI-R) and NEO Five-Factor inventory (NEO-FFI) professional manual.* Odessa, FL: Psychological Assessment Resources.

Côté, S., & Hideg, I. (2011). The ability to influence others via emotion displays: A new dimension of emotional intelligence. *Organizational Psychology Review, 1*, 53–71.

Crossland, C., & Hambrick, D. C. (2007). How national systems differ in their constraints on corporate executives: a study of CEO effects in three countries. *Strategic Management Journal, 28*, 767–89.

Cycyota, C. S., & Harrison, D. A. (2006). What (not) to expect when surveying executives: A meta-analysis of top manager response rates and techniques over time. *Organizational Research Methods, 9*, 133–160.

Daellenbach, U. S., McCarthy, A. M., & Schoenecker, T. S. (1999). Commitment to innovation: The impact of top management team characteristics. *R&D Management, 29*, 199–208.

Daily, C. M., Dalton, D. R. & Canella, A. A. (2003). Corporate governance: Decades of dialogue and data. *Academy of Management Review, 28*, 371–382.

Daniels, K. (1999). Affect and strategic decision making. *The Psychologist, 12*(1), 24–28.

Davis, S. M. (1984). *Managing corporate culture.* New York, NY: Ballinger.

Day, D. V., Gronn, P., & Salas, E. (2004). Leadership capacity in teams. *The Leadership Quarterly, 15*, 857–880.

Day, D. V., Gronn, P., & Salas, E. (2006). Leadership in team-based organizations: On the threshold of a new era. *The Leadership Quarterly, 17*, 211–216.

Day, D. V., & Lord, R. G. (1988). Executive leadership and organizational performance: Suggestions for a new theory and methodology. *Journal of Management, 14*, 453–464.

Day, D. V., & Sin, H. P. (2011). Longitudinal tests of an integrative model of leader development: Charting and understanding developmental trajectories. *The Leadership Quarterly, 22*, 545–560.

DeChurch, L. A., Hiller, N. J., Murase, T., Doty, D., & Salas, E. (2010). Leadership across levels: Levels of leaders and their levels of impact. *The Leadership Quarterly, 21*, 1069–1085.

DeChurch, L. A., & Mesmer-Magnus, J. R. (2010). The cognitive underpinnings of effective teamwork: A meta-analysis. *Journal of Applied Psychology, 95*, 32–53.

Delgado–García, J. B., & De La Fuente–Sabaté, J. M. (2010). How do CEO emotions matter? Impact of CEO affective traits on strategic and performance conformity in the Spanish banking industry. *Strategic Management Journal, 31*, 562–574.

Denis, D. J., & Denis, D. K. (1995). Performance changes following top management dismissals. *Journal of Finance, 50*, 1029–1057.

Denis, J. L., Langley, A., & Sergi, V. (2012). Leadership in the plural. *Academy of Management Annals, 5*, 1–73.

Denison, D. R., Hooijberg, R., & Quinn, R. E. (1995). Paradox and performance: Toward a theory of behavioral complexity in managerial leadership. *Organization Science, 6*, 524–540.

DeRue, D. S., & Wellman, N. (2009). Developing leaders via experience: The role of developmental challenge, learning orientation, and feedback availability. *Journal of Applied Psychology, 94*, 859–875.

Di Zhang, D., & Bruning, E. (2011). Personal characteristics and strategic orientation: Entrepreneurs in Canadian manufacturing companies. *International Journal of Entrepreneurial Behaviour & Research, 17*, 82–103.

Dragoni, L., Tesluk, P. E., Russell, J.E.A., & Oh, I. S. (2009). Understanding managerial developmental assignments, learning orientation, and access to developmental opportunities in predicting managerial competencies. *Academy of Management Journal, 52*, 731–743.

Elfenbein, H. A. (2007). Emotion in organizations: A review and theoretical integration. *Academy of Management Annals, 1*, 371–457.

England, G W. (1975). *The manager and his values.* Cambridge, MA: Ballinger.

Ensley, M. D., Pearson, A. W., & Amason, A. C. (2002). Understanding the dynamics of new venture top management teams: Cohesion, conflict, and new venture performance. *Journal of Business Venturing, 17*, 365–386.

Fama, E. F., & Jensen, M. C. (1983). Separation of ownership and control. *Journal of Law and Economics, 26*, 301–325.

Finkelstein, S. (1992). Power in top management teams: Dimensions, measurement and validation. *Academy of Management Journal, 35*, 505–538.

Finkelstein, S., & Hambrick, D. C. (1990). Top management team tenure and organizational outcomes: The moderating role of managerial discretion. *Administrative Science Quarterly, 35*, 484–503.

Finkelstein, S., & Hambrick, D. C. (2006). Chief executive compensation: A study of the intersection of markets and political processes. *Strategic Management Journal, 10*, 121–134.

Finkelstein, S., Hambrick, D. C., & Cannella, A. A. (2009). *Strategic leadership: Theory and research on executives, top management teams, and boards.* New York, NY: Oxford University Press.

Flood, P. C., Hannan, E., Smith, K. J., Turner, T., West, M. A., & Dawson, J. (2000). Chief executive leadership style, consensus decision making, and top management team effectiveness. *European Journal of Work and Organizational Psychology, 9*, 401–420.

Forbes, D. P., & Milliken, F. J. (1999). Cognition and corporate governance: Understanding boards of directors as strategic decision-making groups. *Academy of Management Review, 24*, 489–505.

Frank, R., Gilovich, T., & Regan, D. (1993). Does studying economics inhibit cooperation? *Journal of Economic Perspectives, 7*, 159–171.

Gerstner, L. V. (2002). *Who said elephants can't dance? Inside IBM's historic turnaround.* London: Harper Collins Publishers.

Giberson, T. R., Resick, C. J., Dickson, M. W., Mitchelson, J. K., Randall, K. R., & Clark, M. A. (2009). Leadership and organizational culture: Linking CEO characteristics to cultural values. *Journal Business Psychology, 24*, 123–137.

Gosling, S. D., Ko, S. J., Mannarelli, T., & Morris, M. E. (2002). A room with a cue: Judgments of personality based on offices and bedrooms. *Journal of Personality and Social Psychology, 82*, 379–398.

Graen, G., & Uhl-Bien, M. (1995). Relationship-based approach to leadership: Development of leader member exchange (LMX) theory of leadership over 25 years: Applying a multi-domain approach. *The Leadership Quarterly, 6,* 219–247.

Grandey, A. (2008). Emotions at work: A review and research agenda. In C. Cooper & J. Barling (Eds.), *The SAGE handbook of organizational behavior* (vol. *1*, pp. 234–261). Thousand Oaks, CA: Sage.

Gupta, A. K., & Govindarajan, V. (1986). Resource sharing among SBUs: Strategic antecedents and administrative implications, *Academy of Management Journal, 29,* 695–714.

Hackner, Y.E.R. (1991). *Integrated complexity and profitability.* Working paper, Case Western Reserve University, Cleveland, OH, Presented at the Academy of Management Conference, Miami, FL.

Hackman, J. R., & Wageman, R. (2005). When and how team leaders matter. *Research in Organizational Behavior, 26,* 37–74.

Haleblian, J., & Finkelstein, S. (1993). Top management team size, CEO dominance, and firm performance: The moderating roles of environmental turbulence and discretion. *Academy of Management Journal, 36,* 844–863.

Halikias, J., & Panayotopoulou, L. (2003), Chief executive personality and export involvement. *Management Decision, 41,* 340–349.

Hambrick, D. C. (1994). Top management groups: A conceptual integration and reconsideration of the "team" label. In B. M. Staw & L. L. Cummings (Eds.), *Research in organizational behavior* (pp. 171–213). Greenwich, CT: JAI Press.

Hambrick, D. C. (1998). Corporate coherence and the top management team. In D. C. Hambrick, D. A. Nadler, & M. L. Tushman (Eds.), *Navigating change: How CEOs, top teams and boards steer transformation* (pp. 123–140). Boston, MA: Harvard Business School Press.

Hambrick, D. C. (2005). Upper echelons theory: Origins, twists and turns, and lessons learned. In K. G. Smith & M. A. Hitt (Eds.), *Great minds in management: The process of theory development* (pp. 109–127). New York, NY: Oxford University Press.

Hambrick, D. (2007). Upper echelons theory: An update. *Academy of Management Review, 32,* 334–343.

Hambrick, D. C., & Abrahamson, E. (1995). Assessing the amount of managerial discretion in different industries: A multimethod approach. *Academy of Management Journal, 38,* 1427–1441.

Hambrick, D. C., & Finkelstein, S. (1987). Managerial discretion: A bridge between polar views of organizations. In L. L. Cummings & B. M. Staw (Eds.), *Research in organizational behavior* (pp. 369–406). Greenwich, CT: JAI Press.

Hambrick, D. C., Geletkanycz, M. A., & Fredrickson, J. W. (1993). Top executive commitment to the status quo: Some tests of its determinants. *Strategic Management Journal, 14,* 401–418.

Hambrick, D. C., & Mason, P. A. (1984). Upper echelons: The organization as a reflection of its top managers. *Academy of Management Review, 9,* 193–206.

Hayward, M.L.A., & Hambrick, D. C. (1997). Explaining the premium paid for large acquisitions: Evidence of CEO hubris. *Administrative Science Quarterly, 42,* 103–127.

Hannan, M. T., & Freeman, J. (1977). The population ecology of organizations. *American Journal of Sociology, 82,* 929–964.

Hannan, M. T., & Freeman, J. (1989). *Organizational Ecology.* Cambridge, MA: Harvard University Press.

Hart, P., & Mellons, J. (1970). Management youth and company growth: A correlation? *Management Decision, 4,* 50–53.

Herrmann, P., & Datta, D. K. (2002). CEO successor characteristics and the choice of foreign market entry mode: an empirical study. *Journal of International Business Studies, 33,* 551–569.

Herrmann, P., & Datta, D. K. (2006). CEO experiences: Effects on the choice of FDI entry mode. *Journal of Management Studies, 43,* 755–778.

Hiller, N. J., Day, D. V., & Vance, R. J. (2006). Collective enactment of leadership roles and team effectiveness: A field study. *The Leadership Quarterly, 17,* 387–397.

Hiller, N. J., DeChurch, L. A., Murase, T., & Doty, D. (2011). Searching for outcomes of leadership: A 25-year review. *Journal of Management, 37,* 1137–1177.

Hiller, N. J., & Hambrick, D. C. (2005). Conceptualizing executive hubris: The role of (hyper) core self-evaluations in strategic decision-making. *Strategic Management Journal, 26,* 297–319.

Hillman, A. J., Withers, M. C., & Collins, B. J. (2009). Resource dependence theory: A review. *Journal of Management, 35,* 1404–1427.

Hitt, M. A., & Tyler, B. B. (1991). Strategic decision models: Integrating different perspectives. *Strategic Management Journal, 12,* 327–351.

Hmieleski, K. M., Cole, M. S., & Baron, R. A. (2012). Shared authentic leadership and new venture performance. *Journal of Management, 38,* 1476–1499.

Hodgkinson, G. P., & Clarke, I. (2007). Conceptual note: Exploring the cognitive significance of organizational strategizing: A dual-process framework and research agenda. *Human Relations, 60,* 243–255.

Hodgkinson, G. P., & Healey, M. P. (2011). Psychological foundations of dynamic capabilities: Reflexion and reflection in strategic management. *Strategic Management Journal, 32,* 1500–1516.

Holland, J. L. (1959). A theory of vocational choice. *Journal of Counseling and Clinical Psychology, 6,* 35–45.

Hollenbeck, J. R., DeRue, D. S., & Mannor, M. (2006). Statistical power and parameter stability when subjects are few and tests are many: Comment on Peterson, Smith, Martorana, and Owens (2003). *Journal of Applied Psychology, 91,* 1–5.

Howell, J. M., & Avolio, B. J. (1993). Transformational leadership, transactional leadership, locus of control, and support for innovation: Key predictors of consolidated-business-unit performance. *Journal of Applied Psychology, 78,* 891–902.

Hutzschenreuter, T., Kleindienst, I., & Greger, C. (2012). How new leaders affect strategic change following a succession event: A critical review of the literature. *The Leadership Quarterly, 23,* 729–755.

Iaquinto, A. L., & Fredrickson, J. W. (1998). Top management team agreement about the strategic decision process: A test of some of its determinants and consequences. *Strategic Management Journal, 18,* 63–75.

Jacobs, T. O., & Jaques, E. (1987). *Leadership in complex systems.* New York, NY: Praeger.

Jaques, E., Clement, S. D., Rigby, C., & Jacobs, T. O. (1986). *Senior leadership performance requirements at the executive level.* US Army Research Institute for the Behavioral and Social Sciences.

Johnson, S. G., Schnatterly, K., & Hill, A. D. (2013). Board composition beyond independence: Social capital, human capital, and demographics. *Journal of Management, 39,* 232–262.

Jones, C. D., & Cannella Jr, A. A. (2011). Alternate configurations in strategic decision making. In M. A. Carpenter (Ed.), *The handbook of research on top management teams* (pp. 15–34). New York, NY: Edward Elgar Publishing.

Judge, T. A., & Bono, J. E. (2000). Five-factor model of personality and transformational leadership. *Journal of Applied Psychology, 85*, 751–765.

Judge, T. A., Erez, A., Bono, J. E., & Thoresen, C. J. (2003). The core self-evaluation scale: Development of a measure. *Personnel Psychology, 56*, 303–331.

Judge, T. A., Locke, E. A., Durham, C. C., & Kluger, A. N. (1998). Dispositional effects on job and life satisfaction: The role of core evaluations. *Journal of Applied Psychology, 83*, 17–34.

Kaiser, R. B., Hogan, R., & Craig, S. B. (2008). Leadership and the fate of organizations. *American Psychologist, 63*, 96–110.

Kaplan, S. (2008). Cognition, capabilities, and incentives: Assessing firm response to the fiber-optic revolution. *Academy of Management Journal, 51*, 672–695.

Karami, A., Analoui, F., & Kakabadse, N. K. (2006). The CEOs characteristics and strategy development in UK SME sector. *Journal of Management Development, 25*, 316–324.

Katz, D., & Kahn, R. L. (1978). *The social psychology of organizations* (2nd ed.). New York, NY: Wiley.

Kimberly, J. R., & Evanisko, M. J. (1981). Organizational innovation: The influence of individual, organizational, and contextual factors on hospital adoption of technological and administrative innovations. *Academy of Management Journal, 24*, 689–713.

Khoo, H. S., & Burch, G. S. J. (2008). The "dark side" of leadership personality and transformational leadership: An exploratory study. *Personality and Individual Differences, 44*, 86–97.

Kraatz, M., & Moore, J. (2002). Executive migration and institutional change. *Academy of Management Journal, 45*, 120–143.

Lamb, M. (2012, August 29). Should the chair and CEO roles be split? *Inside Investor Relations Magazine*. Retrieved from http://www.insideinvestorrelations.com

Lee, D., & Tsang, E. (2001). The effects of entrepreneurial personality, background and network activity on venture growth. *Journal of Management Studies, 38*, 583–602.

Li, J., & Tang, Y. (2010). CEO hubris and firm risk taking in China: The moderating role of managerial discretion. *Academy of Management Journal, 1*, 45–68.

Lieberson, S., & O'Connor, J. (1972). Leadership and organizational performance: A study of large corporations. *American Sociological Review, 37*, 117–130.

Ling, Y., Simsek, Z., Lubatkin, M. H., & Veiga, J. F. (2008). Transformational leadership's role in promoting corporate entrepreneurship: Examining the CEO-TMT interface. *Academy of Management Journal, 51*, 557–576.

Ling, Y., Zhao, H., & Baron, R. A. (2007). Influence of founder-CEOs personal values on firms' performance: Moderating effects of age and size. *Journal of Management, 33*, 673–696.

Locke, E. A. (2003). Foundations for a theory of leadership. In S. E. Murphy, & R. E. Riggio (Eds.), *The future of leadership development* (pp. 29–46). Mahwah, NJ: Lawrence Erlbaum Associates.

Lubatkin, M. H., Simsek, Z., Ling, Y., & Veiga, J. F. (2006). Ambidexterity and performance in small-to medium-sized firms: The pivotal role of top management team behavioral integration. *Journal of Management, 32*, 646–672.

Manner, M. H. (2010). The impact of CEO characteristics on corporate social performance. *Journal of Business Ethics, 93*, 53–72.

March, J. G., & Shapira, Z. (1982). Behavioral decision theory and organizational decision theory. In G. R. Ungson & D. N. Braunstein (Eds.), *Decision making: An interdisciplinary inquiry* (pp. 95–122). Boston, MA: Kent.

Markoczy, L. (1997). Measuring beliefs: Accept no substitutes. *Academy of Management Journal, 40*, 1228–1242.

Marks, M. A., Mathieu, J. E., & Zaccaro, S. J. (2001). A temporally based framework and taxonomy of team processes. *Academy of Management Review, 26*, 356–376.

Mathieu, J. E., Maynard, M. T., Rapp, T. L., & Gilson, L. L. (2008). Team effectiveness 1997–2007: A review of recent advancements and a glimpse into the future. *Journal of Management, 34*, 410–476.

McClelland, D. C. (1961). *The achieving society*. Princeton, NJ: Van Nostrand.

McClelland, P. L., Liang, X., & Barker, V. L. III. (2010). CEO commitment to the status quo: Replication and extension using content analysis. *Journal of Management, 36*, 1251–1277.

Mesmer-Magnus, J. R. & DeChurch, L. A. (2009). Information sharing and team performance: A meta-analysis. *Journal of Applied Psychology, 94*, 535–546.

Miller, C. C., Burke, L. M., & Glick, W. H. (1998). Cognitive diversity among upper-echelon executives: Implications for strategic decision processes. *Strategic Management Journal, 19*, 39–58.

Miller, D., & Droge, C. (1986). Psychological and traditional dimensions of structure. *Administrative Science Quarterly, 31*, 539–560.

Miller, D., Kets de Vries, M. F. R., & Toulouse, J. M. (1982). Top executives locus of control and its relationships to strategy making, structure, and environment. *Academy of Management Journal, 25*, 237–253.

Miller, D., & Toulouse, J. M. (1986a). Chief executive personality and corporate strategy and structure in small firms. *Management Science, 32*, 1389–1409.

Miller, D., & Toulouse, J. M. (1986b). Strategy, structure, CEO personality and performance in small firms. *American Journal of Small Business, 10*, 47–62.

Mintzberg, H. (1973). Strategy-making in three modes. *California Management Review, 15*(2), 44–53.

Mooney, A. C., & Amason, A. C. (2011). In search of the CEO's inner circle and how it is formed. In M. A. Carpenter (Ed.), *The handbook of research on top management teams* (pp. 35–48). New York, NY: Edward Elgar Publishing.

Morgan, G. (1997). *Images of organization* (2nd ed.). Thousand Oaks, CA: Sage Publications.

Morgeson, F. P., DeRue, D. S., & Karam, E. P. (2010). Leadership in teams: A functional approach to understanding leadership structures and processes. *Journal of Management, 36*, 5–39.

Musteen, M., Barker, V. L. I., & Baeten, V. L. (2006). CEO attributes associated with attitude toward change: The direct and moderating effects of CEO tenure. *Journal Business Research, 59*, 604–612.

Nadkarni, S., & Herrmann, P. (2010). CEO personality, strategic flexibility, and firm performance: The case of the Indian BPO industry. *Academy of Management Journal, 53*, 1050–1073.

Nadkarni, S., Perez, P. D., & Morganstein, B. (2006). Mindsets and internationalization success: An exploratory study of the

British retail grocery industry. *Organization Management Journal, 3*, 139–154.
Narayanan, V. K., Zane, L. J., & Kemmerer, B. (2011). The cognitive perspective in strategy: An integrative review. *Journal of Management, 37*, 305–351.
Nelson, T. O. (1996). Consciousness and metacognition. *American Psychologist, 51*, 102–116.
Ng, T. W. H., Sorensen, K. L., & Eby, L. T. (2006). Locus of control at work: A meta-analysis. *Journal of Organizational Behavior, 27*, 1057–1087.
Ochsner, K. N., Bunge, S. A., Gross, J. J., & Gabrieli, J. D. E. (2002). Rethinking feelings: An fMRI study of the cognitive regulation of emotion. *Journal of Cognitive Neuroscience, 14*, 1215–1229.
Oh, I. S., Wang, G., & Mount, M. K. (2011). Validity of observer ratings of the five-factor model of personality traits: A meta-analysis. *Journal of Applied Psychology, 96*, 762–773.
Olguín, D. O., Waber, B. N., Kim, T., Mohan, A., Ara, K., & Pentland, A. (2009). Sensible organizations: Technology and methodology for automatically measuring organizational behavior. *Systems, Man, and Cybernetics, Part B, 39*, 43–55.
Palanski, M. E., & Yammarino, F. J. (2009). Integrity and leadership: A multi-level conceptual framework. *The Leadership Quarterly, 20*, 405–420.
Papadakis, V. M. (2006). Do CEOs shape the process of making strategic decisions? Evidence from Greece. *Management Decision, 44*, 367–394.
Papadakis, V. M., & Bourantas, D. (1998). The chief executive officer as corporate champion of technological innovation: An empirical investigation. *Technology Analysis and Strategic Management, 10*, 89–98.
Paulhus, D. L. (1991). Measurement and control of response bias. In J. P. Robinson, P. R. Shaver, & L. S. Wrightsman (Eds.), *Measures of personality and social psychological attitudes* (pp. 17–59). New York, NY: Academic Press.
Peterson, S. J., Galvin, B. M., & Lange, D. (2012). CEO servant leadership: Exploring executive characteristics and firm performance. *Personnel Psychology, 65*, 565–596.
Peterson, R. S., Smith, D. B., Martorana, P. V., & Owens, P. D. (2003). The impact of chief executive officer personality on top management team dynamics: One mechanism by which leadership affects organizational performance. *Journal of Applied Psychology, 88*, 795–808.
Porac, J. F., & Thomas, H. (2002). Managing cognition and strategy: Issues, trends and future directions. In A. Pettigrew, H. Thomas, & R. Whittington (Eds.), *Handbook of strategy and management* (pp. 165–181). London: Sage.
Porter, M. E., & Nohria, N. (2010). What is leadership? The CEO's role in large, complex organizations. In N. Nohria & R. Khurana (Eds.), *Handbook of leadership theory and practice: A Harvard Business School centennial colloquium* (pp. 433–474). Boston, MA: Harvard Business School Press.
Post, C., Rahman, N., & Rubow, E. (2011). Green governance: Boards of directors' composition and environmental corporate social responsibility. *Business & Society, 50*, 189–223.
Powell, W. W., & DiMaggio, P. J. (1991). *The new institutionalism in organizational analysis*. Chicago, IL: University of Chicago Press.
Ragins, B. R., Townsend, B., & Mattis, M. (1998). Gender gap in the executive suite: CEOs and female executives report on breaking the glass ceiling. *Academy of Management Executive, 12*, 28–42.
Resick, C. J., Whitman, D. S., Weingarden, S. M., & Hiller, N. J. (2009). The bright-side and the dark-side of CEO personality: Examining core self-evaluations, narcissism, transformational leadership, and strategic influence. *Journal of Applied Psychology, 94*, 1365–1381.
Rokeach, M. (1973). *The nature of human values*. New York, NY: Free Press.
Roll, L. (1986). The hubris hypothesis of corporate takeovers. *Journal of Business, 59*, 197–218.
Rosenthal, S. A., & Pittinskya, T. L. (2006). Narcissistic leadership. *The Leadership Quarterly, 17*, 617–633.
Roth, K. (1995). Managing international interdependence: CEO characteristics in a resource-based framework. *Academy of Management Journal, 38*, 200–231.
Rotter, J. B. (1966). Generalized expectancies for internal versus external control of reinforcement. *Psychological Monographs, 80*, 1–28.
Sakano, T., & Lewin, A. Y. (1999). Impact of CEO succession in Japanese companies: A coevolutionary perspective. *Organization Science, 10*, 654–671.
Salancik, G. R., & Pfeffer, J. (1977). An examination of the need–satisfaction models of job attitudes. *Administrative Science Quarterly, 22*, 427–456.
Sanders, W. G., & Carpenter, M. A. (1998). Internationalization and firm governance: The roles of CEO compensation, top team composition, and board structure. *Academy of Management Journal, 41*, 158–178.
Schein, E. (2010). *Organizational culture and leadership* (4th ed.). San Francisco, CA: Jossey-Bass.
Shimizu, K., & Hitt, M. (2005). What constrains or facilitates divestures of formerly acquired firms? The effects of organizational inertia. *Journal of Management, 31*, 50–72.
Sidek, S., & Zainol, F. A. (2011). Psychological traits and business performance of entrepreneurs in small construction industry in Malaysia. *International Business and Management, 2*, 170–185.
Simsek, Z., Heavey, C., & Veiga, J. F. (2010). The impact of CEO core self-evaluation on the firm's entrepreneurial orientation. *Strategic Management Journal, 31*, 110–119.
Simsek, Z., Veiga, J. F., Lubatkin, M., & Dino, R. N. (2005). Modeling the multilevel determinants of top management team behavioral integration. *Academy of Management Journal, 48*, 69–84.
Slater, D. J., & Dixon-Fowler, H. R. (2009). CEO international assignment experience and corporate social performance. *Journal of Business Ethics, 89*, 472–489.
Smith, K. G., Smith, K. A., Olian, J. D., Sims, H. P., O'Bannon, D. P., & Scully, J. A. (1994). Top management team demography and process: The role of social integration and communication. *Administration Science Quarterly, 39*, 412–438.
Sosik, J. J., Gentry, W. A., & Chun, J. U. (2012). The value of virtue in the upper echelons: A multisource examination of executive character strengths and performance. *The Leadership Quarterly, 23*, 367–382.
Stone, W. S., & Tudor, T. R. (2005). The effects of functional background experience, industry experience, generic executive management experience on perceived environmental uncertainty and firm performance. *Advances in Competitiveness Research, 13*, 1–8.
Sully de Luque, M., Washburn, N. T., Waldman, D. A., & House, R. J. (2008). Unrequited profit: How stakeholder and economic values relate to subordinates' perceptions of

leadership and firm performance. *Administrative Science Quarterly, 53*, 626–654.

Taylor, R. N. (1975). Age and experience as determinants of managerial information processing and decision making performance. *Academy of Management Journal, 18*, 74–81.

Tosi, H. L., Misangyi, V. F., Fanelli, A., Waldman, D. A., & Yammarino, F. J. (2004). CEO charisma, compensation, and firm performance. *The Leadership Quarterly, 15*, 405–420.

Tsui, A. S, Zhang, Z. X., Wang, H., Xin, K. R., & Wu, J. B. (2006). Unpacking the relationship between CEO leadership behavior and organizational culture. *The Leadership Quarterly, 17*, 113–137.

Van de Ven, A. H., Hudson, R., & Schroeder, D. M. (1984). Designing new business startups: Entrepreneurial, organizational, and ecological considerations. *Journal of Management, 10*, 87–107.

Vascellaro, J. E. (2010, March 24). Brin drove Google to pull back in China. *The Wall Street Journal*. Retrieved from http://www.wsj.com.

Waldman, D. A., Javidan, M., & Varella, P. (2004). Charismatic leadership at the strategic level: A new application of upper echelons theory. *The Leadership Quarterly, 15*, 355–380.

Waldman, D. A., Ramirez, G. G., House, R. J., & Puranam, P. (2001). Does leadership matter? CEO leadership attributes and profitability under conditions of perceived environmental uncertainty. *Academy of Management Journal, 44*, 134–143.

Waldman, D. A., Siegel, D. S., & Javidan, M. (2006). Components of CEO transformational leadership and corporate social responsibility. *Journal of Management Studies, 43*, 1703–1725.

Wallace, J. C., Little, L. M., Hill, A. D., & Ridge, J. W. (2010). CEO regulatory foci, environmental dynamism, and small firm performance. *Journal of Business Venturing, 48*, 580–604.

Wally, S., & Baum, J. R. (1994). Personal and structural determinants of the pace of strategic decision making. *Academy of Management Journal, 37*, 932–956.

Wang, H., Tsui, A., & Xin, K. (2011). CEO leadership behaviors, organizational performance, and employees' attitudes. *The Leadership Quarterly, 22*, 92–105.

Wasserman, N., Nohria, N., & Anand, B. (2010). When does leadership matter? A contingent opportunities view of CEO leadership, In N. Nohria & R. Khurana (Eds.), *Handbook of leadership theory and practice* (Chapter 2). Cambridge, MA: Harvard Business Publishing.

Weber, M. (1947). *The theory of social and economic organization* (T. Parsons, Trans.). New York, NY: Free Press, Original work published in 1924.

Weisbach, M. (1995). CEO turnover and the firm's investment decisions. *Journal of Financial Economics, 37*, 159–188.

Weng, D. H., & Lin, Z. J. (in press). Beyond CEO tenure: The effect of CEO newness on strategic changes. *Journal of Management.*

Wiersema, M. F. (1995). Executive succession as an antecendent to corporate restructuring. *Human Resource Management, 34*, 185–202.

Wiersema, M. F., & Bantel, K. A. (1992). Top management team demography and corporate strategic change. *Academy of Management Journal, 35*, 95–121.

Yukl, G. (2008). How leaders influence organizational effectiveness. *The Leadership Quarterly, 19*, 708–722.

Zaccaro, S. J. (2001). *The nature of executive leadership: A conceptual and empirical analysis of success.* Washington, DC: APA Books.

Zald, M. (1969). The power and functions of boards of directors: A theoretical synthesis. *American Journal of Sociology, 75*, 97–111.

Zhang, Z., Peterson, S. J., & Reina, C. S. (2013). CEO narcissism and firm performance: The moderating roles of core self-evaluations and organizational identification. Working paper.

PART 7

Emerging Contextual Issues in Leadership

CHAPTER

27 The Context and Leadership

Richard N. Osborn, Mary Uhl-Bien, *and* Ivana Milosevic

Abstract

This chapter explores the role context has played in leadership research over the last 100 years and offers a historical description of diverse perspectives and understandings of this interplay. To this end, it offers three approaches to studying context of leadership: (1) leadership as "nested" in hierarchy; (2) leadership as "pervasive" in social processes; and (3) leadership as a combination of (1) and (2), or "hybrid" approaches. The authors follow the development of each approach from the onset to today and offer alternative avenues for future research. In doing so, they hope not just to challenge some of the current assumptions, but offer a richer theoretical depiction and inspire continuous progress toward a more complete understanding of leadership and leadership effectiveness.

Key Words: Leadership, patterns of influence, context, situational variables, contingency, complexity, contextual, relational, social construction

The purpose of this chapter is to discuss the treatment of context in leadership research. Dating to the 1970s there have been calls for leadership researchers to consider context as a potential factor that may alter leadership and leadership effectiveness (Day, 2000; Fiedler, 1967, 1978; Graen, Alvares, Oris, & Martella, 1970; Hannah, Uhl-Bien, Avolio, & Cavarretta, 2009; House, 1971; Osborn, Hunt, & Jauch; 2002; Osborn & Marion, 2009; Porter & McLaughlin, 2006; Purvanova & Bono, 2009). Looking at the field of leadership, it is comparatively easy to isolate three quite different assumptions on the intertwining of context and leadership. One, context is a potentially important factor, but one that can be circumvented by astute leadership (e.g., "leader-centric" approaches, Avolio & Gardner, 2005; Bass & Avolio, 1994). Two, context alters the impact of leadership on various criteria, often expressed as a contingent relationship involving leadership, context, and criteria (e.g., "situational approaches," Fiedler, 1967, 1978; House, 1971; Liden & Antonakis, 2009). Three, context is a dominant factor that establishes boundary conditions on the type of leadership displayed as well as the effectiveness of leadership (e.g., "contextual approaches," Osborn et al., 2002; and "embedded" approaches, Fairhurst, 2009; Uhl-Bien, 2006).

In overly simplistic terms, we can identify leadership in these approaches according to three main views: (1) leadership as *nested* in hierarchy; (2) leadership as *pervasive* in social processes; and (3) leadership as a combination of (1) and (2), or *hybrid* approaches. In the nested views, leadership is typically envisioned as (a) a real, measurable, commonly observed property or behavior pattern of individuals occupying a formal managerial position or role (e.g., trait, LPC, transformational, and charismatic approaches); or (b) a measurable outcome of hierarchical interaction with others (e.g., LMX, Graen & Uhl-Bien, 1995; and LBDQ, Yunker & Hunt, 1976). In the pervasive views, leadership is typically envisioned as a socially constructed recognizable pattern of influence and order (e.g., romance of leadership, implicit leadership theories, relational leadership, and discursive leadership). In the pervasive view, leadership is not tied to formal positions but emerges (is constructed) in social interactions. In the hybrid view, approaches from both nested and pervasive views are incorporated that recognize the importance of leadership both in the hierarchy and as it emerges in social constructions. Hybrid approaches begin with context in mind.

Premise

The premise of the present chapter is this: *as the view of leadership shifts, so does the concept of context as well as the underlying causal mechanisms evoked and the nature of what is being explained or predicted.* In other words, the perspective of leadership brought by the researcher also partially determines (a) what is to be explained and predicted (criteria), (b) the level of analysis, (c) the contextual conditions being considered, and (d) the causal mechanisms linking leaders (and followers) to the selected criteria. So, for example, at times it appears that leadership is seen as an individual influence attempt by a unit head to stimulate individual performance *nested* deep within a bureaucracy (a nested approach) (e.g., House, 1971), while at other times leadership is viewed in terms of *pervasive* change initiatives emerging from the collective dynamics among individuals to cope with externalities up, down, and across a bureaucracy (a hybrid approach) (e.g., Uhl-Bien & Marion, 2009).

Consequently, in most nested and pervasive cases the contextual elements were derived from the initial view of leadership, and then refined with the selection of a unit of analysis that is accompanied by specific contextual elements and causal mechanisms that link leadership with criteria. Interestingly, with hybrid approaches, the researchers place an equal emphasis on context and influence. Thus, in hybrid approaches some dimensions of leadership stressed in nested or pervasive views are ignored, highlighted, or displaced by leadership dimensions implied by the characterization of the context. For example, how individuals are interconnected in the context and the basic reasons why the members affiliate with the system yields an emphasis on new leadership dimensions, including how networks develop and how individuals in managerial positions balance emergent initiatives and bureaucratic traditions.

Somewhat less familiar to many leadership researchers is a focus on context and causal mechanisms. As used in this chapter, causal mechanisms are the pathways or process by which effect is produced (Gerring, 2010). For us, the causal mechanisms involve the important question of how leadership is linked to other concepts, and why it is important. Of course, causal mechanisms may also be seen as explanations that presume probabilistic, and perhaps highly contingent, causal relationships (Elster, 1998), or as Stinchcombe (2005, p. 17) indicated, "a context dependent (tightly bounded or middle-range) explanation." Since much of the research on leadership pre-dates an emphasis on isolating causal mechanisms, we will identify the major logics used by authors in linking concepts in their analysis of leadership as *causal mechanisms.* With nested models, where leadership is used to predict criteria, this is a comparatively simple process of examining why the authors suggest that specific dimensions of leadership would cause a change in outcomes. In pervasive models where the authors look for a pattern of influence, causal mechanisms are the reasons identified for the emergence of a given pattern. In hybrid models the context itself is used to identify macro relevant causal mechanisms. For example, if the system is in crisis, dealing with the crisis is a central causal mechanism at the system or macro level. When relying upon complexity theory, resolving the tensions in complex adaptive systems is a causal mechanism. Once identified from the context, however, hybrid approaches often use one or more of the conventional causal mechanisms from nested or pervasive views to incorporate more micro mechanisms as well. So, in the case of reliance upon a complexity view, individual desires for achievement could be incorporated.

Scope

Since the discussion of the context of leadership and leadership effectiveness quickly engulfs the researcher in the complexity, inconsistency, and breadth of a vast literature, it is necessary to eliminate all but a fraction of the literature. We concentrate on a comparatively few areas where the context of leadership has received the most attention. We also use a sample of publications as representative of whole research programs and schools of thought. Correspondingly, many areas involving contextual analyses of leadership are not covered because they are separate areas of inquiry, some of which are addressed in separate chapters in this handbook. Predominant among these omissions are analyses that focus on national and societal culture, corporate strategy, spirituality, religion, geography, and physics. We have also eliminated work that focuses on personality, decision making, ancient civilizations, linguistics, gender, demographics, political leaders, social movements, and artificial situations. Moreover, we downplay the potential importance of practice-based enumerations of successful leadership from retrospective accounts, and escalate the potential importance of leadership in and of organizations (Hunt, 1991).

Preview

We start the discussion with an overview of the different approaches to leadership and context identified as nested, pervasive, and hybrid views. We then detail some of the major approaches within each of these three. In many respects, the bulk of the leadership literature is about what we think we know (i.e., proposed models and perspectives) and what we want to know (i.e., open areas for new investigation). Therefore, after discussing each model we follow with an elaboration of a key open area for investigation. In this discussion we identify a "thread" from the initial model to a current open research question.

We begin the discussion with a series of nested views of leadership dating from the 1950s and 1960s to show the development of the literature and the incorporation of contextual variables. For each perspective we highlight the view of leadership, the type of contextual variables mentioned, the criteria to be explained and/or predicted, the unit of analysis (if specified), and the causal mechanisms used (i.e., the links to other concepts such as the criteria that are highlighted by the researcher). At the end of each major view of leadership we note open areas for new work. We repeat this sequence for selected pervasive views and again for the hybrid approaches. We conclude with what we have learned about leadership and context from this discussion, and the implications for where we go from here.

Nested, Pervasive, and Hybrid Views of Leadership

Most leadership researchers begin their analyses with a definition of leadership, often built upon the prior views of fellow researchers. This starting point for analysis has a profound effect on what the researcher sees in terms of both leadership and context. So, for example, if leadership is defined as individual influence over a subordinate, it may be difficult for the researcher to envision the emergence of leadership across individuals within a department. Thus, even if researchers agree that leadership is generally defined in terms of influence (e.g., Bryman, Stephens, & Campo, 1996), with implications of power, control, and/or guidance, there are vast differences across the literature. With different starting points there are may be profound differences in (a) what constitutes leadership (e.g., leadership versus management), (b) why leadership is needed (e.g., to gain higher performance versus coping with inequality), (c) who exercises leadership (e.g., individuals, collectives), (d) when leadership is needed (always versus selectively), and (e) why there is a response to leadership. Rather than addressing each of the questions individually, our review suggests much of the research may be organized into "nested," "pervasive," and "hybrid" views of context and leadership.

Starting with the role holder. In nested views, leadership researchers start the analysis of leadership with individual influence, in general, and the individual influence of a role holder (i.e., manager), in particular. We call these nested views because they are nested in the organizational (i.e., hierarchical) context, so the analysis of leadership and context is virtually identical to the unit of analysis (e.g., House, Rousseau, & Thomas-Hunt, 1995). Researchers starting with a nested view of leadership have examined leadership at almost all organizational levels of analysis (individual, dyad, team/work unit, division, organizational). However, by initially starting with role holders (i.e., managers), it is only natural that the organizational design of the system under investigation guides the definition of the relevant context. So, for instance, the context for leadership among a sample of employees and first-level supervisors would naturally focus on the work unit and organizational conditions immediately facing these role holders. The research would most naturally focus on factors such as size, technology, task, and workflows within and between the units selected for analysis.

Starting with a pattern of influence. The defining element of pervasive views is that leadership is pervasive (not restricted to formal positions) and that context is pervasive in leadership (i.e., leadership is embedded in context). Therefore, in pervasive views leadership can occur and flow throughout a social system (e.g., informal leadership, distributed leadership, emergent leadership). Position holders might, or might not, be identified as engaging in leadership in areas important to members. One of the earliest popular pervasive views was based on the Meindl, Ehrlich, and Dukerich (1985) conception of the romance of leadership. Here, all individuals could be seen as leaders, and leadership was envisioned as emerging naturally from social interaction. When leadership is considered a natural emergent phenomenon, it may be seen as emerging from societally based shared concepts (such as leadership prototypes described by Lord, de Vader, & Alliger, 1986), the interaction of individuals (such as described in Uhl-Bien, 2006; Uhl-Bien, Marion, & McKelvey, 2007), and/or the dynamics of group interaction (e.g., distributed leadership described in Gronn, 2002).

In some pervasive models, the specific concepts of leadership and context stem from a more collective perspective of human activity, including more sociological perspectives (Ospina & Foldy, 2010; Ospina & Sorenson, 2006). For others, leadership is "co-produced" (Shamir, Pillai, Bligh, & Uhl-Bien, 2007) or "co-constructed" (Fairhurst, 2009) in social relations. Therefore, to identify leadership we need to examine its social constructions (e.g., through implicit theories, meaning making, and/or discourse) (Uhl-Bien & Ospina, 2012). Thus, many pervasive views commingle the concepts of leadership and context with an emphasis on social construction (Fairhurst, 2007, 2009; Fairhurst & Grant, 2010)—sometimes within a bureaucracy, and sometimes independent of an institutional referent. As with nested views, there are also wide variations among those adopting a pervasive view in the emphasis on explanation or prediction, why an influence pattern exists or yields outcomes (causal mechanisms), what is to be explained or predicted, and the emphasis placed on the context.

Starting with both context and leadership. Some of the most interesting and newest work on leadership contexts takes a page from both the nested and pervasive views. These we label "hybrid" views (Osborn et al., 2002; Uhl-Bien et al., 2007; Uhl-Bien & Marion, 2009). Here, leadership stems both from individuals acting in bureaucratic settings with defined roles (the formal organization) and from informally networked influence patterns that emerge from interpersonal dynamics emanating from both inside and outside of a system (the informal organization). In these views, context ranges from micro-level (e.g., dyadic, relational contexts) to macro-level (e.g., broader, societal discourses—i.e., "Discourse," Fairhurst, 2007; Foucault, 1972). Like pervasive approaches, hybrid approaches view leadership as *necessarily* embedded in social context. Context is co-defined with leadership, and is a trigger for the emergence of specific aspects of leadership as well as the effectiveness of different leadership dimensions (in some cases where prediction is a goal) (Osborn et al., 2002).

Where you start makes a difference. So what difference does this make in the overall view of context? With nested models, researchers have often drawn on psychology and social psychology literatures closely allied to core concepts such as group composition and group tasks, as well as more general concepts such as power, influence, and control, to isolate key contextual factors found within a bureaucracy (Bass & Bass, 2008; Katz & Kahn, 1978; Selznick 1948). These approaches are most often associated with contingency, or situational, analyses of the context (e.g., context is a variable that interacts with leadership to influence leadership effectiveness) (e.g., Fiedler, 1967; House, 1971). In this nested view, bureaucratic elements of the context are often highlighted (e.g., the power of the position held by the leader and the characteristics of the technology used by the groups under analysis).

With pervasive models, researchers have often drawn from literatures on social construction (Fairhurst & Grant, 2010) and sociology (Ospina & Foldy, 2010) to explain emergent patterns of influence. Here the traditional bureaucratic elements fade in comparison to broader factors underlying social relationships. For example, the presumption that leadership arises through the interactions and negotiation of social order among organizational members (e.g., Fairhurst, 2009) brings characteristics of the social order into consideration as potentially important contextual factors. Similarly, when leadership arises from networked dynamics, characteristics of the social and task networks become important contextual factors (Lichtenstein, Uhl-Bien, Marion, Seers, Orton, & Schreiber, 2006).

It is tempting to presume that hybrid views merely combine all of the aforementioned revealed contextual factors. Such is not the case, as the list would be overwhelming, and the researcher would be left with little more than a laundry list of potentially important factors. Instead, hybrid models most often emphasize a dominant causal mechanism and/or contextual condition that highlights the need for specific aspects of leadership. For instance, a crisis (immediate threat to highly valued goals) might be considered a dominant contextual condition, and the immediate resolution to this crisis might be seen as the dominant causal mechanism (e.g., Osborn et al., 2002). Or in a knowledge organization, complexity might be a dominant contextual condition, and emergence and adaptability are key causal mechanisms (e.g., Uhl-Bien et al., 2007). In hybrid views, as we noted before but need to stress, aspects of leadership found in other nested or contextual views may be seen as either critical, or even negligible, depending upon the characterization of the context. So an emphasis on employee welfare might fade from view in the analysis of a crisis (e.g., Hunt & Ropo, 1995), or consideration of human relations may become less predominant from a complexity view (Uhl-Bien et al., 2007).

History matters. The importance placed on context in leadership research waxes and wanes with the ever-shifting views of leadership itself. Yet, context provides constraints as well as opportunities for organizational behavior in general, and leadership in particular (Johns, 2006). It is instructive, therefore, to provide a historical account of some major perspectives of leadership and context over the last 50 years or so (for additional review see Porter & McLaughlin, 2006). Interestingly, a pattern emerges in much of the 20th-century work of leadership and context: a new vision of leadership emerges, it is elaborated, a few scholars note some potential contextual factors that might be important, contextual analyses proliferate, and another vision of leadership emerges (Reichers & Schneider, 1990). Each once-prominent vision of leadership also leaves behind a series of unanswered questions. While contemporary leadership researchers may want to ignore these unanswered questions, they may provide rich new avenues for a synthesis. Thus, to facilitate the analysis we place the work in a historical context; note that in any one time period there is often a dominant view of leadership or context or both (cf. Aldrich & Pfeffer, 1976) and offer questions that might help those interested in synthesis.

Nested Models

In the last half of the 20th century there was considerable interest in leadership inside organizations to improve the performance of individuals and groups. Although few leadership researchers at the time would have conceded that their work restricted leadership to formal organizational settings, the bulk of the research focused on supervisors deep within the industrial bureaucracies that dominated this era. So, the early work was almost exclusively focused on nested views of leadership.

Great Man Theories and Leader Behavior

After World War II there was a dramatic shift in leadership research away from trait theories of leadership to an emphasis on leader behaviors. In early trait theories such factors as height, weight, insight, originality, and persistence were deemed leader characteristics separating leaders from followers (Bernard, 1926; Bingham, 1927; Kilbourne, 1935). As conflicting findings persisted, Ralph Stogdill (Stogdill, 1948) objected to a sole emphasis on leadership traits thought to separate leaders from non-leaders. He and other researchers at The Ohio State University and the University of Michigan placed the emphasis on leader behaviors and their impact on performance and satisfaction (Likert, 1961; Stogdill, 1974).

Task and people dimensions of leadership. As noted by Stogdill (1974), the earliest studies placing leader behavior on a single continuum ranging from a task to people emphasis were replaced by separate dimensions for task or people. The separation of the dimensions led to the general proposition that more active leaders emphasizing both tasks and people were likely to see higher levels of both performance and satisfaction (e.g., Likert, 1961). In these approaches, stated and sometimes implied casual mechanisms linking leadership and the criteria were comparatively straightforward. Subordinates needed to be told what to do and how to do it. However, it was also argued that employees like to be rewarded and to work for a supervisor who supports them, bringing in the emphasis on the people dimension (Bass & Bass, 2008; Judge, Piccolo, & Ilies, 2004). In sum, the causal mechanism was instrumental—"the deal," or "inducements," versus contributions between leader and subordinate.

Yet, even before much of the disconfirming evidence was published, astute researchers realized that (a) there were boundaries on this simple behavioral emphasis, (b) the causal mechanisms operative in organizations were more multifaceted and complex than considered in the research, and (c) performance and satisfaction did not always go hand in hand (for a review see Larson, Hunt, & Osborn, 1976). Interestingly, elements of the task and people emphasis can still be found in the most recent instruments measuring transformational leadership (e.g. Avolio, Bass, & Jung, 1999; Judge et al., 2004) and in many contemporary leadership studies (e.g., Osborn & Marion, 2009).

Open areas for investigation. At first glance there do not seem to be many open areas for investigation from the old emphasis on leader behavior. Yet, implicit in much of this research is the expectation of the organization for its formally appointed leaders. The work of Jaques and Clement (1991) is an example of a linking thread that eventually re-emerged. Jacques and Clement merged the discussion about large organizational hierarchies with the human side of the enterprise and suggested that organizations exist as a response to societal needs. Hunt (1991) extended the work of Jaques and Clement (Jaques, 1976, 1989; Jaques & Clement, 1991), and introduced a holistic (nested) view of the organization where leadership stretches from the top of the organization to lowest levels (Hunt, 1991). This approach was later combined with complexity theory and organization theory to outline a series of different types of context (to be detailed later in this chapter) (Osborn et al., 2002). What remains unanswered, however, are the emerging demands and constraints on leadership as organizations continue to evolve beyond bureaucratic models (Pettigrew et al., 2003). If the context of the modern organizations is changing, it seems only logical that researchers should be looking for new aspects of leadership to fit organizations' changing needs.

Fiedler's Work

Even as many researchers were concentrating on the task and people dimensions of leadership, the landscape of the leadership literature changed with the advent of situational models, which considered how an element of the context altered the impact of leadership on criteria. The first popular approach to incorporate contextual factors was that of Fred Fiedler (1962). Fielder's contribution lays in his clarification of the context: the causal mechanisms linking leadership, context, and performance in Fiedler's model were at the same time both straightforward and counterintuitive. That is, when the leader provides what the context is missing there will be higher task performance. However, the leader can also change the setting to facilitate the performance, rather than just complement it.

Open areas for investigation. One open research area linking Fiedler's situational model and recent research on organizational change concerns how and if the leader can change the context. The literature focusing on leadership and organizational change often recognizes the role that leaders play in facilitating change processes, mainly through the manipulation of the organization context (Bass & Bass, 2008; Bower & Weinberg, 1988; Conger & Kanungo, 1987; Kavanagh & Ashkanasy, 2006). On the one hand, authors have argued that leaders facilitate change though organizational narrative, rejoicing the new and condemning the old (Bower & Weinberg, 1988; Pettigrew, 1987); others argue that leadership should empower and energize organizational members (Nadler & Tushman, 1989). These approaches all advocate the importance of the leader increasing employees' commitment to new ideas by energizing them to align their self-interest with that of the organization (Bass & Bass, 2008; Burns, 1978; Conger & Kanungo, 1987; House & Shamir, 1993; Sashkin, 1988).

Other approaches recognize that changing the context may present an endeavor requiring destructive and fundamental alterations aimed at the organizational core itself (Pawar & Eastman, 1997). For instance, Pawar and Eastman (1997) presented a view of organizational context that may exist anywhere from a negative polar type, with absolute resistance to leadership efforts, to a positive polar type, where leaders can and should empower and utilize the context for their advantage. This view is analogous to Burn's (1978, p. 170) description of reforming and revolutionary leadership, where "[t]he reformer seeks modifications harmonious with existing trends and consistent with prevailing principles and movements. The revolutionist seeks redirections, arrest or reversal of movements and mutation of principles."

Building on this early insight, new research avenues emerge. In particular, if the leader can and indeed should change the context, the process of how this change progresses over time and how it in turn may change the leadership remains a puzzle. This then sparks yet another avenue for future research, represented in the need for a careful analysis of what leaders can and cannot change.

Path-Goal Leadership

The path-goal model of House and his associates (see Evans, 1970; House, 1971; House & Mitchell, 2007) added considerable sophistication to the definition of the context, the range of leader behaviors considered relevant, and the causal mechanisms linking context and leadership to new criteria. The casual mechanisms evoked by this model involve an instrumental logic, with leaders connecting the effort/desires of subordinates and the demands of the organization by increasing expectancy and instrumentality. Note that this goes beyond just clarification of expectations and providing leader-based rewards to target specific leader behaviors involved in resolving incompatibilities between the subordinate and work requirements. The logic is instrumental in that the justification for the appropriate leader behaviors involves the desirability, achievability, and consequences of externally established goals and paths toward these goals. In this manner the leader's behavior should complement situational contingencies.

Open areas for investigation. More recently, research within the path-goal theory of leadership has suggested that boundary conditions, as well as more fine grained contingencies within this theory, have been largely neglected, leading to, *at best*, mixed results (House, 1996). Specifically, in 1996, House suggested a reformulation of the theory that focused on work unit leadership, specifying leader behaviors that enhance empowerment and satisfaction of subordinates, thereby increasing work unit performance. In doing so, House took a step away from traditional approaches emphasizing task- and person-oriented leader behaviors and toward the subordinates' nonconscious motives and valence. In the words of the author, "The essence of the theory is the meta proposition that leaders, to be effective, engage in behaviors that complement subordinate's environments and abilities in a manner that compensates for deficiencies and is instrumental to subordinate satisfaction and individual and work unit performance" (House, 1996, p. 348).

Of course, it is interesting to note that emphasis on subordinate job satisfaction stressed in House's (1996) extension, as well as many other nested models, also raises the question of what individuals want from their employing organizations. The concept that the work organization is central remains an implicit presumption of most leadership research. But with more organizations drifting away from the more standard bureaucratic idea of Weber (1948) and few opportunities for a lifelong career in one firm, it may be time to reexamine what employees can realistically expect. Perhaps challenge, interest, and relevant experience will be more prominent in an employee's list of desires than easy work, satisfaction, and stable employment. Current research needs to more fully consider whether the expectations of individuals within working organizations are still the same as they were in the 1970s and 1980s (Barbuto & Ramthun, 2011).

Other Nested Contingency Approaches

While the Stogdill, Fiedler, and House perspectives remained dominant in the 1970s and early 1980s, several other models addressing context began to emerge. These approaches also nested leadership within an organization's hierarchy, and generally envisioned the leader as the administrative head of a unit. In addition to the isolation of specific contextual factors that altered leadership effectiveness, several approaches provided a unique perspective that has endured.

Substitutes for leadership. One approach was labeled by Kerr and Jermier (1978) as "substitutes for leadership." These authors suggested that characteristics of the subordinates, the job and/or the organization could substitute for the direct influence of the leader in providing task guidance and incentives to perform. Theoretically, the substitutes model does not specify the relevant contextual dimensions, but focuses instead on a search for factors that could potentially alter the ability of the leader to mold subordinate behavior in desired directions. As with the path-goal approach, the leader is seen as in control and the influence attempts are to be directed toward organizationally mandated objectives. Also similar to the path-goal approach, the leader is to complement the situational contingencies, and not counteract beneficial conditions, for fear of a negative subordinate reaction. Overall, then, the logic from prior leadership approaches is reversed here, as leaders are asked to examine contextual factors altering their ability to provide task guidance or incentives (Podsakoff & MacKenzie, 1997).

Leadership distance. The reversal of logic discussed above, provided some interesting developments in terms of the need for the reexamination of contextual factors that may limit leadership influence. Particularly relevant to the research in the realm of charismatic leadership, contextual factors such as distance may significantly impact a leader's ability to provide task guidance or incentives (Shamir, 1995). More specifically, when leaders are distant (such as organizational leaders), subordinates have less opportunity to critically evaluate leaders' behaviors and characteristics, so the observed charisma is likely viewed as "larger than life" (Hollander, 1978; Katz & Kahn, 1978; Shamir, 1995; Waldman & Yammarino, 1999). However, when the distance is proximal, subordinates have greater opportunity to evaluate leader behavior, and so the behavior itself carries more weight. This categorization of charisma is more applicable to newer theories of charismatic leadership where illusory and unrealistic perception of the leader is not emphasized (Bryman, 1992).

Open areas for investigation. In short, the concept of distance between the leader and follower has evolved from the commonsense notion to a multidimensional construct. Such is also likely for other contextual conditions commonly noted in the literature such as size, subordinate experience, type of industry, and the like. While a reversal of logic (such as in the case of the substitutes for leadership) or the transition of the concept of distance from commonsense notion to multidimensional construct seems natural, what is far from clear is whether greater sophistication and precision is warranted. In particular, given recent developments in the realm of distance between the leader and the follower (Antonakis & Atwater, 2002), we simply do not know the appropriate guidelines for the level of detail needed for the context or specific contextual variables.

The SIU Work

A second nested approach emerged from work at Southern Illinois University (e.g., Martin, Hunt, & Osborn, 1981; Osborn, Hunt & Jauch, 1980). As opposed to prior views, this approach first examined the linkage between contextual factors and outcomes to determine (a) the gaps between context and performance the leader should address, and (b) the relevant range of discretionary and nondiscretionary leadership. The causal mechanisms were again instrumental, and the goals, as well as performance measures, were taken from the expectations of senior executives. To this end, the approach advocated here provides four new features that are more prominent in current thinking. One, important contextual factors are expanded well beyond subordinate and group characteristics to include such factors as the organization's environment, size, technology, and formal structure (Bass, 1997; Den Hartog, House, Hanges, & Ruiz-Quintanilla, 1999; Shamir & Howell, 1999). Two, contextual factors are collapsed into a major force in terms of the complexity facing the leader (e.g., Hunt, Osborn, & Schuler, 1978). Three, contextual factors are expected to have a direct impact on the behavior of the leader and the criteria, as well as a contingent interactive linkage with leadership on the criteria (Hunt et al., 1978). Four, the concept of leadership itself was expanded in two important ways.

Based on an extension of the work of Sayles (1989), the expansion of leadership included horizontal aspects of leader influence, such as reward management (i.e., willingness to adjust to other units and reward them for desired actions), uncertainty reduction (i.e., pressuring other units to provide more predictable flows of resources and information), and network development (i.e., establishing linkages to other units). A distinction was also made between influence attempts embedded in a position (i.e., required leadership) and those under the volition of the leader (i.e., discretionary leadership) (Hunt et al., 1978). Later others (Bedeian & Hunt, 2006) conceptualized the distinction between required and discretionary leadership in terms of management (i.e., required aspects of a position) and leadership (i.e., discretionary aspects).

Open areas for investigation. Clearly one thread from this model to current research is the division between leadership and management (Dachler, 1992; Hosking, 1988; Uhl-Bien, 2006). Whereas management accounts for functional, often position-bound functions that one exercises and may involve a form of manager-subordinate relationship (Graen, 2006; Offstein, Madhavan, & Gnyawali, 2006; Seers, 2004), leadership is often considered as a social dynamic that arises in relationships among people both from within and across traditional hierarchy (Hosking, 1988; Hunt & Dodge, 2000; Uhl-Bien et al., 2007). More specifically, as leadership has been defined and operationalized as the incremental influence above and beyond managerial routines determined through the organizational bureaucracies, it necessarily should be conceptualized as possessing powers beyond those given by the organization (Katz and Kahn, 1978). As such, leadership is necessary in addition to managerial systems to account for and influence various, and often unpredictable, contingencies that exist in complex organization, but cannot be specified through managerial procedures and policies (Katz & Kahn, 1978; Uhl-Bien et al., 2007).

What remains unknown at this point is the relationship between what is labeled management and leadership. From a nested view, this distinction would occur in the leadership role or position (e.g., management). For example if the managerial role requires position holders to cut staff, how would this act influence the perception of their leadership? Is there a natural relationship between the managerial behavior and leadership behavior of manager? To what extent, if any, do the managerial behaviors of the position holders alter their leadership? If leadership also emerges throughout the organization, the issue of traditional managerial and leadership roles becomes even more interesting to investigate. How, for instance, are managerial aspects of leadership altered in the presence of emergent leadership by a nonmanagerial role holder?

Yukl's Multiple Linkage Model

A third model emerged in the late 1970s and early 1980s from the work of Gary Yukl (1981) and was built upon earlier models of leadership and group effectiveness. Here the context was divided into situational variables and intervening variables, with a focus on group performance. The intervening variables are altered by leader behavior and the situational variables are directly linked to group performance. The intervening variables are specified as (a) subordinate effort, (b) role clarity and task skills, (c) organization of work, (d) cohesiveness and cooperation, (e) resources and support services, and (e) external coordination, each of which can be estimated on a favorability scale (Yukl, 1981). The notation of leader behaviors and situational variables is based upon isolating factors that alter the intervening variables. So, for example, if external coordination is poor, the leader should adopt behaviors to improve coordination in the short term and reduce the larger causes of poor coordination in the long term (Yukl, 1981)

Open areas for investigation. While the difference between "situational" and "intervening" variables has not been extensively researched, Yukl (1981) introduced a potentially important distinction that is also reflected in some other models of leadership. First is the notion that broader organizational and societal forces (i.e., "Discourse," Fairhurst, 2007) may shape the types of leadership followers expect and leaders adopt (Schein, 2004; Weick, 1995). The idea that leaders adopt prototypical leader patterns from their larger societal surroundings is also found in the GLOBE studies as well as in expectations of broader differences across societal institutions in the type of leadership one would expected to encounter (House, Hanges, Javidan, Dorfman, & Gupta, 2004). So, few would expect to see the same leadership patterns in a combat setting, R&D labs, universities, or political parties. Not only are these institutional settings quite different, the types of outcomes considered for performance evaluation are also quite different.

Yukl's separation of different kinds of contextual variables raises an important question. Are the contextual factors (a) altering leadership, (b) altering leadership effectiveness, and (c) effectiveness quite distinct? Clearly there are contextual factors far beyond the control or influence of a particular leader that alter the performance of a system. The prior review has suggested a number of contextual factors that alter the linkage between leadership and criteria. And we have shown some linkages between contextual factors and leadership. However, there seems to be little evidence that one particular set of contextual factors alters leadership, leadership effectiveness, and effectiveness in a systematic fashion.

Leadership at Different Echelons

While the development of nested models progressively added, new leadership dimensions and a more comprehensive array of contextual variables, as researchers saw an ever-more sophisticated organizational world, considerable progress in the articulation of the context came from studies of leadership at different echelons. With leadership echelons studies dating to the work of Katz and Kahn (1978), there was a general recognition that leadership at the top, middle, and bottom of large organizations was fundamentally different (Antonakis & Atwater, 2002; Shamir, 1995).

Stratified systems theory. For instance, one of these echelon approaches was based on the work of Elliott Jaques (see Jacob & Jaques, 1987). This work altered the causal mechanism to focus on reducing uncertainty. The approach, labeled Stratified Systems Theory, was based on three core assumptions. One, organizations are required to adapt to the environment to acquire resources and use them. Two, at higher echelons in the organization, there is a greater need for leaders to exercise discretion to cope with greater interdependencies, complexity, and uncertainties. Three, the core function of leaders at higher echelons is to reduce uncertainty via acquiring and interpreting information. The key for leadership was the complexity of the leader and the time span of feedback associated with different echelons. As one moves up the hierarchy, the leader needs to engage in more complex information processing and respond to the ever-increasing time span of feedback. These requirements call for the leader to be cognitively more complex (see Hunt, 1991, for a review of the cognitive complexity used in these models) and explicitly consider a longer time span of feedback.

Open areas for investigation. Studies of leadership at different echelons continued through the 1990s (Gronn, 2002; Hunt, 1991; Phillips & Hunt, 1992; Zaccaro, 1996) and introduced or reinforced, aspects of leadership, contextual factors, and criteria that were not prominent in the more general models. As Gronn (2002) notes, echelon researchers rediscovered the importance of different aspects of shared leadership rather than restricting leadership to a single position holder (for an interesting analysis of this concept at the turn of the century, see Pearce & Conger, 2003). Ropo and Hunt (1999), for instance, took a processual perspective to uncover rotating individual influence patterns as a bank entered different aspects of a dramatic organizational change. They found that the influence patterns of managers were not restricted to direct interpersonal aspects of leadership, but included what many would now call indirect or managerial aspects of influence (e.g., changes in structure, development of rules and procedures, negotiation with external representatives).

While the evolution of echelon studies expanded the range and sophistication of both leadership and contextual analysis, it also left many with a number of unanswered questions regarding the context. For example, what type of context promotes or encourages shared leadership at different echelons? Precisely what combination of contextual conditions and leadership at the top promotes more active leadership toward the bottom of the organization? Are organizational echelons relatively independent of one another as implied by Katz and Kahn (1978) because they have different functions? Or are differences by echelons more a reflection of social strata than organizational necessity? And finally, what leadership is appropriate when the echelons are actually in separate organizational entities as is now common in global manufacturing?

LMX, Transformational and Charismatic Leadership

Even as some researchers moved to incorporate a broader range of influence patterns into leadership, expanded the range of contextual factors and focused on organization-wide change, two more popular approaches became quite fashionable in the United States. These include Leader-Member Exchange (LMX) (Graen & Uhl-Bien, 1995) and transformational leadership (Bass & Avolio, 1994). While there has been some work on contextual factors with LMX and transformational leadership (e.g., see Cogliser & Schriesheim, 2000; Pawar & Eastman, 1997), these models largely adopt "situational" approaches to context, assuming that context is a contingency variable associated with either the antecedents or outcomes of LMX and/or transformational leadership. These studies implicitly or explicitly presume that the leader can overcome contextual constraints to achieve desired results.

We will not have much to say about the enormous volume of work on this and its related cousins because the vast bulk of work on this view does not envision context as a particularly relevant factor. Yet, despite this virtual neglect of context, it is important to note three aspects of transformational leadership. One, the causal mechanism linking leadership and criteria is predominately affective, not instrumental. Two, transformational leadership is not caused by contextual factors but lies in the individual. Three, the transformational leader does not adjust to context but gets subordinates to conquer it.

Nested Models Summary

So in a way we have come full circle with the purely nested models. We started with the individual traits, moved to behavior, and then began the incorporation of contextual variables. Contextual factors started with the incorporation of group setting factors, then characteristics of the subordinates' and group's task as determinants of both leadership and leadership effectiveness. This was followed by a flirting with lateral relationships and organizational factors, and the eventual separation of leadership into managerial-type dimensions and individual influence aspects. Leadership expanded from a few dimensions of interpersonal influence, to multiple aspects of interpersonal influence, to be triggered by contextual factors, and finally to incorporate leadership that altered the context itself. All of this occurred using an instrumentally based causal mechanism to explain and predict outcomes.

By the 1990s research on echelons and leadership had further expanded the concept of leadership and the context as well as the causal mechanisms linking context, leadership, and criteria. Leadership was no longer restricted to vertical interpersonal influence but included shared leadership, rotating leadership, lateral leadership, as well as a host of indirect influence alterations (e.g., changing structure) (Davis & Eisenhardt, 2011 Fischer & Sharp, 1998; Pearce & Conger, 2003; Uhl-Bien, 2006). Beyond instrumentalism came the potential importance of affect, the reduction of uncertainty, and the promotion of interaction as causal mechanisms. Overall, then, as the vision of leadership expanded so did the vision of context and the criteria that might be linked to leadership and context.

Pervasive Perspectives

Beginning in the early to mid-1980s the seeds were planted for new generations of leadership work, as scholars identified alternative ways to explore contextual influences on leadership and leadership effectiveness. We call these perspectives pervasive because they see leadership as pervasive in social systems (e.g., organizations, collectives, societies). These views adopt a social constructionist lens, viewing leadership as a socially constructed recognizable pattern of influence and order (e.g., romance of leadership, relational leadership, discursive leadership). From this perspective, leadership can occur anywhere in social contexts when leadership and followership are constructed.

Unlike nested views, which see leadership and context as separate, pervasive views see leadership and context as largely inseparable: leadership is embedded in context, and cannot be understood absent context. As such, causal mechanisms in pervasive views are less linear than in nested views. Rather than seeing one as preceding the other (as in nested views), pervasive views look to identify social mechanisms (Hedstrom & Swedberg, 1998), or patterns of behaviors that comprise leadership processes. As described by Fairhurst and Grant (2010), social constructionist perspectives can be distinguished into two general types of approaches: those foregrounding perception, emphasizing the cognitive products of social interaction (e.g., cognitive categories, implicit theories, attributions, sense-making) and those foregrounding action, focusing on the interactions and social processes through which leadership is constructed in context (Fairhurst & Grant, 2010). In the discussion below, we begin with the work emphasizing perception (romance of leadership, information-processing approaches) and then describe those focusing on leadership as a co-constructed process (social construction, relational leadership, discursive leadership).

The Romance of Leadership and Implicit Leadership Theories

In the United States, one seed for work on the construction of social reality was planted by Meindl et al. (1985) and labeled the romance of leadership. Rather than viewing leadership from the position of the head nested in an organizational setting, Meindl took a "follower-centered" perspective: leadership is determined by followers' attributions. If the follower sees one who walks like, looks like, talks like, and acts like a leader, the individual is a leader, and when there is success (or failure), it is attributed to the characteristics and actions of the leader.

This was associated with a cognitive revolution in leadership research (Lord, Foti, & de Vader, 1984) that delved deeper into the mental models (e.g., meaning making and attributions) followers develop and evoke in constituting leadership. Going back to earlier view of influence by Sayles (1979, 1989), and Lewin and Gold (1999), others began to throw off the shackles of leader-centric and manager-centric views of leadership and management to open new vistas into the dynamics of leading. This began to shift the center of attention from individual traits and behaviors of leadership to social constructions of followers, bringing attention to the social processes and contexts of leading and following.

Meindl and colleagues' (1985) work on the romance of leadership combined three important elements of the pervasive approaches: (1) any individual could be a leader when others see them as acting like a leader (i.e., leadership as attributions); (2) leadership and followership naturally emerge from social interaction, and (3) to study leadership, researchers must consider the process of social construction. Meindl (1995, p. 330) emphasized that leadership is a "derivative of the constructions made by followers. The behavior of followers is assumed to be much less under the control and influence of the leader, and more under the control and influence of forces that govern the social construction process itself." Leadership is an outcome of the follower's views in a specific context, such that a change in either context or followers may change the revealed leadership (cf. Osborn et al., 2002).

Implicit theories of leadership. The emergent follower-centric perspective is most prominent in the Implicit Leadership Theory (ILT) of Lord and his associates (Lord, 1985; Lord & Emrich, 2000; Lord et al., 1984; Lord & Maher, 1990; Offermann, Kennedy, & Wirtz, 1994) As explained by Felfe and Petersen (2007, p. 2), "there is evidence that the chance to become and to remain an effective leader does not solely depend on the leaders' own behavior but also followers' information processing. The evaluation and acceptance of a leader in a specific situation is determined by followers' mind-sets, which consist of assumptions, beliefs, and expectations regarding the causes, nature, and the consequences of leadership. These mind-sets are regarded as implicit leadership theories" (ILT; Lord & Emrich, 2000).

By stressing the emergent leadership pattern in the minds of followers, these approaches adopted an attributional and sense-making approach to leadership, in which they considered how follower's ILT's identified leadership prototypes. The primary causal mechanisms underlying the development of prototypes are various cognitive attempts of individuals to make sense of their social world (Lord, Brown, Harvey, & Hall, 2001). Leadership prototypes have been investigated as perceptions formed through deliberate, controlled, cognitive-based processes, as well as automatic and spontaneous recognition-based processes (Lord & Maher, 1990). Once formed, such perceptions provide a cognitive framework for the evaluation of future behavior, as well as a basis for attributing the causes of performance.

While there has been little systematic work on context and ILT prototypes (Lord et al., 2001), there have been obvious contextual influences linked to culture (Den Hartog et al.,1999; House, Javidan, Hanges, & Dorfman, 2002), level in an organizational hierarchy (Antonakis & Atwater, 2002; Shamir, 1995) as well as institutional type (e.g., military leaders versus business leaders). In some respects, this work is similar to the research on leadership traits, but from the minds of followers rather than an investigation of leaders.

Open areas for investigation. As with the trait research, those seeking definitive contextual influences find that analyses of ILT prototypes are predominantly about followers' information processes, categorization processes, and/or attributions. Although it would be easy to dismiss the work on prototypes and categorization using a follower view because of such a small emphasis on context, this would be in error for a significant reason. The followers' choice concerning the relevance of a prototype or category is an apparent gestalt of the context. When moving across groups (where individuals within the groups share in a common gestalt), it possible to isolate broad contextual factors that are important in identifying the followers' collective preferred leadership. While the origins of the different prototypes and their relative stability appears to be open questions, the scholar more interested in context also realizes that the profile of contextual conditions evoking different leadership prototypes remains an open question. Is it possible, for instance, for leaders to depict the issue or context in such a way that that their type of leadership seems appropriate, justified, and/or desirable?

Social Constructionist Views

Social constructionist views of leadership evolved out of Berger and Luckman's (1966) work on the social construction of reality. Consistent with Meindl's premise that followers play a large role in determining what gets seen and attributed as leadership, social construction approaches to leadership focuses on actors' (leaders' and followers') constructions of the leadership concept (Fairhurst & Grant, 2010). These approaches see leadership as co-constructed, "a product of sociohistorical and collective meaning making, and negotiated on an ongoing basis through a complex interplay among leadership actors, be they designated or emergent leaders, managers, and/or followers" (Fairhurst & Grant, 2010, p. 173; see also Collinson, 2006; Grint, 2000, 2005; Gronn, 2000, 2002; Meindl, 1995; Vine, Holmes, Marra, Pfeifer, & Jackson, 2008).

Social construction approaches bring to leadership a fully contextual view. They see leadership not as one objective reality but as multiple realities constructed through social processes in which meanings are negotiated, consensus formed, and contestation is possible (Giddens, 1979, 1984). The causal mechanisms are intersubjectively produced meanings (Gioia, 2003). In this way, like follower-centered approaches (Meindl, 1995), social constructionist approaches reject the leader-centric view in which the leaders' personality, style, and/or behavior are the determining influences on follower's thoughts and actions. They go beyond follower-centered approaches, however, by emphasizing the processes and outcomes of all social actors, including leaders *and* followers. Moreover, they focus not on perception and attribution, but on actual interactions as they occur in local cultural-historical contexts to construct leadership (Fairhurst, 2009; Fletcher & Kaufer, 2003; Gergen, 1994, 1995; McNamee & Gergen, 1999; Ospina & Sorenson, 2006).

Open areas for investigation. To those with a nested view, this perspective leaves them short of identifying a definitive series of leadership dimensions related to desired outcomes alone or in combination with the context. Social constructionism does this intentionally, drawing from a different approach to science than that focused on precision and measurement. They presume that "what counts as a 'situation' and what counts as the 'appropriate' way of leading in that situation are interpretive and contestable issues, not issues that can be decided by objective criteria" (Grint, 2000, p. 3, as quoted in Fairhurst & Grant, 2010, p. 175). As a result, this perspective allows the researcher to better understand the emergence of influence patterns and processes, regardless of whether they appear to serve the interests of a particular individual or group. It breaks the iron lock between the presumed interest of the organization or position holders and leadership effectiveness, since leadership effectiveness is itself defined in terms of co-constructions of leaders and followers, whether these are functional or dysfunctional for the organization as a whole.

This newer avenue of research seems to reveal a number of older questions that remain unanswered in current research. Are there common types of negotiations across organizations of a similar size, with similar technologies and similar markets? How is leadership co-constructed, and what is the effect of context in these constructions? What role do leaders and followers play in these processes? What does the presence or absence of agreement on the co-construction of leadership and context mean for different organizational participants?

Relational Leadership

Relational leadership is a view that sees leadership as emerging from social processes and relationships among people (Drath, 2001; Hosking & Morley, 1988; Ospina & Foldy, 2010; Uhl-Bien, 2006; Uhl-Bien & Ospina, 2012). Relational leadership approaches emphasize the study of "relationality" in leadership, the understanding that individuals and collectives constitute *a field of relationships* (Bradbury & Lichtenstein, 2000; Carroll, Levy & Richmond, 2008). Bringing relationality to leadership means "viewing the invisible threads that connect actors engaged in leadership processes and relationships as part of the reality to be studied" (Ospina & Uhl-Bien, 2012).

From this perspective, leadership is still influence but influence from a different lens. Following Uhl-Bien (2006, p. 668), "leadership relationships are identified by interactive dynamics that contribute to emergence or direction of social order and action..., at a collective level deals with 'whole process by which social systems change and...the socially constructed roles and relationships developed that might be labeled leadership'" (Murrell, 1997, p. 39). In relational leadership, all relationships occur in context and this context is important to the study of relational dynamics (cf. Osborn et al., 2002). Since leadership emerges from interacting individuals there are (a) likely different depictions of the social order by different participants; (b) different interpretations of why the social order emerges; and (c) multiple scenarios for the key elements, importance, and shaping of the context. In relational approaches, researchers do not start with an objective reality to be isolated, but rather seek to identify understandings related to how and why organizational members see particular patterns of leadership.

Relational leadership offers a different starting point from nested views, and a new set of contextual influences on leadership. As described by Ospina and Uhl-Bien (2012), relational approaches shift attention from individual to distributed forms of leadership (Gronn, 2002; Mehra, Smith, Dixon & Robertson, 2006), and from the leader and/or the follower to the "reciprocal relationship" as a core target for conceptualizing and studying leadership (Huxham & Vangen, 2000; Shamir, Pillai, Bligh, & Uhl-Bien, 2007). They also shift attention from leadership actors to relational practices as well as communication and organizing processes associated with the emergence of leadership (Dachler & Hosking, 1995; Drath et al., 2008; Fairhurst, 2007; Hosking, 1988, 2007; Ospina & Foldy, 2010).

Open areas for investigation. Relational approaches bring to the fore the issue of context and process in leadership research. By viewing leadership as co-creation, they bring a different focus to followers in the leadership process, seeing them as co-producers of leadership rather than passive recipients. Interesting questions are raised, then, about how context relates to this co-creation process (e.g., status issues, power, culture, norms, and roles). To this end, relational approaches draw attention to the question of how we study relationality in leadership research, how we examine leadership processes as "in relation" (people in relation with one another, leadership actions in relation to context, etc.). Although examining relations among individuals within a single organization has historically been emphasized, we need to enhance understanding of co-production when individuals have different organizational homes (but must work as a unit). In other words, how do individuals quickly coalesce into collections of leaders and followers for the types of temporary work units so common today?

Discursive Leadership Approaches

Others from a postmodernist orientation who adopt a social constructionist approach emphasize the negotiated aspect of the emergent social order to illustrate important underlying contested issues (Fairhurst, 2007, 2009). These discursive scholars treat language as constituting reality. Incorporating a Foucauldian (Foucault, 1972; 1980; 1995) lens, they consider leadership as being negotiated in the context of "Discourse," the historically rooted ideas, assumptions, and talk patterns that serve as the linguistic resources for communicating actors (Fairhurst & Grant, 2010).

This view includes the construction and negotiation of meaning, often around issues involving power and politics. Many of these discursive studies are very rich descriptions of dialogue, where both the definition of context and leadership are unique to the actors. For example, Fairhurst draws from discursive psychology to note the ways in which Discourse can be seen as "an interpretative repertoire" (Potter & Wetherell, 1987; Wetherell,

1998) in the architecture of leadership interaction (Fairhurst & Grant, 2010, p. 183). Because strategic, relational, cultural, and material aspects of power intertwine in dialogue to construct leadership in the situation, many discursive approaches view leaders as receptors of meaning as much as they are managers of it (Fairhurst & Grant, 2010).

Open areas for investigation. While social constructionist assumptions of discursive approaches are quite different from the postpositivist approaches of mainstream leadership researchers, what is revealing for those interested in context is the co-development of relevant leadership and context as selected *by those being investigated* rather than by investigators (who "pre-define" leadership with the questions they ask) (Fairhurst, 2007). Particularly important topics for study are the nature of the issues raised by participants (e.g., what is important and constitutes the context), who helps define these issues (e.g., who is in discourse), and that these are co-determined in the evolution and emergence of leadership. In other terms, the relevant causal mechanisms linking leadership and leadership effectiveness may go far beyond the simple instrumentalism emphasized in many nested models to include the followers' desires for identity, meaning, and power.

Yet, at this stage of development a simple switch of criteria and causal mechanisms seems to leave open a series of questions. For instance, if individuals have a desire for identity and meaning, will they negotiate for a different type of treatment by a superior than if the negotiations are based purely on instrumentalism? To what extent, if any, does the organizational context establish boundaries on who negotiates, what they negotiate, and the type of negotiated outcomes the participants might expect? For instance, the type of negotiated order in the military might be far different from that in a university.

Summary Comparison of Causal Mechanisms in Nested and Pervasive Approaches

The pure nested and pervasive approaches appear to be in stark contrast to one another on a number of fronts. The causal mechanisms underlying leadership are radically different, in one sense, but surprisingly similar in a different sense. While many nested models emphasize instrumentalism, favoring the demands, constraints and opportunities imposed by the larger organization (Stewart, 1982) on both leaders and followers, many of the pervasive approaches stress the development of meaning and sense-making, as followers engage in interactions that construct the realities around them. Yet, a closer examination suggests more of a difference of emphasis rather than a difference of kind. Specifically, instrumentalism is present in many nested approaches simply because the wants, desires, and interests of the followers are not automatically included by an organization in the initial deal between it and the workers. Additional incentives tailored to the context and the worker are needed for superior performance. In many pervasive approaches, it is also implicitly, and sometime explicitly, assumed that the linkages between the organization and the individual are at best incomplete. This is the case because no one organization is capable of providing sufficient meaning, identity, and/or power. Thus, within a single organization, individuals create their own meaning and negotiate for their own interests.

Across these two approaches we see that context and the criteria selected for analysis tilt the balance of how the researcher approaches the study of leadership, driving the assumptions they will make in terms of contextual factors. When the criteria emanate from higher levels in an organization's rigid bureaucracy (as with the classic mechanistic organization of the 1960s, cf. Burns and Stalker, 1961), it seems natural to see the importance of nested models. In this same setting, with a simple change to the interests of the lowest participants, it is easy to see the importance of pervasive views. However, if the criteria for explanation and prediction are slightly modified to consider the organization as a social entity, once-neglected causal mechanisms become more apparent (e.g., interdependence, affiliation, self-interest). These causal mechanisms are addressed in hybrid approaches. Hybrid approaches suggest that current models are not sufficiently robust to understand the dynamics of leadership. Hybrid approaches start with context and consider how, depending upon the context, different aspects of leadership come into play.

Hybrid Approaches

Hybrid approaches go far beyond just a simple combination of pure nested and pervasive approaches. In general, they focus on the context as the triggering mechanisms for leadership and its outcomes, but more important, they also introduce modifications to the leadership dimensions that have already been developed in the nested and contextual views. Perhaps the most profound differences between the hybrid approaches and pure nested or pervasive approaches are in the mix of causal mechanisms triggered by the context that are generated when a focus on different criteria comes into play. Whereas the previous nested and pervasive approaches started with leadership, hybrid approaches generally start with a characterization of the context, emphasizing the demands, constraints, and choices facing a system selected for analysis. Interestingly, such characterizations draw on the character of the *system* under analysis, rather than an individual managerial or worker perspective. By far the most popular characterizations are based on or include complexity theory (see Marion, 1999; Kauffman, 1993; Osborn et al., 2002; Uhl-Bien & Marion, 2009).

The "Contextual View"

Based upon earlier work, Osborn et al. (2002) used a combination of organization theory and complexity theory to propose a "contextual view" of leadership identified by four basic types of organizational contexts with three primary echelons for leadership analysis. Building from more detailed analyses by Jaques (1989) and Hunt (1991), they describe important distinctions among the top, middle, and bottom of systems. With the focus on an entire organization, their view of context combines estimates of volatility and complexity to differentiate among four types of organizational contexts: (a) relative stability, (b) crisis, (c) dynamic equilibrium and (d) the "edge of chaos." This approach emphasizes only one echelon within the hierarchy for the first three contexts. The theory proposes that as the focus of attention and the type of context shifts, so do views of leadership, leadership effectiveness, and the type of criteria typically investigated.

Osborn et al. (2002) examined relative stability at the lowest organizational levels, crisis at the middle, and dynamic equilibrium at the top management level. With stability at the bottom, they placed the emphasis on nested views of leadership, with the criteria mainly from more senior managers and the causal mechanisms stressing instrumentalism. With crisis and the focus on middle management, they noted prior work (Hunt & Ropo, 1995; Ropo & Hunt, 1999) stressing the collective, emergent, and processual aspects of leadership to resolve the crisis. Important in their analysis is the notion that the crisis itself provides an organizing causal mechanism for the analysis of leadership effectiveness. For the context labeled dynamic equilibrium, they suggested that the key aspects of leadership are patterning of attention and network development. These are considered as processually evolving collective aspects of leadership, where the criteria stem from the strategy selected by those under analysis. So the dimensions of leadership fit the nested perspective, while the criteria and causal mechanisms emanate from a pervasive approach cascading down a hierarchy.

Finally, in the analysis of the "edge of chaos," importance is placed on an overall collective view of leaders both "of" the organization and "within" the organization. With this collective view, Osborn et al. (2002) changed the analysis of their leadership dimensions' patterning of attention and network development. They dealt with the overall patterns of network connections to various segments of the organization's environment and within the organization itself, rather than those forged by a particular individual or a small collection of individuals. Regarding the patterning of attention, their analysis highlights the collective mental models of leaders (i.e., a pervasive view of this aspect of leadership, as it emerges from social interaction among organizational participants). The necessity for systemic flexibility and sophistication at the "edge of chaos" is the primary causal mechanism, and it is presumed that the system should seek greater fitness (even though fitness was not clearly defined). Overall, their view of leadership in this "edge of chaos" context stressed pervasive approaches, but the casual mechanism and criteria were taken from complexity theory rather than bureaucracy. They saw emergent strategy as a major mechanism for the systemic adaptation, and suggested several nonlinear linkages among leadership, emergent strategy, and fitness.

Extensions of the "contextual view." In 2007, Osborn & Hunt augmented their earlier analysis of the context by extending Etzioni's (1961, 1975) notion of matching organizational compliance bases and employee responses. Etzioni argued that alienation was in response to coercion, instrumentalism was in response to remuneration, and morality was in response to normative appeals. They suggested that complexity theory (e.g., Marion, 1999) put forth yet another basis for attachment and compliance—affiliation stemming from dialogue and discussion to stimulate emergence (e.g., new solutions to the problems of complexity and volatility coming from deeper within the organization). That is, when individuals are expected to develop, nurture, and cultivate social relationships with others in the organization, rather than stand alone, they would respond to new solutions to complex problems that would make their organizational lives more comfortable.

Later, Hunt, Osborn, and Boal (2009) dealt more specifically with those in near top management positions under conditions of "edge of chaos" to detail their important role in both (a) stimulating emergence, and (b) providing direction and meaning to combine emergent solutions into organization-wide initiatives. Many of these behaviors might be considered management in the nested views, as they involved allocation of resources and other forms of support, but some involved symbolic representation as well.

Open areas for investigation. In contrast to the bulk of the literature cited here, with Osborn et al. (2002), Hunt et al. (2009), and Osborn and Hunt (2007), the context is characterized at the system level rather that specific conditions facing a group or individual leader. With such a macro view, they did not address potentially important micro variations. For example, even with a system "at the edge of chaos," there may be many units and departments that are very stable. Thus, a single description of the overall context could seriously misrepresent the particular context facing a given leader. While these authors stressed collective leadership, they did not clearly articulate the evolution and development of collective leadership or how the context may impact this process. However, as emphasized in this chapter, a critical aspect of the contextual view is the impact of context on leadership. Leaders are expected to effectively respond to the given contextual condition. The important roles of individual initiative and how leaders recognize and specifically address contextual issues were left as open questions for future research.

Complexity Leadership Theory

Another approach applying complexity to leadership is offered by Uhl-Bien and Marion (Marion & Uhl-Bien, 2001; Uhl-Bien et al., 2007; Uhl-Bien & Marion, 2009). Contrary to Osborn and Hunt, who started with nested views and then applied complexity theory (i.e., a pervasive view), Uhl-Bien and Marion started with complexity theory and then brought in nested views. The resulting Complexity Leadership Theory (CLT) is a hybrid view because it is a contextual leadership approach (cf. Osborn et al., 2002) that considers leadership as generated in interactions of informally interacting adaptive leaders (pervasive) operating in tension with one another and with formal managerial leaders (nested).

CLT identifies three forms of leadership: administrative leadership, entrepreneurial leadership, and adaptive leadership. The causal mechanism of CLT is complexity-based, and can be summarized as adaptive tension (i.e., creativity, innovation, learning, and adaptability are generated in the tensions that occur in interactions between interdependent, self-interested local agents brought together by a complex, i.e., adaptive, challenge). This mechanism is triggered under contextual conditions of complexity pressures (e.g., "conflicting constraints"—interdependent heterogeneous relationships created in the face of adaptive challenges) (Uhl-Bien et al., 2007; Uhl-Bien & Marion, 2009).

This approach began with the work of Marion and Uhl-Bien (2001) who identified traditional (nested) models of leadership as suffering from problems of *reductionism*, that is, trying to reduce context down to a few variables and leadership down to actions of individual behavior; and *determinism*, that is, assumptions of linear causality. They argued that complexity, and in particular, the concept of complex adaptive systems (CAS), offers alternate assumptions to help alleviate these problems. Complexity is grounded in principles of interactive dynamics and emergence; according to complexity theory, organizations are self-organizing systems (i.e., CAS) generated by the interactions of members within them as they respond and adapt to contextual conditions (Anderson, 1999). Change occurs nonlinearly rather than being controlled or predetermined by hierarchical leaders (Lichtenstein & Plowman, 2009). Contrary to bureaucratic assumptions of leadership grounded in hierarchy and authority, complexity allowed for more pervasive views of leadership and more embedded views of context.

Extensions of complexity leadership. Recognizing that a CAS-only approach (Marion & Uhl-Bien, 2001) was not sufficient to explain organizational reality, in 2007 Uhl-Bien, Marion, and McKelvey introduced a conceptual framework for complexity leadership that intertwined nested (bureaucratic) and pervasive (interactive) views of leadership and context. This work identified two primary types of functions in organizations: an administrative function and an adaptive function. The administrative function is located in the hierarchical (bureaucratic) systems and structures of the organization and is focused on efficiency and effectiveness. The adaptive function is located in informally network dynamics (i.e., complex adaptive systems) and is focused on innovation, adaptability, and learning. These two functions operate in dynamic equilibrium, and the adaptive tension between them, when adequately balanced in accordance with the notion of requisite complexity (Boisot & McKelvey, 2010), is what generates fitness for the organization. Requisite complexity, adapted from Ross Ashby's (1969) law of requisite variety (i.e., it takes variety to beat variety), says that organizations need to enable complexity to meet the complex needs of the environment.

Adaptive leadership is associated with the adaptive function, and occurs when individuals and collectives, often in the everyday functioning of their jobs (Tsoukas, 1996), take new innovations, learning, and processes (cf. "exploration," March, 1991) generated by entrepreneurial leadership and then work to advance these processes into the formal, organizational system. Administrative leadership occurs in the administrative function and works to coordinate and "exploit" (cf. "exploitation," March, 1991) the innovations and adaptations generated in the entrepreneurial system to convert them to viable products, services, and processes for the firm. A key aspect of administrative leadership is that because it is often focused on alignment (e.g., shared vision) and control (e.g., results orientation), it fails to tap into the complexity dynamics needed for adaptive outcomes. Therefore, adaptive leadership helps to enable the "requisite complexity" needed for the firm to survive and thrive. It does this by managing in the adaptive tension between the administrative and entrepreneurial systems, at times enabling more administrative leadership and at times enabling more entrepreneurial leadership.

Open areas for investigation. Complexity leadership is in its early stages of development, and there is much room for empirical investigation. Initial research is demonstrating support for the basic components of the theory and some revisions. While there are many key questions that need to be addressed, more traditional leadership researchers may be uncomfortable with all of the emphasis on context and highly abstract aspects of leadership. For example, what is the linkage between the complexity view and the traditional nested emphasis on leader behavior? Are there systematic variations in complexity leadership by different echelons? How are various leadership prototypes evoked by employees as individuals engage in adaptive, administrative, and entrepreneurial leadership? Driven by these questions, there is an immediately apparent need for researchers to reconsider traditional research methods with complexity leadership.

The precise desired balance between explanation and prediction in complexity leadership appears to be an open question mainly because the criteria of viability. Following complexity theory, the researcher should expect precise prediction of organizational outcomes as the system seeks viability. On the other hand, it is clear that the ability of the system to gain energy from the environment (a traditional performance measure) is an important feature of maintaining viability. What is an open question is the linkage between the concept of viability and more traditional measures of organizational performance such as those based on strategy, systems goals, or outcome goals (See Osborn et al., 1980). Instead of precise prediction it may be possible to predict the direction of movement from combinations of context and leadership. While managers may not be satisfied with such a vague notion, it may appeal to researchers because it is a more realistic view of the current capability of existing models.

Discussion

As our overview of the vast literature on leadership suggests, leadership researchers often see as important what they want to see. Most often, they do not want to delve into the intricacies of the context nor recognize multiple causal mechanisms, units of analysis, and criteria. However, it would be just as grave an error to suggest that future researchers should simultaneously include all relevant units of analysis, all prior causal mechanisms, and/or criteria as it would be to ignore all of this potential complexity. What is quite apparent is that the definition of leadership and leadership effectiveness is as profoundly influenced by the context and causal mechanisms as the criteria and unit of analysis selected. Yet, as is equally clear from the review, researchers have spent comparatively little time discussing either context or causal mechanisms. One would hope that leadership researchers would not merely repeat the past with the apparent discovery of new leadership dimensions independent of context. The field is ripe for synthesis by exploring open questions emanating from prior work in the new contextual conditions of the 21st century. This synthesis could stem from nested, pervasive, or hybrid models that seriously considered context and the relevant causal mechanisms.

Research Implications from Nested Models

We examined a number of different models where it was implicitly or explicitly presumed that leadership was nested in a single group, unit, division, or organization. What is particularly interesting are the threads to future research drawn from even some of the oldest models. What we do not know would fill volumes, but there are a number of intriguing questions for future research involving changes in context. As for the context itself, there is a clear need to separate contextual factors. Following Yukl's (1981) notions, contextual factors alter (a) criteria, (b) the leader behavior of position holders, and/or (c) the linkage between leadership and criteria.

As organizations are changing, how are the demands, constraints, and choices facing leaders changing to increase or decrease their potential influence? With organizational changes, is the degree to which leaders can change and mold the context expanding or declining? For example, the integrated hierarchical bureaucracy of the 1950s seems less typical in the 21st century than the multifaceted disbursed network organization. Does this imply more or less leadership influence? Is there a change in the areas where leaders can exercise influence? As new generations of individuals populate organizations, do they have different expectations from their organizational experience? For example, if individuals do not expect to have a career within an organization and see work as a series of temporary positions, how will they respond to influence attempts by higher echelons?

Attempting to answer some of the questions will, no doubt, dramatically alter what we research in leadership, what we see as the relevant aspects of the context, and what modifications are needed to the popular causal mechanisms in prior research. Clearly, researchers are moving beyond pure instrumentalism and including a broader range of causal mechanisms. But it is far from clear which causal mechanism or combination of causal mechanisms will be the most useful in future research.

Research Implications from Pervasive Models

While there is little question that nested views of leadership dominated much of the research of the prior century, a whole new series of views emerge when taking the perspective of followers, and not just the dictates of organizational authorities. For example, if organizations are composed of individuals, all individuals are potentially both leaders and followers. In terms used in this chapter, pervasive models of leadership shed a different light on leadership and leadership effectiveness. With emphasis on the social construction of reality, leadership and context were co-defined, sometimes through the lens of followers, and sometimes through the type of dialogue and discussion found in organizational settings.

Again one finds a series of contextually inclusive questions that may well lead future research: If individuals have multiple leadership prototypes, how and why do contextual conditions alter the prototypes evoked by followers? What contextual conditions draw the boundaries for the relevance of specific desired leadership categories or prototypes? And is it possible for a leader to alter the prototypes evoked by followers via highlighting specific contextual factors?

Of course, if context and leadership are socially constructed, again there are a series of contextually based open issues. For example, are there common issues of leadership and context that are negotiated in a wider variety or organizations? To what extent do larger societal issues set the agenda for negotiations and put specific contextual factors into play? To what extent is the construction of meaning at the core of determining the relevance of specific contextual and leadership dimensions? With the history of the predominance of nested views, researchers still need to discover what, if any, commonly identified organizational conditions (e.g., size and technology type), underlie the development of prototypes and the agenda for negotiations. These unknown issues presume that beliefs of followers are critical to understand leadership and leadership effectiveness. These issues also presume that subtle changes in followers and what they want can have a profound impact on the emergence of leadership and leadership effectiveness. Yet these last two presumptions are open research questions themselves.

Research Implications from Hybrid Models

We also identified a number of newly emerging hybrid models containing elements from both the nested and pervasive views. In contrast to the prior models, the existing hybrid models start with the context of leadership and then move to incorporate relevant elements from nested and pervasive models. While the hybrid models provide much more emphasis and detail on the context of leadership, in general, traditional leadership researchers have been more interested in the individual leadership initiatives used to improve specific outcomes. Though hybrid researchers recognize the critical importance of social construction in the analysis of leadership, they also recognize the organizationally based demands and constraints placed on leaders. However, the appropriate balance between contextual pressures and individual initiative, and between organizational "realities" and social construction, remain open questions with profound implications for the type of research in leadership.

It is clear that the more the aspects of the pervasive models are included in a hybrid model, the greater the tilt toward explanation rather than prediction. With hybrid models, there is often an attempt to predict the viability of the system under investigation. However, even without serving the interests of a particular constituency, the concept of viability is itself questionable. In some cases, the criterion of viability is seen as a dynamic, nonpredicable but recurring pattern of adjustment (adjustment could be predicted but the exact type of adjustment could not be predicted). This vague notion of criteria, of course, could easily be a source of frustration to those schooled in nested views of leadership. And no doubt some managers will want to determine not only the types of "progress" pursued but the degree of "progress" attained. However, rather than predicting the level of an outcome desired by managers, perhaps researchers should concentrate more on understanding the mechanisms underlying change processes and emergence of outcomes in organizations.

Research Implications from Units of Analysis and Causal Mechanisms

While leadership researchers are accustomed to dealing with a variety of different units of analysis, they are less familiar with differences in causal mechanisms. In the older nested models, it is clear that the criteria mirrored the leadership dimensions with an emphasis on some type of task completion estimate and some type of employee-centered determination. With the newer pervasive and hybrid models, some models did not attempt to predict but focused on explaining a common pattern of influence from interactions, discourse, and/or negotiation. While most leadership researchers using nested views agree that explaining leadership and leadership effectiveness lies at the heart of research, the question is whether it is sufficient to focus only on prediction, or should researchers also strive to include explanation? If prediction is accepted as a legitimate research goal, whose interests are to be predicted? It is as simplistic to presume that the interests of all involved with organizations are compatible as to assume they are incompatible. For us, an open and important question for future researchers focuses on whose interests are served by concentration on a particular set of criteria.

With a focus on leader behavior, we noted the causal mechanisms highlighted instrumentalism. Later nested models included organizational notions based on uncertainty reduction, while some of the pervasive views stressed the meaning derived from discourse. The few hybrid models included information, affiliation, and achievement based causal mechanisms. Clearly the most powerful causal mechanism was self-interest balanced against organizational interests. With a potentially broader array of causal mechanisms available to future researchers, it is an open question how these will or will not be incorporated into future models. With multiple causal mechanisms operating simultaneously it would seem researchers would be skirting disaster if it came to prediction. It seems more than reasonable to expect that the context itself may have a major impact on the importance of various causal mechanisms. For example, in for-profit organizations the importance of idealism might be limited in the eyes of followers whose leadership prototype might include the expectation of managerial self-interest.

Conclusion

In the introduction we offered the following premise: *as the view of leadership shifts, so does the concept of context as well as the underlying causal mechanisms evoked and the nature of what is being explained or predicted.* We particularly noted that the initial starting point for many leadership researchers, the definition of leadership, often established the unit of analysis, the criteria to be explained and/or predicted, and the causal mechanism used. With the notable exception of some hybrid models, the notion of context was then often derived. To this end, we distinguished between nested, pervasive, and hybrid approaches to show how the vision of leadership also provided specific insight into the context again from the initial perspective of the researcher. What is clear to us, and we hope from this review, is that leadership and context are intricately intertwined. To study leadership is to also study the context of leadership, whether this is recognized by the researcher or not. It is time to stress synthesis based on the inclusion of context.

Selected Questions for Future Research

1. What are the emerging demands and constraints on leadership as organizations continue to evolve beyond bureaucratic models?

2. Is there a natural relationship between the managerial behavior and leadership behavior of manager? To what extent, if any, do the managerial behaviors of the position holders alter their leadership?

3. Are organizational echelons relatively independent of one another, as implied by Katz and Kahn (1978), because they have different functions? Or are differences by echelons more a reflection of social strata than organizational necessity?

4. Is it possible for leaders to depict the issue or context in such a way that their type of leadership seems appropriate, justified, and/or desirable?

5. What does the presence or absence of agreement on the co-construction of leadership and context mean for different organizational participants?

6. If individuals have a desire for identity and meaning, will they negotiate for a different type of treatment by a superior and to what extent, if any, does the organizational context establish boundaries on who negotiates, what they negotiate, and the type of negotiated outcomes the participants might expect?

7. How do individuals quickly coalesce into collections of leaders and followers for the types of temporary work units so common today?

8. If leaders are indeed expected to effectively respond to a given contextual condition, what is the role of individual initiative and how leaders recognize and specifically address the particular contextual issues?

9. What is the linkage between the complexity view and the traditional nested emphasis on leader behavior?

10. How are various leadership prototypes evoked by employees as individuals engage in adaptive, administrative, and complexity leadership?

References

Aldrich, H. E., & Pfeffer, J. (1976). Environments of organizations. *Annual Review of Sociology 2*, 79–105.

Anderson, P. (1999). Complexity theory and organization science. *Organization Science, 10*(3), 216–232.

Antonakis, J., & Atwater, L. (2002). Leader distance: A review and a proposed theory. *The Leadership Quarterly, 13*(6), 673–704.

Ashby, W. R. (1969). Self-regulation and requisite variety. In F. E. Emery (Ed.), *Systems thinking*, (pp. 105–124). Middlesex, England: Penguin Books.

Avolio, B. J., Bass, B. M., & Jung, D. I. (1999). Re-examining the components of transformational and transactional leadership using the Multifactor Leadership Questionnaire. *Journal of Occupational and Organizational Psychology, 72*(4), 441–462.

Avolio, B. J., & Gardner, W. L. (2005). Authentic leadership development: Getting to the root of positive forms of leadership. *The Leadership Quarterly, 16*(3), 315–338.

Barbuto, J. E., & Ramthun, A. J. (2011). *Herzberg revisited: An examination of motivation-hygiene theory fifty years later.* Paper presentation, Midwest Academy of Management Annual Meeting, Omaha, NE, October 20–22.

Bass, B. M. (1997). Does the transactional-transformational leadership paradigm transcend organizational and national boundaries?. *American Psychologist, 52*(2), 130–139.

Bass, B. M., & Avolio, B. J. (Eds.). (1994). *Improving organizational effectiveness through transformational leadership.* Thousand Oaks, CA: Sage Publications.

Bass, B. M., & Bass, R. (2008). *The Bass handbook of leadership: theory, research, and managerial application.* New York, NY: Free Press.

Bedeian, A. G., & Hunt, J. G. (2006). Academic amnesia and vestigial assumptions of our forefathers. *The Leadership Quarterly, 17*(2), 190–205.

Berger, P. L. & Luckman, T. (1966). *The social construction of reality: A treatise in the sociology of knowledge.* Garden City, NY: Doubleday & Company Inc.

Bernard, L. L. (1926). *An introduction to social psychology.* Oxford, England: Holt.

Bingham, W. (1927). *The psychological foundations of management.* New York, NY: Shaw.

Boisot, M., & McKelvey, B. (2010). Integrating modernist and postmodernist perspectives on organizations: A complexity science bridge. *The Academy of Management Review, 35*(3), 415–433.

Bower, J. L., & Weinberg, M. W. (1988). Statecraft, strategy, and corporate leadership. *California Management Review, 30*(2), 39–56.

Bradbury, H., & Lichtenstein, B. (2000). Relationality in organizational research: Exploring the space between. *Organization Science, 11*(5), 551–564.

Bryman, A. (1992). *Charisma and leadership in organizations.* London, England: Sage.

Bryman, A., Stephens, M., & Campo, C.(1996). The importance of context: Qualitative research and the study of leadership. *The Leadership Quarterly, 7*(3), 353–370.

Burns, J. M. (1978). *Leadership.* Oxford, England: Harper & Row.

Burns, T., & Stalker, G. M. (1961). *The management of innovation.* London, England: Tavistock.

Carroll, B., Levy, L., & Richmond, D. (2008). Leadership as practice: Challenging the competency paradigm. *Leadership, 4*(4), 363–379.

Cogliser, C. C., & Schriesheim, C. A. (2000). Exploring work unit context and leader–member exchange: A multi-level perspective. *Journal of Organizational Behavior, 21*(5), 487–511.

Collinson, D. L. (2006). Rethinking followership: A post-structuralist analysis of follower identities. *The Leadership Quarterly, 17*(2), 179–189.

Conger, J. A., & Kanungo, R. N. (1987). Toward a behavioral theory of charismatic leadership in organizational settings. *Academy of Management Review, 12*(4), 637–647.

Dachler, H. P. (1992). Management and leadership as relational phenomena. In M. von Cranach, W. Doise, & G. Mugny (Eds.), *Social representations and the social bases of knowledge* (pp. 169–178). Ashland, OH: Hogrefe & Huber Publishers.

Dachler, H. P., & Hosking, D.-M. (1995). The primacy of relations in socially constructing organizational realities. In D.-M. Hosking, H. P. Dachler, & K. J. Gergen (Eds.), *Management and organization: Relational alternatives to individualism* (pp. 1–28). Brookfield, VT: Avebury/Ashgate Publishing Co.

Davis, J. P., & Eisenhardt, K. M. (2011). Rotating leadership and collaborative innovation recombination processes in symbiotic relationships. *Administrative Science Quarterly, 56*(2), 159–201.

Day, D. V. (2000). Leadership development: A review in context. *The Leadership Quarterly, 11*(4), 581–613.

Den Hartog, D. N., House, R. J., Hanges, P. J., Ruiz-Quintanilla, S. A., & Dorfman, P. W. (1999). Culture specific and cross-culturally generalizable implicit leadership theories: Are attributes of charismatic/transformational leadership universally endorsed? *The Leadership Quarterly, 10*(2), 219–256.

Drath, W. (2001). *The deep blue sea: Rethinking the source of leadership*. San Francisco, CA: Jossey-Bass and Center for Creative Leadership.

Drath, W. H., McCauley, C. D., Palus, C. J., Van Velsor, E., O'Connor, P.M.G., & McGuire, J. B. (2008). Direction, alignment, commitment: Toward a more integrative ontology of leadership. *The Leadership Quarterly, 19*(6), 635–653.

Elster, J. (1998). A plea for mechanisms. In P. Hedstrom & R. Swedberg (Eds.), *Social mechanisms: An analytical approach to social theory* (pp. 45–73). Cambridge, England: Cambridge University Press.

Etzioni, A. (1961). *A comparative analysis of complex organizations*. New York, NY: Free Press.

Etzioni, A. (1975). *A comparative analysis of complex organizations: On power, involvement, and their correlates*. New York, NY: Free Press.

Evans, M. G. (1970). The effects of supervisory behavior on the path-goal relationship. *Organizational Behavior & Human Performance, 5*(3), 277–298.

Fairhurst, G. T. (2007). *Discursive leadership: In conversation with leadership psychology*. Thousand Oaks, CA: Sage Publications.

Fairhurst, G. T. (2009). Considering context in discursive leadership research. *Human Relations, 62*(11), 1607–1633.

Fairhurst, G. T., & Grant, D. (2010). The social construction of leadership: A sailing guide. *Management Communication Quarterly, 24*(2), 171–210.

Felfe, J., & Petersen, L. E. (2007). Romance of leadership and management decision making. *European Journal of Work and Organizational Psychology, 16*(1), 1–24.

Fiedler, F. E. (1962). Leader attitudes, group climate, and group creativity. *The Journal of Abnormal and Social Psychology, 65*(5), 308–318.

Fiedler, F. E. (1967). *A theory of leadership effectiveness*. NewYork, NY: McGraw Hill.

Fiedler, F. E. (1978). The contingency model and the dynamics of the leadership process. *Advanced Experimental Psychology, 11*, 59–112.

Fisher, R., & Sharp, A. (1998). *Getting it done. How to lead when you're not in charge*. New York, NY: HarperBusiness.

Fletcher, J.K. & Kaufer, K. (2003). Shared leadership: paradox and possibility. In C. L. Pearce & J. A. Conger (Eds.), *Shared leadership: Reframing the hows and whys of leadership* (pp. 21–47). Thousand Oaks, CA: Sage Publications.

Foucault, M. (1972). *The archeology of knowledge and the discourse on language*. London, England: Tavistock.

Foucault, M. (1980). *Power/knowledge: Selected interviews and other writings 1972–1977*. New York, NY: Pantheon.

Foucault, M. (1995). *Discipline and punish*. New York, NY: Vintage.

Gergen, K. J. (1994). Exploring the postmodern: Perils or potentials? *American Psychologist, 49*(5), 412–416.

Gergen, K. J. (1995). Social construction and the educational process. In L. P. Steffe & J. E. Gale (Eds.), *Constructivism in education* (pp. 17–39). Hillsdale, NJ: Lawrence Erlbaum Associates, Inc.

Gerring, J. (2010). Causal mechanisms: Yes, but.... *Comparative Political Studies, 43*(11), 1499–1526.

Giddens, A. (1979). *Central problems in social theory*. Berkeley: University of California Press.

Giddens, A. (1984). *The constitution of society*. Berkeley: University of California Press.

Gioia, D. A. (2003). Give it up! Reflections on the interpreted world (A commentary on Meckler and Baillie). *Journal of Management Inquiry, 12*, 285–292.

Graen, G., Alvares, K., Orris, J. B., & Martella, J. A. (1970). Contingency model of leadership effectiveness: Antecedent and evidential results. *Psychological Bulletin, 74*(4), 285–296.

Graen, G. B. (2006). In the eye of the beholder: Cross-cultural lesson in leadership from project GLOBE: A response viewed from the third culture bonding (TCB) model of cross-cultural leadership. *Academy of Management Perspectives, 20*(4), 95–101.

Graen, G. B., & Uhl-Bien, M. (1995). Relationship-based approach to leadership: Development of leader-member exchange (LMX) theory of leadership over 25 years: Applying a multi-level multi-domain perspective. *The Leadership Quarterly, 6*(2), 219–247.

Grint, K. (2000). *The arts of leadership*. Oxford, England: Oxford University Press.

Grint, K. (2005). Problems, problems, problems: The social construction of "leadership." *Human Relations, 58*(11), 1467–1494.

Gronn, P. (2000). Distributed properties: A new architecture for leadership. *Educational Management & Administration, 28*(3), 317–339.

Gronn, P. (2002). Distributed leadership as a unit of analysis. *The Leadership Quarterly, 13*(4), 423–451.

Hannah, S. T., Uhl-Bien, M., Avolio, B. J., & Cavarretta, F. L. (2009). A framework for examining leadership in extreme contexts. *The Leadership Quarterly, 20*(6), 897–919.

Hedström, P., & Swedberg, R. (1998). *Social mechanisms: An analytical approach to social theory*. Cambridge, England: Cambridge University Press.

Hollander, E. P. (1978). *Leadership dynamics: A practical guide to effective relationships*. New York, NY: Free Press.

Hosking, D. M. (1988). Organizing, leadership and skillful process. *Journal of Management Studies, 25*(2), 147–166.

Hosking, D. M. (2007). Not leaders, not followers: A post-modern discourse of leadership processes. In B. Shamir, R. Pillai, M. Bligh, & M. Uhl-Bien (Eds.), *Follower-centered perspectives on leadership: A tribute to the memory of James R. Meindl*. (pp. 243–263). Greenwich, CT: Information Age Publishing.

House, R. J. (1971). A path goal theory of leader effectiveness. *Administrative Science Quarterly, 16*(3), 321–339.

House, R. J. (1996). Path-goal theory of leadership: Lessons, legacy, and a reformulated theory, Editorial. *The Leadership Quarterly*, 323–352.

House, R. J., & Mitchell, T. R. (2007). Path-goal theory of leadership. In R. P. Vecchio (Ed.), *Leadership: Understanding the dynamics of power and influence in organizations* (2nd ed., pp. 241–254). Notre Dame, IN: University of Notre Dame Press.

House, R., Javidan, M., Hanges, P., & Dorfman, P. (2002). Understanding cultures and implicit leadership theories across the globe: An introduction to project GLOBE. *Journal of World Business, 37*(1), 3–10.

House, R. J., Hanges, P. J., Javidan, M., Dorfman, P., & Gupta, V. (Eds.). (2004). *GLOBE, Cultures, Leadership, and Organizations: GLOBE Study of 62 Societies*. Newbury Park, CA: Sage Publications.

House, R. J., & Shamir, B. (1993). Toward the integration of transformational, charismatic, and visionary theories. In M. M. Chemers & R. Ayman (Eds.), *Leadership theory and research: Perspectives and directions* (pp. 81–107). San Diego, CA: Academic Press.

House, R., Rousseau, D. M., & Thomas-Hunt, M. (1995). The meso paradigm: A framework for the integration of micro and macro organizational behavior. *Research in Organizational Behavior, 17,* 71–114.

Hunt, J., & Dodge, G. (2000). Leadership déjà vu all over again. *The Leadership Quarterly, 11*(4), 435–458.

Hunt, J. G. (1991). *Leadership: A new synthesis*. Thousand Oaks, CA: Sage Publications.

Hunt, J. G., Osborn, R. N., & Boal, K. B. (2009). The architecture of managerial leadership: Stimulation and channeling of organizational emergence. *The Leadership Quarterly, 20*(4), 503–516.

Hunt, J. G., Osborn, R. N., & Schuler, R. S. (1978). Relations of discretionary and nondiscretionary leadership to performance and satisfaction in a complex organization. *Human Relations, 31*(6), 507–523.

Hunt, J. G., & Ropo, A. (1995). Multi-level leadership: Grounded theory and mainstream theory applied to the case of general motors. *The Leadership Quarterly, 6*(3), 379–412.

Huxham, C., & Vangen, S. (2000). Leadership in the shaping and implementation of collaboration agendas: How things happen in a (not quite) joined-up world. *Academy of Management Journal, 43*(6), 1159–1175.

Jacobs, T. O., & Jaques, E. (1987) Leadership in complex systems. In J. A. Zeidner (Ed.), *Human productivity enhancement, Volume II: Organizations and personnel* (pp. 7–65). NewYork, NY: Praeger.

Jaques, E. (1976). *A general theory of bureaucracy*. London, England: Heinemann.

Jaques, E. (1989). *Requisite organization: The CEO's guide to creative structure and leadership*. Falls Church, VA: Cason Hall.

Jaques, E., & Clement, S. D. (1991). *Executive leadership: A practical guide to managing complexity*. Arlington, VA: Cason Hall.

Johns, G. (2006). The essential impact of context on organizational behavior. *Academy of Management Review, 31*(2), 386–408.

Judge, T. A., Piccolo, R. F., & Ilies, R. (2004). The forgotten ones? The validity of consideration and initiating structure in leadership research. *Journal of Applied Psychology, 89*(1), 36–51.

Katz, D., & Kahn, R. L. (1978). *The social psychology of organizations* (2nd ed.). New York, NY: Wiley.

Kauffman, S. A. (1993). *The origins of order: Self organization and selection in evolution*. New York, NY: Oxford University Press.

Kavanagh, M. H., & Ashkanasy, N. M. (2006). The impact of leadership and change management strategy on organizational culture and individual acceptance of change during a merger. *British Journal of Management, 17,* S81–S103.

Kerr, S., & Jermier, J. M. (1978). Substitutes for leadership: Their meaning and measurement. *Organizational Behavior & Human Performance, 22*(3), 375–403.

Kilbourne, C. E. (1935). The elements of leadership. *Journal of coast artillery, 78,* 437–439.

Larson, L. L., Hunt, J. G., & Osborn, R. N. (1976). The great hi-hi leader behavior myth: A lesson from Occam's razor. *Academy of Management Journal, 19*(4), 628–641.

Lewin, K., & Gold, M. (1999). *The complete social scientist: A Kurt Lewin reader*. Washington, DC: American Psychological Association.

Lichtenstein, B. B., & Plowman, D. A. (2009). The leadership of emergence: A complex systems leadership theory of emergence at successive organizational levels. *The Leadership Quarterly, 20*(4), 617–630.

Lichtenstein, B. B., Uhl-Bien, M., Marion, R., Seers, A., Orton, J. D., & Schreiber, C. (2006). Complexity leadership theory: An interactive perspective on leading in complex adaptive systems. *Emergence: Complexity & Organization, 8*(4), 2–12.

Liden, R. C., & Antonakis, J. (2009). Considering context in psychological leadership research. *Human Relations, 62*(11), 1587–1605.

Likert, R. (1961). *New patterns of management*. New York, NY: McGraw-Hill.

Lord, R. G. (1985). An information processing approach to social perceptions, leadership and behavioral measurement in organizations. *Research in Organizational Behavior, 7,* 87–128.

Lord, R. G., Brown, D. J., Harvey, J. L., & Hall, R. J. (2001). Contextual constraints on prototype generation and their multilevel consequences for leadership perceptions. *The Leadership Quarterly, 12*(3), 311–338.

Lord, R. G., De Vader, C., & Alliger, G. M. (1986). A meta-analysis of the relation between personality traits and leadership perceptions: An application of validity generalization procedures. *Journal of Applied Psychology, 71*(3), 402–410.

Lord, R. G., & Emrich, C. G. (2000). Thinking outside the box by looking inside the box: Extending the cognitive revolution in leadership research. *The Leadership Quarterly, 11,* 551–579.

Lord, R. G., Foti, R. J., & De Vader, C. L. (1984). A test of leadership categorization theory: Internal structure, information processing, and leadership perceptions. *Organizational Behavior & Human Performance, 34*(3), 343–378.

Lord, R. G., & Maher, K. J. (1990). Alternative information-processing models and their implications for theory, research, and practice. *Academy of Management Review, 15*(1), 9–28.

March, J. G. (1991). Exploration and exploitation in organizational learning. *Organization Science, 2*(1), 71–87.

Marion, R. (1999). *The edge of organization: Chaos and complexity theories of formal social systems*. Thousand Oaks, CA: Sage Publications.

Marion, R., & Uhl-Bien, M. (2001). Leadership in complex organizations. *The Leadership Quarterly, 12*(4), 389–418.

Martin, H. J., Hunt, J. G. & Osborn, R. N. (1981). A macro-organizational approach to leadership. *Academy of Management Proceedings*, 234–238.

McNamee, S., & Gergen, K. J. (1999). *Relational responsibility: Resources for sustainable dialogue*. Thousand Oaks, CA: Sage Publications.

Mehra, A., Smith, B. R., Dixon, A. L., & Robertson, B. (2006). Distributed leadership in teams: The network of leadership perceptions and team performance. *The Leadership Quarterly, 17*(3), 232–245.

Meindl, J. R. (1995). The romance of leadership as a follower-centric theory: A social constructionist approach. *The Leadership Quarterly, 6*(3), 329–341.

Meindl, J. R., Ehrlich, S. B., & Dukerich, J. M. (1985). The romance of leadership. *Administrative Science Quarterly, 30*(1), 78–102.

Murrell, K. L. (1997). Emergent theories of leadership for the next century: Towards relational concepts. *Organization Development Journal, 15*(3), 35–42.

Nadler, D. A., & Tushman, M. L. (1989). Organizational frame bending: Principles for managing reorientation. *Academy of Management Executive, 3*(3), 194–204.

Offermann, L. R., Kennedy, J. K., & Wirtz, P. W. (1994). Implicit leadership theories: Content, structure, and generalizability. *The Leadership Quarterly, 5*(1), 43–58.

Offstein, E. H., Madhavan, R., & Gnyawali, D. R. (2006). Pushing the frontier of LMX research: The contribution of triads. In G. Graen & J. A. Graen (Eds.), *Sharing network leadership* (pp. 95–118). Greenwich, CT: Information Age Publishing.

Osborn, R. N., & Hunt, J. G. (2007). Leadership and the choice of order: Complexity and hierarchical perspectives near the edge of chaos. *The Leadership Quarterly, 18*(4), 319–340.

Osborn, R. N., Hunt, J. G., & Jauch, L. R. (1980). *Organization theory: An integrated approach*. New York, NY: John Wiley.

Osborn, R. N., Hunt, J. G., & Jauch, L. R. (2002). Toward a contextual theory of leadership. *The Leadership Quarterly, 13*(6), 797–837.

Osborn, R. N., & Marion, R. (2009). Contextual leadership, transformational leadership and the performance of international innovation seeking alliances. *The Leadership Quarterly, 20*(2), 191–206.

Ospina, S., & Foldy, E. G. (2010). Building bridges from the margins: The work of leadership in social change organizations. *The Leadership Quarterly, 21*, 292–307.

Ospina, S., & Sorenson, G. L. J. (2006). A constructionist lens on leadership: Charting new territory In G. R. Goethals & G. L. J. Sorenson (Eds.), *The quest for a general theory of leadership* (pp. 188–204). Cheltenham, England: Edward Elgar.

Ospina, S., & Uhl-Bien, M. (2012). Mapping the terrain: Convergence and divergence around relational leadership. In M. Uhl-Bien & S. Ospina (Eds.), *Advancing relational leadership research: A dialogue among perspectives* (pp. xix–xlvii). Charlotte, NC: Information Age Publishers.

Pawar, B. S., & Eastman, K. K. (1997). The nature and implications of contextual influences on transformational leadership: A conceptual examination. *Academy of Management Review, 22*(1), 80–109.

Pearce, C. L., & Conger, J. A. (2003). *Shared leadership: Reframing the hows and whys of leadership*, Thousand Oaks, CA: Sage Publications.

Pettigrew, A. M. (1987). Context and action in the transformation of the firm. *Journal of Management Studies, 24*(6), 649–670.

Pettigrew, A. M., Whittington, R., Melin, L., Sanchez-Runde, C., van den Bosch, F., Ruigrok, W., & Numagami, T. (2003). *Innovative forms of organizing: International perspectives*. London, England: Sage.

Phillips, R. L., & Hunt, J. G. (1992). *Strategic leadership: A multiorganizational-level perspective*. Westport, CT: Quorum Books/Greenwood Publishing Group.

Podsakoff, P. M., & MacKenzie, S. B. (1997). Impact of organizational citizenship behavior on organizational performance: A review and suggestions for future research. *Human Performance, 10*(2), 133–151.

Porter, L. W., & McLaughlin, G. B. (2006). Leadership and the organizational context: Like the weather? *The Leadership Quarterly, 17*(6), 559–576.

Potter, J., & Wetherell, M. (1987). *Discourse and social psychology*. London, England: Sage.

Purvanova, R. K., & Bono, J. E. (2009). Transformational leadership in context: Face-to-face and virtual teams. *The Leadership Quarterly, 20*(3), 343–357.

Reichers, A. E., & Schneider, B. (1990). Climate and culture: An evolution of constructs. In B. Schneider (Ed.), *Organizational climate and culture* (pp. 5–39). San Francisco, CA: Jossey-Bass.

Ropo, A., & Hunt, J. G. (1999). Leadership and organizational change: Some findings from a processual grounded theory study. In J. A. Wagner III (Ed.), *Advances in qualitative organization research* (vol. 2, pp. 169–200). Greenwich, CT: Elsevier Science/JAI Press.

Sashkin, M. (1988). The visionary leader. In J. A. Conger & R. N. Kanungo (Eds.), *Charismatic leadership: The elusive factor in organizational effectiveness* (pp. 122–160). San Francisco, CA: Jossey-Bass.

Sayles, L. R. (1979). *Leadership: What effective managers really do... and how they do it*. New York, NY: McGraw-Hill.

Sayles, L. R. (1989). *Leadership: Managing in real organizations* (2nd ed.). New York, NY: Mcgraw-Hill Book Company.

Schein, E. H. (2004). *Organizational culture and leadership*. San Francisco, CA: Jossey-Bass.

Seers, A. (2004). Leadership and flexible organizational structures: The future is now. In G. B. Graen (Ed.), *New frontiers of leadership* (pp. 1–31). Greenwich, CT: Information Age.

Selznick, P. (1948). Foundations of the theory of organization. *American Sociological Review, 13*, 25–35.

Shamir, B. (1995). Social distance and charisma: Theoretical notes and an exploratory study. *The Leadership Quarterly, 6*(1), 19–47.

Shamir, B., & Howell, J. M. (1999). Organizational and contextual influences on the emergence and effectiveness of charismatic leadership. *The Leadership Quarterly, 10*(2), 257–283.

Shamir, B., Pillai, R., Bligh, M. C., & Uhl-Bien, M. (Eds.). (2007). *Follower-centered perspectives on leadership: A tribute to the memory of James R. Meindl*. Charlotte, NC: Information Age Publishing.

Stewart, R. (1982). *Choices for the manager: A guide to understanding managerial work*. Englewood Cliffs, NJ: Prentice Hall.

Stinchcombe, A. L. (2005). *The logic of social research*. Chicago, IL: University of Chicago Press.

Stogdill, R. M. (1948). Personal factors associated with leadership: A survey of the literature. *Journal of Psychology: Interdisciplinary and Applied, 25*, 35–71.

Stogdill, R. M. (1974). *Handbook of leadership: A survey of theory and research*. New York, NY: Free Press.

Tsoukas, H. (1996). The firm as a distributed knowledge system: A constructionist approach. *Strategic Management Journal, 17*, 11–25.

Uhl-Bien, M. (2006). Relational leadership theory: Exploring the social processes of leadership and organizing. *The Leadership Quarterly, 17*(6), 654–676.

Uhl-Bien, M., & Marion, R. (2009). Complexity leadership in bureaucratic forms of organizing: A meso model. *The Leadership Quarterly, 20*(4), 631–650.

Uhl-Bien, M., Marion, R., & McKelvey, B. (2007). Complexity leadership theory: Shifting leadership from the industrial age to the knowledge era. *The Leadership Quarterly, 18*(4), 298–318.

Uhl-Bien, M., & Ospina, S. (2012). *Advancing relational leadership research: A dialogue among perspectives.* Charlotte, NC: Information Age Publishing.

Vine, B., Holmes, J., Marra, M., Pfeifer, D., & Jackson, B. (2008). Exploring co-leadership talk through interactional sociolinguistics. *Leadership, 4*, 339–360.

Waldman, D. A., & Yammarino, F. J. (1999). CEO charismatic leadership: Levels-of-management and levels-of-analysis effects. *Academy of Management Review, 24*(2), 266–285.

Weber, M. (1948). *From Max Weber: Essays in sociology* (H. Gerth & C. Wright Mills, Eds. & Trans.). London, England: RKP.

Weick, K. E. (1995). *Sensemaking in organizations.* London, England: Sage.

Wetherell, M. (1998). Positioning and interpretative repertoires: Conversation analysis and post-structuralism in dialogue. *Discourse & Society, 9*, 387–412.

Yukl, G. (1981). *Leadership in organizations.* Englewood Cliffs, NJ: Prentice-Hall.

Yunker, G. W., & Hunt, J. G. (1976). An empirical comparison of the Michigan Four-Factor and Ohio State LBDQ leadership scales. *Organizational Behavior & Human Performance, 17*(1), 45–65.

Zaccaro, S. J. (1996). *Models and theories of executive leadership: A conceptual and empirical review and integration.* Alexandria, VA: U.S. Army Research Institute for the Behavioral and Social Sciences.

CHAPTER

28 Leadership in Extreme Contexts

Sean T. Hannah *and* Ken W. Parry

Abstract

Leadership is in all cases inherently contextualized. In extreme contexts, the contextualization of leadership is perhaps more pronounced and should be understood by researchers and incorporated into conceptualizations and models of leadership. This chapter discusses the study and practice of leadership in extreme events and the nesting of those events in extreme contexts, and describes the various unique and significant causations, constraints, contingencies, and other influences that extreme contexts place upon those in leadership positions, their followers, and leadership processes. It proposes that a deeper understanding of the relationships and interactions between leadership and contextual factors are needed, particularly if research is to inform ways to prepare leaders to operate effectively in extreme contexts. It provides numerous directions for future research to advance this nascent area of research, both from theoretical and methodological perspectives.

Key Words: Leadership, extreme context, extreme event, crisis, trauma, high reliability, critical action, leadership development

In this article we discuss the study and practice of leadership in extreme contexts. We take the position that leadership is inherently contextualized and that extreme contexts create unique and significant causations, constraints, contingencies, and other influences on leadership processes. We propose that a deeper understanding of the relationships and interactions between leadership and contextual factors are needed, particularly if research is to inform ways to prepare leaders to operate effectively in extreme contexts.

Osborn, Hunt, and Jauch (2002) propose that leadership is embedded in and "socially constructed in and from a context" (p. 798), yet leadership researchers have continued to note that the field has failed to account for contextual factors in most theories and definitions of leadership (e.g., Avolio, 2007; Boal & Hooijberg, 2000; Tosi, 1991). Porter and McLaughlin (2006, p. 573) note that "it is apparent that the impact of organization context on leadership is an under-researched area." We echo these calls for greater incorporation of context in leadership research in general, and we particularly propose that the unique factors operating in extreme contexts simply cannot be ignored by researchers if theories are to have ecological validity for and be generalized to the more extreme contexts.

Encouragingly, there has been increased interest in studying leadership in extreme contexts, including calls from editors of top-tier journals in the field. For example, Bamberger and Pratt called for researchers to begin "exploring phenomena or relations that are observable or open to discovery in extreme or 'unusual' contexts" (2010, p. 655) and among "those who work in the trenches" (2010, p. 666). Recently researchers have begun to advance frameworks of leadership in extreme contexts (e.g., Baran & Scott, 2010; Fisher, Hutchings, & Sarros, 2010; Hannah,

Campbell, & Matthews, 2010; Hannah, Uhl-Bien, Avolio, & Cavarretta, 2009; Yammarino, Mumford, Connely, & Dionne, 2010). Yet, this work serves as only a starting point and leaves many questions unanswered.

The practical and theoretical significance of advancing research related to leadership in extreme contexts should not be underestimated. First, there are large populations of people working in inherently extreme contexts that can benefit from this work. For example, as reported by the International Institute for Strategic Studies (2010), there are more than 89 million people serving in militaries worldwide. The International Firefighters Association reports that there are 298,000 full-time firefighters serving in Canada and the United States alone, not including volunteer and part-time volunteer firefighters. According to the UN crime database, nearly 4 million police officers serve in just the 10 largest countries alone. There are many other large populations of workers working in other volatile or dangerous contexts.

Second, organizational contexts in general are becoming more volatile and dynamic, and thus the study of extreme contexts might provide findings that can generalize to less extreme yet still turbulent contexts (Hannah et al., 2009). For example, learning how stress influences the formation of trust and group cohesion in extreme contexts may shed some light on trust and cohesion more generally.

Third, we believe that applying our existing theories of leadership to extreme contexts will help illuminate the boundaries of those theories and how they operate under varying contextual conditions. For example, do extrinsic rewards have similar effects in motivating followers facing major physical or psychological threats as they do in less extreme contexts? How do forms of justice operate in a situation where distributed justice cannot be achieved, such as when an Army leader must assign select units to missions where deaths are not only likely, but expected? Is inspirational leadership more or less important in extreme contexts, such that the relationship between inspirational leadership and follower performance is nonlinear, based on varying levels of extremity?

The organization of this article begins with an overview of the categorizations and characteristics of extreme contexts. From this focus on the external context in which leadership is operating, we then describe the internal context by discussing organization types that may operate in extreme contexts and how each uniquely contextualizes leadership. From this understanding of the external and internal context, we then provide numerous future directions along which to study leadership in extreme contexts, including new approaches to methodology.

The External Contextualization of Leadership in Extreme Contexts

Contextual approaches to leadership and organizations are examined in more detail in another chapter in this edited volume. Nonetheless, there is broad consensus that any examination of leadership cannot be divorced from its institutional context (Currie, Lockett, & Suhomlinova, 2009). For example, there is a high degree of similarity in leadership within a particular (cultural) context (Liden & Antonakis, 2009), and leadership styles are "inextricably rooted in contexts" (p. 1590). Osborn et al. (2002) argued that "leadership and its effectiveness, in large part, are dependent upon the context. Change the context and leadership changes" (p. 797). The context leadership is occurring in should thus be a more important component of future research, particularly in contexts noted as being more extreme.

We believe that it is important to take a refined approach when assessing what constitutes extreme contexts, decomposing the context into various layers and forms. First, there are notable differences between extreme contexts and punctuated extreme events. Second, extreme contexts can be defined as more or less proximal related to where leadership is occurring. Third, in many cases there might be a temporal nature to extreme contexts where the level of extremity and how proximal that extremity is to where leadership is occurring varies over time. Fourth, the form of extremity will likely vary across extreme contexts, such as whether the threat being faced is physical, psychological, material, or other. Fifth, what is "extreme" is relative. Thus we will discuss how different types of organizations and their levels of capabilities and preparedness influence levels of extremity.

Extreme Contexts and Extreme Events

It is important to conceptually differentiate *extreme contexts* from *extreme events*. Hannah et al. (2009) defined an extreme event as "a discrete episode or occurrence that may result in an extensive and intolerable magnitude of physical, psychological, or material consequences to—or in close physical or psychosocial proximity to—organization members" (p. 898). Such extreme events can potentially occur to any organization at any time due to fire, natural disaster, crime, terrorist attack, or many other potential calamities that might occur unexpectedly. Importantly, due to their episodic nature, extreme events can occur at a time when the organization is not currently in an extreme context, or at least is not aware that it is in an extreme context. When the first author arrived at work at the Pentagon on the morning of 9/11, he and his coworkers hardly perceived that they were in an extreme context before the extreme event precipitated by the 9:39 a.m. attack occurred. Leadership dynamics then quickly shifted. For example, individuals in formal leadership positions who didn't quickly take positive actions were discounted by followers, and followers looked for direction to other formal and informal leaders who took effective actions and were seen as trustworthy in this type of situation, such as those with prior experience in extreme events. A similar absence of an extreme context prior to the occurrence of an extreme event could be said concerning children attending school the morning of the 1999 Columbine High School massacre in Colorado.

Whether organizations perceive themselves to be in an extreme context thus in large part depends on the probability of extreme events occurring. Accordingly, Hannah et al. (2009) define an extreme context as "an environment where one or more extreme events are occurring or are likely to occur that may exceed the organization's capacity to prevent and result in an extensive and intolerable magnitude of physical, psychological, or material consequences to—or in close physical or psychosocial proximity to—organization members" (p. 898). As a member of the main attack force in Desert Storm, the first author and his infantry unit clearly perceived they were in an extreme context as engagements with the enemy could occur at any moment. Yet, that extreme context was punctuated by two major battles and a series of lesser engagements with the enemy—that is, extreme events that each altered leadership dynamics. Yet, in an extreme context, an extreme event might not occur. Based on ominous weather predictions estimating a direct hit to the city, New York City citizens and emergency responders were in an extreme context during Hurricane Irene in 2011, yet escaping the brunt of the storm that moved east, a major extreme event never occurred to the city.

Further, as they can occur independently or together, it is critical to conceptually separate extreme events from extreme contexts and their independent and combined effects on leadership. Importantly, if an organization is in an extreme context prior to the onset of an extreme event, it has some level of anticipation that an extreme event could occur, and thus has the opportunity to prepare itself and its members to face extreme events if it has effective leadership operating (Pauchant & Mitroff, 1992; Pearson & Mitroff, 1993). In preparation for the launch of the attack in Desert Storm, for example, coalition units had trained for months in the deserts of Saudi Arabia in preparation for battle against a specific enemy under specific terrain and weather conditions. This level of specific preparation reduced the level of extremity of the context relative to the capability of the coalition forces.

Therefore, it is also of note that extreme contexts and extreme events do not necessarily equate to a "crisis." Hermann (1969) defined crisis as "a situation that threatens high priority goals... which suddenly occurs with little or no response time available." Pearson and Clair (1998) further state that crises are "of low probability" and "characterized by ambiguity of cause, effect, and means of resolution" (p. 60). Extreme events can certainly meet these conditions, but do not have to. An extreme event may not only be expected, but be purposely planned, such as a military commander launching an attack at the time and place of his choosing, as we will describe under critical action organizations. Further, extreme events can be of high probability, such as a SWAT team repeatedly being deployed in a high crime area. Extreme events are also not necessarily ambiguous. A trauma surgeon, for example, may fully understand the patient's condition and the exact procedure that is required—yet the execution of that operation may be of high risk and therefore perceived as extreme. Finally, not all crises meet the threshold that we would include in the category of extreme events as we have defined them. Pearson and Clair (1998), for example, include events such as copyright infringement and malicious rumors as crises. Therefore, while extreme events can be of such that they are seen as a "crisis," they are not necessarily so, and not all crises, as have been described in the literature, are extreme events.

In sum, extreme events are often, but not always, nested in extreme contexts. We will also discuss further in the paper that organizations or units can cycle in and out of extreme events and that leadership across these cycles is entrained such that leadership actions in one cycle will influence or constrain leadership actions in later cycles. These realities, coupled with the fact that organizations have differing levels of anticipation for and preparedness to face extreme events, make these situations quite dynamic and necessitate that our research captures such dynamics.

Proximity Factors

This discussion of extreme contexts and extreme events make clear that either can be defined as being more or less proximal to any individual or group, and thus differing in the magnitude of actual or perceived extremeness. We suggest that a context can generally be typified as most extreme when individuals are personally engaged in a volatile or dangerous extreme event, with the level of extremity then varying based on the level of probability that such an event may occur to a particular individual or unit. A wildfire firefighting unit, for example, might not currently be battling a blaze, but know the fire is spreading and that their unit is designated as the next group of firefighters to be activated if the fire spreads further, thus raising their anticipation. A firefighting unit not on the activation list and thus not anticipating as immediate of a threat would tend to perceive less extremity. Proximity in extreme contexts can thus be defined in part by physical location or probability of personal risk. This physical proximity may be an important factor influencing leadership processes. For example, soldiers were found to reevaluate the level that they trusted their leaders prior to deploying for combat operations as well as the level of perceived competence of their leaders (Sweeney, 2010), most likely due to that fact that the context leadership was operating in had changed, and followers were entering into a context where they had higher levels of outcome dependency based on the behaviors of those in leadership positions.

Hannah et al. (2009a) note that proximity, however, can also be defined as psychosocial. Here an individual or unit might not be in harm's way, but others who they are psychologically or socially close to may be. An infantry company, for example, might have one of its platoons cut off and heavily engaged with the enemy, thereby influencing the leadership dynamics occurring in the rest of the company in multiple ways as their "brothers in arms" are in harm's way. For example, it may raise the salience of group cohesion or raise the intrinsic motivation of unit members to support the mission. If those in leadership positions delay or refuse to support the cut-off platoon, we might expect, in example, for followers to more readily challenge their leaders than under situations with less psychosocial proximity. It is even possible that individuals not in physical proximity might experience even greater effects of the extreme context or event than those in physical proximity, highlighting the importance of considering both physical and psychosocial proximity when researching leadership in extreme contexts. A highly trained Special Weapons and Tactics (SWAT) team conducting a forced entry into a building during a hostage rescue, for example, may be calmer than the chief of police who ordered the raid watching as the event unfolds on a televised newscast.

Future research should assess how physical and psychosocial proximity relate or interact to affect leadership processes. For example, we know from leadership research in general that physical distance changes the dynamics of influence processes and how leaders' behaviors are perceived and interpreted by followers (Antonakis & Atwater, 2002). Physical distance can also diminish the quality of social interactions between those in leadership positions and their followers (Bass, 1998; Howell & Hall-Merenda, 1999; Yagil, 1998). For example, physically closer leaders might tend to be seen as more considerate (Shamir, 1995) and leaders rated as more transformational may have a generally more positive impact on follower performance in physically close versus distant positions (Howell, Neufeld, & Avolio, 2005). In extreme contexts, followers personally engaged in the extreme event are likely quite concerned that their leaders "get" what is happening on the ground and are able to make effective decisions on their behalf. This could explain why in combat leaders who are out front sharing risks and hardships with soldiers are seen as more effective and trustworthy (Little, 1964). It is possible, however, that the effects of physical proximity may be moderated by levels of psychosocial proximity. If followers on the front lines have strong social bonds with those in leadership positions, and vice versa, they may more readily assume that those making decisions at higher levels are doing so with empathy and care, even if they are not in close proximity, thus attenuating the otherwise negative effects of physical distance.

Temporal Factors

Organizations thus switch in and out of extreme contexts and extreme events of varying levels of physical and psychosocial proximity, and thereby experience varying levels of extremity. As leadership is entrained across these cycles, temporal phenomena must be considered. A SWAT unit in a high crime city, for example, may oscillate between non-extreme contexts (off duty or training), extreme contexts (on duty and on call), and extreme events (in-situ SWAT operations). This cyclic effect is particularly likely in *action teams*, which operate in extreme contexts as interdependent teams of specialized individuals to accomplish collective tasks and goals (Sundstrom, deMeuse, & Futrell, 1990). Action teams engage in intense yet brief periods of performance, which are often repetitive yet conducted in changing conditions. Examples include surgical teams, military squads, SWAT units, and firefighting units.

When discussing extreme contexts, therefore, we need to consider the microlevel context and its changes over time (Hannah, et al., 2010). Fisher (2000, 2003) found that the work context can have a variable impact upon satisfaction and motivation from minute to minute. Similarly, we suggest that leadership will be affected minute by minute as micro-contexts and extreme events become more or less extreme. Leadership will be affected by the context, and the context will call for changes in how leadership impacts followers. Thus the micro-level context must be considered as organizations or teams/units rotate through cycles that differentiate more extreme micro-contexts from less extreme micro-contexts for leadership. For our purposes, context is not organization or nation or ethnicity—context is (immediate) context. When firefighters are back at their fire house and when soldiers are out of action back at base camp, the extremis nature of the context is less relevant, and a different style of leadership is likely required. When out of action, those in leadership positions can work on climate, culture, ideals, values, and other aspects of leadership that might well assist team functioning and performance when in an actual extreme event. However, the extreme context should be separated from the in-situ extreme event in order to understand the uniqueness of such an extreme event. The question for us is which moderators are relevant to extreme contexts and events, therefore which moderators should be included within our considerations?

Understanding how leadership operates in extreme contexts over time, particularly in organizations that have the probability to engage in repetitive extreme events, thus requires considering temporal effects and the entrainment between leadership constructs. Hannah et al. (2009a) and Palmer, Hannah, and Sosnowik (2011) suggest that extreme contexts should be defined by three phases: (1) anticipation of involvement in an extreme event; (2) effective functioning in situ (i.e., during an extreme event); and (3) post-hoc functioning, which addresses outcomes of involvement in extreme events, such as dealing with stress, sense-making, codifying what was learned, and retraining. Consistent with others (e.g., Bruning, 1964; Leonard & Howitt, 2007), Palmer et al. (2011) suggest that it is important to "recognize that the requirements on leaders may differ substantively across the phases." Therefore, what constitutes effective leadership likely varies over time, and the knowledge, skills, abilities, and attributes required from those in leadership positions would also then vary.

Anticipation phase. During the anticipation phase, if an extreme event is not eminent, leaders may need to intervene to ensure vigilance is maintained (Pauchant & Mitroff, 1992; Pearson & Mitroff, 1993), focusing units on planning, training, and other preparedness efforts (McConnell & Drennan, 2006; Smits & Ally, 2003). During the anticipation stage, those in leadership positions need also to prepare the organization's physical infrastructure, establish monitoring systems, develop redundant essential services and emergency action plans, and develop positive social bonds and social networks and other capacities (Hannah et al., 2009a; Shrivastava, Mitroff, Miller, & Miglani, 1988). Context has a strong impact upon leadership, just as we know from Schein (2010) that organizational culture has a strong impact on leadership. However, although Schein has provided us with ways that leadership can have an impact upon culture, it is less clear intuitively how leadership can have an effect upon the extreme context external to the organization, short of deciding whether or not or the extent with which to engage in that context (e.g., an Army commander deciding whether to attack or not, or a fire chief deciding how many firefighters to deploy). We suspect that leaders largely only react to the external context, but as noted above, they can extensively influence the internal organizational context to enhance its readiness to take on extreme events through training, leader development, establishing cultures and systems that promote adaptability, and other preparedness efforts.

In situ. During an extreme event, in situ or what has been called in extremis (Kolditz, 2007), leaders and followers are dealing with terror and fear, aggression, and other potentially debilitating emotions (e.g., Arndt, Greenberg, Pyszczynski, Solomon, & Simon, 1997; Belenky, Noy, & Solomon, 1985; Foa & Kozak, 1986) as well as managing organizational complexity dynamics (Hannah, Lord, & Pearce, 2011; Marion & Uhl-Bien, 2001), complex knowledge networks and potential information overload, time compression, and many other factors that can reduce performance (Hannah et al., 2009a; Quarantelli, 1988). Leaders who are aggressive and who act quickly to reduce the ambiguity and fear associated with extreme events and who redirect followers toward specific purposeful actions are important in situ (Fodor, 1978). Quarantelli (1988) notes that if leadership is weak during nonstressful periods, "it will prove even weaker when disaster strikes" (p. 379). Due to the need to be responsive to leaders' directives under conditions where there might be little time for dialogue, trust in one's leader becomes paramount when operating in extreme events (Sweeney, Thompson, & Blanton, 2009).

Effectively, leadership can help followers' sense-make and manage the meaning of the complexity and turbulence of extreme contexts. Baran and Scott (2010) concluded this by using grounded theory method to research leadership operating in dangerous contexts. They analyzed 100 reports of "near miss" situations in which firefighters narrowly escaped injury or death, to generate a grounded theory of leadership within extreme events. They found leadership to be a collective sense-making process in which ambiguity is reduced, and consequently salience is promoted in the face of danger, via interactions between leaders and followers. Communication and behavior are parts of the process that they called "organizing ambiguity."

In this way, leaders impact upon the cultural and other characteristics of the context, in order to maximize the impact that leadership can have upon the achievement of outcomes. Faris and Parry (2011) found this phenomenon to be so in less extreme contexts. They found that people demonstrating leadership might reconstruct the context via discourse and narrative as well as by physical restructuring. However, we suggest that in extreme contexts the role of leadership in redefining context and in sense-making is much stronger. This is because extreme contexts and extreme events are by definition non-normal, and thus sense made in normal contexts might no longer apply and new sense-making is required. Sense-making in situ is particularly critical, as noted by Weick (1988, p. 305), because "the less adequate the sense-making process directed at a crisis, the more likely it is that the crisis will get out of control." Weick argues that it is in new or novel situations such as crises that we often learn by doing and then monitoring the effects of our action, adjusting "on the fly." However, those exploratory actions, if ineffective can also exasperate the volatility or extremity of the situation. Leadership influence on sense-making is thus critical in achieving effective and rapid learning to make corrections as needed.

Other phenomena might be operating in situ. For example, when groups operate in extreme events the social distance between followers and those in leadership positions may be reduced if they are sharing risks and hardships (Cole, Bruch, & Shamir, 2009; Little, 1964; Stouffer et al., 1965). The effects of extreme contexts or events on social distance thus may infer a mediated moderated effect, where context influences social distance, which in turn moderates the effects of leadership on outcomes. For example, social distance has been found to moderate the effects of transformational leadership (Howell et al., 2005).

Post hoc. Finally, after extreme events effective leadership might be that which restores systems, procedures, and resources (Porfiriev, 1996), and again assists followers in making sense of the recent experience (Faris & Parry, 2011; Foldy, Goldman, & Ospina, 2008) and that allows followers to reflect in a supportive environment (Moxley & Pulley, 2004). Pearson and Clair (1998) proposed that organizations require "psychic reorganization" after extreme events to restore individuals' assumptions about themselves, their organization, and the way the world works. Trauma from extreme events could threaten individuals' sense of safety (Taylor, 1983) and can create maladies such as battle fatigue or shell-shock (Belenky et al., 1985). After extreme events leadership must thus be concerned with addressing any psychological injuries that might have occurred such as post-traumatic stress disorder (PTSD). Yet through the learning and meaning-making described above, the actions of leadership may be an important factor in whether individuals experience PTSD, or alternatively, post-traumatic growth (PTG) as they grow stronger from challenges faced (Tedeschi & Calhoun, 2004).

During this post-hoc phase, leaders also must regain vigilance and prepare their units for the next extreme event. Part of the essence of leadership in this phase is again sense-making (Pye, 2005), also referred to by Smircich and Morgan (1982) as the management of meaning, and by Parry (1999) as enhancing adaptability. Intuitively, this characteristic of leadership seems to be so much more important in extreme contexts, especially because of the temporal complexity of such contexts. Therefore, an important aspect of leadership in extreme contexts revolves around the ability to (re)define the context such that followers know what is expected of them, and how they should act in similar contexts in the future. Thus, people in leadership positions should focus on individual, team, and organizational learning (Argyris & Schon, 1978; Hannah & Lester, 2008) in the post-hoc phase to prepare followers for extreme contexts by helping them to redefine prior experiences. Here they can prepare followers for those specific potential contexts that they might face, both with the skills and abilities needed for those contexts, but also the psychological preparation needed to succeed under threatening, extreme conditions.

Entrainment of leadership. The transitions between phases noted above make it critical to understand the entrainment of leadership. Collectives such as teams sequence through performance cycles, where the processes the team uses and the emergent states that develop from those processes (e.g., cohesion or team potency) during one performance cycle influence how well the team engages in future performance cycles (Marks, Mathieu, & Zaccaro, 2001). For example, Hannah, Walumbwa, and Fry (2011) investigated action teams operating in an intense military training context and found that teams who shared leadership more and engaged with each other more authentically (e.g., transparently and with moral perspective) displayed higher levels of teamwork and performed better on team tasks over time. Based on the model of Marks et al. (2001), we would expect that the sense of teamwork that these teams built would facilitate performance in the next performance cycle these teams faced. Further, as shared authentic leadership was found to promote performance, we would expect those teams to learn through feedback that sharing such leadership in the future would promote performance, thus sponsoring shared leadership in future team tasks and performance cycles. It is therefore critical to assess the entrained nature of leadership as a collective cycles through the anticipatory, in-situ, and post-hoc phases of extreme contexts by assessing actions taken and processes used, resulting emergent states created, and their effects on future performance cycles. How these entrained effects operate, however, will likely be influenced by the sense-making and learning employed in leadership systems, as described above, and how they influence the interpretation of feedback.

Form of Threat

The final aspect of extreme contexts that we will cover here is the form of risk or threat being faced. Hannah et al. (2009) proposed that "consequences could be classified as physical (e.g., death, injury, exhaustion), psychological (e.g., post-traumatic stress, shell shock), or material (e.g., hurricane or fire damage to a city)" (p. 908). It is likely that each form creates different psychological, physical, and social effects that influence leadership or its effects on individuals, groups, and organizations.

For example, when faced with physical risk mortality salience is heightened and unit members might experience terror and other extreme emotions (Arndt et al., 1997; Bowlby, 1969; Foa & Kozak, 1986; Janoff-Bulman & Freize, 1983; Parks, 1971). Individuals would be unlikely to experience mortality salience when their physical well-being is not at direct risk, and thus would likely face other reactions to material or psychological threats that will differentially influence leadership processes. If a unit is not exposed to direct physical threat but their psychological well-being is threatened, for example, leadership may need to address and will be impacted by other phenomenon. Consider the rescue crews that arrived at the Twin Towers on 9/11 after the primary death and destruction ended and were faced with exposure to intense human suffering and devastation. Here we assume that effective leadership was not that which focused on followers' fear, but that addressed followers' needs for coping (Janoff-Bulman & Frieze, 1983; Moxley & Pulley, 2004) and sense-making (Foldy et al., 2008) among other needs. Finally, threats of material losses might evoke other causal or contingent effects on leadership. A business without insurance or that is underinsured facing destruction in a flood, for example, may create unique influence on leadership processes as the owner, and to lesser extent employees, face financial loss or loss of livelihood. Forms of risk can be manifold, however, as individuals could face physical, psychological, and material risks in tandem. These few examples highlight the various dynamic human reactions to varying forms of threat that researchers need to consider, which might appear separately or in combination.

The Internal Context—Organizational Forms Operating in Extreme Contexts

In thinking about leadership in extreme contexts it is critical to understand that what is perceived to be extreme is comparative or relative to the organization and its level of preparation and potential to address risks that it may face. Leonard and Howitt (2007) discuss that organizations can face *routine* or *non-routine* extreme events. What is considered "routine" is idiosyncratic to individual organizations as outlined above and the frequency they find themselves in a particular extreme context. A large police department with extensive resources, training, experience and expert organizations (e.g., hostage negotiation unit) to deal with hostage situations, for example, would likely perceive a hostage crisis as less extreme than a lesser-resourced or ill-prepared police department in the same situation. Thus we need to not only consider the external context but also the internal context of the organization when assessing what constitutes an extreme context or event.

In the context of disasters, Turner (1976, p. 378) notes that organizations are "cultural mechanisms developed to set collective goals and make arrangements to deploy available resources to attain those goals." Hannah et al. (2009a) note that there are four general types of organizational contexts that each produce unique impacts on leadership when confronting extremity: (1) naïve organizations, (2) trauma organizations, (3) high reliability organizations, and (4) critical action organizations. While there are exceptions, these forms of organizations each likely have general internal characteristics that influence the way they interact with and operate within external extreme contexts. These forms of organizations are described in detail in Hannah et al. (2009a) so are only briefly summarized here.

Naïve Organizations

Naïve organizations are those thrust into extreme contexts or facing extreme events by chance. This could include a building hit by a tornado, a restaurant being robbed, a hotel fire, or similar unexpected events. Naïve organizations normally have only minimal preparations and systems in place to respond to extremity. Pauchant and Mitroff (1992) proposed that such organizations often underestimate potential threats and fail to prepare, thinking "it won't happen to us," and it is difficult for leaders to therefore overcome complacency (e.g., D'Aveni & MacMillan, 1990; Kiesler & Sproull, 1982).

Trauma Organizations

Trauma organizations include hospital emergency rooms, emergency medical technicians and ambulance teams, disaster response units, and similar other organizations that react to extreme events. These organizations are normally highly specialized and are also highly reactive as they have little control over where and when they will face extreme conditions—they are largely "waiting on the call." Trauma organizations must thus always be vigilant and responsive and able to surge their services as needed. They may also operate in extreme events with great frequency. Think of an emergency room in a major city where numerous critical patients might arrive hourly. In general, the more one is exposed to a threat or risk, the less that risk is perceived as threatening (Benner, 1984). Therefore, in those trauma organizations that operate in repetitive cycles of extreme events, what was once seen as extreme can in fact become somewhat "normal," and managers must thus ensure that complacency is prevented and that vigilance is maintained (Pauchant & Mitroff, 1992; Pearson & Mitroff, 1993). This repetition, however, provides the opportunity for high-quality organizational learning and the formation of highly refined team processes and systems.

Another unique aspect of trauma organizations is that the members of the organization are rarely at personal significant risk. While hospital workers might get infected, for example, the incidents are of extremely low base rates. This may create specific causations and contingencies that differ from extreme contexts where organizational members themselves are at primary risk, such as in a military unit. Yet, members of trauma organizations may often have the fate of others (e.g., patients) in their hands, which can create unique psychological processes.

High Reliability Organizations

High reliability organizations (HROs, Weick, 1993; Weick & Sutcliffe, 2001; Weick, Sutcliffe, & Obstfeld, 1999) are those that are largely focused on preventing or containing extreme events. As the title says, they therefore must be highly reliable. Examples are nuclear power plants, disease control organizations, or aircraft carrier flight decks. Hannah et al. (2009a) consider "normal" police operations (e.g., not SWAT, high-risk undercover operations, arrest warrant operations, etc.) in the HRO category. This is because they primarily focus on crime prevention and rarely engage in extreme events. Very few police officers, for example, will ever fire their weapon in the line of duty, much less use deadly force (Geller & Scott, 1992).

HROs or their members can certainly face extreme events when things go amiss as the Fukushima nuclear reactor incident in Japan evidences. As their focus is on prevention of extreme events, HROs tend to be highly administrative and control focused (Weick & Sutcliffe, 2001; Weick, et al., 1999), and tend to focus heavily on risk management systems and on the signal detection of potential systems failures (Glendon, Clarke, & McKenna, 2006).

Critical Action Organizations

Critical action organizations (CAO) is a new categorization proposed by Hannah et al. (2009a) to clearly distinguish organizations that purposely and proactively engage in extreme events from the more prevention-focused HROs. Indeed, Hannah and colleagues note that some organizations may even purposely *create* extreme events, such as an infantry commander launching an attack, a special operations military unit conducting a raid, or a SWAT team raiding a drug lab. The frequency of extreme events that a CAO faces might be of less frequency than a trauma organization such as an ambulance team, but those events are likely marked by two key factors. First, the intensity and potential magnitude of consequences CAOs face, in terms of death, destruction, and other potential outcomes, can be extensive. Second, members of CAOs are more likely placed at personal risk. Whether they are creating or reacting to an extreme event, such as a firefighting unit responding to a major fire, members of CAOs are likely to have "skin in the game," where the outcomes of leadership can influence the safety of team members. This outcome dependency may create unique causations and contingencies than are typically found in other types of organizations where risk to team members may be less probable.

Organizational Composition

Based on the forms of organizations outlined generally above, leadership researchers interested in studying leadership in extreme contexts should also consider the composition of the organization. First, through attraction, selection, and attrition (ASA) processes (Schneider, 1987; Schneider, Goldstein & Smith, 1995) each of the forms of organizations, and more specifically the organizations within them, likely develop unique compositions of people, which in turn influence leadership processes. People attracted to the nursing profession or to be a nuclear reactor engineer, for example, likely differ from those attracted to join the military or firefighting professions on various important physical and psychological dimensions that should be accounted for in research. Many organizations that engage in extreme contexts also have strict entrance requirements (e.g., based on physical, intellectual, moral (e.g., criminal record), age, and gender standards), as well as systems to cull and vet from their ranks those who do not meet standards, thus creating some level of homogeneity in their members over time. These factors should also be accounted for when investigating leadership in extreme contexts. Homogeneity will influence leadership to the extent that diversity influences leadership processes (Milliken & Martins, 1996). Group homogeneity has been linked, for example, to higher levels of member commitment, cohesion, and other desirable social phenomenon; and to reduced levels of intragroup conflict and turnover (see van Knippenberg, De Drue, & Homan, 2004). Accordingly, group homogeneity may facilitate sense-making (Pye, 2005), organizing ambiguity (Baran & Scott, 2010), and enhancing adaptability (Parry, 1999). Yet, homogeneity can also restrict knowledge creation and the introduction of new ideas (Webber & Donohue, 2004).

Yet, broad generalizations should be not be made by researchers, such as lumping all "military" together as if it was a homogeneous category. The composition of an air force financial accounting unit might differ significantly from a U.S. Marine sniper unit or the British SAS. Thus as we proposed earlier, micro-contexts need to be assessed. This is particularly important as the various units inside any organization assume greater or lesser risk of engaging in extreme contexts at the micro-context level. For example, within the larger organization of the "U.S. Military," in Iraq and Afghanistan between October 2001 and June 2010, of the U.S. combat deaths sustained, 73.2 per cent came from the Army and 23 per cent from the Marine Corps. The Navy and Air Force combined represented less than 3 per cent of overall deaths, even though they comprised over 40 per cent of the deployed force (Powers, 2010). At an even more refined micro-context level, infantry and other combat units inside the Army, for example, sustained higher casualty rates than noncombat units. Thus generalizing organizations as being more or less extreme would mask the more refined micro-contexts that should be classified, based on factors such as those we have provided in our framework.

Further, many of the professions that operate in extreme contexts, such as firefighting, law enforcement, or military, are closed systems, as they do not generally allow lateral entry into the profession. Except in rare cases, every police captain started as a patrolman, and every general was once a lieutenant, and worked their way up through the system. This is required due to the need to gain unique professional expertise that is not generally available outside of the profession, and thus must be gained through repetitive practice over many years of a career at successively higher levels. Those in leadership positions at all levels therefore come up through somewhat similar experiences, training, and education. Leaders also often have greater tenure in the organization than followers at lower levels; and this may create unique influence dynamics such as might come from their perceived expert power. In closed systems without lateral entry, members also often stay with the organization for an extended time, which might impact constructs such as organizational identity and organizational commitment. These and other phenomenon can create unique contingencies that influence leadership processes that differ from organizations without closed systems.

Future Research Directions

We have outlined various major factors that can be used to typify external and internal (i.e., intra-organizational) extreme contexts. Researchers can use these factors to help classify and contextualize their theories and investigations. We now present a series of future directions for research that may guide researchers in studying the nascent area of leadership in extreme contexts. These directions are certainly not exhaustive but offer select areas for initial focus.

Developing Individuals for Leadership Positions in Extreme Contexts

Much more research is needed to understand the knowledge, skills, abilities, and attributes needed by formal and informal leaders to be effective in extreme contexts, and how such KSAAs are developed. Indeed, as a field we know very little, empirically, about how leadership is developed in general. DeRue and Wellman (2009), for example, stated, "... we know very little about the processes by which individuals develop the skills and capabilities necessary to lead effectively" (p. 868). Day, Harrison, and Halpin (2009) have created an integrative conceptual model for leader development, stating that their theory "was developed with the U.S. Army in mind" (p. 3). We believe that this well-developed framework can be generalized to other organizations operating in extreme contexts. Yammarino et al. (2010) have provided a multilevel model of team development for extreme contexts, while Palmer et al. (2011) have discussed leader development for extreme contexts, focused on individual leader capacities such as leader self-identity, moral/ethical capacity, cognitive capacity and adaptive expertise, self-regulatory ability, self-efficacy, and goal orientation. Fisher et al. (2010) provides another set of leader attributes thought needed for leading in extremis, as has Kolditz (2007). For parsimony, we will not outline those frameworks in detail here, but do suggest that researchers work to operationalize and test various aspects of these models as a starting point.

We believe that self-identity is a critical component of these frameworks. Fry and Kriger (2009) identified the importance of identity when researching leadership in context. Knowledge, skills, and abilities are linked to identity structures and other deep meta-cognitive structures that facilitate employing those skills in the future (Lord & Hall, 2005). Therefore, who the leader is or perceives themselves to be might be at least as important as the traits or skills that the person possesses or the behaviors that the leader engages in. This issue might be even more important in organizations that prepare for extreme contexts and where skills are determined well in advance and behaviors are trained and practiced in detail, which can lead to highly developed identities related to the expert roles required for extreme contexts. For example, Hannah, Jennings, and Ben-Yoav Nobel (2010) sought to define what constitutes a complex tactical military leader identity. Through three qualitative studies based upon interviews with experienced leaders and using grounded theory analysis, they developed an expert model that outlines five critical identities that expert tactical military leaders possess (i.e., tactical warfighter, nation builder, intelligence gatherer, team leader/developer, and diplomat/negotiator), as well as the associated KSAAs needed to adaptively perform each of those roles. A rich and differentiated identity then facilitates access to and the tailoring of skills to unique leadership role demands (Hannah, Woolfolk, & Lord, 2009; Lord & Hall, 2005), which neuroscience research has shown leads to greater leader adaptability in complex and volatile situations (Hannah, Balthazard, Waldman, Jennings, & Thatcher, 2013). Thus, the difference in the impact of leadership within extreme contexts might well be determined by the identity that is manifested by the person in the leadership role. As (leader) identity is important in this research, so too might be the role of narrative and the assessment of leaders' life stories (Shamir & Eilam, 2005).

From an external perspective, followers have significant outcome dependency stemming from the decisions of their leaders. Thus, the extent to which the person in the leadership role is seen to be (for example) ethical, trustworthy (Fisher et al., 2010; Sweeney, 2010), capable and so on, might determine the impact of their leadership. Certainly, there is a huge need to determine the nuances associated with the relationship between identity and leadership effectiveness in extreme contexts.

Developmental trajectories. Based on our earlier discussion of nonlinearity, such nonlinear effects should also be considered when assessing leader and team development for extreme contexts. Leadership development is idiosyncratic, with different people developing along different trajectories (Day & Sin, 2011). And within person, individuals develop leadership capability nonlinearly over time, requiring a longitudinal approach to assessing development (Day, 2011). We suspect that development in extreme contexts may be particularly nonlinear, due to the inherent discontinuities and jolts that can occur. Developmental trajectories, however, are likely influenced by factors such as the quality of sense-making occurring in the group as outlined earlier (Foldy et al., 2008; Weick, 1988, 1993), and the effectiveness of the organizational learning processes employed (Argyris & Schon, 1978; Hannah & Lester, 2008), which should be assessed as moderators.

We also expect that the four forms of organizations that we outlined might have different learning and development trajectories. A trauma organization, such as a hospital emergency room, might cycle through fairly similar extreme events in a recurring fashion, such as treating heart attack victims, providing such organizations many opportunities to learn in a more incremental manner. An HRO, such as a nuclear power plant, may conduct periodic training drills or simulations for potential catastrophes, but likely will never experience one. If an extreme event does occur, learning and development would likely be quite discontinuous.

Finally, leadership development for extreme contexts is likely heavily influenced by individual differences. Leading in any situation is a risky endeavor, requiring the individual to take on personal responsibility for others and for collective performance (Chan & Drasgow, 2001). In extreme contexts, the outcome dependency placed on the leader can be intense, potentially including the lives of team members. These conditions might well make individual differences critical in predicting the level that leaders pursue tough developmental experiences and the extent that they engage in those experiences. Constructs such as motivation to lead (Chan & Drasgow, 2001) and leader developmental readiness (Avolio & Hannah, 2008; Day et al., 2009; Hannah & Avolio, 2010) may thus be critical factors in such leader engagement, and therefore, the slope of their developmental trajectories. Day and Sin (2011) state, "those individuals with the motivation and ability to learn from experience are most likely to demonstrate the strongest developmental trajectories as leaders over time" (p. 546). Further, leadership efficacy has been proposed to be critical for leader effectiveness under crisis and extreme situations (Hannah, Avolio, Luthans, & Harms, 2008; Hadley, Pittinsky, Sommer, & Zhu, 2011) as empirical research in military units has demonstrated (Hannah, Avolio, Walumbwa, & Chan, 2012).

Developing Collective Requisite Complexity

Extreme events are not only dynamic and unfold over time as we have described, but they are also inherently complex (Hannah et al., 2009). In complex contexts interdependent factors collapse together in unexpected ways and what might appear to be isolated events can interact to generate unpredictable outcomes over time (Cilliers, 1998; Marion & Uhl-Bien, 2001; Uhl-Bien, Marion, & McKelvery, 2007). Future research on leadership in extreme contexts could thus benefit from incorporating complexity theory.

One of the core aspects of complexity leadership theories is that social systems in complex organizational contexts are inherently unpredictable and thus the effects of individual formal and informal leaders on outcomes are rarely directly observable and may not be deterministic (Marion & Uhl-Bien, 2001). Instead, emergent processes occur as the interactions of individuals across levels and social networks produce new patterns of behavior, operating, and organizing that ultimately result in system-level adaptation (Uhl-Bien et al., 2007; Marion & Uhl-Bien, 2001). This "bottom-up" approach is somewhat counter to traditional theorizing on leadership processes. Indeed, largely neglected in leadership research has been research into the impact that individuals have on the context and the impacts of followers who take on informal leadership roles on their leaders and groups (Liden & Antonakis, 2009).

People in leadership positions can certainly influence these bottom-up emergent properties, but not control them. In extreme contexts, particularly, the dynamics of the external context cannot be controlled, and the organization's internal adaptations to those external forces cannot be fully estimated or controlled. Further, events may unfold too quickly where followers and lower-level formal leaders do not have the time to seek guidance when making decisions. Therefore, future research should investigate, based on complexity dynamics, how leaders can set the conditions whereby the organization can adapt effectively to extreme contexts through emergent social dynamics.

Hannah, Lord, and Pearce (2011) described the notion of *collective requisite complexity* (CRC). CRC in essence argues that the group or organization must be able to generate levels of complexity that are requisite to (i.e., that match) the level of complexity in its environment in order to have adaptive capacity. Too little complexity prevents the group from properly assessing and adapting to its environment while too much complexity can lead to chaos and a lack of direction. Hannah et al. (2011) describe CRC as having two aspects. First is *collective static complexity*, which is a product of group composition representing (a) the level of cognitive, social, affective, and self-complexity of each individual (Day & Lance, 2004; Hooijberg, Hunt, & Dodge, 1997; Lord, Hannah, & Jennings, 2011); and (b) the extent that the complexity of the individuals in the group is sufficiently heterogeneous (i.e., not redundant) (Weber & Donahue, 2001; Miliken & Martins, 1996). Collective static complexity, however, only provides opportunity structures that must be leveraged. Therefore, the second aspect of CRC is *collective dynamic complexity*, which can be created through social interactions that not only draw out the complexity of individual group members and promotes (versus excludes or suppresses) their engagement in group leadership processes, but that further cocreates additional complexity in situ as individual's sense-make together and build upon the complexity of each other.

Future research should thus assess how CRC can be developed in organizations operating in extreme situations. Theoretical (e.g., Day & Lance, 2004; Hannah et al., 2009; Lord et al., 2011) and empirical (Hannah, et al., 2010, 2013) research on leader complexity can be leveraged to assess static complexity at the individual level as can work on group composition be used to assess static complexity at the collective level (Miliken & Martins, 1996; van Knippenberg, De Drue, & Homan, 2004; Weber & Donahue, 2001). Dynamic complexity could be informed by research on shared leadership processes (Conger & Pearce, 2003; Pearce, Conger, & Locke, 2008; Pearce & Sims, 2002) through which the capacity of individuals is leveraged such that the right individuals with the right knowledge, skills, abilities, and attributes emerge in serial at the right time and right place to influence the group. Dynamic complexity can also be informed by research on sense-making and sense-giving (Baran & Scott, 2010; Foldy et al., 2008; Gioia & Chittipeddi, 1991; Weick, 1988, 1993), whereby collectives dynamically formulate an understanding of their environment and repertoires of possible solutions to problems.

The challenge for individuals in formal leadership positions, then, is how to establish an adequate level of structure while still generating CRC. Uhl-Bien et al. (2007) suggest that in complex contexts leaders need to establish an effective balance of adaptive versus administrative forms of organizing. What is an effective balance, however, may change across extreme contexts, and we suggest, organizational forms. Some extreme contexts are inherently more controllable, such as a hospital emergency room, as compared to a more dynamic context like military combat. What is clear from the complexity literature, however, is that an excessive use of administrative control suppresses emergence and thus restricts the ability for lower-level units to adapt to complexity dynamics. Further, because we have noted that leadership is contextualized differently before, during, and after extreme events, differing mixes of adaptive and administrative leadership may also be required across time and phases.

Future research is thus needed to determine how senior managers ready their organizations to implement adaptive emergent processes that create CRC, and how they then implement a mix of administrative controls and adaptive organizing during extreme events. Research into organizational readiness might assess what training, education, and development is required, and what types of systems and processes (e.g., command and control and knowledge-sharing systems, and resource allocation processes) best facilitate adaptation. Future work might also assess how various forms and structures of distributed leadership systems operate in extreme contexts. Finally, whether leadership and emergence can be adaptive might depend in part on the type of organizational culture, and whether that culture promotes delegation and initiative.

Effective Leadership across Phases of Extreme Contexts

The discussion of complexity dynamics and administrative and adaptive organizing raise research questions about what type of leadership is most effective across the phases of preparation, in-situ, and post-hoc extreme events. Further, we earlier noted that leadership is entrained across phases, with leadership in one phase influencing leadership in other phases. From a complexity theory perspective, effective leadership might be that which prepares the organization, physically, mentally, emotionally, and culturally, for adaptive response in the preparation phase; that then intervenes to shape but not control emergent dynamics in situ; and that then attempts to make sense out of emergent structures and establish a "new normal" for the organization in the post-hoc phase (Hannah et al., 2009: Uhl-Bien et al., 2007; Uhl-Bien & Marion, 2009). Further, developing requisite collective complexity may require that these various tasks of leadership are shared and performed by systems of formal and informal leaders across the group. There thus are numerous research questions related to leadership operating across these phases. Yet, there are also more refined questions to ask such as what is the best leadership "style" in various extreme contexts, based on the numerous permutations of extreme contexts that can arise based on the external and internal contextual factors outlined earlier.

We know that context imposes contingencies on leadership styles. For example, Currie and Lockett (2007) concluded that context can limit transformational leadership, and that transformational leadership was stronger in public sector than in private sector organizations. Levels and forms of extremeness are just some dimensions of context, and although it is intuitively appealing to suggest that transactional leadership is most effective in extreme contexts, this issue really needs to be tested fully. Situational theories of leadership are probably not relevant because the characteristics of the context can change so quickly. Implicit within situational theories are a level of managerial control over the context, and we have noted that in extreme contexts we are more concerned with high variability.

Limited research has noted that under stress and threat, followers might tend to look to leaders for direction and action guidance, suggesting directive leadership may be more effective during extreme events (Flanagan & Levy, 1952; Gladstein & Reilly, 1985; Isenberg, 1981). For example, Mulder, de Jong, Koppeaar, and Verhage (1986) found that military officers who used consultation in non-extreme situations were seen as more effective by their followers, but in extreme contexts leader consultation behaviors were not correlated with effectiveness. Prior research, however, has not assessed a range of leadership behaviors and how that range relates to outcomes across varying contexts, nor assessed how the leadership style used in one situation is entrained with leadership styles used in previous and future situations. By using a measure reflecting a range of behaviors, such as the eight sets (nine sets in some formulations) of leader behaviors reflected in the Full Range Leadership Model (Avolio, 2011; Bass & Avolio, 2000) (i.e., laissez-faire, management by exception passive and active, transactional, and four transformational dimensions) researchers could conduct refined assessments of the relative effects of various leadership styles across contexts and phases.

Such an investigation using a multifactor measure could also assess the entrainment of leadership styles. One useful theory might be that of *idiosyncrasy credits* (Hollander, 1964). Hannah et al. (2009) suggested that leaders can build "credits" from followers prior to extreme events through demonstrating competence and character, and then have credits to "spend" during extreme events that may allow them to be more directive, built on a prior base of trust. Indeed, leadership during extreme events is thought to normally become more directive and transactional, perhaps out of necessity due to time compression and the inability to collaborate (Dynes, 1983; Perrow, 1984). Therefore, the exemplary actions leaders can take before an extreme event may build idiosyncrasy credits, which then allows them to be more directive during extreme events based on the trust and confidence they have established. A study could, for example, measure the frequency of transformational leadership behaviors used prior to an extreme event (that may have created "credits"), and then use that variable as a moderator of the relationship between transactional leadership and performance outcomes during a subsequent extreme event.

Assessing the Nesting and Temporal Entrainment of Leadership

A logical progression from notions of collective complexity and of the phasing of extreme events is the notion of nesting. We have already identified that extreme events can be nested within certain contexts. For example, the context of firefighting can contain nested within it a number of very different events that have huge leadership implications that are subject to temporal and spatial variability. By contrast, one major firefighting event, for instance a "Black Saturday" event, can have nested within it a number of very different micro-contexts—headquarters leadership, evacuation procedures, and back-burning to name just a few. We proposed that the operation of leadership in extreme events cannot be properly understood without assessing the broader context operating prior to and during engagement in an extreme event. Yet leadership research has tended to not account for context either in theories or assessments of leadership (Avolio, 2007; Porter & McLaughlin, 2006). Nonetheless, the notion of nesting suggests that events can be nested within a context, and that micro-contexts can be nested within events. Therefore, one potential direction for future research is to tease out the relationship between context and event. To provide an example, picture the macro-context of a school. Normally a relatively moderate environment, it might have nested within it a number of extreme events that require leadership. One event could be a death in the playground, another could be a violence-induced school lockdown. Either event might have nested within it a number of micro-contexts, each one characterized by intense dynamic complexity and potentially large degrees of temporal variability.

Properly modeling leadership in extremis will require that the organizational and environmental contexts be considered, within which leadership is nested. We recommend that researchers not only employ standard assessments of various facets of organizational culture and climates (e.g. ethical, safety, or supportive climates), but as we suggested, factors like organization type (HRO, CAO, etc.), level of organizational training and readiness, and levels of adaptive versus administrative organizing. Beyond the organization, facets of the larger operating environment should also be considered, such as levels of stability and volatility, time compression, and other factors that will bear on or constrain leadership.

Further, we noted that individuals at varying levels of an organization are likely experiencing differing levels of physical and psychosocial proximity to an extreme event at any one time, thus there may be different "contexts" (perceived or real) operating at various organization levels. Further, given the time compression and reduced decision-making cycles that often accompany extreme events, the flow of information and decisions across levels may be affected. As described by Bluedorn & Jaussi (2008), time can be viewed in many important ways, such as point in history, duration of event, pace, speed, rhythm, and many other aspects that can inform leadership operating in dynamic extreme contexts. It is thus important that researchers assess leadership as operating as part of a multilevel system and assesses relevant constructs across levels of theory, measurement, and analysis (Yammarino & Dansereau, 2008). The nesting that goes on between events and contexts has huge implications for the modeling of leadership in extremis. The contrast between dynamic and static complexity should be included within this modeling, as should the variation in individual and collective complexity. Overlaying this collective complexity is the temporal variability and complexity of in extremis leadership. The intense variability associated with notions of nesting might lend itself toward "cinematic" method rather than "snap-shot" method. However, this modeling can be researched by a range of methods, as we shall soon see.

Character, Ethics, and Ethos

Extreme contexts and events, by their very definition, involve threat and risk. Therefore the study of ethics and what constitutes extra-ethical, virtuous behavior is an important area of future research. As compared to less extreme contexts, decisions made and actions taken are more likely to have ethical consequences, thus bringing the study of ethics to the forefront.

Members of organizations most likely to operate in extreme contexts largely serve others (e.g., firefighters, law enforcement, military and medical professions). Therefore, they are trustee professions and are expected to serve their "clients" with a certain character and set of values. Such professions are also expected to perform not just ethical, but extra-ethical behaviors. When everyone else is expected to run away from a fire, firefighters are expected to run toward it. When merchant ships are being recalled to harbor due to a storm, Coast Guard rescue ships and units are expected to go into the storm to look for those in trouble. If we are to understand leadership in extreme contexts, therefore, we must understand the character required of members of these organizations that promote "ethics beyond expectation" and the codes such organizations live by and teach to their new members. Along these lines, Wright and Quick (2011) propose that different occupations attract and socialize people with different "profiles in character" (p. 977). Wright and Quick (2011) also argue that high levels of character are required of leaders operating in extreme contexts.

Ethos and virtuous behavior. Organizational behavior and leadership studies have largely defined ethical behavior as doing what is expected morally and not breaking the rules, the absence of commissions of unethical acts. Hannah and Avolio (2011) argue that the leadership field should investigate the criteria space that lies beyond ethical behavior, what they termed "*extra-ethical, super-ethical,* or simply *virtuous* behavior" (p. 991). In the leadership literature, these are also known as supererogatory behaviors—behaviors that are morally commendable, but not morally required. Craig and Gustafson (1998) found a role for supererogatory behaviors when studying perceptions of leader integrity. In extreme contexts, Jennings and Hannah (2011) propose that such supererogatory behaviors must come from a sense of moral aspiration versus mere moral obligation. We believe this matter to be especially important for research on extreme contexts. Hannah and Avolio (2011) argue that such virtuous behavior stems from *ethos.* The term *ethos* is commonly used in military and other dangerous professions to represent the strength of character that compels one to "willingly endure the cognitive, emotional, and physical hardships normally associated with dangerous contexts—and if ultimately needed—to risk physical injury or death; all with little extrinsic reward" (Hannah et al., 2010, p. 180). Hannah and Avolio (2011) define ethos as "Extreme levels of strength of character required to generate and enable extra-ethical, virtuous behavior under conditions of high moral intensity and where personal risk or sacrifice is required in the service of others" (p. 992). Thus far, work on ethos has been theoretical. Future investigations of leadership in extreme contexts should seek to operationalize ethos and determine how ethos is developed in individuals and collectives, and influences virtuous behaviors in situ.

Ethical systems. Beyond the character or actions of specific individuals, the study of leadership systems is important to understand how ethics operate across levels in extreme contexts. Collectives develop collective norms for moral thinking and the ethical actions of group members (Power, Higgins & Kohlberg, 1989; Selznick, 1992). The mechanisms through which leadership can influence such "moral commons," however, require additional research.

Schaubroeck et al. (2012) studied ethical leadership and ethical culture across three distinct hierarchical levels (squad, platoon, and company levels) of U.S. Army combat units operating in Iraq. Their results showed that various follower outcomes related to ethical thoughts and behaviors were influenced by multiple sources of influence, including ethical leadership (Brown, Harrison, & Treviño, 2005) at multiple levels, as well as leaders' influence on ethical cultures at numerous levels. Treviño, Butterfield, and McCabe (1998) defined *ethical culture* as "a subset of organizational culture, representing a multidimensional interplay among various 'formal' and 'informal' systems of behavioral control that are capable of promoting either ethical or unethical behavior" (pp. 451–452). Many of the effects found by Schaubroeck et al. were mediated, or double-mediated through ethical leadership or ethical culture at the same level or one or more lower levels. This is especially important in extreme contexts, due to the inherent time compression for decision making and the often decentralized nature of operations as small specialized action teams operate. The findings of Schaubroeck et al. suggest that it is important that leaders set the context for ethical behavior through their indirect effects such as through establishing ethical culture and the cascading of their influence through leaders at lower levels.

In sum, due to the inherent moral implications of extreme contexts, researchers should assess how leadership impacts and is impacted by the ethical aspects of organizations. Such research should assess not only the character of individuals and collectives, but also the social systems in which they interact related to both leadership and culture. The dependent variables used in these investigations should also assess not just ethical behavior, but the extra-ethical virtuous acts that such extreme contexts may demand.

Leadership Effects on Stress

Extreme contexts, due to the presence of threats, create various physiological responses and introduce stressors (Gunnar & Quevedo, 2007). While a certain level of stress can improve attention and memory, excessive stress or exposure to stressors over extended periods can have negative effects on cognitive functioning (Kalat, 2009), which can reduce effectiveness in extreme contexts such as military combat (Belenky et al., 1985).

Little is known about how leadership can affect stress (Humprey, 2002), making this another critical area of research to advance. Caregivers, for example, have been found to mediate stress responses in youths (Gunnar & Quevedo, 2007). Leaders, like caregivers can provide social and emotional support for followers (Piccolo & Colquitt, 2006; Yukl, 2006), and aid in sense-making (Foldy et al., 2008; Weick, 1988). Future research should thus assess ways leaders can influence followers' physiological responses to threat.

Methods for Studying Leadership in Extreme Contexts

The next new direction we will offer for advancing research on leadership in extreme contexts is methodology, which is robust enough to warrant a new section here. Research in extreme contexts will require that we consider what qualitative and quantitative methodologies and analytic techniques might be best used. Further, it is important that our methods are able to capture the volatility operating in such contexts, such as various forms of nonlinear effects.

Qualitative Methodologies

Qualitative methodologies might be appropriate for the research of in extremis leadership. This is because qualitative methodologies lean toward a subjectivist interpretation of the lived experience of people in these contexts. Such an interpretation is in contrast to the objectivist and arm's length interpretation that usually comes from more quantitative methodologies. Qualitative researchers have been generally reticent to propose the generalizability of their findings from particular contexts; just as many quantitative researchers possibly have been too quick to generalize their findings across contexts. Nonetheless, Liden and Antonakis (2009) suggest that qualitative research, and case study work in particular, is well suited to researching variability in contexts. In the case of extreme contexts; micro-variability in contexts, the nature of specific events, and variation between anticipation, in-situ and post-hoc contexts; seem to be the issue most often in question.

Because extreme contexts might be problematic to create for quasi-experimental research, narrative analysis might provide insight into how leadership operates in such contexts. Narrative analysis can use narrative as data. It can also use narrative for analysis. Finally, it can use narrative as the outcome of the research. Narratives can integrate the range of variables that have an impact upon the process of leadership that is at work, vis-à-vis testing for a small range of predetermined variables. The inherently masculine nature of most extreme contexts lends them to using narrative data, and toward analyzing those data with narrative positivism. The masculine nature of most extreme contexts lends itself to experiences that can be seen, felt, and experienced readily. Narrative positivism uses narrative as data. It utilizes the concepts of masculine positivistic empiricism (Rhodes & Pullen, 2009) in order to code data. Narrative positivism attempts to determine causation (Abbott, 1992) and generalizability (Pentland, 1999), so the outcomes of such research should complement existing leadership research in other organizational settings.

Having said that, there is a role for experimentation, or quasi-experimentation, to enact leadership in extreme contexts and study it. Organizations like the military create extreme situations with which to train their soldiers. Because those situations can be re-created, they are researchable. Researchers can work with organizations to employ varying training or developmental interventions across groups and assess participants' thoughts, emotions, behaviors, or performance in extreme training contexts in comparison to groups in other experimental conditions.

Realism is another issue to be resolved in research on leadership in extreme contexts. The pursuit of realism seeks causal events and how they work out in a particular context (Ackroyd & Fleetwood, 2000). This appears to be the nature of the challenge for researchers here. Realist research, or at least the pursuit of realism, seems to be desirable for leadership in extreme contexts. It might even be considered de rigueur, if not an axiomatic empirical process for researching the extreme context. The pursuit of scientific realism is achieved with the use of positivist or scientific methodology that has dominated leadership research to date. However, critical realism might best be achieved with the use of case study and ethnographic research. Case study research involves intense detailed descriptions of leadership within context, using a range of data sources. Much extant leadership research is actually a form of case study research, although usually not articulated as such when written up.

On the other hand, ethnography involves the immersion of the researcher within the context, in order to generate emotionally rich subjectivist explanations of phenomena. The pursuit of critical realism involves the quest for a pragmatic or practically adequate explanation of phenomena rather than an explanation that is scientifically defensible. Kempster and Parry (2011) have articulated the value of critical realist research for the study of leadership, although no leadership research has yet been undertaken in extreme contexts that fall under this heading. An important component of critical realist research is to undertake the research in iterations, wherein findings are put to participants in order to ascertain the plausibility of the emerging explanation of the phenomenon.

Ethnographic documentaries (Hassard, 2009) are another methodology that has not yet been widely considered for research on leadership in extreme contexts phenomena. Ethnographic documentaries might include actual documentaries about events like 9/11. Other examples might be fictional movies made about events like warfare or firefighting or police work. For example, the movie *Ladder 49* might be used to prompt a focus group of firefighters to relive the leadership that was present in an extreme event that they experienced. The plausibility or otherwise of the visual narrative, along with the prompting of a researcher and the shared recollection of the members present, can generate a theoretical explanation of the ways in which the leadership process was enacted in the contexts that they experienced. The plethora of reality TV shows, including those about police work, customs work and airports, as well as the widespread availability of YouTube, help to provide a visual and audible quasi-reality that can assist participants and researchers to analyze the lived experience of people who experience leadership in extreme contexts.

Realism might be problematic to achieve in these ethnographic documentaries. However, these recreations of in extremis events help to revisit the lived experience of leaders and followers from such events. Researchers then get a richer and more explanatory insight into the lived experience of participants. In addition, the totality of the context can be covered through assessing the perspectives of multiple parties. Covering the totality of the context, behaviors, actions, emotions, and outcomes will result in richer research.

Another way to generate realism from research into leadership in extreme contexts might be with the use of autoethnography. Autoethnography is emotive and subjectivist research, and it is increasingly being integrated into organizational research (Boyle & Parry, 2007), although not yet into research on leadership in extreme contexts. It is hyperreflexive and can provide detailed insights into the lived experience of people in extreme contexts. People who have experienced leadership in extreme contexts might provide detailed narratives of their experiences. Autoethnography provides narratives that are autobiographical narratives that are intensely retrospective, reflexive, and emotive. The intensely emotive nature of many extreme events is brought to life with the autoethnographic narrative, and the role of leadership can be brought to life within these narratives. Boyle and Parry (2007) note that a central feature of autoethnography is the use of an aesthetic style of narrative text. It might take the form of personal essays, poetry, short stories, journals, stream of consciousness, detailed unstructured interview narratives, and other forms of fragmented writing. The sense of a pragmatic realism that is generated within the reader is a strength of this methodology.

Many people have experienced leadership in extreme contexts. Some of those people are researchers. Those people can undertake autoethnographies extremely effectively. The emotive hyperreflexivity of this methodology will provide rich research outcomes. However, it is not restricted to researchers who have experienced leadership in these particular contexts. Coconstructed (or coproduced) autoethnography is perhaps what is needed. Kempster and Stewart (2010) have undertaken it successfully. Stewart, a former Royal Marine and latterly a CEO, was the "auto" part of the research, or the subject of the autoethnography. Kempster was the ethnographer, who researched "over the shoulder" of Stewart as he relived his experiences and drew out a contribution to knowledge and theory. Together, research dyads like this can generate explanatory insights into leadership in extreme contexts. It is the coconstructed autoethnography that perhaps provides the greater opportunity for research of this genre.

The intensely dramatic nature of many extreme events and contexts also makes possible a dramaturgical analysis of these contexts. Most dramaturgical research utilizes Burke's (1975) dramatic pentad as the lens through which to research phenomena. The phenomenon under investigation is presented as a dramatic event or narrative. It is examined according to the following:

- Act—what was or will be done. What is going on?
- Scene—the context of act.
- Agent—who is involved in the action, and the roles of those agents.
- Agency—how the agents act. By what means do they act?
- Purpose—the goal of the act. Why do the agents act?

Gardner and Avolio (1998) theorized about the dramaturgical approach to understanding charismatic leadership. Sinha and Jackson (2006) and Sharma and Grant (2011) conducted dramaturgical research into leadership phenomena, albeit not into explicitly extreme contexts. Micro-narratives about extreme events could potentially be analyzed within the broader macro-narrative of the extreme context.

Quantitative Methodology

A major issue for research on leadership in extreme contexts is that of data. This issue is especially important in light of contemporary fashion for "evidence-based management" (Pfeffer & Sutton, 2006). Data triangulation helps to build methodological rigor into such research. However, gathering clean data, particularly in situ, while rich, can be problematic to obtain. Pre- and post-hoc survey data are clean and convenient, and dominate research on leadership in extreme contexts to date, yet the insight into momentary impact is lost. Bio-monitoring (e.g., heart rate or hormone levels) in situ is feasible in order to gather data about physiological and other similar responses. Secondhand reports are relevant and valid. However, they still are secondhand data creating limitations that must be recognized in analysis and theory building. Such documentary data helps, but that is all.

Further, extreme contexts are inherently variable and unstable and can change from moment to moment as micro-contexts and events change. This will require that our methods and analytical techniques can capture that variability. We need to better understand how leadership is impacted across time—perhaps even minute by minute in extreme contexts, and as a context becomes more or less extreme quite quickly. Therefore, methodologies should be used in the future that can incorporate this temporal variability in extremity. For example, the work of Fisher (2003) and Ilies and Judge (2004), in testing for temporal variability in the relationship between work and job satisfaction, was able to account for this variability. They utilized experience sampling to test momentary job satisfaction. Similarly, the relationship between leadership and context can use such a methodology. This will require that we go beyond traditional approaches and measure the high levels of *variability* and *nonlinearities* operating in extreme contexts. Variability (e.g. Cabral, 2003; Denrell, 2003; Kalnins, 2007; March, 1991; Sørensen, 2002; Taylor & Greve, 2006), and nonlinearities (Baum & McKelvey, 2006; Daft & Lewin, 1990; Starbuck, 2009) have been assessed in areas of research other than that of extreme contexts that could be used as prototype techniques to apply to extreme contexts. Liden and Antonakis (2009) suggest that Social Network Analysis and hierarchical linear modeling are also well suited to testing variability in context.

Variability. Theoretically, variability can be created through phenomenon such as amplifying mechanisms on spirals (George & Jones, 2000; Hackman, 1990; Hambrick & D'Aveni, 1988; Lindsley, Brass, & Thomas, 1995). Lindsley et al. (1995) describe, for example, how through social interactions efficacy can spiral over time to collective levels. Based on the types of team processes used, and the effects of those processes on team emergent states (e.g., team potency or efficacy), teams, for example, over time can get into "self-fueling spirals" that promote performance, or negative downward spirals that lead to failure (Hackman, 1990).

Further, one can imagine how constructs such as high levels of stress or fear operating in an extreme context can create significant levels of variability, such as through spirals over time. Fear can cause erratic behavior, and erratic behavior can create greater volatility in outcomes (e.g., team performance), which produces more fear, and so on. Methodologically, techniques to deal with variability can be gained from the statistics literature (e.g. Tsetlin, Gaba, & Winkler, 2004), with tools such as heteroskedasticity controls (Greene, 2003) and quantile regression (Greene, 2003) but have not generally been used in the leadership literature.

Nonlinearity. Beyond variability effects, various nonlinear phenomena are also operating in extreme contexts that should be assessed and modeled (Meyer, Gaba, & Colwell, 2005). Such nonlinearity has been labeled as discontinuities or jolts (Meyer, 1982), oscillations (Gaba & Meyer, 2008) or hyper-turbulence (Meyer, Brooks, & Goes, 1990). Think of a SWAT team that has a member killed in the line of duty. That "jolt" would likely result in a "spike" in the team's anger and aggression to retaliate, and also perhaps their fear, as the death of a team member might prime members' mortality salience and recognition that they are also in peril.

Besides the discontinuities that can occur moment to moment during extreme events in situ, researchers should assess nonlinearity that occurs as organizations or teams cycle through the anticipatory, in-situ, and post-hoc phases that may occur in extreme contexts outlined earlier. Think of how stress, for example, might operate. We know that a certain level of stress may be beneficial to maintain vigilance and performance up to a certain optimal level, past which point stress becomes detrimental, thus exhibiting a nonlinear relationship with outcomes, such as coping and performance (e.g., Nelson & Sutton, 1990). Yet, what has not been studied to our knowledge is whether what constitutes an optimal stress level shifts over time within person from situation to situation, as units prepare for extreme events, operate within them, and recover, and what the implications for those shifts are. Stress is therefore just one example of phenomenon that may create nonlinear patterns that have significant impacts on leadership processes and effects.

Construct change. Researchers should also consider that the constructs themselves might change between more or less extreme contexts. Constructs can change in measurement along three forms: *alpha*, *beta*, and *gamma* change (Golembiewski & Billingsley, 1980; Golembiewski, Billingsley, & Yeager, 1976; Thompson & Hunt, 1996). Type alpha is the predominant focus of behavioral research, where both the meaning and the measurement of a construct are considered stable. Therefore any changes in participants' ratings on the measure over time are expected to represent actual change along the scale, such as the level of trust in the leader has increased or decreased; or other changes in participants' attitudes, behavior, performance, development, etc., that occur over time.

Beta and gamma changes, however, are rarely theorized or assessed in organizational research, but may be especially important in understanding how constructs operate in extreme contexts. Beta change is represented when the meaning of the construct is unchanged in a respondent's mind, but they alter their measurement scaling. For example, Sweeney (2010) found that prior to deploying to combat, followers reassessed the extent that they trusted their leader and tended to hold them to higher standards. In this case, what they previously considered to be a "2" on a leader trust scale is recalibrated by the respondent to be, for example, a "4."

The third type of potential construct change is gamma change. In gamma change, respondents alter the conceptual meaning of a construct over time. For example, a respondent might have one conceptualization of what constitutes "leader effectiveness" in each of the three phases of preparation for, in-situ operations, and post-hoc recovery from extreme events. Responses to a leader effectiveness measure may thus be conceptually altered based on factors such as respondents' implicit leadership theories at each of these three points in time (Lord, Foti, & DeVader, 1984). Similarly, the conceptualization of what is considered "ethical" may change from a more "normal" context to one where decisions have to be made that might affect lives and well-being and where triage and prioritizations need to be made that force tough decisions where one value or belief has to be traded off for another.

Measuring tradeoffs. The tradeoff decisions that may be faced in extreme contexts suggest that researchers should consider the use of ipsative measures in some cases. Organizational researchers predominantly use normative measures that allow respondents to weigh each of various options independently. Ipsative measures instead require respondents to rank order different options or weight select ones over others (Saville & Willson, 1991). Consider as an example, asking a combat unit normative questions related to their attitudes toward the protection of noncombatants. A measure that instead asks them questions that force them to prioritize the protection of noncombatants versus the protection of their own troops, a situation commonly faced in combat, might illicit a markedly different pattern of results. We suggest that normative and ipsative measures can be used effectually in combination, with the latter reflecting the "hard choices" that need to be made in extreme events, such as an overloaded emergency medical team triaging, deciding which patients to treat or in what order, and which to not or to allow to suffer.

Predictive validity. A final aspect of methodology and analysis that might be considered by researchers is the predictive validity of constructs based on the levels of extremeness of the context. First, some constructs might be exclusively or particularly well suited for extreme contexts. Physical bravery, for example, may not be applicable to an accountant and thus has minimal predictive validity in a "normal" context. Yet, physical bravery could be highly predictive if there is a major fire at that firm, requiring entirely different forms of leadership from that accountant. Other constructs, such as mortality salience, may instantiate primarily only when exposed to physical risks.

Other constructs can be applicable to a greater extent across more and less extreme contexts, but their predictive validity might increase or decrease significantly. For example, group cohesion might be an important factor in any group in any context in predicting performance. Yet, when a group is facing an intense extreme event, the relationship between group cohesion and group performance might increase if maintaining cohesion becomes a critical factor, such as when facing a horrific situation which requires high levels of social support. Extreme contexts and events demand high levels of performance. Thus the literature on typical and maximum performance could be a good starting point to inform ways to assess differing levels of predictive validity across contexts and outcome measures (e.g., Sackett, Zedeck, & Fogli, 1988).

Further, we propose that extreme contexts may create threshold effects in some constructs. For example, a minimally sufficient level of some constructs may simply be a requirement. We could envision, for example, that when lives hold in the balance based on leaders' decisions, that trust in leaders' competence may exhibit such threshold effects. In this case, followers might demand a minimal level of trust, and if that threshold is not met, the leaders' level of influence is marginal at best. We would thus expect a nonlinear relationship between trust in leader, and leader influence, as outlined above. In this case, scores below the threshold and those above the threshold on the trust scale would exhibit quite different patterns of predictive validity.

Summary of Key Future Research Directions

- *Developing individuals for leadership positions in extreme contexts.* What are the knowledge skills, abilities, identity, other attributes, etc., needed to prepare individuals to succeed in formal and informal leadership positions?
- *Developing requisite complexity in organizations/units.* How are systems and networks of formal and informal leaders and systems of leadership created that generate complexity that is requisite to the complexity demands and dynamics of the context?
- *Leadership cycles and entrainment.* How does leadership and its effectiveness change and adjust as organizations cycle and transition from extreme contexts to extreme events and back, and through embedded or nested micro-contexts? How does leadership in one cycle influence leadership in future cycles?
- *Contextualization of leadership based on internal and external context.* How does the form of threat faced, physical and psychosocial proximity, organizational forms and compositions, and other factors internal and external to the organization uniquely contextualize leadership in extreme contexts/events?
- *Character and ethos.* What forms of character and ethos are required at the individual, unit, and organizational levels to sustain units operating in extreme contexts and events? How are individuals, organizational systems, climates, and cultures developed to sustain exemplary behavior under conditions of high moral complexity?

Conclusion

The leadership field has only begun to explore how leadership operates in extreme contexts and the development of individuals and collectives to enact effective leadership in such contexts. As a starting point for advancing this line of research we have argued that "extreme context" is not a general category, but must be decomposed into more refined categories and typologies if we are to better understand the implications for leadership. These categories include dimensions of the external context, including differentiating extreme events from extreme contexts, various forms of threat, issues of physical and psychosocial proximity, and temporal phasing pre-, in-situ, and post-extreme event. Each of these categories, and likely others we have not addressed all work to contextualize leadership uniquely. We also argued that the internal, intra-organizational context should be considered. Factors such as types of organizations, each with unique attraction, selection, and attrition processes should be considered in research, as should levels of organizational preparedness to operate in extreme contexts.

We also noted that pursuing research in extreme contexts will require that we consider the qualitative and quantitative methods that are best to use. Qualitative methods particularly might help us draw out the richness of leadership phenomenon operating in extreme contexts. Concerning quantitative methods, it is critical that our techniques are able to capture the variability in constructs and the nonlinear relationships occurring between contexts that might be accentuated in extreme contexts. Traditional methods and approaches to analysis may indeed misinform our theories if dynamics like threshold effects, spirals, and oscillations are not accounted for, as well as how constructs may change over time as reflected in alpha, beta, and gamma changes. Thus we have offered various ways to approach methodology in extreme contexts.

We have intended for this chapter to inform and promote researchers to conduct research related to leadership in extreme contexts. Toward that end we have identified example areas where additional research is needed. The examples provided, however, reflect only some starting points in this nascent area of research. Pursuing research in this area should not only inform practitioners and scholars on how leadership operates when it is perhaps needed most, but also will allow us to establish the boundaries and contingencies of current models of leadership in the literature that have largely thus far only been tested in relatively normal contexts.

References

Abbott, A. (1992). From causes to events: Notes on narrative positivism. *Sociological Methods and Research, 20*, 428–455.

Ackroyd, S., & Fleetwood, S. (2000). *Realist perspectives on management and organization studies*. London: Routledge.

Antonakis, J., & Atwater, L. (2002). Leader distance: A review and proposed theory. *The Leadership Quarterly, 13*, 673–704.

Argyris, C., & Schon, D. (1978). *Organizational learning*. Reading, MA: Addison Wesley.

Arndt, J., Greenberg, J., Pyszczynski, T., Solomon, S., & Simon, L. (1997). Suppression, accessibility of death-related thoughts, and cultural defense: Exploring the psychodynamics of terror management. *Journal of Personality & Social Psychology, 73*, 5–18.

Avolio, B. J. (2007). Promoting more integrative strategies for leadership theory building. *American Psychologist, 62*, 25–33.

Avolio, B. J. (2011). *Full range leadership development*. Thousand Oaks, CA: Sage.

Avolio, B. J., & Hannah, S. T. (2008). Developmental readiness: Accelerating leader development. *Consulting Psychology Journal, 60*, 331–347.

Bamberger, P. A., & Pratt, M. G. 2010. Moving forward by looking back: Reclaiming unconventional research contexts and samples in organizational scholarship. *Academy of Management Journal, 53*, 665–671.

Baran, B. E., & Scott, C. W. (2010). Organizing ambiguity: A grounded theory of leadership and sense-making within dangerous contexts. *Military Psychology, 22*, 42–69.

Bass, B. M. (1998). *Transformational leadership: Industrial, military, and educational impact*. Mahwah, NJ: Lawrence Erlbaum Associates.

Bass, B. M., & Avolio, B. J. (2000). *MLQ: Multifactor Leadership Questionnaire* (2nd ed.). Redwood City, CA: Mind Garden.

Baum, J. A. C., & McKelvey, B. 2006. Analysis of extremes in management studies. *Research Methodology in Strategy and Management, 3*, 125–199.

Belenky, G. L., Noy, S., & Solomon, Z. (1985). Battle stress: The Israeli experience. *Military Review, July*, 11–20.

Benner, P. E. (1984). *Stress and satisfaction on the job*. New York, NY: Praeger.

Bluedorn, A. C. & Jaussi, K. S. (2008). Leaders, followers, and time. *The Leadership Quarterly, 19*, 654–668.

Boal, K. B., & Hooijberg, R. (2000). Strategic leadership: Moving on. *Leadership Quarterly, 11*, 515–549.

Bowlby, J. (1969). Attachment and loss. *Volume 1: Attachment*. London: Hogarth.

Boyle, M., & Parry, K. W. (2007). Telling the whole story: The case for organizational autoethnography. *Culture & Organization, 13*(3), 185–190.

Brown, M., Harrison, D., & Treviño, L. (2005). Ethical leadership: A social learning perspective for construct development and testing. *Organizational Behavior and Human Decision Processes, 97*, 117–134.

Bruning, J. L. (1964). Leadership in disaster. *Psychology: A journal of human behavior, 1*, 19–23.

Burke, K. (1975). The five key terms of Dramatism. In D. Brissett & C. Edgley (Eds.), *Life as theater: A dramaturgical sourcebook* (pp. 411–418). Chicago, IL: Aldine Press.

Cabral, L.M.B. (2003). R&D competition when firms choose variance. *Journal of Economics & Management Strategy, 12*, 139–150.

Chan, K. Y., & Drasgow, F. (2001). Toward a theory of individual differences and leadership: Understanding the motivation to lead. *Journal of Applied Psychology, 86*, 481–498.

Cilliers, P. (1998). *Complexity and postmodernism: Understanding complex systems*. London: Routledge.

Cole, M. S., Bruch, H., & Shamir, B. (2009). Social distance as a moderator of the effects of transformational leadership: Both neutralizer and enhancer. *Human Relations, 62*, 1697–1733.

Conger, J. A., & Pearce, C. L. (2003). A landscape of opportunities: Future research on shared leadership. In C. L. Pearce & J. A. Conger (Eds.), *Shared leadership: Reframing the hows and whys of leadership* (pp. 285–303). Thousand Oaks, CA: Sage.

Craig, S. B., & Gustafson, S. B. (1998). Perceived leader integrity scale: An instrument for assessing employee perceptions of leader integrity. *The Leadership Quarterly, 9*, 127–145.

Currie, G., & Lockett, A. (2007). A critique of transformational leadership: Moral, professional and contingent dimensions of leadership within public services organizations. *Human Relations, 60*, 341–370.

Daft, R. L., & Lewin, A. Y. (1990). Can organizational studies begin to break out of the normal science straitjacket? An editorial essay. *Organization Science, 1*, 1.

D'Aveni, R. A., & MacMillan, I. C. (1990). Crisis and the content of managerial communications: A study of the focus of attention of top managers in surviving and failing firms. *Administrative Science Quarterly, 35*, 634–657.

Day, D. V. (2011). Integrative perspectives on longitudinal investigations of leader development: From childhood through adulthood. *Leadership Quarterly, 22*, 561–571.

Day, D. V., Harrison, M. M., & Halpin, S. M. (2009). *An integrative approach to leader development: Connecting adult development, identity, and expertise*. New York, NY: Psychology Press.

Day, D. V., & Lance, C. E. (2004). Understanding the development of leadership complexity through latent growth modeling. In D. V. Day, S. J. Zaccaro, & S. M. Halpin (Eds.), *Leader development for transforming organizations* (pp. 41–69). Mahwah, NJ: Lawrence Erlbaum Associates.

Day, D. V., & Sin, H. P. (2011). Longitudinal tests of an integrative model of leader development: Charting and understanding developmental trajectories. *Leadership Quarterly, 22*, 545–560.

Denrell, J. (2003). Vicarious learning, undersampling of failure, and the myths of management. *Organization Science, 14*, 227–243.

DeRue, S. D., & Wellman, N. (2009). Developing leaders via experience: The role of developmental challenge, learning orientation and feedback availability. *Journal of Applied Psychology, 94*, 859–875.

Dynes, R. (1983). Problems in emergency planning. *Energy, 8*, 653–660.

Faris, N., & Parry, K. W. (2011). Islamic organizational leadership within a Western society: The problematic role of external context. *The Leadership Quarterly, 22*(1), 132–151.

Fisher, C. D. (2000). Mood and emotion while working: Missing pieces of job satisfaction? *Journal of Organizational Behavior, 21*, 185–202.

Fisher, C. D. (2003). Why do lay people believe that satisfaction and performance are correlated? Possible sources of a commonsense theory. *Journal of Organizational Behavior, 24*, 753–777.

Fisher, K., Hutchings, K., & Sarros, J. (2010). The "bright" and "shadow" aspects of In Extremis leadership. *Military Psychology, 22*, S89–S116.

Flanagan, J. C., & Levy, S. (1952). *Development of an objective form of the leaders reaction test*. Pittsburgh, PA: American Institute for Research.

Foa, E. B., & Kozak, M. (1986). Emotional processing of fear: Exposure to corrective information. *Psychological Bulletin, 99*, 20–35.

Foldy, E. G., Goldman, L., & Ospina, S. (2008). Sensegiving and the role of cognitive shifts in the work of leadership. *The Leadership Quarterly, 19*, 514–529.

Fry, L., & Kriger, M. (2009). Towards a theory of being-centered leadership: Multiple levels of being as context for effective leadership. *Human Relations, 62*, 1667–1696.

Gaba, V., & Meyer, A. D. (2008). Crossing the organizational species barrier: How venture capital practices infiltrated the information technology sector. *Academy of Management Journal, 51*, 976.

Gardner, W. L., & Avolio, B. J. (1998). The charismatic relationship: A dramaturgical perspective. *Academy of Management Review, 23*, 32–58.

Geller, W., & Scott, M. S. (1992). *Deadly force: What we know*. Washington, DC: Police Executive Research Forum.

George, J. M., & Jones, G. R. (2000). The role of time in theory and theory building. *Journal of Management, 26*, 657–684.

Gioia, D. A., & Chittipeddi, K. (1991). Sensemaking and sensegiving in strategic change initiation. *Strategic Management Journal, 12*, 433–448.

Gladstein, D. L., & Reilly, N. R. (1985). Group decision-making under threat: The tycoon game. *Academy of Management Journal, 28*, 613–627.

Glendon, A. I., Clarke, S. G., & McKenna, E. (2006). *Human safety and risk management* (2nd ed.). Boca Raton, FL: CRC Press LLC.

Golembiewski, R. T., & Billingsley, K. R. (1980). Measuring change in OD panel designs: A response to critics. *Academy of Management Review, 5*, 97.

Golembiewski, R. T., Billingsley, K., & Yeager, S. (1976). The congruence of factor-analytic structures: Comparisons of four procedures and their solutions. *Academy of Management Review, 1*, 27.

Greene, W. H. (2003). *Econometric analysis* (5th ed.). Upper Saddle River, NJ: Prentice Hall.

Gunnar, M., & Quevedo, K. (2007). Biological and genetic processes in development. In S. T. Fiske, A. E. Kasdin, & D. L. Schacter (Eds), *Annual review of psychology* (pp. 145–176). Palo Alto, CA: Annual Reviews.

Hackman, J. R. (1990). *Groups that work (and those that don't): Creating conditions for effective teamwork* (1st ed.). San Francisco, CA: Jossey-Bass.

Hadley, C. N., Pittinsky, T. L., Sommer, S. A., & Zhu, W. (2011). Measuring the efficacy of leaders to assess information and make decisions in a crisis: The C-LEAD scale. *Leadership Quarterly, 22*, 633–648.

Hambrick, D. C., & D'Aveni, R. A. (1988). Large corporate failures as downward spirals. *Administrative Science Quarterly, 33*, 1.

Hannah, S. T., & Avolio, B. J. (2010). Ready or not: How do we accelerate the developmental readiness of leaders? *Journal of Organizational Behavior, 31*, 1181–1187.

Hannah, S. T., & Avolio, B. J. (2011). Leader character, ethos, and virtue: Individual and collective considerations. *The Leadership Quarterly, 22*, 989–994.

Hannah, S. T., Avolio, B. J., Luthans, F., & Harms, P. (2008) Leadership efficacy: Review and future directions. *Leadership Quarterly, 19*, 669–692.

Hannah, S. T., Avolio, B. J., Walumbwa, F., & Chan, A. (2012). Leader self and means efficacy: A multi-component approach. *Organizational Behavior and Human Decision Processes, 118*, 143–161.

Hannah, S. T., Balthazard, P. A., Waldman, D. A., Jennings, P. L., & Thatcher, R. W. (2013). The Psychological and Neurological Bases of Leader Self-Complexity and Effects on Adaptive Decision-Making. *Journal of Applied Psychology*. doi: 10.1037/a0032257

Hannah, S. T., Campbell, D. J., & Matthews, M. D. (2010). Advancing a research agenda for leadership in dangerous contexts. *Military Psychology, 22*, S157–S189.

Hannah, S. T., Jennings, P. L., & Ben-Yoav Nobel, O. (2010). Tactical military leader requisite complexity: Toward a referent structure. *Military Psychology, 22*, 1–38.

Hannah, S. T., & Lester, P. B. (2008). A multilevel approach to building and leading learning organizations. *Leadership Quarterly, 20*, 34–48.

Hannah, S. T., Lord, R. L., & Pearce, C. L. (2011). Leadership and collective requisite complexity. *Organizational Psychology Review, 1*(3), 1–24.

Hannah, S. T., Uhl-Bien, M., Avolio, B. J., & Cavarretta, F. (2009a). A framework for examining leadership in extreme contexts. *Leadership Quarterly, 20*, 897–919.

Hannah, S. T., Woolfolk, R. L., & Lord, R. G. (2009b). Leader self-structure: A framework for positive leadership. *Journal of Organizational Behavior, 30*, 269–290.

Hannah, S. T., Walumbwa, F. O., & Fry, J. (2011). Leadership in action teams: Team leader and members' authenticity, authenticity strength, and performance outcomes. *Personnel Psychology, 64*, 771–801.

Hassard, J. (2009). Researching work and institutions through ethnographic documentaries. Chapter 16 in David Buchanan & Alan Bryman (Eds.), *The Sage handbook of organizational research methods* (pp. 270–280). London: Sage Publications Ltd.

Hooijberg, R., Hunt, J. G., & Dodge, G. E. (1997). Leadership complexity and development of the leaderplex model. *Journal of Management, 23*, 375–408.

Hollander, E. P. (1964). *Leaders, groups, and influence*. New York, NY: Oxford University Press.

Howell, J. M., & Hall-Merenda, K. E. (1999). The ties that bind: The impact of leader–member exchange, transformational and transactional leadership and distance on predicting follower performance. *Journal of Applied Psychology, 84*, 680–694.

Howell, J. M., Neufeld, D. J., & Avolio, B. J. (2005). Leadership at a distance: The effects of physical distance, charismatic leadership, and communication style on predicting business unit performance. *The Leadership Quarterly, 16*, 273–286.

Humprey, R. H. (2002). The many faces of emotional leadership. *Leadership Quarterly, 13*, 493–504.

Ilies, R., & Judge, T. A. (2004). An experience-sampling measure of job satisfaction and its relationships with affectivity, mood at work, job beliefs, and general job satisfaction. *European Journal of Work and Organizational Psychology, 13*(3), 367–389.

International Institute for Strategic Studies. (2010). *The military balance*. London: Routledge.

Isenberg, D. G. (1981). Some effects of time pressure on vertical structure and decision-making accuracy in small groups. *Organizational Behavior and Human Performance, 27*, 119–134.

Janoff-Bulman, R., & Frieze, I. H. (1983). A theoretical perspective for understanding reactions to victimization. *Journal of Social Issues, 39*, 1–17.

Jennings, P. L., & Hannah, S. T. (2011). The moralities of obligation and aspiration: Towards a concept of exemplary military ethics and leadership. *Military Psychology, 23*, 1–22.

Kalat, J. W. (2009). *Biological psychology* (10th ed.). Belmont, CA: Wadsworth.

Kalnins, A. (2007). Sample selection and theory development: implications of firms' varying abilities to appropriately select new ventures. *Academy of Management Review, 32*, 1246–1264.

Kempster, S., & Stewart, J. (2010). Becoming a leader: A co-produced autoethnographic exploration of situated learning of leadership practice. *Management Learning, 41*(2), 205–219.

Kempster, S., & Parry, K. W. (2011). Grounded theory and leadership research: A critical realist perspective. *The Leadership Quarterly, 22*(1), 106–120.

Kiesler, S., & Sproull, L. (1982). Managerial response to changing environments: Perspectives on problem sensing from social cognition. *Administrative Science Quarterly, 27*, 548–570.

Kolditz, T. A. (2007). *In extremis leadership: Leading as if your life depended upon it.* Hoboken, NJ: John Wiley & Sons.

Leonard, H. B., & Howitt, A. M. (2007). Against desperate peril: High performance in emergency preparation and response. In D. E. Gibbons (Ed.), *Communicable crises: Prevention, response and recovery in the global arena* (pp. 1–25). Charlotte, NC: Info Age.

Liden, R. C., & Antonakis, J. (2009). Considering context in psychological leadership research. *Human Relations, 62*(11), 1587–1605.

Lindsley, D. H., Brass, D. J., & Thomas, J. B. (1995). Efficacy-performing spirals: A multilevel perspective. *Academy of Management Review, 20*, 645–678.

Little, R. W. (1964). Buddy relations and combat performance. In M. Janowitz (Ed.), *The new military: Changing patterns of organization.* New York: Russell Sage Foundation.

Lord, R. G., Foti, R. J., & DeVader, C. L. (1984). A test of leadership categorization theory: Internal structure, information processing, and leadership perceptions. *Organizational Behavior and Human Performance, 34*, 343–378.

Lord, R. G., & Hall, R. J. (2005). Identity, deep structure and the development of leadership skills. *Leadership Quarterly, 16*, 591–615.

Lord, R. L., Hannah, S. T., & Jennings, P. L. (2011). A framework for understanding leadership and individual requisite complexity. *Organizational Psychology Review, 1*(2), 104–127.

March, J. G. (1991). Exploration and exploitation in organizational learning. *Organization Science, 2*, 71.

Marion, R., & Uhl-Bien, M. (2001). Leadership in complex organizations. *Leadership Quarterly, 12*, 389–418.

Marks, M. A., Mathieu, J. E., & Zaccaro, S. J. (2001). A temporally based framework and taxonomy of team processes. *Academy of Management Review, 26*, 356–376.

McConnell, A., & Drennan, L. (2006). Mission impossible? Planning and preparing for crisis. *Journal of Contingencies and Crisis Management, 14*, 59–70.

Meyer, A. D. (1982). Adapting to environmental jolts. *Administrative Science Quarterly, 27*, 15.

Meyer, A. D., Brooks, G. R., & Goes, J. B. (1990). Environmental jolts and industry revolutions: Organizational responses to discontinuous change. *Strategic Management Journal, 11*, 93.

Meyer, A. D., Gaba, V., & Colwell, K. A. (2005). Organizing far from equilibrium: Nonlinear change in organizational fields. *Organization Science, 16*, 456–473.

Milliken, F. J., & Martins, L. L. (1996). Searching for common threads: Understanding the multiple effects of diversity in organizational groups. *Academy of Management Review, 21*, 402–433.

Moxley, R., & Pulley, M. L. (2004). Hardships. In C. McCauley & E. Van Velsor (Eds.), *The Center for Creative Leadership handbook of leadership development* (2nd ed.). San Francisco, CA: Jossey-Bass.

Mulder, M., de Jong, R. D., Koppeaar, L., & Verhage, J. (1986). Power, situation and leaders' effectiveness: An organizational field study. *Journal of Applied Psychology, 71*, 566–570.

Nelson, D. L., & Sutton, C. (1990). Chronic work stress and coping: A longitudinal study and suggested new directions. *Academy of Management Journal, 33*, 859.

Osborn, R. N., & Hunt, J. G., & Jauch, L. R. (2002). Toward a contextual theory of leadership. *The Leadership Quarterly, 13*, 797–837.

Palmer, N. F., Hannah, S. T., & Sosnowik, D. E. (2011). Leader development for dangerous contexts. In P. J. Sweeney & P. B. Lester (Eds.), *Leading in dangerous contexts.* Annapolis, MD: Naval Institute Press.

Parks, C. M. (1971). Psycho-social transitions: A field study. *Social Science and Medicine, 5*, 101–115.

Parry, K. (1999). Enhancing adaptability: Leadership strategies to accommodate change in local government settings. *Journal of Organizational Change Management, 12*(2), 134–156.

Pauchant, T., & Mitroff, I. (1992). *Transforming the crisis-prone organization.* San Francisco, CA: Jossey-Bass.

Pearce, C. L., Conger, J. A., & Locke, E. (2008). Shared leadership theory. *Leadership Quarterly, 19*, 622–628.

Pearce, C. L., & Sims, H. P. (2002). Vertical versus shared leadership as predictors of the effectiveness of change management teams: An examination of aversive, directive, transactional, transformational, and empowering leader behaviors. *Group Dynamics, Theory, Research, and Practice, 6*, 172–197.

Pearson, C., & Mitroff, I. (1993). From crisis-prone to crisis-prepared. *Academy of Management Executive, 7*, 48–59.

Pentland, B. T. (1999). Building process theory with narrative. *Academy of Management Review, 24*(4), 711–724.

Perrow, C. (1984). *Normal accidents.* New York, NY: Basic Books.

Pfeffer, J., & Sutton, R. (2006). *Hard facts, dangerous half-truths and total nonsense: Profiting from evidence-based management.* Boston, MA: Harvard Business School Press.

Piccolo, R. F., & Colquitt, J. A. (2006). Transformational leadership and job behaviors: The mediating role of core job characteristics. *Academy of Management Journal, 49*, 327–340.

Porfiriev, B. (1996). Social aftermath and organizational response to a major disaster: The case of the 1995 Sakhalin Earthquake in Russia. *Journal of Contingencies and Crisis Management, 4*, 218–227.

Porter, L. W., & McLaughlin, G. B. (2006). Leadership and the organizational context: Like the weather. *The Leadership Quarterly, 17*, 559–576.

Power, C., Higgins, A., & Kohlberg, L. (1989). The habit of the common life: Building character through democratic community schools. In L. Nucci (Ed.), *Moral development and character education: A aialogue* (pp. 125–143). Berkeley, CA: McCutchan.

Powers, R. (2010, June 19). The cost of war. About.com: U.S. Military. Retrieved November 13, 2010, from http://usmilitary.about.com/od/terrorism/a/iraqdeath1000.htm

Pye, A. (2005). Leadership and organizing: Sense-making in action. *Leadership, 1*(1), 31–50.

Quarantelli, E. L. (1988). Disaster crisis management: A summary of research findings. *Journal of Management Studies, 25*, 373–385.

Rhodes, C., & Pullen, A. (2009). Narrative and stories in organizational research: An exploration of gendered politics in research methodology. Chapter 34 in *The Sage handbook of organizational research methods* (pp. 583–601). London: Sage.

Sackett, P. R., Zedeck, S., & Fogli, L. (1988). Relations between measures of typical and maximum job performance. *Journal of Applied Psychology, 73*, 482–486.

Saville, P., & Willson, E. (1991). The reliability and validity of normative and ipsative approaches in the measurement of personality. *Journal of Occupational Psychology, 64*, 219.

Schaubroeck, J., Hannah, S., Avolio, B. J., Kozlowski, S. W., Lord, R. L., Trevino, L. K., Peng, A. C., & Dimotakas, N. (2012). Embedding ethical leadership within and across organization levels. *Academy of Management Journal, 50*(5), 1053–1078.

Schein, E. H. (2010). *Organizational culture and leadership* (4th ed). San Francisco, CA: Jossey Bass.

Schneider, B. (1987). The people make the place. *Personnel Psychology, 40*, 437–453.

Schneider, B., Goldstein, H. W., & Smith, D. B. (1995). The ASA framework: An update. *Personnel Psychology, 48*, 747–779.

Selznick, P. (1992). *The moral commonwealth*. Berkeley: University of California Press.

Shamir, B. (1995). Social distance and charisma: Theoretical notes and an exploratory study. *The Leadership Quarterly, 6*, 19–47.

Shamir, B., & Eilam, G. (2005). "What's your story?" A life-stoties approach to authentic leadership development. *The Leadership Quarterly, 16*, 395–417.

Sharma, A., & Grant, D. (2011). Narrative, drama and charismatic leadership: The case of Apple's Steve Jobs. *Leadership, 7*(1), 3–26.

Shrivastava, P., Mitroff, I., Miller, D., & Miglani, A. (1988). Understanding industrial crisis. *Journal of Management Studies, 25*, 285–303.

Sinha, P. N., & Jackson, B. (2006). A Burkean inquiry into leader-follower identification motives. *Culture and Organization, 12*(3), 233–247.

Smircich, L., & Morgan, G. (1982). Leadership as the management of meaning. *Journal of Applied Behavioural Science, 18*, 257–273.

Smits, S. J., & Ally, N. E. (2003). "Thinking the unthinkable"—Leadership's role in creating behavioral readiness for crisis management. *Competitiveness Review, 13*, 1–23.

Sørensen, J. B. (2002). The strength of corporate culture and the reliability of firm performance. *Administrative Science Quarterly, 47*, 70.

Starbuck, W. H. (2009). Perspective-cognitive reactions to rare events: Perceptions, uncertainty, and learning. *Organization Science, 20*(5), 925–937.

Sundstrom, E., deMeuse, K. P., & Futrell, D. (1990). Work teams: Applications and effectiveness. *American Psychologist, 45*, 120–133.

Sweeney, P. J. (2010). Do soldiers re-evaluate trust in their leaders prior to combat operations? *Military Psychology, 22*, 70–88.

Sweeney, P. J., Thompson, V., & Blanton, H. (2009). Trust and influence in combat: An interdependence model. *Journal of Applied Social Psychology, 39*, 235–264.

Taylor, S. E. (1983). Adjustment to threatening life events: A theory of cognitive adaptation. *American Psychologist, 38*, 1161–1173.

Taylor, A., & Greve, H. R. (2006). Superman or the fantastic four? Knowledge recombination and experience in innovative teams. *Academy of Management Journal, 49*, 723–740.

Tedeschi, R. G., & Calhoun, L. G. (2004). Posttraumatic growth: Conceptual foundations and empirical evidence. *Psychological Inquiry, 15*, 1–18.

Thompson, R. C., & Hunt, J. G. (1996). Inside the black box of alpha, beta, and gamma change: Using a cognitive-processing model to assess attitude structure. *Academy of Management Review, 21*, 655–690.

Tosi, H. L. (1991). The organization as a context for leadership theory: A multilevel approach. *The Leadership Quarterly, 2*, 205–228.

Treviño, L. K., Butterfield, K. D., & McCabe, D. M. (1998). The ethical context in organizations: Influences on employee attitudes and behaviors. *Business Ethics Quarterly, 8*, 447–476.

Tsetlin, I., Gaba, A., & Winkler, R. L. (2004). Strategic choice of variability in multiround contests and contests with handicaps. *Journal of Risk and Uncertainty, 29*, 143–158.

Turner, B. A. (1976). The organizational and interorganizational development of disasters. *Administrative Science Quarterly, 21*, 378–397.

Uhl-Bien, M., & Marion, R. (2009). Complexity leadership in bureaucratic forms of organizing: A meso model. *The Leadership Quarterly, 20*, 631–650.

Uhl-Bien, M., Marion, R., & McKelvery, B. (2007). Complexity Leadership Theory: Shifting leadership from the industrial age to the knowledge era. *The Leadership Quarterly, 18*, 298–318.

van Knippenberg, D., De Drue, C. K. W., & Homan, A. C. (2004). Work group diversity and group performance: An integrative model and research agenda. *Journal of Applied Psychology, 89*, 1008–1022.

Weber, S. S., & Donahue, L. M. (2001). Impact of highly and less job-related diversity on work group cohesion and performance: A meta-analysis. *Journal of Management, 27*, 141–162.

Weick, K. E. (1988). Enacted sensemaking in crisis situations. *Journal of Management Studies, 25*, 305–317.

Weick, K. E. (1993). The collapse of sensemaking in organizations: The Mann Gulch disaster. *Administrative Science Quarterly, 38*, 628–652.

Weick, K. E., & Sutcliffe, K. M. (2001). *Managing the unexpected: Assuring high performance in an age of complexity*. San Francisco, CA: Jossey-Bass.

Weick, K. E., Sutcliffe, K. M., & Obstfeld, D. (1999). Organizing for high reliability: Processes of collective mindfulness. In R. I. Sutton & B. M. Staw (Eds.), *Research in organizational behavior* (vol. 21, pp. 81–123). Greenwich, CT: Elsevier Science/JAI Press.

Wright, T. A., & Quick, J. C. (2011). The role of character in ethical leadership research. *Leadership Quarterly, 22*, 975–978.

Yagil, D. (1998). Charismatic leadership and organizational hierarchy: Attribution of charisma to close and distant leaders. *The Leadership Quarterly, 9*, 161–176.
Yammarino, F. J., & Dansereau, F. (2008). Multi-level nature of and multi-level approaches to leadership. *The Leadership Quarterly, 19*, 135–141.
Yammarino, F. J., Mumford, M. D., Connely, M. S., & Dionne, S. D. (2010). Leadership and team dynamics for dangerous contexts. *Military Psychology, 22*, S15–S41.
Yukl, G. (2006). *Leadership in organizations* (2nd ed.). Upper Saddle River, NJ: Pearson.

CHAPTER

29 Safety Leadership

Mark A. Griffin *and* Zenobia Talati

Abstract

Safety-critical environments pose a number of complex challenges for leaders. At the interpersonal level, leaders must devote their time to monitoring safety behaviors, providing feedback, setting goals, and providing rewards to improve the behaviors of their followers. At the organizational level, leaders must work to create a positive safety culture where employees feel a sense of trust in management and empowerment. In addition to managing human error, leaders need to maintain the integrity of machines and technology used in the work environment. This chapter demonstrates the positive impact of these leader behaviors on safety performance at different organizational levels. In addition, it reviews how leaders can balance the safety goals intrinsic to high reliability with goals to support a productive and proactive workforce that goes beyond compliance and actively participates in the safety process.

Key Words: empowerment, error management, organizational safety culture, safety leadership, safety participation, safety performance, teams, transactional leadership, transformational leadership, trust

Introduction

The technical and human aspects of managing employee safety have received increasing attention over the past 50 years. In particular, researchers have elaborated the human factors associated with safe working and the organizational strategies that enhance individual knowledge, skill, and motivation for safe working (Reason, 1998). There is now substantial evidence that allocation of resources to organizational safety is associated with measurable safety improvements (Christian, Bradley, Wallace, & Burke, 2009).

Although leadership is an element of various organizational strategies to improve safety, the specific role of leadership for safety has received relatively less attention compared to leadership in other areas of organizational activity (Hofmann & Morgeson, 1999). Nevertheless, some significant studies have been conducted that demonstrate the positive impact of leadership on safety and the processes through which leadership influences safety (Barling, Loughlin, & Kelloway, 2002). In addition, safety leadership is an important element of many organizational training programs, particularly those operating in safety critical and high-hazard industries (Krause, 2005).

The goal of this chapter is to review research addressing safety leadership and integrate this research within a framework that considers wider leadership constructs, organizational research, and practice. The overall framework for integrating research is presented in Figure 29.1, which shows safety leadership as the pivotal link between the safety of individual team members and the safety of the organizational system.

Figure 29.1 depicts two distinct processes through which leaders influence safety within organizations. The first is labeled "Path A: Team Leadership" and

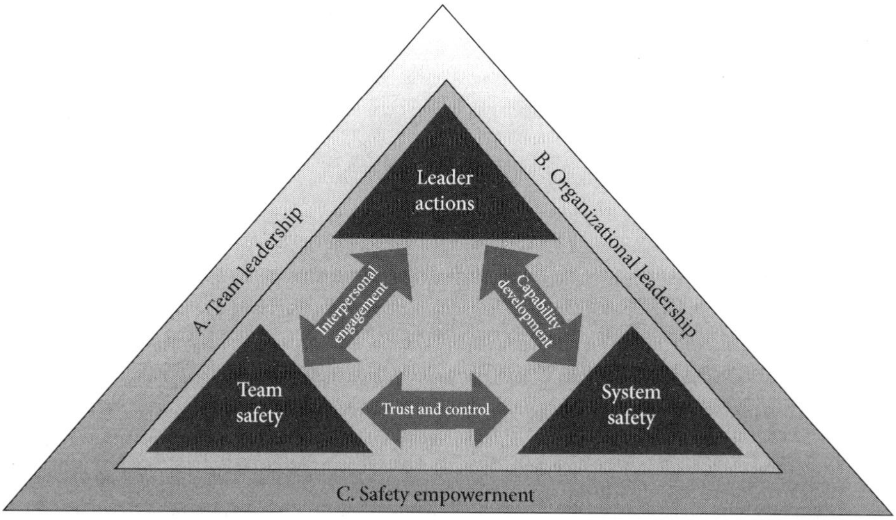

Figure 29.1. Safety Leadership Processes.

involves safety within a work team. We use the term "team" broadly to denote an interpersonal engagement between the leader and team members. The team itself might be a small intact work group or a more complex entity such as a functional area or even a whole organization. Engagement of team members might take the form of daily interaction between a team leader and his or her work group or the communication of an organizational vision for safety by a senior leader. The critical point is that the leader is personally engaged with the team in some way and communicates with team members about safety tasks, roles, and responsibilities.

The second aspect of safety leadership is labeled "Path B: Organizational Leadership" and describes the role that leaders play in building organizational systems that support safety. System safety refers to processes and procedures that constitute organizational capabilities in relation to safety. Organizational leadership is distinguished from team leadership by a focus on actions that enhance overall organizational capabilities for safety rather than actions that involve interpersonal engagement with people.

It is important to note that leader actions can have an indirect but important effect on system safety via their influence on team safety processes. Similarly, leader actions to develop safe systems can have an indirect impact on team safety. This indirect process as "Path C: Safety System Empowerment" is labeled because it requires leaders to develop a synergy between human and organizational capabilities within the organization. This synergy goes beyond the direct impact of a particular leader but is essential for sustaining and improving safety.

Figure 29.1 indicates that there is a bidirectional link between each element of the framework. For example, leaders not only support the team to meet organizational goals but also translate team input into organization processes. However, the focus in this chapter is the processes through which leaders actions can shape team safety and system safety because most research has also adopted this perspective. Ways to expand understanding of the team and organizational factors that shape leadership behavior are considered in the final section on future directions.

The structure of the chapter reflects the aforementioned three aspects of safety leadership. The first section reviews Path A: Team Leadership. This section constitutes the majority of the chapter because past leadership research in the area of workplace safety has focused on the interpersonal process through which leaders influence the safety of individuals in teams. In particular, this research investigates the way leaders communicate with team members to coordinate and motivate the tasks, roles, and responsibilities that support a safe working environment. Less research has directly addressed leadership roles that support safety systems, so the review of Path B: System Leadership is more speculative. This section pays particular attention how leaders contribute to a positive organizational safety culture because the culture reflects the overall effectiveness of underlying safety systems. The processes can be either deliberative or implicit (Reason, 1998). In part, the focus on safety systems involves the management of different types of hazards from those faced in team safety (Hopkins,

2009). Whereas personal injury is a central element of team safety, the focus of process safety are events such as leaks and breaks that are more closely related to asset management.

The third section reviews Path C: System Empowerment. By definition, the actions of leaders are only indirectly related to this process and there is also limited research about the way leaders build empowered safety systems. Nevertheless, system empowerment is an essential concept for sustainable and adaptive safety systems. Therefore, this section reviews how leader actions can support the development of self-sustaining safety systems.

The chapter concludes by exploring the implications of the preceding review for some current issues related to safety leadership: (1) individual differences, (2) safety innovation, (3) balancing safety goals with other goals such as productivity, and (4) the assessment of safety leadership.

Path A: Team Leadership

This section discusses the role of leaders in supporting safe work in teams. It begins by considering what is meant by safe work because a comprehensive view of the work domain is essential for understanding the scope of a leader's influence. A functional approach is then adopted to identify the kinds of activities that leaders undertake to maintain team safety.

What Is Team Safety?

Before considering specific leader functions, we review the meaning of team safety. To ensure the broad domain of safety-relevant activities is included, it is important to go beyond compliance with safety requirements to include factors such as safety innovation and support for team members. Safety in work teams involves the task behaviors of individuals (e.g., following safety procedures with hazardous materials) and the social interactions between individuals (e.g., communicating potential hazards to coworkers). This observation involves a critical distinction between those behaviors that achieve core safety outcomes, termed here "safety task performance," and those behaviors that support the broader safety environment, termed "safety participation." Safety task performance involves compliance with safety rules and procedures such as wearing appropriate protective clothing and following correct lock and tag procedures. Safety participation involves employees engaging in behaviors such as supporting the safety of others or suggesting new ideas for safety (Griffin & Neal, 2000; Neal, Griffin, & Hart, 2000). Safety participation has been linked to lower lost time frequency rates (Shannon et al., 1996). In addition, safety participation has been found to have a greater influence than compliance on overall safety performance (Christian et al., 2009).

The Scope of Team Leadership: A Functional Approach

Leadership actions serve to translate employee performance into effective organizational outcomes. A functional approach seeks to explain the type of leader actions that create effectiveness without specifying all the behaviors or styles a leader might exhibit. Leader functions are best inferred from behaviors (Nealey & Fiedler, 1968), though some functions are more behavior specific than others.

Many frameworks have been proposed to summarize the nature and content of these functions (e.g., Morgeson, DeRue, & Karam, 2010). A fundamental theme of these approaches is that leadership involves attending to events in the internal and external environment, and intervening when action can improve individual or team capacity to achieve effective outcomes (Morgeson, 2005). Attention and intervention are, therefore, primary functional roles of leadership. To describe the focus for leader attention and intervention in relation to safety, we differentiate leader actions along two dimensions that are depicted graphically in Figure 29.2. These dimensions identify the scope of outcomes to which leaders might pay attention and the broad sets of actions that might be used to achieve desired outcomes.

Safety and Avoidance Goals

The first dimension, represented along the horizontal axis, differentiates activities that help move toward valued outcomes versus activities that help to avoid undesirable outcomes. This distinction between approach and avoidance is consistent with the long history of psychological and physiological research supporting the separability of motivational systems in terms such as pleasure/pain, activation/inhibition, and appetitive/aversive motivation (Carver & Scheier, 1978; Elliot, 2006). There is currently broad agreement from both a biological and psychological perspective that positive and negative dimensions of the environment influence distinct motivational systems in individuals (Elliot & Thrash, 2002; Higgins, 2005).

A prevention focus is concerned with "ought" duties and responsibilities achieved through

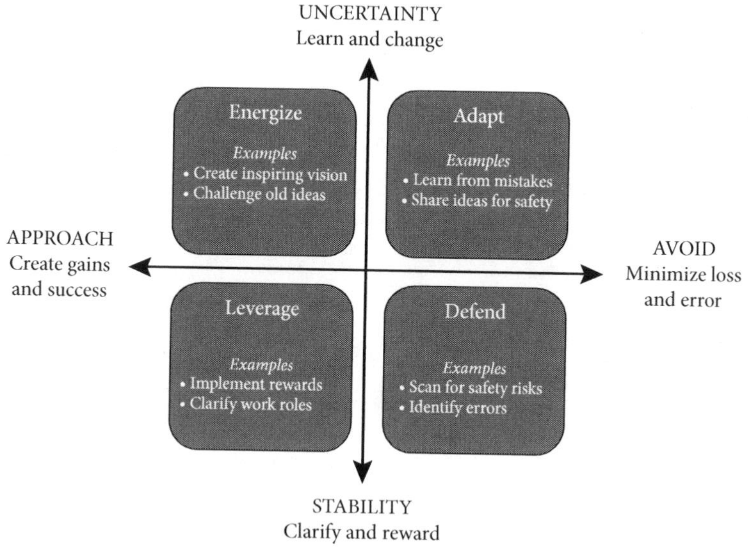

Figure 29.2. Functions of Team Safety Leadership.

vigilance-related goal strategies (Higgins, 1997). A prevention focus of motivation is particularly important for understanding when and how individuals manage threats and risks. A prevention focus is considered to be important for safety because safety behaviors function to avoid or minimize negative outcomes such as harm and injury for the self and others.

The application of regulatory focus theory to safety behavior has received some recent research attention. Wallace and Chen (2006) found that a prevention focus was positively related to supervisor ratings of safety performance. In addition, in a simulation game environment Wallace, Little, and Shull (2008) found that in situations of higher task complexity, a prevention focus had a negative impact on productivity as well as a positive impact on safety.

Stable levels of approach and avoidance motivation vary between individuals as trait differences (Crowe & Higgins, 1997). However, a person's level of approach/avoidance motivation can also be influenced by certain situations. Followers often adopt the regulatory focus of their leaders (Kark & Van Dijk, 2007). In this way, leadership can be a situational variable that influences regulatory focus. Further evidence for the impact of leadership comes from Wallace and Chen (2006), who found that workers who felt that their supervisors promoted safety behaviors and created a safety climate showed a greater prevention focus. This prevention focus, in turn, leads to greater safety performance. The study also found that a prevention focus negatively predicted productivity, although this effect was less for individuals with higher levels of conscientiousness.

Other studies, however, have suggested that a promotion focus may increase safety performance. When Komaki, Barwick, and Scott (1978) provided employees with safety goals to work toward, they found that safety behavior improved substantially. They reasoned that this was because it is easier to work toward the goal of engaging in more safety behaviors than to avoid the punishment of being injured (which does not happen very often). Unfortunately, this study did not include avoidance-oriented goals to allow comparison between the two conditions.

The distinction between approach and avoidance goals suggests important functional roles for safety leadership. Although avoidance goals are clearly important for reducing risks, approach goals are important for motivating safe working practices. The current state of research does not provide clear direction as to when a promotion or prevention focus is best suited for increasing safety behavior. Our framework identifies both goals as important aspects of safe work and suggests ways that leaders can engage with team members to enhance both motivational processes.

Safety under Conditions of Stability and Change

The second dimension of leadership activity is represented by the vertical axis in Figure 29.2 and differentiates leader activities that maintain stability versus those that promote change. Stability and change are fundamental themes within organizations and are intrinsic to safety as well. Most safety research has focused on leader actions that are appropriate in relatively stable environments, that is, an environment in which the link between actions and outcomes is reasonably predictable.

Increasing attention is being paid to the way environments are changing and the requirement for individuals and systems to adapt to ongoing change, anticipate future change, and actively create change in work systems. In the context of change, attention has focused on how organizations can manage safety proactively based on concepts such as resilience (Erik Hollnagel, Woods, & Leveson, 2006) and dynamic capability (Griffin, Cordery, & Soo, 2012). These ideas are discussed in more detail in the section on system safety. For team safety, it is important to recognize that leaders engage with team members about safety in both predictable and unpredictable environments. The appropriateness of leader actions will vary depending on the degree of stability and change in which teams are operating.

Taken together, the dimensions described earlier give rise to four different functional leadership roles as represented by the four quadrants in Figure 29.2. Overall, most safety research has focused on the quadrants labeled "Defend" and "Leverage," which defined activities in more stable environments. The "Defend" quadrant involves leader actions designed to avoid negative outcomes (e.g., preventing errors in the workplace) when the consequences of work behavior are largely predictable. For example, ensuring that team members follow correct safety procedures in hazardous environments is a common and vitally important element of this quadrant. These leader actions are similar to those included in the concept of Active Management by Exception (Bass, 2006) because it involves monitoring and responding to the mistakes and errors of team members.

The "Leverage" quadrant is more closely related to the concept of contingent reward (Podsakoff, Todor, & Skov, 1982) because it is concerned with leader actions that clarify the nature and consequences of team-member safety behaviors with a focus on achieving positive outcomes rather than avoiding negative ones. For example, rewarding employees who display safe working practices would fall in this category.

The "Energize" and "Adapt" quadrants describe leader actions that manage safety under conditions of change and uncertainty. The "Energize" quadrant is similar to the concept of transformational leadership (Dionne, Yammarino, Atwater, & Spangler, 2004; Kark, Shamir, & Chen, 2003; Ozaralli, 2003) because it describes leader actions that motivate employees to achieve new positive outcomes. Recent safety research has drawn a number of parallels between safety leadership and transformational leadership (Barling et al., 2002; Conchie, Taylor, & Donald, 2011; Mullen & Kelloway, 2009). The "Adapt" quadrant describes the management of error and loss when the environment is changing. This topic has received less attention in the safety leadership literature. However, studies of error learning and resilience engineering provide some directions for better understanding the role that leaders play in adapting safety systems to avoid negative outcomes during change.

The next section reviews in more detail the way leaders defend and leverage team safety in four categories: monitoring, feedback, goal setting, and rewards. Leadership activities that energize and adapt safety are then considered.

Team Safety Leadership through Leverage and Defense

MONITORING

Leaders monitor the external environment and work within the team to identify potential hazards and risks. Monitoring is often thought to have negative consequences because it creates a sense of threat and focuses attention on mistakes (Smith, Carayon, Sanders, Lim, & LeGrande, 1992). However, the process of monitoring is also essential for other activities such as feedback and goal setting, so it is important for leaders to undertake monitoring in a way that is appropriate for the team context (Holman, Chissick, & Totterdell, 2002).

Monitoring has been shown to be beneficial across a broad range of leadership contexts (Komaki, 1986; Komaki, Desselles, & Bowman, 1989; Mattila, Hyttinen, & Rantanen, 1994). More specific to the safety context, a number of studies have demonstrated the effectiveness of having trained observers monitor safety performance and provide feedback (Duff, Robertson, Phillips, & Cooper, 1994; Komaki, Heinzmann, & Lawson, 1980; Komaki et al., 1978; Mattila & Hyödynmaa, 1988). To experience the long term benefits of monitoring, it is important to maintain monitoring and feedback after the intervention. For this reason it can be more beneficial for supervisors to monitor performance and provide feedback because they will still be present after intervention.

Management by Walking Around (MBWA) has been proposed as a technique for improving safety monitoring (Peters & Waterman, 1982). As the name suggests, this technique involves leaders spending time interacting with and observing employees at the ground level by informally walking through the work area and having discussions with employees. MBWA is thought to be beneficial for two main reasons. First, it can help leaders build good relationships with their team members by enhancing communication. As described later in the chapter, it is important for team members to feel comfortable discussing safety issues with their manager. Second, MBWA allows leaders to learn more about the functioning of the organizational safety systems. This can take place through their direct observations or through feedback from employees. Recently, Luria and Morag (2012) applied this model to a safety context. They measured SMBWA (Safety Management by Walking Around) in managers and employees at a fabrication company. SMBWA was found to enhance relationships between supervisors and subordinates. There was also a positive correlation between the frequency of a leader's SMBWA and the number of hazards that were identified and/or corrected. However, the greatest gains were seen when SMBWA was combined with an online knowledge sharing system in which managers and employees could enter safety data. Integrating these two aspects proved to be a powerful way to record and analyze safety information.

In the absence of monitoring, leaders may try to gauge safety performance from accident or incident reports. However, accidents occur so infrequently and may be caused by one-off events rather than consistent unsafe behavior. Furthermore, incident reports are generally a voluntary exercise and thus they also do not tell a complete story.

FEEDBACK

Monitoring generates information that is an essential precursor to providing feedback. When leaders provide feedback at regular intervals, employees show observable increases in safety behaviors. For example, Zohar (2002) implemented an intervention in which supervisors emphasized the importance of safety as a priority and provided subordinates with weekly feedback on their levels of safety behavior. The intervention successfully increased supervisors' focus on safety in discussions with their subordinates. More importantly, safety behaviors (measured in terms of earplug use) increased from 25 percent and plateaued at around 73 percent. It remained at this level 5 months after intervention. In addition, there was a significant decrease in the rate of micro accidents (defined as injuries that occurred as the result of unsafe behavior that could require medical attention). The increased safety focus of supervisors, increased earplug use, and reduced micro-accident rate were significantly greater in the experimental group compared to the control group, which did not undergo an intervention. In fact, the micro-accident rate in the control group increased significantly during the post-intervention follow-up.

Komaki et al. (1978) measured baseline levels of safety behavior and then carried out a safety intervention in which they provided employees with safety training followed by a graph displaying changes in the group's safety performance. The graph, which was later displayed in a public place, not only set out current safety performance but also indicated a goal that the employees were to work toward. This was also followed up with supervisors acknowledging employees when they observed them engaging in safe behaviors. This program proved to be successful at increasing safety behaviors and decreasing injury rates. These benefits were maintained a year after withdrawal. Komaki et al. (1978) proposed that one of the reasons for the success of the program was due to the fact that it was based on objective data gathered by outside observers. Employees in the study would have been aware that their behaviors were being monitored by these observers. When employees are aware that they are being evaluated frequently they are likely to perceive feedback as more accurate and fair. This may have motivated them to work toward their safety goals. Furthermore, because feedback was often stated in a positive manner, the authors stated that this acted as reinforcement. Using positive feedback as reinforcement is a more cost-effective and sustainable alternative to using physical reinforcements (discussed later).

The researchers also instituted a reversal phase at the end of the study to determine whether the increase in safety behaviors occurred because the workers knew they were being watched. For a number of weeks after the intervention had run, the observers returned to observe safety behaviors but did not post these on graphs and no feedback was provided. During this period, safety behaviors returned to baseline levels. This indicates that the intervention, rather than the knowledge that they were being observed, motivated the workers to behave more safely.

In a similar, more recent study, Duff et al. (1994) measured safety behavior across a range of construction sites before and after delivering a safety intervention using goal setting followed by feedback. As part of the intervention, employees were shown graphs of their actual levels of safety behavior and the target levels that had been set by the experimenters. Safety behavior rose steadily during the intervention and peaked in the follow-up withdrawal period. Although management and worker attitudes toward the intervention were not formally assessed in this study, the authors made some interesting observations on how these attitudes affected outcomes. The sites that showed the greatest improvements in safety behavior were those in which the management appeared more supportive of the intervention and actively participated in it (e.g., by attending safety meetings). These differences appeared to have an effect even though most of the construction workers were generally positive toward the interventions. This implies that even when people want to behave safely, they are greatly influenced by the attitudes of their supervisor.

In their literature review, McAfee and Winn (1989) found an overwhelmingly positive effect of feedback and incentives on safety performance and accidents. Every study they included in their review found at least a short-term effect of these interventions on at least one safety outcome. As noted previously, a number of studies (e.g., Komaki et al., 1978; Mattila & Hyödynmaa, 1988) use interventions that combine training, goal setting, and feedback. To disentangle the effects of each technique, Komaki et al. (1980) conducted a follow-up study in which they delivered training and feedback separately as part of their intervention and then conducted a component analysis to determine which component of the intervention had the greatest impact. As predicted, training by itself did not have a significant effect on safety behaviors. However, when feedback was added the intervention produced a significant increase in safety behaviors compared to that seen during the baseline period and the training-only period. Ray, Bishop, and Wang (1997) replicated and extended this finding by reporting the levels of safety behavior among workers when they were provided with feedback only or goal setting plus feedback. The combination of goal setting and feedback led to the greatest increase in safety behaviors. Although this still does not tell us if goal setting alone is more effective than feedback alone, it is hard to imagine a situation in which employees can effectively set goals without feedback on their past and current performance. Thus, it seems that one of the best things a leader can do to motivate his or her employees is to provide employees with feedback on their safety performance and have them work toward a goal of higher performance.

GOAL SETTING

Goal setting is one of the most widely studied aspects of safety behaviors. To set goals, however, the leader first needs to provide feedback on current performance. Feedback is also required when tracking employees' progress toward the goal. The studies described in the text that follows all emphasize the role of feedback in the goal setting process.

Komaki, Heinzmann, and Lawson (1980). and Ray et al. (1997) have demonstrated the importance of setting goals when motivating employees to behave safely. In the study of Komaki et al. (1980), employees were shown the mean safety level of their workgroup in graphical form plotted over the last few weeks. Their supervisor then informed the workgroup of the goal they would work toward (e.g., 75 percent safe behaviors).

Whereas being assigned a goal by one's supervisor can increase safety behaviors, there is a greater likelihood of increased safety behavior when employees are involved in setting the goal (Ludwig & Geller, 1997). Furthermore, the effects of participative goal setting appear to last longer than assigned goal setting. Cooper, Phillips, Sutherland, and Makin (1994) had groups of employees set a goal that was difficult but achievable. When group members did not agree (which occurred frequently) the average level of safety behaviors was used as the goal. When comparing the safety behaviors of individual workgroups with their respective goal levels, there were a small number of groups that did not achieve their goals. By way of explanation, the researchers reported that one of the groups that failed to reach its goal was frequently short staffed. In addition, they found a strong positive correlation between absenteeism and accidents. Thus, it appears that goal setting alone cannot increase safety behavior when employees are faced with time pressures and loss in productivity. On the whole, the results of this study were positive as there was a general increase in safety behaviors across the department as a whole.

REWARDS AND INCENTIVES

Safety behaviors can be shaped through operant conditioning. This is the process by which rewards or punishments are provided to reinforce or extinguish certain behaviors. Practicing unsafe behaviors does not always lead to punishment (e.g., in the form of accidents and injury). Furthermore, individuals may feel rewarded when practicing unsafe behavior if it leads to greater productivity, lower levels of discomfort, or perceived acceptance from peers. Thus, there is a need for leaders to provide external rewards to reinforce safe behaviors (Ford & Tetrick, 2008). For example, Fox, Hopkins, and Anger (1987) provided employees with tokens to accompany their monthly paycheck if they had not had any accidents or injuries. They also had the chance to gain tokens if their workgroup had a low level of accidents and injuries or if they made a good suggestion on how to increase safety in the workplace. Their results showed a decrease in money and time lost through accidents and injuries.

One problem with Fox et al.'s (1987) study was that rewards were provided mostly for the absence of accidents rather than the practice of safety behaviors. Although rewarding employees for complying with safety processes has been shown to effectively increase employee safety behaviors (Cameron & Duff, 2007), rewarding low accident rates can provide motivation to not report accidents or injuries (Krause & Hodson, 1998; Pransky, Snyder, Dembe, & Himmelstein, 1999). Peavey (1995) predicts that individuals will be more likely to not report accidents under a group-based rewards system. That is, an individual will be less inclined to report his or her accident if he or she knows the whole work group will be punished. In addition, rewarding low accident rates does not reduce accidents to the same extent as rewarding safety behavior.

Hinze (2002) surveyed a number of organizations on the incentive schemes they used. Of 45 construction firms, they found that only 16 provided rewards for safety behavior whereas the other 29 rewarded low incident rates. The 16 firms awarding safety behavior, however, had the lowest incident rate. Although rewarding low incident rates may have led to underreporting of incidents, these 29 firms still recorded a higher incident rate than the 16 firms that rewarded safety behavior. Thus leaders should focus on rewarding positive and observable, safety behaviors. Motivating employees in this way can be difficult because safety is often perceived as the need to avoid negative outcomes (i.e., accidents, injuries, death). However, leaders can alter this perception so that employees strive to achieve positive outcomes. Zohar and Fussfield (1982), for example, rewarded employees for demonstrating a particular safety behavior (i.e., wearing earplugs).

The types of rewards and the way in which they are offered can have an effect on how employees perceive the reward program. First, it is more effective to provide rewards at variable time intervals. Random allocation of rewards motivates employees to engage in safety behaviors continuously because they cannot know when they will be observed. If observations are conducted at specific times then employees may be more tempted to behave safely only during those times in order to earn the reward. The effectiveness of the variable rewards schedule was illustrated in a study by Zohar and Fussfield (1982), who found that employees' use of personal protective equipment increased substantially after they were offered reward tokens during random inspections.

Second, the length of time in which rewards are distributed should be controlled. Continual use of rewards will eventually become ineffective as the rewards will lose their meaning. It is recommended that mangers follow up the reward program with intrinsic rewards such as praise and feedback. In Zohar and Fussfield's (1982) study, once usage of the safety equipment had increased, leaders provided employees with positive feedback instead of tokens. Providing feedback afterwards maintained high levels of safe behavior. Finally, it is more effective to provide several small rewards rather than one large reward. This is important because it does not distract employees from the purpose of the reward scheme. If a large reward is provided, employees may see their safety behavior as a means to an end in which the end state is to attain a large prize. Even worse, after a large reward is offered, employees may come to expect that more large rewards will be provided. Small rewards, however, are usually sufficient to provide positive reinforcement so that employees will be motivated to repeat their behavior.

Team Safety Leadership through Energizing and Adapting

It is more difficult to standardize safety requirements and contingencies in uncertain environments. If the context of work is changing rapidly because of new technology, methods of working, or means of communicating, then safety requirements are usually changing as well. In this context, it is important that individuals are more proactive and future oriented in their approach to both safety tasks and the social context of safety. Leader actions that energize new ideas and enable flexibility are positive features of leadership in most situations but especially important when considering change.

This section focuses on ways that leaders motivate or energize safety and support learning and adaptability as conditions change.

Many studies find that providing additional safety training fails to improve safety behaviors significantly (Komaki et al., 1980; Ray et al., 1997). One reason for this failure is that there is insufficient attention to the motivational bases of safe work (Christian et al., 2009). Energizing and adapting requires leaders to engage more with the motivational needs of team members to promote more enduring values for safety. Leaders can affect the safety practices of employees by making conscious efforts to discuss safety. Zohar and Luria (2003) monitored supervisory interactions between leaders and subordinates in three workplaces. They provided leaders with regular feedback on the frequency with which they discussed safety behaviors with their subordinates. This feedback intervention resulted in supervisors addressing safety issues with subordinates more frequently. The frequency of safety oriented interactions eventually plateaued and was maintained at the 4-month follow-up. In terms of organizational consequences, the increased attention to safety leads to lower levels of unsafe behavior (as measured by trained observers) and an improvement in the safety climate. Zohar and Luria (2003) explain that the effectiveness of this intervention is due to the strategic targeting of key individuals (viz., supervisors) who can have a large impact on safety behaviors.

In broader terms, transformational leadership is the leadership approach most relevant to energizing and adapting for safety. Studies of transformational leadership consistently link behaviors such as modeling desired behaviors, presenting an inspiring vision, and creating a challenging work environment to positive outcomes for performance and well-being (Judge & Piccolo, 2004). Barling et al. (2002) developed measures of safety-specific transformational leadership and showed that safety-specific transformational leader behaviors were linked to fewer injuries and a more positive safety climate in the organization. The positive impact of safety-specific transformational leadership has been demonstrated in a variety of organizational contexts and observed to influence team members' safety attitudes and behavior (Koster, Stam, & Balk, 2011).

Inness, Turner, Barling, and Stride (2010) found that safety-specific transformational leadership was particularly important for safety participation behaviors compared to safety compliance. Conchie et al. (2011) also found that safety-specific leadership correlated with speaking up about safety issues. These results support the notion that transformational leadership is particularly appropriate for energizing team behaviors, such as promoting safety within the team, that are important during change and uncertainty.

The impact of safety-specific transformational leadership is also consistent with approaches to safety that emphasize safety values over targets and priorities (Geller, 1994, 2001). In unstable and dynamic environments, priorities and goals can readily change, whereas values provide a stable guide for behavior across a range of situations. Maierhofer, Griffin, and Sheehan (2000) found that employees were much more likely to use personal protective equipment when their manager was observed using this equipment. This finding has also been replicated by Harper et al. (1996).

Shannon et al. (1996) surveyed 718 workplaces and found that management attitudes and behaviors in relation to safety significantly contributed to reducing lost time frequency rates (e.g., time lost through worker's compensation). Leaders who expressed the attitude that safety was their responsibility, that it was their moral obligation to keep their workers safe, and acted by attending health and safety meetings had safer workers. Along with expressing attitudes on the importance of safety, leaders can set an example by openly and frequently carrying out safety behaviors.

In addition to the positive impact of safety specific transformational leadership, Kelloway, Mullen, and Francis (2006) found a negative effect of passive leadership on safety. Passive leadership describes a failure to engage with team members and the absence of positive leadership. These results demonstrate that safety-specific transformational leadership does not fully account for leadership effects on team safety. Rather, a lack of any positive leadership can have just as great an impact (in the opposite direction). Most research has focused on leader behaviors most relevant to energizing safety rather than adapting and learning in unstable safety environments. A recent meta-analysis by Burke et al. (2011) showed that hazard and safety training was more effective when it was highly engaging, particularly when employee exposure to hazards were high. The importance of training engagement for learning suggests that leader engagement is also likely to be an influential factor in motivating team members to adapt and learn, but further research is needed to understand this aspect of safety leadership.

Path B: Leadership and Organizational Safety Systems

We next consider safety leadership in terms of more general organizational systems. Although organizational systems are generally more applicable to more senior leaders, it is important to consider how leaders at all levels contribute to safety systems in an organization. We pay most attention to the concept of safety culture, which encompasses a broad variety of practices and processes within organizations. We subsume the concept of safety climate within the broader notion of safety culture. Safety climate refers to the shared understanding that safety is important and valued in an organization (Neal & Griffin, 2004; Zohar, 1980). There has been much discussion about the difference between climate and culture (Denison, 1996; Mearns & Flin, 1999). However, in this chapter we focus on their similar emphasis on shared values for safety within an organization. We first review the role of leadership in developing overall safety culture, and then consider the two specific aspects of safety systems: error management and process safety.

Safety Culture

An organization's culture represents the values and beliefs that are shared by employees about their organization (Guldenmund, 2000). These values and beliefs lead to norms that can inform and guide employee behavior in certain situations (Clarke, 2006; Quick et al., 2008). Reason (1998) argued that a poor safety culture is associated with deficiencies in safety systems that enable defenses-in-depth. High-reliability organizations typically have a number of defensive systems in place to manage and prevent errors. Although this level of defense can be beneficial, it also means that the operator is distanced from the procedures, and might have less appreciation of the risks associated with the safety system. For example, without detailed knowledge about how the machinery functions, the operator is likely to be overreliant on defenses-in-depth and be less able to deal with unexpected situations that occur when the defenses are breached. Investigations of major incidents continue to implicate failures and omissions of safety culture in general and safety leadership in particular. A strong safety culture for motivating sustained safety within organizations is now promoted as an essential element of safety improvement by organizations and researchers alike. Leadership is central to an organization's safety culture, and most practical frameworks for safety management emphasize the role that leaders play in building and sustaining a positive safety culture (Krause, 2005).

An organization's culture can be a major source of motivation and information relevant to safety practices (Nahrgang, Morgeson, & Hofmann, 2008). Longitudinal studies have shown that as an organization develops a safety-oriented work culture over time, teams increase their level of safe behaviors (Cooper & Phillips, 2004; Neal & Griffin, 2006). Leaders at all levels of the organization can influence safety culture and perceptions or organizational systems (Kozlowski & Doherty, 1989)

The most direct impact of senior leaders on safety culture is through the implementation and visible support of safety systems. For example, Hudson (2007) described how a large company implemented a positive health and safety culture. Although the initiative was initiated by senior leaders, multiple levels of leadership played a major role in promoting and developing the culture.

Not only does leader support for a positive safety culture increase overall safety within groups, it also reduces the variability between workgroups in their safety behaviors (Zohar & Luria, 2005). However, it is critical to note that this effect depends on leaders' *enacted* behaviors being consistent with the organization's *espoused* behaviors (Zohar, 2010).

Current organizational strategies encourage leaders to build a positive safety culture, and research confirms a link between a strong safety culture and better safety. However, there remain a number of questions about the specific mechanisms through which leaders can develop overall organizational safety capabilities. The next section explores specific aspects of safety culture that are linked to more specific organizational safety processes. First, error management culture describes how the culture of an organization supports learning from mistakes. Second, process management culture describes the way the culture supports systemic processes intrinsic to an organization's core products rather than the personal safety of team members. Each element of safety culture helps to understand the overall link between safety systems and leader actions.

ERROR MANAGEMENT CULTURE

An error management culture (Van Dyck, Frese, Baer, & Sonnentag, 2005) is one in which the focus is on managing errors once they have occurred. Because it is impossible to eliminate errors completely, it is important to consider how they are responded to and how more positive outcomes can be achieved after error. Central to an error management culture is a mindset in which errors are seen less as negative consequences and more as opportunities to learn. An error management culture has been found to be beneficial for overall performance in a range of organizational settings. For example, Van Dyck et al. (2005) found a strong correlation between managerial support for error management culture and achievement of goals and objective economic performance indicators across a range of organizational settings.

Although error management culture is important for understanding and learning from mistakes, less attention has been paid to the implications of error management in safety-critical environments. Implementing an error management culture in an environment where errors have safety consequences initially seems counterintuitive if errors could result in injuries or fatalities. Encouraging people to make mistakes (Keith & Frese, 2008) is clearly not feasible outside of training simulations in situations in which errors might cause actual harm. Nevertheless, the benefits of incorporating an error management culture into safety have been demonstrated in a number of organizations and industries.

To create an environment that encourages learning from error, it is important that honesty and openness are encouraged when reporting errors rather than fostering guilt and assigning blame. In this way, an error management approach can be seen as the second step in a two-step technique. The first step is to try and prevent errors (as described in the previous sections) whereas the second step is to manage errors once they have been made.

The threat and error management approach presented by Harper and Helmreich (2003) describes this kind of framework for handling errors. The first step in this approach is, after an error has occurred, to identify the behaviors of the workers and any other external threats that contributed to the occurrence of the error. This information is gained from workers involved in the error. Next, a description is obtained on the severity of the error and how the workers managed it. In the final step, corrections and feedback are provided. The threat and error management model has been successfully implemented in the aviation and medical industry (Harper & Helmreich, 2003; Helmreich, 2000).

The Line Operations Safety Audit (LOSA) procedure can be used to measure threats and errors that take place during operations. This technique, now considered the gold standard in the aviation industry, uses external observers to make systematic observations of normal flight operations. The aim is for the observers to understand baseline levels of error during normal operations as well as how these errors are dealt with. Observations are entered into an observation form, which serves as a data collection tool. The data are then analyzed for patterns such as whether errors occur more frequently under certain situations. Finally, the information is provided to the airline so they can amend their procedures, advise their crew on how to deal with high threat situations, or incorporate the findings into their training programs. One benefit of monitoring using the LOSA approach is the access to accurate safety performance data. Helmreich, Klinect, and Wilhelm (2001) argue that monitoring is one of the most effective ways to gain accurate information on crew performance.

Klinect, Wilhelm, and Helmreich (1999) used data from LOSAs conducted on 184 flight crews to determine the types of threats that are frequently encountered, when these threats occur and how they were dealt with by the crew. The data gained from the LOSA monitoring procedure showed that for the majority of errors that occurred, the flight crew failed to respond appropriately. Analysis of crew behavior by experts revealed which crew member behaviors were most adaptive to managing errors (e.g., vigilance, discussing problems, and asking questions around errors). This study is one example of the way in which leaders can utilize "data" gained from behavioral observations of their workgroup.

Using the data gathered from numerous LOSAs, Helmreich et al. (2001) developed recommendations on how to manage errors. They include being proactive in preventing error, managing threats by managing operational complexity and managing threats from not only machinery but also humans. To manage threats, however, the organization must be more interested in using the data from monitoring to learn from error rather than allocate punishments. At the same time, it is important that employees feel they can trust their organization and their leader who is monitoring them to use the data in this way (Klinect, Murray, Merritt, & Helmreich, 2003). Increased trust also leads to an environment in which employees feel comfortable reporting and discussing their errors.

Helmreich, Klinect, Wilhelm, and Merritt (2001) provide guidelines on how an organization can implement an error management culture. Although their guidelines are intended for instructors of training programs, they also provide insight into more systemic interventions from leaders. It is important that everyone in the organization has an understanding of error avoidance, detection, and management strategies. This can be achieved through training programs for employees and managers. Following this, it is important to assess and reinforce observable error detection and management behaviors continually. For example, a leader can praise a team member for sharing their experiences with coworkers so they can avoid making the same errors. At the organizational level, it would be beneficial to establish nonpunitive policies that reward rather than punish employees for sharing error knowledge. Recognizing and reporting errors is only part of the error management culture. What is equally important is how the organization uses error information to increase safety. Ideally there should be a clear process by which this knowledge can be used to inform any changes that should be made to the workplace.

PROCESS SAFETY CULTURE

The Baker panel report into the disaster at BP Texas City highlighted the role of leadership in developing a culture for process safety (Baker et al., 2007). The focus of a process safety culture is the management of hazards that can result from machinery, substances, materials, and work processes (Hopkins, 2009). Since the Baker report, organizations have endeavored to understand how to support process safety as distinct from personal safety. This area is also a focus on asset management—maintaining the integrity of the material assets found in high-risk work environments. In the same way that human-related accidents and incidents do not accurately reflect the state of safety in the workplace, so too do asset-related accidents inaccurately reflect the state of safety in a workplace. As explained in Reason's (1990) Swiss cheese model, there are often a number of factors that come into play simultaneously when an accident occurs. In this analogy, the factors influencing a situation (e.g., operator fatigue, weather conditions) are likened to slices of Swiss cheese. Each slice contains a number of holes and these holes represent weaknesses that could lead to errors. Errors occur when the holes in each slice align, while near misses occur when most, but not all, of the factors necessary for an accident are present.

Owing to the number of variables involved in the lead-up to an accident, it is important to adopt a continuous improvement strategy whereby management remains vigilant for potential hazards (International Association of Oil and Gas Producers, 2011). This can be done by setting process safety Key Performance Indicators (KPIs). These KPIs specify a safe level of operation that is expected from assets. These levels can then be monitored to give an indication of asset integrity. Leaders can be actively involved in process safety by contributing to the KPI statements, monitoring organizational processes, listening to employees' suggestions for improvements, and finding new ways to continuously improve processes (Port, Ashun, & Callaghan, 2010).

Resilience engineering is an approach to understanding risk and safety based on systems thinking and complexity. The research and safety concepts encompassed by the concept of resilience engineering were derived from earlier work in the areas of organizational reliability and human error. A key tenet of the approach is that failure arises from the inability to adapt to complexity rather than as a breakdown or malfunction (Madni & Jackson, 2009). Overall, resilience engineering seeks to describe the ability of an organization to maintain a dynamic stable state in the presence of disruption and threat. For example, Hollnagel, Paries, Woods, and Wreathall (2011) defined resilience engineering as "the intrinsic ability of a system to adjust its functioning prior to, during, or following changes and disturbances, so that it can sustain required operations under both expected and unexpected conditions" (p. 275).

Research in the area of resilience engineering focuses on how to avoid, detect, and recover from errors. In resilience engineering terms, failures are not the result of unpredictable environmental events but rather they occur in systems that cannot adequately deal with unpredictable events in their environment. Disruptions can occur to change the environment in such a way that organizational systems are no longer adaptive. For example, systemic disruptions (Madni & Jackson, 2009) can occur when machinery or technology fail. In these situations, most systems would allow the operator to override the equipment. This is because the operator will generally be better able to process the new unpredictable information than a machine that has never encountered this type of unexpected situation. In this situation, it is important that the operator is trained to act in place of the machinery (e.g., by manually entering in commands).

Path C: Safety Empowerment

The final aspect of safety leadership depicted in Figure 29.1 involves leader support for the link between team safety and system safety. We have described this link as one of empowerment because the functional value of this link resides in the capacity of teams to improve safety systems and the way safety systems enhance team safety. We focus on the nature of empowered teams and how teams actively engaged in safety can contribute to organizational safety systems. We highlight the importance of trust as a foundation for effective empowered teams.

Empowerment and Trust

Empowerment involves employees experiencing authority and control over outcomes in the workplace. Research shows that empowered teams show more safety behaviors and have a better safety record, although this effect tends to diminish as the team gets larger (Hechanova-Alampay & Beehr, 2001). Experiencing confidence to make changes is a key aspect of empowerment for team members (Conger & Kanungo, 1988), and this confidence depends on high levels of trust between leaders and team members (Kirkman & Benson, 1999).

Trust is thought to be the mechanism involved in producing a number of positive organizational safety outcomes. For example, Kath, Magley, and Marmet (2010) found that employee trust in their organization partially mediated the relationship between open communication about safety and safety motivation. That is, when managers communicate openly with employees about safety the employees are likely to place more trust in them. This in turn will increase their motivation to act safely. Creating an environment in which employees feel they can discuss safety issues openly is an essential aspect of an error management culture (Klinect et al., 2003). Hofmann and Morgeson (1999) found that employees felt more comfortable discussing safety issues with their supervisors when they perceived that the organization supported and valued them and when they had a strong positive relationship with their supervisor. Furthermore, leaders who trust their subordinates, and thus are likely to have a strong positive relationship with them, are more likely to ensure the work environment is safe for the subordinates (Luria, 2010). Thus, a trusting relationship between leader and subordinate is important for safety as it motivates both parties to act in ways that minimize risk.

The aforementioned research suggests that if teams are empowered to have control over appropriate decisions and team members experience trust and confidence, they are able to make important contributions to organizational processes.

Teams Support System Safety

Empowered teams can support organizational system safety in a number of ways. First, work teams can be more proactive about solving safety problems and contributing to organizational safety needs. Organizational scholars increasingly recognize the importance of understanding drivers of innovation at different levels of analysis (Baer & Frese, 2003), particularly innovation arising from teams (Hülsheger, Anderson, & Salgado, 2009).

A number of researchers have studied the prerequisites required to form innovative teams. Interestingly, it appears that the group climate is more important in predicting an individual's tendency to be innovative than individual level factors. Innovative teams are generally open to new ideas, highly committed, share information among members, are collaborative, and have a high degree of trust in other team members (Niehoff & Ghartey-Tagoe, 1991). Burningham and West (1995) measured innovation among teams working in a safety context. Their measure consisted of four subscales: vision, participative safety, task orientation, and support for innovation. Task orientation and support for innovation were found to be the strongest predictors of team innovativeness. Also important in predicting innovation was participative decision making and commitment to the team. Given that team culture is a critical determinant of innovativeness, the team leader has an important role to play in creating that culture.

Work Systems Support Team Safety

Finally, it is important for leaders to understand how organizational systems translate into safety within work teams. Recent work in the area of high performance work systems draws a specific link between the quality of an organization's management systems and the safety of team members. Zacharatos, Barling, and Iverson (2005) investigated the link between high- performance work systems (HPWS) and safety outcomes. HPWS include organizational processes and practices such as selective hiring, training, employment security, contingent compensation, and transformational leadership (Huselid, 1995). A study of 136 organizations by Zacharatos et al. (2005) found that higher levels of HPWS across organizations were associated with lower injury rates. They also found that the link between HPWS and safety for individuals was mediated by perceptions of trust.

Changing management behaviors so there is a greater emphasis on safety can impact not only current employees but also new employees. When they first join an organization, new employees go through a process of socialization where norms are learned (Mullen, 2004). This can impact the way they view safety and their subsequent behaviors. Mullen (2004) interviewed a small sample of employees working in dangerous environments and found that formal training programs had less influence on employee behaviors than on the job experiences. In organizations where no training was provided or people frequently engaged in unsafe practices, this became the norm. This research shows that leader efforts to develop effective systems across a range of practices can have a positive impact on team safety. Even when these systems are not directly related to safety they can support team safety by creating trust, enhancing capability, and empowering team members to make effective changes.

Discussion: The Multiple Demands of Safety Leadership

The preceding review outlines the multiple functions and roles involved in safety leadership. Any leadership role is challenging and multifaceted; this chapter highlights the potential demands and complexities of leading in a high-risk environment. In this setting, leaders must maintain their focus across various levels: interpersonal, team, and organizational. At the same time, leaders must balance the priorities of caution and vigilance with requirements for high performance and innovation. Therefore, we conclude by considering how individuals might integrate the many functions reviewed earlier with what is likely to be an already demanding set of goals and expectations. We draw on the idea of ambidextrous leadership as a basis for understanding how leaders can integrate these different demands.

Ambidextrous leadership describes the capacity of leaders to manage simultaneously two or more competing demands. Gibson and Birkinshaw (2004) envision two ways in which leaders can be ambidextrous. First, they could lead one group of employees with a focus on maintaining the efficiency of the current business products while another group focuses on developing new innovative products. Alternatively, leaders can have all employees focus on both objectives simultaneously. Similarly, ambidextrous leaders can simultaneously emphasize the importance of safety behaviors and productivity. One risk here is that employees may experience role ambiguity and the competing demands may lead to intrapersonal and interpersonal conflict.

Time pressure is a well-known threat to safety (Mullen, 2004). Leaders and team members who feel they are under time pressure and rate performance as more important than safety are less likely to engage in safety behaviors (Maierhofer et al., 2000; Mullen, 2004). Conversely, when leaders emphasize that production processes must always be carried out safely, employees show greater levels of safety behavior (Harper et al., 1996). Zohar and Luria (2004) describe the pattern orientation of leaders as the extent to which they routinely emphasize certain goals (such as safety) over other goals (such as productivity).

To date, the effectiveness of ambidexterity in balancing safety goals has not been explored. However, current approaches to ambidexterity in other settings suggest ways that safety might be incorporated in these practices. For example, leaders might work toward developing a culture of ambidexterity. Adler, Goldoftas, and Levine (1999) studied four techniques that managers could use to assist their employees to be explorative and exploitative. These were summarized by Gibson and Birkinshaw (2004) as "(a) meta-routines for systematizing the creative process, (b) job enrichment schemes that provided workers with the skills to become more innovative in their everyday tasks, (c) switching, which refers to individuals moving between different tasks even in the course of a single day's work, and (d) partitioning, which refers to the creation of two activities being done in parallel with different teams" (p. 7).

Smith and Tushman (2005) discuss ways to overcome the paradoxical nature of ambidextrous organizations. Their method involves reframing cognitions in leaders and employees. They describe two team structures in which ambidextrous leadership can occur. In a leader-centric team, leaders come to understand the contradictory goals and make decisions on behalf of the team for how these contradictions will be dealt with. In this situation, team members can work on just one of the multiple goals while the leader acts as an integrator and coordinates the separate actions of team members. Alternatively, in a team-centric team all team members have an understanding of the multiple goals and collectively make decisions on how to achieve these goals. The role of the leader in this team is to manage and capitalize on any conflict among team members. A team-centric model appears to be most suited to a safety setting since it is not possible to divide the goals of productivity and safety among team members. In this case, it is both the leaders and their subordinates who need to be ambidextrous.

Summary and Future Directions

Safety leadership is a multifaceted role that requires personal engagement with team members and a systemic view of organizational safety practices. The complexity of a safety leader's role comes from the many levels on which safety must be managed within an organization. At the interpersonal level, the way in which leaders engage with and motivate employees will vary depending on situational variables such as the stability of the environment which the team is operating in and whether a promotion or prevention focus is ideal.

Implementing an Error Management Culture in a Safety Setting

At the systems level, this chapter described how leaders can be involved in creating a positive safety culture. The culture at an organization creates norms that in turn guide behavior. We proposed that an error management culture would have a positive impact on safety behaviors because this culture encourages people to be open about their errors and learn from them. It is suited to a safety setting where it is crucial that errors actually are reported not repeated. Although there have been a number of studies on error management culture, more studies are needed to examine its impact in a safety setting. Of the few existing studies, most have been carried out in aviation or medicine. The nature of risks, job tasks, and teamwork in these environments varies greatly from those in other high-risk industries such as mining, construction, or offshore drilling.

One important requirement of an error management culture is the presence of trust and empowerment among employees. If employees feel they can't trust their leaders, they are less likely to discuss errors with them for fear of being blamed and punished. Similarly, employees who do not feel empowered and are not involved in the decision-making process will be less motivated to act safely. By fostering an open, trusting, and empowering team environment, leaders are effectively creating the conditions necessary for innovation and safety participation. These behaviors are encompassed under Path C shown in Figure 29.1. There has been less research carried out on this path of the model compared to Paths A and B. More empirical evidence is required to understand better the link between team safety and system safety.

Reciprocal Relationships between Leaders and Teams/Organizations

Figure 29.1 shows that there are reciprocal linkages among leader actions, team safety, and system safety. Our review has focused on the causal flow from leader behaviors to team safety and system safety because most research adopts this perspective. However, it is important to consider how both the organizational system and the team shape the safety behaviors of leaders. The organization plays a direct role in setting the expectations of leaders, defining performance requirements, and managing leader outcomes. This kind of linkage can be understood in terms of the processes already outlined here. More indirect influences not as easily defined.

At the organizational level, the existing safety culture can influence the kind of leaders who are attracted to a particular organization and their early socialization experiences as new members or new leaders, and shape their attitudes and abilities over time. At the team level, it is important to recognize that leadership involves an ongoing relationship between team leaders and members. This process leads to change in leaders as well as members as the relationship develops (Day, Gronn, & Salas, 2006). The study of leader identity is one promising area of research to understand how a leader's safety role might develop over time in response to interactions with team members. A leader's identity describes the meaning a leader attaches to him- or herself in relation to the leadership role (Hannah, Woolfolk, & Lord). This self-concept can influence a wide range of organizational outcomes, although safety has not been the focus of this research to date. DeRue and Ashford (2010) proposed a theoretical process through which leader identity is "co-constructed" via interactions with team members. Such theoretical frameworks indicate useful directions for understanding how teams might shape the safety capabilities of leaders.

Safety and Goal Orientation

There is currently no consensus as to whether a promotion or prevention focus is most effective for increasing safety behavior. This is partly due to the lack of research in this area. On the surface, it seems that a prevention focus would be appropriate in a safety context because there is a focus on avoiding negative outcomes. However, as shown in this chapter, it is equally important for safety to be framed in a positive motivational context. That is, leaders should encourage their employees to participate proactively in the safety process. When safety is framed this way, it is also clearer that a promotion focus may also be beneficial. Clarifying the impact of regulatory focus on safety is one important area for future research.

Transactional Leadership

As shown in Figure 29.2, leaders may focus on energizing, adapting, leveraging, or defending. There are a number of commonalities between our model presented in Figure 29.2 and Bass' (1985) full-range leadership theory. Specifically, the leverage, defend, and energize styles are conceptually similar to the contingent reward, active management by exception, and transformational leadership constructs. Although there has been much research into the impact of transformational leadership in safety settings, there are fewer studies investigating the influence of transactional leadership (i.e., contingent reward and active management by exception) on safety. Future research should consider how these constructs can be applied to a safety setting. This chapter provides a starting point by illustrating how monitoring, feedback, goal setting, and reward behaviors can help leaders to "leverage" and "defend" effectively.

In conclusion, this chapter has drawn on research and practice in the areas of organizational leadership, safety culture, and team performance to provide a comprehensive overview of the various functions of safety leadership. It shows that safety leadership is an integral part of effective leadership in general. Therefore, safety leadership is not an additional set of functions that must be added to an existing list of leader demands and responsibilities. Rather, safety leadership highlights those essential aspects of leadership that minimize risk and harm in any organizational setting. The specific elements of safety leadership will vary in importance depending on multiple factors in the workplace. The importance of leaders understanding the potential for injury and harm, however, is common across all organizations.

References

Adler, P. S., Goldoftas, B., & Levine, D. I. (1999). Flexibility versus efficiency? A case study of model changeovers in the Toyota production system. *Organization Science, 10*(1), 43–68.

Baer, M., & Frese, M. (2003). Innovation is not enough: Climates for initiative and psychological safety, process innovations, and firm performance. *Journal of Organizational Behavior, 24*(1), 45–68.

Baker, J. A., Bowman, F. L., Erwin, G., Gorton, S., Hendershot, D., Leveson, N., et al. (2007). The Report of the BP US Refineries Independent Safety Review Panel. From http://www.bp.com/bakerpanelreport

Barling, J., Loughlin, C., & Kelloway, E. K. (2002). Development and test of a model linking safety-specific transformational leadership and occupational safety. *Journal of Applied Psychology, 87*(3), 488–496.

Bass, B. M. (1985). *Leadership and performance beyond expectations.* New York: Free Press.

Bass, B. M., & Riggio, R. E. (2006). *Transformational leadership* (2nd ed.). Mahwah, NJ: Lawrence Erlbaum.

Burke, M. J., Salvador, R. O., Smith-Crowe, K., Chan-Serafin, S., Smith, A., & Sonesh, S. (2011). The dread factor: How hazards and safety training influence learning and performance. *Journal of Applied Psychology, 96*(1), 46–70.

Burningham, C., & West, M. A. (1995). Individual, climate, and croup interaction processes as predictors of work team innovation. *Small Group Research, 26*(1), 106–117.

Cameron, I., & Duff, R. (2007). A critical review of safety initiatives using goal setting and feedback. *Construction Management and Economics, 25*, 495–508.

Carver, C. S., & Scheier, M. F. (1978). Self-focusing effects of dispositional self-consciousness, mirror presence, and audience presence. *Journal of Personality and Social Psychology, 36*(3), 324–332.

Christian, M. S., Bradley, J. C., Wallace, J. C., & Burke, M. J. (2009). Workplace safety: A meta-analysis of the roles of person and situation factors. *Journal of Applied Psychology, 94*(5), 1103–1127.

Clarke, S. (2006). The relationship between safety climate and safety performance: A meta-analytic review. *Journal of Occupational Health Psychology, 11*(4), 315–327.

Conchie, S. M., Taylor, P. J., & Donald, I. J. (2011). Promoting safety voice with safety-specific transformational leadership: The mediating role of two dimensions of trust. *Journal of Occupational Health Psychology, 17*(1), 105–115.

Conger, J. A., & Kanungo, R. N. (1988). The empowerment process: Integrating theory and practice. *The Academy of Management Review, 13*(3), 471–482.

Cooper, M. D., & Phillips, R. A. (2004). Exploratory analysis of the safety climate and safety behavior relationship. *Journal of Safety Research, 35*(5), 497–512.

Cooper, M. D., Phillips, R. A., Sutherland, V. J., & Makin, P. J. (1994). Reducing accidents using goal setting and feedback: A field study. *Journal of Occupational & Organizational Psychology, 67*(3), 219–240.

Crowe, E., & Higgins, E. T. (1997). Regulatory focus and strategic inclinations: Promotion and prevention in decision-making. *Organizational Behavior and Human Decision Processes, 69*(2), 117–132.

Day, D. V., Gronn, P., & Salas, E. (2006). Leadership in team-based organizations: On the threshold of a new era. *The Leadership Quarterly, 17*(3), 211–216.

Denison, D. R. (1996). What is the difference between organizational culture and organizational climate? A native's point of view on a decade of paradigm Wars. *The Academy of Management Review, 21*(3), 619–654.

DeRue, D. S., & Ashford, S. J. (2010). Who will lead and who will follow? A social process of leadership identity construction in organizations. *The Academy of Management Review, 35*(4), 627–647.

Dionne, S. D., Yammarino, F. J., Atwater, L. E., & Spangler, W. D. (2004). Transformational leadership and team performance. *Journal of Organizational Change Management, 17* (2), 177–193.

Duff, A. R., Robertson, I. T., Phillips, R. A., & Cooper, M. D. (1994). Improving safety by the modification of behaviour. *Construction Management & Economics, 12*(1), 67.

Elliot, A. (2006). The hierarchical model of approach-avoidance motivation. *Motivation and Emotion, 30*(2), 111–116.

Elliot, A. J., & Thrash, T. M. (2002). Approach-avoidance motivation in personality: Approach and avoidance temperaments and goals. *Journal of Personality and Social Psychology, 82*(5), 804-818.

Ford, M. T., & Tetrick, L. E. (2008). Safety motivation and human resource management in North America. *International Journal of Human Resource Management, 19*(8), 1472–1485.

Fox, D. K., Hopkins, B. L., & Anger, W. K. (1987). The long-term effects of a token economy on safety performance in open-pit mining. *Journal of Applied Behavior Analysis, 20*(3), 215–224.

Geller, E. S. (1994). Ten principles for achieving a total safety culture. *Professional Safety, 39*(9), 18–24.

Geller, E. S. (2001). *Building successful safety teams*. Rockville, MD: Government Institutes.

Gibson, C., & Birkinshaw, J. (2004). Contextual determinants of organizational ambidexterity. *The Academy of Management Journal, 47*(2), 209–226.

Griffin, M. A., Cordery, J., & Soo, C. (2012). *Dynamic safety capability: A framework for understanding how safety systems adapt and change*: Working paper, University of Western Australia, Crawley, Australia.

Griffin, M. A., & Neal, A. (2000). Perceptions of safety at work: A framework for linking safety climate to safety performance, knowledge, and motivation. *Journal of Occupational Health Psychology, 5*(3), 347–358.

Guldenmund, F. W. (2000). The nature of safety culture: A review of theory and research. *Safety Science, 34*, 215–257.

Hannah, S. T., Woolfolk, R. L., & Lord, R. G. (2009). Leader self-structure: A framework for positive leadership. *Journal of Organizational Behavior, 30*(2), 269–290.

Harper, A. C., Cordery, J. L., de Klerk, N. H., Sevastos, P., Geelhoed, E., Gunson, C., et al. (1996). Curtin industrial safety trial: Managerial behavior and program effectiveness. *Safety Science, 24*(3), 173–179.

Harper, M. L., & Helmreich, R. L. (2003). *Creating and maintaining a reporting culture*. Paper presented at the Proceedings of the 12th International Symposium on Aviation Psychology, Dayton, OH: The Ohio State University.

Hechanova-Alampay, R., & Beehr, T. A. (2001). Empowerment, span of control, and safety performance in work teams after workforce reduction. *Journal of Occupational Health Psychology, 6*(4), 275–282.

Helmreich, R. L. (2000). On error management: Lessons from aviation. *British Medical Journal, 320*(7237), 781–785.

Helmreich, R. L., Klinect, J. R., & Wilhelm, J. A. (2001). *System safety and threat and error management: The Line Operational Safety Audit (LOSA)*. Paper presented at the The Eleventh International Symposium on Aviation Psychology, Columbus, OH: The Ohio State University.

Helmreich, R. L., Klinect, J. R., Wilhelm, J. A., & Merritt, A. C. (2001). Culture, error and crew resource management. In E. Salas, C. A. Bowers & E. Edens (Eds.), *Improving teamwork in organizations: Applications of resource management training*. Mawah, NJ: Lawrence Erlbaum.

Higgins, E. T. (1997). Beyond pleasure and pain. *American Psychologist, 52*(12), 1280–1300.

Higgins, E. T. (2005). Value from regulatory fit. *Current Directions in Psychological Science, 14*(4), 209–213.

Hinze, J. (2002). Safety incentives: Do they reduce injuries? *Practice Periodical on Structural Design and Construction, 7*(2), 81–84.

Hofmann, D. A., & Morgeson, F. P. (1999). Safety-related behavior as a social exchange: The role of perceived organizational support and leader-member exchange. *Journal of Applied Psychology, 84*(2), 286–296.

Hollnagel, E., Paries, J., Woods, D. D., & Wreathall, J. (2011). *Resilience engineering in practice: A guidebook*. Burlington, VT: Ashgate.

Hollnagel, E., Woods, D. D., & Leveson, N. (2006). *Resilience engineering: Concepts and precepts*. Burlington, VT: Ashgate.

Holman, D., Chissick, C., & Totterdell, P. (2002). The effects of performance monitoring on emotional labor and well-being in call centers. *Motivation & Emotion, 26*(1), 57–81.

Hopkins, A. (2009). Thinking about process safety indicators. *Safety Science, 47*(4), 460–465.

Hudson, P. (2007). Implementing a safety culture in a major multi-national. *Safety Science, 45*(6), 697–722.

Hülsheger, U. R., Anderson, N., & Salgado, J. F. (2009). Team-level predictors of innovation at work: A comprehensive meta-analysis spanning three decades of research. *Journal of Applied Psychology, 94*(5), 1128–1145.

Huselid, M. A. (1995). The impact of human resource management practices on turnover, productivity, and corporate financial performance. *The Academy of Management Journal, 38*(3), 635–672.

Inness, M., Turner, N., Barling, J., & Stride, C. B. (2010). Transformational leadership and employee safety performance: A within-person, between-jobs design. *Journal of Occupational Health Psychology, 15*(3), 279–290.

International Association of Oil and Gas Producers. (2011). *Process safety: Recommended practice on key performance indicators* (No. 456). London, UK: Author.

Judge, T., & Piccolo, R. (2004). Transformational and transactional leadership: A meta-analytic test of their relative validity. *Journal of Applied Psychology, 89*(5), 755–768.

Kark, R., Shamir, B., & Chen, G. (2003). The two faces of transformational leadership: Empowerment and dependency. *Journal of Applied Psychology, 88*(2), 246–255.

Kark, R., & Van Dijk, D. (2007). Motivation to lead, motivation to follow: The role of the self-regulatory focus in leadership processes. *Academy of Management Review, 32*(2), 500–528.

Kath, L. M., Magley, V. J., & Marmet, M. (2010). The role of organizational trust in safety climate's influence on organizational outcomes. *Accident Analysis and Prevention, 42*(5), 1488–1497.

Keith, N., & Frese, M. (2008). Effectiveness of error management training: A meta-analysis. *Journal of Applied Psychology, 93*(1), 59–69.

Kelloway, E. K., Mullen, J., & Francis, L. (2006). Divergent effects of transformational and passive leadership on employee safety. *Journal of Occupational Health Psychology, 11*(1), 76–86.

Kirkman, B. L., & Benson, R. (1999). Beyond self-management: Antecedents and consequences of team empowerment. *The Academy of Management Journal, 42*(1), 58–74.

Klinect, J. R., Murray, P., Merritt, A., & Helmreich, R. (2003). *Line Operations Safety Audit (LOSA): Definition and operating characteristics*. Paper presented at the Proceedings of the 12th International Symposium on Aviation Psychology, Columbus, OH: The Ohio State University.

Klinect, J. R., Wilhelm, J. A., & Helmreich, R. L. (1999). *Threat and error management: Data from line operations safety audits*. Paper presented at the Proceedings of the Tenth International Symposium on Aviation Psychology, Columbus, OH: The Ohio State University.

Komaki, J., Barwick, K. D., & Scott, L. R. (1978). A behavioral approach to occupational safety: Pinpointing and reinforcing safe performance in a food manufacturing plant. *Journal of Applied Psychology, 63*(4), 434–445.

Komaki, J., Heinzmann, A. T., & Lawson, L. (1980). Effect of training and feedback: Component analysis of a behavioral safety program. *Journal of Applied Psychology, 65*(3), 261–270.

Komaki, J. L. (1986). Toward effective supervision: An operant analysis and comparison of managers at work. *Journal of Applied Psychology, 71*(2), 270–279.

Komaki, J. L., Desselles, M. L., & Bowman, E. D. (1989). Definitely not a breeze: Extending an operant model of effective supervision to teams. *Journal of Applied Psychology, 74*(3), 522–529.

Koster, M. B., Stam, D. A., & Balk, B. M. (2011). Accidents happen: The influence of safety-specific transformational leadership, safety consciousness, and hazard reducing systems on warehouse accidents. *Journal of Operations Management, 29*(7-8), 753–765.

Kozlowski, S. W. J., & Doherty, M. L. (1989). Integration of climate and leadership: Examination of a neglected issue. *Journal of Applied Psychology, 74*(4), 546–553.

Krause, T. R. (2005). *Leading with safety.* Hoboken, NJ: Wiley-Interscience.

Krause, T. R., & Hodson, S. J. (1998). A close look at safety incentives. *Occupational Health & Safety, 67*(1), 28–30.

Ludwig, T. D., & Geller, E. S. (1997). Assigned versus participative goal setting and response generalization: Managing injury control among professional pizza deliverers. *Journal of Applied Psychology, 82*(2), 253–261.

Luria, G. (2010). The social aspects of safety management: Trust and safety climate. *Accident Analysis and Prevention, 42*(4), 1288–1295.

Luria, G., & Morag, I. (2012). Safety management by walking around (SMBWA): A safety intervention program based on both peer and manager participation. *Accident Analysis and Prevention, 45*, 248–257.

Madni, A. M., & Jackson, S. (2009). Towards a conceptual framework for resilience engineering. *Systems Journal, IEEE, 3*(2), 181–191.

Maierhofer, N. I., Griffin, M. A., & Sheehan, M. (2000). Linking manager values and behavior with employee values and behavior: A study of values and safety in the hairdressing industry. *Journal of Occupational Health Psychology, 5*(4), 417–427.

Mattila, M., & Hyödynmaa, M. (1988). Promoting job safety in building: An experiment on the behavior analysis approach. *Journal of Occupational Accidents, 9*(4), 255–267.

Mattila, M., Hyttinen, M., & Rantanen, E. (1994). Effective supervisory behaviour and safety at the building site. *International Journal of Industrial Ergonomics, 13*(2), 85–93.

McAfee, R. B., & Winn, A. R. (1989). The use of incentives/feedback to enhance work place safety: A critique of the literature. *Journal of Safety Research, 20*(1), 7–19.

Mearns, K., & Flin, R. (1999). Assessing the state of organizational safety—culture or climate? *Current Psychology, 18*(1), 5–17.

Morgeson, F. P. (2005). The external leadership of self-managing teams: Intervening in the context of novel and disruptive events. *Journal of Applied Psychology, 90*(3), 497–508.

Morgeson, F. P., DeRue, D. S., & Karam, E. P. (2010). Leadership in teams: A functional approach to understanding leadership structures and processes. *Journal of Management, 36*(1), 5–39.

Mullen, J. (2004). Investigating factors that influence individual safety behavior at work. *Journal of Safety Research, 35*(3), 275–285.

Mullen, J. E., & Kelloway, E. K. (2009). Safety leadership: A longitudinal study of the effects of transformational leadership on safety outcomes. *Journal of Occupational and Organizational Psychology, 82*(2), 253–272.

Nahrgang, J. D., Morgeson, F. P., & Hofmann, D. A. (2008). *Predicting safety performance: A meta-analysis of safety and organizational constructs.* Paper presented at the 23rd Annual Meeting of the Society for Industrial and Organizational Psychology, San Francisco, CA.

Neal, A., & Griffin, M. A. (2004). Safety climate and safety at work. In J. Barling (Ed.), *The psychology of workplace safety.* (pp. 15–34). Washington, DC: American Psychological Association.

Neal, A., & Griffin, M. A. (2006). A study of the lagged relationships among safety climate, safety motivation, safety behavior, and accidents at the individual and group levels. *Journal of Applied Psychology, 91*(4), 946–953.

Neal, A., Griffin, M. A., & Hart, P. M. (2000). The impact of organizational climate on safety climate and individual behavior. *Safety Science, 34*(1–3), 99–109.

Nealey, S. M., & Fiedler, F. E. (1968). Leadership functions of middle managers. *Psychological Bulletin, 70*(5), 313–329.

Niehoff, B. P., & Ghartey-Tagoe, A. (1991). *The impact of leader performance monitoring behaviors on employee attitudes, perceptions, and behaviors.* Paper presented at the Annual meeting of the Midwest Academy of Management, Miami, FL.

Ozaralli, N. (2003). Effects of transformational leadership on empowerment and team effectiveness. *Leadership & Organization Development Journal, 24*(5/6), 335–344.

Peavey, B. (1995). Don't reward the safety cover-up. *Occupational Health & Safety, 64*(3), 69–70.

Peters, T., & Waterman, R. (1982). *In search of excellence: Lessons from American's best run companies.* New York, NY: Harper and Row.

Podsakoff, P. M., Todor, W. D., & Skov, R. (1982). Effects of leader contingent and noncontingent reward and punishment behaviors on subordinate performance and satisfaction. *The Academy of Management Journal, 25*(4), 810–821.

Port, T., Ashun, J., & Callaghan, T. J. (2010). A framework for asset management. In J. D. Campbell, A. K. S. Jardine, & J. McGlynn (Eds.), *Asset management excellence* (pp. 23–48). Boca Raton, FL: CRC Press.

Pransky, G., Snyder, T., Dembe, A., & Himmelstein, J. (1999). Under-reporting of work-related disorders in the workplace: A case study and review of the literature. *Ergonomics, 1*, 171–182.

Quick, B. L., Stephenson, M. T., Witte, K., Vaught, C., Booth-Butterfield, S., & Patel, D. (2008). An examination of antecedents to coal miners' hearing protection behaviors: A test of the theory of planned behavior. *Journal of Safety Research, 39*(3), 329–338.

Ray, P. S., Bishop, P. A., & Wang, M. Q. (1997). Efficacy of the components of a behavioral safety program. *International Journal of Industrial Ergonomics, 19*(1), 19–29.

Reason, J. T. (1990). *Human error.* New York, NY: Cambridge University Press.

Reason, J. T. (1998). Achieving a safe culture: theory and practice. *Work and Stress, 12*(3), 293–306.

Shannon, H. S., Walters, V., Lewchuk, W., Richardson, J., Moran, L. A., Haines, T., et al. (1996). Workplace organizational correlates of lost-time accident rates in manufacturing. *American Journal of Industrial Medicine, 29*(3), 258–268.

Smith, M. J., Carayon, P., Sanders, K. J., Lim, S. Y., & LeGrande, D. (1992). Employee stress and health complaints in jobs with and without electronic performance monitoring. *Applied Ergonomics, 23*(1), 17–27.

Smith, W. K., & Tushman, M. L. (2005). Managing strategic contradictions: A top management model for managing innovation streams. *Organization Science, 16*(5), 522–536.

Van Dyck, C., Frese, M., Baer, M., & Sonnentag, S. (2005). Organizational error management culture and its impact on performance: A two-study replication. *Journal of Applied Psychology, 90*(6), 1228–1240.

Wallace, C., & Chen, G. (2006). A multilevel integration of personality, climate, self-regulation, and performance. *Personnel Psychology, 59*(3), 529–557.

Wallace, J. C., Little, L. M., & Shull, A. (2008). The moderating effects of task complexity on the relationship between regulatory foci and safety and production performance. *Journal of Occupational Health Psychology, 13*(2), 95–104.

Williams, J. H., & Geller, E. S. (2000). Behavior-based intervention for occupational safety: Critical impact of social comparison feedback. *Journal of Safety Research, 31*(3), 135–142.

Zacharatos, A., Barling, J., & Iverson, R. D. (2005). High-performance work systems and occupational safety. *Journal of Applied Psychology, 90*(1), 77–93.

Zohar, D. (1980). Safety climate in industrial organizations: Theoretical and applied implications. *Journal of Applied Psychology, 65*(1), 96–102.

Zohar, D. (2002). Modifying supervisory practices to improve subunit safety: A leadership-based intervention model. *Journal of Applied Psychology, 87*(1), 156–163.

Zohar, D. (2010). Thirty years of safety climate research: Reflections and future directions. *Accident Analysis and Prevention, 42*(5), 1517–1522.

Zohar, D., & Fussfield, N. (1982). A systems approach to organizational behavior modification: Theoretical considerations and empirical evidence. *Applied Psychology, 30*(4), 491–504.

Zohar, D., & Luria, G. (2003). The use of supervisory practices as leverage to improve safety behavior: A cross-level intervention model. *Journal of Safety Research, 34*(5), 567–577.

Zohar, D., & Luria, G. (2004). Climate as a socio-cognitive construction of supervisory safety practices: Scripts as proxy of behavior patterns. *Journal of Applied Psychology, 89*(2), 322–333.

Zohar, D., & Luria, G. (2005). A multilevel model of safety climate: Cross-level relationships between organization and group-level climates. *Journal of Applied Psychology, 90*(4), 616–628.

CHAPTER

30 Cross-Cultural and Global Leadership

Felix C. Brodbeck *and* Silke A. Eisenbeiss

Abstract

This chapter summarizes the field of cross-cultural and global leadership research. It starts with a brief historical overview and descriptions of international landmark projects of high impact until today. The progress achieved in the field since about the mid-1990s is critically reviewed along fundamental research questions, for example: which definitions of leadership are appropriate for cross-cultural study? Which approaches to culture are suitable for studying leadership? What is the magnitude of cultural effects on leadership? What is the moderating role of culture on the relationship between leadership and other relevant variables? What methodological issues have been and still need to be resolved in cross-cultural leadership research? With that as a foundation, the chapter delineates how the findings of contemporary cross-cultural leadership research can enhance managerial practice. Targeting the future, seven recommendations are offered that specify fundamental conceptual, theoretical, methodological, and practical issues in which significant progress can be made.

Key Words: Culture, cross-cultural, leadership, global leadership, ethnocentrism, GLOBE, Hofstede, universality, cultural contingency

Introduction

Cross-cultural leadership research considers cultural factors relevant to leadership, its conditions, its processes, and its consequences, in the development of theoretical concepts and the use of research methods. Dickson, Den Hartog, and Mitchelson (2003) noted in their review of the field, "It would be essentially impossible to prepare a single chapter that presented an exhaustive account of the research on cross-cultural issues and leadership" (p. 730). Bass (2008) concluded his more recent review of the field by saying, "I have tried and hope I did not leave out too much" (p. 1047). We agree with both points and therefore restrict the present review to the most noteworthy developments in cross-cultural leadership research and integrate these into a distinctive account of what contemporary cross-cultural leadership research has to offer for future research and practice.

After clarifying some terms and distinctions, we give a brief historical overview and describe landmark projects in this expanding field. We then address basic questions that were, and still are, addressed in cross-cultural leadership research, together with the progress made since about the mid-1990s (for reviews of earlier research, see, e.g., Dorfman, 1996; House, Wright, & Aditya, 1997). Finally, we take a practitioners' perspective, asking the question, what has the field delivered, in practical terms, to resolve "real world" problems of international leadership. The chapter ends with a summary of conclusions and a collection of recommendations addressing future directions and topics that remain to be addressed.

About the Use of Terms

In the literature, you will find several more or less synonymously used terms and expressions, like "cross-cultural", "international", "multinational", "multicultural", or "global", each combined with "leaders", "leadership", "managers", or "management", depending on the authors' preferences, paradigms, and methods used, or on the publication outlet chosen, which might be more practically oriented (e.g., managerial, business-related, political), or more academic in nature (e.g., psychological, sociological, anthropological). No wonder that we found cross-cultural leadership research to be a rather interdisciplinary field. Some disciplines are more dominant, for example, psychological leadership research, cross-cultural psychology, international management, and business research. Each is well represented in journals or periodical book volumes: for example, *Leadership Quarterly*, *The Bass Handbook of Leadership*, *Journal of Cross-Cultural Psychology*, *Journal of Management*, *Journal of International Business Studies*, *Journal of World Business*, or *Mobley's Advances in Global Leadership*, to name just a few.

For the purpose of this chapter, we decided to not engage in scholastic arguments about the correct use of terms and definitional compartmentalization of fields into subfields. In our view, the field of cross-cultural leadership research is not mature enough for such an approach. How could it be, when even the field of leadership research has not yet reached paradigmatic consensus (Glynn & Raffaelli, 2010)? Instead, we take an inclusive approach, and where appropriate, discuss relevant distinctions.

"Cross-Cultural" versus "Global" Leadership Research

Recently, the distinction between cross-cultural and global leadership was pointed out by Avolio, Walumbwa, and Weber (2009) in an *Annual Review of Psychology* article about leadership research. *Cross-cultural leadership* research focuses on the direct or moderating impact of cultural phenomena (often captured in dimensions) on leadership and, for example, the extent to which leadership practices and values that emerge in one culture apply to others. As such, it often takes a comparative approach. The field is mainly represented in the academic literature (for earlier reviews, see Bass, 2008; Dickson et al., 2003). The field of *global leadership* focuses on the more practical problems of international leaders and leading multinational organizations, for example, selection and development of international leaders, the cultural experience and particular competencies necessary for effective international leadership, and international HRM to inform organizations' strategy and international politics. The term "global leadership" is currently mainly represented in the popular literatures (e.g., Green, Hassan, Immelt, Marks, & Meiland, 2003; Kets de Vries & Florent-Treacy, 1999; Lane, 2004) and seldom in more academic outlets (e.g., Kets de Vries & Florent-Treacy, 2002). We found little sound empirical research published under the label "global leadership." A book about various practical issues of global leadership (and management), which is also well informed by empirical cross-cultural research has been presented by Adler (2008). Furthermore, the series "Advances in global leadership" (cf. for the latest volume, Mobley, Li, & Wang, 2011) regularly publishes new developments in the field of cross-cultural and global leadership and leadership development, including empirical studies. The focus of this chapter's review is on the academic field of cross-cultural leadership and its potential application to the field of global leadership.

A Brief Historical Overview

The documented thinking about leadership has a long tradition in the Western and the Eastern cultural hemispheres. In Indian philosophy, the Bhagavad Gita—one of the most famed Hindu texts dated to over 5,000 years ago—includes leadership lessons (Rarick & Nickerson, 2008). In the scripture, in which Lord Krishna explains to Prince Arjuna his duties as a ruler and warrior, leadership is understood as fulfilling one's responsibilities, demonstrating proactivity, and working for the benefit of the greater good. Today, such leadership might be classified as *responsible* and *sustainable*. In the sixth century B.C., the Chinese philosopher Lao-Tzu described ideal leadership as being *invisible* and *empowering* and emphasized the aspect of leader's *humility*: "A leader is best when people barely know he exists. Not so good when people obey and acclaim him, worse when they despise him... But of a good leader, who talks little, when his work is done, his aim fulfilled, they will say, 'We did this ourselves'" (Sergiovanni & Corbally, 1986, p. 216). About the same time, Confucius in China (551–479 B.C.) framed leadership in terms of authentic *role modeling*: "Go before the people with your example, and be laborious in their affairs" (The Analects of Confucius, Book 13). Not very much later, the Greek philosopher Plato (428–348 B.C.) described successful rulers in the "ideal state" (*politeia*) to be *wise* like philosophers. In the second best state (*nomoi*), Plato added citizen *participation*, because he was convinced that unrestricted power will corrupt anyone. Nearly 1,000 years later, Saint Benedict (480–547 A.D.), known as the founder of Western monasticism, noted in the Regula Benedicti (Rule of St. Benedict, published in 540; cf. Saint Benedict, 1981) that the successful abbot is *wise*, *righteous*, *benign*, and *serving* the nature of many, "Let him know that he has undertaken the care of sick souls, and not a tyrannical authority over such as are well" (Ch. 27, Sentence 6)—today one would say *people orientation*. Another 1,000 years later, in his book *Il Principe* (*The Prince*, 1513), Nicolò Machiavelli (1469–1527), a historian, philosopher, Italian state secretary, and one of the founders of modern political science, described the "strive for power in the interest of the lot" as the core of effective leadership, thereby formulating an initial stage of *charismatic leadership*. Its darker side is commonly known as "Machiavellianism"—the tendency to manipulate other people for one's personal gain. Machiavelli also noted, "Everyone sees what you appear to be, few really know what you are" (The Prince, Ch. 18; cf. Machiavelli, 1985). Therewith, he addressed a rather modern perspective on leadership, which has been elaborated within *leadership categorization theory*, namely, "leadership is in the eye of the beholder."

Because leadership has been a long-standing construct of interest in organization studies, beginning in the early 20th century (e.g., Bogardus, 1920), today we can look more closely into and beyond the remarkable insights of the above-cited historical writers (for recent reviews about leadership research in general, not covered in this chapter, see other chapters in this volume, as well as Avolio et al., 2009; Bass & Bass, 2008). However, nearly all leadership research in the 20th century has been conducted from a social science perspective and within single cultures, mainly within North America and some European countries, which has resulted in predominantly Western and ethnocentric approaches to leadership theory and practice.

Ethnocentrism and Parochialism

The insights from the above-cited historical writers are not only influenced by the occupational context of their individual métier, but demonstrably also by the historical, philosophical, religious, political, social, and economic conditions of their cultural epoch. From the perspective of cross-cultural research, the same is the case for contemporary leadership researchers and the way they conceptualize, plan, and conduct leadership studies. Without explicitly considering cultural factors and their interactions with leadership and followership phenomena and the background of the research protagonists, the potential consequences of cultural impact are likely to remain unnoticed and find subliminal entry in leadership theory, empirical results, and global leadership practice. Such *ethnocentrism* has been diagnosed for organizational behavior research in general in the past, although it has decreased lately, to at least some extent (Gelfand, Erez, & Aycan, 2007, p. 496 ff).

A similar and somewhat broader phenomenon is *parochialism*, which means viewing the world only through one's own perspective, thereby neither recognizing nor appreciating the fact that differences in worldview, working, and living can create serious consequences or offer significant opportunities (Adler, 2008, p. 11). As will be discussed in a later section of this chapter, ethnocentrism and parochialism hinder theory development and knowledge integration in leadership research in general.

Leadership in a Global World

Since World War II, an unprecedented globalization of organizations, both private and public, has taken place, requiring leaders to work internationally at particular locations outside their home culture (*expatriate leaders*), often across a diverse set of many different cultures (*global leaders*). The raise of e-communication and the World Wide Web, which took its first steps only about 20 years ago in 1991, made it possible for multinational organizations to literally operate continuously, for example, on global projects, for 24 hours, across all time zones, and across many different cultures around the world. The increasing interest in cross-cultural leadership research is thus also plausible from a practitioners' point of view, resulting in the rise of what has been described above as "global leadership."

As stated in one of the earlier volumes of the Mobley series on global leadership: "Multiple authors... have documented the accelerating globalization of business, the relative dearth of leadership talent, the inadequacy of global leadership development processes and the continued derailment of international executives" (Mobley & Dorfman, 2003, p. ix). Understandably, the selection and development of internationally successful leaders and leadership practices are major goals in the practitioners' world. One way to achieve such practical goals is seen in the advancement of cross-cultural leadership research, by empirical identification of culturally relevant (and irrelevant) antecedents, processes, and consequences of leadership in a global world.

Accordingly, in the present review, we focus on the scientific side of cross-cultural leadership and its consequences for issues in global leadership, rather than on the multitude of practical issues dealt with under the label of global leadership (for an excellent collection of these, see, e.g., Adler, 2008). The extent to which the field of cross-cultural leadership research is up to this challenge will be addressed in a later section.

The Growth of Cross-Cultural Issues in Leadership Research

By now, a substantial body of cross-cultural leadership research is available, as is documented, for example, in the reviews from Bass (2008), Dorfman (2004), and House, Hanges, Javidan, Dorfman, and Gupta (2004). Further extensive reviews exist for cross-cultural research that indirectly links to leadership (e.g., Gelfand et al., 2007; Kirkman, Lowe, & Gibson, 2006; Leung, Bhagat, Buchan, Erez, & Gibson, 2005). Publications about cross-cultural leadership have annually grown fourfold in the second half of the last century (Hofstede, 2001, p. 525). A particular increase is evident from the late 1980s on, the decade in which Hofstede's seminal book "Culture's Consequences" (1980, 1984) was presented, and during the 1990s, when several seminal reviews about cross-cultural leadership were published (e.g., Dorfman, 1996; House et al., 1997) in the same year in which two special issues from *Leadership Quarterly* (Vol. 8 (3/4), 1997) were devoted to original research papers in the field of cross-cultural psychology. Since then, the field has grown continuously.

Landmark Projects

Since Hofstede (1980, 1984) presented his seminal 53 nations study about culture values, it took more than a decade until further studies of similar scope and scale were available: Schwartz's (1992, 1994, 1999) teachers' and students' value survey in 49 nations; Trompenaars' (1993) employee value survey in 46 nations; a 43 nations subsample that was reanalyzed by Smith, Dugan, and Trompenaars (1996); and a student sample value survey comprising 21 countries from especially Asian cultures, conducted by the *Chinese Culture Connection* (CCC, 1987; Bond, 1988). For a review of some earlier mid-scale cultural values studies comprising up to 25 nations, see Ronen and Shenkar (1985). Two recently published cross-cultural studies, one empirical study comprising employee and student samples from 33 nations (Gelfand et al., 2011) and one meta-analysis (Taras, Kirkman, & Steel, 2010) addressing the impact of cultural differences, measured by the Hofstede dimensions, on individual behavior in organizations, are promising candidates for becoming landmark projects in the future.

The above-mentioned projects resolved some major conceptual and methodological shortcomings in comparative cross-cultural research, which usually are evident in small-scale studies, which sample only one or two handful of countries. However, while focusing on culture values, they did not directly investigate leadership phenomena, nor did they take advantage from sampling especially leaders or managers in their various natural habitats. However, they served—and will do so in the future—as a useful context of reference for a multitude of small-scale studies about cross-cultural leadership (for a review, see Bass, 2008).

To our knowledge, only two large-scale multination studies address culture and leadership concordantly, thereby also sampling managerial populations from various organizations. One project began with Smith and Peterson's (1988) early work about leadership, organizations, and culture, along the lines of which an event management evaluation model was developed and refined (e.g., Smith, Wang, & Leung, 1997). Their approach culminates in a 47-nation study about event management styles of nearly 7,000 managers (Smith, Peterson, & Schwartz, 2002). The other project is GLOBE (Global Leadership and Organizational Behaviour Effectiveness), a multination (N = 62), multi-industry (N = 3), multi-organization (N > 900), multilevel (country, industry, organization, N = 17,000 middle-level managers), multi-method (quantitative-comparative and qualitative-interpretative), and multi-investigator study about societal culture, organizational culture, leadership, and performance, with more than 170 management and social scientists participating from the countries studied. It resulted in a multitude of research papers (up to 2003 reviewed by Dickson et al., 2003) and two authoritative book volumes (Chhokar, Brodbeck, & House, 2007; House et al., 2004).

Because most of the recent work in cross-cultural leadership research refers to one or several of the above landmark projects, they are discussed in somewhat more detail: first the large-scale culture values studies, and second, the large-scale cross-cultural leadership studies.

Large-Scale Culture Values Studies

Hofstede's culture dimensions. Hofstede was the first to identify fundamental culture dimensions on the basis of large-scale multination questionnaire studies, which were conducted between 1967 and 1973 with altogether 117,000 IBM employees from originally 66 nations (Hofstede, 1980); later, 40 nations, which were expanded to 53 nations (Hofstede, 1983, 1984). With his seminal research project, Hofstede was the first to actually map the territory of comparative cross-cultural research in a way that advanced the understanding of the societal culture construct at that time, thereby offering new possibilities for hypothesis development and testing in many areas of cross-cultural studies, including leadership research (cf. Kirkman et al., 2006).

Four dimensions were identified (individualism-collectivism, masculinity-femininity, power distance, uncertainty avoidance). A fifth dimension was later added (long-term orientation) in response to the findings from the Chinese Culture Connection (1987), which converged with three of Hofstede's dimensions, but not with uncertainty avoidance. The reliability and validity of Hofstede's four- and five-dimensional models was disputed by several authors (e.g., Kirkman et al., 2006; Sivakumar & Nakata, 2001). For example, it was pointed out that only one company (U.S. based) was studied, that the data was somewhat "old" (reaching into the 1960s), and that individual cultural values within cultures cannot be treated as homogeneous. It was also criticized that the fifth dimension is empirically interrelated with the original four dimensions in a manner that would suggest to replace the uncertainty avoidance dimension by it and not to add it as a fifth dimension to the original model (e.g., McSweeney, 2002; see the rebuttal from Hofstede, 2002). Today, Hofstede's four-dimensional model is the most widely used.

Although there are many problems, for example, the scale construction process, the cultural equivalency of items, and the multilevel nature of the data, to name just a few of the issues that all cross-cultural researchers have to cope with, some respectable correlations between Hofstede's dimensions and other relevant culture dimensions were established in subsequent studies (for reviews to each dimension, see House et al., 2004, chapters 14 to 17 and 19). The largest of these studies, which were conducted about four decades after Hofstede's original study, sampled respondents from many different organizations, and used Hofstede's four- (Gelfand et al., 2011; Smith et al., 2002) and five-dimensional model (House et al., 2004), are described further below.

Schwartz's cultural value types. Schwartz (1999) surveyed individual value preferences (cf. Schwartz, 1992) of some 35,000 individuals from 122 samples of school teachers and college students in altogether 49 nations. He identified seven value types (embeddedness, affective autonomy, intellectual autonomy, hierarchy, egalitarianism, mastery, and harmony), which are structured along three polar dimensions (conservatism versus autonomy [intellectual or affective], hierarchy versus egalitarianism, and mastery versus harmony). The value type approach helped identify groups of national cultures via similarity structure analysis (SSA; Borg & Lingoes, 1987) which, for example, share (or are distinct in) social working norms or values about the centrality of work in life. Schwartz (1999) asserts that the cultural value type approach might fruitfully be further exploited to predict and interpret national differences in managers' behavior toward followers.

Apart from several studies within single cultures (e.g., China: Fu, Tsui, Liu, & Li, 2010) only few mid- to large-scale cross-cultural studies are available, which investigate Schwartz's values together with leadership phenomena (for a large one, see Smith et al., 2002, described below). In a very recent study, comprising over 20,000 participants from 18 countries, Leong and Fischer (2011) used a meta-analytic approach, which is seldom employed in cross-cultural leadership research. They established positive correlations between Schwartz's mastery (-harmony) and egalitarian (-hierarchy) dimensions and transformational leadership, which shared about 25 per cent of the societal cultural variance.

Trompenaars' cultural dimensions. Trompenaars (1993) surveyed the values of more than 11,000 employees in 46 countries (see also Trompenaars & Hampden-Turner, 1998). He identified seven dimensions (orientation in time, attitudes toward the environment, universalism vs. particularism, individualism vs. collectivism, neutral vs. emotional, specific vs. diffuse, and achievement vs. ascription) for understanding cultural diversity in business. Although Trompenaars' dimensions correlate to some extent with culture dimensions of other large-scale studies (e.g., House et al., 2004; Smith et al., 2002), they were disputed extensively. In a review of Trompenaars' (1993) book *Riding the Waves of Culture*, which was titled *Riding the Waves of Commerce*, Hofstede (1996) points out several problems in scale development and construct validity and presents a list of suggestions for improvement. Obviously not hoping to get access to Trompenaars' data base (which only few researchers did, e.g., Smith et al., 1996), he concludes his review by stating that Trompenaars' (1993) work is a "fast food approach to intercultural diversity and communication" (p. 198). Smith et al. (1996) drew a 43-nation data base of about 8,800 managers from Trompenaars' (1993) original databank and applied multidimensional scaling techniques to establish convergence with earlier large-scale surveys (e.g., Hofstede's, Schwartz's, CCC). They ended up simplifying the dimensional space of cultural values into two dimensions (egalitarian commitment vs. conservatism and utilitarian involvement vs. loyal involvement).

Cultural tightness versus looseness. According to Gelfand, Nishii, and Raver (2006), the tightness versus looseness of national cultures is a neglected source of cultural variation that is dominating the geopolitical landscape. Tight cultures have strong norms and a low tolerance of deviant behavior, and loose cultures have weak norms and a high tolerance of deviant behavior. In a recent *Science* article, Gelfand and her colleagues (Gelfand et al., 2011) empirically examined cultural tightness versus looseness and a variety of antecedent and consequent variables across 33 nations. Results speak to the high validity of this culture dimension, in particular its distinctiveness from other culture dimensions such as Hofstede's. Moreover, results support the underlying theoretical model about how culture affects our everyday life and psychological adaptation. Distal factors, such as ecological and historical threads (population density, history of conflict, natural disasters, resources scarcity, human diseases) in combination with sociopolitical institutions (government, education, media, legal, religion) shape the strength of social norms and the tolerance of deviant behavior in a given society (i.e., tightness versus looseness). These in return affect proximal and contemporaneous processes, such as recurrent episodes in local worlds (structure of everyday situations, degree of situational constraint) and our individual psychological adaptation processes within respective social situations (e.g., self-guide, self-regulation, epistemic needs, self-monitoring abilities). The authors further argue that cultural tightness versus looseness has the potential to be a major source of cultural conflict in a global economic and political sphere.

Cultures' consequences meta-analyzed. In a comprehensive meta-analysis of 598 studies, Taras, Kirkman, and Steel (2010) examined the relationship between Hofstede's four cultural value dimensions and various individual-level outcome variables, which are relevant for organizations (e.g., emotions, attitudes, perceptions, behaviors, job performance). All four cultural dimensions have a similar average predictive power at the individual level of analysis ($\rho = .18$). Interestingly, for some dependent variables, namely job performance, absenteeism, and turnover, the cultural effects are significantly weaker than effects attributable to personality traits, demographic characteristics, or general mental ability, whereas, for other dependent variables, such as organizational commitment, identification, citizenship behavior, team-related attitudes, or feedback seeking, the cultural effects are significantly stronger. Furthermore, cultural values were more strongly related to outcomes for particular groups of individuals, for example, for managers (rather than for students), and for older, male, and more educated respondents. Both findings appear to be of relevance to the cross-cultural study of organizations and leadership. It was also found that cultural tightness versus looseness (described above) moderates the relationship between Hofstede's culture dimensions and individual-level outcome variables. The moderator effect speaks to the relative independence of the cultural tightness versus looseness dimension from the established Hofstede dimensions.

Although not directly studying leadership phenomena, all above-described landmark studies of cultural values (Hofstede, CCC, Schwartz, Trompenaars, Smith et al.) stimulated cross-cultural leadership research indirectly. They are often cited and widely used as reference points for cross-cultural studies about different social and organizational phenomena—including leadership. And the last two more recently published studies by Taras et al. (2010) and Gelfand et al. (2011) have the potential to serve as similar reference points in future research.

Large-Scale Cross-Cultural Leadership Studies

Leaders' event management across cultures. Surveying nearly 7,000 middle managers from 47 countries, Smith et al. (2002) aimed to examine how cultural value dimensions identified by Hofstede (1984), Trompenaars (1993), and Schwartz (1999) relate to the sources of guidance that managers use in handling a set of specific work events. The authors focused on investigating sources of guidance as these are more contextualized than are values, and are thus expected to have a closer linkage with actual managerial behavior. The sources of guidance analyzed in the study included sources relevant in vertical organizational relationships (e.g., formal rules and supervisor advice) and other sources such as coworkers, specialists, unwritten rules, and beliefs. The study yielded that cultural values of power distance (Hofstede) and mastery harmony (Schwartz) can predict the managers' reliance on hierarchical sources. However, cultural values were less able to explain the use of lateral and the more tacit sources of guidance.

The GLOBE project. The GLOBE (Global Leadership and Organizational Behavior Effectiveness) project has been described as "the Manhattan Project of the study of the relationship of culture to conceptions of leadership" (Triandis, 2004, p. xv). It investigates the impact of societal and organizational culture on organizational leadership prototypes and performance, thereby testing hypotheses about the link between culture, organization, leadership, and performance derived from leadership categorization or implicit leadership theory (Lord & Maher, 1991), value-belief theory of culture (Hofstede, 1980; Triandis, 1995), implicit motivation theory (McClelland, 1985), and structural contingency theory of organizations (Hickson, Hinings, McMillan, & Schwitter, 1974). Following a quantitative-comparative (*etic*) approach, together with a qualitative-interpretative (*emic*) approach, GLOBE analyzed cultural values in relation to leadership prototypes, thereby distinguishing societal *culture-universal* from societal *culture-specific* leadership attributes and dimensions (cf. Dorfman, Hanges, & Brodbeck, 2004).

By 1997, when a major part of the first GLOBE data set was gathered, the project involved about 170 social scientist and management scholars from more than 62 nations, covering all major regions of the world (Asia, Eastern Europe, Central Europe, Northern Europe, Latin America, North America, North Africa, Middle East, the Pacific Rim, Sub-Sahara Africa). Data from about 17,000 middle-level managers from about 900 organizations across three industries (food processing, financial services, telecommunications) were obtained and validated in the GLOBE phases 1 and 2 (House et al., 2004). Additional qualitative data was gathered by many of GLOBE's country coinvestigators via focus group and individual interviews with leaders, media analysis, participant observations, historical records, and economic databases. All that information has been integrated in each of 25 country chapters as part of GLOBE's second book volume (Chhokar et al., 2007). A third GLOBE volume focusing on CEOs as leaders and organizational effectiveness is currently in preparation (House, Sulley de Luque, Dorfman, Javidan & Hanges, in prep.).

On the basis of previous cultural theorizing and empirical studies about cultural values (see also the review from House et al., 1997), GLOBE developed and validated a set of four types of cultural scales: (a) societal culture, and (b) organizational culture (with equivalent dimensionality for societal and organizational levels), thereby distinguishing (c) cultural values (by using "*should be*"-items), from (d) perceived cultural practices (by using "*as is*"-items) for each of nine cultural dimensions: (1) assertiveness, (2) future orientation, (3) gender egalitarianism, (4) humane orientation, (5) in-group collectivism, (6) institutional collectivism, (7) performance orientation, (8) power distance, and (9) uncertainty avoidance. In addition, country-level measures of leadership prototypes (i.e., culturally endorsed implicit theories of leadership, CLTs; Dorfman et al., 2004) were constructed, based on 112 items comprising cross-culturally equipollent leadership attributes and behaviors. Twenty-one first-order factors emerged that were clustered into six second-order dimensions of leadership: (1) charismatic value-based (transformational), (2) team oriented, (3) humane, (4) participative, (5) autonomous, and (6) self-protective (defensive and hierarchical) leadership. Findings showed that the charismatic and team-oriented leadership dimensions were universally viewed as contributors to effective leadership, whereas the four remaining dimensions were more or less culturally contingent.

GLOBE's newly developed multilevel and multimeasures approach did not remain undisputed. In *Leadership Quarterly*, Peterson and Castro (2006) criticized how level of analysis issues were dealt within GLOBE's scale construction, which was rebutted by Hanges and Dickson (2006). Dansereau and Yammarino (2006) settled the case by presenting a checklist of what a (cross-cultural) researcher needs to consider in testing a multiple levels of analysis theory and focusing on correlations or multiple regression. They examined the design of the GLOBE study and concluded that it satisfies all of the criteria in their checklist.

Fundamental Research Questions and Progress Made

The progress made in the field of cross-cultural leadership research in the past 15 years can be discussed in terms of nine questions: (1) How to define leadership for purposes of cross-cultural study?, (2) Which approach to culture to take for studying leadership?, (3) Should the focus be on leadership differences or communalities across cultures?, (4) What is the magnitude of cultural effects on leadership?, (5) Are there culture-specific dimensions of leadership?, (6) Are there emic "species" of leadership beyond dimensions?, (7) How does culture moderate the relationship between leadership and other variables?, (8) Is leadership culturally contingent or universal or both?, and (9) What are appropriate methodologies for use in cross-cultural leadership research?

How to Define Leadership for Cross-Cultural Study?

Among leadership scholars, there is no consensual agreed-upon definition of leadership (Bass, 2008; House et al., 1997). And even the question, whether this state of affairs is good or bad for leadership research, is controversial. Garry Yukl, who regularly reviewed the field of leadership, takes the position that it is neither feasible nor desirable to attempt to resolve the controversies on the appropriate definition of leadership at this stage (Yukl, 2006, p. 6). This appears plausible when taking the perspective that particular initial definitions of leadership should not predetermine the answer to central practical questions, like "How can leaders be identified?", "How do leaders affect followers?", or "What makes leadership effective?"

Glynn and Raffaelli (2010), who analyzed the field of leadership research between 1957 to 2007 from a theory of science perspective (as an example of a domain with high theoretical pluralism), conclude that the field displays sparse instances of stock taking initiatives and a considerable lack of commensuration by which concepts and theories can be compared or synthesized. The field is seen to be highly pluralistic in concepts and theories that, once suggested, continue to exist, often unchallenged, unshaped, and not integrated with others or substituted by better ones, thereby cluttering the field of scientific inquiry.

Glynn and Raffaelli (2010) conclude that the field of leadership research provides a compartmentalized context of scientific enquiry, in which long existing "stand-alone silos of thought" reflect "incommensuration across theoretical boundaries" (p. 390). From a cross-cultural perspective such a field is likely to be inhabited by parochial and ethnocentric views and attitudes. Over the last 20 years, along the advancements in cross-cultural research, cross-cultural leadership research built up the potential to set an example for the too pluralistic general field of leadership research in how to advance development towards more integrated concepts and theories. To that respect, Glynn and Raffaelli (2010) note that the scientific development of leadership research could indeed profit from a cross-cultural research perspective.

Thus, rather than inherit a multitude of leadership definitions from its mother discipline (and the controversies with them), some cross-cultural leadership researchers began to ask the question of how definitions and theories of leadership should be constructed in order to best suit the purpose of the cross-cultural investigation of leadership phenomena. In that respect, we find two definitional approaches to leadership noteworthy, one is social psychological in nature and addresses leadership as a universal social phenomenon, and one is based on a cross-nationally agreed-upon definition of organizational leadership.

A social psychological "universal" definition of leadership. Because social psychological research is intended to advance universal theories of human experience, emotion, motivation, cognition, and behavior in social situations, it is oriented towards universalistic concepts and definitions of leadership as a social psychological phenomenon (e.g., Bond & Smith, 1996). These are likely to fit the purposes of cross-cultural research. Smith (1995), for example, defines leadership from a social psychological perspective, as "a quality attributed to people as a result of their interrelations with others." This admittedly very abstract and broad definition does not imply that leadership comes with people (e.g., personality characteristics) or a position (e.g., line manager) or the organizational and societal cultural context (e.g., hierarchical values). Instead, personal characteristics, peculiarities of positions, and cultural contexts are seen as conditions that shape, facilitate, or inhibit the expression of leadership and its effectiveness in social contexts, and as such, they are matters for scientific discovery rather than defining constituents of the terms "leader" and "leadership."

One advantage of such an approach is its compatibility with psychological and social psychological theory building, which operates from basically universal concepts of human motivation, cognition, or behavior, for example, the cognitive leadership categorization theory (Lord & Maher, 1991), the propositions of which should principally apply to leadership across all cultures in the world. Smith et al. (2002) argue for the use of a relatively nonspecific social psychological concept of leadership in order to being better able to explore value-behavior linkages by taking a culture general (*etic*) approach.

Another advantage is that a nonspecific social psychological definition is better suited to cross-cultural leadership research than definitions of leadership that make subliminal ethnocentric value assumptions. For example, some authors understand leadership in terms of exercising persuasive (and not coercive) influence on followers, for example, "Leaders are individuals who significantly affect the thoughts and behaviors of others, without using coercion, but rather through persuasion" (Adler, 2002, p. 167). Thereby, it is implied that individuals who rely on coercion and manipulation for influencing followers, although possibly appropriate and effective in some cultures or contexts, are not seen (or categorized by their followers) as "leaders," and respective leadership values and behaviors are likely to be excluded or degraded as subject for scientific inquiry.

A cross-cultural "consensual" definition of organizational leadership. An attempt to define leadership cross-culturally was undertaken by the GLOBE project. In its beginning phase, in 1995, in a meeting of 84 scholars representing 56 countries, a consensual and culture-universal (with respect to the countries represented) definition of "organizational leadership" emerged, that is, "the ability of an individual to influence, motivate, and enable others to contribute to the effectiveness and success of the organizations of which they are members" (House et al., 1997, p. 548). The developmental process was to find consensus among a culturally heterogeneous and large sample of cultural backgrounds of the scholars involved. And, for better comparability across many countries, the focus of inquiry was laid on leadership in business organizations and industries existent in all 61 countries studied; and, for a start, middle managers were used as respondents, because they lead and are being led, and thus have experience with the leader and the follower perspective. Employees or top-level executives would have been an equally appropriate comparison reference across all countries studied. The latter group of managers has lately been investigated in GLOBE phase 3 in relation to organizational effectiveness (see House et al., in prep.).

Which Approach to Culture to Take for Studying Leadership?

As can be seen from the various definitions of culture suggested by prominent social scientists, like with leadership, there is no consensually agreed-upon definition of culture. It has been defined as the man-made part of the environment (Herskovits, 1955); as patterned ways of thinking, feeling, and reacting acquired by human collectives (Kluckhohn & Strodtbeck, 1961); as norms, roles, values, and belief systems that form meaningful wholes (Triandis, 1972); as the collective programming of the mind, which distinguishes the members of one human group from another (Hofstede, 1980); or as standard operating procedures—"the way things are done around here" (e.g., Triandis, 1994). While the meanings of culture as a construct converge, its measurement tends to differ more and more (for a review of current measures, see Tsui, Nifadkar, & Ou, 2007). Although it is often acknowledged that culture operates at multiple levels (e.g., national culture, subcultures, and organizational culture), national culture has been the predominantly used category for cross-cultural leadership research in the past and today. Therefore this review is concerned primarily with national culture and how it relates to leadership.

Cultural values versus cultural practices. It appears that no newer definitions of culture that deviate substantially from the above presented have been suggested lately, except perhaps for one distinction made in the GLOBE study. GLOBE introduced the distinction of cultural values (culture as a normative system of its members—"should be") as compared to cultural practices (culture "as is" experienced by its members) into the cross-cultural research domain (House et al., 1997; House et al., 2004). The cultural values or normative approach is consistent with traditional culture value-belief theory (e.g., Hofstede, 1980; Kluckhohn & Strodtbeck, 1961; Triandis, 1994) that has been widely used in cross-cultural research. According to the experiential ("as is") definition of culture in GLOBE's cultural practices approach, "cultures are distinctive environments about which members share meaning and values, resulting in a compelling model pattern of common affective, attitudinal, and behavioral orientation that is transmitted across generations and that differentiates collectivities from each other" (House et al., 1997, p. 540). Both cultural values and practices measures have been validated on the country level of analysis with different data sets inside and outside from GLOBE (Gupta, Sully de Luque, & House, 2004; Hanges & Dickson, 2004; Javidan & Hauser, 2004).

What the distinction between cultural practices and values actually means is still not fully explored.

Even among GLOBE country coinvestigators, there is considerable disagreement about the meaning of this distinction (e.g., see the country chapters in Chhokar et al., 2007). Whereas the standard cross-cultural literature assumed that societal cultural practices and values are positively correlated on the country level of analysis (e.g., Triandis, 2004), the GLOBE data show that for most dimensions (seven out of nine) negative country-level correlations between their value and practices counterparts are obtained (ranging from $r = -.26$ to $r = -.62$). One explanation for these findings was suggested by Brodbeck, Chhokar, and House (2007) in the form of the *deprivation hypothesis*. For the individual respondent, a disparity between "as is" and "should be" responses to commensurable culture dimensions is based on perceiving certain societal cultural practices as less or more dominant in their society than they think they should be (i.e., deprivation). On the country level, the respondents' shared perceptions of a disparity (negative or positive) between culture practices and values imply a culturally shared "sympathy" with (higher or lower levels of) certain cultural values. It remains to be tested whether the deprivation hypothesis can actually explain or predict cultures' readiness for change toward the implementation of desired cultural values that are deprived (for a more detailed account, see Brodbeck et al., 2007).

With respect to leadership prototypes, the GLOBE results show that cultural and organizational value (should be) dimensions are overall much stronger predictors than culture and organizational practice (as is) dimensions. Given that cultural values reflect an idealized state of what should be in societies and organizations respectively, and that leadership prototypes comprise individuals' implicit beliefs regarding idealized or effective leadership, cultural (should be) values and leadership prototypes ought to correspond more strongly (Dorfman et al., 2004, p. 701ff).

Emic versus etic approach to the study of cross-cultural leadership. There are two basic perspectives that can be employed in the study of a society's cultural system—the point of view of either the outsider or the insider. For that distinction, the linguist and anthropologist Kenneth Pike (1954) coined the neologisms "*etic*" (for an outside view and "*emic*" (for an inside view), which were readily adopted in the cross-cultural literature (cf. Triandis, 1980). Pike derived the terms by analogy from the terms "phonetics" and "phonemics," two subdisciplines in linguistics for the study of languages' sound systems: Phon*etics* asks the question of which phones can be physically expressed by human beings, and phon*emics* asks the question of which meaningful distinctions are referred to by particular phones, and if identified as meaningful, phones become phonemes.

An etic approach to the cross-cultural study of leadership attempts to generalize leadership phenomena and theory across cultures and examines similarities and differences, thereby preferring quantitative and comparative methods. An emic approach focuses on the study of leadership and its meaning within the particular cultural contexts in which it occurs, thereby preferring qualitative, narrative, and interpretative methods. Etic approaches have been more dominant in cross-cultural leadership research than emic approaches. Recently, both approaches were combined in the GLOBE study (Chhokar et al., 2007).

Scandura and Dorfman (2004) pointed out that it is a common misinterpretation in cross-cultural (leadership) research, when "etic" is equated with culture-common or universal leadership phenomena and "emic" with culture-specific ones, because in the distinction in linguistics, "etic" utterances encompass all "emic" utterances, which is not the understanding when culture-universal leadership attributes are differentiated from culture-specific ones. We would not go as far as Dorfman, who suggested "to ditch the terms emic and etic" (Scandura & Dorfman, 2004, p. 288), the use of "etic" for an outer perspective and "emic" for an inner perspective of culture, each in the above-described sense, is still helpful for addressing the particular approach that is taken to the study of cultural issues in leadership.

Should the Field Focus on Leadership Differences or Communalities Across Cultures?

The distinction between culture-specific and culture-universal leadership phenomena addresses a different set of questions than the distinction between emic and etic approaches to the study of cultural issues. Grounded in a basically etic perspective on the cross-cultural study of leadership, *leadership "differs culturally"-approaches* ask the question of whether leadership is culturally contingent and which leadership attributes are most strongly affected by cultural factors. Also grounded in an etic perspective, *leadership "is universal"-approaches*, in contrast, seek to establish leadership and certain leadership attributes as globally concordant phenomena.

The leadership "differs culturally"-approach. Coming from the leadership domain, Yukl (2006) distinguished four types of questions raised in cross-cultural leadership research. Each type of question comprises one theme inherited from general leadership research plus the addendum "*differs culturally*": (a) "How conceptualizations of leadership behavior (e.g., prototypes, descriptions) differ culturally?", (b) "How beliefs about effective leadership differ culturally?", (c) "How actual patterns of leadership behavior differ culturally?", and (d) "How relationships between leadership behavior and outcomes differ across cultures?" Questions like these reflect traditional approaches to the study of cross-cultural leadership, implying that leadership differs across cultures. Studies that take the leadership "differs culturally" approach are often descriptive in nature and usually compare small samples of countries (for a review, see Bass, 2008). Their results yield leadership peculiarities in certain countries and cultural regions as compared to other countries. As in other areas of cross-cultural management research, usual reference points in such comparisons are countries that are of interest for economic reasons: the United States; European countries such as Germany, France, or the United Kingdom; as well as some Asian cultures such as China, India or Japan (cf. Tsui et al., 2007). However, integration of all these findings is a difficult undertaking, because of the multitude of different leadership definitions and concepts used and the often not overlapping sets of countries and groups of respondents studied.

The same approach is taken in studies that are described to establish "main effects of culture" (cf. Gelfand et al., 2007) on leadership, usually evidenced in the amount of variance in leadership phenomena that can be explained by country differences or zero-order correlations between cultural dimensions and leadership phenomena on the country level of analysis (for overviews, see, e.g., Bass, 2008; House et al., 2004). From these studies it is hoped to derive the extent to which findings from leadership research can (or cannot) be transferred or generalized from one culture to another.

The leadership "is universal"-approach. A classic question in cross-cultural leadership is about the universality of leadership and leadership attributes, for example, "is leadership a universal phenomenon?" (Scandura & Dorfman, 2004), is there a "global idea" of leadership? (Peterson & Hunt, 1997). Being aware of the problem to become trapped within the most commonly asked, although often misleading, question of *whether* organizational dynamics (including leadership) are universal or culturally specific, Adler (2008) suggests, from a practitioners' point of view, to focus on the more "crucially important questions of *when* and *how* to be sensitive to culture" (p. 7). This perspective helps to readjust the question of *whether* leadership and leadership attributes are universal or culturally specific into questions like in *which respects* are leadership phenomena more culture specific and in which are they more universal (cf. Scandura & Dorfman, 2004).

Types of universality. Research summarized by Bass (1997, 1999) and GLOBE (cf. Dorfman et al., 2004) suggest that some aspects of leadership, in particular, transformational, charismatic, and team-oriented leadership, may be universal. But what does "universal" mean? Bass (1997) has pointed out that the term can have a variety of meanings when applied to leadership (see also Dickson et al., 2003, p. 732 ff): (a) *simple universal*: a leadership phenomenon or principle that is constant throughout the world (e.g., country level means on leadership prototype dimensions that do not vary across cultures); (b) *variform universal*: a general leadership phenomenon or principle that holds across cultures, but the enactment of it differs across cultures (e.g., various ways of how participative leadership is enacted exist in a set of countries where this principle is equally strongly endorsed, cf. Brodbeck et al., 2007); (c) *functional universal*: when the relationship between two leadership relevant variables is the same across cultures (e.g., within-country correlations are nonvariant across cultures); (d) *variform functional universal*: when a relationship between two leadership relevant variables is found in all cultures, but the strength or direction of the relationship varies across cultures (e.g., collectivistic cultural values strengthen the positive relationship between transformational leadership and employees' job satisfaction, e.g., Walumbwa & Lawler, 2003); and (e) *systematic behavioral universal*: when leadership theory defines a process such as a sequence of behaviors or a structure such as a distinct behavioral cluster that is empirically shown to be constant over cultures.

Dickson et al. (2003) diagnosed a decline in the volume of research focused on identifying simple universals and an increase of attempts to find differences between cultures on leadership traits, characteristics, and relationships that can be explained by the various available sets of cultural dimensions. In our view, this is still the case in principle, although some progress has been made toward the development of cross-culturally more sophisticated leadership theory, which attempts to quantify cultural effects on leadership and to establish more clear-cut distinctions between *near-to-universal* and culture-specific leadership characteristics in several ways: by empirically establishing the magnitude of cultural effects on leadership, by identifying culture-specific leadership dimensions and emic "species" of leadership beyond dimensions in particular groups of countries, by investigating culture as a moderator of the relationships between leadership relevant variables, and by empirically investigating the *culture congruency* proposition (i.e., cultural forces affect the kind of leadership behaviors accepted, enacted, and effective within a particular culture, cf. House et al., 1997, p. 590) in relation to the *universality* proposition of leadership phenomena. Studies and findings as to each of these theoretical questions and propositions are described next.

What Is the Magnitude of Cultural Effects on Leadership?

To empirically quantify the magnitude of cultural effects on leadership phenomena was first suggested by House et al. (1997). Answering this question requires large-scale cross-cultural studies or meta-analytical designs. In their 61 nations study, the GLOBE researchers empirically established effect sizes (coefficient of determination) for cultural (country-level) differences between 14 percent (with respect to autonomous leadership) and 36 percent (with respect to self-protective leadership); 20 percent was obtained for charismatic value-based leadership (Dorfman et al., 2004, p. 697). The latter leadership dimension conceptually overlaps with transformational leadership. Further results of HLM analyses indicate that the six GLOBE leadership dimensions are significantly associated with the nine societal cultural *values* ("should be") scales from GLOBE with an average country-level common variance of about 25 percent (Dorfman et al., 2004, p. 699ff).

Whereas the GLOBE research focused on characteristics of leadership prototypes, Leong and Fischer (2011) focused on transformational leadership behaviors (as assessed with the MLQ) by using a meta-analytical design comprising about 20,000 respondents from N = 18 countries. They found that cultural differences in transformational leadership behavior share up to 50 per cent of the total variability between countries. And similar to the GLOBE findings, they found that about 25 per cent could be explained by cultural value dimensions (from Schwartz and Hofstede). More specifically, Leong and Fischer (2011) report that managers in more egalitarian contexts are seen as engaging more in transformational leadership behaviors. This finding corroborates with the GLOBE findings with respect to charismatic value-based leadership, which relates positively to the GLOBE cultural value scales "in-group collectivism" (r = .41), "gender egalitarianism" (r = .41), and negatively to "power distance" (r = –.57) (Dorfman et al., 2004, p. 699).

Are There Culture-Specific Dimensions of Leadership?

For studying particular leadership phenomena dominant only in certain cultures or groups of countries, specific scales and dimensions have been developed. Two groups of researchers demonstrated that paternalistic leadership has a positive impact on employee attitudes in collectivistic and high-power-distance cultures (Aycan, Kanungo, Mendonca, Yu, & Deller, 2000; Farh & Cheng, 2000). In a study with five nations in North America and Asia, Dorfman, Howell, Hibino, Lee, Tate, and Bautista (1997) showed cultural specificity for directive, participative, and contingent punishment leader behaviors. And, by studying behavioral patterns of leader-follower dyads in China, *guanxi* (i.e., personal relationship characterized by sentiment [*qing*] and obligation [*yi*], cf. Yang, 1994) between supervisor and subordinate was shown to be distinct from the Western concept of leader-member exchange quality (LMX) and to predict supervisor decisions such as promotion or bonus allocation after controlling for performance (Law, Wong, Wang, & Wang, 2000). Interestingly, also, negative effects of *guanxi* practices on trust in management were found and shown to be mediated by perceived (low) procedural justice. In an experimental scenario study, this negative effect was replicated and further relevant moderators were identified, such as favoring a familiar tie (e.g., a family member or a friend), which reduces trust in management to a greater degree than favoring a neutral party (Chen, Chen, & Xin, 2004).

A multidimensional scaling approach (MDS) for identifying culture-specific dimensions of leadership was taken by Brodbeck et al. (2000) who investigated a subset of European countries (N = 22) from the GLOBE study. Three leadership dimensions (interpersonal directness and proximity, modesty, autonomy) were obtained via MDS (cf. Smith et al., 1996), which differentiate well between the European cultural regions (Anglo, Nordic,

Germanic, Latin, Central, South East Europe) identified in earlier studies (cf. Ronen & Shenkar, 1985). Whereas the "interpersonal directness and proximity" leadership dimension is strongly related to Smith et al.'s (1996) culture dimension "egalitarian commitment," and the "modesty" leadership dimension is moderately related to Smith et al.'s (1996) "loyal involvement" dimension, the "autonomy" dimension comes out as a rather distinct facet of leadership. Autonomous leadership is positively endorsed in only a small subset of Central (Germanic) and East European countries (i.e., Germany, German-speaking Switzerland, Austria, Czech Republic, and Georgia). For an in-depth analysis of the Germanic "brands" of autonomous leadership, see Brodbeck, Frese, and Javidan (2002); Brodbeck and Frese (2007); and Szabo, Brodbeck, Den Hartog, Reber, and Weibler (2002).

Are There Emic "Species" of Leadership Beyond Dimensions?

Triandis (1994) pointed out that cultures, on the one hand, can be specified on some common dimension (e.g., collectivism versus individualism), but on the other hand, they differ on additional culturally specific elements of the constructs of interest. He suggested that the cross-cultural construct of interest should be polythetically defined as in zoology: the defining features of the category "bird" are wings and feathers, but distinguishing between different species of birds requires consideration of some further combinations of attributes (e.g., yellow beak, carnivorous). Analogously, for distinguishing between leadership phenomena in societies, cross-culturally valid leadership dimensions constitute a necessary first step, but they are not sufficient. Further theoretical and empirical refinement is necessary.

By combining etic and emic approaches to the study of leadership in 25 countries, Brodbeck et al. (2007) polythetically identified "species" of participative leadership for a subset of countries that all share very high scores on the participative leadership dimension. On the basis of emic accounts of participative leadership in each country, four different "species" of participative leadership were established. Each describes how the high endorsement of participative leadership manifests itself and is rooted in the respective cultures' societal cultural practices and values: (a) as an opposition to nonparticipative, autocratic, or directive leadership without an identifiable prescription of how to practice participative leadership (e.g., Finland, Argentina, France); (b) as a principle to organize interactions at work between "labor and capital" (or management) in a participative way, which is manifest in particular societal and organizational cultural practices, values, and even in legal systems (e.g., Austria, Germany, Switzerland); (c) as a set of personal competencies apparent in leadership conduct, which surfaces, for example, in treating others as equals, being informal and not preoccupied with oneself (e.g., United States); and (d) as a set of communication behaviors like listening and inviting suggestions from others that aligns with societal cultural resentment against formal rules and a preference for open exchange but with few consequences in actual decision-making practices in organizations and society (e.g., Greece). With a purely etic dimensional approach, these different "species" of participative leadership would not have surfaced, because all described societies score in the same high band (i.e., not significantly different from each other) on the GLOBE dimension of participative leadership (cf. Chhokar et al., 2007; House et al., 2004).

Subtle differences and emic leadership practices dominant in certain countries or cultures may even not become apparent until detailed behavioral analysis is undertaken. This was done for some of the above-mentioned European countries by Reber, Jago, Auer-Rizzi, and Szabo (2000) who observed leaders' actual decision-making behavior in leadership training situations derived from Vroom and Yetton's (1973) model of participation. They found that Austrian (similar to German and Swiss) leaders displayed significantly more participative decision-making behavior at work than leaders from Finland, France, Czech Republic, Poland, Turkey, and the United States. Furthermore, Austrian as well as German managers were observed to use participative leadership behavior more often than others to bring information and different perspectives to bear on the task. And even more interesting, Austrian managers responded to and resolved conflicts among subordinates by becoming *more* participative, whereas French, Finnish, American, Polish, and Czech managers displayed more autocratic leadership behaviors when conflicts occurred.

How Does Culture Moderate the Relationship Between Leadership and Other Variables?

Moderating effects of culture have been investigated mainly in small- to mid-scale studies, which were reviewed by Tsui et al. (2007). For example, two different research groups showed that collectivistic (vs. individualistic) cultural values strengthen the relationship between transformational leadership and employees' job satisfaction, organizational attitudes, and turnover intentions (e.g., Spreitzer, Perttula, & Xin, 2005; Walumbwa & Lawler 2003). And, by comparing Sweden and Russia, Elenkov and Manev (2005) found that in Russia innovation was facilitated by active and passive management by exception, charismatic leadership, confidence in, and idealized influence on followers. In contrast, in Sweden only inspirational motivation and intellectual stimulation had similar facilitative effects on innovation. Studies of this type inform global leadership consultants about culture- and country-specific relationships between leadership relevant variables, and they should invite further investigation about the culture-specific enactment, acceptance, and interpretation of leadership characteristics, such as transformational versus transactional leadership, which have been identified as potentially universal leadership characteristics (Bass, 1999; Judge & Piccolo, 2004; Judge, Woolf, Hurst, & Livington, 2006; Leong & Fischer, 2011).

Such further investigation was undertaken in a laboratory study reported by Ensari and Murphy (2003) who examined the interactive effects of two alternative processes of leadership perceptions on attributions of charisma cross-culturally. They found that in individualistic cultures, perception of charisma is based on recognition-based perceptions (i.e., leadership effectiveness is a perception that is based on how well a person fits the characteristics of a "good" or "effective" leader), whereas in collectivistic cultures, it is based on inference-based perceptions (i.e., leadership effectiveness is an inference based on group/organizational performance outcomes). In addition, it was shown that the investigated leaders' prototypical characteristics were more effective in forming a leadership impression in an individualistic culture, whereas collectivistic people made attributions based on the company performance outcome. Even more complex relationships between culture, leadership characteristics, and other relevant variables, like followers' reactions or leader effectiveness, are lurking when, for example, classic propositions such as the *culture congruency proposition* and the *universality proposition* are not only, on plausibility grounds, transferred to other related phenomena than those originally investigated, but when these propositions are directly empirically investigated for the purpose of the development of cross-cultural leadership theory.

Is Leadership Culturally Contingent or Universal or Both?

According to the cultural congruency hypothesis, which has been described as "an article of faith among cultural theorists" (House et al., 1997, p. 590), cultural forces affect the kind of leadership behaviors that are usually accepted, enacted, and effective within a particular cultural collective. Behavior that is consistent with collective values is more acceptable and effective than behavior representing conflicting values. But what actually follows from this for cross-cultural leadership theory? Is perfect cultural congruency always desired, or would it be beneficial to exceed cultural expectations on some dimensions of leadership, as has been formulated in the *cultural differences proposition* (House et al., 1997, p. 591)? Can a leader who violates culturally endorsed leadership expectations still be seen as effective? Are culture-universal leadership characteristics of the simple or variform type? And, do cultural congruency effects hold up in the same way for *variform* cultural-universal as compared to culture-specific dimensions of leadership characteristics and behaviors, or are they of a different type?

Despite wide-ranging differences in cultural norms and values, the *near universality of leadership proposition*, stating that some leadership behaviors are universally or nearly universally accepted, enacted, and effective (cf. House et al., 1997, p. 591), has received some empirical support. Increasing empirical evidence is available that indicates that this proposition holds for attributes of charismatic value-based and transformational leadership (Bass, 1999; Dorfman et al., 2004; Judge et al., 2006) as well as for team-oriented leadership (Dorfman et al., 2004). However, it is a difficult task to empirically establish leadership characteristics and behaviors to be universally endorsed (in the sense of simple universality), because it requires the reverse of the way hypotheses are typically tested—which essentially means testing the null hypothesis, for which very large samples are required. There is always some variance between cultures or countries detectable in the enactment, acceptance, and effectiveness of leadership, which makes it difficult to unequivocally identify certain leadership characteristics as simple universal. Therefore, variform universal characteristics are considered when testing the near-universal proposition empirically. And a thereby important question is, whether the variable components of a variform universal are meaningful with respect to a criterion variable that can be tested empirically in the form of a functional universal.

This reasoning was employed in a recent study presented by Ruderman, Brodbeck, Eckert, Gentry, and Braddy (2011) by testing the cultural congruency proposition and the near-universality proposition concordantly with a set of culture contingent and a set of near-universal leadership characteristics. For this, the authors developed a new 360° feedback instrument (Global Leader View©; Eckert et al., 2011) and analyzed data from N = 1,837 respondents (including N = 316 target leaders) from over 80 countries. By using a different set of items than was used in the GLOBE study, the six GLOBE leadership prototypicality dimensions could be replicated and were shown to be valid on the individual level of analysis. This not only speaks to the robustness of the GLOBE dimensions but also extends the GLOBE scales, which were originally validated only on the country level of analysis, to the individual level of analysis. Each of the items in the new 360° feedback instrument measures characteristics of individual respondents' leadership prototypes (expectations) and also their respective perceptions of their supervisor's (i.e., target leader's) leadership attributes (not measured by GLOBE). As in the GLOBE study, charismatic value-based and team-oriented leadership could be established as characteristics of a universal leadership prototype while other dimensions, notably autonomous and hierarchical leadership, were shown to be culture specific. With polynomial and multiple regression analyses, the culture congruency proposition (for autonomous and hierarchical leadership) and the near-universality proposition (for charismatic and team-oriented leadership) were concordantly tested with leadership effectiveness ratings as the dependent variable.

It was found that for the culture-specific leadership dimensions, the congruency or fit (expressed in a polynomial interaction term) between commensurate leadership expectations and perceptions of a target leader significantly predicted leader effectiveness ratings, which is in line with leadership categorization theory (Lord & Maher, 1991) and the culture congruency proposition (House et al., 1997). In contrast, for the universal leadership dimensions, the congruency between commensurate expectations and perceptions did not relate to leader effectiveness ratings. Instead, leadership perceptions of charismatic and team-oriented leadership significantly predicted leader effectiveness ratings directly. The respective leadership expectations did not seem to matter at all.

The described findings are remarkable in several respects: with respect to near-universal characteristics of leadership prototypes, the results obtained align with the near-universality proposition, but they contradict leadership categorization theory, which up to now was only tested within and not across cultures (e.g., Germany: van Quaquebeke, van Knippenberg, & Brodbeck, 2011; Great Britain: Epitropaki & Martin, 2004, 2005; United States: Lord, Foti, & De Vader, 1984; Offermann, Kennedy, & Wirtz, 1994). More important, whatever amount of cross-cultural variance in leadership expectations about the considered near-to-universal charismatic and team-oriented leadership characteristics may exist, it does not seem to matter for leader effectiveness ratings, neither directly, nor as a part of the interplay between leadership expectations and perceptions. What matters instead only is the variance in perceptions about the target leader. Finally with respect to culture-specific characteristics of leadership prototypes the predictions from both leader categorization theory and the culture congruency proposition hold up.

In summary, from universal leadership characteristics (charismatic and team-oriented leadership), once perceived to be shown by a target leader, leader effectiveness is directly inferred. For culture-specific leadership characteristics (autonomy and hierarchic leadership), leadership expectations and leader perceptions must match for leader effectiveness to be inferred. These findings are an example of how leadership categorization theory, which has been developed and tested in laboratory and monocultural field settings, can be further refined and developed by using cross-cultural leadership studies, thereby also suggesting a solution to the long-standing problems of how universal versus culture-specific leadership characteristics can be empirically differentiated and validated.

Where Do We Stand Regarding Methodological Issues in Cross-Cultural Leadership Research?

From the landmark studies described above and the further mid- to large-scale research programs reviewed, it is apparent that it takes many steps until sound empirical results in cross-cultural leadership research are reportable, not to mention the time and effort necessary for establishing international research networks and larger samples of countries that go beyond convenient assemblies of respondents. It appears, however, that with these programs, long-lasting methodological shortcomings of cross-cultural leadership research, discussed for example by House et al. (1997) and Dickson et al. (2003), have been addressed to a considerable extent during the last 15 years.

In the studies reviewed, effortful attempts and sound approaches to tackle long-standing methodological problems are apparent, like establishing measurement equivalence across cultures (e.g., Hanges & Dickson, 2004); sampling of sufficiently large numbers of countries or cultures and respondents (N > 45; e.g., House et al., 2004; Smith et al., 2002); consideration of multiple levels of analysis and relevant collective units, like country, subcultures per country, industries across countries, organizations, types of respondents (Gelfand et al., 2011; House et al., 2004; House et al., in prep.; Taras et al., 2010); or various managerial levels (Den Hartog, House, Hanges, Ruiz-Quintanilla, & Dorfman, 1999). Sophisticated statistical techniques were used such as multidimensional scaling (Brodbeck et al., 2000; Smith et al., 1996); multilevel confirmatory factor analysis (Hanges & Dickson, 2004); hierarchical linear modeling (Dorfman et al., 2004); polynomial regression with response surface analysis for congruency hypothesis testing (Ruderman et al., 2011); and meta-analysis (e.g., Leong & Fischer, 2011; Taras et al., 2010) to address various important issues, such as construct validity of scales (e.g., Gupta et al., 2004; Gelfand et al., 2011); assessment of effect size estimates, correlations, moderation, and interaction effects, involving leadership relevant variables, as well as a diverse set of qualitative methods and techniques to combine data and results obtained from etic and emic approaches to cross-cultural leadership phenomena (e.g., Brodbeck et al., 2007).

Occasionally, external data sources about countries were also used to triangulate cultural dimensions (e.g., World Values Survey, Human Development Report; cf. Gelfand et al., 2011; Javidan & House, 2004), behavioral observation was undertaken in order to investigate actual participative leadership behavior across several cultures (Reber et al., 2000), or a CEO's rhetoric in speeches for an international audience were analyzed with discourse analysis (Den Hartog, & Verburg, 1997), to name just a few of the more creative approaches to the study of cross-cultural leadership. However, despite the advantage of using multiple methods, survey research is likely to continue to be the dominant research tool in cross-cultural leadership research. The difficulties inherent in conducting qualitative research (cf. Chhokar et al., 2007; House, Spangler, & Woycke, 1991), quasi and field experiments (e.g., Reber et al., 2000) or in-depth content and discourse analysis (Den Hartog & Verburg, 1997) will continue to limit the number of more innovative studies.

In summary, it appears that since the mid '90s not only a raise of large-scale cross-cultural leadership studies is apparent but also an increase in the diversity and sophistication of measurement instruments and statistical analysis. The advantages of large numbers of cross-cultural samples are manifold: they appear to be rather robust against unmatched samples (Smith et al., 1996) and allow the empirical testing of more complex theoretical models. Furthermore, data from large-scale cross-cultural studies can be used as country-level input in other studies, thereby promoting further validation and testing as well as a better integration of cross-cultural empirical findings and leadership theory in general. In the future, small samples of a few countries or cultures would need to be justified by compelling reasons explaining, for example, why the particular countries were selected (Bass, 2008; Scandura & Dorfman, 2004).

Some classic methodological questions still remain to be answered: To what extent are leadership characteristics comparable (e.g., leadership prototypes versus leader behavior perceptions versus actually observed leader behavior)? Are nations suitable units for cultural comparison? Are the leadership phenomena we look at functionally equivalent across cultures? How do we address levels of analysis problems, which arise because of the varying levels of measurement among constructs? For example, societal and organizational culture are by definition aggregated phenomena, but leadership could be an individual, dyadic, team, organization, and/or society level phenomenon (cf. Scandura & Dorfman, 2004).

A Practitioners' Perspective

As organizations increasingly face global markets and operate across national borders, career paths become more and more international, and management assignments are most likely to involve leading in multicultural contexts. Associated with that, managers and human resources practitioners face multiple new challenges: that is, culturally diverse teams have to be managed, people have to be diagnosed for their international leadership potential, professional training programs have to be created in which managers get systematic education on cross-cultural leadership (e.g., Schyns, Kiefer, Kerschreiter, & Tymon, 2011), and—in the case of cross-cultural joint ventures—cultural difference between the partners has to be acknowledged (e.g., Javidan, Stahl, Brodbeck & Wilderom, 2005).

Although cross-cultural research on leadership has generated a substantial amount of knowledge, which may help address these challenges, most research results have not been translated into concrete recommendations and tools for practitioners. Thus, their potential to enhance managerial practice appears to be largely untapped. In the following, we briefly point out some examples of how findings reported in the cross-cultural leadership literature may contribute to resolve practical questions of (1) evaluating and training international managers, (2) selecting international executives, and (3) planning and conducting international joint ventures.

To successfully manage multinational teams and projects, leaders greatly benefit from professional preparation and education programs, in which relevant cultural knowledge is transferred and cross-cultural competencies are developed (Bass, 2008). Black and Mendenhall (1990) showed the general effectiveness of cross-cultural training programs. Programs to equip managers for international projects and assignments should comprise general and culture-specific briefings, which, for instance, could be derived from GLOBE's comparative 61-nations study (House et al., 2004) and in-depth studies of 25 societies (Chhokar et al., 2007), and may start with a sound diagnosis of one's leadership style.

The 360° leadership feedback instruments could be constructed along the lines of empirically established cross-cultural dimensions of leadership (e.g., Ruderman et al., 2011). They can provide leaders with feedback about their own and others' leadership expectations and perceptions in cross-cultural and global contexts, thereby supporting the understanding to what extent "leadership is in the eye of the beholder" and what the role of culturally congruent and near-universal leadership attributes is in this process.

Organizations have to assess and select employees for their potential of international leadership. Spreitzer, McCall, and Mahoney (1997) developed a tool—*Prospector*—that allows for early identification of international executives. The instrument includes 14 dimensions (i.e., sensitive to cultural differences, business knowledge, courage to take a stand, brings out the best in people, acts with integrity, is insightful, is committed to success, takes risks, uses feedback, is culturally adventurous, seeks opportunities to learn, is open to criticism, seeks feedback, is flexible), which measure individuals' relevant competencies and ability to learn from experience.

The concept of "global mindset" may be another fruitful way to approach the selection of international leaders (cf. Beechler & Javidan, 2007). Research established that global mindsets and the cognitive capabilities of senior managers are central to organizational success in international environments (e.g., Gupta & Govindarajan, 2002; Levy, 2005). Integrating different research findings, Levy, Bechler, Taylor, and Boyacigiller (2007) suggested that a global mindset consists of three components: openness to multiple spheres of meaning and action, differentiated articulation of cultural and strategic dynamics on the local and the global level, and integration across these spheres. Organizations may use scales for measuring global mindsets (e.g., Javidan & Teagarden, 2011; Levy, 2005) in their assessment procedures to filter out potential cross-cultural leaders.

Additionally, research on societies' cultural profiles and regional cultural clusters may be helpful in the planning and conduct of international joint ventures. Predictions on the success of joint-venture partnerships frequently built on an index, which determined the cultural similarity between the actors by using the Hofstede dimensions (Kogut & Singh, 1988; for a review of newer indices cf. Magnuson, Wilson, Zdravkovic, Zhou, & Westjohn, 2008). The GLOBE project offers more recent and sophisticated profiles of society culture and cultural clusters, which have been applied for analyzing inhibiting and enhancing cultural factors for cross-cultural joint ventures (Javidan et al., 2005). The indices developed by Smith et al. (1996) in their work on event management reflect what sources of guidance managers use in handling work events and, thereby, are closely related to managerial contexts. And more generally, the culture tightness looseness dimension offered by Gelfand and her colleagues (e.g., Gelfand et al., 2011) provides a further option to systematically compare cultures on grounds that are relevant for global economic and political conduct.

In summary, there appears to be scarce empirical research that measures the impact of cross-cultural leadership research in terms of its practical applications and its usefulness for supporting the above described and further tasks in international human resources management (IHRM) and global leadership development. There is no doubt that the research findings reviewed here and elsewhere are considered to be impactful in an indirect way, for example, in that wide appreciation and acknowledgement of cross-cultural issues in organizations and management is given in practical publications (e.g., Adler, 2008) and recent reviews of cross-cultural organizational behavior (e.g., Gelfand et al., 2007). However, like with the more general endeavor of evidence-based management (e.g., Pfeffer & Sutton, 2006; Rousseau, 2006), which aims to close the gap between theory driven empirical research and practical application in the management domain, empirical studies actually demonstrating the impact and usefulness of concrete interventions in global leadership that have been derived from cross-cultural leadership research are rare.

Conclusions

Rather than being seen as an adjunct to leadership research or an adjunct to cross-cultural research, cross-cultural leadership research today can be seen as a valid and distinct domain of study, even more so than a decade ago (Dickson et al., 2003). As this review illustrates, cross-cultural leadership research is thriving.

Major parts of the progress seem to have been driven by large-scale research programs, notably the GLOBE project, a long-lasting program (since 1994), which is also recognized as a major contributor to cross-cultural leadership in recent reviews of cross-cultural organizational behavior (Gelfand et al., 2007) and leadership research in general (Avolio et al., 2009). The difficulty to integrate single or small-scale culture studies into the broader developments of cross-cultural leadership theory becomes apparent, when comparing Bass's (2008) comprehensive review, which is mainly descriptive rather than integrative in nature, with the present one, in which attempts are made to integrate commensurate research findings and theoretical developments along the lines of central questions of the field. Due to space limitations, we had to be selective in the choice of studies, thereby taking the risk to omit potentially relevant studies and research programs—we apologize for that and urge the reader to cross-check the present review with other available reviews of the field. However, we do hope to have succeeded in stock taking of central questions, theoretical developments, empirical findings, and methodological advancements in the current field from which integrative avenues for its future development can be derived.

Large-scale multination studies conducted by teams of researchers, using the same instruments and construct definitions, are one way to overcome the classic hurdles in cross-cultural leadership research. The present review has demonstrated that such studies emerged and contributed, directly and indirectly, to the progress made in the field during the period sampled here. Several advances in theory development and in the methods of cross-cultural leadership research have been alluded to in this review. Several of these could not have been made without large-scale multinational studies, be they meta-analytic (Leong & Fischer, 2011); quantitative, evaluative, and comparative (e.g., House et al., 2004; Ruderman et al., 2011; Smith et al., 2002); or qualitative, analytic, and culture specific (Chhokar et al., 2007).

Another way to promote theory development in cross-cultural leadership research was shown to come from the employment of multiple and creative approaches, be they large-scale comparative, small-scale culture-specific or quasi experimental, observational, or qualitative in nature, as long as a common basis of commensurate theoretical concepts was identifiable. This was achieved, so to say from scratch, on the basis of universal social psychological or cross-culturally consensual definitions and empirically derived dimensions of culture and leadership and related variables, or, on the shoulders of giants, by using well-established constructs from broader leadership research that appeal to cross-cultural investigation, such as transformational and transactional leadership, leader-member exchange theory (LMX), participative leadership, or leadership categorization theory, to name just a few. From there, several avenues of further inquiry can be distinguished, working toward culture-specific (e.g., *guanxi* in China), culturally contingent (e.g., hierarchic, autonomous), and near-universal (e.g., charismatic, transformational, team-oriented) leadership phenomena, thereby exploring relevant cultural variables as potential direct predictors of cross-cultural leadership phenomena or as moderators of known relationships between leadership and other relevant variables.

A third approach to further the development of cross-cultural leadership theory is seen in testing propositions that are grounded in the field, such as the cultural congruency proposition or the near-universal propositions (cf. House et al., 1997). Both are widely employed in practice, on plausibility grounds, but are rarely tested in relation to leadership theories, which are meant to capture universal characteristics of human information processing and behavior, like leader categorization theory (Lord & Maher, 1991).

As was pointed out in the review by House et al. (1997), an important task in cross-cultural leadership research is to find out about how culture influences human leadership processes and reactions to leadership, via values, beliefs, attitudes, motives, schemata, and other psychological mechanisms that obviously have to be shared by some mechanism (e.g., social norms) to be relevant from a cross-cultural viewpoint. To this respect, it is worthwhile to take a view beyond the fence of leadership research toward other subdomains of organizational behavior and social psychology. There is a wealth of social phenomena relevant to leadership that are strongly related to cultural differences, for example, the strength of social norms (Gelfand et al., 2006; Gelfand et al., 2011), the nature of roles (McAuley, Bond, & Kashima, 2002; Peterson & Smith, 2000), beliefs about the social and the physical world (Leung, Bond, de Carrasquel, Muñoz, & Hernández, 2002), or domain-specific implicit theories (Chiu, Morris, Hong, & Menon, 2000). Gelfand et al. (2007) who reviewed these and other related phenomena point out that cultural differences might also manifest themselves outside of conscious awareness, suggesting the use of nonobtrusive and implicit measures in addition to the usual reactive measures taken. Such approaches are quite uncommon in leadership research (e.g., House et al., 1991) and even less so in cross-cultural leadership research (e.g., Den Hartog & Verburg, 1997).

Our review shows that the integration of cross-cultural issues can help to broaden leadership concepts and theory. As a subdomain of leadership research, cross-cultural leadership appears to offer a viable escape route from too much conceptual and theoretical pluralism and compartmentalization in the general field of leadership. In line with Glynn and Raffaelli (2010), who analyzed the field of leadership research from a theory of science perspective, we see cross-cultural research as a critical ingredient to make leadership research more global and less ethnocentric and to make leadership researchers less parochial in their theoretical and conceptual focus.

One caveat unearthed by this and earlier reviews is the relative lack of empirically demonstrable impact of cross-cultural leadership research in the practical world of global leadership. We do not mean to say that the remarkable work of cross-cultural research, accumulated during the last half century, is not widely acknowledged and used in the practitioners' world. Quite the opposite is the case (e.g., Adler, 2008). But what we do mean to say is that we have found only rare and scarce scientific evidence that cross-cultural leadership theory does indeed make a difference if applied in the practical world (as compared to not), and also making this difference for the reasons and mechanisms specified in the respective cross-cultural leadership theories used. In fact, it appears that we have yet to deliver such theories and the studies for testing and applying them to the practical world.

Tsui et al. (2007) note in their review of 93 cross-cultural management studies in 16 leading management journals, "The 21st century should be, if it is not already, the century of international management research" (p. 427); and, while being aware that cross-cultural research is "not for the faint-hearted" (Smith & Hitt, 2005), the authors salute all cross-cultural researchers for their dedication and contribution to global learning—so do we.

Future Directions

Although significant progress has been made in cross-cultural leadership research, it is overshadowed by some conceptual, theoretical, methodological, and applied science issues. The basic concepts of culture and leadership are not systematically investigated in relation to what is necessary for the study of cross-cultural and global leadership. The welcomed recent raise in large-scale cultural values studies came with a proliferation in overlapping and inconsistent cultural dimensions. And for leadership research in general, an unhealthy pluralism and compartmentalization in leadership theory is apparent, for which cross-cultural leadership research might provide an escape route. However, for this, the apparent ignorance of the fact that culture is not only a differentiator of nations but also of cultures within nations, industries, multinational and domestic organizations, and other social entities (e.g., multinational teams), which are relevant to cross-cultural leadership, needs to be overcome. In most research projects reviewed, the essentially cross-level nature of the phenomena empirically studied is ignored, and respective multilevel theory development in leadership research has not yet taken place to sufficient extent, although asked for about 15 years ago by House et al. (1997). Last but not least, there is no empirical evidence for a direct impact of cross-cultural leadership theory on the applied world of global leadership, perhaps because not very much progress has been made in the development of truly cross-cultural leadership theory in the first place. With the goal to stimulate advances in future research, we offer seven recommendations to address these fundamental issues. Most of our recommendations are not new, which should qualify them as classic issues that no longer should be ignored.

Recommendation 1: Consolidate Culture Values Frameworks

Since the seminal work by Hofstede, several cultural values frameworks have been developed, some of which are directly linked with the cross-cultural study of leadership (House et al., 2004; Smith et al., 2002). This offers an increased choice in cultural frameworks, but it also means the risk of arbitrariness, especially when cultural dimensions are treated as independent measures of culture. By criticizing the dominance of the latter approach, Tsui et al. (2007) advocate a configuration of culture approach that, for organizational cultures, has been shown to predict organizational outcomes differently from independent culture dimensions.

Most definitions of culture comprise a group-level construct. As discussed by Klein and Kozlowski (2000a, 2000b), a group-level construct (e.g., nations) can have three types of properties: global (e.g., GDP), shared (e.g., individual perceptions, cognitions), or configural (e.g., looseness—tightness of cultural norms; Gelfand et al., 2006). Most operationalizations of culture pertain to the shared property type. Configural property means that a cultural value, like collectivism, can have different effects depending on whether respective cultural norms are, for example, tight or loose (Gelfand et al., 2011; Taras et al., 2010). Together with Tsui et al. (2007), we see opportunities for future research by configuration-oriented theorizing and empirically modeling the role of national culture for individual, team, and organizational behavior. This requires multilevel modeling and large-scale studies in the format of Smith et al. (2002) and GLOBE (e.g., Chhokar et al., 2007; House et al., 2004).

Recommendation 2: Make Leadership Concepts More Suitable for Cross-Cultural Study

We have pointed out examples of universal psychological and cross-culturally consensual concepts of leadership, because they offer advantages to the cross-cultural leadership researcher (e.g., less prone to ethnocentrisms, more compatibility with theorizing about human behavior). We also suggest a focus on the integration of current leadership theory and on commensurate findings in (cross-cultural) leadership research, for example, with respect to leadership phenomena that are meant to be universal (e.g., leadership categorization, cf. Lord & Maher, 1991; leader motivation, cf. McClelland, 1985) or have been empirically established as near universals (e.g., team-oriented, charismatic leadership prototypes, Dorfman et al., 2004; transformational leadership behaviors, cf. Bass, 1999). Note that if we wish to make statements about universal leadership characteristics, they need to be phrased in more abstract ways (Bond & Smith, 1999; Smith & Bond, 1999), and if we focus on the culture-specific meaning of these universal characteristics, the specific situations, events, and behaviors relevant to the enactment of these leadership characteristics need to be taken into account (e.g., Brodbeck et al., 2007). For this, a mix of methodological approaches and research designs appears to be helpful, with large-scale comparative studies, preferably repeated over time to gain insights in the changing nature of culture and leadership, on the one extreme; and small-scale studies, which are local, indigenous, and rich in the sense of near to actual behavior and nonobtrusive in nature, on the other extreme.

Recommendation 3: Focus on both Leadership Communalities and Differences across Cultures

The convergence found across cultures with respect to some dimensions and characteristics of leadership is one of the most interesting findings of the last 15 years. This should encourage additional investigations of leadership that can consolidate the previous findings and examine what is unique about leadership in particular cultures. Certainly, there remains the meta-question "if the phenomenon of leadership is universal and found in all societies (Bass, 1990; Murdoch, 1967), to what extent is leadership culturally contingent?" (Scandura & Dorfman, 2004, p. 282). Thus, investigating the causal mechanisms by which organizational behaviors, such as leadership and followership, become culturally contingent (or uniform) would be the next logical step. Both approaches, the "behavioral routines" explanation taken by Peterson and Smith (2000) in their event management studies of leadership (e.g., Smith et al., 2002) and the "cultural values" explanation taken by GLOBE (cf. House et al., 2004) in its leadership prototypes study, constitute viable theoretical pathways along the line of which further progress can be made. The further above-described types of universal (e.g., variform, functional universal) distinguished in the literature can serve as a useful framework to organize respective theoretical developments and empirical findings for their integration in the field.

Recommendation 4: Conduct Country-Specific Research—from a Cross-Cultural Perspective

As Gelfand et al. (2007) point out for organizational behavior, indigenous perspectives are critical for progress in the field and need to be prioritized in the future. This holds true for cross-cultural leadership as well. Taking emic approaches to leadership in particular cultures not only contributes to the development of more universal knowledge by identifying a variety of emic formats of leadership processes and reactions to it (cf. Brodbeck et al., 2007), which might be of benefit in other cultural contexts. If properly transferred (Javidan et al., 2005), they also help us to understand how leadership "works" in other cultures (e.g., Chhokar et al., 2007)—as well as in our own.

Earlier in our review, we discussed the distinctions made between "etic" (i.e., comparative, outer perspective) and "emic" (i.e., indigenous, inner perspective) for the study of culture and leadership. Within etic approaches, a further distinction was made between "leadership is universal"-and "leadership differs"-approaches, to which recommendations are given in the paragraph before. The history of cross-cultural leadership research demonstrates that nearly all etic-comparative approaches, be they universal- or differences-oriented, stem from North America, which is likely to have resulted in North American views on cross-cultural leadership phenomena. Currently, these are supplemented by similar ethnocentric approaches taken from other cultures. The underlying phenomenon is widely discussed in the literature under the terms "ethnocentrism" and "parochialism."

We would like to point out that taking a particular (cultural) lens not only might affect the questions posed, the theoretical understanding taken, and the empirical findings obtained in etic-comparative approaches, but also when emic approaches are taken to the cultural study of leadership. There the risk of holding consistently onto one orientation is that the researchers might not be asking "the right questions," that is, studying issues that may be of low relevance to other cultures. As has been stated by Pruitt (2004, p. xii), "characteristics that are dominant in one culture tend to be recessive in another, and vice-versa. By studying other societies where these features are dominant, they can develop concepts and theories that will eventually be useful for understanding their own." Thus, the investment in more emic studies of leadership should be finished by taking a truly cross-cultural perspective to build a more comprehensive global science of leadership.

Recommendation 5: Engage in Proper Theory Building in (Cross-Cultural) Leadership Research

Proper theory building in cross-cultural leadership research relies on proper theory building in leadership research in general. Yukl (1999, p. 301) asserts, for example, that it is evident that charismatic and transformational leadership theories provide important insights, but some serious conceptual weaknesses need to be corrected to make the theories more useful. Underlying influence processes need to be formulated more clearly, and the leader behaviors related to these processes need to be specified. Such theoretical specification is important to make particular leadership theories more useful for cross-cultural research.

House and colleagues (1997) outlined a basic framework for making progress in building theories in cross-cultural leadership research, which served as a blueprint for the GLOBE study. Among the many suggestions given for how to develop cross-cultural leadership (and organization) theory, they assert that the processes by which cultural entities affect members' psychological states and behavior, and how these relate to cultural differences *and* communalities, are not clear yet and need to be investigated more intensively. A focus might be laid on psychological and social psychological constructs that appeal to cross-cultural leadership, such as shared attitudes, social norms, or motives. These have been studied cross-culturally in the wider realm of organizational behavior and social psychology, as is evident, for example, in the review from Gelfand et al. (2007) and the empirical cross-national study from Gelfand et al. (2011), however, much less so in sufficiently large cross-cultural leadership studies.

To this respect, Glynn and Raffaelli (2010) state in their systematic theory of science review of leadership research in general, "a fairly unexplored territory in leadership is that of international or cross-cultural theorization and methods. Although there have been some initial forays into this area, notably in the GLOBE Research Project on Leadership Worldwide (House et al., 2004; Selznick, 1957, p. 151), there are considerable possibilities for leveraging cultural dimensions to induce new theories of leadership" (p. 394).

Recommendation 6: Make Use of Advanced Methodology, Social Networks, and New Technology

Throughout the review and also in our recommendations, we point out suggestions for analytical methods and design paradigms that are likely to support future progress in cross-cultural leadership research. Rather than repeating them here, we pledge more generally for the use of advanced measures and statistical methodology, international social networks of researchers, and new technologies and point out examples for each.

In order to better "recognize the nature of the beast" (Tsui et al., 2007), cross-level models of statistical analysis should be used to be able to interpret cultural or national effects on the individual, social-interactive, and organizational levels of analysis, which are the common levels of theorizing in leadership research. For a more detailed account of such models, see Tsui et al. (2007), who refer to Klein and Kozlowski (2000b) in their review of levels of analysis in cross-cultural management research. Another pledge is concerned with the focus on cross-cultural construct validity, a sine qua non for cross-cultural theory development. It encompasses such issues as consideration of the "ecological fallacy," semantic and translational equivalence in measurement practice, establishing context-free measures by adaptation, de-contextualization and contextualization (cf. Farh, Canella, & Lee, 2006) or culture-specific scales (e.g., *guanxi*; cf. Chen et al., 2004). Further methodological recommendations along these and here previously discussed lines (e.g., the use of emic and etic items by latent class and variables analysis) are addressed by Tsui et al. (2007).

The necessity of large-scale cross-cultural leadership research requires our attention for how to maintain existing cross-cultural research programs (like the GLOBE 61-nations study or the 47 nations study by Smith et al., 2002) and how to build new social networks that can carry out similar research from new angles in the future. Tsui et al. (2007) calculated a sample of about 300 researchers who would serve the bill. We are confident that 10 times more interested researchers can be counted on worldwide. Beware, such programs may take more effort and resources than originally anticipated (cf. House et al., 2004), especially when the also-needed longitudinal design is to be realized.

While the technological backbone of, for example, the GLOBE program, back in the mid-1990s were fax and postal services supported by literally 10 thousands of e-mails, and lately also an internet portal for the exchange of documents and news, there are more powerful new technologies available today that could be used as support in the future. For example, the availability of already assembled cross-cultural data can be enhanced by the use of professional data banks (e.g., world data bank, world value survey, cf. Javidan & Hauser, 2004), and new technologies like data mining, cloud computing, evaluation polls or decision markets on the internet, to name just a few, could be explored for the cross-cultural study of leadership and related phenomena.

Recommendation 7: Care about the Practical Impact of Your Work

Of course the final question is the question of impact. In our conclusion, we addressed the relative lack of empirically demonstrable impact of cross-cultural leadership research in the practical world of global leadership. This, we think, is partially due to a lack of cross-cultural theory development, which should remind us to Kurt Lewin's word, "there is nothing as practical as a good theory." On the other hand, in numerous conversations we had with practitioners in the field, especially when we reported research results like the ones from GLOBE, there was one common denominator in the reactions among the audience—"so what does this actually mean for our daily work and organizational strategy?" Rather obviously, we should try harder to identify barriers to, and develop ideas about how to encourage the implementation of what follows from our research results. Furthermore, we should assemble existing research and conduct new intervention research to empirically demonstrate the direct impact the field of cross-cultural leadership research has on the practical world.

General Conclusions

With the present review, we aimed to provide a coherent picture of where we stand today in the field of cross-cultural leadership research, with an eye on the more applied field of global leadership, and to set out critical directions for future research. Cross-cultural leadership is a vibrant research arena, becoming even more important in view of rapidly growing globalization. Our review showed that theory development and methodological refinement has moved significantly forward in the last two decades, especially due to large-scale multination studies and the increasing examination of theoretical propositions specific to the cross-cultural leadership domain. We believe that the scientific development of leadership research in general could indeed profit from a cross-cultural research perspective. At the same time, however, several conceptual, theoretical, methodological, and applied science issues still remain unsolved—many of which have been addressed in previous reviews by other eminent authors in the field. In particular, on the basis of our review, we call for further consolidation of cultural value frameworks, investment in proper integrated theory building, and more empirical research about the practical applicability of the results from cross-cultural leadership research.

Acknowledgments

We thank Marian Ruderman and Peter Dorfman for their helpful comments on earlier drafts of this chapter.

References

Adler, N. J. (2002). *International dimensions of organizational behaviour* (4th ed.). Mason, OH: Thomson.

Adler, N. J. (2008). *International dimensions of organizational behavior* (5th ed.). Mason, OH: Thomson.

Avolio, B. J., Walumbwa, F. O., & Weber, T. J. (2009). Leadership: Current theories, research, and future directions. *Annual Review of Psychology, 60*, 421–449.

Aycan, Z., Kanungo, R. N., Mendonca, M., Yu, K., & Deller, J. (2000). Impact of culture on human resource management practices: A 10-country comparison. *Applied Psychology: An International Review, 49*(1), 192–221.

Bass, B. M. (1990). *Bass and Stogdill's handbook of leadership: Theory, research, and managerial applications* (3rd ed.). Binghamton, NY: Free Press.

Bass, B. M. (1997). Does the transactional-transformational leadership paradigm transcend organizational and national boundaries? *American Psychologist, 52*(2), 130–139.

Bass, B. M. (1999). Two decades of research and development in transformational leadership. *European Journal of Work and Organizational Psychology, 8*(1), 9–32.

Bass, B. M. (2008). Globalization and cross national effects. In B. M. Bass & R. Bass (Eds.), *The Bass handbook of leadership: Theory, research, and managerial applications* (pp. 980–1048). New York, NY: Free Press.

Bass, B. M., with Bass, R. (2008). *The Bass handbook of leadership: Theory, research, and managerial applications*. New York, NY: Free Press.

Beechler, S., & Javidan, M. (2007). Leading with a global mindset. In M. Javidan, R. M. Steers, & M. A. Hitt (Eds.), *The global mindset: Advances in international management* (vol. *19*, pp. 131–170). Oxford: Elsevier.

Black, J. S., & Mendenhall, M. (1990). Cross-cultural training effectiveness: A review and a theoretical framework for future research. *Academy of Management Review, 15*(1), 113–136.

Bogardus, E. S. (1920). *The essentials of social psychology*. Los Angeles: University of Southern California Press.

Bond, M. H. (1988). Finding universal dimensions of individual variation in multicultural studies of values: The Rokeach and Chinese value surveys. *Journal of Personality and Social Psychology, 55*, 1009–1015.

Bond, M. H., & Smith, P. B. (1996). Cross-cultural social and organizational psychology. *Annual Review of Psychology, 47*, 205–235.

Borg, I., & Lingoes, J. (1987). *Multidimensional similarity structure analysis*. New York, NY: Springer.

Brodbeck, F. C., Chhokar, J., & House, R. (2007). Culture and leadership in 25 societies: Integration, conclusions, and future directions. In J. Chhokar, F. C. Brodbeck, & R. House (Eds.), *Managerial cultures of the world: A GLOBE report of in-depth studies of the cultures of 25 countries* (pp. 1025–1102). Mahwah, NJ: LEA Publishers.

Brodbeck, F. C., & Frese, M. (2007). Societal culture and leadership in Germany. In J. Chhokar, F. C. Brodbeck, & R. House (Eds.), *Managerial cultures of the world: A GLOBE report of in-depth studies of the cultures of 25 countries* (pp. 147–214). Mahwah, NJ: LEA Publishers.

Brodbeck, F. C., Frese, M., Akerblom, S., Audia, G., Bakacsi, G., & 37 co-authors (2000). Cultural variation of leadership prototypes across 22 European countries. *Journal of Occupational and Organizational Psychology, 73*, 1–29.

Brodbeck, F. C., Frese, M., & Javidan, M. (2002). Leadership made in Germany: Low on compassion, high on performance. *Academy of Management Executive, 16*(1), 16–29.

CCC (Chinese Culture Connection) (1987). Chinese values and the search for culture-free dimensions of culture. *Journal of Cross-Cultural Psychology, 18*(2), 143–164.

Chen, C. C., Chen, Y., & Xin, K. (2004). Guanxi practices and trust in management: A procedural justice perspective. *Organization Science, 15*(2), 200–209.

Chhokar, J. S., Brodbeck, F. C., & House, R. J. (2007). *Culture and leadership around the world: The GLOBE book of in-depth studies of 25 societies*. Mahwah, NJ: LEA Publishers.

Chiu, C., Morris, M. W., Hong, Y., & Menon, T. (2000). Motivated cultural cognition: The impact of implicit cultural theories on dispositional attribution varies as a function of need for closure. *Journal of Personality and Social Psychology, 78*(2), 247–259.

Confucius (500 B. C.). *Confucian Analects* (translated by Legge, J., 1893). Retrieved October 15, 2011, from http://www.sacred-texts.com/cfu/conf1.htm

Dansereau, F., & Yammarino, F. J. (2006). Is more discussion about levels of analysis really necessary? When is such discussion sufficient? *The Leadership Quarterly, 16*, 879–919.

Den Hartog, D. N., House, R. J., Hanges, P. J., Ruiz-Quintanilla, S. A., & Dorfman, P. W. (1999). Culture specific and cross-culturally generalizable implicit leadership theories: Are attributes of charismatic/transformational leadership universally endorsed? *The Leadership Quarterly, 10*(2), 219–256.

Den Hartog, D. N., & Verburg, R. M. (1997). Charisma and rhetoric: Communicative techniques of international business leaders, *The Leadership Quarterly, 8*(4), 355–391.

Dickson, M. W., Den Hartog, D. N., & Mitchelson, J. K. (2003). Research on leadership in a cross-cultural context: Making progress, and raising new questions. *The Leadership Quarterly, 14*, 729–768.

Dorfman, P. W. (1996). International and cross cultural leadership research. In B. J. Punnett & O. Shenkar (Eds.), *Handbook for international management research* (pp. 267–349). Ann Arbor: University of Michigan Press.

Dorfman, P. (2004). International and cross cultural leadership research. In B. J. Punnett & O. Shenkar (Eds.), *Handbook for international management research* (pp. 265–355). Ann Arbor: University of Michigan Press.

Dorfman, P. W., Hanges, P. J., & Brodbeck, F. C. (2004). Leadership and cultural variation. In R. J. House, P. J. Hanges, M. Javidan, P. Dorfman, & V. Gupta (Eds.), Culture, leadership, and organizations: The GLOBE study of 62 societies (pp. 669–719). Thousand Oaks, CA: Sage Publications.

Dorfman, P. W., Howell, J. P., Hibino, S., Lee, J. K., Tate, U., & Bautista, A. (1997). Leadership in Western and Asian countries: Commonalities and differences in effective leadership processes across cultures. *Leadership Quarterly, 8*(3), 233–274.

Eckert, R. H., Ruderman, M. N, Brodbeck, F. C., Gentry, W. A., Leslie, J. B., Braddy, P. W., & Hannum, K. M. (2011) *Global leader view technical manual.* Greensboro, NC: Center for Creative Leadership.

Elenkov, D. S., & Manev, I. M. (2005). Top management leadership and influence on innovation: The role of sociocultural context. *Journal of Management, 31*(3), 381–402.

Ensari, N., & Murphy, S. E. (2003). Cross-cultural variations in leadership perceptions and attribution of charisma to the leader. *Organizational Behavior and Human Decision Processes, 92*(1–2), 52–66.

Epitropaki, O., & Martin, R. (2004). Implicit leadership theories in applied settings: Factor structure, generalizability, and stability over time. *Journal of Applied Psychology, 89*(2), 293–310.

Epitropaki, O., & Martin, R. (2005). From ideal to real: A longitudinal study of the role of implicit leadership theories on leader-member exchanges and employee outcomes. *Journal of Applied Psychology, 90*(4), 659–676.

Farh, J. L., Cannella, A. A., & Lee, C. (2006). Approaches to scale development in Chinese management research. *Management and Organization Review, 2*(3), 301–318.

Farh, J. L., & Cheng, B. S. (2000). A cultural analysis of paternalistic leadership in Chinese organizations. In J. T. Li, A. S. Tsui, & E. Weldon (Eds.), *Management and organizations in the Chinese context* (pp. 84–130). New York, NY: St. Martin's Press.

Fu, P. P., Tsui, A., Liu, J., & Li, L. (2010). Pursuit of whose happiness? Executive leader's transformational behaviors and personal values. *Administrative Science Quarterly, 55*(2), 222–254.

Gelfand, M. J., Erez, M., & Aycan, Z. (2007). Cross-cultural organizational behavior. *Annual Review of Psychology, 58*, 1–35.

Gelfand, M. J., Nishii, L. H., & Raver, J. L. (2006). On the nature and importance of cultural tightness-looseness. *Journal of Applied Psychology, 91*(6), 1225–1244.

Gelfand, M. J., Raver, J. L., Nishii, L., Leslie, L. M., Lun, J., & Lim, B. C. (2011). Differences between tight and loose cultures: A 33-nation study. *Science, 332*, 1100–1104.

Glynn, M. A., & Raffaelli, R. (2010). Uncovering mechanisms of theory development in an academic field: Lessons from leadership research. *Academy of Management Annuals, 4*(1), 359–401.

Green, S., Hassan F., Immelt, J., Marks, M., & Meiland, D. (2003). In search of global leaders. *Harvard Business Review, 81*(8), 38–44.

Gupta, A. K., & Govindarajan, V. (2002). Cultivating a global mindset. *The Academy of Management Executive, 16*(1), 116–126.

Gupta, V., Sully de Luque, M., & House, R. J. (2004). GLOBE unobstrusive measures for societal culture dimensions. In R. J. House, P. J. Hanges, M. Javidan, P. Dorfman, & V. Gupta (Eds.), *Culture, leadership and organizations: The GLOBE study of 62 societies* (pp. 152–177). Thousand Oaks, CA: Sage Publications.

Hanges, P. J., & Dickson, M. W. (2004). The development and validation of the GLOBE culture and leadership scales. In R. J. House, P. J. Hanges, M. Javidan, P. W. Dorfman, & Gupta, V. (Eds.), *Leadership, culture, and organizations: The GLOBE study of 62 societies* (pp. 122–151). Thousand Oaks, CA: Sage Publications.

Hanges, P. J., & Dickson, M. W. (2006). Agitation over aggregation: Clarifying the development of and the nature of the GLOBE scales. *The Leadership Quarterly, 17*, 522–536.

Herskovits, M. J. (1955). *Cultural anthropology: An abridged revision of man and his works.* New York, NY: Knopf.

Hickson, D. J., Hinings, C. R., McMillan, C. J., & Schwitter, J. P. (1974). The culture-free context of organisation structure: A tri-national comparison. *Sociology, 8*, 59–80.

Hofstede, G. (1980). *Culture's consequences: International differences in work-related values.* Beverly Hills, CA: Sage Publications.

Hofstede, G. (1983). Dimensions of national cultures in fifty countries and three regions. In J. Deregowski, S. Dzuirawiec, & R. Annis (Eds.), *Expiscations in cross cultural psychology* (pp. 335–355). Lisse, The Netherlands: Swets, Zeitlinger.

Hofstede, G. (1984). *Culture's consequences: International differences in work-related values.* Newbury Park, CA: Sage Publications.

Hofstede, G. (1996). Riding the waves of commerce: A test of Trompenaars' "model" of national culture differences. *International Journal of Intercultural Relations, 20*(2), 189–198.

Hofstede, G. (2001). *Culture's consequences: Comparing values, behaviors, institutions, and organizations across nations.* Thousand Oaks, CA: Sage Publications.

Hofstede, G. (2002). Dimensions do not exist: A reply to Brendan McSweeney. *Human Relations, 55*(11), 1355–1361.

House, R. J., Hanges, P. J., Javidan, M., Dorfman, P. W., & Gupta, V. (2004). *Culture, leadership, and organizations: The GLOBE study of 62 societies.* Thousand Oaks, CA: Sage Publications.

House, R. J., Spangler, W. D., & Woycke, J. (1991). Personality and charisma in the U. S. presidency: A psychological theory of leader effectiveness. *Administrative Science Quarterly, 36*(3), 364–396.

House, R. J., Sulley de Luque, M., Dorfman, P. W., Javidan, M., & Hanges, P. J. (in prep.). *Strategic leadership: The GLOBE study of CEO effectiveness across cultures.* Thousand Oaks, CA: Sage Publications.

House, R. J., Wright, N., & Aditya, R. A. (1997). Cross-cultural research on organizational leadership: A critical analysis and a proposed theory. In P. C. Earley, & M. Erez (Eds.), *New perspectives on international Industrial/Organizational Psychology* (pp. 535–625). San Francisco, CA: New Lexington Press.

Javidan, M., & Hauser, M. (2004). The linkage between GLOBE findings and other cross cultural information. In R. J. House, P. J. Hanges, M. Javidan, P. W. Dorfman, & V. Gupta (Eds.), *Culture, leadership, and organizations: The GLOBE study of 62 societies* (pp. 102–121). Thousand Oaks, CA: Sage Publications.

Javidan, M., Stahl, G. K., Brodbeck F., & Wilderom, C. P. M. (2005). Cross-border transfer of knowledge: Cultural lessons from project GLOBE. *The Academy of Management Executive, 19*(2), 59–76.

Javidan, M. & Teagarden, M. B. (2011). Conceptualizing and measuring global mindset. In W. H. Mobley, M. Li, & Y. Wang, Y., *Advances in global leadership* (vol. *6*, pp. 13–39). Bingley, UK: Emerald Group Publishing.

Judge, T. A., & Piccolo, R. F. (2004). Transformational and transactional leadership: A meta-analytic test of their relative validity. *Journal of Applied Psychology, 89*(5), 755–768.

Judge, T. A., Woolf, E. C., Hurst, C., & Livingston, B. (2006). Charismatic and transformational leadership: A review and an agenda for future research. *Zeitschrift für Arbeits- und Organisationspsychologie, 50*(4), 203–214.

Kets de Vries, M. F. R., & Florent-Treacy, E. (1999). *The new global leaders: Percy Barnevik, Richard Branson, and David Simon and the making of the international corporation.* San Francisco, CA: Jossey-Bass.

Kets de Vries, M. F. R., & Florent-Treacy, E. (2002). Global leadership from A to Z: Creating high commitment organizations. *Organizational Dynamics, 30*(4), 295–309.

Kirkman B. L., Lowe, K. B., & Gibson, C. B. (2006). A quarter century of culture's consequences: A review of empirical research incorporating Hofstede's cultural values framework. *Journal of International Business Studies, 37*, 285–320.

Klein, K. J., & Kozlowski, S. W. J. (Eds.) (2000a). *Multilevel theory, research, and methods in organizations: Foundations, extensions, and new directions.* San Francisco, CA: Jossey-Bass.

Klein, K. J., & Kozlowski, S. W. J. (2000b). From micro to meso: Critical steps in conceptualizing and conducting multilevel research. *Organizational Research Methods, 3*, 211–236.

Kluckhohn, F. R., & Strodtbeck, F. L. (1961). *Variations in value orientations.* Oxford, England: Row, Peterson.

Kogut, B., & Singh, H. (1988). The effect of national culture on the choice of entry mode. *Journal of International Business Studies, 19*(3), 411–432.

Lane, H. W. (2004). *The Blackwell handbook of global management: A guide to managing complexity.* New York, NY: Blackwell.

Law, K. S., Wong C. S., Wang D., & Wang L. (2000). Effect of supervisor–subordinate guanxi on supervisory decisions in China: An empirical investigation. *The International Journal of Human Resource Management, 11*(4), 751–765.

Leong, L. Y. C., & Fischer, R. (2011). Is transformational leadership universal? A meta-analytical investigation of multifactor leadership questionnaire means across cultures. *Journal of Leadership & Organizational Studies, 18*(2), 164–174.

Leung, K., Bhagat, R. S., Buchan, N. R., Erez, M., & Gibson, C. B. (2005). Culture and international business: Recent advances and their implications for future research. *Journal of International Business Studies, 36*(4), 357–378.

Leung, K., Bond, M. H., de Carrasquel, S. R., Muñoz, C., & Hernández, M. (2002). Social axioms: The search for universal dimensions of general beliefs about how the world functions. *Journal of Cross-Cultural Psychology, 33*(3), 286–302.

Levy, O. (2005). The influence of top management team attention patterns on global strategic posture of firms. *Journal of Organizational Behavior, 26*(7), 797–819.

Levy, O., Bechler, S., Taylor, S., & Boyacigiller, N. (2007). What we talk about when we talk about "global mindset": Managerial cognition in multinational corporations. *Journal of International Business Studies, 38*(2), 231–258.

Lord, R. G., Foti, R., & De Vader, C. (1984). A test of leadership categorization theory: Internal structure, information processing, and leadership perceptions. *Organizational Behavior and Human Performance, 34*, 343–378.

Lord, R. G., & Maher, K. J. (1991). *Leadership and information processing: Linking perceptions and organizational performance.* New York, NY: Routledge, Chapman, Hall.

Machiavelli, N. (1985). *The Prince.* Chicago, IL: University of Chicago Press.

Magnuson, P., Wilson R. T., Zdravkovic, S., Zhou, J. X., & Westjohn, S. A. (2008). Breaking through the cultural clutter: A comparative assessment of multiple cultural and institutional frameworks, *International Marketing Review, 25*(2), 183–201.

McAuley, P. C., Bond, M. H., & Kashima, E. (2002). Toward defining situations objectively: A culture-level analysis of role dyads in Hong Kong and Australia. *Journal of Cross-Cultural Psychology, 33*(4), 363–379.

McClelland, D. C. (1985). How motives, skills, and values determine what people do. *American Psychologist, 40*(7), 812–825.

McSweeney, B. (2002). Hofstede's model of national cultural differences and their consequences: A triumph of faith—a failure of analysis. *Human Relations, 55*(1), 89–118.

Mobley, W. H., & Dorfman, P. W. (2003). *Advances in global leadership* (vol. *3*). Oxford, England: JAI Press.

Mobley, W. H., Li, M., & Wang, Y. (2011). *Advances in global leadership* (vol. *6*). Bingley, UK: Emerald Group Publishing.

Murdoch, G. (1967). *Ethnographic atlas.* Pittsburgh, PA: University of Pittsburgh Press.

Offermann, L. R., Kennedy, J. K., & Wirtz, P. W. (1994). Implicit leadership theories: Content, structure, and generalizability. *The Leadership Quarterly, 5*(1), 43–58.

Peterson, M. F., & Castro, S. L. (2006). Measurement metrics at aggregate levels of analysis: Implications for organization culture research and the GLOBE project, *The Leadership Quarterly, 17*, 506–521.

Peterson, M. F., & Hunt, J. G. J. (1997). International perspectives on international leadership. *The Leadership Quarterly, 8*(3), 203–231.

Peterson, M. F., & Smith, P. B. (2000). Sources of meaning, organizations, and culture: Making sense of organizational events. In N. M. Ashkanasy, C. P. M. Wilderom, & M. F. Peterson (2000), *Handbook of organizational culture and climate* (pp. 101–116). Thousand Oaks, CA: Sage Publications.

Pfeffer, J., & Sutton, R. I. (2006). Evidence-based management. *Harvard Business Review, 84*(1), 62–74.

Pike, K. L. (1954). *Language in relation to a unified theory of the structure of human behavior.* Dallas, TX: Summer Institute of Linguistics.

Pruitt, D. G. (2004). Foreword. In M. J. Gelfand & J. M. Brett (Eds.), *The Handbook of negotiation and culture* (pp. xi–xiii). Stanford, CA: Stanford University Press.

Rarick, C., & Nickerson, I. (2008). Combining classification models for a comprehensive understanding of national culture: Metaphorical analysis and value judgements applied to Burmese cultural assessment. *Journal of Organizational Culture, Communications and Conflict, 12*(2), 9–19.

Reber, G., Jago, A. G., Auer-Rizzi, W., & Szabo, E. (2000). Führungsstile in sieben Ländern Europas—Ein interkultureller Vergleich [Leadership styles in seven European countries—A cross-cultural comparison]. In E. Regnet & L. M. Hofmann (Eds.), *Personalmanagement in Europa [Personnel management in Europe]* (pp. 154–173). Göttingen, Germany: Hogrefe.

Ronen, S., & Shenkar, O. (1985). Clustering countries on attitudinal dimensions: A review and synthesis. *Academy of Management Review, 10*(3), 435–454.

Rousseau, D. M. (2006). Is there such a thing as "evidence-based management"? *Academy of Management Review, 31*(2), 256–269.

Ruderman, M, Brodbeck, F. C., Eckert, R., Gentry, B., & Braddy, P. (2011). *The role of fit in understanding leader*

effectiveness across cultures. Paper and poster presented at the Society of Industrial and Organizational Psychology (SIOP) annual conference, Chicago, April 12–14.
Saint Benedict (1981). *The rule of St. Benedict.* Collegeville, MN: Liturgical Press.
Scandura, T., & Dorfman, P. (2004). Theoretical letters: Leadership research in an international and cross-cultural context. *The Leadership Quarterly, 15*(2), 277–307.
Schwartz, S. H. (1992). Universals in the content and structure of values: Theoretical advances and empirical tests in 20 countries. In M. P. Zanna & P. Mark (Eds.), *Advances in experimental social psychology* (pp. 1–65). San Diego, CA: Academic Press.
Schwartz, S. H. (1994). Are there universal aspects in the structure and contents of human values? *Journal of Social Issues, 50,* 19–45.
Schwartz, S. H. (1999). Cultural value differences: Some implications for work. *Applied Psychology: An International Review, 48,* 23–47.
Schyns, B., Kiefer, T., Kerschreiter, R., & Tymon, A. (2011). Teaching implicit leadership theories to develop leaders and leadership: How and why it can make a difference. *Academy of Management Learning & Education, 10*(3), 397–408.
Selznick, P. (1957). *Leadership and administration: A sociological interpretation.* Evanston, IL: Row, Peterson.
Sergiovanni, T. J., & Corbally, J. E. (Eds.), (1986). *Leadership and organizational culture: New perspectives on administrative theory and practice.* IL: University of Illinois Press.
Sivakumar, K., & Nakata, C. (2001). The Stampede toward Hofstede's framework: Avoiding the sample design pit in cross-cultural research. *Journal of International Business Studies, 32*(3), 555–574.
Smith, P. B., & Bond, M. H. (1999). *Social psychology: Across cultures.* Needham Heights, MA: Allyn, Bacon.
Smith, P. B., Dugan, S., & Trompenaars, F. (1996). National culture and the values of organizational employees. *Journal of Cross-Cultural Psychology, 27*(2), 231–264.
Smith, K. G., & Hitt, M. A. (2005). *Great minds in management: The process of theory development.* New York, NY: Oxford University Press.
Smith, P. B., & Peterson, M. F. (1988). *Leadership, organizations and culture: An event management model.* Thousand Oaks, CA: Sage Publications.
Smith, P. B., Peterson, M. F., & Schwartz, S. H. (2002). Cultural values, sources of guidance, and their relevance to managerial behavior: A 47-nation study. *Journal of Cross-Cultural Psychology, 33*(2), 188–208.
Smith, P. B., Wang, Z. M., & Leung, K. (1997). Leadership, decision-making and cultural context: Event management within Chinese joint ventures. *The Leadership Quarterly, 8*(4), 413–431.
Smith, P. M. (1995). Leadership. In A. S. R. Manstead, & M. Hewstone (Eds.), *The Blackwell encyclopedia of social psychology* (pp. 358–362). Oxford, England: Blackwell.
Spreitzer, G. M., McCall M. W., & Mahoney J. D. (1997). Early identification of international executive potential, *Journal of Applied Psychology, 82,* 6–29.
Spreitzer, G. M., Perttula, K. H., & Xin, K. (2005). Traditionality matters: An examination of the effectiveness of transformational leadership in the United States and Taiwan. *Journal of Organizational Behavior, 26*(3), 205–227.
Szabo, E., Brodbeck, F. C., Den Hartog, D. N., Reber, G., & Weibler, J. (2002). The Germanic Europe cluster: Where employees have a voice. *Journal of World Business, 37*(1), 55–68.
Taras, V., Kirkman, B. L., & Steel, P. (2010). Examining the impact of culture's consequences: A three-decade, multilevel, meta-analytic review of Hofstede's cultural value dimensions. *Journal of Applied Psychology, 95*(3), 405–439.
Triandis, H. C. (1972). *The analysis of subjective culture.* Oxford, England: Wiley-Interscience.
Triandis, H. C. (1980). Reflections on trends in cross-cultural research. *Journal of Cross-Cultural Psychology, 11*(1), 35–58.
Triandis, H. C. (1994). *Culture and social behavior.* New York, NY: McGraw-Hill.
Triandis, H. C. (1995). *Individualism and collectivism.* Boulder, CO: Westview Press.
Triandis, H. C. (2004). Foreword. In R. J. House, P. J. Hanges, M. Javidan, P. W. Dorfman, & V. Gupta (Eds.), *Culture, leadership, and organizations: The GLOBE study of 62 societies* (pp. xv–xix). Thousand Oaks, CA: Sage Publications.
Trompenaars, A. (1993). *Riding the waves of culture: Understanding cultural diversity in business.* London, England: Economist Books.
Trompenaars, A., & Hampden-Turner, C. (1998). *Riding the waves of culture: Understanding cultural diversity in global business.* New York, NY: McGraw Hill.
Tsui, A. S., Nifadkar, S. S., & Ou, A, Y. (2007). Cross-national, cross-cultural organizational behavior research: Advances, gaps, and recommendations. *Journal of Management, 33*(3), 426–478.
Van Quaquebeke, N., Van Knippenberg, D., & Brodbeck, F. C. (2011). More than meets the eye: The role of subordinates' self-perceptions in leader categorization processes. *The Leadership Quarterly, 22*(2), 367–382.
Vroom, V. H., & Yetton, P. W. (1973). *Leadership and decision-making.* Pittsburgh, PA: University of Pittsburgh Press.
Walumbwa, F. O., & Lawler, J. J. (2003). Building effective organizations: Transformational leadership, collectivist orientation, work-related attitudes and withdrawal behaviours in three emerging economies. *The International Journal of Human Resource Management, 14*(7), 1083–1101.
Yang M. M. (1994). *Gifts, favors and banquets: The art of social relationships in China.* Ithaca, NY: Cornell University Press.
Yukl, G. (1999). An evaluation of conceptual weaknesses in transformational and charismatic leadership theories. *The Leadership Quarterly, 10*(2), 285–305.
Yukl, G. (2006). *Leadership in organizations.* Upper Saddle River, NJ: Pearson.

CHAPTER

31 Leadership in a Diverse Workplace

Donna Chrobot-Mason, Marian N. Ruderman, *and* Lisa H. Nishii

Abstract

Although there is a significant need to understand the implications of increasing demographic diversity for leadership, surprisingly little research has been conducted on the topic. This chapter reviews the extant research in this area. The authors organize the review into three sections: how leaders lead themselves, others, and the organization. In the first section, they discuss issues related to social identity and how leaders' social identities interact with those of their employees in influencing what may be required for effective leadership. In the second section, they discuss the qualities that leaders are likely to need when managing employees who are from diverse backgrounds. The authors focus on developing quality relationships, cultivating an inclusive climate, spanning boundaries, and framing of diversity initiatives. In the last section, the authors discuss research related to the role leaders play in setting their organization's diversity strategy, implementing diversity practices, managing conflict, responding to diversity crises, and measuring progress. The chapter ends with suggestions for future research.

Key Words: affirming climate, diversity, identity, inclusion, leader

Introduction

Traditionally, organizational leaders have worked with people who looked like them, shared the same culture, and worked in the same geographic location. Today's organizational leaders find themselves working across a vastly different landscape; workforces characterized by extreme homogeneity are an artifact of the past. With changing social customs and the growth of the internet and its ability to reach all over the globe, the modern environment is asking people of all skin colors, backgrounds, and values to work together in organizations. A challenge to the current reality is that while technology has brought us together, humans still operate with the same stereotypes and mindsets that have torn groups apart throughout history. Thus, contemporary leadership requires the creation of direction, alignment, and commitment across workers who look, speak, and act differently (Drath et al., 2008; McCauley, Van Velsor, & Ruderman, 2010). Leaders in this current environment must engage and manage relationships across diverse coworkers, customers, and suppliers from around the globe. In short, today's leader must encourage cooperation across a vast expanse of geographic, demographic, and functional boundaries to be successful (Ernst & Chrobot-Mason, 2011).

This chapter examines the interface of existing research and theory on leadership with the literature on diversity in the workplace. Although the practical need for understanding the intersection of leadership and diversity is growing every day, this is a topic that hasn't received a great deal of attention from either leadership scholars or diversity scholars. Most discussions of leadership do not involve the heterogeneity of the workforce, and most discussions of diversity overlook the leadership capabilities needed to produce direction, alignment, and commitment in organizations responding to today's dynamic external environment. The two literatures have largely developed independently with few attempts to bring them together.

In the future, we expect to see much more attention given to the interaction of diversity and leadership reflecting both the rapidly changing demographics of the workforce (Eagly & Chin, 2010) and evolving leadership practices. Projections for the year 2018 suggest that the US workforce will be undergoing significant change (Toosi, 2009). The United States is anticipating a large increase in the number of immigrants, and differential fertility rates will compound the rapid diversification of the working population.

At the same time that the workforce is shifting, so is the nature of leadership. People in leadership roles are faced with a highly complicated context. Revolutionary technological changes combined with economic challenges and a trend toward strategic alliances has changed the processes, boundaries, and structures of organizations. Delayering, downsizing, and outsourcing are common practices. Traditional bureaucratic organizations haven't completely gone away but have merged with newer more flexible styles of organizations that allow for greater participation (Graetz & Smith, 2009). According to Ashkenas, Ulrich, Jick, and Kerr (2002), such changes in processes, boundaries, and structure have called for a new set of leadership capabilities that emphasize shared leadership across people and the ability to "connect" people who are very different from one another and separated by geographies or cultures. In an era of rapid change and expectations for greater employee participation, it is essential for leaders to be able to remove the barriers that can inhibit innovation and power sharing within diverse groups. Indeed, with more and more organizations relying on diversity to generate the innovation that is required for survival, understanding and expanding on the intersection of the diversity and leadership literatures is more important than ever.

Crossan, Vera, and Nanjad (2008) offer a cross-level framework for understanding leadership that is particularly useful for highlighting the many places where it is imperative to understand the intersection of diversity and leadership. They argue that in dynamic contexts, such as the 21st century, it is important that leadership requirements be understood in terms of both the micro and macro leadership elements. In addition to looking at leadership at the interpersonal influence of a leader on a team, they incorporate two other levels of leadership—leadership of the self and leadership of the organization. This tri-level model offers a useful lens for examining leadership amidst the growing diversity of the workforce because it acknowledges the differential impact of the dynamics of diversity on the individual (self), group, and organization. Leaders today must have the capacity to lead at all levels and understand the relationships between them. Transcendent leadership refers to the ability to lead at all three levels (Crossan et al., 2008).

At the level of self-management, the chapter summarizes what the literature tells us about how leaders manage their own identity, influence, and effectiveness as either a nontraditional, nondominant leader or a more traditional, dominant leader with greater privilege and power. The role of identity in shaping both leaders and organizational members and some of the diversity-related barriers that have been found to exist are examined. The chapter also explores the literature on leader development and the skill set needed to lead effectively in today's diverse workplace.

Next, the role of leaders in managing relationships with others in a diverse workplace is examined. There is literature that suggests leaders play a critical role in leading across differences that exist both within and between organizational groups. To be able to integrate the perspectives of diverse others, leaders need to develop the capability to build effective relationships and work groups, and to develop others. In relation to leading the organization, the chapter explores how leading a diverse organization requires different strategies, organizational policies, and practices to leverage these differences and take full advantage of the potential that diversity may bring.

At all three levels, leaders are often the key lever in determining whether diversity becomes an organizational liability fraught with miscommunication, distrust, and conflict, or an organizational asset fueled by greater capacity for innovation and creativity. In reviewing current leadership theories about building and maintaining relationships in a diverse work context, three key points are illustrated.

First, research and theory examining leadership in the context of diversity, or at the intersection of diversity and leadership, remains sparse. In 1996, a two-part special issue on diversity leadership was published in *Leadership Quarterly.* At that time DiTomaso and Hooijberg (1996) argued that leaders within the diversity literature were conceived of "more as the targets of influence rather than as agents of influence" (p. 165). In other words, diversity literature at that time focused more on attempting to convince leaders that they should support diversity initiatives rather than on how to accomplish this. As this chapter highlights, this stance has evolved and scholars are focusing more on how leaders can leverage differences rather than whether they should or should not support diversity. A recent special issue in the *American Psychologist* on diversity and leadership clarifies the importance of reexamining existing leadership theory and practice to incorporate issues of equity, diversity, social justice, and inclusion (Chin, 2010). Taken together, even though this literature remains sparse, we believe there is a growing recognition that these two topics are closely linked in the contemporary workplace and that additional research and theory in this area will emerge.

The second key point illustrated in this chapter is that we believe leadership itself is evolving and changing both because of, and in response to, diversity. A heterogeneous workforce demands a different style of leadership and leaders must respond accordingly. Leadership in a diverse context must be more relational in nature than in the past (Chen & Van Velsor, 1996). As we explained later, both leadership theory and practice are evolving in such a way that emphasizes the development of quality relationships, consensual influence, and leadership as a socially constructed process.

The third key point made throughout the chapter is that leadership plays a much more important role in the success or failure of a diverse workforce and diversity initiatives than previous research would suggest. There is a growing recognition in the literature that organizations can leverage differences to become a competitive advantage rather than a liability.

What Is Effective Leadership?

Most research on leadership has addressed the question: What is effective leadership? Traditionally, leadership was thought of as a position in a hierarchical organization held by a manager or supervisor with set responsibilities, authorities, and spans of influence. For many years, the field responded to the question of effective leadership by looking at the characteristics of a leader either naturally in bureaucracies or more systematically in laboratories According to McCauley (2010), answers took the form of personal attributes (e.g., personality and intelligence), roles and behaviors used by leaders (e.g., Mintzberg's [1973] 10 management roles), competencies distinguishing the very best leaders from others (e.g., Boyatzis, 1982), expertise (e.g., tacit knowledge), and mastery of challenging experiences (McCall, 2010). Looking across many definitions of leadership, McCauley (2010) points out that those traditional approaches to leadership have three common elements: (1) they focus on influence as the key leadership process, (2) they examine the characteristics of individual leaders, and (3) they acknowledge that context matters. These models tend to emphasize the relationship between an organizational leader and his or her followers. McCauley also notes that these traditional models have common pitfalls that have recently called them into question. These pitfalls include (1) an overemphasis on the individual at the expense of organizational processes, (2) confusing positional authority with influence, (3) expecting a single individual to have all the necessary capabilities, and (4) ignoring the particular demands of different situations such as the heterogeneity of the workforce. Although there is evidence for all these different theories, they typically don't explain much variance in effectiveness and there has been a realization that leadership as a force does not reside within single individuals in positions of authority.

More recently there has been a trend away from this positional approach to leadership with its emphasis on leader characteristics to a more modern approach that argues that leadership is a shared phenomenon constructed across people (DeRue & Ashford, 2010; Pearce & Conger, 2003). The concept of shared leadership means that there is a social process of group interaction and the development of a shared understanding of the goals and vision of the organization. As such, leadership requires social interactions that allow for the accomplishment of the work of a collective. Leadership is of the organization and not of individuals (Boal & Hooijberg, 2000). At a fundamental level, leadership can be understood as the social process for generating the direction, alignment, and commitment needed by a group to accomplish collective goals (Drath et al., 2008; McCauley et al., 2010). It has to do with leadership functions that encompass the actions of many people, processes, structures, and practices. Leadership also doesn't have to occur within the confines of a formal hierarchy; it can happen anywhere, anytime and is not limited to a particular setting. Over the years, the field has evolved from a focus on the individual to a focus on the actions of a collective. Leadership is now thought of as a relational property rather than as an individual ability. The field now looks at leadership embodied across people rather than a function located in a single individual with authority granted by a bureaucracy to direct a particular group.

It is the socially constructed nature of leadership that makes diversity an important consideration for both today and the future (Chen & Van Velsor, 1996). Leadership is in essence a consensual process endorsed by members of an organization where individuals mutually agree on who will be seen as having an identity as a leader (DeRue & Ashford, 2010). Even if an individual claims to be a leader, it is not so unless others reciprocate by granting or affirming a leader identity on the individual. Within the context of diversity, this framing of a leader identity is strongly impacted by the attitudes and expectations associated with different social identities. This view of leadership as a socially constructed process influences how individuals manage themselves, how they operate when working with others, and how they lead in an organization.

Several different approaches to leadership focus on its shared or connected nature; these theories point to the importance of understanding the intersection of leadership and diversity. Social identity theory helps to explain the importance of diversity at the self-management level by exploring how an identity as a leader is internalized. By explaining the dynamics of stereotyping and prejudice, social identity theory also has implications for leading others so that a group functions effectively. In addition, at the level of leading others, approaches such as Leader–Member Exchange theory, social identity conflict resolution, and boundary spanning behaviors are also quite relevant to understanding how relationships can be best managed within the context of diversity. At the level of the organization, approaches that look at human resources practices, human capital strategies, and organizational learning have important implications for leadership amidst a context of diversity.

Leading Self

Leadership of the self is one of the emerging areas of attention in the leadership literature. As mentioned previously, traditional approaches looked at how demographic, behavioral, and background characteristics impact others. The shift to more contemporary approaches suggests that leaders need to understand the self in the context of a shared leadership environment where many are contributing to adaptive change. It requires being able to be aware of oneself amidst growing diversity in the workplace.

Theoretical Foundations

SELF-PERCEPTION

Leading oneself has to do with the internalization of an identity as a leader. There is a process through which individuals learn to think of themselves as a leader and look to claim leadership responsibilities. Social identity approaches to leadership offer a foundation for understanding what it means to lead oneself in the context of diversity and to internalize a leader identity.

Everyone has both a social identity and a personal identity. An individual's social identity involves group memberships such as nationality, race, gender, language, religion, generation, sexual orientation, and the like. Tajfel and Turner's (1979, 1986) theory of social identity and the associated self-categorization theory (Turner, 1982, 1985, 2004) suggest that these memberships are fundamental to the self, providing both a sense of belonging and a sense of distinctiveness. This distinctiveness means that people distinguish between people like them and people unlike them. Building on this earlier theory, Hogg and his colleagues put forth a social identity theory of leadership (Hogg, 2001; Hogg & van Knippenberg, 2003; Hogg et al., 2005) that emphasizes that social identity is important for understanding who will be accepted and perceived as a leader. In particular, research has established that various features of social identity such as gender, culture, and race influence others' acceptance of leadership behaviors, which is fundamental to developing an identity as someone who leads (Ayman, 1993; Eagly & Karau, 2002; Sy et al., 2010; van Knippenberg, van Knippenberg, De Cremer, & Hogg, 2004).

Lord and Hall (2005) further suggest that the development of a leader identity requires the integration of one's social identities with one's professional and personalidentities. In other words, leaders must understand themselves in terms of their organizational role, social identity, and personal traits. This idea of self-awareness is much broader than the traditional understanding of self-awareness as a function of personality and behaviors. Awareness of social identity suggests that leaders must understand how others react to them and be sensitive to the impact of the social identity of others. From a social identity point of view, leader development is a maturation process merging self and social knowledge with identification as a leader. For example, all three authors of this chapter have had to integrate their identities as leaders of research teams with their own sense of themselves as women and understand how gender may influence how others see and respond to them as leaders. As we have matured, our understanding of leadership has blended with what it means to be female in today's society. As maturity increases, it is easier to facilitate the integration of different aspects of self. And, as a leader gains more experience, the leader identity grows more central to self-concept.

OTHERS' PERCEPTIONS

Developing as a leader requires claiming a leader identity. This, however, is only part of the process. As stated earlier, leadership roles must also be granted by others (DeRue & Ashford, 2010). A socially constructed view of leadership emphasizes that it is important to look at the processes by which people are recognized, accepted, and endorsed as leaders. Over the years, there has been substantial evidence that members of nondominant groups face identity-related obstacles in being granted an identity as a leader. There is a rich literature as to how prejudice seeps into the process of recognizing someone as leader. For example, there have been volumes written about the scarcity of women in top leadership roles as a result of discrimination and bias resulting from the incompatibility of a feminine stereotype with the schemata of a leader. Starting with the work of Virginia Schein (1973, 1975), the "think manager, think male" phenomenon has been identified. Basically, this long line of research points to the fact that the dominant prototype of a leader is male, making it more difficult for perceivers to recognize women as leaders, as they simply do not fit one's schema of a leader. This tendency is robust; it has been documented repeatedly and in multiple countries (Schein, Mueller, Lituchy, & Liu, 1996). More recently, Eagly and Chin (2010) used meta-analytic techniques to account for the underrepresentation of women in the work force as being the result of such discriminatory barriers (Eagly & Chin, 2010). Eagly and Karau (2002) reiterate that prejudice toward women is a function of the mismatch between femininity and expectations for prototypical leaders.

This subtle bias resulting from schema incongruity has received several different names by both scholars and the press over the years. Early on it was called a glass ceiling, or an invisible level above which women cannot rise because of discrimination. More recently, Eagly and Carli (2007) termed it a labyrinth to indicate that there are abrupt stops and turns throughout a woman's journey to the top. Ryan and Haslam (2005) have also identified the glass cliff—the appointment of women to precarious or no-win situations from which a single mishap can send them plummeting from the possibility of successful leadership. We don't mean to imply that these metaphors are all the same; however, they all make the point that discrimination—and not a lack of skills or abilities—is what holds women back. Regardless of the metaphor, the point is that a dominant masculine prototype blocks the recognition of women as leaders, hindering the route to the top.

Moreover, women are only one part of the population impacted by these leader recognition processes. Eagly and Chin (2010) point out that incongruent stereotypes have also created disadvantages for gay men (Madon, 1997), African Americans (Bell & Nkomo, 2001; Livers & Caver, 2003), and Asian-Americans. Livers and Caver refer to the barrier facing African American men and women as miasma, or a general fog that blurs their recognition in leadership positions and makes the path to the top more hazardous and circuitous. The point is that the process of claiming and being granted a leadership identity is much tougher for someone who is not of the dominant leader prototype. The dominant leader prototype may vary from society to society but the ease of a person matching the dominant prototype claiming leadership is a constant. All else being equal, a candidate prototypical of the dominant group appears more qualified to others, regardless of the social identity of the perceiver (i.e., even among women, men appear to be more qualified as leaders than their female counterparts).

Prototypes of leaders are embedded in social systems in organizations and closely tied to power dynamics, with some social identity groups in a society having greater access to resources, status, and privileges than others. Research has pointed out that power differentials are intimately tied to how leadership is claimed and granted with leadership experiences unfolding differently for people in different contexts (Oshry, 2010). In his discussion of the impact of power differentials on behavior, Oshry (2010) points out that people are often blind to the value of status in organizations—both those characterizing their own group and the characteristics of others. People know differences exist but they are blind to the impact of these status differences. Applying a social identity lens to Oshry's work means that people are often blind to the impact of social identity in the context of leadership. This blindness occurs in two different ways: blindness to the context of others and blindness to one's own context.

When people are blind to the social identity of others, there is greater likelihood of misunderstanding and behaving in ways that undermine organizational effectiveness. Not understanding the impact of social hierarchies can make it difficult to provide coaching and mentoring. For example, the prototypical white male boss may not understand the frustration experienced by a female direct report who feels that she isn't granted the same opportunities as the men or may not be as readily accepted as a leader. And the white woman may not understand the difficulty her Asian colleague has in being seen as a leader rather than as an engineer. Despite accumulated research evidence about the deleterious effects of biases in leader categorization (Eagly & Karau, 2002; Ensari & Murphy, 2003; Rosette, Leondardelli, & Phillips, 2008; Schein, 1973; Sy et al., 2010), these dynamics are not always "seen" by members of dominant social identity groups. Rosette et al. (2008) points out that in the United States members of dominant social identity groups give so much weight to individual skills, efforts, and abilities in workplace judgments that they are blind to social identity categories such as race. This can result in interactions that are characterized by attribution biases and misunderstandings.

The other type of blindness is to the impact of one's own identity. Ignorance to the impact of social identity can result in a response that is insensitive to the lack of privileges accorded by society to nondominant groups. Although individuals of dominant social identity groups might be able to recognize that others are disadvantaged, it is rare for them to recognize that they might be advantaged by their position of privilege. For example, some individuals from the dominant group may not be aware of the privileges they have had over the years and may be reluctant to create opportunities for others, attributing their own career progress solely to their own efforts rather than to a combination of effort and social identity-based privileges. Or someone from the dominant group may not be aware that colleagues view him or her as part of the privileged class and not know how to react when associated feelings come into play.

Strategies for Enhancing Leadership of Self

A significant implication of a social identity approach to leadership is that it is important to understand social identity and recognize its impact. Effective management of oneself in a diverse environment requires self-awareness about social identity (Ferdman, 2008): about how you see yourself and others and how others perceive your social identity. Wasserman, Gallegos, and Ferdman (2008) point out that leaders have a responsibility to model the ways in which social identity blindness in themselves, and within organizations more generally, can be addressed. Pretending that organizations are gender, racially, or culturally neutral when they are not limits the effectiveness of leaders to be inclusive (Ayman & Korabik, 2010). As Brewer's well-known optimal distinctiveness theory (1991) has illustrated, people have a dual need for the validation of their uniqueness as well as their belongingness to groups that are composed of individuals to whom they feel similar in some way. Indeed, a recent review of inclusion research (Shore et al., 2011) suggests that achieving both belongingness and uniqueness is key to experiences of inclusion. Thus, the failure of a leader to recognize the gender, racial, or cultural background of an employee potentially limits the employee's felt inclusion. Even if the employee feels a sense of belonging, if his or her unique identity is not acknowledged and accepted, the employee is forced to assimilate to the dominant social identity rather than be truly integrated or included. In situations characterized by heterogeneity it is important to assume that people may have different evaluations of the same experience; although a self-proclaimed leader may perceive assimilation among demographically different employees to be functional, the employees themselves may view their lack of felt belonging as the leader's responsibility, thereby limiting their acceptance of the individual as a leader.

Ferdman (2008) and Hannum (2007) offer similar methodologies for learning about identity: one's own and others'. Their approaches offer the opportunity for leaders to explore how much of their own identity comes from group membership and to appreciate the diversity within groups. They ask the leader to identify their own (multiple) sources of identity and to share it with others. It is followed with a large group discussion with the purposes of understanding the role of identities in interpersonal interactions (Ferdman, 2008). These self-awareness methods help people learn how much diversity there is in identity and the impact of identity on one's perceptions of others and in others' perceptions of oneself. Through this exercise, people consider which of their identities might be the most and least obvious to others at work. The assumption is that by being clear about their own identities and their importance, individuals can more easily avoid confusing their own lenses, feelings, and goals with projections from others. People are also able to see that when certain identities are relatively unimportant to them, they may overlook them in others; likewise, when certain identities are important to them, they may erroneously assume that those identities are important to and recognized by other people. The beauty of this exercise is that it unearths not just the differences across people's identities, but also the overlapping sources of identity among people who had previously assumed themselves to be different.

The identity awareness exercise described by both Ferdman (2008) and Hannum (2007) is useful because it helps people to become more aware of identity perception processes that otherwise often remain implicit. Extending this notion to perceptions of leadership, Rosette et al. (2008) suggest that people should be made aware of the cognitive biases that may lead them to favor people who match the prevailing leader prototype in terms of social identity. Although such awareness may not "correct" the bias, it can at least lead to a better understanding of the impact of social identity on perceptions of leadership. This is one way to address the issue of "blindness" to social identity, particularly on the part of the employees being led.

Leading Self—Future Research

Based on both research and theory highlighted in this section on leading the self, we offer the following research questions for consideration in future research.

- What is the process through which leaders evolve from a mindset in which they view a situation from their own identity and worldview to one in which they are able to view a situation from multiple views and lenses? Although Robert Kegan's work on adult development theory (1982, 1994) provides a framework for this, we still do not know much about what this process involves, and more importantly, how to incorporate this development into current leadership training and development activities.
- How can leaders overcome identity blindness? Throughout this chapter, we have illustrated how powerful issues of identity are in a diverse workplace. Effective leadership requires understanding of one's own identity as well as the identity of others. Although it seems clear that this involves recognition of privilege and social marking (Thomas & Chrobot-Mason, 2005), it is not clear what forms of training and development may be beneficial for helping leaders to overcome their blind spots. Growing research using the implicit association test (e.g., Hofmann, Gawronski, Gschwendner, Le, & Schmitt, 2005) suggests that this may be a useful tool for helping individuals to recognize their implicit biases associated with social identity; however, less is known about the specific training interventions, incentives, and contextual cues that might help leaders to consciously overcome their biases and blind spots.

In the next section, we turn to looking at the literature discussing the impact of diversity on the act of leading others.

Leading Others

In essence, the act of leadership is about guiding and influencing the behavior of others. Indeed, most leadership theory and research has to date focused on leading others. In the cross-level framework of Crossan, Vera, and Nanjad (2008), this level emphasizes the interpersonal influence of leaders. Leaders within organizations are responsible for setting goals and coordinating and managing the work of others to achieve these goals. However, the ability to influence and coordinate the work of others becomes more complex and more challenging within a diverse workplace. When the work group consists of diverse employees, collaboration and integrated efforts toward a common united vision are made more difficult because the leader and the other members of the work group often represent different social identity groups. Thus, the leader and those he or she is leading likely hold different perspectives, values, priorities, and opinions, perhaps speak different languages, live in different parts of the world, and may hold very different positions and type of expertise within the organization. Until recently, leadership theory and research failed to address such complexities and assumed that work groups were homogenous and that leaders could fairly easily influence and exert power over employees. It is only recently that scholars have begun to acknowledge and study leadership within the context of diversity.

Theoretical Foundations

This section highlights two theories that have been examined in the literature from the lens of both leadership and diversity. Social Identity and Leader–Member Exchange (LMX) theory have been used as a theoretical foundation to examine the relational and influence processes involved in leading diverse others.

THE SOCIAL IDENTITY THEORY OF LEADERSHIP

Although the social identity theory of leadership was described in the previous section as it applies to leading oneself and being aware of one's own identity, it is also important to consider the theory as a foundation for understanding how to lead and influence others effectively in the context of diversity. According to Hogg (2001; Hogg & van Knippenberg, 2003), groups more readily grant leadership to someone who is prototypical or representative of the group and leaders have influence over others to the extent they embody the norms and prototype of the group. He describes how three social processes operate in conjunction to determine the level of influence and power a leader develops with respect to others.

The first process Hogg describes is prototypicality. Individuals who are perceived by others to occupy the most prototypical position of the group best embody the behaviors to which others conform. In other words, leaders emerge as having influence and power within a group because they best embody the values, beliefs, vision, and so forth, of the group as a whole. In addition, the more prototypical a leader is, the more likely it is that he or she will be perceived as effective. The second process involves social attraction. When leaders are well-liked and fit with the prototype of the group, others are more likely to accept their ideas and direction. Hogg suggests that the third process is attribution and information processing. When leaders are highly prototypical and socially attractive within a group, others are more likely to attribute their behavior to intrinsic leadership ability or charisma. Such leaders and their suggestions are intrinsically persuasive because they embody the norms of the group. These three social processes combine to create a *cycle of influence*: when leaders embody the norms and prototype of the group, they are endorsed as leaders; their endorsement results in greater power to influence (Hogg, 2001).

The social identity theory of leadership suggests that leader influence and the ability to exert power are largely based on identity and the extent to which the leader embodies the group prototype. However, all three of the social processes described by Hogg are complicated when leaders and work group members are diverse and represent nontraditional or nondominant identities. In fact, Hogg (2001) suggests that one implication is that social minorities may find it more difficult to influence others because they fail to embody the group prototype. Typically, the social identity characteristics of the dominant group in society determine who is recognized as a potential leader. Leader recognition processes also work in reverse: those in top positions in the organization are thought to be characteristic of the organization, or exemplars of the organization. The more representative the person in a top hierarchical role is of the organization at large, the more likely others will identify with this leader and respond positively to leadership attempts. The less representative the person in a top organizational role, the more challenges the leader will face in influencing others. Another consideration is that as leaders and work teams become more diverse and the workplace itself becomes less homogeneous, the range of potential leaders who could embody group norms may actually increase. Thus, although social minorities may be at a disadvantage in assuming leadership roles when they fail to fit the group prototype, we are hopeful that this disadvantage will begin to disappear as the workplace becomes increasingly diverse and people become more aware of and sensitive to identity differences.

Viewing leadership through the lens of social identity suggests that leaders of diverse groups must be aware of their own identity as well as those around them to continually reshape and redefine the group prototype, or as Reicher and Hopkins (1996) suggest, become "entrepreneurs of identity." The important lesson here is that leaders who discover intersectionalities of identity, or identity similarities that cut across simple demographic boundaries (e.g., those defined by race and gender), are more likely to be effective, as the group prototype becomes less simplistic and more likely to capture the multiple identities represented in the group. Another benefit of highlighting cross-cutting identities is that doing so can help to reduce the salience of the demographic categories within the group that might mirror those that are sociohistorically associated with status differences, as these are the ones that can drive negative intragroup dynamics unless actively counteracted (Ridgeway, 1991; Ridgeway & Correll, 2006).

In addition to blurring the distinctions across simple demographic boundaries by highlighting intersectionalities, leaders will also be more effective in leading diverse groups to the extent that their behavior and the norms that they establish delegitimize beliefs that exist in the broader society about the status differences between demographic groups (e.g., men are perceived to be higher status then women, whites have higher status than non-whites, etc.). As described more later, when leaders develop high-quality relationships with individuals of all backgrounds, they help to eliminate the potential salience of sociohistorical status differences, thereby reducing stereotyping and biases related to cultural identities. We now turn our attention to the LMX theory as it emphasizes the development of high-quality relationships and provides a strong theoretical foundation for understanding leading others in a diverse work environment.

LEADER–MEMBER EXCHANGE THEORY

LMX theory suggests that both leaders and their direct reports play a role in the quality of relationship between each superior–subordinate dyad (Graen & Uhl-Bien, 1995). When the relationship is characterized by high levels of trust, interaction, and support (i.e., a "high-quality exchange"), the subordinates in those relationships enjoy positive work outcomes such as higher performance and lower turnover result (Gerstner & Day, 1997). According to Graen and Uhl-Bien (1995), earlier LMX researchers suggested that due to limited time and social resources, work groups would be best served by managers who focused their attention on the most promising of subordinates, whereas more recently researchers have recommended that managers offer all employees access to high-quality LMX relationships by extending an initial offer to develop LMX partnerships with each of them. The expectation was that by doing so, the LMX process would be perceived more equitably by employees, and would also expand the capability of the organization by developing the potential of more employees. Consistent with this, there is now growing empirical evidence to support the notion that when leaders develop quality relationships with each employee, they are more likely to foster high- quality relationships among their work group employees, as manifested in group cohesion, cooperation, and retention (e.g., Ford & Seers, 2006; Liden, Erdogan, Wayne, & Sparrowe, 2006; McClane, 1991; Schyns, Paul, Mohr, & Blank, 2005).

However, there is also evidence to suggest that leaders are more likely to develop high- quality relationships with those who are similar and belong to the same social identity group than with those who belong to another social identity group (Scandura & Lankau, 1996), and that such in-group bias has negative consequences. Scandura and Lankau (1996) describe the tentative nature of the development of a relationship involving cross-race and cross-gender leader–member dyads. Although the demonstration of mutual respect and development of trust are critical to the formation of a high-quality LMX relationship, identity differences often make this more difficult as each member may have a different definition of respect and how it should be demonstrated. If mutual respect is demonstrated, then the next phase in development of the LMX relationship centers on trust. Again, the development of trust is more difficult in diverse dyads because even one violation of trust may destroy the relationship and reinforce negative stereotypes and expectations of discriminatory practices. For this reason, leaders must have a heightened sensitivity to the development of trust when leading diverse employees. Scandura and Lankau (1996) suggest this should be viewed as a fragile process "until norms emerge upon which both members can base expectations of the response and behaviors of the others" (p. 249).

Strategies for Enhancing Leadership

As research on LMX theory suggests, successful leadership of diverse others requires a new set of skills and practices that were not required of leaders when the workplace was homogeneous. Contemporary leaders must create a cohesive team identity despite the fact that work group members vary greatly in their demographic, geographic, and professional identities. They also find themselves in the precarious position of attempting to bridge differences when they themselves may belong to a group that differs from the identity of at least some of their colleagues. Being different themselves can exacerbate the difficulty leaders face in attempting to create a cohesive group identity, as research shows when leaders are a member of the outgroup, this has a negative impact on work group member satisfaction, identification with the organization, and trust and support of leaders (Duck & Fielding, 1999, 2003). Thus, to be effective, leaders in a diverse workplace must first develop a different mindset that includes greater recognition of their own identity as well as the identity of others to understand the differences that exist within their team (as discussed in the previous section), and then develop a set of skills that facilitates the unification of a diverse group of individuals. This skill set needed to lead a diverse workforce may be considered under two broad areas: (1) individualized behaviors or strategies to enhance interactions with individual employees, which include transformational, relational, and inclusive leadership behaviors; and (2) intergroup behaviors or strategies focused on facilitating collaboration across diverse groups, which include creating shared goals, resolving conflict, and fostering collaboration through boundary-spanning leadership. Strategies for leadership development in both areas are discussed in the following subsections.

Individualized Strategies

TRANSFORMATIONAL LEADER BEHAVIORS

As described above, research on LMX has clearly shown that employees who enjoy high-quality relationships with their leader benefit from numerous positive outcomes (Gerstner & Day, 1997). Research on transformational leadership adds to our understanding of effective leadership by specifying the leader behaviors that help leaders to establish an emotional bond with work group members and motivates them to align with the leader's vision (Dvir, Kass, & Shamir, 2004). These behaviors differ significantly from transactional leadership behaviors. While transactional leaders are characterized as engaging in rational social exchange with others, transformational leaders provide inspirational motivation, intellectual stimulation, and show individualized consideration (Bass, 1990; Bass & Avolio, 1994). Recent research suggests that transformational leadership behaviors may be critical for leveraging positive group outcomes like team identity and performance in diverse groups (Kearney & Gebert, 2009; Mitchell & Boyle, 2009). There are two reasons for this. First, transformational leadership behaviors enhance unity and a sense of commitment to the collective. Second, transformational leadership behavior seems to unleash the potential benefits that diversity may bring to the workplace, such as higher quality decision making and greater innovation and creativity (Cox, 1991; Milliken & Martins, 1996; Page, 2007).

For example, when leaders communicate a compelling vision for the team and express confidence in members (i.e., inspirational motivation), they increase trust and commitment among diverse team members (Joshi, Lazarova, & Liao, 2009). When leaders are inspirational, team members begin to trust that their group has the collective skills, expertise, and achievements necessary to accomplish the mission and they also begin to appreciate their teams' accomplishments, thereby building the basis for identification and commitment to the team. When leaders engage in individualized consideration by considering and valuing the unique needs and skills of each employee, they foster mutual respect (Scandura & Lankau, 1996), a sense of collective identity, and trust among group members. As such, Howell and Shamir (2005) suggest that "charismatic leader–employee relationships" result in work group members who are willing to transcend their own self-interests for the sake of the collective team or organization and are highly committed to its vision and goals. Perhaps a key mechanism in this process is that by virtue of treating others with individualized consideration, a leader is able to signal that employees are valued.

Realizing the benefits of diversity seems also to be closely linked to transformational leadership behaviors characterized as intellectual stimulation. In particular, when leaders explicitly encourage questioning and challenging of accepted ideas, research shows that alternative views are more likely to be expressed and considered in the final solution (Mitchell & Boyle, 2009). When leaders show appreciation for employees' contributions and encourage them to provide input, their behaviors promote inclusion (Nembhard & Edmondson, 2006). Kearney and Gebert (2009) found that transformational leadership behaviors that facilitated the elaboration of task-relevant information within the diverse team were positively related to team performance. Their work suggests that leaders may be a key lever in unlocking the greater potential that exists in diverse groups when they engage in behaviors that facilitate the sharing and processing of task-relevant information. In other words, transformational leadership behaviors may account for the difference between a diverse team whose interactions are characterized by miscommunication, distrust, and conflict from one whose interactions lead to the emergence of innovative and creative ideas and solutions that come from a diverse team with varied perspectives, backgrounds, areas of expertise, and the like.

RELATIONAL LEADERSHIP BEHAVIORS

LMX theory described earlier illustrates the importance of developing high-quality relationships in the workplace and the challenge leaders face in attempting to do so within a diverse work context in which there is a natural bias to favor in-group members. In a recent study, Nishii and Mayer (2009) argued that the development of LMX relationships of differential quality is likely to be more harmful for group processes and outcomes in diverse than in homogeneous groups. This is because members of diverse groups are naturally more susceptible to demographically induced status hierarchies, power struggles, and ingroup–outgroup conflicts, and any differential treatment of employees on the part of leaders has the potential to reinforce and perpetuate such status hierarchies. In contrast, leaders who develop high-quality relationships with all of their employees delegitimize sociohistorical status hierarchies by treating employees similarly rather than privileging a select few. As such, they help to establish a level playing field that facilitates positive group processes and lowers group conflict, as evidenced in lower turnover rates. In support of this, they found that when leaders facilitate high levels of inclusion and power sharing within their diverse groups by developing consistently high-quality relationships with employees, they help to attenuate and even reverse the positive relationship that is often observed between group diversity and turnover. However, when leaders are inclusive of only a select few employees, they may exacerbate the relationship between diversity and turnover.

An important implication of this research is that if leaders develop high-quality relationships only with demographically similar others, they will likely pay in the form of higher turnover, which in turn can be detrimental for group performance (Staw, 1980). Thus, leaders should be educated not just about how they can effectively develop high-quality relationships with employees, but also to think about the influence that the overall pattern of LMX relationships across employees (i.e., mean and variance of LMX relationships) may have on the relationship between group diversity and outcomes.

Indeed, developing high-quality relationships in a diverse workplace requires something beyond traditional individual leadership. According to Wasserman et al. (2008), it requires relational leadership and a new set of skills that includes flexibility, self-awareness, and the capacity to be vulnerable. Good leadership embodies relational interactions that are characterized by mutuality and equality (Fletcher, 2010) as well as coordination and shared responsibility with others in service of organizational goals (see Brickson, 2000 and Fletcher, 2010 for a discussion of relational identity orientation). Furthermore, it requires that leaders progress from achieving cultural competence to developing relational eloquence. Relational eloquence is achieved by "continuously attending to how one is making sense of or coordinating meaning with another or others in the relationship" (Wasserman et al., p. 184).

Similar conclusions can be drawn from theoretical work by Shore and her colleagues (2011), who suggest that leaders need to promote inclusion in information sharing and decision making and provide employees with voice in order to enhance inclusion. These inclusive leadership behaviors characterize high, but not low, LMX relationships. The next section elaborates on inclusive behaviors as an effective strategy for enhancing leadership within a diverse work context.

INCLUSIVE LEADERSHIP BEHAVIORS

It is important that leaders operating within a context of difference engage in a set of behaviors that contribute to the creation of a work climate that is inclusive, characterized as being high in respect and trust, and one in which all employees can fully contribute (Nishii, 2010). For purposes of this discussion, Holvino, Ferdman, and Merrill-Sands's (2004) definition of inclusion is used: "equality, justice, and full participation at both the group and individual levels, so that members of different groups not only have equal access to opportunities, decision making, and positions of power, but they are actively sought out *because* of their differences" (p. 248). Leaders play a pivotal role in creating an environment in which diverse employees experience equality, justice, and full participation. At the heart of this lies respect.

In virtually any discussion of creating an inclusive climate, the issue of respect emerges. Therefore, leaders of a diverse workforce must strive to create an environment characterized by high levels of respect. Although the definition of what constitutes respectful behavior varies across cultures, the general concept appears across the literature as a key element in creating a work environment in which differences are valued. Hannum and Glover (2010) examined the role a leader plays in fostering respect in the workplace. They conclude that "at its core, respect is a continuous process of paying attention to someone" (p. 613). It involves understanding and accepting another's viewpoint as valid. They recommend that one demonstrable way leaders can foster a climate of respect is by exhibiting an interest in and appreciation of others' perspectives, knowledge, skills, and abilities. Similarly, Ferdman and his colleagues (Ferdman, Katz, Letchinger, & Thompason, 2009) suggest that leaders who wish to practice inclusion should focus on creating a safe space that invites people to engage and enable true dialogue to occur, showing respect by enabling people to have insight into why and how decisions are made, and being willing to understand and engage people's multiple perspectives. These views are supported by empirical research that has shown that leaders who solicit and appreciate employee input help to create climates that are high in psychological safety (Nembhard & Edmondson, 2006).

When leaders engage in and role model inclusive behavior, a number of positive outcomes are likely to accrue. In particular, there is some evidence to support the link between an inclusive work climate and employee outcomes of well-being, job satisfaction, and organizational commitment (Findler, Wind, & Mor Barak, 2007). There is also some evidence that leaders who facilitate inclusion by being interested in the ideas of employees, listening to them, giving them fair consideration, and taking action to address matters that have been raised, create a climate within which employees are willing to speak up and participate fully in the workplace (Detert & Burris, 2007). Finally, research also suggests that inclusive climates are beneficial not only because they make the attainment of positive outcomes more likely, but also because discrimination and harassment tend to be lower in inclusive climates (Nishii, Langevin, & Bruyere, 2010).

Intergroup Strategies

CREATING SHARED GOALS

Leaders influence the satisfaction and productivity of a diverse work group by fostering high-quality relationships with individuals but also by fostering unity across divergent work groups. At the intergroup level, leaders play an important role in creating or making salient a larger collective identity that encompasses and unites all subgroups (Hogg et al., 2005). This collective or superordinate identity is often the work team or organization itself. As discussed earlier in the section on transformational leadership behaviors, leaders form strong emotional ties with employees in part by communicating and fostering commitment to a vision and set of goals. Likewise, leaders play an important role in creating and strengthening ties between divergent subgroups by focusing on a common mission that serves to bind such groups together in service of common goals.

Along these lines, Pittinsky (2010) suggests that diversity calls for intergroup leadership, which involves behaviors and practices that unite not just individuals but also subgroups in a common goal. He argues that leaders have traditionally attempted to create a collective identity across diverse individuals and groups by focusing on the elimination of negative attitudes and relationships. However, Pittinsky's work on a concept he calls "allophilia," from the Greek meaning love or liking of the other, suggests that leadership in a diverse context requires more than simply reducing negative attitudes; it requires increasing the positive attitudes different subgroups within the collective hold toward one another. He suggests that leadership behaviors that reduce negative attitudes are different from those that increase positive attitudes and that leaders play an important role in facilitating both. Whereas negative attitudes toward members of certain groups are strongly influenced by social norms, positive attitudes represent an individual experience. Through their individual actions, leaders may role model behaviors that go beyond the absence of negative attitudes and treatment toward subgroups and include the development of high-quality positive relationships with all group members and emphasize values of equality (Pittinsky, 2010; Pittinsky & Maruskin, 2008; Pittinsky & Montoya, 2009).

Fiol, Pratt, and O'Connor (2009) also emphasize the importance of creating a superordinate identity while at the same time respecting subgroup identity differences. They too argue that organizational leaders are often a key lever in managing the tension that exists between subgroup identities and encouraging subgroups to focus instead on shared goals and a common mission. Leaders can actively counteract the pervasiveness of sociohistorical biases and stereotypes by treating members of divergent subgroups in a noticeably egalitarian way. By eliminating any threats to subgroup identities by being egalitarian, the leader then makes it possible for group members to work collaboratively toward the accomplishment of shared group goals (Fiolet al., 2009), which is important for fostering positive group identities and outcomes (Brewer & Miller, 1984).

Sociological research on status characteristics theory would suggest that the key is for leaders to be aware of the demographic categories within the group that mirror those that are sociohistorically associated with status differences, as these are the ones that can drive negative intragroup dynamics unless actively counteracted (Ridgeway, 1991; Ridgeway & Correll, 2006). To the extent that a leader's behavior and the norms that he or she establishes legitimize beliefs that exist in the broader society about the status differences between demographic groups (e.g., men are perceived to be higher status then women, whites have higher status than non-whites, etc.), the leader will perpetuate stereotyping and bias related to that cultural identity. When employees do not perceive leaders as promoting or perpetuating arbitrary status hierarchies based on demographic categories, subgroup identities are less likely to be perceived as threatened; this opens up the possibility for employees to transcend their own interests for the sake of the collective (Fiol et al., 2009) and trust the direction and goals the leader has set for the group.

RESOLVING CONFLICT

Even within a highly collaborative work environment, at least some degree of conflict will arise as this is a natural consequence of diversity. As the workplace becomes increasingly diverse, so does the likelihood of identity-based conflict. Ruderman, Glover, Chrobot-Mason, and Ernst (2010) discuss the role of leaders in responding to social identity conflict in the workplace. They suggest that employees hold a strong expectation that someone in a leadership position will respond to situations in which conflict over identity differences emerge in the workplace. However, many leaders fail to act in such instances, likely owing to a lack of confidence in their skills and ability to handle the situation effectively.

Based on their research with organizations across the globe, the authors suggest that the first critical step is for the leader to examine the whole picture and to develop an understanding of the many factors that influence collisions between social identity groups at work (e.g., cultural values, economic and political systems, organizational mission and infrastructure, history of conflict, etc.) and what role he or she plays within the larger picture. Step two is to clarify the message that the leader sends to the groups involved as well as to the organization as a whole. It is important that a leader's actions and words are aligned with his or her personal values as well as the firm's values and mission. Step three involves identifying realistic options for handling the conflict given available resources, and step four involves taking appropriate action. Leaders who intend to send the message that the group should learn from differences and value diversity must select a response to conflicts that conveys this message. In step five, leaders should monitor the situation to determine if the intended outcome has been achieved or if additional action may be needed. Finally, the last step involves reflection and learning once the conflict has been resolved. The authors emphasize the important role that leaders play in helping the team reflect on the conflict and the resolution, to capture the learning that took place during the process, and consider how this can be applied to future social identity difference conflicts that will inevitably arise within a diverse workplace.

Given that leaders cannot possibly be present to monitor and facilitate the resolution of every conflict that emerges, it is also important that they create norms that will operate in their absence. Earlier research focused on the possible benefits of highlighting norms of openness about conflict (Jehn, 1995) and encouraging collaborative strategies (De Dreu & Van Vianen, 2001), but found that neither strategy helps to improve conflict resolution. This may be because these strategies focus on conflict itself, and not the interpersonal context within which the conflicting parties are operating. Indeed, work by Brewer (1999) suggests that if the parties involved in a conflict are of different social status, then highlighting the need for cooperation can backfire because it makes the absence of mutual trust salient. More recent work by Nishii (2010) suggests that in inclusive climates, individuals are more likely to exhibit concern both for themselves and for others and be committed to working through differences as a source of interpersonal learning. As a result, experiences of group conflict in diverse groups with inclusive climates do not negatively impact group morale, as is usually the case in diverse groups (De Dreu & Weingart, 2003). It appears that leaders play an important role in fostering expectations for relational eloquence and authenticity among employees by creating an inclusive climate within which they can forge meaningful relationships and foster dual concern for the self and other, both of which are critical for effective conflict resolution.

FOSTERING COLLABORATION THROUGH BOUNDARY SPANNING LEADERSHIP

Leaders often play the role of boundary spanner in attempting to bridge differences and resolve conflict within their organization or team (Ernst & Chrobot-Mason, 2011). Differences in organizational level, area of expertise, demographic membership, and other boundaries between groups often emerge in the workplace as a border or constraint that limits effective communication and collaboration. However, research suggests that leaders can play an important role in transforming these differences or boundaries from a limitation into an opportunity. In a recent book based on data gathered as part of a multicountry study on leadership across differences conducted by the Center for

Creative Leadership, Ernst and Chrobot-Mason (2011) examine six boundary spanning leadership practices. Following an extensive review of the literature, they conclude that there are three overarching strategies leaders use in attempting to span boundaries.

The first, "managing boundaries," is based on work by Faraj and Yan (2009), who suggest that boundary management is challenging yet critical work that must be done to effectively manage cross-group interactions in the workplace. They argue that boundaries must be managed so that they are porous enough that resources and information can get in, but resistant enough to keep uncertainty and competing demands out. Leaders, therefore, may use strategies such as buffering and reflecting to define and clarify boundaries between groups (Ernst & Chrobot-Mason, 2011). Leaders buffer and protect their direct reports from external threats, competing demands, and other pressures by monitoring and managing the flow of resources, information, people, practices, and perceptions across boundaries. Leaders may also help groups better understand the boundary and differences that exist between them by reflecting-enabling groups to see and understand the needs, goals, values, work styles, preferences, expertise, and experiences of other groups.

The second general strategy for boundary spanning identified by Ernst and Chrobot-Mason (2011) is "forging common ground." This was derived from research based in social identity theory, which suggests that social identity differences, and the conflict this often creates, may be mitigated by emphasizing one-on-one personal interactions rather than group-based interactions (to learn more about this strategy, known as decategorization, see Brewer & Miller, 1984) or by emphasizing a common identity that becomes superordinate to subgroup identities (to learn more about this strategy, known as recategorization, see Gaertner & Dovidio, 2007). Ernst and Chrobot-Mason (2011) recommend that leaders engage in practices such as connecting and mobilizing to forge common ground. Connecting may be accomplished by finding opportunities that allow employees to "step outside" of their boundaries into a neutral zone where people can interact as individuals rather than members who represent their social identity group. The strategy of mobilizing involves created a common mission, vision, or goals that include all employees.

The third overarching strategy is "discovering new frontiers" and focuses on ways to take advantage of both similarities and differences that exist at the boundary between groups to enhance creativity, innovation, and problem-solving capacity. It is largely based on research and theory on subcategorization (Haslam & Ellemers, 2005; Hewstone, & Brown, 1986) as well as cross-cutting (Brewer, 1995). Research has shown that when groups have distinct but complementary roles to contribute toward a common goal, both differences and commonalities are emphasized and this leads to more positive intergroup attitudes and work outcomes (Eggins, Haslam, & Reynolds, 2002; Haslam, Eggins, & Reynolds, 2003). Brewer's (1995) work on cross-cutting suggests that it is important to select team members carefully so that intergroup conflict is minimized. She advocates systematically or randomly crossing work group roles with social identity group membership so that team composition cuts across organizational levels and functions. Based on this work, Ernst and Chrobot-Mason (2011) call out two practices leaders may use to tap into the potential that exists when diverse teams are created in the workplace: weaving and transforming. Leaders who engage in weaving integrate and draw out group differences within a larger whole or common vision. They find ways to capitalize on group differences in service of the larger whole such that subgroups all play an important and unique role in the mission of the entire group. Transforming involves leadership practices and activities that bring members of multiple groups together to create an entirely new social identity group or view a problem in an entirely new way. Both leadership practices attempt to take advantage of both the similarities and the differences that exist between groups to span across boundaries and foster collaboration.

Leading Others–Future Research

This section of the chapter on leadership in a diverse workplace focused on leading others. Overall, the results of our literature review suggest that leaders play a critically important role in creating a work climate that supports and retains a diverse workforce as well as leveraging the potential benefits that diversity may bring. The Social Identity Theory of Leadership and LMX theory provide a useful foundation for understanding key processes involved in the effective management of a diverse workforce. In addition, research on transformational leadership, LMX, and relational leadership, and inclusion provide evidence that specific leader behaviors impact the quality of workplace relationships which ultimately impact employee satisfaction and productivity. Finally, research and theory on intergroup conflict and collaboration suggest that leaders also play an important role in resolving identity-based conflicts, fostering unity, and linking divergent groups in a common mission.

Despite the research and theory on leading diverse others presented here, it is evident that many research questions remain unanswered. We suggest the following questions may serve as a starting point for future research.

- What role do others play in monitoring and holding one another accountable for inclusive behavior? The literature is more informative about the role leaders play in creating an inclusive work environment than the role of other work group members who may be just as important in creating an affirming climate. If leadership is to be viewed as a shared responsibility, then so too should the creation and maintenance of an inclusive climate. Thus, it is important that additional research explore the inclusive behavior and practices required of all work group members, and the implications this may have for diversity and team building initiatives. Special attention needs to be paid to identifying the ways in which group members can formally and informally assess and monitor the inclusiveness of their workgroup and the nonthreatening actions they can take to enforce inclusive standards agreed on by the group.
- How does the social identity theory of leadership and the cycle of influence manifest between the leader and work group members when social identity composition varies? Do the behaviors and strategies required for demonstrating inclusive leadership vary as a function of the demography of the group and the leader's own relational demography vis-à-vis group members? In other words, does or should leadership behavior vary depending on whether the leader is different in terms of identity from some group members versus different from all? It may be the case that leaders must behave or engage in a different set of practices to be recognized as a leader when they are demographically different from some or all other work group members.

Leading the Organization

Diverse organizations face some unique and complex challenges. Organizations may face the challenge of operating in many different countries, employing and coordinating workers from many different cultures and regions of the world, providing a service or product for customers in all corners of the globe, and interacting with stakeholders and suppliers in every time zone. Successful leadership of multicultural organizations operating within a global market requires facilitation and coordination of diverse people, systems, and work. Thus this section examines leadership in a diverse workplace at the organizational level. In the model presented by Crossan et al. (2008), this involves leadership responsibilities such as strategy, structure, rules, and procedures.

Much of what was discussed in the previous section on leading others may also apply when leading a diverse organization. Senior leaders who engage in relational, transformational, inclusive, and boundary spanning leadership behaviors serve as a role model and encourage leaders at all levels of the organization to adopt a similar leadership style and approach to managing diversity. Their potential influence is significant as it becomes aggregated across leadership levels and across managers throughout the organization, which in turn shapes the organizational climate for diversity and inclusion. They often determine (or strongly influence) the diversity strategy and the narrative about why diversity matters. As Crossan et al. (2008) suggest, "leaders are not passive recipients of changes in strategy, organization, and environment, but rather can be dominant forces in affecting their change" (p. 572). This section summarizes literature that has examined leadership of a diverse organization and highlights some key practices leaders must pay particular attention to as they significantly impact the extent to which the organization is able to leverage differences.

Before doing so, however, we wish to clarify the potential costs to overlooking or mismanaging diversity at the organizational level of leadership. Munusamy, Ruderman, and Eckert (2010) identify the four types of capital that may be sacrificed if leaders of organizations discount the importance of diversity to leadership: human, identity, diversity, and social capital. At a very fundamental level, organizations can lose out by not paying attention to the many talented people who might not fit the prototype of the ideal leader. In these days of extreme competition, organizations that want to thrive need to take a highly inclusive approach to the development of the workforce.

Theoretical Foundations

Diversity provides many potential advantages for organizations. It can help organizations to reach out to diverse customer groups and reach new markets. It can also allow for a variety of perspectives. Paying attention to diversity allows a firm to be flexible and withstand changes in the markets and economy. These benefits are referred to as diversity capital (Munusamy, Ruderman, & Eckert, 2010). In the subsections that follow, two theoretical positions are highlighted to explain how leaders accrue diversity capital. The first involves the process by which leaders create and then convey to others a meta-narrative or story about diversity within the organization and the second involves various approaches to managing difference within the organization.

DEVELOPING A META-NARRATIVE

Leaders are unlikely to be successful at creating an inclusive climate for diversity unless they convey a convincing narrative that focuses on the opportunities afforded by successful management of diversity (Wasserman et al., 2008). Through their style, behaviors, and values, leaders shape and then convey a meta-narrative or story for diversity within their organization. Leaders serve as role models who both derive and implement diversity and inclusion policies and practices. Because of their position, expertise, and/or authority, leaders demonstrate for others the extent to which differences are valued, employee subgroups are treated in egalitarian ways, and collaboration is encouraged. Thus, their behavior creates a story for others in the organization to follow.

Nishii and Langevin (2010) adopt the view that leaders play an especially important role as "interpretive filters" of organizational practices (Bowen & Ostroff, 2004). The way that they "sensemake" about practices (Weick, 1979) and in turn provide meaning to their subordinates (i.e., "sensegive") influences the ultimate effectiveness of those practices (Pfeffer, 1981). They showed that managers who attribute the adoption of diversity practices to external compliance motives (like complying with legal standards, keeping up with what competitors are doing, and avoiding looking bad to external stakeholders) fail to implement diversity initiatives effectively, as seen in the high levels of discrimination related to gender, race, age, sexual orientation, and religion (Nishii & Langevin, 2010).

In comparison, managers who attribute the adoption of diversity practices to an internal belief in the opportunities afforded by diversity initiatives (e.g., achieving better strategic outcomes, promoting fairness, enhancing inclusion and well-being) more thoroughly enact change in their units, as seen in the significantly higher reports of inclusion and lower rates of discrimination. They explain their results in terms of the differences that arise from "coaching from compliance" versus "coaching with compassion," the former which focuses on negative affect (e.g., the threat of noncompliance), arouses defensiveness, and induces individuals to achieve the minimum required for compliance, while the latter primes people's "ideal self" and enhances the motivational strength associated with pursuing desired behavioral changes (Boyatzis, 2006). It is also possible that leaders who believe in and are driven by internal motivations for managing diversity are better able to communicate a compelling vision to their employees and provide consistent, reliable diversity leadership; both sets of behaviors are consistent with transformational leadership behaviors as described previously (Kearney & Gebert, 2009). Taken together, this study highlights the fact that the effectiveness of diversity initiatives depends in large part on the way that leaders perceive, make sense of, and implement such initiatives.

APPROACHES TO MANAGING DIFFERENCE

One of the primary ways leaders shape a meta-narrative with respect to diversity is in their approach to managing difference. Research championed by the Center for Creative Leadership reveals that leaders generally engage in one of three ways when addressing tension and conflict that emerges in the workplace as a result of identity differences (Ernst, Hannum, & Ruderman, 2010; Ruderman et al., 2010). Each approach represents underlying beliefs about the organization and its leaders' role in managing cross-group relationships. Some organizations take a "hands-off" or passive approach to managing differences. They may fail to act or intervene for a variety of reasons and beliefs. Many leaders choose to do nothing based on the belief that the workplace is not the appropriate venue for dealing with societal level problems or that the organization is not responsible for intervening in such conflict. Others fail to see that a problem exists and deny the tension between groups. This is common particularly when the leader is a member of the dominant group and his or her own identity becomes a blind spot in the sense that the leader is unable to see issues from other perspectives. Still, other leaders may fail to act out of fear that they may make the situation worse by doing the wrong thing or calling too much attention to the differences that exist.

A second approach to managing differences is "direct and control." Leaders and organizations adopting this approach rely on both formal and informal authority, rewards, and punishments to manage relationships in such a way that the organizational mission and goals are protected. The intent behind the variety of leadership practices using this approach is to prevent or quickly extinguish conflict and tension based on group differences to maintain equilibrium in the organization. For example, some organizations rely on laws and regulations to address differences, while others emphasize a zero-tolerance approach to discrimination and harassment and include diversity policies in their employee handbook.

A third strategy for managing differences is the "cultivate and encourage" approach. The belief underlying this approach is that the organization should create the conditions that cultivate positive interactions among different groups and within which differences are valued. Leaders who adopt this type of approach actively manage differences and engage in, or support, a variety of practices that demonstrate the organization's commitment toward inclusion. Such practices may include diversity training, processes that encourage open dialogue, boundary spanning behavior (as described earlier), and role modeling. Ruderman et al. (2010) reported that the act of apologizing proved to go a long way in cultivating positive cross-group relationships. Recognizing and apologizing for some of the inevitable mistakes that occur when diverse groups interact with one another at work is very important for leaders to consider. Apologies demonstrate shared blame and responsibility, rather than the imposition of one group's interests over another's. They also help to communicate the idea that mistakes are a natural part of the learning process related to diversity. When leaders fail to recognize their own mistakes, they make it more likely that employees become preoccupied with avoiding mistakes rather than learning from them (Dragoni, 2005).

Although these three approaches are descriptive both of leaders as they lead others in their work groups and of more senior leaders who lead the organization, we believe that the approaches set by senior organizational leaders are particularly important because they help set the tone for the entire organization. When senior leaders role model the "cultivate and encourage" approach, they are more likely to cultivate climates for psychological safety, learning, and inclusion, all of which are necessary for optimizing the benefits of diversity. An important requirement is that they guide other leaders throughout the organization to adopt the same approach, and to do so consistently. As Bowen and Ostroff (2004) suggest, intended diversity strategies and approaches need to be communicated by senior leaders in a way that is visible, understandable, and unambiguous, and perceived as relevant to individual employees, with the expected outcomes of diversity strategies being clearly explained. The importance of these messages being directed by senior leaders is underscored by Bowen and Ostroff's (2004) argument that communication originating from sources are perceived as legitimate and authoritative are attended to more by employees. An important consideration, however, is the alignment between senior managers' communications and their behavior (Simons, 2002); the greater the agreement there is among senior leaders in their communications, the more likely it is that line managers and employees will also develop shared understandings of the organization's diversity strategy.

Strategies for Enhancing Leadership

MANAGING FAULTLINES

Just as the faultlines in the earth's crust may be dormant for some time period and then crack apart as a result of tension and pressure underground, so too may differences within the workplace lie dormant until a triggering event brings differences to the forefront. This triggering event may cause a great divide between groups and create significant challenges for leaders who must encourage divergent and distrustful groups to work collaboratively to achieve the organization's mission (Chrobot-Mason, Ruderman, Weber, & Ernst, 2009).

Lau and Murnighan's work on faultlines as well as work in the area of relational demography suggest that workforce composition and the nature and quantity of differences that exist within a work group help determine the strength of a faultline and its potential for polarizing group members. To at least some degree, organizational leaders can influence the composition of their workforce through staffing and affirmative action practices and policies. However, workforce composition is likely to ebb and flow and workgroups may not always engender an ideal diversity mix. Some level of conflict and tension is perhaps inevitable within a diverse organization, and thus it behooves leaders to consider and then determine a strategy for handling differences, disagreements, and conflict that results from diversity.

Gratton, Voigt, and Erickson (2007) examined the role of leaders in bridging faultlines within diverse teams. Based on their assessment of 55 teams from 15 European and American companies, they conclude that although there is a natural tendency when strong faultlines emerge for leaders to encourage team members to connect through meetings and social events, this approach may actually strengthen the faultline if it makes differences more apparent. What they suggest instead is that leading across a strong faultline initially requires a task-oriented style, but that the leader must make a switch to a more relationship-oriented style when the time is right. Beginning with a task-oriented leadership style is important so that the leader can focus on creating energy around the task itself such that collaboration and knowledge sharing is emphasized. In addition, this allows team members the chance to learn about one another's skills and competencies.

However, a relationship-oriented leadership style grows important as the need to deal with the tension and conflict that surround deeper levels of diversity, such as differences in values and priorities, emerges within the group. That is, to transition from an effective to an innovative organization, the leader must learn to surface and openly deal with intergroup tensions and create an environment of deep understanding and respect. Overall, these researchers conclude that although faultlines are a common hazard, there are significant differences between diverse teams in which a faultline leads to productivity declines versus teams that are productive and innovative despite strong faultlines. The determining factor, they argue, is the behavior of the leader.

DEALING WITH DIVERSITY CRISES

There is growing recognition of the fact that espoused strategy, practices, and climate do not always get implemented, and those that do may be implemented in ways that differ from the initial intention (Nishii, Lepak, & Schneider, 2008; Nishii & Wright, 2008). Particularly in the case of diversity management, employees may be looking for evidence of senior leaders' authentic commitment; thus, careful consideration of any misalignment between espoused and implemented strategy may be important for avoiding claims that management "doesn't walk the talk."

Diversity crises represent an opportunity and a challenge, in that how senior leaders respond to crises is very salient to employees and the external public (Bowen & Ostroff, 2004). Crises force leaders to examine the ways in which their espoused diversity strategy may be inappropriate, and/or how their espoused strategy may not be implemented as intended. James and Wooten (2005, 2006) found that when faced with a diversity crisis, many firms maintain a denial stance and demonstrate little openness to communication, while others engage in active organizational learning. Following settlement, these firms adopted change efforts to prevent or more effectively resolve future crises (James & Wooten, 2006). The difference between firms that thrive following crisis versus those that do not is the leadership displayed throughout the process (James & Wooten, 2005). Core competencies for crisis leadership include such things as (1) building a foundation of trust in which leaders communicate openly, honestly, and often; (2) creating a corporate mindset that takes a big-picture approach and considers multiple perspectives of the crisis; (3) making wise and rapid decisions rather than denying or avoiding the crisis; and (4) approaching crisis as an opportunity for growth and change.

IMPLEMENTING HUMAN RESOURCES PRACTICES

Although there are several chapters in the book that deal with HR practices in the context of diversity and readers are referred to such chapters for a detailed discussion of each, we believe it is important to consider these practices with respect to leadership as well. Organizational practices that involve recruitment, hiring, development, and retention of diverse employees are all key "touchpoints" in which leaders play a significant role. At the organizational level, these are the mechanisms though which leaders may impact the extent to which diversity is present, valued, and leveraged. Leadership, defined in this chapter as the social process for generating the direction, alignment, and commitment needed by a group to accomplish collective goals, is enacted through the creation and execution of organizational practices and policies. Leaders throughout the organization, but particularly those at senior levels, serve as role models and provide cues for others about what type of behavior is expected and valued within the organization (Bowen & Ostroff, 2004). For example, senior leaders who fail to hire or promote diversity into the ranks of their senior management team send a strong message to the rest of the organization that he or she does not truly value diversity. Likewise, senior leaders who attend and fully participate in diversity training initiatives send a strong message to their subordinates that they too have something to learn when it comes to managing diversity (Chrobot-Mason, Hays-Thomas, & Wishik, 2008).

Another practice increasingly being used by senior leaders to communicate the importance of diversity is the establishment of employee resource groups. Research by Friedman and colleagues (Friedman & Holtom, 2002; Friedman, Kane, & Cornfield, 1998) has shown that employee network groups have a positive impact on career optimism and retention for minority workers. Network groups can provide nondominant group members the opportunity to meet and exchange knowledge with others belonging to their own demographic group in the company, contributing to their sense of community and belonging. More recently, employee resource groups (ERG) are taking on more strategic roles and are often "sponsored" by a senior leader who is held accountable for achieving goals associated with attracting talent, growing the business (e.g., by marketing more effectively to members of the identity group represented in the ERG), and the professional development of members of the particular identity group.[1] In this way, senior leaders become not just champions of the group, but also help others to see the business value of diversity as reflected in the particular identity group by helping the organization to achieve recruiting and business growth goals. In other words, they play an active role in helping to support the business case for diversity.

PROMOTING A LEARNING CULTURE

Employees carefully observe the pattern of leaders' behaviors in an effort to interpret what priorities are valued by the leader (Zohar & Luria, 2004). When leaders adopt an organizational diversity strategy that exemplifies a learning orientation, they are more likely to capitalize on the potential benefits that diversity brings. To the extent that leaders model, focus feedback efforts around, and reward learning-oriented behaviors, they help to create a learning-oriented organization. Learning-oriented leaders create opportunities for employees to engage in developmental and learning activities; encourage employees to transfer and apply learned skills to their work; model the importance of learning from mistakes; provide and accept constructive feedback on how to improve; and are genuinely open to learning from their interactions with coworkers and direct reports (Dragoni, 2005). By exhibiting these behaviors, leaders encourage organizational members to feel unthreatened by task challenges, value supportive relationships, and focus on organizational improvement (Dragoni, 2005), all of which may be critical for employees to integrate their diverse perspectives and leverage diversity to improve operational functioning.

Leaders also play a key role in fostering a culture of learning by serving in the role of mentor and encouraging others to do so as well (Chao, 2007). Research shows that mentoring for people of color and women helps such workers "break through" existing barriers to reach more senior levels within the organization (Blake-Beard, Murrell, & Thomas, 2007; Giscombe, 2007). Both formal and informal mentoring have potential benefits for employees, and in fact, recent research suggests that it behooves employees to take advantage of the possible benefits of both and foster a "constellation" of developmental relationships (Baugh & Fagenson-Eland, 2007). This may be particularly important for diverse employees, who would benefit from having mentors from within their own demographic group as well as mentors from within the dominant group (Dreher & Cox, 1996; Ibarra, 1992). Although not all leaders may be categorized as mentors, there is considerable overlap between these two roles in terms of the importance of developing high-quality relationships with direct reports (Godshalk & Sosik, 2007). For example, the LMX and transformational theories of leadership overlap with conceptualizations of supervisor mentoring. Thus leaders may foster a learning culture and the career development of minority employees by developing mentoring relationships that facilitate learning by designing assignments and providing ongoing support and performance feedback (Kram, 1985).

Summary

Leading an organization that values diversity requires measuring progress toward diversity goals and rewarding intended behaviors and outcomes. Organizational leaders may measure progress toward diversity goals by measuring change in things such as demographic representation; workforce flow that includes recruitment and retention data; employee opinion data derived from surveys, focus groups, and exit interviews; and litigation activity and costs (Jayne & Dipboye, 2004). When progress is made in these areas and diversity targets and goals are met, organizational leaders must find ways to reward such efforts to continue progress and ensure attention toward diversity efforts are sustained over time.

An important consideration when evaluating the effectiveness of diversity management practices is recent work by Kalev and her colleagues (Kalev, Dobbins, & Kelly, 2006) that suggested that some of the practices that have historically been implemented to increase the representation of women and ethnic minorities in management (e.g., diversity training, mentoring, manager accountability for diversity goals) have not been as effective as hoped. This may be because these practices target moments of personnel decision making (e.g., hiring, promotion), but on their own, fail to alter the everyday sociorelational sources of discrimination that inhibit the full engagement and advancement of members of historically marginalized groups. Thus, for organizational inclusion to be achieved, leaders must focus not just on the effective and fair implementation of HR and diversity practices, but also on the creation of climates that are conducive to personalized interactions and learning from diversity.

Leading the Organization—Future Research

Based on both research and theory highlighted in this section on leading a diverse organization, we offer the following research questions for consideration in future research.

- What are the relative benefits of various diversity initiatives adopted by leaders for creating direction, alignment, and commitment in an organization? Although vitally important to understand the value proposition for investing resources into diversity programs, this is a research question that still has not been adequately addressed in the literature.
- How do organizational leaders learn from diversity crises or conflicts? Does the learning process differ following a positive versus a negative event? How important is it to actively engage in organizational change efforts following an event (such as a change in policy or practice) for learning to occur? Continuous learning is an important part of leading amidst diversity. However, we know less about the situations that teach this than we do about leadership learning in general. It would be worthwhile to understand better how leaders acquire and express the self-understanding necessary to lead in a diverse context.

Summary and Setting the Agenda for Future Research

Although research and theory devoted to the topic of leading within a diverse workplace is still underrepresented in the literature, the current chapter has provided an overview and summary of the extant literature at the intersection of diversity and leadership. Evidence of an evolving definition of effective leadership that is emerging both in response to, and in preparation for, an increasingly diverse workforce has been presented. This emerging definition of leadership differs from the traditional one that viewed leadership as residing within an individual holding a formal position of authority. In contrast, leadership is increasingly now seen as a socially constructed process involving the entire group, and effective leadership is relational in nature. As such, we have argued in this chapter that leaders now play a key role in the ultimate success or failure of a diverse workforce and the organization's ability to leverage differences as a competitive advantage.

By framing our review of the literature based on the cross-level model of Crossan et al. (2008) involving leadership of self, others, and the organization, we have highlighted an important conclusion, which is that effective leadership of a diverse workforce is not the responsibility of the person at the top, but of the entire organization. All employees need to understand the importance of self-leadership. Managers need to understand how this relates to demonstrating interpersonal influence in the leadership of others. Furthermore, executives need to understand issues of equality at the organizational level and that there is a real cost to the organization for overlooking diversity.

Because research on leadership and diversity remains sparse, we feel there are many research questions yet to be addressed and many opportunities for scholars to join this burgeoning research agenda. We suggest that future research in this area should focus on addressing three broad areas: (1) identifying a diversity-leadership mindset; (2) examining the implications of relational leadership in the context of diversity; and (3) exploring innovative and creative strategies for developing leaders with a diversity mindset who engage in relational leadership behavior.

Identifying a Diversity-Leadership Mindset

Research is needed to understand what differentiates the leaders of organizations who are primarily motivated "from the head" to do what is good for their organization from leaders who are committed to real change "from the heart." Even though the number of organizations that have been recognized with corporate diversity awards has grown, these awards have done little to differentiate those organizations that are being led by leaders who believe that their work is done because they have adopted a wide variety of diversity practices and increased diverse representation, from organizations whose leaders have committed to going beyond the adoption of these practices to transforming their organizational cultures to be truly inclusive. Recent research by Catalyst (Prime & Moss-Racusin, 2009) suggests that leaders who are deeply committed to diversity initiatives may be driven by the ideal of equality in a way that is not true of less committed leaders, though more research is needed to bear this out. If a fundamental belief in equality sets effective diversity leaders apart from others, an important issue to understand is whether such beliefs can be cultivated in leaders by their organizations, and if so, how. Although laboratory research has shown that the activation of egalitarian goals can help to prevent the activation of implicit biases (Moskowitz, Gollwitzer, Wasel, & Schaal, 1999), whether including egalitarian goals throughout performance management systems would be sufficient for instilling equality ideals among leaders—and a corresponding internal motivation to lead diversity effectively—remains to be seen.

Examining the Implications of Relational Leadership in the Context of Diversity

Future research should consider whether more stereotypically feminine qualities may be what is needed for successful leadership in a diverse workplace. Recent research by Catalyst revealed that most organizations emphasize stereotypically masculine qualities among their leaders, such as being action-oriented, results-driven, skilled at problem-solving, and assertive (Warren, 2009). However, our review of the existing literature suggests to us that more feminine, relational leadership styles may be better suited for leading diverse groups, as suggested by research on relational self-construal (Gelfand, Major, Raver, Nishii, & O'Brien, 2006). In contrast to a view of the self as largely independent of others, relational self-construal (RSC) reflects a self that is fundamentally connected to other individuals. Leaders who are high in RSC may be more effective at leading diverse groups for a number of reasons. Research suggests that their tendency to engage in perspective taking leads them to see the ways in which they are similar to others, and we see this as an important precondition for being a boundary-spanning leader. In addition, they work hard to develop and affirm connections with others because doing so is an important source of positive emotions and self-esteem, and they tend to adopt numerous tactics for fostering connections with others, such as engaging in personal self-disclosure and considering one's actions in light of the implications for others' needs and feelings. In role-modeling such behaviors for their employees and by prioritizing relationship-building, they are more likely to create the conditions within which employees can see beyond stereotypes and interact with one another more authentically. Furthermore, leaders who are high in RSC are more likely to treat interactions with and among employees as being embedded within a broader temporal context; that is, to see their interactions as having important ramifications for their future relationships with others. As such, they are less likely to try to dominate others and/or leave conflict unresolved, and more likely to gather accurate information about others in an effort to understand others' values and beliefs.

When exhibited by leaders, these behaviors are likely to help employees to believe that their voices are genuinely valued, or in other words to cultivate psychological safety and inclusion (Nembhard & Edmondson, 2006). Leaders who are intrinsically motivated to ask the right questions of others, rather than provide the right answers to others, are much more likely to create the kinds of environments in which employees feel safe to pursue the kind of interpersonal learning that is necessary for the benefits of diversity to emerge. In contrast, when leaders are assertive and overly results-driven, their employees are likely to become more concerned with proving their competence or avoiding failures than with learning from the challenges that may be introduced by diversity.

For organizations, the key is to understand the ways in which beneficial levels of RSC can be primed, or made temporally accessible, among leaders. When features of an organizational context send strong signals about the role appropriateness of behaving relationally, leaders will be induced to behave in the ways described earlier. According to work by Brickson (2000), who has similarly suggested that activating a relational orientation among individuals is critical for promoting the benefits and inhibiting the disadvantages associated with diversity, it is important for organizations to frame task and reward structures around dyads or groups rather than individuals and to promote integrated relationship networks within the organization. Thus, future research should examine how organizational climate may improve if relational leadership became the norm and more feminine leadership characteristics were valued.

Exploring Innovative and Creative Strategies for Developing Leaders of Diversity

Development of leaders with a diversity mindset who understand the value of adopting a relational style of leadership to lead across differences effectively likely occurs not in the workplace, but rather much earlier. This type of leadership development must begin when children are first developing their leadership capacity and skill set. Research on leader development is clear in pointing out that development takes time, motivation, and effort, and cannot be achieved solely by attending a half-day workshop. Developing leaders to lead successfully in a diverse workplace must begin in school and continue throughout an individual's professional career.

More explicit attention to diversity and inclusion within early childhood education is critical such that our leaders of tomorrow rise into their positions equipped with a belief in the ideal of equality. Although there is a relatively well-developed literature on diversity and inclusion within the education field, it has to date remained isolated from the organizational literature. In our future activities, it may behoove us to collaborate with educational researchers to try to understand which educational programs related to diversity and equality are effective not just at reducing diversity-related incidents in schools and enhancing the achievement outcomes of all students, but also in instilling lasting egalitarian ideals in the youth of today.

Future research must begin to view the development of such skills as a collaborative endeavor involving self, others, and organizations not only within the professional context, but also education and society at large. How do we as a society develop and foster leaders who are relational, span boundaries, engage differences and conflict constructively, and ultimately collaborate across differences to resolve society's most challenging issues? Is it outrageous to imagine that if we are successful, we could enjoy a world in which leaders battle less over territorial boundaries and instead collaborate more towards the achievement of global goals?

Note

1. We learned about the more strategic focus of ERGs through a series of focus groups with diversity executives from companies that belong to Cornell University's Center for Advanced Human Resource Studies (conducted in January, 2009).

References

Ashkenas, R., Ulrich, D., Jick, T., & Kerr, S. (2002). *The boundaryless organization: Breaking the chains of organizational structure.* San Francisco, CA: Jossey-Bass.

Ayman, R. (1993). Leadership perception: The role of gender and culture. In M. M. Chemers & R. Ayman (Eds.), *Leadership theory and research: Perspectives and directions* (pp. 137–166). San Diego, CA: Academic Press.

Ayman, R., & Korabik, K. (2010). Leadership: Why gender and culture matter. *American Psychologist, 65*(3), 157–170.

Bass, B. M. (1990). From transactional to transformational leadership: Learning to share the vision. *Organizational Dynamics, 18*(3), 19–31.

Bass, B. M., & Avolio, B. J. (1994). *Improving organizational effectiveness through transformational leadership.* Thousand Oaks, CA: SAGE.

Baugh, S. G., & Fagenson-Eland, E. A. (2007). Formal mentoring programs: A "poor cousin" to informal relationships? In B. R. Ragins & K. E. Kram (Eds.), *The handbook of mentoring at work* (pp. 249–272). Thousand Oaks, CA: SAGE.

Bell, E. L., & Nkomo, S. M. (2001). *Our separate ways: Black and white women and the struggle for professional identity.* Boston, MA: Harvard Business School Press.

Blake-Beard, S. D., Murrell, A., & Thomas, D. (2007). Unfinished business: The impact of race on understanding mentoring relationships. In B. R. Ragins & K. E. Kram (Eds.), *The handbook of mentoring at work* (pp. 223–247). Thousand Oaks, CA: SAGE.

Boal, K. B., & Hooijberg, R. (2000). Strategic leadership research: Moving on. *The Leadership Quarterly, 11*, 515–549.

Bowen, D. E., & Ostroff, C. (2004). Understanding HRM-firm performance linkages: The role of the "strength" of the HRM system. *Academy of Management Review, 29*(2), 203–221.

Boyatzis, R. E. (1982). *The competent manager: A model for effective performance.* New York, NY: John Wiley & Sons.

Boyatzis, R. E. (2006). Intentional change theory from a complexity perspective. *Journal of Management Development, 25*(7), 607–623.

Brewer, M. B. (1991). The social self: On being the same and different at the same time. *Personality and Social Psychology Bulletin, 17*, 475–482.

Brewer, M. B. (1995). Managing diversity: The role of social identities. In S. E. Jackson & M. N. Ruderman (Eds.), *Diversity in work teams* (pp. 47–68). Washington, DC: American Psychological Association.

Brewer, M. B. (1999). The psychology of prejudice: Ingroup love or outgroup hate? *Journal of Social Issues, 55*(3), 429–444.

Brewer, M. B., & Miller, N. (1984). Beyond the contact hypothesis: Theoretical perspectives on desegregation. In N. Miller, & M. B. Brewer (Eds.), *Group in contact: The psychology of desegregation* (pp. 281–302). Orlando, FL: Academic Press.

Brickson, S. (2000). The impact of identity orientation on individual and organizational outcomes in demographically diverse settings. *Academy of Management Review, 25*(1), 82–101.

Chao, G. T. (2007). Mentoring and organizational socialization: Networks for work adjustment. In B. R. Ragins & K. E. Kram (Eds.), *The handbook of mentoring at work* (pp. 179–196). Thousand Oaks, CA: SAGE.

Chen, C. C., & Van Velsor, E. (1996). New directions for research and practice in diversity leadership. *Leadership Quarterly, 7*(2), 285–302.

Chin, L. L. (2010). Introduction to the special issue on diversity and leadership. *American Psychologist, 65*(3), 150–156.

Chrobot-Mason, D., Hays-Thomas, R., & Wishik, H. R. (2008). Understanding and defusing resistance to diversity training and learning. In K. Thomas (Ed)., *Diversity resistance in organizations* (pp. 23–54). Mahwah, NJ: Lawrence Erlbaum.

Chrobot-Mason, D., Ruderman, M. R., Weber, T., & Ernst, C. (2009). The challenge of leading on unstable ground: Triggers that activate social identity faultlines. *Human Relations, 62*(5), 1763–1794.

Cox, T., Jr. (1991). The multicultural organization. *Academy of Management Executive, 5*, 34–47.

Cox, T., Jr. (1994). *Cultural diversity in organizations.* San Francisco, CA: Berrett-Koehler.

Crossan, M., Vera, D., & Nanjad, L. (2008). Transcendent leadership: Strategic leadership in dynamic environments. *The Leadership Quarterly*, 19, 569–581.

DeRue, D. S., & Ashford, S. J. (2010). Who will lead and who will follow? A social process of leadership identity construction in organizations. *Academy of Management Review, 35*, 627–647.

De Dreu, C. K. W., & Van Vianen, A. E. M. (2001). Managing relationship conflict and the effectiveness of organizational teams. *Journal of Organizational Behavior, 22*, 309–328.

De Dreu, C. K. W., & Weingart, L. R. (2003). Task versus relationship conflict, team performance, and team member satisfaction: A meta-analysis. *Journal of Applied Psychology, 88*(4), 741–749.

Detert, J. R., & Burris, E. R. (2007). Leadership behavior and employee voice: Is the door really open? *The Academy of Management Journal, 50*(4), 869–884.

DiTomaso, N., & Hooijberg, R. (1996). Diversity and the demands of leadership. *Leadership Quarterly, 7*, 163–187.

Dragoni, L. (2005). Understanding the emergence of state goal orientation in organizational work groups: The role of leadership and multilevel climate perceptions. *Journal of Applied Psychology, 90*, 1084–1095.

Drath, W. H., McCauley, C. D., Palus, C. J., Van Velsor, E., O'Connor, P. M. G., & McGuire, J. B. (2008). Direction, alignment, commitment: Toward a more integrative ontology of leadership. *Leadership Quarterly, 19*(6), 635–653.

Dreher, G. F., & Cox, T. H. (1996). Race, gender and opportunity: A study of compensation attainment and the establishment of mentoring relationships. *Journal of Applied Psychology, 81*(3), 297–308.

Duck, J. M., & Fielding, K. S. (1999). Leaders and subgroups: One of us or one of them? *Group Processes & Intergroup Relations, 2*, 203–230.

Duck, J. M., & Fielding, K. S. (2003). Leaders and their treatment of subgroups: Implications for evaluations of the leader and the superordinate group. *European Journal of Social Psychology, 33*, 387–401.

Dvir, T., Kass, N., & Shamir, B. (2004). The emotional bond: Vision and organizational commitment among high-tech employees. *Journal of Organizational Change Management, 17*(2), 126–143.

Eagly, A., & Chin, J. L. (2010). Diversity and leadership in a changing world. *American Psychologist, 65*(3), 216–224.

Eagly, A. H., & Carli, L. L. (2007). *Through the labyrinth: The truth about how women become leaders.* Boston, MA: Harvard Business School Press.

Eagly, A. H., & Karau, S. J. (2002). Role congruity theory of prejudice toward female leaders. *Psychological Review, 109*, 573–598.

Eggins, R. A., Haslam, S. A., & Reynolds, K. J. (2002). Social identity and negotiation: Subgroup representation and superordinate consensus. *Personality and Social Psychology Bulletin, 28*, 887–899.

Ensari, N., & Murphy, S. (2003). Cross-cultural variations in leadership perceptions and attribution of charisma to the leader. *Organizational Behavior and Human Decision Processes, 92*(1–2), 52–66.

Ernst, C., & Chrobot-Mason, D. (2011). *Boundary spanning leadership: Six practices for solving problems, driving innovation and transforming organizations.* New York, NY: McGraw-Hill.

Ernst, C., Hannum, K. M., & Ruderman, M. N. (2010). Developing intergroup leadership. In E. Van Velsor, C. D. McCauley, & M. N. Ruderman (Eds.), *The Center for Creative Leadership handbook of leadership development* (3rd ed., pp. 375–404). San Francisco, CA: Jossey-Bass.

Faraj, S., & Yan, S. (2009). Boundary work in knowledge teams. *Journal of Applied Psychology, 94*, 604–617.

Ferdman, B. M. (2008). Who perceives more discrimination? Individual difference predictors among Latinos and Anglos. *The Business Journal of Hispanic Research, 2*(3), 71–75.

Ferdman, B. M., Katz, J., Letchinger, E., & Thompson, C. T. (2009). Inclusive behavior and practices. Unpublished manuscript prepared for the Institute for Inclusion.

Findler, L., Wind, L. H., & Mor Barak, M. E. (2007). The challenge of workforce management in a global society: Modeling the relationship between diversity, inclusion, organizational culture, and employee well-being, job satisfaction and organizational commitment. *Administration in Social Work, 31*(3), 63–94.

Fiol, C. M., Pratt, M. G., & O'Connor, E. J. (2009). Managing intractable identity conflicts. *Academy of Management Review, 34*(1), 32–55.

Fletcher, J. K. (2010). Leadership as relational practice. In K. A. Bunker, D. T. Hall, & K. E. Kram (Eds.), *Extraordinary leadership: Addressing the gaps in senior executive development* (pp. 121–136). San Francisco, CA: Jossey-Bass.

Ford, L. R., & Seers, A. (2006). Relational leadership and team climates: Pitting differentiation versus agreement. *Leadership Quarterly, 17*, 258–270.

Friedman, R. A., & Holtom, B. (2002). The effects of network groups on minority employee turnover intentions. *Human Resource Management, 41*(4), 405–421.

Friedman, R., Kane, M., & Cornfield, D. B. (1998). Social support and career optimism: Examining the effectiveness of network groups among black managers. *Human Relations, 51*(9), 1155–1177.

Gaertner, S., & Dovidio, J. (2007). Addressing contemporary racism: The common intergroup identity model. In C. Willos-Esqueda (Ed.), *Motivational aspects of prejudice and racism* (pp. 111–133). New York, NY: Springer Science+Business Media.

Gelfand, M. J., Major, V. S., Raver, J. L., Nishii, L. H., & O'Brien, K. (2006). Negotiating relationally: The dynamics of the relational self in negotiations. *Academy of Management Review, 31*(2), 427–451.

Gerstner, C. R., & Day, D. V. (1997). Meta-analytic review of leader-member exchange theory: Correlates and construct issues. *Journal of Applied Psychology, 82*, 827–844.

Giscombe, K. (2007). Advancing women through the glass ceiling with formal mentoring. In B. R. Ragins & K. E. Kram (Eds.), *The handbook of mentoring at work* (pp. 549–572). Thousand Oaks, CA: SAGE.

Godshalk, V. M., & Sosik, J. J. (2007). Mentoring and leadership: Standing at the crossroads of theory, research, and practice. In B. R. Ragins & K. E. Kram (Eds.), *The handbook of mentoring at work* (pp. 149–178). Thousand Oaks, CA: SAGE.

Graen, G. B., & Uhl-Bien, M. (1995). Development of leader-member exchange (LMX) theory of leadership over 25 years: Applying a multi-level-multi-domain perspective. *Leadership Quarterly, 6*, 219–247.

Graetz, F., & Smith, A. C. T. (2009).Changing forms of organizing in Australian public companies. *Asia Pacific Journal of Human Resources, 47*(3), 340–360.

Gratton, L., Voigt, A., & Erickson, T. (2007). Bridging faultlines in diverse teams. *MIT Sloan Management Review, 48*(4), 22–29.

Hannum, K. (2007). *Social identity–knowing yourself, leading others*. Greensboro, NC: Center for Creative Leadership.

Hannum, K. M., & Glover, S. L. (2010). Respect. In R. A. Couto (Ed.), *Political and civic leadership* (pp. 611–618). Thousand Oaks, CA: SAGE.

Haslam, S. A., Eggins, R. A., & Reynolds, K. J. (2003). The ASPIRe model: Actualizing social and personal identity resources to enhance organizational outcomes. *Journal of Occupational and Organizational Psychology, 76*, 83–113.

Haslam, S. A., & Ellemers, N. (2005). Social identity in industrial and organizational psychology: Concepts, controversies, and contributions. In G. P. Hodgkinson & J. K. Ford (Eds.), *International review of industrial and organizational psychology* (Vol. 20, pp. 39–118). Hoboken, NJ: John Wiley & Sons.

Hewstone, M., & Brown, R. (1986). Contact is not enough: An intergroup perspective on the contact hypothesis. In R. C. Hewstone & R. J. Brown (Eds.), *Contact and conflict in intergroup encounters* (pp. 1–44). Oxford, UK: Blackwell.

Hofmann, W., Gawronski, B., Gschwendner, T., Le, H., & Schmitt, M. (2005). A meta-analysis on the correlation between the implicit association test and explicit self-report measures. *Personality and Social Psychology Bulletin, 31*(10), 1369–1385.

Hogg, M. A. (2001). A social identity theory of leadership. *Personality and Social Psychology Review, 5*, 184–200.

Hogg, M. A., Martin, R., Epitropaki, O., Mankad, A., Svensson, A., & Weeden, K. (2005). Effective leadership in salient groups: Revisiting leader-member exchange theory from the perspective of the social identity theory of leadership. *Personality and Social Psychology Bulletin, 31*(7), 991–1004.

Hogg, M. A., & van Knippenberg, D. (2003). Social identity and leadership processes in groups. *Advances in Experimental Social Psychology, 35*, 1–52.

Holvino, E., Ferdman, B. M., & Merrill-Sands, D. (2004). Creating and sustaining diversity and inclusion in organizations: Strategies and approaches. In M. S. Stockdale & F. J. Crosby (Eds.), *The psychology and management of workplace diversity* (pp. 245–276). Malden, MA: Blackwell.

Howell, J. M., & Shamir, B. (2005). The role of followers in the charismatic leadership process: Relationships and their consequences. *Academy of Management Review, 30*, 96–112.

Ibarra, H. (1992). Homophily and differential returns: Sex differences in network structure and access in an advertising firm. *Administrative Science Quarterly, 37*(3), 422–447.

James, E. H., & Wooten, L. P. (2005). Leadership as (un) usual: How to display competence in times of crisis. *Organizational Dynamics, 34*(2), 141–152.

James, E. H., & Wooten, L. P. (2006). Diversity crises: How firms manage discrimination lawsuits. *Academy of Management Journal, 49*(6), 1103–1118.

Jayne, M. E. & Dipboye, R. L. (2004). Leveraging diversity to improve business performance: Research findings and recommendations for organizations. *Human Resource Management, 43*, 409–424.

Jehn, K. A. (1995). A multimethod examination of the benefits and detriments of intragroup conflict. *Administrative Science Quarterly, 40*, 256–282.

Joshi, A., Lazarova, M. B., & Liao, H. (2009). Getting everyone on board: The role of inspirational leadership in geographically dispersed teams. *Organization Science, 20*, 240–252.

Kalev, A., Dobbin, F., & Kelly, E. (2006). Best practices or best guesses? Assessing the efficacy of corporate affirmative action and diversity policies. *American Sociological Review, 71*, 589–617.

Kearney, E., & Gebert, D. (2009). Managing diversity and enhancing team outcomes: The promise of transformational leadership. *Journal of Applied Psychology, 94*, 77–89.

Kegan, R. (1982). *The evolving self: Problem and process in human development*. Cambridge, MA: Harvard University Press.

Kegan, R. (1994). *In over our heads: The mental demands of modern life*. Cambridge, MA: Harvard University Press.

Kram, K. E. (1985). *Mentoring at work: Developmental relationships in organizational life*. Glenview, IL: Scott, Foresman.

Liden, R. C., Erdogan, B., Wayne, S. J., & Sparrowe, R. T. (2006). Leader-member exchange, differentiation, and task interdependence: Implications for individual and group performance. *Journal of Organizational Behavior, 27*, 723–746.

Livers, A. B., & Caver, K. A. (2003). *Leading in black and white: Working across the racial divide in corporate America*. San Francisco and Greensboro, NC: Jossey-Bass and Center for Creative Leadership.

Lord, R. G., & Hall, R. J. (2005). Identity, deep structure and the development of leadership skill. *The Leadership Quarterly, 16*(4), 591–615.

Lord, R. G., & Maher, K. J. (1991). *Leadership and information processing: Linking perceptions to performance*. Boston, MA: Unwin Hyman.

Madon, S. (1997). What do people believe about gay males? A study of stereotype content and strength. *Sex Roles, 37*, 663–685.

McCall, M. W. (2010). Recasting leadership development. *Industrial and Organizational Psychology: Perspectives on Science and Practice 3*(1), 3–19.

McCauley, C. D. (2010). Concepts of leadership. In E. Biech (Ed.), *The ASTD leadership handbook* (pp. 1–11). Alexandria, VA: ASTD Press.

McCauley, C. D., Van Velsor, E., & Ruderman, M. N. (2010). Our view of leadership development. In E. Van Velsor, C. D. McCauley, & M. N. Ruderman (Eds.), *The Center for Creative Leadership handbook of leadership development* (3rd ed., pp. 1–26). San Francisco, CA: Jossey-Bass.

McClane, W. E. (1991). Implications of member role differentiation: Analysis of a key concept in the LMX model of leadership. *Group and Organization Studies, 16*, 102–113.

Milliken, F. J., & Martins, L. L. (1996). Searching for common threads: Understanding the multiple effects of diversity in organizational groups. *Academy of Management Review, 21*(2), 402–433.

Mintzberg, H. (1973). *The nature of managerial work*. New York, NY: Harper & Row.

Mitchell, R. J., & Boyle, B. (2009). A theoretical model of transformational leadership's role in diverse teams. *Leadership & Organization Development Journal, 30*(5), 455–474.

Moskowitz, G. B., Gollwitzer, P. M., Wasel, W., & Schaal, B. (1999). Preconsicous control of stereotype activation through chronic egalitarian goals. *Journal of Personality and Social Psychology, 77*(1), 167–184.

Munusamy, V. P., Ruderman, M. N., & Eckert, R. H. (2010). Leader development and social identity. In E. Van Velsor, C. D. McCauley, & M. N. Ruderman (Eds.), *The Center for Creative Leadership handbook of leadership development* (3rd ed., pp. 147–175). San Francisco, CA: Jossey-Bass.

Nembhard, I. M., & Edmondson, A. C. (2006). Making it safe: The effects of leader inclusiveness and professional status on psychological safety and improvement efforts in health care teams. *Journal of Organizational Behavior, 27*(7), 941–966.

Nishii, L. H. (2010). The benefits of climate for inclusion for diverse groups. Unpublished manuscript.

Nishii, L. H., & Langevin, A. (2010). Managers' diversity attributions: Why we should care. Poster presented at the annual conference of the Society for Industrial and Organizational Psychology in Atlanta, GA.

Nishii, L. H. & Langevin, A., & Bruyere, S. (2010). Ageism and the retention of high performers: The positive impact of three forms of inclusion. Technical report submitted to the SHRM Foundation.

Nishii, L. H., Lepak, D. P., & Schneider, B. (2008). Employee attributions of the "why" of HR practices: Their effects on employee attitudes and behaviors, and customer satisfaction. *Personnel Psychology, 61*, 503–545.

Nishii, L. H., & Mayer, D. M. (2009). Do inclusive leaders help to reduce turnover in diverse groups? The moderating role of leader-member exchange in the diversity to turnover relationship. *Journal of Applied Psychology, 94*(6), 1412–1426.

Nishii, L. H., & Wright, P. (2008). Variability within organizations: Implications for strategic human resource management. In D. B. Smith (Ed.), *The people make the place* (pp. 225–248). Mahwah, NJ: Lawrence Erlbaum.

Oshry, B. (2010). People in context. In K. A. Bunker, D. T. Hall & K. E. Kram (Eds.), *Extraordinary leadership: Addressing the gaps in senior executive development* (pp. 175–196). San Francisco, CA: Jossey-Bass.

Page, S. E. (2007). Making the difference: Applying the logic of diversity. *Academy of Management Perspectives, 21*(4), 6–20.

Pearce, C. L., & Conger, J. A. (2003). All those years ago: The historical underpinnings of shared leadership. In C. L. Pearce & J. A. Conger (Eds.), *Shared leadership: Reframing the hows and whys of leadership* (pp. 2–18). Thousand Oaks, CA: SAGE.

Pfeffer, J. (1981). Management as symbolic action: The creation and maintenance of organizational paradigms. In B. B. Staw & L. L. Cummings (Eds.), *Research in organizational behavior* (Vol. 3, pp. 1–52). Greenwich, CT: JAI.

Pittinsky, T. L. (2010). A two-dimensional model of intergroup leadership: The case of national diversity. *American Psychologist, 65*(3), 194–200.

Pittinsky, T. L., & Maruskin, L. (2008). Allophilia: Beyond prejudice. In S. J. Lopez (Ed.), *Positive psychology* (Vol. 2, pp. 141–148). Westport, CT: Praeger.

Pittinsky, T. L., & Montoya, R. M. (2009). Is valuing equality enough? Equality values, allophilia, and social policy support for multiracial individuals. *Journal of Social Issues, 65*, 151–163.

Prime, J., & Moss-Racusin, C. A. (2009). *Engaging men in gender initiatives: What change agents need to know*. New York, NY: Catalyst.

Reicher, S. D., & Hopkins, N. (1996). Seeking influence through characterizing self-categories: An analysis of anti-abortion rhetoric. *British Journal of Social Psychology, 35*, 297–311.

Ridgeway, C. L. (1991). The social construction of status value: Gender and other nominal characteristics. *Social Forces, 70*, 367–386.

Ridgeway, C. L., & Correll, S. J. (2006). Consensus and the creation of status beliefs. *Social Forces, 85*(1), 431–453.

Rosette, A. S., Leonardelli, G. J., & Phillips, K. W. (2008). The white standard: Racial bias in leader categorization. *Journal of Applied Psychology, 93*(4), 758–777.

Ruderman, M. N., Glover, S., Chrobot-Mason, D., & Ernst, C. (2010). Leadership practices across social identity groups. In K. Hannum, B. B. McFeeters, & L. Booysen (Eds.), *Leading across differences* (pp. 95–114). San Francisco, CA: Pfieffer.

Ryan, M., & Haslam, A. (2005). The glass cliff: Evidence that women are over-represented in precarious leadership positions. *British Journal of Management, 15*, 1–10.

Scandura, T. A., & Lankau, M. J. (1996). Developing diverse leaders: A leader-member exchange approach. *Leadership Quarterly, 7*(2), 243–263.

Schein, V. E. (1973). The relationship between sex role stereotypes and requisite management characteristics. *Journal of Applied Psychology, 57*, 95–100.

Schein, V. E. (1975). The relationship between sex role stereotypes and requisite management characteristics among female managers. *Journal of Applied Psychology, 60*, 340–344.

Schein, V., Mueller, R., Lituchy, T., & Liu, J. (1996). Think manager—think male: A global phenomenon? *Journal of Organizational Behavior, 17*(1), 33–41.

Schyns, B., Paul, T., Mohr, G., & Blank, H. (2005). Comparing antecedents and consequences of leader-member exchange in a German working context to findings in the US. *European Journal of Work and Organizational Psychology, 14*, 1–22.

Shore, L. M., Randel, A. E., Chung, B. G., Dean, M. A., Ehrhart, K. H., & Singh, G. (2011). Inclusion and diversity in work groups: A review and model for future research. *Journal of Management, 37*, 1262–1289.

Simons, T. (2002). Behavioral integrity: The perceived alignment between managers' words and deeds as a research focus. *Organizational Science, 13*(1), 18–35.

Staw, B. M. (1980). The consequences of turnover. *Journal of Occupational Behavior, 1*, 253–273.

Sy, T., Shore, L., Strauss, J., Shore, T., Tram, S. & Whiteley, P., & Ikeda-Muromachi, K. (2010). Leadership perceptions as a function of race-occupation fit: The case of Asian Americans. *Journal of Applied Psychology, 95*(5), 902–1010.

Tajfel, H., & Turner, J. C. (1979). An integrative theory of intergroup conflict. In W. S. Austin & S. Worchel (Eds.), *The social psychology of intergroup relations* (pp. 33–47). Monterey, CA: Brooks/Cole.

Tajfel, H., & Turner, J. C. (1986). The social identity theory of inter-group behavior. In S. Worchel & L. W. Austin (Eds.), *Psychology of intergroup relations*. Chicago, IL: Nelson-Hall.

Thomas, K. M., & Chrobot-Mason, D. (2005). Group-level explanations of workplace discrimination. In R. L. Dipboye & A. Colella (Eds.), *Discrimination at work: The psychological and organizational bases* (pp. 63–88). Mahwah, NJ: Lawrence Erlbaum.

Toosi, M. (2009, November). Employment outlook: 2008–18. Labor force projections to 2018: Older workers staying more active. *Monthly Labor Review*, 30–51.

Turner, J. C. (1982). Towards a cognitive redefinition of the group. In H. Tajfel (Ed.), *Social identity and intergroup relations* (pp. 15–40). Cambridge: Cambridge University Press.

Turner, J. C. (1985). Social categorization and the self-concept: A social cognitive theory of group behaviour. In E. J. Lawler (Ed.), *Advances in group processes* (2nd ed., pp. 77–122). Greenwich, CT: JAI Press.

Turner, J. C. (2004). Foreword: What the social identity approach is and why it matters. In S. A Haslam (Ed.), *Psychology in organizations: The social identity approach* (p. xvii). London, UK: SAGE.

Van Knippenberg, D., Van Knippenberg, B., De Cremer, D., & Hogg, M. A. (2004). Leadership, self, and identity: A review and research agenda. *The Leadership Quarterly, 15*, 825–856.

Wasserman, I. C., Gallegos, P. V., & Ferdman, B. M. (2008). Dancing with resistance: Leadership challenges in fostering a culture of inclusion. In K. M. Thomas (Ed.), *Diversity resistance in organizations* (pp. 175–200). New York, NY: Taylor & Francis.

Warren, A. K. (2009). *Cascading gender biases, compounding effects: An assessment of talent management systems*. New York, NY: Catalyst.

Weick, K. M. (1979). *The social psychology of organizing*. Reading, MA: Addison-Wesley.

Zohar, D., & Luria, G. (2004). Climate as a social-cognitive construction of supervisory safety practices: Scripts as proxy for behavioral patterns. *Journal of Applied Psychology, 89*, 322–333.

CHAPTER

32 Changing the Rules: The Implications of Complexity Science for Leadership Research and Practice

James K. Hazy *and* Mary Uhl-Bien

Abstract

Complexity has become an important lens through which to view and understand the causes and potencies of individual action and interaction in organizations as well as their meaning for leadership research and practice. This review of key complexity ideas and their theoretical implications for leadership describes emerging theories in the field, highlights the growing empirical support for these approaches, and sets an agenda for future research. The thesis averred is this: just as complexity has become an overarching theoretical paradigm in the natural sciences, it is providing the basis for a paradigm shift in the social sciences, particularly in leadership and organizational studies. Complex systems leadership theory describes the process whereby the rules governing local interactions are changed in response to and anticipation of changing circumstances. In shifting the focus from the individual to the organizing process itself, the complexity leadership perspective has important implications for both research and practice.

Key Words: Complexity leadership, complex systems leadership theory, human interaction dynamics, generative leadership, adaptive leadership, unifying leadership, adaptation, innovation, chaos theory

Introduction

Complex Systems Leadership Theory (CSLT) is about *interactions* and *emergence*. It is about events and how these shape future action (Lichtenstein et al., 2006), and it is about how human activity is organized into a system of choices and actions when organizations are considered to be complex adaptive systems (Marion & Uhl-Bien, 2001). By describing an overarching dynamic theory of human organizing, CSLT transcends traditional approaches to leadership research by offering a theoretical framework within which prior results can be better understood, evaluated, and integrated into a common view of how human agency drives collective performance and adaptation.

In the complexity approach, "leadership" is not considered to be a person or persons. Rather, it is the recognizable pattern of organizing activity among autonomous heterogeneous individuals as they form into a system of action (Hazy, Goldstein & Lichtenstein, 2007a; Lichtenstein et al., 2006; Uhl-Bien, Marion & McKelvey, 2007). At the same time, for organizing to occur, leadership must perform certain functions, what Katz and Kahn (1966) called the "influential increment."

Interpreting Katz and Kahn (1966), Hazy (2011a) argues that when human interactions are considered as complex systems, leadership performs three functions as it organizes human activity. First, it influences human interactions in ways that *unify* individuals into organized groups. This includes what might be called the strategic functions, such as setting vision and strategy (Boal & Schultz, 2007) and establishing identities and ethics (Hazy, 2011c). Second, leadership changes the rules so as to *generate* a variety of ideas and plans of action (Hazy, 2006) as a mechanism for adapting to changing circumstances (Uhl-Bien et al.,

2007). Creativity and problem solving (Guastello, 2007) are important elements of this function, as are the constraints on action that enable the emergence of novelty (Goldstein, Hazy, & Lichtenstein, 2010). Third, rules are changed though administrative activities in ways that enable the *convergence* of disparate, sometimes conflicting individual perspectives, preferences, and activities into effective and predictable collective action (Dal Forno & Merlone, 2007; Hazy, 2008b; Phelps & Hubler, 2007). In sum, leadership is about changing the rules that guide individual choices and interactions. In complex adaptive systems, "changing the rules of interaction" locally can also change organizational outcomes more globally. CSLT studies this process.

Individuals, of course, enact pieces of this functional puzzle, and as such, the complexity paradigm implies certain things about individuals and their capacity to succeed as they engage in leadership situations (Hannah, Eggers, & Jennings, 2008; Lord, Hannah, & Jennings, 2011). But isolated individual behaviors are not leadership per se. Leadership is in the whole; it serves to form, sustain and grow the system, just as product development or accountability processes are parts of the whole system. No one person is "governance"; likewise, no one person is "leadership." At the same time, individuals must enact the leadership process just as they enact other organizational processes. In this sense, CSLT offers a systems perspective within which traditional views of leadership that include individual skills and actions can be integrated into a process perspective (Hazy, 2011b).

For the purposes of the analysis herein, we define *complex systems leadership* as system processes that *change the rules of interaction* and do so in specific ways that form human interaction dynamics (HID) into a complex adaptive system (Hazy et al., 2007) in a manner analogous to how physical and biological interactions are understood as systems. Core to complexity is the realization that the rules governing the individual human interactions of day-to-day experience are what determine the social structures that emerge (Goldstein, 1989, 2007, 2011; Holland, 1975; McKelvey, 2004). These emergent forms can sometimes be recognized as stable properties; and when they are, *they can be evaluated and managed* within a particular economic, political, social, and technological context.

However, interventions cannot directly cause outcomes to change. Emergent forms can only be affected by judiciously changing the local rules that govern the interactions of others and from which the relevant outcomes emerge (Goldstein et al., 2010). It is within the nexus connecting local rules to emergent forms that leadership gathers its potency. This is why leadership is central to human experience. It is important for both organizing to succeed as a group, and as a means to enable individual success through others. Both of these have been the focus of leadership research. CSLT connects these complementary aspects of leadership within a systems framework.

Leadership guides both performance (i.e., "exploitation," March 1991) and survival of the system in the short term, and adaptation (i.e., "exploration," March 1991) and thus its prospects for survival over the longer term. It does this by processing and using information gathered as feedback from the environment and from within the system itself (Gell-Mann, 2002). It senses this feedback and channels it to individuals who are in a position to use the information it contains to find new ways of organizing in an effort to acquire, store, and allocate resources of all types. As such, complex system leadership theory (CSLT) transcends and integrates prior research and offers a platform for understanding leadership in fundamentally new ways.

Thesis and Overview

Our thesis is summarized as follows: just as complexity has become an overarching theoretical paradigm in the natural sciences, it is serving as the basis for a paradigm shift (Kuhn, 1962) in the social sciences, particularly in the areas of leadership and organizational studies. By shifting the focus from the individual to the organizing process itself, a key value of complexity is its strong implications for practice: individual action must be considered in nonlinear systems terms. In the fast-changing global ecosystem, approaches to management grounded in linear assumptions may overly emphasize applying controls on interactions, thus failing to stimulate information flows, learning, and growth. New techniques that exploit nonlinearities and embrace fast-paced interaction are needed.

To explain this, we begin with some of the challenges a complexity paradigm brings to the field. We then describe how complexity thinking is applied to theorizing about leadership, the growing empirical support for this approach, and the new methods that might change the research process going forward. Because one of the key ideas of complexity is the continual unfolding of newness, we conclude by looking ahead.

Complexity Brings Challenges

The paradigm shift (Kuhn, 1962) toward complexity in leadership research brings with it certain challenges, particularly to those who have traditionally seen leadership as something to be admired in, or executed by, especially gifted or specially trained individuals. In this mindset, individual "leaders" cause things to happen. As these traditional observers might see it, when organizing is needed, that is, when one observes that leadership is necessary, this "leadership vacuum" is translated into the idea that someone, some person, should "step up" to "take charge" causing something to happen (MacGillivray, 2010).

With complexity, however, the scenario is different. While the need for leadership remains, causality—at least much of the causality that really matters—is assumed to be indirect and diffuse (Streatfield, 2001). When circumstances require leadership, individual observations and experiences, connections and shared values, relative status, and the interaction dynamics themselves, force the issue until leadership structures that cross levels-of-analysis emerge through the constructive actions of individuals (Goldstein et al., 2010). These leadership structures provide downward influence on individual interactions even as they are themselves the emergent outcome of those same interactions, in a dynamic process that complexity pioneer Haken (2006) calls circular causality. Certainly people "step up," but they are not seen as providing leadership for others. Rather, they are seen as being drawn into the leadership process along with others. The system properties that begin to emerge are then sustained, evolved, or replaced within the system of interaction, as leadership unfolds dynamically (Panzar, Hazy, McKelvey, & Schwandt, 2007).

One difference in this perspective stems from the fact that complexity science has found that the order we observe and are able to create in the world manifests itself simultaneously at multiple levels of scale. Not only do unique dynamics unfold within individual interactions, but also at the group level, the department level, the firm level, and the institutional level. Each of these levels provides feedback to all of the other levels, influencing the dynamics of the others. These changes, in turn, feed back once again to the other levels, and so on in an ongoing adaptive spiral.

In short, feedback is all over the place and in all kinds of directions, making it exceedingly difficult to meaningfully control events or to cause specific outcomes in the traditional sense (Tobin, 2009). This would seem to account for the common practice in management to attempt to control events by containing the flow of information and thus limiting all diverging nonlinear effects that often accompany reinforcing feedback in complex systems. Because a lot is happening at once, this logic goes, if one doesn't control events and information flows there can be unintended consequences, and it is better to stop them before they happen rather than risk that they might challenge one's assumptions about strategy and direction. CSLT suggests ways for thoughtfully relaxing control and letting constructive deviations build upon their successes, while identifying and reducing destructive deviations before they threaten to pull the organization apart.

A note on terminology: To help clarify for the reader where we are focusing discussion in this paper, we will follow Gell-Mann (2002) and use the term "fine-grained" to refer to individuals interacting with one another, and "coarse-grained" to refer to the higher scale properties of organizations that are of interest to leadership researchers, such as profits, employee turnover, regulatory regimes, or even the leadership capability itself. In truth, however, the experience of leadership floats between the fine- and the coarse- grained levels, crossing scale and effectively becoming scale-free (Boisot & McKelvey, 2007). Organizational life thus challenges people to act both individually and collectively at the same time in the face of this complexity. We describe some of these challenges next.

Stability and Attractors: Coarse-Grained Prediction with Fine-Grained Uncertainty

One of the key insights from complexity science is that organizing, and thus leadership, drives change at the fine-grained level of individual human interaction. Leadership does this by changing the rules that govern the nature of connections and exchanges between individuals. From these fine-grained interactions, persistent patterns emerge as coarse-grained system properties that are sometimes quite stable at a higher level of scale. For example, warehouses and logistics processes that at one point emerged almost by chance may remain at the center of stable activities for months, years, or even decades, attracting behaviors to them (Allen, 2001). Stable properties like these can be recognized and modeled as organizational capabilities (e.g., the logistics example we mentioned, but also accounting or customer service) (Dosi, Nelson, & Winter, 2000; Helfat et al., 2007). To change these coarse-grained properties of organizations, however, one must first change the rules governing fine-grained interactions of the people who are implementing them.

CSLT defines leadership in complex adaptive systems as the social process that changes the rules of interaction across levels of analysis, that is, among individuals, work groups, departments, organizations, and institutions. The leadership meta-capability, in particular, is defined as the routines, knowledge management, and decision-making processes (Helfat et al., 2007) that serve the coarse-grained function of changing the rules of interaction inside the organization or the broader system (Hazy, 2004, 2006; Hazy, Goldstein, & Lichtenstein, 2007b). Thus, coarse-grained properties are changed only indirectly: they change when the rules of interaction are changed at a finer-grained scale. This is an intuitive result: one must change the way that people do what they do in order to change the outcomes they produce. CSLT seeks to discover and specify the mechanisms, both direct and indirect, that enable this top-down/bottom-up iterative process in real organizations, as well as how individuals learn to recognize and become proficient in enacting this capability.

As alluded to above, stable coarse-grained properties are often associated with a dynamical *attractor* within the system of HID, like, for example, the logistics capability described previously (Allen, 2001; Hazy & Ashley, 2011). This complexity term means that there is a subset of all possible coarse-grained states of the system such that the state is "sticky," meaning that these attractor states effectively "pull" the system back to their original state if something disturbs its normal functioning. After a storm that destroys some logistics equipment, for example, activities are "automatically" enacted to return to the "normal" state. As an even more general example, firms that maintain their profitability can be stable for a time. When profits are threatened, they take action to return to profitability. At the same time, firms that lose money will eventually implode or disband. They are not dynamically stable.

Patterns of activity that enable stable profitable operations (i.e., "exploitation," March, 1991) form an attractor of coarse-grained properties. These in turn drive what is happening at the fine-grained interaction level. As individual behavior patterns and choices at the fine-grained level converge towards a pattern of interaction they reinforce the coarse-grained organizing form in what amounts to an iterative stabilizing feedback process that extends back and forth across levels of scale (Hazy & Ashley, 2011). *Convergent* interactions that enable stability and thus predictability are achieved through information feedback processes, wherein coarse-grained structure provides information to individual agents, and their actions in turn influence the specific characteristics of the coarse-grain structures in order maintain their relative stability (Hazy, 2011b).

These feedback loops, both positive or reinforcing and negative or stabilizing, can shape the emergent, dynamically stable coarse-grained state of the system. In turn, coarse-grain stability can imply fine-grained choices and actions, such that their emergent outcomes become to some degree predictable in the aggregate even though any particular event remains difficult to predict, a circumstance that is called statistical complexity (Prokopenko, Boschetti, & Ryan, 2009). For example, one roughly knows what to expect when entering a retail store, a coarse-grained structure. At Wal-Mart, a greeter will greet you somewhere with high probability. At the same time, there is no way to predict exactly when or where such an event will occur. Thus, although there is a level of stability and predictability at the coarse-grained level, there is always unavoidable uncertainty at the fine-grained level. Individual interactions are neither random nor completely predictable. They are constrained, but not determined, by attractors (Hazy & Ashley, 2011; Hazy, 2011b).

Emergence: Fine-Grained Prediction with Coarse-Grained Uncertainty

On the flip side of the comfortable stability and general predictability of familiar coarse-grained aspects of organizational life is the reality that things sometimes change. When this happens, old coarse-grained institutional structures must change as well. This implies a conundrum: If coarse-grained properties are recognizable patterns that emerge from within individual interactions, how does adaptive change actually happen at the coarse-grained level when human interaction is experienced and predicted at the fine-grained level? In evolutionary systems, this occurs through the process of variation, selection, and retention among genetically related but distinct entities over many generations. In cognitively enabled systems, this occurs through an intragenerational learning process whereby organisms learn to respond to stimuli in their environment in a single lifetime. CSLT offers a framework that describes how organizations both evolve through variation, selection, and retention over many generations and also learn to adapt within a single organization in a given generation. How well organizations learn impacts their ability to survive and thus to contribute to the evolution of organizational forms (Hannan & Freeman, 1989).

The process wherein organizing forms evolve and learn is the purview of a key area of complexity research: emergence. Much has been written about emergence as a general matter in complexity (Goldstein, 2007, 2010; Lichtenstein & McKelvey, 2007) as well as with regard to leadership (Lichtenstein & Plowman, 2009; Plowman et al. 2007a, b). The idea is that under certain exogenous constraints, a changing system of fine-grained interactions can cause the emergent coarse-grained properties that are observed to undergo a qualitative transformation in their coarse-grained patterns and structure. Examples of this phenomenon that are taken from the natural sciences—such as the phase transition from liquid to gas—have provided metaphorical insights for leadership researchers.

One important natural science example of emergence is the appearance of what are called dissipative structures (MacIntosh & MacLean, 1999; Prigogine, 1995; Prigogine & Stengers, 1984). An occurrence of this phenomenon is described in some detail by Goldstein et al. (2010) to illustrate how coarse-grained structures emerge in quasi-closed systems of fluids during what are called far-from-equilibrium conditions. In the case described, this type of emergence happens when heat is continually applied to the bottom of a closed container of liquid. As the intensity of heat crosses a certain critical threshold, internal fluctuations interact with one another in the presence of the exogenous force of gravity to cause an observable qualitative shift in the coarse-grained behavior of the system.

The system's dynamic behavior rather suddenly shifts from a relatively calm state where heat is transferred by the mechanism of conduction to an orderly state of circular flow that transfers heat through the mechanism of convection. As this occurs, the emergence of persistent, coarse-grained hexagonal convection cells can be observed. Prigogine (1995) calls these "dissipative structures" because convection dissipates heat more quickly than conduction does. The onset or settling down of this qualitative change in structure can be "toggled" by the experimenter by increasing or decreasing the heat applied to the bottom of the container. Thus, changing patterns in fine-grained interaction behavior among the molecules can be seen to relate to a qualitative change in the coarse-grained properties that emerge in the system, and these are themselves shaped by external constraints on the system, the shape of the container, for example.

Another example of emergence relates to what Haken (2006) calls "order parameters" that emerge through a process of circular causality (Haken, 2006). Using the example of a laser, Haken shows how under the right conditions the light waves emitted by individual atoms eventually synchronize their phases as represented by an order parameter. This occurs as constructive interference reinforces a particular phase determined by interaction with external constraints while destructive interference dampens others that are not reinforced by the environment. This means that bottom-up processes can lead to emerging order. And emergent order places downward pressure on bottom-up events, "enslaving" them to be in phase with the order parameter, a process called "entrainment." This is what is meant by circular causality.

Related to the above, is the subset of systems whose order parameters characterize phase transitions. This well-studied phenomenon of circular causality in natural systems involves a change in physical state as energy that is being added to the system modifies the internal structure of the system to change how the system processes energy and information. Water freezing, iron becoming magnetized, and the onset of superconductivity are examples of this. Well-established mathematical models describe how external constraints—for example, ambient temperature and pressure in the case of water freezing—interact to influence the "order" that emerges within the system of interacting molecules. The progress of these changing dynamics is described by mathematical models that relate an order parameter to the change in state (Goldstein et al., 2010).

Common to these examples is the idea that the breakdown of order within extant coarse-grained properties is a prerequisite for emergence. This condition has been called the "edge of chaos" (Kauffman, 1995; Mitchell, Hraber, & Crutchfield, 1993), "far-from equilibrium" (Meyer, Gaba, & Colwell, 2005; Prigogine, 1995) and "criticality" (Bak & Paczuski, 1995) in varying complexity situations. To emphasize the dynamic nature of this condition and of its potential to enable a qualitative transition from one stability regime to another, we prefer the Goldstein et al. (2010) term for the onset of these conditions: *criticalization.*

The term "criticalization" highlights the potential for change when a certain parameter crosses a critical threshold, what is called a bifurcation in mathematical modeling. In the case where complex systems of human interaction dynamics (HID) experience adaptive tension that pushes the system beyond a critical threshold, Uhl-Bien, Marion, and McKelvey (2007) describe the *requisite complexity* of the system as a prerequisite for the onset of emergence. The interaction between the complexity present in the environment and that which develops within the system has been codified by Boisot & McKelvey (2010) in what they call "Ashby Space," to recognize Ashby's law of requisite variety (1956).

The challenge when going beyond complexity metaphors to develop a theory of emergence in human systems is to explicate the emergence phenomenon in the HID case while taking into account the differences inherent in human interactions when compared to physical systems. Prietula (2011) describes some of the practical differences in the context of agent-based modeling. Hazy and Ashley (2011) explore the implications of these differences when developing a theory of emergence in HID.

According to these researchers, the difference boils down to this: in contrast to physical systems where many agents of a particular class (like water molecules) interact with one another in the same way, human interactions are heterogeneous, each being determined by individual preferences, personal histories, social connections, and perceived difference in power and status, all of which are stored in the individuals' memories. Prediction becomes problematic since these memories are largely hidden from the observer.

Further, human connections are interdependent rather than independent since individuals incorporate into their choices not only information from their direct experiences, but also information and knowledge that is received through communication with others. This interdependent heterogeneity implies that many of the statistical methods used in the natural sciences are not appropriate in the human case since traditional methods assume independence and consistency across time. In many cases, neither of these assumptions is valid with human beings (Hazy & Ashley, 2011). As a result, the development of a well-specified and robust model describing the mechanisms of emergence in HID remains an ongoing challenge for the field (Hazy, 2011b).

Complexity: A Journey from Novelty to New Paradigm

In the late 1980s and 1990s, complexity thinking for organizations had not yet come into sharp focus. Still the application of complexity was all the rage within the social sciences (Anderson, 1999; Cilliers, 1998; Dooley, 1997; Goldstein, 1989; Levinthal, 1997; McKelvey, 1997; Thietart & Forgues, 1995). Exotic concepts that were discovered in the natural sciences, like chaos, strange attractors, and the possibilities implied by emergence—where entirely new order springs forth seemingly in whole cloth—led researchers to look for complexity applications in management and human organizations (Wheatley, 1999). Initial interpretations of complexity often led to an unfortunate tendency to recommend to practitioners a version of laissez-faire leadership—arguing that a hands-off style was all that was needed and that employees would simply "self-organize" to solve business problems.

In contrast, Marion and Uhl-Bien (2001) saw the promise of complexity as beyond metaphoric and suggested specific areas for theoretical exploration and empirical research. This article follows in their direction and that of others (Schneider & Somers, 2006) and reviews what has happened since these early days, and it explores what these activities might mean for the future of leadership research and practice.

Ontological and Epistemological Issues

Relevant to the complexity framing of business and organization has been the distinction between ontology and epistemology. The philosophic challenge is to determine the extent to which the complexity mindset is a reflection of what is real in the world (that is identifiable through observation—ontology) versus the extent to which complexity is just a new or different way of knowing or understanding what is happening or perceived to be happening in the world (Boisot & McKelvey, 2010). In this latter way of thinking, complexity is just an analytical "tool-kit."

The distinction is not a trivial one. It exposes the question of how human beings deal with experienced complexity. As this article explores, some interesting questions this implies include the following: Is the world a complex system? Is it essentially a computation that is unfolding (Dooley, 2007; Richardson, 2010)? If so, what are its algorithms? Are there better, more complex ways to model and predict the world? How does complexity science inform the study of cognitive neuroscience? What about the study and practice of psychology? And of course, what can it tell us about study of leaders and leadership? These concerns can be considered from various philosophical perspectives, for example, as constructionist, constructivist, objective realism, critical realism, etc.

From the practical perspective of epistemology, the increased use of nonlinear techniques and probabilistic prediction models in management are aspects of the complexity revolution in the social sciences that have already established their value in practice. Monte Carlo analyses, information theoretic approaches, game theory modeling, and system dynamics approaches are all now in the mainstream decision support tool-kit in business. All of these are complexity-informed tools that support managers in their decision making. The adoption of these tools, presumably because of their usefulness, supports the notion that ontologically, human organizations appear to act like complex systems. What is missing is a holistic modeling approach—something analogous to a statistical mechanics of HID—that would represent and study organizations using complexity theories framed in a useful epistemology. Such an approach would be invaluable to practice as it would allow managers to forgo their need to apply sub-optimized controls locally, which can dampen both learning and growth in the service of a perceived sense of stability and predictability, a practice that can be counterproductive.

One additional point is relevant here. There are particular ontological implications of the complexity notion of emergence. Does an organization exist ontologically, in other words, does it have agency? There is an argument that insect colonies do in fact exhibit ontological agency. Tens of thousands of honeybees swarm as a collective to find a new nest without central control. Choosing a proper nest is critical for survival of the swarm, and thus for evolutionary adaptation. This is also true for the individual bees, all of which carry the DNA of the queen (Seeley, 2010). Can the same argument be made for a firm or a nation? Does the diversity of DNA in human organizations make the superorganism argument untenable (Nowak, Tarnita, & Wilson, 2010)? This is a fundamental question for leadership researchers. Stated differently, is anthropomorphizing the organization wrongheaded, or forward thinking? Do individuals actually "lead" organizations, or is something else going on, something akin to the emergence of collective agency? If it is the latter, what does this tell us about leadership?

Complexity Approaches to Leadership Research

With the above background, we now turn to the various applications of complexity to leadership. Although there are copious studies that apply conceptual ideas to leadership metaphorically, such as the idea of fractals (Levick & Kuhn, 2007), the onset of chaos (Brown & Eisenhardt, 1998), emergence and attractors (Shoup & Studer, 2010), and sensitivity to initial conditions (Peterson & Meckler, 2001), others have cautioned against such metaphorical applications (Goldstein et al., 2010; Simpson, 2007). Moving beyond metaphor, we focus only on the approaches that uniquely assume a complexity ontology or that apply one of the complexity inspired epistemologies: agent-based modeling (ABM), dynamic network analysis, nonlinear dynamical systems (NDS) modeling, or information theoretic framings such as game theory and non-Gaussian statistical methods. (For a description of these methods see, for example, Boisot & McKelvey, 2007; Guastello, 2002; and Hazy, Millhiser & Solow, 2007).

Because we are for the most part assuming a complex systems perspective,[1] presumably the studies of emergent properties within HID would unfold in a manner analogous to dynamical systems models of weather patterns, ecological models or epidemiology studies, or in the way that agent-based models represent conditions of criticalization or uncertainty that signal an impending phase transition: for example, when a system changes its properties qualitatively—as when water freezes into ice.

As Goldstein et al. (2010) point out, in human systems, situations of "criticalization" occur when conditions in the environment combine with the state of the organization to create uncertainty and unpredictability about where things are going. Researchers studying knowledge generation in organizations describe the unfolding of plans and strategies during everyday practice (Tsoukas, 2005). Often different individuals are observed espousing multiple different plausible futures, and individuals are left to decide which approach is likely to "win" in the end (Hazy & Ashley, 2011). Other authors have referred to conditions like this as "disequilibrium" (Lichtenstein & Plowman, 2009) and identified these conditions as a prerequisite for emergence.

Given how little is known about the relationship between fine-grained interactions and the emergence of coarse-grained properties (Hazy, 2011b), we first explore how leadership can be relevant at the coarse-grained level. We begin with an overarching model as context for the other approaches we will describe.

The Leadership and Capabilities Model (LCM)

Although many articles begin with a statement that the authors are assuming organizations are complex adaptive systems (Boal & Schultz, 2007; Brown & Eisenhardt, 1997; Levinthal, 1997), their use of complexity is usually limited to the assumption that semiautonomous agents interact, and that organizations somehow emerge from this process. Little has been written about the course-grained properties that emerge, how they emerge, and what leadership has to do with this. The Leadership and Capabilities Model (LCM) developed by Hazy (2006, 2011a, 2013) addresses this gap by explicitly describing human organizing as a complex adaptive system of interactions that performs certain functions.

To address the cross-level definitional issue with regard to the term "leadership," Hazy (2006, 2011a) builds upon Katz and Kahn (1966) to define "complex systems leadership" to be a special kind of organizational capability (Dosi et al., 2000; Helfat, et al., 2007) that performs particular system functions wherein the human organization is formed and evolved as a complex adaptive system. In particular, complex systems leadership is the organizational capability that iterates changes to the system's configuration (by changing local rules of interaction) to test its performance in the environment. As such, complex systems leadership is not what individuals do; it represents an organizational capability in the sense described in business strategy (Helfat et al., 2007): it is a set of routines, knowledge management, and decision-making processes that perform leadership functions in the same way that marketing and accounting are capabilities that perform more instrumental system functions. All of these capabilities, including leadership, are enacted by individuals and collectives in furtherance of functional requirements as the system gathers and processes information, resources, and energy to create order. Because complex systems leadership reconfigures other capabilities, Hazy (2006) calls it a meta-capability.

Organizations with well-developed complex systems leadership meta-capabilities are able to iteratively act on the system itself, changing the rules governing fine-grained interactions within the system in response to success or failure (Hazy et al., 2007; Hazy 2011b). The coarse-grained properties that emerge enable subsequent success *of the system* in changing and adapting as the situation develops. The complex systems leadership meta-capability guides this process.

The idea of complex systems leadership as a meta-capability extends the work on organizational capabilities, both dynamic and operational (Barney, 1991; Helfat et al., 2007; Nelson & Winters, 1982; Teece, Pisano, & Shuen, 1997). However, in contrast to the capabilities literature, individuals *in the organization* aren't actualizing these capabilities; rather they are enacting the leadership meta-capability *of the organization* that is acting on the system to test configurations of other capabilities, and to identify those that work better than others.

Using the complex systems agent-based epistemology of system dynamics, Hazy (2004, 2006, 2013) built a computer simulation model of the leadership meta-capability that is called the leadership and capabilities model (LCM). When the model is run, the leadership meta-capability performs an iterated operation on the coarse-grained properties within the system that (i) implements the exploitation (March, 1991) of current capabilities, (ii) promotes the exploration and generative process of new capability creation (March, 1991), and (iii) unifies the system to maintain it as an entity with regard to local and global criticalization conditions as required by the environment. It changes the properties or capabilities that have previously emerged, and presumably it does this by changing local rules of interaction among individuals. By changing the rules, the properties characterizing the system, including its capabilities, also change.

Depending upon the context, the complex systems leadership operation acts on the system to perform three functions: The *convergent* operation within the system adjusts the properties of the system to make them more predictable (Hazy & Ashley, 2011) and thus improve exploitation. Rules are changed to dampen deviations by increasing individual productivity and leveraging cooperative activities with technology and other assets. This is called the exploitation *value-gathering loop* (Hazy, 2011a).

The *generative* operation responds to changing constraints in the environment and promotes exploration, collaboration, creativity, and innovation in system properties (Hazy, 2004, 2006; Surie & Hazy, 2006; Uhl-Bien et al., 2007). If changing constraints on the system implies that a qualitative change in coarse-grained properties is needed, the system often passes through a period of criticalization as requisite complexity is engendered. For this to occur, fine-grained rules of interaction are changed to promote experimentation and to reduce or eliminate premature convergence that might be implied by administrative leadership activities. Because a variety of possible futures coexist, this is a manifestation of Ashby's (1956) notion of requisite variety. The exploration *value-identifying loop* enables adaptation (Hazy, 2011a).

The *unifying* operation of the LCM uses communication and symbolic activities, such as policies and boundary rules for the proprietary use of information, to more clearly specify acceptable and expected rules for system properties by promoting locally stable collective identities and systems of ethics (Hazy, 2011c). This tunes the level of criticalization and requisite complexity (Uhl-Bien & Marion, 2009) both locally and globally within and across the organization. This process allows efficacious experiments and emergent innovations to be integrated into the larger system.

One implication of the LCM is that, just as with other organizational capabilities, individuals learn to implement aspects of the leadership meta-capability in the same way they learn to implement manufacturing, customer service, business planning, or any other capability (Hazy, 2007a, 2008b). The acquisition of leadership skills by individuals is the result of social learning of the meta-capability within organizations, just as the acquisition of marketing skills results from social learning in marketing organizations. Individuals are not born to leadership competency; they learn how to exercise this capability by being involved in organizing efforts that exhibit the coarse-grain property of an effective leadership meta-capability.

Leadership and Emergence

Given how little is known at present about the emergence of coarse-grained properties in the unique manifestation of the distinctly human social context, it is at present difficult to offer specific suggestions about how any given individual should behave. The process of emergence has been explored, however. Lichtenstein and Plowman (2009) draw on case studies of emergent leadership in organizational settings, the case of a mission church (Plowman et al., 2007 a, b) for example, to argue that there are four phases in the emergence process. First there must be *disequilibrium*, unstable conditions that were described in the earlier section as criticalization. During these periods of uncertainty, reinforcing feedback is offered to certain process fluctuations through *amplifying actions* that seem to offer promising new ways to bring back stability. Hazy (2011a) calls these experiments in novelty "constructive deviations" because they deviate from what had previously been the norm, but they do so intentionally and constructively.[2] The constructive deviations that are working are then combined with other fragments of collective activities that are at work in other parts of the organization in a *recombination* process. In this way, new structures grow through the gradual accretion of constructive deviations that work. Eventually, *stabilizing feedback* that operates on this new way of doing things—for example, lack of funds or time limitations, or a saturated market—bring the organization back into a stable, albeit qualitatively different, approach to organizing. In the end, one can observe that distinctly new properties (at the coarse-grained level) have emerged.

As further support for this classification, Beck & Chong (2009) identified these stages in social entrepreneurship ventures they studied in Indonesia. Aspects of these phases were also apparent to Shepherd, and Woods (2011) in a social enterprise that was studied in New Zealand; and Baker, Onyx, and Edwards (2011) found evidence of recombination of network components in a developing community of social enterprises in Australia. The next stage of CSLT research in this area is to uncover the specific mechanisms at work in each of these stages, that is, the mechanisms of emergence at work in HID (Hazy, 2011b).

A series of research projects in Sweden have provided some hints about these mechanisms. These studies explored how first-line managers provide the preconditions to influence both the interactions between individuals and the collective organizing which emerges from them (Backström, 2009; Backström, Hagström, & Göransson, 2011; Backström, Wilhelmson, Olsson, Åteg, & Åberg, 2011). Backström and his colleagues refer to this aspect of management as the "directing task" that focuses on enabling a dynamical balance between the autonomy of individuals and their integration into the emerging organizing structures. The communicative competence of the employees and the reasons, places, and times for them to meet and to communicate were found to be important conditions for the emergence of structures like collective culture and identity, institutionalized collective behavior, and patterns of work relations (Backström, Wilhelmson et al., 2011).

As the above discussion highlights, at present it may be theoretical overreach to posit that any one person is in control of the emergence process whereby the coarse-grained patterns that characterize organizational capabilities come into being, at least as regards what is currently known about complexity (Hazy, 2008b). The assertion that complexity implies a good deal of ambiguity when linking fine-grained action to coarse-grained properties has found support in the literature (Siggelkow & Rivkin, 2005). Morrison (2010) showed how the process of gathering information, analyzing it, recommending approaches, and implementing projects can be a very challenging undertaking for managers. When this occurs within a network of positive and negative feedback loops, as is often the case, the challenge is even more daunting.

There is a point where predicting the resulting outcomes in the face of this nonlinearity is problematic (Morrison, 2010; Siggelkow & Rivkin, 2005). Interdependent, heterogeneous connections between individuals as they interact seem to make each case unique. This is not to say these dynamics are not understandable in a general way, only that they are not yet understood. We next describe work that focuses on discovering additional coarse-grained and fine-grained leadership activities needed in organizations when they are considered to be complex adaptive systems.

Complexity Leadership Theory

An approach that is compatible with, but varies somewhat, from the LCM model just described is Complexity Leadership Theory (CLT) (Uhl-Bien et al., 2007; Uhl-Bien & Marion, 2009, 2011; Uhl-Bien & Arena, 2013). Complexity leadership theory draws from concepts of complex adaptive systems (CAS) to offer a framework for describing how leadership in organizations can enable complexity dynamics that allow the organization to operate as *adaptive*, rather than *bureaucratic*, systems (Uhl-Bien & Arena, 2013).

CLT begins by identifying the systems we have always seen operating in organizations: a formal administrative system and an informal entrepreneurial system (Barnard, 1938; March, 1991; Selznick, 1948). It argues that all organizations start out as entrepreneurial but as they become formalized (e.g., when they go public) they take on an administrative system. Once this happens these two systems go into battle, and almost invariably, administrative wins (Uhl-Bien & Arena, 2013). The result is that organizations are pulled toward equilibrium (stability) rather than adaptability (complexity). The key challenge for organizational leaders, therefore, is how to enable organizations toward adaptability (Uhl-Bien et al., 2007; Uhl-Bien & Arena, 2013).

This challenge can be addressed by understanding leadership in the context of three key systems in organizations. The first, the *administrative system,* represents the exploitation function as identified by March (1991) and modeled in the LCM. Its job is to produce results (i.e., effectiveness) through efficiency and control. Administrative leadership does this through choice, execution and variance reduction (March, 1991). This is the focus in traditional leadership approaches on aligning followers to meet goals using hierarchical leadership and control systems (e.g., Drucker, 1966; Bass, 1985; Bossidy & Charan, 2002). The administrative system is critically important in organizations and must be present for survival. However, because it focuses on reducing variety it reduces complexity (Boisot & McKelvey, 2010), pulling the organization toward stability and equilibrium.

The second, *entrepreneurial system,* represents the exploration function as identified by March (1991) and the LCM. It engages individuals and organizations in search, experimentation, and variation. By engaging in these activities, entrepreneurial leaders help foster innovation, growth and learning in organizations. This is typically a bottom-up process in organizations, and is represented in literature on leadership associated innovation and creative processes (Crossan, Lane & White, 1999; Crossan, Gandz & Seijts, 2010; Hargadon & Bechky, 2006). The entrepreneurial system is also critically important in organizations because it increases variety in ways consistent with complexity in organizations (Boisot & McKelvey, 2010). However, the entrepreneurial system is easily (and often) stifled by administrative leadership activities, which focuses on variety-reducing activities of alignment and control (Uhl-Bien et al., 2007).

Therefore, for organizations to operate as complex adaptive systems they need a third system, the *adaptive system* (Uhl-Bien & Arena, 2013). The adaptive system is one that has not been recognized in previous literature (the LCM refers to a unifying function that manages tensions between exploitation and exploration), and represents a key contribution of complexity approaches to leadership and organization science. Its role is to feed and fuel productive emergence necessary for the fitness and survival of the organization (Uhl-Bien & Arena, 2013). It does this by promoting entrepreneurial leadership and enabling its innovative and adaptive outcomes to be incorporated into administrative systems (Crossan et al., 2010) to become new order for the system. New order is the end state of emergence (Goldstein, 2011) and adaptation.

In this way CLT includes both coarse-grained (administrative) and fine-grained (entrepreneurial) leadership activities. It also recognizes a leadership system associated with the process of enabling emergence of fine-grain into coarse-grain (adaptive). In this way, it adds new understanding of how we can achieve complex adaptive organizing in the context of bureaucratic organizational systems (Uhl-Bien et al., 2007; Uhl-Bien & Arena, 2013).

Leadership and Strategy: The Community-Building Process

One of the anomalies that confronts organizational and leadership researchers is the perception that individuals and, in particular, executive managers, are in charge of organizations—they set the directions; they make things happen. As we can see from the above discussion, this does not square with a complex system viewpoint that organizing patterns emerge through interactions. One point of synthesis, however, is the realization that there are variations in the roles and the impact that individuals have in the system—that is, the influence of all individuals is not equal. Status and reputation differences have significant impacts on outcomes (Axelrod, 1984; Simon, 1997). For example, executives typically set the strategy and direction for the organization; they define the organization's boundaries, its identity, and its ethics; and they hold it together (Hazy, 2011c). In short, executives drive the community-building process at the highest relevant level of coarse-graining. Thus, contrary to the CAS most often studied in the natural sciences, it does appear that in the case of human interactions, through intentional action that recognizes and seeks to exploit emergent patterns, individual agents can make a difference even in properties that are coarse-grained.

STRATEGY, "TAGS," AND THE COMMUNITY-BUILDING PROCESS

For example, Boal and Shultz (2007) focus on the strategic aspects of leadership at the top of the organization. Amid their discussion about how communication strategies and storytelling are core to business strategy making, they assert that individuals performing leadership functions use the complexity idea of "tags," as defined by Holland (1975), to compartmentalize large organizations into differentiated substructures. They argue that this process is useful because, as Holland shows, the use of tags in interactions enables individuals who share the same assumptions and aspirations to identify one another. Tags thus promote higher levels of quality interaction within same-tagged identity groups. The use of tags also results in lower levels of interaction across groups with different tags, which can make communication more efficient.

In a more general sense, the implications of Boal and Schultz (2007) suggest that tags are useful in furthering the community-building process. Tags can be thought of as a mechanism that clarifies and helps resolve *identity tensions* locally and globally, and tunes criticalization conditions locally in the face of further tension between adaptive versus performance concerns. In CLT terms (Uhl-Bien et al., 2007), *administrative leadership* exploits innovations generated by entrepreneurial and adaptive leadership to benefit the firm, which also seems to be relevant to the strategic community-building process that Boal and Schultz describe. Perhaps, the use of tags is a mechanism of leadership that serves to further the community-building process within the organization.

COMMUNITY-BUILDING LEADERSHIP ACROSS SCALE

One might note, however, that the community-building process requires that these activities occur across the organization and are not limited to the actions of top management. They occur at all levels of the organization. To further explore the mechanisms of individual influence within HID, particularly when organizing large-scale efforts, Hunt, Osborne, and Boal (2009) describe the application of complexity to what they call Level VI leadership (Jaques, 1989), the level below strategic leadership. For Jaques, Level VI implies individual cognitive capacity that enables a task horizon and job focus of three to five years for mid-career executives.

Citing the Siggelkow and Rivkin (2005) results, Hazy (2007b) argues that at the senior management level, successful leadership is more about picking strong subordinates and advising and supporting them with resources than it is about choosing actual projects. The process whereby these decisions are taken has recently been explored by Anneloes et al. (2011) in the context of the nature and quality of the interactions between top managers and their middle-management subordinates who are responsible for directly delivering operating results. At this level, it may be more appropriate to worry about picking the right individuals, that is, the right champions, who have proven they can pick and drive winners, than to try to identify winning projects oneself. In CLT terms (Uhl-Bien & Arena, 2013), these are adaptive leaders.

Extending this line of thinking, Hazy (2012) argues that when reputation and status accrue to individuals who are successful, and when these changes are publicized to the organization's members, the organization gets smarter as a system. In his model, relative status and reputation determine relative influence among individuals in a manner analogous to the synaptic weights connecting neurons in the brain. These weightings determine which neurons are activated in response to stimuli in the environment. Similarly, relative status and reputations play a role in determining who is involved and to what degree when an organization is forming a response to events in the environment. In this way, the organization "learns" in a manner analogous to the learning algorithm in the brain's neural network.

As an example, a successful merchant bank in Sweden, with a record of success even during the financial crises, illustrates a complexity-aware structure of this type (Backström et al., 2011). Each department operates as its own company, and each employee has full responsibility for a group of customers. The company's culture unifies these activities as a major mechanism for integrating different groups into the company. Activities such as appointing managers with values that closely match those of the company, and ensuring high-quality communication among individuals were shown to be central for integration into a unified firm with a common identity (Backström et al., 2011). The bank uses a very simple feedback process at the departmental level and uses this to clarify the relative success, and thus the relative status and reputations of departments (and thus of individuals), by publishing a monthly ranking of all departments.

Based upon these complexity ideas, Hazy (2012) argues that one of the most important aspects of effective management is to focus on structuring projects so as to receive clear and unbiased feedback about success or failure and to act on the feedback by adjusting the status and reputations of those involved. Thus, an important imperative of leadership is to hold people to account. This would be an element of administrative leadership (Uhl-Bien et al., 2007; Uhl-Bien & Arena, 2013).

We turn next to the question of what it might take for an individual, a "leader," to differentiate his or her actions in order to successfully engage a system that has complex characteristics.

The Individual in Complex Organizing

Core to the challenge of developing complex systems leadership theory is the unique role played by individual human beings, particularly high-status ones, or powerful ones, in complex organizations (Denis, Langley, & Pineault, 2000). Does complexity suggest what it takes to be a successful individual "leader" in this context? Building on the work of Zaccaro (1999) and Hooijberg (1996), this challenge has been taken up by Hannah, Lord, Jennings, and others (Hannah, Eggers, & Jennings, 2008; Hannah, Jennings, & Nobel, 2010; Hannah, Woolfolk, & Lord, 2009; Lord, Hannah, & Jennings, 2011) to explore the mental characteristics that support success, as well as the potential for bias, for example, gender bias (Hogue & Lord, 2007). These issues become important to researchers for a number of reasons, one being their implications to leadership development programs (Boyatzis, 2008).

As described earlier, Uhl-Bien et al. (2007) extend Ashby's (1956) idea of requisite variety, which says that in a cybernetic system the regulator must be at least as complex as the environment it hopes to regulate, to argue that organizations must likewise match the complexity of the environment, a condition called requisite complexity (Boisot & McKelvey, 2010). In particular, they argue that complexity leaders must structure the organization to enable requisite complexity. To further define this concept, Hannah, Lord, Jennings, and others (Hannah et al., 2010; Hannah et al., 2009; Hannah et al., 2008) have worked to define the characteristics of individuals that enable requisite complexity in action. Most recently, Lord, Hannah, and Jennings (2011) identified two dimensions of complexity, static and dynamic, the latter taking into account the unfolding of complex conditions over time. By analogy, they extend the idea of requisite complexity to groups (Lord, Hannah & Pearce, 2011). The processes of creativity and innovation they describe require different skills, and support the system's functional demand that new information be gathered and synthesized in an ongoing generative process.

Adaptation and Innovation: The Adaptive Process

To sustain itself as an open system (von Bertalanffy, 1950), a complex system needs continuing access to resources within its ecosystem (Hazy, Moskalev, & Torras, 2009, 2010). Since opportunities in an ecosystem ebb and flow, a complex system needs mechanisms to explore the environment, identify resource-gathering opportunities, and construct generative structures within the system to begin to exploit these resources (Garud, Gehman, Kumaraswamy, 2011; Garud, Kumaraswamy, & Sambamurthy, 2006). In short, the organization must balance exploration and exploitation (March, 1991). Since ecologies change, this is not a once-and-done process. This is why Hazy (2011a) calls the value-identifying loop a requisite generative function for complex systems of HID. This system requirement places a functional demand upon the leadership meta-capability: to establish, evolve and regulate this adaptive operation *for the system* by changing the interaction rules among individuals.

Garud et al. (2011) describe the adaptive environment at 3M as what they call "complexity arrangements":

> We conceptualize the different combinations of practices—manifest structure (e.g., products, patents and platforms), relational processes (e.g., interactions between people within and across platforms and businesses), temporal dynamics (e.g., moments of serendipity enabled by the 15% option) and regulative guidelines (e.g., 30% stretch objective)—that are activated at various stages of an innovation journey at 3M as representing *complexity arrangements.* (p. 347)

These "complexity arrangements" enable a generative process of invention, but also innovation, and they are enacted at the individual interaction level. Complexity leadership approaches explore the mechanisms that evolve the rules that govern local interactions to enable the adaptive process of innovation and emergence.

DIVERGENCE THROUGH DISCOVERY

A literal example of this might be the value-identifying loop associated with an as-yet undiscovered oil field in the Gulf of Mexico. Resources are allocated to exploration (March, 1991), albeit with no a priori knowledge of the likelihood that a new field will be discovered at any particular place. Once indications of potential are identified and the probability of success increases (after a geological study, for example), locally specific capabilities must be constructed to explore this possibility further. With additional positive indications, more resources are allocated to take advantage of this potential, and so on, as long as the opportunity remains viable (meaning the probability of success relative to risk remains high).

Complex system leadership evolves local rules of interaction to enact this process. As experiments to acquire resources produce information, feedback (under promising conditions) leads to significant expected value with regard to the resources that could be discovered. This positive feedback loop is generative of possible future ecological niches for the system. However, if risks and rewards are not properly recognized and modeled, this feedback doesn't have to be beneficial for the organization. The unfolding impact of the BP Gulf Oil Spill in 2010 is a value-destroying example of the same positive feedback affect. Thus proper assessment of information about risks and benefits is an important aspect of the interaction rules that are evolved by complex systems leadership.

Events caught up in positive feedback loops can build upon themselves rapidly, and their effects can come to dominate the HID within an organization, as happened at Intel after the discovery of the microprocessor (Hazy, 2008a). Diverging value-identifying loops that build upon themselves exhibit *divergence through discovery* because information about the opportunity grows rapidly after discovery, often feeding upon itself. This information helps individuals to organize the system to deal with rapid growth and expansion. In the above example, this means that the petroleum industry ecosystem began as a dynamically stable system exploiting known resources. Initially the system had no information about this particular oil field (or about the implications of the Deep Water Horizon's blowout in the negative case).

Upon discovery, and assuming continued investment of resources, change unfolds. For example, researchers (Aasen & Berg, 2008; Aasen & Johannessen, 2007; Johannessen & Aasen, 2007) used the complex responsive processes framework to explore the innovation process at a subsea oil recovery case at Statoil ASA a Norwegian oil company. They observed that "innovation emerges from the experiences of everyday social interaction, where patterns gradually perceived as meaningful are created and adopted" (p. 44).

Using system dynamics modeling, the divergence of discovery as a complexity phenomenon was shown to describe organizational transformations at NCR (Hazy, 2006) and the rise of the microprocessor at Intel (Hazy, 2008a). It was also described for an on-line learning company (Hazy, 2008c), and in a case study reported by Surie and Hazy (2006). In the latter case, an Indian manufacturing company was working with foreign partners who were seeking to access production capacity to outsource their manufacturing. During the negotiation process, the

Indian company discovered and exploited entirely new global markets for its products. New information about global markets gradually changed the Indian firm's perception of their potential customer sets. Their visible world diverged from a narrow, traditional, domestic-only market, into the wider visibility of a truly worldwide market.

ECOLOGY OF INNOVATION

What these examples have in common, according to Goldstein et al. (2010), is that they occur in organizations wherein complex systems leadership has managed to position the organization within an "ecology of innovation." This means that the firm is well situated within its network of suppliers, customers, and partnerships and maintains excellent communication across its connections so as to engender knowledge generation, discovery, and thus a level of divergence as new opportunities are discovered. Their point is that leadership occurs at the nexus of interactions, where generative human dynamics lead to creativity and innovation (Andriani, 2011; Beck & Chong, 2009; Garud et al. 2011; Garud et al. 2006; Tapsell & Woods, 2009). The key to this is in the quality of interactions, what Goldstein et al. (2010) call *interaction resonance*, and what Garud et al. (2011) call *relational processes*.

In the Complex Responsive Processes (CRP) perspective, Stacey (1993, 1995) argues that certain conditions are necessary for impactful interactions. These include trust, the holding of anxiety, power relationships that are both cooperative and competitive, and conversational practices that don't block explorations (Simpson, 2007, p.475). These interaction-level tensions must be navigated to achieve a high level of interaction resonance. This in turn implies certain leadership activities that are necessary for adaptation. Complex systems leadership evolves rules of interaction to enable interaction resonance.

Goldstein et al. (2010) go on to argue that conditions of highly resonant interactions, bounded in the right way, can lead the system to *criticalization* in the complexity sense, where the system is poised for a phase transition between two possible dynamic states: one less ordered and thus more symmetric, and one more ordered or organized into specialties and thus less symmetric. The transition from one state to the other can be modeled mathematically if an order parameter can be identified to describe the change (Haken, 2006). Identifying the order parameter for phase transitions in HID remains an open unanswered question in CSLT.

More specifically, on one side of the phase transition, the more ordered case, individuals are oriented in certain roles and tasks, and are thus less interchangeable with others. Some are marketers doing marketing things and are only interchangeable with other marketers; some are accountants doing accounting things and can only be replaced by accountants, and so forth. Because fine-grained elements of the system can be differentiated, there is ordering in the system, and thus there are fewer ways the system is self-similar. It is thus less symmetric. On the other side of the phase transition, everyone does everything and thus, in a certain sense, everyone is interchangeable with everyone else (ignoring for a moment individual heterogeneity). Such a disordered system is thus more symmetric.

This is why qualitative change from one state to the other, called a "phase transition," represents a discontinuous change in the level of order in the system and this change is often referred to as "symmetry breaking" (Guastello, 2002; Haken, 2006). Ecologies of innovation enable symmetry-breaking qualitative change. Generative rules of interaction at the fine-grained level are an enabling prerequisite to innovation reordering of this type (Hazy, 2009).

Performance and Efficiency: The Administrative Process

In addition to unifying HID into communities within CAS, and the exploration and the generative activities that enable organizing in response to opportunities, the system must also converge to stable operations that effectively and efficiently exploit the resources to which it has access. Thus administrative leadership that enables this convergence is the third functional demand placed on the leadership meta-capability as the complex adaptive system (as enacted by its agents) seeks to acquire its requisite resources and to conserve the resources it has accumulated as slack (Cyert & March, 1963).

ADMINISTRATIVE LEADERSHIP FOR PRESERVATION

This functional demand is needed to encourage efficiency and to preserve slack resources (Cyert & March, 1963). In the process, however, potentially productive activities and information about alternative approaches and opportunities are lost (Haken, 2006). The human relations or "consideration" aspects of the administrative leadership process that brings people on-board, and the "initiating structure" elements that enable action-in-concert have long been associated with leadership (Fleishman, 1953; Stogdill, 1974). Individuals who exhibited either or both of these behaviors are called "leaders" by others even though leadership is actually emerging from within the interactions. The tendency to attribute leadership to individuals is a strong one that has also been observed in the complex system leadership context (MacGillivray, 2010).

Complexity ideas and methods have added a perspective on the "how" behind the "what" of these behaviors. Consideration and initiating structure by individual actions enable convergence of a disparate group toward a single, common objective. Convergence of action as enabled through administrative leadership practices satisfies a functional demand of the complex system on the leadership meta-capability as defined by Hazy (2011a). More specifically, Phelps and Hubler (2007) showed how groups could set and choose direction when a single individual was sufficiently motivated to move in a particular direction, essentially shutting out and forgoing other possibilities, including preferences of others. In several experimental settings, the role of individuals in catalyzing convergence toward a particular outcome has also been shown to follow distinctively nonlinear patterns of behavior by Guastello and his colleagues (Guastello, 2002; Guastello, 2007; Guastello & Bond, 2004, 2007a, 2007b; Guastello, Craven, Zygowicz, & Bock, 2005; Guastello & Guastello, 1998).

Complexity researchers have also studied the impact of leadership on group member self-selection across groups. Dal Forno and Merlone (2007) demonstrated both experimentally and computationally that the complex dynamics associated with the distribution of rewards and punishment by individuals on teams had a significant effect on which teams individuals chose to join, and this in turn impacted the projects that were ultimately completed.

Information flow is a critical enabler of project selection and execution. Schreiber and Carley (2006) used data from field observations and dynamic network analysis to study how the flow of information within teams impacted performance. They found that multiple network hubs in the flow of information, rather than a single one, that is, a single "leader," led to better performance when complex functioning was required. Similarly, Solow and Leenawong (2003) used Kauffman's (1995) NK model to show that too much complexity within teams can lead to situations of overload that greatly reduced performance. Insight on the efficacy of a centralized control model versus more distributed decision making was also shown using complexity modeling (Solow & Szmerekovsky, 2006).

Hazy (2007a, 2008b) summarized many of these studies into the theory of complex systems leadership. Synthesizing the studies above as well as others completed at the time, he observed that five distinct aspects of convergent leadership had been identified in these complexity inspired studies. These five mechanisms comprise the leadership response to the requisite system demand for collective convergence within HID toward action-in-concert. These distinct mechanisms include actions or communications by individual agents that

1. Espouse an approach or cooperation strategy for working toward a common objective, a "program of action," such that choosing to participate in the program is an attractor for the individual choices of two or more agents (Phelps & Hubler, 2007).
2. Catalyze social influence conditions such that at least one other agent chooses to participate in the program being espoused rather than continuing to act for its own account or according to an alternative program (Phelps & Hubler, 2007).
3. Catalyze choices and action in other agents intended to navigate complexity and overcome the limits to cognitive capacity in an effort to avoid an interaction catastrophe. This is necessary when there is too much interaction and confusion causing performance to drop precipitously (Solow & Leenawong, 2003).
4. Form a distinct output layer (the Executive Office) that expresses learning and action for the system as a unity in the environment; to do so, the agents disambiguate learning and enable the unambiguous expression of action by the system in the environment (Hazy, 2007b, 2012).
5. Process feedback information regarding success or failure of enactments in the environment or internal to the system, and translate this information into structural changes in the influence network among agents. This is done by changing the reputation and status of participating individuals and thus changing their relative influence (Hazy, 2007b, 2012).

Hazy argues that all of these aspects of leadership are facilitated either directly or indirectly by changing the rules of interaction. A theoretical framework for how these leadership mechanisms are actualized within a group of individuals in an organizational setting is discussed next.

MICROENACTMENTS WITHIN A CAS

By analogy with insect swarming behavior, an emergent process that has been studied intensely (Seeley, 2010), Hazy and Silberstang (2009a) suggest that individual interaction events in groups likewise can be understood as signaling behavior among individuals that culminates in a specific collective action—programs of action (PoAs)—independent of the specific content of the action being considered. Whereas bees swarm in search of a new nest (Seeley, 2010), humans "swarm" in an effort to act in concert with regards to any particular project being considered. Examples of PoAs around which people might "swarm" include the decision to disband a meeting or any social gathering, to initiate a project, or just to meet again the following week. Or they might involve taking a single step in a larger program: to launch as new product development effort, for example. When the relative status and thus influence of the various individuals involved is taken into account, the authors posit that this dance of interaction is actually how decisions are taken when the authority to make a decision is "in the room."

To explore this proposition, the authors go on to describe individual signaling behaviors, called "microenactments" (Hazy & Silberstang, 2009a, 2009b; Silberstang & Hazy, 2008). These include signals that *initiate* a PoA, *reject* it, *accept/imitate* it, *negotiate* to modify it, or *synthesize* it with others to form a qualitatively new project. Together these microenactments constitute a language of interaction that can enable action-in-concert. For efficiency, this language unfolds as separate enactments made by individuals, but they are experienced by others in the context of a shared grammar that enables action-in-concert. Aspects of the grammar might include such rules as when and how to propose new ideas (Beck & Chong, 2009), what constitutes a quorum that enables decisions that are binding on the group (Phelps & Hubler, 2006), and when to accept the decision of a quorum (Goldstein et al., 2010; Guastello, 2007).

Detailed research on the precise nature of the microenactments that individuals display as well as the grammars that enable shared meaning within this communication system might lead to a deeper understanding of human collective behavior. Although the palette might be distinct for each class of problem, there may also be commonalities, and these might shine additional light on the precise nature of leadership in daily practice. In the spirit of the interdisciplinary nature of complexity thinking, this same problem has also been addressed using an ABM framework by Panzar, Hazy, McKelvey, and Schwandt (2007).

Developing fields, like the leadership-as-practice research where the focus is on the dynamic activities of leadership rather than heroic individuals (Raelin, 2011), are linked to the complexity way of thinking. Here we see mutual influence among individuals with common objectives forming into collective action. Research into the precise nature of this process for different classes of problems might lead to a deeper understanding of human collective behavior. Independently, Mangiofico and Feyerherm (2011) have qualitatively identified many of the activities described by Hazy and Silberstang in a nonprofit organization. Likewise, research in shared leadership can be viewed in this way (Lord et al., 2011).

A Contrarian Challenge to Systems Thinking—Complex Responsive Processes

The focus of the complex responsive processes approach to complexity is in understanding the interpretive experience of the individual as human beings interact within complex human organizing activity (Griffin, 2001; Stacey, Griffin & Shaw, 2000). This approach distinguishes human complexity from the "systems approach" (Katz & Kahn, 1966; von Bertalanffy, 1950) arguing, in effect, that human organizing is not appropriately studied using systems models (Stacey, 1995). Instead, as Johannessen (2009) states:

> Taking a complexity approach means that the focus of research attention is drawn towards the exploration of the phenomenon of *human interaction* and *emergence*. Human interaction is the cause of emergence, and human interaction only creates further interaction and emergence. This is what is meant by a radical process view of reality. (p. 217)

The implication of this framing is that the focus of research is on the unfolding of experience, on the narratives themselves, rather than on structures or artifacts that can be modeled and studied using systems approaches.

Although coming from a different theoretical framing, the implications of this research stream are not that different from the system-based approaches described in previous sections. For example, in a case study Mangiofico and Feyerherm (2011) have integrated the notions of complex response processes with the systems perspective of Goldstein et al. (2010) to identify the four leadership skills that are implied by complexity thinking: (i) perpetually scanning the ecology to identify flows of information and resources; (ii) weaving webs of interaction among actors within and across boundaries; (iii) creating coherence among the signals that flow through these networks, what Goldstein, Hazy and Lichtenstein call "interaction resonance"; and (iv) support for expanding innovation by offering stabilizing feedback to converge activity toward a kind of dynamic stability that represents a new way of doing things. In a certain sense, these four principles frame the practical implications of the new perspective that is offered by complexity science.

The Emerging Complexity Paradigm

Figure 32.1 shows a new paradigm that is emerging. Complexity science provides conceptual tools for thinking about organizing (left box in the figure) and identifies key system demands that must be met if a CAS is to be effective at both performance and adaptation (right box). Three organizing mechanisms and their relationship to the leadership process were described in this chapter (center box). These can be used by managers to drive organizational outcomes. At the bottom of the figure we identify the challenges that all of this complexity brings forward for individuals who are asked to manage or to lead. These include complexity within a given situation such as during a large-scale project, as well as complexity that results from changes over time, as might be the case as technology advances more rapidly than ever. Each of these areas has implications for practice and begs further research.

This new paradigm is a significant contribution to leadership research because it begins to connect individual behaviors and actions to system processes, functions, and outcomes. To do so it explores the complexity dynamics within fine-grained HID in areas such as criticalization, and through the study of emergence, it also sheds light on how these might result in beneficial changes to the organization's coarse-grained properties. This perspective is new to leadership research, and it represents a significant advance in understanding that is only beginning to show its promise. A summary of representative empirical studies is shown in Table 32.1.

The Road Ahead

In 2007, Jennings and Dooley used textual analysis to identify the emergence of a new paradigm in complex systems leadership research. Five years later the synthetic analysis described herein has brought this paradigm into clearer focus. A review of the literature shows that a new theory has evolved in what can best be described as the abductive theorizing approach advocated in recent years by Max Boisot (2010). The new paradigm that has emerged both transcends and challenges prior research approaches. It transcends prior approaches in that it represents a general theory of HID consistent with analytical approaches used in the natural sciences. It

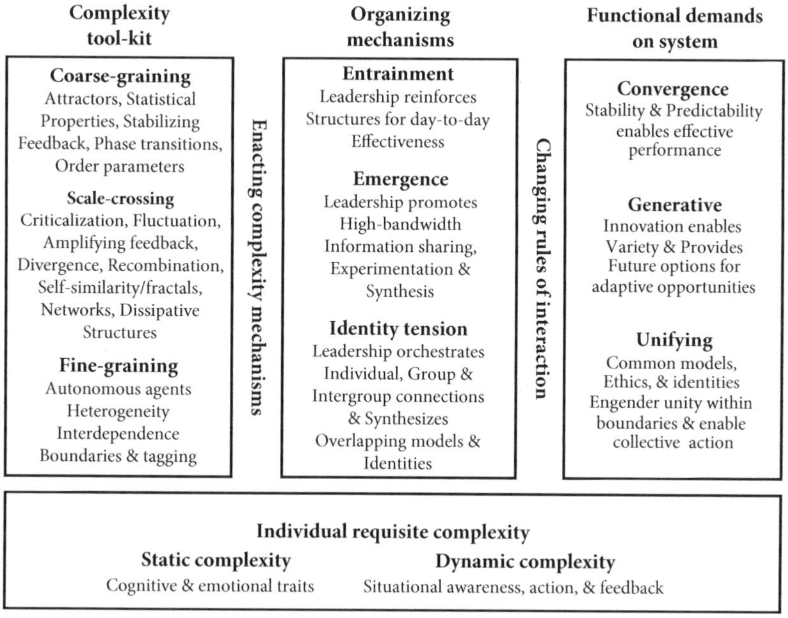

Figure 32.1. A 2013 View of the Emerging Complex Systems Leadership Paradigm Includes a Complexity Tool-kit of Ideas and the Organizing Mechanisms that can be Used to Satisfy the Functional Demands of a Complex Adaptive System.

Table 32.1. Empirical Studies Using Various Methods

Author(s)	Description	Method	Complexity Approach
Aasen & Johannessen (2007) Aasen & Berg (2008)	Innovation in the subsea technology development	Longitudinal industrial case ethnographic	Complex Responsive Processes
Backström (2009)	Resource generation in pharmacies	Case study	CSLT/Directing leadership
Backström, Hagström, & Göransson (2011)	Integration of employees in the company culture of a bank	Network analysis & survey	CSLT/Directing leadership
Backström, Wilhelmson, Olsson, Åteg, & Åberg (2011)	Training of first-line managers	Action learning network, survey and interview	CSLT/Directing leadership
Baker, Onyx, & Edwards (2011)	Community service projects	Network analysis & qualitative case study	CSLT/Generative Leadership
Beck & Chong (2009)	Community groups solving local problems	Action learning & participant observer	CSLT/Leadership of emergence
Buckle, Henning, & Dugan (2007)	Self-organized patterns in the workplace	Grounded Theory	CSLT
Dal Forno & Merlone (2007)	Project team formation and success	Laboratory study & Agent-model	CSLT/Convergent Leadership
Garud, Gehman, & Kumaraswamy (2011)	Innovation process at NCR	Case study	Complexity and innovation
Groot (2009)	Performance improvement at Dutch Railways	Case Study/personal reflection	Complex Responsive Processes
Guastello et al. (2004, 2005, 2007a, b)	Emergence of individuals as team leaders in simulation games	Laboratory Study	Nonlinear dynamical systems/ Game theory
Havermans, Den Hartog, Keegan, & Uhl-Bien (2010)	Leadership practices in project-based organizations	Qualitative/Interviews	Complexity Leadership Theory
Hazy (2008a)	18-month study of 50-person technology firm	Survey/case study	Leadership Meta-capability
Hazy (2004, 2008a)	Organizational Transformations: NCR & Intel	System dynamics modeling of case study	Leadership Meta-capability
MacGillivray (2010)	Leadership in community group	Phenomenographic study	Complexity Leadership Theory
Moerschell (2010)	Leadership emergence in recreational groups	Grounded theory	Complexity and punctuated equilibria
Phelps & Hubler (2007)	Emergent leadership in youth groups	Multi-Case study and agent-based model	Dynamical Systems & Bifurcation Theory
Plowman et al (2007a, b)	Transformation of a mission church	Case study	Leadership of emergence

(continued)

Table 32.1. Continued

Author(s)	Description	Method	Complexity Approach
Schreiber & Carley (2006)	Workgroups at NASA	Network Analysis	Dynamic Network Analysis
Shepherd, & Woods (2011)	Development Entrepreneurial business model	Case study	CSLT/Generative leadership
Surie & Hazy (2006)	Indian Manufacturing Companies	Case studies	CSLT/Generative Leadership
Tapsell & Woods (2009)	Maori of New Zealand	Case study	CSLT/Generative Leadership
Tobin, J. H. (2009)	US Hospital merger	Case study/personal reflection	Complex responsive Processes

challenges them in that its generality implies additional criteria and analytical techniques through which prior results may be evaluated.

Implications for Research

As this theory comes into focus, additional empirical research is needed to inform future iterations of CSLT. In this next phase of abductive theory development, it is increasingly important that quantitative methods be added to the mix so that constructs can be validated and relationships between them identified and tested with statistical methods. However, these methods must be implemented while cognizant of the limitations inherent in traditional methods when events are not independent and where individuals have different preferences, histories, and values.

To do this, a new way of thinking, new methods, and a new set of skills are needed. Tools like ABM, the mathematical treatment of dynamical systems, dynamic network analysis, and power-law analysis can all inform these new techniques. However, because the HID approach is qualitatively different from the interaction dynamics typically modeled in the natural sciences, many new technological advances are also needed (Prietula, 2011).

As a result, quantitative research in CSLT will require advances on many levels, and many of these will need to be built fresh, from the ground up. It will involve changing the rules of interaction among all of those who are engaged in leadership research and practice. This is perhaps the greatest challenge of all: the new paradigm is not just another way of thinking about leadership; it is also a new way of thinking about social science more generally. The magnitude of this challenge is daunting, certainly. But the potential benefits of action—particularly given the many challenges that face the world in the coming decades—make a focused effort toward a new and better way forward not merely a choice to be taken. It is an ethical imperative.

Implications for Practice

These developments also have significant implications for practice and thus for leadership development. One of these is the realization that leadership development must go far beyond the current focus on individual self-understanding and communications skills. In the fast-moving economy of the 21st century, individuals will need tools to help them better understand the nonlinear effects in their ecosystems. These are increasingly being enabled by social media and sociotechnical networks. It would be beneficial to be able to anticipate how various possible interventions might influence emergent outcomes, and then learn to respond quickly and thoughtfully to unfolding events in real-time.

We expect that leadership development programs will increasingly be characterized by computer assisted simulations which express real-life organizations as CAS, in a manner analogous to flight simulators in the airline industry or battlefield simulations in the military. One of the advantages that CSLT provides is a theoretical framework within which one could identify opportunities for management interventions. The potential exists that in the not-too-distant future, computer simulations could be used to evaluate actions of individuals and groups and then present to the user the likely outcomes at the coarse-grained levels under various scenarios.

Not only would this be useful in training, it could also be used to pretest actions to explore possible unintended consequences. With better information, more informed action could be contemplated, and possible contingencies could be better evaluated.

The CSLT approach is a useful and important advance in any case. By making managers aware of the conditions that imply different types of leadership action, and by clarifying what actions lead to which outcomes in a given situation, the process of enacting leadership becomes more understandable as a capability to be learned. This is distinct from more cultish approaches to leadership development that treat "leadership" as a "mysterious" or "authentic" attribute of certain special individuals, one that is hidden deep within a person's soul and can never be fully understood. Rather than leaving us to trust that certain special people will reach inside themselves to lead us where they believe we should go, CSLT exposes the HID that each of us can influence to construct the world in which we choose to live.

Future Directions

The advancement of complex systems leadership theory has brought to the fore several important research questions:

1. How should the ubiquity of interdependent heterogeneity in HID be treated rigorously when modeling complex systems leadership events and when analyzing empirical data? New statistical techniques are needed that take into account individual learning and memory and path dependence with regards human interactions that limit the validity of many traditional methods (Hazy & Ashley, 2010).
2. What are the precise mechanisms of emergence in HID? What is the role of leadership in this process? Can the number and duration of experiments be quantified to determine if potential success is sustained through reinforcing feedback?
3. By what mechanisms do *constraints* on human interaction dynamics imply the particulars of emergent coarse-grained properties? How are constraints and their impacts measured? For example, how are constraints to resources, such as financial, human, temporal, and technological, linked to leadership actions and outcomes? How do changes to the constraints translate into qualitatively different properties? What is the role of leadership in this process?
4. How do individuals who are seeking to have an impact recognize coarse-grain properties, determine the need to change them, and then translate this into complex systems leadership actions that locally change the rules of interaction in ways that alter these emergent properties as intended?
5. By what mechanisms do individual agents influence the local rules of interactions of others? What is the role of identity? Of ethics?
6. By what mechanisms do fine-grained interactions imply specific coarse-grained properties? How do changes in local rules become manifest in qualitative changes in the emergent properties? Is the analogy with phase transitions informative for this?
7. By what mechanisms do coarse-grained properties entrain fine-grained rules of interaction in HID? How is this related to leadership as well as to cultural norms, institutional effects, etc.?
8. When focusing on the rules that govern local interactions, how are these rules recognized, developed, shared, remembered, adapted, and replicated? What role do identities play in storing, sharing, and evolving rules of interaction? How do ethics play into this question?
9. Can examples of collective agency with regard coarse-grained organizing forms in HID be identified and shown to be ontologically distinct from individual intention and action? What would this mean for leadership research?
10. What are the implications of this new paradigm for leadership development programs going forward?

Notes

1. In a later section we describe a competing approach, Complex Responsive Processes (CRP) put forth by Stacey (1993), which challenges the systems approach entirely.
2. Constructive deviations are ad hoc experiments performed with the intention of achieving some purpose; this idea is distinct from the notion of "positive deviance," which is a post hoc analysis and intervention technique used to identify positively performing subgroups (outliers) in populations facing many of the same challenges. The positively deviant solutions are then analyzed and understood before being replicated more broadly across the population (Pascale, Sternin, & Sternin, 2010). This technique could presumably be applied with positive effect to evaluate the relative success of the constructive deviations described herein as they are occurring within organizations that are experiencing criticalization.

References

Aasen, T., & Berg, M. (2008). A complexity perspective on innovation processes for subsea technology development. *International Journal of Learning and Change, 3*(3), 294–307.

Aasen, T.M.B., & Johannessen, S. (2007). Exploring innovation processes from a complexity perspective. Part II: Experiences from the SIOR case. *International Journal of Learning and Change, 2*(4), 434–446.

Allen, P. (2001). What is complexity science? Knowledge of the limits to knowledge. *Emergence: A Journal of Complexity Issues in Organizations and Management, 3*(1), 24–44.

Anderson, P. (1999). Complexity theory and organization science. *Organization Science, 10*(3), 216–232.

Andriani, P. (2011). Complexity and innovation. In P. Allen, S. Maguire, & B. McKelvey (Eds.), *The Sage handbook of complexity and management* (pp 454–470). Los Angeles, CA: SAGE.

Anneloes, M. L. Raes, Heijltjes, M. G., Glunk, U., & Roe, R. A. (2011). The interface of the top management team and middle managers: A process model. *Academy of Management Review, 36*(1), 102–126.

Ashby, W. R. (1956). *An introduction to cybernetics*. London: Chapman and Hall;

Axelrod, R. (1984) *The evolution of cooperation*. New York, NY: Basic Books

Backström, T. (2009). How to organize for local resource generation. *The Learning Organization, 16*(3), 223–236.

Backström, T., Hagström, T., & Göransson, S. (2011). *Communication as a mechanism for culture integration*. Paper presented at the 55th annual meeting of the international society for the system sciences, University of Hull, Hull, UK.

Backström, T., Wilhelmson, L., Olsson, B. K., Åteg, M., & Åberg, M. M. (2011). The role of manager in the post-industrial work system. In E. Seglod, E. Berglund, E. Bjurström, E. Dahlquist, L. Hallén, & E. Johansson (Eds.), *Studies in industrial renewal* (pp. 215–227). Västerås: Mälardalen University Press.

Bak, P., & Paczuski, M. (1995). Complexity, contingency, and criticality. *Proceedings of the National Academy of Sciences of the USA, 92* (15), 6689–6696.

Baker, E., Onyx, J., & Edwards, M. (2011). Emergence, social capital and entrepreneurship: Understanding networks from the inside. *Emergence: Complexity and Organization, 13*(3), 31–45.

Barnard, C. I. (1938). *The functions of the executive*. Cambridge, MA: Harvard University Press.

Barney, J. B. (1991). Firm resources and sustained competitive advantage. *Journal of Management, 17*(1), 99–120.

Beck, D., & Chong, L.C. (2009). Creative interaction in culturally diverse groups. In The emergence of collective identity as a means for creating and sustaining social value. In J. Goldstein, J. K. Hazy, & J. Silberstang (Eds.), *Complexity science and social entrepreneurship* (pp. 487–506). Litchfield Park, AZ: ISCE Publishing.

Boal, K. B., & Schultz, P. L. (2007). Storytelling, time and evolution: The role of strategic leadership in complex adaptive systems. *The Leadership Quarterly, 18*, 411–428.

Boisot, M. (2010). *Connecting the dots before the world does*. Paper presented at the annual meeting of the Academy of Management, Montreal.

Boisot, M., & McKelvey, B. (2007). *Extreme events, power laws, and adaptation: Towards an econphysics of organization*. Academy of Management Conference Best Papers Proceedings, Philadephia, PA, (August 3–8).

Boisot, M., & McKelvey, B. (2010). Integrating modernist and postmodernist perspectives on organizations: A complexity science bridge. *Academy of Management Review, 35*(3), 415–433.

Bossidy, L. & Charan, R. (2002). *Execution: The discipline of getting things done*. New York: Crown Business.

Boyatzis, R. E. (2008). Leadership development from complexity perspective. *Consulting Psychology Journal: Practice and Research, 60*(4), 298–313.

Brown, S., & Eisenhardt, K. (1997). The art of continuous change: Linking complexity theory and time-based evolution in relentlessly shifting organizations. *Administrative Science Quarterly, 42*, 1–34.

Brown, S., & Eisenhardt, K. (1998). *Competing on the edge: Strategy as structured chaos*. Boston, MA: Harvard Business School Press.

Buckle-Henning, P., & Dugan, S. (2007). Leader's detection of problematic self-organized patterns in the Workplace. In J. K. Hazy, J. Goldstein, & B. B. Lichtenstein (Eds.), *Complex systems leadership theory* (pp. 386–412). Mansfield, MA: ISCE Publishing Company.

Cilliers, P. (1998). *Complexity and postmodernism: Understanding complex systems*. London: Routledge.

Crossan, M. M., Lane, H. W., & White, R. E. (1999). An organizational learning framework: From intuition to institution. *Academy of Management Review, 24*(3), 522–537.

Crossan, M., Gandz, J., & Seijts, G. (2010). *Cross-Enterprise Leadership: Business Leadership for the Twenty-First Century*. New Jersey: Wiley.

Cyert, R., & March, J. (1963). *A behavioral theory of the firm*. Englewood Cliffs, NJ: Prentice-Hall.

Dal Forno, A., & Merlone, U. (2007). The emergence of effective leaders: An experimental and computational approach. In J. K. Hazy, J. Goldstein, & B. B. Lichtenstein (Eds.), *Complex systems leadership theory* (pp. 205–226). Mansfield, MA: ISCE Publishing Company.

Denis, J-L., Langley, A., & Pineault, M. (2000). Becoming a leader in complex organizations. *Journal of Management Studies, 37*(8), 1063–1099.

Dooley, K. J. (1997). A complex adaptive systems model of organization change. *Nonlinear Dynamics, Psychology and Life Sciences, 1*(1), 69–97.

Dooley, K. J. (2007). Leadership and a computational model of organizations. In J. K. Hazy, J. Goldstein, & B. B. Lichtenstein (Eds.), *Complex systems leadership theory* (pp. 327–322). Mansfield, MA: ISCE Publishing Company.

Dosi, G., Nelson, R. R., & Winter, S. G. (2000). *The nature and dynamics of organizational capabilities*. Oxford: Oxford University Press.

Drucker, P. F. (1966). *The effective executive*. New York: Harper & Row, Publishers, Inc.

Fleishman, E. A. (1953). The description of supervisory behavior. *Personnel Psychology, 37*, 1–6.

Garud, R., Kumaraswamy, A., & Sambamurthy, V. (2006). Emergent by design: Performance and transformation at Infosys Technologies. *Organization Science, 17*, 277–286.

Garud, R., Gehman, J., & Kumaraswamy, A. (2011). Complexity arrangements for Sustained innovation: Lessons from 3M Corporation. *Organization Studies, 32*, 737–767.

Gell-Mann, M. (2002). What is complexity? In A. Q. Curzio & M. Fortis (Eds.), *Complexity and industrial clusters: Dynamics and models in theory and practice* (pp.13–24). Berlin: Physica-Verlag.

Goldstein, J. (1989). A far-from-equilibrium systems approach to resistance to change. *Organizational Dynamics, 17*, 16–26.

Goldstein, J. A. (2007). A new model of emergence and its leadership implication. In J. K. Hazy, J. Goldstein, & B.

B. Lichtenstein (Eds.), *Complex systems leadership theory* (pp. 61–92). Mansfield, MA: ISCE Publishing Company.

Goldstein, J. A. (2011). Emergence in complex systems. In P. Allen, S. Maguire, & B. McKelvey (Eds.), *The Sage handbook of complexity and management* (pp 65–78). Thousand Oaks, CA: SAGE.

Goldstein, J., Hazy, J. K., & Lichtenstein, B. (2010). *Complexity and the nexus of leadership: Leveraging nonlinear science to create ecologies of innovation.* Englewood Cliffs, NJ: Palgrave Macmillan.

Griffin, D. (2001). *The emergence of leadership: Linking self-organization and ethics.* London: Routledge.

Groot, N. (2009). Senior executives and the emergence of local responsibilities: A complexity approach to identity development and performance improvement. *International Journal of Learning and Change, 3*(3), 264–280.

Guastello, S. J. (2002). *Managing emergent phenomena: Nonlinear dynamics in work organizations.* Mahwah, NJ: Lawrence Erlbaum Associates.

Guastello, S. J. (2007). Nonlinear dynamics and leadership emergence. *The Leadership Quarterly, 18*(4), 357–369.

Guastello, S. J., & Bond, R. W. J. (2004). Coordination learning in Stag Hunt games with application to emergency management. *Nonlinear Dynamics, Psychology, and Life Sciences, 8,* 345–374.

Guastello, S. J., & Bond, R. W. J. (2007a). The emergence of leadership in coordination intensive games. *Nonlinear Dynamics, Psychology, and Life Sciences, 11,* 91–117.

Guastello, S. J., & Bond, R. W. J. (2007b). A swallowtail catastrophe model of leadership in coordination-intensive games. *Nonlinear Dynamics, Psychology, and Life Sciences, 11,* 235–351.

Guastello, S. J., Craven, J., Zygowicz, K. M., & Bock, B. R. (2005). A rugged landscape model for self-organization and emergent leadership in creative problem solving and production groups. *Nonlinear Dynamics, Psychology and Life Sciences, 9*(3), 297–233.

Guastello, S. J., & Guastello, D. D. (1998). Origins of coordination and team effectiveness: A perspective from game theory and non-linear dynamics. *Journal of applied psychology, 83*(3), 423–437.

Haken, H. (2006). *Information and self-organization: A macroscopic approach to complex systems* (3rd ed.). Berlin: Springer.

Hannah, S. T., Eggers, J. T., & Jennings, P. L. (2008). Complex adaptive leadership: Defining what constitutes effective leadership for complex organizational contexts. In G. B. Graen & J. A. Graen (Eds.), *Knowledge-driven corporation: Complex creative destruction* (pp. 79–124). Charlotte, NC: Information Age Publishing.

Hannah, S. T., Jennings, P. L., & Nobel, O. B-Y. (2010). Tactical military leader requisite complexity: Toward a referent Structure. *Military Psychology, 22*(4), 412–449.

Hannah, S. T., Woolfolk, R. L., & Lord, R. G. (2009) Leader self-structure: A framework for positive leadership. *Journal of Organizational Behavior, 30,* 269–290.

Hannan, M. T., & Freeman, J. (1989). *Organizational ecology.* Cambridge, MA: Harvard University Press.

Hargadon, A. B., & Bechky, B. A. (2006). When collections of creatives become creative collectives: A field study of problem solving at work. *Organization Science,* 17(4), 484-500.

Havermans, L., Den Hartog, D., Keegan, A., & Uhl-Bien, M. (2010). *Leadership in project-based organizations: Applying and extending complexity leadership theory through qualitative exploration.* Working Paper.

Hazy, J. K. (2004). *A leadership and capabilities framework for organizational change: Simulating the emergence of leadership as an organizational meta-capability,* Doctoral Dissertation, The George Washington University, Washington, DC.

Hazy, J. K. (2006). Measuring leadership effectiveness in complex socio-technical systems. *Emergence: Complexity and Organization (E:CO), 8*(3), 58–77.

Hazy, J. K. (2007a). Computer models of leadership: Foundation for a new discipline or meaningless diversion? *The Leadership Quarterly, 18*(4), 391–410.

Hazy, J. K. (2007b). *Leading Large: How disambiguation and changing reputations enable back-propagation learning in complex organizations.* Paper presented at the Leadership Quarterly FestSchift in Honor of Dr. Jerry Hunt, Lubbock, TX. (Oct. 12–15, 2007).

Hazy, J. K. (2008a). Leadership or luck? The system dynamics of Intel's shift to microprocessors in the 1970s and 1980s. In M. Uhl-Bien, R. Marion, & P. Hanges (Eds.), *Complexity leadership, part I: Conceptual foundations* (pp. 347–378). Charlotte, NC: Information Age Publishing.

Hazy, J. K. (2008b). Toward a theory of leadership in complex systems: Computational modeling explorations. *Nonlinear Dynamics, Psychology, and Life Sciences, 12*(3) 281–310.

Hazy, J. K. (2008c). Patterns of leadership. The system dynamics of Intel's shift to microprocessors in the 1970s and 1980s. In M. Uhl-Bien, R. Marion, & P. Hanges (Eds.), *Complexity leadership, part I: Conceptual foundations* (pp. 379–390). Charlotte, NC: Information Age Publishing.

Hazy, J. K. (2009). Innovation reordering: Five principles for leading continuous renewal. In S. Schlomer & N. Tomaschek (Eds.), *Leading in complexity: New ways of management* (p. 300). Seiten: Verlag fur Systemische Forschung.

Hazy, J. K. (2011a). Parsing the influential increment in the language of complexity: Uncovering the systemic mechanisms of leadership influence. *International Journal of Complexity in Leadership and Management, 1*(2), 164–192.

Hazy, J. K. (2011b). *Leadership as process: A theory of formal and informal organizing in complex adaptive systems.* Adelphi University School of Business Working Paper: SB-WP-2011-02.

Hazy, J. K. (2011c). Unifying leadership: Shaping identity, ethics and the rules of interaction. *International Journal of Society Systems and Science, 4*(3), 222–241.

Hazy, J. K. (2012). Leading large organizations. *International Journal of Complexity in Leadership and Management, 3*(1/2), 52–71.

Hazy, J. K. (2013). *U.S. Patent No. 8,612,270 B2.* Washington, DC: U.S. Patent and Trademark Office.

Hazy, J. K., & Ashley, A. (2011). Unfolding the future: Bifurcation in organizing form and emergence in social systems. *Emergence: Complexity and organization, 13*(3), 77–91.

Hazy, J. K., Goldstein, J. A., & Lichtenstein, B. B. (Eds.). (2007a). *Complex systems leadership theory.* Mansfield, MA: ISCE Publishing Company.

Hazy, J. K., Goldstein, J., & Lichtenstein, B. B. (2007b). Complex systems leadership theory: An introduction. In J. K. Hazy, J. Goldstein, & B. B. Lichtenstein (Eds.), *Complex systems leadership theory* (pp. 1–17). Mansfield, MA: ISCE Publishing Company.

Hazy, J. K., Millhiser, W. P., & Solow, D. (2007). Mathematical and computational models of leadership: Past and future. In J. K. Hazy, J. Goldstein, & B. B. Lichtenstein (Eds.), *Complex systems leadership theory* (pp. 386–412). Mansfield, MA: ISCE Publishing Company.

Hazy, J. K., Moskalev, S., & Torras, M. (2009). Toward a theory of social value creation: Individual agency and the use of information within nested dynamical systems. In J. A. Goldstein, J. K. Hazy, & J. Silberstang (Eds.), *Complexity science and social entrepreneurship* (pp. 257–281). Litchfield Park, AZ: ISCE Publishing.

Hazy, J. K., Moskalev, S, & Torras, M. (2010). Mechanisms of social value creation: Extending financial modeling to social entrepreneurship and social innovation. *International Journal of Society Systems Science, 2*(2), 134–157.

Hazy, J. K., & Silberstang, J. (2009a). Leadership within emergent events in complex systems: Micro-enactments and the mechanisms of organisational learning and change. *International Journal of Learning and Change, 3*(3), 230–247.

Hazy, J. K., & Silberstang, J. (2009b). The emergence of collective identity as a means for creating and sustsaining social value. In J. A. Goldstein, J. K. Hazy, and J. Silberstang (Eds.), *Complexity science and social entrepreneurship* (pp. 447–470). Litchfield Park, AZ: ISCE Publishing.

Helfat, C. E., Finkelstein, S., Mitchell, W., Peteraf, M. A., Singh, H., Teece, D. J., & Winter, S. G. (2007). *Dynamic capabilities: Understanding strategic change in organizations*. Malden, MA: Blackwell Publishing.

Hogue, M., & Lord, R. G. (2007). A multilevel, complexity theory approach to understanding gender bias in leadership. *The Leadership Quarterly, 18*(4), 370–390.

Holland, J. H. (1975). *Adaptation in natural and artificial systems*. Cambridge, MA: The MIT Press.

Hooijberg, R. (1996). A multidirectional approach to leadership: An extension of the concept of behavioral complexity. *Human Relations, 49*, 917–946.

Hunt, J, G., Osborne, R. N., & Boal, K. B. (2009). The architecture of managerial leadership: Stimulation and channeling of organizational emergence. *The Leadership Quarterly, 20*, 503–516.

Jaques, E. (1989). *Requisite organization*. Arlington, VA: Cason Hall.

Jennings, P. L., & Dooley, K. J. (2007). An emerging complexity paradigm in leadership research. In J. K. Hazy, J. Goldstein, & B. B. Lichtenstein (Eds.), *Complex systems leadership theory* (pp. 17–34). Mansfield, MA: ISCE Publishing Company.

Johannessen, S. (2009). The complexity turn in studies of organisations and leadership: Relevance and implications. *International Journal of Learning and Change, 3*(3), 214–229.

Johannessen, S., & Aasen, T.M.B. (2007). Exploring innovation processes from a complexity perspective, part I: Theoretical and methodological approach. *International Journal of Learning and Change, 2*(4), 420–433.

Katz, D., & Kahn, R. L. (1966). *The social psychology of organizations* (2nd ed.). New York, NY: John Wiley & Sons.

Kauffman, S. (1995). *At home in the universe*. Oxford: Oxford University Press.

Kuhn, T. S. (1962). *The structure of scientific revolutions*. Chicago, IL: University of Chicago Press.

Levick, D., & Kuhn, L. (2007). Fractality, organizational management and creative change. *World Futures, 63*(3–4), 265–274.

Levinthal, D. A. (1997). Adaptation on rugged landscapes. *Management Science, 43*(7), 934–950.

Lichtenstein, B., & McKelvey, B. (2007). Leadership in the four stages of emergence. In J. K. Hazy, J. Goldstein, & B. B. Lichtenstein (Eds.), *Complex systems leadership theory* (pp. 93–108). Mansfield, MA: ISCE Publishing Company.

Lichtenstein, B., & Plowman, D. A. (2009). The leadership of emergence: A complex systems leadership theory of emergence at successive organizational levels. *The Leadership Quarterly, 20*, 651–661.

Lichtenstein, B. B., Uhl-Bien, M., Marion, R., Seers, A., Orton, J. D., & Schreiber, C. (2006). Complexity leadership theory: An interactive process on leading in complex adaptive systems. *Emergence: Complexity and Organization (E:CO), 8*(4), 2–12.

Lord, R. G., Hannah, S. T., & Jennings, P. L. (2011). A framework for understanding leadership and individual complexity. *Organizational Psychology Review, 1*(2), 104–127.

Lord, R. G., Hannah, S. T., & Pearce, C. (2011). A framework for understanding leadership and individual complexity. *Organizational Psychology Review, 1*(2), 104–127.

MacGillivray, A. (2010). Leadership in a network of communities: A phenomenographic study, *The Learning Organization, 17*(1), 24–40.

MacIntosh, R., & MacLean, D. (1999). Conditioned emergence: A dissipative structures approach to transformation. *Strategic Management Journal, 20*, 297–316.

Mangiofico, G., & Feyerherm, A. E. (2011). *The case for using a complexity perspective as applied to leadership*. Working Paper.

March, J. G. (1991). Exploration and exploitation in organizational learning. *Organization Science, 2*, 71–87.

Marion, R., & Uhl-Bien, M. (2001). Leadership in complex organizations. *The Leadership Quarterly, 12*(4), 389–418.

McKelvey, B. (1997). Quasi-natural organization science. *Organization Science, 8*, 352–380.

McKelvey, B. (2004). Toward a complexity science of entrepreneurship. *Journal of Business Venturing, 19*, 313–342.

Meyer, A. D., Gaba, V., & Colwell, K. A. (2005). Organizing far from equilibrium: Nonlinear change in organizational fields. *Organization Science, 16*(5), 456–473.

Mitchell, M., Hraber, P., & Crutchfield, J. P. (1993). Revisiting the edge of chaos: Evolving cellular automata to perform computations. *Complex Systems, 7*, 89–130.

Moerschell, L. (2010). The intersection of punctuated equilibrium and leadership emergence within the framework of naturalistic decision making. *Journal of Outdoor Recreation, Education and Leadership, 2*(2), 1–4.

Morrison, K. (2010). Complexity theory, school leadership and management: Questions for theory and practice. *Educational Management Administration & Leadership, 38*(3), 374–393.

Nelson, R. R., & Winter, S. G. (1982). *An evolutionary theory of economic change*. Cambridge, MA: The Belknap Press of Harvard University Press.

Nowak, M., Tarnita, C. E., & Wilson, E. O. (2010, Aug. 26). The evolution of eusociality. *Nature, 466*, 1057. doi: 10.1038/nature0920

Panzar, C., Hazy, J. K., McKelvey, B., & Schwandt, D. R. (2007). The paradox of complex organizations: Leadership as integrative influence. In J. K. Hazy, J. Goldstein, & B. B. Lichtenstein (Eds.), *Complex systems leadership theory* (pp. 305–326). Mansfield, MA: ISCE Publishing Company.

Pascale, R., Sternin, J., & Sternin, M. (2010). *Power of positive deviance: How unlikely innovators solve the world's toughest problems*. Cambridge, MA: Harvard University Press.

Peterson, M. F., & Meckler, M. R. (2001). Cuban-American entrepreneurs: Chance, complexity and chaos. *Organization Studies, 22*(1), 31–57.

Phelps, K. C,. & Hubler, A. (2007). Toward an understanding on membership and leadership in youth organizations: Sudden changes in average participation due to the behavior of one individual. In J. K. Hazy, J. Goldstein, & B. B. Lichtenstein (Eds.), *Complex systems leadership theory* (pp. 195–204). Mansfield, MA: ISCE Publishing Company.

Plowman, D., Baker, L. T., Beck, T., Kulkarni, M., Solansky, S., & Travis, D. (2007a). Radical change accidentally: The emergence and amplification of small change. *Academy of Management Journal, 50*(3), 515–543.

Plowman, D., Baker, L. T., Beck, T., Kulkarni, M., Solansky, S., & Travis, D. (2007b). The role of leadership in emergent, self-organization. *The Leadership Quarterly, 18*(4), 341–356.

Prietula, M. J. (2011) Thoughts on complexity and computational models. In P. Allen, S. Maguire, & B. McKelvey (Eds.), *The Sage handbook of complexity and management* (pp 93–100). Thousand Oaks, CA: SAGE.

Prigogine, I. (1995). *The end of certainty: Time, chaos, and the new laws of nature.* New York, NY: The Free Press.

Prigogine, I., & Stengers, I. (1984). *Order out of Chaos.* New York, NY: Heinemann.

Prokopenko, M., Boschetti, F., & Ryan, A. J. (2009). An information-theoretic primer on complexity, self-organization and emergence. *Complexity*, ISSN 1099-0526, *15*(1), 11–28.

Raelin, J. (2011). From leadership-as-practice to leaderful practice, *Leadership, 7*(2), 195–211.

Richardson, K. (2010). *Thinking about complexity.* Lichfield Park, AZ: Emergent Publishing.

Schneider, M., & Somers, M. (2006). Organizations as complex adaptive systems: Implications of complexity theory for leadership research. *The Leadership Quarterly, 17*(4), 351–365.

Schreiber, C., & Carley, K. M. (2006). Leadership style as an enabler of organizational complex functioning. *Emergence: Complexity and Organization, 8*(4), 61–76.

Seeley, T. (2010). *Honeybee democracy.* Princeton, NJ: Princeton University press.

Selznick, P. (1948). Foundations of the theory of organizations. *American Sociological Review, 13*, 25–35.

Shepherd, D., & Woods, C. (2011). Developing digital citizenship for digital tots: Hector's World Limited. *Emergence: Complexity and Organization, 13*(3), 16–30.

Shoup, J. R., & Studer, S. C. (2010). *Leveraging choas: The mysteries of leadership and policy revealed.* Lanham, MD: Rowman & Littlefield Education.

Siggelkow, N., & Rivkin, J. (2005). Speed and search: Designing organizations for turbulence and complexity. *Organization Science, 16*, 101–122.

Silberstang, J., & Hazy, J. K. (2008). Toward a micro-enactment theory of leadership and the emergence of innovation. *The Innovation Journal: The Public Sector Innovation Journal, 13*(3), Article 5.

Simpson, P. (2007). Organizing in the mist: A case study of leadership and complexity. *Leadership and Organization Development Journal, 5*, 465–482.

Simon, H. A. (1997). *Administrative behavior: A study of decision-making processes in administrative organizations* (4th ed.). New York, NY: The Free Press.

Solow, D., & Leenawong, C. (2003). Mathematical models for studying the value of cooperative leadership in team replacement. *Computational and Mathematical Organization Theory, 9*(1), 61–81.

Solow, D., & Szmerekovsky, J. G. (2006). The role of leadership: What management science can give back to the study of complex systems. *Emergence: Complexity and organization, 8*(4), 52–60.

Stacey, R. D. (1993). *Strategic management and organization dynamics.* London: Prentice Hall.

Stacey, R. D. (1995). The science of complexity: An alternative perspective for strategic change processes. *Strategic Management Journal, 16*, 477–495.

Stacey, R. D., Griffin, D., & Shaw, P. (2000). *Complexity and management: fad or radical challenge to system thinking?* London: Routledge.

Stogdill, R. M. (1974). *Handbook of leadership: A survey of the literature.* New York, NY: Free Press.

Streatfield, P. J. (2001). *The paradox of control in organizations.* London: Routledge.

Surie, G., & Hazy, J. K. (2006). Generative leadership: Nurturing innovation in complex systems. *Emergence: Complexity and Organization (E:CO), 8*(4), 13–26.

Tapsell, P., & Woods, C. (2009). A spiral of innovation framework for social entrepreneurship: Social innovation at the generational divide in an indigenous context. In J. A. Goldstein, J. K. Hazy & J. Silberstang (Eds.), *Complexity science and social entrepreneurship* (pp. 471ï486). Litchfield Park, AZ: ISCE Publishing.

Teece, D. J., Pisano, G., & Shuen, A. (1997). Dynamic capabilities and strategic management. *Strategic Management Journal, 18*(7), 509–533.

Thietart, R-A., & Forgues, B. (1995). Chaos Theory and Organization. *Organization Science, 6*, 19–31.

Tobin, J. H. (2009). The myth of rational objectivity and leadership: The realities of a hospital merger from a CEO's perspective. *International Journal of Learning and Change, 3*(3), 248–263.

Tsoukas, H. (2005). *Complex knowledge: Studies in organizational epistemology.* Oxford: Oxford University Press.

Uhl-Bien, M., & Arena, M. (2013). Complexity Leadership: Leading the Adaptive Organization. Working paper.

Uhl-Bien, M., & Marion, R. (2009). Complexity leadership in bureaucratic forms of organizing: A meso model. *The Leadership Quarterly, 20*, 631–650.

Uhl-Bien, M., & Marion, R. (2011). Complexity leadership theory. In A. Bryman, D. Collinson, K. Grint, B. Jackson, & M. Uhl-Bien (Eds.), *The Sage Handbook of Leadership* (pp. 468–482). London: Sage.

Uhl-Bien, M., Marion, R., & McKelvey, B. (2007). Complexity leadership theory: Shifting leadership from the industrial age to the knowledge era. *The Leadership Quarterly, 18*, 298–318.

von Bertalanffy, L. (1950). The theory of open systems in physics and biology. *Science, 3*, 23–29.

Wheatley, M. J. (1999). *Leadership and the new science: Discovering order in a chaotic world.* San Francisco, CA: Berrett-Koehler.

Zaccaro, S. J. (1999). Social complexity and the competencies required for effective military leadership. In J. G. Hunt, G. E. Dodge, & L. Wong (Eds.), *Out-of-the-box leadership: Transforming the twenty-first century Army and other top performing organizations* (pp. 131–151). Stamford, CT: JAI Press.

CHAPTER

33 Women and Leadership

Jean Lau Chin

Abstract

Differences and similarities between men and women are identified in the research on women and leadership. The contexts of leadership, including follower perceptions and expectations as well as the nature of the leadership-member relationship are important influences in how women lead. Underrepresentation and the existence of gender bias frame the context of leadership for women. Current theories of leadership typically omit the discussion of gender, feminist values, or principles of diversity. Organizational cultures remain male dominated and do not strive toward gender-equitable work environments although ethics-based leadership, diversity leadership, collaborative leadership, and transformational leadership styles favoring the leadership of women are viewed as important dimensions of leadership today. Although the behavior of men and women leaders is similar, leadership for women remains a different experience. Future directions must consider the importance of leadership contexts and leader identity including work-family interface, affirmative paradigms, lived experience, and multiple dimensions of self-identity.

Key Words: Women and leadership, gender differences, gender bias, collaborative leadership, diversity and leadership, lived experience, leader identity, transformational leadership style, contexts of leadership, Leader-Member relationship

Introduction

Rapid technological advances and social change together with the growing population diversity in the United States and globally demand attention to who our leaders are, who make up their followers, and the contexts in which they lead. In the 21st century, we need to go beyond current leadership paradigms that show a bias (Den Hartog & Dickson, 2004) reflecting organizational structures and cultures of North American organizations run by white Anglo heterosexual males. More women now work outside the home, and have increasingly moved toward greater gender equality at home and in the workplace. Changes in gender roles and lifestyles have occurred with men now sharing more in household chores and childrearing. Social rules of etiquette and gender roles are now more flexible, making equity within the marital relationship more common. So much has changed; yet, so much has not.

Underrepresentation of Women Leaders

When organizational and political leaders in the United States were homogeneously white men, mainly from elite backgrounds, their gender, race, and ethnicity were unremarkable. However, much is changing in the United States and globally. Although white men still predominate as leaders, the increasing presence of women and of racial and ethnic minorities as leaders is unmistakable in the United States. Yet, women are still underrepresented in leadership roles in corporations, institutions of higher education, and the political sector despite their growing presence in the workforce and the gains in equality following the women's movement of the 1960s. For example, among chief executives of all US organizations in the public and private sector, 23 per cent are women, 4 per cent black, 4 per cent Asian, and 5 per cent Hispanic (US Bureau of Labor Statistics, 2009). Only 12 Fortune 500 companies are run by women or 2 per cent. Of the members of the 111th Congress, 17 per cent are women, 8 per cent African American, 1 per cent Asian American, and 6 per cent Hispanic American (Infoplease, 2009).

Women are still considered an anomaly compared to men when in high positions of leadership. Women as chief executives are still a relatively new phenomenon such that they make news or the covers of *Fortune* magazine just by holding the position. Indvik (2004) points to the scarcity of women in higher levels of corporate leadership. While women made up 46.6 per cent of the workforce in the United States, they filled only 15.7 per cent of corporate officer positions in 2002. She suggests that sex differences in worldview, socialization, and life experience may result in different mental models or "implicit theories" of leadership among women.

Women held 23.0 per cent of president positions at all colleges and universities while men held 77.0 per cent in 2006, according to the most recent survey by the American Council on Education (American Council on Education, 2007). Few women reach the top in higher education although women increasingly enter the ranks of academia making up 57 per cent of lecturers and instructors, but only 24 per cent of full professors. As with corporate America, the percentage of women in academic positions drops off the higher they climb.

More women are now heads of state in countries around the world and CEOs of corporations—common definitions of formal leadership positions. *Forbes 2007 Review of the World's Most Powerful Women* identified Chancellor of Germany Angela Merkel in first place; Wu Yi, vice premier of the People's Republic of China in second place, nicknamed the "iron lady" of China. *Forbes* list of the World's Most Powerful Leaders in 2009 identified only 3 women of 61 leaders—Angela Merkel, chancellor of Germany; Hillary Clinton, US secretary of state; and Oprah Winfrey, entertainer.

Access to Leadership Roles

Women and racial/ethnic minorities face barriers in ascending to leadership positions compared with men of comparable strengths and talents—a phenomenon often described as the glass ceiling. Now that more women are in such positions of leadership, Eagly and Carli (2007) has described this process as a "labyrinth" that one must navigate. Once in these roles, women and racial/ethnic leaders in the United States have often been placed in double-bind situations or been victims of double standards used to evaluate their leadership. In a world where male dominance is prevalent in society's institutions, access for women to leadership roles becomes a problem.

We can evaluate the leadership of several significant women leaders throughout history to understand the influence of context, and the perception and expectation of followers on the leadership of women. Empress Dowager Cixi from China (wikipedia, 2007) was a powerful and charismatic figure who became the de facto ruler of the Manchu Qing Dynasty; many considered her reign despotic. Cleopatra VII's (wikipedia, 2007) reign in Egypt marked the end of the Hellenistic Era and the beginning of the Roman Era in the Eastern Mediterranean. She was the last pharaoh of Ancient Egypt; though a powerful political figure, her legend lies in her image as a great seductress who allied herself with two of the most powerful men (Julius Caesar and Mark Antony) of her time. Joan of Arc was a 15th-century national heroine of France, known for her trial and execution for heresy at the age of 19, a judgment that was later overturned by the pope. Her leadership and valor on the battlefield was renown in her attempt to recapture Paris (Wikipedia, 2007).

All three women leaders were noted for their uncharacteristic leadership. Both Cleopatra and Empress Dowager Cixi emerged as leaders by seizing power, ascended to power through their seduction of men, and reigned because of their alliance with the men of their times; their route to power and leadership are generally viewed as invalid, tyrannical, and exercised in a masculinized context. Joan of Arc died a martyr not unlike the victims of the Salem witch hunts, in which women were feared and executed because their "mysterious powers" threatened the power of men. Women before the 20th century were not accepted as leaders in a world that men ruled and dominated, within societies of warrior images, conquerors and imperialism, and subjugation of third world countries through a system of colonialism.

In a review of the 50 most powerful women in business cited by *Fortune* magazine in 2006,

36 per cent have retired or resigned their positions compared to 16 per cent of the 25 most powerful men in business cited by *Fortune* in 2007. Some of the most powerful women leaders in the corporate sector, (e.g., Carol Bartz, CEO of Yahoo; Carly Fiona, former CEO of Hewlett Packard; Cathleen Black, former CEO Hearst) were removed citing their inability to turn things around. Would a man have been forgiven more easily?

Follower-Centric Notions about Women Leaders

These historical images of women leaders reflect how they are marginalized. This has not changed today where women leaders are often described by their clothing fashion in the media rather than by the strength of their leadership. Moreover, their depiction as being "feminine" is often a double-edged sword—to be "too feminine" is to risk being perceived as weak and emotional or as manipulative and devious when exercising leadership; to be "insufficiently feminine" generally results in being labeled as masculine, abrasive, or pushy. When Nancy Pelosi was elected as House Minority leader in 2002, she became the first woman ever to head a party in either chamber of the US legislature. McGrory (Boston Globe, 2002) wrote, "He is called the Hammer. She's a velvet hammer. He is Tom DeLay, the newly elected House majority leader, who is all coercion and threat. She is Nancy Pelosi of California, who is all persuasion and smiles." This description reflects the gender bias and differential language used to describe women leaders in masculinized contexts. Though pointing to Nancy Pelosi's collaborative and interpersonal strengths, the description reflects the tendency to "feminize" women leaders to suggest weakness or incredulity when women behave as decisive and effective leaders. Consider the mixed images about Hillary Clinton, secretary of state, who brought disdain because of her strong, "unfeminine" style, and was "redeemed" during her run for president when she cried and showed emotion.

Bias Toward Women

Followers often associate qualities to leaders that are inherent in the personality of the leader. They may view leaders as and expect them to behave according to their expectations, including (1) role model (i.e., setting an example), (2) talent in having a specific skill for the organization, (3) initiative and entrepreneurial drive, (4) charisma (i.e., attractiveness to others and the ability to leverage this esteem to motivate others), (5) inspirational (i.e., instill passion or cultivating an environment that brings out the best of individuals), and (6) commitment or visionary (i.e., clear sense of purpose or mission driven). However, it is unclear how dimensions of gender, race, and ethnicity confound these assessments of leadership and the conferring of leadership status.

How might we understand the underrepresentation and bias toward women? Researchers have asked whether adjusting for observable human capital variables (e.g., education, training, and job experience) and structural factors (e.g., occupational segregation) would account for the lesser workplace advancement and lower wages among women and minorities. The nearly unanimous conclusions are that such variables account for only a portion of gender and race gaps in wages and promotions and that discrimination is a contributing factor (e.g., Blau & Kahn, 2006; Grodsky & Pager, 2001; Maume, 1999).

In attempting to detect discrimination, researchers have conducted experiments that equate job applicants in all respects other than the attribute (race or gender) that is suspected to trigger discrimination. Although many of these experiments are conducted with resumes presented to students and other participant groups, other experiments are far more naturalistic *audit* studies in which job applications or actual applicants are presented to employers (see Pager, 2007; Riach & Rich, 2002). These experiments reveal discrimination harmful to women, although not in female-dominated jobs such as secretary, where this bias reverses to disadvantage men (see meta-analysis by Davison & Burke, 2000). Experimental studies have shown that discrimination is particularly potent against mothers (Correll, Bernard, & Paik, 2007; Heilman & Okimoto, 2008) and African Americans (e.g., Bertrand & Mullainathan, 2004).

AVERSIVE SEXISM AND STEREOTYPED THREAT

Aversive racism, termed by Dovidio and Gaertner (2004), reflects unintentional or unconscious discriminatory evaluations of racial/ethnic minority individuals because of underlying anxiety about race and ethnicity. Such social perceptions and expectations also apply to women, and often result in more exacting standards for women than those applied to men. Thus, *aversive sexism* influences negative evaluations of women and works to their disadvantage in leadership roles.

These biases and stereotypes associated with gender and race also influence the performance of women and racial/ethnic minorities. Steele (1997) found that diverse individuals might underperform in situations where they are evaluated on a domain in which they are regarded, on the basis of stereotypes, as inferior—which he termed stereotyped threat. Specifically, presenting participants with gender stereotypical portrayals of women prior to a group task caused the women (but not the men) to be less interested in being the group leader and more interested in being a follower (Davies, Spencer, & Steele, 2005).

ROLE INCONGRUITY

It is likely that bias toward women occurs because the roles of women and that of leaders are perceived as incongruous. Eagly and Karau (2002) suggest that perceived incongruity between female gender role and leadership roles leads to two forms of prejudice: (a) perceiving women less favorably than men as potential occupants of leadership roles, and (b) evaluating behavior that fulfills the prescriptions of a leader role less favorably when it is enacted by a woman. Consequently, it is more difficult for women to become leaders and to achieve success in leadership roles.

Eagly (1987) also found that women leaders were evaluated differently and less favorably than men even when performing the same leadership behaviors. They were expected to engage in activities and actions congruent with their culturally defined gender roles; leadership was typically not one of them. Forsyth, Heiney, & Wright (1997) found that group members favor men over women when selecting and evaluating leaders, even when actual leadership behaviors are held constant in a variety of group settings. They examined this role-incongruence hypothesis in small groups led by women who adopted a relationship- or task-oriented leadership style. Group members with liberal attitudes regarding women's roles responded positively to both leadership types. Group members with conservative attitudes felt the task-oriented leader was more effective, but they also rated her more negatively on measures of collegiality. These results suggest that reactions to women leaders are tempered by expectations about the role of women and men in contemporary society.

Evaluations of leaders often include characteristics associated with leaders and leadership, but actually have little to do with effectiveness. Given that white males have typically occupied leadership positions, evaluations of leader effectiveness often favor male characteristics of height, whiteness, and masculinity. Consequently, the context of masculinized norms and the expectations about "what a leader looks like" introduce conditions of bias against women and racial/ethnic minority leaders. It raises challenges that are not faced by white Anglo males.

Perceptions and Expectations of Women Leaders

How do people think about women as leaders? Within the American culture, they are likely to be regarded as un-leader like. Women are more likely to be perceived as communal and interpersonal, possessing traits of warmth and gentleness that appear more tailored for subordinate and service roles (Kite, Deaux, & Haines, 2008; Newport, 2001). This is reflected in the tendency for there to be more women in service professions such as teaching and nursing. Men are more likely to be perceived as task oriented and associated with traits of decisiveness that appear more tailored for leadership roles. While these perceptions may have a basis in actual behaviors, their stereotypic portrayal of men and women results in disadvantaging women. According to the interpersonal interaction leadership perspective, men and women leaders will have different types of social interactions with their men and women supervisors and subordinates, and these will influence the outcomes experienced by each party (Ayman, 1993). A meta-analysis of leader stereotypes (Koenig, 2011) demonstrated that stereotypes of leaders are culturally masculine, with greater agency than communion traits although this masculine construal of leadership is decreasing over time.

IN-GROUP PREFERENCES VS. OUT-GROUP SCAPEGOATING

Pittinsky (2010) frames this as in-group out-group issues in leadership in which positive and negative beliefs toward out-groups often coexist. Given that individuals will deny any conscious belief in stereotypes while harboring unconscious mental associations that affirm stereotypes (described earlier as aversive sexism or racism), fully qualified individuals from "outsider" groups (e.g., women and minorities) will often appear to lack the "right stuff" for leadership. Perceived as deficient in essential qualities for leadership, they have reduced access to leadership (Heilman & Eagly, 2008; Leslie, King, Bradley, & Hebl, 2008).

The tendency to like and associate with others who are similar to oneself (in-group preference) exacerbates the biases stemming from gender and cultural stereotypes (e.g., Byrne & Neuman, 1992), and results in out-group suspicion. As a result, women and minorities are likely to face entry barriers to important networks because they are unlike those within the in-group. Yet, such access to influential social networks is essential to building the social capital that allows people to emerge as leaders and become effective in leader roles (e.g., Brass, 2001). Moreover, women and members of racial or ethnic minority groups who gain positions of leadership are sometimes resented because they overturn the expected and usual hierarchical relations between groups (Sidanius & Pratto, 1999). These perceptions and expectations reduce the access of women and of racial and ethnic minorities to leadership roles.

CREDIBLE LEADERSHIP

These masculinized contexts and biases toward women raise the question of credible leadership. Popular advice to potential leaders often urges them to maintain a leader-like image, and to "dress for success." In an environment where suits and ties dominate, can women dressed in feminine garb or ethnic minorities dressed in ethnic garb be credible, or do they project "un-leader like" images that may, in fact, have little to do with effective leadership? We saw this in the 1980s where women entering the corporate world began wearing pin striped suits with padded shoulders and ties, mimicking the business garb of men. While this phenomenon is less pronounced today, women and ethnic minorities still need to consider whether what they wear could be a distraction from their leadership or fit stereotypic images of being too feminine or too ethnic, and therefore, un-leader like.

Another challenge to credibility is the communication styles of women who tend to have softer, high-pitched voices which may be perceived as being less commanding than a loud, booming male voice. This is reflected in the common observation of their being ignored or not being yielded the floor to speak by others; hence, it serves to disempower women as leaders.

LEADER-CENTRIC APPROACH TO UNDERSTANDING WOMEN AND LEADERSHIP

Much of the research on leadership has been leader-centric in identifying the traits of leaders, and identifying the leadership styles of leaders. Presumably, this leads to selection of those most suited for leadership roles. At a time when leaders were typically white, Anglo males, this approach appeared to reflect the goal of selecting the "best candidates." When attention was directed to dimensions of diversity including gender, race, and class, it results in outcomes that, in effect, exclude women and ethnic minorities. As attention to women and leadership emerged, identifying leader traits shifted to identifying differences between men and women leaders, and a tendency to dichotomize traits that mirror differences between feminine and masculine styles.

Is There a Difference between Women and Men in How They Lead?

Women and leadership has been extensively researched (Eagly & Carli, 2007) and suggest that the answer to this question is complex; Yes and No. Theories of leadership are typically neutral or absent in their attention to gender as if "a leader is a leader" while studies on leadership typically ignore gender differences or mostly study white men. While self-reports of differences between men and women are common, few empirical differences have been found between women and men in the exercise of leadership (Eagly and Johnson 1990); they often show that men and women leaders behave more alike than different when occupying the same positions. Why is it then that the strength of these perceptions persists?

LEADERSHIP TRAITS AND STYLES

We often perceive traits associated with leaders that may not have much with to do effective leadership; these characteristics are often embraced by leaders themselves. Terms like "he looks like a leader"; "he is presidential, charismatic, or a visionary" are all terms used to describe leaders. They often capture what followers want in their leaders—which, in turn, are influenced by social constructions of leadership that do impact leadership styles.

Studies of leadership have been largely confined to men for the simple reason that they have historically held most of the leadership roles in society and its institutions. Although there is general agreement that women face more barriers to becoming leaders than men do, especially for leader roles that are male dominated (Eagly & Carli, 2007), there is much less agreement about how women actually lead.

PERSON ORIENTATION

Several studies (e.g., Bass & Avolio, 1994) found women to be more attentive than men to "the human side of enterprise" (McGregor, 1985), suggesting that female leaders tend to base judgments more on intuition and emotions than on rational calculation of the relationships between means and ends, more toward social stereotypes of being more interpersonal, selfless, and concerned with others. This is often distinguished as a person orientation over task orientation with women viewed as having an advantage.

DEMOCRATIC AND COLLABORATIVE PROCESS

Research thus has demonstrated that women have a somewhat more democratic and participative style than men (Trinidad & Normore, 2005), perhaps because people resist women who take charge in a particularly assertive manner. Female leaders are also somewhat more transformational than male leaders, especially in mentoring and developing workplace colleagues. And somewhat more than men, women adopt a positive managerial approach that trades on rewards rather than a negative approach that trades on reprimands. All of these tendencies have emerged in meta-analyses of studies of the leadership style of women and men (Eagly & Johnson, 1990; Eagly, Johannesen-Schmidt, & van Engen, 2003; van Engen & Willemsen, 2004).

There is strong evidence to support the tendency for women to adopt a more collaborative, cooperative, or democratic leadership style and for men to adopt a more directive, competitive, or autocratic style; this emerged in all types of studies. Even though selection criteria for leadership positions may even out the gender differences, women seem to be intentionally different and more collaborative based on differences in personality and social interpersonal skills. The use of a collaborative process is increasingly central to views of effective leadership.

TRANSFORMATIONAL LEADERSHIP STYLE

A meta-analysis of transformational, transactional, and laissez-fire leadership styles among women (Eagly, Johannesen-Schmidt, & van Engen, 2003) found that female leaders were more transformational than male leaders and also engaged in more of the contingent reward behaviors that are a component of transactional leadership. Male leaders were generally more likely to manifest the other aspects of transactional leadership (active and passive management by exception) and laissez-faire leadership. Although these differences were small, the implications are encouraging because it identifies areas of strength in the leadership styles of women. A transformational style is also consistent with feminist principles of inclusion, collaboration, and social advocacy. Despite stereotype-based suspicions that women might not be effective leaders, these ways that women differ from men in leadership style are generally associated with good managerial practices in current-day organizations (e.g., Judge & Piccolo, 2004).

Lived Experiences of Women Leaders

Given the biases and challenges faced by women leaders, leadership remains a different experience for women and men (Eagly & Carli, 2007, p. xviii) as they "navigate a labyrinth" to reach top leadership positions. As women, their lived experiences include growing up in male-dominant societies and facing social expectations associated with gender roles, and needing to negotiate work-family balance in their lives. As women, they are likely to hold leadership roles through community and service leadership positions as wives and mothers.

Their lived experiences challenge historic theories of leadership drawn primarily from the experiences of white men leading in contexts governed by male values and white middle class norms. Current definitions of leadership in the corporate world include full-time work, and career tracks that do not factor in discontinuities related to childrearing or childbearing responsibilities. Women's time away from their careers are often viewed as reflecting their lesser commitment to the job and disinterest in career advancement. Leadership and leadership styles, as a result, are viewed from a masculine perspective and evaluated against masculine norms. It is increasingly clear that cultural worldviews, socialization of gender roles, and different life experiences do contribute to one's resulting philosophy and style of leadership. Women leaders also face challenges in eliciting more negative nonverbal affect responses from others for the same suggestions and arguments compared to men (Butler & Geis, 1990). There operates a social mechanism that causes devaluation of women's leadership. The implications are that repeated exposure to negative nonverbal affective responses when attempting to exercise leadership could result in women withdrawing from the opportunities when presented. Hence, there are more obstacles making women's journey in navigating the labyrinths more challenging.

Does Difference Make a Difference?

In *Women and Leadership* (Chin, Lott, Rice, & Sanchez-Hucles, 2007), the experience of leadership as different was pronounced among more than 100 feminist women leaders. This includes added stressors of being expected to behave according to gender and race/ethnicity stereotypic norms and managing work-family balance. Case examples suggest that an African American woman may identify with the values of straightforwardness and assertiveness in their leadership style while an Asian American woman may identify with values of respectfulness and unobtrusiveness. However, others may perceive the direct confrontational style of an African American woman as intimidating and deem the use of an indirect and teaching style of an Asian American woman as passive (Sanchez-Hucles, 2003). Hall, Garrett-Akinsanya, & Hucles (2007, p. 283) define black feminist leaders as "Black activists who, from the intersections of race and gender, develop paths, provide a direction, and give voice to black women." Kawahara, Esnil, & Hsu (2007, p. 310), in their interviews, found that Asian American women leaders held a collectivistic view of their leadership styles, and used bicultural values in order to achieve their leadership goals. Native American women described their leadership as "stand[ing] beside, rather than behind, [their] men in their effort to preserve their tribes and treaty rights" (Kidwell, Willis, Jones-Saumty, & Bigfoot, 2007, p. 327). They will not distance themselves from their men because of the inherent threat posed by broader society against their men if they were to distance themselves. These case examples need further investigation, but suggest that different leadership styles are influenced by culture differences.

Diverse women leaders from these racial/ethnic groups defined their leadership relative to their historical experiences and cultural values. They believed that differences do make a difference. They believed their leadership styles were aligned with their worldviews and cultural perspectives, and that being a leader was not divorced from gender and racial/ethnic identities, but rather a dimension of self-identity. However, the significance of this difference in experience compared with white Anglo men is not well understood as to how it influences the exercise of leadership or the interaction between a leader and the group. Because women are the "out-group" relative to men, differences in their exercise of leadership are likely to be viewed as negative or deficient.

Leader Identity

When we ask the question, "Does difference make a difference?," it may be a matter of the leader's identity in which we find little discussion in the literature. A leader's identity is often expected to embody characteristics the group desires, especially when group members view themselves as homogenous. Often these characteristics are tied to social constructions associated with race, ethnicity, and gender. When a leader is perceived as being different from these expectations, gender and racial/ethnic stereotypes may prevail in defining his/her identity and effectiveness as a leader. Men and leaders are often admired for their "assertiveness" defined as being direct and confronting while the same behavior by women may define her as "a bitch," "a dragon lady," or "acting like a man." Witness the public's response to the presidential campaigns of Barack Obama and Hillary Clinton. Both were challenged on traits associated with race and gender as when Barack Obama was called early on to address his views on race (Obama, 2008) and questioned about his birth in the United States, implying that he was a "foreigner" and did not have a right to be president while Hillary was deemed that "iron lady" until she cried. Both were challenged on their competence and deficiencies as leaders based on their lack of experience as US senators—Barack for being a community organizer and Hillary for being first lady. Leader identity can be based not only on these stereotypic notions that constrain behavior, but also on how a leader views his/her sense of self, which will include dimensions of diversity including gender, race, ethnicity, sexual orientation, etc. Yet, theories of leadership would have us believe that gender and ethnicity is inconsequential to leadership.

AUTHENTICITY

Contemporary theories of leadership have begun to consider leader identity by endorsing the importance of authenticity in today's leaders—"in knowing who they are, what they believe and value" (Avolio, Gardner, Walumbwa, Luthans, & May, 2004, p. 803). Avolio (2007) defined authentic leadership development as considering the dynamic interplay between leaders and followers, taking into account the prior, current, and emerging contexts in explaining what actually improves or develops leadership. Feminist leaders would do well to contemplate authenticity in leadership and to realize that achieving authenticity can be a more difficult matter for female than male leaders (Eagly, 2005).

MULTIPLE AND INTERSECTING DIMENSIONS OF IDENTITY

The focus on leader traits and leadership styles does not factor in a leader's identity while women and racial/ethnic minority leaders often find their identities as women, as racial/ethnic individuals, as mothers, etc., important dimensions of their identity as a leader. These multiple dimensions all intersect with one another. For women, the challenges of work-family balance, caretaking responsibilities, gender role expectations, and connectedness are significantly greater than for men. Racial/ethnic minority individuals often have affiliations with multiple communities reflecting their social identities and racial/ethnic affiliations. Maintaining one's authenticity as a leader can be challenging when needing to negotiate these multiple and intersecting dimensions of identities. We need to move beyond single dimensions of identity in our theorizing, and instead investigate multiple and intersecting identities if we are to obtain a more comprehensive understanding of how diversity contributes to important phenomena such as leadership (Chin & Sanchez-Hucles, 2007).

DIVERSE WOMEN LEADERS

In studying diverse women leaders, Chin et al. (2007) found that feminist women often embrace leadership styles that are value driven, ethics based, social change oriented, and transformational. They generally preferred using a collaborative process, empowering followers, and promoting inclusiveness. Their pursuit of an egalitarian model of leadership reflects a desire to level power dynamics inherent in the leader-follower relationship. At the same time, many of these diverse women leaders felt constrained by the masculinized contexts in which leadership was exercised where this is not sanctioned. As a result, they felt the need to use more hierarchical leadership styles to be effective, be viewed as decisive, or as exercising leadership rather than using a more collaborative process.

Many feminist women often sought leadership positions to achieve social justice goals and gender equity, striving to be transformational in their vision, empowering in their actions, and upholding of ethical principles. These principles often were felt to be at odds with strivings for power and status, which they believed to be more commonly associated with men. Many of the women felt constrained to follow institutional rules defined by masculinized norms, and needing to compromise feminist principles in their leadership styles to be effective.

The influence of these identities on leadership is reflected in a comment by Lorene Garrett-Browder (Chin et al., p. 57) who suggests that "African American women throughout history have been able to be effective leaders despite living in oppressive environment and dealing with power structures that do not always include our voice...Consequently, African American women (leaders might tend to use more direct communication styles and) have used our anger as an ally to help us speak the truth...even though it may be unpopular." In a context of oppression and power, value is placed on trust and fairness to accept leadership from an African American perspective. This approach places an emphasis on parity and social justice.

Ann Yabusaki (Chin et al., 2007, p. 55) suggests that Asian American women may use more indirect communication in their leadership styles. In Asian cultures, the balance of opposites and emphasis on the yin and the yang can bring out the best in leadership enriched by different perspectives. She identifies "how the emphasis on hierarchy influences ways in which leaders and authority figures communicate in Asian cultures (resulting in the expectation and tendency of Asian leaders) to teach or convey a moral message when communicating." When this communication operates within a context that values kinship bonds and elders, the concept of benevolent authority is ascribed to leaders in the Asian culture.

These examples suggest that diverse women leaders may hold different views about assertiveness and express their leadership in different ways. Yet, their competence and effectiveness as leaders may be defined by social role stereotypes and expectations. Asian American women may need to learn how to "toot one's horn" without losing one's modesty or to "speak up" although the Asian culture values listening. Native American women may need to learn how to "get a seat at the table", and not wait to be asked. The challenge for diverse women leaders is to learn that it is a different game governed by different rules while transforming the organizational culture in the process.

These racial/ethnic identities that represent people's psychological relationships to their social groups can constrain their behavior (Frable, 1997; Phinney, 1990). For example, Cheung and Halpern (2010) explain how some women import mothering metaphors into their understanding of leadership. Fassinger, Shullman, & Stevenson (2010) discuss whether the assumptions that leaders and followers make about sexuality constrain or enhance the capacities that lesbian and gay leaders bring to leadership. Sanchez-Hucles & Davis (2010) suggest that identities pertaining to race and ethnicity affect the ways in which individuals lead.

Is There a Feminine Advantage?

While an examination of follower-centric approaches reveal biases and perceptions that disadvantage women and racial/ethnic minorities as leaders, researchers of women and leadership have raised the question of a feminine advantage (e.g., Eagly A., 2007). In encountering negative appraisals and portrayals of their effectiveness as leaders, women and diverse leaders may seek to portray themselves from positions of strength while others having little association with these identity group members as leaders may lack insight concerning their potential benefits as leaders (e.g., Ayman & Korabik, 2010; Cheung & Halpern, 2010). In response to such doubts and resistance to their leadership, many have posed the question of a feminine advantage for women leaders compared with men based on their tendencies toward greater connectedness, nurturing, and collaborative styles. For example, several female managerial writers have provided particularly laudatory descriptions of women's leadership styles as interactive and inclusive (e.g., Chin et al., 2007; Helgesen, 1990; Rosener, 1990). Related superiority claims have emerged concerning leadership by African American women (Parker, 2005; Parker & Ogilvie, 1996) and gay men (Snyder, 2006). Such claims of advantage can reflect instances of group pride noted by Pittinsky (2010).

It is also possible that these claims accurately reflect the superior performance that can emerge from having one's abilities challenged on the basis of membership in a group that has usually been excluded from leadership or have been historically oppressed. For example, research has shown that women who are confident about their leadership ability are not deterred by statements that women have less leadership ability than men but instead react by exhibiting even more competence than they do in the absence of an explicit challenge (Hoyt & Blascovich, 2007). In addition, it is plausible that that diverse leaders can perform especially well to the extent that they had to meet a higher standard to attain leadership roles in the first place. A common belief is that women and racial/ethnic minorities must meet higher standards to be accorded competence and agency, a phenomenon that has been demonstrated in many contexts (see reviews by Biernat, 2005; Foschi, 2000).

Yet another rationale for thinking that diverse individuals are often good leaders is that the differences in lived experiences of these individuals do confer special qualities. Individuals from racial and ethnic minority groups, in particular, generally have multicultural experience because they have learned to negotiate both minority and majority cultures. Multicultural competence can foster flexibility and openness to change (Musteen, Barker, & Baeten, 2006), an ability to shift one's thinking between contexts (Molinsky, 2007), and promote creative cognitive processes and problem solving (Leung, Maddux, Galinsky, & Chiu, 2008).

Despite these possible advantages of diverse leaders, their good performance is not necessarily recognized as outstanding (Eagly & Carli, 2007). For example, studies of female and male managers show that, despite women's generally good managerial functioning, they tend to be judged as less effective than men in male-dominated roles and masculine settings. Moreover, female leaders who are made equivalent to male leaders in their qualifications and behavior in controlled experiments receive somewhat lower evaluations than these men, especially if they behave in culturally masculine ways and are portrayed in male-dominated roles (Eagly, Makhijani, & Klonsky, 1992). Such findings demonstrate that leader behavior is only one determinant of their effectiveness. Effective leadership is also related to the transaction between leaders and followers as well as follower expectations and prejudices, and the contexts in which leadership is exercised.

While Vecchio (2003) believes this feminine advantage is overstated, Eagly & Carli (2003) demonstrates the association of female communal style with gains in leader effectiveness, but acknowledges that women also suffer some disadvantages from prejudicial evaluations of their competence as leaders, especially in masculine organizational contexts. Recent findings suggest that once women break through the glass ceiling, they may experience a leadership advantage relative to men. Specifically, when women succeed in top-level positions, they are more likely to be viewed as highly agentic, and their communal characteristics are more likely to be considered beneficial due to the changing construction of what it means to be a good leader. Effective leaders not only need to be achievement oriented, competitive, decisive, and independent but also must recognize the importance of building strong relationships, collaborating with others, and taking care of their employees through coaching and development. That is, when women reside in top leader roles, the successful occupation of the position by a woman conveys information to observers that may augment their evaluation of the woman top leader. Our findings suggest that these enhanced evaluations occurred because women were perceived to face higher standards than men and were expected to engage in increasingly valued feminized management tactics (Rosette & Tost, 2010).

Stressors for Women Leaders

Iwasaki, MacKay, and Ristock (2004) explored the experiences of stress (e.g., negative and positive aspects of stress, different levels of stress, lack of sleep, pressure, financial stressors, being a manager) among both female and male managers. In addition to substantial similarities, a number of important gender differences emerged. Gender continues to be socially constructed in society; specifically, there are differing gender role expectations and responsibilities for women and men. Female managers experienced "emotional stress," primarily because of the pressure to meet expectations of being responsible and caring for people both inside and outside of their home. In contrast, male managers tended to focus on themselves and regard other things as beyond their control or responsibility. These stressors reflect the different experiences of women leaders and the different contexts in which they lead even when all conditions appear to be the same.

Contexts in the Exercise of Leadership

In a meta-analysis of gender and leadership style (Eagly & Johnson, 1990), gender differences did not emerge in organizational studies between interpersonal vs. task-oriented style. However, stereotypic gender differences did emerge in laboratory experiments and assessment studies, that is, studies when participants were not selected for holding a leadership position. Social perceptions and expectations apparently influence the leadership styles of women leaning toward being more relationship based when in situations of self-assessment or when appointed to leadership roles in laboratory studies. Men conformed more toward the social stereotypes of being more task oriented, self-assertive, and motivated to master their environment while women conformed more toward social stereotypes of being more interpersonal, selfless, and concerned with others.

Groups that bring together diverse individuals have been shown to outperform more homogeneous groups because they ordinarily include members with differing ways of representing and solving problems (Hong & Page, 2004; Page, 2007). These multiple perspectives can help deter the dangers of groupthink (Baron, 2004). Diversity in composition of group members brings advantages because the best solutions to complex problems generally result from teams that apply differing tools and skills. The challenge for organizations is to leverage this potential by promoting diversity in groups and its leaders while working to lessen the conflict, communication barriers, and lack of mutual respect that can develop between in-group and out-group members (e.g., Polzer, Milton, & Swann, 2002; see review by Van Knippenberg & Schippers, 2007). Leaders who are themselves from groups traditionally excluded from leadership are likely to have the multicultural competence to manage the challenges of a diverse workgroup to reap its advantages.

Servant and Shared Leadership

Some have attempted to transform these leader-member relationships to more egalitarian ones by redefining the relationship as one of servant leaders to their followers. Servant Leadership was developed by Robert K. Greenleaf (1977) and has become one of the more popular leadership models today. Servant leaders achieve results for their organizations by giving priority attention to the needs of their colleagues and those they serve. They are humble stewards of their organization's resources (human, financial and physical). Servant leadership was made popular with the late Dr. Martin Luther King Jr., and has been described as one of the ways in which President Obama is representative of the modern ethnic minority leader, demonstrating by his work early in his career as a community organizer. He used the community and a sense of purpose beyond himself as he orchestrated one of the most inclusive and expansive presidential campaigns in the history of the United States of America; his message was about the people and the goals he was trying to reach and solve for a collective good.

In most contexts today, top-down, command-and-control leaders no longer provide the most effective or admired type of leadership (Eagly & Carli, 2007; Kanter, 1997). In response to these changes, scholars of leadership have increasingly emphasized that effective leadership emerges from inspiring, motivating, and mentoring followers. Such leadership is embedded in interpersonal exchanges and dialogues in organizations in which leadership is distributed throughout the organization as both followers and leaders take responsibility for adapting to challenges (e.g., Graen & Uhl-Bien, 1995; Spillane, 2006)—often described as shared leadership.

DOUBLE BINDS

Gender biases and attributions constrain women's leadership behaviors and create double-bind situations that may contribute to their feeling marginalized or weak if they behave in feminine ways and criticized if behave in masculine ways. All too often, "feminine" emotionality is rated negatively as a weakness with respect to leadership while "feminine" nurturing is viewed as lacking in substance. Conversely, women leaders adopting "masculine" behaviors are also viewed negatively as aggressive and overbearing while aggressive and direct male leaders are viewed as forthright and taking charge. Much research has shown that task-oriented competencies have come to be associated with leadership success, whereas expressive, person-oriented qualities are generally given low weight in the determination of leadership (Korabik, 1990). Female leaders are often expected to take charge and lead in the same ways as their male colleagues. At the same time, female leaders are expected to be warm and nurturing as culturally prescribed for women. Simultaneously impressing others as a good leader and a good woman is often challenging to achieve with common pitfalls of appearing "too masculine" or "too feminine."

Negotiating between masculine and feminine traits apparently seems to push women leaders toward a relatively androgynous style that incorporates both (Eagly & Karau, 2002). Women also perceive a need to adapt their behavioral style so men do not feel intimidated (Ragins, Townsend, & Mattis 1998) and that a narrower range of behavior is acceptable behavior exists for female leaders than for male leaders (Eagly, Makhijani, & Klonsky, 1992).

MASCULINIZED CONTEXTS

Women leaders more commonly lead in the context of a male advantage, that is, masculinized contexts (Fletcher, 2003a); they are evaluated and perceived differently from men based on our current gender related biases. Ethnic minority women leaders are often questioned in subtle and indirect manners that question their competence or assume they got to where they did because of affirmative action, not because they can do the job.

We need to view leadership as contextual, value driven, diversity inclusive, and collaborative. We look to transform models of leadership—to identify diverse leadership styles across diverse groups, to embrace core values that motivate those in leadership roles, and to identify effective leadership styles for men and women to achieve the outcomes they envision for the organizations and institutions they lead. Transforming leadership is not that men cannot or should not be leaders. It is that women can and should be effective leaders without needing to change their essence or to adopt those values that are not syntonic with their gender or culture. It is about using feminist principles to promote pathways to leadership, recognizing the obstacles, and drawing on its strengths. It is about measuring and identifying effective leadership styles that are not simply based on identifying the characteristics of good male leaders. It is about how issues of power, privilege, and hierarchy that influence the contexts in which leadership occur.

This bias toward women leaders result in double-bind situations when they feel compelled to conform to conflicting role expectations associated with gender and leadership. Are they to be feminine women and be perceived as weak or strong leaders and be perceived as too domineering? Whereas current organizations typically conform to masculinized norms more congruent for men, women leaders can at a disadvantage when exercising behaviors that contradict such expectations or when they are compelled to conform to these norms. The organizational culture, that is, context in which leadership occurs, is important to understand since much of leadership involves managing the organization and realizing its purpose. Women leaders often manage within masculinized contexts and must adapt their leadership styles accordingly. These contexts often constrain women leaders with expectation to behave consistent with their gender roles. At the same time, these same behaviors may be defined as signs of ineffective leadership.

Leadership for the 21st Century

Reflecting the influence of contexts on leadership, leadership theorists are beginning to define criteria for effective leadership in the 21st century and the need to respond to a rapidly changing world. Whereas the 20th century was characterized by the Industrial Revolution in which manufacturing and the production of goods made significant advances, the 21st century has been characterized by the focus on rapid change, a digital age, and the production of services. Advances in technology have reduced the need for physical strength and labor, most jobs have been redefined and depend less on the physical characteristics that differ between men and women. Global concerns in the 21st century include fear of terrorism, global climate change, health care reform, all reflecting the need and wish to create a safe world, and healthy sustainable environments for diverse communities. With the growing presence of multinational organizations, growth in power of former third world countries, and the changing population demographics within countries globally, one might argue that we need public and transformational leaders to govern our nations, thought leaders to plan our future, ethical and authentic leaders in our corporations, and global citizens in higher education able to prepare us for a new future. Leaders in the 21st century will need to motivate change and influence followers to work toward mutual purposes; this has come to mean needing to be visionary, inspirational, authentic, and transformational in their leadership styles. Leaders need to embody and be empathic with the needs and hopes of their followers.

Postindustrial Concepts of Leadership

Rost (1991, p. 102) contributed a postindustrial concept of leadership for the 21st century, which he defined as "an influence relationship among leaders and followers who intend real changes that reflect their mutual purposes." He distinguishes a leader's influence from his authority, having active rather than passive followers, intending real changes from one's that just happen, and mutual purpose as a process. This emphasis expanded the study of leadership traits to a focus on the exchange that occurs between leaders and followers, as in leader-member exchange theories (Graen & Uhl-Bien, 1995), and has the potential for addressing the complexity of how gender and diversity interacts with the exercise of leadership and affect the quality of leader-follower relations. To examine leadership as the interaction between leader and follower in a group, we must ask what types of leadership are needed for what types of groups in today's global and diverse world. A focus on teams—that is, on kinds of teams, dynamics and processes of teams, and member diversity of teams (Rodrigues, 2001)—has become more central to leadership and management training today compared to the emphasis on leader traits (e.g., charismatic leaders) common during the 20th century.

Evolving Contexts of Leadership

Leadership is not divorced from the cultural, social, political, and economic contexts of which it is a part. Leaders often reflect the zeitgeist of the times, the ongoing concerns of the nation, and the group identity of its people. The study of leadership dimensions has mirrored these concerns and the evolving contexts of society; it reflects the interaction of leadership with culture—both within the organizations in which it is exercised, and that of the broader society in which it is embedded.

During the 20th century, interest in democratic vs. autocratic styles of leadership grew post-World War II in response to the military dictatorships of Hitler and Mussolini, and the fear of nuclear war. Military images of command-and-control types of leadership prevailed, embodied in the election of General Dwight Eisenhower as president of the United States. Values of collaboration and empowerment emerged in theories of "shared power" and "servant leader" as the women's movement and civil rights movement of the 1960s raised our consciousness about gender and racial/ethnic inequities and oppression. This shift from power to empowerment and the emergence of social responsibility gained prominence as a concern of leadership.

As we began to see a growing global society undergo rapid social and technological change, transformational leadership styles became popular as the type of leadership needed for the 21st century. Transformational leadership was initially defined by Burns (1978) as a process where leaders and followers engage in a mutual process to raise one another to higher levels of morality and motivation. Transformational leaders raise the bar by appealing to higher ideals and values of followers. In doing so, they may model the values themselves and use charismatic methods to attract people to the values and to the leader. The transformational leader is viewed as promoting change, establishing vision, and using interpersonal relatedness to motivate followers toward a mutual purpose.

The Enron scandal[1] raised calls for ethical leadership. The economic meltdown and crisis in the mortgage and finance industries in the United States due to the subprime lending had global ramifications and raised calls for integrity and authenticity in leadership. These events caused us to pause and think about our leadership in corporations and influenced our theorizing about the type of leadership we need today. It led us to think about the values held by our leaders and how they are transmitted into our organizational cultures.

Looman (2003) suggests that to cope with current complex and volatile environmental and cultural trends, leaders must integrate their cognitive and emotional mental processing systems and function from a metacognitive perspective. They must turn from a profitability-at-all-costs focus toward a focus on environments that encourage development of individual minds and problem solving through humanitarian collaboration and evolutionary progress.

Aligning Leader Identity and Group Identity

If we look at what the group or followers want, we must also examine how the leader embodies what the group wants. This includes how the leader and group identity coalesce. From a group systems perspective, all communities, nations, and cultures operate as groups. Identification of the leader or conferring of leader status is but one dimension of a group's functioning. It is the commonalities among group members that make for group cohesion and identity. It is often the differences between groups that both consolidates group identity and builds cohesion of the "in" group. At the same time, it is the differences that lend themselves to creating the "out" group or marginalized groups—positions in which women and minorities have often ended up. Pittinsky (2010) suggests that these phenomena be addressed through an intergroup leadership model that involves bringing together not only diverse individuals but also the subgroups to which they belong. The model argues that this does not require replacing people's subgroup identities with a superordinate group identity (turning "us" and "them" into "we"), but can be accomplished by promoting positive relations among subgroups, even as their distinctive identities (their senses of "us" and "them") remain. This is reflected in the failed approach of the melting pot myth as the United States tried to deal with the differences in culture and identity brought by the influx of immigrants to this country and the movement toward embracing diversity.

In the 21st century where such groups (i.e., countries, organizations, communities) are now more heterogeneous, alignments between leaders and their groups will change. Whereas group perceptions about the identity of its leader and how a group should be organized often meant having a white, male leader for a majority white group, we will need to consider the interaction of the diversity of leaders and within groups as to how it influences the exercise of leadership.

Global Leadership

As more businesses engage in an international economy and become multinational, they are forced to reexamine the transferability of leadership and management practices across cultures. This has given way to models of collaborative leadership. When Western businesses initially began to outsource their manufacturing to third world countries during the 20th century, Western styles of leadership and management were imposed. Western businesses observed higher levels of productivity of workers in collective societies than they would predict based on their theories of rewards and punishment in vogue at the time, that is, Theory X, which stated that workers inherently dislike and avoid work and must be driven to do it; and Theory Y, which stated that work is natural and can be a source of satisfaction when aimed at higher order human psychological needs. Theory Z, proposed in contrast to Theory X and Y by Ouchi (1981), reflected the "Japanese Management" style popularized during the Asian economic boom of the 1980s, which focused on increasing employee loyalty to the company by providing a job for life with a strong focus on the well-being of the employee, both on and off the job. Promoting stable employment and creating an organization that mirrored the family was believed to result in high productivity, and high employee morale and satisfaction.

Rawlings (2000) suggests that current business trends of globalization, accelerated growth, and reengineering require more cross-functional collaboration and integrated strategies across organizations. Senior and middle management teams are being asked to work together with more interdependence, with shared accountabilities outside their own functions, and with higher levels of trust and participation. This advent of the strategic leadership team does not fit neatly with traditional beliefs about the autocratic nature of teams and team building—these differences have been dichotomized as democratic vs. autocratic styles.

When non-Western businesses in "third world countries" began to seek a place in the international market place, they initially sought to import and emulate Western business management practices, but found themselves identifying dimensions of team and collaborative leadership that were effective but different from models of leadership observed in the United States. Kao, Sinha, and Wilpert (1999) suggest that indigenization in management is an integrative process, and illustrate how cultural values, norms, and expectations are interwoven into managerial styles and organizational functioning. They noted that management and leadership theories fashioned from perspectives rooted cultural contexts of Western societies have limited application in Asian countries, found that non-Western businesses are increasingly shifting from merely adopting Western theories and practices to cherishing their unique social and cultural factors while using applications from Western theories of management.

A Framework for Women and Leadership

When we deconstruct theories of leadership, we find that underrepresentation and the existence of bias frame the context of leadership for women.

Evolving contexts of leadership shape the concerns of scholars of leadership. Current theories of leadership typically omit the discussion of gender or of leader identity, lived experience, and its intersection with multiple dimensions of self-identity. Organizations remain male dominated and do not strive toward gender equitable work environments. Feminist values and principles of inclusion and diversity, while central to the leadership preferences of women, are not included in evaluating leadership or leadership styles. These values are also useful to the leadership of men, but tend not to dominate within masculinized organizational contexts.

Asking New Questions

While studies of women and leadership has been extensive, inclusion of their findings are not reflected in current models of leadership. The literature on women and leadership comprises two strands. The first examines the gendered nature of organizations and reveals a masculine bias in leadership practice that devalues women's ways of leading. The second strand focuses on identifying differences in how women and men lead and suggests that there is a unique women's leadership style (Fine, 2007). In questioning the existence of difference and proving the existence of advantage, we use a comparative paradigm with male leaders remaining the norm. Women leaders are viewed as exceptions and with ambivalence; this is reflected in the article "Power: Do Women Really Want It?," in *Fortune* magazine (Sellers, 2003).

If we are to understand women and leadership, we need to consider its complexity. We need to go beyond underrepresentation and bias, and ask new and different questions. It is time to move from using dichotomous paradigms (e.g., transformational vs. transactional leadership, task-oriented vs. interpersonal leadership styles) to examining multiple and alternative dimensions leadership. We must factor in leadership dimensions that have been outside our purview of the "typical male leader" in a North American and masculinized organizational context. What dimensions of leadership are omitted or need redefinition? We need to factor in the contexts of leadership. How do we address the male-centric and ethnocentric bias that exist or the tendency toward in-group preference vs. out-group scapegoating? How do the lived experiences of women and racial/ethnic minority leaders who have faced the effects of sexism and racism more acutely contribute to how they lead? How do we align women's concerns, identities, and experiences with emerging issues in leadership?

The implications for future directions are significant. We need to move toward questions of greater specificity and complexity. It is time to ask:

- In what contexts and under what circumstances do the strengths of women leaders lead to better outcomes?
- What leadership styles are more effective for what contexts with which followers?
- How might gender alter the exercise of leadership and influence follower expectations of the leader? For example, might a woman president be less confrontational and aggressive during times of crisis, or would she be more like Margaret Thatcher, noted for her toughness?
- Would bicultural individuals be more flexible by virtue of their multiple perspectives (LaFromboise, Coleman, & Gerton, 1994) and therefore be less polarizing in their exercise of leadership?
- Might the emphasis placed on interpersonal relationships in collectivistic cultures such as that of the Chinese (Gao, Ting-Toomey, & Gudykunst, 1996) elicit different types of leadership behavior than the emphasis placed on individualism in the United States and other Western cultures?
- What follows are some dimensions of leadership toward more inclusive, multidimensional, and complex frameworks for leadership and understanding how women exercise leadership. While they are discussed separately for purposes of clarity, we need to recognize how they interact together if we are to realize the complexity of leadership.

Feminist Goals

The research has demonstrated that all the dimensions discussed as important for leadership for the 21st century reflect dimensions in which women leaders have been found to favor. While we examine women and leadership, we need to consider how to incorporate ethics, collaboration, contexts, diversity, and transformational concepts into a new model of feminist leadership. Most important are the values and goals that underlie dimensions of leadership. Porter & Daniel (2007) conceptualized a feminist model of leadership that promotes feminist values as an aspirational goal; it is value based, action oriented, and collaborative, learning from diverse perspectives, with an understanding of power, ethics, and social constructiveness (i.e., VALUES). Using feminist principles to deconstruct principles of leadership, Fletcher (2003a; 2003b) makes the distinction between feminist attributes and feminist goals. While organizations may have feminist attributes such as relational and collaborative processes, environments that ignore gender and power dynamics do not have feminist goals. She advocates trying to create more egalitarian environments, but suggests that organizations need to challenge the power structure and masculinized frameworks in which it operates to do so. Absent that recognition, the rhetoric may sound feminist, but the goal is not there to make it feminist. Consequently, a feminist leadership model needs to have the achievement of feminist values as its goal.

An important distinction from the feminist literature is that "being female" and "being feminist" is not the same. Feminist leadership is both a goal and a style. Feminist women leaders bring these values and characteristics that shape how they lead, but they are also shaped by the environments in which they find themselves. A feminist leadership perspective introduces ethics, social justice, collaboration, and inclusiveness as central to the motivations of women seeking positions of leadership. It includes empowering others through (1) one's stewardship of an organization's resources, (2) creating the vision, (3) social advocacy and change, and (4) promoting feminist policy and a feminist agenda (e.g., family-oriented work environments, wage gap between men and women), (5) changing organizational cultures to create gender equitable environments, and (6) eliminating the need that women leaders need to act like men.

Ethics-Based Leadership

Rost (1991) defined ethical processes as important for the 21st century leader, meaning that leaders and followers must guard against using coercive and authoritarian methods to control the relationship. They must also guard against power wielding, because that only accomplishes the power wielder's objectives, not the recipient's. Ethical leadership adds to the autonomy and value of the individuals who are in the relationship; it does not require that individuals sacrifice some of their integrity to be in the relationship (p. 161).

Fine (2007) points out that the literature on women and leadership tends to focus on how women lead. The characteristics of women's leadership identified (e.g., collaboration, participation, communication, or nurturance) are viewed in terms of how they are used as the means to reach organizational ends. She suggests shifting that focus to the underlying *values* expressed in those means, that is, care for other people, which is consistent with the ethic of care revealed in women's career choices. In her collection of narratives, women discursively constructed leadership through a *moral discourse of leadership* that emphasized (1) leading in order to make a positive contribution in the world; (2) collaboration; (3) open communication; and (4) honesty in relationships—that is, the women imbue *each* element of their leadership with a moral dimension, and place ethics at the center of leadership, a contrast to the most prevalent approaches to leadership. Ethics, as defined by these women is not situational. "Doing good" and "giving back" as the bottom line were core values that these women leaders brought with them regardless of the particular organizational cultures in which they worked. Taken together with the literature on women's leadership styles, the *moral discourse of leadership* found in these narratives offers a way to revision women's leadership specifically and leadership theory more generally.

Collaborative Leadership

Feminist principles value inclusiveness, which translates into involving all in planning and decision making, having consensus building as a goal. As women have been shown to use nurturance and interpersonal connectedness in engaging and communicating with others when they lead, the use of a collaborative process is viewed as essential to a feminist leadership style. It levels the playing field between leader and follower and creates more egalitarian environments; this has come to be described as collaborative or shared leadership. In fact, theorists such as Hollander (2009) has pointed out how followers perceive and respond to a leader, in a two-way influence relationship. Within a particular context, this dynamic process can be called inclusive leadership, which begins with the leader's perceived legitimacy, as in election and appointment. Legitimacy depends on acknowledgment by followers and their response to the leader. The overarching point here is that the leadership process involves more than the leader's qualities alone; it also involves those of followers and their mutual situation.

Collaborative leadership, however, did not emerge out of feminist theory, but from scholars viewing it as essential to the skills of the "modern" leader. Raelin (2003) introduced the Four C's of "Leaderful Practice" and described leadership in the 21st century needing to be concurrent, collective, collaborative, and compassionate. While he recommends a process closely akin to a feminist process, he does not view gender as essential to the process nor does he introduce feminism as among its principles. However, these characteristics have been noted among women leaders who emphasize planning and organizing work using an empathic approach, while placing less emphasis on the "need to win at all costs" compared to men ("Women may make better managers," 1997).

Transformational Leadership

Studies comparing transformational vs. transactional leadership styles have found women to be somewhat more transformational than men in their leadership styles. Transformational leadership styles have been favored as essential to the 21st-century leader. The charisma of a leader who can unite and inspire the group toward a mutual purpose has been cited as one dimension of transformational leadership (see Burns, 1978). Charismatic leadership has been defined as those leaders with a special magnetic charm or appeal arousing special popular loyalty or enthusiasm for a public figure (as a political leader). Gardner and Avolio's (1998) dramaturgical perspective is that charismatic leadership is an impression management process enacted theatrically in acts of *framing, scripting, staging,* and *performing.* Examples of charismatic leadership have generally involved dominant male figures, for example, General Douglas MacArthur, Reverend Martin Luther King, Mahatma Gandhi, Winston Churchill, and Franklin D. Roosevelt. How we would define female charisma is unclear. As cited earlier in the chapter, the description of Nancy Pelosi as a "velvet hammer" who is all "persuasion and smiles" is an ambivalent metaphor of her charisma. It is interesting to note that two women politicians who have risen to charismatic stature, Michelle Bachmann and Sarah Palin, have been conservatives. The metaphors characterizing Sarah Palin's image were those of "hockey mom" and "Mother Grizzly" who abandoned her cubs when she resigned as Governor of Alaska. To understand her charisma, Choi (2006) notes that she gives Tea Party members hope that they have the power to shape the country, and empower them to feel powerful and capable. At the same time, he notes that her charisma is personalized, that is, using her unofficial position of the Tea Party to make money and promote her own image. A predominant image of Palin is that she is not qualified to be president. Two-thirds of registered voters in a new ABC News/ Washington Post poll say she's unqualified for the job, and more than half continue to rate her unfavorably overall. (Mataconis, 2010); she counters this lack of expertise by building a strong interpersonal tie with subordinates (Hughes, Ginnett, & Curphy, 1993)—again drawing on female traits of connectedness to build her charisma.

Diversity Leadership

Diversity leadership would subscribe to principles of inclusiveness, differences, social justice, and ethical values in both the composition of leaders, their relationship to followers, and the exercise of leadership. Attention to diversity is central to the understanding of women and leadership in that bias and lack of inclusiveness have been noted of current leadership models. In the special issue on diversity and leadership (Chin, 2010), we raise questions about the inattention to diversity in the theories and research on leadership. Eagly and Chin (2010) conclude the issue with a call to join the two bodies of theory and research on diversity and leadership to provide guidelines for optimizing leadership in contemporary organizations and nations.

However, attention to diversity is not simply about underrepresentation or about cataloging the presence or absence of women leaders. Attention to diversity and leadership means expanding the traditional leadership paradigms of traits, situations, contexts, and systems to include women and individuals from diverse identity groups. It means examining what leaders from such groups might bring to their exercise of leadership that might be different; it means examining the congruence between perceptions and expectations of diverse leaders with those of more traditional leaders; it means examining how the different cultural and lived experiences of leaders shape their exercise of leadership.

CONTEXTUAL LEADERSHIP

A shift from examining leadership traits and characteristics to examining the contexts of leadership, or the leader-follower relationship influences the types of questions we might ask. If we consider that leadership is cocreated in vivo with the group, then it must be interactive, dynamic, and contextual if it is to meet the needs of a changing world (Klein, 2009). How does a group confer leader status if its views of leadership are rooted in stereotypes and biases about social and gender roles?

While there is a shift toward shared leadership, power structures remain inherent in leadership roles leading some to question if a collaborative process of leadership is possible within existing contexts or organizational cultures, which tend to be hierarchical and masculinized.

Madden (2003) suggests that since leadership behavior occurs within a context that is influenced by the power relationships among the participants, we need to examine the contexts in which women lead, that is, "leadership is contextual." Karakowsky and Siegal (1999) found that the proportional representation of men and women in a work group, along with the gender orientation of the group's task, can significantly influence the kind of leadership behavior exhibited in group activity.

WORK-FAMILY INTERFACE

Kolb & Williams (2000) argue for a fundamental change in organizational cultures, away from masculinized contexts toward gender equitable work environments. In an analysis of 60 prominent women leaders, Erkut (2001) found that obstacles remained in their leadership experiences; although they have diminished but have definitely not disappeared. The identification of "mothering" metaphors for leadership among these women leaders was an unexpected finding. These obstacles are embedded in how work environments are organized that were designed neither with women nor the support of a family structure in mind. Cheung and Halpern (2010) found concerns about the work-family interface for women in top executive and professional roles in China, Hong Kong, and the United States. They found the interplay of personal attributes, processes, and environments as factors associated with successful leadership, and propose an alternative model of leadership that operates in the context of a "culture of gender" that defines expectations for women leaders. Work-family interface is not typically addressed in traditional leadership paradigms. Although the image of a family man is a positive one for male leaders, the challenges of managing a household or being mothers is not included as it is for women leaders.

New Dimensions

Historically, our definitions and views of heroes and leaders have been associated with "masculine" traits of military battle and physical valor. Kidwell, Willis, Jones-Saumty, & Bigfoot (2007) suggests that we rethink these associations of leadership giving as examples Native American women who needed to "stand by their men" to survive in US society as they took on roles of leadership; if we were to interpret these behaviors as ineffective, dependent, or not leadership, we will have missed the point and ignored the contexts in which these women leaders led.

Ayman and Korabik (2010) incorporate gender and culture into existing theories of leadership, viewing these dimensions as the social context for the interaction between leaders and their followers. They propose an integrative model of leadership that considers the complexities and differences among cross-cultural and cross-national groups. Ayman and Chemers (1983) found evidence for a Benevolent Paternalistic leadership dimension in Iran which has been corroborated in other Asian cultures, but yet to be incorporated into current theories of leadership that tend to reflect North American and Western biases. Different from power, this dimension derives from Confucianism within Asian cultures and reflects a patriarchal model of governing social order and leadership by emphasizing virtuous living, extolling the ideal of the (male) scholar-leader and his benevolent rule within a tradition of filial piety. It reflects the willingness of the leader to be benevolent toward his followers and allowing them to emerge; it contrasts with the notion of followers needing to seize power and authority.

AFFIRMATIVE PARADIGMS

Given the bias identified toward women and other minority groups, researchers have underscored affirmative paradigms as central to understanding leadership. Pittinsky (2010) underscores the importance of maintaining people's subgroup identities while creating a superordinate group identity of "we" to address in-group preferences vs. out-group scapegoating. Fassinger, Shullman, and Stevenson (2010) present an affirmative paradigm for understanding the leadership of individuals belonging to sexual minorities—that is, lesbian, gay, bisexual, and transgender people. For groups who have been historically oppressed, such paradigms are central to affirming the strengths that they bring to the exercise of leadership.

Conclusions

When we deconstruct theories of leadership, we find that underrepresentation and the existence of bias frame the context of leadership for women. Evolving contexts of leadership shape the concerns of scholars of leadership. Current theories of leadership, however, typically omit the discussion of gender or of leader identity, lived experience, and its intersection with multiple dimensions of self-identity. Organizations remain male dominated and do not strive toward gender-equitable work environments. Feminist values and principles of inclusion and diversity, while central to the leadership preferences of women, are not included in evaluating leadership or leadership styles.

The "glass ceiling" that many women and minorities face as a barrier to their advancement into top management positions within corporate US society (Morrison and Glinow, 1990) has now been redefined as "navigating a labyrinth" by women blind to the process of getting there (Eagly & Carli, 2007). While the research has noted differences and similarities in how men and women lead, leadership for women is a different experience. As we identify commonalities in lived experience and the group pride that bonds women and other diverse identity groups, we must recognize that diversity becomes central to framing the discussion about leadership.

We need to move toward new questions. There is neither one single type of ideal leader nor a single leadership dimension that is critical for effective leadership. Dimensions are not dichotomous because this approach favors the "in-group" and marginalizes "out-groups." We need to recognize how diversity related to gender, race, ethnicity, sexual orientation, disability, etc., influence who leaders are as well as the composition and distribution of people within a workforce. These dimensions also shape the organizational culture that provides a context for the exercise of leadership and influence the nature of the leader-member relationship.

Several dimensions are central if we are to move toward more inclusive, multidimensional and complex frameworks for leadership relevant in the 21st century and greater understanding of how women exercise leadership. These include feminist goals, ethics-based leadership, collaborative and transformational leadership. Diversity leadership provides a framework for considering the importance of contextual leadership, work-family interface, affirmative paradigms, and the existence of new dimensions in our understanding of leadership.

Future Directions

Future directions for the field are the following:

1. We need to ask different questions. In what contexts and under what circumstances do the strengths of women leaders lead to better outcomes?
2. We need to focus less on representation and who's at the table and more on factors contributing to the exercise of effective leadership in gender equitable environments.
3. We need to expand our understanding of leader identity and lived experiences and how they interact with follower composition and the leader-follower relationship.

These may require paradigm shifts and raise difficult problems to be solved, which include

1. How do we avoid our unconscious biases and inherent tendencies to marginalize out-group members and favor in-group members?
2. How do we change our organizational cultures toward more gender equitable environments?
3. How do we avoid confounding our perceptions and expectations associated with socially constructed gender and racial stereotypes to our appraisals of effective leadership?

This also raises additional topics that remain to be addressed, which include

1. How do different compositions of the diversity of a leader and of followers influence the exercise of leadership and effect outcomes?
2. What are new dimensions to be identified if we go beyond our ethnocentric biases? We cannot find what we do not see.
3. How do we keep ahead of the rapid changes in society without giving in to the popular short-lived trends?
4. How do we evolve a global theory of leadership that is inclusive and diverse for women and other identity groups?

Note

1. Enron scandal, revealed in October 2001, eventually led to the bankruptcy of the Enron Corporation, an American energy company based in Houston, Texas, and the dissolution of Arthur Andersen, which was one of the five largest audit and accountancy partnerships in the world. In addition to being the largest bankruptcy reorganization in American history at that time, Enron was attributed as the biggest audit failure.

References

American Council on Education (2007). *The American College President 2007*. Washington, DC: American Council on Education.

Avolio, B. J. (2007). Promoting more integrative strategies for leadership theory-building. *American Psychologist, 62*, 25–33.

Avolio, B. J., Gardner, W. L., Walumbwa, F. O., Luthans, F., & May, D. R. (2004). Unlocking the mask: A look at the process by which authentic leaders impact follower attitudes and behavior. *The Leadership Quarterly, 15*, 801–823.

Ayman, R. (1993). Leadership perception: The role of gender and culture. In M. M. Chemers & R. Ayman (Eds.), *Leadership theory and research: Perspectives and directions* (pp. 137–166). New York, NY: Academic Press.

Ayman, R., & Chemers, M. M. (1983). Relationship of supervisory behavior ratings to work group effectiveness and subordinate satisfaction among Iranian managers. *Journal of Applied Psychology, 68*, 338–341.

Ayman, R., & Korabik, K. (2010, April). Leadership: Why gender and culture matter. *American Psychologist, 65*(3), 157–170.

Baron, R. S. (2005). So right it's wrong: Groupthink and the ubiquitous nature of polarized group decision making. *Advances in Experimental Social Psychology, 37*, 219–253.

Bass, B. M., & Avolio, B. J. (1994). *Improving organizational effectiveness through transformational leadership*. Thousand Oaks, CA: Sage.

Blau, F. D., & Kahn, L. M. (2006). The gender pay gap: Going, going…but not gone. In F. D. Blau, M. C. Brinton, & D. B. Grusky (Eds.), *The declining significance of gender?* (pp. 37–66). New York, NY: Russell Sage Foundation.

Bertrand, M., & Mullainathan, S. (2004). Are Emily and Greg more employable than Lakisha and Jamal? A field experiment on labor market discrimination. *American Economic Review, 94*, 991–1013.

Biernat, M. (2005). *Standards and expectancies: Contrast and assimilation in judgments of self and others*. New York, NY: Psychology Press.

Brass, D. J. (2001). Social capital and organizational leadership. In S. J. Zaccaro & R. J. Klimoski (Eds.), *The nature of organizational leadership: Understanding the performance imperatives confronting today's leaders* (pp. 132–152). San Francisco, CA: Jossey-Bass.

Burns, J. M. (1978). *Leadership*. New York, NY: Harper Torchbooks, p. 2.

Butler, D., & Geis, F. L. (1990). Nonverbal affect responses to male and female leaders: Implications for leadership evaluations. *Journal of Personality and Social Psychology, 58*, 48–59.

Byrne, D., & Neuman, J. (1992). The implications of attraction research for organizational issues. In K. Kelly (Ed.), *Issues, theory, and research in industrial/organizational psychology* (pp. 29–70). Amsterdam, the Netherlands: Elsevier Science.

Cheung, F. M., & Halpern, D. F. (2010). Women at the top: How successful leaders combine work and family. *American Psychologist, 65*, 182–193.

Chin, J. L. (2010, April). Introduction to the special issue on diversity and leadership. *American Psychologist, 65*(3), 150–156.

Chin, J. L., Lott, B., Rice, J. K., & Sanchez-Hucles, J. (2007). *Women and leadership: Transforming visions and diverse voices*. Malden, MA: Blackwell.

Chin, J. L., & Sanchez-Hucles, J. (2007). Diversity and leadership. *American Psychologist, 62*, 608–609.

Choi, J. (2006). A motivational theory of charismatic leadership: Envisioning, empathy, and empowerment. *Journal of Leadership and Organizational Studies, 13*(1), 24–43.

Correll, S. J., Benard, S., & Paik, I. (2007). Getting a job: Is there a motherhood penalty? *American Journal of Sociology, 112*, 1297–1338.

Davies, P. G., Spencer, S. J., & Steele, C. M. (2005). Clearing the air: Identity safety moderates the effects of stereotype threat on women's leadership aspirations. *Journal of Personality and Social Psychology, 88*, 276–287.

Davison, H. K., & Burke, M. J. (2000). Sex discrimination in simulated employment contexts: A meta-analytic investigation. *Journal of Vocational Behavior, 56*, 225–248.

Den Hartog, D. N., & Dickson, W. (2004). Leadership and culture. In J. Antonakis, A. T. Cianciolo, & R. J. Sternberg (Eds.), *The nature of leadership* (pp. 249–278). Thousand Oaks, CA: Sage.

Dovidio, J. F., & Gaertner, S. L. (2004). Aversive racism. *Advances in Experimental Social Psychology, 36*, 1–52.

Eagly, A. H. (1987). Reporting sex differences. *American Psychologist, 42*, 756–757.

Eagly, A. H. (2005). Achieving relational authenticity in leadership: Does gender matter? *Leadership Quarterly, 16*, 459–474.

Eagly, A. H. (2007). Feminine advantage and disadvantage: Resolving the contradictions. *Psychology of Women Quarterly, 31*, 1–12.

Eagly, A. H., & Carli, L. L. (2003). The female leadership advantage: An evaluation of the evidence. *Leadership Quarterly, 14*(6), 807–834.

Eagly, A. H., & Carli, L. L. (2007). *Through the labyrinth: The truth about how women become leaders*. Boston, MA: Harvard Business School Press.

Eagly, A. H., & Chin, J. L. (2010). Diversity and leadership in a changing world. *American Psychologist, 65*, 216–224.

Eagly, A. H., Johannesen-Schmidt, M. C., & van Engen, M. L. (2003). Transformational, transactional, and laissez-faire leadership styles: A meta-analysis comparing women and men. *Psychological Bulletin, 129*(4), 569–591.

Eagly, A. H., & Johnson, B. T. (1990). Gender and leadership style: A meta-analysis. *Psychological Bulletin, 108*(2), 233–256.

Eagly, A. H., & Karau, S. J. (2002). Role congruity theory of prejudice toward female leaders. *Psychological Review, 109*(3), 573–598.

Eagly, A. H., Makhijani, M. G., & Klonsky, B. G. (1992). Gender and the evaluation of leaders: A meta-analysis. *Psychological Bulletin, 111*(1), 3–22.

Erkut, S. (2001). *Inside women's power: Learning from leaders*. Wellesley, MA: Wellesley Centers for Women.

Fassinger, R. E., Shullman, S. L., & Stevenson, M. R. (2010). Toward an affirmative lesbian, gay, bisexual, and transgender leadership paradigm. *American Psychologist, 65*, 201–215.

Fine, M. G. (2007). Strategic planning: Gender, collaborative leadership, and organizational change. In J. L. Chin, B. Lott, J. K. Rice, & J. Sanchez-Hucles (Eds.). (2007). *Women and leadership: Transforming visions and diverse voices*. Malden, MA: Blackwell.

Fletcher, J. (2003a) The Greatly Exaggerated Demise of Heroic Leadership: Gender, Power, and the Myth of the Female Advantage. http://www.simmons.edu/gsm/cgo/insights13.pdf

Fletcher, J. (2003b). *The different faces of feminist leadership*. Paper presented at the Annual Meeting of the American Psychological Association. Toronto, Canada.

Forsyth, D. R., Heiney, M. M., & Wright, S. S. (1997). Biases in appraisals of women leaders. *Group Dynamics, 1*(1), 98–103.

Foschi, M. (2000). Double standards for competence: Theory and research. *Annual Review of Sociology, 26*, 21–42.

Frable, D.E.S. (1997). Gender, racial, ethnic, sexual, and class identities. *Annual Review of Psychology, 48*, 139–162.

Gao, G., Ting-Toomey, S. & Gudykunst, W. B. (1996). Chinese communication processes. In G. Gao, S. Ting-Toomey, W. B. Gudykunst, M. H. Bond, & M. H. (Eds.), *The handbook of Chinese psychology* (pp. 280–293). New York, NY: Oxford University Press.

Gardner, W., & Avolio, B. J. (1998, Jan.). The charismatic relationship: A dramaturgical perspective. *The Academy of Management Review, 23*(1), 32–58.

Graen, G. B., & Uhl-Bien, M. (1995). Relationship-based approach to leadership: Development of leader-member exchange (LMX) theory of leadership over 25 years: Applying a multilevel multi-domain perspective. *Leadership Quarterly, 6*, 219–247.

Greenleaf, R. K. (1977). *Servant leadership: A journey into the nature of legitimate power and greatness.* New York, NY: Paulist Press.

Grodsky, E., & Pager, D. (2001). The structure of disadvantage: Individual and occupational determinants of the Black–White wage gap. *American Sociological Review, 66*, 542–567.

Hall, R. L., Garrett-Akinsanya, B., & Hucles, M. (2007). Voices of Black feminist leaders: Making spaces for ourselves. In J. L. Chin, B. Lott J. K. Rice, & J. Sanchez-Hucles (Eds.), *Women and leadership: Transforming visions and diverse voices* (pp. 281–296). Malden, MA: Blackwell Publishing.

Heilman, M. E., & Eagly, A. H. (2008). Gender stereotypes are alive, well, and busy producing workplace discrimination. *Industrial and Organizational Psychology: Perspectives on Science and Practice, 1*, 393–398.

Heilman, M. E., & Okimoto, T. G. (2008). Motherhood: A potential source of bias in employment decisions. *Journal of Applied Psychology, 93*, 189–198.

Helgesen, S. (1990). *The female advantage: Women's ways of leadership.* New York, NY: Currency/Doubleday.

Hollander, E. P. (2006). Influence Processes in leadership-followership: Inclusion and the Idiosyncrasy Credit Model. In D. A. Hantula (Ed.), *Advances in social & organizational psychology: A tribute to Ralph Rosnow* (pp. 293–312). Mahwah, NJ: Lawrence Erlbaum & Associates.

Hong, L., & Page, S. E. (2004). Groups of diverse problem solvers can outperform groups of high-ability problem solvers. *Proceedings of the National Academy of Sciences, 101*, 16385–16389.

Hoyt, C. L., & Blascovich, J. (2007). Leadership efficacy and women leaders' responses to stereotype activation. *Group Processes and Intergroup Relations, 10*, 595–616.

Hughes, R. L., Ginnett, R. C., & Curphy, G. J. (1993). *Power, influence, and influence tactics. in leadership: Enhancing the lessons of experience.* NY: Richard D. Irwin, Inc.

Infoplease. (2009). Minorities in the 111th Congress. Retrieved from http://www.infoplease.com/us/government/111-congress-minorities.html

Indvik, J. (2004). Women and leadership. In P. G. Northouse (Ed.), *Leadership: Theory and Practice* (pp.265–299). Thousand Oaks, CA: Sage Publications.

Iwasaki, Y., MacKay, K. J., & Ristock, J. (2004, Feb.). Gender-Based analyses of stress among professional managers: An exploratory qualitative study. *International Journal of Stress Management, 11*(1), 56–79.

Judge, T. A., & Piccolo, R. F. (2004). Transformational and transactional leadership: A meta-analytic test of their relative validity. *Journal of Applied Psychology, 89*, 901–910.

Kanter, R. M. (1997). *Rosabeth Moss Kanter on the frontiers of management.* Boston, MA: Harvard Business School Press.

Kao, H. S. R., Sinha, D., & Wilpert, B. (1999). *Management and cultural values: The indigenization of organizations in Asia.* Thousand Oaks, CA: Sage.

Karakowsky, L., & Siegal, J. P. (1999, Aug.). The effects of proportional representation and gender orientation of the task on emergent leadership behavior in mixed-gender work groups. *Journal of Applied Psychology, 84*(4), 620–631.

Kawahara, D., Esnil, E. M., & Hsu, J. (2007). Asian American women leaders: The intersection of race, gender, and leadership. In J. L. Chin, B. Lott, J. K. Rice, & J. Sanchez-Hucles (Eds.), *Women and leadership: Transforming visions and diverse voices* (pp. 297–313). Malden, MA: Blackwell Publishers.

Kidwell, C. S., Willis, D. J., Jones-Saumty, D., & Bigfoot, D. S. (2006) Feminist leadership among American Indian women. In J. L. Chin, B. Lott, J. Rice, & J. Sanchez-Hucles. (Eds.), *Women and leadership: Transforming visions and diverse voices* (pp. 315–329). New York, NY: Blackwell Publishers.

Kiechel, W., & Sacha, B. (1999). How will we work in the year 2000? *Fortune, 127*, 21–44.

Kite, M. E., Deaux, K., & Haines, E. L. (2008). Gender stereotypes. In F. L. Denmark & M. A. Paludi (Eds.), *Psychology of women: A handbook of issues and theories* (2nd ed., pp. 205–236). Westport, CT: Praeger.

Klein, R. H., Rice, C. A. & Schermer, V. L. (Eds.). (2009). *Leadership in a changing world: Dynamic perspectives on groups and their leaders* (pp. 73-92). Lanham, MD: Lexington Books.

Koenig, A. M., Eagly, A. H., Mitchell, A. A., & Ristikari, T. (2011). Are leader stereotypes masculine? A meta-analysis of three research paradigms. *Psychological Bulletin, 137*(4), 616–642. doi: 10.1037/a0023557

Kolb, D., & Williams, J. (2000) *Shadow Negotiation: How women can master the hidden agendas that determine bargaining success.* New York, NY: Simon & Schuster.

Korabik, K. (1990). Androgyny and leadership style. *Journal of Business Ethics, 9*, 9–18.

LaFromboise, T., Coleman, H. L. K., & Gerton, J. (1994). How is it possible to live biculturally? *Clinician's Research Digest, 12*(4) [American Psychological Association].

Leslie, L. M., King, E. B., Bradley, J. C., & Hebl, M. R. (2008). Triangulation across methodologies: All signs point to persistent stereotyping and discrimination in organizations. *Industrial and Organizational Psychology: Perspectives on Science and Practice, 1*, 399–404.

Leung, A. K., Maddux, W. W., Galinsky, A. D., & Chiu, C. (2008). Multicultural experience enhances creativity: The when and how. *American Psychologist, 63*, 169–181.

Looman, M. D. (2003). Reflective leadership: Strategic planning from the heart and soul. *Journal of Consulting Psychology: Practice & Research, 55*(4), 215–221.

Madden, M. (2003). Management and leadership styles. Retrieved July 2003 from www.feministleadership.com

Mataconis, D. (2010). 67% Of Registered Voters Say Sarah Palin Unqualified To Be President. *Outside the Beltway*, Friday, October 29, 2010. Retrieved July 10, 2011 from http://www.outsidethebeltway.com/67-of-registered-voters-say-sarah-palin-unqualified-to-be-president/.

Maume, D. J. Jr. (1999). Occupational segregation and the career mobility of White men and women. *Social Forces, 77*, 1433–1459.

McGregor, D. (1985). The human side of enterprise. In D. S. (Ed.), *Organization Theory.* London: McGraw Hill.

McGrory, M. (2002, Nov. 16). Pelosi's a salve for a wounded party. *The Boston Globe.* Boston: The Boston Globe.

Molinsky, A. (2007). Cross-cultural code switching: The psychological challenges of adapting behavior in foreign cultural interactions. *Academy of Management Review, 32*, 622–640.

Morrison, A. M., & von Glinow, M. A. (1990). Women and minorities in management. *American Psychologist, 45*(2), 200–208.

Musteen, M., Barker, V. L. III, & Baeten, V. L. (2006). CEO attributes associated with attitude toward change: The direct and moderating effects of CEO tenure. *Journal of Business Research, 59*, 604–612.

Newport, F. (2001, February 21). *Americans see women as emotional and affectionate, men as more aggressive: Gender specific stereotypes persist in recent Gallup poll.* Available from Gallup Brain website: http://brain.gallup.com

Obama, B. H. (2008, March 18). *Obama race speech: Remarks of Senator Barack Obama: "A More Perfect Union."* Retrieved from http://www.huffingtonpost.com/2008/03/18/obama-race-speech-readth_n_92077.html

Ouchi, W. (1981). *Theory Z. Reading.* Boston, MA: Addison-Wesley.

Page, S. E. (2007). *The difference: How the power of diversity creates better groups, firms, schools, and societies.* Princeton, NJ: Princeton University Press.

Pager, D. (2007). The use of field experiments for studies of employment discrimination: Contributions, critiques, and directions for the future. *Annals of the American Academy of Political & Social Science, 609*, 104–133.

Parker, P. S. (2005). *Race, gender, and leadership: Re-envisioning organizational leadership from the perspectives of African American women executives.* Mahwah, NJ: Lawrence Erlbaum & Associates.

Parker, P. S., & Ogilvie, D. T. (1996). Gender, culture, and leadership: Toward a culturally distinct model of African-American women executives' leadership strategies. *Leadership Quarterly, 7*, 189–214.

Phinney, J. S. (1990). Ethnic identity in adolescents and adults: Review of the research. *Psychological Bulletin, 108*, 499–514.

Pittinsky, T. (2010). A two-dimensional theory of intergroup leadership: The case of national diversity. *American Psychologist, 65*, 194–200.

Polzer, J. T., Milton, L. P., & Swann, W. B., Jr. (2002). Capitalizing on diversity: Interpersonal congruence in small work groups. *Administrative Science Quarterly, 47*, 296–324.

Porter, N. & Daniel, J. H. (2007). Developing transformational leaders: Theory to practice. In J. L. Chin, B. Lott, J. K. Rice, & J. Sanchez-Hucles (Eds.), *Women and leadership: Transforming visions and diverse voices* (pp. 245–263). Malden, MA: Blackwell Publishing.

Raelin, J. (2003). *Creating leaderful organizations: How to bring out leadership in everyone.* UK: Berrett-Koehler Pub.

Ragins, B. Townsend, B., & Mattis, M. (1998). Gender gap in the executive suite: CEOs and female executives report on breaking the glass ceiling. *Academy of Management Executive, 12*(1), 28–42.

Rawlings, D. (2000) Collaborative leadership teams: Oxymoron or new paradigm? *Journal of Consulting Psychology: Practice & Research, 52*(1), 36–48.

Riach, P. A., & Rich, J. (2002). Field experiments of discrimination in the market place. *Economic Journal, 112*, F480–F518.

Rodrigues, C. A. (2001). Fayol's 14 principles of management then and now: A framework for managing today's organizations effectively. *Management Decision, 39*, 880–889.

Rosener, J. B. (1990). Ways women lead. *Harvard Business Review, 68*(6), 119–125.

Rosette, A. S., & Tost, L. P. (2010). Agentic women and communal leadership: How role prescriptions confer advantage to top women leaders. *Journal of Applied Psychology, 95*(2), 221–235.

Rost, J. C. (1991). *Leadership in the 21st century.* New York, NY: Praeger.

Sanchez-Hucles, J. (2003, July). Diversity in feminist leadership. www.feministleadership.com

Sanchez-Hucles, J. V., & Davis, D. D. (2010). Women and women of color in leadership: Complexity, identity, and intersectionality. *American Psychologist, 65*, 171–181.

Sellers, P. (2003, Oct. 13) Power: Do women really want it? *Fortune, 148*(8), 80–100.

Sidanius, J., & Pratto, F. (1999). *Social dominance: An intergroup theory of social hierarchy and oppression.* New York, NY: Cambridge University Press.

Snyder, K. (2006). *The G quotient: Why gay executives are excelling as leaders... and what every manager needs to know.* San Francisco, CA: Jossey-Bass.

Spillane, J. P. (2006). *Distributed leadership.* San Francisco, CA: Jossey-Bass.

Steele, C. (1997). Stereotype threat and the intellectual test performance of African Americans. *Journal of Personality and Social Psychology, 69*, 797–811.

Trinidad, C., & Normore, A. H. (2005). Leadership and gender: A dangerous liaison? *Leadership & Organization Development Journal, 26*(7), 574–590.

U.S. Bureau of Labor Statistics. (2009, January). *Household data annual averages: Employed persons by detailed occupation, sex, race, and Hispanic or Latino ethnicity.* Retrieved from http://www.bls.gov/cps/cpsaat11.pdf

van Engen, M. L., & Willemsen, T. M. (2004). Sex and leadership styles: A meta-analysis of research published in the 1990s. *Psychological Reports, 94*, 3–18.

van Knippenberg, D., & Schippers, M. C. (2007). Work group diversity. *Annual Review of Psychology, 58*, 515–541.

Vecchio, R. P. (2003). In search of gender advantage. *Leadership Quarterly, 14*(6), 835–850.

Wikipedia. Cleopatra VII. http://en.wikipedia.org/wiki/Cleopatra; retrieved December 10, 2007.

Wikipedia. Empress Dowager Cixi. http://en.wikipedia.org/wiki/Empress_Dowager_Cixi; retrieved December 10, 2007.

Wikipedia. Joan of Arc. http://en.wikipedia.org/wiki/Joan_of_Arc; retrieved December 10, 2007.

Women may make better managers—Study. (1997, April). *Management, 44*(3), 14.

Yabusaki, A. (2007). Diverse feminist communication styles: Challenges to women and leadership. In J. L. Chin, B. Lott, J. K. Rice, & J. Sanchez-Hucles (Eds.), *Women and leadership: Transforming visions and diverse voices* (pp. 55–68). Malden, MA: Blackwell Publishing.

PART 8

Special Concerns in Leadership

CHAPTER

34 Leading for Creativity: People, Products, and Systems

Michael D. Mumford, Carter Gibson, Vincent Giorgini, *and* Jensen Mecca

Abstract

The success of many organizations depends on creativity, the production of original problem solutions, and innovation—the translation of these solutions into viable new products or processes. Traditionally, it was held that leaders have little influence on the work of creative people. More recent research, however, indicates that leadership may be critical to the success of creative efforts in organizations. This chapter argues that leaders of creative efforts must execute three key functions: (1) directing the work, (2) leading people doing the work, and (3) managing relationships with the organization. Key issues arising in the execution of each of these functions are examined. Directions for future research are discussed.

Key Words: creativity, innovation, leadership, project management, research and development

Leading for Creativity
People, Products, and Systems

Traditionally, creativity, the production of new problem solutions, and innovation, the translation of these problem solutions into viable products, processes, or services, has not been of great concern either to organizations or those who must lead organizations (Mumford, Scott, Gaddis, & Strange, 2002). For three reasons, this negative view of creativity and innovation may have been plausible. First, many organizational strategies do not require creativity and innovation to ensure success (March, 1991; Miles & Snow, 1978). Second, it has been assumed creative problem solutions could be bought if they were needed (Chernow, 1998). Third, creativity, and thus subsequent innovation, were viewed as nonrational processes and hence something outside the ability of leaders to control (Buijs, 2007).

Although one might question whether any of these propositions have, in fact, ever been true (Weightman, 2007), it has become apparent in recent years that creativity and innovation are, in fact, critical to the survival and success of organizations. The importance of creativity and innovation to organizations may be traced to the effects of globalization, the importance of intellectual property to success in more competitive global markets, and the increased rate of technological change (Dess & Pickens, 2000; Gryskiewicz, 1999). Under these conditions, organization success and survival depend on creativity and innovation. As a result, organizations now expect leaders to lead for creativity and innovation (DeCusatis, 2008).

The expectation that leaders, at least some leaders in organizations, must lead for creativity and innovation does not seem misplaced. For example, Chen (2007), in a study of new ventures, found that firm patent rates were positively related to effective leadership. Tierney, Farmer, and Graen (1999) found that perceptions of positive relationships with leaders were positively related to appraisals of employee creativity and invention disclosures. Still other work by Allocca and Kessler (2006) has shown that leader behaviors, such as championing (Howell & Boies, 2004) and goal setting (House, 1996), were positively related to the speed of bringing new products to market. Other research by Amabile, Shatzel, Moneta, and Kramer (2004); Drazin, Glynn, and Kazanjian (1999); Oldham and Cummings (1996); and Pelz (1963) has indicated that effective leadership is related to the production of creative problem solutions and subsequent innovation. Indeed, the magnitude of the relationships obtained in these studies, typically relationships in the .40 range, suggests that effective leadership may be particularly important with respect to the occurrence and success of creative efforts in organizational settings (Mumford et al., 2002).

With this point in mind, our intent in this chapter is to examine the critical functions those asked to lead creative efforts must execute in organizational settings. We begin by describing the nature of creative work and the activities required of the people doing this work. Next we examine three key functions that must be executed by the people asked to lead this work (Mumford, Peterson, & Robledo, 2013; Robledo, Peterson, & Mumford, 2011): (1) leading the work, (2) leading people, and (3) leading organizational systems. Within each of these three functions we discuss the key variables, or mechanisms of influence, on which leaders must act. We then consider some of the practical and substantive implications of these observations for understanding effective leadership of creative efforts and improving the performance of those asked to lead these efforts.

Creativity and Innovation

Creative Problem Solving

Naive conceptions of creativity typically equate creativity with the generation of multiple new ideas (Silva, 2008). Creativity as it is technically defined, however, refers to the production of viable, or workable, new, or original, solutions (Besemer & O'Quin,1999; Hennessey & Amabile, 2010) to complex, novel, ill-defined problems (Mumford & Gustafson, 2007). Thus creativity, and innovations flowing from creative problem solutions, ultimately represents a form of complex cognition.

As might be expected based on our foregoing observations, students of creativity have sought to identify the processes, or mental operations, by which people work with knowledge to generate original problem solutions (Finke, Ward, & Smith, 1992; Merrifield, Guilford, Christensen, & Frick, 1962; Parnes & Noller, 1972). Broadly speaking, the production of creative problem solutions appears to depend on the combination and reorganization of extant knowledge structures (Mobley, Doares, & Mumford, 1992) followed by exploration of the implications of new features emerging from these combination and reorganization efforts (Ward, Smith, & Finke, 1999). Successful efforts with respect to the combination and reorganization of extant knowledge appear to depend on effective execution of eight core processing activities (Mumford, Mobley, Uhlman, Reiter-Palmon, & Doares, 1991): (1) problem definition, (2) information gathering, (3) concept selection, (4) conceptual combination, (5) idea generation, (6) idea evaluation, (7) implementation planning, and (8) mentoring. A series of studies by Mumford and his colleagues (e.g., Dailey & Mumford, 2006; Mumford, Supinski, Baughman, Costanza, & Threlfall, 1997; Osburn & Mumford, 2006) has provided evidence for the unique impact of effective execution of each of these processes on creative problem solving. Effective execution of each of these processes, moreover, depends on use of multiple, viable, problem-solving strategies. For example, creative problem solving improves with appraisal of deficiencies where idea evaluation allows for compensation for these deficiencies (Lonergan, Scott, & Mumford, 2004; Scott, Lonergan, & Mumford, 2005; Vessey & Mumford, 2012).

Creative People

Creative work is, in part, based on expertise. Expertise, however, typically emerges from engagement in a professional field (Zuckerman, 1977)—engagement typically accompanied by extended periods of socialization and mentoring. Moreover, evaluation of creative work is based as much, if not more so, in the professional field than in the organization (Csikszentmihalyi, 1999). The basis of expertise and evaluation within a professional field, along with socialization into this field, has a noteworthy implication for understanding creative people. Creative people's identities will be based as much on the profession and professional status as on the organization. Thus professional achievement will both motivate and direct creative work, with creative people proving especially sensitive to professional appraisals.

Another phenomenon characteristic of creative people arises from the need to invest substantial cognitive resources in creative work. The need to invest resources in creative work suggests that motivational attributes will also characterize creative people (Ma, 2009). In fact, in a meta-analysis of prior studies examining the relationship of personality and motivational variables with creativity and innovation, Fiest and Gorman (1998) found that for creative people, as opposed to less creative counterparts, were characterized by drive/achievement motivation, dominance/arrogance, and autonomy/independence. All these characteristics would, of course, encourage people to invest resources in complex, high-risk, cognitive activities. Moreover, creative people have been found to evidence three characteristics that would lead to them being attracted to, and engaged by, the complex, novel, ill-defined problems that call for creative thought. More specifically, creative people tend to be open and tolerate ambiguity, to be introverted, and to value cognition (Mumford & Gustafson, 1988; Zenasni, Besançon, & Lubart, 2008).

Although all of these characteristics induce attraction to, and motivation for, creative work, it is important to bear in mind another point noted earlier. People make a decision to invest resources in creative work. The discretionary nature of creativity, in turn, implies that how people conceive of themselves vis-à-vis the task at hand will also influence creativity. Thus Jaussi, Randel, and Dionne (2007) asked peers to appraise co-workers' creative behaviors. Behavioral measures of creative personal identity (e.g., creativity is important to who I am) and creative self-efficacy (e.g., I have confidence in my ability to solve problems creatively) were obtained. It was found that both creative self-efficacy and creative identity were positively related ($r = .20$) to peer appraisals of creativity at work. Thus the investment of personal identity in creative work, accompanied by confidence in one's ability to perform creative work, results in people investigating requisite resources in creative activities.

Creative Work

Our stereotype of creative work, a stereotype evident in Einstein (Isaacson, 2007), is that creative work is undertaken by an individual—an individual working alone. Although there is some evidence supporting this assumption with regard to brainstorming or initial idea generation (Litchfield, 2008; Paulus & Brown, 2003), creative efforts in organizations are typically of sufficient complexity that the work of multiple people will be required to produce innovative products. Indeed, Sawyer (2006) has argued that effective collaboration is critical to creative performance and the production of innovative products. This effect can be viewed especially well in the production of knowledge, a highly creative endeavor. Wuchty, Jones, and Uzzi (2007) point out a trend toward larger teams in authoring papers across several academic disciplines. Teams are increasingly accounting for larger amounts of, and higher quality, research.

Although the need for collaborative teamwork in producing creative products seems contradictory to the nature of creative people (Hunter, Thoroughgood, Myer, & Ligon, 2011), the available evidence, in fact, indicates that interactional processes contributing to effective collaboration are critical to innovative work. For example, Taggar (2002) asked people to work in teams on a series of projects where project performance was appraised for creativity. Team process variables were also assessed as team members worked on these projects. He found that team process variables including (1) team citizenship, (2) performance management, (3) effective communication, (4) involving others, (5) providing feedback, (6) reactions to conflict, and (7) avoiding conflict were positively related to the production of creative projects—making a unique contribution to predicting project creativity even when individual-level influences such as motivation and ability were taken into account. Other work by Ancona and Caldwell (1992), Keller (1989), and Madjar, Oldham, and Pratt (2002) also indicates that variables contributing to effective interactions among group members such as cohesiveness, trust, and communication all contribute to the effectiveness of teams working on creative projects.

In addition to effective team interactions two other variables appear to have a marked impact on the success of creative collaborations. The first variable of importance in this regard is the availability of shared mental models (Day, Gronn, & Salas, 2006). In one study along these lines, Mumford, Feldman, Hein, and Nagao (2001) induced shared mental models among team members through a training intervention. In comparison to untrained controls, it was found that trained teams were more likely to produce creative problem solutions. Other qualitative studies, by Dunham and Freeman (2000) and Drazin et al. (1999) of creative work in technical and artistic fields, also indicate that the availability of shared mental models may be critical to creative work, with these shared mental models providing a basis for interpreting events arising in creative efforts, responding to crises, and selecting actions to be taken in responding to events.

A final set of variables that appears critical to creative work refers to perceptions of typical patterns of interpersonal interaction. Studies of characteristic perceptions of interactional patterns have been subsumed under the rubic of climate (Amabile, Conti, Coon, Lazenby, & Herron, 1996; Baer & Frese, 2003; West et al., 2003). Broadly speaking, in these studies, dimensions such as (1) participative safety, (2) supervisory support, (3) organizational support, (4) workgroup support, (5) autonomy, (6) challenging work, (7) clarity of objectives, (8) task orientation, and (9) limited organizational impediments are assessed through climate surveys. In a meta-analysis examining the relationship between appraisals of the work environment with respect to these variables and creative achievement, Hunter, Bedell-Avers, and Mumford (2007) obtained a relationship in the .30-to-.40 range. Thus climate perceptions appear to be strongly related to creative work, especially for creative people (Oldham & Cummings, 1996) when working under unstable, or turbulent, conditions (Hunter et al., 2007). Indeed, climate perceptions may moderate the impact of other variables on creative work. Thus Hsu and Fan (2010) found that time pressure contributed to creativity when the climate was not supportive. However, when climate was supportive, time pressure had little effect on creativity.

Creativity in Organizations

The foregoing observations also suggest that organizational-level influences such as structure, resources, and turbulence might also influence the nature and success of creative work (Damanpour, 1991; Dean and Sharfman, 1996; Nohria & Gulati, 1996). Broadly speaking, creativity in organizations appears to increase when the focus is on the work and customers of the work, rather than finances per se (Nellore & Balachandra, 2001; Sharma, 1999). Moreover, the available evidence indicates that creative work in organizations is more likely to occur when the organization is based on a professional structure where adequate and effective controls have been induced (Cardinal, 2001).

The need for control for creative work in organizational settings may at first glance appear surprising. Indeed, the need for control is inconsistent with creative people's preference for autonomy (Mumford & Hunter, 2005). By the same token, creative work in organizations is costly with respect to both finances and business processes (Jelinek & Schoonhoven, 1990). Creative efforts often fail (Sharma, 1999) and may result in loss of markets for extant products (Chandy & Tellis, 2000). These risks associated with creative ventures imply that organizations must induce adequate control over creative efforts (March, 1991)—with top management involvement and support proving critical to the success of such efforts (Dougherty & Hardy, 1996; Ong, Wan, & Chang, 2003).

The risks associated with creative work at the organizational level and the uncertainty attached to creative work have led to the emergence of a consistent set of organizational strategies for managing creative work. Broadly speaking, creative work in organizations is project based. In project teams, individuals are assembled to work in teams of varying sizes to work on a problem, or set of problems, where new products or new processes must be developed (Dewar & Dutton, 1986). As work on a project proceeds, it is evaluated with respect to various criteria, and projects that meet these evaluation criteria are provided with the resources needed for continuation (Cooper & Kleinschmidt, 2000). What is of note here is that projects appear to progress through different phases of work, with these different phases making different demands for effective work. Thus in a study of project teams, Olson, Walker, Ruekert, and Bonner (2001) found that marketing expertise was important during the early phases of project work while production expertise was important in later stages.

Observations of this sort led Mumford and his colleagues (Mumford, Bedell-Avers, & Hunter, 2008; Mumford et al., 2013; Robledo et al., 2011) to propose a general model of how project work proceeds in organizations. This model is illustrated in Figure 34.1. Broadly speaking, this model holds that creative work in organizations is based on themes—critical technical and functional issues bearing on successful execution of organizational strategy (Hughes, 1989). These themes, in turn, provide a basis for both organizational learning and project definition (Cohen & Levinthal, 1990; Xu & Rickards, 2007). Projects defined within a theme typically begin with scanning, where the critical issues are trend analysis, capability development, and expertise acquisition. Subsequently, projects move to an elaboration phase where the key issues at hand are core technical development, information gathering, gap identification, and parameter testing. In the next phase, development of the innovative product begins where integrated solutions begin to be formulated, a technical core is formulated, early cycle trials are initiated, and cross-functional involvement begins. After initial development, an appraisal stage begins where the critical issues are prototyping, testing, refinement, and preparation. In the fifth and final stage, implementation of the new product or process begins, where the critical

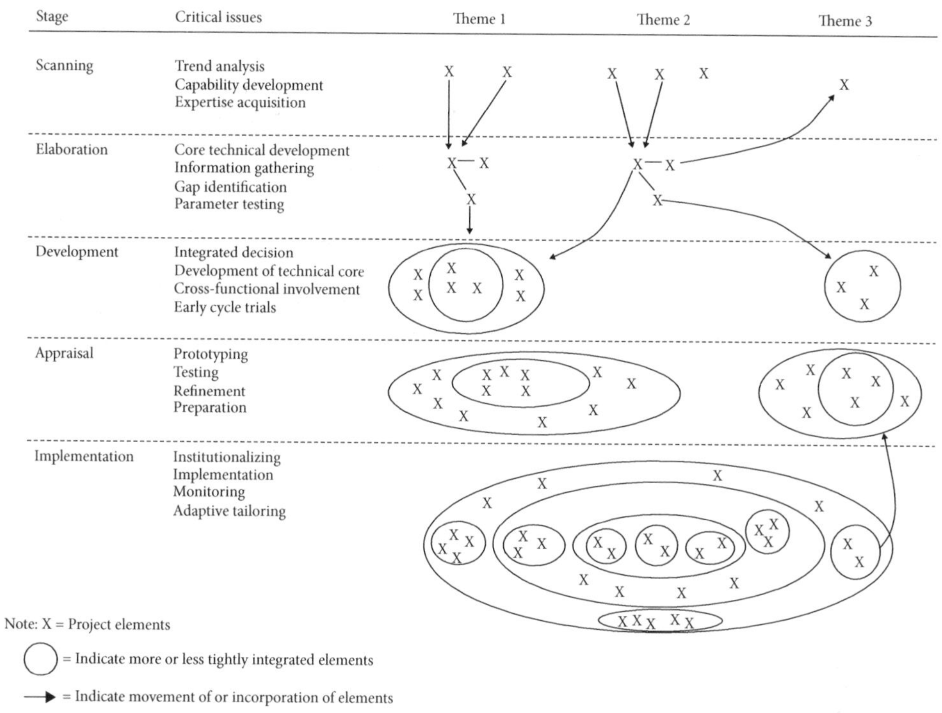

Figure 34.1. General Model of Project Work in Organizations. (Mumford, Bedell-Avers, & Hunter, 2008).

issues include marketing, production, monitoring, and adaptive tailoring.

One critical aspect of this model is that the number of people involved in a project, and the number of different forms of expertise required, generally increases as projects move from early-cycle to late-cycle efforts. Accordingly, project management systems are employed that allow organizations to manage tradeoffs between costs, risk, and learning. For example, a project failure in scanning or elaboration may still allow organizational learning without undue direct, or indirect, costs being attached to the effort. Moreover, as projects move into latter stages of this developmental cycle, cross-functional expertise will prove of greater value (Thamhain, 2003). However, in initial stages cross-functional expertise may prove of less value (Cardinal & Hatfield, 2000). Moreover, the nature of the creative problems presented in early stages may involve gap identification in development of viable production processes. In later stages, however, identification of viable marketing strategies or enhancements in production processes might call for creative thought. Thus, from an organizational perspective, innovative products, processes, or services require a sustained chain of multiple creative efforts.

Leadership

Prior Theories

The nature of creative problem solving, creative people, creative work, and creative work in organizations we have provided is noteworthy, in part, because it points to the difficulty of leading creative work. Implicit in our foregoing observations are a number of seemingly contradictory demands (Hunter et al., 2011; Mumford & Hunter, 2005; Sternberg, 2006). For example, organizations seek control of creative efforts as the individuals doing this work seek autonomy. Dominant, driven individuals must collaborate with others. Creative people seek support from an organization worried about cost and consequences. Although other examples of these fundamental contradictions might be cited (Mumford & Hunter, 2005), these examples serve to illustrate the key problem confronting those asked to lead creative work. How can these contradictory demands be resolved?

One approach that might be used to address this question is to apply an overarching theory of leadership to account for the leadership of creative efforts. One such framework that has proven attractive in this regard is the theory of transformational leadership. In one study along these lines, Shin and Zhou (2003) have provided evidence that leaders evidencing transformational behaviors was positively related to indices of follower creativity. Other studies, however, have indicated that these effects might be moderated by a number of conditions such as anonymity (Jung, 2001) and may be attributable primarily to the effects of transformational leadership on motivation (Sosik, Kahai, & Avolio, 1999) rather than the effectiveness of creative work. In a recent meta-analysis of studies examining the relationship between transformational leadership and innovation, Rosing, Frese, and Bausch (2011) found that the level of leaders was a key moderator of these effects, with transformational leadership exerting stronger effects on creativity when evidenced by upper-level leaders as opposed to those directly responsible for leading the creative effort. Although these relationships might be attributed to the motivation induced by upper-level transformational leaders, or their receptivity to new ideas and approaches, they indicate that transformational leadership may not provide a viable explanation for effective leadership among those asked to direct creative efforts.

Another general leadership model that has been used to account for the leadership of creative efforts may be found in theories of leader–member exchange. The basic assumption underlying this work is that positive exchange relationships between leaders and followers will provide requisite support to those doing creative work, thereby increasing motivation. Some support for this model has been provided by Tierney et al. (1999). They administered a measure of leader–member exchange to 191 employees of a chemical company's research and development department. Positive exchange relationships were found to yield correlations in the mid-.30s with invention disclosures and supervisory appraisals of employee creativity as well as indices of intrinsic motivation. Although those findings point to the potential relevance of positive exchange relationships, causality is ambiguous in this study—for example, creativity may have led to more positive exchange relationships. More centrally, many aspects of creative work, such as the need for critical evaluation (Lonergan et al., 2004) bring into question whether positive exchange relationships can always be established and maintained.

Expertise Leadership

Recognition of these points led Mumford et al. (2002) to argue that the effective leadership of creative efforts is better understood in terms of leader expertise. Some initial support for the proposition that expertise is fundamental to the leadership of creative efforts was provided by Andrews and Farris (1967). They obtained measures of leader technical skills, critical evaluation, motivation, and autonomy granted in a sample of 21 biomedical research teams. They found that leaders' technical skill ($r = .50$) was the best predictor of follower creative performance and a better predictor than other variables such as motivating followers. In another study along these lines, Barnowe (1975) examined the creative achievement of 963 chemists working in 81 research and development teams. Leaders were assessed with respect to (1) technical skill, (2) support, (3) participation, (4) closeness of supervision, and (5) task emphasis. It was found that leader technical skill was the best predictor ($r = .40$) on the part of members of these research and development teams.

Not only do prior studies indicate that professional expertise is critical to the success of those asked to lead creative people, but it also appears critical to exercising the key leadership activity—the exercise of influence (Yukl, 2010). Thamhain and Gemmill (1974) examined the effects of exercising various influence tactics on research and development personnel. Appraisals of managerial effectiveness were obtained along with a manager's use of various influence tactics such as expertise, reward, and coercion. It was found that follower appraisals of leader effectiveness were determined primarily by expertise.

Still another line of evidence pointing to the importance of expertise in the leadership of creative ventures may be found in a study by Keller (1989). Keller examined what research and development employees sought from leaders when working under conditions of uncertainty—bear in mind the point that because creative work is novel, ill-defined, and complex, it is inherently uncertain. When working under conditions of uncertainty, research and development employees, creative people, preferred leaders who initiated structure—and effective initiating structure is held to depend on expertise. In keeping with this observation, Arvey, Dewhirst, and Boling (1976) and Mossholder and Dewhirst (1980) found that scientists and engineers, when appraising leader effectiveness, based these appraisals largely on leader planning skills and clear definition of relevant goals.

A final line of evidence pointing to the importance of expertise in the leadership of creative efforts has been provided in a series of qualitative studies. Kazanjian, Drazin, and Glynn (2000) conducted observations of leaders during the development of a new aircraft. They found that effective leadership was attributable to the leaders' ability to make sense of crises arising in the production of this new product. Similarly, Dunham and Freeman (2000) in a qualitative study of play directors found that sensemaking by the leader was critical to the success of this creative effort. Recently, Marcy and Mumford (2010) examined how sensemaking influences leader performance. In a simulation study, they found that more effective sensemaking was tied to the leader's ability to identify critical causes of performance. What should be remembered here, however, is that identification of critical crises, and thus sensemaking, depends on leader expertise (Mumford, Friedrich, Caughron, & Antes, 2009).

TYPES AND FUNCTIONS OF EXPERTISE

Although the findings obtained in these and other studies (e.g., Chua, & Iyengar, 2008; Hemlin, 2006; Li, Tan, Teo, & Tan, 2006) also point to the importance of expertise in the leadership of creative efforts, two key questions arise as a result of this observation. First, what is the content of the expertise required of those asked to lead creative efforts? Second, how is this expertise employed in leading creative work? Recently, Mumford et al. (2013) and Robledo et al. (2011) have proposed a model of creative leadership that appears to provide plausible answers to both those questions.

As noted earlier, creative work is based on solving novel, ill-defined, and complex problems. In the leadership literature it has long been recognized that when people are asked to perform uncertain tasks, initiating structure is a critical attribute of effective leadership (Yukl, 2010). The initiation of structure when creative work is being conducted, however, implies that a variety of actions that must be taken by leadership. The leader must define or identify the themes and problems that will be pursued (Morgan, 1992) bearing in mind the point that not all themes, and/or projects defined in an attempt to exploit these themes, are of equal value with respect to both the states of the field and the strategy being pursued by the organization (Wise, 1992).

Identification of themes and projects, however, is only one aspect of the structuring activities required of those asked to lead creative efforts. The effective execution of complex, ill-defined projects, even projects in which new ideas will emerge and learning will occur (Patalano & Siefert, 1997), requires planning (Mumford, Hunter, & Van Doorn, 2001). It is through these plans that leaders direct the work of others and define the missions to be pursued by project teams at any given stage of the product development cycle. Planning, however, is a process that is expertise dependent (Thomas & McDaniel, 1990). These plans as formulated with respect to a particular stage of project development provide the basis on which leaders give missions to creative people. The missions provided to creative workers not only direct project work, they provide leaders with the basis for evaluating this work. Thus, Farris (1972) found that creative people sought feedback from leaders with regard to understanding of the mission and appraisal of their work in completing this mission. What should be recognized here, however, is that evaluation of creative work is critical both for enhancing the quality and originality of products (Lonergan et al., 2004) and for minimizing error (Dailey & Mumford, 2006).

Direction of creative work through planning and evaluation is not only necessary given the nature of the work creative people are being asked to accomplish, it will prove useful on a number of other grounds. First, influence is exercised vis-à-vis the technical work being accomplished—and this is the form of influence to which creative people respond. Second, owing to the focus of creative people on the profession, through technical planning and evaluation, leaders can appeal to followers' sense of identity (Kidder, 1981). Third, shared projects provide a basis that allows autonomous, introverted, driven, and arrogant individuals to work together in collaborative fashion. Thus leader structuring serves to help resolve a number of the contradictions evident in creative work.

By this same token, it is not sufficient for leaders simply to focus on structuring the work. As noted earlier, creative work in organizational settings is both costly (Chandy & Tellis, 2000) and potentially disruptive of organizational processes (Tushman & O'Reilly, 1997). The costs associated with creative efforts, along with low probability of success (Sharma, 1999), imply that organizations will not, inherently, be supportive. By the same token top management support is critical to the success of creative efforts. This observation, however, has an important implication. More specifically, leaders of creative efforts must sell their projects to acquire requisite resources—thus project championing is commonly held to be critical to the success of creative efforts (Allocca & Kessler, 2006; Howell & Boies, 2004). As a result, the leaders of creative efforts must not only lead the work, but they must also lead the organization with respect to this work. Indeed, in many cases, they may be the only people who have sufficient understanding of both the organization and the technical field to be capable of leading the organization to pursue certain lines of creative work.

As important as it is for the leaders of creative efforts to be able to sell projects, the resources provided by the organization may not prove fully sufficient. Organizations are loosely coupled social systems where multiple, often conflicting, goals are operating (Katz & Kahn, 1978). As a result, leaders of creative efforts must also build support for projects within other aspects of the system (Ancona & Caldwell, 1992). Thus leaders must communicate with other vested constituencies using this feedback to guide project work. The support leaders build in other organizational entities, in turn, provides a basis for recruiting requisite cross-functional expertise needed as a project proceeds toward development of a new product (Thamhain, 2003).

Not only must the leaders of creative efforts lead the work and organization, but they must also lead the people, or the group, doing this work. In fact, the available evidence indicates that leadership of the project team may be as important as leading the work in the organization (Rego, Sousa, Cunha, Correia, & Saur-Amaral, 2007). In this regard, however, it is important to bear in mind two points noted earlier. First, creative people are autonomous. Second, creative people decide to invest resources in creative work. These points are noteworthy because they suggest that leaders cannot force people to do creative work. Instead, they must select the right people to work on the team—people who possess both requisite expertise and are likely to find the mission being pursued by the team of professional interest.

The indirect leadership of project teams, through project staffing, however, will not prove fully sufficient to allow leaders of creative efforts to lead the group. Leaders must define group processes and create a climate inducing feelings of safety, support, and challenge. Given the known impact of group processes and climate perceptions on creative work (Amabile et al., 2004; Taggar, 2002) and the known impact of leaders in the definition of group process and climate perceptions (Day et al., 2006; James, James, & Ashe, 1990), a case can be made that leader definition of process and climate may be one of the more powerful influences on team creativity (Hunter et al., 2007). Of course, leaders must also interact with team members to establish team processes and climate. These interactions, however, also serve to model appropriate behavior and encourage effective interpersonal exchange (Jaussi & Dionne, 2003; Tierney et al., 1999) while building a sense of creative self-efficacy.

Thus the leaders of creative efforts must lead three distinct functions: (1) the work, (2) the organization, and (3) the people. These observations lead Mumford et al. (2013) and Robledo et al. (2011) to propose their tripartite model of the requirements for effective leadership of creative efforts. This model is presented in Figure 34.2. In the following sections we examine what is known about each of these key functions of creative leadership.

Leading the Work

Scanning and Theme Identification

Leading creative work ultimately depends on information bearing on the technical field and the organization. In keeping with this proposition, Souitaris (2001), in a study of how firms fielding new products used information sources, found that firms fielding new products were likely to use a wide array of sources (e.g., customer feedback, supplier feedback, competitor monitoring, and technology monitoring). Similarly, Koberg, Uhlenbruck, and Sarason (1996) found that among mature high technology firms, the introduction of innovative products was related to the intensity of scanning the firm's external environment. Still other work by Ford and Goia (2000) indicates that scanning the firm's internal environment, specifically issues encountered in day-to-day work, contributes to innovation.

Internal and external scanning by those asked to lead creative efforts serves two critical functions. First, scanning provides leaders with information bearing on emerging issues and technologies applying within the field. Second, it provides leaders with information bearing on the problems being encountered by the organization that might provide a basis for creative work. Although it seems reasonable to expect, based on our foregoing observations, that the leader's ability to synthesize internal and external information would prove critical to creative leadership, evidence bearing on this point is not available. What is clear is that the value of scanning appears to depend on the creative abilities of leaders. Thus Kickul and Gundry (2001) found that the value of scanning for firm innovation was moderated by the creative ability of senior leaders. Similarly, Rodan (2002) has found that senior leaders who initiate creative efforts have a more diverse network of atypical contacts—findings pointing to a broader range of scanning activities on the part of those asked to lead creative efforts.

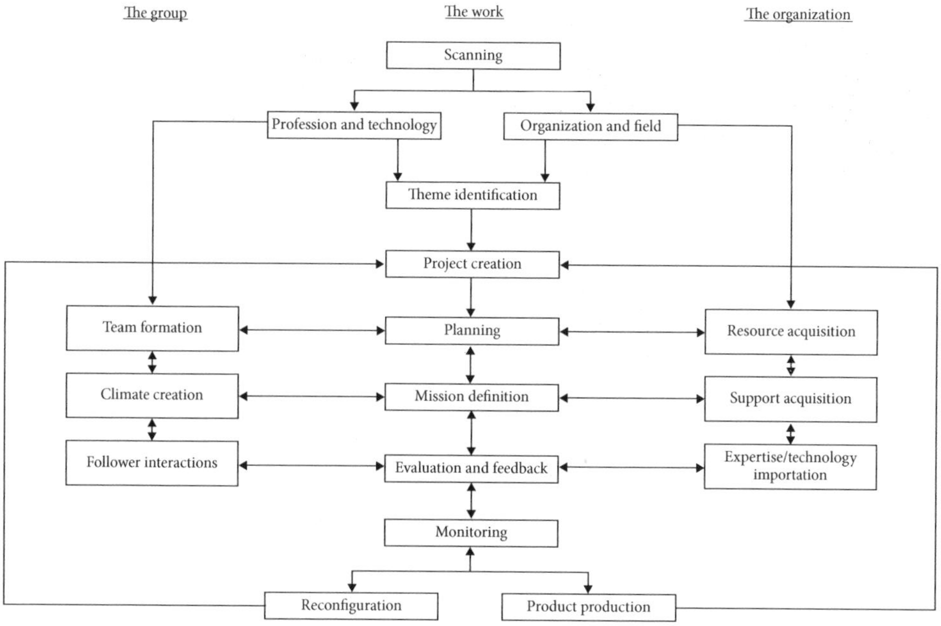

Figure 34.2. Tripartite Model of the Requirements for Effective Leadership of Creative Efforts. (Robledo, Peterson, & Mumford, 2011).

Although more work is needed examining how the information gathered in scanning is used in directing creative efforts (Mumford, Reiter-Palmon, & Redmond, 1999), the importance of scanning has three key implications for creative leadership. First, the leaders of creative efforts will maintain professional contacts—especially contacts with other leaders in the field. Second, the leaders of creative efforts will be actively involved in the work being conducted by the organization, using this involvement to identify critical problems being encountered. Third, leaders of creative efforts can be expected to monitor the technical capabilities and creative efforts being initiated by benchmark competitors.

Scanning is noteworthy not simply because it provides information but also because it provides a basis for identifying the themes to be pursued in subsequent creative work. Thus O'Connor (1998), in a qualitative study of eight leaders who had directed projects resulting in radical innovations, found that those leaders were able to envision, or foresee, the long-term implications of emerging technologies. Similarly, Houndshell (1992), in a historic analysis of DuPont's work on polymer chemistry, found that the leaders of this creative effort identified the key critical themes that might have value to DuPont in pursuing work in organic chemistry. Indeed, in the DuPont case a general goal organized these themes—identify synthetics that mimic the properties of wool.

The fundamental importance of the themes identified in guiding creative work in organizations is noteworthy for a number of reasons. First, given the need for sustained, and stable, investments by the organization, the leaders of creative efforts must build support for pursuing themes among senior leaders vis-à-vis the strategy being pursued by the organization (Hughes, 1989). Second, the leader must identify themes where creative work *might* resolve gaps or produce new knowledge of value to both the field and the firm. Thus, the leaders of creative efforts, in theme identification, do not build products but instead try to build knowledge of value to the firm (Cohen & Levinthal, 1990). Third, in appraising themes, leaders must take into account the firm's ability to exploit the knowledge produced. Thus viable technical themes might be dropped if the firm has neither the capability, nor the expertise, for pursuing emergent ideas.

Project Creation and Project Planning

With the identification of key themes, typically themes that are based on the fundamentals of the field (Mumford et al., 2013), it becomes possible for leaders to identify the projects to be pursued and plan project work. Stockstrom and Herstatt (2008) examined the impact of planning on 475 new product development efforts in electrical and mechanical engineering firms. Research and development directors appraised the success of these efforts, and staff appraised the intensity of planning activities. It was found that the intensity of planning activities was positively related ($r = .30$) to the success of these efforts. In keeping with this observation, Buijs (2008) found that the leaders of research and development efforts see planning as a critical component of their work. Moreover, Gross (2007) found that leaders of research and development efforts are unwilling to delegate planning activities.

Although the aforementioned findings point to the importance of project definition and project planning in the leadership of creative efforts, it should not be assumed that project planning is a simple process (Mumford, Schultz, & Van Doorn, 2001)—indeed planning of creative work makes substantial demands on leaders for complex, creative, thinking (Hemlin, 2009). Planning ultimately involves the mental simulation of future actions and the outcomes of these actions. Planning requires expertise (Bluedorn, 2002) with plan formulation being based on formation of a template mental model. This template model is used to guide the identification of critical causes, resources, restrictions, and contingencies. With the identification of critical plan attributes, an initial, prototype plan is formulated. This prototype plan, in turn, provides a basis for forecasting requisite actions and the outcomes of these actions (Byrne, Shipman, & Mumford, 2010) with plans being extended and revised based on those forecasts. The resulting plan provides a basis for appraising progress *and* effective exploitation of emergent opportunities (Patalano & Siefert, 1997).

In fact, planning and forecasting appear critical to leader performance in a variety of settings (Marta, Leritz, & Mumford, 2005; Shipman, Byrne, & Mumford, 2010). However, planning appears to be particularly important for those asked to lead creative efforts. Thus Farris (1972) studied when scientists and engineers sought to communicate with leaders. He found that scientists and engineers sought to communicate with leaders (1) when initially defining their work and (2) when seeking evaluation of their work. What is noteworthy here is that this pattern of communication suggests creative people seek feedback with respect to integration of their work into plans.

With regard to planning creative work, however, the leaders of creative efforts must take a number of issues into account. Perhaps the most important consideration is the stage of the project (Mumford et al., 2008) given that the issues to be addressed, and the products sought, vary as a function of the stage of the project development. At any given stage, moreover, leaders, in plan formation, must identify the critical resources required for plan execution (Nohria & Gulati, 1994) and the critical causes of effective plan execution that must be controlled (Marcy & Mumford, 2010). What should be recognized here, however, is that as plans progress the critical issues influencing plan execution will shift, typically moving from technical issues in early-stage efforts to organizational issues in latter-stage efforts. As a result, multiple cycles of planning and forecasting will be required of the leaders of creative efforts. As the plans move into the later stages of creative efforts, moreover, a wider array of considerations must be taken into account (e.g., production capacities, marketing strategies). What should be recognized here, however, is that leaders of creative efforts may, or may not, possess the expertise needed to address these issues. As a result, the planning of creative efforts will require leaders to identify gaps in their knowledge and seek information from others who possess requisite expertise. Thus, the leaders of creative efforts will often have extensive networks—networks providing information of value in the planning process. Finally, these plans cannot assume a static environment but instead must take into account likely changes in both the technical environment and the organizational environment that might effect plan execution (Caughron & Mumford, 2008).

Missions

Leaders' plans provide a basis for defining the missions given to the project groups. Missions, of course, imply the assignment of people to certain aspects of project work—the skills people bring to this work are a critical influence of project success. Missions, however, represent something more than work assignments. Mumford et al. (2002) have argued that due to the professional focus of creative people, missions provide both direction and motivation for creative people. Thus, in presenting missions, the leaders of creative efforts must anticipate the implications of the mission for both progress in the technical field and the potential contribution of mission execution for both other teams and the organization as a whole. Thus it is through missions, missions defined based on project plans, that leaders direct project teams.

The role of missions as a vehicle for directing creative workers has an important substantive implication. Missions cannot be vaguely defined. Instead, viable missions must define the work to be conducted, the timeframe in which the work must be completed, and the resources available for completing the work. By the same token, missions cannot be too tightly specified as tightly specified missions result in over-control and a reduction of perceived autonomy on the part of the people doing the work (Andrews & Farris, 1967). Thus mission definitions provided by leaders must be balanced with respect to the amount of direction provided. Moreover, as work progresses, the results flowing from this work must be used by the leader, through the leader's interactions with team members, to refine and revise missions. Thus missions given to project teams are dynamic rather than static entities (Nemanich & Keller, 2007).

Missions as defined, or redefined, however, provide one basis by which leaders direct the work of creative people. One key implication of missions is that they provide leaders with a basis for identifying the resources required of project teams. Missions, moreover, allow leaders to identify critical ambiguities surrounding mission execution. By directing team members' attention to those ambiguities and encouraging technical debate with regard to resolution of these ambiguities, leaders can stimulate creative work by team members. Thus missions provide a basis for structuring the work activities occurring in teams. In fact, studies by Anderson and West (1998); Bain, Mann, and Pirola-Merlo (2001); and Taggar (2001) have all indicated that induction of structure in project teams vis-à-vis the mission being pursued is critical to the success of creative efforts.

In this regard, however, it is important to recognize that the style by which mission direction occurs may be as important as mission content per se. In a series of experimental studies Maier and his colleagues (Hoffman, Hamburg, & Maier, 1962, Maier, 1950, 1953; Maier & Hoffman, 1964, 1965; Maier & Janzen, 1969; Mair & Solom, 1962) have examined how leaders should provide direction with respect to missions. Broadly speaking, the findings obtained in these studies indicate that leaders should (1) request or call for innovative solutions when they are needed, (2) define tasks in terms of technical rather than financial outcomes, (3) encourage group members to consider a variety of factual information bearing on the problem, (4) encourage group members to share factual information, (5) allow disagreements to be voiced but only in the context of the mission, (6) use disagreements to frame integrative solutions, and (7) extend discussions to give creative ideas time to emerge. Other field studies by Andriopoulos and Lowe (2000); Enson, Cottam, and Band (2001); and McGourty, Tarshis, and Dominick (1996) examining effective leadership in new product development efforts all point to the value of this intellectually engaging style of mission direction.

Evaluation and Feedback

Definition of the missions to be pursued by project teams is also used by leaders as a basis for evaluating followers work and providing feedback with regard to this work. Traditionally, evaluation of others' work has not been viewed as an especially demanding activity. Creative work, however, is novel, complex, and ill-defined—as a result, it is often not apparent, even to those doing the work, exactly how it should be appraised. One outcome of this phenomenon is that people doing creative work actively seek evaluative information from leaders (Farris, 1972). A leader's appraisals, moreover, provide a basis for progressive refinement of this work and learning on the part of organizational members (Rickards & Moger, 2006).

What should be recognized here, however, is that the evaluation of creative work is itself an inherently creative activity (Basadur, Runco, & Vega, 2000; Licuanan, Dailey, & Mumford, 2007). A study by Lonergan et al. (2004) has provided some evidence as to how evaluations should occur. They asked undergraduates to assume the roles of a marketing executive appraising ideas of varying quality and originality being proposed for advertising campaigns. Subsequently, a final campaign was to be proposed by the leader. They found that the most creative campaigns emerged under one of two conditions: first, when the leader appraised highly original campaigns with respect to idea quality, and second, when the leader appraised high-quality ideas with respect to originality. Thus leaders of creative efforts must both recognize the strengths and weakness of ideas (Licuanan et al., 2007) and provide compensatory feedback to offset deficiencies in these ideas with respect to the mission at hand and project plans.

Of course, it is not enough simply for a leader to provide compensatory feedback. The leader must give this feedback to a creative person who has a personal and professional investment in the work being evaluated. Sundgren, Selart, Ingelgard, and Bengtson (2005) examined how leaders should provide feedback information to those working on creative projects at five research and development sites. Creativity was assessed through a self-report inventory along with the styles by which leaders provide evaluative feedback: either control- or dialogue-based evaluation. It was found that creativity was positively related to dialogue-based evaluations where ideas and issues were appraised in a developmental fashion. Thus leaders, in providing feedback, cannot base appraisals solely on objective attributes of the idea but must provide followers with feedback that takes into account obstacles encountered, needs for improvement, and potential future directions.

Although evaluation and feedback should be provided as a dialogue between leaders and followers—a dialogue intended to compensate for potential deficiencies in ideas—not all, or, in fact, most ideas will work out. As a result, leaders must be willing to discontinue the work efforts that are unsatisfactory with regard to mission and project plans (Mumford et al., 2008). However, when work is discontinued, appraisals should focus on the mission and/or project rather than deficiencies in the individual or team. Moreover, in making these evaluations it is important for leaders to bear in mind that it is through these evaluative activities that competing needs can be addressed—for example the individual's need to explore versus the organization's need for control (Hunter et al., 2011). Thus in providing evaluative feedback leaders must recognize that they are operating in a boundary-spanning role and clarify to the people doing this work why, or why not, the work being done does, or does not, address the concerns of different stakeholders taking into account shifts in stakeholders, and stakeholder interests, as projects proceed through different stages of development.

Monitoring, Product Production, and Reconfiguration

What should be recognized with regard to evaluation and feedback is that it should not be overly close or tight. Multiple prior studies (Andrews & Farris, 1967; Barnowe, 1975) indicate that overly tight, or close, supervision diminishes the creative work of teams as they pursue a mission. By the same token, however, this statement should not be taken to imply that the leaders of creative efforts do not need to monitor the work of creative people. Rather, the monitoring done by the leaders of creative groups is with respect to the outcomes or implications of creative work rather than how the work is conducted. Not only does outcome-based monitoring preserve the autonomy of creative people (Fiest & Gorman, 1998), but it can also provide creative people with useful feedback information as to how products can be improved.

One implication of this observation is that the leaders of creative efforts in monitoring work being conducted must represent the concerns of critical stakeholders. Thus they might represent manufacturing concerns about product production processes or marketing concerns about unique product features when evaluating the work being conducted by creative people. This representational role in monitoring is noteworthy because it implies that the leaders of creative efforts must understand the concerns of critical stakeholders at a given point in the product development cycle.

Not only must leaders be capable of representing stakeholder concerns, but it should also be recognized that problems, crises, and issues arise continuously in creative work. What is clear is that leaders cannot ignore these crises. Thus Drazin et al. (1999), in a qualitative study of leaders in the production of a new airplane, found that leaders did not penalize followers for bringing crises to their attention. More centrally, in addressing these crises leaders played two key roles. First, they played an active role in helping followers "make sense" of the nature, origins, and significance of the crises. Second, they actively articulated strategies for addressing and/or managing the crisis. As a result, the leaders of creative efforts must engage in active monitoring of project work helping followers make sense of crises and providing frameworks guiding their responses. Thus the leaders of creative efforts must be actively involved in sensemaking and sensegiving as projects proceed through development.

Not only must leaders engage in sensemaking and sensegiving during crises, as projects proceed in response to crises or as a result of stage shifts, projects, and project teams, must be reconfigured. Typically, leaders can be expected to play a key role in reconfiguration activities. In part, the role of leaders in project reconfiguration is technical—how can work or work activities be restructured to enhance the likelihood of project success? In part, however, leaders' efforts in project reconfiguration involve managing the reactions of followers who are invested in their work. Moreover, during project reconfiguration, leaders must use what has been learned both to improve the capabilities of creative teams and to provide a basis for organizational learning. Thus reconfiguration, like monitoring, may make substantial demands on the leaders of creative efforts (Kidder, 1981).

Finally, it should be recognized that creative efforts in organizations are intended to result in new products, processes, or services. Products, processes, and services, however, imply changes in standard organizational operating procedures. Less attention has been given to the role of leaders in fielding new products, processes, and services (Basadur & Basadur, 2011). At a minimum, however, it is clear that leaders must be actively involved in transferring requisite expertise, and knowledge needed, to ensure the success of these efforts. Moreover, during these transition periods leaders must monitor problems encountered, using these problems as a basis for further learning. And, in dealing with problems encountered, the leader must serve as a representative of the creative effort, and the people involved in this effort, helping others understand the nature, significance, and implications of the creative effort for the work of their group.

Leading the People

Earlier we noted that creative people are driven, domineering, and achievement motivated with respect to professional achievement. This pattern of characteristics has an important implication. It is not sufficient for the leaders of creative efforts simply to lead the work. They must also lead the people doing the work. Indeed, historic studies of scientific leaders, for example, Oppenheimer in leading the development of nuclear weapons (Bird & Sherwin, 2005), point to the importance of leading the people. The findings obtained by Oldham and Cummings (1996), moreover, pointing to the environmental sensitivity of creative people leads to a similar conclusion when it is recognized that leader behavior represents a powerful force shaping the environment people experience (Yukl, 2010).

Team Formation

In our description of creative work we noted that creative work in organizations is not typically accomplished by an individual working alone. Rather creative work in organizational settings is accomplished by individuals working in teams. Leaders, of course, establish teams, and reconfigure teams, defining the expectations for team member interactions, all vehicles by which they can exercise influence. In this regard, one rather straightforward activity of leaders is often lost sight of. Here we refer to staffing projects vis-à-vis mission.

Earlier we noted that creative work is expertise dependent. Moreover, the motivation of creative people is often based on recognition for the projects on which they have worked. The need for expertise and the investment of creative people in certain select projects implies that leaders through the selection of project staff may exert a profound impact on the success of creative efforts. In fact, qualitative studies of new product development efforts in information technology point to the importance of staffing (Kidder, 1981). Although studies of project staffing for creative efforts are not available, effective project staffing by leaders is likely to take into account a number of considerations.

First, staffing will be expertise dependent. Thus leaders must appraise the professional knowledge and technical skills of those being selected for a project. This observation is noteworthy because it implies leaders must have an in-depth understanding of both the relevant professional fields and the intellectual demands made by the effort. Second, creative people by virtue of their autonomy and intrinsic interests (Hennessey & Amabile, 2010) cannot simply be assigned to projects. Rather key staff must be *recruited* by leaders based on the technical significance of the mission and its potential impact on their careers. Thus leaders must be able to sell projects, and the value of project work, to creative people. Third, creative work depends on a dynamic interpersonal exchange (Kamoche & Cunha, 2001). As a result, leaders must not only recruit the right staff, but they must also attend to the likely interactions among staff members with respect to the project at hand taking into account the unique knowledge of each individual and likely exchanges among these individuals (Kidder, 1981).

With staff selection the intellectual basis of a team has been established. This statement, however, should not be taken to imply that a team has been formed. Although many variables influence team formation and team performance, the availability of a shared mental model among team members appears to be of special importance (Day et al., 2006). As noted earlier, Mumford et al. (2001), in one study along these lines, induced shared mental models in teams working on a creative problem-solving task through a training intervention. They found that the production of higher quality and more original problem solutions occurred when team members had, as opposed to not having, shared mental models available. These findings are of importance because they suggest that leaders through their interactions with team members must (1) clearly articulate the mission at hand, (2) articulate the key attributes of the technical approach to be applied, (3) articulate noteworthy constraints on this approach, and (4) ensure team members accept this mental model.

In this regard, however, two points should be borne in mind. First, mental models provided by leaders cannot be so tightly defined as to prohibit creative thought. Thus Nyström (1979) found that excessively high levels of cohesion, or trust, could inhibit creativity. Even though lower levels of cohesion may increase stress (Keller, 2001; Murmann & Tushman, 1997), leaders can take actions to minimize stress and interpersonal conflict arising from divergent interpretations of shared mental models. Second, it appears that debate among team members, at least technical as opposed to personal debate, is beneficial with regard to the production of creative products (Isaken, Lauer, & Ekvall, 1999). Thus leaders cannot define team mental models so tightly as to prohibit viable technical debate. Instead, team mental models must provide an overarching structure that promotes rather than inhibits technical debate.

Although leaders by explicitly recognizing the value of intellectual debate with regard to technical issues bearing on shared mental models can encourage creativity (Mumford et al., 2002), the viability of such debates is likely to depend on the processes operating within teams. Thus Taggar (2002) assessed the group processes evident by more and less creative teams working on problem-solving tasks. His findings indicated that more creative teams evidence (1) team citizenship, (2) performance management, (3) effective communication, (4) involving others, (5) providing feedback, and (6) articulating professional conflicts and averting personal conflict. More centrally, Carmeli, Cohen-Meitar, and Elizur (2007) have provided evidence that effective leader behaviors can influence these interactional processes within creative teams. Thus the leaders of creative efforts must seek to ensure viable team processes are operating encouraging exchanges among team members, asking all team members to contribute, and recognizing team citizenship even if the contribution is not necessarily a critical technical input.

Although the operations occurring in teams are important for creative work, creativity in organizational settings increases when communication occurs outside the team. Thus Ancona and Caldwell (1992), in a study of 47 product development teams, found that the extensiveness of communication outside the project teams was positively related to both schedule and budget performance as well as to the creativity of the products produced. Other studies by Andrews and Smith (1996) and Gerstenberger and Allen (1968) point to similar conclusions with regard to the value of external communication. Thus the leaders of creative groups must encourage communication not only within the project team but also between team members and both the profession and other stakeholders in the organization within the scope of the mission being pursued by project teams. Typically, professional communication should be encouraged during early-cycle efforts while organizational communication should be encouraged during late-cycle efforts. Regardless of the specific venues of communication sought, however, the leaders of creative teams cannot allow teams to operate in isolation. Thus leader behaviors that expressly acknowledge the value of relevant external information for team performance and actions taken by the leader to facilitate such communications (e.g., introductions, external speakers, support for conference attendance) will prove of value.

Climate

The descriptions of creative teams presented in the preceding text indicate that leaders must create a cohesive team characterized by trust and positive exchange among team members albeit under conditions where debate can occur and the team is not operating in isolation from either the organization or the profession. By establishing these conditions of team operations, the leader may have done much to help establish a creative climate within the team. By the same token, investment in creative work is selective, especially for creative people (Oldham & Cummings, 1996), and as a result the actions taken by leaders to establish a viable climate, positive perceptions of the value of creativity in the work place, may do much to facilitate creative work.

Over the years, a number of studies have been conducted examining the kind of environments (Abbey & Dickson, 1983; Amabile et al., 1996; Curral, Forrester, Dawson, & West, 2001; Ekvall & Ryhammar, 1999; Lapierre & Giroux, 2003) contributing to creativity. These studies have stressed the importance of a variety of dimensions (Hunter, Bedell, & Mumford, 2005) including (1) positive peer group, (2) positive supervisory relations, (3) resources, (4) challenge, (5) mission clarity, (6) autonomy, (7) positive interpersonal exchange, (8) intellectual stimulation, (9) top management support, (10) reward orientation, (11) flexibility, (12) product emphasis, (13) participations, and (14) organizational integration. Hunter et al. (2007) conducted a meta-analysis of studies examining the relationship between these climate dimensions and creativity, taking into account criteria types (e.g., ratings versus performance) and criterion level (individual, group, organizational). The findings indicated that climate perceptions were positively related to creativity (Δ = .75) with these findings generalizing across criteria but proving especially strong for studies conducted at the group or organizational level (Δ = 1.03). Although all of these climate perceptions proved to be positively related to creativity the strongest relationships resulted from positive interpersonal exchange (Δ = .91), intellectual stimulation (Δ = .88) and challenge (Δ = .85) with these dimensions exerting their strongest efforts when individuals worked in teams in a relatively flat organizational structure.

What should be noted with regard to these findings is that leaders are critical entities shaping positive interpersonal exchange, perceptions of challenge, and feelings of intellectual stimulation in teams. Given the impact of positive interpersonal exchange, it should be recognized that some behaviors exhibited by certain leaders such as sarcasm, personalized criticism, and overly harsh criticism will clearly undermine a positive and effective climate. In this regard, a key aspect of transformational leadership is intellectual stimulation (Bass & Bass, 2008). Moreover, positive leader–member exchange creates conditions giving rise to positive interpersonal exchange within teams (Graen & Uhl-Bien, 1995). Similarly, leaders by defining challenging goals for teams may stimulate feelings of challenge (Shalley, 1995). Thus the behavior of leaders may prove a critical factor shaping climate perceptions. In keeping with this proposition, Jaussi and Dionne (2003), in an experimental study, found that leader role modeling of unconventional behavior could stimulate creative performance in teams. What should be recognized in this regard, however, is that it is not leader role modeling of atypical behavior per se that is critical. Instead, the study of Hunter et al. (2007) indicates that leaders can foster a climate supporting creativity through ongoing behaviors articulating professionally challenging missions, encouraging positive interpersonal exchange around these missions, and by providing followers with intellectual stimulation with regard to these missions. Leader actions in this regard, in turn, create perceptions of a climate where creative work, creative work being accomplished in well-functioning teams, is expected.

In recent years studies of climate have begun to ask another series of questions—asking what variables might mediate the effects of climate perceptions on creative work (Atwater & Carmeli, 2009; Carmeli et al., 2007; Jaussi, Randel, & Dionne, 2007; Tierney & Farmer, 2002). One plausible expectation is that a positive climate might motivate creative work. Atwater and Carmeli (2009), however, found that while positive leader exchanges increased energy invested in creative work these effects hold most strongly for people working on jobs where creativity was not integral to job performance. Thus climate does not appear to motivate creativity per se, rather, the findings obtained in studies by Jaussi, Randell, and Dionne (2007) and Tierney and Farmer (2002) suggest the effects of positive climate perceptions is that it induces feelings of creative self-efficacy with feelings of self-efficacy leading to a willingness to invest resources in creative work.

The potential impact of feelings of creative self-efficacy on subsequent creative work, however, has six important implications for the behavior of those asked to lead creative work. First, leaders should expressly request creative problem solutions from the team. Indeed, prior studies indicate that explicit requests for creativity typically enhance creative production (Barron & Harrington, 1981). Second, leaders should express confidence in the ability of team members to produce creative products (McGourty et al., 1996). Third, leaders should encourage active participation in creative work (Mossholder & Dewhirst, 1980). Fourth, leaders should encourage intellectual engagement in the work being done (Keller, 1997). Fifth leaders should provide requisite time for creative work (Redmond, Mumford, & Teach, 1993). Sixth, leaders should establish conditions such that when creative ideas are broached they are not subject to premature criticism (Andrews & Gordon, 1970; Gallucci, Middleton, & Kline, 2000). These, and other, actions taken by leaders may serve, along with climate perceptions, to build the kind of environments where people believe they are capable of making creative contributions.

Leading the Organization

Traditionally, studies of leadership have viewed the leader as exercising influence only with respect to followers (Yukl, 2010). Clearly, our foregoing observations indicate that the leaders of creative efforts have noteworthy influences on both the work being conducted and followers' investment in creative work. However, in creative efforts a leader's exercise of influence cannot be limited to the work and followers executing this work. Leaders of creative efforts must also exercise influence on the organization (Robledo et al., 2011). The need for leaders to influence the organization arises from three key considerations. First, the leaders of creative efforts may be one of a small group of people who fully understand the implications of the work being conducted (Cohen & Levinthal, 1990). Second, the organization must invest resources in this work (Nohria & Gulati, 1994)—real time and real money. Third, creative work in organizations ultimately involves new product production—and product production will necessarily involve multiple aspects of the organization (Buijs, 2007). As a result leaders must acquire resources, build support for the effort, and import requisite expertise for product production.

Resource Acquisition

Earlier, we noted that creative efforts in organizations are costly with respect to both process disruption and the costs entailed in the creative work. Moreover, creative efforts, by virtue of their novelty, are a high-risk proposition for organizations (Sharma, 1999). As a result, organizations may be unwilling to invest requisite resources in creative efforts. Accordingly, one key requirement imposed on the leaders of creative efforts is acquiring requisite resources. Thus Meyer and Goes (1988) in a study of 12 medical innovations in 25 hospitals found that CEO advocacy of the creative effort was positively related ($r = .30$) to adoption of the innovation and its routine use by hospital staff. Similarly, Maidique and Zirger (1984) surveyed technical, professional, and marketing managers involved in 158 new product introductions in the electronics industry. They found that top management support, support throughout the product development effort, led to successful introduction of new products. Other studies by Dougherty and Hardy (1996), a qualitative investigation, and Ong et al. (2003), a survey study, have also found that leader contact, with, and the engagement of a firm's senior management, with, the creative effort were critical to the successful introduction of new products.

The importance of senior management engagement in acquiring requisite resources, and broader institutional support (Ramus, 2001), has led to the argument that the leaders of creative efforts must be able to sell, or champion, projects (Howell & Higgins, 1988). In fact the available evidence indicates that effective product championing is related to the success of creative efforts in organizations. For example, Allocca and Kessler (2006) studied 158 new product development efforts in several high-technology industries. Senior managers involved in the project development effort were asked to complete surveys examining variables such as goal clarity, cross-functional teamwork, and product championing. It was found that product championing was positively related to both the speed of product development and product success proving especially important for more radical innovations ($b = .46$). Other work by Markham, Green, and Basu (1991) and Markham and Griffin (1998) points to similar conclusions concerning the importance of product championing in the leadership of creative efforts.

Markham and Aiman-Smith (2001) conducted a review of prior studies on product champions, focusing on requisite leader behaviors. The findings obtained in this study indicated that effective championing was based on the availability of an extensive network of contacts throughout the organization. Moreover, effective champions were found to be politically skilled visionaries who were in a position to take risks and evidenced the strong communication skills characteristic of transformation leaders. Thus effective championing may require a networked, politically skilled, transformational leadership.

In another study of product champions, Howell and Boies (2004) contrasted 19 matched pairs of champions and non-champions involved in one of 28 new product development efforts. Interviews conducted with champions and non-champions were content analyzed to assess knowledge, idea promotion, packing, and selling. It was found that contextual knowledge was a powerful influence on both the packaging of ideas and effective sales of these ideas to others.

The findings emerging from the Howell and Boies (2004) study are noteworthy with regard to the leadership of creative efforts for two reasons. First, they indicate that the leaders of creative efforts, to be able to engage in effective championing, must have an in-depth understanding of the strategy being pursued by the organization—including critical differentiators of success and critical competitors (Laugen, Boer, & Acur, 2006). Second, leaders must not only understand broader business strategy, but they must also have an in-depth understanding of day-to-day business practices using this knowledge not only in the development of project plans but also in the championing of projects (Lee & Kelley, 2008). Thus the leaders of creative efforts must know whom to talk to, and how to talk to them, and must have access to networks which allow them to "pitch" projects with respect to broader organizational strategy in practical day-to-day terms.

Support Acquisition

Championing may result in requisite support from top management. However, organizations involve a number of distinct, semi-autonomous, subsystems (Katz & Kahn, 1978). What should be recognized here is that these subsystems may, at least at times, act to block innovative efforts based on their own concerns. Thus Jelinek and Schoonhoven (1990), in a qualitative study of a new product development effort, found that viable new product development efforts could fail as a result of lack of support from key subsystems in organizations. More centrally, in the later stages of new product development efforts, and virtually all process innovations as well, involvement of multiple subsystems is required. Thus production must establish new procedures for producing innovative products, purchasing may need to find new suppliers, and marketing must develop new advertising campaigns.

The acquisition of support from relevant subsystems in organizations, in part, depends on top management support and championing. However, acquisition of support from other organizational units will also involve three other critical activities on the part of those asked to lead creative efforts. More specifically, leaders of creative efforts must (1) establish a sense of shared investment, (2) promote cross-functional learning, and (3) manage demands imposed.

The term "shared investment" is intended to refer to the willingness of other subsystems to see in creative efforts value for the organization as a whole and congruence with the functional requirements imposed on the subsystem. At one level, this statement implies that the leaders of creative efforts must not only champion projects with respect to top management, but they must also champion projects with respect to other critical subsystems within the organization, being able to explain the value of the creative effort for both the organization as a whole and the objectives of the subsystem at hand (Mumford et al., 2013). What should be recognized here, however, is that sales of this sort require attention to costs and benefits of the project vis-à-vis current concerns of the relevant subsystem along with appraisal of the implications of the project for routine functioning of the subsystem. Within subsystems decisions to invest resources in non-normative functions are often based on the appraisals of central, critical, leaders within the subsystem. This observation, in turn, implies that the leaders of creative efforts must engage not only in direct sales to subsystems as a whole, they must also be able to engage in indirect sales by building commitment to the project among individual leaders within the subsystem—often, but not necessarily always, by exploiting personal networks to build support within the subsystem prior to attempts to sell the subsystem as a whole (Kidder, 1981).

In building support among relevant constituencies within an organization, however, leaders must bear in mind the point that any given external subsystem has accountabilities beyond the creative effort. Thus creative efforts that make excessive demands on ongoing subsystem resources and functions are likely to be appraised negatively. Those asked to lead creative efforts must, as a result, manage the demands made on supporting subsystems (Wentroff, 1992). Management of these demands, however, is not simply a matter of limiting requests for support. Rather, it may require the leader of creative efforts to actively work with representatives of other subsystems with the goal of managing the amount and timing of support so as to maximize both the success of the creative effort at hand and the effectiveness of the subsystem providing support. As a result, leaders of creative efforts must help other subsystems solve problems broached for the subsystem by the creative effort.

Finally, efforts to build support among relevant subsystems are noteworthy because they provide a basis for mutual learning. In other words, the leader of the creative effort must acquire an understanding of the other organizational subsystem just as the subsystem must acquire an understanding of the creative effort for operations of the organizational subsystem. Recognition of the importance of shared learning in acquisition of support for creative projects led Xu and Rickards (2007) to argue that organizational learning may be critical to the success of creative efforts. Given the likely impact of organizational learning on building subsystem support, enhancing subsystem functioning to support fielding of the creative effort, and revision of initial appraisals to enhance the workability of the creative effort, it seems reasonable to expect that support acquisition may result in a dynamic exchange critical to successful introduction of new products and processes.

Expertise/Technology Importation

The acquisition of support, and learning in acquiring support, provides leaders with a basis for importing both expertise and technology into creative efforts. In fact, the model of project development cycles presented earlier suggests that as projects proceed into the later stages of development, importing both technology and expertise will be a crucial influence on project success (Mumford et al., 2008). In keeping with this observation a variety of studies examining the success of new product development efforts indicate that the establishment of cross-functional teams may be critical to project success (Allocca & Kessler, 2006; Thamhain, 2003). In one study along those lines, Keller (2001) examined the influence of cross-functional teams on the success of 93 applied research and development teams. His findings indicated that use of cross-functional teams, and thus importation of expertise and technology, was a powerful influence on project performance—both schedule performance and project success.

By the same token, Keller's (2001) findings indicate that cross-functional teams also evidence higher levels of stress and poorer communication. Thus although the creation of cross-functional teams may contribute to project performance, the inclusion of multiple functional perspectives may led to substantial process loss in creative teams. Potential process loss, in turn, implies that leaders of creative efforts must initiate actions intended to minimize process loss arising from cross-functional teams through behaviors intended to clarify goals and establish a shared mission (West, Borrill, Dawson, Brodbeck, & Shapiro, 2003), sensemaking and sensegiving with regard to disagreements emerging among team members (Reiter-Palmon, Herman, & Yammarino, 2008), and balanced evaluation of alternative courses of action being proposed from different functional perspectives (McKenna, Rooney, & Boal, 2009). Thus effective leadership of cross-functional teams may require leaders evidencing substantial wisdom and an ability to help people of different backgrounds understand each other and emerging crises (Drazin et al., 1999).

Although cross-functional teams appear beneficial in the later stages of project development efforts, they may not always prove useful. For example, Cardinal (2001) found that location of early-cycle research and development teams near sites where cross-functional contacts would occur typically inhibited team performance. In an experimental study of creative problem solving, Friedrich and Mumford (2009) introduced divergent ideas at various points as people worked on a creative problem-solving task. They found that introduction of divergent ideas typically resulted in problem solutions of lower, *not* higher, quality and originality. These findings indicate that induction of cross-functional perspective may disrupt early cycle creative efforts.

These findings are noteworthy for two reasons. First, they imply that importation of expertise and technology must be managed by the leaders of creative efforts. New expertise and new technology should be introduced only when it becomes apparent that project performance will suffer without the availability of this expertise or technology. Introduction of new expertise and new technology must therefore be timed to projected needs—otherwise this expertise or technology may prove distracting on tasks that already make substantial resource demands. Thus leaders must appraise the need for new expertise and new technology. Moreover, effective leaders should prepare project teams to incorporate new expertise and new technology—clarifying the potential contributions of this expertise and technology to project success.

Second, it will typically be the leaders of creative efforts who monitor project work vis-à-vis the organization and technical field. Thus leaders must appraise the implications of new technical capabilities and organizational expertise for project performance. These appraisals must, in turn, be used by leaders to appraise the potential value of new expertise and new technologies for project success. These technical and organizational appraisal skills are commonly found to be critical to successful leadership of creative projects in qualitative studies (Bird & Sherwin, 2005). Moreover, such appraisals may require effective forecasting of the implications of inducing new expertise and/or new technologies on project performance (Shipman et al., 2010). By the same token they may also require leaders to dismiss professionally interesting expertise and technologies if they are not relevant to the project at hand (Bird & Sherwin, 2005).

Conclusions

Before proceeding to the broader implications of the present effort certain limitations should be borne in mind. To begin, we have in the present effort focused on conditions where creative work is assumed to be of value to an organization. What should be recognized here, however, is that the need for creative work in organizations varies with certain conditions of the external environment. Thus Wise (1992), in a study of the electrical industry, found that innovations emerged in waves as a function of technological change. Similarly, Hunter et al. (2007) found that creativity was typically of greater value in turbulent, dynamic environments than in more stable environments. Along related lines, it should also be recognized that some business strategies, even strategies employed in turbulent environments, may not require creativity or effective leadership of creative people (Miles & Snow, 1978).

Along related lines, our focus in the present effort has been on a particular level of analysis. More specifically, in the present effort, we have focused on what a leader must do when they take responsibility for a creative effort. Thus the conclusions derived from the present effort were framed with respect to creative problem solving, creative people, creative work, and creativity in organizations. By the same token, however, it must be recognized that a variety of other variables influence creativity and innovation in organizations such as intellectual property rights (Quigg, 1992), alliances (Osborn & Marion, 2009) and capital resources (Dean & Sharfman, 1996). Thus the present effort should not be viewed as providing a comprehensive description of creativity in organizations (Robledo, Hester, Peterson, & Mumford, 2012).

Along somewhat different lines, it should be recognized that we have in the present effort treated all creative efforts in organizations as functionally equivalent. However, distinctions have been drawn between radical and incremental innovations and processes and product innovations (Abbey & Dickson, 1983) in discussions of organizational creativity. As a result, it is possible that the type of innovation of concern may act as a significant contingency on the conclusions drawn about the leadership of creative efforts in the present discussion.

Finally, the requirements imposed on creative problem solving, creative people, and creative work vary as a function of field (Csikszentmihaly, 1999; Simonton, 2012). In the present effort, we have assumed there is sufficient constancy in the requirements for creative work across fields to allow some general conclusions to be drawn about the nature of effective leadership of creative work in organizations. By the same token, however, it should be recognized that the demands made by certain professional fields might also act as noteworthy contingencies on the conclusions emerging from the present effort.

Even bearing these caveats in mind, however, we believe that our observations in the present effort do lead to some noteworthy conclusions about the leadership of creative efforts. Perhaps the first, and most basic, conclusion flowing from the present effort is that the success of creative efforts in organizations strongly depends on effective leadership (Mumford et al., 2002). At one level, the impact of leadership on the success of creative efforts is not surprising. We have long known that leadership is a particularly critical influence on performance whenever multiple people are asked to work on novel, complex, ill-defined tasks associated with substantial risk (Yukl, 2010). At another level, however, this observation suggests our tendency to discount leadership in discussion of creativity in organizations may be a great mistake—a mistake that contradicts both the facts and the theory.

If it is granted that leaders, in fact, make a big difference to the success of creative efforts in organizations, then a new question comes to fore. What makes for effective leadership of creative efforts in organizations? In the present effort we have argued that the leadership of creative work is an unusually complex form of leadership. The demands made on the leaders of creative efforts arise from the fundamental nature of creative work. Creative problem solving is a demanding, resource intensive form of cognition. Creative people are demanding, rather difficult people. However, these demanding, difficult, albeit professionally focused, people must be asked to work together—working together on projects that have a low probability of success where the organization supporting the work must bear the costs and potential disruption.

These characteristics of creative work in organizations are conditions where leadership will prove a powerful influence on the success of creative ventures (Mumford et al., 2002). More centrally, they suggest that leaders, effective leaders, must execute three key functions. They must lead the work. They must lead the people doing this work. And, they must lead the organization.

In recent years, the focus of leadership research has primarily been on leading the people (Gardner, Lowe, Moss, Mahoney, & Cogliser, 2010). Often this is an appropriate approach to take in studies of leadership. Creative people, however, respond to the technical missions associated with the work to be accomplished. In fact, influence can be exercised only through professional expertise (Thamhain & Gemmill, 1974). When these observations are combined with the fact that creative people are being asked to work on complex, novel, ill-defined problems (Mumford & Gustafson, 2007), it implies that leaders must focus on the work being conducted. What should be recognized here, however, is that leadership of the work is an unusually complex activity—requiring scanning of both the organization and professional field, theme identification, planning, mission definition, evaluation and feedback, and ongoing monitoring. These varied activities are noteworthy not only because they demand substantial breadth and depth of expertise but also because they call for substantial creative thought on the part of leaders (Mumford, Connelly, & Gaddis, 2003). Thus leaders are not passive players in creative efforts—they must be actively engaged in the work being conducted, staying focused on the mission at hand.

The leadership of creative efforts, however, is not solely an intellectual matter. As noted earlier, creative people tend to be environmentally sensitive—refusing to invest in creative work when there is no support (Oldham & Cummings, 1996). The leaders need not motivate creative people, people who are already motivated (Fiest & Gorman, 1998), but instead must establish conditions likely to support creative work. Establishing these conditions requires bringing together people with requisite expertise needed at that point in the project development cycle. Thus leaders must be good at appraising others' technical competencies. Leaders, moreover, must establish functional team processes and articulate a mental model that is shared by team members with regard to the mission at hand (Day et al., 2006; Mumford et al., 2001). As team members work on this mission, they must establish a climate likely to promote creative work—a climate characterized by challenge, intellectual stimulation, and positive interpersonal exchange (Hunter et al., 2007). Hence, the leaders of creative efforts need not be supportive of an individual but instead must intellectually challenge followers, promoting debate around mission-critical activities where followers acquire a sense of creative self-efficacy (Tierney & Farmer, 2002).

Often the leaders of creative efforts are comfortable leading the work and the people. In organizations, however, creative work is a costly, high-risk, venture (Sharma, 1999). Thus leaders must be able to sell their projects. Not only must leaders be able to sell their projects to top management, they must be able to build support for the effort throughout the organization. As a result, the leaders of creative efforts must know and understand the organization, both its strategy and its key units, and be able to sell their projects to these groups to acquire requisite support (Howell & Boies, 2004). Indeed, owing to the need to understand both technology and the organization, it may only be the leader who can sell these projects. However important sales work may be unto itself, it should be recognized that it is through sales that leaders acquire the expertise and support needed to import technology and expertise as projects progress to fielding. Moreover, in these "sales" efforts the leader must serve as an internal consultant helping supporting entities address the problems broached by the creative effort. Thus the leaders of creative efforts are a critical factor shaping the absorptive capacity of the organization (Cohen & Levinthal, 1990).

When one considers the complex nature of the activities being conducted by the leaders of creative efforts, it is, in fact, surprising that anyone can actually do this work. In fact, Hauschildt & Kirchmann (2001) have found on successful new product development efforts, different people, different leaders, act to fill each of these three key roles. This finding is of some importance because it suggests that the leaders of creative efforts must be capable of engaging in shared, or collective, leadership (Friedrich, Vessey, Schulke, Ruark, & Mumford, 2009). The identification of these, and other tactics, that might serve to reduce the demands made on the leaders of creative efforts, in fact, might prove of substantial practical value given the complex nature of this form of leadership.

It is important to note that promoting the best engineer, that is, the person with the most technical expertise, is an effective way to ensure those in leadership have some of the skills necessary to manage creative people. Of course, other skills may be important for leadership, such as having an understanding of the organization as well as an articulated technical mission (Mumford, Connelly, & Gaddis, 2003). Thus, it is necessary to provide leaders, and future leaders, of creative efforts with broad exposure and broad understanding (Mumford, 2000).

By the same token, asking leaders to master the work, the people, and the organization suggests that systematic developmental interventions might also prove of value (Mumford et al., 2013; Robledo et al., 2011). For example, rotational assignments that expose potential leaders to broader organizational strategy might have some value both in helping potential leaders establish networks in the organization as well as an understanding of strategic issues facing the organization. Similarly, mentoring programs might prove of value in illustrating to potential leaders of creative efforts how to go about managing teams and establishing viable climates within teams (Mumford, Friedrich,

Caughron, & Byrne, 2007). Finally, encouraging exposure to key professional committees might provide a basis for scanning while ensuring leaders possess requisite technical knowledge.

We do not believe this list of potential developmental interventions to be exhaustive. However, in professional organizations creative people are left to their own to pursue potential developmental experiences. Given the complex nature of the work of creative leaders we believe this is a mistake. In fact, more, and more systematic, developmental interventions may be needed to prepare people to lead creative efforts than is the case in other areas of leadership. We hope the present effort will provide an impetus for future work along these lines—work that recognizes both the complex nature of creative leadership and its exceptional value to organizations.

Acknowledgments

We thank Sam Hunter, Ginamarie Ligon, Katherine Bedell, Isaac Robledo, David Peterson, and Kim Hester for their contributions to the present effort. Correspondences should be addressed to Dr. Michael D. Mumford, Department of Psychology, The University of Oklahoma, Norman, Oklahoma, 73019 or mmumford@ou.edu

References

Abbey, A., & Dickson, J. (1983). R&D work climate and innovation in semiconductors. *Academy of Management Journal, 25*, 362–368.

Allocca, M. A., & Kessler, E. H. (2006). Innovation speed in small and medium-sized enterprises. *Creativity and Innovation Management, 15*, 279–295.

Amabile, T. M., Conti, R., Coon, H., Lazenby, J., & Herron, M. (1996). Assessing the work environment for creativity. *Academy of Management Journal, 39*, 1154–1184.

Amabile, T. M., Shatzel, E. A., Moneta, G. B., & Kramer, S. J. (2004). Leader behaviors and the work environment for creativity: Perceived leader support. *The Leadership Quarterly, 15*, 5–33.

Ancona, D., & Caldwell, D. (1992). Demography and design: Predictors of new product team performance. *Organization Science, 3*, 321–341.

Anderson, N., & West, M. A. (1998). Measuring climate for work group innovation: Development and validation of the team climate inventory. *Journal of Organizational Behavior, 19*, 235–258.

Andrews, F. M., & Farris, G. F. (1967). Supervisory practices and innovation on scientific teams. *Personnel Psychology, 20*, 497–515.

Andrews, F. M., & Gordon, G. (1970). Social and organizational factors affecting innovation research. *Proceedings for the American Psychological Association, 78*, 589–570.

Andrews, J., & Smith, D. C. (1996). In search of marketing imagination: Factors affecting the creativity of marketing programs for the mature products. *Journal of Marketing Research, 33*, 174–187.

Andriopoulos, C., & Lowe, A. (2000). Enhancing organisational creativity: The process of perpetual challenging. *Management Decision, 38*, 734–742.

Arvey, R. D., Dewhirst, H. D., & Boling, J. C. (1976). Relationships between goal clarity, participation in goal setting, and personality characteristics on job satisfaction in a scientific organization. *Journal of Applied Psychology, 61*, 103–105.

Atwater, L., & Carmeli, A. (2009). Leader-member exchange, feelings of energy, and involvement in creative work. *The Leadership Quarterly, 20*, 264–275.

Baer, M., & Frese, M. (2003). Innovation is not enough: Climates for initiative and psychological safety, process innovations, and firm performance. *Journal of Organizational Behavior, 24*, 45–68.

Bain, P. G., Mann, L., & Pirola-Merlo, A. (2001). The innovation imperative: The relationships between team climate, innovation, and performance in research and development teams. *Small Group Research, 32*, 55–73.

Barnowe, J. T. (1975). Leadership and performance outcomes in research organizations. *Organizational Behavior and Human Performance, 14*, 264–280.

Barron, F., & Harrington, D. (1981). Creativity, intelligence, and personality. *Annual Review of Psychology, 32*, 434–476.

Basadur, M. S., & Basadur, T. M. (2011). Where are the generators? *Psychology of Aesthetics, Creativity and the Arts, 5*, 29–42.

Basadur, M., Runco, M. A., & Vega, L. A. (2000). Understanding how creative thinking skills, attitudes and behaviors work together: A causal process model. *Journal of Creative Behavior, 34*, 77–100.

Bass, B. M., & Bass, R. (2008). *The Bass handbook of leadership: Theory, research, and managerial applications*. New York, NY: Free Press.

Besemer, S. P., & O'Quin, K. (1999). Confirming the three-factor creative product analysis matrix model in an American sample. *Creativity Research Journal, 12*, 287–296.

Bird, B., & Sherwin, M. J. (2005). *American Prometheus: The triumph and tragedy of J. Robert Oppenheimer*. New York, NY: Random House.

Bluedorn, A. C. (2002). *The human organization of time: Temporal realities and experience*. Stanford, CA: Stanford Business Books.

Buijs, J. (2007). Innovation leaders should be controlled schizophrenics. *Creativity & Innovation Management, 16*, 203–210.

Buijs, J. (2008). Action planning for new product development projects. *Creativity and Innovation Management, 17*, 319–333.

Byrne, C. L. Shipman, A. S., & Mumford, M. D. (2010). The effects of forecasting on creative problem-solving: An experimental study. *Creativity Research Journal, 22*, 119–138.

Cardinal, L. B. (2001). Technological innovation in the pharmaceutical industry: The use of organizational control on managing research and development. *Organization Science, 12*, 19–37.

Cardinal, L. B., & Hatfield, D. E. (2000). Internal knowledge generation: The research laboratory and innovative productivity in the pharmaceutical industry. *Journal of Engineering & Technology Management, 17*, 247–272.

Carmeli, A., Cohen-Meitar, A., & Elizur, D. (2007). The role of job challenge and organizational identification in enhancing creative behavior among employees in the workplace. *Journal of Creative Behavior, 41*, 75–90.

Caughron, J. J., & Mumford, M. D. (2008). Project planning: The effects of using formal planning techniques on creative problem-solving. *Creativity and Innovation Management, 17*, 204–215.

Chandy, R. K., & Tellis, G. J. (2000). The incumbent's curse? Incumbency, size and radical innovation. *Journal of Marketing, 64,* 1–17.
Chen, M. (2007). Entrepreneurial leadership and new ventures: Creativity in entrepreneurial teams. *Creativity and Innovation Management, 16,* 239–249.
Chernow, R. (1998). *Titan: The life of John D. Rockefeller, Sr.* New York, NY: Vintage.
Chua, R. Y. J., & Iyengar, S. S. (2008). Creativity as a matter of choice: Prior experience and task instruction as boundary conditions for the positive effect of choice on creativity. *Journal of Creative Behavior, 42,* 164–180.
Cohen, W. M., & Levinthal, D. A. (1990). Absorptive capacity: A new perspective on learning and innovation. *Administrative Science Quarterly, 35,* 128–152.
Cooper, R. G., & Kleinschmidt, E. J. (2000). New product performance: What distinguishes the star products. *Australian Journal of Management, 25,* 17–46.
Csikszentmihalyi, M. (1999). Implications of a system's perspective for the study of creativity. In R. J. Sternberg (Ed.), *Handbook of creativity* (pp. 313–338). Cambridge, UK: Cambridge University Press.
Curral, L. A., Forrester, R. H., Dawson, J. F., & West, M. A. (2001). It's what you do and the way that you do it: Team task, team size, and innovation-related group processes. *European Journal of Work and Organizational Psychology, 10,* 187–204.
Dailey, L., & Mumford, M. D. (2006). Evaluative aspects of creative thought: Errors in appraising the implications of new ideas. *Creativity Research Journal, 18,* 367–384.
Damanpour, F. (1991). Organizational innovation: A meta-analysis of effects of determinants and moderators. *Academy of Management Journal, 34,* 555–590.
Day, D. V., Gronn, P., & Salas, E. (2006). Leadership in team-based organizations: On the threshold of a new era. *The Leadership Quarterly, 17,* 211–216.
Dean, J. W., & Sharfman, M. P. (1996). Does decision process matter: A study of strategic decision making effectiveness. *Academy of Management Journal, 39,* 368–396.
DeCusatis, C. (2008). Creating, growing and sustaining efficient innovation teams. *Creativity & Innovation Management, 17,* 155–164.
Dess, G. G., & Pickens, J. C. (2000). Changing roles: Leadership in the 21st century. *Organizational Dynamics, 28,* 18–34.
Dewar, R. D., & Dutton, J. E. (1986). The adoption of radical and incremental innovations: An empirical analysis. *Management Science, 32,* 1422–1433.
Dougherty, D., & Hardy, B. F. (1996). Sustained innovation production in large mature organizations: Overcoming organization problems. *Academy of Management Journal, 39,* 826–851.
Drazin, R., Glynn, M. A., & Kazanjian, R. K. (1999). Multi-level theorizing about creativity in organizations: A sensemaking perspective. *Academy of Management Review, 24,* 286–329.
Dunham, L., & Freeman, R. E. (2000). There is business like show business: Leadership lessons from the theater. *Organizational Dynamics, 29,* 108–122.
Ekvall, G., & Ryhammar, L. (1999). The creative climate: Its determinants and effects at a Swedish University. *Creativity Research Journal, 12,* 303–310.
Enson, J., Cottam, A., & Band, C. (2001). Fostering knowledge management through the creative work environment: A portable model from the advertising industry. *Journal of Information Science, 27,* 147–155.
Farris, G. F. (1972). The effect of individual role on performance in innovative groups. *R & D Management, 3,* 23–28.
Fiest, G. J., & Gorman, M. E. (1998). The psychology of science: Review and integration of a nascent discipline. *Review of General Psychology, 2,* 3–47.
Finke, R. A., Ward, T. B., & Smith, S. M. (1992). *Creative cognition: Theory, research, and applications.* Cambridge, MA: The MIT Press.
Ford, C., & Goia, D. (2000). Factors influencing creativity in the domain of managerial decision making. *Journal of Management, 26,* 705–732.
Friedrich, T. L., & Mumford, M. D. (2009). The effects of conflicting information on creative thought: A source of performance or performance decrements? *Creativity Research Journal, 21,* 265–281.
Friedrich, T. L., Vessey, W. B., Schuelke, M. J., Ruark, G. A., & Mumford, M. D. (2009). A framework for understanding collective leadership: The selective utilization of leader and team expertise within networks. *The Leadership Quarterly, 20,* 933–958.
Gallucci, N. T., Middleton, G., & Kline, A. (2000). Perfectionism and creative strivings. *Journal of Creative Behavior, 34,* 135–141.
Gardner, W. L., Lowe, K., Moss, T. W., Mahoney, K., & Cogliser, C. (2010). Scholarly leadership of the study of leadership: A review of The Leadership Quarterly's second decade, 2000-2009. *The Leadership Quarterly, 21,* 922–958.
Gerstenberger, P. C., & Allen, T. J. (1968). Criteria used by research and development engineers in the selection of an information source. *Journal of Applied Psychology, 52,* 272–279.
Graen, G. B., & Uhl-Bien, M. (1995). Relationship-based approach to leadership: Development of leader-member exchange (LMX) theory of leadership over 25 years: Applying a multilevel multi-domain perspective. *The Leadership Quarterly, 6,* 219–247.
Gross, D. (2007). Leadership in R&D projects. *Creativity and Innovation Management, 16,* 447–456.
Gryskiewicz, S. (1999). *Positive turbulence: Developing climates for creativity, innovation, and renewal.* San Francisco, CA: Jossey-Bass.
Hauschildt, J., & Kirchmann, E. (2001). Teamwork for innovation—the "troika" of promotors. *R&D Management, 31,* 41–49.
Hemlin, S. (2006). Creative knowledge environments for research groups in biotechnology. The influence of leadership and organizational support in universities and business companies. *Scientometrics, 67,* 121–42.
Hemlin, S. (2009). Creative knowledge environments: An interview study with group members and group leaders of university and industry R&D groups in biotechnology. *Creativity and Innovation Management, 18,* 278–285.
Hennessey, B. A., & Amabile, T. M. (2010). Creativity. *Annual Review of Psychology, 61,* 569–598.
Hoffman, L. R., Hamburg, E., & Maier, N. (1962). Differences and disagreements as factors in creative problem solving. *Journal of Abnormal and Social Psychology, 64,* 20–214.
Houndshell, E. A. (1992). Invention in the industrial research laboratory: Individual or collective process? In R. J. Weber, & D. N. Perkins (Eds.), *Inventive minds: Creativity in technology* (pp. 273–91). New York, NY: Oxford University Press.
House, R. J. (1996). Path-goal theory of leadership: Lessons, legacy, and a reformulated theory. *The Leadership Quarterly, 7,* 323–352.

Howell, J. M., & Boies, K. (2004). Champions of technological innovation: The influence of contextual knowledge, role orientation, idea generation, and idea promotion on champion emergence. *The Leadership Quarterly, 15*, 130–149.
Howell, J. M., & Higgins, C. A. (1988). Champions of technological innovation. *Administrative Science Quarterly, 35*, 317–341.
Hsu, M. L., & Fan, H. L. (2010). Organizational innovation climate and creative outcomes: Exploring the moderating effect of time pressure. *Creativity Research Journal, 22*, 378–386.
Hughes, T. P. (1989). *American genesis: A history of the American genius for invention*. New York, NY: Penguin.
Hunter, S. T., Bedell, K. E., & Mumford, M. D. (2005). Dimensions of creative climate: A general taxonomy. *Korean Journal of Thinking and Problem Solving, 15*, 97–116.
Hunter, S. T., Bedell-Avers, K. E., & Mumford, M. D. (2007). Climate for creativity: A quantitative review. *Creativity Research Journal, 19*, 69–90.
Hunter, S. T., Thoroughgood, C., Myers, A., & Ligon, G. S. (2012). Managing the paradoxes of leading for innovation, *Psychology of Aesthetics, Creativity, and the Arts, 5*, 54–66.
Isaacson, W. (2007). *Einstein: His life and universe*. New York, NY: Simon & Schuster.
Isaken, S. G., Lauer, K. J., & Ekvall, G. (1999). Situational Outlook Questionnaire: A measure of the climate for creativity and change. *Psychological Reports, 85*, 665–674.
James, L. R., James, L. A., & Ashe, D. K. (1990). The meaning of organizations: The role of cognition and values. In B. Schneider (Ed.), *Organizational climate and culture* (pp. 40–84). San Francisco, CA: Jossey-Bass.
Jaussi, K. S., & Dionne, S. D. (2003). Leading for creativity: The role of unconventional behavior. *The Leadership Quarterly, 14*, 351–368.
Jaussi, K., Randel, A., & Dionne, S. (2007). I am, I think I can, and I do: The role of personal identity, self-efficacy, and cross-application of experiences in creativity at work. *Creativity Research Journal, 19*, 247–258.
Jelinek, M., & Schoonhoven, C. B. (1990). *The innovation marathon: Lessons learned from high technology firms*. Oxford, England: Blackwell.
Jung, D. I. (2001). Transformational and transactional leadership and their effects on creativity in groups. *Creativity Research Journal, 13*, 185–195.
Kamoche, K., & Cunha, M. (2001). Minimal structures: From jazz improvisation to product innovation. *Organization Studies, 22*, 733–764.
Katz, D., & Kahn, R. L. (1978). *The social psychology of organizations*. New York, NY: John Wiley & Sons.
Kazanjian, R. K., Drazin, R., & Glynn, M. A. (2000). Creativity and technological learning: The roles of organization, architecture, and crisis in large-scale projects. *Journal of Engineering Technology Management, 17*, 273–298.
Keller, R. T. (1989). A test of the path-goal theory of leadership with need for clarity as a moderator in research and development organizations. *Journal of Applied Psychology, 74*, 208–212.
Keller, R. T. (1997). Job involvement and organizational commitment as longitudinal predictors of job performance: A study of scientists and engineers. *Journal of Applied Psychology, 82*, 539–545.
Keller, R. T. (2001). Cross-functional project groups in research and new product development: Diversity, communications, job stress, and outcomes. *Academy of Management Journal, 44*, 547–559.
Kickul, J., & Gundry, L. K. (2001). Breaking through boundaries for organizational innovation: New managerial roles and practices in e-commerce firms. *Journal of Management, 27*, 347–361.
Kidder, T. (1981). *The sole of a new machine*. New York, NY: Avon.
Koberg, C. S., Uhlenbruck, N., & Sarason, Y. (1996). Facilitators of organizational innovation: The role of life-cycle stage. *Journal of Business Venturing, 11*, 133–149.
Lapierre, J., & Giroux, V. (2003). Creativity and work environment in a high-tech context. *Creativity and Work Environment, 12*, 11–23.
Laugen, B. T., Boer, H., & Acur, N. (2006). The new product development improvement motives and practices of Miles and Snow's prospectors, analysers and defenders. *New Product Development Improvement Motives and Practices, 15*, 85–95.
Lee, H., & Kelley, D. (2008). Building dynamic capabilities for innovation: An exploratory study of key management practices. *R&D Management, 38*, 155–168.
Li, Y., Tan, C. -H., Teo, H. -H., & Tan, B. C. Y. (2006). Innovative usage of information technology in Singapore organizations: Do CIO characteristics make a difference? *IEEE Transactions on Engineering Management, 53*, 177–190.
Licuanan, B., Dailey, L., & Mumford, M. D. (2007). Idea evaluation: Errors in evaluating highly original ideas. *Journal of Creative Behavior, 18*, 367–384.
Litchfield, R. (2008). Brainstorming reconsidered: A goal-based view. *Academy of Management Review, 33*, 649–668.
Lonergan, D. C., Scott, G. M., & Mumford, M. D. (2004). Evaluative aspects of creative thought: Effects of idea appraisal and revision standards. *Creativity Research Journal, 16*, 231–246.
Ma, H. (2009). The effect size of variables associated with creativity: A meta-analysis. *Creativity Research Journal, 21*, 30–42.
Madjar, N., Oldham, G. R., Pratt, M. G. (2002). There's no place like home? The contributions of work and nonwork creativity support to employees' creative performance. *Academy of Management Journal, 45*, 757–767.
Maidique, M., & Zirger, B. J. (1984). A study of success and failure in product innovation: The case of the U.S. electronics industry. *IEEE Transactions in Engineering Management, 31*, 192–203.
Maier, N. R. (1950). The quality of group discussions as influenced by the discussion leader. *Human Relations, 3*, 155–174.
Maier, N. R. (1953). An experimental test of the effect of training on discussion leadership. *Human Relations, 6*, 161–173.
Maier, N. R. F., & Hoffman, L. R. (1964). Financial incentives and group decision in motivating change. *Journal of Social Psychology, 64*, 161–378.
Maier, N. R. F., & Hoffman, L. R. (1965). Acceptance and quality of solutions as related to leaders' attitudes toward disagreement in group problem-solving. *Journal of Applied Behavioral Science, 1*, 373–386.
Maier, N. R, & Janzen, J. C. (1969). Are good problem solvers also creative? *Psychological Reports, 24*, 139–146.
Maier, N. R. F., & Solem, A. R. (1962). Improving solutions by turning choice situations and problems. *Personnel Psychology, 15*, 151–157.
March, J. G. (1991). Exploration and exploitation in organizational learning. *Organization Science, 2*, 71–87.

Marcy, R. A., & Mumford, M. D. (2010). Leader cognition: Improving leader performance through causal analysis. *The Leadership Quarterly, 21*, 1–19.

Markham, S. K., & Aiman-Smith, L. A. (2001). Product champions: Truths, myths and management. *Research Technology Management, 44*, 44–55.

Markham, S. K., Green, S., & Basu, R. (1991). Champions and antagonists: Relationships with R & D project characteristics and management. *Journal of Engineering and Technology, 8*, 217–242.

Markham, S. K., & Griffin, A. (1998). The breakfast of champions: Associations between champions and product development, environments, practices, and performance. *Journal of Product Innovation Management, 15*, 436–454.

Marta, S., Leritz, L. E., & Mumford, M. D. (2005). Leadership skills and group performance: Situational demands, behavioral requirements, and planning. *The Leadership Quarterly, 16*, 97–120.

McGourty, J., Tarshis, L. A., & Dominick, P. (1996). Managing innovation: Lessons from world class organizations. *International Journal of Technology Management, 11*, 354–368.

McKenna, B., Rooney, D., & Boal, K. B. (2009). Wisdom principles as a meta-theoretical basis for evaluating leadership. *The Leadership Quarterly, 20*, 177–190.

Merrifield, P. R., Guilford, J. P., Christensen, P. R., & Frick, J. W. (1962). Interrelationships between certain abilities and certain traits of motivation and temperament. *Journal of General Psychology, 65*, 57–74.

Meyer, A. D., & Goes, J. B. (1988). Organizational assimilation of innovations. *Academy of Management Journal, 31*, 897–923.

Miles, R. E., & Snow, C. C., (1978). *Organizational strategy, structure and process*. New York, NY: McGraw-Hill.

Mobley, M. I., Doares, L., & Mumford, M. D. (1992). Process analytic models of creative capacities: Evidence for the combination and reorganization process. *Creativity Research Journal, 5*, 125–156.

Morgan, P. W. (1992). Discovery and invention in polymer chemistry. In R. J. Weber & D. N. Perkins (Eds.), *Inventive minds: Creativity in technology* (pp. 178–193). New York, NY: Oxford University Press.

Mossholder, K. W., & Dewhirst, H. D. (1980). The appropriateness of management-by-objectives for development and research personnel. *Journal of Management, 6*, 145–156.

Mumford, M. D. (2000). Managing creative people: Strategy and tactics for innovation. *Human Resource Management Review, 10*, 1–29.

Mumford, M. D., Bedell-Avers, K. E., & Hunter, S. T. (2008). Planning for innovation: A multi-level perspective. In M. D. Mumford, S. T. Hunter, & K. E. Bedell-Avers (Eds.), *Innovation in organizations: A multi-level perspective* (pp. 107–154). Oxford, England: Elsevier.

Mumford, M. D., Connelly, M. S., & Gaddis, B. (2003). How creative leaders think: Experimental findings and cases. *The Leadership Quarterly, 14*, 411–432.

Mumford, M. D., Feldman, J. M., Hein, M. B., & Nagao, D. J. (2001). Tradeoffs between ideas and structure: Individual versus group performance in creative problem-solving. *Journal of Creative Behavior, 35*, 1–23.

Mumford, M. D., Friedrich, T. L., Caughron, J. J., & Antes, A. (2009). Leadership research: Traditions, developments and current directions. In D. A. Buchanan & A. Bryman (Eds.), *Handbook of organizational research methods* (pp. 111–127). Thousand Oaks, CA: SAGE.

Mumford, M. D., Friedrich, T. L., Caughron, J. J., & Byrne, C. L. (2007). Leader cognition in real-world settings: How do leaders think about crises? *The Leadership Quarterly, 18*, 515–543.

Mumford, M. D., & Gustafson, S. B. (1988). Creativity syndrome: Integration, application, and innovation. *Psychological Bulletin, 103*, 27–43.

Mumford, M. D., & Gustafson, S. B. (2007). Creative thought: Cognition and problem-solving in a dynamic system. In M. A. Runco (Ed.), *Creativity research handbook*, Vol. II. (pp. 33–77). Cresskill, NJ: Hampton.

Mumford, M. D., & Hunter, S. T. (2005). Innovation in organizations: A multi-level perspective on creativity. In F. Dansereau & F. J. Yammarino (Eds.), *Research in multi-level issues*, Vol. IV (pp. 11–74). Oxford, England: Elsevier.

Mumford, M. D., Mobley, M. I., Uhlman, C. E., Reiter-Palmon, R., & Doares, L. (1991). Process analytic models of creative capacities. *Creativity Research Journal, 4*, 91–122.

Mumford, M. D., Peterson, D., & Robledo I. (2013). Leading scientists and engineers: Cognition in a socio-technical context. In S. Hemlin, C. M. Allwood, B. Martin, & M. D. Mumford (Eds.), *Creativity and leadership in science technology and innovation* (pp.29–57).:London, England: Taylor & Francis.

Mumford, M. D., Reiter-Palmon, R., & Redmond, M. R. (1994). Problem construction and cognition: Applying problem representations in ill-defined domains. In M. A. Runco, (Ed.). *Problem finding, problem solving, and creativity* (pp. 3–39). Westport, CT: Ablex.

Mumford, M. D., Schultz, R. A., & Van Doorn, J. R. (2001). Performance in planning: Processes, requirements, and errors. *Review of General Psychology, 5*, 213–240.

Mumford, M. D., Scott, G. M., Gaddis, B., & Strange, J. M. (2002). Leading creative people: Orchestrating expertise and relationships. *The Leadership Quarterly, 13*, 705–750.

Mumford, M. D., Supinski, E. P., Baughman, W. A., Costanza, D. P., & Threlfall, K. V. (1997). Process-based measures of creative problem-solving skills: V. Overall prediction. *Creativity Research Journal, 10*, 77–85.

Murmann, J. P., & Tushman, M. L. (1997). Organizational responsiveness to environmental shock as an indication of foresight and oversight: The role of executive team characteristics and organizational content. In R. Garud & P. R. Nayer (Eds.), *Technological innovations: Oversights and foresights* (pp. 260–278). New York, NY: Cambridge University Press.

Nellore, R., & Balachandra, R. (2001). Factors influencing success in integrated product development (IPD) projects. *IEEE Transactions on Engineering Management, 48*, 164–173.

Nemanich, L. A., & Keller R. T. (2007). Transformational leadership in an acquisition: A field study of employees. *The Leadership Quarterly, 18*, 49–68.

Nohria, N., & Gulati, R. (1994). Firms and their environments. In N. Smelser & R. Swedberg (Eds.), *Handbook of economic sociology* (pp. 529–555). Princeton, NJ: Princeton University Press.

Nohria, K., & Gulati, D. (1996). Is slack good or bad for innovation? *Academy of Management Journal, 39*, 799–825.

Nyström, H. (1979). *Creativity and innovation*. London, UK: John Wiley & Sons.

O'Connor, G. C. (1998). Market learning and radical innovation: A cross case comparison of eight radical innovation

projects. *Journal of Product Innovation Management, 15,* 151–166.
Oldham, G. R., & Cummings, A. (1996). Employee creativity: Personal and contextual factors at work. *Academy of Management Journal, 39,* 607–634.
Olson, E. M., Walker, O. C., Ruekert, R. W., & Bonner, J. M. (2001). Patterns of cooperation during new product development among marketing, operations, and R&D. *Journal of Product Development Management, 18,* 258–271.
Ong, C. H., Wan, D., & Chang, S. H. (2003). Factors affecting individual innovation: An examination within a Japanese subsidiary in Singapore. *Technovation, 23,* 617–633.
Osborn, R. N., & Marion, R. (2009). Contextual leadership, transformational leadership and the performance of international innovation seeking alliances. *The Leadership Quarterly, 20,* 191–206.
Osburn, H., & Mumford, M. (2006). Creativity and planning: Training interventions to develop creative problem-solving skills. *Creativity Research Journal, 18,* 173–190.
Parnes, S. J., & Noller, R. B. (1972). Applied creativity: The creative studies project—Part II: Results of the two year program. *Journal of Creative Behavior, 6,* 164–186.
Patalano, A. L., & Siefert, C. M. (1997). Opportunistic planning: Being reminded of pending goals. *Cognitive Psychology, 34,* 1–36.
Paulus, P. B., & Brown, V. R. (2003). Enhancing ideational creativity in groups: Lessons from research on brainstorming. In P. B. Paulus, B. A. Nijstad, P. B. Paulus, & B. A. Nijstad (Eds.), *Group creativity: Innovation through collaboration* (pp. 110–136). New York, NY: Oxford University Press.
Pelz, D. C. (1963). Relationships between measures of scientific performance and other variables. In C. W. Taylor & F. Barron (Eds.), *Scientific creativity: Its recognition and development* (pp. 302–310). New York, NY: John Wiley & Sons.
Quigg, D. J. (1992). The role of patents. In R. J. Weber & D. N. Perkins (Eds.), *Inventive minds: Creativity in technology* (pp. 311–317). Oxford, England: Oxford University Press.
Ramus, C. A. (2001). Organizational support for employees: Encouraging creative ideas for environmental sustainability. *California Management Review, 43,* 85–105.
Redmond, M. R., Mumford, M. D., & Teach, R. J. (1993). Putting creativity to work: Leader influences on subordinate creativity. *Organizational Behavior and Human Decision Processes, 55,* 120–151.
Rego, A., Sousa, F., Cunha, M., Correia, A., & Saur-Amaral, I. (2007). Leader self-reported emotional intelligence and perceived employee creativity: An exploratory study. *Creativity and Innovation Management, 16,* 250–264.
Reiter-Palmon, R., Herman, A. E., & Yammarino, F. J. (2008). Creativity and cognitive processes: Multilevel linkages between individual and team cognition. In M. D. Mumford, S. T. Hunter, & K. E. Bedell-Avers (Eds.), *Multilevel issues in creativity and innovation*: Vol. VII (pp. 203–267). Oxford, England: Elsevier.
Rickards, T., & Moger, S. (2006). Creative leaders: A decade of contributions from *Creativity and Innovation Management* journal. *Creativity and Management, 15,* 4–18.
Robledo, I., Hester, K., Peterson, D., & Mumford, M. D. (2012). Creativity in organizations: Conclusions. In M. D. Mumford (Ed.), *Handbook of organizational creativity* (pp. 707–725). Oxford, UK: Elsevier Science.
Robledo, I., Peterson, D., & Mumford, M. D. (2011). Leadership of scientists and engineers: A three-vector model. *Journal of Organizational Behavior, 33,* 140–147.
Rodan, S. (2002). Innovation and heterogeneous knowledge in managerial contact networks. *Journal of Knowledge Management, 6,* 152–163.
Rosing, K., Frese, M., & Bausch, A. (2011). Explaining the heterogeneity of the leadership-innovation relationship: Ambidextrous leadership. *The Leadership Quarterly, 22,* 956–974.
Sawyer, R. K. (2006). Group creativity: Musical performance and collaboration. *Psychology of Music, 34,* 148–165.
Scott, G. M., Lonergan, D. C., & Mumford, M. D. (2005). Conceptual combination: Alternative knowledge structures, alternative heuristics. *Creativity Research Journal, 17,* 79–98.
Shalley, C. E. (1995). Effects of coaction, expected evaluation, and goal setting on creativity and productivity. *Academy of Management Journal, 38,* 483–503.
Sharma, A. (1999). Central dilemmas of managing innovation in large firms. *California Management Review, 41,* 65–85.
Shin, S. J., & Zhou, J. (2003). Transformational leadership, conservation, and creativity: Evidence from Korea. *Academy of Management Journal, 46,* 703–714.
Shipman, A. L., Byrne, C. L., & Mumford, M. D. (2010). Vision formation and forecasting: The effects of forecasting extent, resources, and time frame. *The Leadership Quarterly, 21,* 439–456.
Silva, P. (2008). Another look at creativity and intelligence: Exploring higher-order models and probably counfounds. *Personality and Individual Differences, 44,* 1012–1021.
Simonton, D. K. (2012). Fields, domains, and individuals. In M. D. Mumford (Ed.), *Handbook of organizational creativity* (pp. 67–86). Oxford, UK: Elsevier Science.
Sosik, J. J., Kahai, S. S., & Avolio, B. J. (1999). Leadership style, anonymity, and creativity in group decision support systems: The mediating role of optimal flow. *Journal of Creative Behavior, 33,* 227–256.
Souitaris, V. (2001). External communication determinants of innovation in the context of a newly industrialised country: A comparison of objective and perceptual results from Greece. *Technovation, 21,* 25–34.
Sternberg, R. (2006). The nature of creativity. *Creativity Research Journal, 18,* 87–98.
Stockstrom, C., & Herstatt, C. (2008). Planning and uncertainty in new product development. *R&D Management, 38,* 480–490.
Sundgren, M., Selart, M., Ingelgard, A., & Bengtson, C. (2005). Dialogue-based evaluation as a creative climate indicator: Evidence from the pharmaceutical industry. *Creativity and Innovation Management, 14,* 84–98.
Taggar, S. (2001). Group composition, creative synergy, and group performance. *Journal of Creative Behavior, 35,* 261–286.
Taggar, S. (2002). Individual creativity and group ability to utilize individual creative resources: A multilevel model. *Academy of Management Journal, 45,* 315–330.
Thamhain, H. J. (2003). Managing innovative R&D teams. *R&D Management, 33,* 297–311.
Thamhain, H. J., & Gemmill, G. R. (1974). Influence styles of project managers: Some project performance correlates. *Academy of Management Journal, 17,* 216–224.
Thomas, J. B., & McDaniel, R. R. (1990). Interpreting strategic issues: Effects of strategy and the information-processing structure of top management teams. *Academy of Management Journal, 33,* 286–306.

Tierney, P., & Farmer, S. M. (2002). Creative self-efficacy: Its potential antecedents and relationship to creative performance. *Academy of Management Journal, 45*, 1137.

Tierney, P., Farmer, S. M., & Graen, G. B. (1999). An examination of leadership and employee creativity: The relevance of traits and relationships. *Personnel Psychology, 52*, 591–620.

Tushman, M. L., & O'Reilly, C. A. (1997). *Winning through innovation*. Boston, MA: Harvard Business School Press.

Vessey, W. B., & Mumford, M. D. (2012). Heuristics as a basis for assessing creative potential: Measures, methods, and contingencies. *Creativity Research Journal, 24*, 41–54.

Ward, T. B., Smith, S. M., & Finke, R. A. (1999). Creative cognition. In R. J. Sternberg (Ed.), *Handbook of creativity* (pp. 189–213). Cambridge, England: Cambridge University Press.

Weightman, G. (2007). *The industrial revolutionaries*. New York, NY: Grove Press.

West, M. A., Borrill, C. S., Dawson, J. F., Brodbeck, F., Shapiro, D. A., & Haward, B. (2003). Leadership clarity and team innovation in health care. *The Leadership Quarterly, 14*, 393–410.

Wentroff, R.H. (1992). The synthesis of diamonds. In R. J. Weber & D. N. Perkins (Eds.), *Inventive minds: Creativity in technology* (pp. 154–310). New York, NY: Oxford University Press.

Wise, G. (1992). Inventions and corporations in the maturing electrical industry. In R. J. Weber & D. N. Perkins (Eds.), *Inventive minds: Creativity in technology* (pp. 291–310). New York, NY: Oxford University Press.

Wuchty, S., Jones, B. F., & Uzzi, B. (2007). The increasing dominance of teams in production of knowledge. *Science, 316*, 1036–1039.

Xu, F., & Rickards, T. (2007). Creative management: A predicted development from research into creativity and management. *Creativity and Innovation Management, 16*, 216–228.

Yukl, G. (2010). *Leadership in Organizations* (7th ed.). Upper Saddle River, NJ: Prentice Hall.

Zenasni, F., Besançon, M., & Lubart, T. (2008). Creativity and tolerance of ambiguity: An empirical study. *Journal of Creative Behavior, 42*, 61–73.

Zuckerman, H. (1977). *The scientific elite*. New York, NY: Free Press.

CHAPTER

35 Leadership and Emotion: A Multilevel Perspective

Neal M. Ashkanasy *and* Ronald H. Humphrey

Abstract

This chapter presents a model of five levels of leadership and emotional organizing. At Level 1, leaders generate and manage "affective events" that result in emotional states leading to positive or negative attitudes and behaviors. At Level 2, leaders exhibit individual differences in their ability to perceive and manage emotions, usually referred to as "emotional intelligence." At Level 3, leadership effectiveness is associated with "leading with emotional labor," in which a leader's ability to manage followers is determined by modeling the right type and amount of emotion, as reflected in authentic leadership. At Level 4, group leadership and the processes of emotional contagion are important, as in charismatic leadership. At Level 5, emotions and leadership are viewed as organization-wide processes. As such, leaders create positive outcomes for the organization by promoting a positive work environment and organizational culture. The chapter concludes with a discussion of future research directions.

Key Words: Multilevel, emotions, emotional intelligence, emotional contagion, positive work environment

The year 1995 marks a watershed year for both popular and scholarly interest in the role that emotions play in leadership. From a popular perspective, a book by Daniel Goleman (1995) titled *Emotional Intelligence: Why It Can Matter More Than IQ*, was a *NY Times* best seller and even featured as a *Time Magazine* cover story. On the scholarly side, Ashforth and Humphrey (1995), in a seminal article, questioned why leadership scholars seemed to have ignored the emotional dimension.

Following these publications, mainstream leadership scholars began to take a closer look at emotions. For example, Gary Yukl, at the time the leading textbook author in leadership, called in 1999 for a reexamination of the prevailing theories of leadership, with a view to including the effects and consequences of emotions. Yukl (1999) noted in particular that contemporary theories of charismatic and transformational leadership at the time needed to focus more on understanding the role of emotion in interpersonal processes underlying leader–member relationships.

In response to these calls, leadership scholarship by the end of the 1990s started to regard emotions as an inherent component of effective leadership. For example, Shamir and Howell (1999) posited that emotion is a central component of charismatic leadership, and Ashkanasy and Tse (2000) outlined a model of transformational leadership based on individual, interpersonal, and group theories of emotion. Other models of leadership to incorporate emotions around this time included Barbuto and Burbach (2006); Caruso, Mayer, and Salovey (2002), and George (2000). Empirical studies followed (e.g., Gardner & Stough 2002; Wolff, Pescosolido, & Druskat, 2002; Wong & Law, 2002), although these tended to emphasize emotional intelligence. In introducing a Special Issue of

The Leadership Quarterly devoted to the topic, for example, Humphrey (2002) commented that there was already a sea-change in scholarly attitudes about the role played by emotions in leadership.

The lack of attention paid to emotions in leadership up until the end of the twentieth century, as noted by Ashforth and Humphrey (1995), appeared to be a strange anomaly, possibly a symptom of a pervasive view at the time that organizational management must be largely governed by the laws of rational thinking. By the latter part of the century, however, this view had begun to break down. Even economists had begun to acknowledge that rational theories were too limiting to understand human behavior at work (Mumby & Putnam, 1992; Simon, 1976) and that, after all, emotions might play a key role in management and leadership.

Of course, it is axiomatic that organizational leadership had always been underpinned by emotions. Leadership is, like any form of behavior, based on the decisions the leader makes and, as Damasio (1994) conclusively demonstrated, all human decision making is underpinned by emotional states. In this respect, Damasio coined the term "somatic marker" to describe the bodily feelings that are an integral component of human decision making. In one memorable passage in his book, Damasio outlined how "Patient Elliott," who had a high IQ but suffered from a brain injury that prevented him from accessing his bodily emotional states, was unable to make even a simple decision.

More recently, Niedenthal and her colleagues (Niedenthal, Barsalou, Winkielman, Krauth-Gruber, & Ric, 2005; Niedenthal, Winkielman, Mondillon, & Vermeulen, 2009) found experimental support for the role of bodily feelings (which they refer to as "the embodiment of emotions," Niedenthal et al., 2009, p. 1120) in everyday thinking. In their research, Niedenthal et al. measured facial muscle movements in subjects who were asked to evaluate the emotional connotations of different words and found that people who evaluated words with emotional meanings actually activated facial muscles associated with emotion display. Niedenthal and her associates concluded that common higher level cognitive activities—like reading words—involves partial reactivations of sensory motor states. In other words, whether we like it or not, emotions are an integral part of human thought processes.

Referring specifically to the role of emotions in leadership, Mastenbroek (2000) outlined the detailed history of emotion in organizational management since Aristotle and described the pervasive effect of emotions in work and organizational settings for more than 2,000 years. Interestingly, early leadership scholars seemed to have no problem grasping this idea. For example, Redl (1942) described how the emotional makeup of workgroups was conditioned by leaders. And pioneering management theorists such as Fayol (1916/1949) seemed to understand that effective leadership relied on an ability to understand psychology and to manage followers' emotional states. Weiss and Brief (2001), in a historical review of emotions in organizational behavior scholarship, noted that the early studies of leadership invariably included full consideration of the role played by emotions. As we noted earlier, however, and rather surprisingly in view of this early recognition, scholars of leadership and organizational behavior more generally appeared for many years to have forgotten all about emotions.

In the years following Ashforth and Humphrey's (1995) call, however, leadership scholars still seemed to be reluctant to incorporate emotions fully into their models. Ashkanasy and Jordan (2008) commented, for example, that incorporation of emotional dimensions into leadership theories tended to take a "tack on" approach, such as incorporating aspects of emotional intelligence into existing theories of leadership. Citing the Five-Level Model of emotion in organizations proposed by Ashkanasy (2003*a*), Ashkanasy and Jordan urged scholars to take a broader view of emotions and to consider the influence of emotion in leadership across all levels of organizational analysis (see also Ashkanasy & Humphrey, 2011).

In this chapter, therefore, we follow suit and adopt Ashkanasy's (2003*a*) Five-Level Model as our overarching framework. Moreover, in this chapter, we address some of the more recent work that has supported the multilevel framework, including the nexus of emotional intelligence, emotional labor, and leadership. We also expand on some of the more recent work that has identified the role leaders play in establishing a positive work environment (Härtel & Ashkanasy, 2011).

Five Levels of Organizational Analysis

In Figure 35.1, we depict the five levels of organizational analysis proposed by Ashkanasy (2003*a*). These are (1) within person (temporal variations), (2) between persons (individual differences), (3) interpersonal interactions (dyadic relationships), (4) group dynamics and leadership, and

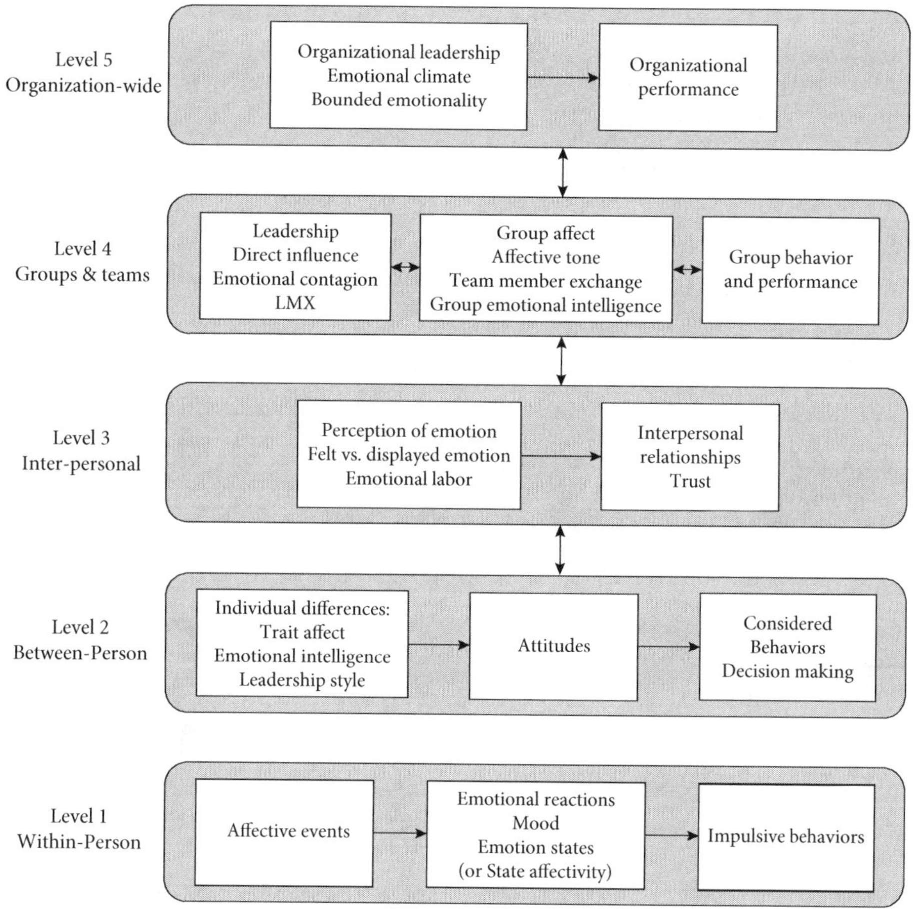

Figure 35.1. The Five-Level Model of Emotion in Organizations. (From Ashkanasy & Jordan, 2008)

(5) emotional climate at the organization level. In a rejoinder to commentary on this article, Ashkanasy (2003*b*) noted that the biological basis of emotional neurobiology serves to integrate the various theories across all five levels. For example, temporal variations in emotional states (Level 1) are associated with changes in electroencephalographic brain activity, which in turn are associated with the neural processes behind emotion recognition (Level 3, see Ekman, 1999) and emotional contagion (Level 4, see Hatfield, Cacioppo, & Rapson, 1993).

At the most fundamental level of analysis (Level 1), emotion and emotional experiences, or "feelings," vary within an individual moment by moment. Weiss and Cropanzano (1996) noted that this variation is an essential consideration in our understanding of the role of emotion in organizations. Organizational members experience changing mood in the longer term, for example, on returning from a vacation (Kuehnel & Sonnentag, 2011) and also during the day (Clark, Watson, & Leeka, 1989). Fritz and Sonnentag (2009) found, in particular, that hassles and uplifts throughout the working day cause emotional states to vary rapidly on a moment-by-moment basis. Although one might think that the intensity of emotional experiences would have the largest effects, Weiss and Cropanzano note especially that emotional states are most affected by the accumulation of frequent "affective events and that it is these emotional states that drive attitudes and behavior in the workplace" (see also Fisher, 2000).

Between-person individual differences in predispositions and attitudes are considered at Level 2 in the Five-Level Model. Trait effects include emotional intelligence (Mayer & Salovey, 1997) and positive-negative trait affectivity (Watson & Tellegen, 1985). Also included at Level 2 are relatively stable attitudes such as job satisfaction and affective attitudes to work (as a between-person variable, see Fisher, 2000), as well as job and organizational commitment (Meyer & Allen, 1997).

The focus at Level 3 shifts to consideration of dyadic interactions. This encompasses all facets of recognizing emotional states in others, including facial emotion displays (Ekman, 1984; 1999), emotional labor (Hochschild, 1983), and emotional regulation (Gross, 2006). Especially pertinent at Level 2 is the idea of emotional labor, usually applied in the context of service provision (e.g., see Rafaeli & Sutton, 1987) and where employees are remunerated for displaying particular emotional states, which can have health consequences for the "emotional laborer" (e.g., see Grandey, 2003; Mann, 1997; 1999).

At Level 4 of the model, attention broadens to address emotions in teams and groups, reflected for example in group affective tone (George, 1990). A key mechanism at this level is *emotional contagion* (Hatfield et al., 1993), in which the emotional state of one individual in a group is "caught" by other members. Barsade (2002; see also Kelly & Barsade, 2001), for example, found that contagion processes ultimately affect group mood and performance. From a leadership perspective, Sy, Côté, & Saavedra (2005) found that emotional contagion can flow from the leader to subordinates. Dasborough, Ashkanasy, Tee, and Tse (2009) argue further that contagion can flow both ways: from followers to the leader, as well as from leader to followers (see also Tee, Ashkanasy, & Paulsen, 2013). This idea is supported by Graen and Uhl-Bien (1995), who posited that one of the central roles played by group leaders is communication of emotional states.

Finally, at Level 5, we are concerned with emotion reflected in organizational culture and climate (e.g., see Härtel & Ashkanasy, 2011). Ashkanasy (2003*a*) in particular quoted from De Rivera (1992), who defined emotional climate as "an objective group phenomenon that can be palpably sensed—as when one enters a party or a city and feels an attitude of gaiety or depression, openness or fear" (p. 197).

In the following section of this chapter, therefore, we provide an outline of Ashkanasy and Jordan's (2008) model of leadership effectiveness and its relationship to emotion at each of the five levels we have outlined. Table 35.1 illustrates the characteristics of effective leaders at each of the levels in the Ashkanasy and Jordan model as further developed here. This table will be explained in more detail in the following sections.

Table 35.1. Characteristics of Effective Leaders at the Five Levels of Emotions in Organizations

Level 1: Within-Person
Effective Leaders: Long periods of peak positive moods; peak moods timed with work and leadership activities; greater resilience helps them overcome the mood-dampening effects of negative events; takes responsibility for creating positive affective events for followers; helps subordinates interpret workplace events and change feelings of frustration to optimism
Level 2: Between-Persons (Individual Differences)
Effective Leaders: More likely to have average emotional baselines in the positive range; generally higher activity levels for positive emotions and less extreme or intense for negative emotions; more likely to access "gut feelings" when making decisions; higher emotional intelligence, self-awareness, and empathy
Level 3: Interpersonal
Effective Leaders: Take initiative in expressing emotions; accurately recognize followers' emotions; use emotional labor and regulation to express appropriate and genuine emotions; develop authentic relationships based on trust
Level 4: Groups and Teams
Effective Leaders: Focus on the management of group members' moods and affective climate; express appropriate (usually positive) emotions and create emotional contagion among team members; they form groups with high average group emotional intelligence
Level 5: Organization-Wide
Effective Leaders: Create appropriate emotional display rules; create organizational cultures with positive emotional climates

Level 1: Within-Person

Located at the base of the Five Level Model is within-person temporal variation in emotion. Natural biorhythms influence the moods that people feel throughout the day; for example, some people feel their best in the mornings, whereas others feel their best in the afternoons or evenings (Clark et al., 1989). Most people have some up-and-down patterns in their moods throughout the day. Effective leaders may have their peak energy levels and positive moods timed to when they most need to feel their best in order to carry out their leadership duties. In addition, effective leaders may have longer periods of peak positive moods and overall stamina.

In a seminal article, Weiss and Cropanzano (1996) introduced the concept of the "affective event," in which occurrences (i.e., "events") in the organizational environment are perceived by organizational members who experience an "affective reaction" leading to an emotional response. In this respect, emotions are relatively short-lived, acute, and event-orientated. In other words, people experience emotions in relation to an object in their environment. For example, anger at an injustice or sadness following a loss. This concept has come to be known as *affective events theory* (AET).

According to Weiss and Cropanzano (1996), the resulting moods and emotions have two behavioral effects. The first is proximal and comprises of immediate behavioral responses such as violent outbursts or spontaneous helping. The second is distal and is mediated by the formation of affect-driven attitudes such as job satisfaction and commitment; these in turn lead to what Weiss and Cropanzano refer to as "judgment-driven behavior" and include deciding either to remain with or to quit the organization or to engage in either productive or counterproductive work behavior.

Ashkanasy and Tse (2000) noted that leaders form a key part of the organizational environment and, as such, form an important source of affective events for organizational members. Moreover, and despite the implicit assumption in traditional theories of leadership that leaders are somehow more emotionally stable than their subordinates, leaders themselves are also subject to affective events. For example, Tee and his colleagues (2013) recently demonstrated that leaders can be subject to "upward" emotional contagion from their subordinates and that this is then reflected in the leader's performance. Moreover, leaders can become a conduit for internal and external affective events (Ashton-James & Ashkanasy, 2008), such as organizational change events; external economic, legal, and political events; and negotiation with the environment, including other organizations and organizational units. Ashton-James and Ashkanasy argue that leaders' affective states are especially pertinent because their decision making is strongly shaped by their affective state at the time (Forgas, 1995), which can have both micro- and macroimpacts on the organization and its members. Thus, because leaders are buffeted by the same negative affective events that influence the moods of their subordinates, effective leaders need to be higher on emotional resiliency (a Level 2 personality trait) in order to help both themselves and their subordinates cope with these negative events.

In this chapter, we apply AET to leadership on the basis that leaders have the capacity to influence employees' moods at work (e.g., see Humphrey, 2002; Pescosolido, 2002). Indeed, research into AET has confirmed that employees experience workplace events (hassles and uplifts) throughout the day that impact their positive and negative mood states (Weiss & Cropanzano, 1996; Weiss, Nichols, & Daus, 1999). Thus, leaders might have a special role to buffer these effects. This effect was demonstrated in a study by Pirola-Merlo, Härtel, Mann, and Hirst (2002) who found that leaders with facilitative and transformational styles were able to improve both their subordinates' moods and performance. Pirola-Merlo and his colleagues demonstrated in particular that these leaders were effective because they were able to help their subordinates overcome the damaging effects of workplace aggravations. The authors concluded that a key role of leaders therefore is to help followers to cope with the frustrations they experience in everyday work.

In another study, this time focusing in particular on transformational leadership, McColl-Kennedy and Anderson (2002) found that effective transformational leaders boosted their followers' optimistic moods. In effect, these leaders helped their followers to transform their feelings of frustration into an optimistic outlook on the challenging goals facing them, leading to more effective follower performance. Similar effects have been demonstrated in studies by Bono, Foldes, Vinson, and Muros (2007). Moreover, the results of these studies confirmed that subordinates' improved mood states persisted long after the leader's intervention, resulting in an improved performance throughout the day (see also Ashkanasy & Daus, 2002), especially reflected in more positive moods when interacting with customers and each other.

More support for the proposition that effective leadership involves mood repair comes from a study by Pescosolido (2002) involving jazz musicians and sports teams. In line with the tenets of AET, Pescosolido reasoned that a key role of leaders is to model positive responses to an ambiguous workplace. For example, a sporting team that suffers a setback on the field when the opposition scores a goal can be inspired by a coach who reframes the event as an incentive for the team to redouble their effort.

The foregoing examples demonstrate that the process of managing mood and emotion is not straightforward, however. Although considerable research demonstrates that positive moods usually increase performance (e.g., see Judge & Kammeyer-Muellar, 2008; Wagner & Ilies, 2008), there are times when negative moods might be useful. Indeed, Jordan, Lawrence, and Troth (2006) demonstrated that, depending on circumstances, negative moods can serve to promote performance. This idea is consistent with research by George and Zhou (2007), who found that group effectiveness was most likely to be maximized when members experience a combination of positive and negative mood. Thus, a high-performing team working on an important project may experience a combination of exhilaration coupled with an anticipatory fear that a deadline is looming. In this situation, consistent with Pescosolido's (2002) findings, leaders have a particular responsibility to model appropriate emotional responses and moods.

In summary of Level 1, we have argued that a leader's ability to model emotional responses that are appropriate to complex work situations involves considerable skill and judgment. In particular, the leader needs to be able to perceive the emotional states of her or his followers and then take the requisite actions to manage followers' mood states in a way most consistent with high performance. In this respect, some leaders are likely to be more skilled than others; which brings us to the next level in our model: between-person effects.

Level 2: Between-Persons

At Level 2, the focus shifts to between-person phenomena such as personality, trait affect, and cognitive and emotional intelligence. This level also includes relatively stable attitudinal variables such as job satisfaction and job commitment. From the perspective of research into leadership effectiveness, we have long known that assertiveness, decisiveness, and dependability play a role, although the role of individual differences in emotional competency has only recently been recognized (e.g., see Bass & Bass, 2008).

The role played by individual differences in leadership effectiveness, however, was for many years downplayed in subsequent movements that were based in behavioral, contingency, and transformational theories of leadership (Bass, 1990; Bass & Avolio, 1990; Bass & Bass, 2008). For example, Bass (1990) proposed a model of transformational leadership that focuses on behavior and its cognitive antecedents, including the "Four I's:" (1) individualized consideration, (2) idealized influence, (3) intellectual stimulation, and (4) inspirational motivation. With the notable exception of House and Howell (1992), leadership scholars of this period tended to ignore individual differences and to portray charisma in terms of transactional/transformational behaviors. It was not until House, Shane, and Harold (1996) declared that "Rumors of the death of dispositional research are vastly exaggerated" (p. 203) that individual differences returned to center stage in leadership research.

Affective event theorists have emphasized the importance of individual differences in average emotional baselines (Weiss & Cropanzano, 1996). For instance, some people typically feel positive emotions most of the time and thus are high on positive affectivity and have an average emotional baseline in the positive range. In contrast, others are high in negative affectivity and have an average emotional baseline in the negative range. In addition, people also differ in how intensely and actively they feel emotions; some people typically feel active and energetic and feel intense emotions such as excitement and enthusiasm, whereas others might feel less active positive emotions like contentment. Likewise, some might feel mild negative emotions, whereas others might often feel intense emotions like anger. Effective leaders should be more likely to have positive average emotional baselines and to experience active positive emotions while at the same time experiencing negative, unproductive emotions less intensely.

Unsurprisingly, the individual difference variable that has recently attracted the most intention in respect of emotions and leadership is emotional intelligence. Emotional intelligence may in particular help leaders make better decisions, and leaders are, if nothing else, decision makers. As mentioned earlier, Damasio (1994) argued that effective thinkers rely on their "somatic markers," or bodily reactions and gut instincts, to help them make crucial decisions. By listening to their gut instincts, leaders are able to access important feelings and emotions to help them make decisions consistent with their values. Indeed, on the basis that emotional intelligence involves the ability to access emotional information and to incorporate this information in thinking (Mayer & Salovey, 1997), it follows logically that emotional intelligence should be associated with leadership.

It is also not surprising that authors have connected emotional intelligence and transformational leadership (e.g., see Ashkanasy & Tse, 2000; Gardner & Stough, 2002; George, 2000), a link that has subsequently been supported in empirical research (e.g., see Barling, Slater, & Kelloway, 2000; Daus & Ashkanasy, 2005; Rosete & Ciarrochi, 2005). More recently, meta-analyses by Joseph and Newman (2010) and O'Boyle, Humphrey, Pollack, Hawver, and Story (2011) have demonstrated more conclusively the link between emotional intelligence and work performance. Nonetheless, this idea has attracted considerable and trenchant criticism (e.g., see Antonakis, 2004; Antonakis, Ashkanasy, & Dasborough, 2009; Locke, 2005), largely on the basis of exaggerated claims for the emotional construct literature that have been made in the popular literature. Goleman (1995), for example, initially claimed that emotional intelligence accounted for the majority of the variance in personal life success.

In fact, the construct of emotional intelligence has been with us for 20 years now, since Salovey and Mayer's (1990) published the seminal article and defined emotional intelligence as perceiving, understanding, and managing emotions in self and others.[1] Mayer and Salovey (1997) subsequently added a fourth component, emotional assimilation. They referred to this as the "four-branch" model and, together with Caruso, developed an IQ-style ability measure, the Mayer-Salovey-Caruso Emotional Intelligence Test (MSCEIT; see Mayer, Salovey, & Caruso, 2002). The current version of this scale is a 141-item measure (MSCEIT V2.0; Mayer, Salovey, Caruso, & Sitarenios, 2003) and is designed to rate each of the four "branches": (1) perception, (2) assimilation, (3) understanding, and (4) management of emotions. Because it is an ability measure, the MSCEIT rates the correctness of responses. In this case, the authors used two different ways of determining the "right" answers. The first is a consensus sample of 5,000 English-speaking lay people; the second was a group of 80 experts who were members at the time of the International Society for Research on Emotions (ISRE). With regard to the first dimension, the ability to perceive emotions, there are a number of other specific scales that measure this ability. A recent meta-analysis found that objective measures of the ability to perceive emotions (as portrayed by videotapes, still photos, or vocal recordings) is positively correlated with workplace effectiveness (Elfenbein, Foo, White, Tan, & Aik, 2007). As we discuss later, the ability to perceive others' emotions plays a major role at Level 3 of the model because it helps leaders develop positive interpersonal relationships.

In addition to the MSCEIT, other measures have been developed that use self- or peer ratings of emotional intelligence. Ashkanasy and Daus (2005) categorized the emotional intelligence measures into three "streams." Stream 1 is represented by the MSCEIT. Stream 2 measures are self- or peer-report measures based on the Mayer and Salovey four-branch definition. Examples include the Emotional Intelligence Scale (EIS; Schutte et al., 1998), the Workgroup Emotional Intelligence Profile (WEIP; Jordan, Ashkanasy, Härtel, & Hooper, 2002), and the Wong and Law Emotional Intelligence Scale (WLEIS; Wong & Law, 2002). Stream 3 measures are based on other definitions of the construct and include the Bar-On EQ-I (Bar-On, 1997) and the Trait Emotional Intelligence Questionnaire (TEIQue; Petrides, 2009). Ashkanasy and Daus refer to the MSCEIT as the "gold standard" of emotional intelligence measures and state that Stream 2 measures are acceptable in some circumstances. With respect to Stream 3 measures, Ashkanasy and Daus recommend against their use. Recent meta-analyses of emotional intelligence and performance (Joseph & Newman, 2010; O'Boyle et al., 2011) indicate, however, that although Stream 3 measures tend to overlap existing measures of personality, they can still exhibit predictive validity.

As we mentioned earlier, evidence from meta-analytic studies (e.g., Joseph & Newman, 2010; O'Boyle et al., 2011; Van Rooy & Viswesvaran, 2004) has consistently confirmed that emotional intelligence is associated with work performance. The rapid growth in the field is shown by the increase in studies in the 2011 meta-analysis done by O'Boyle and his colleagues compared to the meta-analysis published in 2010 by Joseph and Newman (based on data they had gathered for a 2007 conference paper). Compared to the earlier study, the O'Boyle et al. (2011) article examined the relationship between emotional intelligence and job performance for 65 percent more studies with twice the sample size (43 studies with a total sample size of 5,795). In particular, O'Boyle and his colleagues found support for incremental validity of emotional intelligence over and above IQ and Big Five personality. By using a technique called *dominance analysis* (aka "relative importance analysis") these researchers determined that emotional intelligence and competency measures were either the second or third most important predictors of job performance (depending on the emotional intelligence/competency measure used). The three most important predictors were cognitive intelligence, emotional intelligence/competency, and conscientiousness.

In terms of specific studies, Law, Wong, and Song (2004) found in a field study involving Chinese participants that, after controlling for Big Five personality, coworker ratings of an employee's emotional intelligence predicted supervisors' ratings of the employees' performance. In another telling study, Brackett, Mayer, and Warner (2004) found that emotional intelligence was positively associated with college grade point average (GPA). Brackett and his colleagues also reported that low emotional intelligence was associated with deviant behavior, including drug taking.

The link between emotional intelligence and effective leadership has been and continues to be controversial (e.g., see Antonakis et al., 2009). Nonetheless, the weight of recently emerging empirical evidence seems to be tipping the balance toward recognition that the link between emotional intelligence and leadership is both credible and substantial. Walter, Cole, and Humphrey (2011) summarized the research on leadership and emotional intelligence/competency with regard to leadership emergence, leadership behaviors, and leadership effectiveness. They found that 100 percent of the studies supported the role of emotional intelligence and related competencies in leadership emergence. Moreover, 81 percent of the studies fully or partially supported the belief that emotionally intelligent/competent leaders were more likely to use transformational leadership or other effective leadership behaviors. Finally, 87.5 percent of the studies fully or partially supported the hypothesis that emotionally intelligent/competent leaders had higher overall leadership effectiveness.

Moreover, we are beginning to gain a better understanding of how the association between emotional intelligence and leadership works, and especially the nexus of emotional and cognitive intelligence in leadership. For example, although Kellett and her colleagues (2002; 2006) confirmed that emotional intelligence predicted emergent leadership, they also reported some interesting individual differences. For example, whereas some leaders relied more on empathetic (i.e., emotional) skills, others relied on cognitive skills, especially in high task complexity situations. A similar finding was reported by Côté and Miners (2006). These studies seem to imply a contingency relationship whereby leaders use cognitive versus emotional skills, depending on the task being undertaken. As a general rule, emotional intelligence skills are needed for work requiring more group interaction, whereas cognitive skills are required for work that does not require social interaction.

In a similar vein, Jordan and Troth (2004) and Offermann, Bailey, Vasilopoulos, Seal, and Sass (2004), in separate but similar studies of team performance, found that cognitive intelligence predicted individual work performance whereas emotional intelligence predicted team performance and ratings of leadership. Aydin, Leblebici, Arslan, Kilic, and Oktem (2005) found that the highest levels of leader performance tend to be associated with high scores on both cognitive and emotional intelligence.

A question remains, however, as to whether there is evidence that emotional intelligence is directly associated with better supervisory performance. In fact, results of empirical research have also consistently supported this idea. Wong and Law (2002), for example, reported in a study of Chinese workers that leaders with high emotional intelligence engender job satisfaction and extra-role performance. Moreover, Sy, Tram, and O'Hara (2006) found in a field study of food-processing workers that managers' emotional intelligence was associated with greater follower job satisfaction, especially when the followers themselves were low on emotional intelligence. Rosete and Ciarrochi (2005) studied a sample of senior executives in Australia and found that executives with higher emotional intelligence tended to be given higher performance appraisal ratings by both superiors and subordinates and achieved higher business productivity. These findings held up over and above the effect of IQ and the Big Five personality traits.

It is also worthwhile for us to consider the role of empathy in leadership. Distinct from emotional intelligence, empathetic skill is an emotion-related construct defined by Salovey and Mayer (1990, pp. 194–195) as "the ability to comprehend another's feelings and to re-experience them oneself."

Salovey and Mayer included empathy in their initial definition of emotional intelligence. Subsequently, however, they came to see empathy as a differentiated construct (see Mayer & Salovey, 1997; although it is included in some Stream 3 models of emotional intelligence, e.g., see Goleman, Boyatzis, & McKee, 2002; Wolff et al., 2002). Although many definitions of empathy describe a passive type in which perceivers re-experience others' emotions, Kellett et al. (2006) argued that leaders need to take the initiative in creating a two-way emotional bond in which leaders not only feel others' emotions but also influence others' emotions. Based on this distinction, Kellett et al. (2006) developed a measure of interactive empathy and found in an assessment center study that interactive empathy predicted leadership emergence. Interestingly, they found that interactive empathy was the best predictor of leadership emergence in the study (even better than cognitive intelligence) and that it mediated the ability to perceive others' emotions and partially mediated the ability to express one's emotions.

Finally, we note that relevant individual personality factors may help leaders regulate both their own moods and the moods of their followers. Leader self-awareness would seem to be important in this respect. For example, Sosik and Megerian (1999) found that leader self-awareness is associated with the leader's performance and subordinate positive regard so that leaders who under- or overestimate their own abilities tend to be poorly regarded as leaders by their subordinates (Dasborough et al., 2009; Yammarino & Atwater, 1997). Based on this evidence, Ashkanasy and Jordan (2008) concluded that leadership effectiveness is critically dependent on the leader's recognition of her or his capabilities and limitations. In particular, leaders who lack self-awareness are likely to be prone to react inappropriately to affective events. For example, a leader who laughs at a subordinate who has failed to accomplish a particular task when other team members feel that the member deserves sympathy, possibly because the failure was externally caused, would be seen by other members to be out of touch.

In summary of Level 2, the evidence seems to suggest that effective leaders differ from ineffective ones and from followers in several affect-related ways. First, effective leaders are likely to be high on positive affectivity and to have average emotional baselines in the positive range. This helps them overcome the effects of negative affective events and negative emotional contagion that may influence followers and less effective managers. The effective leaders are also likely to experience more active, high-arousal positive emotions and less active, lower arousal negative emotions. The more effective leaders should also be better at accessing their gut feelings when making decisions. People high on emotional intelligence should also be more likely to emerge as leaders, to use effective leadership behaviors such as transformational leadership behaviors, and to have overall higher leadership effectiveness. Effective leaders should also be high on self-awareness and empathy.

Level 3: Interpersonal Relationships

Yukl (2001) defined organizational leadership as a process of managing interpersonal relationships at work. A similar perspective is reflected in the *leader–member exchange* (LMX) theory of leadership (see Graen & Uhl-Bien, 1995). In this instance, leadership has a place at Level 3 of the multilevel model, where the central focus is on communication of emotion in interpersonal exchanges. Moreover, as Ashkanasy and Jordan (2008) point out, leadership involves much more than just managing others. Citing Mumby and Putnam (1992), Ashkanasy and Jordan argue that organizational life is intrinsically reflected in the expression and control of emotions. Mumby and Putnam refer to this as "bounded emotionality." In other words, just as human decision making is subject to "bounded rationality" (Simon, 1976), human relationships at work are constrained in terms of the way people express and deal with their emotions. As a corollary of this, effective leaders regulate relationships with their followers as a means to develop and enhance their relationships with them. In effect, and as Martin, Knopoff, and Beckman (1998) have noted, this means that managing emotional states and emotional expression is a key aspect of effective leadership.

Consistent with this idea, Humphrey (2006) posited the idea of "leading with emotional labor" (see also Humphrey, 2005; 2008; Humphrey, Pollack, & Hawver, 2008; Ashkanasy & Humphrey, 2011). Hochschild (1983) defined emotional labor as "management of feeling to create a publicly observable facial and bodily display" (p. 7). Although Hochschild originally cast this idea in the context of service work, where service employees are remunerated in part for managing their emotional displays in the presence of customers, the idea can apply equally well to leadership in the sense that leaders "serve" their subordinates (e.g., as reflected in the idea of "servant leadership," see Greenleaf, 1977).

The basis of emotional labor according to Hochschild (1983) is that service employees, as a component of their employment contract, are required to express particular emotions as part of their job duties. Usually, the emotion expressed by employees toward customers needs to be positive (Ashforth & Humphrey, 1993; Brotheridge & Grandey, 2002; Pugh, 2001; Rafaeli & Sutton, 1987; Van Dijk & Kirk-Brown, 2006), but not necessarily. Sutton (1991), for example, studied the need for bill collectors to display a range of emotions, including irritation, anger, and even sadness. Pugh (2001), in a study of bank tellers, concluded moreover that emotional labor serves to improve task effectiveness in that the customer sees the emotional expression he or she expects. As a result, the server–customer relationship is not distracted from the task at hand. Ashforth and Humphrey (1993) stress this aspect of emotional labor. Thus, when people interacting at work do not have to deal with out-of-character emotional expressions (e.g., laughter when something goes wrong), things tend to run more smoothly.

Unsurprisingly, given Hochschild's (1983) original focus, early work in emotional labor tended to focus on service settings. Notable exceptions, however, were studies by Brotheridge and Grandey (2002) and Mann (1997). Brotheridge and Grandey examined emotional labor in five occupations, focusing on managers' regulation of their emotional displays, and confirmed that the managers performed emotional labor just as frequently as sales/service and human services workers. The same phenomenon was reported by Mann, who studied managers in the British nuclear industry. Similar to Brotheridge and Grandey, Mann found that emotional labor effects could be found at all levels of organizational communication and especially in manager–subordinate relationships.

The notion that emotional labor can be important in nonservice situations obtained further support in research by Lewis (2000), who examined emotional expression in a field setting and reported that, when leaders' displays of negative emotions were inappropriate (i.e., situationally incongruent) subordinate ratings of their effectiveness were lowered. Newcombe and Ashkanasy (2002) found the same effect in a laboratory study. Based on these data, Humphrey (2005) proposed that emotional labor may be a critical ingredient of transformational leadership. In effect, leaders who employ emotional labor would be more likely to be perceived as transformational leaders. This idea has since been supported in a study by Epitropaki (2006), who reported higher subordinate ratings on transformational leadership for leaders who employed emotional labor when interacting with their followers.

To understand this phenomenon in more detail, Humphrey et al. (2008) proposed that emotional labor can be categorized into three types: (1) customer service, (2) caring professions, and (3) social control situations. Thus, consistent with Hochschild's (1983) original conceptualization, service employees typically are expected to express pleasant emotions, demonstrated through smiling and behaving in an open, friendly manner. Interestingly, and as Grandey (2003) subsequently demonstrated empirically, employees who are required to exhibit such positive emotions, irrespective of the pace and affective tone of their work surroundings, suffer a good deal of stress. This stress in turn makes it harder for them to display (incongruent) emotional expressions, thus further deepening their stress (Grandey, 2000).

Employees in the caring professions, such as nurses, health care workers, social workers, and childcare workers, also have to deal with their displays of emotional expression under sometimes trying circumstances. For example, they have to convey sympathy for sick patients or clients who might have deep personal problems that are difficult to deal with. This has been associated with the high rate of burnout in the caring professions (Maslach, 1982).

Finally, we note that social control agents, such as bouncers, policemen, and bill collectors, also have to display emotions, but this time the emotions that they need to display are negative. As we noted earlier, for example, Sutton (1991) found that bill collectors need to express just the right amount of irritation and that this can be a source of further work stress for these employees.

Humphrey et al. (2008) argue that, because of the complexity of what they do, leaders need to employ *all three types* of emotional labor when interacting with their subordinates. Moreover, leaders need also to consider carefully which type of emotional labor is appropriate in a given situation. For example, in a service setting, the leader might have to set an example by acting cheerful and enthusiastic when employees are feeling bored. On the other hand, when s/he needs to deal with a difficult situation, the leader might need to express sympathy and support to frustrated subordinates. Or, in situations in which employees need to be disciplined, the leader might need to display stern disapproval. Moreover, and in view of the complexity of everyday work situations, a leader might need to deal with a mixture of these situations. For example, there may be a need to display sympathy for the personal problems that might have resulted in an employee arriving late, but, at the same time, make it clear that on-time arrival is critical, especially for a job that entails interactions with customers who expect agents to be there at the opening bell.

Iszatt-White's (2009) study of college leaders demonstrates that even positive, supportive leaders still have to use emotional labor tactics to display a range of emotions. Although the leaders in her sample preferred to use genuine and natural emotional labor, at times, they had to use either surface acting or deep acting to express more positive emotions than they were feeling at the time or to express tougher emotions than what they usually preferred to feel and express. In the course of their interviews with Iszatt-White, the leaders made clear that they had to exercise judgment about the best possible emotions to display for each situation they encountered. This would seem to further underline the need for researchers to understand emotional intelligence as a potential and important determining factor in effective leadership.

A key distinction in the emotional labor literature is between *surface acting*, in which the actors change their outward emotional expressions without changing their actual feelings ("felt emotions"), and *deep acting*, in which the actors recall their feelings toward a past object or person and then use these inner feelings as a means to govern their outward displays of emotion (Grandey, 2000; Hochschild, 1983). Although the latter is usually construed as more "authentic" than the former, both types of emotional labor can create feelings of inauthenticity, often referred to as "emotional dissonance." Subsequent research (e.g., see Bono & Vey, 2005; Bryant & Cox, 2006; Brotheridge & Grandey, 2002; Van Dijk & Kirk-Brown, 2006) has found that, although the strength of the effect is less in the instance of deep acting, both forms can have negative psychological consequences, including stress and burnout.

In addition to these types of emotional labor, Ashforth and Humphrey (1993) identified a third mode, namely *naturally expressed emotion*. According to Ashforth and Humphrey (1993), these are the emotional expressions that employees express as a result of feeling genuine emotions. For example, a service employee who really enjoys dealing with a particular customer has no need to engage in either surface or deep acting. Subsequent research by Glomb and Tews (2004) and Diefendorff, Croyle, and Gosserand (2005) has supported the existence of this form of emotional display. The question, however, arises as to whether this can be described as "labor" per se. In this respect, Hennig-Thurau, Groth, Paul, and Gremler (2006) found support for the idea that it can be so regarded, so long as it is consistent with the organization's display rules. In particular, Hennig-Thurau and his colleagues found that customers respond more positively to this kind of natural emotional labor so long as it is consistent with the organization's emotional display rules.

Turning now to consider how leaders may engage in the three types of emotional labor, we note that leader authenticity is a major issue here. Avolio, Gardner, Walumbwa, Luthans, and May (2004), for example, suggest that a critical element of "authentic leadership" involves not masking the leader's true intensions through overuse of impression management (see also Newcombe & Ashkanasy, 2002). More recently, Hunt, Gardner, and Fischer (2008) developed a typology based on the three types of emotional labor as they relate to authentic leadership. Hunt and his associates reasoned that two factors determine the effectiveness or otherwise of a leader's emotional labor. The first is whether the leader's emotional display is consistent with the organization's display rules. The second is the physical and/or psychological distance between a leader and her or his followers. For example, a leader who displays genuine anger contrary to a close employee's social expectations may be perceived as authentic but yet generate unfavorable impressions. Dasborough and Ashkanasy (2005) refer to this as "emotional ambivalence." Thus, although it is probably true that, in comparison to, say, service workers, leaders have more freedom to choose the valance and intensity of their emotional expressions, this is going to be constrained by the nature of the leader's position in the organization and also by her or his relationship with followers (Humphrey et al., 2008).

Hunt at al. (2008) argue further that the type of emotional labor a leader uses to influence followers' perceptions of leader authenticity and trustworthiness is also is a function of the leader's closeness to her or his subordinate, suggesting a deeper issue of ethical leadership. More recently, Gardner, Fischer, and Hunt (2009) developed this idea further and concluded that genuine emotional expression (as a form of emotional labor) is a prerequisite for authentic leadership (see also Dasborough & Ashkanasy, 2005).

In this respect, leaders also need to balance the power relationships that they have with their followers. Thus, leaders need simultaneously to balance their (downward) displays of relationship leadership with their need to display appropriate (upward) demeanors to their own superiors (Cowsill & Grint, 2008). This represents yet a further complication in the process of leading with emotional labor that we discussed in the previous section. It is little wonder then that research (e.g., see Ashforth & Humphrey, 1993; Brotheridge & Grandey, 2002; Brotheridge & Lee, 2008; Hochschild,1983; Pugh, 2001; Rafaeli & Sutton, 1987; Van Dijk & Kirk-Brown, 2006) has consistently found that leaders suffer from a range of stress-related issues that ultimately affect their ability to lead and, ultimately, their own well-being. Moreover, the emotional labor literature, as well as the related literature on emotion regulation, has categorized a number of techniques that people can use to help them both feel and express appropriate emotions. Thus, applying the concepts from research on emotional labor may prove beneficial to leadership researchers (Humphrey, 2005; 2008).

Considering further the specific effect of emotional labor on leader stress, the emotional labor literature (e.g., see Grandey, 1999; 2000) tells us that surface acting is likely to be more stressful for leaders than deep acting or genuine emotional expression. In this respect, Humphrey et al. (2008) argued that it is important for leaders to portray a positive outlook (e.g., optimism, hope, confidence) in the face of morale-defeating events that might lead their subordinates to lose confidence. In this instance, it is incumbent on the leader to employ surface or deep emotional labor strategies as a means to portray confidence, in the hope that this will be picked up by followers through a processes of emotional contagion (see also Dasborough et al., 2009; Tee et al., 2013).

This idea is also consistent with the emerging concepts of positive leadership and psychological capital (Hannah & Luthans, 2008). Moreover, recent research by Jones, Visio, Wilberding, and King (2008) appears to indicate that leaders' emotive awareness may influence whether they find performing emotional labor to be stressful. In sum, although the extant research suggests that deep acting and genuine emotional expression are the preferred modes for effective leadership, the effect of emotional labor on leaders appears to be more complex than originally envisaged. Clearly, this is a field that needs to be investigated further.

Another issue to be considered here concerns the broader issue of emotion regulation strategies (Grandey, 2000). In this instance, emotional regulation encompasses a broad spectrum of behaviors in addition to emotional labor (Gross, 1998; 2006). Mikolajczak, Tran, and Brotheridge (2008) recently classified a range of emotional regulation in work settings in addition to the three emotional labor strategies we have outlined in this chapter. This work suggests that leaders might employ a broader range of emotional regulation strategies in their interactions with others in the organization, including superiors, peers, and subordinates. These also imply that emotional regulation can play an expanded role in controlling the leader's own emotion, as well as influencing the moods, emotions, and performance of followers.

Finally, we note that there is an inevitable overlap between Level 2 and Level 3. In particular, a leader's individual differences, such as emotional intelligence and trait affect, might affect which of the three types of emotional labor a leader might apply, as well as how skillfully the leader can use each approach (Salovey, Hsee, & Mayer, 1993). In support of this idea, Brotheridge (2006) found that emotional intelligence predicted undergraduate students' use of emotional labor strategies. More recently, Jordan, Soutar, and Kiffin-Petersen (2008) found in a field study that, although only 4 percent of employees could be categorized as "chameleons," able to display three types of emotional labor depending on circumstances, another 28 percent could be categorized as "empathists," possessing an ability to employ deep acting and genuine emotional expression in interactions with others. Clearly, this is an area ripe for additional research.

In summary of Level 3, we have argued that, in order to establish effective interpersonal relationships, leaders need to be able to perceive others' true emotions and also be able to effectively communicate their own feelings. Leaders also have to make sure that their expressed emotions match organizational and societal expectations and norms. To express appropriate emotions, leaders may have to use emotional labor and regulation tactics to manage both their own emotions and their expressed emotions. Leaders high on emotional intelligence, self-awareness, and positive affectivity should be better at establishing authentic, trusting relationships with followers.

Level 4: Groups

In the original five-level model, based on the tenets of LMX theory, Ashkanasy (2003*a*) envisaged that leadership is a Level 4 phenomenon. In other words, leaders' interactions with group members ultimately determine the affective tone of the group (see also George, 2000; Pescosolido, 2002; Pirola-Merlo et al., 2002). As we outline here, however, there is also a good deal of overlap between leadership at Levels 3 and 4.

An intriguing additional ingredient in leadership at the group level is emotional contagion. Ashkanasy and Jordan (2008), for example, cited Barsade's (2002) research on emotional contagion processes in groups to illustrate how a leader can set the emotional tone in the group he or she is leading (see also Bono & Ilies, 2006; Cherulnik, Donley, Wiewel, & Miller, 2001; Kelly & Barsade, 2001; Sy et al., 2005). Thus, and consistent with the tenets of bounded emotionality, a key leader's role is to be a facilitator of group emotions. This effect was demonstrated in a field study by Tse, Dasborough, and Ashkanasy (2008), who found that LMX contributes to the quality of team members' exchanges only in a positive affective team climate. In another field study, Sy, Côté, and Saavedra (2005) demonstrated that group positive group affect is a direct outcome of leader positive display (i.e., an example of leading with emotions labor, as discussed earlier). These authors reported further that the group's positive affect was associated with team coordination task effectiveness. On the other hand, Fitness (2000) reported that, if the leader engages in unwarranted displays of negative emotion, such as anger, the group affective tone can easily turn negative.

Humphrey and his colleagues (see Ashkanasy & Humphrey, 2011; Humphrey, 2005; 2006; 2008; Humphrey et al., 2008) posit further that this process is intrinsically tied to emotional labor. In effect, leaders can both gain control of their own emotions and use emotional contagion to influence the emotions and moods of their coworkers and subordinates through appropriate use of emotional labor. In support of this idea, Jones, Kane, Russo, and Walmsley (2008) found in a field study that emotional contagion processes depended on the subordinates' perceptions of the leaders and concluded that this is an instance of leading with emotional labor.

The key issue here is that a leader needs to display the *right* emotion at the *right* intensity to be effective. In this respect, Dasborough and Ashkanasy (2002; 2005) developed a model in which follower attributions to a leader's influence attempts results in positive or negative emotional responses. Thus, the manner in which followers attribute sincere versus manipulative intentions to their leader is critical in that followers' subsequent emotional responses serve to drive followers' perceptions of leader trustworthiness and their behavioral and attitudinal reactions to the leader's influence attempt. As we noted earlier, this is critically dependent on the leader's appropriate use of emotional labor. For example, in Newcombe and Ashkanasy's (2002) experiential study, followers in a performance appraisal situation were asked to rate the LMX of their appraiser. Lowest ratings were given to leaders who attempted to convey a positive appraisal message while at the same time displaying negative facial affect.

Of special relevance at Level 4 is the notion of leader charisma. We discussed this earlier as a Level 2 (individual difference) phenomenon, but the effects of charisma are also felt at the group level. In this respect, scholars of leadership charisma seem to understand that emotion is a critical ingredient in leader–follower relationships (for a review, see Bratton, Grint, & Nelson, 2005), and early charisma theorists such as Conger and Kanungo (1987) and Gardner and Avolio (1998) recognized that charismatic leaders influence their followers' emotions. These authors, however, viewed this as a mainly attributional process and an example of (cognitive) impression management.

More recently, however, scholars have begun to recognize that the emotional component of charisma can be important in its own right. In particular, the emergence of contagion processes in the literature has provided a new lens on charismatic leadership. Cherulnik, Donley, Wiewel, and Miller (2001), for example, found that videotapes of a leader displaying positive nonverbal emotional expressions such as smiling was reproduced in observers' facial expressions. Goleman, Boyatzis, and McKee (2002) developed a theory of "emotional resonance" to explain this kind of effect. In their model, an effective leader serves to create an emotional resonance that "synchronizes" the emotions of both leaders and followers.

Leaders' use of emotionally arousing language has also been shown to play a role here. For example, Mio, Riggio, Levin, and Reese (2005) demonstrated that charismatic leaders use more emotionally engaging metaphors than do their less charismatic peers. Bono and Ilies (2006) also found in an extensive field investigation of charisma and emotional contagion that followers gave higher ratings to more emotionally expressive leaders and rated their intention to be influenced by expressive leaders more highly than less expressive leaders. Bono and Ilies reported further that these effects held even after controlling for vision statements and other nonaffective characteristics of charismatic leaders. In another study, Waples and Connelly (2008) found followers' "vision-related performance" was influenced more by leaders who used "active emotions," irrespective of whether the leaders' emotional valence was positive or negative. Waples and Connelly reported that subordinates' ratings of the leader as transformational was higher for the leaders who conveyed active emotions. This effect was particularly evident for low emotional competence followers, suggesting that such followers are more susceptible to leaders who convey active emotions.

In the Sy et al. (2005) study we referred to earlier, the authors examined in particular the extent to which leaders' moods "infected" group members through emotional contagion and subsequently influenced their performance. Sy and his associates reported that this is exactly what they found: the leaders' mood did in fact determine to a large extent group members' positive or negative mood. Moreover, groups led by the positive mood leaders performed better than the negative leader groups, both in terms of coordination and in effort required to achieve task goals. This finding parallels similar results by De Hoogh and colleagues (2005), who reported that the charismatic leaders in their study performed more effectively than noncharismatic leaders through improving their subordinates' work attitudes.

There is, however, also evidence of a Level 2 cross-over effect on leader charisma and its effects at Level 4. Thus, individuals might differ in their ability to be charismatic because of differences in their ability to display emotions. In demonstration of this effect, Groves (2005) found in a field study that whether the leaders were perceived as charismatic depended on their level of perceived emotional expressiveness. There is also evidence that emotional expressiveness may be required for appointment to leadership roles in the first instance. Thus, Kellett et al. (2006) found that leadership emergence in a group task accomplishment situation was predicated on the leader's ability to express appropriate emotions.

Results of the Kellett et al. (2006) study suggest further that, while a leader's ability to express emotions might have a direct effect, for example, through expressing tough, nonempathetic emotions, there might also be an indirect effect through leader empathy on both relations leadership and task leadership. These results imply that leaders need to express situationally congruent emotions. Thus, although the leader needs to, in general, convey positive emotions, expression of negative emotions when the situation calls for it is viewed positively. This is consistent with Newcombe and Ashkanasy's (2002) finding that negative emotions tend to be viewed as appropriate when situational contingencies are congruent.

Leaders may also improve performance by selecting group members who are high in emotional intelligence. For example, Jordan et al. (2002) found that teams whose members had higher average emotional intelligence were more effective at quickly establishing effective work groups.

To summarize Level 4, we argue that leaders influence the group affective tone by expressing appropriate emotions and by controlling emotional contagion processes. Leaders who express appropriate emotions establish better LMX processes and are also more likely to be seen as charismatic leaders. Leaders can also improve performance by selecting team members who have high emotional intelligence.

Level 5: Organization-Wide

At Level 5, we address the leader's role in shaping the organization's culture and the climate of the organization (De Rivera, 1992; Schein, 1992). In this respect, Schein emphasized that the founder of an organization most often sets the tone for its subsequent culture, which then becomes embedded in the organization's values and basic assumptions and is reflected in observable artifacts and patterns of behavior. Within this framework, Härtel and Ashkanasy (2011) adopted the metaphor of culture as a "fossilification" of human patterns of relating. Thus, like a fossil record, culture contains within it the evolution of an organization, including evolution of the norms of emotional expression and rules governing social interactions between organizational members.

Härtel and Ashkanasy (2011) emphasize in particular the leader's role in shaping a positive work environments that in turn derives from social environments characterized by a positive emotional climate, social inclusion, and human flourishing (Sekerka & Fredrickson, 2008). They argue further that an understanding of the culture of positive work environments requires consideration not only of the cultural constituents, but how people interpret the organization's culture (i.e., its organizational climate).

In fact, the idea that organizational culture has an emotional dimension is not all that new. Authors such as Beyer and Niño (2001), Fineman (2001), and Van Maanen and Kunda (1989) have written on this. Others, including Hochschild (1983), Rafaeli and Sutton (1987; 1989) have emphasized how culture is embodied in emotional display rules. Ashkanasy (2003*a*) argued further, consistent with De Rivera (1992), that organizational culture can determine in the way organizational members experience emotions on a day-to-day basis. In this regard, Härtel (2008) identified emotions as central to a culture being healthy or toxic. For example, individual customers and clients can detect if the climate in the back office of a store or restaurant is healthy and positive or toxic and negative. Similarly, clients in business-to-business settings who deal with organizations operated by effective lean teams come to pick up the "vibes" or indicators of positive/negative climate. Moreover, cultures can go either way: positive or negative. Many of the authors listed above describe such "toxic" cultures.

Härtel and Ashkanasy (2011) used the term "positive work environment" (PWE) to refer to the contextual factors and work conditions associated with well-being and positive organizational behavior. As noted by Härtel (2008), a PWE exists when employees see their workplace as positive, respectful, inclusive, and psychologically safe; leaders and co-workers as trustworthy, fair, and open to diversity; and characterized by just policies and decision making. Moreover, a PWE is also manifested through objective criteria including physical and neurological measures of well-being and safety audits.

A further key characteristic of a PWE is that it provides the set of emotional experiences necessary for human flourishing. According to Fredrickson's (2001) broaden and build theory, "experiences of positive emotions broaden people's momentary thought-action repertoires, which in turn serves to build their enduring personal resources, ranging from physical and intellectual resources to psychological resources" (p. 218). In a similar vein, other studies have linked positive emotions to greater sociability, improved social interactions (Burger & Caldwell, 2000; Cunningham, 1988; Isen, 1970), and closer friendships (Berry, Willingham, & Thayer, 2000).

Based on the foregoing, it is clear that leaders must play a key role in developing and maintaining a PWE. At the same time, the leader cannot ignore the reality of negative emotion. In this respect, and as Van Maanen and Kunda (1989) demonstrate, negative emotion is an inevitable part of organizational life, even in organizations like Disney that set out to show an exclusively positive face to the world. Härtel and Ashkanasy (2011) argue, however, that negative emotions need not automatically equate to subsequent negative outcomes, just as positive emotions do not automatically equate to positive outcomes following the emotional experience. These authors point out that negative emotion often provides important signals about moral dilemmas and areas where learning is required. Thus, the ability to respond constructively to negative emotions depends on other factors, including, for example, how frequently we are exposed to negative emotional experiences.

Positive emotions play an important role in this because they have the capacity to buffer the impact of negative emotions on people, to build psychological resiliency toward negative events (Tugade & Fredrickson, 2004), and to promote the adoption of functional coping strategies (Härtel, 2008). In this instance, a leader has responsibility to establish an emotional climate that promotes human flourishing, one where positive emotional experiences outweigh negative emotional experiences.

In summary of Level 5, we have argued here that leaders play a crucial role in determining an organization's culture and affective climate. In this respect, culture is a kind of fossilized relic of entrenched patterns of behaving, and this is then reflected in the affective tone within the organization. Thus, leaders have a special role to play in organizations, fostering and modeling positive patterns of behavior that result in a PWE, which is then, in turn, related to more effective organizational outcomes.

Conclusion

In the course of this chapter, and based in Ashkanasy's (2003*a*) five-level model of emotion in organizations, we have argued that leadership and emotion are intimately connected at all levels of organizing. At Level 1, corresponding to within-personal temporal variability in feelings and behavior, leaders generate and manage "affective events" for their followers that result in emotional states calling forth attitudes and behaviors that can be positive or negative. At Level 2, we address individual differences in leaders' ability to perceive and manage emotions, both in themselves and in their followers, usually referred to as emotional intelligence, and detail the growing volume of empirical evidence that supports the notion that emotional intelligence is related to both leadership and employee effectiveness. At Level 3, which concerns interpersonal relationships, we identified that leadership effectiveness can be found in "leading with emotional labor," in which a leader's ability to manage followers is determined in part by the leader's ability to model the right type and amount of emotion in the right circumstance. The result is reflected in what has come to be called "authentic leadership." Emotion as a group phenomenon is the focus of Level 4, and here processes of emotional contagion are important. Charismatic leadership, in particular, is reflected in an ability to "infect" members of a group with an emotional state that is right for the situation. Finally, at Level 5, we address emotions and leadership as an organization-wide process. Culture in particular is seen as a fossilization of patterns of behavior. A particular feature of the model is that many of the effects we discuss operate at the "meso-level" (cf. House, Rousseau, & Thomas-Hunt, 1995). As such, leaders have a responsibility to engender a PWE, resulting in positive outcomes for the organization as a whole.

Before we finish, however, we acknowledge that the leadership style we have advocated can also be misused. Emotion is a powerful motivating force in determining human behavior (Frijda, 1987). Although we have stressed the positive role that leaders can adopt, there is also a potential "dark side." For example, transformational leaders can manipulate their followers to engage in evil and/or self-destructive behavior (Conger, 1990). Also, Fineman (2004) argues that emotional intelligence can easily become a form of manipulation, in which top management seeks to control employees for their own selfish ends. In this chapter, however, and in line with Bass, Avolio, and Atwater (1996), we have focused on situations in which a leader seeks to engage in genuine emotional expression, with a view to advancing the interests of all stakeholders, including employees, customers, and the community at large.

We also acknowledge that there are national cultural differences in both leadership and the expression of emotion. In this respect, Elfenbein and Ambady (2002) demonstrated that, although the physical expression of emotion is universal (Ekman, 1984), cultural rules and norms governing the expression and even the experience of emotion are in part culturally determined. Similarly, rules of leadership can vary across cultures (see den Hartog et al., 1999).

In this chapter, we have mentioned several intriguing possibilities for future research; we would like to highlight the following:

Leading with emotional labor. Research by Humphrey and his associates (Humphrey, 2005; 2006; 2008; Humphrey et al., 2008; Ashkanasy & Humphrey, 2011) has drawn attention to the fact that leaders use emotional labor in their interactions with their subordinates. As we discuss earlier in this chapter, however, emotional labor can be stressful, with some individuals more prone to experiencing stress than others. Possibly, emotional intelligence may also hold the key here (e.g., see Waples & Connelly, 2008). Clearly, research is needed to investigate the effects of emotional labor on both the leaders themselves and on leadership effectiveness.

Embodiment of emotions, emotional tagging, and leadership. Research by Damasio (1994) has demonstrated that people access their bodily reactions, or gut feelings, to help them make decisions. Experiments by Niedenthal and her colleagues (Niedenthal et al., 2005; 2009) have shown in particular that we access bodily reactions through partial reactivation of sensory motor states even when evaluating the emotional connotations of words. Judging the emotional connotation of words involves a fairly low level of emotional arousal and intensity. In contrast, leaders often have to make judgments under conditions of considerable stress or emotional arousal. Case studies by Finkelstein, Whitehead, and Campbell (2009) suggest that a related concept, emotional tagging, also influences leaders' judgments about mergers and acquisitions, responses to crisis situations, and other important decisions. Emotional tagging occurs when memories that are part of our pattern recognition processes are tagged with positive, negative, or neutral emotional associations. As Finkelstein and his associates argue, these emotional tags aid in making most decisions by alerting the decision maker to the importance of an issue. Important issues are tagged with strong positive or negative emotions, whereas trivial issues have largely neutral tags. Problems occur, however, when emotional tags are attached to misleading experiences. Together, these studies suggest that bodily reactions and emotional tagging can have a strong influence on how leaders make decisions; however, more research is needed using both field and experimental simulations to verify this.

Emotional intelligence, cognitive intelligence, the Big Five, and leadership. Walter, Cole, and Humphrey's (2011) review found consistent results for the importance of emotional intelligence to leader emergence, leader behaviors, and leadership effectiveness. They argued, however, that more leadership studies are needed to include measures of the three major types of predictors of leadership *simultaneously*; viz. emotional intelligence, cognitive intelligence, and the Big Five personality measures. Moreover, we need additional research to uncover the underlying mechanisms of individual differences such as these. Only by including all three types of predictors can we know for sure the relative importance of each one.

Cross-level aspects of leadership. The model we have based this analysis on also emphasizes cross-level (or meso-level) effects (e.g., see Dasborough et al., 2009). In this respect, Ashkanasy (2003*a*; 2003*b*) also stressed how processes at each level cross over to other levels. For example, we have argued that leadership, which is essentially a group (Level 4) phenomenon, is strongly influenced by individual differences such as emotional intelligence (Level 2) and notions of emotional labor and leader–member exchange (at Level 3). Leaders also play a central role as shapers of organizational culture and climate (Level 5) and as generators of affective events (Level 1, Weiss & Cropanzano, 1996). As Dasborough and her colleague point out, "What goes around, comes around" (p. 571); what leaders do at one level is ultimately reflected in variability at the other four levels. For example, a leader who is perceived as unfair by group members not only engenders negative emotions in the group, but also sets up a dynamic whereby top management becomes aware of the issue and loses confidence in the leader's abilities to do her or his job. Dasborough et al. framed their model around the idea of emotional contagion, but this has yet to be investigated as a cross-level phenomenon. Clearly, research is needed to identify the nature of this kind of process and its effects.

To conclude, we have presented the view in this chapter that leadership is intrinsically a process of managing emotions. To do this, leaders need to recognize that they are a source of affective events for their followers, and that the resulting affective reactions determine how their followers subsequently form attitudes and behave. As such, it seems leaders may well need to possess the emotional intelligence necessary to execute "leading with emotional labor" resulting in positive work environments and organizational outcomes.

Note

1. The first use of the term "emotional intelligence" was in a PhD dissertation by Payne (1986), but Payne did not formally define the construct.

References

Antonakis, J. J. (2004). On why "Emotional Intelligence" will not predict leadership effectiveness beyond IQ or the "Big Five": An extension and rejoinder. *Organizational Analysis, 12*, 171–182.

Antonakis, J., Ashkanasy, N. M., & Dasborough, M. T. (2009). Does leadership need emotional intelligence? *Leadership Quarterly, 20*, 247–261.

Ashforth, B. E., & Humphrey, R. H. (1993). Emotional labor in service roles: The influence of identity. *Academy of Management Review, 18*, 88–115.

Ashforth, B. E., & Humphrey, R. H. (1995). Emotion in the workplace: A reappraisal. *Human Relations, 48*, 97–125.

Ashkanasy, N. M. (2003*a*). Emotions in organizations: A multilevel perspective. In F. Dansereau & F. J. Yammarino (Eds.), *Research in multi-level issues: Multi-level issues in organizational behavior and strategy* (vol. 2, pp. 9–54). Oxford: Elsevier/JAI Press.

Ashkanasy, N. M. (2003b). Emotions at multiple levels: An integration. In F. Dansereau & F. J. Yammarino (Eds.), *Research in multi-level issues: Multi-level issues in organizational behavior and strategy* (vol. 2, pp. 71–81). Oxford: Elsevier/JAI Press.

Ashkanasy, N. M., & Daus, C. S. (2002). Emotion in the workplace: The new challenge for managers. *Academy of Management Executive, 16*(*1*), 76–86.

Ashkanasy, N. M., & Daus, C. S. (2005). Rumors of the death of emotional intelligence in organizational behavior are vastly exaggerated. *Journal of Organizational Behavior, 26*, 441–452.

Ashkanasy, N. M., & Humphrey, R. H. (2011). A multi-level view of leadership and emotions: Leading with emotional labor. In A. Bryman, D. Collinson, K. Grint, B. Jackson, & M. Uhl-Bien (Eds.), *The Sage handbook of leadership* (pp. 363–377). London: Sage.

Ashkanasy, N. M., & Jordan, P. J. (2008). A multi-level view of leadership and emotion. In R. H. Humphrey (Ed.), *Affect and emotion: New directions in management theory and research* (pp. 17–39). Charlotte, NC: Information Age Publishing.

Ashkanasy, N. M., & Tse, B. (2000). Transformational leadership as management of emotion. In N. M. Ashkanasy, C. E. J. Härtel, & W. Zerbe (Eds.), *Emotions in the workplace: Research, theory, and practice* (pp. 221–235). Westport, CT: Quorum Books.

Ashton-James, C. E., & Ashkanasy, N. M. (2008). Affective events theory: A strategic perspective. In W. J. Zerbe, C. E. J. Härtel, & N. M. Ashkanasy. *Research on emotion in organizations: Emotions, ethics, and decision-making* (vol. 4, pp. 1–34). Bingley: Emerald Group Publishing/JAI Press.

Avolio, B. J., Gardner, W. L., Walumbwa, F. O., Luthans, F., & May, D. R. (2004). Unlocking the mask: A look at the process by which authentic leaders impact follower attitudes and behaviors. *Leadership Quarterly, 15*, 801–823

Aydin, M., Leblebici, D., Arslan, M., Kilic M., & Oktem, M. (2005). The impact of IQ and EQ on pre-eminent achievement in organizations: Implications for the hiring decisions of HRM specialists. *International Journal of Human Resource Management, 16*, 701–719.

Bar-On, R. (1997). *Bar-On Emotional Quotient Inventory technical manual.* Toronto: Multi-Health Systems.

Barbuto, J. E., Jr., & Burbach, M. E. M. (2006). The emotional intelligence of transformational leaders: A field study of elected officials, *Journal of Social Psychology, 146*, 51–64.

Barling, J., Slater, F., & Kelloway, E. K. (2000). Transformational leadership and emotional intelligence: An exploratory study. *Leadership and Organizational Development Journal, 21*, 157–161.

Barsade, S. G. (2002). The ripple effect: Emotional contagion and its influence on group behavior. *Administrative Science Quarterly, 47*, 644–675.

Bass, B. M. (1990). From transactional to transformational leadership: Learning to share the vision. *Organizational Dynamics, 18*(3), 19–36.

Bass, B. M., & Avolio, B. J. (1990). The implications of transactional and transformational leadership for individual, team, and organizational development. *Research in Organizational Change and Development, 4*, 231–272.

Bass, B. M., Avolio, B. J., & Atwater, L. (1996). The transformational and transactional leadership of men and women. *Applied Psychology. An International Review, 45*, 5–34.

Bass, B. M., & Bass, R. (2008). *The Bass handbook of leadership: Theory, research and managerial applications.* New York: Free Press.

Berry, D. S., Willingham, J. K., & Thayer, C. A. (2000). Affect and personality as predictors of conflict and closeness in young adults' friendships. *Journal of Research in Personality, 34*, 84–107.

Beyer, J., & Niño, D. (2001). Culture as a source, expression, and reinforcer of emotions in organizations. In R. L. Payne & C. L. Cooper (Eds.), *Emotions at work: Theory, research, and applications for management* (pp. 173–197). Chichester, UK: John Wiley & Sons.

Bono, J. E., & Ilies, R. (2006). Charisma, positive emotions, and mood contagion. *Leadership Quarterly, 17*, 317–334.

Bono, J. E., Foldes, H. J., Vinson, G., & Muros, J. P. (2007). Workplace emotions: The role of supervision and leadership. *Journal of Applied Psychology*, 92, 1357–1367.

Bono, J. E., & Vey, M. A. (2005). Toward understanding emotional management at work: A quantitative review of emotional labor research," in C. E. J. Härtel, W. J. Zerbe, & N. M. Ashkanasy (Eds.), *Emotions in organizational behavior* (pp. 213–233). Mahwah, NJ: Lawrence Erlbaum Associates.

Brackett, M. A., Mayer, J. D., & Warner, R. M. (2004). Emotional intelligence and its relation to everyday behavior. *Personality and Individual Differences*, 36, 1387–1402.

Bratton, J., Grint, K., & Nelson, D. (2005). *Organizational leadership.* Mason, OH: Thomson/South-Western.

Brotheridge, C. M. (2006). The role of emotional intelligence and other individual difference variables in predicting emotional labor relative to situational demands. *Psicothema, 18*, 139–144.

Brotheridge, C. M., & Grandey, A. A. (2002). Emotional labor and burnout: Comparing two perspectives of "People Work." *Journal of Vocational Behavior, 60*, 17–39.

Brotheridge, C. M., & Lee, R. T. (2008). The emotions of managing: An introduction to the special issue. *Journal of Managerial Psychology, 23*, 108–117.

Bryant, M., & Cox, J. W. (2006). The expression of suppression: Loss and emotional labour in narratives of organizational change. *Journal of Management & Organization, 12*, 116–130.

Burger, J. M., & Caldwell, D. F. (2000). Personality, social activities, job-search behavior and interview success: Distinguishing between PANAS trait positive affect and NEO extraversion. *Motivation and Emotion, 24*, 51–62.

Caruso, D. R., Mayer, J. D., & Salovey, P. (2002). Emotional intelligence and emotional leadership. In F. J. Pirozzolo (Ed.), *Multiple intelligences and leadership.* Mahwah, NJ: Lawrence Erlbaum Associates.

Cherulnik, P. D., Donley, K. A., Wiewel, T. S. R., & Miller, S. R. (2001). Charisma is contagious: The effect of leaders' charisma on observers' affect. *Journal of Applied Social Psychology, 31*, 2149–2159.

Clark, L. A., Watson, D., & Leeka, J. (1989). Diurnal variation in the positive affects. *Motivation and Emotion, 13*, 205–234.

Conger, J. A. (1990). The dark side of leadership. *Organizational Dynamics, 19*, 44–55.

Conger, J. A., & Kanungo, R. N. (1987). Toward a behavioral theory of charismatic leadership in organizational settings. *Academy of Management Review, 12*, 637–647.

Côté, S., & Miners, C. (2006). Emotional intelligence, cognitive intelligence, and job performance. *Administrative Science Quarterly, 51*, 1–26.

Cowsill, R., & Grint, K. (2008). Leadership, task and relationship: Orpheus, Prometheus and Janus. *Human Resource Management Journal, 18*, 188–195.

Cunningham, M. R. (1988). Does happiness mean friendliness? Induced mood and heterosexual self-disclosure. *Personality and Social Psychology Bulletin, 14*, 283–297.

Damasio, A. R. (1994). *Descartes' error: Emotion, reason, and the human brain.* New York: Putnam.

Dasborough, M. T., & Ashkanasy, N. M. (2002). Emotion and attribution of intentionality in leader-member relationships. *Leadership Quarterly, 13*, 615–634.

Dasborough, M. T., & Ashkanasy, N. M. (2005). Follower emotional reactions to authentic and inauthentic leadership influence. In Gardner, W. L., Avolio, B. J., & Walumbwa, F. O. (Eds.), *Monographs in leadership and management, volume 3: Authentic leadership theory and practice: Origins, effects and development* (pp. 281–300). Oxford: Elsevier/JAI Press.

Dasborough, M. T., Ashkanasy, N. M., Tee, E. E. J., & Tse, H. H. M. (2009). What goes around comes around: How meso-level negative emotional contagion can ultimately determine organizational attitudes toward leaders. *Leadership Quarterly, 20*, 571–585.

Daus, C. S., & Ashkanasy, N. M. (2005). The case for an ability-based model of emotional intelligence in organizational behavior. *Journal of Organizational Behavior, 26*, 453–466.

De Hoogh, A. H. B., Den Hartog, D. N., Kopman, P. L., Thierry, H., Van den Berg, P. T., Van der Weide, J. G., & Wilderom, C. P. M. (2005). Leader motives, charismatic leadership, and subordinates' work attitudes in the profit and voluntary sector. *Leadership Quarterly, 16*, 17–38.

den Hartog, D. N., House, R. J., Hanges, P. J., Dorfman, P. W., Ruiz-Quintana, A., Ashkanasy, N. M., & GLOBE Associates. (1999). Culture specific and cross-culturally generalizable implicit leadership theories: Are attributes of charismatic/transformational leadership universally endorsed? *Leadership Quarterly, 10*, 219–256.

De Rivera, J. (1992). Emotional climate: Social structure and emotional dynamics. *International Review of Studies of Emotion, 2*, 197–218.

Diefendorff, J. M., Croyle, M. H., & Gosserand, R. H. (2005). The dimensionality and antecedents of emotional labor strategies. *Journal of Vocational Behavior, 66*, 339–357.

Elfenbein, H. A., & Ambady, N. (2002). On the universality and cultural specificity of emotion recognition: A meta-analysis. *Psychological Bulletin, 128*, 203–235.

Elfenbein, H. A., Foo, M. D., White, J., Tan, H. H., & Aik, V. C. (2007). Reading your counterpart: The benefit of

emotion recognition accuracy for effectiveness in negotiation. *Journal of Nonverbal Behavior, 31*, 205–223.
Ekman, P. (1984). Expression and the nature of emotion. In: K. R. Scherer & P. Ekman (Eds.), *Approaches to emotion* (pp. 319–343). Hillsdale, NJ: Lawrence Erlbaum.
Ekman, P. (1999). Facial expressions. In T. Dalgleish & M. J. Power (Eds.), *Handbook of cognition and emotion* (pp. 301–320). New York: John Wiley and Sons.
Epitropaki, O. (2006). "Leading the show": The impact of leader's emotional labor on subordinates' transformation leadership perceptions and collective emotional labor. Paper presentation, *The Academy of Management*, Atlanta, GA.
Fayol, H. (1916/1949). *General and industrial management*. Translated from the French edition (Dunod) by C. Storrs. London: Pitman.
Fineman, S. (2001). Emotions and organizational control. In R. L. Payne & C. L. Cooper (Eds.), *Emotions at work: Theory, research, and applications for management* (pp. 219–240). Chichester, UK: Wiley.
Fineman, S. (2004). Getting the measure of emotion—and the cautionary tale of emotional intelligence. *Human Relations, 57*, 719–740.
Finkelstein, S., Whitehead, J., & Campbell, A. (2009). *Think again: Why good leaders make bad decisions and how to keep it from happening to you*. Boston, MA: Harvard Business Press.
Fisher, C. D. (2000). Mood and emotions while working: Missing pieces of job satisfaction? *Journal of Organizational Behavior, 21*, 185–202.
Fitness, J. (2000). Anger in the workplace: An emotion script approach to anger episodes between workers and their superiors, co-workers and subordinates. *Journal of Organizational Behavior, 21*, 147–162.
Forgas, J. P. (1995). Mood and judgment: The Affect Infusion Model (AIM). *Psychological Bulletin, 117*, 39–66.
Fredrickson, B. L. (2001). The role of positive emotions in positive psychology: The broaden-and-build theory of positive emotions. *American Psychologist, 56*, 218–226.
Frijda, N. H. (1987). The emotions: Studies in emotion and social interaction. New York: Cambridge University Press.
Fritz, C., & Sonnentag, S. (2009). Antecedents of day-level proactive behavior: A look at job stressors and positive affect during the workday. *Journal of Management, 35*, 94–111.
Gardner, W. L., & Avolio, B. J. (1998). The charismatic relationship: A dramaturgical perspective. *Academy of Management Review, 23*, 32–58.
Gardner, W. L., Fischer, D., & Hunt, J. G. (2009). Emotional labor and leadership: A threat to authenticity? *Leadership Quarterly, 20*, 466–482.
Gardner, W. L., & Stough, C. (2002). Examining the relationship between leadership and emotional intelligence in senior level managers. *Leadership & Organization Development Journal, 23*(2), 68–78.
George, G. M. (1990). Personality, affect, and behavior in groups. *Journal of Applied Psychology, 76*, 299–307.
George, J. M. (2000). Emotions and leadership: The role of emotional intelligence. *Human Relations, 53*, 1027–1055.
George, J. M., & Zhou, J. (2007). Dual tuning in a supportive context: Joint contributions of positive mood, negative mood, and supervisory behaviors to employee creativity. *Academy of Management Journal, 50*, 605–622.
Glomb, T. M., & Tews, M. J. (2004). Emotional labor: A conceptualization and scale development. *Journal of Vocational Behavior, 64*, 1–23.
Goleman, D. (1995). *Emotional intelligence: Why it can matter more than IQ*. New York: Bantam.
Goleman, D., Boyatzis, R., & McKee, A. (2002). *Primal leadership*. Harvard Business School Press, Cambridge, MA.
Graen, G. B., & Uhl-Bien, M. (1995). Relationship-based approach to leadership: Development of leader–member exchange LMX theory of leadership over 25 years: Applying a multi-level multi-domain perspective. *Leadership Quarterly, 6*, 219–247.
Grandey, A. A. (2000). Emotion regulation in the workplace: A new way to conceptualize emotional labor. *Journal of Occupational Health Psychology, 5*, 59–100
Grandey, A. A. (2003). When "the show must go on": Surface acting and deep acting as determinants of emotional exhaustion and peer-rated service delivery. *Academy of Management Journal, 46*, 86–96.
Greenleaf, R. K. (1977). *Servant leadership: A journey into the nature of legitimate power and greatness*. New York: Paulist Press.
Gross, J. J. (1998). The emerging field of emotion regulation: An integrative review. *Review of General Psychology, 2*, 271–299.
Gross, J. J. (2006). *Handbook of emotion regulation*. New York: Guilford Press.
Groves, K. S. (2005), Linking leader skills, follower attitudes, and contextual variables via an integrated model of charismatic leadership, *Journal of Management, 31*, 255–277.
Hannah, S. T., & Luthans, F. (2008). A cognitive affective processing explanation of positive leadership: Toward theoretical understanding of the role of psychological capital. In R. H. Humphrey (Ed.), *Affect and emotion: New directions in management theory and research* (pp. 97–136). Charlotte, NC: Information Age Publishing.
Härtel, C. E. J. (2008). How to build a healthy emotional culture and avoid a toxic culture. In C. L. Cooper & N. M. Ashkanasy (Eds.), *Research companion to emotion in organizations* (pp. 575–588). Cheltenham, UK: Edwin Elgar.
Härtel, C. E. J., & Ashkanasy, N. M. (2011). Healthy human cultures as positive work environments. In N. M. Ashkanasy, C. E. P. Wilderom, & M. F. Peterson (Eds.), *The handbook of organizational culture and climate, second edition* (pp. 85–100). Thousand Oaks, CA: Sage.
Hatfield, E., Cacioppo, J. T., & Rapson, R. L. (1993). Emotional contagion. *Current Directions in Psychological Science, 2*, 96–99.
Hennig-Thurau, T., Groth, M., Paul, M., & Gremler, D. D. (2006). Are all smiles created equal? How emotional contagion and emotional labor affect service relationships. *Journal of Marketing, 70*, 58–73.
Hochschild, A. R. (1983). *The managed heart: Commercialization of human feeling*. Berkeley: University of California Press.
House, R. J., & Howell, J. M. (1992). Personality and charismatic leadership. *Leadership Quarterly*, 3, 81–108.
House, R., Rousseau, D. M., & Thomas-Hunt, M. (1995). The meso paradigm: A framework for the integration of micro and macro organizational behavior. In L. L. Cummings & B. M. Staw (Eds.), *Research in organizational behavior* (vol. 17, pp. 71–114). Greenwich, CT: JAI Press.
House, R. J., Shane, S. A., & Harold, D. J. (1996). Rumors of the death of dispositional research are vastly exaggerated. *Academy of Management Review, 21*, 203–224.
Humphrey, R. H. (2002). The many faces of emotional leadership. *Leadership Quarterly, 13*, 493–504.
Humphrey, R. H. (2005). Empathy, emotional expressiveness, and leadership. *Proceedings of the Southern Management Association*, 1–6. Charleston, SC.

Humphrey, R. H. (2006, August). Leading with emotional labor. Paper presented at the annual meetings of the Academy of Management Conference, Atlanta, GA.

Humphrey, R. H. (2008). The right way to lead with emotional labor. In R. H. Humphrey (Ed.), *Affect and emotion: New directions in management theory and research* (pp. 1–17). Charlotte, NC: Information Age Publishing.

Humphrey, R. H., Pollack, J. M., & Hawver, T. H. (2008). Leading with emotional labor. *Journal of Managerial Psychology, 23,* 151–168.

Hunt, J. G., Gardner, W. L., & Fischer, D. (2008). Leader emotional displays from near and far: The implications of close versus distant leadership. In R. H. Humphrey (Ed.), *Affect and emotion: New directions in management theory and research* (pp. 42–65). Charlotte, NC: Information Age Publishing.

Isen, A. M. (1970). Success, failure, attention, and reactions to others: The warm glow of success. *Journal of Personality and Social Psychology, 25,* 294–301.

Iszatt-White, M. (2009). Leadership as emotional labour: The effortful accomplishment of valuing practices. *Leadership, 5,* 447–467.

Jones, R. G., Kane, T., Russo, J., & Walmsley, P. (2008). *What you see is what you feel: Leader emotional labor is in the eye of the beholder.* A symposium presentation at The Sixth International Conference on Emotions and Organizational Life (EMONET VI), Fontainbleau, France.

Jones, R. G., Visio, M., Wilberding, K., & King, H. (2008). *Leader emotive awareness, emotional labor, burnout and work-family conflict.* A symposium presentation at The Sixth International Conference on Emotions and Organizational Life (EMONET VI), Fontainbleau, France.

Jordan, C., Soutar, G., & Kiffin-Petersen, S. (2008). *Are there different "types" of emotional laborers?* Paper presented at The Sixth International Conference on Emotions and Organizational Life (EMONET VI), Fontainbleau, France.

Jordan, P. J., Ashkanasy, N. M., Härtel, C. E. J., & Hooper, G. S. (2002). Workgroup emotional intelligence: Scale development and relationship to team process effectiveness and goal focus. *Human Resource Management Review, 12,* 195–214.

Jordan, P. J., Lawrence, S. A., & Troth, A. C. (2006). The impact of negative mood on team performance. *Journal of Management & Organization, 12,* 131–145.

Jordan, P. J., & Troth, A. C. (2004). Managing emotions during team problem solving: Emotional intelligence and conflict resolution. *Human Performance, 17,* 195–218.

Joseph, D. L., & Newman, D. A. (2010). Emotional intelligence: An integrative meta-analysis and cascading model. *Journal of Applied Psychology, 95,* 54–78.

Judge, T. A., & Kammeyer-Muellar, J. D. (2008). Affect, satisfaction, and performance. In N. M. Ashkanasy & C. L. Cooper (Eds.), *Research Companion to Emotion in Organizations* (pp. 136–151). Cheltenham, UK: Edward Elgar Publishing Limited.

Kellett, J. B., Humphrey, R. H., & Sleeth, R. G. (2002). Empathy and complex task performance: Two routes to leadership. *Leadership Quarterly, 13,* 523–544.

Kellett, J. B., Humphrey, R. H., & Sleeth, R. G. (2006). Empathy and the emergence of task and relations leaders. *Leadership Quarterly, 17,* 146–162.

Kelly, J. R., & Barsade, S. G. (2001). Mood and emotions in small groups and work teams. *Organizational Behavior and Human Decision Processes, 86,* 99–130.

Kuehnel, J., & Sonnentag, S. (2011). How long do you benefit from vacation? A closer look at the fade-out of vacation effects. *Journal of Organizational Behavior, 32,* 125–143.

Law, K. S., Wong, C. S., & Song, L. J. (2004). The construct and criterion validity of emotional intelligence and its potential utility for management studies. *Journal of Applied Psychology, 89,* 483–496.

Lewis, K. M. (2000). When leaders display emotion: How followers respond to negative emotional expression of male and female leaders. *Journal of Organizational Behavior, 21,* 221–234.

Locke, E. A. (2005). Why emotional intelligence is an invalid concept. *Journal of Organizational Behavior, 26,* 425–431.

Mann, S. (1997). Emotional labour in organizations. *Leadership & Organization Development Journal, 18,* 4–12.

Mann, S. (1999). *Hiding what we feel, faking what we don't: Understanding the role of your emotions at work.* New York: Harper-Collins.

Martin, J., Knopoff, K., & Beckman, C. (1998). An alternative to bureaucratic impersonality and emotional labor: Bounded emotionality at The Body Shop. *Administrative Science Quarterly, 43,* 429–469.

Maslach, C. (1982). *Burnout: The cost of caring.* Hillsdale, NJ: Prentice-Hall.

Mastenbroek, W. (2000). Organizational behavior as emotion management. In N. M. Ashkanasy, W. Zerbe, & C. E. J. Härtel (Eds.), *Emotions in the workplace: Research, theory, and practice* (pp. 19–35). Westport, CT: Quorum Books.

Mayer, J., & Salovey, P. (1997). What is emotional intelligence? In P. Salovey & D. Sluyter (Eds.), *Emotional development and emotional intelligence: Implications for educators* (pp. 3–31). New York: Basic Books.

Mayer, J. D., Salovey, P., & Caruso, D. (2002). *Mayer-Salovey-Caruso Emotional Intelligence Test (MSCEIT): User's manual.* Toronto, ON: Multi-Health Systems.

Mayer, J. D., Salovey, P., Caruso, D., & Sitarenios, G. (2003). Measuring emotional intelligence with the MSCEI V2.0. *Emotion,* 3, 97–105.

McColl-Kennedy, J. R., & Anderson, R. D. (2002). Impact of leadership style and emotions on subordinate performance. *Leadership Quarterly, 13*(5), 545–559.

Meyer, J. P., & Allen, N. J. (1997). *Commitment in the workplace: Theory, research and application.* Thousand Oaks, CA: Sage Publications.

Mikolajczak, M., Tran, V., & Brotheridge, C. M. (2008). *From emotional labour to emotion regulation: Enlarging the perspective on emotion management in the workplace.* A symposium presentation at The Sixth International Conference on Emotions and Organizational Life (EMONET VI), Fontainbleau, France.

Mio, J. S., Riggio, R. E., Levin, S., & Reese, R. (2005). Presidential leadership and charisma: The effects of metaphor. *Leadership Quarterly, 16,* 287–294.

Mumby, D. K., & Putnam, L. A. (1992). The politics of emotion: A feminist reading of bounded rationality. *Academy of Management Review, 17,* 465–486.

Newcombe, M. J., & Ashkanasy, N. M. (2002). The role of affect and affective congruence in perceptions of leaders: An experimental study. *Leadership Quarterly, 13,* 601–614.

Niedenthal, P. M., Barsalou, L. W., Winkielman, P., Krauth-Gruber, S., & Ric, F. (2005). Embodiment in attitudes, social perception, and emotion. *Personality and Social Psychology Review, 9,* 184–211.

Niedenthal, P. M., Winkielman, P., Mondillon, L., & Vermeulen, N. (2009). Embodiment of emotion concepts. *Journal of Personality and Social Psychology, 96*, 1120–1136.

O'Boyle, E. H. Jr., Humphrey, R. H., Pollack, J. M., Hawver, T. H., & Story, P. A. (2011). The relation between emotional intelligence and job performance: A meta-analysis. *Journal of Organizational Behavior, 32*, 788–818.

Offermann, L., Bailey, J. R., Vasilopoulos, N. L., Seal, C., & Sass, M. (2004). The relative contribution of emotional competence and cognitive ability to individual and team performance. *Human Performance, 17*, 219–243.

Payne, W. L. (1986). A study of emotion: Developing emotional intelligence; self integration; relating to fear, pain and desire. *Dissertation Abstracts International, 47*, 203A (University microfilms No. AAC 8605928).

Pescosolido, A. T. (2002). Emergent leaders as managers of group emotion. *Leadership Quarterly, 13*, 583–599.

Petrides, K. V. (2009). *Technical manual for the Trait Emotional Intelligence Questionnaires (TEIQue).* London: London Psychometric Laboratory.

Pirola-Merlo, A., Härtel, C. E. J., Mann, L., & Hirst, G. (2002). How leaders influence the impact of affective events on team climate and performance in R&D teams. *Leadership Quarterly, 13*, 561–581.

Pugh, S. D. (2001). Service with a smile: Emotional contagion in the service encounter. *Academy of Management Journal, 44*, 1018–1027.

Rafaeli, A., & Sutton, R. I. (1987). Expression of emotion as part of the work role. *Academy of Management Review, 12*, 23–37.

Rafaeli, A., & Sutton, R. I. (1989). The expression of emotion in organizational life. In L. L. Cummings & B. M. Staw (Eds.), *Research in organizational behavior* (vol. 11, pp. 1–42). Greenwich, CT: JAI Press.

Redl, F. (1942). Group emotion and leadership. *Psychiatry: Journal for the Study of Interpersonal Processes, 5*, 573–596.

Rosete, D., & Ciarrochi, J. (2005). Emotional intelligence and its relationship to workplace performance outcomes of leadership effectiveness. *Leadership & Organization Development Journal, 26*, 388–399.

Salovey, P., Hsee, C. K., & Mayer, J. D. (1993). Emotional intelligence and the self-regulation of affect. In D, M. Wegner & J. W. Pennebaker (Eds.), *Handbook of mental control* (pp. 258–277). Englewood Cliffs, NJ: Prentice-Hall.

Salovey, P., & Mayer, J. D. (1990). Emotional intelligence. *Imagination, Cognition and Personality*, 9(3), 185–211.

Schein, E. (1992). *Organizational culture and leadership.* San Francisco: Jossey-Bass.

Schutte, N. S., Malouff, J. M., Hall, L. E., Haggerty, D. J., Cooper, J. T., Golden, C. J., & Dornheim, L. (1998). Development and validation of a measure of emotional intelligence. *Personality and Individual Differences, 25*, 167–177.

Sekerka, L. E., & Fredrickson, B. L. (2008). Establishing positive emotional climates to advance organizational transformation. In N. M. Ashkanasy & C. L. Cooper (Eds.), *Research companion to emotion in organizations* (pp. 531–545). Cheltenham, UK: Edward Elgar. Niedenthalmeso-level.

Shamir, B., & Howell, J. M. (1999). Organizational and contextual influences on the emergence and effectiveness of charismatic leadership. *Leadership Quarterly, 10*, 257–283.

Simon, H. A. (1976). *Administrative behavior: A study of decision-making processes in administrative organization, 3rd edition.* New York: Free Press.

Sosik, J. J., & Megerian, L. E. (1999). Understanding leader emotional intelligence and performance: The role of self-other agreement on transformational leadership perceptions. *Group and Organization Management, 24*, 367–390.

Sutton, R. I. (1991), "Maintaining norms about expressed emotions: The case of bill collectors," *Administrative Science Quarterly, 36*, 245–268.

Sy, T., Côté, S., & Saavedra, R. (2005). The contagious leader: Impact of the leader's mood on the mood of group members, group affective tone, and group processes. *Journal of Applied Psychology, 90*, 295–305.

Sy, T., Tram, S., & O'Hara, L. A. (2006). Relation of employee and manager emotional intelligence to job satisfaction and performance. *Journal of Vocational Behavior, 68*, 461–473.

Tee, E. Y. J., Ashkanasy, N. M., & Paulsen, N. (2013). The influence of follower mood on leader mood and task performance: Evidence for an affective, follower-centric perspective of leadership. *The Leadership Quarterly, 24*, 496–515.

Tse, H, H. M., Dasborough, M. T., & Ashkanasy, N. M. (2008). A multi-level analysis of team climate and interpersonal exchange relationships at work. *Leadership Quarterly, 19*, 195–211.

Tugade, M. M., & Fredrickson B. L. (2004). Resilient individuals use positive emotions to bounce back from negative emotional experiences. *Journal of Personality and Social Psychology, 86*, 320–333.

Van Dijk, P. A., & Kirk-Brown, A. (2006). Emotional labor and negative job outcomes: An evaluation of the mediating role of emotional dissonance. *Journal of Management & Organization, 12*, 101–115.

Van Maanen, J., & Kunda, G. (1989). "Real feelings": Emotional expression and organizational culture. In L. L. Cummings and B. A. Staw (Eds.), *Research in organizational behavior* (vol.11, pp. 43–103). Greenwich, CT: JAI Press.

Van Rooy, D., & Viswesvaran, C. (2004). Emotional intelligence: A meta-analytic investigation of predictive validity and nomological net. *Journal of Vocational Behavior, 65*, 71–95.

Wagner, D. T., & Illes, R. (2008). Affective influences on employee satisfaction and performance. In N. M. Ashkanasy & C. L. Cooper (Eds.), *Research companion to emotion in organizations* (pp. 152–169), Cheltenham, UK: Edward Elgar.

Walter, F., Cole, M. S., & Humphrey, R. H. (2011). Leadership and emotional intelligence: Past findings, current criticisms, and future directions. Emotional Intelligence: sine qua non of leadership or folderol? *Academy of Management Perspectives, 25*, 45–59.

Waples, E. P., & Connelly, S. (2008). Leader emotions and vision implementation: Effects of activation potential and valence. In R. H. Humphrey (Ed.), *Affect and emotion: New directions in management theory and research* (pp. 66–96). Charlotte, NC: Information Age Publishing.

Watson, D., & Tellegen, A. (1985). Towards a consensual structure of mood. *Psychological Bulletin, 98*, 219–235.

Weiss, H. M., & Brief, A. (2001). Affect at work: A historical perspective. In R. L. Payne & C. L. Cooper (Eds.), *Emotions at work: Theory, research and applications for management* (pp. 133–172). Chichester, UK: John Wiley and Sons.

Weiss, H. M., & Cropanzano, R. (1996). Affective events theory: A theoretical discussion of the structure, causes, and consequences of affective experiences at work. In B. M. Staw & L. L. Cummings (Eds.), *Research in organizational behavior* (vol. 18, pp. 1–74). Greenwich, CT: JAI Press.

Weiss, H. M., Nichols, J. P., & Daus, C. S. (1999). An examination of the joint effects of affective experiences and job beliefs on job satisfaction and variations in affective experiences over time. *Organizational Behavior and Human Decision Processes, 78*, 1–24.

Wolff, S. B., Pescosolido, A. T., & Druskat, V. U. (2002). Emotional intelligence as the basis of leadership emergence in self-managing teams. *Leadership Quarterly, 13*, 505–522.

Wong, C. S., & Law, K. S. (2002). The effects of leader and follower emotional intelligence on performance and attitude: An exploratory study. *Leadership Quarterly, 13*, 243–274.

Yammarino, F. J., & Atwater, L. E. (1997). Do managers see themselves as others see them? Implications of self-other ratings agreement for human resources management, *Organizational Dynamics, 25*, 35–44.

Yukl, G. A. (1999). An evaluation of conceptual weaknesses in transformational and charismatic leadership theories. *Leadership Quarterly, 10*, 285–305.

Yukl, G. A. (2001). *Leadership in organizations.* Englewood Cliffs, NJ: Prentice Hall.

CHAPTER

36 Student Leadership Development: Theory, Research, and Practice

Susan R. Komives *and* John P. Dugan

Abstract

This chapter advances a life span approach to the process of leadership development through the exploration of educational contexts experienced by youth and college students as powerful venues for building leadership capacity. Considerations from developmental psychology are positioned as critical influences on the processes of leadership development. The chapter synthesizes existing theories, research, and practical applications designed specifically for youth and college student populations.

Key Words: co-curricular activities, college student leadership, extracurricular activities, high-impact practices, high school student leadership, leader development, leader identity development, leadership development, life span leadership development, social change model, youth leadership

Until the turn of the 21st century, the study of leadership focused predominately on adult populations (MacNeil, 2006; Murphy, 2011). Early classic studies examined antecedents to adult leadership (e.g., Bray, Campbell, & Grant, 1974) demonstrating the positive role of college activities in later work place leadership effectiveness. This contributed to increased study of the nature of antecedents as well as how to integrate them effectively into college contexts as a means to target leadership development prior to entry into the workforce. A growing interest in life span approaches to leader development (Day, Harrison, & Halpin, 2009; Lord, Hall, & Halpin, 2011; Murphy & Johnson, 2011; Summers, 2000; Van Velsor & Drath, 2004) validated these efforts and offered justification for the process of leadership development beginning even prior to college (Day, 2011; Gottfried & Gottfried, 2011). Indeed, leadership is now understood to be happening at all ages and stages in the life span.

Drawing on the life span perspective, this chapter first briefly provides an overview of psychological aspects of development as a critical contextual influence for understanding leader development. The concept of the development of leader identity is explored in association with other social identities. This chapter then presents the evolution of both youth and college student leadership including developmental models as well as related theoretical and conceptual leadership models, research and scholarship, and examples of common practices. The differential effect on and experiences of diverse students, particularly females and students of color, are noted throughout. Given the core purpose of educational systems is focused on learning and development, this chapter approaches leadership development primarily from the perspective of how to leverage learning within these contexts. Interventions associated with each educational level reflect the increasing acknowledgment that developmental sequencing is critical (Avolio & Vogelgesang, 2011; Brungardt, 1996; Dugan, 2011a; Lord & Hall, 2005). The chapter concludes with observations on challenges in leadership development for youth and college students and recommendations for future directions. Key resources are identified that will lead readers to supplemental materials.

Several terms and concepts are critical to reading this chapter. The term "youth leadership" refers to adolescents enrolled in middle school and high school and does not address leadership in childhood. "College student leadership" refers to late adolescents, young adults, and other adults enrolled in colleges and universities. The term "leader" refers to anyone engaged in the process of influencing others toward change. This use of the term does not require that the person hold a positional leadership role. Finally, the terms "internal" and "external" are used throughout the chapter to refer to those experiences, interventions, and group memberships that either occur as a sanctioned part of the student-school experience (i.e., internal) or supplemental to the student experience via community-based organizations (i.e., external).

Dimensions of Development

A paradigm shift from viewing leadership as an adult phenomenon involves a growing acceptance that leadership is exhibited by and among people at all stages of the life span including among children (Avolio & Vogelgesang, 2011; Komives, Owen, Longerbeam, Mainella, & Osteen, 2005; Murphy, 2011). Perhaps even more importantly, this life span perspective finds that "beginnings matter" and those with early experiences in leader development have more complex leadership skills as adults (Avolio & Vogelgesang, 2011, p. 179). Because leadership develops in the context of other dimensions of human development, an overview of these dimensions will add context to the leadership development process.

Overview

The stages of life span development typically include the developmental processes of early childhood (ages 2–6), middle and late childhood (ages 6–11), early and late adolescence (ages 12–19) the early adult years (ages 19–22), and beyond (Arnett, 2006; Erikson, 1968; Murphy, 2011). Each of these stages comprises developmental tasks addressed by a person that contribute to increasingly complex ways of making meaning and solidification of one's core sense of self. This occurs through a process of differentiation and integration (Erikson, 1968). Helsing (2010) observes that these "age/phasic models" are useful, yet may be limited in explaining differences among individual adults and groups of adults specifically not accounting for culture and other dimensions of experience (p. 679).

Erikson (1968) describes that the work, or *tasks,* of these stages lead to healthy development if accomplished successfully, but if left unresolved may contribute to dysfunction or dissonance. For example, in the life span stages addressed in this chapter, adolescents deal with identity versus role confusion as they wrestle with integrating many new roles into a personal self-image particularly in light of peer relationships. Their key question at this stage is: Who am I and where am I going? Young adults deal with intimacy versus isolation examining the question, Am I loved and wanted? Cooperation is central to this stage allowing young adults to move beyond dependence and independence to value interdependence with others. A detailed explanation of these stages of development is beyond the scope of this chapter, yet informs the context of leader identity development and youth and college student leadership. For more information regarding youth and college student development see Boyd and Bee (2009); Erikson (1968); Evans, Forney, Guido, Renn, and Patton (2010); or Sigelman and Rider (2009). Childhood and youth are widely studied in general, but until recently these studies have not focused on leadership or factors that predict leadership outcomes.

Leader Identity

A life span perspective of leadership is informed by an understanding of how identity forms and develops over time. Identity is described as a stable and congruent inner sense of self that is confirmed by societal norms and expectations in relationship to external others (Bronfenbrenner, 1979; Erikson, 1968). Identity is intertwined with the psychosocial tasks frequently described for adolescents and young adults noted earlier and may occur best when youth engage in intentional self-reflection and receive useful feedback in environments that are safe and where there is trust in the adults involved in those environments (Day et al., 2009; Komives et al., 2005).

An individual's identity includes relevant social identities, which reflect socially constructed group membership related to race, gender, sexual orientation, or other designated groups. Social identity may also include membership in a group such as being a Boy Scout, an athlete, a graduate student, or a member of a specific profession (Hogg & Terry, 2001; van Knippenberg, van Kippenberg, De Cremer, & Hogg, 2005). Likewise one may develop a leader identity as a social identity through working with others in group settings (Hall, 2004; Hogg, 2001;

Komives et al., 2005). "A leader identity is an important component of the self, especially with regard to continuous and ongoing leader development" (Day et al., 2009, p. 68). Leader identity assumes more meaning when considered in the intersectionality of other social identities (Hall, 2004; Ibarra, Snook, & Guillen Ramo, 2010). For a more detailed treatment of leader identity see Chapter 16. See also Day et al. (2009) and Day, Zaccaro, and Halpin (2004).

Komives et al. (2005; Komives, Longerbeam, Mainella, Osteen, & Owen, 2006) used life narrative interviews with 13 diverse college students to develop a grounded theory of leader identity development (LID) that encompassed participant reflection on their youth. The six-stage model is described in Table 36.1 and includes transitions between stages when the previous stage no longer "fits" and the student is drawn into new meanings in the next stage. Findings from this study suggest that leader identity begins in stage 1 (Awareness) when the youth does not adopt a leader identity, but is aware of others, particularly adults, in leader roles. In stage 2 (Exploration/Engagement) the student joins groups and is aware of working with friends and peers in mutually chosen contexts (e.g., scouts, church choir, swim club) in which positional leaders may now be older peers. In the first two stages, the student is largely dependent on others and follows their guidance and direction. Stage 3 (Leader Identified) is a leader-centric stage where the positional leader does leadership and others are followers helping the leader get the job done. Leadership is viewed as behaviors of the positional leader. This hierarchical view of leadership is commonly embraced in Western culture in which leadership is viewed largely in an organizational context (Wielkiewicz, 2000). In this stage the student feels independent from others when serving in a positional leader role and shifts to assuming dependence in the follower role. In the research of Komives et al. (2006), this stage appeared to emerge in high school and carried into the college years. The authors further speculated that this view is held by most college students and carries well into adulthood.

Table 36.1. Stages in Leader Identity Development

Stage 1:	Dependent	Awareness—A childhood perspective when there is the recognition that there are such people as leaders, usually parents, teachers, or other authority and historical or even mythical figures (e.g., presidents of the United States, Superman).
Stage 2:		Exploration/Engagement—A time of experiencing groups, expanding interpersonal relationships, taking on responsibilities (although perhaps not in a formal leadership position), and engaging in institutional involvement with clubs (e. g., Boy Scouts), student organizations (student council), or sports teams
Stage 3:	Independent & Dependent	Leader Identified—A leader-centric stage in which participants understand that groups are composed of leaders and followers and that it was the leaders who did the leadership. Someone was a leader only if he or she occupied a formal leadership role; furthermore there was only one leader per group. Komives and colleagues (2005) proposed that all or nearly all students enter college with this perspective on leadership.
Stage 4:	Interdependent	Leadership Differentiated—Students begin to differentiate leadership beyond the role of a formal leader and begin to see leadership as non-positional, i.e., "I can be A leader even if I am not THE leader." This stage is included an emerging recognition that leadership was a process between and among people and anyone in the group could take part in leadership. Teamwork is valued.
Stage 5:		Generativity—Becoming actively committed to a larger purpose as well as commitment to the groups and individuals who are involved in that purpose. The core values and beliefs embedded in the group's purpose begin to be internalized by students. Mentoring others is valued.
Stage 6:		Integration/Synthesis—A time of continuous active engagement with leadership as a daily process—as part of self-identity. Students demonstrate increasing intrinsic confidence and strive for congruence and integrity.

Source: Adapted from Day, Harrison, and Halpin (2009) and Komives, Owen, Longerbeam, Mainella, & Osteen (2005).

A critical transition happens from stage three when the student embraces interdependence, realizes tasks are too complex for any one leader to accomplish, and begins to see leadership as something an individual does whether in a positional or nonpositional role. In the later three stages of the model, the predominate belief in interdependence differentiates leadership (stage 4) as nonpositional, shared, and focusing on the processes of teamwork and the importance of relational skills. Expanding on the view of leader now as a dimension of personal identity, in stage 5 (generativity) the student mentors and teaches younger group members and is devoted to the commitment and passions of the groups of which he or she is a part. As they leave college, some students in stage 6 experienced an integration of their leader identify with their other social identities and, as one participant observed, "I see leadership now as an everyday thing" (Komives et al., 2005, p. 607).

In the LID model, a student's identity as a leader shifted from a focus on the individual, to a relational focus on others, and then a view that leadership involves everyone (Komives, 2011b; Komives et al., 2005, 2006). The student shifts from being dependent on others as a follower, to being independent of others when serving as a leader, and eventually to recognizing interdependence with others in a more complex relational leader identity. This shifting complexity of view is evident in viewing leadership as hierarchical in stage 3 to valuing a systems perspective in the interdependent stages of the model. As Day et al. (2009) observe, the LID model is congruent with Lord and Hall's (2005) assertion that leader identity develops from "individual to relational to collective identities" (Day et al., p. 67). This move from "me," "you and me," to "us" appears to be a developmental process (Komives, Lucas, & McMahon, 2007; Lord & Hall, 2005).

LID reflects identity based on evolving levels of consciousness. Kegan's (1994) holistic view of development (i.e., constructive-developmental theory) observes that meaning-making process involves more complex levels of consciousness. This process involves a subject–object shift when one can see past behaviors and attitudes as "object" and make meaning of self in the past. "Subject" views of self are the lived experience in the present and harder to make meaning or view with perspective. Kegan's subject–object shift question related to LID would be to ask, "What did you used to think leadership was and what do you think it is now?" A response such as, "I used to think leadership was what the person in charge did and now I see it is what we all do" shows a constructive-developmental shift in one's stage of consciousness about leadership and signals a new identity perspective. Indeed as Helsing (2010) observes the benefits of constructive-developmental theories that "... consider the ways in which our beliefs *construct* the reality in which we live and the ways in which these beliefs can change or *develop* over time" (p. 679). That complexity is central to the development of a leader identity.

Youth Leadership Context

The evolution of both the scholarship and practices of youth leadership are best understood in the context of youth development. In 1988, Avolio and Gibbons observed, "Although there are exceptions, the majority of leadership studies have not examined leadership within lifespan and developmental frameworks" (p. 276). Youth leadership is a focus of youth programs both internal and external to school systems.

Asserting that "leadership, in its simplest form, is an exercise of social influence that is manifested in various ways at each developmental stage of a person's life" Murphy (2011, p. 5) along with other scholars (Avolio & Gibbons, 1988; Komives et al., 2005; Lord & Hall, 2005) endorsed a life span approach to leadership development. Leadership is exhibited at all stages across the life span. Murphy (2011) proposed the tasks and skills in each of these youth stages that relate to leadership development. See Table 36.2.

Leadership Binaries

A review of the status of youth leadership reveals dynamic tensions in the study and evolution of leadership for youth and adolescents (Klau, Boyd, Luckow, & Associates, 2006). Viewing these tensions as binaries obfuscates the enrichment of "and-ing" these constructs. These binaries are not discrete, but do illustrate these extant tensions.

VIEWING LEADERSHIP AS AN AUTHORITY POSITION OR AS AN ACTIVITY FOR EVERYONE

Scholars note distinctions between adult leadership and approaches to youth leadership, notably differentiating authority from leadership. Adult leadership approaches and definitions are typically hierarchical and managerial positioning the leader with the authority to act, yet youth are rarely in any position of power or authority (MacNeil, 2006). A decade-long study of youth leadership in

Table 36.2. Leadership Tasks and Skills for Youth

Age Range	New Leadership Tasks and Skills
Preschool Years (Ages 2–5)	Influencing others; Getting others to like you; Communicating wishes; Modeling adults; Increased need for emotional intelligence in interactions with others (reading the emotions of others, delaying gratification)
Elementary School (Ages 6–11)	Early school leadership tasks (e.g., classroom monitor, teacher's helper, bus patrol); Fundraising (e.g., selling candy, wrapping paper); Coordinating others in teams; Public speaking to express ideas; Increased need for social intelligence in interactions with others (understanding social situations and acting appropriately); Begin joining groups (e.g., Cub Scouts)
Middle School–Early Adolescence (Ages 12–14)	Coordinating teams for fundraising or student projects; Self-management (e.g., goal setting, self-observation, and evaluation); Serving in elected office and other student government activities; Public speaking as a leader to gain support for a cause; Playing team sports
High School–Late Adolescence (Ages 15–19)	Organizing complex projects (e.g., school newspaper, choir trips); Participating in classroom group projects; Motivating team members; Organizational skills required by after-school or summer jobs; Working with others to complete a work product in after-school or summer jobs
College–Young Adulthood (Ages 19–22)	Establishing grassroots organizations; Complex supervisory skills required during internships; Serving as a leader with multiple constituents; Being a responsible participant

Note: The tasks important at an earlier age are still appropriate at older ages. The tasks listed for older ages are those more unique to that developmental stage. Adapted from Murphy (2011).

underserved and at-risk communities found that youth leadership focuses:

> On how leadership happens, not on who leaders are as power figures, skillful managers, or individuals bearing specific traits. These perspectives from youth carry strong links to recent work in cognitive psychology and organizational sociology that maintains the key importance of adaptation, engagement with situation, and distribution of knowledge and roles. (Roach et al., 1999, p. 13)

ELITE LEADERSHIP ("A SELECT FEW CAN BE LEADERS") OR EGALITARIAN LEADERSHIP ("EVERYONE CAN BE A LEADER")

Those youth who do hold authoritative, positional roles in formal organizations are identified in the literature as representing elite models of leadership. Youth leaders are frequently the high-achieving or overachieving students, typically from gifted and talented programs, largely from middle-class backgrounds, and often representing privileged classes in society with disproportionate access to resources (Kress, 2006). Often tapped by adults for key positional roles, they are called "elites." Although some scholars distinguish the leaders from the led and advocate for developing leaders, others note issues of access that prohibit more diverse students from participating in the various organizations where they could practice leadership (Kress, 2006) or be tapped for special leadership development experiences. Just as perspectives of leadership among adults have evolved to see leadership as nonpositional and as process, there is a growing perspective that all youth can exhibit leadership even if not in an authority role, which broadens the settings for where leadership development may occur.

LEADERSHIP FOR NOW OR CREATING LEADERS FOR LATER

Perhaps unintentionally, much of the scholarship about youth leadership advances a case for building leaders for tomorrow and developing the youth generation for assuming their leadership roles as adults. Others contest this delayed or deferred approach to leadership and acknowledge youth leadership is needed in their everyday lived experience and personal context as youth shape their organizations, families, and communities (Kress, 2006; Murphy, 2011). Kress (2006) concluded "youth often fail to see themselves as actors in decision-making processes today" because of the framing adults overlay on the youth experience (p. 54). A critical lens would reveal that too often there is even a negative portrayal of youth by adults as liabilities and problems to be fixed (MacNeil, 2006). This "adultism" perspective views youth as a:

> Problem time, to be suffered through, rather than as a positive stage of life development. Young people,

then, are silenced and "warehoused" in schools or youth programs until they are old enough to join society. Clearly, this attitude is not one that encourages either young people or adults to see youth as being organizational or community leaders. (MacNeil, 2006, p. 33)

However, there is growing awareness that people exhibit leadership across the life span (Day et al., 2009; Komives et al., 2005, 2006; Murphy & Reichart, 2011), including during childhood and adolescence. Rich opportunities may exist if developmental leadership interventions capitalized on this.

Theoretical and Conceptual Approaches to Leadership

There have not been exhaustive studies of diverse youth leadership programs, and perhaps because of this leadership educators (Klau, 2006) lament that few programs are based on any definition of leadership and rarely use any specific leadership theories or models. Klau (2006) reports on a Carnegie Foundation study that reviewed 120 youth organizations over a 10-year period observing they were typically based on "unexamined ideas" about how youth develop leadership (p. 60). Indeed, there is controversy on whether "adult" leadership models are even transferable to youth contexts, particularly those models that are based on the leader having authority and power to act (MacNeil, 2006). MacNeil (2006) particularly challenges those adult models that emphasize authority (e.g., "voice, influence, and decision-making power") as not applicable to youth leadership practices that focus on ability (e.g., "skills, knowledge, and talent;" p. 27).

A 10-year study of 30,000 youth engaged in leadership in external organizations such as 4-H and boy's clubs shows that youth emphasize the process of leadership particularly "adaptation, engagement with situation, and distribution of knowledge and roles" instead of traditional adult leadership models that focus on power, management, or trait approaches (Roach et al., 1999). A 2003 Social Policy Research Associates study (cited in Conner & Strobel, 2007) observed a similar phenomenon among the 12 organizational participants in the Youth Leadership Development Initiative. Youth leadership in these civic contexts relates to participating in "group process, build consensus, and subsume personal interests and ideas to those of the collective" (p. 7). These approaches to youth leadership development appear to be more aligned with contemporary adult leadership theories focused on collaboration and shared leadership.

Despite the general lack of theoretical grounding, there are a number of nationally based leadership programs with theoretical foundations. Whitehead (2009) advocated for authentic leadership (Chapter 18) and observes the pro-social outcomes of that approach in the Future Farmers of American (FFA) and Junior Reserve Officer Training Corps (JROTC). The National Youth Leadership Council has adopted Greenleaf's (1977) servant leadership approach (Libby, Sedonaen, & Bliss, 2006). The nationally based Hugh O'Brien Youth leadership (HOBY) program revised their curriculum in 2008 to be based on the social change model of leadership development (Higher Education Research Institute [HERI], 1996) also widely used in college student leadership programs (Kezar, Carducci, Contreras-McGavin, 2006; Komives, Wagner, & Associates, 2009). FFA bases their program on the psychosocial work of Chickering and Reisser (1993) and the social change model (HERI, 1996). FFA advocates for 16 precepts of essential learning that advance quality leadership, personal growth, and career success. The 16 precepts are addressed in their four-stage "me-we-do-serve" model and developed through their LifeKnowledge instructional materials. They assert that all 16 precepts build leadership with a focus on the precepts of action, relationships, vision, character, awareness, and continuous improvement. Emphasizing that youth need to learn they are part of something bigger than themselves, many youth leadership programs connect youth to their communities through service, community organizing, and community change conceptual models (Deschenes, McLaughlin, & Newman, 2008; Nitzberg, 2005; Yu, Lewis-Charp, & Gambone, 2007).

The character education movement (e.g., Character Counts! charactercounts.org/) promotes ethical decision making with leadership from the Josephson Institute. The Institute has both curricular and co-curricular materials based on their six pillars of trustworthiness, respect, responsibility, fairness, caring, and citizenship. Character education programs uniformly produce pro-social outcomes (Berkowitz & Bier, 2004). Research studies published on the Josephson website attest to program impact in academic achievement, behaviors, and attitudes (http://charactercounts.org/research/summary.html). In a similar vein of building character that informs healthy leadership, a large number of high schools have adopted Covey's

(1989) *7 Habits of Highly Effective People* for use in school curricula (www.whig.com/story/news/Habits-Conference-062111).

Even though many programs are anti-theoretical or atheoretical with regard to a foundational grounding in leadership studies, they are concerned about pedagogical practices and largely use an experiential learning pedagogical framework for program delivery. Kress (2006) summarized the basic findings and experiential learning principles involved in general youth development programs:

> Some things cannot be taught but must be learned through experience, experiences are transformed by the individuals who participate in them, development occurs when a person is at a level that she or he can only achieve with help from another person, and we can learn from observing others and their actions. (pp. 49–50)

For more information on school programs, external programs, and national programs see van Linden and Fertman (1998) or Rice (2011).

Research and Scholarship

Despite the "extensive educational infrastructure" (Klau et al., 2006, p. 3) surrounding youth leadership both inside schools and outside the school environment, the effectiveness of youth leadership educational interventions is largely understudied and atheoretical (Klau et al., 2006). Libby et al. (2006) observed that studies of youth leadership development have only recently emerged and are often embedded in other constructs such as character education, community engagement, and life preparation. In the literature, leadership means both holding positional leadership roles as well as enhancing leadership-related skills and capacities (e.g., communication, interpersonal relationships) regardless of leadership role (Conner & Strobel, 2007).

The scholarship of youth development, in general, has historically focused on personal circumstances, motivations, and mediating experiences that predict negative outcomes such as alcohol and drug use, suicide, bullying, and delinquency (Eccles, 2005). Interventions including participation in youth programs such as extracurricular school activities have been shown to reduce risky behaviors and are related to pro-social behaviors such as lowering alcohol consumption, reducing truancy, and developing positive outcomes like initiative (Larson, 2000) and leadership (Eccles, Barber, Stone, & Hunt, 2003; Fredricks & Eccles, 2006, 2008).

EXTRACURRICULAR ACTIVITIES

Eccles (2005; Barber, Eccles, & Stone, 2001; Eccles & Barber, 1999; Mahoney, Larson, & Eccles, 2005) and other researchers support that organized activities are clearly developmental contexts for student growth. A meta-analysis noting methodological limitations in studying the role of extracurricular activities in schools on educational outcomes such as academic achievement shows some noncausal relationships, with small effect sizes (Shulruf, 2010). Extracurricular activities provide a context for potential adult supervision and structure as well as frequently emphasizing skill building, resilience, and competency building (Roth & Brooks-Gunn, 2003). Breadth of participation (i.e., the number of different activities) generally shows less positive outcomes at extremely low or extremely high levels (Fredricks & Eccles, 2006; Marsh & Kleitman, 2002). Involvement in extracurricular activities is more highly correlated with future leadership than is high school academic achievement (Karnes & Bean, 1990).

Involvement in extracurricular activities demonstrates long-term effects (Komives & Johnson, 2009). Fredricks and Eccles (2006) found that extracurricular activity participation predicted "school belonging, psychological resilience, a positive peer context, and lower distress 1 year later" (p. 307). Further study showed 11th graders' breadth of involvement also predicted civic engagement two years out of high school (Fredricks & Eccles, 2008, 2010). According to Zaff, Malanchuk, and Eccles (2008):

> [S]ocial interactions with peers, parent modeling of civic behaviors, and cultural factors, such as ethnicity-specific practices, cumulatively result in a higher level of civic activities among youth and that a continued context that includes these factors results in a higher level of civic activities into adulthood. (p. 38)

Other studies of specific extracurricular involvements such a 4-H (Anderson, Bruce, & Mouton, 2010) show that they have a cumulative impact and are credited as the source of pro-social development by involved students (Feldman & Matjasko, 2005).

School-based extracurricular activities (ESAs) have been found to be more beneficial than external activities (Marsh & Kleitman, 2002). In addition to select academic activities, Marsh and Kleitman (2002) found benefit from such internal activities such as "student government, school publications, and performing arts" (p. 464). Enhanced leadership is typically found as an outcome of participation in extracurricular activities including high school sports (Dubosz & Beaty, 1999). It must be noted that "sport's potential to actually develop leadership in any context depends on it consciously being administered with educational ends in mind" (Reid, 2010, p. 1034).

It is of note that Marsh and Kleitman (2002) found ESAs were of benefit "particularly for socioeconomically disadvantaged students who are least well served by the traditional educational curriculum" (p. 464). Organized activities are typically voluntary and therefore bring challenges and critique regarding access (Brown & Evans, 2002). Creating access is critical because they appear to make a greater contribution to lower income youth than those with higher incomes. Extracurricular activities "foster school identification/commitment that benefits diverse academic outcomes, particularly for socioeconomically disadvantaged students" (Marsh & Kleitman, p. 464). Thus, the relative accessibility of antecedents of leadership development reflect the complex systems of social stratification in society offering systematic advantage and disadvantage based on social status.

ASSET PERSPECTIVE

Moving away from a deficit model approach, more recent research and scholarship in youth development have taken a positive, asset-development perspective (Benson, Scales, Hamilton, & Sesma, 2006; Klau, 2006). This newer movement is to encourage "opportunity and resilience over preventing delinquency and failure" (Kress, 2006, p. 45). Involvement in "effective youth-based organizations" contributes significantly to pro-civic and pro-social values, task efficacy, commitment to service, stronger locus of control, and "desire to work to correct economic inequalities" (Roach et al., 1999, p. 22).

A synthesis of the emergent, positive, asset-based youth development work by Benson et al. (2006) does not reveal a consensus among numerous definitions, but does identify five core constructs guiding the evolution of this asset-based approach. These constructs are (1) the context for development (e.g., places, relationships), (2) the nature of the child, (3) the child's attributes and strengths, (4) lowering of high risk behaviors, and (5) increase in thriving behaviors (Benson et al., 2006). The Search Institute (Benson et al., 2006) identified 40 developmental assets for adolescents (i.e., age 12–18) that contribute to healthy youth development. These assets represent external and internal domains and are further categorized into four subsets in each domain. External assets include support (e.g., family support, caring neighborhood, caring school climate), empowerment (e.g., view of youth as resources, safety, service to others), boundaries and expectations (e.g., family boundaries, adult role models, high expectations), and constructive use of time (e.g., creative activities, religious community). The internal assets include the subset of commitment to learning (e.g., school engagement, achievement motivation), positive values (e.g., caring, equality and social justice, integrity), social competencies (e.g., cultural competence, peaceful conflict resolution), and positive identity (e.g., self-esteem, sense of purpose, personal power). Research on engagement with these assets shows a significant positive correlation between engagement with designated assets and positive youth behavior and outcomes (Benson et al., 2006). According to MacNeil (2006):

> This asset development movement directly connects to the positive outcomes of youth leadership. From a positive youth development perspective, leadership development experiences are good for all youth, providing them with supportive relationships and opportunities to see themselves (and be seen by others) as having valuable contributions to make to the world. Further, their active engagement can help them develop self-esteem, confidence, and essential social and intellectual competencies and can provide an important foundation for future civic involvement. (p. 31)

Furthermore, newer directions in youth development and youth leadership development focus "on the role of youth as problem solvers, not problems to be solved; youth as assets to communities, not liabilities" (MacNeil, 2006, p. 31). These newer frameworks view youth as talent to contribute to community action and not as problems the community needs to address.

LONGITUDINAL STUDIES

Leadership scholars have recently joined the three-decade-long Fullerton Longitudinal Study adding such leadership variables as adult leader emergence (self-reported) and transformational leadership in the current adult development phase of the study (Gottfried et al., 2011; Guerin et al., 2011; Reichard et al., 2011). The Fullerton Study covered ages 2 to 29 with a variety of variables such as gifted motivation (Gottfried & Gottfried, 2011), including intelligence and extraversion as a personality indicator that are now being examined for their early roots of leadership. Using structural equation modeling with an ongoing sample of 106 participants, researchers examined the effects of extraversion and intelligence (IQ) on adult social skills and various leadership potential measures (Guerin et al., 2011). They found that the relationship "between adolescent extraversion and adult leadership potential was completely mediated by adult social skills. Adolescent IQ had neither a direct nor an indirect relationship with adult leadership potential, nor did it interact with extraversion in predicting adult leadership potential" (Guerin et al., 2011, p. 482). Reichard et al. (2011) examined the same personality and intelligence data collected at age 17 and multiple measures of self-reported adult leader emergence and transformational leadership at age 29. "Results indicated a significant relationship between adolescent extraversion and adult workplace leader emergence and transformational leadership above and beyond adolescent intelligence, across a 12-year span" (Reichard et al., 2011, p. 471). Guerin et al. (2011) also used the longitudinal data to examine pathways to adult leadership and identified "a pathway beginning in early childhood with temperamental approach/withdrawal shows stability throughout childhood and leads to extraversion in adolescence, which in turn relates to leadership potential in adulthood via adult social skills" (p. 482).

Practices of Youth Leadership

INTERNAL AND EXTERNAL EXPERIENCES

Although the scholarship on youth leadership is scarce and largely emergent, programs and practices designed to support youth leadership development have existed both inside school systems and outside of schools in communities for many decades (Libby et al., 2006). Conner and Strobel (2007) observed that more than 500,000 high school students engage in some kind of youth leadership activity annually although "the field of youth leadership remains on the margins of educational theory and research" (p. 276). The desirability of developing youth as citizens willing to engage in community life is a common purpose of these programs (McLaughlin, 2000). Support for youth leadership is "woven into the fabric of community life" (McLaughlin, 2000, p. 16).

Most internal experiences are offered through school-based organizations. There are few academic or curricular leadership studies offerings and no known national association to support school-based leadership educators. Some long-term, school-based curricular programs include the program at John F. Kennedy High School in Montgomery County, Maryland, founded in 1994 (Kretman, 1996). Internal school-based student organizations include Key Club, FFA (Horstmeier & Nall, 2007), JROTC, band, student councils, and athletic teams. External or outside organizations include 4-H (Woyach & Cox, 1992), Boy Scouts, Girl Scouts, Junior Achievement, and church youth groups that provide adult-sponsored and supervised experience for youth as they learn to engage with peers around group goals. Numerous regional and national organizations also provide youth leadership experiences such as the Congressional Youth Leadership Council, Hugh O'Brien Youth Foundation, Innovation Center for Community and Youth Development (Wheeler, 2006), National Conference for Community and Justice (Matsudaira, 2006), and the Youth Leadership Institute (Libby et al., 2006). It is surprising that so little study of the leadership impact of these experiences has occurred to date.

In addition to non–school-based experiences, Libby et al. (2006) assert that truly "outside" leadership development includes involvement in social movements seeking equity and justice in their local communities such as Latino students involved with the DREAM Act. They observe that outside strategies are often based on "contestation and conflict" challenging insiders to do more to transform systems and processes to address societal needs (Libby et al., p. 17). Inside programs typically do not reform their systems, but deliver programs to maintain and support existing systems. Students may be involved in either or both approaches.

YOUTH–ADULT PARTNERSHIPS

Noam and Fiore (2004) and others (Culp & Cox, 2002; Libby, Rosen, & Sedonaen, 2005) explored the profound impact of youth–adult relationships framed as "partnerships" in the youth development literature. Partnerships offer the reciprocity of benefit to both youth and adults involved in a shared experience. In these approaches, adults serve as mentors to youth and have a great impact as role models (Berkowitz & Bier, 2004). Both parties contribute their skills and learn from each other, a model that is well evidenced in service learning experience (Marais, Yang, & Farzanehkia, 2000). Students must be active partners in this civic engagement process (Zlotkowski, Horowitz, & Benson, 2011; Zlotkowski, Longo, & Williams, 2006). "Caring, capable, and committed adults invested in the lives of young people... are the most important developmental asset" contributing to positive developmental outcomes including leadership (Lerner, Brittian, & Fay, 2007, p. 4).

Adults often wrestle with how much authority to turn over to youth in partnership models. An empowerment model would turn over authority and control for group decision making to youth, yet may be too much autonomy overwhelming positional youth leaders who need more support to learn and practice how to lead. "This autonomy is often nothing more than abandonment by adults who are unsure how to partner effectively with young leaders" (Kress, 2006, p. 52). Instead, Kress (2006) recommends that adults interested in supporting youth leadership:

> Focus on creating environments in which youth matter and are part of a supportive group that knows them well enough to recognize the optimal zone where they can achieve more only with help from other people—environments where youth skill development is encouraged through hands-on participation and by recognizing that experiences are transformed by the youth who participate in them. (pp. 54–55)

ADDRESSING REAL PROBLEMS

Critics of youth and college student programs (MacNeil, 2006) encourage meaningful involvement of youth in real problems attempting real change. One of the most developmentally powerful activities is service learning and community based action. Community service consistently relates to numerous outcomes including identity formation (McIntosh, Metz, & Youniss, 2005) and leadership (Zlotkowski et al., 2011). Educators (Villarruel, Montero-Sieburth, Dunbar, & Outley, 2005) particularly argue for community-based models emphasizing service learning to build on the assets of youth of color to learn leadership as they contribute to their communities.

Summary

A life span approach to leader development brings the recognition that youth are being engaged at a very early age in leadership through their lived experiences and that it develops over time and experience. Civilizations construct educational systems and community support processes to prepare youth to take on the complex responsibilities of adulthood. Internal and external extracurricular activities are critical to this development. The seeds of effective leadership are planted in the developmental tasks associated with youth. Educators must learn to maximize learning in this context or forfeit critical developmental opportunities to cultivate leadership early in the life span.

College Student Leadership Context

Leadership has been both an explicit and implicit goal over the 375-year history of American higher education in which leadership is often thought to be an outcome of a liberal arts education (Brungardt, Gould, Moore, & Potts, 1997; Riggio, Ciulla, & Sorenson, 2003). Until the last 50 years, preparing students to assume leadership roles in their professions and public life was most frequently a privilege accessible only to elite college students elected or selected for positional roles (Komives, 2011a). At elite selective colleges it was assumed that all students were already leaders. When leadership began to be viewed as something any student could learn, leadership became a disciplinary-based outcome (Sharp, Komives, & Fincher, 2011) and co-curricular programs were broadened to include any student, not just elites such as those in honors programs or those who were officers in student organizations (Komives, 2011a). College student leadership interventions occur in the curriculum (e.g., leadership majors, minors, certificate programs, and courses) as well as in the co-curriculum (e.g., identity-based retreats, alternative spring break service experiences, and internships) and are often delivered as an academic affairs and student affairs partnership. For an overview of how the field of leadership education has professionalized in the last 40 years to include an extensive body of scholarship, theoretical and conceptual models, professional associations, and a growing body of research on the college student leadership development experience see Komives (2011a). This section presents college student development theory as a context for leadership development, explores theoretical and conceptual models used in college leadership education, an overview of research and scholarship in this context, and common leadership development practices.

College Student Development

Psychologist Erik Erikson (1968) first outlined the epigenetic principle that human development reflects the complex interaction of the biological and the environmental. Perhaps nowhere is this interaction more profound than when the powerful influences of the collegiate environment intersect with the biological changes associated with late adolescence and young adulthood. Certainly, either influence on its own (the collegiate environment or late adolescent) creates the context for potentially powerful developmental consequences for individuals. The combination, though, has been the source of interest for scholars across a variety of disciplines (Evans et al., 2010).

The body of literature commonly referred to as student development theory explores development during college and is grounded in classic theories of developmental psychology (e.g., Bandura, 1997; Erikson, 1968; Kegan, 1982, 1994; Kohlberg, 1975; Piaget, 1977). This burgeoning body of literature is generally segmented into three distinct domains exploring psychosocial, social identity, and cognitive dimensions of development (see Evans et al., 2010). Contemporary theory and research extending this work increasingly push for more holistic approaches that integrate the three domains in recognition of their shared influences (Baxter Magolda, 2009; Jones & Abes, 2010). A full review of student development theories is beyond the scope of this chapter, but each domain is defined in the sections that follow along with key suppositions and theorists.

PSYCHOSOCIAL

Psychosocial theories are grounded in the work of Erikson (1968) and explore the content of development. Development is framed as an age-based, sequential process addressing critical developmental tasks that emerge across the life span as an individual interacts with various environments (Evans et al., 2010; Jones & Abes, 2010). Key psychosocial theorists extending the work of Erikson include Chickering and Reisser (1993), Josselson (1978/1991), and Marcia (1966). The most applied of these theories in the college context is Chickering and Reisser's work exploring the influences of higher education on college students' search for identity. The theory posits seven developmental vectors each having magnitude and direction (i.e., developing competence, managing emotions, moving through autonomy toward interdependence, developing mature interpersonal relationships, establishing identity, developing purpose, and developing integrity) along with specific environmental influences on students' growth. The content of psychosocial development undergirds core tenets of contemporary leadership theories through a focus on increasing self-awareness and interpersonal competence.

COGNITIVE

Theories of cognitive development are traditionally built from the foundations of Piaget's (1977) work on intellectual and moral development and explore the process of making-meaning. Development is typically hierarchical and sequential with higher stages reflecting increasingly complex ways of interpreting knowledge, experiences, and events (Evans et al., 2010; Jones & Abes, 2010). Cognitive and moral development theorists extending the work of Piaget include Baxter Magolda (1992); Belenky, Clinchy, Goldberger, and Tarule (1986); Gilligan (1982, 1993); King and Kitchener (1994), Kohlberg (1975); and Perry (1968). The extension and application of cognitive and moral development theories within the college context is vast. Love and Guthrie (1999) suggest that across most theories a similar developmental trajectory emerges reflecting movement from absolute knowing predicated on authoritative expertise and rigid dualism through subjective knowing (i.e., opinions as authoritative in absence of certainty) to generative knowing grounded in an acceptance of ambiguity and constructivist ways of making meaning. Critical to cognitive development during college is the "Grand Accommodation," which Love and Guthrie suggest occurs "when the individual comes to realize that uncertainty is neither anomalous nor restricted to certain knowledge domains—that it is evident everywhere" (p. 79). Cognitive and moral development theories inherently connect to leadership via the exploration of how individuals make meaning of critical leadership issues associated with power, authority, complexity, adaptation, and negotiating the common good.

SOCIAL IDENTITY

Theories of social identity represent a sub-dimension of psychosocial theories that attend to issues of identity formation with a specific focus on the influences of privilege and oppression derived from socially constructed identities (e.g., race, gender, sexual orientation, socioeconomic status; Evans et al., 2010; Jones & Abes, 2010). These theories explore both discrete dimensions of an individual's social identity and intersecting influences of multiple identities. Theorists address developmental trajectories associated with race (Cross, 1991; Helms, 1995; Wijeyesinghe & Jackson, 2001), ethnicity (Phinney, 1990), gender (Bem, 1983; Downing & Roush, 1985), sexual identity (Cass, 1979; D'Augelli, 1994; Fassinger, 1998), and many others including the integration of multiple identities (Jones & McEwen, 2000; Poston, 1990; Renn, 2004; Root, 1996). Development typically reflects movement through recognition of membership within a particular identity group (either internally or externally prescribed) through immersion in learning about the group to integrating the identity as a key component of one's overarching self-concept (Evans et al., 2010; Jones & Abes, 2010). Through this process individuals must develop the necessary coping mechanisms to deal with the consequences of unearned privilege and/or internalized oppression. The focus of social identity theories on self-awareness, intergroup dynamics, and navigating social systems that systematically oppress and privilege various groups connects directly to leadership via the exploration of contextual and identity-based influences. A discussion of leader identity development was presented earlier in this chapter.

HOLISTIC DEVELOPMENT

Increasing exploration of integrated models exploring multiple domains of development simultaneously offer insights into the shared influences of the intrapsychic and the social as well as the cognitive and the affective on one's overall development (Evans et al., 2010; Jones & Abes, 2010). Grounded in the work of Kegan (1982, 1994), holistic theories posit development as a function of an individual's subjective (i.e., embedded within) and objective (i.e., distinct from) meaning-making models that directly shape how they engage with others, experiences various environments, navigate developmental tasks, and concretize a sense of identity. Integrating psychosocial, social identity, and cognitive dimensions, Kegan presents five orders of mind through which a person develops to make meaning of their world and adopt more inclusive worldviews. Several scholars offer theories of holistic development extending or complementing the work of Kegan including Abes, Jones, and McEwen (2007); Bandura (1997); Baxter Magolda (2001); Bronfenbrenner (1979); and Parks (2000). Baxter Magolda (2009) suggested that the primary theme emergent in holistic studies is the "gradual emergence of an internal voice to coordinate external influence and manage one's life. Before the cultivation of this internal voice, one's personal voice is an echo of the voice of external authority" (p. 628). This process is labeled as self-authorship and connects directly to leadership through the recognition of complex and intertwined developmental influences on the process of developing leadership capacity.

Association of Student Development Theory to Leadership Development

Developmental psychology situates growth as a function of the complex interactions of human biology within an environment. Leadership development mirrors this. Brain-based learning and maturation associated with age are tied to clear alterations in how individuals potentially view leadership (Rock & Schwartz, 2006; Waldman, Balthazard, & Peterson, 2011), but this must be complemented by disequilibrium capable of disrupting the tendency for homeostasis to optimize leadership development (Day et al., 2009). The collegiate environment provides a laboratory for the introduction of novel situations that can potentially create the dissonance necessary to leverage the increasingly complex ways of making meaning and sophisticated integration of identity necessary for leadership development to occur. Table 36.3 provides some dimensions of psychological development that may contribute to leadership development and the formation of a leader identity.

Theoretical and Conceptual Models of Leadership

Although many college leadership curricular or co-curricular programs are atheoretical, models do exist that were created specifically for use in the college context. These theoretical models range from leader-centric management approaches to relational, systems approaches (Owen, 2009). Adult leadership theories and models are also frequently used at the college level. Komives and Dugan (2010) observed that common themes among contemporary leadership models include the importance of self-awareness, an emphasis on ethics, moral leadership and social responsibility, as well as the redistribution of power and collaborative or shared leadership. For an overview of these theories see Dugan and Komives (2011) and Komives and Dugan (2010).

Extending Burns's (1978) work on transforming leadership and Bass's (1985) work on transformational leadership, Kouzes and Posner's (2008) five exemplary leadership practices (i.e., model the way, encourage the heart, challenge the process, enable others to act, and inspire a shared vision) from the *Leadership Challenge* are widely used in both curriculum and co-curriculum (See chapter 13). Greenleaf's (1977) servant leadership is also widely embraced in the collegiate context particularly in programs fostering social change using service learning pedagogies including graduate-level leadership degrees (See chapter 19). Both models have been the focus of extensive research and application in college student leadership programs.

Table 36.3. Dimensions of Psychological Development and Connections to Leadership

Domain of Development	Developmental Issue	Relationship to Leadership
Psychosocial	Moving from Autonomy Toward Interdependence	• Recognition of membership in broader communities for which individuals have responsibility • Connected to increased problem-solving abilities • Understanding systems perspectives • Understands and values team work and collaboration
	Developing Competence	• Links directly to perceptions of self-efficacy • Connected to increased capacity for interpersonal competence necessary for leadership
	Managing Emotions/ Developing Mature Interpersonal Relationships	• Consistent with dimensions of leadership associated with emotional intelligence • Links to appreciation of differences and ability to work with broad constituencies
Cognitive	Generative Knowing	• Necessary to move beyond simple power and control models of leadership predicated on authority
	Complex Moral Reasoning	• Necessary for exploration of ethical components of leadership • Relates to higher order cognitive skills associated with social perspective-taking and other critical leadership capacities
Social Identity	Immersion/ Emersion in Group Membership	• Particular stages are characterized by strong in-group/ out-group differentiation divisive in contemporary conceptualizations of leadership
	Identity Integration	• Increases capacity for collaborative partnerships across in and out groups • Characterized by necessary coping mechanisms to avoid internalization of negative experiences, avoid stereotype threat, and navigate hostile environments
Holistic	Self-Authorship	• Predicated on deep sense of self-awareness necessary for authentic interactions

Co-curricular leadership programs often incorporate the relational leadership model of Komives et al. (2007), which emphasized being purposeful, inclusive, empowering, ethical, and process-oriented defining leadership as "a relational and ethical process of people together attempting to accomplish positive change" (p. 74; see also chapter 18 and chapter 27). Programs also use concepts of emotional intelligence (Bar-On, 2007; Goleman, 1998; Goleman, Boyatzis & McKee, 2002; Shankman & Allen, 2008). Building on principles from positive psychology, there is also growing interest in asset-based approaches to leadership such as strengths development (e.g., Buckingham & Clifton, 2001; Rath & Conchie, 2009).

However, the social change model of leadership development (HERI, 1996) is the most widely used in co-curricular programs, as both a philosophy of leadership and a framing structure for program design (Kezar et al., 2006; Owen, 2009). Developed by a group of scholars and leadership educators in the mid-1990s, this model "approaches leadership as a purposeful, collaborative, values-based process that results in positive social change" (Komives et al., 2009, p. xii). The seven values associated with the model are clustered into individual, group, and societal/community domains. The individual values are conscious of self, congruence, and commitment; group values are common purpose, collaboration, and controversy with civility; and the societal/community value is citizenship. The model is focused on enhancing students' capacities to engage in social change for the common good (HERI, 1996; Komives et al., 2009; See also chapter 18, chapter 20, and chapter 23). Leadership scholars Kezar et al. (2006) assessed that "The social change model of leadership development and seven C's of social change have played a prominent role in shaping the curricula and formats of undergraduate leadership education initiatives in colleges and universities throughout the country" (p. 142).

Research and Scholarship

Empirical research on college student leadership is largely focused on understanding predictors of leadership development and the role of leadership as a positive intermediate outcome in shaping other desirable educational outcomes (e.g., persistence, complex cognitive skills, academic achievement). The nature of this research is largely quantitative, and the vast majority has emerged in the last 20 years as institutions of higher education began attending more purposefully to the cultivation of leadership capacity as a critical college outcome. Avolio et al. (2005) astutely noted, however, that much of the empirical research on leadership in general is in essence college student leadership research given its reliance on samples comprised predominantly of undergraduate students. Unfortunately, most of this research interpreted findings in the context of leadership themes more broadly, neglecting to interpret findings using student development theory or provide unique implications for developing college students' leadership capacities. Thus, the content of this section reviews only those studies in which the authors' primary interests targeted understanding college student leadership development. The evolution of this literature clusters around three distinct phases of inquiry reflecting higher education's increasing alignment with leadership studies.

NATURE OF EVOLVING RESEARCH ON COLLEGE STUDENT LEADERSHIP DEVELOPMENT

Increasingly complex approaches to the study of college student leadership reflect a movement from research designs and definitional parameters focused almost entirely on atheoretical positional authority to those examining theoretically grounded, process orientations. Three distinct phases capture both the prevailing assumptions regarding the role of leadership development in the higher education context as well as the nature of leadership.

Phase 1: Industrial Approaches

Alexander Astin (1993b) deserves significant credit for the early measurement of leadership as a critical college outcome and the general effects of college on its development. Using multi-institutional, longitudinal samples derived from the Cooperative Institutional Research Program (CIRP), Astin and colleagues established that college students' gains in leadership reflected more than simple maturation along with the critical role that institutions of higher education could play in cultivating future leaders. CIRP scholarship led to the identification of a student typological category labeled as "Leader" (Astin, 1993a) employed in extension research to examine the relationships between high leadership capacity and other educational outcomes (e.g., cognitive skills) as well as collegiate experiences that predicted gains in leader development (Antonio, 2001; Astin, 1993b; Cress, Astin, Zimmerman-Oster, & Burkhardt, 2001; Kezar & Moriarty, 2000; Smart, Ethington, Riggs, & Thompson, 2002). This early research, however, was atheoretical and highly leader-centric, reflecting more industrial conceptualizations of leadership predicated on management and social persuasion. Definitional parameters for the term leadership were largely absent and almost no linkages were made to the established leadership studies literature. Furthermore, variables comprising leadership constructs reflected participants' perceptions of their popularity, experiences holding positional roles, and degree of ambition. Interestingly, other measures employed in CIRP research labeled as student activism were more closely aligned with contemporary conceptualizations of leadership than the ones directly labeled as leader or leadership constructs. As CIRP research evolved, scholars attempted to include additional measures that were more congruent with contemporary leadership scholarship (e.g., understanding of self, commitment to civic values). However, the core constructs remained the same and the findings from these studies eventually shepherded in a second phase of empirical inquiry. Nevertheless, this work provided a critical foundation validating the need for the purposeful development of college students' leadership abilities and contributed to the proliferation of co-curricular leadership education programs in particular.

Phase 2: Positional Emphases

The second phase of scholarship on college student leadership evolved from foundational CIRP work, but connected more directly to the broader leadership studies literature through the increasing use of theoretically grounded research designs. This collection of studies continued, however, to reflect the leader-centric orientation of previous research by maintaining a distinct focus on the identification of leadership styles related almost exclusively to positional leaders or drawing clear distinctions between leaders and non-leaders (Hall, Scott, & Borsz, 2008; Logue, Hutchens, & Hector, 2005; Posner, 2004). The adaptation of Kouzes and Posner's (2003) Leadership Practices Inventory (LPI) for use with the college population was particularly significant as both a training tool and for generating theoretically grounded scholarship. Studies using the LPI provided rich descriptive information regarding the leadership styles and behavioral norms for students in a variety of positional leadership roles (e.g., fraternity and sorority leaders, student organization presidents, resident assistants) as well as correlations between leadership styles and positional experiences (Posner, 2004). Occasionally, research also explored the unique experiences of women and students of color, but typically did so with a distinct focus on samples of students selected from those solely within positional roles rather than the general student population (Arminio et al., 2000; Kimbrough, 1995; Romano, 1996). These studies advanced the importance of connecting college student research to the broader leadership studies literature, but in some cases the exclusive focus on positional leaders belied the very beliefs of contemporary theories positing the need to develop leadership capacity among the broadest range of constituents possible.

Phase 3: Human Capacity Building

Contemporary scholarship on college student leadership continues to generate at least some research consistent with the orientations of the previous two phases. An emergent phase, however, seems to reflect a consistent grounding in the leadership studies literature, an examination of *both* positional leaders *and* college students in general, and an emphasis on understanding the process of human capacity building. Evidence of this is present in research using the LPI in a longitudinal design (Posner, 2009), examinations of influences associated with hierarchical versus systemic thinking orientations (Wielkiewicz, 2000), and the integration of Bandura's (1997) social cognitive theory to explore leadership efficacy (Chemers, Watson, & May, 2000; Dugan & Komives, 2010; McCormick & Tanguma, 2007; McCormick, Tanguma, & López-Forment, 2002). Each of these works advances a more complex understanding of how to develop college students' leadership capacities.

The emphasis on human capacity building stems at least partially from the leadership identity development model (Komives et al., 2005, 2006), which identified critical developmental influences associated with building leadership capacity. This shifted the focus from the examination of simple predictors of leadership to a more complex understanding that leadership development is a function of human development. As such, researchers began examining the leadership development *process* along with influences associated with other developmental constructs (e.g., efficacy, cognition, identity; Dugan, 2011a; Dugan & Komives, 2010; McCormick & Tanguma, 2007; McCormick et al., 2002). The focus on social construction also contributed to a greater emphasis on social justice and led to the disaggregation of data sets and the increased use of qualitative techniques to explore better the unique needs of often marginalized student populations (Boatwright & Egidio, 2003; Dugan, 2011b; Renn, 2007; Renn & Ozaki, 2010). This phase also marked some of the first ventures into examining college student leadership in a broader global context (Dugan, Rossetti Morosini, & Beazley, 2011; Renn & Lytle, 2010).

THEMES FROM COLLEGE STUDENT LEADERSHIP RESEARCH

A thematic analysis of scholarship across the three phases of college student leadership research surfaces several themes related to consistent predictors, *how* development occurs, and the nature of educational interventions that matter most in facilitating learning. Each is explored in the following sections.

Development Occurs Across Interrelated Domains

Perhaps one of the most important themes from college student leadership scholarship is the recognition that leadership development occurs across a number of distinct, yet interrelated, domains. Emergent across this body of research is clear evidence of the unique constructs of leadership efficacy (i.e., personal beliefs in one's capacity to lead; Hannah, Avolio, Luthans, & Harms, 2008), leadership capacity (i.e., the knowledge, skills, and attitudes associated with one's ability to engage in the process of leadership; Day et al., 2009; Dugan, 2011b; Hannah et al., 2008), leadership behaviors (i.e., the actions one takes in the pursuit of leadership), and leadership motivations/aspirations (i.e., an individual's underlying desire to engage in leadership processes, attain leadership positions, and demonstrate a positive influence in their personal and professional career domains; Chan & Drasgow, 2001; Kark & Van Dijk, 2007). Empirical research typically treats leadership capacity, behaviors, efficacy, and motivations/aspirations as mutually exclusive constructs despite emerging evidence of shared influences (Dugan, 2011a; Dugan & Komives, 2010; Hannah et al., 2008). Research indicates that leadership efficacy is a powerful predictor of leadership capacity explaining up to 13 percent of the variance in students' capacities for socially responsible leadership (Dugan & Komives, 2010). Leadership aspirations are also influenced significantly by leadership efficacy (McCormick et al., 2002), as are leadership behaviors (Chemers et al., 2000; McCormick et al., 2002), but relationships between aspirations, capacity, and behaviors remain relatively unexplored in the literature.

Predictors/Interventions

The distinctiveness of the four domains of leadership development is supported by empirical research identifying a variety of unique predictors from the collegiate environment. Analyses across leadership domains and phases of research elicit a relatively stable set of experiences from the collegiate environment with the potential to influence development positively. In a review of empirical research on college student leadership, Dugan (2011b) identified these experiences as including community service, interactions across and discussions about difference, mentoring relationships, internships, involvement in student clubs and organizations, positional leadership roles, and formal leadership training. Important to note, however, are the varied effects of formal leadership training programs. Contradictory research indicated that these experiences had either strong positive effects, no effects, or potentially negative effects on developmental gains. A recent study examined the direct effect of these experiences and determined that the relative efficacy of the interventions was less about the platform of delivery and more about the degree to which high-impact learning pedagogies (e.g., interactions across difference, service learning, efficacy-building techniques, experiential learning) were embedded in the design (Dugan, Bohle et al., 2011).

Influences of Identity

Evolving literature on college student leadership has traditionally afforded little attention toward the influences of social identity (Dugan, 2011b; Munin & Dugan, 2011). Similar omissions are present in the broader leadership studies literature, which Ospina and Foldy (2009) accurately described as color-blind in its attention to complex issues associated with race. Similar neglect is present in the treatment and consideration of other social identities based on gender, sexual orientation, ability status, and socioeconomic status. Research on issues of gender in college student leadership generally identified a female proclivity for leadership capacity and behaviors when defined using contemporary theoretical principals of collaboration, reciprocity, and process-orientations (Dugan, 2011b). This proclivity did not persist in studies examining leadership efficacy, which found college women demonstrated lower levels than their male peers (Dugan, 2011b).

Research on race in college student leadership typically yields differential results depending on the methodology employed. Qualitative studies identified significant influences of race on leadership perceptions, development, and outcomes (Arminio et al., 2000; Komives et al., 2005; Renn & Ozaki, 2010), while quantitative studies have not identified a significant influence (Cress et al., 2001; Dugan & Komives, 2010; Posner, 2004). Dugan (2011b) summarized a recent study that addressed Ospina and Foldy's (2009) critique regarding the lack of complexity in research on the influences of race on leadership. The researchers tested the hypothesis that variation in results between qualitative and quantitative studies reflected quantitative researchers' overreliance on categorical markers of race as proxies for the more powerful constructs associated with racial identity. Results confirmed that the incorporation of more complex racial identity measures explained significantly more of the variance in students' leadership capacities above and beyond the use of racial categories alone. In addition, the inclusion of these measures differentiated predictors emerging from the collegiate environment across racial groups. Emerging research on the influences of social identity on college student leadership is also beginning to also address a broader range of identity perspectives (Dugan, 2011b).

Developmental Sequencing and Readiness

Supporting the importance of leadership development across the life span, students' pre-college exposure to leadership learning is the greatest predictor of variance in students' abilities during their final year in college (Antonio, 2001; Dugan & Komives, 2010; Kezar & Moriarty, 2000; Smart et al., 2002). Furthermore, emerging research grounded in the social change model points to the critical roles of developmental sequencing and readiness. Bohle, Woelker, Cooney, and Dugan (2011) examined the relationships between three dimensions of leadership capacity and found no direct relationship between individual capacities (i.e., self awareness, values congruence, commitment) and citizenship capacity (i.e., the degree to which individuals' have the knowledge, skills, and attitudes necessary to have a positive influence on their communities). Students' capacities for citizenship were a direct function of group-related leadership capacities (i.e., collaboration, navigating conflict with civility). The findings suggest the importance of sequencing interventions in the process of human capacity building along with the recognition that developmental readiness plays a critical role in shaping the efficacy of learning opportunities (Bohle et al., 2011; Day et al., 2009).

The collective body of literature on college student leadership development has grown exponentially in the last decade reflecting a shift to more complex measurement approaches and a deeper grounding in the leadership studies literature. Findings illustrate the potential for significantly enhancing the leadership development of college students when interventions target multiple domains (i.e., leadership capacity, efficacy, behaviors, and motivations/ aspirations), employ evidence-based approaches in the design and delivery of educational interventions, and account for considerations associated with social identity. The section that follows provides several frameworks for engaging in this work that can enhance the overall efficacy of curricular and co-curricular leadership development programs.

Practices in College Student Leadership

Leadership programs can be thought of as having a focus on leadership training, education, or development (Roberts & Ullom, 1989). *Leadership training* encompasses those programs designed to build knowledge and skills in those who hold a specific leadership role (e.g., presidents, treasurers, resident assistants). *Leadership education* focuses on leadership studies and building a knowledge base about leadership (e.g., academic courses), whereas *leadership development* builds on knowledge bases with specific experiential and other learning activities including reflection and feedback to enhance a student's leadership capacity and self-efficacy (Council for the Advancement of Standards in Higher Education [CAS], 2012). When institutions assert their responsibility for shaping leadership development as a critical college outcome, all sectors should work together to accomplish that goal; typically these activities are organized separately and on occasion in partnership between academic affairs and student affairs units within a college environment.

GUIDELINES FOR PRACTICE

The professionalization of leadership education (see Komives, 2011a) has led to co-curricular standards of practice for student leadership programs (i.e., CAS, 2012), numerous co-curricular competency models (e.g., National Association of Campus Activities; University of Arizona Competency Project), as well as guiding questions to frame curricular leadership courses and certificates, programs, minors, and majors (e.g., International Leadership Association; Ritch, 2008). This section briefly overviews developments in curricular and co-curricular leadership programs. Readers are referred to the National Clearinghouse for Leadership Programs (www.nclp.edu) and the International Leadership Association (ILA; www.ila-net.org) for additional resources; see also the *Handbook for Student Leadership Programs* (Komives, Dugan, Owen, Slack, & Wagner, 2011).

CURRICULAR PRACTICES

Curricular approaches to leadership exist as stand-alone courses (Howe, 1997), minors and academic certifications, as well as leadership majors (Brungardt, Greenleaf, Brungardt, & Arensdorf, 2006; Mainella & Love, 2011). ILA lists more than 1500 leadership majors, minors, and academic certificates on their website. Leadership studies programs usually do not advance one theory or model of leadership, but explore the evolution of leadership as a socially constructed phenomena or view leadership as good management (Rost, 1991). The first undergraduate leadership major was established in 1992 at the Jepson School of Leadership Studies at the University of Richmond as an interdisciplinary major (Klenke, 1993). Other early undergraduate leadership majors include those at Fort Hayes State University and the McDonough Center at Marietta College as well as early graduate program programs such as the University of San Diego (Troyer, 2004). A study of the learning outcomes from 37 academic disciplines reveals that most require the development of student leadership capacity for the accreditation of those majors (Sharp et al., 2011). Specific skills noted included collaboration, teamwork, and managing people effectively.

Leadership is not owned by any one discipline. Curricular leadership educators debate if leadership is or should be a discipline in itself. Leadership course work may occur targeting a specific major (e.g., engineers, agricultural extension), be the focus of specific programs such as nonprofit leadership, living-learning programs, or problem-based learning communities (e.g., leadership for environmental sustainability), or be generic majors or minors open to the whole student body and often delivered in partnership with educators in student affairs. Common textbooks used in leadership courses are included in the references at the end of the chapter.

It is well established that leadership can be taught (Parks, 2005; Wren, 1994). Pedagogically leadership is often approached through group work or teamwork in laboratories, problem-based learning, ropes courses, internships, study abroad, or service learning (Meixner & Rosch, 2011). Parks studied the case-in-point pedagogy used by Ronald Heifitz at the Kennedy School to illustrate this point. In the early 1990s, Frankin University (IN) mainstreamed leadership throughout their curriculum using direct and indirect methods such as student-centered classroom management techniques. Leadership is also a focus of capstone courses in majors often focusing on ethical decision-making practices in a given profession.

CO-CURRICULAR PRACTICES

Leadership programs exist in numerous student affairs functions most frequently through the office of student activities, student involvement, civic engagement, or multicultural programs (Smist, 2011). Leadership may be an incidental or indirect outcome of student involvement or may be intentional through the complex design of a multiyear sequenced program built around a developmental model like LID with a designated theoretical framework like the social change model (Eich, 2008; Komives et al., 2009).

Leadership experiences exist across the institution ranging from student employment positions to participation in curricular and co-curricular activities. Hundreds of diverse student organizations (e.g., intramurals, fraternities and sororities, social identity groups, academic and professional clubs, political and activist groups) exist within the vast diversity of types of institutions of post-secondary education. These organizations are largely student-led with advising and coaching from educators at the institution. Leadership development is a direct or indirect outcome from this participation particularly when these experiences include such high impact practices as those identified in the research section of this chapter, notably, mentoring, discussions of sociocultural issues, service learning, and internships. Grounded in principles of experiential learning, student affairs educators and faculty advisors facilitate student learning through reflection and engaged practice. Many of these organizations are chapters of national organizations bringing a connection to other students and alumni engaged in the work of that organization; typically those organizations (such as fraternities and sororities) have elaborate systems of leader education with role-differentiated experiences.

OTHER SETTINGS

Commuter students and part-time students also frequently engage in leadership experiences in the community including Parent–Teacher Associations, church and other religious groups, Kiwanis, Zonta, or Rotary clubs through work, as well as professional associations. Collaborative gaming is another nontraditional setting in which leadership may develop. Although understudied, massively multiplayer on-line experiences (MMO) such as Second Life and World of Warcraft create communal frameworks and strategies. World of Warcraft has 11.4 million registered users (http://wow.joystiq.com/2011/05/09/world-of-warcraft-dips-to-a-mere-11-4-million-subscribers/), more than the population of an entire country like Greece. Researching these experiences may reveal unique contributions to leadership outcomes (O'Connor & Menaker, 2008; Siitonen, 2011).

Summary

Focused efforts on college student leadership in the last 20 years have resulted in the growth in leadership courses, degree program offerings, and co-curricular leadership programs accessible to diverse students. Research on college student leadership now includes studies with theoretical focus and the examination of interventions that contribute to leadership outcomes This professionalizing of leadership education (Komives, 2011a) bodes well for the continued role of leadership outcomes in college and university practices.

Overall Conclusions

The purpose of this chapter was to position leadership development using a life span approach that allowed for a more comprehensive consideration of contributions associated with young adulthood. Specific attention was paid to developmental considerations associated with social psychology originating with the works of Erickson and Piaget. Given the epigenetic nature of developmental growth, the chapter highlighted age-related patterns while also examining influences from the environment. These environmental influences largely stem from engagement with educational environments and the variety of opportunities and interventions available to maximize developmental growth. Empirical research offers insights into the types of experiences and interventions that seem most salient for cultivating leadership development, which often is a function of developmental gains in areas such as cognition and identity.

Looking Forward

The growing recognition that leadership is happening across the life span brings a critical imperative to develop theoretically grounded, evidence-based practices that are developmental appropriate particularly for children, youth, and college students. Any nation, any community, any profession, and any group working together for a shared purpose depends on individuals who can work effectively together to accomplish those shared goals. Nevertheless, there remain challenges and unanswered questions that require further exploration to better accomplish the youth and college student leadership development agenda.

Challenges

THEORY

Youth leadership educators need theoretical models that apply to the experiences in this youth dimension of the life span. Asset-based models and those that describe shared, relational leadership hold promise for application in youth contexts. These models should be appropriate for culturally diverse students and accommodate the intersectionality of a leader identity with other social identities.

RESEARCH

Research on youth leadership has numerous methodological challenges. More differentiation among elements of activities (e.g., nature of adult involvement, distribution of power, access, nature of peer relationships) is needed to understand the differential effect on specific groups of students (e.g., youth of color, gender; Eccles, 2005). Additional challenges include other variables (such as motivation to participate) that need to be controlled in research designs as a means to better isolate and understand contributions to outcome achievement (Eccles, 2005). Studies that demonstrate the long-term impact of leadership education and experience are needed at all levels of the life span, particularly from college into post-college experience of work and community engagement.

PRACTICE

Critical challenges exist to make leadership experiences and leadership education accessible to youth who may be excluded (e.g., lack resources) or for whom current approaches to leadership are too conventional to apply to their context. In addition, leadership educators are challenged to increase the leadership efficacy of students in addition to the emphasis now placed on enhancing their leadership capacity (e.g., competencies and skills).

Recommended Future Directions

CONTENT

Leadership programs for youth and college students should bring a global perspective to all content (See chapter 34). Exposing students to understanding diverse worldviews (e.g., religion, nationalism) and exploring shared issues (e.g., poverty, health) will help them develop social perspective-taking and learn to develop frameworks from which to examine complex, ill-structured problems. Concepts such as spirituality should be explored in both the meaning making needed in leadership as well as a source for inner values and beliefs that may shape developing authentic relationships. Finally, enormous potential exists for integrating the growing arena of brain-based research from neuroscience with leadership development. This line of inquiry may unlock critical information related to how best educators can sequence learning experiences to capitalize on developmental readiness. The principles of epigenetic development are most often addressed in leadership education through recognition of influences from the environment. Epigenetics, however, also suggests the need to address age-based development. Brain-based approaches may offer insights into how biological maturation should frame the sequencing of leadership development.

PROCESS

Leader development needs more evidence on how to sequence interventions developmentally to maximize learning. This includes enhancing the understanding of key knowledge, skills, and attitudes that undergird broader leadership capacities such as citizenship and systems-thinking. Further, leadership education is largely individually focused, working with individuals to enhance their efficacy and capacity to be leaders or to engage in leadership. This work needs to expand to address better collective development (e.g., how the group does leadership together as a group process) and the outcomes that are derived from this. Finally, an antecedent to the design and delivery of educationally meaningful work in leadership development is the adequate preparation to do so. Intuitive design of education experiences lacking theoretical and/or pedagogical grounding, replication of best practices neglecting contextual influences, and oversimplification of the process of leadership development represent problematic approaches to curricular and co-curricular leadership education. These issues most often arise when leadership educators do not have specific training in leadership or in designing leadership development experiences. Professional associations and educational preparation programs are encouraged to meet this need through the development of resources and focused professional development opportunities.

Select Resources

In addition to the educational resources available in the broader field of the leadership industry such as *Leadership Quarterly*, there is a wealth of resources for youth and college student leadership educators, researchers, and scholars. For an overview of the evolution of resources in college student leadership see Komives (2011a). The resources noted in Table 36.4 focus on youth or college students or are used in curricular approaches; there are many other resources such as the Center for Creative Leadership for the broader field of leadership education

Table 36.4. Youth and College Student Leadership Development Resources

Journals and Magazines	
Journal of College Student Development	Research journal from ACPA: College Student Educators International: www.jcsdonline.org/
Journal of Leadership Education	On-line journal of the Association of Leadership Educators: www.ale.org
Journal of Leadership Studies	A Wiley journal that seeks to promote interdisciplinary inquiry on the study of leadership: onlinelibrary.wiley.com/journal/10.1002/
Journal of Leadership & Organizational Studies	A SAGE publisher journal for business and management programs: jlo.sagepub.com/
The Journal of Research in Character Education	A journal from the Character Education Partnership: www.character.org/journalofresearchincharactereducation2
Journal of Student Affairs Research and Practice	Journal from NASPA: National Association of Student Affairs Administrators: journals.naspa.org/jsarp/
Leadership for Student Activities	Magazine published by the National Association of Secondary School Principals and is the official publication of National Honor Society, National Junior Honor Society, National Association of Student Councils: www.nassp.org/
Professional associations	
American Student Government Association (ASGA)	A professional association serving and supporting college student government leaders and advisors. www.asgaonline.com/
Association of Leadership Educators (ALE)	Founded in 1987 primarily by scholars and practitioners within agricultural extension, the association hosts an annual conference and publishes the *Journal of Leadership Education*. http://leadershipeducators.org
International Leadership Association (ILA)	Open to a broad base of those who study and practice leadership world-wide, ILA has member interest groups including leadership education and leadership development. www.ila-net.org/
National Association of Secondary School Principals (NASSP)	Focused on school leadership, NASSP sponsors youth leadership programs and publications including the National Association of Student Councils (www.nassp.org)

(continued)

Table 36.4. Continued

Journals and Magazines	
National Clearinghouse for Leadership Programs (NCLP)	Founded in 1989, this college student leadership clearinghouse produces three annual issues of a theme based publication, Concepts & Connections, and a monograph series called Insights & Applications. NCLP projects include the Multi-institutional Study of Leadership (www.leadershipstudy.net) and the site license of the Socially Responsible Leadership Scale designed to measure the social change model of leadership development. www.nclp.umd.edu
Student Affairs professional associations	Several student affairs associations have internal entities for leadership educators. ACPA has a commission on student involvement with a focus on leadership. NASPA has a student leadership programs knowledge community. The National Association of Campus Activities has an emphasis on co-curricular involvement and leadership.
Other college associations	Leadership programs and initiatives exist in such co-curricular entities as the National Collegiate Athletics Association (NCAA), fraternal and sorority organizations, Association of College Unions International (ACUI) as well as disciplinary based academic associations such as in engineering and business management.

Select Books for Leadership Educators

Bordas, J. (2007). *Salsa, soul, and spirit: New approaches to leadership from Latino, Black, and American Indian communities*. San Francisco, CA: Berrett-Koehler.

Daft, R. L. (2008). *The leadership experience* (5th ed.). Mason, OH: South-Western Cengage Learning.

Day, D. V., & Antonakis, J. (2012). *The nature of leadership* (2nd ed.). Los Angeles, CA: SAGE.

Higher Education Research Institute [HERI]. (1996) *Collaborative leadership for social change—Guidebook* (Version III). Los Angeles: UCLA Higher Education Research Institute.

Johnson, D. W., & Johnson, F. P. (2008). *Joining together: Group theory and group skills* (10th ed.). Boston, MA: Allyn & Bacon.

Hannum, K. M., Martineau, J. W., & Reinelt, C. (2007). *The handbook of leadership development evaluation*. San Francisco, CA: Jossey-Bass.

Kezar, A. J., Carducci, R., & Contreras-McGavin, M. (2006). *Rethinking the "L" Word in Higher Education: The Revolution of Research on Leadership*. ASHE Higher Education Report (J-B ASHE Higher Education Report Series (ASHE). San Francisco, CA: Jossey-Bass.

Komives, S. R., Dugan, J., Owen, J. E., Slack, C., & Wagner, W. (Eds). (2011). *Handbook for student leadership development* (2nd ed.). A publication of the National Clearinghouse for Leadership Programs. San Francisco, CA: Jossey-Bass.

Parks, S. D. (2005). *Leadership can be taught: A bold approach for a complex world*. Boston, MA: Harvard Business School Press.

Roberts, D. R. (2007). *Deeper learning in leadership: Helping college students find the potential within*. San Francisco, CA: Jossey-Bass.

Zimmerman-Oster, K., & Burkhardt, J. C. (1999). *Leadership in the making: Impact and insights from leadership development programs in U. S. colleges and universities*. Battle Creek, MI: W. K. Kellogg Foundation.

Select college student textbooks and other resources:

Hughes, R. L., Ginnett, R. C., & Curphy, G. J. (2006). *Leadership: Enhancing the lessons of experience* (5th ed.). New York, NY: McGraw-Hill/Irwin.

Komives, S. R., Lucas, N., & McMahon, T. R. (2013) *Exploring leadership: For college students who want to make a difference* (3rd ed.). San Francisco, CA: Jossey-Bass.

Komives, S. R., Wagner, W., & Associates. (2009). *Leadership for a better world: Understanding the social change model of leadership development*. San Francisco, CA: Jossey-Bass.

Kouzes, J. M., & Posner, B. Z. (2008). *The student leadership challenge: Five practices for exemplary leaders*. San Francisco: Jossey-Bass.

Marshall, S. M. & Hornak, A. M. (2008), *A day in the life of a college student leader: Case studies for undergraduate leaders*. Sterling, VA: Stylus.

Northouse, P. G. (2008). *Introduction to leadership: Concepts and practice*. Thousand Oaks, CA: SAGE.

Northouse, P. G. (2010). *Leadership: Theory and practice* (5th ed.). Thousand Oaks, SA: SAGE.

Osland, J. S., Kolb, D. A., Rubin, I. M., & Turner, M. (2006). *Organizational behavior: An experiential approach* (8th ed.). Upper Saddle River, NJ: Prentice Hall.

Rath, T. & Conchie, B. (2009). *Strengths-based leadership*. New York, NY: Gallup Press.

Shankman, M. L., & Allen, S. J. (2008). *Emotionally intelligent leadership: A guide for college students*. San Francisco, CA: Jossey-Bass.

Yukl, G. A. (2010). *Leadership in organizations* (7th ed). Englewood Cliffs: Prentice-Hall.

and practice. It is of note that most resources are designed for leadership educators and fewer are designed for direct use with students.

References

Abes, E. S., Jones, S. R., & McEwen, M. K. (2007). Reconceptualizing the model of multiple dimensions of identity: The role of meaning-making capacity in the construction of multiple identities. *Journal of College Student Development, 48*, 1–22.

Anderson, J., Bruce, J., & Mouton, L (2010). 4-H made me a leader: A college-level alumni perspective of leadership life skill development. *Journal of Leadership Education, 9*(2), 35–49.

Antonio, A. L. (2001). The role of interracial interaction in the development of leadership skills and cultural knowledge and understanding. *Research in Higher Education, 42*, 593–617.

Arminio, J. L., Carter, S., Jones, S. E., Kruger, K., Lucas, N., Washington, J... Scott, A. (2000). Leadership experiences of students of color. *NASPA Journal, 37*, 496–510.

Arnett, J. J. (2006). Emerging adulthood: Understanding the new way of coming of age. In J. J. Arnett, & J. L. Tanner (Eds.), *Emerging adults in America: Coming of age in the 21st century* (pp. 3–20). Washington, DC: American Psychological Association.

Astin, A. W. (1993a). An empirical typology of college students. *Journal of College Student Development, 34*, 36–46.

Astin, A. W. (1993b). *What matters in college.* San Francisco, CA: Jossey-Bass.

Avolio, B. J., Chan, A., Chan N., Galanhxi-Janaqi, H., Gitlitz, J., Hannah, S.... Zhu, W. (2005). 100 year review of leadership intervention research: Briefings report 2004-01, Gallup Leadership Institute. *Leadership Review, 5*, 7–13.

Avolio, B. J., & Gibbons, T. C. (1988). Developing transformational leaders: A life span approach. In J. A. Conger, R. N. Kanungo, & Associates (Eds.), *Charismatic leadership* (pp. 276–308). San Francisco, CA: Jossey-Bass.

Avolio, B. J., & Vogelgesang, G. R. (2011). Beginnings matter in genuine leadership development. In S. E. Murphy, & R. J. Reichard (Eds.), *Early development and leadership: Building the next generation of leaders* (pp. 179–204). New York, NY: Psychology Press/Routledge.

Bandura, A. (1997). *Self-efficacy: The exercise of control.* New York, NY: Harper Collins.

Barber, B. L., Eccles, J. S., & Stone, M. R. (2001). Whatever happened to the jock, the brain, and the princess? Young adult pathways linked to adolescent activity involvement and social identity. *Journal of Adolescent Research, 16*, 429–455.

Bar-On, R. (2007). The Bar-On model of emotional intelligence: A valid, robust and applicable EI model. *Organizations & People, 14*, 27–34.

Bass, B. M. (1985). *Leadership and performance beyond expectations.* New York, NY: Free Press.

Baxter Magolda, M. B. (1992). *Knowing and reasoning in college: Gender-based patterns in students' intellectual development.* San Francsico, CA: Jossey-Bass.

Baxter Magolda, M. B. (2001). Making their own way: Narratives for transforming higher education to promote self-development. Sterling, VA: Stylus.

Baxter Magolda, M. B. (2009). The activity of meaning making: A holistic perspective on college student development. *Journal of College Student Development, 50*, 621–639.

Belenky, M. F., Clinchy, B. M., Goldberger, N. R., & Tarule, J. M. (1986). *Women's ways of knowing: The development of self, voice, and mind.* New York, NY: Basic Books.

Bem, S. L. (1983). Gender schema theory and its implications for child development: Raising gender-aschematic children in a gender-schematic society. *Signs, 8*(4), 598–616.

Benson, P. L., Scales, P. C., Hamilton, S. F., & Sesma, A., Jr. (with Hong, K. L., & Roehlkepartain, E. C.). (2006). Positive youth development so far: Core hypotheses and their implications for policy and practice. *Search Institute Insights & Evidence, 3*(1), 1–13.

Berkowitz, M. W., & Bier, M. C. (2004). Research-based character education. *The ANNALS of the American Academy of Political and Social Science, 591*, 72–85.

Boatwright, K. J., & Egidio, R. K. (2003). Psychological predictors of college women's leadership aspirations. *Journal of College Student Development, 44*, 653–669.

Bohle, C. W., Woelker, L., Cooney, M. A., & Dugan, J. P. (2011, March). *The role of social perspective-taking in developing students' leadership capacities.* Unpublished research paper presented at the ACPA: College Student Educators International Annual Convention, Baltimore, MD.

Boyd, D., & Bee, H. (2009) *Lifespan development* (5th ed.). Boston, MA: Allyn & Bacon.

Bray, D. W., Campbell, R. J., & Grant, D. L. (1974). *Formative years in business: A long-term AT&T study of managerial lives.* New York, NY: John Wiley & Sons.

Bronfenbrenner, U. (1979). *The ecology of human development: Experiments by nature and design.* Cambridge, MA: Harvard University Press.

Brown, R., & Evans, W. P. (2002). Extracurricular activity and ethnicity: Creating greater school connection among diverse student populations. *Urban Education, 37*(1), 41–58.

Brungardt, C. (1996). The making of leaders: A review of the research in leadership development and education. *Journal of Leadership Studies, 3*, 81–95.

Brungardt, C. L., Gould, L. V., Moore, R., & Potts, J. (1997). The emergence of leadership studies: Linking the traditional outcomes of liberal education with leadership development. *Journal of Leadership Studies, 4*, 53–67.

Brungardt, C., Greenleaf, J., Brungardt, C., & Arensdorf, J. (2006). Majoring in leadership: A review of undergraduate leadership degree programs. *Journal of Leadership Education, 5*, 4–25.

Buckingham, M., & Clifton, D. O. (2001). *Now, discover your strengths.* New York, NY: Free Press.

Burns, J. M. (1978). *Leadership.* New York, NY: Harper and Row.

Cass, V. C. (1979). Homosexual identity formation: A theoretical model. *Journal of Homosexuality, 4*(3), 219–235.

Chan, K. Y., & Drasgow, F. (2001). Toward a theory of individual differences and leadership: Understanding the motivation to lead. *Journal of Applied Psychology, 86*, 481–498.

Chemers, M. M., Watson, C. B., & May S. T. (2000). Dispositional affect and leadership effectiveness: A comparison of self-esteem, optimism, and efficacy. *Personality & Social Psychology Bulletin, 26*, 267–277.

Chickering, A. W., & Reisser, L. (1993). Education and identity (2nd ed.). San Francisco, CA: Jossey-Bass.

Conner, J. O., & Strobel (2007). Leadership development: An examination of individual and programmatic growth. *Journal of Adolescent Research, 22*, 275–296.

Council for the Advancement of Standards in Higher Education [CAS]. (2012). Student leadership programs. In *CAS professional standards for higher education* (8th ed.). Washington, DC: Author.

Covey, S. R. (1989). *The 7 habits of highly effective people.* New York, NY: Simon & Schuster.

Cress, C. M., Astin, H. S., Zimmerman-Oster, K., & Burkhardt, J. C. (2001). Developmental outcomes of college students' involvement in leadership activities. *Journal of College Student Development, 42*, 15–27.

Cross, W. E., Jr. (1991). *Shades of Black: Diversity in African-American identity.* Philadelphia, PA: Temple University Press.

Culp, K., & Cox, K. J. (2002). Developing leadership through adult and adolescent partnerships in the third millennium. *Journal of Leadership Education, 1*(1), 41–57.

D'Augelli, A. R. (1994). Identity development and sexual orientation: Toward a model of lesbian, gay, and bisexual development. In E. J. Trickett, R. J. Watts, & D. Birman (Eds.), *Human diversity* (pp. 312–333). San Francisco, CA: Jossey-Bass.

Day, D. V. (2011). Integrative perspectives on longitudinal investigations of leader development: From childhood through adulthood. *Leadership Quarterly, 22*, 561–571.

Day, D. V., Harrison, M. M., & Halpin, S. (2009). *An integrative approach to leader development: Connecting adult development, identity, and expertise*. New York, NY: Routledge.

Day, D. V., Zaccaro, S. J., & Halpin, S. M. (Eds.). (2004). *Leader development for transforming organizations: Growing leaders for tomorrow* (pp. 3–22). Mahwah, NJ: Lawrence Erlbaum.

Deschenes, S., McLaughlin, M. W., & Newman, A. (Eds.) (2008). *Community organizing and youth advocacy*. New Directions for Youth Development, No. 117. San Francisco, CA: Jossey-Bass.

Downing, N. E., & Roush, K. L. (1985). From passive acceptance to active commitment: A model of feminist identity development for women. *The Counseling Psychologist, 13*, 695–709.

Dubosz, R. P., & Beaty, L. A. (1999). The relationship between athletic participation and high school students' leadership ability. *Adolescence, 34*, 215–220.

Dugan, J. P. (2011a). Pervasive myths in leadership development: Unpacking constraints on leadership learning. *Journal of Leadership Studies, 5*(2), 79–84.

Dugan, J. P. (2011b). Research on college student leadership development. In S. R. Komives, J. P. Dugan, J. E. Owen, C. Slack, & W. Wagner, & Associates. *Handbook for student leadership development* (2nd ed., pp. 59–84). San Francisco, CA: Jossey-Bass.

Dugan, J. P., Bohle, C. W., Gebhardt, M., Hofert, M., Wilk, E., & Cooney, M. A. (2011). Influences of leadership program participation on students' capacities for socially responsible leadership. *Journal for Student Affairs Research and Practice, 48*, 65–84.

Dugan, J. P., & Komives, S. R. (2010). Influences on college students' capacity for socially responsible leadership. *Journal of College Student Development, 51*, 525–549.

Dugan, J. P., & Komives, S. R. (2011). Leadership theories. In S. R. Komives, J. P. Dugan, J. E. Owen, C. Slack, W. Wagner, & Associates (Eds.), *The handbook for student leadership development* (2nd ed., pp. 35–57). San Francisco, CA: Jossey-Bass.

Dugan, J. P., Rossetti Morosini, A. M., & Beazley, M. R. (2011). Cultural transferability of socially responsible leadership: Findings from the United States and Mexico. *Journal of College Student Development, 52*, 456–474.

Eccles, J. S. (2005). The present and future of research on activity settings as developmental contexts. In J. L. Mahoney, R. W. Larson, & J. S. Eccles (Edss), (2005). *Organized activities as contexts of development* (pp. 353–371). Mahwah, NJ: Lawrence Erlbaum.

Eccles, J. S., & Barber, B. L. (1999). Student council, volunteering, basketball, or marching band: What kind of extracurricular involvement matters? *Journal of Adolescent Research, 14*(1), 10–3.

Eccles, J. S., Barber, B.L., Stone, M., & Hunt, J. (2003). Extracurricular activities and adolescent development. *Journal of Social Issues, 59*, 865–889.

Eich, D. (2008). A grounded theory of high-quality leadership programs: Perspectives from student leadership development programs in higher education. *Journal of Leadership & Organizational Studies, 15*(2), 176–187.

Erikson, E. (1968). *Identity: Youth and crisis*. New York, NY: W. W. Norton.

Evans, N. J., Forney, D. S., Guido, F. M., Renn, K. A., & Patton, L. D. (2010). *Student development in college* (2nd ed.). San Francisco, CA: Jossey-Bass.

Fassinger, R. E. (1998). Lesbian, gay, and bisexual identity and student development theory. In R. L. Sanlo (Ed.), *Working with lesbian, gay, bisexual, and transgender college students: A handbook for faculty and administrators* (pp. 12–22). Westport, CT. Greenwood Press.

Feldman, A. F., & Matjasko, J. L. (2005). The role of school-based extracurricular activities in adolescent development: A comprehensive review and future directions. *Review of Educational Research, 75*, 159–210.

Fredricks, J. A., &, Eccles, J. S. (2006). Is extracurricular participation associated with beneficial outcomes? Concurrent and longitudinal relations. *Developmental Psychology, 42*, 698–713.

Fredricks, J. A., & Eccles, J. S. (2008). Participation in extracurricular activities in the middle school years: Are there developmental benefits for African American and European American youth? *Journal of Youth and Adolescence, 37*, 1029–1043.

Fredricks, J. A., & Eccles, J. (2010). Breadth of extracurricular participation and adolescent adjustment among African-American and European-American youth. *Journal of Research on Adolescence*, 20, 307–333.

Gilligan, C. (1982/ 1993). *In a different voice: Psychological theory and women's development*. Cambridge, MA: Harvard University Press.

Goleman, D. (1998). *Working with emotional intelligence*. New York, NY: Bantam Books.

Goleman, D., Boyatzis, R., & McKee, A. (2002). *Primal leadership: Realizing the power of emotional intelligence*. Boston, MA: Harvard Business School Press.

Gottfried, A., & Gottfried, A. (2011). Paths from gifted motivation to leadership. In S. E. Murphy, & R. J. Reichard (Eds.), *Early development and leadership: Building the next generation of leaders* (pp. 71–91). New York, NY: Psychology Press/ Routledge.

Gottfried, A. E., Gottfried, A. W., Reichard, R. J., Guerin, D. W., Oliver, P. H., & Riggio, R. E. (2011). Motivational roots of leadership: A longitudinal study from childhood through adulthood. *Leadership Quarterly, 22*, 510–519.

Greenleaf, R. K. (1977). *Servant leadership*. New York, NY: Paulist Press.

Guerin, D. W., Oliver, P. H., Gottfried, A. W., Gottfried, A. E., Reichard, R. J., & Riggio, R. E. (2011). Childhood and adolescent antecedents of social skills and leadership potential in adulthood: Temperamental approach/withdrawal and extraversion. *Leadership Quarterly, 22*, 482–494.

Hall, D. T. (2004). Self awareness, identity, and leader development. In D. V. Day, A. J. Zaccaro, & S. M. Halpin (Eds.), *Leadership development for transforming organizations: Growing leadership for tomorrow* (pp. 153–176). Mahwah, NJ: Lawrence Erlbaum.

Hall, S. L., Scott, F., & Borsz, M. (2008). A constructivist case study of undergraduate students in campus recreational sports. *Journal of College Student Development, 49*, 125–140.

Hannah, S, T., Avolio, B. J., Luthans, F., & Harms, P. D. (2008). Leadership efficacy: Review and future directions. *Leadership Quarterly, 19*, 669–692.

Helms, J. E. (1995). An update of Helms's White and People of Color racial identity models. In J. G. Ponterotto, J. M. Casas, L. A. Suzuki, & C. M. Alexander (Eds.), *Handbook of multicultural counseling* (pp. 181–198). Thousand Oaks, CA: SAGE.

Helsing, D. (2010). Human development. In R. A. Couto (Ed.), *Political and civic leadership: A reference handbook* (pp. 678–687). Thousand Oaks, CA: SAGE.

Higher Education Research Institute [HERI]. (1996). *A social change model of leadership development: Guidebook version III.* College Park, MD: National Clearinghouse for Leadership Programs.

Hogg, M. A. (2001). A social identity theory of leadership. *Personality and Social Psychology Review, 5*, 184–200.

Hogg, M. A., & Terry, D. J. (2001). *Social identity processes in organizational contexts.* Philadelphia, PA: Psychology Press.

Horstmeier, R. P., & Nall, M. A. (2007). Youth leadership development: A national analysis of FFA member role and activity context. *Journal of Leadership Education 6*(1), 141–157.

Howe, W. (1997). Leadership education: A look across the courses. In F. Freeman et al. (Eds.), *Leadership education*, (6th ed., Vol. 2). Greensboro, NC: Center for Creative Leadership.

Ibarra, H., Snook, S., & Guillen Ramo, L. (2010). Identity-based leader development. In N. Nohria, & R. Khurana (Eds.), *Handbook of leadership theory and practice: A Harvard business school centennial* (pp. 657–678). Boston, MA: Harvard Business School.

Jones, S. R., & Abes, E. S. (2010). Theories about college students, environments, and organizations. In J. Schuh, S. R. Jones, & S. Harper (Eds.), *Student services: A handbook for the profession* (5th ed.; pp. 138–148). San Francisco, CA: Jossey-Bass.

Jones, S. R., & McEwen, M. K. (2000). A conceptual model of multiple dimensions of identity. *Journal of College Student Development, 41*, 405–414.

Josselson, R. E. (1978/ 1991). *Finding herself: Pathways to identity development in women.* San Francisco, CA: Jossey-Bass.

Kark, R., & Van Dijk, D. (2007). Motivation to lead, motivation to follow: The role of the self-regulatory focus in leadership processes. *Academy of Management Review, 32*, 500–528.

Karnes, F., & Bean, S. M. (1990). *Developing leadership in gifted youth.* ERIC Digest #E485. Council for Exceptional Children, Reston, VA.

Kegan, R. (1982). *The evolving self.* Cambridge, MA: Harvard University Press.

Kegan, R. (1994). *In over our heads: The mental demands of modern life.* Cambridge, MA: Harvard University Press.

Kezar, A. J., Carducci, R., & Contreras-McGavin, M. (2006). *Rethinking the "L" word in higher education: The revolution in research on leadership.* ASHE Higher Education Report, *31*(6). San Francisco, CA: Jossey-Bass.

Kezar, A., & Moriarty, D. (2000). Expanding our understanding of student leadership development: A study exploring gender and ethnic identity. *Journal of College Student Development, 41*, 55–68.

Kimbrough, W. M. (1995). Self-assessment, participation, and value of leadership skills, activities, and experiences for Black students relative to their membership in historically Black fraternities and sororities. *The Journal of Negro Education, 64*(1), 63–74.

King, P. M., & Kitchener, K. S. (1994). *Developing reflective judgment: Understanding and promoting intellectual growth and critical thinking in adolescents and adults.* San Francisco, CA: Jossey-Bass.

Klau, M. (2006). Exploring youth leadership in theory and practice: An empirical study. In M. Klau, S. Boyd, L. Luckow, & Associates. *Youth leadership.* New Directions for Youth Development No. 109 (pp. 57–87). San Francisco, CA: Jossey-Bass.

Klau, M., Boyd, S., Luckow, L., & Associates (2006). *Youth leadership.* New Directions for Youth Development No. 109. San Francisco, CA: Jossey-Bass.

Klenke, K. (1993). Leadership education at the great divide: Crossing into the twenty-first century. *The Journal of Leadership Studies, 1*(1). 111–127.

Kohlberg, L. (1975). The cognitive developmental approach to moral education. *Phi Delta Kappa, 56*, 670–677.

Komives, S. R. (2011a). Advancing leadership education. In S. R. Komives, J. P. Dugan, J. E. Owen, C. Slack, W. Wagner, & Associates (Eds.), *The handbook for student leadership development* (2nd ed., pp. 1–32). San Francisco, CA: Jossey-Bass.

Komives. S. R. (2011b). College student leadership identity development. In S. E. Murphy, & R. J. Reichard (Eds.), *Early development and leadership: Building the next generation of leaders* (pp. 273–292). New York, NY: Psychology Press/ Routledge.

Komives, S. R., & Dugan, J. P. (2010). Contemporary leadership theories. In R. A. Couto (Ed.), *Political and civic leadership: A reference handbook* (pp. 111–120). Thousand Oaks, CA: SAGE.

Komives, S. R., Dugan, J., Owen, J. E., Slack, C., & Wagner, W. (Eds). (2011). *Handbook for student leadership development* (2nd ed.). San Francisco, CA: Jossey-Bass.

Komives, S. R., & Johnson, M. (2009). The role of high school experience in college student leadership development. *Educational Considerations, 37*(1), 30–39.

Komives, S. R., Longerbeam, S. D., Mainella, F., Osteen, L., Owen, J. E., & Wagner, W. (2009). Leadership identity development: Challenges in applying a developmental model. *Journal of Leadership Education, 8*(1), 11–47.

Komives, S. R., Longerbeam, S., Owen, J. E., Mainella, F. C., & Osteen, L. (2006). A leadership identity development model: Applications from a grounded theory. *Journal of College Student Development, 47*, 401–420.

Komives, S. R., Lucas, N., & McMahon, T. R. (2007). *Exploring leadership: For college students who want to make a difference* (2nd ed.). San Francisco, CA: Jossey-Bass.

Komives, S. R., Owen, J. E., Longerbeam, S. D., Mainella, F. C., & Osteen, L. (2005). Developing a leadership identity: A grounded theory. *Journal of College Student Development, 46*, 593–611.

Komives, S. R., Wagner, W., & Associates. (2009). *Leadership for a better world: Understanding the social change model of leadership development.* A publication of the National Clearinghouse for Leadership Programs. San Francisco, CA: Jossey-Bass.

Kouzes, J. M., & Posner, B. Z. (2003/2008). *The student leadership challenge: Five practices for exemplary leaders.* San Francisco, CA: Jossey-Bass.

Kress, C. A. (2006). Youth leadership and youth development: Connections and questions. In M. Klau, S. Boyd, L. Luckow, & Associates. *Youth leadership.* New Directions for Youth Development No. 109 (pp. 45–56). San Francisco, CA: Jossey-Bass.

Kretman, K. P. (Ed.). (1996). *Learning leadership: A curriculum guide for a new generation grades k-12.* A CivicQuest Project. College Park, MD: Center for Political Leadership and Participation and John F. Kennedy High School.

Larson, R. W. (2000). Toward a psychology of positive youth development. *American Psychologist, 55*, 170–183.

Lerner, R. M., Brittian, A. S., & Fay, K. E. (2007). *Mentoring: A key resource for promoting positive youth development.* Research in Action No. 1. Alexandria, VA: MENTOR/National Mentoring Partnership.

Libby, M., Rosen, M., & Sedonaen, M. (2005). Building youth-adult partnerships for community change: Lessons from the Youth Leadership Institute and the Ford Foundation. *Journal of Community Psychology, 33*(1), 111–120.

Libby, M., Sedonaen, M., & Bliss, S. (2006). The mystery of youth leadership development. The path to just communities. In M. Klau, S. Boyd, L. Luckow, & Associates. *Youth leadership.* New Directions for Youth Development No. 109 (pp. 13–26). San Francisco, CA: Jossey-Bass.

Logue, C. T., Hutchens, T. A., & Hector, M. A. (2005). Student leadership: A phenomenological exploration of post-secondary experiences. *Journal of College Student Development, 46,* 393–408.

Lord, R. G., & Hall, R. J. (2005). Identity, deep structure and the development of leadership skill. *The Leadership Quarterly, 16,* 591–615.

Lord, R. G., Hall, R. J., & Halpin, S. M. (2011). Leadership skill development and divergence: A model for the early effects of gender and race on leadership development In S. E. Murphy, & R. J. Reichard (Eds.), *Early development and leadership: Building the next generation of leaders* (pp. 229–252). New York, NY: Psychology Press/Routledge.

Love, P. G., & Guthrie, V. L. (1999). *Understanding and applying cognitive development. New Directions for Student Services* (No. 88). San Francisco, CA: Jossey Bass.

MacNeil, C. A. (2006). Bridging generations: Applying "adult" leadership theories to youth leadership development. In M. Klau, S. Boyd, L. Luckow, & Associates. *Youth leadership.* New Directions for Youth Development No. 109 (pp. 27–44). San Francisco, CA: Jossey-Bass.

Mahoney, J. L., Larson, R. W., & Eccles, J. S. (Eds). (2005). *Organized activities as contexts of development: Extracurricular activities, after-school and community programs.* Mahwah, NJ: Lawrence Erlbaum.

Mainella, F., & Love, M. M. (2011). Curricular programs. In S. R. Komives, J. P. Dugan, J. E. Owen, C. Slack, W. Wagner, & Associates. *Handbook for student leadership development* (2nd ed.; pp. 259–286). San Francisco, CA: Jossey-Bass.

Marais, J. D., Yang, Y., & Farzanehkia, F. (2000). Service-learning leadership development for youths. *Phi Delta Kappan, 81*(9), 678–680.

Marcia, J. E. (1966). Development and validation of ego-identity status. *Journal of Personality and Social Psychology, 3,* 551–559.

Matsudaira, J. (2006). Anytown: NCCJ's youth leadership experience in social justice. In M. Klau, S. Boyd, L. Luckow, & Associates. *Youth leadership.* New Directions for Youth Development No. 109 (pp. 107–116). San Francisco, CA: Jossey-Bass.

Marsh, H. W. & Kleitman, S. W. (2002). Extracurricular school activities: The good, the bad, and the nonlinear. *Harvard Educational Review, 72,* 464–514.

McCormick, M. J., & Tanguma, J. (2007). The constraining effect of pre-training leadership self-efficacy beliefs on change in post-training leadership self-efficacy beliefs. *Journal of Leadership Education, 6*(1), 108–126.

McCormick, M. J., Tanguma, J., & López-Forment, A. S. (2002). Extending self-efficacy theory to leadership: A review and empirical test. *Journal of Leadership Education, 1,* 1–15.

McIntosh, H., Metz, E., & Youniss, J. (2005). Community service and identity formation in adolescents. In J. L. Mahoney, R. W. Larson, & J. S. Eccles (Eds). *Organized activities as contexts of development* (pp. 331–351). Mahwah, NJ: Lawrence Erlbaum.

McLaughlin, M. (2000). *Community counts: How organizations matter for youth development.* Washington, DC: Public Education Network.

Meixner, C. & Rosch, D. (2011). Powerful pedagogies. In S. R. Komives, J. P. Dugan, J. E. Owen, C. Slack, W. Wagner, & Associates. *Handbook for student leadership development* (2nd ed., pp. 307–338). San Francisco, CA: Jossey-Bass.

Munin, A., & Dugan, J. P. (2011). Inclusive design in leadership program development. In S. R. Komives, J. P. Dugan, J. E. Owen, W. Wagner, C. Slack, & Associates, *Handbook for student leadership development* (pp. 157–176). San Francisco, CA: Jossey-Bass.

Murphy, S. E. (2011). Providing a foundation for leadership development. In S. E. Murphy, & R. J. Reichard (Eds.), *Early development and leadership: Building the next generation of leaders* (pp. 3–37). New York, NY: Psychology Press/Routledge.

Murphy, S. E., & Johnson, S. K. (2011). The benefits of a long-lens approach to leader development: Understanding the seeds of leadership. *Leadership Quarterly, 22,* 459–470.

Murphy, S. E., & Reichard, R. J. (Eds.) (2011). *Early development and leadership: Building the next generation of leaders.* New York, NY: Psychology Press/Routledge.

Nitzberg, J. (Ed.). (2005). *Putting youth at the center of community building.* New Directions for Youth Development No. 106. San Francisco, CA: Jossey-Bass.

Noam, G. G., & Fiore, N. (Eds.). (2004). *The transforming power of adult-youth relationships.* New Directions for Youth Development No. 103. San Francisco, CA: Jossey-Bass.

O'Connor, D. L., & Menaker, E. S. (2008). Can massively multiplayer online gaming environments support team training? *Performance Improvement Quarterly, 21*(3), 23–41.

Ospina, S., & Foldy, E. (2009). A critical review of race and ethnicity in the leadership literature: Surfacing context, power and the collective dimensions of leadership. *Leadership Quarterly, 20,* 876–896.

Owen, J. E. (2009). A snapshot of collegiate leadership programs. *Concepts & Connections, 16*(3) 1, 3–6.

Parks, S. D. (2000). *Big questions, worthy dreams: Mentoring young adults in their search for meaning, purpose, and faith.* San Francisco, CA: Jossey-Bass.

Parks, S. D. (2005). *Leadership can be taught: A bold approach for a complex world.* Boston, MA: Harvard Business School Press.

Perry, W. G., Jr. (1968/1970). *Forms of intellectual and ethical development in the college years: A scheme.* New York, NY: Holt, Rinehart and Winston.

Phinney, J. S. (1990). Ethnic identity in adolescents and adults: Review of research. *Psychological Bulletin, 108,* 499–514.

Piaget, J. (1977). *The moral judgment of the child.* Harmondsforth, England: Penguin.

Posner, B. Z. (2004). A leadership development instrument for students: Updated. *Journal of College Student Development, 45,* 443–456.

Posner, B. Z. (2009). A longitudinal study examining changes in students' leadership behavior. *Journal of College Student Development, 50,* 551–563.

Poston, W. S. C. (1990). The biracial identity development model: A needed addition. *Journal of Counseling and Development, 69*, 152–155.
Rath, T., & Conchie, B. (2009). *Strengths-based leadership.* New York, NY: Gallup Press.
Reichard, R. J., Riggio, R. E., Guerin, D. W., Oliver, P. H., Gottfried, A. W., & Gottfried, A. E. (2011). A longitudinal analysis of relationships between adolescent personality and intelligence with adult leader emergence and transformational leadership. *Leadership Quarterly, 22*, 471–481.
Reid, H. L. (2010). Leadership and sport. In R. A. Couto (Ed.), *Political and civic leadership: A reference handbook* (pp. 1034–1039). Thousand Oaks, CA: SAGE.
Renn, K. A. (2004). *Mixed race students in college: The ecology of race, identity, and community on campus.* Albany, NY: State University of New York Press.
Renn, K. A. (2007). LGBT student leaders and queer activists: Identities of lesbian, gay, bisexual, transgender, and queer identified college student leaders and activists. *Journal of College Student Development, 48*, 311–330.
Renn, K. A., & Lytle, J. H. (2010). Student leaders at women's post-secondary institutions: A global perspective. *Journal of Student Affairs Research and Practice, 47*, 215–232.
Renn, K. A., & Ozaki, C. C. (2010). Psychosocial and leadership identities among leaders of identity-based campus organizations. *Journal of Diversity in Higher Education, 3*, 14–26.
Rice, D. (2011). Qualities that exemplify student leadership. *Techniques, 86*(5), 28–31.
Riggio, R. E., Ciulla, J., & Sorenson, G. (2003). Leadership education at the undergraduate level: A liberal arts approach to leadership development. In S. E. Murphy, & R. E. Riggio (Eds.), *The future of leadership development* (pp. 223–236). Mahwah, NJ: Lawrence Erlbaum.
Ritch, S. (2008). *Guidelines for leadership education learning community.* Retrieved from http://www.ila-net.org/Communities/LC/Guidelines.htm
Roach, A. A., Wyman, L. T., Brookes, H., Chavez, C., Heath, S. B., & Valdes, G. (1999). Leadership giftedness: Models revisited. *Gifted Child Quarterly, 43*, 13–24.
Roberts, D. C & Ullom C. (1989) Student leadership program model. *NASPA Journal, 25*, 67–74.
Rock, D., & Schwartz, J. (2006). The neuroscience of leadership. *Strategy & Business, 43*, 71–79.
Romano, C.R. (1996). A qualitative study of women student leaders. *Journal of College Student Development*, 37,676–683.
Root, M. P. P. (1996). The multiracial experience: Racial borders as a significant frontier in race relations. In M. P. P. Root (Ed.), *The multiracial experience: Racial borders as the new frontier* (pp. xiii–xxviii). Thousand Oaks, CA: SAGE.
Rost, J. C. (1991). *Leadership for the twenty-first century.* Westport, CT: Praeger.
Roth, J. L., & Brooks-Gunn, J. (2003). What exactly is a youth development program? Answers from research and practice. *Applied Developmental Science, 7*, 94–111.
Shankman M. L., & Allen, S. J. (2008). *Emotionally intelligent leadership: A guide for college students.* San Francisco, CA: Jossey-Bass.
Sharp, M. D., Komives, S. R., & Fincher, J. (2011). Learning outcomes in academic disciplines: Identifying common ground. *Journal of Student Affairs Research and Practice. 48*, 481–504.
Shulruf, B. (2010). Do extra-curricular activities in schools improve educational outcomes? A critical review and meta-analysis of the literature. *International Review of Education, 56*, 591–612.
Sigelman, C. K., & Rider, E. A. (2009). *Life-span human development* (6th ed.). Belmont, CA: Wadsworth Cengage Learning.
Siitonen, M. (2011). Leadership in an online, multiplayer strategy game: Case—Illuria. *International Journal of Arts and Technology, 4*, 315–325.
Smart, J. C., Ethington, C. A., Riggs, R. O., & Thompson, M. D. (2002). Influences of institutional expenditure patterns on the development of students' leadership competencies. *Research in Higher Education, 43*, 115–132.
Smist, J. A. (2011). Curricular programs. In S. R. Komives, J. P. Dugan, J. E. Owen, C. Slack, W. Wagner, & Associates. *Handbook for student leadership development* (2nd ed.; pp. 287–306). San Francisco, CA: Jossey-Bass.
Summers, P. P. (2000). The roots of leadership. *Psychology: A Journal of Human Behavior, 37*(1), 27–36.
Troyer, M. J. (2004). The challenges of leadership: A study of an emerging field (Doctoral dissertation). Retrieved from *Dissertations & Theses (ProQuest).* (AAT 3127817)
van Knippenberg, B., van Kippenberg, D., De Cremer, D., & Hogg, M. A. (2005). Research in leadership, self, and identity: A sample of the present and a glimpse of the future. *Leadership Quarterly, 16*, 495–499.
van Linden, J. A. & Fertman, C. I. (1998). *Youth leadership—A guide to understanding leadership development in adolescents.* San Francisco, CA: Jossey-Bass.
Van Velsor, E., & Drath, W. H. (2004). A lifelong developmental perspective on leader development. In C. D. McCauley, & E. V. Velsor (Eds.), *The Center for Creative Leadership handbook of leadership development* (pp. 383–414). San Francisco, CA: Jossey-Bass.
Villarruel, F. A., Montero-Sieburth, M., Dunbar, C., & Outley, C. W. (2005). Dorothy, there is no yellow brick road: The paradox of community youth development approaches for Latino and African American urban youth. In J. L. Mahoney, R. W. Larson, & J. S. Eccles (Eds). (2005). *Organized activities as contexts of development: Extracurricular activities, after-school and community programs* (pp. 111–129). Mahwah, NJ: Lawrence Erlbaum.
Waldman, D. A., Balthazard, P. A., & Peterson, S. J. (2011). Leadership and neuroscience: Can we revolutionize the way that inspirational leaders are identified and developed? *Academy of Management Perspectives, 25*, 60–74.
Wheeler, W. (2006). Leading, learning, and unleashing potential: Youth leadership and civic engagement. In M. Klau, S. Boyd, L. Luckow, & Associates. *Youth leadership.* New Directions for Youth Development No. 109 (pp. 89–97). San Francisco, CA: Jossey-Bass.
Whitehead, G. (2009). Adolescent leadership development: Building a case for an authenticity framework. *Educational Management Administration & Leadership, 37*, 847–871.
Wielkiewicz, R. M. (2000). The Leadership Attitudes and Beliefs Scale: An instrument for evaluating college students' thinking about leadership and organizations. *Journal of College Student Development, 41*, 335–347.
Wijeyesinghe, C. L., & Jackson, B. W. (2001), *New perspectives on racial identity development: A theoretical and practical anthology.* New York, NY: New York University Press.
Woyach, R. B., & Cox, K. J. (1992). *Principles for youth leadership development. 4-H teen leadership handbook.* Columbus, OH: Ohio State University Extension.

Wren, J. T. (1994). Teaching leadership: The art of the possible. *Journal of Leadership Studies, 1*, 73–93.

Yu, H. C., Lewis-Charp, H. K., & Gambone, M. A. (2007). Evaluating youth leadership development through civic activism. In K. M. Hannum, J. W. Martineau, & C. Reinelt (Eds), *The handbook of leadership development evaluation* (pp. 377–402). San Francisco, CA: Jossey-Bass.

Zaff, J. F., Malanchuk, O., & Eccles, J. S. (2008). Predicting positive citizenship from adolescence to young adulthood: The effects of a civic context. *Applied Developmental Science, 12*(1), 38–53.

Zlotkowski, E., Horowitz, K., & Benson, S (2011). The potential of service-learning for student leadership. In N. V. Longo, & C. M. Gibson (Eds.), *From command to community: A new approach to leadership education in colleges and universities* (pp. 45–64). Medford, MA: Tufts University Press.

Zlotkowski, E., Longo, N. V., & Williams, J. R. (Eds). (2006). *Students as colleagues: Expanding the circle of service-learning leadership*. Providence, RI: Campus Compact.

CHAPTER

37 Leadership Development: A Review and Agenda for Future Research

D. Scott DeRue *and* Christopher G. Myers

Abstract

This chapter develops a conceptual framework that helps organize and synthesize key insights from the literature on leadership development. In this framework, called PREPARE, the authors call attention to the strategic purpose and desired results of leadership development in organizations. They emphasize how organizations can deliberately and systematically leverage a range of developmental experiences for enhancing the leadership capabilities of individuals, relationships, and collectives. Finally, they highlight how individuals and organizations vary in their approach to and support for leadership development, and how these differences explain variation in leadership development processes and outcomes. As an organizing mechanism for the existing literature, the PREPARE framework advances our understanding of what individuals and organizations can do to develop leadership talent, and highlights important questions for future research.

Key Words: Leadership, leadership development, leader development, training, learning, experience, coaching, feedback

Introduction

Contemporary organizations operate in environments characterized by rapid change and increasing complexity. Indeed, some historians believe that our world is undergoing a transformation more profound and far-reaching than any experienced since the Industrial Revolution (Daft, 2008). Advancements in technology are creating opportunities for new business models that can dramatically shift the competitive landscape of entire industries. Globalization and shifting geopolitical forces are permanently altering the boundaries of interorganizational collaboration and competition. In addition, a myriad of economic, environmental, and ethical crises are directly challenging the role of corporations in society, and highlighting the interdependence among business, government and social sectors. The result is organizations around the world and across a broad array of domains—industry, government, military, not-for-profit, health care, and education—are adapting their strategies, structures, and practices with the intent of becoming more agile and responsive to these dynamic environments.

Because of these ongoing organizational transformations, effective leadership is needed more than ever. Leadership is one of the most important predictors of whether groups and organizations are able to effectively adapt to and perform in dynamic environments (Mintzberg & Waters, 1982; Peterson, Smith, Martorana, & Owens, 2003; Peterson, Walumbwa, Byron, & Myrowitz, 2009; Thomas, 1988; Waldman, Ramirez, House, & Puranam, 2001). As Bass and Bass (2008, p. 11) concluded, "when an organization must be changed to reflect changes in technology, the environment, and the completion of programs, its leadership is critical in orchestrating that process." Consequently, organizations are designating leadership as a top strategic priority and potential source of competitive advantage, and are investing in its development accordingly (Day, Harrison, & Halpin, 2009). For example, in 2009, almost a quarter of the $50 billion that U.S. organizations spent on learning and development was targeted at leadership development (O'Leonard, 2010).

Despite the fact that organizations are increasing their investments in leadership development, there is an emerging consensus that the supply of leadership talent is insufficient to meet the leadership needs of contemporary organizations. According to a survey of 1,100 U.S.-based organizations, 56 per cent of employers report a dearth of leadership talent, and 31 per cent of organizations expect to have a shortage of leaders that will impede performance in the next four years (Adler & Mills, 2008). Likewise, a survey of 13,701 managers and HR professionals across 76 countries found that individuals' confidence in their leaders declined by 25 per cent from 1999–2007, and that 37 per cent of respondents believe those who hold leadership positions fail to achieve their position's objectives (Howard & Wellins, 2009). These data allude to an emerging leadership talent crisis where the need and demand for leadership surpass our ability to develop effective leadership talent.

Ironically, this leadership talent crisis is emerging at the same time the pace of scholarly research on leadership development is reaching a historical peak. Conceptual and empirical research on leadership development has proliferated through the publication of a number of books, including the *Center for Creative Leadership Handbook of Leadership Development* (Van Velsor, McCauley, & Ruderman, 2010), Day and colleagues' (2009) *Integrated Approach to Leader Development*, and Avolio's (2005) *Leadership Development in Balance.* Likewise, reviews of the leadership development literature point to rapid growth in the base of scholarly research on leadership development over the past 20 years (Collins & Holton, 2004; Day, 2000; Hernez-Broome & Hughes, 2004; McCall, 2004), and numerous special issues in management and psychology journals have been dedicated to the topic (DeRue, Sitkin, & Podolny, 2011; Pearce, 2007; Riggio, 2008). All of this scholarly literature is notwithstanding the thousands of popular press books and articles that have been written on the topic.

Indeed, the depth and richness of the existing literature has produced an array of important insights about leadership development in organizations. For example, drawing from experiential learning theories (Dewey, 1938; Kolb, 1984), scholars have documented how lived experiences that are novel, of high significance to the organization, and require people to manage change with diverse groups of people and across organizational boundaries are important sources of leadership development (DeRue & Wellman, 2009; McCall & Hollenbeck, 2002; McCall, Lombardo, & Morrison, 1988; McCauley, Ruderman, Ohlott, & Morrow, 1994). Indeed, it was this research that led McCall (2004, p. 127) to conclude that "the primary source of learning to lead, to the extent that leadership can be learned, is experience." In addition, scholars have identified an array of personal attributes (e.g., learning orientation, developmental readiness) and situational characteristics (e.g., feedback, coaching, reflection practices) that influence how much leadership development occurs via these lived experiences (Avolio & Hannah, 2008; Alimo-Metcalfe, 1998; DeRue & Wellman, 2009; Dragoni, Tesluk, Russell, & Oh, 2009; Hirst, Mann, Bain, Pirola-Merlo, & Richver, 2004; Ting & Scisco, 2006). Moving beyond the sources and predictors of leadership development, researchers have also examined a multitude of outcomes associated with leadership development, including but not limited to the development of individuals' leadership knowledge, skills, abilities, motivations, and identities (Chan & Drasgow, 2001; Day & Harrison, 2007; DeRue & Ashford, 2010a; Mumford, Campion, & Morgeson, 2007; Mumford, Zaccaro, Harding, Jacobs, & Fleishman, 2000). Altogether, these conceptual articles and empirical studies provide substantial insight into a complex and multifaceted leadership development process, and point to various ways in which individuals and organizations can enhance (and impair) leadership development.

Despite notable progress in our understanding of leadership development, there are at least three reasons why this body of literature has not yielded the insights and breakthroughs that are needed to sufficiently inform and address the emerging leadership talent crisis. First, the existing literature is predominantly focused on individual leader development, at the expense of understanding the evolution of leading-following processes and the construction of leadership relationships and structures in groups and organizations (DeRue, 2011; DeRue & Ashford, 2010a). This focus on individuals as the target of development may stem from the broader leadership literature, which has traditionally endorsed an individualistic and hierarchical conception of leadership (Bedeian & Hunt, 2006). However, there is an emerging shift toward thinking of leadership as a shared activity or process that anyone can participate in, regardless of their formal position or title (Charan, 2007; Day, Gronn, & Salas, 2004; Morgeson, DeRue & Karam, 2010; Quinn, 1996; Pearce & Conger, 2003). In turn, the leadership development literature needs to explain how these collective leadership processes develop and evolve over time.

Second, consistent with the focus on individuals, the existing literature generally endorses a narrow focus on the knowledge, skills, and abilities (KSAs) required for effective leadership (Mumford, Campion, & Morgeson, 2007; Mumford et al., 2000). One potential reason for the focus on KSAs is that much of the existing literature on leadership development is framed within the domain of human resource management, which often focuses on the training and transfer of KSAs (Saks & Belcourt, 2006). Another potential reason is that scholars have developed coherent theories and taxonomies of leadership KSAs, and there is clear evidence linking these leadership KSAs to individual leader effectiveness (Connelly et al., 2000; Mumford et al., 2007). Only recently have scholars begun to explore a wider range of leadership development outcomes, including individuals' self-concept and identity (Day & Harrison, 2007; DeRue & Ashford, 2010a; Lord & Hall, 2005), motivations related to leadership (Barbuto, 2005; Chan & Drasgow, 2001), and mental models of leadership (Lord, Brown, Harvey & Hall, 2001; Epitropaki & Martin, 2004; Lord, Foti, & De Vader, 1984). These alternative outcomes are important to understanding leadership development because it is possible that individuals are developing the KSAs necessary for effective leadership, but are choosing not to take on leadership roles because they do not see themselves as leaders, or they are not motivated to lead given the risks associated with it (Heifetz & Linsky, 2002). Although these leadership identities, motivations, and mental models could be the target of leadership development interventions, it is not clear based on the current research how malleable these attributes are, or what types of experiences or interventions would develop them.

Finally, consistent with Avolio's (2007) call for more integrative theory building in the leadership literature, our field lacks a coherent and integrative framework for organizing the existing literature on leadership development. With respect to the emerging leadership talent crisis, this lack of an integrative, organizing framework is limiting progress in two ways. First, without an integrative understanding of the inputs, processes, and outcomes associated with leadership development, organizations are forced to speculate or rely on intuition as to what to develop, how to develop it, where and when it should be developed, and who is ready (or not ready) for development. Second, it remains unclear what the critical knowledge gaps are related to leadership development, and where future research needs to focus in order to help organizations more effectively identify and develop future leadership talent.

Thus, the aim of this chapter is to develop an organizing framework for the inputs, processes, and outcomes associated with leadership development, synthesize key insights from the existing literature, and identify critical knowledge gaps that can serve as the impetus for future research on leadership development. We seek to accomplish these goals, as well as complement and extend prior reviews of this literature (Brungardt, 1997; Day, 2000), by first defining leadership development and articulating some of the key assumptions associated with this definition. We then introduce an organizing framework called PREPARE, and use this framework to integrate key insights from the existing literature. We conclude by summarizing an agenda for future research based on the PREPARE framework, with the purpose of extending existing theories of leadership development and advancing our understanding of what individuals and organizations can do to identify and develop leadership talent.

Leadership Development: A Definition

Leadership is a social and mutual influence process where multiple actors engage in leading-following interactions in service of accomplishing a collective goal (Bass & Bass, 2008; Yukl, 2010). In his oft-cited review of the leadership development literature, Day (2000) distinguishes between two forms of development. Individual leader development focuses on an individual's capacity to participate in leading-following processes and generally presumes that developing an individual's leadership KSAs will result in more effective leadership. A key limitation of this perspective is that it does not account for leadership as a complex and interactive process among multiple actors who are both leading and following, or that the relationships that are created and maintained within the social context can have a strong influence on how leadership processes emerge and evolve (Day & Halpin, 2004; DeRue, 2011). The second form, leadership development, focuses on developing the capacity of collectives to engage in the leadership process. Whereas leader development focuses on individuals and the development of human capital, leadership development attends to the interpersonal dynamics of leadership and focuses on the development of social capital. Specifically, leadership development refers to building the mutual commitments and interpersonal relationships that are necessary for leading-following processes to unfold effectively within a given social context.

Historically, the existing literature has focused on individual leader development at the expense of understanding and explaining leadership development (Day, 2000; Drath et al., 2008; Van Velsor, McCauley, & Ruderman, 2010). In fact, because of the dearth of research on leadership development, prior reviews of the existing literature have been forced to acknowledge the importance of leadership development but then go on to narrowly focus on individual leader development (e.g., Day, 2000; McCauley, 2008). This narrow focus on leader development is unfortunate because both leader and leadership development are necessary but insufficient for understanding and explaining how leadership capacity is developed, especially as organizations embrace more collective and shared models of leadership (Pearce & Conger, 2003).

In the present article, we broaden the definition of leadership development to include both individual and collective forms of development. Specifically, we define leadership development as the process of preparing individuals and collectives to effectively engage in leading-following interactions. Several assumptions are embedded in this definition. First, we assume that both leader and leadership development are essential for enabling more effective leadership processes in organizations. Individuals need the leadership KSAs, motivations, and beliefs necessary to effectively participate in the leading-following process, but effective leading-following interactions also involve the emergence of leader-follower relationships and collective leadership structures. In addition, we assume that leader and leadership development are interdependent. Developmental experiences or interventions designed to promote more effective leadership relationships will also affect individuals' KSAs, beliefs, and motivations. Likewise, actions taken to enhance individual leadership capabilities will indirectly alter the landscape of leading-following relationships among actors. Therefore, the conceptual model we use to structure our literature review will incorporate both individual leader development and the development of leadership relationships and collective structures.

Our expectation is that the framework developed herein will be used by researchers in several ways. First, as noted above, the framework is purposefully integrative across a range of levels of analysis and developmental approaches, with the intent of motivating scholars to adopt a more integrative approach to studying leadership development. For example, scholars might use the framework to emphasize the intersection of individual leader development with more relational or collective forms of development, or ways in which formal training might complement informal, on-the-job development. Second, researchers can use the framework to conceptualize a broader range of outcomes associated with leadership development. Historically, leadership development research has focused narrowly on the development of individual skills or competencies, but this framework emphasizes a range of individual, relational, and collective outputs of leadership development. Finally, we expect scholars can use the framework to situate their individual studies within a broader nomological network of research on leadership development, which in turn will identify key gaps in the literature and advance the accumulation of knowledge related to leadership development.

PREPARE: An Organizing Framework

As illustrated in Figure 37.1, PREPARE is an acronym that refers to the individual components of our organizing framework. The PREPARE framework consists of seven key components: (1) Purpose, (2) Result, (3) Experience, (4) Point of Intervention, (5) Architecture, (6) Reinforcement, and (7) Engagement.

Purpose refers to why an organization is engaging in leadership development: in particular the role that leadership development plays in enabling an organization to achieve its strategic objectives and performance goals. The *Result* component refers to the desired outcome, what is actually trying to be developed, such as individuals' cognitive schemas related to leadership (e.g., implicit leadership theory), the affective or relational ties among group members (e.g., trust), or the organizational climate for shared leadership. *Experience* refers to the mechanism through which leadership development occurs, specifically what experiences (e.g., formal training, on-the-job assignments) will serve as the basis for challenging individuals and/or collectives

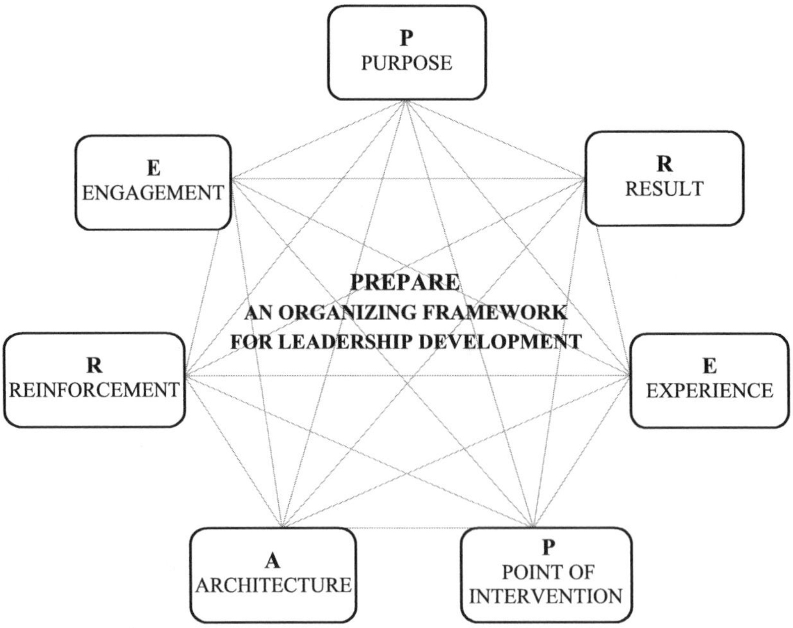

Figure 37.1. PREPARE Framework for Leadership Development.

to improve their leadership capacity. These experiences vary in their formality (e.g., on-the-job assignments, classroom experiences), mode (e.g., direct or vicarious) and content (e.g., the degree of developmental challenge). The *Point of Intervention* component represents the intended target of leadership development (i.e., who is being developed), and the attributes associated with that target. The target can be at the individual level (e.g., developing an individual's skills), the relational level (e.g., developing the leading-following relationship among actors), or the collective level (e.g., shared team leadership). *Architecture* refers to features of the organizational context (e.g., practices, processes, climate) that are designed to facilitate and support leadership development. The *Reinforcement* components refer to the temporal sequencing of developmental experiences, and the timing of those experiences. Finally, the *Engagement* component refers to the ways in which individuals and collectives enter, go through, and reflect on the leadership development process.

Each of these seven dimensions receives a different level of attention in the existing literature. For example, scholars frequently examine how the organizational architecture (e.g., 360° feedback, mentoring, and coaching programs) supports individual leader development (e.g., Alimo-Metcalfe, 1998; Brungardt, 1997), but few scholars consider the purpose of leadership development or how leadership development is aligned (or not aligned) with organizational strategy. Likewise, scholars rarely theorize or empirically examine how developmental experiences should be sequenced so that they are reinforcing over time. Our contention is that each of these dimensions is an essential ingredient to successful leadership development, and that the design of effective leadership development systems must address each of these components. Our hope is that the PREPARE framework helps organize key insights from the existing literature in a way that synthesizes what is known about leadership development, highlights questions that need to be addressed in future research, and provides guidance to individuals and organizations looking to improve their leadership talent. In the sections that follow, we review the base of scholarly research for each of the PREPARE dimensions, and identify key knowledge gaps that can serve as the impetus for future research.

Purpose: Aligning Leadership Development and Organizational Strategy

Theories of strategic human resource management explain how different patterns of human resource management (HRM) practices and activities enable organizations to achieve their strategic objectives and goals (Wright & McMahan, 1992; Wright & Snell, 1998). Drawing from theories of fit and congruence (Nadler & Tushman, 1980;

Venkatraman, 1989), these strategic HRM theories emphasize that organizational performance is in part a function of the alignment between HRM practices and the organization's strategy (Schuler & Jackson, 1987). Indeed, empirical research has established that a key predictor of organizational productivity and performance is the alignment between firm strategy and the configuration of HRM practices (Delery & Doty, 1996; Youndt, Snell, Dean & Lepak, 1996).

With respect to leadership development practices, organizations often speculate that alignment between organizational strategy and leadership development practices is important for maximizing the return on investment in leadership development (Zenger, Ulrich, & Smallwood, 2000). For example, in their report on the *Top Companies for Leaders*, Hewitt & Associates (2009) concluded that "... HR leaders and senior management are finding they must rethink leadership selection and development strategies—to better align with organizational goals, cost pressures, and competing resources." Similarly, in a review of best-practices research on leadership development, McCauley (2008) underscored how, in best-practice organizations, leadership development practices are closely tied to the vision, values, and goals of the business, and that leadership development is a core part of the organization's strategic planning processes. These conclusions are consistent with McCall and Hollenbeck's (2002) contention that global leaders are best developed through challenging experiences and assignments that are tied to the strategic imperatives of the business.

Despite the fact that organizations are emphasizing strategic alignment with leadership development practices, there is currently a lack of scholarly research on the mechanisms through which leadership development can support organizational goals and strategies, or the implications of alignment in terms of return on investments in leadership development. The research on strategic HRM suggests that alignment with organizational strategy will be essential for developing leadership development systems that promote and enhance organizational effectiveness, but research is needed to connect these insights about general HRM practices to leadership development specifically. Currently, the field of leadership development studies lacks a theoretical or empirical basis for explaining how organizations can achieve strategic alignment with leadership development practices, or why strategic alignment enhances the value of leadership development to the organization.

In fact, there are some trends in the leadership development literature that suggest a sort of duality with respect to aligning leadership development with organizational strategy. On the one hand, scholars suggest that an important source of leadership development is having individuals and groups engage in challenging assignments that are directly linked to firm strategy and the future directions of the business (McCall et al., 1988; McCall & Hollenbeck, 2002). On the other hand, organizations are increasing outsourcing leadership development by placing employees in challenging, developmental experiences that are outside of the organization and have very little to do with the organization's strategy (e.g., IBM's Peace Corps; Colvin, 2009). There are likely benefits to both approaches. Strategic alignment should not only enhance employees' leadership development but also directly contribute to the business needs of the organization. Yet, enabling employees to explore developmental opportunities outside of the core business may also broaden the employee's perspective and introduce motivational benefits that might not be possible within the context of the core business. Future research that examines the value of strategic alignment in leadership development, and how best to balance developmental experiences that are inside the organization's core business with experiences outside of the core business, would be particularly noteworthy. This research would go a long way toward helping organizations explain and understand the business returns associated with leadership development.

Result: Identifying the Desired Outcome of Leadership Development

Organizations invest considerable resources into identifying the "holy grail" of leadership competencies that are needed for success in their organization (Alldredge & Nilan, 2000; Intagliata, Ulrich, & Smallwood, 2000). As described by Intagliata et al. (2000, p. 12), "This holy grail, when found, would identify a small set of attributes that successful leaders possess, articulate them in ways that could be transferred across all leaders, and create leadership development experiences to ensure that future leaders possess these attributes." Indeed, organizations routinely use their leadership competency models not only for leadership development but also for performance management, recruiting and staffing, and succession planning (Gentry & Leslie, 2007; McCauley, 2008). The challenge, however, is that it is unclear whether there is such a "holy grail," or even a coherent set of attributes or competencies that are needed for effective leadership.

Scholarly research on leadership development has considered a range of development outcomes, including leadership KSAs (Hulin, Henry & Noon, 1990; Mumford et al., 2007), forms of cognition such as leadership schemas and identities (Day & Harrison, 2007; DeRue, Ashford, & Cotton, 2009; Shamir & Eilam, 2005), and the motivations associated with taking on leadership roles and responsibilities (Chan & Drasgow, 2001; Kark & Van Dijk, 2007). In addition, scholars have looked beyond individual attributes and examined the development and evolution of leader-follower relationships (DeRue & Ashford, 2010a; Nahrgang, Morgeson, & Ilies, 2009). Although we do not intend to discover the "holy grail" of leadership competencies in this chapter, we can identify three broad themes of development outcomes in the existing literature: behavioral, affective/motivational, and cognitive. Further, each of these themes can be conceptualized at the individual, relational, or collective level of analysis, although most existing research is at the individual level.

Behavioral. We conceptualize behavioral outcomes in leadership development as the acquisition of leadership KSAs that are necessary for the performance of specific leadership behaviors, or positive changes in the performance of actual leadership behaviors. In the current literature, leadership development scholars have considered a wide range of these behavioral outcomes. One influential article in this domain is Mumford et al.'s (2007) leadership skills strataplex. In this article, the authors identify four distinct categories of leadership skill requirements: cognitive skills, interpersonal skills, business skills, and strategic skills. Then, in a sample of 1023 professional employees in an international agency of the U.S. government, the authors find empirical support for the four distinct categories of leadership skill requirements, and show that different categories of leadership skill requirements emerge at different hierarchical levels of organizations. For example, basic cognitive skills are required across all hierarchical levels, but strategic skills become important only once employees reach senior-level positions.

Moving beyond the acquisition of leadership skills, leadership scholars have also examined changes in the performance of actual leadership behaviors. For example, Barling, Weber, and Kelloway (1996) conducted a field experiment of 20 managers randomly assigned to either a control condition or a leadership training condition. In the training group, managers received a one-day training seminar on transformational leadership, followed by four booster training sessions on a monthly basis. The control group received no such training. Drawing upon subordinates' perceptions of transformational leadership behaviors, results showed that participants in the training group improved their performance of transformational leadership behaviors more so than participants in the control group. In a similar study design, Dvir and colleagues (2002) examined the impact of transformational leadership training on follower development and performance. In a sample of 54 military leaders, their results establish that transformational leadership training can increase leaders' display of transformational leadership behaviors, which in turn have a positive effect on follower motivation, morality, empowerment, and performance.

Affect/Motivational. Most of the existing research has conceptualized and empirically studied leadership development in terms of behavioral outcomes, but scholars have recently begun to examine how individuals' affective states and their motivations related to leadership influence how they engage in, go through, and process leadership experiences. For example, individuals' positive and negative affective states explain not only their leadership effectiveness, but also how leaders influence followers' affect and behavior (Bono & Ilies, 2006; Damen, Van Knippenberg, & Van Knippenberg, 2008; Ilies, Judge, & Wagner, 2006). Similarly, emotional intelligence, or the ability to understand and manage moods and emotions in the self and others (Mayer, Salovey, Caruso, & Sitarenios, 2001), can contribute to effective leadership in organizations (George, 2000; Prati, Douglas, Ferris, Ammeter, & Buckley, 2003). In terms of motivation, scholars have suggested and found some empirical support for the notion that individuals have different levels of motivation for leadership, and that these motivations can impact participation in leadership roles and leadership potential (Chan & Drasgow, 2001; Kark & van Dijk, 2007).

However, in contrast to behavioral outcomes, there is very little empirical research on how individuals or collectives develop the affective or motivational attributes that promote effective leadership. Rather, most of the existing research focuses on how these affective and motivational attributes influence the leadership process or the individual's effectiveness as a leader (e.g., Atwater, Dionne, Avolio, Camobreco, & Lau, 1999; Chemers, Watson, &

May, 2000). The antecedents to these attributes or the processes through which these attributes are developed generally remain a mystery. Notable exceptions include Chan and Drasgow's (2001) study of Singaporean military cadets, where they find that personality, cultural values such as collectivism and individualism, and prior leadership experience predict whether individuals are motivated to take on leadership roles and responsibilities. Likewise, Boyce, Zaccaro, and Wisecarver (2010), in their study of junior-military cadets, find that individuals who have a mastery and learning orientation are more motivated than people without this orientation to engage in leadership development activities, and in addition, are more skilled at self-regulatory, learning processes. Yet, the developmental implications of these studies are unclear given that attributes such as personality and values can be fixed properties of a person (Costa & McCrae, 1994; Schwartz, 1994). Another exception is Shefy and Sadler-Smith's (2006) case study of a management development program implemented in a technology company, whereby focusing on non-Western principles of human development (e.g., harmony and balance), the program enhanced individuals' emotional awareness and interpersonal sensitivity.

Notwithstanding these few exceptions, there is a considerable need for research on the development of the affective and motivational attributes that enable individuals to effectively participate in the leadership process. For example, affective events theory (Weiss & Cropanzano, 1996) explains how work events interact with dispositional characteristics and situational factors to influence individuals' affective states. This focus on event-level phenomena is consistent with the notion that discrete work events and experiences are the primary source of leadership development (McCall, 2004), yet these two literatures have yet to be integrated. Future research that explains how work events and experiences influence the development of particular affective states, and how these affective states enable more effective leadership and leadership development processes, would help integrate and extend theories of affect and leadership development. Likewise, a fundamentally important question that needs to be explored further is why some people are more motivated than others to take on leadership roles and responsibilities, even when they are not designated as a formal leader. This research needs to move beyond a focus on stable individuals' differences, and consider how the social and organizational context enables (or constrains) individual motivation for leadership. In particular, this research could build on prior theories of the rewards and risks associated with leadership (Heifetz & Linsky, 2002) to understand how people process, cognitively and emotionally, the rewards and risks of assuming leadership roles and responsibilities in different group and organizational contexts.

Cognitive. Cognitive outcomes refer to the mental models and structures that individuals and collectives rely on to participate in and carry out leadership processes. In this sense, individuals and collectives develop their capacity for effective leadership by expanding or changing their conceptual models and mental structures of what it means to lead, the way in which leading-following processes unfold, and/or their conception of themselves as leaders and followers. Indeed, a commonly espoused purpose of using multi-rater feedback for leadership development is to create self-awareness and stimulate reflection related to what leadership means in a given setting and to expand people's conceptions of their roles as leaders (Yammarino & Atwater, 1993). Developing these cognitive models and mental structures are important because they impact how people engage in leadership processes (Shamir & Eilam, 2005).

In the existing literature, there are at least three cognitive outcomes that seem particularly important for leadership development, especially as organizations embrace collective and shared forms of leadership. First, an individual's self-concept or identity as a leader is important for determining how that person will engage in the leadership process (Day & Harrison, 2007; DeRue & Ashford, 2010a; DeRue, Ashford & Cotton, 2009; Hall, 2004; Shamir & Eilam, 2005). Developmental experiences allow individuals to create, modify, and adapt their identities as leaders by "trying on" different possible self-concepts (Ibarra, 1999) and engaging in the identity work that is necessary to clarify one's self-concept (Kreiner, Hollensbe, & Sheep, 2006). Importantly, this identity development is not limited to the individual level, as leadership development can help individuals construct leadership identities at the relational and collective levels of analysis, which then become the basis for the formation of effective leading-following relationships (DeRue & Ashford, 2010a). In addition, with the increasing interest in ethical leadership and moral psychology (Aquino & Reed, 2002; Mayer, Kuenzi, Greenbaum, Bardes, & Salvador, 2009), research on the development of individual and collective levels of moral identity may prove to be particularly important as leadership development outcomes.

Another potentially important cognitive outcome for leadership development is individuals' implicit theories of leadership. Implicit leadership theories (ILTs) refer to people's cognitive schemas for what personal attributes and behavioral tendencies make for an effective leader, and these ILTs can have a significant impact on individuals' perceptions of who is (and is not) a leader in a given context (Epitropaki & Martin, 2004; Lord, Foti, & De Vader, 1984; Rush, Thomas, & Lord, 1977). There is some research evidence supporting the idea that these ILTs emerge as a result of cultural background (House, Javidan, Hanges, & Dorfman, 2002), media influence (Holmberg & Akerblom, 2001), and life experience (Keller, 2003). However, much more research is needed to clarify the origin of these beliefs about prototypical leaders, as well as what organizations can do to modify these beliefs. It is quite possible that many people choose not to take on leadership roles because they perceive a misfit between their own self-concept and what they believe to be prototypical of an effective leader. However, it is also possible that organizations can change these perceptions and create a fit between people's self-concept and their ILT, thereby engendering a greater propensity to step up and take on leadership.

Finally, scholars are beginning to suggest that individuals not only have implicit theories about who is prototypical of an effective leader, but that individuals also have implicit theories about how leadership is structured in groups. For example, DeRue and Ashford (2010a) proposed the concept of a leadership-structure schema, which refers to whether individuals conceptualize leadership as zero-sum and reserved for a single individual within a group (often the designated leader), or whether leadership can be shared among multiple group members. Following up on this proposition, there is emerging empirical evidence suggesting that not only do individuals possess different leadership-structure schemas, but also that these schemas are malleable and can be developed (Hinrichs, Carson, Li, & Porter, 2011; Wellman, Ashford, DeRue, & Sanchez-Burks, 2011). Future research that examines the developmental interventions that alter the leadership-structure schemas of individuals and collectives, and the implications for group process and performance, would be particularly important for promoting more shared leadership in organizations.

In addition to behavioral, affective/motivational, and cognitive development outcomes, leadership development scholars have also examined changes in overall leadership performance or leadership emergence (e.g., Atwater, Dionne, Avolio, Camobreco, & Lau, 1999). Given that it is rare for empirical studies to model changes in leadership behavior or performance, these studies offer valuable insight into the predictors of leadership development. However, because they focus on overall performance changes and rarely experimentally manipulate the developmental intervention, these studies offer less insight into what is actually being developed or causing the observed change in leadership performance. On the one hand, it might be that individuals are developing new leadership skills or motivations. On the other hand, it is also possible that the context is changing in ways that enable individuals' to engage in more effective leadership behavior, but that no meaningful development is occurring. For future research, we recommend scholars assess change over time in specific behavioral, affective/motivational, and/or cognitive outcomes, which will provide more insight into the underlying mechanisms explaining improvements in leadership performance or emergence.

Experience: Developing Leadership through Lived Experience

Drawing on experiential learning theories (Dewey, 1938; Knowles, 1970; Kolb, 1984), scholars at the Center for Creative Leadership conducted the early research on the role of experience in leadership development (McCall et al., 1988). This research then spawned a multitude of follow-up studies exploring a range of leadership development experiences, and there is now considerable consensus in the existing literature that the primary source of leadership development is experience (McCall, 2004; Ohlott, 2004; Van Velsor & Drath, 2004). As Mumford and colleagues (2000) note, without appropriate developmental experience, even the most intelligent and motivated individuals are unlikely to be effective leaders.

The existing research on experience-based leadership development spans across a wide range of different types of experiences, including informal on-the-job assignments (McCall et al., 1988), coaching and mentoring programs (Ting & Sciscio, 2006), and formal training programs (Burke & Day, 1986). A common assumption in the existing literature is that 70 per cent of leadership development occurs via on-the-job assignments, 20 per cent through working with and learning from other people (e.g., learning from bosses or coworkers), and 10 per cent through formal programs such as training, mentoring, or coaching programs (McCall et al., 1988; Robinson & Wick, 1992). Despite the popularity of this assumption, there are four fundamental problems with framing developmental experiences in this way. First and foremost, there is actually no empirical evidence supporting this assumption, yet scholars and practitioners frequently quote it as if it is fact. Second, as McCall (2010) appropriately points out, this assumption is misleading because it suggests informal, on-the-job experiences, learning from other people, and formal programs are independent. Yet, these different forms of experience can occur in parallel, and it is possible (and likely optimal) that learning in one form of experience can complement and build on learning in another form of experience. Third, it is inconsistent with the fact that a large portion of organizational investments are directed at formal leadership development programs (O'Leonard, 2010). It is certainly possible that organizations are misguided in their focus on and deployment of these programs (Conger & Toegel, 2003), but we are not ready to condemn formal programs given the lack of empirical evidence. Finally, it is possible that the "70:20:10" assumption leads organizations to prioritize informal, on-the-job experience over all other forms of developmental experiences, which some scholars argue allows leadership development to become a "haphazard process" (Conger, 1993, p. 46) without sufficient notice to intentionality, accountability, and formal evaluation (Day, 2000).

We offer an integrative framework for conceptualizing the different forms of developmental experience, including both formal and informal developmental experiences. Specifically, we propose that developmental experiences are best described and understood in terms of three dimensions: formality, mode, and content.

Formality. The formality dimension ranges from formal to informal. Formal developmental experiences are activities designed with the intended purpose of leadership development, which would include leadership training programs and interventions. In contrast, informal developmental experiences occur within the normal context of everyday life and are often not designed for the specific purpose of leadership development. Another way the formal versus informal distinction appears in the literature is when Avolio and colleagues discuss planned and unplanned events that serve as "developmental triggers" (Avolio, 2004; Avolio & Hannah, 2008). These trigger events are experiences that prompt a person to focus attention on the need to learn and develop, but as Avolio and his colleagues propose, formal training that is planned and informal experiences that are unplanned can both serve as developmental triggers.

One assumed benefit of formal developmental experiences is that they allow individuals to spend time away from the workplace, where they are free to challenge existing ways of thinking and reflect more deeply on the lessons of experience (Fulmer, 1997). Indeed, meta-analyses by Burke and Day (1986) and Collins and Holton (2004) suggest that formal leadership programs have a positive impact on employees' acquisition of new knowledge, behavior change, and performance. However, as noted by Collins and Holton (2004), formal development programs have a stronger, positive effect on knowledge outcomes in comparison to behavior or performance outcomes. One reason for this differential effect could be that program participants acquire new knowledge and skills, but then encounter barriers to transferring those lessons to their actual jobs (Belling, James, & Ladkin, 2004).

For example, in a study of 95 managers engaged in a formal development program in the United Kingdom, Belling and her colleagues (2004) found that participants perceived significant barriers to their ability to transfer lessons from the program back to the workplace. These barriers included individuals' lack of motivation, as well as organizational factors such as time constraints, lack of managerial support, and a lack of opportunity to apply new skills. Similar barriers appear in McAlearney's (2006) interviews with 160 health care managers, where program participants report that variability in organizational commitment to leadership development has a strong influence on whether they will be able to transfer new knowledge to their actual work. Similarly, Gilpin-Jackson and Bushe's (2007) case study of 18 participants in a Canadian leadership development program reinforces these findings. In this study, participants reported fears about violating organizational norms by applying new techniques learned in the program. To address these barriers, a common suggestion in recent research on formal leadership development programs is to have intact teams from the same organization participate in the program together, which might help develop a common understanding of the lessons learned and increase the likelihood that behavior changes would be welcomed upon returning to the workplace (Conger & Benjamin, 1999; Umble et al., 2005).

In part to address the barriers associated with formal leadership development programs, and in part realizing the potential learning value of on-the-job experience, scholars have also investigated the developmental value of informal, on-the-job experiences (Davies & Easterby-Smith, 1984; DeRue & Wellman, 2009; Dragoni et al., 2009; McCall et al., 1988; McCauley et al., 1994; Morrison & Hock, 1986; Ohlott, 2004; Wick, 1989). According to Murphy and Young (1995), informal learning refers to learning that takes place outside of organized, structured learning processes such as institutionally based degree or training programs. These informal developmental experiences occur within the normal course of work and life, and it is this contextual groundedness that scholars believe provides greater developmental "punch" relative to formal programs (Day, 2000; Dotlich & Noel, 1998).

For example, DeRue and Wellman (2009) examined how challenging, on-the-job experiences promote the acquisition of cognitive, interpersonal, business, and strategic leadership skills. Based on a sample of 225 on-the-job experiences across 60 managers from a range of organizations, the results of this study demonstrate that the relationship between developmentally challenging experiences and leadership skill development exhibits a pattern of diminishing returns, such that on-the-job experiences are developmental but can become too challenging and actually impair an employee's development. This research refines the common assumption that challenging employees beyond their current skill set promotes leadership development—there is such thing as "too much" challenge. Consistent with these findings, research suggests that many of the same organizational factors that enhance the efficacy of formal programs are necessary for enabling informal learning through experience, including organizational commitment, feedback, managerial support, and a climate promoting learning and experimentation (Mumford, 1980; Robinson & Wick, 1992).

Mode. Learning can occur as individuals directly engage and participate in developmental experiences, but learning can also occur vicariously through observing others and learning from their experiences. Indeed, scholars have long argued that one of humankind's differentiating cognitive capabilities is the ability to learn vicariously (Anderson & Cole, 1990; Bandura, 1986). The mode dimension reflects whether the developmental experience is characterized by direct or vicarious learning. Both direct and vicarious learning are possible in either formal or informal developmental experiences. For example, in a formal development program, vicarious learning can occur through observing other participants engage in various elements of the program. Likewise, in informal experiences, individuals can be directly involved, but it is also possible that significant learning can occur by observing and modeling others.

Most of the existing literature on leadership development focuses on a direct learning mode, specifically on how individuals develop leadership capabilities as they engage in and solve real-life organizational problems (Revans, 1980). As Smith (2001, p. 36) advocates, "we can only learn about [something] by doing it, and then thinking over carefully what happened, making sense of the lessons, and working through how the learning can be built on and used next time around." Examples of direct learning approaches to the study of leadership development not only include recent research on the role of experience in leadership development (e.g., DeRue & Wellman, 2009; Dragoni et al., 2009), but also studies investigating how individuals and groups develop leadership capacity through direct involvement in formal training programs.

Although most of the existing literature focuses on a direct mode of experience, there are several noteworthy exceptions that emphasize the developmental value of observational learning. For example, McCall and colleagues (1988) emphasized that "notable people" can be an important source of learning about leadership and management; in most cases, these notable people included bosses who were deviant from the norm, either as exceptional performers or shockingly poor performers. Likewise, in interviews with six directors of a European, multinational company, Kempster (2006) found that observational learning was an important source of leadership development, although interviewees had a difficult time immediately recognizing the value of these indirect or vicarious forms of learning. Based on this research, it is possible that indirect forms of experience are more valuable than what is actually recognized in practice, and future research needs to further investigate how vicarious and observational learning can augment and/or complement direct forms of developmental experience.

Content. The final dimension along which developmental experiences vary is with respect to their content. The interest in experience as a vehicle for learning dates back to ancient philosophy—for example, Aristotle's claim that "... for the things we have to learn before we can do them, we learn by doing them." However, it is not until recently that scholars have begun to develop a theory explaining how the content of lived experiences influences the developmental value of those experiences. In particular, experiences that present individuals with novel and ambiguous challenges force individuals to extend and refine their existing knowledge structures and skills (McCall et al., 1988). These different forms of challenge represent the content of experience.

For example, in a study of 692 managers from 5 large corporations and 1 governmental agency, McCauley and colleagues (1994) demonstrated that most development occurred in experiences consisting of significant job transitions (e.g., unfamiliar responsibilities), or task-related challenges such as creating change, managing large amounts of scope and scale, and/or influencing people without authority. Likewise, other studies exploring similar forms of experience content have linked these content dimensions to enhanced individual motivation and more creative decision making (Thompson, Hochwarter, & Mathys, 1997), as well as greater individual flexibility and adaptability (Campion, Cheraskin, & Stevens, 1994). Indeed, one reason scholars advocate the developmental value of international assignments is that the content of international assignments includes unfamiliar responsibilities, numerous task-related challenges, and a variety of challenges related to cultural diversity and assimilation (Caligiuri, 2006; McCall & Hollenbeck, 2002).

Beyond these positive content dimensions, scholars have also identified ways in which the content of experiences can detract from or impair leadership development outcomes. For example, in the same McCauley et al. (1994) study, experiences that were comprised of obstacles such as a difficult boss or a lack of top-management support detracted from individual learning. In addition, it is possible that the same content dimensions that promote learning and development can become overwhelming and impair learning. In their study, DeRue and Wellman (2009) showed that, when the content of an experience presents individuals with demands that far exceed their current capabilities, individuals get cognitively and emotionally overwhelmed, and as a result, leadership development suffers. From these studies, a number of interesting research questions emerge. For example, it is not clear when and why these particular types of challenges overwhelm individuals and detract from learning, as opposed to stretching employees in positive, developmental ways. One possible explanation is that people vary as to whether they see challenging experiences as having potential for growth and mastery, or the potential for personal harm or loss (Folkman & Lazarus, 1985), and these different orientations influence how people go through their experiences and ultimately what they gain from those experiences. Future research that investigates the personal and situational factors that explain these differences in orientation across different content dimensions would help organizations construct experiences and allocate people to experiences in ways that reduce perceptions of threat and enhance the perceived developmental value of experience. This research could also help address concerns over high rates of voluntary turnover after employees engage in challenging, on-the-job experiences such as expatriate assignments (Black, Gregersen, & Mendenhall, 1992).

Point of Intervention: Determining the Level of Analysis in Leadership Development

The current literature on leadership development spans across three levels of analysis. In particular, the point of intervention for leadership development initiatives can be at the individual level, the relational level, or the collective level. By a large margin, most of the existing research on leadership development is conducted at the individual level. In these studies, development is generally conceptualized as a positive change in the leadership capabilities of individuals, and there is a predominant focus on how individual attributes (e.g., KSAs, personality, prior experience) impact individual-level learning and development. For example, Mumford et al. (2000) examined how the ability, personality, and motivation of junior Army officers explain their leadership development, which in this case was operationalized as individual career success (i.e., reaching senior-level management positions). More recently, scholars have begun to examine how individuals vary in their readiness for leadership development (Avolio & Hannah, 2008), and these different levels of readiness are based on individual differences such as learning orientation, self-concept clarity, and efficacy beliefs. Indeed, several studies have empirically documented how different facets of developmental readiness can accelerate or accentuate learning in the context of developmental experiences. For instance, in a sample of 218 junior-level managers from a wide range of firms and industries, Dragoni et al. (2009) showed how learning orientation enhances the developmental value of individuals' on-the-job experiences. All of these examples portray leadership development in terms of individual-level abilities and performance.

Despite the value of understanding leadership development at the individual level, there are several reasons why our field needs to further extend the research on leadership development to relational and collective levels of analysis. First, leadership theory and research have widely adopted more relational and collective forms of leadership (e.g., Carson et al., 2007; Pearce & Conger, 2003), but the leadership development literature has yet to develop the conceptual or empirical knowledge base necessary for understanding how relational or collective forms of leadership develop. Second, organizations are shifting toward more collective forms of leadership development—for example, developing cohorts of managers or intact teams altogether (Conger & Benjamin, 1999)—but these decisions about how best to develop leadership talent lack a theoretical or empirical basis. Third, most research on leadership development draws on human learning theories that were developed to explain how individuals learn (e.g., Dewey, 1938; Knowles, 1970; Kolb, 1984), but it is not clear that these individual-level learning theories will be able to fully account for the group dynamics involved in relational or collective leadership development.

More recently, however, there is an emerging trend toward the study of relational and collective forms of leadership development. At the relational level, leadership development can be conceptualized as the emergence and development of leadership (leader-follower) relationships (DeRue & Ashford, 2010a). The origin of this perspective can be traced back to the initial work on leader-member exchange (LMX), where scholars explained how leader-follower relationships and structures are a function of interactional processes (Dienesch & Liden, 1986; Graen & Scandura, 1987). Although most of the subsequent LMX research focused on the effects of LMX rather than the development of these relationships, there are a few exceptions (Bauer & Green, 1996). For example, Nahrgang et al. (2009) examined the development of 330 leader-follower dyads over 8 weeks in the context of MBA-student teams. Their findings suggest that leaders and followers form initial perceptions of relationship quality based on different personality characteristics, but over time, both leaders and followers refine their perceptions of the leader-follower relationship based on the performance of their dyadic partner.

Beyond the relational level, there is also an emerging shift in the literature toward understanding how collective leadership structures emerge and develop over time (Mehra, Dixon, Brass & Robertson, 2006; Mehra, Smith, Dixon, & Robertson, 2006; Pearce & Conger, 2003; Sivasubramaniam et al., 2002). For example, Day, Gronn, and Salas (2004) theorize that collective or shared leadership in teams is a function of group dynamics and interactional processes, as opposed to the characteristics of individual team members. Providing empirical support for this idea, Carson et al. (2007) investigated the antecedents to shared leadership in 59 MBA-student consulting teams. The consulting teams were comprised of five to seven team members and worked with their corporate clients for five months. The results of the study emphasized three distinct antecedents to shared leadership in teams. Specifically, teams with a shared purpose, social support, and opportunities for participation and voice from all group members were much more likely to develop shared leadership structures than teams without these characteristics. These data suggest that the development of collective leadership structures is not simply a function of the aggregation of individuals' leadership attributes, but rather is a function of the social interactions among group members.

These studies of relational and collective leadership development mark an important change of direction in the study of leadership development—from a focus on individuals independent of any social context to the study of a contextualized and emergent leadership development process. Drawing from this perspective, new and interesting research questions emerge about the development of leadership in organizations. For example, research is needed to explain how the pattern of interactions among group members—for example, in terms of communication, conflict, or trust—influences the structural pattern of leadership that develops in the group. For questions about how group dynamics influence the emergence and development of relational or collective leadership, we expect applying models of group development (Kozlowski et al., 1996) to understand the evolution of leadership roles and networks of relationships will be especially constructive. This research will also need to parse out the influence of formal hierarchical structures from the informal relationships and patterns of interaction that emerge in the leadership development process. Furthermore, it is not yet clear what underlying mechanisms explain how different patterns of leadership relationships and structures emerge. On the one hand, leadership theories are often grounded in the concept of social exchange (e.g., Kellerl & Dansereaul, 1995), suggesting that leader-follower relationships develop as group members exchange resources (e.g., control, liking) for compliance or following direction. On the other hand, identity-based theories of leadership development (Day, Harrison, & Halpin, 2009; DeRue, 2011; DeRue & Ashford, 2010a) suggest that leadership relationships and structures develop as individuals, through interaction, socially negotiate meaning and reciprocal identities as leaders and followers. Research that empirically tests and documents these divergent explanatory mechanisms would significantly advance our field's understanding of how relational and collective forms of leadership develop in groups and organizations.

Architecture: Developing a Social and Organizational Context That Enables Leadership Development

We define architecture as the organizational practices, structures, and cultural factors that influence the leadership development process. Examples include practices such as feedback or reflection interventions that are designed to enhance employee learning from experience (Daudelin, 1996; Densten & Gray, 2001), structures such as on-boarding or job rotation policies that are intended to accelerate employee learning and development (Campion, Cheraskin, & Stevens, 1996; Conger & Fishel, 2007), and cultural factors such as an organizational climate for learning (Lim & Morris, 2006; Rouiller & Goldstein, 1993). In practice, it is often posited that these architectural features enhance employees' motivation for engaging in leadership development activities, their access to developmental opportunities, and their ability to learn from experience. Yet, though organizations increasingly invest in these architectures to support and enhance leadership development (Hernez-Broome & Hughes, 2004), the conceptual and empirical basis for these investments has historically been dubious. Recent studies, however, offer important insights about how these architectures can promote leadership development within organizations.

For example, the positive effect of coaching and mentoring on employee career development is well established (e.g., Kram, 1983; Levinson, Darrow, Klein, Levinson, & McKee, 1978 Ragins & Cotton, 1999; Seibert, 1999), but scholars are only beginning to examine the value of coaching and mentoring in leadership development (Hall, Otazo, & Hollenbeck, 1999; Ting & Hart, 2004). In their quasi-experimental study of 1361 senior managers in a global financial services company, Smither and colleagues (2003) provided all managers multisource feedback related to their performance. However, a subset of managers also worked with a coach to interpret the feedback results, link the feedback to the business plan, create a self-development plan, and use the feedback to solicit input from employees on how to improve their leadership performance. Managers who worked with a coach were more likely to set goals for their development, solicit ideas for improvement, and improve their performance based on ratings from their direct reports and supervisors.

Unfortunately, studies that examine coaching and/or mentoring in the context of management or leadership development are rare. In fact, in their meta-analysis of the management development literature, Collins and Holton (2004) could not identify enough studies on the role of mentoring or coaching to include these practices in their analysis. Relative to the frequency with which coaching and mentoring are used in practice for leadership development, there is a significant need for more theory development and empirical research on how personal, situational, and organizational factors explain how coaching and mentoring influence the leadership development process. For example, it is possible that coaching or mentoring can enable individuals or groups to more effectively learn from their experiences, but it is also possible that these practices can create a sense of dependency that detracts from employees engaging in self-development activities (Bushardt, Fretwell, & Holdnak, 1991; Kram, 1983; North, Johnson, Knotts, & Whelan, 2006). The current literature has only begun to unpack the mechanisms through which coaching and mentoring influence leadership development, and future research is needed to inform how individuals and organizations can fully realize the value of practices such as mentoring and coaching.

Beyond coaching and mentoring, there is also an emerging literature on the role of reflection in employee learning and development, and scholars are beginning to extend this feature of the organizational architecture to the context of leadership development. In field experiments with members of the Israel Defense Forces and in laboratory experiments with undergraduate students, Ellis and colleagues (Ellis & Davidi, 2005; Ellis, Ganzach, Castle, & Sekely, 2010; Ellis, Mendel, & Nir, 2006) have documented how structured reflection practices can enhance individuals' mental models of their experiences, promote more internal attributions for performance, and produce greater performance improvements than if employees are to process and reflect on their experiences without any formal structure or guidance. Likewise, Anseel and colleagues (2009) showed in both field and laboratory settings that reflection combined with feedback results in greater performance improvements than feedback alone. DeRue and colleagues (DeRue, Nahrgang, Hollenbeck, & Workman, 2012) have extended these findings to a leadership development context, where they show in a nine-month field experiment that structured reflection enhances leadership development for people who are conscientious, open to experience, emotionally stable, and have a rich base of prior developmental experiences.

Finally, after decades of research on how organizational climate and culture can influence learning at the individual, group, and organizational levels of analysis (Argyris, 1993; Edmondson, 1999; Hofmann & Stetzer, 1996; Rouiller & Goldstein, 1993; Weick, 1993), scholars are beginning to explore how organizational climate and culture influence leadership development. For example, international assignments are often used for leadership development purposes (Kohonen, 2005; Pucik & Saba, 1998), and in a study of 58 expatriates from 4 multinational firms, Lazarova and Caligiuri (2001) found that a climate of organizational support increases expatriate commitment to the organization and reduces turnover intentions. Similarly, in the context of a large, U.S.-based hospital, Tansky and Cohen (2001) found that a climate of organizational support enhanced the degree to which employees were satisfied with their opportunities for personal growth and career development. Altogether, these results suggest that building a culture that supports learning and development not only enhances employee learning, but also the likelihood that organizations' best leadership talent will be retained and continue to invest in the organization.

Reinforcement: Creating Positive Feedback Loops in Leadership Development

Leadership development is a dynamic and cyclical process of human growth and development (McCauley, Moxley, & Van Velsor, 1998; Van Velsor, Moxley, & Bunker, 2004). At individual, relational and group levels of analysis, the capacity for leadership develops in different ways, at different times, and at different rates—ultimately forming positive or negative feedback loops that, over time, emerge as different trajectories of development (Day et al., 2009; Day & Lance, 2004; Halpern, 2004). Historically, scholarly research has offered limited insight into these longitudinal patterns and trajectories of leadership development, but a recent special issue in *Leadership Quarterly* focused entirely on the topic (Riggio & Mumford, 2011). For example, in this issue, Day and Sin (2011) demonstrated in a sample of 1315 students from the Pacific Rim that an individual's leader identity predicts the rate of change in leadership effectiveness over time. Likewise, several articles in this issue establish empirically how aspects of individuals' childhood and adolescent experiences predict and explain their motivation to lead and leadership potential in adulthood (Gottfried et al., 2011; Oliver et al., 2011). Our hope is that studies such as these into the rate of growth and patterns of development are only the beginning of a shift in the field toward more longitudinal investigations of leadership development.

To help motivate research on reinforcement and feedback loops in the trajectories of leadership development, we highlight two issues that, based on recent theory in developmental psychology (Adolph, Robinson, Young, & Gill-Alvarez, 2008), should be important in explaining whether positive or negative developmental trajectories emerge in leadership development. The first issue is related to how developmental experiences are sequenced over time, while the second issue is concerned with the pace and timing of specific developmental experiences.

Theories of human development emphasize that the sequencing or temporal order of lived experiences is an important factor in explaining how much learning occurs from experience, what people learn, and whether those lessons are internalized or quickly forgotten (Riegel, 1976). Likewise, experiential learning theories describe a learning process where lessons are learned within experiences, but then those lessons are refined and internalized through experimentation, repetition, and reinforcement across experiences (Kolb, 1984). Drawing from these theoretical perspectives, we contend that the sequencing of developmental experiences will be an important consideration in leadership development.

Developmental experiences that reinforce and extend the lessons learned from prior experiences are the building blocks to a positive leadership development trajectory (DeRue & Workman, 2011). When learning is reinforced across developmental experiences, people are able to refine and internalize the lessons of experience in ways that are not possible within a single experience. Moreover, developmental experiences that are disconnected or do not reinforce the lessons of past experience can interrupt the development process, and it is possible that individuals could even regress and retreat back to old, ineffective habits and behaviors. Consistent with this perspective, research in cognitive psychology has empirically documented how reinforcing experiences enable individuals to recognize patterns across experiences, and as a result, more effectively recall the lessons of experience (Bechtel & Abrahamsen, 1991; Reed, 1972). Similarly, research on expertise suggests that people become experts in a particular domain through repetition over long periods of time and across many reinforcing developmental experiences (Ericsson & Charness, 1994; Ericsson & Lehmann, 1996). Unfortunately, the leadership development literature has yet to develop a theoretical or empirical basis for understanding how the sequence of experiences impacts leadership development. Most research on experience-based leadership development examines the developmental value of a single experience or job (e.g., DeRue & Wellman, 2009; Dragoni et al., 2009), and thus the optimal sequence of experiences remains a mystery. Whereas Ericsson's research (Ericsson & Charness, 1994; Ericsson & Lehmann, 1996) on expertise suggests sequencing experiences so that individuals are able to practice a particular skill repeatedly until it is perfected, leadership requires a complex constellation of skills, and the skills required for effective performance will ebb and flow with variability in situations (e.g., Mumford et al., 2000; Mumford et al., 2007). Indeed, some scholars have expressed concerns about too much repetition and suggested that employees should be rotated regularly to avoid the narrowing of their leadership skills (Hall, 2002). Thus, it is not clear that the principles of repetition and deliberate practice will generalize to leadership development where the skills requirements are more fluid, and future research that clarifies how developmental experiences should be sequenced will be particularly valuable.

In addition to the sequencing of developmental experiences, the timing of particular experiences will also be important for understanding the emergence of positive feedback loops and developmental trajectories. While sequencing refers to the order of potential developmental experience, issues of timing revolve around the pacing of developmental experiences, as well as the identification of particular moments in an individual's career that are more or less suited for development. In addition to an appropriate sequence of developmental challenges, individuals need sufficient time in each experience in order to maximize the learning and development that can be gleaned from the challenge (Gabarro, 1987; McCall et al., 1988). For example, Eisenhardt and Martin (2000) asserted that experience that comes too fast can overwhelm the individual, creating a barrier to their ability to capture their experience and shape it into meaningful learning. However, on the other end of the spectrum, Argote (1999) argued that infrequent experience can lead individuals to forget what was learned in the prior experience, hindering the ability to accumulate knowledge. These two perspectives suggest that organizations must seek to find an optimal balance, providing developmentally challenging experiences often enough to accumulate learning and knowledge, but not so often as to run into the problem of diminishing returns from an overwhelming amount of experience (e.g., DeRue &Wellman, 2009).

In addition to these questions of pace, research has explored the specific moments in an individual's career progression where developmental experiences are most suitable. Through interviews with representatives from 13 different organizations, Karaevli and Hall (2006) posit that variety of developmental experiences is particularly beneficial early in an individual's career. Specifically, they contend that developmental challenges at this early stage enable managers to establish their competence and an identity as a professional (Hall, 1976; Levinson et al., 1978). Likewise, research suggests that developmental challenge and variety in experience early in an individual's career enhances adaptability and openness to change, and enables individuals to develop more effectively later in their careers (Bunker & Webb, 1992; McCall, 1998). These insights highlight the long-term benefits that early-career challenges can have for leadership development.

Engagement: Learning to Learn Leadership

In his seminal article on organizational learning, de Geus (1988, p. 71) claimed that the "...only enduring source of competitive advantage is an organization's relative ability to learn faster than its competition." The same may very well be true for leadership development. Given the importance of learning from experience in leadership development (McCall, 2004; McCall et al., 1988; McCauley et al., 1994; Ohlott, 2004), both human resource professionals and scholars are turning their attention toward understanding what enables individuals and collectives to effectively learn from developmental experiences. In the current literature, concepts such as the ability to learn (Ohlott, 2004), learning agility (Lombardo & Eichinger, 2000), and mindful engagement (DeRue & Ashford, 2010b) all speak to the attributes, practices and strategies that enable individuals to effectively learn from their experiences. The common theme across these concepts is an assumption that learning from experience is, in part, a function of how individuals and collective engage in the experience.

For example, Lombardo and Eichinger (2000, p. 323) define learning agility as "the willingness and ability to learn from experience, and subsequently apply that learning to perform successfully under new or first-time conditions." The concept of learning agility is derived from insights about how individuals learn from and draw patterns across developmental experiences (McCall et al., 1988), as well as the literature on learning orientation (Dweck, 1986) and adaptive performance (Pulakos, Arad, Donovan, & Plamondon, 2000). Although conceptual development and empirical research on learning agility are in their infancy, some interesting insights are emerging from the current research (De Meuse, Dai, & Hallenbeck, 2010). In a series of studies using the CHOICES measure of learning agility, findings suggest that learning agility is empirically distinct from related concepts such as cognitive ability, goal orientation, and openness to experience, and that learning agility is associated with higher promotability and performance (Connolly & Viswesvaran, 2002; Eichinger & Lombardo, 2004). Building on these findings, our hope is that scholars will heed recent calls for further theory development and research on learning agility (DeRue, Ashford, & Myers, 2012), with the goal of understanding how the learning agility concept contributes to the field's understanding of how people learn leadership via experience.

In addition, scholars are beginning to identify the behavioral practices and strategies that people can employ as they engage in key developmental experiences. For example, in interviews with 100 senior pastors, McKenna, Boyd and Yost (2007) found that pastors engaged in a series of personal strategies that helped them navigate through and learn from their experiences. These strategies included adopting a learning orientation, relying on personal character and values, establishing and managing relationships, relying on their faith and calling, and using their expertise and knowledge. Similarly, DeRue and Ashford (2010b) outlined a set of practices that individuals can engage in to enhance the developmental value of experience, including approaching experiences with a learning orientation and specific goals for their development, engaging in active experimentation and feedback seeking during the experience, and systematically and critically reflecting on the successes and failures of any given experience.

These few studies on the ability to learn from experience are only the beginning. Indeed, much more research is needed on the antecedents to understanding the ability to learn from experience for both individuals and collectives. For example, there may be a range of cognitive abilities (e.g., practical intelligence, wisdom; Sternberg, 2007), or different sources of motivation for learning (e.g., extrinsic vs. intrinsic, self vs. other; DeRue & Myers, 2011), that explain why some people are more effective at learning from experience than others. In addition, research is needed to further develop, both conceptually and empirically, the behavioral practices and strategies that enable individuals and collectives to learn from experience. Thus far, the current literature has largely overlooked how the social context shapes the behaviors and practices that enable individuals and collectives to learn from experience, and research that develops a more contextually embedded model of ability to learn would be particularly helpful for advancing theories of experience-based leadership development. Indeed, this research could ultimately shift organizations' leadership selection, staffing and succession planning processes away from a singular focus on who has performed well in prior leadership roles, and expand these processes to consider who is better equipped to learn from future experiences that might require fundamentally different modes of leadership. As John Ryan (2009, p. 7), the president and CEO of The Center for Creative Leadership, stated: "To succeed in a world where our work is always changing, where challenges are unpredictable and competition abounds, we need to be agile learners."

Concluding Remarks: Key Insights and Next Steps

The scientific study of leadership enjoys a rich tradition of theoretical development and empirical research (Avolio, Walumbwa, & Weber, 2009;

Bass & Bass, 2008), but most of this research has emphasized the effects of leadership rather than the development of leadership. However, in the past two decades, scholars have developed a wealth of ideas and theories about how leadership capacity develops in organizational settings. In addition, working across a variety of organizational and cultural contexts, scholars have employed a diverse set of research methods to empirically examine the antecedents and processes associated with leadership development. Based on this research, a range of key insights have emerged. For instance, leadership development occurs primarily through action-based learning and experience, but not all experiences are equally developmental; and challenging assignments can be formal or informal, direct or indirect, and vary greatly in terms of their content. In addition, it is clear that leadership development is not simply about developing leadership knowledge and skills, but also about developing people's motivation to lead, their affect toward the rewards and risks associated with leadership, their identity as leaders, as well as their cognitive schemas about what it means to participate in a leadership process. Indeed, leadership development has become a topic of interest for scholars across a range of disciplines, and the diversity of theories and research emerging on leadership development is stimulating new and exciting ideas on the topic.

At the same time, however, a number of important knowledge gaps remain in the field's understanding of leadership development. Indeed, based on the present literature review, there are aspects of the PREPARE framework that lack the necessary theoretical or empirical grounding, and thus represent opportunities for future research. Herein, we review several of these knowledge gaps and explain how they provide a foundation for new and interesting research on leadership development.

An Agenda for Future Research

• Considering Multiple *Points of Intervention*: Integrating Leader and Leadership Development

Most research has focused on individual leaders as the point of intervention for leadership development, but based on the current literature, the process by which organizations develop leadership relationships and collective leadership structures remains an open question. Leader and leadership development have historically been treated as distinct concepts, but as Day (2000, p. 605) noted, the "preferred approach is to link leader development with leadership development such that the development of leadership transcends but does not replace the development of individual leaders." Instead of treating these concepts as independent, future research should provide a more integrative account of how leader and leadership development can be complementary in building the capacity for more effective leadership processes. In particular, an important research question is how organizations can develop effective leader-follower relationships and collective leadership structures, while also cultivating individuals who effectively participate in these leadership processes. The two concepts are interdependent and likely complementary.

• Aligning Strategy and *Purpose*: Syncing Leadership Development Efforts with Strategic Goals

Despite a wealth of theory and empirical research on the value of strategic alignment in HRM practices (Delery & Doty, 1996; Wright & McMahan, 1992), there is very little research on how leadership development can be effectively aligned with the strategic priorities of organizations, or what the value of that strategic alignment might be for organizations. For instance, research is needed to determine the appropriate balance between developmental experiences that align directly with an organization's goals or strategy and developmental experiences that are *not* aligned with strategy, but which may bring new insights and broaden an individual's perspective on leadership. Understanding the various mechanisms by which leadership development efforts can be shaped to both support and broaden organizational strategies will contribute significantly to the field's understanding of the organizational-level impact of leadership development.

• Unpacking Developmental *Engagement*: Understanding what Motivates and Triggers Leaders to Develop From Experiences

Though research has begun to explore some of the antecedents to learning from experience, this research has largely focused on individuals' cognitive abilities and behavioral approaches to learning, with much less attention paid to individuals' motivations for learning or the process by which these individuals come to recognize an experience as an opportunity for development. Indeed, individuals may be equally able to learn from experience, but may differ substantially in why they would be motivated to develop (i.e., they may have different motives for learning; DeRue & Myers, 2011), and this difference in the source of their motivation may lead to differing levels of engagement in a developmental experience. Likewise, certain events or situations may serve as "developmental triggers" (Avolio, 2004), focusing an individual's attention on the need for development. The current literature offers little insight into why some people can see an experience as an opportunity for learning (and thus a trigger for development), whereas other people may see that same experience as a problem or risk that needs to be solved or minimized. Future research that explores the consequences of individuals' motives for leadership development, and the anatomy of events that trigger a focus on learning, would be particularly helpful in advancing the field's understanding of leadership development in organizational contexts.

• Promoting *Reinforcement*: Considering Leadership Development as a Sequence of Developmental Experiences

In spite of considerable recognition that leadership development is a temporal and cyclical process, there is a dearth of research on how developmental experiences should be arranged over time, how these experiences can reinforce each other, how different trajectories of development emerge and evolve, or how the timing and pace of experiences affect development. Conceptualizing leaders' development in terms of the trajectory of development over time (e.g., steep, flat, linear, exponential) opens up a new set of questions about the nature of time and cumulative experience in the developmental process, which are only beginning to be explored in empirical research, and require researchers to develop new theories that specify the duration of change, the predictors of change, the form or pattern of change, and the level of change expected (Ployhart & Vandenberg, 2010). Drawing from exemplars such as Day and Sin's (2011) study of developmental trajectories, future research needs to unpack the temporal cycles and processes involved in leadership development.

To address these questions, scholars will need to employ a diverse range of research methods and approaches. At its core, leadership development is about change (in knowledge, skills, motivation, identity, process, structure, etc.); thus studying a leadership development process requires modeling change processes over time, whether it be at the individual, relational, or group level of analysis. Accordingly, scholars will need to carefully craft research designs, determining the number of measurement occasions and observations necessary for testing the proposed theory of development (i.e., change). In addition, these future research designs will need to either use experimental methods with a control group, or introduce the appropriate time lags between intervals to address issues of causality. Indeed, as our theories of leadership development advance and become more refined, our methods for studying leadership development will also need to advance and become more sophisticated. Our hope is that by acknowledging these opportunities for future research, the current chapter not only provides a substantive review of the current literature, but also serves as a source of inspiration and guidance as scholars seek to build and test new theories of leadership development.

References

Adler, S., & Mills, A. (2008). *Controlling leadership talent risk: An enterprise imperative*: Aon Consulting.

Adolph, K. E., Robinson, S. R., Young, J. W., & Gill-Alvarez, F. (2008). What is the shape of developmental change? *Psychological Review, 115*, 527–543.

Alimo-Metcalfe, B. (1998). 360 degree feedback and leadership development. *International Journal of Selection and Assessment, 6*(1), 35–44.

Alldredge, M. E., & Nilan, K. J. (2000). 3M's leadership competency model: An internally developed solution. *Human Resource Management, 39*(2/3), 133–146.

Anderson, S. M. & Cole, S. T. (1990). Do I know you? The role of significant others in general social perception. *Journal of Personality and Social Psychology, 59*(3), 384–399.

Anseel, F., Lievens, F., & Schollaert E. (2009). Reflection as a strategy to enhance task performance after feedback. *Organizational Behavior and Human Decision Processes, 110*, 23–35.

Aquino, K., & Reed, A. (2002). The self-importance of moral identity. *Journal of Personality and Social Psychology, 83*, 1423–1440.

Argote, L. (1999). *Organizational learning: Creating, retaining and transferring knowledge*. Norwell, MA: Kluwer.

Argyris, C. (1993). *Knowledge for action: A guide to overcoming barriers to organizational change*. San Francisco, CA: Jossey-Bass.

Atwater, L. E., Dionne, S. D., Avolio, B., Camobreco, J. F., & Lau, A. W. (1999). A longitudinal study of the leadership development process: Individual differences predicting leader effectiveness. *Human Relations, 52*, 1543–1562.

Avolio, B. J. (2004). Examining the Full Range Model of leadership: Looking back to transform forward. In D. V. Day, S. J. Zaccaro, & S. M. Halpin (Eds.), *Leader development for transforming organizations: Growing leaders for tomorrow* (pp. 71–98). Mahwah, NJ: Erlbaum & Associates.

Avolio, B. J. (2005). *Leadership development in balance: Made/Born*. Mahwah, NJ: Erlbaum & Associates.

Avolio, B. J. (2007). Promoting more integrative strategies for leadership theory-building. *American Psychologist, 62*, 25–33.

Avolio, B. J., & Hannah, S. T. (2008). Developmental readiness: Accelerating leader development. *Consulting Psychology Journal: Research and Practice, 60*, 331–347.

Avolio, B. J., Walumbwa, F. O., & Weber, T. J. (2009). Leadership: Current theories, research, and future directions. *Annual Review of Psychology, 60*, 421–449.
Bandura, A. (1986). *Social foundations of thought and action: A social cognitive theory*. Englewood Cliffs, NJ: Prentice-Hall.
Barbuto, J. E. Jr. (2005). Motivation and transactional, charismatic, and transformational leadership: A test of antecedents. *Journal of Leadership and Organizational Studies, 11*, 26–40.
Barling, J., Weber, T., & Kelloway, E. K. (1996). Effects of transformational leadership training on attitudinal and financial outcomes: A field experiment. *Journal of Applied Psychology 81*, 827–832.
Bass, B. M, & Bass, R. (2008). *The Bass handbook of leadership* (4th ed). New York: NY: Free Press.
Bauer, T. N., & Green, S. G. (1996). Development of leader member exchange: A longitudinal test. *Academy of Management Journal, 39*, 1538–1567.
Bechtel, W., & Abrahamsen, A. (1991). *Connectionism and the mind: An introduction to parallel processing in networks*. Cambridge, MA: Blackwell.
Bedeian, A. G., & Hunt, J. G. (2006). Academic amnesia and vestigial assumptions of our forefathers. *Leadership Quarterly, 17*(2), 190–205.
Belling, R., James, K., & Ladkin, D. (2004). Back to the workplace: How organisations can improve their support for management learning and development. *Journal of Management Development, 23*(3), 234–255.
Black, J. S., Gregersen, H. B., & Mendenhall, M. E. (1992). Toward a theoretical framework of repatriation adjustment. *Journal of International Business Studies, 23*(4), 737–760.
Bono, J. E., & Ilies, R. (2006). Charisma, positive emotions and mood contagion. *Leadership Quarterly, 17*, 317–334.
Boyce, L. A., Zaccaro, S. J., & Wisecarver, M. Z. (2010). Propensity for self-development of leadership attributes: Understanding, predicting, and supporting leader self-development performance. *Leadership Quarterly, 21*(1), 159–178.
Brungardt, C. (1997). The making of leaders: A review of the research in leadership development and education. *The Journal of Leadership Studies, 3*(3), 81–95.
Bunker, K. A., & Webb, A. D. (1992). *Learning how to learn from experience: Impact of stress and coping* (Tech. Rep. No. 154). Greensboro, NC: Center for Creative Leadership.
Burke, M. J., & Day, D. V. (1986). A cumulative study of the effectiveness of managerial training. *Journal of Applied Psychology, 71*, 232–245.
Bushardt, S. C., Fretwell, C., & Holdnak, B. J. (1991). The mentor/protege relationship: A biological perspective. *Human Relations, 44*(6), 619–639.
Caligiuri, P. (2006). Developing global leaders. *Human Resource Management Review, 16*(2), 219–228.
Campion, M. A., Cheraskin, L., & Stevens, M. S. (1994). Career-related antecedents and outcomes of job rotation. *Academy of Management Journal, 37*, 1518–1542.
Carson, J. B., Tesluk, P. E., & Marrone, J. A. (2007). Shared leadership in teams: An investigation of antecedent conditions and performance. *Academy of Management Journal, 50*, 1217–1234.
Chan, K. Y. & Drasgow, F. (2001). Toward a theory of individual differences and leadership: Understanding the motivation to lead. *Journal of Applied Psychology, 86*(3): 481–498.
Charan, R. (2007). *Leaders at all levels: Deepening your talent pool to solve the succession crisis*. San Francisco, CA: Jossey-Bass.
Chemers, M. M., Watson, C. B., & May, S. T. (2000). Dispositional affect and leadership effectiveness: A comparison of self-esteem, optimism, and efficacy. *Personality and Social Psychology Bulletin, 26*, 267–277.
Collins, D. B., & Holton, E. F. (2004). The effectiveness of managerial leadership development programs: A meta-analysis of studies from 1982 to 2001. *Human Resource Development Quarterly, 15*, 217–248.
Colvin, G. (2009). How to build great leaders [Electronic Version]. *Fortune* from http://money.cnn.com/2009/11/19/news/companies/leadership_companies_colvin.fortune/index.htm
Conger, J. A. (1993). The brave new world of leadership training. *Organizational Dynamics, 21*(3), 46–58.
Conger, J. A., & Benjamin, B. (1999). *Building leaders: How successful companies develop the next generation*. San Francisco, CA: Jossey-Bass.
Conger, J. A., & Fishel, B. (2007). Accelerating leadership performance at the top: Lessons from the Bank of America's executive on-boarding process. *Human Resource Management Review, 17*(4): 442–454.
Conger, J., & Toegel, G. (2003). Action learning and multi-rater feedback as leadership development interventions: Popular but poorly deployed. *Journal of Change Management, 3*(4), 332–348.
Connolly, J. A., & Viswesvaran, C. (2002). *Assessing the construct validity of a measure of learning agility*. Paper presented at the Annual Conference of the Society for Industrial and Organizational Psychology, Toronto.
Costa, P. T. Jr, & McCrae, R. R. (1994). Set like plaster: Evidence for the stability of adult personality. In T. F. Heatherton & J. L. Weinberger (Eds.), *Can personality change?* (pp. 21–40). Washington, DC: American Psychological Association.
Daft, R. L. (2008). *The leadership experience* (4th ed.). Mason, OH: Thomson South-Western.
Damen, F., van Knippenberg, B., & van Knippenberg, D. (2008). Affective match: Leader emotional displays, follower positive affect, and follower performance. *Journal of Applied Social Psychology, 38*, 868–902.
Daudelin, M. W. (1996). Learning from experience through reflection. *Organizational Dynamics, 24*(3): 36–48.
Davies, J., & Easterby-Smith, M. (1984). Learning and developing from managerial work experiences. *Journal of Management Studies, 21*(2): 169–183.
Day, D. V. (2000). Leadership development: A review in context. *Leadership Quarterly, 11*, 581–613.
Day, D. V., Gronn, P., & Salas, E. (2004). Leadership capacity in teams. *Leadership Quarterly, 15*(6), 857–880.
Day, D. V., & Halpin, S. M. (2004). Growing leaders for tomorrow: An introduction. In D. V. Day, S. J. Zacarro, & S. M. Halpin (Eds.), *Leader development for transforming organizations: Growing leaders for tomorrow* (pp. 3–22). Mahwah, NJ: Erlbaum & Associates.
Day, D. V., & Harrison, M. M. (2007). A multilevel, identity-based approach to leadership development. *Human Resource Management Review, 17*, 360–373.
Day, D. V., Harrison, M. M., & Halpin, S. M. (2009). *An integrative approach to leader development: Connecting adult development, identity, and expertise*. New York, NY: Psychology Press.
Day, D. V., & Sin, H. P. (2011). Longitudinal tests of an integrative model of leader development: Charting and understanding developmental trajectories. *Leadership Quarterly, 22*, 545–560.

De Geus, A. P. (1988). Planning as learning. *Harvard Business Review, 66*(2), 70–74.
Delery, J. E., & Doty, D. H. (1996). Modes of theorizing in strategic human resource management: Tests of universalistic, contingency, and configurational performance predictions. *Academy of Management Journal, 39*(4), 802–835.
Delery, J. E., & Doty, D. H. (1996). Modes of theorizing in strategic human resource management: Tests of universalistic, contingency, and configurational performance predictions. *Academy of Management Journal, 39*, 802–835.
De Meuse, K. P., Dai, G., & Hallenbeck, G. S. (2010). Learning agility: A construct whose time has come. *Consulting Psychology Journal: Practice and Research, 62*(2), 119–130.
Densten, I. L., & Gray, J. H. (2001). Leadership development and reflection: What is the connection? *International Journal of Educational Management, 15*(3), 119–124.
DeRue, D. S. (2011). Adaptive leadership theory: Leading and following as a complex adaptive process. *Research in Organizational Behavior, 31*, 125–150.
DeRue, D. S., & Ashford, S. J. (2010a). Who will lead and who will follow? A social process of leadership identity construction in organizations. *Academy of Management Review, 35*, 627–647.
DeRue, D. S., & Ashford, S. J. (2010b). Power to the people: Where has personal agency gone in leadership development? *Industrial and Organizational Psychology, 3*(1), 24–27.
DeRue, D. S., Ashford, S. J., & Cotton, N. C. (2009). Assuming the mantle: Unpacking the process by which individuals internalize a leader identity. In L. M. Roberts & J. E. Dutton (Eds.), *Exploring positive identities and organizations: Building a theoretical and research foundation* (pp. 217–236). New York, NY: Routledge.
DeRue, D. S., Ashford, S. J., & Myers, C. G. (2012). Learning agility: In search of conceptual clarity and theoretical grounding. *Industrial and Organizational Psychology, 5(3)*, 258–279.
DeRue, D. S., & Myers, C. G. (2011). *What is your motivation for learning? Cultural differences and the impact on leader development.* Paper presented at the 2011 Annual Meeting of the Academy of Management, San Antonio, TX.
DeRue, D. S., Nahrgang, J. D., Hollenbeck, J. R., & Workman, K. (2012). A quasi-experimental study of after-event reviews and leadership development. *Journal of Applied Psychology, 97(5)*, 997–1015.
DeRue, D. S., & Wellman, N. (2009). Developing leaders via experience: The role of developmental challenge, learning orientation, and feedback availability. *Journal of Applied Psychology, 94*, 859–875.
DeRue, D. S., & Workman, K. M. (2011). Toward a positive and dynamic theory of leadership development. In K. Cameron & G. Spreitzer (Eds.), *The Oxford handbook of positive organizational scholarship*. New York, NY: Oxford University Press.
DeRue, D. S., Sitkin, S. B., & Podolny, J. M. (2011). Teaching leadership-issues and insights. *Academy of Management Learning & Education, 10*, 369–372.
Dewey, J. (1938). *Experience and education*. New York, NY: Macmillan.
Dienesch, R. M., & Liden, R. C. (1986). Leader-member exchange model of leadership: A critique and further development. *Academy of Management Review, 11*, 618–634.
Dotlich, D. L., & Noel, J. L. (1998). *Action learning: How the world's top companies are recreating their leaders and themselves* (1st ed.). San Francisco, CA: Jossey-Bass.
Dragoni, L., Tesluk, P. E., Russell, J.E.A., & Oh, I. S. (2009). Understanding managerial development: Integrating developmental assignments, learning orientation, and access to developmental opportunities in predicting managerial competencies. *Academy of Management Journal, 52*, 731–743.
Drath, W. H., McCauley, C. D., Palus, C. J., Van Velsor, E., O'Connor, P., & McGuire, J. B. (2008). Direction, alignment, commitment: Toward a more integrative ontology of leadership. *The Leadership Quarterly, 19*(6), 635–653.
Dvir, T., Eden, D., Avolio, B. J., & Shamir, B. (2002). Impact of transformational leadership on follower development and performance: A field experiment. *Academy of Management Journal, 45*, 735–744.
Dweck, C. S. (1986). Motivational processes affecting learning. *American Psychologist, 41*(10), 1040–1048.
Edmondson, A. (1999). Psychological safety and learning behavior in work teams. *Administrative Science Quarterly, 44*, 350–383.
Eichinger, R. W., & Lombardo, M. M. (2004). Learning agility as a prime indicator of potential. *Human Resource Planning, 27*, 12–16.
Eisenhardt, K. M., & Martin, J. A. 2000. Dynamic capabilities: What are they? *Strategic Management Journal, 21*, 1105–1121.
Ellis, S., & Davidi, I. (2005). After-event reviews: Drawing lessons from successful and failed experience. *Journal of Applied Psychology, 90*(5), 857–871.
Ellis, S., Ganzach, Y., Castle, E., & Sekely, G. (2010). The effect of filmed versus personal after-event reviews on task performance: The mediating and moderating role of self-efficacy. *Journal of Applied Psychology, 95*, 122–131.
Ellis, S., Mendel, R., & Nir, M. (2006). Learning from successful and failed experience: The moderating role of kind of after-event review. *Journal of Applied Psychology, 91*, 669–680.
Epitropaki, O., & Martin, R. (2004). Implicit leadership theories in applied settings: Factor structure, generalizability and stability over time. *Journal of Applied Psychology, 89*, 293–310.
Ericsson, K. A., and Charness, N. (1994). Expert performance: Its structure and acquisition. *American Psychologist, 49*, 725–747.
Ericsson, K. A. & Lehmann, A. C. (1996). Expert and exceptional performance: Evidence of maximal adaptation to task constraints. *Annual Review of Psychology, 47*, 273–305.
Folkman, S., & Lazarus, R. S. (1985). If it changes it must be a process. Study of emotion and coping during three stages of a college examination. *Journal of Personality and Social Psychology, 48*, 150–170.
Fulmer, R. M. (1997). The evolving paradigm of leadership development. *Organizational Dynamics, 25*(4), 59–72.
Gentry, W., & Leslie, J. (2007). Competencies for leadership development: What's hot and what's not when assessing leadership—Implications for organizational development. *Organizational Development Journal, 25*(1), 37–46.
George, J. M. (2000). Emotions and leadership: The role of emotional intelligence. *Human Relations, 53*(8): 1027–1055.
Gilpin-Jackson, Y., & Bushe, G. R. (2007). Leadership development training transfer: A case study of post-training determinants. *Journal of Management Development, 26*(10): 980–1004.
Gottfried, A. E., Gottfried, A. W., Reichard, R. J., Guerin, D. W., Oliver, P. H., & Riggio, R. E. (2011). Motivational roots of leadership: A longitudinal study from childhood through adulthood. *Leadership Quarterly, 22*(3), 510–519.

Graen, G. B., & Scandura, T. (1987). Toward a psychology of dyadic organizing. In B. Staw & L. L. Cumming (Eds.), *Research in organizational behavior* (vol. 9, pp. 175–208). Greenwich, CT: JAI Press.

Hall, D. T. (1976). *Careers in organizations*. Pacific Palisades, CA. Goodyear Publishing.

Hall, D. T. (2002). *Careers in and out of organizations*. Thousands Oak, CA: Sage Publications.

Hall, D. T. (2004). Self-awareness, identity, and leader development. In D. V. Day, S. J. Zaccaro, & S. M. Halpin (Eds.), *Leader development for transforming organizations* (pp. 153–176). Mahwah, NJ: Erlbaum & Associates.

Hall, D. T., Otazo, K. L., & Hollenbeck, G. P. (1999). Behind closed doors: What really happens in executive coaching. *Organizational Dynamics, 29*(Winter), 39–53.

Heifetz, R. A., & Linsky, M. (2002). *Leadership on the line: Staying alive through the dangers of leading*. Boston, MA: Harvard Business School Press.

Hernez-Broome, G., & Hughes, R. L. (2004). Leadership development: Past, present, and future. *Human Resource Planning, 27*, 24–32.

Hewitt Associates. (2009). *Top companies for leaders for 2009* [Electronic Version] from https://rblip.s3.amazonaws.com/Articles/TCFL-%20Research%20Highlights.pdf

Hinrichs, A. T., Carson, J. B., Li, N., & Porter, C.O.L.H. (2011). *Orientation toward leadership: A study of leadership beliefs and leader emergence in teams*. Paper presented at the 2011 Annual Meeting of the Academy of Management, San Antonio, TX.

Hirst, G., Mann, L., Bain, P., Pirola-Merlo, A., & Richver, A. (2004). Learning to lead: The development and testing of a model of leadership learning. *Leadership Quarterly, 15*, 311–327.

Hofmann, D. A., & Stetzer, A. (1996). A cross level investigation of factors influencing unsafe behavior and accidents. *Personnel Psychology, 49*, 307–339.

Holmberg, I., & Åkerblom, S. (2001). The production of outstanding leadership—An analysis of leadership images expressed in Swedish media. *Scandinavian Journal of Management, 1*(17), 67–85.

House, R., Javidan, M., Hanges, P., & Dorfman, P. (2002). Understanding cultures and implicit leadership theories across the globe: An introduction to project GLOBE. *Journal of World Business, 37*, 3–10.

Howard, A., & Wellins, R. S. (2009). *Global leadership forecast: Overcoming the shortfalls in developing leaders*. Pittsburgh, PA: Development Dimensions International.

Hulin, C. L., Henry, R. A., & Noon, S. L. (1990). Adding a dimension: Time as a factor in the generalizability of predictive relationships. *Psychological Bulletin, 107*, 328–340.

Ibarra, H. (1999). Provisional selves: Experimenting with image and identity in professional adaptation. *Administrative Science Quarterly, 44*, 764–791.

Ilies, R., Judge, T., & Wagner, D. (2006). Making sense of motivational leadership: The trail from transformational leaders to motivated followers. *Journal of Leadership and Organizational Studies, 13*(1), 1–22.

Intagliata, J., Smallwood, N., & Ulrich, D. (2000). Leveraging leadership competencies to produce leadership brand: Creating distinctiveness by focusing on strategy and results. *Human Resource Planning, 23*, 12–23.

Karaevli, A., & Hall, D. T. T. (2006). How career variety promotes the adaptability of managers: A theoretical model. *Journal of Vocational Behavior, 69*(3), 359–373.

Kark, R., & Van Dijk, D. (2007). Motivation to lead, motivation to follow: The role of the self-regulatory focus in leadership processes. *Academy of Management Review, 32*, 500–528.

Keller, T. (2003). Parental images as a guide to leadership sensemaking: An attachment perspective on implicit leadership theories. *Leadership Quarterly, 14*, 141–160.

Kempster, S. (2006). Leadership learning through lived experience: A process of apprenticeship? *Journal of Management & Organization, 12*(1): 4–22.

Knowles, M. (1970). *The modern practice of adult education: Andragogy versus pedagogy*. New York, NY: Associated Press.

Kohonen, E. (2005). Developing global leaders through international assignments: An identity construction perspective. *Personnel Review, 34*(1), 22–36.

Kolb, D. A. (1984). *Experiential learning: Experience as the source of learning and development*. Englewood Cliffs, NJ: Prentice-Hall.

Kozlowski, S. W. J., Gully, S. M., McHugh, P. P., Salas, E., & Cannon-Bowers, J. A. (1996). A dynamic theory of leadership and team effectiveness: Developmental and task contingent leader roles. In G. R. Ferris (Ed.), *Research in personnel and human resource management* (vol. 14, pp. 253–305). Greenwich, CT: JAI.

Kram, K. E. (1983). Phases of the mentor relationship. *Academy of Management Journal, 26*, 608–625.

Kreiner, G. E., Hollensbe, E. C., & Sheep M. L. (2006). Where is the "me" among the "we"? Identity work and the search for optimal balance. *Academy of Management Journal, 49*, 1031–1057.

Lazarova, M., & Caligiuri, P. (2001). Retaining repatriates: The role of organizational support practices. *Journal of World Business, 36*, 389–402.

Levinson, D. J., Darrow, C. N., Klein, E. B., Levinson, M. A., & McKee, B. (1978). *Seasons of a man's life*. New York, NY: Knopf.

Lim, D. H., & Morris, M. L. (2006). Influence of trainee characteristics, instructional satisfaction, and organizational climate on perceived learning and transfer training. *Human Resource Development Quarterly, 17*, 85–115.

Lombardo, M. M., & Eichinger, R. W. (2000). High potentials as high learners. *Human Resource Management, 39*, 321–330.

Lord, R. G., & Hall, R. J. (2005). Identity, deep structure and the development of leadership skill. *Leadership Quarterly, 16*, 561–615.

Lord, R. G., Brown, D. J., Harvey, J. L., & Hall, R. J. (2001). Contextual constraints on prototype generation and their multilevel consequences for leadership perceptions. *Leadership Quarterly, 12*, 311–338.

Lord, R. G., Foti, R. J., & De Vader, C. L. (1984). A test of leadership categorization theory: Internal structure, information processing, and leadership perceptions. *Organizational Behavior and Human Performance, 34*, 343–378.

Mayer, D., Kuenzi, M., Greenbaum, M., Bardes, R., & Salvador, M. R. (2009). How low does ethical leadership flow? Test of a trickle-down model. *Organizational Behavior and Human Decision Processes, 108*, 1–13.

Mayer, J. D., Salovey, P., Caruso, D. L., & Sitarenios, G. (2001). Emotional intelligence as a standard intelligence. *Emotion, 1*, 232–242.

McAlearney, A. S. (2006). Leadership development in healthcare: A qualitative study. *Journal of Organizational Behavior, 27*(7), 967–982.

McCall, M. W. (1998). *High flyers: Developing the next generation of leaders*. Boston, MA: Harvard Business School Press.

McCall, M. W. (2004). Leadership development through experience. *Academy of Management Executive, 18*, 127–130.

McCall, M. W. (2010). Recasting leadership development. *Industrial and Organizational Psychology, 3*, 3–19.

McCall, M. W., & Hollenbeck, G. P. (2002). *Developing global executives: The lessons of international experience*. Boston, MA: Harvard Business School Press.

McCall, M. W., Lombardo, M. M., & Morrison, A. M. (1988). *The lessons of experience: How successful executives develop on the job*. Lexington, MA: Lexington Books.

McCauley, C. D. (2008). Leader development: A review of research. *Center for Creative Leadership*. Online at shrm.org

McCauley, C. D., Moxley, R. S., & Van Velsor, E. (Eds.). (1998). *The Center for Creative Leadership handbook of leadership development*. San Francisco, CA: Jossey-Bass.

McCauley, C. D., Ruderman, M. N., Ohlott, P. J., & Morrow, J. E. (1994). Assessing the developmental components of managerial jobs. *Journal of Applied Psychology, 79*, 544–560.

McKenna, R. B., Boyd, T. N., & Yost, P. R. (2007). Learning agility in clergy: Understanding the personal strategies and situational factors that enable pastors to learn from experience. *Journal of Psychology and Theology, 35*(3), 179–189.

Mehra, A., Dixon, A. L., Brass, D. J., & Robertson, B. (2006). The social network ties of group leaders: Implications for group performance and leadership reputation. *Organization Science, 17*, 64–79.

Mehra, A., Smith, B. R., Dixon, A. L., & Robertson, B. (2006). Distributed leadership in teams: The network of leadership perceptions and team performance. *Leadership Quarterly, 17*(3): 232–245.

Mintzberg H., & Waters, J. (1982). Tracking strategy in an entrepreneurial firm. *Academy of Management Journal, 25*, 465–499.

Morgeson, F. P., DeRue, D. S, & Karam, E. (2010). Leadership in teams: A functional approach to understanding leadership structures and processes. *Journal of Management, 36*, 5–39.

Morrison, R. F., & Hock, R. R. (1986). Career building: Learning from cumulative work experiences. In D. T. Hall & Associates (Eds.), *Career development in organizations* (pp. 236–273). San Francisco, CA: Jossey-Bass.

Mumford, A. (1980). *Making experience pay*. Berkshire, UK: McGraw-Hill.

Mumford, M. D., Zaccaro, S. J., Harding, F. D., Jacobs, T. O., & Fleishman, E. A. (2000). Leadership skills for a changing world: Solving complex social problems. *Leadership Quarterly, 11*, 11–35.

Mumford, T. V., Campion, M. A., & Morgeson, F. P. (2007). The leadership skills strataplex: Leadership skill requirements across organizational levels. *Leadership Quarterly, 18*, 154–166.

Murphy, H. J., & Young, J. D. (1995). Management self-development and small business: Exploring emergent issues. *Management Learning, 26*(3), 319–330.

Nadler, D., & Tushman, M. (1980). A model for diagnosing organizational behavior: Applying a congruence perspective. *Organizational Dynamics, 9*(3), 35–51.

Nahrgang, J. D., Morgeson, F. P., & Ilies, R. (2009). The development of leader-member exchanges: Exploring how personality and performance influence leader and member relationships over time. *Organizational Behavior and Human Decision Processes, 108*, 256–266.

North, A., Johnson, J., Knotts, K., & Whelan, L. (2006). Ground instability with mentoring. *Nursing Management*, 16–17.

O'Leonard, K. (2010). *The corporate learning factbook 2009: Benchmarks, trends and analysis of the U.S. Training Market*. Oakland, CA: Bersin & Associates.

Ohlott, P. J. (2004). Job assignments. In C. McCauley & E. V. Velsor (Eds.), *The Center for Creative Leadership handbook of leadership development* (2nd ed., pp. 151–182). San Francisco, CA: Jossey-Bass.

Oliver, P. H., Gottfried, A. W., Guerin, D. W., Gottfried, A. E., Reichard, R. J., & Riggio, R. E. (2011). Adolescent family environmental antecedents to transformational leadership potential: A longitudinal mediational analysis. *Leadership Quarterly, 22*(3), 535–544.

Pearce, C. L. (2007). The future of leadership development: The importance of identity, multi-level approaches, self-leadership, physical fitness, shared leadership, networking, creativity, emotions, spirituality and on-boarding processes. *Human Resource Management Review, 17*, 355–359.

Pearce, C. L., & Conger, J. A. (2003). *Shared leadership: Reframing the hows and whys of leadership*. Thousand Oaks, CA: Sage.

Peterson, R. S., Smith, D. B., Martorana, P. V., & Owens, P. D. (2003). The impact of chief executive officer personality on top management team dynamics. *Journal of Applied Psychology, 88*, 795–808.

Peterson, S. J., Walumbwa, F. O., Byron, K, & Myrowitz, J. (2009). CEO positive psychological traits, transformational leadership, and firm performance in high-technology start-up and established firms. *Journal of Management, 35*, 348–368.

Ployhart, R. E., & Vandenberg, R. J. (2010). Longitudinal research: The theory, design, and analysis of change. *Journal of Management, 36*, 94–120.

Prati, L., Ferris, D. C., Ammeter, A. P., & Buckley, M. R. (2003). Emotional intelligence, leadership effectiveness, and team outcomes. *International Journal of Organizational Analysis, 11*, 21–40.

Pucik, V., & Saba, T. (1998). Selecting and developing the global versus the expatriate manager: A review of the state-of-the-art. *Human Resource Planning, 21*(4), 40–53.

Pulakos, E. D., Arad, S., Donovan, M. A., & Plamondon, K. E. (2000). Adaptability in the workplace: Development of a taxonomy of adaptive performance. *Journal of Applied Psychology, 85*(4), 612–624.

Quinn, R. E. (1996). *Deep change: Discovering the leader within*. San Francisco, CA: Jossey-Bass.

Ragins, B. R., & Cotton, J. L. (1999). Mentor functions and outcomes: A comparison of men and women in formal and informal mentoring relationships. *Journal of Applied Psychology, 84*, 529–550.

Reed, S. K. (1972). Pattern recognition and categorization. *Cognitive Psychology, 3*, 382–407.

Revans, R. W. (1980). *Action learning: New techniques for management*. London: Blond & Briggs.

Riegel, K. F. (1976). The dialectics of human development. *American Psychologist, 31*, 689–700.

Riggio, R. E. (2008). Leadership development: The current state and future expectations. *Consulting Psychology Journal: Practice and Research, 60*(4), 383–392.

Riggio, R. E., & Mumford, M. D. (2011). Introduction to the special issue: Longitudinal studies of leadership development. *Leadership Quarterly, 22*, 453–456.

Robinson, G., & Wick, C. (1992). Executive development that makes a business difference. *Human Resource Planning, 15*(1), 63–76.

Rouiller, J. Z., & Goldstein, I. L. (1993). The relationship between organizational transfer climate and positive transfer of training. *Human Resources Development Quarterly, 4*, 377–390.

Rush, M. C, Thomas, J. C., & Lord, R. L. (1977). Implicit leadership theory: A potential threat to the internal validity of leader behavior questionnaires. *Organizational Behavior and Human Performance, 20*, 92–110.

Ryan, J. R. (2009). *Accelerating performance: Five leadership skills you and your organization can't do without.* Greensboro, NC: Center for Creative Leadership.

Saks, A., & Belcourt, M. (2006). An investigation of training activities and transfer of training in organizations. *Human Resources Management, 45*(4), 629–648.

Schuler, R. S., & Jackson, S. E. (1987). Linking competitive strategies with human resource management practices. *Academy of Management Executive, 1*(3), 207–219.

Schwartz, S. H. (1994). Are there universal aspects in the structure and contents of human values? *Journal of Social Issues, 50*(4), 19–46.

Seibert, S. (1999). The effectiveness of facilitated mentoring: A longitudinal quasi-experiment. *Journal of Vocational Behavior, 54*, 483–502.

Shamir, B., & Eilam, G. (2005). What's your story?: A life-stories approach to authentic leadership development. *Leadership Quarterly, 16*, 395–417.

Shefy, E., & Sadler-Smith, E. (2006). Applying holistic principles in management development. *Journal of Management Development, 25*(4), 368–385.

Sivasubramaniam, N., Murry, W. D., Avolio, B. J., & Jung, D. I. (2002). A longitudinal model of the effects of team leadership and group potency on group performance. *Group & Organization Management, 27*, 66–96.

Smith, P. A. C. (2001). Action learning and reflective practice in project environments that are related to leadership development. *Management Learning, 32*(1): 31–48.

Smither, J. W., London, M., Flautt, R., Vargas, Y., & Kucine, I. (2003). Can working with an executive coach improve multisource feedback ratings over time? A quasi-experimental study. *Personnel Psychology, 56*, 23–44.

Sternberg, R. J. (2007). A systems model of leadership—WICS. *American Psychologist, 62*(1), 34–42.

Tansky, J., & Cohen, D. (2001). The relationship between organizational support, employee development, and organizational commitment: An empirical study. *Human Resource Development Quarterly, 12*, 285–300.

Thomas, A. B. (1988). Does leadership make a difference in organizational performance? *Administrative Science Quarterly, 33*, 388–400.

Thompson, K. R., Hochwarter, W. A., & Mathys, N. J. (1997). Stretch targets: What makes them effective? *The Academy of Management Executive, 11*(3), 48–60.

Ting, S., & Hart, E. W. (2004). Formal coaching. In C. D. McCauley & E. Van Velsor (Eds.), *The Center for Creative Leadership handbook of leadership development* (pp. 116–150). San Francisco, CA: John Wiley & Sons

Ting, S., & Scisco, P. (Eds.) (2006). *The Center for Creative Leadership handbook of coaching: A guide for the leader coach.* San Francisco, CA: Jossey-Bass.

Umble, K., Steffen, D., Porter, J., Miller, D., Hummer-McLaughlin, K., Lowman, A., Zelt, S. (2005). The National Public Health Leadership Institute: Evaluation of a team-based approach to developing collaborative public health leaders. *American Journal of Public Health, 95*(4), 641–644.

Van Velsor, E., & Drath, W. H. (2004). A lifelong developmental perspective on leader development. In C. D. McCauley & E. Van Velsor (Eds.), *The Center for Creative Leadership handbook of leadership development* (pp. 383–414). San Francisco, CA: Jossey-Bass.

Van Velsor, E., McCauley, C. D., & Ruderman, M. N. (2010). *The Center for Creative Leadership handbook of leadership development.* San Francisco, CA: Jossey-Bass.

Van Velsor, E., Moxley, R. S., & Bunker, K. A. (2004). The leadership development process. In C. McCauley & E. Van Velsor (Eds.), *The Center for Creative Leadership handbook of leadership development* (2nd ed., pp. 204–233). San Francisco, CA: Jossey-Bass.

Venkatraman, N. (1989). The concept of fit in strategy research: Toward a verbal and statistical correspondence. *Academy of Management Review, 14*, 423–444.

Waldman, D. A., Ramirez, G. G., House, R. J., & Puranam, P. (2001). Does leadership matter? CEO leadership attributes and profitability under conditions of perceived environmental uncertainty. *Academy of Management Journal, 44*, 134–143.

Weick, K. E. (1993). The collapse of sensemaking in organizations: The Mann Gulch disaster. *Administrative Science Quarterly, 38*, 628–652.

Weiss, H. M., & Cropanzano, R. (1996). Affective events theory: A theoretical discussion of the structure, causes and consequences of affective experiences at work. In B. M. Staw & L. L. Cummings (Eds.), *Research in organization behavior: An annual series of analytical essays and critical reviews* (vol. 18, pp. 1–74). Greenwich, CT: JAI.

Wellman, N., Ashford, S. J., DeRue, D. S., & Sanchez-Burks, J. (2011). *To lead or not to lead? The impact of alternative leadership-structure schemas on leadership behavior.* Paper presented at the 2011 Annual Meeting of the Academy of Management, San Antonio, TX.

Wick, C. W. (1989). How people develop: An in-depth look. *HR Report, 6*(1), 1–3.

Wright, P. M., & McMahan, G. C. (1992). Theoretical perspectives for strategic human resource management. *Journal of Management, 18*(2), 295–320.

Wright, P. M., & Snell, S. A. (1998). Toward a unifying framework for exploring fit and flexibility in strategic human resource management. *Academy of Management Review, 23*, 756–772.

Yammarino, F. J., & Atwater, L. E. (1993). Understanding self-perception accuracy: Implications for human resource management. *Human Resource Management, 32*, 231-247.

Youndt, M. A., Snell, S. A., Dean, J. W. Jr., & Lepak, D. P. (1996). Human resource management, manufacturing strategy, and firm performance. *Academy of Management Journal, 39*, 836–866.

Yukl, G. (2010). *Leadership in organizations* (7th ed.). Upper Saddle River, NJ: Prentice Hall.

Zenger, J., Ulrich, D., & Smallwood, N. (2000). The new leadership development. *Training and Development, 54*(3), 22.

PART 9

Future of Leadership

CHAPTER

38 The Future of Leadership: Challenges and Prospects

David V. Day

Abstract

This concluding handbook chapter addresses the future of leadership from a scholarly research and theory perspective. Challenges or shortcomings in the leadership field pertaining to construct redundancy, mediators and moderators, multidimensionality and higher order factors, and leadership questionnaires are discussed. Turning to the future of leadership, issues pertaining to leadership theory (construct definitions, process models, development, and time) and leadership methods (causality and temporal design issues) are addressed. By embracing better theory and more rigorous methods, the future of leadership appears to be very bright.

Key Words: leadership, constructs, mediators, moderators, multidimensionality, leadership questionnaires, causality, leader development, process models, temporal design, intensive longitudinal data

This final handbook chapter addresses the future of leadership from a scholarly research and theory perspective. In that spirit, I hope to be more forward looking than backward looking in my comments and observations. Therefore, this will not attempt to be a summary of all of the ideas and topics presented in the previous chapters. Instead, I first comment on some of the challenges or shortcomings in the leadership field as I see them. Although there are a great many positive features associated with the present state of leadership theory and research (much of which is presented in this handbook), there are also some distinct challenges for the future.

It is evident from the many different perspectives on leadership represented in this handbook that it is a diverse and varied field. In some ways, this makes the field appear unorganized or, as some of have called it, "curiously unformed" (Hackman & Wageman, 2007, p. 43). Nonetheless, it is a basic tenet of systems theory that differentiation always precedes integration (Gharajedaghi, 1999; Katz & Kahn, 1978). Considering the field of leadership as one type of system—as we should—we see a great deal of differentiation and relatively little integration. Thus, one way forward is to work toward greater integration and synthesis across these various topics in the field to provide a more cohesive and integrated leadership science for the future. This is a commendable overarching objective, but there are a number of underlying issues that need to be addressed before a meaningful systems perspective on leadership can be developed. Some of these additional challenges are addressed in the next section.

Challenges to the Present State of Leadership Research and Theory

Construct Redundancy

Something that we can say with certainty is that leadership matters in terms of shaping individual, team, and organizational outcomes. It is also the case that individual leaders matter. It is less clear what particular skills and competencies are needed to be effective as a leader and how these vary across different contexts. Related to this gap in our understanding is a tendency to reinvent the wheel in some ways with regard to various leadership styles or functions. For example, there is a very large literature on transformational leadership theory demonstrating that it is related to a variety of outcomes (see Bass & Riggio, 2006). But there are also emerging literatures on related styles pertaining to authentic leadership, ethical leadership, and servant leadership, among others. A pertinent question is how these various styles differ from transformational leadership and differ from each other theoretically and empirically. Although there is some literature suggesting incremental contributions of something like servant leadership above and beyond what can be explained by transformational leadership and leader–member exchange (LMX) (Liden, Wayne, Zhao, & Henderson, 2008), this has been the exception rather than the rule. The potential concern is that by simply placing a new but related leadership construct into a conceptual framework in which another construct has already demonstrated empirical relationships, we may not be learning much that is new about the content or consequences of leadership.

On Moderators and Mediators

The various approaches of transformational, authentic, ethical, and servant leadership all have a conceptual foundation in what might be called a universal style of leadership. An approach such as transformational leadership is thought to be a preferred leadership orientation or "style" pretty much regardless of culture or context. But what has emerged in the guise of theoretical advances in these approaches is to hypothesize and test specific kinds of moderators of the effects of leadership on relevant outcomes, sometimes through the hypothesized effects of mediators. Whereas developments in conceptualizing and testing sophisticated models, such as those dealing with mediated moderation or moderated mediation (Edwards & Lambert, 2007; Preacher, Rucker, & Hayes, 2007; Zyphur, Barsky, & Zhang, 2012), are commendable in terms of incorporating varied influences associated with leadership, there are also some potential risks that have not been discussed widely in the literature.

If a model is proposed in which a contextual factor is hypothesized to moderate the relationship between a universal leadership construct and a mediator or outcome, this is essentially proposing a contingency model of leadership that was originally conceptualized as universal. No doubt this development is due in part to the publish-or-perish reality of academic careers and the corresponding pressure to more finely mince a particular topic; however, this is a slippery slope of sorts in terms of reconceptualizing these various leadership approaches in ways that were not intended originally (and without acknowledging the theoretical implications). There are also concerns about just how much meaningful incremental variance can be explained by adding moderators to existing leadership models. Mediators have the advantage of potentially explaining how, in a causal fashion, leadership effects ultimately shape relevant outcomes; however, most of these studies are conducted in a cross-sectional manner. Little if any kind of causal inference can be drawn from such cross-sectional designs—with or without mediators (Smith, 2012).

I am not arguing that we must have greater simplification in our leadership theories and models. Rather, what I am suggesting is that there a good deal of potential redundancy in what is proposed and tested, and some of what is being tested is inherently inconsistent with how it was developed theoretically. It is also the case that there is too much piecemeal theory and research in the leadership field. An example of this can be found once again in various mediation models of leadership. A typical example is when one set of researchers proposes and tests a particular mediator of the relationship between a particular form of leadership and organizational outcomes and another set of researchers proposes and tests a different mediator of the same relationship, ignoring what has already been established. Again, to what extent does this enhance our understanding of leadership? That is not at all clear. The focal question at hand is whether this second mediator would provide any additional insights into the causes or consequences of leadership if the first mediator had also been considered in the model. Unfortunately, this is something that too few researchers consider.

Multidimensionality

Another disconcerting trend in the leadership literature is when multidimensional or multifaceted leadership constructs (as theorized) are rolled up into a second-order higher level factor using the various dimensions as construct indicators. This is usually based on confirmatory factor analysis results indicating an acceptably fitting higher order factor. Unfortunately, this practice is creating a significant (and serious) disconnection between leadership theory and tests of that theory. It is important to keep in mind that transformational leadership was originally conceptualized in terms of four different factors (i.e., idealized influence, inspirational motivation, individualized consideration, and intellectual stimulation; Bass & Riggio, 2006) or as many as nine different factors (Antonakis, Avolio, & Sivasubramaniam, 2003); authentic leadership was proposed as composed of four unique factors (i.e., self-awareness, relational transparency, internalized moral perspective, and balanced processing; Walumba, Avolio, Gardner, Wernsing, & Peterson, 2008); and servant leadership comprises seven factors (i.e., putting subordinates first, helping subordinates grow and succeed, empowering, emotional healing, creating value for the community, behaving ethically, and conceptual skills; Liden et al., 2008).

A potential problem occurs if a particular leadership construct is conceptualized theoretically to be multidimensional; it then makes little sense to combine it into a single factor, regardless of what is suggested empirically. Put bluntly: is it a multidimensional construct or not? Of course, engaging in this second-order construct modeling practice makes sense pragmatically because it is easier to include a single-order construct in a structural model than a multifaceted construct. But pragmatics aside, it is not good measurement practice or good science. It is also the case that what is proposed as a multidimensional construct morphs into a second-order construct with the various dimensions used as first-order indicators. This makes it essentially no different from a construct with individual item indicators, given that the dimensions are averages of the scale items. This strikes me as serious misunderstanding on the part of researchers who engage in such practices in terms of the meaning and appropriate use of higher-order constructs (see Johnson, Rosen, & Chang, 2011; Johnson, Rosen, Chang, Djurdjevic, & Taing, 2012, for additonal discussion and recommendations on the practice of high-order construct modeling).

Counter-arguments to this noted concern may claim that since confirmatory factor analytic results suggest that if the factors all hang together as indicators of a second-order construct, then it is appropriate to model it as such. That is not a compelling argument. One reason that the factors might all intercorrelate at a very high level is because of common source method bias (Johnson, Rosen, & Djurdjevic, 2011). It also assumes that the higher order construct *causes* its facet indicators, which simply does not pass the sniff test for something like authentic leadership. Specifically, it is unclear how authentic leadership could cause something like internalized moral perspective or balanced processing. It seems much more likely that these are not effects indicators of a reflective construct but causal indicators of formative construct (see Avolio & Walumbwa, this volume, for a counter-explanation). That is, self-awareness, relational transparency, internalized moral perspective, and balanced processing combine to form authentic leadership; authentic leadership does not cause any of those particular facets or dimensions.

In short, all of the theoretical work done to develop these and other multidimensional leadership constructs is ignored when it comes to subsequent measurement and modeling practices. For that reason, it is unclear what the literature actually reveals with regard to these and other multidimensional leadership constructs that are operationalized in terms of a single, higher order factor. Researchers need to think very carefully about the potential implications of specifying multidimensional leadership constructs into single, higher order factors.

Leadership Questionnaires

Central to measurement concerns are serious limitations associated with the use of leadership questionnaires. One of the assumptions underlying the use of questionnaires to measure leadership is that the individuals completing those measures store in memory and recall instances (i.e., behaviors) related to the respective leadership construct under study. The available research evidence suggests that this is an erroneous assumption. When forming impressions observers tend to quickly categorize and characterize (i.e., attach trait labels) to observed behaviors and then correct those trait-based inferences in an effortful manner, provided there are adequate cognitive resources to do so (Gilbert, 1998). One implication of this aspect of person perception is that behaviors consistent with an impression of a target person will be endorsed or rated favorably even if they never occurred (Sulsky & Day, 1992). As I have noted elsewhere (Day, 2012), researchers are fooling themselves if they believe that responses to leadership questionnaires accurately reflect observed leader behavior and only leader behavior.

Another limitation associated with most of the questionnaire-based leadership research is that it tends to use cross-sectional designs, which makes it impossible to rule out potential alternative explanations that performance information available in the social environment causes the ratings (i.e., reverse causality). Research has shown that it is likely that people reason backward from outcomes to the leadership ratings that they provide. In experimental research in which individuals were told that the videotaped group that they had viewed was either second-best or second-worst of all the groups studied in terms of performance were later shown to provide ratings of the group leader that were biased in the direction of that performance cue feedback despite seeing identical leader behaviors (e.g., Lord, Binning, Rush, & Thomas, 1978; Mitchell, Larson, & Green, 1977). It appears that raters infer effective leadership from good group performance and ineffective leadership from poor performance regardless of what they actually see. This type of looking backward in providing leadership ratings is open to innumerable potential biases.

Nonetheless, questionnaires remain a popular (if misguided) approach to studying leadership. If you design and publish a brief, easy-to-administer survey questionnaire, there is little doubt that researchers will use it. But we should not lose sight of the fact that the map is not the territory, and simply labeling a questionnaire as a measure of leadership does not mean that it actually measures leadership.

Despite these and other challenges to the leadership field, overall, there appears to be much promise for the scholarly study of leadership. There is a receptive audience for leadership research, and, after some challenging times in which it was thought that leadership was "dead" as a scholarly discipline, there is unprecedented research activity. The following sections identify a few of the areas that need to be addressed through research and theory development in shaping the future of leadership studies. The focus is on two core aspects of science: theory and methods. If there is an implicit message in these identified areas for future attention it is that the era of low-hanging fruit with regard to contributions to the leadership field is probably over. After more than a century of study, the leadership field has entered into a mature stage. Thus, what will contribute (i.e., be published) in the future will need to be significantly more sophisticated than what was published in the past. Overall, this is how science develops and progresses.

The Future of Leadership Theory[1]

Construct Definitions

A foundation of high-quality research rests on strong theory. The leadership field is (or should be) no different. Although there is no shortage of available leadership theory, questions might be raised as to what extent the research base is truly theoretically grounded. It seems that publishing a leadership measure (with the disturbing trend of then copyrighting it) is a gateway to establishing a particular leadership theory, whether it is transformational leadership, authentic, servant, ethical, LMX, or other. It is important to keep in mind that the foundation of theory is constructs, not measures (Bacharach, 1989), and clearly defined and accurate terms are at the core of strong constructs (Suddaby, 2010). Constructs are not the same thing as theory, but they are necessary but insufficient considerations for a theory to take reasonable form and have merit. Without getting into what it takes to develop clear theory (which could be the topic of an entire handbook), one particular area that needs greater attention is the role of construct definitions.

Clearly defining the underlying construct and being able to capture the essence of a construct coherently are hallmarks of sound theory, yet they are historical weaknesses in the leadership field. A sound construct definition also avoids tautology or circularity, which occurs when elements of the term being defined are included in the definition of the construct. Another form of tautological definition occurs when it includes hypothesized antecedents and outcomes as part of the definition. An example from the leadership literature involves definitions of charisma, which define charisma or charismatic leadership in terms of its antecedents, outcomes, or by exemplars, thus ignoring the underlying theme of the focal phenomenon (Antonakis, Fenley, & Liechti, 2011). It can be a very difficult exercise to propose concise definitions, in that it risks proposing something overly narrow, which compromises construct generalizability and relevance (Suddaby, 2010). Nonetheless, further evolution of the leadership field requires that much closer attention be paid to how carefully we define the core theoretical constructs in the discipline.

Process Models

Interest continues to grow in conceptualizing mediators and moderators of leadership effects within multilevel frameworks (e.g., Chen, Farh, Campbell-Bush, Wu, & Wu, in press; Chen, Kirkman, Kanfer, Allen, & Rosen, 2007). One likely reason for this interest is due to the significant advances made in making accessible various multilevel modeling techniques that can accurately estimate and partition within- and between-level effects. This is now possible even in complex cases involving moderated mediation and mediated moderation models (Edwards & Lambert, 2007;

Preacher, Rucker, & Hayes, 2007), as well as multilevel mediation (Preacher, Zyphur, & Zhang, 2010).

In cases in which sophisticated modeling techniques and related software become accepted and accessible, researchers gravitate to using them to test complex models that were difficult if not impossible to test with previously existing techniques. Just as meta-analysis revolutionized quantitative review approaches, hierarchical linear modeling (Raudenbush & Bryk, 2002) and related approaches have done the same for testing multilevel models appropriately. Analytical techniques and statistical packages aside, it is the quality of the underlying model and associated data that matters the most in terms of making a contribution to the leadership literature and enhancing our understanding of leadership processes.

Something that the field continues to overlook despite cautions made over a half-century ago (Hollander & Julian, 1969) is that leadership is a process and not a person or a position. Thus, we should be proposing and testing insightful process models of leadership. By that, I mean those that include underlying causes of other variables in the model. Failing to do so runs the risk of introducing endogeneity (i.e., a predictor that correlates with the model's error term), which undermines any unequivocal causal inferences that might be drawn (see Antonakis, Bendahan, Jacquart, & Lalive, this volume). This is a particular risk when estimating and testing models based on nonexperimental methods, which is typical of the leadership field. Because of its fundamental importance to the future of leadership research, this topic is elaborated on in more detail in the section addressing the future of leadership methods.

In sum, process theories propose that deep determinants, such as personality traits or general mental ability, *cause* observable behaviors that form a particular leadership style that in turn shapes leader emergence and effectiveness outcomes. Proposing and testing these kinds of process models are the future of leadership because they allow researchers to identify causal effects associated with deep-level leader characteristics (e.g., personality traits) given that they are exogenous so long as they have strong heritability influences.

Development

There is more than a century of leadership research and theory to draw from, and, as noted in this handbook, the foundation of theory and evidence continues to evolve. But comparatively little attention has been given to the important role of theory in predicting how leaders and leadership develop. In a paper drawing attention to this oversight, I made a distinction between leader development based on the acquisition of individual knowledge, skills, and other characteristics needed to be effective in leadership roles and processes from leadership development that focuses on the networked interrelationships among a broader collective (Day, 2000). This is hardly "strong theory," and greater efforts are needed to develop a theoretical foundation(s) regarding how individual leaders, or more collective leadership processes, develop over time.

This has been a critical omission in the literature, especially from a practical impact perspective. Most organizations care relatively little about which particular leadership theory has the most research support, but they do care a great deal about how to best develop leaders and leadership. Correspondingly, an overly short-term perspective on leadership training has emerged. What this perspective does not fully consider is that leadership training is a short-term proposition designed to provide proven solutions to known problems. Conversely, leader development is something that unfolds over a much longer time period, perhaps across the entire lifespan. Put somewhat differently, development is about enhancing the potential or capacity of an individual to be effective in situations where there is no agreed-upon solution and where even the challenge itself may be completely novel. There is no proven solution because there is no history of experience with the particular leadership challenge.

This development imperative was the basis for an integrative theory of leader development incorporating aspects of expertise and expert performance at the most observable level, self-regulation and identity at the middle or meso level, all of which are supported by adult development processes at the deepest level (Day, Harrison, & Halpin, 2009). The focus of this approach is agnostic or eclectic with regard to any particular leadership theory. Instead, it emphasizes various developmental processes that ultimately result in developing more skilled (i.e., expert) leaders.

There are other theoretical frameworks of leader and leadership development in the literature, including those that are summarized in the present volume; however, very few have been tested empirically. Looking to the future, the topics of leader and leadership development represent promising emerging pathways for the future of the field. Organizations are keen to develop leaders and leadership and to do so efficiently and effectively. Accelerating leader development is very much on the minds of those in organizations who are responsible for such practices and programs. Adopting more theoretically based approaches to test how this occurs can only help to build a better science and practice of leader development that will also enhance the broader leadership discipline.

Time and Leadership

It is a given that leadership takes time because it takes a period of time to be seen by others as a leader and to influence them, as well as to develop leadership skills and competencies. As noted previously, leadership is a process not a position, and process implies time. Thus, developing process models of leadership should incorporate time into them. For this reason, leadership and time should be inherently intertwined in theory and research. Unfortunately, the treatment of time in the leadership literature has been cursory at best. And when it is addressed, it is mainly at a theoretical rather than empirical level.

As others have noted, the role of time in studying, understanding, and practicing leadership is critically important, yet it continues to be "an unexplored dimension in leadership studies" (Shamir, 2011, p. 307). This is troubling because what we think we know about leadership may not be as robust as we believe. Results from cross-sectional research may not generalize longitudinally, and if those results do generalize, we need to understand the timeframe under which they operate. These are just a few of the many questions that are raised when we fail to consider time in leadership theory and research.

This may seem like an obvious point, but it is necessary to address time lags in assessing the effects of anything—especially leadership—because "it takes time for causes to have effects" (Gollub & Reichardt, 1987, p. 80). Time matters, especially when the focus of study is leadership, especially from a process perspective. The point about time and leadership is not a new one, but it is critically important if the field is to progress beyond the present state, which is mainly based on cross-sectional "snapshots" using almost entirely self-reported, survey questionnaire data. We need to do much better as theorists and researchers (especially), and taking time seriously is one area where greater attention is needed.

The Future of Leadership Methods

Integral to better theorizing about leadership and improving the model specification of leadership research is better model testing. Clear definitions and strong theory must be followed by robust measurement and testing. This is an area where leadership research has not yet fully delivered on its potential. Nonetheless, the future of leadership needs to be focused on stronger testing if it is to continue to advance as a scholarly discipline. One of the biggest methodological challenges facing leadership research is how to deal with endogeneity and, more specifically, devise ways to correctly estimate multilevel models. These two problems are related (as explained below) and are poised to become highly salient issues in leadership research in the coming years. For example, a review of 110 randomly sampled papers published in top-level journals indicated that researchers failed to address nearly all (90 percent) of the design and estimation conditions that make for confounded interpretations (Antonakis, Bendahan, Jacquart, & Lalive, 2010). This is a very serious concern for the future of leadership research.

Causality

The holy grail of science is the ability to draw strong causal inferences. By a strong causal inference I mean the ability to confidently claim that an independent variable or predictor (x) causes/influences/affects a dependent variable or criterion (y). To draw such a strong causal inference means that all other possible explanations for this relationship can be ruled out. A relevant question to consider is whether we can make such strong causal claims with regard to leadership research. Reviews of the evidence suggest this may not always or even usually be the case. This is important not simply from a scientific perspective. If an important objective in taking ideas into action is for relevant policies and practices to be correctly informed by leadership research, then we need to be able to draw strong causal inferences. Furthermore, resources need to be wisely invested in research activities and practical interventions.

For these and other reasons, it is important to identify variables that form part of a theory and to know how these variables are causally related. Policy and practice have to rely on research to know whether implementing certain actions would likely result in desired outcomes (i.e., basing decisions on clear evidence that x causes y). The implications of knowing such relationships with a level of certainty are critical in terms of making sound investments in selection, training, and organizational design.

A dependable way to know whether systems of variables are causally related is to manipulate the relevant independent variable(s), as is done in an experiment; however, much of what is studied in leadership is difficult (but not impossible) to manipulate. In cases in which experimental methods are infeasible, researchers have to rely on observational and correlational methods to better understand causal relationships in leadership.

A challenge of using observational methods is that merely observing a correlation between two variables does not provide much, if any, causal insight because of the potential problem of endogeneity. That is, a leadership predictor could cause an organizational outcome, but the opposite also could be true if potential endogeneity concerns are not addressed. Another possibility is that these variables share a common third cause and are related because they covary as a function of this third variable. A straightforward example is the near-perfect correlation observed between the number of churches and number of taverns in US cities. Does religion (*x*) drive a person to drink (*y*), or does drinking (*y*) cause people to find religion (*x*)? The correct inference is neither of these: the relationship is entirely due to a third (exogenous) causal variable of city size. As the population of a city gets larger, both the number of churches and taverns increases. Once the effect of the common cause (city population) is removed there is no relationship between *x* and *y*. Thus, it is not clear what the true nature the relationship between two variables is when one observes a correlation in a model that does not include exogenous sources of variance to identify the true causal effects. In other words, if the predictor is endogenous, correlating it with anything will yield inaccurate estimates (i.e., result in an endogeneity confound) that cannot help science or practice advance.

In general, endogeneity issues are not given much if any attention by leadership researchers. A typical scenario goes something like this: leadership ratings are provided by followers, and these ratings are correlated with some available criterion measure (outcome), or regression analyses or path analyses are conducted. Statistically significant results are taken to mean that leadership caused the outcome (while at the same time acknowledging that these are correlational data). No attention is given to including exogenous factors such as leader intelligence or personality. The future of leadership will need to involve more robust model testing to allow researchers, practitioners, and policy makers to have greater faith in the veracity of leadership research findings and to be able to draw meaningful and appropriate causal inferences.

Temporal Design Issues

Another methods theme for the future of leadership research will be on giving greater consideration to temporal design concerns involving the sampling of measurement waves (Collins & Graham, 2002). In particular, research design issues associated with determining how many times to measure and the appropriate intervals between measurement periods deserve greater consideration when designing and conducting leadership research. This is a natural methodological follow-on to the previous theoretical issue involving time and leadership.

The importance of temporal design issues in research was illustrated in a creative way by Gollub and Reichardt (1987). Those authors provide an example of taking aspirin to reduce the pain associated with a headache. The effect of aspirin on a headache may be zero after two minutes, relatively substantial after thirty minutes, near maximum effect after two or three hours, much reduced after five hours, and near zero again after twenty-four hours. As this straightforward example illustrates, understanding an effect size depends on knowing—or hypothesizing—the time lag involved. Because different time lags have different effects, varied time scales need to be studied to understand causal effects fully. This is an interesting example to consider within the realm of leader development, where it is commonly assumed that the effects of an intervention will continue indefinitely over time. But it could also apply to the study of leader behavior. Just how long-lasting are instances of something like inspirational motivation or intellectual stimulation within the broader concern of transformational leadership? I do not believe such research has ever been conducted.

Not only do the effects of leadership take time to be fully known, but if leadership is essentially about change and change requires time, then time is fully implicated as a component of leadership research. Others have made related points about the need to more carefully consider the effects of time with regard to research on leadership (Bluedorn & Jaussi, 2008; Shamir, 2011). Therefore, a very modest proposal would be to encourage researchers and authors to be very clear in stating the temporal parameters under which their leadership research was conducted. Along with the particular temporal design specification that was used, also including a brief discussion of the potential primary benefits and limitations of the time scales that were adopted would have at least a couple of advantages. Stating the time parameters under study more clearly and explicitly will help with future meta-analytic studies of various leadership phenomena and may yield insights into the role of time at a between-study level. Including a brief statement on the implications and potential limitations of the time scale used in a study might also help keep the issue salient in the minds of researchers and possibly generate additional ideas for future research. But again, these are modest proposals for a scholarly area in which big changes are needed.

One such change of a larger scope is to consider using inductive research designs based on intensive longitudinal data (ILD; Tan, Shiyko, Li, Li, & Dierker, 2012) in addition to more deductive or theory-based approaches to leadership research. ILD involve temporal designs with substantially larger numbers of observations for each participant compared to traditional longitudinal designs. Although there is no fixed number of observations needed for ILD, ten or more observations is suggested as a reasonable number to be effectively modeled with appropriate procedures (Tan et al., 2012). These kinds of dense time scales are driven by different types of research questions that focus on fine-grained temporal changes in human behavior or psychosocial processes, with particular attention paid to issues of covariation and causation. ILD contain detailed information about change that requires flexible statistical approaches. Because the recommended analytic approach by Tan et al. is nonparametric and therefore does not impose strict assumptions regarding the nature (i.e., form) of change, it offers greater modeling flexibility.

Another advantage to ILD is that, rather than having to rely on prior knowledge about the shape of change or rely on ill-defined or unreliable theory, this approach offers an inductive alternative. The shape of change is learned directly from data. This potentially accelerates the iterative learning process needed in understanding the nature of change. Dense observations yielding data containing fine-grained information about the change and appropriate statistical models and estimation techniques help to speed up this learning process.

Conclusion

In closing, a relevant question to pose concerns what is needed to help the leadership field to continue to evolve and be accepted among scientists and practitioners, rather than becoming obsolete and irrelevant. At one point in time, obsolescence was a distinct possibility. It may be difficult to believe, but a moratorium was proposed for the entire leadership discipline (Miner, 1975). Reasons for this call included that leadership research was so poorly designed and the construct itself so nebulous and ill-defined that it was thought (at least by some) that there was nothing to be gained from further research. So, although it is tempting to recommend a halt to all cross-sectional leadership research in order to encourage more process models and research, there are more measured actions that can be taken. At the top of that list is for researchers to take a more dynamic and systems-level perspective (i.e., include time and exogenous variables) in all aspects of leadership research. Another suggestion is to consider inductive research designs that incorporate intensive time scales and that do not value only theoretically driven, deductive research.

The greater part of this closing chapter focused on two areas that are elemental to all scientific fields, including that of leadership—theory and method. If there is a take-away message from this focus, it is that the future of leadership does not reside (solely) in identifying additional content topic domains. Instead, the field needs to attend to some of the basic concerns of science. Without more clearly defined constructs and tightly focused theories, the future of leadership study will be limited. Without more careful consideration of the factors that limit or otherwise undermine the kinds of causal inferences that are the hallmark of good science, the leadership field will be unable to fully inform business and education practices or public policy issues. Leadership can be a potent force in shaping the experiences and effectiveness of individuals, groups, organizations, and societies. But to fully realize this potential, leadership needs to be conceptualized and studied in the most rigorous ways possible.

In conclusion, the future prospects of leadership appear hopeful. The leadership field has demonstrated a remarkable adaptability and tenacity despite its many detractors. It is a good thing that we can now say with reasonable scientific (i.e., evidence-based) certainty that leadership matters, and by embracing better theory and more rigorous methods, the future of leadership is indeed very bright. Although there are challenges and obstacles, as noted in this chapter, the potential benefits are far stronger. It is hoped that this handbook will serve as both a guide and an inspiration for leadership scholars and those aspiring leadership scholars well into the twenty-first century.

Note

1. Portions of this section draw from earlier work by Day and Antonakis (2013) and Day (2014).

References

Antonakis, J., Avolio, B. J., & Sivasubramaniam, N. (2003). Context and leadership: An examination of the nine-factor Full-Range Leadership Theory using the Multifactor Leadership Questionnaire. *Leadership Quarterly, 14*, 261–295.

Antonakis, J., Bendahan, S., Jacquart, P., & Lalive, R. (2010). On making causal claims: A review and recommendations. *Leadership Quarterly, 21*, 1086–1120.

Antonakis, J., Fenley, M., & Liechti, S. U. E. (2011). Can charisma be taught? Tests of two interventions. *Academy of Management Learning & Education, 10*, 374–396.

Bacharach, S. B. (1989). Organizational theories: Some criteria for evaluation. *Academy of Management Review, 14*, 496–515.

Bass, B. M., & Riggio, R. E. (2006). *Transformational leadership* (2nd ed.). Mahwah, NJ: Erlbaum.

Bluedorn, A. C., & Jaussi, K. S. (2008). Leaders, followers, and time. *Leadership Quarterly, 19*, 654–668.

Chen, G., Farh, J.-L., Campbell-Bush, E. M., Wu, Z., & Wu, X. (in press). Teams as innovative systems: Multilevel motivational antecedents of innovation in R&D teams. *Journal of Applied Psychology*. doi: 10.1037/a0032663.

Chen, G., Kirkman, B. L., Kanfer, R., Allen, D., & Rosen, B. (2007). A multilevel study of leadership, empowerment, and performance in teams. *Journal of Applied Psychology, 92*, 331–346.

Collins, L. M., & Graham, J. W. (2002). The effect of the timing and spacing of observations in longitudinal studies of tobacco and other drug use: Temporal design considerations. *Drug and Alcohol Dependence, 68*, Supplement, 85–96.

Day, D. V. (2000). Leadership development: A review in context. *Leadership Quarterly, 11*, 581–613.

Day, D. V. (2012). Leadership. In S. W. J. Kozlowski (Ed.), *The Oxford handbook of organizational psychology* (vol. 1, pp. 696–729). New York: Oxford University.

Day, D. V. (2014). Time and leadership. In A. J. Shipp & Y. Fried (Eds.), *Time and work* (vol. 2, pp. 30–52). New York: Psychology Press.

Day, D. V., & Antonakis, J. (2013). The future of leadership. In H. S. Leonard, R. Lewis, A. M. Freedman & J. Passmore (Eds.), *The Wiley-Blackwell handbook of the psychology of leadership, change, and organizational development* (pp. 221–235). London: Wiley-Blackwell.

Day, D. V., Harrison, M. M., & Halpin, S. M. (2009). *An integrative approach to leader development: Connecting adult development, identity, and expertise*. New York: Routledge.

Edwards, J. R., & Lambert, L. S. (2007). Methods for integrating moderation and mediation: A general analytical framework using moderated path analysis. *Psychological Methods, 12*, 1–22.

Gharajedaghi, J. (1999). *Systems thinking: Managing chaos and complexity*. Boston: Butterworth Heinemann.

Gilbert, D. T. (1998). Ordinary personology. In D. T. Gilbert, S. T. Fiske & G. Lindzey (Eds.), *The handbook of social psychology* (4th ed., vol. 2, pp. 89–150). Boston, MA: McGraw-Hill.

Gollub, H. F., & Reichardt, C. S. (1987). Taking account of time lags in causal models. *Child Development, 58*, 80–92.

Hackman, J. R., & Wageman, R. (2007). Asking the right questions about leadership. *American Psychologist, 62*, 43–47.

Hollander, E. P., & Julian, J. W. (1969). Contemporary trends in the analysis of leadership processes. *Psychological Bulletin, 71*, 387–397.

Johnson, R. E., Rosen, C. C., & Chang, C.-H. D. (2011). To aggregate or not to aggregate: Steps for developing and validating higher-order multidimensional constructs. *Journal of Business Psychology, 26*, 241–248.

Johnson, R. E., Rosen, C. C., & Djurdjevic, E. (2011). Assessing the impact of common method variance on higher order multidimensional constructs. *Journal of Applied Psychology, 96*, 744–761.

Johnson, R. E., Rosen, C. C., Chang, C.-H. D., Djurdjevic, E., & Taing, M. U. (2012). Recommendations for improving the construct clarity of higher-order multidimensional constructs. *Human Resource Management Review, 22*, 62–72.

Katz, D., & Kahn, R. L. (1978). *The social psychology of organizations* (2nd ed.). New York: Wiley.

Liden, R. C., Wayne, S. J., Zhao, H., & Henderson, D. (2008). Servant leadership: Development of a multidimensional measure and multi-level assessment. *Leadership Quarterly, 19*, 161–177.

Lord, R. G., Binning, J. F., Rush, M. C., & Thomas, J. C. (1978). The effect of performance cues and leader behavior on questionnaire ratings of leadership behavior. *Organizational Behavior and Human Performance, 21*, 27–39.

Miner, J. B. (1975). The uncertain future of the leadership concept: An overview. In J. G. Hunt & L. L. Larson (Eds.), *Leadership frontiers* (pp. 197–208). Kent, OH: Kent State University.

Mitchell, T. R., Larson, J. R., Jr., & Green, S. G. (1977). Leader behavior, situational moderators, and group performance: An attributional analysis. *Organizational Behavior and Human Performance, 18*, 254–268.

Preacher, K. J., Rucker, D. D., & Hayes, A. F. (2007). Addressing moderated mediation hypotheses: Theory, methods, and prescriptions. *Multivariate Behavioral Research, 42*, 185–227.

Preacher, K. J., Zyphur, M. J., & Zhang, Z. (2010). A general multilevel SEM framework for assessing multilevel mediation. *Psychological Methods, 15*, 209–233.

Raudenbush, S. W., & Bryk, A. S. (2002). *Hierarchical linear models: Applications and data analysis methods* (2nd ed.). Thousand Oaks, CA: Sage.

Shamir, B. (2011). Leadership takes time: Some implications of (not) taking time seriously in leadership research. *The Leadership Quarterly, 22*, 307–315.

Smith, E. R. (2012). Editorial. *Journal of Personality & Social Psychology, 102*, 1–3.

Suddaby, R. (2010). Editor's comments: Construct clarity in theories of management and organization. *Academy of Management Review, 35*, 346–357.

Sulsky, L. M., & Day, D. V. (1992). Frame-of-reference training and cognitive categorization: An empirical investigation of rater memory issues. *Journal of Applied Psychology, 77*, 501–510.

Tan, X., Shiyko, M. P., Li, R., Li, Y., & Dierker, L. (2012). A time-varying effect model for intensive longitudinal data. *Psychological Methods, 17*, 61–77.

Walumba, F. O., Avolio, B. J., Gardner, W. L., Wernsing, T. S., & Peterson, S. J. (2008). Authentic leadership: Development and validation of a theory-based measure. *Journal of Management, 34*, 89–126.

Zyphur, M. J., Barsky, A. P., & Zhang, Z. (2012). Advances in leadership research methods. In D. V. Day & J. Antonakis (Eds.), *The nature of leadership* (2nd ed., pp. 66–107). Los Angeles: Sage.

INDEX

Page numbers followed by *f* and *t* in italics refer to figures and tables page numbers respectively.

C

D

F

M

Q

R

W

Y

Z